BOB
BIBLE
ANAGRAMS
ROBERT GILLIS

10 9 8 7 6 5 4 3 2 1
First Edition

For additional titles, see:
http://wordbooks.homestead.com

Some books are also available **coil bound** *or* **hardcover**
from
http://lulu.com/wordplay

Bob's Backwards Bible – Words arranged by ending letters! 460 pp.
Bob's Bible Stems – All 6 letter stems to make 6s, 7s & 8s – 1368 pp. 2 Vol.
Bobs' Bible: Volume 2 – 9 to 15 letter words with Hooks & Anagrams – 240 pp.
Bob's Bible By Length – 2-9 Letters in 9 Sections by Word Length 460 pp.
Top Anamonics 2007 – Best 996 7s for making 8s with Mnemonics 300 pp.
Bob's British Bible – SOWPODS differences marked - 2007 edition 470pp
Complete 3-4-5-Letter Study Guide – Quiz all 3-4-5s & 3-4-5s to make 4-5-6s 470 pp.
Complete 6-Letter Study Guide – Quiz on all 6s & 6s to make 7s 470 pp.
Complete 7-Letter Study Guides – Quiz on all 7s & 7s to make 8s 700pp in 2Vol.

.

Or write:

bible@hiwaay.net

Robert Gillis
Huntsville, AL

ISBN **978-0-9719473-0-6**

Who is Bob's Bible School Edition for?

Bob's Bible is for all school-age crossword game players who have always wanted a word game reference & don't mind learning a little extra each time they check whether a word is in the dictionary. Guide words at the bottom of each page help you flip to the right page quickly. The School Edition leaves out euphemisms such as FATSO and other words labelled as offensive in collegiate dictionaries.

What is in Bob's Bible:

Bob's Bible contains every 2 to 8 letter word deemed acceptable by the National SCRABBLE® Association for School Tournament play in alphabetical order. For each of these words, all of the *hooks* and *anagrams* are also listed. A *hook*, in tournament parlance, is a single letter that can be appended to a word to form another acceptable word. For example, the entry

CX **EROTIC** AS indicates that CEROTIC, XEROTIC, EROTIC, EROTICA and EROTICS are all acceptable.

The entry for ABLE looks like this:

CFG **ABLE** RS
ST BALE
BLAE

This indicates that ABLE can be hooked on the left with C, F, G, S or T to make CABLE, FABLE, GABLE, SABLE or TABLE or on the right with R or S to form ABLER or ABLES. The lightface BALE and BLAE tell us that the letters in **ABLE** can be rearranged to make the words BALE and BLAE as well as ABLE.

Hooks of all eight-letter words are also included, to indicate the acceptable nine-letter words that can be formed.

Any word that has an acceptable anagram (a word with exactly the same letters in a different order) will have each of its anagrams listed below it. Thus, a word such as SENATOR will also appear under ATONERS, SANTERO and TREASON.

When to use the Bible:

Use the bible whenever you encounter an unfamiliar word. You can quickly check its validity, and if it is indeed an acceptable word, you will immediately see all of its hooks and anagrams, so you can safely add it to your crossword game repertoire.

You can also browse the Bible to scan for interesting hooks and anagrams. The format is designed to make words with hooks and/or anagrams stand out. This edition of the Bible contains several special browsing categories plus self-quizzing sections for all the multiple-angram 2, 3, 4, 5, 7 and 8 letter words as well as the most likely 7 and 8 letter words. Enjoy!

See previous page for other Bob's Bible titles! Order direct and save.

Table of Contents

Added in 2006

2-letter Words

Q

QI S

3-letter Words

Q

QAT S
QIS

S

SUQ S

4-letter Words

Q

QADI S
QAID S
QATS
QOPH S

S

SUQS

5-letter Words

B

BURQA S

F

FAQIR S

Q

QADIS
QAIDS
QANAT S
QOPHS
QUBIT S
QURSH

T

TRANQ S

U

UMIAQ S

6-letter Words

B

BUQSHA S
BURQAS

C

CLIQUY

E

EXEQUY

F

FAQIRS

Q

QABALA HS
QANATS
QINDAR S
QINTAR S
QIVIUT S
QUBITS
QUBYTE S
QURUSH
QWERTY S

S

SHEQEL S
SQUUSH

T

TRANQS

U

UMIAQS

7-letter Words

B

BUQSHAS

O

OBLOQUY
OBSEQUY

Q

QABALAH S
QABALAS
QINDARS
QINTARS
QIVIUTS
QUBYTES
QURSHES
QWERTYS

S

SHEQELS

8-letter Words

C

COLLOQUY

M

MBAQANGA S

Q

QABALAHS
QINDARKA
QURUSHES

S

SHEQALIM
SQUUSHED
SQUUSHES

9-letter Words

M

MBAQANGAS

S

SOLILOQUY
SQUUSHING

11-letter Words

V

VENTRILOQUY

Vowel Heavy Words

2-letter Words

B **AA** HLS
GHK MNS TW **AE**
R **AI** DLMNRST
DFH JRT VW **OE** S
KP **OI** L

3-letter Words

AAH S
AHA
B **AAL** S
ALA
BK **AAS**
B **ABA** S
BAA
DFL MPR T **ACE** DS
DF **ADO** S
ODA
GRS **AGA** RS
CGM PRS W **AGE** DERS
GAE
DS **AGO** GN
GOA
H **AHA**
AAH
AHI S
CLM PQR S **AID** ES
BFH JKM NPR STV W **AIL** S
M **AIM** S
AMI
CFG KLM PRS TVW **AIN** S
ANI
FHL MPV W **AIR** NSTY
RAI RIA
DR **AIS**
BGW **AIT** S
GNT **ALA** ENRS
AAL
BDG HKM PRS TVW **ALE** CEFS
LEA
GLM **AMA** HS
KR **AMI** ADENRS
AIM
AMU S
KMN **ANA** LS
BCF GJK LMP SVW **ANE** SW
NAE
BR **ANI** LS
AIN
CGJ NRT **APE** DRSX
PEA
C **APO** DS

BCD FHM PRT WY **ARE** AS
EAR ERA
BCD FGH LMP RST **ATE** S
EAT ETA TAE TEA
JW **AUK** S
FJK L **AVA**
CEF GHL NPR SW **AVE** RS
AVO SW
OVA
AWA Y
AWE DES
WAE
AXE DLS
AYE S
YEA
AZO N
ZOA
BAA LS
ABA
BEE FNPRST
BIO GS
OBI
BOA RST
OBA
BOO BKMNRST
CEE S
COO FKLNPST
CUE DS
ECU
DEE DMPRST
DIE DLST
DOE RS
ODE
DUE LST
DUI T
DUO S
OUD UDO
BDF GHL NPR STW Y **EAR** LNS
ARE ERA
BFH MNP ST **EAT** HS
ATE ETA TAE TEA
B **EAU** X
ECU S
CUE
GKL MPR SW **EEK**
EKE
FHK PRS TW **EEL** SY
LEE
S **EGO** S
DLP **EKE** DS
EEK
DFH MS **EME** SU
EMU S
AJN P **EON** S
ONE
SV **ERA** S
ARE EAR
CDF HMP SW **ERE**
REE
BFG MSZ **ETA** S
ATE EAT TAE TEA
N **EVE** NRS
VEE

EWE RS
WEE
EYE DNRS
FEE BDLST
FEU DS
FIE F
FOE S
FOU LR
GAE DNS
AGE
AO **GEE** DKSZ
GIE DNS
GOA DLST
AGO
GOO DFKNPS
T **HAE** DMNST
C **HAO**
HIE DS
S **HOE** DRS
HUE DS
BDF LMN PRS V **ICE** DS
CLP **ION** S
CDF HLM STW **IRE** DS
REI
A **JEE** DPRSZ
JEU X
JOE SY
KAE S
KEA
KEA S
KAE
KOA NS
OAK OKA
KOI S
KUE S
UKE
FIO P **LEA** DFKLNPR S
ALE
AFG **LEE** KRST
EEL
LEI S
LIE
LEU D
P **LIE** DFNRSU
LEI
LOO FKMNPST
MAE S
MOA NST
MOO DLNRST
NAE
ANE
K **NEE** DMP
NOO KN
ONO
L **OAF** S
S **OAK** SY
KOA OKA
BHR S **OAR** S
ORA
BCD GM **OAT** HS
TAO
S **OBA** S
BOA
LR **OBE** SY
OBI AST
BIO
CLS **OCA** S
CS **ODA** HS
ADO
BCL MNR **ODE** AS
DOE

DFG HJN RTV W **OES**
OSE
BC **OHO**
OOH
BCF MNR ST **OIL** SY
OKA SY
KOA OAK
CHJ MPS TWY **OKE** HS
BCD HJM PRS TV **OLE** AOS
BCD GHL NPS TZ **ONE** S
EON
M **ONO** S
NOO
P **OOH** S
OHO
BCF HLM RST **OOT** S
TOO
CDH LMN PRT **OPE** DNS
BFH KMS T **ORA** DL
OAR
BCD FGK LMP STW Y **ORE** S
ROE
DHL NPR **OSE** S
OES
L **OUD** S
DUO UDO
DFH LPS TY **OUR** S
BGL PRT **OUT** S
N **OVA** L
AVO
HLY **OWE** DS
WOE
OXO
PEA GKLNRST
APE
E **PEE** KLNPRS
PIA LNS
PIE DRS
PIU
POI S
A **QUA** DGIY
RAI ADLNS
AIR RIA
BDF GPT **REE** DFKLS
ERE
REI FNS
IRE
A **RIA** LS
AIR RAI
F **ROE** S
ORE
GT **RUE** DRS
SAE
SEA
SAU L
A **SEA** LMRST
SAE
SEE DKLMNPR S
SEI FS
SOU KLPRS
SUE DRST
USE

TAE L
ATE EAT ETA TEA
TAO S
OAT
TAU ST
UTA
TEA KLMRST
ATE EAT ETA TAE
TEE DLMNS
TIE DRS
TOE ADS
TOO KLMNT
OOT
EP **TUI** S
JK **UDO** NS
DUO OUD
CDJ NP **UKE** S
KUE
LS **ULU** S
UPO N
FMR **USE** DRS
SUE
UTA S
TAU
BCJ LM **UTE** S
VAU S
VEE PRS
EVE
VIA L
VIE DRSW
VOE S
T **WAE** S
AWE
AT **WEE** DKLNPRS T
EWE
WOE S
OWE
WOO DFLS
YEA HNRS
AYE
YOU RS
ZEE S
ZOA
AZO
ZOO MNS

4-letter Words

P **AEON** S
AERO
R **AGEE**
AGIO S
V **AGUE** S
AIDE DRS
IDEA
AJEE
R **AKEE** S
ALAE
ALEE
ALOE S
OLEA
LZ **AMIA** S
MR **AMIE** S
ANOA S
AQUA ES
AREA ELS
MV **ARIA** S
RAIA
ASEA
L **AURA** ELRS
AUTO S

AWEE
BEAU STX
CIAO
CFL PT **EASE** DLS
B **EAUX**
DHL RW **EAVE** DS
EIDE R
EMEU S
T **EPEE** S
ETUI S
EURO S
ROUE
IDEA LS
AIDE
P **ILEA** CL
CM **ILIA** CDL
INIA
B **IOTA** S
IXIA S
JIAO
LIEU S
LUAU S
MEOU S
MOUE
MOUE S
MEOU
NAOI
C **OBIA** S
OBOE S
ODEA
Y **OGEE** S
OHIA S
OLEA
ALOE
OLEO S
FP **OLIO** S
B **OOZE** DS
OUZO S
QUAI LS
RAIA S
ARIA
ROUE NS
EURO
TOEA S
UNAI S
UNAU S
UREA LS
UVEA LS
ZOEA ELS

5-letter Words

AALII S
ADIEU SX
AECIA L
F **AERIE** DRS
AIOLI S
AQUAE
AREAE
AUDIO S
L **AURAE**
AUREI
URAEI
COOEE DS

P **EERIE** R
BF **LOOIE** S
LOUIE S
MIAOU S
OIDIA
OORIE
OURIE
QUEUE DRS
URAEI
AUREI
ZOEAE

6-letter Words

AALIIS
ABASIA S
ABELIA NS
ABULIA S
ACACIA S
ACAJOU S
ACEDIA S
ACUATE
ACULEI
ADAGIO S
ADIEUS
ADIEUX
AECIAL
AECIUM
AEDILE S
AEDINE
AENEUS
UNEASE
AEONIC
AERATE DS
AERIAL S
REALIA
AERIED
DEARIE
REDIAE
AERIER
F **AERIES** T
EASIER
AEROBE S
AERUGO S
AGAPAE
AGAPAI
AGORAE
AGOUTI S
AIKIDO S
AIOLIS
H **AIRIER**
ALEXIA S
ALODIA L
ALULAE
AMADOU S
AMEBAE
AMOEBA ENS
AMUSIA S
ANEMIA S
ANOMIE S
ANOPIA S
ANOXIA S
ANURIA S
URANIA
AORTAE
AOUDAD S
APIECE
APNOEA LS
APOGEE S
APORIA S
AREOLA ERS
AREOLE S
ARIOSE
ARIOSI

ARIOSO S
C AROUSE DRS
ATAXIA S
ATONIA S
AUBADE S
AUCUBA S
AUDIAL
AUDILE S
AUDIOS
AUGITE S
V AUNTIE S
AURATE D
AUREUS
URAEUS
AURORA ELS
AUROUS
AUSUBO S
H AUTEUR S
AUTOED
AVENUE S
AVIATE DS
AZALEA S

BAILEE S
BAILIE S
BATEAU X
BAUBEE S
BEANIE S
BEEBEE S
BLOOIE
BOOBOO S
BOOCOO S
BOOGIE DS
BOOHOO S
BOOKIE S
BOOKOO S
BOOTEE S
BOOTIE S
BOUBOU S
BOUGIE S
BUREAU SX

CAEOMA S
CAIQUE S
COATEE S
CODEIA S
COOCOO
COOEED
COOEES
COOKIE S
COOLIE S
COOTIE S
COTEAU X
COULEE S
CURIAE

DAIMIO S
DAUTIE S
DEARIE S
AERIED
REDIAE
DOOBIE S
DOODOO S
DOOLEE S
DOOLIE S
DOOZIE S

EASIER
AERIES
EASIES T
EELIER
BL EERIER
EIDOLA
EKUELE
ELODEA S
ELUATE S
ELUVIA L
EMEUTE S
EOCENE
A EOLIAN
A EONIAN
EOSINE S
EPIZOA

EPOPEE S
EQUATE DS
EQUINE S
ETOILE S
EUPNEA S
EUREKA
EURIPI
EXODOI
EXUVIA EL

FACIAE
FAERIE S
FERIAE
FAUNAE
FEIJOA S
FEIRIE
FERIAE
FAERIE
FLOOIE
FOODIE S
FOOTIE RS
FOVEAE

GALEAE
GATEAU SX
GIAOUR S
GOALIE S
GOATEE DS
GOODIE S
GOOIER
GOONIE RS
NOOGIE
GUAIAC S
GUINEA S

HEAUME S
HEINIE S
HOAGIE S
HOODIE RS
HOODOO S
HOOLIE
HOOPOE S
HOOPOO S

IDEATE DS
IGUANA S
IODATE DS
IODIDE S
IODINE S
IODISE DS
IODIZE DRS
IODOUS
ODIOUS
IOLITE S
L IONISE DS
IONIUM S
L IONIZE DRS
IONONE S

KOODOO S
KOOKIE R
KOUROI

LAMIAE
LAOGAI S
LAURAE
LEAGUE DRS
LIAISE DS
LOOIES
LOONIE RS
LOUIES

MEALIE RS
MEANIE S
MEDIAE
MEINIE S
MEOUED
MIAOUS
MILIEU SX
MOIRAI
MUUMUU S

NAUSEA S

NOOGIE S
GOONIE

OAKIER
L OBELIA S
OCREAE
ODIOUS
IODOUS
OEDEMA S
OEUVRE S
OIDIUM
R OILIER
OLEATE S
OLEINE S
OOLITE S
OOMIAC KS
OOMIAK S
W OORALI S
BW OOZIER
ZOOIER
OPAQUE DRS
OPIATE DS
OPIOID S
OREIDE S
ORIOLE S
OROIDE S
OTIOSE
OURARI S
OUREBI S
OUTAGE S
OUTATE
OUTEAT
OUTEAT S
OUTATE
OUTLIE RS
OUTSEE NS
OUTVIE DS

PALEAE
PEERIE S
PEEWEE S
PEREIA

QUAERE S
QUALIA
QUELEA S
QUEUED
QUEUER S
QUEUES
QUINOA S

REALIA
AERIAL
REDIAE
AERIED
DEARIE
RESEAU SX
UREASE
ROADEO S
ROADIE S
ROOFIE S
B ROOKIE RS
ROOMIE RS

SOIREE S
SOUARI S

TAENIA ES
TEEPEE S
TENIAE
TIBIAE
TOONIE S
TOUPEE S

UAKARI S
UBIQUE
UNCIAE
UNEASE S
AENEUS
UNIQUE RS
URAEUS
AUREUS
URANIA S
ANURIA
UREASE S
RESEAU

UREDIA L
UREIDE S
UREMIA S
UTOPIA NS
UVEOUS
UVULAE

VEEPEE S
VOODOO S

WEENIE RS
WEEPIE RS
WEEWEE DS
WIENIE S
WOODIE RS
WOOLIE RS

YAUTIA S

ZAIKAI S
ZOARIA L
ZOECIA
ZOOIER
OOZIER
ZOUAVE S

7-letter Words

ABOULIA S
ACEQUIA S
AECIDIA L
AENEOUS
AEOLIAN
AEONIAN
AEROBIA
ALIENEE S
AMOEBAE
ANAEMIA S
AQUARIA LN
AQUEOUS
AREOLAE
AUDITEE S
L AUREATE
AUREOLA ES
AUREOLE DS
AURORAE

COUTEAU X

EPINAOI
EUCAINE S
EUGENIA S
EULOGIA ES
EUPNOEA S
EVACUEE S
EXUVIAE

IPOMOEA S

MIAOUED

NOUVEAU

OIDIOID
OOGONIA L
OUABAIN S
OUGUIYA S

ROULEAU SX

SEQUOIA S

TAENIAE

URAEMIA S

ZOOECIA

8-letter Words

ABOIDEAU SX
ABOITEAU SX
ABOULIAS
ACADEMIA S
ACAUDATE
ACAULINE
ACAULOSE
ACAULOUS
ACEQUIAS
ACICULAE
ACIDEMIA S
ACIDURIA S
ACIERATE DS
ACOELOUS
ACQUIREE S
ACTINIAE
V ACUITIES
ACULEATE D
ADEQUATE
ADULARIA S
AECIDIAL
AECIDIUM
AEQUORIN S
AERATION S
AERIFIED
AERIFIES
AEROBIUM
AEROFOIL S
AEROLITE S
AERONAUT S
AGENESIA S
AGIOTAGE S
AGOUTIES
AGUACATE S
AGUELIKE
AGUEWEED S
AIGUILLE S
AKINESIA S
ALEHOUSE S
ALEURONE S
ALIENAGE S
ALIENATE DS
ALIENEES
ALLELUIA S
ALOPECIA S
AMEERATE S
AMOEBEAN
AMOEBOID
ANABAENA S
ANAEMIAS
ANAEROBE S
ANALOGUE S
ANOOPSIA S
ANOREXIA S
ANOXEMIA S
APIARIAN S
APIARIES
APIMANIA S
APOLOGIA ES
APOLOGUE S
AQUACADE S
AQUANAUT S
AQUARIAL
AQUARIAN S
AQUARIUM S
AQUATONE S
AQUILINE
QUINIELA
ARACEOUS
ARAPAIMA S
AREOLATE D
ATARAXIA S
AUBRETIA S
AUBRIETA
AUBRIETA S
AUBRETIA
AUDIENCE S
AUDITEES

AUDITION S
AUDITIVE S
AUGURIES
AUREOLAE
AUREOLAS
AUREOLED
AUREOLES
AURICULA ER S
AUROREAN
AUTACOID S
AUTOCADE S
AUTOCOID S
AUTOGIRO S
AUTOMATA
AUTOMATE D S
AUTOSOME S
AUTUNITE S
AVIANIZE DS
AVIARIES
AVIATION S
AVIFAUNA EL S

AZOTEMIA S
AZOTURIA S

BAUHINIA S
BEAUCOUP S
BEAUTIES
BIUNIQUE
BOISERIE S
BOOHOOED
BOUSOUKI AS
BOUTIQUE SY
BOUZOUKI AS

CAESURAE
CAPOEIRA S
CAUSERIE S
CAUTIOUS
COEQUATE D S

COOEEING
COUMAROU S
COUTEAUX

DAIQUIRI S
DEAERATE DS
DECIDUAE
DEIONIZE DR S

DETAINEE S
DIALOGUE DR S

DIAPAUSE DS
DIECIOUS
DIOECIES
DIOICOUS
DOUPIONI S
DUOLOGUE S

EARPIECE S
EATERIES
ECAUDATE
EDACIOUS
EGOMANIA CS
ELUVIATE DS
EMACIATE DS
EMEERATE S
EMERITAE
ENCAENIA
EOLIPILE S
EOLOPILE S
EPICEDIA
EPIFAUNA EL S

EPIGEOUS
EPILOGUE DS
EPIZOITE S
EPOPOEIA S
EQUALISE DR S

EQUALIZE DR S

EQUATION S
EQUIPAGE S
EQUISETA
EQUITIES
EQUIVOKE S
R ERADIATE DS
P ETIOLATE DS
ETOUFFEE S
EUCAINES
EUDAEMON S
EUDAIMON S
EUGENIAS
EULOGIAE
EULOGIAS
EULOGIES
EULOGISE
EULOGISE DS
EULOGIES
EULOGIUM S
EULOGIZE DR S

EUPEPSIA S
EUPHORIA S
EUPNOEAS
EUPNOEIC
EUROKIES
EUROKOUS
EUROPIUM S
EUSOCIAL
EUTAXIES
EUXENITE S
EVACUATE DS
EVACUEES
DR EVALUATE DS
EXAMINEE S
EXEQUIAL
EXEQUIES
EXIGUOUS
EXIMIOUS
EXONUMIA
EXUVIATE DS
EYEPIECE S

FACETIAE
FAUTEUIL S
FILARIAE
FOVEOLAE

GAIETIES
GUAIACOL S
GUAIACUM S
GUAIOCUM S

HEMIOLIA S
HETAERAE
HETAIRAI
HOODOOED

IBOGAINE S
ICEHOUSE S
IDEALISE DS
IDEALIZE DR S

IDEATION S
IODINATE
IDEATIVE
IDIOCIES
IDONEOUS
IGUANIAN S
INERTIAE
INFAUNAE
INITIATE DS
IODATION S
IODINATE DS
IDEATION
IPOMOEAS
ISOLOGUE S

JALOUSIE DS

KAMAAINA S

LAUREATE DS
LEUCEMIA S
LEUKEMIA S

MAIASAUR AS
MAIEUTIC
MAIOLICA S
MAUSOLEA N
MAZAEDIA
MEUNIERE
MIAOUING
MILIARIA LS
MINUTIAE
MOIETIES
MOVIEOLA S

NAUSEATE DS
NAUSEOUS
NEURULAE

OCEANAUT S
OEDEMATA
OEDIPEAN
OEILLADE S
OITICICA S
OLIGURIA S
Z OOGAMETE S
OOGAMIES
OOGAMOUS
Z OOGENIES
OOGONIAL
OOGONIUM S
Z OOLOGIES
OOTHECAE
OPTIONEE S
ORATORIO S
OUABAINS
OUGUIYAS
OUISTITI S
OUTARGUE D S

OUTEATEN
OUTGUIDE DS
OUTHOUSE S
OUTQUOTE D S
OUTRAISE DS
SAUTOIRE
OUTVALUE DS
OUTVOICE DS
OVARIOLE S

PAHOEHOE S
PARANOEA S
PARANOIA CS
PATOOTIE S
PEEKABOO S
PEEKAPOO S
POACEOUS
PRIEDIEU SX

QUAALUDE S
QUEASIER
QUEAZIER
QUEUEING
QUIETUDE S
QUILLAIA S
QUINIELA S
AQUILINE

RADIALIA
REAROUSE D S
RETIARII
ROULEAUS
ROULEAUX
T ROUSSEAU S

SAUTOIRE S
OUTRAISE
SEAPIECE S
SEAQUAKE S

SEQUELAE
SEQUOIAS
SILIQUAE
SQUEEGEE D S

TAQUERIA S
TEAHOUSE S
THIOUREA S
TOEPIECE S
TOXAEMIA S

D UBIETIES
UINTAITE S
UNEASIER
UNIAXIAL
UNIDEAED
UNIONISE DS
UNIONIZE DR S

URAEMIAS
URAEUSES
UREDINIA L
URINEMIA S
USQUABAE S
USQUEBAE S
USURIOUS
UXORIOUS

VOODOOED

WEIGELIA S

ZABAIONE S
ZOOECIUM
ZOOGLEAE
ZOOGLOEA E L S

ZOOMANIA S

No Vowel Words

2-letter Words

A BY ES

O HM M

HU MM
MY C

A SH AEHY

3-letter Words

BRR R
A BYS

S CRY
CWM S

DRY S

FLY
FRY

GYM S
GYP S

HMM
HYP EOS

MYC S

NTH

PHT
PLY
S PRY
PST
PYX

SHH
A SHY
SKY
SLY
E SPY
STY E
SYN CE

THY
TRY
TSK S

WHY S
A WRY
WYN DNS

ZZZ

4-letter Words

BRRR
BYRL S

CWMS
CYST S

DRYS

GYMS
GYPS Y

HYMN S
HYPS
SYPH

LYCH
LYNX

MYCS
MYTH SY

PFFT
PSST

RYND S

SCRY
SPRY
SYNC HS
SYPH S
HYPS

TSKS
TYPP S
TYPY

WHYS
WYCH
WYND S
WYNN S
WYNS

XYST IS

5-letter Words

BYRLS

CRWTH S
CRYPT OS
CYSTS

DRYLY

FLYBY S

GHYLL S
GLYPH S
GYPSY

HYMNS

LYMPH S
LYNCH

MYRRH S
MYTHS
MYTHY
THYMY

NYMPH AOS

PHPHT
PSYCH EOS
PYGMY

RYNDS

SHYLY
SLYLY
STYMY
SYLPH SY
SYNCH S
SYNCS
SYNTH S

SYPHS

THYMY
MYTHY
TRYST ES
TYPPS

WRYLY
WYNDS
WYNNS

XYLYL S
XYSTS

6-letter Words

CRWTHS
CRYPTS

FLYBYS
FLYSCH

GHYLLS
GLYCYL S
GLYPHS

LYMPHS

MYRRHS

NYMPHS

PSYCHS

RHYTHM S

SPHYNX
SPRYLY
SYLPHS
SYLPHY
SYNCHS
SYNTHS
SYZYGY

TRYSTS
TSKTSK S

XYLYLS

7-letter Words

GLYCYLS

RHYTHMS

TSKTSKS

2-letter Words

B **AA** HLS

CDF **AB** ASY
GJK
LNS
TW

BCD **AD** DOSZ
FGH
LMP
RST
W

GHK **AE**
MNS
TW

BDF **AG** AEOS
GHJ
LMN
RST
WYZ

ABD **AH** AIS
HNP
RY

R **AI** DLMNRST

ABD **AL** ABELPST
GPS

BCD **AM** AIPU
GHJ
LNP
RTY

BCD **AN** ADEITY
FGM
NPR
TVW

BCE **AR** BCEFKMST
FGJ
LMO
PTV
WY

ABF **AS** HKPS
GHK
LMP
RTV
WZ

BCE **AT** ET
FGH
KLM
OPQ
RST
VW

CDH **AW** AELN
JLM
NPR
STV
WY

FLM **AX** E
PRS
TWZ

BCD **AY** ES
FGH
JKL
MNP
RSW
Y

AO **BA** ADGHLMNP RSTY

O **BE** DEGLNSTY

O **BI** BDGNOSTZ

A **BO** ABDGOPST WXY

A **BY** ES

O **DE** BEFLNVWX Y

AU **DO** CEGLMNRS TW

BFG **ED** HS
LMP
RTW
Z

DKR **EF** FST

FHP **EH**
Y

BCD **EL** DFKLMS
EGM
ST

FGH **EM** ESU
MR

BDF **EN** DGS
GHK
MPS
TWY

FHP **ER** AEGNRS
S

BFH **ES** S
LOP
RY

BFG **ET** AH
HJL
MNP
RST
VWY

DHK **EX**
LRS
V

AE **GO** ABDORSTX Y

ASW **HA** DEGHJMOP STWY

ST **HE** HMNPRSTW XY

ACG **HI** CDEMNPST
KP

O **HM** M

MOR **HO** BDEGNPST WY
TW

ABD **ID** S
FGH
KLM
RVY

DKR **IF** FS

ABD **IN** KNS
FGH
JKL
PRS
TWY
Z

ABC **IS** M
DHK
LMP
QST
VWX

ABD **IT** S
FGH
KLN
PST
WZ

OS **KA** BEFSTY

S **KI** DFNPRST

A **LA** BCDGMPRS TVWXY

A **MA** CDEGNPRS TWXY

E **ME** DGLMNTW

A **MI** BCDGLMRS X

HU **MM**

AE **MU** DGMNST

A **NA** BEGHMNPW Y

AO **NE** BEGTW

O **NO** BDGHMORS TW

G **NU** BNST

BCG **OD** ADES
HMN
PRS
TY

DFH **OE** S
JRT
VW

FNO **OH** MOS
P

KP **OI** L

DMN **OM** S
PRS
TY

CDE **ON** EOS
FHI
MST
WY

BCF **OP** EST
HKL
MPS
TW

CDF **OR** ABCEST
GKM
NT

BCD **OS** E
GHK
MNS
W

BCD **OW** ELN
HJL
MNP
RST
VWY

BCF **OX** OY
GLP
SV

BCF **OY**
GHJ
ST

S **PA** CDHLMNPR STWXY

AO **PE** ACDEGHNP RSTW

AEI **RE** BCDEFGIM PSTVX
O

A **SH** AEHY

P **SI** BCMNPRST X

EU **TA** BDEGJMNO PRSTUVWX

DH **UH**

BCG **UM** MP
HLM
RSV
Y

BDF **UN** S
GHJ
MNP
RST

CDH **UP** OS
PST
Y

BJM **US** E
NP

BCG **UT** AES
HJM
NOP
RT

AEO **WE** BDENT

T **WO** EKNOSTW

PR **YA** GHKMPRWY

ABD **YE** AHNPSTW
EKL
PRT
W

3-letter Words

B **AAL** S

BK **AAS**

B **ABA** S

CDF **ABS**
GJK
LNS
TW

BG **ABY** ES

DFL **ACE** DS
MPR
T

FPT **ACT** AS

DF **ADO** S

BCD **ADS**
FGL
MPR
TW

BCD **AFF**
GNR
WY

DHR **AFT**
W

GRS **AGA** RS

CGM **AGE** DERS
PRS
W

DS **AGO** GN

BDF **AGS**
GHJ
LMN
RST
WYZ

H **AHA**

ADH **AHS**

CLM **AID** ES
PQR
S

BFH **AIL** S
JKM
NPR
STV
W

M **AIM** S

CFG **AIN** S
KLM
PRS
TVW

FHL **AIR** NSTY
MPV
W

DR **AIS**

BGW **AIT** S

GNT **ALA** ENRS

BDG **ALE** CEFS
HKM
PRS
TVW

BCF **ALL** SY
GHL
MPS
TW

PS **ALP** S

ABD **ALS** O
GPS

HMS **ALT** OS

GLM **AMA** HS

KR **AMI** ADENRS

CDG **AMP** S
LRS
TV

KMN **ANA** LS

BHL **AND** S
RSW

BCF **ANE** SW
GJK
LMP
SVW

BR **ANI** LS

CHP **ANT** AEIS
RW

MWZ **ANY**

CGJ **APE** DRSX
NRT

C **APO** DS

R **APT**

BCD **ARB** S
G

MN **ARC** HOS

BCD **ARE** AS
FHM
PRT
WY

BZ **ARF** S

BCD **ARK** S
HLM
NPS
W

BFH **ARM** SY
W

BCE **ARS**
GJL
MOP
TVW

CDF **ART** SY
HKM
PTW

BCD **ASH** Y
FGH
LMP
RSW

BCM **ASK** S
T

GHR **ASP** S
W

BLM **ASS**
PST

BCD **ATE** S
FGH
LMP
RST

BMW **ATT**

JW **AUK** S

FJK **AVA**
L

CEF **AVE** RS
GHL
NPR
SW

BPW **AWL** S
Y

DFL **AWN** SY
MPS
Y

BCD **AYS**
FGH
JKL
MNP
RSW
Y

K **BAR** BDEFKMN S

AO **BAS** EHKST

A **BED** SU

O **BES** T

A **BET** AHS

O **BEY** S

IO **BIS** EK

O **BIT** EST

A **BOS** HKS

A **BUT** EST

A **BYE** S

A **BYS**

S **CAB** S

S **CAD** EIS

S **CAM** EOPS

S **CAN** EST

S **CAR** BDEKLNP RST

S **CAT** ES

I **CON** EIKNSY

S **COP** ESY

S **COT** ES

S **COW** LSY

E **CRU** DSX

S **CRY**

S **CUD** S

S **CUM**

S **CUP** S

S **CUT** ES

O **DAH** LS

AE **DIT** AESZ

I **DOL** ELST

U **DON** AEGS

O **DOR** EKMPRSY

AU **DOS** EST

BDF **EAR** LNS
GHL
NPR
STW
Y

BFH **EAT** HS
MNP
ST

B **EAU** X

BFG **EDS**
MPR
TWZ

GKL **EEK**
MPR
SW

FHK **EEL** SY
PRS
TW

T **EFF** S

KR **EFS**

DHL **EFT** S
RW

TY **EGG** SY

S **EGO** S

DLP **EKE** DS

GHM **ELD** S
VWY

DPS **ELF**

Y **ELK** S

BCD **ELL** S
FHJ
MST
WY

H **ELM** SY

BCD **ELS** E
EGM
ST

DFH **EME** SU
MS

FGH **EMS**
MR

BFL **END** S
MPR
STV
W

BDF **ENS**
GHK
LPT
WY

AJN **EON** S
P

SV **ERA** S

CDF **ERE**
HMP
SW

B **ERG** OS

FHK **ERN** ES
T

HS **ERS** T

CFJ **ESS**
LMN

BFG **ETA** S
MSZ

BHM **ETH** S
T

N **EVE** NRS

A **FAR** DELMOT

O **FAY** S

E **GAD** IS

E **GAL** AELS

O **GAM** ABEPSY

A **GAR** BS

A **GAS** HPT

A **GED** S

AO **GEE** DKSZ

A **GIN** KS

E **GOS** H

CS **HAD** EJ

T **HAE** DMNST

S **HAG** S

S **HAH** AS

CSW **HAM** ES

C **HAO**

CW **HAP** S

CGK **HAT** EHS
PST
W

CST **HAW** KS

CS **HAY** S

AT **HEM** EPS

TW **HEN** ST

S **HES** T

KW **HET** HS

CPS **HEW** NS
TW

TW **HEY**

C **HIC** K

CW **HID** E

SW **HIM** S

CST **HIN** DST
W

CSW **HIP** S

ACG **HIS** NST
KPT

CSW **HIT** S

S **HOD** S

S **HOE** DRS

S **HOG** GS

CP **HON** EGKS

CSW **HOP** ES

PS **HOT** S

CDS **HOW** EFKLS

A **HOY** AS

C **HUB** S

CT **HUG** ES

C **HUM** PS

S **HUN** GHKST

W **HUP**

BPS **HUT** S

BDF **ICE** DS
LMN
PRS
V

LRW **ICH** S

DHK **ICK** Y
LMN
PRS
TW

ABF **IDS**
GKL
MRV
Y

BDJ **IFF** Y
MRT

DKR **IFS**

M **IGG** S

BMS **ILK** AS

BDF **ILL** SY
GHJ
KMN
PRS
TVW
YZ

GJL **IMP** IS
PSW

DFG **INK** SY
JKL
MOP
RSW

JL **INN** S

ABD **INS**
FGH
JKL
PRS
TWY
Z

CLP **ION** S

CDF **IRE** DS
HLM
STW

BDK **IRK** S
M

J **ISM** S

Bob's Bible: Words With Front Hooks

ABDFGHKLNPSTWZ **ITS**
JT **IVY**

A **JAR** LS
A **JEE** DPRSZ
D **JIN** KNSX

OS **KAS**
IS **KAT** AS
O **KAY** OS
S **KEG** S
S **KEP** IST
S **KID** S
AS **KIN** ADEGKOS
S **KIP** S
S **KIS** ST
S **KIT** EHS

BFS **LAB** S
CG **LAD** ESY
CFS **LAG** S
BCFGS **LAM** ABEPS
CFS **LAP** S
A **LAR** DIKS
A **LAS** EHST
BFPS **LAT** EHISU
BCFS **LAW** NS
F **LAX**
CFPS **LAY** S
FIOP **LEA** DFKLNPRS
BFGPS **LED**
AFG **LEE** KRST
G **LEG** S
B **LET** S
FIP **LEX**
FG **LEY** S
G **LIB** S
S **LID** OS
P **LIE** DFNRSU
B **LIN** EGKNOSTY
BCFS **LIP** AES
AFS **LIT** ESU
BGS **LOB** EOS
BCFS **LOG** EOSY
CFGPS **LOP** ES
BCPS **LOT** AHIS
ABFGPS **LOW** ENS
GPS **LUG** ES
AGPS **LUM** APS
F **LUX** E

A **MAS** AHKST
AO **MEN** DOU
S **MEW** LS
E **MIC** AES
AI **MID** IS
AE **MIR** EIKSY
A **MIS** EOST
S **MOG** S
S **MUG** GS
AE **MUS** EHKST
S **MUT** EST

S **NAG** S
KS **NAP** AES
GS **NAW**
K **NEE** DMP
AK **NEW** ST

S **NIB** S
A **NIL** LS
S **NIP** AS
KSU **NIT** ES
KS **NOB** S
S **NOG** GS
O **NOS** EHY
KS **NOT** AE
EKS **NOW** ST
S **NUB** S
AGO **NUS**

L **OAF** S
S **OAK** SY
BHRS **OAR** S
BCDGM **OAT** HS
S **OBA** S
LR **OBE** SY
CLS **OCA** S
CS **ODA** HS
BCLMNR **ODE** AS
BCGHMNPRSTY **ODS**
DFGHJNRTVW **OES**
BCDT **OFF** S
CLST **OFT**
BC **OHO**
O **OHS**
BCFMNRST **OIL** SY
CHJMPSTWY **OKE** HS
BCFGHMSTW **OLD** SY
BCDHJMPRSTV **OLE** AOS
DMNPRST **OMS**
BCDGHLNPSTZ **ONE** S
M **ONO** S
CDEFHIMPSTW **ONS**
P **OOH** S
BCFHLMRST **OOT** S
CDHLMNPRT **OPE** DNS
BCFHKLMOPSTW **OPS**
BFHKMST **ORA** DL
FS **ORB** SY
T **ORC** AS
BCDFGKLMPSTWY **ORE** S
CDKMT **ORS**
BFMPSTW **ORT** S

DHLNPR **OSE** S
L **OUD** S
DFHLPSTY **OUR** S
BGLPRT **OUT** S
N **OVA** L
HLY **OWE** DS
BCFHJY **OWL** S
DGLMST **OWN** S
BDFP **OXY**

O **PAH**
O **PAL** ELMPSY
S **PAM** S
S **PAN** EGST
S **PAR** ADEKRST
SU **PAS** EHST
S **PAT** EHSY
S **PAY** S
S **PEC** HKS
AOS **PED** S
E **PEE** KLNPRS
O **PEN** DST
A **PER** EIKMPTV
AO **PES** OT
S **PEW** S
ES **PIC** AEKS
S **PIN** AEGKSTY
S **PIT** AHSY
A **POD** S
S **POT** S
S **PRY**
S **PUD** S
S **PUN** AGKSTY
S **PUR** EILRS
O **PUS** HS

A **QUA** DGIY

BGOT **RAD** S
BCDF **RAG** AEGIS
CDGPT **RAM** IPS
BG **RAN** DGIKT
CFTW **RAP** EST
BE **RAS** EHP
BDFGP **RAT** EHOS
BCD **RAW** S
BDFGPT **RAY** AS
BCI **RED** DEOS
BDFGPT **REE** DFKLS
T **REF** ST
D **REG** S
P **REP** OPS
AIOT **RES** HT
FT **RET** ES
P **REX**
A **RIA** LS
CD **RIB** S
AGI **RID** ES
BFGPT **RIG** S
BGPT **RIM** ESY
BG **RIN** DGKS
DGT **RIP** ES
C **ROC** KS
PT **ROD** ES
F **ROE** S
FP **ROM** PS
GT **ROT** AEILOS

BCFGPTV **ROW** S
DG **RUB** ESY
GT **RUE** DRS
DFT **RUG** AS
ADG **RUM** PS
B **RUT** HS

A **SEA** LMRST
U **SER** AEFS
A **SHY**
P **SIS**
E **SPY**

S **TAB** SU
S **TAG** S
A **TAP** AES
S **TAR** ENOPST
EU **TAS** KS
S **TAT** ES
S **TAW** S
S **TET** HS
S **TEW** S
EO **TIC** KS
A **TOM** BES
AS **TOP** EHIOS
S **TOT** ES
S **TOW** NSY
S **TUB** AES
EP **TUI** S
S **TUN** AEGS
S **TYE** ERS

JK **UDO** NS
PSV **UGH** S
CDJNP **UKE** S
LS **ULU** S
M **UMM**
BDHJLMPRST **UMP** S
BDFGHMNPRST **UNS**
CDPSTY **UPS**
BC **URB** S
BCNST **URD** S
BCDT **URN** S
B **URP** S
FMR **USE** DRS
BCJLM **UTE** S
BCGHJMNOPRT **UTS**

K **VAS** AET
A **VID** ES
A **VOW** S
O **VUM**

S **WAB** S
T **WAE** S
S **WAG** ES
HS **WAN** DEKSTY
S **WAP** S
T **WAS** HPT
ST **WAT** ST
AS **WAY** S
AO **WED** S
AT **WEE** DKLNPRST
ST **WIG** S
T **WIN** DEGKOSY
IY **WIS** EHPST
T **WIT** EHS
T **WOS** T

S **WOT** S
A **WRY**

A **XIS**

A **YAH**
K **YAK** S
K **YAR** DEN
E **YEN** S
ABDEKLOPRTW **YES**
APT **YIN** S

4-letter Words

B **AALS**
B **ABAS** EH
S **ABED**
CFGST **ABLE** DRS
FLMPR **ACED**
DFLMPRT **ACES**
CMT **ACHE** DS
N **ACRE** DS
FPT **ACTS**
DF **ADOS**
P **AEON** S
F **AERY**
RS **AGAS**
CGPRW **AGED**
R **AGEE**
CEGJLPSWY **AGER** S
CGMPRSW **AGES**
F **AGIN** G
M **AGMA** S
W **AGON** ESY
V **AGUE** S
A **AHED**
CMQRS **AIDS**
BFHJKMNPRSTVW **AILS**
M **AIMS**
CGKMPRSTW **AINS**
BC **AIRN** S
FHLMPVW **AIRS**
DFH **AIRY**
BGW **AITS**
R **AKEE** S
T **AKIN**
MT **ALAR** MY
BGNT **ALAS**
BDGHKMPRSTVW **ALES**
CK **ALIF** S
BT **ALKY** DL
BCFGHLMPTW **ALLS**
BDGPRSTW **ALLY** L
H **ALMA** HS
BCHMP **ALMS**
PS **ALPS**
HMS **ALTS**
CGLM **AMAS** S
MS **AMBO** S
RY **AMEN** DST
LZ **AMIA** S
MR **AMIE** S
G **AMIN** EOS
T **AMIS** S
CDGLRSTV **AMPS**

RW **AMUS** E
BC **ANAL**
KMN **ANAS**
BHLRSW **ANDS**
BCFJKLMPSVW **ANES**
FMPST **ANGA** S
R **ANIS** E
CM **ANNA** LS
CF **ANON**
H **ANSA** E
M **ANTA** ES
CHPRW **ANTS** Y
M **ANUS**
CGJRT **APED**
CGJPRT **APER** SY
CGJNRT **APES**
C **APOS**
L **APSE** S
BCDG **ARBS**
LMP **ARCH**
N **ARCO**
MN **ARCS**
BCDFHLMNPRTW **ARES**
BZ **ARFS**
MV **ARIA** S
BCDHLMNPSW **ARKS**
BFHW **ARMS**
B **ARMY**
CDFHKMPTW **ARTS** Y
PTW **ARTY**
L **ARUM** S
P **ARVO** S
DMW **ASHY**
BCMT **ASKS**
GHRW **ASPS**
W **ATAP** S
BCDFGHMNPRST **ATES**
JW **AUKS**
CFY **AULD**
DGHJTV **AUNT** SY
L **AURA** ELRS
CHLPRSW **AVER** ST
CEFHLNOPRSW **AVES**
P **AVID**
CDHJLMPSTY **AWED**
BPWY **AWLS**
DFLPY **AWNS**
FLT **AWNY**
FMRTW **AXED**
FLMPRSTWZ **AXES**
MT **AXIS**

T AXON ES
R AYAH S
LZ AYIN S
H AZAN S

A BACK S
K BARS
A BASE DRS
A BASH
A BATE DS
A BEAM SY
A BETS
O BEYS
O BIAS
A BIDE DRST
O BITS Y
A BLED
A BODE DS
A BOIL S
O BOLE S
E BONY
E BOOK S
A BOON S
A BORT SYZ
A BOUT S
A BRIS KS
A BUTS
A BUZZ
A BYES

S CABS
S CADS
S CALL AS
S CAMP IOSY
S CAMS
S CANS OT
S CANT OSY
S CAPE DRS
S CARE DRSTX
S CARP IS
S CARS E
S CART ES
S CATS
S CENT OSU
S CION S
Y CLAD ES
A COCK SY
S COFF S
AS COLD S
S CONE DSY
I CONS
S COOP ST
S COOT S
S COPE DNRS
S COPS E
S CORE DRS
AS CORN SUY
S COTS
S COWL S
S COWS
S CRAG S
S CRAM PS
S CRAP ES
A CRED OS
S CREW S
E CRUS EHT
S CUDS
S CUFF S
S CULL SY
S CUPS
S CURF S
AS CUTE RSY
S CUTS

O DAHS
I DEAL ST
A DEEM S
AE DITS Y
I DOLS
U DONS Y
A DORE
O DORS A
O DOUR A
A DOWN SY
A DOZE DNRS
E DUCE S
E DUCT S
A DUST SY

BLP EACH
RT
P EARL SY
LY EARN S
BDF EARS
GHL
NPR
STW
Y
CFL EASE DLS
PT
BFL EAST S
Y
DHN EATH
BFH EATS
MNP
ST
B EAUX
DHL EAVE DS
RW
W ECHT
NT EDDY
HKL EDGE DRS
SW
HLS EDGY
W
FHK EELS
PRS
T
S EELY
BLP EERY
V
T EFFS
HLW EFTS
LR EGAL
L EGER S
TY EGGS
L EGGY
A EGIS
S EGOS
D EKED
DP EKES
GMV ELDS
W
Y ELKS
BCD ELLS
FHJ
MST
WY
H ELMS
DFH EMES
MS
DH EMIC
DR EMIT S
GJ EMMY S
BFL ENDS
MPR
STV
W
ANP EONS
T EPEE S
S EPIC S
PR EPOS
B ERGS
KT ERNE S
FHK ERNS
T
CHZ EROS E
V ERST
BLY ESES
M ESNE S
BFG ETAS
Z
FKL ETCH
RV
BHM ETHS
T
S EVEN ST
FLN EVER TY
S
N EVES
DK EVIL S
FHN EWER S
S
HSV EXED
DHK EXES
LRS
V
K EYED
F EYER S

O FAYS
A FIRE DRS
A FOOT SY
A FORE S
A FOUL S
A FRIT HSTZ

E GADS
A GAIN S
A GAMA SY
O GAMS
A GAPE DRS
A GARS
A GATE DRS
A GAVE L
A GAZE DRS
O GEES ET
A GENE ST
A GENT S
E GEST ES
A GIST S
O GIVE NRS
O GLED ES
A GLEE DKST
A GLEY S
A GLOW S
A GONE FR
A GREE DKNST

STW HACK S
S HADE DS
S HAFT S
S HAGS
S HAHS
C HAIR SY
S HAKE S
SW HALE DRS
S HALL OS
S HALT S
S HAME S
CSW HAMS
BCW HANG S
ST HANK SY
C HANT S
CW HAPS
CS HARD SY
CS HARE DMS
CS HARK S
CT HARM S
S HARP SY
C HART S
G HAST EY
CGK HATS
W
S HAUL MS
G HAUT E
S HAVE NRS
CST HAWS E
CS HAYS
A HEAD SY
SW HEAL S
C HEAP SY
S HEAR DST
CW HEAT HS
C HECK S
W HEEL S
T HEFT SY
T HEIR S
S HELL OS
W HELM S
W HELP S
RT HEME S
TW HENS
S HENT S
S HERD S
TW HERE S
T HERM AS
C HEST S
CK HETH S
KW HETS
S HEWN
CST HEWS
W
CT HICK S
C HIDE DRS
S HIED
S HIES
T HIGH ST
C HILI
CST HILL OSY
SW HIMS
CST HINS
W
CSW HIPS
S HIRE DERS
SW HIST S
CSW HITS
CS HIVE DS
CS HOCK S
S HOED
S HOER S
S HOES
S HOGS
C HOKE DSY
A HOLD S
DTW HOLE DSY
PS HONE DRSY
T HONG IS
P HONS
W HOOF S
CS HOOK ASY
W HOOP S
BS HOOT SY
CSW HOPS
ST HORN SY
CTW HOSE DLNRSY
G HOST AS
PS HOTS
S HOVE LR
CDS HOWS
C HUBS
CS HUCK S
C HUFF SY
CT HUGS
A HULL OS
CTW HUMP HSY
C HUMS
CT HUNK SY
S HUNS
S HUNT S
CT HURL SY
S HUSH
BPS HUTS
P HYLA S

DRV ICED
BDF ICES
RSV
DKP ICKY
ABH IDES
NRS
TW
S IDLE DRS
BJM IFFY
M IGGS
E IKON S
P ILEA CL
S ILEX
CM ILIA CDL
BMS ILKS
BDF ILLS
GHJ
KMN
PRS
TVW
YZ
BDF ILLY
GHS
W
T IMID EOS
J IMMY
GLP IMPS
SW
CFP INCH
W
DFG INKS
JKL
MOP
RSW
DHK INKY
LPZ
JL INNS
P INTO
CLP IONS
B IOTA S
AFH IRED
MST
W
CFH IRES
MST
VW
V IRID S
BDK IRKS
M
G IRON ESY
AL ISLE DST
J ISMS
ABD ITCH Y
FHP
W
K IWIS
S IZAR S

D JINN IS
D JINS
A JUGA L

IS KATS
O KAYS
S KEEN S
S KEET S
S KEGS
S KELP SY
S KEPS
S KIDS
S KIER S
S KILL S
E KING S
S KINK SY
S KINS
S KIPS
S KITE DRS
S KITS

BFS LABS
GP LACE DRSY
ABC LACK S
FPS
BCG LADE DNRS
CG LADS
G LADY
CFS LAGS
P LAID
BEP LAIN
S
FG LAIR DS
FS LAKE DRS
F LAKY
LU LAMA S
BF LAME DRS
C LAMP S
BCF LAMS
GS
ABE LAND S
G
AP LANE S
ACS LANG
BCF LANK Y
PS
CFS LAPS E
B LASE DRS
CFP LASH
S
CG LASS IO
BC LAST S
ABE LATE DNRX
PS
BFP LATS
S
CS LAVE DRS
B LAWN SY
BCF LAWS
S
CFP LAYS
S
BG LAZE DS
G LAZY
P LEAD SY
B LEAK SY
I LEAL
CG LEAN ST
BC LEAR NSY
FP LEAS EHT
CGS LEEK S
F LEER SY
FG LEES
FGS LEET S
C LEFT SY
B LEND S
G LENS E
B LENT O
CS LEPT A
B LESS
B LEST
B LETS
FG LEYS
S LICE
CFK LICK S
S
FP LIED
A LIEN S
FPS LIER S
FP LIES
C LIFT S
A LIKE DNRS
S LILY
C LIMB AIOSY
CGS LIME DNSY
B LIMP AS
BS LIMY
AC LINE DNRSY
CFS LING AOSY
BCP LINK SY
S
EFG LINT SY
S LIPE
BCF LIPS
S
A LIST S
BEF LITE R
FS LITS
AO LIVE DNRS
G LOAM SY
G LOBE DS
BGS LOBS
BCF LOCK S
A LOFT SY
BCF LOGS
S
O LOGY
S LOID S
AE LOIN S
AC LONE R
AFK LONG ES
AK LOOF AS
BG LOOM S
BS LOOP SY
C LOOT S
ES LOPE DRS
CFG LOPS
PS
G LORY
C LOSE LRS
FG LOSS Y
G LOST
F LOTA HS
CS LOTH
BCP LOTS
S
AC LOUD
CF LOUR SY
CFG LOUT S
CG LOVE DRS
BCF LOWN
BFG LOWS E
PS
CP LUCK SY
E LUDE S
BCF LUES
GS
BFS LUFF AS
K LUGE DRS
GPS LUGS
CFP LUMP SY
S
AGP LUMS
S
CFS LUNG EIS
CFP LUNK S
S
B LUNT S
BFP LUSH
S
EFG LUTE ADS
K LUTZ

S MACK S
I MAGE S
E MAIL ELS
A MAIN S
S MALL S
S MALT SY
S MART S
O MASA S
S MASH Y
A MASS AEY
AS MAZE DRS
S MEEK
O MEGA
S MELL S
S MELT SY
AE MEND S
S MERK S
S MEWS
A MICE
AI MIDS T
S MILE RS
AI MINE DRS
S MIRK SY
AE MIRS
A MISS Y
S MITE RS
A MITY
S MOCK S
S MOGS
S MOKE S
A MOLE S
S MOLT OS
A MORT S
ES MOTE LSTY
A MUCK SY
A MUSE DRS
S MUSH Y
S MUTS

S NAGS
S NAIL S
J NANA S
KS NAPS
S NARK SY
U NARY
K NAVE LS
S NEAP S
A NEAR S
S NECK S
K NEED SY
E NEMA S
S NIBS

S NICK S
S NIDE DS
A NILS
S NIPS
U NITE RS
KSU NITS
KS NOBS
K NOCK S
A NODE S
S NOGS
G NOME NS
S NOOK S
E NORM S
EKS NOWS
S NUBS
K NURL S

L OAFS
S OAKS
BHR OARS
S
BCR OAST S
T
L OATH S
BCD OATS
GM
S OBAS
LR OBES E
C OBIA S
CS OCAS
CS ODAS
BCL ODES
MNR
IS ODIC
BCD OFFS
T
Y OGEE S
B OGLE DRS
O OHED
BCF OILS
MNR
ST
DNR OILY
B OINK S
T OKAY S
CHJ OKES
MPS
TY
BCF OLDS
GHM
W
M OLDY
BCD OLES
HJM
PRS
TV
FP OLIO S
H OLLA S
NW OMEN S
CGH OMER S
V
V OMIT S
NP ONCE T
BCH ONES
JNP
STZ
S ONLY
M ONOS
C ONTO
BCT ONUS
P OOHS
CGH OOPS
LPW
BCF OOTS
HLM
RST
B OOZE DS
BDW OOZY
CN OPAL S
CDH OPED
LMR
T
C OPEN S
CDH OPES
LMP
RT

BCG ORAL S
HLM
FS ORBS
CF ORBY
T ORCS
F ORDO S
BCF ORES
GLM
PST
Y
P ORGY
BFM ORTS
PST
W
CDH OSES
LNP
R
F OSSA
L OTIC
LMP OTTO S
CMP OUCH
TV
FHL OURS
PST
Y
JR OUST S
BGL OUTS
PRT
CDR OVEN S
W
CHL OVER ST
MR
BCD OWED
JLM
RST
VWY
HLY OWES
BCF OWLS
HJY
DGT OWNS
BDL OWSE N
BCF OXES
GLP
CFT OYER S

AS PACE DRSY
E PACT S
S PACY
S PAIL S
S PALE ADRST
S PALL SY
O PALS Y
S PAMS
S PANG AS
S PANS Y
S PARE DORSU
S PARK AS
S PARS E
A PART SY
S PATE DNRS
S PATS Y
S PAWN S
S PAYS
AS PEAK SY
S PEAN S
S PEAR LST
S PECK SY
S PECS
A PEEK S
S PEEL S
S PEER SY
E PEES
S PELT S
SU PEND S
O PENS
S PENT
S PERM S
S PEWS
A PHIS
A PIAN OS
S PICA LS
S PICE
S PICK SY
ES PICS
S PIED

S PIER S
S PIES
S PIKE DRS
S PILE ADIS
S PILL S
OS PINE DSY
AO PING OS
S PINS
S PINY
A PISH
S PITS
S PLAT ESY
S PLAY AS
A PODS
S POKE DRSY
S POOF
S POOL S
S POON S
S POOR I
S PORE DS
AS PORT S
S POTS Y
S POUT SY
E POXY
S PRAT ES
S PRAY S
S PREE DNS
S PRIG S
A PSIS
S PUDS
S PUNK ASY
S PURS EY

S QUAD S
ES QUID S
E QUIP SU

BGT RACE DRS
CTW RACK S
BG RADS
D RAFF S
CDG RAFT S
K
T RAGI S
BCD RAGS
F
B RAID S
BDF RAIL S
GT
BDG RAIN SY
T
BCD RAKE DERS
CGT RAMP S
CDG RAMS
PT
BG RAND SY
OPW RANG EY
BCD RANK S
FPT
BG RANT S
CDG RAPE DRS
CFT RAPS
W
TW RAPT
U RARE DRS
EPU RASE DRS
BCT RASH
G RASP SY
CGI RATE DLRS
OPU
W RATH E
BDF RATS
P
BCD RAVE DLNRS
GT
BCD RAWS
BDF RAYS
GPT
BCG RAZE DERS
BDO READ DSY
T
AU REAL MS
BCD REAM S
D REAR MS

DW RECK S
B REDE DS
CU REDO NSX
C REDS
BCD REED SY
FGP
T
CG REEK SY
C REEL S
BDF REES T
GPT
D REGS
T REND S
B RENT ES
P REPS
F RESH
CDP REST S
W
A RETE M
FT RETS
TU RIAL S
A RIAS
CD RIBS
PT RICE DRS
BCP RICK S
TW
BGP RIDE RS
GI RIDS
AO RIEL S
G RIFF S
DG RIFT S
BFG RIGS
PT
BDF RILL ES
GKP
T
CGP RIME DRS
BPT RIMS
G RIMY
G RIND SY
BIW RING S
BDP RINK S
BG RINS E
G RIOT S
CGT RIPE DNRS
DGT RIPS
AFP RISE NRS
BF RISK SY
TW RITE S
F RITZ Y
D RIVE DNRST
B ROAD S
G ROAN S
P ROBE DS
BCF ROCK SY
T
C ROCS
ET RODE OS
P RODS
F ROES
B ROIL SY
P ROLE S
DT ROLL S
T ROMP S
P ROMS
B ROOD S
P ROOF S
BC ROOK SY
BGV ROOM SY
GT ROPE DRSY
ABE ROSE DST
P
BP ROSY
W ROTE S
GT ROTS
CG ROUP SY
GT ROUT EHS
DGP ROVE DNRS
T
BCF ROWS
GPT
V
DG RUBS
CT RUCK S

CP RUDE R
T RUED
T RUER S
GT RUES
G RUFF ES
DFT RUGS
B RUIN GS
T RULY
CFG RUMP S
T
AD RUMS
P RUNE S
BW RUNG S
BG RUNT SY
CD RUSE S
BC RUSH Y
B RUSK S
CT RUST SY
T RUTH S
B RUTS

T SADE S
T SADI S
U SAGE RS
E SCAR EFPSTY
AE SCOT S
U SERS
P SHAW LMNS
A SHED S
A SHES
A SIDE DS
U SING ES
A SKEW S
I SLED S
A STIR KPS
E STOP EST
T SUBA HS

S TABS
S TACK SY
S TAGS
S TAIN ST
S TAKE NRS
S TALE RS
S TALK SY
S TALL SY
S TAMP S
S TANG AOSY
S TANK AS
E TAPE DRS
A TAPS
S TARE DS
S TARS I
S TART SY
S TATE RS
S TATS
S TEAK S
S TEAL S
S TEAM S
S TEED
S TEEL S
S TELA E
S TELE SX
S TENT HSY
S TERN ES
S TETS
S TEWS
S TICK S
S TIED
S TIES
S TIFF S
SU TILE DRS
S TILL S
AS TILT HS
S TIME DRS
S TING ES
S TINT S
S TOKE DNRS
S TOLE DS
A TOLL S
A TOMS
AS TONE DRSY

AS TONY
S TOOK
S TOOL S
S TOPE DERS
S TOPS
S TORE S
S TORY
S TOSS
S TOTS
S TOUR S
S TOUT S
S TOWS
S TRAP ST
S TRAY S
AS TRIP ES
S TROP E
S TROW S
S TROY S
S TUBS
S TUCK S
S TUFF S
E TUIS
S TUMP S
S TUNG S
S TUNS
E TWEE DNT
S TYES

JK UDOS
SV UGHS
CDJ UKES
NP
Y ULAN S
LS ULUS
V ULVA S
DGJ UMBO S
BDH UMPS
JLM
PRS
T
BJ UNCO SY
JP UNTO
P UPAS
JY UPON
BC URBS
BCH URDS
NST
GPS URGE DRS
A URIC
BCD URNS
T
BT URPS
B URSA E
GK URUS
BFM USED
M USER S
BFM USES
PR
BCJ UTES
LM

A VAIL S
O VARY
A VAST SY
U VEAL SY
E VENT S
AEO VERT SU
E VERY
I VIED
I VIES
O VINE DS
AO VOID S
A VOWS

S WABS
T WAES
S WAGE DRS
S WAGS
S WAIL S
ST WAIN S
A WAIT S
A WAKE DNRS
S WALE DRS
S WANS

S WAPS
AS WARD S
AS WARE DS
S WARM S
S WART SY
AS WASH Y
ST WATS
S WAYS
T WEAK
S WEAR SY
T WEED SY
T WEEN SY
S WEEP SY
S WEER
ST WEET S
DS WELL SY
D WELT S
S WEPT
ST WIGS
ST WILL SY
DGS WINE DSY
T
AOS WING SY
S WINK S
T WINS
T WINY
S WIPE DRS
S WISH A
S WISS
T WIST S
S WITH EY
T WITS
S WIVE DRS
A WOKE N
S WORD SY
S WORE
S WORN
S WOTS

K YACK S
K YAKS
L YARD S
AP YINS
X YLEM S

A ZINE BS
A ZOIC
O ZONE DRS

New 2006

5-letter Words

K ABAKA S
K ABAYA S
CFG ABLED
T
CF ABLER
CFG ABLES T
ST
BG ABOON
BC ACHED
BCL ACHES
MNT
FLM ACING
PR
H ACKEE S
NS ACRED
N ACRES
F ACTOR S
GMP ADDED
RW
BGL ADDER S
MPS
W
DPR ADDLE DS
SW
R ADIOS
BM ADMAN
BM ADMEN
P AEONS
F AERIE DRS
DHR AFTER S
W
CEG AGERS
JLP
WY
BDG AGGER S
JLN
STW
B AGGIE S
V AGILE
CGP AGING S
RW
E AGLET S
M AGMAS
W AGONS
A AHING
R AIDED
R AIDER S
BFH AILED
JMN
RST
VW
M AIMED
M AIMER S
FHL AIRED
PW
F AIRER S
BC AIRNS
NW AIVER S
R AKEES
S ALARY
MP ALATE DS
B ALDER S
CK ALIFS
M ALIGN S
MSV ALINE DRS
T ALKIE S
CM ALLEE S
GV ALLEY S
BH ALLOT S
CFH ALLOW S
MST
W
H ALMAS
H ALOES
K ALONG
FHP ALTER S
S
C AMASS
CL AMBER SY
G AMBIT S
GRW AMBLE DRS
MS AMBOS
Y AMENS
L AMENT S
LZ AMIAS
MR AMIES
FG AMINE S
G AMINS
CDL AMPED
RTV
S AMPLE R
D AMPLY
R ANCHO RS
FMP ANGAS
S
M ANGEL S
BDG ANGER S
HMR
S
BDJ ANGLE DRS
MTW
FW ANION S
R ANKLE DST
CM ANNAS
T ANNOY S
M ANTAS
CHP ANTED
RW
M ANTES
CM ANTIC KS
M ANTIS
MTY ANTRA L
C ANYON ES
CGJ APERS
PRT
JNP APERY
R APHIS
GJR APING
T
R APPEL S
D APPLE ST
L APSES
R APTLY
H ARBOR S
F ARCED
G ARGLE DS
J ARGON S
V ARIAS
CFP ARLES
FHW ARMED
FHW ARMER S
BFH ARROW SY
MNY
CMP ARSES
P ARSON S
H ARTAL
C ARTEL S
L ARUMS
L ARVAL
P ARVOS
M ASCOT S
BCD ASHED
FGH
LMP
SW
BCD ASHES
FGH
LMP
RSW
BCM ASKED
T
M ASKER S
GJR ASPER S
BGL ASSES S
MPS
T
BT ASSET S
BCE ASTER NS
FGL
MPR
TVW
W ATAPS
B ATMAN S
L ATRIA L
C AUDAD S
GMS AUGER S
CNT AUGHT S
W
DHJ AUNTS
TV
JV AUNTY
L AURAE
L AURAS
K AURIS T
S AVANT
DHM AVENS
R
CHL AVERS E
PRS
W
V AWARD S
L AWFUL
CDH AWING
JLM
PST
Y
DFP AWNED
Y
FMR AXING
TW
T AXITE S
T AXMAN
T AXMEN
T AXONS
R AYAHS
LZ AYINS
H AZANS

A BASED
A BASER
A BASES T
A BATED
A BATES
O BENTO S
I BICES
A BIDED
A BIDER S
A BIDES
I BISES
O BLAST SY
AO BLATE
A BLAZE DRS
A BLEST
A BLOOM SY
A BLUSH
A BOARD S
A BODED
A BODES
O BOLES
O BOLUS
E BOOKS
A BORAL S
A BORTS
A BOUND S
A BROAD S
A BUSED
A BUSES

S CABBY
S CALLS
S CAMPI
S CAMPS
S CANTS
S CANTY
S CAPED
S CAPES
S CARED
S CARER S
S CARES S
S CARPS
S CARRY
E CARTE DLRS
S CARTS
S CATTY
O CELLI
S CENTS
E CHARD S
S CIONS
Y CLEPT
S COFFS
S COLDS
IS CONES
I CONIC S
S COOCH
S COOPS
S COOTS
S COPED
S COPES
S CORED
S CORER S
S CORES
S CORIA
AS CORNS
S COUTH S
S COWED
S COWLS
S CRAGS
S CRAMS
S CRAPE DS
S CRAPS
S CRAWL SY
S CREAK SY
S CREAM SY
S CREED S
S CREWS
S CRIED
S CRIES
S CRIMP SY
A CROSS E
S CUFFS
S CULCH
S CULLS
S CURFS
S CURRY
S CURVY
S CUTCH
A CUTER
AS CUTES TY

I DEALS
A DEEMS
A DRIFT SY
A DROIT S
E DUCES
E DUCTS

M EAGER S
B EAGLE DST
M EAGRE S
FGN EARED
RST
P EARLS
DNP EARLY
Y
LY EARNS
DH EARTH SY
CFL EASED
T
TW EASEL S
CFL EASES
PT
BFL EASTS
Y
BN EATEN
BFH EATER SY
NS
DHL EAVED
RW
DHL EAVES
RW
W EBBED
R EBOOK S
LPT ECHED
L ECHES
O EDEMA S
HKW EDGED
HL EDGER S
HKL EDGES
SW
AS EDILE S
DRS EDUCE DS
D EDUCT S
P EERIE R
L EGERS
BS EGGAR S
BKL EGGED
PV
K EGGER S
R EGRET S
HW EIGHT HSY
DR EJECT AS
D EKING
R ELAND S
DGR ELATE DRS
V
GMW ELDER S
S ELECT S
P ELITE S
D ELUDE DRS
D ELVER S
DHP ELVES
S
R EMAIL S
M EMBER S
R EMEND S
DR EMITS
H EMMER S
DGR EMOTE DRS
S ENATE S
BFM ENDED
PRS
TVW
BFG ENDER S
LMR
STV
V ENDUE DS
CRT ENTER AS
V
GS ENTRY
T ENURE DS
R ENVOI S
T EPEES
KT ERNES
R EROSE S
T ERROR S
PV ERSES
A ERUGO S
M ESNES
CFJ ESSES
MNY
FJN ESTER S
PRT
WYZ
R ETAPE S
ANT ETHER S
W
M ETHYL S
S EVENS
R EVERT S
R EVERY
DK EVILS
R EVOKE DRS
HS EWERS
R EXINE S
HSV EXING
S EXIST S
K EYING

A FIELD S
A FLAME DNRS
A FLOAT SY
A FRESH
A FRITS

A GAMAS
A GAMIC
A GAPES
A GATES
A GENES
A GENTS
E GESTS
A GHAST
A GISTS
O GIVES
A GLARE DS
A GLEAM SY
A GOUTY
A GREED SY
A GREES

STW HACKS
S HADED
S HADES
S HAFTS
C HAIRS
S HAKES
SW HALED
TW HALER SU
SW HALES T
S HAMES
CSW HAMMY
C HANCE S
S HANDY
BCW HANGS
ST HANKS
C HANTS
CS HARDS
CS HARED
CS HARES
CS HARKS
CT HARMS
S HARPS
S HARPY
CG HARRY
C HARTS
C HASTE DNS
T HATCH
S HAUGH S
S HAULS
C HAUNT S
S HAVEN S
S HAVER S
S HAVES
CST HAWED
C HAZAN S
SW HEALS
C HEAPS
S HEARS E
S HEATH SY
CW HEATS
S HEAVE DNRS
C HECKS
C HEDER S
W HEELS
W HEEZE DS
T HEFTS
T HEIRS
T HEIST S
S HELLS
W HELMS
W HELPS
S HELVE DS
RT HEMES
C HEMIC
TW HENCE
S HERDS
TW HERES Y
T HERMS
CSW HERRY
C HESTS
CK HETHS
S HEUCH S
S HEUGH S
CS HEWED
CS HEWER S
CT HICKS
C HIDED
C HIDER S
C HIDES
T HIGHS
CST HILLS
C HILLY
W HINGE DRS
C HINKY
SW HINNY
C HINTS
CW HIPPY
S HIRES
SW HISTS
CS HIVES
CS HOCKS
S HOERS
C HOKED
C HOKES
C HOKEY
A HOLDS
T HOLED
DTW HOLES
C HOLLA S
W HOLLY
P HONED
P HONES T
P HONEY S
T HONGS
P HOOEY S
W HOOFS
CS HOOKS
D HOOLY
W HOOPS
BS HOOTS
C HOPPY
C HORAL
T HORNS
T HORNY
A HORSE DSY
C HOSEN
C HOSES
G HOSTS
C HOUSE DLRS
S HOVEL S
S HOVER S
C HUBBY
CS HUCKS
C HUFFS
C HUFFY
CTW HUMPS
CT HUNKS
C HUNKY
S HUNTS
CT HURLS
S HYING

D ICIER
DRV ICING S
BDK ICKER S
LNP
STW
R ICTUS
S IDLED
S IDLER S
S IDLES T
DFG IGGED
JPR
WZ
E IKONS
P ILEUM
P ILEUS
F ILIAL
CM ILIUM
BFG ILLER
HKM
STW
L IMBED S
GLP IMPED E
W
DJL IMPLY
PS
W INDOW S
DJM INGLE S
ST
MP INION S
DFJ INKED
KLO
PW
JLP INKER S
STW
TW INKLE S
BDF INNED
GPS
TW
DGP INNER S
STW
HLM INTER NS
STW
BP IONIC S

New 2006

B IOTAS
T IRADE S
P IRATE R
AFH IRING
MST
W
D IRKED
G IRONS
AM ISLED
AL ISLES
T ISSUE DRS
BFP ITCHY
W
CDE ITHER
HLM
TWZ
C IVIES
S IZARS

D JEBEL S
D JINNI S
D JINNS

S KEENS
S KEETS
S KELPS
S KERRY
S KETCH
S KIDDY
S KIERS
S KILLS
S KINKS
S KITED
S KITES

P LACED
P LACER S
GP LACES
BCF LACKS
PS
B LADED
B LADER S
BCG LADES
FG LAIRS
FS LAKED
FS LAKER S
FS LAKES
LU LAMAS
BF LAMED HS
BF LAMER
BF LAMES T
C LAMPS
G LANCE DRST
AEG LANDS
FP LANES
C LANKY
E LAPSE DRS
BFG LARES
A LARUM S
BC LASTS
KS LATCH
AEP LATED
S
P LATEN ST
EPS LATER
S LAVED
CS LAVER S
CS LAVES
BCF LAWED
F LAXES T
CFP LAYED
S
FPS LAYER S
BG LAZED
BG LAZES
BP LEACH Y
P LEADS
B LEAKS
CG LEANS
BC LEARS
B LEARY
P LEASE DRS
CS LEAVE DNRS
FPS LEDGE RS

F LEDGY
F LEECH
CGS LEEKS
F LEERS
FGS LEETS
C LEFTS
E LEGIT S
B LENDS
F LENSE DS
F LETCH
C LEVER S
A LEVIN S
C LEVIS
FIP LEXES
E LICIT
CFK LICKS
S
A LIENS
FP LIERS
S LIEVE R
C LIFTS
ABF LIGHT S
PS
C LIMBS
GS LIMED
CGS LIMES
B LIMEY S
B LIMPS Y
A LINED
A LINER S
AC LINES
O LINGO
CFS LINGS
C LINGY
BCP LINKS
S
S LINKY
EFG LINTS
FG LINTY
FS LIPPY
B LITHE R
S LIVER SY
O LIVES T
G LOAMS
GS LOBBY
G LOBED
G LOBES
BCF LOCKS
S LOGAN S
C LOGGY
S LOIDS
AE LOINS
C LONER S
FK LONGS
BF LOOEY S
K LOOFS
BF LOOIE S
BG LOOMS
BS LOOPS
C LOOTS
ES LOPED
ES LOPER S
ES LOPES
FGS LOPPY
F LORAL
C LOSER S
C LOSES
FG LOSSY
F LOTAS
B LOTTO S
CPS LOUGH S
CF LOURS
F LOURY
B LOUSE DS
B LOUSY
CFG LOUTS
G LOVED
CGP LOVER S
CG LOVES
BFG LOWED
PS
BFG LOWER SY
PS

S LOWLY
CP LUCKS
P LUCKY
E LUDES
BFS LUFFS
K LUGED
K LUGES
CFP LUMPS
S
CG LUMPY
G LUNCH
BP LUNGE DERS
CFP LUNKS
B LUNTS
EF LUTED
EFG LUTES
F LUXES
FP LYING S

S MACKS
I MAGES
E MAILS
S MALLS
S MALTS
S MARTS
A MAZED
AS MAZES
S MELLS
S MELTS
AE MENDS
O MENTA L
E MERGE DERS
S MERKS
S MIDGE ST
A MIDST S
S MILER S
S MILES
AI MINES
S MIRKS
S MIRKY
S MITER S
S MITES
S MOCKS
S MOGGY
S MOKES
A MOLES T
S MOLTS
S MOOCH
A MORAL ES
E MOTES
A MOUNT S
A MUCKS
A MUSED
A MUSER S
A MUSES
S MUTCH

S NAGGY
S NAILS
S NAKED
J NANAS
S NAPPY
S NARES
S NARKS
S NARKY
S NATCH
E NATES
G NATTY
K NAVES
S NEAPS
A NEARS
S NECKS
E NEMAS
I NERTS
S NICKS
K NIGHT SY
S NIPPY
U NITER SY
U NITES
KS NOBBY
K NOCKS
A NODAL

A NODES
G NOMES
S NOOKS
G NOSES
KS NUBBY
K NURLS

RS OARED
BCR OASTS
T
BC OATER S
LS OAVES
C OBIAS
GH OBOES
T OCHER SY
CDH OCKER S
LMR
L OCULI
CDF ODDER
N
PS ODIUM S
BD OFFED
CDG OFFER S
S OFTEN
LS OFTER
Y OGEES
B OGLES
O OHING
BCD OILED
FMR
ST
BCM OILER S
T
B OINKS
T OKAYS
GH OLDEN
BCF OLDER
GHM
PS
FP OLIOS
H OLLAS
O OLOGY
BCS OMBER S
HS OMBRE S
CGH OMERS
V
V OMITS
GR ONION SY
CGI ONIUM
P OOHED
B OOZED
B OOZES
CN OPALS
C OPENS
CDH OPING
LMR
T
BCG ORALS
M
B ORATE DS
S ORBED
BC ORDER S
M ORGAN AS
DFW ORMER S
M ORRIS
CHN OSIER S
R
C OSMIC S
BMN OTHER S
PT
C OTTAR S
CDH OTTER S
JLP
RT
LMP OTTOS
BDF OUGHT S
NS
BJP OUNCE S
H OUSEL S
JR OUSTS
LPR OUTED
T
CPR OUTER S
ST
C OVARY

CDW OVENS
CHL OVERS
MR
C OVERT
B OVINE S
BCD OWING
JLM
RST
VWY
H OWLET S
DG OWNED
D OWNER S
FT OYERS

S PACED
S PACER S
S PACES
S PACEY
E PACTS
S PAILS
S PALES T
S PALLS
E PARCH
S PARED
S PARER S
S PARES
S PARGE DST
S PARKS
S PARRY
S PARSE CDRS
U PASES
S PATES
S PAVIN GS
S PAWNS
S PAYED
S PEAKS
S PEANS
S PEARS
S PECKS
S PEELS
S PEERS
S PEISE DS
S PELTS
S PENCE L
SU PENDS
S PERMS
AE PICAL
S PICAS
S PICKS
A PIECE DRS
S PIERS
S PIKED
S PIKER S
S PIKES
S PILED
S PILES
S PILLS
OS PINED
OS PINES
S PINNY
S PINTO S
S PLASH Y
S PLATS
S PLAYS
U PLINK S
S POKED
S POKES
S POOLS
S POONS
S PORED
S PORES
S PORTS
E POSES
S POTTY
S POUTS
S PRANG S
U PRATE DRS
S PRATS
S PRAYS
S PREES
S PRIER S
S PRIGS
S PRINT S

U PRISE DS
U PROSE DRS
S PRYER S
S PUNKS
S PUNKY
S PURGE DRS
O PUSES

S QUADS
S QUARE
S QUARK S
S QUASH
E QUATE
ES QUIDS
S QUILL S
S QUINT AES
E QUIPS
S QUIRE DS
S QUIRT S

A RABIC
BGT RACED
BT RACER S
BGT RACES
CTW RACKS
D RAFFS
CDG RAFTS
K
D RAGEE S
BCD RAGGY
B RAIDS
BDF RAILS
GT
BDG RAINS
T
BG RAINY
BFP RAISE DRS
B RAKED
BCD RAKES
O RALLY E
CGT RAMPS
PT RANCE S
BC RANCH O
BG RANDS
B RANDY
GO RANGE DRS
O RANGY
BCF RANKS
PT
BG RANTS
CD RAPED
D RAPER S
CDG RAPES
T
U RARES T
E RASED
E RASER S
CEP RASES
U
G RASPS
C RATCH
CGO RATED
P
CFG RATER S
IKP
CGO RATES
PU
B RATTY
BCG RAVED
GT RAVEL S
CG RAVEN S
BCG RAVER S
BCG RAVES
T
BD RAWER
BCD RAWLY
P RAXES
BDF RAYED
GP
C RAYON S
BCG RAZED
BG RAZER S
BCG RAZES
BP REACH

P REACT S
BDO READS
T
B READY
BCD REAMS
P REARM S
D REARS
G REAVE DRS
P REBID S
P REBUY S
DW RECKS
P RECUT S
B REDES
U REDIA ELS
CU REDOS
P REDRY
BCG REEDS
G REEDY
BC REEKS
C REELS
F REEST S
P REFER S
P REFIX
B REGMA
P REMAN DS
P REMIX T
T RENDS
B RENTS
P REPAY S
P RESET S
CPW RESTS
P RETAX
W RETCH
BT REVET S
P REVUE S
BC REWED S
P REXES
TU RIALS
BT RIBES
PT RICED
P RICER S
PT RICES
BCP RICKS
TW
A RIDER S
BGI RIDES
P
BF RIDGE DLS
AO RIELS
G RIFFS
T RIFLE DRS
DG RIFTS
ABF RIGHT OSY
W
F RIGID
A RILED
G RILLE DST
BDF RILLS
GKP
T
GP RIMED
PT RIMER S
CGP RIMES
G RINDS
BW RINGS
BDP RINKS
G RIOTS
G RIPED
G RIPER
CGT RIPES T
A RISEN
ABC RISES
FIK
P
BF RISKS
F RISKY
FW RITES
D RIVEN
D RIVER S
D RIVES
GPT RIVET S
B ROACH
B ROADS
G ROANS

P ROBED
P ROBES
BCF ROCKS
T
E RODES
BD ROGUE DS
B ROILS
P ROLES
DT ROLLS
T ROMPS
B ROODS
P ROOFS
BC ROOKS
BGV ROOMS
B ROOMY
G ROPED
GP ROPER SY
GT ROPES
P ROSED
BEP ROSES
C ROTCH E
T ROUGH SY
AG ROUND S
CG ROUPS
C ROUPY
ACG ROUSE DRS
C ROUTE DRS
D ROUTH S
GT ROUTS
DGP ROVED
P ROVEN
DPT ROVER S
DGP ROVES
T
C ROWDY
BCT ROWED
T ROWEL S
CGP ROWER S
GT ROWTH S
G RUBBY
CT RUCKS
C RUDDY
C RUDER Y
T RUFFE DS
G RUFFS
F RUGAL
T RUING
B RUINS
C RUMMY
CFG RUMPS
T
P RUNES
BG RUNTS
C RURAL
CDU RUSES
B RUSHY
CT RUSTS
CT RUSTY
T RUTHS

U SABLE S
T SADES
T SADIS MT
U SAGES T
I SATIN GSY
E SCAPE DS
E SCARP HS
E SCARS
A SCEND S
A SCENT S
AE SCOTS
E SCUDO
P SHAWS
A SHIER S
A SHORE DS
A SIDES
A SLANT SY
A SLEEP SY
I SLING S
A SLOPE DRS
A SLOSH Y
T SORES T
E SPIED
E SPIES
A SPIRE ADMS
E SPRIT ESZ
E STATE DRS
O STEAL S
A STERN AS
A STONY
E STOPS
AE STRAY S
E STRUM AS
U SURER
A SWARM S
A SWIRL SY
A SWOON SY

S TABLE DST
S TACKS
S TAINS
S TAKES
S TALER S
S TALES
S TALKS
S TALKY
S TALLS
E TALON S
S TAMPS
S TANGS
S TANKS
ES TAPES
S TARED
S TARES
S TARRY
S TARTS
S TATER S
S TATES
S TEAKS
S TEALS
S TEAMS
S TEELS
S TELAE
S TELES
AS TELIC
S TENCH
S TENTS
E TERNE S
S TERNS
S TEWED
E THANE S
S TICKS
S TIFFS
S TILES
S TILLS
S TILTS
S TIMES
S TINGS
S TINTS
O TITIS
E TOILE DRST
S TOKED
S TOKER S
S TOKES
S TOLED O
S TOLES
A TOLLS
A TONAL
AS TONED
AS TONER S
AS TONES
S TONEY
A TONIC S
S TOOLS
S TOPED
S TOPER S
S TOPES
A TOPIC S
S TORES
S TOURS
S TOUTS
S TOWED
S TRAIN S
S TRAIT S
S TRAPS
S TRASS
S TRAYS
S TRESS Y
S TREWS
A TRIAL S
S TRICK SY
S TRIKE S
S TRIPE S
S TRIPS
S TRODE
S TROKE DS
S TROLL SY
S TROVE RS
S TROWS
S TROYS
S TRUCK S
S TUBBY
S TUFFS
S TUMPS
A TWAIN S
A TWEEN SY
S TYING
A TYPIC

BJM UDDER S
R
Y ULANS
V ULVAS
CDL UMBER S
N
DGJ UMBOS
BDH UMPED
JLM
PT
N UNCLE S
BJ UNCOS
FS UNDER
B UNION S
DG UNITE DRS
R UNLET
S UNLIT
G UNMAN S
S UNSET S
A UNTIE DS
CDP UPPED
ST
CS UPPER S
C URARE S
CO URARI S
AC URATE S
RT URBAN E
GPS URGED
BPS URGER S
GPS URGES
BC URIAL S
MP URINE S
B URPED
B URSAE
M USERS
BGL USHER S
MPR
BFM USING
FR UTILE
BCG UTTER S
MNP

A VAILS
K VASES
A VAUNT SY
A VENGE DS
E VENTS
A VENUE S
A VERSE DRST
AE VERTS
K VETCH
E VILER
O VINES
AO VOIDS
A VOUCH
A VOWED
A VOWER S

S WAGED
S WAGER S
S WAGES
S WAILS
ST WAINS
A WAITS
A WAKED
A WAKEN S
A WAKES
S WALES
AS WARDS
S WARMS
S WARTY
S WATCH
S WEARS
A WEARY
T WEEDS
T WEEDY
T WEENS Y
ST WEENY
S WEEPS
S WEEPY
ST WEETS
A WEIGH ST
DS WELLS
A WHILE DS
A WHIRL SY
T WIGGY
ST WILLS
DT WINED
DT WINES
S WINGS
S WINGY
S WINKS
S WIPED
S WIPES
T WISTS
ST WITCH Y
S WITHE DRS
S WIVED
S WIVES
A WOKEN
S WOOPS
S WOOSH
S WORDS
S WOUND S

A XENIC

K YACKS
C YESES
X YLEMS

A ZINES
A ZONAL
O ZONES

6-letter Words

K ABAKAS
K ABAYAS
B ABYING
BC ACHING
H ACKEES
T ACNODE S
FPT ACTION S
F ACTORS
FT ACTUAL
V ACUITY
GLM ADDERS
PW
GMP ADDING
RW
DPR ADDLED
SW
DPR ADDLES
SW
F AERIES T
HRW AFTERS
H AGGADA HS
BDG AGGERS
JLN
STW
BJR AGGIES
P AGINGS
E AGLETS
M AGNATE S
R AIDERS
R AIDING
BFH AILING
JMN
RST
VW
M AIMERS
M AIMING
F AIREST
H AIRIER
FLP AIRING S
W
F AIRWAY S
W AIVERS
MP ALATES
V ALGOID
M ALIGNS
MSV ALINES
T ALIPED S
T ALKIES
CM ALLEES
GV ALLEYS
DGR ALLIED
ST
BDG ALLIES
RST
W
GP ALLIUM S
B ALLOTS
FGH ALLOWS
MST
W
FHP ALTERS
S
CL AMBERS
G AMBITS
GRW AMBLED
GR AMBLER S
GRW AMBLES
L AMENTS
FG AMINES
CDL AMPING
RTV
S AMPLER
W AMUSES
B ANALLY
R ANCHOS
P ANELED
M ANGELS
BDG ANGERS
HMR
S
DJM ANGLED
TW
DJM ANGLER S
TW
BDJ ANGLES
MTW
FW ANIONS
R ANKLED
R ANKLES
T ANNOYS
P ANTHER S
CHP ANTING S
RW
T ANTRUM S
C ANYONS
N APHTHA E
H APLITE S
R APPELS
D APPLES
P APPOSE DRS
P ARABLE S
H ARBORS
H ARBOUR S
MP ARCHED
M ARCHER SY
LMP ARCHES
F ARCING
M ARGENT S
G ARGLED
G ARGLES
J ARGONS
P ARISES
B ARISTA ES
FHW ARMERS
H ARMFUL S
FHW ARMING S
C AROUSE DRS
BC ARRACK S
W ARRANT
BFH ARROWS
MNY
M ARROWY
P ARSONS
C ARTELS
PTW ARTIER
T ARTILY
N ASCENT S
M ASCOTS
CDW ASHIER
BCD ASHING
FGH
LMP
SW
M ASKERS
BCG ASKING S
MT
GJR ASPERS E
RW ASPISH
W ASSAIL S
BT ASSETS
B ASSIST S
EP ASTERN
BCE ASTERS
GLM
PRT
W
G ASTRAL S
N ATRIUM S
FW ATTEST S
L AUDING S
GS AUGERS
NW AUGHTS
V AUNTIE S
G AUNTLY
H AUTEUR S
V AWARDS
JL AWLESS
DFP AWNING S
Y
M AXILLA ERS
T AXITES
W AXLIKE

A BASHED
A BASHES
A BASING
A BATING
O BENTOS
A BETTED
A BETTER S
A BETTOR S
A BIDERS
A BIDING
A BIOTIC S
O BLASTS
A BODING S
A BOUGHT
A BOUNDS
A BREAST S
A BRIDGE DS
A BROACH
A BUBBLE DRS
A BUSING S
A BUTTED
A BUTTER SY
A BYSSAL

S CABBED
S CAMPED
S CAMPER S
S CANNED
S CANNER SY
S CANTED
S CANTER S
A CANTHI
S CARERS
O CARINA ELS
S CARING
S CARPED
S CARPER S
S CARTED
E CARTES
S CARVES
S CATTED
A CAUDAL
O CELLAR S
A CERATE DS
A CEROUS
E CHARDS
A CHIRAL
Y CLEPED
A CLINIC S
S COFFER S
S COLDER
S COLLOP S
S COOPED
S COOPER SY
S COOTER S
S COPING S
S COPULA ERS
S CORERS
S CORING
AS CORNED
S CORNER S
E COTYPE S
S COUTER S
S COUTHS
S COWING
S COWLED
S CRAGGY
S CRAPED
S CRAPES
S CRAPPY
S CRATCH
S CRAWLS
S CRAWLY
S CREAKS
S CREAKY
S CREAMS
O CREATE DS
S CREEDS
S CREWED
S CRIMPS
S CRIMPY
S CRUNCH Y
S CRYING

S CUFFED
S CULLED
S CULLER S
S CULTCH
S CUMMER S
S CUNNER S
S CUPPER S
A CUTELY
A CUTEST
S CUTTER S
S CUTTLE DS
A CYCLIC

A DEEMED
O DONATE DS

B EAGLES
FT EARFUL S
BFG EARING S
HNR
STW
LY EARNED
LY EARNER S
DH EARTHS
TW EASELS
CFL EASING
T
F EASTER NS
BHS EATERS
BHS EATING S
W EBBING
R EBOOKS
LP ECHING
NT EDDIES
O EDEMAS
HL EDGERS
HLS EDGIER
W
HKW EDGING S
A EDILES
DRS EDUCED
DRS EDUCES
D EDUCTS
BL EERIER
L EERILY
BS EGGARS
K EGGERS
BKL EGGING
PV
A EGISES
R EGRESS
R EGRETS
H EIGHTH S
HW EIGHTS
W EIGHTY
N EITHER
D EJECTA
DR EJECTS
R ELANDS
R ELAPSE DS
BDG ELATED
R
R ELATER S
DGR ELATES
GMW ELDERS
S ELECTS
S ELFISH
PV ELITES
D ELUDED
D ELUDER S
D ELUDES
D ELVERS
R EMAILS
M EMBERS
R EMENDS
DR EMERGE DS
N EMESES
N EMESIS
H EMMERS
D EMOTED
R EMOTER S
DGR EMOTES
T ENABLE DRS

PS ENATES
V ENATIC
BFG ENDERS
LMR
STV
BFL ENDING S
MPR
STV
W
V ENDUES
T ENFOLD S
K ENOSIS
PT ENSILE DS
C ENSURE DRS
V ENTAIL S
CRT ENTERS
V
T ENURED
T ENURES
R ENVOIS
A EOLIAN
N EOLITH S
A EONIAN
P EONISM S
DR EPOSES
T ERBIUM S
X EROSES
CX EROTIC AS
H ERRING
T ERRORS
A ERUGOS
GRT ESTATE DS
FJN ESTERS
PRT
WZ
V ESTRAL
O ESTRIN S
O ESTRUM S
O ESTRUS
R ETAPES
FLR ETCHED
T
F ETCHER S
FKL ETCHES
RV
M ETHANE S
ATW ETHERS
M ETHOXY L
M ETHYLS
R EVERTS
R EVILER
R EVOKED
R EVOKER S
R EVOKES
DR EVOLVE DRS
R EXINES
S EXISTS
S EXTANT

A FEARED

A GAINST
A GAMETE S
A GENTRY
A GINNER S
A GROUND S

STW HACKED
W HACKER S
S HACKLE DRS
S HADING
S HAFTED
S HAGGED
C HAIRED
TW HALERS
W HALING
C HALLAH S
CS HALLOT H
S HALLOW S
C HALUTZ
SW HAMMED
S HAMMER S
C HAMPER S
C HANCES

CW HANGED
C HANGER S
ST HANKED
T HANKER S
C HANTED
CW HAPPED
CS HARING
CS HARKED
C HARMED
C HARMER S
S HARPED
S HARPER S
C HASTEN S
C HATTED
CPS HATTER S
S HAUGHS
S HAULED
C HAUNTS
S HAVERS
S HAVING
CST HAWING
C HAZANS
C HAZZAN S
C HEAPER S
S HEARER S
C HEATED
CT HEATER S
S HEATHS
S HEAVED
S HEAVES
C HEDERS
W HEELED
W HEELER S
W HEEZED
W HEEZES
T HEISTS
S HELLED
S HELLER ISY
W HELMED
W HELPED
S HELVED
S HELVES
TW HEREAT
TW HEREBY
TW HEREIN
TW HEREOF
TW HEREON
TW HERETO
T HERMAE
T HERMIT S
S HEUCHS
S HEUGHS
CS HEWERS
CS HEWING
C HIDDEN
C HIDERS
C HIDING S
CS HILLED
C HILLER S
W HINGED
W HINGER S
W HINGES
CSW HIPPED
CSW HIPPER
C HIPPIE RS
W HISTED
TW HITHER
CW HITTER S
CS HOCKED
S HOCKER S
S HODDEN S
S HOEING
S HOGGED
C HOKIER
C HOKING
T HOLING
W HOLISM S
C HOLLAS
P HONEYS
P HONIED
P HONING
W HOOFED

W HOOPED
W HOOPER S
W HOOPLA S
S HOOTER S
CSW HOPPED
CSW HOPPER S
C HORDED
T HORNED
G HOSTED
G HOSTLY
S HOTTED
C HOUSED
C HOUSER S
C HOUSES
S HOVELS
S HOVERS
C HUCKLE S
C HUFFED
C HUGGED
C HUGGER S
C HUMMED
CTW HUMPED
T HUMPER S
S HUNTED
CS HUNTER S
C HUPPAH S
S HUSHED
S HUSHES
C HUTZPA HS

D ICIEST
BDK ICKERS
LNP
TW
DKP ICKIER
S IDLERS
S IDLING
M IFFIER
BDF IGGING
GJP
RWZ
DLS IGNIFY
L IGNITE DRS
S IGNORE DRS
S ILEXES
T ILLITE S
GJ IMMIES
GLP IMPING ES
W
W IMPISH
DPR IMPLED
W
CPW INCHED
PW INCHER S
CFP INCHES
W
Z INCITE DRS
L INDIES
W INDIGO S
W INDOWS
P INFOLD S
DJM INGLES
ST
MP INIONS
JLP INKERS
STW
DHK INKIER
DFJ INKING
KLO
PSW
TW INKLES S
P INNATE
DGP INNERS
STW
BDF INNING S
GPR
STW
HLM INTERS
STW
B IONICS
L IONISE DS
L IONIZE DRS
T IRADES
D IREFUL
E IRENIC S

D IRKING
T ISSUED
T ISSUES
BDH ITCHED
PW
ABD ITCHES
FHP
W
G IZZARD S

D JEBELS

S KELPED
S KELTER S
S KIDDED
S KIDDER S
S KILLED
S KINKED
S KIPPED
S KIPPER S
S KITING
S KITTLE DRS

P LACERS
G LACIER
P LACING S
BCF LACKED
S
BCS LACKER S
BG LADDER S
B LADERS
B LADING S
CFS LAGGED
F LAGGER S
G LAIRED
FS LAKERS
F LAKIER
FS LAKING S
C LAMBER ST
BF LAMING
CFS LAMMED
C LAMPED
P LANATE D
G LANCED
G LANCER S
G LANCES
BS LANDER S
BF LANKER
B LANKLY
P LANNER S
CFS LAPPED
CFS LAPPER S
E LAPSED
E LAPSES
A LARUMS
CFP LASHED
S
CFP LASHER S
S
CFP LASHES
S
CG LASSES
G LASSIE S
C LASSIS
B LASTED
BP LASTER S
P LATENS
BS LATHER SY
P LATINA S
F LATTEN S
BCF LATTER
P
CS LAVERS
S LAVING
S LAVISH
BCF LAWING S
FPS LAYERS
CFP LAYING
S
P LAYOFF S
G LAZIER
G LAZILY
BG LAZING
P LEADED

P LEADER S
B LEAKER S
CG LEANED
CG LEANER S
C LEANLY
P LEASED
P LEASER S
P LEASES
CS LEAVED
C LEAVER S
CS LEAVES
F LECHES
E LECTOR S
P LEDGER S
FPS LEDGES
F LEERED
E LEGIST S
E LEGITS
BS LENDER S
F LENSED
F LENSES
B LESSER
P LESSOR S
A LEVINS
P LIABLE
C LICHES
CFS LICKED
CFS LICKER S
ABF LIGHTS
PS
C LIMBED
C LIMBER S
S LIMIER
GS LIMING
GS LIMMER S
S LIMPSY
A LINERS
CFS LINGER S
A LINING S
BCP LINKED
S
BCP LINKER S
FG LINTED
BCF LIPPED
S
CFS LIPPER S
G LISTEN S
BGK LISTER S
BS LITHER
FGS LITTER SY
CS LIVERS
G LOBATE D
B LOBBED
CS LOBBER S
G LOBULE S
BCF LOCKED
BC LOCKER S
S LOGANS
CFS LOGGED
BCF LOGGER S
S
C LONERS
BG LOOMED
B LOOPED
B LOOPER S
ES LOPERS
ES LOPING
CFG LOPPED
PS
F LOPPER S
G LORIES
C LOSERS
C LOSING S
FG LOSSES
BCP LOTTED
S
BPS LOTTER SY
CPS LOUGHS
CF LOURED
B LOUSED
B LOUSES
CFG LOUTED
CGP LOVERS

G LOVING
P LOWBOY S
BFG LOWERS
P
F LOWERY
S LOWEST
BFG LOWING S
PS
S LOWISH
BCF LUBBER S
S
CP LUCKED
BFS LUFFED
GPS LUGGED
PS LUGGER S
K LUGING
CPS LUMBER S
A LUMINA L
F LUMMOX
CFP LUMPED
S
P LUMPEN S
P LUMPER S
BP LUNGED
BP LUNGER S
BP LUNGES
CFP LUNKER S
B LUNTED
BFS LUSHED
BFP LUSHER
BFP LUSHES T
S
P LUSHLY
BCF LUSTER S
G LUTEAL
EF LUTING S
F LUTIST S
K LUTZES
F LYINGS

E MAILED
S MARTED
S MARTEN S
S MASHED
S MASHER S
S MASHES
A MASSED
A MASSES
S MATTER SY
A MAZING
S MELLED
S MELTED
S MELTER S
AE MENDED
AE MENDER S
O MENTAL
O MENTUM
A MERCER SY
A MERCES
E MERGED
E MERGES
O MICRON S
S MIDGES
O MIKRON S
S MILERS
S MIRKER
S MITERS
S MITTEN S
S MOCKED
S MOLDER S
A MONGST
S MOTHER SY
AE MOTION S
E MOTIVE DS
A MOUNTS
S MUGGER S
A MUSERS
S MUSHED
S MUSHES
A MUSING S

S NAGGED
S NAILED

O **NANISM** S
KS **NAPPED**
KS **NAPPER** S
E **NATION** S
A **NEARED**
U **NEATEN** S
S **NIBBED**
S **NICKED**
S **NICKER** S
S **NIFFER** S
S **NIGGLE** DRS
K **NIGHTS**
S **NIPPED**
S **NIPPER** S
U **NITERS**
K **NOCKED**
S **NOGGED**
A **NOTHER**
K **NURLED**

RS **OARING**
BC **OATERS**
L **OBELIA** S
T **OCHERS**
CDH **OCKERS**
LMR
JL **OCULAR** S
L **OCULUS**
PS **ODIUMS**
CDG **OFFERS**
BCD **OFFING** S
S **OFTEST**
BCM **OILERS**
T
R **OILIER**
BCF **OILING**
MRS
T'
B **OINKED**
BCG **OLDEST**
C **OLDISH**
BC **OMBERS**
H **OMBRES**
LMT **OMENTA** L
R **ONIONS**
BNT **ONUSES**
BDN **OODLES**
P
Z **OOGENY**
P **OOHING**
Z **OOLOGY**
W **OORALI** S
BW **OOZIER**
BW **OOZILY**
B **OOZING**
C **ORACLE** S
M **ORALLY**
B **ORATED**
B **ORATES**
S **ORBING**
BC **ORDERS**
B **ORDURE** S
M **ORGANS**
P **ORGIES**
F **ORGONE** S
DFW **ORMERS**
M **ORPHIC**
H **OSIERS**
HJ **OSTLER** S
BMP **OTHERS**
C **OTTARS**
CDJ **OTTERS**
LPR
T
CDM **OUCHED**
PTV
CDM **OUCHES**
PRT
V
N **OUGHTS**
BJP **OUNCES**
H **OUSELS**
JR **OUSTED**
JR **OUSTER** S

CPR **OUTERS**
ST
LPR **OUTING** S
T
CH **OVERED**
L **OVERLY**
B **OVINES**
H **OWLETS**
D **OWNERS**
DG **OWNING**
BF **OXLIKE**
F **OXTAIL** S
R **OYSTER** S

S **PACERS**
S **PACIER**
O **PACIFY**
S **PACING**
S **PALLED**
S **PANNED**
S **PANNER** S
S **PARERS**
S **PARGED**
S **PARGES**
S **PARING** S
S **PARKED**
S **PARKER** S
S **PARRED**
S **PARSER** S
S **PARTAN** S
S **PATTED**
S **PATTER** NS
S **PAVINS**
S **PAWNED**
S **PAWNER** S
S **PAYING**
S **PECKED**
S **PEELED**
S **PEERED**
S **PEISES**
S **PELTER** S
U **PENDED**
A **PHASIC**
A **PHONIC** S
A **PHOTIC** S
S **PIKERS**
S **PIKING**
S **PILING** S
S **PILLED**
S **PINIER**
O **PINING**
O **PINION** S
S **PINNER** S
S **PINTOS**
S **PITTED**
S **PLASHY**
S **PLAYED**
A **PLENTY**
U **PLIGHT** S
U **PLINKS**
S **POKING**
S **PONGED**
S **POOLED**
S **POOLER** S
S **PORING**
S **PORTED**
S **PORTER** S
O **POSSUM** S
S **POTTED**
S **POTTER** SY
S **POUTED**
S **POUTER** S
U **PRAISE** DRS
S **PRANGS**
U **PRATED**
U **PRATES**
S **PRAYED**
S **PRAYER** S
U **PREACH** Y
S **PRIEST** S
S **PRINTS**
U **PRISES**
S **PUNKIE** RS

S **PURGES**
S **PURRED**
S **PUTTER** S

S **QUARKS**
S **QUILLS**
S **QUINTS**
S **QUIRED**
S **QUIRES**
S **QUIRTS**
A **QUIVER** SY

D **RABBET** S
BDG **RABBLE** DRS
BT **RACERS**
B **RACHET** S
BGT **RACING** S
CTW **RACKED**
CT **RACKER** S
B **RACKET** SY
CG **RACKLE**
B **RADDED**
CDG **RAFTED**
CDG **RAFTER** S
D **RAGEES**
BCD **RAGGED** Y
F
D **RAGGLE** S
B **RAIDED**
B **RAIDER** S
BT **RAILED**
FT **RAILER** S
BDG **RAINED**
T
BP **RAISED**
P **RAISER** S
BFP **RAISES**
B **RAKING**
B **RAMBLE** DRS
CDT **RAMMED**
C **RAMMER** S
CT **RAMPED**
PT **RANCES**
P **RANGED**
G **RANGER** S
GO **RANGES**
CFP **RANKED**
CF **RANKER** S
C **RANKLE** DS
CF **RANKLY**
T **RANSOM** S
G **RANTED**
G **RANTER** S
D **RAPERS**
G **RAPIER** S
CD **RAPING**
CFT **RAPPED**
W
CTW **RAPPER** S
E **RASERS**
BCT **RASHER** S
BCT **RASHES** T
B **RASHLY**
E **RASING**
G **RASPED**
G **RASPER** S
W **RASSLE** DS
E **RASURE** S
CFG **RATERS**
KP
G **RATIFY**
G **RATINE** S
CGO **RATING** S
P
O **RATION** S
D **RATTED**
BP **RATTLE** DRS
C **RAUNCH** Y
GT **RAVELS**
C **RAVENS**
BCG **RAVERS**
BCG **RAVING** S
B **RAWEST**

BDF **RAYING**
GP
C **RAYONS**
BG **RAZERS**
BCG **RAZING**
P **REACTS**
T **READER** S
A **REALLY**
BCD **REAMED**
CD **REAMER** S
P **REARMS**
T **REASON** S
G **REAVED**
P **REAVER** S
G **REAVES**
P **REBIDS**
P **REBILL** S
P **REBIND** S
P **REBOIL** S
P **REBOOK** S
P **REBUYS**
P **RECAST** S
P **RECEDE** DS
P **RECENT**
P **RECEPT** S
P **RECESS**
P **RECIPE** S
W **RECKED**
P **RECODE** DS
P **RECOOK** S
P **RECOUP** ES
E **RECTOR** SY
P **RECUTS**
P **REDATE** DS
T **REDDLE** DS
PU **REDIAL** S
P **REEDIT** S
C **REELED**
P **REFACE** DS
P **REFECT** S
P **REFERS**
P **REFILE** DS
P **REFIRE** DS
P **REFORM** S
P **REFUND** S
P **REHEAT** S
P **RELATE** DRS
P **RELOAD** S
P **REMADE**
C **REMATE** DS
P **REMEET** S
P **REMISE** DS
P **REMISS**
P **REMIXT**
P **REMOLD** S
T **RENAIL** S
P **RENAME** DS
T **RENDED**
P **REPACK** S
P **REPAID**
P **REPAVE** DS
P **REPAYS**
P **REPLAN** ST
P **REPPED**
P **RESALE** S
P **RESELL** S
P **RESENT** S
P **RESETS**
F **RESHES**
P **RESHIP** S
P **RESHOW** NS
P **RESIDE** DRS
P **RESIFT** S
P **RESOAK** S
P **RESOLD**
P **RESORT** S
CW **RESTED**
PW **RESTER** S
P **RESUME** DRS
P **RETAPE** DS
P **RETELL** S
P **RETEST** S

P **RETOLD**
P **RETRIM** S
F **RETTED**
P **RETYPE** DS
P **REVERB** S
BT **REVETS**
P **REVIEW** S
P **REVISE** DRS
P **REVUES**
P **REWARM** S
P **REWASH**
P **REWIRE** DS
P **REWORK** S
P **REWORN**
P **REWRAP** ST
CD **RIBBED**
C **RIBBER** S
D **RIBLET** S
P **RICERS**
PT **RICING**
BCP **RICKED**
TW
C **RICKEY** S
G **RIDDED**
G **RIDDER** S
G **RIDDLE** DRS
T **RIDENT**
B **RIDGED**
BF **RIDGES**
GP **RIDING** S
G **RIEVER** S
T **RIFLED**
T **RIFLER** SY
T **RIFLES**
DG **RIFTED**
FPT **RIGGED**
T **RIGGER** S
BFW **RIGHTS**
DFG **RILLED**
PT
G **RILLES**
PT **RIMERS**
G **RIMIER**
GP **RIMING**
BPT **RIMMED**
BCG **RIMMER** S
KPT
C **RIMPLE** DS
BG **RINDED**
CFW **RINGED**
BCW **RINGER** S
G **RIPING**
DGT **RIPPED**
DGT **RIPPER** S
CG **RIPPLE** DRST
AIP **RISING** S
BF **RISKED**
BF **RISKER** S
CFG **RITTER** S
F **RITZES**
D **RIVERS**
GPT **RIVETS**
D **RIVING**
P **ROBAND** S
P **ROBING**
C **ROCHET** S
CFT **ROCKED**
BC **ROCKET** S
P **RODDED**
E **RODENT** S
BD **ROGUES**
B **ROILED**
DT **ROLLED**
DT **ROLLER** S
T **ROMPED**
P **ROOFED**
P **ROOFER** S
BC **ROOKED**
B **ROOKIE** RS
BGV **ROOMED**
G **ROOMER** S
GP **ROPERS**
G **ROPING**

C **ROQUET** S
CP **ROSIER**
P **ROSILY**
P **ROSING**
T **ROTTED**
T **ROTTER** S
O **ROTUND** A
T **ROUBLE** S
T **ROUGHS**
G **ROUNDS**
GT **ROUPED**
AG **ROUSED**
AGT **ROUSER** S
AG **ROUSES**
G **ROUTED**
G **ROUTER** S
C **ROUTES**
D **ROUTHS**
DPT **ROVERS**
DP **ROVING** S
T **ROWELS**
CG **ROWERS**
CGT **ROWING** S
GT **ROWTHS**
DG **RUBBED**
DG **RUBBER** SY
T **RUCKED**
T **RUCKLE** DS
C **RUDELY**
P **RUDERY**
C **RUDEST**
G **RUFFED**
T **RUFFES**
T **RUFFLE** DRS
G **RUFFLY**
DF **RUGGED**
A **RUGOLA** S
CDG **RUMBLE** DRS
CG **RUMBLY**
DG **RUMMER** S
C **RUMPLE** DS
C **RUMPLY**
T **RUNDLE** ST
T **RUNNEL** S
BC **RUSHED**
BC **RUSHER** S
BC **RUSHES**
CT **RUSTED**

P **SALTER** NS
I **SATINS**
E **SCAPED**
E **SCAPES**
A **SCARED**
E **SCARPS**
A **SCENDS**
A **SCENTS**
A **SCRIBE** DRS
A **SEPSES**
A **SEPSIS**
A **SEPTIC** S
E **SERINE** S
A **SEXUAL**
A **SHAMED**
P **SHAWED**
A **SHIEST**
A **SOCIAL** S
I **SOLATE** DS
A **SPIRED**
A **SPIRES**
E **SPOUSE** DS
E **SPRITS**
E **SPYING**
A **SQUINT** SY
E **SQUIRE** DS
E **STATED**
E **STATES**
A **STATIC** ES
A **STOUND** S
E **STRAYS**
A **STRICT**
A **STRIDE** RS

E **STRUMS**
A **STYLAR**
A **SUNDER** S

S **TABBED**
S **TABLED**
S **TABLES**
S **TACKED**
S **TACKER** S
A **TACTIC** S
S **TAGGED**
S **TAGGER** S
S **TAKING** S
S **TALKED**
S **TALKER** S
E **TALONS**
S **TAMPED**
S **TAMPER** S
S **TANGED**
S **TANNIC**
S **TARING**
S **TARRED**
S **TARTED**
S **TARTER**
S **TATERS**
A **TAXIES**
S **TEAMED**
S **TEWING**
E **THANES**
A **THEISM** S
A **THEIST** S
A **THIRST** SY
A **THWART** S
S **TIBIAL**
S **TICKED**
S **TICKER** S
S **TICKLE** DRS
S **TIFFED**
S **TILLED**
S **TILLER** S
S **TILTED**
A **TINGLE** DRS
S **TINKER** S
S **TINTED**
S **TINTER** S
S **TIPPLE** DRS
E **TOILES**
S **TOKERS**
S **TOKING**
AS **TONERS**
A **TONICS**
S **TONIER**
AS **TONING**
S **TONISH**
S **TOOLED**
S **TOPERS**
S **TOPING**
S **TOPPED**
S **TOPPER** S
S **TOPPLE** DS
S **TORIES**
S **TOTTED**
S **TOUTER** S
S **TOWAGE** S
S **TOWING**
S **TRAINS**
S **TRAITS**
S **TRICKS** Y
S **TRIKES**
S **TRIPES**
S **TROKED**
S **TROKES**
S **TROLLS**
A **TROPHY**
A **TROPIN** ES
S **TROWED**
S **TUBBED**
S **TUMBLE** DRS
S **TUMPED**
S **TUNNED**

D **UBIETY**

BJM UDDERS
R
S ULLAGE DS
CLN UMBERS
BFH UMBLES
JMN
RT
BDH UMPING
JLM
PT
T UNABLE
S UNBELT S
N UNCLES
F UNFAIR
B UNIONS
DG UNITES
GRS UNLESS
NS UNLIKE D
G UNLOCK S
S UNROOF S
S UNSETS
G UNSHIP S
AP UNTIES
S UNWISE R
E UPHROE S
CS UPPERS
CDP UPPING S
ST
P URANIC
C URARES
CO URARIS
C URATES
T URGENT
BPS URGERS
GPS URGING
B URIALS
MP URINES
B URPING
M USEFUL
BGM USHERS
PR
O UTMOST S
BCG UTTERS
MNP

A VAILED
E VANISH
O VARIES
A VENGED
A VENGES
A VENUES
O VERBID S
O VERSET S
A VIATIC A
A VIATOR S
E VICTOR SY
E VILEST
A VOIDED
A VOIDER S
E VOLUTE DS
A VOWERS
A VOWING

ST WADDLE DRS
S WAGERS
S WAGGED
S WAGGER SY
S WAGING
A WAITED
A WAITER S
A WAKENS
A WAKING
S WALLOW S
T WANGLE DRS
S WANNED
S WAPPED
AS WARDED
A WARDER S
S WARMED
S WARMER S
S WASHED
S WASHER S
S WASHES
S WATTER
T WATTLE DS
S WEARER S
S WEEPER S
T WEETED
DS WELLED
S WELTER S
T WIDDLE DS
ST WIGGED
ST WILLED
S WILLER S
DS WINDLE DS
ST WINGED
S WINGER S
T WINIER
DT WINING
S WINISH
S WINKED
T WINKLE DS
T WINNED
S WIPING
S WISHED
S WISHER S
S WISHES
S WISSES
T WISTED
T WITCHY
S WITHER S
T WITTED
S WIVING
S WOTTED
S WOUNDS

O YESSES

T ZADDIK
O ZONATE D

7-letter Words

L ABILITY
LM ACERATE D
T ACNODES
T ACONITE S
FPT ACTIONS
DPR ADDLING
SW
M ADWOMAN
M ADWOMEN
W AGELESS
H AGGADAH S
H AGGADAS
H AGGADIC
H AGGADOT H
V AGILITY
M AGNATES
B AILMENT S
H AIRIEST
FP AIRINGS
H AIRLESS
H AIRLIKE
H AIRLINE RS
F AIRWAYS
H ALATION S
K ALEWIFE
M ALIGNED
M ALIGNER S
P ALIMONY
T ALIPEDS
GP ALLIUMS
FHS ALLOWED
TW
DGR ALLYING
ST
FHP ALTERED
FP ALTERER S
C AMASSES
GR AMBLERS
GRW AMBLING
H AMBONES
B ANALITY
P ANELING
D ANGERED
DJM ANGLERS
TW
DGJ ANGLING S
MTW
S ANGUINE
L ANGUISH
R ANKLING
T ANNATES
C ANNULAR
P ANTHERS
T ANTRUMS
T APELIKE
JN APERIES
R APHIDES
H APLITES
C APSIDAL
R APTNESS
P ARABLES
H ARBORED
H ARBOURS
M ARCHERS
MP ARCHING S
M ARGENTS
G ARGLING
B ARISTAS
F ARMINGS
H ARMLESS
C AROUSAL S
C AROUSED
C AROUSER S
C AROUSES
BC ARRACKS
FHM ARROWED
N
P ARTICLE DS
TW ARTIEST
BP ARTISAN S
W ARTLESS
H ARUSPEX
DW ASHIEST
CS ASHLESS
GM ASKINGS
W ASSAILS
B ASSISTS
Y ATAGHAN S
N ATRIUMS
L AUREATE
H AUTEURS
T AUTONYM S
L AWFULLY
M AXILLAE
M AXILLAS
L AZURITE S

A BASHING S
A BEGGING
A BETTERS
A BETTING
A BETTORS
A BOUNDED
A BRACHIA L
A BRIDGED
A BRIDGES
A BUTTALS
A BUTTERS
A BUTTING

S CABBING
S CAMPERS
S CAMPING S
S CANDENT
S CANNERS
S CANNING S
A CANTHUS
S CANTING
O CARINAS
S CARIOUS
S CARLESS
S CARPERS
S CARPING S
S CARRIER S
S CARTING
S CATTIER
S CATTING
AE CAUDATE DS
A CAULINE
A CENTRIC
A CERATED
S CHILLER S
A CHROMIC
S COFFERS
S COFFING
S COLLOPS
I CONICAL
S COOCHES
S COOPERS
S COOPING
S COOTERS
S COPULAE
S COPULAS
S CORNERS
S CORNING
E COTYPES
S COUTERS
S COUTHER
S COWLING S
S CRAGGED
S CRAMMED
S CRAPING
S CRAPPED
S CRAWLED
S CRAWLER S
S CREAKED
S CREAMED
S CREAMER SY
S CREWING
S CRIMPED
S CRIMPER S
S CRUNCHY
S CUFFING
S CULCHES
S CULLERS
S CULLING
S CULLION S
S CUMMERS
S CUNNERS
S CUPPERS
S CURRIED
S CURRIES
S CURVIER
S CUTCHES
S CUTTERS
S CUTTLED
S CUTTLES
S CUTWORK S

A DEEMING
E DENTATE D
O DONATES
A DYNAMIC S

M EAGERLY
WY EANLING S
T EARDROP S
BGH EARINGS
FGT EARLESS
NP EARLIER
LY EARNERS
LY EARNING S
TW EASELED
F EASTERS
FY EASTING S
BH EATABLE S
BS EATINGS
O ECOLOGY
P ECTASES
O EDEMATA
HLS EDGIEST
W
S EDITION S
DRS EDUCING
R EDUCTOR S
BL EERIEST
H EIGHTHS
DR EJECTED
R EJECTOR S
R ELAPSED
R ELAPSES
R ELATERS
DGR ELATING
DGR ELATION S
R ELATIVE S
S ELECTED
S ELECTEE S
S ELECTOR S
D ELUDERS
D ELUDING
D ELUSION S
D ELUSIVE
D ELUSORY
R EMAILED
R EMENDED
DR EMERGED
DR EMERGES
M EMETICS
DR EMITTED
R EMITTER S
D EMOTING
DR EMOTION S
V ENATION S
P ENCHANT S
M ENDINGS
B ENDWAYS
B ENDWISE
T ENFOLDS
MOP ENOLOGY
V
DR ENOUNCE DS
C ENSURED
C ENSURER S
C ENSURES
V ENTAILS
CT ENTERED
GS ENTRIES
T ENURING
N EOLITHS
P EONISMS
L EPIDOTE S
D EPILATE DS
R EQUITES
T ERBIUMS
MV ERISTIC S
B ESPOUSE DR
S

GR ESTATED
GRT ESTATES
A ESTHETE S
AF ESTIVAL
O ESTRINS
O ESTRIOL S
O ESTRONE S
O ESTROUS
O ESTRUMS
K ETAMINE S
F ETCHERS
FLR ETCHING S
M ETHANES
M ETHANOL S
A ETHERIC
M ETHOXYL S
M ETHYLIC
R EVERTED
R EVOKERS
R EVOKING
R EVOLUTE S
DR EVOLVED
R EVOLVER S
DR EVOLVES
R EVULSED
H EXAMINE DER
S

H EXARCHY

A FEBRILE
A FLUTTER SY

A GAMETES
A GENESES
A GENESIS
A GENETIC S
A GINNERS
A GLIMMER S
A GLITTER SY
A GNOSTIC S
A GRAPHIC S
A GREEING

W HACKERS
STW HACKING
S HACKLED
S HACKLER S
S HACKLES
C HADARIM
S HADDOCK S
S HAFTING
S HAGGING
C HALLAHS
C HALLOTH
S HALLOWS
S HAMMERS
SW HAMMING
C HAMPERS
C HANDLER S
C HANGERS
CW HANGING S
T HANKERS
ST HANKING
C HANTING
CW HAPPING
CS HARKING
C HARMERS
CP HARMING
S HARPERS
S HARPIES
S HARPING S
C HARRIER S
G HARRIES
C HASTENS
T HATCHED
T HATCHER SY
T HATCHES
CS HATTERS
C HATTING
S HAULING
C HAUNTED
C HAUNTER S
C HAZANIM
C HAZZANS
S HEALING
S HEARERS
S HEARING S
CT HEATERS
S HEATHER SY
C HEATING
S HEAVING
W HEELERS
W HEELING S
W HEEZING
S HELLERS
S HELLING
W HELMING
W HELPING S
S HELVING
RT HEMATIC S
T HERMITS
W HERRIED
CSW HERRIES
C HEWABLE
T HICKISH
C HICKORY
C HILDING S
C HILLERS
C HILLIER
CS HILLING
W HINGERS
W HINGING
C HINKIER
SW HINNIED
SW HINNIES
S HIPLESS
W HIPLIKE
CW HIPPIER
C HIPPIES T
CSW HIPPING
W HISTING
S HITLESS
CW HITTERS
S HITTING
S HOCKERS
CS HOCKING
S HOGGING
C HOKIEST
W HOLISMS
P HONEYED
W HOOFING
W HOOPERS
W HOOPING
W HOOPLAS
S HOOTERS
S HOOTING
CSW HOPPERS
C HOPPIER
CSW HOPPING S
C HORDING
T HORNIER
T HORNILY
T HORNING S
G HOSTING
S HOTTING
C HOUSERS
C HOUSING S
S HOVELED
C HUCKLES
C HUFFIER
C HUFFING

C HUGGERS
C HUGGING
C HUMMING
T HUMPERS
CTW HUMPING
C HUNKIER
CS HUNTERS
S HUNTING S
C HUPPAHS
D HURRIES
S HUSHING
S HUTTING
C HUTZPAH S
C HUTZPAS

V ICELESS
DKP ICKIEST
R ICTUSES
M IFFIEST
L IGNEOUS
L IGNITES
T ILLITES
PW INCHERS
CPW INCHING
Z INCITES
W INDIGOS
W INDOWED
P INFOLDS
DHK INKIEST
TW INKLING S
GW INNINGS
L IONISED
L IONISES
L IONIZED
L IONIZER S
L IONIZES
FTW IRELESS
M ISOGAMY
T ISSUING
BPW ITCHIER
BP ITCHILY
BDH ITCHING S
PW
L ITERATE DS
G IZZARDS

D JELLABA S

S KELPING
S KELTERS
S KERRIES
S KETCHES
S KIDDERS
S KIDDING
S KILLING S
A KINETIC S
S KINKING
S KINLESS
S KIPPERS
S KIPPING
S KITTLES T

FG LABELLA
CS LACKERS
BCF LACKING
S
B LADDERS
B LADINGS
F LAGGERS
BCF LAGGING S
S
G LAIRING
F LAKIEST
C LAMBERS
CFS LAMMING
C LAMPERS
C LAMPING
G LANCERS
G LANCING
GS LANDERS
B LANKEST
C LANKIER
P LANNERS
CFS LAPPERS
CFS LAPPING
E LAPSING
CFP LASHERS
S
CFP LASHING S
S
G LASSIES
BP LASTERS
B LASTING S
KS LATCHES
BS LATHERS
P LATINAS
F LATTENS
CF LAWLESS
C LAWLIKE
P LAYOFFS
G LAZIEST
BP LEACHED
B LEACHER S
BP LEACHES
P LEADERS
P LEADING S
CG LEANERS
C LEANEST
CG LEANING S
B LEARIER
P LEASERS
P LEASING S
P LEATHER NSY
C LEAVERS
CS LEAVING S
EF LECTION S
E LECTORS
P LEDGERS
F LEDGIER
F LEECHED
F LEECHES
F LEERING
E LEGISTS
B LENDERS
B LENDING
F LENSING
P LESSORS
F LETCHED
F LETCHES
E LEVATOR S
CFS LICKERS
CFS LICKING S
ABF LIGHTED
PS
BPS LIGHTER S
S LIGHTLY
C LIMBERS
C LIMBING
S LIMIEST
GS LIMMERS
CFS LINGERS
C LINGIER
BCP LINKERS
BCP LINKING
S
FG LINTIER
FG LINTING
S LIPLESS
CFS LIPPERS
S LIPPIER
BCF LIPPING S
S
G LISTENS
BGK LISTERS
B LITHELY
B LITHEST
C LITORAL
FGS LITTERS
G LITTERY
S LIVERED
G LOAMING
G LOBATED
CS LOBBERS
B LOBBING
G LOBULAR
G LOBULES
B LOCKAGE S
BC LOCKERS
BCF LOCKING
BCF LOGGERS
S
C LOGGIER
BCF LOGGING S
S
A LOGICAL
BG LOOMING
B LOOPERS
B LOOPING
F LOPPERS
FGS LOPPIER
CFG LOPPING
PS
C LOSABLE
C LOSINGS
BPS LOTTERS
BCP LOTTING
S
CF LOURING
B LOUSIER
B LOUSILY
B LOUSING
CFG LOUTING
B LOWBALL S
P LOWBOYS
BS LOWDOWN S
FG LOWERED
P LOWLAND S
S LOWNESS
BCF LUBBERS
S
P LUCKIER
P LUCKILY
CP LUCKING
BFS LUFFING
PS LUGGERS
GPS LUGGING
P LUMBAGO S
CPS LUMBERS
P LUMPENS
P LUMPERS
CG LUMPIER
G LUMPILY
CFP LUMPING
S
CP LUMPISH
G LUNCHED
G LUNCHES
BP LUNGERS
BP LUNGING
CFP LUNKERS
B LUNTING
FP LUSHEST
BFS LUSHING
BCF LUSTERS
F LUTINGS
F LUTISTS
P LYINGLY

E MAILING S
S MARTENS
S MARTING
S MASHERS
S MASHING
A MASSING
S MATTERS
A MAZEDLY
S MELLING
S MELTERS
S MELTING
AE MENDERS
AE MENDING S
A MERCERS
E MERGING
O MICRONS
A MIDSHIP S
E MIGRANT S
E MIGRATE DS
O MIKRONS
S MIRKIER
S MIRKILY
EO MISSION S
EO MISSIVE S
S MITHERS
A MITOSES
A MITOSIS
A MITOTIC
S MOCKING
S MOLDERS
S MOOCHED
S MOOCHER S
S MOOCHES
A MORALLY
A MORTISE DRS
S MOTHERS
S MOTHERY
AE MOTIONS
S MOULDER S
A MOUNTED
S MUSHING
S MUTCHES

S NAGGIER
S NAGGING
S NAILING
O NANISMS
S NAPLESS
KS NAPPERS
S NAPPIER
KS NAPPING
E NATIONS
G NATTIER
A NEARING
E NERVATE
S NIBBING
KS NICKERS
S NICKING
S NIFFERS
S NIGGLED
S NIGGLER S
S NIGGLES
K NIGHTLY
S NIPPERS
S NIPPIER
S NIPPILY
S NIPPING
KS NOBBIER
S NOBBILY
K NOCKING
A NODALLY
S NOGGING S
KS NUBBIER
K NURLING

B OARFISH
BGM OATLIKE
L OBELIAS
T OCHERED
C OCREATE
CG OFFERED
S OFTENER
R OILIEST
B OINKING
BC OLDNESS
O OLOGIES
O OLOGIST S
D OLOROSO S
LMT OMENTUM S
DGL ONENESS
Z ONETIME
Z OOLOGIC
Z OOPHYTE S
W OORALIS
Z OOSPERM S
Z OOSPORE S
BW OOZIEST
C ORACLES
M ORALISM S
M ORALIST S
M ORALITY
B ORATING
M ORATORY
B ORDERED
B ORDERER S
S ORDINES
B ORDURES
H OROLOGY
M ORRISES
C OSMOSES
HJ OSTLERS
P OSTMARK S
CDM OUCHING
PTV
Y OURSELF
JR OUSTERS
JR OUSTING
C OVARIES
N OVATION S
C OVERAGE DS
C OVERALL S
H OVERFLY
CH OVERING
C OVERLET S
C OVERTLY
B OWLLIKE
F OXTAILS
R OYSTERS

S PACIEST
S PALLING
S PANNERS
S PANNING
S PARABLE S
S PARGING S
S PARKERS
S PARKING S
S PARLING
S PARRIER S
S PARRING
S PATTERS
S PATTING
S PAWNERS
S PAWNING
S PEAKING
S PECKING
S PECTATE S
S PEELING S
S PEERING
S PELTERS
SU PENDING
A PHONICS
E PHORATE S
S PILINGS
S PILLAGE DRS
S PILLING
S PINIEST
O PINIONS
S PINNERS
S PINNIES
S PINNING
S PITTING S
S PLASHED
S PLASHER S
S PLASHES
A PLASTIC S
S PLATTED
S PLATTER S
S PLAYING
U PLIGHTS
U PLINKED
S PONGING
S PONTOON S
S POOLERS
S POOLING
S PORTERS
S PORTING
O POSSUMS
S POTTERS
S POTTIER
S POTTING
S POUTERS
S POUTING
A PRACTIC E
U PRAISED
U PRAISER S
U PRAISES
U PRATING
S PRATTLE DRS
S PRAYERS
S PRAYING
S PRIGGED
S PRINTED
S PRINTER SY
U PRISING
S PUDDING S
S PUNKIER
S PUNKIES T
S PURRING
S PUTTERS
A PYRETIC

S QUADDED
E QUALITY
S QUASHED
S QUASHER S
S QUASHES
E QUIPPED
E QUIPPER S
S QUIRING
S QUIRTED

D RABBETS
BDG RABBLED
BG RABBLER S
BDG RABBLES
B RACHETS
B RACHIAL
BT RACINGS
CT RACKERS
B RACKETS
W RACKFUL S
CTW RACKING
B RADDING
E RADIATE DS
D RAFFISH
CDG RAFTERS
CDG RAFTING
BDF RAGGING
D RAGGLES
B RAIDERS
B RAIDING
T RAILERS
BT RAILING S
BG RAINIER
B RAINILY
BDG RAINING
T
P RAISERS
BP RAISING S
B RAMBLED
B RAMBLES
C RAMMERS
CDT RAMMING
CT RAMPING
BC RANCHED
BCT RANCHES
B RANDIES T
G RANGERS
O RANGIER
P RANGING
F RANKERS
CF RANKEST
CFP RANKING S
CP RANKISH
C RANKLED
C RANKLES S
T RANSOMS
G RANTERS
G RANTING
G RANULAR
CTW RAPPERS
CFT RAPPING
W
CT RASHERS
B RASHEST
G RASPERS
G RASPING S
W RASSLED
W RASSLES
E RASURES
C RATCHES
G RATINGS
O RATIONS
B RATTIER
D RATTING
B RATTISH
BP RATTLED
P RATTLER S
BP RATTLES
GT RAVELED
T RAVELER S
G RAVELLY
C RAVENED
C RAVINGS
BP REACHED
BP REACHER S
BP REACHES
P REACTED
P READAPT S
T READERS
BDT READING S
P READMIT S
P READOPT S
P REALLOT S
P REALTER S
CD REAMERS
BCD REAMING
P REAPPLY
P REARMED
T REASONS
P REAVERS
P REBILLS
P REBINDS
P REBIRTH S
P REBOARD S
P REBOILS
P REBOOKS
P REBOUND S
P REBUILD S
P REBUILT
P RECASTS
P RECEDED
P RECEDES
P RECEPTS
P RECHECK S
P RECHOSE N
P RECIPES
P RECITED
W RECKING
P RECLEAN S
P RECODED
P RECODES
P RECOOKS
E RECTORS
P REDATED
P REDATES
T REDDLED
T REDDLES
P REDRAFT S
P REDRIED
P REDRIES
P REDRILL S
G REEDIER
G REEDILY
B REEDING S
P REEDITS
F REEDMAN
F REEDMEN
P REELECT S
C REELING S
P REENACT S
P REERECT S
P REFACED
P REFACES
P REFECTS
P REFIGHT S
P REFILED
P REFILES
P REFIRED

P REFIRES
P REFIXED
P REFIXES
P REFOCUS
P REFORMS
P REFROZE N
P REFUNDS
B REGMATA
P REGNANT
P REHEATS
P REJUDGE DS
P RELATES
P RELIVES
P RELOADS
C REMAINS
C REMATED
C REMATES
P REMISED
P REMISES
P REMIXED
P REMIXES
P REMOLDS
P REMORSE S
T RENAILS
P RENAMES
T RENDING
P REORDER S
P REPACKS
P REPAVED
P REPAVES
P REPLACE DRS
P REPLANS
P REPLANT S
P REPPING
P REPRESS
P REPRICE DS
P REPRINT S
P RESALES
P RESCIND S
P RESCORE DS
P RESELLS
P RESENTS
P RESERVE DRS
P RESHAPE DRS
P RESHIPS
P RESHOWN
P RESHOWS
P RESIDED
P RESIDER S
P RESIDES
P RESIFTS
P RESOAKS
P RESOLVE DRS
P RESORTS
P RESPLIT S
P RESTAMP S
PW RESTERS
CW RESTING
P RESTORE DRS
P RESUMED
P RESUMER S
P RESUMES
P RETAPED
P RETAPES
P RETASTE DS
W RETCHED
W RETCHES
P RETELLS
P RETESTS
P RETRAIN S
P RETREAT S
P RETRIAL S
P RETRIMS
F RETTING
P RETYPED
P RETYPES
P REUNION S
P REUNITE DRS
P REVALUE DS
P REVERBS
P REVIEWS

P REVISED
P REVISES
P REVISIT S
P REVISOR SY
P REWARMS
P REWEIGH S
P REWIRED
P REWIRES
P REWORKS
P REWRAPS
C RIBBERS
CD RIBBING S
D RIBLETS
CP RICKETS
BCPTW RICKING
G RIDDERS
G RIDDLED
G RIDDLES
B RIDGING
G RIEVERS
T RIFLERS
T RIFLING S
DG RIFTING
T RIGGERS
FPT RIGGING S
F RIGHTED
B RIGHTER S
B RIGHTLY
F RIGIDLY
DFGPT RILLING
G RIMIEST
B RIMLESS
BCKT RIMMERS
BPT RIMMING
C RIMPLED
C RIMPLES
BCW RINGERS
BCFW RINGING
G RINNING
DGT RIPPERS
DGT RIPPING
C RIPPLED
C RIPPLER S
C RIPPLES
F RISKERS
F RISKIER
F RISKILY
BF RISKING
CFG RITTERS
B ROACHED
B ROACHES
P ROBANDS
C ROCHETS
C ROCKERY
BC ROCKETS
CFT ROCKING
P RODDING
B ROGUERY
B ROGUISH
B ROILING
T ROLLERS
DT ROLLING S
T ROMPING
P ROOFERS
P ROOFING S
C ROOKERY
B ROOKIES T
BC ROOKING
G ROOMERS
B ROOMIER
BGV ROOMING
C ROQUETS
P ROSIEST
C ROTCHES
T ROTTERS
T ROTTING
T ROUBLES
CG ROUCHES
G ROUNDED

G ROUNDER S
C ROUPIER
C ROUPILY
GT ROUPING
AGT ROUSERS
AG ROUSING
G ROUTERS
G ROUTING
G ROWABLE
C ROWDIES T
T ROWELED
DG RUBBERS
DG RUBBING S
T RUCKING
T RUCKLED
T RUCKLES
C RUDDIER
G RUFFING
T RUFFLED
T RUFFLES
DF RUGGING
A RUGOLAS
CDG RUMBLED
G RUMBLER S
CDG RUMBLES
D RUMMERS
G RUMMEST
C RUMMIER
C RUMMIES T
C RUMPLED
C RUMPLES S
T RUNDLES
T RUNNELS
BC RUSHERS
B RUSHIER
BC RUSHING S
CT RUSTIER
CT RUSTILY
CT RUSTING
T RUTHFUL

P SALTERS
E SCALADE S
E SCALLOP S
E SCAPING
E SCARPED
A SCENDED
A SCRIBED
A SCRIBES
E SERINES
P SHAWING
I SLANDER S
A SOCIALS
I SOLATED
I SOLATES
A SPARKLE DRST
E SPECIAL S
A SPHERIC S
A SPIRANT S
A SPIRING
E SPOUSAL S
E SPOUSED
E SPOUSES
E SQUIRED
E SQUIRES
E STATING
A STERNAL
A STEROID S
A STHENIA S
A STHENIC
O STOMATE S
A STONISH
E STOPPED
A STOUNDS
E STOVERS
E STRANGE RS
E STRAYED

S TABBING
S TABLING
S TACKERS

S TACKING
S TAGGERS
S TAGGING
S TAKEOUT S
S TALKERS
S TALKIER
S TALKING S
S TAMPERS
S TAMPING
S TANGING
S TARRIER S
S TARRING
S TARTING
S TEAMING
A TECHNIC S
S TENCHES
A THEISMS
A THEISTS
S TICKERS
S TICKING S
S TICKLED
S TICKLER S
S TICKLES
S TIFFING
S TILLING
S TILTING
S TINGING
S TINKERS
S TINTERS
S TINTING S
S TIPPLED
S TIPPLER S
S TIPPLES
S TOCCATA S
A TONALLY
S TONIEST
S TOOLING S
S TOPPERS
S TOPPING S
S TOPPLED
S TOPPLES
S TOTTING
S TOWABLE
S TOWAGES
S TOWAWAY S
S TRAINED
S TRAINER S
S TRAPPED
S TRAPPER S
S TRASSES
A TREMBLE DRS
S TRESSED
S TRESSES
S TRICKLE DS
S TRIDENT S
S TRIPPED
S TRIPPER S
S TROKING
S TROLLED
S TROLLER S
AS TROPHIC
A TROPINE S
A TROPINS
A TROPISM S
S TROWING
S TRUMPET S
S TUBBIER
S TUBBING
S TUMBLED
S TUMBLER S
S TUMBLES
S TUMPING
S TUNNING
A TWITTER SY
A TYPICAL

S ULLAGES
CLN UMBERED
S UNBAKED
S UNBELTS
S UNBLOCK S
S UNBURNT

S UNCHOKE DS
FJ UNCTION S
S UNDRESS
F UNHOUSE DS
C UNIFORM S
P UNITIVE
G UNLOCKS
S UNROOFS
R UNROUND S
G UNSHIPS
E UPHROES
C UPPINGS
R URALITE S
T URGENCY
F USELESS
F UTILITY
BGMP UTTERED
MP UTTERER S

A VAILING
E VALUATE DS
A VARICES
O VARIOLE S
A VENGING
A VENTAIL S
O VERBIDS
O VERSETS
AE VERSION S
K VETCHES
A VIATORS
E VICTORS
E VOCABLE S
A VOIDERS
A VOIDING
E VOLUTES
A VOUCHED
A VOUCHER S
A VOUCHES

ST WADDLED
T WADDLER S
ST WADDLES
S WAGGERS
S WAGGING
A WAITERS
A WAITING S
A WAKENED
A WAKENER S
S WALLOWS
S WAMPISH
T WANGLED
T WANGLER S
T WANGLES
S WANNING
S WAPPING
A WARDERS
AS WARDING
S WARMERS
S WARMING
S WASHERS
S WASHING S
S WATCHES
T WATTLED
T WATTLES S
S WEARERS
S WEARING
A WEATHER S
T WEEDIER
ST WEENIES T
S WEEPERS
S WEEPIER
S WEEPING S
ST WEETING
DS WELLING
S WELTERS
T WIDDLED
T WIDDLES
T WIGGIER
ST WIGGING S
T WIGLESS
T WIGLIKE

S WILLERS
ST WILLING
DS WINDLED
DS WINDLES S
S WINGERS
S WINGIER
ST WINGING
S WINGMAN
S WINGMEN
T WINIEST
S WINKING
T WINKLED
T WINKLES
T WINNING S
S WISHERS
S WISHING
T WISTING
ST WITCHED
ST WITCHES
S WITHERS
T WITTING S
S WOOSHED
S WOOSHES
S WOTTING
S WOUNDED

O ZONATED
A ZYGOSES

8-letter Words

LM ACERATED
T ACONITES
M ACRODONT S
FT ACTUALLY
V ACUITIES
H AGGADAHS
H AGGADOTH
B AILMENTS
H AIRBRUSH
H AIRINESS
H AIRLINES
H ALATIONS
K ALEWIVES
M ALIGNERS
M ALIGNING
D ALLIANCE S
FHSTW ALLOWING
FP ALTERERS
FHP ALTERING
D ANGERING
C ANNULATE D
G ANTELOPE S
N APHTHOUS
H ARBOROUS
H ARBOURED
H ARMONICA S
C AROUSALS
C AROUSERS
C AROUSING
H ARQUEBUS
FHMN ARROWING
P ARTICLES
T ARTINESS
BP ARTISANS
W ASHINESS
W ASSAILED
W ASSAILER S
Y ATAGHANS
T AUTONYMS
N AVICULAR
N AVIGATOR S
M AXILLARY
L AZURITES

A BASEMENT S
A BIOGENIC
A BOUNDING
A BRIDGING S
A BUILDING S

S CANNINGS
S CATTIEST
A CELLULAR S
A CEPHALIC
S CHILLERS
S CHILLING
A CHROMOUS
I CONICITY
S COPULATE DS
S CORELESS
S CRAGGIER
S CRAGGILY
S CRAMMING
S CRAPPIER
S CRAPPING
S CRATCHES
S CRAWLERS
S CRAWLIER
S CRAWLING
S CREAKING
S CREAMERS
S CREAMING
S CRIBBLED
S CRIMPERS
S CRIMPIER
S CRIMPING

A CRITICAL
S CRUNCHED
S CRUNCHES
S CULLIONS
S CULTCHES
S CURRYING
S CURVIEST
A CUTENESS
S CUTTLING
S CUTWORKS

WY EANLINGS
T EARDROPS
NP EARLIEST
LY EARNINGS
B EASTINGS
S EDITIONS
DRS EDUCIBLE
DRS EDUCTION S
DRS EDUCTIVE
R EDUCTORS
BL EERINESS
R EGRESSED
R EGRESSES
DR EJECTING
DR EJECTION S
R EJECTIVE S
R EJECTORS
R ELAPSING
BR ELATEDLY
DGR ELATIONS
R ELATIVES
S ELECTEES
S ELECTING
S ELECTION S
S ELECTIVE S
S ELECTORS
S ELFISHLY
D ELUSIONS
R EMAILING
R EMENDING
DR EMERGING
R EMIGRATE DS
DR EMISSION S
R EMISSIVE
R EMITTERS
DR EMITTING
DR EMOTIONS
D EMULSIFY
V ENATIONS
P ENCHANTS
D ENERVATE DS
OX ENOPHILE S
K ENOSISES
DR ENOUNCED
DR ENOUNCES
C ENSURERS
C ENSURING
P ENTANGLE DRS

CT ENTERING
N EOLITHIC
L EPIDOTES
D EPILATED
D EPILATES
D EPILATOR S
R ERADIATE DS
O ESOPHAGI
B ESPOUSED
B ESPOUSES
H ESSONITE S
GR ESTATING
A ESTHESIA S
A ESTHETES
A ESTHETIC S
A ESTIVATE DS
O ESTRIOLS
O ESTROGEN S
O ESTRONES
O ESTRUSES
K ETAMINES
M ETHANOLS

A ETHEREAL
M ETHYLATE DS
M ETHYLENE S
P ETIOLATE DS
A ETIOLOGY
DR EVALUATE DS
N EVERMORE
R EVERSION S
R EVERTING
R EVOCABLE
R EVOLVERS
DR EVOLVING
R EVULSION S
H EXAMINES
D EXTRORSE

A FOREHAND S
A FORESAID
A FORETIME S
S FORZANDI
S FORZANDO S

A GENTRIES
A GNOSTICS
S GRAFFITI S
S GRAFFITO

S HACKLERS
S HACKLING
S HADDOCKS
S HALLOWED
S HALLOWER S
C HALUTZIM
C HANDLERS
C HARMLESS
C HASTENED
C HASTENER S
T HATCHERS
T HATCHING S
C HAUNTERS
C HAUNTING
C HAZZANIM
S HEARINGS
C HEATABLE
S HEATHERS
W HEATLESS
W HEELINGS
W HEELLESS
S HELLFIRE S
W HELPLESS
T HEMATICS
C HEMOSTAT S
TW HEREINTO
TW HEREUNTO
TW HEREUPON
TW HEREWITH
W HERRYING
C HILLIEST
C HINKIEST
SW HINNYING
CW HIPPIEST
A HISTORIC
T HITHERTO
W HOLISTIC
P HONEYING
C HOPPIEST
S HOPPINGS
T HORNIEST
T HORNLESS
T HORNLIKE
S HOVELING
S HOVELLED
C HUFFIEST
C HUNKIEST
C HUTZPAHS

P ICKINESS
M IFFINESS
DLS IGNIFIED
DLS IGNIFIES
L IMITABLE
V INDICATE DS

W INDOWING
P INFOLDED
K INKINESS
T INKLINGS
P INNATELY
P INSETTER S
L IONISING
L IONIZERS
L IONIZING
D IREFULLY
E IRENICAL
BPW ITCHIEST
W ITCHINGS
L ITERATES

E JACULATE DS
D JELLABAS

S KILLINGS
S KIPPERED

F LABELLUM
P LACELESS
A LACKADAY
BF LAGGINGS
G LANDLESS
S LANGUAGE S
C LANKIEST
B LANKNESS
C LAPBOARD S
FS LASHINGS
B LASTINGS
E LATERITE S
BS LATHERED
B LATHERER S
P LATINIZE DS
P LATITUDE S
S LAUGHTER S
C LAVATION S
S LAVISHLY
G LAZINESS
B LEACHERS
BP LEACHING
P LEADINGS
G LEANINGS
C LEANNESS
B LEARIEST
P LEATHERS
EF LECTIONS
F LEDGIEST
F LEECHING
F LETCHING
E LEVATORS
A LIENABLE
BPS LIGHTERS
S LIGHTEST
ABFPS LIGHTING S
A LIKENESS
S LIMINESS
S LIMPSIER
C LINGIEST
FG LINTIEST
S LIPPERED
S LIPPIEST
C LIPPINGS
G LISTENED
A LITERACY
A LITERATE S
FG LITTERED
A LIVENESS
S LIVERING
B LOCKABLE
B LOCKAGES
E LOCUTION S
C LOGGIEST
BF LOGGINGS
A LONENESS
FGS LOPPIEST
B LOUSIEST
B LOWBALLS
BS LOWDOWNS

FG LOWERING
P LOWLANDS
P LUCKIEST
P LUMBAGOS
S LUMBERED
S LUMBERER S
A LUMINOUS
F LUMMOXES
CG LUMPIEST
G LUNCHING
FP LUSHNESS
BCF LUSTERED

S MATTERED
AE MENDABLE
E MERGENCE S
A MIDSHIPS
E MIGRANTS
E MIGRATED
E MIGRATES
S MIRKIEST
EO MISSIONS
S MOLDERED
S MOOCHERS
S MOOCHING
A MORALISM S
A MORALITY
A MORTISED
A MORTISES
S MOTHERED
E MOTIONAL
E MOTIVITY
S MOULDERS
A MOUNTING S
A MUSINGLY
A MYOTONIA S

S NAGGIEST
S NAPPIEST
G NATTIEST
P NEUMATIC
S NICKERED
S NIGGLERS
S NIGGLING S
S NIPPIEST
KS NOBBIEST
KS NUBBIEST
E NUCLEATE DS
E NUMERATE DS

T OCHERING
J OCULARLY
I ODOMETRY
P OENOLOGY
CG OFFERING S
O OLOGISTS
LM OMENTUMS
Z OOGAMETE S
Z OOGENIES
Z OOLOGIES
Z OOLOGIST S
Z OOPHYTES
Z OOPHYTIC
Z OOSPERMS
N OOSPHERE S
Z OOSPORES
Z OOSPORIC
BW OOZINESS
M ORALISMS
M ORALISTS
B ORDERERS
B ORDERING
P OSTMARKS
N OVATIONS
C OVERABLE
C OVERAGES
C OVERALLS
C OVERLETS
C OVERSLIP ST
C OVERTURE DS
R OYSTERED

O PACIFIED
O PACIFIER S
O PACIFIES
S PARABLES
A PATHETIC
S PATTERED
S PECTATES
S PECULATE DS
A PERIODIC
A PETALOUS
A PHERESES
A PHERESIS
E PHORATES
E PICRITIC
S PILLAGES
S PINDLING
S PINELIKE
O PINIONED
S PLASHERS
S PLASHIER
S PLASHING
S PLATTERS
S PLATTING
U PLIGHTED
U PLINKING
S PONTOONS
S POTTIEST
U PRAISERS
U PRAISING
S PRATTLED
S PRATTLES
U PREACHED
U PREACHES
S PRIGGING
S PRINTERS
S PRINTING S
A PRIORITY
S PUNKIEST
S PUTTERED
S PUTTERER S

S QUADDING
S QUASHERS
S QUASHING
E QUIPPERS
E QUIPPING
S QUIRTING

BG RABBLERS
BDG RABBLING
B RACKETED
E RADIATED
E RADIATES
E RADICATE DS
CD RAFTSMAN
CD RAFTSMEN
T RAILHEAD S
T RAINBAND S
BG RAINIEST
BG RAINLESS
B RAINWASH
B RAMBLING
BC RANCHING
O RANGIEST
C RANKLING
F RANKNESS
B RASHNESS
W RASSLING
G RATIFIED
G RATIFIER S
G RATIFIES
B RATTIEST
P RATTLERS
BP RATTLING S
C RAUNCHES
T RAVELERS
GT RAVELING S
GT RAVELLED
T RAVELLER S
C RAVENING S
P REABSORB S

P REACCUSE DS
BP REACHERS
BP REACHING
P REACTING
P READAPTS
P READJUST S
P READMITS
P READOPTS
P REALLOTS
P REALTERS
P REARMING
P REASSIGN S
P REASSURE DS

P REBIDDEN
P REBILLED
P REBIRTHS
P REBOARDS
P REBOILED
P REBOOKED
P REBOUGHT
P REBUILDS
P REBUYING
P RECEDING
P RECENSOR S
P RECEPTOR S
P RECESSED
P RECESSES
P RECHARGE DRS

P RECHECKS
P RECHOOSE S
P RECHOSEN
P RECISION S
P RECLEANS
P RECODING
P RECOOKED
P REDATING
T REDDLING
P REDEFINE DS
P REDIGEST S
P REDRILLS
P REDRYING
G REEDIEST
B REEDINGS
P REEDITED
P REELECTS
P REENACTS
G REENGAGE DS

P REERECTS
P REEXPOSE DS

P REFACING
P REFERRED
P REFERRER S
P REFIGURE DS
P REFILING
P REFILLED
P REFIRING
P REFIXING
P REFORMAT ES

P REFORMED
P REFREEZE S
P REFROZEN
P REFUNDED
P REGNANCY
P REGROWTH S
P REHANDLE DS

P REHARDEN S
P REHEATED
P REHEATER S
P REHIRING
P REIMPOSE DS
P REINFORM S
P REINSERT S
P REINVITE DS
P REJUDGED
P REJUDGES
P RELAUNCH

P RELOADED
P RELOCATE DES

P REMARKET S
C REMATING
P REMISING
P REMIXING
P REMODIFY
P REMOLDED
C RENATURE DS

P RENOTIFY
P RENUMBER S
P REOBTAIN S
P REOCCUPY
P REORDAIN S
P REORDERS
P REPACKED
P REPASTED
P REPAVING
P REPAYING
P REPLACED
P REPLACES
P REPRICED
P REPRICES
P REPRINTS
P RERECORD S
P REREVIEW S
P RESCHOOL S
P RESCINDS
P RESCORED
P RESCORES
P RESCREEN S
P RESCRIPT S
P RESEASON S
P RESELECT S
P RESENTED
P RESERVED
P RESERVER S
P RESERVES
P RESETTLE DS
P RESHAPED
P RESHAPES
P RESHOWED
P RESIDENT S
P RESIDERS
P RESIDING
P RESIFTED
P RESOAKED
P RESOLVED
P RESOLVES
P RESORTED
P RESTAMPS
C RESTLESS
P RESTORED
P RESTORES
P RESTRESS
P RESTRIKE S
P RESUMERS
P RESUMING
P RESURVEY S
P RETAPING
P RETASTED
P RETASTES
P RETESTED
C RETINOID S
P RETRAINS
P RETREATS
P RETRIALS
P RETYPING
P REUNIONS
P REUNITED
P REUNITES
P REVALUED
P REVALUES
B REVETTED
P REVIEWED
P REVIEWER S
P REVISING
P REVISION S
P REVISITS
P REVISORS
P REWARMED

New 2006

Bob's Bible: Words With Front Hooks

P REWASHED
P REWASHES
P REWEIGHS
P REWIRING
P REWORKED
C RIBBINGS
G RIDDLING
T RIFLINGS
B RIGHTEST
F RIGHTFUL
F RIGHTING
F RIGIDITY
T RIMESTER S
G RIMINESS
C RIMPLING
C RIPPLERS
C RIPPLING
F RISKIEST
B ROACHING
B ROADSIDE S
C ROCKETED
F ROCKLESS
T ROLLINGS
B ROOMIEST
C ROQUETED
C ROQUETTE S
P ROSINESS
P ROSTRATE
G ROUNDERS
G ROUNDING
C ROUPIEST
T ROUSSEAU S
T ROWELING
T ROWELLED
D RUBBINGS
T RUCKLING
C RUDDIEST
C RUDENESS
P RUDERIES
G RUMBLERS
CDG RUMBLING S
C RUMMIEST
C RUMPLIER
C RUMPLING
B RUSHIEST
T RUSTABLE
CT RUSTIEST
CT RUSTLESS
T RUTHLESS

E SCALADES
E SCALLOPS
E SCARPING
A SCENDING
A SCRIBING
A SEXUALLY
A SKEWNESS
I SLANDERS
I SOLATING
I SOLATION S
A SPIRANTS
E SPOUSALS
E SPOUSING
E SQUIRING
E STABLISH
A STEROIDS
A STHENIAS
A STOMATAL
O STOMATES
E STOPPAGE S
E STOPPING
A STOUNDED
A STRADDLE DR
S
E STRANGER S
E STRANGES T
E STRAYING
A STRINGED
A SYLLABIC S
A SYMMETRY
A SYNAPSES
A SYNAPSIS
A SYNDETIC

S TACKLESS
S TAKEOUTS
S TALKIEST
S TALKINGS
S TARRIEST
A TEMPORAL S
A THEISTIC
E THIONINE S
S TICKLERS
S TICKLING
S TICKSEED S
S TIPPLERS
S TIPPLING
S TOCCATAS
A TONALITY
A TONICITY
S TOPPLING
S TOWAWAYS
S TRAINERS
S TRAINING S
S TRAPPERS
S TRAPPING S
S TRICKLED
S TRICKLES
S TRIPLING
S TRIPPERS
S TRIPPING S
S TROLLERS
S TROLLING S
A TROPHIED
A TROPHIES
A TROPINES
A TROPISMS
S TRUMPETS
S TUBBIEST
S TUMBLERS
S TUMBLING S

D UBIETIES
CLN UMBERING
S UNBATHED
S UNBLOCKS
S UNBONNET S
S UNBURNED
S UNCHOKES
R UNCINATE
FJ UNCTIONS
G UNFOUGHT
P UNGENTLY
F UNHOUSES
C UNIFORMS
R UNROUNDS
S UNTANNED
C UPBEARER S
R URALITES
B URSIFORM
P USTULATE
MP UTTERERS
BGM UTTERING
P

E VAGINATE D
E VALUABLE S
E VALUATED
E VALUATES
E VALUATOR S
E VANISHED
E VANISHES
O VARIOLES
A VASCULAR
A VENGEFUL
A VENTAILS
E VENTLESS
AE VERSIONS
E VINCIBLE
A VIRULENT
AE VOCATION S
E VOCATIVE S
A VOIDABLE
A VOIDANCE S
E VOLUTION S
A VOUCHERS
A VOUCHING

T WADDLERS
ST WADDLING
A WAKENERS
A WAKENING S
S WALLOWED
S WALLOWER S
T WANGLERS
T WANGLING
T WATTLING
T WEEDIEST
S WEEPIEST
S WEEPINGS
S WELLHEAD S
S WELTERED
T WIDDLING
T WIGGIEST
DS WINDLING S
S WINGIEST
T WINKLING
T WINNINGS
T WITCHIER
ST WITCHING S
S WITHERED
S WOOSHING
S WORDPLAY S
S WOUNDING

T ZADDIKIM
O ZONATION S

2-letter Words

B **AA** HLS
CDFGJKLNSTW **AB** ASY
BCDFGHLMPRSTW **AD** DOSZ
BDFGHJLMNRSTWYZ **AG** AEOS
ABDHNPRY **AH** AIS
R **AI** DLMNRST
ABDGPS **AL** ABELPST
BCDGHJLNPRTY **AM** AIPU
BCDFGMNPRTVW **AN** ADEITY
BCEFGJLMOPTVWY **AR** BCEFKMST
ABFGHKLMPRTVWZ **AS** HKPS
BCEFGHKLMOPQRSTVW **AT** ET
CDHJLMNPRSTVWY **AW** AELN
FLMPRSTWZ **AX** E
BCDFGHJKLMNPRSWY **AY** ES
AO **BA** ADGHLMNPRSTY
O **BE** DEGLNSTY
O **BI** BDGNOSTZ
A **BO** ABDGOPSTWXY
A **BY** ES
O **DE** BEFLNVWXY
AU **DO** CEGLMNRSTW
BFGLMPRTWZ **ED** HS
DKR **EF** FST
BCDEGMST **EL** DFKLMS
FGHMR **EM** ESU
BDFGHKMPSTWY **EN** DGS
FHPS **ER** AEGNRS
BFHLOPRY **ES** S
BFGHJLMNPRSTVWY **ET** AH
FA BDGNRSTXY
FE DEHMNRSTUWYZ
AE **GO** ABDORSTXY
ASW **HA** DEGHJMOPSTWY
ST **HE** HMNPRSTWXY
ACGKP **HI** CDEMNPST
O **HM** M
MORTW **HO** BDEGNPSTWY
DKR **IF** FS
ABDFGHJKLPRSTWYZ **IN** KNS
ABCDHKLMPQSTVWX **IS** M
JO BEGTWY
OS **KA** BEFSTY
S **KI** DFNPRST
A **LA** BCDGMPRSTVWXY
LI BDENPST
LO BGOPTWX
A **MA** CDEGNPRSTWXY
E **ME** DGLMNTW
A **MI** BCDGLMRSX
MO ABCDGLMNOPRSTW
AE **MU** DGMNST
MY C
A **NA** BEGHMNPWY
AO **NE** BEGTW
O **NO** BDGHMORSTW
G **NU** BNST
BCGHMNPRSTY **OD** ADES
OF FT
FNOP **OH** MOS
KP **OI** L
CDEFHIMSTWY **ON** EOS
BCFHKLMPSTW **OP** EST
CDFGKMNT **OR** ABCEST
BCDGHKMNSW **OS** E
BCDHJLMNPRSTVWY **OW** ELN
BCFGLPSV **OX** OY
S **PA** CDHLMNPRSTWXY
AO **PE** ACDEGHNPRSTW
PI ACEGNPSTUX
AEIO **RE** BCDEFGIMPSTVX
A **SH** AEHY
P **SI** BCMNPRSTX
SO BDLMNPSTUWXY
EU **TA** BDEGJMNOPRSTUVWX
TI CELNPST
TO DEGMNOPRTWY
BCGHLMRSVY **UM** MP
CDHPSTY **UP** OS
BJMNP **US** E
BCGHJMNOPRT **UT** AES
AEO **WE** BDENT
T **WO** EKNOSTW
PR **YA** GHKMPRWY
ABDEKLPRTW **YE** AHNPSTW
YO BDKMNUW
ZA GPSX

3-letter Words

BG **ABY** ES
FPT **ACT** AS
DF **ADO** S
ADZ E
GRS **AGA** RS
CGMPRSW **AGE** DERS
DS **AGO** GN
CLMPQRS **AID** ES
FHLMPVW **AIR** NSTY
GNT **ALA** ENRS
ALB AS
BDGHKMPRSTVW **ALE** CEFS
BCFGHLMPSTW **ALL** SY
ABDGPS **ALS** O
HMS **ALT** OS
GLM **AMA** HS
KR **AMI** ADENRS
KMN **ANA** LS
BCFGJKLMPSVW **ANE** SW
BR **ANI** LS
CHPRW **ANT** AEIS
CGJNRT **APE** DRSX
C **APO** DS
MN **ARC** HOS
BCDFHMPRTWY **ARE** AS
BFHW **ARM** SY
BCEGJLMOPTVW **ARS**
CDFHKMPTW **ART** SY
BCDFGHLMPRSW **ASH** Y
CEFGHLNPRSW **AVE** RS
AVO SW
AWA Y
AWE DES
DFLMPSY **AWN** SY
AXE DLS
AZO N
BAA LS
BAD ES
BAH T
BAL DEKLMS
BAN DEGIKS
K **BAR** BDEFKMNS
AO **BAS** EHKST
BAT EHST
A **BED** SU
BEE FNPRST
BEL LST
BEN DEST
O **BES** T
A **BET** AHS
BIB BS
BID EIS
BIN DEST
BIO GS
IO **BIS** EK
O **BIT** EST
BIZ E
BOA RST
BOD ESY
BOG SY
BOO BKMNRST
A **BOS** HKS
BOT AHST
BOW LS
BOX Y
BOY OS
BRA DEGNSTWY
BRO OSW
BRR R
BUB OSU
BUM FPS
BUN ADGKNST
BUR ABDGLNPRSY
BUS HKSTY
A **BUT** EST
S **CAD** EIS
S **CAM** EOPS
S **CAN** EST
CAP EHOS
S **CAR** BDEKLNPRST
S **CAT** ES
CEL LST
CEP ES
CHI ACDNPST
CIS T
COB BS
COD AES
COL ADESTY
I **CON** EIKNSY
COO FKLNPST
S **COP** ESY
COR DEFKMNSY
COS HSTY
S **COT** ES
S **COW** LSY
COX A
COZ Y
E **CRU** DSX
CUB ES
CUR BDEFLNRST
S **CUT** ES
DAD AOS
DAG OS
O **DAH** LS
DAL ES
DAM ENPS
DAN GKS
DAW KNST
DEB ST
DEE DMPRST
DEF ITY
DEL EFILST
DEN EISTY
DEV AS
DEW SY
DEX Y
DID OY
DIE DLST
DIF FS
DIM ES
DIN EGKOST
DIP ST
DIS CHKS
AE **DIT** AESZ
DOC KS
DOG ESY
I **DOL** ELST
DOM ES
U **DON** AEGS
O **DOR** EKMPRSY
AU **DOS** EST
DOT EHSY
DOW NS
DUD ES
DUE LST
DUI T
DUN EGKST
DUO S
DUP ES
BDFGHLNPRSTWY **EAR** LNS
BFHMNPST **EAT** HS
B **EAU** X
FHKPRSTW **EEL** SY
TY **EGG** SY
S **EGO** S
H **ELM** SY
BCDEGMST **ELS** E
DFHMS **EME** SU
B **ERG** OS
FHKT **ERN** ES
HS **ERS** T
N **EVE** NRS
EWE RS
EYE DNRS
FAD EOS
FAN EGOS
A **FAR** DELMOT
FAS HT
FAT ES
FEE BDLST
FEM ES
FEN DS
FER EN
FES ST
FET AES
FEU DS
FID OS
FIE F
FIL AELMOS
FIN DEKOS
FIR EMNS
FIX T
FIZ Z
FLU BESX
FOG SY
FOH N
FON DST
FOR ABDEKMT
FOU LR
FOX Y
FRO EGMW
FUG SU
FUN DKS
FUR LSY
GAB SY
E **GAD** IS
GAE DNS
GAG AES
E **GAL** AELS
O **GAM** ABEPSY
GAN EG
GAP ESY
A **GAR** BS
A **GAS** HPT
GAT ES
AO **GEE** DKSZ
GEL DST
GEN ESTU
GET AS
GIB ES
GIE DNS
GIG AS
A **GIN** KS
GIT ES
GOA DLST
GOB OSY
GOO DFKNPS
GOR EMPY
E **GOS** H
GOT H
GUL FLPS
GUN KS
CS **HAD** EJ
T **HAE** DMNST
S **HAH** AS
HAJ IJ
CSW **HAM** ES
HAS HPT
CGKPSTW **HAT** EHS
CST **HAW** KS
AT **HEM** EPS
TW **HEN** ST
HER BDELMNOS
S **HES** T
KW **HET** HS
CPSTW **HEW** NS
C **HIC** K
CW **HID** E
CSTW **HIN** DST
ACGKPT **HIS** NST
HOB OS
S **HOG** GS
CP **HON** EGKS
CSW **HOP** ES
CDS **HOW** EFKLS
A **HOY** AS
CT **HUG** ES
C **HUM** PS
S **HUN** GHKST
HYP EOS
DHKLMNPRSTW **ICK** Y
BDJMRT **IFF** Y
BMS **ILK** AS
BDFGHJKMNPRSTVWYZ **ILL** SY
GJLPSW **IMP** IS
DFGJKLMOPRSW **INK** SY
JAG GS
JAM BS
A **JAR** LS
A **JEE** DPRSZ
JET ES
JEU X
JIB BES
D **JIN** KNSX
JOE SY
JOT AS
JOW LS
JUG AS

New 2006

Bob's Bible: Words With Interesting Back Hooks

JUN K
JUS T
JUT ES

IS **KAT** AS
O **KAY** OS
KEN OST
S **KEP** IST
AS **KIN** ADEGKOS
KIR KNS
S **KIS** ST
S **KIT** EHS
KOA NS
KOB OS
KOP HS
KOR AES
KOS S

LAC EKSY
CG **LAD** ESY
BCFGS **LAM** ABEPS
A **LAR** DIKS
A **LAS** EHST
BFPS **LAT** EHISU
LAV AES
BCFS **LAW** NS
FIOP **LEA** DFKLNPRS
AFG **LEE** KRST
LEK ESU
LEU D
LEV AOY
S **LID** OS
P **LIE** DFNRSU
B **LIN** EGKNOSTY
BCFS **LIP** AES
LIS PT
AFS **LIT** ESU
BGS **LOB** EOS
BCFS **LOG** EOSY
LOO FKMNPST
CFGPS **LOP** ES
BCPS **LOT** AHIS
ABFGPS **LOW** ENS
GPS **LUG** ES
AGPS **LUM** APS
F **LUX** E

MAC EHKS
MAD ES
MAG EIS
MAN AEOSY
MAR ACEKLST
A **MAS** AHKST
MAT EHST
MAW NS
MAX I
MAY AOS
MEG AS
MEL DLST
MEM EOS
AO **MEN** DOU
MET AEH
S **MEW** LS
MHO S
E **MIC** AES
AI **MID** IS
MIG GS
MIL DEKLOST
MIM E
AE **MIR** EIKSY
A **MIS** EOST
MIX T
MOA NST
MOC KS

MOD EIS
MOL ADELSTY
MOM EIS
MON KOSY
MOO DLNRST
MOP ESY
MOR AENST
MOS HKST
MOT EHST
MOW NS
S **MUG** GS
MUM MPSU
MUN IS
AE **MUS** EHKST
S **MUT** EST

NAB ES
NAM E
NAN AS
KS **NAP** AES
K **NEE** DMP
NET ST
AK **NEW** ST
A **NIL** LS
S **NIP** AS
KSU **NIT** ES
NIX EY
NOD EIS
S **NOG** GS
NOM AES
NOO KN
NOR IM
O **NOS** EHY
KS **NOT** AE
EKS **NOW** ST

S **OAK** SY
BCDGM **OAT** HS
LR **OBE** SY
OBI AST
CS **ODA** HS
BCLMNR **ODE** AS
BCFMNRST **OIL** SY
OKA SY
CHJMPSTWY **OKE** HS
BCFGHMSTW **OLD** SY
BCDHJMPRSTV **OLE** AOS
M **ONO** S
CDHLMNPRT **OPE** DNS
BFHKMST **ORA** DL
FS **ORB** SY
T **ORC** AS
N **OVA** L

PAC AEKSTY
PAD IS
O **PAL** ELMPSY
S **PAN** EGST
PAP AS
S **PAR** ADEKRST
SU **PAS** EHST
S **PAT** EHSY
PAW LNS
PEA GKLNRST
S **PEC** HKS
E **PEE** KLNPRS
O **PEN** DST
PEP OS
A **PER** EIKMPTV
AO **PES** OT

PHI SZ
PIA LNS
ES **PIC** AEKS
PIE DRS
S **PIN** AEGKSTY
PIP ESY
PIS HO
S **PIT** AHSY
PIX Y
POL ELOSY
POP ES
POX Y
PRO ADFGMPSW
PUG HS
PUL AEILPS
S **PUN** AGKSTY
PUP ASU
S **PUR** EILRS
O **PUS** HS
PUT STZ

A **QUA** DGIY

BCDF **RAG** AEGIS
RAI ADLNS
RAJ A
CDGPT **RAM** IPS
BG **RAN** DGIKT
CFTW **RAP** EST
BE **RAS** EHP
BDFGP **RAT** EHOS
BDFGPT **RAY** AS
REC KS
BCI **RED** DEOS
BDFGPT **REE** DFKLS
T **REF** ST
REI FNS
P **REP** OPS
AIOT **RES** HT
FT **RET** ES
RHO S
A **RIA** LS
AGI **RID** ES
RIF EFST
BGPT **RIM** ESY
BG **RIN** DGKS
DGT **RIP** ES
ROB ES
C **ROC** KS
PT **ROD** ES
FP **ROM** PS
GT **ROT** AEILOS
DG **RUB** ESY
DFT **RUG** AS
ADG **RUM** PS
RUN EGST
B **RUT** HS

SAB ES
SAC KS
SAD EI
SAG AEOSY
SAL ELPST
SAT EI
SAU L
SAW NS
A **SEA** LMRST
SEC ST
SEE DKLMNPRS
SEG OS
SEI FS
SEL FLS
SEN DET
U **SER** AEFS
SET AST

SEW NS
SEX TY
SHA DGHMWY
SHE ADSW
SIB BS
SIC EKS
SIM APS
SIN EGHKS
SIP ES
SIR ES
SIT EHS
SKA GST
SKI DMNPST
SOB AS
SOD AS
SOL ADEIOS
SOM AES
SON EGS
SOP HS
SOT HS
SOU KLPRS
SOW NS
SOY AS
SPA EMNRSTY
STY E
SUB AS
SUE DRST
SUM OPS
SUN GKNS
SUP ES
SYN CE

S **TAB** SU
TAE L
TAM EPS
TAN GKS
TAO S
A **TAP** AES
S **TAR** ENOPST
EU **TAS** KS
S **TAT** ES
TAU ST
TAX AI
TEA KLMRST
TEE DLMNS
TEG GS
TEL AELS
TEN DST
S **TET** HS
THE EMNWY
THO U
EO **TIC** KS
TIL ELST
TIN EGSTY
TIP IS
TIT IS
TOD SY
TOE ADS
TOG AS
A **TOM** BES
TON EGSY
TOO KLMNT
AS **TOP** EHIOS
TOR ACEINORSTY
S **TOT** ES
S **TOW** NSY
TOY OS
S **TUB** AES
S **TUN** AEGS
TUT SU
TWA ES
TWO S
S **TYE** ERS

JK **UDO** NS
UPO N

VAN EGS
VAR ASY
K **VAS** AET
VAT SU
VEE PRS

VET OS
VEX T
VIA L
A **VID** ES
VIE DRSW
VIG AS
VIS AE
VUG GHS

WAD EISY
S **WAG** ES
HS **WAN** DEKSTY
WAR DEKMNPSTY
T **WAS** HPT
ST **WAT** ST
WAW LS
WAX Y
AT **WEE** DKLNPRST
WEN DST
WHA MPT
WHO AMP
T **WIN** DEGKOSY
IY **WIS** EHPST
T **WIT** EHS
WOK ES
WON KST
WOO DFLS
T **WOS** T
WYN DNS

YAG IS
K **YAR** DEN
YAW LNPS
YEA HNRS
YET IT
YIP ES
YOD HS
YOK ES
YON DI
YOU RS
YOW ELS

ZIN CEGS
ZIT IS
ZOO MNS

4-letter Words

B **ABAS** EH
ABBE SY
CFGST **ABLE** DRS
ABYS MS
ACID SY
F **AGIN** G
AGIO S
W **AGON** ESY
AIRT HS
ALAN DEGST
MT **ALAR** MY
ALGA ELS
BT **ALKY** DL
BDGPRSTW **ALLY** L
H **ALMA** HS
ALME HS
ALTO S
CGLM **AMAS** S
MS **AMBO** S
RY **AMEN** DST
AMID EOS
G **AMIN** EOS
T **AMIS** S
AMMO S
RW **AMUS** E
ANIL ES
R **ANIS** E
CM **ANNA** LS
H **ANSA** E
M **ANTA** ES
ANTI CS
CHPRW **ANTS** Y
CGJPRT **APER** SY
AQUA ES
AREA ELS
CDFHKMPTW **ARTS** Y
P **ARVO** S
ATMA NS
ATOM SY
ATOP Y
DGHJTV **AUNT** SY
L **AURA** ELRS
AUTO S
CHLPRSW **AVER** ST
AXIL ES
T **AXON** ES

BABE LS
BABU LS
BAFF SY
BAIT HS
BALD SY
BALK SY
BALL SY
BALM SY
BALS A
BAND ASY
BARB ES
BARD ES
BARE DRS
BARK SY
BARM SY
BARN SY
A **BASE** DRS
BASS IOY
BAST ES
BATH ES
BATT SUY
BAWD SY

BEAD SY
BEAK SY
A **BEAM** SY
BEAN OS
BEAR DS
BEAU STX
BEEF SY
BEER SY
BELL ESY
BEND SY
BENT OS
BERM ES
BICE PS
A **BIDE** DRST
BIFF SY
BILL SY
BIMA HS
BIND IS
BINE RS
BIRL ES
BIRO S
O **BITS** Y
BITT SY
BLAM ES
BLAT ES
BLAW NS
BLIN DIK
BLOC KS
BLOW NSY
BLUE DRSTY
BLUR BST
BOAR DST
BOAS T
BOFF OS
BOHO S
BOLA RS
BOLO S
BOMB ES
BONE DRSY
BONG OS
BOOB SY
BOOM SY
BOOS T
BOOT HSY
BORA LSX
BORN E
A **BORT** SYZ
BOSK SY
BOSS Y
BOTH Y
BOWS E
BOYO S
BOZO S
BRAN DKST
BRAS HS
BRAW LNS
BRED E
BREN ST
BRIE FRS
BRIN EGKSY
BRIO S
A **BRIS** KS
BRIT HST
BROO DKMS
BROS EY
BROW NS
BRUT ES
BUCK OS
BUFF IOSY
BULK SY
BULL ASY
BUMP HSY
BUND ST
BUNK OS
BUNN SY
BURA NS
BURG HS
BURL SY
BURN ST
BURR OSY
BURS AET
BUSH Y

Bob's Bible: Words With Interesting Back Hooks

Front	Word	Back
	BUST	SY
	BUTE	OS
	BUTT	ESY
	CACA	OS
	CADE	ST
	CAGE	DRSY
	CAKE	DSY
S	CALL	AS
	CALO	S
	CAME	LOS
	CAMO	S
S	CAMP	IOSY
S	CANS	OT
S	CANT	OSY
S	CAPE	DRS
	CAPO	NS
	CARB	OS
S	CARE	DRSTX
	CARL	ES
	CARN	SY
S	CARP	IS
	CARR	SY
S	CARS	E
S	CART	ES
	CASK	SY
	CAST	ES
	CATE	RS
	CAUL	DKS
	CECA	L
	CEIL	IS
	CELL	AIOS
S	CENT	OSU
	CERO	S
	CHAI	NRS
	CHAM	PS
	CHAO	S
	CHAP	EST
	CHAR	DEKMRS TY
	CHEW	SY
	CHIA	OS
	CHIC	AKOS
	CHID	E
	CHIN	AEKOS
	CHUM	PS
Y	CLAD	ES
	CLAM	PS
	CLAN	GKS
	CLAP	ST
	CLEF	ST
	CLIP	ST
	CLON	EKS
	CLOT	HS
	COAL	ASY
	COAT	IS
	COBB	SY
A	COCK	SY
	COCO	AS
	CODE	CDNRSX
	COHO	GS
	COMA	ELS
	COMB	EOS
	COME	RST
	COMP	OST
S	CONE	DSY
	CONI	CN
	CONK	SY
	COOK	SY
	COOL	SY
S	COOP	ST
S	COPE	DNRS
S	COPS	E
S	CORE	DRS
	CORK	SY
AS	CORN	SUY
	CORS	E
	COST	AS
	COUP	ES
	COVE	DNRSTY
	COXA	EL
S	CRAM	PS
S	CRAP	ES
	CRAW	LS
A	CRED	OS
	CRIS	P
	CROC	IKS
	CROW	DNS
	CRUD	ES
E	CRUS	EHT
	CUBE	BDRS
S	CULL	SY
	CULT	IS
	CURD	SY
	CURE	DRST
	CURL	SY
	CURR	SY
	CURS	ET
	CUSS	O
AS	CUTE	RSY
	CYAN	OS
	CYMA	ERS
	DADO	S
	DAFF	SY
	DAIS	Y
	DARK	S
	DASH	IY
	DATO	S
	DAUB	ESY
I	DEAL	ST
	DEAR	SY
	DECO	RSY
	DEED	SY
	DELF	ST
	DELL	SY
	DELT	AS
	DEMO	BNS
	DENI	M
	DENS	E
	DERM	AS
	DICE	DRSY
	DICK	SY
	DIDO	S
	DIKE	DRSY
	DILL	SY
	DIME	RS
	DING	EOSY
	DINK	SY
	DINO	S
	DIPS	O
	DIRE	R
	DIRT	SY
	DISC	IOS
	DISH	Y
AE	DITS	Y
	DITZ	Y
	DIVA	NS
	DJIN	NS
	DODO	S
	DOES	T
	DOGE	SY
	DOJO	S
	DOLL	SY
	DONE	E
	DONG	AS
U	DONS	Y
	DOOM	SY
	DOPE	DRSY
	DORK	SY
	DORM	SY
O	DORS	A
	DOUM	AS
O	DOUR	A
	DOVE	NS
A	DOWN	SY
	DOWS	E
A	DOZE	DNRS
	DRAM	AS
	DRAW	LNS
	DRIP	ST
	DROP	ST
	DUCK	SY
	DULL	SY
	DUMB	OS
	DUMP	SY
	DUNG	SY
	DURA	LS
	DURO	CS
	DURR	AS
	DUSK	SY
A	DUST	SY
	DYKE	DSY
	DYNE	LS
P	EARL	SY
CFL PT	EASE	DLS
	EBON	SY
	ECHO	S
HKL SW	EDGE	DRS
	EIDE	R
	ELAN	DS
	EMYD	ES
	EPHA	HS
	ERAS	E
	ERGO	T
CHZ	EROS	E
	EURO	S
S	EVEN	ST
FLN S	EVER	TY
	EXPO	S
	EYAS	S
	FACE	DRST
	FADO	S
	FAIN	T
	FAIR	SY
	FAKE	DRSY
	FANG	AS
	FANO	NS
	FARL	ES
	FARO	S
	FATS	O
	FAUN	AS
	FAWN	SY
	FELL	ASY
	FERN	SY
	FESS	E
	FETA	LS
	FIDO	S
	FILA	R
	FILE	DRST
	FILL	EOSY
	FILM	ISY
	FILO	S
	FINE	DRS
	FINO	S
	FIRS	T
	FISH	Y
	FIVE	RS
	FIZZ	Y
	FLAK	EY
	FLAM	ESY
	FLAN	KS
	FLAW	SY
	FLAX	Y
	FLEA	MS
	FLEE	RST
	FLIC	KS
	FLIR	ST
	FLIT	ES
	FLOC	KS
	FLOW	NS
	FLUS	H
	FOAM	SY
	FOLK	SY
	FOND	SU
A	FOOT	SY
	FORA	MY
	FORB	SY
	FORD	OS
	FORK	SY
	FORM	ES
	FORT	EHSY
	FOSS	AE
	FREE	DRS
A	FRIT	HSTZ
	FRIZ	Z
	FROW	NS
	FUBS	Y
	FUGU	ES
	FULL	SY
	FUME	DRST
	FUND	IS
	FUNK	SY
	FUSE	DELS
	FUSS	Y
	FUZE	DES
	FUZZ	Y
	GADI	DS
	GAFF	ES
	GALA	HSX
	GALE	AS
	GALL	SY
A	GAMA	SY
	GAMB	AES
	GAME	DRSY
	GANE	FV
A	GATE	DRS
	GAUD	SY
	GAUN	T
A	GAVE	L
	GAWK	SY
	GECK	OS
	GEEK	SY
O	GEES	ET
A	GENE	ST
	GENU	AS
	GERM	SY
E	GEST	ES
	GILL	SY
	GIMP	SY
	GIPS	Y
	GIRL	SY
	GIRO	NS
	GIRT	HS
O	GIVE	NRS
	GLAD	ESY
O	GLED	ES
A	GLEE	DKST
	GLIA	LS
	GLIM	ES
	GLOB	ES
	GLUE	DRSY
	GLUM	ES
	GLUT	ES
	GNAR	LRS
	GNAW	NS
	GOBO	S
	GOGO	S
A	GONE	FR
	GOOD	SY
	GOOF	SY
	GOOK	SY
	GOON	SY
	GOOP	SY
	GOOS	EY
	GOUT	SY
	GRAD	ES
	GRAM	APS
	GRAN	ADST
	GRAT	E
A	GREE	DKNST
	GRID	ES
	GRIM	EY
	GRIN	DS
	GRIP	ESTY
	GRIT	HS
	GROW	LNS
	GRUE	LS
	GRUM	EP
	GUAN	OS
	GUAR	DS
	GUID	ES
	GULF	SY
	GULL	SY
	GULP	SY
	GUNK	SY
	GUSH	Y
	GUST	OSY
	GUTS	Y
	GYPS	Y
	GYRO	NS
	HADJ	I
	HAIK	ASU
C	HAIR	SY
	HAJJ	I
SW	HALE	DRS
S	HALL	OS
	HALM	AS
	HALO	NS
	HAND	SY
ST	HANK	SY
CS	HARD	SY
CS	HARE	DMS
S	HARP	SY
G	HAST	EY
S	HAUL	MS
G	HAUT	E
S	HAVE	NRS
CST	HAWS	E
	HAZE	DLRS
A	HEAD	SY
C	HEAP	SY
S	HEAR	DST
CW	HEAT	HS
T	HEFT	SY
S	HELL	OS
	HELO	ST
	HEMP	SY
	HERB	SY
T	HERM	AS
	HERO	NS
T	HIGH	ST
	HILA	R
CST	HILL	OSY
S	HIRE	DERS
	HISS	Y
	HOAR	DSY
	HOBO	S
C	HOKE	DSY
DTW	HOLE	DSY
	HOME	DRSY
	HOMO	S
PS	HONE	DRSY
T	HONG	IS
	HONK	SY
	HOOD	SY
CS	HOOK	ASY
BS	HOOT	SY
	HORA	HLS
ST	HORN	SY
CTW	HOSE	DLNRSY
G	HOST	AS
	HOUR	IS
S	HOVE	LR
	HOWF	FS
C	HUFF	SY
	HUGE	R
	HULK	SY
A	HULL	OS
CTW	HUMP	HSY
CT	HUNK	SY
CT	HURL	SY
	HUSK	SY
	HYPO	S
	IAMB	IS
	IDEA	LS
S	IDLE	DRS
	IDYL	LS
P	ILEA	CL
CM	ILIA	CDL
T	IMID	EOS
	INBY	E
	INFO	S
G	IRON	ESY
AL	ISLE	DST
ABD FHP W	ITCH	Y
	JACK	SY
	JAGG	SY
	JAMB	ES
	JATO	S
	JAZZ	Y
	JELL	OSY
	JERK	SY
	JESS	E
	JIFF	SY
	JIMP	Y
D	JINN	IS
	JIVE	DRSY
	JOCK	OS
	JOIN	ST
	JOKE	DRSY
	JOLT	SY
	JOWL	SY
	JUCO	S
	JUDO	S
A	JUGA	L
	JUMP	SY
	JUNK	SY
	JURA	LT
	KAMI	K
	KAYO	S
S	KELP	SY
	KEMP	ST
	KENO	S
	KENT	E
	KERN	ES
	KETO	L
	KHET	HS
	KIBE	IS
	KICK	SY
	KILO	S
	KILT	SY
S	KINK	SY
	KINO	S
	KISS	Y
	KITH	ES
	KNEE	DLS
	KNOW	NS
	KNUR	LS
	KOBO	S
	KOLO	S
	KOOK	SY
	KORA	IST
	KOTO	SW
	KUDO	S
	KVAS	S
GP	LACE	DRSY
BCG	LADE	DNRS
	LAIC	HS
FG	LAIR	DS
FS	LAKE	DRS
	LAMB	SY
BF	LAME	DRS
BCF PS	LANK	Y
CFS	LAPS	E
	LARD	SY
	LARK	SY
B	LASE	DRS
CG	LASS	IO
ABE PS	LATE	DNRX
	LATH	EISY
CS	LAVE	DRS
B	LAWN	SY
P	LEAD	SY
	LEAF	SY
B	LEAK	SY
CG	LEAN	ST
	LEAP	ST
BC	LEAR	NSY
FP	LEAS	EHT
F	LEER	SY
C	LEFT	SY
	LENO	S
G	LENS	E
B	LENT	O
CS	LEPT	A
	LIAR	DS
	LICH	IT
	LIDO	S
	LIFE	R
A	LIKE	DNRS
	LILO	S
	LIMA	NS
C	LIMB	AIOSY
CGS	LIME	DNSY
	LIMO	S
B	LIMP	AS
AC	LINE	DNRSY
CFS	LING	AOSY
BCP S	LINK	SY
	LINO	S
EFG	LINT	SY
BEF	LITE	R
AO	LIVE	DNRS
G	LOAM	SY
	LOBO	S
	LOCA	L
	LOCO	S
	LODE	NS
A	LOFT	SY
	LOGO	INS
	LOLL	SY
AFK	LONG	ES
AK	LOOF	AS
	LOON	SY
BS	LOOP	SY
	LOOS	E
C	LOSE	LRS
FG	LOSS	Y
F	LOTA	HS
	LOTI	C
	LOUP	ES
CF	LOUR	SY
	LOWE	DRS
BFG PS	LOWS	E
CP	LUCK	SY
BFS	LUFF	AS
CFP S	LUMP	SY
	LUNA	RS
	LUNE	ST
CFS	LUNG	EIS
	LURE	DRSX
	LUST	SY
EFG	LUTE	ADS
	MACE	DRS
	MACH	EOS
	MAGI	C
E	MAIL	ELS
	MAKO	S
	MALM	SY
S	MALT	SY
	MANA	ST
	MANO	RS
	MANS	E
	MARC	HS
	MARK	AS
	MARL	SY
	MARS	EH
S	MASH	Y
A	MASS	AEY
	MATE	DRSY
	MATT	ES
	MAUN	D
	MAXI	MS
	MAYA	NS
	MAYO	RS
	MAYS	T
AS	MAZE	DRS
	MEAL	SY
	MEAN	STY
	MEAT	SY

Bob's Bible: Words With Interesting Back Hooks

S MELT SY
MEMO S
MERC HSY
MERE RS
MERL ES
MESH Y
MESS Y
META L
METE DRS
AI MIDS T
MIFF SY
MILK SY
MILL ES
MILO S
MILT SY
MIME DORS
MINA ES
MINI MS
MINK ES
MINT SY
MIRE DSX
MIRI N
S MIRK SY
MISO S
A MISS Y
MIST SY
S MITE RS
MODE LMS
MOJO S
MOLA LRS
MOLD SY
MOLL SY
S MOLT OS
MONO S
MOOD SY
MOOL AS
MOON SY
MOOR SY
MOOS E
MOPE DRSY
MORA ELSY
MORE LS
MORS E
MOSS OY
MOST ES
ES MOTE LSTY
MOTH SY
MOTT EOS
MOZO S
MUCH O
A MUCK SY
MUGG SY
MULE DSY
MULL AS
MUMM SY
MURA LS
MURE DSX
MURK SY
MURR AESY
S MUSH Y
MUSK SY
MUSS Y
MUST HSY
MUTE DRS
MYNA HS
MYTH SY

NARC OS
S NARK SY
K NAVE LS
NEAT HS
K NEED SY
NERD SY
NETT SY
NEUM ES
NEVE RS
NEWS Y
NICE R
NIGH ST
U NITE RS
NOIL SY
NOLO S

NOMA DS
G NOME NS
NONE ST
S NOOK S
NORI AS
NOSE DSY
NOTA L
NOVA ES
NUDE RS
NUTS Y

LR OBES E
OBOL EIS
ODYL ES
OLEO S
FP OLIO S
NP ONCE T
F ORDO S
ORZO S
LMP OTTO S
OUPH ES
OUZO S
CHL MR OVER ST
BDL OWSE N
OXID ES
OXIM ES

AS PACE DRSY
PAGE DRS
PAIN ST
S PALE ADRST
S PALL SY
PALM SY
PALP IS
O PALS Y
PANE DLS
S PANG AS
S PANS Y
PANT OSY
PAPA LSW
PARA ES
PARD ISY
S PARE DORSU
S PARK AS
PARR SY
S PARS E
A PART SY
PASE OS
PASH A
PASS E
PAST AESY
S PATE DNRS
S PATS Y
PEAG ES
AS PEAK SY
S PEAR LST
PEAS E
PEAT SY
S PECK SY
S PEER SY
PEON SY
PEPO S
PERE AS
PERI LS
PERK SY
PESO S
PEST OSY
PHON EOSY
PHOT OS
A PIAN OS
S PICA LS
S PICK SY
S PIKE DRS
S PILE ADIS
OS PINE DSY
AO PING OS
PINK OSY
PINT AOS
PIPE DRST
PISO S
PITH SY
PLAN EKST

S PLAT ESY
S PLAY AS
PLEA DST
PLEB ES
PLOT SZ
PLUM BEPSY
PLUS H
POCK SY
POIS E
S POKE DRSY
POLO S
POLY PS
POMO S
S POOF
S POOR I
POPS Y
PORK SY
PORN OSY
S POTS Y
POUF FS
S POUT SY
PRAO S
S PRAT ES
S PREE DNS
PREX Y
PRIM AEIOPS
PROM OS
PROS EOSTY
PROW LS
PUCK AS
PUFF SY
PUJA HS
PULI KS
PULP SY
PULS E
S PUNK ASY
PUNT OSY
PUPA ELS
PURE ER
PURI NS
S PURS EY
PUSH Y
PUSS Y
PUTT IOSY
PYRE SX
PYRO S

QUAI LS
QUIN ST
E QUIP SU
QUIT ES

RAGE DES
RAGG SY
BDG T RAIN SY
RAIS E
RAJA HS
BCD RAKE DERS
RAMI E
BG RAND SY
OPW RANG EY
RANI DS
U RARE DRS
G RASP SY
CGI OPU RATE DLRS
W RATH E
RATO S
BCD GT RAVE DLNRS
RAYA HS
BCG RAZE DERS
BDO T READ DSY
AU REAL MS
D REAR MS
CU REDO NSX
BCD FGP T REED SY
REEF SY
CG REEK SY

BDF GPT REES T
REIF SY
REIN KS
B RENT ES
REPO ST
A RETE M
PT RICE DRS
RIFE R
RILE DSY
BDF GKP T RILL ES
G RIND SY
BG RINS E
CGT RIPE DNRS
AFP RISE NRS
BF RISK SY
F RITZ Y
D RIVE DNRST
BCF T ROCK SY
ET RODE OS
B ROIL SY
BC ROOK SY
BGV ROOM SY
ROOT SY
GT ROPE DRSY
ABE P ROSE DST
ROTO RS
ROUE NS
CG ROUP SY
GT ROUT EHS
DGP T ROVE DNRS
RUBE LS
RUDD SY
CP RUDE R
G RUFF ES
RUGA EL
B RUIN GS
BG RUNT SY
BC RUSH Y
CT RUST SY

SABE DRS
SAFE RS
U SAGE RS
SAGO S
SAIN ST
SAKE RS
SALE PS
SALL Y
SALP AS
SALS A
SALT SY
SAME K
SAND SY
SANE DRS
SANG AH
SARI NS
SARK SY
SASS Y
SATE DMS
SATI NS
SAUL ST
SAYS T
SCAM PS
SCAN ST
E SCAR EFPSTY
SCAT ST
SCOP ES
SCOW LS
SCUD IOS
SCUT AES
SEAM SY
SEED SY
SEEL SY
SEEP SY
SEGO S
SEIS EM
SELL ES

SEME NS
SENT EI
SEPT AS
SERA CIL
SERE DRS
SETA EL
SEXT OS
SHAD ESY
SHAM ES
P SHAW LMNS
SHEA FLRS
SHEW NS
SHIN ESY
SHIV AES
SHOG IS
SHOO KLNST
SHOT EST
SHOW NSY
SHUL NS
SHUN ST
SHUT ES
SICK OS
SIDH E
SIGH ST
SIGN AS
SIKE RS
SILK SY
SILL SY
SILO S
SILT SY
SIMA RS
SINE SW
U SING ES
SIRE DENS
SIZE DRS
SKAT ES
SKEE DNST
SKIM PS
SKIN KST
SKIT ES
SLAT ESY
SLID E
SLIM ESY
SLIP EST
SLOP ES
SLOT HS
SLUM PS
SLUR BPS
SMIT EH
SNIP ES
SNOW SY
SOAP SY
SOCK OS
SOFA RS
SOFT ASY
SOLA NR
SOLD IO
SOLE DIS
SOLI D
SOLO NS
SOMA NS
SONS Y
SOOT HSY
SOPH SY
SORE DLRS
SORT AS
SOUP SY
SOUS E
SPAN GKS
SPAR EKS
SPAS M
SPAT ES
SPEC KS
SPIN ESY
SPIT ESZ
SPUN K
SPUR NST
STAG ESY
STAR EKST
STAT ES
STEW SY
A STIR KPS

STOA EIST
E STOP EST
STOT ST
STOW PS
STUD SY
STUM PS
STUN GKST
T SUBA HS
SUCK SY
SUDS Y
SUED E
SUET SY
SUIT ES
SULK SY
SUMO S
SUNN ASY
SUPE RS
SURA HLS
SURE R
SURF SY
SWAG ES
SWAM IPY
SWAN GKS
SWAT HS
SYCE ES
SYNC HS

TABU NS
TACE ST
TACH ES
S TACK SY
TACO S
S TAIN ST
S TAKE NRS
TALA RS
S TALE RS
S TALK SY
S TALL SY
TAME DRS
S TANG AOSY
S TANK AS
TANS Y
TARO CKST
S TARS I
S TART SY
TASS E
S TATE RS
TAWS E
TEAR SY
TEAS E
TECH SY
TEEN SY
S TELA E
S TELE SX
TELL SY
TEMP IOST
TEND SU
TENS E
S TENT HSY
TEPA LS
S TERN ES
TEST ASY
THAN EK
THEM E
THEW SY
THIN EGKS
THIO L
THIR DL
THRO BEW
THRU M
AS TILT HS
TINE ADS
S TING ES
TIPS Y
TIRO S
TOAD SY
TOFF SY
TOGA ES
TOIL ES
S TOKE DNRS
TOLA NRS
AS TONE DRSY

TONG AS
TOOT HS
S TOPE DERS
TOPH EIS
TOPI CS
TOPO IS
TORA HS
TORC HS
TORI CI
TORO ST
TORS EIKO
TORT AES
TOTE DMRS
TOWN SY
TOYO NS
TRAD E
TRAM PS
S TRAP ST
TREE DNS
TRES S
TRIG OS
TRIO LS
AS TRIP ES
TROD E
S TROP E
TROT HS
TRUE DRS
TUBA ELS
TUBE DRS
TUFT SY
TURF SY
TUSH Y
E TWEE DNT
TWIN ESY
TYIN G
TYPE DSY
TYPO S
TYRO S

ULNA DERS
DGJ UMBO S
UNCI A
BJ UNCO SY
UNDE ER
UNIT ESY
UPBY E
UPDO S
UREA LS
B URSA E
UVEA LS

VALE ST
VAMP SY
VASA L
A VAST SY
U VEAL SY
VEER SY
VEIN SY
VELA R
VELD ST
VENA EL
AEO VERT SU
VEST AS
VIDE O
VIEW SY
VILE R
VILL AIS
VINA LS
VINO S
VINY L
VIOL AS
VITA EL
VOLT AEIS
VUGG SY

WACK EOSY
S WAGE DRS
A WAKE DNRS
S WALE DRS
WALL ASY
WANE DSY
S WART SY
AS WASH Y

WASP SY
WAST ES
WAVE DRSY
WEAL DS
S WEAR SY
T WEED SY
T WEEN SY
S WEEP SY
WEES T
WEIR DS
DS WELL SY
WHAM OS
WHEE LNP
WHIN ESY
WHIP ST
WHIR LRS
WHIT ESY
WHIZ Z
WHOM P
WIDE NRS
WIFE DSY
ST WILL SY
WIMP SY
WIND SY
DGST WINE DSY
AOS WING SY
WINO S
WISE DRS
S WISH A
WISP SY
S WITH EY
S WIVE DRS
A WOKE N
WOMB SY
WONK SY
WOOD SY
WOOL SY
WOOS H
S WORD SY
WORM SY
WORT HS
WOVE N
WRAP ST
WRIT ES
WUSS Y

XYST IS

YARE R
YEAR NS
YEAS T
YECH SY
YEUK SY
YOGI CNS
YOKE DLS
YOLK SY
YONI CS
YOUR NS
YOUS E
YUCK SY
YURT AS

ZERO S
ZEST SY
ZINC SY
A ZINE BS
ZING SY
ZOEA ELS
ZONA EL
ZORI LS

5-letter Words

ABBES S
CFGST ABLES T
ABMHO S
ACARI D
ACETA L
ACINI C
ACTIN GS
ACUTE RS
ADIEU SX
ADMIX T
ADOBO S
AECIA L
F AERIE DRS
AGGRO S
AGHAS T
AGORA ES
ALAMO S
ALIYA HS
ALMUD ES
ALULA ER
CL AMBER SY
AMEBA ENS
AMIDO L
AMIDS T
AMIGO S
AMNIO NS
S AMPLE R
AMPUL ES
R ANCHO RS
ANCON E
ANDRO S
ANGLO S
ANIMA LS
R ANKLE DST
ANKUS H
ANNEX E
ANNUL IS
CM ANTIC KS
MTY ANTRA L
C ANYON ES
AORTA ELS
APNEA LS
APPAL LS
D APPLE ST
ARGAL AIS
ARISE NS
ARMOR SY
ARPEN ST
BFHMNY ARROW SY
ASPIS H
ASSAI LS
BGLMPST ASSES S
BCEFGLMPRTVW ASTER NS
L ATRIA L
AUDIO S
AUGUR SY
K AURIS T
CHLPRSW AVERS E
AVISO S
AWAKE DNS
AWOKE N

BABOO LNS
BACCA E
BADGE DRS
BAKER SY
BALLS Y
BALSA MS
BANCO S
BANJO S
BARBE DLRST
BARES T
BARGE DES
BARON GSY
BARRE DLNST
BASAL T
A BASES T
BASIN GS
BASSO S
BATTU E
BAULK SY
BAZOO S
BEACH Y
BEANO S
BEAUT SY
BEDEL LS
BEECH Y
BELIE DFRS
BELON GS
BEMIX T
BENNE ST
O BENTO S
BERTH AS
BETON SY
BIJOU SX
BILBO AS
BIMBO S
BINGO S
BITCH Y
O BLAST SY
A BLAZE DRS
BLEAR SY
BLEND ES
BLOCK SY
BLOND ES
BLOOD SY
A BLOOM SY
BLOWS Y
BLUES TY
BOCCI AES
BOFFO S
BONGO S
BONNE ST
BONZE RS
BOSOM SY
BOTCH Y
BOUGH ST
BOURN ES
BOWER SY
BOYAR DS
BRAIN SY
BRAND SY
BRASH Y
BRASS Y
BRAVE DRS
BRAVO S
BRAWL SY
BRAWN SY
BRAZE DNRS
BREAD SY
BREVE ST
BRIAR DSY
BRIBE DERS
BRICK SY
BRIER SY
BRILL OS
BROKE NR
BROMO S
BRONC OS
BROOD SY
BROOM SY
BROTH SY
BROWN SY
BROWS E
BRUSH Y
BUBAL ES
BUCKO S
BUDGE DRST
BUFFO S
BULGE DRS
BULLA E
BUNCH Y
BUNCO S
BUNKO S
BURRO SW
BURSA ELRS
BUTEO S
BUTLE DRS
BUTTE DRS

CABAL AS
CABLE DRST
CACAO S
CACHE DST
CAECA L
CAIRN SY
CALLA NS
CAMAS S
CAMEO S
CAMPO S
CANSO S
CANTO NRS
CARAT ES
CARBO NSY
S CARES S
CARGO S
CAROL IS
E CARTE DLRS
CARVE DLNRS
CASTE RS
CATCH Y
CAUSE DRSY
CAVER NS
CEDAR NSY
CELLA ER
CELLO S
CENSE DRS
CENTO S
CENTU M
CHAFE DRS
CHAFF SY
CHAIN ES
CHAIS E
CHALK SY
CHAMP SY
CHANG ES
CHANT SY
CHAPE LS
CHARK AS
CHARR OSY
CHASM SY
CHEAP OS
CHEEK SY
CHEER OSY
CHELA ES
CHEMO S
CHERT SY
CHEST SY
CHIAS M
CHICO S
CHIEL DS
CHILD E
CHILL ISY
CHINK SY
CHINO S
CHIRO S
CHIRP SY
CHIRR ES
CHOKE DRSY
CHOLO S
CHORE ADS
CHOSE NS
CHOWS E
CHUCK SY
CHUFF SY
CHUNK SY
CHURR OS
CISCO S
CLANK SY
CLARO S
CLASP ST
CLASS Y
CLAVE RS
CLIFF SY
CLING SY
CLOSE DRST
CLOTH ES
CLOUD SY
CLOVE NRS
CLUMP SY
CLUNK SY
CNIDA E
COCCI CD
COHOS HT
COIGN ES
COLON EISY
COMBO S
COMET HS
COMPO S
CONCH AOSY
CONDO MRS
CONGE ERS
CONGO SU
CONIN EGS
CONTO S
COOMB ES
COPAL MS
COPRA HS
CORNU AS
CORPS E
CORSE ST
COSIE DRS
COSTA ELR
COTTA ERS
COUNT SY
COVER ST
COVIN GS
COZIE DRS
CRACK SY
CRAFT SY
CRAMP SY
CRANK SY
CRATE DRS
CRAVE DNRS
S CRAWL SY
S CREAK SY
S CREAM SY
CREDO S
CREEP SY
CREPE DSY
CRESS Y
S CRIMP SY
CRISP SY
CROAK SY
A CROSS E
CROUP ESY
CROWD SY
CROZE RS
CRUDE RS
CRUMB SY
CRURA L
CRUSE ST
CRUST SY
CRYPT OS
CUBIT IS
CULPA E
CULTI C
CURIA EL
CURIO S
CURVE DSTY
CUSSO S
AS CUTES TY
CYCLO S

DANIO S
DATTO S
DEATH SY
DEBAR KS
DEKKO S
DELIS HT
DEMUR ES
DENAR ISY
DENSE R
DERAT ES
DERMA LS
DILDO ES
DINER OS
DINGE DRSY
DIPSO S
DISCO S
DITTO S
DIVER ST
DIVES T
DJINN ISY
DOBRO S
DODGE DMRS
DOLMA NS
DONNE DE
DORSA DL
DOUGH STY
DOURA HS
DOWER SY
DRAFF SY
DRAFT SY
DRAPE DRSY
DRAWL SY
DREAM STY
DREAR SY
DRECK SY
DRESS Y
DRIES T
A DRIFT SY
DRIVE LNRS
DROLL SY
DROOL SY
DROOP SY
DROPS Y
DROSS Y
DROVE DRS
DROWN DS
DUMBO S
DUOMO S
DUPER SY
DUPLE X
DURES S
DWEEB SY

B EAGLE DST
DH EARTH SY
BFHNS EATER SY
P EERIE R
EGEST AS
HW EIGHT HSY
DR EJECT AS
DGRV ELATE DRS
EMBAR KS
ENROL LS
CRTV ENTER AS
ENZYM ES
EOSIN ES
EPHOR IS
A ERUGO S
ESCAR PS
EXACT AS
EXPOS E
EXTOL LS

FACET ES
FACIA ELS
FAKER SY
FALSE R
FARCE DRS
FARCI E
FAULT SY
FAUNA ELS
FEIST SY
FELLA HS
FELON SY
FERIA ELS
FIDGE DST
FILLE DRST
FILLO S
FILMI CS
FILOS E
FILTH SY
FINAL ES
FINER Y
FINES T
FINIS H
FITCH Y
FIXIT Y
FLAKE DRSY
A FLAME DNRS
FLASH Y
FLECK SY
FLESH Y
FLIES T
FLINT SY
FLIRT SY
A FLOAT SY
FLOCK SY
FLORA ELS
FLOSS Y
FLOUR SY
FLUFF SY
FLUKE DSY
FLUNK SY
FLUTE DRSY
FOLIA R
FOLIO S
FOLKS Y
FONDU ES
FOOTS Y
FORBY E
FORES T
FORGE DRST
FORGO T
FORME DERS
FOSSA ES
FOVEA ELS
FREAK SY
FREES T
FRIAR SY
FRILL SY
FRISE ES
FRISK SY
FRIZZ Y
FROST SY
FROTH SY
FROWS TY
FROZE N
FRUIT SY
FRUMP SY
FUGIO S
FUNDI C
FUNGI C
FURAN ES
FUROR ES
FUSIL ES

GAFFE DRS
GAINS T
GALAX Y
GALEA ES
GAMES T
GAMIN EGS
GANJA HS
GARDA I
GECKO S
GEMMA E
GEMOT ES
GENOM ES
GENRO S
GHOST SY
GISMO S
GIZMO S
GLAIR ESY
GLASS Y
GLAZE DRS
A GLEAM SY
GLEBA E
GLEET SY
GLIDE DRS
GLINT SY
GLITZ Y
GLOOM SY
GLOSS AY
GLOVE DRS

GLUTE INS
GNARL SY
GOBAN GS
GOMBO S
GONIF FS
GOOSE DSY
GORGE DRST
GOURD ES
GOWAN SY
GRAIN SY
GRAMP AS
GRAPE SY
GRASS Y
GRAVE DLNRS
A **GREED** SY
GREEN SY
GREGO S
GRIFF ES
GRILL ES
GRIPE DRSY
GROSZ EY
GROUT SY
GROVE DLS
GROWL SY
GRUFF SY
GRUMP SY
GUACO S
GUANO S
GUILT SY
GUIRO S
GUMBO S
GUTTA E
GYROS E

HALAL AS
TW **HALER** SU
SW **HALES** T
HALID ES
HALLO AOSTW
HALVA HS
HAMZA HS
HANSE LS
C **HASTE** DNS
HAULM SY
HAWSE RS
S **HEARS** E
HEART HSY
S **HEATH** SY
S **HEAVE** DNRS
HEIGH T
HELIO S
HELLO S
TW **HERES** Y
HERMA EI
HEXAD ES
HIGHT HS
HIJRA HS
HILLO AS
HIPPO S
HOARS E
HOLLO AOSW
HOMIE RS
P **HONES** T
HOOKA HS
A **HORSE** DSY
HORST ES
C **HOUSE** DLRS
HULLO AOS
HUMAN ES
HUZZA HS
HYDRA ES
HYDRO S
HYPHA EL

IAMBI C
S **IDLES** T
IGLOO S
IMAGO S
GLPW **IMPED** E
IMPIS H
INANE RS
INCUS E

INDOL ES
HLMSTW **INTER** NS
INTRO NS
IODID ES
IODIN ES
P **IRATE** R
IROKO S
IRONE DRS

JALOP SY
JAPER SY
JAUNT SY
JELLO S
JOCKO S
JUICE DRS
JUMBO S
JUNCO S
JUNTO S

KALPA CKS
KAPUT T
KARAT ES
KAROO S
KAVAS S
KAZOO S
KENDO S
KERNE DLS
KHEDA HS
KIBBE HS
KIBLA HS
KIDDO S
KINAS E
KLUTZ Y
KNAWE LS
KNOLL SY
KNURL SY
KORUN AY
KRONE NR
KROON IS
KULAK IS
KUSSO S

LABIA L
BF **LAMED** HS
BF **LAMES** T
LAMIA ES
G **LANCE** DRST
LARGE RS
LARGO S
LARVA ELS
LASSI ES
LASSO S
P **LATEN** ST
LATHE DRS
LATTE NRS
LAURA ES
LAVAS H
F **LAXES** T
LAYIN GS
BP **LEACH** Y
LEARN ST
CS **LEAVE** DNRS
FPS **LEDGE** RS
LEMON SY
LENTO S
LIBRA ES
S **LIEVE** R
LIGAN DS
LIKES T
LIMBI C
LIMBO S
B **LIMPS** Y
LINEN SY
LINGA MS
LININ GS
LIPID ES
LIROT H
B **LITHE** R
LITHO S
S **LIVER** SY
O **LIVES** T
LLANO S

LOATH E
LOCAL ES
LOCUS T
LOOFA HS
LOOSE DNRS
B **LOTTO** S
LOUPE DNS
BFGPS **LOWER** SY
LOWES T
BP **LUNGE** DERS
LUPIN ES
LUTEA L
LYSIN EGS
LYTTA ES

MACHO S
MACRO NS
MADAM ES
MALIC E
MAMBO S
MAMMA ELS
MANGE LRSY
MANGO S
MANIA CS
MANNA NS
MARSH Y
MATIN GS
MATTE DRS
MATZA HS
MATZO HST
MAUND SY
MAXIM AS
MEDIA DELNS
MEDIC KOS
MENSA ELS
O **MENTA** L
MERES T
E **MERGE** DERS
METRO S
MEZZO S
MIASM AS
MICRO NS
S **MIDGE** ST
MIGHT SY
MILLE DRST
MIMEO S
MINIM AS
MINIS H
MIRIN GS
MISER SY
MODES T
MOIRA I
A **MOLES** T
MONDO S
MONGO ELS
MOOLA HS
MOPER SY
A **MORAL** ES
MORAS S
MORPH OS
MORRO SW
MORSE L
MOTTO S
MOULD SY
MOUSE DRSY
MOUTH SY
MULLA HS
MUNGO S
MURRE SY
MUSCA ET
MUSIC KS
MUTES T

NACHO S
NAIVE RS
NARCO S
NEROL IS
K **NIGHT** SY
U **NITER** SY
NITRO S
NOBLE RS
NUCHA EL

NUDES T
NURSE DRS
NYMPH AOS

OBELI A
T **OCHER** SY
OCHRE ADS
OCREA E
OCTAN EST
OGRES S
OLEIN ES
GR **ONION** SY
ORACH E
ORANG ESY
M **ORGAN** AS
ORPIN ES
OSMOL ES
OUTBY E
OVOLO S

PAGOD AS
PAINT SY
PAISA NS
PALEA EL
S **PALES** T
PANTO S
PAPER SY
PARDI E
PAREO S
S **PARGE** DST
PARGO S
PARIS H
PARLE DSY
PAROL ES
S **PARSE** CDRS
PARVO S
PASEO S
PASSE DELRS
PASTE DLRS
PATCH Y
PATEN ST
PATIN AES
PATIO S
PAVAN ES
S **PAVIN** GS
PAVIS E
PEACH Y
PEARL SY
PEASE NS
PEDAL OS
PEDRO S
S **PENCE** L
PENGO S
PENNA E
PENNI AS
PERDU ES
PERIS H
PESTO S
PETIT E
PHONE DSY
PHONO NS
PHOTO GNS
PHYLA ER
PIANO S
PILAF FS
PINGO S
PINKO S
PINNA ELS
S **PINTO** S
PIQUE DST
PIROG I
PISCO S
PITCH Y
PIZZA SZ
PLACE DRST
PLAIN ST
PLANE DRST
S **PLASH** Y
PLASM AS
PLATE DNRS
PLEAS E
PLICA EL
PLUCK SY

PLUNK SY
PLUSH Y
POACH Y
POINT ESY
POLIO S
POLIS H
POLYP IS
PORNO S
POSSE ST
POTTO S
POUCH Y
POUFF ESY
PRESE T
PREST OS
PRICE DRSY
PRICK SY
PRIES T
PRIMA LS
PRIME DRS
PRIMO S
PRIOR SY
PRISS Y
PROLE GS
PROMO S
U **PROSE** DRS
PROSO S
PROVE DNRS
PRUTA H
PSEUD OS
PSYCH EOS
PULSE DRS
PUNCH Y
PUNKA HS
PUNTO S
PURDA HS
PURIN ES
PURIS MT
PURSE DRS
PUTTI E

QUACK SY
QUALM SY
QUANT AS
QUART EOSZ
QUINS Y
S **QUINT** AES
QUIRK SY
QUOTH A

RABAT OS
RABBI NST
RADIO S
RAKIS H
O **RALLY** E
BC **RANCH** O
GO **RANGE** DRS
U **RARES** T
RATAN SY
RATHE R
RATIO NS
RAVIN EGS
REBEC KS
RECIT ES
RECTA L
RECTO RS
U **REDIA** ELS
REDIP ST
REDON ES
REFEL LST
REGAL E
REGNA L
RELIC ST
P **REMAN** DS
P **REMIX** T
REPIN ES
REPOS E
REPRO S
RESAW NS
RESEE DKNS
RESEW NS
RESID ES
RESIN SY
RESIT ES

RESOW NS
RETIA L
RETRO S
REWIN DS
RHEUM SY
RHINO S
RHOMB IS
RHUMB AS
RICIN GS
BF **RIDGE** DLS
ABFW **RIGHT** OSY
G **RILLE** DST
CGT **RIPES** T
ROBIN GS
RODEO S
ROMAN OS
ROMEO S
RONDO S
GP **ROPER** SY
ROQUE ST
ROSIN GSY
C **ROTCH** E
ROTTE DNRS
T **ROUGH** SY
C **ROUTE** DRS
C **RUDER** Y

SABIN ES
SACRA L
T **SADIS** MT
SAFES T
U **SAGES** T
SAITH E
SALPA ES
SALVE DRS
SALVO RS
SAMBA LRS
SAMBO S
SAMEK HS
SANES T
SANGA RS
SANTO LS
SARGO S
SAROD ES
I **SATIN** GSY
SAUCE DRS
SAUGH SY
SAVIN EGS
SAVOR SY
SCAMP IS
SCANT SY
SCARE DRSY
E **SCARP** HS
SCATT SY
SCHMO ES
SCHUL NS
SCOUT HS
SCRAP ES
SCREE DNS
SCREW SY
SCRIM PS
SCRIP ST
SCULP ST
SCURF SY
SCUZZ Y
SECCO S
SEGNO S
SENOR AS
SENSE DIS
SEPTA L
SERAI LS
SERES T
SERGE DRS
SERIN EGS
SERVO S
SEVER ES
SEXTO NS
SHACK OS
SHAKE NRS
SHAKO S
SHALE DSY
SHAPE DNRS

SHARN SY
SHARP SY
SHAVE DNRS
SHEEN SY
SHEIK HS
SHELL SY
SHIEL DS
SHIES T
SHIFT SY
SHIRT SY
SHIVA HS
SHIVE RS
SHLEP PS
SHOAL SY
SHORT SY
SHOVE DLRS
SHREW DS
SICKO S
SIGNA L
SILVA ENS
SINEW SY
SIRRA HS
SIRUP SY
SIXMO S
SKANK SY
SKEAN ES
SKIMP SY
SKUNK SY
SLANG SY
A **SLANT** SY
SLATE DRSY
SLAVE DRSY
SLEEK SY
A **SLEEP** SY
SLEET SY
SLIMS Y
SLINK SY
A **SLOSH** Y
SLUSH Y
SMALT IOS
SMARM SY
SMART SY
SMEAR SY
SMELL SY
SMILE DRSY
SMIRK SY
SMITH SY
SMOKE DRSY
SNAKE DSY
SNARK SY
SNARL SY
SNATH ES
SNEAK SY
SNEER SY
SNIDE R
SNIFF SY
SNOOP SY
SNOOT SY
SNOUT SY
SNUFF SY
SODOM SY
SOLAN DOS
SOLID IS
SONDE RS
SOOTH ES
SOREL SY
T **SORES** T
SORGO S
SOUGH ST
SOZIN ES
SPACE DRSY
SPARK SY
SPARS E
SPEED OSY
SPELT SZ
SPEND SY
SPICA ES
SPICE DRSY
SPIFF SY
SPIKE DRSY
SPILT H
SPINE DLST

New 2006

A SPIRE ADMS
SPOIL ST
SPOKE DNS
SPOOF SY
SPOOK SY
SPOON SY
SPORT SY
E SPRIT ESZ
SPUNK SY
STAGE DRSY
STALE DRS
STALK SY
STEAD SY
STEAM SY
STEEL SY
STELA EIR
STENO S
STERE OS
A STERN AS
STICK SY
STILL SY
STING OSY
STINK OSY
STIPE DLS
STOCK SY
STOLE DNS
STOMA LS
STONE DRSY
STORE DRSY
STORM SY
STOUR ESY
STOVE RS
STRAW SY
STREW NS
STRIA E
STRIP ESTY
STROW NS
E STRUM AS
STUFF SY
STUMP SY
STYLE DRST
SUAVE R
SUGAR SY
SUITE DRS
SUMAC HS
SUMMA ES
SUNNA HS
SUPER BS
SWAMP SY
SWANK SY
SWART HY
SWATH ES
SWEAT SY
SWEEP SY
SWING ESY
A SWIRL SY
SWISH Y
SWITH E
SWIVE DLST
A SWOON SY
SWOOP SY
SWOUN DS
SYLPH SY
SYLVA ENS
SYRUP SY

S TABLE DST
TABOO S
TAKIN GS
TALUK AS
TAMAL ES
TAMES T
TANGO S
TARGE ST
TARSI A
TASSE LST
TEASE DLRS
TECTA L
TEENS Y
TEETH E
TELCO S
TELIA L

TEMPO S
TENIA ES
TENSE DRS
TERCE LST
TERGA L
TERRA ES
TERSE R
TESTA E
TETRA DS
THECA EL
THEIN ES
THERM ES
THORN SY
THORO N
THORP ES
THRAW NS
THREE PS
THROW NS
THYME SY
THYMI C
TIBIA ELS
TINEA LS
TOAST SY
E TOILE DRST
TOLAN ES
S TOLED O
TONDO S
TONNE RS
TOOTH SY
TOOTS Y
TOQUE ST
TORCH Y
TOROS E
TOROT H
TORSO S
TORTE NS
TOUCH EY
TOUGH SY
TOWER SY
TOXIN ES
TRAGI C
TRAMP SY
TRASH Y
TRAVE LS
TREAT SY
TREND SY
S TRESS Y
TRICE DPS
S TRICK SY
TRIGO NS
TRIOS E
TRITE R
S TROLL SY
TROMP ES
TROUT SY
S TROVE RS
TRUES T
TRUST SY
TRYST ES
TUNIC AS
TURBO ST
TUYER ES
TWANG SY
TWEAK SY
TWEED SY
A TWEEN SY
TWIRL SY
TWIST SY

UMBRA ELS
UMIAC KS
UNCIA EL
UNCUT E
UNFIX T
UNMIX T
UNPEN ST
UNRIP ES
UNSEW NS
UNSEX Y
RT URBAN E
UREAS E
UREDO S

UVULA ERS

VAGUE R
VANDA LS
VAPOR SY
VAULT SY
A VAUNT SY
VENIN ES
VERGE DRS
A VERSE DRST
VERSO S
VERST ES
VERVE ST
VESTA LS
VIDEO S
VILLA ES
VIREO S
VIRTU ES
VITTA E
VODOU NS
VOMIT OS
VULVA ELRS

WACKE RS
WACKO S
WAFER SY
WAHOO S
WAIVE DRS
WALLA HS
WATAP ES
WATER SY
WAUGH T
WAVER SY
WEDEL NS
T WEENS Y
A WEIGH ST
WEIRD OSY
WHACK OSY
WHALE DRS
WHELK SY
WHIMS Y
WHINE DRSY
A WHIRL SY
WHIRR SY
WHISH T
WHISK SY
WHITE DNRSY
WHIZZ Y
WICCA NS
WIDES T
WIELD SY
WINCE DRSY
WISES T
ST WITCH Y
S WITHE DRS
WIVER NS
WOODS Y
WORSE NRST
WORTH SY
WRATH SY
WRIES T
WRIST SY

XENIA LS

YAHOO S
YEAST SY
YOBBO S
YOGIN IS

ZEBEC KS
ZIBET HS
ZIZIT H
ZOMBI ES

6-letter Words

AARRGH H
ABELIA NS
ABOLLA E
ABOMAS AI
ABRADE DRS
ACUTES T
ADAGIO S
ADDEND AS
ADJOIN ST
ADNEXA L
ADVISE DERS
F AERIES T
AERUGO S
AFFAIR ES
AFGHAN IS
H AGGADA HS
AGOROT H
AIKIDO S
ALANIN ES
ALBEDO S
ALBINO S
ALEXIN ES
ALIDAD ES
ALKALI CNS
ALKANE ST
ALMOND SY
ALNICO S
ALODIA L
ALUMIN AES
ALUMNA E
AMIDIN ES
AMOEBA ENS
AMTRAC KS
ANALOG SY
ANARCH SY
ANATTO S
ANGINA LS
ANILIN ES
ANIMIS MT
ANLAGE NS
N APHTHA E
APNOEA LS
APOLLO S
APOLOG SY
ARABIC A
M ARCHER SY
AREOLA ERS
ARIOSO S
B ARISTA ES
ARISTO S
ARMOUR SY
ARROYO S
ARTIST ES
GJR ASPERS E
ATTACH E
ATTAIN ST
ATTRIT ES
AURORA ELS
AUSUBO S
M AXILLA ERS

BABIES T
BAGASS E
BAGGIE RS
BAGNIO S
BALLAD ES
BAMBOO S
BANDIT OS
BARBEL LS
BARMIE R
BARRIO S
BASSET ST
BATEAU X
BATTER SY
BAYAMO S
BEDLAM PS
BEGGAR SY
BEGRIM ES

BEIGNE ST
BELDAM ES
BELEAP ST
BENZIN ES
BENZOL ES
BERLIN ES
BETAKE NS
BEWRAP ST
BIBBER SY
BIBLES S
BICORN ES
BIFFIN GS
BIGGIN GS
BILLOW SY
BINDER SY
BIOGEN SY
BISTRO S
BITTER NS
BLIGHT SY
BLINTZ E
BLITHE R
BLONDE RS
BLOTCH Y
BLUDGE DRS
BOBBER SY
BOBBIN GS
BOFFIN S
BOLERO S
BONITO S
BONNIE R
BONOBO S
BOOBOO S
BOOCOO S
BOOHOO S
BOOKOO S
BORSCH T
BOSQUE ST
BRACER OS
BRANCH Y
BRAVER SY
BRAVES T
BREATH ESY
BREWER SY
BRIBER SY
BRILLO S
BROMID ES
BROMIN ES
BRONCO S
BRUCIN ES
BRUISE DRS
A BUBBLE DRS
BUCKLE DRS
BUGGER SY
BUREAU SX
BURGOO S
BURSAR SY
BUSHWA HS
BUSIES T
BUSKIN GS
BUTLER SY
A BUTTER SY
BUTTON SY
BUZUKI AS

CADDIS H
CALICO S
CALKIN GS
CALLAN ST
CALPAC KS
CAMBIA L
CAMERA ELS
CANDID AS
S CANNER SY
CANNIE R
CANTAL AS
CANULA ERS
CANVAS S
CAPITA L
CAPRIC E
CARDIA CES
O CARINA ELS
CARLES S

CARLIN EGS
CAROCH E
CARPAL ES
CARREL LS
CARROT SY
CASERN ES
CASHOO S
CASINO S
CATALO GS
CATENA ES
CATLIN GS
CATTIE RS
CAVIAR ES
CEMENT AS
CENTRA L
CESTOI D
CESURA ES
CHAETA EL
CHALLA HS
CHALOT H
CHANCE DLRS
CHARRO S
CHASTE NR
CHEAPO S
CHEERO S
CHEQUE RS
CHEVRE ST
CHIASM AIS
CHIMER AES
CHINCH Y
CHINTZ Y
CHIRRE DNS
CHOANA E
CHOICE RS
CHOLER AS
CHOOSE RSY
CHOPIN ES
CHORAL ES
CHOREA LS
CHRISM AS
CHROMO S
CHROMY L
CHUKKA RS
CHUPPA HS
CHURCH Y
CHURRO S
CICADA ES
CICERO S
CINDER SY
CINEOL ES
CIRCLE DRST
CIRCUS Y
CITHER NS
CITRIN ES
CITRUS Y
CLAQUE RS
CLEANS E
CLEAVE DRS
CLIQUE DSY
CLOACA ELS
CLOSES T
CLOVER SY
CLUTCH Y
COARSE NR
COBBLE DRS
COCAIN ES
CODEIN AES
CODLIN GS
COELOM ES
COFFIN GS
COGITO S
COHERE DRS
COLLAR DS
COLLIE DRS
COLONE LS
COLONI C
COLUGO S
COMEDO S
COMMIX T
COMPAS S
COMPOS ET
CONCHA ELS

CONCHO S
CONGES T
CONSOL ES
CONSUL ST
CONTES T
COOKER SY
S COOPER SY
COPPER SY
S COPULA ERS
CORNEA LS
CORNUA L
CORONA ELS
CORTIN AS
CORYZA LS
COSIES T
COSTAR DS
COTEAU X
COTING A
COTTON SY
COUPLE DRST
COZIES T
CRAMBO S
CRANIA L
CRISSA L
CRISTA E
CROSSE DRS
CRUDES T
CRUISE DRS
S CRUNCH Y
CRYPTO S
CUATRO S
CUCKOO S
CULVER ST
CUPULA ER
CURIOS A
CURRAN ST
CURSOR SY
CUTLAS S
CUTLER SY
CYANID ES
CYANIN ES
CYCLER SY
CYCLIN GS
CYMLIN GS
CYPRES S

DACOIT SY
DACTYL IS
DAIMIO S
DAIMYO S
DAKOIT SY
DAUBER SY
DEJECT AS
DEMURE R
DENARI I
DENTIN EGS
DEODAR AS
DETENT ES
DEVISE DERS
DEVOTE DES
DHOOTI ES
DIAMIN ES
DIAZIN ES
DICKIE RS
DIDDLE DRSY
DINERO S
DIOXAN ES
DIOXID ES
DISCUS S
DISTIL LS
DITHER SY
DIVERS E
DIVINE DRS
DODDER SY
DODGER SY
DOGGER SY
DOGGIE RS
DOMAIN ES
DOMINO S
DOODOO S
DORADO S
DOUBLE DRST

DOUGHT Y
DRACHM AS
DRAPER SY
DROMON DS
DRONGO S
DROUTH SY
DUBBIN GS
DUCKIE RS
DUELLO S
DYNAMO S
DYNAST SY

EASIES T
F EASTER NS
ELUVIA L
EMBOLI C
EMBRYO NS
EMETIN ES
EMPLOY ES
ENCINA LS
ENDURO S
ENHALO S
ENNUYE E
ENTERA L
ENVIRO NS
EPARCH SY
EPHEBI C
EPIGON EIS
EPIMER ES
EPONYM SY
ERINGO S
CX EROTIC AS
ERYNGO S
ESCAPE DERS
ESCUDO S
ETAMIN ES
M ETHOXY L
EXARCH SY
EXEDRA E
EXOTIC AS
EXTERN ES
EXUVIA EL

FACTOR SY
FACULA ER
FAGGOT SY
FASCIA ELS
FECULA E
FEEBLE R
FEMORA L
FERRET SY
FERULA ES
FIANCE ES
FIASCO S
FIBULA ERS
FICKLE R
FIDGET SY
FIERCE R
FISHER SY
FLAMBE ES
FLAUNT SY
FLAVIN ES
FLAVOR SY
FLIGHT SY
FLOWER SY
FOLIOS E
FOLKIE RS
FOOTIE RS
FORBAD E
FOREBY E
FORGER SY
FORMAT ES
FORMIC A
FREEZE RS
FRESCO S
FRIJOL E
FROWST SY
FUGATO S
FULFIL LS
FULLER SY
FURROW SY

GABBRO S
GADGET SY
GALAGO S
GALLET AS
GALLIC A
GALOSH E
GARGET SY
GASHES T
GASKIN GS
GATEAU SX
GAUCHE R
GAUCHO S
GAZABO S
GAZEBO S
GELATI NS
GELATO S
GENERA L
GENTIL E
GENTLE DRS
GENTOO S
GEODES Y
GERMAN ES
GHETTO S
GIGOLO S
GINGAL LS
GINGER SY
GINGKO S
GINKGO S
GIRLIE RS
GITANO S
GITTIN G
GLITCH Y
GLOBIN GS
GLOSSA ELS
GLYCIN ES
GOBBLE DRS
GOLOSH E
GOODBY ES
GOONIE RS
GOSSIP SY
GRADIN EGS
GRAMMA RS
GRATIN EGS
GRAVEL SY
GRAVES T
GRAVID A
GROCER SY
GROTTO S
GROUCH Y
GROWTH SY
GRUNGE RS
GUANIN ES
GUNNER SY
GURGLE DST
GUTTER SY
GWEDUC KS

HAGGIS H
HAIRDO S
HALALA HS
HALLOO S
CS HALLOT H
HALTER ES
HAPTEN ES
HARMIN EGS
HARPIN GS
HEALTH SY
HEIGHT HS
S HELLER ISY
HEMPIE R
HERNIA ELS
HEROIN ES
HETERO S
C HIPPIE RS
HOARSE NR
HOLIES T
HOLLOO S
HOMAGE DRS
HOMIES T
HONCHO S
HONEST Y
HOODIE RS
HOODOO S
HOOPOO S
HOSIER SY
HULLOO S
HUMANE R
C HUTZPA HS
HYALIN ES
HYDRAS E
HYDRIA E
HYDRID ES

IMAGER SY
GLPW IMPING ES
IMPROV ES
IMPURE R
INANES T
W INDIGO S
INFANT AES
INGEST AS
TW INKLES S
INSANE R
INSIDE RS
INSTAL LS
INSTIL LS
INTERN ES
INTIMA ELS
INVITE DERS
INWOVE N
ISATIN ES
ISCHIA L
ISOBAR ES
ISOGON ESY
ISTHMI C

JAGGER SY
JARGON SY
JASMIN ES
JASPER SY
JAZZBO S
JEJUNA L
JERKIN GS
JIGSAW NS
JINGAL LS
JITTER SY
JOBBER SY
JOINER SY
JOURNO S
JUBILE ES
JUGULA R
JUNKIE RS

KAINIT ES
KAKAPO S
KAOLIN ES
KARROO S
KERMES S
KHALIF AS
KIMONO S
KITSCH Y
S KITTLE DRS
KLEPTO S
KLUDGE DSY
KOLHOZ Y
KOLKOZ Y
KOODOO S
KOOKIE R
KOUMIS S
KOUMYS S
KOUSSO S
KVETCH Y

LACUNA ELRS
LADINO S
LADRON ES
LALLAN DS
C LAMBER ST
LAMBIE RS
LAMINA ELRS
LANGUE ST
LANUGO S
LARGES ST
BS LATHER SY
LATIGO S
LATINO S
LAVABO S
LAZIES T
LEAGUE DRS
LECHER SY
LEGATE DES
LEGATO RS
LEGGIN GS
LENGTH SY
LEUCIN ES
LEXICA L
LIBIDO S
LIGULA ERS
LIMINA L
LINGUA EL
LISSOM E
FGS LITTER SY
LITTLE RS
LOCHIA L
LOCUST AS
LOGGIE R
LOLLOP SY
LOMENT AS
LONGES T
LOONIE RS
LOOSES T
LORICA E
BPS LOTTER SY
LUCERN ES
LUCKIE RS
A LUMINA L
LUNIES T
LUNULA ER
LURDAN ES
BFPS LUSHES T
LUSTRA L

MACACO S
MACULA ERS
MADRAS A
MADURO S
MAGGOT SY
MAGNET OS
MANCHE ST
MANIOC AS
MANITO SU
MANTLE DST
MANTRA MPS
MARINE RS
MARKKA AS
MARLIN EGS
MARQUE ES
MARROW SY
MARTIN GIS
MARTYR SY
MASTER SY
S MATTER SY
MATTIN GS
MATURE DRS
MATZOT H
MAXIMA L
MEADOW SY
MEALIE RS
MEDIAN ST
MEDICO S
MEDUSA ELNS
MEGASS E
MEGILP HS
MENSCH Y
MENUDO S
A MERCER SY
MERINO S
MEZUZA HS
MIASMA LS
MICELL AES
MICKLE RS
MIDDLE DRS
MIKADO S
MIKVOT H
MILDEW SY
MILIEU SX
MINIMA LX
MINUTE DRS
MISTER MS
MOCKER SY
MODERN ES
MODEST Y
MOMENT AOS
MORASS Y
MORPHO S
MORTAR SY
MORULA ERS
S MOTHER SY
MUCOSA ELS
MUFFIN GS
MUFFLE DRS
MUMMER SY
MUNTIN GS
MUSKIE RS
MUTTON SY
MYELIN ES

NAIVES T
NANDIN AS
NAPPIE RS
NARCOS E
NAUGHT SY
NEBULA ERS
NECTAR SY
NEURON ES
NEWSIE RS
NIELLO S
NIMBLE R
NITRID ES
NITRIL ES
NITROS O
NOBLES T
NOGGIN GS
NOMINA L
NONEGO S
NOVENA ES
NUCLEI N
NUGGET SY
NUNCIO S
NURSER SY
NYMPHA EL
NYMPHO S

OBENTO S
OBLAST IS
OBLIGE DERS
OBTUSE R
OCHREA E
OCTAVO S
OFFICE RS
OLEFIN ES
OLINGO S
LMT OMENTA L
OOMIAC KS
OPAQUE DRS
OPTIMA L
ORANGE SY
ORATOR SY
OSCULA R
OSMUND AS
OUTLIE RS
OUTRAN GK
OUTRUN GS
OUTSEE NS
OUTSIN GS
OUTWAR DS
OUTWIT HS
OVERDO G
OVULAR Y

PAESAN IOS
PAISAN AOS
PALLIA L
PALMAR Y
PAMPER OS
PANGEN ES
PAPAYA NS
PAPULA ER
PARAMO S
PAROLE DES
PARROT SY
PARVIS E
PASTER NS
PASTIE RS
PATINA ES
S PATTER NS
PAUNCH Y
PAVISE RS
PEDALO S
PEDLAR SY
PEDLER SY
PENSIL ES
PEPINO S
PEPPER SY
PEPSIN ES
PEPTID ES
PERSON AS
PHALLI C
PHLEGM SY
PHYLLO S
PIAFFE DRS
PICARO S
PICKAX E
PIGGIE RS
PIGGIN GS
PILLOW SY
PINKEY ES
PIPPIN GS
PISTOL ES
PIZAZZ Y
PIZZAZ Z
PLAGUE DRSY
PLANCH E
PLATAN ES
PLEDGE DERST
PLEURA ELS
POKIES T
POLEAX E
POLITE R
POMELO S
PONCHO S
POORIS H
POSSES S
POSTER NS
POSTIN GS
POTHER BS
S POTTER SY
POWDER SY
U PREACH Y
PRECIS E
PREMIE RS
PREMIX T
PRESTO S
PREWAR MN
PRIAPI C
PRIMER OS
PROBIT SY
PROPYL AS
PROTEA NS
PROTEI DN
PROTYL ES
PROVER BS
PRUTOT H
PSEUDO S
PSYCHO S
PUCKER SY
PUEBLO S
PUFFER SY
PUFFIN GS
PUMELO S
PUMMEL OS
S PUNKIE RS
PURLIN EGS
PURPLE DRS
PUZZLE DRS
PYLORI C
PYRROL ES

QABALA HS
QUANGO S
QUANTA L
QUARTE RST
QUARTO S
QUAVER SY
QUININ AES
QUINTA LNRS
QUINTE ST
A QUIVER SY

RABATO S
RABBIT SY
BDG RABBLE DRS
B RACKET SY
RADIAL ES
RADIAN ST
RADULA ERS
BCDF RAGGED Y
RAISIN GSY
RANCHO S
RANULA RS
BCT RASHES T
RATLIN ES
C RAUNCH Y
REALES T
REBATO S
REBOZO S
P RECOUP ES
E RECTOR SY
REDRAW NS
REFLOW NS
REFUGE DES
REGIME NS
REGINA ELS
REGIVE NS
REGROW NS
REHEAR DS
REMOTE RS
P REPLAN ST
RERISE NS
RESEAU SX
P RESHOW NS
RETAKE NRS
RETINA ELS
RETIRE DERS
REVERS EO
REWAKE DNS
REWOKE N
REWOVE N
P REWRAP ST
REZERO S
RHOMBI C
RIALTO S
RIBBON SY
RICHES T
RIFFLE DRS
T RIFLER SY
RIPOST ES
CG RIPPLE DRST
RIPSAW NS
ROADEO S
ROBALO S
ROBBER SY
ROBBIN GS
ROBUST A
ROCKER SY
ROCOCO S
ROMANO S
B ROOKIE RS
ROOMIE RS
ROOTLE DST
ROSTRA L
O ROTUND A
RUBATO S
DG RUBBER SY
RUBIES T
RUBIGO S
RUMINA L
T RUNDLE ST
RUSSET SY

SABBAT HS
SAFROL ES
SAGGAR DS
SALLOW SY

P SALTER NS
SALTIE RS
SATRAP SY
SAVAGE DRS
SAVOUR SY
SCALAR ES
SCARCE R
SCHIZO S
SCHLEP PS
SCHNOZ Z
SCLERA ELS
SCORIA E
SCRAWL SY
SCREAK SY
A SCRIBE DRS
SCRIMP SY
SCROTA L
SCRUFF SY
SEALER SY
SEAWAN ST
SECOND EIOS
SECRET ES
SECURE DRS
SEDATE DRS
SEISIN GS
SEIZIN GS
SEMINA LR
SENHOR AS
SENSOR SY
SEQUEL AS
SERENE RS
SERING A
SEROSA ELS
SEVERE DR
SEXTAN ST
SHACKO S
SHADOW SY
SHANTI HS
SHARIA HS
SHEATH ES
SHERIF FS
SHIKAR IS
SHIVER SY
SHLOCK SY
SHLUMP SY
SHOWER SY
SHRIEK SY
SHRILL SY
SHRIMP SY
SHRIVE DLNRS
SHTICK SY
SIERRA NS
SIGNOR AEISY
SILKIE RS
SILVER NSY
SIMPLE RSX
SINGLE DST
SIZZLE DRS
SKATOL ES
SKETCH Y
SKIDOO S
SLAVER SY
SLEIGH ST
SLOUCH Y
SLOUGH SY
SMALTO S
SMIDGE NS
SMOOCH Y
SMOOTH SY
SMUTCH Y
SNATCH Y
SOCAGE RS
SOIGNE E
SOLANO S
SONSIE R
SORGHO S
SPARES T
SPARSE R
SPAVIE ST
SPEEDO S
SPENCE RS

SPICER SY
SPIDER SY
SPINTO S
SPIREM ES
SPLASH Y
SPLEEN SY
SPRAWL SY
SPRING ESY
SPRUCE DRS
SQUALL SY
SQUAMA E
SQUARE DRS
SQUASH Y
SQUEAK SY
SQUILL AS
A SQUINT SY
SQUIRM SY
SQUISH Y
STABLE DRS
STALES T
STAPLE DRS
STARCH Y
STARTS Y
A STATIC ES
STATIN GS
STATUS Y
STELLA RS
STENCH Y
STEREO S
STERNA L
STIGMA LS
STINGO S
STRANG E
STRATA LS
STREAK SY
STREAM SY
STRING SY
STRIPE DRS
STRIVE DNRS
STROMA L
STRUMA ES
STUCCO S
STUDIO S
SUBPAR T
SUBTLE R
SUCCOR SY
SUKKOT H
SULFID ES
SULFUR SY
SULTAN AS
SUMMER SY
SUPPLE DRS
SURGER SY
SVELTE R
SWARTH SY
SWITHE R
SYLVIN ES
SYNURA E

TAENIA ES
TALKIE RS
TALLIS H
TALLIT HS
TALLOW SY
TAMARI NS
TAMBUR AS
TANNER SY
TANNIN GS
TAPALO S
TAPETA L
TARTAN AS
TARTAR ES
TATTIE RS
TATTOO S
TAVERN AS
TECHIE RS
TECHNO S
TEETHE DRS
TEMPER AS
TEMPLE DST
TENNIS T
TENSES T

TENTIE R
TENUTO S
TEREDO S
THALLI C
THATCH Y
THERME LS
A THIRST SY
THOUGH T
THREAD SY
THRIFT SY
THRIVE DNRS
THROAT SY
TIDIES T
TIERCE DLS
TIFFIN GS
TIMBAL ES
TIMBER SY
TIMBRE LS
TINDER SY
TISSUE DSY
TOLEDO S
TOLUID ES
TOLUOL ES
TOMBAC KS
TOPFUL L
TORERO S
TORULA ES
TOTTER SY
TRACER SY
TRAMEL LS
TREPAN GS
S TRICKS Y
TRIPLE DSTX
TRIPOD SY
TRITON ES
TRIVIA L
TROCHE ES
A TROPIN ES
TROUPE DRS
TRUDGE DNRS
TUNICA E
TUPELO S
TURACO SU
TURBIT HS
TURNER SY
TUSSOR ES
TUXEDO S
TWEEZE DRS
TWIBIL LS
TWITCH Y
TYMPAN AIOSY

UGLIES T
UNDRAW NS
UNGULA ER
UNHAND SY
UNLADE DNS
UNREAD Y
UNRIPE R
UNROVE N
UNTRUE R
S UNWISE R
UNWOVE N
UPGROW NS
UPLEAP ST
UPRISE NRS
URBANE R
UREDIA L
UTOPIA NS

VAGINA ELS
VAPOUR SY
VELCRO S
VELVET SY
VERISM OS
VESICA EL
A VIATIC A
VIBRIO NS
E VICTOR SY
VIMINA L
VIRAGO S
VOLANT E

VOMICA E
VOMITO S
VOODOO S

WACKES T
WADMOL LS
S WAGGER SY
WASTER SY
WAVIES T
WEALTH SY
WEASEL SY
WEDGIE RS
WEENIE RS
WEEPIE RS
WEEVIL SY
WEIGHT SY
WEIRDO S
WESTER NS
WHACKO S
WHITES T
WILLOW SY
WINDOW SY
WINTER SY
WITHIN GS
WOODIE RS
WOOLIE RS
WREATH ESY
WRITHE DNRS

YELLOW SY
YESTER N

ZANIES T
ZEBRAS S
ZITHER NS
ZOARIA L
ZOCALO S
ZONULA ERS
ZYDECO S

7-letter Words

ABOMASA L
ABSINTH ES
ACALEPH ES
ACANTHA E
ACICULA ERS
ACQUIRE DERS

ACROMIA L
ACTINIA ENS
ACTRESS Y
ADVISOR SY
AECIDIA L
H AGGADOT H
AGITATO R
AGLYCON ES
H AIRLINE RS
ALEURON ES
ALFAQUI NS
ALKALIN E
ALKALIS E
ALLEGRO S
ALLODIA L
ALLUVIA L
ALMANAC KS
AMMONIA CS
AMNESIA CS
AMPHORA ELS
AMPULLA ER
ANAPHOR AS
ANCILLA ES
ANETHOL ES
ANGELIC A
ANIMATO R
ANNATTO S
ANTEFIX A
ANTENNA ELS
ANTIGEN ES
ANTILOG SY
ANTONYM SY
APAREJO S
APHASIA CS
APHELIA N
APOCARP SY
AQUARIA LN
ARCADIA NS
ARCHAEA LN
ARMIGER OS
ARMILLA ES
ARNATTO S
ARNOTTO S
ASCIDIA N
ASPIRIN GS
ATOMISE DRS
ATOMIZE DRS
ATROPIN ES
AUDITOR SY
AUREOLA ES
AUSTERE R
AUTARCH SY
AUTOMAT AES

AVELLAN E
AVOCADO S
AXILLAR SY
AZULEJO S

BACALAO S
BACCARA ST
BACKBIT E
BAGGIES T
BALDRIC KS
BAMBINO S
BANDEAU SX
BANDITO S
BARYTON ES
BASEMEN T
BASIDIA L

BASILAR Y
BASILIC A
BASTARD SY
BATTEAU X
BAWDIES T
BEEFALO S
BEGORRA H
BENEFIC E
BESPOKE N
BESTREW NS
BESTRID E
BESTROW NS
BIENNIA L
BISCUIT SY
BIZARRO S
BLADDER SY
BLASTIE RS
BLISTER SY
BLONDES T
BLOOMER SY
BLOSSOM SY
BLUBBER SY
BLUSTER SY
BOHEMIA NS
BONIATO S
BOSSIES T
BOTANIC A
BOTCHER SY
BOULDER SY
BRACERO S
A BRACHIA L
BRAILLE DRS
BRASHES T
BRASSIE RS
BRAVADO S
BRAWLIE R
BRECCIA LS
BRIMFUL L
BRINIES T
BRITTLE DRS
BROADAX E
BROIDER SY
BRONCHI A
BRONCHO S
BROWNIE RS
BRUSQUE R
BUFFALO S
BUGABOO S
BUGGIES T
BULIMIA CS
BULLIES T
BULLOCK SY
BUMMALO S
BURGLAR SY
BURRITO S
BUSHIDO S
BUTCHER SY

CABBAGE DSY

CABBALA HS
CABEZON ES
CABILDO S
CACONYM SY
CAESURA ELS

CAFFEIN ES
CAJOLER SY
CALAMAR ISY

CALYPSO S
CANDIDA LS
CANNULA ERS
CANZONE ST
CAPABLE R
CARABAO S
CARABIN ES
CARACOL ES
CAROUSE DLRS

CARTOON SY
CASSINO S
CATTALO S

CATTIES T
CAVETTO S
CEMBALO S
CENTAUR SY
CENTAVO S
CENTIMO S
CEREBRA L
CHALAZA ELS
CHALLOT H
CHAMISO S
CHAMPAC AS
CHANCER SY
CHAPEAU SX
CHARISM AS
CHARQUI DS
CHATEAU SX
CHATTER SY
CHEDDAR SY
CHEERIO S
CHIASMA LS
CHIASMI C
CHICANO S
CHIPPIE RS
CHIRRUP SY
CHITLIN GS
CHLORID ES
CHLORIN ES
CHOICES T
CHORAGI C
CHORIZO S
CHRISMA L
CHUTZPA HS
CINEAST ES
CINGULA R
CIRCUIT SY
CISTERN AS
CITATOR SY
CLASSIC OS
CLASSIS MT
CLATTER SY
CLUSTER SY
CLUTTER SY
COCHLEA ERS

CODRIVE NRS
COLICIN ES
COLLAGE DNS
COLLEGE RS
COLLIDE DRS
COLLIER SY
COMITIA L
COMMAND OS
COMMUTE DRS

COMPLIN ES
COMPUTE DRS

CONCEPT IS
CONCERT IOS

CONCISE R
CONIDIA LN
CONJOIN ST
CONTRAS T
COQUITO S
CORANTO S
CORNUTO S
CORPORA L
COSINES S
COSTUME DRSY

COTHURN IS
COTTAGE RSY

COURANT EOS

COUTEAU X
COUTHIE R
CRANNOG ES
CRAPPIE RS
CRAZIES T
S CREAMER SY
CREATIN EGS

CREEPIE RS
CRIOLLO S
CROCEIN ES
CROOKER Y
CROSSES T
CRUMMIE RS
CRUSADO S
CRUZADO S
CRYOGEN SY
CURACAO S
CURRIER SY
CUSHION SY
CUSTARD SY
CUTESIE R
CYPSELA E
CYSTEIN ES

DACTYLI C
DANDIES T
DAUPHIN ES
DEBOUCH E
DECIDUA ELS
DECLASS E
DELIVER SY
DEMAGOG SY
DEMERGE DRS
DEVELOP ES
DEXTRIN ES
DIABOLO S
DIALYSE DRS
DIALYZE DRS
DIASTEM AS
DICKIES T
DILATOR SY
DILUVIA LN
DINGIES T
DINKIES T
DIPLOID SY
DIPLOMA ST
DIPTERA LN
DIRTIES T
DISJOIN ST
DIVINES T
DIVORCE DERS
DIZZIES T
DOGGIES T
DOMICIL ES
DOVECOT ES
DOWDIES T
DRACHMA EIS
DRAUGHT SY
DRIBBLE DRST
DROLLER Y
DROUGHT SY
DRUDGER SY
DRUGGIE RS
DUCKIES T
DUODENA L
DUUMVIR IS
DUVETYN ES
DYSPNEA LS

ECDYSON ES
ECHIDNA ES
ECTOZOA N
EIGHTVO S
ELECTRO NS
ELENCHI C
EMERITA ES
EMPLOYE DERS
EMPTIES T
ENACTOR SY
ENDARCH Y
ENDOGEN SY
ENDORSE DERS
ENLARGE DRS
ENTHRAL LS
ENTOZOA LN
ENTREAT SY
ENVELOP ES
EPIGONI C
EROTICA L
ESCALOP ES
ESPARTO S
EULOGIA ES
EUPLOID SY
H EXAMINE DERS
EXCRETA L
EXEMPLA R
EXHEDRA E
EXORDIA L
EXPRESS O
EXTREME RS

FABLIAU X
FANCIES T
FARRIER SY
FATTIES T
FEATHER SY
FEDAYEE N
FILARIA ELN
FIMBRIA EL
FINALIS EMT
FINIKIN G
FISTULA ERS
FLAMING O
FLATTER SY
FLAVOUR SY
FLICKER SY
FLOSSIE RS
FLUORID ES
FLUORIN ES
FLUSHES T
A FLUTTER SY
FLYBLOW NS
FOLKIES T
FOLKMOT ES
FOOTIES T
FOOTLES S
FORERAN K
FORESEE NRS
FORGIVE NRS
FORMULA ES
FORSAKE NRS
FOVEOLA ERS
FOVEOLE ST
FRACTUR ES
FRENULA R
FRESHES T
FUCHSIN ES
FUNNIES T
FURCULA ER
FURRIER SY

GALANGA LS
GALLICA NS
GAMBADO S
GAMINES S
GANGLIA LR
GARBAGE SY
GARBLES S
GAUDIES T
GAWKIES T
GELATIN EGS
GENTLES T
GERMINA L
GESTAPO S
GIDDIES T
GIMMICK SY
GINGIVA EL
GIRASOL ES
GIRLIES T
GLASSIE RS
GLAZIER SY
GLIADIN ES
A GLITTER SY
GLUTTON SY
GONIDIA L
GOONIES T
GRAMARY E
GRANDAM ES
GRAPLIN ES
GRATINE E
GRAVIDA ES
GREENER Y
GREENIE RS
GRILLER SY
GRINDER SY
GROSSES T
GUANACO S
GYRATOR SY

HABITAN ST
HACKSAW NS
HAFTARA HS
HAGGADA HS
HALAKHA HS
HALIDOM ES
HANDCAR ST
HANDLES S
HAPKIDO S
HAPLOID SY
HARDIES T
T HATCHER SY
S HEATHER SY
HEAVIES T
HEGEMON SY
HEGUMEN ESY
HEMATIN ES
HEPATIC AS
HETAERA ES
HETAIRA IS
HEXAPLA RS
HEXAPOD SY
HIDALGO S
HILLOCK SY
C HIPPIES T
HISSIES T
HOMINES S
HOMOLOG SY
HOMONYM SY
HOODIES T
HOOKIES T
HORNITO S
HOSANNA HS
HUMBLES T
HUMMOCK SY
HURTLES S
HUSKIES T
HYDRANT HS
HYDROPS Y
HYDROXY L
HYMENIA L
HYPOGEA LN
HYPONYM SY

ILLUVIA L
IMMENSE R
IMPASTO S
IMPERIA L
INCISOR SY
INDAMIN ES
INDICAN ST
INDIGEN EST
INDORSE DERS
INDULIN ES
INDUSIA L
INERTIA ELS
INFAUNA ELS
INFERNO S
INHUMAN E
INTAGLI O
INTENSE R
INTERNE DES
INTHRAL LS
ISOCHOR ES

JACINTH ES
JAGGIES T
JAMBEAU X
JAMMIES T
JAVELIN AS
JEALOUS Y
JEOPARD SY
JERKIES T
JETTIES T
JOLLIES T
JUGGLER SY
JUNKIES T

KABBALA HS
KASHRUT HS
KERMESS E
KILLDEE RS
KINDLES S
S KITTLES T
KNACKER SY
KNUCKLE DRS
KOLKHOS Y
KOLKHOZ Y

LACUNAR SY
LAMBAST ES
LAMBIES T
LAMELLA ERS
LAMINAR Y
LANOLIN ES
LARGESS E
P LEATHER NSY
LEGGIER O
LICENCE DERS
LICENSE DERS
LIGROIN ES
LINGULA ER
LITTLES T
LIXIVIA L
LOCUSTA EL
LOONIES T
LOWLIFE RS
LUCKIES T
P LUMBAGO S
LYSOGEN SY

MADRASA HS
MADRONO S
MAESTRO S
MAFIOSO S
MAGNETO NS
MAHJONG GS
MALARIA LNS
MANDRIL LS
MANTEAU SX
MARABOU ST
MARCATO S
MARCHES AEI
MARQUES S
MARQUIS E
MARRANO S
MARSHAL LS
MASTABA HS
MATELOT ES
MATURES T
MAXILLA ES
MEALIES T
MEDULLA ERS
MEGAPOD ES
MEGILLA HS
MELODIC A
MEMENTO S
MENDIGO S
MESHUGA H
MESQUIT ES
MESTESO S
MESTINO S
MESTIZO S
METAMER ES
METAZOA LN
METHOXY L
METONYM SY
MEZQUIT ES
MEZUZOT H
MICELLA ER
MICKLES T
MIDLIFE R
MINICAM PS
MINUTES T
MINUTIA EL
MISDEAL ST
MISDRAW NS
MISGIVE NS
MISGROW NS
MISHEAR DS
MISKNOW NS
MISPLAN ST
MISTAKE NRS
MISWRIT E
MODERNE RS
MOLLUSC AS
MOMENTO S
MONARCH SY
MONITOR SY
MONOLOG SY
MONOPOD ESY
MONSTER AS
MONTERO S
MORCEAU X
MORELLO S
MOROCCO S
MORPHIN EGS
MUDDIES T
MULATTO S
MULLOCK SY
MUSICAL ES
MUSKIES T
MUSTARD SY
MYCELIA LN

NAPPIES T
NARCEIN ES
NARGILE HS
NARWHAL ES
NASTIES T
NEBBISH Y
NEEDLES S
NEGLIGE ES
NELUMBO S
NEURULA ERS
NEWSIES T
NICOTIN ES
NIFTIES T
NITPICK SY
NOCTURN ES
NOMARCH SY
NORTHER NS
NOUMENA L

OBSCENE R
OBSCURE DRS
OCTUPLE DSTX
D OLOROSO S
OOGONIA L
OOTHECA EL
OPAQUES T
OREGANO S
OUTBURN ST
OUTCAST ES
OUTCHID E
OUTCROW DS
OUTDRAW NS
OUTFLOW NS
OUTGIVE NS
OUTGNAW NS
OUTGROW NS
OUTHEAR DS
OUTLEAP ST
OUTRANG E
OUTRIDE RS
OUTWEAR SY
OUTWRIT E
OVERMAN SY
OVERRAN K
OVERSEE DNRS
OVERSEW NS
OXIDISE DRS
OXIDIZE DRS
OXYPHIL ES

PACHUCO S
PAESANO S
PAISANO S
PALAZZO S
PAMPERO S
PANACEA NS
PAPILLA ER
PAPPIES T
PARCHES I
PARTAKE NRS
PARVENU ES
PASSADO S
PASTIES T
PATAGIA L
PATELLA ERS
PEACOCK SY
PECULIA R
PEDAGOG SY
PEDDLER SY
PEKEPOO S
PELORIA NS
PENSION ES
PERFECT AOS
PERIDIA L
PERINEA L
PEROXID ES
PERSONA ELS
PFENNIG ES
PHONIES T
PICACHO S
PICCOLO S
PICOLIN ES
PIGGIES T
PIGNOLI AS
PIMENTO S
PINNULA ER
PINTADO S
PINTANO S
PISCINA ELS
PIZZAZZ Y
PLACEBO S
PLANCHE ST
PLANULA ER
PLASTER SY
PLATEAU SX
PLATIES T
PLIMSOL ELS
PLUMBER SY
PLUSHES T
POBLANO S
PODAGRA LS
POLITIC KOS
POLYGON SY
POLYPOD SY
POMPANO S
PORKIES T
PORTICO S
POTLACH E
POTTIES T
POULARD ES
A PRACTIC E
PRECAVA EL
PRECISE DRS
PREMIER ES
PREPLAN ST
PREPPIE RS
PREPUPA ELS
PRESHOW NS
PRIMERO S
PRINCES S
S PRINTER SY
PRIVATE RS
PRIVIES T
PROLONG ES
PROMISE DERS
PROSOMA LS
PROTEAS E
PROTEGE ES
PROTEID ES
PROVISO S
PRURIGO S
PSALTER SY
PTERYLA E
PTOMAIN ES
PUDENDA L
PUMMELO S
S PUNKIES T
PUPARIA L
PUPILAR Y
PURPLES T
PUSSIES T
PYGIDIA L
PYREXIA LS

QUADRAT ES
QUARTER NS
QUILLAI AS
QUOMODO S

RANCHER OS
B RANDIES T
C RANKLES S
RAVELIN GS
READIES T
REAWAKE DNS
REAWOKE N
P RECHOSE N
RECOVER SY
REDREAM ST
REDRIVE NS
REFINER SY
P REFROZE N
REGIMEN ST
REHEARS E
RELAXIN GS
RELEARN ST
RELIEVO S
RELLENO S
REMOTES T
RESHAVE DNS
RESIDUA L
RESILIN GS
RESPOKE N
REVENUE DRS
REVERSO S
P REVISOR SY
REVOLVE DRS
RHABDOM ES
RICKSHA SW
RIDOTTO S
RIPIENO S
RISOTTO S
ROCKABY E
ROLLICK SY
RONDEAU X
B ROOKIES T
ROOMIES T
ROOTLES S
ROSARIA N
ROSEOLA RS
ROSOLIO S
ROTATOR SY
ROULEAU SX
C ROWDIES T
RUBABOO S
RUBBISH Y
RUBEOLA RS
C RUMMIES T
C RUMPLES S
RUSTLES S

SACRIST SY
SADDLER SY
SAGUARO S

New 2006

Bob's Bible: Words With Interesting Back Hooks

- SAHUARO S
- SALICIN ES
- SALTIES T
- SALVAGE DERS
- SANDBUR RS
- SANTERO S
- SAPHENA ES
- SAPONIN ES
- SAPSAGO S
- SARCINA ES
- SARMENT AS
- SASSIES T
- SAUTOIR ES
- SAVAGER Y
- SAVAGES T
- SAVANNA HS
- SAVVIES T
- SAWDUST SY
- SCALADO S
- SCAPULA ERS
- SCHERZO S
- SCHLOCK SY
- SCHLUMP SY
- SCHMALZ Y
- SCHMOOS E
- SCIATIC AS
- SCOPULA ES
- SCRATCH Y
- SCREECH Y
- SCRUNCH Y
- SCULLER SY
- SCULPIN GS
- SCURRIL E
- SECRETE DRS
- SECURES T
- SEDATES T
- SEMIMAT T
- SEMINAR SY
- SEMIPRO S
- SENECIO S
- SENTIMO S
- SEQUELA E
- SERENES T
- SERPIGO S
- SERRANO S
- SFUMATO S
- SHAMMAS H
- SHAMPOO S
- SHELLAC KS
- SHIMMER SY
- SHIPMEN T
- SHMALTZ Y
- SHOEPAC KS
- SHUDDER SY
- SIGNIOR ISY
- SILICON ES
- SILIQUA E
- SILKIES T
- SILLIES T
- SIMPLES T
- SINCERE R
- SIROCCO S
- SISSIES T
- SKIDDOO S
- SKITTER SY
- SLABBER SY
- SLIPPER SY
- SLITHER SY
- SLOBBER SY
- SLUMBER SY
- SMARAGD ES
- SMELTER SY
- SMOTHER SY
- SNICKER SY
- SNIPPET SY
- SNUGGER Y
- SOLANIN ES
- SOLDIER SY
- SOOTHES T
- SOPRANO S
- SOUTHER NS
- SOVKHOZ Y
- A SPARKLE DRST
- SPATULA RS
- SPECTRA L
- SPECULA R
- SPICULA ER
- SPINACH Y
- SPINNER SY
- SPINULA E
- SPIRULA ES
- SPLENIA L
- SPLOTCH Y
- SPONGIN GS
- SPOOFER SY
- SPRUCES T
- SPUNKIE RS
- SPUTTER SY
- SQUARES T
- SQUELCH Y
- SQUILLA ES
- SQUOOSH Y
- STABLES T
- STAGGER SY
- STAGGIE RS
- STAMINA LS
- STAMPED E
- STEALTH SY
- STEARIN ES
- STEELIE RS
- STEMMER SY
- STOMACH SY
- STOMATA L
- E STRANGE RS
- STRETCH Y
- STRETTO S
- STROBIL AEIS
- SUBLIME DRS
- SUBTILE R
- SUCCUBA ES
- SUCKLES S
- SULFURY L
- SULKIES T
- SULPHID ES
- SULPHUR SY
- SUNBATH ES
- SUNBEAM SY
- SUNBURN ST
- SUPPLES T
- SUPREME RS
- SUPREMO S
- SYLLABI C
- SYMBION ST
- SYMBIOT ES
- SYNCARP SY
- SYNCHRO S
- SYNONYM ESY
- SYNOVIA LS
- SYNTAGM AS
- TABLEAU SX
- TABORIN EGS
- TACHISM ES
- TACHIST ES
- TACKLES S
- TAILLES S
- TALKIES T
- TALLYHO S
- TAMANDU AS
- TAMARAO S
- TAMARIN DS
- TAMARIS K
- TAMBOUR AS
- TANDOOR IS
- TANGELO S
- TARDIES T
- TARRIES T
- TATTIES T
- TAWNIES T
- TECHIES T
- TEENAGE DR
- TEGMINA L
- TEGUMEN T
- TESSERA E
- TESTUDO S
- THALAMI C
- THEOLOG SY
- THEORBO S
- THERIAC AS
- THERMIT ES
- THIAMIN ES
- THIAZIN ES
- THIAZOL ES
- THICKET SY
- THIONIN ES
- THROMBI N
- THUNDER SY
- TITULAR SY
- TOBACCO S
- TOLIDIN ES
- TOMBOLO S
- TONNEAU SX
- TOPONYM SY
- TORNADO S
- TORPEDO S
- TOSTADO S
- TOURACO S
- TOURIST ASY
- TRACHEA ELS
- TRAVOIS E
- TREMOLO S
- TRIAZIN ES
- TRICKER SY
- TRICKIE R
- TRICORN ES
- TRIOXID ES
- TRIPTAN ES
- TROCHIL IS
- TROLLOP SY
- TRUMEAU X
- TSUNAMI CS
- TUSSOCK SY
- TUTELAR SY
- A TWITTER SY
- TYMPANA L
- TYMPANI C
- TZITZIT H
- UNBROKE N
- UNCLOUD SY
- UNDERDO G
- UNDERGO D
- UNFROZE N
- UNGUENT AS
- UNIQUES T
- UNLEARN ST
- UNLOOSE DNS
- UNSPOKE N
- UPSTATE RS
- UPTEMPO S
- UPTHROW NS
- URETHAN ES
- URETHRA ELS
- VACCINA LS
- VACCINE ES
- VALVULA ER
- VAQUERO S
- VARIOLA RS
- VARNISH Y
- VASCULA R
- VEINULE ST
- VERANDA HS
- VERISMO S
- VERRUCA ES
- VERTIGO S
- VETIVER ST
- VEXILLA R
- VIATICA L
- VIBRATO RS
- VILLAIN SY
- VINEGAR SY
- VISCERA L
- VITAMIN ES
- VOLCANO S
- WANNABE ES
- WARRANT SY
- T WATTLES S
- WEARIES T
- WEDGIES T
- ST WEENIES T
- WEEPIES T
- WENDIGO S
- WHIPSAW NS
- WHISKER SY
- WHISPER SY
- WINDIGO S
- DS WINDLES S
- WINSOME R
- WITHIES T
- WOODBIN DES
- WOODIES T
- WOOLIES T
- WREATHE DNRS
- WUSSIES T
- XANTHIN ES
- XYLIDIN ES
- YESHIVA HS
- YUMMIES T
- ZAMARRO S
- ZAPATEO S
- ZEBRANO S
- ZECCHIN IOS
- ZEMSTVO S
- ZOOGLEA ELS
- ZORILLO S
- ZYMOGEN ES

8-letter Words

- ABDOMINA L
- ABOIDEAU SX
- ABOITEAU SX
- ABSCISIN GS
- ABSCISSA ES
- ACETAMID ES
- ADULATOR SY
- ALIZARIN ES
- ALLOPATH SY
- AMARETTO S
- AMBROSIA LNS
- AMORETTO S
- AMPHIBIA N
- AMPULLAR Y
- AMYGDALA E
- ANAPHORA LS
- ANECDOTA L
- ANGELICA LS
- ANTEFIXA EL
- ANTIMONY L
- ANTIPHON SY
- ANTISTAT ES
- APOLOGIA ES
- APPRAISE DERS
- ARGUMENT AS
- ARMIGERO S
- ARPEGGIO S
- ASPHYXIA LS
- ASPIRATA E
- ASTRAGAL IS
- ATAMASCO S
- AURICULA ERS
- AUTOGIRO S
- AUTOGYRO S
- AVIFAUNA ELS
- BACCHANT ES
- BACILLAR Y
- BACKDROP ST
- BACKSLID E
- BACTERIA LS
- BALLISTA E
- BALLYHOO S
- BANDEROL ES
- BARBASCO S
- BARGELLO S
- BARRANCO S
- BASILICA ELNS
- BASOPHIL ES
- BENZIDIN ES
- BERBERIN ES
- BLASTEMA LS
- BLASTIES T
- BLASTULA ERS
- BLIZZARD SY
- BLOODIES T
- BOCACCIO S
- BORDELLO S
- BOTANICA LS
- BOUSOUKI AS
- BOUTIQUE SY
- BOUZOUKI AS
- BRANCHIA EL
- BRASSIER E
- BRASSIES T
- BRIMFULL Y
- BRITTLES T
- BRONCHIA L
- BROWNIES T
- BRUCELLA ES
- BUBBLIES T
- BUCKAROO S
- BUCKAYRO S
- BUCKEROO S
- BULLETIN GS
- CABESTRO S
- CABRESTO S
- CABRIOLE ST
- CACOMIXL ES
- CALCANEA L
- CALLALOO S
- CALVARIA LNS
- CAMISADO S
- CAPITULA R
- CAPRICCI O
- CAPSOMER ES
- CARETAKE NRS
- CARTOUCH E
- CASTRATO RS
- CATHEDRA ELS
- CAUDILLO S
- CAVALERO S
- CERCARIA ELNS
- CHANDLER SY
- CHAPERON ES
- CHARCOAL SY
- CHECHAKO S
- CHICANER SY
- CHILLIES T
- CHIPPIES T
- CHLORDAN ES
- CHOCKFUL L
- CHUBASCO S
- CICISBEO S
- CILANTRO S
- CINNAMON SY
- CIOPPINO S
- CIRRIPED ES
- CISTERNA EL
- CLAUSTRA L
- COCKAPOO S
- COCKATOO S
- COCOBOLO S
- COLLEGIA LN
- COLLUVIA L
- COLOPHON SY
- COMATULA E
- COMMANDO S
- COMPLAIN ST
- CONCERTO S
- CONCOURS E
- CONFERVA ELS
- CONJUNTO S
- CONNIVER SY
- CONTINUA L
- CONTINUO S
- CONTRAST SY
- CONVERSO S
- COSTUMER SY
- COURANTO S
- CRAPPIES T
- CREEPIES T
- CREMATOR SY
- CRITERIA L
- CROTCHET SY
- CRUMMIES T
- CRUZEIRO S
- CURCULIO S
- CUTICULA ER
- CYANAMID ES
- DAINTIES T
- DANDRUFF SY
- DAYDREAM STY
- DEBONAIR E
- DEBUTANT ES
- DECEMVIR IS
- DECENNIA L
- DEDICATE DES
- DELEGATE DES
- DEMENTIA LS
- DEMERARA NS
- DEMIVOLT ES
- DEVIATOR SY
- DIARRHEA LS
- DICHASIA L
- DIPLOMAT AES
- DIRECTOR SY
- DISCOVER STY
- DISPROVE DNRS
- DISSEISE DES
- DISSEIZE DES
- DISTRAIN ST
- DISTRAIT E
- DISULFID ES
- DJELLABA HS
- DOGGONES T
- DOLCETTO S
- DREARIES T
- DRUGGIES T
- DUECENTO S
- DYSTOPIA NS
- ECCLESIA EL
- EDUCATOR SY
- EFFLUVIA L
- EGOMANIA CS
- EMBRACER SY
- EMPHASIS E
- ENDAMEBA ES
- ENDOSTEA L
- ENSHEATH ES
- ENSHRINE DES
- ENSORCEL LS
- ENTAMEBA ES
- EPHEDRIN ES
- EPHEMERA ELS
- EPIFAUNA ELS
- EPIGRAPH SY
- ESOTERIC A
- ESPRESSO S
- ETHNARCH SY
- EUCALYPT IS
- EXANTHEM AS
- EXECUTOR SY
- EXEMPLAR SY
- EXPIATOR SY
- EXPRESSO S
- EXTREMES T
- FALSETTO S
- FANDANGO S
- FAROLITO S
- FELLATIO NS
- FENESTRA EL
- FIBRILLA ER
- FINICKIN G
- FINOCHIO S
- FLAGELLA R
- FLAMBEAU SX
- FLAMENCO S
- FLAMINGO S
- FLIMSIES T
- FLOPPIES T
- FLOSSIES T
- FORAMINA L
- FOREKNOW NS
- FORESHOW NS
- FORESTAL L
- S FORZANDO S
- FRIZZIES T
- FROSTBIT E
- GALABIYA HS
- GARBANZO S
- GASTRULA ERS
- GAZPACHO S
- GESNERIA D
- GLABELLA ER
- GLADIOLA RS
- GLASSIES T
- GLOSSIES T
- GLYCERIN ES
- GOLLIWOG GS
- GOSSAMER SY
- GRACIOSO S
- GRANDSIR ES
- GREENIES T
- GUACHARO S
- GUANIDIN ES
- GYMNASIA L

HABANERO S
HAFTAROT H
HAFTOROT H
HAGGADOT H
HALACHOT H
HALAKHOT H
HANDWRIT E
HAPHTARA HS
HARMONIC AS
HAWTHORN SY
HEADACHE SY
HEARTIES T
HEPATICA ES
HEPTARCH SY
HERBARIA L
HIERARCH SY
HISTAMIN ES
HISTIDIN ES
HUARACHO S
HYPODERM AS

IMMODEST Y
IMPETIGO S
INNUENDO S
INSHEATH ES
INSOMNIA CS
INTAGLIO S
INTERVAL ES
INTIFADA HS
INVENTOR SY
INVERTIN GS
ISOCHRON ES

JACKAROO S
JACKEROO S
JALAPENO S
JEWELLER SY

KAKEMONO S
KANGAROO S

LANDSLID E
LAUDATOR SY
LAVALIER ES
LAVISHES T
LIBECCIO S
LIBRETTO S
LICHENIN GS
LITERATI M
LOCOFOCO S
LOGOMACH SY
LOTHARIO S
LOVELIES T

MACARONI CS
MACHISMO S
MADRASSA HS
MAESTOSO S
MAGDALEN ES
MAGNESIA NS
MAGNIFIC O
MAHARAJA HS
MAIASAUR AS
MAKIMONO S
MALVASIA NS
MAMMILLA E
MANDATOR SY
MANDOLIN ES
MANIFEST OS
MANUBRIA L
MARGARIN ES
MARSUPIA L
MARTELLO S
MASTODON ST
MAUSOLEA N
MEDIATOR SY
MEDULLAR Y
MENSTRUA L
MESHUGGA H
MESOGLEA LS
MESOPHYL LS
METHADON ES
MICROMHO S
MIGRATOR SY
MILESIMO S
MILIARIA LS
MILLEPED ES
MILLIMHO S
MILLINER SY
MILLIPED ES
MISCHOSE N
MISDRIVE NS
MISENROL LS
MISLEARN ST
MISSHAPE DNRS
MISSPOKE N
MISTHROW NS
MODERATO RS
MODERNES T
MOLLUSCA N
MORTGAGE DERS
MOSCHATE L
MOSQUITO S
MOUNTAIN SY
MRIDANGA MS
MUCHACHO S
MULTIPED ES
MULTIPLE STX
MULTITON E
MUNDUNGO S
MYSTAGOG SY
MYXAMEBA ES

NERVINES S
NEUROMAS T
NEUTRINO S
NIGROSIN ES
NONSTICK Y
NOPALITO S

OBLIGATO RS
OBSCURES T
OCCIPITA L
OCOTILLO S
OKEYDOKE Y
OLIGARCH SY
OPERCULA R
OPUSCULA R
ORATORIO S
ORTHODOX Y
OSTINATO S
OSTRACOD ES
OUTDOORS Y
OUTDREAM ST
OUTDRIVE NS
OUTLEARN ST
OUTSPOKE N
OUTTHROW NS
OVERBLOW NS
OVERBORN E
OVERBURN ST
OVERDRAW NS
OVERFLOW NS
OVERGROW NS
OVERHEAR DS
OVERLADE DNS
OVERLEAP ST
OVERPLAN ST
C OVERSLIP ST
OVERTAKE NS
OVERTHIN K
OVERWEAR SY

PACHINKO S
PALESTRA ELS
PALMETTO S
PALOMINO S
PALPATOR SY
PALPEBRA ELS
PAPILLAR Y
PARAFFIN ES
PARAMENT AS
PARANOIA CS
PARASHOT H
PARVOLIN ES
PASTICCI O
PASTITSO S
PASTORAL EIS
PATHOGEN ESY
PECORINO S
PEDERAST SY
PEEKABOO S
PEEKAPOO S
PENTARCH SY
PENUMBRA ELS
PEREGRIN ES
PERFECTO S
PERFUMER SY
PETECHIA EL
PHANTASM AS
PHENAZIN ES
PHENETOL ES
PHILOMEL AS
PHOSPHID ES
PHOSPHIN ES
PHOSPHOR EIS
PIMIENTO S
PISCATOR SY
PLACEMEN T
PLACENTA ELS
PLANARIA NS
PLOTTIES T
PLUMBAGO S
POLITICO S
POLYMATH SY
POSTCAVA ELS
POZZOLAN AS
PRECHOSE N
PRECISES T
PREDATOR SY
PREFROZE N
PREPPIES T
PRESIDIA L
PRESIDIO S
PRETERIT ES
PRETTIES T
PRIEDIEU SX
PRINCESS E
PRINCIPI A
PRISSIES T
PRIVATES T
PROCURES S
PROLAMIN ES
PROTAMIN ES
PROTOXID ES
PROTOZOA LN
PRUNELLO S
PTERYGIA L
PUERPERA EL
PULSATOR SY
PYCNIDIA L
PYORRHEA LS

QUADRIGA E
QUINOLIN ES

RACHILLA E
RAKEHELL SY
RANCHERO S
RATIONAL ES
P REFORMAT ES
P RELOCATE DES
RENEGADO S
REPLICAS E
REPTILIA N
RESTRAIN ST
RESTRIVE NS
RETICULA R
RETINULA ERS
RHEOPHIL E
RHIZOBIA L
RHODAMIN ES
RICERCAR EIS
ROSTELLA R
ROUGHHEW NS
RUBBABOO S

SACRARIA L
SAFRANIN ES
SALTINES S
SANNYASI NS
SARABAND ES
SARGASSO S
SAVORIES T
SCANTIES T
SCAPULAR SY
SCENARIO S
SCHLIERE N
SCHMALTZ Y
SCHNECKE N
SCIROCCO S
SCURVIES T
SCUTELLA R
SECRETES T
SECRETIN GS
SECRETOR SY
SEICENTO S
SEIGNEUR SY
SEIGNIOR SY
SEMIHOBO S
SEMIMATT E
SEMINOMA DS
SENSILLA E
SENSORIA L
SEPTARIA N
SEPTUPLE DST
SERAGLIO S
SERGEANT SY
SERJEANT SY
SEXTUPLE DST
SFORZATO S
SHEEPCOT ES
SHIGELLA ES
SHILLALA HS
SHODDIES T
SICKLIES T
SIGHTSEE NRS
SILICULA E
SINGSONG SY
SKIFFLES S
SMOOTHES T
SNAKEBIT E
SOAPSUDS Y
SOLFEGGI O
SOLIDAGO S
SOMBRERO S
SOUVLAKI AS
SPICCATO S
SPIFFIES T
SPLINTER SY
SPLUTTER SY
SPOONIES T
SPOROZOA LN
SPRINGAL DS
SPUNKIES T
SQUIRREL SY
STACCATO S
STAGGIES T
STANCHES T
STEADIES T
STEELIES T
STICKIES T
STILETTO S
STITCHER SY
STOCCADO S
STOMODEA L
E STRANGES T
STROBILA ER
STRONGYL ES
STRONTIA NS
STURDIES T
SUBLIMES T
SUBLIMIT SY
SUBLUNAR Y
SUBPHYLA R
SUPEREGO S
SUPERPRO S
SUPREMES T
SYMPODIA L
SYMPOSIA C
SYNCYTIA L

TALEGGIO S
TAPADERO S
TAUTONYM SY
TAWDRIES T
TEGMENTA L
TELEPATH SY
TELESTIC HS
TENTORIA L
TERRAZZO S
TETRARCH SY
TETROXID ES
THEREFOR E
THERIACA LS
THIOPHEN ES
THYROXIN ES
TOLUIDIN ES
TORCHIER ES
TORNILLO S
TRANSFIX T
TRAPEZIA L
TRAPUNTO S
TREADLES S
TRECENTO S
TRENDIES T
TRICHINA ELS
TRIENNIA L
TRIHEDRA L
TRIPLOID SY
TRIUMVIR IS
TROCHLEA ERS
TRUSTIES T
TURQUOIS E
TWELVEMO S

UNCHASTE R
UNTIDIES T
UREDINIA L
UROPYGIA L

VACCINIA LS
VERATRIN ES
VERTEBRA ELS
VESICULA ER
VESTIGIA L
VEXILLAR Y
VIBRATOR SY
VIBRISSA EL
VIDEOTEX T
VIGILANT E
VILLAGER SY
VINDALOO S
VIRTUOSI C
VIRTUOSO S
VISCOUNT SY
VITELLIN ES
VITILIGO S

WALLAROO S
WANDEROO S
WATERLOO S
WHINNIES T
WHIRLIES T
WINDBURN ST
WIREDRAW NS
WITHDRAW NS
WOBBLIES T
WOOLLIES T
WORTHIES T

YESHIVOT H

ZAMINDAR IS
ZECCHINO S
ZEMINDAR SY
ZOOGLOEA ELS

Added in 2006

2-letter Words

FE DEHMNRST / EF UWYZ
S **KI** DFNPRST
KP **OI** L
QI S
ZA GPSX

3-letter Words

BDF GHJ LMN RST WYZ **AGS** GAS SAG
AHI S
ADH **AHS** ASH HAS SHA
C **APO** DS
APP S PAP
O **BES** T
CIG S
E **CRU** DSX CUR
DAN GKS AND
DEF ITY FED
DIF FS FID
DUH
BFG MPR TWZ **EDS**
GKL MPR SW **EEK** EKE
FAB S
FES ST EFS
E **GOS** H
M **IGG** S GIG
S **KIS** ST SKI
KYE S KEY
MEG AS GEM
E **MIC** AES
MYC S
NEG S ENG GEN
S **OBA** S BOA
CS **ODA** HS ADO
M **ONO** S NOO
PST
QIS
RAI ADLNS AIR RIA
SOM AES MOS OMS
SUK S
B **URP** S PUR
BCJ LM **UTE** S
A **VID** ES
O **VUM**
YAG IS GAY
ZAS
ZEP S
ZUZ
ZZZ

4-letter Words

A **AHED** HADE HAED HEAD
AHIS
C **APOS** SOAP
APPS PAPS
BERK S KERB
BIDI S
BIOG S
BIRO S BRIO
BLOG S GLOB
BOHO S HOBO
BORK S
BRUX
BUBU S
BUNA S
BURB S
CAMO S COMA
CHAI NRS CHIA
CIGS
COKY YOCK
CORS E ORCS ROCS
A **CRED** OS
CRIT S
DANS ANDS SAND
DELT AS
DENI M DINE NIDE
DIFF S
DIFS FIDS
DINO S NODI
W **ECHT** ETCH TECH
GJ **EMMY** S
ENUF
M **ESNE** S SEEN SENE
HSV **EXED**
FABS
FEEB S BEEF
FEST S EFTS FETS
FLIR ST
GITE S
GLAM S
GORM S
GOTH S
GROK S
HAKU S
SW **HIMS** SHIM
M **IGGS** GIGS
JIVY
JUCO S
JUKU S
KELT S
KLIK S
KOIS
KOJI S
KORA IST OKRA
KUFI S
KUNA
KUNE NEUK NUKE
KYES KEYS SYKE
LATU
LILO S
LIPA PAIL PIAL
S **LIPE** PILE PLIE
S **LOID** S DIOL IDOL LIDO
LUMA S ALUM MAUL
LYCH
MARA S MAAR
O **MASA** S AMAS
MEDS
O **MEGA** GAME MAGE
MEGS GEMS
MEME S
MERC HSY
MICS
MIPS IMPS SIMP
MOSH MHOS OHMS SHMO
MYCS
NAFF S
NALA S ALAN ANAL
NAPA S
NEGS ENGS GENS
OAKY KAYO OKAY
S **OBAS** BOAS SOBA
ODAH S
CS **ODAS** ADOS SODA
M **ONOS** SOON
S **PACY**
PERE AS PEER PREE
PERP S PREP REPP
PERV S
PLEX
POMO S
E **POXY**
PTUI
PUPU S
PYRO S ROPY
QADI S QAID
RAGG SY
RAIS E AIRS RIAS SARI
RAKU S
SHWA S HAWS SHAW WASH
SIDH E DISH
SIKA S SAKI
SOBA S BOAS OBAS
SOCA S OCAS
SOMS MOSS
SPAM S AMPS MAPS PAMS SAMP
STOT ST TOST TOTS
SUKS
TECH SY ECHT ETCH
TEGG S
TOPO IS
TRES S ERST REST RETS
TROG S GROT
TYIN G TINY
UDON S UNDO
BT **URPS** PURS SPUR
BCJ LM **UTES** SUET
VIDS
WHUP S
YAGS GAYS SAGY
YEPS ESPY PYES
YOUS E
YUTZ
ZEPS
A **ZINE** BS ZEIN
ZONA EL AZON
ZOUK S

5-letter Words

K **ABAYA** S
CFG T **ABLED** BALED BLADE
ADZED DAZED
AGITA S TAIGA
A **AHING**
T **ALKIE** S ALIKE
AMNIO NS AMINO
CDL RTV **AMPED**
R **ANCHO** RS NACHO
ANDRO S ADORN RADON
ANGLO S ALONG LOGAN
C **ANYON** ES ANNOY
ARAME S
ARENE S RANEE
AREPA S PARAE
AZUKI S
BANDA S
BARCA S
BEEDI
BELON GS NOBLE
O **BENTO** S BETON
BERKS KERBS
BESES
BICEP S
BIDIS
BIGGY
BIGOS BIOGS
BILBY
BINER S BRINE
BIOGS BIGOS
BIROS BRIOS
BLAFF S
BLOGS GLOBS
BOHOS HOBOS
BORKS
BRISS
BRITH S BIRTH
BRUNG
BRUTS BURST
BUBUS
BUNAS
BUPPY
BURKA S
BURQA S
BUTES TUBES
CALOS COALS COLAS
CAMOS COMAS
CAPIZ
CEILI S
CENTU M
CHAIS E CHIAS
CHICA S
CHIRU S
CHOLA S LOACH
CNIDA E CANID NICAD
COLBY S
COPAY S
CREDS
CRITS
CUVEE S
CYBER
DEBAG S BADGE
DELTS
DEMIC MEDIC
DENAR ISY REDAN
DIFFS
DINOS
DIRAM S
DOBRO S BROOD
DOODY
DOULA S ALOUD
DROID S
DUFUS
DUMBO S
R **EBOOK** S
R **EMAIL** S MAILE
EMMYS
M **ESNES** SENSE
HSV **EXING**
EYASS ESSAY
FEDEX
FEEBS BEEFS
FESTS
FEZZY
FILMI CS
FINCA S
FLIRS
FOLEY S
FOLIC
FUDDY
GARDA I
GATER S GRATE GREAT RETAG TARGE TERGA
GITES
GLAMS
GLUMS
GLUTE INS
GOMER S
GOPIK
GORMS
GOTHS GHOST
GRODY
GROKS
GWINE
GYOZA S
HAINT S
HAKUS
HALAL AS
HALON S
HAYEY
HEAPY
HENGE S
HIJAB S
HIJRA HS
C **HINKY**
HIPLY
HIREE S
HOMIE RS
HONGI OHING
HOSER S HEROS HOERS HORSE SHOER SHORE
HOSEY S
DFG JPR WZ **IGGED**
INRUN S INURN
JELLO S
JIGGY
JOMON
JUCOS
JUKUS
KANZU S
KELTS
KENTE S
KLICK S
KLIKS
KNAWE LS WAKEN
KOBOS BOOKS
KOJIS
KOMBU S
KORAS OKRAS
KORMA S
KREWE S
KUFIS
KVELL S
LASSI ES SAILS SIALS SISAL
F **LAXES** T AXELS AXLES
LAYIN GS INLAY
C **LEVIS** EVILS LIVES VEILS
LILOS
LOGIN S LINGO
LOGON S
S **LOIDS** DIOLS IDOLS LIDOS SLOID SOLDI SOLID
LOUMA S
LUBED BLUED
LUMAS ALUMS MAULS
LUREX
LYCRA S CLARY
MANAT S ATMAN MANTA
MANGA S
MARAS MAARS
MARKA S KARMA MAKAR
MASAS AMASS MASSA
MAXED
MELTY
MEMES
MENSH
MERCH
MERCS
METOL S MOTEL
MILDS
MIRIN GS
MUCHO MOUCH
MYLAR S MARLY
NAFFS
NAIRU S
NAKFA S
NALAS ALANS ANLAS NASAL
NAPAS
NAPPA S
NEDDY
NENES
ODAHS
ONCET CENTO CONTE
ONLAY S
ORLON S
S **PACEY**
PARAE AREPA
PERES PEERS PERSE PREES PRESE SPEER SPREE
PERPS PREPS REPPS
PERVS
PITTA S
PLEON S PELON
POBOY S
POMOS
PREOP S
PUNJI S
PUPUS

Added in 2006

Bob's Bible: Words Added in 2006

PURTY
PYREX
PREXY
PYROS
PROSY

QADIS
QAIDS
QUBIT S
QUOLL S

RAGGS
RAITA S
ATRIA RIATA
TIARA
RAKUS
RAMAL
ALARM MALAR
RAMEN
NAMER REMAN
RECIT ES
CITER RECTI
TRICE
REJIG S
RESAT
ASTER RATES
STARE TARES
TEARS
RESIT ES
RITES TIERS
TIRES TRIES
RHEME S
REHEM
RINDY
E **RODES**
DOERS DOSER
REDOS RESOD
ROSED SORED
ROSHI S
G **RUBBY**
RUBEL S
BLUER RUBLE

SABAL S
ALBAS BAALS
BALAS BALSA
BASAL
SARGO S
SAYED S
SCUZZ Y
SHLUB S
BLUSH BUHLS
SHOGI S
SHWAS
SHAWS SWASH
SIDHE
HIDES SHIED
SIGLA
GLIAS
SIGNA L
GAINS
SIKAS
SAKIS
SKANK SY
SKELL S
SKORT S
STORK TORSK
SMUSH
SNARF S
SOBAS
BASSO
SOCAS
SOMAN S
MANOS MASON
MOANS MONAS
NOMAS
SORED
DOERS DOSER
REDOS RESOD
RODES ROSED
SORTA
RATOS ROAST
ROTAS TAROS
TORAS
SPAMS
SAMPS SPASM
STENT S
NETTS TENTS
STEWY
WYTES
STOTS
STOTT S

SUCKY
YUCKS

TAKAS
KATAS
S **TALLS**
STALL
TANGA
TAUON S
TAXOL S
TECHS
CHEST
TEGGS
TELCO S
TENDU S
TUNED
TENGE
GENET
TETRI S
TITER TITRE
TRITE
THESP S
TIKKA S
TOEAS
STOAE
TOLAR S
TORRS
TORTA S
OTTAR TAROT
TROGS
GROTS
TYIYN

UDONS
NODUS SOUND
UMAMI S
IMAUM
UNJAM S
UNWET
B **URPED**
DRUPE DUPER
PERDU PRUDE
URSID S

VAMPY
VEGES
VENUS
NEVUS
VIGIA S
VOCAB S
VODOU NS

WHUPS
WICCA NS
WIFEY S
WOMYN
WUSHU

YABBY
YAWEY
YCLAD
YEAHS
YUKKY
YUPPY

A **ZINES**
ZEINS
ZONAE
ZOOEY
ZOUKS
ZUZIM

6-letter Words

K **ABAYAS**
ADZING
DAZING
AGAMID S
AGAPES
H **AGGADA** HS
AGITAS
TAIGAS
AIRBAG S
AMNIOS
CDL RTV **AMPING**

R **ANCHOS**
NACHOS
ANDROS
ADORNS
RADONS
ANGLOS
LOGANS
SLOGAN
ANNONA S
C **ANYONS**
ANNOYS
APORIA S
APPLET S
LAPPET
ARAMES
ARENES
RANEES
AREPAS
SARAPE
ARIARY
ARRIBA
ASLOSH
SHOALS
ATONIA S
ATTRIT ES
AUTIST S
AZUKIS

BABIER
BARBIE
BANDAS
BANKIT S
BARBIE S
BABIER
BARCAS
SCARAB
BARNED
BANDER
BARNEY S
NEARBY
BEADER S
BEIGNE ST
BELONS
NOBLES
O **BENTOS**
BETONS
BERMED
BINERS
BRINES
BITMAP S
BLADER S
BALDER
BLARED
BLAFFS
BLUDGE DRS
BUGLED
BULGED
BOGART S
BOINGS
BINGOS
GIBSON
BONOBO S
BOOCOO S
BOOJUM S
BOOKOO S
BOREAS
BORKED
BOUDIN S
BOXILY
BRILLO S
BRISES
BIRSES
BRITHS
BIRTHS
BRUXED
BRUXES
EXURBS
BUBKES
BUCKOS
BUDDHA S
BUGOUT S
BUPKES
BUPKUS
BURKAS
BURQAS
BUYOFF S
A **BYSSAL**
BASSLY

CABLER S
CALLEE S
CELLAE
CAMMIE S
CANOER S
CORNEA
CANTAL AS
CARDIO
CARDON S
CANDOR
DACRON
CECITY
CEDARY
CEILIS
CENTAI
ACETIN
ENATIC
CENTAS
ASCENT
ENACTS
SECANT
STANCE
CERCAL
CARCEL
CHEFED
CHICAS
CHILIS
LICHIS
CHIRUS
CHOLAS
CHROMY L
CHUPPA HS
CHURRO S
CISTED
EDICTS
CLANKY
CNIDAE
COLBYS
COMPAS S
CAMPOS
CONCHO S
COPAYS
COPOUT S
CORVID S
COSMID S
COVARY
CRAMPY
CRESSY
CROUTE S
COUTER
CUATRO S
TURACO
CUBITI
CUMBIA S
CUSPAL
CUVEES
CYCLIN GS

DACITE S
DACRON S
CANDOR
CARDON
DADGUM
DAMMIT
DANGLY
DARBAR S
DEBAGS
BADGES
DEFFER
REFFED
DEFRAG S
DEFUEL S
FUELED
DELISH
SHIELD
DEMOED
DEMODE
DENARI I
RAINED
DENARS
REDANS
SANDER
SNARED
DIEOFF S
DIRAMS
DISARM
DISEUR S
DOBROS
BROODS

DONGLE S
GOLDEN
LONGED
DOOBIE S
DOODOO S
DOOWOP S
DOPILY
PLOIDY
DOULAS
DROIDS
SORDID
DROOLY
DUETED
DUMBOS
DWEEBY

EAGLED
EARBUD S
DAUBER
R **EBOOKS**
ECESIC
R **EMAILS**
MAILES
MESIAL
SAMIEL
EMDASH
MASHED
SHAMED
ENDASH
ENVIRO NS
RENVOI
EOCENE
EVULSE DS
EXILER S
EXONYM S

FABBER
FACIAE
FADEIN S
FANFIC S
FELSIC
FERALS
FALSER
FARLES
FLARES
FILMIS
FINCAS
FINITO
FLAUTA S
FLUISH
FOLDUP S
UPFOLD
FOLEYS
FRIGES
GRIEFS
FRISEE S
FRITES
REFITS
RESIFT
RIFEST
SIFTER
STRIFE
FUNDER S
REFUND
FUSUMA
FYNBOS

GARDAI
GATERS
GASTER
GRATES
GREATS
RETAGS
STAGER
TARGES
GAYDAR S
GEEKED
GELCAP S
GIFTEE S
GITTED
GLINTY
TINGLY
GLUTES
GOMERS
GORMED
GOTCHA S
GRAMMA RS
GRAMPA S

GYOZAS
AZYGOS
GYTTJA S

HAIKUS
HAINTS
SHANTI
HALALS
HALLAL
HALONS
HAMMAM S
HANDAX
HANDER S
HARDEN
HAWALA S
HAZMAT S
MATZAH
C **HEAPER** S
HENGES
HENLEY S
HEPPER
HICKIE S
HIJABS
HIJRAH S
HIJRAS
HIREES
HITMAN
HITMEN
HOBBER S
HOMEYS
HOMIES T
HOOVER S
HOSERS
HORSES
SHOERS
SHORES
HOSEYS
HOTTIE S
HRYVNA S
HULLOO S
T **HUMPER** S
C **HUPPAH** S
HYPERS
SPHERY
SYPHER

BDF GJP RWZ **IGGING**
ILLUDE DS
DUELLI
DPR W **IMPLED**
DIMPLE
LIMPED
INCENT S
PW **INCHER** S
ENRICH
RICHEN
INFILL
MP **INIONS**
INNAGE S
INRUNS
INURNS

JAZZBO S
JEANED
JELLOS
JETLAG S
JETWAY S
JIMMIE DS
JINNIS
JOURNO S

KALPAC S
KANZUS
KAONIC
KEGGED
KEGGER S
KENTES
KEWPIE S
KEYPAL S
KINARA S
KITBAG S
KLEPTO S
KLICKS
KLUDGY

KLUGED
KLUDGE
KNAWES
WAKENS
KOMBUS
KORMAS
KREWES
SKEWER
KVELLS

LAOGAI S
C **LASSIS**
SISALS
P **LATINA** S
LAVASH
HALVAS
LAYINS
INLAYS
LEKKED
LENITE DS
LEPTIN S
PINTLE
LIGNAN S
FG **LINTED**
DENTIL
LOGINS
LOSING
SOLING
LOGONS
LOIDED
DILDOE
DOILED
LOONIE RS
BPS **LOTTER** SY
LOUMAS
LUBING
BLUING
LUCITE S
LUETIC
K **LUGING**
GLUING
LULLER S
LYCHES
CHYLES
LYCRAS

MADTOM S
MAMZER S
MANATS
ATMANS
MANTAS
MANGAS
GASMAN
MARKAS
KARMAS
MAKARS
MASALA S
SALAAM
MATIER
IMARET
MAXING
MEGARA
MEHNDI S
MELENA S
ENAMEL
MENTEE S
MENUDO S
A **MERCES**
CREMES
MERGEE S
EMERGE
METOLS
MOLEST
MOTELS
MIDCAP
MIKVOS
MIKVOT H
MILDED
MIDDLE
MIRINS
MISFED
MIZUNA S
MODALS
DOLMAS
MOGHUL S
MOHAWK S
MOONER S
MOSHED
MOSHER S
HOMERS

MOSHES
SHMOES
MUDBUG S
MUDHEN S
MUGHAL S
MUSICK S
MUSKOX
MYLARS

NAFFED
NAIRAS
NAIRUS
NAKFAS
NAPPAS
NAYSAY S
NEOCON S
NEPETA S
NEWBIE S
NIDATE DS
DETAIN
NIGGLY
NOOGIE S
GOONIE
NUBUCK S

OAKIER
OBENTO S
OCICAT S
OLINGO S
LOGION
LOOING
ONLAYS
ONLINE
ONLOAD S
ORISHA S
ORLONS
OSETRA S
OATERS
ORATES
OUTLED
LOUTED
OUTRIG S
OUTSAY S
BF **OXLIKE**
OYEZES
OZALID S

S **PACIER**
PAKORA S
PALAPA S
PALPED
DAPPLE
LAPPED
PANINI
PANINO
S **PANNER** S
PEPINO S
PERITI
PITIER
PERNIO
ORPINE
PERNOD S
PONDER
PHREAK S
PHYTIN S
PISHER S
PERISH
RESHIP
PISTOU S
PITAYA S
PITTAS
PIZZAZ Z
PIZAZZ
PLEONS
PLEXES
EXPELS
PLUNKY
POBOYS
POLIES
PILOSE
POLEIS
POLYOL S
S **POOLER** S
LOOPER
PORKED
POSOLE S

POSTIE S
POTSIE
SOPITE
POSTOP S
POTHOS
PHOTOS
POUFFY
POXIER
POZOLE S
PRAJNA S
PREBID S
PREBUY S
PREDRY
PRELAW
PREOPS
PROGUN
PSYOPS
PTOOEY
PUNJIS
PUTTIE DRS
PYJAMA S

QABALA HS
QUACKY
QUBITS
QUBYTE S
QUELEA S
QUIPPY
QUOLLS

RAITAS
ARISTA
RIATAS
TARSIA
TIARAS
RAMADA S
ARMADA
RAMBLA S
RAMONA S
RECITS
CITERS
STERIC
TRICES
RECOAT S
COATER
REFLAG S
REJIGS
REKNOT S
RELAND S
DARNEL
LANDER
REPLOW S
PLOWER
RERENT S
RENTER
RESITS
RESIST
SISTER
REWEAR S
WEARER
REWORE
P **REWORN**
REXINE S
REZERO S
RHEMES
REHEMS
RHOTIC
THORIC
RIFLIP S
RISTRA S
ROMAJI S
ROOFIE S
ROOTLE DST
LOOTER
RETOOL
TOOLER
ROSHIS
ROUGHY
RUBATI
RUBELS
RUBLES
P **RUDERY**

SABALS
BALSAS
SAMBAL S
BALSAM
SARGOS
SAYEDS

SCHLUB S
SCHULS
SCOOCH
SCULCH
SEITAN S
TENIAS
TINEAS
TISANE
SELKIE S
SENSEI S
SEINES
SERGED
EDGERS
GREEDS
SERGER S
SHARIA HS
SHAZAM
HAMZAS
SHEESH
SHLUBS
SHOGIS
SIGLUM
SILKIE RS
SISSES
SKANKS
SKANKY
SKELLS
SKORTS
STORKS
TORSKS
SKUNKY
SLIEVE S
LEVIES
SLITTY
SMOOSH
SNARFS
SNEERY
SOMANS
MASONS
SOMONI
SIMOON
SPENDY
SPHYNX
SPIVVY
SQUARK S
QUARKS
STANOL S
SANTOL
TALONS
TOLANS
STATIN GS
TAINTS
TANIST
TITANS
STENTS
STORER S
RESORT
RETROS
ROSTER
SORTER
STOTIN S
STOTTS
SUNRAY S
SYNURA
SWANNY
SWOONY
SWOOPY

TANNOY S
TATSOI S
TAUONS
TAXOLS
TECHNO S
TEFLON S
TEKKIE S
TELCOS
CLOSET
TELNET S
NETTLE
TENDUS
NUDEST
TETRIS
SITTER
TITERS
TITRES
TRISTE
THEBES
BEHEST
THESPS

TICCED
TIKKAS
TINPOT
TOLARS
TOONIE S
TORICS
TORTAS
OTTARS
STATOR
TAROTS
TRAMPY
TRANNY
TRICEP S
TURION S
TURNON S
UNTORN
TUSSES
TUTUED
TWEENS
NEWEST

UAKARI S
UMAMIS
IMAUMS
UNAXED
UNBALE DS
NEBULA
UNABLE
UNCAST
CANTUS
UNJAMS
UNSNAG S
UPSIZE DS
UPTALK S
B **URPING**
URSIDS

VARIAS
VEGGED
VELCRO S
CLOVER
VENENE S
VETTER S
TREVET
VIGIAS
VOCABS
VODOUS
VOUDON S
VODOUN

WACKER
WAFFLY
WAKAME S
WEAKON S
AWOKEN
WEBCAM S
WEBLOG S
BOWLEG
WHIZZY
WICCAN S
WICCAS
WIFEYS
WILDED
WIDDLE
WIMMIN
WIMPED
WITANS
TWAINS
WIZZES

YABBIE S
YAKUZA
YARDER S
DREARY
YUTZES

ZOCALO S
ZOOIER
OOZIER
ZOONED

7-letter Words

ABLATOR S
ABLEISM S
LAMBIES
ABLEIST S
ALBITES
ASTILBE
BASTILE
BESTIAL
BLASTIE
STABILE
ABORTUS
ROBUSTA
RUBATOS
TABOURS
ACANTHA E
ACHIRAL
RACHIAL
ACORNED
ACTORLY
M **ADWOMAN**
M **ADWOMEN**
WOMANED
AEROBAT S
AGAMIDS
AGEMATE S
AGAMETE
AGENTED
NEGATED
H **AGGADAH** S
HAGGADA
H **AGGADAS**
H **AGGADOT** H
AIRBAGS
AIRSHOT S
SHORTIA
THORIAS
AIRSHOW S
ALFREDO
ALMONDY
ALNICOS
OILCANS
AMARONE S
ANALYTE S
ANIMACY
ANNONAS
ANTIFOG
APORIAS
APPLETS
LAPPETS
ARCHAEA LN
ARCHEAN
ARCHFOE S
ARRASES
ASCARED
ARCADES
ASHCAKE S
ATONIAS
ATRESIC
CRISTAE
RACIEST
STEARIC
ATRETIC
CATTIER
CITRATE
ATTRITS
AUDITEE S
AUTARCH SY
AUTISTS
AUTOMAT AE S
T **AUTONYM** S
AUTOPEN S
AVERTER S
AVIATIC
VIATICA
AZULEJO S

BAASKAP S
BABIEST
TABBIES
BABYSAT
BABYSIT S
BAGLIKE
BANDAID
BANDITO S
BANDSAW S
BANKITS
BARBIES
RABBIES
BARISTA S
BARNEYS
BARNING
BARYTON ES
BATGIRL S
BATIKED
BEADERS
DEBASER
SABERED
BEEDIES
BEIGNES
BELAYER S
BENDIER
INBREED
BENTHON S
BERMING
BHANGRA S
BIALIES
ALIBIES
BAILIES
BICORNS
BICRONS
BIGOSES
BIGTIME
BILBIES
BILEVEL S
BINGOES
BIOGENS
BIOFILM S
BIOFUEL S
BIRDDOG S
BIRIANI S
BIRYANI S
BITCHEN
BENTHIC
BITMAPS
BAPTISM
BITSIER
BIZARRO S
BLADERS
BLADING S
BALDING
BLEEPER S
BLITZER S
BLOGGER S
BOGGLER
BLUDGED
BLUDGES
BOGARTS
BOGUSLY
BOHRIUM S
BOMBLET S
BONEYER
BONIATO S
BONOBOS
BOOBIRD S
BOOCOOS
BOOJUMS
BOOKOOS
BORKING
BROKING
BOSONIC
BOUDINS
BOURSIN S
BOXBALL S
BREWPUB S
BREWSKI S
BRILLOS
BRUXING
BUDDHAS
BUFFEST
BUFFETS
BUGOUTS
BULGHUR S
BUMELIA S
BUMMALO S
BUSGIRL S
BUSTLER S
BLUSTER
BUTLERS
SUBTLER
BUYOFFS
BUZZCUT S
BYCATCH

CABBAGY
CABLERS
CACONYM SY
CALLEES
CALPAIN S
CAMELID S
CLAIMED
DECIMAL
DECLAIM
MEDICAL
CAMMIES
CAMPOUT S
CANOERS
COARSEN
CORNEAS
NARCOSE
CANOLAS
CANOPIC
CANTALS
CANULAR
LACUNAR
CAPIZES
CAPSIZE
CARDONS
CANDORS
DACRONS
CARJACK S
CASSENA S
CASSENE S
ENCASES
SEANCES
SENECAS
CASSINA S
CASSINE S
CASEINS
INCASES
CATJANG S
CATSUIT S
CEILIDH S
CELOTEX
CERVEZA S
CHACHKA S
CHAEBOL S
CHALUPA S
CHAMISA S
CHIASMA
CHANCER SY
CHANCRE
CHANOYU S
CHAPPIE S
CHEFING
CHEVRET S
CHIANTI S
CHILLIS
CHINWAG S
CHAWING
CHIRREN
CHORTEN S
NOTCHER
CHUNNEL S
CHUPPAH S
CHUPPAS
CHURROS
CHYTRID S
CLADDED
CLADISM S
CLASSON S
CLOSEUP S
COUPLES
CLOVERY
CONCHAS
CONCHOS
COOKOFF S
COPOUTS
OCTOPUS
CORNIFY
CORTINA S
CAROTIN
CORVIDS
COSMIDS
COTINGA S
COATING
COXLESS
CRAFTER S
REFRACT
CRAPOLA S
CAPORAL
CREEPED
PRECEDE
CREMINI S
CRIMINE
MINCIER

Added in 2006

CREWCUT S
CRIMINE
CREMINI
MINCIER
CRIMINI S
CRIMINY
CRONISH
CROOKER Y
CROUTES
COUTERS
SCOUTER
CUATROS
SURCOAT
TURACOS
CUBITUS
CULEXES
CUMBIAS
CYCLINS

DACITES
DACRONS
CANDORS
CARDONS
DAMIANA S
DANAZOL S
DARBARS
DAYCARE S
DEADMAN
DEADMEN
AMENDED
DEBEARD S
BEARDED
BREADED
DEFFEST
DEFRAGS
DEFUELS
DEFUSER S
REFUSED
DEKEING
DEMOING
MENDIGO
DENIMED
DICAMBA S
DIEOFFS
OFFSIDE
DISEURS
SUDSIER
DIVULSE DS
DOMAINE S
AMIDONE
DONGLES
DOOBIES
DOODIES
DOODOOS
DOOMIER
MOIDORE
MOODIER
DOOWOPS
DOPINGS
PONGIDS
DOWNBOW S
DRACENA S
DRAMADY
DRYWELL S
DUBNIUM S
DUETING
DUFUSES
DYNEINS

EAGLING
EARBUDS
DAUBERS
TW **EASELED**
EBONICS
ECOTAGE S
ECOTOUR S
EDITRIX
R **EMAILED**
LIMEADE
EMANANT
ENDPLAY S
ENDURER S
ENVIROS
RENVOIS
VERSION
D **EPILATE** DS
PILEATE
ERRABLE

EUSTASY
R **EVULSED**
EVULSES
EXABYTE S
EXAPTED
EXHEDRA E
EXILERS
EXONYMS
EYASSES
EYEFOLD S
EYELIFT S

FABBEST
FADEINS
FADEOUT S
FADLIKE
FANFICS
FAREBOX
FARTLEK S
FEDEXED
FEDEXES
FENNIER
FIBSTER S
FIRRIER
FJORDIC
FLAREUP S
FLAUTAS
FLEHMEN S
FLEURON S
FLOSSER S
FLUFFER S
FLUKILY
FLUNKIE S
FOLDUPS
UPFOLDS
FOLKIER
FONDUED
FOUNDED
FOOTBAG S
FORBARE
FORBEAR
FORMICA S
ACIFORM
FORNENT
FRISBEE S
FRISEES
FROGLET S
FROTHER S
FRYABLE
FUDDIES
FUNDERS
REFUNDS
FUNFEST S
FUNKILY
FUNPLEX
FUSARIA

GALANGA LS
GALETTE S
GALLICA NS
GLACIAL
GAMETAL
GANGSTA S
GAPLESS
GARBAGY
GASEITY
GATEAUS
GATINGS
GASTING
STAGING
GAYDARS
GEEKDOM S
GELATIS
AIGLETS
LIGATES
GELCAPS
GIARDIA S
GIFTEES
GINGKOS
GINKGOS
GIRLIER
GIROLLE S
GITTING
GLAZILY
GLITZED
GODETIA S

GOLIATH S
GOMBEEN S
GOONIER
GORDITA S
GORMING
GOTCHAS
GRAMMAS
GRAMPAS
GRIDDED
GRISTER S
GRITTER S
GRODIER
GROKKED
GRUNGER S
GUARANA S
GUMBALL S
GUMLINE S
LEGUMIN
GUNKIER
GYTTJAS

HAFIZES
HAIMISH
HAMMAMS
HANDERS
HARDENS
HAPKIDO S
HARISSA S
SHARIAS
HASSIUM S
HAWALAS
HAZMATS
MATZAHS
HEADEND S
HEADFUL S
HEAPERS
RESHAPE
HEGEMON SY
HENLEYS
HENNISH
HEPPEST
HEXYLIC
HIGHTOP S
HIJRAHS
C **HINKIER**
HISSIER
HOBBERS
HOMERIC
HONGIED
HONGIES
SHOEING
HOOCHIE S
HOOVERS
HOSEYED
HOTLINK S
HOTSPOT S
POTSHOT
HOTTIES
HRYVNAS
HRYVNIA S
HULLOOS
HUMIDEX
T **HUMPERS**
C **HUPPAHS**
HYPONYM SY

IGUANID S
ILLUDED
ILLUDES
SULLIED
IMPURER
INCENTS
PW **INCHERS**
RICHENS
INLYING
INNAGES
INOSINE S
IRONMAN
IRONMEN
ISLETED
ISOFORM S

JACUZZI S
JAGGIES T
JAMLIKE
JARGONY

JAWLESS
JAZZBOS
JETFOIL S
JETLAGS
JETWAYS
JIGGIER
JIGGISH
JIGLIKE
JOHNNIE S
JONESED
JOURNOS
SOJOURN

KALPACS
KATSURA S
KEGGERS
KEGGING
KEWPIES
KEYPALS
KICKBOX
KINARAS
S **KINLESS**
INKLESS
KITBAGS
KLEENEX
KLEPTOS
KLUDGED
KLUDGEY
KLUGING
KOPIYKA S
KUCHENS
KVELLED
KWACHAS
HACKSAW

LADDISH
LADHOOD S
LAKEBED S
LALIQUE S
LAMBADA S
LAMININ S
LAOGAIS
LARCHEN
CHARNEL
LATILLA S
P **LATINAS**
LEADENS
LEKKING
LENITED
LENITES
LISENTE
SETLINE
TENSILE
LEPTINS
PINTLES
PLENIST
LIGNANS
LINSANG
LINGULA ER
LINGUAL
FG **LINTING**
LIPREAD S
PREDIAL
LIRIOPE S
LITHOPS
S **LIVERED**
DELIVER
RELIVED
REVILED
LOCKSET S
LOCKETS
LOGGISH
LOIDING
LOLLOPY
LOOKISM S
LOOKIST S
LOONILY
LOOPILY
BPS **LOTTERS**
SETTLOR
SLOTTER
LOWLILY
LUCITES
LUETICS
LULLERS
LUREXES

LUTFISK S
KISTFUL
LYRICON S
CORNILY

MADRASA HS
ARMADAS
RAMADAS
MADTOMS
MAGALOG S
MAMZERS
MANTRAM S
MAQUILA S
MASALAS
SALAAMS
MATIEST
ETATISM
MAYBIRD S
MEDIGAP S
MEDIVAC S
MEGARON
MARENGO
MEGILLA HS
MILLAGE
MEHNDIS
MEISTER S
METIERS
REEMITS
RETIMES
TRISEME
MELENAS
ENAMELS
MENSCHY
MENSHEN
MENSHES
MENTEES
MENUDOS
MERCHES
SCHEMER
SCHMEER
MERGEES
EMERGES
MESCLUN S
METATAG S
MIDLIST S
MILDING
MIMESES
MINIBAR S
MINICAM PS
MIOCENE
MISFEED S
MIXEDLY
MIZUNAS
MOBBISM S
MODEMED
MOGHULS
MOGULED
MOHAWKS
MONOPOD ES
Y

MOONERS
MORPHED
MOSHERS
MOSHING S
GNOMISH
MOUSAKA S
MUDBUGS
MUDFLAP S
MUDHENS
MUGHALS
MUNGOES
MURALED
MUSICKS
MUTUALS
UMLAUTS

NAFFING
NARCOMA S
NAYSAID
NAYSAYS
NEATNIK S
NEDDIES
NEOCONS
NEOGENE
NEPETAS
PENATES
NETIZEN S

NEUSTIC
NEWBIES
NICOISE
EOSINIC
NIDATED
NIDATES
DESTAIN
DETAINS
INSTEAD
SAINTED
STAINED
NIGELLA S
GALLEIN
NIOBITE S
NONCORE
NONDRIP
NONORAL
NONWAGE
NONWOOL
NOOGIES
GOONIES
ISOGONE
NOPALES
ESPANOL
NOPLACE
NUBUCKS

OAKIEST
OBENTOS
OCICATS
OFFLINE
OIDIOID
OLESTRA S
OLICOOK S
OLINGOS
LOGIONS
LOOSING
SOLOING
ONLOADS
ORBLESS
ORGIAST S
ORISHAS
ORPHISM S
ROMPISH
OSETRAS
OSSETRA
OSIERED
OREIDES
OSSETRA S
OSETRAS
OSTRAKA
OUTCALL S
OUTCITY
OUTGAZE DS
OUTLEAD S
OUTRIGS
OUTSAID
OUTSAYS
OUTWITH
WITHOUT
OVERFIT
OZALIDS

S **PACIEST**
ASEPTIC
SPICATE
PAGEFUL S
PAKORAS
PALAPAS
PALEATE
PALMFUL S
PALMTOP S
PALPING
LAPPING
PANGRAM S
S **PANNERS**
SPANNER
PAPADAM S
PAPADOM S
PAPADUM S
PARBAKE DS
PARKADE S
S **PARRIER** S
PAVISSE S
PASSIVE
PAVISES
SPAVIES

PEDALER S
PEARLED
PLEADER
REPLEAD
PEKEPOO S
PELOTON S
PEPINOS
PEPTALK S
PEREONS
OPENERS
REOPENS
PERFUMY
PERITUS
PERMIAN
PERNODS
PONDERS
RESPOND
PERSPEX
PHATTER
PHORESY
PHREAKS
PHYTINS
PICANTE
PICCATA
PIEHOLE S
PINGOES
EPIGONS
PIGEONS
PISHERS
RESHIPS
PISTOUS
PITAYAS
PIZZAZZ Y
PLEONAL
PLEONIC
PINOCLE
PLUMMER
POBLANO S
POCOSEN S
POCOSON S
POKABLE
POLICER S
PELORIC
POLYOLS
POLYPED S
S **POOLERS**
LOOPERS
RESPOOL
SPOOLER
PORKING
POSABLE
POSOLES
POSTIES
POTSIES
SOPITES
POSTOPS
POUTINE S
POXIEST
EXPOSIT
POZOLES
PRAJNAS
PREBADE
BEDRAPE
PREBIDS
PREBUYS
PREFUND S
PRELOAD S
LEOPARD
PAROLED
PREORAL
PERORAL
PREPAVE DS
PREPUPA ELS
PRESHIP S
SHIPPER
PRETELL S
PRETOLD
DROPLET
PREVERB S
PREWIRE DS
PREWORN
PRICILY
PRODRUG S
PROMOED
PROPRIA
PURFLER S
PURTIER

Added in 2006

PUTDOWN S
PYREXES

QABALAH S
QABALAS
QUBYTES
QUELEAS
SEQUELA

RAMADAS
ARMADAS
MADRASA
RAMBLAS
RAMONAS
OARSMAN
G RANULAR
REALTOR S
RELATOR
REBLENT
RECLADS
CRADLES
RECOATS
COASTER
COATERS
REFLAGS
REKNOTS
RELANDS
DARNELS
LANDERS
SLANDER
SNARLED
RELLENO S
REPLOWS
PLOWERS
P REPPING
RERENTS
RENTERS
STERNER
RESHOED
RESILIN GS
INLIERS
RESPOOL S
LOOPERS
POOLERS
SPOOLER
RETALLY
ALERTLY
RETOTAL S
REWEARS
SWEARER
WEARERS
REXINES
REZEROS
RIFLIPS
RIMSHOT S
RIPSAWN
INWRAPS
RISTRAS
ROGERED
ROMAJIS
ROOFIES
ROOTCAP S
ROOTLED
ROOTLES S
LOOTERS
RETOOLS
TOOLERS
ROSACEA S
ROSEHIP S
RUBBIES

SAMADHI S
SAMBALS
BALSAMS
SAMOYED S
SOMEDAY
SANTERA S
SANTERO S
ATONERS
SENATOR
TREASON
SANTIMU
MANITUS
TSUNAMI
SANTOOR S
RATOONS
SARCINA ES
ACRASIN
ARNICAS
CARINAS

SARSNET S
SAUNAED
SAVVILY
SCAMMER S
SCARFER S
FARCERS
SCENICS
SCHLUBS
SCOOTCH
SCUBAED
ABDUCES
SCUFFER S
SCULTCH
SCUZZES
SEALIFT S
FETIALS
SECONAL S
SEITANS
ENTASIS
NASTIES
SESTINA
TANSIES
TISANES
SELKIES
SELLOFF S
SENSEIS
SEPTAGE S
SERGERS
REGRESS
SEROVAR S
SAVORER
SHACKED
SHARIAH S
SHARIAS
HARISSA
SHEQELS
SHIVITI S
SHLOCKY
SHYLOCK
SHNAPPS
SHOEBOX
SHTICKY
KITSCHY
SHUSHER S
SIEVERT S
RESTIVE
VERIEST
VERITES
SIRUPED
UPDRIES
SKANKED
SKANKER S
KRAKENS
SKYLIKE
KYLIKES
SKYSURF S
SLANTLY
SLICKEN S
NICKELS
NICKLES
SLIEVES
SLOTTER S
LOTTERS
SETTLOR
SLUDGED
SMILEYS
MESSILY
SMUSHED
SMUSHES
SNACKER S
CANKERS
SNARFED
SNIFFLY
SNIGLET S
GLISTEN
SINGLET
TINGLES
SNOWCAT S
SOFABED S
SOLUNAR
SOUKOUS
SOUSLIK S
SPAMBOT S
SPAMMED
SPAMMER S
SPASMED

SPOOLER S
LOOPERS
POOLERS
RESPOOL
SPURTER S
SQUARKS
STANOLS
SANTOLS
STATINS
TANISTS
STETSON S
TESTONS
STOPOFF S
STORERS
RESORTS
ROSTERS
SORTERS
STOTINS
STOTTED
STRAPPY
STRIATA
SUCKIER
SUGARER S
ARGUERS
SUMOIST S
MISSOUT
SUNRAYS
SURFMAN
SURFMEN
FRENUMS
SURIMIS
SWEENEY S
SYNTAGM AS
GYMNAST
SYRETTE S
SYRUPED

TACRINE S
CERATIN
CERTAIN
CREATIN
TAGGANT S
TAGLINE S
ATINGLE
ELATING
GELATIN
GENITAL
TAILFIN S
TALLITS
TANKINI S
TANNOYS
TARDIVE
TARTARE
TARTIER
RATTIER
TARTILY
TASKBAR S
TATSOIS
TECHNOS
NOTCHES
TECTUMS
TEFLONS
TEKKIES
TELECOM S
TELEFAX
TELNETS
NETTLES
THALWEG S
THERIAN S
HAIRNET
INEARTH
THERMIT ES
TICCING
TIMBERY
TOFUTTI S
TOOLBAR S
TOONIES
ISOTONE
S TOWABLE
TEABOWL
TOWSACK S
TRASHER S
TRIBALS
TRILITH S
TRIPTAN ES
TSADDIK
TSATSKE S
TSOURIS
SUITORS

TUMESCE DS
TURIONS
NITROUS
TURNONS
TUSHERY
TWEENER S
TWINKIE S
TWOONIE S

UAKARIS
UNADDED
UNADEPT
UNAWAKE D
UNBALED
UNBALES
NEBULAS
UNBEING
UNCEDED
UNCHAIR S
UNCLEFT
UNGATED
UNIBODY
UNISIZE
UNLIKED
UNSLICK
UNSNAGS
UNSPOOL S
UNTIMED
MINUTED
MUTINED
UNTRACK S
UPCOURT
UPSIZED
UPSIZES
UPSLOPE
UPTALKS
UPTEMPO S

VAMPIER
VAMPIRE
VANLOAD S
VEGGING
VELCROS
CLOVERS
VENENES
VENUSES
VETTERS
TREVETS
VOTIVES
VOUDONS
VODOUNS
VOUDOUN S

WACKEST
WAIFISH
WAITRON S
WAKAMES
WANNABE ES
WAVICLE S
WAXABLE
WEAKONS
WEBCAMS
WEBCAST S
WEBLOGS
BOWLEGS
WEBPAGE S
WEBSITE S
WEIRDED
WETSUIT S
WETWARE S
WHINGER S
WHOOPIE S
WHUPPED
WICCANS
WIMPING
WINDOWY
WINESAP S
WISEGUY S

XENOPUS

YABBIES
YARDERS
YOHIMBE S
YUKKIER
YUPPIFY

ZEBRANO S
ZEPPOLE S
ZEPPOLI
ZESTILY
STYLIZE
ZIPLOCK
ZOCALOS
ZOOGENY
ZOOIEST
OOZIEST
ZOONING

8-letter Words

ABDUCTEE S
ABEGGING
ABLATORS
ABLEISMS
MISSABLE
ABLEISTS
ASTILBES
BASTILES
BLASTIES
STABILES
ACANTHAE
ACARBOSE S
ACOELOUS
ACQUIREE S
ACTIONER S
ANORETIC
CREATION
REACTION
ADMASSES
ADMITTEE S
MEDITATE
AEROBATS
AGEMATES
AGAMETES
H AGGADAHS
HAGGADAS
H AGGADOTH
HAGGADOT
AGUACATE S
AIRSHOTS
SHORTIAS
AIRSHOWS
AKINESIA S
AKINETIC
ALACHLOR S
ALDICARB S
ALIASING S
ALLOSAUR S
ALLSORTS
ALMANACK S
ALTERITY
AMARONES
ANALYTES
ANTHEMIC
ANTIACNE
ANTIGANG
ANTIMINE
ANTINOME S
NOMINATE
ANTISPAM
APOAPSES
AQUAFARM S
AQUALUNG S
ARCHAEAL
ARCHAEAN S
ARCHAEON
ARCHFOES
ASHCAKES
ASOCIALS
ASSUAGER S
ATABRINE S
ATENOLOL S
ATTAGIRL
ATTICIZE DS
ATTRITES
RATTIEST
TARTIEST
TITRATES
TRISTATE

AUDIBLED
BUDDLEIA
AUDITEES
AURALITY
AUTARCHS
AUTOHARP S
AUTOMATS
T AUTONYMS
AUTOPENS
AVERTERS
TRAVERSE
AZULEJOS

BAASKAPS
BAASSKAP
BAASSKAP S
BAASKAPS
BABBITRY
BABYDOLL S
BABYSITS
BACKFLIP S
BACKHOED
BACKLOAD S
BACLOFEN S
BAGPIPED
BAITFISH
BAKELITE S
BAKEWARE S
BALLYARD S
BALLADRY
BANDITOS
BANDMATE S
BANDSAWS
BANNABLE
BAREHAND S
BARISTAS
BAROSAUR S
BARYTONS
BASHINGS
BASILECT S
BATGIRLS
BATIKING
BATTERER S
BARRETTE
BERRETTA
BEDBOARD S
BEHEADAL S
BEHEADER S
BELAYERS
BELLINGS
BENADRYL S
BENCHTOP
BENDIEST
BENTHONS
BERIMBAU S
BESTOWER S
BHANGRAS
BIGSTICK
BILEVELS
BIMBETTE S
BINARISM S
MINIBARS
BIOFILMS
BIOFUELS
BIOMETER S
BIOMORPH S
BIOSOLID S
BIRDDOGS
BIRDFEED S
BIRDLIFE
BIRIANIS
BIRYANIS
BISCOTTI
BISCOTTO
BISCUITY
BITSIEST
BIZARROS
BLADINGS
BLAGGING S
BLAZERED
BLEBBING S
BLEEPERS
BLINDGUT S
BLITZERS

BLOGGERS
BOGGLERS
BLOGGING S
BOGGLING
BLONDINE DS
BLUDGING
BLUEBEAT S
BLURBIST S
BOATLIFT S
BOATNECK S
BOBBYSOX
BOGARTED
BOHRIUMS
BOILOVER S
OVERBOIL
BOLTLESS
BLOTLESS
BOLTLIKE
BOMBABLE
BOMBLETS
BONDLESS
BOLDNESS
BONEYEST
BONIATOS
BOOBIRDS
BOONLESS
BOREASES
BORNITIC
BORRELIA S
BOURSINS
BOXBALLS
BRAILLER S
BRAINIAC S
BREWPUBS
BREWSKIS
BRUNCHER S
BULGHURS
BUMELIAS
BUMMALOS
BUSGIRLS
BUSHVELD S
BUSTLERS
BLUSTERS
BUTTHEAD S
BUZZCUTS

CABBAGEY
CACONYMS
CACONYMY
CADDISED
CAFTANED
CAGELIKE
CAKINESS
CALABAZA S
CALAMATA S
CALKINGS
SLACKING
CALPAINS
CAMELIDS
DECIMALS
DECLAIMS
MEDICALS
CAMPOUTS
CANCERED
CANDIDAL
CANISTEL S
CANNOLIS
CAPOEIRA S
CARCERAL
CARJACKS
CASSENAS
CASSENES
CASSINAS
CASSINES
CATJANGS
CATSUITS
CECITIES
CECROPIA S
CEILIDHS
CENOZOIC
CERAMIDE S
MEDICARE
CERVEZAS
CHACHKAS
CHAEBOLS

Bob's Bible: Words Added in 2006

CHALUPAS
CHAMISAS
CHIASMAS
CHAMPACA S
CHANCERS
CHANCRES
CRANCHES
CHANGEUP S
CHANOYUS
CHAPPIES
CHATROOM S
CHECKSUM S
CHEDDARY
CHESHIRE S
CHESTILY
LECYTHIS
CHEVRETS
CHIANTIS
CHICHIER
CHINWAGS
CHIPOTLE S
HELICOPT
CHORTENS
NOTCHERS
CHROMIER
CHUNNELS
CHUPPAHS
CHYTRIDS
CINGULAR
CIPHERER S
CLADDAGH S
CLADISMS
CLAFOUTI S
CLAMLIKE
MILLCAKE
CLANKIER
CLASSONS
CLAWBACK S
CLEARCUT S
CLOGGILY
CLOSEUPS
CLOVERED
CLUBFACE S
CLUBHEAD S
COCOPLUM S
COINFECT S
COKELIKE
COLORWAY S
COLUMNEA S
COMMUNER S
COMORBID
CONCEPTI
CONCOURS E
CONJUNTO S
CONTEMPO
CONTESSA S
CONVERSO S
COOKOFFS
COPYABLE
COPYGIRL S
COPYLEFT S
CORPUSES
CORTINAS
CAROTINS
COSTALLY
COTINGAS
AGNOSTIC
COASTING
COATINGS
COTININE S
NICOTINE
COTURNIX
COVARIED
COVARIES
VARICOSE
COWBOYED
COWRITER S
CRABLIKE
CRAFTERS
REFRACTS
CRAMPIER
CRAPOLAS
CAPORALS
CRAYONER S
CREMINIS
CRENSHAW S

CREWCUTS
CRIMINIS
CROCKPOT S
CROOKEST
CROSTINI
CROSTINO
CRYOBANK S
CUFFLINK S
CYBERSEX
CYCLEWAY S
CYCLOPES

DAEMONES
DAIDZEIN S
DAMIANAS
DANAZOLS
DANEGELT S
DANGLIER
DRAGLINE
DANISHES
SHANDIES
DATEBOOK S
DAYCARES
DEBAGGED
DEBARKER S
DEBEARDS
DEEJAYED
DEFENCED
DEFORCER S
DEFUELED
DEFUSERS
DEGENDER S
GENDERED
DEICTICS
DEMISTER S
DEMERITS
DIMETERS
DEPEOPLE DS
DEPLETER S
PELTERED
DEPLOYER S
REDEPLOY
DEPORTER S
PORTERED
REPORTED
DEPRENYL S
DERANGER S
GARDENER
GARNERED
DESPISAL S
DETHATCH
THATCHED
DEVONIAN
DIAPSIDS
DICAMBAS
DIGERATI
DIGESTIF S
DIPLEGIC
DIPROTIC
DIOPTRIC
TRIPODIC
DISABLER S
BEDRAILS
DIVULSED
DIVULSES
DOCTORLY
DOLCETTO S
DOLMENIC
DOMAINES
AMIDONES
DAIMONES
DOOMIEST
MOODIEST
SODOMITE
DORMERED
DOWNBOWS
DOWNLESS
DOWNLIKE
DOWNSPIN S
DOWNZONE DS
DRACENAS
DRIPPILY
DROOLIER
DRYWELLS
DUBNIUMS
DUMPSITE S
DUMPIEST

DUMPSTER S
DUSTINGS
DWEEBIER
DWEEBISH

ECLIPSER S
PRESLICE
RESPLICE
ECOTAGES
ECOTOURS
OUTSCORE
EGGFRUIT S
R EMAILING
EMDASHES
EMERITAS
EMIRATES
STEAMIER
EMOTICON S
ENCLAVED
ENDASHES
DASHEENS
ENDLEAFS
ENDPLAYS
DYSPNEAL
ENDURERS
SUNDERER
OX ENOPHILE S
ENTERICS
ENTICERS
SECRETIN
ENURESES
D EPILATED
DEPILATE
PILEATED
D EPILATES
D EPILATOR S
PETIOLAR
ERODABLE
LEEBOARD
ESCALOPE DS
OPALESCE
ESCHEWER S
ETHNONYM S
ETHOGRAM S
EUDAIMON S
EUGLENID S
EUSOCIAL
EVULSING
EXABYTES
EXAHERTZ
EXAPTIVE
EXHEDRAE
EXILABLE
EXOCYTIC
EXPECTER S
EXTRANET S
EYEBLACK S
EYEBLINK S
EYEFOLDS
EYELIFTS
EYESHINE S

FABULATE DS
FACELIFT S
FACEMASK S
FADEOUTS
FAIRGOER S
FALAFELS
FARFALLE
FAROLITO S
FARTLEKS
FASCITIS
FATHOMER S
FEDEXING
FEEDYARD S
DEFRAYED
FEISTILY
FELAFELS
FENNIEST
FENTANYL S
FERNINST
FETIDITY
FIBSTERS
FILENAME S
FILLABLE
FALLIBLE
FILMLESS

FILMLIKE
FIRESHIP S
FIREWALL S
FIRRIEST
FISHKILL S
FISSURAL
FLAPERON S
FLAREUPS
FLATLINE DRS
FLEHMENS
FLESHILY
ELFISHLY
FLEURONS
FLIPBOOK S
FLIPFLOP S
FLOSSERS
FLUFFERS
FLYSHEET S
FOGEYISH
FOGEYISM S
FOLKIEST
FOLKSONG S
FOLLOWUP S
FONDUING
FOUNDING
FOOSBALL S
FOOTBAGS
FORMABLY
FORMICAS
S FORZANDI
FOUREYED
FRANCIZE DS
FREEWARE S
FRENULAR
FRISBEES
FRIZZIES T
FROGLETS
FRONTMAN
FRONTMEN
FROSTNIP S
FROTHERS
FRYBREAD S
FUNFESTS
FUNHOUSE S
FUSARIUM
FUSELIKE
FUSIONAL
FUZZTONE S

GALANGAS
GALETTES
GALLICAS
GANGSTAS
GARBAGEY
GARRETED
GARTERED
REGRATED
GEARHEAD S
HEADGEAR
GEEKDOMS
GEMATRIA S
GENNAKER S
GENOGRAM S
GENOMICS
GERMLIKE
GEWGAWED
GIARDIAS
GIFTABLE S
GIFTWRAP S
GIGAFLOP S
GIRLIEST
GIROLLES
GLINTIER
RETILING
TINGLIER
GLITZING
GLOPPIER
GLUHWEIN S
GLUINESS
UGLINESS
GLUTENIN S
A GNOSTICS
GOBSHITE S
GODETIAS

GOLDTONE
GOLIATHS
GOMBEENS
GOONIEST
GORDITAS
GOSPELLY
GREENLIT
GRILLERY
GRISTERS
GRITTERS
GRODIEST
DIGESTOR
STODGIER
GROKKING
GROTTOED
GRUNGERS
GUARANAS
GUARDDOG S
GULLWING
GUMBALLS
GUMLINES
LEGUMINS
GUNKIEST

HABANERO S
HACKABLE
HACKSAWN
HAFTOROS
HAGRIDER S
HALACHIC
HALAKHAH S
HALAKHIC
HALFPIPE S
HALLUCAL
HANDAXES
HANDCLAP S
HAPKIDOS
HARDPACK S
HARISSAS
HASSIUMS
HAZARDER S
HEADENDS
HEADFULS
HEGEMONS
HELLERIS
SHELLIER
HERBAGED
HIERURGY
HIGHRISE S
HIGHTOPS
HIGHSPOT
C HINKIEST
HISSIEST
HITTABLE
TITHABLE
HOLDDOWN S
HOLOCENE
HOMEBREW S
HOMEGIRL S
HOMEPAGE S
HONEYPOT S
HONGIING
HOOCHIES
HOODMOLD S
HOOVERED
HOPINGLY
HORDEOLA
HORNINGS
HORRIDER
HOSELIKE
HOSEYING
HOTLINKS
HOTSPOTS
POTSHOTS
HOURLIES
HOURLONG
HOVERFLY
HRYVNIAS
VARNISHY
HULLOOED
HUMITURE S
HYDRILLA S
HYPHENIC
HYPONYMS
SYMPHONY

HYPONYMY

ICEMAKER S
IDIOTYPE S
IGUANIDS
ILLUDING
IMPUREST
IMPUTERS
STUMPIER
INCENTED
INDECENT
INEDIBLY
INFOBAHN S
INGROUND
ROUNDING
INHOLDER S
INOSINES
INPUTTER S
INTACTLY
INTERMAT S
MARTINET
INTIFADA HS
INTRANET S
INVERSED
INVERTIN GS
ISOBUTYL S
ISOFORMS
ISOSTACY

JACUZZIS
JADELIKE
JAILABLE
JAMMABLE
JETFOILS
JIGGIEST
JOLLIERS
JONESING
JUMPABLE
JURASSIC
JURYLESS
JUTELIKE

KABALISM S
KALIMBAS
KABALIST S
KAFFIYAH S
KALAMATA S
KATSURAS
KEFFIYAH S
KAFFIYEH
KEIRETSU S
KERNELLY
KERYGMAS
KETAMINE S
KILLABLE
KILTLIKE
KLEZMERS
KLONDIKE S
KLUDGIER
KLUDGING
KNEESIES
KOPIYKAS
KREPLECH
KRUMKAKE S
KURTOSES
KVELLING
KVETCHER S

LADHOODS
LAKEBEDS
LALIQUES
SQUILLAE
LAMBADAS
LAMINALS
MANILLAS
LAMININS
LASTBORN S
LATILLAS
LAVASHES
LEADENED
LEFTMOST S
LENITING
LENTOIDS
LIFECARE S
LIFESPAN S
LINGUICA S

LINGUISA S
LINGULAE
LINGULAR
ALLURING
LINOTYPE DRS
LIPREADS
PARSLIED
SPIRALED
LIRIOPES
LISTERIA S
LITENESS
SETLINES
S LIVERING
RELIVING
REVILING
LOCKSETS
LONGJUMP S
LONGNECK S
LOOKISMS
LOOKSISM
LOOKISTS
LOOKSISM S
LOOKISMS
LOSSLESS
LOVEFEST S
LOVESEAT S
LUMBERLY
LUNCHBOX
LURINGLY
LUTFISKS
KISTFULS
LYRICONS

MACHOISM S
MACHISMO
MADERIZE DS
MADRASAH S
MADRASAS
MADRASSA
MADRASSA HS
MADRASAS
MAFIOSOS
MAGALOGS
MAIASAUR AS
MAILGRAM S
MAILROOM S
MALLINGS
MANGANIN S
MANTRAMS
MAQUILAS
MARCATOS
MASHGIAH
MASONITE S
AMNIOTES
MISATONE
MATURERS
MAYBIRDS
MAZELTOV
MBAQANGA S
MECHITZA S
MEDICANT S
MEDICIDE S
MEDIGAPS
MISPAGED
MEDIVACS
MEGAFLOP S
MEGAPLEX
MEGILLAS
LEGALISM
MILLAGES
MEISTERS
MISSTEER
TRISEMES
MEMETICS
MESCLUNS
MESOZOAN S
MESOZOIC
METATAGS
METRAZOL S
MICROCAP
MIDLIFER S
MIDLISTS
MILESIAN
ALIENISM
MILKLESS
MINIBARS
BINARISM
MINICAMS

MINIDISC S
MINIPILL S
MIREPOIX
MISALLOT S
MAILLOTS
MISCHOSE N
ECHOISMS
MISFEEDS
MISSTAMP S
MITTENED
MOBBISMS
MOCKTAIL S
MODEMING
MODERNES T
MODULARS
MOLLUSCA N
MONOKINE S
MONOPODS
MOONROOF S
MOOTNESS
MOONSETS
MOPINESS
PEONISMS
MORENESS
MORPHING S
MOSHINGS
MOUSAKAS
MOUSSAKA
MOUSEPAD S
MUDFLAPS
MULTIDAY
MURALLED
MEDULLAR
MUSICKED
MUSKOXEN
MUSKROOT S
MUSTELID S
MYXAMEBA ES

NANNYISH
NANOTECH S
NANOTUBE S
BUTANONE
NAPROXEN S
NARCOMAS
NASALISM S
NEATNIKS
NETIZENS
NEURULAR
NEWSBEAT S
NEWSDESK S
NEWSGIRL S
NEWSWIRE S
NEWWAVER S
NIDATING
NIDATION S
NIGELLAS
GALLEINS
NIGGLIER
NIOBITES
NONCOLAS
NONINERT
NONLEVEL
NONLOYAL
NONLYRIC
NONNASAL
NONNOBLE
NONSTOPS
NONTONIC
NONVITAL
NOPALITO S
OPTIONAL
NOSEDOVE
NOTECARD S
CARTONED
NUMCHUCK S

OLESTRAS
OLICOOKS
ONLOADED
ONSCREEN
ORDUROUS
OREODONT S
ORGASMED
ORGIASTS
ORIENTER S
REORIENT
ORPHISMS
OSSATURE S
OSSETRAS
OSTINATI
OSTOMATE S
TOMATOES
OSTRAKON
OTITISES
OSTEITIS
OUGUIYAS
OUTBULGE DS
OUTCALLS
LOCUSTAL
OUTCROWD S
OUTFENCE DS
OUTFLOAT S
OUTGAZED
OUTGAZES
OUTGLEAM S
OUTLEADS
OUTPLACE DS
COPULATE
OUTPUPIL S
OUTSMELL S
OUTSMELT
OUTSWEEP S
OUTWEEPS
OUTSWEPT
OUTSWING S
OUTSWUNG
OVERARMS
OVERDYER S
OVERPACK S
OVOIDALS
OXIMETER S
OXIMETRY

PAGEFULS
PALLETED
PETALLED
PALMFULS
PALMTOPS
LAMPPOST
PANELESS
PALENESS
PANGRAMS
PANTALET S
PAPADAMS
PAPADOMS
PAPADUMS
PAPPADAM S
PARAFOIL S
PARASAIL S
PARASHOT H
PARBAKED
PARBAKES
PARCLOSE S
PARKADES
PARKETTE S
PARMESAN S
SPEARMAN
PAROSMIA S
MARIPOSA
PARRIERS
SPARRIER
PASHMINA S
PASTITSO S
PASTORLY
PATINAED
PATOOTIE S
PATRIATE DS
PATTENED
PATENTED
PAVISSES
PASSIVES
PEARWOOD S
PEDALERS
PLEADERS
RELAPSED
REPLEADS
PEDALLER S
PREDELLA
PEEKAPOO S
PEKEPOOS
PELAGICS
PELOTONS
PELTLESS
PEPTALKS
PEREIONS
ISOPRENE
PIONEERS
PETABYTE S
PETNAPER S
PETTABLE
PHARMING S
PHATTEST
A **PHERESES**
A **PHERESIS**
PERISHES
PHREAKED
PHREAKER S
PICOWAVE DS
PIEHOLES
PISOLITH S
PITAHAYA S
PIZZAZES
PIZAZZES
PIZZAZZY
PIZZELLE S
PLEATHER S
PLIOCENE
PLIOFILM S
PLUMMEST
PLUMMETS
PLUNKIER
POBLANOS
POCOSENS
POCOSONS
POLICERS
POLYPEDS
PONCHOED
CHENOPOD
POPLITEI
POPPADOM S
POPPADUM S
POPSICLE S
PORCINIS
PORTSIDE
DIOPTERS
DIOPTRES
PERIDOTS
PROTEIDS
RIPOSTED
TOPSIDER
POSTGRAD S
POSTPOSE DS
POSTPUNK
POTBOUND
POUTINES
PREALTER S
PALTERER
PREAPPLY
PREBIRTH S
PREBOARD S
PREBUILD S
PREBUILT
PRECHOSE N
PREDEATH S
THREAPED
PREDELLA S
PEDALLER
PREDRAFT
PREDRIED
PREDRIES
PRESIDER
REPRISED
RESPIRED
PREFUNDS
PREGAMES
PREGUIDE DS
PRELOADS
LEOPARDS
PREOWNED
PREPAVED
PREPAVES
PREPRESS
PREPUBES
PREPUBIS
PREPUPAE
PREPUPAS
PRERADIO
PRESALES
PLEASERS
RELAPSES
PRESHIPS
SHIPPERS
PRESOLVE DS
PRESTORE DS
PRETELLS
PRETERMS
PREVALUE DS
PREVERBS
PREVISIT S
PRIVIEST
PREWEIGH S
PREWIRED
PREWIRES
PREWORKS
PRODRUGS
PROFORMA
PROMOING
PROPRIUM
PROTEOME S
PROTRADE
PARROTED
PREDATOR
PRORATED
TEARDROP
PUERPERA EL
PURFLERS
PURLINGS
SLURPING
PURTIEST
PUTTIERS
PUTDOWNS

QABALAHS
QUACKIER
QUARTIER S
QUINSIED
QUIPPIER

RACEWALK S
RACHETED
DETACHER
RAMTILLA S
RANKLESS
RASPINGS
PINGRASS
RATABLES
ARBALEST
REALTORS
RELATORS
RESTORAL
RECARPET S
RECEMENT S
CEMENTER
CEREMENT
P **RECENSOR** S
RECOATED
DECORATE
RECONFER S
CONFRERE
ENFORCER
RECONNED
REDLINER S
REELINGS
REJIGGED
JIGGERED
RELANDED
RELLENOS
REPLETES
REPLOWED
REPTILIA N
RERENTED
TENDERER
P **RESELECT** S
REELECTS
RESHOWER S
SHOWERER
RESILINS
RESOFTEN S
SOFTENER
RESPOOLS
SPOOLERS
RESTABLE DS
ARBELEST
BLEATERS
RETABLES
RETIEING
REIGNITE
RETOTALS
RETRACER S
RETRONYM S
REUPTAKE S
REZEROED
REZEROES
RIBOZYME S
RIDGETOP S
RIMSHOTS
RINDLESS
RIPSAWED
ROCKABLE
ROGERING
GORGERIN
ROOTCAPS
COPASTOR
ROOTLING
ROOTWORM S
MOORWORT
TOMORROW
WORMROOT
C **ROQUETTE** S
ROSACEAS
ROSEHIPS
ROUGHIES
RUBBOARD S
P **RUDERIES**
RUGALACH
RUGELACH

SAILLESS
SAMADHIS
SAMOYEDS
SANDABLE
SANDLESS
SANIDINE S
SANTERAS
SANTERIA S
ANTISERA
RATANIES
SEATRAIN
SANTEROS
ASSENTOR
SENATORS
STARNOSE
TREASONS
SANTOORS
SAPHENAS
SAPIENTS
STEAPSIN
SARCINAE
ACARINES
CANARIES
CESARIAN
SARCINAS
ACRASINS
SARDINED
SARSNETS
SASHLESS
SAUCEPOT S
OUTPACES
SAUCIERS
SAUNAING
SAWDUSTY
SCAMMERS
SCAMSTER S
SCAREDER
SCARFERS
SCHLUMPY
SCHMATTE S
SCHMOOZY
SCHNOZES
SCOMBRID S
SCOOCHED
SCOOCHES
SCRIBBLY
SCRUNCHY
SCUBAING
SCUFFERS
SCULCHES
SCUMLESS
SCUMMILY
SCUTWORK S
CUTWORKS
SEAHORSE S
SEASHORE
SEALIFTS
SEATBACK S
BACKSEAT
SEATBELT S
TESTABLE
SEATROUT S
OUTRATES
OUTSTARE
SECONALS
SELLOFFS
SEMILLON S
SEMIMILD
SEMINOMA DS
SEMIOPEN
SEMIOVAL
SEPTAGES
SEROTINY
TYROSINE
SEROVARS
SAVORERS
SERPIGOS
GOSSIPER
SHACKING
SHADKHAN S
SHAMABLY
SHAMISEN S
SHARIAHS
SHEKALIM
SHEKELIM
SHIPLESS
SHIVITIS
SHNORRER S
SHOTHOLE S
SHOWTIME S
SHUSHERS
SHUTTLER S
SIDEARMS
MISREADS
SIEVERTS
VESTRIES
SILURIAN
SIRUPIER
SIRUPING
UPRISING
SKANKERS
SKANKIER
SKANKING
SKULLING
SKUNKIER
SKYBOARD S
SKYSURFS
SLALOMER S
SLAYABLE
SALEABLY
SLEAZOID S
DIAZOLES
SLEEKERS
SLICKENS
SLIPPILY
SLITLIKE
SLITTIER
SLOTTERS
SETTLORS
SLUDGING
SMIRKILY
SMOOCHER S
MOOCHERS
SMOOSHED
SMOOSHES
SMUSHING
SNACKERS
SNAKEPIT S
SNARFING
SNARKILY
SNEERIER
SNIGLETS
GLISTENS
SINGLETS
SNOWCATS
SOFABEDS
SOFTCORE
SOLEUSES
SOTTEDLY
SOULMATE S
SOUPLESS
SOUPLIKE
SOUSLIKS
SPALDEEN S
DEPLANES
SPAMBOTS
SPAMMERS
SPAMMING
SPANSULE S
SPARKLET S
SPARTINA S
ASPIRANT
PARTISAN
SPASMING
SPATZLES
SPENDIER
SPHYNXES
SPIFFIED
SPIFFIES T
SPODOSOL S
SPOOLERS
RESPOOLS
SPURTERS
SPUTTERY
STAMENED
STANDUPS
DUSTPANS
UPSTANDS
STELLITE S
STETSONS
STEWABLE
STICKIES T
EKISTICS
STOCKAGE S
STOPOFFS
STOPWORD S
STOTINOV
STOTTING
E **STRANGES** T
STRIATUM
SUBAURAL
SUBCLAIM S
SUBDWARF S
SUBFUSCS
SUBLIMIT SY
MISBUILT
SUBOCEAN
SUBVIRUS
SUCCUBAS
SUCKIEST
SUGARERS
SUMOISTS
MISSOUTS
SUNDRILY
SUPERBUG S
SUPREMES T
PRESUMES
SURFSIDE
FISSURED
SURTITLE S
SLUTTIER
SWEENEYS
SWOONIER
SWOOPIER
SYNGENIC
ENSIGNCY
SYNKARYA
SYNTAGMS
GYMNASTS
SYNTHPOP S
SYRETTES
SYRUPIER
SYRUPING
SYSADMIN S

TABOULEH S
TACRINES
CANISTER
CERATINS
CISTERNA
CREATINS
SCANTIER
TAGGANTS
TAGLINES
GELATINS
GENITALS
STEALING
TAILFINS
FINALIST
TALEGGIO S
TALKBACK S

TALLISES
TAILLESS
TALLITHS
TANDOORS
DONATORS
ODORANTS
TORNADOS
TANKINIS
TANKLESS
TANTRISM S
TRANSMIT
TAPEABLE
TAPENADE S
TAPPABLE
TAQUERIA S
TARTIEST
ATTRITES
RATTIEST
TITRATES
TRISTATE
TASKBARS
TEASABLE
EATABLES
TEDDERED
TELECOMS
TELESHOP S
HEELPOST
PESTHOLE
TELETYPE DS
TELNETED
TENTORIA L
TENURING
RETUNING
TERABYTE S
TERAFLOP S
TERYLENE S
TEVATRON S
THALWEGS
THERIANS
HAIRNETS
INEARTHS
THERMITS
THISAWAY
TIEBREAK S
TINSNIPS
TIPSHEET S
EPITHETS
TITUBANT
TOFUTTIS
TOLARJEV
TOOLBARS
BARSTOOL
TOTEABLE
TOUCHPAD S
TOURISTA S
TOWPLANE S
TOWSACKS
TRACKPAD S
TRAMPIER
IMPARTER
TRANNIES
ENTRAINS
TRASHERS
TRENDOID S
TREVALLY S
TRIASSIC
TRILITHS
TRIPTANS
TRUANTLY
TSATSKES
TUBEWORM S
TUFTINGS
TUMESCED
TUMESCES
TWEENERS
TWEENESS
SWEETENS
TWINKIES
TWOONIES

UNACIDIC
UNAGREED
DUNGAREE
UNDERAGE
UNAMAZED
UNARCHED
UNBALING
UNBANDED
UNBASTED
UNBOBBED
UNBOILED
UNILOBED
UNBONDED
UNBOOTED
UNBOTTLE DS
UNBOWING
UNCANNED
UNCARDED
UNCARTED
UNCRATED
UNDERACT
UNTRACED
UNCARVED
UNCHAIRS
UNCLASSY
UNCLAWED
UNCLOUDY
UNCREWED
UNDENTED
UNTENDED
UNDERUSE DS
UNFELTED
UNFLAWED
UNFLUTED
UNGARBED
UNGAZING
UNGELDED
UNGIVING
UNHAIRER S
UNIRONIC
UNJAMMED
UNKEELED
UNMAILED
UNPADDED
UNPITTED
INPUTTED
UNPURELY
UNRETIRE DS
REUNITER
UNRIBBED
UNSPOOLS
UNTIEING
UNTRACKS
UNUNBIUM S
UNVESTED
UPLINKED
UPSIZING
UPSTAGER S
UPTALKED
UPTEMPOS
URINATOR S
USERNAME S

VALLEYED
VAMPIEST
VANLOADS
VASELINE S
VENOLOGY
VERRUCAS
VIRILIZE DS
VIRUSOID S
VOCALESE S
VOGUINGS
VOICINGS
VOUDOUNS

WAFFLIER
WAGGLIER
WAITERED
WAITLIST S
WAITRONS
WANNABEE S
WANNABES
WARDLESS
WRASSLED
WATERBUS
WATERHEN S
WREATHEN
WATERJET S
WATERSKI S
WAVICLES
WAYPOINT S
WEBCASTS
WEBPAGES
WEBSITES
WEIRDING
WETSUITS
WETWARES
WHINGERS
SHREWING
WHIZZIER
WHOOPIES
WHUPPING
WICKLESS
WIDEBODY
WILDCARD S
WINDBELL S
WINESAPS
WISEGUYS
WITHEROD S
WOFULLER
WOMANISM S
WOMANIST S
WOODTONE S
WOODNOTE
WORKABLY
WORKFLOW S
WORKHOUR S
WORMGEAR S
WREATHER S
WRENCHER S
WURTZITE S

YOHIMBES
YUKKIEST

ZEBRANOS
ZEBRINES
ZEPPOLES
ZIGZAGGY
ZIRCALOY S
ZUGZWANG S

2-letter Words

FLMPRSTWZ **AX** E
DHKLRSV **EX**
JO BEGTWY
BCFGLPSV **OX** OY
QI S
XI S
XU
ZA GPSX

3-letter Words

ADZ E
AXE DLS
AZO N
ZOA
BIZ E
BOX Y
COX A
COZ Y
DEX Y
FAX
FEZ
FIX T
FIZ Z
FOX Y
GOX
HAJ IJ
HEX
JAB S
JAG GS
JAM BS
A **JAR** LS
RAJ
JAW S
JAY S
A **JEE** DPRSZ
JET ES
JEU X
JIB BES
JIG S
D **JIN** KNSX
JOB S
JOE SY
JOG S
JOT AS
JOW LS
JOY S
JUG AS
JUN K
JUS T
JUT ES
KEX
F **LAX**
FIP **LEX**
LOX
F **LUX** E
MAX I
MIX T
NIX EY
OXO
BDFP **OXY**
PAX
PIX Y
POX Y
PYX
QAT S
QIS
A **QUA** DGIY
RAJ A
JAR
RAX
P **REX**
SAX
SEX TY
SIX
XIS
SOX
SUQ S
TAJ
TAX AI
TUX
VEX T
VOX
WAX Y
WIZ
A **XIS**
SIX
ZAG S
ZAP S
ZAS
ZAX
ZED S
ZEE S
ZEK S
ZEP S
ZIG S
ZIN CEGS
ZIP S
ZIT IS
ZOA
AZO
ZOO MNS
ZUZ
ZZZ

4-letter Words

ADZE DS
DAZE
AJAR
RAJA
AJEE
APEX
AQUA ES
AXAL
FMRTW **AXED**
AXEL S
AXLE
FLMPRSTWZ **AXES**
AXIL ES
MT **AXIS**
AXLE DS
AXEL
T **AXON** ES
H **AZAN** S
AZON S
ZONA
BIZE S
BOXY
BOZO S
BRUX
A **BUZZ**
CALX
CHEZ
COAX
COXA
COXA EL
COAX
COZY
CRUX
CZAR S
DAZE DS
ADZE
DEXY
DITZ Y
DJIN NS
DOJO S
DOUX
DOXY
A **DOZE** DNRS
DOZY
B **EAUX**
EXAM S
EXEC S
HSV **EXED**
DHKLRSV **EXES**
EXIT S
EXON S
OXEN
EXPO S
FALX
FLAX
FAUX
FAZE DS
FIXT
FIZZ Y
FLAX Y
FALX
FLEX
FLUX
FOXY
FOZY
FRIZ Z
FUJI S
FUTZ
FUZE DES
FUZZ Y
A **GAZE** DRS
GEEZ
HADJ I
HAJI S
HAJJ I
HAZE DLRS
HAZY
HOAX
IBEX
S **ILEX**
IXIA S
S **IZAR** S
JABS
JACK SY
JADE DS
JAGG SY
JAGS
JAIL S
JAKE S
JAMB ES
JAMS
JANE S
JEAN
JAPE DRS
JARL S
JARS
JATO S
JOTA
JAUK S
JAUP S
PUJA
JAVA S
JAWS
JAYS
JAZZ Y
JEAN S
JANE
JEED
JEEP S
JEER S
JEES
JEEZ
JEFE S
JEHU S
JELL OSY
JEON
JERK SY
JESS E
JEST S
JETS
JETE S
JETS
JEST
JEUX
JIAO
JIBB S
JIBE DRS
JIBS
JIFF SY
JIGS
JILL S
JILT S
JIMP Y
JINK S
D **JINN** IS
D **JINS**
JINX
JIVE DRSY
JIVY
JOBS
JOCK OS
JOES
JOEY S
JOGS
JOHN S
JOIN ST
JOKE DRSY
JOKY
JOLE S
JOLT SY
JOSH
JOSS
JOTA S
JATO
JOTS
JOUK S
JOWL SY
JOWS
JOYS
JUBA S
JUBE S
JUCO S
JUDO S
A **JUGA** L
JUGS
JUJU S
JUKE DS
JUKU S
JUMP SY
JUNK SY
JUPE S
JURA LT
JURY
JUST S
JUTS
JUTE S
JUTS
JUST
KOJI S
BG **LAZE** DS
ZEAL
G **LAZY**
K **LUTZ**
LUXE S
LYNX
MAXI MS
AS **MAZE** DRS
MAZY
MEZE S
MINX
MIXT
MOJO S
MOXA S
MOZO S
ZOOM
NAZI S
NEXT
NIXE DS
NIXY
ONYX
B **OOZE** DS
BDW **OOZY**
ORYX
ORZO S
OUZO S
OXEN
EXON
BCFGLP **OXES**
OXID ES
OXIM ES
OYEZ
PHIZ
PIXY
PLEX
E **POXY**
PREX Y
PREZ
PUJA HS
JAUP
PUTZ
QADI S
QAID
QAID S
QADI
QATS
QOPH S
S **QUAD** S
QUAG S
QUAI LS
QUAY S
QUEY S
ES **QUID** S
QUIN ST
E **QUIP** SU
QUIT ES
QUIZ
QUOD S
RAJA HS
AJAR
BCG **RAZE** DERS
RAZZ
F **RITZ** Y
ROUX
SEXT OS
SEXY
SIZE DRS
SIZY
SOJA S
SUQS
TAXA
TAXI S
TEXT S
TZAR S
VEXT
WAXY
WHIZ Z
XYST IS
YUTZ
ZAGS
ZANY
ZAPS
ZARF S
ZEAL S
LAZE
ZEBU S
ZEDS
ZEES
ZEIN S
ZINE
ZEKS
ZEPS
ZERK S
ZERO S
ZEST SY
ZETA S
ZIGS
ZILL S
ZINC SY
A **ZINE** BS
ZEIN
ZING SY
ZINS
ZIPS
ZITI S
ZITS
ZOEA ELS
A **ZOIC**
ZONA EL
AZON
O **ZONE** DRS
ZONK S
ZOOM S
MOZO
ZOON S
ZOOS
ZORI LS
ZOUK S
ZYME S

5-letter Words

ABUZZ
ADDAX
ADMIX T
ADOZE
ADZED
DAZED
ADZES
DAZES
AFFIX
AGAZE
AJIVA S
AJUGA S
AMAZE DS
ANNEX E
AQUAE
AQUAS
ATAXY
AUXIN S
AXELS
AXLES LAXES
AXIAL
AXILE
AXILS
FMRTW **AXING**
AXIOM S
AXION S
T **AXITE** S
AXLED
AXLES
AXELS LAXES
T **AXMAN**
T **AXMEN**
AXONE S
T **AXONS**
H **AZANS**
AZIDE S
AZIDO
DIAZO
AZINE S
AZLON S
ZONAL
AZOIC
AZOLE S
ZOEAL
AZONS
AZOTE DS
AZOTH S
AZUKI S
AZURE S
BAIZA S
BAIZE S
BANJO S
BAZAR S
BRAZA
BAZOO S
BEAUX
BEMIX T
BEZEL S
BEZIL S
BIJOU SX
BIZES
A **BLAZE** DRS
BLITZ
BONZE RS
BOOZE DRS
BOOZY
BORAX
BORTZ
BOXED
BOXER S
BOXES
BOZOS
BRAXY
BRAZA S
BAZAR
BRAZE DNRS
ZEBRA
BURQA S
BUXOM
CAJON
CALIX
CALYX
CAPIZ
CAREX
CIMEX
CLOZE S
CODEX
COXED
COLZA S
COMIX
COXAE
COXAL
COXED
CODEX
COXES
COZEN S
COZES
COZEY S
COZIE DRS
CRAZE DS
CRAZY
CROZE RS
CULEX
CYLIX
CZARS
DAZED
ADZED
DAZES
ADZES
DEOXY
DESEX
DEXES SEXED
DETOX
DEWAX
WAXED
DEXES
DESEX SEXED
DEXIE S

Bob's Bible: Words Containing J Q X or Z by Word-Length

DIAZO
AZIDO
DITZY
DIXIT S
DIZEN S
DIZZY
DJINN ISY
DJINS
DOJOS
DOOZY
DOXIE S
OXIDE
DOZED
DOZEN S
ZONED
DOZER S
DOZES

DR EJECT AS
ENJOY S
ENZYM ES
EPOXY
EQUAL S
QUALE
EQUID S
EQUIP S
PIQUE
EXACT AS
EXALT S
LATEX
EXAMS
MAXES
EXCEL S
EXECS
EXERT S
EXILE DRS
R EXINE S
HSV EXING
S EXIST S
EXITS SIXTE
EXITS
EXIST SIXTE
EXONS
EXPAT S
EXPEL S
EXPOS E
POXES
EXTOL LS
EXTRA S
RETAX TAXER
EXUDE DS
EXULT S
EXURB S

FAQIR S
FAXED
FAXES
FAZED
FAZES
FEAZE DS
FEDEX
FEEZE DS
FEZES
FEZZY
FIQUE S
FIXED
FIXER S
REFIX
FIXES
FIXIT Y
FIZZY
FJELD S
FJORD S
FLAXY
FOXED
FOXES
FRITZ
FRIZZ Y
FROZE N
FUJIS
FURZE S
FURZY
FUZED
FUZEE S
FUZES
FUZIL S

FUZZY

GALAX Y
GANJA HS
GAUZE S
GAUZY
GAZAR S
GAZED
GAZER S
GRAZE
GAZES
GHAZI S
GIZMO S
GLAZE DRS
GLAZY
GLITZ Y
GLOZE DS
GONZO
GOXES
GRAZE DRS
GAZER
GROSZ EY
GYOZA S

HADJI S
JIHAD
HAFIZ
HAJES
HAJIS
HAJJI S
HAMZA HS
HAPAX
C HAZAN S
HAZED
HAZEL S
HAZER S
HAZES
W HEEZE DS
HELIX
HERTZ
HEXAD ES
HEXED
HEXER S
HEXES
HEXYL S
HIJAB S
HIJRA HS
HUZZA HS
HYRAX

IMMIX
INDEX
NIXED
INFIX
IXIAS
IXORA S
IXTLE S
S IZARS
SIZAR

JABOT S
JACAL S
JACKS
JACKY
JADED
JADES
JAGER S
JAGGS
JAGGY
JAGRA S
JAILS
JAKES
JALAP S
JALOP SY
JAMBE DS
JAMBS
JAMMY
JANES
JEANS
JANTY
JAPAN S
JAPED
JAPER SY
JAPES
JARLS

JATOS
JOTAS
JAUKS
JAUNT SY
JUNTA
JAUPS
PUJAS
JAVAS
JAWAN S
JAWED
JAZZY
JEANS
JANES
D JEBEL S
JEEPS
JEERS
JEFES
JEHAD S
JEHUS
JELLO S
JELLS
JELLY
JEMMY
JENNY
JERID S
JERKS
JERKY
JERRY
JESSE DS
JESTS
JETES
JETON S
JETTY
JEWEL S
JIBBS
JIBED
JIBER S
JIBES
JIFFS
JIFFY
JIGGY
JIHAD S
HADJI
JILLS
JILTS
JIMMY
JIMPY
JINGO
JINKS
D JINNI S
D JINNS
JIVED
JIVER S
JIVES
JIVEY
JNANA S
JOCKO S
JOCKS
JOEYS
JOHNS
JOINS
JOINT S
JOIST S
JOKED
JOKER S
JOKES
JOKEY
JOLES
JOLLY
JOLTS
JOLTY
JOMON
JONES
JORAM S
MAJOR
JORUM S
JOTAS
JATOS
JOTTY
JOUAL S
JOUKS
JOULE S
JOUST S
JOWAR S

JOWED
JOWLS
JOWLY
JOYED
JUBAS
JUBES
JUCOS
JUDAS
JUDGE DRS
JUDOS
JUGAL
JUGUM S
JUICE DRS
JUICY
JUJUS
JUKED
JUKES
JUKUS
JULEP S
JUMBO S
JUMPS
JUMPY
JUNCO S
JUNKS
JUNKY
JUNTA S
JAUNT
JUNTO S
JUPES
JUPON S
JURAL
JURAT S
JUREL S
JUROR S
JUSTS
JUTES
JUTTY

KANJI S
KANZU S
KAZOO S
KEXES
KLUTZ Y
KOJIS
KOPJE S
KUDZU S
KYLIX

LATEX
EXALT
LAXER
RELAX
F LAXES T
AXELS AXLES
LAXLY
LAZAR S
BG LAZED
BG LAZES
ZEALS
FIP LEXES
LEXIS
SILEX
LOXED
LOXES
LUREX
F LUXES

MAIZE S
MAJOR S
JORAM
MAQUI S
UMIAQ
MATZA HS
MATZO HST
MAXED
MAXES
EXAMS
MAXIM AS
MAXIS
A MAZED
MAZER S
AS MAZES
SMAZE
MEZES
MEZZO S

MIREX
MIXER REMIX
MIRZA S
ZIRAM
MIXED
MIXER S
MIREX REMIX
MIXES
MIXUP S
MIZEN S
MOJOS
MOXAS
MOXIE S
OXIME
MOZOS
ZOOMS
MUJIK S
MUREX
MUZZY

NAZIS
NERTZ
NEXUS
UNSEX
NINJA S
NIXED
INDEX
NIXES
NIXIE S
NIZAM S
NUDZH

OBJET S
B OOZED
B OOZES
ORZOS
OUZEL S
OUZOS
OXBOW S
OXEYE S
OXIDE S
DOXIE
OXIDS
OXIME S
MOXIE
OXIMS
SIXMO
OXLIP S
OXTER S
OZONE S

PAXES
PHLOX
PIQUE DST
EQUIP
PIXEL S
PIXES
PIXIE S
PIZZA SZ
PLAZA S
PLOTZ
POXED
POXES
EXPOS
PREXY
PYREX
PRIZE DRS
PROXY
PUJAH S
PUJAS
JAUPS
PUNJI S
PYREX
PREXY
PYXES
PYXIE S
PYXIS

QADIS
QAIDS
QAIDS
QADIS
QANAT S
QOPHS
QUACK SY
S QUADS
SQUAD
QUAFF S

QUAGS
QUAIL S
QUAIS
QUASI
QUAKE DRS
QUAKY
QUALE
EQUAL
QUALM SY
QUANT AS
S QUARE
S QUARK S
QUART EOSZ
S QUASH
QUASI
QUAIS
QUASS
E QUATE
QUAYS
QUBIT S
QUEAN S
QUEEN S
QUEER S
QUELL S
QUERN S
QUERY
QUEST S
QUEUE DRS
QUEYS
QUICK S
ES QUIDS
SQUID
QUIET S
QUITE
QUIFF S
S QUILL S
QUILT S
QUINS Y
S QUINT AES
E QUIPS
QUIPU S
S QUIRE DS
QUIRK SY
S QUIRT S
QUITE
QUIET
QUITS
QUODS
QUOIN S
QUOIT S
QUOLL S
QUOTA S
QUOTE DRS
TOQUE
QUOTH A
QURSH

RADIX
RAJAH S
RAJAS
RAJES
RAXED
P RAXES
BCG RAZED
RAZEE DS
BG RAZER S
BCG RAZES
RAZOR S
REDOX
REDUX
P REFIX
FIXER
REJIG S
RELAX
LAXER
REMEX
P REMIX T
MIREX MIXER
P RETAX
EXTRA TAXER
REWAX
WAXER
P REXES
RIOJA S
RITZY

ROQUE ST

SAJOU S
SAXES
SCUZZ Y
SEIZE DRS
SEXED
DESEX DEXES
SEXES
SEXTO NS
SEXTS
SHOJI S
SILEX
LEXIS
SIXES
SIXMO S
OXIMS
SIXTE S
EXIST EXITS
SIXTH S
SIXTY
XYSTI
SIZAR S
IZARS
SIZED
SIZER S
SIZES
SLOJD S
SMAZE S
MAZES
SOJAS
SOYUZ
SOZIN ES
SPITZ
SQUAB S
SQUAD S
QUADS
SQUAT S
SQUEG S
SQUIB S
SQUID S
QUIDS

TAJES
TAXED
TAXER S
EXTRA RETAX
TAXES
TEXAS
TAXIS
TAXOL S
TAXON S
TAXUS
TAZZA S
TAZZE
TELEX
TEXAS
TAXES
TEXTS
THUJA S
TIZZY
TOPAZ
TOQUE ST
QUOTE
TOXIC S
TOXIN ES
TRANQ S
TROOZ
TUQUE S
TUXES
TWIXT
TZARS

UMIAQ S
MAQUI
UNBOX
UNFIX T
UNJAM S
UNMIX T
UNSEX Y
NEXUS
UNZIP S
USQUE S

VARIX
VEXED
VEXER S

2006 Addition

VEXES
VEXIL S
VIXEN S
VIZIR S
VIZOR S

WALTZ
WAXED
DEWAX
WAXEN
WAXER S
REWAX
WAXES
WHIZZ Y
WINZE S
WIZEN
WIZEN S
WINZE
WIZES
WOOZY

XEBEC S
XENIA LS
A XENIC
XENON S
XERIC
XEROX
XERUS
XYLAN S
XYLEM S
XYLOL S
XYLYL S
XYSTI
SIXTY
XYSTS

ZAIRE S
ZAMIA S
ZANZA S
ZAPPY
ZARFS
ZAXES
ZAYIN S
ZAZEN S
ZEALS
LAZES
ZEBEC KS
ZEBRA S
BRAZE
ZEBUS
ZEINS
ZINES
ZERKS
ZEROS
ZESTS
ZESTY
ZETAS
ZIBET HS
ZILCH
ZILLS
ZINCS
ZINCY
ZINEB S
A ZINES
ZEINS
ZINGS
ZINGY
ZINKY
ZIPPY
ZIRAM S
MIRZA
ZITIS
ZIZIT H
ZLOTE
ZLOTY S
ZOEAE
ZOEAL
AZOLE
ZOEAS
ZOMBI ES
ZONAE
A ZONAL
AZLON
ZONED
DOZEN
ZONER S
O ZONES
ZONKS
ZOOEY
ZOOID S
ZOOKS
ZOOMS
MOZOS
ZOONS
ZOOTY
ZORIL S
ZORIS
ZOUKS
ZOWIE
ZUZIM
ZYMES

6-letter Words

ABJECT
ABJURE DRS
ABLAZE
ACAJOU S
ACQUIT S
ADIEUX
ADJOIN ST
ADJURE DRS
ADJUST S
ADMIXT
ADNEXA L
ADZING
DAZING
ADZUKI S
AFFLUX
AGNIZE DS
AJIVAS
AJOWAN S
AJUGAS
ALEXIA S
ALEXIN ES
XENIAL
ALKOXY
AMAZED
AMAZES
AMAZON S
ANNEXE DS
ANOXIA S
ANOXIC
AXONIC
APEXES
ASSIZE S
ATAXIA S
ATAXIC S
AUSPEX
AUXINS
AXEMAN
AXEMEN
EXAMEN
AXENIC
M AXILLA ERS
AXIOMS
AXIONS
AXISED
AXISES
T AXITES
TAXIES
W AXLIKE
AXONAL
AXONES
AXONIC
ANOXIC
AXSEED S
AZALEA S
AZIDES
AZINES
ZANIES
AZLONS
AZOLES
SLEAZO
AZONAL
AZONIC
AZOTED
AZOTES
AZOTHS
AZOTIC
AZUKIS
AZURES
AZYGOS
GYOZAS

BAIZAS
BAIZES
BANJAX
BANJOS
BANZAI S
BARQUE S
BASQUE S
BAZAAR S
BAZARS
BRAZAS
BAZOOS
BEEZER S
BREEZE
BEGAZE DS
BEMIXT
BENZAL
BENZIN ES
BENZOL ES
BENZYL S
BEZANT S
BEZAZZ
BEZELS
BEZILS
BEZOAR S
BIAXAL
BIFLEX
BIJOUS
BIJOUX
BISQUE S
BIZONE S
BIZZES
BLAZED
BLAZER S
BLAZES
BLAZON S
BLINTZ E
BLOWZY
BOLLIX
BOLLOX
BOMBAX
BOMBYX
BONZER
BRONZE
BONZES
BOOJUM S
BOOZED
BOOZER S
REBOZO
BOOZES
BORZOI S
BOSQUE ST
BOXCAR S
BOXERS
BOXFUL S
BOXIER
BOXILY
BOXING S
BRAIZE S
BRAZAS
BAZARS
BRAZED
BRAZEN S
BRAZER S
BRAZES
ZEBRAS
BRAZIL S
BREEZE DS
BEEZER
BREEZY
BRONZE DRS
BONZER
BRONZY
BRUXED
BRUXES
EXURBS
BUQSHA S
BURQAS
BUZUKI AS
BUZZED
BUZZER S
BUZZES
BYZANT S

CAIQUE S
CAJOLE DRS
CALQUE DS
CLAQUE
CALXES
CASQUE DS
SACQUE
CAUDEX
CERVIX
CHAZAN S
CHEQUE RS
CHINTZ Y
CINQUE S
QUINCE
CIRQUE S
CLAQUE RS
CALQUE
CLAXON S
CLIMAX
CLIQUE DSY
CLIQUY
CLOQUE S
CLOZES
COAXAL
COAXED
COAXER S
COAXES
COCCYX
COJOIN S
COLZAS
COMMIX T
CONVEX
COQUET S
CORTEX
CORYZA LS
COWPOX
COXING
COZENS
COZEYS
COZIED
COZIER
COZIES T
COZILY
COZZES
CRAZED
CRAZES
CROJIK S
CROZER S
CROZES
CRUXES

DAZING
ADZING
DAZZLE DRS
DEEJAY S
DEFUZE DS
DEIXIS
DEJECT AS
DELUXE
DESOXY
DEXIES
DEXTER
DEXTRO
DEZINC S
ZINCED
DIAZIN ES
DIOXAN ES
DIOXID ES
IXODID
DIOXIN S
DIPLEX
DIQUAT S
DITZES
DIXITS
DIZENS
DJEBEL S
DJINNI
DJINNS
DJINNY
DONJON S
DONZEL S
DOOZER S
DOOZIE S
DOXIES
OXIDES
DOZENS
DOZERS
DOZIER
DOZILY
DOZING
DUPLEX

EARWAX
ECZEMA S
EFFLUX
D EJECTA
DR EJECTS
ELIXIR S
ENJOIN S
ENJOYS
ENZYME S
ENZYMS
EPIZOA
EQUALS
SQUEAL
EQUATE DS
EQUIDS
EQUINE S
EQUIPS
PIQUES
EQUITY
ERSATZ
M ETHOXY L
EUTAXY
EVZONE S
EXACTA S
EXACTS
EXALTS
LAXEST
EXAMEN S
AXEMEN
EXARCH SY
EXCEED S
EXCELS
EXCEPT S
EXPECT
EXCESS
EXCIDE DS
EXCISE DS
EXCITE DRS
EXCUSE DRS
EXEDRA E
EXEMPT S
EXEQUY
EXERTS
EXSERT
EXEUNT
EXHALE DS
EXHORT S
EXHUME DRS
EXILED
EXILER S
EXILES
ILEXES
EXILIC
R EXINES
S EXISTS
SEXIST
SIXTES
EXITED
EXODOI
EXODOS
EXODUS
EXOGEN S
EXONIC
EXONYM S
EXOTIC AS
EXPAND S
EXPATS
EXPECT S
EXCEPT
EXPELS
PLEXES
EXPEND S
EXPERT S
EXPIRE DRS
EXPIRY
EXPORT S
EXPOSE DRS
EXSECT S
EXSERT S
EXERTS
S EXTANT
EXTEND S
EXTENT S
EXTERN ES
EXTOLL S
EXTOLS
EXTORT S
EXTRAS
TAXERS
EXUDED
EXUDES
EXULTS
EXURBS
BRUXES
EXUVIA EL

FAJITA S
FANJET S
FAQIRS
FAQUIR S
FAXING
FAZING
FEAZED
FEAZES
FEEZED
FEEZES
FEIJOA S
FEZZED
FEZZES
FIQUES
FIXATE DS
FIXERS
FIXING S
FIXITY
FIXURE S
FIZGIG S
FIZZED
FIZZER S
FIZZES
FIZZLE DS
FJELDS
FJORDS
FLAXEN
FLAXES
FLEXED
FLEXES
FLEXOR S
FLOOZY
FLUXED
FLUXES
FOOZLE DRS
FORNIX
FOXIER
FOXILY
FOXING S
FOZIER
FRAZIL S
FREEZE RS
FRENZY
FRIEZE S
FRIJOL E
FRIZED
FRIZER S
FRIZES
FRIZZY
FROUZY
FROWZY
FROZEN
FURZES
FUTZED
FUTZES
FUZEES
FUZILS
FUZING
FUZZED
FUZZES

GAIJIN
GALAXY
GANJAH S
GANJAS
GAUZES
GAZABO S
GAZARS
GAZEBO S
GAZERS
GRAZES
GAZING
GAZUMP S
GEEZER S
GHAZIS
GIZMOS
GLAZED
GLAZER S
GLAZES
GLITZY
GLOZED
GLOZES
GRAZED
GRAZER S
GRAZES
GAZERS
GROSZE
GROSZY
GUZZLE DRS
GYOZAS
AZYGOS
GYTTJA S

HADJEE S
HADJES
JEHADS
HADJIS
JADISH
JIHADS
HAJJES
HAJJIS
HALLUX
C HALUTZ
HAMZAH S
HAMZAS
SHAZAM
HANDAX
HATBOX
C HAZANS
HAZARD S
HAZELS
HAZERS
HAZIER
HAZILY
HAZING S
HAZMAT S
MATZAH
C HAZZAN S
W HEEZED
W HEEZES
HEJIRA S
HEXADE S
HEXADS
HEXANE S
HEXERS
HEXING
HEXONE S
HEXOSE S
HEXYLS
HIJABS
HIJACK S
HIJRAH S
HIJRAS
HOAXED
HOAXER S
HOAXES
HOTBOX
C HUTZPA HS
HUZZAH S
HUZZAS

IBEXES
ICEBOX
S ILEXES
EXILES
INFLUX
INJECT S

Bob's Bible: Words Containing J Q X or Z by Word-Length

INJURE DRS
INJURY
INKJET
IODIZE DRS
L IONIZE DRS
IXODID S
DIOXID
IXORAS
IXTLES
G IZZARD S

JABBED
JABBER S
JABIRU S
JABOTS
JACALS
JACANA S
JACKAL S
JACKED
JACKER S
JACKET S
JADING
JADISH
HADJIS
JIHADS
JAEGER S
JAGERS
JAGGED
JAGGER SY
JAGRAS
JAGUAR S
JAILED
JAILER S
JAILOR S
JALAPS
JALOPS
JALOPY
JAMBED
JAMBES
JAMMED
JAMMER S
JANGLE DRS
JANGLY
JAPANS
JAPERS
JASPER
JAPERY
JAPING
JARFUL S
JARGON SY
JARINA S
JARRAH S
JARRED
JARVEY S
JASMIN ES
JASPER SY
JAPERS
JASSID S
JAUKED
JAUNCE DS
JAUNTS
JUNTAS
JAUNTY
JAUPED
JAWANS
JAWING
JAYGEE S
JAYVEE S
VEEJAY
JAZZBO S
JAZZED
JAZZER S
JAZZES
JEANED
D JEBELS
JEEING
JEEPED
JEERED
JEREED
JEERER S
JEHADS
HADJES
JEJUNA L
JEJUNE
JELLED
JELLOS
JENNET S
JERBOA S
JEREED S
JEERED
JERIDS
JERKED
JERKER S
JERKIN GS
JINKER
JERRID S
JERSEY S
JESSED
JESSES
JESTED
JESTER S
JETLAG S
JETONS
JETSAM S
JETSOM S
JETTED
JETTON S
JETWAY S
JEWELS
JEZAIL S
JIBBED
JIBBER S
JIBERS
JIBING
JICAMA S
JIGGED
JIGGER S
JIGGLE DS
JIGGLY
JIGSAW NS
JIHADS
HADJIS
JADISH
JILTED
JILTER S
JIMINY
JIMMIE DS
JIMPER
JIMPLY
JINGAL LS
JINGKO
JOKING
JINGLE DRS
JINGLY
JINKED
JINKER S
JERKIN
JINNEE
JINNIS
JINXED
JINXES
JITNEY S
JITTER SY
TRIJET
JIVERS
JIVIER
JIVING
JNANAS
JOBBED
JOBBER SY
JOCKEY S
JOCKOS
JOCOSE
JOCUND
JOGGED
JOGGER S
JOGGLE DRS
JOHNNY
JOINED
JOINER SY
REJOIN
JOINTS
JOISTS
JOJOBA S
JOKERS
JOKIER
JOKILY
JOKING
JINGKO
JOLTED
JOLTER S
JORAMS
MAJORS
JORDAN S
JORUMS
JOSEPH S
JOSHED
JOSHER S
JOSHES
JOSSES
JOSTLE DRS
JOTTED
JOTTER S
JOUALS
JOUKED
JOULES
JOUNCE DS
JOUNCY
JOURNO S
JOUSTS
JOVIAL
JOWARS
JOWING
JOWLED
JOYFUL
JOYING
JOYOUS
JOYPOP S
JUBBAH S
JUBHAH S
JUBILE ES
JUDDER S
JUDGED
JUDGER S
JUDGES
JUDOKA S
JUGATE
JUGFUL S
JUGGED
JUGGLE DRS
JUGULA R
JUGUMS
JUICED
JUICER S
JUICES
JUJUBE S
JUKING
JULEPS
JUMBAL S
JUMBLE DRS
JUMBOS
JUMPED
JUMPER S
JUNCOS
JUNGLE DS
JUNGLY
JUNIOR S
JUNKED
JUNKER S
JUNKET S
JUNKIE RS
JUNTAS
JAUNTS
JUNTOS
JUPONS
JURANT S
JURATS
JURELS
JURIED
JURIES
JURIST S
JURORS
JUSTED
JUSTER S
JUSTLE DS
JUSTLY
JUTTED

KANJIS
KANZUS
KAZOOS
KHAZEN S
KIBITZ
KLAXON S
KLUTZY
KOLHOZ Y
KOLKOZ Y
KOPJES
KUDZUS
KUVASZ
KWANZA S

LARYNX
LAXEST
EXALTS
LAXITY
LAZARS
LAZIED
G LAZIER
LAZIES T
G LAZILY
BG LAZING
LAZULI S
LEXEME S
LEXICA L
LIQUID S
LIQUOR S
LIZARD S
LOGJAM S
LOQUAT S
LOXING
F LUMMOX
K LUTZES
LUXATE DS
LUXURY
LYNXES

MAHZOR S
MAIZES
MAJORS
JORAMS
MAMZER S
MANQUE
MAQUIS
UMIAQS
MARQUE ES
MASJID S
MASQUE RS
MASTIX
MATRIX
MATZAH S
HAZMAT
MATZAS
MATZOH S
MATZOS
MATZOT H
MAXIMA L
MAXIMS
MAXING
MAXIXE S
MAZARD S
MAZERS
MAZIER
MAZILY
A MAZING
MAZUMA S
MENINX
MEZCAL S
MEZUZA HS
MEZZOS
MINXES
MIRZAS
ZIRAMS
MIXERS
MIXING
MIXUPS
MIZENS
MIZUNA S
MIZZEN S
MIZZLE DS
MIZZLY
MOJOES
MOMZER S
MOSQUE S
MOUJIK S
MOXIES
OXIMES
MUJIKS
MUSJID S
MUSKOX
MUZHIK S
MUZJIK S
MUZZLE DRS
MYXOID
MYXOMA S

NAZIFY
NINJAS
NIXIES
NIXING
NIZAMS
NONTAX
NOZZLE S
NUZZLE DRS

OBJECT S
OBJETS
ONYXES
BW OOZIER
ZOOIER
BW OOZILY
B OOZING
OPAQUE DRS
ORYXES
OUTBOX
OUTFOX
OUTJUT S
OUZELS
OXALIC
OXALIS
OXBOWS
OXCART S
OXEYES
OXFORD S
OXIDES
DOXIES
OXIDIC
OXIMES
MOXIES
BF OXLIKE
OXLIPS
F OXTAIL S
OXTERS
OXYGEN S
OYEZES
OZALID S
OZONES
SNOOZE
OZONIC

PAJAMA S
PANZER S
PATZER S
PAXWAX
PAZAZZ
PEGBOX
PEROXY
PHENIX
PHIZES
PIAZZA S
PIAZZE
PICKAX E
PIQUED
PIQUES
EQUIPS
PIQUET S
PIXELS
PIXIES
PIZAZZ Y
PIZZAZ
PIZZAS
PIZZAZ Z
PIZAZZ
PIZZLE S
PLAQUE S
PLAZAS
PLEXAL
PLEXES
EXPELS
PLEXOR S
PLEXUS
PODZOL S
POLEAX E
POLLEX
POTZER S
POXIER
POXING
POZOLE S
PRAJNA S
PRAXES
PRAXIS
PREFIX
PREMIX T
PRETAX
PREXES
PREZES
PRIZED
PRIZER S
PRIZES
PROJET S
PROLIX
PUJAHS
PULQUE S
PUNJIS
PUTZED
PUTZES
PUZZLE DRS
PYJAMA S
PYXIES

QABALA HS
QANATS
QINDAR S
QINTAR S
QIVIUT S
QUACKS
QUACKY
QUAERE S
QUAFFS
QUAGGA S
QUAGGY
QUAHOG S
QUAICH S
QUAIGH S
QUAILS
QUAINT
QUINTA
QUAKED
QUAKER S
QUAKES
SQUEAK
QUALIA
QUALMS
QUALMY
QUANGO S
QUANTA L
QUANTS
S QUARKS
SQUARK
QUARRY
QUARTE RST
QUATRE
QUARTO S
QUARTS
QUARTZ
QUASAR S
QUATRE S
QUARTE
QUAVER SY
QUBITS
QUBYTE S
QUEANS
QUEASY
QUEAZY
QUEENS
QUEERS
QUELEA S
QUELLS
QUENCH
QUERNS
QUESTS
QUEUED
QUEUER S
QUEUES
QUEZAL S
QUICHE S
QUICKS
QUIETS
QUIFFS
S QUILLS
SQUILL
QUILTS
QUINCE S
CINQUE
QUINIC
QUININ AES
QUINOA S
QUINOL S
QUINSY
QUINTA LNRS
QUAINT
QUINTE ST
S QUINTS
SQUINT
QUIPPU S
QUIPPY
QUIPUS
S QUIRED
S QUIRES
RISQUE
SQUIRE
QUIRKS
QUIRKY
S QUIRTS
SQUIRT
QUITCH
A QUIVER SY
QUOHOG S
QUOINS
QUOITS
QUOKKA S
QUOLLS
QUORUM S
QUOTAS
QUOTED
QUOTER S
ROQUET
TORQUE
QUOTES
TOQUES
QUOTHA
QURUSH
QWERTY S

RAJAHS
RAMJET S
RAXING
RAZEED
RAZEES
BG RAZERS
BCG RAZING
RAZORS
RAZZED
RAZZES
REBOZO S
BOOZER
REFLEX
REFLUX
REJECT S
REJIGS
REJOIN S
JOINER
P REMIXT
REQUIN S
RESIZE DS
SEIZER
REXINE S
REZERO S
REZONE DS
RIOJAS
RISQUE
QUIRES
SQUIRE
F RITZES
ROMAJI S
ROQUES
C ROQUET S
QUOTER
TORQUE
ROZZER S

SACQUE S
CASQUE
SAJOUS
SANJAK S
SAXONY
SCHIZO S
SCHIZY
SCHNOZ Z
SCOLEX
SCUZZY
SEIZED
SEIZER S
RESIZE
SEIZES
SEIZIN GS
SEIZOR S
SEJANT
SEQUEL AS
SEQUIN S
SEXIER
SEXILY
SEXING
SEXISM S
SEXIST S
EXISTS
SIXTES
SEXPOT S
SEXTAN ST
SEXTET S
SEXTON S
SEXTOS
A SEXUAL
SHAZAM
HAMZAS
SHEQEL S
SHOJIS
SILVEX
VEXILS
SIXMOS
SIXTES
EXISTS
SEXIST
SIXTHS
SIZARS
SIZERS
SIZIER
SIZING S
SIZZLE DRS
SKYBOX
SLEAZE S
SLEAZO
AZOLES
SLEAZY
SLOJDS
SMAZES
SMILAX
SNAZZY
SNEEZE DRS
SNEEZY
SNOOZE DRS
OZONES
SNOOZY
SOZINE S
SOZINS
SPADIX
SPELTZ
SPHINX
SPHYNX
SPRITZ
SQUABS
SQUADS
SQUALL SY
SQUAMA E
SQUARE DRS
SQUARK S
QUARKS
SQUASH Y
SQUATS
SQUAWK S
SQUEAK SY
QUAKES
SQUEAL S
EQUALS
SQUEGS

SQUIBS
SQUIDS
SQUILL AS
QUILLS
A SQUINT SY
QUINTS
E SQUIRE DS
QUIRES
RISQUE
SQUIRM SY
SQUIRT S
QUIRTS
SQUISH Y
SQUUSH
STANZA S
STORAX
STYRAX
SUBFIX
SUFFIX
SURTAX
SVARAJ
SWARAJ
SYNTAX
SYRINX
SYZYGY

TARZAN S
TAXEME S
TAXERS
EXTRAS
TAXIED
A TAXIES
AXITES
TAXING
TAXITE S
TAXMAN
TAXMEN
TAXOLS
TAXONS
TAZZAS
TEABOX
TEAZEL S
TEAZLE
TEAZLE DS
TEAZEL
THORAX
THUJAS
TOQUES
QUOTES
TOQUET S
TORQUE DRS
QUOTER
ROQUET
TOUZLE DS
TOXICS
TOXINE S
TOXINS
TOXOID S
TRANQS
TRIJET S
JITTER
TUQUES
TUXEDO S
TWEEZE DRS
TZETZE S
TZURIS

UBIQUE
UMIAQS
MAQUIS
UNAXED
UNFIXT
UNIQUE RS
UNISEX
UNJAMS
UNJUST
UNMIXT
UNSEXY
UNVEXT
UNZIPS
UPGAZE DS
UPSIZE DS
URTEXT S
USQUES

VEEJAY S
JAYVEE
VERNIX
VERTEX
VEXERS
VEXILS
SILVEX
VEXING
VIXENS
VIZARD S
VIZIER S
VIZIRS
VIZORS
VIZSLA S
VOLVOX
VORTEX

WAXERS
WAXIER
WAXILY
WAXING S
WHEEZE DRS
WHEEZY
WHIZZY
WINZES
WIZENS
WIZARD S
WIZENS
WINZES
WIZZEN S
WIZZES
WURZEL S

XEBECS
XENIAL
ALEXIN
XENIAS
XENONS
XYLANS
XYLEMS
XYLENE S
XYLOID
XYLOLS
XYLOSE S
XYLYLS
XYSTER S
XYSTOI
XYSTOS
XYSTUS

YAKUZA
YANQUI S
YUTZES

T ZADDIK
ZAFFAR S
ZAFFER S
ZAFFRE
ZAFFIR S
ZAFFRE S
ZAFFER
ZAFTIG
ZAGGED
ZAIKAI S
ZAIRES
ZAMIAS
ZANANA S
ZANDER S
ZANIER
ZANIES T
AZINES
ZANILY
ZANZAS
ZAPPED
ZAPPER S
ZAREBA S
ZARIBA S
ZAYINS
ZAZENS
ZEALOT S
ZEATIN S
ZEBECK S
ZEBECS
ZEBRAS S
BRAZES

ZECHIN S
ZENANA S
ZENITH S
ZEPHYR S
ZEROED
ZEROES
ZEROTH
ZESTED
ZESTER S
ZEUGMA S
ZIBETH S
ZIBETS
ZIGGED
ZIGZAG S
ZILLAH S
ZINCED
DEZINC
ZINCIC
ZINCKY
ZINEBS
ZINGED
ZINGER S
ZINNIA S
ZIPPED
ZIPPER S
ZIRAMS
MIRZAS
ZIRCON S
ZITHER NS
ZIZITH
ZIZZLE DS
ZLOTYS
ZOARIA L
ZOCALO S
ZODIAC S
ZOECIA
ZOFTIG
ZOMBIE S
ZOMBIS
ZONARY
O ZONATE D
ZONERS
ZONING
ZONKED
ZONULA ERS
ZONULE S
ZOOIDS
ZOOIER
OOZIER
ZOOMED
ZOONAL
ZOONED
ZORILS
ZOSTER S
ZOUAVE S
ZOUNDS
ZOYSIA S
ZYDECO S
ZYGOID
ZYGOMA S
ZYGOSE S
ZYGOTE S
ZYMASE S

7-letter Words

ABAXIAL
ABAXILE
ABJURED
ABJURER S
ABJURES
ACAJOUS
ACEQUIA S
ACQUEST S
ACQUIRE DER S

ACQUITS
ADAXIAL
ADDAXES
ADJOINS
ADJOINT S
ADJOURN S
ADJUDGE DS
ADJUNCT S
ADJURED
ADJURER S
ADJURES
ADJUROR S
ADJUSTS
ADMIXED
ADMIXES
ADNEXAL
ADZUKIS
AFFIXAL
AFFIXED
AFFIXER S
REAFFIX
AFFIXES
AGATIZE DS
AGENIZE DS
AGNIZED
AGNIZES
AGONIZE DS
AJOWANS
ALBIZIA S
ALCAZAR S
ALEXIAS
ALEXINE S
ALEXINS
ALFAQUI NS
ALFORJA S
ALIQUOT S
ALLOXAN S
AMAZING
AMAZONS
ANALYZE DRS
ANNEXED
ANNEXES
ANODIZE DS
ANOREXY
ANOXIAS
ANTEFIX A
ANTHRAX
ANTIJAM
ANTIQUE DRS
QUINATE
ANTISEX
SEXTAIN
ANTITAX
ANXIETY
ANXIOUS
APAREJO S
APPRIZE DRS
ZAPPIER
APRAXIA S
APRAXIC
APTERYX
AQUARIA LN
AQUATIC S
AQUAVIT S
AQUEOUS
AQUIFER S
AQUIVER
ARABIZE DS
H ARUSPEX
ASEXUAL
ASPHYXY
ASQUINT
QUINTAS
ASSIZES
ATARAXY
ATAXIAS
ATAXICS
ATAXIES
ATOMIZE DRS
AUXESES
AUXESIS
AUXETIC S
AUXINIC
AXIALLY
M AXILLAE
AXILLAR SY
M AXILLAS
AXOLOTL S

AXONEME S
AXSEEDS
AZALEAS
AZIMUTH S
AZOTISE DS
AZOTIZE DS
AZULEJO S
L AZURITE S
AZYGOUS

BANDBOX
BANJOES
BANQUET S
BANZAIS
BAPTIZE DRS
BAROQUE S
BARQUES
BASENJI S
BASQUES
BATEAUX
BAUXITE S
BAZAARS
BAZOOKA S
BEDIZEN S
BEESWAX
BEEZERS
BREEZES
BEGAZED
BEGAZES
BEJESUS
BEJEWEL S
BEMIXED
BEMIXES
BENZENE S
BENZINE S
BENZINS
BENZOIC
BENZOIN S
BENZOLE S
BENZOLS
BENZOYL S
BENZYLS
BEQUEST S
BETAXED
BETWIXT
BEZANTS
BEZIQUE S
BEZOARS
BEZZANT S
BIAXIAL
BISQUES
BIZARRE S
BRAZIER
BIZARRO S
BIZNAGA S
BIZONAL
BIZONES
BLAZERS
BLAZING
BLAZONS
BLINTZE S
BLITZED
BLITZER S
BLITZES
BLOWZED
BLUEJAY S
BONANZA S
BOOJUMS
BOOMBOX
BOOZERS
REBOZOS
BOOZIER
BOOZILY
BOOZING
BORAXES
BORTZES
BORZOIS
BOSQUES
BOSQUET S
BOUQUET S
BOXBALL S
BOXCARS
BOXFISH

BOXFULS
BOXHAUL S
BOXIEST
BOXINGS
BOXLIKE
BOXWOOD S
WOODBOX
BRAIZES
BRAXIES
BRAZENS
BRAZERS
BRAZIER S
BIZARRE
BRAZILS
BRAZING
BREEZED
BREEZES
BEEZERS
BRIQUET S
BRITZKA S
BROADAX E
BROMIZE DS
BRONZED
BRONZER S
BRONZES
BRULZIE S
BRUSQUE R
BRUXING
BRUXISM S
BUQSHAS
BUREAUX
BUXOMER
BUXOMLY
BUZUKIA
BUZUKIS
BUZZARD S
BUZZCUT S
BUZZERS
BUZZING
BUZZWIG S
BYZANTS

CABEZON ES
CACHEXY
CACIQUE S
CADENZA S
CAIQUES
CAJAPUT S
CAJEPUT S
CAJOLED
CAJOLER SY
CAJOLES
CAJONES
CAJUPUT S
CALQUED
CALQUES
CLAQUES
CALYXES
CALZONE S
CANZONA S
CANZONE ST
CANZONI
CAPIZES
CAPSIZE
CAPSIZE DS
CAPIZES
CARAPAX
CARJACK S
CASHBOX
CASQUED
CASQUES
SACQUES
CATJANG S
CAZIQUE S
CELOTEX
CERVEZA S
CHALAZA ELS
CHALUTZ
CHAMOIX
CHARQUI DS
CHAZANS
CHAZZAN S
CHAZZEN S
CHEQUER S

CHEQUES
CHINTZY
CHORIZO S
CHUTZPA HS
CINQUES
QUINCES
CIRQUES
CITIZEN S
ZINCITE
CLAQUER S
LACQUER
CLAQUES
CALQUES
CLAXONS
CLIQUED
CLIQUES
CLIQUEY
CLOQUES
COALBOX
COANNEX
COAXERS
COAXIAL
COAXING
COEQUAL S
COEXERT S
COEXIST S
EXOTICS
COGNIZE DRS
COJOINS
COMMIXT
COMPLEX
CONFLUX
CONJOIN ST
CONJURE DRS
CONQUER S
CONTEXT S
COQUETS
COQUINA S
COQUITO S
CORYZAL
CORYZAS
COTEAUX
COXALGY
COXCOMB S
COXITIS
COXLESS
COZENED
COZENER S
COZIEST
COZYING
CRAZIER
CRAZIES T
CRAZILY
CRAZING
CROJIKS
CROQUET S
CROQUIS
CROZERS
CROZIER S
CRUZADO S
CULEXES
CUMQUAT S
CYCLIZE DS
CZARDAS
CZARDOM S
CZARINA S
CZARISM S
CZARIST S

DAMOZEL S
DANAZOL S
DAZEDLY
DAZZLED
DAZZLER S
DAZZLES
DEEJAYS
DEFUZED
DEFUZES
DEGLAZE DS
DEJECTA
DEJECTS
DENIZEN S
DESEXED
DESEXES
DETOXED
DETOXES
DEUTZIA S
DEWAXED
DEWAXES
DEXTRAL
DEXTRAN S
DEXTRIN ES
DEZINCS
DIALYZE DRS
DIAZINE S
DIAZINS
DIAZOLE S
DIGOXIN S
DIOXANE S
DIOXANS
DIOXIDE S
DIOXIDS
IXODIDS
DIOXINS
DIQUATS
DISJECT S
DISJOIN ST
DITZIER
DIZENED
DIZZIED
DIZZIER
DIZZIES T
DIZZILY
DJEBELS
DONJONS
DONZELS
DOOZERS
DOOZIES
DOZENED
DOZENTH S
DOZIEST
DRIZZLE DS
DRIZZLY
DUALIZE DS

EBONIZE DS
ECTOZOA N
ECZEMAS
EDITRIX
DR EJECTED
R EJECTOR S
ELEGIZE DS
ELIXIRS
EMBLAZE DRS
EMPRIZE S
ENJOINS
ENJOYED
ENJOYER S
REENJOY
ENQUIRE DS
ENQUIRY
ENTOZOA LN
OZONATE
ENZYMES
ENZYMIC
EPAZOTE S
EPITAXY
EPIZOIC
EPIZOON
EPOXIDE S
EPOXIED
EPOXIED
EPOXIDE
EPOXIES
EPOXYED
EQUABLE
EQUABLY
EQUALED
EQUALLY
EQUATED
EQUATES
EQUATOR S
EQUERRY
EQUINES
EQUINOX
R EQUITES
EROTIZE DS
ESQUIRE DS
QUERIES
M METHOXYL S
EVZONES
EXABYTE S
EXACTAS
EXACTED
EXACTER S
EXCRETA
EXACTLY
EXACTOR S
EXALTED
EXALTER S
EXAMENS
H EXAMINE DERS
EXAMPLE DS
EXEMPLA
EXAPTED
EXARCHS
H EXARCHY
EXCEEDS
EXCEPTS
EXPECTS
EXCERPT S
EXCIDED
EXCIDES
EXCISED
EXCIMER S
EXCIPLE S
EXCISED
EXCIDES
EXCISES
EXCITED
EXCITER S
EXCITES
EXCITON S
EXCITOR S
XEROTIC
EXCLAIM S
EXCLAVE S
EXCLUDE DRS
EXCRETA L
EXACTER
EXCRETE DRS
EXCUSED
EXCUSER S
EXCUSES
EXECUTE DRS
EXEDRAE
EXEGETE S
EXEMPLA R
EXAMPLE
EXEMPTS
EXERGUE S
EXERTED
EXHALED
EXHALES
EXHAUST S
EXHEDRA E
EXHIBIT S
EXHORTS
EXHUMED
EXHUMER S
EXHUMES
EXIGENT
EXILERS
EXILIAN
EXILING
EXISTED
EXITING
EXOCARP S
EXODERM S
EXOGAMY
EXOGENS
EXONYMS
EXORDIA L
EXOSMIC
EXOTICA
EXOTICS
COEXIST
EXOTISM S
EXPANDS
SPANDEX
EXPANSE S
EXPECTS
EXCEPTS
EXPENDS
EXPENSE DS
EXPERTS
EXPIATE DS
EXPIRED
EXPIRER S
EXPIRES
PREXIES
EXPLAIN S
EXPLANT S
EXPLODE DRS
EXPLOIT S
EXPLORE DRS
EXPORTS
EXPOSAL S
EXPOSED
EXPOSER S
EXPOSES
EXPOSIT S
POXIEST
EXPOUND S
EXPRESS O
EXPULSE DS
EXPUNGE DRS
EXSCIND S
EXSECTS
EXSERTS
EXTENDS
EXTENTS
EXTERNE S
EXTERNS
EXTINCT S
EXTOLLS
EXTORTS
EXTRACT S
EXTREMA
EXTREME RS
EXTRUDE DRS
EXUDATE S
EXUDING
EXULTED
EXURBAN
EXURBIA S
EXUVIAE
EXUVIAL
EXUVIUM

FAJITAS
FANJETS
FANZINE S
FAQUIRS
FAREBOX
FAZENDA S
FEAZING
FEDEXED
FEDEXES
FEEDBOX
FEEZING
FEIJOAS
FIREBOX
FIXABLE
FIXATED
FIXATES
FIXATIF S
FIXEDLY
FIXINGS
FIXTURE S
FIXURES
FIZGIGS
FIZZERS
FRIZZES
FIZZIER
FIZZING
FIZZLED
FIZZLES
FJORDIC
FLAXIER
FLEXILE
FLEXING
FLEXION S
FLEXORS
FLEXURE S
FLOOZIE S
FLUMMOX
FLUXING
FLUXION S
FOOZLED
FOOZLER S
FOOZLES
FOWLPOX
FOXFIRE S
FOXFISH
FOXHOLE S
FOXHUNT S
FOXIEST
FOXINGS
FOXLIKE
FOXSKIN S
FOXTAIL S
FOXTROT S
FOZIEST
FRAZILS
FRAZZLE DS
FREEZER S
FREEZES
FRIEZES
FRIJOLE S
FRITZES
FRIZERS
FRIZING
FRIZZED
FRIZZER S
FRIZZES
FIZZERS
FRIZZLE DRS
FRIZZLY
FUNPLEX
FURZIER
FUTZING
FUZZIER
FUZZILY
FUZZING

GALAXES
GANJAHS
GATEAUX
GAUZIER
GAUZILY
GAZABOS
GAZANIA S
GAZEBOS
GAZELLE S
GAZETTE DS
GAZUMPS
GEARBOX
GEEZERS
GHAZIES
GIZZARD S
GJETOST S
GLAZERS
GLAZIER SY
GLAZILY
GLAZING S
GLITZED
GLITZES
GLOZING
GRAVLAX
GRAZERS
GRAZIER S
GRAZING S
GRECIZE DS
GRIZZLE DRS
GRIZZLY
GUZZLED
GUZZLER S
GUZZLES
GYTTJAS

HADJEES
HAFIZES
HAMZAHS
HAPAXES
HARIJAN S
C HAZANIM
HAZARDS
HAZELLY
HAZIEST
HAZINGS
HAZMATS
MATZAHS
C HAZZANS
W HEEZING
HEJIRAS
HELIXES
HELLBOX
HEROIZE DS
HERTZES
HEXADES
HEXADIC
HEXAGON S
HEXANES
HEXAPLA RS
HEXAPOD SY
HEXEREI S
HEXONES
HEXOSAN S
HEXOSES
HEXYLIC
HIJACKS
HIJINKS
HIJRAHS
HOATZIN S
HOAXERS
HOAXING
HOMOSEX
HORIZON S
HUMIDEX
C HUTZPAH S
C HUTZPAS
HUZZAED
HUZZAHS
HYDROXY L
HYPOXIA S
HYPOXIC
HYRAXES

IDOLIZE DRS
IMBLAZE DS
IMMIXED
IMMIXES
INDEXED
INDEXER S
REINDEX
INDEXES
INDOXYL S
INEXACT
INFIXED
INFIXES
INJECTS
INJURED
INJURER S
INJURES
INQUEST S
QUINTES
INQUIET S
INQUIRE DRS
INQUIRY
IODIZED
IODIZER S
IODIZES
L IONIZED
L IONIZER S
IRONIZE
L IONIZES
IRONIZE DS
IONIZER
ISOZYME S
ITEMIZE DRS
IXODIDS
DIOXIDS
G IZZARDS

JABBERS
JABBING
JABIRUS
JACALES
JACAMAR S
JACANAS
JACINTH ES
JACKALS
JACKASS
JACKDAW S
JACKERS
JACKETS
JACKIES
JACKING
JACKLEG S
JACKPOT S
JACOBIN S
JACOBUS
JACONET S
JACUZZI S
JADEDLY
JADEITE S
JADITIC
JAEGERS
JAGGARY
JAGGERS
JAGGERY
JAGGIER
JAGGIES T
JAGGING
JAGLESS
JAGUARS
JAILERS
JAILING
JAILORS
JALAPIC
JALAPIN S
JALOPPY
JAMBEAU X
JAMBING
JAMLIKE
JAMMERS
JAMMIER
JAMMIES T
JAMMING
JANGLED
JANGLER S
JANGLES
JANITOR S
JARFULS
JARSFUL
JARGONS
JARGONY
JARGOON S
JARHEAD S
JARINAS
JARLDOM S
JARRAHS
JARRING
JARSFUL
JARFULS
JARVEYS
JASMINE S
JASMINS
JASPERS
JASPERY
JASSIDS
JAUKING
JAUNCED
JAUNCES
JAUNTED
JAUPING
JAVELIN AS
JAWBONE DRS
JAWLESS
JAWLIKE
JAWLINE S
JAYBIRD S
JAYGEES
JAYVEES
VEEJAYS
JAYWALK S
JAZZBOS
JAZZERS
JAZZIER
JAZZILY
JAZZING
JAZZMAN

JAZZMEN
JEALOUS Y
JEEPERS
JEEPING
JEEPNEY S
JEERERS
JEERING
JEJUNAL
JEJUNUM
D JELLABA S
JELLIED
JELLIES
JELLIFY
JELLING
JEMADAR S
JEMIDAR S
JEMMIED
JEMMIES
JENNETS
JENNIES
JEOPARD SY
JERBOAS
JEREEDS
JERKERS
JERKIER
JERKIES T
JERKILY
JERKING
JERKINS
JINKERS
JERREED S
JERRIDS
JERRIES
JERSEYS
JESSANT
JESSING
JESTERS
JESTFUL
JESTING S
JETBEAD S
JETFOIL S
JETLAGS
JETLIKE
JETPORT S
JETSAMS
JETSOMS
JETTIED
JETTIER
JETTIES T
JETTING
JETTONS
JETWAYS
JEWELED
JEWELER S
JEWELRY
JEWFISH
JEZAILS
JEZEBEL S
JIBBERS
JIBBING
JIBBOOM S
JICAMAS
JIFFIES
JIGGERS
JIGGIER
JIGGING
JIGGISH
JIGGLED
JIGGLES
JIGLIKE
JIGSAWN
JIGSAWS
JILLION S
JILTERS
JILTING
JIMJAMS
JIMMIED
JIMMIES
JIMMINY
JIMPEST
JINGALL S
JINGALS
JINGLED

JINGLER S
JINGLES
JINGOES
JINKERS
JERKINS
JINKING
JINXING
JITNEYS
JITTERS
TRIJETS
JITTERY
JIVEASS
JIVIEST
JOANNES
JOBBERS
JOBBERY
JOBBING
JOBLESS
JOBNAME S
JOCKEYS
JOCULAR
JODHPUR S
JOGGERS
JOGGING S
JOGGLED
JOGGLER S
JOGGLES
JOHNNIE S
JOINDER S
JOINERS
REJOINS
JOINERY
JOINING S
JOINTED
JOINTER S
JOINTLY
JOISTED
JOJOBAS
JOKIEST
JOLLIED
JOLLIER S
JOLLIES T
JOLLIFY
JOLLILY
JOLLITY
JOLTILY
JOLTERS
JOSTLER
JOLTIER
JOLTILY
JOLLITY
JOLTING
JONESED
JONESES
JONQUIL S
JORDANS
JOSEPHS
JOSHERS
JOSHING
JOSTLED
JOSTLER S
JOLTERS
JOSTLES
JOTTERS
JOTTING S
JOUKING
JOUNCED
JOUNCES
JUNCOES
JOURNAL S
JOURNEY S
JOURNOS
SOJOURN
JOUSTED
JOUSTER S
JOWLIER
JOYANCE S
JOYLESS
JOYPOPS
JOYRIDE RS
JOYRODE
JUBBAHS
JUBHAHS
JUBILEE S
JUBILES

JUDASES
JUDDERS
JUDGERS
JUDGING
JUDOIST S
JUDOKAS
JUGFULS
JUGSFUL
JUGGING
JUGGLED
JUGGLER SY
JUGGLES
JUGHEAD S
JUGSFUL
JUGFULS
JUGULAR S
JUGULUM
JUICERS
JUICIER
JUICILY
JUICING
JUJITSU S
JUJUIST
JUJUBES
JUJUISM S
JUJUIST S
JUJITSU
JUJUTSU S
JUKEBOX
JUMBALS
JUMBLED
JUMBLER S
JUMBLES
JUMBUCK S
JUMPERS
JUMPIER
JUMPILY
JUMPING
JUMPOFF S
JUNCOES
JOUNCES
JUNGLED
JUNGLES
JUNIORS
JUNIPER S
JUNKERS
JUNKETS
JUNKIER
JUNKIES T
JUNKING
JUNKMAN
JUNKMEN
JURALLY
JURANTS
JURIDIC
JURISTS
JURYING
JURYMAN
JURYMEN
JUSSIVE S
JUSTERS
JUSTEST
JUSTICE S
JUSTIFY
JUSTING
JUSTLED
JUSTLES
JUTTIED
JUTTIES
JUTTING
JUVENAL S

KAJEPUT S
KHAZENS
KIBBITZ
KIBBUTZ
KICKBOX
KILLJOY S
KLAXONS
KLEENEX
KLEZMER S
KLUTZES
KOLHOZY
KOLKHOZ Y

KOLKOZY
KREUZER S
KUMQUAT S
KUNZITE S
KWANZAS
KYANIZE DS

LACQUER S
CLAQUER
LACQUEY S
LAICIZE DS
LALIQUE S
LATEXES
LAXNESS
LAZARET S
G LAZIEST
LAZULIS
LAZYING
LAZYISH
LEXEMES
LEXEMIC
LEXICAL
LEXICON S
LIONIZE DRS
LIQUATE DS
TEQUILA
LIQUEFY
LIQUEUR S
LIQUIDS
LIQUIFY
LIQUORS
LIXIVIA L
LIZARDS
LOCKBOX
LOCKJAW S
LOGJAMS
LOQUATS
LOZENGE S
LUREXES
LUXATED
LUXATES

MACAQUE S
MACHZOR S
MADZOON S
MAHJONG GS
MAHZORS
MAILBOX
MAJAGUA S
MAJESTY
MAJORED
MAJORLY
MAMZERS
MAQUILA S
MARQUEE S
MARQUES S
MASQUER
MARQUIS E
MASJIDS
MASQUER S
MARQUES
MASQUES
MATZAHS
HAZMATS
MATZOHS
MATZOON S
MATZOTH
MAXILLA ES
MAXIMAL S
MAXIMIN S
MINIMAX
MAXIMUM S
MAXIXES
MAXWELL S
MAZARDS
A MAZEDLY
MAZIEST
MESTIZA
MAZUMAS
MAZURKA S
MAZZARD S
MENAZON S
MESQUIT ES
MESTIZA S
MAZIEST

MESTIZO S
METAZOA LN
METHOXY L
MEZCALS
MEZQUIT ES
MEZUZAH S
MEZUZAS
MEZUZOT H
MIDSIZE D
MILIEUX
MINIMAX
MAXIMIN
MINXISH
MIREXES
REMIXES
MISJOIN S
MITZVAH S
MIXABLE
MIXEDLY
MIXIBLE
MIXTURE S
MIZUNAS
MIZZENS
MIZZLED
MIZZLES
MOJARRA S
MOMZERS
MONAXON S
MOSQUES
MOUJIKS
MOZETTA S
MOZETTE
MUEZZIN S
MUNTJAC S
MUNTJAK S
MUREXES
MUSJIDS
MUZHIKS
MUZJIKS
MUZZIER
MUZZILY
MUZZLED
MUZZLER S
MUZZLES
MYXOMAS

NARTHEX
NETIZEN S
NEXUSES
UNSEXES
NONJURY
NONZERO
NOXIOUS
NOZZLES
NUDZHED
NUDZHES
NUZZLED
NUZZLER S
NUZZLES

OBELIZE DS
OBJECTS
OBLIQUE DS
OBLOQUY
OBSEQUY
ODORIZE DS
BW OOZIEST
ZOOIEST
OPAQUED
OPAQUER
OPAQUES T
OQUASSA S
ORATRIX
ORGANZA S
OUTGAZE DS
OUTJINX
OUTJUMP S
OUTJUTS
OUTSIZE DS
OVERJOY S
OVERLAX
OVERMIX
OVERTAX
OXALATE DS

OXAZINE S
OXBLOOD S
OXCARTS
OXFORDS
OXHEART S
OXIDANT S
OXIDASE S
OXIDATE DS
OXIDISE DRS
OXIDIZE DRS
F OXTAILS
OXYACID S
OXYGENS
OXYMORA
OXYPHIL ES
OXYSALT S
OXYSOME S
OXYTONE S
OZALIDS
OZONATE DS
ENTOZOA
OZONIDE S
OZONISE DS
OZONIZE DRS
OZONOUS

PACKWAX
PAJAMAS
PALAZZI
PALAZZO S
PANCHAX
PANZERS
PARADOX
PARQUET S
PASQUIL S
PATZERS
PECTIZE DS
PEMPHIX
PEPTIZE DRS
PERIQUE S
REEQUIP
PERJURE DRS
PERJURY
PEROXID ES
PERPLEX
PERSPEX
PHALANX
PHARYNX
PHENOXY
PHLOXES
PHOENIX
PIAZZAS
PICKAXE DS
PICQUET S
PILLBOX
PIQUANT
PIQUETS
PIQUING
PIROJKI
PIROQUE S
PIXYISH
PIZAZZY
PIZZAZZ Y
PIZZLES
PLAQUES
PLEXORS
PLOTZED
PLOTZES
PODZOLS
POETIZE DRS
POLEAXE DS
POSTBOX
POSTFIX
POSTTAX
POTZERS
POXIEST
EXPOSIT
POZOLES
PRAJNAS
PREMIXT
PREQUEL S
PRETEXT S
PRETZEL S

PREXIES
EXPIRES
PRINCOX
PRIZERS
PRIZING
PROJECT S
PROJETS
PROPJET S
PROXIES
PROXIMO
PULQUES
PUTZING
PUZZLED
PUZZLER S
PUZZLES
PYJAMAS
PYREXES
PYREXIA LS
PYREXIC
PYXIDES
PYXIDIA

QABALAH S
QABALAS
QINDARS
QINTARS
QIVIUTS
QUACKED
S QUADDED
QUADRAT ES
QUADRIC S
QUAERES
QUAFFED
QUAFFER S
QUAGGAS
QUAHAUG S
QUAHOGS
QUAICHS
QUAIGHS
QUAILED
QUAKERS
QUAKIER
QUAKILY
QUAKING
QUALIFY
E QUALITY
QUAMASH
QUANGOS
QUANTAL
QUANTED
QUANTIC S
QUANTUM
QUARREL S
QUARTAN S
QUARTER NS
QUARTES
QUATRES
QUARTET S
QUARTIC S
QUARTOS
QUASARS
S QUASHED
S QUASHER S
S QUASHES
QUASSES
QUASSIA S
QUASSIN S
QUATRES
QUARTES
QUAVERS
QUAVERY
QUAYAGE S
QUBYTES
QUEENED
QUEENLY
QUEERED
QUEERER
QUEERLY
QUELEAS
SEQUELA
QUELLED
QUELLER S
QUERIDA S

QUERIED
QUERIER S
REQUIRE
QUERIES
ESQUIRE
QUERIST S
QUESTED
QUESTER S
REQUEST
QUESTOR S
QUOTERS
ROQUETS
TORQUES
QUETZAL S
QUEUERS
QUEUING
QUEZALS
QUIBBLE DRS
QUICHES
QUICKEN S
QUICKER
QUICKIE S
QUICKLY
QUIETED
QUIETEN S
QUIETER S
REQUITE
QUIETLY
QUIETUS
QUILLAI AS
QUILLED
QUILLET S
QUILTED
QUILTER S
QUINARY
QUINATE
ANTIQUE
QUINCES
CINQUES
QUINELA S
QUININA S
QUININE S
QUININS
QUINNAT S
QUINTAN
QUINOAS
QUINOID S
QUINOLS
QUINONE S
QUINTAL S
QUINTAN S
QUINNAT
QUINTAR S
QUINTAS
ASQUINT
QUINTES
INQUEST
QUINTET S
QUINTIC S
QUINTIN S
E QUIPPED
E QUIPPER S
QUIPPUS
S QUIRING
QUIRKED
S QUIRTED
QUITTED
QUITTER S
QUITTOR S
QUIVERS
QUIVERY
QUIXOTE S
QUIZZED
QUIZZER S
QUIZZES
QUOHOGS
QUOINED
QUOITED
QUOKKAS
QUOMODO S
QUONDAM
QUORUMS

QUOTERS
QUESTOR
ROQUETS
TORQUES
QUOTING
QURSHES
QWERTYS

RACQUET S
RADIXES
RAMJETS
RAZORED
RAZZING
REAFFIX
AFFIXER
REALIZE DRS
REANNEX
REBOZOS
BOOZERS
RECTRIX
REDOXES
REEJECT S
REENJOY S
ENJOYER
REEQUIP S
PERIQUE
REEXPEL S
P REFIXED
P REFIXES
P REFROZE N
REGLAZE DS
REINDEX
INDEXER
REJECTS
REJOICE DRS
REJOINS
JOINERS
P REJUDGE DS
RELAXED
RELAXER S
RELAXES
RELAXIN GS
RELIQUE S
P REMIXED
P REMIXES
MIREXES
REQUEST S
QUESTER
REQUIEM S
REQUINS
REQUIRE DRS
QUERIER
REQUITE DRS
QUIETER
RESEAUX
RESEIZE DS
RESIZED
RESIZES
SEIZERS
RESOJET S
RETAXED
RETAXES
REWAXED
REWAXES
REXINES
REZEROS
REZONED
REZONES
RHIZOID S
RHIZOMA
RHIZOME S
RHIZOPI
RITZIER
RITZILY
ROMAJIS
C ROQUETS
QUESTOR
QUOTERS
TORQUES
RORQUAL S
ROZZERS

SACQUES
CASQUES
SALPINX
SALTBOX

SANDBOX
SANJAKS
SAPAJOU S
SAXHORN S
SAXTUBA S
SUBTAXA
SCHERZI
SCHERZO S
SCHIZOS
SCHIZZY
SCHMALZ Y
SCHNOZZ
SCUZZES
SEIZERS
RESIZES
SEIZING S
SEIZINS
SEIZORS
SEIZURE S
SEJEANT
SELTZER S
SEQUELA E
QUELEAS
SEQUELS
SEQUENT S
SEQUINS
SEQUOIA S
SEXIEST
SEXISMS
SEXISTS
SEXLESS
SEXPOTS
SEXTAIN S
ANTISEX
SEXTANS
SEXTANT S
SEXTETS
SEXTILE S
SEXTONS
SHEQELS
SHIATZU S
SHMALTZ Y
SHMOOZE DS
SHOEBOX
SHOWBIZ
SILEXES
SILIQUA E
SILIQUE S
SIMPLEX
SIXFOLD
SIXTEEN S
SIXTHLY
SIXTIES
SIZABLE
SIZABLY
SIZIEST
SIZINGS
SIZZLED
SIZZLER S
SIZZLES
SJAMBOK S
SKYJACK S
SLEAZES
SNEEZED
SNEEZER S
SNEEZES
SNOOZED
SNOOZER S
SNOOZES
SNOOZLE DS
SOAPBOX
SOJOURN S
JOURNOS
SONOVOX
SOVKHOZ Y
SOYUZES
SOZINES
SOZZLED
SPANDEX
EXPANDS
SPATZLE S
SPITZES
SQUABBY
SQUALID

SQUALLS
SQUALLY
SQUALOR S
SQUAMAE
SQUARED
SQUARER S
SQUARES T
SQUARKS
SQUASHY
SQUATLY
SQUATTY
SQUAWKS
SQUEAKS
SQUEAKY
SQUEALS
SQUEEZE DRS
SQUELCH Y
SQUIFFY
SQUILLA ES
SQUILLS
SQUINCH
SQUINNY
SQUINTS
SQUINTY
E SQUIRED
E SQUIRES
SQUIRMS
SQUIRMY
SQUIRTS
SQUISHY
SQUOOSH Y
STANZAS
STYLIZE DRS
ZESTILY
SUBJECT S
SUBJOIN S
SUBTAXA
SAXTUBA
SUBTEXT S
SUBZERO
SUBZONE S
SWIZZLE DRS
SYZYGAL

TARZANS
TAXABLE S
TAXABLY
TAXEMES
TAXEMIC
TAXICAB S
TAXIING
TAXIMAN
TAXIMEN
TAXITES
TAXITIC
TAXIWAY S
TAXLESS
TAXPAID
TAXWISE
WAXIEST
TAXYING
TEAZELS
TEAZLES
TEAZLED
TEAZLES
TEAZELS
TECTRIX
TELEFAX
TELEXED
TELEXES
TEQUILA S
LIQUATE
TEXASES
TEXTILE S
TEXTUAL
TEXTURE DS
THIAZIN ES
THIAZOL ES
TIZZIES
TOOLBOX
TOPAZES
TOQUETS
TORQUED
TORQUER S

TORQUES
QUESTOR
QUOTERS
ROQUETS
TORTRIX
TOUZLED
TOUZLES
TOXEMIA S
TOXEMIC
TOXICAL
TOXINES
TOXOIDS
TRAJECT S
TRAPEZE S
TRIAZIN ES
TRIJETS
JITTERS
TRIOXID ES
TRIPLEX
TUBIFEX
TUXEDOS
TWEEZED
TWEEZER S
TWEEZES
TWINJET S
TZADDIK
TZARDOM S
TZARINA S
TZARISM S
TZARIST S
TZETZES
TZIGANE S
TZIMMES
TZITZIS
TZITZIT H

ULEXITE S
UNBOXED
UNBOXES
UNCRAZY
UNEQUAL S
UNFAZED
UNFIXED
UNFIXES
UNFROZE N
UNIQUER
UNIQUES T
UNISIZE
UNITIZE DRS
UNJADED
UNJOINT S
UNMIXED
UNMIXES
UNQUIET S
UNQUOTE DS
UNRAZED
UNSEXED
UNSEXES
NEXUSES
UNSIZED
UNTAXED
UNVEXED
UNWAXED
UNZONED
UPGAZED
UPGAZES
UPSIZED
UPSIZES
URTEXTS
UTILIZE DRS
UXORIAL

VAQUERO S
VEEJAYS
JAYVEES
VEXEDLY
VEXILLA R
VIXENLY
VIZARDS
VIZIERS
VIZORED
VIZSLAS

WALTZED

WALTZER S
WALTZES
WAXABLE
WAXBILL S
WAXIEST
TAXWISE
WAXINGS
WAXLIKE
WAXWEED S
WAXWING S
WAXWORK S
WAXWORM S
WEAZAND S
WHEEZED
WHEEZER S
WHEEZES
WHIZZED
WHIZZER S
WHIZZES
WIZARDS
WIZENED
WIZZENS
WOADWAX
WOODBOX
BOXWOOD
WOODWAX
WOOZIER
WOOZILY
WORKBOX
WURZELS

XANTHAN S
XANTHIC
XANTHIN ES
XENOPUS
XERARCH
XEROSES
XEROSIS
XEROTIC
EXCITOR
XEROXED
XEROXES
XERUSES
XIPHOID S
XYLENES
XYLIDIN ES
XYLITOL S
XYLOSES
XYSTERS

YANQUIS

ZACATON S
ZADDICK
ZAFFARS
ZAFFERS
ZAFFRES
ZAFFIRS
ZAFFRES
ZAFFERS
ZAGGING
ZAIKAIS
ZAMARRA S
ZAMARRO S
ZANANAS
ZANDERS
ZANIEST
ZEATINS
ZANYISH
ZAPATEO S
ZAPPERS
ZAPPIER
APPRIZE
ZAPPING
ZAPTIAH S
ZAPTIEH S
ZAREBAS
ZAREEBA S
ZARIBAS
ZEALOTS
ZEALOUS
ZEATINS
ZANIEST
ZEBECKS
ZEBRAIC

ZEBRANO S
ZEBRASS
ZEBRINE S
ZEBROID
ZECCHIN IOS
ZECHINS
ZEDOARY
ZELKOVA S
ZEMSTVA
ZEMSTVO S
ZENAIDA S
ZENANAS
ZENITHS
ZEOLITE S
ZEPHYRS
ZEPPOLE S
ZEPPOLI
ZEROING
ZESTERS
ZESTFUL
ZESTIER
ZESTILY
STYLIZE
ZESTING
ZEUGMAS
ZIBETHS
ZIGGING
ZIGZAGS
ZIKURAT S
ZILCHES
ZILLAHS
ZILLION S
ZINCATE S
ZINCIFY
ZINCING
ZINCITE S
CITIZEN
ZINCKED
ZINCOID
ZINCOUS
ZINGANI
ZINGANO
ZINGARA
ZINGARE
ZINGARI
ZINGARO
ZINGERS
ZINGIER
ZINGING
ZINKIFY
ZINNIAS
ZIPLESS
ZIPLOCK
ZIPPERS
ZIPPIER
ZIPPING
ZIRCONS
ZITHERN S
ZITHERS
ZIZZLED
ZIZZLES
ZLOTIES
ZLOTYCH
ZOARIAL
ZOARIUM
ZOCALOS
ZODIACS
ZOECIUM
ZOISITE S
ZOMBIES
ZOMBIFY
ZONALLY
O ZONATED
ZONKING
ZONULAE
ZONULAR
ZONULAS
ZONULES
ZOOECIA
ZOOGENY
ZOOGLEA EL S
ZOOIDAL

2006 Addition

Bob's Bible: Words Containing J Q X or Z by Word-Length

ZOOIEST
OOZIEST
ZOOLOGY
ZOOMING
ZOONING
ZOOTIER
ZOOTOMY
ZORILLA S
ZORILLE S
ZORILLO S
ZOSTERS
ZOUAVES
ZOYSIAS
ZYDECOS
ZYGOMAS
A ZYGOSES
ZYGOSIS
ZYGOTES
ZYGOTIC
ZYMASES
ZYMOGEN ES
ZYMOSAN S
ZYMOSES
ZYMOSIS
ZYMOTIC
ZYMURGY
ZYZZYVA S

8-letter Words

ABJECTLY
ABJURERS
ABJURING
ACEQUIAS
ACETOXYL S
ACQUAINT S
ACQUESTS
ACQUIRED
ACQUIREE S
ACQUIRER S
ACQUIRES
ACTIVIZE DS
ADEQUACY
ADEQUATE
ADJACENT
ADJOINED
ADJOINTS
ADJOURNS
ADJUDGED
ADJUDGES
ADJUNCTS
ADJURERS
ADJURING
ADJURORS
ADJUSTED
ADJUSTER S
READJUST
ADJUSTOR S
ADJUTANT S
ADJUVANT S
ADMIXING
AEQUORIN S
AFFIXERS
AFFIXIAL
AFFIXING
AFFLUXES
AFTERTAX
AGATIZED
AGATIZES
AGENIZED
AGENIZES
AGNIZING
AGONIZED
AGONIZES
ALBIZIAS
ALBIZZIA S
ALCAZARS
ALEXINES
ALFAQUIN S
ALFAQUIS
ALFORJAS
ALIQUANT
ALIQUOTS
ALIZARIN ES
ALKALIZE DRS
ALKOXIDE S
ALLOXANS
AMAZEDLY
AMORTIZE DS
ATOMIZER
AMPHIOXI
AMPLEXUS
ANALYZED
ANALYZER S
ANALYZES
ANATOXIN S
ANNEXING
ANODIZED
ANODIZES
ANOREXIA S
ANOREXIC S
ANOXEMIA S
ANOXEMIC
ANTEFIXA EL
ANTHELIX
ANTIQUED
ANTIQUER S
QUAINTER
ANTIQUES
APAREJOS
APHORIZE DRS
APOMIXES
APOMIXIS
APOPLEXY
APPENDIX
APPLIQUE DS
APPRIZED
APPRIZER S
APPRIZES
APRAXIAS
AQUACADE S
AQUAFARM S
AQUALUNG S
AQUANAUT S
AQUARIAL
AQUARIAN S
AQUARIST S
AQUARIUM S
AQUATICS
AQUATINT S
AQUATONE S
AQUAVITS
AQUEDUCT S
AQUIFERS
AQUILINE
QUINIELA
ARABIZED
ARABIZES
ARBORIZE DS
ARCHAIZE DRS
H ARQUEBUS
ARRHIZAL
ASPHYXIA LS
ATARAXIA S
ATARAXIC S
ATOMIZED
ATOMIZER S
AMORTIZE
ATOMIZES
ATRAZINE S
ATTICIZE DS
AUTOLYZE DS
AUXETICS
AVIANIZE DS
AVIATRIX
AXIALITY
AXILLARS
M AXILLARY
AXIOLOGY
AXLETREE S
AXOLOTLS
AXONEMAL
AXONEMES
AXOPLASM S
AZIMUTHS
AZOTEMIA S
AZOTEMIC
METAZOIC
AZOTISED
AZOTISES
AZOTIZED
AZOTIZES
AZOTURIA S
AZULEJOS
L AZURITES
AZYGOSES

BANALIZE DS
BANDEAUX
BANJAXED
BANJAXES
BANJOIST S
BANQUETS
BAPTIZED
BAPTIZER S
BAPTIZES
BARBEQUE DS
BAROQUES
BARTIZAN S
BASENJIS
BATTEAUX
BAUXITES
BAUXITIC
BAZOOKAS
BEDAZZLE DS
BEDIZENS
BEDQUILT S
BEGAZING
BEJABERS
BEJEEZUS
BEJEWELS
BEJUMBLE DS
BELIQUOR S
BEMIXING
BEMUZZLE DS
BENJAMIN S
BENZENES
BENZIDIN ES
BENZINES
BENZOATE S
BENZOINS
BENZOLES
BENZOYLS
BENZYLIC
BEQUEATH S
BEQUESTS
BEZAZZES
BEZIQUES
BEZZANTS
BICONVEX
BIJUGATE
BIJUGOUS
BIOTOXIN S
BISEXUAL S
BIUNIQUE
BIZARRES
BRAZIERS
BIZARROS
BIZNAGAS
BLAZERED
BLAZONED
BLAZONER S
BLAZONRY
BLINTZES
BLITZERS
BLITZING
BLIZZARD SY
BLOWZIER
BLOWZILY
BLUEJACK S
BLUEJAYS
BOBBYSOX
BOLLIXED
BOLLIXES
BOLLOXED
BOLLOXES
BOMBYXES
BONANZAS
BOOTJACK S
JACKBOOT
BOOZIEST
BORDEAUX
BOSQUETS
BOTANIZE DRS
BOUQUETS
BOUTIQUE SY
BOUZOUKI AS
BOXBALLS
BOXBERRY
BOXBOARD S
BOXHAULS
BOXINESS
BOXTHORN S
BOXWOODS
BRAZENED
BRAZENLY
BRAZIERS
BIZARRES
BRAZILIN S
BREADBOX
BREEZIER
BREEZILY
BREEZING
BRIQUETS
BRITZKAS
BRITZSKA
BRITZSKA S
BRITZKAS
BROADAXE S
BROMIZED
BROMIZES
BRONZERS
BRONZIER
BRONZING S
BRULZIES
BRUNIZEM S
BRUSQUER
BRUXISMS
BRYOZOAN S
BULLDOZE DRS
BUXOMEST
BUZZARDS
BUZZCUTS
BUZZWIGS
BUZZWORD S

CABEZONE S
CABEZONS
CACHEXIA S
CACHEXIC
CACIQUES
CACOMIXL ES
CADENZAS
CAJAPUTS
CAJEPUTS
CAJOLERS
CAJOLERY
CAJOLING
CAJUPUTS
CALABAZA S
CALORIZE DS
CALQUING
CALZONES
CANALIZE DS
CANONIZE DRS
CANZONAS
CANZONES
CANZONET S
CAPONIZE DS
CAPSIZED
CAPSIZES
CARBOXYL S
CARCAJOU S
CARJACKS
CATALYZE DRS
CATHEXES
CATHEXIS
CATJANGS
CAUDEXES
CAZIQUES
CENOZOIC
CERVEZAS
CERVIXES
CHALAZAE
CHALAZAL
CHALAZAS
CHALAZIA
CHAPEAUX
CHAQUETA S
CHARQUID
CHARQUIS
CHATEAUX
CHAZANIM
CHAZZANS
CHAZZENS
CHEQUERS
CHINTZES
CHORIZOS
CHROMIZE DS
CHRONAXY
CHUTZPAH S
CHUTZPAS
CICATRIX
CINQUAIN S
CITIZENS
ZINCITES
CIVILIZE DRS
CLAQUERS
LACQUERS
CLAQUEUR S
CLIMAXED
CLIMAXES
EXCLAIMS
CLIQUIER
CLIQUING
CLIQUISH
COCCYXES
COENZYME S
COEQUALS
COEQUATE DS
COEXERTS
CORTEXES
COEXISTS
COEXTEND S
COGNIZED
COGNIZER S
COGNIZES
COJOINED
COLLOQUY
COLONIZE DRS
COLORIZE DRS
COMMIXED
COMMIXES
COMPRIZE DS
CONJOINS
CONJOINT
CONJUGAL
CONJUNCT S
CONJUNTO S
CONJURED
CONJURER S
CONJURES
CONJUROR S
CONQUERS
CONQUEST S
CONQUIAN S
CONTEXTS
CONVEXES
CONVEXLY
COQUETRY
COQUETTE DS
COQUILLE S
COQUINAS
COQUITOS
CORTEXES
COEXERTS
COTQUEAN S
COTURNIX
COUTEAUX
COWPOXES
COXALGIA S
COXALGIC
COXCOMBS
COXSWAIN S
COZENAGE S
COZENERS
COZENING
COZINESS
CRAZIEST
CREDENZA S
CREOLIZE DS
CRITIQUE DS
CROQUETS
CROZIERS
CRUCIFIX
CRUZADOS
CRUZEIRO S
CUMQUATS
CURARIZE DS
CURTALAX
CUTINIZE DS
CYBERSEX
CYCLIZED
CYCLIZES
CZARDOMS
CZAREVNA S
CZARINAS
CZARISMS
CZARISTS
CZARITZA S

DAIDZEIN S
DAIQUIRI S
DAMOZELS
DANAZOLS
DAZZLERS
DAZZLING
DEEJAYED
DEFLEXED
DEFUZING
DEGLAZED
DEGLAZES
DEIONIZE DRS
DEIXISES
DEJECTED
DEJEUNER S
DEMIJOHN S
DEMONIZE DS
DENAZIFY
DENIZENS
DEPUTIZE DS
DESEXING
DETOXIFY
DETOXING
DEUTZIAS
DEWAXING
DEXTRANS
DEXTRINE S
DEXTRINS
DEXTROSE S
DEXTROUS
DEZINCED
DIALYZED
DIALYZER S
DIALYZES
DIAZEPAM S
DIAZINES
DIAZINON S
DIAZOLES
SLEAZOID
DIGITIZE DRS
DIGOXINS
DIMERIZE DS
DIOXANES
DIOXIDES
OXIDISED
DIPLEXER S
DISJECTS
DISJOINS
DISJOINT S
DISJUNCT S
DISPRIZE DS
DISQUIET S
DISSEIZE DES
DITZIEST
DIVINIZE DS
DIZENING
DIZYGOUS
DIZZIEST
DIZZYING
DJELLABA HS
DOORJAMB S
DOUZEPER S
DOWNSIZE DS
DOWNZONE DS
DOXOLOGY
DOZENING
DOZENTHS
DOZINESS
DRIZZLED
DRIZZLES
DUALIZED
DUALIZES
DUPLEXED
DUPLEXER S
DUPLEXES
EXPULSED
DUXELLES
DYSLEXIA S
DYSLEXIC S
DYSTAXIA S

EARWAXES
EBONIZED
EBONIZES
ECONOBOX
ECTOZOAN S
ECTOZOON
EFFLUXES
DR EJECTING
DR EJECTION S
R EJECTIVE S
R EJECTORS
EKTEXINE S
ELEGIZED
ELEGIZES
ELOQUENT
EMBEZZLE DRS
EMBLAZED
EMBLAZER S
EMBLAZES
EMBLAZON S
EMPRIZES
ENDEXINE S
ENDOZOIC
ENERGIZE DRS
ENJAMBED
ENJOINED
ENJOINER S
ENJOYERS
REENJOYS
ENJOYING
ENQUIRED
ENQUIRES
SQUIREEN
ENTOZOAL
ENTOZOAN S
ENTOZOIC
ENZOOTIC
ENTOZOON
ENZOOTIC S
ENTOZOIC
EPAZOTES
EPICALYX
EPITAXIC
EPIZOISM S
EPIZOITE S
EPIZOOTY
EPOXIDES
EPOXYING
EQUALING
EQUALISE DRS
EQUALITY
EQUALIZE DRS
EQUALLED
EQUATING
EQUATION S
EQUATORS
QUAESTOR
EQUINELY

EQUINITY
INEQUITY
EQUIPAGE S
EQUIPPED
EQUIPPER S
EQUISETA
EQUITANT
EQUITIES
EQUIVOKE S
EROTIZED
EROTIZES
ERSATZES
ESQUIRED
ESQUIRES
ETERNIZE DS
ETHERIZE DRS
ETHICIZE DS
ETHOXIES
ETHOXYLS
EULOGIZE DRS
EUTAXIES
EUXENITE S
EXABYTES
EXACTERS
EXACTEST
EXACTING
EXACTION S
EXACTORS
EXAHERTZ
EXALTERS
EXALTING
EXAMINED
EXAMINEE S
EXAMINER S
H EXAMINES
EXAMPLED
EXAMPLES
EXANTHEM AS
EXAPTIVE
EXARCHAL
EXCAVATE DS
EXCEEDED
EXCEEDER S
EXCELLED
EXCEPTED
EXPECTED
EXCERPTS
EXCESSED
EXCESSES
EXCHANGE DRS
EXCIDING
EXCIMERS
EXCIPLES
EXCISING
EXCISION S
EXCITANT S
EXCITERS
EXCITING
EXCITONS
EXCITORS
EXORCIST
EXCLAIMS
CLIMAXES
EXCLAVES
EXCLUDED
EXCLUDER S
EXCLUDES
EXCRETAL
EXCRETED
EXCRETER S
EXCRETES
EXCURSUS
EXCUSERS
EXCUSING
EXECRATE DS
EXECUTED
EXECUTER S
EXECUTES
EXECUTOR SY
EXEGESES
EXEGESIS
EXEGETES
EXEGETIC S

EXEMPLAR SY
EXEMPLUM
EXEMPTED
EXEQUIAL
EXEQUIES
EXERCISE DRS
EXERGUAL
EXERGUES
EXERTING
EXERTION S
EXERTIVE
EXHALANT S
EXHALENT S
EXHALING
EXHAUSTS
EXHEDRAE
EXHIBITS
EXHORTED
EXHORTER S
EXHUMERS
EXHUMING
EXIGENCE S
EXIGENCY
EXIGIBLE
EXIGUITY
EXIGUOUS
EXILABLE
EXIMIOUS
EXISTENT S
EXISTING
EXITLESS
SEXTILES
EXOCARPS
EXOCRINE S
EXOCYTIC
EXODERMS
EXODUSES
EXOERGIC
EXOGAMIC
EXONUMIA
EXORABLE
EXORCISE DRS
EXORCISM S
EXORCIST S
EXCITORS
EXORCIZE DS
EXORDIAL
EXORDIUM S
EXOSMOSE S
EXOSPORE S
EXOTERIC
EXOTISMS
EXOTOXIC
EXOTOXIN S
EXPANDED
EXPANDER S
EXPANDOR S
EXPANSES
EXPECTED
EXCEPTED
EXPECTER S
EXPEDITE DRS
EXPELLED
EXPELLEE S
EXPELLER S
EXPENDED
EXPENDER S
EXPENSED
EXPENSES
EXPERTED
EXPERTLY
EXPIABLE
EXPIATED
EXPIATES
EXPIATOR SY
EXPIRERS
EXPIRIES
EXPIRING
EXPLAINS
EXPLANTS
EXPLICIT S
EXPLODED

EXPLODER S
EXPLORED
EXPLODES
EXPLOITS
EXPLORED
EXPLODER
EXPLORER S
EXPLORES
EXPONENT S
EXPORTED
EXPORTER S
REEXPORT
EXPOSALS
EXPOSERS
EXPRESSO
EXPOSING
EXPOSITS
EXPOSURE S
EXPOUNDS
EXPRESSO S
EXPOSERS
EXPULSED
DUPLEXES
EXPULSES
PLEXUSES
EXPUNGED
EXPUNGER S
EXPUNGES
EXSCINDS
EXSECANT S
EXSECTED
EXSERTED
EXTENDED
EXTENDER S
EXTENSOR S
EXTERIOR S
EXTERNAL S
EXTERNES
EXTINCTS
EXTOLLED
EXTOLLER S
EXTORTED
EXTORTER S
EXTRACTS
EXTRADOS
EXTRANET S
EXTREMER
EXTREMES T
EXTREMUM
D EXTRORSE
EXTRUDED
EXTRUDER S
EXTRUDES
EXTUBATE DS
EXUDATES
EXULTANT
EXULTING
EXURBIAS
EXUVIATE DS

FABLIAUX
FANZINES
FARADIZE DRS
FAZENDAS
FEDEXING
FEMINIZE DS
FIBERIZE DS
FINALIZE DRS
FIXATIFS
FIXATING
FIXATION S
FIXATIVE S
FIXITIES
FIXTURES
FIZZIEST
FIZZLING
FLAPJACK S
FLAXIEST
FLAXSEED S
FLEXAGON S
FLEXIBLE
FLEXIBLY
FLEXIONS
FLEXTIME RS
FLEXUOSE

FLEXUOUS
FLEXURAL
FLEXURES
REFLUXES
FLOOZIES
FLUIDIZE DRS
FLUXGATE S
FLUXIONS
FOCALIZE DS
FOOZLERS
FOOZLING
FORJUDGE DS
S FORZANDI
S FORZANDO S
FOURPLEX
FOXFIRES
FOXGLOVE S
FOXHOLES
FOXHOUND S
FOXHUNTS
FOXINESS
FOXSKINS
FOXTAILS
FOXTROTS
FOZINESS
FRABJOUS
FRANCIZE DS
FRAZZLED
FRAZZLES
FREEZERS
FREEZING
FRENZIED
FRENZIES
FRENZILY
FREQUENT S
FRIJOLES
FRIZETTE S
FRIZZERS
FRIZZIER
FRIZZIES T
FRIZZILY
FRIZZING
FRIZZLED
FRIZZLER S
FRIZZLES
FROUZIER
FROWZIER
FROWZILY
FROZENLY
FURZIEST
FUZZIEST
FUZZTONE S

GADZOOKS
GALAXIES
GARBANZO S
GAUZIEST
GAZABOES
GAZANIAS
GAZEBOES
GAZELLES
GAZETTED
GAZETTES
GAZOGENE S
GAZPACHO S
GAZUMPED
GAZUMPER S
GEOTAXES
GEOTAXIS
GIZZARDS
GJETOSTS
GLAZIERS
GLAZIERY
GLAZIEST
GLAZINGS
GLITZIER
GLITZING
GLOXINIA S
GRAECIZE DS
GRAZABLE
GRAZIERS
GRAZINGS
GRAZIOSO

GRECIZED
GRECIZES
GRIZZLED
GRIZZLER S
GRIZZLES
GUZZLERS
GUZZLING

HALAZONE S
C HALUTZIM
HANDAXES
HARIJANS
HARUSPEX
HATBOXES
HAZARDED
HAZARDER S
HAZELHEN S
HAZELNUT S
HAZINESS
C HAZZANIM
HEBRAIZE DS
HEMOLYZE DS
HENEQUEN S
HENEQUIN S
HENIQUEN
HENIQUEN S
HENEQUIN
HEPATIZE DS
HERETRIX
HERITRIX
HEROIZED
HEROIZES
HEXAGONS
HEXAGRAM S
HEXAMINE S
HEXAPLAR
HEXAPLAS
HEXAPODS
HEXAPODY
HEXARCHY
HEXEREIS
HEXOSANS
HIGHJACK S
HIJACKED
HIJACKER S
HIZZONER S
HOACTZIN S
HOATZINS
HOLOZOIC
HOMEOBOX
HOMINIZE DS
HORIZONS
HORSEPOX
HOTBOXES
HOWITZER S
HUMANIZE DRS
C HUTZPAHS
HUZZAHED
HUZZAING
HYDROXYL S
HYLOZOIC
HYPOXIAS

ICEBOXES
IDEALIZE DRS
IDOLIZED
IDOLIZER S
IDOLIZES
ILLIQUID
IMBLAZED
IMBLAZES
IMMIXING
IMMUNIZE DRS
INDEXERS
INDEXING S
INDOXYLS
INEQUITY
EQUINITY
INEXPERT S
INFIXING
INFIXION S
INFLEXED
INFLUXES

INIQUITY
INJECTED
INJECTOR S
INJURERS
INJURIES
INJURING
INQUESTS
INQUIETS
INQUIRED
INQUIRER S
INQUIRES
INTERMIX
INTERREX
INTERSEX
IODIZERS
IODIZING
L IONIZERS
IRONIZES
L IONIZING
IRONIZED
IRONIZES
IONIZERS
ISOZYMES
ISOZYMIC
ITEMIZED
ITEMIZER S
ITEMIZES

JABBERED
JABBERER S
JACAMARS
JACINTHE S
JACINTHS
JACKAROO S
JACKBOOT S
BOOTJACK
JACKDAWS
JACKEROO S
JACKETED
JACKFISH
JACKLEGS
JACKPOTS
JACKROLL S
JACKSTAY S
JACOBINS
JACONETS
JACQUARD S
E JACULATE DS
JACUZZIS
JADEITES
JADELIKE
JADISHLY
JAGGEDER
JAGGEDLY
JAGGHERY
JAGGIEST
JAILABLE
JAILBAIT
JAILBIRD S
JALAPENO S
JALAPINS
JALOPIES
JALOUSIE DS
JAMBEAUX
JAMBOREE S
JAMMABLE
JAMMIEST
JANGLERS
JANGLIER
JANGLING
JANIFORM
JANISARY
JANITORS
JANIZARY
JAPANIZE DS
JAPANNED
JAPANNER S
JAPERIES
JAPINGLY
JAPONICA S
JARGONED
JARGONEL S
JARGOONS

JARHEADS
JARLDOMS
JAROSITE S
JAROVIZE DS
JASMINES
JAUNCING
JAUNDICE DS
JAUNTIER
JAUNTILY
JAUNTING
JAVELINA S
JAVELINS
JAWBONED
JAWBONER S
JAWBONES
JAWLINES
JAYBIRDS
JAYWALKS
JAZZIEST
JAZZLIKE
JEALOUSY
JEEPNEYS
JEJUNELY
JEJUNITY
D JELLABAS
JELLYING
JELUTONG S
JEMADARS
JEMIDARS
JEMMYING
JEOPARDS
JEOPARDY
JEREMIAD S
JERKIEST
JEROBOAM S
JERREEDS
JERRICAN S
JERRYCAN S
JERSEYED
JESTINGS
JETBEADS
JETFOILS
JETLINER S
JETPORTS
JETTIEST
JETTISON S
JETTYING
JEWELERS
JEWELING
JEWELLED
JEWELLER SY
JEZEBELS
JIBBOOMS
JIBINGLY
JIGGERED
REJIGGED
JIGGIEST
JIGGLIER
JIGGLING
JIGSAWED
JILLIONS
JIMMYING
JINGALLS
JINGKOES
JINGLERS
JINGLIER
JINGLING
JINGOISH
JINGOISM S
JINGOIST S
JOISTING
JIPIJAPA S
JITTERED
JIUJITSU S
JIUJUTSU S
JOBNAMES
JOCKETTE S
JOCKEYED
JOCOSELY
JOCOSITY
JOCUNDLY
JODHPURS
JOGGINGS

JOGGLERS
JOGGLING
JOHANNES
JOHNBOAT S
JOHNNIES
JOINABLE
JOINDERS
JOININGS
JOINTERS
JOINTING
JOINTURE DS
JOISTING
JINGOIST
JOKESTER S
JOKINESS
JOKINGLY
JOLLIERS
JOLLIEST
JOLLYING
JOLTIEST
JONESING
JONGLEUR S
JONQUILS
JOSTLERS
JOSTLING
JOTTINGS
JOUNCIER
JOUNCING
JOURNALS
JOURNEYS
JOUSTERS
JOUSTING
JOVIALLY
JOVIALTY
JOWLIEST
JOYANCES
JOYFULLY
JOYOUSLY
JOYRIDER S
JOYRIDES
JOYSTICK S
JUBILANT
JUBILATE DS
JUBILEES
JUDDERED
JUDGMENT S
JUDICIAL
JUDOISTS
JUGGLERS
JUGGLERY
JUGGLING S
JUGHEADS
JUGULARS
JUGULATE DS
JUICIEST
JUJITSUS
JUJUISTS
JUJUISMS
JUJUISTS
JUJITSUS
JUJUTSUS
JULIENNE DS
JUMBLERS
JUMBLING
JUMBUCKS
JUMPABLE
JUMPIEST
JUMPOFFS
JUMPSUIT S
JUNCTION S
JUNCTURE S
JUNGLIER
JUNIPERS
JUNKETED
JUNKETER S
JUNKIEST
JUNKYARD S
JURASSIC
JURATORY
JURISTIC
JURYLESS
JUSSIVES
JUSTICES
JUSTLING
JUSTNESS
JUTELIKE
JUTTYING
JUVENALS
JUVENILE S

KABELJOU S
KAJEPUTS
KAMIKAZE S
KAZACHKI
KAZACHOK
KAZATSKI
KAZATSKY
KHAZENIM
KIBITZED
KIBITZER S
KIBITZES
KILLJOYS
KINKAJOU S
KLEZMERS
KLUTZIER
KOLHOZES
KOLKHOZY
KOLKOZES
KREUTZER S
KREUZERS
KUMQUATS
KUNZITES
KUVASZOK
KYANIZED
KYANIZES

LACQUERS
CLAQUERS
LACQUEYS
LAICIZED
LAICIZES
LALIQUES
SQUILLAE
LARYNXES
LATERIZE DS
P LATINIZE DS
LAXATION S
LAXATIVE S
LAXITIES
LAZARETS
G LAZINESS
LAZULITE S
LAZURITE S
LEGALIZE DRS
LEXICONS
LIONIZED
LIONIZER S
LIONIZES
LIQUATED
LIQUATES
TEQUILAS
LIQUEURS
LIQUIDLY
LIQUORED
LIXIVIAL
LIXIVIUM S
LOCALIZE DRS
LOCKJAWS
LOGICIZE DS
LONGJUMP S
LOZENGES
F LUMMOXES
LUNCHBOX
LUXATING
LUXATION S
LUXURIES
LYRICIZE DS
LYSOZYME S

MACAQUES
MACHZORS
MADERIZE DS
MADZOONS
MAGAZINE S
MAHARAJA HS
MAHJONGG S
MAHJONGS
MAHZORIM
MAJAGUAS
MAJESTIC
MAJOLICA S
MAJORING
MAJORITY
MANTEAUX
MAQUETTE S
MAQUILAS
MARJORAM S
MARQUEES
MARQUESS
MASQUERS
MARQUISE S
MARYJANE S
MARZIPAN S
MASQUERS
MARQUESS
MASTIXES
MATCHBOX
MATRIXES
MATZOONS
MAXICOAT S
MAXILLAE
MAXILLAS
MAXIMALS
MAXIMINS
MAXIMISE DS
MAXIMITE S
MAXIMIZE DRS
MAXIMUMS
MAXWELLS
MAZAEDIA
MAZELIKE
MAZELTOV
MAZINESS
MAZOURKA S
MAZURKAS
MAZZARDS
MBAQANGA S
MECHITZA S
MEGAPLEX
MELANIZE DS
MELODIZE DRS
MEMORIZE DRS
MENAZONS
MESOZOAN S
MESOZOIC
MESQUITE S
MESQUITS
MESTIZAS
MESTIZOS
METALIZE DS
METAZOAL
METAZOAN S
METAZOIC
AZOTEMIC
METAZOON
METHOXYL
METRAZOL S
MEZEREON S
MEZEREUM S
MEZQUITE S
MEZQUITS
MEZUZAHS
MEZUZOTH
MICROLUX
MIDSIZED
MIJNHEER S
MILLILUX
MINIMIZE DRS
MIQUELET S
MIREPOIX
MISJOINS
MISJUDGE DS
MISPRIZE DRS
MISQUOTE DRS
MITZVAHS
MITZVOTH
MIXOLOGY
MIXTURES
MIZZLING
MOBILIZE DRS
MOJARRAS
MONAXIAL
MONAXONS
MONAZITE S
MONETIZE DS
ZONETIME
MONOXIDE S
MOQUETTE S
MORALIZE DRS
MORCEAUX
MORESQUE S
MOSQUITO S
MOTORIZE DS
MOZETTAS
MOZZETTA S
MOZZETTE
MUEZZINS
MULTIJET
MUNTJACS
MUNTJAKS
MUSKOXEN
MUSQUASH
MUZZIEST
MUZZLERS
MUZZLING
MYSTIQUE S
MYXAMEBA ES
MYXEDEMA S
MYXOCYTE S
MYXOMATA

NALOXONE S
NAPROXEN S
NASALIZE DS
NAZIFIED
NAZIFIES
NEBULIZE DRS
NETIZENS
NEURAXON S
NEXTDOOR
NIGHTJAR S
NIZAMATE S
NONEQUAL S
NONJUROR S
NONMAJOR S
NONQUOTA
NONTAXES
NONTOXIC
NOTARIZE DS
NOVELIZE DRS
NUDZHING
NUZZLERS
NUZZLING

OBELIZED
OBELIZES
OBJECTED
OBJECTOR S
OBLIQUED
OBLIQUES
OCTUPLEX
ODORIZED
ODORIZES
OLDSQUAW S
BW OOZINESS
OZONISES
OPAQUELY
OPAQUEST
OPAQUING
OPSONIZE DS
OPTIMIZE DRS
OQUASSAS
ORGANIZE DRS
ORGANZAS
ORTHODOX Y
OTOTOXIC
OUTBLAZE DS
OUTBOXED
OUTBOXES
OUTFOXED
OUTFOXES
OUTGAZED
OUTGAZES
OUTJUMPS
OUTQUOTE DS
OUTSIZED
OUTSIZES
OVERJOYS
OVERJUST
OVERSIZE DS
OVERZEAL S
OXALATED
OXALATES
OXALISES
OXAZEPAM S
OXAZINES
OXBLOODS
OXHEARTS
THORAXES
OXIDABLE
OXIDANTS
OXIDASES
OXIDASIC
OXIDATED
OXIDATES
OXIDISED
DIOXIDES
OXIDISER S
OXIDISES
OXIDIZED
OXIDIZER S
OXIDIZES
OXIMETER S
OXIMETRY
OXPECKER S
OXTONGUE S
OXYACIDS
OXYGENIC
OXYMORON S
OXYPHILE S
OXYPHILS
OXYSALTS
OXYSOMES
OXYTOCIC S
OXYTOCIN S
OXYTONES
OZONATED
OZONATES
OZONIDES
OZONISED
OZONISED
OZONIDES
OZONISES
OOZINESS
OZONIZED
OZONIZER S
OZONIZES

PAGANIZE DRS
PAJAMAED
PALAZZOS
PANMIXES
PANMIXIA S
PANMIXIS
PARALLAX
PARALYZE DRS
PARAQUAT S
PARAQUET S
PARAZOAN S
PAROQUET S
PAROXYSM S
PARQUETS
PARTIZAN S
PASQUILS
PATINIZE DS
PAXWAXES
PAZAZZES
PECTIZED
PECTIZES
PEGBOXES
PENALIZE DS
PEPTIZED
PEPTIZER S
PEPTIZES
PERIQUES
REEQUIPS
PERJURED
PERJURER S
PERJURES
PEROXIDE DS
PEROXIDS
PETUNTZE S
PHENAZIN ES
PHENIXES
PHYLAXIS
PHYSIQUE DS
PICKAXED
PICKAXES
PICQUETS
PINTSIZE D
PIQUANCE S
PIQUANCY
PIROQUES
PIROZHKI
PIROZHOK
PIXIEISH
PIXINESS
PIZAZZES
PIZZAZES
PIZZAZES
PIZAZZES
PIZZAZZY
PIZZELLE S
PIZZERIA S
PLATEAUX
PLEXUSES
EXPULSES
PLOTZING
PODZOLIC
POETIZED
POETIZER S
POETIZES
POLARIZE DRS
POLEAXED
POLEAXES
POLEMIZE DS
POLYZOAN S
POLYZOIC
PONTIFEX
POPINJAY S
POSTIQUE S
POXVIRUS
POZZOLAN AS
PRATIQUE S
PRAXISES
PREAXIAL
PRECIEUX
PREEXIST S
PREFIXAL
PREFIXED
PREFIXES
PREFROZE N
PREJUDGE DRS
PREMIXED
PREMIXES
PREQUELS
PRETEXTS
PRETZELS
PROJECTS
PROLIXLY
PROPJETS
PROTOXID ES
PROTOZOA LN
PROXEMIC S
PROXIMAL
PULSEJET S
PULSOJET S
PUZZLERS
PUZZLING
PYREXIAL
PYREXIAS
PYROLIZE DS
PYROLYZE DRS
PYROXENE S
PYXIDIUM

QABALAHS
QINDARKA
QUAALUDE S
QUACKERY
QUACKIER
QUACKING
QUACKISH
QUACKISM S
S QUADDING
QUADPLEX
QUADRANS
QUADRANT S
QUADRATE DS
QUADRATS
QUADRICS
QUADRIGA E
QUADROON S
QUAESTOR S
EQUATORS
QUAFFERS
QUAFFING
QUAGGIER
QUAGMIRE S
QUAGMIRY
QUAHAUGS
QUAICHES
QUAILING
QUAINTER
ANTIQUER
QUAINTLY
QUAKIEST
QUALMIER
QUALMISH
QUANDANG S
QUANDARY
QUANDONG S
QUANTICS
QUANTIFY
QUANTILE S
QUANTING
QUANTITY
QUANTIZE DRS
QUANTONG S
QUARRELS
QUARRIED
QUARRIER S
QUARRIES
QUARTANS
QUARTERN S
QUARTERS
QUARTETS
SQUATTER
QUARTICS
QUARTIER S
QUARTILE S
REQUITAL
QUARTZES
S QUASHERS
SQUASHER
S QUASHING
QUASSIAS
QUASSINS
QUATORZE S
QUATRAIN S
QUAVERED
QUAVERER S
QUAYAGES
QUAYLIKE
QUAYSIDE S
QUEASIER
QUEASILY
QUEAZIER
QUEENDOM S
QUEENING
QUEEREST
QUEERING
QUEERISH
QUELLERS
QUELLING
QUENCHED
QUENCHER S
QUENCHES
QUENELLE S
QUERCINE
QUERIDAS

QUERIERS
REQUIRES
QUERISTS
QUERYING
QUESTERS
REQUESTS
QUESTING
QUESTION S
QUESTORS
QUETZALS
QUEUEING
QUEZALES
QUIBBLED
QUIBBLER S
QUIBBLES
QUICKENS
QUICKEST
QUICKSET
QUICKIES
QUICKSET S
QUICKEST
QUIDDITY
QUIDNUNC S
QUIETENS
QUIETERS
REQUITES
QUIETEST
QUIETING
QUIETISM S
QUIETIST S
QUIETUDE S
QUILLAIA S
QUILLAIS
QUILLAJA S
QUILLETS
QUILLING S
QUILTERS
QUILTING S
QUINCUNX
QUINELAS
QUINELLA S
QUINIELA S
AQUILINE
QUININAS
QUININES
QUINNATS
QUINTANS
QUINOIDS
QUINOLIN ES
QUINONES
QUINSIED
QUINSIES
QUINTAIN S
QUINTALS
QUINTANS
QUINNATS
QUINTARS
QUINTETS
QUINTICS
QUINTILE S
QUINTINS
E QUIPPERS
QUIPPIER
E QUIPPING
QUIPPISH
QUIPSTER S
QUIRKIER
QUIRKILY
QUIRKING
QUIRKISH
S QUIRTING
QUISLING S
QUITCHES
QUITRENT S
QUITTERS
QUITTING
QUITTORS
QUIVERED
QUIVERER S
QUIXOTES
QUIXOTIC
QUIXOTRY
QUIZZERS
QUIZZING

QUOINING
QUOITING
QUOMODOS
QUOTABLE
QUOTABLY
QUOTIENT S
QURUSHES

RACEMIZE DS
RACQUETS
RAMEQUIN S
RAZEEING
RAZORING
P READJUST S
ADJUSTER
REALIZED
REALIZER S
REALIZES
SLEAZIER
REEJECTS
REENJOYS
ENJOYERS
REEQUIPS
PERIQUES
REEXPELS
REEXPORT S
EXPORTER
P REEXPOSE DS
P REFIXING
REFLEXED
REFLEXES
REFLEXLY
REFLUXED
REFLUXES
FLEXURES
P REFREEZE S
P REFROZEN
REGLAZED
REGLAZES
REINJECT S
REINJURE DS
REINJURY
REJACKET S
REJECTED
REJECTEE S
REJECTER S
REJECTOR S
REJIGGED
JIGGERED
REJIGGER S
REJOICED
REJOICER S
REJOICES
REJOINED
P REJUDGED
P REJUDGES
REJUGGLE DS
RELAXANT S
RELAXERS
RELAXING
RELAXINS
RELIQUES
REMARQUE S
P REMIXING
RENDZINA S
REOBJECT S
REQUESTS
QUESTERS
REQUIEMS
REQUIRED
REQUIRER S
REQUIRES
QUERIERS
REQUITAL S
QUARTILE
REQUITED
REQUITER S
REQUITES
QUIETERS
RESEIZED
RESEIZES
RESIZING
RESOJETS
RETAXING
REWAXING

REZEROED
REZEROES
REZONING
RHIZOBIA L
RHIZOIDS
RHIZOMES
RHIZOMIC
RHIZOPOD S
RHIZOPUS
RIBOZYME S
RITZIEST
ROBOTIZE DS
ROMANIZE DS
RONDEAUX
C ROQUETED
C ROQUETTE S
RORQUALS
ROULEAUX
RURALIZE DS

SALINIZE DS
SAMIZDAT S
SANITIZE DRS
SAPAJOUS
SARDONYX
SATIRIZE DRS
SAUCEBOX
SAXATILE
SAXHORNS
SAXONIES
SAXTUBAS
SCHERZOS
SCHIZIER
SCHIZOID S
SCHIZONT S
SCHMALTZ Y
SCHMALZY
SCHMELZE S
SCHMOOZE DRS
SCHMOOZY
SCHNOZES
SCRAMJET S
SCUZZIER
SEAQUAKE S
SEIZABLE
SIZEABLE
SEIZINGS
SEIZURES
SELTZERS
SEQUELAE
SEQUENCE DRS
SEQUENCY
SEQUENTS
SEQUINED
SEQUITUR S
SEQUOIAS
SERJEANT SY
SEXINESS
SEXOLOGY
SEXTAINS
SEXTANTS
SEXTARII
SEXTETTE S
SEXTILES
EXITLESS
SEXTUPLE DST
SEXTUPLY
A SEXUALLY
SFORZATO S
SHEQALIM
SHIATZUS
SHMALTZY
SHMOOZED
SHMOOZES
SIEROZEM S
SILIQUAE
SILIQUES
SILOXANE S
SILVEXES
SIMAZINE S
SIMONIZE DS
SINICIZE DS
SITZMARK S

SIXPENCE S
SIXPENNY
SIXTEENS
SIXTIETH S
SIXTYISH
SIZEABLE
SEIZABLE
SIZEABLY
SIZINESS
SIZZLERS
SIZZLING
SJAMBOKS
SKIJORER S
SKIPJACK S
SKYBOXES
SKYJACKS
SLAPJACK S
SLEAZIER
REALIZES
SLEAZILY
SLEAZOID S
DIAZOLES
SMALLPOX
SMILAXES
SNAZZIER
SNEEZERS
SNEEZIER
SNEEZING
SNOOZERS
SNOOZIER
SNOOZING
SNOOZLED
SNOOZLES
SNUFFBOX
SOBERIZE DS
SODOMIZE DS
SOJOURNS
SOLARIZE DS
SOLECIZE DS
SOLIQUID S
SOLONETZ
SOUNDBOX
SOVKHOZY
SPADIXES
SPAETZLE S
SPATZLES
SPELTZES
SPHINXES
SPHYNXES
SPINIFEX
SPOROZOA LN
SPRITZED
SPRITZER S
SPRITZES
SQUABBLE DRS
SQUADDED
SQUADRON S
SQUALENE S
SQUALLED
SQUALLER S
SQUALORS
SQUAMATE S
SQUAMOSE
SQUAMOUS
SQUANDER S
SQUARELY
SQUARERS
SQUAREST
SQUARING
SQUARISH
SQUASHED
SQUASHER S
QUASHERS
SQUASHES
SQUATTED
SQUATTER S
QUARTETS
SQUAWKED
SQUAWKER S
SQUEAKED
SQUEAKER S
SQUEALED
SQUEALER S

SQUEEGEE DS
SQUEEZED
SQUEEZER S
SQUEEZES
SQUEGGED
SQUELCHY
SQUIBBED
SQUIDDED
SQUIFFED
SQUIGGLE DS
SQUIGGLY
SQUILGEE DS
SQUILLAE
LALIQUES
SQUILLAS
SQUINTED
SQUINTER S
SQUIREEN S
ENQUIRES
E SQUIRING
SQUIRISH
SQUIRMED
SQUIRMER S
SQUIRREL SY
SQUIRTED
SQUIRTER S
SQUISHED
SQUISHES
SQUOOSHY
SQUUSHED
SQUUSHES
STANZAED
STANZAIC
STARGAZE DRS
STORAXES
STYLIZED
STYLIZER S
STYLIZES
STYRAXES
SUBAXIAL
SUBERIZE DS
SUBFIXES
SUBINDEX
SUBJECTS
SUBJOINS
SUBOXIDE S
SUBTAXON S
SUBTEXTS
SUBZONES
SUFFIXAL
SUFFIXED
SUFFIXES
SUPERFIX
SUPERJET S
SUPERSEX
SUPERTAX
SURPRIZE DS
SURTAXED
SURTAXES
SUZERAIN S
SVARAJES
SWARAJES
SWEATBOX
SWINEPOX
SWIZZLED
SWIZZLER S
SWIZZLES
SYNTAXES
SYRINXES
SYZYGIAL
SYZYGIES

TABLEAUX
TAQUERIA S
TAXABLES
TAXATION S
TAXICABS
TAXINGLY
TAXIWAYS
TAXONOMY
TAXPAYER S
TEABOXES
TEAZELED

TEAZLING
TELETEXT S
TELEXING
TEQUILAS
LIQUATES
TERRAZZO S
TETANIZE DS
TETROXID ES
TEXTBOOK S
TEXTILES
TEXTLESS
TEXTUARY
TEXTURAL
TEXTURED
TEXTURES
THEORIZE DRS
THIAZIDE S
THIAZINE S
THIAZINS
THIAZOLE S
THIAZOLS
THORAXES
OXHEARTS
THYROXIN ES
TOADFLAX
TOLARJEV
TONNEAUX
TOPAZINE
TORQUATE
TORQUERS
TORQUING
TOTALIZE DRS
TOUZLING
TOXAEMIA S
TOXAEMIC
TOXEMIAS
TOXICANT S
TOXICITY
TRAJECTS
TRANQUIL
TRANSFIX T
TRAPEZES
TRAPEZIA L
TRAPEZII
TRIAXIAL
TRIAZINE S
TRIAZINS
TRIAZOLE S
TRIOXIDE S
TRIOXIDS
TRISTEZA S
TRUMEAUX
TSARITZA S
TURBOJET S
TURQUOIS E
TUXEDOED
TUXEDOES
TWEEZERS
TWEEZING
TWINJETS
TZARDOMS
TZAREVNA S
TZARINAS
TZARISMS
TZARISTS
TZARITZA S
TZIGANES
TZITZITH

UBIQUITY
ULEXITES
UNAMAZED
UNBOXING
UNDERJAW S
UNDERTAX
UNEQUALS
UNEXOTIC
UNEXPERT
UNFIXING
UNFLEXED
UNFREEZE S
UNFROZEN
UNGAZING

UNGLAZED
UNIAXIAL
UNIONIZE DRS
UNIQUELY
UNIQUEST
UNQUIETS
UNISEXES
UNITIZED
UNITIZER S
UNITIZES
UNJAMMED
UNJOINED
UNJOINTS
UNJOYFUL
UNJUDGED
UNJUSTLY
UNMIXING
UNMUZZLE DS
UNPRIZED
UNPUZZLE DS
UNQUIETS
UNIQUEST
UNQUOTED
UNQUOTES
UNSEIZED
UNSEXING
UNSEXUAL
UNZIPPED
UPGAZING
UPSIZING
URBANIZE DS
USQUABAE S
USQUEBAE S
UTILIZED
UTILIZER S
UTILIZES
UXORIOUS

VALORIZE DS
VANQUISH
VAPORIZE DRS
VAQUEROS
VELARIZE DS
VERJUICE S
VERNIXES
VERTEXES
VEXATION S
VEXILLAR Y
VEXILLUM
VEXINGLY
VIDEOTEX T
VIRILIZE DS
VITALIZE DRS
VIXENISH
VIZARDED
VIZCACHA S
VIZIRATE S
VIZIRIAL
VIZORING
VOCALIZE DRS
VOLVOXES
VORTEXES
VOWELIZE DS

WALTZERS
WALTZING
WATERJET S
WAXBERRY
WAXBILLS
WAXINESS
WAXPLANT S
WAXWEEDS
WAXWINGS
WAXWORKS
WAXWORMS
WEAZANDS
WHEEZERS
WHEEZIER
WHEEZILY
WHEEZING
WHIZBANG S
WHIZZERS
WHIZZIER

WHIZZING
WIZARDLY
WIZARDRY
WIZENING
WOMANIZE DRS
WOOZIEST
WURTZITE S

XANTHANS
XANTHATE S
XANTHEIN S
XANTHINE
XANTHENE S
XANTHINE S
XANTHEIN
XANTHINS
XANTHOMA S
XANTHONE S
XANTHOUS
XENOGAMY
XENOGENY
XENOLITH S
XEROSERE S
XEROXING
XIPHOIDS
XYLIDINE S
XYLIDINS
XYLITOLS
XYLOCARP S
XYLOTOMY

YAHRZEIT S
YOKOZUNA S

ZABAIONE S
ZABAJONE S
ZACATONS
T ZADDIKIM
ZAIBATSU
ZAMARRAS
ZAMARROS
ZAMINDAR IS
ZANINESS
ZAPATEOS
ZAPPIEST
ZAPTIAHS
ZAPTIEHS
ZARATITE S
ZAREEBAS
ZARZUELA S
ZASTRUGA
ZASTRUGI
ZEALOTRY
ZEBRANOS
ZEBRINES
ZECCHINI
ZECCHINO S
ZECCHINS
ZELKOVAS
ZEMINDAR SY
ZEMSTVOS
ZENAIDAS
ZENITHAL
ZEOLITES
ZEOLITIC
ZEPPELIN S
ZEPPOLES
ZESTIEST
ZESTLESS
ZIBELINE S
ZIGGURAT S
ZIGZAGGY
ZIKKURAT S
ZIKURATS
ZILLIONS
ZINCATES
ZINCITES
CITIZENS
ZINCKING
ZINGIEST
ZIPPERED
ZIPPIEST
ZIRCALOY S
ZIRCONIA S
ZIRCONIC
ZITHERNS
ZIZZLING
ZODIACAL
ZOISITES
ZOMBIISM S
O ZONATION S
ZONELESS
ZONETIME S
MONETIZE
ZOOCHORE S
ZOOECIUM
ZOOGENIC
ZOOGLEAE
ZOOGLEAL
ZOOGLEAS
ZOOGLOEA ELS
ZOOLATER S
ZOOLATRY
ZOOLOGIC
ZOOMANIA S
ZOOMETRY
ZOOMORPH S
ZOONOSES
ZOONOSIS
ZOONOTIC
ZOOPHILE S
ZOOPHILY
ZOOPHOBE S
ZOOPHYTE S
ZOOSPERM S
ZOOSPORE S
ZOOTIEST
ZOOTOMIC
ZORILLAS
ZORILLES
ZORILLOS
ZUCCHINI S
ZUGZWANG S
ZWIEBACK S
ZYGOMATA
ZYGOSITY
ZYGOTENE S
ZYMOGENE S
ZYMOGENS
ZYMOGRAM S
ZYMOLOGY
ZYMOSANS
ZYZZYVAS

2-letter Words

B **AA** HLS
CDF GJK LNS TW **AB** AOSY
BCD FGH LMP RST W **AD** DOSZ
GHK MNS TW **AE**
BDF GHJ LMN RST WYZ **AG** AEOS
ABD HNP RY **AH** AIS
R **AI** DLMNR ST
ABD GPS **AL** ABELP ST
BCD GHJ LNP RTY **AM** AIPU
BCD FGM NPR TVW **AN** ADEIT Y
BCE FGJ LMO PTV WY **AR** BCEFK MST
ABF GHK LMP RTV WZ **AS** HKPS
BCE FGH KLM OPQ RST VW **AT** ET
CDH JLM NPR STV WY **AW** AELN
FLM PRS TWZ **AX** E
BCD FGH JKL MNP RSW Y **AY** ES
AO **BA** ADGHL MNPRS TY
O **BE** DEGLN STY
O **BI** BDGNO STZ
A **BO** ABDGO PSTWX Y
A **BY** ES
O **DE** BEFLN VWXY
AU **DO** CEGLM NRSTW
BFG LMP RTW Z **ED** HS
DKR **EF** FST
FHP Y **EH**
BCD EGM ST **EL** DFKLM S
FGH MR **EM** ESU
BDF GHK MPS TWY **EN** DGS
FHP S **ER** AEGNR S
BFH LOP RY **ES** S
BFG HJL MNP RST VWY **ET** AH
DHK LRS V **EX**
FA BDGNR STXY
FE DEHMN RSTUW YZ
AE **GO** ABDOR STXY
ASW **HA** DEGHJ MOPST WY
ST **HE** HMNPR STWXY
ACG KP **HI** CDEMN PST
O **HM** M
MOR TW **HO** BDEGN PSTWY
ABD FGH KLM RVY **ID** S
DKR **IF** FS
ABD FGH JKL PRS TWY Z **IN** KNS
ABC DHK LMP QST VWX **IS** M
ABD FGH KLN PST WZ **IT** S
JO BEGTW Y
OS **KA** BEFST Y
S **KI** DFNPR ST
A **LA** BCDGM PRSTV WXY
LI BDENP ST
LO BGOPT WX
A **MA** CDEGN PRSTW XY
E **ME** DGLMN TW
A **MI** BCDGL MRSX
HU **MM**
MO ABCDG LMNOP RSTW
AE **MU** DGMNS T
MY C
A **NA** BEGHM NPWY
AO **NE** BEGTW
O **NO** BDGHM ORSTW
G **NU** BNST
BCG HMN PRS TY **OD** ADES
DFH JRT VW **OE** S
OF FT
FNO P **OH** MOS
KP **OI** L
DMN PRS TY **OM** S
CDE FHI MST WY **ON** EOS
BCF HKL MPS TW **OP** EST
CDF GKM NT **OR** ABCES T
BCD GHK MNS W **OS** E
BCD HJL MNP RST VWY **OW** ELN
BCF GLP SV **OX** OY
BCF GHJ ST **OY**
S **PA** CDHLM NPRST WXY
AO **PE** ACDEG HNPRS TW
PI ACEGN PSTUX
QI S
AEI O **RE** BCDEF GIMPS TVX
A **SH** AEHY
P **SI** BCMNP RSTX
SO BDLMN PSTUW XY
EU **TA** BDEGJ MNOPR STUVW X
TI CELNP ST
TO DEGMN OPRTW Y
DH **UH**
BCG HLM RSV Y **UM** MP
BDF GHJ MNP RST **UN** S
CDH PST Y **UP** OS
BJM NP **US** E
BCG HJM NOP RT **UT** AES
AEO **WE** BDENT
T **WO** EGKNO PSTW
XI S
XU
PR **YA** GHKMP RWY
ABD EKL PRT W **YE** AHNPS TW
YO BDKMN UW
ZA GPSX

3-letter Words

AAH S
B **AAL** S
BK **AAS**
B **ABA** S
ABO S
CDF GJK LNS TW **ABS**
BG **ABY** ES
DFL MPR T **ACE** DS
FPT **ACT** AS
ADD S
DF **ADO** S
BCD FGL MPR TW **ADS**
ADZ E
BCD GNR WY **AFF**
DHR W **AFT**
GRS **AGA** RS
CGM PRS W **AGE** DERS
DS **AGO** GN
BDF GHJ LMN RST WYZ **AGS**
H **AHA**
AHI S
ADH **AHS**
CLM PQR S **AID** ES
BFH JKM NPR STV W **AIL** S
M **AIM** S
CFG KLM PRS TVW **AIN** S
FHL MPV W **AIR** NSTY
DR **AIS**
BGW **AIT** S
GNT **ALA** ENRS
ALB AS
BDG HKM PRS TVW **ALE** CEFS
BCF GHL MPS TW **ALL** SY
PS **ALP** S
ABD GPS **ALS** O
HMS **ALT** OS
GLM **AMA** HS
KR **AMI** ADEN RS
CDG LRS TV **AMP** S
AMU S
KMN **ANA** LS
BHL RSW **AND** S
BCF GJK LMP SVW **ANE** SW
BR **ANI** LS
CHP RW **ANT** AEIS
MWZ **ANY**
CGJ NRT **APE** DRSX
C **APO** DS
APP S
R **APT**
BCD G **ARB** S
MN **ARC** HOS
BCD FHM PRT WY **ARE** AS
BZ **ARF** S
BCD HLM NPS W **ARK** S
BFH W **ARM** SY
BCE GJL MOP TVW **ARS** E
CDF HKM PTW **ART** SY
BCD FGH LMP RSW **ASH** Y
BCM T **ASK** S
GHR W **ASP** S
BLM PST **ASS**
BCD FGH LMP RST **ATE** S
BMW **ATT**
JW **AUK** S
FJK L **AVA**
CEF GHL NPR SW **AVE** RS
AVO SW
AWA Y
AWE DES
BPW Y **AWL** S
DFL MPS Y **AWN** SY
AXE DLS
AYE S
BCD FGH JKL MNP RSW Y **AYS**
AZO N
BAA LS
BAD ES
BAG S
BAH T
BAL DEKL MS
BAM S
BAN DEGI KS
BAP S
K **BAR** BDEF KMNS
AO **BAS** EHKS T
BAT EHST
BAY S
A **BED** SU
BEE FNPR ST
BEG S
BEL LST
BEN DEST
O **BES** T
A **BET** AHS
O **BEY** S
BIB BS
BID EIS
BIG S
BIN DEST
BIO GS
IO **BIS** EK
O **BIT** EST
BIZ E
BOA RST
BOB S
BOD ESY
BOG SY
BOO BKMN RST
BOP S
A **BOS** HKS
BOT AHST
BOW LS
BOX Y
BOY OS
BRA DEGN STWY
BRO OSW
BRR R
BUB OSU
BUD S
BUG S
BUM FPS
BUN ADGK NST
BUR ABDG LNPR SY
BUS HKST Y
A **BUT** EST
BUY S
A **BYE** S
A **BYS**
S **CAB** S
S **CAD** EIS
S **CAM** EOPS
S **CAN** EST
CAP EHOS
S **CAR** BDEK LNPR ST
S **CAT** ES
CAW S
CAY S
CEE S
CEL LST
CEP ES
CHI ACDN PST
CIG S
CIS T
COB BS
COD AES
COG S
COL ADES TY
I **CON** EIKN SY
COO FKLN PST
S **COP** ESY
COR DEFK MNSY
COS HSTY
S **COT** ES
S **COW** LSY
COX A
COY S
COZ Y
E **CRU** DSX
S **CRY**
CUB ES
S **CUD** S
CUE DS
S **CUM**
S **CUP** S
CUR BDEF LNRS T
S **CUT** ES
CWM S
DAB S
DAD AOS
DAG OS
O **DAH** LS
DAK S
DAL ES
DAM ENPS
DAN GKS
DAP S
DAW KNST
DAY S
DEB ST
DEE DMPR ST
DEF ITY
DEL EFIL ST
DEN EIST Y
DEV AS
DEW SY
DEX Y
DEY S
DIB S
DID OY
DIE DLST
DIF FS
DIG S
DIM ES
DIN EGKO ST
DIP ST
DIS CHKS
AE **DIT** AESZ
DOC KS
DOE RS
DOG ESY
I **DOL** ELST
DOM ES
U **DON** AEGS
O **DOR** EKMP RSY
AU **DOS** EST
DOT EHSY
DOW NS
DRY S
DUB S
DUD ES
DUE LST
DUG S
DUH
DUI T
DUN EGKS T
DUO S
DUP ES
DYE DRS
BDF GHL NPR STW Y **EAR** LNS
BFH MNP ST **EAT** HS
B **EAU** X
EBB S
ECU S
EDH S
BFG MPR TWZ **EDS**
GKL MPR SW **EEK**
FHK PRS TW **EEL** SY
T **EFF** S
KR **EFS**
DHL RW **EFT** S
TY **EGG** SY
S **EGO** S
DLP **EKE** DS
GHM VWY **ELD** S
DPS **ELF**
Y **ELK** S
BCD FHJ MST WY **ELL** S
H **ELM** SY
BCD EGM ST **ELS** E
DFH MS **EME** SU
FGH MR **EMS**
EMU S
BFL MPR STV W **END** S
ENG S
BDF GHK LPT WY **ENS**
AJN P **EON** S
SV **ERA** S
CDF HMP SW **ERE**
B **ERG** OS
FHK T **ERN** ES
ERR S
HS **ERS** T
CFJ LMN **ESS**
BFG MSZ **ETA** S
BHM T **ETH** S
N **EVE** NRS
EWE RS
EYE DNRS
FAB S
FAD EOS
FAG S
FAN EGOS
A **FAR** DELM OT
FAS HT
FAT ES
FAX
O **FAY** S
FED S
FEE BDLS T
FEH S
FEM ES
FEN DS
FER EN
FES ST
FET AES
FEU DS
FEW
FEY
FEZ
FIB S

Front	Word	Back
	FID	OS
	FIE	F
	FIG	S
	FIL	AELMOS
	FIN	DEKOS
	FIR	EMNS
	FIT	S
	FIX	T
	FIZ	Z
	FLU	BESX
	FLY	
	FOB	S
	FOE	S
	FOG	SY
	FOH	N
	FON	DST
	FOP	S
	FOR	ABDEKMT
	FOU	LR
	FOX	Y
	FOY	S
	FRO	EGMW
	FRY	
	FUB	S
	FUD	S
	FUG	SU
	FUN	DKS
	FUR	LSY
	GAB	SY
E	GAD	IS
	GAE	DNS
	GAG	AES
E	GAL	AELS
O	GAM	ABEPSY
	GAN	EG
	GAP	ESY
A	GAR	BS
A	GAS	HPT
	GAT	ES
	GAY	S
A	GED	S
AO	GEE	DKSZ
	GEL	DST
	GEM	S
	GEN	ESTU
	GET	AS
	GEY	
	GHI	S
	GIB	ES
	GID	S
	GIE	DNS
	GIG	AS
A	GIN	KS
	GIP	S
	GIT	ES
	GNU	S
	GOA	DLST
	GOB	OSY
	GOD	S
	GOO	DFKNPS
	GOR	EMPY
E	GOS	H
	GOT	H
	GOX	
	GOY	S
	GUL	FLPS
	GUM	S
	GUN	KS
	GUT	S
	GUV	S
	GUY	S
	GYM	S
	GYP	S
CS	HAD	EJ
T	HAE	DMNST
S	HAG	S
S	HAH	AS
	HAJ	IJ
CSW	HAM	ES
C	HAO	
CW	HAP	S
	HAS	HPT
CGKPSTW	HAT	EHS
CST	HAW	KS
CS	HAY	S
	HEH	S
AT	HEM	EPS
TW	HEN	ST
	HEP	
	HER	BDELMNOS
S	HES	T
KW	HET	HS
CPSTW	HEW	NS
	HEX	
TW	HEY	
C	HIC	K
CW	HID	E
	HIE	DS
SW	HIM	S
CSTW	HIN	DST
CSW	HIP	S
ACGKPT	HIS	NST
CSW	HIT	S
	HMM	
	HOB	OS
S	HOD	S
S	HOE	DRS
S	HOG	GS
CP	HON	EGKS
CSW	HOP	ES
MR	HOS	ET
PS	HOT	S
CDS	HOW	EFKLS
A	HOY	AS
C	HUB	S
	HUE	DS
CT	HUG	ES
	HUH	
C	HUM	PS
S	HUN	GHKST
W	HUP	
BPS	HUT	S
	HYP	EOS
BDFLMNPRSV	ICE	DS
LRW	ICH	S
DHKLMNPRSTW	ICK	Y
	ICY	
ABFGKLMRVY	IDS	
BDJMRT	IFF	Y
DKR	IFS	
M	IGG	S
BMS	ILK	AS
BDFGHJKMNPRSTVWYZ	ILL	SY
GJLPSW	IMP	IS
DFGJKLMOPRSW	INK	SY
JL	INN	S
ABDFGHJKLPRSTWYZ	INS	
CLP	ION	S
CDFHLMSTW	IRE	DS
BDKM	IRK	S
J	ISM	S
ABDFGHKLNPSTWZ	ITS	
JT	IVY	
	JAB	S
	JAG	GS
	JAM	BS
A	JAR	LS
	JAW	S
	JAY	S
A	JEE	DPRSZ
	JET	ES
	JEU	X
	JEW	S
	JIB	BES
	JIG	S
D	JIN	KNSX
	JOB	S
	JOE	SY
	JOG	S
	JOT	AS
	JOW	LS
	JOY	S
	JUG	AS
	JUN	K
	JUS	T
	JUT	ES
	KAB	S
	KAE	S
	KAF	S
OS	KAS	
IS	KAT	AS
O	KAY	OS
	KEA	S
	KEF	S
S	KEG	S
	KEN	OST
S	KEP	IST
	KEX	
	KEY	S
	KHI	S
S	KID	S
	KIF	S
AS	KIN	ADEGKOS
S	KIP	S
	KIR	KNS
S	KIS	ST
S	KIT	EHS
	KOA	NS
	KOB	OS
	KOI	S
	KOP	HS
	KOR	AES
	KOS	S
	KUE	S
	KYE	S
BFS	LAB	S
	LAC	EKSY
CG	LAD	ESY
CFS	LAG	S
BCFGS	LAM	ABEPS
CFS	LAP	S
A	LAR	DIKS
A	LAS	EHST
BFPS	LAT	EHISU
	LAV	AES
BCFS	LAW	NS
F	LAX	
CFPS	LAY	S
FIOP	LEA	DFKLNPRS
BFGPS	LED	
AFG	LEE	KRST
G	LEG	S
	LEI	S
	LEK	ESU
AO	LES	ST
B	LET	S
	LEU	D
	LEV	AOY
FIP	LEX	
FG	LEY	S
	LEZ	
G	LIB	S
S	LID	OS
P	LIE	DFNRSU
B	LIN	EGKNOSTY
BCFS	LIP	AES
	LIS	PT
AFS	LIT	ESU
BGS	LOB	EOS
BCFS	LOG	EOSY
	LOO	FKMNPST
CFGPS	LOP	ES
BCPS	LOT	AHIS
ABFGPS	LOW	ENS
	LOX	
GPS	LUG	ES
AGPS	LUM	APS
	LUV	S
F	LUX	E
	LYE	S
	MAC	EHKS
	MAD	ES
	MAE	S
	MAG	EIS
	MAN	AEOSY
	MAP	S
	MAR	ACEKLST
A	MAS	AHKST
	MAT	EHST
	MAW	NS
	MAX	I
	MAY	AOS
	MED	S
	MEG	AS
	MEL	DLST
	MEM	EOS
AO	MEN	DOU
	MET	AEH
S	MEW	LS
	MHO	S
	MIB	S
E	MIC	AEKS
AI	MID	IS
	MIG	GS
	MIL	DEKLOST
	MIM	E
AE	MIR	EIKSY
A	MIS	EOST
	MIX	T
	MOA	NST
	MOB	S
	MOC	KS
	MOD	EIS
S	MOG	S
	MOL	ADELSTY
	MOM	EIS
	MON	KOSY
	MOO	DLNRST
	MOP	ESY
	MOR	AENST
	MOS	HKST
	MOT	EHST
	MOW	NS
	MUD	S
S	MUG	GS
	MUM	MPSU
	MUN	IS
AE	MUS	EHKST
S	MUT	EST
	MYC	S
	NAB	ES
	NAE	
S	NAG	S
	NAH	
	NAM	E
	NAN	AS
KS	NAP	AES
GS	NAW	
	NAY	S
	NEB	S
K	NEE	DMP
	NEG	S
	NET	ST
AK	NEW	ST
S	NIB	S
A	NIL	LS
	NIM	S
S	NIP	AS
KSU	NIT	ES
	NIX	EY
KS	NOB	S
	NOD	EIS
S	NOG	GS
	NOH	
	NOM	AES
	NOO	KN
	NOR	IM
O	NOS	EHY
KS	NOT	AE
EKS	NOW	ST
	NTH	
S	NUB	S
	NUN	S
AGO	NUS	
	NUT	S
L	OAF	S
S	OAK	SY
BHRS	OAR	S
BCDGM	OAT	HS
S	OBA	S
LR	OBE	SY
	OBI	AST
CLS	OCA	S
CS	ODA	HS
	ODD	S
BCLMNR	ODE	AS
BCGHMNPRSTY	ODS	
DFGHJNRTVW	OES	
BCDT	OFF	S
CLST	OFT	
	OHM	S
BC	OHO	
O	OHS	
BCFMNRST	OIL	SY
	OKA	SY
CHJMPSTWY	OKE	HS
BCFGHMSTW	OLD	SY
BCDHJMPRSTV	OLE	AOS
DMNPRST	OMS	
BCDGHLNPSTZ	ONE	S
M	ONO	S
CDEFHIMPSTW	ONS	
P	OOH	S
BCFHLMRST	OOT	S
CDHLMNPRT	OPE	DNS
BCFHKLMOPSTW	OPS	
	OPT	S
BFHKMST	ORA	DL
FS	ORB	SY
T	ORC	AS
BCDFGKLMPSTWY	ORE	S
CDKMT	ORS	
BFMPSTW	ORT	S
DHLNPR	OSE	S
L	OUD	S
DFHLPSTY	OUR	S
BGLPRT	OUT	S
N	OVA	L
HLY	OWE	DS
BCFHJY	OWL	S
DGLMST	OWN	S
	OXO	
BDFP	OXY	
	PAC	AEKSTY
	PAD	IS
O	PAH	
O	PAL	ELMPSY
S	PAM	S
S	PAN	EGST
	PAP	AS
S	PAR	ADEKRST
SU	PAS	EHST
S	PAT	EHSY
	PAW	LNS
	PAX	
S	PAY	S
	PEA	GKLNRST
S	PEC	HKS
AOS	PED	S
E	PEE	DKLNPRS
	PEG	S
	PEH	S
O	PEN	DST
	PEP	OS
A	PER	EIKMPTV
AO	PES	OT
	PET	S
S	PEW	S
	PHI	SZ
	PHT	
	PIA	LNS
ES	PIC	AEKS
	PIE	DRS
	PIG	S
S	PIN	AEGKSTY
	PIP	ESY
	PIS	HOS
S	PIT	AHSY
	PIU	
	PIX	Y
	PLY	
A	POD	S
	POH	
	POI	S
	POL	ELOSY
	POM	EOPS
	POO	DFHLNPRS
	POP	ES
S	POT	S
	POW	S
	POX	Y
	PRO	ADFGMPSW
S	PRY	
	PSI	S
	PST	
	PUB	S
S	PUD	S
	PUG	HS
	PUL	AEILPS
S	PUN	AGKSTY
	PUP	ASU
S	PUR	EILRS
O	PUS	HS
	PUT	STZ
	PYA	S
	PYE	S
	PYX	
	QAT	S
	QIS	
A	QUA	DGIY
BGOT	RAD	S
BCDF	RAG	AEGIS
	RAH	
	RAI	ADLNS
	RAJ	A
CDGPT	RAM	IPS
BG	RAN	DGIKT
CFTW	RAP	EST
BE	RAS	EHP
BDFGP	RAT	EHOS
BCD	RAW	S
	RAX	
BDFGPT	RAY	AS
	REB	S
	REC	KS
BCI	RED	DEOS
BDFGPT	REE	DFKLS
T	REF	ST
D	REG	S
	REI	FNS
	REM	S
P	REP	OPS
AIOT	RES	HT
FT	RET	ES
	REV	S
P	REX	
	RHO	S
A	RIA	LS
CD	RIB	S
AGI	RID	ES
	RIF	EFST
BFGPT	RIG	S
BGPT	RIM	ESY
BG	RIN	DGKS
DGT	RIP	ES
	ROB	ES
C	ROC	KS
PT	ROD	ES
F	ROE	S
FP	ROM	PS
GT	ROT	AEILOS
BCFGPTV	ROW	S
DG	RUB	ESY
GT	RUE	DRS
DFT	RUG	AS
ADG	RUM	PS
	RUN	EGST
B	RUT	HS
	RYA	S
	RYE	S
	SAB	ES
	SAC	KS
	SAD	EI
	SAE	
	SAG	AEOSY
	SAL	ELPST
	SAP	S
	SAT	EI
	SAU	L
	SAW	NS
	SAX	
	SAY	S
A	SEA	LMRST
	SEC	ST
	SEE	DKLMNPRS
	SEG	OS
	SEI	FS
	SEL	FLS
	SEN	DET
U	SER	AEFS
	SET	AST
	SEW	NS
	SEX	TY
	SHA	DGHMTWY
	SHE	ADSW
	SHH	
A	SHY	
	SIB	BS
	SIC	EKS
	SIM	APS
	SIN	EGHKS
	SIP	ES
	SIR	ES
P	SIS	
	SIT	EHS
	SIX	
	SKA	GST
	SKI	DMNPST
	SKY	
	SLY	
	SOB	AS
	SOD	AS
	SOL	ADEIOS
	SOM	AES
	SON	EGS
	SOP	HS
	SOS	
	SOT	HS
	SOU	KLPRS
	SOW	NS
	SOX	
	SOY	AS
	SPA	EMNRSTYZ
E	SPY	
	SRI	S
	STY	E
	SUB	AS
	SUE	DRST
	SUK	S
	SUM	OPS
	SUN	GKNS
	SUP	ES
	SUQ	S
	SYN	CE
S	TAB	SU
	TAD	S
	TAE	L
S	TAG	S
	TAJ	
	TAM	EPS
	TAN	GKS
	TAO	S
A	TAP	AES
S	TAR	ENOPST
EU	TAS	KS
S	TAT	ES
	TAU	ST
	TAV	S
S	TAW	S
	TAX	AI
	TEA	KLMRST
	TED	S
	TEE	DLMNS
	TEG	GS
	TEL	AELS
	TEN	DST
S	TET	HS
S	TEW	S
	THE	EMNWY
	THO	U
	THY	
EO	TIC	KS
	TIE	DRS
	TIL	ELST

2006 Addition

TIN EGSTY
TIP IS
TIS
TIT IS
TOD SY
TOE ADS
TOG AS
A **TOM** BES
TON EGSY
TOO KLMNT
AS **TOP** EHIOS
TOR ACEINORSTY
S **TOT** ES
S **TOW** NSY
TOY OS
TRY
TSK S
S **TUB** AES
TUG S
EP **TUI** S
S **TUN** AEGS
TUP S
TUT SU
TUX
TWA EST
TWO S
S **TYE** ERS
JK **UDO** NS
PSV **UGH** S
CDJNP **UKE** S
LS **ULU** S
M **UMM**
BDHJLMPRST **UMP** S
BDFGHMNPRST **UNS**
UPO N
CDPSTY **UPS**
BC **URB** S
BCNST **URD** S
BCDT **URN** S
B **URP** S
FMR **USE** DRS
UTA S
BCJLM **UTE** S
BCGHJMNOPRT **UTS**
VAC S
VAN EGS
VAR ASY
K **VAS** AET
VAT SU
VAU S
VAV S
VAW S
VEE PRS
VEG
VET OS
VEX T
VIA L
A **VID** ES
VIE DRSW
VIG AS
VIM S
VIS AE
VOE S
A **VOW** S
VOX
VUG GHS
O **VUM**
S **WAB** S
WAD EISY
T **WAE** S
S **WAG** ES
HS **WAN** DEKSTY
S **WAP** S
WAR DEKMNPSTY
T **WAS** HPT
ST **WAT** ST
WAW LS
WAX Y
AS **WAY** S
WEB S
AO **WED** S
AT **WEE** DKLNPRST
WEN DST
WET S
WHA MPT
WHO AMP
WHY S
ST **WIG** S
T **WIN** DEGKOSY
IY **WIS** EHPST
T **WIT** EHS
WIZ
WOE S
WOG S
WOK ES
WON KST
WOO DFLS
S **WOP** S
T **WOS** T
S **WOT** S
WOW S
A **WRY**
WUD
WYE S
WYN DNS
A **XIS**
YAG IS
A **YAH**
K **YAK** S
YAM S
YAP S
K **YAR** DEN
YAW LNPS
YAY S
YEA HNRS
YEH
E **YEN** S
YEP S
ABDEKLOPRTW **YES**
YET IT
YEW S
YID S
APT **YIN** S
YIP ES
YOB S
YOD HS
YOK ES
YOM
YON DI
YOU RS
YOW ELS
YUK S
YUM
YUP S
ZAG S
ZAP S
ZAS
ZAX
ZED S
ZEE S
ZEK S
ZEP S
ZIG S
ZIN CEGS
ZIP S
ZIT IS
ZOA
ZOO MNS
ZUZ
ZZZ

4-letter Words

AAHS
B **AALS**
B **ABAS** EH
ABBA S
ABBE SY
S **ABED**
ABET S
CFGST **ABLE** DRS
ABLY
ABOS
ABRI S
ABUT S
ABYE S
ABYS MS
FLMPR **ACED**
DFLMPRT **ACES**
CMT **ACHE** DS
ACHY
ACID SY
ACME S
ACNE DS
N **ACRE** DS
ACTA
FPT **ACTS**
ACYL S
ADDS
ADIT S
DF **ADOS**
ADZE DS
P **AEON** S
AERO
F **AERY**
AFAR S
AGAR S
RS **AGAS**
CGPRW **AGED**
R **AGEE**
CEGJLPSWY **AGER** S
CGMPRSW **AGES**
AGHA S
F **AGIN** G
AGIO S
AGLY
M **AGMA** S
AGOG
W **AGON** ESY
V **AGUE** S
A **AHED**
AHEM
AHIS
AHOY
AIDE DRS
CMQRS **AIDS**
BFHJKMNPRSTVW **AILS**
M **AIMS**
CGKMPRSTW **AINS**
BC **AIRN** S
FHLMPVW **AIRS**
AIRT HS
DFH **AIRY**
BGW **AITS**
AJAR
AJEE
R **AKEE** S
T **AKIN**
ALAE
ALAN DEGST
MT **ALAR** MY
BGNT **ALAS**
ALBA S
ALBS
ALEC S
ALEE
ALEF S
BDGHKMPRSTVW **ALES**
ALFA S
ALGA ELS
CK **ALIF** S
ALIT
BT **ALKY** DL
BCFGHLMPTW **ALLS**
BDGPRSTW **ALLY** L
H **ALMA** HS
ALME HS
BCHMP **ALMS**
ALOE S
ALOW
PS **ALPS**
ALSO
ALTO S
HMS **ALTS**
ALUM S
AMAH S
CGLM **AMAS** S
MS **AMBO** S
RY **AMEN** DST
LZ **AMIA** S
AMID EOS
MR **AMIE** S
G **AMIN** EOS
AMIR S
T **AMIS** S
AMMO S
AMOK S
CDGLRSTV **AMPS**
RW **AMUS** E
AMYL S
BC **ANAL**
KMN **ANAS**
BHLRSW **ANDS**
BCFJKLMPSVW **ANES**
ANEW
FMPST **ANGA** S
ANIL ES
R **ANIS** E
ANKH S
CM **ANNA** LS
ANOA S
CF **ANON**
H **ANSA** E
M **ANTA** ES
ANTE DS
ANTI CS
CHPRW **ANTS** Y
M **ANUS**
CGJRT **APED**
CGJPRT **APER** SY
CGJNRT **APES**
APEX
APOD S
C **APOS**
APPS
L **APSE** S
AQUA ES
ARAK S
BCDG **ARBS**
LMP **ARCH**
N **ARCO**
MN **ARCS**
AREA ELS
BCDFHLMNPRTW **ARES**
BZ **ARFS**
MV **ARIA** S
ARID
ARIL S
BCDHLMNPSW **ARKS**
BFHW **ARMS**
B **ARMY**
CMP **ARSE** S
CDFHKMPTW **ARTS** Y
PTW **ARTY**
L **ARUM** S
P **ARVO** S
ARYL S
ASCI
ASEA
DMW **ASHY**
BCMT **ASKS**
GHRW **ASPS**
W **ATAP** S
BCDFGHMNPRST **ATES**
ATMA NS
ATOM SY
ATOP Y
JW **AUKS**
CFY **AULD**
DGHJTV **AUNT** SY
L **AURA** ELRS
AUTO S
CHLPRSW **AVER** ST
CEFHLNOPRSW **AVES**
P **AVID**
AVOS
AVOW S
AWAY
CDHJLMPSTY **AWED**
AWEE
AWES
BPWY **AWLS**
DFLPY **AWNS**
FLT **AWNY**
AWOL S
AWRY
AXAL
FMRTW **AXED**
AXEL S
FLMPRSTWZ **AXES**
AXIL ES
MT **AXIS**
AXLE DS
T **AXON** ES
R **AYAH** S
AYES
LZ **AYIN** S
H **AZAN** S
AZON S
BAAL S
BAAS
BABA S
BABE LS
BABU LS
BABY
BACH
A **BACK** S
BADE
BADS
BAFF SY
BAGS
BAHT S
BAIL S
BAIT HS
BAKE DRS
BALD SY
BALE DRS
BALK SY
BALL SY
BALM SY
BALS A
BAMS
BAND ASY
BANE DS
BANG S
BANI
BANK S
BANS
BAPS
BARB ES
BARD ES
BARE DRS
BARF S
BARK SY
BARM SY
BARN SY
K **BARS**
A **BASE** DRS
A **BASH**
BASK S
BASS IOY
BAST ES
A **BATE** DS
BATH ES
BATS
BATT SUY
BAUD S
BAWD SY
BAWL S
BAYS
BEAD SY
BEAK SY
A **BEAM** SY
BEAN OS
BEAR DS
BEAT S
BEAU STX
BECK S
BEDS
BEDU
BEEF SY
BEEN
BEEP S
BEER SY
BEES
BEET S
BEGS
BELL ESY
BELS
BELT S
BEMA S
BEND SY
BENE S
BENS
BENT OS
BERG S
BERK S
BERM ES
BEST S
BETA S
BETH S
A **BETS**
BEVY
O **BEYS**
BHUT S
O **BIAS**
BIBB S
BIBS
BICE PS
A **BIDE** DRST
BIDI S
BIDS
BIER S
BIFF SY
BIGS
BIKE DRS
BILE S
BILK S
BILL SY
BIMA HS
BIND IS
BINE RS
BINS
BINT S
BIOG S
BIOS
BIRD S
BIRK S
BIRL ES
BIRO S
BIRR S
BISE S
BISK S
BITE RS
O **BITS** Y
BITT SY
BIZE S
BLAB S
BLAE
BLAH S
BLAM ES
BLAT ES
BLAW NS
BLEB S
A **BLED**
BLET S
BLEW
BLIN DIK
BLIP S
BLOB S
BLOC KS
BLOG S
BLOT S
BLOW NSY
BLUB S
BLUE DRSTY
BLUR BST
BOAR DST
BOAS T
BOAT S
BOBS
BOCK S
A **BODE** DS
BODS
BODY
BOFF OS
BOGS
BOGY
BOHO S
A **BOIL** S
BOLA RS
BOLD S
O **BOLE** S
BOLL S
BOLO S
BOLT S
BOMB ES
BOND S
BONE DRSY
BONG OS
BONK S
E **BONY**
BOOB SY
E **BOOK** S
BOOM SY
A **BOON** S
BOOR S
BOOS T
BOOT HSY
BOPS
BORA LSX
BORE DRS
BORK S
BORN E
A **BORT** SYZ
BOSH
BOSK SY
BOSS Y
BOTA S
BOTH Y
BOTS
BOTT S
A **BOUT** S
BOWL S
BOWS E
BOXY
BOYO S
BOYS
BOZO S
BRAD S
BRAE S
BRAG S
BRAN DKST
BRAS HS
BRAT S
BRAW LNS
BRAY S
BRED E
BREE DS
BREN ST
BREW S
BRIE FRS
BRIG S
BRIM S
BRIN EGKSY
BRIO S
A **BRIS** KS
BRIT HST
BROO DKMS
BROS EY
BROW NS
BRRR
BRUT ES
BRUX
BUBO
BUBS
BUBU S
BUCK OS
BUDS
BUFF IOSY
BUGS
BUHL S
BUHR S
BULB S
BULK SY

BULL ASY
BUMF S
BUMP HSY
BUMS
BUNA S
BUND ST
BUNG S
BUNK OS
BUNN SY
BUNS
BUNT S
BUOY S
BURA NS
BURB S
BURD S
BURG HS
BURL SY
BURN ST
BURP S
BURR OSY
BURS AET
BURY
BUSH Y
BUSK S
BUSS
BUST SY
BUSY
BUTE OS
A **BUTS**
BUTT ESY
BUYS
A **BUZZ**
A **BYES**
BYRE S
BYRL S
BYTE S

S **CABS**
CACA OS
CADE ST
CADI S
S **CADS**
CAFE S
CAFF S
CAGE DRSY
CAGY
CAID S
CAIN S
CAKE DSY
CAKY
CALF S
CALK S
S **CALL** AS
CALM S
CALO S
CALX
CAME LOS
CAMO S
S **CAMP** IOSY
S **CAMS**
CANE DRS
S **CANS** OT
S **CANT** OSY
S **CAPE** DRS
CAPH S
CAPO NS
CAPS
CARB OS
CARD S
S **CARE** DRSTX
CARK S
CARL ES
CARN SY
S **CARP** IS
CARR SY
S **CARS** E
S **CART** ES
CASA S
CASE DS
CASH

CASK SY
CAST ES
CATE RS
S **CATS**
CAUL DKS
CAVE DRS
CAVY
CAWS
CAYS
CECA L
CEDE DRS
CEDI S
CEES
CEIL IS
CELL AIOS

CELS
CELT S
S **CENT** OSU
CEPE S
CEPS
CERE DS
CERO S
CESS
CETE S
CHAD S
CHAI NRS
CHAM PS
CHAO S
CHAP EST
CHAR DEKMRSTY

CHAT S
CHAW S
CHAY S
CHEF S
CHEW SY
CHEZ
CHIA OS
CHIC AKOS
CHID E
CHIN AEKOS
CHIP S
CHIS
CHIT S
CHON
CHOP S
CHOW S
CHUB S
CHUG S
CHUM PS
CIAO
CIGS
CINE S
S **CION** S
CIRE S
CIST S
CITE DRS
CITY
Y **CLAD** ES
CLAG S
CLAM PS
CLAN GKS
CLAP ST
CLAW S
CLAY S
CLEF ST
CLEW S
CLIP ST
CLOD S
CLOG S
CLON EKS
CLOP S
CLOT HS
CLOY S
CLUB S
CLUE DS
COAL ASY
COAT IS
COAX

COBB SY
COBS
COCA S
A **COCK** SY
COCO AS
CODA S
CODE CDNRSX

CODS
COED S
S **COFF** S
COFT
COGS
COHO GS
COIF S
COIL S
COIN S
COIR S
COKE DS
COKY
COLA S
AS **COLD** S
COLE DS
COLS
COLT S
COLY
COMA ELS
COMB EOS
COME RST
COMP OST
S **CONE** DSY
CONI CN
CONK SY
CONN S
I **CONS**
CONY
COOF S
COOK SY
COOL SY
COON S
S **COOP** ST
COOS
S **COOT** S
S **COPE** DNRS
S **COPS** E
COPY
CORD S
S **CORE** DRS
CORF
CORK SY
CORM S
AS **CORN** SUY
CORS E
CORY
COSH
COSS
COST AS
COSY
COTE DS
S **COTS**
COUP ES
COVE DNRSTY
S **COWL** S
S **COWS**
COWY
COXA EL
COYS
COZY
CRAB S
S **CRAG** S
S **CRAM** PS
S **CRAP** ES
CRAW LS
A **CRED** OS
S **CREW** S
CRIB S
CRIS P
CRIT S
CROC IKS
CROP S
CROW DNS

CRUD ES
E **CRUS** EHT
CRUX
CUBE BDRS

CUBS
S **CUDS**
CUED
CUES
S **CUFF** S
CUIF S
CUKE S
S **CULL** SY
CULM S
CULT IS
CUNT S
S **CUPS**
CURB S
CURD SY
CURE DRST
S **CURF** S
CURL SY
CURN S
CURR SY
CURS ET
CURT
CUSK S
CUSP S
CUSS O
AS **CUTE** RSY
S **CUTS**
CWMS
CYAN OS
CYMA ERS
CYME S
CYST S
CZAR S

DABS
DACE S
DADA S
DADO S
DADS
DAFF SY
DAFT
DAGO S
DAGS
DAHL S
O **DAHS**
DAIS Y
DAKS
DALE S
DALS
DAME S
DAMN S
DAMP S
DAMS
DANG S
DANK
DANS
DAPS
DARB S
DARE DRS
DARK SY
DARN S
DART S
DASH IY
DATA
DATE DRS
DATO S
DAUB ESY
DAUT S
DAVY
DAWK S
DAWN S
DAWS
DAWT S
DAYS
DAZE DS
DEAD S
DEAF
I **DEAL** ST

DEAN S
DEAR SY
DEBS
DEBT S
DECK S
DECO RSY
DEED SY
A **DEEM** S
DEEP S
DEER S
DEES
DEET S
DEFI S
DEFT
DEFY
DEIL S
DEKE DS
DELE DS
DELF ST
DELI S
DELL SY
DELS
DELT AS
DEME S
DEMO BNS
DEMY
DENE S
DENI M
DENS E
DENT S
DENY
DERE
DERM AS
DESK S
DEVA S
DEVS
DEWS
DEWY
DEXY
DEYS
DHAK S
DHAL S
DHOW S
DIAL S
DIBS
DICE DRSY
DICK SY
DIDO S
DIDY
DIED
DIEL
DIES
DIET S
DIFF S
DIFS
DIGS
DIKE DRSY
DILL SY
DIME RS
DIMS
DINE DRS
DING EOSY
DINK SY
DINO S
DINS
DINT S
DIOL S
DIPS O
DIPT
DIRE R
DIRK S
DIRL S
DIRT SY
DISC IOS
DISH Y
DISK S
DISS
DITA S
DITE S
AE **DITS** Y

DITZ Y
DIVA NS
DIVE DRS
DJIN NS
DOAT S
DOBY
DOCK S
DOCS
DODO S
DOER S
DOES T
DOFF S
DOGE SY
DOGS
DOGY
DOIT S
DOJO S
DOLE DS
DOLL SY
I **DOLS**
DOLT S
DOME DS
DOMS
DONA S
DONE E
DONG AS
U **DONS** Y
DOOM SY
DOOR S
DOPA S
DOPE DRSY
DOPY
A **DORE**
DORK SY
DORM SY
DORP S
DORR S
O **DORS** A
DORY
DOSE DRS
DOSS
DOST
DOTE DRS
DOTH
DOTS
DOTY
DOUM AS
O **DOUR** A
DOUX
DOVE NS
A **DOWN** SY
DOWS E
DOXY
A **DOZE** DNRS
DOZY
DRAB S
DRAG S
DRAM AS
DRAT S
DRAW LNS
DRAY S
DREE DS
DREG S
DREK S
DREW
DRIB S
DRIP ST
DROP ST
DRUB S
DRUG S
DRUM S
DRYS
DUAD S
DUAL S
DUBS
E **DUCE** S
DUCI
DUCK SY
E **DUCT** S
DUDE DS
DUDS

DUEL S
DUES
DUET S
DUFF S
DUGS
DUIT S
DUKE DS
DULL SY
DULY
DUMA S
DUMB OS
DUMP SY
DUNE S
DUNG SY
DUNK S
DUNS
DUNT S
DUOS
DUPE DRS
DUPS
DURA LS
DURE DS
DURN S
DURO CS
DURR AS
DUSK SY
A **DUST** SY
DUTY
DYAD S
DYED
DYER S
DYES
DYKE DSY
DYNE LS

BLPRT **EACH**
P **EARL** SY
LY **EARN** S
BDFGHLNPRSTWY **EARS**
CFLPT **EASE** DLS
BFLY **EAST** S
EASY
DHN **EATH**
BFHMNPST **EATS**
B **EAUX**
DHLRW **EAVE** DS
EBBS
EBON SY
ECHE DS
ECHO S
W **ECHT**
ECRU S
ECUS
EDDO
NT **EDDY**
HKLSW **EDGE** DRS
HLSW **EDGY**
EDHS
EDIT S
FHKPRST **EELS**
S **EELY**
BLPV **EERY**
T **EFFS**
HLW **EFTS**
EGAD S
LR **EGAL**
L **EGER** S
TY **EGGS**
L **EGGY**
A **EGIS**

S **EGOS**
EIDE R
D **EKED**
DP **EKES**
ELAN DS
GMVW **ELDS**
ELHI
Y **ELKS**
BCDFHJMSTWY **ELLS**
H **ELMS**
ELMY
ELSE
DFHMS **EMES**
EMEU S
DH **EMIC**
EMIR S
DR **EMIT** S
GJ **EMMY** S
EMUS
EMYD ES
BFLMPRSTVW **ENDS**
ENGS
ENOL S
ENOW S
ENUF
ENVY
ANP **EONS**
T **EPEE** S
EPHA HS
S **EPIC** S
PR **EPOS**
ERAS E
ERGO T
B **ERGS**
KT **ERNE** S
FHKT **ERNS**
CHZ **EROS** E
ERRS
V **ERST**
BLY **ESES**
M **ESNE** S
ESPY
BFGZ **ETAS**
FKLRV **ETCH**
BHMT **ETHS**
ETIC
ETNA S
ETUI S
EURO S
S **EVEN** ST
FLNS **EVER** TY
N **EVES**
DK **EVIL** S
FHNS **EWER** S
EWES
EXAM S
EXEC S
HSV **EXED**
DHKLRSV **EXES**
EXIT S
EXON S
EXPO S
EYAS S
K **EYED**
EYEN
F **EYER** S
EYES
EYNE
EYRA S

EYRE S
EYRY

FABS
FACE DRST
FACT S
FADE DRS
FADO S
FADS
FAGS
FAIL S
FAIN T
FAIR SY
FAKE DRSY
FALL S
FALX
FAME DS
FANE S
FANG AS
FANO NS
FANS
FARD S
FARE DRS
FARL ES
FARM S
FARO S
FART S
FASH
FAST S
FATE DS
FATS O
FAUN AS
FAUX
FAVA S
FAVE S
FAWN SY
O **FAYS**
FAZE DS
FEAL
FEAR S
FEAT S
FECK S
FEDS
FEEB S
FEED S
FEEL S
FEES
FEET
FEHS
FELL ASY
FELT S
FEME S
FEMS
FEND S
FENS
FEOD S
FERE S
FERN SY
FESS E
FEST S
FETA LS
FETE DS
FETS
FEUD S
FEUS
FIAR S
FIAT S
FIBS
FICE S
FICO
FIDO S
FIDS
FIEF S
FIFE DRST
FIGS
FILA R
FILE DRST
FILL EOSY
FILM ISY

FILO S
FILS
FIND S
FINE DRS
FINK S
FINO S
FINS
A FIRE DRS
FIRM S
FIRN S
FIRS T
FISC S
FISH Y
FIST S
FITS
FIVE RS
FIXT
FIZZ Y
FLAB S
FLAG S
FLAK EY
FLAM ESY
FLAN KS
FLAP S
FLAT S
FLAW SY
FLAX Y
FLAY S
FLEA MS
FLED
FLEE RST
FLEW S
FLEX
FLEY S
FLIC KS
FLIP S
FLIR ST
FLIT ES
FLOC KS
FLOE S
FLOG S
FLOP S
FLOW NS
FLUB S
FLUE DS
FLUS H
FLUX
FOAL S
FOAM SY
FOBS
FOCI
FOES
FOGS
FOGY
FOHN S
FOIL S
FOIN S
FOLD S
FOLK SY
FOND SU
FONS
FONT S
FOOD S
FOOL S
A FOOT SY
FOPS
FORA MY
FORB SY
FORD OS
A FORE S
FORK SY
FORM ES
FORT EHS Y
FOSS AE Y
A FOUL S
FOUR S
FOWL S
FOXY
FOYS
FOZY
FRAE

FRAG S
FRAP S
FRAT S
FRAY S
FREE DRS
FRET S
FRIG S
A FRIT HST Z
FRIZ Z
FROE S
FROG S
FROM
FROW NS
FRUG S
FUBS Y
FUCI
FUCK S
FUDS
FUEL S
FUGS
FUGU ES
FUJI S
FULL SY
FUME DRS T
FUMY
FUND IS
FUNK SY
FUNS
FURL S
FURS
FURY
FUSE DEL S
FUSS Y
FUTZ
FUZE DES
FUZZ Y
FYCE S
FYKE S
GABS
GABY
GADI DS
E GADS
GAED
GAEN
GAES
GAFF ES
GAGA
GAGE DRS
GAGS
A GAIN S
GAIT S
GALA HSX
GALE AS
GALL SY
GALS
A GAMA SY
GAMB AES
GAME DRS Y
GAMP S
O GAMS
GAMY
GANE FV
GANG S
GAOL S
A GAPE DRS
GAPS
GAPY
GARB S
A GARS
GASH
GASP S
GAST S
A GATE DRS
GATS
GAUD SY
GAUM S
GAUN T
GAUR S

A GAVE L
GAWK SY
GAWP S
GAYS
A GAZE DRS
GEAR S
GECK OS
GEDS
GEED
GEEK SY
O GEES ET
GEEZ
GELD S
GELS
GELT S
GEMS
A GENE ST
GENS
A GENT S
GENU AS
GERM SY
E GEST ES
GETA S
GETS
GEUM S
GHAT S
GHEE S
GHIS
GIBE DRS
GIBS
GIDS
GIED
GIEN
GIES
GIFT S
GIGA S
GIGS
GILD S
GILL SY
GILT S
GIMP SY
GINK S
GINS
GIPS Y
GIRD S
GIRL SY
GIRN S
GIRO NS
GIRT HS
A GIST S
GITE S
GITS
O GIVE NRS
GLAD ESY
GLAM S
O GLED ES
A GLEE DKS T
GLEG
GLEN S
A GLEY S
GLIA LS
GLIB
GLIM ES
GLOB ES
GLOM S
GLOP S
A GLOW S
GLUE DRS Y
GLUG S
GLUM ES
GLUT ES
GNAR LRS
GNAT S
GNAW NS
GNUS
GOAD S
GOAL S
GOAS
GOAT S
GOBO S
GOBS

GOBY
GODS
GOER S
GOES
GOGO S
GOLD S
GOLF S
A GONE FR
GONG S
GOOD SY
GOOF SY
GOOK SY
GOON SY
GOOP SY
GOOS EY
GORE DS
GORM S
GORP S
GORY
GOSH
GOTH S
GOUT SY
GOWD S
GOWK S
GOWN S
GOYS
GRAB S
GRAD ES
GRAM APS
GRAN ADS T
GRAT E
GRAY S
A GREE DKN ST
GREW
GREY S
GRID ES
GRIG S
GRIM EY
GRIN DS
GRIP EST Y
GRIT HS
GROG S
GROK S
GROT S
GROW LNS
GRUB S
GRUE LS
GRUM EP
GUAN OS
GUAR DS
GUCK S
GUDE S
GUFF S
GUID ES
GULF SY
GULL SY
GULP SY
GULS
GUMS
GUNK SY
GUNS
GURU S
GUSH Y
GUST OSY
GUTS Y
GUVS
GUYS
GYBE DS
GYMS
GYPS Y
GYRE DS
GYRI
GYRO NS
GYVE DS
HAAF S
HAAR S
HABU S
STW HACK S
S HADE DS

HADJ I
HAED
HAEM S
HAEN
HAES
HAET S
S HAFT S
S HAGS
HAHA S
S HAHS
HAIK ASU
HAIL S
C HAIR SY
HAJI S
HAJJ I
S HAKE S
HAKU S
SW HALE DRS
HALF
S HALL OS
HALM AS
HALO NS
S HALT S
S HAME S
CSW HAMS
HAND SY
BCW HANG S
ST HANK SY
C HANT S
CW HAPS
CS HARD SY
CS HARE DMS
CS HARK S
HARL S
CT HARM S
S HARP SY
C HART S
HASH
HASP S
G HAST EY
HATE DRS
HATH
CGK W HATS
S HAUL MS
G HAUT E
S HAVE NRS
HAWK S
CST HAWS E
CS HAYS
HAZE DLR S
HAZY
A HEAD SY
SW HEAL S
C HEAP SY
S HEAR DST
CW HEAT HS
T HEBE S
C HECK S
HEED S
W HEEL S
T HEFT SY
HEHS
HEIL S
T HEIR S
HELD
S HELL OS
W HELM S
HELO ST
W HELP S
RT HEME S
HEMP SY
HEMS
TW HENS
S HENT S
HERB SY
S HERD S
TW HERE S
HERL S
T HERM AS
HERN S
HERO NS

HERS
C HEST S
CK HETH S
KW HETS
S HEWN
CST W HEWS
CT HICK S
C HIDE DRS
S HIED
S HIES
T HIGH ST
HIKE DRS
HILA R
C HILI
CST HILL OSY
HILT S
SW HIMS
HIND S
CST W HINS
HINT S
CSW HIPS
S HIRE DER S
HISN
HISS Y
SW HIST S
CSW HITS
CS HIVE DS
HOAR DSY
HOAX
HOBO S
HOBS
CS HOCK S
HODS
S HOED
S HOER S
S HOES
HOGG S
S HOGS
C HOKE DSY
A HOLD S
DTW HOLE DSY
HOLK S
HOLM S
HOLP
HOLS
HOLT S
HOLY
HOME DRS Y
HOMO S
HOMY
PS HONE DRS Y
T HONG IS
HONK SY
P HONS
HOOD SY
W HOOF S
CS HOOK ASY
W HOOP S
BS HOOT SY
HOPE DRS
CSW HOPS
HORA HLS
ST HORN SY
CTW HOSE DLN RSY
G HOST AS
PS HOTS
HOUR IS
S HOVE LR
HOWE S
HOWF FS
HOWK S
HOWL S
CDS HOWS
HOYA S
HOYS
C HUBS
CS HUCK S

HUED
HUES
C HUFF SY
HUGE R
CT HUGS
HUIC
HULA S
HULK SY
A HULL OS
CTW HUMP HSY
C HUMS
HUNG
HUNH
CT HUNK SY
S HUNS
S HUNT S
CT HURL SY
HURT S
S HUSH
HUSK SY
BPS HUTS
HWAN
P HYLA S
HYMN S
HYPE DRS
HYPO S
HYPS
HYTE
IAMB IS
IBEX
IBIS
DRV ICED
BDF RSV ICES
ICHS
DKP ICKY
ICON S
IDEA LS
IDEM
ABH NRS TW IDES
S IDLE DRS
IDLY
IDOL S
IDYL LS
BJM IFFY
M IGGS
IGLU S
IKAT S
E IKON S
P ILEA CL
S ILEX
CM ILIA CDL
ILKA
BMS ILKS
BDF GHJ KMN PRS TVW YZ ILLS
BDF GHS W ILLY
IMAM S
T IMID EOS
J IMMY
IMPI S
GLP SW IMPS
INBY E
CFP W INCH
INFO S
INIA
DFG JKL MOP RSW INKS
DHK LPZ INKY
INLY
JL INNS

INRO
INTI S
P INTO
CLP IONS
B IOTA S
AFH MST W IRED
CFH MST VW IRES
V IRID S
IRIS
BDK M IRKS
G IRON ESY
ISBA S
AL ISLE DST
J ISMS
ABD FHP W ITCH Y
ITEM S
K IWIS
IXIA S
S IZAR S
JABS
JACK SY
JADE DS
JAGG SY
JAGS
JAIL S
JAKE S
JAMB ES
JAMS
JANE S
JAPE DRS
JARL S
JARS
JATO S
JAUK S
JAUP S
JAVA S
JAWS
JAYS
JAZZ Y
JEAN S
JEED
JEEP S
JEER S
JEES
JEEZ
JEFE S
JEHU S
JELL OSY
JEON
JERK SY
JESS E
JEST S
JETE S
JETS
JEUX
JEWS
JIAO
JIBB S
JIBE DRS
JIBS
JIFF SY
JIGS
JILL S
JILT S
JIMP Y
JINK S
D JINN IS
D JINS
JINX
JISM S
JIVE DRS Y
JIVY
JOBS
JOCK OS
JOES

JOEY S
JOGS
JOHN S
JOIN ST
JOKE DRS Y
JOKY
JOLE S
JOLT SY
JOSH
JOSS
JOTA S
JOTS
JOUK S
JOWL SY
JOWS
JOYS
JUBA S
JUBE S
JUCO S
JUDO S
A JUGA L
JUGS
JUJU S
JUKE DS
JUKU S
JUMP SY
JUNK SY
JUPE S
JURA LT
JURY
JUST S
JUTE S
JUTS
KAAS
KABS
KADI S
KAES
KAFS
KAGU S
KAIF S
KAIL S
KAIN S
KAKA S
KAKI S
KALE S
KAME S
KAMI K
KANA S
KANE S
KAON S
KAPA S
KAPH S
KARN S
KART S
KATA S
IS KATS
KAVA S
KAYO S
O KAYS
KBAR S
KEAS
KECK S
KEEF S
KEEK S
KEEL S
S KEEN S
KEEP S
S KEET S
KEFS
S KEGS
KEIR S
S KELP SY
KELT S
KEMP ST
KENO S
KENS
KENT E
KEPI S
S KEPS
KEPT

KERB S
KERF S
KERN ES
KETO L
KEYS
KHAF S
KHAN S
KHAT S
KHET HS
KHIS
KIBE IS
KICK SY
S KIDS
KIEF S
S KIER S
KIFS
KIKE S
S KILL S
KILN S
KILO S
KILT SY
KINA S
KIND S
KINE S
E KING S
S KINK SY
KINO S
S KINS
S KIPS
KIRK S
KIRN S
KIRS
KISS Y
KIST S
S KITE DRS
KITH ES
S KITS
KIVA S
KIWI S
KLIK S
KNAP S
KNAR S
KNEE DLS
KNEW
KNIT S
KNOB S
KNOP S
KNOT S
KNOW NS
KNUR LS
KOAN S
KOAS
KOBO S
KOBS
KOEL S
KOHL S
KOIS
KOJI S
KOLA S
KOLO S
KONK S
KOOK SY
KOPH S
KOPS
KORA IST
KORE
KORS
KOSS
KOTO SW
KRIS
KUDO S
KUDU S
KUES
KUFI S
KUNA
KUNE
KURU S
KVAS S
KYAK S
KYAR S
KYAT S
KYES
KYTE S
BFS LABS
GP LACE DRSY
ABCFPS LACK S
LACS
LACY
BCG LADE DNRS
CG LADS
G LADY
CFS LAGS
LAIC HS
P LAID
BEPS LAIN
FG LAIR DS
FS LAKE DRS
LAKH S
F LAKY
LALL S
LU LAMA S
LAMB SY
BF LAME DRS
C LAMP S
BCFGS LAMS
ABEG LAND S
AP LANE S
ACS LANG
BCFPS LANK Y
CFS LAPS E
LARD SY
LARI S
LARK SY
LARS
B LASE DRS
CFPS LASH
CG LASS IO
BC LAST S
ABEPS LATE DNRX
LATH EISY
LATI
BFPS LATS
LATU
LAUD S
LAVA S
CS LAVE DRS
LAVS
B LAWN SY
BCFS LAWS
CFPS LAYS
BG LAZE DS
G LAZY
P LEAD SY
LEAF SY
B LEAK SY
I LEAL
CG LEAN ST
LEAP ST
BC LEAR NSY
FP LEAS EHT
LECH
CGS LEEK S
F LEER SY
FG LEES
FGS LEET S
C LEFT SY
LEGS
LEHR S
LEIS
LEKE
LEKS
LEKU
B LEND S
LENO S
G LENS E
B LENT O
CS LEPT A
B LESS
B LEST
B LETS
LEUD S
LEVA
LEVO
LEVY
LEWD
FG LEYS
LIAR DS
LIBS
S LICE
LICH IT
CFKS LICK S
LIDO S
LIDS
FP LIED
LIEF
A LIEN S
FPS LIER S
FP LIES
LIEU S
LIFE R
C LIFT S
A LIKE DNRS
LILO S
LILT S
S LILY
LIMA NS
C LIMB AIOSY
CGS LIME DNSY
LIMN S
LIMO S
B LIMP AS
BS LIMY
AC LINE DNRSY
CFS LING AOSY
BCPS LINK SY
LINN S
LINO S
LINS
EFG LINT SY
LINY
LION S
LIPA
S LIPE
BCFS LIPS
LIRA S
LIRE
LIRI
LISP S
A LIST S
BEF LITE R
FS LITS
LITU
AO LIVE DNRS
LOAD S
LOAF S
G LOAM SY
LOAN S
G LOBE DS
LOBO S
BGS LOBS
LOCA L
LOCH S
LOCI
BCF LOCK S
LOCO S
LODE NS
A LOFT SY
LOGE S
LOGO INS
BCFS LOGS
O LOGY
S LOID S
AE LOIN S
LOLL SY
AC LONE R
AFK LONG ES
AK LOOF AS
LOOK S
BG LOOM S
LOON SY
BS LOOP SY
LOOS E
C LOOT S
ES LOPE DRS
CFGPS LOPS
LORD S
LORE S
LORN
G LORY
C LOSE LRS
FG LOSS Y
G LOST
F LOTA HS
CS LOTH
LOTI C
BCPS LOTS
AC LOUD
LOUP ES
CF LOUR SY
CFG LOUT S
CG LOVE DRS
LOWE DRS
BCF LOWN
BFGPS LOWS E
LUAU S
LUBE DS
LUCE S
CP LUCK SY
E LUDE S
BCFGS LUES
BFS LUFF AS
K LUGE DRS
GPS LUGS
LULL S
LULU S
LUMA S
CFPS LUMP SY
AGPS LUMS
LUNA RS
LUNE ST
CFS LUNG EIS
CFPS LUNK S
B LUNT S
LUNY
LURE DRSX
LURK S
BFPS LUSH
LUST SY
EFG LUTE ADS
K LUTZ
LUVS
LUXE S
LWEI S
LYCH
LYES
LYNX
LYRE S
LYSE DS
MAAR S
MABE S
MACE DRS
MACH EOS
S MACK S
MACS
MADE
MADS
MAES
I MAGE S
MAGI C
MAGS
MAID S
E MAIL ELS
MAIM S
A MAIN S
MAIR S
MAKE RS
MAKO S
MALE S
S MALL S
MALM SY
S MALT SY
MAMA S
MANA ST
MANE DS
MANO RS
MANS E
MANY
MAPS
MARA S
MARC HS
MARE S
MARK AS
MARL SY
MARS EH
S MART S
O MASA S
S MASH Y
MASK S
A MASS AEY
MAST S
MATE DRSY
MATH S
MATS
MATT ES
MAUD S
MAUL S
MAUN D
MAUT S
MAWN
MAWS
MAXI MS
MAYA NS
MAYO RS
MAYS T
AS MAZE DRS
MAZY
MEAD S
MEAL SY
MEAN STY
MEAT SY
MEDS
MEED S
S MEEK
MEET S
O MEGA
MEGS
MELD S
S MELL S
MELS
S MELT SY
MEME S
MEMO S
MEMS
AE MEND S
MENO
MENU S
MEOU S
MEOW S
MERC HSY
MERE RS
S MERK S
MERL ES
MESA S
MESH Y
MESS Y
META L
METE DRS
METH S
MEWL S
S MEWS
MEZE S
MHOS
MIBS
MICA S
A MICE
MICK S
MICS
MIDI S
AI MIDS T
MIEN S
MIFF SY
MIGG S
MIGS
MIKE DS
MILD S
S MILE RS
MILK SY
MILL ES
MILO S
MILS
MILT SY
MIME DORS
MINA ES
MIND S
AI MINE DRS
MINI MS
MINK ES
MINT SY
MINX
MIPS
MIRE DSX
MIRI N
S MIRK SY
AE MIRS
MIRY
MISE RS
MISO S
A MISS Y
MIST SY
S MITE RS
MITT S
A MITY
MIXT
MOAN S
MOAS
MOAT S
MOBS
S MOCK S
MOCS
MODE LMS
MODI
MODS
S MOGS
MOIL S
MOJO S
S MOKE S
MOLA LRS
MOLD SY
A MOLE S
MOLL SY
MOLS
S MOLT OS
MOLY
MOME S
MOMI
MOMS
MONK S
MONO S
MONS
MONY
MOOD SY
MOOL AS
MOON SY
MOOR SY
MOOS E
MOOT S
MOPE DRSY
MOPS
MOPY
MORA ELSY
MORE LS
MORN S
MORS E
A MORT S
MOSH
MOSK S
MOSS OY
MOST ES
ES MOTE LSTY
MOTH SY
MOTS
MOTT EOS
MOUE S
MOVE DRS
MOWN
MOWS
MOXA S
MOZO S
MUCH O
A MUCK SY
MUDS
MUFF S
MUGG SY
MUGS
MULE DSY
MULL AS
MUMM SY
MUMP S
MUMS
MUMU S
MUNI S
MUNS
MUON S
MURA LS
MURE DSX
MURK SY
MURR AESY
A MUSE DRS
S MUSH Y
MUSK SY
MUSS Y
MUST HSY
MUTE DRS
S MUTS
MUTT S
MYCS
MYNA HS
MYTH SY
NAAN S
NABE S
NABS
NADA S
NAFF S
S NAGS
NAIF S
S NAIL S
NALA S
NAME DRS
J NANA S
NANS
NAOI
NAOS
NAPA S
NAPE S
KS NAPS
NARC OS
NARD S
S NARK SY
U NARY
K NAVE LS
NAVY
NAYS
NAZI S
S NEAP S
A NEAR S
NEAT HS
NEBS
S NECK S
K NEED SY
NEEM S
NEEP S
NEGS
NEIF S
E NEMA S
NENE S
NEON S
NERD SY
NESS
NEST S
NETS
NETT SY
NEUK S
NEUM ES
NEVE RS
NEVI
NEWS Y
NEWT S
NEXT
S NIBS
NICE R
S NICK S
S NIDE DS
NIDI
NIGH ST
NILL S
A NILS
NIMS
NINE S
NIPA S
S NIPS
NISI
U NITE RS
KSU NITS
NIXE DS
NIXY
KS NOBS
K NOCK S
A NODE S
NODI
NODS
NOEL S
NOES
NOGG S
S NOGS
NOIL SY
NOIR S
NOLO S
NOMA DS
G NOME NS
NOMS
NONA S
NONE ST
S NOOK SY
NOON S
NOPE
NORI AS
E NORM S
NOSE DSY
NOSH
NOSY
NOTA L
NOTE DRS
NOUN S
NOUS
NOVA ES
EKS NOWS
NOWT S
S NUBS
NUDE RS
NUKE DS
NULL S
NUMB S
NUNS
NURD S
K NURL S
NUTS Y
L OAFS
S OAKS
OAKY
BHRS OARS
BCRT OAST S
L OATH S
BCDGM OATS
S OBAS
LR OBES E
OBEY S
C OBIA S
OBIS
OBIT S
OBOE S
OBOL EIS
CS OCAS
ODAH S
CS ODAS
ODDS
ODEA
BCLMNR ODES
IS ODIC
ODOR S
ODYL ES
OFAY S
BCDT OFFS
OGAM S
Y OGEE S
B OGLE DRS
OGRE S
O OHED
OHIA S
OHMS
BCFMNRST OILS
DNR OILY
B OINK S
OKAS
T OKAY S
OKEH S
CHJMPSTY OKES
OKRA S
BCFGHMW OLDS
M OLDY
OLEA
OLEO S
BCDHJMPRSTV OLES
FP OLIO S
H OLLA S
NW OMEN S
CGHV OMER S
V OMIT S
NP ONCE T
BCHJNPSTZ ONES
S ONLY
M ONOS
C ONTO
BCT ONUS
ONYX
P OOHS
CGHLPW OOPS
BCFHLMRST OOTS

2006 Addition

B OOZE DS
BDW OOZY
OPAH S
CN OPAL S
CDHLMRT OPED
C OPEN S
CDHLMPRT OPES
OPTS
OPUS
ORAD
BCGHLM ORAL S
FS ORBS
CF ORBY
ORCA S
T ORCS
F ORDO S
BCFGLMPSTY ORES
P ORGY
ORLE S
ORRA
BFMPSTW ORTS
ORYX
ORZO S
OSAR
CDHLNPR OSES
F OSSA
L OTIC
LMP OTTO S
CMPTV OUCH
OUDS
OUPH ES
FHLPSTY OURS
JR OUST S
BGLPRT OUTS
OUZO S
OVAL S
CDRW OVEN S
CHLMR OVER ST
OVUM
BCDJLMRSTVWY OWED
HLY OWES
BCFHJY OWLS
DGT OWNS
BDL OWSE N
OXEN
BCFGLP OXES
OXID ES
OXIM ES
CFT OYER S
OYES
OYEZ
PACA S
AS PACE DRSY
PACK S
PACS
E PACT S
S PACY
PADI S
PADS
PAGE DRS
PAID

PAIK S
S PAIL S
PAIN ST
PAIR S
S PALE ADRST
S PALL SY
PALM SY
PALP IS
O PALS Y
PALY
S PAMS
PANE DLS
S PANG AS
S PANS Y
PANT OSY
PAPA LSW
PAPS
PARA ES
PARD ISY
S PARE DORSU
S PARK AS
PARR SY
S PARS E
A PART SY
PASE OS
PASH A
PASS E
PAST AESY
S PATE DNRS
PATH S
S PATS Y
PATY
PAVE DRS
PAWL S
S PAWN S
PAWS
S PAYS
PEAG ES
AS PEAK SY
PEAL S
S PEAN S
S PEAR LST
PEAS E
PEAT SY
PECH S
S PECK SY
S PECS
PEDS
S PEED
A PEEK S
S PEEL S
PEEN S
PEEP S
S PEER SY
E PEES
PEGS
PEHS
PEIN S
PEKE S
PELE S
PELF S
S PELT S
SU PEND S
O PENS
S PENT
PEON SY
PEPO S
PEPS
PERE AS
PERI LS
PERK SY
S PERM S
PERP S
PERT
PERV S
PESO S
PEST OSY
PETS
S PEWS

PFFT
PFUI
PHAT
PHEW
A PHIS
PHIZ
PHON EOSY
PHOT OS
PHUT S
PIAL
A PIAN OS
PIAS
S PICA LS
S PICE
S PICK SY
ES PICS
S PIED
S PIER S
S PIES
PIGS
PIKA S
S PIKE DRS
PIKI S
S PILE ADIS
PILI S
S PILL S
PILY
PIMA S
PIMP S
PINA S
OS PINE DSY
AO PING OS
PINK OSY
S PINS
PINT AOS
S PINY
PION S
PIPE DRST
PIPS
PIPY
PIRN S
A PISH
PISO S
PISS
PITA S
PITH SY
S PITS
PITY
PIXY
PLAN EKST
S PLAT ESY
S PLAY AS
PLEA DST
PLEB ES
PLED
PLEW S
PLEX
PLIE DRS
PLOD S
PLOP S
PLOT SZ
PLOW S
PLOY S
PLUG S
PLUM BEPSY
PLUS H
POCK SY
POCO
A PODS
POEM S
POET S
POGY
POIS E
S POKE DRSY
POKY
POLE DRS
POLL S

POLO S
POLS
POLY PS
POME S
POMO S
POMP S
POMS
POND S
PONE S
PONG S
PONS
PONY
POOD S
S POOF SY
POOH S
S POOL S
S POON S
POOP S
S POOR I
POOS
POPE S
POPS Y
S PORE DS
PORK SY
PORN OSY
AS PORT S
POSE DRS
POSH
POST S
POSY
S POTS Y
POUF FS
POUR S
S POUT SY
POWS
E POXY
PRAM S
PRAO S
S PRAT ES
PRAU S
S PRAY S
S PREE DNS
PREP S
PREX Y
PREY S
PREZ
S PRIG S
PRIM AEIOPS
PROA S
PROD S
PROF S
PROG S
PROM OS
PROP S
PROS EOSTY
PROW LS
A PSIS
PSST
PTUI
PUBS
PUCE S
PUCK AS
S PUDS
PUFF SY
PUGH
PUGS
PUJA HS
PUKE DS
PULA
PULE DRS
PULI KS
PULL S
PULP SY
PULS E
PUMA S
PUMP S
PUNA S
PUNG S
S PUNK ASY
PUNS
PUNT OSY

PUNY
PUPA ELS
PUPS
PUPU S
PURE ER
PURI NS
PURL S
PURR S
S PURS EY
PUSH Y
PUSS Y
PUTS
PUTT IOSY
PUTZ
PYAS
PYES
PYIC
PYIN S
PYRE SX
PYRO S

QADI S
QAID S
QATS
QOPH S
S QUAD S
QUAG S
QUAI LS
QUAY S
QUEY S
ES QUID S
QUIN ST
E QUIP SU
QUIT ES
QUIZ
QUOD S

BGT RACE DRS
CTW RACK S
RACY
BG RADS
D RAFF S
CDGK RAFT S
RAGA S
RAGE DES
RAGG SY
T RAGI S
BCDF RAGS
RAIA S
B RAID S
BDFGT RAIL S
BDGT RAIN SY
RAIS E
RAJA HS
BCD RAKE DERS
RAKI S
RAKU S
RALE S
RAMI E
CGT RAMP S
CDGPT RAMS
BG RAND SY
OPW RANG EY
RANI DS
BCDFPT RANK S
BG RANT S
CDG RAPE DRS
CFTW RAPS
TW RAPT
U RARE DRS
EPU RASE DRS
BCT RASH
G RASP SY
CGIOPU RATE DLRS

W RATH E
RATO S
BDFP RATS
BCDGT RAVE DLNRS
BCD RAWS
RAYA HS
BDFGPT RAYS
BCG RAZE DERS
RAZZ
BDOT READ DSY
AU REAL MS
BCD REAM S
REAP S
D REAR MS
REBS
DW RECK S
RECS
REDD S
B REDE DS
CU REDO NSX
C REDS
BCDFGPT REED SY
REEF SY
CG REEK SY
C REEL S
BDFGPT REES T
REFS
REFT
D REGS
REIF SY
REIN KS
REIS
RELY
REMS
T REND S
B RENT ES
REPO ST
REPP S
P REPS
F RESH
CDPW REST S
A RETE M
FT RETS
REVS
RHEA S
RHOS
RHUS
TU RIAL S
A RIAS
CD RIBS
PT RICE DRS
RICH
BCPTW RICK S
BGP RIDE RS
GI RIDS
AO RIEL S
RIFE R
G RIFF S
RIFS
DG RIFT S
BFGPT RIGS
RILE DSY
BDFGKPT RILL ES
CGP RIME DRS
BPT RIMS
G RIMY
G RIND SY
BIW RING S
BDP RINK S
BG RINS E
G RIOT S

CGT RIPE DNRS
DGT RIPS
AFP RISE NRS
BF RISK SY
TW RITE S
F RITZ Y
D RIVE DNRST
B ROAD S
ROAM S
G ROAN S
ROAR S
P ROBE DS
ROBS
BCFT ROCK SY
C ROCS
ET RODE OS
P RODS
F ROES
B ROIL SY
P ROLE S
ROLF S
DT ROLL S
T ROMP S
P ROMS
B ROOD S
P ROOF S
BC ROOK SY
BGV ROOM SY
ROOT SY
GT ROPE DRSY
ROPY
ABEP ROSE DST
BP ROSY
ROTA S
W ROTE S
ROTI S
ROTL S
ROTO RS
GT ROTS
ROUE NS
CG ROUP SY
GT ROUT EHS
ROUX
DGPT ROVE DNRS
BCFGPTV ROWS
RUBE LS
DG RUBS
RUBY
CT RUCK S
RUDD SY
CP RUDE R
T RUED
T RUER S
GT RUES
G RUFF ES
RUGA EL
DFT RUGS
B RUIN GS
RULE DRS
T RULY
CFGT RUMP S
AD RUMS
P RUNE S
BW RUNG S
RUNS
BG RUNT SY
CD RUSE S
BC RUSH Y
B RUSK S
CT RUST SY
T RUTH S
B RUTS
RYAS
RYES
RYKE DS

RYND S
RYOT S

SABE DRS
SABS
SACK S
SACS
T SADE S
T SADI S
SAFE RS
SAGA S
U SAGE RS
SAGO S
SAGS
SAGY
SAID S
SAIL S
SAIN ST
SAKE RS
SAKI S
SALE PS
SALL Y
SALP AS
SALS A
SALT SY
SAME K
SAMP S
SAND SY
SANE DRS
SANG AH
SANK
SANS
SAPS
SARD S
SARI NS
SARK SY
SASH
SASS Y
SATE DMS
SATI NS
SAUL ST
SAVE DRS
SAWN
SAWS
SAYS T
SCAB S
SCAD S
SCAG S
SCAM PS
SCAN ST
E SCAR EFPSTY
SCAT ST
SCOP ES
AE SCOT S
SCOW LS
SCRY
SCUD IOS
SCUM S
SCUP S
SCUT AES
SEAL S
SEAM SY
SEAR S
SEAS
SEAT S
SECS
SECT S
SEED SY
SEEK S
SEEL SY
SEEM S
SEEN
SEEP SY
SEER S
SEES
SEGO S
SEGS
SEIF S
SEIS EM
SELF S
SELL ES

SELS
SEME NS
SEMI S
SEND S
SENE
SENT EI
SEPT AS
SERA CIL
SERE DRS
SERF S
U SERS
SETA EL
SETS
SETT S
SEWN
SEWS
SEXT OS
SEXY
SHAD ESY
SHAG S
SHAH S
SHAM ES
SHAT
P SHAW LMNS
SHAY S
SHEA FLRS
A SHED S
A SHES
SHEW NS
SHIM S
SHIN ESY
SHIP S
SHIT S
SHIV AES
SHMO
SHOD
SHOE DRS
SHOG IS
SHOO KLNST
SHOP S
SHOT EST
SHOW NSY
SHRI S
SHUL NS
SHUN ST
SHUT ES
SHWA S
SIAL S
SIBB S
SIBS
SICE S
SICK OS
SICS
A SIDE DS
SIDH E
SIFT S
SIGH ST
SIGN AS
SIKA S
SIKE RS
SILD S
SILK SY
SILL SY
SILO S
SILT SY
SIMA RS
SIMP S
SIMS
SINE SW
U SING ES
SINH S
SINK S
SINS
SIPE DS
SIPS
SIRE DENS
SIRS
SITE DS
SITH

SITS
SIZE DRS
SIZY
SKAG S
SKAS
SKAT ES
SKEE DNST
SKEG S
SKEP S
A SKEW S
SKID S
SKIM OPS
SKIN KST
SKIP S
SKIS
SKIT ES
SKUA S
SLAB S
SLAG S
SLAM S
SLAP S
SLAT ESY
SLAW S
SLAY S
I SLED S
SLEW S
SLID E
SLIM ESY
SLIP EST
SLIT S
SLOB S
SLOE S
SLOG S
SLOP ES
SLOT HS
SLOW S
SLUB S
SLUE DS
SLUG S
SLUM PS
SLUR BPS
SLUT S
SMEW S
SMIT EH
SMOG S
SMUG
SMUT S
SNAG S
SNAP S
SNAW S
SNED S
SNIB S
SNIP ES
SNIT S
SNOB S
SNOG S
SNOT S
SNOW SY
SNUB S
SNUG S
SNYE S
SOAK S
SOAP SY
SOAR S
SOBA S
SOBS
SOCA S
SOCK OS
SODA S
SODS
SOFA RS
SOFT ASY
SOIL S
SOJA S
SOKE S
SOLA NR
SOLD IO
SOLE DIS
SOLI D
SOLO NS
SOLS

SOMA NS
SOME
SOMS
SONE S
SONG S
SONS Y
SOOK S
SOON
SOOT HSY
SOPH SY
SOPS
SORA S
SORB S
SORD S
SORE DLRS
SORI
SORN S
SORT AS
SOTH S
SOTS
SOUK S
SOUL S
SOUP SY
SOUR S
SOUS E
SOWN
SOWS
SOYA S
SOYS
SPAE DS
SPAM S
SPAN GKS
SPAR EKS
SPAS M
SPAT ES
SPAY S
SPAZ Z
SPEC KS
SPED
SPEW S
A SPIC AEKSY
SPIK ESY
SPIN ESY
SPIT ESZ
SPIV S
SPOT S
SPRY
SPUD S
SPUE DS
SPUN K
SPUR NST
SRIS
STAB S
STAG ESY
STAR EKST
STAT ES
STAW
STAY S
STEM S
STEP S
STET S
STEW SY
STEY
A STIR KPS
STOA EIST
STOB S
E STOP EST
STOT ST
STOW PS
STUB S
STUD SY
STUM PS
STUN GKST
STYE DS
T SUBA HS
SUBS
SUCH
SUCK SY

SUDD S
SUDS Y
SUED E
SUER S
SUES
SUET SY
SUGH S
SUIT ES
SUKS
SULK SY
SULU S
SUMO S
SUMP S
SUMS
SUNG
SUNK
SUNN ASY
SUNS
SUPE RS
SUPS
SUQS
SURA HLS
SURD S
SURE R
SURF SY
SUSS
SWAB S
SWAG ES
SWAM IPY
SWAN GKS
SWAP S
SWAT HS
SWAY S
SWIG S
SWIM S
SWOB S
SWOP S
SWOT S
SWUM
SYBO
SYCE ES
SYKE S
SYLI S
SYNC HS
SYNE
SYPH S
S TABS
TABU NS
TACE ST
TACH ES
S TACK SY
TACO S
TACT S
TADS
TAEL S
S TAGS
TAHR S
TAIL S
S TAIN ST
TAKA S
S TAKE NRS
TALA RS
TALC S
S TALE RS
TALI
S TALK SY
S TALL SY
TAME DRS
S TAMP S
TAMS
S TANG AOSY
S TANK AS
TANS Y
TAOS
TAPA S
E TAPE DRS
A TAPS
S TARE DS
TARN S
TARO CKST

TARP S
S TARS I
S TART SY
TASK S
TASS E
S TATE RS
S TATS
TAUS
TAUT S
TAVS
TAWS E
TAXA
TAXI S
S TEAK S
S TEAL S
S TEAM S
TEAR SY
TEAS E
TEAT S
TECH SY
TEDS
S TEED
S TEEL S
TEEM S
TEEN SY
TEES
TEFF S
TEGG S
TEGS
S TELA E
S TELE SX
TELL SY
TELS
TEMP IOST
TEND SU
TENS E
S TENT HSY
TEPA LS
TERM S
S TERN ES
TEST ASY
TETH S
S TETS
S TEWS
TEXT S
THAE
THAN EK
THAT
THAW S
THEE
THEM E
THEN S
THEW SY
THEY
THIN EGKS
THIO L
THIR DL
THIS
THOU S
THRO BEW
THRU M
THUD S
THUG S
THUS
S TICK S
TICS
TIDE DS
TIDY
S TIED
TIER S
S TIES
S TIFF S
TIKE S
TIKI S
SU TILE DRS
S TILL S
TILS
AS TILT HS
S TIME DRS
TINE ADS
S TING ES

TINS
S TINT S
TINY
TIPI S
TIPS Y
TIRE DS
TIRL S
TIRO S
TITI S
TITS
TIVY
TOAD SY
TOBY
TODS
TODY
TOEA S
TOED
TOES
TOFF SY
TOFT S
TOFU S
TOGA ES
TOGS
TOIL ES
TOIT S
S TOKE DNRS
TOLA NRS
TOLD
S TOLE DS
A TOLL S
TOLU S
TOMB S
TOME S
A TOMS
AS TONE DRSY
TONG AS
TONS
AS TONY
S TOOK
S TOOL S
TOOM
TOON S
TOOT HS
S TOPE DERS
TOPH EIS
TOPI CS
TOPO IS
S TOPS
TORA HS
TORC HS
S TORE S
TORI CI
TORN
TORO ST
TORR S
TORS EIKO
TORT AES
S TORY
TOSH
S TOSS
TOST
TOTE DMRS
S TOTS
S TOUR S
S TOUT S
TOWN SY
S TOWS
TOWY
TOYO NS
TOYS
TRAD E
TRAM PS
S TRAP ST
S TRAY S
TREE DNS
TREF
TREK S
TRES S

TRET S
TREY S
TRIG OS
TRIM S
TRIO LS
AS TRIP ES
TROD E
TROG S
S TROP E
TROT HS
S TROW S
S TROY S
TRUE DRS
TRUG S
TSAR S
TSKS
TUBA ELS
TUBE DRS
S TUBS
S TUCK S
TUFA S
S TUFF S
TUFT SY
TUGS
E TUIS
TULE S
S TUMP S
TUNA S
TUNE DRS
S TUNG S
S TUNS
TUPS
TURD S
TURF SY
TURK S
TURN S
TUSH Y
TUSK S
TUTS
TUTU S
TWAE S
TWAS
TWAT S
E TWEE DNT
TWIG S
TWIN ESY
TWIT S
TWOS
TYEE S
TYER S
S TYES
TYIN G
TYKE S
TYNE DS
TYPE DSY
TYPO S
TYPP S
TYPY
TYRE DS
TYRO S
TZAR S
UDON S
JK UDOS
SV UGHS
UGLY
CDJNP UKES
Y ULAN S
ULNA DERS
LS ULUS
V ULVA S
DGJ UMBO S
BDHJLMPRST UMPS
UNAI S
UNAU S
UNBE
UNCI A
BJ UNCO SY

UNDE ER
UNDO
UNDY
UNIT ESY
JP UNTO
P UPAS
UPBY E
UPDO S
JY UPON
BC URBS
BCHNST URDS
UREA LS
GPS URGE DRS
A URIC
BCDT URNS
BT URPS
B URSA E
GK URUS
BFM USED
M USER S
BFMPR USES
UTAS
BCJLM UTES
UVEA LS
VACS
VAGI
A VAIL S
VAIN
VAIR S
VALE ST
VAMP SY
VANE DS
VANG S
VANS
VARA S
VARS
O VARY
VASA L
VASE S
A VAST SY
VATS
VATU S
VAUS
VAVS
VAWS
U VEAL SY
VEEP S
VEER SY
VEES
VEIL S
VEIN SY
VELA R
VELD ST
VENA EL
VEND S
E VENT S
VERA
VERB S
AEO VERT SU
E VERY
VEST AS
VETO
VETS
VEXT
VIAL S
VIBE S
VICE DS
VIDE O
VIDS
I VIED
VIER S
I VIES
VIEW SY
VIGA S
VIGS
VILE R
VILL AIS
VIMS

VINA LS
O VINE DS
VINO S
VINY L
VIOL AS
VIRL S
VISA S
VISE DS
VITA EL
VIVA S
VIVE
VOES
AO VOID S
VOLE DS
VOLT AEIS
VOTE DRS
A VOWS
VROW S
VUGG SY
VUGH S
VUGS
S WABS
WACK EOSY
WADE DRS
WADI S
WADS
WADY
T WAES
WAFF S
WAFT S
S WAGE DRS
S WAGS
WAIF S
S WAIL S
ST WAIN S
WAIR S
A WAIT S
A WAKE DNRS
S WALE DRS
WALK S
WALL ASY
WALY
WAME S
WAND S
WANE DSY
S WANK S
S WANS
WANT S
WANY
S WAPS
AS WARD S
AS WARE DS
WARK S
S WARM S
WARN S
WARP S
WARS
S WART SY
WARY
AS WASH Y
WASP SY
WAST ES
ST WATS
WATT S
WAUK S
WAUL S
WAUR
WAVE DRSY
WAVY
WAWL S
WAWS
WAXY
S WAYS
T WEAK
WEAL DS
WEAN S
S WEAR SY
WEBS

WEDS
T WEED SY
WEEK S
WEEL
T WEEN SY
S WEEP SY
S WEER
WEES T
ST WEET S
WEFT S
WEIR DS
WEKA S
WELD S
DS WELL SY
D WELT S
WEND S
WENS
WENT
S WEPT
WERE
WERT
WEST S
WETS
WHAM OS
WHAP S
WHAT S
WHEE LNP
WHEN S
WHET S
WHEW S
WHEY S
WHID S
WHIG S
WHIM S
WHIN ESY
WHIP ST
WHIR LRS
WHIT ESY
WHIZ Z
WHOA
WHOM P
WHOP S
WHUP S
WHYS
WICH
WICK S
WIDE NRS
WIFE DSY
ST WIGS
WILD S
WILE DS
ST WILL SY
WILT S
WILY
WIMP SY
WIND SY
DGST WINE DSY
AOS WING SY
S WINK S
WINO S
T WINS
T WINY
S WIPE DRS
WIRE DRS
WIRY
WISE DRS
S WISH A
WISP SY
S WISS
T WIST S
WITE DS
S WITH EY
T WITS
S WIVE DRS
WOAD S
WOES
WOGS
A WOKE N
WOKS
WOLD S
WOLF S

WOMB SY
WONK SY
WONS
WONT S
WOOD SY
WOOF S
WOOL SY
WOOS H
S WOPS
S WORD SY
S WORE
WORK S
WORM SY
S WORN
WORT HS
WOST
S WOTS
WOVE N
WOWS
WRAP ST
WREN S
WRIT ES
WUSS Y
WYCH
WYES
WYLE DS
WYND S
WYNN S
WYNS
WYTE DS

XYST IS

K YACK S
YAFF S
YAGI S
YAGS
K YAKS
YALD
YAMS
YANG S
YANK S
YAPS
L YARD S
YARE R
YARN S
YAUD S
YAUP S
YAWL S
YAWN S
YAWP S
YAWS
YAYS
YEAH S
YEAN S
YEAR NS
YEAS T
YECH SY
YEGG S
YELD
YELK S
YELL S
YELP S
YENS
YEPS
YERK S
YETI S
YETT S
YEUK SY
YEWS
YIDS
YILL S
AP YINS
YIPE S
YIPS
YIRD S
YIRR S
X YLEM S
YOBS
YOCK S
YODH S
YODS
YOGA S
YOGH S
YOGI CNS
YOKE DLS
YOKS
YOLK SY
YOND
YONI CS
YORE S
YOUR NS
YOUS E
YOWE DS
YOWL S
YOWS
YUAN S
YUCA S
YUCH
YUCK SY
YUGA S
YUKS
YULE S
YUPS
YURT AS
YUTZ
YWIS

ZAGS
ZANY
ZAPS
ZARF S
ZEAL S
ZEBU S
ZEDS
ZEES
ZEIN S
ZEKS
ZEPS
ZERK S
ZERO S
ZEST SY
ZETA S
ZIGS
ZILL S
ZINC SY
A ZINE BS
ZING SY
ZINS
ZIPS
ZITI S
ZITS
ZOEA ELS
A ZOIC
ZONA EL
O ZONE DRS
ZONK S
ZOOM S
ZOON S
ZOOS
ZORI LS
ZOUK S
ZYME S

5-letter Words

AAHED
AALII S
AARGH
ABACA S
ABACI
ABACK
ABAFT
K ABAKA S
ABAMP S
ABASE DRS
ABASH
ABATE DRS
K ABAYA S
ABBAS
ABBES S
ABBEY S
ABBOT S
ABEAM
ABELE S
ABETS
ABHOR S
ABIDE DRS
CFG ABLED T
CF ABLER
CFGST ABLES T
ABMHO S
ABODE DS
ABOHM S
ABOIL
ABOMA S
BG ABOON
ABORT S
ABOUT
ABOVE S
ABRIS
ABUSE DRS
ABUTS
ABUZZ
ABYES
ABYSM S
ABYSS
ACARI D
ACERB
ACETA L
BC ACHED
BCLMNT ACHES
ACHOO
ACIDS
ACIDY
FLMPR ACING
ACINI C
H ACKEE S
ACMES
ACMIC
ACNED
ACNES
ACOCK
ACOLD
ACORN S
NS ACRED
N ACRES
ACRID
ACTED
ACTIN GS
F ACTOR S
ACUTE RS
ACYLS
ADAGE S
ADAPT S
ADDAX
GMPRW ADDED
BGLMPSW ADDER S
DPRSW ADDLE DS
ADEEM S
ADEPT S
ADIEU SX
R ADIOS
ADITS
BM ADMAN
BM ADMEN
ADMIT S
ADMIX T
ADOBE S
ADOBO S
ADOPT S
ADORE DRS
ADORN S
ADOWN
ADOZE
ADULT S
ADUNC
ADUST
ADYTA
ADZED
ADZES
AECIA L
AEDES
AEGIS
P AEONS
F AERIE DRS
AFARS
AFFIX
AFIRE
AFOOT
AFORE
AFOUL
AFRIT S
DHRW AFTER S
AGAIN
AGAMA S
AGAPE S
AGARS
AGATE S
AGAVE S
AGAZE
AGENE S
AGENT S
CEGJLPWY AGERS
BDGJLNSTW AGGER S
B AGGIE S
AGGRO S
AGHAS T
V AGILE
CGPRW AGING S
AGIOS
AGISM S
AGIST S
AGITA S
AGLEE
E AGLET S
AGLEY
AGLOW
M AGMAS
AGONE S
W AGONS
AGONY
AGORA ES
AGREE DS
AGRIA S
AGUES
AHEAD
A AHING
AHOLD S
AHULL
R AIDED
R AIDER S
AIDES
BFHJMNRSTVW AILED
M AIMED
M AIMER S
AIOLI S
FHLPW AIRED
F AIRER S
BC AIRNS
AIRTH S
AIRTS
AISLE DS
AITCH
NW AIVER S
AJIVA S
AJUGA S
R AKEES
AKELA S
AKENE S
ALACK
ALAMO S
ALAND S
ALANE
ALANG
ALANS
ALANT S
ALARM S
S ALARY
MP ALATE DS
ALBAS
ALBUM S
ALCID S
B ALDER S
ALDOL S
ALECS
ALEFS
ALEPH S
ALERT S
ALFAS
ALGAE
ALGAL
ALGAS
ALGID
ALGIN S
ALGOR S
ALGUM S
ALIAS
ALIBI S
ALIEN S
CK ALIFS
M ALIGN S
ALIKE
MSV ALINE DRS
ALIST
ALIVE
ALIYA HS
T ALKIE S
ALKYD S
ALKYL S
ALLAY S
CM ALLEE S
GV ALLEY S
ALLOD S
BH ALLOT S
CFHMSTW ALLOW S
ALLOY S
ALLYL S
ALMAH S
H ALMAS
ALMEH S
ALMES
ALMUD ES
ALMUG S
H ALOES
ALOFT
ALOHA S
ALOIN S
ALONE
K ALONG
ALOOF
ALOUD
ALPHA S
ALTAR S
FHPS ALTER S
ALTHO
ALTOS
ALULA ER
ALUMS
ALWAY S
AMAHS
AMAIN
C AMASS
AMAZE DS
CL AMBER SY
G AMBIT S
GRW AMBLE DRS
MS AMBOS
AMBRY
AMEBA ENS
AMEER S
AMEND S
Y AMENS
L AMENT S
LZ AMIAS
AMICE S
AMICI
AMIDE S
AMIDO L
AMIDS T
MR AMIES
AMIGA S
AMIGO S
FG AMINE S
AMINO
G AMINS
AMIRS
AMISS
AMITY
AMMOS
AMNIA
AMNIC
AMNIO NS
AMOKS
AMOLE S
AMONG
AMORT
AMOUR S
CDLRTV AMPED
S AMPLE R
D AMPLY
AMPUL ES
AMUCK S
AMUSE DRS
AMYLS
R ANCHO RS
ANCON E
ANDRO S
ANEAR S
ANELE DS
ANENT
FMPS ANGAS
M ANGEL S
BDGHMRS ANGER S
BDJMTW ANGLE DRS
ANGLO S
ANGRY
ANGST S
ANILE
ANILS
ANIMA LS
ANIME S
ANIMI S
FW ANION S
ANISE S
ANKHS
R ANKLE DST
ANKUS H
ANLAS
ANNAL S
CM ANNAS
ANNEX E
T ANNOY S
ANNUL IS
ANOAS
ANODE S
ANOLE S
ANOMY
ANSAE
ANTAE
M ANTAS
CHPRW ANTED
M ANTES
CM ANTIC KS
M ANTIS
MTY ANTRA L
ANTRE S
ANTSY
ANVIL S
C ANYON ES
AORTA ELS
APACE
APART
APEAK
APEEK
CGJPRT APERS
JNP APERY
APHID S
R APHIS
APIAN
GJRT APING
APISH
APNEA LS
APODS
APORT
APPAL LS
R APPEL S
D APPLE ST
APPLY
APRES
APRON S
L APSES
APSIS
APTER
R APTLY
AQUAE
AQUAS
ARAKS
ARAME S
H ARBOR S
F ARCED
ARCUS
ARDEB S
ARDOR S
AREAE
AREAL
AREAS
ARECA S
AREIC
ARENA S
ARENE S
AREPA S
ARETE S
ARGAL AIS
ARGIL S
G ARGLE DS
ARGOL S
J ARGON S
ARGOT S
ARGUE DRS
ARGUS
ARHAT S
V ARIAS
ARIEL S
ARILS
ARISE NS
CFP ARLES
FHW ARMED
FHW ARMER S
ARMET S
ARMOR SY
AROID S
AROMA S
AROSE
ARPEN ST
ARRAS
ARRAY S
ARRIS
BFHMNY ARROW SY
CMP ARSES
ARSIS
P ARSON S
H ARTAL S
C ARTEL S
ARTSY
L ARUMS
L ARVAL
P ARVOS
ARYLS
ASANA S
M ASCOT S
ASCUS
ASDIC S
BCDFGHLMPSW ASHED
ASHEN
BCDFGHLMPRSW ASHES
ASIDE S
BCMT ASKED
M ASKER S
ASKEW
ASKOI
ASKOS
ASPEN S
GJR ASPER S
ASPIC S
ASPIS H
ASSAI LS
ASSAY S
BGLMPST ASSES S
BT ASSET S
BCEFGLMPRTVW ASTER NS
ASTIR
ASYLA
W ATAPS
ATAXY
ATILT
ATLAS
B ATMAN S
ATMAS
ATOLL S
ATOMS
ATOMY
ATONE DRS
ATONY
ATOPY
L ATRIA L
ATRIP
ATTAR S
ATTIC S
C AUDAD S
AUDIO S
AUDIT S
GMS AUGER S
CNTW AUGHT S
AUGUR SY
AULIC
DHJTV AUNTS
JV AUNTY
L AURAE
AURAL
AURAR
L AURAS
AUREI
AURES
AURIC
K AURIS T
AURUM S
AUTOS
AUXIN S
AVAIL S
S AVANT
AVAST
DHMR AVENS
CHLPRSW AVERS E
AVERT S
AVGAS
AVIAN S
AVION S
AVISO S
AVOID S
AVOWS
AWAIT S
AWAKE DNS
V AWARD S
AWARE
AWASH
L AWFUL
CDHJLMPSTY AWING
DFPY AWNED
AWOKE N
AWOLS
AXELS
AXIAL
AXILE
AXILS
FMRTW AXING
AXIOM S
AXION S
T AXITE S
AXLED
AXLES
T AXMAN
T AXMEN
AXONE S
T AXONS
R AYAHS
LZ AYINS
H AZANS
AZIDE S
AZIDO
AZINE S
AZLON S
AZOIC
AZOLE S
AZONS
AZOTE DS
AZOTH S
AZUKI S
AZURE S

BAAED
BAALS
BABAS
BABEL S
BABES
BABKA S
BABOO LNS
BABUL S
BABUS
BACCA E
BACKS
BACON S
BADDY
BADGE DRS
BADLY
BAFFS
BAFFY
BAGEL S
BAGGY
BAHTS
BAILS
BAIRN S
BAITH
BAITS
BAIZA S
BAIZE S
BAKED
BAKER SY
BAKES
BALAS
BALDS
BALDY
BALED
BALER S
BALES
BALKS
BALKY
BALLS Y
BALLY
BALMS
BALMY
BALSA MS
BANAL
BANCO S
BANDA S
BANDS
BANDY
BANED
BANES
BANGS
BANJO S
BANKS
BANNS
BANTY
BARBE DLRST
BARBS
BARCA S
BARDE DS
BARDS
BARED
BARER
BARES T
BARFS
BARGE DES
BARIC
BARKS
BARKY
BARMS
BARMY
BARNS
BARNY
BARON GSY
BARRE DLNST
BARYE S
BASAL T
A BASED
A BASER
A BASES T
BASIC S
BASIL S
BASIN GS
BASIS
BASKS
BASSI
BASSO S
BASSY
BASTE DRS
BASTS
BATCH
A BATED
A BATES
BATHE DRS
BATHS
BATIK S
BATON S
BATTS
BATTU E
BATTY
BAUDS
BAULK SY
BAWDS
BAWDY
BAWLS
BAWTY
BAYED
BAYOU S
BAZAR S
BAZOO S
BEACH Y
BEADS
BEADY
BEAKS
BEAKY
BEAMS
BEAMY
BEANO S
BEANS
BEARD S
BEARS
BEAST S
BEATS
BEAUS
BEAUT SY
BEAUX
BEBOP S
BECAP S
BECKS
BEDEL LS
BEDEW S
BEDIM S
BEECH Y
BEEDI
BEEFS
BEEFY
BEEPS
BEERS
BEERY
BEETS
BEFIT S
BEFOG S
BEGAN
BEGAT
BEGET S
BEGIN S
BEGOT
BEGUM S
BEGUN
BEIGE S
BEIGY
BEING S
BELAY S
BELCH
BELGA S
BELIE DFRS
BELLE DS
BELLS
BELLY
BELON GS
BELOW S
BELTS
BEMAS
BEMIX T
BENCH
BENDS
BENDY S
BENES
BENNE ST
BENNI S
BENNY
O BENTO S
BENTS
BERET S
BERGS
BERKS
BERME DS
BERMS
BERRY
BERTH AS
BERYL S
BESES
BESET S
BESOM S
BESOT S
BESTS
BETAS
BETEL S
BETHS
BETON SY
BETTA S
BEVEL S
BEVOR S
BEWIG S
BEZEL S
BEZIL S
BHANG S
BHOOT S
BHUTS
BIALI S
BIALY S
BIBBS
BIBLE S
BICEP S
I BICES
BIDDY
A BIDED
A BIDER S
A BIDES
BIDET S
BIDIS
BIELD S
BIERS
BIFFS
BIFFY
BIFID
BIGGY
BIGHT S
BIGLY
BIGOS
BIGOT S
BIJOU SX
BIKED
BIKER S
BIKES
BIKIE S
BILBO AS
BILBY
BILES
BILGE DS
BILGY
BILKS
BILLS
BILLY
BIMAH S
BIMAS
BIMBO S
BINAL
BINDI S
BINDS
BINER S
BINES
BINGE DRS
BINGO S
BINIT S
BINTS
BIOGS
BIOME S
BIONT S
BIOTA S
BIPED S
BIPOD S
BIRCH
BIRDS
BIRKS
BIRLE DRS
BIRLS
BIROS
BIRRS
BIRSE S
BIRTH S
I BISES
BISKS
BISON S
BITCH Y
BITER S
BITES
BITSY
BITTS
BITTY
BIZES
BLABS
BLACK S
BLADE DRS
BLAFF S
BLAHS
BLAIN S
BLAME DRS
BLAMS
BLAND
BLANK S
BLARE DS
BLASE
O BLAST SY
AO BLATE
BLATS
BLAWN
BLAWS
A BLAZE DRS
BLEAK S
BLEAR SY
BLEAT S
BLEBS
BLEED S
BLEEP S
BLEND ES
BLENT
BLESS
A BLEST
BLETS
BLIMP S
BLIMY
BLIND S
BLINI S
BLINK S
BLIPS
BLISS
BLITE S
BLITZ
BLOAT S
BLOBS
BLOCK SY
BLOCS
BLOGS
BLOKE S
BLOND ES
BLOOD SY
A BLOOM SY
BLOOP S
BLOTS
BLOWN
BLOWS Y
BLOWY
BLUBS
BLUED
BLUER
BLUES TY
BLUET S
BLUEY S
BLUFF S
BLUME DS
BLUNT S
BLURB S
BLURS
BLURT S
A BLUSH
BLYPE S
A BOARD S
BOARS
BOART S
BOAST S
BOATS
BOBBY
BOCCE S
BOCCI AES
BOCHE S
BOCKS
A BODED
A BODES
BOFFO S
BOFFS
BOGAN S
BOGEY S
BOGGY
BOGIE S
BOGLE S
BOGUS
BOHEA S
BOHOS
BOILS
BOING S
BOINK S
BOITE S
BOLAR
BOLAS
BOLDS
O BOLES
BOLLS
BOLOS
BOLTS
O BOLUS
BOMBE DRS
BOMBS
BONDS
BONED
BONER S
BONES
BONEY
BONGO S
BONGS
BONKS
BONNE ST
BONNY
BONUS
BONZE RS
BOOBS
BOOBY
BOODY
BOOED
BOOGY
E BOOKS
BOOMS
BOOMY
BOONS
BOORS
BOOST S
BOOTH S
BOOTS
BOOTY
BOOZE DRS
BOOZY
A BORAL S
BORAS
BORAX
BORED
BORER S
BORES
BORIC
BORKS
BORNE
BORON S
A BORTS
BORTY
BORTZ
BOSKS
BOSKY
BOSOM SY
BOSON S
BOSSY
BOSUN S
BOTAS
BOTCH Y
BOTEL S
BOTHY
BOTTS
BOUGH ST
BOULE S
A BOUND S
BOURG S
BOURN ES
BOUSE DS
BOUSY
BOUTS
BOVID S
BOWED
BOWEL S
BOWER SY
BOWLS
BOWSE DS
BOXED
BOXER S
BOXES
BOYAR DS
BOYLA S
BOYOS
BOZOS
BRACE DRS
BRACH S
BRACT S
BRADS
BRAES
BRAGS
BRAID S
BRAIL S
BRAIN SY
BRAKE DS
BRAKY
BRAND SY
BRANK S
BRANS
BRANT S
BRASH Y
BRASS Y
BRATS
BRAVA S
BRAVE DRS
BRAVI
BRAVO S
BRAWL SY
BRAWN SY
BRAWS
BRAXY
BRAYS
BRAZA S
BRAZE DNRS
BREAD SY
BREAK S
BREAM S
BREDE S
BREED S
BREES
BRENS
BRENT S
BREVE ST
BREWS
BRIAR DSY
BRIBE DERS
BRICK SY
BRIDE S
BRIEF S
BRIER SY
BRIES
BRIGS
BRILL OS
BRIMS
BRINE DRS
BRING S
BRINK S
BRINS
BRINY
BRIOS
BRISK S
BRISS
BRITH S
BRITS
BRITT S
A BROAD S
BROCK S
BROIL S
BROKE NR
BROME S
BROMO S
BRONC OS
BROOD SY
BROOK S
BROOM SY
BROOS
BROSE S
BROSY
BROTH SY
BROWN SY
BROWS E
BRUGH S
BRUIN S
BRUIT S
BRUME S
BRUNG
BRUNT S
BRUSH Y
BRUSK
BRUTE DS
BRUTS
BUBAL ES
BUBBA S
BUBBY
BUBUS
BUCKO S
BUCKS
BUDDY
BUDGE DRST
BUFFI
BUFFO S
BUFFS
BUFFY
BUGGY
BUGLE DRS
BUHLS
BUHRS
BUILD S
BUILT
BULBS
BULGE DRS
BULGY
BULKS
BULKY
BULLA E
BULLS
BULLY
BUMFS
BUMPH S
BUMPS
BUMPY
BUNAS
BUNCH Y
BUNCO S
BUNDS
BUNDT S
BUNGS
BUNKO S
BUNKS
BUNNS
BUNNY
BUNTS
BUNYA S
BUOYS
BUPPY
BURAN S
BURAS
BURBS
BURDS
BURET S
BURGH S
BURGS
BURIN S
BURKA S
BURKE DRS
BURLS
BURLY
BURNS
BURNT
BURPS
BURQA S
BURRO SW
BURRS
BURRY
BURSA ELRS
BURSE S
BURST S
BUSBY
A BUSED
A BUSES
BUSHY
BUSKS
BUSTS
BUSTY
BUTCH
BUTEO S
BUTES
BUTLE DRS
BUTTE DRS
BUTTS
BUTTY
BUTUT S
BUTYL S
BUXOM
BUYER S
BWANA S
BYLAW S
BYRES
BYRLS
BYSSI
BYTES
BYWAY S
CABAL AS
S CABBY
CABER S
CABIN S
CABLE DRST
CABOB S
CACAO S
CACAS
CACHE DST
CACTI
CADDY
CADES
CADET S
CADGE DRS
CADGY
CADIS
CADRE S
CAECA L
CAFES
CAFFS
CAGED
CAGER S
CAGES
CAGEY
CAHOW S
CAIDS
CAINS
CAIRD S
CAIRN SY
CAJON
CAKED
CAKES
CAKEY
CALFS
CALIF S
CALIX
CALKS
CALLA NS
S CALLS
CALMS
CALOS
CALVE DS
CALYX
CAMAS S
CAMEL S
CAMEO S
CAMES
CAMOS
S CAMPI
CAMPO S
S CAMPS
CAMPY
CANAL S
CANDY
CANED
CANER S
CANES
CANID S
CANNA S
CANNY
CANOE DRS
CANON S
CANSO S
CANST
CANTO NRS
S CANTS
S CANTY
S CAPED
CAPER S
S CAPES
CAPHS
CAPIZ
CAPON S
CAPOS
CAPUT
CARAT ES
CARBO NSY
CARBS
CARDS
S CARED
S CARER S
S CARES S
CARET S
CAREX
CARGO S
CARKS

CARLE S
CARLS
CARNS
CARNY
CAROB S
CAROL IS
CAROM S
CARPI
S CARPS
CARRS
S CARRY
CARSE S
E CARTE DLRS
S CARTS
CARVE DLNRS

CASAS
CASED
CASES
CASKS
CASKY
CASTE RS
CASTS
CASUS
CATCH Y
CATER S
CATES
S CATTY
CAULD S
CAULK S
CAULS
CAUSE DRSY

CAVED
CAVER NS
CAVES
CAVIE S
CAVIL S
CAWED
CEASE DS
CEBID S
CECAL
CECUM
CEDAR NSY

CEDED
CEDER S
CEDES
CEDIS
CEIBA S
CEILI S
CEILS
CELEB S
CELLA ER
O CELLI
CELLO S
CELLS
CELOM S
CELTS
CENSE DRS

CENTO S
S CENTS
CENTU M
CEORL S
CEPES
CERCI S
CERED
CERES
CERIA S
CERIC
CEROS
CESTA S
CESTI
CETES
CHADS
CHAFE DRS

CHAFF SY
CHAIN ES
CHAIR S

CHAIS E
CHALK SY
CHAMP SY
CHAMS
CHANG ES
CHANT SY
CHAOS
CHAPE LS
CHAPS
CHAPT
E CHARD S
CHARE DS
CHARK AS
CHARM S
CHARR OSY

CHARS
CHART S
CHARY
CHASE DRS

CHASM SY
CHATS
CHAWS
CHAYS
CHEAP OS
CHEAT S
CHECK S
CHEEK SY
CHEEP S
CHEER OSY

CHEFS
CHELA ES
CHEMO S
CHERT SY
CHESS
CHEST SY
CHETH S
CHEVY
CHEWS
CHEWY
CHIAO
CHIAS M
CHICA S
CHICK S
CHICO S
CHICS
CHIDE DRS

CHIEF S
CHIEL DS
CHILD E
CHILE S
CHILI S
CHILL ISY

CHIMB S
CHIME DRS

CHIMP S
CHINA S
CHINE DS
CHINK SY
CHINO S
CHINS
CHIPS
CHIRK S
CHIRM S
CHIRO S
CHIRP SY
CHIRR ES
CHIRU S
CHITS
CHIVE S
CHIVY
CHOCK S
CHOIR S
CHOKE DRSY

CHOKY
CHOLA S
CHOLO S

CHOMP S
CHOOK S
CHOPS
CHORD S
CHORE ADS

CHOSE NS
CHOTT S
CHOWS E
CHUBS
CHUCK SY
CHUFA S
CHUFF SY
CHUGS
CHUMP S
CHUMS
CHUNK SY
CHURL S
CHURN S
CHURR OS
CHUTE DS
CHYLE S
CHYME S
CIBOL S
CIDER S
CIGAR S
CILIA
CIMEX
CINCH
CINES
S CIONS
CIRCA
CIRES
CIRRI
CISCO S
CISSY
CISTS
CITED
CITER S
CITES
CIVET S
CIVIC S
CIVIE S
CIVIL
CIVVY
CLACH S
CLACK S
CLADE S
CLADS
CLAGS
CLAIM S
CLAMP S
CLAMS
CLANG S
CLANK SY
CLANS
CLAPS
CLAPT
CLARO S
CLARY
CLASH
CLASP ST
CLASS Y
CLAST S
CLAVE RS
CLAVI
CLAWS
CLAYS
CLEAN S
CLEAR S
CLEAT S
CLEEK S
CLEFS
CLEFT S
CLEPE DS
Y CLEPT
CLERK S
CLEWS
CLICK S
CLIFF SY
CLIFT S
CLIMB S

CLIME S
CLINE S
CLING SY
CLINK S
CLIPS
CLIPT
CLOAK S
CLOCK S
CLODS
CLOGS
CLOMB
CLOMP S
CLONE DRS

CLONK S
CLONS
CLOOT S
CLOPS
CLOSE DRST

CLOTH ES
CLOTS
CLOUD SY
CLOUR S
CLOUT S
CLOVE NRS

CLOWN S
CLOYS
CLOZE S
CLUBS
CLUCK S
CLUED
CLUES
CLUMP SY
CLUNG
CLUNK SY
CNIDA E
COACH
COACT S
COALA S
COALS
COALY
COAPT S
COAST S
COATI S
COATS
COBBS
COBBY
COBIA S
COBLE S
COBRA S
COCAS
COCCI CD
COCKS
COCKY
COCOA S
COCOS
CODAS
CODEC S
CODED
CODEN S
CODER S
CODES
CODEX
CODON S
COEDS
S COFFS
COGON S
COHOG S
COHOS HT
COIFS
COIGN ES
COILS
COINS
COIRS
COKED
COKES
COLAS
COLBY S
S COLDS
COLED
COLES

COLIC S
COLIN S
COLLY
COLOG S
COLON EISY

COLOR S
COLTS
COLZA S
COMAE
COMAL
COMAS
COMBE DRS

COMBO S
COMBS
COMER S
COMES
COMET HS
COMFY
COMIC S
COMIX
COMMA S
COMMY
COMPO S
COMPS
COMPT S
COMTE S
CONCH AOSY

CONDO MRS

CONED
IS CONES
CONEY S
CONGA S
CONGE ERS

CONGO SU
I CONIC S
CONIN EGS

CONKS
CONKY
CONNS
CONTE S
CONTO S
CONUS
S COOCH
COOED
COOEE DS
COOER S
COOEY S
COOFS
COOKS
COOKY
COOLS
COOLY
COOMB ES
COONS
S COOPS
COOPT S
S COOTS
COPAL MS
COPAY S
S COPED
COPEN S
COPER S
S COPES
COPRA HS
COPSE S
CORAL S
CORBY
CORDS
S CORED
S CORER S
S CORES
CORGI S
S CORIA
CORKS
CORKY
CORMS
AS CORNS

CORNU AS
CORNY
CORPS E
CORSE ST
COSEC S
COSES
COSET S
COSEY S
COSIE DRS

COSTA ELR

COSTS
COTAN S
COTED
COTES
COTTA ERS

COUCH
COUDE
COUGH S
COULD
COUNT SY
COUPE DS
COUPS
COURT S
S COUTH S
COVED
COVEN S
COVER ST
COVES
COVET S
COVEY S
COVIN GS
S COWED
COWER S
S COWLS
COWRY
COXAE
COXAL
COXED
COXES
COYED
COYER
COYLY
COYPU S
COZEN S
COZES
COZEY S
COZIE DRS

CRAAL S
CRABS
CRACK SY
CRAFT SY
S CRAGS
CRAKE S
CRAMP SY
S CRAMS
CRANE DS
CRANK SY
S CRAPE DS
S CRAPS
CRASH
CRASS
CRATE DRS

CRAVE DNRS

S CRAWL SY
CRAWS
CRAZE DS
CRAZY
S CREAK SY
S CREAM SY
CREDO S
CREDS
S CREED S
CREEK S
CREEL S
CREEP SY
CREME S

CREPE DSY

CREPT
CREPY
CRESS Y
CREST S
S CREWS
CRIBS
CRICK S
S CRIED
CRIER S
S CRIES
CRIME S
S CRIMP SY
CRIPE S
CRISP SY
CRITS
CROAK SY
CROCI
CROCK S
CROCS
CROFT S
CRONE S
CRONY
CROOK S
CROON S
CROPS
CRORE S
A CROSS E
CROUP ESY

CROWD SY
CROWN S
CROWS
CROZE RS
CRUCK S
CRUDE RS
CRUDS
CRUEL
CRUET S
CRUMB SY
CRUMP S
CRUOR S
CRURA L
CRUSE ST
CRUSH
CRUST SY
CRWTH S
CRYPT OS
CUBBY
CUBEB S
CUBED
CUBER S
CUBES
CUBIC S
CUBIT IS
CUDDY
S CUFFS
CUIFS
CUING
CUISH
CUKES
S CULCH
CULET S
CULEX
S CULLS
CULLY
CULMS
CULPA E
CULTI C
CULTS
CUMIN S
CUNTS
CUPEL S
CUPID S
CUPPA S
CUPPY
CURBS
CURCH
CURDS
CURDY
CURED
CURER S

CURES
CURET S
S CURFS
CURIA EL
CURIE S
CURIO S
CURLS
CURLY
CURNS
CURRS
S CURRY
CURSE DRS

CURST
CURVE DSTY

S CURVY
CUSEC S
CUSHY
CUSKS
CUSPS
CUSSO S
S CUTCH
A CUTER
AS CUTES TY
CUTEY S
CUTIE S
CUTIN S
CUTIS
CUTTY
CUTUP S
CUVEE S
CYANO
CYANS
CYBER
CYCAD S
CYCAS
CYCLE DRS

CYCLO S
CYDER S
CYLIX
CYMAE
CYMAR S
CYMAS
CYMES
CYMOL S
CYNIC S
CYSTS
CYTON S
CZARS

DACES
DACHA S
DADAS
DADDY
DADOS
DAFFS
DAFFY
DAGGA S
DAGOS
DAHLS
DAILY
DAIRY
DAISY
DALES
DALLY
DAMAN S
DAMAR S
DAMES
DAMNS
DAMPS
DANCE DRS

DANDY
DANGS
DANIO S
DARBS
DARED
DARER S
DARES
DARIC S
DARKS

DARKY
DARNS
DARTS
DASHI S
DASHY
DATED
DATER S
DATES
DATOS
DATTO S
DATUM S
DAUBE DRS

DAUBS
DAUBY
DAUNT S
DAUTS
DAVEN S
DAVIT S
DAWED
DAWEN
DAWKS
DAWNS
DAWTS
DAZED
DAZES
DEADS
DEAIR S
I DEALS
DEALT
DEANS
DEARS
DEARY
DEASH
DEATH SY
DEAVE DS
DEBAG S
DEBAR KS
DEBIT S
DEBTS
DEBUG S
DEBUT S
DEBYE S
DECAF S
DECAL S
DECAY S
DECKS
DECOR S
DECOS
DECOY S
DECRY
DEDAL
DEEDS
DEEDY
A DEEMS
DEEPS
DEERS
DEETS
DEFAT S
DEFER S
DEFIS
DEFOG S
DEGAS
DEGUM S
DEICE DRS

DEIFY
DEIGN S
DEILS
DEISM S
DEIST S
DEITY
DEKED
DEKES
DEKKO S
DELAY S
DELED
DELES
DELFS
DELFT S
DELIS HT
DELLS
DELLY

DELTA S
DELTS
DELVE DRS
DEMES
DEMIC
DEMIT S
DEMOB S
DEMON S
DEMOS
DEMUR ES
DENAR ISY
DENES
DENIM S
DENSE R
DENTS
DEOXY
DEPOT S
DEPTH S
DERAT ES
DERAY S
DERBY
DERMA LS
DERMS
DERRY
DESEX
DESKS
DETER S
DETOX
DEUCE DS
DEVAS
DEVEL S
DEVIL S
DEVON S
DEWAN S
DEWAR S
DEWAX
DEWED
DEXES
DEXIE S
DHAKS
DHALS
DHOBI S
DHOLE S
DHOTI S
DHOWS
DHUTI S
DIALS
DIARY
DIAZO
DICED
DICER S
DICES
DICEY
DICKS
DICKY
DICOT S
DICTA
DICTY
DIDIE S
DIDOS
DIDST
DIENE S
DIETS
DIFFS
DIGHT S
DIGIT S
DIKED
DIKER S
DIKES
DIKEY
DILDO ES
DILLS
DILLY
DIMER S
DIMES
DIMLY
DINAR S
DINED
DINER OS
DINES

DINGE DRSY
DINGO
DINGS
DINGY
DINKS
DINKY
DINOS
DINTS
DIODE S
DIOLS
DIPPY
DIPSO S
DIRAM S
DIRER
DIRGE S
DIRKS
DIRLS
DIRTS
DIRTY
DISCI
DISCO S
DISCS
DISHY
DISKS
DISME S
DITAS
DITCH
DITES
DITSY
DITTO S
DITTY
DITZY
DIVAN S
DIVAS
DIVED
DIVER ST
DIVES T
DIVOT S
DIVVY
DIWAN S
DIXIT S
DIZEN S
DIZZY
DJINN ISY
DJINS
DOATS
DOBBY
DOBIE S
DOBLA S
DOBRA S
DOBRO S
DOCKS
DODGE DMRS
DODGY
DODOS
DOERS
DOEST
DOETH
DOFFS
DOGES
DOGEY S
DOGGO
DOGGY
DOGIE S
DOGMA S
DOILY
DOING S
DOITS
DOJOS
DOLCE
DOLCI
DOLED
DOLES
DOLLS
DOLLY
DOLMA NS
DOLOR S
DOLTS
DOMAL
DOMED

DOMES
DOMIC
DONAS
DONEE S
DONGA S
DONGS
DONNA S
DONNE DE
DONOR S
DONSY
DONUT S
DOODY
DOOLY
DOOMS
DOOMY
DOORS
DOOZY
DOPAS
DOPED
DOPER S
DOPES
DOPEY
DORKS
DORKY
DORMS
DORMY
DORPS
DORRS
DORSA DL
DORTY
DOSED
DOSER S
DOSES
DOTAL
DOTED
DOTER S
DOTES
DOTTY
DOUBT S
DOUCE
DOUGH STY
DOULA S
DOUMA S
DOUMS
DOURA HS
DOUSE DRS
DOVEN S
DOVES
DOWDY
DOWED
DOWEL S
DOWER SY
DOWIE
DOWNS
DOWNY
DOWRY
DOWSE DRS
DOXIE S
DOYEN S
DOYLY
DOZED
DOZEN S
DOZER S
DOZES
DRABS
DRAFF SY
DRAFT SY
DRAGS
DRAIL S
DRAIN S
DRAKE S
DRAMA S
DRAMS
DRANK
DRAPE DRSY
DRATS
DRAVE
DRAWL SY
DRAWN

DRAWS
DRAYS
DREAD S
DREAM STY
DREAR SY
DRECK SY
DREED
DREES
DREGS
DREKS
DRESS Y
DREST
DRIBS
DRIED
DRIER S
DRIES T
A DRIFT SY
DRILL S
DRILY
DRINK S
DRIPS
DRIPT
DRIVE LNRS
DROID S
A DROIT S
DROLL SY
DRONE DRS
DROOL SY
DROOP SY
DROPS Y
DROPT
DROSS Y
DROUK S
DROVE DRS
DROWN DS
DRUBS
DRUGS
DRUID S
DRUMS
DRUNK S
DRUPE S
DRUSE S
DRYAD S
DRYER S
DRYLY
DUADS
DUALS
DUCAL
DUCAT S
E DUCES
DUCHY
DUCKS
DUCKY
E DUCTS
DUDDY
DUDED
DUDES
DUELS
DUETS
DUFFS
DUFUS
DUITS
DUKED
DUKES
DULIA S
DULLS
DULLY
DULSE S
DUMAS
DUMBO S
DUMBS
DUMKA
DUMKY
DUMMY
DUMPS
DUMPY
DUNAM S
DUNCE S
DUNCH

DUNES
DUNGS
DUNGY
DUNKS
DUNTS
DUOMI
DUOMO S
DUPED
DUPER SY
DUPES
DUPLE X
DURAL
DURAS
DURED
DURES S
DURNS
DUROC S
DUROS
DURRA S
DURRS
DURST
DURUM S
DUSKS
DUSKY
DUSTS
DUSTY
DUTCH
DUVET S
DWARF S
DWEEB SY
DWELL S
DWELT
DWINE DS
DYADS
DYERS
DYING S
DYKED
DYKES
DYKEY
DYNEL S
DYNES
M EAGER S
B EAGLE DST
M EAGRE S
FGNRST EARED
P EARLS
DNPY EARLY
LY EARNS
DH EARTH SY
CFLT EASED
TW EASEL S
CFLPT EASES
BFLY EASTS
BN EATEN
BFHNS EATER SY
DHLRW EAVED
DHLRW EAVES
W EBBED
EBBET S
EBONS
EBONY
R EBOOK S
LPT ECHED
L ECHES
ECHOS
ECLAT S
ECRUS
O EDEMA S
HKW EDGED
HL EDGER S
HKLSW EDGES
EDICT S
EDIFY

AS EDILE S
EDITS
DRS EDUCE DS
D EDUCT S
P EERIE R
EGADS
L EGERS
EGEST AS
BS EGGAR S
BKLPV EGGED
K EGGER S
R EGRET S
EIDER S
EIDOS
HW EIGHT HSY
EIKON S
DR EJECT AS
D EKING
ELAIN S
R ELAND S
ELANS
DGRV ELATE DRS
ELBOW S
GMW ELDER S
S ELECT S
ELEGY
ELEMI S
ELFIN S
ELIDE DS
ELINT S
P ELITE S
ELOIN S
ELOPE DRS
D ELUDE DRS
ELUTE DS
D ELVER S
DHPS ELVES
R EMAIL S
EMBAR KS
EMBAY S
EMBED S
M EMBER S
EMBOW S
EMCEE DS
EMEER S
R EMEND S
EMERY
EMEUS
EMIRS
DR EMITS
H EMMER S
EMMET S
EMMYS
DGR EMOTE DRS
EMPTY
EMYDE S
EMYDS
ENACT S
S ENATE S
BFMPRSTVW ENDED
BFGLMRSTV ENDER S
ENDOW S
V ENDUE DS
ENEMA S
ENEMY
ENJOY S
ENNUI S
ENOKI S
ENOLS
ENORM
ENOWS
ENROL LS
ENSKY

ENSUE DS
CRTV ENTER AS
ENTIA
GS ENTRY
T ENURE DS
R ENVOI S
ENVOY S
ENZYM ES
EOSIN ES
EPACT S
T EPEES
EPHAH S
EPHAS
EPHOD S
EPHOR IS
EPICS
EPOCH S
EPODE S
EPOXY
EQUAL S
EQUID S
EQUIP S
ERASE DRS
ERECT S
ERGOT S
ERICA S
KT ERNES
ERODE DS
R EROSE S
ERRED
T ERROR S
PV ERSES
ERUCT S
A ERUGO S
ERUPT S
ERVIL S
ESCAR PS
ESCOT S
ESKAR S
ESKER S
M ESNES
ESSAY S
CFJMNY ESSES
FJNPRTWYZ ESTER S
ESTOP S
R ETAPE S
ANTW ETHER S
ETHIC S
ETHOS
M ETHYL S
ETNAS
ETUDE S
ETUIS
ETWEE S
ETYMA
EUROS
EVADE DRS
S EVENS
EVENT S
R EVERT S
R EVERY
EVICT S
DK EVILS
EVITE DS
R EVOKE DRS
HS EWERS
EXACT AS
EXALT S
EXAMS
EXCEL S
EXECS
EXERT S
EXILE DRS
R EXINE S
HSV EXING

S EXIST S
EXITS
EXONS
EXPAT S
EXPEL S
EXPOS E
EXTOL LS
EXTRA S
EXUDE DS
EXULT S
EXURB S
EYASS
EYERS
K EYING
EYRAS
EYRES
EYRIE S
EYRIR
FABLE DRS
FACED
FACER S
FACES
FACET ES
FACIA ELS
FACTS
FADDY
FADED
FADER S
FADES
FADGE DS
FADOS
FAENA S
FAERY
FAGGY
FAGIN S
FAGOT S
FAILS
FAINT S
FAIRS
FAIRY
FAITH S
FAKED
FAKER SY
FAKES
FAKEY
FAKIR S
FALLS
FALSE R
FAMED
FAMES
FANCY
FANES
FANGA S
FANGS
FANNY
FANON S
FANOS
FANUM S
FAQIR S
FARAD S
FARCE DRS
FARCI E
FARCY
FARDS
FARED
FARER S
FARES
FARLE S
FARLS
FARMS
FAROS
FARTS
FASTS
FATAL
FATED
FATES
FATLY
FATSO S
FATTY

FATWA S
FAUGH
FAULD S
FAULT SY
FAUNA ELS
FAUNS
FAUVE S
FAVAS
FAVES
FAVOR S
FAVUS
FAWNS
FAWNY
FAXED
FAXES
FAYED
FAZED
FAZES
FEARS
FEASE DS
FEAST S
FEATS
FEAZE DS
FECAL
FECES
FECKS
FEDEX
FEEBS
FEEDS
FEELS
FEEZE DS
FEIGN S
FEINT S
FEIST SY
FELID S
FELLA HS
FELLS
FELLY
FELON SY
FELTS
FEMES
FEMME S
FEMUR S
FENCE DRS
FENDS
FENNY
FEODS
FEOFF S
FERAL S
FERES
FERIA ELS
FERLY
FERMI S
FERNS
FERNY
FERRY
FESSE DS
FESTS
FETAL
FETAS
FETCH
FETED
FETES
FETID
FETOR S
FETUS
FEUAR S
FEUDS
FEUED
FEVER S
FEWER
FEYER
FEYLY
FEZES
FEZZY
FIARS
FIATS
FIBER S
FIBRE S
FICES

FICHE S
FICHU S
FICIN S
FICUS
FIDGE DST
FIDOS
FIEFS
A FIELD S
FIEND S
FIERY
FIFED
FIFER S
FIFES
FIFTH S
FIFTY
FIGHT S
FILAR
FILCH
FILED
FILER S
FILES
FILET S
FILLE DRST
FILLO S
FILLS
FILLY
FILMI CS
FILMS
FILMY
FILOS E
FILTH SY
FILUM
FINAL ES
FINCA S
FINCH
FINDS
FINED
FINER Y
FINES T
FINIS H
FINKS
FINNY
FINOS
FIORD S
FIQUE S
FIRED
FIRER S
FIRES
FIRMS
FIRNS
FIRRY
FIRST S
FIRTH S
FISCS
FISHY
FISTS
FITCH Y
FITLY
FIVER S
FIVES
FIXED
FIXER S
FIXES
FIXIT Y
FIZZY
FJELD S
FJORD S
FLABS
FLACK S
FLAGS
FLAIL S
FLAIR S
FLAKE DRSY
FLAKY
A FLAME DNRS
FLAMS
FLAMY
FLANK S
FLANS
FLAPS
FLARE DS
FLASH Y
FLASK S
FLATS
FLAWS
FLAWY
FLAXY
FLAYS
FLEAM S
FLEAS
FLECK SY
FLEER S
FLEES
FLEET S
FLESH Y
FLEWS
FLEYS
FLICK S
FLICS
FLIED
FLIER S
FLIES T
FLING S
FLINT SY
FLIPS
FLIRS
FLIRT SY
FLITE DS
FLITS
A FLOAT SY
FLOCK SY
FLOCS
FLOES
FLOGS
FLONG S
FLOOD S
FLOOR S
FLOPS
FLORA ELS
FLOSS Y
FLOTA S
FLOUR SY
FLOUT S
FLOWN
FLOWS
FLUBS
FLUED
FLUES
FLUFF SY
FLUID S
FLUKE DSY
FLUKY
FLUME DS
FLUMP S
FLUNG
FLUNK SY
FLUOR S
FLUSH
FLUTE DRSY
FLUTY
FLUYT S
FLYBY S
FLYER S
FLYTE DS
FOALS
FOAMS
FOAMY
FOCAL
FOCUS
FOEHN S
FOGEY S
FOGGY
FOGIE S
FOHNS
FOILS
FOINS
FOIST S
FOLDS
FOLEY S
FOLIA R
FOLIC
FOLIO S
FOLKS Y
FOLKY
FOLLY
FONDS
FONDU ES
FONTS
FOODS
FOOLS
FOOTS Y
FOOTY
FORAM S
FORAY S
FORBS
FORBY E
FORCE DRS
FORDO
FORDS
FORES T
FORGE DRST
FORGO T
FORKS
FORKY
FORME DERS
FORMS
FORTE S
FORTH
FORTS
FORTY
FORUM S
FOSSA ES
FOSSE S
FOULS
FOUND S
FOUNT S
FOURS
FOVEA ELS
FOWLS
FOXED
FOXES
FOYER S
FRAGS
FRAIL S
FRAME DRS
FRANC S
FRANK S
FRAPS
FRASS
FRATS
FRAUD S
FRAYS
FREAK SY
FREED
FREER S
FREES T
FREMD
FRENA
FRERE S
A FRESH
FRETS
FRIAR SY
FRIED
FRIER S
FRIES
FRIGS
FRILL SY
FRISE ES
FRISK SY
FRITH S
A FRITS
FRITT S
FRITZ
FRIZZ Y
FROCK S
FROES
FROGS
FROND S
FRONS
FRONT S
FRORE
FROSH
FROST SY
FROTH SY
FROWN S
FROWS TY
FROZE N
FRUGS
FRUIT SY
FRUMP SY
FRYER S
FUBAR
FUBSY
FUCKS
FUCUS
FUDDY
FUDGE DS
FUELS
FUGAL
FUGGY
FUGIO S
FUGLE DS
FUGUE DS
FUGUS
FUJIS
FULLS
FULLY
FUMED
FUMER S
FUMES
FUMET S
FUNDI C
FUNDS
FUNGI C
FUNGO
FUNKS
FUNKY
FUNNY
FURAN ES
FURLS
FUROR ES
FURRY
FURZE S
FURZY
FUSED
FUSEE S
FUSEL S
FUSES
FUSIL ES
FUSSY
FUSTY
FUTON S
FUZED
FUZEE S
FUZES
FUZIL S
FUZZY
FYCES
FYKES
FYTTE S
GABBY
GABLE DS
GADDI S
GADID S
GADIS
GADJE
GADJO
GAFFE DRS
GAFFS
GAGED
GAGER S
GAGES
GAILY
GAINS T
GAITS
GALAH S
GALAS
GALAX Y
GALEA ES
GALES
GALLS
GALLY
GALOP S
A GAMAS
GAMAY S
GAMBA S
GAMBE S
GAMBS
GAMED
GAMER S
GAMES T
GAMEY
A GAMIC
GAMIN EGS
GAMMA S
GAMMY
GAMPS
GAMUT S
GANEF S
GANEV S
GANGS
GANJA HS
GANOF S
GAOLS
GAPED
GAPER S
A GAPES
GAPPY
GARBS
GARDA I
GARNI
GARTH S
GASES
GASPS
GASSY
GASTS
GATED
GATER S
A GATES
GATOR S
GAUDS
GAUDY
GAUGE DRS
GAULT S
GAUMS
GAUNT
GAURS
GAUSS
GAUZE S
GAUZY
GAVEL S
GAVOT S
GAWKS
GAWKY
GAWPS
GAWSY
GAYAL S
GAYER
GAYLY
GAZAR S
GAZED
GAZER S
GAZES
GAZOO S
GEARS
GECKO S
GECKS
GEEKS
GEEKY
GEESE
GEEST S
GELDS
GELEE S
GELID
GELTS
GEMMA E
GEMMY
GEMOT ES
A GENES
GENET S
GENIC
GENIE S
GENII
GENIP S
GENOA S
GENOM ES
GENRE S
GENRO S
A GENTS
GENUA
GENUS
GEODE S
GEOID S
GERAH S
GERMS
GERMY
GESSO
GESTE S
E GESTS
GETAS
GETUP S
GEUMS
A GHAST
GHATS
GHAUT S
GHAZI S
GHEES
GHOST SY
GHOUL S
GHYLL S
GIANT S
GIBED
GIBER S
GIBES
GIDDY
GIFTS
GIGAS
GIGHE
GIGOT S
GIGUE S
GILDS
GILLS
GILLY
GILTS
GIMEL S
GIMME S
GIMPS
GIMPY
GINKS
GINNY
GINZO
GIPON S
GIPSY
GIRDS
GIRLS
GIRLY
GIRNS
GIRON S
GIROS
GIRSH
GIRTH S
GIRTS
GISMO S
A GISTS
GITES
GIVEN S
GIVER S
O GIVES
GIZMO S
GLACE S
GLADE S
GLADS
GLADY
GLAIR ESY
GLAMS
GLAND S
GLANS
A GLARE DS
GLARY
GLASS Y
GLAZE DRS
GLAZY
A GLEAM SY
GLEAN S
GLEBA E
GLEBE S
GLEDE S
GLEDS
GLEED S
GLEEK S
GLEES
GLEET SY
GLENS
GLEYS
GLIAL
GLIAS
GLIDE DRS
GLIFF S
GLIME DS
GLIMS
GLINT SY
GLITZ Y
GLOAM S
GLOAT S
GLOBE DS
GLOBS
GLOGG S
GLOMS
GLOOM SY
GLOPS
GLORY
GLOSS AY
GLOST S
GLOUT S
GLOVE DRS
GLOWS
GLOZE DS
GLUED
GLUER S
GLUES
GLUEY
GLUGS
GLUME S
GLUMS
GLUON S
GLUTE INS
GLUTS
GLYPH S
GNARL SY
GNARR S
GNARS
GNASH
GNATS
GNAWN
GNAWS
GNOME S
GOADS
GOALS
GOATS
GOBAN GS
GOBOS
GODET S
GODLY
GOERS
GOFER S
GOGOS
GOING S
GOLDS
GOLEM S
GOLFS
GOLLY
GOMBO S
GOMER S
GONAD S
GONEF S
GONER S
GONGS
GONIA
GONIF FS
GONOF S
GONZO
GOODS
GOODY
GOOEY
GOOFS
GOOFY
GOOKS
GOOKY
GOONS
GOONY
GOOPS
GOOPY
GOOSE DSY
GOOSY
GOPIK
GORAL S
GORED
GORES
GORGE DRST
GORMS
GORPS
GORSE S
GORSY
GOTHS
GOUGE DRS
GOURD ES
GOUTS
A GOUTY
GOWAN SY
GOWDS
GOWKS
GOWNS
GOXES
GOYIM
GRAAL S
GRABS
GRACE DS
GRADE DRS
GRADS
GRAFT S
GRAIL S
GRAIN SY
GRAMA S
GRAMP AS
GRAMS
GRANA
GRAND S
GRANS
GRANT S
GRAPE SY
GRAPH S
GRAPY
GRASP S
GRASS Y
GRATE DRS
GRAVE DLNRS
GRAVY
GRAYS
GRAZE DRS
GREAT S
GREBE S
A GREED SY
GREEK
GREEN SY
A GREES
GREET S
GREGO S
GREYS
GRIDE DS
GRIDS
GRIEF S
GRIFF ES
GRIFT S
GRIGS
GRILL ES
GRIME DS
GRIMY
GRIND S
GRINS
GRIOT S
GRIPE DRSY
GRIPS
GRIPT
GRIPY
GRIST S
GRITH S
GRITS
GROAN S
GROAT S
GRODY
GROGS
GROIN S
GROKS
GROOM S
GROPE DRS
GROSS
GROSZ EY
GROTS
GROUP S
GROUT SY
GROVE DLS
GROWL SY
GROWN
GROWS
GRUBS
GRUEL S
GRUES
GRUFF SY
GRUME S
GRUMP SY
GRUNT S
GUACO S
GUANO S
GUANS
GUARD S
GUARS
GUAVA S
GUCKS
GUDES
GUESS
GUEST S
GUFFS
GUIDE DRS
GUIDS
GUILD S
GUILE DS
GUILT SY
GUIRO S
GUISE DS
GULAG S
GULAR
GULCH
GULES
GULFS
GULFY
GULLS
GULLY
GULPS
GULPY
GUMBO S
GUMMA S
GUMMY
GUNKS
GUNKY
GUNNY
GUPPY
GURGE DS
GURRY
GURSH
GURUS
GUSHY
GUSSY
GUSTO

GUSTS
GUSTY
GUTSY
GUTTA E
GUTTY
GUYED
GUYOT S
GWINE
GYBED
GYBES
GYOZA S
GYPSY
GYRAL
GYRED
GYRES
GYRON S
GYROS E
GYRUS
GYVED
GYVES

HAAFS
HAARS
HABIT S
HABUS
HACEK S
STW HACKS
HADAL
S HADED
S HADES
HADJI S
HADST
HAEMS
HAETS
HAFIZ
S HAFTS
HAHAS
HAIKA
HAIKS
HAIKU S
HAILS
HAINT S
C HAIRS
HAIRY
HAJES
HAJIS
HAJJI S
S HAKES
HAKIM S
HAKUS
HALAL AS
SW HALED
TW HALER SU
SW HALES T
HALID ES
HALLO AOSTW

HALLS
HALMA S
HALMS
HALON S
HALOS
HALTS
HALVA HS
HALVE DS
HAMAL S
S HAMES
CSW HAMMY
HAMZA HS
C HANCE S
HANDS
S HANDY
BCW HANGS
ST HANKS
HANKY
HANSA S
HANSE LS
C HANTS
HAOLE S
HAPAX
HAPLY
HAPPY
CS HARDS
HARDY
CS HARED
HAREM S
CS HARES
CS HARKS
HARLS
CT HARMS
S HARPS
S HARPY
CG HARRY
HARSH
C HARTS
HASPS
C HASTE DNS

HASTY
T HATCH
HATED
HATER S
HATES
S HAUGH S
HAULM SY
S HAULS
C HAUNT S
HAUTE
S HAVEN S
S HAVER S
S HAVES
HAVOC S
CST HAWED
HAWKS
HAWSE RS
HAYED
HAYER S
HAYEY
C HAZAN S
HAZED
HAZEL S
HAZER S
HAZES
HEADS
HEADY
SW HEALS
C HEAPS
HEAPY
HEARD
S HEARS E
HEART HSY
S HEATH SY
CW HEATS
S HEAVE DNRS
HEAVY
T HEBES
C HECKS
C HEDER S
HEDGE DRS
HEDGY
HEEDS
W HEELS
W HEEZE DS
T HEFTS
HEFTY
HEIGH T
HEILS
T HEIRS
T HEIST S
HELIO S
HELIX
HELLO S
S HELLS
W HELMS
HELOS
HELOT S
W HELPS
S HELVE DS
HEMAL
RT HEMES
C HEMIC
HEMIN S
HEMPS
HEMPY
TW HENCE
HENGE S
HENNA S
HENRY S
HENTS
HERBS
HERBY
S HERDS
TW HERES Y
HERLS
HERMA EI
T HERMS
HERNS
HERON S
HEROS
CSW HERRY
HERTZ
C HESTS
CK HETHS
S HEUCH S
S HEUGH S
CS HEWED
CS HEWER S
HEXAD ES
HEXED
HEXER S
HEXES
HEXYL S
CT HICKS
C HIDED
C HIDER S
C HIDES
T HIGHS
HIGHT HS
HIJAB S
HIJRA HS
HIKED
HIKER S
HIKES
HILAR
HILLO AS
CST HILLS
C HILLY
HILTS
HILUM
HILUS
HINDS
W HINGE DRS
C HINKY
SW HINNY
C HINTS
HIPLY
HIPPO S
CW HIPPY
HIRED
HIREE S
HIRER S
S HIRES
HISSY
SW HISTS
HITCH
HIVED
CS HIVES
HOAGY
HOARD S
HOARS E
HOARY
HOBBY
HOBOS
CS HOCKS
HOCUS
HODAD S
S HOERS
HOGAN S
HOGGS
HOICK S
HOISE DS
HOIST S
C HOKED
C HOKES
C HOKEY
HOKKU
HOKUM S
A HOLDS
T HOLED
DTW HOLES
HOLEY
HOLKS
C HOLLA S
HOLLO AOSW
W HOLLY
HOLMS
HOLTS
HOMED
HOMER S
HOMES
HOMEY S
HOMIE RS
HOMOS
HONAN S
HONDA S
P HONED
HONER S
P HONES T
P HONEY S
HONGI
T HONGS
HONKS
HONKY
HONOR S
HOOCH
HOODS
HOODY
P HOOEY S
W HOOFS
HOOKA HS
CS HOOKS
HOOKY
D HOOLY
W HOOPS
BS HOOTS
HOOTY
HOPED
HOPER S
HOPES
C HOPPY
HORAH S
C HORAL
HORAS
HORDE DS
T HORNS
T HORNY
A HORSE DY

HORST ES
HORSY
HOSED
HOSEL S
C HOSEN
HOSER S
C HOSES
HOSEY S
HOSTA S
G HOSTS
HOTCH
HOTEL S
HOTLY
HOUND S
HOURI S
HOURS
C HOUSE DLRS
S HOVEL S
S HOVER S
HOWDY
HOWES
HOWFF S
HOWFS
HOWKS
HOWLS
HOYAS
HOYLE S
C HUBBY
CS HUCKS
C HUFFS
C HUFFY
HUGER
HULAS
HULKS
HULKY
HULLO AOS

HULLS
HUMAN ES
HUMIC
HUMID
HUMOR S
HUMPH S
CTW HUMPS
HUMPY
HUMUS
HUNCH
CT HUNKS
C HUNKY
S HUNTS
HURDS
CT HURLS
HURLY
HURRY
HURST S
HURTS
HUSKS
HUSKY
HUSSY
HUTCH
HUZZA HS
HYDRA ES
HYDRO S
HYENA S
S HYING
HYLAS
HYMEN S
HYMNS
HYOID S
HYPED
HYPER S
HYPES
HYPHA EL
HYPOS
HYRAX
HYSON S

IAMBI C
IAMBS
ICHOR S
D ICIER
ICILY
DRV ICING S
BDKLNPSTW ICKER S

ICONS
ICTIC
R ICTUS
IDEAL S
IDEAS
IDIOM S
IDIOT S
S IDLED
S IDLER S
S IDLES T
IDOLS
IDYLL S
IDYLS
DFGJPRWZ IGGED

IGLOO S
IGLUS
IHRAM S
IKATS
E IKONS
ILEAC
ILEAL
P ILEUM
P ILEUS
ILIAC
ILIAD S
F ILIAL
CM ILIUM
BFGHKMSTW ILLER

IMAGE DRS

IMAGO S
IMAMS
IMAUM S
L IMBED S
IMBUE DS
IMIDE S
IMIDO
IMIDS
IMINE S
IMINO
IMMIX
GLPW IMPED E

IMPEL S
IMPIS H
DJLPS IMPLY

INANE RS
INAPT
INARM S
INBYE
INCOG S
INCUR S
INCUS E
INDEX
INDIE S
INDOL ES
W INDOW S
INDRI S
INDUE DS
INEPT
INERT S
INFER S
INFIX
INFOS
INFRA
DJMST INGLE S

INGOT S
MP INION S
DFJKLOPW INKED

JLPSTW INKER S
TW INKLE S
INLAY S
INLET S
BDFGPSTW INNED

DGPSTW INNER S

INPUT S
INRUN S
INSET S
HLMSTW INTER NS

INTIS
INTRO NS
INURE DS
INURN S
INVAR S
IODIC
IODID ES
IODIN ES
BP IONIC S
B IOTAS
T IRADE S
P IRATE R
IRIDS
AFHMSTW IRING
D IRKED
IROKO S
IRONE DRS

G IRONS
IRONY
ISBAS
AM ISLED
AL ISLES
ISLET S
ISSEI S
T ISSUE DRS

ISTLE S
BFPW ITCHY

ITEMS
CDEHLMTWZ ITHER

IVIED
C IVIES
IVORY
IXIAS
IXORA S
IXTLE S
S IZARS

JABOT S
JACAL S
JACKS
JACKY
JADED
JADES
JAGER S
JAGGS
JAGGY
JAGRA S
JAILS
JAKES
JALAP S
JALOP SY
JAMBE DS
JAMBS
JAMMY
JANES
JANTY
JAPAN S
JAPED
JAPER SY
JAPES
JARLS
JATOS
JAUKS
JAUNT SY
JAUPS
JAVAS
JAWAN S
JAWED
JAZZY
JEANS
D JEBEL S
JEEPS
JEERS
JEFES
JEHAD S
JEHUS
JELLO S
JELLS
JELLY
JEMMY
JENNY
JERID S
JERKS
JERKY
JERRY
JESSE DS
JESTS
JETES
JETON S
JETTY
JEWED
JEWEL S
JIBBS
JIBED
JIBER S
JIBES
JIFFS
JIFFY
JIGGY
JIHAD S
JILLS
JILTS
JIMMY
JIMPY
JINGO
JINKS
D JINNI S
D JINNS
JISMS
JIVED
JIVER S
JIVES
JIVEY
JNANA S
JOCKO S
JOCKS
JOEYS
JOHNS
JOINS
JOINT S
JOIST S
JOKED
JOKER S
JOKES
JOKEY
JOLES
JOLLY
JOLTS
JOLTY
JOMON
JONES
JORAM S
JORUM S
JOTAS
JOTTY
JOUAL S
JOUKS
JOULE S
JOUST S
JOWAR S
JOWED
JOWLS
JOWLY
JOYED
JUBAS
JUBES
JUCOS
JUDAS
JUDGE DRS

JUDOS
JUGAL
JUGUM S
JUICE DRS

JUICY
JUJUS
JUKED
JUKES
JUKUS
JULEP S
JUMBO S
JUMPS
JUMPY
JUNCO S
JUNKS
JUNKY
JUNTA S
JUNTO S
JUPES
JUPON S
JURAL
JURAT S
JUREL S
JUROR S
JUSTS
JUTES
JUTTY

KABAB S
KABAR S
KABOB S
KADIS
KAFIR S
KAGUS
KAIAK S
KAIFS
KAILS
KAINS
KAKAS
KAKIS
KALAM S
KALES
KALIF S
KALPA CKS

KAMES
KAMIK S
KANAS
KANES
KANJI S
KANZU S
KAONS
KAPAS
KAPHS
KAPOK S
KAPPA S
KAPUT T
KARAT ES
KARMA S
KARNS
KAROO S
KARST S
KARTS
KASHA S
KATAS
KAURI S
KAURY
KAVAS S
KAYAK S
KAYOS
KAZOO S
KBARS
KEBAB S
KEBAR S
KEBOB S
KECKS
KEDGE DS
KEEFS
KEEKS
KEELS
S KEENS
KEEPS
S KEETS
KEEVE S
KEFIR S
KEIRS
KELEP S
KELIM S
KELLY
S KELPS
KELPY
KELTS
KEMPS
KEMPT
KENAF S
KENCH
KENDO S
KENOS
KENTE S
KEPIS
KERBS
KERFS
KERNE DLS

KERNS
S KERRY
S KETCH

KETOL S
KEVEL S
KEVIL S
KEXES
KEYED
KHADI S
KHAFS
KHAKI S
KHANS
KHAPH S
KHATS
KHEDA HS
KHETH S
KHETS
KHOUM S
KIANG S
KIBBE HS
KIBBI S
KIBEI S
KIBES
KIBLA HS
KICKS
KICKY
KIDDO S
S KIDDY
KIEFS
S KIERS
KIKES
KILIM S
S KILLS
KILNS
KILOS
KILTS
KILTY
KINAS E
KINDS
KINES
KINGS
KININ S
S KINKS
KINKY
KINOS
KIOSK S
KIRKS
KIRNS
KISSY
KISTS
S KITED
KITER S
S KITES
KITHE DS
KITHS
KITTY
KIVAS
KIWIS
KLICK S
KLIKS
KLONG S
KLOOF S
KLUGE DS
KLUTZ Y
KNACK S
KNAPS
KNARS
KNAUR S
KNAVE S
KNAWE LS
KNEAD S
KNEED
KNEEL S
KNEES
KNELL S
KNELT
KNIFE DR S
KNISH
KNITS
KNOBS
KNOCK S
KNOLL SY
KNOPS
KNOSP S

KNOTS
KNOUT S
KNOWN S
KNOWS
KNURL SY
KNURS
KOALA S
KOANS
KOBOS
KOELS
KOHLS
KOINE S
KOJIS
KOLAS
KOLOS
KOMBU S
KONKS
KOOKS
KOOKY
KOPEK S
KOPHS
KOPJE S
KOPPA S
KORAI
KORAS
KORAT S
KORMA S
KORUN AY
KOTOS
KOTOW S
KRAAL S
KRAFT S
KRAIT S
KRAUT S
KREEP S
KREWE S
KRILL S
KRONA
KRONE NR
KROON IS
KRUBI S
KUDOS
KUDUS
KUDZU S
KUFIS
KUGEL S
KUKRI S
KULAK IS
KUMYS
KURTA S
KURUS
KUSSO S
KVASS
KVELL S
KYACK S
KYAKS
KYARS
KYATS
KYLIX
KYRIE S
KYTES
KYTHE DS

LAARI
LABEL S
LABIA L
LABOR S
LABRA
P LACED
P LACER S
GP LACES
LACEY
BCF LACKS PS
B LADED
LADEN S
B LADER S
BCG LADES
LADLE DR S
LAEVO
LAGAN S
LAGER S

LAHAR S
LAICH S
LAICS
LAIGH S
LAIRD S
FG LAIRS
LAITH
LAITY
FS LAKED
FS LAKER S
FS LAKES
LAKHS
LALLS
LU LAMAS
LAMBS
LAMBY
BF LAMED HS
BF LAMER
BF LAMES T
LAMIA ES
C LAMPS
LANAI S
G LANCE DR ST
AEG LANDS
FP LANES
C LANKY
LAPEL S
LAPIN S
LAPIS
E LAPSE DR S
LARCH
LARDS
LARDY
LAREE S
BFG LARES
LARGE RS
LARGO S
LARIS
LARKS
LARKY
A LARUM S
LARVA EL S
LASED
LASER S
LASES
LASSI ES
LASSO S
BC LASTS
KS LATCH
AEP LATED S
P LATEN ST
EPS LATER
LATEX
LATHE DR S
LATHI S
LATHS
LATHY
LATKE S
LATTE NR S
LAUAN S
LAUDS
LAUGH S
LAURA ES
LAVAS H
S LAVED
CS LAVER S
CS LAVES
BCF LAWED
LAWNS
LAWNY
LAXER
F LAXES T
LAXLY
CFP LAYED S
FPS LAYER S
LAYIN GS

LAYUP S
LAZAR S
BG LAZED
BG LAZES
BP LEACH Y
P LEADS
LEADY
LEAFS
LEAFY
B LEAKS
LEAKY
CG LEANS
LEANT
LEAPS
LEAPT
LEARN ST
BC LEARS
B LEARY
P LEASE DR S
LEASH
LEAST S
CS LEAVE DN RS
LEAVY
LEBEN S
FPS LEDGE RS
F LEDGY
F LEECH
CGS LEEKS
F LEERS
LEERY
FGS LEETS
C LEFTS
LEFTY
LEGAL S
LEGER S
LEGES
LEGGY
E LEGIT S
LEHRS
LEHUA S
LEMAN S
LEMMA S
LEMON SY
LEMUR S
B LENDS
LENES
LENIS
LENOS
F LENSE DS
LENTO S
LEONE S
LEPER S
LEPTA
LESBO S
LESES
F LETCH
LETHE S
LETUP S
LEUDS
LEVEE DS
LEVEL S
C LEVER S
A LEVIN S
C LEVIS
LEWIS
FIP LEXES
LEXIS
LEZZY
LIANA S
LIANE S
LIANG S
LIARD S
LIARS
LIBEL S
LIBER S
LIBRA ES
LIBRI
LICHI S
LICHT S
E LICIT

CFK LICKS S
LIDAR S
LIDOS
LIEGE S
A LIENS
FP LIERS
LIEUS
S LIEVE R
LIFER S
C LIFTS
LIGAN DS
LIGER S
ABF LIGHT S PS
LIKED
LIKEN S
LIKER S
LIKES T
LILAC S
LILOS
LILTS
LIMAN S
LIMAS
LIMBA S
LIMBI C
LIMBO S
C LIMBS
LIMBY
GS LIMED
LIMEN S
CGS LIMES
B LIMEY S
LIMIT S
LIMNS
LIMOS
LIMPA S
B LIMPS Y
LINAC S
LINDY
A LINED
LINEN SY
A LINER S
AC LINES
LINEY
LINGA MS
O LINGO
CFS LINGS
C LINGY
LININ GS
BCP LINKS S
S LINKY
LINNS
LINOS
EFG LINTS
FG LINTY
LINUM S
LIONS
LIPID ES
LIPIN S
FS LIPPY
LIRAS
LIROT H
LISLE S
LISPS
LISTS
LITAI
LITAS
LITER S
B LITHE R
LITHO S
LITRE S
LIVED
LIVEN S
S LIVER SY
O LIVES T
LIVID
LIVRE S
LLAMA S
LLANO S
LOACH
LOADS

LOAFS
G LOAMS
LOAMY
LOANS
LOATH E
LOBAR
GS LOBBY
G LOBED
G LOBES
LOBOS
LOCAL ES
LOCHS
BCF LOCKS
LOCOS
LOCUM S
LOCUS T
LODEN S
LODES
LODGE DR S
LOESS
LOFTS
LOFTY
S LOGAN S
LOGES
C LOGGY
LOGIA
LOGIC S
LOGIN S
LOGOI
LOGON S
LOGOS
S LOIDS
AE LOINS
LOLLS
LOLLY
C LONER S
LONGE DR S
FK LONGS
LOOBY
LOOED
BF LOOEY S
LOOFA HS
K LOOFS
BF LOOIE S
LOOKS
BG LOOMS
LOONS
LOONY
BS LOOPS
LOOPY
LOOSE DN RS
C LOOTS
ES LOPED
ES LOPER S
ES LOPES
FGS LOPPY
F LORAL
LORAN S
LORDS
LORES
LORIS
LORRY
LOSEL S
C LOSER S
C LOSES
FG LOSSY
LOTAH S
F LOTAS
LOTIC
LOTOS
LOTTE DR S
B LOTTO S
LOTUS
CPS LOUGH S
LOUIE S
LOUIS
LOUMA S
LOUPE DN S

LOUPS
CF LOURS
F LOURY
B LOUSE DS
B LOUSY
CFG LOUTS
LOVAT S
G LOVED
CGP LOVER S
CG LOVES
BFG LOWED PS
BFG LOWER SY PS
LOWES T
S LOWLY
LOWSE
LOXED
LOXES
LOYAL
LUAUS
LUBED
LUBES
LUCES
LUCID
CP LUCKS
P LUCKY
LUCRE S
E LUDES
LUDIC
LUFFA S
BFS LUFFS
K LUGED
LUGER S
K LUGES
LULLS
LULUS
LUMAS
LUMEN S
CFP LUMPS S
CG LUMPY
LUNAR S
LUNAS
G LUNCH
LUNES
LUNET S
BP LUNGE DE RS
LUNGI S
LUNGS
CFP LUNKS
B LUNTS
LUPIN ES
LUPUS
LURCH
LURED
LURER S
LURES
LUREX
LURID
LURKS
LUSTS
LUSTY
LUSUS
LUTEA L
EF LUTED
EFG LUTES
F LUXES
LWEIS
LYARD
LYART
LYASE S
LYCEA
LYCEE S
LYCRA S
FP LYING S
LYMPH S
LYNCH
LYRES
LYRIC S
LYSED
LYSES

LYSIN EG S
LYSIS
LYSSA S
LYTIC
LYTTA ES

MAARS
MABES
MACAW S
MACED
MACER S
MACES
MACHE S
MACHO S
MACHS
S MACKS
MACLE DS
MACON S
MACRO NS
MADAM ES
MADLY
MADRE S
MAFIA S
MAFIC
I MAGES
MAGIC S
MAGMA S
MAGOT S
MAGUS
MAHOE S
MAIDS
MAILE DR S
MAILL S
E MAILS
MAIMS
MAINS
MAIRS
MAIST S
MAIZE S
MAJOR S
MAKAR S
MAKER S
MAKES
MAKOS
MALAR S
MALES
MALIC E
S MALLS
MALMS
MALMY
S MALTS
MALTY
MAMAS
MAMBA S
MAMBO S
MAMEY S
MAMIE S
MAMMA EL S
MAMMY
MANAS
MANAT S
MANED
MANES
MANGA S
MANGE LR SY
MANGO S
MANGY
MANIA CS
MANIC S
MANLY
MANNA NS
MANOR S
MANOS
MANSE S
MANTA S
MANUS
MAPLE S
MAQUI S
MARAS

MARCH
MARCS
MARES
MARGE S
MARIA
MARKA S
MARKS
MARLS
MARLY
MARRY
MARSE S
MARSH Y
S MARTS
MARVY
MASAS
MASER S
MASHY
MASKS
MASON S
MASSA S
MASSE DS
MASSY
MASTS
MATCH
MATED
MATER S
MATES
MATEY S
MATHS
MATIN GS
MATTE DR S
MATTS
MATZA HS
MATZO HS T
MAUDS
MAULS
MAUND SY
MAUTS
MAUVE S
MAVEN S
MAVIE S
MAVIN S
MAVIS
MAWED
MAXED
MAXES
MAXIM AS
MAXIS
MAYAN
MAYAS
MAYBE S
MAYED
MAYOR S
MAYOS
MAYST
A MAZED
MAZER S
AS MAZES
MBIRA S
MEADS
MEALS
MEALY
MEANS
MEANT
MEANY
MEATS
MEATY
MECCA S
MEDAL S
MEDIA DE LN S
MEDIC KO S
MEDII
MEEDS
MEETS
MEINY
MELDS
MELEE S
MELIC

S MELLS
MELON S
S MELTS
MELTY
MEMES
MEMOS
MENAD S
AE MENDS
MENSA ELS
MENSE DS
MENSH
O MENTA L
MENUS
MEOUS
MEOWS
MERCH
MERCS
MERCY
MERDE S
MERER
MERES T
E MERGE DERS
MERIT S
S MERKS
MERLE S
MERLS
MERRY
MESAS
MESHY
MESIC
MESNE S
MESON S
MESSY
METAL S
METED
METER S
METES
METHS
METIS
METOL S
METRE DS
METRO S
MEWED
MEWLS
MEZES
MEZZO S
MIAOU S
MIAOW S
MIASM AS
MIAUL S
MICAS
MICHE DS
MICKS
MICRA
MICRO NS
MIDDY
S MIDGE ST
MIDIS
A MIDST S
MIENS
MIFFS
MIFFY
MIGGS
MIGHT SY
MIKED
MIKES
MIKRA
MILCH
MILDS
S MILER S
S MILES
MILIA
MILKS
MILKY
MILLE DRST
MILLS
MILOS
MILPA S
MILTS
MILTY

MIMED
MIMEO S
MIMER S
MIMES
MIMIC S
MINAE
MINAS
MINCE DRS
MINCY
MINDS
MINED
MINER S
AI MINES
MINGY
MINIM AS
MINIS H
MINKE S
MINKS
MINNY
MINOR S
MINTS
MINTY
MINUS
MIRED
MIRES
MIREX
MIRIN GS
S MIRKS
S MIRKY
MIRTH S
MIRZA S
MISDO
MISER SY
MISES
MISOS
MISSY
MISTS
MISTY
S MITER S
S MITES
MITIS
MITRE DS
MITTS
MIXED
MIXER S
MIXES
MIXUP S
MIZEN S
MOANS
MOATS
MOCHA S
S MOCKS
MODAL S
MODEL S
MODEM S
MODES T
MODUS
S MOGGY
MOGUL S
MOHEL S
MOHUR S
MOILS
MOIRA I
MOIRE S
MOIST
MOJOS
S MOKES
MOLAL
MOLAR S
MOLAS
MOLDS
MOLDY
A MOLES T
MOLLS
MOLLY
MOLTO
S MOLTS
MOMES
MOMMA S
MOMMY
MOMUS

MONAD S
MONAS
MONDE S
MONDO S
MONEY S
MONGO ELS
MONIE DS
MONKS
MONOS
MONTE S
MONTH S
S MOOCH
MOODS
MOODY
MOOED
MOOLA HS
MOOLS
MOONS
MOONY
MOORS
MOORY
MOOSE
MOOTS
MOPED S
MOPER SY
MOPES
MOPEY
MORAE
A MORAL ES
MORAS S
MORAY S
MOREL S
MORES
MORNS
MORON S
MORPH OS
MORRO SW
MORSE L
MORTS
MOSEY S
MOSKS
MOSSO
MOSSY
MOSTE
MOSTS
MOTEL S
E MOTES
MOTET S
MOTEY
MOTHS
MOTHY
MOTIF S
MOTOR S
MOTTE S
MOTTO S
MOTTS
MOUCH
MOUES
MOULD SY
MOULT S
MOUND S
A MOUNT S
MOURN S
MOUSE DRSY
MOUSY
MOUTH SY
MOVED
MOVER S
MOVES
MOVIE S
MOWED
MOWER S
MOXAS
MOXIE S
MOZOS
MUCHO
MUCID
MUCIN S
A MUCKS
MUCKY
MUCOR S

MUCRO
MUCUS
MUDDY
MUDRA S
MUFFS
MUFTI S
MUGGS
MUGGY
MUHLY
MUJIK S
MULCH
MULCT S
MULED
MULES
MULEY S
MULLA HS
MULLS
MUMMS
MUMMY
MUMPS
MUMUS
MUNCH
MUNGO S
MUNIS
MUONS
MURAL S
MURAS
MURED
MURES
MUREX
MURID S
MURKS
MURKY
MURRA S
MURRE SY
MURRS
MURRY
MUSCA ET
A MUSED
A MUSER S
A MUSES
MUSHY
MUSIC KS
MUSKS
MUSKY
MUSSY
MUSTH S
MUSTS
MUSTY
S MUTCH
MUTED
MUTER
MUTES T
MUTON S
MUTTS
MUZZY
MYLAR S
MYNAH S
MYNAS
MYOID
MYOMA S
MYOPE S
MYOPY
MYRRH S
MYSID S
MYTHS
MYTHY

NAANS
NABES
NABIS
NABOB S
NACHO S
NACRE DS
NADAS
NADIR S
NAEVI
NAFFS
S NAGGY
NAIAD S
NAIFS
S NAILS

NAIRA S
NAIRU S
NAIVE RS
S NAKED
NAKFA S
NALAS
NALED S
NAMED
NAMER S
NAMES
J NANAS
NANCE S
NANCY
NANNY
NAPAS
NAPES
NAPPA S
NAPPE DRS
S NAPPY
NARCO S
NARCS
NARDS
S NARES
NARIC
NARIS
S NARKS
S NARKY
NASAL S
NASTY
NATAL
S NATCH
E NATES
G NATTY
NAVAL
NAVAR S
NAVEL S
K NAVES
NAVVY
NAWAB S
NAZIS
S NEAPS
A NEARS
NEATH
NEATS
S NECKS
NEDDY
NEEDS
NEEDY
NEEMS
NEEPS
NEGUS
NEIFS
NEIGH S
NEIST
NELLY
E NEMAS
NENES
NEONS
NERDS
NERDY
NEROL IS
I NERTS
NERTZ
NERVE DS
NERVY
NESTS
NETOP S
NETTS
NETTY
NEUKS
NEUME S
NEUMS
NEVER
NEVES
NEVUS
NEWEL S
NEWER
NEWIE S
NEWLY
NEWSY
NEWTS

NEXUS
NGWEE
NICAD S
NICER
NICHE DS
S NICKS
NICOL S
NIDAL
NIDED
NIDES
NIDUS
NIECE S
NIEVE S
NIFTY
NIGHS
K NIGHT SY
NIHIL S
NILLS
NIMBI
NINES
NINJA S
NINNY
NINON S
NINTH S
NIPAS
S NIPPY
NISEI S
NISUS
U NITER SY
U NITES
NITID
NITON S
NITRE S
NITRO S
NITTY
NIVAL
NIXED
NIXES
NIXIE S
NIZAM S
KS NOBBY
NOBLE RS
NOBLY
K NOCKS
A NODAL
NODDY
A NODES
NODUS
NOELS
NOGGS
NOHOW
NOILS
NOILY
NOIRS
NOISE DS
NOISY
NOLOS
NOMAD S
NOMAS
NOMEN
G NOMES
NOMOI
NOMOS
NONAS
NONCE S
NONES
NONET S
NONYL S
S NOOKS
NOOKY
NOONS
NOOSE DRS
NOPAL S
NORIA S
NORIS
NORMS
NORTH S
NOSED
G NOSES
NOSEY
NOTAL

NOTCH
NOTED
NOTER S
NOTES
NOTUM
NOUNS
NOVAE
NOVAS
NOVEL S
NOWAY S
NOWTS
KS NUBBY
NUBIA S
NUCHA EL
NUDER
NUDES T
NUDGE DRS
NUDIE S
NUDZH
NUKED
NUKES
NULLS
NUMBS
NUMEN
NURDS
K NURLS
NURSE DRS
NUTSY
NUTTY
NYALA S
NYLON S
NYMPH AOS

OAKEN
OAKUM S
RS OARED
OASES
OASIS
BCRT OASTS
OATEN
BC OATER S
OATHS
LS OAVES
OBEAH S
OBELI A
OBESE
OBEYS
C OBIAS
OBITS
OBJET S
GH OBOES
OBOLE S
OBOLI
OBOLS
OCCUR S
OCEAN S
T OCHER SY
OCHRE ADS
OCHRY
CDHLMR OCKER S
OCREA E
OCTAD S
OCTAL
OCTAN EST
OCTET S
OCTYL S
L OCULI
ODAHS
CDFN ODDER
ODDLY
ODEON S
ODEUM S
ODIST S
PS ODIUM S
ODORS
ODOUR S

ODYLE S
ODYLS
OFAYS
OFFAL S
BD OFFED
CDG OFFER S
S OFTEN
LS OFTER
OGAMS
Y OGEES
OGHAM S
OGIVE S
OGLED
OGLER S
B OGLES
OGRES S
OHIAS
O OHING
OHMIC
OIDIA
BCDFMRST OILED
BCMT OILER S
B OINKS
OKAPI S
T OKAYS
OKEHS
OKRAS
GH OLDEN
BCFGHMPS OLDER
OLDIE S
OLEIC
OLEIN ES
OLEOS
OLEUM S
FP OLIOS
OLIVE S
H OLLAS
O OLOGY
OMASA
BCS OMBER S
HS OMBRE S
OMEGA S
OMENS
CGHV OMERS
V OMITS
ONCET
ONERY
GR ONION SY
CGI ONIUM
ONLAY S
ONSET S
ONTIC
P OOHED
OOMPH S
OORIE
OOTID S
B OOZED
B OOZES
OPAHS
CN OPALS
C OPENS
OPERA S
OPINE DS
CDHLMRT OPING
OPIUM S
OPSIN S
OPTED
OPTIC S
ORACH E
BCGM ORALS
ORANG ESY
B ORATE DS
S ORBED
ORBIT S

ORCAS
ORCIN S
BC ORDER S
ORDOS
OREAD S
M ORGAN AS
ORGIC
ORIBI S
ORIEL S
ORLES
ORLON S
ORLOP S
DFW ORMER S
ORNIS
ORPIN ES
M ORRIS
ORTHO
ORZOS
CHNR OSIER S
C OSMIC S
OSMOL ES
OSSIA
OSTIA
BMNPT OTHER S
C OTTAR S
CDHJLPRT OTTER S
LMP OTTOS
BDFNS OUGHT S
BJP OUNCE S
OUPHE S
OUPHS
OURIE
H OUSEL S
JR OUSTS
OUTBY E
OUTDO
LPRT OUTED
CPRST OUTER S
OUTGO
OUTRE
OUZEL S
OUZOS
OVALS
C OVARY
OVATE
CDW OVENS
CHLMR OVERS
C OVERT
B OVINE S
OVOID S
OVOLI
OVOLO S
OVULE S
BCDJLMRSTVWY OWING
H OWLET S
DG OWNED
D OWNER S
OWSEN
OXBOW S
OXEYE S
OXIDE S
OXIDS
OXIME S
OXIMS
OXLIP S
OXTER S
FT OYERS
OZONE S

PACAS
S PACED
S PACER S
S PACES

S PACEY
PACHA S
PACKS
E PACTS
PADDY
PADIS
PADLE S
PADRE S
PADRI
PAEAN S
PAEON S
PAGAN S
PAGED
PAGER S
PAGES
PAGOD AS
PAIKS
S PAILS
PAINS
PAINT SY
PAIRS
PAISA NS
PAISE
PALEA EL
PALED
PALER
S PALES T
PALET S
S PALLS
PALLY
PALMS
PALMY
PALPI
PALPS
PALSY
PAMPA S
PANDA S
PANDY
PANED
PANEL S
PANES
PANGA S
PANGS
PANIC S
PANNE DRS
PANSY
PANTO S
PANTS
PANTY
PAPAL
PAPAS
PAPAW S
PAPER SY
PAPPI
PAPPY
PARAE
PARAS
E PARCH
PARDI E
PARDS
PARDY
S PARED
PAREO S
S PARER S
S PARES
PAREU S
S PARGE DST
PARGO S
PARIS H
PARKA S
S PARKS
PARLE DSY
PAROL ES
PARRS
S PARRY
S PARSE CDRS
PARTS
PARTY
PARVE

PARVO S
PASEO S
U PASES
PASHA S
PASSE DELRS
PASTA S
PASTE DLRS
PASTS
PASTY
PATCH Y
PATED
PATEN ST
PATER S
S PATES
PATHS
PATIN AES
PATIO S
PATLY
PATSY
PATTY
PAUSE DRS
PAVAN ES
PAVED
PAVER S
PAVES
PAVID
S PAVIN GS
PAVIS E
PAWED
PAWER S
PAWKY
PAWLS
S PAWNS
PAXES
S PAYED
PAYEE S
PAYER S
PAYOR S
PEACE DS
PEACH Y
PEAGE S
PEAGS
S PEAKS
PEAKY
PEALS
S PEANS
PEARL SY
S PEARS
PEART
PEASE NS
PEATS
PEATY
PEAVY
PECAN S
PECHS
S PECKS
PECKY
PEDAL OS
PEDES
PEDRO S
PEEKS
S PEELS
PEENS
PEEPS
S PEERS
PEERY
PEEVE DS
PEINS
S PEISE DS
PEKAN S
PEKES
PEKIN S
PEKOE S
PELES
PELFS
PELON
S PELTS
PENAL

S PENCE L
SU PENDS
PENES
PENGO S
PENIS
PENNA E
PENNE DR
PENNI AS
PENNY
PEONS
PEONY
PEPLA
PEPOS
PEPPY
PERCH
PERDU ES
PERDY
PEREA
PERES
PERIL S
PERIS H
PERKS
PERKY
S PERMS
PERPS
PERRY
PERSE S
PERVS
PESKY
PESOS
PESTO S
PESTS
PESTY
PETAL S
PETER S
PETIT E
PETTI
PETTO
PETTY
PEWEE S
PEWIT S
PHAGE S
PHASE DS
PHIAL S
PHLOX
PHONE DSY
PHONO NS
PHONS
PHONY
PHOTO GNS
PHOTS
PHPHT
PHUTS
PHYLA ER
PHYLE
PIANO S
PIANS
PIBAL S
AE PICAL
S PICAS
S PICKS
PICKY
PICOT S
PICUL S
A PIECE DRS
S PIERS
PIETA S
PIETY
PIGGY
PIGMY
PIING
PIKAS
S PIKED
S PIKER S
S PIKES
PIKIS
PILAF FS
PILAR
PILAU S
PILAW S

PILEA
S PILED
PILEI
S PILES
PILIS
S PILLS
PILOT S
PILUS
PIMAS
PIMPS
PINAS
PINCH
OS PINED
OS PINES
PINEY
PINGO S
PINGS
PINKO S
PINKS
PINKY
PINNA ELS
S PINNY
PINON S
PINOT S
PINTA S
S PINTO S
PINTS
PINUP S
PIONS
PIOUS
PIPAL S
PIPED
PIPER S
PIPES
PIPET S
PIPIT S
PIQUE DST
PIRNS
PIROG I
PISCO S
PISOS
PISTE S
PITAS
PITCH Y
PITHS
PITHY
PITON S
PITTA S
PIVOT S
PIXEL S
PIXES
PIXIE S
PIZZA SZ
PLACE DRST
PLACK S
PLAGE S
PLAID S
PLAIN ST
PLAIT S
PLANE DRST
PLANK S
PLANS
PLANT S
S PLASH Y
PLASM AS
PLATE DNRS
S PLATS
PLATY S
PLAYA S
S PLAYS
PLAZA S
PLEAD S
PLEAS E
PLEAT S
PLEBE S
PLEBS
PLENA
PLEON S

PLEWS
PLICA EL
PLIED
PLIER S
PLIES
U PLINK S
PLODS
PLONK S
PLOPS
PLOTS
PLOTZ
PLOWS
PLOYS
PLUCK SY
PLUGS
PLUMB S
PLUME DS
PLUMP S
PLUMS
PLUMY
PLUNK SY
PLUSH Y
PLYER S
POACH Y
POBOY S
POCKS
POCKY
PODGY
PODIA
POEMS
POESY
POETS
POGEY S
POILU S
POIND S
POINT ESY
POISE DRS
S POKED
POKER S
S POKES
POKEY S
POLAR S
POLED
POLER S
POLES
POLIO S
POLIS H
POLKA S
POLLS
POLOS
POLYP IS
POLYS
POMES
POMMY
POMOS
POMPS
PONCE DS
PONDS
PONES
PONGS
POOCH
POODS
POOED
S POOFS
S POOFY
POOHS
S POOLS
S POONS
POOPS
POORI S
POOVE S
POPES
POPPA S
POPPY
POPSY
PORCH
S PORED
S PORES
PORGY
PORKS
PORKY

PORNO S
PORNS
PORNY
S PORTS
POSED
POSER S
E POSES
POSIT S
POSSE ST
POSTS
POTSY
POTTO S
S POTTY
POUCH Y
POUFF ESY
POUFS
POULT S
POUND S
POURS
S POUTS
POUTY
POWER S
POXED
POXES
POYOU S
PRAAM S
PRAHU S
PRAMS
S PRANG S
PRANK S
PRAOS
PRASE S
U PRATE DRS
S PRATS
PRAUS
PRAWN S
S PRAYS
PREED
PREEN S
S PREES
PREOP S
PREPS
PRESA
PRESE T
PRESS
PREST OS
PREXY
PREYS
PRICE DRSY
PRICK SY
PRICY
PRIDE DS
PRIED
S PRIER S
PRIES T
S PRIGS
PRILL S
PRIMA LS
PRIME DRS
PRIMI
PRIMO S
PRIMP S
PRIMS
PRINK S
S PRINT S
PRION S
PRIOR SY
U PRISE DS
PRISM S
PRISS Y
PRIVY
PRIZE DRS
PROAS
PROBE DRS
PRODS
PROEM S
PROFS

PROGS
PROLE GS
PROMO S
PROMS
PRONE
PRONG S
PROOF S
PROPS
U PROSE DRS
PROSO S
PROSS
PROST
PROSY
PROUD
PROVE DNRS
PROWL S
PROWS
PROXY
PRUDE S
PRUNE DRS
PRUTA H
S PRYER S
PSALM S
PSEUD OS
PSHAW S
PSOAE
PSOAI
PSOAS
PSYCH EOS
PUBES
PUBIC
PUBIS
PUCES
PUCKA
PUCKS
PUDGY
PUDIC
PUFFS
PUFFY
PUGGY
PUJAH S
PUJAS
PUKED
PUKES
PUKKA
PULED
PULER S
PULES
PULIK
PULIS
PULLS
PULPS
PULPY
PULSE DRS
PUMAS
PUMPS
PUNAS
PUNCH Y
PUNGS
PUNJI S
PUNKA HS
S PUNKS
S PUNKY
PUNNY
PUNTO S
PUNTS
PUNTY
PUPAE
PUPAL
PUPAS
PUPIL S
PUPPY
PUPUS
PURDA HS
PUREE DS
PURER
S PURGE DRS

PURIN ES
PURIS MT
PURLS
PURRS
PURSE DRS
PURSY
PURTY
O PUSES
PUSHY
PUSSY
PUTON S
PUTTI E
PUTTO
PUTTS
PUTTY
PYGMY
PYINS
PYLON S
PYOID
PYRAN S
PYRES
PYREX
PYRIC
PYROS
PYXES
PYXIE S
PYXIS

QADIS
QAIDS
QANAT S
QOPHS
QUACK SY
S QUADS
QUAFF S
QUAGS
QUAIL S
QUAIS
QUAKE DRS
QUAKY
QUALE
QUALM SY
QUANT AS
S QUARE
S QUARK S
QUART EOSZ
S QUASH
QUASI
QUASS
E QUATE
QUAYS
QUBIT S
QUEAN S
QUEEN S
QUEER S
QUELL S
QUERN S
QUERY
QUEST S
QUEUE DRS
QUEYS
QUICK S
ES QUIDS
QUIET S
QUIFF S
S QUILL S
QUILT S
QUINS Y
S QUINT AES
E QUIPS
QUIPU S
S QUIRE DS
QUIRK SY
S QUIRT S
QUITE
QUITS
QUODS
QUOIN S

QUOIT S
QUOLL S
QUOTA S
QUOTE DRS
QUOTH A
QURSH

RABAT OS
RABBI NST
A RABIC
RABID
BGT RACED
BT RACER S
BGT RACES
CTW RACKS
RACON S
RADAR S
RADII
RADIO S
RADIX
RADON S
D RAFFS
CDGK RAFTS
RAGAS
RAGED
D RAGEE S
RAGES
RAGGS
BCD RAGGY
RAGIS
RAIAS
B RAIDS
BDFGT RAILS
BDGT RAINS
BG RAINY
BFP RAISE DRS
RAITA S
RAJAH S
RAJAS
RAJES
B RAKED
RAKEE S
RAKER S
BCD RAKES
RAKIS H
RAKUS
RALES
O RALLY E
RALPH S
RAMAL
RAMEE S
RAMEN
RAMET S
RAMIE S
RAMMY
CGT RAMPS
RAMUS
PT RANCE S
BC RANCH O
BG RANDS
B RANDY
RANEE S
GO RANGE DRS
O RANGY
RANID S
RANIS
BCFPT RANKS
BG RANTS
CD RAPED
D RAPER S
CDGT RAPES
RAPHE S
RAPID S
RARED
RARER

U RARES T
E RASED
E RASER S
CEPU RASES
G RASPS
RASPY
RATAL S
RATAN SY
C RATCH
CGOP RATED
RATEL S
CFGIKP RATER S
CGOPU RATES
RATHE R
RATIO NS
RATOS
B RATTY
BCG RAVED
GT RAVEL S
CG RAVEN S
BCG RAVER S
BCGT RAVES
RAVIN EGS
BD RAWER
RAWIN S
BCD RAWLY
RAXED
P RAXES
RAYAH S
RAYAS
BDFGP RAYED
C RAYON S
BCG RAZED
RAZEE DS
BG RAZER S
BCG RAZES
RAZOR S
BP REACH
P REACT S
READD S
BDOT READS
B READY
REALM S
REALS
BCD REAMS
REAPS
P REARM S
D REARS
REATA S
G REAVE DRS
REBAR S
REBBE S
REBEC KS
REBEL S
P REBID S
REBOP S
REBUS
REBUT S
P REBUY S
RECAP S
RECCE S
RECIT ES
DW RECKS
RECON S
RECTA L
RECTI
RECTO RS
RECUR S
P RECUT S
REDAN S
REDDS
REDED
B REDES
U REDIA ELS
REDID
REDIP ST
REDLY
REDON ES
CU REDOS
REDOX
P REDRY
REDUB S
REDUX
REDYE DS
BCG REEDS
G REEDY
REEFS
REEFY
BC REEKS
REEKY
C REELS
F REEST S
REEVE DS
REFED
REFEL LST
P REFER S
REFIT S
P REFIX
REFLY
REFRY
REGAL E
REGES
B REGMA
REGNA L
REHAB S
REHEM S
REIFS
REIFY
REIGN S
REINK S
REINS
REIVE DRS
REJIG S
REKEY S
RELAX
RELAY S
RELET S
RELIC ST
RELIT
P REMAN DS
REMAP S
REMET
REMEX
REMIT S
P REMIX T
RENAL
T RENDS
RENEW S
RENIG S
RENIN S
RENTE DRS
B RENTS
REOIL S
P REPAY S
REPEG S
REPEL S
REPIN ES
REPLY
REPOS E
REPOT S
REPPS
REPRO S
RERAN
RERIG S
RERUN S
RESAT
RESAW NS
RESAY S
RESEE DKNS
P RESET S
RESEW NS
RESID ES
RESIN SY
RESIT ES
RESOD S
RESOW NS
CPW RESTS
RETAG S
P RETAX
W RETCH
RETEM S
RETIA L
RETIE DS
RETRO S
RETRY
REUSE DS
REVEL S
BT REVET S
P REVUE S
REWAN
REWAX
BC REWED S
REWET S
REWIN DS
REWON
P REXES
RHEAS
RHEME S
RHEUM SY
RHINO S
RHOMB IS
RHUMB AS
RHYME DRS
RHYTA
TU RIALS
RIANT
RIATA S
RIBBY
BT RIBES
PT RICED
P RICER S
PT RICES
RICIN GS
BCPTW RICKS
A RIDER S
BGIP RIDES
BF RIDGE DLS
RIDGY
AO RIELS
RIFER
G RIFFS
T RIFLE DRS
DG RIFTS
ABFW RIGHT OSY
F RIGID
RIGOR S
A RILED
RILES
RILEY
G RILLE DST
BDFGKPT RILLS
GP RIMED
PT RIMER S
CGP RIMES
G RINDS
RINDY
BW RINGS
BDP RINKS
RINSE DRS
RIOJA S
G RIOTS
G RIPED
RIPEN S
G RIPER
CGT RIPES T
A RISEN
RISER S
ABCFIKP RISES
RISHI S
BF RISKS
F RISKY
RISUS
FW RITES
RITZY
RIVAL S
RIVED
D RIVEN
D RIVER S
D RIVES
GPT RIVET S
RIYAL S
B ROACH
B ROADS
ROAMS
G ROANS
ROARS
ROAST S
P ROBED
P ROBES
ROBIN GS
ROBLE S
ROBOT S
BCFT ROCKS
ROCKY
RODEO S
E RODES
ROGER S
BD ROGUE DS
B ROILS
ROILY
P ROLES
ROLFS
DT ROLLS
ROMAN OS
ROMEO S
T ROMPS
RONDO S
B ROODS
P ROOFS
BC ROOKS
ROOKY
BGV ROOMS
B ROOMY
ROOSE DRS
ROOST S
ROOTS
ROOTY
G ROPED
GP ROPER SY
GT ROPES
ROPEY
ROQUE ST
P ROSED
BEP ROSES
ROSET S
ROSHI S
ROSIN GSY
ROTAS
C ROTCH E
ROTES
ROTIS
ROTLS
ROTOR S
ROTOS
ROTTE DNRS
ROUEN S
ROUES
ROUGE DS
T ROUGH SY
AG ROUND S
CG ROUPS
C ROUPY
ACG ROUSE DRS
ROUST S
C ROUTE DRS
D ROUTH S
GT ROUTS
DGP ROVED
P ROVEN
DPT ROVER S
DGPT ROVES
ROWAN S
C ROWDY
BCT ROWED
T ROWEL S
ROWEN S
CGP ROWER S
GT ROWTH S
ROYAL S
RUANA S
G RUBBY
RUBEL S
RUBES
RUBLE S
RUBUS
RUCHE DS
CT RUCKS
RUDDS
C RUDDY
C RUDER Y
RUERS
T RUFFE DS
G RUFFS
RUGAE
F RUGAL
RUGBY
T RUING
B RUINS
RULED
RULER S
RULES
RUMBA S
RUMEN S
C RUMMY
RUMOR S
CFGT RUMPS
P RUNES
RUNGS
RUNIC
RUNNY
BG RUNTS
RUNTY
RUPEE S
C RURAL
CDU RUSES
B RUSHY
RUSKS
CT RUSTS
CT RUSTY
T RUTHS
RUTIN S
RUTTY
RYKED
RYKES
RYNDS
RYOTS
SABAL S
SABED
SABER S
SABES
SABIN ES
SABIR S
U SABLE S
SABOT S
SABRA S
SABRE DS
SACKS
SACRA L
T SADES
SADHE S
SADHU S
T SADIS MT
SADLY
SAFER
SAFES T
SAGAS
SAGER
U SAGES T
SAGGY
SAGOS
SAGUM
SAHIB S
SAICE S
SAIDS
SAIGA S
SAILS
SAINS
SAINT S
SAITH E
SAJOU S
SAKER S
SAKES
SAKIS
SALAD S
SALAL S
SALEP S
SALES
SALIC
SALLY
SALMI S
SALOL S
SALON S
SALPA ES
SALPS
SALSA S
SALTS
SALTY
SALVE DRS
SALVO RS
SAMBA LRS
SAMBO S
SAMEK HS
SAMPS
SANDS
SANDY
SANED
SANER
SANES T
SANGA RS
SANGH S
SANTO LS
SAPID
SAPOR S
SAPPY
SARAN S
SARDS
SAREE S
SARGE S
SARGO S
SARIN S
SARIS
SARKS
SARKY
SAROD ES
SAROS
SASIN S
SASSY
SATAY S
SATED
SATEM
SATES
I SATIN GSY
SATIS
SATYR S
SAUCE DRS
SAUCH S
SAUCY
SAUGH SY
SAULS
SAULT S
SAUNA S
SAURY
SAUTE DS
SAVED
SAVER S
SAVES
SAVIN EGS
SAVOR SY
SAVOY S
SAVVY
SAWED
SAWER S
SAXES
SAYED S
SAYER S
SAYID S
SAYST
SCABS
SCADS
SCAGS
SCALD S
SCALE DRS
SCALL S
SCALP S
SCALY
SCAMP IS
SCAMS
SCANS
SCANT SY
E SCAPE DS
SCARE DRSY
SCARF S
E SCARP HS
E SCARS
SCART S
SCARY
SCATS
SCATT SY
SCAUP S
SCAUR S
SCENA S
A SCEND S
SCENE S
A SCENT S
SCHAV S
SCHMO ES
SCHUL NS
SCHWA S
SCION S
SCOFF S
SCOLD S
SCONE S
SCOOP S
SCOOT S
SCOPE DS
SCOPS
SCORE DRS
SCORN S
AE SCOTS
SCOUR S
SCOUT HS
SCOWL S
SCOWS
SCRAG S
SCRAM S
SCRAP ES
SCREE DNS
SCREW SY
SCRIM PS
SCRIP ST
SCROD S
SCRUB S
SCRUM S
SCUBA S
SCUDI
E SCUDO
SCUDS
SCUFF S
SCULK S
SCULL S
SCULP ST
SCUMS
SCUPS
SCURF SY
SCUTA
SCUTE S
SCUTS
SCUZZ Y
SEALS
SEAMS
SEAMY
SEARS
SEATS
SEBUM S
SECCO S
SECTS
SEDAN S
SEDER S
SEDGE S
SEDGY
SEDUM S
SEEDS
SEEDY
SEEKS
SEELS
SEELY
SEEMS
SEEPS
SEEPY
SEERS
SEGNI
SEGNO S
SEGOS
SEGUE DS
SEIFS
SEINE DRS
SEISE DRS
SEISM S
SEIZE DRS
SELAH S
SELFS
SELLE RS
SELLS
SELVA S
SEMEN S
SEMES
SEMIS
SENDS
SENGI
SENNA S
SENOR AS
SENSA
SENSE DIS
SENTE
SENTI
SEPAL S
SEPIA S
SEPIC
SEPOY S
SEPTA L
SEPTS
SERAC S
SERAI LS
SERAL
SERED
SERER
SERES T
SERFS
SERGE DRS
SERIF S
SERIN EGS
SEROW S
SERRY
SERUM S
SERVE DRS
SERVO S
SETAE
SETAL
SETON S
SETTS
SETUP S
SEVEN S
SEVER ES
SEWAN S
SEWAR S
SEWED
SEWER S
SEXED
SEXES
SEXTO NS
SEXTS
SHACK OS
SHADE DRS
SHADS
SHADY
SHAFT S
SHAGS
SHAHS
SHAKE NRS
SHAKO S
SHAKY
SHALE DSY
SHALL
SHALT
SHALY
SHAME DS
SHAMS
SHANK S
SHAPE DNRS
SHARD S
SHARE DRS
SHARK S
SHARN SY
SHARP SY
SHAUL S
SHAVE DNRS
SHAWL S
SHAWM S
SHAWN
P SHAWS
SHAYS
SHEAF S
SHEAL S
SHEAR S
SHEAS
SHEDS
SHEEN SY
SHEEP
SHEER S
SHEET S
SHEIK HS
SHELF
SHELL SY
SHEND S
SHENT
SHEOL S
SHERD S
SHEWN
SHEWS
SHIED
SHIEL DS
A SHIER S
SHIES T
SHIFT SY
SHILL S
SHILY
SHIMS
SHINE DRS
SHINS
SHINY
SHIPS

SHIRE S
SHIRK S
SHIRR S
SHIRT SY
SHIST S
SHITS
SHIVA HS
SHIVE RS
SHIVS
SHLEP PS
SHLUB S
SHOAL SY
SHOAT S
SHOCK S
SHOED
SHOER S
SHOES
SHOGI S
SHOGS
SHOJI S
SHONE
SHOOK S
SHOOL S
SHOON
SHOOS
SHOOT S
SHOPS
A SHORE DS
SHORL S
SHORN
SHORT SY
SHOTE S
SHOTS
SHOTT S
SHOUT S
SHOVE DL RS
SHOWN
SHOWS
SHOWY
SHOYU S
SHRED S
SHREW DS
SHRIS
SHRUB S
SHRUG S
SHTIK S
SHUCK S
SHULN
SHULS
SHUNS
SHUNT S
SHUSH
SHUTE DS
SHUTS
SHWAS
SHYER S
SHYLY
SIALS
SIBBS
SIBYL S
SICES
SICKO S
SICKS
SIDED
A SIDES
SIDHE
SIDLE DR S
SIEGE DS
SIEUR S
SIEVE DS
SIFTS
SIGHS
SIGHT S
SIGIL S
SIGLA
SIGMA S
SIGNA L
SIGNS
SIKAS
SIKER
SIKES

SILDS
SILEX
SILKS
SILKY
SILLS
SILLY
SILOS
SILTS
SILTY
SILVA EN S
SIMAR S
SIMAS
SIMPS
SINCE
SINES
SINEW SY
SINGE DR S
SINGS
SINHS
SINKS
SINUS
SIPED
SIPES
SIRED
SIREE S
SIREN S
SIRES
SIRRA HS
SIRUP SY
SISAL S
SISES
SISSY
SITAR S
SITED
SITES
SITUP S
SITUS
SIVER S
SIXES
SIXMO S
SIXTE S
SIXTH S
SIXTY
SIZAR S
SIZED
SIZER S
SIZES
SKAGS
SKALD S
SKANK SY
SKATE DR S
SKATS
SKEAN ES
SKEED
SKEEN S
SKEES
SKEET S
SKEGS
SKEIN S
SKELL S
SKELM S
SKELP S
SKENE S
SKEPS
SKEWS
SKIDS
SKIED
SKIER S
SKIES
SKIEY
SKIFF S
SKILL S
SKIMO S
SKIMP SY
SKIMS
SKINK S
SKINS
SKINT
SKIPS
SKIRL S

SKIRR S
SKIRT S
SKITE DS
SKITS
SKIVE DR S
SKOAL S
SKORT S
SKOSH
SKUAS
SKULK S
SKULL S
SKUNK SY
SKYED
SKYEY
SLABS
SLACK S
SLAGS
SLAIN
SLAKE DR S
SLAMS
SLANG SY
SLANK
A SLANT SY
SLAPS
SLASH
SLATE DR SY
SLATS
SLATY
SLAVE DR SY
SLAWS
SLAYS
SLEDS
SLEEK SY
A SLEEP SY
SLEET SY
SLEPT
SLEWS
SLICE DR S
SLICK S
SLIDE RS
SLIER
SLILY
SLIME DS
SLIMS Y
SLIMY
I SLING S
SLINK SY
SLIPE DS
SLIPS
SLIPT
SLITS
SLOBS
SLOES
SLOGS
SLOID S
SLOJD S
SLOOP S
A SLOPE DR S
SLOPS
A SLOSH Y
SLOTH S
SLOTS
SLOWS
SLOYD S
SLUBS
SLUED
SLUES
SLUFF S
SLUGS
SLUMP S
SLUMS
SLUNG
SLUNK
SLURB S
SLURP S
SLURS
SLUSH Y

SLUTS
SLYER
SLYLY
SLYPE S
SMACK S
SMALL S
SMALT IO S
SMARM SY
SMART SY
SMASH
SMAZE S
SMEAR SY
SMEEK S
SMELL SY
SMELT S
SMERK S
SMEWS
SMILE DR SY
SMIRK SY
SMITE RS
SMITH SY
SMOCK S
SMOGS
SMOKE DR SY
SMOKY
SMOLT S
SMOTE
SMUSH
SMUTS
SNACK S
SNAFU S
SNAGS
SNAIL S
SNAKE DS Y
SNAKY
SNAPS
SNARE DR S
SNARF S
SNARK SY
SNARL SY
SNASH
SNATH ES
SNAWS
SNEAK SY
SNEAP S
SNECK S
SNEDS
SNEER SY
SNELL S
SNIBS
SNICK S
SNIDE R
SNIFF SY
SNIPE DR S
SNIPS
SNITS
SNOBS
SNOGS
SNOOD S
SNOOK S
SNOOL S
SNOOP SY
SNOOT SY
SNORE DR S
SNORT S
SNOTS
SNOUT SY
SNOWS
SNOWY
SNUBS
SNUCK
SNUFF SY
SNUGS
SNYES
SOAKS
SOAPS

SOAPY
SOARS
SOAVE S
SOBAS
SOBER S
SOCAS
SOCKO
SOCKS
SOCLE S
SODAS
SODDY
SODIC
SODOM SY
SOFAR S
SOFAS
SOFTA S
SOFTS
SOFTY
SOGGY
SOILS
SOJAS
SOKES
SOKOL S
SOLAN DO S
SOLAR
SOLDI
SOLDO
SOLED
SOLEI
SOLES
SOLID IS
SOLON S
SOLOS
SOLUM S
SOLUS
SOLVE DR S
SOMAN S
SOMAS
SONAR S
SONDE RS
SONES
SONGS
SONIC S
SONLY
SONNY
SONSY
SOOEY
SOOKS
SOOTH ES
SOOTS
SOOTY
SOPHS
SOPHY
SOPOR S
SOPPY
SORAS
SORBS
SORDS
SORED
SOREL SY
SORER
T SORES T
SORGO S
SORNS
SORRY
SORTA
SORTS
SORUS
SOTHS
SOTOL S
SOUGH ST
SOUKS
SOULS
SOUND S
SOUPS
SOUPY
SOURS
SOUSE DS
SOUTH S
SOWAR S
SOWED

SOWER S
SOYAS
SOYUZ
SOZIN ES
SPACE DR SY
SPACY
SPADE DR S
SPADO
SPAED
SPAES
SPAHI S
SPAIL S
SPAIT S
SPAKE
SPALE S
SPALL S
SPAMS
SPANG
SPANK S
SPANS
SPARE DR S
SPARK SY
SPARS E
SPASM S
SPATE S
SPATS
SPAWN S
SPAYS
SPAZZ
SPEAK S
SPEAN S
SPEAR S
SPECK S
SPECS
SPEED OS Y
SPEEL S
SPEER S
SPEIL S
SPEIR S
SPELL S
SPELT SZ
SPEND SY
SPENT
SPERM S
SPEWS
SPICA ES
SPICE DR SY
SPICK S
A SPICS
SPICY
E SPIED
SPIEL S
SPIER S
E SPIES
SPIFF SY
SPIKE DR SY
SPIKS
SPIKY
SPILE DS
SPILL S
SPILT H
SPINE DL ST
SPINS
SPINY
A SPIRE AD MS
SPIRT S
SPIRY
SPITE DS
SPITS
SPITZ
SPIVS
SPLAT S
SPLAY S
SPLIT S
SPODE S
SPOIL ST

SPOKE DN S
SPOOF SY
SPOOK SY
SPOOL S
SPOON SY
SPOOR S
SPORE DS
SPORT SY
SPOTS
SPOUT S
SPRAG S
SPRAT S
SPRAY S
SPREE S
SPRIG S
E SPRIT ES Z
SPRUE S
SPRUG S
SPUDS
SPUED
SPUES
SPUME DS
SPUMY
SPUNK SY
SPURN S
SPURS
SPURT S
SPUTA
SQUAB S
SQUAD S
SQUAT S
SQUAW KS
SQUEG S
SQUIB S
SQUID S
STABS
STACK S
STADE S
STAFF S
STAGE DR SY
STAGS
STAGY
STAID
STAIG S
STAIN S
STAIR S
STAKE DS
STALE DR S
STALK SY
STALL S
STAMP S
STAND S
STANE DS
STANG S
STANK S
STAPH S
STARE DR S
STARK
STARS
START S
STASH
E STATE DR S
STATS
STAVE DS
STAYS
STEAD SY
STEAK S
O STEAL S
STEAM SY
STEED S
STEEK S
STEEL SY
STEEP S
STEER S
STEIN S
STELA EI R

STELE S
STEMS
STENO S
STENT S
STEPS
STERE OS
A STERN AS
STETS
STEWS
STEWY
STICH S
STICK SY
STIED
STIES
STIFF S
STILE S
STILL SY
STILT S
STIME S
STIMY
STING OS Y
STINK OS Y
STINT S
STIPE DL S
STIRK S
STIRP S
STIRS
STOAE
STOAI
STOAS
STOAT S
STOBS
STOCK SY
STOGY
STOIC S
STOKE DR S
STOLE DN S
STOMA LS
STOMP S
STONE DR SY
A STONY
STOOD
STOOK S
STOOL S
STOOP S
STOPE DR S
E STOPS
STOPT
STORE DR SY
STORK S
STORM SY
STORY
STOSS
STOTS
STOTT S
STOUP S
STOUR ES Y
STOUT S
STOVE RS
STOWP S
STOWS
STRAP S
STRAW SY
AE STRAY S
STREP S
STREW NS
STRIA E
STRIP ES TY
STROP S
STROW NS
STROY S
E STRUM AS
STRUT S
STUBS

STUCK
STUDS
STUDY
STUFF SY
STULL S
STUMP SY
STUMS
STUNG
STUNK
STUNS
STUNT S
STUPA S
STUPE S
STURT S
STYED
STYES
STYLE DR ST
STYLI
STYMY
SUAVE R
SUBAH S
SUBAS
SUBER S
SUCKS
SUCKY
SUCRE S
SUDDS
SUDOR S
SUDSY
SUEDE DS
SUERS
SUETS
SUETY
SUGAR SY
SUGHS
SUING
SUINT S
SUITE DR S
SUITS
SULCI
SULFA S
SULFO
SULKS
SULKY
SULLY
SULUS
SUMAC HS
SUMMA ES
SUMOS
SUMPS
SUNNA HS
SUNNS
SUNNY
SUNUP S
SUPER BS
SUPES
SUPRA
SURAH S
SURAL
SURAS
SURDS
U SURER
SURFS
SURFY
SURGE DR S
SURGY
SURLY
SURRA S
SUSHI S
SUTRA S
SUTTA S
SWABS
SWAGE DR S
SWAGS
SWAIL S
SWAIN S
SWALE S
SWAMI S
SWAMP SY

SWAMY
SWANG
SWANK SY
SWANS
SWAPS
SWARD S
SWARE
SWARF S
A SWARM S
SWART HY
SWASH
SWATH ES
SWATS
SWAYS
SWEAR S
SWEAT SY
SWEDE S
SWEEP SY
SWEER
SWEET S
SWELL S
SWEPT
SWIFT S
SWIGS
SWILL S
SWIMS
SWINE
SWING ESY
SWINK S
SWIPE DS
A SWIRL SY
SWISH Y
SWISS
SWITH E
SWIVE DLST
SWOBS
A SWOON SY
SWOOP SY
SWOPS
SWORD S
SWORE
SWORN
SWOTS
SWOUN DS
SWUNG
SYCEE S
SYCES
SYKES
SYLIS
SYLPH SY
SYLVA ENS
SYNCH S
SYNCS
SYNOD S
SYNTH S
SYPHS
SYREN S
SYRUP SY
SYSOP S
TABBY
TABER S
TABES
TABID
TABLA S
S TABLE DST
TABOO S
TABOR S
TABUN S
TABUS
TACES
TACET
TACHE S
TACHS
TACIT
S TACKS
TACKY
TACOS
TACTS
TAELS
TAFFY
TAFIA S
TAHRS
TAIGA S
TAILS
S TAINS
TAINT S
TAJES
TAKAS
TAKEN
TAKER S
S TAKES
TAKIN GS
TALAR S
TALAS
TALCS
S TALER S
S TALES
S TALKS
S TALKY
S TALLS
TALLY
E TALON S
TALUK AS
TALUS
TAMAL ES
TAMED
TAMER S
TAMES T
TAMIS
TAMMY
S TAMPS
TANGA
TANGO S
S TANGS
TANGY
TANKA S
S TANKS
TANSY
TANTO
TAPAS
TAPED
TAPER S
ES TAPES
TAPIR S
TAPIS
TARDO
TARDY
S TARED
S TARES
TARGE ST
TARNS
TAROC S
TAROK S
TAROS
TAROT S
TARPS
TARRE DS
S TARRY
TARSI A
S TARTS
TARTY
TASKS
TASSE LST
TASTE DRS
TASTY
TATAR S
S TATER S
S TATES
TATTY
TAUNT S
TAUON S
TAUPE S
TAUTS
TAWED
TAWER S
TAWIE
TAWNY
TAWSE DS
TAXED
TAXER S
TAXES
TAXIS
TAXOL S
TAXON S
TAXUS
TAZZA S
TAZZE
TEACH
S TEAKS
S TEALS
S TEAMS
TEARS
TEARY
TEASE DLRS
TEATS
TECHS
TECHY
TECTA L
TEDDY
S TEELS
TEEMS
TEENS Y
TEENY
TEETH E
TEFFS
TEGGS
TEGUA S
TEIID S
TEIND S
S TELAE
TELCO S
S TELES
TELEX
TELIA L
AS TELIC
TELLS
TELLY S
TELOI
TELOS
TEMPI
TEMPO S
TEMPS
TEMPT S
S TENCH
TENDS
TENDU S
TENET S
TENGE
TENIA ES
TENON S
TENOR S
TENSE DRS
TENTH S
S TENTS
TENTY
TEPAL S
TEPAS
TEPEE S
TEPID
TEPOY S
TERAI S
TERCE LST
TERGA L
TERMS
E TERNE S
S TERNS
TERRA ES
TERRY
TERSE R
TESLA S
TESTA E
TESTS
TESTY
TETHS
TETRA DS
TETRI S
TEUCH
TEUGH
S TEWED
TEXAS
TEXTS
THACK S
E THANE S
THANK S
THARM S
THAWS
THEBE S
THECA EL
THEFT S
THEGN S
THEIN ES
THEIR S
THEME DS
THENS
THERE S
THERM ES
THESE S
THESP S
THETA S
THEWS
THEWY
THICK S
THIEF
THIGH S
THILL S
THINE
THING S
THINK S
THINS
THIOL S
THIRD S
THIRL S
THOLE DS
THONG S
THORN SY
THORO N
THORP ES
THOSE
THOUS
THRAW NS
THREE PS
THREW
THRIP S
THROB S
THROE S
THROW NS
THRUM S
THUDS
THUGS
THUJA S
THUMB S
THUMP S
THUNK S
THURL S
THUYA S
THYME SY
THYMI C
THYMY
TIARA S
TIBIA ELS
TICAL S
S TICKS
TIDAL
TIDED
TIDES
TIERS
S TIFFS
TIGER S
TIGHT S
TIGON S
TIKES
TIKIS
TIKKA S
TILAK S
TILDE S
TILED
TILER S
S TILES
S TILLS
TILTH S
S TILTS
TIMED
TIMER S
S TIMES
TIMID
TINCT S
TINEA LS
TINED
TINES
TINGE DS
S TINGS
TINNY
S TINTS
TIPIS
TIPPY
TIPSY
TIRED
TIRES
TIRLS
TIROS
TITAN S
TITER S
TITHE DRS
O TITIS
TITLE DS
TITRE S
TITTY
TIZZY
TOADS
TOADY
TOAST SY
TODAY S
TODDY
TOEAS
TOFFS
TOFFY
TOFTS
TOFUS
TOGAE D
TOGAS
TOGUE S
E TOILE DRST
TOILS
TOITS
TOKAY S
S TOKED
TOKEN S
S TOKER S
S TOKES
TOLAN ES
TOLAR S
TOLAS
S TOLED O
S TOLES
A TOLLS
TOLUS
TOLYL S
TOMAN S
TOMBS
TOMES
TOMMY
A TONAL
TONDI
TONDO S
AS TONED
AS TONER S
AS TONES
S TONEY
TONGA S
TONGS
A TONIC S
TONNE RS
TONUS
S TOOLS
TOONS
TOOTH SY
TOOTS Y
TOPAZ
S TOPED
TOPEE S
S TOPER S
S TOPES
TOPHE S
TOPHI
TOPHS
A TOPIC S
TOPIS
TOPOI
TOPOS
TOQUE ST
TORAH S
TORAS
TORCH Y
TORCS
S TORES
TORIC S
TORII
TOROS E
TOROT H
TORRS
TORSE S
TORSI
TORSK S
TORSO S
TORTA S
TORTE NS
TORTS
TORUS
TOTAL S
TOTED
TOTEM S
TOTER S
TOTES
TOUCH EY
TOUGH SY
S TOURS
TOUSE DS
S TOUTS
S TOWED
TOWEL S
TOWER SY
TOWIE S
TOWNS
TOWNY
TOXIC S
TOXIN ES
TOYED
TOYER S
TOYON S
TOYOS
TRACE DRS
TRACK S
TRACT S
TRADE DRS
TRAGI C
TRAIK S
TRAIL S
S TRAIN S
S TRAIT S
TRAMP SY
TRAMS
TRANK S
TRANQ S
TRANS
S TRAPS
TRAPT
TRASH Y
S TRASS
TRAVE LS
TRAWL S
S TRAYS
TREAD S
TREAT SY
TREED
TREEN S
TREES
TREKS
TREND SY
S TRESS Y
TRETS
S TREWS
TREYS
TRIAC S
TRIAD S
A TRIAL S
TRIBE S
TRICE DPS
S TRICK SY
TRIED
TRIER S
TRIES
TRIGO NS
TRIGS
S TRIKE S
TRILL S
TRIMS
TRINE DS
TRIOL S
TRIOS E
S TRIPE S
S TRIPS
TRITE R
TROAK S
TROCK S
S TRODE
TROGS
TROIS
S TROKE DS
S TROLL SY
TROMP ES
TRONA S
TRONE S
TROOP S
TROOZ
TROPE S
TROTH S
TROTS
TROUT SY
S TROVE RS
S TROWS
S TROYS
TRUCE DS
S TRUCK S
TRUED
TRUER
TRUES T
TRUGS
TRULL S
TRULY
TRUMP S
TRUNK S
TRUSS
TRUST SY
TRUTH S
TRYMA
TRYST ES
TSADE S
TSADI S
TSARS
TSKED
TSUBA
TUBAE
TUBAL
TUBAS
S TUBBY
TUBED
TUBER S
TUBES
TUCKS
TUFAS
S TUFFS
TUFTS
TUFTY
TULES
TULIP S
TULLE S
TUMID
TUMMY
TUMOR S
S TUMPS
TUNAS
TUNED
TUNER S
TUNES
TUNGS
TUNIC AS
TUNNY
TUPIK S
TUQUE S
TURBO ST
TURDS
TURFS
TURFY
TURKS
TURNS
TURPS
TUSHY
TUSKS
TUTEE S
TUTOR S
TUTTI S
TUTTY
TUTUS
TUXES
TUYER ES
TWAES
A TWAIN S
TWANG SY
TWATS
TWEAK SY
TWEED SY
A TWEEN SY
TWEET S
TWERP S
TWICE
TWIER S
TWIGS
TWILL S
TWINE DRS
TWINS
TWINY
TWIRL SY
TWIRP S
TWIST SY
TWITS
TWIXT
TWYER S
TYEES
TYERS
S TYING
TYIYN
TYKES
TYNED
TYNES
TYPAL
TYPED
TYPES
TYPEY
A TYPIC
TYPOS
TYPPS
TYRED
TYRES
TYROS
TYTHE DS
TZARS
BJMR UDDER S
UDONS
UHLAN S
UKASE S
ULAMA S
Y ULANS
ULCER S
ULEMA S
ULNAD
ULNAE
ULNAR
ULNAS
ULPAN
ULTRA S
V ULVAS
UMAMI S
UMBEL S
CDLN UMBER S
DGJ UMBOS
UMBRA ELS
UMIAC KS
UMIAK S
UMIAQ S
BDHJLMPT UMPED
UNAIS
UNAPT
UNARM S
UNARY
UNAUS
UNBAN S
UNBAR S
UNBID
UNBOX
UNCAP S
UNCIA EL
N UNCLE S
BJ UNCOS
UNCOY
UNCUS
UNCUT E
UNDEE
FS UNDER
UNDID
UNDUE
UNFED
UNFIT S
UNFIX T
UNGOT
UNHAT S
UNHIP
UNIFY
B UNION S
DG UNITE DRS
UNITS
UNITY
UNJAM S
UNLAY S
UNLED
R UNLET
S UNLIT
G UNMAN S
UNMET
UNMEW S
UNMIX T
UNPEG S
UNPEN ST
UNPIN S
UNRIG S
UNRIP ES
UNSAY S
S UNSET S
UNSEW NS
UNSEX Y
A UNTIE DS
UNTIL
UNWED
UNWET
UNWIT S
UNWON
UNZIP S
UPBOW S
UPBYE
UPDOS
UPDRY
UPEND S
UPLIT
CDPST UPPED
CS UPPER S
UPSET S
URAEI
C URARE S
CO URARI S
URASE S
AC URATE S

RT URBAN E
URBIA S
UREAL
UREAS E
UREDO S
UREIC
GPS URGED
BPS URGER S
GPS URGES
BC URIAL S
MP URINE S
B URPED
B URSAE
URSID S
USAGE S
M USERS
BGLMPR USHER S
BFM USING
USNEA S
USQUE S
USUAL S
USURP S
USURY
UTERI
FR UTILE
BCGMNP UTTER S
UVEAL
UVEAS
UVULA ERS

VACUA
VAGAL
VAGUE R
VAGUS
A VAILS
VAIRS
VAKIL S
VALES
VALET S
VALID
VALOR S
VALSE S
VALUE DRS
VALVE DS
VAMPS
VAMPY
VANDA LS
VANED
VANES
VANGS
VAPID
VAPOR SY
VARAS
VARIA S
VARIX
VARNA S
VARUS
VARVE DS
VASAL
K VASES
VASTS
VASTY
VATIC
VATUS
VAULT SY
A VAUNT SY
VEALS
VEALY
VEENA S
VEEPS
VEERS
VEERY
VEGAN S
VEGES
VEGIE S
VEILS
VEINS
VEINY
VELAR S

VELDS
VELDT S
VELUM
VENAE
VENAL
VENDS
A VENGE DS
VENIN ES
VENOM S
E VENTS
A VENUE S
VENUS
VERBS
VERGE DRS
A VERSE DRST
VERSO S
VERST ES
AE VERTS
VERTU S
VERVE ST
VESTA LS
VESTS
K VETCH
VEXED
VEXER S
VEXES
VEXIL S
VIALS
VIAND S
VIBES
VICAR S
VICED
VICES
VICHY
VIDEO S
VIERS
VIEWS
VIEWY
VIGAS
VIGIA S
VIGIL S
VIGOR S
E VILER
VILLA ES
VILLI
VILLS
VIMEN
VINAL S
VINAS
VINCA S
VINED
O VINES
VINIC
VINOS
VINYL S
VIOLA S
VIOLS
VIPER S
VIRAL
VIREO S
VIRES
VIRGA S
VIRID
VIRLS
VIRTU ES
VIRUS
VISAS
VISED
VISES
VISIT S
VISOR S
VISTA S
VITAE
VITAL S
VITTA E
VIVAS
VIVID
VIXEN S
VIZIR S
VIZOR S
VOCAB S

VOCAL S
VOCES
VODKA S
VODOU NS
VODUN S
VOGIE
VOGUE DRS
VOICE DRS
AO VOIDS
VOILA
VOILE S
VOLAR
VOLED
VOLES
VOLTA
VOLTE S
VOLTI
VOLTS
VOLVA S
VOMER S
VOMIT OS
VOTED
VOTER S
VOTES
A VOUCH
A VOWED
VOWEL S
A VOWER S
VROOM S
VROUW S
VROWS
VUGGS
VUGGY
VUGHS
VULGO
VULVA ELRS
VYING

WACKE RS
WACKO S
WACKS
WACKY
WADDY
WADED
WADER S
WADES
WADIS
WAFER SY
WAFFS
WAFTS
S WAGED
S WAGER S
S WAGES
WAGON S
WAHOO S
WAIFS
S WAILS
ST WAINS
WAIRS
WAIST S
A WAITS
WAIVE DRS
A WAKED
A WAKEN S
WAKER S
A WAKES
WALED
WALER S
S WALES
WALKS
WALLA HS
WALLS
WALLY
WALTZ
WAMES
WAMUS
WANDS
WANED
WANES

WANEY
S WANKS
WANLY
WANTS
AS WARDS
WARED
WARES
WARKS
S WARMS
WARNS
WARPS
WARTS
S WARTY
WASHY
WASPS
WASPY
WASTE DRS
WASTS
WATAP ES
S WATCH
WATER SY
WATTS
WAUGH T
WAUKS
WAULS
WAVED
WAVER SY
WAVES
WAVEY S
WAWLS
WAXED
WAXEN
WAXER S
WAXES
WAZOO S
WEALD S
WEALS
WEANS
S WEARS
A WEARY
WEAVE DRS
WEBBY
WEBER S
WECHT S
WEDEL NS
WEDGE DS
WEDGY
T WEEDS
T WEEDY
WEEKS
T WEENS Y
ST WEENY
S WEEPS
S WEEPY
WEEST
ST WEETS
WEFTS
A WEIGH ST
WEIRD OSY
WEIRS
WEKAS
WELCH
WELDS
DS WELLS
WELLY
WELSH
WELTS
WENCH
WENDS
WENNY
WESTS
WETLY
WHACK OSY
WHALE DRS
WHAMO
WHAMS
WHANG S
WHAPS

WHARF S
WHATS
WHAUP S
WHEAL S
WHEAT S
WHEEL S
WHEEN S
WHEEP S
WHELK SY
WHELM S
WHELP S
WHENS
WHERE S
WHETS
WHEWS
WHEYS
WHICH
WHIDS
WHIFF S
WHIGS
A WHILE DS
WHIMS Y
WHINE DRSY
WHINS
WHINY
WHIPS
WHIPT
A WHIRL SY
WHIRR SY
WHIRS
WHISH T
WHISK SY
WHIST S
WHITE DNRSY
WHITS
WHITY
WHIZZ Y
WHOLE S
WHOMP S
WHOOF S
WHOOP S
WHOPS
WHORE DS
WHORL S
WHORT S
WHOSE
WHOSO
WHUMP S
WHUPS
WICCA NS
WICKS
WIDDY
WIDEN S
WIDER
WIDES T
WIDOW S
WIDTH S
WIELD SY
WIFED
WIFES
WIFEY S
WIFTY
WIGAN S
T WIGGY
WIGHT S
WILCO
WILDS
WILED
WILES
ST WILLS
WILLY
WILTS
WIMPS
WIMPY
WINCE DRSY
WINCH
WINDS
WINDY
DT WINED

DT WINES
WINEY
S WINGS
S WINGY
S WINKS
WINOS
WINZE S
S WIPED
WIPER S
S WIPES
WIRED
WIRER S
WIRES
WIRRA
WISED
WISER
WISES T
WISHA
WISPS
WISPY
T WISTS
WITAN S
ST WITCH Y
WITED
WITES
S WITHE DRS
WITHY
WITTY
S WIVED
WIVER NS
S WIVES
WIZEN S
WIZES
WOADS
WOALD S
WODGE S
WOFUL
A WOKEN
WOLDS
WOLFS
WOMAN S
WOMBS
WOMBY
WOMEN
WOMYN
WONKS
WONKY
WONTS
WOODS Y
WOODY
WOOED
WOOER S
WOOFS
WOOLS
WOOLY
S WOOPS
S WOOSH
WOOZY
S WORDS
WORDY
WORKS
WORLD S
WORMS
WORMY
WORRY
WORSE NRST
WORST S
WORTH SY
WORTS
WOULD
S WOUND S
WOVEN S
WOWED
WRACK S
WRANG S
WRAPS
WRAPT
WRATH SY
WREAK S
WRECK S
WRENS

WREST S
WRICK S
WRIED
WRIER
WRIES T
WRING S
WRIST SY
WRITE RS
WRITS
WRONG S
WROTE
WROTH
WRUNG
WRYER
WRYLY
WURST S
WUSHU
WUSSY
WYLED
WYLES
WYNDS
WYNNS
WYTED
WYTES

XEBEC S
XENIA LS
A XENIC
XENON S
XERIC
XEROX
XERUS
XYLAN S
XYLEM S
XYLOL S
XYLYL S
XYSTI
XYSTS

YABBY
YACHT S
K YACKS
YAFFS
YAGER S
YAGIS
YAHOO S
YAIRD S
YAMEN S
YAMUN S
YANGS
YANKS
YAPOK S
YAPON S
YARDS
YARER
YARNS
YAUDS
YAULD
YAUPS
YAWED
YAWEY
YAWLS
YAWNS
YAWPS
YCLAD
YEAHS
YEANS
YEARN S
YEARS
YEAST SY
YECCH S
YECHS
YECHY
YEGGS
YELKS
YELLS
YELPS
YENTA S
YENTE S
YERBA S
YERKS
C YESES

YETIS
YETTS
YEUKS
YEUKY
YIELD S
YIKES
YILLS
YINCE
YIPES
YIRDS
YIRRS
YIRTH S
X YLEMS
YOBBO S
YOCKS
YODEL S
YODHS
YODLE DRS
YOGAS
YOGEE S
YOGHS
YOGIC
YOGIN IS
YOGIS
YOKED
YOKEL S
YOKES
YOLKS
YOLKY
YOMIM
YONIC
YONIS
YORES
YOUNG S
YOURN
YOURS
YOUSE
YOUTH S
YOWED
YOWES
YOWIE S
YOWLS
YUANS
YUCAS
YUCCA S
YUCCH
YUCKS
YUCKY
YUGAS
YUKKY
YULAN S
YULES
YUMMY
YUPON S
YUPPY
YURTA
YURTS

ZAIRE S
ZAMIA S
ZANZA S
ZAPPY
ZARFS
ZAXES
ZAYIN S
ZAZEN S
ZEALS
ZEBEC KS
ZEBRA S
ZEBUS
ZEINS
ZERKS
ZEROS
ZESTS
ZESTY
ZETAS
ZIBET HS
ZILCH
ZILLS
ZINCS
ZINCY

ZINEB S
A ZINES
ZINGS
ZINGY
ZINKY
ZIPPY
ZIRAM S
ZITIS
ZIZIT H
ZLOTE
ZLOTY S
ZOEAE
ZOEAL
ZOEAS
ZOMBI ES
ZONAE
A ZONAL
ZONED
ZONER S
O ZONES
ZONKS
ZOOEY
ZOOID S
ZOOKS
ZOOMS
ZOONS
ZOOTY
ZORIL S
ZORIS
ZOUKS
ZOWIE
ZUZIM
ZYMES

Bob's Bible Quiz: All Multi-Anagram 2-5 Letter Words

2

AB AB BA
AH AH HA
AL AL LA
AM AM MA
AN AN NA
AT AT TA
AY AY YA
DE DE ED
DO DO OD
EF EF FE
EH EH HE
EM EM ME
EN EN NE
ER ER RE
HO HO OH
IS IS SI
IT IT TI
MO MO OM
MU MU UM
NO NO ON
NU NU UN
OS OS SO
OW OW WO
OY OY YO

3

AET ATE EAT ETA TAE TEA
AHS AHS ASH HAS SHA
APS ASP PAS SAP SPA
ARY RAY RYA YAR
BOR BRO ORB ROB
BRU BUR RUB URB
DOS DOS ODS SOD
OTW TOW TWO WOT
ABL ALB BAL LAB
ABO BOA OBA
ABR ARB BAR BRA
ABS ABS BAS SAB
ADS ADS SAD
AEK KAE KEA
AEN ANE NAE
AER ARE EAR ERA
AES SAE SEA
AEY AYE YEA
AFR ARF FAR
AGS AGS GAS SAG
AIR AIR RAI RIA
AKO KOA OAK OKA
AKS ASK KAS SKA
ALP ALP LAP PAL
ALS ALS LAS SAL
AMN MAN NAM
AMP AMP MAP PAM
AMR ARM MAR RAM
ANT ANT TAN
ANW AWN NAW WAN
APT APT PAT TAP
APY PAY PYA YAP
ARS ARS RAS
ART ART RAT TAR
ATW TAW TWA WAT
BIO BIO OBI
BOS BOS SOB
CHI CHI HIC ICH
COR COR ORC ROC
CRU CRU CUR
DEL DEL ELD LED
DEN DEN END
DLO DOL OLD
DOR DOR ROD
DOU DUO OUD UDO
EFR FER REF
EFT EFT FET
EGN ENG GEN NEG
EHS HES SHE
EHT ETH HET THE
EHY HEY YEH
EKU KUE UKE
ELS ELS SEL
ELT LET TEL
EOR ORE ROE
EPR PER REP
ERS ERS RES SER
ETW TEW WET
EWY WYE YEW
FOR FOR FRO
HMO MHO OHM
HOO OHO OOH
HOP HOP POH
IKS KIS SKI
IMS ISM MIS SIM
INS INS SIN
IPS PIS PSI SIP
IST ITS SIT TIS
MOS MOS OMS SOM
NOO NOO ONO
NOS NOS ONS SON
NOW NOW OWN WON
NRU RUN URN
NSU NUS SUN UNS
OPS OPS SOP
OPT OPT POT TOP
ORT ORT ROT TOR
PSU PUS SUP UPS
AAB ABA BAA
AAH AAH AHA
AAL AAL ALA
ABD BAD DAB
ABG BAG GAB
ABN BAN NAB
ABT BAT TAB
ABY ABY BAY
ACM CAM MAC
ACP CAP PAC
ACR ARC CAR
ACT ACT CAT
ADD ADD DAD
ADG DAG GAD
ADH DAH HAD
ADL DAL LAD
ADM DAM MAD
ADN AND DAN
ADO ADO ODA
ADP DAP PAD
ADW DAW WAD
AEG AGE GAE
AEL ALE LEA
AEP APE PEA
AEW AWE WAE
AFT AFT FAT
AGL GAL LAG
AGM GAM MAG
AGN GAN NAG
AGO AGO GOA
AGR GAR RAG
AGT GAT TAG
AGY GAY YAG
AHP HAP PAH
AHW HAW WHA
AHY HAY YAH
AIM AIM AMI
AIN AIN ANI
AJR JAR RAJ
AKY KAY YAK
ALT ALT LAT
ALW AWL LAW
AMT MAT TAM
AMY MAY YAM
ANP NAP PAN
ANY ANY NAY
AOR OAR ORA
AOT OAT TAO
AOV AVO OVA
AOZ AZO ZOA
APP APP PAP
APR PAR RAP
APW PAW WAP
ARW RAW WAR
AST SAT TAS
ASW SAW WAS
ASY AYS SAY
ATT ATT TAT
ATU TAU UTA
ATV TAV VAT
AWY WAY YAW
BDE BED DEB
BDI BID DIB
BDU BUD DUB
BEN BEN NEB
BEY BEY BYE
BGI BIG GIB
BGO BOG GOB
BIN BIN NIB
BIS BIS SIB
BNU BUN NUB
BOY BOY YOB
BSU BUS SUB
BTU BUT TUB
CDO COD DOC
CEP CEP PEC
CEU CUE ECU
CIS CIS SIC
DEF DEF FED
DEO DOE ODE
DEW DEW WED
DEY DEY DYE
DFI DIF FID
DGI DIG GID
DGO DOG GOD
DIM DIM MID
DIS DIS IDS
DMO DOM MOD
DNO DON NOD
DOT DOT TOD
DPU DUP PUD
EEK EEK EKE
EEL EEL LEE
EER ERE REE
EEV EVE VEE
EEW EWE WEE
EFS EFS FES
EGL GEL LEG
EGM GEM MEG
EGR ERG REG
EGT GET TEG
EHP HEP PEH
EIL LEI LIE
EIR IRE REI
EKL ELK LEK
EKY KEY KYE
ELM ELM MEL
ELY LEY LYE
ENO EON ONE
ENS ENS SEN
ENT NET TEN
ENW NEW WEN
EOS OES OSE
EOW OWE WOE
EPY PYE YEP
ESU SUE USE
ETY TYE YET
FIR FIR RIF
GGI GIG IGG
GHU HUG UGH
GIP GIP PIG
GLU GUL LUG
GMU GUM MUG
GNU GNU GUN
GOT GOT TOG
GTU GUT TUG
GUV GUV VUG
HIP HIP PHI
HNO HON NOH
HOT HOT THO
HOW HOW WHO
IKN INK KIN
IKR IRK KIR
ILN LIN NIL
ILT LIT TIL
IMR MIR RIM
INP NIP PIN
INT NIT TIN
IPT PIT TIP
IRS SIR SRI
ISX SIX XIS
LOP LOP POL
LOW LOW OWL
MMU MUM UMM
MNO MON NOM
MOR MOR ROM
MOT MOT TOM
MSU MUS SUM
NOT NOT TON
NTU NUT TUN
OOT OOT TOO
OSW SOW WOS
PRU PUR URP
PTU PUT TUP

4

AEST ATES EAST EATS ETAS SATE SEAT SETA TEAS
AELR EARL LEAR RALE REAL
AERS ARES EARS ERAS RASE SEAR SERA
AILR ARIL LAIR LARI LIAR LIRA RAIL RIAL
OSTW STOW SWOT TOWS TWOS WOST WOTS
ADER DARE DEAR READ
ADIS AIDS DAIS SADI SAID
AELM ALME LAME MALE MEAL
AELS ALES LASE LEAS SALE SEAL
AELT LATE TAEL TALE TEAL TELA
AELV LAVE LEVA VALE VEAL VELA
AIRS AIRS RAIS RIAS SARI
APST PAST PATS SPAT TAPS
ARST ARTS RATS STAR TARS TSAR
ASTW STAW SWAT TAWS TWAS WAST WATS
DEER DEER DERE DREE REDE REED
DEIL DEIL DELI DIEL IDLE LIED
DEOR DOER DORE REDO RODE
EELS EELS ELSE LEES SEEL
EEMS EMES SEEM SEME
EORS EROS ORES ROES ROSE SORE
ERSU RUES RUSE SUER SURE USER
OPST OPTS POST POTS SPOT STOP TOPS
ABEL ABLE BALE BLAE
ACLO CALO COAL COLA LOCA
AEGN GAEN GANE
AEGR AGER GEAR RAGE
AEHT EATH HAET HATE HEAT THAE
AELP LEAP PALE PEAL PLEA
AEMN AMEN MANE MEAN NAME NEMA
AEMS MAES MESA SAME SEAM
AEMT MATE MEAT META TAME TEAM
AENS ANES SANE
AEPR APER PARE PEAR RAPE REAP
AEPS APES APSE PASE PEAS SPAE
AERY AERY EYRA YARE YEAR
AIKN AKIN KAIN KINA
ALPS ALPS LAPS PALS SALP SLAP
ALST ALTS LAST LATS SALT SLAT
AMPS AMPS MAPS PAMS SAMP SPAM
ANSW AWNS SAWN SNAW SWAN WANS
AOST OAST OATS STOA TAOS
APRT PART PRAT RAPT TARP TRAP
APSW PAWS SWAP WAPS WASP
BORS BROS ORBS ROBS SORB
DEIT DIET DITE EDIT TIDE TIED
DENS DENS ENDS SEND SNED
DILO DIOL IDOL LIDO LOID
EENS ESNE SEEN SENE
EFIN FINE NEIF
EGOR ERGO GOER GORE OGRE
EILR LIER LIRE RIEL RILE
EILS ISLE LEIS LIES
EILV EVIL LIVE VEIL VILE
EIMR EMIR MIRE RIME
EIRS IRES REIS RISE SIRE
EKSY KEYS KYES SYKE
ELNO ENOL LENO LONE NOEL
ENOS EONS NOES NOSE ONES SONE
ENST NEST NETS SENT TENS
ENSY SNYE SYNE YENS
EPST PEST PETS SEPT STEP
ESTW STEW TEWS WEST WETS
HINS HINS HISN SHIN SINH
HIST HIST HITS SITH THIS
HMOS MHOS MOSH OHMS SHMO
HOPS HOPS POSH SHOP SOPH
HOST HOST HOTS SHOT SOTH TOSH
ILST LIST LITS SILT SLIT TILS
INOR INRO IRON NOIR NORI
IORT RIOT ROTI TIRO TORI TRIO
MSTU MUST MUTS SMUT STUM
NOSW NOWS OWNS SNOW SOWN WONS
ORST ORTS ROTS SORT TORS
AALM ALMA LAMA
AALN ALAN ANAL NALA
AAMS AMAS MASA
AANN ANNA NAAN NANA
ABDR BARD BRAD DARB DRAB
ABET ABET BATE BEAT BETA
ABKR BARK KBAR
ABLS ALBS BALS LABS SLAB
ABOS BOAS OBAS SOBA
ABST BAST BATS STAB TABS
ABTU ABUT TABU TUBA
ACDE ACED CADE DACE
ACER ACRE CARE RACE
ACES ACES CASE
ACOT COAT TACO
ACST ACTS CAST CATS SCAT
ADEG AGED EGAD GAED
ADEH AHED HADE HAED HEAD
ADEL DALE DEAL LADE LEAD
ADHS DAHS DASH SHAD
ADLU AULD DUAL LAUD
ADNS ANDS DANS SAND
ADOS ADOS ODAS SODA
AEFL ALEF FEAL FLEA LEAF
AEGM GAME MAGE MEGA
AEKS KAES KEAS SAKE
AELN ELAN LANE LEAN
AENP NAPE NEAP PANE PEAN
AENR EARN NEAR
AENT ANTE ETNA NEAT
AENW ANEW WANE WEAN
AEPT PATE PEAT TAPE TEPA
AERT RATE TARE TEAR
AERV AVER RAVE VERA
AESV AVES SAVE VASE
AESY AYES EASY EYAS YEAS
AGNS NAGS SANG SNAG
AGST GAST GATS STAG TAGS
AHPS HAPS HASP PASH
AHRT HART RATH TAHR
AHST HAST HATS
AHSW HAWS SHAW SHWA WASH
AHSY ASHY HAYS SHAY
AIKL ILKA KAIL
AILP LIPA PAIL PIAL
AILS AILS SAIL SIAL
AILT ALIT LATI TAIL TALI
AIMN AMIN MAIN MINA
AIMR AMIR MAIR RAMI
AIMS AIMS AMIS SIMA
AINP NIPA PAIN PIAN PINA
AINS AINS ANIS SAIN
AIST AITS SATI
AKNR KARN KNAR NARK RANK
AKOS KOAS OAKS OKAS SOAK
AKST KATS SKAT TASK
ALMS ALMS LAMS SLAM
AMNO MANO MOAN NOMA
ANPS NAPS PANS SNAP SPAN
ANST ANTS TANS
AOPS APOS SOAP
AORS OARS OSAR SOAR SORA
AORT RATO ROTA TARO TORA
APRS PARS RAPS RASP SPAR
APSS ASPS PASS SAPS SPAS
APSY PAYS PYAS SPAY YAPS
BLOO BOLO LOBO OBOL
BRSU BURS RUBS URBS
BSTU BUST BUTS STUB TUBS
CDEI CEDI DICE ICED
CDEO CODE COED DECO
CEIR CIRE RICE
CINO CION COIN CONI ICON
COST COST COTS SCOT
CRSU CRUS CURS
DEIN DENI DINE NIDE
DEIS DIES IDES SIDE
DELS DELS ELDS SLED
DELU DUEL LEUD LUDE
DERU DURE RUDE RUED
DESU DUES SUED USED
DHOS HODS SHOD
DLOS DOLS OLDS SOLD
DOOR DOOR ODOR ORDO ROOD
DORS DORS RODS SORD
EEFR FERE FREE REEF
EEMT MEET METE TEEM
EERS REES SEER SERE
EESS ESES SEES
EFIR FIRE REIF RIFE
EFRT FRET REFT TREF
EFST EFTS FEST FETS
EGLO LOGE OGLE
EGOS EGOS GOES SEGO
EHST ETHS HEST HETS
EILW LWEI WILE
EIMT EMIT ITEM MITE TIME
EIPS PIES SIPE
EIRT RITE TIER TIRE
ELMY ELMY YLEM
ELOR LORE ORLE ROLE
ELOS LOSE OLES SLOE SOLE
ELOV LEVO LOVE VOLE
ELST LEST LETS TELS
ELSY LEYS LYES LYSE
ENOP NOPE OPEN PEON PONE
EOPS EPOS OPES PESO POSE
EPSY ESPY PYES YEPS
ERST ERST REST RETS TRES
ERTY TREY TYER TYRE
ESTT SETT STET TEST TETS
ESTY STEY STYE TYES
ESWY WYES YEWS
GHSU GUSH HUGS SUGH
GINS GINS SIGN SING
GNOS NOGS SNOG SONG

Bob's Bible Quiz: All Multi-Anagram 2-5 Letter Words

GNSU GNUS GUNS SNUG SUNG
HIPS HIPS PHIS PISH SHIP
HOOS OOHS SHOO
HSTU HUTS SHUT THUS TUSH
IKNS INKS KINS SINK SKIN
IKRS IRKS KIRS KRIS RISK
ILNO LINO LION LOIN NOIL
ILOS OILS SILO SOIL SOLI
IMPS IMPS MIPS SIMP
INPS NIPS PINS SNIP SPIN
LOSW LOWS OWLS SLOW
OPRY PYRO ROPY
OPSW POWS SWOP
ORTY RYOT TORY TROY TYRO
ABCS CABS SCAB
ABDE ABED BADE BEAD
ABDU BAUD DAUB
ABEM BEAM BEMA MABE
ABEN BANE BEAN NABE
ABER BARE BEAR BRAE
ABGR BRAG GARB GRAB
ABHT BAHT BATH
ABLM BALM BLAM LAMB
ABNS BANS NABS
ABRS ARBS BARS BRAS
ACDI ACID CADI CAID
ACEM ACME CAME MACE
ACEN ACNE CANE
ACHR ARCH CHAR
ACLY ACYL CLAY LACY
ACMS CAMS MACS SCAM
ACNR CARN NARC
ACRS ARCS CARS SCAR
ADEM DAME MADE MEAD
ADEW AWED WADE
ADGR DRAG GRAD
ADIL DIAL LAID
ADIR ARID RAID
ADNR DARN NARD RAND
ADOT DATO DOAT TOAD
ADRS RADS SARD
ADRT DART DRAT TRAD
ADRY DRAY YARD
ADSW DAWS WADS
AEFR FARE FEAR FRAE
AEFT FATE FEAT FETA
AEGL EGAL GALE
AEGP GAPE PAGE PEAG
AEGS AGES GAES SAGE
AEGT GATE GETA
AEHM AHEM HAEM HAME
AEHR HARE HEAR RHEA
AEKL KALE LAKE LEAK
AEKT TAKE TEAK
AEKW WAKE WEAK WEKA
AELW WALE WEAL
AENV NAVE VANE VENA
AERW WARE WEAR
AESW AWES WAES
AETT TATE TEAT
AFIL ALIF FAIL FILA
AFOR FARO FORA
AFRT FRAT RAFT
AFST FAST FATS
AGHS GASH HAGS SHAG
AGLS GALS LAGS SLAG
AGNR GNAR GRAN RANG
AGNT GNAT TANG
AGPS GAPS GASP
AGRU GAUR GUAR RUGA
AGSY GAYS SAGY YAGS
AHHS HAHS HASH SHAH
AHKN ANKH HANK KHAN
AHMS HAMS MASH SHAM
AHNT HANT THAN
AHOR HOAR HORA
AIKS SAKI SIKA
AILM LIMA MAIL
AILN ANIL LAIN NAIL
AILV VAIL VIAL
AINR AIRN RAIN RANI
AKOR KORA OKRA
AKOY KAYO OAKY OKAY
AKRS ARKS SARK
ALMO LOAM MOLA
ALMU ALUM LUMA MAUL
ALNU LUNA ULAN ULNA
ALOT ALTO LOTA TOLA
ALSW AWLS LAWS SLAW
AMOR MORA ROAM
AMRS ARMS MARS RAMS
AMST MAST MATS TAMS
AMSW MAWS SWAM
ANNO ANON NONA
ANTU AUNT TUNA
ANWY AWNY WANY YAWN
ARSU SURA URSA
ARSY RAYS RYAS
ASTU TAUS UTAS
ASTV TAVS VAST VATS
ASWY SWAY WAYS YAWS
BEER BEER BREE
BEIR BIER BRIE
BENS BENS NEBS
BGOY BOGY GOBY
BHOO BOHO HOBO
BHOS BOSH HOBS
BINS BINS NIBS SNIB
BIOS BIOS OBIS
BKOO BOOK KOBO
BKOS BOSK KOBS
BNSU BUNS NUBS SNUB
BOSY BOYS SYBO YOBS
CEHT ECHT ETCH TECH
CEIL CEIL LICE
CEIT CITE ETIC
CEPS CEPS PECS SPEC
CERU CURE ECRU
CFIO COIF FICO FOCI
CHIS CHIS ICHS
CHIT CHIT ITCH
CIST CIST TICS
CORS CORS ORCS ROCS
CPSU CUPS CUSP SCUP
DEEK DEKE EKED
DEEM DEEM DEME MEED
DEEN DENE NEED
DEHI HIDE HIED
DEIR DIRE IRED RIDE
DEIV DIVE VIDE VIED
DELO DOLE LODE
DEMO DEMO DOME MODE
DENO DONE NODE
DENR NERD REND
DENU DUNE NUDE UNDE
DENY DENY DYNE
DEOS DOES DOSE ODES
DESY DEYS DYES
DIKS DISK KIDS SKID
DILS LIDS SILD SLID
DLOY ODYL OLDY
DNOS DONS NODS
DNOU UDON UNDO
DNRU DURN NURD
DOPR DORP DROP PROD
DOSS DOSS SODS
DOST DOST DOTS TODS
DOSU DUOS OUDS UDOS
DPSU DUPS PUDS SPUD
DRSU SURD URDS
EEGR EGER GREE
EEKL KEEL LEEK LEKE
EEKP KEEP PEEK PEKE
EEKS EKES SEEK SKEE
EELP PEEL PELE
EELR LEER REEL
EELT LEET TEEL TELE
EENP NEEP PEEN
EENV EVEN NEVE
EEPR PEER PERE PREE
EERT RETE TREE
EERV EVER VEER
EERW EWER WEER WERE
EERY EERY EYER EYRE
EESW EWES WEES
EFIL FILE LIEF LIFE
EFOR FORE FROE
EGLU GLUE LUGE
EGNS ENGS GENS NEGS
EGST GEST GETS TEGS
EHOR HERO HOER
EHOS HOES HOSE SHOE
EHRS HERS RESH
EIKP KEPI PIKE
EIKR KEIR KIER
EILP LIPE PILE PLIE
EILT LITE TILE
EIMN MIEN MINE
EINP PEIN PINE
EINV NEVI VEIN VINE
EIPR PERI PIER RIPE
EIRV RIVE VIER
EIST SITE TIES
EKNU KUNE NEUK NUKE
EKOS OKES SOKE
EKPS KEPS SKEP
EKSU KUES UKES
ELOP LOPE POLE
ELSU LUES SLUE
EMNO MENO NOME OMEN
EMOP MOPE POEM POME
EMOR MORE OMER
EMSU EMUS MUSE
EMSW MEWS SMEW
ENSW NEWS SEWN WENS
EOPP PEPO POPE
EOPR PORE REPO ROPE
EOPT POET TOPE
EOSW OWES OWSE WOES
EPPR PERP PREP REPP
EPRY PREY PYRE
FINO FINO FOIN INFO
FIRS FIRS RIFS
FIST FIST FITS SIFT
FLOW FLOW FOWL WOLF
GHOS GOSH HOGS SHOG
GINR GIRN GRIN RING
GIRT GIRT GRIT TRIG
GIST GIST GITS
GLSU GULS LUGS
GMSU GUMS MUGS SMUG
GORY GORY GYRO ORGY
GSTU GUST GUTS TUGS
HRTU HURT RUTH THRU
IKLS ILKS SILK
IKNO IKON KINO OINK
IKPS KIPS SKIP
IKST KIST KITS SKIT
ILLY ILLY LILY YILL
ILMO LIMO MILO MOIL
ILPS LIPS LISP SLIP
IMRS MIRS RIMS
IMSS ISMS MISS SIMS
IMST MIST SMIT
INST NITS SNIT TINS
IPSS PSIS SIPS
IPST PITS SPIT TIPS
ISTU SUIT TUIS
KOOT KOTO TOOK
LOOP LOOP POLO POOL
LOOS LOOS SOLO
LOOT LOOT TOOL
LOPS LOPS POLS SLOP
LOST LOST LOTS SLOT
MOOT MOOT TOOM
MOST MOST MOTS TOMS
NOOS ONOS SOON
NOOT ONTO TOON
NOST SNOT TONS
NOTW NOWT TOWN WONT
NRSU RUNS URNS
NSTU NUTS STUN TUNS
OORT ROOT ROTO TORO
OPSU OPUS SOUP
ORTW TROW WORT
OSTT STOT TOST TOTS
OSTU OUST OUTS
PRSU PURS SPUR URPS
AABB ABBA BABA
AABL ALBA BAAL
AABS ABAS BAAS
AAGL ALGA GALA
AAGM AGMA GAMA
AAGR AGAR RAGA
AAGS AGAS SAGA
AAIR ARIA RAIA
AAJR AJAR RAJA
AAKT KATA TAKA
AALS AALS ALAS
AAMR MAAR MARA
AANS ANAS ANSA
AAPT ATAP TAPA
ABBE ABBE BABE
ABCR CARB CRAB
ABDS BADS DABS
ABEK BAKE BEAK
ABES BASE SABE
ABGS BAGS GABS
ABIM BIMA IAMB
ABIS BIAS ISBA
ABKS BASK KABS
ABLW BAWL BLAW
ABNR BARN BRAN
ABOR BOAR BORA
ABOT BOAT BOTA
ABSS BASS SABS
ABSW SWAB WABS
ABSY ABYS BAYS
ACDS CADS SCAD
ACEF CAFE FACE
ACEH ACHE EACH
ACEL ALEC LACE
ACEP CAPE PACE
ACET CATE TACE
ACHI CHAI CHIA
ACHM CHAM MACH
ACHP CAPH CHAP
ACHT CHAT TACH
ACHY ACHY CHAY
ACKL CALK LACK
ACKR CARK RACK
ACKS CASK SACK
ACKY CAKY YACK
ACLM CALM CLAM
ACMO CAMO COMA
ACMR CRAM MARC
ACNS CANS SCAN
ACOR ARCO ORCA
ACOS OCAS SOCA
ACOX COAX COXA
ACPR CARP CRAP
ACPS CAPS PACS
ADDS ADDS DADS
ADEF DEAF FADE
ADEI AIDE IDEA
ADEZ ADZE DAZE
ADGS DAGS GADS
ADHL DAHL DHAL
ADIM AMID MAID
ADIP PADI PAID
ADIQ QADI QAID
ADIT ADIT DITA
ADIV AVID DIVA
ADLS DALS LADS
ADLY LADY YALD
ADMS DAMS MADS
ADMU DUMA MAUD
ADNW DAWN WAND
ADOP APOD DOPA
ADOR ORAD ROAD
ADPS DAPS PADS
ADRW DRAW WARD
AEHL HALE HEAL
AEHP EPHA HEAP
AEHS HAES SHEA
AEJN JANE JEAN
AEKM KAME MAKE
AELO ALOE OLEA
AELX AXEL AXLE
AELZ LAZE ZEAL
AEMR MARE REAM
AERR RARE REAR
AFIN FAIN NAIF
AFIR FAIR FIAR
AFLO FOAL LOAF
AFLX FALX FLAX
AFOS OAFS SOFA
AGIN AGIN GAIN
AGIV VAGI VIGA
AGLO GAOL GOAL
AGMS GAMS MAGS
AGNU GAUN GUAN
AGOS GOAS SAGO
AGOT GOAT TOGA
AGRS GARS RAGS
AGSW SWAG WAGS
AHIL HAIL HILA
AHLT HALT LATH
AHLU HAUL HULA
AHOY AHOY HOYA
AHPT PATH PHAT
AHTW THAW WHAT
AIKP PAIK PIKA
AIMM IMAM MAIM
AINT ANTI TAIN
AINV VAIN VINA
AJOT JATO JOTA
AJPU JAUP PUJA
AKLY ALKY LAKY
AKMO AMOK MAKO
AKNO KAON KOAN
AKSS ASKS SKAS
AKSU AUKS SKUA
AKSY KAYS YAKS
ALLS ALLS SALL
ALMP LAMP PALM
ALOS ALSO SOLA
ALOW ALOW AWOL
ALPY PALY PLAY
ALSS LASS SALS
ALSY LAYS SLAY
ALWY WALY YAWL
AMNY MANY MYNA
AMOS MOAS SOMA
AMOT ATOM MOAT
AMPR PRAM RAMP
AMRT MART TRAM
AMRU ARUM MURA
AMSY MAYS YAMS
ANOZ AZON ZONA
ANRT RANT TARN
ANRY NARY YARN
AOPR PRAO PROA
AORR ORRA ROAR
APPS APPS PAPS
APRW WARP WRAP
ARSW RAWS WARS
ARTY ARTY TRAY
ARWY AWRY WARY
ASTT STAT TATS
BBIS BIBS SIBB
BBLU BLUB BULB
BDES BEDS DEBS
BDIR BIRD DRIB
BDIS BIDS DIBS
BDOY BODY DOBY
BDRU BURD DRUB
BDSU BUDS DUBS
BEEF BEEF FEEB
BEEN BEEN BENE
BEIK BIKE KIBE
BEKR BERK KERB
BELO BOLE LOBE
BELT BELT BLET
BELU BLUE LUBE
BENO BONE EBON
BEOR BORE ROBE
BEST BEST BETS
BESY BEYS BYES
BETU BUTE TUBE
BGIS BIGS GIBS
BGLO BLOG GLOB
BGOS BOGS GOBS
BGRU BURG GRUB
BHSU BUSH HUBS
BIOR BIRO BRIO
BIRS BRIS RIBS
BKNO BONK KNOB
BLOS LOBS SLOB
BLOT BLOT BOLT
BLOW BLOW BOWL
BLRU BLUR BURL
BNOS NOBS SNOB
BOOR BOOR BROO
BOSS BOSS SOBS
BOST BOTS STOB
BOSW BOWS SWOB
BRUY BURY RUBY
BSSU BUSS SUBS
BSUY BUSY BUYS
CDEU CUED DUCE
CDLO CLOD COLD
CDOS CODS DOCS
CDRU CRUD CURD
CDSU CUDS SCUD
CEIM EMIC MICE
CEIN CINE NICE
CEIP EPIC PICE
CEIS ICES SICE
CELU CLUE LUCE
CENO CONE ONCE
CEOR CERO CORE
CESS CESS SECS
CESU CUES ECUS
CFIU CUIF FUCI
CHIN CHIN INCH
CHMU CHUM MUCH
CILO COIL LOCI
CKNO CONK NOCK
CKOR CORK ROCK
CKOY COKY YOCK
CKSU CUSK SUCK
CLOO COOL LOCO
CLOT CLOT COLT
CLOY CLOY COLY
COOP COOP POCO
COPS COPS SCOP
COSW COWS SCOW
COSY COSY COYS
CSTU CUTS SCUT
DDEY DYED EDDY
DDSU DUDS SUDD
DEEG EDGE GEED
DEES DEES SEED
DEET DEET TEED
DEFL DELF FLED
DEGL GELD GLED
DEHO HOED OHED
DEHS EDHS SHED
DEIM DIME IDEM
DELW LEWD WELD
DEMY DEMY EMYD
DENT DENT TEND
DEOP DOPE OPED
DEOT DOTE TOED
DEPS PEDS SPED
DESW DEWS WEDS
DFIS DIFS FIDS
DGIR GIRD GRID
DGIS DIGS GIDS
DGOS DOGS GODS
DHIS DISH SIDH
DIIM IMID MIDI
DIKN DINK KIND
DILY IDLY IDYL
DIMS DIMS MIDS
DINO DINO NODI
DLOT DOLT TOLD
DMOO DOOM MOOD
DMOS DOMS MODS
DORU DOUR DURO
DOTY DOTY TODY
DSTU DUST STUD
EEFL FEEL FLEE
EEFT FEET FETE
EEKN KEEN KNEE
EENY EYEN EYNE
EEPS PEES SEEP
EESV EVES VEES
EETW TWEE WEET
EFFI FIEF FIFE
EFLT FELT LEFT
EFLU FLUE FUEL
EFRS REFS SERF
EFSU FEUS FUSE
EGGY EGGY YEGG
EGIS EGIS GIES
EGKS KEGS SKEG
EGLS GELS LEGS
EGMS GEMS MEGS
EGRS ERGS REGS
EGRU GRUE URGE
EGRY GREY GYRE
EHIL ELHI HEIL
EHIR HEIR HIRE
EHKO HOKE OKEH
EHLO HELO HOLE
EHLR HERL LEHR
EHMS HEMS MESH
EHMT METH THEM
EHNT HENT THEN
EHNW HEWN WHEN
EHSW HEWS SHEW
EHTW THEW WHET
EHTY HYTE THEY
EIKT KITE TIKE
EILM LIME MILE
EILN LIEN LINE
EIMS MISE SEMI
EINT NITE TINE
EINZ ZEIN ZINE
EIRW WEIR WIRE
EISV VIES VISE
EIVW VIEW WIVE
EJST JEST JETS
EKLS ELKS LEKS
EKOT KETO TOKE
EKRY RYKE YERK
EKTY KYTE TYKE
ELLS ELLS SELL
ELMS ELMS MELS
ELPT LEPT PELT
ELRU LURE RULE

ELRY LYRE RELY
ELSS LESS SELS
ELTU LUTE TULE
EMMO MEMO MOME
EMNU MENU NEUM
EMOT MOTE TOME
EMOU MEOU MOUE
ENNO NEON NONE
ENOT NOTE TONE
ENOX EXON OXEN
ENRT RENT TERN
ENTT NETT TENT
ENTW NEWT WENT
EORT ROTE TORE
EORU EURO ROUE
EORV OVER ROVE
EORY OYER YORE
EOTV VETO VOTE
EPSU SPUE SUPE
EPSW PEWS SPEW
ESSU SUES USES
ESTU SUET UTES
ESTV VEST VETS
FGLO FLOG GOLF
FILO FILO FOIL
FILT FLIT LIFT
FIRT FRIT RIFT
FLOO FOOL LOOF
FMOR FORM FROM
FRSU FURS SURF
GGIS GIGS IGGS
GGNO GONG NOGG
GHIS GHIS SIGH
GIKN GINK KING
GIPR GRIP PRIG
GIPS GIPS PIGS
GISW SWIG WIGS
GLOS LOGS SLOG
GLPU GULP PLUG
GMOS MOGS SMOG
GOPR GORP PROG
GORT GROT TROG
GSUV GUVS VUGS
HIMS HIMS SHIM
HINT HINT THIN
HITW WHIT WITH
HKLO HOLK KOHL
HLOT HOLT LOTH
HLSU LUSH SHUL
HMSU HUMS MUSH
HNOS HONS NOSH
HNSU HUNS SHUN
HOOP HOOP POOH
HOPT PHOT TOPH
HOSW HOWS SHOW
HPSY HYPS SYPH
HRSU RHUS RUSH
IKLN KILN LINK
IKNR KIRN RINK
IKSS KISS SKIS
ILLS ILLS SILL
ILLT LILT TILL
ILMS MILS SLIM
ILNS LINS NILS
ILNY INLY LINY
ILOT LOTI TOIL
IMRY MIRY RIMY
INPY PINY PYIN
INTY TINY TYIN
IOPS PISO POIS
IRSS SIRS SRIS
ISTW WIST WITS
JSTU JUST JUTS
KLOO KOLO LOOK
KNOW KNOW WONK
LMOO LOOM MOOL
LMPU LUMP PLUM
LMSU LUMS SLUM
LNOO LOON NOLO
LOPY PLOY POLY
LOSS LOSS SOLS
LOTU LOUT TOLU
LPSU PLUS PULS
LSTU LUST SLUT
LSUU SULU ULUS
MNOO MONO MOON
MNOR MORN NORM
MNOS MONS NOMS
MOOR MOOR ROOM
MOOZ MOZO ZOOM
MOPR PROM ROMP
MORS MORS ROMS
MOSS MOSS SOMS
MPSU SUMP UMPS
MSSU MUSS SUMS
NNSU NUNS SUNN
NOSU NOUS ONUS
NPSU PUNS SPUN
NRTU RUNT TURN
OOST OOTS SOOT
OOTT OTTO TOOT
OPRT PORT TROP
OPRU POUR ROUP
ORSU OURS SOUR
ORTT TORT TROT
ORTU ROUT TOUR
OSST SOTS TOSS
PSSU PUSS SUPS
PSTU PUTS TUPS
RSTU RUST RUTS

5

AEPRS APERS APRES ASPER PARES PARSE PEARS PRASE PRESA RAPES REAPS SPARE SPEAR
AERST ASTER RATES RESAT STARE TARES TEARS
AELST LEAST SETAL SLATE STALE STEAL STELA TAELS TALES TEALS TESLA
AELPS LAPSE LEAPS PALES PEALS PLEAS SALEP SEPAL SPALE
EERST ESTER REEST RESET STEER STERE TERSE TREES
ACERS ACRES CARES CARSE ESCAR RACES SCARE SERAC
AELRS ARLES EARLS LARES LASER LEARS RALES REALS SERAL
AIRST AIRTS ASTIR SITAR STAIR STRIA TARSI
DEILS DEILS DELIS IDLES ISLED SIDLE SLIDE
DEORS DOERS DOSER REDOS RESOD RODES ROSED SORED
EIPRS PERIS PIERS PRIES PRISE RIPES SPEIR SPIER SPIRE
IORST RIOTS ROTIS TIROS TORSI TRIOS TROIS
ABEST ABETS BASTE BATES BEAST BEATS BETAS TABES
AELMS ALMES LAMES MALES MEALS
AELPT LEAPT LEPTA PALET PETAL PLATE PLEAT TEPAL
AELSV LAVES SALVE SELVA SLAVE VALES VALSE VEALS
AEMNS AMENS MANES MANSE MEANS MENSA NAMES NEMAS
AENPS ASPEN NAPES NEAPS PANES PEANS SNEAP SPEAN
AEPRT APTER PATER PEART PRATE TAPER
AEPST PASTE PATES PEATS SEPTA SPATE TAPES TEPAS
ACERT CARET CARTE CATER CRATE REACT RECTA TRACE
ACOST ASCOT COAST COATS COSTA TACOS
ADERS DARES DEARS RASED READS
AEHLS HALES HEALS LEASH SELAH SHALE SHEAL
AEKRS ASKER ESKAR RAKES SAKER
AERSW RESAW SAWER SEWAR SWARE SWEAR WARES WEARS
AILRS ARILS LAIRS LARIS LIARS LIRAS RAILS RIALS
AKNRS KARNS KNARS NARKS RANKS SNARK
APRST PARTS PRATS SPRAT STRAP TARPS TRAPS
CEIRS CIRES CRIES RICES
DEERS DEERS DREES REDES REEDS SEDER SERED
DEIST DEIST DIETS DITES EDITS SITED STIED TIDES
DILOS DIOLS IDOLS LIDOS LOIDS SLOID SOLDI SOLID
EEMST MEETS METES TEEMS
EENST SENTE TEENS TENSE
EEPRS PEERS PERES PERSE PREES PRESE SPEER SPREE
EGORS GOERS GORES GORSE OGRES
EILST ISLET ISTLE STILE TILES
EILSV EVILS LEVIS LIVES VEILS
EIMST EMITS ITEMS METIS MITES SMITE STIME TIMES
EINRS REINS RESIN RINSE RISEN SERIN SIREN
EINST INSET NEIST NITES SENTI STEIN TINES
EIRST RESIT RITES TIERS TIRES TRIES
ELORS LORES LOSER ORLES ROLES SOREL
EOPST ESTOP PESTO POETS STOPE TOPES
EORST ROSET ROTES STORE TORES TORSE
EORSW RESOW SEROW SOWER SWORE WORSE
AABLS ALBAS BAALS BALAS BALSA BASAL SABAL
AAIRT ATRIA RAITA RIATA TIARA
ABDER ARDEB BARDE BARED BEARD BREAD DEBAR
ABDOR BOARD BROAD DOBRA
ABELR ABLER BALER BLARE BLEAR
ABELS ABLES BALES BLASE SABLE
ABERS BARES BASER BEARS BRAES SABER SABRE
ACDER ACRED ARCED CADRE CARED CEDAR RACED
ADDER ADDER DARED DREAD READD
ADEHS ASHED DEASH HADES HEADS SADHE SHADE
ADELS DALES DEALS LADES LASED LEADS
ADEMN ADMEN AMEND MANED MENAD NAMED
ADERT DATER DERAT RATED TARED TRADE TREAD
ADEST DATES SATED STADE STEAD TSADE
AEGRS AGERS GEARS RAGES SAGER SARGE
AEGRT GATER GRATE GREAT RETAG TARGE TERGA
AEHST HAETS HASTE HATES HEATS
AEKST SKATE STAKE STEAK TAKES TEAKS
AELRT ALERT ALTER ARTEL LATER RATEL TALER
AEMST MATES MEATS SATEM STEAM TAMES TEAMS
AENRS EARNS NARES NEARS SANER SNARE
AENST ANTES ETNAS NATES NEATS STANE
AERSY EYRAS RESAY SAYER YEARS
AESTT STATE TASTE TATES TEATS TESTA
AINPS NIPAS PAINS PIANS PINAS
AINST ANTIS SAINT SATIN STAIN TAINS
AMNOS MANOS MASON MOANS MONAS NOMAS SOMAN
ANSTU AUNTS TUNAS
AOPRS PRAOS PROAS SAPOR
AORST RATOS ROAST ROTAS SORTA TAROS TORAS
BEIRS BIERS BIRSE BRIES RIBES
CERSU CRUSE CURES CURSE ECRUS SUCRE
CERTU CRUET CURET CUTER ERUCT RECUT TRUCE
DEINS DINES NIDES SNIDE
DELOS DOLES LODES SOLED
DELSU DUELS DULSE LEUDS LUDES SLUED
DEPRU DRUPE DUPER PERDU PRUDE URPED
EEGRS EGERS GREES REGES SERGE
EELST LEETS SLEET STEEL STELE TEELS TELES
EFIRS FIRES FRIES FRISE REIFS SERIF
EHORS HEROS HOERS HORSE HOSER SHOER SHORE
EILNS LENIS LIENS LINES
EILPS PILES PLIES SLIPE SPEIL SPIEL SPILE
EILRS LIERS RIELS RILES SLIER
EIMRS EMIRS MIRES MISER RIMES
EIRSW WEIRS WIRES WISER WRIES
ENORS SENOR SNORE
ENOST NOTES ONSET SETON STENO STONE TONES
EOPRS PORES POSER PROSE REPOS ROPES SPORE
EPRSU PURSE SPRUE SUPER
INORS IRONS NOIRS NORIS ORNIS ROSIN
LOOST LOOTS LOTOS SOTOL STOOL TOOLS
OORST ROOST ROOTS ROTOS TOROS TORSO
ORSTU ROUST ROUTS STOUR TORUS TOURS
ORSTY RYOTS STORY STROY TROYS TYROS
AALNS ALANS ANLAS NALAS NASAL
AAMSS AMASS MASAS MASSA
ABOST BOAST BOATS BOTAS SABOT
ABSTU ABUTS TABUS TSUBA TUBAS
ACENR CANER CRANE NACRE RANCE
ACEST CASTE CATES CESTA TACES
ADEIR AIDER AIRED DEAIR IRADE REDIA
ADERY DEARY DERAY RAYED READY
AEEGR AGREE EAGER EAGRE RAGEE
AEFLS ALEFS FALSE FLEAS LEAFS
AEFST FATES FEAST FEATS FETAS
AEGLR ARGLE GLARE LAGER LARGE REGAL
AEHRS HARES HEARS RHEAS SHARE SHEAR
AEHRT EARTH HATER HEART RATHE
AEILN ALIEN ALINE ANILE ELAIN LIANE
AELNS ELANS LANES LEANS
AELPR PALER PARLE PEARL
AELRY EARLY LAYER LEARY RELAY
AELSS LASES SALES SEALS
AELSW SWALE WALES WEALS
AEMRS MARES MARSE MASER REAMS SMEAR
AEMRT ARMET MATER RAMET TAMER
AEMSS MASSE MESAS SEAMS
AERSS ARSES RASES SEARS
AESST ASSET EASTS SATES SEATS TASSE
AESTW SWEAT TAWSE TWAES WASTE
AGILN ALGIN ALIGN LIANG LIGAN LINGA
AGLOR ALGOR ARGOL GORAL LARGO
AGNOR ARGON GROAN ORANG ORGAN
AGNST ANGST GNATS STANG TANGS
AHRST HARTS TAHRS TRASH
AIKNS KAINS KINAS
AINRS AIRNS NARIS RAINS RANIS SARIN
ALOST ALTOS LOTAS TOLAS
AMRSU ARUMS MURAS RAMUS
ARSTW STRAW SWART WARTS
CDEIR CIDER CRIED DICER RICED
CEOST COSET COTES ESCOT
CINOS CIONS COINS ICONS SCION SONIC
DEENS DENES DENSE NEEDS
DEHIS HIDES SHIED SIDHE
DEIRS DRIES RESID RIDES SIRED
DENRU NUDER UNDER
DOORS DOORS ODORS ORDOS ROODS
EEFRS FERES FREES REEFS
EELPS PEELS PELES SLEEP SPEEL
EEMNS MENSE MESNE NEEMS SEMEN
EERSV SERVE SEVER VEERS VERSE
EFINS FINES NEIFS
EGINR REIGN RENIG
EGLOS LOGES OGLES
EGNOR GENRO GONER
EHIRS HEIRS HIRES SHIER SHIRE
EIKRS KEIRS KIERS SIKER SKIER
EILNT ELINT INLET
EILRV ERVIL LIVER LIVRE VILER
EILSW LEWIS LWEIS WILES
EIMRT MERIT MITER MITRE REMIT TIMER
EINPS PEINS PENIS PINES SNIPE SPINE
EINRT INERT INTER NITER NITRE TRINE
EKRSY RYKES YERKS
ELNOS ENOLS LENOS NOELS
ELOPS LOPES POLES SLOPE
ELOSV LOVES SOLVE VOLES
ELPSU PULES PULSE
EMORS MORES MORSE OMERS
EMOST MOSTE MOTES SMOTE TOMES
ENORT NOTER TENOR TONER TRONE
ERSSU RUSES SUERS USERS
ERSTY TREYS TYERS TYRES
GIRST GIRTS GRIST GRITS TRIGS
HISTW SWITH WHIST WHITS
HORTW ROWTH THROW WHORT WORTH WROTH
INOPT PINOT PINTO PITON POINT
IPRST SPIRT SPRIT STIRP STRIP TRIPS
LOOPS LOOPS POLOS POOLS SLOOP SPOOL
NOSTU SNOUT TONUS
ORSTW STROW TROWS WORST WORTS
AAIMN AMAIN AMNIA ANIMA MANIA
AALMS ALMAS LAMAS
AALRT ALTAR ARTAL RATAL TALAR
ABCER ACERB BRACE CABER
ABCOR CARBO CAROB COBRA
ABDRS BARDS BRADS DARBS DRABS
ABEGL BAGEL BELGA GABLE GLEBA
ABEKR BAKER BRAKE BREAK KEBAR
ABELT ABLET BLATE BLEAT TABLE
ABEMR AMBER BREAM EMBAR
ABIRS ABRIS SABIR
ABKRS BARKS KBARS
ABLOR BOLAR BORAL LABOR LOBAR
ACDES CADES CASED DACES
ACDIR ACRID CAIRD DARIC
ACDIS ACIDS ASDIC CADIS CAIDS
ACEHT CHEAT TACHE TEACH THECA
ACELR CARLE CLEAR LACER
ACELS ALECS LACES SCALE
ACEMS ACMES CAMES MACES
ACEPR CAPER CRAPE PACER RECAP
ACEPS CAPES PACES SCAPE SPACE
ACERV CARVE CAVER CRAVE
ACIPS ASPIC PICAS SPICA
ACLOS CALOS COALS COLAS
ACLPS CLAPS CLASP SCALP
ACMSU MUSCA SUMAC
ACNOT CANTO COTAN OCTAN
ACNRS CARNS NARCS
ACPRS CARPS CRAPS SCARP SCRAP
ADDEL ADDLE DEDAL LADED
ADEGR GRADE RAGED
ADEKR DRAKE RAKED
ADELN ELAND LADEN NALED
ADELP PADLE PALED PEDAL PLEAD
ADELW LAWED WALED WEALD
ADEMR ARMED DERMA DREAM MADRE
ADENS DEANS SANED SEDAN
ADENW AWNED DAWEN DEWAN WANED
ADEPR DRAPE PADRE PARED RAPED
ADEPT ADEPT PATED TAPED
ADERR DARER DREAR RARED
ADILR DRAIL LAIRD LIARD LIDAR
ADINR DINAR DRAIN NADIR RANID
ADISS SADIS SAIDS
ADIST ADITS DITAS STAID TSADI
ADORS DORSA ROADS SAROD
ADRST DARTS DRATS
AEELS EASEL LEASE
AEEMR AMEER RAMEE
AEERS ERASE SAREE
AEFRS FARES FEARS SAFER
AEGLN ANGEL ANGLE GLEAN
AEGMR GAMER MARGE REGMA
AEGNR ANGER RANGE REGNA
AEGPR GAPER GRAPE PAGER PARGE
AEGST GATES GETAS STAGE
AEHPS EPHAS HEAPS PHASE SHAPE
AEIMR AIMER RAMIE
AEIRS ARISE RAISE SERAI
AEKLS KALES LAKES LEAKS SLAKE
AEKMS KAMES MAKES SAMEK
AEKNS KANES SKEAN SNAKE SNEAK
AELNP PANEL PENAL PLANE PLENA
AEMNR NAMER RAMEN REMAN
AEMNT AMENT MEANT MENTA
AENSS SANES SENSA
AEPSS APSES PASES PASSE SPAES
AERRS RARES RASER REARS
AERRT RATER TARRE TERRA
AERSU AURES URASE UREAS URSAE
AERSV AVERS RAVES SAVER
AERTT TATER TETRA TREAT
AGINR GARNI GRAIN
AGIST AGIST GAITS STAIG
AGLMU ALGUM ALMUG
AGLNO ALONG ANGLO LOGAN
AGRSU ARGUS GAURS GUARS SUGAR
AHKNS ANKHS HANKS KHANS SHANK
AHLOS HALOS SHOAL
AHNST HANTS SNATH
AHOST HOSTA OATHS SHOAT
AILMS LIMAS MAILS SALMI
AILNS ANILS NAILS SLAIN SNAIL

Bob's Bible Quiz: All Multi-Anagram 2-5 Letter Words

AILPS LAPIS PAILS SPAIL
AILSS LASSI SAILS SIALS SISAL
AILSV SILVA VAILS VIALS
AIMNS AMINS MAINS MINAS
AIMRS AMIRS MAIRS SIMAR
AIMSS AMISS SIMAS
AINPT INAPT PAINT PATIN PINTA
AIPST PITAS SPAIT TAPIS
AKRST KARST KARTS STARK
AKRSY KYARS SARKY
ALMPS LAMPS PALMS PLASM PSALM
ALNOS LOANS SALON SOLAN
ALNOT NOTAL TALON TOLAN TONAL
ALPST PLATS SPLAT
ALPSY PALSY PLAYS SPLAY
ALPTY APTLY PATLY PLATY TYPAL
AMNOR MANOR ROMAN
ANRST RANTS TARNS TRANS
AORTT OTTAR TAROT TORTA
AOSST OASTS STOAS
APSTU SPUTA STUPA
ARSTY ARTSY SATYR STRAY TRAYS
BDEIR BIDER BRIDE REBID
BDEOR BORED ORBED ROBED
BDOOR BROOD DOBRO
BEEMR BERME EMBER
BELRU BLUER RUBEL RUBLE
BEORS BORES BROSE ROBES SOBER
BERSU BURSE REBUS RUBES SUBER
BERTU BRUTE BURET REBUT TUBER
BLOOS BOLOS LOBOS OBOLS
CDEOR CODER CORED CREDO DECOR
CDEOS CODES COEDS DECOS
CEILS CEILS SLICE
CEIRT CITER RECIT RECTI TRICE
CENOS CONES SCONE
CEORS CEROS CORES CORSE SCORE
CHOTU COUTH TOUCH
COOST COOTS SCOOT
DEESW SEWED SWEDE WEEDS
DEFIL FELID FIELD FILED FLIED
DEGIR DIRGE GRIDE RIDGE
DEINW DWINE WIDEN WINED
DEIPR PRIDE PRIED REDIP RIPED
DEIRR DIRER DRIER RIDER
DEIRV DIVER DRIVE RIVED
DEIRW WEIRD WIDER WIRED WRIED
DELOW DOWEL LOWED
DEMOS DEMOS DOMES MODES
DENOR DRONE REDON
DEOPR DOPER PEDRO PORED ROPED
DEOPT DEPOT OPTED TOPED
DERSU DRUSE DURES
DMOOS DOOMS MOODS SODOM
DNOSU NODUS SOUND UDONS
DOPRS DORPS DROPS PRODS
EEFRR FREER FRERE REFER
EEHRS HERES SHEER
EEHST SHEET THESE
EEKNS KEENS KNEES SKEEN SKENE
EEKRS ESKER REEKS
EELRS LEERS REELS
EEMRT METER METRE REMET RETEM
EEMSS SEEMS SEMES
EENRT ENTER RENTE TERNE TREEN
EENSV EVENS NEVES SEVEN
EERSS ERSES SEERS SERES
EERSW EWERS RESEW SEWER SWEER
EESTW SWEET WEEST WEETS
EFILR FILER FLIER LIFER RIFLE
EFILS FILES FLIES
EGLSU GLUES GULES LUGES
EGORU ERUGO ROGUE ROUGE
EHLOS HELOS HOLES HOSEL SHEOL
EIKPS KEPIS PIKES SPIKE
EILMS LIMES MILES SLIME SMILE
EILRT LITER LITRE RELIT TILER
EINSW SINEW SWINE WINES
EIPST PISTE SPITE STIPE
EIRSV RIVES SIVER VIERS VIRES
EIRTT TETRI TITER TITRE TRITE
ELOSS LOESS LOSES SLOES SOLES
ELOST STOLE TELOS TOLES
EMRSU MURES MUSER SERUM
ENNOT NONET TENON TONNE
ENOPS OPENS PEONS PONES
ENOSW ENOWS OWSEN
ENRST NERTS RENTS STERN TERNS
EOPRR REPRO ROPER
EOPRT REPOT TOPER TROPE
EOPSS PESOS POSES POSSE
EOPSY POESY SEPOY
EORSV OVERS ROVES SERVO VERSO
EORTT OTTER ROTTE TORTE TOTER
EPRST PREST STREP
EPRSY PREYS PYRES
EPSST PESTS SEPTS STEPS
FIRST FIRST FRITS RIFTS
HOOST HOOTS SHOOT SOOTH
HOSTU SHOUT SOUTH THOUS
IKNOS IKONS KINOS OINKS
IKNST KNITS SKINT STINK
ILNOS LINOS LIONS LOINS NOILS
IMOST MOIST OMITS
KLOOS KOLOS LOOKS SOKOL
LMOOS LOOMS MOOLS OSMOL
LNOOS LOONS NOLOS SNOOL SOLON
NOOPS POONS SNOOP SPOON
NOSTW NOWTS TOWNS WONTS
OOPRS PROSO SOPOR SPOOR
OOPST STOOP TOPOS
OPRST PORTS PROST SPORT STROP
AABRZ BAZAR BRAZA
AAGNS ANGAS SANGA
AAHLM ALMAH HALMA HAMAL
AAKMR KARMA MAKAR MARKA
AALMR ALARM MALAR RAMAL
AALRV ARVAL LARVA
AALST ATLAS TALAS
AAMNT ATMAN MANAT MANTA
AANNS ANNAS NAANS NANAS
AANRT ANTRA RATAN
AANRV NAVAR VARNA
AAPST ATAPS PASTA TAPAS
ABCRS CARBS CRABS
ABDEG BADGE DEBAG
ABDEL ABLED BALED BLADE
ABDES BASED BEADS SABED
ABDLY BADLY BALDY
ABDSU BAUDS DAUBS
ABEMS BEAMS BEMAS MABES
ABEMY BEAMY EMBAY MAYBE
ABENS BANES BEANS NABES
ABERR BARER BARRE REBAR
ABERY BARYE YERBA
ABESS BASES SABES
ABETU BEAUT TUBAE
ABGNO BOGAN GOBAN
ABGRS BRAGS GARBS GRABS
ABHSU HABUS SUBAH
ABILS BAILS BASIL
ABIMS BIMAS IAMBS
ABINR BAIRN BRAIN
ABINS BASIN NABIS SABIN
ABISS BASIS BASSI ISBAS
ABLMS BALMS BLAMS LAMBS
ABMOS AMBOS SAMBO
ABNRU BURAN UNBAR URBAN
ABORT ABORT BOART TABOR
ABRSU BURAS BURSA
ACDEL CLADE DECAL LACED
ACDEN ACNED CANED DANCE
ACDIN CANID CNIDA NICAD
ACEHP CHAPE CHEAP PEACH
ACEHR CHARE REACH
ACEIR AREIC CERIA ERICA
ACEKR CRAKE CREAK
ACELM CAMEL MACLE
ACELN CLEAN LANCE
ACELT CLEAT ECLAT
ACELV CALVE CLAVE
ACEMR CREAM MACER
ACENS ACNES CANES SCENA
ACERR CARER RACER
ACHMS CHAMS CHASM MACHS
ACHST CHATS TACHS
ACILS LAICS SALIC
ACKLS CALKS LACKS SLACK
ACLOR CAROL CLARO CORAL
ACLST CLAST TALCS
ACLSY ACYLS CLAYS SCALY
ACMOR CAROM MACRO
ACMRS CRAMS MARCS SCRAM
ACNOR ACORN NARCO RACON
ACNST CANST CANTS SCANT
ACRST CARTS SCART
ADEEV DEAVE EAVED EVADE
ADEGS DEGAS EGADS
ADEHR HARED HEARD
ADEIL AILED IDEAL
ADEIM AIMED AMIDE MEDIA
ADEIS AIDES ASIDE IDEAS
ADELR ALDER LADER
ADELT DEALT DELTA LATED
ADELY DELAY LAYED LEADY
ADEMS DAMES MEADS
ADENR DENAR REDAN
ADEOR ADORE OARED OREAD
ADEPS SPADE SPAED
ADERW DEWAR WADER WARED
ADESV DEVAS SAVED
ADESW SAWED WADES
ADGRS DRAGS GRADS
ADIPR PADRI PARDI RAPID
ADIRY DAIRY DIARY YAIRD
ADLMO DOLMA DOMAL MODAL
ADLSU DUALS LAUDS
ADMNU DUNAM MAUND
ADMSU DUMAS MAUDS
ADNOR ADORN ANDRO
ADNRS DARNS NARDS RANDS
ADOPS APODS DOPAS SPADO
ADOST DATOS DOATS TOADS
ADRSW DRAWS SWARD WARDS
AEENV VEENA VENAE
AEERT ARETE EATER
AEFLM FLAME FLEAM
AEFLR FARLE FERAL FLARE
AEGGR AGGER EGGAR GAGER
AEGMS GAMES MAGES
AEGPS GAPES PAGES PEAGS
AEGRU ARGUE AUGER RUGAE
AEGRY GAYER YAGER
AEHMS HAEMS HAMES SHAME
AEHNT NEATH THANE
AEHSV HAVES SHAVE
AEIMN AMINE ANIME MINAE
AEINT ENTIA TENIA TINEA
AEINV NAEVI NAIVE
AEIRT IRATE RETIA TERAI
AEKPS PEAKS SPAKE SPEAK
AEKSW ASKEW WAKES WEKAS
AELMP AMPLE MAPLE
AELMR LAMER REALM
AELNR LEARN RENAL
AELNV NAVEL VENAL
AELPP APPEL APPLE PEPLA
AELRV LAVER RAVEL VELAR
AELSX AXELS AXLES LAXES
AEMTY ETYMA MATEY MEATY
AENSV AVENS NAVES VANES
AENSW SEWAN WANES WEANS
AEOPR OPERA PAREO
AEORT OATER ORATE
AEPRV PARVE PAVER
AEPRY APERY PAYER REPAY
AERTV AVERT TRAVE
AERTW TAWER WATER
AERTX EXTRA RETAX TAXER
AFILR FILAR FLAIR FRAIL
AFLOT ALOFT FLOAT FLOTA
AFORS FAROS SOFAR
AFRST FRATS RAFTS
AGHNS GNASH HANGS SANGH
AGHST GHAST GHATS
AGILR ARGIL GLAIR GRAIL
AGILS GLIAS SIGLA
AGLRU GULAR RUGAL
AGMNO AMONG MANGO
AGMSU GAUMS MAGUS SAGUM
AGNOW GOWAN WAGON
AGNSW GNAWS SWANG
AGORT ARGOT GATOR GROAT
AHILT LAITH LATHI
AHIPS APHIS APISH SPAHI
AHLOT ALTHO LOATH LOTAH
AHLST HALTS LATHS SHALT
AHLSU HAULS HULAS SHAUL
AHMSW SHAWM WHAMS
AHORS HOARS HORAS
AHSSW SHAWS SHWAS SWASH
AHSTW SWATH THAWS WHATS
AILNV ANVIL NIVAL VINAL
AILRT TRAIL TRIAL
AILST ALIST LITAS TAILS
AILSW SWAIL WAILS
AIMMS IMAMS MAIMS MIASM
AINRT RIANT TRAIN
AINTT TAINT TITAN
AIOST IOTAS OSTIA STOAI
AIPRT ATRIP TAPIR
AIRSS ARSIS SARIS
AIRSZ IZARS SIZAR
AKLOS KOLAS SKOAL
AKNOS KAONS KOANS
AKNST STANK TANKS
AKORT KORAT TAROK TROAK
ALMOR MOLAR MORAL
ALMOS LOAMS MOLAS
ALMRU LARUM MURAL
ALMSU ALUMS LUMAS MAULS
ALNRU LUNAR ULNAR
ALNSU LUNAS ULANS ULNAS
ALOPR PAROL POLAR
ALORS ORALS SOLAR
ALORV VALOR VOLAR
ALSST LASTS SALTS SLATS
AMORS MORAS ROAMS
AMOST ATOMS MOATS STOMA
AMPSS SAMPS SPAMS SPASM
AMRST MARTS SMART TRAMS
AMRSW SWARM WARMS
ANORS ARSON ROANS SONAR
ANSTY ANTSY NASTY TANSY
AOPSS PSOAS SOAPS
AORSS SAROS SOARS SORAS
AORSV ARVOS SAVOR
APRSY PRAYS RASPY SPRAY
APSST PASTS SPATS
APSSW SWAPS WASPS
APSTY PASTY PATSY
ARSST STARS TRASS TSARS
ARSTT START TARTS
ASSTW SWATS WASTS
ASTTU SUTTA TAUTS
BBLSU BLUBS BULBS
BDEEL BEDEL BLEED
BDEIT BIDET DEBIT
BDELU BLUED LUBED
BEERS BEERS BREES
BEEST BEETS BESET
BEFIR BRIEF FIBER FIBRE
BEGIN BEGIN BEING BINGE
BEIRT BITER TRIBE
BELMU BLUME UMBEL
BELOS BOLES LOBES
BELOW BELOW BOWEL ELBOW
BELST BELTS BLEST BLETS
BELSU BLUES LUBES
BEMOR BROME OMBER OMBRE
BEMRU BRUME UMBER
BHLSU BLUSH BUHLS SHLUB
BHOOS BOHOS HOBOS
BHRSU BRUSH BUHRS SHRUB
BIKRS BIRKS BRISK
BINRU BRUIN BURIN
BKOOS BOOKS KOBOS
BLRSU BLURS BURLS SLURB
BNOSU BONUS BOSUN
BOORS BOORS BROOS
BRSTU BRUTS BURST
CDEER CEDER CERED CREED
CDEIS CEDIS DICES
CDEIT CITED EDICT
CDLOS CLODS COLDS SCOLD
CEEPR CREEP CREPE
CEERS CERES SCREE
CEHIL CHIEL CHILE
CEHIM CHIME HEMIC MICHE
CEHOR CHORE OCHER OCHRE
CEHOS CHOSE ECHOS
CEIPS EPICS SEPIC SPICE
CEIST CESTI CITES
CELOS CLOSE COLES SOCLE
CELRU CRUEL LUCRE ULCER
CENOR CRONE RECON
CENOT CENTO CONTE ONCET
CEOPS COPES COPSE SCOPE
CHIOR CHIRO CHOIR ICHOR
CHIST CHITS STICH
CINTU CUTIN TUNIC
CIOPT OPTIC PICOT TOPIC
CISTU CUTIS ICTUS
CLOSW COWLS SCOWL
CNOSU CONUS UNCOS
DDEER DREED REDED
DEEFR DEFER FREED REFED
DEEGL GLEDE GLEED LEDGE
DEEMS DEEMS DEMES MEEDS
DEEPS DEEPS PEDES SPEED
DEEST DEETS STEED
DEESX DESEX DEXES SEXED
DEGLO LODGE OGLED
DEHOS HOSED SHOED
DEHRS HERDS SHERD SHRED
DEIKR DIKER IRKED
DEILP PILED PLIED
DEILT TILDE TILED
DEILV DEVIL LIVED
DEILW WIELD WILED
DEIMR DIMER MIRED RIMED
DEIMS DEISM DIMES DISME
DEINT TEIND TINED
DEIPS SIPED SPIED
DEIRT TIRED TRIED
DEISW WIDES WISED
DELOY ODYLE YODEL YODLE
DELPU DUPLE PULED
DENOS NODES NOSED SONDE
DENOW ENDOW OWNED
DENRS NERDS RENDS
DENST DENTS TENDS
DEOPS DOPES POSED SPODE
DEORT DOTER TRODE
DEORV DROVE ROVED
DEOST DOEST DOTES
DEPSU DUPES PSEUD SPUED
DERRY DERRY DRYER REDRY
DIIMO IDIOM IMIDO
DLOOR DOLOR DROOL
DNOOR DONOR RONDO
DNRSU DURNS NURDS
DORSW SWORD WORDS
DORWY DOWRY ROWDY WORDY
EEFRY FEYER REEFY
EEGNR GENRE GREEN
EEGST EGEST GEEST GESTE
EEHRT ETHER THERE THREE
EEKLS KEELS LEEKS SLEEK
EEKPS KEEPS PEEKS PEKES
EEKST KEETS SKEET STEEK
EELRV ELVER LEVER REVEL
EENPS NEEPS PEENS PENES
EENRS ERNES SNEER
EENRV NERVE NEVER
EENSS ESNES SENSE
EFIRR FIRER FRIER RIFER
EFLRY FERLY FLYER REFLY
EFLSU FLUES FUELS FUSEL
EFLTY FLYTE LEFTY
EFORS FORES FROES
EFORT FETOR FORTE OFTER
EFRRY FERRY FRYER
EGGOR GORGE GREGO
EGHIN HINGE NEIGH
EGINS SENGI SINGE
EGLRU GLUER GRUEL LUGER
EGMNO GENOM GNOME
EGOSS GESSO SEGOS
EGRSU GRUES SURGE URGES
EHILS HEILS SHIEL
EHLOT HELOT HOTEL THOLE
EHLPS HELPS SHLEP
EHNOR HERON HONER
EHNOS HONES HOSEN SHONE
EHNST HENTS SHENT THENS
EHOST ETHOS SHOTE THOSE
EIKNO EIKON ENOKI KOINE
EIKST KITES SKITE TIKES
EILOR OILER ORIEL REOIL
EILPR PERIL PLIER
EIMNS MIENS MINES
EIMRX MIREX MIXER REMIX
EIMSS MISES SEISM SEMIS
EINSV VEINS VINES
EIPSS SIPES SPIES
EIRSS RISES SIRES
EIRTW TWIER WRITE
EISTX EXIST EXITS SIXTE
EISVW SWIVE VIEWS WIVES
EKLPS KELPS SKELP
EKSTY KYTES TYKES
ELNOR ENROL LONER NEROL
ELOOS LOOSE OLEOS
ELOPR LOPER POLER PROLE
ELORW LOWER ROWEL
ELOSU LOUSE OUSEL
ELOSW LOWES LOWSE
ELPST PELTS SLEPT SPELT
ELRSU LURES RULES
EMNOS MESON NOMES OMENS
EMOPR MOPER PROEM
EMOPS MOPES POEMS POMES
EMOSU MEOUS MOUES MOUSE
EMOTT MOTET MOTTE TOTEM
EMPRS PERMS SPERM
ENNOS NEONS NONES
ENORW OWNER REWON ROWEN
ENOSS NOSES SONES
ENSTT NETTS STENT TENTS
ENSTU TUNES UNSET
EOPPS PEPOS POPES
EORSU EUROS ROUES ROUSE
EORTU OUTER OUTRE ROUTE
EORTV OVERT TROVE VOTER
EORTW TOWER WROTE
EPPRS PERPS PREPS REPPS
EPRRY PERRY PRYER
EPSSU PUSES SPUES SUPES
EPSTU SETUP STUPE UPSET
EPSTY PESTY TYPES
ERRTY RETRY TERRY
ERSTW STREW TREWS WREST
ESSTT SETTS STETS TESTS
ESTTY TESTY YETTS
FINOS FINOS FOINS INFOS
FLORU FLOUR FLUOR
FLOSW FLOWS FOWLS WOLFS
GHINO HONGI OHING
GHIRT GIRTH GRITH RIGHT
GHOST GHOST GOTHS
GINOP GIPON OPING PINGO
GINOT INGOT TIGON
GINRS GIRNS GRINS RINGS
GINSS SIGNS SINGS
GIPRS GRIPS PRIGS SPRIG
GOPRS GORPS PROGS
HILOT LITHO THIOL
HISST HISTS SHIST
HOOPS HOOPS POOHS

Bob's Bible Quiz: All Multi-Anagram 2-5 Letter Words

HOOSW WHOSO WOOSH
HOPSS SHOPS SOPHS
HOSST HOSTS SHOTS SOTHS
HRSTU HURST HURTS RUTHS
IKLNS KILNS LINKS SLINK
ILLST LILTS STILL TILLS
ILLSY SILLY SLILY YILLS
ILMOS LIMOS MILOS MOILS
ILOPS POLIS SPOIL
ILORS LORIS ROILS
ILPST SLIPT SPILT SPLIT
ILSST LISTS SILTS SLITS
INOPR ORPIN PRION
INOPS OPSIN PIONS
INPSY PYINS SPINY
INSTU SUINT UNITS
KNOPS KNOPS KNOSP
KNOSW KNOWS WONKS
KOOST KOTOS STOOK
KORST SKORT STORK TORSK
LMPSU LUMPS PLUMS SLUMP
LOPSY PLOYS POLYS
LOSTU LOTUS LOUTS TOLUS
MNOOS MONOS MOONS NOMOS
MNOTU MOUNT MUTON NOTUM
MOORS MOORS ROOMS
MSSTU MUSTS SMUTS STUMS
NOOST SNOOT TOONS

OPPSY POPSY SOPPY
OPRSY PROSY PYROS
OPSST POSTS SPOTS STOPS
OPSTU POUTS SPOUT STOUP
OPSTY POTSY TYPOS
RSTTU STRUT STURT TRUST
AABBK BABKA KABAB
AABBS ABBAS BABAS
AABEM ABEAM AMEBA
AABNW BWANA NAWAB
AADEH AAHED AHEAD
AADMN ADMAN DAMAN
AADMR DAMAR DRAMA
AAEGL ALGAE GALEA
AAENP APNEA PAEAN
AAENR ANEAR ARENA
AAEPR AREPA PARAE
AAGIT AGITA TAIGA
AAGLN ALANG LAGAN
AAGLR ARGAL GRAAL
AAGLS ALGAS GALAS
AAGMM GAMMA MAGMA
AAGMS AGMAS GAMAS
AAGNP PAGAN PANGA
AAGRS AGARS RAGAS
AAILN LANAI LIANA
AAIRS ARIAS RAIAS
AAKST KATAS TAKAS
AALNT ALANT NATAL
AALPP APPAL PAPAL
AALRU AURAL LAURA
AALSV LAVAS VASAL

AAMRS MAARS MARAS
AARTT ATTAR TATAR
ABBES ABBES BABES
ABBLU BABUL BUBAL
ABCIR BARIC RABIC
ABCNO BACON BANCO
ABDEO ABODE ADOBE
ABDEY BAYED BEADY
ABDIR BRAID RABID
ABEHO BOHEA OBEAH
ABEKS BAKES BEAKS
ABELM AMBLE BLAME
ABERZ BRAZE ZEBRA
ABESU ABUSE BEAUS
ABHIT BAITH HABIT
ABHMO ABMHO ABOHM
ABHST BAHTS BATHS
ABIIL ALIBI BIALI
ABILN BINAL BLAIN
ABILR BRAIL LIBRA
ABKRY BARKY BRAKY
ABLMY BALMY LAMBY
ABLST BLAST BLATS
ABLSW BAWLS BLAWS
ABMRU RUMBA UMBRA
ABMRY AMBRY BARMY
ABNRS BARNS BRANS
ABORS BOARS BORAS
ABOSS BASSO SOBAS
ABSST BASTS STABS
ABSSY ABYSS BASSY
ACDEF DECAF FACED
ACDEG CADGE CAGED

ACDEP CAPED PACED
ACDET ACTED CADET
ACDLS CLADS SCALD
ACDLU CAULD DUCAL
ACEFR FACER FARCE
ACEFS CAFES FACES
ACEGR CAGER GRACE
ACEHL CHELA LEACH
ACEHS ACHES CHASE
ACELY LACEY LYCEA
ACEMO CAMEO COMAE
ACENO CANOE OCEAN
ACESU CAUSE SAUCE
ACETT TACET TECTA
ACGIM GAMIC MAGIC
ACGRS CRAGS SCRAG
ACHIN CHAIN CHINA
ACHIS CHAIS CHIAS
ACHKS HACKS SHACK
ACHLO CHOLA LOACH
ACHMO MACHO MOCHA
ACHMR CHARM MARCH
ACHNO ANCHO NACHO
ACHNT CHANT NATCH
ACHOR ORACH ROACH
ACHPS CAPHS CHAPS
ACHPT CHAPT PATCH
ACHRS CHARS CRASH
ACHRT CHART RATCH
ACHSW CHAWS SCHWA
ACIIL CILIA ILIAC
ACILM CLAIM MALIC
ACILP PICAL PLICA

ACILV CAVIL CLAVI
ACIMN AMNIC MANIC
ACINR CAIRN NARIC
ACINT ACTIN ANTIC
ACIRU AURIC CURIA
ACITT ATTIC TACIT
ACKMS MACKS SMACK
ACKRS CARKS RACKS
ACKSS CASKS SACKS
ACKST STACK TACKS
ACKSY CASKY YACKS
ACLLS CALLS SCALL
ACLMS CALMS CLAMS
ACLRY CLARY LYCRA
ACMOS CAMOS COMAS
ACMPS CAMPS SCAMP
ACNNO ANCON CANON
ACORT ACTOR TAROC
ACRSS CRASS SCARS
ACRSU ARCUS SCAUR
ACSST CASTS SCATS
ACSSU ASCUS CASUS
ACSTT SCATT TACTS
ACSUY SAUCY YUCAS
ADDEW DAWED WADED
ADDEZ ADZED DAZED
ADDGI GADDI GADID
ADEEM ADEEM EDEMA
ADEES AEDES EASED
ADEFR FADER FARED
ADEFT DEFAT FATED
ADEGP GAPED PAGED
ADEHT DEATH HATED

ADEHY HAYED HEADY
ADEKN KNEAD NAKED
ADELM LAMED MEDAL
ADEMT MATED TAMED
ADENV DAVEN VANED
ADERV DRAVE RAVED
ADESZ ADZES DAZES
ADEWX DEWAX WAXED
ADGNO DONGA GONAD
ADHIJ HADJI JIHAD
ADHLS DAHLS DHALS
ADHRS HARDS SHARD
ADHRY HARDY HYDRA
ADHSY DASHY SHADY
ADIMS AMIDS MAIDS
ADINV DIVAN VIAND
ADIOR AROID RADIO
ADIOZ AZIDO DIAZO
ADIPS PADIS SAPID
ADIPV PAVID VAPID
ADIQS QADIS QAIDS
ADISY DAISY SAYID
ADLLO ALDOL ALLOD
ADLOU ALOUD DOULA
ADLRY LARDY LYARD
ADMNO MONAD NOMAD
ADNSW DAWNS WANDS
ADOTY TOADY TODAY
ADQSU QUADS SQUAD
ADRSY DRAYS YARDS
ADSTU ADUST DAUTS
AEEGL AGLEE EAGLE
AEELT ELATE TELAE

AEENR ARENE RANEE
AEENT EATEN ENATE
AEEST SETAE TEASE
AEFIR AFIRE FERIA
AEFKR FAKER FREAK
AEGNO AGONE GENOA
AEGNV GANEV VEGAN
AEGRZ GAZER GRAZE
AEGSS GASES SAGES
AEGSU AGUES USAGE
AEGSW SWAGE WAGES
AEHKS HAKES SHAKE
AEHLM ALMEH HEMAL
AEHLW WHALE WHEAL
AEHMR HAREM HERMA
AEHNS ASHEN HANSE
AEHSS ASHES SHEAS
AEIKL ALIKE ALKIE
AEILM EMAIL MAILE
AEIPS PAISE SEPIA
AEIRU AUREI URAEI
AEJNS JANES JEANS
AEKNW KNAWE WAKEN
AEKRW WAKER WREAK
AELNO ALONE ANOLE
AELNT LATEN LEANT
AELOZ AZOLE ZOEAL
AELQU EQUAL QUALE
AELRX LAXER RELAX
AELSZ LAZES ZEALS
AELTX EXALT LATEX
AELUV UVEAL VALUE
AELVY LEAVY VEALY

AEMNY MEANY YAMEN
AEMRR ARMER REARM
AEMSX EXAMS MAXES
AEMSZ MAZES SMAZE
AENNP PANNE PENNA
AENOT ATONE OATEN
AEOPS PASEO PSOAE
AEOST STOAE TOEAS
AEOSV OAVES SOAVE
AEPRR PARER RAPER
AERWX REWAX WAXER
AESSV SAVES VASES
AESSY ESSAY EYASS
AESTV STAVE VESTA
AESTX TAXES TEXAS
AESUV SUAVE UVEAS
AFHST HAFTS SHAFT
AFIKR FAKIR KAFIR
AFILS ALIFS FAILS
AFIRS FAIRS FIARS
AFLOO ALOOF LOOFA
AFLOS FOALS LOAFS
AFNSU FAUNS SNAFU
AFOSS FOSSA SOFAS
AGHTU AUGHT GHAUT
AGIMO AMIGO IMAGO
AGIMS AGISM SIGMA
AGINS GAINS SIGNA
AGINW AWING WIGAN
AGLNS GLANS SLANG
AGLOS GAOLS GOALS
AGLRY GLARY GYRAL
AGLSS GLASS SLAGS

AGNOT TANGO TONGA
AGNPS PANGS SPANG
AGNRS GNARS GRANS
AGNRY ANGRY RANGY
AGOST GOATS TOGAS
AGPRS GRASP SPRAG
AGSST GASTS STAGS
AHKRS HARKS SHARK
AHLLO HALLO HOLLA
AHLLS HALLS SHALL
AHLPY HAPLY PHYLA
AHLSY HYLAS SHALY
AHMRS HARMS MARSH
AHMSS SHAMS SMASH
AHNTU HAUNT UNHAT
AHPRS HARPS SHARP
AHPST PATHS STAPH
AHPSW PSHAW WHAPS
AHRTW THRAW WRATH
AIKPS PAIKS PIKAS
AIKRT KRAIT TRAIK
AIKSS SAKIS SIKAS
AILMP LIMPA MILPA
AILNP LAPIN PLAIN
AILNY INLAY LAYIN
AILOV VIOLA VOILA
AILPP PALPI PIPAL
AILRV RIVAL VIRAL
AIMMU IMAUM UMAMI
AIMNO AMINO AMNIO
AIMQU MAQUI UMIAQ
AIMRZ MIRZA ZIRAM
AIMST MAIST TAMIS

AINRV INVAR RAVIN
AINSS SAINS SASIN
AINSV SAVIN VINAS
AINSW SWAIN WAINS
AINTW TWAIN WITAN
AIOSS OASIS OSSIA
AIPRS PAIRS PARIS
AIPSS APSIS ASPIS
AIQSU QUAIS QUASI
AIRRS ARRIS SIRRA
AISTW WAIST WAITS
AJMOR JORAM MAJOR
AJNTU JAUNT JUNTA
AJOST JATOS JOTAS
AJPSU JAUPS PUJAS
AKLST STALK TALKS
AKMOS AMOKS MAKOS
AKNPS KNAPS SPANK
AKNSY SNAKY YANKS
AKORS KORAS OKRAS
AKOSS ASKOS SOAKS
AKOSY KAYOS OKAYS
AKPRS PARKS SPARK
AKRTU KRAUT KURTA
AKSST SKATS TASKS
ALLMS MALLS SMALL
ALLOS OLLAS SALOL
ALLOT ALLOT ATOLL
ALLOY ALLOY LOYAL
ALLPS PALLS SPALL
ALLST STALL TALLS
ALMPY AMPLY PALMY
ALMRY MARLY MYLAR

ALMST MALTS SMALT
ALNOZ AZLON ZONAL
ALNUY UNLAY YULAN
ALNWY LAWNY WANLY
ALOSV OVALS SALVO
ALOTV LOVAT VOLTA
ALPSS SALPS SLAPS
ALSSY LYSSA SLAYS
ALSTU SAULT TALUS
ALSTY SALTY SLATY
ALSUU LUAUS USUAL
AMORY MAYOR MORAY
AMPRS PRAMS RAMPS
AMPST STAMP TAMPS
ANNOY ANNOY ANYON
ANPSS SNAPS SPANS
ANPSW PAWNS SPAWN
ANSSW SNAWS SWANS
ANSUY UNSAY YUANS
AOPRV PARVO VAPOR
AOSTT STOAT TOAST
APRSS RASPS SPARS
APRSU PRAUS SUPRA
APRSW WARPS WRAPS
APSWY WASPY YAWPS
ARTTY RATTY TARTY
ASSTY SAYST STAYS
BBOOY BOOBY YOBBO
BCMOO COMBO COOMB
BCRSU CURBS SCRUB
BDEER BREDE BREED
BDEEW BEDEW DWEEB
BDEGU BUDGE DEBUG

BDEIM BEDIM IMBED
BDETU DEBUT TUBED
BDIRS BIRDS DRIBS
BDRSU BURDS DRUBS
BEEFS BEEFS FEEBS
BEELP BLEEP PLEBE
BEGLO BOGLE GLOBE
BEGLU BUGLE BULGE
BEIIK BIKIE KIBEI
BEIKS BIKES KIBES
BEILR BIRLE LIBER
BEINR BINER BRINE
BEKRS BERKS KERBS
BELNO BELON NOBLE
BELTU BLUET BUTLE
BENOR BONER BORNE
BENOS BONES EBONS
BENOT BENTO BETON
BENOY BONEY EBONY
BEOPR PROBE REBOP
BERUY BUYER REBUY
BESTU BUTES TUBES
BGHRU BRUGH BURGH
BGILY BIGLY BILGY
BGINO BINGO BOING
BGIOS BIGOS BIOGS
BGLOS BLOGS GLOBS
BGRSU BURGS GRUBS
BHIRT BIRTH BRITH
BHOOT BHOOT BOOTH
BHORT BROTH THROB
BILMY BLIMY LIMBY
BIORS BIROS BRIOS

BKNOS BONKS KNOBS
BLOST BLOTS BOLTS
BLOSW BLOWS BOWLS
BMOOR BROMO BROOM
BMOOS BOOMS BOSOM
BNOOS BOONS BOSON
BNRTU BRUNT BURNT
BOOST BOOST BOOTS
BOSUY BOUSY BUOYS
BSSTU BUSTS STUBS
CCEIR CERCI CERIC
CCEOS COSEC SECCO
CDEEU DEUCE EDUCE
CDEIM DEMIC MEDIC
CDELO COLED DOLCE
CDENO CODEN CONED
CDEOU COUDE DOUCE
CDEOX CODEX COXED
CDEOY COYED DECOY
CDERU CRUDE CURED
CDERY CYDER DECRY
CDILU LUCID LUDIC
CDIOS DISCO SODIC
CDIPU CUPID PUDIC
CDLOU CLOUD COULD
CDNOO CODON CONDO
CDORS CORDS SCROD
CDRSU CRUDS CURDS
CEENS CENSE SCENE
CEERT ERECT TERCE
CEFHI CHIEF FICHE
CEHIN CHINE NICHE
CEHRT CHERT RETCH

CEHST CHEST TECHS
CEHTU CHUTE TEUCH
CEILM CLIME MELIC
CEINS CINES SINCE
CEIPR CRIPE PRICE
CEIRR CRIER RICER
CEIRU CURIE UREIC
CEITV CIVET EVICT
CEKNS NECKS SNECK
CEKPS PECKS SPECK
CELSU CLUES LUCES
CEMOT COMET COMTE
CENOP COPEN PONCE
CENST CENTS SCENT
CEORR CORER CRORE
CEOSV COVES VOCES
CERRU CURER RECUR
CERSW CREWS SCREW
CESTU CUTES SCUTE
CFFOS COFFS SCOFF
CFFSU CUFFS SCUFF
CFISU CUIFS FICUS
CFRSU CURFS SCURF
CGINO COIGN INCOG
CGIOR CORGI ORGIC
CGNOO COGON CONGO
CHIIL CHILI LICHI
CHIVY CHIVY VICHY
CHKOS HOCKS SHOCK
CHKSU HUCKS SHUCK
CHLRU CHURL LURCH
CHMOU MOUCH MUCHO
CHORT ROTCH TORCH

CIKLS LICKS SLICK
CIKNS NICKS SNICK
CIKST STICK TICKS
CILNO COLIN NICOL
CIMNU CUMIN MUCIN
CINOT ONTIC TONIC
CINRU INCUR RUNIC
CIPRS CRISP SCRIP
CIPRY PRICY PYRIC
CKLSU LUCKS SCULK
CKMOS MOCKS SMOCK
CKNOS CONKS NOCKS
CKOOS COOKS SOCKO
CKORS CORKS ROCKS
CKORY CORKY ROCKY
CKSSU CUSKS SUCKS
CKSTU STUCK TUCKS
CKSUY SUCKY YUCKS
CLLSU CULLS SCULL
CLOOS COOLS LOCOS
CLOST CLOTS COLTS
CMORU MUCOR MUCRO
CNORS CORNS SCORN
CNORY CORNY CRONY
COOPS COOPS SCOOP
COPRS CORPS CROPS
COSST COSTS SCOTS
CPSSU CUSPS SCUPS
CRSTU CRUST CURST
DDEIN DINED NIDED
DDEIR DRIED REDID
DDERU DURED UDDER
DEEGR EDGER GREED

DEEGS EDGES SEDGE
DEEIL EDILE ELIDE
DEEKS DEKES SKEED
DEELV DELVE DEVEL
DEENU ENDUE UNDEE
DEERT DETER TREED
DEERY REDYE REEDY
DEETW TEWED TWEED
DEFIN FIEND FINED
DEFIR FIRED FRIED
DEFIY DEIFY EDIFY
DEFSU FEUDS FUSED
DEGIL GELID GLIDE
DEGIN DEIGN DINGE
DEGIO DOGIE GEOID
DEGLS GELDS GLEDS
DEGLU GLUED LUGED
DEHIR HIDER HIRED
DEHLO DHOLE HOLED
DEHOP EPHOD HOPED
DEIIM IMIDE MEDII
DEIKS DIKES SKIED
DEILO OILED OLDIE
DEILR IDLER RILED
DEIMN DENIM MINED
DEIMT DEMIT TIMED
DEINU INDUE NUDIE
DEINX INDEX NIXED
DEIOX DOXIE OXIDE
DEISV DIVES VISED
DEKSY DYKES SKYED
DELNO LODEN OLDEN
DELOP LOPED POLED

DELOV LOVED VOLED
DELRU LURED RULED
DEMNO DEMON MONDE
DEMRU DEMUR MURED
DEMSU MUSED SEDUM
DENOT NOTED TONED
DENOV DEVON DOVEN
DENOZ DOZEN ZONED
DENPS PENDS SPEND
DENSS SENDS SNEDS
DENSU DUNES NUDES
DENTU TENDU TUNED
DEORW DOWER ROWED
DEOSW DOWSE SOWED
DFNOU FONDU FOUND
DGINO DINGO DOING
DGINY DINGY DYING
DGIRS GIRDS GRIDS
DIIMS IMIDS MIDIS
DIKNS DINKS KINDS
DIKSS DISKS SKIDS
DILLY DILLY IDYLL
DIMOU DUOMI ODIUM
DIOST DOITS ODIST
DIQSU QUIDS SQUID
DLOSY ODYLS SLOYD
DMOOY DOOMY MOODY
DMOSU DOUMS MODUS
DNOSY DONSY SYNOD
DORSS DROSS SORDS
DORSU DUROS SUDOR
DSSTU DUSTS STUDS
DSTUY DUSTY STUDY

EEFLR FLEER REFEL
EEFLS FEELS FLEES
EEGLS GLEES LEGES
EEGNT GENET TENGE
EEGRT EGRET GREET
EEHMR REHEM RHEME
EEHRW HEWER WHERE
EEKRY REEKY REKEY
EEKSS SEEKS SKEES
EELNS LENES LENSE
EELPR LEPER REPEL
EENRW NEWER RENEW
EENTY TEENY YENTE
EEPRU PUREE RUPEE
EEPSW SWEEP WEEPS
EERSY EYERS EYRES
EERTV EVERT REVET
EERVY EVERY VEERY
EFFIS FIEFS FIFES
EFGOR FORGE GOFER
EFHLS FLESH SHELF
EFILT FILET FLITE
EFINR FINER INFER
EFIRX FIXER REFIX
EFIRY FIERY REIFY
EFLST FELTS LEFTS
EFMRU FEMUR FUMER
EGILM GIMEL GLIME
EGIOV OGIVE VOGIE
EGKLU KLUGE KUGEL
EGNSU GENUS NEGUS
EGRSY GREYS GYRES
EHIKS HIKES SHEIK

EHINT THEIN THINE
EHIRT ITHER THEIR
EHISV HIVES SHIVE
EHITW WHITE WITHE
EHKOS HOKES OKEHS
EHLLS HELLS SHELL
EHLOY HOLEY HOYLE
EHLRS HERLS LEHRS
EHNSW SHEWN WHENS
EHOPR EPHOR HOPER
EHORT OTHER THROE
EHOSS HOSES SHOES
EHOSW HOWES WHOSE
EHSTW THEWS WHETS
EIKLN INKLE LIKEN
EIKNR INKER REINK
EIKNS KINES SKEIN
EIKRT KITER TRIKE
EIKSS SIKES SKIES
EIKSY SKIEY YIKES
EILLR ILLER RILLE
EILNO ELOIN OLEIN
EILNV LEVIN LIVEN
EILOT TELOI TOILE
EILOV OLIVE VOILE
EILSU ILEUS LIEUS
EILSX LEXIS SILEX
EIMOX MOXIE OXIME
EINNR INNER RENIN
EINOS EOSIN NOISE
EINOV ENVOI OVINE
EINPR REPIN RIPEN
EINRU INURE URINE

EINSZ ZEINS ZINES
EINTU UNITE UNTIE
EINWZ WINZE WIZEN
EIPQU EQUIP PIQUE
EIPRR PRIER RIPER
EIPSW SWIPE WIPES
EIPTT PETIT PETTI
EIQTU QUIET QUITE
EIRRW WIRER WRIER
EISST SITES STIES
EISTU ETUIS SUITE
EKMOS MOKES SMOKE
EKMRS MERKS SMERK
EKNSU NEUKS NUKES
EKOPS POKES SPOKE
EKORT TOKER TROKE
EKOST STOKE TOKES
ELLMS MELLS SMELL
ELLSW SWELL WELLS
ELMNO LEMON MELON
ELMOT METOL MOTEL
ELMST MELTS SMELT
ELNOP PELON PLEON
ELNTU LUNET UNLET
ELOTW OWLET TOWEL
ELPRY PLYER REPLY
ELPSY SLYPE YELPS
ELRRU LURER RULER
ELRSY LYRES SLYER
ELSTU LUTES TULES
EMMOS MEMOS MOMES
EMNSU MENUS NEUMS
EMOPY MOPEY MYOPE

EMORV MOVER VOMER
ENRSU NURSE RUNES
ENSUV NEVUS VENUS
ENSUX NEXUS UNSEX
ENTTY NETTY TENTY
EOPSX EXPOS POXES
EOQTU QUOTE TOQUE
EORSS ROSES SORES
EORSY OYERS YORES
EOSTV STOVE VOTES
EPRXY PREXY PYREX
ERRSU RUERS SURER
ERSST RESTS TRESS
ERSTV VERST VERTS
ESSTW STEWS WESTS
ESTWY STEWY WYTES
FFIST STIFF TIFFS
FFLSU LUFFS SLUFF
FFSTU STUFF TUFFS
FGLOS FLOGS GOLFS
FHIRT FIRTH FRITH
FHORT FORTH FROTH
FILOS FILOS FOILS
FILST FLITS LIFTS
FISST FISTS SIFTS
FLOOS FOOLS LOOFS
FLOSU FOULS SULFO
FLTUY FLUTY FLUYT
FNOTU FOUNT FUTON
FORST FORTS FROST
GGNOS GONGS NOGGS
GHHIT HIGHT THIGH
GHINT NIGHT THING

GHLOU GHOUL LOUGH
GHOTU OUGHT TOUGH
GHRSU GURSH SHRUG
GIKNS GINKS KINGS
GILNO LINGO LOGIN
GILNS LINGS SLING
GILNY LINGY LYING
GILOO IGLOO LOGOI
GIMPY GIMPY PIGMY
GINOR GIRON GROIN
GINRU RUING UNRIG
GINST STING TINGS
GINSU SUING USING
GINSW SWING WINGS
GIORT GRIOT TRIGO
GLNSU LUNGS SLUNG
GLOSS GLOSS SLOGS
GLPSU GULPS PLUGS
GNORW GROWN WRONG
GNOSS SNOGS SONGS
GNSTU STUNG TUNGS
GORST GROTS TROGS
GORSY GORSY GYROS
GOSTU GOUTS GUSTO
GOTUY GOUTY GUYOT
GRSUY GYRUS SURGY
GSTUY GUSTY GUTSY
HIKST KITHS SHTIK
HILLS HILLS SHILL
HINSS SHINS SINHS
HINST HINTS THINS
HITWY WHITY WITHY
HKLOS HOLKS KOHLS

HKMOU HOKUM KHOUM
HKOOS HOOKS SHOOK
HLOST HOLTS SLOTH
HLSSU SHULS SLUSH
HMORU HUMOR MOHUR
HMTYY MYTHY THYMY
HNORS HORNS SHORN
HNORT NORTH THORN
HNSTU HUNTS SHUNT
HOORT ORTHO THORO
HOPST PHOTS TOPHS
HOPSY HYPOS SOPHY
HORST HORST SHORT
IKKNS KINKS SKINK
IKLLS KILLS SKILL
IKMRS MIRKS SMIRK
IKNRS KIRNS RINKS
IKNSS SINKS SKINS
IKNSW SWINK WINKS
IKRST SKIRT STIRK
IKSST KISTS SKITS
ILLPS PILLS SPILL
ILLSW SWILL WILLS
ILNTU UNLIT UNTIL
ILORT LIROT TRIOL
ILOSS SILOS SOILS
ILPSS LISPS SLIPS
ILPSU PILUS PULIS
ILPTU TULIP UPLIT
ILSSY LYSIS SYLIS
ILSTT STILT TILTS
ILSTY SILTY STYLI
IMNSU MINUS MUNIS

IMOSX OXIMS SIXMO
IMPRS PRIMS PRISM
IMSTY MISTY STIMY
INNRU INRUN INURN
INORT INTRO NITRO
INOSY NOISY YONIS
INPRU PURIN UNRIP
INPSS SNIPS SPINS
INSSU NISUS SINUS
INSTT STINT TINTS
IOPST POSIT TOPIS
IPRSU PURIS SIRUP
IRSTW WRIST WRITS
ISSTU SITUS SUITS
ISTTW TWIST TWITS
ISTXY SIXTY XYSTI
KLNSU LUNKS SLUNK
KMSUY KUMYS MUSKY
KNOOS NOOKS SNOOK
KNPSU PUNKS SPUNK
KOSSU KUSSO SOUKS
LMOST MOLTS SMOLT
LMPUY LUMPY PLUMY
LNNOY NONYL NYLON
LOPPY LOPPY POLYP
LOSSU SOLUS SOULS
LPRSU PURLS SLURP
LSSTU LUSTS SLUTS
LSSUU LUSUS SULUS
MNORS MORNS NORMS
MOORY MOORY ROOMY
MOOSZ MOZOS ZOOMS
MOPRS PROMS ROMPS

MORST MORTS STORM
MPSTU STUMP TUMPS
NOPTU PUNTO PUTON
NRSTU RUNTS TURNS
OOPSW SWOOP WOOPS
OOSTT OTTOS TOOTS
OOSTY SOOTY TOYOS
OPRSU POURS ROUPS
ORSSU SORUS SOURS
ORSTT TORTS TROTS
ORTTU TROUT TUTOR
OSSTW STOWS SWOTS
OSTTU STOUT TOUTS
PRSTU SPURT TURPS
PRSUY PURSY SYRUP
RSSTU RUSTS TRUSS
RSTUY RUSTY YURTS

Bob's Bible Bonus: Top 7s Single Anagram Quiz

7-letter Words

ADEINOR ANEROID
AEINORS ERASION
AEINOST ATONIES
ADEILOR DARIOLE
ADEIORS ROADIES
AEILNOS ANISOLE
AEILOST ISOLATE
AENORTU OUTEARN
EILNORT RETINOL
EINORTU ROUTINE
AEIINRT INERTIA
AEEILNR ALIENER
AEEILNT LINEATE
AEEILRT ATELIER
AEEINST ETESIAN
AAEILNO AEOLIAN
AEINNOT ENATION
ABEINOT NIOBATE
ACEINOT ACONITE
ACEIORT EROTICA
AEIMNOT AMNIOTE
AEENORS ARENOSE
AEEORST ROSEATE
EEILNOR ELOINER
AAEEINT TAENIAE
ADEGIOT GODETIA
AEGNORT NEGATOR
EGINORT GENITOR
ADEINTU AUDIENT
AEILNTU ALUNITE
AEILRTU URALITE
ADINORT DIATRON
AINORTU RAINOUT
AEEGINR REGINAE
ADEILOS ISOLEAD
AADEINR ARANEID
ADEIINR DENARII
ADEIINT INEDITA
AEIILNR AIRLINE
AEIINRS SENARII
AEIINST ISATINE
AEIIRST AIRIEST
ADELNOR LADRONE

ADELNOT TALONED
ADENORU RONDEAU
ADENOST DONATES
AELNORU ALEURON
AELORTU TORULAE
AENORSU ARENOUS
AENOSTU SOUTANE
DEILNOT LENTOID
DEIORTU OUTRIDE
EILNORS NEROLIS
EILNOST ENTOILS
EILORTU OUTLIER
EINORSU URINOSE
EIORSTU STOURIE
AELORST OLESTRA
ADEEILR LEADIER
ADEEINS ANISEED
ADEEIST IDEATES
AEEILRS REALISE
ADEEITU AUDITEE
AEINNRT ENTRAIN
AEFINRT FAINTER
AAEORST AEROSAT
DEIINOT EDITION
DEIIORT DIORITE
EIINOST INOSITE
ADEGIRT TRIAGED
AEGINTU UNITAGE
ABEIORS ISOBARE
ACDEINO CODEINA
ACEILOT ALOETIC
ACEINOS ACINOSE
ACEIORS SCORIAE
ADEINOV NAEVOID
ADEIOPT OPIATED
AEFILOT FOLIATE
AEHILOR AIRHOLE
AEILMOR LOAMIER
AEILNOP OPALINE
AEILOPR PELORIA
AEILORV VARIOLE
AEILOTV VIOLATE
AEIMNOS ANOMIES
AEINOSV EVASION
AEIOPRS SOAPIER

AEIORSV OVARIES
AINOORT ORATION
AGINORT ORATING
AEELNOS ENOLASE
AEELORS AREOLES
AEELORU AUREOLE
AEELOST OLEATES
AEENOSU AENEOUS
DEEILNO ELOINED
DEEILOR REOILED
EEILNOS OLEINES
EEILOST ETOILES
EINORTT TRITONE
ACENORT ENACTOR
AEHNORT ANOTHER
AEMNORT TONEARM
BEINORT BORNITE
DEENORT ERODENT
EENORST ESTRONE
EEIINRT NITERIE
ADEGILO GEOIDAL
AEGILOU EULOGIA
ABEEINT BETAINE
AEEHINR HERNIAE
AEEINPR PERINEA
AEEINTV NAIVETE
AEEIPRT PEATIER
AEEIRRT TEARIER
AAEGINR ANERGIA
ADENOOT ODONATE
EILNOOR LOONIER
EINOORS EROSION
EIOORST SOOTIER
ADEGNOR GROANED
ADEGNOT TANGOED
ADEGORT GAROTED
AEGLNOT TANGELO
AEGNOST ONSTAGE
AEGORTU OUTRAGE
DEGINOT INGOTED
EGILNOT LENTIGO
EGIORTU GOUTIER
ADEILRU UREDIAL
ADEIRSU RESIDUA
ADEISTU DAUTIES

AEILNSU INULASE
AABEIOR AEROBIA
AEIINOP EPINAOI
AAEINNO AEONIAN
ADENRST STANDER
AELNRTU NEUTRAL
DEINRST TINDERS
EILNRST LINTERS
AAEELOR AREOLAE
ADILNOR ORDINAL
ADILORT DILATOR
ADIORTU AUDITOR
AILNOTU OUTLAIN
AIORSTU SAUTOIR
AEEGILN LINEAGE
AEEGILT EGALITE
AEEGINU EUGENIA
ACEENOT ACETONE
ACEEORT OCREATE
AEEOPRT OPERATE
BEEINOT EBONITE
CEEIORT COTERIE
EEHINOR HEROINE
EEIMNOT ONETIME
AEENNOT NEONATE
EEINORR ONERIER
AADEILR RADIALE
AADEINS NAIADES
AAEILRS AERIALS
ADEIILR DELIRIA
AEIILST LAITIES
ADELORU ROULADE
ADELOST SOLATED
ADEORSU AROUSED
DEILNOS INDOLES
DEILNOU UNOILED
DEILOTU TOLUIDE
EILNOSU ELUSION
EILOSTU OUTLIES
AEEEILN ALIENEE
AAENRST SANTERA
ADELOTU OUTLEAD
ABEGINO BEGONIA
ACEGINO COINAGE
AAILNOT ALATION

AAINOST ATONIAS
ADEEGOT GOATEED
AEEGLOR AEROGEL
AEEGOST GOATEES
ADEEILS AEDILES
EEEINRT TEENIER
ADEINNR NARDINE
ADEINTT TAINTED
ADEIRTT ATTIRED
AEILRTT TERTIAL
AEINNRU ANEURIN
AEINRRS SIERRAN
ABDEINR BRAINED
ACDEINR CAIRNED
ACEILNR CARLINE
ACEINTU TUNICAE
ADEHINR HANDIER
ADEHIRT AIRTHED
ADEIMNR INARMED
ADEIMNT MEDIANT
ADEIMRT READMIT
ADEINPR PARDINE
ADEINTV DEVIANT
ADEIRTY DIETARY
AEFILNT INFLATE
AEFINRS INFARES
AEFINST FAINEST
AEFIRST FAIREST
AEHILRT LATHIER
AEHINRS HERNIAS
AEHIRST HASTIER
AEILNPT PANTILE
AEILNRV RAVELIN
AEILNRY INLAYER
AEILNTV VENTAIL
AEIMRTU MURIATE
AEINPTU PETUNIA
AEINRSV RAVINES
AEINTUV VAUNTIE
ADEELNR LEARNED
ADEELNT LATENED
ADEENRS ENDEARS
ADEENST STANDEE
AEELNRS LEANERS
AEERSTU AUSTERE

DEEILRT RETILED
DEEINTU DETINUE
DEEIRTU ERUDITE
DEEILNT LENITED
ABINORT TABORIN
AINOPRT ATROPIN
ADEIRTV TARDIVE
AEGNOOR OREGANO
AEGOORT ROOTAGE
AAELORS AREOLAS
AAELORU AUREOLA
AEIKNRT KERATIN
EGINOOR GOONIER
ADEGILT LIGATED
ADEGIRU GAUDIER
ADEGIST AGISTED
AEGILRS GLAIRES
AEGINSU GUINEAS
AEGISTU AUGITES
AINORTW WAITRON
AEGLNRT TANGLER
AEGNRTU GAUNTER
EGINRTU TRUEING
ABEILOS OBELIAS
ACDEIOS CODEIAS
ACEILOS CELOSIA
ADEILMO MELODIA
ADEILOP OEDIPAL
ADEIMOU MIAOUED
ADEIOPS ADIPOSE
ADGINOR ADORING
ADGINOT DOATING
AGILNOT ANTILOG
ADEELOS ELODEAS
DEEILOS OILSEED
AAEIRTT ARIETTA
AEIINRR RAINIER
AAEHIRT HETAIRA
AAEIMRT AMIRATE
AAEINPT PATINAE
AAEIPRT APTERIA
AAEIRTV VARIATE
AAEIRTW AWAITER
AEIIMNT INTIMAE
AEIIMRT AIRTIME

ADENOTT NOTATED
ADEORTT ROTATED
AENNOTU TONNEAU
AENORRS SERRANO
AENOSTT NOTATES
AEORRST ROASTER
AEORTTU OUTRATE
DEINNOT INTONED
DEIORTT DOTTIER
EILNORR LORINER
EINNORU REUNION
EINORRS IRONERS
EINOSTT TONIEST
AELORTT RETOTAL
ABELNOT NOTABLE
ABELORT BLOATER
ABENORS BORANES
ACDENOT TACNODE
ACELNOR CORNEAL
ACELNOT LACTONE
ACELORT LOCATER
ACENOST OCTANES
ACEORTU OUTRACE
ADEMNOR MADRONE
ADENOPT NOTEPAD
AEHORST EARSHOT
AEHORTU OUTHEAR
AELMNOR ALMONER
AELNOPT POLENTA
AELNOTV VOLANTE
AELNOTY ANOLYTE
AELOPRT PROLATE
AELORTV LEVATOR
AEMNOTU AUTOMEN
AEMORST MAESTRO
AENOPRS PERSONA
AENOPST TEOPANS
AEORTUV OUTRAVE
AEORTUW OUTWEAR
BEINOST BONIEST
BEIORST ORBIEST
CDEIORT CORDITE
CEILNOT LECTION
CEINORU COENURI
CEIORST EROTICS

DEHINOR HORDEIN
DEHIORT THEROID
DEIMNOR MINORED
DEINOPT POINTED
DEINORW DOWNIER
EFIORST FORTIES
EFIORTU OUTFIRE
EILMORT MOTLIER
EILNOPR PROLINE
EILNOTV VIOLENT
EILNOTW TOWLINE
EILORTV OVERLIT
EIMNORS MERINOS
EINOPRS ORPINES
EINORSW SNOWIER
EINOSTW TOWNIES
EIOPRTU POUTIER
ADDEINO ADENOID
ADDEIOR RADIOED
AADEENR ANEARED
AADEERT AERATED
AAEERST AERATES
AAEERTU AUREATE
EEIINST SIENITE
DEENORS ENDORSE
DEENOST DENOTES
EELNOTU TOLUENE
EELORST SOLERET
EENOSTU OUTSEEN
ADGIORT GORDITA
AGIORST ORGIAST
ADINRTU UNITARD
AILNRST RATLINS
AINRSTU NUTRIAS
ADEINOX DIOXANE
ADEINOZ ANODIZE
ADEIORX EXORDIA
ADEIOTX OXIDATE
AEIKLNO KAOLINE
AEIKLOR OARLIKE
AEIOSTZ AZOTISE
ADEEINN ADENINE
ADEEIRR READIER
AEEIRRS RERAISE
ACDENOR ACORNED

AENOPTU AUTOPEN
EINOPTU POUTINE
ABDEEIR BEADIER
ABEEINS BEANIES
ABEEIST BEASTIE
ACDEEIR DECIARE
ACEEINU EUCAINE
ADEEHIR HEADIER
ADEEIMT MEDIATE
ADEEIRW WEARIED
ADEEITV DEVIATE
AEEILMR MEALIER
AEEILNP ELAPINE
AEEILTV ELATIVE
AEEIMNS MEANIES
AEEIPRS APERIES
AEEIRSW WEARIES
AAEGILR REGALIA
EIJNORT JOINTER
ADEOORS ROADEOS
DEILNOO EIDOLON
DEIOORS OROIDES
DEIOOST OSTEOID
EILNOOS LOONIES
EILOORS ORIOLES
ADEGLOT GLOATED
ADEGORS DOGEARS
ADEGOST DOTAGES
AEGORSU AERUGOS
AEGOSTU OUTAGES
DEGILNO GLENOID
DEGINOS DINGOES
EGILORS GLORIES
EGILOST LOGIEST
EGINOSU IGNEOUS
AEENRRT TERRANE
EEINNRT INTERNE
ADEILSU AUDILES
AAEGNRT TANAGER
ENOORST ENROOTS
EGNORST TONGERS
ADELNTU LUNATED
ADELRST DARTLES
ADENSTU UNSATED
AELNSTU ELUANTS

DEILNST DENTILS
DEILNTU DILUENT
DEILRTU DILUTER
DEINRSU INSURED
DEINSTU DUNITES
AEIKOST OAKIEST
AAEORRT AERATOR
CEIINOR ONEIRIC
EIINOPR RIPIENO
ADILNOS LADINOS
ADILOTU OUTLAID
AILOSTU OUTSAIL
AADINRT RADIANT
AABEORT AEROBAT
AAEMNOR AMARONE
BEIINOT NIOBITE
ABEGINR BEARING
ABEGINT BEATING
ACEGINR ANERGIC
ACEGIRT CIGARET
AEFGINR FEARING
AEFGIRT FRIGATE
AEGHINR HEARING
AEGINPR REAPING
AEGINRW WEARING
AEGINTV VINTAGE
AEGIRTV VIRGATE
AEEGLNT ELEGANT
AEEGNRS ENRAGES
AEEGNRU UNEAGER
AEEGNST NEGATES
EEGILNT GENTILE
EEGINRS GREISEN
ADLNORT TROLAND
ADNORTU ROTUNDA
ANORSTU SANTOUR
ILNORST NOSTRIL
AEHIORR HOARIER
AEIMORR ARMOIRE
ADIOSTU OUTSAID
EEILNNO LEONINE
ABEELOR EARLOBE
ABEEORS AEROBES
ACEEORS ACEROSE
ADEEOPT ADOPTEE

AEELOPR PAROLEE
AEENOPU EUPNOEA
AEEORSV OVERSEA
CDEEINO CODEINE
CEEILNO CINEOLE
CEEINOS SENECIO
CEEIOST COESITE
DEEIMOR EMEROID
DEEIOPT EPIDOTE
EEFILNO OLEFINE
EEILOPT PETIOLE
EEINOPS PEONIES
EEIOPST POETISE
EEIORSV EROSIVE
ABCEIOR AEROBIC
ABCEIOT ICEBOAT
ABEIOTV OBVIATE
ACEHIOT ACHIOTE
ACEIMNO ENCOMIA
ACEIMOR COREMIA
ACEINOP APNOEIC
ACEIOPT ECTOPIA
AEFIMOR FOAMIER
AAEGORS AGAROSE
EEFNORT OFTENER
EEHNORT THEREON
AADELNR ADRENAL
AADELNT LANATED
AADELRT LATERAD
AADENST ANSATED
AADERTU AURATED
AAELNRS ARSENAL
AAELNST SEALANT
DEIINRS INSIDER
DEIINRU URIDINE
EIILNST LINIEST
EIILNTU INUTILE
EIILRST SILTIER
EIINSTU UNITIES
EEIORTZ EROTIZE
DELNORS RONDELS
DELNORU ROUNDEL
DELORST OLDSTER
DENOSTU SNOUTED
AAILORS SOLARIA

AAILOST SOLATIA
ADIILNO LIANOID
AIILNOS LIAISON
AEFGILO FOLIAGE
AEGHIOS HOAGIES
AEGIMOS IMAGOES
EIOORRT ROOTIER
DEEEINR NEEDIER
EEEINRS ESERINE
EEEIRST EERIEST
AEGNORR GROANER
AEGORRT GARROTE
AEGORTT GAROTTE
EGINNOR NEGRONI
EGINORR IGNORER
ACENOOR CORONAE
AEMOORT TEAROOM
BEINOOT EOBIONT
CEINOOT COONTIE
EFIOORT FOOTIER
EHIOORT HOOTIER
EIMNOOT EMOTION
AAIINRT ANTIAIR
ADEILRR LARDIER
ADEIRRS RAIDERS
AEILRRS RAILERS
AEISTTU SITUATE
DIINORT DINITRO
IINORST IRONIST
ABEGNOR BEGROAN
ACEGNOR ACROGEN
AEFGORT FAGOTER
AEGNORW WAGONER
AEGNORY ORANGEY
AEGOPRT PORTAGE
CEGINOR COREIGN
CEGIORT ERGOTIC
EFGINOR FOREIGN
EGINORV OVERING
EGINOTV VETOING
EGIORTV VERTIGO
EEGLNOR ERELONG
ABDEIRU DAUBIER
ABEILNS LESBIAN
ABEILRS BAILERS

Bob's Bible Bonus: Top 7s Single Anagram Quiz

ACDEILN INLACED	ABDENRT BARTEND	AEIKLNT ANTLIKE	AADEITW AWAITED	AELOPTU OUTLEAP	AAEMNRT RAMENTA	AEFIRTT FATTIER	AEEFRTU FEATURE	ABCEINR CARBINE	AAEORRU AURORAE	DILORTU DILUTOR	AEMNOTT TOMENTA
ACEILNU CAULINE	ABENRST BANTERS	AEIKNRS SNAKIER	AAEILMN LAMINAE	AELOSTV SOLVATE	AAENRTV TAVERNA	AEIMNNT MANNITE	AEEHLNT LETHEAN	ABCEINT CABINET	EIILORR ROILIER	ILORSTU TROILUS	AENNORY ANNOYER
ACEILRU AURICLE	ACDENRT TRANCED	AEIKNST INTAKES	AAEIMRU URAEMIA	AELOTUV OVULATE	EFIINRT NIFTIER	AEIMNRR MARINER	AEEHNST ETHANES	ABEFIRT BAREFIT	AEEEGNT TEENAGE	ABDEGIN BEADING	AENORRV OVERRAN
ACEIRSU SAUCIER	ACELNRT CENTRAL	AEIKNTU UNAKITE	AAEINPS PAESANI	BDEILOR BROILED	EHIINRT INHERIT	AEINNPR PANNIER	AEELMNT TELEMAN	ABEIMNT AMBIENT	AEEEGRT ETAGERE	ABEGINS SABEING	BEINNOR BONNIER
ADEFIRS FARSIDE	ADENRTV VERDANT	AEILNRX RELAXIN	AAEIPRS SPIRAEA	BDEINOU BEDOUIN	EIINRTW TWINIER	AEINNPT PINNATE	AEELNPR REPANEL	ABEINPT BEPAINT	EEEGINR GREENIE	ACDEGIN INCAGED	BEIORRT ORBITER
ADEHILN INHALED	AEHLNRT ENTHRAL	AEIRTUZ AZURITE	AAEISTV AVIATES	BEIORSU OUREBIS	ADEGNTU UNGATED	AEINPTT PATIENT	AEELNRW RENEWAL	ABEIRTV VIBRATE	DELOORT ROOTLED	ACEGIST CAGIEST	CEINORR CORNIER
ADEILNP PLAINED	AELNRTV VENTRAL	ADEGISU GAUDIES	ACEIILT CILIATE	CEILOST CITOLES	DEGINTU DUETING	AEIPRRT PARTIER	AEEMNST MEANEST	ACEFINR FANCIER	ADELRSU LAUDERS	ADEGHIN HEADING	CEINOTT TONETIC
ADEILNV ANVILED	AENRSTW WANTERS	ADEGLNT TANGLED	ADEIIPR PERIDIA	DEFIOST FOISTED	ADILNRS ALDRINS	AEIPRTT PARTITE	AEENRSW WEANERS	ACEHINR ARCHINE	ADEEIJT JADEITE	ADEGHIR HAGRIDE	CEIORTT COTTIER
ADEILRV RIVALED	AENRTUV VAUNTER	ADEGNST STANGED	AEFIILT FILIATE	DEHILOT LITHOED	ADILNRU DIURNAL	AEIRRTW WARTIER	AEERSTW SWEATER	ACEHIRT THERIAC	AEEIKLR LEAKIER	ADEGINW WINDAGE	EFINNOR INFERNO
ADEILRY READILY	DEINPRT PRINTED	AEGLNRS ANGLERS	AEFIIRS FAIRIES	DEHINOS HOIDENS	ADINRSU DURIANS	AEIRRTY RETIARY	BEEILNR BERLINE	ACEIMNR CARMINE	AEEIKLT TEALIKE	AEFGILR FRAGILE	EFIORRT ROTIFER
ADEIMNU UNAIMED	DEINRTY TINDERY	AEGLNRU GRANULE	AEIILMR RAMILIE	DEHIOST HOISTED	AILRSTU RITUALS	DEILOOS DOOLIES	CDEEINT ENTICED	ACEIMNT NEMATIC	AEEILNX ALEXINE	AEFGINS FEASING	EHINORR HORNIER
ADEINPS PANDIES	EFINRST SNIFTER	AEGLNTU LANGUET	AEIILRV VIRELAI	DEHIOTU HIDEOUT	AABIORT AIRBOAT	ACELNOS SECONAL	CEEILNR RECLINE	ACEINPR CAPRINE	AEEILRZ REALIZE	AEFGIRU REFUGIA	EHIORRT HERITOR
ADEINSV INVADES	EHINRST HINTERS	AEGLRST LARGEST	AEIIMST AMITIES	DEILMOR MOLDIER	AACINOR OCARINA	ADEFLOR ALFREDO	CEEINRS SINCERE	ACEINTV VENATIC	AABELNO ABALONE	AEFGITU FATIGUE	EHIORTT THORITE
ADEIRSV ADVISER	EILNRTY INERTLY	AEGLRTU TEGULAR	AEIIRSW AIRWISE	DEILOPR LEPORID	AAIMNOT ANIMATO	ADEFOTU FADEOUT	CEEINST ENTICES	ACEINTY CYANITE	AACELOR ACEROLA	AEGHILN HEALING	EIMNNOT MENTION
AEFILNS FINALES	EINPRST PTERINS	DEGINRU DUNGIER	AAGINRT GRANITA	DEILOPT PILOTED	AAINORV OVARIAN	ADEENTT DENTATE	CEEIRTU EUCRITE	AEFIMNR FIREMAN	AADEMNO ADENOMA	AEGILMN GEMINAL	EIMORTT OMITTER
AEFILRU FAILURE	EINRTUV VENTURI	DEGINST NIDGETS	AGIINRT AIRTING	DEIMORS MISDOER	AAIORTV AVIATOR	ADEERTT TREATED	DEEFINT FEINTED	AEFINPR FIREPAN	AAELMOT OATMEAL	AEGILMR GREMIAL	EINNOPT PONTINE
AEHILNS INHALES	AEGINOZ AGONIZE	EGILNTU ELUTING	ALNOORT ORTOLAN	DEIOPRS PERIODS	ADDENOR ADORNED	AEENNST NEATENS	DEEHINR INHERED	AEFINRW FAWNIER	AAELNOP APNOEAL	AEGILNY YEALING	EINNORV ENVIRON
AEHILRU HAULIER	ADEELNS LEADENS	EGINRSU REUSING	AADEELT DEALATE	DEIOTUV OUTVIED	ADDENOT DONATED	AEENNTU UNEATEN	DEEHIRT DIETHER	AEHIMNR HARMINE	CDEIIOR ERICOID	AEGIRSW EARWIGS	EINOPRR PORNIER
AEILMNU ALUMINE	DEEILST ISLETED	EGINSTU GUNITES	DEEIIST DEITIES	DEIOTUW WIDEOUT	AELLORT REALLOT	AEENSTT NEATEST	DEEIMNR ERMINED	AEHIMNT HEMATIN	DEIIMNO DOMINIE	AEGNNRT REGNANT	EIOPRTT POTTIER
AEILNSW LAWINES	DEENRST TENDERS	ABDINOT BANDITO	ABDELOR LABORED	EFILNOS OLEFINS	AIIMNOR AMORINI	DEEINNT DENTINE	DEEINTV EVIDENT	AEHINPR HEPARIN	EIILNOV OLIVINE	AEGINNS INNAGES	ABGINOT BOATING
AEILNSY ELYSIAN	ADDEINT NIDATED	AILOORS OORALIS	ABDEOST BOASTED	EHINOSU HEINOUS	DDEINOT DENTOID	DEEINTT DINETTE	DEEIPRT PREEDIT	AEIMNRV VERMIAN	EIILORV RILIEVO	AACEORS ROSACEA	ACGINOR ORGANIC
AEILNUW LAUWINE	AEEGIMR REIMAGE	AIJNORT JANITOR	ABELORU RUBEOLA	EILMNOS LOMEINS	EINOSST NOSIEST	EEILNNT LENIENT	DEEIRTV RIVETED	AEIMNRW WIREMAN	EIINOPS SINOPIE	EIILOPR LIRIOPE	ACGIORT ARGOTIC
AEILRSV REVISAL	AEEGINP EPIGEAN	AAEILNN ALANINE	ACDELNO CELADON	EILMORS MOILERS	BENORST SORBENT	EEILNTT ENTITLE	EEFILRT FERTILE	AEIMPRT PRIMATE	EIIORSV IVORIES	AAILNST LATINAS	AGIMNOR ROAMING
AEILRSW WAILERS	ABDINOR INBOARD	AAEISTT SATIATE	ACDELOR CAROLED	EILMOST MOTILES	CENORST CORNETS	EEILRTT RETITLE	EEFINRS REFINES	AEIMRTV VITAMER	ADEGINN DEANING	ACEINPT PICANTE	AGIMNOT MOATING
AEILSTV ESTIVAL	ABILORT ORBITAL	AEIILNN ANILINE	ACDELOT LOCATED	EILOPRS SPOILER	DEFNORT FRONTED	EEINNRU NEURINE	EEHILNT THEELIN	AEIMRTW WARTIME	AEGILRR GLARIER	AEIMNPR PERMIAN	AGINOPR PIGNORA
AEIMRSU UREMIAS	ACDIORT CAROTID	AEIINNS ASININE	ACDEOST COASTED	EILOSTV VIOLETS	DEMNORT MORDENT	EEINRRS RERISEN	EEHINST THEINES	AEINTVW VAWNTIE	AEEKNRT RETAKEN	AGINNOT ATONING	ABDEIMO AMEBOID
AEIPRSU UPRAISE	ACILNOR CLARION	ADGILNO LOADING	ACEOSTU ACETOUS	EILOTUV OUTLIVE	EFNORST FRONTES	EEIRSTT TESTIER	EEHIRST HEISTER	AEINTVY NAIVETY	EEIKNRT KERNITE	AGINORR ROARING	ADEHIMO HAEMOID
EINOOTW TWOONIE	ADHINOT ANTHOID	ADGILOR GOLIARD	ADEFLOT FLOATED	EILOTUW OUTWILE	EFNORTU FORTUNE	ADEKORT TROAKED	EEILNPT PENLITE	AEIPRTV PRIVATE	DENRSTU UNDREST	AIMNOOR AMORINO	ADEIMOW MIAOWED
ADEELST DELATES	ADINOPT PINTADO	ADGINOS GANOIDS	ADEFORS FEDORAS	EIMORSU MOUSIER	ELNORTY ELYTRON	ADENOTZ ZONATED	EEILNRV LIVENER	AEIPRTW WIRETAP	ELNRSTU RUNLETS	AIMNOOT AMOTION	AEHILMO HEMIOLA
ADEESTU SAUTEED	ADIOPRT PAROTID	AGIORSU GIAOURS	ADEHLOT LOATHED	EIMOSTU TIMEOUS	ENOPRST POSTERN	AEOQRTU EQUATOR	EEILNTV VEINLET	AEIRTVY VARIETY	AADINRS RADIANS	AINOOTV OVATION	AACEENT CATENAE
AEELSTU ELUATES	AFINORS INSOFAR	AGIOSTU AGOUTIS	ADELMOR EARLDOM	EIOPRSU SOUPIER	ENORTUY TOURNEY	DEIJNOR JOINDER	EEIMNRS ERMINES	ACEEGOT ECOTAGE	ADIINST DISTAIN	EEGLNRT GENTLER	AACEERT ACERATE
DEEILRS RESILED	AFIORTU FAITOUR	ADELOTT TOTALED	ADELOPT TADPOLE	EIOPSTU PITEOUS	AEEGNOP PEONAGE	DEIJNOT JOINTED	EEIMNST EMETINS	AADGIOT AGATOID	ADIIRST DIARIST	EINNOTT TONTINE	AAEEFRT RATAFEE
EEILRSU LEISURE	AILORTY ORALITY	ADEOSTT TOASTED	ADEMORS RADOMES	EIOSTUV OUTVIES	AEEGORV OVERAGE	EIJLORT JOLTIER	EEINSTV TENSIVE	AAGILNO LOGANIA	AIILNTU NAUTILI	AEFGNRT ENGRAFT	AAEEHRT HETAERA
AELNNRT LANTERN	AIMNOST MANITOS	ADEOTTU OUTDATE	ADENOPS DAPSONE	DEELORS RESOLED	EEGINOP EPIGONE	EINOSTX TOXINES	EEINSTY SYENITE	AAGILOT OTALGIA	AEEGLNU EUGLENA	AEGNPRT TREPANG	AAEEMRT AMREETA
AENNRST TANNERS	AIMORST AMORIST	AELOTTU TOLUATE	ADENOSY NOYADES	DEELORU URODELE	AEIIKNT KAINITE	ABEELNR ENABLER	ADDEEIT IDEATED	AAGINOS AGNOSIA	AEEGLRU LEAGUER	AEGNRTW TWANGER	AAEERTW TEAWARE
AENRTTU TAUNTER	AINOPRS SOPRANI	AEORRSU AROUSER	ADEOPST PODESTA	AAENRRT NARRATE	ADEILOZ DIAZOLE	ABEELNT TENABLE	AEEISST EASIEST	ADGIINO GONIDIA	DEEGILN DELEING	AEGNRTY AGENTRY	CEEIINR EIRENIC
DEINRTT TRIDENT	AINORSW WARISON	AEOSTTU OUTEATS	ADEORSW REDOWAS	EIINNRT TINNIER	ADEIOSX OXIDASE	ACDEENR RECANED	AADEGRT GRADATE	DEGNOTU TONGUED	DEEGILR LEDGIER	EGINRTY RETYING	EEIIMRT EMERITI
EINRRTU RUNTIER	AIOPRST AIRPOST	DEIOSTT DOTIEST	AEFLOST FOLATES	AGNORTU OUTRANG	AEIOQSU SEQUOIA	ACDEENT ENACTED	AAEGNST AGNATES	DEGORTU GROUTED	DEEGINS SEEDING	ADEEMOS OEDEMAS	EEIINRV VEINIER
EINRTTU NUTTIER	AIORSTY OSTIARY	EILORRS LORRIES	AEHLNOS ENHALOS	DENNORT DONNERT	ABEEILS BAILEES	ACEELRT TREACLE	DEGIINR DINGIER	EGLNORS LONGERS	DEEGIRS SEDGIER	BEEILOS OBELISE	EEIINTV INVITEE
ADINNOR ANDIRON	EGIOORS GOOSIER	AABEILN ABELIAN	AEHLORS SHOALER	ENNORST TONNERS	ADEEISV ADVISEE	ACEENTU CUNEATE	EGIILNR LINGIER	EGLNORU LOUNGER	DEEGIST EDGIEST	CDEEIOS DIOCESE	ALNORSU SOLUNAR
AILNNOT ANTLION	EGIOOST GOOIEST	AABEILT LABIATE	AEHLOST LOATHES	ENNORTU NEUTRON	AEEILMS MEALIES	ADEEFRT DRAFTEE	EGIILNT LIGNITE	EGLNOST LONGEST	EEGILNS SEELING	DEEIOPS EPISODE	DEEORTT TETRODE
AINOSTT STATION	ACDEIST DACITES	AACDEIR CARDIAE	AELMORS MORALES	ENORRST SNORTER	ABEINRR BARNIER	ADEEMRT REMATED	EGIINST IGNITES	EGNORSU SURGEON	ADLNORU NODULAR	ABENNOR BARONNE	EENNORU NEURONE
AEILLNR RALLINE	ADEFINS FADEINS	AADEHIR AIRHEAD	AELMORU MORULAE	ENORSTT STENTOR	ACEINNT ANCIENT	ADEENRV RAVENED	DENOOST SNOOTED	EGNOSTU TONGUES	ADLNOTU OUTLAND	ACENNOT CONNATE	EEORRST RESTORE
AEINRSS ARSINES	ADEIKRT TRAIKED	AADEIMR MADEIRA	AELMOST MALTOSE	AABENRT ANTBEAR	AEFINNT INFANTE	ADEERTV AVERTED	DEOORST ROOSTED	EIINNOS INOSINE	ADNOSTU ASTOUND	AEFNORR FORERAN	EEORRTU REROUTE
AEIRSST SATIRES	AEIKLNR LANKIER	AADEITV AVIATED	AELNOPU APOLUNE	AACENRT CATERAN	AEFINRR REFRAIN	AEEFLRT REFLATE	ENOORSU ONEROUS	AAELORR AREOLAR	ALORSTU TORULAS	AEMNNOR MONERAN	EEORSTT ROSETTE

Bob's Bible Bonus: Top 7s Single Anagram Quiz

ABINOOT BONIATO
AINRSTT TRANSIT
BEENOST BONESET
CEENORU COENURE
CEENOST CENOTES
DEEMNOR MODERNE
DEEMNOT DEMETON
DEENOPT PENTODE
DEEORTV REVOTED
DEEORTW TOWERED
EEHNORS RESHONE
EEHORST HETEROS
EELORTV OVERLET
EEMNORS MOREENS
EEMNOST TONEMES
EENOSTW TOWNEES
AEEORSS SEROSAE
EEINOSS EOSINES
EEIORSS SOIREES
ABEMNOT BOATMEN
ABEMORT BROMATE
ABENOTY BAYONET
ABEOPRT PROBATE
ACEMNOR ROMANCE
ACENOTV CENTAVO
ACEORTV OVERACT
AEFMORT FORMATE
AEFNOPR PROFANE
AEFORTV OVERFAT
AEHMNOR MENORAH
AEHMORT TERAOHM
AEHOPRT PHORATE
AEMNOPR MANROPE
AEMNORV OVERMAN
AEMNORY ANYMORE
AEOPRTV OVERAPT
BCEINOR BICORNE
BEFINOR BONFIRE
BEIMNOR BROMINE
BEINORW BROWNIE
CEHINOR CHORINE
CEIMNOR INCOMER
CEIMORT MORTICE
CEINOPR PORCINE
CEINORV CORVINE

CEIORTV EVICTOR
CEIORTW COWRITE
EFIMNOR FERMION
EHIMORT MOTHIER
EHINOPR PHONIER
EIMNOPR PROMINE
EIMNOPT PIMENTO
EIMORTV VOMITER
EIOPRTV OVERTIP
AEGINRZ ZINGARE
AEGINTZ TZIGANE
AEGISTY GASEITY
EIMNNOR IRONMEN
AADELRU RADULAE
AADELTU ADULATE
DEIILNS LINDIES
EIILSTU UTILISE
ABINRST BRISANT
ACINRST NARCIST
ACINRTU CURTAIN
ADFINRT INDRAFT
AFINRTU ANTIFUR
AHILNRT INTHRAL
AHINRST TARNISH
AILNRTY RIANTLY
AIMNRST MARTINS
AIMNRTU NATRIUM
AINPRST SPIRANT
AINPRTU PURITAN
AINRTUY UNITARY
AEEIMNN ENAMINE
AEEIMTT TEATIME
AEEIRRW WEARIER
ADIILOS SIALOID
EEIKLOT TOELIKE
EEIKNOS EIKONES
EEILOTZ ZEOLITE
AAEGITT AGITATE
EINNOOS IONONES
EIOOSTT TOOTSIE
AEEELRS RELEASE
DEEEIRS SEEDIER
AFGINOT ANTIFOG
ADEGOTT TOGATED
AEGNNOS NONAGES

EGIORRS GORSIER
EGIOSTT EGOTIST
AADENSU SAUNAED
ABDEOOT TABOOED
ABEOOST SEABOOT
AEMOOST OSTEOMA
BEINOOS BOONIES
BEIOOST BOOTIES
CEIOOST COOTIES
DEHIOOR HOODIER
DEHIOOT DHOOTIE
DEIOORW WOODIER
EILMNOO OINOMEL
EILNOOV VIOLONE
EILOOPR LOOPIER
EILOORW WOOLIER
EIMNOOS NOISOME
EIMOORS ROOMIES
EIOOPST ISOTOPE
ABEEIMR BEAMIER
AEEHIRV HEAVIER
AEEINVW INWEAVE
AAEGINV VAGINAE
AEGIIMN IMAGINE
ACEIOTX EXOTICA
AEIMOTX TOXEMIA
AEIMOTZ ATOMIZE
AAEEGLT GALEATE
GINOORT ROOTING
AALORST ALASTOR
DIILNOT TOLIDIN
DIINORS SORDINI
IILNORS SIRLOIN
DEEENRT ENTERED
EEGLNOU EUGENOL
EGNNORT RONTGEN
ABEGLOT GLOBATE
ABEGNOS NOSEBAG
ABEGORS BORAGES
ACDEGOR CORDAGE
ACEGLNO CONGEAL
ACEGORU COURAGE
ADEFGOR FORAGED
ADEFGOT FAGOTED
ADEGHOR HAGRODE

ADEGNOV DOGVANE
AEFGLOT FLOTAGE
AEFGORS FORAGES
AEGHLNO HALOGEN
AEGHOST HOSTAGE
AEGLOPR PERGOLA
AEGLORV VORLAGE
AEGLOTV VOLTAGE
AEGMNOS MANGOES
AEGNOSY NOSEGAY
AEGOTUV OUTGAVE
BDEGIOT BIGOTED
BEGILNO IGNOBLE
BEGILOR OBLIGER
CDEGINO COIGNED
CDEGIOR ERGODIC
DEFGIOR FIREDOG
DEGHIOT HOGTIED
DEGIOPR PODGIER
EGHIORS OGREISH
EGHIOST HOGTIES
EGHIOTU TOUGHIE
EGILMOR GOMERIL
EGILNOP ELOPING
EGIMNOU MEOUING
EGIMORS OGREISM
EGIMOST EGOTISM
EGINOSW WIGEONS
EGINOSY ISOGENY
EGIOTUV OUTGIVE
CENOORT CORONET
EMNOORT MONTERO
DEGIORR GRODIER
ADGINTU DAUTING
AGIRSTU GUITARS
ABDEILU AUDIBLE
ABDEISU SUBIDEA
ADEHILS HALIDES
ADEILMU MIAULED
ADEILSV DEVISAL
ADEILSY DIALYSE
ADELRTT RATTLED
ADENSTT ATTENDS
AELNNRU UNLEARN
AELNNTU ANNULET

AELNRRS SNARLER
AELRTTU TUTELAR
AERSTTU STATURE
DEINNRU INURNED
DEINNTU DUNNITE
EILNNST LINNETS
EINNSTU TUNNIES
EIRRSTU RUSTIER
EFIORTV OVERFIT
EFIOORS ROOFIES
AILNNOS SOLANIN
AILOSTT ALTOIST
AIORRSU OURARIS
ADDEILT DILATED
ADDEINS DANDIES
ADDEINU UNAIDED
ADDEITU AUDITED
ADEILLT TALLIED
ADEISST DISSEAT
AEILLNS AINSELL
AEILSST SALTIES
AEIRSSU SAURIES
DEELNST NESTLED
EELNRSU UNREELS
EIOORTZ ZOOTIER
ABDELNR BLANDER
ABDENRS BANDERS
ABDENTU UNBATED
ABDERST DABSTER
ABELNRU NEBULAR
ABENRSU UNBEARS
ABENSTU BUTANES
ACDELNR CANDLER
ACDENRS DANCERS
ACDENRU DURANCE
ACDENTU UNACTED
ACELNRS LANCERS
ACENSTU NUTCASE
ACERSTU CURATES
ADEFRST STRAFED
ADEHLNR HANDLER
ADEHNRU UNHEARD
ADEHNST HANDSET
ADEHNTU HAUNTED
ADELMNR MANDREL

ADELMNT MANTLED
ADELNPT PLANTED
ADELNTW WETLAND
ADELRTW TRAWLED
ADELRTY LYRATED
ADEMNST TANDEMS
ADEMRST SMARTED
ADEMRTU MATURED
ADENPRS PANDERS
ADENPRU UNDRAPE
ADENRUY UNREADY
ADENSTV ADVENTS
ADENTUV VAUNTED
ADERSTY STRAYED
AEFLRST FALTERS
AEFNRSU FURANES
AEHLNST HANTLES
AELMNRS ALMNERS
AELMNRU NUMERAL
AELNSTV LEVANTS
AELRTUV VAULTER
AENPSTU PEANUTS
AENRSUW UNSWEAR
AENRSUY SYNURAE
AERSTUY ESTUARY
BDEILRT DRIBLET
BDEIRTU BRUITED
BEILNRS BERLINS
BEILRTU REBUILT
CDEINRU INDUCER
CEILRST RELICTS
CEILRTU UTRICLE
DEFILNR FLINDER
DEFILNT FLINTED
DEFINRU UNFIRED
DEFIRTU FRUITED
DEHILRT THIRLED
DEHINRU UNHIRED
DEHIRST DITHERS
DEILPRT TRIPLED
DEILRTW TWIRLED
DEILRTY TIREDLY
DEIMNRU UNRIMED
DEINPRS PINDERS
DEINRSV VERDINS

EFILRTU FLUTIER
EFINRSU INFUSER
EHILRST SLITHER
EHILRTU LUTHIER
EHIRSTU HIRSUTE
EILMRST MILTERS
EILNPRS PILSNER
EILNPRU PURLINE
EILNRSV SILVERN
EILNSTW WINTLES
EILRTUV RIVULET
EIMRSTU MUSTIER
EINRSUW UNWISER
ACEEGIL ELEGIAC
AEEGILM MILEAGE
AEEGILP EPIGEAL
AEEGILW WEIGELA
DEGIOOS GOODIES
EGILOOS OLOGIES
ABDILOR LABROID
ABDILOT TABLOID
ABILNOS ALBINOS
ABILORS BAILORS
ABILOST OBLASTI
ACDILNO NODICAL
ACDILOR CORDIAL
ACDILOT COTIDAL
ACDIORS SARCOID
ACDIOST DACOITS
ACILNOU INOCULA
ACINOSU ACINOUS
ADHIORS HAIRDOS
ADHIOST TOADISH
ADILOPR DIPOLAR
ADIOPRS SPAROID
ADIORSV ADVISOR
AILMNOS MALISON
AILMORS ORALISM
AILMOST SOMITAL
AIOPSTU UTOPIAS
AEEGNTT TENTAGE
EEGIRTT TERGITE
INNORST INTRONS
AACINRT ANTICAR
AAINRTV VARIANT

AAINRTW ANTIWAR
AIIMNRT MARTINI
AIINRTV VITRAIN
EGINORZ ZEROING
ABEEGNR REBEGAN
ADDINOR ANDROID
AEEGHNT THENAGE
AEEGMNR GERMANE
AEEGMNT GATEMEN
AEEGNTV VENTAGE
AILLORT LITORAL
BEEGINR REBEGIN
BEEGINT BEIGNET
CEEGINR GENERIC
CEEGINT GENETIC
EEGHINR REHINGE
EEGIMNR REGIMEN
EEGINTW WEETING
DEGHINO HONGIED
EGNOORS ORGONES
EGNOOST GENTOOS
EGNOOTU OUTGONE
ACNORTU COURANT
ADNORTY TARDYON
AFLNORT FRONTAL
AHLNORT ALTHORN
AMNORTU ROMAUNT
ANORSTY AROYNTS
CINORTU RUCTION
FINORST FORINTS
HINORST HORNIST
INOPRST TROPINS
AENRSST SARSNET
ADEIQRU QUERIDA
ADEIRSX RADIXES
ADEITUZ DEUTZIA
AEIJLRS JAILERS
AEIKLNS ALKINES
AEIKLNU UNALIKE
AEIKRSU KAURIES
AEILNQU QUINELA
AEILNSX ALEXINS
AEILSTZ LAZIEST
AEEMNNO ANEMONE
AEENNOV NOVENAE

EEIMNNO NOMINEE
ADEGNSU AUGENDS
DEGILRU GUILDER
DEGINSU SUEDING
DEGIRSU GUIDERS
EGILRSU LIGURES
ADENRTX DEXTRAN
DEINRTX DEXTRIN
EIKLNRT TINKLER
ADEFNRS SNARFED
ADENPTU UNADEPT
CEINSTU NEUSTIC
EIPRSTU PERITUS
AEEGINZ AGENIZE
ACEEHOR OCHREAE
AEEFOTV FOVEATE
AEEMOPT METOPAE
AEEORVW OVERAWE
CEEHIOR CHEERIO
CEEIOPT PICOTEE
CEEIORV REVOICE
EEIMOPT EPITOME
EEIMOTV EMOTIVE
AAEGNOP APOGEAN
EGIINOP EPIGONI
EGIIOPR PIEROGI
ADIJNOT ADJOINT
ADINOTX OXIDANT
AIKNOST KATIONS
AIKORST TROIKAS
ADGILOS DIALOGS
AABDEIS DIABASE
AABEILS ABELIAS
AACDEIL ALCAIDE
AACDEIS ACEDIAS
AADEIMS AMIDASE
AAEILMS MALAISE
ABDEIIL ALIBIED
ACEIILS LAICISE
AAGINRS SANGRIA
AAGINRU GUARANI
ADGIINR RAIDING
ADLNOOR LARDOON
AOORSTU OUTSOAR
ILNOORS ROSINOL

IOORSTU RIOTOUS
EGLNRTU GRUNTLE
EGNRSTU GURNETS
AADENNT ANDANTE
AAELNTT TETANAL
AAENNST ANNATES
AAERRST ERRATAS
AAERTTU TUATERA
DEIIRRT DIRTIER
EIILNTT INTITLE
EIINNST INTINES
EIINSTT TINIEST
DEELOSU DELOUSE
ADGLNOR GOLDARN
ADGNORS DRAGONS
ADGNORU AGROUND
ADGORTU OUTDRAG
AGLNORU LANGUOR
AGNORSU OURANGS
AGORSTU RAGOUTS
DGILNOR LORDING
GILNORU LOURING
GILNOST TIGLONS
GILNOTU LOUTING
DELORTT DOTTREL
DENNOST TENDONS
DENNOTU UNNOTED
DENORRS DRONERS
DEORSTT DOTTERS
DEORTTU TUTORED
ELNNORS RONNELS
ELNOSTT TONLETS
ENNOSTU NEUSTON
ABDELOS ALBEDOS
ADEHLOS SHOALED
ADELMOS DAMOSEL
ADELOSV SALVOED
BDEILOS BOLIDES
DEHIOSU HIDEOUS
DEILOPU EUPLOID
DEILOSY DOYLIES
DEIOSUV DEVIOUS
EILOPSU PILEOUS
AABELRT RATABLE
AACELNT LACTEAN

AACENST CATENAS
AACERST CARATES
AACERTU ARCUATE
AADEMNT MANDATE
AADENRV VERANDA
AAEHLRT TREHALA
AAELNPR PREANAL
AAELPRT APTERAL
AAEMNTU MANTEAU
AAEMRTU AMATEUR
AAENRUW UNAWARE
AAENSTW SEAWANT
AAIORRS ROSARIA
BEIINRS BRINIES
BEIINST STIBINE
CDEIINR DINERIC
CDEIIRT DICTIER
CEIINST INCITES
CEIIRST ERISTIC
DEIIMRT TIMIDER
DEIINRV DIVINER
DEIINRW WINDIER
DEIINTV INVITED
EFIILRT FIRELIT
EFIINRU UNIFIER
EHIINRS SHINIER
EIINSTW WINIEST
EIINTUV UNITIVE
EIIRSTW WIRIEST
ADILNSU SUNDIAL
AABINOU OUABAIN
AABIORS ABROSIA
AACDIOR ACAROID
AADIMOR DIORAMA
AAILNOV VALONIA
AAIMNOS ANOSMIA
ACDIINO CONIDIA
ADDENOU DUODENA
ADDEORS DEODARS
ADEORSS SARODES
AELORUU ROULEAU
AELOSST SOLATES
AEORSSU AROUSES
AFIILOR AIRFOIL
AIILORV RAVIOLI

AIINOPS SINOPIA
DDEILOT DELTOID
DDEINOS NODDIES
DDEIOST TODDIES
DEIORSS DOSSIER
EILLNOS NIELLOS
EILLORU ROUILLE
EIORSSU SERIOUS
AEIMOOP IPOMOEA
EEEIMNT EMETINE
EEEIMRT EREMITE
EEEINRW WEENIER
EEEIRRT RETIREE
BDELNOR BLONDER
BDENORS BONDERS
BDEORST DEBTORS
BELNOST NOBLEST
BELORTU TROUBLE
BENOSTU SUBTONE
BEORSTU OBTUSER
CDENORS SCORNED
CDENORU CRUNODE
CDENOST DOCENTS
CDENOTU COUNTED
CELNOTU NOCTULE
CENOSTU CONTUSE
DEFLNOR FONDLER
DEFLNOT TENFOLD
DEFLORT TELFORD
DEFNOST FONDEST
DEHNORS DEHORNS
DEHNORU HOUNDER
DELNOTW LETDOWN
DELNOTY NOTEDLY
DEMNORU MOURNED
DEMNOST ENDMOST
DEMORST STORMED
DENORSV VENDORS
DENORUW REWOUND
DEOPRTU TROUPED
DEORTUW OUTDREW
EFLORTU FLOUTER
EHNORSU UNHORSE
ELMNORS MERLONS
ELMORTU MOULTER

Bob's Bible Bonus: Top 7s Single Anagram Quiz

ELNOPRU PLEURON
ELNOPST LEPTONS
ELNOPTU OPULENT
ELNOSTV SOLVENT
ELOPRTU POULTER
ELORSTV REVOLTS
ELORSTW TROWELS
EMORSTU OESTRUM
ENORSUV NERVOUS
ENORSUW UNSWORE
AANORTT ARNATTO
IINORTT INTROIT
CEEIMNO MIOCENE
AEEGOPS APOGEES
BEEGILO OBLIGEE
ADNRSTU TUNDRAS
AADEINZ ZENAIDA
AAEISTX ATAXIES
ADEIINZ DIAZINE
AEIIKLR AIRLIKE
AEIILNX EXILIAN
BEENOOT BOTONEE
CEENOOT ECOTONE
EEHNOOR HONOREE
CIINORT NORITIC
DDENORT TRODDEN
ABDEIRR BRAIDER
ABEIRRS BRASIER
ACDEITT DICTATE
ACEILNN ENCINAL
ADEIRRV ARRIVED
AEFILRR FRAILER
AEFINNS FANNIES
AEFISTT FATTIES
AEHIRRS HARRIES
AEILMRR MARLIER
AEILNNY INANELY
AEIMRRS MARRIES
AEIPSTT PATTIES
AEISTTV STATIVE
AEISTTY SATIETY
ACEGIOP APOGEIC
ADEENNS ENNEADS
ADEESTT ESTATED
AEERRSU ERASURE

DEEINNS INDENES
EEILRRS RELIERS
AGINNRT RANTING
AGINRRT TARRING
AACDENR DRACENA
AAELNTY ANALYTE
BEIIRST BITSIER
GIORSTU OUTRIGS
AENNRTT ENTRANT
CEEGORT CORTEGE
EEGOPRT PROTEGE
AAIOPRS APORIAS
AEKLOST SKATOLE
AELNOUZ ZONULAE
AELOSTZ ZEALOTS
DEIJOST JOISTED
DEIKLOR RODLIKE
DEIKNOS DOESKIN
DEINOQU QUOINED
DEIOQTU QUOITED
DEIOSTZ DOZIEST
EIKLNOS SONLIKE
EILOSTZ ZLOTIES
EIOSTUZ OUTSIZE
ABDEELN ENABLED
ABDEELR BLEARED
ABEELNU NEBULAE
ACDEELT CLEATED
ACDEETU EDUCATE
ACEELST CELESTA
ACEERSU CESURAE
ADEEFLN ENDLEAF
ADEEFLR FEDERAL
ADEEFLT DEFLATE
ADEEFNS DEAFENS
ADEEHNS DASHEEN
ADEEHST HEADSET
ADEELMN LEADMEN
ADEELMR EMERALD
ADEELMT METALED
ADEELRV RAVELED
ADEELRW LEEWARD
ADEELTV VALETED
ADEEMRS SMEARED
ADEEMST STEAMED

ADEENSW DEEWANS
ADEESTW SWEATED
ADEESTY YEASTED
AEEFLRU FERULAE
AEEHLRS HEALERS
AEELMTU EMULATE
AEELNPS SPELEAN
AEELPRU PLEURAE
AEELPTU EPAULET
AEELRSY SEALERY
AEELRUV REVALUE
AEEMRSU MEASURE
AEENPSU EUPNEAS
AEENSUV AVENUES
BDEEIRS DERBIES
BDEEIST BETIDES
BEEILRS BELIERS
CDEEILN DECLINE
CDEEIST DECEITS
CEEILNU LEUCINE
CEEILRS CEILERS
CEEILST SECTILE
CEEILTU LEUCITE
CEEISTU CUTESIE
DEEFILT FILETED
DEEFINS DEFINES
DEEHIST HEISTED
DEEILNV LIVENED
DEEILNY NEEDILY
DEEILRW WIELDER
DEEIMNS SIDEMEN
DEEIMRS REMISED
DEEIPST DESPITE
DEEISTW DEWIEST
EEFILNS FELINES
EEHILST SHELTIE
EEILMST ELMIEST
EEILNPS PENSILE
EEILNSY YEELINS
EEILNUV VEINULE
EEILPRU PUERILE
DEOOSTU OUTDOES
ELNOOSU UNLOOSE
ELOOSTU OUTSOLE
AADEGNS AGENDAS

AAEGNSU GUANASE
DEGIILN ELIDING
DEGIINS DINGIES
EGIILRS GIRLIES
AIORRTT TRAITOR
AEMNNRT REMNANT
AENNRTY TANNERY
AENPRRT PARTNER
AENRRTY TERNARY
BEINRTT BITTERN
CEINRTT CITTERN
EHINNRT THINNER
EINNRTV VINTNER
EINRTTW WRITTEN
AGINRTW RINGTAW
EELNRTT NETTLER
ABCDEIN CABINED
ABCDEIR CARBIDE
ABCEILT CITABLE
ABDEHIT HABITED
ABDEIRW BAWDIER
ABEFILN FINABLE
ABEFILR FRIABLE
ABEHILR HIRABLE
ABEHINS BANSHIE
ABEHIRS BEARISH
ABEHITU HABITUE
ABEILMN MINABLE
ABEILNP BIPLANE
ABEILRY BILAYER
ABEIMRS AMBRIES
ABEIPST BAPTISE
ABEISTW BAWTIES
ACDEHIR CHAIRED
ACDEINY CYANIDE
ACDEIPR PERACID
ACDEITY EDACITY
ACEFINU UNIFACE
ACEHILR CHARLIE
ACEHILT ETHICAL
ACEHINS CHAINES
ACEILMN MELANIC
ACEILPT PLICATE
ACEILRY CLAYIER
ACEIMRU URAEMIC

ACEIMST SEMATIC
ACEINPS INSCAPE
ACEISTV ACTIVES
ADEFHIT FAITHED
ADEHIPR RAPHIDE
ADEHIPT PITHEAD
ADEHIRW RAWHIDE
ADEIMRY MIDYEAR
ADEIMTY DAYTIME
ADEITWY TIDEWAY
AEFILMN INFLAME
AEFILMR FLAMIER
AEFILNV FLAVINE
AEFILPT FLEAPIT
AEFILRW FLAWIER
AEFIMNS FAMINES
AEFINSW FANWISE
AEHILNY HYALINE
AEHILPR HARELIP
AEHILPT HAPLITE
AEHILTY HYALITE
AEHIMNS HAEMINS
AEHIMRS MISHEAR
AEHIMST ATHEISM
AEHINPS INPHASE
AEHINSW WAHINES
AEILMTY MEATILY
AEILNPW PINWALE
AEILNVY NAIVELY
AEILPRV PREVAIL
AEILRVY VIRELAY
AEILRWY WEARILY
AEILTVY VILAYET
AEIMNSW MANWISE
AEIMPRS IMPRESA
AEIMRSV MISAVER
AEIMRSW SEMIRAW
AEINSWY ANYWISE
AEIPRSW WASPIER
AEIPSTV SPAVIET
AEIPSTW TAWPIES
AEIRSVW WAIVERS
AEISTVW WAVIEST
AADGIOS ADAGIOS
ACINORR CARRION

ACINOTT TACTION
AFINNOT FONTINA
AIMORTT TRITOMA
AINNOPT PINTANO
AINOPTT ANTIPOT
AIOPRRT AIRPORT
AIOPRTT PATRIOT
AEEEGLT LEGATEE
EGINNOO IONOGEN
DEGLNOU LOUNGED
DEGLORS LODGERS
DEGLOST GOLDEST
DEGLOTU GLOUTED
EGLNOSU LOUNGES
AACDEII AECIDIA
DDEEINT ENDITED
EEINSST SESTINE
EEIRSST RESITES
EFLNORU FLEURON
EFLNOST TEFLONS
CEELNRT LECTERN
DEENPRT PRETEND
EENRSTV VENTERS
EENRSTW WESTERN
EENRTUV VENTURE
AAGIINT IGNATIA
ACENRTY NECTARY
AEHNPRT PANTHER
AEMNRTV VARMENT
EHINRTV THRIVEN
EHINRTW WRITHEN
EINRTWY WINTERY
AADELMO ALAMODE
CDEIILO EIDOLIC
AEFGOOT FOOTAGE
AEGMOOR MOORAGE
EFGIOOR GOOFIER
EGIOOPR GOOPIER
AAGLNOR GRANOLA
AAGNORS ANGORAS
GIILNOT TOILING
AAEGSTU GATEAUS
ABCINOR CORBINA
ABCINOT BOTANIC
ABHIORT BOTHRIA

ABINORW RAINBOW
ABIORTV VIBRATO
ACFINOT FACTION
ACIMNOR MINORCA
ACINORV CORVINA
AHIMNOT MANIHOT
AIMNOPR RAMPION
AIOPRTY TOPIARY
AADILRS RADIALS
AADIRSU SUDARIA
ADIILST DIALIST
ADIINSU INDUSIA
AAGILOS LAOGAIS
DELNRSU RUNDLES
AIMNNOR IRONMAN
ADEERTX RETAXED
AEEJNST SEJEANT
AEEKLNT KANTELE
AEEKNRS SNEAKER
AEEKRST RETAKES
AEELRTX EXALTER
AEERSTX RETAXES
DEEIKNR REINKED
EEIKLNT NETLIKE
EEINQRU ENQUIRE
EEINQTU QUIETEN
EEINSTX SIXTEEN
EEIRSTZ ZESTIER
AADDEOR DEODARA
EIINOSS IONISES
AAAENST ANATASE
ADEEGLU LEAGUED
AEEGLSU LEAGUES
ADLNOSU UNLOADS
ADLORSU SUDORAL
DILNOSU UNSOLID
DILOSTU TOLUIDS
AEGLNTT GANTLET
AEGNNST GANNETS
AEGNNTU TUNNAGE
AEGRSTT TARGETS
DEGIRTT GRITTED
EGILNTT LETTING
EGILRTT GLITTER
EGINNRS GINNERS

EGINNRU ENURING
EGINRRS RINGERS
BEELNRT REBLENT
ADEGILV GLAIVED
ADEGIMS DEGAMIS
ADEGISV VISAGED
AEGILMS MILAGES
AEGILSV GLAIVES
AALNRTU NATURAL
DIINRST NITRIDS
IILNRST NITRILS
AEGGIOS ISAGOGE
DEGLNOS DONGLES
AGILNNO LOANING
ABEIKNT BEATNIK
ACEIKRT TACKIER
ACEINTX INEXACT
ACEINTZ ZINCATE
AEFINTX ANTEFIX
AEIKMNR RAMEKIN
AEIKNPR RANPIKE
AEIKNTY KYANITE
AEIMNTX TAXIMEN
AEINTXY ANXIETY
ADIOOPR PARODOI
AILOORW WOORALI
AAEFIRR AIRFARE
AAEIPRR PAREIRA
AAEIPTT APATITE
ABEIINN BIENNIA
AEHIIRR HAIRIER
AEIIMTT IMITATE
AEIIPRR PRAIRIE
AEIIRRV RIVIERA
AEIITTV VITIATE
AEGILLT TILLAGE
AEGIRSS GASSIER
DEEGLNT GENTLED
DEEGNRS GENDERS
EEGLNST GENTLES
EEGLRST REGLETS
EEGRSTU GESTURE
AAELOTX OXALATE
DEIINOZ IONIZED
DEIIORZ IODIZER

EIILNOZ LIONIZE
EIINOSZ IONIZES
EIIOSTZ ZOISITE
ADEFGRT GRAFTED
ADEGNPR PRANGED
ADEGNTW TWANGED
AEFGLNR FLANGER
AEGHNST STENGAH
AEGHRST GATHERS
AEGLMNR MANGLER
AEGLNPR GRAPNEL
AEGLNRY ANGERLY
AEGLNTW TWANGLE
AEGLRTY GREATLY
AEGMNST MAGNETS
AEGNRSW GNAWERS
AEGPRST PARGETS
AEGRSTV GRAVEST
BEGILNT BELTING
BEGILRT GILBERT
BEGINRS BINGERS
BEGINST BESTING
CDEGINR CRINGED
CEGINRS CRINGES
DEFGINR FRINGED
DEFGIRT GRIFTED
DEGHINR HERDING
DEGINTW TWINGED
EFGILNR FLINGER
EFGILNT FELTING
EFGINRU GUNFIRE
EGHILNT LIGHTEN
EGHINRS HINGERS
EGHINST NIGHEST
EGILMNT MELTING
EGILNPT PELTING
EGILNRY RELYING
EGINRSY SYRINGE
EGINSTV VESTING
EGIRSTV GRIVETS
AEINPSW WINESAP
INOORTT TORTONI
ABELORR LABORER
ABELOTT TOTABLE
ABEORRS ARBORES

ACDEORR CORRADE
ACELNNO ALENCON
ACELORR CAROLER
ACELOTT CALOTTE
ACEORRS COARSER
ACEOSTT COSTATE
ADEHORR HOARDER
ADEMORR ARMORED
ADEOPRR EARDROP
ADEORRW ARROWED
AEHORRS HOARSER
AELMOTT MATELOT
AELOPTT PALETOT
AEMNNOS MANNOSE
AEMNNOU NOUMENA
AEMOSTT STOMATE
AENNOSV NOVENAS
AEOPSTT TEAPOTS
BDEIORR BROIDER
BEILORR BROILER
BEINNOS BENISON
CEINNOS CONINES
CEIORRU COURIER
CEIOSTT SCOTTIE
DEIMORR REMORID
DEIMOTT OMITTED
DEIOPTT TIPTOED
EFILNNO NONLIFE
EHIORRS HORSIER
EILMORR LORIMER
EIMOTTU TIMEOUT
EINNOSV VENISON
EIOPRRS PROSIER
EIOPRRU ROUPIER
EIORRSV REVISOR
EIORRSW WORRIES
EGIRRST GRISTER
AEIKNNT NEATNIK
DEENNOS DONNEES
DEEORRS REREDOS
EELOSTT TELEOST
AGNORRT GRANTOR
GINORTT ROTTING
AABEELT EATABLE
AACEEST CASEATE

AADEEFR AFEARED
AADEEMT EDEMATA
AADEERW AWARDEE
AAEELMT MALEATE
AAEERSW SEAWARE
CDEEIIT EIDETIC
DEEIIRW WEIRDIE
EEFIIRS REIFIES
EEHIINS HEINIES
EEIIMNS MEINIES
EEIIMST ITEMISE
EEIIPST PIETIES
ABDGINO ABODING
ABGILOR GARBOIL
ACDGINO GONADIC
ACGILNO COALING
ACGILOT OTALGIC
AGHILNO HALOING
AGHIOST GOATISH
AGILMNO LOAMING
AGILOPT GALIPOT
AGILORW AIRGLOW
AGIMORS ISOGRAM
AGIMORU GOURAMI
AGINOPS SOAPING
AGIORSV VIRAGOS
EKNORST REKNOTS
BINOORT BIOTRON
HINOORT HORNITO
IMNOORT MONITOR
INOOPRT PORTION
ENORRTT TORRENT
AACEIMN ANAEMIC
AAEIMTV AMATIVE
AAEIRVW AIRWAVE
AEIIMPR IMPERIA
AEIIMRV VIREMIA
ADINNRS INNARDS
ADINSTT DISTANT
ADIRRST RITARDS
AILNSTT LATTINS
AILRSTT STARLIT
AILRTTU TITULAR
AIRSTTU TURISTA
BDEENOS DEBONES

BEELOST BOLETES
CDEEORS RECODES
CEELNOS ENCLOSE
CEELORS CREOLES
DEEFLOT FEEDLOT
DEELOPR DEPLORE
DEELORY YODELER
DEELOTW TOWELED
DEEMNOU EUDEMON
DEEMORS EMERODS
DEEMOST DEMOTES
DEEORSW RESOWED
DEEORUV OVERDUE
DEEOSTV DEVOTES
EEFLNOS ONESELF
EEFLOTU OUTFEEL
EEHORSU REHOUSE
EELNOSV ELEVONS
EELOPTU EELPOUT
EELORSV RESOLVE
EELORSY EROSELY
EEOPSTU TOUPEES
ABEILLO LOBELIA
ABEIOSS ABIOSES
ADDEIOV AVOIDED
AEILLOV ALVEOLI
EMNORTT TORMENT
ENOPRTT PORTENT
EEINRSX REXINES
GINOPRT PORTING
GINORTW TROWING
ABCDEOR BROCADE
ABCENOS BEACONS
ABCEORS BORACES
ABDEFOR FORBADE
ABDEMNO ABDOMEN
ABDEORV BRAVOED
ABELNOW OWNABLE
ABELNOY BALONEY
ABELOPR ROPABLE
ABELOPT POTABLE
ABELORW ROWABLE
ABELOTV VOTABLE
ABEMOTU OUTBEAM
ABENOSY SOYBEAN

Bob's Bible Bonus: Top 7s Single Anagram Quiz

- **ABEOPRS** SAPROBE
- **ABEORSV** BRAVOES
- **ABEORSY** ROSEBAY
- **ACDEHOR** ROACHED
- **ACDEHOT** CATHODE
- **ACDEOPT** COAPTED
- **ACEFOTU** OUTFACE
- **ACEHLNO** CHALONE
- **ACEHLOT** CHOLATE
- **ACELOPT** POLECAT
- **ACELORY** CALOYER
- **ACELOTY** ACOLYTE
- **ACEMORU** MORCEAU
- **ACEMOST** COMATES
- **ACEOPTU** OUTPACE
- **ADEFORV** FAVORED
- **ADEHOPT** POTHEAD
- **ADEHOTW** TOWHEAD
- **ADEOPRV** VAPORED
- **AEFLMOR** FEMORAL
- **AEFLNOV** FLAVONE
- **AEFMORS** FOAMERS
- **AEFORSW** FORESAW
- **AEHLMNO** MANHOLE
- **AEHLMOR** ARMHOLE
- **AEHLOPR** EPHORAL
- **AEHLOPT** TAPHOLE
- **AEHOPST** TEASHOP
- **AELMOPR** RAMPOLE
- **AELMORV** REMOVAL
- **AELOPRV** OVERLAP
- **AELOTVY** OVATELY
- **AEMORSW** WOMERAS
- **AEMOSTW** TWASOME
- **AENOPSW** WEAPONS
- **AEOPSTY** TEAPOYS
- **BCEILNO** BINOCLE
- **BCEIORS** CORBIES
- **BDEIMOR** BROMIDE
- **BDEIORV** OVERBID
- **BEFILNO** LOBEFIN
- **BEHIOST** BOTHIES
- **BEILMOR** EMBROIL
- **BEILNOW** BOWLINE
- **BEILOPR** PREBOIL
- **BEILORW** BLOWIER
- **BEINOSV** BOVINES
- **BEIORUV** BOUVIER
- **BEIOSTY** OBESITY
- **CDEFINO** CONFIDE
- **CDEHINO** HEDONIC
- **CDEHIOR** CHOIRED
- **CDEIMNO** DEMONIC
- **CDEIMOR** DORMICE
- **CDEIMOT** DEMOTIC
- **CDEIOPR** PERCOID
- **CDEIOPT** PICOTED
- **CDEIORW** CROWDIE
- **CEHIOTU** COUTHIE
- **CEILMOT** TELOMIC
- **CEINOSV** NOVICES
- **CEINOUV** UNVOICE
- **CEIOPRS** COPIERS
- **CEIOPST** POETICS
- **CEIORSV** VOICERS
- **CEIORSW** COWRIES
- **CEIOSTV** COSTIVE
- **CEIOSTW** COWIEST
- **CEIOSTY** SOCIETY
- **DEFIMOR** DEIFORM
- **DEHIMOR** HEIRDOM
- **DEHIMOT** ETHMOID
- **DEHINOP** PHONIED
- **DEHINOY** HYENOID
- **DEIMNOP** IMPONED
- **DEIOPRV** PROVIDE
- **DEIOPTV** PIVOTED
- **EFILMOT** FILEMOT
- **EFILOPR** PROFILE
- **EFIMOST** FOMITES
- **EHILNOP** PINHOLE
- **EHILOPT** HOPLITE
- **EHIMNOS** HOMINES
- **EHIMORS** HEROISM
- **EHIMOST** HOMIEST
- **EHINOPS** PHONIES
- **EHIOPST** OPHITES
- **EHIORSW** SHOWIER
- **EHIORSY** HOSIERY
- **EHIOSTY** ISOHYET
- **EILMOPR** IMPLORE
- **EIMNOSW** WINSOME
- **EIMORSV** VERISMO
- **EIMOSTV** MOTIVES
- **EINOPSW** WINESOP
- **EIOPSTY** ISOTYPE
- **EIOPTUW** WIPEOUT
- **AAEELPT** PALEATE
- **ADEGINZ** AGNIZED
- **AEGIKNS** SINKAGE
- **AEGILRZ** GLAZIER
- **AEGINSZ** AGNIZES
- **AEGIRUZ** GAUZIER
- **ABDINRS** RIBANDS
- **ABDINRU** UNBRAID
- **ABDINST** BANDITS
- **ACDILRT** TRICLAD
- **ACDINRU** IRACUND
- **ACDINST** DISCANT
- **ACDIRST** DRASTIC
- **ACDIRTU** DATURIC
- **ACILNRS** CARLINS
- **ACILNTU** LUNATIC
- **ACILRST** CITRALS
- **ACILRTU** CURTAIL
- **ADILRTY** TARDILY
- **ADIMNST** MANTIDS
- **ADINRSW** INWARDS
- **ADIPRST** DISPART
- **ADIRSTY** SATYRID
- **AFILNTU** ANTIFLU
- **AFINSTU** FUSTIAN
- **AHINRSU** UNHAIRS
- **AILMNRS** MARLINS
- **AILMNRU** RUMINAL
- **AILNPST** PLAINTS
- **AILRSTY** TRYSAIL
- **AILRTUV** VIRTUAL
- **AIMNRSU** URANISM
- **AIMRSTU** ATRIUMS
- **AIPRSTU** UPSTAIR
- **DDEENOT** DENOTED
- **EENORSS** SENORES
- **EEORSST** STEREOS
- **EHIOSTT** HOTTIES
- **EELLNOR** RELLENO
- **BEHNORT** BETHORN
- **CENORTV** CONVERT
- **CENORTW** CROWNET
- **EFNORTW** FORWENT
- **ENOPRTY** ENTROPY
- **EIKNNOR** EINKORN
- **ADEEELS** EASELED
- **EFNNORT** FORNENT
- **ADEFOOS** SEAFOOD
- **BEILOOS** LOOBIES
- **CDEILOO** OCELOID
- **CEILOOS** COOLIES
- **DEFILOO** FOLIOED
- **DEFIOOS** FOODIES
- **DEHIOOS** HOODIES
- **DEIOOSW** WOODIES
- **EILOOSW** WOOLIES
- **ABEERRT** REBATER
- **ACEENNT** CANTEEN
- **AEEFRRT** FERRATE
- **AEENRRV** RAVENER
- **AEENRRY** YEARNER
- **AEENTTV** NAVETTE
- **AEERRTW** WATERER
- **CEEIRRT** RECITER
- **EEFIRRT** FERRITE
- **EEHINRR** ERRHINE
- **EEIMNNT** EMINENT
- **EEINNRW** WENNIER
- **EEINNTW** ENTWINE
- **EEIPRTT** PETTIER
- **EEIRRTV** RIVETER
- **EEIRRTW** REWRITE
- **DEELOOS** DOOLEES
- **AALORSU** AROUSAL
- **GINOORS** ROOSING
- **GINOOST** SOOTING
- **AGINORZ** ZINGARO
- **ACEEILP** CALIPEE
- **ACEEISV** VESICAE
- **AEEFILW** ALEWIFE
- **AEEHISV** HEAVIES
- **AEEIPSV** PEAVIES
- **AAEGNNT** TANNAGE
- **AAEGNRR** ARRANGE
- **AAEGRTT** REGATTA
- **DEEHORS** RESHOED
- **DEEELNR** NEEDLER
- **EEELNST** STELENE
- **DEOORRT** REDROOT
- **ENOOSTT** TESTOON
- **EOORSTT** TOOTERS
- **AGHILOT** GOLIATH
- **DEEKNOT** TOKENED
- **DEENORZ** REZONED
- **EEJORST** RESOJET
- **EEKNOST** KETONES
- **EEKORST** RESTOKE
- **EENORSZ** REZONES
- **AEFIJOS** FEIJOAS
- **EGORRTU** GROUTER
- **AAGIOTT** AGITATO
- **BELNOOR** BORNEOL
- **CDENOOR** CROONED
- **CELNOOR** CORONEL
- **DEFNOOR** FORDONE
- **DEHNOOR** HONORED
- **DEMNOOR** DOORMEN
- **DEMOORT** MOTORED
- **EFLOORT** FOOTLER
- **EHNOORS** ONSHORE
- **ELMNOOT** MOONLET
- **ELMOORT** TREMOLO
- **EMNOOST** MOONSET
- **EMOORST** MOOTERS
- **ENOORSW** SWOONER
- **EOORTUW** OUTWORE
- **ABDEGOS** BODEGAS
- **ACDEGLO** DECALOG
- **ADEGLOP** GALOPED
- **AEGHLOS** GALOSHE
- **AEGLMOU** MOULAGE
- **AEGLOSV** LOVAGES
- **BDEGILO** OBLIGED
- **BEGILOS** OBLIGES
- **BEGIOSU** BOUGIES
- **EGHILOU** GHOULIE
- **EGILMOS** SEMILOG
- **EGILOPS** EPILOGS
- **AACEGNR** CARNAGE
- **AACEGRT** CARTAGE
- **AAEGHNT** THANAGE
- **AAEGMNR** MANAGER
- **AAEGMRT** REGMATA
- **AAEGNPT** PAGEANT
- **AAEGNTV** VANTAGE
- **AAEGNTW** WANTAGE
- **EGHIINR** HEIRING
- **EGHIINT** NIGHTIE
- **EGIIMNR** MINGIER
- **EGIIMNT** ITEMING
- **EGIINRV** REIVING
- **EGIINRW** WINGIER
- **EGIINTV** EVITING
- **ABEEHNT** BENEATH
- **ABEEHRT** BREATHE
- **ABEENRV** VERBENA
- **ABEENRY** BEANERY
- **ACEEMNR** MENACER
- **ACEEMNT** CEMENTA
- **ACEEMRT** CREMATE
- **AEEFMRT** FERMATE
- **AEEHMNT** METHANE
- **AEEHMRT** THERMAE
- **AEEHNTW** WHEATEN
- **AEEHPRT** PREHEAT
- **AEEMNPR** PRENAME
- **AEEMPRT** TEMPERA
- **BCEEIRT** TEREBIC
- **BEEFINT** BENEFIT
- **CEEIMNT** CENTIME
- **CEEINRV** CERVINE
- **CEEIPRT** RECEIPT
- **EEFHIRT** HEFTIER
- **EEFIMNR** FIREMEN
- **EEHINRW** WHEREIN
- **EEHIPRT** PRITHEE
- **EEHIRTW** THEWIER
- **EEIMNRW** WIREMEN
- **EEIMPRT** EMPTIER
- **EEIPRTY** YPERITE
- **AEERRTV** AVERTER
- **EEFINNR** FENNIER
- **ADELNNU** UNLADEN
- **ADELRRS** LARDERS
- **ADELRRU** RUDERAL
- **ADELSTT** SLATTED
- **ADENNSU** DUENNAS
- **ADESTTU** STATUED
- **AELRRSU** SURREAL
- **DEILNNS** LINDENS
- **DEILNNU** UNLINED
- **DEINNSU** UNDINES
- **DEIRRSU** DURRIES
- **EILRRSU** SURLIER
- **AEIRRRT** TARRIER
- **ADGINSU** AUDINGS
- **ADGIRSU** GUISARD
- **AGILNSU** NILGAUS
- **AINQRST** QINTARS
- **AINQRTU** QUINTAR
- **BEIIOTT** BIOTITE
- **CEIINNO** CONIINE
- **ACEJNOT** JACONET
- **ACEORTX** EXACTOR
- **AEHORTX** OXHEART
- **AENORXY** ANOREXY
- **AEORTVX** OVERTAX
- **BEIKORT** REITBOK
- **CEINOTX** EXCITON
- **EIJNORY** JOINERY
- **EIKMNOR** MONIKER
- **EIKNORV** INVOKER
- **EIKNORW** WONKIER
- **AAGIMNO** ANGIOMA
- **AEGLLOR** ALLEGRO
- **AEGLLOT** TOLLAGE
- **AGIIMOR** ORIGAMI
- **DDEGIOR** DODGIER
- **ABILRST** TRIBALS
- **AAAEIMN** ANAEMIA
- **BEGNORU** BURGEON
- **CEGNORS** CONGERS
- **CEGNOST** CONGEST
- **DEGHNOT** THONGED
- **DEGNOPR** PRONGED
- **DEGNORW** WRONGED
- **EFGORST** FORGETS
- **EFGORTU** FOREGUT
- **EGHLNOR** LEGHORN
- **EGHNORS** GORHENS
- **EGHNORU** ROUGHEN
- **EGHNOTU** TOUGHEN
- **EGHORTU** TOUGHER
- **EGLMNOR** MONGREL
- **EGMORTU** GOURMET
- **EGNORSV** GOVERNS
- **EGNORUY** YOUNGER
- **EGORTUW** OUTGREW
- **ADDEILS** LADDIES
- **ADEILSS** AIDLESS
- **DEELSTU** TELEDUS
- **ACELNOP** NOPLACE
- **BCEINOS** EBONICS
- **EHIOPRS** ROSEHIP
- **ELNNRTU** TRUNNEL
- **ENNRSTU** STUNNER
- **GINRSTU** RUSTING
- **AAILRTT** RATTAIL
- **AAINSTT** ATTAINS
- **AIINSTT** TITIANS
- **ABDELRU** DURABLE
- **ABDELTU** ABLUTED
- **ABELSTU** SUBLATE
- **ACDELNU** UNLACED
- **ACDELST** CASTLED
- **ACDENSU** UNCASED
- **ACDERSU** CRUSADE
- **ACELSTU** SULCATE
- **ADEFLRS** FARDELS
- **ADEFLRU** DAREFUL
- **ADEFNSU** SNAFUED
- **ADEHLRS** HERALDS
- **ADEHLST** DALETHS
- **ADELMRS** MEDLARS
- **ADELMST** MALTEDS
- **ADELNSY** ADENYLS
- **ADELPRS** PEDLARS
- **ADELPST** STAPLED
- **ADELRSW** WARSLED
- **ADELTUV** VAULTED
- **ADEMNSU** MEDUSAN
- **ADEMRSU** REMUDAS
- **ADENSUV** UNSAVED
- **ADENSUW** UNSAWED
- **ADEPSTU** UPDATES
- **ADERSUY** DASYURE
- **AEFLSTU** SULFATE
- **AEHLNSU** UNLEASH
- **AEHLRSU** HAULERS
- **AELPSTU** PULSATE
- **AELRSUV** VALUERS
- **BDEILNS** BINDLES
- **BDEILRS** BRIDLES
- **BDEILST** BILSTED
- **BDEINSU** BEDUINS
- **BDEISTU** SUBEDIT
- **BEILNSU** SUBLINE
- **BEILSTU** SUBTILE
- **CDEILRS** CLERIDS
- **CDEILST** DELICTS
- **CDEILTU** DUCTILE
- **CDEIRSU** CRUISED
- **CEILNSU** LEUCINS
- **DEFILRU** DIREFUL
- **DEFILST** STIFLED
- **DEFINSU** INFUSED
- **DEFISTU** FEUDIST
- **DEHILRS** HIRSLED
- **DEHIRSU** HURDIES
- **DEILMNS** MILDENS
- **DEILMST** MILDEST
- **DEILNPU** UNPILED
- **DEILNSY** SNIDELY
- **DEILNUV** UNLIVED
- **DEILRSV** DRIVELS
- **DEILRSY** RIDLEYS
- **DEILSTW** WILDEST
- **DEIMSTU** TEDIUMS
- **DEIPSTU** DISPUTE
- **EFILSTU** SULFITE
- **EHILRSU** HURLIES
- **EILMRSU** MISRULE
- **EILPSTU** STIPULE
- **EILRSUV** SURVEIL
- **DEINOOZ** OZONIDE
- **DEIOORZ** ODORIZE
- **EIKNOOS** NOOKIES
- **EIKOORS** ROOKIES
- **EINOOSZ** OZONISE
- **AAEGITZ** AGATIZE
- **AABEMNO** AMOEBAN
- **AACEHNO** CHOANAE
- **AACEOPT** PEACOAT
- **AAEMOTY** ATEMOYA
- **CEFIIOR** ORIFICE
- **CEIIMOT** MEIOTIC
- **CEIINOV** INVOICE
- **AAIRSTT** STRIATA
- **ADEEGRR** REGRADE
- **AEEGLRR** REGALER
- **AEEGRRU** REARGUE
- **AEEGSTT** GESTATE
- **EEGINNS** ENGINES
- **ADLNNOR** NORLAND
- **ALORRST** ROSTRAL
- **DIORRST** STRIDOR
- **DIORSTT** DISTORT
- **ILNNORU** LINURON
- **INNOSTU** NONSUIT
- **IORSTTU** TOURIST
- **ABEGINN** BEANING
- **AEGIMNN** MEANING
- **AEGIMRR** ARMIGER
- **AEGINNW** WEANING
- **AEGINNY** YEANING
- **AEGIPRR** GRAPIER
- **ABEEIKR** BEAKIER
- **AEEIKPR** PEAKIER
- **AEEIMNX** EXAMINE
- **AEEIPTX** EXPIATE
- **ADHILOS** HALOIDS
- **ADILMOS** AMIDOLS
- **ADILMOU** ALODIUM
- **ADIOPSU** ADIPOUS
- **AABDINT** TABANID
- **AABINST** ABSTAIN
- **AACDINT** ANTACID
- **AACILNT** ACTINAL
- **AACINST** SATANIC
- **AACIRST** CARITAS
- **AADINPT** PINTADA
- **AAFINRS** FARINAS
- **AAHINST** SHAITAN
- **AAILMNR** LAMINAR
- **AAILMNT** MATINAL
- **AAILNPT** PLATINA
- **AAILNRY** LANIARY
- **AAILNTV** VALIANT
- **AAILNTY** ANALITY
- **AAILPRT** PARTIAL
- **AAILRTV** TRAVAIL
- **AAIMNRS** MARINAS
- **AAIMNST** STAMINA
- **AAIMRTU** TIMARAU
- **AAINRSV** SAVARIN
- **ACIIRST** SATIRIC
- **ADDELNR** DANDLER
- **ADDELRT** DARTLED
- **ADDENRS** DANDERS
- **ADDENRU** DAUNDER
- **ADDERST** ADDREST
- **ADELLNR** LANDLER
- **ADENRSS** SANDERS
- **ADIIRTY** ARIDITY
- **AELLRST** STELLAR
- **AELNRUU** NEURULA
- **AENSSTU** UNSEATS
- **AERSTUU** AUTEURS
- **AFIILRT** AIRLIFT
- **AHIINST** TAHINIS
- **AIILMNT** INTIMAL
- **AIILNPT** PINTAIL
- **AIILNRY** RAINILY
- **AIILNTV** INVITAL
- **AIILNTY** ANILITY
- **AIILRTV** TRIVIAL
- **AIIMNTU** MINUTIA
- **AIIMRST** SIMITAR
- **AIINPRS** ASPIRIN
- **AIINPST** PIANIST
- **AIINRSY** RAISINY
- **DDEILRT** TIDDLER
- **DDEINRU** UNDRIED
- **DDEINST** DISTEND
- **DEILLRT** TRILLED
- **EIRSSTU** SUITERS
- **BENOOST** OBENTOS
- **CEOORTU** ECOTOUR
- **ELNOOPT** PELOTON
- **EMNOORS** MOONERS
- **EGILLOR** GIROLLE
- **BELNRTU** BLUNTER
- **CENRSTU** ENCRUST
- **DEHNRTU** THUNDER
- **EHLNRTU** LUTHERN
- **ELNRSTY** STERNLY
- **AEEGILL** GALILEE
- **AEEGISS** AEGISES
- **AILORSS** SAILORS
- **AIORSSU** SOUARIS
- **DEGNOOS** NOODGES
- **DEGOOST** STOOGED
- **EGLOORS** REGOSOL
- **EGOOSTU** OUTGOES
- **AEEGLTT** GALETTE
- **ABEEGLT** GETABLE
- **ABEEGRU** AUBERGE
- **ACDEEGN** ENCAGED
- **ACEEGNS** ENCAGES
- **ADEEGMN** ENDGAME
- **ADEEGNV** AVENGED
- **ADEEGPR** PREAGED
- **ADEEGRV** GREAVED
- **AEEFGLN** FENAGLE
- **AEEFGRS** SERFAGE
- **AEEGLMR** GLEAMER
- **AEEGLMT** MELTAGE
- **AEEGLNV** EVANGEL
- **AEEGLRY** EAGERLY
- **AEEGLTV** VEGETAL
- **AEEGPRS** PRESAGE
- **AEEGPRU** PUGAREE
- **AEEGRSV** GREAVES
- **BEEGINU** BEGUINE
- **CEEGINU** EUGENIC
- **DEEGHIR** HEDGIER
- **DEEGIMN** DEEMING
- **DEEGINW** WEEDING
- **DEEGIRW** WEDGIER
- **EEGHILN** HEELING
- **EEGILNP** PEELING
- **EEGILRV** VELIGER
- **EEGIMNS** SEEMING

Bob's Bible Bonus: Top 7s Single Anagram Quiz

EEGINPS SEEPING
EEGISTV VESTIGE
ABDNORS ROBANDS
ABLNOTU BUTANOL
ABLORST BORSTAL
ACDLNOR CALDRON
ACDNORU CANDOUR
ACDORST COSTARD
ACLORST SCROTAL
ADFNOST FANTODS
ADHNORS HADRONS
ADHNOTU HANDOUT
ADNOPRS PARDONS
ADNOPRU PANDOUR
ADNOPST DOPANTS
ADNORSW ONWARDS
ADORSTW TOWARDS
AHLORST HARLOTS
AHORSTU AUTHORS
ALMNORS NORMALS
ALMNORU UNMORAL
ALMORTU TUMORAL
ALNOPRS PROLANS
ALNOPTU OUTPLAN
ANOPSTU OUTSPAN
AORSTUW OUTWARS
BILNOTU BOTULIN
CILNOTU LINOCUT
CILORST LICTORS
CINOSTU SUCTION
CIORSTU CITROUS
DFILORT TRIFOLD
DFINOTU OUTFIND
DHINORS DRONISH
DILNOPT DIPLONT
DINOTUW OUTWIND
FILNORS FLORINS
FILNORU FLUORIN
FILORST FLORIST
FILORTU FLORUIT
HILORTU UROLITH
HINORSU NOURISH
ILMORTU TURMOIL
ILNOPRU PURLOIN
ILNOPST PONTILS

ILNOTUV VOLUTIN
IMORSTU TOURISM
INOPRSU INPOURS
INOPSTU SPINOUT
EGIJNOS JINGOES
AEINOXZ OXAZINE
ADEILQU QUAILED
ADEILUZ DUALIZE
ABEGIMN BEAMING
ABEGIMR GAMBIER
ABEGIMT MEGABIT
ACEGIMR GRIMACE
ACEGIMT GAMETIC
ACEGINP PEACING
ACEGINY GYNECIA
AEGHIMT MEGAHIT
AEGHINP HEAPING
AEGHINV HEAVING
AEGIMRY IMAGERY
AEGINVW WEAVING
EEGHNRT GREENTH
AINNRTT INTRANT
AABIRST BARISTA
AFIILNT TAILFIN
BEENORR ENROBER
CEEORRT ERECTOR
EEHORTT THERETO
EEMORRT REMOTER
EENNOTY NEOTENY
EENOPTT POTTEEN
EEORRTV EVERTOR
EEORRTW REWROTE
EFGLORT FROGLET
AAEGLOP APOGEAL
ADEJNTU JAUNTED
ADEKLNR RANKLED
ADEKNRS DARKENS
ADEKNRU UNRAKED
ADEKNST DANKEST
ADELRTX DEXTRAL
ADENQTU QUANTED
ADENRSZ ZANDERS
ADENRUZ UNRAZED
ADENTUX UNTAXED
AEKLNRS RANKLES

DEIJNRU INJURED
DEIKLNR KINDLER
DEIKLNT TINKLED
DEIKLRT KIRTLED
DEIKNRS REDSKIN
DEIKNST KINDEST
DEIKRST SKIRTED
DEIQRTU QUIRTED
EIJLRST JILTERS
EIJNRSU INJURES
EIKLNRU URNLIKE
EIKLNTU NUTLIKE
EILQRTU QUILTER
EINQRSU REQUINS
EIQRSTU QUERIST
ABEEFLO BEEFALO
ACDEEMO CAMEOED
AEEMOSW AWESOME
CDEEIOV DEVOICE
EEIMOPS EPISOME
AAINRTZ TZARINA
AIINRTZ TRIAZIN
ABDELNU UNBALED
ABDELRS BLADERS
ADELMRU MURALED
DILNOOS OODLINS
AAGILNS AGNAILS
AAGILRS ARGALIS
AAGINSU IGUANAS
ADGIILT DIGITAL
ADGIINS SIGANID
ADIJNOS ADJOINS
ADIKLOR KILORAD
ADIKNOS DAIKONS
ADIKOST DAKOITS
ADINOSX DIOXANS
AIJLORS JAILORS
AIKLNOS KAOLINS
AILOQTU ALIQUOT
AILORUX UXORIAL
AILOSTX OXTAILS
AINOQSU QUINOAS
AINOSUX ANXIOUS
ACINRTT TANTRIC
AINRRTY TRINARY

AADERRS ARRASED
AAELNNS ANNEALS
EIILSTT ELITIST
DEGRSTU TRUDGES
EGLNRSU LUNGERS
ABENORZ ZEBRANO
BEEORTV OVERBET
CEEFNOR ENFORCE
CEEHORT TROCHEE
CEENOPT POTENCE
CEEORTV COVETER
EEFHORT THEREOF
EEFMNOR FOREMEN
EEHMORT THEOREM
EEHNOPT POTHEEN
EEHORTW WHERETO
EEMNORY MONEYER
EENOPTY NEOTYPE
EEORTVW OVERWET
AEEGPST SEPTAGE
BEEGINS BEIGNES
EEFGIST GIFTEES
EEGIJNR JEERING
EEGIKNR REEKING
EEGINTX EXIGENT
ABCEIMO AMOEBIC
ABEHIMO BOHEMIA
ACEIMOV VOMICAE
DEORRSU ORDURES
DEOSTTU TESTUDO
ELOSTTU OUTLETS
AADDEIL ALIDADE
AAEILSS ALIASES
ADDEIIS DAISIED
ADEIISS DAISIES
AGLNOSU LANUGOS
AGLORSU RUGOLAS
DGILOST DIGLOTS
GILNOSU LOUSING
AKNORTU OUTRANK
AABDENU BANDEAU
AABDERS ABRADES
AABELRS ARABLES
AABELST ABLATES
AABELTU TABLEAU

AABERSU SUBAREA
AACDETU CAUDATE
AACELNS ANLACES
AACELRS SCALARE
AACERSU CAESURA
AADELMN LEADMAN
AADELMR ALARMED
AADELRY ALREADY
AADENSW WEASAND
AADEPRS PARADES
AADERSW SEAWARD
AADERSY DARESAY
AAEHLST ALTHEAS
AAELMNU ALUMNAE
AAELNSY ANALYSE
AAELPRS EARLAPS
AAELPST PALATES
AAELPTU PLATEAU
AAELTUV VALUATE
BDEIIRS BIRDIES
BEIILRS RISIBLE
CEIILST ELICITS
CEIINSU CUISINE
DEFIINU UNIFIED
DEFIIST FIDEIST
DEHIIRS DISHIER
DEIILMN MIDLINE
DEIINSV DIVINES
DEIISTV VISITED
EFIINSU UNIFIES
EIILNPS SPLENII
EIILRSV LIVIERS
EIILSTW WILIEST
EIISTUV UVEITIS
DNOORTU OROTUND
NOORSTU UNROOTS
AADGNRT GARDANT
GIILNRT TIRLING
DEEEIRR REEDIER
EEEILRR LEERIER
BINORSU BOURSIN
AEEELTV ELEVATE
BEEEILN BEELINE
DEEEIRW WEEDIER
EEEHINS SHEENIE

EEEILRV RELIEVE
EEEIMNS ENEMIES
EEEIMRS EMERIES
EEEINSW WEENIES
EEEIPST EPEEIST
EEEIRSV VEERIES
EEEISTW SWEETIE
AABILOU ABOULIA
AACILOS ASOCIAL
ADIIMOS DAIMIOS
DDEILOS DILDOES
DEILLOS DOLLIES
ABINRTV VIBRANT
ACIMNRT MANTRIC
ACINPRT CANTRIP
AIMNRTV VARMINT
AGINOOP POGONIA
AAIINTT TITANIA
ADLNOOS ONLOADS
AANOSTT ANATTOS
IILNNOT NITINOL
IINOTTU TUITION
AACIINT ACTINIA
AAELLRT LATERAL
DDEIINT INDITED
DDEIIRT DIRTIED
ADGIINU IGUANID
BDELNOS BLONDES
BDELNOU UNLOBED
BDELORS BORDELS
BDELOST BOLDEST
BDELOTU DOUBLET
BDEORSU ROSEBUD
BELORSU ROUBLES
BELOSTU BOLETUS
CDELORS SCOLDER
CDELORU CLOURED
CDELOST COLDEST
CDELOTU CLOUTED
CDEOSTU SCOUTED
DEFLORU FLOURED
DEFLOTU FLOUTED
DEFNOSU FONDUES
DEHLNOS HONDLES
DEHLORS HOLDERS

DELMNOS DOLMENS
DELMORU MOULDER
DELMOTU MOULTED
DELNOUV UNLOVED
DELORSW WELDORS
DELORSY YODLERS
DELORUV LOUVRED
DELOTUV VOLUTED
DENOPSU UNPOSED
DEORSUV DEVOURS
EFLNOSU SULFONE
EFLORSU OURSELF
EFLOSTU FOULEST
ELOPSTU TUPELOS
ELORSUY ELUSORY
ELOSTUV VOLUTES
AINPRTT TRIPTAN
DEEGNNO ENDOGEN
ADLNRSU LURDANS
DILNSTU INDULTS
ABEGORR BEGORRA
ACEGOTT COTTAGE
AEFGORR FORAGER
AEGOPTT POTTAGE
AEGOTTV GAVOTTE
EGHIOTT GOTHITE
EGIMNNO OMENING
EGINNOP OPENING
BEEOOST BOOTEES
EEHOOST TOESHOE
EELMNOO OENOMEL
EEMNOOS SOMEONE
EEOOPRS OPEROSE
AAAILRT TALARIA
AIIILNT INITIAL
AACEEGR ACREAGE
AAEEGRV AVERAGE
AEEKORW REAWOKE
AEEMNOX AXONEME
AEEOPTZ EPAZOTE
BEEINOZ EBONIZE
CEEIJOR REJOICE
EEHIORZ HEROIZE
EEIOPTZ POETIZE
AABDNOR BANDORA

AABNOST SABATON
AACNOST SACATON
AACORST OSTRACA
AADMORT MATADOR
AADNOPR PANDORA
AADOPRT ADAPTOR
AAMNOTU AUTOMAN
BIINOST BIOTINS
CDIINOR CRINOID
CDIINOT DICTION
CIINORS INCISOR
CIIORST SORITIC
DDELORT TODDLER
DDENORS NODDERS
DELLORT TROLLED
DENORSS SONDERS
DIIMNOR MIDIRON
ELLNORS ENROLLS
ELLNOST STOLLEN
ELLORST TOLLERS
ELNOSST TELSONS
ENOSSTU TONUSES
ENOSTUU TENUOUS
FIILNOT TINFOIL
HIINORS NOIRISH
IILNOPT PINITOL
IILOPRT TRIPOLI
IILORTV VITRIOL
IINORSV VIRIONS
IIORSTV VISITOR
AEGOTUZ OUTGAZE
EGINOSZ GINZOES
AAEILSX ALEXIAS
ABEOOTV OBOVATE
ACEHOOT OOTHECA
AEMOORW WOOMERA
BEIMOOR BOOMIER
BEIOOPT BIOTOPE
EEHILOP PIEHOLE
ADGINNR DARNING
AGINNRS SNARING
AGINNTU ANTIGUN
AGINTTU TAUTING
AELRRTT RATTLER
EINNRRU RUNNIER

EIRRTTU RUTTIER
AEGGIRU GARIGUE
AEGGIST STAGGIE
CDEEGNO CONGEED
CEEGNOS CONGEES
EEFGLOR FORELEG
EEGLMOR GOMEREL
EEGMNOS GENOMES
EEGMOST GEMOTES
EEGNOPS PONGEES
DEEGORR ROGERED
EEENRTW TWEENER
AAEKLNT ALKANET
AAEKRST KARATES
AAELRTZ LAZARET
AEILLRR RALLIER
AEINNSS SIENNAS
DEIIKNR DINKIER
DEIIRTZ DITZIER
EIIKLNT TINLIKE
EIIKNST INKIEST
EIINQRU INQUIRE
EIINQTU INQUIET
EIINTUZ UNITIZE
BEENORY BONEYER
AADEGLS GELADAS
ABDEELS BEADLES
ABEELSU USEABLE
ACEELSU EUCLASE
ADEEFLS DEFLEAS
ADEEHLS LEASHED
ADEELMS MEASLED
ADEELSV SLEAVED
ADEELUV DEVALUE
ADEEMSU MEDUSAE
AEEFLSU EASEFUL
BDEEILS EDIBLES
CDEEILS DECILES
DEEFILS DEFILES
DEEILMS DELIMES
EEILSUV ELUSIVE
DEELNTT NETTLED
DEENRRS RENDERS
DEENSTT DETENTS
DEERTTU UTTERED

EELNTTU LUNETTE
EENRRSU ENSURER
EERRSTU URETERS
EERSTTU TRUSTEE
ABDENNR BRANNED
ABDENRR BRANDER
ABENNRS BANNERS
ABENNST BANNETS
ABENRRS BARRENS
ABENRRU URBANER
ABENSTT BATTENS
ABERSTT BATTERS
ABERTTU ABUTTER
ACDENNT CANDENT
ACDERTT DETRACT
ACELRTT CLATTER
ACENNST NASCENT
ACERSTT SCATTER
ACERTTU CURTATE
ADENNPT PENDANT
ADENPRR PARDNER
ADENRRW REDRAWN
ADENRRY REYNARD
AEFLNTT FLATTEN
AEFLRTT FLATTER
AEFNNRS FANNERS
AEFNSTT FATTENS
AEFRTTU TARTUFE
AEHRRTU URETHRA
AELMNTT MANTLET
AELMRTT MARTLET
AELNNPR PLANNER
AELRRTW TRAWLER
AEMNNRS MANNERS
AEMNNTU UNMEANT
AEMNRRU MANURER
AEMNTTU NUTMEAT
AENNRSV VANNERS
AENNSTW WANNEST
AENRRSY YARNERS
AEPRRST PRATERS
AEPRRTU RAPTURE
AERRSTV STARVER
AERRSTY STRAYER
AERSTTW SWATTER

AERSTTY YATTERS
BEILRTT BRITTLE
BEINRRS BRINERS
BEIRRTU BRUITER
BEIRSTT BITTERS
BEIRTTU TRIBUTE
CDEINTT TINCTED
CEINRRU REINCUR
CEIRRTU RECRUIT
CEIRSTT TRISECT
DEFIRRT DRIFTER
DEFIRTT FRITTED
DEHINNT THINNED
DEINNTW TWINNED
EFILRTT FLITTER
EFINNRU FUNNIER
EFIRTTU TUFTIER
EILNNRY INNERLY
EILPRTT TRIPLET
EILRRTW TWIRLER
EIMNRRU MURRINE
EIMRSTT METRIST
EINNPRU PUNNIER
EINNPST TENPINS
EINNRSW WINNERS
EINNSTV INVENTS
EINNTUW UNTWINE
EINPRRU UNRIPER
EINSTTY TENSITY
EINTTUY TENUITY
EIPRRST STRIPER
EIPRTTU PUTTIER
EIRRSTV STRIVER
EIRRSTW WRITERS
EIRSTTV TRIVETS
AABEEMO AMOEBAE
ADEKLOS SKOALED
AEJLOSU JEALOUS
AELOSUZ ZEALOUS
DEIKLOS KELOIDS
ABEGHOR BEGORAH
ABEGMOR EMBARGO
AEFGMOR FROMAGE
AEFGORV FORGAVE
AEGHMNO HOGMANE

AEGHMOR HOMAGER
AEGORVY VOYAGER
BEGIORV OVERBIG
CEGHINO ECHOING
CEGHIOR CHOREGI
CEGIMNO GENOMIC
EFGIORV FORGIVE
EGHIOTV EIGHTVO
EGIMNOW MEOWING
AAILORZ ZOARIAL
AAINOSX ANOXIAS
ABDGINT DINGBAT
ABDGIRT DIRTBAG
ABGILNR BLARING
ABGILNT TABLING
ABGINRS SABRING
ABGINST BASTING
ACDGINR CARDING
ACGILNR CARLING
ADFGINR FARDING
ADGINPR DRAPING
ADGINTW DAWTING
AFGILNR FLARING
AFGILNT FATLING
AFGINST FASTING
AGHILRT ALRIGHT
AGHINST HASTING
AGILMNR MARLING
AGILMNT MALTING
AGILNPT PLATING
AGILNRY ANGRILY
AGINPST PASTING
AGINRSV RAVINGS
AGINRSY SYRINGA
AGINSTV STAVING
ABIORRS BARRIOS
ACDINNO NONACID
ACDIORR CORRIDA
ACILNNO CANNOLI
ACIORRS CORSAIR
ADIMORR MIRADOR
ADIMOTT MATTOID
ADIOPRR AIRDROP
AFINNOS FANIONS
AILMNNO NOMINAL

Bob's Bible Bonus: Top 8s Single Anagram Quiz

8-letter Words

- AAEINORT AERATION
- AEEILORT AEROLITE
- ADEILNOT DELATION
- ADEINORS ANEROIDS
- ADEIORST ASTEROID
- AEINORTT TENTORIA
- AEINORRT ANTERIOR
- AEEIINRT INERTIAE
- AEHINORT ANTIHERO
- AEINOPRT ATROPINE
- DEEINORT ORIENTED
- ADEGINOR ORGANDIE
- AEGINORS ORGANISE
- ADEILORS DARIOLES
- ADEIINRT DAINTIER
- AEIILNRT INERTIAL
- AELNORTU OUTLEARN
- AENORSTU OUTEARNS
- EILNORST RETINOLS
- EILNORTU OUTLINER
- ADEEILNR RENAILED
- ADEEINST ANDESITE
- AEEILNRS ALIENERS
- AEEINRSU UNEASIER
- AAENORTU AERONAUT
- DEIINORT RETINOID
- ADEIORRT ADROITER
- ADEIORTT TERATOID
- AEILORRT RETAILOR
- AEINNORS RAISONNE
- AEIORRST ROTARIES
- AEIORSTT TOASTIER
- AADEEIRT ERADIATE
- AAEEILNT ALIENATE
- ADEENORS REASONED
- ADEENOST ENDOSTEA
- AEELNORU ALEURONE
- AEELORST OLEASTER
- DEEINORS INDORSEE
- EEILNORS ELOINERS
- ABDEINOR DEBONAIR
- ABDEINOT OBTAINED
- ABEILNOT TAILBONE
- ABEILORT LABORITE
- ACDEINOT CATENOID
- ACDEIORT CERATOID
- ACEINORS SCENARIO
- ADEIMNOR RADIOMEN
- ADEIMNOT DOMINATE
- ADEIMORT MEDIATOR
- ADEINOPT ANTIPODE
- ADEINOTV DONATIVE
- ADEIORTV DEVIATOR
- AEFILORT FLOATIER
- AEFINORS FARINOSE
- AEHILORT AEROLITH
- AEHIORST HOARIEST
- AEHIORTU THIOUREA
- AEILNOPR PELORIAN
- AEILNOPT ANTIPOLE
- AEILNORV OVERLAIN
- AEILORTV VIOLATER
- AEINOPST SAPONITE
- AEINORSV AVERSION
- AEEINRRT RETAINER
- ADEGILOR DIALOGER
- AEGILNOS GASOLINE
- AEGIOSTU AGOUTIES
- AEINORTZ NOTARIZE
- AEEHINRT HERNIATE
- AEEIMNRT ANTIMERE
- AEEINPRT APERIENT
- AAEGINRT AERATING
- ADENOORT RATOONED
- EINOORST SNOOTIER
- ADEGNORT DRAGONET
- AEGNORTU OUTRANGE
- EGINORST GENITORS
- ADEGIOST GODETIAS
- ADEILNRS ISLANDER
- AEILRSTU URALITES
- AAEELORT AREOLATE
- ADEEGINR REGAINED
- AEEGILNR ALGERINE
- ADILNORT TRINODAL
- ADINORTU DURATION
- AILNORST TONSILAR
- AINORSTU RAINOUTS
- AEEILOTT ETIOLATE
- ADEEINOP OEDIPEAN
- EEINORTT TENORITE
- ACEENORT CAROTENE
- EEHINORT HEREINTO
- AADEILNT DENTALIA
- AADEILRT LARIATED
- AADEINRS ARANEIDS
- ADEIINRU UREDINIA
- AEIILNRS AIRLINES
- AEIILRST LISTERIA
- ADELNORU UNLOADER
- AELORSTU ROSULATE
- DEILNOTU OUTLINED
- DEILORST STOLIDER
- EILORSTU OUTLIERS
- ADEEEINT DETAINEE
- AEEEIRST EATERIES
- AEEGILOU EULOGIAE
- AEGINNOT NEGATION
- AEGINORR ORANGIER
- AADINORT ANTIDORA
- DEILNOST LENTOIDS
- ADEEGNOR RENEGADO
- ADEEGORT DEROGATE
- AEEGLNOT ELONGATE
- EEGILNOR ELOIGNER
- EEGINORS ERINGOES
- EEGINOST EGESTION
- AEGIORTV RAVIGOTE
- ADEEILNS DELAINES
- ADEEILST LEADIEST
- ADEINRTT NITRATED
- AEILNNRT INTERNAL
- ADEEISTU AUDITEES
- ADEELNRT ANTLERED
- AEENRSTU SAUTERNE
- ACDEINRT DICENTRA
- ACEILNRT CLARINET
- ACEINRTU ANURETIC
- ADEHINRT ANTHERID
- ADEINPRT DIPTERAN
- AEFILNRT INFLATER
- AEFINRST FAINTERS
- AEILNRTV INTERVAL
- AEILNRTY INTERLAY
- AEIMNRTU RUMINATE
- AEINRSTW TINWARES
- DEIILNOT TOLIDINE
- DEIIORST DIORITES
- EIILNORS LIONISER
- EIILORST ROILIEST
- ADEGILNT DELATING
- AEGILRST GLARIEST
- AEGILRTU LIGATURE
- ADEILNNO NONIDEAL
- AEILNNOS SOLANINE
- AEILOSTT TOTALISE
- ADINOORT TANDOORI
- AINOORST ORATIONS
- AEIINNRT TRIENNIA
- ADEELORU AUREOLED
- ADEELOST DESOLATE
- AEELORSU AUREOLES
- DEEILNOS LESIONED
- ADENNORT NONRATED
- ADENORTT ATTORNED
- AELNORTT TOLERANT
- AENNORST RESONANT
- AENNORTU UNORNATE
- AENORRST ANTRORSE
- DEINNORT INDENTOR
- DEINORTT INTORTED
- EILNORTT TROTLINE
- EINNORTU NEUTRINO
- EINORRST INTRORSE
- AGILNORT TRIGONAL
- ABDEINOS BEDSONIA
- ACDEIORS IDOCRASE
- ADEFILOT FOLIATED
- ADEFIORS FORESAID
- ADEHINOS ADHESION
- ADEILMNO MELANOID
- ADEILNOP PALINODE
- ADEILOPT PETALOID
- ADEILORV OVERLAID
- ADEIMOST ATOMISED
- ADEIOPST DIOPTASE
- AEFILORS FORESAIL
- AEFILOST FOLIATES
- AEILMORS MORALISE
- AEILMOST LOAMIEST
- AEILNOPS OPALINES
- AEILOPST SPOLIATE
- AEILOSTV VIOLATES
- AAEINPRT ANTIRAPE
- AAEINRTW ANTIWEAR
- AEIINPRT PAINTIER
- EEIINRST NITERIES
- ADDEINOR ORDAINED
- AEINOSST ASTONIES
- DEENORTU DEUTERON
- EELNORST ENTRESOL
- ABENORST BARONETS
- ADENOPRT PRONATED
- ADENORTY AROYNTED
- AEFNORST SEAFRONT
- AELNORTY ORNATELY
- AEMNORTU ROUTEMAN
- BEINORST BORNITES
- DEIMNORT DORMIENT
- DEINOPRT DIPTERON
- EILNOPRT TERPINOL
- EINOPRTU ERUPTION
- EINORSTV INVESTOR
- AABEINRT ATABRINE
- ADEEIRTT ITERATED
- AEEILNRR NEARLIER
- AEEILRRT RETAILER
- AEEINNRS ANSERINE
- AEEIRRST ARTERIES
- ADEIMNOU EUDAIMON
- ADEGILOU DIALOGUE
- AEGILOSU EULOGIAS
- ADENOOST ODONATES
- EILOORST OESTRIOL
- ABDEEIRT REBAITED
- ABEEILRT LIBERATE
- ABEEINST BETAINES
- ACEEILNR RELIANCE
- ACEEINRS INCREASE
- ACEEINST CINEASTE
- ADEEIMNR REMAINED
- ADEEIMNT DEMENTIA
- ADEEIMRT DIAMETER
- ADEEINRV REINVADE
- ADEEINTW ANTIWEED
- ADEEIRTV DERIVATE
- AEEFILNR FLANERIE
- AEEFILRT FEATLIER
- AEEHIRST HEARTIES
- AEEILMNT MELANITE
- AEEILMRT MATERIEL
- AEEILNPR PERINEAL
- AEEILPRT PEARLITE
- AEEINPRS NAPERIES
- AEEINSTV NAIVETES
- AEEIPRST PARIETES
- AEEIRSTY YEASTIER
- AADEGINT INDAGATE
- AAEGILNR GERANIAL
- ADEGIINR DEAIRING
- ADEGIINT IDEATING
- AEGIILNR GAINLIER
- ADEIKORT KERATOID
- AEIJORST JAROSITE
- AEILORTZ TRIAZOLE
- AEINOQRU AEQUORIN
- AEINOQTU EQUATION
- ADEGIIRT DIGERATI
- AEGLNOST TANGELOS
- AEGLORTU OUTGLARE
- AEGORSTU OUTRAGES
- DEGINORS NEGROIDS
- DEGINORU GUERIDON
- EGILNORS RESOLING
- ADEILRSU RESIDUAL
- ADEEIRTW WAITERED
- AAEELORU AUREOLAE
- AABEIOTU ABOITEAU
- AGIINORT RIGATONI
- EIINORRT INTERIOR
- ADELNRTU DENTURAL
- AELNRSTU NEUTRALS
- DEILNRTU UNDERLIT
- DEINRSTU INTRUDES
- EILNRSTU INSULTER
- AAEMNORT EMANATOR
- EFIINORT NOTIFIER
- EIINOPRT POINTIER
- AEEIKNRT ANKERITE
- ADEEGIRS DISAGREE
- AEEGILRS GASELIER
- AEEGILST EGALITES
- AEEGINSU EUGENIAS
- ADILNORS ORDINALS
- ADILORST DILATORS
- ADINORSU DINOSAUR
- ADINOSTU SUDATION
- ADIORSTU AUDITORS
- AEINNOTT INTONATE
- AEEGLNRT REGENTAL
- EEGINRTU GENITURE
- AAEINORX ANOREXIA
- ADEENOTT DETONATE
- AEELORTT TOLERATE
- AEENNOST NEONATES
- AEENORRS REASONER
- AEENOTTU OUTEATEN
- EEILNNOT NONELITE
- EEILORRT LOITERER
- ABEINORR AIRBORNE
- ACEINOTT TACONITE
- AEFINOTT FETATION
- AEHINOTT THIONATE
- AEIMORTT AMORETTI
- AEINORRW IRONWARE
- AEIOPRRT PRIORATE
- AEIORTTV ROTATIVE
- AACEEIRT ACIERATE
- EEGILNRT GREENLIT
- ABEENORS SEABORNE
- ACDEENOT ANECDOTE
- ADEEFORT FOREDATE
- ADEEHNOT HEADNOTE
- ADEEMNOT NEMATODE
- ADEEMORT MODERATE
- ADEENORV ENDEAVOR
- ADEENORY AERODYNE
- ADEEOPRT OPERATED
- AEEHLNOT ANETHOLE
- AEELNOPR PERONEAL
- AEELNOPT ANTELOPE
- AEENOPRS PERSONAE
- AEEORSTV OVEREATS
- BDEEINOT OBEDIENT
- CDEEINOR RECOINED
- CEEILNOT ELECTION
- CEEINOST SEICENTO
- DEEIMNOR DOMINEER
- DEEINORW IRONWEED
- DEEINOTV DENOTIVE
- DEEIOPRT PROTEIDE
- DEEIORTV OVEREDIT
- EEHILORT HOTELIER
- EEHINORS HEROINES
- EEILNOPR LEPORINE
- EEIMNORS EMERSION
- EEIMORST TIRESOME
- EEINORSV EVERSION
- EGIINORS SEIGNIOR
- AADEILRS SALARIED
- ADEIILST IDEALIST
- ABCEIORT BORACITE
- ABEIORTV ABORTIVE
- ACEHINOT INCHOATE
- ACEIMNOT COINMATE
- ACEINORV VERONICA
- ACEIOPRT OPERATIC
- AEFINOPR PINAFORE
- AEFIORTV FAVORITE
- AEIMNOPT PTOMAINE
- AEIMNORW AIRWOMEN
- AEEEILNS ALIENEES
- ADELORSU ROULADES
- AAELNRST ASTERNAL
- DEIINRTU UNTIDIER
- EIILNRST NITRILES
- EIINRSTU NEURITIS
- AEGINNOS ANGINOSE
- AAEEGILN ALIENAGE
- AAEEGINS AGENESIA
- AEEGIIST GAIETIES
- AEFILOOR AEROFOIL
- AEILOORV OVARIOLE
- AAILNORS ORINASAL
- AAILNOST ALATIONS
- ADIILNOT DILATION
- ADIINOTU AUDITION
- AGINOORT ROGATION
- AEEELNRT LATEENER
- AEEENRST SERENATE
- AENOORRT RATOONER
- DELNORTU ROUNDLET
- ELNORSTU TURNSOLE
- EEINORTX EXERTION
- AEEGLNOS GASOLENE
- AEEGLORS AEROGELS
- DEEGILNO ELOIGNED
- AEGNNORT NEGATRON
- AEGNORTT TETRAGON
- EGINNORT NITROGEN
- ADELOSTU OUTLEADS
- DEENOORT ENROOTED
- EENOORST OESTRONE
- ACENOORT CORONATE
- AEMNOORT ANTEROOM
- ADEILNNR INLANDER
- ADEILNNT DENTINAL
- ADEILRTT DETRITAL
- ADEINNRS INSNARED
- ADEINNTU INUNDATE
- ADEINSTT INSTATED
- AEILNRRS SNARLIER
- AEILRRTU RURALITE
- AEILRSTT TERTIALS
- AEINNRSU ANEURINS
- ABEGILOT OBLIGATE
- ABEGINOS BEGONIAS
- ACEGINOS COINAGES
- ADEGIMNO AMIDOGEN
- ADEGIMOR IDEOGRAM
- AEGILOPT PILOTAGE
- AEGIORSV VIRAGOES
- EEGNORST ESTROGEN
- ADEENSTU UNSEATED
- AEELRSTU RESALUTE
- DEEILNRS REDLINES
- DEEILNRU UNDERLIE
- DEEILRST RELISTED
- DEEINSTU DETINUES
- AEFGNORT FRONTAGE
- CEGINORT GERONTIC
- EGINORTV REVOTING
- EGINORTW TOWERING
- AABEENOR ANAEROBE
- ABDEILNR BILANDER
- ABDEILNT BIDENTAL
- ABDEILRT LIBRATED
- ABDEINRS BRANDIES
- ABEILNRS RINSABLE
- ABEILNRU RUINABLE
- ABEILNST INSTABLE
- ABEINRSU URBANISE
- ACDEINST DISTANCE
- ACDEINTU INCUDATE
- ACDEIRST ACRIDEST
- ACEILRTU RETICULA
- ACEIRSTU SURICATE
- ADEFILNT INFLATED
- ADEHILNR HARDLINE
- ADEHINRU UNHAIRED
- ADEHINST HANDIEST
- ADEHIRST HARDIEST
- ADEILNPT PANTILED
- ADEILNTV DIVALENT
- ADEIMNRU MURAENID
- ADEIMNST MEDIANTS
- ADEIMRTU MURIATED
- ADEINPRS SPRAINED
- ADEINPST DEPAINTS
- ADEINRSV INVADERS
- ADEINRUV UNVARIED
- ADEINSTV DEVIANTS
- ADEIRSTW TAWDRIES
- ADEIRTUV DURATIVE
- AEFILNRU FRAULEIN
- AEFILNST INFLATES
- AEFILRST FRAILEST
- AEHILNRS INHALERS
- AEHILNRU INHAULER
- AEHIRSTU THESAURI
- AEILNPRS PRALINES
- AEILNRSV RAVELINS
- AEILNRSY INLAYERS
- AEILNSTV VENTAILS
- AEILRTUV VAULTIER
- AEIMNRSU ANEURISM
- AEIMRSTU MURIATES
- AEEGINNT ANTIGENE
- AEEGINRR REGAINER
- AEEGIRTT AIGRETTE
- AINORSTT STRONTIA
- AINORRTU URINATOR
- AAELORSU AUREOLAS
- DEIILNOS LIONISED
- DEIILORS IDOLISER
- AEGNOORS OREGANOS
- AEGOORST ROOTAGES
- DEGINOOR RODEOING
- ACEEGINT AGENETIC
- AEEFGIRT FIGEATER
- AEEGHIRT HERITAGE
- AEEGIMNT GEMINATE
- AEEGIMRT EMIGRATE
- AEEGINPR PERIGEAN
- AEEGIRTV ERGATIVE
- ABINORST TABORINS
- ACDINORT TORNADIC
- AHILNORT HORNTAIL
- AINOPRST ATROPINS
- AEGINORZ ORGANIZE
- EGINOOST GOONIEST
- ACEILNST CANISTEL
- ADEGILST GLADIEST
- ADEGISTU GAUDIEST
- AAEGIMNO EGOMANIA
- ABEGIINO IBOGAINE
- AEIJNRTU JAUNTIER
- AEIKNRST KERATINS
- ADEEIILS IDEALISE
- ADILNOOR DOORNAIL
- AILNOOST SOLATION
- AADEINTT ATTAINED
- AAEILRRT ARTERIAL
- AEIILNRR AIRLINER
- AEIILRTT LITERATI
- AEIINNRS SIRENIAN
- AEIINTTU UINTAITE
- AEIIRRST RARITIES
- DEGINRST STRINGED
- AINORSTW WAITRONS
- ADELNNOT LENTANDO
- ADENNOTU UNATONED
- ADEORRST ROADSTER

Bob's Bible Bonus: Top 8s Single Anagram Quiz

AELNNORU	NEURONAL
AENNORSU	UNREASON
AENNOSTU	TONNEAUS
DEILNNOT	INDOLENT
DEINNORU	UNIRONED
DEINORRS	INDORSER
DEIORRTU	OUTRIDER
EILNNOST	INSOLENT
EILNORRS	LORINERS
EILORRTU	ULTERIOR
EILORSTT	TRIOLETS
EINNORSU	REUNIONS
ADGINORU	RIGAUDON
AGINORSU	AROUSING
AGINOSTU	OUTGAINS
AAEELRTU	LAUREATE
AAEENSTU	NAUSEATE
DEEIIRST	SIDERITE
EEIILNST	LENITIES
AABEILNR	INARABLE
AACDEINR	RADIANCE
AACDEIRT	RADICATE
AACEILRT	TAILRACE
AACEINST	ESTANCIA
AADEIMNR	MARINADE
AADEIRTV	VARIATED
AAEFINST	FANTASIE
AAEHILNT	ANTHELIA
AAEHINST	ASTHENIA
AAEHIRST	HETAIRAS
AAEILMRT	MATERIAL
AAEILNPR	AIRPLANE
AAEILNPT	PALATINE
AAEILNRV	VALERIAN
AAEILNTV	AVENTAIL
AAEILPRT	PARIETAL
AAEILRTV	VARIETAL
AAEIMRST	AMIRATES
AAEINSTV	SANATIVE
AAEIRSTV	VARIATES
AAEIRSTW	AWAITERS
ABDEIIRT	DIATRIBE
ABEIILNR	BILINEAR
ABEIINRS	BINARIES
ACDEIINR	ACRIDINE
ACDEIIRT	RATICIDE
ACEIILNR	IRENICAL
ACEIINST	CANITIES
ADEFIIRT	RATIFIED
ADEIIMNR	MERIDIAN
ADEIINTV	VANITIED
AEFIILNT	ANTILIFE
AEFIIRST	RATIFIES
AEHIILNR	HAIRLINE
AEHIIRST	HAIRIEST
AEIIMNRU	URINEMIA
AEIIMNTU	MINUTIAE
AEIINSTV	VANITIES
AEIIPRST	PARITIES
AEIIRSTW	WISTERIA
ACDEIOSU	EDACIOUS
ADEILMOS	MELODIAS
ADEILOPS	SEPALOID
AEEEIMRT	EMERITAE
AELORSTT	RETOTALS
EELNOSTU	TOLUENES
EELORSTU	RESOLUTE
ADDEINOS	ADENOIDS
ADDEIORS	ROADSIDE
ADEILLOR	ARILLODE
AEILNOSS	ANISOLES
AEILORSS	SOLARISE
AEILOSST	ISOLATES
AIINORTT	ANTIRIOT
ABDELNOR	BANDEROL
ABDEORST	BROADEST
ABEORSTU	SABOTEUR
ACDENORS	ENDOSARC
ACDEORST	REDCOATS
ACELNOST	LACTONES
ACENORSU	NACREOUS
ACEORSTU	OUTRACES
ADEFLNOR	FORELAND
ADEFLORT	DEFLATOR
ADEHNORS	HARDNOSE
ADELNORV	OVERLAND
ADELOPRT	PORTALED
ADELORTW	LEADWORT
ADEMNOTU	AMOUNTED
ADEMORTU	OUTDREAM
ADENOPST	NOTEPADS
ADENOTUY	AUTODYNE
ADEORTUV	OUTRAVED
AEFLNORS	FARNESOL
AEFNORSU	FURANOSE
AEHORSTU	OUTHEARS
AELMNORS	ALMONERS
AELMORTU	EMULATOR
AELNOPST	POLENTAS
AELNOSTY	ANOLYTES
AEMNOSTU	SEAMOUNT
AENORSUV	RAVENOUS
AEOPRSTU	APTEROUS
AEORSTUV	OUTRAVES
BDEILORT	TRILOBED
BDEINOTU	BOUNTIED
BDEIORST	DEORBITS
BDEIORTU	TUBEROID
BEILORST	STROBILE
BEINOSTU	BOUNTIES
CDEINORS	CONSIDER
CDEINORU	DECURION
CDEINOTU	EDUCTION
CDEIORST	CORDITES
CDEIORTU	OUTCRIED
CEINORSU	COINSURE
CEINOSTU	COUNTIES
DEFILNOR	INFOLDER
DEFIORTU	OUTFIRED
DEHINORS	HORDEINS
DEHINOST	HEDONIST
DEILORTY	ELYTROID
DEIMNOST	DEMONIST
DEIMORST	MORTISED
DEINOPRS	PRISONED
DEINOPRU	INPOURED
DEINOSTW	DOWNIEST
DEINOTUV	INDEVOUT
DEIORTUV	OUTDRIVE
EFILNORU	FLUORINE
EFILORST	TREFOILS
EFILORTU	FLUORITE
EFIORSTU	OUTFIRES
EHILNORU	UNHOLIER
EHINOSTU	OUTSHINE
EILMNORS	MISENROL
EILNOPRS	PROLINES
EILNOPTU	UNPOLITE
EILNOSTV	NOVELIST
EILNOSTW	TOWLINES
EILNOTUV	INVOLUTE
EILOPRST	POITRELS
EILORTUV	OUTLIVER
EIMNORSU	MONSIEUR
EINOPRSU	PRUINOSE
EINORSUV	SOUVENIR
EIOPRSTU	ROUPIEST
EEGINORR	ERIGERON
ADINRSTU	UNITARDS
EEINOOPT	OPTIONEE
AEINNRTT	INTRANET
AADEINPT	PATINAED
AEIILPRT	REPTILIA
AACINORT	RAINCOAT
AAIMNORT	ANIMATOR
EINORSST	OESTRINS
ADEEINNS	ADENINES
AEEILRRS	REALISER
ADGIORST	GORDITAS
AEINNRRT	INERRANT
AEINRRTT	RETIRANT
DDEINORT	TRENDOID
CEEGINOR	EROGENIC
DEINOOSU	IDONEOUS
ACEILOSU	EUSOCIAL
AEELNNRT	LANNERET
AEELNRRT	RELEARNT
AEENRRST	TERRANES
AEENRRTU	RENATURE
DEEINRTT	RETINTED
EEILNRTT	NETTLIER
AADEGILT	GLADIATE
AAEGILRS	GASALIER
ADEGIILN	GLIADINE
ABDEEILN	DENIABLE
ABDEEILR	RIDEABLE
ABDEEILT	EDITABLE
ABEEILNS	BASELINE
ABEEISTU	BEAUTIES
ACDEEILT	DELICATE
ACDEEINU	AUDIENCE
ACDEEIRS	DECIARES
ACEEILNS	SALIENCE
ACEEINSU	EUCAINES
ACEEIRSU	CAUSERIE
ADEEFILN	ENFILADE
ADEEFIST	SAFETIED
ADEEHILN	HEADLINE
ADEEHIST	HEADIEST
ADEEILMN	ENDEMIAL
ADEEILPR	PEDALIER
ADEEIMST	MEDIATES
ADEEIPRS	AIRSPEED
AEEFILRS	FILAREES
AEEILMRS	MEASLIER
AEEILPRS	ESPALIER
AEEILRSY	YEARLIES
AEEILTUV	ELUVIATE
AAEINRTZ	ATRAZINE
AEIINRTZ	TRIAZINE
ACEINRTT	INTERACT
AEIMNNRT	TRAINMEN
AEINPRTT	TRIPTANE
AEINRRTV	VERATRIN
AEINRRTW	INTERWAR
ADEIKLOT	TOADLIKE
ADEILORX	EXORDIAL
ADEINOSX	DIOXANES
ADEINOSZ	ANODIZES
ADEIOSTX	OXIDATES
ADEIOSTZ	AZOTISED
AEIKLNOS	KAOLINES
AEIKLOST	KEITLOAS
AEILNOSX	SILOXANE
AEILORSZ	SOLARIZE
ADDEEINT	DETAINED
AEEILLNT	TENAILLE
AEEILLRT	LAETRILE
AEEIRSST	SERIATES
AENOPSTU	AUTOPENS
DEHILNOR	INHOLDER
EINOPSTU	POUTINES
ADIINOOT	IODATION
DENOORTU	UNROOTED
ENOORSTU	OUTSNORE
AEGLNOSU	ANGULOSE
DEGILNOS	SIDELONG
DEGILOST	GODLIEST
EGILNOSU	LIGNEOUS
EGILOSTU	EULOGIST
AAEGLNRT	ARGENTAL
AAEGNRST	TANAGERS
AAEGNRTU	RUNAGATE
EGIINRTU	INTRIGUE
ABDEENRT	BANTERED
ABEELNRT	RENTABLE
ABEENRST	ABSENTER
ACEENRTU	UNCREATE
ADEENPRT	PARENTED
AEEHLNRT	LEATHERN
AEEHNRTU	URETHANE
AEELMNRT	LAMENTER
AEELNRTW	TREELAWN
AEEMNRTU	NUMERATE
AEENRSTV	VETERANS
BDEEINRT	INTERBED
DEEIMNRT	REMINTED
DEEINRTV	INVERTED
DEEINRTW	WINTERED
EEIMNRST	MISENTER
EEIMNRTU	MUTINEER
EEINPRTU	PREUNITE
EEINRSTY	SERENITY
EEGINOOS	OOGENIES
EIJNORST	JOINTERS
EIJNORTU	JOINTURE
EIKNORST	INSTROKE
AAELNNOT	NEONATAL
AAENORRU	AUROREAN
AAEORRST	AERATORS
AAEORSTT	AEROSTAT
EIILNNOT	LENITION
EIILORTT	TROILITE
ADGIINOR	RADIOING
ADGIINOT	IODATING
AGIILNOR	ORIGINAL
AABDEIOU	ABOIDEAU
AACEIINT	ACTINIAE
AAEHIIRT	HETAIRAI
AEEILNSV	VASELINE
AEEILPST	EPILATES
ABCEINRT	BACTERIN
ACEINRTV	NAVICERT
AEHINPRT	PERIANTH
AEIMNRTY	TYRAMINE
DEGNORTU	TRUDGEON
EGNORSTU	STURGEON
ADELNSTU	UNSALTED
AABDEORT	TEABOARD
AABELNOT	ATONABLE
AACDENOT	ANECDOTA
AACENOTU	OCEANAUT
AADEOPRT	TAPADERO
AAELORTY	ALEATORY
BEIINORS	BRIONIES
CEIILORT	ELICITOR
DEFIINOT	NOTIFIED
DEIINOTY	IDONEITY
EFIINOST	NOTIFIES
EIILMNOT	LIMONITE
EIINOPRS	RIPIENOS
EIINORSV	REVISION
AEGILNNR	LEARNING
AEGILNRR	GNARLIER
AEGILRTT	AGLITTER
AEEIKNRS	SNEAKIER
AEEILRTZ	LATERIZE
AADINRST	RADIANTS
ADIINRST	DISTRAIN
AINOORTT	ROTATION
ADEEGLNR	ENLARGED
ADEEGRST	RESTAGED
AEEGLRTU	REGULATE
DEEGILNT	DELETING
EEGILNRU	REGULINE
EEGINRSU	SEIGNEUR
EEGINSTU	EUGENIST
ADLNORST	TROLANDS
ADNORSTU	ROTUNDAS
ADEELORR	RELOADER
AEEORRSU	REAROUSE
DEEILOTT	TOILETED
AABEORST	AEROBATS
AAEMNORS	AMARONES
BEIINOST	NIOBITES
AGINNORT	IGNORANT
AGINORTT	ROTATING
ABDEGINT	DEBATING
ABEGILNR	BLEARING
ABEGINST	BEATINGS
ACEGILNT	CLEATING
ACEGINRS	CREASING
ADEFGIRT	DRIFTAGE
ADEGHINR	ADHERING
ADEGIMRT	MIGRATED
ADEGINRY	READYING
AEFGILNR	FINAGLER
AEFGINST	FEASTING
AEFGIRST	FRIGATES
AEGHILNT	ATHELING
AEGHINST	GAHNITES
AEGILNPT	PLEATING
AEGILNRV	RAVELING
AEGILNTV	VALETING
AEGILRTY	REGALITY
AEGIMNRS	SMEARING
AEGIMNRU	GERANIUM
AEGINPRS	SPEARING
AEGINRSV	VINEGARS
AEGINSTV	VINTAGES
AEGINSTW	SWEATING
AEGINSTY	YEASTING
AEGIPRST	GRAPIEST
AEGIRSTV	VIRGATES
ADEEFIIR	AERIFIED
ADEEIITV	IDEATIVE
AEEFIIRS	AERIFIES
ACEILORR	CARRIOLE
ACEINNOS	CANONISE
ADEHIOTT	ATHETOID
ADEIMNNO	DEMONIAN
ADEIMORR	AIRDROME
AEINNOPS	SAPONINE
AEIORRSV	SAVORIER
ABINOORT	ABORTION
AAEENRTT	ANTEATER
ADEEILLO	OEILLADE
ADEEGLNT	DANEGELT
EEGILNRS	REELINGS
AAEGLNOU	ANALOGUE
DEGIINOS	INDIGOES
ABEELORS	EARLOBES
ACEELORS	ESCAROLE
ADEEFLOR	FREELOAD
ADEEHLNO	ENHALOED
ADEEHORS	SOREHEAD
ADEELMNO	LEMONADE
ADEELMOR	REMOLADE
ADEELORV	OVERLADE
ADEEMNOU	EUDAEMON
ADEEMORS	SEADROME
ADEEOPST	ADOPTEES
AEEHLNOS	ENHALOES
AEEHOSTU	TEAHOUSE
AEELOPRS	PAROLEES
AEELORSV	OVERSALE
AEENOPSU	EUPNOEAS
BDEEINOS	EBONISED
BDEEIORS	REBODIES
BEEILORS	EROSIBLE
CDEEILOR	RECOILED
CDEEINOS	CODEINES
CEEILNOS	CINEOLES
CEEILORS	CREOLISE
DEEFIORS	FORESIDE
DEEIMNOS	DEMONISE
DEEIMORS	EMEROIDS
DEEINOSV	NOSEDIVE
DEEIORSV	OVERSIDE
EEILNOSV	NOVELISE
EEILOPST	PETIOLES
ABENORTT	BETATRON
AEMNNORT	ORNAMENT
AENNORTW	WANTONER
AENOPRTT	PATENTOR
AENORTTY	ATTORNEY
CEINORRT	TRICORNE
CEINORTT	CONTRITE
EFINORRT	FRONTIER
EHINNORT	INTHRONE
EHINORRT	THORNIER
EINNORTV	INVENTOR
EINORRTV	INVERTOR
EINORRTW	INTERROW
CEEIINRT	REINCITE
EEIINRTV	REINVITE
AGINORTV	GRAVITON
AGINORTY	GYRATION
EEILLNOR	LONELIER
EEINOSST	ESSONITE
ABEILORR	BORRELIA
ADEINNOV	DEVONIAN
ADEIOPRR	PRERADIO
ABCEIORS	AEROBICS
ABCEIOST	ICEBOATS
ABDEIMOR	AMBEROID
ABDEIOTV	OBVIATED
ABEFILOT	LIFEBOAT
ABEILOTV	BLOVIATE
ABEIMORS	BIRAMOSE
ABEIMORU	AEROBIUM
ABEIOSTV	OBVIATES
ACDEINOP	CANOPIED
ACDEINOV	VOIDANCE
ACEHILOR	HEROICAL
ACEHIOST	ACHIOTES
ACEILOPR	CAPRIOLE
ACEILOPT	POETICAL
ACEILOTV	LOCATIVE
ACEINOPS	CANOPIES
ACEIOPST	ECTOPIAS
ADEHIMOT	HEMATOID
ADEHINOP	DIAPHONE
ADEHINOY	HYOIDEAN
ADEIMNOP	DOPAMINE
ADEIOPRV	OVERPAID
ADEIOPTV	ADOPTIVE
AEFIMOST	FOAMIEST
AEHIOPRS	APHORISE
AEHIOPRU	EUPHORIA
AEILMOPR	PROEMIAL
AEIMNOSW	WOMANISE
AEIMOPRS	MEROPIAS
AEIOPRSV	VAPORISE
CEELNORT	ELECTRON
EEFNORTU	FOURTEEN
EEHNORST	HONESTER
EEHNORTU	HEREUNTO
EELNOPRT	PETRONEL
EELNORTV	OVERLENT
EEMNORTU	ROUTEMEN
EENOPRTU	OUTPREEN
AADELNRS	ADRENALS
DEIINRSU	URIDINES
EIILRSTU	UTILISER
AENORTTV	TEVATRON
ADEEENRS	SERENADE
ADEEERST	RESEATED
AEEELNST	SELENATE
AEEELRST	TEASELER
DEEEINST	NEEDIEST
DEEEIRST	REEDIEST
ABEEIRTT	BATTERIE
ACEEINNR	NARCEINE
AEEFIRTT	FETERITA
AEEINNTV	VENETIAN
AEEIRRTW	WATERIER
ABENORTV	BEVATRON
ABENORTY	BARYTONE
ACEHNORT	ANCHORET
ACENORTY	ENACTORY
AEMNORTY	MONETARY
CEFINORT	INFECTOR
CEIMNORT	INTERCOM
CEINORTV	CONTRIVE
EFINORTY	RENOTIFY
EHIMNORT	THERMION
EHINORTV	OVERTHIN
EIMNOPRT	ORPIMENT
EIMNORTW	TIMEWORN
EIMNORTY	ENORMITY
ADEOORRT	TOREADOR
AEOORRST	SORORATE
DEINNOOT	NOONTIDE
ADEEMNOS	DAEMONES
AEELOSTV	LOVESEAT
AAEGINNR	ANEARING
AEGIINNR	ARGININE
AEGIINRR	GRAINIER
AEGIIRRT	IRRIGATE
ADGINOOR	RIGADOON
AGIOORTU	AUTOGIRO
AEGIKNRT	RETAKING
AEGINRTX	RETAXING
AAIINRST	INTARSIA

Bob's Bible Bonus: Top 8s Single Anagram Quiz

ADEGNNOR ANDROGEN
ADEGORRT GARROTED
ADEGORTT GAROTTED
AEGLNNOR NONGLARE
AEGNORRS GROANERS
AEGORRST GARROTES
AEGORSTT GAROTTES
AEGORTTU TUTORAGE
DEGINNOT DENOTING
DEGINORR ORDERING
EGINNORS NEGRONIS
EGINORRS IGNORERS
EGIORRTU GROUTIER
DEELOORT RETOOLED
EELNOORS LOOSENER
AADEEGNR GADARENE
AAEEGNRS SANGAREE
EEGIILNR LINGERIE
AEEKORST KERATOSE
DEEIJNOR REJOINED
DEEIORTZ EROTIZED
EEIKLORT LORIKEET
EEIKNORS KEROSINE
EEIORSTZ EROTIZES
ACELNOOT ECOTONAL
ADEMNOOR MAROONED
ADEMOORT MODERATO
ADENOORW WANDEROO
AELOORTW WATERLOO
AEMOORST TEAROOMS
AENOOPST TEASPOON
CDEIOORT COEDITOR
CEINOOST COONTIES
DEINOOPT OPTIONED
DEINOOTV DEVOTION
EFILNOOR ROOFLINE
EILOORTV OVERTOIL
ADEILNNU UNNAILED
ADEISTTU SITUATED
AEILRRSU RURALISE
AAEGINPT PAGINATE
ACEGIINR REAGINIC
ABEEHINT THEBAINE
ACEEHINT ECHINATE
ACEEINPT PATIENCE

ACEEINTV ENACTIVE
ADEFGILO FOLIAGED
ADEGILOY IDEALOGY
AEFGILOS FOLIAGES
AEGILOPS SPOILAGE
DEEGLNOR GOLDENER
EEGNORSU GENEROUS
AEGINOSS AGONISES
AEGIORSS ARGOSIES
DEEILRSU LEISURED
ACDEIORV COVARIED
ADENRRST STRANDER
ADENRTTU TRUANTED
AELNNRST LANTERNS
AELNNRTU UNLEARNT
AELNRSTT SLATTERN
AENRSTTU TAUNTERS
DEINNRTU INTURNED
DEINRRTU INTRUDER
EINNRSTU RUNNIEST
EINRSTTU RUNTIEST
AADEEMOT OEDEMATA
BEEIIORS BOISERIE
EEIIMOST MOIETIES
ABEINOTZ BOTANIZE
ACEINORX ANOREXIC
ACEINOTX EXACTION
AEIMNORZ ROMANIZE
AEIMNOTZ MONAZITE
AEINOPTZ TOPAZINE
AEINOTVX VEXATION
AEIOPRTX EXPIATOR
ABEGNORS BEGROANS
ACEGLNOT OCTANGLE
ACEGNORS ACROGENS
ACEGORST ESCARGOT
ADEGHORT GOATHERD
ADEGMNOR DRAGOMEN
ADEGMNOT MONTAGED
ADEGNOPR DOGNAPER
ADEGOPRT PORTAGED
ADEGORTW WATERDOG
AEFGORST FAGOTERS
AEGHORST SHORTAGE
AEGLNOPT GANTLOPE

AEGLNORY YEARLONG
AEGLORTV TRAVELOG
AEGLORTW WATERLOG
AEGNORSW WAGONERS
AEGNOTUY AUTOGENY
AEGOPRST PORTAGES
BEGINORS SOBERING
CDEGINOR RECODING
CEGINOST ESCOTING
DEGIMNOT DEMOTING
DEGINORV RINGDOVE
DEGINORW DOWERING
DEGINOTV DEVOTING
EFGILNOR FLORIGEN
EGHILORT REGOLITH
EGHINOST HISTOGEN
EGHIORST GHOSTIER
EGILMNOT LONGTIME
EGILNOTW TOWELING
EGILORTV OVERGILT
EGIMNOST MITOGENS
EGIMORST ERGOTISM
EGINORSW RESOWING
EGINORSY SEIGNORY
EGINOTUV OUTGIVEN
EGIORSTV VERTIGOS
ADGILNRT DARTLING
ADGINRTU ANTIDRUG
AGILNRST STARLING
AEEGIRRS GREASIER
ADILNNOT NONTIDAL
ADINNORS ANDIRONS
AILNNOST ANTLIONS
AILNNOTU LUNATION
AILORTTU TUTORIAL
AINOSTTU TITANOUS
EINOORSW SWOONIER
EINOOSTW TWOONIES
ABDEILTU DUTIABLE
ABDEINSU UNBIASED
ABDEIRSU DAUBRIES
ABDEISTU DAUBIEST
ABEILSTU SUITABLE
ACDEILNU DULCINEA
ACDEILRU AURICLED

ACEILNSU LUNACIES
ACEILRSU AURICLES
ADEHILNU UNHAILED
ADEILMRS DISMALER
ADEILNPS SANDPILE
ADEILPRU EPIDURAL
ADEILPST TALIPEDS
ADEILRSY DIALYSER
ADEILSTY STEADILY
ADEIMNSU MAUNDIES
ADEIPRSU UPRAISED
AEFILRSU FAILURES
AEFILSTU FISTULAE
AEHILRSU HAULIERS
AEILMNSU ALUMINES
AEILMSTU SIMULATE
AEILNPSU SPINULAE
AEILNSUW LAUWINES
AEILNSUY UNEASILY
AEILPRSU SPIRULAE
DEELNRTU UNDERLET
ADDEILNT TIDELAND
ADDEINST DANDIEST
ADDEIRST DISRATED
AEILLRTU TAILLEUR
AEILNRSS RAINLESS
AEINSSTU SINUATES
AAEGIMRT GEMATRIA
EEGINNRT ENTERING
DEGILOOR GOODLIER
AIORSTTU TOURISTA
ABDENRST BARTENDS
ABELNRTU TURNABLE
ABENRSTU URBANEST
ACELNRST CENTRALS
ADEHNRTU UNTHREAD
ADELNRTY ARDENTLY
ADEMNRTU UNDREAMT
ADENPRTU UNPARTED
AEFLNRTU FLAUNTER
AEHLNRST ENTHRALS
AELNRSTV VENTRALS
AEMNRSTU MENSTRUA
AENRSTUV VAUNTERS
CDEINRTU REINDUCT

DEILNRTY TRENDILY
DEINPRST SPRINTED
EILMNRST MINSTREL
EILNPRST SPLINTER
EILNRTUV VIRULENT
EINPRSTU UNRIPEST
EINRSTUV VENTURIS
ACEEGINS AGENCIES
ADEEGIMN ADEEMING
ADEEGIMR REIMAGED
AEEFGILR FILAGREE
AEEGILMN LIEGEMAN
AEEGILMR GLEAMIER
AEEGILPR PERIGEAL
AEEGILTV LEVIGATE
AEEGIMRS REIMAGES
AEEGINSV ENVISAGE
AEEGISTY GAYETIES
ADDEINRS SARDINED
ABDINORS INBOARDS
ABDINORU AIRBOUND
ACDILNOR IRONCLAD
ACDILORT DICROTAL
ACDINORS SARDONIC
ACDIORST CAROTIDS
ACILNORS CLARIONS
ADILNOTY NODALITY
ADIMNOST SAINTDOM
ADINOPRS PONIARDS
ADINOSTY DYSTONIA
ADIORTUY AUDITORY
AFIORSTU FAITOURS
AILMORST MORALIST
AILNOPRU UNIPOLAR
AILNOSTY LANOSITY
AILOPRTU TROUPIAL
AILORTUV OUTRIVAL
AIORSTUV VIRTUOSA
AADEEERT DEAERATE
AILLNORT ANTIROLL
AINORSST ARSONIST
ADEGINOZ AGONIZED
AEGIKLOT GOATLIKE
AEGINOSZ AGONIZES
AEGIOSTX GEOTAXIS

EEGINPRT PETERING
EEGINRTV EVERTING
DEEENORS ENDORSEE
DEEEORST STEREOED
AEENORRV OVERNEAR
AEEOPRRT PERORATE
AEEOPRTT OPERETTA
AEEORRTV OVERRATE
CEEINNOT NEOTENIC
EEIOPRRT PORTIERE
EEIORRTV OVERTIRE
EEIORRTW TOWERIER
AAEGORRT ARROGATE
ABDEGORT BOGARTED
DEGIOPRT RIDGETOP
AACEIOPR CAPOEIRA
ADEILMNU UNMAILED
AADEILTT DILATATE
AADEISTT SATIATED
AAEILNNS ALANINES
AEIILNNS ANILINES
ADEIINNS SANIDINE
ADEINQTU ANTIQUED
AEIKLNST LANKIEST
AEIKLNTU AUNTLIKE
AEIKNSTU UNAKITES
AEILNQTU QUANTILE
AEILNRSX RELAXINS
AEILRTUZ LAZURITE
AEINQSTU ANTIQUES
AEINRSUZ SUZERAIN
AEIRSTUZ AZURITES
AEGLNRSU GRANULES
AEGLNSTU LANGUETS
AEGLRSTU GESTURAL
DEGILNRU INDULGER
DEGINSTU DUNGIEST
ADEOSTTU OUTDATES
AELNNOSU ANNULOSE
AELOSTTU TOLUATES
AABEGNOR BARONAGE
AABEGORT ABROGATE
EGIINOPR PEIGNOIR
AADEELST DEALATES
DEEIILNS SIDELINE

AADENRRT NARRATED
AAENRRST NARRATES
EIINRSTT NITRITES
ALNOORST ORTOLANS
ABEEORTV OVERBEAT
ACEENOPT CONEPATE
AEEFMNOR FORENAME
AEEHNOPR EARPHONE
AEEHOPRT EPHORATE
AEEMORTV OVERTAME
AEENORVW OVENWARE
BCEEINOT CENOBITE
BEEIORTV OVERBITE
CEEHINOR COINHERE
CEEIMORT METEORIC
CEEINORV OVERNICE
CEEINOTV EVECTION
CEEIORTV ORECTIVE
EEFIMORT FORETIME
EEIMORTV OVERTIME
EEINOPTY EYEPOINT
AAGINRST GRANITAS
ADGILNOS LOADINGS
ADGILORS GOLIARDS
ABDINOST BANDITOS
AABDEILR RADIABLE
AABDEILT LABIATED
AABEILRS RAISABLE
AACEILNS CANALISE
AACEILNU ACAULINE
AADEFILR FAIRLEAD
AADEHILN NAILHEAD
AADEHILR RAILHEAD
AADEHIRS AIRHEADS
AADEILPR PRAEDIAL
AADEILPT LAPIDATE
AADEILTV VALIDATE
AADEIMRS MADEIRAS
AADEIPRS PARADISE
AAEILPST STAPELIA
AAEILRSV REAVAILS
AAEIMRSU URAEMIAS
ABEIILST SIBILATE
ACDEIILN ALCIDINE
ACDEIILT CILIATED

ACDEIINS SCIAENID
ACEIILNS SALICINE
ACEIISTU ACUITIES
ADEFIILN FINIALED
ADEFIILR AIRFIELD
ADEFIILT FILIATED
ADEIILPR PERIDIAL
ADEIILTV DILATIVE
ADEIILTY IDEALITY
ADEIIMRS SEMIARID
ADEIIPRS PRESIDIA
ADEIITUV AUDITIVE
AEFIILNS FINALISE
AEIILMRS RAMILIES
AEIILRSV VIRELAIS
AEIILSTV VITALISE
AEEGINRZ RAZEEING
AADINNOT ADNATION
AADIORRT RADIATOR
AAILNNOT NATIONAL
AAINNOST SONATINA
AAINORRS ROSARIAN
AIIORRST SARTORII
DEELNOSU ENSOULED
AIJNORST JANITORS
ADIINNOT NIDATION
AIINOSTT OSTINATI
ENNORSTU NEUTRONS
AADDEIRT RADIATED
AAEILLNT ALLANITE
AAEILLRT ARILLATE
AAEINSST ENTASIAS
AEIINRSS AIRINESS
AEIIRSST SATIRISE
AABENRTU ARBUTEAN
AACENRST CATERANS
AAEHLNRT ANTHERAL
AAELMNRT MATERNAL
AAEMNRST SARMENTA
BEIINRST BRINIEST
CEIINRTU NEURITIC
DEIIMNRT DIRIMENT
DEIINPRT INTREPID
EFIILNRT FLINTIER
EHIINRST INHERITS

EIINPRST PRISTINE
ABEEENRT TENEBRAE
AEIOOPTT PATOOTIE
ABDELNOU UNDOABLE
ABDELORU LABOURED
ABELORSU RUBEOLAS
ABELOSTU ABSOLUTE
ACDELNOS CELADONS
ACDEORSU CAROUSED
ACELNOSU LACUNOSE
ACELORSU CAROUSEL
ADELMORS EARLDOMS
ADELMOTU MODULATE
ADELOPRU POULARDE
ADELOPST TADPOLES
ADELOSTV SOLVATED
ADELOTUV OVULATED
ADELOTUW OUTLAWED
ADEOPRSU UPSOARED
ADEORSUV SAVOURED
AELMNOSU MELANOUS
AELMORSU RAMULOSE
AELNOPSU APOLUNES
AELOSTUV OVULATES
AELOSTUY AUTOLYSE
BDEINOSU BEDOUINS
BEILNOSU NUBILOSE
BEILORSU BLOUSIER
CDEILNOS INCLOSED
CDEILORS SCLEROID
CDEILORU CLOUDIER
DEFILNOU UNFOILED
DEFILORU FLUORIDE
DEFILOTU OUTFIELD
DEHIOSTU HIDEOUTS
DEILOPRS LEPORIDS
DEILOPST PISTOLED
DEILORSY SOLDIERY
DEILOTUV OUTLIVED
DEILOTUW OUTWILED
DEILOTUY OUTYIELD
DEIMORSU DIMEROUS
DEINOPSU UNPOISED
DEIOSTUW WIDEOUTS
EFILOSTU OUTFLIES

EILMNOSU EMULSION
EILMOSTU OUTSMILE
EILNOSUV EVULSION
EILOPRSU PERILOUS
EILORSUV RIVULOSE
EILOSTUV OUTLIVES
EILOSTUW OUTWILES
ADILNRSU DIURNALS
EENNOORT ROTENONE
ACEGINNO CANOEING
ACEGIOTT COGITATE
AEGIMNNO NONIMAGE
AEGIMORR ARMIGERO
AEGIOPRR PROGERIA
AEINNRRS INSNARER
AEINNSTT STANNITE
AABILNOR BARONIAL
AABILNOT ABLATION
AABINORS ABRASION
AABIORST AIRBOATS
AACINORS OCARINAS
AADHINOT ANTHODIA
AADIMNOR RADIOMAN
AADIMNOT MANATOID
AADINOPR PARANOID
AADINOPT ADAPTION
AAHILNOT HALATION
AAILNOPT TALAPOIN
AAILNOTV LAVATION
AAIORSTV AVIATORS
ABDIIORT ORIBATID
ABIILNOT LIBATION
ACIILNOR IRONICAL
ACIIORST AORISTIC
ADDEORTU OUTDARED
AENOSSTU SOUTANES
AIIORSTV OVARITIS
DDEINORS INDORSED
DEILLORT TROLLIED
DEIORSST STEROIDS
EILLNOTU LUTEOLIN
EILLORST TROLLIES
EILORSST ESTRIOLS
EEGNNORT ROENTGEN
BENORSTU BURSTONE

DEFNORTU FORTUNED
DEMNORST MORDENTS
DENORSTY DRYSTONE
DENORTUW UNDERTOW
EFNORSTU FORTUNES
EHNORSTU SOUTHERN
ENORSTUY TOURNEYS
EENOORTV OVERTONE
ADEEGHOR GHERAOED
ADEEGORV OVERAGED
AEEGHLOT HELOTAGE
AEEGHORS GHERAOES
AEEGNOPS PEONAGES
AEEGORSV OVERAGES
CDEEGINO GENOCIDE
CDEEGIOT GEODETIC
CEEGILOT ECLOGITE
EEGINOPS EPIGONES
ADEELNTT TALENTED
ADEELRRT TREADLER
ADEENNRS ENSNARED
ADEENNRU UNEARNED
ADEENTTU TAUTENED
AEELRRTU URETERAL
AEELRSTT ALERTEST
DEEILNTT ENTITLED
DEEIRRST DESTRIER
DEEIRSTT TIREDEST
EEILNNST SENTINEL
EEILNSTT ENTITLES
EEILRSTT RETITLES
EEINNRSU NEURINES
EEINRRSU REINSURE
BEEIMORT BIOMETER
AELORSST OLESTRAS
AEORSSTU OSSATURE
ADEEILMS LIMEADES
ADEEILPS PLEIADES
ABDEINNR ENDBRAIN
ABEILRTT TITRABLE
ABEINNRU INURBANE
ABEINTTU INTUBATE
ABEIRSTT BIRETTAS
ACDEINNR CRANNIED
ACDEINNT INCANTED

Bob's Bible Bonus: Top 8s Single Anagram Quiz

ACDEINTT NICTATED
ACEILRTT TRACTILE
ACEINNTU UNCINATE
ACEINRRU CURARINE
ACEINTTU TUNICATE
ACEIRRST ERRATICS
ACEIRTTU URTICATE
ADEFINRR INFRARED
ADEFIRRT DRAFTIER
ADEHIRRT TRIHEDRA
ADEIMRTT ADMITTER
ADEINNPT PINNATED
ADEIRRTW TAWDRIER
AEFILNNR INFERNAL
AEFILNTT ANTILEFT
AEFILRTT FILTRATE
AEFINNST INFANTES
AEFINRRS REFRAINS
AEFINRRU UNFAIRER
AEFINSTT FAINTEST
AEHINSTT HESITANT
AEHIRRST TRASHIER
AEILMRTT REMITTAL
AEILNNTY INNATELY
AEILNPTT TINPLATE
AEILRRTY LITERARY
AEIMNNRS REINSMAN
AEIMNNST MANNITES
AEIMNRRS MARINERS
AEINNPRS PANNIERS
AEINPRRU UNREPAIR
AEINPSTT PATIENTS
AEINRRUW UNWARIER
AEINSTTW TAWNIEST
AEIPRRST PARTIERS
AEIRRSTW STRAWIER
AEIRSTTW WARTIEST
DEEILNRR REDLINER
AAEIKLNT ANTILEAK
AEIIKNRS KAISERIN
AEIIKNST KAINITES
AEIILNTZ LATINIZE
AEIINSTZ SANITIZE
AEIIRSTX SEXTARII
AEIIRSTZ SATIRIZE

AINORRTT NITRATOR
ADDEEILN DEADLINE
ADDEEILT DETAILED
ADDEEINU UNIDEAED
ADDEEIST STEADIED
ADEEINSS ANISEEDS
ADEEISST STEADIES
AEEILLST LEALTIES
AEEILRSS REALISES
AEFGIORR FAIRGOER
DENOOSTU DUOTONES
DEOORSTU OUTDOERS
ACEGIMNO CAMEOING
ACEGINOY GYNOECIA
AEIJLOSU JALOUSIE
AADEGRST GRADATES
AADEGRTU GRADUATE
AAEGLNTU ANGULATE
AAEGLRST AGRESTAL
DEGIILNT DILIGENT
DEGIINST DINGIEST
DEGIIRST RIDGIEST
EGIILRTU GUILTIER
ABDEENRU UNBEARED
ABDEENST ABSENTED
ABEELNRS ENABLERS
ABEELNST NESTABLE
ABEELNTU TUNEABLE
ACDEELNR CALENDER
ACDEELNT LANCETED
ACDEELRT DECRETAL
ACDEENTU CUNEATED
ACEELNRU CERULEAN
ACEELNST CLEANEST
ACEELNTU NUCLEATE
ACEELRTU ULCERATE
ACEERSTU SECATEUR
ADEEFNRU UNFEARED
ADEEFNST FASTENED
ADEEFRST DRAFTEES
ADEEFRTU FEATURED
ADEEHLNR REHANDLE
ADEEHNST HASTENED
ADEEHNTU UNHEATED
ADEEHRST HEADREST

ADEELMNR ALDERMEN
ADEELMNT LAMENTED
ADEELMRT TRAMELED
ADEELNPT ENDPLATE
ADEELNRV LAVENDER
ADEELNTV LEVANTED
ADEELRTV TRAVELED
ADEENRSW ANSWERED
ADEENRSY YEARENDS
ADEENSTY ANDESYTE
ADEEPRTU DEPURATE
ADEERSTY ESTRAYED
AEEFLNRU FUNEREAL
AEEFLRST REFLATES
AEEFRSTU FEATURES
AEELMNST TALESMEN
AEELNPRS REPANELS
AEELNRSV ENSLAVER
AEELNRSW RENEWALS
AEELNRUV REVENUAL
AEELNTUV EVENTUAL
AEELRSTY EASTERLY
BDEEINRS INBREEDS
BEEILNRS BERLINES
CDEEILNT DENTICLE
CDEEILRT DERELICT
CDEEINRU REINDUCE
CDEEINTU INDUCTEE
CDEEIRTU DEUTERIC
CEEILNST CENTILES
CEEILRTU RETICULE
DEEFILRT FILTERED
DEEFINRS DEFINERS
DEEFINST INFESTED
DEEFIRST RESIFTED
DEEHINRS RESHINED
DEEHIRST DIETHERS
DEEIMNST SEDIMENT
DEEINSTV INVESTED
DEEINTUV DUVETINE
DEEIRSTW WEIRDEST
EEFINRSU REINFUSE
EEHILNST THEELINS
EEILNPRS PILSENER
EEILNPRU PERILUNE

EEILNSTV VEINLETS
EEILNTUV VEINULET
EEIMRSTU EMERITUS
EEINRSUV UNIVERSE
ADEEEGNR RENEGADE
ADEEEGNT TEENAGED
EEEGILRT GLEETIER
DEIIOSTT OTITIDES
EIINNOSU UNIONISE
ADEFOSTU FADEOUTS
AELMOSTU SOULMATE
EHILORSU HOURLIES
AAGILOST OTALGIAS
ADGIILNO GONIDIAL
AGIILORU OLIGURIA
DDEEINRT DENDRITE
EEINRSST SENTRIES
AAEFIILR FILARIAE
AAEIIPRS APIARIES
AAEIIRSV AVIARIES
ACINORRT CARROTIN
ACINORTT TRACTION
AINNOPRT ANTIPORN
AEGIMOOS OOGAMIES
ADENORUX RONDEAUX
ADEORSTX EXTRADOS
DEIJNORS JOINDERS
DEIKORST DORKIEST
EINOQSTU QUESTION
ACEEGOST ECOTAGES
DEGNORSU GUERDONS
EGLNORSU LOUNGERS
AEHINRRU UNHAIRER
AEILRTTY ALTERITY
ABCEINST CABINETS
ABCEINTU INCUBATE
ABDEIPRT BIPARTED
ABDEIRTV VIBRATED
ABEHILNR HIBERNAL
ABEHINRS BANISHER
ABEHINST ABSINTHE
ABEILMNT BAILMENT
ABEILNTV BIVALENT
ABEILNTY BINATELY
ABEILPRT PARTIBLE

ABEILRTW WRITABLE
ABEIMNST AMBIENTS
ABEIMRST BARMIEST
ABEINPST BEPAINTS
ABEIRSTV VIBRATES
ACDEHINR INARCHED
ACDEHIRT TRACHEID
ACDEIMRT TIMECARD
ACDEINPT PEDANTIC
ACDEIPRT PICRATED
ACEFINRS FANCIERS
ACEFINST FANCIEST
ACEHILNT ETHNICAL
ACEILMRT METRICAL
ACEILRTV VERTICAL
ACEILRTY LITERACY
ACEIMNRU MANICURE
ACEIMNTU NEUMATIC
ACEIMRTU MURICATE
ACEINSTV VESICANT
ACEINSTY CYANITES
ACEIRTUV CURATIVE
ADEFINPR PANFRIED
ADEIMNRY DAIRYMEN
ADEIMNTY DYNAMITE
ADEINRVY VINEYARD
AEFILMNT FILAMENT
AEFIMNST MANIFEST
AEFINSTW FAWNIEST
AEHIMNRS HARMINES
AEHIMNST HEMATINS
AEHINPST THESPIAN
AEHINSTW INSWATHE
AEHIPRST TRIPHASE
AEHIRSTW WATERISH
AEHIRSTY HYSTERIA
AEILNPTY PENALITY
AEILPRTV LIVETRAP
AEILRTWY WATERILY
AEIMNRSY SEMINARY
AEIMPRST PRIMATES
AEIMPRTU APTERIUM
AEIMRSTV VITAMERS
AEIMRSTW WARTIMES
AEINPSTY EPINASTY

AEIPRSTV PRIVATES
AEIPRSTW WIRETAPS
AEIPRSTY ASPERITY
AEIRSTVY VESTIARY
AAGNORTU ARGONAUT
GIINORST IGNITORS
EGIILRST GIRLIEST
AABDELOR ADORABLE
AABDEORS SEABOARD
AABELNOS ABALONES
AACDEOTU AUTOCADE
AACELORS ACEROLAS
AACELOST CATALOES
AACEORSU ARACEOUS
AADEMNOS ADENOMAS
AAELMOST OATMEALS
AAELOPRS PSORALEA
CDEIILNO INDOCILE
CDEIILOT IDIOLECT
CDEIINOS DECISION
DEFIILNO DIOLEFIN
DEIIMNOS DOMINIES
DEIINOSV VISIONED
DEIIOPRS PRESIDIO
EIILNOSV OLIVINES
AEFGOORT FOOTGEAR
CEGINOOR OROGENIC
ADEGILNN LADENING
AEGILNNU UNGENIAL
AEGIRRSU SUGARIER
AADILNRS LANIARDS
AADILRST DIASTRAL
ADEEIJST JADEITES
ADEEILRZ REALIZED
AEEIKLST LEAKIEST
AEEILNSX ALEXINES
AEEIQRSU QUEASIER
AEEIQSTU EQUISETA
AEEISTUX EUTAXIES
AAEORSST AEROSATS
AAIINOTV AVIATION
ADEEMNST STAMENED
AEEMNRSU USERNAME
BDEEINST BENDIEST
DEEINPRS SPENDIER

DEEINRSV INVERSED
AAEIQRTU TAQUERIA
ADINNOOT DONATION
ADINOOTT DOTATION
AILNNOOT NOTIONAL
AINOOSTT OSTINATO
AEIIRRTT IRRITATE
ACFINORT FRACTION
ACHINORT ANORTHIC
ACIMNORT ROMANTIC
ACINORTY CARYOTIN
AIMNOPRT PROTAMIN
AIMNORTY MINATORY
AINORTVY VANITORY
AEEGLNSU EUGLENAS
AEEGLRSU LEAGUERS
DEEGILNS SEEDLING
DEEGILST LEDGIEST
DEGINNRT TRENDING
EGINRSTT GITTERNS
EGINRTTU UTTERING
ADLNOSTU OUTLANDS
DILORSTU DILUTORS
AEEJNRST SERJEANT
AEELNRTX EXTERNAL
DEEIKNRT TINKERED
DEEINRTX DEXTRINE
EEIJLNRT JETLINER
EEIKNRST KERNITES
EEINRSTX INTERSEX
AEORRSTT ROSTRATE
EILNNOTT NONTITLE
EIORRTTU TROUTIER
ADGINNOR ADORNING
ADGINNOT DONATING
AGILNOTT TOTALING
AGINOSTT TOASTING
AIILNRSU SILURIAN
AADEENTT ANTEDATE
AAEELNNR ANNEALER
AAEERSTT STEARATE
EEIINSTT ENTITIES
AAEFINNT FAINEANT
AAEHIRTT HATTERIA
AAEIMRTT AMARETTI

AAEINPTT PATINATE
AAEINRRW RAINWEAR
AAEIRRTV VERATRIA
ABEIINRR BRAINIER
ACEIIRRT CRITERIA
AEFIIRRT RATIFIER
AEIIMNTT INTIMATE
ABDEGILN BLINDAGE
ABEGILNS SINGABLE
ACDEGINU GUIDANCE
ACDEGIRS DISGRACE
ACEGILST GESTICAL
ADEFGILN FINAGLED
ADEFGIRU ARGUFIED
ADEFGITU FATIGUED
ADEGHIRS HAGRIDES
ADEGILNY DELAYING
ADEGIMRS MISGRADE
ADEGINSW WINDAGES
AEFGILNS FINAGLES
AEFGIRSU ARGUFIES
AEFGISTU FATIGUES
AEGILMRS GREMIALS
AEGILMTU MULTIAGE
AEGILNSY YEALINGS
AEGILRSY GREASILY
ACILNOOT LOCATION
ADINOOPT ADOPTION
ADIOOPRT PAROTOID
AHILOORT LOTHARIO
AILMNOOR MONORAIL
AILMNOOT MOTIONAL
AILOOPRT TROOPIAL
AILOORTV VIOLATOR
AIMNOOST AMOTIONS
AINOOSTV OVATIONS
EIILOPRS LIRIOPES
AEGGINOS SEAGOING
AEGILLNR ALLERGIN
AEILLNNO LANOLINE
AEIORRSS ROSARIES
DEELORTT DOTTEREL
DEENORRS ENDORSER
DEEORRTU REROUTED
DEEORSTT TETRODES

EELORTTU ROULETTE
EENNORSU NEURONES
EEORRSTU REROUTES
EEORSTTU OUTSTEER
AACDEERT ACERATED
AACEELRT LACERATE
AACEENRS CESAREAN
AADEEMNT EMANATED
AAEEFRST RATAFEES
AAEEHRST HETAERAS
AAEELNPT PANETELA
AAEELRTV VALERATE
AAEEMRST AMREETAS
CDEEIINT INDICTEE
CDEEIIRT DIERETIC
CEEIINST NICETIES
DEEFIINT DEFINITE
EEFIINRS FINERIES
EEIILMRT TIMELIER
EEIILNTV LENITIVE
EEIIMNST ENMITIES
EEIINPRS PINERIES
EEIINRSV VINERIES
EEIINRSW WINERIES
EEIIRSTV VERITIES
ABDEELOS ALBEDOES
ADEELMOS SOMEDEAL
AEEHLOSU ALEHOUSE
BDEEILOS OBELISED
ABELNNOR BANNEROL
ABENNORS BARONNES
ABEORRTU TABOURER
ACDENNOR ORDNANCE
ACDENNOT CANTONED
ACDENORR RANCORED
ACDENOTT COATTEND
ACDEORRT REDACTOR
ADEHORTT THROATED
ADEMNNOR NORMANDE
ADEMORRT MORTARED
ADENNOTW WANTONED
ADENOPRR PARDONER
ADENORRW NARROWED
ADEOPRTT TETRAPOD
AEFLNNOT FONTANEL

AEHORSTT RHEOSTAT
AELMNNOT NONMETAL
AELNNOPT PENTANOL
AEMNNOST MONTANES
AEMNORRS RANSOMER
AEMORRST REARMOST
AEMORTTU TAUTOMER
AENNOPST PENTOSAN
AENNORSY ANNOYERS
AEOPRSTT PROSTATE
BEINNOST BONNIEST
BEIORRST ORBITERS
CEINNORU NEURONIC
CEINNOTU CONTINUE
CEINORRS RESORCIN
CEIORRTU COURTIER
CEIORSTT COTTIERS
CEIORTTU TOREUTIC
DEINNOPT ENDPOINT
DEIORRTW WORRITED
EFINNORS INFERNOS
EFINOSTT FISTNOTE
EFIORTTU REOUTFIT
EHIORRST HERITORS
EILOPRRT PORTLIER
EILOPRTT PLOTTIER
EILORTTY TOILETRY
EIMNNOST MENTIONS
EIMORSTT OMITTERS
EINNOPRU PREUNION
EINNORSV ENVIRONS
EINOPRRS PRISONER
EINOPSTT NEPOTIST
EIOPRSTT SPOTTIER
EIORTTUW OUTWRITE
AACEINNT ANTIACNE
AAEIPRTT PATRIATE
AEIIMNNT ANTIMINE
AEFGNRST ENGRAFTS
AEGLNRTW TWANGLER
AEGNPRST TREPANGS
AEGNRSTW TWANGERS
BEGILNRT TREBLING
CEGINRST CRESTING
CEGINRTU ERUCTING

EFGINRTU REFUTING
DEEGILNU EUGLENID
ACDEIMNT MEDICANT
AAENOQTU AQUATONE
DEIINORZ IRONIZED
DEIIORTX TRIOXIDE
EIIKLNOR IRONLIKE
EIILNORZ LIONIZER
AEIKNRTW KNITWEAR
AILNRTTU RUTILANT
AINNRSTU INSURANT
ADDEELOR RELOADED
AEELNOSS ENOLASES
DEEILLNO NIELLOED
ABDGINOR BOARDING
ABGILNOR LABORING
ABGILNOT BLOATING
ACGILNOR CAROLING
ACGILNOT LOCATING
ACGINORS ORGANICS
ACGIORST ORGASTIC
ADGHINOR HOARDING
ADGINOPT ADOPTING
ADGINOTY TOADYING
AFGILNOT FLOATING
AFGIORST ISOGRAFT
AGHILNOR LONGHAIR
AGHILNOT LOATHING
AGHINORS ORANGISH
AGILNOPR PAROLING
AGILNOTY ANTILOGY
AGIMNORS ORGANISM
AGIMNORU ORIGANUM
AGIMNOST ANTISMOG
AGINORSV SAVORING
AABCEINR CARABINE
AABCEIRT BACTERIA
AABEIMNR AMBERINA
AACEHIRT THERIACA
AACEINRV VARIANCE
AACEINTV CAVATINE
AACEIRTV VICARATE
AAEHINPT APHANITE
AAEIMNPR PEARMAIN
ABCEIIRT RABIETIC

Bob's Bible Bonus: Top 8s Single Anagram Quiz

Alphagram	Word
ACEFIIRT	ARTIFICE
ACEHIINT	ETHICIAN
ACEHIIRT	HIERATIC
ACEIINTV	INACTIVE
AEFIINRV	VINIFERA
AEFIIPRT	APERITIF
AEHIIMNT	THIAMINE
AEIIMNTV	VITAMINE
AEGGILOT	TALEGGIO
BDEEORST	BESTRODE
BDEEORTU	OUTBREED
BEENOSTU	TUBENOSE
BEEORSTU	TUBEROSE
CDEENORU	COENDURE
CDEENOTU	DUECENTO
CEENORSU	COENURES
DEEFLNOR	ENFOLDER
DEEFNOST	SOFTENED
DEELNORV	OVERLEND
DEELORTV	REVOLTED
DEELORTW	TROWELED
DEEMNOST	DEMETONS
DEEMORST	MODESTER
DEEMORTU	UDOMETER
DEENOPST	PENTODES
DEEOPRST	DOPESTER
DEEORTUV	DEVOUTER
EEFLNORU	FLUORENE
EEFLNOST	FELSTONE
EEHLORST	HOSTELER
EELMNORS	SOLEMNER
EELMORST	MOLESTER
EELORSTV	OVERLETS
EEORSTUV	OUTSERVE
ABINOOST	BONIATOS
AFILOORT	FAROLITO
ABCEILOS	SOCIABLE
ABDEILOV	VOIDABLE
ACDEILMO	MELODICA
ACEFILOS	FOCALISE
ACEILMOS	CAMISOLE
ACEILOSV	VOCALISE
ADEHILMO	HALIDOME
AEHILMOS	HEMIOLAS
AEILMOPS	EPISOMAL
AEILMOSW	WAILSOME
ABEIORSS	ISOBARES
ACEILLOR	ROCAILLE
ACEIORSS	SCARIOSE
ADDEIOPR	PARODIED
AEFILLOT	FELLATIO
AEILLOTV	VOLATILE
AEIMNOSS	ANEMOSIS
AEINOPSS	SENOPIAS
AEINOSSV	EVASIONS
AEIOPSST	SOAPIEST
AEIORSSV	SAVORIES
AADELSTU	ADULATES
DEIILSTU	UTILISED
AADEENPT	TAPENADE
ADEEELST	TEASELED
DEEEILNS	SELENIDE
EENORSST	ESTRONES
AELOORRS	ROSEOLAR
AADEGIRR	GERARDIA
AADEGITT	AGITATED
AAEGILTT	TAILGATE
AAEGISTT	AGITATES
ADEGIITT	DIGITATE
AEGIILNN	ALIENING
AEGIILRR	GLAIRIER
AEGIILTT	LITIGATE
AEENRRTT	RATTENER
EEINNRTT	RENITENT
ABEEILNN	BIENNALE
ABEEILRR	BLEARIER
ACEEIRRS	CREASIER
ADEEFIRR	RAREFIED
ADEEIMRR	DREAMIER
AEEFIRRS	RAREFIES
AEEHISTT	HESITATE
AEEILPRR	PEARLIER
AEEILTTV	LEVITATE
AEEIMNNS	ENAMINES
AEEIMRRS	SMEARIER
AEEIPSTT	PEATIEST
AEEISTTV	ESTIVATE
AGILNOOS	ISOGONAL
AEEGGINR	AGREEING
ABINRSTU	URBANIST
ACINRSTU	CURTAINS
ADFINRST	INDRAFTS
AFILNRTU	TRAINFUL
AHILNRST	INTHRALS
AINPRSTU	PURITANS
ABCELORT	BROCATEL
ABDEMNOR	BOARDMEN
ABDEMORT	BROMATED
ABDENORW	RAWBONED
ABDENORY	BONEYARD
ABDENOTW	DOWNBEAT
ABDEOPRT	PROBATED
ABELOPRT	PORTABLE
ABEMNOST	BOATSMEN
ABEMNOTU	UMBONATE
ABEMORST	BROMATES
ABENOSTY	BAYONETS
ABEOPRST	PROBATES
ABEORTUV	OUTBRAVE
ACDEFORT	FACTORED
ACDEHNOR	ANCHORED
ACDEHORT	CHORDATE
ACDEMNOR	ROMANCED
ACDEMORT	DEMOCRAT
ACDENOPR	ENDOCARP
ACDEORTV	CAVORTED
ACEFLNOR	FALCONER
ACEFORST	FORECAST
ACEHORST	THORACES
ACEHORTU	OUTREACH
ACELNOPT	CONEPATL
ACELNORV	NOVERCAL
ACELNOTV	COVALENT
ACELOPRT	PECTORAL
ACEMNORS	ROMANCES
ACENOSTV	CENTAVOS
ACEOPRST	POSTRACE
ACEOPRTU	OUTCAPER
ADEFHNOR	FOREHAND
ADEFNOPR	PROFANED
ADEHMNOT	METHADON
ADEHNOPR	ORPHANED
ADEHNOPT	PHONATED
ADEMNOPR	POMANDER
ADEMNOPT	TAMPONED
ADEMORTW	DAMEWORT
AEFHLNOT	HALFTONE
AEFLNOPT	PANTOFLE
AEFLORTW	FLEAWORT
AEFMNORS	FORAMENS
AEFNOPRS	PROFANES
AEFOPRST	FOREPAST
AEFORSTV	OVERFAST
AEFORSTW	SOFTWARE
AEFORSTY	FORESTAY
AEHLOPRT	PLETHORA
AEHMORST	TERAOHMS
AEHOPRST	PHORATES
AELMOPRT	TEMPORAL
AELNOPRV	OVERPLAN
AEMNOPRS	MANROPES
AEMNORSV	OVERMANS
AENOPRSY	PYRANOSE
AEOPRSTV	OVERPAST
AEORSTVY	OVERSTAY
BCEINORS	BICORNES
BCEINORU	BOUNCIER
BCEIORST	BISECTOR
BDEIMNOT	INTOMBED
BDEINORV	OVENBIRD
BEFINORS	BONFIRES
BEILMNOR	BROMELIN
BEIMNORS	BROMINES
BEINORSW	BROWNIES
BEINORSY	BRYONIES
BEIORSTY	SOBRIETY
CDEFINOR	CONFIDER
CDEIMORT	MORTICED
CDEINORV	CODRIVEN
CDEIOPRT	DEPICTOR
CEFILNOT	FLECTION
CEHILNOR	CHLORINE
CEHINORS	CHORINES
CEHINORU	UNHEROIC
CEILNOPR	REPLICON
CEILNOPT	LEPTONIC
CEILORTY	CRYOLITE
CEIMNOST	CENTIMOS
CEIMORST	MORTICES
CEINOPTU	UNPOETIC
CEINOSTY	CYTOSINE
CEIOPRTU	OUTPRICE
CEIORSTW	COWRITES
DEFIMNOR	INFORMED
DEHIOPRT	TROPHIED
DEHIORTY	THYREOID
DEIMNOPT	PIEDMONT
DEIMNOTW	DOWNTIME
DEIMOPRT	IMPORTED
DEINOPRY	PYRENOID
DEINORVW	OVERWIND
EFIMORST	SETIFORM
EHILNOPT	THOLEPIN
EHILOPRT	HELIPORT
EHILORTY	RHYOLITE
EHIMORST	ISOTHERM
EHIMORTU	MOUTHIER
EHINOPST	PHONIEST
EHIOPRST	TROPHIES
EHIORSTW	WORTHIES
EILMNOTY	MYLONITE
EILOPRTW	PILEWORT
EIMNOPRS	PROMINES
EIMNORSW	WINSOMER
EIMOPRST	IMPOSTER
EIMORSTV	VOMITERS
EIMORSTY	ISOMETRY
EINOPRSV	OVERSPIN
EINOSTVY	VENOSITY
AEILOTTZ	TOTALIZE
DEILOORR	DROOLIER
DEEELNRT	RELENTED
DEEENRTU	NEUTERED
DEELNOOS	LOOSENED
AEGIJLNR	JANGLIER
AEGIKLNT	GNATLIKE
AEGILNRX	RELAXING
AEGILNTX	EXALTING
AEGILNTZ	TEAZLING
AEGINQTU	EQUATING
AEGINSTZ	TZIGANES
AADEEGLR	LAAGERED
AADEEGLT	GALEATED
AAEEGLST	STEALAGE
EGINNOSU	ENGINOUS
EGIOSTTU	GOUTIEST
EGIINRRT	RETIRING
ABEENNRT	BANNERET
ABEENRRT	BANTERER
ABEENRTT	BATTENER
ACEENNRT	ENTRANCE
AEEFNRTT	FATTENER
AEEHNRTT	THREATEN
AEEMNNRT	REMANENT
AEENNRTV	REVENANT
AEENRRTV	TAVERNER
AEENRTTV	ANTEVERT
AEENRTTY	ENTREATY
CEEINNRT	INCENTER
CEEINRTT	RETICENT
EEHINNRT	INHERENT
EEHINRTT	THIRTEEN
EEINRRTV	INVERTER
EEINRRTW	WINTERER
AADLORST	LOADSTAR
DIILNOST	TOLIDINS
DIILORTU	UTILIDOR
GINOORST	ROOSTING
ACDELNOO	CANOODLE
ADEHLOOT	TOOLHEAD
ADELOORV	OVERLOAD
ADELOOTW	LATEWOOD
ADEMOOST	STOMODEA
AEFLOORS	SEAFLOOR
AELMOORS	SALEROOM
AEMOOSTU	AUTOSOME
BDEILOOR	BLOODIER
BDEINOOS	NOBODIES
CDEIOORS	CORODIES
DEILMOOT	DOLOMITE
DEIMOORS	MOIDORES
DEINOOPS	POISONED
DEIOORSW	WOODSIER
DEIOOSTW	WOODIEST
EILMOOST	TOILSOME
EILNOOSV	VIOLONES
EILOOPST	LOOPIEST
EILOOSTW	WOOLIEST
EILOOSTY	OTIOSELY
EIKNORTT	KNOTTIER
ADEEKORS	RESOAKED
EEIKLNOS	NOSELIKE
EEIKLORS	ROSELIKE
EEIKORSU	EUROKIES
EEILOSTZ	ZEOLITES
DEEMNORS	MODERNES
AABDEGIN	BADINAGE
AABDEGIR	BIGARADE
AABEGILN	GAINABLE
AABEGILT	AGITABLE
AACEGILN	ANGELICA
AACEGILT	GLACIATE
AADEGIRV	GRAVIDAE
AADEGITV	DIVAGATE
AAEGIMNS	MAGNESIA
AAEGINPS	PAGANISE
AAEGIRSV	VAGARIES
ADEGIIMN	IMAGINED
AEFGIIRS	GASIFIER
AEGIILMR	REMIGIAL
AEGIILTV	LIGATIVE
AEGIIMNS	IMAGINES
AEGIISTV	VESTIGIA
AAGINNOT	AGNATION
AAGIORTT	AGITATOR
AAENNOTT	ANNOTATE
AAEGGIOT	AGIOTAGE
ABDEEIPR	BEDIAPER
ABEEFILN	FINEABLE
ABEEFILT	FLEABITE
ABEEFIRS	FIREBASE
ABEEHILR	HIREABLE
ABEEILMN	MINEABLE
ABEEILNP	PLEBEIAN
ABEEILNV	ENVIABLE
ABEEILRW	BEWAILER
ABEEILTV	EVITABLE
ABEEIMRS	AMBERIES
ABEEIMST	BEAMIEST
ACDEEFIN	DEFIANCE
ACDEEHIN	ECHIDNAE
ACDEEINV	DEVIANCE
ACEEHILR	LEACHIER
ACEEIMRS	CASIMERE
ACEEINPS	SAPIENCE
ACEEIPST	SPECIATE
ACEEIRSW	WISEACRE
ACEEISTV	VESICATE
ADEEINVW	INWEAVED
AEEHILNP	ELAPHINE
AEEHIPRS	PHARISEE
AEEHIRSV	SHIVAREE
AEEHISTV	HEAVIEST
AEEILRVW	REVIEWAL
AEEINSVW	INWEAVES
EINOORSS	EROSIONS
EINOOSST	ISOTONES
EEGLNOSU	EUGENOLS
EGNNORST	RONTGENS
EGNORRST	STRONGER
ADDEGILO	DIALOGED
AEGILOSS	SOILAGES
AEIIINTT	INITIATE
AEIIIRRT	RETIARII
AGIKNORT	TROAKING
AELLNOOT	ATENOLOL
EENORSTX	EXTENSOR
CDENOORT	CREODONT
CENOORST	CORONETS
ADELRRTU	ULTRARED
ADELRSTT	STARTLED
AELNNRSU	UNLEARNS
AELNNSTU	ANNULETS
DEINNRSU	UNRINSED
DEINNSTU	DUNNITES
DEIRRSTU	STURDIER
DEIRSTTU	DETRITUS
EILNNSTU	UNSILENT
EILNSTTU	LUTENIST
EILRRSTU	SULTRIER
CEGIINRT	RECITING
EGIINRTV	RIVETING
CDEEIIOS	DIOECIES
AEEGMOOT	OOGAMETE
CEEGINOO	COOEEING
AABEORRT	ARBORETA
EFIINORR	INFERIOR
EHIINNOT	THIONINE
EIINOPTT	PETITION
GILNOORT	ROOTLING
ABCEENRT	CABERNET
ACEENPRT	PREENACT
AEEHMNRT	EARTHMEN
AEEMNPRT	PERMEANT
AEEMNRTV	AVERMENT
AEEMNRTW	WATERMEN
EEHIMNRT	THEREMIN
EEHINRTW	WHITENER
ADGILNRS	DARLINGS
AGILNRSU	SINGULAR
AGILNSTU	SALUTING
AEEINTTZ	TETANIZE
ABDEGLOT	GLOBATED
ACDEGNOS	DECAGONS
ACDEGORS	CORDAGES
ACEGLNOS	CONGEALS
ACEGORSU	COURAGES
ADEFGLOT	GATEFOLD
ADEGLNOP	ANGLEPOD
ADEGLORV	OVERGLAD
ADEGNOPU	POUNDAGE
ADEGNOSV	DOGVANES
AEFGLOST	FLOTAGES
AEGHLNOS	HALOGENS
AEGLMORS	GOMERALS
AEGLOPRS	PERGOLAS
AEGLORSV	VORLAGES
AEGLOSTV	VOLTAGES
BEGILORS	OBLIGERS
DEFGIORS	FIREDOGS
DEGHIORU	DOUGHIER
DEGILMNO	MODELING
DEGILNOW	DOWELING
DEGILNOY	YODELING
DEGILORV	OVERGILD
DEGINOPS	DEPOSING
DEGIOPST	PODGIEST
EGHIOSTU	TOUGHIES
EGILMORS	GOMERILS
EGILNOSW	LONGWISE
EGINOPSU	EPIGONUS
EGIORSUV	GRIEVOUS
EGIOSTUV	OUTGIVES
AILNNOSU	UNISONAL
AACGINOT	CONTAGIA
AAGIORTV	AVIGATOR
AEGORSST	STORAGES
AEGORTUU	OUTARGUE
AGIIMNOR	IGNORAMI
AGIINOPT	OPIATING
EGINORSS	GORINESS
ABEIJLNO	JOINABLE
ABEIKLOT	BOATLIKE
ACEILORZ	CALORIZE
ADEIMOTZ	ATOMIZED
AEHILOTZ	THIAZOLE
AEIKLMOT	MOATLIKE
AEIKLNOV	NOVALIKE
AEILMORZ	MORALIZE
AEILOPRZ	POLARIZE
AEILORVZ	VALORIZE
AEIMNOUX	EXONUMIA
AEIMOSTX	TOXEMIAS
AEIMOSTZ	ATOMIZES
AEILMOSV	SEMIOVAL
ABDEILSU	AUDIBLES
ADEILSUV	DISVALUE
AACEILOP	ALOPECIA
AEHIILMO	HEMIOLIA
ADEILLNU	UNALLIED
AEILNSSU	INULASES
ADEHLOOR	HORDEOLA
ADEEGNNR	ENDANGER
ADEEGRTT	TARGETED
AEEGLNNT	ENTANGLE
AEEGLNRR	ENLARGER
AEEGNSTT	TENTAGES
AEEGRRST	REGRATES
AEEGRSTT	GREATEST
DEEGINRR	DERINGER
EEGILNRR	LINGERER
EEGINNRS	SNEERING
EEGINRRS	RESIGNER
EEGIRRST	REGISTER
BEGNORTU	BURGONET
DEGHNORT	THRONGED
EGNORSTW	WRONGEST
AEFLNOPR	FLAPERON
AEFLOPRT	TERAFLOP
AELNOPTW	TOWPLANE
DEHIORTW	WITHEROD
EILNOPTY	LINOTYPE
EGILOOSU	ISOLOGUE
CEIJNORT	INJECTOR
AEGIILMN	EMAILING
ABDELNST	BLANDEST
ACDELNRS	CANDLERS
ACDENRSU	DURANCES
ACDERSTU	TRADUCES
ACELNRSU	LUCARNES
ADEFLNTU	FLAUNTED
ADEHLNRS	HANDLERS
ADEHLNST	SHETLAND
ADEHNRSU	UNSHARED
ADELMNRS	MANDRELS
ADELNPRS	SPANDREL
ADELNRUY	UNDERLAY
ADELNSTW	WETLANDS
ADELPRTU	PREADULT
ADELRTUY	ADULTERY
ADENPRSU	UNDRAPES
ADENSTUW	UNWASTED
AEFLRSTU	REFUTALS
AELMRSTU	STAUMREL
AELNRSUV	UNRAVELS
BDEILNRU	UNBRIDLE
BDEILNST	BLINDEST
BEILNSTU	BUSTLINE
CDEINRSU	INDUCERS
DEFILNRS	FLINDERS
DEFILNRU	UNRIFLED
DEFINSTU	UNSIFTED
DEILNPRS	SPINDLER
DEILNPRU	UNDERLIP
DEILNPST	SPLINTED
DEILNRSW	SWINDLER
DEILNTUY	UNITEDLY
DEIMNSTU	MISTUNED
DEIMRSTU	DIESTRUM
EHILRSTU	LUTHIERS
EILNPRSU	PURLINES
EILRSTUV	RIVULETS
AEEGILSW	WEIGELAS
AACEORTV	CAVEATOR
AAEHMORT	ATHEROMA

Bob's Bible Bonus: Top 8s Single Anagram Quiz

CEIINOPR PECORINI
CEIINOTV EVICTION
CEIIOPRT PERIOTIC
EIIMNOPT PIMIENTO
EIIMNOTV MONITIVE
ABEGINTT ABETTING
ACEGINNR RECANING
ACEGINNT ENACTING
AEGHINNT NAETHING
AEGHINTT GNATHITE
AEGIMNNR RENAMING
AEGIMNRR REARMING
AEGINNRV RAVENING
AEGINNRY YEARNING
AEGINRRV AVERRING
ADENOOTZ OZONATED
AELNOOTZ ENTOZOAL
AELOORTZ ZOOLATER
AENOOSTZ OZONATES
EIKLOORT ROOTLIKE
EIKOORST ROOKIEST
EINOORSZ SNOOZIER
AABILNRT BRANTAIL
AABINRST BARTISAN
AADIMNRT TAMARIND
AADINRTY INTRADAY
AAINRSTV VARIANTS
AAINRSTY SANITARY
ACIINRTU URANITIC
ADENRSST STANDERS
AELNRSST SALTERNS
AIINRSTV VITRAINS
DDEILNRT TRINDLED
DDEINRST STRIDDEN
DDEINRTU INTRUDED
AACEEINN ENCAENIA
ABDILORS LABROIDS
ABDILOST TABLOIDS
ACDILORS CORDIALS
ACILNOSU UNSOCIAL
ADILMNOS SALMONID
ADILORSY SOLIDARY
ADILOSTY SODALITY
AILMNOSU LAMINOUS
AILMORSU SOLARIUM

AILMOSTU SOLATIUM
AILNOSUV AVULSION
ACEEFILR LIFECARE
AEEFILMN FILENAME
DEGNOOST STEGODON
ADDINORS ANDROIDS
ADINORSS SADIRONS
ADIORSST SARODIST
AILLNOST STALLION
AILORSST ORALISTS
AIORSSTU SAUTOIRS
AEEIKRTW TWEAKIER
AEEIMNRX EXAMINER
EENORRTT ROTTENER
EGIILNNO ELOINING
ABEEGRST ABSTERGE
ADEEGHNR REHANGED
ADEEGHRT GATHERED
ADEEGMNR GENDARME
ADEEGNRV ENGRAVED
ADEEGPRT PARGETED
AEEGHNRS SHAGREEN
AEEGHNST THENAGES
AEEGLMRT TELEGRAM
AEEGMRST GAMESTER
AEEGNSTV VENTAGES
BEEGILNT BEETLING
BEEGINRS REBEGINS
BEEGINST BEIGNETS
CDEEGINR RECEDING
CEEGILNR CREELING
CEEGILNT ELECTING
CEEGINRS GENERICS
CEEGINST GENETICS
DEEFGINR FINGERED
DEEFGIRT FIDGETER
DEEGHINR REHINGED
DEEGINRY REDYEING
EEFGILNR FLEERING
EEFGILNT FLEETING
EEFGINRS FEIGNERS
EEGILRTY LEGERITY
EEGIMNRS REGIMENS
EEGIMNRU MERINGUE
EEGIMNST MEETINGS

EEGIMRST GERMIEST
EEGINPRS SPEERING
EEGINPRU PUREEING
EEGINPST STEEPING
EEGINRSV SEVERING
EEGINSTV STEEVING
EEGINSTW SWEETING
EEGIPRST PRESTIGE
DEEIINOZ DEIONIZE
AEELMOTT MATELOTE
AEELOPTT TOEPLATE
AEEMNNOS ANEMONES
CEEILORR RECOILER
DEEIORRV OVERRIDE
EEILMNNO LIMONENE
EEIMNNOS NOMINEES
EEINNOPS PENSIONE
EEIOPRRS ROPERIES
ADEGIKLO GOADLIKE
ACLNORTU CALUTRON
ACNORSTU COURANTS
ADMNORST MORDANTS
ADNORSTW SANDWORT
ADNORSTY TARDYONS
AFLNORST FRONTALS
AHLNORST ALTHORNS
ALNOPRST PLASTRON
AMNORSTU ROMAUNTS
CDINORTU INDUCTOR
CINORSTU RUCTIONS
ILNORSTY NITROSYL
AACEEFIT FACETIAE
AACEEIMT EMACIATE
ADEGMORS ORGASMED
AEGLMOTU OUTGLEAM
EGHIORSU ROUGHIES
ACEIMNNO MONECIAN
AEFIMORR AERIFORM
AEHIOPTT THIOTEPA
AEIMOTTV MOTIVATE
AEINNOPV PAVONINE
AEIOPRRW AIRPOWER
AEIOPTTV OPTATIVE
ADEGJNOR JARGONED
AEGJLNOR JARGONEL

DEGINOTX DETOXING
CEENNORT CRETONNE
CEENORTT TRECENTO
EEHNNORT ENTHRONE
EENOPRTT ENTREPOT
ABEGIMNR BREAMING
ABEGINRW BEWARING
ACEFGINR REFACING
ACEFGINT FACETING
ACEGHINR REACHING
ACEGIMNT MAGNETIC
ACEGINPR CAPERING
AEFGHINR HANGFIRE
AEFGINRW WAFERING
AEFGIRTW GIFTWARE
AEGHINRV HAVERING
AEGHIPRT GRAPHITE
AEGINPRV REPAVING
AEGINPRY REPAYING
AEGINPTY EGYPTIAN
AEGINRVW WAVERING
AEGINRVY VINEGARY
AEGINRWY WEARYING
AEGIPRTY PTERYGIA
EINNNORT NONINERT
ADEIKLNS SANDLIKE
ADEILQTU LIQUATED
ADEIQRSU QUERIDAS
ADEISTUZ DEUTZIAS
AEILNQSU QUINELAS
DEGILNSU INDULGES
EEEINRRS SNEERIER
DEGLNOOT GOLDTONE
AABEINOZ ZABAIONE
AAEIMNOX ANOXEMIA
AAEIMOTX TOXAEMIA
AAEIMOTZ AZOTEMIA
AADENNST ANDANTES
AAELNNTU ANNULATE
AAELNSTT ATLANTES
AAENNSTU NAUSEANT
DEIILNTT INTITLED
DEIINTTU INTUITED
DEIIRSTT DIRTIEST
EIILNTTU INTITULE

ABEELOTT TOTEABLE
AABEGOST SABOTAGE
AAEFGLOT FLOATAGE
AAEGMORS SAGAMORE
CEGIINOS ISOGENIC
CEGIIOST EGOISTIC
EGIIOPRS PIROGIES
ADLNOORS LARDOONS
ILNOOSTU SOLUTION
AADGINRU GUARDIAN
AAGINRSU GUARANIS
ADGIILNT DILATING
ADGIINTU AUDITING
AGIILNRS RAILINGS
AGIILNST TAILINGS
AABEHNOR HABANERO
AACEHNOR ARCHAEON
ABCDEENO BEACONED
ABDEEHNO BONEHEAD
ABDEEMNO BEMOANED
ABEEHORS RHEOBASE
ABEELMNO BONEMEAL
ABEELOPR OPERABLE
ABEELORV OVERABLE
ABEELOTV VOTEABLE
ACEEMORS RACEMOSE
ADEEFHOR FOREHEAD
ADEEFMOR DEFOAMER
ADEEFOTV FOVEATED
ADEEHORV OVERHEAD
ADEENOPW WEAPONED
AEEFLORV OVERLEAF
AEEFMORS FEARSOME
AEELOPRV OVERLEAP
AEEORSVW OVERAWES
AEEORSVY OVEREASY
BDEEIMOR EMBODIER
BEEIORSW BOWERIES
CDEEIMOR MEDIOCRE
CDEEIOPR RECOPIED
CEEHIORS CHEERIOS
CEEILMOR COMELIER
CEEILNOV VIOLENCE
CEEINOPU EUPNOEIC
CEEIOPRS RECOPIES

CEEIOPST PICOTEES
CEEIORSV REVOICES
DEEIORVW OVERWIDE
EEHILMOR HOMELIER
EEHIMOST HOMESITE
EEILMNOP PEMOLINE
EEIORSVW OVERWISE
ADEEENNT NEATENED
ADEEENRR REEARNED
AEEERRST ARRESTEE
DEEEINRR REINDEER
EEEINSTT TEENIEST
EEEIRRST RETIREES
ABDENSTU UNBASTED
AACDEILS ALCAIDES
AADEHILS HEADSAIL
AADEILMS MALADIES
AADEILPS PALISADE
AADEILSV VEDALIAS
AADEIPSU DIAPAUSE
ACDEIILS LAICISED
ADEFIILS SALIFIED
AADILORR RAILROAD
AAILORRS RASORIAL
EIILRSTT SLITTIER
ADENRSTX DEXTRANS
ADENRTUX UNDERTAX
DEINRSTX DEXTRINS
EIKLNRST TINKLERS
EINQRSTU SQUINTER
ADEEGINZ AGENIZED
AEEGIKLT GATELIKE
AEEGINSZ AGENIZES
DEGLNRTU GRUNTLED
DEGNRSTU TRUDGENS
EGLNRSTU GRUNTLES
DELORSTT DOTTRELS
DENNOSTU UNSTONED
AFILNOSU FUSIONAL
AADEISST DIASTASE
AAEILNSS NASALISE
AAIINNRT ANTIARIN
ADIJNOST ADJOINTS
ADINOSTX OXIDANTS
AILNOTUX LUXATION

EGIORRTT GROTTIER
BEENORTV VERBOTEN
CEEHNORT COHERENT
EEFMNORT FOMENTER
EEFNORTW FOREWENT
ADGLNORS GOLDARNS
ADGORSTU OUTDRAGS
AGLNORSU LANGUORS
DGILNORS LORDINGS
GILNOSTU TOUSLING
ABEEENST ABSENTEE
ACDEEENR CAREENED
ACDEEENT ANTECEDE
ADEEEHRT REHEATED
ADEEEMNT EMENDATE
ADEEEMRT RETEAMED
AEEEHLRT ETHEREAL
AEEELMNR ENAMELER
AEEELNRV VENEREAL
AEEEMNST EASEMENT
BEEEIRST BEERIEST
CEEEILRT ERECTILE
DEEEFINR REDEFINE
DEEEINTV EVENTIDE
DEEEIRTW TWEEDIER
EEEFIRST REEFIEST
EEEHINRS SHEENIER
EEEILNPR PELERINE
EEEILNRY EYELINER
EEEIMNRU MEUNIERE
EEEIMNST EMETINES
EEEIMRST EREMITES
EEEINRSV VENERIES
EEEINRSW WEENSIER
EEIJNNOR ENJOINER
EEIORRTX EXTERIOR
AAAENOPR PARANOEA
AABDELRT TRADABLE
AABDENTU UNABATED
AACDELNR CALENDAR
AACDENTU ADUNCATE
AACDERTU ARCUATED
AACELNST ANALECTS
AADELMNR ALDERMAN
AADEMNST MANDATES

AADENRSV VERANDAS
AADENSTY ASYNDETA
AAEHLRST TREHALAS
AAEHRSTU ARETHUSA
AAELMNST TALESMAN
AAELNRSY ANALYSER
AAELPRST PALESTRA
AAEMNSTU MANTEAUS
AAEMRSTU AMATEURS
AAENRSUW UNAWARES
BEIILNRS RINSIBLE
BEIILRST TRILBIES
CDEIIRTU DIURETIC
CEIINSTU CUTINISE
DEFIINTU FINITUDE
DEHIIRST DISHERIT
DEIIMNTU MUTINIED
DEIINPRS INSPIRED
DEIINPTU UNPITIED
DEIINRSV DIVINERS
DEIINSTV DIVINEST
DEIINSTW WINDIEST
EFIILRST FILISTER
EFIINRSU UNIFIERS
EIILMRST LIMITERS
EIILNSTY SENILITY
EIILNTUV VITULINE
EIIMNSTU MUTINIES
EIIPRSTU PURITIES
AANORSTT ARNATTOS
IINORSTT INTROITS
ACEOORTT COROTATE
AEMOORTT AMORETTO
AEOOPRRT OPERATOR
EHIOORTT TOOTHIER
EIMNNOOT NOONTIME
EEGINRTX EXERTING
AEEGIILW WEIGELIA
ABLNORST LASTBORN
DEILMOSU EMULSOID
DEILOPSU EUPLOIDS
DDEIINRT NITRIDED
ABCEFINO BONIFACE
ABEHIMNO BOHEMIAN
ABEHIORV BEHAVIOR

ACEHIOPR POACHIER
ACEIMOPR COPREMIA
AABILOST SAILBOAT
AABINOSU OUABAINS
AACDILNO DIACONAL
AACDIOTU AUTACOID
AADIMORS DIORAMAS
AADINOPS DIAPASON
AADIOPRS DIASPORA
AAILNOSV VALONIAS
AAILORSV VARIOLAS
ABDIINOS OBSIDIAN
ACDIILNO CONIDIAL
ADELORSS ROADLESS
ADELOSST TOADLESS
AELORSUU ROULEAUS
AFIILORS AIRFOILS
AIILNOSV VISIONAL
AIILORSV RAVIOLIS
DDEILOST DELTOIDS
DEILLORU LOUDLIER
DEILORSS SOLDIERS
DEILOSST SOLIDEST
DEIORSSU DESIROUS
DEIOSSTU OUTSIDES
EILLORSU ROUILLES
EILNOSSU ELUSIONS
EILORSSU SOILURES
EILOSSTU LOUSIEST
ABGINOOR BIGAROON
ABGINOOT TABOOING
ABEEIKRT TIEBREAK
AEEIKMNT KETAMINE
ADDIINOT ADDITION
AIILLNOT ILLATION
AAENRSST SANTERAS
ABDEIMOO AMOEBOID
AEILMOOV MOVIEOLA
AEIMOOPS IPOMOEAS
BDEEOORT REBOOTED
CEENOOST ECOTONES
CEEOORST CREOSOTE
DEEFNOOR FOREDONE
DEEMOORT ODOMETER
DEENOORV OVERDONE

DEENOORW WOODENER
EEHNOORS HONOREES
EEOOPRST PROTEOSE
ADEELNNU UNANELED
AABEEGNT ABNEGATE
AACEEGNR CARAGEEN
AAEEGRTW WATERAGE
EEGIINTV GENITIVE
BDELNOST BLONDEST
BDELNOTU UNBOLTED
BDELORTU TROUBLED
BELORSTU TROUBLES
CDELORTU CLOTURED
CDENORSU CRUNODES
CDENOSTU CONTUSED
CDEORSTU EDUCTORS
CELNOSTU NOCTULES
DEFLNORS FONDLERS
DEFLNOST TENFOLDS
DEFLORST TELFORDS
DELNOPRS SPLENDOR
DELNOSTW LETDOWNS
DELOPRST DROPLETS
DENOPRSU POUNDERS
EFLORSTU FLOUTERS
ELMORSTU MOULTERS
ELNOPSTU PLEUSTON
ELOPRSTU POULTERS
AENNRSTT ENTRANTS
EINNRTTU NUTRIENT
ADEEGMOS MEGADOSE
AEEGLMOS MESOGLEA
BEEGILOS OBLIGEES
CDEEGIOS GEODESIC
EEGILMOS EGLOMISE
EEGILOPU EPILOGUE
EEGIOPSU EPIGEOUS
ACEGNNOR CRANNOGE
ACEGORTT COTTAGER
AEFGORTT FROTTAGE
AEGMNNOT MAGNETON
AEGMNORR RENOGRAM
AEGNNOPT PENTAGON
AEGNOPRR PARERGON
AEGNORRY ORANGERY

BEGINORR REBORING
CEGINNOR ENCORING
EGINNORV VIGNERON
EGIORRTV OVERGIRT
AADMNORT MANDATOR
AALMNORT MATRONAL
AALNOPRT PATRONAL
CDIINORT INDICTOR
CIILNORT NITROLIC
ENORSSTU TONSURES
FIINORTU FRUITION
IILMNORT MIRLITON
ADGINRTT DRATTING
AGILNRTT RATTLING
AGINRRST STARRING
AGINRSTT STARTING
ADDEEGOR DOGEARED
EEGINOSS GENOISES
ADIORRTT TRADITOR
AINNOTTU NUTATION
AIORRSTT TRAITORS
ABDEIRRS BRAIDERS
ABEILRRU REBURIAL
ACDEILTT LATTICED
ACDEISTT DICTATES
ACEILSTT LATTICES
ACEINNSU NUISANCE
ACEISTTU EUSTATIC
ADEILNNP PINELAND
ADEILRRW DRAWLIER
ADEILRRY DREARILY
ADEIPTTU APTITUDE
AEHILSTT LATHIEST
AEILNNPU PINNULAE
AEILNNSY INSANELY
AEILPRRS REPRISAL
AEILPSTT PLATIEST
AEIPRRSU UPRAISER
ABEFOORT BAREFOOT
ACEFOORT FOOTRACE
ACEMNOOR COENAMOR
AEFOORTW FOOTWEAR
AEMNOORY AERONOMY
CEINOOPR PECORINO
EIMNOORV OMNIVORE

Bob's Bible Bonus: Complete 7-letter Multi-Anagram Quiz

7-letter Words

AEINRST
ANESTRI ANTSIER NASTIER RATINES RETAINS RETINAS RETSINA STAINER STEARIN

AEGINST
EASTING EATINGS INGATES INGESTA SEATING TEASING

AEGINRS
EARINGS ERASING GAINERS REAGINS REGAINS REGINAS SEARING SERINGA

ADEIRST
ARIDEST ASTRIDE DIASTER DISRATE STAIDER TARDIES TIRADES

AEILNST
ELASTIN ENTAILS NAILSET SALIENT SALTINE SLAINTE TENAILS

EORSSTU
ESTROUS OESTRUS OUSTERS SOUREST SOUTERS STOURES TUSSORE

EIPRSST
ESPRITS PERSIST PRIESTS SPRIEST SPRITES STIRPES STRIPES

DEIORST
EDITORS SORTIED STEROID STORIED TRIODES

AEGIRST
AIGRETS GAITERS SEAGIRT STAGIER TRIAGES

AEIRSTT
ARTIEST ARTISTE ATTIRES IRATEST RATITES STRIATE TASTIER

AEIPRST
PARTIES PASTIER PIASTER PIASTRE PIRATES TRAIPSE

ADEERST
DEAREST DERATES REDATES SEDATER

ABEILST
ABLEIST ALBITES ASTILBE BASTILE BESTIAL BLASTIE STABILE

AEERSST
EASTERS RESEATS SEAREST SEATERS TEASERS TESSERA

EEIMPRS
EMPIRES EMPRISE EPIMERS IMPRESE PREMIES PREMISE SPIREME

ADEINST
DESTAIN DETAINS INSTEAD NIDATES SAINTED STAINED

ACEINRT
CERATIN CERTAIN CREATIN TACRINE

ADEGINR
DERAIGN GRADINE GRAINED READING

AEGILNR
ALIGNER ENGRAIL NARGILE REALIGN REGINAL

AEIMRST
IMARETS MAESTRI MISRATE SMARTIE

CEINORS
COINERS CRONIES ORCEINS RECOINS

ACENRST
CANTERS CARNETS NECTARS RECANTS SCANTER TANRECS TRANCES

AENPRST
ARPENTS ENTRAPS PARENTS PASTERN TREPANS

EIORSST
ROSIEST SORITES SORTIES STORIES TRIOSES

ADEILPS
ALIPEDS ELAPIDS LAPIDES PALSIED PLEIADS

DEGILRS
GILDERS GIRDLES GLIDERS REGILDS RIDGELS

EOPRSTU
PETROUS POSTURE POUTERS PROTEUS SPOUTER TROUPES

ACELPRS
CARPELS CLASPER PARCELS PLACERS RECLASP SCALPER

AEILNRT
LATRINE RATLINE RELIANT RETINAL TRENAIL

EINORST
NORITES OESTRIN ORIENTS STONIER

AEILRST
REALIST RETAILS SALTIER SALTIRE SLATIER TAILERS

DEINORS
DINEROS INDORSE ORDINES ROSINED SORDINE

AEINRTT
INTREAT ITERANT NATTIER NITRATE TERTIAN

EEINRST
ENTIRES ENTRIES RETINES TRIENES

AEIMNST
ETAMINS INMATES TAMEINS

EIOPRST
PROSTIE REPOSIT RIPOSTE ROPIEST

ACENORS
CANOERS COARSEN CORNEAS NARCOSE

ADELNRS
DARNELS LANDERS RELANDS SLANDER SNARLED

DEORSTU
DETOURS DOUREST REDOUTS ROUSTED

ABDEIRS
ABIDERS BRAISED DARBIES SEABIRD SIDEBAR

AEINSST
ENTASIS NASTIES SEITANS SESTINA TANSIES TISANES

ACELORS
CLAROES COALERS ESCOLAR ORACLES RECOALS SOLACER

DEIOPST
DEPOSIT DOPIEST PODITES POSITED SOPITED TOPSIDE

EEIRRST
RETIRES RETRIES TERRIES

ADEEMNR
AMENDER MEANDER REEDMAN RENAMED

EEIMRST
MEISTER METIERS REEMITS RETIMES TRISEME

AEEGLST
EAGLETS GELATES LEGATES SEGETAL TELEGAS

EILRSTT
LITTERS SLITTER TILTERS

ADEHRST
DEARTHS HARDEST HARDSET HATREDS THREADS TRASHED

AELPRST
PALTERS PERSALT PLASTER PLATERS PSALTER STAPLER

DEILOPS
DESPOIL DIPLOES DIPOLES SPOILED

AEIPRRS
ASPIRER PARRIES PRAISER RAPIERS RASPIER REPAIRS

ACEEHRT
CHEATER HECTARE RECHEAT RETEACH TEACHER

AEIMSST
MISEATS MISSEAT SAMITES TAMISES

ACDEILM
CAMELID CLAIMED DECIMAL DECLAIM MEDICAL

CEHORST
HECTORS ROCHETS ROTCHES TOCHERS TORCHES TROCHES

CEORSST
CORSETS COSTERS ESCORTS SCOTERS SECTORS

EOPRSST
POSTERS PRESTOS RESPOTS STOPERS

AEEPRSS
ASPERSE PARESES SERAPES

CEEPRST
RECEPTS RESPECT SCEPTER SCEPTRE SPECTER SPECTRE

ELRSSTU
LUSTERS LUSTRES RESULTS RUSTLES SUTLERS ULSTERS

AEHPRSS
PHRASES SERAPHS SHAPERS SHERPAS

AEGINRT
GRANITE GRATINE INGRATE TANGIER TEARING

AEGILNT
ATINGLE ELATING GELATIN GENITAL TAGLINE

EINOPRT
POINTER PROTEIN TROPINE

DEGINOR
ERODING GROINED IGNORED NEGROID REDOING

AELNRST
ANTLERS RENTALS SALTERN STERNAL

DEINRTU
INTRUDE TURDINE UNTIRED UNTRIED

ADEELRT
ALERTED ALTERED RELATED TREADLE

AEELRST
ELATERS REALEST RELATES RESLATE STEALER

DEEIRST
DIESTER DIETERS REEDITS RESITED

AEGILST
AIGLETS GELATIS LIGATES

ABEORST
BOASTER BOATERS BORATES REBATOS SORBATE

EGILNOS
ELOIGNS LEGIONS LINGOES LONGIES

AEGINNR
AGINNER EARNING ENGRAIN GRANNIE NEARING

AEGINRR
ANGRIER EARRING GRAINER RANGIER REARING

AEGIMNR
GERMINA MANGIER REAMING

ADEEGNR
ANGERED DERANGE ENRAGED GRANDEE GRENADE

DEEGINR
DREEING ENERGID REEDING REIGNED

ABDEILR
BEDRAIL BRAILED RIDABLE

ACEILST
ELASTIC LACIEST LATICES

ADEIMNS
MAIDENS MEDIANS MEDINAS SIDEMAN

ADEIMRS
ADMIRES MISREAD SEDARIM SIDEARM

AGINRST
GASTRIN GRATINS RATINGS STARING

EGILNST
GLISTEN SINGLET SNIGLET TINGLES

ACELOST
LACTOSE LOCATES TALCOSE

ADEMNOS
DAEMONS MASONED MONADES

ABDEERT
BERATED DEBATER REBATED TABERED

ACDEERT
CATERED CERATED CREATED REACTED

DEEIMRT
DEMERIT DIMETER MERITED MITERED RETIMED

EEINRSV
ENVIERS INVERSE VEINERS VENIRES VERSINE

EEIRSTV
RESTIVE SIEVERT VERIEST VERITES

EENOPRS
OPENERS PEREONS REOPENS

AGILNST
LASTING SALTING SLATING STALING

ADERRST
DARTERS RETARDS STARRED TRADERS

AELRSTT
RATTLES STARLET STARTLE

AENSTTU
ATTUNES NUTATES TAUTENS TETANUS UNSTATE

AEILRSS
AIRLESS RESAILS SAILERS SERAILS SERIALS

ABELRST
BLASTER LABRETS STABLER

ACELRST
CARTELS CLARETS CRESTAL SCARLET

AEHLRST
HALTERS HARSLET LATHERS SLATHER THALERS

EIMNSTU
MINUETS MINUTES MISTUNE MUTINES

AGIINRS
AIRINGS ARISING RAISING

EORRSTU
ROUSTER ROUTERS TOURERS TROUSER

ADEERRS
READERS REDEARS REREADS

DEEIRRS
DERRIES DESIRER REDRIES RESIDER SERRIED

ACEELRS
CEREALS RELACES RESCALE SCLERAE

ADEEHRS
ADHERES HEADERS HEARSED SHEARED

AEELPRS
LEAPERS PLEASER PRESALE RELAPSE REPEALS

AEELRSV
LAVEERS LEAVERS REVEALS SEVERAL VEALERS

EEILRSV
LEVIERS RELIVES REVILES SERVILE VEILERS

AAEGLNS
ANLAGES GALENAS LASAGNE

ACEILRV
CAVILER CLAVIER VALERIC

AEENSST
ENTASES SATEENS SENATES SENSATE

EHOORST
HOOTERS RESHOOT SHEROOT SHOOTER SOOTHER

ACELNSU
CENSUAL LACUNES LAUNCES UNLACES

AELRSST
ARTLESS LASTERS SALTERS SLATERS

BENRSTU
BRUNETS BUNTERS BURNETS SUBRENT

ABORSTU
ABORTUS ROBUSTA RUBATOS TABOURS

EELRSTT
LETTERS SETTLER STERLET TRESTLE

AEELRSS
EARLESS LEASERS RESALES RESEALS SEALERS

EEILNSS
ENISLES ENSILES SENILES

AEIPRSS
ASPIRES PARESIS PARISES PRAISES SPIREAS

ACEHRST
CHASTER RACHETS RATCHES

ACIMNOS
ANOSMIC CAMIONS MANIOCS MASONIC

EOPRRST
PORTERS PRESORT PRETORS REPORTS SPORTER

GILNOOS
LOGIONS LOOSING OLINGOS SOLOING

ACEEPRS
ESCAPER RESPACE

EIOPSST
POSTIES POTSIES SOPITES

CELRSTU
CLUSTER CUTLERS RELUCTS

CEEHORS
CHEEROS COHERES ECHOERS RECHOSE

ABELSTT
BATTLES TABLETS

CDEERSU
RECUSED REDUCES RESCUED SECURED SEDUCER

AEILPSS
ESPIALS LAPISES LIPASES PALSIES

ABELMRS
AMBLERS BLAMERS LAMBERS MARBLES RAMBLES

AELPRSY
PARLEYS PARSLEY PLAYERS REPLAYS SPARELY

BEIRSST
BESTIRS BISTERS BISTRES

ACEKRST
RACKETS RESTACK RETACKS STACKER TACKERS

DEEEMRS
EMERSED REDEEMS

ACERSSU
ARCUSES CAUSERS CESURAS SAUCERS SUCRASE

CEORSSU
COURSES SOURCES SUCROSE

EERSSTT
RETESTS SETTERS STREETS TERSEST TESTERS

AEPRRSS
PARSERS RASPERS SPARERS SPARSER

CEERSSU
CERUSES RECUSES RESCUES SECURES

ACEPRSS
ESCARPS PARSECS SCRAPES SECPARS SPACERS

AEHMRSS
MARSHES MASHERS SHMEARS SMASHER

AEINRTU
RUINATE TAURINE URANITE URINATE

AENORST
ATONERS SANTERO SENATOR TREASON

ADEORST
ROASTED TORSADE

AEELNRT
ENTERAL ETERNAL TELERAN

AEENRST
EARNEST EASTERN NEAREST

EEINRTU
RETINUE REUNITE UTERINE

EIINORS
IRONIES NOISIER

ACEILOR
CALORIE CARIOLE COALIER LORICAE

AEIMOST
AMOSITE ATOMIES ATOMISE

AEGORST
GAROTES ORGEATS STORAGE

EGINORS
ERINGOS IGNORES REGIONS SIGNORE

ADEILRS
DERAILS DIALERS REDIALS

ADENRTU
DAUNTER NATURED UNRATED UNTREAD

AILORST
ORALIST RIALTOS TAILORS

AEEGNRT
GRANTEE GREATEN NEGATER REAGENT

EEGINRT
INTEGER TREEING

ADEIIRS
DAIRIES DIARIES

AEIRRST
ARTSIER TARRIES TARSIER

ABEINST
BANTIES BASINET

ABEIRST
BAITERS BARITES REBAITS TERBIAS

ACEINRS
ARCSINE ARSENIC CARNIES

AEILMNR
MANLIER MARLINE MINERAL

AEIMNRS
MARINES REMAINS SEMINAR

AEINPST
PANTIES PATINES SAPIENT SPINATE

AEINSTW
TAWNIES WANIEST

AEIRSTW
WAISTER WAITERS WARIEST WASTRIE

EEILNST
LENITES LISENTE SETLINE TENSILE

ACEIRST
ATRESIC CRISTAE RACIEST STEARIC

AGINORS
ORIGANS SIGNORA SOARING

ADENOPR
APRONED OPERAND PADRONE PANDORE

DEIOPRT
DIOPTER DIOPTRE PERIDOT PROTEID

EHIORST
HERIOTS HOISTER SHORTIE

EILNOPT
POTLINE TOPLINE

EIMNOST
MESTINO MOISTEN SENTIMO

EIMORST
EROTISM MOISTER MORTISE TRISOME

EEINRRT
REINTER RENTIER TERRINE

EILNSTU
LUNIEST LUTEINS UTENSIL

DENORSU
ENDUROS RESOUND SOUNDER UNDOERS

AEGMNOT
MAGNETO MEGATON MONTAGE

ACDEILT
CITADEL DELTAIC DIALECT EDICTAL

ACDEIRS
RADICES SIDECAR

ADEHIRS
AIRSHED DASHIER HARDIES SHADIER

ADEIPRS
ASPIRED DESPAIR DIAPERS PRAISED

AEILMNS
MALINES MENIALS SEMINAL

AEILNPS
ALPINES PINEALS SPANIEL SPLENIA

AEILPST
APLITES PALIEST PLATIES TALIPES

EINRSTT
RETINTS STINTER TINTERS

AEHNRTU
HAUNTER UNEARTH URETHAN

AEMNRST
MARTENS SARMENT SMARTEN

EIMNRST
MINSTER MINTERS REMINTS

EIMNRTU
MINUTER UNMITER UNMITRE

EENRSTU
NEUTERS RETUNES TENURES TUREENS

ADNOORT
DONATOR ODORANT TANDOOR TORNADO

DEIMOST
DISTOME MODISTE

DEIORSV
DEVISOR DEVOIRS VISORED VOIDERS

GINORST
SORTING STORING TRIGONS

GINORTU
OUTGRIN OUTRING ROUTING TOURING

CEIINRT
CITRINE CRINITE INCITER NERITIC

EINORSS
SENIORS SONSIER

CENORTU
CORNUTE COUNTER RECOUNT TROUNCE

DEHNORT
THORNED THRONED

EHNORST
HORNETS SHORTEN THRONES

AEELRRT
ALERTER ALTERER REALTER RELATER

ACEENRS
CAREENS CASERNE RECANES

ACEERST
CERATES CREATES ECARTES

ADEENRY
DEANERY YEAREND YEARNED

ADEEPRT
ADEPTER PREDATE RETAPED TAPERED

AEELPRT
PETRALE PLEATER PRELATE REPLATE

AEEMRST
REMATES RETEAMS STEAMER

DEEFINR
DEFINER REFINED

ELOORST
LOOTERS RETOOLS ROOTLES TOOLERS

AEGILNN
ANELING EANLING LEANING

AEGIMNS
ENIGMAS GAMINES SEAMING

AEGIMRS
GISARME IMAGERS MIRAGES

EENOPST
OPENEST PENTOSE POSTEEN POTEENS

EEORSTV
OVERSET REVOTES VETOERS

ADEILMS
MEDIALS MISDEAL MISLEAD

ACELNST
CANTLES CENTALS LANCETS

ADEMNRS
DAMNERS REMANDS

ADEMNRU
DURAMEN MANURED MAUNDER UNARMED

AELMRST
ARMLETS LAMSTER TRAMELS

AEPRSTU
PASTURE UPRATES UPSTARE UPTEARS

CEIRSTU
CURITES ICTERUS

DEFINRS
FINDERS FRIENDS REDFINS REFINDS

DEIMNTU
MINUTED MUTINED UNTIMED

EFILRST
FILTERS LIFTERS STIFLER TRIFLES

EEFGINR
FEIGNER FREEING REEFING

ACNORST
CANTORS CARTONS CONTRAS CRATONS

CINORST
CISTRON CITRONS CORTINS

ADEGLNS
DANGLES GLANDES LAGENDS SLANGED

DEGILNS
DINGLES ENGILDS SINGLED

EIKNRST
REKNITS STINKER TINKERS

AAGINST
AGAINST ANTISAG

GINOSTU
OUSTING OUTINGS OUTSING TOUSING

EIINPRS
INSPIRE SPINIER

AELORSS
LASSOER OARLESS SEROSAL

EILNOSS
INSOLES LESIONS LIONESS

BDEORTU
DOUBTER OBTRUDE OUTBRED REDOUBT

CELORST
COLTERS CORSLET COSTREL LECTORS

ELORSTT
LOTTERS SETTLOR SLOTTER

ACDEELR
CLEARED CREEDAL DECLARE RELACED

ACEELNS
CLEANSE ENLACES SCALENE

ADEEFST
DEAFEST DEFEATS FEASTED

ADEELPR
PEARLED PEDALER PLEADER REPLEAD

DEEFILR
DEFILER FIELDER REFILED

DEEILRV
DELIVER LIVERED RELIVED REVILED

DEEIPRS
PRESIDE SPEIRED SPIERED

DEEIRSV
DERIVES DEVISER DIVERSE REVISED

EEFILRS
FERLIES REFILES REFLIES RELIEFS

EEILSTV
EVILEST LIEVEST VELITES

ABCEIRS
ASCRIBE CARIBES

ABEILMR
BALMIER LAMBIER

ACEILMR
CLAIMER MIRACLE RECLAIM

ACEIRSV
VARICES VISCERA

AEILMPR
IMPALER IMPEARL LEMPIRA PALMIER

EENPRST
PENSTER PRESENT REPENTS SERPENT

ACIOPRT
APRICOT APROTIC PAROTIC

AIMNOPT
MAINTOP PTOMAIN TAMPION TIMPANO

AEGHNRS
HANGERS REHANGS

ABDEORR
ARBORED BOARDER BROADER REBOARD

CEIORRS
CIRROSE CORRIES CROSIER ORRICES

ACEERRT
CATERER RECRATE RETRACE TERRACE

AAEGMNT
GATEMAN MAGENTA MAGNATE NAMETAG

CEEHIRT
ERETHIC ETHERIC HERETIC TECHIER

ADEILLS
DALLIES SALLIED

CDEINSU
INCUDES INCUSED INDUCES

EILNPSU
LINEUPS LUPINES SPINULE UNPILES

AACINRS
ACRASIN ARNICAS CARINAS SARCINA

AAINPST
PASTINA PATINAS PINATAS TAIPANS

EILLRST
RILLETS STILLER TILLERS TRELLIS

EILNSST
ENLISTS LISTENS SILENTS TINSELS

DELMORS
MOLDERS REMOLDS SMOLDER

ELOPRSU
LEPROUS PELORUS SPORULE

EEENRRT
ENTERER REENTER TERREEN TERRENE

AADMNOR
MADRONA MONARDA

ADEELPS
ELAPSED PLEASED SEPALED

AEHRSTT
HATTERS SHATTER THREATS

ACGINRS
RACINGS SACRING SCARING

AGINPRS
PARINGS PARSING RASPING SPARING

Bob's Bible Bonus: Complete 7-letter Multi-Anagram Quiz

AGINSTW TAWSING WASTING
DDEEIRS DERIDES DESIRED RESIDED
EELMRST MELTERS REMELTS RESMELT SMELTER
EELPRST PELTERS PETRELS RESPELT SPELTER
AEIPSST PASTIES PATSIES PETSAIS TAPISES
EOQRSTU QUESTOR QUOTERS ROQUETS TORQUES
ACEPRST CARPETS PREACTS PRECAST SPECTRA
AEHLRTY EARTHLY LATHERY
AELPRTY PEARTLY PEYTRAL PTERYLA
AEMPRST RESTAMP STAMPER TAMPERS
CEINPST INCEPTS INSPECT PECTINS
EENRSST NESTERS RENESTS RESENTS
ACDIMNO MONACID MONADIC NOMADIC
ACILOPT CAPITOL COALPIT OPTICAL TOPICAL
ACIMOST ATOMICS OSMATIC SOMATIC
DEEGLRS GELDERS LEDGERS REDLEGS
AEGILSS GLASSIE LIGASES SILAGES
EORRSTT RETORTS ROTTERS STERTOR
EGINRSS INGRESS RESIGNS SIGNERS SINGERS
GINOPRS PROSING SPORING
BEILMOS MOBILES OBELISM
EEIPRRS PERRIES PRISERE REPRISE RESPIRE
EEIRRSV REIVERS REVISER RIEVERS
CDELOOR COLORED DECOLOR

ELOOPRS LOOPERS POOLERS RESPOOL SPOOLER
CEEIPRS PIECERS PIERCES PRECISE RECIPES
AAILMNS ANIMALS LAMINAS MANILAS
BELRSTU BLUSTER BUSTLER BUTLERS SUBTLER
AANPRST PARTANS SPARTAN TARPANS TRAPANS
ACLORSU CAROLUS OCULARS OSCULAR
AEEHPRS HEAPERS RESHAPE
GIILNST LISTING SILTING TILINGS
ADERRSW DRAWERS REDRAWS REWARDS WARDERS
EFIRRSU FRISEUR SURFIER
AEGGRST GAGSTER GARGETS STAGGER TAGGERS
EGGINRS GINGERS SERGING SNIGGER
AERSSTT STARETS STATERS TASTERS
DEEPRSU PERDUES PERUSED SUPERED
AEILMSS AIMLESS SAMIELS SEISMAL
AELMPRS LAMPERS PALMERS SAMPLER
EILMPRS LIMPERS PRELIMS RIMPLES SIMPLER
ABERSST BASTERS BREASTS
EIRSSTV STIVERS STRIVES VERISTS
AGIKNST SKATING STAKING TAKINGS TASKING
GILNOSW LOWINGS SLOWING
AACELMR CAMERAL CARAMEL CERAMAL
EORRSST RESORTS ROSTERS SORTERS STORERS
GINORSS GRISONS SIGNORS SORINGS

EFLORSW FLOWERS FOWLERS REFLOWS WOLFERS
DDEEIRR DERIDER REDRIED
EEIMNSS NEMESIS SIEMENS
EEIMRSS MERISES MESSIER REMISES
ACEENSS CASSENE ENCASES SEANCES SENECAS
AIRSSTT ARTISTS STRAITS TSARIST
CDEEERS DECREES RECEDES SECEDER
DEEERSW RESEWED SEWERED WEEDERS
ACEHOPS CHEAPOS POACHES SHOEPAC
EGGILNS LEGGINS NIGGLES SNIGGLE
AELSSTT LATESTS SALTEST STALEST
ABERSSU ABUSERS RUBASSE SURBASE
ACELLRS CALLERS CELLARS RECALLS SCLERAL
ACELRSS CARLESS CLASSER SCALERS SCLERAS
AEHLRSS ASHLERS LASHERS SLASHER
AELRSSV SALVERS SERVALS SLAVERS
CEISSTU CUTISES ICTUSES
ACELPSU CAPSULE SCALEUP SPECULA UPSCALE
AEKRSST SKATERS STRAKES STREAKS
GHIINST HISTING INSIGHT
GIIMNST MISTING SMITING TIMINGS
GHNOSTU GUNSHOT HOGNUTS NOUGHTS SHOTGUN
ELOSSTY SYSTOLE TOYLESS
ABGILMN AMBLING BLAMING LAMBING
AGHINPS HASPING PASHING PHASING SHAPING

EELMPST PELMETS TEMPLES
CEENRSS CENSERS SCREENS SECERNS
CEERSST CRESSET RESECTS SECRETS
EERSSTV REVESTS VERSETS VERSTES
AEIPSSV PASSIVE PAVISES PAVISSE SPAVIES
ACEHMRS MARCHES MESARCH SCHMEAR
CELOPSU CLOSEUP COUPLES
ACGIKNR ARCKING CARKING RACKING
AEGLLRY ALLERGY GALLERY LARGELY REGALLY
AENPPRS NAPPERS SNAPPER
CGINOPS COPINGS SCOPING
GILNPSU PULINGS PULSING
BELMRSU LUMBERS RUMBLES SLUMBER
EEERRSV RESERVE REVERES REVERSE SEVERER
GIILNPS LISPING PILINGS SLIPING SPILING
GIIKNRS GRISKIN RISKING
EIMPRSS IMPRESS PREMISS SIMPERS SPIREMS
CEORRSS CROSSER RECROSS SCORERS
IPRSSTU PURISTS UPSTIRS
EGGLRSU GURGLES LUGGERS SLUGGER
ABCEHMR BECHARM BRECHAM CHAMBER
AACLRSS LASCARS RASCALS SACRALS SCALARS
BBELRSU BURBLES LUBBERS RUBBLES SLUBBER
ELPPRSU PULPERS PURPLES SUPPLER
AEHLSSS ASHLESS HASSELS HASSLES SLASHES

AEILNOR AILERON ALIENOR
AEEINRT ARENITE RETINAE TRAINEE
ADEINRT ANTIRED DETRAIN TRAINED
ADEILRT DILATER REDTAIL TRAILED
ADEINRS RANDIES SANDIER SARDINE
AEILNRS ALINERS NAILERS RENAILS
AADEIRT AIRDATE RADIATE TIARAED
AAEIRST ARISTAE ASTERIA ATRESIA
ADEORTU OUTDARE OUTREAD READOUT
AELNORS LOANERS RELOANS
EILORST ESTRIOL LOITERS TOILERS
AEINRRT RETRAIN TERRAIN TRAINER
AEHINRT HAIRNET INEARTH THERIAN
AEIMNRT MINARET RAIMENT
AEINPRT PAINTER PERTAIN REPAINT
EINNORT INTONER TERNION
AENOPRT OPERANT PRONATE PROTEAN
CEINORT COINTER NOTICER
AEEIMRT EMERITA EMIRATE MEATIER
EGIORST GOITERS GOITRES GORIEST
AENRSTU NATURES SAUNTER
EINRSTU NUTSIER TRIUNES UNITERS
ADINORS INROADS ORDAINS SADIRON
ADELORS LOADERS ORDEALS RELOADS
EILORSU LOUSIER SOILURE
AEILRRT RETRIAL TRAILER
AEINNST INANEST STANINE
ABEILRT LIBRATE TRIABLE

ACEILRT ARTICLE RECITAL
ACEINST ACETINS CINEAST
ADEINPT DEPAINT PAINTED PATINED
ADEIPRT DIPTERA PARTIED PIRATED
AEILMRT MALTIER MARLITE
AEILNPR PLAINER PRALINE
AEILRTY IRATELY REALITY TEARILY
AEINSTV NAIVEST NATIVES VAINEST
AEIRSTV VASTIER VERITAS
AEELNST LATEENS LEANEST
DEEINRS DENIERS NEREIDS RESINED
DEEINST DESTINE ENDITES
EEILRST LEISTER RETILES STERILE
EIILNOS ELISION ISOLINE LIONISE
ADEGILN ALIGNED DEALING LEADING
AEGILNS LEASING LINAGES SEALING
AEGNRST ARGENTS GARNETS STRANGE
EGILNRT RINGLET TINGLER
EIORRST RIOTERS ROISTER
ABDEORT ABORTED BORATED TABORED
ACEORST COASTER COATERS RECOATS
AEFLORT FLOATER REFLOAT
AELMNOT LOMENTA OMENTAL TELAMON
AEMNORS ENAMORS MOANERS OARSMEN
AEOPRST ESPARTO PROTEAS SEAPORT
BDEIORT DEORBIT ORBITED
CDEINOT CTENOID DEONTIC NOTICED
EINOPST PINTOES POINTES

DEEORST OERSTED TEREDOS
EINORSV ENVIROS RENVOIS VERSION
AEEFIRS FAERIES FREESIA
EILOOST OOLITES OSTIOLE STOOLIE
DEGILOR GLORIED GODLIER
AEENRTT ENTREAT RATTEEN TERNATE
ACEENRT CENTARE CRENATE REENACT
AEENRTV NERVATE VETERAN
EGIINRT IGNITER TIERING
ADELNRU LAUNDER LURDANE
ADENRSU ASUNDER DANSEUR
DEIRSTU DUSTIER STUDIER
EILRSTU LUSTIER RULIEST RUTILES
AEGINNT ANTEING ANTIGEN GENTIAN
AAINRST ANTIARS ARTISAN TSARINA
AEGIMNT MINTAGE TEAMING TEGMINA
AEEGLNR ENLARGE GENERAL GLEANER
ADEIILS DAILIES LIAISED SEDILIA
DEIIRST DIRTIES DITSIER TIDIERS
EGINOPR PERIGON PIROGEN
ACDEILR DECRIAL RADICEL RADICLE
ACEILNS INLACES SANICLE SCALENI
ACEILRS CLARIES ECLAIRS SCALIER
ADEISTV DATIVES VISTAED
AEILMRS MAILERS REALISM REMAILS
ADEELRS DEALERS LEADERS
DEEILNS ENISLED ENSILED LINSEED
AINNOST ANOINTS NATIONS ONANIST

AEILLRT LITERAL TALLIER
ACENRTU CENTAUR UNCRATE
AEHNRST ANTHERS THENARS
AELNPRT PLANTER REPLANT
AENRSTV SERVANT TAVERNS VERSANT
BEINRTU TRIBUNE TURBINE
DEENRTU DENTURE RETUNED TENURED
EELNRST NESTLER RELENTS
ABINOST BASTION BONITAS OBTAINS
ACINOST ACTIONS ATONICS CATIONS
EGINOOS GOONIES ISOGONE NOOGIES
ADEILPR LIPREAD PREDIAL
ADEGNRS DANGERS GANDERS GARDENS
AEGLNST GELANTS TANGLES
EGILNRS LINGERS SLINGER
AHIORST AIRSHOT SHORTIA THORIAS
AGILOST GALIOTS LATIGOS
INOORST NITROSO TORSION
ADELOPR LEOPARD PAROLED PRELOAD
BEILORS BOILERS REBOILS
CDEINOS CODEINS SECONDI
CDEIOST CESTOID COEDITS
CEILNOS CINEOLS INCLOSE
DEIMNOS DOMINES EMODINS MISDONE
DEIORSW DOWRIES ROWDIES WEIRDOS
EHILOST EOLITHS HOLIEST HOSTILE
EINOSUV ENVIOUS NIVEOUS
EIINRTT NITRITE NITTIER
EIIMNRT INTERIM MINTIER TERMINI
EMNORST MENTORS MONSTER

EMNORTU MOUNTER REMOUNT
AEIRRTT RATTIER TARTIER
ABEIRTT BATTIER BIRETTA
AEERRST RETEARS SERRATE TEARERS
AEERSTT ESTREAT RESTATE RETASTE
DEEIRRT RETIRED RETRIED TIREDER
ABEERST BEATERS BERATES REBATES
ADEERTW DEWATER TARWEED WATERED
AEEHRST AETHERS HEATERS REHEATS
CEEIRST CERITES RECITES TIERCES
EEHINRS HENRIES INHERES RESHINE
EEINRSW NEWSIER WEINERS WIENERS
AAEGRST GASTREA TEARGAS
DEGIINT DIETING EDITING IGNITED
ACEIRTT ATRETIC CATTIER CITRATE
DEGNORU GUERDON UNDERGO
CEIINOS EOSINIC NICOISE
AEENPST NEPETAS PENATES
AAINRSU ANURIAS SAURIAN URANIAS
ADEEGLN ANGELED GLEANED
ADEEGLT GELATED LEGATED
ACEGILN ANGELIC ANGLICE GALENIC
AEFGILN FINAGLE LEAFING
AEGHIRS HEGARIS HEGIRAS
AEGILNP LEAPING PEALING
AEGINPS SPAEING SPINAGE
AEGIRSV GRAVIES RIVAGES
EGINNRT RENTING RINGENT
AEGMNRT GARMENT MARGENT

ABEORRT ABORTER TABORER
ABEORTT ABETTOR TABORET
ACEORRT CREATOR REACTOR
EIOPRRT PIERROT PRERIOT
AAEEMNT EMANATE ENEMATA MANATEE
BDEENOR DEBONER ENROBED REDBONE
EEMORST EMOTERS METEORS REMOTES
CEFINOR COINFER CONIFER
CEIMNOT CENTIMO TONEMIC
DELNOSU LOUDENS NODULES
DELOSTU LOUDEST TOUSLED
EFIOOST FOOTIES FOOTSIE
EEENRST ENTREES RETENES TEENERS
ACEGORS CARGOES CORSAGE SOCAGER
AEGOPST GESTAPO POSTAGE POTAGES
DEGINOW WENDIGO WIDGEON
EGINOPS EPIGONS PIGEONS PINGOES
ABDEILS BALDIES DISABLE
ADENRRS DARNERS ERRANDS
ADENTTU ATTUNED NUTATED TAUNTED
AELNSTT LATENTS LATTENS TALENTS
DEINNST DENTINS INDENTS INTENDS
DEINSTT DENTIST DISTENT STINTED
EINNRSU SUNNIER UNRISEN
DEIMOOR DOOMIER MOIDORE MOODIER
ADEILLR DALLIER DIALLER RALLIED
AEILLST TAILLES TALLIES
DEELNRS LENDERS RELENDS SLENDER
ABERSTU ARBUTES BURSATE

ACDENST DECANTS DESCANT SCANTED
ACELNRU LUCARNE NUCLEAR UNCLEAR
ADENRSW WANDERS WARDENS
ADEPRST DEPARTS PETARDS
ADERSTW STEWARD STRAWED
AEFLNRU FLANEUR FRENULA FUNERAL
AELMNST LAMENTS MANTELS MANTLES
AELRSTV TRAVELS VARLETS VESTRAL
AELRSTW WARSTLE WASTREL WRASTLE
AEMNRSU MANURES SURNAME
BDEINRS BINDERS INBREDS REBINDS
BEILRST BLISTER BRISTLE RIBLETS
BEINRSU BURNIES SUBERIN
CDEINRS CINDERS DISCERN RESCIND
CEILNST CLIENTS LECTINS STENCIL
CEILNTU CUTLINE LINECUT TUNICLE
DEHINRS HINDERS NERDISH SHRINED
DEIRSTV DIVERTS STRIVED
EILPRST RESPLIT TRIPLES
EIMNRSU MUREINS MURINES
EINPRSU PURINES UPRISEN
EIRSTUV REVUIST STUIVER VIRTUES
ABILOTU BAILOUT TABOULI
ADIMNOS DAIMONS DOMAINS
ANORSTT ATTORNS RATTONS
EINRSST ESTRINS INSERTS SINTERS
AIORSST AORISTS ARISTOS SATORIS
EEGINRV REEVING REGIVEN VEERING

ANOPRST PARTONS PATRONS TARPONS
AEGLNSU ANGELUS LAGUNES LANGUES
DEGILNU DUELING ELUDING INDULGE
AEKNRST RANKEST TANKERS
EILNPST LEPTINS PINTLES PLENIST
ABEIILS ALIBIES BAILIES BIALIES
AGIILNR LAIRING RAILING
DENORRU RONDURE ROUNDER
EORSTTU OUTSERT STOUTER TOUTERS
DEILMOS MELOIDS MIDSOLE
AAELNPT PLANATE PLATANE
CEIINRS IRENICS SERICIN
EIIMRST MIRIEST MISTIER RIMIEST
EIINPST PINIEST PINITES TIEPINS
EIIRSTV REVISIT VISITER
AAINOPS ANOPIAS ANOPSIA PAISANO
EILORSS LORISES RISSOLE
BDENORU BOUNDER REBOUND UNROBED
BELORST BOLSTER BOLTERS LOBSTER
BENORSU BOURNES UNROBES UNSOBER
CELORTU CLOTURE CLOUTER COULTER
CEORSTU COUTERS CROUTES SCOUTER
DEOPRST DEPORTS REDTOPS SPORTED
DEORSTY DESTROY STROYED
ENORSST NESTORS STONERS TENSORS
ACEINNS CANINES ENCINAS
ACEISTT CATTIES STATICE
ADEIMRR ADMIRER MARRIED

ADEIPRR PARRIED RAPIDER
AEIMSTT ETATISM MATIEST
ACDEELN CLEANED ENLACED
ACDEERS CREASED DECARES
ADEELRY DELAYER LAYERED RELAYED
ADEEMNS DEMEANS SEEDMAN
ADEEPRS RESPADE SPEARED
CEEILNS LICENSE SELENIC SILENCE
EEFILST FELSITE LEFTIES LIEFEST
ACGINRT CARTING CRATING TRACING
AFGINRT INGRAFT RAFTING
AGINPRT PARTING PRATING
EENRRST RENTERS RERENTS STERNER
EENRSTT NETTERS TENTERS
ABEILMT BIMETAL LIMBATE TIMBALE
ACEFINS FANCIES FASCINE FIANCES
ACEHIRS CAHIERS CASHIER
ACEILNP CAPELIN PANICLE PELICAN
ACEIPRS SCRAPIE SPACIER
ACEIPST ASEPTIC PACIEST SPICATE
ACINNOT ACTINON CONTAIN
DEGORSU DROGUES GOURDES GROUSED
ADDEERT DERATED REDATED TREADED
EEINRSS SEINERS SEREINS SERINES
DENOPRS PERNODS PONDERS RESPOND
CEENRST CENTERS CENTRES TENRECS
GIINORS ORIGINS SIGNIOR SIGNORI
ABDEERS BEADERS DEBASER SABERED

DELRSTU LUSTRED RUSTLED STRUDEL
AEGRRST GARRETS GARTERS GRATERS
EGINNST NESTING TENSING
AEGMNRS ENGRAMS GERMANS MANGERS
AEGRSTY GRAYEST GYRATES
EGILMNR GREMLIN MINGLER
EGINPRS PINGERS SPRINGE
EGINSTW STEWING TWINGES WESTING
DEIORRW ROWDIER WORDIER WORRIED
EINNOPS PENSION PINONES
EIOPSTT POTTIES TIPTOES
DEEFIIR DEIFIER EDIFIER REIFIED
CDEEOST CESTODE ESCOTED
ACEHLOR CHOLERA CHORALE CHOREAL
ACEHORS CHOREAS ORACHES ROACHES
ACEOPST CAPOTES TOECAPS
AEORSVW AVOWERS OVERSAW REAVOWS
CEIMNOS INCOMES MESONIC
EIMOPRS IMPOSER PROMISE SEMIPRO
EIMOPST MOPIEST OPTIMES
AILNPTU NUPTIAL UNPLAIT
AIMNSTU MANITUS SANTIMU TSUNAMI
AINRSST INSTARS SANTIRS STRAINS
AEERRTT RETREAT TREATER
AEEHRTT THEATER THEATRE THEREAT
EEINNRV INNERVE NERVINE
DEEENRS NEEDERS SNEERED
EOORRST ROOSTER ROOTERS TOREROS
EFOORST FOETORS FOOTERS

Bob's Bible Bonus: Complete 7-letter Multi-Anagram Quiz

EOOPRST POOREST, STOOPER
AEEHNPT HAPTENE, HEPTANE, PHENATE
AEEHRTW WEATHER, WHEREAT, WREATHE
AEIRTTT ATTRITE, TATTIER, TITRATE
ABDELST BALDEST, BLASTED, STABLED
ABDERSU DAUBERS, EARBUDS
ACDELRS CRADLES, RECLADS
ACELRSU RECUSAL, SECULAR
AEFLRSU EARFULS, FERULAS, REFUSAL
AELPRSU PERUSAL, PLEURAS
BDEILRU BUILDER, REBUILD
DEILNPS SPINDLE, SPLINED
AACILNR CARINAL, CRANIAL
ACDIIRT TRIACID, TRIADIC
AIIMNST ANIMIST, INTIMAS, SANTIMI
DEINSST DISSENT, SNIDEST
EILLNST LENTILS, LINTELS
DENPRTU PRUDENT, UPTREND
EHNRSTU HUNTERS, SHUNTER
EMNRSTU MUNSTER, STERNUM
ABEEGRS BAREGES, BARGEES
EEGIMRS EMIGRES, REGIMES, REMIGES
ACDNORS CANDORS, CARDONS, DACRONS
ACNOSTU CONATUS, TOUCANS
AMNOSTU AMOUNTS, OUTMANS
DIOPRST DISPORT, TORPIDS, TRIPODS
ADEKRST DARKEST, STRAKED
AEKLNST ANKLETS, LANKEST
AEQRSTU QUARTES, QUATRES
EIKLNRS LINKERS, RELINKS

EIKLRST KILTERS, KIRTLES, KLISTER
DEIPRSU SIRUPED, UPDRIES
ADGIILN DIALING, GLIADIN
AGIILNS NILGAIS, SAILING
DEIISTT DITTIES, TIDIEST
DEGNRSU GERUNDS, NUDGERS
DELOSTT DOTTELS, DOTTLES, SLOTTED
AACDELN CANALED, CANDELA, DECANAL
AAELMST MALATES, MALTASE, TAMALES
DEIIMST MISEDIT, STIMIED
EIILMST ELITISM, LIMIEST, LIMITES
ACORSTU CUATROS, SURCOAT, TURACOS
ACFINRT FRANTIC, INFARCT, INFRACT
CDEORSU COURSED, SCOURED, SOURCED
ELORSUV LOUVERS, LOUVRES, VELOURS
DDENORU REDOUND, ROUNDED, UNDERDO
ELORSST OSTLERS, STEROLS
AERRSTT RATTERS, RESTART, STARTER
AEIRRSS ARRISES, RAISERS, SIERRAS
DEEILPS SPEILED, SPIELED
ABELRTT BATTLER, BLATTER, BRATTLE
ACERRST CARTERS, CRATERS, TRACERS
AEFRRST FRATERS, RAFTERS, STRAFER
AELPRTT PARTLET, PLATTER, PRATTLE
AEPRSTT PATTERS, SPATTER, TAPSTER
EFIRRTU FRUITER, TURFIER
EIPRSTT SPITTER, TIPSTER
EIRSTTW RETWIST, TWISTER

AGHINRS GARNISH, SHARING
AGIMNST MASTING, MATINGS
AIMNNOS AMNIONS, MANSION, ONANISM
ADDEEST DEADEST, SEDATED, STEADED
AEERSSU RESEAUS, UREASES
EEILSST LISTEES, TELESIS, TIELESS
EEFLRST REFLETS, TELFERS
EELRSTW SWELTER, WELTERS, WRESTLE
ABEIRSS BRAISES, BRASSIE
ACEINSS CASEINS, CASSINE, INCASES
AEFISST FIESTAS, FISSATE
AEINPSS PANSIES, SAPIENS
ABEHRST BATHERS, BERTHAS, BREATHS
AEFHRST FATHERS, HAFTERS
AEHPRST TEPHRAS, THREAPS
AEHRSTW SWATHER, THAWERS, WREATHS
AEMRSTY MASTERY, STREAMY
AENPRSW ENWRAPS, PAWNERS, SPAWNER
BEIMRST TIMBERS, TIMBRES
CEHIRST CITHERS, RICHEST
CEINPRS CRISPEN, PINCERS, PRINCES
EHIRSTW SWITHER, WITHERS, WRITHES
EGINNSU ENSUING, GUNNIES
AGIINNR INGRAIN, RAINING
ACDEGLN CLANGED, GLANCED
ADEGPRS GRASPED, SPARGED
AEGLPRU EARPLUG, GRAUPEL, PLAGUER
DEGILMN MELDING, MINGLED
INOOPST OPTIONS, POTIONS
ABEILMS ABLEISM, LAMBIES

EHORRST RHETORS, SHORTER
EMORRST TERMORS, TREMORS
EOPRSTT POTTERS, PROTEST, SPOTTER
CEHINRS INCHERS, RICHENS
BGINORS BORINGS, SORBING
GINOPRU INGROUP, POURING, ROUPING
AABCERT ABREACT, BEARCAT, CABARET
ABDILRS BRIDALS, RIBALDS
ABDDEOR BOARDED, ROADBED
CEINOSS CESSION, COSINES, OSCINES
EIMORSS ISOMERS, MOSSIER
CEHORTU COUTHER, RETOUCH, TOUCHER
CEORSTV CORVETS, COVERTS, VECTORS
CEORTUV CUTOVER, OVERCUT
EHMORST MOTHERS, SMOTHER, THERMOS
EHOPRST POTHERS, STROPHE, THORPES
ADEEMRR DREAMER, REARMED, REDREAM
AEEHRRS HEARERS, REHEARS, SHEARER
DEEFIRR FERRIED, REFIRED, REFRIED
DEEIRRV DERIVER, REDRIVE
EEFIRRS FERRIES, REFIRES, REFRIES
DEEELST DELETES, SLEETED, STEELED
EGIINNS INSIGNE, SEINING
EGILMNU GUMLINE, LEGUMIN
DEFLOOR FLOODER, FLOORED, REFLOOD
AAEGMNS MANAGES, SAGAMEN
ABDEEMN BEADMEN, BEDEMAN, BENAMED
ABEEHNS BANSHEE, SHEBEAN

ABEEMNS BASEMEN, BEMEANS, BENAMES
ABEEMRS AMBEERS, BESMEAR
ACDEEMR AMERCED, CREAMED, RACEMED
ACEEHST ESCHEAT, TEACHES
ACEEMRS AMERCES, RACEMES
ADEEPRV DEPRAVE, PERVADE, REPAVED
BDEEFIR BRIEFED, DEBRIEF, FIBERED
BEEIMRS BEMIRES, BERIMES, BIREMES
DEEIMPR DEMIREP, EPIDERM, IMPEDER
DEEIPRV DEPRIVE, PREDIVE
AEERRSW REWEARS, SWEARER, WEARERS
CEIIMNR CREMINI, CRIMINE, MINCIER
ENOORSS NOOSERS, SOONERS
CEIOSTX COEXIST, EXOTICS
GILNSTU LUSTING, LUTINGS
AACDIRS ACARIDS, ASCARID, CARDIAS
ACIILNS INCISAL, SALICIN
ADDELRS LADDERS, RADDLES, SADDLER
DDEILRS DREIDLS, RIDDLES
AANRSTT RATTANS, TANTRAS, TARTANS
BELNSTU SUNBELT, UNBELTS, UNBLEST
EFLRSTU FLUSTER, FLUTERS, RESTFUL
EEGINSS GENESIS, SEEINGS, SIGNEES
EFGHIRT FIGHTER, FREIGHT, REFIGHT
EGIMNPR GRIPMEN, IMPREGN, PERMING
EGIMNPT PIGMENT, TEMPING
AHIRSTT ATHIRST, RATTISH, TARTISH
BEEORSV OBSERVE, OBVERSE, VERBOSE

CDEEHOR COHERED, OCHERED
CDEEOPR PRECODE, PROCEED
AHIMRST THAIRMS, THIRAMS
AIMPRST ARMPITS, IMPARTS, MISPART
EEEMRST MEETERS, REMEETS, TEEMERS
EEENRSV EVENERS, VENEERS
DELORSS DORSELS, RODLESS, SOLDERS
ELOSSTU LOTUSES, SOLUTES, TOUSLES
BEIRRSU BRUISER, BURIERS
CEIRRSU CRUISER, CURRIES
EHILSTT LITHEST, THISTLE
AEGGNRS GANGERS, GRANGES, NAGGERS
AGILNPS LAPSING, PALINGS, SAPLING
AGILNSV SALVING, SLAVING
DEEILSS DIESELS, IDLESSE, SEIDELS
AERRSST ARRESTS, RASTERS, STARERS
CCEINOR CORNICE, CROCEIN, CROCINE
EEFLRSU FERULES, FUELERS, REFUELS
DEENRSS REDNESS, RESENDS, SENDERS
DEERSST DESERTS, DESSERT, TRESSED
ACDEPRS REDCAPS, SCARPED, SCRAPED
ACEHLRS CLASHER, LARCHES
ACEHLST CHALETS, LATCHES, SATCHEL
ACELRSV CARVELS, CLAVERS
BEIMRSU ERBIUMS, IMBRUES
EIMPRSU SPUMIER, UMPIRES
EIMPSTU IMPETUS, IMPUTES, UPTIMES
ACENSST ASCENTS, SECANTS, STANCES

ACERSST ACTRESS, CASTERS, RECASTS
AEHNSST HASTENS, SNATHES
AEHRSST RASHEST, TRASHES
AELLRTY ALERTLY, RETALLY
AENPSST APTNESS, PATNESS
AEPRSST PASTERS, REPASTS, SPAREST
AERSSTY ESTRAYS, STAYERS
EFIRSST RESIFTS, SIFTERS, STRIFES
ADHILOY HOLIDAY, HYALOID, HYOIDAL
ACINOSS CAISSON, CASINOS, CASSINO
AEKRRST KRATERS, STARKER
EIKRRST SKIRRET, SKIRTER, STRIKER
ACHNORS ANCHORS, ARCHONS, RANCHOS
AMNOPST POSTMAN, TAMPONS
FIOPRST PROFITS, SPORTIF
EEKLRST KELTERS, KESTREL, SKELTER
AABGINS ABASING, BISNAGA
AEGRSSU ARGUSES, SAUGERS
DDEGILR GIRDLED, GRIDDLE
CEIKRST RICKETS, STICKER, TICKERS
CEORRSU COURSER, SCOURER
CNOORTU CONTOUR, CORNUTO, CROUTON
BGILNOS GLOBINS, GOBLINS
CDEILLO COLLIDE, COLLIED
ENOSSTT STETSON, TESTONS
AEEGGRS RAGGEES, REGGAES
ADNPSTU DUSTPAN, STANDUP, UPSTAND
CEHORSU CHOUSER, ROUCHES
CEOPRSU CROUPES, RECOUPS
BEORSST SORBETS, STROBES

EEIRRSS RERISES, SERRIES, SIRREES
EEPRSTT PERTEST, PETTERS, PRETEST
CEEHILS HELICES, LICHEES
EEEGNRR GREENER, REGREEN, RENEGER
AAEGLLT GALLATE, GALLETA, TALLAGE
ABDDEER BEARDED, BREADED, DEBEARD
AERSTTT STRETTA, TARTEST, TATTERS
EIRSTTT STRETTI, TITTERS, TRITEST
ACGHINR ARCHING, CHAGRIN, CHARING
AEKORSS ARKOSES, RESOAKS, SOAKERS
ADIILMS MILADIS, MISDIAL, MISLAID
CEKORST RESTOCK, ROCKETS, STOCKER
ACEHPRT CHAPTER, PATCHER, REPATCH
CEHINPR NEPHRIC, PHRENIC, PINCHER
AALNPST PLATANS, SALTPAN
AEEKPRS RESPEAK, SPEAKER
EEIPQRU PERIQUE, REEQUIP
AEIMMST MISMATE, SEMIMAT, TAMMIES
EGHINSW SHEWING, WHINGES
EGINPSY ESPYING, PIGSNEY
AGGINST GASTING, GATINGS, STAGING
EORSTTT STRETTO, TOTTERS
DEEEHRS HEEDERS, HEREDES, SHEERED
EEELPRS PEELERS, SLEEPER
ABCEERR ACERBER, CEREBRA
CEEIPRR CREPIER, PIERCER, REPRICE
ERRSTTU TRUSTER, TURRETS
BDEMOOR BEDROOM, BOREDOM, BROOMED

ADEGGLR DRAGGLE, GARGLED
AEGGLRS GARGLES, LAGGERS, RAGGLES
CERSTTU CURTEST, CUTTERS, SCUTTER
DDEENSU DENUDES, DUDEENS, DUENDES
GHINSTU SHUTING, TUSHING, UNSIGHT
ACIKNST ANTICKS, CATKINS
ADDELRW DAWDLER, DRAWLED, WADDLER
ADEPRSS SPADERS, SPREADS
AEFLSST FALSEST, FATLESS
AEHLSST HASLETS, HATLESS, SHELTAS
AELRSSW WARLESS, WARSLES, WRASSLE
AEMRSSU AMUSERS, ASSUMER, MASSEUR
EFIRSSU FISSURE, FUSSIER
EILNPSS PENSILS, SPINELS, SPLINES
EIMRSSU MISUSER, MUSSIER, SURMISE
EIPRSSU PUSSIER, SUSPIRE, UPRISES
DEILMPS DIMPLES, MISPLED
EHILMSU HELIUMS, MUHLIES
EMPRSTU STUMPER, SUMPTER
EIKLSTT KITTLES, SKITTLE
ACHLORS CHORALS, SCHOLAR
INOPSST PISTONS, POSTINS, SPINTOS
GIINNRU INURING, RUINING
AEGLLSU SEAGULL, SULLAGE, ULLAGES
BDEGRSU BEDRUGS, BUDGERS, REDBUGS
BEGLRSU BUGLERS, BULGERS, BURGLES
EGGLOST GOGLETS, LOGGETS, TOGGLES
GIINPRS PRISING, SPIRING

ACEKLRS CALKERS, LACKERS, SLACKER
CEIKLNS NICKELS, NICKLES, SLICKEN
CEIKLRS LICKERS, SLICKER
CEIKLST STICKLE, TICKLES
CELORSS CLOSERS, CRESOLS
CIIMOST MIOTICS, SOMITIC
ELOPRSS PLESSOR, SLOPERS, SPLORES
AGINNSW AWNINGS, SNAWING
CDEHOSU CHOUSED, DOUCHES, HOCUSED
CEERRSU RESCUER, SECURER
ACEPRRS CARPERS, SCARPER, SCRAPER
AEHPRRS HARPERS, SHARPER
AEMRRSW REWARMS, SWARMER, WARMERS
AEPRRSY PRAYERS, RESPRAY, SPRAYER
EHISTTW WETTISH, WHITEST
AEELPSS ELAPSES, PLEASES
BDEEILL BELLIED, LIBELED
EGGINRY GINGERY, GREYING
CEIIKST EKISTIC, ICKIEST
ACGHINS CASHING, CHASING
AGHINSW SHAWING, WASHING
ABCEISS ABSCISE, SCABIES, SEBASIC
CDEKOST DOCKETS, STOCKED
ABCEMRS CAMBERS, CRAMBES
CEHILTY ETHYLIC, LECYTHI, TECHILY
CEHIPRS CERIPHS, CIPHERS, SPHERIC
ABBERST BARBETS, RABBETS, STABBER
AEFFRST RESTAFF, STAFFER
EILPPRT RIPPLET, TIPPLER
FGILNOW FLOWING, FOWLING, WOLFING

GHIMNOS GNOMISH, MOSHING
CEHIKNT KITCHEN, THICKEN
ACHNSTU CANTHUS, CHAUNTS, STAUNCH
CELSTTU CUTLETS, CUTTLES, SCUTTLE
EINOSSS ESSOINS, OSSEINS, SESSION
AACFILS FACIALS, FASCIAL
ADDELSW DAWDLES, SWADDLE, WADDLES
EOPPRST STOPPER, TOPPERS
AELLSST SALLETS, STELLAS
AACMRST AMTRACS, TARMACS
AACNPST CAPSTAN, CAPTANS, CATNAPS
EMRSSTU ESTRUMS, MUSTERS
ACLOPSU COPULAS, CUPOLAS, SCOPULA
ACHISTT CATTISH, TACHIST
BDEEERR BREEDER, REBREED
EIKLNSS INKLESS, KINLESS
DGHIINS DISHING, HIDINGS, SHINDIG
GIILMNS SLIMING, SMILING
EIILMSS MISLIES, MISSILE, SIMILES
BELLOSU BOULLES, LOBULES, SOLUBLE
ACHIMRS CHARISM, CHIMARS, CHRISMA
ACERRSS CRASSER, SCARERS
DEEPRSS DEPRESS, PRESSED
EELLPRS PRESELL, RESPELL, SPELLER
ACEHRSS CHASERS, CRASHES, ESCHARS
AEHRSSW HAWSERS, SWASHER, WASHERS
EFHIRSS FISHERS, SERFISH, SHERIFS
AEKPRRS PARKERS, REPARKS, SPARKER
ACGIKNS CASKING, SACKING

ABBDELR DABBLER, DRABBLE, RABBLED
ABBELRS BARBELS, RABBLES, SLABBER
ACCERSU ACCRUES, ACCUSER
AELPPRS LAPPERS, RAPPELS, SLAPPER
EILPPRS LIPPERS, RIPPLES, SLIPPER
EIMMRSU IMMURES, RUMMIES
BGINOSS BOSSING, GIBSONS
EEGIMMR GEMMIER, GREMMIE, IMMERGE
EHIPRSS PISHERS, RESHIPS
ABCEKST BACKSET, SETBACK
IMRSSTU SISTRUM, TRISMUS, TRUISMS
AFLMRSU ARMFULS, ARMSFUL, FULMARS
CILNPSU INSCULP, SCULPIN, UNCLIPS
CEKORRS CORKERS, RECORKS, ROCKERS
AELPPST APPLETS, LAPPETS
EFFIIST FIFTIES, IFFIEST
DGGIINR GIRDING, GRIDING, RIDGING
AAILSSV SALIVAS, SALVIAS
AAHLPST ASPHALT, SPATHAL
CDDELRU CUDDLER, CURDLED
CELLRSU CULLERS, SCULLER
DENPSSU SENDUPS, SUSPEND, UPSENDS
EHLSSTU HUSTLES, LUSHEST, SLEUTHS
CEHKORS CHOKERS, HOCKERS, SHOCKER
OPRSSTU SPROUTS, STUPORS
AGGINPS GASPING, PAGINGS
AAABLST ALBATAS, ATABALS, BALATAS
AAADMRS ARMADAS, MADRASA, RAMADAS

CEEHMRS MERCHES, SCHEMER, SCHMEER
CEKLRSU RUCKLES, SCULKER, SUCKLER
ACIMSST MASTICS, MISACTS, MISCAST
EGHHIST EIGHTHS, HEIGHTS, HIGHEST
AEGGRSS AGGRESS, SAGGERS, SEGGARS
AEEPPRR PAPERER, PREPARE, REPAPER
EILMSSY MESSILY, SMILEYS
EOOPPRS OPPOSER, PROPOSE
HNOPSTY PHYTONS, PYTHONS, TYPHONS
GIINPSW SWIPING, WISPING
ADELPPS DAPPLES, SLAPPED
AELPPSU APPULSE, PAPULES, UPLEAPS
EHIKRSS SHRIEKS, SHRIKES
EFFRSTU RESTUFF, STUFFER, TRUFFES
EEPRRSS PRESSER, REPRESS
IKLNPSU LINKUPS, UPLINKS
AEMPPRS MAPPERS, PAMPERS, PREAMPS
EEEKRSS RESEEKS, SEEKERS
AAACMRS MARACAS, MARASCA, MASCARA
ERSSSTU RUSSETS, TRUSSES, TUSSERS
GIIKLNN INKLING, KILNING, LINKING
BBDELRU BLURBED, BURBLED, RUBBLED
GIIKNPS PIGSKIN, SPIKING
ACEHMSS SACHEMS, SAMECHS, SCHEMAS
CGHIINN CHINING, INCHING, NICHING
HOOPSTT HOTSPOT, POTSHOT
ELPSSUY PUSLEYS, PUSSLEY
ACCEKLR CACKLER, CLACKER, CRACKLE

AAAMRSS ASRAMAS, SAMARAS, SAMSARA
DEFFLSU DUFFELS, DUFFLES, SLUFFED
IMMSSTU MUTISMS, SUMMITS
ABBBELR BABBLER, BLABBER, BRABBLE
AEILNOT ELATION, TOENAIL
ADEIOST IODATES, TOADIES
AEEIRST AERIEST, SERIATE
AEIMNOR MORAINE, ROMAINE
AEGINOS AGONIES, AGONISE
ADEINRU UNAIRED, URANIDE
AEINSTU AUNTIES, SINUATE
AINORST AROINTS, RATIONS
AAEINST ENTASIA, TAENIAS
ADELORT DELATOR, LEOTARD
AELNOST ETALONS, TOLANES
DEINORU DOURINE, NEUROID
EILNOTU ELUTION, OUTLINE
ADEEILN ALIENED, DELAINE
ADEEIRS DEARIES, READIES
AEINRTW TAWNIER, TINWARE
ADEIMNO AMIDONE, DOMAINE
ADEIORV AVODIRE, AVOIDER
AEINOPS EPINAOS, SENOPIA
AEIOPST ATOPIES, OPIATES
DEEIORS OREIDES, OSIERED
ABENORT BARONET, REBOANT
AEGILOS GOALIES, SOILAGE
AEEIMNT ETAMINE, MATINEE
AEEIRTT ARIETTE, ITERATE
EINOOST ISOTONE, TOONIES
AEGLORT GLOATER, LEGATOR
AEGNORS ONAGERS, ORANGES
ADEILNS DENIALS, SNAILED

Bob's Bible Bonus: Complete 7-letter Multi-Anagram Quiz

ADEILNU	**AGINOST**	**EEHINRT**	**ADGINRT**	**ADEORSV**	**CEEILNT**	**AEGILNV**	**AELNNRS**	**EILMNRS**	**ENOSTTU**	**ACEIRRS**	**ABCEILR**	**EGINSTT**	**DEENOPS**
ALIUNDE	AGONIST	NEITHER	DARTING	OVERSAD	CENTILE	LEAVING	ENSNARL	LIMNERS	STOUTEN	CARRIES	CALIBER	SETTING	DEPONES
UNIDEAL	GITANOS	THEREIN	TRADING	SAVORED	LICENTE	VEALING	LANNERS	MERLINS	TENUTOS	SCARIER	CALIBRE	TESTING	SPONDEE
ADEILST	**AGINOTU**	**AEEILPT**	**AENRRST**	**AEFLORS**	**CEEILRT**	**AEGIMST**	**DEINNRS**	**EINPSTU**	**ACDELOS**	**ADEHIRR**	**ABEILRW**	**EGIRTTU**	**DEEOPRS**
DETAILS	AUTOING	EPILATE	ERRANTS	LOAFERS	RETICLE	GAMIEST	DINNERS	PUNIEST	COLEADS	HARDIER	BRAWLIE	GUTTIER	DEPOSER
DILATES	OUTGAIN	PILEATE	RANTERS	SAFROLE	TIERCEL	SIGMATE	ENDRINS	PUNTIES	SOLACED	HARRIED	WIRABLE	TURGITE	REPOSED
DEILNRT	**AACEINR**	**ADELNST**	**AENRSTT**	**AELNOPS**	**DEEINPR**	**AEGNRRT**	**DEIRRST**	**ACILOST**	**ADELOPS**	**AEHISTT**	**ACDEFIN**	**AEGILLN**	**EELMOST**
TENDRIL	ACARINE	DENTALS	NATTERS	ESPANOL	REPINED	GRANTER	STIRRED	CITOLAS	DEPOSAL	ATHEIST	FACIEND	GALLEIN	OMELETS
TRINDLE	CARINAE	SLANTED	RATTENS	NOPALES	RIPENED	REGRANT	STRIDER	STOICAL	PEDALOS	STAITHE	FANCIED	NIGELLA	TELOMES
AILNOST	**AAEIMNT**	**AELRSTU**	**EINNRST**	**AELOPRS**	**DEEINRW**	**EGINRTT**	**EINRRSU**	**ACIORSU**	**AABERST**	**AEILMNN**	**ACDEHIN**	**AEGISST**	**EELOPRS**
LATINOS	AMENTIA	ESTRUAL	INTERNS	PAROLES	REWIDEN	GITTERN	INSURER	CARIOUS	ABATERS	LINEMAN	CHAINED	AGEISTS	ELOPERS
TALIONS	ANIMATE	SALUTER	TINNERS	REPOSAL	WIDENER	RETTING	RUINERS	CURIOSA	ABREAST	MELANIN	ECHIDNA	SAGIEST	LEPROSE
AEEORTV	**ADENORR**	**AEGHINT**	**ADDEINR**	**AELOPST**	**EEILPRT**	**EIINORZ**	**AEILLRS**	**ADIMOST**	**AADEPRT**	**AEIRRSV**	**ACEFIRS**	**ABEGNRS**	**EELOTUV**
OVERATE	ADORNER	GAHNITE	DANDIER	APOSTLE	PERLITE	IONIZER	RALLIES	DIATOMS	ADAPTER	ARRIVES	FARCIES	BANGERS	EVOLUTE
OVEREAT	READORN	HEATING	DRAINED	PELOTAS	REPTILE	IRONIZE	SALLIER	MASTOID	READAPT	VARIERS	FIACRES	GRABENS	VELOUTE
EEINOPR	**AEORSTT**	**AEGIMRT**	**CEINRST**	**BDEIORS**	**EEINPRS**	**EEGNRST**	**AEILNSS**	**AILOPST**	**AAENPST**	**AEGGINR**	**ACEHIST**	**ACEGLNR**	**EEORSUV**
PEREION	ROTATES	MIGRATE	CISTERN	BORIDES	EREPSIN	GERENTS	SALINES	APOSTIL	ANAPEST	GEARING	ACHIEST	CLANGER	OEUVRES
PIONEER	TOASTER	RAGTIME	CRETINS	DISROBE	REPINES	REGENTS	SILANES	TOPSAIL	PEASANT	NAGGIER	AITCHES	GLANCER	OVERUSE
DEILORS	**EILORTT**	**AEGINRV**	**EINRSTV**	**CEILORS**	**EEIPRST**	**EGIMNRT**	**DEENRSU**	**AIORSUV**	**CDEIINT**	**AGINRTT**	**ACEILMT**	**ADEGRTY**	**EFNORRT**
SOLDIER	TORTILE	REAVING	INVERTS	COILERS	PESTIER	METRING	ENDURES	SAVIOUR	IDENTIC	RATTING	CLIMATE	GYRATED	FRONTER
SOLIDER	TRIOLET	VINEGAR	STRIVEN	RECOILS	RESPITE	TERMING	ENSURED	VARIOUS	INCITED	TARTING	METICAL	TRAGEDY	REFRONT
DEIOSTU	**EINNOST**	**AEEGRST**	**EINRSTW**	**EILNOPS**	**ADDEEIR**	**AEMNNOT**	**EELNSTU**	**AEEGRRT**	**DEIIPRT**	**ADEEISS**	**ACEILPR**	**AEGLNRW**	**EHNORRT**
OUTSIDE	INTONES	ERGATES	TWINERS	EPSILON	DEAIRED	MONTANE	ELUENTS	GREATER	RIPTIDE	DISEASE	CALIPER	WANGLER	HORRENT
TEDIOUS	TENSION	RESTAGE	WINTERS	PINOLES	READIED	NONMEAT	UNSTEEL	REGRATE	TIDERIP	SEASIDE	REPLICA	WRANGLE	NORTHER
DEIINRT	**AELORRT**	**EEGILNR**	**ACINOTU**	**EILOPST**	**DENOOTU**	**AEOPRRT**	**AENOOTZ**	**ANNORST**	**EFIINST**	**ABDEELT**	**ACEIMNS**	**AEGMNTU**	**ABELOTW**
INDITER	REALTOR	LEERING	AUCTION	PIOLETS	DUOTONE	PRAETOR	ENTOZOA	NATRONS	FINITES	BELATED	AMNESIC	AUGMENT	TEABOWL
NITRIDE	RELATOR	REELING	CAUTION	PISTOLE	OUTDONE	PRORATE	OZONATE	NONARTS	NIFTIES	BLEATED	CINEMAS	MUTAGEN	TOWABLE
EIILNRT	**ABDENOR**	**INORSTU**	**ADINOPR**	**EIINRTV**	**DEOORTU**	**ACGINOT**	**ABELNTU**	**INORSTT**	**EIILMRT**	**ABDEEST**	**ADEHINP**	**CEGILNR**	**ABEMNOS**
LINTIER	BANDORE	NITROUS	PADRONI	INVITER	OUTDOER	COATING	ABLUENT	INTORTS	LIMITER	BESTEAD	HEADPIN	CLINGER	AMBONES
NITRILE	BROADEN	TURIONS	PONIARD	VITRINE	OUTRODE	COTINGA	TUNABLE	TRITONS	MILTIER	DEBATES	PINHEAD	CRINGLE	BEMOANS
DENORST	**ACDEORT**	**ADEEGNT**	**AIMNOTU**	**AILNRSU**	**ACEIPRT**	**DEENNOT**	**ACDERST**	**AAIMNRT**	**EIINSTV**	**ABEELNS**	**ADEHIRY**	**DEGHIRT**	**ACDEMOR**
RODENTS	CORDATE	AGENTED	MANITOU	INSULAR	PARETIC	ENDNOTE	REDACTS	MARTIAN	INVITES	BALEENS	HAYRIDE	GIRTHED	CAROMED
SNORTED	REDCOAT	NEGATED	TINAMOU	URINALS	PICRATE	TENONED	SCARTED	TAMARIN	VINIEST	ENABLES	HYDRIAE	RIGHTED	COMRADE
ENORSTU	**ADEOPRT**	**ACEEOST**	**AINOPTU**	**AENORSS**	**AEIMNTY**	**BEENORS**	**ACDERTU**	**AEEGNRV**	**EIIPRST**	**ACDEENS**	**AEHINSV**	**DEGINRW**	**ACEOSTV**
TENOURS	ADOPTER	ACETOSE	OPUNTIA	REASONS	AMENITY	BOREENS	CURATED	AVENGER	PITIERS	DECANES	EVANISH	REDWING	AVOCETS
TONSURE	READOPT	COATEES	UTOPIAN	SENORAS	ANYTIME	ENROBES	TRADUCE	ENGRAVE	TIPSIER	ENCASED	VAHINES	WRINGED	OCTAVES
EEGINOS	**AEHLNOT**	**BEEINOS**	**AIORSTV**	**DENOPRT**	**ADEEILM**	**CDEENOR**	**ADEMNTU**	**EEGIMNT**	**ADILSTU**	**ADEELNP**	**AEHIPRS**	**EFGINRS**	**ADEFORY**
GENOISE	ANETHOL	EBONIES	TRAVOIS	PORTEND	EMAILED	ENCODER	UNMATED	MEETING	DUALIST	DEPLANE	HARPIES	FINGERS	FEODARY
SOIGNEE	ETHANOL	EBONISE	VIATORS	PROTEND	LIMEADE	ENCORED	UNTAMED	TEEMING	TULADIS	PANELED	SHARPIE	FRINGES	FORAYED
ADEINRR	**AEHLORT**	**EEILORV**	**DEIILOS**	**AEORSST**	**ADELNSU**	**CEELORT**	**ADENPST**	**EEGINPR**	**AAILORV**	**ADEELPT**	**AEHIRSW**	**EGHILRT**	**AELORVY**
DRAINER	LOATHER	OVERLIE	DOILIES	OSETRAS	UNLADES	ELECTOR	PEDANTS	PEERING	OVARIAL	PETALED	WASHIER	LIGHTER	LAYOVER
RANDIER	RATHOLE	RELIEVO	IDOLISE	OSSETRA	UNLEADS	ELECTRO	PENTADS	PREEING	VARIOLA	PLEATED	WEARISH	RELIGHT	OVERLAY
ADEIRRT	**AEHNORS**	**AEIMOPR**	**AEIKLRT**	**ABEIRRT**	**ADELSTU**	**CEENORS**	**ADEPRTU**	**BEGINOS**	**CDEORTU**	**ADEENPS**	**AEILMNP**	**EGHIRST**	**BCEILOR**
TARDIER	HOARSEN	EMPORIA	RATLIKE	ARBITER	AULDEST	ENCORES	UPDATER	BINGOES	COURTED	SNEAPED	IMPANEL	RESIGHT	BRICOLE
TARRIED	SENHORA	MEROPIA	TALKIER	RAREBIT	SALUTED	NECROSE	UPRATED	BIOGENS	EDUCTOR	SPEANED	MANIPLE	SIGHTER	CORBEIL
AEINNRS	**AEMNORU**	**EENNORT**	**AEINQTU**	**ACEINNR**	**DEILSTU**	**DEENORW**	**ADERSTV**	**DEGIMNO**	**CELNORS**	**ADEERSV**	**AEIMPST**	**EGILNTW**	**CDEIORV**
INSANER	ENAMOUR	ENTERON	ANTIQUE	CANNIER	DILUTES	ENDOWER	ADVERTS	DEMOING	CLONERS	ADVERSE	IMPASTE	WELTING	CODRIVE
INSNARE	NEUROMA	TENONER	QUINATE	NARCEIN	DUELIST	REENDOW	STARVED	MENDIGO	CORNELS	EVADERS	PASTIME	WINGLET	DIVORCE
AEINSTT	**CEINOST**	**DEIINST**	**AEINSTX**	**ACEINTT**	**AAENOPS**	**AEFMNOR**	**AEFLRTU**	**EGHINOS**	**DEFNORU**	**ADEERSW**	**AEIPRSV**	**EGINRSV**	**CEHILNO**
INSTATE	NOTICES	INDITES	ANTISEX	NICTATE	APNOEAS	FORAMEN	REFUTAL	HONGIES	FOUNDER	DRAWEES	PARVISE	SERVING	CHOLINE
SATINET	SECTION	TINEIDS	SEXTAIN	TETANIC	PAESANO	FOREMAN	TEARFUL	SHOEING	REFOUND	RESAWED	PAVISER	VERSING	HELICON
ABDEIRT	**EFILORT**	**EIILNRS**	**AEINSTZ**	**ACEIRRT**	**BDEEINR**	**AEHNOPT**	**AELNPRS**	**ADMNORT**	**DEFORST**	**AEELMNS**	**ACIORTT**	**EGINRSW**	**CEHIORS**
REDBAIT	LOFTIER	INLIERS	ZANIEST	CIRRATE	BENDIER	PHAETON	PLANERS	DORMANT	DEFROST	ENAMELS	CITATOR	SWINGER	COHEIRS
TRIBADE	TREFOIL	RESILIN	ZEATINS	ERRATIC	INBREED	PHONATE	REPLANS	MORDANT	FROSTED	MELENAS	RICOTTA	WINGERS	HEROICS
ADEFINT	**EHILNOT**	**AEGNNOT**	**ADEGLNR**	**ADEERRT**	**GIINORT**	**CEINOPT**	**AELNPST**	**AMNORST**	**DEHORST**	**AEELNSV**	**CDEENRT**	**ANOORTT**	**CEILNOP**
DEFIANT	HOTLINE	NEGATON	DANGLER	RETREAD	IGNITOR	ENTOPIC	PLANETS	MATRONS	DEHORTS	ENSLAVE	CENTRED	ARNOTTO	PINOCLE
FAINTED	NEOLITH	TONNAGE	GNARLED	TREADER	RIOTING	NEPOTIC	PLATENS	TRANSOM	SHORTED	LEAVENS	CREDENT	RATTOON	PLEONIC
ADEINRV	**EHINORS**	**EIMNOOR**	**DEGILNT**	**AEELNRR**	**AEGINNU**	**EFIOPRT**	**AELNRUV**	**AEIKLST**	**DELOPRT**	**CDEEIRS**	**EENRSTY**	**ACENNOS**	**CEILOPR**
INVADER	HEROINS	IONOMER	GLINTED	LEARNER	ANGUINE	FIREPOT	UNRAVEL	LAKIEST	DROPLET	DECRIES	STYRENE	ANCONES	PELORIC
RAVINED	INSHORE	MOONIER	TINGLED	RELEARN	GUANINE	PIEFORT	VENULAR	TALKIES	PRETOLD	DEICERS	YESTERN	SONANCE	POLICER
AEHILNR	**EHINOST**	**ADEILNN**	**DEGINRS**	**AEENNRS**	**DELNRTU**	**EEEILST**	**AEMRSTU**	**AEILQTU**	**DEMNORS**	**DEEFIRS**	**ACEHNRT**	**ADENNOY**	**DEIMOTV**
HERNIAL	ETHIONS	ANNELID	DINGERS	ENSNARE	RUNDLET	EELIEST	MATURES	LIQUATE	MODERNS	DEFIERS	CHANTER	ANNOYED	MOTIVED
INHALER	HISTONE	LINDANE	ENGIRDS	RENNASE	TRUNDLE	STEELIE	STRUMAE	TEQUILA	RODSMEN	SERIFED	TRANCHE	ANODYNE	VOMITED
AEHINST	**EILOPRT**	**ACEGNOT**	**EGILRST**	**AEENRRS**	**AADILNR**	**ACEEFIN**	**BDEILNR**	**ADEGRSU**	**DEMNOTU**	**DEEILPR**	**CEHINRT**	**AELOPRR**	**EIMNOPS**
SHEITAN	POITREL	COAGENT	GLISTER	EARNERS	LANIARD	FAIENCE	BLINDER	DESUGAR	DEMOUNT	PERILED	CITHERN	PERORAL	IMPONES
STHENIA	POLITER	COGNATE	GRISTLE	REEARNS	NADIRAL	FIANCEE	BRINDLE	SUGARED	MOUNTED	REPLIED	CITHREN	PREORAL	PEONISM
AEILMNT	**ADDEIOT**	**AEGMNOR**	**EGIRSTU**	**DEEINRR**	**AAILRST**	**ABDEGNO**	**BDEIRST**	**EGILSTU**	**DENOPRU**	**DEEILRY**	**GIILNOR**	**AEMORRS**	**AEGIKLN**
AILMENT	IODATED	MARENGO	GUSTIER	DERNIER	LARIATS	BONDAGE	BESTRID	GLUIEST	POUNDER	REEDILY	LIGROIN	REMORAS	LEAKING
ALIMENT	TOADIED	MEGARON	GUTSIER	NERDIER	LATRIAS	DOGBANE	BISTRED	UGLIEST	UNROPED	YIELDER	ROILING	ROAMERS	LINKAGE
AEILPRT	**AEIKLOT**	**EGIMNOT**	**AGILORS**	**EEINNST**	**ADEEGLR**	**ACDEGNO**	**BEIRSTU**	**ADEHNRS**	**DENORSW**	**DEEINSV**	**ACHIORT**	**AEORRSV**	**AEGIKLT**
PLAITER	KEITLOA	EMOTING	GIRASOL	INTENSE	LAGERED	CONGAED	BUSTIER	HANDERS	DOWNERS	DEVEINS	CHARIOT	SAVORER	GLAIKET
PLATIER	OATLIKE	MITOGEN	GLORIAS	TENNIES	REGALED	DECAGON	RUBIEST	HARDENS	WONDERS	ENDIVES	HARICOT	SEROVAR	TAGLIKE
AEINPRS	**AEEILRR**	**ABDEINS**	**ADEORRS**	**EIJNORS**	**ADEEGRS**	**ADEGNOW**	**CDEIRST**	**ACILNOS**	**DEORSTW**	**DEEINSW**	**ACINOPT**	**EEIINSW**	**ACILNST**
PANIERS	EARLIER	BANDIES	ADORERS	JOINERS	DRAGEES	GOWANED	CREDITS	ALNICOS	STROWED	ENDWISE	CAPTION	EISWEIN	CATLINS
RAPINES	LEARIER	BASINED	DROSERA	REJOINS	GREASED	WAGONED	DIRECTS	OILCANS	WORSTED	SINEWED	PACTION	WIENIES	TINCALS
DEEILNR	**AEEFILR**	**ACDEINS**	**EILOSTT**	**ABEELRT**	**AEEGLRS**	**ADEGORW**	**DEFILRT**	**AADEILV**	**EFLORST**	**EEILPRS**	**ADEEKNR**	**ABGINOS**	**ADILMNR**
REDLINE	FILAREE	CANDIES	LITOTES	BLEATER	GALERES	DOWAGER	FLIRTED	AVAILED	FLORETS	REPLIES	KNEADER	BAGNIOS	MANDRIL
RELINED	LEAFIER	INCASED	TOILETS	RETABLE	REGALES	WORDAGE	TRIFLED	VEDALIA	LOFTERS	SPIELER	NAKEDER	GABIONS	RIMLAND
EEILNRS	**AEEILRV**	**ADEILPT**	**AAEILRV**	**ACEELNR**	**EEGILST**	**AEGLMOR**	**DEILNTW**	**AGIILNT**	**EHLORST**	**EEILPST**	**DEEINRX**	**AFGILNO**	**ADINPST**
LIERNES	LEAVIER	PLAITED	REAVAIL	CLEANER	ELEGIST	GLOMERA	INDWELT	INTAGLI	HOLSTER	EPISTLE	INDEXER	FOALING	PANDITS
RELINES	VEALIER	TALIPED	VELARIA	RECLEAN	ELEGITS	GOMERAL	WINTLED	TAILING	HOSTLER	PELITES	REINDEX	LOAFING	SANDPIT
ACINORT	**AEEIMRS**	**ADEIMST**	**AAEIMNS**	**ACEENST**	**ADLNORS**	**AEGOSTW**	**DEIMNRS**	**DINOORS**	**EHORSTU**	**DELNOOS**	**EEIKRST**	**ACNOORT**	**AILMRST**
CAROTIN	SEAMIER	DIASTEM	AMNESIA	CETANES	LADRONS	STOWAGE	MINDERS	INDOORS	SHOUTER	NOODLES	KEISTER	CARTOON	MISTRAL
CORTINA	SERIEMA	MISDATE	ANEMIAS	TENACES	LARDONS	TOWAGES	REMINDS	SORDINO	SOUTHER	SNOOLED	KIESTER	CORANTO	RAMTILS
DEIINOS	**AELOORS**	**ADEISTW**	**ADEIIMN**	**ADEEHRT**	**ADLNOST**	**CEGINOS**	**DEIMNST**	**DIOORST**	**ELMNOST**	**DELOOST**	**EEIQRTU**	**ANOOPRT**	**AILNSTY**
IODINES	AEROSOL	DAWTIES	AMIDINE	EARTHED	DALTONS	COGNISE	MINDSET	DISROOT	LOMENTS	STOOLED	QUIETER	PATROON	NASTILY
IONISED	ROSEOLA	WAISTED	DIAMINE	HEARTED	SANDLOT	COIGNES	MISTEND	TOROIDS	MELTONS	TOLEDOS	REQUITE	PRONOTA	SAINTLY
EIILOST	**AEGLORS**	**AEFILST**	**ANOORST**	**AEEFRST**	**DINORSU**	**EGIOPRS**	**DEINPST**	**ILNOOST**	**ELMORST**	**AAEGLRS**	**ADEGNRR**	**AACEIRV**	**EFILOOS**
IOLITES	GALORES	FETIALS	RATOONS	AFREETS	DIURONS	PORGIES	DIPNETS	LOTIONS	MERLOTS	ALEGARS	GNARRED	AVARICE	FLOOSIE
OILIEST	GAOLERS	SEALIFT	SANTOOR	FEASTER	DURIONS	SERPIGO	STIPEND	SOLITON	MOLTERS	LAAGERS	GRANDER	CAVIARE	FOLIOSE
ADEGILR	**AEGLOST**	**AEHILRS**	**ABDELOT**	**AEEHLRT**	**ABDEGIR**	**EGIOPRU**	**DEINRSW**	**DEGNRTU**	**ELOPRST**	**AENPRTT**	**AEGNRRS**	**BDEEORS**	**ABEERTT**
GLADIER	GELATOS	HAILERS	BLOATED	HALTERE	ABRIDGE	GROUPIE	REWINDS	GRUNTED	PETROLS	PATTERN	GARNERS	BEDSORE	ABETTER
GLAIRED	LEGATOS	SHALIER	LOBATED	LEATHER	BRIGADE	PIROGUE	WINDERS	TRUDGEN	REPLOTS	REPTANT	RANGERS	SOBERED	BERETTA
AEGILNU	**EEINRTT**	**AEHILST**	**ABELOST**	**AEEMNRS**	**ACEGILR**	**ADGILNR**	**DEINSTY**	**AGNOSTU**	**ABEISTT**	**EINPRRT**	**DEGINNR**	**CDEENOS**	**AEENNPT**
LINGUAE	NETTIER	HALITES	BOATELS	MEANERS	GLACIER	DARLING	DENSITY	NOUGATS	BATISTE	PRINTER	GRINNED	ENCODES	PENNATE
UNAGILE	TENTIER	HELIAST	OBLATES	RENAMES	GRACILE	LARDING	DESTINY	OUTSANG	BISTATE	REPRINT	RENDING	SECONDE	PENTANE
ADEGNRT	**AEEHNRT**	**AEILNSV**	**ACDENOS**	**AEEPRST**	**ACEGINS**	**ADGINRS**	**DEIPRST**	**GINORSU**	**ACDEIRR**	**AGIMNRT**	**DEGINNT**	**DEELMOR**	**AEEPRRT**
DRAGNET	EARTHEN	ALEVINS	ACNODES	REPEATS	CEASING	DARINGS	SPIRTED	ROUSING	ACRIDER	MARTING	DENTING	MODELER	PEARTER
GRANTED	HEARTEN	VALINES	DEACONS	RETAPES	INCAGES	GRADINS	STRIPED	SOURING	CARRIED	MIGRANT	TENDING	REMODEL	TAPERER
EGINRST	**CEEINRT**	**DEEIRSU**	**ACEORSU**	**CDEEIRT**	**ADEGINV**	**ADERSTT**	**EFIRSTU**	**ENNORSU**	**ACEILTT**	**EENNRST**	**DEGINRR**	**DEELORW**	**EEFINRR**
RESTING	ENTERIC	RESIDUE	ACEROUS	RECITED	DEAVING	STARTED	FUSTIER	NEURONS	LATTICE	RENNETS	GRINDER	LOWERED	FERNIER
STINGER	ENTICER	UREIDES	CAROUSE	TIERCED	EVADING	TETRADS	SURFEIT	NONUSER	TACTILE	TENNERS	REGRIND	ROWELED	REFINER

Bob's Bible Bonus: Complete 7-letter Multi-Anagram Quiz

EEIMRRT	**ADEHLNS**	**ADMNORS**	**ADELOSS**	**EFIRSTT**	**DEEPRTU**	**EHILPRT**	**ACLNOOT**	**CEOPRST**	**CEEIRSV**	**EHLRSTU**	**AINPRSW**	**EILSTTY**	**ADEHPST**
MITERER	HANDLES	RANDOMS	ALDOSES	FITTERS	ERUPTED	PHILTER	COOLANT	COPTERS	SCRIEVE	HURTLES	INWRAPS	STYLITE	HEPTADS
TRIREME	HANDSEL	RODSMAN	LASSOED	TITFERS	REPUTED	PHILTRE	OCTANOL	PROSECT	SERVICE	HUSTLER	RIPSAWN	TESTILY	SPATHED
EEIMRTT	**AELMRSU**	**ADMORST**	**BDELORU**	**EHIRSTT**	**DEERSTW**	**EHIMNRU**	**ACNOORS**	**EMOPRST**	**EEFILPR**	**AAIRSST**	**BEIMORW**	**EIPRRSU**	**ADEMPST**
EMITTER	MAULERS	STARDOM	BOULDER	HITTERS	STREWED	INHUMER	CORONAS	STOMPER	PREFILE	ARISTAS	IMBOWER	PURSIER	DAMPEST
TERMITE	SERUMAL	TSARDOM	DOUBLER	TITHERS	WRESTED	RHENIUM	RACOONS	TROMPES	PRELIFE	TARSIAS	WOMBIER	UPRISER	STAMPED
EEINPRR	**AELMSTU**	**ADORTUW**	**CELNOSU**	**EILRTTY**	**EEFLNRS**	**EHIMRST**	**ADMNOOR**	**EOPRSTW**	**EEIMPST**	**AEFGRRT**	**CEHINOP**	**ABDGILN**	**AEHLPRS**
REPINER	AMULETS	OUTDRAW	COUNSEL	LITTERY	FLENSER	HERMITS	DOORMAN	POWTERS	EMPTIES	GRAFTER	CHOPINE	BALDING	PLASHER
RIPENER	MULETAS	OUTWARD	UNCLOSE	TRITELY	FRESNEL	MITHERS	MADRONO	PROWEST	SEPTIME	REGRAFT	PHOCINE	BLADING	SPHERAL
EEINRRV	**BDEIRSU**	**ALMORST**	**CELORSU**	**EIMNSTT**	**EELRSTY**	**EIMPRST**	**AMNOORS**	**AEKOTTU**	**EEINPSV**	**ABDNOSU**	**BDELOSU**	**ACGILNS**	**CDEHIRS**
NERVIER	BRUISED	MORTALS	CLOSURE	MITTENS	RESTYLE	IMPREST	MAROONS	OUTTAKE	PENSIVE	ABOUNDS	BLOUSED	LACINGS	CHIDERS
VERNIER	BURDIES	STROMAL	COLURES	SMITTEN	TERSELY	PERMITS	ROMANOS	TAKEOUT	VESPINE	BAUSOND	DOUBLES	SCALING	HERDICS
ADGNOOR	**CDEILNU**	**ALOPRST**	**DEFLNOS**	**EIMRRST**	**ABEILLR**	**AEIKRRS**	**AEGRSST**	**AMNRSTU**	**EEIRSVW**	**ABLORSU**	**DEEEMNR**	**ACGINSU**	**CDEIPST**
DRAGOON	INCLUDE	PATROLS	ENFOLDS	RETRIMS	BRAILLE	KERRIAS	GASTERS	ANTRUMS	REVIEWS	LABOURS	EMENDER	CAUSING	DEPICTS
GADROON	NUCLIDE	PORTALS	FONDLES	TRIMERS	LIBERAL	SARKIER	STAGERS	UNSMART	VIEWERS	SUBORAL	REEDMEN	SAUCING	DISCEPT
GILNOOT	**DEILNSW**	**BILORST**	**DEFLORS**	**EINNPRS**	**ACEISST**	**ABILOPR**	**DDEGINR**	**ACEERRS**	**ADEGOSS**	**ACLOSTU**	**EEELMNT**	**ADGHINS**	**CEFILRU**
LOOTING	SWINDLE	BRISTOL	FOLDERS	PINNERS	ASCITES	BIPOLAR	GRINDED	CAREERS	DOSAGES	LOCUSTA	ELEMENT	DASHING	FLUERIC
TOOLING	WINDLES	STROBIL	REFOLDS	SPINNER	ECTASIS	PARBOIL	REDDING	CREASER	SEADOGS	TALCOUS	TELEMEN	SHADING	LUCIFER
EGIINNR	**DEILRSW**	**CDINOTU**	**DEHOSTU**	**EINSTTW**	**AEILLPR**	**ACDIOPR**	**EGILLNT**	**ADEEHRR**	**AINQSTU**	**ADLMNOS**	**EEENRUV**	**AGHILNU**	**CEILNPS**
GINNIER	SWIRLED	CONDUIT	SHOUTED	ENTWIST	PALLIER	PARODIC	GILLNET	ADHERER	ASQUINT	ALMONDS	REVENUE	HAULING	PENCILS
REINING	WILDERS	NOCTUID	SOUTHED	TWINSET	PERILLA	PICADOR	TELLING	REHEARD	QUINTAS	DOLMANS	UNREEVE	NILGHAU	SPLENIC
DEEERST	**EILNSUV**	**DIMNORS**	**DELOPRS**	**BEGINOY**	**AEIMNSS**	**ACIOPRS**	**EGINSST**	**AEELPTT**	**EIKMORS**	**ALOSTUY**	**AADILLO**	**AGILMNS**	**CEIMRSU**
REESTED	UNLIVES	DORMINS	POLDERS	BIOGENY	INSEAMS	PICAROS	INGESTS	PALETTE	IRKSOME	LAYOUTS	ALLODIA	LINGAMS	CERIUMS
STEERED	UNVEILS	NIMRODS	PRESOLD	OBEYING	SAMISEN	PROSAIC	SIGNETS	PELTATE	SMOKIER	OUTLAYS	ALODIAL	MALIGNS	MURICES
ELOORTT	**EIOOSTZ**	**ILNOSTY**	**DENOSUW**	**ABDGINR**	**AEINSSV**	**DDEIIOS**	**EHIKNRT**	**AEEMRRS**	**EIOPSTX**	**ILNOPSU**	**CENOORR**	**AEGHMOS**	**DEHIRSV**
ROOTLET	OOZIEST	STONILY	SWOUNED	BARDING	SAVINES	IODIDES	RETHINK	REAMERS	EXPOSIT	PULSION	CORONER	HOMAGES	DERVISH
TOOTLER	ZOOIEST	TYLOSIN	UNSOWED	BRIGAND	VINASSE	IODISED	THINKER	SMEARER	POXIEST	UPSILON	CROONER	OHMAGES	SHRIVED
BEOORST	**AEEGRRS**	**AEGIMPR**	**DEOPSTU**	**ABGINTU**	**EJLORST**	**AENNPRS**	**BELORTT**	**AEEPRRS**	**DENNSTU**	**ACEERTX**	**AACLOST**	**AGGILNO**	**DEIMPRU**
BOOSTER	GREASER	EPIGRAM	OUTSPED	ANTIBUG	JOLTERS	PANNERS	BLOTTER	REAPERS	DUNNEST	EXACTER	CATALOS	GAOLING	DUMPIER
REBOOTS	REGEARS	PRIMAGE	SPOUTED	TABUING	JOSTLER	SPANNER	BOTTLER	SPEARER	STUNNED	EXCRETA	COASTAL	GOALING	UMPIRED
CEOORST	**DEEGINN**	**EEOPRTT**	**AEGMNNO**	**ACGILNT**	**DEEEGNR**	**AEELSTZ**	**CENORRS**	**DEEHIRR**	**DENSTTU**	**AEEKNRW**	**AADLMNO**	**CCEIORT**	**EFILMRS**
COOTERS	ENGINED	PROETTE	AGNOMEN	CATLING	GREENED	TEAZELS	CORNERS	HERRIED	STUDENT	REWAKEN	MANDOLA	CEROTIC	FILMERS
SCOOTER	NEEDING	TREETOP	NONGAME	TALCING	RENEGED	TEAZLES	SCORNER	REHIRED	STUNTED	WAKENER	MONADAL	ORECTIC	REFILMS
DEOOPRT	**EEGINNU**	**AEKLRST**	**AAEEGMT**	**ACGINST**	**DEEEGRT**	**DEEIKNS**	**ENNORSW**	**DEEIRRW**	**CEGORSU**	**DEGIKLO**	**CIILOST**	**DEELRSW**	**EFILMST**
TORPEDO	GENUINE	STALKER	AGAMETE	ACTINGS	DETERGE	ENSKIED	RENOWNS	REWIRED	SCOURGE	DOGLIKE	COLITIS	REWELDS	FILMSET
TROOPED	INGENUE	TALKERS	AGEMATE	CASTING	GREETED	SKEINED	WONNERS	WEIRDER	SCROUGE	GODLIKE	SOLICIT	WELDERS	LEFTISM
EFNOOST	**CEHNORT**	**EIKLNST**	**EEENPRT**	**ACGIRST**	**GIILNOS**	**EEIQRSU**	**ENORRUV**	**EEHIRRS**	**DEGHOTU**	**DDEEGIN**	**DHIILOT**	**EELMRSU**	**EILMPRU**
EFTSOON	CHORTEN	LENTISK	PRETEEN	GASTRIC	SILOING	ESQUIRE	OVERRUN	HERRIES	OUGHTED	DEEDING	DITHIOL	LEMURES	LUMPIER
FESTOON	NOTCHER	TINKLES	TERPENE	TRAGICS	SOILING	QUERIES	RUNOVER	REHIRES	TOUGHED	DEIGNED	LITHOID	RELUMES	PLUMIER
ENOOPRS	**AAFILNT**	**EINQSTU**	**AABORST**	**ADGINRW**	**ABEHLRT**	**EIKNRTT**	**EORRSTY**	**EEINNPS**	**EGLORSV**	**EEFIIRR**	**DIIORSV**	**ADEISSV**	**EILMPST**
OPERONS	FANTAIL	INQUEST	ABATORS	DRAWING	BLATHER	KNITTER	ROYSTER	PENNIES	GLOVERS	FIERIER	DIVISOR	ADVISES	LIMPEST
SNOOPER	TAILFAN	QUINTES	RABATOS	WARDING	HALBERT	TRINKET	STROYER	PINENES	GROVELS	REIFIER	VIROIDS	DISSAVE	LIMPETS
AEEFHRT	**AAILMRT**	**CEILSTU**	**AAMNORS**	**ADGINRY**	**ABERSTY**	**ADEGRRS**	**ABGNORS**	**ADGLNOO**	**EGLORSW**	**ALNOSST**	**ELLOSTU**	**AGILNNS**	**EILMRSY**
FEATHER	MARITAL	LUCITES	OARSMAN	DRAYING	BARYTES	GRADERS	BARONGS	DONGOLA	GLOWERS	SANTOLS	OUTSELL	LIGNANS	MISERLY
TEREFAH	MARTIAL	LUETICS	RAMONAS	YARDING	BETRAYS	REGARDS	BROGANS	GONDOLA	REGLOWS	STANOLS	SELLOUT	LINSANG	MISRELY
AEEFMNR	**AAIMRST**	**EGLNSTU**	**AGINNST**	**AGHILNT**	**ACDEFRT**	**AEGRRSU**	**BGILNOT**	**AEEIMSS**	**EGMORSU**	**ANORSUU**	**IIMNOSU**	**EGNOPRY**	**EILRSVY**
ENFRAME	AMRITAS	ENGLUTS	ANTINGS	HALTING	CRAFTED	ARGUERS	BILTONG	MISEASE	GRUMOSE	ANUROUS	IONIUMS	PROGENY	LIVYERS
FREEMAN	TAMARIS	GLUTENS	STANING	LATHING	FRACTED	SUGARER	BOLTING	SIAMESE	MORGUES	URANOUS	NIMIOUS	PYROGEN	SILVERY
DEILSTT	**AAINPRS**	**EEHNORW**	**AGINSTT**	**AGILNPR**	**ACDEHNR**	**DEGINNS**	**CGINOST**	**AEISTTT**	**CEENPRT**	**INORSUU**	**GIMNOOR**	**ACORRST**	**ACENRSS**
SLITTED	PARIANS	NOWHERE	STATING	GRAPLIN	ENDARCH	ENDINGS	COSTING	ETATIST	PERCENT	RUINOUS	MOORING	CARROTS	ANCRESS
STILTED	PIRANAS	WHEREON	TASTING	PARLING	RANCHED	SENDING	GNOSTIC	TATTIES	PRECENT	URINOUS	ROOMING	TROCARS	CASERNS
ADGILNS	**ADDENTU**	**EEMNORV**	**AENNSTT**	**AGIMNRS**	**ACEFRTU**	**DEEGLRU**	**GHINORS**	**CDENOOS**	**ACEHIPT**	**IORSSTU**	**DEEIOPX**	**AOPRRST**	**AEFNSST**
LADINGS	DAUNTED	OVERMEN	TANNEST	ARMINGS	FACTURE	GRUELED	HORSING	CONDOES	APHETIC	SUITORS	EPOXIDE	PARROTS	FASTENS
LIGANDS	UNDATED	VENOMER	TENANTS	MARGINS	FURCATE	REGLUED	SHORING	SECONDO	HEPATIC	TSOURIS	EPOXIED	RAPTORS	FATNESS
ADGILNU	**DEIRSST**	**EENORVW**	**EINNSTT**	**AGINSTY**	**ACEHLNR**	**EGNRTTU**	**GINOPST**	**CELNOOS**	**ACDELSU**	**AEGIMPS**	**ABEFORR**	**DDEENRU**	**AEMRSST**
LANGUID	DISSERT	OVERNEW	INTENTS	STAYING	CHARNEL	GRUTTEN	POSTING	COLONES	CAUDLES	MAGPIES	FORBARE	DENUDER	MASTERS
LAUDING	STRIDES	REWOVEN	TENNIST	STYGIAN	LARCHEN	TURGENT	STOPING	CONSOLE	CEDULAS	MISPAGE	FORBEAR	ENDURED	STREAMS
CEIKNOT	**EILRSST**	**AEIILSS**	**EIRRSTT**	**EEEGILS**	**ACENRSV**	**AEIMSTZ**	**EHIIRTW**	**CELOORS**	**ADELMSU**	**DEIRSSU**	**EGNORRW**	**DDEERST**	**AENRSSW**
KENOTIC	LISTERS	LIAISES	RITTERS	ELEGIES	CAVERNS	MAZIEST	WHITIER	COOLERS	ALMUDES	DISEURS	REGROWN	REDDEST	ANSWERS
KETONIC	RELISTS	SILESIA	TERRITS	ELEGISE	CRAVENS	MESTIZA	WITHIER	CREOSOL	MEDUSAL	SUDSIER	WRONGER	TEDDERS	RAWNESS
CEIORTX	**EINRSSU**	**DGINOSU**	**AEGGINS**	**ADINNOP**	**ADEHRTW**	**AEISTWX**	**ACELOSV**	**CELOOST**	**EGINNTT**	**BEEORRS**	**EEIRRRT**	**EELLRST**	**AIIMNPT**
EXCITOR	INSURES	DOUSING	AGEINGS	DIPNOAN	THRAWED	TAXWISE	ALCOVES	COOLEST	NETTING	REBORES	RETIRER	RETELLS	IMPAINT
XEROTIC	SUNRISE	GUIDONS	SIGNAGE	NONPAID	WRATHED	WAXIEST	COEVALS	OCELOTS	TENTING	SOBERER	TERRIER	TELLERS	TIMPANI
AEGLLNO	**ENPRSTU**	**AABDELT**	**AEGGIRS**	**DEEIRSS**	**ADEHRTY**	**ACEGNSU**	**BCDEIOS**	**DENOOPS**	**ADEMOSY**	**AEFORRV**	**EEJNORY**	**EELNSST**	**CEINSST**
ALLONGE	PUNSTER	ABLATED	RAGGIES	DESIRES	HYDRATE	CANGUES	BODICES	SNOOPED	SAMOYED	FAVORER	ENJOYER	NESTLES	INCESTS
GALLEON	PUNTERS	DATABLE	SAGGIER	RESIDES	THREADY	UNCAGES	CEBOIDS	SPOONED	SOMEDAY	OVERFAR	REENJOY	NETLESS	INSECTS
EGIOSST	**AINOSSU**	**AACDELR**	**ACCEINO**	**EEILRSS**	**ADEMNRY**	**AEGLMNS**	**CDEIMOS**	**AADEGRY**	**ADIIMNS**	**DEIKLNS**	**EHMNOOR**	**EELRSST**	**EFINSST**
EGOISTS	SANIOUS	CALDERA	COCAINE	IRELESS	DRAYMEN	MANGELS	MEDICOS	DRAYAGE	AMIDINS	KINDLES	HORMONE	STREELS	FITNESS
STOGIES	SUASION	CRAALED	OCEANIC	RESILES	YARDMEN	MANGLES	MISCODE	YARDAGE	DIAMINS	SLINKED	MOORHEN	TRESSEL	INFESTS
EGMNORS	**ADEEGRW**	**AACDERS**	**DEEILSY**	**EEIRSSU**	**ADENPRW**	**AEGLRSV**	**ABILRSU**	**AAEGRSV**	**AELLRSU**	**DEIKRSU**	**ABDELTT**	**ABCERSU**	**EHINRSS**
MONGERS	RAGWEED	ARCADES	EYELIDS	REISSUE	PRAWNED	GRAVELS	BURIALS	RAVAGES	ALLURES	DUIKERS	BATTLED	RUBACES	SHINERS
MORGENS	WAGERED	ASCARED	SEEDILY	SEISURE	PREDAWN	VERGLAS	RAILBUS	SAVAGER	LAURELS	DUSKIER	BLATTED	SUBRACE	SHRINES
EGNOPRS	**AEEGLMN**	**AACELNU**	**EELNSTT**	**ABDEILP**	**AEFRSTW**	**BDEGIRS**	**AHILSTU**	**EGIINSV**	**AELNSSU**	**ACINNST**	**ACDERRS**	**ABDELMR**	**EIMRSST**
PRESONG	GLEEMAN	CANULAE	NETTLES	BIPEDAL	FRETSAW	BEGIRDS	HALITUS	SIEVING	SENSUAL	INCANTS	CARDERS	MARBLED	MISTERS
SPONGER	MELANGE	LACUNAE	TELNETS	PIEBALD	WAFTERS	BRIDGES	THULIAS	VISEING	UNSEALS	STANNIC	SCARRED	RAMBLED	SMITERS
EGNORSY	**AEEGMNS**	**AACELST**	**ABERRST**	**ACEILPS**	**AEHMNST**	**CDEGINU**	**AILNPSU**	**ABDEEPR**	**AELSSTU**	**EEOPSTY**	**ACESTTU**	**ABDELRW**	**EINPSST**
ERYNGOS	MANEGES	ACETALS	BARRETS	PLAICES	ANTHEMS	DEUCING	PAULINS	BEDRAPE	SALUTES	EYESPOT	ACUTEST	BRAWLED	INSTEPS
GROYNES	MENAGES	LACTASE	BARTERS	SPECIAL	HETMANS	EDUCING	SPINULA	PREBADE	TALUSES	PEYOTES	SCUTATE	WARBLED	SPINETS
DEELRSU	**AEEGMST**	**AADEMNS**	**ACENNRS**	**ADEHIPS**	**AEHNSTY**	**DEGHILT**	**AELLORV**	**ACDEEFR**	**AFIILNS**	**EEGIKNS**	**ADEMNNU**	**ABELRSW**	**EINSSTW**
DUELERS	GAMETES	ANADEMS	CANNERS	APHIDES	ASTHENY	DELIGHT	ALLOVER	DEFACER	FINALIS	SEEKING	MUNDANE	BAWLERS	WISENTS
ELUDERS	METAGES	MAENADS	SCANNER	DIPHASE	SHANTEY	LIGHTED	OVERALL	REFACED	FINIALS	SKEEING	UNNAMED	WARBLES	WITNESS
ADEMNOW	**AEEGNSV**	**CDEIINS**	**ADEFRRT**	**ADEILMP**	**AEHRSTV**	**DEGINSY**	**AEOPSST**	**ACEEHNS**	**DDEILNS**	**AACDELS**	**ADEPRRS**	**ACDEHRS**	**BEGOORS**
ADWOMEN	AVENGES	INCISED	DRAFTER	IMPALED	HARVEST	DINGEYS	PETASOS	ACHENES	DINDLES	ALCADES	DRAPERS	CRASHED	BOOGERS
WOMANED	GENEVAS	INDICES	REDRAFT	IMPLEAD	THRAVES	DYEINGS	SAPOTES	ENCHASE	SLIDDEN	SCALADE	SPARRED	ECHARDS	GOOBERS
ENRRSTU	**DEEFGIN**	**CDEIIST**	**AEMRRST**	**ADEISWY**	**AELMPRT**	**EGHILNS**	**BEIORSS**	**ACEELNV**	**DDEISTU**	**DEFNRSU**	**AELSTTY**	**ACELMST**	**DEGOORV**
RETURNS	FEEDING	DEISTIC	ARMREST	SIDEWAY	TEMPLAR	ENGLISH	BOSSIER	ENCLAVE	STUDDIE	FUNDERS	STATELY	CALMEST	GROOVED
TURNERS	FEIGNED	DICIEST	SMARTER	WAYSIDE	TRAMPLE	SHINGLE	RIBOSES	VALENCE	STUDIED	REFUNDS	STYLATE	CAMLETS	OVERDOG
ENRSTTU	**DEEGHIN**	**DEFIILN**	**AEMRRTU**	**BDEELNR**	**AELNPTY**	**EGHIRSU**	**EIMOSST**	**ACEELPR**	**DEILRSS**	**AEIMPRV**	**AEPRRSU**	**ACELNPS**	**EGLNOOY**
ENTRUST	HEEDING	INFIDEL	ERRATUM	BLENDER	APLENTY	GRUSHIE	MITOSES	PERCALE	SIDLERS	VAMPIER	PARURES	ENCLASP	ENOLOGY
NUTTERS	NEIGHED	INFIELD	MATURER	REBLEND	PENALTY	GUSHIER	SOMITES	REPLACE	SLIDERS	VAMPIRE	UPREARS	SPANCEL	NEOLOGY
ABDENSU	**DEEGIRV**	**DEIILMT**	**AEMRSTT**	**BEELRST**	**BEIMRTU**	**EGILNSW**	**EIOPRSS**	**AEEHRSV**	**DEISSTU**	**EEENRRS**	**CDEIRRU**	**ACELPST**	**EIJRSTT**
SUBDEAN	DIVERGE	DELIMIT	MATTERS	BELTERS	IMBRUTE	SLEWING	POISERS	HEAVERS	STUDIES	SERENER	CURDIER	CAPLETS	JITTERS
UNBASED	GRIEVED	LIMITED	SMATTER	TREBLES	TERBIUM	SWINGLE	PROSSIE	RESHAVE	TISSUED	SNEERER	CURRIED	PLACETS	TRIJETS
ABELNSU	**EEFGILN**	**EIILMRS**	**AENPSTT**	**BEENSTU**	**CEHINST**	**GINNORS**	**AINSSTU**	**AEELMNP**	**AEEIKLP**	**ACIMNRU**	**DEHIRRU**	**ACEPRSU**	**EEGHIRW**
NEBULAS	FEELING	MILREIS	PATENTS	BUTENES	ETHNICS	SNORING	ISSUANT	EMPANEL	APELIKE	CRANIUM	DHURRIE	APERCUS	REWEIGH
UNBALES	FLEEING	SLIMIER	PATTENS	SUBTEEN	STHENIC	SORNING	SUSTAIN	EMPLANE	PEALIKE	CUMARIN	HURRIED	SCAUPER	WEIGHER
ACDELNS	**EEGIRSV**	**EEEIPRS**	**AENRRSW**	**CDEENST**	**CEINSTY**	**DEEFIIS**	**CDENORW**	**AEELMPR**	**BDELNRU**	**AHIRSTW**	**DEIMNNU**	**ACEPSTU**	**ABCNORS**
CALENDS	GRIEVES	PEERIES	WARNERS	DESCENT	CYSTEIN	DEIFIES	CROWNED	EMPALER	BLUNDER	TRISHAW	MINUEND	CUSPATE	CARBONS
CANDLES	REGIVES	SEEPIER	WARRENS	SCENTED	CYSTINE	EDIFIES	DECROWN	PREMEAL	BUNDLER	WRAITHS	UNMINED	TEACUPS	CORBANS
ADEFLTU	**ACLNORU**	**EIMOORR**	**EFILRRT**	**DEEMNRS**	**CEIPRTU**	**ABDNOOR**	**CEHNOST**	**BDEEIMR**	**CDERSTU**	**AILNPTY**	**EHIRRSU**	**ADEHPRS**	**AHLNOPT**
DEFAULT	CORNUAL	MOORIER	FLIRTER	MENDERS	CUPRITE	BRADOON	NOTCHES	BEMIRED	CRUDEST	INAPTLY	HURRIES	PHRASED	HAPLONT
FAULTED	COURLAN	ROOMIER	TRIFLER	REMENDS	PICTURE	ONBOARD	TECHNOS	BERIMED	CRUSTED	PTYALIN	RUSHIER	SHARPED	NAPHTOL

Bob's Bible Bonus: Complete 7-letter Multi-Anagram Quiz

CILNORY	**ENORRSS**	**CDEEILP**	**EHIMRTY**	**CGHINOR**	**CEHOORS**	**ADDEMNS**	**AAMNPRT**	**AADGMNR**	**ELLOPRS**	**IILNNSU**	**CINOOPS**	**AGILLSU**	**ACORSSU**
CORNILY	SNORERS	PEDICEL	MYTHIER	CHORING	CHOOSER	DEMANDS	MANTRAP	GRANDAM	POLLERS	INSULIN	OPSONIC	LIGULAS	SARCOUS
LYRICON	SORNERS	PEDICLE	THYMIER	OCHRING	SOROCHE	MADDENS	RAMPANT	GRANDMA	REPOLLS	INULINS	POCOSIN	LUGSAIL	SOUCARS
CIMNORS	**GINOSST**	**EEEGRRT**	**EKLOORS**	**AINSSTT**	**CEOOPRS**	**ADDERSW**	**AEEMMRT**	**DGIINTY**	**CDEFOSU**	**DEGLOSS**	**ABGIKNR**	**CEEHISV**	**AFLLOTU**
CRIMSON	STINGOS	GREETER	LOOKERS	STATINS	COOPERS	SWARDED	AMMETER	DIGNITY	DEFOCUS	GLOSSED	BARKING	CHEVIES	FALLOUT
MICRONS	TOSSING	REGREET	RELOOKS	TANISTS	SCOOPER	WADDERS	METAMER	TIDYING	FOCUSED	GODLESS	BRAKING	SEVICHE	OUTFALL
IMOPRST	**ACELLOS**	**ACEHRRT**	**AEGNNPS**	**ACHILRS**	**CEOOSTY**	**ADEHRSS**	**ABDORSY**	**FGIILNT**	**ELMOPSU**	**EEPRSST**	**AEISSST**	**EGGNRSU**	**AOPRSSU**
IMPORTS	CALLOSE	CHARTER	PANGENS	ARCHILS	COYOTES	DASHERS	BOYARDS	FLITING	PLUMOSE	PESTERS	SIESTAS	GRUNGES	SAPOURS
TROPISM	LOCALES	RECHART	PENANGS	CARLISH	OOCYTES	SHADERS	BYROADS	LIFTING	PUMELOS	PRESETS	TASSIES	SNUGGER	UPSOARS
AGIILNN	**ADEHLLO**	**ACEHRTT**	**AEGPRRS**	**ACILNPS**	**DEHNOOW**	**ADEMNSS**	**ACFLNOS**	**FGIINST**	**EEFLSTT**	**ACEHILL**	**AEGPRSS**	**IINSTTW**	**AORSSUY**
ALINING	HALLOED	CHATTER	GRASPER	CAPLINS	HOEDOWN	DESMANS	FALCONS	FISTING	FETTLES	CHALLIE	GASPERS	INTWIST	OSSUARY
NAILING	HOLLAED	RATCHET	SPARGER	INCLASP	WOODHEN	MADNESS	FLACONS	SIFTING	LEFTEST	HELICAL	SPARGES	NITWITS	SUASORY
EEQRSTU	**EHILLOS**	**AENPRRW**	**AABDRST**	**ADHIMRS**	**AAEGTWY**	**AEFLLRS**	**AHOSTUW**	**GIILNTW**	**AESTTTU**	**AEHIMSS**	**EGHIRSS**	**GGIINRT**	**IMOSSTU**
QUESTER	HILLOES	PRAWNER	BASTARD	DIRHAMS	GATEWAY	FALLERS	OUTWASH	WILTING	STATUTE	MASHIES	GIRSHES	GIRTING	MISSOUT
REQUEST	HOLLIES	PREWARN	TABARDS	MIDRASH	GETAWAY	REFALLS	WASHOUT	WITLING	TAUTEST	MESSIAH	SIGHERS	RINGGIT	SUMOIST
DEEFRSU	**AEELQSU**	**DDELOOR**	**AADHNRS**	**ADILPRY**	**ADEGGST**	**AELMSST**	**AOPSTUY**	**ACDEKLT**	**AAEGSSU**	**AEIMSSV**	**EGINSSW**	**BBDEILO**	**CILOPSU**
DEFUSER	QUELEAS	DOODLER	DARSHAN	PYRALID	GADGETS	MATLESS	AUTOPSY	TACKLED	ASSUAGE	MASSIVE	SEWINGS	BILOBED	OILCUPS
REFUSED	SEQUELA	DROOLED	DHARNAS	RAPIDLY	STAGGED	SAMLETS	PAYOUTS	TALCKED	SAUSAGE	MAVISES	SWINGES	LOBBIED	UPCOILS
ADLMOOR	**ACLRSTU**	**ELOOSST**	**DENRSSU**	**AILMNPS**	**DEGGILN**	**AELPSST**	**DHIMORU**	**ACELQRU**	**ABELMRR**	**AOPRRTY**	**EGILMPS**	**BBEILOS**	**GIILNNS**
LORDOMA	CRUSTAL	LOOSEST	SUNDERS	MISPLAN	GELDING	PASTELS	HUMIDOR	CLAQUER	MARBLER	PARROTY	GLIMPSE	BILBOES	LIGNINS
MALODOR	CURTALS	LOTOSES	UNDRESS	PLASMIN	NIGGLED	STAPLES	RHODIUM	LACQUER	RAMBLER	PORTRAY	MEGILPS	LOBBIES	LININGS
ILOOPST	**ADMRSTU**	**CEIINTZ**	**DERSSTU**	**DEEEFRS**	**EEKORSV**	**AELRSSY**	**DILORWY**	**ADENPSX**	**ABELRRW**	**AGIKNNR**	**DEIMMRT**	**AEORSSS**	**ACEIPSZ**
POLOIST	DURMAST	CITIZEN	DUSTERS	FEEDERS	EVOKERS	RAYLESS	ROWDILY	EXPANDS	BRAWLER	NARKING	MIDTERM	SAROSES	CAPIZES
TOPSOIL	MUSTARD	ZINCITE	TRUSSED	REFEEDS	REVOKES	SLAYERS	WORDILY	SPANDEX	WARBLER	RANKING	TRIMMED	SEROSAS	CAPSIZE
AAGIMNS	**ADNRSUW**	**ABEELLR**	**ACFIMOR**	**DEEEHST**	**EGGILNU**	**BEILLRS**	**DEGLTTU**	**AEKPSTU**	**ACEFRRS**	**EKORSST**	**EFFINRS**	**CGIKNOR**	**BNORTUU**
MAGIANS	SUNWARD	LABELER	ACIFORM	SEETHED	GLUEING	BILLERS	GLUTTED	TAKEUPS	FARCERS	STOKERS	NIFFERS	CORKING	BURNOUT
SIAMANG	UNDRAWS	RELABEL	FORMICA	SHEETED	LUGEING	REBILLS	GUTTLED	UPTAKES	SCARFER	STROKES	SNIFFER	ROCKING	OUTBURN
ADDEGLN	**BDINSTU**	**ADDEEHR**	**ACIMOPT**	**DEEELRV**	**AGIKNOY**	**BEISSTU**	**ACORSST**	**AEMQRSU**	**ACEHLTT**	**DDEFNOU**	**EINPPRS**	**GILSTUY**	**ABEEKPR**
DANGLED	BUNDIST	ADHERED	APOMICT	LEVERED	KAYOING	BUSIEST	CASTORS	MARQUES	CHATTEL	FONDUED	NIPPERS	GUSTILY	BARKEEP
GLADDEN	DUSTBIN	REDHEAD	POTAMIC	REVELED	OKAYING	SUBSITE	COSTARS	MASQUER	LATCHET	FOUNDED	SNIPPER	GUTSILY	PREBAKE
AGHIILN	**ILNPSTU**	**ADDEEMN**	**ADLNOSS**	**DEEEMNS**	**AERRSSU**	**DDEILNW**	**AMNORSS**	**CDEIKLN**	**ACEHRRS**	**CDEKORS**	**APRSTTU**	**AGLLNTU**	**CEEIKPR**
HAILING	UNSPILT	AMENDED	SOLANDS	DEMESNE	ASSURER	DWINDLE	RAMSONS	CLINKED	ARCHERS	DOCKERS	STARTUP	GALLNUT	PECKIER
NILGHAI	UNSPLIT	DEADMEN	SOLDANS	SEEDMEN	RASURES	WINDLED	RANSOMS	NICKLED	CRASHER	REDOCKS	UPSTART	NUTGALL	PICKEER
AGIILNV	**EERRTTU**	**AEEFLLT**	**ABEEKRS**	**DEEEPRS**	**DEILLRR**	**DEIMNSS**	**CINOSST**	**CDEIKNS**	**ACERRSV**	**CEJNOSU**	**IPRRSTU**	**CEEFPRT**	**DEFFIOS**
VAILING	REUTTER	FELLATE	BEAKERS	SPEEDER	DRILLER	DIMNESS	CONSIST	DICKENS	CARVERS	JOUNCES	IRRUPTS	PERFECT	DIEOFFS
VIALING	UTTERER	LEAFLET	BERAKES	SPEERED	REDRILL	MISSEND	TOCSINS	SNICKED	CRAVERS	JUNCOES	STIRRUP	PREFECT	OFFSIDE
EGILLRS	**BCDENOU**	**BDDEEIT**	**ADEEKRW**	**DEEEPST**	**EEEKNST**	**DEIPRSS**	**INOPRSS**	**CDEIKST**	**AEFMRRS**	**CEKLORS**	**EFMORRS**	**DGGILNO**	**AAHIRSS**
GILLERS	BOUNCED	BETIDED	REWAKED	DEEPEST	KEENEST	PRISSED	PRISONS	DETICKS	FARMERS	LOCKERS	FORMERS	GODLING	HARISSA
GRILLES	BUNCOED	DEBITED	WREAKED	STEEPED	KETENES	SPIDERS	SPINORS	STICKED	FRAMERS	RELOCKS	REFORMS	LODGING	SHARIAS
ACEKNRS	**BCEORSU**	**CDDEEIR**	**EEIMRSX**	**DEEERSV**	**EEEKRST**	**EFILLRS**	**CEEORRV**	**CEINQSU**	**AEPRRSW**	**CEKLOST**	**DDEEOPS**	**BEGLOSW**	**ACILTTY**
CANKERS	BESCOUR	DECIDER	MIREXES	DESERVE	KEESTER	FILLERS	COVERER	CINQUES	REWRAPS	LOCKETS	DEPOSED	BOWLEGS	CATTILY
SNACKER	OBSCURE	DECRIED	REMIXES	SEVERED	SKEETER	REFILLS	RECOVER	QUINCES	WARPERS	LOCKSET	SEEDPOD	WEBLOGS	TACITLY
AEHKNRS	**BDELORW**	**AELRTTT**	**EEIPRSX**	**EEEFLRS**	**ACEEHPR**	**EHILRSS**	**AGIKLNS**	**DEIKNSY**	**CEIPRRS**	**ACDEHMR**	**DEEOPSS**	**AACILPS**	**EEEHSTT**
HANKERS	BOWLDER	TARTLET	EXPIRES	FEELERS	CHEAPER	HIRSELS	LAKINGS	DINKEYS	CRISPER	CHARMED	DEPOSES	APICALS	ESTHETE
HARKENS	LOWBRED	TATTLER	PREXIES	REFEELS	PEACHER	HIRSLES	SLAKING	KIDNEYS	PRICERS	MARCHED	SPEEDOS	SPACIAL	TEETHES
CEIKLNR	**BELORSW**	**ACGINPR**	**ACEFRRT**	**EEEHLRS**	**AGILLNU**	**EILLRSW**	**EEGIKNN**	**EIKLNSW**	**ABDEESS**	**ACEHPRS**	**AEHIKSW**	**ACDELSS**	**DNOOSUV**
CLINKER	BLOWERS	CARPING	CRAFTER	HEELERS	LINGUAL	SWILLER	KEENING	WELKINS	DEBASES	EPARCHS	HAWKIES	CLASSED	VODOUNS
CRINKLE	BOWLERS	CRAPING	REFRACT	REHEELS	LINGULA	WILLERS	KNEEING	WINKLES	SEABEDS	PARCHES	WEAKISH	DECLASS	VOUDONS
CEIKLRT	**CEFORSU**	**ACGINRV**	**AEIMMNS**	**ABBEIRS**	**CENNRSU**	**EILMRSS**	**GIILNTT**	**EIKNPSU**	**ADDEELP**	**ACEHPST**	**ACCDIOT**	**ADEHLSS**	**ABGGINR**
TICKLER	FOCUSER	CARVING	AMMINES	BARBIES	CUNNERS	RIMLESS	TILTING	PUNKIES	PEDALED	HEPCATS	CACTOID	HASSLED	BARGING
TRICKLE	REFOCUS	CRAVING	MISNAME	RABBIES	SCUNNER	SMILERS	TITLING	SPUNKIE	PLEADED	PATCHES	OCTADIC	SLASHED	GARBING
CEIKNRS	**CELOPTU**	**AFGIMNR**	**AEINPPS**	**ABBEIST**	**ENNPSTU**	**EILNSSY**	**AADEGGR**	**EILSTYZ**	**AEELSSW**	**ACEMPRS**	**ACCILNO**	**ADEMSSU**	**AHIIKRS**
NICKERS	COUPLET	FARMING	NAPPIES	BABIEST	PUNNETS	LINSEYS	AGGRADE	STYLIZE	AWELESS	CAMPERS	CONICAL	ASSUMED	RIKISHA
SNICKER	OCTUPLE	FRAMING	PINESAP	TABBIES	UNSPENT	LYSINES	GARAGED	ZESTILY	WEASELS	SCAMPER	LACONIC	MEDUSAS	SHIKARI
BDELOTT	**CELORSV**	**AGIMNPR**	**AEIPPRS**	**ACIRSST**	**ENPRRSU**	**EILPSST**	**AEIKLSS**	**AABORRS**	**DDEEFIL**	**AEMPRSV**	**EGHLNTY**	**AAILLMN**	**DDEIKRS**
BLOTTED	CLOVERS	GRIPMAN	APPRISE	RACISTS	PRUNERS	STIPELS	ALSIKES	ARROBAS	DEFILED	REVAMPS	LENGTHY	LAMINAL	KIDDERS
BOTTLED	VELCROS	RAMPING	SAPPIER	SACRIST	SPURNER	TIPLESS	ASSLIKE	RASBORA	FIELDED	VAMPERS	THEGNLY	MANILLA	SKIDDER
BDENNOU	**DEFMORS**	**BEERSTW**	**GHINOTT**	**AHINRSS**	**EPRSTTU**	**EILRSSV**	**DEEORRR**	**ELLORRS**	**DDEEIMS**	**CEHINPS**	**BGILNOW**	**ADDENSS**	**ABCCEIR**
BOUNDEN	DEFORMS	BESTREW	HOTTING	ARSHINS	PUTTERS	SILVERS	ORDERER	REROLLS	DEMISED	PINCHES	BLOWING	DESANDS	ACERBIC
UNBONED	SERFDOM	WEBSTER	TONIGHT	SHAIRNS	SPUTTER	SLIVERS	REORDER	ROLLERS	MISDEED	SPHENIC	BOWLING	SADDENS	BRECCIA
BEGLNRU	**ELOPRSW**	**CEEHRST**	**DEILLSU**	**CELOORR**	**DDEELRS**	**EINPSSU**	**EGILLSU**	**EOSSTTU**	**AACIITV**	**AACLNSU**	**BGINOSW**	**AIIMNSS**	**ACCEIMR**
BLUNGER	PLOWERS	ETCHERS	ILLUDES	COLORER	REDDLES	PUISNES	GULLIES	OUTSETS	AVIATIC	CANULAS	BOWINGS	SAIMINS	CERAMIC
BUNGLER	REPLOWS	RETCHES	SULLIED	RECOLOR	SLEDDER	SUPINES	LIGULES	SETOUTS	VIATICA	LACUNAS	BOWSING	SIMIANS	RACEMIC
CDEORRS	**EFORSST**	**EEFHRST**	**NORSTUU**	**EFOORRS**	**ADDEILL**	**ABCDESU**	**ALNOOSS**	**AACHILR**	**DEEEGMR**	**EGINNSS**	**AABCEMR**	**NORTTUU**	**ACEIPPR**
CORDERS	FORESTS	FRESHET	OUTRUNS	REROOFS	DALLIED	ABDUCES	SALOONS	ACHIRAL	DEMERGE	ENSIGNS	MACABER	OUTTURN	CRAPPIE
RECORDS	FOSTERS	HEFTERS	RUNOUTS	ROOFERS	DIALLED	SCUBAED	SOLANOS	RACHIAL	EMERGED	SENSING	MACABRE	TURNOUT	EPICARP
DENNOUW	**EHNORSS**	**EEIQRRU**	**CIMNOOR**	**CEILMOP**	**ACOSTTU**	**ABDELMS**	**CDNOORS**	**CEEMOPR**	**EEEGMRS**	**ACHIMOS**	**ACDDIST**	**AABMNST**	**EGLNSSU**
ENWOUND	NOSHERS	QUERIER	MORONIC	COMPILE	OUTACTS	BEDLAMS	CONDORS	COMPEER	EMERGES	CHAMISO	ADDICTS	BANTAMS	GUNLESS
UNOWNED	SENHORS	REQUIRE	OMICRON	POLEMIC	OUTCAST	BELDAMS	CORDONS	COMPERE	MERGEES	CHAMOIS	DIDACTS	BATSMAN	GUNSELS
EFORRSU	**EORSSTV**	**DGINOPS**	**ABEGLMR**	**ACEEMRR**	**ENRRTUU**	**ACDELPS**	**DOOPRTU**	**EEHORVW**	**EGMOORR**	**AALRSST**	**AHILSST**	**AACFLRT**	**EGLSSTU**
FERROUS	STOVERS	DOPINGS	GAMBLER	AMERCER	NURTURE	CLASPED	DROPOUT	HOWEVER	GROOMER	ASTRALS	SALTISH	FLATCAR	GUTLESS
FURORES	VOTRESS	PONGIDS	GAMBREL	CREAMER	UNTRUER	SCALPED	OUTDROP	WHOEVER	REGROOM	TARSALS	TAHSILS	FRACTAL	TUGLESS
EOPRRSU	**EORSSTY**	**EGLORSS**	**BDEGHIT**	**ACEEPRR**	**BGINSTU**	**ACELMSU**	**FNOORSU**	**AAELLRY**	**ABGILNW**	**EEIKNSS**	**AILPSST**	**AADMNRY**	**DEGGLOS**
POURERS	OYSTERS	GLOSSER	BEDIGHT	CAPERER	BUSTING	ALMUCES	SUNROOF	ALLAYER	BAWLING	ENSKIES	PASTILS	DRAYMAN	DOGLEGS
REPOURS	STOREYS	REGLOSS	BIGHTED	PRERACE	TUBINGS	MACULES	UNROOFS	AREALLY	BLAWING	KINESES	SPITALS	YARDMAN	SLOGGED
CNOORST	**BCINORS**	**ABCEILM**	**ADGGINR**	**CGILNOO**	**GGINORU**	**ADELMPS**	**MNOORSU**	**CEIINSS**	**ACGINPS**	**EEIRSSZ**	**ADHILSY**	**BDELMRU**	**LLOORTU**
CONSORT	BICORNS	ALEMBIC	GRADING	COOLING	ROGUING	PSALMED	SUNROOM	ICINESS	SCAPING	RESIZES	LADYISH	DRUMBLE	OUTROLL
CROTONS	BICRONS	CEMBALI	NIGGARD	LOCOING	ROUGING	SAMPLED	UNMOORS	INCISES	SPACING	SEIZERS	SHADILY	RUMBLED	ROLLOUT
AAGMNRT	**EERRSTW**	**ADELLSU**	**AGGILNR**	**GILNOOP**	**AACIMNS**	**BEFILSU**	**BDEGLNU**	**EIIMSST**	**AGHIMNS**	**ACEKRRT**	**DEEERSS**	**BELMSTU**	**GIILLNT**
TANGRAM	STREWER	ALLUDES	ARGLING	LOOPING	CAIMANS	FUSIBLE	BLUNGED	MITISES	MASHING	RETRACK	RESEEDS	STUMBLE	LILTING
TRANGAM	WRESTER	ALUDELS	GLARING	POOLING	MANIACS	SUBFILE	BUNGLED	STIMIES	SHAMING	TRACKER	SEEDERS	TUMBLES	TILLING
BEEEFIR	**EERSTTV**	**CEKNORS**	**DGIILNS**	**AEGILLM**	**AAHIPRS**	**CDEHILS**	**BDEGLRU**	**AAANRTT**	**AGILMNP**	**CDEEISX**	**BCEMORS**	**ELMNPSU**	**ACELQSU**
BEEFIER	TREVETS	CONKERS	SIDLING	MEGILLA	PARIAHS	CHIELDS	BLUDGER	TANTARA	LAMPING	EXCIDES	COMBERS	LUMPENS	CALQUES
FREEBIE	VETTERS	RECKONS	SLIDING	MILLAGE	RAPHIAS	CHILDES	BURGLED	TARTANA	PALMING	EXCISED	RECOMBS	PLENUMS	CLAQUES
EEEIMPR	**DELOOPS**	**ABEIKRR**	**BDEELOW**	**AINNQTU**	**ABDERSS**	**BCERSTU**	**BEGLNSU**	**EEGIKNP**	**EIJKNRS**	**EEGNSSU**	**CDEHORW**	**ELMPRSU**	**CDEIKLS**
EPIMERE	POODLES	BARKIER	BOWELED	QUINNAT	BRASSED	BECRUST	BLUNGES	KEEPING	JERKINS	GENUSES	CHOWDER	LUMPERS	SICKLED
PREEMIE	SPOOLED	BRAKIER	ELBOWED	QUINTAN	SERDABS	BECURST	BUNGLES	PEEKING	JINKERS	NEGUSES	COWHERD	RUMPLES	SLICKED
ADGHNOS	**AAEGLSV**	**ABEIRRZ**	**CENORRW**	**CEIKORR**	**ABELLRU**	**BELMRTU**	**DEGLNPU**	**AACLOPR**	**BDEEMRU**	**ACHMNOR**	**EFLORVY**	**ABEEGLL**	**BEEHOPS**
HAGDONS	LAVAGES	BIZARRE	CROWNER	CORKIER	RUBELLA	TUMBLER	PLUNGED	CAPORAL	EMBRUED	MONARCH	FLYOVER	GABELLE	EPHEBOS
SANDHOG	SALVAGE	BRAZIER	RECROWN	ROCKIER	RULABLE	TUMBREL	PUNGLED	CRAPOLA	UMBERED	NOMARCH	OVERFLY	GELABLE	PHOEBES
CDGILNO	**ABCDEEL**	**ABCEHRT**	**DEKLNRU**	**EGOPRRU**	**ABELLTU**	**BELRTUY**	**EGLNPSU**	**CELOSST**	**CDEEFLT**	**ACCEILS**	**EHMNOPS**	**AEEGMSS**	**EEEPRSW**
CODLING	BELACED	BATCHER	KNURLED	GROUPER	BALLUTE	BRUTELY	PLUNGES	CLOSEST	CLEFTED	CALICES	PHENOMS	MEGASSE	SWEEPER
LINGCOD	DEBACLE	BRACHET	RUNKLED	REGROUP	BULLATE	BUTLERY	PUNGLES	CLOSETS	DEFLECT	CELIACS	SHOPMEN	MESSAGE	WEEPERS
AACESTV	**ABDEELY**	**ACEHMRT**	**EKLNRSU**	**EGORRSW**	**ABELRSS**	**CELRTUY**	**EGLPRSU**	**CIILNOP**	**DEEMPRS**	**DDEEFII**	**EERSTTT**	**BEKOORS**	**EFOOPRR**
CAVEATS	BELAYED	MATCHER	LUNKERS	GROWERS	BARLESS	CRUELTY	GULPERS	CIPOLIN	DEPERMS	DEIFIED	STRETTE	BOOKERS	PROOFER
VACATES	DYEABLE	REMATCH	RUNKLES	REGROWS	BRALESS	CUTLERY	SPLURGE	PICOLIN	PREMEDS	EDIFIED	TETTERS	REBOOKS	REPROOF
EIIMPRS	**AEELSWY**	**BCEHINT**	**AACLNRU**	**BELMOOR**	**ACENSSU**	**CERSTUY**	**CEEERRT**	**DDEHNOS**	**EEFHLRS**	**BCILOOR**	**DEOOPSW**	**BEOORSZ**	**GNOSTUU**
PISMIRE	LEEWAYS	BENTHIC	CANULAR	BLOOMER	UNCASES	CURTESY	ERECTER	HODDENS	FLESHER	BICOLOR	SWOOPED	BOOZERS	OUTGUNS
PRIMSIE	WEASELY	BITCHEN	LACUNAR	REBLOOM	USANCES	CURTSEY	REERECT	SHODDEN	HERSELF	BROCOLI	WOOPSED	REBOZOS	OUTSUNG
DDENNOR	**BEEILMS**	**CEFIRTY**	**CDDEEOR**	**CDEOORV**	**ACESSTU**	**EFMNRSU**	**EGGLORS**	**DEORSSW**	**EEMPRSU**	**CDHIOOR**	**ADEGGLS**	**CEKOORS**	**AKLOTUW**
DENDRON	BESLIME	CERTIFY	DECODER	CODROVE	CAESTUS	FRENUMS	LOGGERS	DOWSERS	PRESUME	CHOROID	DAGGLES	COOKERS	OUTWALK
DONNERD	BESMILE	RECTIFY	RECODED	VOCODER	CUESTAS	SURFMEN	SLOGGER	DROWSES	SUPREME	OCHROID	SLAGGED	RECOOKS	WALKOUT

Bob's Bible Bonus: Complete 7-letter Multi-Anagram Quiz

BELOSSU CEIPSST BBINORS DDEHLRU DEELOVV LLOOPRT AACLMSU CGHIKNO CGHIIMN AHILPPS AACKMNP BBBDELU
BLOUSES CESSPIT RIBBONS HUDDLER DEVOLVE ROLLTOP CALAMUS CHOKING CHIMING PALSHIP MANPACK BLUBBED
BOLUSES SEPTICS ROBBINS HURDLED EVOLVED TROLLOP MACULAS HOCKING MICHING SHIPLAP PACKMAN BUBBLED

CDDELOS EHIRSSV ACEKPRS DEPRSUU BEEERSZ CNOOPSU ALMSTUU EHIPPRS ACCELSY ADDDELW ACHKOSS
CODDLES SHIVERS PACKERS PURSUED BEEZERS COUPONS MUTUALS PRESHIP CALYCES DAWDLED HASSOCK
SCOLDED SHRIVES REPACKS USURPED BREEZES SOUPCON UMLAUTS SHIPPER CYCLASE WADDLED SHACKOS

CDELLOU EHIRSSW CEFIKLR ELMSTUU BDEELSS EGHRSSU AFJLRSU AABHMRS AEHPPSU AELPSSS CFFOSTU
COLLUDE SWISHER FICKLER MUTUELS BEDLESS GURSHES JARFULS BRAHMAS SHAPEUP PASSELS CUTOFFS
LOCULED WISHERS FLICKER MUTULES BLESSED GUSHERS JARSFUL SAMBHAR UPHEAPS SAPLESS OFFCUTS

CELLOSU ACDEMPS CEIKPST ELPSTUU CDDEESU ABBDELS FIKLSTU AACLRVY CCEHILS AAHMSTZ CKNSTUU
LOCULES DECAMPS PICKETS PLUTEUS DEDUCES DABBLES KISTFUL CALVARY CHICLES HAZMATS UNSTUCK
OCELLUS SCAMPED SKEPTIC PUSTULE SEDUCED SLABBED LUTFISK CAVALRY CLICHES MATZAHS UNTUCKS

DEOPSSU EFHILMS GNOPRUW ACKNSTU EELLRSS ABBELSU BBEIRRS AALMPRY GGIINNS GINPPSU GGGINRU
PSEUDOS FLEMISH GROWNUP UNSTACK RESELLS BAUBLES BRIBERS PALMARY SIGNING SUPPING GURGING
SPOUSED HIMSELF UPGROWN UNTACKS SELLERS BUBALES RIBBERS PALMYRA SINGING UPPINGS RUGGING

ABIMPST NNOOPST ALMRTUU ACEHPRY AEFFIRX DEIMMSU DHLOPSU BEHRSSU ACPSSTU FGIIKNN ACCELLY
BAPTISM NONSTOP MUTULAR EPARCHY AFFIXER DUMMIES HOLDUPS BRUSHES CATSUPS FINKING CALYCLE
BITMAPS PONTONS TUMULAR PREACHY REAFFIX MEDIUMS UPHOLDS BUSHERS UPCASTS KNIFING CECALLY

GHINOOP ACEKRRS BILNTUU CDEFKOR AEIPPRZ EILPPSU AGILNPP CEPRSSU BCISSTU GIIKNNP ACCHOPU
HOOPING RACKERS TUBULIN DEFROCK APPRIZE PILEUPS LAPPING PERCUSS BUSTICS KINGPIN CAPOUCH
POOHING RERACKS UNBUILT FROCKED ZAPPIER UPPILES PALPING SPRUCES CUBISTS PINKING PACHUCO

DDENOSS AEKMRRS ABLMRSU ADDDEER GHINPSU ACEKRSS AEIPSSS BBCELOR AEGLSSS IMMNOSS EIKKLSY
ODDNESS MARKERS LABRUMS DREADED GUNSHIP SACKERS ASEPSIS CLOBBER GASLESS MONISMS KYLIKES
SODDENS REMARKS LUMBARS READDED PUSHING SCREAKS ASPISES COBBLER GLASSES NOMISMS SKYLIKE

BGIKNOR GHIINTT ACFLNSU NOPSSTU GILMNPU AEHKRSS AGGILLN BBEMORS ABBOSTY ALMSSUY AGGGINN
BORKING HITTING CANFULS SUNSPOT LUMPING KASHERS GALLING BOMBERS BATBOYS ALYSSUM GANGING
BROKING TITHING CANSFUL UNSTOPS PLUMING SHAKERS GINGALL MOBBERS BOBSTAY ASYLUMS NAGGING

DEERRSS ABCMOST AFHLSTU ABEEKPS GIMNPSU EEFFORR AHMOOPS CEFFORS ACFFOST BDILPUU CHIKSST
DRESSER COMBATS HATFULS BESPAKE IMPUGNS OFFERER OOMPAHS COFFERS CASTOFF BUILDUP SCHTIKS
REDRESS TOMBACS HATSFUL BESPEAK SPUMING REOFFER SHAMPOO SCOFFER OFFCAST UPBUILD SHTICKS

GIIKLNT ACHOPRS DINPSUW AEEJSVY ACCEHNR EFFLRTU CEEPSTX EHOPPRS ADFFHNO BEFFRSU AAABCSS
KILTING CARHOPS UPWINDS JAYVEES CHANCER FRETFUL EXCEPTS HOPPERS HANDOFF BUFFERS CASABAS
KITLING COPRAHS WINDUPS VEEJAYS CHANCRE TRUFFLE EXPECTS SHOPPER OFFHAND REBUFFS CASSABA

EELORVV CHINOPS CEOPRSS AEELMPX ACESSUY ACDEHKL AEKKNRS AHLLOSW BBGIINR CEMMRSU AAACSSV
EVOLVER CHOPINS CORPSES EXAMPLE CAUSEYS CHALKED KRAKENS HALLOWS BRIBING CUMMERS CASAVAS
REVOLVE PHONICS PROCESS EXEMPLA CAYUSES HACKLED SKANKER SHALLOW RIBBING SCUMMER CASSAVA

AEHRRSS DHIOPTY EHORSSW EEESSTT AEHLPSS ACEHKLS AABSTUX BEKRRSU FFGIINR CEPPRSU EEIPPPR
RASHERS PHYTOID RESHOWS SETTEES HAPLESS HACKLES SAXTUBA BRUSKER GRIFFIN CUPPERS PEPPIER
SHARERS TYPHOID SHOWERS TESTEES PLASHES SHACKLE SUBTAXA BURKERS RIFFING SCUPPER PREPPIE

CEMNOOY JNOORSU EEFHRRS AAGLRUU CEIMSSU EERRSSV ACCEHST ADDDELS KLOOOTU EMPPRSU ABCKSUW
ECONOMY JOURNOS FRESHER ARUGULA CESIUMS SERVERS CACHETS DADDLES LOOKOUT PUMPERS BUCKSAW
MONOECY SOJOURN REFRESH AUGURAL MISCUES VERSERS CATCHES SADDLED OUTLOOK REPUMPS SAWBUCK

ABEGGRS DILMOOY CDEHOSW DGIINSS EFHILSS BCIIOPS ACEHHST AACCILS DDEGGRU FHLRTUU ELMSSSU
BAGGERS DOOMILY CHOWSED DISSING HISSELF BIOPICS CHETAHS ALCAICS DRUGGED HURTFUL MUSSELS
BEGGARS MOODILY COWSHED SIDINGS SELFISH BIOPSIC HATCHES CICALAS GRUDGED RUTHFUL SUMLESS

AEGGRSW ABGIKNS BDDELOO ACCEHIL CEFFIOS CEFOSSU AEHMMRS CEEPPRT OPSTTUU GIINPPS AAADGGH
SWAGGER BAKINGS BLOODED CALICHE COIFFES FOCUSES HAMMERS PERCEPT OUTPUTS PIPINGS AGGADAH
WAGGERS BASKING BOODLED CHALICE OFFICES FUCOSES SHAMMER PRECEPT PUTOUTS SIPPING HAGGADA

EGGILNY ACGIKLN AABEGSS ACCEIPS EHRSSTY CEHOSSU AEPPRSY BCLOOSU EFFOSST EESSSTT GGGINNO
GINGELY CALKING BAGASSE ICECAPS SHYSTER CHOUSES PREPAYS COLOBUS OFFSETS SESTETS GONGING
GLEYING LACKING SEABAGS IPECACS THYRSES HOCUSES YAPPERS SUBCOOL SETOFFS TSETSES NOGGING

EGGILRW AGIKMNS AAEGSSV EFMOPRR DGIINNW AACHIMS CEILPPR BCEEEHS AAHMSST AIIMMNX EEEMMSS
WIGGLER MAKINGS AVGASES PERFORM DWINING CHAMISA CLIPPER BEECHES ASTHMAS MAXIMIN MESEEMS
WRIGGLE MASKING SAVAGES PREFORM WINDING CHIASMA CRIPPLE BESEECH MATSAHS MINIMAX SEMEMES

CDEEEPR AERSSST EKORRSW DEEEHLW AHLLOTY AACGILL CDEKLSU ACEQSSU BEHLSSU GNOPPSU AACHKSW
CREEPED ASSERTS REWORKS WHEEDLE LOATHLY GALLICA SCULKED CASQUES BLUSHES OPPUGNS HACKSAW
PRECEDE TRASSES WORKERS WHEELED TALLYHO GLACIAL SUCKLED SACQUES BUSHELS POPGUNS KWACHAS

CDEELPU EIRSSST AEEHPSS CDDEEER ALLOTWY NPRSTUU GGIINNR IJLLOTY ELLPSUW AABLLSY CCEEHKR
CUPELED RESISTS APHESES DECREED TALLOWY TURNUPS GIRNING JOLLITY UPSWELL BASALLY CHECKER
DECUPLE SISTERS SPAHEES RECEDED TOLLWAY UPTURNS RINGING JOLTILY UPWELLS SALABLY RECHECK

BEERSSU EOPRRSS ACEHMRR EEEMSST CIMOSST ABCKOTU AEGRSSS ACCISTT AEFFRSZ AABLMSS DEGGGLU
REBUSES PRESSOR CHARMER ESTEEMS COSMIST BACKOUT GASSERS TACTICS ZAFFERS BALSAMS GLUGGED
SUBSERE PROSERS MARCHER MESTEES SITCOMS OUTBACK GRASSES TICTACS ZAFFRES SAMBALS GUGGLED

CDDEENS ADENPPS AAGGRST EEESSTV HINOPSS ACKLMOR CGIKNNO IKLMOSY EIKPPRS ACCDEKL CHKLOSY
DESCEND APPENDS RAGTAGS STEEVES SIPHONS ARMLOCK CONKING SMOKILY KIPPERS CACKLED SHLOCKY
SCENDED SNAPPED TAGRAGS VESTEES SONSHIP LOCKRAM NOCKING SOYMILK SKIPPER CLACKED SHYLOCK

EEHLLRS AEFFLRS HIMOPRS AADOPSS IMOPSST ADKORWY ABHMRSU GIIKNSV CIKPSTU LLOPTUU CCIKLOY
HELLERS FARFELS ORPHISM PASSADO IMPOSTS DAYWORK RHUMBAS SKIVING STICKUP OUTPULL COCKILY
SHELLER RAFFLES ROMPISH POSADAS MISSTOP WORKDAY SAMBHUR VIKINGS UPTICKS PULLOUT COLICKY

AFFINRU AEMMSTU BEGGLOR ACILMPS BCELMRU KOORTUW EOPPRRS GINOOPP AEPPRRW BEFFSTU BDOOOWX
FUNFAIR MAUMETS BLOGGER PLASMIC CLUMBER OUTWORK PROPERS POGONIP PREWRAP BUFFEST BOXWOOD
RUFFIAN SUMMATE BOGGLER PSALMIC CRUMBLE WORKOUT PROSPER POOPING WRAPPER BUFFETS WOODBOX

ACHNNOS AEPPSTU CEEHLRY ADHIMPS BELMPRU AACCDES EPRRSUU AACLSSU BOSTUUY GGHIINN BFLLOWY
CHANSON PASTEUP CHEERLY DAMPISH PLUMBER CASCADE PURSUER CASUALS BUYOUTS HINGING BLOWFLY
NONCASH PUPATES LECHERY PHASMID REPLUMB SACCADE USURPER CAUSALS OUTBUYS NIGHING FLYBLOW

ADFORRW BBDEILR CEEHRSW AILPSWY EENSSUX CCEIILS DFLOPSU GIINNNS CHLOSUY AAALMSS CFLPSUU
FORWARD DIBBLER CHEWERS SLIPWAY NEXUSES CILICES FOLDUPS INNINGS CHYLOUS MASALAS CUPFULS
FROWARD DRIBBLE RECHEWS WASPILY UNSEXES ICICLES UPFOLDS SINNING SLOUCHY SALAAMS CUPSFUL

AGMNSTY CCEILRS ACGHINW ACHNRUY AHLLOOS DGGIILN BBGINOS GGIKNOS CCEEHRS CCDEKLO ABBBDEL
GYMNAST CIRCLES CHAWING RAUNCHY HALLOOS GILDING GIBBONS GINGKOS CRECHES CLOCKED BABBLED
SYNTAGM CLERICS CHINWAG UNCHARY HOLLOAS GLIDING SOBBING GINKGOS SCREECH COCKLED BLABBED

BGINRUY EILMMRS EEGRRSS GIIKLNS AGIKNSS COOPSTU FFGINOS DGGINNU CIIILLT CKOOOTU ACCKOSS
BURYING LIMMERS REGRESS LIKINGS ASKINGS COPOUTS GONIFFS DUNGING ILLICIT COOKOUT CASSOCK
RUBYING SLIMMER SERGERS SILKING GASKINS OCTOPUS OFFINGS NUDGING ILLITIC OUTCOOK COSSACK

ACCEHOR EILNPPS BBELORS CCENNOT CDEEKLS CEEHLSW EGGMRSU AGINSSS AACCLRU BCILMPU BBBDELO
CAROCHE LIPPENS LOBBERS CONCENT DECKELS LECHWES MUGGERS ASSIGNS ACCRUAL PLUMBIC BLOBBED
COACHER NIPPLES SLOBBER CONNECT DECKLES WELCHES SMUGGER SASSING CARACUL UPCLIMB BOBBLED

CCEHIOR EILPPST DEFFNOS ABBEGLR AAFFIRS AACCORU BGINSSU ANNPSSU AACHKRS EFIRSZZ DELOPPP
CHOICER STIPPLE OFFENDS GABBLER AFFAIRS CURACAO BUSINGS SANNUPS CHAKRAS FIZZERS PLOPPED
CHOREIC TIPPLES SENDOFF GRABBLE RAFFIAS CURACOA BUSSING UNSNAPS CHARKAS FRIZZES POPPLED

AACHIPR GHIINTW ELOPPRS AEGMMRS ACCIIST DEORSSS GIMNSSU BOOPSTY HIIKNPS CLLOOPS FGJLSUU
CHARPAI WHITING LOPPERS GAMMERS ASCITIC DOSSERS MUSINGS POSTBOY KINSHIP COLLOPS JUGFULS
HAIRCAP WITHING PROPELS GRAMMES SCIATIC DROSSES MUSSING POTBOYS PINKISH SCOLLOP JUGSFUL

ABEHRSS HIOTTUW ELOPPST BBEGILR DDDEILR ELNOSSS DDGGINO BGGILNU CCEKORS CHIKSTY IJJSTUU
BASHERS OUTWITH STOPPLE GLIBBER DIDDLER LESSONS DODGING BUGLING COCKERS KITSCHY JUJITSU
BRASHES WITHOUT TOPPLES GRIBBLE RIDDLED SONLESS GODDING BULGING RECOCKS SHTICKY JUJUIST

ACEHSST AEEGMMT BDDERSU DEGHHIT EIRSSSU DGGNOSU DDIIOSX FGGILNU GIIKNSS ELNSSSY BBBELRU
SACHETS GEMMATE BUDDERS HIGHTED ISSUERS DUGONGS DIOXIDS FUGLING KISSING SELSYNS BLUBBER
SCATHES TAGMEME REDBUDS THIGHED RISUSES GUNDOGS IXODIDS GULFING SKIINGS SLYNESS BUBBLER

AERSSWY CEHIISV BELSSTU EGIPPRS EISSSTU AALLNSY ABFGLSU GGHINSU BBGIMNO ALLOSWW AAAHHKL
SAWYERS CHIVIES BUSTLES GIPPERS SITUSES ALANYLS BAGFULS GUSHING BOMBING SWALLOW HALAKAH
SWAYERS VICHIES SUBLETS GRIPPES TISSUES NASALLY BAGSFUL SUGHING MOBBING WALLOWS HALAKHA

8-letter Words

AEGINRST: ANGRIEST ASTRINGE GANISTER GANTRIES GRANITES INGRATES RANGIEST
ACEINRST: CANISTER CERATINS CISTERNA CREATINS SCANTIER TACRINES
AEGILNRS: ALIGNERS ENGRAILS NARGILES REALIGNS SIGNALER SLANGIER
AEEGNRST: ESTRANGE GRANTEES GREATENS NEGATERS REAGENTS SERGEANT
DEIOPRST: DIOPTERS DIOPTRES PERIDOTS PORTSIDE PROTEIDS RIPOSTED TOPSIDER
AEILNRST: ENTRAILS LATRINES RATLINES RETINALS TRENAILS
AEGILNRT: ALERTING ALTERING INTEGRAL RELATING TANGLIER TRIANGLE
AEINRSST: ARTINESS RETSINAS STAINERS STEARINS
EIOPRSST: PROSIEST PROSTIES REPOSITS RIPOSTES TRIPOSES
AEINORST: NOTARIES SENORITA
AAEINRST: ANTISERA RATANIES SANTERIA SEATRAIN
AEINRRST: RESTRAIN RETRAINS STRAINER TERRAINS TRAINERS
AEINPRST: PAINTERS PANTRIES PERTAINS PINASTER PRISTANE REPAINTS
EGIINRST: IGNITERS RESITING STINGIER
AEILNSST: ELASTINS NAILSETS SALIENTS SALTINES
ADEERRST: ARRESTED RETREADS SERRATED TREADERS

AEGINSST: EASTINGS GIANTESS SEATINGS
CEFINORS: COINFERS CONIFERS FORENSIC FORNICES
ACINNOST: ACTINONS CANONIST CONTAINS SANCTION SONANTIC
ABEILSST: ABLEISTS ASTILBES BASTILES BLASTIES STABILES
EEIMPRSS: EMPRISES IMPRESES PREMISES SPIREMES
AEEINRST: ARENITES ARSENITE RESINATE STEARINE TRAINEES
AEEILRST: ATELIERS EARLIEST LEARIEST REALTIES
AEGNORST: ESTRAGON NEGATORS
AEINRSTT: INTREATS NITRATES STRAITEN TERTIANS
DEEINRST: INSERTED NERDIEST RESIDENT SINTERED TRENDIES
AEGILNST: GELATINS GENITALS STEALING TAGLINES
ADEIMNOS: AMIDONES DAIMONES DOMAINES
EINOPRST: POINTERS PORNIEST PROTEINS TROPINES
AEEIRSTT: ARIETTES ITERATES TEARIEST TREATIES TREATISE
EEGINRST: GENTRIES INTEGERS REESTING STEERING
ACEGINRT: ARGENTIC CATERING CREATING REACTING
ABDEIRST: REDBAITS TRIBADES
ACEILRST: ARTICLES RECITALS STERICAL
ADEIPRST: RAPIDEST TRAIPSED
AEILMNST: AILMENTS ALIMENTS MANLIEST MELANIST SMALTINE
AEILMRST: LAMISTER MARLIEST MARLITES MISALTER

EGILNRST: RINGLETS STERLING TINGLERS
AENORSST: ASSENTOR SANTEROS SENATORS STARNOSE TREASONS
EEINRRST: INSERTER REINSERT REINTERS RENTIERS TERRINES
EEINRSTT: INSETTER INTEREST STERNITE TRIENTES
ACDEENRT: CANTERED CRENATED DECANTER RECANTED
ACEENRST: CENTARES REASCENT REENACTS SARCENET
EGIILNRT: GLINTIER RETILING TINGLIER
CEEINRST: ENTERICS ENTICERS SECRETIN
ADEEGNRU: DUNGAREE UNAGREED UNDERAGE
DEEGINRS: DESIGNER ENERGIDS REDESIGN REEDINGS RESIGNED
AEGIMNST: MANGIEST MINTAGES MISAGENT STEAMING
DELNORSU: ROUNDELS UNSOLDER
DEENRSTU: DENTURES SEDERUNT UNDERSET UNRESTED
ADEILPRS: LIPREADS PARSLIED SPIRALED
GINORSTU: OUTGRINS OUTRINGS ROUSTING TOURINGS
CENORSTU: CONSTRUE COUNTERS RECOUNTS TROUNCES
ABEELRST: ARBELEST BLEATERS RESTABLE RETABLES
EEILPRST: EPISTLER PELTRIES PERLITES REPTILES
ACEIPRST: CRISPATE PARETICS PICRATES PRACTISE
ADEOPRRT: PARROTED PREDATOR PRORATED PROTRADE TEARDROP

AEINSSTT: ANTSIEST INSTATES NASTIEST SATINETS TITANESS
AEIMRSST: ASTERISM MISRATES SMARTIES
AEIPRSST: PASTRIES PIASTERS PIASTRES RASPIEST TRAIPSES
AEORRSST: ASSERTOR ASSORTER ORATRESS REASSORT ROASTERS
AEIRSTTT: ATTRITES RATTIEST TARTIEST TITRATES TRISTATE
ACEEHRST: CHEATERS HECTARES RECHEATS TEACHERS
EEENRRST: ENTERERS REENTERS TERREENS TERRENES
AELPRSTT: PARTLETS PLATTERS PRATTLES SPLATTER SPRATTLE
EEILRRSV: RESILVER REVILERS SILVERER SLIVERER
DEEIMPRS: DEMIREPS EPIDERMS IMPEDERS PREMISED SIMPERED
DEEERSTT: DETESTER RETESTED
AEELMNSS: LAMENESS MALENESS MANELESS NAMELESS SALESMEN
EEILNSSV: EVILNESS LIVENESS VEINLESS VILENESS
EHOORSST: ORTHOSES RESHOOTS SHEROOTS SHOOTERS SOOTHERS
CEHIISTT: CHITTIES ETHICIST ITCHIEST THEISTIC
EILPPRST: PRESPLIT RIPPLETS STIPPLER TIPPLERS
CEEPRSST: RESPECTS SCEPTERS SCEPTRES SPECTERS SPECTRES
ADEINORT: AROINTED ORDINATE RATIONED
ABEINORT: BARITONE OBTAINER REOBTAIN TABORINE

ACEINORT: ACTIONER ANORETIC CREATION REACTION
ADEINRTU: INDURATE RUINATED URINATED
AEINRSTU: RUINATES TAURINES URANITES URINATES
ADEILOST: DIASTOLE ISOLATED SODALITE
ADEEINRS: ARSENIDE NEARSIDE
ADEEIRST: READIEST SERIATED STEADIER
ADEGINRT: DERATING GRADIENT REDATING TREADING
ABEINOST: BOTANIES BOTANISE NIOBATES OBEISANT
ACEILNOR: ACROLEIN COLINEAR
AEIMNOST: AMNIOTES MASONITE MISATONE
ACEEINRT: CENTIARE CREATINE INCREATE ITERANCE
DEIORSTU: OUTRIDES OUTSIDER
EEILNRST: ENLISTER LISTENER REENLIST SILENTER
EEINRSTU: ESURIENT RETINUES REUNITES
DEIINORS: DERISION IRONSIDE RESINOID
AEILORSV: VALORISE VARIOLES
ACENORST: ANCESTOR ENACTORS
AEMNORST: MONSTERA ONSTREAM TONEARMS
CEINORST: COINTERS CORNIEST NOTICERS
AEEIMNST: ETAMINES MATINEES MISEATEN
AEEIRSTW: SWEATIER WASTERIE WEARIEST
AEEIMRST: EMERITAS EMIRATES STEAMIER
AEGINRTV: AVERTING GRIEVANT VINTAGER
DEIINRST: DISINTER INDITERS NITRIDES
DEEILNST: ENLISTED LISTENED TINSELED

AACEINRS: ACARINES CANARIES CESARIAN SARCINAE
ACDEIINT: ACTINIDE CTENIDIA INDICATE
ADEOPRST: ADOPTERS PASTORED READOPTS
CEILORST: CLOISTER COISTREL COSTLIER
EILNOPST: POTLINES TOPLINES
ADEEHNRT: ADHERENT NEATHERD
EEINRSTV: NERVIEST REINVEST SIRVENTE
AEGINNRS: AGINNERS EARNINGS ENGRAINS GRANNIES
AEGIMRST: MAGISTER MIGRATES RAGTIMES STERIGMA
DEIINSTU: DISUNITE NUDITIES UNTIDIES
AEGMNOST: MAGNETOS MEGATONS MONTAGES
ADEIRSST: DIASTERS DISASTER DISRATES
AEILRSST: REALISTS SALTIERS SALTIRES
ACENRSTU: CENTAURS RECUSANT UNCRATES
AEHNRSTU: HAUNTERS UNEARTHS URETHANS
EIMNRSTU: TERMINUS UNMITERS UNMITRES
ACDENRTU: UNCARTED UNCRATED UNDERACT UNTRACED
ADNOORST: DONATORS ODORANTS TANDOORS TORNADOS
AEIINSST: ISATINES SANITIES SANITISE TENIASIS
AAELNPRT: PARENTAL PARLANTE PATERNAL PRENATAL
ACEINNST: ANCIENTS CANNIEST INSECTAN INSTANCE
ACEINSTT: ENTASTIC NICTATES TETANICS
ADEEPRST: PEDERAST PREDATES REPASTED TRAPESED

AEELPRST: PETRALES PLEATERS PRELATES REPLATES
CEEILRST: RETICLES SCLERITE TIERCELS TRISCELE
DEEIMRST: DEMERITS DEMISTER DIMETERS
EEEGINRS: ENERGIES ENERGISE GREENIES RESEEING
ACEIMRST: CERAMIST MATRICES MISTRACE SCIMETAR
AEGINRSS: ASSIGNER REASSIGN SERINGAS
EEIILMNT: ILMENITE MELINITE TIMELINE
ACGINOST: AGNOSTIC COASTING COATINGS COTINGAS
CDEENORS: CENSORED ENCODERS NECROSED SECONDER
CEELORST: CORSELET ELECTORS ELECTROS SELECTOR
AEIMOSST: AMITOSES AMOSITES ATOMISES
AEEIMSTT: ESTIMATE MEATIEST TEATIMES
AEHMNORS: HORSEMAN MENORAHS RHAMNOSE
EIOPRSTV: OVERTIPS SORPTIVE SPORTIVE
DEELRSTU: DELUSTER LUSTERED RESULTED
DEEILRSV: DELIVERS DESILVER SILVERED SLIVERED
AEELRSST: RESLATES STEALERS TEARLESS
DEEIRSST: DIESTERS EDITRESS RESISTED SISTERED
ABEINSST: BASINETS BASSINET
ACEINRSS: ARCSINES ARSENICS RACINESS
AEHINSST: ANTHESIS SHANTIES SHEITANS STHENIAS
ABEILMST: BALMIEST BIMETALS LAMBIEST TIMBALES
ACEILMST: CLEMATIS CLIMATES METICALS

ACEILRSV: CAVILERS CLAVIERS VISCERAL
EIILNOSS: ELISIONS ISOLINES LIONISES OILINESS
ACEHNRST: CHANTERS SNATCHER STANCHER TRANCHES
CEHINRST: CHRISTEN CITHERNS CITHRENS SNITCHER
ADEELPRS: PEDALERS PLEADERS RELAPSED REPLEADS
AEGILNSS: GAINLESS GLASSINE LEASINGS
CEGINRSU: RECUSING RESCUING SECURING
EGINRSST: STINGERS TRIGNESS
AEHORSST: EARSHOTS HOARSEST
AEOPRSST: ESPARTOS PROTASES SEAPORTS
EHIORSST: HOISTERS HORSIEST SHORTIES
ACDEERRT: CRATERED RECRATED RETRACED TERRACED
ACEERRST: CATERERS RECRATES RETRACES TERRACES
EEIMRRST: MERRIEST MITERERS RIMESTER TRIREMES
EEIRRSTV: RESTRIVE RIVETERS
AEEHNPST: HAPTENES HEPTANES PHENATES
CDEEHINR: ENRICHED RICHENED
ACDIIRST: CARDITIS TRIACIDS TRIADICS
AIILNPST: ALPINIST ANTISLIP PINTAILS TAILSPIN
DEIRSSTU: DIESTRUS STUDIERS STURDIES
ADDEEGNR: DANGERED DERANGED GANDERED GARDENED
AADMNORS: MADRONAS MONARDAS
CEIPRSTU: CUPRITES PICTURES PIECRUST
AIOPRSST: AIRPOSTS PROSAIST PROTASIS

ACDEILMS: CAMELIDS DECIMALS DECLAIMS MEDICALS
AABCERST: ABREACTS BEARCATS CABARETS CABRESTA
ACELOSST: COATLESS LACTOSES
AEERRSST: ASSERTER REASSERT SERRATES TERRASES
AEKOSTTU: OUTSKATE OUTTAKES STAKEOUT TAKEOUTS
ADDEEMNR: DAMNEDER DEMANDER REDEMAND REMANDED
DEEIPRRS: PREDRIES PRESIDER REPRISED RESPIRED
ACEHIMST: HEMATICS MASTICHE MISTEACH TACHISME
ACEHIPRS: ASPHERIC PARCHESI SERAPHIC
CDEEERST: RESECTED SECRETED
ACEMOPRS: CAPSOMER COMPARES MESOCARP
AGILNSST: LASTINGS SALTINGS SLATINGS
AELPRSST: PERSALTS PLASTERS PSALTERS STAPLERS
AELRSSTW: WARSTLES WARTLESS WASTRELS WRASTLES
CEIRSSTU: CITRUSES CURTSIES RICTUSES
CEEFNORR: CONFRERE ENFORCER RECONFER
CNOORSTU: CONTOURS CORNUTOS CROUTONS OUTSCORN
EEEIMPRS: EMPERIES EPIMERES PREEMIES
AABELPRS: PARABLES PARSABLE PREBASAL SPARABLE
CEIKLRST: STICKLER STRICKLE TICKLERS TRICKLES
DEEIRRSS: DERRISES DESIRERS DRESSIER RESIDERS
EOPRSSTU: OUTPRESS POSTURES SPOUTERS

AAEGLLST: GALLATES GALLETAS TALLAGES
ADEEPRSS: ASPERSED REPASSED RESPADES
DEEIRSSV: DEVISERS DISSERVE DISSEVER
CEHIRSTT: CHITTERS RESTITCH STITCHER
EENPRSST: PENSTERS PERTNESS PRESENTS SERPENTS
AEHOPSST: PATHOSES POTASHES SPATHOSE TEASHOPS
GIILNSTT: SLITTING STILTING
EEIMMRST: MERISTEM STEMMIER
ABCELMRS: CLAMBERS SCRAMBLE
CEHIKNST: KITCHENS THICKENS
AGHILNSS: HASSLING LASHINGS SLASHING
GIMNOSSU: MOUSINGS MOUSSING
CHINOPTY: HYPNOTIC PHYTONIC PYTHONIC TYPHONIC
MOOORRTW: MOORWORT ROOTWORM TOMORROW WORMROOT
AEILNORT: ORIENTAL RELATION
AEILNORS: AILERONS ALIENORS
AEILNOST: ELATIONS INSOLATE TOENAILS
AEEILNRT: ELATERIN ENTAILER TREENAIL
ADEIINOT: IDEATION IODINATE
AEINNORT: ANOINTER REANOINT
ADEINRST: DETRAINS RANDIEST STRAINED
AEILNRTU: AUNTLIER RETINULA TENURIAL
ADEEILNT: DATELINE ENTAILED LINEATED
ADEEILRT: DETAILER ELATERID RETAILED
ACEINOST: ACONITES CANOEIST SONICATE
AEIMNORS: MORAINES ROMAINES ROMANISE

AEIORSTV: TRAVOISE VIATORES VOTARIES
AEGILORS: GASOLIER GIRASOLE SERAGLIO
ADEILRST: DILATERS LARDIEST REDTAILS
ADEINRSU: DENARIUS UNRAISED URANIDES
AEEGILNT: GALENITE GELATINE LEGATINE
AADEIRST: AIRDATES DATARIES RADIATES
AEIILNST: ALIENIST LITANIES
ADELORST: DELATORS LEOTARDS LODESTAR
ADEORSTU: OUTDARES OUTREADS READOUTS
ADEEILRS: REALISED RESAILED SIDEREAL
ADEENRTU: DENATURE UNDERATE UNDEREAT
AEELNRST: ETERNALS TELERANS
ABEINRST: BANISTER BARNIEST
AEHINRST: HAIRNETS INEARTHS THERIANS
AEILNPRT: INTERLAP TRAPLINE TRIPLANE
AEIMNRST: MINARETS RAIMENTS
ADEGINRS: DERAIGNS GRADINES READINGS
EINNORST: INTONERS TERNIONS
EINORSTT: SNOTTIER TENORIST TRITONES
ADEGILNR: DANGLIER DRAGLINE
ACDEINOS: CODEINAS DIOCESAN
ACEILORS: CALORIES CARIOLES
ACEILOST: COALIEST SOCIETAL
AEILMNOS: LAMINOSE SEMOLINA
AENOPRST: OPERANTS PRONATES PROTEANS
AEEINSTT: ANISETTE TETANIES TETANISE
AADEGINR: DRAINAGE GARDENIA
AAEGINRS: ANERGIAS ANGARIES ARGINASE

DEGIORST: DIGESTOR GRODIEST STODGIER
ADENRSTU: DAUNTERS TRANSUDE UNTREADS
DEILNRST: TENDRILS TRINDLES
AEGINRTT: GNATTIER TREATING
ABEGINRT: BERATING REBATING TABERING
AEGHINRT: EARTHING HEARTING INGATHER
EEHIORST: ISOTHERE THEORIES THEORISE
EEINOPRS: ISOPRENE PEREIONS PIONEERS
EGIILNOR: LIGROINE RELIGION REOILING
ACEINOPR: APOCRINE CAPONIER PROCAINE
DEILNOSU: DELUSION INSOULED UNSOILED
DENORSTU: ROUNDEST TONSURED UNSORTED
ADEIRSTT: STRIATED TARDIEST
AEILRRST: RETRIALS TRAILERS
ADEELRST: DESALTER RESLATED TREADLES
ADEENRSU: UNDERSEA UNERASED UNSEARED
ABEILRST: BLASTIER LIBRATES
ADEIMRST: MISRATED READMITS
AEILMNRS: MARLINES MINERALS MISLEARN
AEILNPST: PANELIST PANTILES PLAINEST
AEILPRST: PILASTER PLAISTER PLAITERS
ACINORST: CAROTINS CORTINAS
ADEGILNS: DEALINGS LEADINGS SIGNALED
AAEINSTT: ASTATINE SANITATE
AEGLNRST: STRANGLE TANGLERS
AEORSTTU: OUTRATES OUTSTARE SEATROUT
AGILNOST: ANTILOGS SOLATING
AAEILMNT: ANTIMALE LAMINATE

Bob's Bible Bonus: Complete 8-letter Multi-Anagram Quiz

AAEIPRST
ASPIRATE
PARASITE
SEPTARIA

AELORRST
REALTORS
RELATORS
RESTORAL

ADEINOSS
ADENOSIS
ADONISES

ABELNOST
NOTABLES
STONABLE

ABELORST
BLOATERS
SORTABLE
STORABLE

ACDEORTU
AERODUCT
EDUCATOR
OUTRACED

ADEMNORS
MADRONES
RANSOMED

ADENOPRS
OPERANDS
PADRONES
PANDORES

AEFLORST
FLOATERS
FORESTAL
REFLOATS

AELOPRST
PETROSAL
POLESTAR

AEORSTUW
OUTSWARE
OUTSWEAR
OUTWEARS

EHILNOST
HOLSTEIN
HOTLINES
NEOLITHS

EIORSTUV
VIRTUOSE
VITREOUS

ADEENRTT
ATTENDER
NATTERED
RATTENED

DEEINNRT
INDENTER
INTENDER
INTERNED

ADEEILPT
DEPILATE
EPILATED
PILEATED

AEEFILST
FEALTIES
FETIALES
LEAFIEST

AEEILNPS
PENALISE
SEPALINE

AEEILSTV
ELATIVES
LEAVIEST
VEALIEST

AEEFNRST
FASTENER
FENESTRA
REFASTEN

AEEEGNRT
GENERATE
TEENAGER

AGIILNOT
INTAGLIO
LIGATION

ADELNRSU
LAUNDERS
LURDANES

DEILNSTU
DILUENTS
INSULTED
UNLISTED

DEILRSTU
DILUTERS
STUDLIER

AEGINNST
ANTIGENS
GENTIANS

ADEEGNRS
DERANGES
GRANDEES
GRENADES

AEEGLNRS
ENLARGES
GENERALS
GLEANERS

DEEGILNR
ENGIRDLE
LINGERED
REEDLING

DEEGINST
INGESTED
SIGNETED

DEEGIRST
DIGESTER
REDIGEST

EEGILNST
GENTILES
SLEETING
STEELING

ABEGILNT
BLEATING
TANGIBLE

ACEGIRST
AGRESTIC
CIGARETS
ERGASTIC

ADEGIMNR
DREAMING
MARGINED
MIDRANGE

AEGHINRS
HEARINGS
HEARSING
SHEARING

AEGILMNR
GERMINAL
MALIGNER
MALINGER

AEGILMNT
LIGAMENT
METALING
TEGMINAL

AEGILNRY
LAYERING
RELAYING
YEARLING

AEGINRSW
RESAWING
SWEARING

EEILORSV
OVERLIES
RELIEVOS
VOLERIES

ABGINORT
ABORTING
BORATING
TABORING

ABCEILOR
ALBICORE
BRACIOLE
CABRIOLE

ACDEIMNO
COMEDIAN
DAEMONIC
DEMONIAC

EEEILRST
LEERIEST
SLEETIER
STEELIER

CEINOPRT
ENTROPIC
INCEPTOR

EEFNORST
RESOFTEN
SOFTENER

EIMOORST
MOORIEST
MOTORISE
ROOMIEST

EINOOPRS
POISONER
SNOOPIER
SPOONIER

CEGINORS
COREIGNS
COSIGNER

EGINOPRS
PERIGONS
REPOSING
SPONGIER

ABDEILRS
BEDRAILS
DISABLER

ACDEILRS
DECRIALS
RADICELS
RADICLES

AEILLRST
LITERALS
TALLIERS

AELNPRST
PLANTERS
REPLANTS

ABILORST
ORBITALS
STROBILA

ACINOSTU
AUCTIONS
CAUTIONS

ADILORTY
ADROITLY
DILATORY
IDOLATRY

AEIKLRST
LARKIEST
STALKIER
STARLIKE

AAELNRTT
ALTERANT
TARLETAN

AABEILST
LABIATES
SATIABLE

ADEILOSS
ASSOILED
ISOLEADS

CDEIINRT
INDICTER
INDIRECT
REINDICT

CEIINRST
CITRINES
CRINITES
INCITERS

EIIMNRST
INTERIMS
MINISTER
MISINTER

EIINRSTV
INVITERS
VITRINES

ACELOSTU
LACTEOUS
LOCUSTAE
OSCULATE

CDEILNOU
NUCLEOID
UNCOILED
UNDOCILE

DEILMOST
MELODIST
MODELIST
MOLDIEST

AEIRRSTT
STRAITER
TARRIEST

EMNORSTU
MOUNTERS
REMOUNTS

ADEERSTT
RESTATED
RETASTED

AEELRRST
ALTERERS
REALTERS
RELATERS

ABEIRRST
ARBITERS
RAREBITS

ACDEIRTT
CITRATED
TETRACID
TETRADIC

ACEIRSTT
CITRATES
CRISTATE
SCATTIER

ADDEEILR
DEADLIER
DERAILED
REDIALED

DEGIINRS
DESIRING
RESIDING
RINGSIDE

ABDEERST
BREASTED
DEBATERS

ACEELNRS
CLEANERS
CLEANSER
RECLEANS

ACEELRST
CLEAREST
TREACLES

ADEEFLRT
DEFLATER
FALTERED
REFLATED

ADEEMNRS
AMENDERS
MEANDERS

ADEERSTW
DEWATERS
TARWEEDS

CDEEIRST
DESERTIC
DISCREET
DISCRETE

CEEILNRS
LICENSER
RECLINES
SILENCER

CEEIRSTU
CERUSITE
CUTESIER
EUCRITES

DEEIPRST
PREEDITS
PRIESTED
RESPITED

AEEEGLRT
EGLATERE
REGELATE
RELEGATE

AEEEGRST
EAGEREST
ETAGERES
STEERAGE

AEENRSST
ASSENTER
EARNESTS
SARSENET

ACEHIRST
CHARIEST
THERIACS

AEHINPRS
HEPARINS
SERAPHIN

AEGNRRST
GRANTERS
REGRANTS
STRANGER

EGINRRST
RESTRING
STRINGER

ADEGHINS
DEASHING
HEADINGS

AEGHILNS
LEASHING
SHEALING

ABILNOOT
BOLTONIA
LOBATION
OBLATION

DEEORRST
RESORTED
RESTORED

EEFIIRST
FEISTIER
FERITIES
FIERIEST

ABEORRST
ABORTERS
TABORERS

ABEORSTT
ABETTORS
TABORETS

ACEORRST
CREATORS
REACTORS

CEINOSTT
STENOTIC
TONETICS

AEGMNRST
GARMENTS
MARGENTS

EIINORSZ
IONIZERS
IRONIZES

ABGINOST
BOASTING
BOATINGS

CDEEORST
CORSETED
ESCORTED
SECTORED

DEEFORST
DEFOREST
FORESTED
FOSTERED

DEENORSW
ENDOWERS
REENDOWS
WORSENED

ACEHLORT
CHELATOR
CHLORATE
TROCHLEA

AEFMORST
FOREMAST
FORMATES

AEHNOPST
PHAETONS
PHONATES
STANHOPE

CEIMNORS
INCOMERS
SERMONIC

EFIOPRST
FIREPOTS
PIEFORTS
POSTFIRE

EIMNOPST
NEPOTISM
PIMENTOS

CEILNOOS
COLONIES
COLONISE
ECLOSION

ABEEFILR
AFEBRILE
BALEFIRE
FIREABLE

ACDEEIMT
DECIMATE
MEDICATE

EGIIMNRT
MERITING
MITERING
RETIMING

CEEFINRT
FRENETIC
INFECTER
REINFECT

EEHINPRT
NEPHRITE
TREPHINE

CDEGINOS
CODESIGN
COGNISED
COSIGNED

DEIMOOST
DOOMIEST
MOODIEST
SODOMITE

ADELNPRU
PENDULAR
UNDERLAP
UPLANDER

ADEMNRSU
DURAMENS
MAUNDERS
SURNAMED

ADEPRSTU
PASTURED
UPDATERS
UPSTARED

CDEIRSTU
CRUDITES
CURDIEST
CURTSIED

CEILNSTU
CUTLINES
LINECUTS
TUNICLES

AAINPRST
ASPIRANT
PARTISAN
SPARTINA

AEEGINSS
AGENESIS
ASSIGNEE

ADEEGNRR
DERANGER
GARDENER
GARNERED

ADEEGRRT
GARRETED
GARTERED
REGRATED

BDEEGINR
BERINGED
BREEDING

EEGHINRS
GREENISH
REHINGES
SHEERING

EEGINRSW
RESEWING
SEWERING

ADEEORRV
OVERDARE
OVERDEAR

AEEHNRTW
WATERHEN
WREATHEN

ACEGIMNR
AMERCING
CREAMING
GERMANIC

CDEEIORV
CODERIVE
DIVORCEE
REVOICED

EEIMOPRS
MOPERIES
PROMISEE
REIMPOSE

EEIMOPST
EPISTOME
EPITOMES

DENORRSU
RONDURES
ROUNDERS

AAEILRSS
ASSAILER
REASSAIL
SALARIES

ADEEEFRT
DEFEATER
FEDERATE
REDEFEAT

AACELNTU
CANULATE
LACUNATE
TENACULA

DEIIPRST
RIPTIDES
SPIRITED
TIDERIPS

BDENORSU
BOUNDERS
REBOUNDS
SUBORNED

BDEORSTU
DOUBTERS
OBTRUDES
REDOUBTS

CELORSTU
CLOTURES
CLOUTERS
COULTERS

DEHNORSU
ENSHROUD
HOUNDERS
UNHORSED

DEOPRSTU
POSTURED
PROUDEST
SPROUTED

ELORSTUY
ELYTROUS
UROSTYLE

ADEIMRRS
ADMIRERS
DISARMER
MARRIEDS

AEILMSTT
MALTIEST
METALIST
SMALTITE

AEGGILNR
GANGLIER
LAGERING
REGALING

AEGGILNT
GELATING
LEGATING

AEGGINRS
GEARINGS
GREASING
SNAGGIER

AEIRSSTT
ARTISTES
ARTSIEST
STRIATES

ADEELMNS
DALESMEN
LEADSMEN

CDEEILNS
DECLINES
LICENSED
SILENCED

DEEHILRS
HIRSELED
RELISHED
SHIELDER

AENPRSTT
PATTERNS
TRANSEPT
TRAPNEST

EINPRRST
PRINTERS
REPRINTS
SPRINTER

ADEENSST
ASSENTED
SENSATED
STANDEES

EEILRSST
LEISTERS
TIRELESS

AFGINRST
INGRAFTS
STRAFING

AGINRSTW
RINGTAWS
STRAWING

AEFINRSS
FAIRNESS
SANSERIF

AEIRSSTW
WAISTERS
WAITRESS
WASTRIES

ACEILMNS
MELANICS
MENISCAL

ACEILMRS
CLAIMERS
MIRACLES
RECLAIMS

ACEILNPS
CAPELINS
PANICLES
PELICANS

ACEILPRS
CALIPERS
REPLICAS
SPIRACLE

ACEILPST
SEPTICAL
TIECLASP

ADEHINPS
DEANSHIP
HEADPINS
PINHEADS

AEFILMNS
FLAMINES
INFLAMES

AEHILPRS
EARLSHIP
HARELIPS
PLASHIER

AEILMPRS
IMPALERS
IMPEARLS
LEMPIRAS

AEILMSTY
STEAMILY
TALEYSIM

ACHIORST
ACTORISH
CHARIOTS
HARICOTS

AIMNOPST
MAINTOPS
PTOMAINS
TAMPIONS

EEINQRSU
ENQUIRES
SQUIREEN

AEGILLST
LEGALIST
TILLAGES

DEEFIIRS
DEIFIERS
EDIFIERS
FIRESIDE

ABDEORRS
ADSORBER
BOARDERS
REBOARDS

EILOPSTT
PLOTTIES
POLITEST

ACNOORST
CARTOONS
CORANTOS
OSTRACON

INOOPRST
PORTIONS
POSITRON
SORPTION

AILRSTTU
ALTRUIST
TITULARS
ULTRAIST

EGHILRST
LIGHTERS
RELIGHTS
SLIGHTER

EGILMNRS
GREMLINS
MINGLERS

EGILNSTW
WELTINGS
WINGLETS

EGINPRSU
PERUSING
SUPERING

EIORRSST
RESISTOR
ROISTERS
SORRIEST

ABEIKRST
BARKIEST
BRAKIEST

ACDEIITV
CAVITIED
VATICIDE

AGINORSS
ASSIGNOR
SIGNORAS
SOARINGS

DEELMORS
MODELERS
MORSELED
REMODELS

EELOPSTU
EELPOUTS
OUTSLEEP

AEERRSTT
RETREATS
TREATERS

GINORSTY
STORYING
STROYING

AILMRSTU
ALTRUISM
MURALIST
ULTRAISM

AILNPSTU
NUPTIALS
UNPLAITS

AACIMNOR
ARMONICA
MACARONI
MAROCAIN

EIMNOSST
MESTINOS
MOISTENS
SENTIMOS

EIMORSST
EROTISMS
MORTISES
TRISOMES

ABELOSTW
BESTOWAL
STOWABLE
TEABOWLS

ACEHLOST
CHOLATES
ESCHALOT

CDEIORSV
CODRIVES
DISCOVER
DIVORCES

DEHINOPS
SIPHONED
SPHENOID

EHILOPST
HELISTOP
HOPLITES
ISOPLETH

EIOPRSUV
PERVIOUS
PREVIOUS
VIPEROUS

DEGIINNT
ENDITING
INDIGENT

AEEHRSTT
EARTHSET
THEATERS
THEATRES

EEFILRRT
FILTERER
REFILTER

EEINPRRS
PRERINSE
REPINERS
RIPENERS

GILNOOST
STOOLING
TOOLINGS

AAEGMNST
MAGENTAS
MAGNATES
NAMETAGS

EGHIINST
HEISTING
NIGHTIES

CDEEIPRT
DECREPIT
DEPICTER
PRECITED

CDEILNSU
INCLUDES
NUCLIDES
UNSLICED

CEIKORST
CORKIEST
ROCKIEST
STOCKIER

ACEGILNN
CLEANING
ENLACING

ACEHIPRT
CHAPITER
PATCHIER
PHREATIC

EGIILNRV
LIVERING
RELIVING
REVILING

EEGILNPS
PEELINGS
SLEEPING
SPEELING

CDINOSTU
CONDUITS
DISCOUNT
NOCTUIDS

EEFORRST
FORESTER
FOSTERER
REFOREST

EFIMNORR
INFORMER
REINFORM
RENIFORM

DEEOPRRT
DEPORTER
PORTERED
REPORTED

DEIINSST
INSISTED
TIDINESS

ACEEIMRR
CREAMIER
REARMICE
RECAMIER

CDEEENRT
CENTERED
DECENTER
DECENTRE

EEENPRST
PRETEENS
PRETENSE
TERPENES

DELMORSU
MOULDERS
SMOULDER

DENORSSU
DOURNESS
RESOUNDS
SOUNDERS

ABELRSTT
BATTLERS
BLATTERS
BRATTLES

AEPRRSTU
PASTURER
RAPTURES

EFIRRSTU
FRUITERS
FURRIEST

ADEELSST
DATELESS
DETASSEL
TASSELED

DEEIRSSU
DIURESES
REISSUED
RESIDUES

ABGILNST
BLASTING
STABLING

ACGILNST
CASTLING
CATLINGS

ADGINRSW
DRAWINGS
SWARDING

AGILNPRS
GRAPLINS
SPARLING
SPRINGAL

AGILNPST
PLATINGS
STAPLING

ABEILLRS
BRAILLES
LIBERALS

ACEILSST
ELASTICS
SCALIEST

EIMNRSST
MINSTERS
TRIMNESS

AELPRSTY
PEYTRALS
PLASTERY
PSALTERY

BEIMRSTU
IMBRUTES
RESUBMIT
TERBIUMS

ACILOPST
CAPITOLS
COALPITS

AGIINNST
SAINTING
STAINING

AEEEPRRT
REPARTEE
REPEATER
REREPEAT

AACDGINR
ARCADING
CARANGID
CARDIGAN

AGIINPRS
ASPIRING
PAIRINGS
PRAISING

EGILNSST
GLISTENS
SINGLETS
SNIGLETS

EGILRSST
GLISTERS
GRISTLES

AEGLPRSU
EARPLUGS
GRAUPELS
PLAGUERS

AACEILLN
ALLIANCE
ANCILLAE
CANAILLE

EOPRRSTU
POSTURER
RESPROUT
TROUPERS

CGINORSU
COURSING
SCOURING
SOURCING

DGINORSW
DROWSING
WORDINGS

GHINOSTU
SHOUTING
SOUTHING

CEIIMRST
MERISTIC
SCIMITER
TRISEMIC

EIMPRSTU
IMPUREST
IMPUTERS
STUMPIER

ACELORSS
ESCOLARS
LACROSSE
SOLACERS

DDEINOSW
DISENDOW
DISOWNED
DOWNSIDE

AEELRRSV
RAVELERS
REVERSAL
SLAVERER

DEEGGINR
GINGERED
RENIGGED

AEENNRSS
ENSNARES
NEARNESS
RENNASES

AEERSSTT
ESTREATS
RESTATES
RETASTES

CEHORSTU
SCOUTHER
TOUCHERS

CEORSTUV
CUTOVERS
OVERCUTS

GIINNORS
IRONINGS
NIGROSIN
ROSINING

DEFLOORS
FLOODERS
REFLOODS

AADEGMRS
DAMAGERS
SMARAGDE

EGILMNSU
GUMLINES
LEGUMINS

AEEMRSST
MASSETER
SEAMSTER
STEAMERS

AEELMNPS
EMPANELS
EMPLANES
ENSAMPLE

CDEEIRSV
SCRIEVED
SERVICED

DDEGNORU
GROUNDED
UNDERDOG
UNDERGOD

EIIMNOSS
EMISSION
SIMONIES

ACEHIMRS
CHIMERAS
MARCHESI

ACEHIPST
HEPATICS
PASTICHE
PISTACHE

EEIMRSST
MEISTERS
MISSTEER
TRISEMES

EEIRSSTV
SIEVERTS
VESTRIES

EGINPRRS
RESPRING
SPRINGER

AEEGLRSS
EELGRASS
GEARLESS
LARGESSE

ACHIMNOR
HARMONIC
OMNIARCH

CEEORRSU
RECOURSE
RESOURCE

ADEEHKNR
DAKERHEN
HANKERED
HARKENED

CEEILPRS
ECLIPSER
PRESLICE
RESPLICE

GHINNORT
NORTHING
THORNING
THRONING

EIMOPRRS
PRIMEROS
PRIMROSE
PROMISER

AEIMMRST
MARMITES
RAMMIEST

ABEERRTT
BARRETTE
BATTERER
BERRETTA

EFGHIRST
FIGHTERS
FREIGHTS
REFIGHTS

DEEFLORW
DEFLOWER
FLOWERED
REFLOWED

EEHLOPST
HEELPOST
PESTHOLE
TELESHOP

CDEEENRS
SCREENED
SECERNED

GHINORTW
INGROWTH
THROWING
WORTHING

EFGIINNR
INFRINGE
REFINING

DEEELPRT
DEPLETER
PELTERED

AELRSSTT
STARLETS
STARTLES

EOOPRSTV
OVERTOPS
STOPOVER

AGHILNSU
LANGUISH
NILGHAUS
SHAULING

AEILLNSS
AINSELLS
SENSILLA

AEILLSST
TAILLESS
TALLISES

ADEILMSS
MISDEALS
MISLEADS

CCEINORS
CONCISER
CORNICES
CROCEINS

AHIIMNST
HISTAMIN
ISTHMIAN
THIAMINS

EEORRRST
RESORTER
RESTORER
RETRORSE

ACDHLNOR
CHALDRON
CHLORDAN

AABELSTT
ABETTALS
STATABLE
TASTABLE

AGIKLNST
STALKING
TALKINGS

DDEGILNU
DELUDING
INDULGED

BDEORRSU
BORDURES
SUBORDER

EORRSSTU
ROUSTERS
TRESSOUR
TROUSERS

AGINNTTU
ATTUNING
NUTATING
TAUNTING

CDGILNOS
CODLINGS
LINGCODS
SCOLDING

AACELMRS
CARAMELS
CERAMALS

CEEEMNRT
CEMENTER
CEREMENT
RECEMENT

DEILOPSS
DESPOILS
DIPLOSES

CEIRRSTT
CRITTERS
RESTRICT
STRICTER

EEEGNRRS
REGREENS
RENEGERS

CDIIOPRT
DIOPTRIC
DIPROTIC
TRIPODIC

CELORSST
CORSLETS
COSTRELS
CROSSLET

CIIMNOST
MONISTIC
NOMISTIC

AEHISSTT
ATHEISTS
HASTIEST
STAITHES

AEIMSSTT
ETATISMS
MISSTATE

DELOORSS
DOORLESS
LORDOSES
ODORLESS

AEELMSST
MATELESS
MEATLESS
TAMELESS

AEELPRSS
PLEASERS
PRESALES
RELAPSES

Bob's Bible Bonus: Complete 8-letter Multi-Anagram Quiz

CEEILNSS LICENSES SILENCES
DEEIPRSS DESPISER DISPERSE PRESIDES
ACEHRRST CHARTERS RECHARTS
CDEEILPS ECLIPSED PEDICELS PEDICLES
CEIINSTZ CITIZENS ZINCITES
ACGHINRS ARCHINGS CHAGRINS CRASHING
ACGINPRS CARPINGS SCARPING SCRAPING
AGHINPRS HARPINGS PHRASING SHARPING
ABEILLRY BLEARILY RELIABLY
ACEIPSST ESCAPIST SPACIEST
AEIMPRSS IMPRESAS MISPARSE
AEIMPSST IMPASTES PASTIMES
EEHILLRS HELLERIS SHELLIER
GHINOSTT SHOTTING TONIGHTS
AEGILLMS LEGALISM MEGILLAS MILLAGES
EEIKLPST SPIKELET STEPLIKE
EEIPQRSU PERIQUES REEQUIPS
GILNNOOS GLONOINS SNOOLING
EGINPRSS PRESSING SPRINGES
BEGIMNSU BEMUSING MISBEGUN
CEELORSS CORELESS SCLEROSE
ACEEHRRS REACHERS RESEARCH SEARCHER
ACEEMRRS AMERCERS CREAMERS SCREAMER
CEEIPRRS PIERCERS PRECISER REPRICES
EEIMPRRS PREMIERS SIMPERER
EIMOPRSS IMPOSERS PROMISES SEMIPROS
CEILMOPS COMPILES COMPLIES POLEMICS
DEGGILNS GELDINGS SLEDGING SNIGGLED
ADDEEGRR DEGRADER REGARDED REGRADED

ACEEHMRS CASHMERE MACHREES MARCHESE
ACCIINOT ACONITIC CATIONIC
AAIMNSST MANTISSA SATANISM STAMINAS
ADDELRSW DAWDLERS WADDLERS
AELOPPRS PROLAPSE SAPROPEL
DEILNSSW SWINDLES WILDNESS WINDLESS
CEGHORSU CHOREGUS COUGHERS GROUCHES
BELMRSTU STUMBLER TUMBLERS TUMBRELS
CEEERRST ERECTERS REERECTS SECRETER
AAANRSTT TANTARAS TARANTAS TARTANAS
AADGMNRS GRANDAMS GRANDMAS
BGIILNRS BIRLINGS BRISLING
GILNPRSU PURLINGS SLURPING
DEIILMSV MIDLIVES MISLIVED
CDIIMNOU CONIDIUM MUCINOID ONCIDIUM
CELNOSSU CLONUSES COUNSELS UNCLOSES
CIILNOPS CIPOLINS PICOLINS PSILOCIN
CIILOPST COLPITIS POLITICS PSILOTIC
EELRSSTT SETTLERS STERLETS TRESTLES
AEMRSSTT MATTRESS SMARTEST SMATTERS
DEEFFNOR FOREFEND OFFENDER
EENOPPRS PROPENES PROPENSE
AGINPRSS PINGRASS RASPINGS
EEFLNRSS FERNLESS FLENSERS FRESNELS
EELMRSST RESMELTS SMELTERS TERMLESS
ACGILNPS CLASPING SCALPING
AGILMNPS PSALMING SAMPLING
ACEHNSST CHASTENS SNATCHES STANCHES

ACIIMNTY INTIMACY MINACITY
AABEELLS LEASABLE SALEABLE SEALABLE
EOPRRSST PORTRESS PRESORTS SPORTERS
DEEELNSS LESSENED NEEDLESS
GINOPSST POSTINGS SIGNPOST
EEIPRRSS PRISERES REPRISES RESPIRES
EHLRSSTU HURTLESS HUSTLERS RUTHLESS
DEEERRSV DESERVER RESERVED REVERSED
AGGINPRS GRASPING PARGINGS SPARGING
EEEHRSST SHEEREST SHEETERS
ADEERRRW REDRAWER REREWARD REWARDER
AEHIPPST EPITAPHS HAPPIEST
CEIRRSSU CRUISERS SCURRIES
EIPRRSSU SPURRIES SURPRISE UPRISERS
EGGINRSS SERGINGS SNIGGERS
AGILLNSY SALLYING SIGNALLY SLANGILY
AACHIMRS ARCHAISM CHARISMA
ACELPRSS CLASPERS RECLASPS SCALPERS
GIIMNNTU MINUTING MUTINING
EIKRRSST SKIRRETS SKIRTERS STRIKERS
EIIPSSTT PIETISTS STIPITES TIPSIEST
CEMPRSTU CRUMPETS SPECTRUM
CEORRSSU COURSERS SCOURERS
ADNPSSTU DUSTPANS STANDUPS UPSTANDS
CEEILSSV CLEVISES VESICLES VICELESS
ACEIMPSS ESCAPISM MISSPACE SCAMPIES
AEHIMPSS EMPHASIS MISSHAPE
ABCEHMRS BECHARMS BRECHAMS CHAMBERS

AEIMSSST MASSIEST MISSEATS
EEELPRSS PEERLESS SLEEPERS
AEEPPRRS PAPERERS PREPARES REPAPERS
ACELPSSU CAPSULES SCALEUPS UPSCALES
EMPRSSTU STUMPERS SUMPTERS
ACCEHNRS CHANCERS CHANCRES CRANCHES
AEGLLSSU GALLUSES SEAGULLS SULLAGES
AAEEPPRR RAPPAREE REAPPEAR
CCEEIRSV CERVICES CRESCIVE CREVICES
BDEEGGRU BEGRUDGE BUGGERED DEBUGGER
CEHIKSTT THICKEST THICKETS THICKSET
CEIMMRSU CRUMMIES SCUMMIER
ACGGILNN CLANGING GLANCING
AEEPRSSS ASPERSES REPASSES
EELLPRSS PRESELLS RESPELLS SPELLERS
CGIIKLNS LICKINGS SICKLING SLICKING
EEERRRSV RESERVER REVERERS REVERSER
BBGILNRU BLURBING BURBLING RUBBLING
AACCOSTT STACCATO STOCCATA TOCCATAS
CEHIKRSS KIRSCHES SHICKERS
ACCEKLRS CACKLERS CLACKERS CRACKLES
AACCLRSU ACCRUALS CARACULS SACCULAR
EELPSSUX EXPULSES PLEXUSES
GIILNPPS LIPPINGS SLIPPING
AAACMRSS MARASCAS MASCARAS
ABBBELRS BABBLERS BLABBERS BRABBLES
ADEILORT IDOLATER TAILORED
ADEINOST ASTONIED SEDATION
AEIORSTU OUTRAISE SAUTOIRE

ADEEINRT DETAINER RETAINED
AEENORST EARSTONE RESONATE
EEINORST ONERIEST SEROTINE
AEGILNOR GERANIOL REGIONAL
AEGILNOT GELATION LEGATION
AEEGINRT GRATINEE INTERAGE
AEIINRST INERTIAS RAINIEST
EINORSTU ROUTINES SNOUTIER
ADEINNOT ANOINTED ANTINODE
ADEINORR ORDAINER REORDAIN
ADEINOTT ANTIDOTE TETANOID
AEINNOST ENATIONS SONATINE
ADEELNOR OLEANDER RELOANED
DEEILNOT DELETION ENTOILED
DEEILORT DOLERITE LOITERED
ABEINORS BARONIES SEAROBIN
ACEILORT EROTICAL LORICATE
AEILMORT AMITROLE ROLAMITE
AEIMORST AMORTISE ATOMISER
AEILOPRT EPILATOR PETIOLAR
ADEGINOS AGONISED DIAGNOSE
AEGILOST LATIGOES OTALGIES
ADEINSTU AUDIENTS SINUATED
AEILNSTU ALUNITES INSULATE
AEEGINRS ANERGIES GESNERIA
ADINORST DIATRONS INTRADOS
EEINORRT ORIENTER REORIENT
AEENORTV OVERNEAT RENOVATE
CEEINORT ERECTION NEOTERIC
ADEIINST ADENITIS DAINTIES
ADELNORS LADRONES SOLANDER
AELNORSU ALEURONS NEUROSAL
DEINORSU DOURINES SOURDINE
EILNOSTU ELUTIONS OUTLINES

AAILNORT NOTARIAL RATIONAL
AEINNRST ENTRAINS TRANNIES
DEEINRTU RETINUED REUNITED
ABEINRTU BRAUNITE URBANITE
AEILMNRT TERMINAL TRAMLINE
DEIINOST EDITIONS SEDITION
ADEGINST SEDATING STEADING
AEGINSTU SAUTEING UNITAGES
AAEINRTT ATTAINER REATTAIN
AGINORST ORGANIST ROASTING
ADEILOTV DOVETAIL VIOLATED
ADEIOPRS DIASPORE PARODIES
ADEIORSV AVODIRES AVOIDERS
AEHILORS AIRHOLES SHOALIER
AEILOPRS PELORIAS POLARISE
AACEINRT CARINATE CRANIATE
AAEIMNRT ANIMATER MARINATE
AAEENRST ARSENATE SERENATA
AEINORSS ERASIONS SENSORIA
DEELNORT REDOLENT RONDELET
ACDENORT CARTONED NOTECARD
ACENORTU COURANTE OUTRANCE
ADENORTW DANEWORT TEARDOWN
CDEINORT CENTROID DOCTRINE
CEINORTU NEUROTIC UNEROTIC
EHINORST HORNIEST ORNITHES
AEEILRTT LATERITE LITERATE
EILNOOST LOONIEST OILSTONE
AEEILNPT PETALINE TAPELINE
AEEILRTV LEVIRATE RELATIVE
AAEGILNT AGENTIAL ALGINATE
EINORSTY SEROTINY TYROSINE
ADEGORTU OUTRAGED RAGOUTED
AEGLORST GLOATERS LEGATORS

AEEGILNS ENSILAGE LINEAGES
AEGIMNRT EMIGRANT REMATING
AEGINPRT RETAPING TAPERING
AEGINRTW TWANGIER WATERING
EEINOSTT NOISETTE TEOSINTE
AEINNOTV INNOVATE VENATION
ACDEEORT DECORATE RECOATED
ACEELORT CORELATE RELOCATE
ACEENOST ACETONES NOTECASE
ADEEMNOR DEMEANOR ENAMORED
AEELORTV ELEVATOR OVERLATE
AEEOPRST OPERATES PROTEASE
BEEINOST BETONIES EBONITES
CEEIORST COTERIES ESOTERIC
EEIMNOST MONETISE SEMITONE
EEIOPRST POETISER POETRIES
AEIMNNOT ANTINOME NOMINATE
ABEFIORT BIFORATE FIREBOAT
ACEINOTV CONATIVE INVOCATE
DEILOSTU SOLITUDE TOLUIDES
EEEINRST ETERNISE TEENSIER
EEGIINRT REIGNITE RETIEING
EIMNOORT MOTIONER REMOTION
ADEINRRS DRAINERS SERRANID
ACDEILRT ARTICLED LACERTID
ACEILNRS CARLINES LANCIERS
ADEILPRT DIPTERAL TRIPEDAL
ADEINPRU UNPAIRED UNREPAID
ADEIPRTU EUPATRID PREAUDIT
AEFILRTU FAULTIER FILATURE
AEINPSTU PETUNIAS SUPINATE
AEEGINTV AGENTIVE NEGATIVE
ACILNORT CILANTRO CONTRAIL
AFILNORT FLATIRON INFLATOR

AEINQRTU ANTIQUER QUAINTER
ADILOORT IDOLATOR TOROIDAL
AILOORST ISOLATOR OSTIOLAR
AAEIRSTT ARIETTAS ARISTATE
ADEGNRST DRAGNETS GRANDEST
ADENORRS ADORNERS READORNS
ADEORTTU OUTRATED OUTTRADE
AABEIRTU AUBRETIA AUBRIETA
AACEILNT ANALCITE LAITANCE
AADEIMNT ANIMATED DIAMANTE
AAEIMNST AMENTIAS ANIMATES
AEIIMRST AIRTIMES SERIATIM
ABDENORS BANDORES BROADENS
ABDEORTU OBDURATE TABOURED
ACDELNOR COLANDER CONELRAD
ACDENOST ENDOCAST TACNODES
ACDENOTU OUTDANCE UNCOATED
ACELORST LOCATERS SECTORAL
ADEHORTU AUTHORED OUTHEARD
AEHLNOST ANETHOLS ETHANOLS
AEHLORST LOATHERS RATHOLES
AELNOPRS PERSONAL PSORALEN
AELORSTV LEVATORS OVERSALT
AEMNORSU ENAMOURS NEUROMAS
CEILNORS INCLOSER LICENSOR
CEILNOST LECTIONS TELSONIC
CEIORSTU CITREOUS OUTCRIES
DEIORSTW ROWDIEST WORDIEST
EIMORSTU MISROUTE MOISTURE
ADEEIRRS DREARIES RERAISED
DEILNOOS EIDOLONS SOLENOID
AEENRSTT ENTREATS RATTEENS
DEEINRRT INTERRED TRENDIER
EEINNRST INTENSER INTERNES

EEINRRTU REUNITER UNRETIRE
ABDEEIST BEADIEST DIABETES
ADEEILMR REMAILED REMEDIAL
ADEEISTV DEVIATES SEDATIVE
AEEILMST MEALIEST METALISE
AEINPRRT PRETRAIN TERRAPIN
AEEINSST ETESIANS TENIASES
AEEHNRST HASTENER HEARTENS
AEELNRTV LEVANTER RELEVANT
CEEINRTU CEINTURE ENURETIC
EEFINRST FERNIEST INFESTER
EEILNRTY ENTIRELY LIENTERY
AEIMNRTT INTERMAT MARTINET
CEIINORS RECISION SORICINE
AEGILNNT GANTLINE LATENING
AEGINRRS EARRINGS GRAINERS
AEGINSTT ESTATING TANGIEST
ABDEGINR BEARDING BREADING
ABEGINRS BEARINGS SABERING
ACEGILNR CLEARING RELACING
AEFGIRTU FIGURATE FRUITAGE
AEGHILNR NARGHILE NARGILEH
AEGHILRT LITHARGE THIRLAGE
AEGILNPR GRAPLINE PEARLING
AEGIMNTU TEGUMINA UMANGITE
AEGINRSY RESAYING SYNERGIA
AEIMORRS ARMOIRES ARMORIES
EEIINRTT INTERTIE RETINITE
EENNORST ENTERONS TENONERS
ACDEELOR COLEADER RECOALED
BDEEILOR ERODIBLE REBOILED
DEEILOPT LEPIDOTE PETIOLED
DEEILORV EVILDOER OVERIDLE
DEEIOPST EPIDOTES POETISED

DEEIORSW DOWERIES WEIRDOES
EEFILNOS FELONIES OLEFINES
AEENORSS RESEASON SEASONER
ABCEILNO BIOCLEAN COINABLE
ACDEIMOR COADMIRE RACEMOID
AEHILNOP APHELION PHELONIA
DEEHNORT DETHRONE THRENODE
DEEMNORT ENTODERM MENTORED
DEEEINRS NEREIDES REDENIES
EEEILNST ENLISTEE SELENITE
AEEHIRRT EARTHIER HEARTIER
ACENOPRT COPARENT PORTANCE
EIOORSTT ROOTIEST TORTOISE
ABDEELOR ERODABLE LEEBOARD
EEGILOSU EULOGIES EULOGISE
AEGNNOST NEGATONS TONNAGES
BEINOOST BONITOES EOBIONTS
DEIMNOOT DEMOTION MOTIONED
EIMNOORS IONOMERS MOONRISE
EIMNOOST EMOTIONS MOONIEST
ADEILNNS ANNELIDS LINDANES
ADEILTTU ALTITUDE LATITUDE
AAEGIMNT AGMINATE ENIGMATA
AAEGINTV NAVIGATE VAGINATE
AEGIIMNR IMAGINER MIGRAINE
ACEEHIRT AETHERIC HETAERIC
ACEEIRTV CREATIVE REACTIVE
AEEHIMNT HEMATEIN HEMATINE
ADEELNSU UNLEASED UNSEALED
ACEIORSV COVARIES VARICOSE
DEINRSTT STRIDENT TRIDENTS
AEIMORTZ AMORTIZE ATOMIZER
ACEGNOST COAGENTS COGNATES
EGILNORW LOWERING ROWELING

ACDEILST CITADELS DIALECTS
ADEILMST MEDALIST MISDEALT
ADEINRSS ARIDNESS SARDINES
ADEINSST DESTAINS SANDIEST
AEINRSSU ANURESIS SENARIUS
ABDENRTU BREADNUT TURBANED
BEINRSTU TRIBUNES TURBINES
DEIMNRTU RUDIMENT UNMITRED
ABILNOTU ABLUTION ABUTILON
ACDILNOT ANTICOLD DALTONIC
ADILOPRT DIOPTRAL TRIPODAL
ADINOPST PINTADOS SATINPOD
ADIOPRST PARODIST PAROTIDS
AILORSTY ROYALIST SOLITARY
AIMNOSTU MANITOUS TINAMOUS
AINOPSTU OPUNTIAS UTOPIANS
CEEGINRT ERECTING GENTRICE
EEGIMNRT METERING REGIMENT
AEILQRTU QUARTILE REQUITAL
ADEGLNRS DANGLERS GLANDERS
AEEHORTV OVERHATE OVERHEAT
EEIMNORV OVERMINE VOMERINE
AGIILNRT RINGTAIL TRAILING
AADEFIRS FARADISE SAFARIED
AADEIMST ADAMSITE DIASTEMA
AAEILSTV AESTIVAL SALIVATE
ACEIILST CILIATES SILICATE
ADEIIMNS AMIDINES DIAMINES
AEFIILST FETIALIS FILIATES
AEIILMNS ALIENISM MILESIAN
DEELORSU DELOUSER URODELES
EEEINNRT INTERNEE RETINENE
AAEIRSST ASTERIAS ATRESIAS
AABENRST ANTBEARS RATSBANE

AAENRSTV TAVERNAS TSAREVNA
AEEENRTV ENERVATE VENERATE
ADELOPRS LEOPARDS PRELOADS
AELOPSTU OUTLEAPS PETALOUS
DEILMORU LEMUROID MOULDIER
AAILMNOR MANORIAL MORAINAL
ACDIINOT ACTINOID DIATONIC
ADEORSST ASSORTED TORSADES
AELLORST REALLOTS ROSTELLA
AENORSSU ANSEROUS ARSENOUS
DEINORSS INDORSES SORDINES
EINORSSU NEUROSIS RESINOUS
CDENORTU CORNUTED TROUNCED
DENOPRST PORTENDS PROTENDS
AEELNRRS LEARNERS RELEARNS
AEERRSTU AUSTERER TREASURE
DEEILRTT LITTERED RETITLED
DEEINNST DENTINES DESINENT
DEEINSTT DINETTES INSETTED
ABDEEILS ABSEILED BELADIES
ACEINNRS CRANNIES NARCEINS
AEILPRRT PALTRIER PRETRIAL
AEIMRSTT MISTREAT TERATISM
ADEILOSZ DIAZOLES SLEAZOID
EGIILNRS RESILING RIESLING
EGIILNST LIGNITES LINGIEST
ACDEENRS ASCENDER REASCEND
ADEEHLRT HALTERED LATHERED
ADEELPRT PALTERED REPLATED
ADEEMRST MASTERED STREAMED
AEEHLRST HALTERES LEATHERS
BDEEILNR LINEBRED RENDIBLE
BDEEIRST BESTRIDE BISTERED
BEEILNST STILBENE TENSIBLE

Bob's Bible Bonus: Complete 8-letter Multi-Anagram Quiz

CDEEILNR DECLINER RECLINED
CEEINRSU INSECURE SINECURE
DEEINRSW REWIDENS WIDENERS
EEILMNRU LEMURINE RELUMINE
EEILNPST PENLITES PLENTIES
EEILNRSV LIVENERS SNIVELER
EEINPRSU PENURIES RESUPINE
BDEILNOU UNBOILED UNILOBED
AADGILNO DIAGONAL GONADIAL
AEOQRSTU EQUATORS QUAESTOR
ABCEINRS BRISANCE CARBINES
ABEIRSTY BESTIARY SYBARITE
ACEHINRS ARCHINES INARCHES
ACEHINST ASTHENIC CHANTIES
ACEILPRT PARTICLE PRELATIC
ACEIMNRS CARMINES CREMAINS
ACEIMNST AMNESTIC SEMANTIC
ADEIMPRT IMPARTED PREADMIT
AEFILMNR INFLAMER RIFLEMAN
AEFINPRS FIREPANS PANFRIES
AEHILRTY EARTHILY HEARTILY
AEHINRSV ENRAVISH VANISHER
AEILNTVY NATIVELY VENALITY
CEIILNOS ISOCLINE SILICONE
EIILOPST PISOLITE POLITIES
AEGILNNS EANLINGS LEANINGS
AEGINNSU GUANINES SANGUINE
AEEILRSZ REALIZES SLEAZIER
EIINOSST INOSITES NOISIEST
DELNRSTU RUNDLETS TRUNDLES
EGINNRTU RETUNING TENURING
EINNOSTT TINSTONE TONTINES
AGINORRS GARRISON ROARINGS
EEIINNST EINSTEIN NINETIES

ABDEGINS BEADINGS DEBASING
ABDEGIRS ABRIDGES BRIGADES
ACEGILRS GLACIERS GRACILES
ADEGHILT ALIGHTED GILTHEAD
ADEGILMN MALIGNED MEDALING
ADEGILNP PEDALING PLEADING
AEGILNPS ELAPSING PLEASING
AEGILNSV LEAVINGS SLEAVING
ADDEGINR DREADING READDING
DEENNOST ENDNOTES SONNETED
AABEELRT RATEABLE TEARABLE
AAEEMNST EMANATES MANATEES
AAEEPRST ASPERATE SEPARATE
AAEERSTW SEAWATER TEAWARES
EEIINSTV INVITEES VEINIEST
DEEILMOS MELODIES MELODISE
ABENNOTU BUTANONE NANOTUBE
ABEORTTU OBTURATE TABOURET
AEMNNORS MONERANS SONARMEN
AEOPRRST PRAETORS PRORATES
BEILORTT BLOTTIER LIBRETTO
CDEIORRT CREDITOR DIRECTOR
EFIORRST FROSTIER ROTIFERS
EHIORSTT THEORIST THORITES
EIMORRST MORTISER STORMIER
EIOPRRST PIERROTS SPORTIER
EIORRSTV OVERSTIR SERVITOR
AEGMNRTU ARGENTUM ARGUMENT
EGINPRTU ERUPTING REPUTING
EGINRSTW STREWING WRESTING
AINRSTTU ANTIRUST NATURIST
ADEENOSS ADENOSES SEASONED
AAEHIMNT ANTHEMIA HAEMATIN
BDEENORS DEBONERS REDBONES

CEELNORS ENCLOSER ENSORCEL
DEEORSTY OYSTERED STOREYED
EELORTUV REVOLUTE TRUELOVE
AILNOOPT NOPALITO OPTIONAL
ACEILLOT LOCALITE TEOCALLI
ADEEELRS RELEASED RESEALED
ACDEEINN DECENNIA ENNEADIC
ADEEIPRR RAPIERED REPAIRED
ABILNRTU TRIBUNAL TURBINAL
AIMNRSTU NATRIUMS NATURISM
ABCEORST CABESTRO CABRESTO
ACDENORY CRAYONED DEACONRY
ACEFLNOT CONFLATE FALCONET
ACELMNOR AMELCORN CORNMEAL
ACENOPST CAPSTONE OPENCAST
ACEORSTV OVERACTS OVERCAST
ADEHNORV HANDOVER OVERHAND
AEHLMNOT HOTELMAN METHANOL
AEORTUWY OUTWEARY ROUTEWAY
CEHILORT CHLORITE CLOTHIER
CEHIORTU COUTHIER TOUCHIER
CEILOPRT LEPROTIC PETROLIC
CEINOPRS CONSPIRE INCORPSE
CEIORSTV EVICTORS VORTICES
DEFIOPRT PIEDFORT PROFITED
EFIMNORS ENSIFORM FERMIONS
EIMORSTW MISWROTE WORMIEST
DEEENRST RENESTED RESENTED
ACEENRRT RECANTER RECREANT
EEINNRTV INVENTER REINVENT
EEINRTTY ENTIRETY ETERNITY
AADLORTU ADULATOR LAUDATOR
DIILNOTU DILUTION TOLUIDIN
DEHIOOST DHOOTIES HOODIEST

DEIMNOOS DOMINOES MONODIES
EILMNOOS OINOMELS SIMOLEON
ADEEIMTT ADMITTEE MEDITATE
ABCEEILT CELIBATE CITEABLE
ACEEFINS FAIENCES FIANCEES
EMNOORST MESOTRON MONTEROS
ADENSTTU UNSTATED UNTASTED
AELRSTTU LUSTRATE TUTELARS
DEILNTTU UNTILTED UNTITLED
EILRSTTU SLUTTIER SURTITLE
AAEMORTT AMARETTO TERATOMA
CEEINPRT PRENTICE TERPENIC
ABDEGNOS BONDAGES DOGBANES
ADEGHLNO HEADLONG LONGHEAD
ADEGORSW DOWAGERS WORDAGES
DEGIMNOS MENDIGOS SMIDGEON
DEGINOSW WENDIGOS WIDGEONS
EGIOPRSU GROUPIES PIROGUES
EGIORSST GORSIEST STRIGOSE
ADDEILNS ISLANDED LANDSIDE
ADEILLRS DALLIERS DIALLERS
ADEIRSSU RADIUSES SUDARIES
EEGIRSTT GRISETTE TERGITES
CEIINNOT COTININE NICOTINE
ABELNSTU ABLUENTS UNSTABLE
ABELRSTU BALUSTER RUSTABLE
ADELRSTW WARSTLED WRASTLED
ADENSTUY UNSTAYED UNSTEADY
AEFLNRSU FLANEURS FUNERALS
AELMNRSU MENSURAL NUMERALS
AELNPRSU PURSLANE SUPERNAL
AELRSTUV VAULTERS VESTURAL
BDEILNRS BLINDERS BRINDLES
BDEILRST BRISTLED DRIBLETS

BEILRSTU BURLIEST SUBTILER
CEILRSTU CURLIEST UTRICLES
DEIPRSTU DISPUTER STUPIDER
ACEEGILS ELEGIACS LEGACIES
AEEGILMS GELSEMIA MILEAGES
AAIMNRST MARTIANS TAMARINS
ADDENRST DARNDEST STRANDED
AENRSSTU ANESTRUS SAUNTERS
AIIMNRST MARTINIS MISTRAIN
ABILOSTU BAILOUTS TABOULIS
ACDEEIMR CERAMIDE MEDICARE
AEEGNRSV AVENGERS ENGRAVES
EEGHINST SEETHING SHEETING
EEGILNRV LEVERING REVELING
ADNORTUW OUTDRAWN UNTOWARD
ACEGHINT CHEATING TEACHING
AEILQSTU LIQUATES TEQUILAS
DEGILRSU GUILDERS SLUDGIER
AAERSTTU SATURATE TUATERAS
EIILNSTT INTITLES LINTIEST
ABEELNOP BEANPOLE OPENABLE
ADEEORVW OVERAWED REAVOWED
ADEEENTT ATTENDEE EDENTATE
ADEIILMS IDEALISM MILADIES
AEGORRTT GAROTTER GARROTTE
ADEEEPRT DEPARTEE REPEATED
EEEINSTW TWEENIES WEENIEST
AABELRST ARBALEST RATABLES
AACDERST CADASTER CADASTRE
AADEPRST ADAPTERS READAPTS
AADERSTW EASTWARD RADWASTE
AAELNPST PLATANES PLEASANT
CEIINRSU INCISURE SCIURINE
EIINRSST INSISTER SINISTER

ADDELNOU DUODENAL UNLOADED
DEFLNORU FLOUNDER UNFOLDER
DEFNORSU FOUNDERS REFOUNDS
DEMNOSTU DEMOUNTS MUDSTONE
DENOPSTU OUTSPEND UNPOSTED
BEGINNOR ENROBING RINGBONE
AEILMNNS LINESMAN MELANINS
AEILMTTU MUTILATE ULTIMATE
ACEOORTV EVOCATOR OVERCOAT
AEIILNQU AQUILINE QUINIELA
AEINNSST INSANEST STANINES
AEEKORTV OVERTAKE TAKEOVER
EEIMNOTZ MONETIZE ZONETIME
DELNOOSU NODULOSE UNLOOSED
ACDEELRS DECLARES RESCALED
ADEELMRS DEMERSAL EMERALDS
ADEELNPS DEPLANES SPALDEEN
DEEFILRS DEFILERS FIELDERS
DEEILNUV UNLEVIED UNVEILED
CEINRSTT CENTRIST CITTERNS
CEINRTTU INTERCUT TINCTURE
ACINNOTU CONTINUA COUNTIAN
ACINOSTT OSCITANT TACTIONS
ACIORSTT CITATORS RICOTTAS
AILNNORV NONRIVAL NONVIRAL
ACGINRST SCARTING TRACINGS
AGIMNRST MIGRANTS SMARTING
AGINRSTY STINGRAY STRAYING
AEGHNOPT HEPTAGON PATHOGEN
AEGHNORV HANGOVER OVERHANG
AEGMNORV MANGROVE VENOGRAM
CEGHINOR COHERING OCHERING
ACDDEINR CANDIDER RIDDANCE
ACEINSST CINEASTS SCANTIES

AEIMNSST MANTISES MATINESS
EEILNSST LITENESS SETLINES
ABCDEIRS ASCRIBED CARBIDES
ABCEILRS CALIBERS CALIBRES
ABEILMNS BAILSMEN BIMENSAL
ADEHIMRS MISHEARD SEMIHARD
ADEHIRSW DISHWARE RAWHIDES
ADEILMNY MAIDENLY MEDIANLY
AEFILSTW FLATWISE FLAWIEST
AEHILRSV LAVISHER SHRIEVAL
AEILMNPS IMPANELS MANIPLES
AEGLOORY AEROLOGY AREOLOGY
EGILMOOR GLOOMIER OLIGOMER
DEGINRRS GRINDERS REGRINDS
ACINOPST CAPTIONS PACTIONS
ACIOPRST APRICOTS PISCATOR
AFILMNOR FORMALIN INFORMAL
AILMORTY MOLARITY MORALITY
AIMOPRST ATROPISM PASTROMI
ANOORSTT ARNOTTOS RATTOONS
DEEIKLNR REKINDLE RELINKED
EEIQRSTU QUIETERS REQUITES
AEFIIRRS FRIARIES RARIFIES
AEINPSST SAPIENTS STEAPSIN
DEELORRS RESOLDER SOLDERER
ADEGILLR GLADLIER GRILLADE
AEGILLNS GALLEINS NIGELLAS
AABEELST EATABLES TEASABLE
AAEELNPS SEAPLANE SPELAEAN
ABELORRU LABOURER RUBEOLAR
BDEIORRS BROIDERS DISROBER
EIMOSTTU TIMEOUTS TITMOUSE
ACEGLNRS CLANGERS GLANCERS
AEGLNRSW WANGLERS WRANGLES

AEGMNSTU AUGMENTS MUTAGENS
CEGILNRS CLINGERS CRINGLES
DEGINRSY SYNERGID SYRINGED
EFGINRSU GUNFIRES REFUSING
ABEIKNST BEATNIKS SNAKEBIT
AACEILMN ANALCIME CALAMINE
AACEILNV VALENCIA VALIANCE
AACEIPRS AIRSCAPE AIRSPACE
AACEIRSV AVARICES CAVIARES
BEELNOSU BLUENOSE NEBULOSE
EELOSTUV EVOLUTES VELOUTES
BENORTTU BUTTONER REBUTTON
ENORRTUV OVERTURN TURNOVER
ABEILLOS ISOLABLE LOBELIAS
DEELLNOR ENROLLED RONDELLE
DEEORSST DOSSERET OERSTEDS
EELNOSST NOTELESS TONELESS
GINORSTW STROWING WORSTING
ABEIRRTT BIRRETTA BRATTIER
ACILNSTU LUNATICS SULTANIC
ACILRSTU CURTAILS RUSTICAL
ADILMNRS MANDRILS RIMLANDS
ABEORSST BOASTERS SORBATES
ACENORSS COARSENS NARCOSES
ACEORSST COARSEST COASTERS
AEHNORSS HOARSENS SENHORAS
AENOPRSS PERSONAS RESPONSA
ACEHLORS CHOLERAS CHORALES
ACEHOSTU CATHOUSE SOUTACHE
ACELOPTU COPULATE OUTPLACE
ACELORSY CALOYERS COARSELY
ACEOPSTU OUTPACES SAUCEPOT
AEFLMORU FORMULAE FUMAROLE
AEHOPSTU PHASEOUT TAPHOUSE

AELMNOPS NEOPLASM PLEONASM
AELORSVY LAYOVERS OVERLAYS
BCEILORS BRICOLES CORBEILS
CDEIMOST DEMOTICS DOMESTIC
CEHILNOS CHOLINES HELICONS
DEHIMNOS HEDONISM MONISHED
DEIOPRSV DISPROVE PROVIDES
EHILOPRS POLISHER REPOLISH
EILMOPST MILEPOST POLEMIST
EILOPRSV OVERSLIP SLIPOVER
ELOORSTT ROOTLETS TOOTLERS
ABEERSTT ABETTERS BERETTAS
ADEEHNRR HARDENER REHARDEN
ADEEHRRT RETHREAD THREADER
ADEEMNNR MANNERED REMANNED
ADEENPTT PATENTED PATTENED
AEELPRRT PALTERER PREALTER
AEEMRRST REMASTER STREAMER
AEEPRSTT PEARTEST PRETASTE
CDEEIRRT DIRECTER REDIRECT
DEEIMNRR REMINDER REREMIND
DEEIRRTV DIVERTER VERDITER
EEIMRSTT EMITTERS TERMITES
EEINNRSV INNERVES NERVINES
EEINNSTW ENTWINES WENNIEST
ADGNOORS DRAGOONS GADROONS
AEGIKLNS LINKAGES SNAGLIKE
BENORSTW BESTROWN BROWNEST
EIKNNORS EINKORNS NONSKIER
AELOORSS AEROSOLS ROSEOLAS
EILOOSST OSTIOLES STOOLIES
ADEIRTTT ATTRITED TITRATED
AEIRRRST STARRIER TARRIERS
DEGNORRU GROUNDER REGROUND

ACEHIRTT CHATTIER THEATRIC
AEIMPRRT IMPARTER TRAMPIER
ACEEILPS CALIPEES ESPECIAL
ABEEILLN LIENABLE LINEABLE
CELNOORS CONSOLER CORONELS
DEOOPRST DOORSTEP TORPEDOS
AAGNORRT ARROGANT TARRAGON
CEIINNOS CONIINES OSCININE
BDEGIINT BETIDING DEBITING
EGHIIRST RIGHTIES TIGERISH
EGIINPRS SPEIRING SPIERING
AEERRSTV AVERTERS TRAVERSE
CDEEINNT INCENTED INDECENT
ACDEEHRT DETACHER RACHETED
ACDEENRV CAVERNED CRAVENED
ACDEEPRT CARPETED PREACTED
ADEEFMNR ENFRAMED FREEDMAN
AEEHNSTW ENSWATHE WHEATENS
AEEHRSTW WEATHERS WREATHES
AEEMNPRS PRENAMES SPEARMEN
CEEHIRST CHESTIER HERETICS
CEEIMNST CENTIMES TENESMIC
CEEIPRST CREPIEST RECEIPTS
AEGLLNOS ALLONGES GALLEONS
ADEEGRRU REARGUED REDARGUE
EEGINNSU INGENUES UNSEEING
ADNOSTTU OUTSTAND STANDOUT
GILNRSTU LUSTRING RUSTLING
EGHORSTU RESOUGHT ROUGHEST
ADEFLSTU DEFAULTS SULFATED
BDEILRSU BUILDERS REBUILDS
ABEKORTU BREAKOUT OUTBREAK
AEHORSTX OXHEARTS THORAXES
CEIORSTX EXCITORS EXORCIST

AAFILNST FANTAILS TAILFANS
AAILMNST STAMINAL TALISMAN
AFIILNST FINALIST TAILFINS
DDEIRSTU RUDDIEST STURDIED
DEINRSSU INSUREDS SUNDRIES
AEGINNPS SNEAPING SPEANING
CEIIMOST COMITIES SEMIOTIC
ABEIMRTV AMBIVERT VERBATIM
AEEGILLS GALILEES LEGALISE
DEINOOSZ OZONIDES OZONISED
AAINRSST ARTISANS TSARINAS
CEOORSTU ECOTOURS OUTSCORE
CEHNORST CHORTENS NOTCHERS
ACDLNORU CAULDRON CRUNODAL
ACLNORSU CONSULAR COURLANS
ADHNOSTU HANDOUTS THOUSAND
ADORSTUW OUTDRAWS OUTWARDS
ALOPRSTU POSTURAL PULSATOR
ADEEHPRT PREDEATH THREAPED
CDEEORTT COTTERED DETECTOR
CEEORRST ERECTORS SECRETOR
DEEOPRTT POTTERED REPOTTED
EENOPSTT POSTTEEN POTTEENS
EEOPRSTT PROETTES TREETOPS
EEORRSTV EVERTORS RESTROVE
EEORRTUV OVERTURE TROUVERE
ACDEGIMR DECIGRAM GRIMACED
AEGIMPRS EPIGRAMS PRIMAGES
AACEEMRT MACERATE RACEMATE
AAEEHRTW AWEATHER WHEATEAR
ADGIILNS DIALINGS GLIADINS
AEORSTTT ATTESTOR TESTATOR
ACINRTTU TACITURN URTICANT
CEHIORRT RHETORIC TORCHIER

EIMOPRRT IMPORTER REIMPORT
DEEENRRT RERENTED TENDERER
BEGHINRT BERTHING BRIGHTEN
ADEJRSTU ADJUSTER READJUST
ADEEELRV LAVEERED REVEALED
BDEEMNOT BODEMENT ENTOMBED
CDEEHORT HECTORED TOCHERED
CEENORSV CONSERVE CONVERSE
EELMORTY MOTLEYER REMOTELY
AADELMNS DALESMAN LEADSMAN
DEFIILNS INFIDELS INFIELDS
DEIILMST DELIMITS LIMITEDS
ADDEEENR DEADENER ENDEARED
AEEERSST ESTERASE TESSERAE
EEEINRSS EERINESS ESERINES
DEEENPRT REPENTED REPETEND
ABEHIMOS BOHEMIAS OBEAHISM
DEEMNOOS ENDOSOME MOONSEED
DEEOORSV OVERDOES OVERDOSE
EELMNOOS LONESOME OENOMELS
AEEHORSS SEAHORSE SEASHORE
AELRRSTT RATTLERS STARTLER
AACEEGRS ACREAGES GEARCASE
AAEEGMST AGAMETES AGEMATES
ACFINRST INFARCTS INFRACTS
AIMNRSTT TANTRISM TRANSMIT
BDELORSU BOULDERS DOUBLERS
CIILORST CLITORIS COISTRIL
DELLORST DROLLEST STROLLED
ADEGOPRR DRAGROPE PROGRADE
AEGOPSTT GATEPOST POTTAGES
ACEHNOPR CANEPHOR CHAPERON
CEHIMORT CHROMITE TRICHOME
AEMOOSTT OSTOMATE TOMATOES

Bob's Bible Bonus: Complete 8-letter Multi-Anagram Quiz

EELNSTTU LUNETTES UNSETTLE
CEHIOORS CHOOSIER ISOCHORE
ADEISSTT DISTASTE STAIDEST
AEILSSTT SALTIEST SLATIEST
DEEGLORW GLOWERED REGLOWED
ABEGIKNR BERAKING BREAKING
AEGIKNRW REWAKING WREAKING
ACEELOPS ESCALOPE OPALESCE
ADEFRRST DRAFTERS REDRAFTS
ADEMNRRU UNDERARM UNMARRED
AELMRSTT MALTSTER MARTLETS
AELNPTTU PATULENT PETULANT
AELRRSTW TRAWLERS WARSTLER
AEMNRRSU MANURERS SURNAMER
BEIRRSTU BRUITERS BURRIEST
CEIRRSTU CRUSTIER RECRUITS
DEINPTTU INPUTTED UNPITTED
EFILRRST FLIRTERS TRIFLERS
EILPRSTT SPLITTER TRIPLETS
ACEEHIRV ACHIEVER CHIVAREE
DEEILNSS IDLENESS LINSEEDS
DEENRRSU ENDURERS SUNDERER
AADEEGHR GEARHEAD HEADGEAR
AILLORTT LITTORAL TORTILLA
BDEELNRS BLENDERS REBLENDS
CDEELRTU LECTURED RELUCTED
CEELRSTU CRUELEST LECTURES
DEEMRSTU DEMUREST MUSTERED
DEENRSUV UNSERVED UNVERSED
AEEGHRRT GATHERER REGATHER
BEGILNOW BOWELING ELBOWING
CDEGINOY DECOYING GYNECOID
ABDEIRSS SEABIRDS SIDEBARS
ABEILLST BASTILLE LISTABLE

ACEILNSS LACINESS SANICLES
ACEISSTU SAUCIEST SUITCASE
ADEHIRSS AIRSHEDS RADISHES
ADEHISST DASHIEST SHADIEST
ADEIMRSS MISREADS SIDEARMS
ADEIMSST DIASTEMS MISDATES
AEHILSST HELIASTS SHALIEST
AEILLPST PALLIEST PASTILLE
AEILNPSS PAINLESS SPANIELS
ADEILMPS IMPLEADS MISPLEAD
CCEINORT CONCERTI NECROTIC
ACEIMOTZ AZOTEMIC METAZOIC
AEMNRSST SARMENTS SMARTENS
AENPRSST PASTERNS RAPTNESS
AENRSSTV SERVANTS VERSANTS
ABEHLRST BLATHERS HALBERTS
ACDEHNST SNATCHED STANCHED
ACEFRSTU FACTURES FURCATES
ACEHLNRU LAUNCHER RELAUNCH
ACEHNSTU NAUTCHES UNCHASTE
ACELPRST SCEPTRAL SPECTRAL
AELMPRST TEMPLARS TRAMPLES
AEMPRSTU TEMPURAS UPSTREAM
CDEIPRST PREDICTS SCRIPTED
EHILPRST PHILTERS PHILTRES
EHIMNRSU INHUMERS RHENIUMS
EILMNTUY MINUTELY UNTIMELY
BEILOORV BOILOVER OVERBOIL
EIPRSTTU PURTIEST PUTTIERS
ABINOSST ANTIBOSS BASTIONS
CEINOOTZ ENTOZOIC ENZOOTIC
ACDIOPRS PICADORS SPORADIC
ACILMNOS LACONISM LIMACONS
ACIOPSTU AUTOPSIC CAPTIOUS

BEEFGINR BEFINGER BEFRINGE
EIKNRSTT KNITTERS TRINKETS
EGNRRSTU GRUNTERS RESTRUNG
ADEHINSS DANISHES SHANDIES
AACERSTT CASTRATE TEACARTS
ABLOORST BARSTOOL TOOLBARS
ACLNOOST COOLANTS OCTANOLS
CILNOOST COLONIST STOLONIC
CILOORST COLORIST CORTISOL
AACILOTT COATTAIL TAILCOAT
ADELLOTT ALLOTTED TOTALLED
AFIINNOS SAINFOIN SINFONIA
EINNOSSU NONISSUE UNSONSIE
AABGILNT ABLATING BANGTAIL
AAGILMNR ALARMING MARGINAL
AAGIRSTV GRAVITAS STRAVAIG
AGIILNRV RIVALING VIRGINAL
AGIINSTW WAISTING WAITINGS
DEGHILST DELIGHTS SLIGHTED
AEIKRSST ASTERISK SARKIEST
AGILNOSS GLOSSINA LASSOING
AHIORSST AIRSHOTS SHORTIAS
AEIILLMR MILLIARE RAMILLIE
BELORSTT BLOTTERS BOTTLERS
ENORRSUV OVERRUNS RUNOVERS
BDGINORS BIRDSONG SONGBIRD
AABCELNR BALANCER BARNACLE
AABCELRT BRACTEAL CARTABLE
AABELRTY BETRAYAL RATEABLY
CEIIPRST PICRITES PRICIEST
EFHIINRS FINISHER REFINISH
EFIILNTY FELINITY FINITELY
DGINNORU INGROUND ROUNDING
EHIKNRST RETHINKS THINKERS

AEGGINNR ANGERING ENRAGING
AEGGINNT AGENTING NEGATING
AAIMOPRS MARIPOSA PAROSMIA
ABDDEORS ADSORBED ROADBEDS
ACDELLOR CAROLLED COLLARED
ADENOPSS DAPSONES SPADONES
AELLORSV ALLOVERS OVERALLS
CEILOSST SOLECIST SOLSTICE
DEIMOSST DISTOMES MODISTES
DEIOPRSS DISPOSER DROPSIES
DEIOPSST DEPOSITS TOPSIDES
EGIILNNS ENISLING ENSILING
ADEEMRRS DREAMERS REDREAMS
ADEEPRRS RESPREAD SPREADER
AEELPRRS PEARLERS RELAPSER
CDEEIRRS DECRIERS DESCRIER
CEEILSTT TELESTIC TESTICLE
DEEINNUV UNENVIED UNVEINED
DEEIRRSV DERIVERS REDRIVES
CDEILOPU CLUPEOID UPCOILED
DEHILOPS DEPOLISH POLISHED
ADGLNOOS DONGOLAS GONDOLAS
ADDEENTT ATTENDED DENTATED
DDEEINNT INDENTED INTENDED
EEIRRSST RESISTER TRESSIER
BDENOPRU PREBOUND UNPROBED
CDEFNORU FROUNCED UNFORCED
CEMNORSU CONSUMER MUCRONES
CEMORSTU COSTUMER CUSTOMER
ELOPRSTY PROSTYLE PROTYLES
ACEHILTT ATHLETIC THETICAL
ACEIRRSW AIRCREWS AIRSCREW
CCEEINOR CICERONE CROCEINE
CDELNOOS CONDOLES CONSOLED

CDELOORU COLOURED DECOLOUR
DEHLOOST TOEHOLDS TOOLSHED
CIINOOST COITIONS ISOTONIC
AADEGRSY DRAYAGES YARDAGES
DEFGIILN DEFILING FIELDING
EGIILNPS SPEILING SPIELING
EIIOSSTT OSTEITIS OTITISES
ACDDEENT DECADENT DECANTED
ACEERSST CATERESS CERASTES
ADDEEHNR ADHEREND HARDENED
ADDEEPRT DEPARTED PREDATED
CDDEEIRT CREDITED DIRECTED
EEINPRSS EREPSINS RIPENESS
EEINRSSV INVERSES VERSINES
ABDEEMNS BEADSMEN BEDESMAN
ABDEEPRS BEDRAPES BESPREAD
ACDEEHNS ENCASHED ENCHASED
ACDEEHST DETACHES SACHETED
ACDEELPR PARCELED REPLACED
ACDEEPRS ESCARPED RESPACED
ACEELNSV ENCLAVES VALENCES
ACEELPRS PERCALES REPLACES
ACEELRSV CERVELAS CLEAVERS
ADEEHPRS EPHEDRAS RESHAPED
ADEELPRY PARLEYED REPLAYED
ADEEMPST STAMPEDE STEPDAME
ADEEPRSV DEPRAVES PERVADES
AEELMPRS EMPALERS RESAMPLE
BDEEIMST BEDTIMES BEMISTED
CEEHILRS CHISELER SCHLIERE
DEEFILPR PILFERED PREFILED
DEEHIRSV SHIVERED SHRIEVED
DEEIPRSV DEPRIVES PREVISED
ABEELSTT SEATBELT TESTABLE

ACIORTTY ATROCITY CITATORY
AIMNNOTY ANTIMONY ANTINOMY
AAEMNPRS PARMESAN SPEARMAN
EIIPRSTV PREVISIT PRIVIEST
AGHINRTW THRAWING WRATHING
CEENPRST PERCENTS PRECENTS
AEEKRRST RETAKERS STREAKER
GIINOPST POSITING SOPITING
CDEGORSU SCOURGED SCROUGED
ACEIMPRS PARECISM SAPREMIC
ACEIMPST CAMPIEST CAMPSITE
AEHIMPRS SAMPHIRE SERAPHIM
AEHIMPST MATESHIP SHIPMATE
BDELNRSU BLUNDERS BUNDLERS
AEFGRRST GRAFTERS REGRAFTS
DEGINRRY GRINDERY REDRYING
ADEEGRSS DEGASSER DRESSAGE
EGGINORR GORGERIN ROGERING
ABEHILTT HITTABLE TITHABLE
AEHINNTX XANTHEIN XANTHINE
ABEEILSZ SEIZABLE SIZEABLE
AACEIPTT APATETIC CAPITATE
AACEITTV ACTIVATE CAVITATE
EGIIKLNR KINGLIER RINGLIKE
BDEEOSTT BESOTTED OBTESTED
CDEENNOU DENOUNCE ENOUNCED
DEEORRUV DEVOURER OVERRUDE
DDEENNOR DONNERED REDONNED
EELLNORR ENROLLER REENROLL
ACDEEKRT RACKETED RETACKED
AEEKNRSW REWAKENS WAKENERS
ABDDEGIR ABRIDGED BRIGADED
AEGINPSS SPAEINGS SPINAGES
AABDEERY BAYADEER BAYADERE

AABEEHLT HATEABLE HEATABLE
AABEELMN AMENABLE NAMEABLE
ACNOORTY CARTOONY OCTONARY
IMNOORTY MONITORY MORONITY
ABDEHORR ABHORRED HARBORED
ABDEORRW DRAWBORE WARDROBE
AELMOPRR PREMOLAR PREMORAL
CDEIORRV CODRIVER DIVORCER
AEEPRRTT PATTERER PRETREAT
EEIMRRTT REMITTER TRIMETER
EEIPRRTT PRETERIT PRETTIER
BEGIMNRU EMBRUING UMBERING
EGHINRSW SHREWING WHINGERS
EGIMNPST EMPTINGS PIGMENTS
EENOPSST PENTOSES POSTEENS
EEORSSTV ESTOVERS OVERSETS
CDEEFORS DEFORCES FRESCOED
CDEEOPRS PRECODES PROCEEDS
CEELOPRU OPERCULE RECOUPLE
DEEHORSW RESHOWED SHOWERED
EIOOSSTT SOOTIEST TOOTSIES
CEEELRST REELECTS RESELECT
DEEENRUV REVENUED UNREEVED
EEENRSUV REVENUES UNREEVES
ACCINORT CRATONIC NARCOTIC
CENOORRS CORONERS CROONERS
ENOOPSTT POTSTONE TOPSTONE
EOORTTUW OUTTOWER OUTWROTE
EFGIINRR FRINGIER REFIRING
EGIINNPR REPINING RIPENING
AEERRRST ARRESTER REARREST
EEINSTTT NETTIEST TENTIEST
EEIRRRST RETIRERS TERRIERS
ACILNRUY CULINARY URANYLIC

ACIMNRSU CRANIUMS CUMARINS
AILMNPST IMPLANTS MISPLANT
ADGILNNS LANDINGS SANDLING
ABEERRTY BETRAYER TEABERRY
BGINOOST BONGOIST BOOSTING
GHINOOST SHOOTING SOOTHING
ACDEMOPR COMPADRE COMPARED
BEFHINOS BONEFISH FISHBONE
CEHILNOP PHENOLIC PINOCHLE
CEHIOPRU EUPHORIC POUCHIER
CEHIOPST POSTICHE POTICHES
CEILMOPR COMPILER COMPLIER
CEILOPTY EPICOTYL LIPOCYTE
AAEEKNRW AWAKENER REAWAKEN
AEMOOSST MAESTOSO OSTEOMAS
GINNRSTU TURNINGS UNSTRING
DEEEIKLR DEERLIKE REEDLIKE
AENSSTTU TAUTNESS UNSTATES
AIINSTTV NATIVIST VISITANT
EIRSSTTU RUSTIEST TRUSTIES
EHMNOORS HORMONES MOORHENS
EHMOORST RESMOOTH SMOOTHER
EGGILNRS NIGGLERS SNIGGLER
EGGILNRU GRUELING REGLUING
BEGIIMNR BEMIRING BERIMING
ADEGIMPS MEDIGAPS MISPAGED
AGILLNRU ALLURING LINGULAR
BEEKNOST BETOKENS STEENBOK
CEEORSTX COEXERTS CORTEXES
EEJNORSY ENJOYERS REENJOYS
EEKNOSTY KEYNOTES KEYSTONE
DEELPRSU PRELUDES REPULSED
ACEGORSS CORSAGES SOCAGERS
AEGOPSST GESTAPOS POSTAGES

EGIOPRSS GOSSIPER SERPIGOS
DDEENRSU DENUDERS SUNDERED
EELNSSTU TUNELESS UNSTEELS
DEELOPRY DEPLOYER REDEPLOY
EEOPSTUW OUTSWEEP OUTWEEPS
ACEEFPRT PERFECTA PRAEFECT
ABDEISSU DISABUSE SUBIDEAS
ACCENOST COENACTS COSECANT
ACCEORTU ACCOUTER ACCOUTRE
EGHNORUV HUNGOVER OVERHUNG
AACHIRST ARCHAIST CITHARAS
AACILMNT CALAMINT CLAIMANT
ABELRSST BLASTERS STABLERS
ABHIINRS BAIRNISH BRAINISH
AEHLRSST HARSLETS SLATHERS
AELLNRUY NEURALLY UNREALLY
AELMRSST LAMSTERS TRAMLESS
AEPRSSTU PASTURES UPSTARES
AILLMRTY LIMITARY MILITARY
AIIMNPST IMPAINTS MISPAINT
AIIMNSTV NATIVISM VITAMINS
BEILRSST BLISTERS BRISTLES
CDEINRSS DISCERNS RESCINDS
DEIMNSST MINDSETS MISTENDS
EFILRSST RIFTLESS STIFLERS
EFIRSSTU SURFEITS SURFIEST
EILLNSTY SILENTLY TINSELLY
EILRSSTY SISTERLY STYLISER
EIRSSTUV REVUISTS STUIVERS
ABELMNSU ALBUMENS BLUESMAN
ACELMSTU CALUMETS MUSCATEL
ADELNPSY DYSPNEAL ENDPLAYS
CEFILRSU FLUERICS LUCIFERS
DEFILMNU FULMINED UNFILMED

DEIMPSTU DUMPIEST DUMPSITE
EILMPSTU LUMPIEST PLUMIEST
AILLMOST MAILLOTS MISALLOT
AILMORSS ORALISMS SOLARISM
AILOPSST APOSTILS TOPSAILS
ADHILOPS HAPLOIDS SHIPLOAD
ADHILOSY HOLIDAYS HYALOIDS
ADILMOPS DIPLOMAS PLASMOID
AEKMORTW TEAMWORK WORKMATE
ADEEGMNY GANYMEDE MEGADYNE
AEEGLMRY MEAGERLY MEAGRELY
BDEEGINW BEDEWING BEWINGED
EEGHIRSW REWEIGHS WEIGHERS
EEGINPSW SWEEPING WEEPINGS
AEQRSTTU QUARTETS SQUATTER
DGINNOSU SOUNDING UNDOINGS
ADHOPRST HARDTOPS POTSHARD
ADMNORSW SANDWORM SWORDMAN
AHLNOPST HAPLONTS NAPHTOLS
DHIORSTY THYROIDS THYRSOID
HILNOSTY THIONYLS TONISHLY
HIMORSTU HUMORIST THORIUMS
DEHIISTT DITHEIST STITHIED
EIILMSTT MILTIEST MISTITLE
CEHILOPT CHIPOTLE HELICOPT
AAIIMNNT AMANITIN MAINTAIN
ADLMOORS LORDOMAS MALODORS
ABDDEILU AUDIBLED BUDDLEIA
ADEGLLNU GLANDULE UNGALLED
ADEGRSSU DESUGARS GRADUSES
AGIILMNS MAILINGS MISALIGN
DEEOORRV OVERDOER OVERRODE
ELOPSTTU OUTSLEPT OUTSPELT
AACORTTU ACTUATOR AUTOCRAT

ELLORRST STROLLER TROLLERS
ELORSSTT SETTLORS SLOTTERS
ENNOSSTU NEUSTONS SUNSTONE
EORSSTTU OUTSERTS TUTORESS
ABEGKORS BROKAGES GROSBEAK
ABDEEERV BEAVERED BEREAVED
CDEEEIRV DECEIVER RECEIVED
CEEEILTV CLEVEITE ELECTIVE
AAACDINR ACARIDAN ARCADIAN
AAGMNRST TANGRAMS TRANGAMS
FGIILNRT FLIRTING TRIFLING
GIINPRST SPIRTING STRIPING
BEGLNRSU BLUNGERS BUNGLERS
ABIIMNRS BINARISM MINIBARS
AEEIPRRR RARERIPE REPAIRER
EERRSTTU REUTTERS UTTERERS
DGILLNOR DROLLING LORDLING
AAENPSST ANAPESTS PEASANTS
EIIMNRSS MIRINESS RIMINESS
EIIRSSTV REVISITS VISITERS
AEGGILNN ANGELING GLEANING
AABELMST BLASTEMA LAMBASTE
AACDEHRS CHARADES HARDCASE
AACDENSV ADVANCES CANVASED
AACELNPS CAPELANS SCALEPAN
DEFHIINS FIENDISH FINISHED
EIILMPRS IMPERILS LIMPSIER
DEEGHOTT DOGTEETH GHETTOED
CEENORVY CONVEYER RECONVEY
AAINOPSS ANOPSIAS PAISANOS
ABEKLNST BLANKEST BLANKETS
AEKMNRSU UNMAKERS UNMASKER
CEIKLNRS CLINKERS CRINKLES
EIKLNPRS PLINKERS SPRINKLE

ABCDIILO BIOCIDAL DIABOLIC
AELOPSSU ESPOUSAL SEPALOUS
DDEILOPS DISPLODE LOPSIDED
AEERRSSU ERASURES REASSURE
GLNORSTY STRONGLY STRONGYL
EEEGRRST GREETERS REGREETS
EGILNSSU GLUINESS UGLINESS
ABGILNTT BATTLING BLATTING
AGIMNNRU MANURING UNARMING
AABMORTU MARABOUT TAMBOURA
BELORSST BOLSTERS LOBSTERS
CDHIIORT HIDROTIC TRICHOID
CENORSUU CERNUOUS COENURUS
CENOSSTU CONTUSES COUNTESS
CEORSSTU CRUSTOSE SCOUTERS
CEORSTUU COUTURES OUTCURSE
CHIIORST HISTORIC ORCHITIS
DEFORSST DEFROSTS FROSTEDS
EHLORSST HOLSTERS HOSTLERS
EHNORSSU ONRUSHES UNHORSES
EHORSSTU SHOUTERS SOUTHERS
EMORSSTU OESTRUMS STRUMOSE
BDEERTTU BUTTERED REBUTTED
CDELNOSY CONDYLES SECONDLY
CELOPSTU COUPLETS OCTUPLES
ABEIRRSS BRASIERS BRASSIER
AEIPRRSS ASPIRERS PRAISERS
AEISSTTV STATIVES VASTIEST
AELRSTTT TARTLETS TATTLERS
EEIMMORS MEMORIES MEMORISE
ACEGGILN CAGELING GLACEING
ABDEESST BASSETED BESTEADS
ABEELLRS LABELERS RELABELS
ACDEELLR CELLARED RECALLED

Bob's Bible Bonus: Complete 8-letter Multi-Anagram Quiz

- **ACEELRSS** CARELESS RESCALES
- **ADEEHNSS** DASHEENS ENDASHES
- **AEEFLLST** FELLATES LEAFLETS
- **AEELNPSS** PALENESS PANELESS
- **AEEMRSSU** MEASURES REASSUME
- **BDDEEIRS** BIRDSEED DEBRIDES
- **CDDEEIRS** DECIDERS DESCRIED
- **DEEINSSW** DEWINESS WIDENESS
- **DEEIPSST** DESPITES SIDESTEP
- **EEHILRSS** HEIRLESS RELISHES
- **ACEHRSTT** CHATTERS RATCHETS
- **AENPRRSW** PRAWNERS PREWARNS
- **CEIPRRST** RESCRIPT SCRIPTER
- **BDEEILMS** BESLIMED BESMILED
- **DENOOOTW** WOODNOTE WOODTONE
- **GIILNOPS** PIGNOLIS SPOILING
- **EIINQTUY** EQUINITY INEQUITY
- **EEIQRRSU** QUERIERS REQUIRES
- **ABGILMNR** MARBLING RAMBLING
- **ABGILNRW** BRAWLING WARBLING
- **ACGINRSV** CARVINGS CRAVINGS
- **AFGIMNRS** FARMINGS FRAMINGS
- **DDEIIOPS** DIOPSIDE DIPODIES
- **ABEHINSS** BANISHES BANSHIES
- **ACEHIRSS** CASHIERS RACHISES
- **ACEILLMR** MICELLAR MILLRACE
- **AEHIMRSS** MARISHES MISHEARS
- **AEHIPRSS** PARISHES SHARPIES
- **AEIPRSSV** PARVISES PAVISERS
- **ABEGMNOY** BOGEYMAN MONEYBAG
- **AALPRSTU** PASTURAL SPATULAR
- **AGIINNPT** PAINTING PATINING
- **ADEELLPR** PEDALLER PREDELLA
- **ADEELLPT** PALLETED PETALLED
- **ABCEHNRS** BRANCHES BRECHANS
- **ABCEHRST** BATCHERS BRACHETS
- **ACEHPRST** CHAPTERS PATCHERS
- **CEHINPRS** PINCHERS PINSCHER
- **ABEIRRSZ** BIZARRES BRAZIERS
- **EEIKRSST** KEISTERS KIESTERS
- **ACILMOPR** PICLORAM PROCLAIM
- **AHIMOPRS** APHORISM MORPHIAS
- **BGILNOTT** BLOTTING BOTTLING
- **AACEHRTT** ATTACHER REATTACH
- **CEFIIRRT** FERRITIC TERRIFIC
- **ACEFRRST** CRAFTERS REFRACTS
- **AEGILLPS** PILLAGES SPILLAGE
- **ACENNOSS** CANONESS SONANCES
- **AEORRSSV** SAVORERS SEROVARS
- **BEINNOSS** BENISONS BONINESS
- **ACOOPRST** COPASTOR ROOTCAPS
- **CHINOORS** CHORIONS ISOCHRON
- **IOOPRSTY** ISOTROPY POROSITY
- **GIIJNOST** JINGOIST JOISTING
- **EGHIRSST** RESIGHTS SIGHTERS
- **EEGGINNR** GREENING RENEGING
- **ACCEILNS** CALCINES SCENICAL
- **ACCEIRSU** CAESURIC CURACIES
- **AGHILLNO** HALLOING HOLLAING
- **ABEGLMRS** GAMBLERS GAMBRELS
- **BEELNOSS** BONELESS NOBLESSE
- **CDEEOSST** CESTODES COSSETED
- **DDEELMOR** MOLDERED REMOLDED
- **DEELLORW** ROWELLED WELLDOER
- **EEOPRSSU** ESPOUSER REPOUSSE
- **CENORRSW** CROWNERS RECROWNS
- **CDEEELST** DESELECT SELECTED
- **DEEELPST** DEPLETES STEEPLED
- **CELOORRS** COLORERS RECOLORS
- **ACCDINOR** CANCROID DRACONIC
- **ACEHIKLR** CHALKIER HACKLIER
- **ACEELPRR** PRECLEAR REPLACER
- **ACEEPSTT** PECTATES SPECTATE
- **ADEEPRRV** DEPRAVER PERVADER
- **AEEHPRRS** REPHRASE RESHAPER
- **AEELMPTT** PALMETTE TEMPLATE
- **CEEHISTT** ESTHETIC TECHIEST
- **EEHIPSTT** EPITHETS TIPSHEET
- **BDGILNOO** BLOODING BOODLING
- **ABELLOTY** LOBATELY OBLATELY
- **ACELLORV** COVERALL OVERCALL
- **AEOPRSSV** OVERPASS PASSOVER
- **EHIMNOSS** HOMINESS MONISHES
- **ACEIRRRS** CARRIERS SCARRIER
- **ADEHLLOO** HALLOOED HOLLOAED
- **ABDEHOSW** BESHADOW BOWHEADS
- **CDEILMOP** COMPILED COMPLIED
- **CEEHNRRT** RETRENCH TRENCHER
- **AINNQSTU** QUINNATS QUINTANS
- **EGOPRRSU** GROUPERS REGROUPS
- **AACILSTT** CATTAILS STATICAL
- **DEILLRRS** DRILLERS REDRILLS
- **ABEEILLV** LEVIABLE LIVEABLE
- **EFNOOSST** EFTSOONS FESTOONS
- **EMNOOSST** MOONSETS MOOTNESS
- **ENOOPRSS** POORNESS SNOOPERS
- **AIIRSSTT** SATIRIST SITARIST
- **BDEMOORS** BEDROOMS BOREDOMS
- **BELMOORS** BLOOMERS REBLOOMS
- **CEHOORSU** OCHEROUS OCHREOUS
- **DEHLOORV** HOLDOVER OVERHOLD
- **DEHNOOSW** HOEDOWNS WOODHENS
- **EHLOOPST** POSTHOLE POTHOLES
- **EHOOPSTU** HOUSETOP POTHOUSE
- **AAEGSTWY** GATEWAYS GETAWAYS
- **DEFGIINY** DEIFYING EDIFYING
- **DEGIIMNP** IMPEDING IMPINGED
- **AEIPRRRS** PARRIERS SPARRIER
- **AAENPPRT** APPARENT TRAPPEAN
- **DEELOPRX** EXPLODER EXPLORED
- **ABCDEEHR** BERDACHE BREACHED
- **ABCDEEMR** CAMBERED EMBRACED
- **ACEEHPRS** PEACHERS PREACHES
- **AEEHLMNW** WHALEMEN WHEELMAN
- **CDEEHIPR** CIPHERED DECIPHER
- **CEEFHIST** CHIEFEST FETICHES
- **ALOPRRSU** PARLOURS SPORULAR
- **EINOSSST** SONSIEST STENOSIS
- **GHILNSTU** HUSTLING SUNLIGHT
- **GIIMNOTV** MOTIVING VOMITING
- **AACINRSS** ACRASINS SARCINAS
- **AEEHKNRR** HANKERER HARKENER
- **AEEKMRRT** MARKETER REMARKET
- **DNNORTUW** DOWNTURN TURNDOWN
- **AABCILST** BASALTIC CABALIST
- **AACILPST** APLASTIC CAPITALS
- **ABBELORS** BELABORS SORBABLE
- **ABIILMNS** ALBINISM MINILABS
- **ACDDERSU** ADDUCERS CRUSADED
- **ACELRSSU** RECUSALS SECULARS
- **ADDELPRS** PADDLERS SPRADDLE
- **ADEHLNSS** HANDLESS HANDSELS
- **ADELLMRU** MEDULLAR MURALLED
- **AEFLSSTU** FLATUSES SULFATES
- **BDEIRSSU** DISBURSE SUBSIDER
- **DDEILNPS** SPINDLED SPLENDID
- **DDEILNSW** DWINDLES SWINDLED
- **DEFIRSSU** FISSURED SURFSIDE
- **DEILMNSS** MILDNESS MINDLESS
- **EILNPSSU** SPINULES SPLENIUS
- **EINOOSSZ** OOZINESS OZONISES
- **EIMNOPSS** MOPINESS PEONISMS
- **ACDELPSU** CAPSULED UPSCALED
- **DEILMPSU** DISPLUME IMPULSED
- **CEHIIMOS** ISOCHEIM ISOCHIME
- **EEELRRTT** LETTERER RELETTER
- **CENRSSTU** CURTNESS ENCRUSTS
- **EHNRSSTU** HUNTRESS SHUNTERS
- **EMNRSSTU** MUNSTERS STERNUMS
- **IIMNPRST** IMPRINTS MISPRINT
- **AEEGPRSS** ASPERGES PRESAGES
- **DEEORRRS** ORDERERS REORDERS
- **EFGINRRY** FERRYING REFRYING
- **ACEHIMPT** EMPATHIC EMPHATIC
- **ADMORSST** STARDOMS TSARDOMS
- **BILORSST** BRISTOLS STROBILS
- **CEFIKLOR** FIRELOCK FLOCKIER
- **CEEORRSV** COVERERS RECOVERS
- **DEEFMORR** DEFORMER REFORMED
- **EEFLORRW** FLOWERER REFLOWER
- **EEMOPRRS** EMPERORS PREMORSE
- **EIILSSTT** ELITISTS SILTIEST
- **ABFLOSTU** BOASTFUL BOATFULS
- **DHIMORSU** HUMIDORS RHODIUMS
- **ACCEELNR** CANCELER CLARENCE
- **AEEHHNST** ENSHEATH HEATHENS
- **AEEHHRST** HEATHERS SHEATHER
- **AEEMMRST** AMMETERS METAMERS
- **AEEPPRST** PREPASTE PRETAPES
- **CCEEILNR** ENCIRCLE LICENCER
- **ACDENNNO** CANNONED NONDANCE
- **AADEGGRS** AGGRADES SAGGARED
- **CEEELRTT** ELECTRET TERCELET
- **CEEENRRS** RESCREEN SCREENER
- **AABDLORR** LABRADOR LARBOARD
- **IIMNNOSU** MISUNION UNIONISM
- **DOOPRSTU** DROPOUTS OUTDROPS
- **ABDEEEFL** BEFLEAED FEEDABLE
- **EEEIPSST** EPEEISTS SEEPIEST
- **ADELRSSW** WARDLESS WRASSLED
- **AACDELLN** CALENDAL CANALLED
- **EIILMSST** ELITISMS SLIMIEST
- **EINQSTUU** UNIQUEST UNQUIETS
- **DEFIILMS** MISFIELD MISFILED
- **CDEEEFRT** REDEFECT REFECTED
- **ACCEHINR** CHANCIER CHICANER
- **ACCEHINT** ATECHNIC CATECHIN
- **CDEEMOPT** COEMPTED COMPETED
- **CEEMOPRS** COMPEERS COMPERES
- **EELMOPRY** EMPLOYER REEMPLOY
- **AERRSSTT** RESTARTS STARTERS
- **ACELQRSU** CLAQUERS LACQUERS
- **EFIKLSTU** FLUKIEST LUTEFISK
- **EEHORRSW** RESHOWER SHOWERER
- **AGILNNUY** UNGAINLY UNLAYING
- **EEOPRRTX** EXPORTER REEXPORT
- **CDEERRSU** CURSEDER REDUCERS
- **AACLOPRS** CAPORALS CRAPOLAS
- **BDELNOSS** BOLDNESS BONDLESS
- **CDELORSS** CORDLESS SCOLDERS
- **CELORSSU** CLOSURES SCLEROUS
- **EFLNOSSU** FOULNESS SULFONES
- **ELLOPSTU** OUTSPELL POLLUTES
- **EEINOSSS** ENOSISES NOESISES
- **AAINSTTT** ANTISTAT ATTAINTS
- **AEGGISST** SAGGIEST STAGGIES
- **AAEIKLLS** ALKALIES ALKALISE
- **AEPRSSTT** SPATTERS TAPSTERS
- **EINSSTTW** ENTWISTS TWINSETS
- **EIPRSSTT** SPITTERS TIPSTERS
- **EIRSSTTW** RETWISTS TWISTERS
- **DDEENNTU** UNDENTED UNTENDED
- **AAADELMS** ALAMEDAS SALAAMED
- **GIINPRSU** SIRUPING UPRISING
- **ABELMRRS** MARBLERS RAMBLERS
- **ABELRRSW** BRAWLERS WARBLERS
- **ACEFRRSU** FARCEURS SURFACER
- **ACEHLSTT** CHATTELS LATCHETS
- **ACELRRSW** CRAWLERS SCRAWLER
- **GIIKNRST** SKIRTING STRIKING
- **EGMOORRS** GROOMERS REGROOMS
- **AIMNNOSS** MANSIONS ONANISMS
- **EHMNOOTW** HOMETOWN TOWNHOME
- **DDEEFNRU** REFUNDED UNDERFED
- **EELRSSTW** SWELTERS WRESTLES
- **EEMNSSTU** MUTENESS TENESMUS
- **AEILLQSU** LALIQUES SQUILLAE
- **DDEEEGNR** DEGENDER GENDERED
- **AGHILNSW** SHAWLING WHALINGS
- **AGILNPSY** PALSYING SPLAYING
- **ACEILPSS** SLIPCASE SPECIALS
- **ADEISSWY** SIDEWAYS WAYSIDES
- **AABEEGKR** BRAKEAGE BREAKAGE
- **EGISSTTU** GUSTIEST GUTSIEST
- **AELLMNTY** MENTALLY TALLYMEN
- **AEMPRSST** RESTAMPS STAMPERS
- **CEHINSST** CHINTSES SNITCHES
- **CEINPRSS** CRISPENS PRINCESS
- **CEINSSTY** CYSTEINS CYSTINES
- **EGHLOOTY** ETHOLOGY THEOLOGY
- **ACILLOTY** COITALLY LOCALITY
- **CCEHINOR** CORNICHE ENCHORIC
- **CEEEHIRR** CHEERIER REECHIER
- **EEEIRRVW** REREVIEW REVIEWER
- **EEILSSTX** EXITLESS SEXTILES
- **EHIISTTW** WHITIEST WITHIEST
- **EFMNRTUY** FRUMENTY FURMENTY
- **ACEKRRST** RETRACKS TRACKERS
- **EGGIINRV** GRIEVING REGIVING
- **ADEISSST** ASSISTED DISSEATS
- **AHINRSVY** HRYVNIAS VARNISHY
- **ACDMNORY** DORMANCY MORDANCY
- **ACHMNORS** MONARCHS NOMARCHS
- **ACHMORTU** OUTCHARM OUTMARCH
- **ACMNOPRS** CORPSMAN CRAMPONS
- **CFIMNORU** CUNIFORM UNCIFORM
- **BCILOORS** BICOLORS BROCOLIS
- **CILMOORS** COLORISM MISCOLOR
- **ILNOOPSY** SNOOPILY SPOONILY
- **DEEGGIRR** DREGGIER RERIGGED
- **BEGILNSS** BLESSING GLIBNESS
- **EGILNSSW** SWINGLES WINGLESS
- **BDEEKNRU** BUNKERED DEBUNKER
- **DDEIIOSX** DIOXIDES OXIDISED
- **EOPRSSTT** PROTESTS SPOTTERS
- **EORRSSTY** ROYSTERS STROYERS
- **AACEHILL** ACHILLEA HELIACAL
- **CDEOPRRU** PROCURED PRODUCER
- **CEHNNOSU** NONESUCH UNCHOSEN
- **ACGIKLNT** TACKLING TALCKING
- **AGIKNPRS** PARKINGS SPARKING
- **ABEIKLLN** BALKLINE LINKABLE
- **AEHIKSST** SHAKIEST SHITAKES
- **ABEILMSS** ABLEISMS MISSABLE
- **ABBDERST** DRABBEST DRABBETS
- **BBEIRSTU** STUBBIER SUBTRIBE
- **ACEELLRR** CELLARER RECALLER
- **ACEERRSS** CARESSER CREASERS
- **ACEESSTT** CASETTES CASSETTE
- **AEELLPTT** PALLETTE PLATELET
- **AEEPRRSS** ASPERSER SPEARERS
- **CEEINNSS** INCENSES NICENESS
- **ADIMMNOS** MONADISM NOMADISM
- **AABEFLMR** FARMABLE FRAMABLE
- **CEIIMPRS** EMPIRICS MISPRICE
- **CGHINOSU** CHOUSING HOCUSING
- **CGILNOSW** COWLINGS SCOWLING
- **GILNOPSY** POSINGLY SPONGILY
- **ABCDEIKS** BACKSIDE DIEBACKS
- **ACEILMSX** CLIMAXES EXCLAIMS
- **ACELLOPS** COLLAPSE ESCALLOP
- **AACEKRTT** ATTACKER REATTACK
- **DFGINNOU** FONDUING FOUNDING
- **BEEMNRRU** NUMBERER RENUMBER
- **ABCEKRST** BACKREST BRACKETS
- **CILRSTUY** CRUSTILY RUSTICLY
- **AACHMORT** ACHROMAT TRACHOMA
- **EHOPRSST** HOTPRESS STROPHES
- **BDELLOOR** BORDELLO DOORBELL
- **CELNOOSS** CONSOLES COOLNESS
- **CELOORSS** COLESSOR CREOSOLS
- **BELMORSY** SOMBERLY SOMBRELY
- **BEORSUVY** OVERBUSY OVERBUYS
- **CDEHORSW** CHOWDERS COWHERDS
- **CEHILSTY** CHESTILY LECYTHIS
- **ABDDEEMN** BEDAMNED BEMADDEN
- **ABEEHNSS** BANSHEES SHEBEANS
- **ACEEHNSS** ENCASHES ENCHASES
- **ACEEPRSS** ESCAPERS RESPACES
- **ADDEEFRY** DEFRAYED FEEDYARD
- **ADDEEPRV** DEPRAVED PERVADED
- **CEEIRSSV** SCRIEVES SERVICES
- **EEHIPRSS** PERISHES PHERESIS
- **ACEHRTTY** CHATTERY TRACHYTE
- **EGGIKNOS** GINGKOES GINKGOES
- **EGGLRSTU** GURGLETS STRUGGLE
- **AGLLNSTU** GALLNUTS NUTGALLS
- **DGGILNOS** GODLINGS LODGINGS
- **CEGORSSU** SCOURGES SCROUGES
- **NORSTTUU** OUTTURNS TURNOUTS
- **CEEFPRST** PERFECTS PREFECTS
- **CEEHNRSW** WENCHERS WRENCHES
- **EEHINNQU** HENEQUIN HENIQUEN
- **ACGHIMNR** CHARMING MARCHING
- **ACGHINPT** NIGHTCAP PATCHING
- **ADEEISSS** DISEASES SEASIDES
- **ELOOPRSS** RESPOOLS SPOOLERS
- **ABDEEGLL** BEGALLED GABELLED
- **AACFLRST** FLATCARS FRACTALS
- **BELRSSTU** BLUSTERS BUSTLERS
- **EFLRSSTU** FLUSTERS TURFLESS
- **EFLRSTUU** FRUSTULE SULFURET
- **EMMNORSU** RESUMMON SUMMONER
- **CEGINNSY** ENSIGNCY SYNGENIC
- **ACLLOSTU** LOCUSTAL OUTCALLS
- **AFLLOSTU** FALLOUTS OUTFALLS
- **CILLNOSU** CULLIONS SCULLION
- **ILNOPSSU** PULSIONS UPSILONS
- **BDEEERRS** BREEDERS REBREEDS
- **ABEKLMOS** ABELMOSK SMOKABLE
- **ADEELPPR** LAPPERED RAPPELED
- **DEEIMMRS** IMMERSED SIMMERED
- **BNORSTUU** BURNOUTS OUTBURNS
- **AAILLMNS** LAMINALS MANILLAS
- **LLOORSTU** OUTROLLS ROLLOUTS
- **GINNOOPS** SNOOPING SPOONING
- **ACHINNSU** ANCHUSIN UNCHAINS
- **ACDEEESS** DECEASES SEEDCASE
- **ADEEESSW** SEAWEEDS SEESAWED
- **GIINSSTU** SUITINGS TISSUING
- **ACMNOOPR** CRAMPOON MONOCARP
- **ABDEEKMR** BEDMAKER EMBARKED
- **ABEEKPRS** BARKEEPS PREBAKES
- **AGGILNRY** GRAYLING RAGINGLY
- **GINNSTTU** NUTTINGS STUNTING
- **DEHIILLS** HILLSIDE SIDEHILL
- **CEEERSST** SECRETES SESTERCE
- **DDEEEFNR** DEFENDER FENDERED
- **EEENSSTW** SWEETENS TWEENESS
- **BEEORSSV** OBSERVES OBVERSES
- **CDEEEHLR** CHEERLED LECHERED
- **EFOOPRRS** PROOFERS REPROOFS
- **ACEIPPRS** CRAPPIES EPICARPS
- **CIILOSST** SCIOLIST SOLICITS
- **ELLOSSTU** OUTSELLS SELLOUTS
- **AHIPRSST** HARPISTS STARSHIP
- **GINOOPSW** SWOOPING WOOPSING
- **ACCHIORT** THORACIC TROCHAIC
- **CGINSTTU** CUTTINGS TUNGSTIC
- **GHINNSTU** HUNTINGS SHUNTING
- **AKLOSTUW** OUTWALKS WALKOUTS
- **ADEELLSS** ALLSEEDS LEADLESS
- **ABCEFIKR** BACKFIRE FIREBACK
- **ABBEORRS** ABSORBER REABSORB
- **ACIIMSTT** ATTICISM MASTITIC
- **AABEEKMT** BAKEMEAT MAKEBATE
- **GIIKLNST** KILTINGS KITLINGS
- **AEGGRSST** GAGSTERS STAGGERS
- **CDEHNOOP** CHENOPOD PONCHOED
- **CDEMNOOW** COMEDOWN DOWNCOME
- **CEHMOORS** MOOCHERS SMOOCHER
- **EELORSVV** EVOLVERS REVOLVES
- **CEELRSSU** CURELESS RECLUSES
- **ADDGILNW** DAWDLING WADDLING
- **GIINNSTT** STINTING TINTINGS
- **EGGILRSW** WIGGLERS WRIGGLES
- **EMPRSTTU** STRUMPET TRUMPETS
- **ACDDEISS** CADDISES DISCASED
- **CDEIIKLS** DISCLIKE SICKLIED
- **GGHINOTU** OUGHTING TOUGHING
- **CGHINRSU** CRUSHING RUCHINGS
- **AFFINRSU** FUNFAIRS RUFFIANS
- **CDEEORRR** RECORDER RERECORD
- **AACDHIMR** CHADARIM DRACHMAI
- **AACDIMNY** ADYNAMIC CYANAMID
- **AACHIPRS** CHARPAIS HAIRCAPS
- **ABELLMRU** UMBELLAR UMBRELLA
- **ACEHLSST** SATCHELS SLATCHES
- **ACELNPSS** ENCLASPS SPANCELS
- **ADENPSSY** DYSPNEAS SYNAPSED
- **AEHLPRSS** PLASHERS SPLASHER
- **AELPRSSY** PARSLEYS SPARSELY
- **CEHILLRS** CHILLERS SCHILLER
- **CEIRSSUV** CURSIVES SCURVIES
- **EFILMSST** FILMSETS LEFTISMS
- **EILMNPSS** LIMPNESS PLENISMS
- **EILMPSST** MISSPELT SIMPLEST
- **GIINPSTT** PITTINGS SPITTING

Bob's Bible Bonus: Complete 8-letter Multi-Anagram Quiz

GIINSTTW TWISTING WITTINGS
AHILOPSS ALPHOSIS HAPLOSIS
GGIINNOR GROINING IGNORING
ACCEHORS CAROCHES COACHERS
CEFFIORU COIFFEUR COIFFURE
CEIMMNOU ENCOMIUM MECONIUM
CEEEELST ELECTEES SELECTEE
EIIMSSTT MISTIEST SEMITIST
EEEMPRRT RETEMPER TEMPERER
ABEHORRR ABHORRER HARBORER
ADDLNOOW DOWNLOAD WOODLAND
ILOOPSST POLOISTS TOPSOILS
ABCEKOOS BOOKCASE CASEBOOK
AAGIMNSS AMASSING SIAMANGS
AAGINSSY ASSAYING GAINSAYS
EEKLRSST KESTRELS SKELTERS
EEQRSSTU QUESTERS REQUESTS
ADLNOPWY DOWNPLAY PLAYDOWN
BCIOPSTU SUBOPTIC SUBTOPIC
CILOPRUY CROUPILY POLYURIC
ACCEEPRT ACCEPTER REACCEPT
AABFLOTT FALTBOAT FLATBOAT
DEIRSSST DISSERTS DISTRESS
EEFLRSUX FLEXURES REFLUXES
ACHIPRRT PARRITCH PHRATRIC
CGHIILNT CHITLING LICHTING
FGHIINST INFIGHTS SHIFTING
GHIINSTW WHISTING WHITINGS
DEEEGMRR DEMERGER REMERGED
ABBDELRS DABBLERS DRABBLES
AEFFLSTU FEASTFUL SUFFLATE
BBDEILRS DIBBLERS DRIBBLES
ACELLOSS CALLOSES COALLESS
ACEKRSST RESTACKS STACKERS
BEIKRSST BRISKEST BRISKETS
AEEGMMST GEMMATES TAGMEMES
EEGIMMRS GREMMIES IMMERGES
EERRSSTW STREWERS WRESTERS
ADMRSSTU DURMASTS MUSTARDS
BDINSSTU BUNDISTS DUSTBINS
EEMPRRSU PRESUMER SUPREMER
AGINNPSW SPAWNING WINGSPAN
ADFHLNSU HANDFULS HANDSFUL
BCEORSSU BESCOURS OBSCURES
CEHORSSU CHORUSES CHOUSERS
EMOPRSSU SPERMOUS SUPREMOS
ACEHKLRS HACKLERS SHACKLER
ADKLOORW WOODLARK WORKLOAD
ABEELMSS ASSEMBLE BEAMLESS
AEEFLMSS FAMELESS SELFSAME
AEELLSWY WALLEYES WEASELLY
BEEILMSS BESLIMES BESMILES
DEEILLMP IMPELLED MILLEPED
DGGIILNR GIRDLING RIDGLING
ACEHMRRS CHARMERS MARCHERS
CEIMPRRS CRIMPERS SCRIMPER
EHIMSTTY MYTHIEST THYMIEST
BEERSSTW BESTREWS WEBSTERS
EEFHRSST FRESHEST FRESHETS
BEGGLORS BLOGGERS BOGGLERS
ACGIMNPS CAMPINGS SCAMPING
AABCEKST BACKSEAT SEATBACK
AGGILNNS ANGLINGS SLANGING
AEGPRRSS GRASPERS SPARGERS
AABDHRSU BAHADURS SUBAHDAR
AACLPRSU CAPSULAR SCAPULAR
BIILMSTU MISBUILT SUBLIMIT
DEFLRSUU DESULFUR SULFURED
DEEGGIJR JIGGERED REJIGGED
ADDDEENS DESANDED SADDENED
EEIRSSSU REISSUES SEISURES
ACGIKLNS CALKINGS SLACKING
CEKORSST RESTOCKS STOCKERS
AEPPRRST STRAPPER TRAPPERS
EIPPRRST STRIPPER TRIPPERS
BCGINNOU BOUNCING BUNCOING
AEEKPRSS RESPEAKS SPEAKERS
CEHKNOSU SUNCHOKE UNCHOKES
AEHINSSS ASHINESS HESSIANS
CDEEERSS RECESSED SECEDERS
DEEEMNSS DEMESNES SEEDSMEN
AHMNNSTU HUNTSMAN MANHUNTS
ACHMNORY MONARCHY NOMARCHY
DOOOPRST DOORPOST DOORSTOP
BDEELLOW BELLOWED BOWELLED
EFMOPRRS PERFORMS PREFORMS
CEEHKRST RESKETCH SKETCHER
ABDEILMM DIMMABLE IMBALMED
ACCEHILS CALICHES CHALICES
ABDILLRY BRIDALLY RIBALDLY
AILMNPSS MISPLANS PLASMINS
AILMPSST PALMISTS PSALMIST
ACCEHRST CATCHERS CRATCHES
ACDGHOTW DOGWATCH WATCHDOG
ABBIMNOS BAMBINOS NABOBISM
CEHIMOSS ECHOISMS MISCHOSE
EELNOSSS NOSELESS SOLENESS
CEHOORSS CHOOSERS SOROCHES
EEEKRSST KEESTERS SKEETERS
EGGINSSU GUESSING SNUGGIES
BDENNRUU UNBURDEN UNBURNED
ENPRRSSU PRESSRUN SPURNERS
CCENNOST CONCENTS CONNECTS
ABBEGLRS GABBLERS GRABBLES
AEFFGRSU GAUFFERS SUFFRAGE
EGIMMSTU GUMMIEST GUMMITES
GGHIINRT GIRTHING RIGHTING
EEOPRSSX EXPOSERS EXPRESSO
ADEEPPRR DAPPERER PREPARED
GHINSSTU HUSTINGS UNSIGHTS
GINPRSUU PURSUING USURPING
CEINOSSS CESSIONS COSINESS
AABCILLR BACILLAR CABRILLA
AIIMNPSS PIANISMS SINAPISM
GINOPPST STOPPING TOPPINGS
FGHILNSU FLUSHING LUNGFISH
BDEEKMOS BESMOKED EMBOSKED
AAGHMNOY HOGMANAY MAHOGANY
AABCILMS BALSAMIC CABALISM
AACHILPS CALIPASH PASHALIC
ABCELSSU BASCULES SUBSCALE
BEILMSSU LIMBUSES SUBLIMES
AEEIMSSS MISEASES SIAMESES
GIKLNNRU KNURLING RUNKLING
EEEPRRSV PERVERSE PRESERVE
ABIKLMNS LAMBKINS LAMBSKIN
ACEIPPRR CRAPPIER PERICARP
AEFFIMRR AFFIRMER REAFFIRM
BCELMRSU CLUMBERS CRUMBLES
BELMPRSU PLUMBERS REPLUMBS
CCEHORST CROCHETS CROTCHES
CGIMNNOO GNOMONIC ONCOMING
ADEEMPPR PAMPERED REMAPPED
CEKRRSTU RESTRUCK TRUCKERS
DEELPSUX DUPLEXES EXPULSED
FHLORTUW WORTHFUL WROTHFUL
AABELLSY SALEABLY SLAYABLE
EFIILMSS FLIMSIES MISFILES
EEFFORRS OFFERERS REOFFERS
GHNOSSTU GUNSHOTS SHOTGUNS
CEERRSSU RESCUERS SECURERS
DDEEMRRU DEMURRED MURDERED
EEPRRSSU PERUSERS PRESSURE
ACEKLSST SLACKEST TACKLESS
AEHQRSSU QUASHERS SQUASHER
AEMQRSSU MARQUESS MASQUERS
CEIKLSST SLICKEST STICKLES
BELLOSST BLOTLESS BOLTLESS
ABIKLOSS KOLBASIS KOLBASSI
DDEEEGMR DEGERMED DEMERGED
DDEEIPSS DEPSIDES DESPISED
EEILLPSS ELLIPSES PILELESS
ACEPRRSS SCARPERS SCRAPERS
AEPRRSSY RESPRAYS SPRAYERS
ABIKRSTZ BRITZKAS BRITZSKA
AADGGHOT AGGADOTH HAGGADOT
KOORSTUW OUTWORKS WORKOUTS
ABCKOSTU BACKOUTS OUTBACKS
ACKLMORS ARMLOCKS LOCKRAMS
ADKORSWY DAYWORKS WORKDAYS
EEMPRSSU PRESUMES SUPREMES
CGIIKNST STICKING TICKINGS
AGHINSSW SWASHING WASHINGS
CEIIKNSS ICKINESS KINESICS
CEIIKSST EKISTICS STICKIES
INNOOPSS OPSONINS SPONSION
DDIIMRSU DRUIDISM SIDDURIM
ACHOTTUW OUTWATCH WATCHOUT
CHIOPTTU OUTPITCH PITCHOUT
AACCORSU CURACAOS CURACOAS
AGMMNOOR MONOGRAM NOMOGRAM
GGILNTTU GLUTTING GUTTLING
DEERSSST DESSERTS STRESSED
EELRSSST RESTLESS TRESSELS
BBEILRRU BURBLIER RUBBLIER
APRSSTTU STARTUPS UPSTARTS
CEIKQSTU QUICKEST QUICKSET
AEPRSSST SPARSEST TRESPASS
DEEMRRRU DEMURRER MURDERER
ACGINNNS CANNINGS SCANNING
ACINOSSS CAISSONS CASSINOS
AACCHINR ANARCHIC CHARACIN
AEFFRSST RESTAFFS STAFFERS
AEHHRSST HARSHEST THRASHES
GGIILNNT GLINTING TINGLING
AFILLPSU PAILFULS PAILSFUL
ACGHIKLN CHALKING HACKLING
ABEIKLLM BALMLIKE LAMBLIKE
ABBCELRS CLABBERS SCRABBLE
ACELPPRS CLAPPERS SCRAPPLE
CEILPPRS CLIPPERS CRIPPLES
ABLMNRUU ALBURNUM LABURNUM
BCEEMRRU CEREBRUM CUMBERER
CENOPSSY PYCNOSES SYNCOPES
CCEORRSU REOCCURS SUCCORER
GGILNOSS GLOSSING GOSLINGS
DDGINPSU PUDDINGS SPUDDING
EGMMRSTU GRUMMEST GRUMMETS
AGGHINNS GNASHING HANGINGS
EEERRSSV RESERVES REVERSES
NNOOOPST PONTOONS SPONTOON
ADDDEEMN DEMANDED MADDENED
EEHISSST ESTHESIS HESSITES
EEIMSSST MESSIEST METISSES
BBCELORS CLOBBERS COBBLERS
BBELORSY LOBBYERS SLOBBERY
CCEHORSU COUCHERS CROUCHES
BGIILNSS BLISSING SIBLINGS
ACEIKLLM CLAMLIKE MILLCAKE
CEEPPRST PERCEPTS PRECEPTS
AHIIKRSS RIKISHAS SHIKARIS
GIIKLNNS INKLINGS SLINKING
CGIKLNSU SCULKING SUCKLING
CIIKNPST NITPICKS STICKPIN
ACCEHILM ALCHEMIC CHEMICAL
ACCHNOOR COANCHOR CORONACH
ACEHHRTY HATCHERY THEARCHY
BCEKLRSU BUCKLERS SUBCLERK
CKORSTUW CUTWORKS SCUTWORK
CDEEEPTX EXCEPTED EXPECTED
DEEEFRRR DEFERRER REFERRED
AGMNSSTY GYMNASTS SYNTAGMS
AEEHMMRR HAMMERER REHAMMER
GINOOPPS OPPOSING POGONIPS
EFHILLSY ELFISHLY FLESHILY
AABIKLMS KABALISM KALIMBAS
ABERSSSU RUBASSES SURBASES
ACELRSSS CLASSERS SCARLESS
AELNPSSS SNAPLESS SPANLESS
AEMRSSSU ASSUMERS MASSEURS
EIMRSSSU MISUSERS SURMISES
BFHILOSW BLOWFISH FISHBOWL
GGIILNNS SINGLING SLINGING
ABBELRSS BARBLESS SLABBERS
BCIKOSTT BITSTOCK BITTOCKS
CCDEEKOR COCKERED RECOCKED
CEIKKLOR CORKLIKE ROCKLIKE
ADDNORWW DOWNWARD DRAWDOWN
CILNPSSU INSCULPS SCULPINS
FILLNSUY SINFULLY SULFINYL
ABCEKSST BACKSETS SETBACKS
KLOOOSTU LOOKOUTS OUTLOOKS
CCEHRSTU CRUTCHES SCUTCHER
ALMOPPST LAMPPOST PALMTOPS
CEEHMNSS CHESSMEN MENSCHES
CEEHMRSS SCHEMERS SCHMEERS
ABCKMOST BACKMOST TOMBACKS
ELNOSSSW SLOWNESS SNOWLESS
AABCCELS CASCABEL CASCABLE
AABDLLRY BALLADRY BALLYARD
AAEGSSSU ASSUAGES SAUSAGES
HOOOSTTU OUTSHOOT SHOOTOUT
AAOSTWWY STOWAWAY TOWAWAYS
EOPPRSSU PURPOSES SUPPOSER
ACEHHSTT HATCHETS THATCHES
AEPPRRSW PREWRAPS WRAPPERS
ABEFILLL FALLIBLE FILLABLE
AEIPSSSV PASSIVES PAVISSES
BDEEFFRU BUFFERED REBUFFED
AAADMRSS MADRASAS MADRASSA
CEKLRSSU SCULKERS SUCKLERS
CIIKLPST LICKSPIT LIPSTICK
GIIKLLNS KILLINGS SKILLING
CEHMOOSS SCHMOOSE SMOOCHES
EELOPPSS PEPLOSES POPELESS
ACHIMMOS MACHISMO MACHOISM
ACDEHHTT DETHATCH THATCHED
BCKLNOSU SUNBLOCK UNBLOCKS
CGILMNUU CINGULUM GLUCINUM
BEOORSSS OBSESSOR SORBOSES
EOOPPRSS OPPOSERS PROPOSES
GHHIOPST HIGHSPOT HIGHTOPS
GHINOPPS HOPPINGS SHOPPING
AAABIPSS PIASABAS PIASSABA
AAAIPSSV PIASAVAS PIASSAVA
EILLSSST LISTLESS SLITLESS
AEEGMSSS MEGASSES MESSAGES
IMOSSSTU MISSOUTS SUMOISTS
ACCDESUU CADUCEUS CAUCUSED
CGIIKLNN CLINKING NICKLING
GIIKNNPS KINGPINS PINKINGS
EFFRSSTU RESTUFFS STUFFERS
BDILPSUU BUILDUPS UPBUILDS
AACHIMSS CHAMISAS CHIASMAS
GLMNOOOY MONOLOGY NOMOLOGY
AAKMOSSU MOUSAKAS MOUSSAKA
DLNOOSWW LOWDOWNS SLOWDOWN
CCEHLSTU CLUTCHES CULTCHES
AACCDESS CASCADES SACCADES
AAORSSVV VAVASORS VAVASSOR
AACLLSUY CASUALLY CAUSALLY
BGGILNNU BLUNGING BUNGLING
GGILNNPU PLUNGING PUNGLING
LLOPSTUU OUTPULLS PULLOUTS
FIKLSSTU KISTFULS LUTFISKS
AGGGILNS LAGGINGS SLAGGING
IKLMOOSS LOOKISMS LOOKSISM
ELMMPSTU PLUMMEST PLUMMETS
EPRRSSUU PURSUERS USURPERS
BEGILLLU BLUEGILL GULLIBLE
AAHHKLOT HALAKHOT HALAKOTH
CKOOOSTU COOKOUTS OUTCOOKS
GGGILNOS LOGGINGS SLOGGING
ACCGIKLN CACKLING CLACKING
EHIPPRSS PRESHIPS SHIPPERS
ABCJKOOT BOOTJACK JACKBOOT
AABCDKRW BACKWARD DRAWBACK
AABCFKST FASTBACK FATBACKS
CCGIKLNO CLOCKING COCKLING
ACDDHKOS HADDOCKS SHADDOCK
HPRSTTUU THRUPUTS UPTHRUST
DGGGINRU DRUGGING GRUDGING
HOOPSSTT HOTSPOTS POTSHOTS
AEFFHIKY KAFFIYEH KEFFIYAH
ACFFOSST CASTOFFS OFFCASTS
AACCELLY CAECALLY CALYCEAL
FIKKLNOS KINFOLKS KINSFOLK
AAADGGHS AGGADAHS HAGGADAS
GGGINNOS NOGGINGS SNOGGING
ACILMSSS CLASSISM MISCLASS
AHILPPSS PALSHIPS SHIPLAPS
GLOOPTYY LOGOTYPY TYPOLOGY
CCEEHKRS CHECKERS RECHECKS
FFKLORSU FORKFULS FORKSFUL
BGGGILNO BLOGGING BOGGLING
HIILLMMO MILLIMHO MILLIOHM
ACFKLSSU SACKFULS SACKSFUL
CEFFLSSU CUFFLESS SCUFFLES
DMOOORWW WOODWORM WORMWOOD
AABCCKST BACKCAST SCATBACK
GGGIINSW SWIGGING WIGGINGS
ABBBGILN BABBLING BLABBING
ABCKSSUW BUCKSAWS SAWBUCKS
BBBGILNO BLOBBING BOBBLING
GILNOPPP PLOPPING POPPLING
HMNOPSYY HYPONYMS SYMPHONY
BBBELRSU BLUBBERS BUBBLERS
AAAHHKLS HALAKAHS HALAKHAS
AAABKPSS BAASKAPS BAASSKAP
ACCEHHKT CHATCHKE HATCHECK
BBBGILNU BLUBBING BUBBLING
IJJSSTUU JUJITSUS JUJUISTS
ACCKOSSS CASSOCKS COSSACKS
AEIPSZZZ PIZAZZES PIZZAZES
GGGGILNU GLUGGING GUGGLING

A

B AA HLS
AAH S
AHA
AAHED
AHEAD
AAHING
AAHS
B AAL S
ALA
AALII S
AALIIS
B AALS
ALAS
AARDVARK S
AARDWOLF
AARGH
AARRGH H
AARRGHH
BK AAS
AASVOGEL S
CDFGJKLNSTW AB ASY
BA
B ABA S
BAA
ABACA S
ABACAS
CASABA
ABACI
ABACK
ABACUS
ABACUSES
ABAFT
K ABAKA S
K ABAKAS
ABALONE S
ABALONES
ABAMP S
ABAMPERE S
ABAMPS
ABANDON S
ABANDONS
ABAPICAL
B ABAS EH
BAAS
ABASE DRS
ABASED
ABASEDLY
ABASER S
ABASERS
ABASES
BAASES
ABASH
ABASHED
ABASHES
ABASHING
ABASIA S
ABASIAS
ABASING
BISNAGA
ABATABLE
ABATE DRS
ABATED
ABATER S
ABATERS
ABREAST
ABATES
ABATING
ABATIS
ABATISES
ABATOR S
RABATO
ABATORS
RABATOS
ABATTIS
ABATTOIR S
ABAXIAL
ABAXILE
K ABAYA S
K ABAYAS
ABBA S
BABA
ABBACIES
ABBACY

ABBAS
BABAS
ABBATIAL
ABBE SY
BABE
ABBES S
BABES
ABBESS
ABBESSES
ABBEY S
ABBEYS
ABBOT S
ABBOTCY
ABBOTS
ABDICATE DS
ABDOMEN S
ABDOMENS
ABDOMINA L
ABDUCE DS
ABDUCED
ABDUCENS
ABDUCENT
ABDUCES
SCUBAED
ABDUCING
ABDUCT S
ABDUCTED
ABDUCTEE S
ABDUCTOR S
ABDUCTS
ABEAM
AMEBA
S ABED
BADE BEAD
ABEGGING
ABELE S
ABELES
ABELIA NS
ABELIAN
ABELIAS
ABELMOSK S
SMOKABLE
ABERRANT S
ABET S
BATE BEAT
BETA
ABETMENT S
ABETS
BASTE BATES
BEAST BEATS
BETAS TABES
ABETTAL S
ABETTALS
STATABLE
TASTABLE
ABETTED
ABETTER S
BERETTA
ABETTERS
BERETTAS
ABETTING
ABETTOR S
TABORET
ABETTORS
TABORETS
ABEYANCE S
ABEYANCY
ABEYANT
ABFARAD S
ABFARADS
ABHENRY S
ABHENRYS
ABHOR S
ABHORRED
HARBORED
ABHORRER S
HARBORER
ABHORS
ABIDANCE S
ABIDE DRS
ABIDED
BADDIE
ABIDER S
ABIDERS
BRAISED
DARBIES
SEABIRD
SIDEBAR
ABIDES
BIASED

ABIDING
ABIGAIL S
ABIGAILS
L ABILITY
ABIOSES
ABIOSIS
ABIOTIC
ABJECT
ABJECTLY
ABJURE DRS
ABJURED
ABJURER S
ABJURERS
ABJURES
ABJURING
ABLATE DS
ABLATED
DATABLE
ABLATES
ABLATING
BANGTAIL
ABLATION S
ABLATIVE S
ABLATOR S
ABLATORS
ABLAUT S
ABLAUTS
ABLAZE
CFGST ABLE DRS
BALE BLAE
CFGT ABLED
BALED BLADE
ABLEGATE S
ABLEISM S
LAMBIES
ABLEISMS
MISSABLE
ABLEIST S
ALBITES
ASTILBE
BASTILE
BESTIAL
BLASTIE
STABILE
ABLEISTS
ASTILBES
BASTILES
BLASTIES
STABILES
CF ABLER
BALER BLARE
BLEAR
CFGST ABLES T
BALES BLASE
SABLE
ABLEST
BLEATS
STABLE
TABLES
ABLINGS
ABLINS
BLAINS
ABLOOM
ABLUENT S
TUNABLE
ABLUENTS
UNSTABLE
ABLUSH
ABLUTED
ABLUTION S
ABUTILON
ABLY
ABMHO S
ABOHM
ABMHOS
ABOHMS
ABNEGATE DS
ABNORMAL S
ABOARD
ABROAD
ABODE DS
ADOBE
ABODED
ABODES
ADOBES
ABODING
ABOHM S
ABMHO
ABOHMS
ABMHOS
ABOIDEAU SX

ABOIL
ABOITEAU SX
ABOLISH
ABOLLA E
ABOLLAE
ABOMA S
ABOMAS AI
ABOMASA L
ABOMASAL
ABOMASI
ABOMASUM
ABOMASUS
BG ABOON
ABORAL
ABORALLY
ABORNING
ABORT S
BOART TABOR
ABORTED
BORATED
TABORED
ABORTER S
TABORER
ABORTERS
TABORERS
ABORTING
BORATING
TABORING
ABORTION S
ABORTIVE
ABORTS
BOARTS
TABORS
ABORTUS
ROBUSTA
RUBATOS
TABOURS
ABOUGHT
ABOULIA S
ABOULIAS
ABOULIC
ABOUND S
ABOUNDED
ABOUNDS
BAUSOND
ABOUT
ABOVE S
ABOVES
ABRACHIA S
ABRADANT S
ABRADE DRS
ABRADED
ABRADER S
ABRADERS
ABRADES
ABRADING
ABRASION S
ABRASIVE S
ABREACT S
BEARCAT
CABARET
ABREACTS
BEARCATS
CABARETS
CABRESTA
ABREAST
ABATERS
ABRI S
ABRIDGE DRS
BRIGADE
ABRIDGED
BRIGADED
ABRIDGER S
ABRIDGES
BRIGADES
ABRIS
SABIR
ABROACH
ABROAD
ABOARD
ABROGATE DS
ABROSIA S
ABROSIAS
ABRUPT
ABRUPTER
ABRUPTLY

CDFGJKLNSTW ABS
BAS SAB
ABSCESS
ABSCISE DS
SCABIES
SEBASIC
ABSCISED
ABSCISES
ABSCISIN GS
ABSCISSA ES
ABSCOND S
ABSCONDS
ABSEIL S
ABSEILED
BELADIES
ABSEILS
ABSENCE S
ABSENCES
ABSENT S
ABSENTED
ABSENTEE S
ABSENTER S
ABSENTLY
ABSENTS
ABSINTH ES
ABSINTHE S
ABSINTHS
ABSOLUTE RS
ABSOLVE DRS
ABSOLVED
ABSOLVER S
ABSOLVES
ABSONANT
ABSORB S
ABSORBED
ABSORBER S
REABSORB
ABSORBS
ABSTAIN S
ABSTAINS
ABSTERGE DS
ABSTRACT S
ABSTRICT S
ABSTRUSE R
ABSURD S
ABSURDER
ABSURDLY
ABSURDS
ABUBBLE
ABULIA S
ABULIAS
ABULIC
ABUNDANT
ABUSABLE
ABUSE DRS
BEAUS
ABUSED
DAUBES
ABUSER S
BURSAE
ABUSERS
RUBASSE
SURBASE
ABUSES
SUBSEA
ABUSING
ABUSIVE
ABUT S
TABU TUBA
ABUTILON S
ABLUTION
ABUTMENT S
ABUTS
TABUS TSUBA
TUBAS
ABUTTAL S
ABUTTALS
ABUTTED
ABUTTER S
ABUTTERS
ABUTTING
ABUZZ
ABVOLT S
ABVOLTS
ABWATT S

ABWATTS
BG ABY ES
BAY
ABYE S
ABYES
B ABYING
BAYING
ABYS MS
BAYS
ABYSM S
ABYSMAL
ABYSMS
ABYSS
BASSY
ABYSSAL
ABYSSES
ACACIA S
ACACIAS
ACADEME S
ACADEMES
ACADEMIA S
ACADEMIC S
ACADEMY
ACAJOU S
ACAJOUS
ACALEPH ES
ACALEPHE S
ACALEPHS
ACANTHA E
ACANTHAE
ACANTHI
ACANTHUS
ACAPNIA S
ACAPNIAS
ACARBOSE S
ACARI D
ACARID S
CARDIA
ACARIDAN S
ARCADIAN
ACARIDS
ASCARID
CARDIAS
ACARINE S
CARINAE
ACARINES
CANARIES
CESARIAN
SARCINAE
ACAROID
ACARPOUS
ACARUS
ACAUDAL
ACAUDATE
ACAULINE
ACAULOSE
ACAULOUS
ACCEDE DRS
ACCEDED
ACCEDER S
ACCEDERS
ACCEDES
ACCEDING
ACCENT S
ACCENTED
ACCENTOR S
ACCENTS
ACCEPT S
ACCEPTED
ACCEPTEE S
ACCEPTER S
REACCEPT
ACCEPTOR S
ACCEPTS
ACCESS
ACCESSED
ACCESSES
ACCIDENT S
ACCIDIA S
ACCIDIAS
ACCIDIE S
ACCIDIES
ACCLAIM S
ACCLAIMS
ACCOLADE DS
ACCORD S
ACCORDED

ACCORDER S
ACCORDS
ACCOST S
COACTS
ACCOSTED
ACCOSTS
ACCOUNT S
ACCOUNTS
ACCOUTER S
ACCOUTRE
ACCOUTRE DS
ACCOUTER
ACCREDIT S
ACCRETE DS
ACCRETED
ACCRETES
ACCRUAL S
CARACUL
ACCRUALS
CARACULS
SACCULAR
ACCRUE DS
ACCRUED
ACCRUES
ACCUSER
ACCRUING
ACCURACY
ACCURATE
ACCURSED
ACCURST
ACCUSAL S
ACCUSALS
ACCUSANT S
ACCUSE DRS
ACCUSED
ACCUSER S
ACCRUES
ACCUSERS
ACCUSES
ACCUSING
ACCUSTOM S
DFLMPRT ACE DS
FLMPR ACED
CADE DACE
ACEDIA S
ACEDIAS
ACELDAMA S
ACENTRIC
ACEQUIA S
ACEQUIAS
LM ACERATE D
LM ACERATED
ACERB
BRACE CABER
ACERBATE DS
ACERBER
CEREBRA
ACERBEST
ACERBIC
BRECCIA
ACERBITY
ACEROLA S
ACEROLAS
ACEROSE
ACEROUS
CAROUSE
ACERVATE
ACERVULI
DFLMPRT ACES
CASE
ACESCENT S
ACETA L
ACETAL S
ACETALS
LACTASE
ACETAMID ES
ACETATE DS
ACETATED
ACETATES
ACETIC
ACETIFY
ACETIN S
CENTAI
ENATIC
ACETINS
CINEAST

ACETONE S
ACETONES NOTECASE
ACETONIC
ACETOSE COATEES
ACETOUS
ACETOXYL S
ACETUM
ACETYL S
ACETYLIC
ACETYLS
CMT ACHE DS EACH
BC ACHED
ACHENE S
ACHENES ENCHASE
ACHENIAL
BCL MNT ACHES CHASE
ACHIER CAHIER
ACHIEST AITCHES
ACHIEVE DRS
ACHIEVED
ACHIEVER S CHIVAREE
ACHIEVES
ACHILLEA S HELIACAL
ACHINESS
BC ACHING
ACHINGLY
ACHIOTE S
ACHIOTES
ACHIRAL RACHIAL
ACHOLIA S
ACHOLIAS
ACHOO
ACHROMAT S TRACHOMA
ACHROMIC
ACHY CHAY
ACICULA ERS
ACICULAE
ACICULAR
ACICULAS
ACICULUM S
ACID SY CADI CAID
ACIDEMIA S
ACIDHEAD S
ACIDIC
ACIDIFY
ACIDITY
ACIDLY
ACIDNESS
ACIDOSES
ACIDOSIS
ACIDOTIC
ACIDS ASDIC CADIS CAIDS
ACIDURIA S
ACIDY
ACIERATE DS
ACIFORM FORMICA
ACINAR ARNICA CARINA CRANIA
FLM PR ACING
ACINI C
ACINIC
ACINOSE
ACINOUS
ACINUS
H ACKEE S
H ACKEES
ACLINIC
ACMATIC
ACME S CAME MACE

ACMES CAMES MACES
ACMIC
ACNE DS CANE
ACNED CANED DANCE
ACNES CANES SCENA
T ACNODE S CANOED DEACON
T ACNODES DEACONS
ACOCK
ACOELOUS
ACOLD
ACOLYTE S
ACOLYTES
T ACONITE S
T ACONITES CANOEIST SONICATE
ACONITIC CATIONIC
ACONITUM S
ACORN S NARCO RACON
ACORNED
ACORNS NARCOS RACONS
ACOUSTIC S
ACQUAINT S
ACQUEST S
ACQUESTS
ACQUIRE DER S
ACQUIRED
ACQUIREE S
ACQUIRER S
ACQUIRES
ACQUIT S
ACQUITS
ACRASIA S
ACRASIAS
ACRASIN S ARNICAS CARINAS SARCINA
ACRASINS SARCINAS
N ACRE DS CARE RACE
ACREAGE S
ACREAGES GEARCASE
NS ACRED ARCED CADRE CARED CEDAR RACED
N ACRES CARES CARSE ESCAR RACES SCARE SERAC
ACRID CAIRD DARIC
ACRIDER CARRIED
ACRIDEST
ACRIDINE S
ACRIDITY
ACRIDLY
ACRIMONY
ACROBAT S
ACROBATS
M ACRODONT S
ACROGEN S
ACROGENS
ACROLECT S
ACROLEIN S COLINEAR
ACROLITH S
ACROMIA L
ACROMIAL
ACROMION
ACRONIC
ACRONYM S
ACRONYMS
ACROSOME S

ACROSS
ACROSTIC S
ACROTIC
ACROTISM S
ACRYLATE S
ACRYLIC S
ACRYLICS
FPT ACT AS CAT
ACTA
ACTABLE
ACTED CADET
ACTIN GS ANTIC
ACTINAL
ACTING S
ACTINGS CASTING
ACTINIA ENS
ACTINIAE
ACTINIAN S
ACTINIAS
ACTINIC
ACTINIDE S CTENIDIA INDICATE
ACTINISM S
ACTINIUM S
ACTINOID S DIATONIC
ACTINON S CONTAIN
ACTINONS CANONIST CONTAINS SANCTION SONANTIC
ACTINS ANTICS NASTIC
FPT ACTION S ATONIC CATION
ACTIONER S ANORETIC CREATION REACTION
FPT ACTIONS ATONICS CATIONS
ACTIVATE DS CAVITATE
ACTIVE S
ACTIVELY
ACTIVES
ACTIVISM S
ACTIVIST S
ACTIVITY
ACTIVIZE DS
F ACTOR S TAROC
ACTORISH CHARIOTS HARICOTS
ACTORLY
F ACTORS CASTOR COSTAR SCROTA TAROCS
ACTRESS Y CASTERS RECASTS
ACTRESSY
FPT ACTS CAST CATS SCAT
FT ACTUAL
FT ACTUALLY
ACTUARY
ACTUATE DS
ACTUATED
ACTUATES
ACTUATOR S AUTOCRAT
ACUATE
V ACUITIES
V ACUITY
ACULEATE D

ACULEI
ACULEUS
ACUMEN S
ACUMENS
ACUTANCE S
ACUTE RS
ACUTELY
ACUTER CURATE
ACUTES T CUESTA
ACUTEST SCUTATE
ACYCLIC
ACYL S CLAY LACY
ACYLATE DS
ACYLATED
ACYLATES
ACYLOIN S
ACYLOINS
ACYLS CLAYS SCALY
BCD FGH LMP RST W AD DOSZ
ADAGE S
ADAGES
ADAGIAL
ADAGIO S
ADAGIOS
ADAMANCE S
ADAMANCY
ADAMANT S
ADAMANTS
ADAMSITE S DIASTEMA
ADAPT S
ADAPTED
ADAPTER S READAPT
ADAPTERS READAPTS
ADAPTING
ADAPTION S
ADAPTIVE
ADAPTOR S
ADAPTORS
ADAPTS
ADAXIAL
ADD S DAD
ADDABLE
ADDAX
ADDAXES
GMP RW ADDED
ADDEDLY
ADDEND AS
ADDENDA
ADDENDS
ADDENDUM S
BGL MPS W ADDER S DARED DREAD READD
GLM PW ADDERS DREADS READDS SADDER
ADDIBLE
ADDICT S DIDACT
ADDICTED
ADDICTS DIDACTS
GMP RW ADDING
ADDITION S
ADDITIVE S
ADDITORY
DPR SW ADDLE DS DEDAL LADED
DPR SW ADDLED DADDLE
DPR SW ADDLES SADDLE

DPR SW ADDLING
ADDRESS
ADDREST
ADDS DADS
ADDUCE DRS
ADDUCED
ADDUCENT
ADDUCER S
ADDUCERS CRUSADED
ADDUCES
ADDUCING
ADDUCT S
ADDUCTED
ADDUCTOR S
ADDUCTS
ADEEM S EDEMA
ADEEMED
ADEEMING
ADEEMS EDEMAS SEAMED
ADENINE S
ADENINES
ADENITIS DAINTIES
ADENOID S
ADENOIDS
ADENOMA S
ADENOMAS
ADENOSES SEASONED
ADENOSIS ADONISES
ADENYL S
ADENYLS
ADEPT S PATED TAPED
ADEPTER PREDATE RETAPED TAPERED
ADEPTEST
ADEPTLY
ADEPTS PASTED
ADEQUACY
ADEQUATE
ADHERE DRS HEADER
ADHERED REDHEAD
ADHEREND S HARDENED
ADHERENT S NEATHERD
ADHERER S REHEARD
ADHERERS
ADHERES HEADERS HEARSED SHEARED
ADHERING
ADHESION S
ADHESIVE S
ADHIBIT S
ADHIBITS
ADIEU SX
ADIEUS
ADIEUX
R ADIOS
ADIPIC
ADIPOSE S
ADIPOSES
ADIPOSIS
ADIPOUS
ADIT S DITA
ADITS DITAS STAID TSADI
ADJACENT
ADJOIN ST
ADJOINED
ADJOINS

ADJOINT S
ADJOINTS
ADJOURN S
ADJOURNS
ADJUDGE DS
ADJUDGED
ADJUDGES
ADJUNCT S
ADJUNCTS
ADJURE DRS
ADJURED
ADJURER S
ADJURERS
ADJURES
ADJURING
ADJUROR S
ADJURORS
ADJUST S
ADJUSTED
ADJUSTER S READJUST
ADJUSTOR S
ADJUSTS
ADJUTANT S
ADJUVANT S
BM ADMAN DAMAN
ADMASS
ADMASSES
BM ADMEN AMEND MANED MENAD NAMED
ADMIRAL S
ADMIRALS
ADMIRE DRS
ADMIRED
ADMIRER S MARRIED
ADMIRERS DISARMER MARRIEDS
ADMIRES MISREAD SEDARIM SIDEARM
ADMIRING
ADMIT S
ADMITS AMIDST
ADMITTED
ADMITTEE S MEDITATE
ADMITTER S
ADMIX T
ADMIXED
ADMIXES
ADMIXING
ADMIXT
ADMONISH
ADNATE
ADNATION S
ADNEXA L
ADNEXAL
ADNOUN S
ADNOUNS
DF ADO S ODA
ADOBE S ABODE
ADOBES ABODES
ADOBO S
ADOBOS
ADONIS DANIOS
ADONISES ADENOSIS
ADOPT S
ADOPTED
ADOPTEE S
ADOPTEES
ADOPTER S READOPT
ADOPTERS PASTORED READOPTS
ADOPTING
ADOPTION S

ADOPTIVE
ADOPTS
ADORABLE
ADORABLY
ADORE DRS OARED OREAD
ADORED DEODAR
ADORER S ROARED
ADORERS DROSERA
ADORES OREADS SARODE SOARED
ADORING
ADORN S ANDRO RADON
ADORNED
ADORNER S READORN
ADORNERS READORNS
ADORNING
ADORNS ANDROS RADONS
DF ADOS ODAS SODA
ADOWN
ADOZE
ADRENAL S
ADRENALS
ADRIFT
ADROIT
ADROITER
ADROITLY DILATORY IDOLATRY
BCD FGL MPR TW ADS SAD
ADSCRIPT S
ADSORB S BOARDS BROADS DOBRAS
ADSORBED ROADBEDS
ADSORBER S BOARDERS REBOARDS
ADSORBS
ADULARIA S
ADULATE DS
ADULATED
ADULATES
ADULATOR SY LAUDATOR
ADULT S
ADULTERY
ADULTLY
ADULTS
ADUMBRAL
ADUNC
ADUNCATE
ADUNCOUS
ADUST DAUTS
ADVANCE DRS
ADVANCED
ADVANCER S
ADVANCES CANVASED
ADVECT S
ADVECTED
ADVECTS
ADVENT S
ADVENTS
ADVERB S BRAVED
ADVERBS
ADVERSE EVADERS
ADVERT S
ADVERTED
ADVERTS STARVED

ADVICE S
ADVICES
ADVISE DERS
DAVIES
VISAED
ADVISED
ADVISEE S
ADVISEES
ADVISER S
ADVISERS
ADVISES
DISSAVE
ADVISING
ADVISOR SY
ADVISORS
ADVISORY
ADVOCACY
ADVOCATE DS
ADVOWSON S
M ADWOMAN
M ADWOMEN
WOMANED
ADYNAMIA S
ADYNAMIC
CYANAMID
ADYTA
ADYTUM
ADZ E
ADZE DS
DAZE
ADZED
DAZED
ADZES
DAZES
ADZING
DAZING
ADZUKI S
ADZUKIS
GHK MNS TW AE
AECIA L
AECIAL
AECIDIA L
AECIDIAL
AECIDIUM
AECIUM
AEDES
EASED
AEDILE S
AEDILES
AEDINE
AEGIS
AEGISES
AENEOUS
AENEUS
UNEASE
AEOLIAN
P AEON S
AEONIAN
AEONIC
P AEONS
AEQUORIN S
AERATE DS
AERATED
AERATES
AERATING
AERATION S
AERATOR S
AERATORS
AERIAL S
REALIA
AERIALLY
AERIALS
F AERIE DRS
AERIED
DEARIE
REDIAE
AERIER
F AERIES T
EASIER
AERIEST
SERIATE
AERIFIED
AERIFIES
AERIFORM
AERIFY
AERILY

AERO
AEROBAT S
AEROBATS
AEROBE S
AEROBES
AEROBIA
AEROBIC S
AEROBICS
AEROBIUM
AERODUCT S
EDUCATOR
OUTRACED
AERODYNE S
AEROFOIL S
AEROGEL S
AEROGELS
AEROGRAM S
AEROLITE S
AEROLITH S
AEROLOGY
AREOLOGY
AERONAUT S
AERONOMY
AEROSAT S
AEROSATS
AEROSOL S
ROSEOLA
AEROSOLS
ROSEOLAS
AEROSTAT S
AERUGO S
AERUGOS
F AERY
EYRA YARE
YEAR
AESTHETE S
AESTIVAL
SALIVATE
AETHER S
HEATHER
HEREAT
REHEAT
AETHERIC
HETAERIC
AETHERS
HEATHERS
REHEATS
AFAR S
AFARS
AFEARD
AFEARED
AFEBRILE
BALEFIRE
FIREABLE
BCD GNR WY AFF
AFFABLE
AFFABLY
AFFAIR ES
RAFFIA
AFFAIRE S
AFFAIRES
AFFAIRS
RAFFIAS
AFFECT S
AFFECTED
AFFECTER S
AFFECTS
AFFERENT S
AFFIANCE DS
AFFIANT S
AFFIANTS
AFFICHE S
AFFICHES
AFFINAL
AFFINE DS
AFFINED
AFFINELY
AFFINES
AFFINITY
AFFIRM S
AFFIRMED
AFFIRMER S
REAFFIRM
AFFIRMS
AFFIX
AFFIXAL

AFFIXED
AFFIXER S
REAFFIX
AFFIXERS
AFFIXES
AFFIXIAL
AFFIXING
AFFLATUS
AFFLICT S
AFFLICTS
AFFLUENT S
AFFLUX
AFFLUXES
AFFORD S
AFFORDED
AFFORDS
AFFOREST S
AFFRAY S
AFFRAYED
AFFRAYER S
AFFRAYS
AFFRIGHT S
AFFRONT S
AFFRONTS
AFFUSION S
AFGHAN IS
AFGHANI S
AFGHANIS
AFGHANS
AFIELD
FAILED
AFIRE
FERIA
AFLAME
AFLOAT
AFLUTTER
AFOOT
AFORE
AFOUL
AFRAID
AFREET S
FEATER
AFREETS
FEASTER
AFRESH
AFRIT S
AFRITS
DHR W AFT
FAT
DHR W AFTER S
HRW AFTERS
FASTER
STRAFE
AFTERTAX
AFTMOST
AFTOSA S
AFTOSAS
BDF GHJ LMN RST WYZ AG AEOS
GRS AGA RS
AGAIN
AGAINST
ANTISAG
AGALLOCH S
AGALWOOD S
AGAMA S
AGAMAS
AGAMETE S
AGEMATE
AGAMETES
AGEMATES
AGAMIC
AGAMID S
AGAMIDS
AGAMOUS
AGAPAE
AGAPAI
AGAPE S
AGAPEIC
AGAPES
AGAR S
RAGA
AGARIC S

AGARICS
AGAROSE S
AGAROSES
AGARS
RAGAS
RS AGAS
SAGA
AGATE S
AGATES
AGATIZE DS
AGATIZED
AGATIZES
AGATOID
AGAVE S
AGAVES
SAVAGE
AGAZE
CGM PRS W AGE DERS
GAE
CGP RW AGED
EGAD GAED
AGEDLY
AGEDNESS
R AGEE
AGEING S
GAEING
AGEINGS
SIGNAGE
AGEISM S
IMAGES
AGEISMS
AGEIST S
AGEISTS
SAGIEST
W AGELESS
AGELONG
AGEMATE S
AGAMETE
AGEMATES
AGAMETES
AGENCIES
AGENCY
AGENDA S
AGENDAS
AGENDUM S
AGENDUMS
AGENE S
AGENES
SENEGA
AGENESES
AGENESIA S
AGENESIS
ASSIGNEE
AGENETIC
AGENIZE DS
AGENIZED
AGENIZES
AGENT S
AGENTED
NEGATED
AGENTIAL
ALGINATE
AGENTING S
NEGATING
AGENTIVE S
NEGATIVE
AGENTRY
AGENTS
CEG JLP SWY AGER S
GEAR RAGE
AGERATUM S
CEG JLP WY AGERS
GEARS RAGES
SAGER SARGE
CGM PRS W AGES
GAES SAGE
H AGGADA HS
H AGGADAH S
HAGGADA
H AGGADAHS
HAGGADAS
H AGGADAS
H AGGADIC
H AGGADOT H
H AGGADOTH
HAGGADOT

BDG JLN STW AGGER S
EGGAR GAGER
BDG JLN STW AGGERS
EGGARS
GAGERS
SAGGER
SEGGAR
B AGGIE S
BJR AGGIES
AGGRADE DS
GARAGED
AGGRADED
AGGRADES
SAGGARED
AGGRESS
SAGGERS
SEGGARS
AGGRIEVE DS
AGGRO S
AGGROS
AGHA S
AGHAS T
AGHAST
V AGILE
AGILELY
V AGILITY
F AGIN G
GAIN
CGP RW AGING S
P AGINGS
AGINNER S
EARNING
ENGRAIN
GRANNIE
NEARING
AGINNERS
EARNINGS
ENGRAINS
GRANNIES
AGIO S
AGIOS
AGIOTAGE S
AGISM S
SIGMA
AGISMS
SIGMAS
AGIST S
GAITS STAIG
AGISTED
AGISTING
AGISTS
STAIGS
AGITA S
TAIGA
AGITABLE
AGITAS
TAIGAS
AGITATE DS
AGITATED
AGITATES
AGITATO R
AGITATOR S
AGITPROP S
AGLARE
ALEGAR
LAAGER
AGLEAM
AGLEE
EAGLE
E AGLET S
E AGLETS
AGLEY
AGLIMMER
AGLITTER
AGLOW
AGLY
AGLYCON ES
AGLYCONE S
AGLYCONS
M AGMA S
GAMA
M AGMAS
GAMAS
AGMINATE
ENIGMATA
AGNAIL S
AGNAILS
M AGNATE S

M AGNATES
AGNATIC
AGNATION S
AGNIZE DS
AGNIZED
AGNIZES
AGNIZING
AGNOMEN S
NONGAME
AGNOMENS
AGNOMINA
AGNOSIA S
AGNOSIAS
AGNOSTIC S
COASTING
COATINGS
COTINGAS
DS AGO GN
GOA
AGOG
W AGON ESY
AGONAL
ANALOG
AGONE S
GENOA
AGONES
GENOAS
AGONIC
AGONIES
AGONISE
AGONISE DS
AGONIES
AGONISED
DIAGNOSE
AGONISES
AGONIST S
GITANOS
AGONISTS
AGONIZE DS
AGONIZED
AGONIZES
W AGONS
AGONY
AGORA ES
AGORAE
AGORAS
AGOROT H
AGOROTH
AGOUTI S
AGOUTIES
AGOUTIS
AGOUTY
AGRAFE S
AGRAFES
AGRAFFE S
AGRAFFES
AGRAPHA
AGRAPHIA S
AGRAPHIC
AGRARIAN S
AGRAVIC
AGREE DS
EAGER EAGRE
RAGEE
AGREED
DRAGEE
GEARED
AGREEING
AGREES
EAGERS
EAGRES
GREASE
RAGEES
AGRESTAL
AGRESTIC
CIGARETS
ERGASTIC
AGRIA S
AGRIAS
AGRIMONY
AGROLOGY
AGRONOMY
AGROUND
AGRYPNIA S
BDF GHJ LMN RST WYZ AGS
GAS SAG

AGUACATE S
V AGUE S
AGUELIKE
AGUES
USAGE
AGUEWEED S
AGUISH
AGUISHLY
ABD HNP RY AH AIS
HA
H AHA
AAH
AHCHOO
AHEAD
AAHED
A AHED
HADE HAED
HEAD
AHEM
HAEM HAME
AHI S
AHIMSA S
AHIMSAS
A AHING
AHIS
AHOLD S
AHOLDS
AHORSE
ASHORE
HOARSE
AHOY
HOYA
ADH AHS
ASH HAS
SHA
AHULL
R AI DLMNRST
AIBLINS
CLM PQR S AID ES
AIDE DRS
IDEA
R AIDED
R AIDER S
AIRED DEAIR
IRADE REDIA
R AIDERS
DEAIRS
IRADES
RAISED
REDIAS
RESAID
AIDES
ASIDE IDEAS
AIDFUL
R AIDING
AIDLESS
AIDMAN
AIDMEN
DAIMEN
MAIDEN
MEDIAN
MEDINA
CMQ RS AIDS
DAIS SADI
SAID
AIGLET S
GELATI
LIGATE
AIGLETS
GELATIS
LIGATES
AIGRET S
GAITER
TRIAGE
AIGRETS
GAITERS
SEAGIRT
STAGIER
TRIAGES
AIGRETTE S
AIGUILLE S
AIKIDO S
AIKIDOS
BFH JKM NPR STV W AIL S

2006 addition

BFH **AILED**
JMN IDEAL
RST
VW
AILERON S
ALIENOR
AILERONS
ALIENORS
BFH **AILING**
JMN NILGAI
RST
VW
B **AILMENT** S
ALIMENT
B **AILMENTS**
ALIMENTS
MANLIEST
MELANIST
SMALTINE
BFH **AILS**
JKM SAIL SIAL
NPR
STV
W
M **AIM** S
AMI
M **AIMED**
AMIDE MEDIA
M **AIMER** S
RAMIE
M **AIMERS**
ARMIES
RAMIES
AIMFUL
FAMULI
AIMFULLY
M **AIMING**
AIMLESS
SAMIELS
SEISMAL
M **AIMS**
AMIS SIMA
CFG **AIN** S
KLM ANI
PRS
TVW
CGK **AINS**
MPR ANIS SAIN
STW
AINSELL S
AINSELLS
SENSILLA
AIOLI S
AIOLIS
FHL **AIR** NSTY
MPV RAI
W RIA
AIRBAG S
AIRBAGS
AIRBOAT S
AIRBOATS
AIRBORNE
AIRBOUND
H **AIRBRUSH**
AIRBURST S
AIRBUS
URBIAS
AIRBUSES
AIRCHECK S
AIRCOACH
AIRCRAFT
AIRCREW S
AIRCREWS
AIRSCREW
AIRDATE S
RADIATE
TIARAED
AIRDATES
DATARIES
RADIATES
AIRDROME S
AIRDROP S
AIRDROPS
FHL **AIRED**
PW AIDER DEAIR
IRADE REDIA
F **AIRER** S
AIRERS
RAISER
SIERRA

F **AIREST**
SATIRE
STRIAE
TERAIS
AIRFARE S
AIRFARES
AIRFIELD S
AIRFLOW S
AIRFLOWS
AIRFOIL S
AIRFOILS
AIRFRAME S
AIRGLOW S
AIRGLOWS
AIRHEAD S
AIRHEADS
AIRHOLE S
AIRHOLES
SHOALIER
H **AIRIER**
H **AIRIEST**
AIRILY
H **AIRINESS**
FLP **AIRING** S
W
FP **AIRINGS**
ARISING
RAISING
H **AIRLESS**
RESAILS
SAILERS
SERAILS
SERIALS
AIRLIFT S
AIRLIFTS
H **AIRLIKE**
H **AIRLINE** RS
AIRLINER S
H **AIRLINES**
AIRMAIL S
AIRMAILS
AIRMAN
MARINA
AIRMEN
MARINE
REMAIN
BC **AIRN** S
RAIN RANI
BC **AIRNS**
NARIS RAINS
RANIS SARIN
AIRPARK S
AIRPARKS
AIRPLANE S
AIRPLAY S
AIRPLAYS
AIRPORT S
AIRPORTS
AIRPOST S
AIRPOSTS
PROSAIST
PROTASIS
AIRPOWER S
AIRPROOF S
FHL **AIRS**
MPV RAIS RIAS
W SARI
AIRSCAPE S
AIRSPACE
AIRSCREW S
AIRCREWS
AIRSHED S
DASHIER
HARDIES
SHADIER
AIRSHEDS
RADISHES
AIRSHIP S
AIRSHIPS
AIRSHOT S
SHORTIA
THORIAS
AIRSHOTS
SHORTIAS
AIRSHOW S
AIRSHOWS
AIRSICK
AIRSPACE S
AIRSCAPE
AIRSPEED S

AIRSTRIP S
AIRT HS
AIRTED
TIRADE
AIRTH S
AIRTHED
AIRTHING
AIRTHS
AIRTIGHT
AIRTIME S
AIRTIMES
SERIATIM
AIRTING
AIRTS
ASTIR SITAR
STAIR STRIA
TARSI
AIRWARD
AIRWAVE S
AIRWAVES
F **AIRWAY** S
F **AIRWAYS**
AIRWISE
AIRWOMAN
AIRWOMEN
DFH **AIRY**
DR **AIS**
AISLE DS
AISLED
DEASIL
IDEALS
LADIES
SAILED
AISLES
LASSIE
AISLEWAY S
BGW **AIT** S
AITCH
AITCHES
ACHIEST
BGW **AITS**
SATI
NW **AIVER** S
W **AIVERS**
VARIES
AJAR
RAJA
AJEE
AJIVA S
AJIVAS
AJOWAN S
AJOWANS
AJUGA S
AJUGAS
R **AKEE** S
R **AKEES**
AKELA S
AKELAS
AKENE S
AKENES
SKEANE
AKIMBO
T **AKIN**
KAIN KINA
AKINESIA S
AKINETIC
AKVAVIT S
AKVAVITS
ABD **AL** ABELPST
GPS LA
GNT **ALA** ENRS
AAL
ALACHLOR S
ALACK
ALACRITY
ALAE
ALAMEDA S
ALAMEDAS
SALAAMED
ALAMO S
ALAMODE S
ALAMODES
ALAMOS
ALAN DEGST
ANAL NALA
ALAND S
ALANDS
SANDAL

ALANE
ALANG
LAGAN
ALANIN ES
ALANINE S
ALANINES
ALANINS
ALANS
ANLAS NALAS
NASAL
ALANT S
NATAL
ALANTS
ASLANT
ALANYL S
ANALLY
ALANYLS
NASALLY
MT **ALAR** MY
ALARM S
MALAR RAMAL
ALARMED
ALARMING
MARGINAL
ALARMISM S
ALARMIST S
ALARMS
MALARS
ALARUM S
ALARUMED
ALARUMS
S **ALARY**
BGN **ALAS**
T AALS
ALASKA S
ALASKAS
ALASTOR S
ALASTORS
MP **ALATE** DS
ALATED
MP **ALATES**
H **ALATION** S
H **ALATIONS**
ALB AS
BAL
LAB
ALBA S
BAAL
ALBACORE S
ALBAS
BAALS BALAS
BALSA BASAL
SABAL
ALBATA S
ATABAL
BALATA
ALBATAS
ATABALS
BALATAS
ALBEDO S
DOABLE
ALBEDOES
ALBEDOS
ALBEIT
ALBITE
ALBICORE S
BRACIOLE
CABRIOLE
ALBINAL
ALBINIC
ALBINISM S
MINILABS
ALBINO S
ALBINOS
ALBITE S
ALBEIT
ALBITES
ABLEIST
ASTILBE
BASTILE
BESTIAL
BLASTIE
STABILE
ALBITIC
ALBIZIA S
ALBIZIAS
ALBIZZIA S
ALBS
BALS LABS
SLAB
ALBUM S

ALBUMEN S
ALBUMENS
BLUESMAN
ALBUMIN S
ALBUMINS
ALBUMOSE S
ALBUMS
ALBURNUM S
LABURNUM
ALCADE S
ALCADES
SCALADE
ALCAHEST S
ALCAIC S
CICALA
ALCAICS
CICALAS
ALCAIDE S
ALCAIDES
ALCALDE S
ALCALDES
ALCAYDE S
ALCAYDES
ALCAZAR S
ALCAZARS
ALCHEMIC
CHEMICAL
ALCHEMY
ALCHYMY
ALCID S
ALCIDINE
ALCIDS
ALCOHOL S
ALCOHOLS
ALCOVE DS
COEVAL
ALCOVED
ALCOVES
COEVALS
ALDEHYDE S
B **ALDER** S
LADER
ALDERFLY
ALDERMAN
ALDERMEN
ALDERS
LADERS
ALDICARB S
ALDOL S
ALLOD
ALDOLASE S
ALDOLS
ALLODS
ALDOSE S
ALDOSES
LASSOED
ALDRIN S
ALDRINS
BDG **ALE** CEFS
HKM LEA
PRS
TVW
ALEATORY
ALEC S
LACE
ALECS
LACES SCALE
ALEE
ALEF S
FEAL FLEA
LEAF
ALEFS
FALSE FLEAS
LEAFS
ALEGAR S
AGLARE
LAAGER
ALEGARS
LAAGERS
ALEHOUSE S
ALEMBIC S
CEMBALI
ALEMBICS
ALENCON S
ALENCONS
ALEPH S
ALEPHS
ALERT S
ALTER ARTEL
LATER RATEL
TALER

ALERTED
ALTERED
RELATED
TREADLE
ALERTER
ALTERER
REALTER
RELATER
ALERTEST
ALERTING
ALTERING
INTEGRAL
RELATING
TANGLIER
TRIANGLE
ALERTLY
RETALLY
ALERTS
ALTERS
ARTELS
ESTRAL
LASTER
RATELS
SALTER
SLATER
STALER
STELAR
TALERS
BDG **ALES**
HKM LASE LEAS
PRS SALE SEAL
TVW
ALEURON ES
ALEURONE S
ALEURONS
NEUROSAL
ALEVIN S
ALVINE
VALINE
VEINAL
VENIAL
VINEAL
ALEVINS
VALINES
K **ALEWIFE**
K **ALEWIVES**
ALEXIA S
ALEXIAS
ALEXIN ES
XENIAL
ALEXINE S
ALEXINES
ALEXINS
ALFA S
ALFAKI S
ALFAKIS
ALFALFA S
ALFALFAS
ALFAQUI NS
ALFAQUIN S
ALFAQUIS
ALFAS
ALFORJA S
ALFORJAS
ALFREDO
ALFRESCO
ALGA ELS
GALA
ALGAE
GALEA
ALGAL
ALGAROBA S
ALGAS
GALAS
ALGEBRA S
ALGEBRAS
ALGERINE S
ALGICIDE S
ALGID
ALGIDITY
ALGIN S
ALIGN LIANG
LIGAN LINGA
ALGINATE S
AGENTIAL

ALGINS
ALIGNS
LASING
LIANGS
LIGANS
LINGAS
SIGNAL
V **ALGOID**
DIALOG
ALGOLOGY
ALGOR S
ARGOL GORAL
LARGO
ALGORISM S
ALGORS
ARGOLS
GORALS
LARGOS
ALGUM S
ALMUG
ALGUMS
ALMUGS
ALIAS
ALIASES
ALIASING S
ALIBI S
BIALI
ALIBIED
ALIBIES
BAILIES
BIALIES
ALIBIING
ALIBIS
BIALIS
ALIBLE
LABILE
LIABLE
ALIDAD ES
ALIDADE S
ALIDADES
ALIDADS
ALIEN S
ALINE ANILE
ELAIN LIANE
ALIENAGE S
ALIENATE DS
ALIENED
DELAINE
ALIENEE S
ALIENEES
ALIENER S
ALIENERS
ALIENING
ALIENISM S
MILESIAN
ALIENIST S
LITANIES
ALIENLY
ALIENOR S
AILERON
ALIENORS
AILERONS
ALIENS
ALINES
ELAINS
LIANES
SALINE
SILANE
CK **ALIF** S
FAIL FILA
ALIFORM
CK **ALIFS**
FAILS
ALIGHT S
ALIGHTED
GILTHEAD
ALIGHTS
M **ALIGN** S
ALGIN LIANG
LIGAN LINGA
M **ALIGNED**
DEALING
LEADING
M **ALIGNER** S
ENGRAIL
NARGILE
REALIGN
REGINAL

M **ALIGNERS**
ENGRAILS
NARGILES
REALIGNS
SIGNALER
SLANGIER
M **ALIGNING**
M **ALIGNS**
ALGINS
LASING
LIANGS
LIGANS
LINGAS
SIGNAL
ALIKE
ALKIE
ALIMENT S
AILMENT
ALIMENTS
AILMENTS
MANLIEST
MELANIST
SMALTINE
P **ALIMONY**
MSV **ALINE** DRS
ALIEN ANILE
ELAIN LIANE
ALINED
DENIAL
NAILED
ALINER S
LARINE
LINEAR
NAILER
RENAIL
ALINERS
NAILERS
RENAILS
MSV **ALINES**
ALIENS
ELAINS
LIANES
SALINE
SILANE
ALINING
NAILING
T **ALIPED** S
ELAPID
PLEIAD
T **ALIPEDS**
ELAPIDS
LAPIDES
PALSIED
PLEIADS
ALIQUANT
ALIQUOT S
ALIQUOTS
ALIST
LITAS TAILS
ALIT
LATI TAIL
TALI
ALIUNDE
UNIDEAL
ALIVE
ALIYA HS
ALIYAH S
ALIYAHS
ALIYAS
ALIYOS
ALIYOT
ALIZARIN ES
ALKAHEST S
ALKALI CNS
ALKALIC
ALKALIES
ALKALISE
ALKALIFY
ALKALIN E
ALKALINE
ALKALIS E
ALKALISE DS
ALKALIES
ALKALIZE DR S
ALKALOID S
ALKANE ST
ALKANES
ALKANET S
ALKANETS
ALKENE S

ALKENES
T **ALKIE** S
ALIKE
T **ALKIES**
ALSIKE
ALKINE S
ALKINES
ALKOXIDE S
ALKOXY
BT **ALKY** DL
LAKY
ALKYD S
ALKYDS
ALKYL S
ALKYLATE DS
ALKYLIC
ALKYLS
ALKYNE S
ALKYNES
BCF GHL MPS TW **ALL** SY
ALLANITE S
ALLAY S
ALLAYED
ALLAYER S
AREALLY
ALLAYERS
ALLAYING
ALLAYS
CM **ALLEE** S
CM **ALLEES**
ALLEGE DRS
ALLEGED
ALLEGER S
ALLEGERS
ALLEGES
ALLEGING
ALLEGORY
ALLEGRO S
ALLEGROS
ALLELE S
ALLELES
ALLELIC
ALLELISM S
ALLELUIA S
ALLERGEN S
ALLERGIC
ALLERGIN S
ALLERGY
GALLERY
LARGELY
REGALLY
GV **ALLEY** S
GV **ALLEYS**
ALLEYWAY S
ALLHEAL S
ALLHEALS
ALLIABLE
D **ALLIANCE** S
ANCILLAE
CANAILLE
ALLICIN S
ALLICINS
DGR ST **ALLIED**
BDG RST W **ALLIES**
GP **ALLIUM** S
GP **ALLIUMS**
ALLOBAR S
ALLOBARS
ALLOCATE DS
ALLOD S
ALDOL
ALLODIA L
ALODIAL
ALLODIAL
ALLODIUM
ALLODS
ALDOLS
ALLOGAMY
ALLONGE S
GALLEON
ALLONGES
GALLEONS

ALLONYM S
ALLONYMS
ALLOPATH SY
ALLOSAUR S
BH **ALLOT** S
ATOLL
B **ALLOTS**
ATOLLS
ALLOTTED
TOTALLED
ALLOTTEE S
ALLOTTER S
ALLOTYPE S
ALLOTYPY
ALLOVER S
OVERALL
ALLOVERS
OVERALLS
CFH MST W **ALLOW** S
FHS TW **ALLOWED**
FHS TW **ALLOWING**
FGH MST W **ALLOWS**
SALLOW
ALLOXAN S
ALLOXANS
ALLOY S
LOYAL
ALLOYED
ALLOYING
ALLOYS
BCF GHL MPT W **ALLS**
SALL
ALLSEED S
ALLSEEDS
LEADLESS
ALLSORTS
ALLSPICE S
ALLUDE DS
ALUDEL
ALLUDED
ALLUDES
ALUDELS
ALLUDING
ALLURE DRS
LAUREL
ALLURED
ALLURER S
ALLURERS
ALLURES
LAURELS
ALLURING
LINGULAR
ALLUSION S
ALLUSIVE
ALLUVIA L
ALLUVIAL S
ALLUVION S
ALLUVIUM S
BDG PRS TW **ALLY** L
DGR ST **ALLYING**
ALLYL S
ALLYLIC
ALLYLS
H **ALMA** HS
LAMA
ALMAGEST S
ALMAH S
HALMA HAMAL
ALMAHS
HALMAS
HAMALS
ALMANAC KS
ALMANACK S
ALMANACS
H **ALMAS**
LAMAS
ALME HS
LAME MALE
MEAL
ALMEH S
HEMAL

ALMEHS
ALMEMAR S
ALMEMARS
ALMES
LAMES MALES
MEALS
ALMIGHTY
ALMNER S
ALMNERS
ALMOND SY
DOLMAN
ALMONDS
DOLMANS
ALMONDY
ALMONER S
ALMONERS
ALMONRY
ALMOST
SMALTO
STOMAL
BCH MP **ALMS**
LAMS SLAM
ALMSMAN
ALMSMEN
ALMUCE S
MACULE
ALMUCES
MACULES
ALMUD ES
ALMUDE S
MAULED
ALMUDES
MEDUSAL
ALMUDS
ALMUG S
ALGUM
ALMUGS
ALGUMS
ALNICO S
OILCAN
ALNICOS
OILCANS
ALODIA L
ALODIAL
ALLODIA
ALODIUM
ALOE S
OLEA
H **ALOES**
ALOETIC
ALOFT
FLOAT FLOTA
ALOGICAL
ALOHA S
ALOHAS
ALOIN S
ALOINS
ALONE
ANOLE
K **ALONG**
ANGLO LOGAN
ALOOF
LOOFA
ALOOFLY
ALOPECIA S
ALOPECIC
ALOUD
DOULA
ALOW
AWOL
PS **ALP** S
LAP
PAL
ALPACA S
ALPACAS
ALPHA S
ALPHABET S
ALPHAS
ALPHORN S
ALPHORNS
ALPHOSIS
HAPLOSIS
ALPHYL S
ALPHYLS
ALPINE S
PENIAL
PINEAL
ALPINELY

ALPINES
PINEALS
SPANIEL
SPLENIA
ALPINISM S
ALPINIST S
ANTISLIP
PINTAILS
TAILSPIN
PS **ALPS**
LAPS PALS
SALP SLAP
ALREADY
ALRIGHT
ABD GPS **ALS** O
LAS
SAL
ALSIKE S
ALKIES
ALSIKES
ASSLIKE
ALSO
SOLA
HMS **ALT** OS
LAT
ALTAR S
ARTAL RATAL
TALAR
ALTARS
ASTRAL
RATALS
TALARS
TARSAL
FHP S **ALTER** S
ALERT ARTEL
LATER RATEL
TALER
ALTERANT S
TARLETAN
FHP **ALTERED**
ALERTED
RELATED
TREADLE
FP **ALTERER** S
ALERTER
REALTER
RELATER
FP **ALTERERS**
REALTERS
RELATERS
FHP **ALTERING**
ALERTING
INTEGRAL
RELATING
TANGLIER
TRIANGLE
ALTERITY
FHP S **ALTERS**
ALERTS
ARTELS
ESTRAL
LASTER
RATELS
SALTER
SLATER
STALER
STELAR
TALERS
ALTHAEA S
ALTHAEAS
ALTHEA S
ALTHEAS
ALTHO
LOATH LOTAH
ALTHORN S
ALTHORNS
ALTHOUGH
ALTITUDE S
LATITUDE
ALTO S
LOTA TOLA
ALTOIST S
ALTOISTS
ALTOS
LOTAS TOLAS
ALTRUISM S
MURALIST
ULTRAISM
ALTRUIST S
TITULARS
ULTRAIST

HMS **ALTS**
LAST LATS
SALT SLAT
ALUDEL S
ALLUDE
ALUDELS
ALLUDES
ALULA ER
ALULAE
ALULAR
ALUM S
LUMA MAUL
ALUMIN AES
ALUMNI
LUMINA
ALUMINA S
ALUMINAS
ALUMINE S
ALUMINES
ALUMINIC
ALUMINS
ALUMINUM S
ALUMNA E
MANUAL
ALUMNAE
ALUMNI
ALUMIN
LUMINA
ALUMNUS
ALUMROOT S
ALUMS
LUMAS MAULS
ALUNITE S
ALUNITES
INSULATE
ALVEOLAR S
ALVEOLI
ALVEOLUS
ALVINE
ALEVIN
VALINE
VEINAL
VENIAL
VINEAL
ALWAY S
ALWAYS
ALYSSUM S
ASYLUMS
ALYSSUMS
BCD GHJ LNP RTY **AM** AIPU
MA
GLM **AMA** HS
AMADAVAT S
AMADOU S
AMADOUS
AMAH S
AMAHS
AMAIN
AMNIA ANIMA
MANIA
AMALGAM S
AMALGAMS
AMANDINE
AMANITA S
AMANITAS
AMANITIN S
MAINTAIN
AMARANTH S
AMARELLE S
AMARETTI
AMARETTO S
TERATOMA
AMARNA
AMARONE S
AMARONES
CGL M **AMAS** S
MASA
C **AMASS**
MASAS MASSA
AMASSED
AMASSER S
AMASSERS
C **AMASSES**
AMASSING
SIAMANGS
AMATEUR S
AMATEURS

AMATIVE
AMATOL S
AMATOLS
AMATORY
AMAZE DS
AMAZED
AMAZEDLY
AMAZES
AMAZING
AMAZON S
AMAZONS
AMBAGE S
AMBAGES
AMBARI S
AMBARIES
AMBARIS
AMBARY
AMBEER S
AMBEERS
BESMEAR
CL **AMBER** SY
BREAM EMBAR
AMBERIES
AMBERINA S
AMBEROID S
CL **AMBERS**
BREAMS
EMBARS
AMBERY
AMBIANCE S
AMBIENCE S
AMBIENT S
AMBIENTS
G **AMBIT** S
AMBITION S
G **AMBITS**
AMBIVERT S
VERBATIM
GRW **AMBLE** DRS
BLAME
GRW **AMBLED**
BEDLAM
BELDAM
BLAMED
LAMBED
GR **AMBLER** S
BLAMER
LAMBER
MARBLE
RAMBLE
GR **AMBLERS**
BLAMERS
LAMBERS
MARBLES
RAMBLES
GRW **AMBLES**
BLAMES
GRW **AMBLING**
BLAMING
LAMBING
MS **AMBO** S
AMBOINA S
AMBOINAS
H **AMBONES**
BEMOANS
MS **AMBOS**
SAMBO
AMBOYNA S
AMBOYNAS
AMBRIES
AMBROID S
AMBROIDS
AMBROSIA LN S
AMBRY
BARMY
AMBSACE S
AMBSACES
AMBULANT
AMBULATE DS
AMBUSH
AMBUSHED
AMBUSHER S
AMBUSHES
AMEBA ENS
ABEAM
AMEBAE
AMEBAN
AMEBAS

AMEBEAN
AMEBIC
AMEBOID
AMEER S
RAMEE
AMEERATE S
AMEERS
RAMEES
SEAMER
AMELCORN S
CORNMEAL
RY **AMEN** DST
MANE MEAN
NAME NEMA
AMENABLE
NAMEABLE
AMENABLY
AMEND S
ADMEN MANED
MENAD NAMED
AMENDED
DEADMEN
AMENDER S
MEANDER
REEDMAN
RENAMED
AMENDERS
MEANDERS
AMENDING
AMENDS
DESMAN
MENADS
AMENITY
ANYTIME
Y **AMENS**
MANES MANSE
MEANS MENSA
NAMES NEMAS
L **AMENT** S
MEANT MENTA
AMENTIA S
ANIMATE
AMENTIAS
ANIMATES
L **AMENTS**
MANTES
STAMEN
AMERCE DRS
RACEME
AMERCED
CREAMED
RACEMED
AMERCER S
CREAMER
AMERCERS
CREAMERS
SCREAMER
AMERCES
RACEMES
AMERCING
CREAMING
GERMANIC
AMESACE S
AMESACES
AMETHYST S
KR **AMI** ADENRS
AIM
LZ **AMIA** S
AMIABLE
AMIABLY
AMIANTUS
LZ **AMIAS**
AMICABLE
AMICABLY
AMICE S
AMICES
CAMISE
AMICI
AMICUS
UMIACS
AMID EOS
MAID
AMIDASE S
AMIDASES
AMIDE S
AIMED MEDIA
AMIDES
MEDIAS
AMIDIC
AMIDIN ES
DIAMIN
AMIDINE S
DIAMINE

AMIDINES
DIAMINES
AMIDINS
DIAMINS
AMIDO L
AMIDOGEN S
AMIDOL S
AMIDOLS
~~**AMIDONE**~~ S
DOMAINE
AMIDONES
DAIMONES
DOMAINES
AMIDS T
MAIDS
AMIDSHIP S
AMIDST
ADMITS
MR **AMIE** S
MR **AMIES**
AMIGA S
AMIGAS
AMIGO S
IMAGO
AMIGOS
IMAGOS
G **AMIN** EOS
MAIN MINA
FG **AMINE** S
ANIME MINAE
FG **AMINES**
ANIMES
INSEAM
MESIAN
SEMINA
AMINIC
AMINITY
AMINO
AMNIO
G **AMINS**
MAINS MINAS
AMIR S
MAIR RAMI
AMIRATE S
AMIRATES
AMIRS
MAIRS SIMAR
T **AMIS** S
AIMS SIMA
AMISS
SIMAS
AMITIES
AMITOSES
AMOSITES
ATOMISES
AMITOSIS
AMITOTIC
AMITROLE S
ROLAMITE
AMITY
AMMETER S
METAMER
AMMETERS
METAMERS
AMMINE S
IMMANE
AMMINES
MISNAME
AMMINO
AMMO S
AMMOCETE S
AMMONAL S
AMMONALS
AMMONIA CS
AMMONIAC S
AMMONIAS
AMMONIC
AMMONIFY
AMMONITE S
AMMONIUM S
AMMONO
AMMONOID S
AMMOS
AMNESIA CS
ANEMIAS
AMNESIAC S
AMNESIAS
AMNESIC S
CINEMAS
AMNESICS
AMNESTIC
SEMANTIC

AMNESTY
AMNIA
AMAIN ANIMA
MANIA
AMNIC
MANIC
AMNIO NS
AMINO
AMNION S
NOMINA
AMNIONIC
AMNIONS
MANSION
ONANISM
AMNIOS
AMNIOTE S
AMNIOTES
MASONITE
MISATONE
AMNIOTIC
AMOEBA ENS
AMOEBAE
AMOEBAN
AMOEBAS
AMOEBEAN
AMOEBIC
AMOEBOID
AMOK S
MAKO
AMOKS
MAKOS
AMOLE S
AMOLES
AMONG
MANGO
AMONGST
AMORAL
AMORALLY
AMORETTI
AMORETTO S
AMORINI
AMORINO
AMORIST S
AMORISTS
AMOROSO
AMOROUS
AMORT
AMORTISE DS
ATOMISER
AMORTIZE DS
ATOMIZER
AMOSITE S
ATOMIES
ATOMISE
AMOSITES
AMITOSES
ATOMISES
AMOTION S
AMOTIONS
AMOUNT S
OUTMAN
AMOUNTED
AMOUNTS
OUTMANS
AMOUR S
AMOURS
RAMOUS
CDG **AMP** S
LRS MAP
TV PAM
CDL **AMPED**
RTV
AMPERAGE S
AMPERE S
AMPERES
AMPHIBIA N
AMPHIOXI
AMPHIPOD S
AMPHORA ELS
AMPHORAE
AMPHORAL
AMPHORAS
CDL **AMPING**
RTV
S **AMPLE** R
MAPLE
S **AMPLER**
PALMER
AMPLEST
AMPLEXUS

AMPLIFY
D **AMPLY**
PALMY
AMPOULE S
AMPOULES
CDG **AMPS**
LRS MAPS PAMS
TV SAMP SPAM
~~**AMPUL**~~ ES
AMPULE S
AMPULES
AMPULLA ER
AMPULLAE
AMPULLAR Y
AMPULS
AMPUTATE DS
AMPUTEE S
AMPUTEES
AMREETA S
AMREETAS
AMRITA S
TAMARI
AMRITAS
TAMARIS
AMTRAC KS
TARMAC
AMTRACK S
AMTRACKS
AMTRACS
TARMACS
AMU S
AMUCK S
AMUCKS
AMULET S
MULETA
AMULETS
MULETAS
RW **AMUS** E
AMUSABLE
AMUSE DRS
AMUSED
MEDUSA
AMUSEDLY
AMUSER S
AMUSERS
ASSUMER
MASSEUR
W **AMUSES**
ASSUME
AMUSIA S
AMUSIAS
AMUSING
AMUSIVE
AMYGDALA E
AMYGDALE S
AMYGDULE S
AMYL S
AMYLASE S
AMYLASES
AMYLENE S
AMYLENES
AMYLIC
AMYLOGEN S
AMYLOID S
AMYLOIDS
AMYLOSE S
AMYLOSES
AMYLS
AMYLUM S
AMYLUMS
BCD **AN** ADEITY
FGM NA
NPR
TVW
KMN **ANA** LS
ANABAENA S
ANABAS
ANABASES
ANABASIS
ANABATIC
ANABLEPS
ANABOLIC
ANACONDA S
ANADEM S
MAENAD
ANADEMS
MAENADS
ANAEMIA S

ANAEMIAS
ANAEMIC
ANAEROBE S
ANAGLYPH S
ANAGOGE S
ANAGOGES
ANAGOGIC
ANAGOGY
ANAGRAM S
ANAGRAMS
BC **ANAL**
ALAN NALA
ANALCIME S
CALAMINE
ANALCITE S
LAITANCE
ANALECTA
ANALECTS
ANALEMMA S
ANALGIA S
ANALGIAS
B **ANALITY**
B **ANALLY**
ALANYL
ANALOG SY
AGONAL
ANALOGIC
ANALOGS
ANALOGUE S
ANALOGY
ANALYSE DRS
ANALYSED
ANALYSER S
ANALYSES
ANALYSIS
ANALYST S
ANALYSTS
ANALYTE S
ANALYTES
ANALYTIC S
ANALYZE DRS
ANALYZED
ANALYZER S
ANALYZES
ANANKE S
ANANKES
ANAPAEST S
ANAPEST S
PEASANT
ANAPESTS
PEASANTS
ANAPHASE S
ANAPHOR AS
ANAPHORA LS
ANAPHORS
ANARCH SY
ANARCHIC
CHARACIN
ANARCHS
ANARCHY
KMN **ANAS**
ANSA
ANASARCA S
ANATASE S
ANATASES
ANATHEMA S
ANATOMIC
ANATOMY
ANATOXIN S
ANATTO S
ANATTOS
ANCESTOR S
ENACTORS
ANCESTRY
R **ANCHO** RS
NACHO
ANCHOR S
ARCHON
RANCHO
ANCHORED
ANCHORET S
ANCHORS
ARCHONS
RANCHOS
R **ANCHOS**
NACHOS
ANCHOVY
ANCHUSA S

ANCHUSAS
ANCHUSIN S
UNCHAINS
ANCIENT S
ANCIENTS
CANNIEST
INSECTAN
INSTANCE
ANCILLA ES
ANCILLAE
ALLIANCE
CANAILLE
ANCILLAS
ANCON E
CANON
ANCONAL
ANCONE S
ANCONEAL
ANCONES
SONANCE
ANCONOID
ANCRESS
CASERNS
BHL **AND** S
RSW DAN
ANDANTE S
ANDANTES
ANDESITE S
ANDESYTE S
ANDIRON S
ANDIRONS
ANDRO S
ADORN RADON
ANDROGEN S
ANDROID S
ANDROIDS
ANDROS
ADORNS
RADONS
BHL **ANDS**
RSW DANS SAND
BCF **ANE** SW
GJK NAE
LMP
SVW
ANEAR S
ARENA
ANEARED
ANEARING
ANEARS
ARENAS
ANECDOTA L
ANECDOTE S
ANECHOIC
ANELE DS
P **ANELED**
LEADEN
LEANED
ANELES
P **ANELING**
EANLING
LEANING
ANEMIA S
ANEMIAS
AMNESIA
ANEMIC
CINEMA
ICEMAN
ANEMONE S
ANEMONES
ANEMOSES
ANEMOSIS
ANENST
ANENT
ANERGIA S
ANERGIAS
ANGARIES
ARGINASE
ANERGIC
ANERGIES
GESNERIA
ANERGY
ANEROID S
ANEROIDS
BCF **ANES**
JKL SANE
MPS
VW

ANESTRI
ANTSIER
NASTIER
RATINES
RETAINS
RETINAS
RETSINA
STAINER
STEARIN
ANESTRUS
SAUNTERS
ANETHOL ES
ETHANOL
ANETHOLE S
ANETHOLS
ETHANOLS
ANEURIN S
ANEURINS
ANEURISM S
ANEURYSM S
ANEW
WANE WEAN
FMP **ANGA** S
ST
ANGAKOK S
ANGAKOKS
ANGARIA S
ANGARIAS
ANGARIES
ANERGIAS
ARGINASE
ANGARY
FMP **ANGAS**
S SANGA
M **ANGEL** S
ANGLE GLEAN
ANGELED
GLEANED
ANGELIC A
ANGLICE
GALENIC
ANGELICA LS
ANGELING
GLEANING
M **ANGELS**
ANGLES
GLEANS
ANGELUS
LAGUNES
LANGUES
BDG **ANGER** S
HMR RANGE REGNA
S
D **ANGERED**
DERANGE
ENRAGED
GRANDEE
GRENADE
D **ANGERING**
ENRAGING
ANGERLY
BDG **ANGERS**
HMR RANGES
S SANGER
ANGINA LS
ANGINAL
ANGINAS
ANGINOSE
ANGINOUS
ANGIOMA S
ANGIOMAS
BDJ **ANGLE** DRS
MTW ANGEL GLEAN
DJM **ANGLED**
TW DANGLE
LAGEND
ANGLEPOD S
DJM **ANGLER** S
TW REGNAL
DJM **ANGLERS**
TW
BDJ **ANGLES**
MTW ANGELS
GLEANS
ANGLICE
ANGELIC
GALENIC
DGJ **ANGLING** S
MTW
ANGLINGS
SLANGING

ANGLO S
ALONG LOGAN
ANGLOS
LOGANS
SLOGAN
ANGORA S
ORGANA
ANGORAS
ANGRIER
EARRING
GRAINER
RANGIER
REARING
ANGRIEST
ASTRINGE
GANISTER
GANTRIES
GRANITES
INGRATES
RANGIEST
ANGRILY
ANGRY
RANGY
ANGST S
GNATS STANG
TANGS
ANGSTROM S
ANGSTS
STANGS
S ANGUINE
GUANINE
L ANGUISH
ANGULAR
ANGULATE DS
ANGULOSE
ANGULOUS
ANHINGA S
ANHINGAS
BR ANI LS
AIN
ANIL ES
LAIN NAIL
ANILE
ALIEN ALINE
ELAIN LIANE
ANILIN ES
ANILINE S
ANILINES
ANILINS
ANILITY
ANILS
NAILS SLAIN
SNAIL
ANIMA LS
AMAIN AMNIA
MANIA
ANIMACY
ANIMAL S
LAMINA
MANILA
ANIMALIC
ANIMALLY
ANIMALS
LAMINAS
MANILAS
ANIMAS
MANIAS
ANIMATE DRS
AMENTIA
ANIMATED
DIAMANTE
ANIMATER S
MARINATE
ANIMATES
AMENTIAS
ANIMATO R
ANIMATOR S
ANIME S
AMINE MINAE
ANIMES
AMINES
INSEAM
MESIAN
SEMINA
ANIMI S
ANIMIS MT
SAIMIN
SIMIAN
ANIMISM S
ANIMISMS

ANIMIST S
INTIMAS
SANTIMI
ANIMISTS
ANIMUS
ANIMUSES
FW ANION S
ANIONIC
FW ANIONS
NASION
R ANIS E
AINS SAIN
ANISE S
ANISEED S
ANISEEDS
ANISES
SANIES
SANSEI
ANISETTE S
TETANIES
TETANISE
ANISIC
CASINI
ANISOLE S
ANISOLES
ANKERITE S
ANKH S
HANK KHAN
ANKHS
HANKS KHANS
SHANK
R ANKLE DST
R ANKLED
R ANKLES
ANKLET S
ANKLETS
LANKEST
R ANKLING
ANKUS H
ANKUSES
ANKUSH
ANKUSHES
ANKYLOSE DS
ANLACE S
ANLACES
ANLAGE NS
GALENA
ANLAGEN
ANLAGES
GALENAS
LASAGNE
ANLAS
ALANS NALAS
NASAL
ANLASES
CM ANNA LS
NAAN NANA
ANNAL S
ANNALIST S
ANNALS
CM ANNAS
NAANS NANAS
T ANNATES
ANNATTO S
ANNATTOS
ANNEAL S
ANNEALED
ANNEALER S
ANNEALS
ANNELID S
LINDANE
ANNELIDS
LINDANES
ANNEX E
ANNEXE DS
ANNEXED
ANNEXES
ANNEXING
ANNONA S
ANNONAS
ANNOTATE DS
ANNOUNCE DR S
T ANNOY S
ANYON
ANNOYED
ANODYNE
ANNOYER S
ANNOYERS

ANNOYING
T ANNOYS
ANYONS
ANNUAL S
ANNUALLY
ANNUALS
ANNUITY
ANNUL IS
C ANNULAR
C ANNULATE D
ANNULET S
ANNULETS
ANNULI
UNNAIL
ANNULLED
ANNULOSE
ANNULS
ANNULUS
ANOA S
ANOAS
ANODAL
ANODALLY
ANODE S
ANODES
ANODIC
ANODIZE DS
ANODIZED
ANODIZES
ANODYNE S
ANNOYED
ANODYNES
ANODYNIC
ANOINT S
NATION
ANOINTED
ANTINODE
ANOINTER S
REANOINT
ANOINTS
NATIONS
ONANIST
ANOLE S
ALONE
ANOLES
LANOSE
ANOLYTE S
ANOLYTES
ANOMALY
ANOMIC
CAMION
MANIOC
ANOMIE S
ANOMIES
ANOMY
CF ANON
NONA
ANONYM S
ANONYMS
ANOOPSIA S
ANOPIA S
ANOPIAS
ANOPSIA
PAISANO
ANOPSIA S
ANOPIAS
PAISANO
ANOPSIAS
PAISANOS
ANORAK S
ANORAKS
ANORETIC S
ACTIONER
CREATION
REACTION
ANOREXIA S
ANOREXIC S
ANOREXY
ANORTHIC
ANOSMIA S
ANOSMIAS
ANOSMIC
CAMIONS
MANIOCS
MASONIC
ANOTHER
ANOVULAR
ANOXEMIA S
ANOXEMIC
ANOXIA S

ANOXIAS
ANOXIC
AXONIC
H ANSA E
ANAS
ANSAE
ANSATE D
ANSATED
ANSERINE S
ANSEROUS
ARSENOUS
ANSWER S
RESAWN
ANSWERED
ANSWERER S
ANSWERS
RAWNESS
CHP RW ANT AEIS
TAN
M ANTA ES
ANTACID S
ANTACIDS
ANTAE
ANTALGIC S
M ANTAS
ANTBEAR S
ANTBEARS
RATSBANE
ANTE DS
ETNA NEAT
ANTEATER S
ANTECEDE DS
CHP RW ANTED
ANTEDATE DS
ANTEED
ANTEFIX A
ANTEFIXA EL
ANTEING
ANTIGEN
GENTIAN
G ANTELOPE S
ANTENNA ELS
ANTENNAE
ANTENNAL
ANTENNAS
ANTEPAST S
ANTERIOR
ANTEROOM S
M ANTES
ETNAS NATES
NEATS STANE
ANTETYPE S
ANTEVERT S
ANTHELIA
ANTHELIX
ANTHEM S
HETMAN
ANTHEMED
ANTHEMIA
HAEMATIN
ANTHEMIC
ANTHEMS
HETMANS
P ANTHER S
THENAR
ANTHERAL
ANTHERID S
P ANTHERS
THENARS
ANTHESES
ANTHESIS
SHANTIES
SHEITANS
STHENIAS
ANTHILL S
ANTHILLS
ANTHODIA
ANTHOID
ANTHRAX
ANTI CS
TAIN
ANTIACNE
ANTIAIR
ANTIAR S
ANTIARIN S
ANTIARS
ARTISAN
TSARINA

ANTIATOM S
ANTIBIAS
ANTIBODY
ANTIBOSS
BASTIONS
ANTIBUG
TABUING
CM ANTIC KS
ACTIN
ANTICAR
ANTICITY
ANTICK S
CATKIN
ANTICKED
ANTICKS
CATKINS
ANTICLY
ANTICOLD
DALTONIC
ANTICS
ACTINS
NASTIC
ANTICULT S
ANTIDORA
ANTIDOTE DS
TETANOID
ANTIDRUG
ANTIFAT
ANTIFLU
ANTIFOAM
ANTIFOG
ANTIFUR
ANTIGANG
ANTIGAY
ANTIGEN ES
ANTEING
GENTIAN
ANTIGENE S
ANTIGENS
GENTIANS
ANTIGUN
ANTIHERO
ANTIJAM
ANTIKING S
ANTILEAK
ANTILEFT
ANTILIFE R
ANTILOCK
ANTILOG SY
ANTILOGS
SOLATING
ANTILOGY
ANTIMALE
LAMINATE
ANTIMAN
ANTIMASK S
ANTIMERE S
ANTIMINE
ANTIMONY L
ANTINOMY
CHP RW ANTING S
ANTINGS
STANING
ANTINODE S
ANOINTED
ANTINOME S
NOMINATE
ANTINOMY
ANTIMONY
ANTINUKE RS
ANTIPHON SY
ANTIPILL
ANTIPODE S
ANTIPOLE S
ANTIPOPE S
ANTIPORN
ANTIPOT
ANTIPYIC S
ANTIQUE DRS
QUINATE
ANTIQUED
ANTIQUER S
QUAINTER
ANTIQUES
ANTIRAPE
ANTIRED
DETRAIN
TRAINED
ANTIRIOT

ANTIROCK
ANTIROLL
ANTIRUST S
NATURIST
M ANTIS
SAINT SATIN
STAIN TAINS
ANTISAG
AGAINST
ANTISERA
RATANIES
SANTERIA
SEATRAIN
ANTISEX
SEXTAIN
ANTISHIP
ANTISKID
ANTISLIP
ALPINIST
PINTAILS
TAILSPIN
ANTISMOG
ANTISMUT
ANTISNOB S
ANTISPAM
ANTISTAT ES
ATTAINTS
ANTITANK
ANTITAX
ANTITYPE S
ANTIWAR
ANTIWEAR
ANTIWEED
ANTLER S
LEARNT
RENTAL
ANTLERED
ANTLERS
RENTALS
SALTERN
STERNAL
ANTLIKE
ANTLION S
ANTLIONS
ANTONYM SY
ANTONYMS
ANTONYMY
MTY ANTRA L
RATAN
ANTRAL
TARNAL
ANTRE S
ANTRES
ASTERN
STERNA
ANTRORSE
T ANTRUM S
T ANTRUMS
UNSMART
CHP RW ANTS Y
TANS
ANTSIER
ANESTRI
NASTIER
RATINES
RETAINS
RETINAS
RETSINA
STAINER
STEARIN
ANTSIEST
INSTATES
NASTIEST
SATINETS
TITANESS
ANTSY
NASTY TANSY
ANURAL
RANULA
ANURAN S
ANURANS
ANURESES
ANURESIS
SENARIUS
ANURETIC
ANURIA S
URANIA
ANURIAS
SAURIAN
URANIAS

ANURIC
URANIC
ANUROUS
URANOUS
M ANUS
ANUSES
USNEAS
ANVIL S
NIVAL VINAL
ANVILED
ANVILING
ANVILLED
ANVILS
SILVAN
VINALS
ANVILTOP S
ANXIETY
ANXIOUS
MWZ ANY
NAY
ANYBODY
ANYHOW
ANYMORE
C ANYON ES
ANNOY
ANYONE
C ANYONS
ANNOYS
ANYPLACE
ANYTHING S
ANYTIME
AMENITY
ANYWAY S
ANYWAYS
ANYWHERE S
ANYWISE
AORIST S
ARISTO
RATIOS
SATORI
AORISTIC
AORISTS
ARISTOS
SATORIS
AORTA ELS
AORTAE
AORTAL
AORTAS
AORTIC
AOUDAD S
AOUDADS
APACE
APACHE S
APACHES
APAGOGE S
APAGOGES
APAGOGIC
APANAGE S
APANAGES
APAREJO S
APAREJOS
APART
APATETIC
CAPITATE
APATHIES
APATHY
APATITE S
APATITES
CGJ NRT APE DRSX
PEA
APEAK
CGJ RT APED
APEEK
T APELIKE
PEALIKE
CGJ PRT APER SY
PARE PEAR
RAPE REAP
APERCU S
APERCUS
SCAUPER
APERIENT S
JN APERIES
APERITIF S

2006 addition

CGJ APERS
PRT APRES ASPER
PARES PARSE
PEARS PRASE
PRESA RAPES
REAPS SPARE
SPEAR
APERTURE DS
JNP APERY
PAYER REPAY
CGJ APES
NRT APSE PASE
PEAS SPAE
APETALY
APEX
APEXES
APHAGIA S
APHAGIAS
APHANITE S
APHASIA CS
APHASIAC S
APHASIAS
APHASIC S
APHASICS
APHELIA N
APHELIAN
APHELION S
PHELONIA
APHESES
SPAHEES
APHESIS
APHETIC
HEPATIC
APHID S
R APHIDES
DIPHASE
APHIDIAN S
APHIDS
R APHIS
APISH SPAHI
APHOLATE S
APHONIA S
APHONIAS
APHONIC S
APHONICS
APHORISE DS
APHORISM S
MORPHIAS
APHORIST S
APHORIZE DR S
APHOTIC
N APHTHA E
APHTHAE
N APHTHOUS
APHYLLY
APIAN
APIARIAN S
APIARIES
APIARIST S
APIARY
PIRAYA
APICAL S
APICALLY
APICALS
SPACIAL
APICES
SPICAE
APICULI
APICULUS
APIECE
APIMANIA S
GJR APING
T
APIOLOGY
APISH
APHIS SPAHI
APISHLY
APLASIA S
APLASIAS
APLASTIC
CAPITALS
APLENTY
PENALTY
H APLITE S
H APLITES
PALIEST
PLATIES
TALIPES

APLITIC
APLOMB S
APLOMBS
APNEA LS
PAEAN
APNEAL
APNEAS
PAEANS
PAESAN
APNEIC
APNOEA LS
APNOEAL
APNOEAS
PAESANO
APNOEIC
C APO DS
APOAPSES
APOAPSIS
APOCARP SY
APOCARPS
APOCARPY
APOCOPE S
APOCOPES
APOCOPIC
APOCRINE
CAPONIER
PROCAINE
APOD S
DOPA
APODAL
APODOSES
APODOSIS
APODOUS
APODS
DOPAS SPADO
APOGAMIC
APOGAMY
APOGEAL
APOGEAN
APOGEE S
APOGEES
APOGEIC
APOLLO S
APOLLOS
APOLOG SY
APOLOGAL
APOLOGIA ES
APOLOGS
APOLOGUE S
APOLOGY
APOLUNE S
APOLUNES
APOMICT S
POTAMIC
APOMICTS
APOMIXES
APOMIXIS
APOPHONY
APOPHYGE S
APOPLEXY
APORIA S
APORIAS
APORT
C APOS
SOAP
APOSPORY
APOSTACY
APOSTASY
APOSTATE S
APOSTIL S
TOPSAIL
APOSTILS
TOPSAILS
APOSTLE S
PELOTAS
APOSTLES
APOTHECE S
APOTHEGM S
APOTHEM S
APOTHEMS
APP S
PAP
APPAL LS
PAPAL
APPALL S
PALPAL
APPALLED
APPALLS

APPALS
APPANAGE S
APPARAT S
APPARATS
APPAREL S
APPARELS
APPARENT
TRAPPEAN
APPEAL S
APPEALED
APPEALER S
APPEALS
APPEAR S
APPEARED
APPEARS
APPEASE DRS
APPEASED
APPEASER S
APPEASES
R APPEL S
APPLE PEPLA
APPELLEE S
APPELLOR S
R APPELS
APPLES
APPEND S
NAPPED
APPENDED
APPENDIX
APPENDS
SNAPPED
APPESTAT S
APPETENT
APPETITE S
APPLAUD S
APPLAUDS
APPLAUSE S
D APPLE ST
APPEL PEPLA
D APPLES
APPELS
APPLET S
LAPPET
APPLETS
LAPPETS
APPLIED
APPLIER S
APPLIERS
APPLIES
APPLIQUE DS
APPLY
APPLYING
APPOINT S
APPOINTS
P APPOSE DRS
APPOSED
APPOSER S
APPOSERS
APPOSES
APPOSING
APPOSITE
APPRAISE DE RS
APPRISE DRS
SAPPIER
APPRISED
APPRISER S
APPRISES
APPRIZE DRS
ZAPPIER
APPRIZED
APPRIZER S
APPRIZES
APPROACH
APPROVAL S
APPROVE DRS
APPROVED
APPROVER S
APPROVES
APPS
PAPS
APPULSE S
PAPULES
UPLEAPS
APPULSES
APRACTIC
APRAXIA S
APRAXIAS

APRAXIC
APRES
APERS ASPER
PARES PARSE
PEARS PRASE
PRESA RAPES
REAPS SPARE
SPEAR
APRICOT S
APROTIC
PAROTIC
APRICOTS
PISCATOR
APRON S
APRONED
OPERAND
PADRONE
PANDORE
APRONING
APRONS
PARSON
APROPOS
APROTIC
APRICOT
PAROTIC
L APSE S
APES PASE
PEAS SPAE
L APSES
PASES PASSE
SPAES
C APSIDAL
APSIDES
APSIS
ASPIS
R APT
PAT TAP
APTER
PATER PEART
PRATE TAPER
APTERAL
APTERIA
APTERIUM
APTEROUS
APTERYX
APTEST
APTITUDE S
R APTLY
PATLY PLATY
TYPAL
R APTNESS
PATNESS
APYRASE S
APYRASES
APYRETIC
AQUA ES
AQUACADE S
AQUAE
AQUAFARM S
AQUALUNG S
AQUANAUT S
AQUARIA LN
AQUARIAL
AQUARIAN S
AQUARIST S
AQUARIUM S
AQUAS
AQUATIC S
AQUATICS
AQUATINT S
AQUATONE S
AQUAVIT S
AQUAVITS
AQUEDUCT S
AQUEOUS
AQUIFER S
AQUIFERS
AQUILINE
QUINIELA
AQUIVER
BCE AR BCEFKMST
FGJ
LMO
PTV
WY
ARABESK S
ARABESKS
ARABIC A
ARABICA S

ARABICAS
ARABIZE DS
ARABIZED
ARABIZES
P ARABLE S
P ARABLES
ARACEOUS
ARACHNID S
ARAK S
ARAKS
ARAME S
ARAMES
ARAMID S
ARAMIDS
ARANEID S
ARANEIDS
ARAPAIMA S
ARAROBA S
ARAROBAS
BCD ARB S
G BAR
BRA
ARBALEST S
RATABLES
ARBALIST S
ARBELEST S
BLEATERS
RESTABLE
RETABLES
ARBITER S
RAREBIT
ARBITERS
RAREBITS
ARBITRAL
H ARBOR S
ARBOREAL
H ARBORED
BOARDER
BROADER
REBOARD
ARBORES
ARBORETA
ARBORIST S
ARBORIZE DS
H ARBOROUS
H ARBORS
H ARBOUR S
H ARBOURED
H ARBOURS
BCD ARBS
G BARS BRAS
ARBUSCLE S
ARBUTE S
ARBUTEAN
ARBUTES
BURSATE
ARBUTUS
MN ARC HOS
CAR
ARCADE DS
ARCADED
ARCADES
ASCARED
ARCADIA NS
ARCADIAN S
ACARIDAN
ARCADIAS
ARCADING S
CARANGID
CARDIGAN
ARCANA
ARCANE
ARCANUM S
ARCANUMS
ARCATURE S
F ARCED
ACRED CADRE
CARED CEDAR
RACED
LMP ARCH
CHAR
ARCHAEA LN
ARCHAEAL
ARCHAEAN S
ARCHAEON
ARCHAIC
ARCHAISE DS

ARCHAISM S
CHARISMA
ARCHAIST S
CITHARAS
ARCHAIZE DR
S
ARCHDUKE S
ARCHEAN
MP ARCHED
CHARED
ECHARD
M ARCHER SY
M ARCHERS
CRASHER
ARCHERY
LMP ARCHES
CHARES
CHASER
ESCHAR
SEARCH
ARCHFOE S
ARCHFOES
ARCHIL S
CHIRAL
ARCHILS
CARLISH
ARCHINE S
ARCHINES
INARCHES
MP ARCHING S
CHAGRIN
CHARING
ARCHINGS
CHAGRINS
CRASHING
ARCHIVAL
ARCHIVE DS
ARCHIVED
ARCHIVES
ARCHLY
ARCHNESS
ARCHON S
ANCHOR
RANCHO
ARCHONS
ANCHORS
RANCHOS
ARCHWAY S
ARCHWAYS
ARCIFORM
F ARCING
CARING
RACING
ARCKED
CARKED
DACKER
RACKED
ARCKING
CARKING
RACKING
N ARCO
ORCA
MN ARCS
CARS SCAR
ARCSINE S
ARSENIC
CARNIES
ARCSINES
ARSENICS
RACINESS
ARCTIC S
ARCTICS
ARCUATE D
ARCUATED
ARCUS
SCAUR
ARCUSES
CAUSERS
CESURAS
SAUCERS
SUCRASE
ARDEB S
BARDE BARED
BEARD BREAD
DEBAR
ARDEBS
BARDES
BEARDS
BREADS
DEBARS
SABRED
SERDAB

ARDENCY
ARDENT
RANTED
ARDENTLY
ARDOR S
ARDORS
ARDOUR S
ARDOURS
ARDUOUS
BCD ARE AS
FHM EAR
PRT ERA
WY
AREA ELS
AREAE
AREAL
AREALLY
ALLAYER
AREAS
AREAWAY S
AREAWAYS
ARECA S
ARECAS
CAESAR
AREIC
CERIA ERICA
ARENA S
ANEAR
ARENAS
ANEARS
ARENE S
RANEE
ARENES
RANEES
ARENITE S
RETINAE
TRAINEE
ARENITES
ARSENITE
RESINATE
STEARINE
TRAINEES
ARENOSE
ARENOUS
AREOLA ERS
AREOLAE
AREOLAR
AREOLAS
AREOLATE D
AREOLE S
AREOLES
AREOLOGY
AEROLOGY
AREPA S
PARAE
AREPAS
SARAPE
BCD ARES
FHL EARS ERAS
MNP RASE SEAR
RTW SERA
ARETE S
EATER
ARETES
EASTER
EATERS
RESEAT
SEATER
TEASER
ARETHUSA S
BZ ARF S
FAR
BZ ARFS
ARGAL AIS
GRAAL
ARGALA S
ARGALAS
ARGALI S
ARGALIS
ARGALS
GRAALS
M ARGENT S
GARNET
ARGENTAL
ARGENTIC
CATERING
CREATING
REACTING
M ARGENTS
GARNETS
STRANGE

ARGENTUM S
ARGUMENT
ARGIL S
GLAIR GRAIL
ARGILS
GLAIRS
GRAILS
ARGINASE S
ANERGIAS
ANGARIES
ARGININE S
G ARGLE DS
GLARE LAGER
LARGE REGAL
G ARGLED
GLARED
G ARGLES
GLARES
LAGERS
LARGES
G ARGLING
GLARING
ARGOL S
ALGOR GORAL
LARGO
ARGOLS
ALGORS
GORALS
LARGOS
J ARGON S
GROAN ORANG
ORGAN
ARGONAUT S
J ARGONS
GROANS
ORANGS
ORGANS
SARONG
ARGOSIES
ARGOSY
ARGOT S
GATOR GROAT
ARGOTIC
ARGOTS
GATORS
GROATS
ARGUABLE
ARGUABLY
ARGUE DRS
AUGER RUGAE
ARGUED
ARGUER S
ARGUERS
SUGARER
ARGUES
AUGERS
SAUGER
ARGUFIED
ARGUFIER S
ARGUFIES
ARGUFY
ARGUING
ARGUMENT AS
ARGENTUM
ARGUS
GAURS GUARS
SUGAR
ARGUSES
SAUGERS
ARGYLE S
ARGYLES
ARGYLL S
ARGYLLS
ARHAT S
ARHATS
MV ARIA S
RAIA
ARIARY
V ARIAS
RAIAS
ARID
RAID
ARIDER
RAIDER
ARIDEST
ASTRIDE
DIASTER
DISRATE
STAIDER
TARDIES
TIRADES
ARIDITY

ARIDLY
ARIDNESS
SARDINES
ARIEL S
ARIELS
RESAIL
SAILER
SERAIL
SERIAL
ARIETTA S
ARIETTAS
ARISTATE
ARIETTE S
ITERATE
ARIETTES
ITERATES
TEARIEST
TREATIES
TREATISE
ARIGHT
ARIL S
LAIR LARI
LIAR LIRA
RAIL RIAL
ARILED
DERAIL
DIALER
LAIRED
RAILED
REDIAL
RELAID
ARILLATE
ARILLODE S
ARILLOID
ARILS
LAIRS LARIS
LIARS LIRAS
RAILS RIALS
ARIOSE
ARIOSI
ARIOSO S
ARIOSOS
ARISE NS
RAISE SERAI
ARISEN
ARSINE
P ARISES
RAISES
SERAIS
ARISING
AIRINGS
RAISING
B ARISTA ES
RAITAS
RIATAS
TARSIA
TIARAS
ARISTAE
ASTERIA
ATRESIA
B ARISTAS
TARSIAS
ARISTATE
ARIETTAS
ARISTO S
AORIST
RATIOS
SATORI
ARISTOS
AORISTS
SATORIS
BCD HLM NPS W ARK S
ARKOSE S
RESOAK
SOAKER
ARKOSES
RESOAKS
SOAKERS
ARKOSIC
BCD HLM NPS W ARKS
SARK
CFP ARLES
EARLS LARES
LASER LEARS
RALES REALS
SERAL

BFH W ARM SY
MAR
RAM
ARMADA S
RAMADA
ARMADAS
MADRASA
RAMADAS
ARMAGNAC S
ARMAMENT S
ARMATURE DS
ARMBAND S
ARMBANDS
ARMCHAIR S
FHW ARMED
DERMA DREAM
MADRE
FHW ARMER S
REARM
FHW ARMERS
REARMS
ARMET S
MATER RAMET
TAMER
ARMETS
MASTER
MATERS
MATRES
RAMETS
STREAM
TAMERS
H ARMFUL S
FULMAR
ARMFULS
ARMSFUL
FULMARS
ARMHOLE S
ARMHOLES
ARMIES
AIMERS
RAMIES
ARMIGER OS
ARMIGERO S
ARMIGERS
ARMILLA ES
ARMILLAE
ARMILLAS
FHW ARMING S
MARGIN
F ARMINGS
MARGINS
H ARMLESS
ARMLET S
TRAMEL
ARMLETS
LAMSTER
TRAMELS
ARMLIKE
ARMLOAD S
ARMLOADS
ARMLOCK S
LOCKRAM
ARMLOCKS
LOCKRAMS
ARMOIRE S
ARMOIRES
ARMORIES
H ARMONICA S
MACARONI
MAROCAIN
ARMOR SY
ARMORED
ARMORER S
ARMORERS
ARMORIAL S
ARMORIES
ARMOIRES
ARMORING
ARMORS
ARMORY
ARMOUR SY
ARMOURED
ARMOURER S
ARMOURS
ARMOURY
ARMPIT S
IMPART
ARMPITS
IMPARTS
MISPART

ARMREST S
SMARTER
ARMRESTS
BFH W ARMS
MARS RAMS
ARMSFUL
ARMFULS
FULMARS
ARMURE S
ARMURES
B ARMY
ARMYWORM S
ARNATTO S
ARNATTOS
ARNICA S
ACINAR
CARINA
CRANIA
ARNICAS
ACRASIN
CARINAS
SARCINA
ARNOTTO S
RATTOON
ARNOTTOS
RATTOONS
AROID S
RADIO
AROIDS
RADIOS
AROINT S
RATION
AROINTED
ORDINATE
RATIONED
AROINTS
RATIONS
AROMA S
AROMAS
AROMATIC S
AROSE
AROUND
C AROUSAL S
C AROUSALS
C AROUSE DRS
C AROUSED
C AROUSER S
C AROUSERS
C AROUSES
C AROUSING
AROYNT S
NOTARY
AROYNTED
AROYNTS
ARPEGGIO S
ARPEN ST
ARPENS
ARPENT S
ENRAPT
ENTRAP
PARENT
TREPAN
ARPENTS
ENTRAPS
PARENTS
PASTERN
TREPANS
H ARQUEBUS
BC ARRACK S
BC ARRACKS
ARRAIGN S
ARRAIGNS
ARRANGE DRS
ARRANGED
ARRANGER S
ARRANGES
W ARRANT
ARRANTLY
ARRAS
ARRASED
ARRASES
ARRAY S
ARRAYAL S
ARRAYALS
ARRAYED
ARRAYER S
ARRAYERS
ARRAYING
ARRAYS

ARREAR S
ARREARS
ARREST S
RAREST
RASTER
RATERS
STARER
TARRES
TERRAS
ARRESTED
RETREADS
SERRATED
TREADERS
ARRESTEE S
ARRESTER S
REARREST
ARRESTOR S
ARRESTS
RASTERS
STARERS
ARRHIZAL
ARRIBA
ARRIS
SIRRA
ARRISES
RAISERS
SIERRAS
ARRIVAL S
ARRIVALS
ARRIVE DRS
VARIER
ARRIVED
ARRIVER S
ARRIVERS
ARRIVES
VARIERS
ARRIVING
ARROBA S
ARROBAS
RASBORA
ARROGANT
TARRAGON
ARROGATE DS
BFH MNY ARROW SY
FHM N ARROWED
FHM N ARROWING
BFH MNY ARROWS
M ARROWY
YARROW
ARROYO S
ARROYOS
BCE GJL MOP TVW ARS
RAS
ARSENAL S
ARSENALS
ARSENATE S
SERENATA
ARSENIC S
ARCSINE
CARNIES
ARSENICS
ARCSINES
RACINESS
ARSENIDE S
NEARSIDE
ARSENITE S
ARENITES
RESINATE
STEARINE
TRAINEES
ARSENO
REASON
SENORA
ARSENOUS
ANSEROUS
CMP ARSES
RASES SEARS
ARSHIN S
SHAIRN
ARSHINS
SHAIRNS
ARSINE S
ARISEN
ARSINES
ARSINO
NORIAS

ARSIS
SARIS
P ARSON S
ROANS SONAR
ARSONIST S
ARSONOUS
P ARSONS
SONARS
CDF HKM PTW ART SY
RAT
TAR
H ARTAL
ALTAR RATAL
TALAR
ARTEFACT S
C ARTEL S
ALERT ALTER
LATER RATEL
TALER
C ARTELS
ALERTS
ALTERS
ESTRAL
LASTER
RATELS
SALTER
SLATER
STALER
STELAR
TALERS
ARTERIAL S
ARTERIES
ARTERY
ARTFUL
ARTFULLY
P ARTICLE DS
RECITAL
ARTICLED
LACERTID
P ARTICLES
RECITALS
STERICAL
PTW ARTIER
IRATER
TW ARTIEST
ARTISTE
ATTIRES
IRATEST
RATITES
STRIATE
TASTIER
ARTIFACT S
ARTIFICE RS
T ARTILY
T ARTINESS
RETSINAS
STAINERS
STEARINS
BP ARTISAN S
ANTIARS
TSARINA
BP ARTISANS
TSARINAS
ARTIST ES
STRAIT
STRATI
TRAITS
ARTISTE S
ARTIEST
ATTIRES
IRATEST
RATITES
STRIATE
TASTIER
ARTISTES
ARTSIEST
STRIATES
ARTISTIC
ARTISTRY
ARTISTS
STRAITS
TSARIST
W ARTLESS
LASTERS
SALTERS
SLATERS
CDF HKM PTW ARTS Y
RATS STAR
TARS TSAR
ARTSIER
TARRIES
TARSIER

ARTSIEST
ARTISTES
STRIATES
ARTSY
SATYR STRAY
TRAYS
ARTWORK S
ARTWORKS
PTW ARTY
TRAY
ARUGOLA S
ARUGOLAS
ARUGULA S
AUGURAL
ARUGULAS
L ARUM S
MURA
L ARUMS
MURAS RAMUS
H ARUSPEX
L ARVAL
LARVA
P ARVO S
P ARVOS
SAVOR
ARYL S
ARYLS
ARYTHMIA S
ARYTHMIC
ABF GHK LMP RTV WZ AS HKPS
ASANA S
ASANAS
ASARUM S
ASARUMS
ASBESTIC
ASBESTOS
ASBESTUS
ASCARED
ARCADES
ASCARID S
ACARIDS
CARDIAS
ASCARIDS
ASCARIS
ASCEND S
DANCES
ASCENDED
ASCENDER S
REASCEND
ASCENDS
N ASCENT S
CENTAS
ENACTS
SECANT
STANCE
ASCENTS
SECANTS
STANCES
ASCESES
ASCESIS
ASCETIC S
ASCETICS
ASCI
ASCIDIA N
ASCIDIAN S
ASCIDIUM
ASCITES
ECTASIS
ASCITIC
SCIATIC
ASCOCARP S
ASCORBIC
M ASCOT S
COAST COATS
COSTA TACOS
M ASCOTS
COASTS
ASCRIBE DS
CARIBES
ASCRIBED
CARBIDES
ASCRIBES
ASCUS
CASUS
ASDIC S
ACIDS CADIS
CAIDS

2006 addition

ASDICS
ASEA
ASEPSES
ASEPSIS
ASPISES
ASEPTIC
PACIEST
SPICATE
ASEXUAL
BCD ASH Y
FGH AHS
LMP HAS
RSW SHA
ASHAMED
ASHCAKE S
ASHCAKES
ASHCAN S
NACHAS
ASHCANS
BCD ASHED
FGH DEASH HADES
LMP HEADS SADHE
SW SHADE
ASHEN
HANSE
BCD ASHES
FGH SHEAS
LMP
RSW
ASHFALL S
ASHFALLS
CDW ASHIER
DW ASHIEST
W ASHINESS
HESSIANS
BCD ASHING
FGH
LMP
SW
ASHLAR S
LAHARS
ASHLARED
ASHLARS
ASHLER S
HALERS
LASHER
ASHLERED
ASHLERS
LASHERS
SLASHER
CS ASHLESS
HASSELS
HASSLES
SLASHES
ASHMAN
SHAMAN
ASHMEN
ASHORE
AHORSE
HOARSE
ASHPLANT S
ASHRAM S
ASHRAMS
ASHTRAY S
ASHTRAYS
DMW ASHY
HAYS SHAY
ASIDE S
AIDES IDEAS
ASIDES
DAISES
DASSIE
ASININE
BCM ASK S
T KAS
SKA
ASKANCE
ASKANT
TANKAS
BCM ASKED
T
M ASKER S
ESKAR RAKES
SAKER
M ASKERS
ESKARS
SAKERS
ASKESES
ASKESIS
ASKEW
WAKES WEKAS

BCG ASKING S
MT GASKIN
KIANGS
GM ASKINGS
GASKINS
ASKOI
ASKOS
SOAKS
BCM ASKS
T SKAS
ASLANT
ALANTS
ASLEEP
ELAPSE
PLEASE
ASLOPE
ASLOSH
SHOALS
ASOCIAL S
ASOCIALS
GHR ASP S
W PAS
SAP
SPA
ASPARKLE
ASPECT S
EPACTS
ASPECTS
ASPEN S
NAPES NEAPS
PANES PEANS
SNEAP SPEAN
ASPENS
SNEAPS
SPEANS
GJR ASPER S
APERS APRES
PARES PARSE
PEARS PRASE
PRESA RAPES
REAPS SPARE
SPEAR
ASPERATE DS
SEPARATE
ASPERGES
PRESAGES
ASPERITY
GJR ASPERS E
PARSES
PASSER
PRASES
REPASS
SPARES
SPARSE
SPEARS
ASPERSE DRS
PARESES
SERAPES
ASPERSED
REPASSED
RESPADES
ASPERSER S
SPEARERS
ASPERSES
REPASSES
ASPERSOR S
ASPHALT S
SPATHAL
ASPHALTS
ASPHERIC
PARCHESI
SERAPHIC
ASPHODEL S
ASPHYXIA LS
ASPHYXY
ASPIC S
PICAS SPICA
ASPICS
SPICAS
ASPIRANT S
PARTISAN
SPARTINA
ASPIRATA E
ASPIRATE DS
PARASITE
SEPTARIA
ASPIRE DRS
PARIES
PRAISE
SPIREA

ASPIRED
DESPAIR
DIAPERS
PRAISED
ASPIRER S
PARRIES
PRAISER
RAPIERS
RASPIER
REPAIRS
ASPIRERS
PRAISERS
ASPIRES
PARESIS
PARISES
PRAISES
SPIREAS
ASPIRIN GS
ASPIRING
PAIRINGS
PRAISING
ASPIRINS
ASPIS H
APSIS
ASPISES
ASEPSIS
RW ASPISH
PHASIS
SPAHIS
GHR ASPS
W PASS SAPS
SPAS
ASQUINT
QUINTAS
ASRAMA S
SAMARA
ASRAMAS
SAMARAS
SAMSARA
BLM ASS
PST
ASSAGAI S
ASSAGAIS
ASSAI LS
W ASSAIL S
W ASSAILED
W ASSAILER S
REASSAIL
SALARIES
W ASSAILS
ASSAIS
ASSASSIN S
ASSAULT S
ASSAULTS
ASSAY S
ASSAYED
ASSAYER S
ASSAYERS
ASSAYING
GAINSAYS
ASSAYS
ASSEGAI S
ASSEGAIS
ASSEMBLE DR
BEAMLESS S
ASSEMBLY
ASSENT S
SANEST
STANES
ASSENTED
SENSATED
STANDEES
ASSENTER S
EARNESTS
SARSENET
ASSENTOR S
SANTEROS
SENATORS
STARNOSE
TREASONS
ASSENTS
ASSERT S
ASTERS
STARES
ASSERTED
ASSERTER S
REASSERT
SERRATES
TERRASES

ASSERTOR S
ASSORTER
ORATRESS
REASSORT
ROASTERS
ASSERTS
TRASSES
BGL ASSES S
MPS
T
ASSESS
SASSES
ASSESSED
ASSESSES
ASSESSOR S
BT ASSET S
EASTS SATES
SEATS TASSE
BT ASSETS
STASES
TASSES
ASSIGN S
ASSIGNAT S
ASSIGNED
ASSIGNEE S
AGENESIS
ASSIGNER S
REASSIGN
SERINGAS
ASSIGNOR S
SIGNORAS
SOARINGS
ASSIGNS
SASSING
B ASSIST S
STASIS
ASSISTED
DISSEATS
ASSISTER S
ASSISTOR S
B ASSISTS
ASSIZE S
ASSIZES
ASSLIKE
ALSIKES
ASSOIL S
ASSOILED
ISOLEADS
ASSOILS
ASSONANT S
ASSORT S
ROASTS
ASSORTED
TORSADES
ASSORTER S
ASSERTOR
ORATRESS
REASSORT
ROASTERS
ASSORTS
ASSUAGE DRS
SAUSAGE
ASSUAGED
ASSUAGER S
ASSUAGES
SAUSAGES
ASSUME DRS
AMUSES
ASSUMED
MEDUSAS
ASSUMER S
AMUSERS
MASSEUR
ASSUMERS
MASSEURS
ASSUMES
ASSUMING
ASSURE DRS
URASES
ASSURED S
ASSUREDS
ASSURER S
RASURES
ASSURERS
ASSURES
ASSURING
ASSUROR S
ASSURORS
ASSWAGE DS
ASSWAGED
ASSWAGES
ASTASIA S

ASTASIAS
ASTATIC
ASTATINE S
SANITATE
BCE ASTER NS
FGL RATES RESAT
MPR STARE TARES
TVW TEARS
ASTERIA S
ARISTAE
ATRESIA
ASTERIAS
ATRESIAS
ASTERISK S
SARKIEST
ASTERISM S
MISRATES
SMARTIES
EP ASTERN
ANTRES
STERNA
ASTERNAL
ASTEROID S
BCE ASTERS
GLM ASSERT
PRT STARES
W
ASTHENIA S
ASTHENIC S
CHANTIES
ASTHENY
SHANTEY
ASTHMA S
MATSAH
ASTHMAS
MATSAHS
ASTIGMIA S
ASTILBE S
ABLEIST
ALBITES
BASTILE
BESTIAL
BLASTIE
STABILE
ASTILBES
ABLEISTS
BASTILES
BLASTIES
STABILES
ASTIR
AIRTS SITAR
STAIR STRIA
TARSI
ASTOMOUS
ASTONIED
SEDATION
ASTONIES
ASTONISH
ASTONY
ASTOUND S
ASTOUNDS
ASTRAGAL IS
G ASTRAL S
ALTARS
RATALS
TALARS
TARSAL
ASTRALLY
ASTRALS
TARSALS
ASTRAY
ASTRICT S
ASTRICTS
ASTRIDE
ARIDEST
DIASTER
DISRATE
STAIDER
TARDIES
TIRADES
ASTRINGE DS
ANGRIEST
GANISTER
GANTRIES
GRANITES
INGRATES
RANGIEST
ASTUTE
STATUE
ASTUTELY
ASTYLAR

ASUNDER
DANSEUR
ASWARM
ASWIRL
ASWOON
ASYLA
ASYLUM S
ASYLUMS
ALYSSUM
ASYNDETA
BCE AT ET
FGH TA
KLM
OPQ
RST
VW
ATABAL S
ALBATA
BALATA
ATABALS
ALBATAS
BALATAS
ATABRINE S
ATACTIC
Y ATAGHAN S
Y ATAGHANS
ATALAYA S
ATALAYAS
ATAMAN S
ATAMANS
ATAMASCO S
W ATAP S
TAPA
W ATAPS
PASTA TAPAS
ATARAXIA S
ATARAXIC S
ATARAXY
ATAVIC
ATAVISM S
ATAVISMS
ATAVIST S
ATAVISTS
ATAXIA S
ATAXIAS
ATAXIC S
ATAXICS
ATAXIES
ATAXY
BCD ATE S
FGH EAT
LMP ETA
RST TAE
TEA
ATECHNIC
CATECHIN
ATELIC
ATELIER S
ATELIERS
EARLIEST
LEARIEST
REALTIES
ATEMOYA S
ATEMOYAS
ATENOLOL S
BCD ATES
FGH EAST EATS
MNP ETAS SATE
RST SEAT SETA
TEAS
ATHANASY
ATHEISM S
ATHEISMS
ATHEIST S
STAITHE
ATHEISTS
HASTIEST
STAITHES
ATHELING S
ATHENEUM S
ATHEROMA S
ATHETOID
ATHIRST
RATTISH
TARTISH
ATHLETE S
ATHLETES
ATHLETIC S
THETICAL

ATHODYD S
ATHODYDS
ATHWART
ATILT
ATINGLE
ELATING
GELATIN
GENITAL
TAGLINE
ATLANTES
ATLAS
TALAS
ATLASES
ATLATL S
ATLATLS
ATMA NS
B ATMAN S
MANAT MANTA
ATMANS
MANATS
MANTAS
ATMAS
ATOLL S
ALLOT
ATOLLS
ALLOTS
ATOM SY
MOAT
ATOMIC S
ATOMICAL
ATOMICS
OSMATIC
SOMATIC
ATOMIES
AMOSITE
ATOMISE
ATOMISE DRS
AMOSITE
ATOMIES
ATOMISED
ATOMISER S
AMORTISE
ATOMISES
AMITOSES
AMOSITES
ATOMISM S
ATOMISMS
ATOMIST S
ATOMISTS
ATOMIZE DRS
ATOMIZED
ATOMIZER S
AMORTIZE
ATOMIZES
ATOMS
MOATS STOMA
ATOMY
ATONABLE
ATONAL
ATONALLY
ATONE DRS
OATEN
ATONED
DONATE
ATONER S
ORNATE
ATONERS
SANTERO
SENATOR
TREASON
ATONES
ATONIA S
ATONIAS
ATONIC S
ACTION
CATION
ATONICS
ACTIONS
CATIONS
ATONIES
ATONING
ATONY
ATOP Y
ATOPIC
ATOPIES
OPIATES
ATOPY
ATRAZINE S
ATREMBLE

ATRESIA S
ARISTAE
ASTERIA
ATRESIAS
ASTERIAS
ATRESIC
CRISTAE
RACIEST
STEARIC
ATRETIC
CATTIER
CITRATE
L ATRIA L
RAITA RIATA
TIARA
ATRIAL
LARIAT
LATRIA
ATRIP
TAPIR
N ATRIUM S
N ATRIUMS
ATROCITY
CITATORY
ATROPHIA S
ATROPHIC
ATROPHY
ATROPIN ES
ATROPINE S
ATROPINS
ATROPISM S
PASTROMI
BMW ATT
TAT
ATTABOY
ATTACH E
ATTACHE DRS
ATTACHED
ATTACHER S
REATTACH
ATTACHES
ATTACK S
ATTACKED
ATTACKER S
REATTACK
ATTACKS
ATTAGIRL
ATTAIN ST
ATTAINED
ATTAINER S
REATTAIN
ATTAINS
ATTAINT S
ATTAINTS
ANTISTAT
ATTAR S
TATAR
ATTARS
STRATA
TATARS
ATTEMPER S
ATTEMPT S
ATTEMPTS
ATTEND S
ATTENDED
DENTATED
ATTENDEE S
EDENTATE
ATTENDER S
NATTERED
RATTENED
ATTENDS
ATTENT
FW ATTEST S
ATTESTED
ATTESTER S
ATTESTOR S
TESTATOR
ATTESTS
ATTIC S
TACIT
ATTICISM S
MASTITIC
ATTICIST S
ATTICIZE DS
ATTICS
STATIC
ATTIRE DS
RATITE
ATTIRED

ATTIRES
ARTIEST
ARTISTE
IRATEST
RATITES
STRIATE
TASTIER
ATTIRING
ATTITUDE S
ATTORN S
RATTON
ATTORNED
ATTORNEY S
ATTORNS
RATTONS
ATTRACT S
ATTRACTS
ATTRIT ES
ATTRITE DS
TATTIER
TITRATE
ATTRITED
TITRATED
ATTRITES
RATTIEST
TARTIEST
TITRATES
TRISTATE
ATTRITS
ATTUNE DS
NUTATE
TAUTEN
ATTUNED
NUTATED
TAUNTED
ATTUNES
NUTATES
TAUTENS
TETANUS
UNSTATE
ATTUNING
NUTATING
TAUNTING
ATWAIN
ATWEEN
ATWITTER
ATYPIC
ATYPICAL
AUBADE S
AUBADES
AUBERGE S
AUBERGES
AUBRETIA S
AUBRIETA
AUBRIETA S
AUBRETIA
AUBURN S
AUBURNS
AUCTION S
CAUTION
AUCTIONS
CAUTIONS
AUCUBA S
AUCUBAS
AUDACITY
C AUDAD S
AUDADS
AUDIAL
AUDIBLE DS
AUDIBLED
BUDDLEIA
AUDIBLES
AUDIBLY
AUDIENCE S
AUDIENT S
AUDIENTS
SINUATED
AUDILE S
AUDILES
L AUDING S
AUDINGS
AUDIO S
AUDIOS
AUDIT S
AUDITED
AUDITEE S
AUDITEES
AUDITING
AUDITION S

AUDITIVE S
AUDITOR SY
AUDITORS
AUDITORY
AUDITS
AUGEND S
UNAGED
AUGENDS
GMS AUGER S
ARGUE RUGAE
GS AUGERS
ARGUES
SAUGER
CNT AUGHT S
W GHAUT
NW AUGHTS
GHAUTS
AUGITE S
AUGITES
AUGITIC
AUGMENT S
MUTAGEN
AUGMENTS
MUTAGENS
AUGUR SY
AUGURAL
ARUGULA
AUGURED
AUGURER S
AUGURERS
AUGURIES
AUGURING
AUGURS
AUGURY
AUGUST
AUGUSTER
AUGUSTLY
JW AUK S
AUKLET S
AUKLETS
JW AUKS
SKUA
CFY AULD
DUAL LAUD
AULDER
LAUDER
AULDEST
SALUTED
AULIC
DGH AUNT SY
JTV TUNA
AUNTHOOD S
V AUNTIE S
AUNTIES
SINUATE
AUNTLIER
RETINULA
TENURIAL
AUNTLIKE
G AUNTLY
DHJ AUNTS
TV TUNAS
JV AUNTY
L AURA ELRS
L AURAE
AURAL
LAURA
AURALITY
AURALLY
AURAR
L AURAS
AURATE D
AURATED
L AUREATE
AUREI
URAEI
AUREOLA ES
AUREOLAE
AUREOLAS
AUREOLE DS
AUREOLED
AUREOLES
AURES
URASE UREAS
URSAE
AUREUS
URAEUS
AURIC
CURIA
AURICLE DS

AURICLED
AURICLES
AURICULA ER
S
AURIFORM
K AURIS T
AURIST S
AURISTS
AUROCHS
AURORA ELS
AURORAE
AURORAL
AURORAS
AUROREAN
AUROUS
AURUM S
AURUMS
AUSFORM S
AUSFORMS
AUSPEX
AUSPICE S
AUSPICES
AUSTERE R
AUSTERER
TREASURE
AUSTRAL S
AUSTRALS
AUSUBO S
AUSUBOS
AUTACOID S
AUTARCH SY
AUTARCHS
AUTARCHY
AUTARKIC
AUTARKY
AUTECISM S
H AUTEUR S
H AUTEURS
AUTHOR S
AUTHORED
OUTHEARD
AUTHORS
AUTISM S
AUTISMS
AUTIST S
AUTISTIC S
AUTISTS
AUTO S
AUTOBAHN S
AUTOBUS
AUTOCADE S
AUTOCOID S
AUTOCRAT S
ACTUATOR
AUTODYNE S
AUTOED
AUTOGAMY
AUTOGENY
AUTOGIRO S
AUTOGYRO S
AUTOHARP S
AUTOING
OUTGAIN
AUTOLYSE DS
AUTOLYZE DS
AUTOMAN
AUTOMAT AES
AUTOMATA
AUTOMATE DS
AUTOMATS
AUTOMEN
AUTONOMY
T AUTONYM S
T AUTONYMS
AUTOPEN S
AUTOPENS
AUTOPSIC
CAPTIOUS
AUTOPSY
PAYOUTS
AUTOS
AUTOSOME S
AUTOTOMY
AUTOTYPE S
AUTOTYPY

AUTUMN S
AUTUMNAL
AUTUMNS
AUTUNITE S
AUXESES
AUXESIS
AUXETIC S
AUXETICS
AUXIN S
AUXINIC
AUXINS
FJK AVA
L
AVADAVAT S
AVAIL S
AVAILED
VEDALIA
AVAILING
AVAILS
SALIVA
SALVIA
S AVANT
AVARICE S
CAVIARE
AVARICES
CAVIARES
AVAST
AVATAR S
AVATARS
AVAUNT
CEF AVE RS
GHL
NPR
SW
AVELLAN E
AVELLANE
AVENGE DRS
GENEVA
AVENGED
AVENGER S
ENGRAVE
AVENGERS
ENGRAVES
AVENGES
GENEVAS
AVENGING
DHM AVENS
R NAVES VANES
AVENSES
AVENTAIL S
AVENUE S
AVENUES
CHL AVER ST
PRS RAVE VERA
W
AVERAGE DS
AVERAGED
AVERAGES
AVERMENT S
AVERRED
AVERRING
CHL AVERS E
PRS RAVES SAVER
W
AVERSE
REAVES
AVERSELY
AVERSION S
AVERSIVE S
AVERT S
TRAVE
AVERTED
AVERTER S
AVERTERS
TRAVERSE
AVERTING
GRIEVANT
VINTAGER
AVERTS
STARVE
TRAVES
VASTER
CEF AVES
HLN SAVE VASE
OPR
SW
AVGAS
AVGASES
SAVAGES
AVGASSES

AVIAN S
AVIANIZE DS
AVIANS
AVIARIES
AVIARIST S
AVIARY
AVIATE DS
AVIATED
AVIATES
AVIATIC
VIATICA
AVIATING
AVIATION S
AVIATOR S
AVIATORS
AVIATRIX
N AVICULAR
P AVID
DIVA
AVIDIN S
AVIDINS
AVIDITY
AVIDLY
AVIDNESS
AVIFAUNA EL
S
N AVIGATOR S
AVION S
AVIONIC S
AVIONICS
AVIONS
AVISO S
AVISOS
AVO SW
OVA
AVOCADO S
AVOCADOS
AVOCET S
OCTAVE
AVOCETS
OCTAVES
AVODIRE S
AVOIDER
AVODIRES
AVOIDERS
AVOID S
AVOIDED
AVOIDER S
AVODIRE
AVOIDERS
AVODIRES
AVOIDING
AVOIDS
AVOS
AVOSET S
AVOSETS
AVOUCH
AVOUCHED
AVOUCHER S
AVOUCHES
AVOW S
AVOWABLE
AVOWABLY
AVOWAL S
AVOWALS
AVOWED
AVOWEDLY
AVOWER S
REAVOW
AVOWERS
OVERSAW
REAVOWS
AVOWING
AVOWS
AVULSE DS
VALUES
AVULSED
AVULSES
AVULSING
AVULSION S
CDH AW AELN
JLM
NPR
STV
WY
AWA Y
AWAIT S
AWAITED

AWAITER S
AWAITERS
AWAITING
AWAITS
AWAKE DNS
AWAKED
AWAKEN S
AWAKENED
AWAKENER S
REAWAKEN
AWAKENS
AWAKES
AWAKING
V AWARD S
AWARDED
AWARDEE S
AWARDEES
AWARDER S
AWARDERS
AWARDING
V AWARDS
AWARE
AWASH
AWAY
AWAYNESS
AWE DES
WAE
AWEARY
AWEATHER
WHEATEAR
CDH AWED
JLM WADE
PST
Y
AWEE
AWEIGH
AWEING
AWELESS
WEASELS
AWES
WAES
AWESOME
L AWFUL
AWFULLER
L AWFULLY
AWHILE
AWHIRL
CDH AWING
JLM WIGAN
PST
Y
AWKWARD
BPW AWL S
Y LAW
JL AWLESS
SWALES
BPW AWLS
Y LAWS SLAW
AWLWORT S
AWLWORTS
AWMOUS
DFL AWN SY
MPS NAW
Y WAN
DFP AWNED
Y DAWEN DEWAN
WANED
DFP AWNING S
Y WANING
AWNINGED
AWNINGS
SNAWING
AWNLESS
DFL AWNS
PY SAWN SNAW
SWAN WANS
FLT AWNY
WANY YAWN
AWOKE N
AWOKEN
WEAKON
AWOL S
ALOW
AWOLS
AWRY
WARY
FLM AX E
PRS
TWZ
AXAL

AXE DLS
FMR **AXED**
TW
AXEL S
AXLE
AXELS
AXLES LAXES
AXEMAN
AXEMEN
EXAMEN
AXENIC
FLM **AXES**
PRS
TWZ
AXIAL
AXIALITY
AXIALLY
AXIL ES
AXILE
M **AXILLA** ERS
M **AXILLAE**
AXILLAR SY
AXILLARS
M **AXILLARY**
M **AXILLAS**
AXILS
FMR **AXING**
TW
AXIOLOGY
AXIOM S
AXIOMS
AXION S
AXIONS
MT **AXIS**
AXISED
AXISES
T **AXITE** S
T **AXITES**
TAXIES
AXLE DS
AXEL
AXLED
AXLES
AXELS LAXES
AXLETREE S
W **AXLIKE**
T **AXMAN**
T **AXMEN**
AXOLOTL S
AXOLOTLS
T **AXON** ES
AXONAL
AXONE S
AXONEMAL
AXONEME S
AXONEMES
AXONES
AXONIC
ANOXIC
T **AXONS**
AXOPLASM S
AXSEED S
AXSEEDS
BCD **AY** ES
FGH YA
JKL
MNP
RSW
Y
R **AYAH** S
R **AYAHS**
AYE S
YEA
AYES
EASY EYAS
YEAS
LZ **AYIN** S
LZ **AYINS**
BCD **AYS**
FGH SAY
JKL
MNP
RSW
Y
AYURVEDA S
AZALEA S
AZALEAS
H **AZAN** S
H **AZANS**

AZIDE S
AZIDES
AZIDO
DIAZO
AZIMUTH S
AZIMUTHS
AZINE S
AZINES
ZANIES
AZLON S
ZONAL
AZLONS
AZO N
ZOA
AZOIC
AZOLE S
ZOEAL
AZOLES
SLEAZO
AZON S
ZONA
AZONAL
AZONIC
AZONS
AZOTE DS
AZOTED
AZOTEMIA S
AZOTEMIC
METAZOIC
AZOTES
AZOTH S
AZOTHS
AZOTIC
AZOTISE DS
AZOTISED
AZOTISES
AZOTIZE DS
AZOTIZED
AZOTIZES
AZOTURIA S
AZUKI S
AZUKIS
AZULEJO S
AZULEJOS
AZURE S
AZURES
L **AZURITE** S
L **AZURITES**
AZYGOS
GYOZAS
AZYGOSES
AZYGOUS

B

AO **BA** ADGHLMNP
AB RSTY
BAA LS
ABA
BAAED
BAAING
BAAL S
ALBA
BAALIM
BAALISM S
BAALISMS
BAALS
ALBAS BALAS
BALSA BASAL
SABAL
BAAS
ABAS
BAASES
ABASES
BAASKAAP S
BAASKAP S
BAASKAPS
BAASSKAP
BAASSKAP S
BAASKAPS
BABA S
ABBA
BABAS
ABBAS
BABASSU S
BABASSUS
BABBITRY
BABBITT S
BABBITTS
BABBLE DRS

BABBLED
BLABBED
BABBLER S
BLABBER
BRABBLE
BABBLERS
BLABBERS
BRABBLES
BABBLES
BABBLING S
BLABBING
BABE LS
ABBE
BABEL S
BABELS
BABES
ABBES
BABESIA S
BABESIAS
BABICHE S
BABICHES
BABIED
BABIER
BARBIE
BABIES T
BABIEST
TABBIES
BABIRUSA S
BABKA S
KABAB
BABKAS
KABABS
BABOO LNS
BABOOL S
BABOOLS
BABOON S
BABOONS
BABOOS
BABU LS
BABUL S
BUBAL
BABULS
BUBALS
BABUS
BABUSHKA S
BABY
BABYDOLL S
BABYHOOD S
BABYING
BABYISH
BABYSAT
BABYSIT S
BABYSITS
BACALAO S
BACALAOS
BACCA E
BACCAE
BACCARA ST
BACCARAS
BACCARAT S
BACCATE D
BACCATED
BACCHANT ES
BACCHIC
BACCHII
BACCHIUS
BACH
BACHED
BACHELOR S
BACHES
BACHING
BACILLAR Y
CABRILLA
BACILLI
BACILLUS
A **BACK** S
BACKACHE S
BACKBEAT S
BACKBEND S
BACKBIT E
BACKBITE RS
BACKBONE DS
BACKCAST S
SCATBACK
BACKCHAT S
BACKDATE DS
BACKDOOR
BACKDROP ST

BACKED
BACKER S
BACKERS
BACKFILL S
BACKFIRE DS
FIREBACK
BACKFIT S
BACKFITS
BACKFLIP S
BACKFLOW S
BACKHAND S
BACKHAUL S
BACKHOE DS
BACKHOED
BACKHOES
BACKING S
BACKINGS
BACKLAND S
BACKLASH
BACKLESS
BACKLIST S
BACKLIT
BACKLOAD S
BACKLOG S
BACKLOGS
BACKMOST
TOMBACKS
BACKOUT S
OUTBACK
BACKOUTS
OUTBACKS
BACKPACK S
BACKREST S
BRACKETS
BACKROOM S
BACKRUSH
BACKS
BACKSAW S
BACKSAWS
BACKSEAT S
SEATBACK
BACKSET S
SETBACK
BACKSETS
SETBACKS
BACKSIDE S
DIEBACKS
BACKSLAP S
BACKSLID E
BACKSPIN S
BACKSTAB S
BACKSTAY S
BACKSTOP S
BACKUP S
BACKUPS
BACKWARD S
DRAWBACK
BACKWASH
BACKWOOD S
BACKWRAP S
BACKYARD S
BACLOFEN S
BACON S
BANCO
BACONS
BANCOS
BACTERIA LS
BACTERIN S
BACULA
BACULINE
BACULUM S
BACULUMS
BAD ES
DAB
BADDER
BARDED
BADDEST
BADDIE S
ABIDED
BADDIES
BADDY
BADE
ABED BEAD
BADGE DRS
DEBAG
BADGED
BADGER S
BARGED
GARBED

BADGERED
BADGERLY
BADGERS
BADGES
DEBAGS
BADGING
BADINAGE DS
BADLAND S
BADLANDS
BADLY
BALDY
BADMAN
BADMEN
BEDAMN
BADMOUTH S
BADNESS
BADS
DABS
BAFF SY
BAFFED
BAFFIES
BAFFING
BAFFLE DRS
BAFFLED
BAFFLER S
BAFFLERS
BAFFLES
BAFFLING
BAFFS
BAFFY
BAG S
GAB
BAGASS E
BAGASSE S
SEABAGS
BAGASSES
BAGEL S
BELGA GABLE
GLEBA
BAGELS
BELGAS
GABLES
BAGFUL S
BAGFULS
BAGSFUL
BAGGAGE S
BAGGAGES
BAGGED
BAGGER S
BEGGAR
BAGGERS
BEGGARS
BAGGIE RS
BAGGIER
BAGGIES T
BAGGIEST
BAGGILY
BAGGING S
BAGGINGS
BAGGY
BAGHOUSE S
BAGLIKE
BAGMAN
BAGMEN
BAGNIO S
GABION
BAGNIOS
GABIONS
BAGPIPE DRS
BAGPIPED
BAGPIPER S
BAGPIPES
BAGS
GABS
BAGSFUL
BAGFULS
BAGUET S
BAGUETS
BAGUETTE S
BAGWIG S
BAGWIGS
BAGWORM S
BAGWORMS
BAH T
BAHADUR S
BAHADURS
SUBAHDAR
BAHT S
BATH

BAHTS
BATHS
BAIDARKA S
BAIL S
BAILABLE
BAILED
BAILEE S
BAILEES
BAILER S
LIBRAE
BAILERS
BAILEY S
BAILEYS
BAILIE S
BAILIES
ALIBIES
BIALIES
BAILIFF S
BAILIFFS
BAILING
BAILMENT S
BAILOR S
BAILORS
BAILOUT S
TABOULI
BAILOUTS
TABOULIS
BAILS
BASIL
BAILSMAN
BAILSMEN
BIMENSAL
BAIRN S
BRAIN
BAIRNISH
BRAINISH
BAIRNLY
BAIRNS
BRAINS
BAIT HS
BAITED
BAITER S
BARITE
REBAIT
TERBIA
BAITERS
BARITES
REBAITS
TERBIAS
BAITFISH
BAITH
HABIT
BAITING
BAITS
BAIZA S
BAIZAS
BAIZE S
BAIZES
BAKE DRS
BEAK
BAKED
BAKELITE S
BAKEMEAT S
MAKEBATE
BAKER SY
BRAKE BREAK
KEBAR
BAKERIES
BAKERS
BRAKES
BREAKS
KEBARS
BAKERY
BAKES
BEAKS
BAKESHOP S
BAKEWARE S
BAKING S
BAKINGS
BASKING
BAKLAVA S
BAKLAVAS
BAKLAWA S
BAKLAWAS
BAKSHISH
BAL DEKLMS
ALB
LAB
BALANCE DRS
BALANCED

BALANCER S
BARNACLE
BALANCES
BALAS
ALBAS BAALS
BALSA BASAL
SABAL
BALASES
BALATA S
ALBATA
ATABAL
BALATAS
ALBATAS
ATABALS
BALBOA S
BALBOAS
BALCONY
BALD SY
BALDED
BLADED
BALDER
BLADER
BLARED
BALDEST
BLASTED
STABLED
BALDHEAD S
BALDIES
DISABLE
BALDING
BLADING
BALDISH
BALDLY
BALDNESS
BALDPATE DS
BALDRIC KS
BALDRICK S
BALDRICS
BALDS
BALDY
BADLY
BALE DRS
ABLE BLAE
BALED
ABLED BLADE
BALEEN S
ENABLE
BALEENS
ENABLES
BALEFIRE S
AFEBRILE
FIREABLE
BALEFUL
BALER S
ABLER BLARE
BLEAR
BALERS
BLARES
BLEARS
BALES
ABLES BLASE
SABLE
BALING
BALISAUR S
BALK SY
BALKED
BALKER S
BALKERS
BALKIER
BALKIEST
BALKILY
BALKING
BALKLINE S
LINKABLE
BALKS
BALKY
BALL SY
BALLAD ES
BALLADE S
BALLADES
BALLADIC
BALLADRY
BALLYARD
BALLADS
BALLAST S
BALLASTS
BALLED
BALLER S
BALLERS
BALLET S

BALLETIC
BALLETS
BALLGAME S
BALLHAWK S
BALLIES
BALLING
BALLISTA E
BALLON S
BALLONET S
BALLONNE S
BALLONS
BALLOON S
BALLOONS
BALLOT S
BALLOTED
BALLOTER S
BALLOTS
BALLPARK S
BALLROOM S
BALLS Y
BALLUTE S
BULLATE
BALLUTES
BALLY
BALLYARD S
BALLADRY
BALLYHOO S
BALLYRAG S
BALM SY
BLAM LAMB
BALMIER
LAMBIER
BALMIEST
BIMETALS
LAMBIEST
TIMBALES
BALMILY
BALMLIKE
LAMBLIKE
BALMORAL S
BALMS
BLAMS LAMBS
BALMY
LAMBY
BALNEAL
BALONEY S
BALONEYS
BALS A
ALBS LABS
SLAB
BALSA MS
ALBAS BAALS
BALAS BASAL
SABAL
BALSAM S
SAMBAL
BALSAMED
BALSAMIC
CABALISM
BALSAMS
SAMBALS
BALSAS
SABALS
BALUSTER S
RUSTABLE
BAM S
BAMBINI
BAMBINO S
BAMBINOS
NABOBISM
BAMBOO S
BAMBOOS
BAMMED
BAMMING
BAMS
BAN DEGIKS
NAB
BANAL
BANALITY
BANALIZE DS
BANALLY
BANANA S
BANANAS
BANAUSIC
BANCO S
BACON
BANCOS
BACONS
BAND ASY
BANDA S
BANDAGE DRS
BANDAGED
BANDAGER S
BANDAGES
BANDAID
BANDANA S
BANDANAS
BANDANNA S
BANDAS
BANDBOX
BANDEAU SX
BANDEAUS
BANDEAUX
BANDED
BANDER S
BARNED
BANDEROL ES
BANDERS
BANDIED
BANDIES
BASINED
BANDING
BANDIT OS
BANDITO S
BANDITOS
BANDITRY
BANDITS
BANDITTI
BANDMATE S
BANDOG S
BANDOGS
BANDORA S
BANDORAS
BANDORE S
BROADEN
BANDORES
BROADENS
BANDS
BANDSAW S
BANDSAWS
BANDSMAN
BANDSMEN
BANDY
BANDYING
BANE DS
BEAN NABE
BANED
BANEFUL
BANES
BEANS NABES
BANG S
BANGED
BANGER S
GRABEN
BANGERS
GRABENS
BANGING
BANGKOK S
BANGKOKS
BANGLE S
BANGLES
BANGS
BANGTAIL S
ABLATING
BANI
BANIAN S
BANIANS
BANING
BANISH
BANISHED
BANISHER S
BANISHES
BANSHIES
BANISTER S
BARNIEST
BANJAX
BANJAXED
BANJAXES
BANJO S
BANJOES
BANJOIST S
BANJOS
BANK S
BANKABLE
BANKBOOK S
BANKCARD S
BANKED
BANKER S
BANKERLY
BANKERS
BANKING S
BANKINGS
BANKIT S
BANKITS
BANKNOTE S
BANKROLL S
BANKRUPT S
BANKS
BANKSIA S
BANKSIAS
BANKSIDE S
BANNABLE
BANNED
BANNER S
BANNERED
BANNERET S
BANNEROL S
BANNERS
BANNET S
BANNETS
BANNING
BANNOCK S
BANNOCKS
BANNS
BANQUET S
BANQUETS
BANS
NABS
BANSHEE S
SHEBEAN
BANSHEES
SHEBEANS
BANSHIE S
BANSHIES
BANISHES
BANTAM S
BATMAN
BANTAMS
BATSMAN
BANTENG S
BANTENGS
BANTER S
BANTERED
BANTERER S
BANTERS
BANTIES
BASINET
BANTLING S
BANTY
BANYAN S
BANYANS
BANZAI S
BANZAIS
BAOBAB S
BAOBABS
BAP S
BAPS
BAPTISE DS
BAPTISED
BAPTISES
BAPTISIA S
BAPTISM S
BITMAPS
BAPTISMS
BAPTIST S
BAPTISTS
BAPTIZE DRS
BAPTIZED
BAPTIZER S
BAPTIZES
K BAR BDEFKMN
ARB S
BRA
BARATHEA S
BARB ES
BARBAL
BARBARIC
BARBASCO S
BARBATE
BARBE DLRST
BARBECUE DR S
BARBED
DABBER
BARBEL LS
RABBLE
BARBELL S
BARBELLS
BARBELS
RABBLES
SLABBER
BARBEQUE DS
BARBER S
BARBERED
BARBERRY
BARBERS
BARBES
BARBET S
RABBET
BARBETS
RABBETS
STABBER
BARBETTE S
BARBICAN S
BARBICEL S
BARBIE S
BABIER
BARBIES
RABBIES
BARBING
BARBITAL S
BARBLESS
SLABBERS
BARBS
BARBULE S
BARBULES
BARBUT S
BARBUTS
BARBWIRE S
BARCA S
BARCAS
SCARAB
BARCHAN S
BARCHANS
BARD ES
BRAD DARB
DRAB
BARDE DS
ARDEB BARED
BEARD BREAD
DEBAR
BARDED
BADDER
BARDES
ARDEBS
BEARDS
BREADS
DEBARS
SABRED
SERDAB
BARDIC
BARDING
BRIGAND
BARDS
BRADS DARBS
DRABS
BARE DRS
BEAR BRAE
BAREBACK
BAREBOAT S
BARED
ARDEB BARDE
BEARD BREAD
DEBAR
BAREFIT
BAREFOOT
BAREGE S
BARGEE
BAREGES
BARGEES
BAREHAND S
BAREHEAD
BARELY
BARLEY
BLEARY
BARENESS
BARER
BARRE REBAR
BARES T
BASER BEARS
BRAES SABER
SABRE
BARESARK S
BAREST
BASTER
BREAST
TABERS
BARF S
BARFED
BARFING
BARFLIES
BARFLY
BARFS
BARGAIN S
BARGAINS
BARGE DES
BARGED
BADGER
GARBED
BARGEE S
BAREGE
BARGEES
BAREGES
BARGELLO S
BARGEMAN
BARGEMEN
BARGES
BARGHEST S
BARGING
GARBING
BARGUEST S
BARHOP S
BARHOPS
BARIC
RABIC
BARILLA S
BARILLAS
BARING
BARISTA S
BARISTAS
BARITE S
BAITER
REBAIT
TERBIA
BARITES
BAITERS
REBAITS
TERBIAS
BARITONE S
OBTAINER
REOBTAIN
TABORINE
BARIUM S
BARIUMS
BARK SY
KBAR
BARKED
BRAKED
DEBARK
BARKEEP S
PREBAKE
BARKEEPS
PREBAKES
BARKER S
BARKERS
BARKIER
BRAKIER
BARKIEST
BRAKIEST
BARKING
BRAKING
BARKLESS
BARKS
KBARS
BARKY
BRAKY
BARLEDUC S
BARLESS
BRALESS
BARLEY S
BARELY
BLEARY
BARLEYS
BARLOW S
BARLOWS
BARM SY
BARMAID S
BARMAIDS
BARMAN
BARMEN
BARMIE R
BARMIER
BARMIEST
BARMS
BARMY
AMBRY
BARN SY
BRAN
BARNACLE DS
BALANCER
BARNED
BANDER
BARNEY S
NEARBY
BARNEYS
BARNIER
BARNIEST
BANISTER
BARNING
BARNLIKE
BARNS
BRANS
BARNY
BARNYARD S
BAROGRAM S
BARON GSY
BARONAGE S
BARONESS
BARONET S
REBOANT
BARONETS
BARONG S
BROGAN
BARONGS
BROGANS
BARONIAL
BARONIES
SEAROBIN
BARONNE S
BARONNES
BARONS
BARONY
BARYON
BAROQUE S
BAROQUES
BAROSAUR S
BAROUCHE S
BARQUE S
BARQUES
BARRABLE
BARRACK S
BARRACKS
BARRAGE DS
BARRAGED
BARRAGES
BARRANCA S
BARRANCO S
BARRATER S
BARRATOR S
BARRATRY
BARRE DLNST
BARER REBAR
BARRED
BARREL S
BARRELED
BARRELS
BARREN S
BARRENER
BARRENLY
BARRENS
BARRES
REBARS
BARRET S
BARTER
BARRETOR S
BARRETRY
BARRETS
BARTERS
BARRETTE S
BATTERER
BERRETTA
BARRIER S
BARRIERS
BARRING
BARRIO S
BARRIOS
BARROOM S
BARROOMS
BARROW S
BARROWS
K BARS
ARBS BRAS
BARSTOOL S
TOOLBARS
BARTEND S
BARTENDS
BARTER S
BARRET
BARTERED
BARTERER S
BARTERS
BARRETS
BARTISAN S
BARTIZAN S
BARWARE S
BARWARES
BARYE S
YERBA
BARYES
YERBAS
BARYON S
BARONY
BARYONIC
BARYONS
BARYTA S
BARYTAS
BARYTE S
BETRAY
BARYTES
BETRAYS
BARYTIC
BARYTON ES
BARYTONE S
BARYTONS
AO BAS EHKST
ABS
SAB
BASAL T
ALBAS BAALS
BALAS BALSA
SABAL
BASALLY
SALABLY
BASALT S
TABLAS
BASALTES
BASALTIC
CABALIST
BASALTS
BASCULE S
BASCULES
SUBSCALE
A BASE DRS
SABE
BASEBALL S
BASEBORN
A BASED
BEADS SABED
BASELESS
BASELINE RS
BASELY
BELAYS
BASEMAN
BASEMEN T
BEMEANS
BENAMES
A BASEMENT S
BASENESS
BASENJI S
BASENJIS
A BASER
BARES BEARS
BRAES SABER
SABRE
A BASES T
SABES
BASEST
BASSET
BASTES
BEASTS
A BASH
BASHAW S
BASHAWS
A BASHED
BASHER S
REHABS
BASHERS
BRASHES
A BASHES
BASHFUL
A BASHING S
BASHINGS
BASHLYK S

BASHLYKS
BASIC S
BASICITY
BASICS
BASIDIA L
BASIDIAL
BASIDIUM
BASIFIED
BASIFIER S
BASIFIES
BASIFY
BASIL S
BAILS
BASILAR Y
BASILARY
BASILECT S
BASILIC A
BASILICA EL NS
BASILISK S
BASILS
BASIN GS
NABIS SABIN
BASINAL
BASINED
BANDIES
BASINET S
BANTIES
BASINETS
BASSINET
BASINFUL S
A BASING
BASINS
SABINS
BASION S
BONSAI
BASIONS
BASIS
BASSI ISBAS
BASK S
KABS
BASKED
BASKET S
BASKETRY
BASKETS
BASKING
BAKINGS
BASKS
BASMATI S
BASMATIS
BASOPHIL ES
BASQUE S
BASQUES
BASS IOY
SABS
BASSES
BASSET ST
BASEST
BASTES
BEASTS
BASSETED
BESTEADS
BASSETS
BASSETT S
BASSETTS
BASSI
BASIS ISBAS
BASSINET S
BASINETS
BASSIST S
BASSISTS
BASSLY
BYSSAL
BASSNESS
BASSO S
SOBAS
BASSOON S
BASSOONS
BASSOS
BASSWOOD S
BASSY
ABYSS
BAST ES
BATS STAB
TABS
BASTARD SY
TABARDS
BASTARDS
BASTARDY

BASTE DRS
ABETS BATES
BEAST BEATS
BETAS TABES
BASTED
BASTER S
BAREST
BREAST
TABERS
BASTERS
BREASTS
BASTES
BASEST
BASSET
BEASTS
BASTILE S
ABLEIST
ALBITES
ASTILBE
BESTIAL
BLASTIE
STABILE
BASTILES
ABLEISTS
ASTILBES
BLASTIES
STABILES
BASTILLE S
LISTABLE
BASTING S
BASTINGS
BASTION S
BONITAS
OBTAINS
BASTIONS
ANTIBOSS
BASTS
STABS
BAT EHST
TAB
BATBOY S
BATBOYS
BOBSTAY
BATCH
BATCHED
BATCHER S
BRACHET
BATCHERS
BRACHETS
BATCHES
BATCHING
A BATE DS
ABET BEAT
BETA
BATEAU X
BATEAUX
A BATED
A BATES
ABETS BASTE
BEAST BEATS
BETAS TABES
BATFISH
BATFOWL S
BATFOWLS
BATGIRL S
BATGIRLS
BATH ES
BAHT
BATHE DRS
BATHED
BATHER S
BERTHA
BREATH
BATHERS
BERTHAS
BREATHS
BATHES
BATHETIC
BATHING
BATHLESS
BATHMAT S
BATHMATS
BATHOS
BATHOSES
BATHROBE S
BATHROOM S
BATHS
BAHTS
BATHTUB S
BATHTUBS
BATHYAL

BATIK S
BATIKED
BATIKING
BATIKS
A BATING
BATISTE S
BISTATE
BATISTES
BATLIKE
BATMAN
BANTAM
BATMEN
BATON S
BATONS
BATS
BAST STAB
TABS
BATSMAN
BANTAMS
BATSMEN
BATT SUY
BATTALIA S
BATTEAU X
BATTEAUX
BATTED
BATTEN S
BATTENED
BATTENER S
BATTENS
BATTER SY
BATTERED
BATTERER S
BARRETTE
BERRETTA
BATTERIE S
BATTERS
BATTERY
BATTIER
BIRETTA
BATTIEST
BATTIK S
BATTIKS
BATTING S
BATTINGS
BATTLE DRS
TABLET
BATTLED
BLATTED
BATTLER S
BLATTER
BRATTLE
BATTLERS
BLATTERS
BRATTLES
BATTLES
TABLETS
BATTLING
BLATTING
BATTS
BATTU E
BATTUE S
TUBATE
BATTUES
BATTY
BATWING
BAUBEE S
BAUBEES
BAUBLE S
BUBALE
BAUBLES
BUBALES
BAUD S
DAUB
BAUDEKIN S
BAUDRONS
BAUDS
DAUBS
BAUHINIA S
BAULK SY
BAULKED
BAULKIER
BAULKING
BAULKS
BAULKY
BAUSOND
ABOUNDS
BAUXITE S
BAUXITES
BAUXITIC

BAWBEE S
BAWBEES
BAWCOCK S
BAWCOCKS
BAWD SY
BAWDIER
BAWDIES T
BAWDIEST
BAWDILY
BAWDRIC S
BAWDRICS
BAWDRIES
BAWDRY
BAWDS
BAWDY
BAWL S
BLAW
BAWLED
BLAWED
BAWLER S
WARBLE
BAWLERS
WARBLES
BAWLING
BLAWING
BAWLS
BLAWS
BAWSUNT
BAWTIE S
BAWTIES
BAWTY
BAY S
ABY
BAYADEER S
BAYADERE
BAYADERE S
BAYADEER
BAYAMO S
BAYAMOS
BAYARD S
BAYARDS
BAYBERRY
BAYED
BEADY
BAYING
ABYING
BAYMAN
BAYMEN
BYNAME
BAYONET S
BAYONETS
BAYOU S
BAYOUS
BAYS
ABYS
BAYWOOD S
BAYWOODS
BAZAAR S
BAZAARS
BAZAR S
BRAZA
BAZARS
BRAZAS
BAZOO S
BAZOOKA S
BAZOOKAS
BAZOOS
BDELLIUM S
O BE DEGLNSTY
BEACH Y
BEACHBOY S
BEACHED
BEACHES
BEACHIER
BEACHING
BEACHY
BEACON S
BEACONED
BEACONS
BEAD SY
ABED BADE
BEADED
BEADER S
BEADERS
DEBASER
SABERED
BEADIER
BEADIEST
DIABETES

BEADILY
BEADING S
BEADINGS
DEBASING
BEADLE S
BEADLES
BEADLIKE
BEADMAN
BEADMEN
BEDEMAN
BENAMED
BEADROLL S
BEADS
BASED SABED
BEADSMAN
BEADSMEN
BEDESMAN
BEADWORK S
BEADY
BAYED
BEAGLE S
GLEBAE
BEAGLES
BEAK SY
BAKE
BEAKED
DEBEAK
BEAKER S
BERAKE
BEAKERS
BERAKES
BEAKIER
BEAKIEST
BEAKLESS
BEAKLIKE
BEAKS
BAKES
BEAKY
A BEAM SY
BEMA MABE
BEAMED
BEAMIER
BEAMIEST
BEAMILY
BEAMING
BEAMISH
BEAMLESS
ASSEMBLE
BEAMLIKE
BEAMS
BEMAS MABES
BEAMY
EMBAY MAYBE
BEAN OS
BANE NABE
BEANBAG S
BEANBAGS
BEANBALL S
BEANED
BEANERY
BEANIE S
BEANIES
BEANING
BEANLIKE
BEANO S
BEANOS
BEANPOLE S
OPENABLE
BEANS
BANES NABES
BEAR DS
BARE BRAE
BEARABLE
BEARABLY
BEARCAT S
ABREACT
CABARET
BEARCATS
ABREACTS
CABARETS
CABRESTA
BEARD S
ARDEB BARDE
BARED BREAD
DEBAR
BEARDED
BREADED
DEBEARD
BEARDING
BREADING

BEARDS
ARDEBS
BARDES
BREADS
DEBARS
SABRED
SERDAB
BEARER S
BEARERS
BEARHUG S
BEARHUGS
BEARING S
BEARINGS
SABERING
BEARISH
BEARLIKE
BEARS
BARES BASER
BRAES SABER
SABRE
BEARSKIN S
BEARWOOD S
BEAST S
ABETS BASTE
BATES BEATS
BETAS TABES
BEASTIE S
BEASTIES
BEASTLY
BEASTS
BASEST
BASSET
BASTES
BEAT S
ABET BATE
BETA
BEATABLE
BEATEN
BEATER S
BERATE
REBATE
BEATERS
BERATES
REBATES
BEATIFIC
BEATIFY
BEATING S
BEATINGS
BEATLESS
BEATNIK S
BEATNIKS
SNAKEBIT
BEATS
ABETS BASTE
BATES BEAST
BETAS TABES
BEAU STX
BEAUCOUP S
BEAUISH
BEAUS
ABUSE
BEAUT SY
TUBAE
BEAUTIES
BEAUTIFY
BEAUTS
BEAUTY
BEAUX
BEAVER S
BEAVERED
BEREAVED
BEAVERS
BEBEERU S
BEBEERUS
BEBLOOD S
BEBLOODS
BEBOP S
BEBOPPER S
BEBOPS
BECALM S
BECALMED
BECALMS
BECAME
BECAP S
BECAPPED
BECAPS
BECARPET S
BECAUSE
BECHALK S

BECHALKS
BECHAMEL S
BECHANCE DS
BECHARM S
BRECHAM
CHAMBER
BECHARMS
BRECHAMS
CHAMBERS
BECK S
BECKED
BEDECK
BECKET S
BECKETS
BECKING
BECKON S
BECKONED
BECKONER S
BECKONS
BECKS
BECLAMOR S
BECLASP S
BECLASPS
BECLOAK S
BECLOAKS
BECLOG S
BECLOGS
BECLOTHE DS
BECLOUD S
BECLOUDS
BECLOWN S
BECLOWNS
BECOME S
BECOMES
BECOMING S
BECOWARD S
BECRAWL S
BECRAWLS
BECRIME DS
BECRIMED
BECRIMES
BECROWD S
BECROWDS
BECRUST S
BECURST
BECRUSTS
BECUDGEL S
BECURSE DS
BECURSED
BECURSES
BECURST
BECRUST
A BED SU
DEB
BEDABBLE DS
BEDAMN S
BADMEN
BEDAMNED
BEMADDEN
BEDAMNS
BEDARKEN S
BEDAUB S
BEDAUBED
BEDAUBS
BEDAZZLE DS
BEDBOARD S
BEDBUG S
BEDBUGS
BEDCHAIR S
BEDCOVER S
BEDDABLE
BEDDED
BEDDER S
BEDDERS
BEDDING S
BEDDINGS
BEDEAFEN S
BEDECK S
BECKED
BEDECKED
BEDECKS
BEDEL LS
BLEED
BEDELL S
BELLED
BEDELLS

BEDELS
BLEEDS
BEDEMAN
BEADMEN
BENAMED
BEDEMEN
BEDESMAN
BEADSMEN
BEDESMEN
BEDEVIL S
BEDEVILS
BEDEW S
DWEEB
BEDEWED
BEDEWING
BEWINGED
BEDEWS
DWEEBS
BEDFAST
BEDFRAME S
BEDGOWN S
BEDGOWNS
BEDIAPER S
BEDIGHT S
BIGHTED
BEDIGHTS
BEDIM S
IMBED
BEDIMMED
BEDIMPLE DS
BEDIMS
IMBEDS
BEDIRTY
BEDIZEN S
BEDIZENS
BEDLAM PS
AMBLED
BELDAM
BLAMED
LAMBED
BEDLAMP S
BEDLAMPS
BEDLAMS
BELDAMS
BEDLESS
BLESSED
BEDLIKE
BEDMAKER S
EMBARKED
BEDMATE S
BEDMATES
BEDOTTED
BEDOUIN S
BEDOUINS
BEDPAN S
BEDPANS
BEDPLATE S
BEDPOST S
BEDPOSTS
BEDQUILT S
BEDRAIL S
BRAILED
RIDABLE
BEDRAILS
DISABLER
BEDRAPE DS
PREBADE
BEDRAPED
BEDRAPES
BESPREAD
BEDRENCH
BEDRID
BIDDER
BIRDED
BEDRIVEL S
BEDROCK S
BEDROCKS
BEDROLL S
BEDROLLS
BEDROOM S
BOREDOM
BROOMED
BEDROOMS
BOREDOMS
BEDRUG S
BUDGER
REDBUG
BEDRUGS
BUDGERS
REDBUGS

BEDS
DEBS
BEDSHEET S
BEDSIDE S
BEDSIDES
BEDSIT S
BIDETS
DEBITS
BEDSITS
BEDSONIA S
BEDSORE S
SOBERED
BEDSORES
BEDSTAND S
BEDSTEAD S
BEDSTRAW S
BEDTICK S
BEDTICKS
BEDTIME S
BEDTIMES
BEMISTED
BEDU
BEDUIN S
BEDUINS
BEDUMB S
BEDUMBED
BEDUMBS
BEDUNCE DS
BEDUNCED
BEDUNCES
BEDWARD S
BEDWARDS
BEDWARF S
BEDWARFS
BEE FNPRST
BEEBEE S
BEEBEES
BEEBREAD S
BEECH Y
BEECHEN
BEECHES
BESEECH
BEECHIER
BEECHNUT S
BEECHY
BEEDI
BEEDIES
BEEF SY
FEEB
BEEFALO S
BEEFALOS
BEEFCAKE S
BEEFED
BEEFIER
FREEBIE
BEEFIEST
BEEFILY
BEEFING
BEEFLESS
BEEFS
FEEBS
BEEFWOOD S
BEEFY
BEEHIVE S
BEEHIVES
BEELIKE
BEELINE DS
BEELINED
BEELINES
BEEN
BENE
BEEP S
BEEPED
BEEPER S
BEEPERS
BEEPING
BEEPS
BEER SY
BREE
BEERIER
BEERIEST
BEERS
BREES
BEERY
BEES
BEESWAX
BEESWING S

BEET S
BEETLE DRS
BEETLED
BEETLER S
BEETLERS
BEETLES
BEETLING
BEETROOT S
BEETS
BESET
BEEVES
BEEYARD S
BEEYARDS
BEEZER S
BREEZE
BEEZERS
BREEZES
BEFALL S
BEFALLEN
BEFALLS
BEFELL
BEFINGER S
BEFRINGE
BEFIT S
BEFITS
BEFITTED
BEFLAG S
BEFLAGS
BEFLEA S
BEFLEAED
FEEDABLE
BEFLEAS
BEFLECK S
BEFLECKS
BEFLOWER S
BEFOG S
BEFOGGED
BEFOGS
BEFOOL S
BEFOOLED
BEFOOLS
BEFORE
BEFOUL S
BEFOULED
BEFOULER S
BEFOULS
BEFRET S
BEREFT
BEFRETS
BEFRIEND S
BEFRINGE DS
BEFINGER
BEFUDDLE DS
BEG S
BEGALL S
BEGALLED
GABELLED
BEGALLS
BEGAN
BEGAT
BEGAZE DS
BEGAZED
BEGAZES
BEGAZING
BEGET S
BEGETS
BEGETTER S
BEGGAR SY
BAGGER
BEGGARED
BEGGARLY
BEGGARS
BAGGERS
BEGGARY
BEGGED
A BEGGING
BEGIN S
BEING BINGE
BEGINNER S
BEGINS
BEINGS
BINGES
BEGIRD S
BRIDGE
BEGIRDED
BEGIRDLE DS
BEGIRDS
BRIDGES

BEGIRT
BEGLAD S
GABLED
BEGLADS
BEGLAMOR S
BEGLOOM S
BEGLOOMS
BEGONE
BEGONIA S
BEGONIAS
BEGORAH
BEGORRA H
BEGORRAH
BEGOT
BEGOTTEN
BEGRIM ES
BEGRIME DS
BEGRIMED
BEGRIMES
BEGRIMS
BEGROAN S
BEGROANS
BEGRUDGE DR
BUGGERED S
DEBUGGER
BEGS
BEGUILE DRS
BEGUILED
BEGUILER S
BEGUILES
BEGUINE S
BEGUINES
BEGULF S
BEGULFED
BEGULFS
BEGUM S
BEGUMS
BEGUN
BEHALF
BEHALVES
BEHAVE DRS
BEHAVED
BEHAVER S
BEHAVERS
BEHAVES
BEHAVING
BEHAVIOR S
BEHEAD S
BEHEADAL S
BEHEADED
BEHEADER S
BEHEADS
BEHELD
BEHEMOTH S
BEHEST S
THEBES
BEHESTS
BEHIND S
BEHINDS
BEHOLD S
BEHOLDEN
BEHOLDER S
BEHOLDS
BEHOOF
BEHOOVE DS
BEHOOVED
BEHOOVES
BEHOVE DS
BEHOVED
BEHOVES
BEHOVING
BEHOWL S
BEHOWLED
BEHOWLS
BEIGE S
BEIGES
BEIGNE ST
BEIGNES
BEIGNET S
BEIGNETS
BEIGY
BEING S
BEGIN BINGE

BEINGS
BEGINS
BINGES
BEJABERS
BEJEEZUS
BEJESUS
BEJEWEL S
BEJEWELS
BEJUMBLE DS
BEKISS
BEKISSED
BEKISSES
BEKNIGHT S
BEKNOT S
BEKNOTS
BEL LST
BELABOR S
BELABORS
SORBABLE
BELABOUR S
BELACED
DEBACLE
BELADIED
BELADIES
ABSEILED
BELADY
DYABLE
BELATED
BLEATED
BELAUD S
BELAUDED
BELAUDS
BELAY S
BELAYED
DYEABLE
BELAYER S
BELAYERS
BELAYING
BELAYS
BASELY
BELCH
BELCHED
BELCHER S
BELCHERS
BELCHES
BELCHING
BELDAM ES
AMBLED
BEDLAM
BLAMED
LAMBED
BELDAME S
BELDAMES
BELDAMS
BEDLAMS
BELEAP ST
BELEAPED
BELEAPS
BELEAPT
BELFRIED
BELFRIES
BELFRY
BELGA S
BAGEL GABLE
GLEBA
BELGAS
BAGELS
GABLES
BELIE DFRS
BELIED
EDIBLE
BELIEF S
BELIEFS
BELIER S
BELIERS
BELIES
BELIEVE DRS
BELIEVED
BELIEVER S
BELIEVES
BELIKE
BELIQUOR S
BELITTLE DR
S
BELIVE
BELL ESY
BELLBIRD S
BELLBOY S

BELLBOYS
BELLE DS
BELLED
BEDELL
BELLEEK S
BELLEEKS
BELLES
BELLHOP S
BELLHOPS
BELLIED
LIBELED
BELLIES
BELLING S
BELLINGS
BELLMAN
BELLMEN
BELLOW S
BELLOWED
BOWELLED
BELLOWER S
BELLOWS
BELLPULL S
BELLS
BELLWORT S
BELLY
BELLYFUL S
BELLYING
BELON GS
NOBLE
BELONG S
BELONGED
BELONGS
BELONS
NOBLES
BELOVED S
BELOVEDS
BELOW S
BOWEL ELBOW
BELOWS
BOWELS
ELBOWS
BELS
BELT S
BLET
BELTED
BELTER S
TREBLE
BELTERS
TREBLES
BELTING S
BELTINGS
BELTLESS
BELTLINE S
BELTS
BLEST BLETS
BELTWAY S
BELTWAYS
BELUGA S
BELUGAS
BELYING
BEMA S
BEAM MABE
BEMADAM S
BEMADAMS
BEMADDEN S
BEDAMNED
BEMAS
BEAMS MABES
BEMATA
BEMEAN S
BENAME
BEMEANED
BEMEANS
BASEMEN
BENAMES
BEMINGLE DS
BEMIRE DS
BERIME
BIREME
BEMIRED
BERIMED
BEMIRES
BERIMES
BIREMES
BEMIRING
BERIMING
BEMIST S
BEMISTED
BEDTIMES
BEMISTS

BEMIX T
BEMIXED
BEMIXES
BEMIXING
BEMIXT
BEMOAN S
BEMOANED
BEMOANS
AMBONES
BEMOCK S
BEMOCKED
BEMOCKS
BEMUDDLE DS
BEMURMUR S
BEMUSE DS
BEMUSED
BEMUSES
BEMUSING
MISBEGUN
BEMUZZLE DS
BEN DEST
NEB
BENADRYL S
BENAME DS
BEMEAN
BENAMED
BEADMEN
BEDEMAN
BENAMES
BASEMEN
BEMEANS
BENAMING
BENCH
BENCHED
BENCHER S
BENCHERS
BENCHES
BENCHING
BENCHTOP
BEND SY
BENDABLE
BENDAY S
BENDAYED
BENDAYS
BENDED
BENDEE S
BENDEES
BENDER S
BENDERS
BENDIER
INBREED
BENDIEST
BENDING
BENDS
BENDWAYS
BENDWISE
BENDY S
BENDYS
BENE S
BEEN
BENEATH
BENEDICK S
BENEDICT S
BENEFIC E
BENEFICE DS
BENEFIT S
BENEFITS
BENEMPT
BENES
BENIGN
BENIGNLY
BENISON S
BENISONS
BONINESS
BENJAMIN S
BENNE ST
BENNES
BENNET S
BENNETS
BENNI S
BENNIES
BENNIS
BENNY
BENOMYL S
BENOMYLS
BENS
NEBS

BENT OS
BENTHAL
BENTHIC
BITCHEN
BENTHON S
BENTHONS
BENTHOS
O **BENTO** S
BETON
O **BENTOS**
BETONS
BENTS
BENTWOOD S
BENUMB S
BENUMBED
BENUMBS
BENZAL
BENZENE S
BENZENES
BENZIDIN ES
BENZIN ES
BENZINE S
BENZINES
BENZINS
BENZOATE S
BENZOIC
BENZOIN S
BENZOINS
BENZOL ES
BENZOLE S
BENZOLES
BENZOLS
BENZOYL S
BENZOYLS
BENZYL S
BENZYLIC
BENZYLS
BEPAINT S
BEPAINTS
BEPIMPLE DS
BEQUEATH S
BEQUEST S
BEQUESTS
BERAKE DS
BEAKER
BERAKED
BERAKES
BEAKERS
BERAKING
BREAKING
BERASCAL S
BERATE DS
BEATER
REBATE
BERATED
DEBATER
REBATED
TABERED
BERATES
BEATERS
REBATES
BERATING
REBATING
TABERING
BERBERIN ES
BERBERIS
BERCEUSE S
BERDACHE S
BREACHED
BEREAVE DRS
BEREAVED
BEAVERED
BEREAVER S
BEREAVES
BEREFT
BEFRET
BERET S
BERETS
BERETTA S
ABETTER
BERETTAS
ABETTERS
BERG S
BERGAMOT S
BERGERE S
BERGERES
BERGS
BERHYME DS
BERHYMED
BERHYMES
BERIBERI S
BERIMBAU S
BERIME DS
BEMIRE
BIREME
BERIMED
BEMIRED
BERIMES
BEMIRES
BIREMES
BERIMING
BEMIRING
BERINGED
BREEDING
BERK S
KERB
BERKS
KERBS
BERLIN ES
BERLINE S
BERLINES
BERLINS
BERM ES
BERME DS
EMBER
BERMED
BERMES
EMBERS
BERMING
BERMS
BERMUDAS
BERNICLE S
BEROBED
BEROUGED
BERRETTA S
BARRETTE
BATTERER
BERRIED
BERRIES
BERRY
BERRYING
BERSEEM S
BERSEEMS
BERSERK S
BERSERKS
BERTH AS
BERTHA S
BATHER
BREATH
BERTHAS
BATHERS
BREATHS
BERTHED
BERTHING
BRIGHTEN
BERTHS
BERYL S
BERYLINE
BERYLS
O **BES** T
BESCORCH
BESCOUR S
OBSCURE
BESCOURS
OBSCURES
BESCREEN S
BESEECH
BEECHES
BESEEM S
BESEEMED
BESEEMS
BESES
BESET S
BEETS
BESETS
BESETTER S
BESHADOW S
BOWHEADS
BESHAME DS
BESHAMED
BESHAMES
BESHIVER S
BESHOUT S
BESHOUTS
BESHREW S
BESHREWS
BESHROUD S
BESIDE S
BESIDES
BESIEGE DRS
BESIEGED
BESIEGER S
BESIEGES
BESLAVED
BESLIME DS
BESMILE
BESLIMED
BESMILED
BESLIMES
BESMILES
BESMEAR S
AMBEERS
BESMEARS
BESMILE DS
BESLIME
BESMILED
BESLIMED
BESMILES
BESLIMES
BESMIRCH
BESMOKE DS
BESMOKED
EMBOSKED
BESMOKES
BESMOOTH S
BESMUDGE DS
BESMUT S
BESMUTS
BESNOW S
BESNOWED
BESNOWS
BESOM S
BESOMS
EMBOSS
BESOOTHE DS
BESOT S
BESOTS
BESOTTED
OBTESTED
BESOUGHT
BESPAKE
BESPEAK
BESPEAK S
BESPAKE
BESPEAKS
BESPOKE N
BESPOKEN
BESPOUSE DS
BESPREAD S
BEDRAPES
BESPRENT
BEST S
BETS
BESTEAD S
DEBATES
BESTEADS
BASSETED
BESTED
BESTIAL
ABLEIST
ALBITES
ASTILBE
BASTILE
BLASTIE
STABILE
BESTIARY
SYBARITE
BESTING
BESTIR S
BISTER
BISTRE
BITERS
TRIBES
BESTIRS
BISTERS
BISTRES
BESTOW S
BESTOWAL S
STOWABLE
TEABOWLS
BESTOWED
BESTOWER S
BESTOWS
BESTREW NS
WEBSTER
BESTREWN
BESTREWS
WEBSTERS
BESTRID E
BISTRED
BESTRIDE S
BISTERED
BESTRODE
BESTROW NS
BESTROWN
BROWNEST
BESTROWS
BESTS
BESTUD S
BUSTED
DEBUTS
BESTUDS
BESWARM S
BESWARMS
A **BET** AHS
BETA S
ABET BATE
BEAT
BETAINE S
BETAINES
BETAKE NS
BETAKEN
BETAKES
BETAKING
BETAS
ABETS BASTE
BATES BEAST
BEATS TABES
BETATRON S
BETATTER S
BETAXED
BETEL S
BETELNUT S
BETELS
BETH S
BETHANK S
BETHANKS
BETHEL S
BETHELS
BETHESDA S
BETHINK S
BETHINKS
BETHORN S
BETHORNS
BETHS
BETHUMP S
BETHUMPS
BETIDE DS
BETIDED
DEBITED
BETIDES
BETIDING
DEBITING
BETIME S
BETIMES
BETISE S
BETISES
BETOKEN S
BETOKENS
STEENBOK
BETON SY
BENTO
BETONIES
EBONITES
BETONS
BENTOS
BETONY
BETOOK
BETRAY S
BARYTE
BETRAYAL S
RATEABLY
BETRAYED
BETRAYER S
TEABERRY
BETRAYS
BARYTES
BETROTH S
BETROTHS
A **BETS**
BEST
BETTA S
BETTAS
A **BETTED**
A **BETTER** S
BETTERED
A **BETTERS**
A **BETTING**
A **BETTOR** S
A **BETTORS**
BETWEEN
BETWIXT
BEUNCLED
BEVATRON S
BEVEL S
BEVELED
BEVELER S
BEVELERS
BEVELING
BEVELLED
BEVELLER S
BEVELS
BEVERAGE S
BEVIES
BEVOMIT S
BEVOMITS
BEVOR S
BEVORS
BEVY
BEWAIL S
BEWAILED
BEWAILER S
BEWAILS
BEWARE DS
BEWARED
BEWARES
BEWARING
BEWEARY
BEWEEP S
BEWEEPS
BEWEPT
BEWIG S
BEWIGGED
BEWIGS
BEWILDER S
BEWINGED
BEDEWING
BEWITCH
BEWORM S
BEWORMED
BEWORMS
BEWORRY
BEWRAP ST
BEWRAPS
BEWRAPT
BEWRAY S
BEWRAYED
BEWRAYER S
BEWRAYS
O **BEY** S
BYE
BEYLIC S
BEYLICS
BEYLIK S
BEYLIKS
BEYOND S
BEYONDS
O **BEYS**
BYES
BEZANT S
BEZANTS
BEZAZZ
BEZAZZES
BEZEL S
BEZELS
BEZIL S
BEZILS
BEZIQUE S
BEZIQUES
BEZOAR S
BEZOARS
BEZZANT S
BEZZANTS
BHAKTA S
BHAKTAS
BHAKTI S
BHAKTIS
BHANG S
BHANGRA S
BHANGRAS
BHANGS
BHARAL S
BHARALS
BHEESTIE S
BHEESTY
BHISTIE S
BHISTIES
BHOOT S
BOOTH
BHOOTS
BOOTHS
BHUT S
BHUTS
O **BI** BDGNOSTZ
BIACETYL S
BIALI S
ALIBI
BIALIES
ALIBIES
BAILIES
BIALIS
ALIBIS
BIALY S
BIALYS
BIANNUAL
O **BIAS**
ISBA
BIASED
ABIDES
BIASEDLY
BIASES
BIASING
BIASNESS
BIASSED
BIASSES
BIASSING
BIATHLON S
BIAXAL
BIAXIAL
BIB BS
BIBASIC
BIBB S
BIBBED
BIBBER SY
BIBBERS
BIBBERY
BIBBING
BIBBS
BIBCOCK S
BIBCOCKS
BIBELOT S
BIBELOTS
BIBLE S
BIBLES S
BIBLESS
BIBLICAL
BIBLIKE
BIBLIST S
BIBLISTS
BIBS
SIBB
BIBULOUS
BICARB S
BICARBS
BICAUDAL
BICE PS
BICEP S
BICEPS
BICEPSES
I **BICES**
BICHROME
BICKER S
BICKERED
BICKERER S
BICKERS
BICOLOR S
BROCOLI
BICOLORS
BROCOLIS
BICOLOUR S
BICONVEX
BICORN ES
BICRON
BICORNE S
BICORNES
BICORNS
BICRONS
BICRON S
BICORN
BICRONS
BICORNS
BICUSPID S
BICYCLE DRS
BICYCLED
BICYCLER S
BICYCLES
BICYCLIC
BID EIS
DIB
BIDARKA S
BIDARKAS
BIDARKEE S
BIDDABLE
BIDDABLY
BIDDEN
BIDDER S
BEDRID
BIRDED
BIDDERS
BIDDIES
BIDDING S
BIDDINGS
BIDDY
A **BIDE** DRST
A **BIDED**
BIDENTAL
A **BIDER** S
BRIDE REBID
A **BIDERS**
BRIDES
DEBRIS
REBIDS
A **BIDES**
BIDET S
DEBIT
BIDETS
BEDSIT
DEBITS
BIDI S
A **BIDING**
BIDIS
BIDS
DIBS
BIELD S
BIELDED
BIELDING
BIELDS
BIENNALE S
BIENNIA L
BIENNIAL S
BIENNIUM S
BIER S
BRIE
BIERS
BIRSE BRIES
RIBES
BIFACE S
BIFACES
BIFACIAL
BIFF SY
BIFFED
BIFFIES
BIFFIN GS
BIFFING
BIFFINS
BIFFS
BIFFY
BIFID
BIFIDITY
BIFIDLY
BIFILAR
BIFLEX
BIFOCAL S
BIFOCALS
BIFOLD
BIFORATE
FIREBOAT
BIFORKED
BIFORM
BIFORMED
BIG S
GIB
BIGAMIES
BIGAMIST S
BIGAMOUS

BIGAMY
BIGARADE S
BIGAROON S
BIGEMINY
BIGEYE S
BIGEYES
BIGFEET
BIGFOOT S
BIGFOOTS
BIGGER
BIGGEST
BIGGETY
BIGGIE S
BIGGIES
BIGGIN GS
GIBING
BIGGING S
BIGGINGS
BIGGINS
BIGGISH
BIGGITY
BIGGY
BIGHEAD S
BIGHEADS
BIGHORN S
BIGHORNS
BIGHT S
BIGHTED
BEDIGHT
BIGHTING
BIGHTS
BIGLY
BILGY
BIGMOUTH S
BIGNESS
BIGNONIA S
BIGOS
BIOGS
BIGOSES
BIGOT S
BIGOTED
BIGOTRY
BIGOTS
BIGS
GIBS
BIGSTICK
BIGTIME
BIGWIG S
BIGWIGS
BIHOURLY
BIJOU SX
BIJOUS
BIJOUX
BIJUGATE
BIJUGOUS
BIKE DRS
KIBE
BIKED
BIKER S
BIKERS
BIKES
KIBES
BIKEWAY S
BIKEWAYS
BIKIE S
KIBEI
BIKIES
KIBEIS
BIKING
BIKINI S
BIKINIED
BIKINIS
BILABIAL S
BILANDER S
BILAYER S
BILAYERS
BILBERRY
BILBIES
BILBO AS
BILBOA S
BILBOAS
BILBOES
LOBBIES
BILBOS
BILBY
BILE S
BILES
BILEVEL S
BILEVELS
BILGE DS
BILGED
BILGES
BILGIER
BILGIEST
BILGING
BILGY
BIGLY
BILIARY
BILINEAR
BILIOUS
BILK S
BILKED
BILKER S
BILKERS
BILKING
BILKS
BILL SY
BILLABLE
BILLBUG S
BILLBUGS
BILLED
BILLER S
REBILL
BILLERS
REBILLS
BILLET S
BILLETED
BILLETER S
BILLETS
BILLFISH
BILLFOLD S
BILLHEAD S
BILLHOOK S
BILLIARD S
BILLIE S
BILLIES
BILLING S
BILLINGS
BILLION S
BILLIONS
BILLON S
BILLONS
BILLOW SY
BILLOWED
BILLOWS
BILLOWY
BILLS
BILLY
BILLYCAN S
BILOBATE D
BILOBED
LOBBIED
BILSTED S
BILSTEDS
BILTONG S
BOLTING
BILTONGS
BIMA HS
IAMB
BIMAH S
BIMAHS
BIMANOUS
BIMANUAL
BIMAS
IAMBS
BIMBETTE S
BIMBO S
BIMBOES
BIMBOS
BIMENSAL
BAILSMEN
BIMESTER S
BIMETAL S
LIMBATE
TIMBALE
BIMETALS
BALMIEST
LAMBIEST
TIMBALES
BIMETHYL S
BIMODAL
BIMORPH S
BIMORPHS
BIN DEST
NIB
BINAL
BLAIN
BINARIES
BINARISM S
MINIBARS
BINARY
BRAINY
BINATE
BINATELY
BINAURAL
BIND IS
BINDABLE
BINDER SY
BRINED
INBRED
REBIND
BINDERS
INBREDS
REBINDS
BINDERY
BINDI S
BINDING S
BINDINGS
BINDIS
BINDLE S
BINDLES
BINDS
BINDWEED S
BINE RS
BINER S
BRINE
BINERS
BRINES
BINES
BINGE DRS
BEGIN BEING
BINGED
BINGEING
BINGER S
BINGERS
BINGES
BEGINS
BEINGS
BINGING
BINGO S
BOING
BINGOES
BIOGENS
BINGOS
BOINGS
GIBSON
BINIT S
BINITS
BINNACLE S
BINNED
BINNING
BINOCLE S
BINOCLES
BINOCS
BINOMIAL S
BINS
NIBS SNIB
BINT S
BINTS
BIO GS
OBI
BIOASSAY S
BIOCHIP S
BIOCHIPS
BIOCIDAL
DIABOLIC
BIOCIDE S
BIOCIDES
BIOCLEAN
COINABLE
BIOCYCLE S
BIOETHIC S
BIOFILM S
BIOFILMS
BIOFUEL S
BIOFUELS
BIOG S
BIOGAS
BIOGASES
BIOGEN SY
A BIOGENIC
BIOGENS
BINGOES
BIOGENY
OBEYING
BIOGS
BIGOS
BIOHERM S
BIOHERMS
BIOLOGIC S
BIOLOGY
BIOLYSES
BIOLYSIS
BIOLYTIC
BIOMASS
BIOME S
BIOMES
BIOMETER S
BIOMETRY
BIOMORPH S
BIONIC S
NIOBIC
BIONICS
BIONOMIC S
BIONOMY
BIONT S
BIONTIC
BIONTS
BIOPIC S
BIOPICS
BIOPSIC
BIOPLASM S
BIOPSIC
BIOPICS
BIOPSIED
BIOPSIES
BIOPSY
BIOPTIC
BIOS
OBIS
BIOSCOPE S
BIOSCOPY
BIOSOLID S
BIOTA S
BIOTAS
BIOTECH S
BIOTECHS
A BIOTIC S
BIOTICAL
BIOTICS
BIOTIN S
BIOTINS
BIOTITE S
BIOTITES
BIOTITIC
BIOTOPE S
BIOTOPES
BIOTOXIN S
BIOTRON S
BIOTRONS
BIOTYPE S
BIOTYPES
BIOTYPIC
BIOVULAR
BIPACK S
BIPACKS
BIPAROUS
BIPARTED
BIPARTY
BIPED S
BIPEDAL
PIEBALD
BIPEDS
BIPHASIC
BIPHENYL S
BIPLANE S
BIPLANES
BIPOD S
BIPODS
BIPOLAR
PARBOIL
BIRACIAL
BIRADIAL
BIRAMOSE
BIRAMOUS
BIRCH
BIRCHED
BIRCHEN
BIRCHES
BIRCHING
BIRD S
DRIB
BIRDBATH S
BIRDCAGE S
BIRDCALL S
BIRDDOG S
BIRDDOGS
BIRDED
BEDRID
BIDDER
BIRDER S
BIRRED
BIRDERS
BIRDFARM S
BIRDFEED S
BIRDIE DS
BIRDIED
BIRDIES
BIRDING S
BIRDINGS
BIRDLIFE
BIRDLIKE
BIRDLIME DS
BIRDMAN
BIRDMEN
BIRDS
DRIBS
BIRDSEED S
DEBRIDES
BIRDSEYE S
BIRDSHOT
BIRDSONG S
SONGBIRD
BIREME S
BEMIRE
BERIME
BIREMES
BEMIRES
BERIMES
BIRETTA S
BATTIER
BIRETTAS
BIRIANI S
BIRIANIS
BIRK S
BIRKIE S
BIRKIES
BIRKS
BRISK
BIRL ES
BIRLE DRS
LIBER
BIRLED
BRIDLE
BIRLER S
BIRLERS
BIRLES
LIBERS
BIRLING S
BIRLINGS
BRISLING
BIRLS
BIRO S
BRIO
BIROS
BRIOS
BIRR S
BIRRED
BIRDER
BIRRETTA S
BRATTIER
BIRRING
BIRROTCH
BIRRS
BIRSE S
BIERS BRIES
RIBES
BIRSES
BRISES
BIRTH S
BRITH
BIRTHDAY S
BIRTHED
BIRTHING S
BIRTHS
BRITHS
BIRYANI S
BIRYANIS
IO BIS EK
SIB
BISCOTTI
BISCOTTO
BISCUIT SY
BISCUITS
BISCUITY
BISE S
BISECT S
BISECTED
BISECTOR S
BISECTS
I BISES
BISEXUAL S
BISHOP S
BISHOPED
BISHOPS
BISK S
BISKS
BISMUTH S
BISMUTHS
BISNAGA S
ABASING
BISNAGAS
BISON S
BISONS
BISQUE S
BISQUES
BISTATE
BATISTE
BISTER S
BESTIR
BISTRE
BITERS
TRIBES
BISTERED
BESTRIDE
BISTERS
BESTIRS
BISTRES
BISTORT S
BISTORTS
BISTOURY
BISTRE DS
BESTIR
BISTER
BITERS
TRIBES
BISTRED
BESTRID
BISTRES
BESTIRS
BISTERS
BISTRO S
ORBITS
BISTROIC
BISTROS
O BIT EST
BITABLE
BITCH Y
BITCHED
BITCHEN
BENTHIC
BITCHERY
BITCHES
BITCHIER
BITCHILY
BITCHING
BITCHY
BITE RS
BITEABLE
BITER S
TRIBE
BITERS
BESTIR
BISTER
BISTRE
TRIBES
BITES
BITEWING S
BITING
BITINGLY
BITMAP S
BITMAPS
BAPTISM
O BITS Y
BITSIER
BITSIEST
BITSTOCK S
BITTOCKS
BITSY
BITT SY
BITTED
BITTEN
BITTER NS
BITTERED
BITTERER
BITTERLY
BITTERN S
BITTERNS
BITTERS
BITTIER
BITTIEST
BITTING S
BITTINGS
BITTOCK S
BITTOCKS
BITSTOCK
BITTS
BITTY
BITUMEN S
BITUMENS
BIUNIQUE
BIVALENT S
BIVALVE DS
BIVALVED
BIVALVES
BIVINYL S
BIVINYLS
BIVOUAC S
BIVOUACS
BIWEEKLY
BIYEARLY
BIZ E
BIZARRE S
BRAZIER
BIZARRES
BRAZIERS
BIZARRO S
BIZARROS
BIZE S
BIZES
BIZNAGA S
BIZNAGAS
BIZONAL
BIZONE S
BIZONES
BIZZES
BLAB S
BLABBED
BABBLED
BLABBER S
BABBLER
BRABBLE
BLABBERS
BABBLERS
BRABBLES
BLABBING
BABBLING
BLABBY
BLABS
BLACK S
BLACKBOY S
BLACKCAP S
BLACKED
BLACKEN S
BLACKENS
BLACKER
BLACKEST
BLACKFIN S
BLACKFLY
BLACKGUM S
BLACKING S
BLACKISH
BLACKLEG S
BLACKLY
BLACKOUT S
BLACKS
BLACKTOP S
BLADDER SY
BLADDERS
BLADDERY

BLADE DRS
ABLED BALED
BLADED
BALDED
BLADER S
BALDER
BLARED
BLADERS
BLADES
BLADING S
BALDING
BLADINGS
BLAE
ABLE BALE
BLAFF S
BLAFFS
BLAGGING S
BLAH S
BLAHS
BLAIN S
BINAL
BLAINS
ABLINS
BLAM ES
BALM LAMB
BLAMABLE
BLAMABLY
BLAME DRS
AMBLE
BLAMED
AMBLED
BEDLAM
BELDAM
LAMBED
BLAMEFUL
BLAMER S
AMBLER
LAMBER
MARBLE
RAMBLE
BLAMERS
AMBLERS
LAMBERS
MARBLES
RAMBLES
BLAMES
AMBLES
BLAMING
AMBLING
LAMBING
BLAMS
BALMS LAMBS
BLANCH
BLANCHED
BLANCHER S
BLANCHES
BLAND
BLANDER
BLANDEST
BLANDISH
BLANDLY
BLANK S
BLANKED
BLANKER
BLANKEST
BLANKETS
BLANKET S
BLANKETS
BLANKEST
BLANKING
BLANKLY
BLANKS
BLARE DS
ABLER BALER
BLEAR
BLARED
BALDER
BLADER
BLARES
BALERS
BLEARS
BLARING
BLARNEY S
BLARNEYS
BLASE
ABLES BALES
SABLE
O BLAST SY
BLATS
BLASTED
BALDEST
STABLED

BLASTEMA LS
LAMBASTE
BLASTER S
LABRETS
STABLER
BLASTERS
STABLERS
BLASTIE RS
ABLEIST
ALBITES
ASTILBE
BASTILE
BESTIAL
STABILE
BLASTIER
LIBRATES
BLASTIES T
ABLEISTS
ASTILBES
BASTILES
STABILES
BLASTING S
STABLING
BLASTOFF S
BLASTOMA S
O BLASTS
BLASTULA ER S
BLASTY
STABLY
BLAT ES
BLATANCY
BLATANT
AO BLATE
BLEAT TABLE
BLATHER S
HALBERT
BLATHERS
HALBERTS
BLATS
BLAST
BLATTED
BATTLED
BLATTER S
BATTLER
BRATTLE
BLATTERS
BATTLERS
BRATTLES
BLATTING
BATTLING
BLAUBOK S
BLAUBOKS
BLAW NS
BAWL
BLAWED
BAWLED
BLAWING
BAWLING
BLAWN
BLAWS
BAWLS
A BLAZE DRS
BLAZED
BLAZER S
BLAZERED
BLAZERS
BLAZES
BLAZING
BLAZON S
BLAZONED
BLAZONER S
BLAZONRY
BLAZONS
BLEACH
BLEACHED
BLEACHER S
BLEACHES
BLEAK S
BLEAKER
BLEAKEST
BLEAKISH
BLEAKLY
BLEAKS
BLEAR SY
ABLER BALER
BLARE
BLEARED
BLEARIER
BLEARILY
RELIABLY

BLEARING
BLEARS
BALERS
BLARES
BLEARY
BARELY
BARLEY
BLEAT S
BLATE TABLE
BLEATED
BELATED
BLEATER S
RETABLE
BLEATERS
ARBELEST
RESTABLE
RETABLES
BLEATING
TANGIBLE
BLEATS
ABLEST
STABLE
TABLES
BLEB S
BLEBBING S
BLEBBY
BLEBS
A BLED
BLEED S
BEDEL
BLEEDER S
BLEEDERS
BLEEDING S
BLEEDS
BEDELS
BLEEP S
PLEBE
BLEEPED
BLEEPER S
BLEEPERS
BLEEPING
BLEEPS
PLEBES
BLELLUM S
BLELLUMS
BLEMISH
BLENCH
BLENCHED
BLENCHER S
BLENCHES
BLEND ES
BLENDE DRS
BLENDED
BLENDER S
REBLEND
BLENDERS
REBLENDS
BLENDES
BLENDING
BLENDS
BLENNIES
BLENNY
BLENT
BLESBOK S
BLESBOKS
BLESBUCK S
BLESS
BLESSED
BEDLESS
BLESSER S
BLESSERS
BLESSES
BLESSING S
GLIBNESS
A BLEST
BELTS BLETS
BLET S
BELT
BLETHER S
BLETHERS
BLETS
BELTS BLEST
BLEW
BLIGHT SY
BLIGHTED
BLIGHTER S
BLIGHTS
BLIGHTY
BLIMEY
BLIMP S

BLIMPISH
BLIMPS
BLIMY
LIMBY
BLIN DIK
BLIND S
BLINDAGE S
BLINDED
BLINDER S
BRINDLE
BLINDERS
BRINDLES
BLINDEST
BLINDGUT S
BLINDING
BLINDLY
BLINDS
BLINI S
BLINIS
BLINK S
BLINKARD S
BLINKED
BLINKER S
BLINKERS
BLINKING
BLINKS
BLINTZ E
BLINTZE S
BLINTZES
BLIP S
BLIPPED
BLIPPING
BLIPS
BLISS
BLISSED
BLISSES
BLISSFUL
BLISSING
SIBLINGS
BLISTER SY
BRISTLE
RIBLETS
BLISTERS
BRISTLES
BLISTERY
BLITE S
BLITES
BLITHE R
BLITHELY
BLITHER S
BLITHERS
BLITHEST
BLITZ
BLITZED
BLITZER S
BLITZERS
BLITZES
BLITZING
BLIZZARD SY
BLOAT S
BLOATED
LOBATED
BLOATER S
BLOATERS
SORTABLE
STORABLE
BLOATING
BLOATS
OBLAST
BLOB S
BLOBBED
BOBBLED
BLOBBING
BOBBLING
BLOBS
BLOC KS
BLOCK SY
BLOCKADE DR S
BLOCKAGE S
BLOCKED
BLOCKER S
BLOCKERS
BLOCKIER
BLOCKING
BLOCKISH
BLOCKS

BLOCKY
BLOCS
BLOG S
GLOB
BLOGGER S
BOGGLER
BLOGGERS
BOGGLERS
BLOGGING S
BOGGLING
BLOGS
GLOBS
BLOKE S
BLOKES
BLOND ES
BLONDE RS
BLONDER
BLONDES T
BLONDEST
BLONDINE DS
BLONDISH
BLONDS
BLOOD SY
BLOODED
BOODLED
BLOODFIN S
BLOODIED
BLOODIER
BLOODIES T
BLOODILY
BLOODING S
BOODLING
BLOODRED
BLOODS
BLOODY
BLOOEY
BLOOIE
A BLOOM SY
BLOOMED
BLOOMER SY
REBLOOM
BLOOMERS
REBLOOMS
BLOOMERY
BLOOMIER
BLOOMING
BLOOMS
BLOOMY
BLOOP S
BLOOPED
BLOOPER S
BLOOPERS
BLOOPING
BLOOPS
BLOSSOM SY
BLOSSOMS
BLOSSOMY
BLOT S
BOLT
BLOTCH Y
BLOTCHED
BLOTCHES
BLOTCHY
BLOTLESS
BOLTLESS
BLOTS
BOLTS
BLOTTED
BOTTLED
BLOTTER S
BOTTLER
BLOTTERS
BOTTLERS
BLOTTIER
LIBRETTO
BLOTTING
BOTTLING
BLOTTO
BLOTTY
BLOUSE DS
BOULES
OBELUS
BLOUSED
DOUBLES
BLOUSES
BOLUSES
BLOUSIER
BLOUSILY
BLOUSING

BLOUSON S
BLOUSONS
BLOUSY
BLOVIATE DS
BLOW NSY
BOWL
BLOWBACK S
BLOWBALL S
BLOWBY S
WOBBLY
BLOWBYS
BLOWDOWN S
BLOWED
BOWLED
BLOWER S
BOWLER
BLOWERS
BOWLERS
BLOWFISH
FISHBOWL
BLOWFLY
FLYBLOW
BLOWGUN S
BLOWGUNS
BLOWHARD S
BLOWHOLE S
BLOWIER
BLOWIEST
BLOWING
BOWLING
BLOWN
BLOWOFF S
BLOWOFFS
BLOWOUT S
BLOWOUTS
BLOWPIPE S
BLOWS Y
BOWLS
BLOWSED
BLOWSIER
BLOWSILY
BLOWSY
BLOWTUBE S
BLOWUP S
BLOWUPS
BLOWY
BLOWZED
BLOWZIER
BLOWZILY
BLOWZY
BLUB S
BULB
BLUBBED
BUBBLED
BLUBBER SY
BUBBLER
BLUBBERS
BUBBLERS
BLUBBERY
BLUBBING
BUBBLING
BLUBS
BULBS
BLUCHER S
BLUCHERS
BLUDGE DRS
BUGLED
BULGED
BLUDGED
BLUDGEON S
BLUDGER S
BURGLED
BLUDGERS
BLUDGES
BLUDGING
BLUE DRSTY
LUBE
BLUEBALL S
BLUEBEAT S
BLUEBELL S
BLUEBILL S
BLUEBIRD S
BLUEBOOK S
BLUECAP S
BLUECAPS
BLUECOAT S
BLUED
LUBED
BLUEFIN S

BLUEFINS
BLUEFISH
BLUEGILL S
GULLIBLE
BLUEGUM S
BLUEGUMS
BLUEHEAD S
BLUEING S
BLUEINGS
BLUEISH
BLUEJACK S
BLUEJAY S
BLUEJAYS
BLUELINE RS
BLUELY
BLUENESS
BLUENOSE DS
NEBULOSE
BLUER
RUBEL RUBLE
BLUES TY
LUBES
BLUESIER
BLUESMAN
ALBUMENS
BLUESMEN
BLUEST
BLUETS
BUSTLE
BUTLES
SUBLET
SUBTLE
BLUESTEM S
BLUESY
BLUEYS
BLUET S
BUTLE
BLUETICK S
BLUETS
BLUEST
BUSTLE
BUTLES
SUBLET
SUBTLE
BLUEWEED S
BLUEWOOD S
BLUEY S
BLUEYS
BLUESY
BLUFF S
BLUFFED
BLUFFER S
BLUFFERS
BLUFFEST
BLUFFING
BLUFFLY
BLUFFS
BLUING S
LUBING
BLUINGS
BLUISH
BLUME DS
UMBEL
BLUMED
BLUMES
UMBELS
UMBLES
BLUMING
BLUNDER S
BUNDLER
BLUNDERS
BUNDLERS
BLUNGE DRS
BUNGLE
BLUNGED
BUNGLED
BLUNGER S
BUNGLER
BLUNGERS
BUNGLERS
BLUNGES
BUNGLES
BLUNGING
BUNGLING
BLUNT S
BLUNTED
BLUNTER
BLUNTEST
BLUNTING
BLUNTLY

BLUNTS
BLUR BST
BURL
BLURB S
BLURBED
BURBLED
RUBBLED
BLURBING
BURBLING
RUBBLING
BLURBIST S
BLURBS
BLURRED
BLURRIER
BLURRILY
BLURRING
BLURRY
BLURS
BURLS SLURB
BLURT S
BLURTED
BLURTER S
BLURTERS
BLURTING
BLURTS
A BLUSH
BUHLS SHLUB
BLUSHED
BLUSHER S
BLUSHERS
BLUSHES
BUSHELS
BLUSHFUL
BLUSHING
BLUSTER SY
BUSTLER
BUTLERS
SUBTLER
BLUSTERS
BUSTLERS
BLUSTERY
BLYPE S
BLYPES
A BO ABDGOPST WXY
BOA RST
OBA
BOAR DST
BORA
A BOARD S
BROAD DOBRA
BOARDED
ROADBED
BOARDER S
ARBORED
BROADER
REBOARD
BOARDERS
ADSORBER
REBOARDS
BOARDING S
BOARDMAN
BOARDMEN
BOARDS
ADSORB
BROADS
DOBRAS
BOARFISH
BOARISH
BOARS
BORAS
BOART S
ABORT TABOR
BOARTS
ABORTS
TABORS
BOAS T
OBAS SOBA
BOAST S
BOATS BOTAS
SABOT
BOASTED
BOASTER S
BOATERS
BORATES
REBATOS
SORBATE
BOASTERS
SORBATES
BOASTFUL
BOATFULS
BOASTING
BOATINGS
BOASTS
SABOTS
BOAT S
BOTA
BOATABLE
BOATBILL S
BOATED
BOATEL S
LOBATE
OBLATE
BOATELS
OBLATES
BOATER S
BORATE
REBATO
BOATERS
BOASTER
BORATES
REBATOS
SORBATE
BOATFUL S
BOATFULS
BOASTFUL
BOATHOOK S
BOATING S
BOATINGS
BOASTING
BOATLIFT S
BOATLIKE
BOATLOAD S
BOATMAN
BOATMEN
BOATNECK S
BOATS
BOAST BOTAS
SABOT
BOATSMAN
BOATSMEN
BOATYARD S
BOB S
BOBBED
BOBBER SY
BOBBERS
BOBBERY
BOBBIES
BOBBIN GS
BOBBINET S
BOBBING
BOBBINS
BOBBLE DS
BOBBLED
BLOBBED
BOBBLES
BOBBLING
BLOBBING
BOBBY
BOBBYSOX
BOBCAT S
BOBCATS
BOBECHE S
BOBECHES
BOBOLINK S
BOBS
BOBSLED S
BOBSLEDS
BOBSTAY S
BATBOYS
BOBSTAYS
BOBTAIL S
BOBTAILS
BOBWHITE S
BOCACCIO S
BOCCE S
BOCCES
BOCCI AES
BOCCIA S
BOCCIAS
BOCCIE S
BOCCIES
BOCCIS
BOCK S
BOCKS
BOD ESY
A BODE DS
A BODED
BODEGA S
BODEGAS
BODEMENT S
ENTOMBED
A BODES
BODHRAN S
BODHRANS
BODICE S
CEBOID
BODICES
CEBOIDS
BODIED
BODIES
DOBIES
BODILESS
BODILY
A BODING S
BODINGLY
BODINGS
BODKIN S
BODKINS
BODS
BODY
DOBY
BODYING
BODYSUIT S
BODYSURF S
BODYWORK S
BOEHMITE S
BOFF OS
BOFFIN S
BOFFINS
BOFFO S
BOFFOLA S
BOFFOLAS
BOFFOS
BOFFS
BOG SY
GOB
BOGAN S
GOBAN
BOGANS
GOBANS
BOGART S
BOGARTED
BOGARTS
BOGBEAN S
BOGBEANS
BOGEY S
BOGEYED
BOGEYING
BOGEYMAN
MONEYBAG
BOGEYMEN
BOGEYS
BOGGED
BOGGIER
BOGGIEST
BOGGING
BOGGISH
BOGGLE DRS
BOGGLED
BOGGLER S
BLOGGER
BOGGLERS
BLOGGERS
BOGGLES
BOGGLING
BLOGGING
BOGGY
BOGIE S
BOGIES
GOBIES
BOGLE S
GLOBE
BOGLES
GLOBES
BOGS
GOBS
BOGUS
BOGUSLY
BOGWOOD S
BOGWOODS
BOGY
GOBY
BOGYISM S
BOGYISMS
BOGYMAN
BOGYMEN
BOHEA S
OBEAH
BOHEAS
OBEAHS
BOHEMIA NS
BOHEMIAN S
BOHEMIAS
OBEAHISM
BOHO S
HOBO
BOHOS
HOBOS
BOHRIUM S
BOHRIUMS
A BOIL S
BOILABLE
BOILED
BOLIDE
BOILER S
REBOIL
BOILERS
REBOILS
BOILING
BOILOFF S
BOILOFFS
BOILOVER S
OVERBOIL
BOILS
BOING S
BINGO
BOINGS
BINGOS
GIBSON
BOISERIE S
BOITE S
BOITES
SOBEIT
TOBIES
BOLA RS
BOLAR
BORAL LABOR
LOBAR
BOLAS
BOLASES
BOLD S
BOLDER
BORDEL
BOLDEST
BOLDFACE DS
BOLDLY
BOLDNESS
BONDLESS
BOLDS
O BOLE S
LOBE
BOLERO S
BOLEROS
O BOLES
LOBES
BOLETE S
BOLETES
BOLETI
BOLETUS
BOLIDE S
BOILED
BOLIDES
BOLIVAR S
BOLIVARS
BOLIVIA S
BOLIVIAS
BOLL S
BOLLARD S
BOLLARDS
BOLLED
BOLLING
BOLLIX
BOLLIXED
BOLLIXES
BOLLOCKS
BOLLOX
BOLLOXED
BOLLOXES
BOLLS
BOLLWORM S
BOLO S
LOBO OBOL
BOLOGNA S
BOLOGNAS
BOLONEY S
BOLONEYS
BOLOS
LOBOS OBOLS
BOLSHIE S
BOLSHIES
BOLSHY
BOLSON S
BOLSONS
BOLSTER S
BOLTERS
LOBSTER
BOLSTERS
LOBSTERS
BOLT S
BLOT
BOLTED
BOLTER S
BOLTERS
BOLSTER
LOBSTER
BOLTHEAD S
BOLTHOLE S
BOLTING
BILTONG
BOLTLESS
BLOTLESS
BOLTLIKE
BOLTONIA S
LOBATION
OBLATION
BOLTROPE S
BOLTS
BLOTS
O BOLUS
BOLUSES
BLOUSES
BOMB ES
BOMBABLE
BOMBARD S
BOMBARDS
BOMBAST S
BOMBASTS
BOMBAX
BOMBE DRS
BOMBED
MOBBED
BOMBER S
MOBBER
BOMBERS
MOBBERS
BOMBES
BOMBESIN S
BOMBING S
MOBBING
BOMBINGS
BOMBLET S
BOMBLETS
BOMBLOAD S
BOMBS
BOMBYCID S
BOMBYX
BOMBYXES
BONACI S
BONACIS
BONANZA S
BONANZAS
BONBON S
BONBONS
BOND S
BONDABLE
BONDAGE S
DOGBANE
BONDAGES
DOGBANES
BONDED
BONDER S
BONDERS
BONDING S
BONDINGS
BONDLESS
BOLDNESS
BONDMAID S
BONDMAN
BONDMEN
BONDS
BONDSMAN
BONDSMEN
BONDUC S
BONDUCS
BONE DRSY
EBON
BONED
BONEFISH
FISHBONE
BONEHEAD S
BONELESS
NOBLESSE
BONEMEAL S
BONER S
BORNE
BONERS
BONES
EBONS
BONESET S
BONESETS
BONEY
EBONY
BONEYARD S
BONEYER
BONEYEST
BONFIRE S
BONFIRES
BONG OS
BONGED
BONGING
BONGO S
BONGOES
BONGOIST S
BOOSTING
BONGOS
BONGS
BONHOMIE S
BONIATO S
BONIATOS
BONIER
BONIEST
BONIFACE S
BONINESS
BENISONS
BONING
BONITA S
OBTAIN
BONITAS
BASTION
OBTAINS
BONITO S
BONITOES
EOBIONTS
BONITOS
BONK S
KNOB
BONKED
BONKERS
BONKING
BONKS
KNOBS
BONNE ST
BONNES
BONNET S
BONNETED
BONNETS
BONNIE R
BONNIER
BONNIEST
BONNILY
BONNOCK S
BONNOCKS
BONNY
BONOBO S
BONOBOS
BONSAI
BASION
BONSPELL S
BONSPIEL S
BONTEBOK S
BONUS
BOSUN
BONUSES
E BONY
BONZE RS
BONZER
BRONZE
BONZES
BOO BKMNRST
BOOB SY
BOOBED
BOOBIES
BOOBING
BOOBIRD S
BOOBIRDS
BOOBISH
BOOBOO S
BOOBOOS
BOOBS
BOOBY
YOBBO
BOOCOO S
BOOCOOS
BOODLE DRS
BOODLED
BLOODED
BOODLER S
BOODLERS
BOODLES
BOODLING
BLOODING
BOOED
BOOGER S
GOOBER
BOOGERS
GOOBERS
BOOGEY S
BOOGEYED
BOOGEYS
BOOGIE DS
BOOGIED
BOOGIES
BOOGY
BOOGYING
BOOGYMAN
BOOGYMEN
BOOHOO S
BOOHOOED
BOOHOOS
BOOING
BOOJUM S
BOOJUMS
E BOOK S
KOBO
BOOKABLE
BOOKCASE S
CASEBOOK
BOOKED
BOOKEND S
BOOKENDS
BOOKER S
REBOOK
BOOKERS
REBOOKS
BOOKFUL S
BOOKFULS
BOOKIE S
BOOKIES
BOOKING S
BOOKINGS
BOOKISH
BOOKLET S
BOOKLETS
BOOKLICE
BOOKLORE S
BOOKMAN
BOOKMARK S
BOOKMEN
BOOKOO S
BOOKOOS
BOOKRACK S
BOOKREST S
E BOOKS
KOBOS
BOOKSHOP S
BOOKWORM S
BOOM SY
BOOMBOX
BOOMED
BOOMER S
BOOMERS
BOOMIER
BOOMIEST
BOOMING
BOOMKIN S
BOOMKINS
BOOMLET S
BOOMLETS

BOOMS
BOSOM
BOOMTOWN S
BOOMY
A BOON S
BOONDOCK S
BOONIES
BOONLESS
BOONS
BOSON
BOOR S
BROO
BOORISH
BOORS
BROOS
BOOS T
BOOST S
BOOTS
BOOSTED
BOOSTER S
REBOOTS
BOOSTERS
BOOSTING
BONGOIST
BOOSTS
BOOT HSY
BOOTABLE
BOOTED
BOOTEE S
BOOTEES
BOOTERY
BOOTH S
BHOOT
BOOTHS
BHOOTS
BOOTIE S
BOOTIES
BOOTING
BOOTJACK S
JACKBOOT
BOOTLACE S
BOOTLEG S
BOOTLEGS
BOOTLESS
BOOTLICK S
BOOTS
BOOST
BOOTY
BOOZE DRS
BOOZED
BOOZER S
REBOZO
BOOZERS
REBOZOS
BOOZES
BOOZIER
BOOZIEST
BOOZILY
BOOZING
BOOZY
BOP S
BOPEEP S
BOPEEPS
BOPPED
BOPPER S
BOPPERS
BOPPING
BOPS
BORA LSX
BOAR
BORACES
BORACIC
BORACITE S
BORAGE S
BORAGES
A BORAL S
BOLAR LABOR
LOBAR
BORALS
LABORS
BORANE S
BORANES
BORAS
BOARS
BORATE DS
BOATER
REBATO

BORATED
ABORTED
TABORED
BORATES
BOASTER
BOATERS
REBATOS
SORBATE
BORATING
ABORTING
TABORING
BORAX
BORAXES
BORDEAUX
BORDEL S
BOLDER
BORDELLO S
DOORBELL
BORDELS
BORDER S
BORDERED
BORDERER S
BORDERS
BORDURE S
BORDURES
SUBORDER
BORE DRS
ROBE
BOREAL
BOREAS
BOREASES
BORECOLE S
BORED
ORBED ROBED
BOREDOM S
BEDROOM
BROOMED
BOREDOMS
BEDROOMS
BOREEN S
ENROBE
BOREENS
ENROBES
BOREHOLE S
BORER S
BORERS
RESORB
BORES
BROSE ROBES
SOBER
BORESOME
BORIC
BORIDE S
BORIDES
DISROBE
BORING S
ORBING
ROBING
BORINGLY
BORINGS
SORBING
BORK S
BORKED
BORKING
BROKING
BORKS
BORN E
BORNE
BONER
BORNEOL S
BORNEOLS
BORNITE S
BORNITES
BORNITIC
BORON S
BORONIC
BORONS
BOROUGH S
BOROUGHS
BORRELIA S
BORROW S
BORROWED
BORROWER S
BORROWS
BORSCH T
BORSCHES
BORSCHT S
BORSCHTS

BORSHT S
BROTHS
THROBS
BORSHTS
BORSTAL S
BORSTALS
A BORT SYZ
A BORTS
BORTY
BORTZ
BORTZES
BORZOI S
BORZOIS
A BOS HKS
SOB
BOSCAGE S
BOSCAGES
BOSCHBOK S
BOSH
HOBS
BOSHBOK S
BOSHBOKS
BOSHES
BOSHVARK S
BOSK SY
KOBS
BOSKAGE S
BOSKAGES
BOSKER
BOSKET S
BOSKETS
BOSKIER
BOSKIEST
BOSKS
BOSKY
BOSOM SY
BOOMS
BOSOMED
BOSOMING
BOSOMS
BOSOMY
BOSON S
BOONS
BOSONIC
BOSONS
BOSQUE ST
BOSQUES
BOSQUET S
BOSQUETS
BOSS Y
SOBS
BOSSDOM S
BOSSDOMS
BOSSED
BOSSES
OBSESS
BOSSIER
RIBOSES
BOSSIES T
BOSSIEST
BOSSILY
BOSSING
GIBSONS
BOSSISM S
BOSSISMS
BOSSY
BOSTON S
BOSTONS
BOSUN S
BONUS
BOSUNS
BOT AHST
BOTA S
BOAT
BOTANIC A
BOTANICA LS
BOTANIES
BOTANISE
NIOBATES
OBEISANT
BOTANISE DS
BOTANIES
NIOBATES
OBEISANT
BOTANIST S
BOTANIZE DRS
BOTANY

BOTAS
BOAST BOATS
SABOT
BOTCH Y
BOTCHED
BOTCHER SY
BOTCHERS
BOTCHERY
BOTCHES
BOTCHIER
BOTCHILY
BOTCHING
BOTCHY
BOTEL S
BOTELS
BOTFLIES
BOTFLY
BOTH Y
BOTHER S
BOTHERED
BOTHERS
BOTHIES
BOTHRIA
BOTHRIUM S
BOTHY
BOTONEE
BOTONNEE
BOTRYOID
BOTRYOSE
BOTRYTIS
BOTS
STOB
BOTT S
BOTTLE DRS
BOTTLED
BLOTTED
BOTTLER S
BLOTTER
BOTTLERS
BLOTTERS
BOTTLES
BOTTLING S
BLOTTING
BOTTOM S
BOTTOMED
BOTTOMER S
BOTTOMRY
BOTTOMS
BOTTS
BOTULIN S
BOTULINS
BOTULISM S
BOUBOU S
BOUBOUS
BOUCHEE S
BOUCHEES
BOUCLE S
BOUCLES
BOUDIN S
BOUDINS
BOUDOIR S
BOUDOIRS
BOUFFANT S
BOUFFE S
BOUFFES
BOUGH ST
BOUGHED
BOUGHPOT S
BOUGHS
A BOUGHT
BOUGHTEN
BOUGIE S
BOUGIES
BOUILLON S
BOULDER SY
DOUBLER
BOULDERS
DOUBLERS
BOULDERY
BOULE S
BOULES
BLOUSE
OBELUS
BOULLE S
LOBULE

BOULLES
LOBULES
SOLUBLE
BOUNCE DRS
BOUNCED
BUNCOED
BOUNCER S
BOUNCERS
BOUNCES
BOUNCIER
BOUNCILY
BOUNCING
BUNCOING
BOUNCY
A BOUND S
BOUNDARY
A BOUNDED
BOUNDEN
UNBONED
BOUNDER S
REBOUND
UNROBED
BOUNDERS
REBOUNDS
SUBORNED
A BOUNDING
A BOUNDS
BOUNTIED
BOUNTIES
BOUNTY
BOUQUET S
BOUQUETS
BOURBON S
BOURBONS
BOURDON S
BOURDONS
BOURG S
BOURGEON S
BOURGS
BOURN ES
BOURNE S
UNROBE
BOURNES
UNROBES
UNSOBER
BOURNS
SUBORN
BOURREE S
BOURREES
BOURRIDE S
BOURSE S
BOURSES
BOURSIN S
BOURSINS
BOURTREE S
BOUSE DS
BOUSED
BOUSES
BOUSING
BOUSOUKI AS
BOUSY
BUOYS
A BOUT S
BOUTIQUE SY
BOUTON S
BOUTONS
BOUTS
BOUVIER S
BOUVIERS
BOUZOUKI AS
BOVID S
BOVIDS
BOVINE S
BOVINELY
BOVINES
BOVINITY
BOW LS
BOWED
BOWEL S
BELOW ELBOW
BOWELED
ELBOWED
BOWELING
ELBOWING
BOWELLED
BELLOWED

BOWELS
BELOWS
ELBOWS
BOWER SY
BOWERED
BOWERIES
BOWERING
BOWERS
BROWSE
BOWERY
BOWYER
BOWFIN S
BOWFINS
BOWFRONT
BOWHEAD S
BOWHEADS
BESHADOW
BOWING S
BOWINGLY
BOWINGS
BOWSING
BOWKNOT S
BOWKNOTS
BOWL S
BLOW
BOWLDER S
LOWBRED
BOWLDERS
BOWLED
BLOWED
BOWLEG S
WEBLOG
BOWLEGS
WEBLOGS
BOWLER S
BLOWER
BOWLERS
BLOWERS
BOWLESS
BOWLFUL S
BOWLFULS
BOWLIKE
BOWLINE S
BOWLINES
BOWLING S
BLOWING
BOWLINGS
BOWLLIKE
BOWLS
BLOWS
BOWMAN
BOWMEN
ENWOMB
BOWPOT S
BOWPOTS
BOWS E
SWOB
BOWSE DS
BOWSED
BOWSES
BOWSHOT S
BOWSHOTS
BOWSING
BOWINGS
BOWSPRIT S
BOWWOW S
BOWWOWED
BOWWOWS
BOWYER S
BOWERY
BOWYERS
BOX Y
BOXBALL S
BOXBALLS
BOXBERRY
BOXBOARD S
BOXCAR S
BOXCARS
BOXED
BOXER S
BOXERS
BOXES
BOXFISH
BOXFUL S
BOXFULS
BOXHAUL S
BOXHAULS
BOXIER
BOXIEST

BOXILY
BOXINESS
BOXING S
BOXINGS
BOXLIKE
BOXTHORN S
BOXWOOD S
WOODBOX
BOXWOODS
BOXY
BOY OS
YOB
BOYAR DS
BOYARD S
BYROAD
BOYARDS
BYROADS
BOYARISM S
BOYARS
BOYCHICK S
BOYCHIK S
BOYCHIKS
BOYCOTT S
BOYCOTTS
BOYHOOD S
BOYHOODS
BOYISH
BOYISHLY
BOYLA S
BOYLAS
BOYO S
BOYOS
BOYS
SYBO YOBS
BOZO S
BOZOS
BRA DEGNSTW
ARB Y
BAR
BRABBLE DRS
BABBLER
BLABBER
BRABBLED
BRABBLER S
BRABBLES
BABBLERS
BLABBERS
BRACE DRS
ACERB CABER
BRACED
BRACELET S
BRACER OS
BRACERO S
BRACEROS
BRACERS
BRACES
CABERS
BRACH S
BRACHES
BRACHET S
BATCHER
BRACHETS
BATCHERS
A BRACHIA L
BRACHIAL S
BRACHIUM
BRACHS
BRACING S
BRACINGS
BRACIOLA S
BRACIOLE S
ALBICORE
CABRIOLE
BRACKEN S
BRACKENS
BRACKET S
BRACKETS
BACKREST
BRACKISH
BRACONID S
BRACT S
BRACTEAL
CARTABLE
BRACTED
BRACTLET S
BRACTS
BRAD S
BARD DARB
DRAB

BRADAWL S
BRADAWLS
BRADDED
BRADDING
BRADOON S
ONBOARD
BRADOONS
BRADS
BARDS DARBS DRABS
BRAE S
BARE BEAR
BRAES
BARES BASER BEARS SABER SABRE
BRAG S
GARB GRAB
BRAGGART S
BRAGGED
BRAGGER S
BRAGGERS
BRAGGEST
BRAGGIER
BRAGGING
BRAGGY
BRAGS
GARBS GRABS
BRAHMA S
BRAHMAS
SAMBHAR
BRAID S
RABID
BRAIDED
BRAIDER S
BRAIDERS
BRAIDING S
BRAIDS
DISBAR
BRAIL S
LIBRA
BRAILED
BEDRAIL RIDABLE
BRAILING
BRAILLE DRS
LIBERAL
BRAILLED
BRAILLER S
BRAILLES
LIBERALS
BRAILS
BRASIL LIBRAS
BRAIN SY
BAIRN
BRAINED
BRAINIAC S
BRAINIER
BRAINILY
BRAINING
BRAINISH
BAIRNISH
BRAINPAN S
BRAINS
BAIRNS
BRAINY
BINARY
BRAISE DS
RABIES
BRAISED
ABIDERS DARBIES SEABIRD SIDEBAR
BRAISES
BRASSIE
BRAISING
BRAIZE S
BRAIZES
BRAKE DS
BAKER BREAK KEBAR
BRAKEAGE S
BREAKAGE
BRAKED
BARKED DEBARK
BRAKEMAN
BRAKEMEN
BRAKES
BAKERS BREAKS KEBARS
BRAKIER
BARKIER
BRAKIEST
BARKIEST
BRAKING
BARKING
BRAKY
BARKY
BRALESS
BARLESS
BRAMBLE DS
BRAMBLED
BRAMBLES
BRAMBLY
BRAN DKST
BARN
BRANCH Y
BRANCHED
BRANCHES
BRECHANS
BRANCHIA EL
BRANCHY
BRAND SY
BRANDED
BRANDER S
BRANDERS
BRANDIED
BRANDIES
BRANDING S
BRANDISH
BRANDS
BRANDY
BRANK S
BRANKS
BRANNED
BRANNER S
BRANNERS
BRANNIER
BRANNING
BRANNY
BRANS
BARNS
BRANT S
BRANTAIL S
BRANTS
BRAS HS
ARBS BARS
BRASH Y
BRASHER
BRASHES T
BASHERS
BRASHEST
BRASHIER
BRASHLY
BRASHY
BRASIER S
BRASIERS
BRASSIER
BRASIL S
BRAILS LIBRAS
BRASILIN S
BRASILS
BRASS Y
BRASSAGE S
BRASSARD S
BRASSART S
BRASSED
SERDABS
BRASSES
BRASSICA S
BRASSIE RS
BRAISES
BRASSIER E
BRASIERS
BRASSIES T
BRASSILY
BRASSING
BRASSISH
BRASSY
BRAT S
BRATS
BRATTICE DS
BRATTIER
BIRRETTA
BRATTISH
BRATTLE DS
BATTLER BLATTER
BRATTLED
BRATTLES
BATTLERS BLATTERS
BRATTY
BRAUNITE S
URBANITE
BRAVA S
BRAVADO S
BRAVADOS
BRAVAS
BRAVE DRS
BRAVED
ADVERB
BRAVELY
BRAVER SY
BRAVERS
BRAVERY
BRAVES T
BRAVEST
BRAVI
BRAVING
BRAVO S
BRAVOED
BRAVOES
BRAVOING
BRAVOS
BRAVURA S
BRAVURAS
BRAVURE
BRAW LNS
BRAWER
BRAWEST
BRAWL SY
BRAWLED
WARBLED
BRAWLER S
WARBLER
BRAWLERS
WARBLERS
BRAWLIE R
WIRABLE
BRAWLIER
BRAWLING
WARBLING
BRAWLS
BRAWLY
BRAWN SY
BRAWNIER
BRAWNILY
BRAWNS
BRAWNY
BRAWS
BRAXIES
BRAXY
BRAY S
BRAYED
BREADY REDBAY
BRAYER S
BRAYERS
BRAYING
BRAYS
BRAZA S
BAZAR
BRAZAS
BAZARS
BRAZE DNRS
ZEBRA
BRAZED
BRAZEN S
BRAZENED
BRAZENLY
BRAZENS
BRAZER S
BRAZERS
BRAZES
ZEBRAS
BRAZIER S
BIZARRE
BRAZIERS
BIZARRES
BRAZIL S
BRAZILIN S
BRAZILS
BRAZING
BREACH
BREACHED
BERDACHE
BREACHER S
BREACHES
BREAD SY
ARDEB BARDE BARED BEARD DEBAR
BREADBOX
BREADED
BEARDED DEBEARD
BREADING
BEARDING
BREADNUT S
TURBANED
BREADS
ARDEBS BARDES BEARDS DEBARS SABRED SERDAB
BREADTH S
BREADTHS
BREADY
BRAYED REDBAY
BREAK S
BAKER BRAKE KEBAR
BREAKAGE S
BRAKEAGE
BREAKER S
BREAKERS
BREAKING S
BERAKING
BREAKOUT S
OUTBREAK
BREAKS
BAKERS BRAKES KEBARS
BREAKUP S
BREAKUPS
BREAM S
AMBER EMBAR
BREAMED
BREAMING
BREAMS
AMBERS EMBARS
A **BREAST** S
BAREST BASTER TABERS
BREASTED
DEBATERS
BREASTS
BASTERS
BREATH ESY
BATHER BERTHA
BREATHE DRS
BREATHED
BREATHER S
BREATHES
BREATHS
BATHERS BERTHAS
BREATHY
BRECCIA LS
ACERBIC
BRECCIAL
BRECCIAS
BRECHAM S
BECHARM CHAMBER
BRECHAMS
BECHARMS CHAMBERS
BRECHAN S
BRECHANS
BRANCHES
BRED E
BREDE S
BREED
BREDES
BREEDS
BREE DS
BEER
BREECH
BREECHED
BREECHES
BREED S
BREDE
BREEDER S
REBREED
BREEDERS
REBREEDS
BREEDING S
BERINGED
BREEDS
BREDES
BREEKS
BREES
BEERS
BREEZE DS
BEEZER
BREEZED
BREEZES
BEEZERS
BREEZIER
BREEZILY
BREEZING
BREEZY
BREGMA
BREGMATA
BREGMATE
BREN ST
BRENS
BRENT S
BRENTS
BRETHREN
BREVE ST
BREVES
BREVET S
BREVETCY
BREVETED
BREVETS
BREVIARY
BREVIER S
BREVIERS
BREVITY
BREW S
BREWAGE S
BREWAGES
BREWED
BREWER SY
BREWERS
BREWERY
BREWING S
BREWINGS
BREWIS
BREWISES
BREWPUB S
BREWPUBS
BREWS
BREWSKI S
BREWSKIS
BRIAR DSY
BRIARD S
BRIARDS
BRIARS
BRIARY
BRIBABLE
BRIBE DERS
BRIBED
DIBBER RIBBED
BRIBEE S
BRIBEES
BRIBER SY
RIBBER
BRIBERS
RIBBERS
BRIBERY
BRIBES
BRIBING
RIBBING
BRICK SY
BRICKBAT S
BRICKED
BRICKIER
BRICKING
BRICKLE S
BRICKLES
BRICKS
BRICKY
BRICOLE S
CORBEIL
BRICOLES
CORBEILS
BRIDAL S
RIBALD
BRIDALLY
RIBALDLY
BRIDALS
RIBALDS
BRIDE S
BIDER REBID
BRIDES
BIDERS DEBRIS REBIDS
A **BRIDGE** DS
BEGIRD
A **BRIDGED**
A **BRIDGES**
BEGIRDS
A **BRIDGING** S
BRIDLE DRS
BIRLED
BRIDLED
BRIDLER S
BRIDLERS
BRIDLES
BRIDLING
BRIDOON S
BRIDOONS
BRIE FRS
BIER
BRIEF S
FIBER FIBRE
BRIEFED
DEBRIEF FIBERED
BRIEFER S
BRIEFERS
BRIEFEST
BRIEFING S
BRIEFLY
BRIEFS
FIBERS FIBRES
BRIER SY
BRIERS
BRIERY
BRIES
BIERS BIRSE RIBES
BRIG S
BRIGADE DS
ABRIDGE
BRIGADED
ABRIDGED
BRIGADES
ABRIDGES
BRIGAND S
BARDING
BRIGANDS
BRIGHT S
BRIGHTEN S
BERTHING
BRIGHTER
BRIGHTLY
BRIGHTS
BRIGS
BRILL OS
BRILLO S
BRILLOS
BRILLS
BRIM S
BRIMFUL L
BRIMFULL Y
BRIMLESS
BRIMMED
BRIMMER S
BRIMMERS
BRIMMING
BRIMS
BRIN EGKSY
BRINDED
BRINDLE DS
BLINDER
BRINDLED
BRINDLES
BLINDERS
BRINE DRS
BINER
BRINED
BINDER INBRED REBIND
BRINER S
BRINERS
BRINES
BINERS
BRING S
BRINGER S
BRINGERS
BRINGING
BRINGS
BRINIER
BRINIES T
BRINIEST
BRINING
BRINISH
BRINK S
BRINKS
BRINS
BRINY
BRIO S
BIRO
BRIOCHE S
BRIOCHES
BRIONIES
BRIONY
BRIOS
BIROS
BRIQUET S
BRIQUETS
A **BRIS** KS
RIBS
BRISANCE S
CARBINES
BRISANT
BRISES
BIRSES
BRISK S
BIRKS
BRISKED
BRISKER
BRISKEST
BRISKETS
BRISKET S
BRISKETS
BRISKEST
BRISKING
BRISKLY
BRISKS
BRISLING S
BIRLINGS
BRISS
BRISSES
BRISTLE DS
BLISTER RIBLETS
BRISTLED
DRIBLETS
BRISTLES
BLISTERS
BRISTLY
BRISTOL S
STROBIL
BRISTOLS
STROBILS
BRIT HST
BRITCHES
BRITH S
BIRTH
BRITHS
BIRTHS
BRITS
BRITSKA S
BRITSKAS
BRITT S
BRITTLE DRS
BRITTLED
BRITTLER
BRITTLES T
BRITTLY
BRITTS
BRITZKA S
BRITZKAS
BRITZSKA

BRITZSKA S
BRITZKAS
BRO OSW
ORB
ROB
A BROACH
BROACHED
BROACHER S
BROACHES
A BROAD S
BOARD DOBRA
BROADAX E
BROADAXE S
BROADEN S
BANDORE
BROADENS
BANDORES
BROADER
ARBORED
BOARDER
REBOARD
BROADEST
BROADISH
BROADLY
BROADS
ADSORB
BOARDS
DOBRAS
BROCADE DS
BROCADED
BROCADES
BROCATEL S
BROCCOLI S
BROCHE
BROCHURE S
BROCK S
BROCKAGE S
BROCKET S
BROCKETS
BROCKS
BROCOLI S
BICOLOR
BROCOLIS
BICOLORS
BROGAN S
BARONG
BROGANS
BARONGS
BROGUE S
BROGUERY
BROGUES
BROGUISH
BROIDER SY
BROIDERS
DISROBER
BROIDERY
BROIL S
BROILED
BROILER S
BROILERS
BROILING
BROILS
BROKAGE S
BROKAGES
GROSBEAK
BROKE NR
BROKEN
BROKENLY
BROKER S
BROKERED
BROKERS
BROKING S
BORKING
BROKINGS
BROLLIES
BROLLY
BROMAL S
BROMALS
BROMATE DS
BROMATED
BROMATES
BROME S
OMBER OMBRE
BROMELIN S
BROMES
OMBERS
OMBRES
SOMBER
SOMBRE

BROMIC
BROMID ES
MORBID
BROMIDE S
BROMIDES
BROMIDIC
BROMIDS
BROMIN ES
BROMINE S
BROMINES
BROMINS
BROMISM S
BROMISMS
BROMIZE DS
BROMIZED
BROMIZES
BROMO S
BROOM
BROMOS
BROOMS
BRONC OS
BRONCHI A
BRONCHIA L
BRONCHO S
BRONCHOS
BRONCHUS
BRONCO S
BRONCOS
BRONCS
BRONZE DRS
BONZER
BRONZED
BRONZER S
BRONZERS
BRONZES
BRONZIER
BRONZING S
BRONZY
BROO DKMS
BOOR
BROOCH
BROOCHES
BROOD SY
DOBRO
BROODED
BROODER S
BROODERS
BROODIER
BROODILY
BROODING
BROODS
DOBROS
BROODY
BROOK S
BROOKED
BROOKIE S
BROOKIES
BROOKING
BROOKITE S
BROOKLET S
BROOKS
BROOM SY
BROMO
BROOMED
BEDROOM
BOREDOM
BROOMIER
BROOMING
BROOMS
BROMOS
BROOMY
BROOS
BOORS
BROS EY
ORBS ROBS
SORB
BROSE S
BORES ROBES
SOBER
BROSES
SOBERS
BROSY
BROTH SY
THROB
BROTHEL S
BROTHELS
BROTHER S
BROTHERS

BROTHS
BORSHT
THROBS
BROTHY
BROUGHAM S
BROUGHT
BROUHAHA S
BROW NS
BROWBAND S
BROWBEAT S
BROWED
BROWLESS
BROWN SY
BROWNED
BROWNER
BROWNEST
BESTROWN
BROWNIE RS
BROWNIER
BROWNIES T
BROWNING
BROWNISH
BROWNOUT S
BROWNS
BROWNY
BROWS E
BROWSE DRS
BOWERS
BROWSED
BROWSER S
BROWSERS
BROWSES
BROWSING
BRR R
BRRR
BRUCELLA ES
BRUCIN ES
BRUCINE S
BRUCINES
BRUCINS
BRUGH S
BURGH
BRUGHS
BURGHS
BRUIN S
BURIN
BRUINS
BURINS
BRUISE DRS
BURIES
BUSIER
RUBIES
BRUISED
BURDIES
BRUISER S
BURIERS
BRUISERS
BRUISES
BRUISING
BRUIT S
BRUITED
BRUITER S
BRUITERS
BURRIEST
BRUITING
BRUITS
BRULOT S
BRULOTS
BRULYIE S
BRULYIES
BRULZIE S
BRULZIES
BRUMAL
LABRUM
LUMBAR
UMBRAL
BRUMBIES
BRUMBY
BRUME S
UMBER
BRUMES
UMBERS
BRUMOUS
BRUNCH
BRUNCHED
BRUNCHER S
BRUNCHES

BRUNET S
BUNTER
BURNET
BRUNETS
BUNTERS
BURNETS
SUBRENT
BRUNETTE S
BRUNG
BRUNIZEM S
BRUNT S
BURNT
BRUNTS
BRUSH Y
BUHRS SHRUB
BRUSHED
BRUSHER S
BRUSHERS
BRUSHES
BUSHERS
BRUSHIER
BRUSHING
BRUSHOFF S
BRUSHUP S
BRUSHUPS
BRUSHY
BRUSK
BRUSKER
BURKERS
BRUSKEST
BRUSQUE R
BRUSQUER
BRUT ES
BRUTAL
BRUTALLY
BRUTE DS
BURET REBUT
TUBER
BRUTED
BRUTELY
BUTLERY
BRUTES
BURETS
BUSTER
REBUTS
TUBERS
BRUTIFY
BRUTING
BRUTISH
BRUTISM S
BRUTISMS
BRUTS
BURST
BRUX
BRUXED
BRUXES
EXURBS
BRUXING
BRUXISM S
BRUXISMS
BRYOLOGY
BRYONIES
BRYONY
BRYOZOAN S
BUB OSU
BUBAL ES
BABUL
BUBALE S
BAUBLE
BUBALES
BAUBLES
BUBALINE
BUBALIS
BUBALS
BABULS
A BUBBLE DRS
BUBBLED
BLUBBED
BUBBLER S
BLUBBER
BUBBLERS
BLUBBERS
BUBBLES
BUBBLIER
BUBBLIES T
BUBBLING
BLUBBING
BUBBLY
BUBINGA S
BUBINGAS

BUBKES
BUBO
BUBOED
BUBOES
BUBONIC
BUBS
BUBU S
BUBUS
BUCCAL
BUCCALLY
BUCK OS
BUCKAROO S
BUCKAYRO S
BUCKBEAN S
BUCKED
BUCKEEN S
BUCKEENS
BUCKER S
BUCKEROO S
BUCKERS
BUCKET S
BUCKETED
BUCKETS
BUCKEYE S
BUCKEYES
BUCKING
BUCKISH
BUCKLE DRS
BUCKLED
BUCKLER S
BUCKLERS
SUBCLERK
BUCKLES
BUCKLING
BUCKO S
BUCKOES
BUCKOS
BUCKRAM S
BUCKRAMS
BUCKS
BUCKSAW S
SAWBUCK
BUCKSAWS
SAWBUCKS
BUCKSHEE S
BUCKSHOT
BUCKSKIN S
BUCKTAIL S
BUCOLIC S
BUCOLICS
BUD S
DUB
BUDDED
BUDDER S
REDBUD
BUDDERS
REDBUDS
BUDDHA S
BUDDHAS
BUDDIED
BUDDIES
BUDDING S
BUDDINGS
BUDDLE S
BUDDLEIA S
AUDIBLED
BUDDLES
BUDDY
BUDDYING
BUDGE DRST
DEBUG
BUDGED
BUDGER S
BEDRUG
REDBUG
BUDGERS
BEDRUGS
REDBUGS
BUDGES
DEBUGS
BUDGET S
BUDGETED
BUDGETER S
BUDGETS
BUDGIE S
BUDGIES
BUDGING

BUDLESS
BUDLIKE
BUDS
DUBS
BUDWORM S
BUDWORMS
BUFF IOSY
BUFFABLE
BUFFALO S
BUFFALOS
BUFFED
BUFFER S
REBUFF
BUFFERED
REBUFFED
BUFFERS
REBUFFS
BUFFEST
BUFFETS
BUFFET S
BUFFETED
BUFFETER S
BUFFETS
BUFFEST
BUFFI
BUFFIER
BUFFIEST
BUFFING
BUFFO S
BUFFOON S
BUFFOONS
BUFFOS
BUFFS
BUFFY
BUG S
BUGABOO S
BUGABOOS
BUGBANE S
BUGBANES
BUGBEAR S
BUGBEARS
BUGEYE S
BUGEYES
BUGGED
BUGGER SY
BUGGERED
BEGRUDGE
DEBUGGER
BUGGERS
BUGGERY
BUGGIER
BUGGIES T
BUGGIEST
BUGGING
BUGGY
BUGHOUSE S
BUGLE DRS
BULGE
BUGLED
BLUDGE
BULGED
BUGLER S
BULGER
BURGLE
BUGLERS
BULGERS
BURGLES
BUGLES
BULGES
BUGLING
BULGING
BUGLOSS
BUGOUT S
BUGOUTS
BUGS
BUGSEED S
BUGSEEDS
BUGSHA S
BUGSHAS
BUHL S
BUHLS
BLUSH SHLUB
BUHLWORK S
BUHR S
BUHRS
BRUSH SHRUB
BUILD S
BUILDED

BUILDER S
REBUILD
BUILDERS
REBUILDS
A BUILDING S
BUILDS
BUILDUP S
UPBUILD
BUILDUPS
UPBUILDS
BUILT
BUIRDLY
BULB S
BLUB
BULBAR
BULBED
BULBEL S
BULBELS
BULBIL S
BULBILS
BULBLET S
BULBLETS
BULBOUS
BULBS
BLUBS
BULBUL S
BULBULS
BULGE DRS
BUGLE
BULGED
BLUDGE
BUGLED
BULGER S
BUGLER
BURGLE
BULGERS
BUGLERS
BURGLES
BULGES
BUGLES
BULGHUR S
BULGHURS
BULGIER
BULGIEST
BULGING
BUGLING
BULGUR S
BULGURS
BULGY
BULIMIA CS
BULIMIAC
BULIMIAS
BULIMIC S
BULIMICS
BULK SY
BULKAGE S
BULKAGES
BULKED
BULKHEAD S
BULKIER
BULKIEST
BULKILY
BULKING
BULKS
BULKY
BULL ASY
BULLA E
BULLACE S
BULLACES
BULLAE
BULLATE
BALLUTE
BULLBAT S
BULLBATS
BULLDOG S
BULLDOGS
BULLDOZE DR S
BULLED
BULLET S
BULLETED
BULLETIN GS
BULLETS
BULLFROG S
BULLHEAD S
BULLHORN S
BULLIED
BULLIER

2006 addition

BULLIES T
BULLIEST
BULLING
BULLION S
BULLIONS
BULLISH
BULLNECK S
BULLNOSE S
BULLOCK SY
BULLOCKS
BULLOCKY
BULLOUS
BULLPEN S
BULLPENS
BULLPOUT S
BULLRING S
BULLRUSH
BULLS
BULLSHOT S
BULLWEED S
BULLWHIP S
BULLY
BULLYBOY S
BULLYING
BULLYRAG S
BULRUSH
BULWARK S
BULWARKS
BUM FPS
BUMBLE DRS
BUMBLED
BUMBLER S
BUMBLERS
BUMBLES
BUMBLING S
BUMBOAT S
BUMBOATS
BUMELIA S
BUMELIAS
BUMF S
BUMFS
BUMKIN S
BUMKINS
BUMMALO S
BUMMALOS
BUMMED
BUMMER S
BUMMERS
BUMMEST
BUMMING
BUMP HSY
BUMPED
BUMPER S
BUMPERED
BUMPERS
BUMPH S
BUMPHS
BUMPIER
BUMPIEST
BUMPILY
BUMPING
BUMPKIN S
BUMPKINS
BUMPS
BUMPY
BUMS
BUN ADGKNST
NUB
BUNA S
BUNAS
BUNCH Y
BUNCHED
BUNCHES
BUNCHIER
BUNCHILY
BUNCHING
BUNCHY
BUNCO S
BUNCOED
BOUNCED
BUNCOING
BOUNCING
BUNCOMBE S
BUNCOS

BUND ST
BUNDIST S
DUSTBIN
BUNDISTS
DUSTBINS
BUNDLE DRS
BUNDLED
BUNDLER S
BLUNDER
BUNDLERS
BLUNDERS
BUNDLES
BUNDLING S
BUNDS
BUNDT S
BUNDTS
BUNG S
BUNGALOW S
BUNGED
BUNGEE S
BUNGEES
BUNGHOLE S
BUNGING
BUNGLE DRS
BLUNGE
BUNGLED
BLUNGED
BUNGLER S
BLUNGER
BUNGLERS
BLUNGERS
BUNGLES
BLUNGES
BUNGLING S
BLUNGING
BUNGS
BUNION S
BUNIONS
BUNK OS
BUNKED
DEBUNK
BUNKER S
BUNKERED
DEBUNKER
BUNKERS
BUNKING
BUNKMATE S
BUNKO S
BUNKOED
BUNKOING
BUNKOS
BUNKS
BUNKUM S
BUNKUMS
BUNN SY
BUNNIES
BUNNS
BUNNY
BUNRAKU S
BUNRAKUS
BUNS
NUBS SNUB
BUNT S
BUNTED
BUNTER S
BRUNET
BURNET
BUNTERS
BRUNETS
BURNETS
SUBRENT
BUNTING S
BUNTINGS
BUNTLINE S
BUNTS
BUNYA S
BUNYAS
BUOY S
BUOYAGE S
BUOYAGES
BUOYANCE S
BUOYANCY
BUOYANT
BUOYED
BUOYING
BUOYS
BOUSY
BUPKES

BUPKUS
BUPPIE S
BUPPIES
BUPPY
BUQSHA S
BUQSHAS
BUR ABDGLNP
RUB RSY
URB
BURA NS
BURAN S
UNBAR URBAN
BURANS
UNBARS
BURAS
BURSA
BURB S
BURBLE DRS
LUBBER
RUBBLE
BURBLED
BLURBED
RUBBLED
BURBLER S
BURBLERS
BURBLES
LUBBERS
RUBBLES
SLUBBER
BURBLIER
RUBBLIER
BURBLING
BLURBING
RUBBLING
BURBLY
RUBBLY
BURBOT S
BURBOTS
BURBS
BURD S
DRUB
BURDEN S
BURNED
UNBRED
BURDENED
BURDENER S
BURDENS
BURDIE S
BURIED
RUBIED
BURDIES
BRUISED
BURDOCK S
BURDOCKS
BURDS
DRUBS
BUREAU SX
BUREAUS
BUREAUX
BURET S
BRUTE REBUT
TUBER
BURETS
BRUTES
BUSTER
REBUTS
TUBERS
BURETTE S
BURETTES
BURG HS
GRUB
BURGAGE S
BURGAGES
BURGEE S
BURGEES
BURGEON S
BURGEONS
BURGER S
BURGERS
BURGESS
BURGH S
BRUGH
BURGHAL
BURGHER S
BURGHERS
BURGHS
BRUGHS
BURGLAR SY
BURGLARS
BURGLARY

BURGLE DS
BUGLER
BULGER
BURGLED
BLUDGER
BURGLES
BUGLERS
BULGERS
BURGLING
BURGONET S
BURGOO S
BURGOOS
BURGOUT S
BURGOUTS
BURGRAVE S
BURGS
GRUBS
BURGUNDY
BURIAL S
BURIALS
RAILBUS
BURIED
BURDIE
RUBIED
BURIER S
RUBIER
BURIERS
BRUISER
BURIES
BRUISE
BUSIER
RUBIES
BURIN S
BRUIN
BURINS
BRUINS
BURKA S
BURKAS
BURKE DRS
BURKED
BURKER S
BURKERS
BRUSKER
BURKES
BUSKER
BURKING
BURKITE S
BURKITES
BURL SY
BLUR
BURLAP S
BURLAPS
BURLED
BURLER S
BURLERS
BURLESK S
BURLESKS
BURLEY S
BURLEYS
BURLIER
BURLIEST
SUBTILER
BURLILY
BURLING
BURLS
BLURS SLURB
BURLY
BURN ST
BURNABLE S
BURNED
BURDEN
UNBRED
BURNER S
BURNERS
BURNET S
BRUNET
BUNTER
BURNETS
BRUNETS
BUNTERS
SUBRENT
BURNIE S
BURNIES
SUBERIN
BURNING S
BURNINGS
BURNISH
BURNOOSE DS
BURNOUS

BURNOUT S
OUTBURN
BURNOUTS
OUTBURNS
BURNS
BURNT
BRUNT
BURP S
BURPED
BURPING
BURPS
BURQA S
BURQAS
BURR OSY
BURRED
BURRER S
BURRERS
BURRIER
BURRIEST
BRUITERS
BURRING
BURRITO S
BURRITOS
BURRO SW
BURROS
BURROW S
BURROWED
BURROWER S
BURROWS
BURRS
BURRY
BURS AET
RUBS URBS
BURSA ELRS
BURAS
BURSAE
ABUSER
BURSAL
BURSAR SY
BURSARS
BURSARY
BURSAS
BURSATE
ARBUTES
BURSE S
REBUS RUBES
SUBER
BURSEED S
BURSEEDS
BURSERA
BURSES
SUBERS
BURSITIS
BURST S
BRUTS
BURSTED
BURSTER S
BURSTERS
BURSTING
BURSTONE S
BURSTS
BURTHEN S
BURTHENS
BURTON S
BURTONS
BURWEED S
BURWEEDS
BURY
RUBY
BURYING
RUBYING
BUS HKSTY
SUB
BUSBAR S
BUSBARS
BUSBIES
BUSBOY S
BUSBOYS
BUSBY
A BUSED
A BUSES
BUSGIRL S
BUSGIRLS
BUSH Y
HUBS
BUSHBUCK S
BUSHED
BUSHEL S

BUSHELED
BUSHELER S
BUSHELS
BLUSHES
BUSHER S
BUSHERS
BRUSHES
BUSHES
BUSHFIRE S
BUSHGOAT S
BUSHIDO S
BUSHIDOS
BUSHIER
BUSHIEST
BUSHILY
BUSHING S
BUSHINGS
BUSHLAND S
BUSHLESS
BUSHLIKE
BUSHMAN
BUSHMEN
BUSHPIG S
BUSHPIGS
BUSHTIT S
BUSHTITS
BUSHVELD S
BUSHWA HS
BUSHWAH S
BUSHWAHS
BUSHWAS
BUSHY
BUSIED
BUSIER
BRUISE
BURIES
RUBIES
BUSIES T
BUSIEST
SUBSITE
BUSILY
BUSINESS
A BUSING S
BUSINGS
BUSSING
BUSK S
BUSKED
BUSKER S
BURKES
BUSKERS
BUSKIN GS
BUSKINED
BUSKING
BUSKINS
BUSKS
BUSLOAD S
BUSLOADS
BUSMAN
BUSMEN
BUSS
SUBS
BUSSED
BUSSES
BUSSING S
BUSINGS
BUSSINGS
BUST SY
BUTS STUB
TUBS
BUSTARD S
BUSTARDS
BUSTED
BESTUD
DEBUTS
BUSTER S
BRUTES
BURETS
REBUTS
TUBERS
BUSTERS
BUSTIC S
CUBIST
CUBITS
BUSTICS
CUBISTS
BUSTIER S
RUBIEST
BUSTIERS

BUSTIEST
BUSTING
TUBINGS
BUSTLE DRS
BLUEST
BLUETS
BUTLES
SUBLET
SUBTLE
BUSTLED
BUSTLER S
BLUSTER
BUTLERS
SUBTLER
BUSTLERS
BLUSTERS
BUSTLES
SUBLETS
BUSTLINE S
BUSTLING
BUSTS
STUBS
BUSTY
BUSULFAN S
BUSY
BUYS
BUSYBODY
BUSYING
BUSYNESS
BUSYWORK S
A BUT EST
TUB
BUTANE S
BUTANES
BUTANOL S
BUTANOLS
BUTANONE S
NANOTUBE
BUTCH
BUTCHER SY
BUTCHERS
BUTCHERY
BUTCHES
BUTE OS
TUBE
BUTENE S
BUTENES
SUBTEEN
BUTEO S
BUTEOS
OBTUSE
BUTES
TUBES
BUTLE DRS
BLUET
BUTLED
BUTLER SY
BUTLERS
BLUSTER
BUSTLER
SUBTLER
BUTLERY
BRUTELY
BUTLES
BLUEST
BLUETS
BUSTLE
SUBLET
SUBTLE
BUTLING
A BUTS
BUST STUB
TUBS
BUTT ESY
A BUTTALS
BUTTE DRS
A BUTTED
A BUTTER SY
BUTTERED
REBUTTED
A BUTTERS
BUTTERY
BUTTES
BUTTHEAD S
BUTTIES
A BUTTING
BUTTOCK S
BUTTOCKS
BUTTON SY
BUTTONED

BUTTONER S
REBUTTON
BUTTONS
BUTTONY
BUTTRESS
BUTTS
BUTTY
BUTUT S
BUTUTS
BUTYL S
BUTYLATE DS
BUTYLENE S
BUTYLS
SUBTLY
BUTYRAL S
BUTYRALS
BUTYRATE S
BUTYRIC
BUTYRIN S
BUTYRINS
BUTYROUS
BUTYRYL S
BUTYRYLS
BUXOM
BUXOMER
BUXOMEST
BUXOMLY
BUY S
BUYABLE
BUYBACK S
BUYBACKS
BUYER S
REBUY
BUYERS
REBUYS
BUYING
BUYOFF S
BUYOFFS
BUYOUT S
OUTBUY
BUYOUTS
OUTBUYS
BUYS
BUSY
BUZUKI AS
BUZUKIA
BUZUKIS
A BUZZ
BUZZARD S
BUZZARDS
BUZZCUT S
BUZZCUTS
BUZZED
BUZZER S
BUZZERS
BUZZES
BUZZING
BUZZWIG S
BUZZWIGS
BUZZWORD S
BWANA S
NAWAB
BWANAS
NAWABS
A BY ES
BYCATCH
A BYE S
BEY
BYELAW S
BYELAWS
A BYES
BEYS
BYGONE S
BYGONES
BYLAW S
BYLAWS
BYLINE DRS
BYLINED
BYLINER S
BYLINERS
BYLINES
BYLINING
BYNAME S
BAYMEN
BYNAMES
BYPASS
BYPASSED

BYPASSES
BYPAST
BYPATH S
BYPATHS
BYPLAY S
BYPLAYS
BYRE S
BYRES
BYRL S
BYRLED
BYRLING
BYRLS
BYRNIE S
BYRNIES
BYROAD S
BOYARD
BYROADS
BOYARDS
A BYS
A BYSSAL
BASSLY
BYSSI
BYSSUS
BYSSUSES
BYSTREET S
BYTALK S
BYTALKS
BYTE S
BYTES
BYWAY S
BYWAYS
BYWORD S
BYWORDS
BYWORK S
BYWORKS
BYZANT S
BYZANTS

C

S CAB S
CABAL AS
CABALA S
CABALAS
CABALISM S
BALSAMIC
CABALIST S
BASALTIC
CABALLED
CABALS
CABANA S
CABANAS
CABARET S
ABREACT
BEARCAT
CABARETS
ABREACTS
BEARCATS
CABRESTA
CABBAGE DSY
CABBAGED
CABBAGES
CABBAGEY
CABBAGY
CABBALA HS
CABBALAH S
CABBALAS
S CABBED
CABBIE S
CABBIES
S CABBING
S CABBY
CABER S
ACERB BRACE
CABERNET S
CABERS
BRACES
CABESTRO S
CABRESTO
CABEZON ES
CABEZONE S
CABEZONS
CABILDO S
CABILDOS
CABIN S
CABINED
CABINET S

CABINETS
CABINING
CABINS
CABLE DRST
CABLED
CABLER S
CABLERS
CABLES
CABLET S
CABLETS
CABLEWAY S
CABLING
CABMAN
CABMEN
CABOB S
CABOBS
CABOCHED
CABOCHON S
CABOMBA S
CABOMBAS
CABOODLE S
CABOOSE S
CABOOSES
CABOSHED
CABOTAGE S
CABRESTA S
ABREACTS
BEARCATS
CABARETS
CABRESTO S
CABESTRO
CABRETTA S
CABRILLA S
BACILLAR
CABRIOLE ST
ALBICORE
BRACIOLE
S CABS
SCAB
CABSTAND S
CACA OS
CACAO S
CACAOS
CACAS
CACHALOT S
CACHE DST
CACHED
CACHEPOT S
CACHES
CACHET S
CACHETED
CACHETS
CATCHES
CACHEXIA S
CACHEXIC
CACHEXY
CACHING
CACHOU S
CACHOUS
CACHUCHA S
CACIQUE S
CACIQUES
CACKLE DRS
CACKLED
CLACKED
CACKLER S
CLACKER
CRACKLE
CACKLERS
CLACKERS
CRACKLES
CACKLES
CACKLING
CLACKING
CACODYL S
CACODYLS
CACOMIXL ES
CACONYM SY
CACONYMS
CACONYMY
CACTI
CACTOID
OCTADIC
CACTUS
CACTUSES
S CAD EIS

CADASTER S
CADASTRE
CADASTRE S
CADASTER
CADAVER S
CADAVERS
CADDICE S
CADDICES
CADDIE DS
CADDIED
CADDIES
CADDIS H
CADDISED
CADDISES
DISCASED
CADDISH
CADDY
CADDYING
CADE ST
ACED DACE
CADELLE S
CADELLES
CADENCE DS
CADENCED
CADENCES
CADENCY
CADENT
CANTED
DECANT
CADENZA S
CADENZAS
CADES
CASED DACES
CADET S
ACTED
CADETS
CADGE DRS
CAGED
CADGED
CADGER S
GRACED
CADGERS
CADGES
CADGING
CADGY
CADI S
ACID CAID
CADIS
ACIDS ASDIC
CAIDS
CADMIC
CADMIUM S
CADMIUMS
CADRE S
ACRED ARCED
CARED CEDAR
RACED
CADRES
CEDARS
SACRED
SCARED
S CADS
SCAD
CADUCEAN
CADUCEI
CADUCEUS
CAUCUSED
CADUCITY
CADUCOUS
CAECA L
CAECAL
CAECALLY
CALYCEAL
CAECUM
CAEOMA S
CAEOMAS
CAESAR S
ARECAS
CAESARS
CAESIUM S
CAESIUMS
CAESTUS
CUESTAS
CAESURA ELS
CAESURAE
CAESURAL
CAESURAS
CAESURIC
CURACIES

CAFE S
FACE
CAFES
FACES
CAFF S
CAFFEIN ES
CAFFEINE S
CAFFEINS
CAFFS
CAFTAN S
CAFTANED
CAFTANS
CAGE DRSY
CAGED
CADGE
CAGEFUL S
CAGEFULS
CAGELIKE
CAGELING S
GLACEING
CAGER S
GRACE
CAGERS
GRACES
CAGES
CAGEY
CAGIER
CAGIEST
CAGILY
CAGINESS
CAGING
CAGY
CAHIER S
ACHIER
CAHIERS
CASHIER
CAHOOT S
CAHOOTS
CAHOW S
CAHOWS
CAID S
ACID CADI
CAIDS
ACIDS ASDIC
CADIS
CAIMAN S
MANIAC
CAIMANS
MANIACS
CAIN S
CAINS
CAIQUE S
CAIQUES
CAIRD S
ACRID DARIC
CAIRDS
DARICS
CAIRN SY
NARIC
CAIRNED
CAIRNS
CAIRNY
CAISSON S
CASINOS
CASSINO
CAISSONS
CASSINOS
CAITIFF S
CAITIFFS
CAJAPUT S
CAJAPUTS
CAJEPUT S
CAJEPUTS
CAJOLE DRS
CAJOLED
CAJOLER SY
CAJOLERS
CAJOLERY
CAJOLES
CAJOLING
CAJON
CAJONES
CAJUPUT S
CAJUPUTS
CAKE DSY
CAKED
CAKES
CAKEWALK S
CAKEY

CAKIER
CAKIEST
CAKINESS
CAKING
CAKY
YACK
CALABASH
CALABAZA S
CALADIUM S
CALAMAR ISY
CALAMARI S
CALAMARS
CALAMARY
CALAMATA S
CALAMI
CAMAIL
CALAMINE DS
ANALCIME
CALAMINT S
CLAIMANT
CALAMITE S
CALAMITY
CALAMUS
MACULAS
CALANDO
CALASH
CALASHES
CALATHI
CALATHOS
CALATHUS
CALCANEA L
CALCANEI
CALCAR S
CALCARIA
CALCARS
CALCEATE
CALCES
CALCIC
CALCIFIC
CALCIFY
CALCINE DS
CALCINED
CALCINES
SCENICAL
CALCITE S
CALCITES
CALCITIC
CALCIUM S
CALCIUMS
CALCSPAR S
CALCTUFA S
CALCTUFF S
CALCULI
CALCULUS
CALDARIA
CALDERA S
CRAALED
CALDERAS
CALDRON S
CALDRONS
CALECHE S
CALECHES
CALENDAL
CANALLED
CALENDAR S
CALENDER S
CALENDS
CANDLES
CALESA S
CALESAS
CALF S
CALFLIKE
CALFS
CALFSKIN S
CALIBER S
CALIBRE
CALIBERS
CALIBRES
CALIBRE DS
CALIBER
CALIBRED
CALIBRES
CALIBERS
CALICES
CELIACS
CALICHE S
CHALICE

CALICHES
CHALICES
CALICLE S
CALICLES
CALICO S
CALICOES
CALICOS
CALIF S
CALIFATE S
CALIFS
FISCAL
CALIPASH
PASHALIC
CALIPEE S
CALIPEES
ESPECIAL
CALIPER S
REPLICA
CALIPERS
REPLICAS
SPIRACLE
CALIPH S
CALIPHAL
CALIPHS
CALISAYA S
CALIX
CALK S
LACK
CALKED
LACKED
CALKER S
LACKER
RACKLE
CALKERS
LACKERS
SLACKER
CALKIN GS
CALKING S
LACKING
CALKINGS
SLACKING
CALKINS
CALKS
LACKS SLACK
S CALL AS
CALLA NS
CALLABLE
CALLALOO S
CALLAN ST
CALLANS
CALLANT S
CALLANTS
CALLAS
CALLBACK S
CALLBOY S
CALLBOYS
CALLED
CALLEE S
CELLAE
CALLEES
CALLER S
CELLAR
RECALL
CALLERS
CELLARS
RECALLS
SCLERAL
CALLET S
CALLETS
CALLING S
CALLINGS
CALLIOPE S
CALLIPEE S
CALLIPER S
CALLOSE S
LOCALES
CALLOSES
COALLESS
CALLOUS
CALLOW
CALLOWER
S CALLS
SCALL
CALLUS
SULCAL
CALLUSED
CALLUSES
CALM S
CLAM

CALMED
MACLED
CALMER
MARCEL
CALMEST
CAMLETS
CALMING
CALMLY
CALMNESS
CALMS
CLAMS
CALO S
COAL COLA
LOCA
CALOMEL S
CALOMELS
CALORIC S
CALORICS
CALORIE S
CARIOLE
COALIER
LORICAE
CALORIES
CARIOLES
CALORIZE DS
CALORY
CALOS
COALS COLAS
CALOTTE S
CALOTTES
CALOTYPE S
CALOYER S
CALOYERS
COARSELY
CALPAC KS
CALPACK S
CALPACKS
CALPACS
CALPAIN S
CALPAINS
CALQUE DS
CLAQUE
CALQUED
CALQUES
CLAQUES
CALQUING
CALTHROP S
CALTRAP S
CALTRAPS
CALTROP S
CALTROPS
CALUMET S
CALUMETS
MUSCATEL
CALUMNY
CALUTRON S
CALVADOS
CALVARIA LN S
CALVARY
CAVALRY
CALVE DS
CLAVE
CALVED
CALVES
CLAVES
CALVING
CALX
CALXES
CALYCATE
CALYCEAL
CAECALLY
CALYCES
CYCLASE
CALYCINE
CALYCLE S
CECALLY
CALYCLES
CALYCULI
CALYPSO S
CALYPSOS
CALYPTER S
CALYPTRA S
CALYX
CALYXES
CALZONE S
CALZONES
S CAM EOPS
MAC

CAMAIL S
CALAMI
CAMAILED
CAMAILS
CAMAS S
CAMASES
CAMASS
CAMASSES
CAMBER S
CRAMBE
CAMBERED
EMBRACED
CAMBERS
CRAMBES
CAMBIA L
CAMBIAL
CAMBISM S
CAMBISMS
CAMBIST S
CAMBISTS
CAMBIUM S
CAMBIUMS
CAMBOGIA S
CAMBRIC S
CAMBRICS
CAME LOS
ACME MACE
CAMEL S
MACLE
CAMELEER S
CAMELIA S
CAMELIAS
CAMELID S
CLAIMED
DECIMAL
DECLAIM
MEDICAL
CAMELIDS
DECIMALS
DECLAIMS
MEDICALS
CAMELLIA S
CAMELS
MACLES
MESCAL
CAMEO S
COMAE
CAMEOED
CAMEOING
CAMEOS
CAMERA ELS
CAMERAE
CAMERAL
CARAMEL
CERAMAL
CAMERAS
CAMES
ACMES MACES
CAMION S
ANOMIC
MANIOC
CAMIONS
ANOSMIC
MANIOCS
MASONIC
CAMISA S
CAMISADE S
CAMISADO S
CAMISAS
CAMISE S
AMICES
CAMISES
CAMISIA S
CAMISIAS
CAMISOLE S
CAMLET S
CAMLETS
CALMEST
CAMMIE S
CAMMIES
CAMO S
COMA
CAMOMILE S
CAMORRA S
CAMORRAS
CAMOS
COMAS
S CAMP IOSY
CAMPAGNA
CAMPAGNE

CAMPAIGN S
S CAMPED
DECAMP
S CAMPER S
S CAMPERS
SCAMPER
CAMPFIRE S
CAMPHENE S
CAMPHINE S
CAMPHIRE S
CAMPHOL S
CAMPHOLS
CAMPHOR S
CAMPHORS
S CAMPI
CAMPIER
CAMPIEST
CAMPSITE
CAMPILY
S CAMPING S
CAMPINGS
SCAMPING
CAMPION S
CAMPIONS
CAMPO S
CAMPONG S
CAMPONGS
CAMPOREE S
CAMPOS
COMPAS
CAMPOUT S
CAMPOUTS
S CAMPS
SCAMP
CAMPSITE S
CAMPIEST
CAMPUS
CAMPUSED
CAMPUSES
CAMPY
S CAMS
MACS SCAM
CAMSHAFT S
S CAN EST
CANAILLE S
ALLIANCE
ANCILLAE
CANAKIN S
CANAKINS
CANAL S
CANALED
CANDELA
DECANAL
CANALING
CANALISE DS
CANALIZE DS
CANALLED
CALENDAL
CANALLER S
CANALS
CANAPE S
CANAPES
CANARD S
CANARDS
CANARIES
ACARINES
CESARIAN
SARCINAE
CANARY
CANASTA S
CANASTAS
CANCAN S
CANCANS
CANCEL S
CANCELED
CANCELER S
CLARENCE
CANCELS
CANCER S
CANCERED
CANCERS
CANCHA S
CANCHAS
CANCROID S
DRACONIC
CANDELA S
CANALED
DECANAL

CANDELAS
S CANDENT
CANDID AS
CANDIDA LS
CANDIDAL
CANDIDAS
CANDIDER
RIDDANCE
CANDIDLY
CANDIDS
CANDIED
CANDIES
INCASED
CANDLE DRS
LANCED
CANDLED
CANDLER S
CANDLERS
CANDLES
CALENDS
CANDLING
CANDOR S
CARDON
DACRON
CANDORS
CARDONS
DACRONS
CANDOUR S
CANDOURS
CANDY
CANDYING
CANE DRS
ACNE
CANED
ACNED DANCE
CANELLA S
CANELLAS
CANEPHOR S
CHAPERON
CANER S
CRANE NACRE
RANCE
CANERS
CASERN
CRANES
NACRES
RANCES
CANES
ACNES SCENA
CANEWARE S
CANFIELD S
CANFUL S
CANFULS
CANSFUL
CANGUE S
UNCAGE
CANGUES
UNCAGES
CANID S
CNIDA NICAD
CANIDS
NICADS
CANIKIN S
CANIKINS
CANINE S
CANNIE
ENCINA
CANINES
ENCINAS
CANING
CANINITY
CANISTEL S
CANISTER S
CERATINS
CISTERNA
CREATINS
SCANTIER
TACRINES
CANITIES
CANKER S
CANKERED
CANKERS
SNACKER
CANNA S
CANNABIC
CANNABIN S
CANNABIS
CANNAS
S CANNED
CANNEL S
CANNELON S

CANNELS
S CANNER SY
S CANNERS
SCANNER
CANNERY
CANNIBAL S
CANNIE R
CANINE
ENCINA
CANNIER
NARCEIN
CANNIEST
ANCIENTS
INSECTAN
INSTANCE
CANNIKIN S
CANNILY
S CANNING S
S CANNINGS
SCANNING
CANNOLI S
CANNOLIS
CANNON S
CANNONED
NONDANCE
CANNONRY
CANNONS
CANNOT
CANTON
CANNULA ERS
CANNULAE
CANNULAR
CANNULAS
CANNY
CANOE DRS
OCEAN
CANOED
ACNODE
DEACON
CANOEING
CANOEIST S
ACONITES
SONICATE
CANOER S
CORNEA
CANOERS
COARSEN
CORNEAS
NARCOSE
CANOES
OCEANS
CANOLA S
CANOLAS
CANON S
ANCON
CANONESS
SONANCES
CANONIC
CANONISE DS
CANONIST S
ACTINONS
CONTAINS
SANCTION
SONANTIC
CANONIZE DR S
CANONRY
CANONS
CANOODLE DS
CANOPIC
CANOPIED
CANOPIES
CANOPY
CANOROUS
S CANS OT
SCAN
CANSFUL
CANFULS
CANSO S
CANSOS
CANST
CANTS SCANT
S CANT OSY
CANTAL AS
CANTALA S
CANTALAS
CANTALS
CANTATA S
CANTATAS
CANTDOG S

CANTDOGS
S CANTED
CADENT
DECANT
CANTEEN S
CANTEENS
S CANTER S
CARNET
CENTRA
NECTAR
RECANT
TANREC
TRANCE
CANTERED
CRENATED
DECANTER
RECANTED
CANTERS
CARNETS
NECTARS
RECANTS
SCANTER
TANRECS
TRANCES
CANTHAL
A CANTHI
A CANTHUS
CHAUNTS
STAUNCH
CANTIC
CANTICLE S
CANTINA S
CANTINAS
S CANTING
CANTLE S
CENTAL
LANCET
CANTLES
CENTALS
LANCETS
CANTO NRS
COTAN OCTAN
CANTON S
CANNOT
CANTONAL
CANTONED
CANTONS
CANTOR S
CARTON
CONTRA
CRATON
CANTORS
CARTONS
CONTRAS
CRATONS
CANTOS
COTANS
OCTANS
CANTRAIP S
CANTRAP S
CANTRAPS
CANTRIP S
CANTRIPS
S CANTS
CANST SCANT
CANTUS
UNCAST
S CANTY
CANULA ERS
LACUNA
CANULAE
LACUNAE
CANULAR
LACUNAR
CANULAS
LACUNAS
CANULATE DS
LACUNATE
TENACULA
CANVAS S
CANVASED
ADVANCES
CANVASER S
CANVASES
CANVASS
CANYON S
CANYONS
CANZONA S
CANZONAS
CANZONE ST
CANZONES

CANZONET S
CANZONI
CAP EHOS
PAC
CAPABLE R
CAPABLER
CAPABLY
CAPACITY
S CAPE DRS
PACE
S CAPED
PACED
CAPELAN S
CAPELANS
SCALEPAN
CAPELET S
CAPELETS
CAPELIN S
PANICLE
PELICAN
CAPELINS
PANICLES
PELICANS
CAPER S
CRAPE PACER
RECAP
CAPERED
CAPERER S
PRERACE
CAPERERS
CAPERING
CAPERS
CRAPES
ESCARP
PACERS
PARSEC
RECAPS
SCRAPE
SECPAR
SPACER
S CAPES
PACES SCAPE
SPACE
CAPESKIN S
CAPEWORK S
CAPFUL S
CAPFULS
CAPH S
CHAP
CAPHS
CHAPS
CAPIAS
CAPIASES
CAPITA L
CAPITAL S
CAPITALS
APLASTIC
CAPITATE D
APATETIC
CAPITOL S
COALPIT
OPTICAL
TOPICAL
CAPITOLS
COALPITS
CAPITULA R
CAPIZ
CAPIZES
CAPSIZE
CAPLESS
CAPLET S
PLACET
CAPLETS
PLACETS
CAPLIN S
CAPLINS
INCLASP
CAPMAKER S
CAPO NS
CAPOEIRA S
CAPON S
CAPONATA S
CAPONIER S
APOCRINE
PROCAINE
CAPONIZE DS
CAPONS
CAPORAL S
CRAPOLA
CAPORALS
CRAPOLAS

CAPOS
CAPOTE S
TOECAP
CAPOTES
TOECAPS
CAPOUCH
PACHUCO
CAPPED
CAPPER S
CAPPERS
CAPPING S
CAPPINGS
CAPRIC E
CAPRICCI O
CAPRICE S
CAPRICES
CAPRIFIG S
CAPRINE
CAPRIOLE DS
CAPRIS
CAPROCK S
CAPROCKS
CAPS
PACS
CAPSICIN S
CAPSICUM S
CAPSID S
CAPSIDAL
CAPSIDS
CAPSIZE DS
CAPIZES
CAPSIZED
CAPSIZES
CAPSOMER ES
COMPARES
MESOCARP
CAPSTAN S
CAPTANS
CATNAPS
CAPSTANS
CAPSTONE S
OPENCAST
CAPSULAR
SCAPULAR
CAPSULE DS
SCALEUP
SPECULA
UPSCALE
CAPSULED
UPSCALED
CAPSULES
SCALEUPS
UPSCALES
CAPTAIN S
CAPTAINS
CAPTAN S
CATNAP
CAPTANS
CAPSTAN
CATNAPS
CAPTION S
PACTION
CAPTIONS
PACTIONS
CAPTIOUS
AUTOPSIC
CAPTIVE S
CAPTIVES
CAPTOR S
CARTOP
CAPTORS
CAPTURE DRS
CAPTURED
CAPTURER S
CAPTURES
CAPUCHE DS
CAPUCHED
CAPUCHES
CAPUCHIN S
CAPUT
CAPYBARA S
S **CAR** BDEKLNP RST
ARC
CARABAO S
CARABAOS
CARABID S
CARABIDS
CARABIN ES
CARABINE RS

CARABINS
CARACAL S
CARACALS
CARACARA S
CARACK S
CARACKS
CARACOL ES
CARACOLE DR S
CARACOLS
CARACUL S
ACCRUAL
CARACULS
ACCRUALS
SACCULAR
CARAFE S
CARAFES
CARAGANA S
CARAGEEN S
CARAMBA
CARAMEL S
CAMERAL
CERAMAL
CARAMELS
CERAMALS
CARANGID S
ARCADING
CARDIGAN
CARAPACE DS
CARAPAX
CARASSOW S
CARAT ES
CARATE S
CARATES
CARATS
CARAVAN S
CARAVANS
CARAVEL S
CARAVELS
CARAWAY S
CARAWAYS
CARB OS
CRAB
CARBAMIC
CARBAMYL S
CARBARN S
CARBARNS
CARBARYL S
CARBIDE S
CARBIDES
ASCRIBED
CARBINE S
CARBINES
BRISANCE
CARBINOL S
CARBO NSY
CAROB COBRA
CARBOLIC S
CARBON S
CORBAN
CARBONIC
CARBONS
CORBANS
CARBONYL S
CARBORA S
CARBORAS
CARBOS
CAROBS
COBRAS
CARBOXYL S
CARBOY S
CARBOYED
CARBOYS
CARBS
CRABS
CARBURET S
CARCAJOU S
CARCANET S
CARCASE S
CARCASES
CARCASS
CARCEL S
CERCAL
CARCELS
CARCERAL
CARD S
CARDAMOM S
CARDAMON S

CARDAMUM S
CARDCASE S
CARDED
CARDER S
CARDERS
SCARRED
CARDIA CES
ACARID
CARDIAC S
CARDIACS
CARDIAE
CARDIAS
ACARIDS
ASCARID
CARDIGAN S
ARCADING
CARANGID
CARDINAL S
CARDING S
CARDINGS
CARDIO
CARDIOID S
CARDITIC
CARDITIS
TRIACIDS
TRIADICS
CARDON S
CANDOR
DACRON
CARDONS
CANDORS
DACRONS
CARDOON S
CARDOONS
CARDS
S **CARE** DRSTX
ACRE RACE
S **CARED**
ACRED ARCED
CADRE CEDAR
RACED
CAREEN S
RECANE
CAREENED
CAREENER S
CAREENS
CASERNE
RECANES
CAREER S
CAREERED
CAREERER S
CAREERS
CREASER
CAREFREE
CAREFUL
CARELESS
RESCALES
S **CARER** S
RACER
S **CARERS**
RACERS
SCARER
S **CARES** S
ACRES CARSE
ESCAR RACES
SCARE SERAC
CARESS
CARSES
CRASES
ESCARS
SCARES
SERACS
CARESSED
CARESSER S
CREASERS
CARESSES
CARET S
CARTE CATER
CRATE REACT
RECTA TRACE
CARETAKE NR S
CARETOOK
CARETS
CARTES
CASTER
CATERS
CRATES
REACTS
RECAST
TRACES

CAREWORN
CAREX
CARFARE S
CARFARES
CARFUL S
FULCRA
CARFULS
CARGO S
CARGOES
CORSAGE
SOCAGER
CARGOS
CARHOP S
COPRAH
CARHOPS
COPRAHS
CARIBE S
CARIBES
ASCRIBE
CARIBOU S
CARIBOUS
CARICES
CARIED
CARIES
CERIAS
ERICAS
CARILLON S
O **CARINA** ELS
ACINAR
ARNICA
CRANIA
CARINAE
ACARINE
CARINAL
CRANIAL
O **CARINAS**
ACRASIN
ARNICAS
SARCINA
CARINATE D
CRANIATE
S **CARING**
ARCING
RACING
CARIOCA S
CARIOCAS
CARIOLE S
CALORIE
COALIER
LORICAE
CARIOLES
CALORIES
S **CARIOUS**
CURIOSA
CARITAS
CARJACK S
CARJACKS
CARK S
RACK
CARKED
ARCKED
DACKER
RACKED
CARKING
ARCKING
RACKING
CARKS
RACKS
CARL ES
CARLE S
CLEAR LACER
CARLES S
CLEARS
LACERS
SCALER
SCLERA
S **CARLESS**
CLASSER
SCALERS
SCLERAS
CARLIN EGS
CARLINE S
CARLINES
LANCIERS
CARLING S
CARLINGS
CARLINS
CARLISH
ARCHILS
CARLOAD S
CARLOADS
CARLS

CARMAKER S
CARMEN
CARMINE S
CARMINES
CREMAINS
CARN SY
NARC
CARNAGE S
CARNAGES
CARNAL
CARNALLY
CARNAUBA S
CARNET S
CANTER
CENTRA
NECTAR
RECANT
TANREC
TRANCE
CARNETS
CANTERS
NECTARS
RECANTS
SCANTER
TANRECS
TRANCES
CARNEY S
CARNEYS
CARNIE S
CARNIES
ARCSINE
ARSENIC
CARNIFY
CARNIVAL S
CARNS
NARCS
CARNY
CAROACH
CAROB S
CARBO COBRA
CAROBS
CARBOS
COBRAS
CAROCH E
CAROCHE S
COACHER
CAROCHES
COACHERS
CAROL IS
CLARO CORAL
CAROLED
CAROLER S
CAROLERS
CAROLI
LORICA
CAROLING
CAROLLED
COLLARED
CAROLLER S
CAROLS
CLAROS
CORALS
CAROLUS
OCULARS
OSCULAR
CAROM S
MACRO
CAROMED
COMRADE
CAROMING
CAROMS
MACROS
CAROTENE S
CAROTID S
CAROTIDS
CAROTIN S
CORTINA
CAROTINS
CORTINAS
CAROUSAL S
CAROUSE DLR
ACEROUS S
CAROUSED
CAROUSEL S
CAROUSER S
CAROUSES
S **CARP** IS
CRAP
CARPAL ES
CARPALE

CARPALIA
CARPALS
S **CARPED**
CRAPED
REDCAP
CARPEL S
PARCEL
PLACER
CARPELS
CLASPER
PARCELS
PLACERS
RECLASP
SCALPER
S **CARPER** S
S **CARPERS**
SCARPER
SCRAPER
CARPET S
PREACT
CARPETED
PREACTED
CARPETS
PREACTS
PRECAST
SPECTRA
CARPI
S **CARPING** S
CRAPING
CARPINGS
SCARPING
SCRAPING
CARPOOL S
CARPOOLS
CARPORT S
CARPORTS
S **CARPS**
CRAPS SCARP
SCRAP
CARPUS
CARR SY
CARRACK S
CARRACKS
CARREL LS
CARRELL S
CARRELLS
CARRELS
CARRIAGE S
CARRIED
ACRIDER
S **CARRIER** S
CARRIERS
SCARRIER
CARRIES
SCARIER
CARRIOLE S
CARRION S
CARRIONS
CARRITCH
CARROCH
CARROM S
CARROMED
CARROMS
CARROT SY
TROCAR
CARROTIN S
CARROTS
TROCARS
CARROTY
CARRS
S **CARRY**
CARRYALL S
CARRYING
CARRYON S
CARRYONS
CARRYOUT S
S **CARS** E
ARCS SCAR
CARSE S
ACRES CARES
ESCAR RACES
SCARE SERAC
CARSES
CARESS
CRASES
ESCARS
SCARES
SERACS
CARSICK
S **CART** ES

CARTABLE
BRACTEAL
CARTAGE S
CARTAGES
E **CARTE** DLRS
CARET CATER
CRATE REACT
RECTA TRACE
S **CARTED**
CRATED
REDACT
TRACED
CARTEL S
CLARET
RECTAL
CARTELS
CLARETS
CRESTAL
SCARLET
CARTER S
CRATER
TRACER
CARTERS
CRATERS
TRACERS
E **CARTES**
CARETS
CASTER
CATERS
CRATES
REACTS
RECAST
TRACES
S **CARTING**
CRATING
TRACING
CARTLOAD S
CARTON S
CANTOR
CONTRA
CRATON
CARTONED
NOTECARD
CARTONS
CANTORS
CONTRAS
CRATONS
CARTOON SY
CORANTO
CARTOONS
CORANTOS
OSTRACON
CARTOONY
OCTONARY
CARTOP
CAPTOR
CARTOUCH E
S **CARTS**
SCART
CARUNCLE S
CARVE DLNRS
CAVER CRAVE
CARVED
CRAVED
CARVEL S
CLAVER
CARVELS
CLAVERS
CARVEN
CAVERN
CRAVEN
CARVER S
CRAVER
CARVERS
CRAVERS
S **CARVES**
CAVERS
CRAVES
CARVING S
CRAVING
CARVINGS
CRAVINGS
CARWASH
CARYATIC
CARYATID S
CARYOTIN S
CASA S
CASABA S
ABACAS
CASABAS
CASSABA
CASAS
CASAVA S

CASAVAS
CASSAVA
CASBAH S
CASBAHS
CASCABEL S
CASCABLE
CASCABLE S
CASCABEL
CASCADE DS
SACCADE
CASCADED
CASCADES
SACCADES
CASCARA S
CASCARAS
CASE DS
ACES
CASEASE S
CASEASES
CASEATE DS
CASEATED
CASEATES
CASEBOOK S
BOOKCASE
CASED
CADES DACES
CASEFIED
CASEFIES
CASEFY
CASEIC
CASEIN S
INCASE
CASEINS
CASSINE
INCASES
CASELOAD S
CASEMATE DS
CASEMENT S
CASEOSE S
CASEOSES
CASEOUS
CASERN ES
CANERS
CRANES
NACRES
RANCES
CASERNE S
CAREENS
RECANES
CASERNES
CASERNS
ANCRESS
CASES
CASETTE S
CASETTES
CASSETTE
CASEWORK S
CASEWORM S
CASH
CASHABLE
CASHAW S
CASHAWS
CASHBOOK S
CASHBOX
CASHED
CHASED
CASHES
CHASES
CHASSE
CASHEW S
CASHEWS
CASHIER S
CAHIERS
CASHIERS
RACHISES
CASHING
CHASING
CASHLESS
CASHMERE S
MACHREES
MARCHESE
CASHOO S
CASHOOS
CASIMERE S
CASIMIRE S
CASING S
CASINGS
CASINI
ANISIC
CASINO S

CASINOS
CAISSON
CASSINO
CASITA S
CASITAS
CASK SY
SACK
CASKED
SACKED
CASKET S
CASKETED
CASKETS
CASKING
SACKING
CASKS
SACKS
CASKY
YACKS
CASQUE DS
SACQUE
CASQUED
CASQUES
SACQUES
CASSABA S
CASABAS
CASSABAS
CASSATA S
CASSATAS
CASSAVA S
CASAVAS
CASSAVAS
CASSENA S
CASSENAS
CASSENE S
ENCASES
SEANCES
SENECAS
CASSENES
CASSETTE S
CASETTES
CASSIA S
CASSIAS
CASSINA S
CASSINAS
CASSINE S
CASEINS
INCASES
CASSINES
CASSINO S
CAISSON
CASINOS
CASSINOS
CAISSONS
CASSIS
CASSISES
CASSOCK S
COSSACK
CASSOCKS
COSSACKS
CAST ES
ACTS CATS
SCAT
CASTABLE
CASTANET S
CASTAWAY S
CASTE RS
CATES CESTA
TACES
CASTEISM S
CASTER S
CARETS
CARTES
CATERS
CRATES
REACTS
RECAST
TRACES
CASTERS
ACTRESS
RECASTS
CASTES
CESTAS
CASTING S
ACTINGS
CASTINGS
CASTLE DS
CLEATS
ECLATS
CASTLED
CASTLES
CASTLING
CATLINGS

CASTOFF S
OFFCAST
CASTOFFS
OFFCASTS
CASTOR S
ACTORS
COSTAR
SCROTA
TAROCS
CASTORS
COSTARS
CASTRATE DR
TEACARTS S
CASTRATI
CASTRATO RS
CASTS
SCATS
CASUAL S
CAUSAL
CASUALLY
CAUSALLY
CASUALS
CAUSALS
CASUALTY
CASUIST S
CASUISTS
CASUS
ASCUS
S CAT ES
ACT
CATACOMB S
CATALASE S
CATALO GS
CATALOES
CATALOG S
CATALOGS
CATALOS
COASTAL
CATALPA S
CATALPAS
CATALYST S
CATALYZE DR S
CATAMITE S
CATAPULT S
CATARACT S
CATARRH S
CATARRHS
CATAWBA S
CATAWBAS
CATBIRD S
CATBIRDS
CATBOAT S
CATBOATS
CATBRIER S
CATCALL S
CATCALLS
CATCH Y
CATCHALL S
CATCHER S
CATCHERS
CRATCHES
CATCHES
CACHETS
CATCHFLY
CATCHIER
CATCHING
CATCHUP S
CATCHUPS
CATCHY
CATCLAW S
CATCLAWS
CATE RS
TACE
CATECHIN S
ATECHNIC
CATECHOL S
CATECHU S
CATECHUS
CATEGORY
CATENA ES
CATENAE
CATENARY
CATENAS
CATENATE DS
CATENOID S

CATER S
CARET CARTE
CRATE REACT
RECTA TRACE
CATERAN S
CATERANS
CATERED
CERATED
CREATED
REACTED
CATERER S
RECRATE
RETRACE
TERRACE
CATERERS
RECRATES
RETRACES
TERRACES
CATERESS
CERASTES
CATERING
ARGENTIC
CREATING
REACTING
CATERS
CARETS
CARTES
CASTER
CRATES
REACTS
RECAST
TRACES
CATES
CASTE CESTA
TACES
CATFACE S
CATFACES
CATFALL S
CATFALLS
CATFIGHT S
CATFISH
CATGUT S
CATGUTS
CATHEAD S
CATHEADS
CATHECT S
CATHECTS
CATHEDRA EL S
CATHETER S
CATHEXES
CATHEXIS
CATHODAL
CATHODE S
CATHODES
CATHODIC
CATHOLIC S
CATHOUSE S
SOUTACHE
CATION S
ACTION
ATONIC
CATIONIC
ACONITIC
CATIONS
ACTIONS
ATONICS
CATJANG S
CATJANGS
CATKIN S
ANTICK
CATKINS
ANTICKS
CATLIKE
CATLIN GS
TINCAL
CATLING S
TALCING
CATLINGS
CASTLING
CATLINS
TINCALS
CATMINT S
CATMINTS
CATNAP S
CAPTAN
CATNAPER S
CATNAPS
CAPSTAN
CAPTANS
CATNIP S

CATNIPS
S CATS
ACTS CAST
SCAT
CATSPAW S
CATSPAWS
CATSUIT S
CATSUITS
CATSUP S
UPCAST
CATSUPS
UPCASTS
CATTAIL S
CATTAILS
STATICAL
CATTALO S
CATTALOS
S CATTED
CATTERY
CATTIE RS
S CATTIER
ATRETIC
CITRATE
CATTIES T
STATICE
S CATTIEST
CATTILY
TACITLY
S CATTING
CATTISH
TACHIST
CATTLE
TECTAL
CATTLEYA S
S CATTY
CATWALK S
CATWALKS
CAUCUS
CAUCUSED
CADUCEUS
CAUCUSES
CAUDAD
A CAUDAL
CAUDALLY
AE CAUDATE DS
CAUDATED
CAUDATES
CAUDEX
CAUDEXES
CAUDICES
CAUDILLO S
CAUDLE S
CEDULA
CAUDLES
CEDULAS
CAUGHT
CAUL DKS
CAULD S
DUCAL
CAULDRON S
CRUNODAL
CAULDS
CAULES
CLAUSE
CAULICLE S
A CAULINE
CAULIS
CAULK S
CAULKED
CAULKER S
CAULKERS
CAULKING S
CAULKS
CAULS
CAUSABLE
CAUSAL S
CASUAL
CAUSALLY
CASUALLY
CAUSALS
CASUALS
CAUSE DRSY
SAUCE
CAUSED
SAUCED
CAUSER S
CESURA
SAUCER
CAUSERIE S

CAUSERS
ARCUSES
CESURAS
SAUCERS
SUCRASE
CAUSES
SAUCES
CAUSEWAY S
CAUSEY S
CAYUSE
CAUSEYS
CAYUSES
CAUSING
SAUCING
CAUSTIC S
CAUSTICS
CAUTERY
CAUTION S
AUCTION
CAUTIONS
AUCTIONS
CAUTIOUS
CAVALERO S
CAVALIER S
CAVALLA S
CAVALLAS
CAVALLY
CAVALRY
CALVARY
CAVATINA S
CAVATINE
CAVE DRS
CAVEAT S
VACATE
CAVEATED
CAVEATOR S
CAVEATS
VACATES
CAVED
CAVEFISH
CAVELIKE
CAVEMAN
CAVEMEN
CAVER NS
CARVE CRAVE
CAVERN S
CARVEN
CRAVEN
CAVERNED
CRAVENED
CAVERNS
CRAVENS
CAVERS
CARVES
CRAVES
CAVES
CAVETTI
CAVETTO S
CAVETTOS
CAVIAR ES
CAVIARE S
AVARICE
CAVIARES
AVARICES
CAVIARS
CAVICORN
CAVIE S
CAVIES
VESICA
CAVIL S
CLAVI
CAVILED
CAVILER S
CLAVIER
VALERIC
CAVILERS
CLAVIERS
VISCERAL
CAVILING
CAVILLED
CAVILLER S
CAVILS
CAVING S
CAVINGS
CAVITARY
CAVITATE DS
ACTIVATE
CAVITIED
VATICIDE
CAVITIES
CAVITY

CAVORT S
CAVORTED
CAVORTER S
CAVORTS
CAVY
CAW S
CAWED
CAWING
CAWS
CAY S
CAYENNE DS
CAYENNED
CAYENNES
CAYMAN S
CAYMANS
CAYS
CAYUSE S
CAUSEY
CAYUSES
CAUSEYS
CAZIQUE S
CAZIQUES
CEASE DS
CEASED
CEASES
CEASING
INCAGES
CEBID S
CEBIDS
CEBOID S
BODICE
CEBOIDS
BODICES
CECA L
CECAL
CECALLY
CALYCLE
CECITIES
CECITY
CECROPIA S
CECUM
CEDAR NSY
ACRED ARCED
CADRE CARED
RACED
CEDARN
CRANED
DANCER
NACRED
CEDARS
CADRES
SACRED
SCARED
CEDARY
CEDE DRS
CEDED
CEDER S
CERED CREED
CEDERS
CREEDS
SCREED
CEDES
CEDI S
DICE ICED
CEDILLA S
CEDILLAS
CEDING
CEDIS
DICES
CEDULA S
CAUDLE
CEDULAS
CAUDLES
CEE S
CEES
CEIBA S
CEIBAS
CEIL IS
LICE
CEILED
DECILE
CEILER S
CEILERS
CEILI S
CEILIDH S
CEILIDHS
CEILING S
CEILINGS
CEILIS

CEILS
SLICE
CEINTURE S
ENURETIC
CEL LST
CELADON S
CELADONS
CELEB S
CELEBS
CELERIAC S
CELERIES
CELERITY
CELERY
CELESTA S
CELESTAS
CELESTE S
CELESTES
CELIAC S
CICALE
CELIACS
CALICES
CELIBACY
CELIBATE S
CITEABLE
CELL AIOS
CELLA ER
CELLAE
CALLEE
O **CELLAR** S
CALLER
RECALL
CELLARED
RECALLED
CELLARER S
RECALLER
CELLARET S
CELLARS
CALLERS
RECALLS
SCLERAL
CELLED
O **CELLI**
CELLING
CELLIST S
CELLISTS
CELLMATE S
CELLO S
CELLOS
CELLS
A **CELLULAR** S
CELLULE S
CELLULES
CELOM S
CELOMATA
CELOMS
CELOSIA S
CELOSIAS
CELOTEX
CELS
CELT S
CELTS
CEMBALI
ALEMBIC
CEMBALO S
CEMBALOS
CEMENT AS
CEMENTA
CEMENTED
CEMENTER S
CEREMENT
RECEMENT
CEMENTS
CEMENTUM S
CEMETERY
CENACLE S
CENACLES
CENOBITE S
CENOTAPH S
CENOTE S
CENOTES
CENOZOIC
CENSE DRS
SCENE
CENSED
CENSER S
SCREEN
SECERN

CENSERS
SCREENS
SECERNS
CENSES
SCENES
CENSING
CENSOR S
CRONES
RECONS
CENSORED
ENCODERS
NECROSED
SECONDER
CENSORS
CENSUAL
LACUNES
LAUNCES
UNLACES
CENSURE DRS
CENSURED
CENSURER S
CENSURES
CENSUS
CENSUSED
CENSUSES
S **CENT** OSU
CENTAI
ACETIN
ENATIC
CENTAL S
CANTLE
LANCET
CENTALS
CANTLES
LANCETS
CENTARE S
CRENATE
REENACT
CENTARES
REASCENT
REENACTS
SARCENET
CENTAS
ASCENT
ENACTS
SECANT
STANCE
CENTAUR SY
UNCRATE
CENTAURS
RECUSANT
UNCRATES
CENTAURY
CENTAVO S
CENTAVOS
CENTER S
CENTRE
RECENT
TENREC
CENTERED
DECENTER
DECENTRE
CENTERS
CENTRES
TENRECS
CENTESES
CENTESIS
CENTIARE S
CREATINE
INCREATE
ITERANCE
CENTILE S
LICENTE
CENTILES
CENTIME S
CENTIMES
TENESMIC
CENTIMO S
TONEMIC
CENTIMOS
CENTNER S
CENTNERS
CENTO S
CONTE ONCET
CENTONES
CENTOS
CONTES

CENTRA L
CANTER
CARNET
NECTAR
RECANT
TANREC
TRANCE
CENTRAL S
CENTRALS
CENTRE DS
CENTER
RECENT
TENREC
CENTRED
CREDENT
CENTRES
CENTERS
TENRECS
A **CENTRIC**
CENTRING S
CENTRISM S
CENTRIST S
CITTERNS
CENTROID S
DOCTRINE
CENTRUM S
CENTRUMS
S **CENTS**
SCENT
CENTU M
CENTUM S
CENTUMS
CENTUPLE DS
CENTURY
CEORL S
CEORLISH
CEORLS
CLOSER
CRESOL
CEP ES
PEC
CEPE S
CEPES
CEPHALAD
A **CEPHALIC**
CEPHALIN S
CEPHEID S
CEPHEIDS
CEPS
PECS SPEC
CERAMAL S
CAMERAL
CARAMEL
CERAMALS
CARAMELS
CERAMIC S
RACEMIC
CERAMICS
CERAMIDE S
MEDICARE
CERAMIST S
MATRICES
MISTRACE
SCIMETAR
CERASTES
CATERESS
A **CERATE** DS
CREATE
ECARTE
A **CERATED**
CATERED
CREATED
REACTED
CERATES
CREATES
ECARTES
CERATIN S
CERTAIN
CREATIN
TACRINE
CERATINS
CANISTER
CISTERNA
CREATINS
SCANTIER
TACRINES
CERATOID
CERCAL
CARCEL
CERCARIA EL NS

CERCI S
CERIC
CERCIS
CERCISES
CERCUS
CRUCES
CERE DS
CEREAL S
RELACE
CEREALS
RELACES
RESCALE
SCLERAE
CEREBRA L
ACERBER
CEREBRAL S
CEREBRIC
CEREBRUM S
CUMBERER
CERED
CEDER CREED
CEREMENT S
CEMENTER
RECEMENT
CEREMONY
CERES
SCREE
CEREUS
CERUSE
RECUSE
RESCUE
SECURE
CEREUSES
CERIA S
AREIC ERICA
CERIAS
CARIES
ERICAS
CERIC
CERCI
CERING
CRINGE
CERIPH S
CIPHER
CERIPHS
CIPHERS
SPHERIC
CERISE S
CERISES
CERITE S
RECITE
TIERCE
CERITES
RECITES
TIERCES
CERIUM S
UREMIC
CERIUMS
MURICES
CERMET S
CERMETS
CERNUOUS
COENURUS
CERO S
CORE
CEROS
CORES CORSE
SCORE
CEROTIC
ORECTIC
CEROTYPE S
A **CEROUS**
COURSE
CROUSE
SOURCE
CERTAIN
CERATIN
CREATIN
TACRINE
CERTES
ERECTS
RESECT
SECRET
TERCES
CERTIFY
RECTIFY
CERULEAN S
CERUMEN S
CERUMENS
CERUSE S
CEREUS
RECUSE
RESCUE
SECURE

CERUSES
RECUSES
RESCUES
SECURES
CERUSITE S
CUTESIER
EUCRITES
CERVELAS
CLEAVERS
CERVELAT S
CERVEZA S
CERVEZAS
CERVICAL
CERVICES
CRESCIVE
CREVICES
CERVID
CERVINE
CERVIX
CERVIXES
CESAREAN S
CESARIAN S
ACARINES
CANARIES
SARCINAE
CESIUM S
MISCUE
CESIUMS
MISCUES
CESS
SECS
CESSED
CESSES
CESSING
CESSION S
COSINES
OSCINES
CESSIONS
COSINESS
CESSPIT S
SEPTICS
CESSPITS
CESSPOOL S
CESTA S
CASTE CATES
TACES
CESTAS
CASTES
CESTI
CITES
CESTODE S
ESCOTED
CESTODES
COSSETED
CESTOI D
CESTOID S
COEDITS
CESTOIDS
CESTOS
COSETS
COSSET
ESCOTS
CESTUS
SCUTES
CESTUSES
CESURA ES
CAUSER
SAUCER
CESURAE
CESURAS
ARCUSES
CAUSERS
SAUCERS
SUCRASE
CETACEAN S
CETANE S
TENACE
CETANES
TENACES
CETE S
CETES
CETOLOGY
CEVICHE S
CEVICHES
CHABLIS
CHABOUK S
CHABOUKS
CHABUK S
CHABUKS
CHACHKA S
CHACHKAS

CHACMA S
CHACMAS
CHACONNE S
CHAD S
CHADAR S
CHADARIM
DRACHMAI
CHADARS
CHADLESS
CHADOR S
CHADORS
CHADRI
CHADS
CHAEBOL S
CHAEBOLS
CHAETA EL
CHAETAE
CHAETAL
CHAFE DRS
CHAFED
CHAFER S
CHAFERS
CHAFES
CHAFF SY
CHAFFED
CHAFFER S
CHAFFERS
CHAFFIER
CHAFFING
CHAFFS
CHAFFY
CHAFING
CHAGRIN S
ARCHING
CHARING
CHAGRINS
ARCHINGS
CRASHING
CHAI NRS
CHIA
CHAIN ES
CHINA
CHAINE DS
CHAINED
ECHIDNA
CHAINES
CHAINING
CHAINMAN
CHAINMEN
CHAINS
CHINAS
CHAINSAW S
CHAIR S
CHAIRED
CHAIRING
CHAIRMAN S
CHAIRMEN
CHAIRS
RACHIS
CHAIS E
CHIAS
CHAISE S
CHAISES
CHAKRA S
CHARKA
CHAKRAS
CHARKAS
CHALAH S
CHALAHS
CHALAZA ELS
CHALAZAE
CHALAZAL
CHALAZAS
CHALAZIA
CHALCID S
CHALCIDS
CHALDRON S
CHLORDAN
CHALEH S
CHALEHS
CHALET S
THECAL
CHALETS
LATCHES
SATCHEL
CHALICE DS
CALICHE
CHALICED

CHALICES
CALICHES
CHALK SY
CHALKED
HACKLED
CHALKIER
HACKLIER
CHALKING
HACKLING
CHALKS
CHALKY
HACKLY
CHALLA HS
CHALLAH S
CHALLAHS
CHALLAS
CHALLIE S
HELICAL
CHALLIES
CHALLIS
CHALLOT H
CHALLOTH
CHALLY
CHALONE S
CHALONES
CHALOT H
CHALOTH
CHALUPA S
CHALUPAS
CHALUTZ
CHAM PS
MACH
CHAMADE S
CHAMADES
CHAMBER S
BECHARM
BRECHAM
CHAMBERS
BECHARMS
BRECHAMS
CHAMBRAY S
CHAMFER S
CHAMFERS
CHAMFRON S
CHAMISA S
CHIASMA
CHAMISAS
CHIASMAS
CHAMISE S
CHAMISES
CHAMISO S
CHAMOIS
CHAMISOS
CHAMMIED
CHAMMIES
CHAMMY
CHAMOIS
CHAMISO
CHAMOIX
CHAMP SY
CHAMPAC AS
CHAMPACA S
CHAMPACS
CHAMPAK S
CHAMPAKS
CHAMPED
CHAMPER S
CHAMPERS
CHAMPING
CHAMPION S
CHAMPS
CHAMPY
CHAMS
CHASM MACHS
CHANCE DLRS
CHANCED
CHANCEL S
CHANCELS
CHANCER SY
CHANCRE
CHANCERS
CHANCRES
CRANCHES
CHANCERY
CHANCES
CHANCIER
CHICANER
CHANCILY
CHANCING

CHANCRE S
CHANCER
CHANCRES
CHANCERS
CRANCHES
CHANCY
CHANDLER SY
CHANFRON S
CHANG ES
CHANGE DRS
CHANGED
CHANGER S
CHANGERS
CHANGES
CHANGEUP S
CHANGING
CHANGS
CHANNEL S
CHANNELS
CHANOYU S
CHANOYUS
CHANSON S
NONCASH
CHANSONS
CHANT SY
NATCH
CHANTAGE S
CHANTED
CHANTER S
TRANCHE
CHANTERS
SNATCHER
STANCHER
TRANCHES
CHANTEY S
CHANTEYS
CHANTIES
ASTHENIC
CHANTING
CHANTOR S
CHANTORS
CHANTRY
CHANTS
SNATCH
STANCH
CHANTY
CHAO S
CHAOS
CHAOSES
CHAOTIC
CHAP EST
CAPH
CHAPATI S
CHAPATIS
CHAPATTI S
CHAPBOOK S
CHAPE LS
CHEAP PEACH
CHAPEAU SX
CHAPEAUS
CHAPEAUX
CHAPEL S
PLEACH
CHAPELS
CHAPERON ES
CANEPHOR
CHAPES
CHEAPS
CHAPITER S
PATCHIER
PHREATIC
CHAPLAIN S
CHAPLET S
CHAPLETS
CHAPMAN
CHAPMEN
CHAPPATI S
CHAPPED
CHAPPIE S
CHAPPIES
CHAPPING
CHAPS
CAPHS
CHAPT
PATCH
CHAPTER S
PATCHER
REPATCH
CHAPTERS
PATCHERS
CHAQUETA S
CHAR DEKMRS
ARCH TY
CHARACID S
CHARACIN S
ANARCHIC
CHARADE S
CHARADES
HARDCASE
CHARAS
CHARASES
CHARCOAL SY
E CHARD S
E CHARDS
CHARE DS
REACH
CHARED
ARCHED
ECHARD
CHARES
ARCHES
CHASER
ESCHAR
SEARCH
CHARGE DRS
CHARGED
CHARGER S
CHARGERS
CHARGES
CHARGING
CHARIER
CHARIEST
THERIACS
CHARILY
CHARING
ARCHING
CHAGRIN
CHARIOT S
HARICOT
CHARIOTS
ACTORISH
HARICOTS
CHARISM AS
CHIMARS
CHRISMA
CHARISMA S
ARCHAISM
CHARISMS
CHARITY
CHARK AS
CHARKA S
CHAKRA
CHARKAS
CHAKRAS
CHARKED
CHARKHA S
CHARKHAS
CHARKING
CHARKS
CHARLADY
CHARLEY S
CHARLEYS
CHARLIE S
CHARLIES
CHARLOCK S
CHARM S
MARCH
CHARMED
MARCHED
CHARMER S
MARCHER
CHARMERS
MARCHERS
CHARMING
MARCHING
CHARMS
CHARNEL S
LARCHEN
CHARNELS
CHARPAI S
HAIRCAP
CHARPAIS
HAIRCAPS
CHARPOY S
CHARPOYS
CHARQUI DS
CHARQUID
CHARQUIS
CHARR OSY
CHARRED
CHARRIER
CHARRING
CHARRO S
CHARROS
CHARRS
CHARRY
CHARS
CRASH
CHART S
RATCH
CHARTED
CHARTER S
RECHART
CHARTERS
RECHARTS
CHARTING
CHARTIST S
CHARTS
STARCH
CHARY
CHASE DRS
ACHES
CHASED
CASHED
CHASER S
ARCHES
CHARES
ESCHAR
SEARCH
CHASERS
CRASHES
ESCHARS
CHASES
CASHES
CHASSE
CHASING S
CASHING
CHASINGS
CHASM SY
CHAMS MACHS
CHASMAL
CHASMED
CHASMIC
CHASMS
CHASMY
CHASSE DS
CASHES
CHASES
CHASSED
CHASSES
CHASSEUR S
CHASSIS
CHASTE NR
CHEATS
SACHET
SCATHE
TACHES
CHASTELY
CHASTEN S
CHASTENS
SNATCHES
STANCHES
CHASTER
RACHETS
RATCHES
CHASTEST
CHASTISE DR S
CHASTITY
CHASUBLE S
CHAT S
TACH
CHATCHKA S
CHATCHKE S
HATCHECK
CHATEAU SX
CHATEAUS
CHATEAUX
CHATROOM S
CHATS
TACHS
CHATTED
CHATTEL S
LATCHET
CHATTELS
LATCHETS
CHATTER SY
RATCHET
CHATTERS
RATCHETS
CHATTERY
TRACHYTE
CHATTIER
THEATRIC
CHATTILY
CHATTING
CHATTY
CHAUFER S
CHAUFERS
CHAUFFER S
CHAUNT S
NAUTCH
CHAUNTED
CHAUNTER S
CHAUNTS
CANTHUS
STAUNCH
CHAUSSES
CHAW S
CHAWED
CHAWER S
CHAWERS
CHAWING
CHINWAG
CHAWS
SCHWA
CHAY S
ACHY
CHAYOTE S
CHAYOTES
CHAYS
CHAZAN S
CHAZANIM
CHAZANS
CHAZZAN S
CHAZZANS
CHAZZEN S
CHAZZENS
CHEAP OS
CHAPE PEACH
CHEAPEN S
CHEAPENS
CHEAPER
PEACHER
CHEAPEST
CHEAPIE S
CHEAPIES
CHEAPISH
CHEAPLY
CHEAPO S
CHEAPOS
POACHES
SHOEPAC
CHEAPS
CHAPES
CHEAT S
TACHE TEACH
THECA
CHEATED
CHEATER S
HECTARE
RECHEAT
RETEACH
TEACHER
CHEATERS
HECTARES
RECHEATS
TEACHERS
CHEATING
TEACHING
CHEATS
CHASTE
SACHET
SCATHE
TACHES
CHEBEC S
CHEBECS
CHECHAKO S
CHECK S
CHECKED
CHECKER S
RECHECK
CHECKERS
RECHECKS
CHECKING
CHECKOFF S
CHECKOUT S
CHECKROW S
CHECKS
CHECKSUM S
CHECKUP S
CHECKUPS
CHEDDAR SY
CHEDDARS
CHEDDARY
CHEDDITE S
CHEDER S
CHEDERS
CHEDITE S
CHEDITES
CHEEK SY
CHEEKED
CHEEKFUL S
CHEEKIER
CHEEKILY
CHEEKING
CHEEKS
CHEEKY
CHEEP S
CHEEPED
CHEEPER S
CHEEPERS
CHEEPING
CHEEPS
SPEECH
CHEER OSY
CHEERED
CHEERER S
CHEERERS
CHEERFUL
CHEERIER
REECHIER
CHEERILY
CHEERING
CHEERIO S
CHEERIOS
CHEERLED
LECHERED
CHEERLY
LECHERY
CHEERO S
COHERE
ECHOER
REECHO
CHEEROS
COHERES
ECHOERS
RECHOSE
CHEERS
CREESH
CHEERY
REECHY
CHEESE DS
CHEESED
CHEESES
CHEESIER
CHEESILY
CHEESING
CHEESY
CHEETAH S
CHEETAHS
CHEF S
CHEFDOM S
CHEFDOMS
CHEFED
CHEFFED
CHEFFING
CHEFING
CHEFS
CHEGOE S
CHEGOES
CHELA ES
LEACH
CHELAE
CHELAS
LACHES
CHELATE DS
CHELATED
CHELATES
CHELATOR S
CHLORATE
TROCHLEA
CHELIPED S
CHELOID S
CHELOIDS
CHEMIC S
CHEMICAL S
ALCHEMIC
CHEMICS
CHEMISE S
CHEMISES
CHEMISM S
CHEMISMS
CHEMIST S
CHEMISTS
CHEMO S
CHEMOS
SCHMOE
CHEMURGY
CHENILLE S
CHENOPOD S
PONCHOED
CHEQUE RS
CHEQUER S
CHEQUERS
CHEQUES
CHERISH
CHEROOT S
CHEROOTS
CHERRIES
CHERRY
CHERT SY
RETCH
CHERTIER
CHERTS
CHERTY
CHERUB S
CHERUBIC
CHERUBIM S
CHERUBS
CHERVIL S
CHERVILS
CHESHIRE S
CHESS
CHESSES
CHESSMAN
CHESSMEN
MENSCHES
CHEST SY
TECHS
CHESTED
CHESTFUL S
CHESTIER
HERETICS
CHESTILY
LECYTHIS
CHESTNUT S
CHESTS
CHESTY
SCYTHE
CHETAH S
CHETAHS
HATCHES
CHETH S
CHETHS
CHETRUM S
CHETRUMS
CHEVALET S
CHEVERON S
CHEVIED
CHEVIES
SEVICHE
CHEVIOT S
CHEVIOTS
CHEVRE ST
CHEVRES
CHEVRET S
CHEVRETS
CHEVRON S
CHEVRONS
CHEVY
CHEVYING
CHEW SY
CHEWABLE
CHEWED
CHEWER S
RECHEW
CHEWERS
RECHEWS
CHEWIER
CHEWIEST
CHEWING
CHEWINK S
CHEWINKS
CHEWS
CHEWY
CHEZ
CHI ACDNPST
HIC
ICH
CHIA OS
CHAI
CHIANTI S
CHIANTIS
CHIAO
CHIAS M
CHAIS
CHIASM AIS
CHIASMA LS
CHAMISA
CHIASMAL
CHIASMAS
CHAMISAS
CHIASMI C
CHIASMIC
CHIASMS
CHIASMUS
CHIASTIC
CHIAUS
CHIAUSES
CHIBOUK S
CHIBOUKS
CHIC AKOS
CHICA S
CHICANE DRS
CHICANED
CHICANER SY
CHANCIER
CHICANES
CHICANO S
CHICANOS
CHICAS
CHICCORY
CHICER
CHICEST
CHICHI S
CHICHIER
CHICHIS
CHICK S
CHICKEE S
CHICKEES
CHICKEN S
CHICKENS
CHICKORY
CHICKPEA S
CHICKS
CHICLE S
CLICHE
CHICLES
CLICHES
CHICLY
CHICNESS
CHICO S
CHICORY
CHICOS
CHICS
CHID E
CHIDDEN
CHIDE DRS
CHIDED
CHIDER S
DREICH
HERDIC
CHIDERS
HERDICS
CHIDES
CHIDING
CHIEF S
FICHE
CHIEFDOM S
CHIEFER
CHIEFEST
FETICHES
CHIEFLY
CHIEFS
FICHES
CHIEL DS
CHILE
CHIELD S
CHILDE

CHIELDS
CHILDES
CHIELS
CHILES
CHISEL
LICHES
CHIFFON S
CHIFFONS
CHIGETAI S
CHIGGER S
CHIGGERS
CHIGNON S
CHIGNONS
CHIGOE S
CHIGOES
CHILD E
CHILDBED S
CHILDE S
CHIELD
CHILDES
CHIELDS
CHILDING
CHILDISH
CHILDLY
CHILDREN
CHILE S
CHIEL
CHILES
CHIELS
CHISEL
LICHES
CHILI S
LICHI
CHILIAD S
CHILIADS
CHILIASM S
CHILIAST S
CHILIDOG S
CHILIES
CHILIS
LICHIS
CHILL ISY
CHILLED
S CHILLER S
S CHILLERS
SCHILLER
CHILLEST
CHILLI S
CHILLIER
CHILLIES T
CHILLILY
S CHILLING
CHILLIS
CHILLS
CHILLUM S
CHILLUMS
CHILLY
CHILOPOD S
CHIMAERA S
CHIMAR S
CHIMARS
CHARISM
CHRISMA
CHIMB S
CHIMBLEY S
CHIMBLY
CHIMBS
CHIME DRS
HEMIC MICHE
CHIMED
MICHED
CHIMER AES
CHIMERA S
CHIMERAS
MARCHESI
CHIMERE S
CHIMERES
CHIMERIC
CHIMERS
CHIMES
MICHES
CHIMING
MICHING
CHIMLA S
CHIMLAS
CHIMLEY S
CHIMLEYS
CHIMNEY S

CHIMNEYS
CHIMP S
CHIMPS
CHIN AEKOS
INCH
CHINA S
CHAIN
CHINAS
CHAINS
CHINBONE S
CHINCH Y
CHINCHES
CHINCHY
CHINE DS
NICHE
CHINED
INCHED
NICHED
CHINES
INCHES
NICHES
CHINING
INCHING
NICHING
CHINK SY
CHINKED
CHINKIER
CHINKING
CHINKS
CHINKY
CHINLESS
CHINNED
CHINNING
CHINO S
CHINONE S
CHINONES
CHINOOK S
CHINOOKS
CHINOS
CHINS
CHINTS
SNITCH
CHINTSES
SNITCHES
CHINTZ Y
CHINTZES
CHINTZY
CHINWAG S
CHAWING
CHINWAGS
CHIP S
CHIPMUCK S
CHIPMUNK S
CHIPOTLE S
HELICOPT
CHIPPED
CHIPPER S
CHIPPERS
CHIPPIE RS
CHIPPIER
CHIPPIES T
CHIPPING
CHIPPY
CHIPS
A CHIRAL
ARCHIL
CHIRK S
CHIRKED
CHIRKER
CHIRKEST
CHIRKING
CHIRKS
KIRSCH
SCHRIK
CHIRM S
CHIRMED
CHIRMING
CHIRMS
CHRISM
SMIRCH
CHIRO S
CHOIR ICHOR
CHIROS
CHOIRS
ICHORS
ORCHIS
CHIRP SY
CHIRPED
CHIRPER S

CHIRPERS
CHIRPIER
CHIRPILY
CHIRPING
CHIRPS
CHIRPY
CHIRR ES
CHIRRE DNS
RICHER
CHIRRED
CHIRREN
CHIRRES
CHIRRING
CHIRRS
CHIRRUP SY
CHIRRUPS
CHIRRUPY
CHIRU S
CHIRUS
CHIS
ICHS
CHISEL S
CHIELS
CHILES
LICHES
CHISELED
CHISELER S
SCHLIERE
CHISELS
CHIT S
ITCH
CHITAL
CHITCHAT S
CHITIN S
CHITINS
CHITLIN GS
CHITLING S
LICHTING
CHITLINS
CHITON S
CHITONS
CHITOSAN S
CHITS
STICH
CHITTER S
CHITTERS
RESTITCH
STITCHER
CHITTIES
ETHICIST
ITCHIEST
THEISTIC
CHITTY
CHIVALRY
CHIVAREE DS
ACHIEVER
CHIVARI
CHIVE S
CHIVES
CHIVIED
CHIVIES
VICHIES
CHIVVIED
CHIVVIES
CHIVVY
CHIVY
VICHY
CHIVYING
CHLAMYS
CHLOASMA S
CHLORAL S
CHLORALS
CHLORATE S
CHELATOR
TROCHLEA
CHLORDAN ES
CHALDRON
CHLORIC
CHLORID ES
CHLORIDE S
CHLORIDS
CHLORIN ES
CHLORINE S
CHLORINS
CHLORITE S
CLOTHIER
CHLOROUS
CHOANA E

CHOANAE
CHOCK S
CHOCKED
CHOCKFUL L
CHOCKING
CHOCKS
CHOICE RS
ECHOIC
CHOICELY
CHOICER
CHOREIC
CHOICES T
CHOICEST
CHOIR S
CHIRO ICHOR
CHOIRBOY S
CHOIRED
CHOIRING
CHOIRS
CHIROS
ICHORS
ORCHIS
CHOKE DRSY
CHOKED
HOCKED
CHOKER S
HOCKER
CHOKERS
HOCKERS
SHOCKER
CHOKES
CHOKEY
HOCKEY
CHOKIER
CHOKIEST
CHOKING
HOCKING
CHOKY
CHOLA S
LOACH
CHOLAS
CHOLATE S
CHOLATES
ESCHALOT
CHOLENT S
CHOLENTS
CHOLER AS
CHOLERA S
CHORALE
CHOREAL
CHOLERAS
CHORALES
CHOLERIC
CHOLERS
CHOLINE S
HELICON
CHOLINES
HELICONS
CHOLLA S
CHOLLAS
CHOLO S
CHOLOS
SCHOOL
CHOMP S
CHOMPED
CHOMPER S
CHOMPERS
CHOMPING
CHOMPS
CHON
CHOOK S
CHOOKS
CHOOSE RSY
CHOOSER S
SOROCHE
CHOOSERS
SOROCHES
CHOOSES
CHOOSEY
CHOOSIER
ISOCHORE
CHOOSING
CHOOSY
CHOP S
CHOPIN ES
PHONIC
CHOPINE S
PHOCINE
CHOPINES

CHOPINS
PHONICS
CHOPPED
CHOPPER S
CHOPPERS
CHOPPIER
CHOPPILY
CHOPPING
CHOPPY
CHOPS
CHORAGI C
CHORAGIC
CHORAGUS
CHORAL ES
CHORALE S
CHOLERA
CHOREAL
CHORALES
CHOLERAS
CHORALLY
CHORALS
SCHOLAR
CHORD S
CHORDAL
CHORDATE S
CHORDED
CHORDING
CHORDS
SCHROD
CHORE ADS
OCHER OCHRE
CHOREA LS
OCHREA
ORACHE
CHOREAL
CHOLERA
CHORALE
CHOREAS
ORACHES
ROACHES
CHORED
OCHRED
CHOREGI
CHOREGUS
COUGHERS
GROUCHES
CHOREIC
CHOICER
CHOREMAN
CHOREMEN
CHOREOID
CHORES
COSHER
OCHERS
OCHRES
CHORIAL
CHORIAMB S
CHORIC
CHORINE S
CHORINES
CHORING
OCHRING
CHORIOID S
CHORION S
CHORIONS
ISOCHRON
CHORIZO S
CHORIZOS
CHOROID S
OCHROID
CHOROIDS
CHORTEN S
NOTCHER
CHORTENS
NOTCHERS
CHORTLE DRS
CHORTLED
CHORTLER S
CHORTLES
CHORUS
CHORUSED
CHORUSES
CHOUSERS
CHOSE NS
ECHOS
CHOSEN
CHOSES
COSHES
CHOTT S
CHOTTS

CHOUGH S
CHOUGHS
CHOUSE DRS
OUCHES
CHOUSED
DOUCHES
HOCUSED
CHOUSER S
ROUCHES
CHOUSERS
CHORUSES
CHOUSES
HOCUSES
CHOUSH
CHOUSHES
CHOUSING
HOCUSING
CHOW S
CHOWCHOW S
CHOWDER S
COWHERD
CHOWDERS
COWHERDS
CHOWED
CHOWING
CHOWS E
CHOWSE DS
CHOWSED
COWSHED
CHOWSES
CHOWSING
CHOWTIME S
CHRESARD S
CHRISM AS
CHIRMS
SMIRCH
CHRISMA L
CHARISM
CHIMARS
CHRISMAL
CHRISMON S
CHRISMS
CHRISOM S
CHRISOMS
CHRISTEN S
CITHERNS
CITHRENS
SNITCHER
CHRISTIE S
CHRISTY
CHROMA S
CHROMAS
CHROMATE S
CHROME DS
CHROMED
CHROMES
A CHROMIC
CHROMIDE S
CHROMIER
CHROMING S
CHROMITE S
TRICHOME
CHROMIUM S
CHROMIZE DS
CHROMO S
CHROMOS
A CHROMOUS
CHROMY L
CHROMYL S
CHROMYLS
CHRONAXY
CHRONIC S
CHRONICS
CHRONON S
CHRONONS
CHTHONIC
CHUB S
CHUBASCO S
CHUBBIER
CHUBBILY
CHUBBY
CHUBS
CHUCK SY
CHUCKED
CHUCKIES
CHUCKING
CHUCKLE DRS
CHUCKLED

CHUCKLER S
CHUCKLES
CHUCKS
CHUCKY
CHUDDAH S
CHUDDAHS
CHUDDAR S
CHUDDARS
CHUDDER S
CHUDDERS
CHUFA S
CHUFAS
CHUFF SY
CHUFFED
CHUFFER
CHUFFEST
CHUFFIER
CHUFFING
CHUFFS
CHUFFY
CHUG S
CHUGALUG S
CHUGGED
CHUGGER S
CHUGGERS
CHUGGING
CHUGS
CHUKAR S
CHUKARS
CHUKKA RS
CHUKKAR S
CHUKKARS
CHUKKAS
CHUKKER S
CHUKKERS
CHUM PS
MUCH
CHUMMED
CHUMMIER
CHUMMILY
CHUMMING
CHUMMY
CHUMP S
CHUMPED
CHUMPING
CHUMPS
CHUMS
CHUMSHIP S
CHUNK SY
CHUNKED
CHUNKIER
CHUNKILY
CHUNKING
CHUNKS
CHUNKY
CHUNNEL S
CHUNNELS
CHUNTER S
CHUNTERS
CHUPPA HS
CHUPPAH S
CHUPPAHS
CHUPPAS
CHURCH Y
CHURCHED
CHURCHES
CHURCHLY
CHURCHY
CHURL S
LURCH
CHURLISH
CHURLS
CHURN S
CHURNED
CHURNER S
CHURNERS
CHURNING S
CHURNS
CHURR OS
CHURRED
CHURRING
CHURRO S
CHURROS
CHURRS

2006 addition

CHUTE DS
TEUCH
CHUTED
CHUTES
TUSCHE
CHUTING
CHUTIST S
CHUTISTS
CHUTNEE S
CHUTNEES
CHUTNEY S
CHUTNEYS
CHUTZPA HS
CHUTZPAH S
CHUTZPAS
CHYLE S
CHYLES
LYCHES
CHYLOUS
SLOUCHY
CHYME S
CHYMES
CHYMIC S
CHYMICS
CHYMIST S
CHYMISTS
CHYMOSIN S
CHYMOUS
CHYTRID S
CHYTRIDS
CIAO
CIBOL S
CIBOLS
CIBORIA
CIBORIUM
CIBOULE S
CIBOULES
CICADA ES
CICADAE
CICADAS
CICALA S
ALCAIC
CICALAS
ALCAICS
CICALE
CELIAC
CICATRIX
CICELIES
CICELY
CICERO S
CICERONE S
CROCEINE
CICERONI
CICEROS
CICHLID S
CICHLIDS
CICISBEI
CICISBEO S
CICOREE S
CICOREES
CIDER S
CRIED DICER
RICED
CIDERS
DICERS
SCRIED
CIG S
CIGAR S
CIGARET S
CIGARETS
AGRESTIC
ERGASTIC
CIGARS
CIGS
CILANTRO S
CONTRAIL
CILIA
ILIAC
CILIARY
CILIATE DS
CILIATED
CILIATES
SILICATE
CILICE S
ICICLE
CILICES
ICICLES
CILIUM

CIMBALOM S
CIMEX
CIMICES
CINCH
CINCHED
CINCHES
CINCHING
CINCHONA S
CINCTURE DS
CINDER SY
CINDERED
CINDERS
DISCERN
RESCIND
CINDERY
CINE S
NICE
CINEAST ES
ACETINS
CINEASTE S
CINEASTS
SCANTIES
CINEMA S
ANEMIC
ICEMAN
CINEMAS
AMNESIC
CINEOL ES
ENOLIC
CINEOLE S
CINEOLES
CINEOLS
INCLOSE
CINERARY
CINERIN S
CINERINS
CINES
SINCE
CINGULA R
CINGULAR
CINGULUM
GLUCINUM
CINNABAR S
CINNAMIC
CINNAMON SY
CINNAMYL S
CINQUAIN S
CINQUE S
QUINCE
CINQUES
QUINCES
S CION S
COIN CONI
ICON
S CIONS
COINS ICONS
SCION SONIC
CIOPPINO S
CIPHER S
CERIPH
CIPHERED
DECIPHER
CIPHERER S
CIPHERS
CERIPHS
SPHERIC
CIPHONY
CIPOLIN S
PICOLIN
CIPOLINS
PICOLINS
PSILOCIN
CIRCA
CIRCLE DRST
CLERIC
CIRCLED
CIRCLER S
CIRCLERS
CIRCLES
CLERICS
CIRCLET S
CIRCLETS
CIRCLING
CIRCUIT SY
CIRCUITS
CIRCUITY
CIRCULAR S
CIRCUS Y
CIRCUSES
CIRCUSY

CIRE S
RICE
CIRES
CRIES RICES
CIRQUE S
CIRQUES
CIRRATE
ERRATIC
CIRRI
CIRRIPED ES
CIRROSE
CORRIES
CROSIER
ORRICES
CIRROUS
CIRRUS
CIRSOID
CIS T
SIC
CISCO S
CISCOES
CISCOS
CISLUNAR
CISSIES
CISSOID S
CISSOIDS
CISSY
CIST S
TICS
CISTED
EDICTS
CISTERN AS
CRETINS
CISTERNA EL
CANISTER
CERATINS
CREATINS
SCANTIER
TACRINES
CISTERNS
CISTRON S
CITRONS
CORTINS
CISTRONS
CISTS
CISTUS
CISTUSES
CITABLE
CITADEL S
DELTAIC
DIALECT
EDICTAL
CITADELS
DIALECTS
CITATION S
CITATOR SY
RICOTTA
CITATORS
RICOTTAS
CITATORY
ATROCITY
CITE DRS
ETIC
CITEABLE
CELIBATE
CITED
EDICT
CITER S
RECIT RECTI
TRICE
CITERS
RECITS
STERIC
TRICES
CITES
CESTI
CITHARA S
CITHARAS
ARCHAIST
CITHER NS
THRICE
CITHERN S
CITHREN
CITHERNS
CHRISTEN
CITHRENS
SNITCHER
CITHERS
RICHEST
CITHREN S
CITHERN

CITHRENS
CHRISTEN
CITHERNS
SNITCHER
CITIED
CITIES
ICIEST
CITIFIED
CITIFIES
CITIFY
CITING
CITIZEN S
ZINCITE
CITIZENS
ZINCITES
CITOLA S
COITAL
CITOLAS
STOICAL
CITOLE S
CITOLES
CITRAL S
RICTAL
CITRALS
CITRATE DS
ATRETIC
CATTIER
CITRATED
TETRACID
TETRADIC
CITRATES
CRISTATE
SCATTIER
CITREOUS
OUTCRIES
CITRIC
CRITIC
CITRIN ES
NITRIC
CITRINE S
CRINITE
INCITER
NERITIC
CITRINES
CRINITES
INCITERS
CITRININ S
CITRINS
CITRON S
CORTIN
CITRONS
CISTRON
CORTINS
CITROUS
CITRUS Y
RICTUS
RUSTIC
CITRUSES
CURTSIES
RICTUSES
CITRUSY
CITTERN S
CITTERNS
CENTRIST
CITY
CITYFIED
CITYWARD
CITYWIDE
CIVET S
EVICT
CIVETS
EVICTS
CIVIC S
CIVICISM S
CIVICS
CIVIE S
CIVIES
CIVIL
CIVILIAN S
CIVILISE DS
CIVILITY
CIVILIZE DR S
CIVILLY
CIVISM S
CIVISMS
CIVVIES
CIVVY
CLABBER S
CLABBERS
SCRABBLE

CLACH S
CLACHAN S
CLACHANS
CLACHS
CLACK S
CLACKED
CACKLED
CLACKER S
CACKLER
CRACKLE
CLACKERS
CACKLERS
CRACKLES
CLACKING
CACKLING
CLACKS
Y CLAD ES
CLADDAGH S
CLADDED
CLADDING S
CLADE S
DECAL LACED
CLADES
DECALS
SCALED
CLADISM S
CLADISMS
CLADIST S
CLADISTS
CLADODE S
CLADODES
CLADS
SCALD
CLAFOUTI S
CLAG S
CLAGGED
CLAGGING
CLAGS
CLAIM S
MALIC
CLAIMANT S
CALAMINT
CLAIMED
CAMELID
DECIMAL
DECLAIM
MEDICAL
CLAIMER S
MIRACLE
RECLAIM
CLAIMERS
MIRACLES
RECLAIMS
CLAIMING
CLAIMS
CLAM PS
CALM
CLAMANT
CLAMBAKE S
CLAMBER S
CLAMBERS
SCRAMBLE
CLAMLIKE
MILLCAKE
CLAMMED
CLAMMER S
CLAMMERS
CLAMMIER
CLAMMILY
CLAMMING
CLAMMY
CLAMOR S
CLAMORED
CLAMORER S
CLAMORS
CLAMOUR S
CLAMOURS
CLAMP S
CLAMPED
CLAMPER S
CLAMPERS
CLAMPING
CLAMPS
CLAMS
CALMS
CLAMWORM S
CLAN GKS
CLANG S

CLANGED
GLANCED
CLANGER S
GLANCER
CLANGERS
GLANCERS
CLANGING
GLANCING
CLANGOR S
CLANGORS
CLANGOUR S
CLANGS
CLANK SY
CLANKED
CLANKIER
CLANKING
CLANKS
CLANKY
CLANNISH
CLANS
CLANSMAN
CLANSMEN
CLAP ST
CLAPPED
CLAPPER S
CLAPPERS
SCRAPPLE
CLAPPING
CLAPS
CLASP SCALP
CLAPT
CLAPTRAP S
CLAQUE RS
CALQUE
CLAQUER S
LACQUER
CLAQUERS
LACQUERS
CLAQUES
CALQUES
CLAQUEUR S
CLARENCE S
CANCELER
CLARET S
CARTEL
RECTAL
CLARETS
CARTELS
CRESTAL
SCARLET
CLARIES
ECLAIRS
SCALIER
CLARIFY
CLARINET S
CLARION S
CLARIONS
CLARITY
CLARKIA S
CLARKIAS
CLARO S
CAROL CORAL
CLAROES
COALERS
ESCOLAR
ORACLES
RECOALS
SOLACER
CLAROS
CAROLS
CORALS
CLARY
LYCRA
CLASH
CLASHED
CLASHER S
LARCHES
CLASHERS
CLASHES
CLASHING
CLASP ST
CLAPS SCALP
CLASPED
SCALPED
CLASPER S
CARPELS
PARCELS
PLACERS
RECLASP
SCALPER

CLASPERS
RECLASPS
SCALPERS
CLASPING
SCALPING
CLASPS
SCALPS
CLASPT
CLASS Y
CLASSED
DECLASS
CLASSER S
CARLESS
SCALERS
SCLERAS
CLASSERS
SCARLESS
CLASSES
CLASSIC OS
CLASSICO
CLASSICS
CLASSIER
CLASSIFY
CLASSILY
CLASSING
CLASSIS MT
CLASSISM S
MISCLASS
CLASSIST S
CLASSON S
CLASSONS
CLASSY
CLAST S
TALCS
CLASTIC S
CLASTICS
CLASTS
CLATTER SY
CLATTERS
CLATTERY
CLAUCHT
CLAUGHT S
CLAUGHTS
CLAUSAL
CLAUSE S
CAULES
CLAUSES
CLAUSTRA L
CLAVATE
CLAVE RS
CALVE
CLAVER S
CARVEL
CLAVERED
CLAVERS
CARVELS
CLAVES
CALVES
CLAVI
CAVIL
CLAVICLE S
CLAVIER S
CAVILER
VALERIC
CLAVIERS
CAVILERS
VISCERAL
CLAVUS
CLAW S
CLAWBACK S
CLAWED
DECLAW
CLAWER S
CLAWERS
CLAWING
CLAWLESS
CLAWLIKE
CLAWS
CLAXON S
CLAXONS
CLAY S
ACYL LACY
CLAYBANK S
CLAYED
CLAYEY
CLAYIER
CLAYIEST
CLAYING
CLAYISH

CLAYLIKE
CLAYMORE S
CLAYPAN S
CLAYPANS
CLAYS
ACYLS SCALY
CLAYWARE S
CLEAN S
LANCE
CLEANED
ENLACED
CLEANER S
RECLEAN
CLEANERS
CLEANSER
RECLEANS
CLEANEST
CLEANING
ENLACING
CLEANLY
CLEANS E
LANCES
CLEANSE DRS
ENLACES
SCALENE
CLEANSED
CLEANSER S
CLEANERS
RECLEANS
CLEANSES
CLEANUP S
CLEANUPS
CLEAR S
CARLE LACER
CLEARCUT S
CLEARED
CREEDAL
DECLARE
RELACED
CLEARER S
CLEARERS
CLEAREST
TREACLES
CLEARING S
RELACING
CLEARLY
CLEARS
CARLES
LACERS
SCALER
SCLERA
CLEAT S
ECLAT
CLEATED
CLEATING
CLEATS
CASTLE
ECLATS
CLEAVAGE S
CLEAVE DRS
CLEAVED
CLEAVER S
CLEAVERS
CERVELAS
CLEAVES
CLEAVING
CLEEK S
CLEEKED
CLEEKING
CLEEKS
CLEF ST
CLEFS
CLEFT S
CLEFTED
DEFLECT
CLEFTING
CLEFTS
CLEIDOIC
CLEMATIS
CLIMATES
METICALS
CLEMENCY
CLEMENT
CLENCH
CLENCHED
CLENCHER S
CLENCHES
CLEOME S
CLEOMES
CLEPE DS
Y CLEPED
CLEPES
CLEPING
Y CLEPT
CLERGIES
CLERGY
CLERIC S
CIRCLE
CLERICAL S
CLERICS
CIRCLES
CLERID S
CLERIDS
CLERIHEW S
CLERISY
CLERK S
CLERKDOM S
CLERKED
CLERKING
CLERKISH
CLERKLY
CLERKS
CLEVEITE S
ELECTIVE
CLEVER
CLEVERER
CLEVERLY
CLEVIS
CLEVISES
VESICLES
VICELESS
CLEW S
CLEWED
CLEWING
CLEWS
CLICHE DS
CHICLE
CLICHED
CLICHES
CHICLES
CLICK S
CLICKED
CLICKER S
CLICKERS
CLICKING
CLICKS
CLIENT S
LECTIN
LENTIC
CLIENTAL
CLIENTS
LECTINS
STENCIL
CLIFF SY
CLIFFIER
CLIFFS
CLIFFY
CLIFT S
CLIFTS
CLIMATAL
CLIMATE S
METICAL
CLIMATES
CLEMATIS
METICALS
CLIMATIC
CLIMAX
CLIMAXED
CLIMAXES
EXCLAIMS
CLIMB S
CLIMBED
CLIMBER S
CLIMBERS
CLIMBING
CLIMBS
CLIME S
MELIC
CLIMES
CLINAL
CLINALLY
CLINCH
CLINCHED
CLINCHER S
CLINCHES
CLINE S
CLINES
CLING SY
CLINGED
CLINGER S
CRINGLE
CLINGERS
CRINGLES
CLINGIER
CLINGING
CLINGS
CLINGY
GLYCIN
A CLINIC S
CLINICAL
CLINICS
CLINK S
CLINKED
NICKLED
CLINKER S
CRINKLE
CLINKERS
CRINKLES
CLINKING
NICKLING
CLINKS
CLIP ST
CLIPPED
CLIPPER S
CRIPPLE
CLIPPERS
CRIPPLES
CLIPPING S
CLIPS
CLIPT
CLIQUE DSY
CLIQUED
CLIQUES
CLIQUEY
CLIQUIER
CLIQUING
CLIQUISH
CLIQUY
CLITELLA
CLITIC S
CLITICS
CLITORAL
CLITORIC
CLITORIS
COISTRIL
CLIVERS
CLIVIA S
CLIVIAS
CLOACA ELS
CLOACAE
CLOACAL
CLOACAS
CLOAK S
CLOAKED
CLOAKING
CLOAKS
CLOBBER S
COBBLER
CLOBBERS
COBBLERS
CLOCHARD S
CLOCHE S
CLOCHES
CLOCK S
CLOCKED
COCKLED
CLOCKER S
CLOCKERS
CLOCKING
COCKLING
CLOCKS
CLOD S
COLD
CLODDIER
CLODDISH
CLODDY
CLODPATE S
CLODPOLE S
CLODPOLL S
CLODS
COLDS SCOLD
CLOG S
CLOGGED
CLOGGER S
CLOGGERS
CLOGGIER
CLOGGILY
CLOGGING
CLOGGY
CLOGS
CLOISTER S
COISTREL
COSTLIER
CLOMB
CLOMP S
CLOMPED
CLOMPING
CLOMPS
CLON EKS
CLONAL
CLONALLY
CLONE DRS
CLONED
CLONER S
CORNEL
CLONERS
CORNELS
CLONES
CLONIC
CLONING S
CLONINGS
CLONISM S
CLONISMS
CLONK S
CLONKED
CLONKING
CLONKS
CLONS
CLONUS
CONSUL
CLONUSES
COUNSELS
UNCLOSES
CLOOT S
CLOOTS
CLOP S
CLOPPED
CLOPPING
CLOPS
CLOQUE S
CLOQUES
CLOSABLE
CLOSE DRST
COLES SOCLE
CLOSED
CLOSELY
CLOSEOUT S
CLOSER S
CEORLS
CRESOL
CLOSERS
CRESOLS
CLOSES T
SOCLES
CLOSEST
CLOSETS
CLOSET S
TELCOS
CLOSETED
CLOSETS
CLOSEST
CLOSEUP S
COUPLES
CLOSEUPS
CLOSING S
CLOSINGS
CLOSURE DS
COLURES
CLOSURED
CLOSURES
SCLEROUS
CLOT HS
COLT
CLOTH ES
CLOTHE DS
CLOTHED
CLOTHES
CLOTHIER S
CHLORITE
CLOTHING S
CLOTHS
CLOTS
COLTS
CLOTTED
CLOTTING
CLOTTY
CLOTURE DS
CLOUTER
COULTER
CLOTURED
CLOTURES
CLOUTERS
COULTERS
CLOUD SY
COULD
CLOUDED
CLOUDIER
CLOUDILY
CLOUDING
CLOUDLET S
CLOUDS
CLOUDY
CLOUGH S
CLOUGHS
CLOUR S
CLOURED
CLOURING
CLOURS
CLOUT S
CLOUTED
CLOUTER S
CLOTURE
COULTER
CLOUTERS
CLOTURES
COULTERS
CLOUTING
CLOUTS
LOCUST
CLOVE NRS
CLOVEN
CLOVER SY
VELCRO
CLOVERED
CLOVERS
VELCROS
CLOVERY
CLOVES
CLOWDER S
CLOWDERS
CLOWN S
CLOWNED
CLOWNERY
CLOWNING
CLOWNISH
CLOWNS
CLOY S
COLY
CLOYED
CLOYING
CLOYS
CLOZE S
CLOZES
CLUB S
CLUBABLE
CLUBBED
CLUBBER S
CLUBBERS
CLUBBIER
CLUBBING
CLUBBISH
CLUBBY
CLUBFACE S
CLUBFEET
CLUBFOOT
CLUBHAND S
CLUBHAUL S
CLUBHEAD S
CLUBMAN
CLUBMEN
CLUBROOM S
CLUBROOT S
CLUBS
CLUCK S
CLUCKED
CLUCKING
CLUCKS
CLUE DS
LUCE
CLUED
CLUEING
CLUELESS
CLUES
LUCES
CLUING
CLUMBER S
CRUMBLE
CLUMBERS
CRUMBLES
CLUMP SY
CLUMPED
CLUMPIER
CLUMPING
CLUMPISH
CLUMPS
CLUMPY
CLUMSIER
CLUMSILY
CLUMSY
MUSCLY
CLUNG
CLUNK SY
CLUNKED
CLUNKER S
CLUNKERS
CLUNKIER
CLUNKING
CLUNKS
CLUNKY
CLUPEID S
CLUPEIDS
CLUPEOID S
UPCOILED
CLUSTER SY
CUTLERS
RELUCTS
CLUSTERS
CLUSTERY
CLUTCH Y
CULTCH
CLUTCHED
CLUTCHES
CULTCHES
CLUTCHY
CLUTTER SY
CLUTTERS
CLUTTERY
CLYPEAL
CLYPEATE
CLYPEI
CLYPEUS
CLYSTER S
CLYSTERS
CNIDA E
CANID NICAD
CNIDAE
COACH
COACHED
COACHER S
CAROCHE
COACHERS
CAROCHES
COACHES
COACHING
COACHMAN
COACHMEN
COACT S
COACTED
COACTING
COACTION S
COACTIVE
COACTOR S
COACTORS
COACTS
ACCOST
COADMIRE DS
RACEMOID
COADMIT S
COADMITS
COAEVAL S
COAEVALS
COAGENCY
COAGENT S
COGNATE
COAGENTS
COGNATES
COAGULA
COAGULUM S
COAL ASY
CALO COLA
LOCA
COALA S
COALAS
COALBIN S
COALBINS
COALBOX
COALED
COLEAD
COALER S
ORACLE
RECOAL
COALERS
CLAROES
ESCOLAR
ORACLES
RECOALS
SOLACER
COALESCE DS
COALFISH
COALHOLE S
COALIER
CALORIE
CARIOLE
LORICAE
COALIEST
SOCIETAL
COALIFY
COALING
COALLESS
CALLOSES
COALPIT S
CAPITOL
OPTICAL
TOPICAL
COALPITS
CAPITOLS
COALS
CALOS COLAS
COALSACK S
COALSHED S
COALY
COALYARD S
COAMING S
COAMINGS
COANCHOR S
CORONACH
COANNEX
COAPPEAR S
COAPT S
COAPTED
COAPTING
COAPTS
COARSE NR
COARSELY
CALOYERS
COARSEN S
CANOERS
CORNEAS
NARCOSE
COARSENS
NARCOSES
COARSER
COARSEST
COASTERS
COASSIST S
COASSUME DS
COAST S
ASCOT COATS
COSTA TACOS
COASTAL
CATALOS
COASTED
COASTER S
COATERS
RECOATS
COASTERS
COARSEST
COASTING S
AGNOSTIC
COATINGS
COTINGAS
COASTS
ASCOTS
COAT IS
TACO
COATED
COATEE S
COATEES
ACETOSE

COATER S
RECOAT
COATERS
COASTER
RECOATS
COATI S
COATING S
COTINGA
COATINGS
AGNOSTIC
COASTING
COTINGAS
COATIS
SCOTIA
COATLESS
LACTOSES
COATRACK S
COATROOM S
COATS
ASCOT COAST
COSTA TACOS
COATTAIL S
TAILCOAT
COATTEND S
COATTEST S
COAUTHOR S
COAX
COXA
COAXAL
COAXED
COAXER S
COAXERS
COAXES
COAXIAL
COAXING
COB BS
COBALT S
COBALTIC
COBALTS
COBB SY
COBBER S
COBBERS
COBBIER
COBBIEST
COBBLE DRS
COBBLED
COBBLER S
CLOBBER
COBBLERS
CLOBBERS
COBBLES
COBBLING
COBBS
COBBY
COBIA S
COBIAS
COBLE S
COBLES
COBNUT S
COBNUTS
COBRA S
CARBO CAROB
COBRAS
CARBOS
CAROBS
COBS
COBWEB S
COBWEBBY
COBWEBS
COCA S
COCAIN ES
COCAINE S
OCEANIC
COCAINES
COCAINS
COCAS
COCCAL
COCCI CD
COCCIC
COCCID S
COCCIDIA
COCCIDS
COCCOID S
COCCOIDS
COCCOUS
COCCUS
COCCYGES
COCCYX
COCCYXES
COCHAIR S
COCHAIRS
COCHIN S
COCHINS
COCHLEA ERS
COCHLEAE
COCHLEAR
COCHLEAS
COCINERA S
A **COCK** SY
COCKADE DS
COCKADED
COCKADES
COCKAPOO S
COCKATOO S
COCKBILL S
COCKBOAT S
COCKCROW S
COCKED
COCKER S
RECOCK
COCKERED
RECOCKED
COCKEREL S
COCKERS
RECOCKS
COCKEYE DS
COCKEYED
COCKEYES
COCKIER
COCKIEST
COCKILY
COLICKY
COCKING
COCKISH
COCKLE DS
COCKLED
CLOCKED
COCKLES
COCKLIKE
COCKLING
CLOCKING
COCKLOFT S
COCKNEY S
COCKNEYS
COCKPIT S
COCKPITS
COCKS
COCKSHUT S
COCKSHY
COCKSPUR S
COCKSURE
COCKTAIL S
COCKUP S
COCKUPS
COCKY
COCO AS
COCOA S
COCOANUT S
COCOAS
COCOBOLA S
COCOBOLO S
COCOMAT S
COCOMATS
COCONUT S
COCONUTS
COCOON S
COCOONED
COCOONS
COCOPLUM S
COCOS
COCOTTE S
COCOTTES
COCOYAM S
COCOYAMS
COCREATE DS
COD AES
DOC
CODA S
CODABLE
CODAS
CODDED
CODDER S
CORDED
CODDERS
CODDING
CODDLE DRS
CODDLED
CODDLER S
CODDLERS
CODDLES
SCOLDED
CODDLING
CODE CDNRSX
COED DECO
CODEBOOK S
CODEBTOR S
CODEC S
CODECS
CODED
CODEIA S
CODEIAS
CODEIN AES
COINED
CODEINA S
CODEINAS
DIOCESAN
CODEINE S
CODEINES
CODEINS
SECONDI
CODELESS
CODEN S
CONED
CODENS
SECOND
CODER S
CORED CREDO
DECOR
CODERIVE DS
DIVORCEE
REVOICED
CODERS
CREDOS
DECORS
SCORED
CODES
COEDS DECOS
CODESIGN S
COGNISED
COSIGNED
CODEX
COXED
CODFISH
CODGER S
CODGERS
CODICES
CODICIL S
CODICILS
CODIFIED
CODIFIER S
CODIFIES
CODIFY
CODING
CODIRECT S
CODLIN GS
CODLING S
LINGCOD
CODLINGS
LINGCODS
SCOLDING
CODLINS
CODON S
CONDO
CODONS
CONDOS
CODPIECE S
CODRIVE NRS
DIVORCE
CODRIVEN
CODRIVER S
DIVORCER
CODRIVES
DISCOVER
DIVORCES
CODROVE
VOCODER
CODS
DOCS
COED S
CODE DECO
COEDIT S
COEDITED
COEDITOR S
COEDITS
CESTOID
COEDS
CODES DECOS
COEFFECT S
COELIAC
COELOM ES
COELOME S
COELOMES
COELOMIC
COELOMS
COEMBODY
COEMPLOY S
COEMPT S
COEMPTED
COMPETED
COEMPTS
COENACT S
COENACTS
COSECANT
COENAMOR S
COENDURE DS
COENURE S
COENURES
COENURI
COENURUS
CERNUOUS
COENZYME S
COEQUAL S
COEQUALS
COEQUATE DS
COERCE DRS
COERCED
COERCER S
COERCERS
COERCES
COERCING
COERCION S
COERCIVE
COERECT S
COERECTS
COESITE S
COESITES
COEVAL S
ALCOVE
COEVALLY
COEVALS
ALCOVES
COEVOLVE DS
COEXERT S
COEXERTS
CORTEXES
COEXIST S
EXOTICS
COEXISTS
COEXTEND S
COFACTOR S
S **COFF** S
COFFEE S
COFFEES
S **COFFER** S
COFFERED
S **COFFERS**
SCOFFER
COFFIN GS
COFFINED
S **COFFING**
COFFINS
COFFLE DS
COFFLED
COFFLES
COFFLING
COFFRET S
COFFRETS
S **COFFS**
SCOFF
COFOUND S
COFOUNDS
COFT
COG S
COGENCY
COGENT
COGENTLY
COGGED
COGGING
COGITATE DS
COGITO S
COGITOS
COGNAC S
COGNACS
COGNATE S
COAGENT
COGNATES
COAGENTS
COGNISE DS
COIGNES
COGNISED
CODESIGN
COSIGNED
COGNISES
COGNIZE DRS
COGNIZED
COGNIZER S
COGNIZES
COGNOMEN S
COGNOVIT S
COGON S
CONGO
COGONS
CONGOS
COGS
COGWAY S
COGWAYS
COGWHEEL S
COHABIT S
COHABITS
COHEAD S
COHEADED
COHEADS
COHEIR S
HEROIC
COHEIRS
HEROICS
COHERE DRS
CHEERO
ECHOER
REECHO
COHERED
OCHERED
COHERENT
COHERER S
COHERERS
COHERES
CHEEROS
ECHOERS
RECHOSE
COHERING
OCHERING
COHESION S
COHESIVE
COHO GS
COHOBATE DS
COHOG S
COHOGS
COHOLDER S
COHORT S
COHORTS
COHOS HT
COHOSH
COHOSHES
COHOST S
COHOSTED
COHOSTS
COHUNE S
COHUNES
COIF S
FICO FOCI
COIFED
COIFFE DS
OFFICE
COIFFED
COIFFES
OFFICES
COIFFEUR S
COIFFURE
COIFFING
COIFFURE DS
COIFFEUR
COIFING
COIFS
COIGN ES
INCOG
COIGNE DS
COIGNED
COIGNES
COGNISE
COIGNING
COIGNS
COSIGN
INCOGS
COIL S
LOCI
COILED
DOCILE
COILER S
RECOIL
COILERS
RECOILS
COILING
COILS
COIN S
CION CONI
ICON
COINABLE
BIOCLEAN
COINAGE S
COINAGES
COINCIDE DS
COINED
CODEIN
COINER S
ORCEIN
RECOIN
COINERS
CRONIES
ORCEINS
RECOINS
COINFECT S
COINFER S
CONIFER
COINFERS
CONIFERS
FORENSIC
FORNICES
COINHERE DS
COINING
COINMATE S
COINS
CIONS ICONS
SCION SONIC
COINSURE DR
S
COINTER S
NOTICER
COINTERS
CORNIEST
NOTICERS
COINVENT S
COIR S
COIRS
COISTREL S
CLOISTER
COSTLIER
COISTRIL S
CLITORIS
COITAL
CITOLA
COITALLY
LOCALITY
COITION S
COITIONS
ISOTONIC
COITUS
COITUSES
COJOIN S
COJOINED
COJOINS
COKE DS
COKED
COKEHEAD S
COKELIKE
COKES
COKING
COKY
YOCK
COL ADESTY
COLA S
CALO COAL
LOCA
COLANDER S
CONELRAD
COLAS
CALOS COALS
COLBY S
COLBYS
AS **COLD** S
CLOD
COLDCOCK S
S **COLDER**
COLDEST
COLDISH
COLDLY
COLDNESS
S **COLDS**
CLODS SCOLD
COLE DS
COLEAD S
COALED
COLEADER S
RECOALED
COLEADS
SOLACED
COLED
DOLCE
COLES
CLOSE SOCLE
COLESEED S
COLESLAW S
COLESSEE S
COLESSOR S
CREOSOLS
COLEUS
OSCULE
COLEUSES
COLEWORT S
COLIC S
COLICIN ES
COLICINE S
COLICINS
COLICKY
COCKILY
COLICS
COLIES
COLIFORM S
COLIN S
NICOL
COLINEAR
ACROLEIN
COLINS
NICOLS
COLISEUM S
COLISTIN S
COLITIC
COLITIS
SOLICIT
COLLAGE DNS
COLLAGED
COLLAGEN S
COLLAGES
COLLAPSE DS
ESCALLOP
COLLAR DS
COLLARD S
COLLARDS
COLLARED
CAROLLED
COLLARET S
COLLARS
COLLATE DS
COLLATED
COLLATES
COLLATOR S
COLLECT S
COLLECTS
COLLEEN S
COLLEENS
COLLEGE RS
COLLEGER S
COLLEGES
COLLEGIA LN
COLLET S
COLLETED
COLLETS
COLLIDE DRS
COLLIED
COLLIDED
COLLIDER S
COLLIDES
COLLIE DRS
OCELLI
COLLIED
COLLIDE
COLLIER SY
COLLIERS
COLLIERY
COLLIES
COLLINS
COLLOGUE DS

2006 addition

COLLOID S
COLLOIDS
S COLLOP S
S COLLOPS
SCOLLOP
COLLOQUY
COLLUDE DRS
LOCULED
COLLUDED
COLLUDER S
COLLUDES
COLLUVIA L
COLLY
COLLYING
COLLYRIA
COLOBI
COLOBOMA
COLOBUS
SUBCOOL
COLOCATE DS
COLOG S
COLOGNE DS
COLOGNED
COLOGNES
COLOGS
COLON EISY
COLONE LS
COLONEL S
COLONELS
COLONES
CONSOLE
COLONI C
COLONIAL S
COLONIC S
COLONICS
COLONIES
COLONISE
ECLOSION
COLONISE DS
COLONIES
ECLOSION
COLONIST S
STOLONIC
COLONIZE DRS
COLONS
CONSOL
COLONUS
COLONY
COLOPHON SY
COLOR S
COLORADO
COLORANT S
COLORED
DECOLOR
COLORER S
RECOLOR
COLORERS
RECOLORS
COLORFUL
COLORING S
COLORISM S
MISCOLOR
COLORIST S
CORTISOL
COLORIZE DRS
COLORMAN
COLORMEN
COLORS
COLORWAY S
COLOSSAL
COLOSSI
COLOSSUS
COLOTOMY
COLOUR S
COLOURED
DECOLOUR
COLOURER S
COLOURS
COLPITIS
POLITICS
PSILOTIC
COLS
COLT S
CLOT
COLTER S
LECTOR

COLTERS
CORSLET
COSTREL
LECTORS
COLTISH
COLTS
CLOTS
COLUBRID S
COLUGO S
COLUGOS
COLUMBIC
COLUMEL S
COLUMELS
COLUMN S
COLUMNAL
COLUMNAR
COLUMNEA S
COLUMNED
COLUMNS
COLURE S
COLURES
CLOSURE
COLY
CLOY
COLZA S
COLZAS
COMA ELS
CAMO
COMADE
COMAE
CAMEO
COMAKE RS
COMAKER S
COMAKERS
COMAKES
COMAKING
COMAL
COMANAGE DRS
COMAS
CAMOS
COMATE S
COMATES
COMATIC
COMATIK S
COMATIKS
COMATOSE
COMATULA E
COMB EOS
COMBAT S
TOMBAC
COMBATED
COMBATER S
COMBATS
TOMBACS
COMBE DRS
COMBED
COMBER S
RECOMB
COMBERS
RECOMBS
COMBES
COMBINE DRS
COMBINED S
COMBINER S
COMBINES
COMBING S
COMBINGS
COMBLIKE
COMBO S
COOMB
COMBOS
COOMBS
COMBS
COMBUST S
COMBUSTS
COME RST
COMEBACK S
COMEDIAN S
DAEMONIC
DEMONIAC
COMEDIC
COMEDIES
COMEDO S
COMEDOS
COMEDOWN S
DOWNCOME
COMEDY

COMELIER
COMELILY
COMELY
COMEMBER S
COMER S
COMERS
COMES
COMET HS
COMTE
COMETARY
COMETH
COMETHER S
COMETIC
COMETS
COMTES
COMFIER
COMFIEST
COMFIT S
COMFITS
COMFORT S
COMFORTS
COMFREY S
COMFREYS
COMFY
COMIC S
COMICAL
COMICS
COSMIC
COMING S
GNOMIC
COMINGLE DS
COMINGS
COMITIA L
COMITIAL
COMITIES
SEMIOTIC
COMITY
MYOTIC
COMIX
COMMA S
COMMAND OS
COMMANDO S
COMMANDS
COMMAS
COMMATA
COMMENCE DRS
COMMEND S
COMMENDS
COMMENT S
COMMENTS
COMMERCE DS
COMMIE S
COMMIES
COMMIT S
COMMITS
COMMIX T
COMMIXED
COMMIXES
COMMIXT
COMMODE S
COMMODES
COMMON S
COMMONER S
COMMONLY
COMMONS
COMMOVE DS
COMMOVED
COMMOVES
COMMUNAL
COMMUNE DRS
COMMUNED
COMMUNER S
COMMUNES
COMMUTE DRS
COMMUTED
COMMUTER S
COMMUTES
COMMY
COMORBID
COMOSE
COMOUS
COMP OST
COMPACT S
COMPACTS

COMPADRE S
COMPARED
COMPANY
COMPARE DRS
COMPARED
COMPADRE
COMPARER S
COMPARES
CAPSOMER
MESOCARP
COMPART S
COMPARTS
COMPAS S
CAMPOS
COMPASS
COMPED
COMPEER S
COMPERE
COMPEERS
COMPERES
COMPEL S
COMPELS
COMPEND S
COMPENDS
COMPERE DS
COMPEER
COMPERED
COMPERES
COMPEERS
COMPETE DS
COMPETED
COEMPTED
COMPETES
COMPILE DRS
POLEMIC
COMPILED
COMPLIED
COMPILER S
COMPLIER
COMPILES
COMPLIES
POLEMICS
COMPING
COMPLAIN ST
COMPLEAT
COMPLECT S
COMPLETE DRS
COMPLEX
COMPLICE S
COMPLIED
COMPILED
COMPLIER S
COMPILER
COMPLIES
COMPILES
POLEMICS
COMPLIN ES
COMPLINE S
COMPLINS
COMPLOT S
COMPLOTS
COMPLY
COMPO S
COMPONE
COMPONY
COMPORT S
COMPORTS
COMPOS ET
COMPOSE DRS
COMPOSED
COMPOSER S
COMPOSES
COMPOST S
COMPOSTS
COMPOTE S
COMPOTES
COMPOUND S
COMPRESS
COMPRISE DS
COMPRIZE DS
COMPS
COMPT S
COMPTED
COMPTING
COMPTS
COMPUTE DRS
COMPUTED
COMPUTER S

COMPUTES
COMRADE S
CAROMED
COMRADES
COMTE S
COMET
COMTES
COMETS
I CON EIKNSY
CONATION S
CONATIVE
INVOCATE
CONATUS
TOUCANS
CONCAVE DS
CONCAVED
CONCAVES
CONCEAL S
CONCEALS
CONCEDE DRS
CONCEDED
CONCEDER S
CONCEDES
CONCEIT S
CONCEITS
CONCEIVE DRS
CONCENT S
CONNECT
CONCENTS
CONNECTS
CONCEPT IS
CONCEPTI
CONCEPTS
CONCERN S
CONCERNS
CONCERT IOS
CONCERTI
NECROTIC
CONCERTO S
CONCERTS
CONCH AOSY
CONCHA ELS
CONCHAE
CONCHAL
CONCHAS
CONCHES
CONCHIE S
CONCHIES
CONCHO S
CONCHOID S
CONCHOS
CONCHS
CONCHY
CONCISE R
CONCISER
CORNICES
CROCEINS
CONCLAVE S
CONCLUDE DRS
CONCOCT S
CONCOCTS
CONCORD S
CONCORDS
CONCOURS E
CONCRETE DS
CONCUR S
CONCURS
CONCUSS
CONDEMN S
CONDEMNS
CONDENSE DRS
CONDIGN
CONDO MRS
CODON
CONDOES
SECONDO
CONDOLE DRS
CONDOLED
CONDOLER S
CONDOLES
CONSOLED
CONDOM S
CONDOMS
CONDONE DRS
CONDONED

CONDONER S
CONDONES
CONDOR S
CORDON
CONDORES
CONDORS
CORDONS
CONDOS
CODONS
CONDUCE DRS
CONDUCED
CONDUCER S
CONDUCES
CONDUCT S
CONDUCTS
CONDUIT S
NOCTUID
CONDUITS
DISCOUNT
NOCTUIDS
CONDYLAR
CONDYLE S
CONDYLES
SECONDLY
S CONE DSY
ONCE
CONED
CODEN
CONELRAD S
COLANDER
CONENOSE S
CONEPATE S
CONEPATL S
IS CONES
SCONE
CONEY S
CONEYS
CONFAB S
CONFABS
CONFECT S
CONFECTS
CONFER S
CONFEREE S
CONFERS
CONFERVA ELS
CONFESS
CONFETTI
CONFETTO
CONFIDE DRS
CONFIDED
CONFIDER S
CONFIDES
CONFINE DRS
CONFINED
CONFINER S
CONFINES
CONFIRM S
CONFIRMS
CONFIT S
CONFITS
CONFLATE DS
FALCONET
CONFLICT S
CONFLUX
CONFOCAL
CONFORM S
CONFORMS
CONFOUND S
CONFRERE S
ENFORCER
RECONFER
CONFRONT S
CONFUSE DS
CONFUSED
CONFUSES
CONFUTE DRS
CONFUTED
CONFUTER S
CONFUTES
CONGA S
CONGAED
DECAGON
CONGAING
CONGAS
GASCON
CONGE ERS
CONGEAL S

CONGEALS
CONGEE DS
CONGEED
CONGEES
CONGENER S
CONGER S
CONGERS
CONGES T
CONGEST S
CONGESTS
CONGII
CONGIUS
CONGLOBE DS
CONGO SU
COGON
CONGOES
CONGOS
COGONS
CONGOU S
CONGOUS
CONGRATS
CONGRESS
CONI CN
CION COIN
ICON
I CONIC S
I CONICAL
LACONIC
I CONICITY
CONICS
CONIDIA LN
CONIDIAL
CONIDIAN
CONIDIUM
MUCINOID
ONCIDIUM
CONIES
COSINE
ICONES
OSCINE
CONIFER S
COINFER
CONIFERS
COINFERS
FORENSIC
FORNICES
CONIINE S
CONIINES
OSCININE
CONIN EGS
CONINE S
CONINES
CONING
CONINS
CONIOSES
CONIOSIS
CONIUM S
MUONIC
CONIUMS
CONJOIN ST
CONJOINS
CONJOINT
CONJUGAL
CONJUNCT S
CONJUNTO S
CONJURE DRS
CONJURED
CONJURER S
CONJURES
CONJUROR S
CONK SY
NOCK
CONKED
NOCKED
CONKER S
RECKON
CONKERS
RECKONS
CONKING
NOCKING
CONKS
NOCKS
CONKY
CONN S
CONNATE
CONNECT S
CONCENT
CONNECTS
CONCENTS

CONNED
CONNER S
CONNERS
CONNING
CONNIVE DRS
CONNIVED
CONNIVER SY
CONNIVES
CONNOTE DS
CONNOTED
CONNOTES
CONNS
CONODONT S
CONOID S
CONOIDAL
CONOIDS
CONQUER S
CONQUERS
CONQUEST S
CONQUIAN S
I CONS
CONSENT S
CONSENTS
CONSERVE DR
CONVERSE S
CONSIDER S
CONSIGN S
CONSIGNS
CONSIST S
TOCSINS
CONSISTS
CONSOL ES
COLONS
CONSOLE DRS
COLONES
CONSOLED
CONDOLES
CONSOLER S
CORONELS
CONSOLES
COOLNESS
CONSOLS
CONSOMME S
CONSORT S
CROTONS
CONSORTS
CONSPIRE DR
INCORPSE S
CONSTANT S
CONSTRUE DR
COUNTERS S
RECOUNTS
TROUNCES
CONSUL ST
CLONUS
CONSULAR
COURLANS
CONSULS
CONSULT S
CONSULTS
CONSUME DRS
CONSUMED
CONSUMER S
MUCRONES
CONSUMES
CONTACT S
CONTACTS
CONTAGIA
CONTAIN S
ACTINON
CONTAINS
ACTINONS
CANONIST
SANCTION
SONANTIC
CONTE S
CENTO ONCET
CONTEMN S
CONTEMNS
CONTEMPO
CONTEMPT S
CONTEND S
CONTENDS
CONTENT S
CONTENTS
CONTES T
CENTOS
CONTESSA S
CONTEST S

CONTESTS
CONTEXT S
CONTEXTS
CONTINUA L
COUNTIAN
CONTINUE DR
S
CONTINUO S
CONTO S
CONTORT S
CONTORTS
CONTOS
NOSTOC
CONTOUR S
CORNUTO
CROUTON
CONTOURS
CORNUTOS
CROUTONS
OUTSCORN
CONTRA S
CANTOR
CARTON
CRATON
CONTRACT S
CONTRAIL S
CILANTRO
CONTRARY
CONTRAS T
CANTORS
CARTONS
CRATONS
CONTRAST SY
CONTRITE
CONTRIVE DR
S
CONTROL S
CONTROLS
CONTUSE DS
CONTUSED
CONTUSES
COUNTESS
CONUS
UNCOS
CONVECT S
CONVECTS
CONVENE DRS
CONVENED
CONVENER S
CONVENES
CONVENOR S
CONVENT S
CONVENTS
CONVERGE DS
CONVERSE DR
CONSERVE S
CONVERSO S
CONVERT S
CONVERTS
CONVEX
CONVEXES
CONVEXLY
CONVEY S
CONVEYED
CONVEYER S
RECONVEY
CONVEYOR S
CONVEYS
CONVICT S
CONVICTS
CONVINCE DR
S
CONVOKE DRS
CONVOKED
CONVOKER S
CONVOKES
CONVOLVE DS
CONVOY S
CONVOYED
CONVOYS
CONVULSE DS
CONY
COO FKLNPST
S COOCH
S COOCHES
COOCOO
COOED
COOEE DS

COOEED
COOEEING
COOEES
COOER S
COOERS
ROSCOE
COOEY S
COOEYED
COOEYING
COOEYS
COOF S
COOFS
COOING
COOINGLY
COOK SY
COOKABLE
COOKBOOK S
COOKED
COOKER SY
RECOOK
COOKERS
RECOOKS
COOKERY
COOKEY S
COOKEYS
COOKIE S
COOKIES
COOKING S
COOKINGS
COOKLESS
COOKOFF S
COOKOFFS
COOKOUT S
OUTCOOK
COOKOUTS
OUTCOOKS
COOKS
SOCKO
COOKSHOP S
COOKTOP S
COOKTOPS
COOKWARE S
COOKY
COOL SY
LOCO
COOLANT S
OCTANOL
COOLANTS
OCTANOLS
COOLDOWN S
COOLED
LOCOED
COOLER S
COOLERS
CREOSOL
COOLEST
OCELOTS
COOLIE S
COOLIES
COOLING
LOCOING
COOLISH
COOLLY
COOLNESS
CONSOLES
COOLS
LOCOS
COOLTH S
COOLTHS
COOLY
COOMB ES
COMBO
COOMBE S
COOMBES
COOMBS
COMBOS
COON S
COONCAN S
COONCANS
COONS
COONSKIN S
COONTIE S
COONTIES
S COOP ST
POCO
S COOPED
S COOPER SY
COOPERED

S COOPERS
SCOOPER
COOPERY
S COOPING
S COOPS
SCOOP
COOPT S
COOPTED
COOPTING
COOPTION S
COOPTS
COOS
S COOT S
S COOTER S
S COOTERS
SCOOTER
COOTIE S
COOTIES
S COOTS
SCOOT
S COP ESY
COPAIBA S
COPAIBAS
COPAL MS
COPALM S
COPALMS
COPALS
COPARENT S
PORTANCE
COPASTOR S
ROOTCAPS
COPATRON S
COPAY S
COPAYS
S COPE DNRS
COPECK S
COPECKS
S COPED
COPEMATE S
COPEN S
PONCE
COPENS
PONCES
COPEPOD S
COPEPODS
COPER S
COPERS
CORPSE
S COPES
COPSE SCOPE
COPIED
COPIER S
COPIERS
COPIES
COPIHUE S
COPIHUES
COPILOT S
COPILOTS
S COPING S
COPINGS
SCOPING
COPIOUS
COPLANAR
COPLOT S
COPLOTS
COPOUT S
COPOUTS
OCTOPUS
COPPED
COPPER SY
COPPERAH S
COPPERAS
COPPERED
COPPERS
COPPERY
COPPICE DS
COPPICED
COPPICES
COPPING
COPPRA S
COPPRAS
COPRA HS
COPRAH S
CARHOP
COPRAHS
CARHOPS
COPRAS
COPREMIA S

COPREMIC
COPRINCE S
S COPS E
SCOP
COPSE S
COPES SCOPE
COPSES
SCOPES
COPTER S
COPTERS
PROSECT
S COPULA ERS
CUPOLA
S COPULAE
COPULAR
S COPULAS
CUPOLAS
SCOPULA
S COPULATE DS
OUTPLACE
COPURIFY
COPY
COPYABLE
COPYBOOK S
COPYBOY S
COPYBOYS
COPYCAT S
COPYCATS
COPYDESK S
COPYEDIT S
COPYGIRL S
COPYHOLD S
COPYING
COPYIST S
COPYISTS
COPYLEFT S
COPYREAD S
COQUET S
COQUETRY
COQUETS
COQUETTE DS
COQUILLE S
COQUINA S
COQUINAS
COQUITO S
COQUITOS
COR DEFKMNS
ORC Y
ROC
CORACLE S
CORACLES
CORACOID S
CORAL S
CAROL CLARO
CORALS
CAROLS
CLAROS
CORANTO S
CARTOON
CORANTOS
CARTOONS
OSTRACON
CORBAN S
CARBON
CORBANS
CARBONS
CORBEIL S
BRICOLE
CORBEILS
BRICOLES
CORBEL S
CORBELED
CORBELS
CORBIE S
CORBIES
CORBINA S
CORBINAS
CORBY
CORD S
CORDAGE S
CORDAGES
CORDATE
REDCOAT
CORDED
CODDER
CORDELLE DS
CORDER S
RECORD
CORDERS
RECORDS

CORDIAL S
CORDIALS
CORDING S
CORDINGS
CORDITE S
CORDITES
CORDLESS
SCOLDERS
CORDLIKE
CORDOBA S
CORDOBAS
CORDON S
CONDOR
CORDONED
CORDONS
CONDORS
CORDOVAN S
CORDS
SCROD
CORDUROY S
CORDWAIN S
CORDWOOD S
S CORE DRS
CERO
S CORED
CODER CREDO
DECOR
COREDEEM S
COREIGN S
COREIGNS
COSIGNER
CORELATE DS
RELOCATE
S CORELESS
SCLEROSE
COREMIA
COREMIUM
S CORER S
CRORE
S CORERS
CRORES
SCORER
S CORES
CEROS CORSE
SCORE
CORF
CORGI S
ORGIC
CORGIS
S CORIA
S CORING
CORIUM
CORK SY
ROCK
CORKAGE S
CORKAGES
CORKED
DOCKER
REDOCK
ROCKED
CORKER S
RECORK
ROCKER
CORKERS
RECORKS
ROCKERS
CORKIER
ROCKIER
CORKIEST
ROCKIEST
STOCKIER
CORKING
ROCKING
CORKLIKE
ROCKLIKE
CORKS
ROCKS
CORKWOOD S
CORKY
ROCKY
CORM S
CORMEL S
CORMELS
CORMLIKE
CORMOID
CORMOUS
CORMS
AS CORN SUY
CORNBALL S
CORNCAKE S
CORNCOB S

CORNCOBS
CORNCRIB S
CORNEA LS
CANOER
CORNEAL
CORNEAS
CANOERS
COARSEN
NARCOSE
AS CORNED
CORNEL S
CLONER
CORNELS
CLONERS
CORNEOUS
S CORNER S
CORNERED
S CORNERS
SCORNER
CORNET S
CORNETCY
CORNETS
CORNFED
CORNHUSK S
CORNICE DS
CROCEIN
CROCINE
CORNICED
CORNICES
CONCISER
CROCEINS
CORNICHE S
ENCHORIC
CORNICLE S
CORNIER
CORNIEST
COINTERS
NOTICERS
CORNIFY
CORNILY
LYRICON
S CORNING
CORNMEAL S
AMELCORN
CORNPONE S
CORNROW S
CORNROWS
AS CORNS
SCORN
CORNU AS
CORNUA L
CORNUAL
COURLAN
CORNUS
CORNUSES
CORNUTE D
COUNTER
RECOUNT
TROUNCE
CORNUTED
TROUNCED
CORNUTO S
CONTOUR
CROUTON
CORNUTOS
CONTOURS
CROUTONS
OUTSCORN
CORNY
CRONY
CORODIES
CORODY
COROLLA S
COROLLAS
CORONA ELS
RACOON
CORONACH S
COANCHOR
CORONAE
CORONAL S
CORONALS
CORONARY
CORONAS
RACOONS
CORONATE DS
CORONEL S
CORONELS
CONSOLER
CORONER S
CROONER

CORONERS
CROONERS
CORONET S
CORONETS
CORONOID
COROTATE DS
CORPORA L
CORPORAL S
CORPS E
CROPS
CORPSE S
COPERS
CORPSES
PROCESS
CORPSMAN
CRAMPONS
CORPSMEN
CORPUS
CROUPS
CORPUSES
CORRADE DS
CORRADED
CORRADES
CORRAL S
CORRALS
CORRECT S
CORRECTS
CORRIDA S
CORRIDAS
CORRIDOR S
CORRIE S
ORRICE
CORRIES
CIRROSE
CROSIER
ORRICES
CORRIVAL S
CORRODE DS
CORRODED
CORRODES
CORRODY
CORRUPT S
CORRUPTS
CORS E
ORCS ROCS
CORSAC S
CORSACS
CORSAGE S
CARGOES
SOCAGER
CORSAGES
SOCAGERS
CORSAIR S
CORSAIRS
CORSE ST
CEROS CORES
SCORE
CORSELET S
ELECTORS
ELECTROS
SELECTOR
CORSES
CROSSE
SCORES
CORSET S
COSTER
ESCORT
RECTOS
SCOTER
SECTOR
CORSETED
ESCORTED
SECTORED
CORSETRY
CORSETS
COSTERS
ESCORTS
SCOTERS
SECTORS
CORSLET S
COLTERS
COSTREL
LECTORS
CORSLETS
COSTRELS
CROSSLET
CORTEGE S
CORTEGES
CORTEX
CORTEXES
COEXERTS

CORTICAL
CORTICES
CORTIN AS
CITRON
CORTINA S
CAROTIN
CORTINAS
CAROTINS
CORTINS
CISTRON
CITRONS
CORTISOL S
COLORIST
CORULER S
CORULERS
CORUNDUM S
CORVEE S
CORVEES
CORVES
COVERS
CORVET S
COVERT
VECTOR
CORVETS
COVERTS
VECTORS
CORVETTE S
CORVID S
CORVIDS
CORVINA S
CORVINAS
CORVINE
CORY
CORYBANT S
CORYMB S
CORYMBED
CORYMBS
CORYPHEE S
CORYZA LS
CORYZAL
CORYZAS
COS HSTY
COSCRIPT S
COSEC S
SECCO
COSECANT S
COENACTS
COSECS
SECCOS
COSES
COSET S
COTES ESCOT
COSETS
CESTOS
COSSET
ESCOTS
COSEY S
COSEYS
COSH
COSHED
COSHER S
CHORES
OCHERS
OCHRES
COSHERED
COSHERS
COSHES
CHOSES
COSHING
COSIE DRS
COSIED
COSIER
COSIES T
COSIEST
COSIGN S
COIGNS
INCOGS
COSIGNED
CODESIGN
COGNISED
COSIGNER S
COREIGNS
COSIGNS
COSILY
COSINE S
CONIES
ICONES
OSCINE

COSINES S
CESSION
OSCINES
COSINESS
CESSIONS
COSMETIC S
COSMIC
COMICS
COSMICAL
COSMID S
COSMIDS
COSMISM S
COSMISMS
COSMIST S
SITCOMS
COSMISTS
COSMOS
COSMOSES
COSS
COSSACK S
CASSOCK
COSSACKS
CASSOCKS
COSSET S
CESTOS
COSETS
ESCOTS
COSSETED
CESTODES
COSSETS
COST AS
COTS SCOT
COSTA ELR
ASCOT COAST
COATS TACOS
COSTAE
COSTAL
COSTALLY
COSTAR DS
ACTORS
CASTOR
SCROTA
TAROCS
COSTARD S
COSTARDS
COSTARS
CASTORS
COSTATE
COSTED
COSTER S
CORSET
ESCORT
RECTOS
SCOTER
SECTOR
COSTERS
CORSETS
ESCORTS
SCOTERS
SECTORS
COSTING
GNOSTIC
COSTIVE
COSTLESS
COSTLIER
CLOISTER
COISTREL
COSTLY
OCTYLS
COSTMARY
COSTREL S
COLTERS
CORSLET
LECTORS
COSTRELS
CORSLETS
CROSSLET
COSTS
SCOTS
COSTUME DRS
Y
COSTUMED
COSTUMER SY
CUSTOMER
COSTUMES
COSTUMEY
COSY
COYS
COSYING
S COT ES
COTAN S
CANTO OCTAN

COTANS
CANTOS
OCTANS
COTE DS
COTEAU X
COTEAUX
COTED
COTENANT S
COTERIE S
COTERIES
ESOTERIC
COTES
COSET ESCOT
COTHURN IS
COTHURNI
COTHURNS
COTIDAL
COTILLON S
COTING A
COTINGA S
COATING
COTINGAS
AGNOSTIC
COASTING
COATINGS
COTININE S
NICOTINE
COTQUEAN S
S COTS
COST SCOT
COTTA ERS
COTTAE
COTTAGE RSY
COTTAGER S
COTTAGES
COTTAGEY
COTTAR S
COTTARS
COTTAS
COTTER S
COTTERED
DETECTOR
COTTERS
COTTIER S
COTTIERS
COTTON SY
COTTONED
COTTONS
COTTONY
COTURNIX
COTYLOID
E COTYPE S
E COTYPES
COUCH
COUCHANT
COUCHED
COUCHER S
COUCHERS
CROUCHES
COUCHES
COUCHING S
COUDE
DOUCE
COUGAR S
COUGARS
COUGH S
COUGHED
COUGHER S
COUGHERS
CHOREGUS
GROUCHES
COUGHING
COUGHS
COULD
CLOUD
COULDEST
COULDST
COULEE S
COULEES
COULIS
COULISSE S
COULOIR S
COULOIRS
COULOMB S
COULOMBS
COULTER S
CLOTURE
CLOUTER

COULTERS
CLOTURES
CLOUTERS
COUMARIC
COUMARIN S
COUMAROU S
COUNCIL S
COUNCILS
COUNSEL S
UNCLOSE
COUNSELS
CLONUSES
UNCLOSES
COUNT SY
COUNTED
COUNTER S
CORNUTE
RECOUNT
TROUNCE
COUNTERS
CONSTRUE
RECOUNTS
TROUNCES
COUNTESS
CONTUSES
COUNTIAN S
CONTINUA
COUNTIES
COUNTING
COUNTRY
COUNTS
COUNTY
COUP ES
COUPE DS
COUPED
COUPES
COUPING
COUPLE DRST
COUPLED
COUPLER S
COUPLERS
COUPLES
CLOSEUP
COUPLET S
OCTUPLE
COUPLETS
OCTUPLES
COUPLING S
COUPON S
COUPONS
SOUPCON
COUPS
COURAGE S
COURAGES
COURANT EOS
COURANTE S
OUTRANCE
COURANTO S
COURANTS
COURIER S
COURIERS
COURLAN S
CORNUAL
COURLANS
CONSULAR
COURSE DRS
CEROUS
CROUSE
SOURCE
COURSED
SCOURED
SOURCED
COURSER S
SCOURER
COURSERS
SCOURERS
COURSES
SOURCES
SUCROSE
COURSING S
SCOURING
SOURCING
COURT S
COURTED
EDUCTOR
COURTER S
COURTERS
COURTESY
COURTIER S
COURTING
COURTLY

COURTS
COUSCOUS
COUSIN S
COUSINLY
COUSINRY
COUSINS
COUTEAU X
COUTEAUX
S COUTER S
CROUTE
S COUTERS
CROUTES
SCOUTER
S COUTH S
TOUCH
S COUTHER
RETOUCH
TOUCHER
COUTHEST
COUTHIE R
COUTHIER
TOUCHIER
S COUTHS
SCOUTH
COUTURE S
COUTURES
OUTCURSE
COUVADE S
COUVADES
COVALENT
COVARIED
COVARIES
VARICOSE
COVARY
COVE DNRSTY
COVED
COVEN S
COVENANT S
COVENS
COVER ST
COVERAGE S
COVERALL S
OVERCALL
COVERED
COVERER S
RECOVER
COVERERS
RECOVERS
COVERING S
COVERLET S
COVERLID S
COVERS
CORVES
COVERT S
CORVET
VECTOR
COVERTLY
COVERTS
CORVETS
VECTORS
COVERUP S
COVERUPS
COVES
VOCES
COVET S
COVETED
COVETER S
COVETERS
COVETING
COVETOUS
COVETS
COVEY S
COVEYS
COVIN GS
COVING S
COVINGS
COVINS
S COW LSY
COWAGE S
COWAGES
COWARD S
COWARDLY
COWARDS
COWBANE S
COWBANES
COWBELL S
COWBELLS
COWBERRY

COWBIND S
COWBINDS
COWBIRD S
COWBIRDS
COWBOY S
COWBOYED
COWBOYS
S COWED
COWEDLY
COWER S
COWERED
COWERING
COWERS
ESCROW
COWFISH
COWFLAP S
COWFLAPS
COWFLOP S
COWFLOPS
COWGIRL S
COWGIRLS
COWHAGE S
COWHAGES
COWHAND S
COWHANDS
COWHERB S
COWHERBS
COWHERD S
CHOWDER
COWHERDS
CHOWDERS
COWHIDE DS
COWHIDED
COWHIDES
COWIER
COWRIE
COWIEST
S COWING
COWINNER S
S COWL S
S COWLED
COWLICK S
COWLICKS
S COWLING S
COWLINGS
SCOWLING
S COWLS
SCOWL
COWMAN
COWMEN
COWORKER S
COWPAT S
COWPATS
COWPEA S
COWPEAS
COWPIE S
COWPIES
COWPLOP S
COWPLOPS
COWPOKE S
COWPOKES
COWPOX
COWPOXES
COWRIE S
COWIER
COWRIES
COWRITE RS
COWRITER S
COWRITES
COWROTE
COWRY
S COWS
SCOW
COWSHED S
CHOWSED
COWSHEDS
COWSKIN S
COWSKINS
COWSLIP S
COWSLIPS
COWY
COX A
COXA EL
COAX
COXAE
COXAL

COXALGIA S
COXALGIC
COXALGY
COXCOMB S
COXCOMBS
COXED
  CODEX
COXES
COXING
COXITIS
COXLESS
COXSWAIN S
COY S
COYDOG S
COYDOGS
COYED
  DECOY
COYER
COYEST
COYING
COYISH
COYLY
COYNESS
COYOTE S
  OOCYTE
COYOTES
  OOCYTES
COYPOU S
COYPOUS
COYPU S
COYPUS
COYS
  COSY
COZ Y
COZEN S
COZENAGE S
COZENED
COZENER S
COZENERS
COZENING
COZENS
COZES
COZEY S
COZEYS
COZIE DRS
COZIED
COZIER
COZIES T
COZIEST
COZILY
COZINESS
COZY
COZYING
COZZES
CRAAL S
CRAALED
  CALDERA
CRAALING
CRAALS
  LASCAR
  RASCAL
  SACRAL
  SCALAR
CRAB S
  CARB
CRABBED
CRABBER S
CRABBERS
CRABBIER
CRABBILY
CRABBING
CRABBY
CRABLIKE
CRABMEAT S
CRABS
  CARBS
CRABWISE
CRACK SY
CRACKED
CRACKER S
CRACKERS
CRACKING S
CRACKLE DS
  CACKLER
  CLACKER
CRACKLED
CRACKLES
  CACKLERS
  CLACKERS
CRACKLY
CRACKNEL S
CRACKPOT S
CRACKS
CRACKUP S
CRACKUPS
CRACKY
CRADLE DRS
  CREDAL
  RECLAD
CRADLED
CRADLER S
CRADLERS
CRADLES
  RECLADS
CRADLING
CRAFT SY
CRAFTED
  FRACTED
CRAFTER S
  REFRACT
CRAFTERS
  REFRACTS
CRAFTIER
CRAFTILY
CRAFTING
CRAFTS
CRAFTY
S **CRAG** S
S **CRAGGED**
S **CRAGGIER**
S **CRAGGILY**
S **CRAGGY**
S **CRAGS**
  SCRAG
CRAGSMAN
CRAGSMEN
CRAKE S
  CREAK
CRAKES
  CREAKS
  SACKER
  SCREAK
S **CRAM** PS
  MARC
CRAMBE S
  CAMBER
CRAMBES
  CAMBERS
CRAMBO S
CRAMBOES
CRAMBOS
S **CRAMMED**
CRAMMER S
CRAMMERS
S **CRAMMING**
CRAMOISY
CRAMP SY
CRAMPED
CRAMPIER
CRAMPING
CRAMPIT S
CRAMPITS
CRAMPON S
CRAMPONS
  CORPSMAN
CRAMPOON S
  MONOCARP
CRAMPS
CRAMPY
S **CRAMS**
  MARCS SCRAM
CRANCH
CRANCHED
CRANCHES
  CHANCERS
  CHANCRES
CRANE DS
  CANER NACRE
  RANCE
CRANED
  CEDARN
  DANCER
  NACRED
CRANES
  CANERS
  CASERN
  NACRES
  RANCES
CRANIA L
  ACINAR
  ARNICA
  CARINA
CRANIAL
  CARINAL
CRANIATE S
  CARINATE
CRANING
CRANIUM S
  CUMARIN
CRANIUMS
  CUMARINS
CRANK SY
CRANKED
CRANKER
CRANKEST
CRANKIER
CRANKILY
CRANKING
CRANKISH
CRANKLE DS
CRANKLED
CRANKLES
CRANKLY
CRANKOUS
CRANKPIN S
CRANKS
CRANKY
CRANNIED
CRANNIES
  NARCEINS
CRANNOG ES
CRANNOGE S
CRANNOGS
CRANNY
S **CRAP** ES
  CARP
S **CRAPE** DS
  CAPER PACER
  RECAP
S **CRAPED**
  CARPED
  REDCAP
S **CRAPES**
  CAPERS
  ESCARP
  PACERS
  PARSEC
  RECAPS
  SCRAPE
  SECPAR
  SPACER
S **CRAPING**
  CARPING
CRAPOLA S
  CAPORAL
CRAPOLAS
  CAPORALS
S **CRAPPED**
CRAPPIE RS
  EPICARP
S **CRAPPIER**
  PERICARP
CRAPPIES T
  EPICARPS
S **CRAPPING**
S **CRAPPY**
S **CRAPS**
  CARPS SCARP
  SCRAP
CRASES
  CARESS
  CARSES
  ESCARS
  SCARES
  SERACS
CRASH
  CHARS
CRASHED
  ECHARDS
CRASHER S
  ARCHERS
CRASHERS
CRASHES
  CHASERS
  ESCHARS
CRASHING
  ARCHINGS
  CHAGRINS
CRASIS
  CRISSA
CRASS
  SCARS
CRASSER
  SCARERS
CRASSEST
CRASSLY
S **CRATCH**
S **CRATCHES**
  CATCHERS
CRATE DRS
  CARET CARTE
  CATER REACT
  RECTA TRACE
CRATED
  CARTED
  REDACT
  TRACED
CRATER S
  CARTER
  TRACER
CRATERED
  RECRATED
  RETRACED
  TERRACED
CRATERS
  CARTERS
  TRACERS
CRATES
  CARETS
  CARTES
  CASTER
  CATERS
  REACTS
  RECAST
  TRACES
CRATING
  CARTING
  TRACING
CRATON S
  CANTOR
  CARTON
  CONTRA
CRATONIC
  NARCOTIC
CRATONS
  CANTORS
  CARTONS
  CONTRAS
CRAUNCH
CRAVAT S
CRAVATS
CRAVE DNRS
  CARVE CAVER
CRAVED
  CARVED
CRAVEN S
  CARVEN
  CAVERN
CRAVENED
  CAVERNED
CRAVENLY
CRAVENS
  CAVERNS
CRAVER S
  CARVER
CRAVERS
  CARVERS
CRAVES
  CARVES
  CAVERS
CRAVING S
  CARVING
CRAVINGS
  CARVINGS
CRAW LS
CRAWDAD S
CRAWDADS
CRAWFISH
S **CRAWL** SY
S **CRAWLED**
S **CRAWLER** S
S **CRAWLERS**
  SCRAWLER
S **CRAWLIER**
S **CRAWLING**
S **CRAWLS**
  SCRAWL
CRAWLWAY S
S **CRAWLY**
CRAWS
CRAYFISH
CRAYON S
CRAYONED
  DEACONRY
CRAYONER S
CRAYONS
CRAZE DS
CRAZED
CRAZES
CRAZIER
CRAZIES T
CRAZIEST
CRAZILY
CRAZING
CRAZY
S **CREAK** SY
  CRAKE
S **CREAKED**
CREAKIER
CREAKILY
S **CREAKING**
S **CREAKS**
  CRAKES
  SACKER
  SCREAK
S **CREAKY**
S **CREAM** SY
  MACER
S **CREAMED**
  AMERCED
  RACEMED
S **CREAMER** SY
  AMERCER
S **CREAMERS**
  AMERCERS
  SCREAMER
CREAMERY
CREAMIER
  REARMICE
  RECAMIER
CREAMILY
S **CREAMING**
  AMERCING
  GERMANIC
S **CREAMS**
  MACERS
  SCREAM
CREAMY
CREASE DRS
CREASED
  DECARES
CREASER S
  CAREERS
CREASERS
  CARESSER
CREASES
CREASIER
CREASING
CREASY
  SCAREY
O **CREATE** DS
  CERATE
  ECARTE
CREATED
  CATERED
  CERATED
  REACTED
CREATES
  CERATES
  ECARTES
CREATIN EGS
  CERATIN
  CERTAIN
  TACRINE
CREATINE S
  CENTIARE
  INCREATE
  ITERANCE
CREATING
  ARGENTIC
  CATERING
  REACTING
CREATINS
  CANISTER
  CERATINS
  CISTERNA
  SCANTIER
  TACRINES
CREATION S
  ACTIONER
  ANORETIC
  REACTION
CREATIVE S
  REACTIVE
CREATOR S
  REACTOR
CREATORS
  REACTORS
CREATURE S
CRECHE S
CRECHES
  SCREECH
A **CRED** OS
CREDAL
  CRADLE
  RECLAD
CREDENCE S
CREDENDA
CREDENT
  CENTRED
CREDENZA S
CREDIBLE
CREDIBLY
CREDIT S
  DIRECT
  TRICED
CREDITED
  DIRECTED
CREDITOR S
  DIRECTOR
CREDITS
  DIRECTS
CREDO S
  CODER CORED
  DECOR
CREDOS
  CODERS
  DECORS
  SCORED
CREDS
S **CREED** S
  CEDER CERED
CREEDAL
  CLEARED
  DECLARE
  RELACED
S **CREEDS**
  CEDERS
  SCREED
CREEK S
CREEKS
CREEL S
CREELED
CREELING
CREELS
CREEP SY
  CREPE
CREEPAGE S
CREEPED
  PRECEDE
CREEPER S
CREEPERS
CREEPIE RS
CREEPIER
CREEPIES T
CREEPILY
CREEPING
CREEPS
  CREPES
CREEPY
  CREPEY
CREESE S
CREESES
CREESH
  CHEERS
CREESHED
CREESHES
CREMAINS
  CARMINES
CREMATE DS
CREMATED
CREMATES
CREMATOR SY
CREME S
CREMES
  MERCES
CREMINI S
  CRIMINE
  MINCIER
CREMINIS
CRENATE D
  CENTARE
  REENACT
CRENATED
  CANTERED
  DECANTER
  RECANTED
CRENEL S
CRENELED
CRENELLE DS
CRENELS
CRENSHAW S
CREODONT S
CREOLE S
CREOLES
CREOLISE DS
CREOLIZE DS
CREOSOL S
  COOLERS
CREOSOLS
  COLESSOR
CREOSOTE DS
CREPE DSY
  CREEP
CREPED
CREPES
  CREEPS
CREPEY
  CREEPY
CREPIER
  PIERCER
  REPRICE
CREPIEST
  RECEIPTS
CREPING
CREPON S
CREPONS
CREPT
CREPY
CRESCENT S
CRESCIVE
  CERVICES
  CREVICES
CRESOL S
  CEORLS
  CLOSER
CRESOLS
  CLOSERS
CRESS Y
CRESSES
CRESSET S
  RESECTS
  SECRETS
CRESSETS
CRESSY
CREST S
CRESTAL
  CARTELS
  CLARETS
  SCARLET
CRESTED
CRESTING S
CRESTS
CRESYL S
CRESYLIC
CRESYLS
CRETIC S
CRETICS
CRETIN S
CRETINS
  CISTERN
CRETONNE S
CREVALLE S
CREVASSE DS
CREVICE DS
CREVICED
CREVICES
  CERVICES
  CRESCIVE
S **CREW** S
CREWCUT S
CREWCUTS
S **CREWED**
CREWEL S
CREWELS
S **CREWING**
CREWLESS
CREWMAN

2006 addition

CREWMATE S
CREWMEN
CREWNECK S
S CREWS
SCREW
CRIB S
CRIBBAGE S
CRIBBED
CRIBBER S
CRIBBERS
CRIBBING S
S CRIBBLED
CRIBROUS
CRIBS
CRIBWORK S
CRICETID S
CRICK S
CRICKED
CRICKET S
CRICKETS
CRICKEY
CRICKING
CRICKS
CRICOID S
CRICOIDS
S CRIED
CIDER DICER
RICED
CRIER S
RICER
CRIERS
RICERS
S CRIES
CIRES RICES
CRIKEY
RICKEY
CRIME S
CRIMES
CRIMINAL S
CRIMINE
CREMINI
MINCIER
CRIMINI S
CRIMINIS
CRIMINY
CRIMMER S
CRIMMERS
S CRIMP SY
S CRIMPED
S CRIMPER S
S CRIMPERS
SCRIMPER
S CRIMPIER
S CRIMPING
CRIMPLE DS
CRIMPLED
CRIMPLES
S CRIMPS
SCRIMP
S CRIMPY
CRIMSON S
MICRONS
CRIMSONS
CRINGE DRS
CERING
CRINGED
CRINGER S
CRINGERS
CRINGES
CRINGING
CRINGLE S
CLINGER
CRINGLES
CLINGERS
CRINITE S
CITRINE
INCITER
NERITIC
CRINITES
CITRINES
INCITERS
CRINKLE DS
CLINKER
CRINKLED
CRINKLES
CLINKERS
CRINKLY
CRINOID S
CRINOIDS

CRINUM S
CRINUMS
CRIOLLO S
CRIOLLOS
CRIPE S
PRICE
CRIPES
PRECIS
PRICES
SPICER
CRIPPLE DRS
CLIPPER
CRIPPLED
CRIPPLER S
CRIPPLES
CLIPPERS
CRIS P
CRISES
SCRIES
CRISIC
CRISIS
CRISP SY
SCRIP
CRISPATE D
PARETICS
PICRATES
PRACTISE
CRISPED
CRISPEN S
PINCERS
PRINCES
CRISPENS
PRINCESS
CRISPER S
PRICERS
CRISPERS
CRISPEST
CRISPIER
CRISPILY
CRISPING
CRISPLY
CRISPS
SCRIPS
CRISPY
CRISSA L
CRASIS
CRISSAL
CRISSUM
CRISTA E
RACIST
TRIACS
CRISTAE
ATRESIC
RACIEST
STEARIC
CRISTATE D
CITRATES
SCATTIER
CRIT S
CRITERIA L
CRITIC S
CITRIC
A CRITICAL
CRITICS
CRITIQUE DS
CRITS
CRITTER S
CRITTERS
RESTRICT
STRICTER
CRITTUR S
CRITTURS
CROAK SY
CROAKED
CROAKER S
CROAKERS
CROAKIER
CROAKILY
CROAKING
CROAKS
CROAKY
CROC IKS
CROCEIN ES
CORNICE
CROCINE
CROCEINE S
CICERONE
CROCEINS
CONCISER
CORNICES

CROCHET S
CROCHETS
CROTCHES
CROCI
CROCINE
CORNICE
CROCEIN
CROCK S
CROCKED
CROCKERY
CROCKET S
CROCKETS
CROCKING
CROCKPOT S
CROCKS
CROCOITE S
CROCS
CROCUS
OCCURS
SUCCOR
CROCUSES
CROFT S
CROFTER S
CROFTERS
CROFTS
CROJIK S
CROJIKS
CROMLECH S
CRONE S
RECON
CRONES
CENSOR
RECONS
CRONIES
COINERS
ORCEINS
RECOINS
CRONISH
CRONY
CORNY
CRONYISM S
CROOK S
CROOKED
CROOKER Y
CROOKERY
CROOKEST
CROOKING
CROOKS
CROON S
CROONED
CROONER S
CORONER
CROONERS
CORONERS
CROONING
CROONS
CROP S
CROPLAND S
CROPLESS
CROPPED
CROPPER S
CROPPERS
CROPPIE S
CROPPIES
CROPPING
CROPS
CORPS
CROQUET S
CROQUETS
CROQUIS
CRORE S
CORER
CRORES
CORERS
SCORER
CROSIER S
CIRROSE
CORRIES
ORRICES
CROSIERS
A CROSS E
CROSSARM S
CROSSBAR S
CROSSBOW S
CROSSCUT S
CROSSE DRS
CORSES
SCORES

CROSSED
CROSSER S
RECROSS
SCORERS
CROSSERS
CROSSES T
CROSSEST
CROSSING S
CROSSLET S
CORSLETS
COSTRELS
CROSSLY
CROSSTIE DS
CROSSWAY S
CROSTINI
CROSTINO
CROTCH
CROTCHED
CROTCHES
CROCHETS
CROTCHET SY
CROTON S
CROTONS
CONSORT
CROUCH
CROUCHED
CROUCHES
COUCHERS
CROUP ESY
CROUPE S
RECOUP
CROUPES
RECOUPS
CROUPIER S
CROUPILY
POLYURIC
CROUPOUS
CROUPS
CORPUS
CROUPY
CROUSE
CEROUS
COURSE
SOURCE
CROUSELY
CROUTE S
COUTER
CROUTES
COUTERS
SCOUTER
CROUTON S
CONTOUR
CORNUTO
CROUTONS
CONTOURS
CORNUTOS
OUTSCORN
CROW DNS
CROWBAR S
CROWBARS
CROWD SY
CROWDED
CROWDER S
CROWDERS
CROWDIE S
CROWDIES
CROWDING
CROWDS
CROWDY
CROWED
CROWER S
CROWERS
CROWFEET
CROWFOOT S
CROWING
CROWN S
CROWNED
DECROWN
CROWNER S
RECROWN
CROWNERS
RECROWNS
CROWNET S
CROWNETS
CROWNING
CROWNS
CROWS
CROWSTEP S
CROZE RS

CROZER S
CROZERS
CROZES
CROZIER S
CROZIERS
E CRU DSX
CUR
CRUCES
CERCUS
CRUCIAL
CRUCIAN S
CRUCIANS
CRUCIATE
CRUCIBLE S
CRUCIFER S
CRUCIFIX
CRUCIFY
CRUCK S
CRUCKS
CRUD ES
CURD
CRUDDED
CRUDDIER
CRUDDING
CRUDDY
CRUDE RS
CURED
CRUDELY
CRUDER
CURRED
CRUDES T
CURSED
CRUDEST
CRUSTED
CRUDITES
CURDIEST
CURTSIED
CRUDITY
CRUDS
CURDS
CRUEL
LUCRE ULCER
CRUELER
CRUELEST
LECTURES
CRUELLER
CRUELLY
CRUELTY
CUTLERY
CRUET S
CURET CUTER
ERUCT RECUT
TRUCE
CRUETS
CRUSET
CURETS
ERUCTS
RECTUS
RECUTS
TRUCES
CRUISE DRS
CURIES
CRUISED
CRUISER S
CURRIES
CRUISERS
SCURRIES
CRUISES
CRUISING S
CRULLER S
CRULLERS
CRUMB SY
CRUMBED
CRUMBER S
CRUMBERS
CRUMBIER
CRUMBING
CRUMBLE DS
CLUMBER
CRUMBLED
CRUMBLES
CLUMBERS
CRUMBLY
CRUMBS
CRUMBUM S
CRUMBUMS
CRUMBY
CRUMHORN S
CRUMMIE RS
CRUMMIER

CRUMMIES T
SCUMMIER
CRUMMY
CRUMP S
CRUMPED
CRUMPET S
CRUMPETS
SPECTRUM
CRUMPING
CRUMPLE DS
CRUMPLED
CRUMPLES
CRUMPLY
CRUMPS
S CRUNCH Y
S CRUNCHED
CRUNCHER S
S CRUNCHES
S CRUNCHY
CRUNODAL
CAULDRON
CRUNODE S
CRUNODES
CRUOR S
CRUORS
CURSOR
CRUPPER S
CRUPPERS
CRURA L
CRURAL
E CRUS EHT
CURS
CRUSADE DRS
CRUSADED
ADDUCERS
CRUSADER S
CRUSADES
CRUSADO S
CRUSADOS
CRUSE ST
CURES CURSE
ECRUS SUCRE
CRUSES
CURSES
CUSSER
SUCRES
CRUSET S
CRUETS
CURETS
ERUCTS
RECTUS
RECUTS
TRUCES
CRUSETS
CRUSH
CRUSHED
CRUSHER S
CRUSHERS
CRUSHES
CRUSHING
RUCHINGS
CRUSILY
CRUST SY
CURST
CRUSTAL
CURTALS
CRUSTED
CRUDEST
CRUSTIER
RECRUITS
CRUSTILY
RUSTICLY
CRUSTING
CRUSTOSE
SCOUTERS
CRUSTS
CRUSTY
CURTSY
CRUTCH
CRUTCHED
CRUTCHES
SCUTCHER
CRUX
CRUXES
CRUZADO S
CRUZADOS
CRUZEIRO S
CRWTH S
CRWTHS

S CRY
CRYBABY
S CRYING
CRYINGLY
CRYOBANK S
CRYOGEN SY
CRYOGENS
CRYOGENY
CRYOLITE S
CRYONIC S
CRYONICS
CRYOSTAT S
CRYOTRON S
CRYPT OS
CRYPTAL
CRYPTIC
CRYPTO S
CRYPTOS
CRYPTS
CRYSTAL S
CRYSTALS
CTENIDIA
ACTINIDE
INDICATE
CTENOID
DEONTIC
NOTICED
CUATRO S
TURACO
CUATROS
SURCOAT
TURACOS
CUB ES
CUBAGE S
CUBAGES
CUBATURE S
CUBBIES
CUBBISH
CUBBY
CUBE BDRS
CUBEB S
CUBEBS
CUBED
CUBER S
CUBERS
CUBES
CUBIC S
CUBICAL
CUBICITY
CUBICLE S
CUBICLES
CUBICLY
CUBICS
CUBICULA
CUBIFORM
CUBING
CUBISM S
CUBISMS
CUBIST S
BUSTIC
CUBITS
CUBISTIC
CUBISTS
BUSTICS
CUBIT IS
CUBITAL
CUBITI
CUBITS
BUSTIC
CUBIST
CUBITUS
CUBOID S
CUBOIDAL
CUBOIDS
CUBS
CUCKOLD S
CUCKOLDS
CUCKOO S
CUCKOOED
CUCKOOS
CUCUMBER S
CUCURBIT S
S CUD S
CUDBEAR S
CUDBEARS
CUDDIE S

CUDDIES
CUDDLE DRS
CUDDLED
CUDDLER S
CURDLED
CUDDLERS
CUDDLES
CUDDLIER
CUDDLING
CUDDLY
CUDDY
CUDGEL S
CUDGELED
CUDGELER S
CUDGELS
S CUDS
SCUD
CUDWEED S
CUDWEEDS
CUE DS
ECU
CUED
DUCE
CUEING
CUES
ECUS
CUESTA S
ACUTES
CUESTAS
CAESTUS
S CUFF S
S CUFFED
S CUFFING
CUFFLESS
SCUFFLES
CUFFLINK S
S CUFFS
SCUFF
CUIF S
FUCI
CUIFS
FICUS
CUING
CUIRASS
CUISH
CUISHES
CUISINE S
CUISINES
CUISSE S
CUISSES
CUITTLE DS
CUITTLED
CUITTLES
CUKE S
CUKES
S CULCH
S CULCHES
CULET S
CULETS
CULEX
CULEXES
CULICES
CULICID S
CULICIDS
CULICINE S
CULINARY
URANYLIC
S CULL SY
CULLAY S
CULLAYS
S CULLED
S CULLER S
S CULLERS
SCULLER
CULLET S
CULLETS
CULLIED
CULLIES
S CULLING
S CULLION S
S CULLIONS
SCULLION
CULLIS
CULLISES
S CULLS
SCULL
CULLY
CULLYING

CULM S
CULMED
CULMING
CULMS
CULOTTE S
CULOTTES
CULPA E
CULPABLE
CULPABLY
CULPAE
CULPRIT S
CULPRITS
CULT IS
S CULTCH
CLUTCH
S CULTCHES
CLUTCHES
CULTI C
CULTIC
CULTIGEN S
CULTISH
CULTISM S
CULTISMS
CULTIST S
CULTISTS
CULTIVAR S
CULTLIKE
CULTRATE D
CULTS
CULTURAL
CULTURE DS
CULTURED
CULTURES
CULTUS
CULTUSES
CULVER ST
CULVERIN S
CULVERS
CULVERT S
CULVERTS
S CUM
CUMARIN S
CRANIUM
CUMARINS
CRANIUMS
CUMBER S
CUMBERED
CUMBERER S
CEREBRUM
CUMBERS
CUMBIA S
CUMBIAS
CUMBROUS
CUMIN S
MUCIN
CUMINS
MUCINS
S CUMMER S
S CUMMERS
SCUMMER
CUMMIN S
CUMMINS
CUMQUAT S
CUMQUATS
CUMSHAW S
CUMSHAWS
CUMULATE DS
CUMULI
CUMULOUS
CUMULUS
CUNDUM S
CUNDUMS
CUNEAL
LACUNE
LAUNCE
UNLACE
CUNEATE D
CUNEATED
CUNEATIC
CUNIFORM S
UNCIFORM
S CUNNER S
S CUNNERS
SCUNNER
CUNNING S
CUNNINGS
S CUP S

CUPBOARD S
CUPCAKE S
CUPCAKES
CUPEL S
CUPELED
DECUPLE
CUPELER S
CUPELERS
CUPELING
CUPELLED
CUPELLER S
CUPELS
CUPFUL S
CUPFULS
CUPSFUL
CUPID S
PUDIC
CUPIDITY
CUPIDS
CUSPID
CUPLIKE
CUPOLA S
COPULA
CUPOLAED
CUPOLAS
COPULAS
SCOPULA
CUPPA S
CUPPAS
CUPPED
S CUPPER S
S CUPPERS
SCUPPER
CUPPIER
CUPPIEST
CUPPING S
CUPPINGS
CUPPY
CUPREOUS
CUPRIC
CUPRITE S
PICTURE
CUPRITES
PICTURES
PIECRUST
CUPROUS
CUPRUM S
CUPRUMS
S CUPS
CUSP SCUP
CUPSFUL
CUPFULS
CUPULA ER
CUPULAE
CUPULAR
CUPULATE
CUPULE S
CUPULES
CUR BDEFLNR
CRU ST
CURABLE
CURABLY
CURACAO S
CURACOA
CURACAOS
CURACOAS
CURACIES
CAESURIC
CURACOA S
CURACAO
CURACOAS
CURACAOS
CURACY
CURAGH S
CURAGHS
CURARA S
CURARAS
CURARE S
CURARES
CURARI S
CURARINE S
CURARIS
CURARIZE DS
CURASSOW S
CURATE DS
ACUTER
CURATED
TRADUCE
CURATES

CURATING
CURATIVE S
CURATOR S
CURATORS
CURB S
CURBABLE
CURBED
CURBER S
CURBERS
CURBING S
CURBINGS
CURBS
SCRUB
CURBSIDE S
CURCH
CURCHES
CURCULIO S
CURCUMA S
CURCUMAS
CURD SY
CRUD
CURDED
CURDIER
CURRIED
CURDIEST
CRUDITES
CURTSIED
CURDING
CURDLE DRS
CURLED
CURDLED
CUDDLER
CURDLER S
CURDLERS
CURDLES
CURDLING
CURDS
CRUDS
CURDY
CURE DRST
ECRU
CURED
CRUDE
CURELESS
RECLUSES
CURER S
RECUR
CURERS
CURSER
RECURS
CURES
CRUSE CURSE
ECRUS SUCRE
CURET S
CRUET CUTER
ERUCT RECUT
TRUCE
CURETS
CRUETS
CRUSET
ERUCTS
RECTUS
RECUTS
TRUCES
CURETTE DS
CURETTED
CURETTES
S CURF S
CURFEW S
CURFEWS
S CURFS
SCURF
CURIA EL
AURIC
CURIAE
CURIAL
URACIL
CURIE S
UREIC
CURIES
CRUISE
CURING
CURIO S
CURIOS A
CURIOSA
CARIOUS
CURIOUS
CURITE S
URETIC
CURITES
ICTERUS

CURIUM S
CURIUMS
CURL SY
CURLED
CURDLE
CURLER S
CURLERS
CURLEW S
CURLEWS
CURLICUE DS
CURLIER
CURLIEST
UTRICLES
CURLILY
CURLING S
CURLINGS
CURLS
CURLY
CURLYCUE S
CURN S
CURNS
CURR SY
CURRACH S
CURRACHS
CURRAGH S
CURRAGHS
CURRAN ST
CURRANS
CURRANT S
CURRANTS
CURRED
CRUDER
CURRENCY
CURRENT S
CURRENTS
CURRICLE S
CURRIE DRS
S CURRIED
CURDIER
CURRIER SY
CURRIERS
CURRIERY
S CURRIES
CRUISER
CURRING
CURRISH
CURRS
S CURRY
S CURRYING
CURS ET
CRUS
CURSE DRS
CRUSE CURES
ECRUS SUCRE
CURSED
CRUDES
CURSEDER
REDUCERS
CURSEDLY
CURSER S
CURERS
RECURS
CURSERS
CURSES
CRUSES
CUSSER
SUCRES
CURSING
CURSIVE S
CURSIVES
SCURVIES
CURSOR SY
CRUORS
CURSORS
CURSORY
CURST
CRUST
CURT
CURTAIL S
CURTAILS
RUSTICAL
CURTAIN S
CURTAINS
CURTAL S
CURTALAX
CURTALS
CRUSTAL
CURTATE
CURTER

CURTEST
CUTTERS
SCUTTER
CURTESY
CURTSEY
CURTLY
CURTNESS
ENCRUSTS
CURTSEY S
CURTESY
CURTSEYS
CURTSIED
CRUDITES
CURDIEST
CURTSIES
CITRUSES
RICTUSES
CURTSY
CRUSTY
CURULE
CURVE DSTY
CURVED
CURVEDLY
CURVES
CURVET S
CURVETED
CURVETS
CURVEY
S CURVIER
S CURVIEST
CURVING
S CURVY
CUSCUS
CUSCUSES
CUSEC S
CUSECS
CUSHAT S
CUSHATS
CUSHAW S
CUSHAWS
CUSHIER
CUSHIEST
CUSHILY
CUSHION SY
CUSHIONS
CUSHIONY
CUSHY
CUSK S
SUCK
CUSKS
SUCKS
CUSP S
CUPS SCUP
CUSPAL
CUSPATE D
TEACUPS
CUSPATED
CUSPED
CUSPID S
CUPIDS
CUSPIDAL
CUSPIDES
CUSPIDOR S
CUSPIDS
CUSPIS
CUSPS
SCUPS
CUSS O
CUSSED
CUSSEDLY
CUSSER S
CRUSES
CURSES
SUCRES
CUSSERS
CUSSES
CUSSING
CUSSO S
CUSSOS
CUSSWORD S
CUSTARD SY
CUSTARDS
CUSTARDY
CUSTODES
CUSTODY
CUSTOM S
CUSTOMER S
COSTUMER

CUSTOMS
CUSTOS
SCOUTS
CUSTUMAL S
S CUT ES
CUTAWAY S
CUTAWAYS
CUTBACK S
CUTBACKS
CUTBANK S
CUTBANKS
S CUTCH
CUTCHERY
S CUTCHES
CUTDOWN S
CUTDOWNS
AS CUTE RSY
A CUTELY
A CUTENESS
A CUTER
CRUET CURET
ERUCT RECUT
TRUCE
AS CUTES TY
SCUTE
CUTESIE R
CUTESIER
CERUSITE
EUCRITES
A CUTEST
CUTESY
CUTEYS
CUTEY S
CUTEYS
CUTESY
CUTGRASS
CUTICLE S
CUTICLES
CUTICULA ER
CUTIE S
CUTIES
CUTIN S
TUNIC
CUTINISE DS
CUTINIZE DS
CUTINS
TUNICS
CUTIS
ICTUS
CUTISES
ICTUSES
CUTLAS S
CUTLASES
CUTLASS
CUTLER SY
RELUCT
CUTLERS
CLUSTER
RELUCTS
CUTLERY
CRUELTY
CUTLET S
CUTTLE
CUTLETS
CUTTLES
SCUTTLE
CUTLINE S
LINECUT
TUNICLE
CUTLINES
LINECUTS
TUNICLES
CUTOFF S
OFFCUT
CUTOFFS
OFFCUTS
CUTOUT S
CUTOUTS
CUTOVER S
OVERCUT
CUTOVERS
OVERCUTS
CUTPURSE S
S CUTS
SCUT
CUTTABLE
CUTTAGE S
CUTTAGES
S CUTTER S

S CUTTERS
CURTEST
SCUTTER
CUTTIES
CUTTING S
CUTTINGS
TUNGSTIC
S CUTTLE DS
CUTLET
S CUTTLED
S CUTTLES
CUTLETS
SCUTTLE
S CUTTLING
CUTTY
CUTUP S
CUTUPS
CUTWATER S
S CUTWORK S
S CUTWORKS
SCUTWORK
CUTWORM S
CUTWORMS
CUVEE S
CUVEES
CUVETTE S
CUVETTES
CWM S
CWMS
CYAN OS
CYANAMID ES
ADYNAMIC
CYANATE S
CYANATES
CYANIC
CYANID ES
CYANIDE DS
CYANIDED
CYANIDES
CYANIDS
CYANIN ES
CYANINE S
CYANINES
CYANINS
CYANITE S
CYANITES
CYANITIC
CYANO
CYANOGEN S
CYANOSED
CYANOSES
CYANOSIS
CYANOTIC
CYANS
CYBER
CYBERSEX
CYBORG S
CYBORGS
CYCAD S
CYCADS
CYCAS
CYCASES
CYCASIN S
CYCASINS
CYCLAMEN S
CYCLASE S
CALYCES
CYCLASES
CYCLE DRS
CYCLECAR S
CYCLED
CYCLER SY
CYCLERS
CYCLERY
CYCLES
CYCLEWAY S
A CYCLIC
CYCLICAL S
CYCLICLY
CYCLIN GS
CYCLING S
CYCLINGS
CYCLINS
CYCLIST S
CYCLISTS
CYCLITOL S

CYCLIZE DS
CYCLIZED
CYCLIZES
CYCLO S
CYCLOID S
CYCLOIDS
CYCLONAL
CYCLONE S
CYCLONES
CYCLONIC
CYCLOPES
CYCLOPS
CYCLOS
CYCLOSES
CYCLOSIS
CYDER S
DECRY
CYDERS
DESCRY
CYESES
SYCEES
CYESIS
CYGNET S
CYGNETS
CYLICES
CYLINDER S
CYLIX
CYMA ERS
CYMAE
CYMAR S
CYMARS
CYMAS
CYMATIA
CYMATIUM
CYMBAL S
CYMBALER S
CYMBALOM S
CYMBALS
CYMBIDIA
CYMBLING S
CYME S
CYMENE S
CYMENES
CYMES
CYMLIN GS
CYMLING S
CYMLINGS
CYMLINS
CYMOGENE S
CYMOID
CYMOL S
CYMOLS
CYMOSE
CYMOSELY
CYMOUS
CYNIC S
CYNICAL
CYNICISM S
CYNICS
CYNOSURE S
CYPHER S
CYPHERED
CYPHERS
CYPRES S
CYPRESES
CYPRESS
CYPRIAN S
CYPRIANS
CYPRINID S
CYPRUS
SPRUCY
CYPRUSES
CYPSELA E
CYPSELAE
CYST S
CYSTEIN ES
CYSTINE
CYSTEINE S
CYSTEINS
CYSTINES
CYSTIC
CYSTINE S
CYSTEIN
CYSTINES
CYSTEINS
CYSTITIS

CYSTOID S
CYSTOIDS
CYSTS
CYTASTER S
CYTIDINE S
CYTOGENY
CYTOKINE S
CYTOLOGY
CYTON S
CYTONS
CYTOSINE S
CYTOSOL S
CYTOSOLS
CZAR S
CZARDAS
CZARDOM S
CZARDOMS
CZAREVNA S
CZARINA S
CZARINAS
CZARISM S
CZARISMS
CZARIST S
CZARISTS
CZARITZA S
CZARS

D

DAB S
BAD
DABBED
DABBER S
BARBED
DABBERS
DABBING
DABBLE DRS
DABBLED
DABBLER S
DRABBLE
RABBLED
DABBLERS
DRABBLES
DABBLES
SLABBED
DABBLING S
DABCHICK S
DABS
BADS
DABSTER S
DABSTERS
DACE S
ACED CADE
DACES
CADES CASED
DACHA S
DACHAS
DACITE S
DACITES
DACKER S
ARCKED
CARKED
RACKED
DACKERED
DACKERS
DACOIT SY
DACOITS
DACOITY
DACRON S
CANDOR
CARDON
DACRONS
CANDORS
CARDONS
DACTYL IS
DACTYLI C
DACTYLIC S
DACTYLS
DACTYLUS
DAD AOS
ADD
DADA S
DADAISM S
DADAISMS
DADAIST S
DADAISTS
DADAS
DADDIES

DADDLE DS
ADDLED
DADDLED
DADDLES
SADDLED
DADDLING
DADDY
DADGUM
DADO S
DADOED
DADOES
DADOING
DADOS
DADS
ADDS
DAEDAL
DAEMON S
MOANED
DAEMONES
DAEMONIC
COMEDIAN
DEMONIAC
DAEMONS
MASONED
MONADES
DAFF SY
DAFFED
DAFFIER
DAFFIEST
DAFFILY
DAFFING
DAFFODIL S
DAFFS
DAFFY
DAFT
DAFTER
RAFTED
DAFTEST
DAFTLY
DAFTNESS
DAG OS
GAD
DAGGA S
DAGGAS
DAGGER S
RAGGED
DAGGERED
DAGGERS
DAGGLE DS
LAGGED
DAGGLED
DAGGLES
SLAGGED
DAGGLING
DAGLOCK S
DAGLOCKS
DAGOBA S
DAGOBAS
DAGS
GADS
DAGWOOD S
DAGWOODS
O DAH LS
HAD
DAHABEAH S
DAHABIAH S
DAHABIEH S
DAHABIYA S
DAHL S
DHAL
DAHLIA S
DAHLIAS
DAHLS
DHALS
DAHOON S
DAHOONS
O DAHS
DASH SHAD
DAIDZEIN S
DAIKER S
DAIKERED
DAIKERS
DAIKON S
DAIKONS
DAILIES
LIAISED
SEDILIA
DAILY

DAIMEN
AIDMEN
MAIDEN
MEDIAN
MEDINA
DAIMIO S
DAIMIOS
DAIMON S
DOMAIN
DAIMONES
AMIDONES
DOMAINES
DAIMONIC
DAIMONS
DOMAINS
DAIMYO S
DAIMYOS
DAINTIER
DAINTIES T
ADENITIS
DAINTILY
DAINTY
DAIQUIRI S
DAIRIES
DIARIES
DAIRY
DIARY YAIRD
DAIRYING S
DAIRYMAN
DAIRYMEN
DAIS Y
AIDS SADI
SAID
DAISES
ASIDES
DASSIE
DAISHIKI S
DAISIED
DAISIES
DAISY
SAYID
DAK S
DAKERHEN S
HANKERED
HARKENED
DAKOIT SY
DAKOITS
DAKOITY
DAKS
DAL ES
LAD
DALAPON S
DALAPONS
DALASI S
DALASIS
DALE S
DEAL LADE
LEAD
DALEDH S
DALEDHS
DALES
DEALS LADES
LASED LEADS
DALESMAN
LEADSMAN
DALESMEN
LEADSMEN
DALETH S
HALTED
LATHED
DALETHS
DALLES
LADLES
DALLIED
DIALLED
DALLIER S
DIALLER
RALLIED
DALLIERS
DIALLERS
DALLIES
SALLIED
DALLY
DALLYING
DALMATIC S
DALS
LADS
DALTON S
DALTONIC
ANTICOLD
DALTONS
SANDLOT

DAM ENPS
MAD
DAMAGE DRS
DAMAGED
DAMAGER S
DAMAGERS
SMARAGDE
DAMAGES
DAMAGING
DAMAN S
ADMAN
DAMANS
DAMAR S
DRAMA
DAMARS
DRAMAS
MADRAS
DAMASK S
DAMASKED
DAMASKS
DAME S
MADE MEAD
DAMES
MEADS
DAMEWORT S
DAMIANA S
DAMIANAS
DAMMAR S
DAMMARS
DAMMED
DAMMER S
RAMMED
DAMMERS
DAMMING
DAMMIT
DAMN S
DAMNABLE
DAMNABLY
DAMNDEST S
DAMNED
DEMAND
MADDEN
DAMNEDER
DEMANDER
REDEMAND
REMANDED
DAMNER S
REMAND
DAMNERS
REMANDS
DAMNIFY
DAMNING
DAMNS
DAMOSEL S
DAMOSELS
DAMOZEL S
DAMOZELS
DAMP S
DAMPED
DAMPEN S
DAMPENED
DAMPENER S
DAMPENS
DAMPER S
RAMPED
DAMPERS
DAMPEST
STAMPED
DAMPING S
DAMPINGS
DAMPISH
PHASMID
DAMPLY
DAMPNESS
DAMPS
DAMS
MADS
DAMSEL S
LAMEDS
MEDALS
DAMSELS
DAMSON S
MONADS
NOMADS
DAMSONS
DAN GKS
AND
DANAZOL S
DANAZOLS

DANCE DRS
ACNED CANED
DANCED
DANCER S
CEDARN
CRANED
NACRED
DANCERS
DANCES
ASCEND
DANCING
DANDER S
DARNED
DANDERED
DANDERS
DANDIER
DRAINED
DANDIES T
DANDIEST
DANDIFY
DANDILY
DANDLE DRS
LANDED
DANDLED
DANDLER S
DANDLERS
DANDLES
DANDLING
DANDRIFF S
DANDRUFF SY
DANDY
DANDYISH
DANDYISM S
DANEGELD S
DANEGELT S
DANEWEED S
DANEWORT S
TEARDOWN
DANG S
DANGED
DANGER S
GANDER
GARDEN
RANGED
DANGERED
DERANGED
GANDERED
GARDENED
DANGERS
GANDERS
GARDENS
DANGING
DANGLE DRS
ANGLED
LAGEND
DANGLED
GLADDEN
DANGLER S
GNARLED
DANGLERS
GLANDERS
DANGLES
GLANDES
LAGENDS
SLANGED
DANGLIER
DRAGLINE
DANGLING
DANGLY
DANGS
DANIO S
DANIOS
ADONIS
DANISH
SANDHI
DANISHES
SHANDIES
DANK
DANKER
DARKEN
NARKED
RANKED
DANKEST
DANKLY
DANKNESS
DANS
ANDS SAND
DANSEUR S
ASUNDER
DANSEURS
DANSEUSE S

DAP S
PAD
DAPHNE S
DAPHNES
DAPHNIA S
DAPHNIAS
DAPPED
DAPPER
RAPPED
DAPPERER
PREPARED
DAPPERLY
DAPPING
DAPPLE DS
LAPPED
PALPED
DAPPLED
DAPPLES
SLAPPED
DAPPLING
DAPS
PADS
DAPSONE S
DAPSONES
SPADONES
DARB S
BARD BRAD
DRAB
DARBAR S
DARBARS
DARBIES
ABIDERS
BRAISED
SEABIRD
SIDEBAR
DARBS
BARDS BRADS
DRABS
DARE DRS
DEAR READ
DARED
ADDER DREAD
READD
DAREFUL
DARER S
DREAR RARED
DARERS
DREARS
DARES
DEARS RASED
READS
DARESAY
DARIC S
ACRID CAIRD
DARICS
CAIRDS
DARING S
GRADIN
DARINGLY
DARINGS
GRADINS
DARIOLE S
DARIOLES
DARK S
DARKED
DARKEN S
DANKER
NARKED
RANKED
DARKENED
DARKENER S
DARKENS
DARKER
DARKEST
STRAKED
DARKING
DARKISH
DARKLE DS
LARKED
DARKLED
DARKLES
DARKLIER
DARKLING S
DARKLY
DARKNESS
DARKROOM S
DARKS
DARKSOME
DARLING S
LARDING
DARLINGS

DARN S
NARD RAND
DARNDEST S
STRANDED
DARNED
DANDER
DARNEDER
DARNEL S
LANDER
RELAND
DARNELS
LANDERS
RELANDS
SLANDER
SNARLED
DARNER S
ERRAND
DARNERS
ERRANDS
DARNING S
DARNINGS
DARNS
NARDS RANDS
DARSHAN S
DHARNAS
DARSHANS
DART S
DRAT TRAD
DARTED
TRADED
DARTER S
RETARD
TARRED
TRADER
DARTERS
RETARDS
STARRED
TRADERS
DARTING
TRADING
DARTLE DS
DARTLED
DARTLES
DARTLING
DARTS
DRATS
DASH IY
DAHS SHAD
DASHED
SHADED
DASHEEN S
DASHEENS
ENDASHES
DASHER S
SHADER
SHARED
DASHERS
SHADERS
DASHES
SADHES
SASHED
SHADES
DASHI S
DASHIER
AIRSHED
HARDIES
SHADIER
DASHIEST
SHADIEST
DASHIKI S
DASHIKIS
DASHING
SHADING
DASHIS
DASHPOT S
DASHPOTS
DASHY
SHADY
DASSIE S
ASIDES
DAISES
DASSIES
DASTARD S
DASTARDS
DASYURE S
DASYURES
DATA
DATABANK S
DATABASE DS
DATABLE
ABLATED

DATARIES
AIRDATES
RADIATES
DATARY
DATCHA S
DATCHAS
DATE DRS
DATEABLE
DATEBOOK S
DATED
DATEDLY
DATELESS
DETASSEL
TASSELED
DATELINE DS
ENTAILED
LINEATED
DATER S
DERAT RATED
TARED TRADE
TREAD
DATERS
DERATS
STARED
TRADES
TREADS
DATES
SATED STADE
STEAD TSADE
DATING
DATIVAL
DATIVE S
DATIVELY
DATIVES
VISTAED
DATO S
DOAT TOAD
DATOS
DOATS TOADS
DATTO S
DATTOS
DATUM S
DATUMS
DATURA S
DATURAS
DATURIC
DAUB ESY
BAUD
DAUBE DRS
DAUBED
DAUBER SY
EARBUD
DAUBERS
EARBUDS
DAUBERY
DAUBES
ABUSED
DAUBIER
DAUBIEST
DAUBING
DAUBRIES
DAUBRY
DAUBS
BAUDS
DAUBY
DAUGHTER S
DAUNDER S
DAUNDERS
DAUNT S
DAUNTED
UNDATED
DAUNTER S
NATURED
UNRATED
UNTREAD
DAUNTERS
TRANSUDE
UNTREADS
DAUNTING
DAUNTS
DAUPHIN ES
DAUPHINE S
DAUPHINS
DAUT S
DAUTED
DAUTIE S
DAUTIES
DAUTING
DAUTS
ADUST

DAVEN S
VANED
DAVENED
DAVENING
DAVENS
DAVIES
ADVISE
VISAED
DAVIT S
DAVITS
DAVY
DAW KNST
WAD
DAWDLE DRS
WADDLE
DAWDLED
WADDLED
DAWDLER S
DRAWLED
WADDLER
DAWDLERS
WADDLERS
DAWDLES
SWADDLE
WADDLES
DAWDLING
WADDLING
DAWED
WADED
DAWEN
AWNED DEWAN
WANED
DAWING
WADING
DAWK S
DAWKS
DAWN S
WAND
DAWNED
DAWNING
DAWNLIKE
DAWNS
WANDS
DAWS
WADS
DAWT S
DAWTED
DAWTIE S
WAITED
DAWTIES
WAISTED
DAWTING
DAWTS
DAY S
DAYBED S
DAYBEDS
DAYBOOK S
DAYBOOKS
DAYBREAK S
DAYCARE S
DAYCARES
DAYDREAM ST Y
DAYFLIES
DAYFLY
DAYGLOW S
DAYGLOWS
DAYLIGHT S
DAYLILY
DAYLIT
DAYLONG
DAYMARE S
DAYMARES
DAYROOM S
DAYROOMS
DAYS
DAYSIDE S
DAYSIDES
DAYSMAN
DAYSMEN
DAYSTAR S
DAYSTARS
DAYTIME S
DAYTIMES
DAYWORK S
WORKDAY
DAYWORKS
WORKDAYS
DAZE DS
ADZE

DAZED
ADZED
DAZEDLY
DAZES
ADZES
DAZING
ADZING
DAZZLE DRS
DAZZLED
DAZZLER S
DAZZLERS
DAZZLES
DAZZLING
O DE BEFLNVWX
ED Y
DEACON S
ACNODE
CANOED
DEACONED
DEACONRY
CRAYONED
DEACONS
ACNODES
DEAD S
DEADBEAT S
DEADBOLT S
DEADEN S
DEANED
DEADENED
DEADENER S
ENDEARED
DEADENS
DEADER
DEADEST
SEDATED
STEADED
DEADEYE S
DEADEYES
DEADFALL S
DEADHEAD S
DEADLIER
DERAILED
REDIALED
DEADLIFT S
DEADLINE DS
DEADLOCK S
DEADLY
DEADMAN
DEADMEN
AMENDED
DEADNESS
DEADPAN S
DEADPANS
DEADS
DEADWOOD S
DEAERATE DS
DEAF
FADE
DEAFEN S
DEAFENED
DEAFENS
DEAFER
FEARED
DEAFEST
DEFEATS
FEASTED
DEAFISH
DEAFLY
FLAYED
DEAFNESS
DEAIR S
AIDER AIRED
IRADE REDIA
DEAIRED
READIED
DEAIRING
DEAIRS
AIDERS
IRADES
RAISED
REDIAS
RESAID
I DEAL ST
DALE LADE
LEAD
DEALATE DS
DEALATED
DEALATES
DEALER S
LEADER

DEALERS
LEADERS
DEALFISH
DEALING S
ALIGNED
LEADING
DEALINGS
LEADINGS
SIGNALED
I DEALS
DALES LADES
LASED LEADS
DEALT
DELTA LATED
DEAN S
DEANED
DEADEN
DEANERY
YEAREND
YEARNED
DEANING
DEANS
SANED SEDAN
DEANSHIP S
HEADPINS
PINHEADS
DEAR SY
DARE READ
DEARER
READER
REARED
REDEAR
REREAD
DEAREST
DERATES
REDATES
SEDATER
DEARIE S
AERIED
REDIAE
DEARIES
READIES
DEARLY
DEARNESS
DEARS
DARES RASED
READS
DEARTH S
HATRED
THREAD
DEARTHS
HARDEST
HARDSET
HATREDS
THREADS
TRASHED
DEARY
DERAY RAYED
READY
DEASH
ASHED HADES
HEADS SADHE
SHADE
DEASHED
DEASHES
DEASHING
HEADINGS
DEASIL
AISLED
IDEALS
LADIES
SAILED
DEATH SY
HATED
DEATHBED S
DEATHCUP S
DEATHFUL
DEATHLY
DEATHS
HASTED
DEATHY
DEAVE DS
EAVED EVADE
DEAVED
EVADED
DEAVES
EVADES
DEAVING
EVADING
DEB ST
BED
DEBACLE S
BELACED
DEBACLES

DEBAG S
BADGE
DEBAGGED
DEBAGS
BADGES
DEBAR KS
ARDEB BARDE
BARED BEARD
BREAD
DEBARK S
BARKED
BRAKED
DEBARKED
DEBARKER S
DEBARKS
DEBARRED
DEBARS
ARDEBS
BARDES
BEARDS
BREADS
SABRED
SERDAB
DEBASE DRS
SEABED
DEBASED
DEBASER S
BEADERS
SABERED
DEBASERS
DEBASES
SEABEDS
DEBASING
BEADINGS
DEBATE DRS
DEBATED
DEBATER S
BERATED
REBATED
TABERED
DEBATERS
BREASTED
DEBATES
BESTEAD
DEBATING
DEBAUCH
DEBEAK S
BEAKED
DEBEAKED
DEBEAKS
DEBEARD S
BEARDED
BREADED
DEBEARDS
DEBILITY
DEBIT S
BIDET
DEBITED
BETIDED
DEBITING
BETIDING
DEBITS
BEDSIT
BIDETS
DEBONAIR E
DEBONE DRS
DEBONED
DEBONER S
ENROBED
REDBONE
DEBONERS
REDBONES
DEBONES
DEBONING
DEBOUCH E
DEBOUCHE DS
DEBRIDE DS
DEBRIDED
DEBRIDES
BIRDSEED
DEBRIEF S
BRIEFED
FIBERED
DEBRIEFS
DEBRIS
BIDERS
BRIDES
REBIDS
DEBRUISE DS
DEBS
BEDS
DEBT S

DEBTLESS
DEBTOR S
DEBTORS
DEBTS
DEBUG S
BUDGE
DEBUGGED
DEBUGGER S
BEGRUDGE
BUGGERED
DEBUGS
BUDGES
DEBUNK S
BUNKED
DEBUNKED
DEBUNKER S
BUNKERED
DEBUNKS
DEBUT S
TUBED
DEBUTANT ES
DEBUTED
DEBUTING
DEBUTS
BESTUD
BUSTED
DEBYE S
DEBYES
DECADAL
DECADE S
DECADENT S
DECANTED
DECADES
DECAF S
FACED
DECAFS
DECAGON S
CONGAED
DECAGONS
DECAGRAM S
DECAL S
CLADE LACED
DECALOG S
DECALOGS
DECALS
CLADES
SCALED
DECAMP S
CAMPED
DECAMPED
DECAMPS
SCAMPED
DECANAL
CANALED
CANDELA
DECANE S
DECANES
ENCASED
DECANT S
CADENT
CANTED
DECANTED
DECADENT
DECANTER S
CANTERED
CRENATED
RECANTED
DECANTS
DESCANT
SCANTED
DECAPOD S
DECAPODS
DECARE S
DECARES
CREASED
DECAY S
DECAYED
DECAYER S
DECAYERS
DECAYING
DECAYS
DECEASE DS
DECEASED
DECEASES
SEEDCASE
DECEDENT S
DECEIT S
DECEITS
DECEIVE DRS
DECEIVED

DECEIVER S
RECEIVED
DECEIVES
DECEMVIR IS
DECENARY
DECENCY
DECENNIA L
ENNEADIC
DECENT
DECENTER S
CENTERED
DECENTRE
DECENTLY
DECENTRE DS
CENTERED
DECENTER
DECERN S
DECERNED
DECERNS
DECIARE S
DECIARES
DECIBEL S
DECIBELS
DECIDE DRS
DEICED
DECIDED
DECIDER S
DECRIED
DECIDERS
DESCRIED
DECIDES
DECIDING
DECIDUA ELS
DECIDUAE
DECIDUAL
DECIDUAS
DECIGRAM S
GRIMACED
DECILE S
CEILED
DECILES
DECIMAL S
CAMELID
CLAIMED
DECLAIM
MEDICAL
DECIMALS
CAMELIDS
DECLAIMS
MEDICALS
DECIMATE DS
MEDICATE
DECIPHER S
CIPHERED
DECISION S
DECISIVE
DECK S
DECKED
DECKEL S
DECKLE
DECKELS
DECKLES
DECKER S
RECKED
DECKERS
DECKHAND S
DECKING S
DECKINGS
DECKLE S
DECKEL
DECKLES
DECKELS
DECKS
DECLAIM S
CAMELID
CLAIMED
DECIMAL
MEDICAL
DECLAIMS
CAMELIDS
DECIMALS
MEDICALS
DECLARE DRS
CLEARED
CREEDAL
RELACED
DECLARED
DECLARER S
DECLARES
RESCALED

DECLASS E
CLASSED
DECLASSE DS
DECLAW S
CLAWED
DECLAWED
DECLAWS
DECLINE DRS
DECLINED
DECLINER S
RECLINED
DECLINES
LICENSED
SILENCED
DECO RSY
CODE COED
DECOCT S
DECOCTED
DECOCTS
DECODE DRS
DECODED
DECODER S
RECODED
DECODERS
DECODES
DECODING
DECOLOR S
COLORED
DECOLORS
DECOLOUR S
COLOURED
DECOR S
CODER CORED
CREDO
DECORATE DS
RECOATED
DECOROUS
DECORS
CODERS
CREDOS
SCORED
DECORUM S
DECORUMS
DECOS
CODES COEDS
DECOUPLE DR
S
DECOY S
COYED
DECOYED
DECOYER S
DECOYERS
DECOYING
GYNECOID
DECOYS
DECREASE DS
DECREE DRS
RECEDE
DECREED
RECEDED
DECREER S
DECREERS
DECREES
RECEDES
SECEDER
DECREPIT
DEPICTER
PRECITED
DECRETAL S
DECRIAL S
RADICEL
RADICLE
DECRIALS
RADICELS
RADICLES
DECRIED
DECIDER
DECRIER S
DECRIERS
DESCRIER
DECRIES
DEICERS
DECROWN S
CROWNED
DECROWNS
DECRY
CYDER
DECRYING
DECRYPT S
DECRYPTS
DECUMAN

DECUPLE DS
CUPELED
DECUPLED
DECUPLES
DECURIES
DECURION S
DECURVE DS
DECURVED
DECURVES
DECURY
DEDAL
ADDLE LADED
DEDANS
DESAND
SADDEN
SANDED
DEDICATE DE
S
DEDUCE DS
DEUCED
EDUCED
DEDUCED
DEDUCES
SEDUCED
DEDUCING
DEDUCT S
DUCTED
DEDUCTED
DEDUCTS
DEE DMPRST
DEED SY
DEEDED
DEEDIER
DEEDIEST
DEEDING
DEIGNED
DEEDLESS
DEEDS
DEEDY
DEEJAY S
DEEJAYED
DEEJAYS
A **DEEM** S
DEME MEED
A **DEEMED**
A **DEEMING**
A **DEEMS**
DEMES MEEDS
DEEMSTER S
DEEP S
DEEPEN S
PEENED
DEEPENED
DEEPENER S
DEEPENS
DEEPER
PEERED
DEEPEST
STEEPED
DEEPLY
YELPED
DEEPNESS
DEEPS
PEDES SPEED
DEER S
DERE DREE
REDE REED
DEERFLY
DEERLIKE
REEDLIKE
DEERS
DREES REDES
REEDS SEDER
SERED
DEERSKIN S
DEERWEED S
DEERYARD S
DEES
SEED
DEET S
TEED
DEETS
STEED
DEEWAN S
WEANED
DEEWANS
DEF ITY
FED
DEFACE DRS
DEFACED

DEFACER S
REFACED
DEFACERS
DEFACES
DEFACING
DEFAME DRS
DEFAMED
DEFAMER S
DEFAMERS
DEFAMES
DEFAMING
DEFANG S
FANGED
DEFANGED
DEFANGS
DEFAT S
FATED
DEFATS
FASTED
DEFATTED
DEFAULT S
FAULTED
DEFAULTS
SULFATED
DEFEAT S
DEFEATED
DEFEATER S
FEDERATE
REDEFEAT
DEFEATS
DEAFEST
FEASTED
DEFECATE DS
DEFECT S
DEFECTED
DEFECTOR S
DEFECTS
DEFENCE DS
DEFENCED
DEFENCES
DEFEND S
FENDED
DEFENDED
DEFENDER S
FENDERED
DEFENDS
DEFENSE DS
DEFENSED
DEFENSES
DEFER S
FREED REFED
DEFERENT S
DEFERRAL S
DEFERRED
DEFERRER S
REFERRED
DEFERS
DEFFER
REFFED
DEFFEST
DEFI S
DEFIANCE S
DEFIANT
FAINTED
DEFICIT S
DEFICITS
DEFIED
DEFIER S
DEFIERS
SERIFED
DEFIES
DEFILADE DS
DEFILE DRS
DEFILED
FIELDED
DEFILER S
FIELDER
REFILED
DEFILERS
FIELDERS
DEFILES
DEFILING
FIELDING
DEFINE DRS
DEFINED
DEFINER S
REFINED
DEFINERS
DEFINES
DEFINING

DEFINITE
DEFIS
DEFLATE DRS
DEFLATED
DEFLATER S
FALTERED
REFLATED
DEFLATES
DEFLATOR S
DEFLEA S
LEAFED
DEFLEAED
DEFLEAS
DEFLECT S
CLEFTED
DEFLECTS
DEFLEXED
DEFLOWER S
FLOWERED
REFLOWED
DEFOAM S
FOAMED
DEFOAMED
DEFOAMER S
DEFOAMS
DEFOCUS
FOCUSED
DEFOG S
DEFOGGED
DEFOGGER S
DEFOGS
DEFORCE DRS
DEFORCED
DEFORCER S
DEFORCES
FRESCOED
DEFOREST S
FORESTED
FOSTERED
DEFORM S
FORMED
DEFORMED
DEFORMER S
REFORMED
DEFORMS
SERFDOM
DEFRAG S
DEFRAGS
DEFRAUD S
DEFRAUDS
DEFRAY S
FRAYED
DEFRAYAL S
DEFRAYED
FEEDYARD
DEFRAYER S
DEFRAYS
DEFROCK S
FROCKED
DEFROCKS
DEFROST S
FROSTED
DEFROSTS
FROSTEDS
DEFT
DEFTER
DEFTEST
DEFTLY
FLYTED
DEFTNESS
DEFUEL S
FUELED
DEFUELED
DEFUELS
DEFUNCT
DEFUND S
FUNDED
DEFUNDED
DEFUNDS
DEFUSE DRS
DEFUSED
DEFUSER S
REFUSED
DEFUSERS
DEFUSES
DEFUSING
DEFUZE DS
DEFUZED
DEFUZES
DEFUZING

DEFY
DEFYING
DEGAGE
DEGAME S
DEGAMES
DEGAMI S
IMAGED
DEGAMIS
DEGAS
EGADS
DEGASES
DEGASSED
DEGASSER S
DRESSAGE
DEGASSES
DEGAUSS
DEGENDER S
GENDERED
DEGERM S
MERGED
DEGERMED
DEMERGED
DEGERMS
DEGLAZE DS
DEGLAZED
DEGLAZES
DEGRADE DRS
DEGRADED
DEGRADER S
REGARDED
REGRADED
DEGRADES
DEGREASE DR
S
DEGREE DS
DEGREED
DEGREES
DEGUM S
DEGUMMED
DEGUMS
SMUDGE
DEGUST S
GUSTED
DEGUSTED
DEGUSTS
DEHISCE DS
DEHISCED
DEHISCES
DEHORN S
HORNED
DEHORNED
DEHORNER S
DEHORNS
DEHORT S
DEHORTED
DEHORTS
SHORTED
DEICE DRS
DEICED
DECIDE
DEICER S
DEICERS
DECRIES
DEICES
DEICIDAL
DEICIDE S
DEICIDES
DEICING
DEICTIC S
DEICTICS
DEIFIC
DEIFICAL
DEIFIED
EDIFIED
DEIFIER S
EDIFIER
REIFIED
DEIFIERS
EDIFIERS
FIRESIDE
DEIFIES
EDIFIES
DEIFORM
DEIFY
EDIFY
DEIFYING
EDIFYING
DEIGN S
DINGE

DEIGNED
DEEDING
DEIGNING
DEIGNS
DESIGN
DINGES
SIGNED
SINGED
DEIL S
DELI DIEL
IDLE LIED
DEILS
DELIS IDLES
ISLED SIDLE
SLIDE
DEIONIZE DR S
DEISM S
DIMES DISME
DEISMS
DISMES
MISSED
DEIST S
DIETS DITES
EDITS SITED
STIED TIDES
DEISTIC
DICIEST
DEISTS
DESIST
DEITIES
DEITY
DEIXIS
DEIXISES
DEJECT AS
DEJECTA
DEJECTED
DEJECTS
DEJEUNER S
DEKAGRAM S
DEKARE S
DEKARES
DEKE DS
EKED
DEKED
DEKEING
DEKES
SKEED
DEKING
KINGED
DEKKO S
DEKKOS
DEL EFILST
ELD
LED
DELAINE S
ALIENED
DELAINES
DELATE DS
ELATED
DELATED
DELATES
DELATING
DELATION S
DELATOR S
LEOTARD
DELATORS
LEOTARDS
LODESTAR
DELAY S
LAYED LEADY
DELAYED
DELAYER S
LAYERED
RELAYED
DELAYERS
DELAYING
DELAYS
SLAYED
DELE DS
DELEAD S
LEADED
DELEADED
DELEADS
DELEAVE DS
DELEAVED
DELEAVES
DELED
DELEGACY
DELEGATE DE S

DELEING
DELES
DELETE DS
DELETED
DELETES
SLEETED
STEELED
DELETING
DELETION S
ENTOILED
DELF ST
FLED
DELFS
DELFT S
DELFTS
DELI S
DEIL DIEL
IDLE LIED
DELICACY
DELICATE S
DELICT S
DELTIC
DELICTS
DELIGHT S
LIGHTED
DELIGHTS
SLIGHTED
DELIME DS
DELIMED
DELIMES
DELIMING
DELIMIT S
LIMITED
DELIMITS
LIMITEDS
DELIRIA
DELIRIUM S
DELIS HT
DEILS IDLES
ISLED SIDLE
SLIDE
DELISH
SHIELD
DELIST S
IDLEST
LISTED
SILTED
TILDES
DELISTED
DELISTS
DELIVER SY
LIVERED
RELIVED
REVILED
DELIVERS
DESILVER
SILVERED
SLIVERED
DELIVERY
DELL SY
DELLIES
DELLS
DELLY
DELOUSE DRS
DELOUSED
DELOUSER S
URODELES
DELOUSES
DELPHIC
DELS
ELDS SLED
DELT AS
DELTA S
DEALT LATED
DELTAIC
CITADEL
DIALECT
EDICTAL
DELTAS
DESALT
LASTED
SALTED
SLATED
STALED
DELTIC
DELICT
DELTOID S
DELTOIDS
DELTS

DELUDE DRS
DUELED
ELUDED
DELUDED
DELUDER S
DELUDERS
DELUDES
DELUDING
INDULGED
DELUGE DS
DELUGED
DELUGES
DELUGING
DELUSION S
INSOULED
UNSOILED
DELUSIVE
DELUSORY
DELUSTER S
LUSTERED
RESULTED
DELUXE
DELVE DRS
DEVEL
DELVED
DELVER S
DELVERS
DELVES
DEVELS
DELVING
DEMAGOG SY
DEMAGOGS
DEMAGOGY
DEMAND S
DAMNED
MADDEN
DEMANDED
MADDENED
DEMANDER S
DAMNEDER
REDEMAND
REMANDED
DEMANDS
MADDENS
DEMARCHE S
DEMARK S
MARKED
DEMARKED
DEMARKS
DEMAST S
MASTED
DEMASTED
DEMASTS
DEME S
DEEM MEED
DEMEAN S
DEMEANED
DEMEANOR S
ENAMORED
DEMEANS
SEEDMAN
DEMENT S
DEMENTED
DEMENTIA LS
DEMENTS
DEMERARA NS
DEMERGE DRS
EMERGED
DEMERGED
DEGERMED
DEMERGER S
REMERGED
DEMERGES
DEMERIT S
DIMETER
MERITED
MITERED
RETIMED
DEMERITS
DEMISTER
DIMETERS
DEMERSAL
EMERALDS
DEMES
DEEMS MEEDS
DEMESNE S
SEEDMEN
DEMESNES
SEEDSMEN
DEMETON S
DEMETONS

DEMIC
MEDIC
DEMIES
DEMISE
DEMIGOD S
DEMIGODS
DEMIJOHN S
DEMILUNE S
DEMIREP S
EPIDERM
IMPEDER
DEMIREPS
EPIDERMS
IMPEDERS
PREMISED
SIMPERED
DEMISE DS
DEMIES
DEMISED
MISDEED
DEMISES
DEMISING
DEMISTER S
DEMERITS
DIMETERS
DEMIT S
TIMED
DEMITS
MISTED
DEMITTED
DEMIURGE S
DEMIVOLT ES
DEMO BNS
DOME MODE
DEMOB S
DEMOBBED
DEMOBS
DEMOCRAT S
DEMODE D
DEMOED
DEMODED
DEMOED
DEMODE
DEMOING
MENDIGO
DEMOLISH
DEMON S
MONDE
DEMONESS
DEMONIAC S
COMEDIAN
DAEMONIC
DEMONIAN
DEMONIC
DEMONISE DS
DEMONISM S
DEMONIST S
DEMONIZE DS
DEMONS
MONDES
DEMOS
DOMES MODES
DEMOSES
DEMOTE DS
EMOTED
DEMOTED
DEMOTES
DEMOTIC S
DEMOTICS
DOMESTIC
DEMOTING
DEMOTION S
MOTIONED
DEMOTIST S
DEMOUNT S
MOUNTED
DEMOUNTS
MUDSTONE
DEMPSTER S
DEMUR ES
MURED
DEMURE R
DEMURELY
DEMURER
DEMUREST
MUSTERED
DEMURRAL S
DEMURRED
MURDERED
DEMURRER S
MURDERER
DEMURS

DEMY
EMYD
DEN EISTY
END
DENAR ISY
REDAN
DENARI I
RAINED
DENARII
DENARIUS
UNRAISED
URANIDES
DENARS
REDANS
SANDER
SNARED
DENARY
YARNED
DENATURE DS
UNDERATE
UNDEREAT
DENAZIFY
DENDRITE S
DENDROID
DENDRON S
DONNERD
DENDRONS
DENE S
NEED
DENES
DENSE NEEDS
DENGUE S
DENGUES
DENI M
DINE NIDE
DENIABLE
DENIABLY
DENIAL S
ALINED
NAILED
DENIALS
SNAILED
DENIED
INDEED
DENIER S
NEREID
REINED
DENIERS
NEREIDS
RESINED
DENIES
DIENES
SEINED
DENIM S
MINED
DENIMED
DENIMS
DENIZEN S
DENIZENS
DENNED
DENNING
DENOTE DS
DENOTED
DENOTES
DENOTING
DENOTIVE
DENOUNCE DR
ENOUNCED S
DENS E
ENDS SEND
SNED
DENSE R
DENES NEEDS
DENSELY
DENSER
ENDERS
RESEND
SENDER
DENSEST
DENSIFY
DENSITY
DESTINY
DENT S
TEND
DENTAL S
DENTALIA
DENTALLY
DENTALS
SLANTED
E **DENTATE** D
DENTATED
ATTENDED

DENTED
TENDED
DENTICLE S
DENTIL S
LINTED
DENTILED
DENTILS
DENTIN EGS
INDENT
INTEND
TINNED
DENTINAL
DENTINE S
DENTINES
DESINENT
DENTING
TENDING
DENTINS
INDENTS
INTENDS
DENTIST S
DISTENT
STINTED
DENTISTS
DENTOID
DENTS
TENDS
DENTURAL
DENTURE S
RETUNED
TENURED
DENTURES
SEDERUNT
UNDERSET
UNRESTED
DENUDATE DS
DENUDE DRS
DUDEEN
DUENDE
ENDUED
DENUDED
DENUDER S
ENDURED
DENUDERS
SUNDERED
DENUDES
DUDEENS
DUENDES
DENUDING
DENY
DYNE
DENYING
DEODAND S
DEODANDS
DEODAR AS
ADORED
DEODARA S
DEODARAS
DEODARS
DEONTIC
CTENOID
NOTICED
DEORBIT S
ORBITED
DEORBITS
DEOXY
DEPAINT S
PAINTED
PATINED
DEPAINTS
DEPART S
PARTED
PETARD
PRATED
DEPARTED
PREDATED
DEPARTEE S
REPEATED
DEPARTS
PETARDS
DEPEND S
PENDED
DEPENDED
DEPENDS
DEPEOPLE DS
DEPERM S
PERMED
PREMED
DEPERMED
DEPERMS
PREMEDS
DEPICT S

DEPICTED
DEPICTER S
DECREPIT
PRECITED
DEPICTOR S
DEPICTS
DISCEPT
DEPILATE DS
EPILATED
PILEATED
DEPLANE DS
PANELED
DEPLANED
DEPLANES
SPALDEEN
DEPLETE DRS
DEPLETED
DEPLETER S
PELTERED
DEPLETES
STEEPLED
DEPLORE DRS
DEPLORED
DEPLORER S
DEPLORES
DEPLOY S
PLOYED
DEPLOYED
DEPLOYER S
REDEPLOY
DEPLOYS
DEPLUME DS
DEPLUMED
DEPLUMES
DEPOLISH
POLISHED
DEPONE DS
OPENED
DEPONED
DEPONENT S
DEPONES
SPONDEE
DEPONING
DEPORT S
PORTED
REDTOP
DEPORTED
DEPORTEE S
DEPORTER S
PORTERED
REPORTED
DEPORTS
REDTOPS
SPORTED
DEPOSAL S
PEDALOS
DEPOSALS
DEPOSE DRS
EPODES
SPEEDO
DEPOSED
SEEDPOD
DEPOSER S
REPOSED
DEPOSERS
DEPOSES
SPEEDOS
DEPOSING
DEPOSIT S
DOPIEST
PODITES
POSITED
SOPITED
TOPSIDE
DEPOSITS
TOPSIDES
DEPOT S
OPTED TOPED
DEPOTS
DESPOT
POSTED
STOPED
DEPRAVE DRS
PERVADE
REPAVED
DEPRAVED
PERVADED
DEPRAVER S
PERVADER
DEPRAVES
PERVADES
DEPRENYL S

DEPRESS
PRESSED
DEPRIVAL S
DEPRIVE DRS
PREDIVE
DEPRIVED
DEPRIVER S
DEPRIVES
PREVISED
DEPSIDE S
DEPSIDES
DESPISED
DEPTH S
DEPTHS
DEPURATE DS
DEPUTE DS
DEPUTED
DEPUTES
DEPUTIES
DEPUTING
DEPUTIZE DS
DEPUTY
DERAIGN S
GRADINE
GRAINED
READING
DERAIGNS
GRADINES
READINGS
DERAIL S
ARILED
DIALER
LAIRED
RAILED
REDIAL
RELAID
DERAILED
DEADLIER
REDIALED
DERAILS
DIALERS
REDIALS
DERANGE DRS
ANGERED
ENRAGED
GRANDEE
GRENADE
DERANGED
DANGERED
GANDERED
GARDENED
DERANGER S
GARDENER
GARNERED
DERANGES
GRANDEES
GRENADES
DERAT ES
DATER RATED
TARED TRADE
TREAD
DERATE DS
REDATE
TEARED
DERATED
REDATED
TREADED
DERATES
DEAREST
REDATES
SEDATER
DERATING
GRADIENT
REDATING
TREADING
DERATS
DATERS
STARED
TRADES
TREADS
DERATTED
DERAY S
DEARY RAYED
READY
DERAYS
DERBIES
DERBY
DERE
DEER DREE
REDE REED
DERELICT S
DERIDE DRS
DERIDED
DERIDER S
REDRIED
DERIDERS
DERIDES
DESIRED
RESIDED
DERIDING
DERINGER S
DERISION S
IRONSIDE
RESINOID
DERISIVE
DERISORY
DERIVATE S
DERIVE DRS
REIVED
DERIVED
DERIVER S
REDRIVE
DERIVERS
REDRIVES
DERIVES
DEVISER
DIVERSE
REVISED
DERIVING
DERM AS
DERMA LS
ARMED DREAM
MADRE
DERMAL
MARLED
MEDLAR
DERMAS
DREAMS
MADRES
DERMIC
DERMIS
DIMERS
DERMISES
DERMOID S
DERMOIDS
DERMS
DERNIER
NERDIER
DEROGATE DS
DERRICK S
DERRICKS
DERRIERE S
DERRIES
DESIRER
REDRIES
RESIDER
SERRIED
DERRIS
DRIERS
RIDERS
DERRISES
DESIRERS
DRESSIER
RESIDERS
DERRY
DRYER REDRY
DERVISH
SHRIVED
DESALT S
DELTAS
LASTED
SALTED
SLATED
STALED
DESALTED
DESALTER S
RESLATED
TREADLES
DESALTS
DESAND S
DEDANS
SADDEN
SANDED
DESANDED
SADDENED
DESANDS
SADDENS
DESCANT S
DECANTS
SCANTED
DESCANTS
DESCEND S
SCENDED
DESCENDS
DESCENT S
SCENTED
DESCENTS
DESCRIBE DR S
DESCRIED
DECIDERS
DESCRIER S
DECRIERS
DESCRIES
DESCRY
CYDERS
DESELECT S
SELECTED
DESERT S
DETERS
RESTED
DESERTED
DESERTER S
DESERTIC
DISCREET
DISCRETE
DESERTS
DESSERT
TRESSED
DESERVE DRS
SEVERED
DESERVED
DESERVER S
RESERVED
REVERSED
DESERVES
DESEX
DEXES SEXED
DESEXED
DESEXES
DESEXING
DESIGN S
DEIGNS
DINGES
SIGNED
SINGED
DESIGNED
DESIGNEE S
DESIGNER S
ENERGIDS
REDESIGN
REEDINGS
RESIGNED
DESIGNS
DESILVER S
DELIVERS
SILVERED
SLIVERED
DESINENT
DENTINES
DESIRE DRS
EIDERS
RESIDE
DESIRED
DERIDES
RESIDED
DESIRER S
DERRIES
REDRIES
RESIDER
SERRIED
DESIRERS
DERRISES
DRESSIER
RESIDERS
DESIRES
RESIDES
DESIRING
RESIDING
RINGSIDE
DESIROUS
DESIST S
DEISTS
DESISTED
DESISTS
DESK S
DESKMAN
DESKMEN
DESKS
DESKTOP S
DESKTOPS
DESMAN S
AMENDS
MENADS
DESMANS
MADNESS
DESMID S
DESMIDS
DESMOID S
DESMOIDS
DESOLATE DR S
DESORB S
SORBED
DESORBED
DESORBS
DESOXY
DESPAIR S
ASPIRED
DIAPERS
PRAISED
DESPAIRS
DESPATCH
DESPISAL S
DESPISE DRS
DESPISED
DEPSIDES
DESPISER S
DISPERSE
PRESIDES
DESPISES
DESPITE DS
DESPITED
DESPITES
SIDESTEP
DESPOIL S
DIPLOES
DIPOLES
SPOILED
DESPOILS
DIPLOSES
DESPOND S
DESPONDS
DESPOT S
DEPOTS
POSTED
STOPED
DESPOTIC
DESPOTS
DESSERT S
DESERTS
TRESSED
DESSERTS
STRESSED
DESTAIN S
DETAINS
INSTEAD
NIDATES
SAINTED
STAINED
DESTAINS
SANDIEST
DESTINE DS
ENDITES
DESTINED
DESTINES
DESTINY
DENSITY
DESTRIER S
DESTROY S
STROYED
DESTROYS
DESTRUCT S
DESUGAR S
SUGARED
DESUGARS
GRADUSES
DESULFUR S
SULFURED
DETACH
DETACHED
DETACHER S
RACHETED
DETACHES
SACHETED
DETAIL S
DILATE
TAILED
DETAILED
DETAILER S
ELATERID
RETAILED
DETAILS
DILATES
DETAIN S
NIDATE
DETAINED
DETAINEE S
DETAINER S
RETAINED
DETAINS
DESTAIN
INSTEAD
NIDATES
SAINTED
STAINED
DETASSEL S
DATELESS
TASSELED
DETECT S
DETECTED
DETECTER S
DETECTOR S
COTTERED
DETECTS
DETENT ES
NETTED
TENTED
DETENTE S
DETENTES
DETENTS
DETER S
TREED
DETERGE DRS
GREETED
DETERGED
DETERGER S
DETERGES
DETERRED
DETERRER S
DETERS
DESERT
RESTED
DETEST S
TESTED
DETESTED
DETESTER S
RETESTED
DETESTS
DETHATCH
THATCHED
DETHRONE DR S
THRENODE
DETICK S
TICKED
DETICKED
DETICKER S
DETICKS
STICKED
DETINUE S
DETINUES
DETONATE DS
DETOUR S
REDOUT
ROUTED
TOURED
DETOURED
DETOURS
DOUREST
REDOUTS
ROUSTED
DETOX
DETOXED
DETOXES
DETOXIFY
DETOXING
DETRACT S
DETRACTS
DETRAIN S
ANTIRED
TRAINED
DETRAINS
RANDIEST
STRAINED
DETRITAL
DETRITUS
DETRUDE DS
DETRUDED
DETRUDES
DEUCE DS
EDUCE
DEUCED
DEDUCE
EDUCED
DEUCEDLY
DEUCES
EDUCES
SEDUCE
DEUCING
EDUCING
DEUTERIC
DEUTERON S
DEUTZIA S
DEUTZIAS
DEV AS
DEVA S
DEVALUE DS
DEVALUED
DEVALUES
DEVAS
SAVED
DEVEIN S
ENDIVE
ENVIED
VEINED
DEVEINED
DEVEINS
ENDIVES
DEVEL S
DELVE
DEVELED
DEVELING
DEVELOP ES
DEVELOPE DR S
DEVELOPS
DEVELS
DELVES
DEVERBAL S
DEVEST S
VESTED
DEVESTED
DEVESTS
DEVIANCE S
DEVIANCY
DEVIANT S
DEVIANTS
DEVIATE DS
DEVIATED
DEVIATES
SEDATIVE
DEVIATOR SY
DEVICE S
DEVICES
DEVIL S
LIVED
DEVILED
DEVILING
DEVILISH
DEVILKIN S
DEVILLED
DEVILRY
DEVILS
DEVILTRY
DEVIOUS
DEVISAL S
DEVISALS
DEVISE DERS
SIEVED
VISEED
DEVISED
DEVISEE S
DEVISEES
DEVISER S
DERIVES
DIVERSE
REVISED
DEVISERS
DISSERVE
DISSEVER
DEVISES
DEVISING
DEVISOR S
DEVOIRS
VISORED
VOIDERS
DEVISORS
DEVOICE DS
DEVOICED
DEVOICES
DEVOID
VOIDED
DEVOIR S
VOIDER
DEVOIRS
DEVISOR
VISORED
VOIDERS
DEVOLVE DS
EVOLVED
DEVOLVED
DEVOLVES
DEVON S
DOVEN
DEVONIAN
DEVONS
DOVENS
DEVOTE DES
VETOED
DEVOTED
DEVOTEE S
DEVOTEES
DEVOTES
DEVOTING
DEVOTION S
DEVOUR S
DEVOURED
DEVOURER S
OVERRUDE
DEVOURS
DEVOUT
DEVOUTER
DEVOUTLY
DEVS
DEW SY
WED
DEWAN S
AWNED DAWEN
WANED
DEWANS
SNAWED
DEWAR S
WADER WARED
DEWARS
WADERS
DEWATER S
TARWEED
WATERED
DEWATERS
TARWEEDS
DEWAX
WAXED
DEWAXED
DEWAXES
DEWAXING
DEWBERRY
DEWCLAW S
DEWCLAWS
DEWDROP S
DEWDROPS
DEWED
DEWFALL S
DEWFALLS
DEWIER
DEWIEST
DEWILY
WIDELY
WIELDY
DEWINESS
WIDENESS
DEWING
WINGED
DEWLAP S
DEWLAPS
DEWLESS
DEWOOL S
WOOLED
DEWOOLED
DEWOOLS
DEWORM S
WORMED
DEWORMED
DEWORMER S
DEWORMS
DEWS
WEDS
DEWY
DEX Y
DEXES
DESEX SEXED
DEXIE S
DEXIES
DEXTER
DEXTRAL

DEXTRAN S
DEXTRANS
DEXTRIN ES
DEXTRINE S
DEXTRINS
DEXTRO
DEXTROSE S
DEXTROUS
DEXY
DEY S
DYE
DEYS
DYES
DEZINC S
ZINCED
DEZINCED
DEZINCS
DHAK S
DHAKS
DHAL S
DAHL
DHALS
DAHLS
DHARMA S
DHARMAS
DHARMIC
DHARNA S
DHARNAS
DARSHAN
DHOBI S
DHOBIS
DHOLE S
HOLED
DHOLES
DHOOLIES
DHOOLY
DHOORA S
DHOORAS
DHOOTI ES
DHOOTIE S
DHOOTIES
HOODIEST
DHOOTIS
DHOTI S
DHOTIS
DHOURRA S
DHOURRAS
DHOW S
DHOWS
DHURNA S
DHURNAS
DHURRIE S
HURRIED
DHURRIES
DHUTI S
DHUTIS
DIABASE S
DIABASES
DIABASIC
DIABETES
BEADIEST
DIABETIC S
DIABLERY
DIABOLIC
BIOCIDAL
DIABOLO S
DIABOLOS
DIACETYL S
DIACID S
DIACIDIC
DIACIDS
DIACONAL
DIADEM S
MEDIAD
DIADEMED
DIADEMS
DIAGNOSE DS
AGONISED
DIAGONAL S
GONADIAL
DIAGRAM S
DIAGRAMS
DIAGRAPH S
DIAL S
LAID

DIALECT S
CITADEL
DELTAIC
EDICTAL
DIALECTS
CITADELS
DIALED
LADDIE
DIALER S
ARILED
DERAIL
LAIRED
RAILED
REDIAL
RELAID
DIALERS
DERAILS
REDIALS
DIALING S
GLIADIN
DIALINGS
GLIADINS
DIALIST S
DIALISTS
DIALLAGE S
DIALLED
DALLIED
DIALLEL
DIALLER S
DALLIER
RALLIED
DIALLERS
DALLIERS
DIALLING S
DIALLIST S
DIALOG S
ALGOID
DIALOGED
DIALOGER S
DIALOGIC
DIALOGS
DIALOGUE DR S
DIALS
DIALYSE DRS
DIALYSED
DIALYSER S
DIALYSES
DIALYSIS
DIALYTIC
DIALYZE DRS
DIALYZED
DIALYZER S
DIALYZES
DIAMANTE S
ANIMATED
DIAMETER S
DIAMIDE S
DIAMIDES
DIAMIN ES
AMIDIN
DIAMINE S
AMIDINE
DIAMINES
AMIDINES
DIAMINS
AMIDINS
DIAMOND S
DIAMONDS
DIANTHUS
DIAPASON S
DIAPAUSE DS
DIAPER S
PAIRED
PARDIE
REPAID
DIAPERED
DIAPERS
ASPIRED
DESPAIR
PRAISED
DIAPHONE S
DIAPHONY
DIAPIR S
DIAPIRIC
DIAPIRS
DIAPSID S
DIAPSIDS
DIARCHIC
DIARCHY

DIARIES
DAIRIES
DIARIST S
DIARISTS
DIARRHEA LS
DIARY
DAIRY YAIRD
DIASPORA S
DIASPORE S
PARODIES
DIASTASE S
DIASTEM AS
MISDATE
DIASTEMA S
ADAMSITE
DIASTEMS
MISDATES
DIASTER S
ARIDEST
ASTRIDE
DISRATE
STAIDER
TARDIES
TIRADES
DIASTERS
DISASTER
DISRATES
DIASTOLE S
ISOLATED
SODALITE
DIASTRAL
DIATOM S
DIATOMIC
DIATOMS
MASTOID
DIATONIC
ACTINOID
DIATRIBE S
DIATRON S
DIATRONS
INTRADOS
DIAZEPAM S
DIAZIN ES
DIAZINE S
DIAZINES
DIAZINON S
DIAZINS
DIAZO
AZIDO
DIAZOLE S
DIAZOLES
SLEAZOID
DIB S
BID
DIBASIC
DIBBED
DIBBER S
BRIBED
RIBBED
DIBBERS
DIBBING
DIBBLE DRS
DIBBLED
DIBBLER S
DRIBBLE
DIBBLERS
DRIBBLES
DIBBLES
DIBBLING
DIBBUK S
DIBBUKIM
DIBBUKS
DIBS
BIDS
DICAMBA S
DICAMBAS
DICAST S
DICASTIC
DICASTS
DICE DRSY
CEDI ICED
DICED
DICENTRA S
DICER S
CIDER CRIED
RICED
DICERS
CIDERS
SCRIED
DICES
CEDIS

DICEY
DICHASIA L
DICHOTIC
DICHROIC
DICIER
DICIEST
DEISTIC
DICING
DICK SY
DICKENS
SNICKED
DICKER S
RICKED
DICKERED
DICKERS
DICKEY S
DICKEYS
DICKIE RS
DICKIER
DICKIES T
DICKIEST
DICKS
DICKY
DICLINY
DICOT S
DICOTS
DICOTYL S
DICOTYLS
DICROTAL
DICROTIC
DICTA
DICTATE DS
DICTATED
DICTATES
DICTATOR S
DICTIER
DICTIEST
DICTION S
DICTIONS
DICTUM S
DICTUMS
DICTY
DICYCLIC
DICYCLY
DID OY
DIDACT S
ADDICT
DIDACTIC S
DIDACTS
ADDICTS
DIDACTYL
DIDAPPER S
DIDDLE DRSY
LIDDED
DIDDLED
DIDDLER S
RIDDLED
DIDDLERS
DIDDLES
DIDDLEY S
DIDDLEYS
DIDDLIES
DIDDLING
DIDDLY
DIDIE S
DIDIES
DIDO S
DIDOES
DIODES
DIDOS
DIDST
DIDY
DIDYMIUM S
DIDYMOUS
DIDYNAMY
DIE DLST
DIEBACK S
DIEBACKS
BACKSIDE
DIECIOUS
DIED
DIEHARD S
DIEHARDS
DIEING

DIEL
DEIL DELI
IDLE LIED
DIELDRIN S
DIEMAKER S
DIENE S
DIENES
DENIES
SEINED
DIEOFF S
DIEOFFS
OFFSIDE
DIERESES
DIERESIS
DIERETIC
DIES
IDES SIDE
DIESEL S
EDILES
ELIDES
SEDILE
SEIDEL
DIESELED
DIESELS
IDLESSE
SEIDELS
DIESES
SEISED
DIESIS
DIESTER S
DIETERS
REEDITS
RESITED
DIESTERS
EDITRESS
RESISTED
SISTERED
DIESTOCK S
DIESTRUM S
DIESTRUS
STUDIERS
STURDIES
DIET S
DITE EDIT
TIDE TIED
DIETARY
DIETED
EDITED
DIETER S
REEDIT
RETIED
TIERED
DIETERS
DIESTER
REEDITS
RESITED
DIETETIC S
DIETHER S
DIETHERS
DIETING
EDITING
IGNITED
DIETS
DEIST DITES
EDITS SITED
STIED TIDES
DIF FS
FID
DIFF S
DIFFER S
RIFFED
DIFFERED
DIFFERS
DIFFRACT S
DIFFS
DIFFUSE DRS
DIFFUSED
DIFFUSER S
DIFFUSES
DIFFUSOR S
DIFS
FIDS
DIG S
GID
DIGAMIES
DIGAMIST S
DIGAMMA S
DIGAMMAS
DIGAMOUS
DIGAMY
DIGERATI

DIGEST S
DIGESTED
DIGESTER S
REDIGEST
DIGESTIF S
DIGESTOR S
GRODIEST
STODGIER
DIGESTS
DIGGED
DIGGER S
RIGGED
DIGGERS
DIGGING S
DIGGINGS
DIGHT S
DIGHTED
DIGHTING
DIGHTS
DIGIT S
DIGITAL S
DIGITALS
DIGITATE D
DIGITIZE DR S
DIGITS
DIGLOT S
DIGLOTS
DIGNIFY
DIGNITY
TIDYING
DIGOXIN S
DIGOXINS
DIGRAPH S
DIGRAPHS
DIGRESS
DIGS
GIDS
DIHEDRAL S
DIHEDRON S
DIHYBRID S
DIHYDRIC
DIKDIK S
DIKDIKS
DIKE DRSY
DIKED
DIKER S
IRKED
DIKERS
RISKED
DIKES
SKIED
DIKING
DIKTAT S
DIKTATS
DILATANT S
DILATATE
DILATE DRS
DETAIL
TAILED
DILATED
DILATER S
REDTAIL
TRAILED
DILATERS
LARDIEST
REDTAILS
DILATES
DETAILS
DILATING
DILATION S
DILATIVE
DILATOR SY
DILATORS
DILATORY
ADROITLY
IDOLATRY
DILDO ES
DILDOE S
DOILED
LOIDED
DILDOES
DILDOS
DILEMMA S
DILEMMAS
DILEMMIC
DILIGENT
DILL SY

DILLED
DILLIES
DILLS
DILLY
IDYLL
DILUENT S
DILUENTS
INSULTED
UNLISTED
DILUTE DRS
DILUTED
DILUTER S
DILUTERS
STUDLIER
DILUTES
DUELIST
DILUTING
DILUTION S
TOLUIDIN
DILUTIVE
DILUTOR S
DILUTORS
DILUVIA LN
DILUVIAL
DILUVIAN
DILUVION S
DILUVIUM S
DIM ES
MID
DIME RS
IDEM
DIMER S
MIRED RIMED
DIMERIC
DIMERISM S
DIMERIZE DS
DIMEROUS
DIMERS
DERMIS
DIMES
DEISM DISME
DIMETER S
DEMERIT
MERITED
MITERED
RETIMED
DIMETERS
DEMERITS
DEMISTER
DIMETHYL S
DIMETRIC
DIMINISH
DIMITIES
DIMITY
DIMLY
DIMMABLE
IMBALMED
DIMMED
DIMMER S
RIMMED
DIMMERS
DIMMEST
DIMMING
DIMNESS
MISSEND
DIMORPH S
DIMORPHS
DIMOUT S
DIMOUTS
DIMPLE DS
IMPLED
LIMPED
DIMPLED
DIMPLES
MISPLED
DIMPLIER
DIMPLING
DIMPLY
DIMS
MIDS
DIMWIT S
DIMWITS
DIN EGKOST
DINAR S
DRAIN NADIR
RANID
DINARS
DRAINS
NADIRS
RANIDS

DINDLE DS
DINDLED
DINDLES
SLIDDEN
DINDLING
DINE DRS
DENI NIDE
DINED
NIDED
DINER OS
DINERIC
DINERO S
IRONED
DINEROS
INDORSE
ORDINES
ROSINED
SORDINE
DINERS
RINSED
SNIDER
DINES
NIDES SNIDE
DINETTE S
DINETTES
INSETTED
DING EOSY
DINGBAT S
DINGBATS
DINGDONG S
DINGE DRSY
DEIGN
DINGED
DINGER S
ENGIRD
GIRNED
REDING
RINGED
DINGERS
ENGIRDS
DINGES
DEIGNS
DESIGN
SIGNED
SINGED
DINGEY S
DYEING
DINGEYS
DYEINGS
DINGHIES
DINGHY
DINGIER
DINGIES T
DINGIEST
DINGILY
DINGING
DINGLE S
ENGILD
DINGLES
ENGILDS
SINGLED
DINGO
DOING
DINGOES
DINGS
DINGUS
DINGUSES
DINGY
DYING
DINING
INDIGN
NIDING
DINITRO
DINK SY
KIND
DINKED
DINKEY S
KIDNEY
DINKEYS
KIDNEYS
DINKIER
DINKIES T
DINKIEST
DINKING
DINKLY
KINDLY
DINKS
KINDS
DINKUM S
DINKUMS
DINKY
DINNED

DINNER S
ENDRIN
DINNERS
ENDRINS
DINNING
DINO S
NODI
DINOS
DINOSAUR S
DINS
DINT S
DINTED
DINTING
DINTS
DIOBOL S
DIOBOLON S
DIOBOLS
DIOCESAN S
CODEINAS
DIOCESE S
DIOCESES
DIODE S
DIODES
DIDOES
DIOECIES
DIOECISM S
DIOECY
DIOICOUS
DIOL S
IDOL LIDO
LOID
DIOLEFIN S
DIOLS
IDOLS LIDOS
LOIDS SLOID
SOLDI SOLID
DIOPSIDE S
DIPODIES
DIOPTASE S
DIOPTER S
DIOPTRE
PERIDOT
PROTEID
DIOPTERS
DIOPTRES
PERIDOTS
PORTSIDE
PROTEIDS
RIPOSTED
TOPSIDER
DIOPTRAL
TRIPODAL
DIOPTRE S
DIOPTER
PERIDOT
PROTEID
DIOPTRES
DIOPTERS
PERIDOTS
PORTSIDE
PROTEIDS
RIPOSTED
TOPSIDER
DIOPTRIC S
DIPROTIC
TRIPODIC
DIORAMA S
DIORAMAS
DIORAMIC
DIORITE S
DIORITES
DIORITIC
DIOXAN ES
DIOXANE S
DIOXANES
DIOXANS
DIOXID ES
IXODID
DIOXIDE S
DIOXIDES
OXIDISED
DIOXIDS
IXODIDS
DIOXIN S
DIOXINS
DIP ST
DIPHASE
APHIDES
DIPHASIC
DIPHENYL S

DIPLEGIA S
DIPLEGIC
DIPLEX
DIPLEXER S
DIPLOE S
DIPOLE
DIPLOES
DESPOIL
DIPOLES
SPOILED
DIPLOIC
DIPLOID SY
DIPLOIDS
DIPLOIDY
DIPLOMA ST
DIPLOMAS
PLASMOID
DIPLOMAT AE S
DIPLONT S
DIPLONTS
DIPLOPIA S
DIPLOPIC
DIPLOPOD S
DIPLOSES
DESPOILS
DIPLOSIS
DIPNET S
DIPNETS
STIPEND
DIPNOAN S
NONPAID
DIPNOANS
DIPODIC
DIPODIES
DIOPSIDE
DIPODY
DIPOLAR
DIPOLE S
DIPLOE
DIPOLES
DESPOIL
DIPLOES
SPOILED
DIPPABLE
DIPPED
DIPPER S
RIPPED
DIPPERS
DIPPIER
DIPPIEST
DIPPING
DIPPY
DIPROTIC
DIOPTRIC
TRIPODIC
DIPS O
DIPSADES
DIPSAS
DIPSO S
DIPSOS
DIPSTICK S
DIPT
DIPTERA LN
PARTIED
PIRATED
DIPTERAL
TRIPEDAL
DIPTERAN S
DIPTERON
DIPTYCA S
DIPTYCAS
DIPTYCH S
DIPTYCHS
DIQUAT S
DIQUATS
DIRAM S
DIRAMS
DISARM
DIRDUM S
DIRDUMS
DIRE R
IRED RIDE
DIRECT S
CREDIT
TRICED
DIRECTED
CREDITED
DIRECTER
REDIRECT

DIRECTLY
DIRECTOR SY
CREDITOR
DIRECTS
CREDITS
DIREFUL
DIRELY
RIDLEY
DIRENESS
DIRER
DRIER RIDER
DIREST
DRIEST
STRIDE
DIRGE S
GRIDE RIDGE
DIRGEFUL
DIRGES
GRIDES
RIDGES
DIRHAM S
DIRHAMS
MIDRASH
DIRIMENT
DIRK S
DIRKED
KIDDER
DIRKING
DIRKS
DIRL S
DIRLED
DREIDL
RIDDLE
DIRLING
DIRLS
DIRNDL S
DIRNDLS
DIRT SY
DIRTBAG S
DIRTBAGS
DIRTIED
DIRTIER
DIRTIES T
DITSIER
TIDIERS
DIRTIEST
DIRTILY
DIRTS
DIRTY
DIRTYING
DIS CHKS
IDS
DISABLE DRS
BALDIES
DISABLED
DISABLER S
BEDRAILS
DISABLES
DISABUSE DS
SUBIDEAS
DISAGREE DS
DISALLOW S
DISANNUL S
DISARM S
DIRAMS
DISARMED
DISARMER S
ADMIRERS
MARRIEDS
DISARMS
DISARRAY S
DISASTER S
DIASTERS
DISRATES
DISAVOW S
DISAVOWS
DISBAND S
DISBANDS
DISBAR S
BRAIDS
DISBARS
DISBOSOM S
DISBOUND
DISBOWEL S
DISBUD S
DISBUDS
DISBURSE DR S
SUBSIDER
DISC IOS
DISCANT S

DISCANTS
DISCARD S
DISCARDS
DISCASE DS
DISCASED
CADDISES
DISCASES
DISCED
DISCEPT S
DEPICTS
DISCEPTS
DISCERN S
CINDERS
RESCIND
DISCERNS
RESCINDS
DISCI
DISCING
DISCIPLE DS
DISCLAIM S
DISCLIKE
SICKLIED
DISCLOSE DR S
DISCO S
SODIC
DISCOED
DISCOID S
DISCOIDS
DISCOING
DISCOLOR S
DISCORD S
DISCORDS
DISCOS
DISCOUNT S
CONDUITS
NOCTUIDS
DISCOVER ST Y
CODRIVES
DIVORCES
DISCREET
DESERTIC
DISCRETE
DISCRETE
DESERTIC
DISCREET
DISCROWN S
DISCS
DISCUS S
DISCUSES
DISCUSS
DISDAIN S
DISDAINS
DISEASE DS
SEASIDE
DISEASED
DISEASES
SEASIDES
DISENDOW S
DISOWNED
DOWNSIDE
DISEUR S
DISEURS
SUDSIER
DISEUSE S
DISEUSES
DISFAVOR S
DISFROCK S
DISGORGE DS
DISGRACE DR S
DISGUISE DR S
DISGUST S
DISGUSTS
DISH Y
SIDH
DISHED
DISHELM S
DISHELMS
DISHERIT S
DISHES
HISSED
DISHEVEL S
DISHFUL S
DISHFULS
DISHIER
DISHIEST

DISHING
HIDINGS
SHINDIG
DISHLIKE
DISHONOR S
DISHPAN S
DISHPANS
DISHRAG S
DISHRAGS
DISHWARE S
RAWHIDES
DISHY
DISINTER S
INDITERS
NITRIDES
DISJECT S
DISJECTS
DISJOIN ST
DISJOINS
DISJOINT S
DISJUNCT S
DISK S
KIDS SKID
DISKED
DISKETTE S
DISKING
DISKLIKE
DISKS
SKIDS
DISLIKE DRS
DISLIKED
DISLIKER S
DISLIKES
DISLIMN S
DISLIMNS
DISLODGE DS
DISLOYAL
DISMAL S
DISMALER
DISMALLY
DISMALS
DISMAST S
DISMASTS
DISMAY S
DISMAYED
DISMAYS
DISME S
DEISM DIMES
DISMES
DEISMS
MISSED
DISMISS
DISMOUNT S
DISOBEY S
DISOBEYS
DISOMIC
DISORDER S
DISOWN S
INDOWS
DISOWNED
DISENDOW
DOWNSIDE
DISOWNS
DISPART S
DISPARTS
DISPATCH
DISPEL S
LISPED
SLIPED
SPILED
DISPELS
DISPEND S
DISPENDS
DISPENSE DR S
DISPERSE DR S
DESPISER
PRESIDES
DISPIRIT S
DISPLACE DR S
DISPLANT S
DISPLAY S
DISPLAYS
DISPLODE DS
LOPSIDED
DISPLUME DS
IMPULSED

DISPORT S
TORPIDS
TRIPODS
DISPORTS
DISPOSAL S
DISPOSE DRS
DISPOSED
DISPOSER S
DROPSIES
DISPOSES
DISPREAD S
DISPRIZE DS
DISPROOF S
DISPROVE DN RS
PROVIDES
DISPUTE DRS
DISPUTED
DISPUTER S
STUPIDER
DISPUTES
DISQUIET S
DISRATE DS
ARIDEST
ASTRIDE
DIASTER
STAIDER
TARDIES
TIRADES
DISRATED
DISRATES
DIASTERS
DISASTER
DISROBE DRS
BORIDES
DISROBED
DISROBER S
BROIDERS
DISROBES
DISROOT S
TOROIDS
DISROOTS
DISRUPT S
DISRUPTS
DISS
DISSAVE DS
ADVISES
DISSAVED
DISSAVES
DISSEAT S
DISSEATS
ASSISTED
DISSECT S
DISSECTS
DISSED
DISSEISE DE S
DISSEIZE DE S
DISSENT S
SNIDEST
DISSENTS
DISSERT S
STRIDES
DISSERTS
DISTRESS
DISSERVE DS
DEVISERS
DISSEVER
DISSES
DISSEVER S
DEVISERS
DISSERVE
DISSING
SIDINGS
DISSOLVE DR S
DISSUADE DR S
DISTAFF S
DISTAFFS
DISTAIN S
DISTAINS
DISTAL
DISTALLY
DISTANCE DS
DISTANT
DISTASTE DS
STAIDEST
DISTAVES
DISTEND S

DISTENDS
DISTENT
DENTIST
STINTED
DISTICH S
DISTICHS
DISTIL LS
DISTILL S
DISTILLS
DISTILS
DISTINCT
DISTOME S
MODISTE
DISTOMES
MODISTES
DISTORT S
DISTORTS
DISTRACT S
DISTRAIN ST
DISTRAIT E
DISTRESS
DISSERTS
DISTRICT S
DISTRUST S
DISTURB S
DISTURBS
DISULFID ES
DISUNION S
DISUNITE DR
NUDITIES S
UNTIDIES
DISUNITY
DISUSE DS
ISSUED
DISUSED
DISUSES
DISUSING
DISVALUE DS
DISYOKE DS
DISYOKED
DISYOKES
AE DIT AESZ
DITA S
ADIT
DITAS
ADITS STAID
TSADI
DITCH
DITCHED
DITCHER S
DITCHERS
DITCHES
DITCHING
DITE S
DIET EDIT
TIDE TIED
DITES
DEIST DIETS
EDITS SITED
STIED TIDES
DITHEISM S
DITHEIST S
STITHIED
DITHER SY
DITHERED
DITHERER S
DITHERS
DITHERY
DITHIOL
LITHOID
AE DITS Y
DITSIER
DIRTIES
TIDIERS
DITSIEST
DITSY
DITTANY
DITTIES
TIDIEST
DITTO S
DITTOED
DITTOING
DITTOS
DITTY
DITZ Y
DITZES
DITZIER
DITZIEST

DITZY
DIURESES
REISSUED
RESIDUES
DIURESIS
DIURETIC S
DIURNAL S
DIURNALS
DIURON S
DURION
DIURONS
DURIONS
DIVA NS
AVID
DIVAGATE DS
DIVALENT
DIVAN S
VIAND
DIVANS
VIANDS
DIVAS
DIVE DRS
VIDE VIED
DIVEBOMB S
DIVED
DIVER ST
DRIVE RIVED
DIVERGE DS
GRIEVED
DIVERGED
DIVERGES
DIVERS E
DRIVES
DIVERSE
DERIVES
DEVISER
REVISED
DIVERT S
DIVERTED
DIVERTER S
VERDITER
DIVERTS
STRIVED
DIVES T
VISED
DIVEST S
DIVESTED
DIVESTS
DIVIDE DRS
DIVIDED
DIVIDEND S
DIVIDER S
DIVIDERS
DIVIDES
DIVIDING
DIVIDUAL
DIVINE DRS
DIVINED
DIVINELY
DIVINER S
DIVINERS
DIVINES T
DIVINEST
DIVING
DIVINING
DIVINISE DS
DIVINITY
DIVINIZE DS
DIVISION S
DIVISIVE
DIVISOR S
VIROIDS
DIVISORS
DIVORCE DER
CODRIVE S
DIVORCED
DIVORCEE S
CODERIVE
REVOICED
DIVORCER S
CODRIVER
DIVORCES
CODRIVES
DISCOVER
DIVOT S
DIVOTS
DIVULGE DRS
DIVULGED
DIVULGER S

DIVULGES
DIVULSE DS
DIVULSED
DIVULSES
DIVVIED
DIVVIES
DIVVY
DIVVYING
DIWAN S
DIWANS
DIXIT S
DIXITS
DIZEN S
DIZENED
DIZENING
DIZENS
DIZYGOUS
DIZZIED
DIZZIER
DIZZIES T
DIZZIEST
DIZZILY
DIZZY
DIZZYING
DJEBEL S
DJEBELS
DJELLABA HS
DJIN NS
DJINN ISY
DJINNI
DJINNS
DJINNY
DJINS
AU DO CEGLMNRS
OD TW
DOABLE
ALBEDO
DOAT S
DATO TOAD
DOATED
DOATING
DOATS
DATOS TOADS
DOBBER S
ROBBED
DOBBERS
DOBBIES
DOBBIN S
DOBBINS
DOBBY
DOBIE S
DOBIES
BODIES
DOBLA S
DOBLAS
DOBLON S
DOBLONES
DOBLONS
DOBRA S
BOARD BROAD
DOBRAS
ADSORB
BOARDS
BROADS
DOBRO S
BROOD
DOBROS
BROODS
DOBSON S
DOBSONS
DOBY
BODY
DOC KS
COD
DOCENT S
DOCENTS
DOCETIC
DOCILE
COILED
DOCILELY
DOCILITY
DOCK S
DOCKAGE S
DOCKAGES
DOCKED

DOCKER S
CORKED
REDOCK
ROCKED
DOCKERS
REDOCKS
DOCKET S
DOCKETED
DOCKETS
STOCKED
DOCKHAND S
DOCKING
DOCKLAND S
DOCKS
DOCKSIDE S
DOCKYARD S
DOCS
CODS
DOCTOR S
DOCTORAL
DOCTORED
DOCTORLY
DOCTORS
DOCTRINE S
CENTROID
DOCUMENT S
DODDER SY
RODDED
DODDERED
DODDERER S
DODDERS
DODDERY
DODGE DMRS
DODGED
GODDED
DODGEM S
DODGEMS
DODGER SY
DODGERS
DODGERY
DODGES
DODGIER
DODGIEST
DODGING
GODDING
DODGY
DODO S
DODOES
DODOISM S
DODOISMS
DODOS
DOE RS
ODE
DOER S
DORE REDO
RODE
DOERS
DOSER REDOS
RESOD RODES
ROSED SORED
DOES T
DOSE ODES
DOESKIN S
DOESKINS
DOEST
DOTES
DOETH
DOFF S
DOFFED
DOFFER S
DOFFERS
DOFFING
DOFFS
DOG ESY
GOD
DOGBANE S
BONDAGE
DOGBANES
BONDAGES
DOGBERRY
DOGCART S
DOGCARTS
DOGDOM S
DOGDOMS
DOGE SY
DOGEAR S
DOGEARED
DOGEARS
DOGEDOM S

DOGEDOMS
DOGES
DOGESHIP S
DOGEY S
DOGEYS
DOGFACE S
DOGFACES
DOGFIGHT S
DOGFISH
DOGGED
DOGGEDLY
DOGGER SY
GORGED
DOGGEREL S
DOGGERS
DOGGERY
DOGGIE RS
DOGGIER
DOGGIES T
DOGGIEST
DOGGING
DOGGISH
DOGGO
DOGGONE DRS
DOGGONED
DOGGONER
DOGGONES T
DOGGREL S
DOGGRELS
DOGGY
DOGHOUSE S
DOGIE S
GEOID
DOGIES
GEOIDS
DOGLEG S
LOGGED
DOGLEGS
SLOGGED
DOGLIKE
GODLIKE
DOGMA S
DOGMAS
DOGMATA
DOGMATIC S
DOGNAP S
DOGNAPED
DOGNAPER S
DOGNAPS
DOGS
GODS
DOGSBODY
DOGSLED S
DOGSLEDS
DOGTEETH
GHETTOED
DOGTOOTH
DOGTROT S
DOGTROTS
DOGVANE S
DOGVANES
DOGWATCH
WATCHDOG
DOGWOOD S
DOGWOODS
DOGY
DOILED
DILDOE
LOIDED
DOILIES
IDOLISE
DOILY
DOING S
DINGO
DOINGS
DOSING
DOIT S
DOITED
DOITS
ODIST
DOJO S
DOJOS
I DOL ELST
OLD
DOLCE
COLED
DOLCETTO S
DOLCI

DOLDRUMS
DOLE DS
LODE
DOLED
DOLEFUL
DOLERITE S
LOITERED
DOLES
LODES SOLED
DOLESOME
DOLING
DOLL SY
DOLLAR S
DOLLARS
DOLLED
DOLLIED
DOLLIES
DOLLING
DOLLISH
DOLLOP S
DOLLOPED
DOLLOPS
DOLLS
DOLLY
DOLLYING
DOLMA NS
DOMAL MODAL
DOLMADES
DOLMAN S
ALMOND
DOLMANS
ALMONDS
DOLMAS
MODALS
DOLMEN S
DOLMENIC
DOLMENS
DOLOMITE S
DOLOR S
DROOL
DOLOROSO
DOLOROUS
DOLORS
DROOLS
DOLOUR S
DOLOURS
DOLPHIN S
DOLPHINS
I DOLS
OLDS SOLD
DOLT S
TOLD
DOLTISH
DOLTS
DOM ES
MOD
DOMAIN ES
DAIMON
DOMAINE S
AMIDONE
DOMAINES
AMIDONES
DAIMONES
DOMAINS
DAIMONS
DOMAL
DOLMA MODAL
DOME DS
DEMO MODE
DOMED
DOMELIKE
DOMES
DEMOS MODES
DOMESDAY S
DOMESTIC S
DEMOTICS
DOMIC
DOMICAL
DOMICIL ES
DOMICILE DS
DOMICILS
DOMINANT S
DOMINATE DS
DOMINE S
EMODIN
MONIED
DOMINEER S
DOMINES
EMODINS
MISDONE

DOMING
DOMINICK S
DOMINIE S
DOMINIES
DOMINION S
DOMINIUM S
DOMINO S
DOMINOES
MONODIES
DOMINOS
DOMS
MODS
U DON AEGS
NOD
DONA S
DONAS
O DONATE DS
ATONED
DONATED
O DONATES
DONATING
DONATION S
DONATIVE S
DONATOR S
ODORANT
TANDOOR
TORNADO
DONATORS
ODORANTS
TANDOORS
TORNADOS
DONE E
NODE
DONEE S
DONEES
DONENESS
DONG AS
DONGA S
GONAD
DONGAS
GONADS
DONGLE S
GOLDEN
LONGED
DONGLES
DONGOLA S
GONDOLA
DONGOLAS
GONDOLAS
DONGS
DONJON S
DONJONS
DONKEY S
DONKEYS
DONNA S
DONNAS
DONNE DE
DONNED
DONNEE S
NEONED
DONNEES
DONNERD
DENDRON
DONNERED
REDONNED
DONNERT
DONNIKER S
DONNING
DONNISH
DONOR S
RONDO
DONORS
RONDOS
U DONS Y
NODS
DONSIE
NOISED
ONSIDE
DONSY
SYNOD
DONUT S
DONUTS
STOUND
DONZEL S
DONZELS
DOOBIE S
DOOBIES
DOODAD S
DOODADS
DOODIES

DOODLE DRS
DOODLED
DOODLER S
DROOLED
DOODLERS
DOODLES
DOODLING
DOODOO S
DOODOOS
DOODY
DOOFUS
DOOFUSES
DOOLEE S
DOOLEES
DOOLIE S
DOOLIES
DOOLY
DOOM SY
MOOD
DOOMED
DOOMFUL
DOOMIER
MOIDORE
MOODIER
DOOMIEST
MOODIEST
SODOMITE
DOOMILY
MOODILY
DOOMING
DOOMS
MOODS SODOM
DOOMSDAY S
DOOMSTER S
DOOMY
MOODY
DOOR S
ODOR ORDO
ROOD
DOORBELL S
BORDELLO
DOORJAMB S
DOORKNOB S
DOORLESS
LORDOSES
ODORLESS
DOORMAN
MADRONO
DOORMAT S
DOORMATS
DOORMEN
DOORNAIL S
DOORPOST S
DOORSTOP
DOORS
ODORS ORDOS
ROODS
DOORSILL S
DOORSTEP S
TORPEDOS
DOORSTOP S
DOORPOST
DOORWAY S
DOORWAYS
DOORYARD S
DOOWOP S
DOOWOPS
DOOZER S
DOOZERS
DOOZIE S
DOOZIES
DOOZY
DOPA S
APOD
DOPAMINE S
DOPANT S
DOPANTS
DOPAS
APODS SPADO
DOPE DRSY
OPED
DOPED
DOPEHEAD S
DOPER S
PEDRO PORED
ROPED
DOPERS
PEDROS
PROSED
SPORED

DOPES
POSED SPODE
DOPESTER S
DOPEY
DOPIER
PERIOD
DOPIEST
DEPOSIT
PODITES
POSITED
SOPITED
TOPSIDE
DOPILY
PLOIDY
DOPINESS
DOPING S
PONGID
DOPINGS
PONGIDS
DOPY
O DOR EKMPRSY
ROD
DORADO S
DORADOS
DORBUG S
DORBUGS
A DORE
DOER REDO
RODE
DORHAWK S
DORHAWKS
DORIES
DORK SY
DORKIER
DORKIEST
DORKS
DORKY
DORM SY
DORMANCY
MORDANCY
DORMANT
MORDANT
DORMER S
DORMERED
DORMERS
DORMICE
DORMIE
DORMIENT
DORMIN S
NIMROD
DORMINS
NIMRODS
DORMOUSE
DORMS
DORMY
DORNECK S
DORNECKS
DORNICK S
DORNICKS
DORNOCK S
DORNOCKS
DORP S
DROP PROD
DORPER S
DORPERS
DORPS
DROPS PRODS
DORR S
DORRS
O DORS A
RODS SORD
DORSA DL
ROADS SAROD
DORSAD
DORSAL S
DORSALLY
DORSALS
DORSEL S
RESOLD
SOLDER
DORSELS
RODLESS
SOLDERS
DORSER S
ORDERS
DORSERS
DORSUM
DORTY
DORY

AU DOS EST
ODS
SOD
DOSAGE S
SEADOG
DOSAGES
SEADOGS
DOSE DRS
DOES ODES
DOSED
DOSER S
DOERS REDOS
RESOD RODES
ROSED SORED
DOSERS
DOSSER
RESODS
DOSES
DOSING
DOINGS
DOSS
SODS
DOSSAL S
DOSSALS
DOSSED
DOSSEL S
DOSSELS
DOSSER S
DOSERS
RESODS
DOSSERET S
OERSTEDS
DOSSERS
DROSSES
DOSSES
DOSSIER S
DOSSIERS
DOSSIL S
SLOIDS
SOLIDS
DOSSILS
DOSSING
DOST
DOTS TODS
DOT EHSY
TOD
DOTAGE S
TOGAED
DOTAGES
DOTAL
DOTARD S
DOTARDLY
DOTARDS
DOTATION S
DOTE DRS
TOED
DOTED
DOTER S
TRODE
DOTERS
SORTED
STORED
STRODE
DOTES
DOEST
DOTH
DOTIER
EDITOR
RIOTED
TRIODE
DOTIEST
DOTING
DOTINGLY
DOTS
DOST TODS
DOTTED
DOTTEL S
DOTTLE
LOTTED
DOTTELS
DOTTLES
SLOTTED
DOTTER S
ROTTED
DOTTEREL S
DOTTERS
DOTTIER
DOTTIEST
DOTTILY
DOTTING

DOTTLE S
DOTTEL
LOTTED
DOTTLES
DOTTELS
SLOTTED
DOTTREL S
DOTTRELS
DOTTY
DOTY
TODY
DOUBLE DRST
DOUBLED
DOUBLER S
BOULDER
DOUBLERS
BOULDERS
DOUBLES
BLOUSED
DOUBLET S
DOUBLETS
DOUBLING
DOUBLOON S
DOUBLURE S
DOUBLY
DOUBT S
DOUBTED
DOUBTER S
OBTRUDE
OUTBRED
REDOUBT
DOUBTERS
OBTRUDES
REDOUBTS
DOUBTFUL
DOUBTING
DOUBTS
DOUCE
COUDE
DOUCELY
DOUCEUR S
DOUCEURS
DOUCHE DS
OUCHED
DOUCHED
DOUCHES
CHOUSED
HOCUSED
DOUCHING
DOUGH STY
DOUGHBOY S
DOUGHIER
DOUGHNUT S
DOUGHS
DOUGHT Y
DOUGHTY
DOUGHY
DOULA S
ALOUD
DOULAS
DOUM AS
DOUMA S
DOUMAS
DOUMS
MODUS
DOUPIONI S
O DOUR A
DURO
DOURA HS
DOURAH S
DOURAHS
DOURAS
DOURER
ORDURE
DOUREST
DETOURS
REDOUTS
ROUSTED
DOURINE S
NEUROID
DOURINES
SOURDINE
DOURLY
DOURNESS
RESOUNDS
SOUNDERS
DOUSE DRS
DOUSED

DOUSER S
ROUSED
SOURED
UREDOS
DOUSERS
DOUSES
SOUSED
DOUSING
GUIDONS
DOUX
DOUZEPER S
DOVE NS
DOVECOT ES
DOVECOTE S
DOVECOTS
DOVEKEY S
DOVEKEYS
DOVEKIE S
DOVEKIES
DOVELIKE
DOVEN S
DEVON
DOVENED
DOVENING
DOVENS
DEVONS
DOVES
DOVETAIL S
VIOLATED
DOVISH
DOW NS
DOWABLE
DOWAGER S
WORDAGE
DOWAGERS
WORDAGES
DOWDIER
DOWDIES T
DOWDIEST
DOWDILY
DOWDY
DOWDYISH
DOWED
DOWEL S
LOWED
DOWELED
DOWELING
DOWELLED
DOWELS
SLOWED
DOWER SY
ROWED
DOWERED
DOWERIES
WEIRDOES
DOWERING
DOWERS
DOWSER
DROWSE
DOWERY
DOWIE
DOWING
A DOWN SY
DOWNBEAT S
DOWNBOW S
DOWNBOWS
DOWNCAST S
DOWNCOME S
COMEDOWN
DOWNED
DOWNER S
WONDER
DOWNERS
WONDERS
DOWNFALL S
DOWNHAUL S
DOWNHILL S
DOWNIER
DOWNIEST
DOWNING
DOWNLAND S
DOWNLESS
DOWNLIKE
DOWNLINK S
DOWNLOAD S
WOODLAND
DOWNPIPE S
DOWNPLAY S
PLAYDOWN

DOWNPOUR S
DOWNS
DOWNSIDE S
DISENDOW
DISOWNED
DOWNSIZE DS
DOWNSPIN S
DOWNTICK S
DOWNTIME S
DOWNTOWN S
DOWNTROD
DOWNTURN S
TURNDOWN
DOWNWARD S
DRAWDOWN
DOWNWASH
DOWNWIND
DOWNY
DOWNZONE DS
DOWRIES
ROWDIES
WEIRDOS
DOWRY
ROWDY WORDY
DOWS E
DOWSABEL S
DOWSE DRS
SOWED
DOWSED
DOWSER S
DOWERS
DROWSE
DOWSERS
DROWSES
DOWSES
DOWSING
DOXIE S
OXIDE
DOXIES
OXIDES
DOXOLOGY
DOXY
DOYEN S
DOYENNE S
DOYENNES
DOYENS
DOYLEY S
DOYLEYS
DOYLIES
DOYLY
A DOZE DNRS
DOZED
DOZEN S
ZONED
DOZENED
DOZENING
DOZENS
DOZENTH S
DOZENTHS
DOZER S
DOZERS
DOZES
DOZIER
DOZIEST
DOZILY
DOZINESS
DOZING
DOZY
DRAB S
BARD BRAD
DARB
DRABBED
DRABBER
DRABBEST
DRABBETS
DRABBET S
DRABBETS
DRABBEST
DRABBING
DRABBLE DS
DABBLER
RABBLED
DRABBLED
DRABBLES
DABBLERS
DRABLY
DRABNESS

DRABS
BARDS BRADS
DARBS
DRACAENA S
DRACENA S
DRACENAS
DRACHM AS
DRACHMA EIS
DRACHMAE
DRACHMAI
CHADARIM
DRACHMAS
DRACHMS
DRACONIC
CANCROID
DRAFF SY
DRAFFIER
DRAFFISH
DRAFFS
DRAFFY
DRAFT SY
DRAFTED
DRAFTEE S
DRAFTEES
DRAFTER S
REDRAFT
DRAFTERS
REDRAFTS
DRAFTIER
DRAFTILY
DRAFTING S
DRAFTS
DRAFTY
DRAG S
GRAD
DRAGEE S
AGREED
GEARED
DRAGEES
GREASED
DRAGGED
DRAGGER S
DRAGGERS
DRAGGIER
DRAGGING
DRAGGLE DS
GARGLED
DRAGGLED
DRAGGLES
DRAGGY
DRAGLINE S
DANGLIER
DRAGNET S
GRANTED
DRAGNETS
GRANDEST
DRAGOMAN S
DRAGOMEN
DRAGON S
DRAGONET S
DRAGONS
DRAGOON S
GADROON
DRAGOONS
GADROONS
DRAGROPE S
PROGRADE
DRAGS
GRADS
DRAGSTER S
DRAIL S
LAIRD LIARD
LIDAR
DRAILS
LAIRDS
LIARDS
LIDARS
DRAIN S
DINAR NADIR
RANID
DRAINAGE S
GARDENIA
DRAINED
DANDIER
DRAINER S
RANDIER
DRAINERS
SERRANID
DRAINING

DRAINS
DINARS
NADIRS
RANIDS
DRAKE S
RAKED
DRAKES
DRAM AS
DRAMA S
DAMAR
DRAMADY
DRAMAS
DAMARS
MADRAS
DRAMATIC S
DRAMEDY
DRAMMED
DRAMMING
DRAMMOCK S
DRAMS
DRAMSHOP S
DRANK
DRAPABLE
DRAPE DRSY
PADRE PARED
RAPED
DRAPED
PADDER
DRAPER SY
PARRED
DRAPERS
SPARRED
DRAPERY
DRAPES
PADRES
PARSED
RASPED
SPADER
SPARED
SPREAD
DRAPEY
PRAYED
DRAPING
DRASTIC
DRAT S
DART TRAD
DRATS
DARTS
DRATTED
DRATTING
DRAUGHT SY
DRAUGHTS
DRAUGHTY
DRAVE
RAVED
DRAW LNS
WARD
DRAWABLE
DRAWBACK S
BACKWARD
DRAWBAR S
DRAWBARS
DRAWBORE S
WARDROBE
DRAWDOWN S
DOWNWARD
DRAWEE S
DRAWEES
RESAWED
DRAWER S
REDRAW
REWARD
WARDER
WARRED
DRAWERS
REDRAWS
REWARDS
WARDERS
DRAWING S
WARDING
DRAWINGS
SWARDING
DRAWL SY
DRAWLED
DAWDLER
WADDLER
DRAWLER S
DRAWLERS
DRAWLIER
DRAWLING
DRAWLS
DRAWLY
DRAWN
DRAWS
SWARD WARDS
DRAWTUBE S
DRAY S
YARD
DRAYAGE S
YARDAGE
DRAYAGES
YARDAGES
DRAYED
YARDED
DRAYING
YARDING
DRAYMAN
YARDMAN
DRAYMEN
YARDMEN
DRAYS
YARDS
DREAD S
ADDER DARED
READD
DREADED
READDED
DREADFUL S
DREADING
READDING
DREADS
ADDERS
READDS
SADDER
DREAM STY
ARMED DERMA
MADRE
DREAMED
DREAMER S
REARMED
REDREAM
DREAMERS
REDREAMS
DREAMFUL
DREAMIER
DREAMILY
DREAMING
MARGINED
MIDRANGE
DREAMS
DERMAS
MADRES
DREAMT
MARTED
DREAMY
DREAR SY
DARER RARED
DREARIER
DREARIES T
RERAISED
DREARILY
DREARS
DARERS
DREARY
YARDER
DRECK SY
DRECKS
DRECKY
DREDGE DRS
DREDGED
DREDGER S
DREDGERS
DREDGES
DREDGING S
DREE DS
DEER DERE
REDE REED
DREED
REDED
DREEING
ENERGID
REEDING
REIGNED
DREES
DEERS REDES
REEDS SEDER
SERED
DREG S
DREGGIER
RERIGGED
DREGGISH
DREGGY
DREGS
DREICH
CHIDER
HERDIC
DREIDEL S
DREIDELS
DREIDL S
DIRLED
RIDDLE
DREIDLS
RIDDLES
DREIGH
DRIEGH
DREK S
DREKS
DRENCH
DRENCHED
DRENCHER S
DRENCHES
DRESS Y
DRESSAGE S
DEGASSER
DRESSED
DRESSER S
REDRESS
DRESSERS
DRESSES
DRESSIER
DERRISES
DESIRERS
RESIDERS
DRESSILY
DRESSING S
DRESSY
DREST
DREW
DRIB S
BIRD
DRIBBED
DRIBBING
DRIBBLE DRS
DIBBLER T
DRIBBLED
DRIBBLER S
DRIBBLES
DIBBLERS
DRIBBLET S
DRIBBLY
DRIBLET S
DRIBLETS
BRISTLED
DRIBS
BIRDS
DRIED
REDID
DRIEGH
DREIGH
DRIER S
DIRER RIDER
DRIERS
DERRIS
RIDERS
DRIES T
RESID RIDES
SIRED
DRIEST
DIREST
STRIDE
A **DRIFT** SY
DRIFTAGE S
DRIFTED
DRIFTER S
DRIFTERS
DRIFTIER
DRIFTING
DRIFTPIN S
DRIFTS
DRIFTY
DRILL S
DRILLED
DRILLER S
REDRILL
DRILLERS
REDRILLS
DRILLING S
DRILLS
DRILY
DRINK S
DRINKER S
DRINKERS
DRINKING S
DRINKS
DRIP ST
DRIPLESS
DRIPPED
DRIPPER S
DRIPPERS
DRIPPIER
DRIPPILY
DRIPPING S
DRIPPY
DRIPS
DRIPT
DRIVABLE
DRIVE LNRS
DIVER RIVED
DRIVEL S
DRIVELED
DRIVELER S
DRIVELS
DRIVEN
VERDIN
DRIVER S
DRIVERS
DRIVES
DIVERS
DRIVEWAY S
DRIVING S
DRIVINGS
DRIZZLE DS
DRIZZLED
DRIZZLES
DRIZZLY
DROGUE S
GOURDE
ROGUED
ROUGED
DROGUES
GOURDES
GROUSED
DROID S
DROIDS
SORDID
A **DROIT** S
DROITS
DROLL SY
DROLLED
DROLLER Y
DROLLERY
DROLLEST
STROLLED
DROLLING
LORDLING
DROLLS
DROLLY
LORDLY
DROMON DS
DROMOND S
DROMONDS
DROMONS
DRONE DRS
REDON
DRONED
NODDER
DRONER S
DRONERS
DRONES
REDONS
SNORED
SONDER
SORNED
DRONGO S
DRONGOS
DRONING
DRONISH
DROOL SY
DOLOR
DROOLED
DOODLER
DROOLIER
DROOLING
DROOLS
DOLORS
DROOLY
DROOP SY
DROOPED
DROOPIER
DROOPILY
DROOPING
DROOPS
DROOPY
DROP ST
DORP PROD
DROPHEAD S
DROPKICK S
DROPLET S
PRETOLD
DROPLETS
DROPOUT S
OUTDROP
DROPOUTS
OUTDROPS
DROPPED
DROPPER S
DROPPERS
DROPPING S
DROPS Y
DORPS PRODS
DROPSHOT S
DROPSIED
DROPSIES
DISPOSER
DROPSY
DROPT
DROPWORT S
DROSERA S
ADORERS
DROSERAS
DROSHKY
DROSKIES
DROSKY
DROSS Y
SORDS
DROSSES
DOSSERS
DROSSIER
DROSSY
DROUGHT SY
DROUGHTS
DROUGHTY
DROUK S
DROUKED
DROUKING
DROUKS
DROUTH SY
DROUTHS
DROUTHY
DROVE DRS
ROVED
DROVED
DROVER S
DROVERS
DROVES
DROVING
DROWN DS
DROWND S
DROWNDED
DROWNDS
DROWNED
DROWNER S
DROWNERS
DROWNING
DROWNS
DROWSE DS
DOWERS
DOWSER
DROWSED
DROWSES
DOWSERS
DROWSIER
DROWSILY
DROWSING
WORDINGS
DROWSY
DRUB S
BURD
DRUBBED
DRUBBER S
DRUBBERS
DRUBBING S
DRUBS
BURDS
DRUDGE DRS
DRUDGED
DRUDGER SY
DRUDGERS
DRUDGERY
DRUDGES
DRUDGING
DRUG S
DRUGGED
GRUDGED
DRUGGET S
DRUGGETS
DRUGGIE RS
DRUGGIER
DRUGGIES T
DRUGGING
GRUDGING
DRUGGIST S
DRUGGY
DRUGS
DRUID S
DRUIDESS
DRUIDIC
DRUIDISM S
SIDDURIM
DRUIDS
SIDDUR
DRUM S
DRUMBEAT S
DRUMBLE DS
RUMBLED
DRUMBLED
DRUMBLES
DRUMFIRE S
DRUMFISH
DRUMHEAD S
DRUMLIER
DRUMLIKE
DRUMLIN S
DRUMLINS
DRUMLY
DRUMMED
DRUMMER S
DRUMMERS
DRUMMING
DRUMROLL S
DRUMS
DRUNK S
DRUNKARD S
DRUNKEN
DRUNKER
DRUNKEST
DRUNKS
DRUPE S
DUPER PERDU
PRUDE URPED
DRUPELET S
DRUPES
DUPERS
PERDUS
PRUDES
PURSED
DRUSE S
DURES
DRUSES
DURESS
SUDSER
DRUTHERS
DRY S
DRYABLE
DRYAD S
DRYADES
DRYADIC
DRYADS
DRYER S
DERRY REDRY
DRYERS
DRYEST
DRYING
DRYISH
DRYLAND
DRYLOT S
DRYLOTS
DRYLY
DRYNESS
DRYPOINT S
DRYS
DRYSTONE
DRYWALL S
DRYWALLS
DRYWELL S
DRYWELLS
DUAD S
DUADS
DUAL S
AULD LAUD
DUALISM S
DUALISMS
DUALIST S
TULADIS
DUALISTS
DUALITY
DUALIZE DS
DUALIZED
DUALIZES
DUALLY
DUALS
LAUDS
DUB S
BUD
DUBBED
DUBBER S
RUBBED
DUBBERS
DUBBIN GS
DUBBING S
DUBBINGS
DUBBINS
DUBIETY
DUBIOUS
DUBNIUM S
DUBNIUMS
DUBONNET S
DUBS
BUDS
DUCAL
CAULD
DUCALLY
DUCAT S
DUCATS
E **DUCE** S
CUED
E **DUCES**
DUCHESS
DUCHIES
DUCHY
DUCI
DUCK SY
DUCKBILL S
DUCKED
DUCKER S
RUCKED
DUCKERS
DUCKIE RS
DUCKIER
DUCKIES T
DUCKIEST
DUCKING
DUCKLING S
DUCKPIN S
DUCKPINS
DUCKS
DUCKTAIL S
DUCKWALK S
DUCKWEED S
DUCKY
E **DUCT** S
DUCTAL
DUCTED
DEDUCT
DUCTILE
DUCTING S
DUCTINGS
DUCTLESS
E **DUCTS**
DUCTULE S
DUCTULES
DUCTWORK S
DUD ES
DUDDIE
DUDDY
DUDE DS
DUDED
DUDEEN S
DENUDE
DUENDE
ENDUED

DUDEENS
DENUDES
DUENDES
DUDES
DUDGEON S
DUDGEONS
DUDING
DUDISH
DUDISHLY
DUDS
SUDD
DUE LST
DUECENTO S
DUEL S
LEUD LUDE
DUELED
DELUDE
ELUDED
DUELER S
ELUDER
DUELERS
ELUDERS
DUELING
ELUDING
INDULGE
DUELIST S
DILUTES
DUELISTS
DUELLED
DUELLER S
DUELLERS
DUELLI
ILLUDE
DUELLING
DUELLIST S
DUELLO S
DUELLOS
DUELS
DULSE LEUDS
LUDES SLUED
DUENDE S
DENUDE
DUDEEN
ENDUED
DUENDES
DENUDES
DUDEENS
DUENESS
DUENNA S
DUENNAS
DUES
SUED USED
DUET S
DUETED
DUETING
DUETS
DUETTED
DUETTING
DUETTIST S
DUFF S
DUFFEL S
DUFFLE
LUFFED
DUFFELS
DUFFLES
SLUFFED
DUFFER S
RUFFED
DUFFERS
DUFFLE S
DUFFEL
LUFFED
DUFFLES
DUFFELS
SLUFFED
DUFFS
DUFUS
DUFUSES
DUG S
DUGONG S
GUNDOG
DUGONGS
GUNDOGS
DUGOUT S
DUGOUTS
DUGS
DUH
DUI T
DUIKER S
DUIKERS
DUSKIER

DUIT S
DUITS
DUKE DS
DUKED
DUKEDOM S
DUKEDOMS
DUKES
DUKING
DULCET S
DULCETLY
DULCETS
DULCIANA S
DULCIFY
DULCIMER S
DULCINEA S
DULIA S
DULIAS
DULL SY
DULLARD S
DULLARDS
DULLED
DULLER
DULLEST
DULLING
DULLISH
DULLNESS
DULLS
DULLY
DULNESS
DULSE S
DUELS LEUDS
LUDES SLUED
DULSES
DULY
DUMA S
MAUD
DUMAS
MAUDS
DUMB OS
DUMBBELL S
DUMBCANE S
DUMBED
DUMBER
DUMBEST
DUMBHEAD S
DUMBING
DUMBLY
DUMBNESS
DUMBO S
DUMBOS
DUMBS
DUMDUM S
DUMDUMS
DUMFOUND S
DUMKA
DUMKY
DUMMIED
DUMMIES
MEDIUMS
DUMMKOPF S
DUMMY
DUMMYING
DUMP SY
DUMPCART S
DUMPED
DUMPER S
DUMPERS
DUMPIER
UMPIRED
DUMPIEST
DUMPSITE
DUMPILY
DUMPING S
DUMPINGS
DUMPISH
DUMPLING S
DUMPS
DUMPSITE S
DUMPIEST
DUMPSTER S
DUMPY
DUN EGKST
DUNAM S
MAUND
DUNAMS
MAUNDS

DUNCE S
DUNCES
SECUND
DUNCH
DUNCHES
DUNCICAL
DUNCISH
DUNE S
NUDE UNDE
DUNELAND S
DUNELIKE
DUNES
NUDES
DUNG SY
DUNGAREE DS
UNAGREED
UNDERAGE
DUNGED
NUDGED
DUNGEON S
DUNGEONS
DUNGHILL S
DUNGIER
DUNGIEST
DUNGING
NUDGING
DUNGS
DUNGY
DUNITE S
UNITED
UNTIED
DUNITES
DUNITIC
DUNK S
DUNKED
DUNKER S
DUNKERS
DUNKING
DUNKS
DUNLIN S
DUNLINS
DUNNAGE S
DUNNAGES
DUNNED
DUNNER
DUNNESS
DUNNEST
STUNNED
DUNNING
DUNNITE S
DUNNITES
DUNS
DUNT S
DUNTED
DUNTING
DUNTS
DUO S
OUD
UDO
DUODENA L
DUODENAL
UNLOADED
DUODENUM S
DUOLOG S
DUOLOGS
DUOLOGUE S
DUOMI
ODIUM
DUOMO S
DUOMOS
DUOPOLY
DUOPSONY
DUOS
OUDS UDOS
DUOTONE S
OUTDONE
DUOTONES
DUP ES
PUD
DUPABLE
DUPE DRS
DUPED
DUPER SY
DRUPE PERDU
PRUDE URPED
DUPERIES

DUPERS
DRUPES
PERDUS
PRUDES
PURSED
DUPERY
DUPES
PSEUD SPUED
DUPING
DUPLE X
PULED
DUPLEX
DUPLEXED
DUPLEXER S
DUPLEXES
EXPULSED
DUPPED
DUPPING
DUPS
PUDS SPUD
DURA LS
DURABLE S
DURABLES
DURABLY
DURAL
DURAMEN S
MANURED
MAUNDER
UNARMED
DURAMENS
MAUNDERS
SURNAMED
DURANCE S
DURANCES
DURAS
DURATION S
DURATIVE S
DURBAR S
DURBARS
DURE DS
RUDE RUED
DURED
UDDER
DURES S
DRUSE
DURESS
DRUSES
SUDSER
DURESSES
DURIAN S
DURIANS
DURING
UNGIRD
DURION S
DIURON
DURIONS
DIURONS
DURMAST S
MUSTARD
DURMASTS
MUSTARDS
DURN S
NURD
DURNDEST
DURNED
DURNEDER
DURNING
DURNS
NURDS
DURO CS
DOUR
DUROC S
DUROCS
DUROS
SUDOR
DURR AS
DURRA S
DURRAS
DURRIE S
DURRIES
DURRS
DURST
DURUM S
DURUMS
DUSK SY
DUSKED
DUSKIER
DUIKERS
DUSKIEST
DUSKILY

DUSKING
DUSKISH
DUSKS
DUSKY
A **DUST** SY
STUD
DUSTBIN S
BUNDIST
DUSTBINS
BUNDISTS
DUSTED
DUSTER S
RUDEST
RUSTED
DUSTERS
TRUSSED
DUSTHEAP S
DUSTIER
STUDIER
DUSTIEST
DUSTILY
DUSTING S
DUSTINGS
DUSTLESS
DUSTLIKE
DUSTMAN
DUSTMEN
DUSTOFF S
DUSTOFFS
DUSTPAN S
STANDUP
UPSTAND
DUSTPANS
STANDUPS
UPSTANDS
DUSTRAG S
DUSTRAGS
DUSTS
STUDS
DUSTUP S
DUSTUPS
DUSTY
STUDY
DUTCH
DUTCHMAN
DUTCHMEN
DUTEOUS
DUTIABLE
DUTIES
SUITED
DUTIFUL
DUTY
DUUMVIR IS
DUUMVIRI
DUUMVIRS
DUVET S
DUVETINE S
DUVETS
DUVETYN ES
DUVETYNE S
DUVETYNS
DUXELLES
DWARF S
DWARFED
DWARFER
DWARFEST
DWARFING
DWARFISH
DWARFISM S
DWARFS
DWARVES
DWEEB SY
BEDEW
DWEEBIER
DWEEBISH
DWEEBS
BEDEWS
DWEEBY
DWELL S
DWELLED
DWELLER S
DWELLERS
DWELLING S
DWELLS
DWELT
DWINDLE DS
WINDLED
DWINDLED

DWINDLES
SWINDLED
DWINE DS
WIDEN WINED
DWINED
WINDED
DWINES
WIDENS
DWINING
WINDING
DYABLE
BELADY
DYAD S
DYADIC S
DYADICS
DYADS
DYARCHIC
DYARCHY
DYBBUK S
DYBBUKIM
DYBBUKS
DYE DRS
DEY
DYEABLE
BELAYED
DYED
EDDY
DYEING S
DINGEY
DYEINGS
DINGEYS
DYER S
DYERS
DYES
DEYS
DYESTUFF S
DYEWEED S
DYEWEEDS
DYEWOOD S
DYEWOODS
DYING S
DINGY
DYINGS
DYKE DSY
DYKED
DYKES
SKYED
DYKING
A **DYNAMIC** S
DYNAMICS
DYNAMISM S
DYNAMIST S
DYNAMITE DR S
DYNAMO S
DYNAMOS
DYNAST SY
DYNASTIC
DYNASTS
DYNASTY
DYNATRON S
DYNE LS
DENY
DYNEIN S
DYNEINS
DYNEL S
DYNELS
DYNES
DYNODE S
DYNODES
DYSGENIC S
DYSLEXIA S
DYSLEXIC S
DYSPEPSY
DYSPNEA LS
DYSPNEAL
ENDPLAYS
DYSPNEAS
SYNAPSED
DYSPNEIC
DYSPNOEA S
DYSPNOIC
DYSTAXIA S
DYSTOCIA S
DYSTONIA S
DYSTONIC
DYSTOPIA NS
DYSURIA S
DYSURIAS

DYSURIC
DYVOUR S
DYVOURS

E

BLPRT **EACH**
ACHE
M **EAGER** S
AGREE EAGRE
RAGEE
EAGERER
EAGEREST
ETAGERES
STEERAGE
M **EAGERLY**
EAGERS
AGREES
EAGRES
GREASE
RAGEES
B **EAGLE** DST
AGLEE
EAGLED
B **EAGLES**
EAGLET S
GELATE
LEGATE
TELEGA
EAGLETS
GELATES
LEGATES
SEGETAL
TELEGAS
EAGLING
M **EAGRE** S
AGREE EAGER
RAGEE
EAGRES
AGREES
EAGERS
GREASE
RAGEES
WY **EANLING** S
ANELING
LEANING
WY **EANLINGS**
LEANINGS
BDFGHLNPRSTWY **EAR** LNS
ARE ERA
EARACHE S
EARACHES
EARBUD S
DAUBER
EARBUDS
DAUBERS
T **EARDROP** S
T **EARDROPS**
EARDRUM S
EARDRUMS
FGNRST **EARED**
EARFLAP S
EARFLAPS
FT **EARFUL** S
FERULA
EARFULS
FERULAS
REFUSAL
BFGHNRSTW **EARING** S
GAINER
REAGIN
REGAIN
REGINA
BGH **EARINGS**
ERASING
GAINERS
REAGINS
REGAINS
REGINAS
SEARING
SERINGA
P **EARL** SY
LEAR RALE
REAL
EARLAP S
EARLAPS
EARLDOM S
EARLDOMS

FGT **EARLESS**
LEASERS
RESALES
RESEALS
SEALERS
NP **EARLIER**
LEARIER
NP **EARLIEST**
ATELIERS
LEARIEST
REALTIES
EARLOBE S
EARLOBES
EARLOCK S
EARLOCKS
P **EARLS**
ARLES LARES
LASER LEARS
RALES REALS
SERAL
EARLSHIP S
HARELIPS
PLASHIER
DNPY **EARLY**
LAYER LEARY
RELAY
EARMARK S
EARMARKS
EARMUFF S
EARMUFFS
LY **EARN** S
NEAR
LY **EARNED**
ENDEAR
NEARED
LY **EARNER** S
NEARER
REEARN
LY **EARNERS**
REEARNS
EARNEST S
EASTERN
NEAREST
EARNESTS
ASSENTER
SARSENET
LY **EARNING** S
AGINNER
ENGRAIN
GRANNIE
NEARING
LY **EARNINGS**
AGINNERS
ENGRAINS
GRANNIES
LY **EARNS**
NARES NEARS
SANER SNARE
EARPHONE S
EARPIECE S
EARPLUG S
GRAUPEL
PLAGUER
EARPLUGS
GRAUPELS
PLAGUERS
EARRING S
ANGRIER
GRAINER
RANGIER
REARING
EARRINGS
GRAINERS
BDFGHLNPRSTWY **EARS**
ARES ERAS
RASE SEAR
SERA
EARSHOT S
EARSHOTS
HOARSEST
EARSTONE S
RESONATE
DH **EARTH** SY
HATER HEART
RATHE
EARTHED
HEARTED
EARTHEN
HEARTEN
EARTHIER
HEARTIER
EARTHILY
HEARTILY

EARTHING
HEARTING
INGATHER
EARTHLY
LATHERY
EARTHMAN
EARTHMEN
EARTHNUT S
EARTHPEA S
DH **EARTHS**
HATERS
HEARTS
EARTHSET S
THEATERS
THEATRES
EARTHY
HEARTY
EARWAX
EARWAXES
EARWIG S
EARWIGS
EARWORM S
EARWORMS
CFLPT **EASE** DLS
CFLT **EASED**
AEDES
EASEFUL
TW **EASEL** S
LEASE
TW **EASELED**
TW **EASELS**
LEASES
EASEMENT S
CFLPT **EASES**
EASIER
AERIES
EASIES T
EASIEST
EASILY
EASINESS
CFLT **EASING**
BFLY **EAST** S
ATES EATS
ETAS SATE
SEAT SETA
TEAS
F **EASTER** NS
ARETES
EATERS
RESEAT
SEATER
TEASER
EASTERLY
EASTERN
EARNEST
NEAREST
F **EASTERS**
RESEATS
SEAREST
SEATERS
TEASERS
TESSERA
FY **EASTING** S
EATINGS
INGATES
INGESTA
SEATING
TEASING
B **EASTINGS**
GIANTESS
SEATINGS
BFLY **EASTS**
ASSET SATES
SEATS TASSE
EASTWARD S
RADWASTE
EASY
AYES EYAS
YEAS
BFHMNPST **EAT** HS
ATE
ETA
TAE
TEA
BH **EATABLE** S
EATABLES
TEASABLE
BN **EATEN**
ENATE

BFHNS **EATER** SY
ARETE
EATERIES
BHS **EATERS**
ARETES
EASTER
RESEAT
SEATER
TEASER
EATERY
DHN **EATH**
HAET HATE
HEAT THAE
BHS **EATING** S
INGATE
BS **EATINGS**
EASTING
INGATES
INGESTA
SEATING
TEASING
BFHMNPST **EATS**
ATES EAST
ETAS SATE
SEAT SETA
TEAS
B **EAU** X
B **EAUX**
DHLRW **EAVE** DS
DHLRW **EAVED**
DEAVE EVADE
DHLRW **EAVES**
EBB S
W **EBBED**
EBBET S
EBBETS
W **EBBING**
EBBS
EBON SY
BONE
EBONICS
EBONIES
EBONISE
EBONISE DS
EBONIES
EBONISED
EBONISES
EBONITE S
EBONITES
BETONIES
EBONIZE DS
EBONIZED
EBONIZES
EBONS
BONES
EBONY
BONEY
R **EBOOK** S
R **EBOOKS**
ECARTE S
CERATE
CREATE
ECARTES
CERATES
CREATES
ECAUDATE
ECBOLIC S
ECBOLICS
ECCLESIA EL
ECCRINE
ECDYSES
ECDYSIAL
ECDYSIS
ECDYSON ES
ECDYSONE S
ECDYSONS
ECESIC
ECESIS
ECESISES
ECHARD S
ARCHED
CHARED
ECHARDS
CRASHED
ECHE DS
LPT **ECHED**
ECHELLE S
ECHELLES

ECHELON S
ECHELONS
L **ECHES**
ECHIDNA ES
CHAINED
ECHIDNAE
ECHIDNAS
ECHINATE D
LP **ECHING**
ECHINI
ECHINOID S
ECHINUS
ECHO S
ECHOED
ECHOER S
CHEERO
COHERE
REECHO
ECHOERS
CHEEROS
COHERES
RECHOSE
ECHOES
ECHOEY
ECHOGRAM S
ECHOIC
CHOICE
ECHOING
ECHOISM S
ECHOISMS
MISCHOSE
ECHOLESS
ECHOS
CHOSE
W **ECHT**
ETCH TECH
ECLAIR S
LACIER
ECLAIRS
CLARIES
SCALIER
ECLAT S
CLEAT
ECLATS
CASTLE
CLEATS
ECLECTIC S
ECLIPSE DRS
ECLIPSED
PEDICELS
PEDICLES
ECLIPSER S
PRESLICE
RESPLICE
ECLIPSES
ECLIPSIS
ECLIPTIC S
ECLOGITE S
ECLOGUE S
ECLOGUES
ECLOSION S
COLONIES
COLONISE
ECOCIDAL
ECOCIDE S
ECOCIDES
ECOFREAK S
ECOLOGIC
O **ECOLOGY**
ECONOBOX
ECONOMIC S
ECONOMY
MONOECY
ECOTAGE S
ECOTAGES
ECOTONAL
ECOTONE S
ECOTONES
ECOTOUR S
ECOTOURS
OUTSCORE
ECOTYPE S
ECOTYPES
ECOTYPIC
ECRASEUR S
ECRU S
CURE
ECRUS
CRUSE CURES
CURSE SUCRE

ECSTASY
ECSTATIC S
P **ECTASES**
ECTASIS
ASCITES
ECTATIC
ECTHYMA
ECTODERM S
ECTOMERE S
ECTOPIA S
ECTOPIAS
ECTOPIC
ECTOSARC S
ECTOZOA N
ECTOZOAN S
ECTOZOON
ECTYPAL
ECTYPE S
ECTYPES
ECU S
CUE
ECUMENIC S
ECUS
CUES
ECZEMA S
ECZEMAS
BFGLMPRTWZ **ED** HS
DE
EDACIOUS
EDACITY
EDAPHIC
EDDIED
NT **EDDIES**
EDDO
EDDOES
NT **EDDY**
DYED
EDDYING
O **EDEMA** S
ADEEM
O **EDEMAS**
ADEEMS
SEAMED
O **EDEMATA**
EDENIC
EDENTATE S
ATTENDEE
HKLSW **EDGE** DRS
GEED
HKW **EDGED**
EDGELESS
HL **EDGER** S
GREED
HL **EDGERS**
GREEDS
SERGED
HKLSW **EDGES**
SEDGE
EDGEWAYS
EDGEWISE
HLSW **EDGIER**
HLSW **EDGIEST**
EDGILY
EDGINESS
HKW **EDGING** S
EDGINGS
HLSW **EDGY**
EDH S
EDHS
SHED
EDIBLE S
BELIED
EDIBLES
EDICT S
CITED
EDICTAL
CITADEL
DELTAIC
DIALECT
EDICTS
CISTED
EDIFICE S
EDIFICES
EDIFIED
DEIFIED

EDIFIER S
DEIFIER
REIFIED
EDIFIERS
DEIFIERS
FIRESIDE
EDIFIES
DEIFIES
EDIFY
DEIFY
EDIFYING
DEIFYING
AS **EDILE** S
ELIDE
A **EDILES**
DIESEL
ELIDES
SEDILE
SEIDEL
EDIT S
DIET DITE
TIDE TIED
EDITABLE
EDITED
DIETED
EDITING
DIETING
IGNITED
S **EDITION** S
S **EDITIONS**
SEDITION
EDITOR S
DOTIER
RIOTED
TRIODE
EDITORS
SORTIED
STEROID
STORIED
TRIODES
EDITRESS
DIESTERS
RESISTED
SISTERED
EDITRIX
EDITS
DEIST DIETS
DITES SITED
STIED TIDES
BFGMPRTWZ **EDS**
EDUCABLE S
EDUCATE DS
EDUCATED
EDUCATES
EDUCATOR SY
AERODUCT
OUTRACED
DRS **EDUCE** DS
DEUCE
DRS **EDUCED**
DEDUCE
DEUCED
DRS **EDUCES**
DEUCES
SEDUCE
DRS **EDUCIBLE**
DRS **EDUCING**
DEUCING
D **EDUCT** S
DRS **EDUCTION** S
DRS **EDUCTIVE**
R **EDUCTOR** S
COURTED
R **EDUCTORS**
D **EDUCTS**
GKLMPRSW **EEK**
EKE
FHKPRSTW **EEL** SY
LEE
EELGRASS
GEARLESS
LARGESSE
EELIER
EELIEST
STEELIE
EELLIKE
EELPOUT S
EELPOUTS
OUTSLEEP

FHKPRST **EELS**
ELSE LEES
SEEL
EELWORM S
EELWORMS
S **EELY**
P **EERIE** R
BL **EERIER**
BL **EERIEST**
L **EERILY**
BL **EERINESS**
ESERINES
BLPV **EERY**
EYER EYRE
DKR **EF** FST
FE
T **EFF** S
EFFABLE
EFFACE DRS
EFFACED
EFFACER S
EFFACERS
EFFACES
EFFACING
EFFECT S
EFFECTED
EFFECTER S
EFFECTOR S
EFFECTS
EFFENDI S
EFFENDIS
EFFERENT S
EFFETE
EFFETELY
EFFICACY
EFFIGIAL
EFFIGIES
EFFIGY
EFFLUENT S
EFFLUVIA L
EFFLUX
EFFLUXES
EFFORT S
EFFORTS
T **EFFS**
EFFULGE DS
EFFULGED
EFFULGES
EFFUSE DS
EFFUSED
EFFUSES
EFFUSING
EFFUSION S
EFFUSIVE
KR **EFS**
FES
DHLRW **EFT** S
FET
HLW **EFTS**
FEST FETS
EFTSOON S
FESTOON
EFTSOONS
FESTOONS
EGAD S
AGED GAED
EGADS
DEGAS
LR **EGAL**
GALE
EGALITE S
EGALITES
L **EGER** S
GREE
L **EGERS**
GREES REGES
SERGE
EGEST AS
GEEST GESTE
EGESTA
EGESTED
EGESTING
EGESTION S
EGESTIVE
EGESTS
GEESTS
GESTES
TY **EGG** SY

BS **EGGAR** S
AGGER GAGER
BS **EGGARS**
AGGERS
GAGERS
SAGGER
SEGGAR
EGGCUP S
EGGCUPS
BKL PV **EGGED**
K **EGGER** S
K **EGGERS**
EGGFRUIT S
EGGHEAD S
EGGHEADS
BKL PV **EGGING**
EGGLESS
EGGNOG S
EGGNOGS
EGGPLANT S
TY **EGGS**
EGGSHELL S
L **EGGY**
YEGG
A **EGIS**
GIES
A **EGISES**
SIEGES
EGLATERE S
REGELATE
RELEGATE
EGLOMISE
S **EGO** S
EGOISM S
EGOISMS
EGOIST S
STOGIE
EGOISTIC
EGOISTS
STOGIES
EGOLESS
EGOMANIA CS
S **EGOS**
GOES SEGO
EGOTISM S
EGOTISMS
EGOTIST S
EGOTISTS
R **EGRESS**
SERGES
R **EGRESSED**
R **EGRESSES**
R **EGRET** S
GREET
R **EGRETS**
GREETS
EGYPTIAN S
FHP Y **EH**
HE
EIDE R
EIDER S
EIDERS
DESIRE
RESIDE
EIDETIC
EIDOLA
EIDOLIC
EIDOLON S
EIDOLONS
SOLENOID
EIDOS
HW **EIGHT** HSY
EIGHTEEN S
H **EIGHTH** S
HEIGHT
EIGHTHLY
H **EIGHTHS**
HEIGHTS
HIGHEST
EIGHTIES
HW **EIGHTS**
EIGHTVO S
EIGHTVOS
W **EIGHTY**
EIKON S
ENOKI KOINE
EIKONES

EIKONS
ENOKIS
KOINES
EINKORN S
EINKORNS
NONSKIER
EINSTEIN S
NINETIES
EIRENIC
EISWEIN S
WIENIES
EISWEINS
N **EITHER**
DR **EJECT** AS
D **EJECTA**
DR **EJECTED**
DR **EJECTING**
DR **EJECTION** S
R **EJECTIVE** S
R **EJECTOR** S
R **EJECTORS**
DR **EJECTS**
DLP **EKE** DS
EEK
D **EKED**
DEKE
DP **EKES**
SEEK SKEE
D **EKING**
EKISTIC S
ICKIEST
EKISTICS
STICKIES
EKPWELE S
EKPWELES
EKTEXINE S
EKUELE
BCD EGM ST **EL** DFKLMS
ELAIN S
ALIEN ALINE
ANILE LIANE
ELAINS
ALIENS
ALINES
LIANES
SALINE
SILANE
ELAN DS
LANE LEAN
R **ELAND** S
LADEN NALED
R **ELANDS**
LADENS
NALEDS
SENDAL
ELANS
LANES LEANS
ELAPHINE
ELAPID S
ALIPED
PLEIAD
ELAPIDS
ALIPEDS
LAPIDES
PALSIED
PLEIADS
ELAPINE
R **ELAPSE** DS
ASLEEP
PLEASE
R **ELAPSED**
PLEASED
SEPALED
R **ELAPSES**
PLEASES
R **ELAPSING**
PLEASING
ELASTASE S
ELASTIC S
LACIEST
LATICES
ELASTICS
SCALIEST
ELASTIN S
ENTAILS
NAILSET
SALIENT
SALTINE
SLAINTE
TENAILS

ELASTINS
NAILSETS
SALIENTS
SALTINES
DGR V **ELATE** DRS
TELAE
BDG R **ELATED**
DELATE
BR **ELATEDLY**
R **ELATER** S
RELATE
ELATERID S
DETAILER
RETAILED
ELATERIN S
ENTAILER
TREENAIL
R **ELATERS**
REALEST
RELATES
RESLATE
STEALER
DGR **ELATES**
STELAE
TEASEL
DGR **ELATING**
ATINGLE
GELATIN
GENITAL
TAGLINE
DGR **ELATION** S
TOENAIL
DGR **ELATIONS**
INSOLATE
TOENAILS
R **ELATIVE** S
R **ELATIVES**
LEAVIEST
VEALIEST
ELBOW S
BELOW BOWEL
ELBOWED
BOWELED
ELBOWING
BOWELING
ELBOWS
BELOWS
BOWELS
GHM VWY **ELD** S
DEL
LED
GMW **ELDER** S
ELDERLY
GMW **ELDERS**
ELDEST
ELDRESS
ELDRICH
ELDRITCH
GMV W **ELDS**
DELS SLED
S **ELECT** S
S **ELECTED**
S **ELECTEE** S
S **ELECTEES**
SELECTEE
S **ELECTING**
S **ELECTION** S
S **ELECTIVE** S
CLEVEITE
S **ELECTOR** S
ELECTRO
S **ELECTORS**
CORSELET
ELECTROS
SELECTOR
ELECTRET S
TERCELET
ELECTRIC S
ELECTRO NS
ELECTOR
ELECTRON S
ELECTROS
CORSELET
ELECTORS
SELECTOR
ELECTRUM S
S **ELECTS**
SELECT
ELEGANCE S
ELEGANCY
ELEGANT
ELEGIAC S

ELEGIACS
LEGACIES
ELEGIES
ELEGISE
ELEGISE DS
ELEGIES
ELEGISED
ELEGISES
ELEGIST S
ELEGITS
ELEGISTS
ELEGIT S
ELEGITS
ELEGIST
ELEGIZE DS
ELEGIZED
ELEGIZES
ELEGY
ELEMENT S
TELEMEN
ELEMENTS
ELEMI S
ELEMIS
ELENCHI C
ELENCHIC
ELENCHUS
ELENCTIC
ELEPHANT S
ELEVATE DS
ELEVATED S
ELEVATES
ELEVATOR S
OVERLATE
ELEVEN S
ELEVENS
ELEVENTH S
ELEVON S
ELEVONS
DPS **ELF**
ELFIN S
ELFINS
S **ELFISH**
S **ELFISHLY**
FLESHILY
ELFLIKE
ELFLOCK S
ELFLOCKS
ELHI
HEIL
ELICIT S
ELICITED
ELICITOR S
ELICITS
ELIDE DS
EDILE
ELIDED
ELIDES
DIESEL
EDILES
SEDILE
SEIDEL
ELIDIBLE
ELIDING
ELIGIBLE S
ELIGIBLY
ELINT S
INLET
ELINTS
ENLIST
INLETS
LISTEN
SILENT
TINSEL
ELISION S
ISOLINE
LIONISE
ELISIONS
ISOLINES
LIONISES
OILINESS
P **ELITE** S
PV **ELITES**
LISTEE
ELITISM S
LIMIEST
LIMITES
ELITISMS
SLIMIEST
ELITIST S

ELITISTS
SILTIEST
ELIXIR S
ELIXIRS
Y **ELK** S
LEK
ELKHOUND S
Y **ELKS**
LEKS
BCD FHJ MST WY **ELL** S
ELLIPSE S
ELLIPSES
PILELESS
ELLIPSIS
ELLIPTIC
BCD FHJ MST WY **ELLS**
SELL
H **ELM** SY
MEL
ELMIER
ELMIEST
H **ELMS**
MELS
ELMY
YLEM
ELODEA S
ELODEAS
ELOIGN S
LEGION
ELOIGNED
ELOIGNER S
ELOIGNS
LEGIONS
LINGOES
LONGIES
ELOIN S
OLEIN
ELOINED
ELOINER S
ELOINERS
ELOINING
ELOINS
INSOLE
LESION
OLEINS
ELONGATE DS
ELOPE DRS
ELOPED
ELOPER S
ELOPERS
LEPROSE
ELOPES
ELOPING
ELOQUENT
BCD EGM ST **ELS** E
SEL
ELSE
EELS LEES
SEEL
ELUANT S
LUNATE
ELUANTS
ELUATE S
ELUATES
D **ELUDE** DRS
D **ELUDED**
DELUDE
DUELED
D **ELUDER** S
DUELER
D **ELUDERS**
DUELERS
D **ELUDES**
LEUDES
D **ELUDING**
DUELING
INDULGE
ELUENT S
ELUENTS
UNSTEEL
D **ELUSION** S
D **ELUSIONS**
D **ELUSIVE**
D **ELUSORY**
ELUTE DS

ELUTED
TELEDU
ELUTES
ELUTING
ELUTION S
OUTLINE
ELUTIONS
OUTLINES
ELUVIA L
ELUVIAL
ELUVIATE DS
ELUVIUM S
ELUVIUMS
D **ELVER** S
LEVER REVEL
D **ELVERS**
LEVERS
REVELS
DHP S **ELVES**
ELVISH
ELVISHLY
ELYSIAN
ELYTRA
LYRATE
REALTY
ELYTROID
ELYTRON
ELYTROUS
UROSTYLE
ELYTRUM
FGH MR **EM** ESU
ME
EMACIATE DS
R **EMAIL** S
MAILE
R **EMAILED**
LIMEADE
R **EMAILING**
R **EMAILS**
MAILES
MESIAL
SAMIEL
EMANANT
EMANATE DS
ENEMATA
MANATEE
EMANATED
EMANATES
MANATEES
EMANATOR S
EMBALM S
EMBALMED
EMBALMER S
EMBALMS
EMBANK S
EMBANKED
EMBANKS
EMBAR KS
AMBER BREAM
EMBARGO
EMBARK S
EMBARKED
BEDMAKER
EMBARKS
EMBARRED
EMBARS
AMBERS
BREAMS
EMBASSY
EMBATTLE DS
EMBAY S
BEAMY MAYBE
EMBAYED
EMBAYING
EMBAYS
MAYBES
EMBED S
EMBEDDED
EMBEDS
M **EMBER** S
BERME
M **EMBERS**
BERMES
EMBEZZLE DR S
EMBITTER S
EMBLAZE DRS
EMBLAZED
EMBLAZER S

EMBLAZES
EMBLAZON S
EMBLEM S
EMBLEMED
EMBLEMS
EMBODIED
EMBODIER S
EMBODIES
EMBODY
EMBOLDEN S
EMBOLI C
MOBILE
EMBOLIC
EMBOLIES
EMBOLISM S
EMBOLUS
EMBOLY
EMBORDER S
EMBOSK S
EMBOSKED
BESMOKED
EMBOSKS
EMBOSOM S
EMBOSOMS
EMBOSS
BESOMS
EMBOSSED
EMBOSSER S
EMBOSSES
EMBOW S
EMBOWED
EMBOWEL S
EMBOWELS
EMBOWER S
EMBOWERS
EMBOWING
EMBOWS
EMBRACE DRS
EMBRACED
CAMBERED
EMBRACER SY
EMBRACES
EMBROIL S
EMBROILS
EMBROWN S
EMBROWNS
EMBRUE DS
EMBRUED
UMBERED
EMBRUES
EMBRUING
UMBERING
EMBRUTE DS
EMBRUTED
EMBRUTES
EMBRYO NS
EMBRYOID S
EMBRYON S
EMBRYONS
EMBRYOS
EMCEE DS
EMCEED
EMCEEING
EMCEES
EMDASH
MASHED
SHAMED
EMDASHES
DFH MS **EME** SU
EMEER S
EMEERATE S
EMEERS
SEEMER
R **EMEND** S
EMENDATE DS
R **EMENDED**
EMENDER S
REEDMEN
EMENDERS
R **EMENDING**
R **EMENDS**
MENSED
EMERALD S
EMERALDS
DEMERSAL

DR EMERGE DS
MERGEE
DR EMERGED
DEMERGE
EMERGENT S
DR EMERGES
MERGEES
DR EMERGING
EMERIES
EMERITA ES
EMIRATE
MEATIER
EMERITAE
EMERITAS
EMIRATES
STEAMIER
EMERITI
EMERITUS
EMEROD S
EMERODS
EMEROID S
EMEROIDS
EMERSED
REDEEMS
EMERSION S
EMERY
DFHMS EMES
SEEM SEME
N EMESES
N EMESIS
EMETIC S
M EMETICS
EMETIN ES
EMETINE S
EMETINES
EMETINS
EMEU S
EMEUS
EMEUTE S
EMEUTES
DH EMIC
MICE
EMIGRANT S
REMATING
R EMIGRATE DS
EMIGRE S
REGIME
EMIGRES
REGIMES
REMIGES
EMINENCE S
EMINENCY
EMINENT
EMIR S
MIRE RIME
EMIRATE S
EMERITA
MEATIER
EMIRATES
EMERITAS
STEAMIER
EMIRS
MIRES MISER
RIMES
EMISSARY
DR EMISSION S
SIMONIES
R EMISSIVE
DR EMIT S
ITEM MITE
TIME
DR EMITS
ITEMS METIS
MITES SMITE
STIME TIMES
DR EMITTED
R EMITTER S
TERMITE
R EMITTERS
TERMITES
DR EMITTING
H EMMER S
H EMMERS
EMMET S
EMMETS
GJ EMMY S
EMMYS
EMODIN S
DOMINE
MONIED
EMODINS
DOMINES
MISDONE
DGR EMOTE DRS
D EMOTED
DEMOTE
R EMOTER S
METEOR
REMOTE
EMOTERS
METEORS
REMOTES
DGR EMOTES
EMOTICON S
D EMOTING
MITOGEN
DR EMOTION S
DR EMOTIONS
MOONIEST
EMOTIVE
EMPALE DRS
EMPALED
EMPALER S
PREMEAL
EMPALERS
RESAMPLE
EMPALES
EMPALING
EMPANADA S
EMPANEL S
EMPLANE
EMPANELS
EMPLANES
ENSAMPLE
EMPATHIC
EMPHATIC
EMPATHY
EMPERIES
EPIMERES
PREEMIES
EMPEROR S
EMPERORS
PREMORSE
EMPERY
EMPHASES
EMPHASIS E
MISSHAPE
EMPHATIC
EMPATHIC
EMPIRE S
EPIMER
PREMIE
EMPIRES
EMPRISE
EPIMERS
IMPRESE
PREMIES
PREMISE
SPIREME
EMPIRIC S
EMPIRICS
MISPRICE
EMPLACE DS
EMPLACED
EMPLACES
EMPLANE DS
EMPANEL
EMPLANED
EMPLANES
EMPANELS
ENSAMPLE
EMPLOY ES
EMPLOYE DER S
EMPLOYED
EMPLOYEE S
EMPLOYER S
REEMPLOY
EMPLOYES
EMPLOYS
EMPOISON S
EMPORIA
MEROPIA
EMPORIUM S
EMPOWER S
EMPOWERS
EMPRESS
EMPRISE S
EMPIRES
EPIMERS
IMPRESE
PREMIES
PREMISE
SPIREME
EMPRISES
IMPRESES
PREMISES
SPIREMES
EMPRIZE S
EMPRIZES
EMPTIED
EMPTIER S
EMPTIERS
EMPTIES T
SEPTIME
EMPTIEST
EMPTILY
EMPTINGS
PIGMENTS
EMPTINS
EMPTY
EMPTYING
EMPURPLE DS
EMPYEMA S
EMPYEMAS
EMPYEMIC
EMPYREAL
EMPYREAN S
FGHMR EMS
EMU S
EMULATE DS
EMULATED
EMULATES
EMULATOR S
EMULOUS
D EMULSIFY
EMULSION S
EMULSIVE
EMULSOID S
EMUS
MUSE
EMYD ES
DEMY
EMYDE S
EMYDES
EMYDS
BDFGHKMPSTWY EN DGS
NE
T ENABLE DRS
BALEEN
ENABLED
ENABLER S
ENABLERS
ENABLES
BALEENS
ENABLING
ENACT S
ENACTED
ENACTING
ENACTIVE
ENACTOR SY
ENACTORS
ANCESTOR
ENACTORY
ENACTS
ASCENT
CENTAS
SECANT
STANCE
ENAMEL S
MELENA
ENAMELED
ENAMELER S
ENAMELS
MELENAS
ENAMINE S
ENAMINES
ENAMOR S
MOANER
ENAMORED
DEMEANOR
ENAMORS
MOANERS
OARSMEN
ENAMOUR S
NEUROMA
ENAMOURS
NEUROMAS
S ENATE S
EATEN
PS ENATES
SATEEN
SENATE
V ENATIC
ACETIN
CENTAI
V ENATION S
V ENATIONS
SONATINE
ENCAENIA
ENCAGE DS
ENCAGED
ENCAGES
ENCAGING
ENCAMP S
ENCAMPED
ENCAMPS
ENCASE DS
SEANCE
SENECA
ENCASED
DECANES
ENCASES
CASSENE
SEANCES
SENECAS
ENCASH
HANCES
NACHES
ENCASHED
ENCHASED
ENCASHES
ENCHASES
ENCASING
ENCEINTE S
ENCHAIN S
ENCHAINS
P ENCHANT S
P ENCHANTS
ENCHASE DRS
ACHENES
ENCHASED
ENCASHED
ENCHASER S
ENCHASES
ENCASHES
ENCHORIC
CORNICHE
ENCINA LS
CANINE
CANNIE
ENCINAL
ENCINAS
CANINES
ENCIPHER S
ENCIRCLE DS
LICENCER
ENCLASP S
SPANCEL
ENCLASPS
SPANCELS
ENCLAVE DS
VALENCE
ENCLAVED
ENCLAVES
VALENCES
ENCLITIC S
ENCLOSE DRS
ENCLOSED
ENCLOSER S
ENSORCEL
ENCLOSES
ENCODE DRS
ENCODED
ENCODER S
ENCORED
ENCODERS
CENSORED
NECROSED
SECONDER
ENCODES
SECONDE
ENCODING
ENCOMIA
ENCOMIUM S
MECONIUM
ENCORE DS
ENCORED
ENCODER
ENCORES
NECROSE
ENCORING
ENCROACH
ENCRUST S
ENCRUSTS
CURTNESS
ENCRYPT S
ENCRYPTS
ENCUMBER S
ENCYCLIC S
ENCYST S
ENCYSTED
ENCYSTS
BFLMPRSTVW END S
DEN
ENDAMAGE DS
ENDAMEBA ES
ENDANGER S
ENDARCH Y
RANCHED
ENDARCHY
ENDASH
ENDASHES
DASHEENS
ENDBRAIN S
ENDEAR S
EARNED
NEARED
ENDEARED
DEADENER
ENDEARS
ENDEAVOR S
BFMPRSTVW ENDED
ENDEMIAL
ENDEMIC S
ENDEMICS
ENDEMISM S
BFGLMRSTV ENDER S
ENDERMIC
BFGLMRSTV ENDERS
DENSER
RESEND
SENDER
ENDEXINE S
ENDGAME S
ENDGAMES
BFLMPRSTVW ENDING S
GINNED
M ENDINGS
SENDING
ENDITE DS
ENDITED
ENDITES
DESTINE
ENDITING
INDIGENT
ENDIVE S
DEVEIN
ENVIED
VEINED
ENDIVES
DEVEINS
ENDLEAF S
ENDLEAFS
ENDLESS
ENDLONG
ENDMOST
ENDNOTE S
TENONED
ENDNOTES
SONNETED
ENDOCARP S
ENDOCAST S
TACNODES
ENDODERM S
ENDOGAMY
ENDOGEN SY
ENDOGENS
ENDOGENY
ENDOPOD S
ENDOPODS
ENDORSE DER S
ENDORSED
ENDORSEE S
ENDORSER S
ENDORSES
ENDORSOR S
ENDOSARC S
ENDOSMOS
ENDOSOME S
MOONSEED
ENDOSTEA L
ENDOW S
OWNED
ENDOWED
ENDOWER S
REENDOW
ENDOWERS
REENDOWS
WORSENED
ENDOWING
ENDOWS
SNOWED
ENDOZOIC
ENDPAPER S
ENDPLATE S
ENDPLAY S
ENDPLAYS
DYSPNEAL
ENDPOINT S
ENDRIN S
DINNER
ENDRINS
DINNERS
BFLMPRSTVW ENDS
DENS SEND
SNED
V ENDUE DS
UNDEE
ENDUED
DENUDE
DUDEEN
DUENDE
V ENDUES
ENSUED
ENDUING
ENDURE DRS
ENURED
ENDURED
DENURED
ENDURER S
ENDURERS
SUNDERER
ENDURES
ENSURED
ENDURING
ENDURO S
UNDOER
ENDUROS
RESOUND
SOUNDER
UNDOERS
B ENDWAYS
B ENDWISE
SINEWED
ENEMA S
ENEMAS
MENSAE
SEAMEN
ENEMATA
EMANATE
MANATEE
ENEMIES
ENEMY
ENERGID S
DREEING
REEDING
REIGNED
ENERGIDS
DESIGNER
REDESIGN
REEDINGS
RESIGNED
ENERGIES
ENERGISE
GREENIES
RESEEING
ENERGISE DS
ENERGIES
GREENIES
RESEEING
ENERGIZE DR S
ENERGY
GREENY
GYRENE
D ENERVATE DS
VENERATE
ENFACE DS
ENFACED
ENFACES
ENFACING
ENFEEBLE DR S
ENFEOFF S
ENFEOFFS
ENFETTER S
ENFEVER S
ENFEVERS
ENFILADE DS
ENFLAME DS
ENFLAMED
ENFLAMES
T ENFOLD S
FONDLE
ENFOLDED
ENFOLDER S
T ENFOLDS
FONDLES
ENFORCE DRS
ENFORCED
ENFORCER S
CONFRERE
RECONFER
ENFORCES
ENFRAME DS
FREEMAN
ENFRAMED
FREEDMAN
ENFRAMES
ENG S
GEN
NEG
ENGAGE DRS
ENGAGED
ENGAGER S
ENGAGERS
ENGAGES
ENGAGING
ENGENDER S
ENGILD S
DINGLE
ENGILDED
ENGILDS
DINGLES
SINGLED
ENGINE DS
ENGINED
NEEDING
ENGINEER S
ENGINERY
ENGINES
ENGINING
ENGINOUS
ENGIRD S
DINGER
GIRNED
REDING
RINGED
ENGIRDED
ENGIRDLE DS
LINGERED
REEDLING
ENGIRDS
DINGERS
ENGIRT
ENGLISH
SHINGLE
ENGLUT S
GLUTEN
ENGLUTS
GLUTENS
ENGORGE DS
ENGORGED
ENGORGES
ENGRAFT S
ENGRAFTS

ENGRAIL S
ALIGNER
NARGILE
REALIGN
REGINAL
ENGRAILS
ALIGNERS
NARGILES
REALIGNS
SIGNALER
SLANGIER
ENGRAIN S
AGINNER
EARNING
GRANNIE
NEARING
ENGRAINS
AGINNERS
EARNINGS
GRANNIES
ENGRAM S
GERMAN
MANGER
RAGMEN
ENGRAMME S
ENGRAMS
GERMANS
MANGERS
ENGRAVE DRS
AVENGER
ENGRAVED
ENGRAVER S
ENGRAVES
AVENGERS
ENGROSS
ENGS
GENS NEGS
ENGULF S
ENGULFED
ENGULFS
ENHALO S
ENHALOED
ENHALOES
ENHALOS
ENHANCE DRS
ENHANCED
ENHANCER S
ENHANCES
ENIGMA S
GAMINE
ENIGMAS
GAMINES
SEAMING
ENIGMATA
AGMINATE
ENISLE DS
ENSILE
SENILE
ENISLED
ENSILED
LINSEED
ENISLES
ENSILES
SENILES
ENISLING
ENSILING
ENJAMBED
ENJOIN S
ENJOINED
ENJOINER S
ENJOINS
ENJOY S
ENJOYED
ENJOYER S
REENJOY
ENJOYERS
REENJOYS
ENJOYING
ENJOYS
ENKINDLE DR S
ENLACE DS
ENLACED
CLEANED
ENLACES
CLEANSE
SCALENE
ENLACING
CLEANING
ENLARGE DRS
GENERAL
GLEANER

ENLARGED
ENLARGER S
ENLARGES
GENERALS
GLEANERS
ENLIST S
ELINTS
INLETS
LISTEN
SILENT
TINSEL
ENLISTED
LISTENED
TINSELED
ENLISTEE S
SELENITE
ENLISTER S
LISTENER
REENLIST
SILENTER
ENLISTS
LISTENS
SILENTS
TINSELS
ENLIVEN S
ENLIVENS
ENMESH
ENMESHED
ENMESHES
ENMITIES
ENMITY
ENNEAD S
ENNEADIC
DECENNIA
ENNEADS
ENNEAGON S
ENNOBLE DRS
ENNOBLED
ENNOBLER S
ENNOBLES
ENNUI S
ENNUIS
ENNUYE E
ENNUYEE
ENOKI S
EIKON KOINE
ENOKIS
EIKONS
KOINES
ENOL S
LENO LONE
NOEL
ENOLASE S
ENOLASES
ENOLIC
CINEOL
MOP **ENOLOGY**
V NEOLOGY
ENOLS
LENOS NOELS
OX **ENOPHILE** S
ENORM
ENORMITY
ENORMOUS
K **ENOSIS**
EOSINS
ESSOIN
NOESIS
NOISES
OSSEIN
SONSIE
K **ENOSISES**
NOESISES
ENOUGH S
ENOUGHS
DR **ENOUNCE** DS
DR **ENOUNCED**
DENOUNCE
DR **ENOUNCES**
ENOW S
ENOWS
OWSEN
ENPLANE DS
ENPLANED
ENPLANES
ENQUIRE DS
ENQUIRED
ENQUIRES
SQUIREEN
ENQUIRY

ENRAGE DS
GENERA
ENRAGED
ANGERED
DERANGE
GRANDEE
GRENADE
ENRAGES
ENRAGING
ANGERING
ENRAPT
ARPENT
ENTRAP
PARENT
TREPAN
ENRAVISH
VANISHER
ENRICH
INCHER
RICHEN
ENRICHED
RICHENED
ENRICHER S
ENRICHES
ENROBE DRS
BOREEN
ENROBED
DEBONER
REDBONE
ENROBER S
ENROBERS
ENROBES
BOREENS
ENROBING
RINGBONE
ENROL LS
LONER NEROL
ENROLL S
ENROLLED
RONDELLE
ENROLLEE S
ENROLLER S
REENROLL
ENROLLS
ENROLS
LONERS
NEROLS
ENROOT S
ENROOTED
ENROOTS
BDF GHK LPT WY **ENS**
SEN
ENSAMPLE S
EMPANELS
EMPLANES
ENSCONCE DS
ENSCROLL S
ENSEMBLE S
ENSERF S
ENSERFED
ENSERFS
ENSHEATH ES
HEATHENS
ENSHRINE DE S
ENSHROUD S
HOUNDERS
UNHORSED
ENSIFORM
FERMIONS
ENSIGN S
ENSIGNCY
SYNGENIC
ENSIGNS
SENSING
ENSILAGE DS
LINEAGES
PT **ENSILE** DS
ENISLE
SENILE
ENSILED
ENISLED
LINSEED
ENSILES
ENISLES
SENILES
ENSILING
ENISLING
ENSKIED
SKEINED
ENSKIES
KINESES

ENSKY
ENSKYED
ENSKYING
ENSLAVE DRS
LEAVENS
ENSLAVED
ENSLAVER S
ENSLAVES
ENSNARE DRS
RENNASE
ENSNARED
ENSNARER S
ENSNARES
NEARNESS
RENNASES
ENSNARL S
LANNERS
ENSNARLS
ENSORCEL LS
ENCLOSER
ENSOUL S
ENSOULED
ENSOULS
ENSPHERE DS
ENSUE DS
ENSUED
ENDUES
ENSUES
ENSUING
GUNNIES
C **ENSURE** DRS
ENURES
C **ENSURED**
ENDURES
C **ENSURER** S
C **ENSURERS**
C **ENSURES**
C **ENSURING**
ENSWATHE DS
WHEATENS
V **ENTAIL** S
TENAIL
TINEAL
ENTAILED
DATELINE
LINEATED
ENTAILER S
ELATERIN
TREENAIL
V **ENTAILS**
ELASTIN
NAILSET
SALIENT
SALTINE
SLAINTE
TENAILS
ENTAMEBA ES
P **ENTANGLE** DR S
ENTASES
SATEENS
SENATES
SENSATE
ENTASIA S
TAENIAS
ENTASIAS
ENTASIS
NASTIES
SEITANS
SESTINA
TANSIES
TISANES
ENTASTIC
NICTATES
TETANICS
ENTELLUS
ENTENTE S
ENTENTES
CRT V **ENTER** AS
RENTE TERNE
TREEN
ENTERA L
NEATER
ENTERAL
ETERNAL
TELERAN
CT **ENTERED**
ENTERER S
REENTER
TERREEN
TERRENE

ENTERERS
REENTERS
TERREENS
TERRENES
ENTERIC S
ENTICER
ENTERICS
ENTICERS
SECRETIN
CT **ENTERING**
ENTERON S
TENONER
ENTERONS
TENONERS
CRT V **ENTERS**
NESTER
RENEST
RENTES
RESENT
TENSER
TERNES
TREENS
ENTHALPY
ENTHETIC
ENTHRAL LS
ENTHRALL S
ENTHRALS
ENTHRONE DS
ENTHUSE DS
ENTHUSED
ENTHUSES
ENTIA
TENIA TINEA
ENTICE DRS
ENTICED
ENTICER S
ENTERIC
ENTICERS
ENTERICS
SECRETIN
ENTICES
ENTICING
ENTIRE S
RETINE
TRIENE
ENTIRELY
LIENTERY
ENTIRES
ENTRIES
RETINES
TRIENES
ENTIRETY
ETERNITY
ENTITIES
ENTITLE DS
ENTITLED
ENTITLES
ENTITY
ENTODERM S
MENTORED
ENTOIL S
ENTOILED
DELETION
ENTOILS
ENTOMB S
ENTOMBED
BODEMENT
ENTOMBS
ENTOPIC
NEPOTIC
ENTOZOA LN
OZONATE
ENTOZOAL
ENTOZOAN S
ENTOZOIC
ENZOOTIC
ENTOZOON
ENTRAILS
LATRINES
RATLINES
RETINALS
TRENAILS
ENTRAIN S
ENTRAINS
TRANNIES
ENTRANCE DS
ENTRANT S
ENTRANTS

ENTRAP S
ARPENT
ENRAPT
PARENT
TREPAN
ENTRAPS
ARPENTS
PARENTS
PASTERN
TREPANS
ENTREAT SY
RATTEEN
TERNATE
ENTREATS
RATTEENS
ENTREATY
ENTREE S
ETERNE
RETENE
TEENER
ENTREES
RETENES
TEENERS
ENTRENCH
ENTREPOT S
ENTRESOL S
GS **ENTRIES**
ENTIRES
RETINES
TRIENES
ENTROPIC
INCEPTOR
ENTROPY
ENTRUST S
NUTTERS
ENTRUSTS
GS **ENTRY**
ENTRYWAY S
ENTWINE DS
ENTWINED
ENTWINES
WENNIEST
ENTWIST S
TWINSET
ENTWISTS
TWINSETS
ENUF
T **ENURE** DS
T **ENURED**
ENDURE
T **ENURES**
ENSURE
ENURESES
ENURESIS
ENURETIC S
CEINTURE
T **ENURING**
ENVELOP ES
ENVELOPE DR S
ENVELOPS
ENVENOM S
ENVENOMS
ENVIABLE
ENVIABLY
ENVIED
DEVEIN
ENDIVE
VEINED
ENVIER S
VEINER
VENIRE
ENVIERS
INVERSE
VEINERS
VENIRES
VERSINE
ENVIES
NIEVES
ENVIOUS
NIVEOUS
ENVIRO NS
RENVOI
ENVIRON S
ENVIRONS
ENVIROS
RENVOIS
VERSION
ENVISAGE DS
ENVISION S
R **ENVOI** S
OVINE

R **ENVOIS**
OVINES
ENVOY S
ENVOYS
ENVY
ENVYING
ENWHEEL S
ENWHEELS
ENWIND S
WINNED
ENWINDS
ENWOMB S
BOWMEN
ENWOMBED
ENWOMBS
ENWOUND
UNOWNED
ENWRAP S
PAWNER
ENWRAPS
PAWNERS
SPAWNER
ENZOOTIC S
ENTOZOIC
ENZYM ES
ENZYME S
ENZYMES
ENZYMIC
ENZYMS
EOBIONT S
EOBIONTS
BONITOES
EOCENE
EOHIPPUS
A **EOLIAN**
EOLIPILE S
N **EOLITH** S
N **EOLITHIC**
N **EOLITHS**
HOLIEST
HOSTILE
EOLOPILE S
AJN **EON** S
P ONE
A **EONIAN**
P **EONISM** S
MONIES
P **EONISMS**
ANP **EONS**
NOES NOSE
ONES SONE
EOSIN ES
NOISE
EOSINE S
EOSINES
EOSINIC
NICOISE
EOSINS
ENOSIS
ESSOIN
NOESIS
NOISES
OSSEIN
SONSIE
EPACT S
EPACTS
ASPECT
EPARCH SY
PREACH
EPARCHS
PARCHES
EPARCHY
PREACHY
EPAULET S
EPAULETS
EPAZOTE S
EPAZOTES
T **EPEE** S
EPEEIST S
EPEEISTS
SEEPIEST
T **EPEES**
EPEIRIC
EPENDYMA S
EPERGNE S
EPERGNES
EPHA HS
HEAP
EPHAH S
EPHAHS

EPHAS HEAPS PHASE SHAPE
EPHEBE S
EPHEBES
EPHEBI C
EPHEBIC
EPHEBOI
EPHEBOS PHOEBES
EPHEBUS
EPHEDRA S
EPHEDRAS RESHAPED
EPHEDRIN ES
EPHEMERA EL S
EPHOD S HOPED
EPHODS
EPHOR IS HOPER
EPHORAL
EPHORATE S
EPHORI
EPHORS HOPERS POSHER
EPIBLAST S
EPIBOLIC
EPIBOLY
S **EPIC** S PICE
EPICAL PLAICE PLICAE
EPICALLY
EPICALYX
EPICARP S CRAPPIE
EPICARPS CRAPPIES
EPICEDIA
EPICENE S
EPICENES
EPICLIKE
EPICOTYL S LIPOCYTE
EPICS SEPIC SPICE
EPICURE S
EPICURES
EPICYCLE S
EPIDEMIC S
EPIDERM S DEMIREP IMPEDER
EPIDERMS DEMIREPS IMPEDERS PREMISED SIMPERED
L **EPIDOTE** S
L **EPIDOTES** POETISED
EPIDOTIC
EPIDURAL S
EPIFAUNA EL S
EPIFOCAL
EPIGEAL
EPIGEAN
EPIGEIC
EPIGENE
EPIGENIC
EPIGEOUS
EPIGON EIS PIGEON
EPIGONE S
EPIGONES
EPIGONI C
EPIGONIC
EPIGONS PIGEONS PINGOES
EPIGONUS
EPIGRAM S PRIMAGE
EPIGRAMS PRIMAGES
EPIGRAPH SY
EPIGYNY
D **EPILATE** DS PILEATE
D **EPILATED** DEPILATE PILEATED
D **EPILATES**
D **EPILATOR** S PETIOLAR
EPILEPSY
EPILOG S
EPILOGS
EPILOGUE DS
EPIMER ES EMPIRE PREMIE
EPIMERE S PREEMIE
EPIMERES EMPERIES PREEMIES
EPIMERIC
EPIMERS EMPIRES EMPRISE IMPRESE PREMIES PREMISE SPIREME
EPIMYSIA
EPINAOI
EPINAOS SENOPIA
EPINASTY
EPIPHANY
EPIPHYTE S
EPISCIA S
EPISCIAS
EPISCOPE S
EPISODE S
EPISODES
EPISODIC
EPISOMAL
EPISOME S
EPISOMES
EPISTASY
EPISTLE RS PELITES
EPISTLER S PELTRIES PERLITES REPTILES
EPISTLES
EPISTOME S EPITOMES
EPISTYLE S
EPITAPH S
EPITAPHS HAPPIEST
EPITASES
EPITASIS
EPITAXIC
EPITAXY
EPITHET S
EPITHETS TIPSHEET
EPITOME S
EPITOMES EPISTOME
EPITOMIC
EPITOPE S
EPITOPES
EPIZOA
EPIZOIC
EPIZOISM S
EPIZOITE S
EPIZOON
EPIZOOTY
EPOCH S
EPOCHAL
EPOCHS
EPODE S
EPODES DEPOSE SPEEDO
EPONYM SY
EPONYMIC
EPONYMS
EPONYMY
EPOPEE S
EPOPEES
EPOPOEIA S
PR **EPOS** OPES PESO POSE
DR **EPOSES**
EPOXIDE S EPOXIED
EPOXIDES
EPOXIED EPOXIDE
EPOXIES
EPOXY
EPOXYED
EPOXYING
EPSILON S PINOLES
EPSILONS
EQUABLE
EQUABLY
EQUAL S QUALE
EQUALED
EQUALING
EQUALISE DR S
EQUALITY
EQUALIZE DR S
EQUALLED
EQUALLY
EQUALS SQUEAL
EQUATE DS
EQUATED
EQUATES
EQUATING
EQUATION S
EQUATOR S
EQUATORS QUAESTOR
EQUERRY
EQUID S
EQUIDS
EQUINE S
EQUINELY
EQUINES
EQUINITY INEQUITY
EQUINOX
EQUIP S PIQUE
EQUIPAGE S
EQUIPPED
EQUIPPER S
EQUIPS PIQUES
EQUISETA
EQUITANT
R **EQUITES**
EQUITIES
EQUITY
EQUIVOKE S
FHP S **ER** AEGNRS RE
SV **ERA** S ARE EAR
R **ERADIATE** DS
ERAS E ARES EARS RASE SEAR SERA
ERASABLE
ERASE DRS SAREE
ERASED RESEDA SEARED
ERASER S SEARER
ERASERS
ERASES SAREES
ERASING EARINGS GAINERS REAGINS REGAINS REGINAS SEARING SERINGA
ERASION S SENSORIA
ERASIONS
ERASURE S
ERASURES REASSURE
T **ERBIUM** S IMBRUE
T **ERBIUMS** IMBRUES
CDF HMP SW **ERE** REE
ERECT S TERCE
ERECTED
ERECTER S REERECT
ERECTERS REERECTS SECRETER
ERECTILE
ERECTING GENTRICE
ERECTION S NEOTERIC
ERECTIVE
ERECTLY
ERECTOR S
ERECTORS SECRETOR
ERECTS CERTES RESECT SECRET TERCES
ERELONG
EREMITE S
EREMITES
EREMITIC
EREMURI
EREMURUS
ERENOW
EREPSIN S REPINES
EREPSINS RIPENESS
ERETHIC ETHERIC HERETIC TECHIER
ERETHISM S
EREWHILE S
B **ERG** OS REG
ERGASTIC AGRESTIC CIGARETS
ERGATE S
ERGATES RESTAGE
ERGATIVE S
ERGO T GOER GORE OGRE
ERGODIC
ERGOT S
ERGOTIC
ERGOTISM S
ERGOTS
B **ERGS** REGS
ERICA S AREIC CERIA
ERICAS CARIES CERIAS
ERICOID
ERIGERON S
ERINGO S IGNORE REGION
ERINGOES
ERINGOS IGNORES REGIONS SIGNORE
MV **ERISTIC** S
ERISTICS
ERLKING S
ERLKINGS
ERMINE DS
ERMINED
ERMINES
FHK T **ERN** ES
KT **ERNE** S
KT **ERNES** SNEER
FHK T **ERNS**
ERODABLE LEEBOARD
ERODE DS
ERODED
ERODENT
ERODES REDOES
ERODIBLE REBOILED
ERODING GROINED IGNORED NEGROID REDOING
EROGENIC
CHZ **EROS** E ORES ROES ROSE SORE
R **EROSE** S
EROSELY
X **EROSES**
EROSIBLE
EROSION S
EROSIONS
EROSIVE
CX **EROTIC** AS
EROTICA L
EROTICAL LORICATE
EROTICS
EROTISM S MOISTER MORTISE TRISOME
EROTISMS MORTISES TRISOMES
EROTIZE DS
EROTIZED
EROTIZES
ERR S
ERRABLE
ERRANCY
ERRAND S DARNER
ERRANDS DARNERS
ERRANT S RANTER
ERRANTLY
ERRANTRY
ERRANTS RANTERS
ERRATA S
ERRATAS
ERRATIC S CIRRATE
ERRATICS
ERRATUM MATURER
ERRED
ERRHINE S
ERRHINES
H **ERRING** RINGER
ERRINGLY
T **ERROR** S
T **ERRORS**
ERRS
HS **ERS** T RES SER
ERSATZ
ERSATZES
PV **ERSES** SEERS SERES
V **ERST** REST RETS TRES
ERUCT S CRUET CURET CUTER RECUT TRUCE
ERUCTATE DS
ERUCTED
ERUCTING
ERUCTS CRUETS CRUSET CURETS RECTUS RECUTS TRUCES
ERUDITE
A **ERUGO** S ROGUE ROUGE
A **ERUGOS** GROUSE ROGUES ROUGES RUGOSE
ERUMPENT
ERUPT S
ERUPTED REPUTED
ERUPTING REPUTING
ERUPTION S
ERUPTIVE S
ERUPTS PUREST
ERVIL S LIVER LIVRE VILER
ERVILS LIVERS LIVRES SILVER SLIVER
ERYNGO S GROYNE
ERYNGOES
ERYNGOS GROYNES
ERYTHEMA S
ERYTHRON S
BFH LOP RY **ES** S
ESCALADE DR S
ESCALATE DS
ESCALLOP S COLLAPSE
ESCALOP ES
ESCALOPE DS OPALESCE
ESCALOPS
ESCAPADE S
ESCAPE DERS PEACES
ESCAPED
ESCAPEE S
ESCAPEES
ESCAPER S RESPACE
ESCAPERS RESPACES
ESCAPES
ESCAPING
ESCAPISM S MISSPACE SCAMPIES
ESCAPIST S SPACIEST
ESCAR PS ACRES CARES CARSE RACES SCARE SERAC
ESCARGOT S
ESCAROLE S
ESCARP S CAPERS CRAPES PACERS PARSEC RECAPS SCRAPE SECPAR SPACER
ESCARPED RESPACED
ESCARPS PARSECS SCRAPES SECPARS SPACERS
ESCARS CARESS CARSES CRASES SCARES SERACS
ESCHALOT S CHOLATES
ESCHAR S ARCHES CHARES CHASER SEARCH
ESCHARS CHASERS CRASHES
ESCHEAT S TEACHES
ESCHEATS
ESCHEW S
ESCHEWAL S
ESCHEWED
ESCHEWER S
ESCHEWS
ESCOLAR S CLAROES COALERS ORACLES RECOALS SOLACER
ESCOLARS LACROSSE SOLACERS
ESCORT S CORSET COSTER RECTOS SCOTER SECTOR
ESCORTED CORSETED SECTORED
ESCORTS CORSETS COSTERS SCOTERS SECTORS
ESCOT S COSET COTES
ESCOTED CESTODE
ESCOTING
ESCOTS CESTOS COSETS COSSET
ESCROW S COWERS
ESCROWED
ESCROWS
ESCUAGE S
ESCUAGES
ESCUDO S
ESCUDOS
ESCULENT S
ESERINE S
ESERINES EERINESS
BLY **ESES** SEES
ESKAR S ASKER RAKES SAKER
ESKARS ASKERS SAKERS

ESKER S
REEKS
ESKERS
M ESNE S
SEEN SENE
M ESNES
SENSE
O ESOPHAGI
ESOTERIC A
COTERIES
ESPALIER S
ESPANOL
NOPALES
ESPARTO S
PROTEAS
SEAPORT
ESPARTOS
PROTASES
SEAPORTS
ESPECIAL
CALIPEES
ESPIAL S
LIPASE
ESPIALS
LAPISES
LIPASES
PALSIES
ESPIED
PEISED
ESPIEGLE
ESPIES
PEISES
SPEISE
ESPOUSAL S
SEPALOUS
B ESPOUSE DRS
B ESPOUSED
ESPOUSER S
REPOUSSE
B ESPOUSES
ESPRESSO S
ESPRIT S
PRIEST
RIPEST
SPRITE
STRIPE
TRIPES
ESPRITS
PERSIST
PRIESTS
SPRIEST
SPRITES
STIRPES
STRIPES
ESPY
PYES YEPS
ESPYING
PIGSNEY
ESQUIRE DS
QUERIES
ESQUIRED
ESQUIRES
CFJ LMN ESS
ESSAY S
EYASS
ESSAYED
ESSAYER S
ESSAYERS
ESSAYING
ESSAYIST S
ESSAYS
ESSENCE S
ESSENCES
CFJ MNY ESSES
ESSOIN S
ENOSIS
EOSINS
NOESIS
NOISES
OSSEIN
SONSIE
ESSOINS
OSSEINS
SESSION
H ESSONITE S
ESTANCIA S
GRT ESTATE DS
TESTAE
GR ESTATED
GRT ESTATES

GR ESTATING
TANGIEST
ESTEEM S
MESTEE
ESTEEMED
ESTEEMS
MESTEES
FJN PRT WYZ ESTER S
REEST RESET
STEER STERE
TERSE TREES
ESTERASE S
TESSERAE
ESTERIFY
FJN PRT WZ ESTERS
REESTS
RESETS
SEREST
STEERS
STERES
ESTHESES
A ESTHESIA S
ESTHESIS
HESSITES
A ESTHETE S
TEETHES
A ESTHETES
A ESTHETIC S
TECHIEST
ESTIMATE DS
MEATIEST
TEATIMES
AF ESTIVAL
A ESTIVATE DS
ESTOP S
PESTO POETS
STOPE TOPES
ESTOPPED
ESTOPPEL S
ESTOPS
PESTOS
POSSET
PTOSES
STOPES
ESTOVERS
OVERSETS
ESTRAGON S
NEGATORS
V ESTRAL
ALERTS
ALTERS
ARTELS
LASTER
RATELS
SALTER
SLATER
STALER
STELAR
TALERS
ESTRANGE DRS
GRANTEES
GREATENS
NEGATERS
REAGENTS
SERGEANT
ESTRAY S
STAYER
YAREST
ESTRAYED
ESTRAYS
STAYERS
ESTREAT S
RESTATE
RETASTE
ESTREATS
RESTATES
RETASTES
O ESTRIN S
INERTS
INSERT
INTERS
NITERS
NITRES
SINTER
TRIENS
TRINES
O ESTRINS
INSERTS
SINTERS
O ESTRIOL S
LOITERS
TOILERS
O ESTRIOLS

O ESTROGEN S
O ESTRONE S
O ESTRONES
O ESTROUS
OESTRUS
OUSTERS
SOUREST
SOUTERS
STOURES
TUSSORE
ESTRUAL
SALUTER
O ESTRUM S
MUSTER
O ESTRUMS
MUSTERS
O ESTRUS
RUSSET
SUREST
TUSSER
O ESTRUSES
ESTUARY
ESURIENT
RETINUES
REUNITES
BFG HJL MNP RST VWY ET AH
BFG MSZ ETA S
ATE
EAT
TAE
TEA
ETAGERE S
ETAGERES
EAGEREST
STEERAGE
ETALON S
TOLANE
ETALONS
TOLANES
ETAMIN ES
INMATE
TAMEIN
K ETAMINE S
MATINEE
K ETAMINES
MATINEES
MISEATEN
ETAMINS
INMATES
TAMEINS
R ETAPE S
R ETAPES
PESETA
BFG Z ETAS
ATES EAST
EATS SATE
SEAT SETA
TEAS
ETATISM S
MATIEST
ETATISMS
MISSTATE
ETATIST
TATTIES
ETCETERA S
FKL RV ETCH
ECHT TECH
ETCHANT S
ETCHANTS
FLR T ETCHED
TECHED
F ETCHER S
F ETCHERS
RETCHES
FKL RV ETCHES
FLR ETCHING S
ETCHINGS
ETERNAL S
ENTERAL
TELERAN
ETERNALS
TELERANS
ETERNE
ENTREE
RETENE
TEENER
ETERNISE DS
TEENSIER

ETERNITY
ENTIRETY
ETERNIZE DS
ETESIAN S
ETESIANS
TENIASES
BHM T ETH S
HET
THE
M ETHANE S
M ETHANES
M ETHANOL S
ANETHOL
M ETHANOLS
ANETHOLS
ETHENE S
ETHENES
ETHEPHON S
ANT W ETHER S
THERE THREE
A ETHEREAL
A ETHERIC
ERETHIC
HERETIC
TECHIER
ETHERIFY
ETHERISH
ETHERIZE DR S
ATW ETHERS
THERES
THREES
ETHIC S
ETHICAL S
ETHICALS
ETHICIAN S
ETHICIST S
CHITTIES
ITCHIEST
THEISTIC
ETHICIZE DS
ETHICS
ITCHES
ETHINYL S
ETHINYLS
ETHION S
ETHIONS
HISTONE
ETHMOID S
ETHMOIDS
ETHNARCH SY
ETHNIC S
ETHNICAL
ETHNICS
STHENIC
ETHNONYM S
ETHNOS
HONEST
ETHNOSES
ETHOGRAM S
ETHOLOGY
THEOLOGY
ETHOS
SHOTE THOSE
ETHOSES
ETHOXIES
M ETHOXY L
M ETHOXYL S
ETHOXYLS
BHM T ETHS
HEST HETS
M ETHYL S
M ETHYLATE DS
M ETHYLENE S
M ETHYLIC
LECYTHI
TECHILY
M ETHYLS
SHELTY
ETHYNE S
ETHYNES
ETHYNYL S
ETHYNYLS
ETIC
CITE
P ETIOLATE DS
A ETIOLOGY
ETNA S
ANTE NEAT

ETNAS
ANTES NATES
NEATS STANE
ETOILE S
ETOILES
ETOUFFEE S
ETUDE S
ETUDES
ETUI S
ETUIS
SUITE
ETWEE S
ETWEES
ETYMA
MATEY MEATY
ETYMON S
ETYMONS
EUCAINE S
EUCAINES
EUCALYPT IS
EUCHARIS
EUCHRE DS
EUCHRED
EUCHRES
EUCHRING
EUCLASE S
EUCLASES
EUCRITE S
EUCRITES
CERUSITE
CUTESIER
EUCRITIC
EUDAEMON S
EUDAIMON S
EUDEMON S
EUDEMONS
EUGENIA S
EUGENIAS
EUGENIC S
EUGENICS
EUGENIST S
EUGENOL S
EUGENOLS
EUGLENA S
EUGLENAS
EUGLENID S
EULACHAN S
EULACHON S
EULOGIA ES
EULOGIAE
EULOGIAS
EULOGIES
EULOGISE
EULOGISE DS
EULOGIES
EULOGIST S
EULOGIUM S
EULOGIZE DR S
EULOGY
EUNUCH S
EUNUCHS
EUONYMUS
EUPATRID S
PREAUDIT
EUPEPSIA S
EUPEPSY
EUPEPTIC
EUPHENIC S
EUPHONIC
EUPHONY
EUPHORIA S
EUPHORIC
POUCHIER
EUPHOTIC
EUPHRASY
EUPHROE S
EUPHROES
EUPHUISM S
EUPHUIST S
EUPLOID SY
EUPLOIDS
EUPLOIDY
EUPNEA S
EUPNEAS
EUPNEIC

EUPNOEA S
EUPNOEAS
EUPNOEIC
EUREKA
EURIPI
EURIPUS
EURO S
ROUE
EUROKIES
EUROKOUS
EUROKY
EUROPIUM S
EUROS
ROUES ROUSE
EURYBATH S
EURYOKY
EURYTHMY
EUSOCIAL
EUSTACY
EUSTASY
EUSTATIC
EUSTELE S
EUSTELES
EUTAXIES
EUTAXY
EUTECTIC S
EUTROPHY
EUXENITE S
EVACUANT S
EVACUATE DS
EVACUEE S
EVACUEES
EVADABLE
EVADE DRS
DEAVE EAVED
EVADED
DEAVED
EVADER S
REAVED
EVADERS
ADVERSE
EVADES
DEAVES
EVADIBLE
EVADING
DEAVING
DR EVALUATE DS
EVANESCE DS
EVANGEL S
EVANGELS
EVANISH
VAHINES
EVASION S
EVASIONS
EVASIVE
N EVE NRS
VEE
EVECTION S
S EVEN ST
NEVE
EVENED
VENDEE
EVENER S
VENEER
EVENERS
VENEERS
EVENEST
EVENFALL S
EVENING S
EVENINGS
EVENLY
EVENNESS
S EVENS
NEVES SEVEN
EVENSONG S
EVENT S
EVENTFUL
EVENTIDE S
EVENTS
EVENTUAL
FLN S EVER TY
VEER
N EVERMORE
R EVERSION S
R EVERT S
REVET
R EVERTED
R EVERTING

EVERTOR S
EVERTORS
RESTROVE
R EVERTS
REVEST
REVETS
VERSET
VERSTE
R EVERY
VEERY
EVERYDAY S
EVERYMAN
EVERYMEN
EVERYONE
EVERYWAY
N EVES
VEES
EVICT S
CIVET
EVICTED
EVICTEE S
EVICTEES
EVICTING
EVICTION S
EVICTOR S
EVICTORS
VORTICES
EVICTS
CIVETS
EVIDENCE DS
EVIDENT
DK EVIL S
LIVE VEIL
VILE
EVILDOER S
OVERIDLE
R EVILER
LEVIER
LIEVER
RELIVE
REVILE
VEILER
EVILEST
LIEVEST
VELITES
EVILLER
EVILLEST
EVILLY
LIVELY
VILELY
EVILNESS
LIVENESS
VEINLESS
VILENESS
DK EVILS
LEVIS LIVES
VEILS
EVINCE DS
EVINCED
EVINCES
EVINCING
EVINCIVE
EVITABLE
EVITE DS
EVITED
EVITES
EVITING
R EVOCABLE
EVOCATOR S
OVERCOAT
R EVOKE DRS
R EVOKED
R EVOKER S
REVOKE
R EVOKERS
REVOKES
R EVOKES
R EVOKING
R EVOLUTE S
VELOUTE
EVOLUTES
VELOUTES
DR EVOLVE DRS
DR EVOLVED
DEVOLVE
R EVOLVER S
REVOLVE
R EVOLVERS
REVOLVES
DR EVOLVES
DR EVOLVING

EVONYMUS
EVULSE DS
R EVULSED
EVULSES
EVULSING
R EVULSION S
EVZONE S
EVZONES
EWE RS
WEE
FHN EWER S
S WEER WERE
HS EWERS
RESEW SEWER SWEER
EWES
WEES
DHK LRS V EX

EXABYTE S
EXABYTES
EXACT AS
EXACTA S
EXACTAS
EXACTED
EXACTER S
EXCRETA
EXACTERS
EXACTEST
EXACTING
EXACTION S
EXACTLY
EXACTOR S
EXACTORS
EXACTS
EXAHERTZ
EXALT S
LATEX
EXALTED
EXALTER S
EXALTERS
EXALTING
EXALTS
LAXEST
EXAM S
EXAMEN S
AXEMEN
EXAMENS
H EXAMINE DER S
EXAMINED
EXAMINEE S
EXAMINER S
H EXAMINES
EXAMPLE DS
EXEMPLA
EXAMPLED
EXAMPLES
EXAMS
MAXES
EXANTHEM AS
EXAPTED
EXAPTIVE
EXARCH SY
EXARCHAL
EXARCHS
H EXARCHY
EXCAVATE DS
EXCEED S
EXCEEDED
EXCEEDER S
EXCEEDS
EXCEL S
EXCELLED
EXCELS
EXCEPT S
EXPECT
EXCEPTED
EXPECTED
EXCEPTS
EXPECTS
EXCERPT S
EXCERPTS
EXCESS
EXCESSED
EXCESSES

EXCHANGE DR S
EXCIDE DS
EXCIDED
EXCIDES
EXCISED
EXCIDING
EXCIMER S
EXCIMERS
EXCIPLE S
EXCIPLES
EXCISE DS
EXCISED
EXCIDES
EXCISES
EXCISING
EXCISION S
EXCITANT S
EXCITE DRS
EXCITED
EXCITER S
EXCITERS
EXCITES
EXCITING
EXCITON S
EXCITONS
EXCITOR S
XEROTIC
EXCITORS
EXORCIST
EXCLAIM S
EXCLAIMS
CLIMAXES
EXCLAVE S
EXCLAVES
EXCLUDE DRS
EXCLUDED
EXCLUDER S
EXCLUDES
EXCRETA L
EXACTER
EXCRETAL
EXCRETE DRS
EXCRETED
EXCRETER S
EXCRETES
EXCURSUS
EXCUSE DRS
EXCUSED
EXCUSER S
EXCUSERS
EXCUSES
EXCUSING
EXEC S
EXECRATE DS
EXECS
EXECUTE DRS
EXECUTED
EXECUTER S
EXECUTES
EXECUTOR SY
HSV EXED
EXEDRA E
EXEDRAE
EXEGESES
EXEGESIS
EXEGETE S
EXEGETES
EXEGETIC S
EXEMPLA R
EXAMPLE
EXEMPLAR SY
EXEMPLUM
EXEMPT S
EXEMPTED
EXEMPTS
EXEQUIAL
EXEQUIES
EXEQUY
EXERCISE DR S
EXERGUAL
EXERGUE S
EXERGUES
EXERT S
EXERTED

EXERTING
EXERTION S
EXERTIVE
EXERTS
EXSERT
DHK LRS V EXES
EXEUNT
EXHALANT S
EXHALE DS
EXHALED
EXHALENT S
EXHALES
EXHALING
EXHAUST S
EXHAUSTS
EXHEDRA E
EXHEDRAE
EXHIBIT S
EXHIBITS
EXHORT S
EXHORTED
EXHORTER S
EXHORTS
EXHUME DRS
EXHUMED
EXHUMER S
EXHUMERS
EXHUMES
EXHUMING
EXIGENCE S
EXIGENCY
EXIGENT
EXIGIBLE
EXIGUITY
EXIGUOUS
EXILABLE
EXILE DRS
EXILED
EXILER S
EXILERS
EXILES
ILEXES
EXILIAN
EXILIC
EXILING
EXIMIOUS
R EXINE S
R EXINES
HSV EXING
S EXIST S
EXITS SIXTE
EXISTED
EXISTENT S
EXISTING
S EXISTS
SEXIST
SIXTES
EXIT S
EXITED
EXITING
EXITLESS
SEXTILES
EXITS
EXIST SIXTE
EXOCARP S
EXOCARPS
EXOCRINE S
EXOCYTIC
EXODERM S
EXODERMS
EXODOI
EXODOS
EXODUS
EXODUSES
EXOERGIC
EXOGAMIC
EXOGAMY
EXOGEN S
EXOGENS
EXON S
OXEN
EXONIC
EXONS
EXONUMIA

EXONYM S
EXONYMS
EXORABLE
EXORCISE DR S
EXORCISM S
EXORCIST S
EXCITORS
EXORCIZE DS
EXORDIA L
EXORDIAL
EXORDIUM S
EXOSMIC
EXOSMOSE S
EXOSPORE S
EXOTERIC
EXOTIC AS
EXOTICA
EXOTICS
COEXIST
EXOTISM S
EXOTISMS
EXOTOXIC
EXOTOXIN S
EXPAND S
EXPANDED
EXPANDER S
EXPANDOR S
EXPANDS
SPANDEX
EXPANSE S
EXPANSES
EXPAT S
EXPATS
EXPECT S
EXCEPT
EXPECTED
EXCEPTED
EXPECTER S
EXPECTS
EXCEPTS
EXPEDITE DR S
EXPEL S
EXPELLED
EXPELLEE S
EXPELLER S
EXPELS
PLEXES
EXPEND S
EXPENDED
EXPENDER S
EXPENDS
EXPENSE DS
EXPENSED
EXPENSES
EXPERT S
EXPERTED
EXPERTLY
EXPERTS
EXPIABLE
EXPIATE DS
EXPIATED
EXPIATES
EXPIATOR SY
EXPIRE DRS
EXPIRED
EXPIRER S
EXPIRERS
EXPIRES
PREXIES
EXPIRIES
EXPIRING
EXPIRY
EXPLAIN S
EXPLAINS
EXPLANT S
EXPLANTS
EXPLICIT S
EXPLODE DRS
EXPLODED
EXPLODER S
EXPLORED
EXPLODES
EXPLOIT S
EXPLOITS

EXPLORE DRS
EXPLORED
EXPLODER
EXPLORER S
EXPLORES
EXPO S
EXPONENT S
EXPORT S
EXPORTED
EXPORTER S
REEXPORT
EXPORTS
EXPOS E
POXES
EXPOSAL S
EXPOSALS
EXPOSE DRS
EXPOSED
EXPOSER S
EXPOSERS
EXPRESSO
EXPOSES
EXPOSING
EXPOSIT S
POXIEST
EXPOSITS
EXPOSURE S
EXPOUND S
EXPOUNDS
EXPRESS O
EXPRESSO S
EXPOSERS
EXPULSE DS
EXPULSED
DUPLEXES
EXPULSES
PLEXUSES
EXPUNGE DRS
EXPUNGED
EXPUNGER S
EXPUNGES
EXSCIND S
EXSCINDS
EXSECANT S
EXSECT S
EXSECTED
EXSECTS
EXSERT S
EXERTS
EXSERTED
EXSERTS
S EXTANT
EXTEND S
EXTENDED
EXTENDER S
EXTENDS
EXTENSOR S
EXTENT S
EXTENTS
EXTERIOR S
EXTERN ES
EXTERNAL S
EXTERNE S
EXTERNES
EXTERNS
EXTINCT S
EXTINCTS
EXTOL LS
EXTOLL S
EXTOLLED
EXTOLLER S
EXTOLLS
EXTOLS
EXTORT S
EXTORTED
EXTORTER S
EXTORTS
EXTRA S
RETAX TAXER
EXTRACT S
EXTRACTS
EXTRADOS
EXTRANET S
EXTRAS
TAXERS
EXTREMA
EXTREME RS

EXTREMER
EXTREMES T
EXTREMUM
D EXTRORSE
EXTRUDE DRS
EXTRUDED
EXTRUDER S
EXTRUDES
EXTUBATE DS
EXUDATE S
EXUDATES
EXUDE DS
EXUDED
EXUDES
EXUDING
EXULT S
EXULTANT
EXULTED
EXULTING
EXULTS
EXURB S
EXURBAN
EXURBIA S
EXURBIAS
EXURBS
BRUXES
EXUVIA EL
EXUVIAE
EXUVIAL
EXUVIATE DS
EXUVIUM
EYAS S
AYES EASY
YEAS
EYASES
EYASS
ESSAY
EYASSES
EYE DNRS
EYEABLE
EYEBALL S
EYEBALLS
EYEBAR S
EYEBARS
EYEBEAM S
EYEBEAMS
EYEBLACK S
EYEBLINK S
EYEBOLT S
EYEBOLTS
EYEBROW S
EYEBROWS
EYECUP S
EYECUPS
K EYED
EYEDNESS
EYEDROPS
EYEFOLD S
EYEFOLDS
EYEFUL S
EYEFULS
EYEGLASS
EYEHOLE S
EYEHOLES
EYEHOOK S
EYEHOOKS
EYEING
EYELASH
EYELESS
EYELET S
EYELETS
EYELID S
EYELIDS
SEEDILY
EYELIFT S
EYELIFTS
EYELIKE
EYELINER S
EYEN
EYNE
EYEPIECE S
EYEPOINT S
F EYER S
EERY EYRE
EYERS
EYRES

EYES
EYESHADE S
EYESHINE S
EYESHOT S
EYESHOTS
EYESIGHT S
EYESOME
EYESORE S
EYESORES
EYESPOT S
PEYOTES
EYESPOTS
EYESTALK S
EYESTONE S
EYETEETH
EYETOOTH
EYEWASH
EYEWATER S
EYEWEAR
EYEWINK S
EYEWINKS
K EYING
EYNE
EYEN
EYRA S
AERY YARE
YEAR
EYRAS
RESAY SAYER
YEARS
EYRE S
EERY EYER
EYRES
EYERS
EYRIE S
EYRIES
EYRIR
EYRY

F

FA BDGNRSTX Y
FAB S
FABBER
FABBEST
FABLE DRS
FABLED
FABLER S
FABLERS
FABLES
FABLIAU X
FABLIAUX
FABLING
FABRIC S
FABRICS
FABS
FABULAR
FABULATE DS
FABULIST S
FABULOUS
FACADE S
FACADES
FACE DRST
CAFE
FACEABLE
FACED
DECAF
FACEDOWN S
FACELESS
FACELIFT S
FACEMASK S
FACER S
FARCE
FACERS
FARCES
FACES
CAFES
FACET ES
FACETE D
FACETED
FACETELY
FACETIAE
FACETING
FACETS
FACETTED
FACEUP
FACIA ELS

FACIAE
FACIAL S
FACIALLY
FACIALS
FASCIAL
FACIAS
FASCIA
FACIEND S
FANCIED
FACIENDS
FACIES
FACILE
FECIAL
FACILELY
FACILITY
FACING S
FACINGS
FACT S
FACTFUL
FACTION S
FACTIONS
FACTIOUS
FACTOID S
FACTOIDS
FACTOR SY
FACTORED
FACTORS
FACTORY
FACTOTUM S
FACTS
FACTUAL
FACTURE S
FURCATE
FACTURES
FURCATES
FACULA ER
FAUCAL
FACULAE
FACULAR
FACULTY
FAD EOS
FADABLE
FADDIER
FADDIEST
FADDISH
FADDISM S
FADDISMS
FADDIST S
FADDISTS
FADDY
FADE DRS
DEAF
FADEAWAY S
FADED
FADEDLY
FADEIN S
FADEINS
FADELESS
FADEOUT S
FADEOUTS
FADER S
FARED
FADERS
FADES
FADGE DS
FADGED
FADGES
FADGING
FADING S
FADINGS
FADLIKE
FADO S
FADOS
FADS
FAECAL
FAECES
FAENA S
FAENAS
FAERIE S
FERIAE
FAERIES
FREESIA
FAERY
FAG S
FAGGED
FAGGING
FAGGOT SY
FAGGOTED
FAGGOTS
FAGIN S
FAGINS
FAGOT S
FAGOTED
FAGOTER S
FAGOTERS
FAGOTING S
FAGOTS
FAGS
FAHLBAND S
FAIENCE S
FIANCEE
FAIENCES
FIANCEES
FAIL S
ALIF FILA
FAILED
AFIELD
FAILING S
FAILINGS
FAILLE S
FAILLES
FAILS
ALIFS
FAILURE S
FAILURES
FAIN T
NAIF
FAINEANT S
FAINER
INFARE
FAINEST
FAINT S
FAINTED
DEFIANT
FAINTER S
FAINTERS
FAINTEST
FAINTING
FAINTISH
FAINTLY
FAINTS
FAIR SY
FIAR
FAIRED
FAIRER
FAIREST
FAIRGOER S
FAIRIES
FAIRING S
FAIRINGS
FAIRISH
FAIRLEAD S
FAIRLY
FAIRNESS
SANSERIF
FAIRS
FIARS
FAIRWAY S
FAIRWAYS
FAIRY
FAIRYISM S
FAITH S
FAITHED
FAITHFUL S
FAITHING
FAITHS
FAITOUR S
FAITOURS
FAJITA S
FAJITAS
FAKE DRSY
FAKED
FAKEER S
FAKEERS
FAKER SY
FREAK
FAKERIES
FAKERS
FREAKS
FAKERY
FREAKY
FAKES
FAKEY
FAKING
FAKIR S
KAFIR
FAKIRS
KAFIRS
FALAFEL S
FALAFELS
FALBALA S
FALBALAS
FALCATE D
FALCATED
FALCES
FALCHION S
FALCON S
FLACON
FALCONER S
FALCONET S
CONFLATE
FALCONRY
FALCONS
FLACONS
FALDERAL S
FALDEROL S
FALL S
FALLACY
FALLAL S
FALLALS
FALLAWAY S
FALLBACK S
FALLEN
FALLER S
REFALL
FALLERS
REFALLS
FALLFISH
FALLIBLE
FILLABLE
FALLIBLY
FALLING
FALLOFF S
FALLOFFS
FALLOUT S
OUTFALL
FALLOUTS
OUTFALLS
FALLOW S
FALLOWED
FALLOWS
FALLS
FALSE R
ALEFS FLEAS
LEAFS
FALSELY
FALSER
FARLES
FERALS
FLARES
FALSEST
FATLESS
FALSETTO S
FALSIE S
FALSIES
FALSIFY
FALSITY
FALTBOAT S
FLATBOAT
FALTER S
FALTERED
DEFLATER
REFLATED
FALTERER S
FALTERS
FALX
FLAX
FAME DS
FAMED
FAMELESS
SELFSAME
FAMES
FAMILIAL
FAMILIAR S
FAMILIES
FAMILISM S
FAMILY
FAMINE S
FAMINES
FAMING
FAMISH
FAMISHED
FAMISHES
FAMOUS
FAMOUSLY
FAMULI
AIMFUL
FAMULUS
FAN EGOS
FANATIC S
FANATICS
FANCIED
FACIEND
FANCIER S
FANCIERS
FANCIES T
FASCINE
FIANCES
FANCIEST
FANCIFUL
FANCIFY
FANCILY
FANCY
FANCYING
FANDANGO S
FANDOM S
FANDOMS
FANE S
FANEGA S
FANEGADA S
FANEGAS
FANES
FANFARE S
FANFARES
FANFARON S
FANFIC S
FANFICS
FANFOLD S
FANFOLDS
FANG AS
FANGA S
FANGAS
FANGED
DEFANG
FANGLESS
FANGLIKE
FANGS
FANION S
FANIONS
FANJET S
FANJETS
FANLIGHT S
FANLIKE
FANNED
FANNER S
FANNERS
FANNIES
FANNING
FANNY
FANO NS
FANON S
FANONS
FANOS
FANS
FANTAIL S
TAILFAN
FANTAILS
TAILFANS
FANTASIA S
FANTASIE DS
FANTASM S
FANTASMS
FANTAST S
FANTASTS
FANTASY
FANTOD S
FANTODS
FANTOM S
FANTOMS
FANUM S
FANUMS
FANWISE
FANWORT S
FANWORTS
FANZINE S
FANZINES
FAQIR S
FAQIRS
FAQUIR S
FAQUIRS
A FAR DELMOT
ARF
FARAD S
FARADAIC
FARADAY S
FARADAYS
FARADIC
FARADISE DS
SAFARIED
FARADISM S
FARADIZE DR S
FARADS
FARAWAY
FARCE DRS
FACER
FARCED
FARCER S
FARCERS
SCARFER
FARCES
FACERS
FARCEUR S
FARCEURS
SURFACER
FARCI E
FARCICAL
FARCIE S
FIACRE
FARCIES
FIACRES
FARCING
FARCY
FARD S
FARDED
FARDEL S
FLARED
FARDELS
FARDING
FARDS
FARE DRS
FEAR FRAE
FAREBOX
FARED
FADER
FARER S
FARERS
FARES
FEARS SAFER
FAREWELL S
FARFAL S
FARFALLE
FARFALS
FARFEL S
RAFFLE
FARFELS
RAFFLES
FARINA S
FARINAS
FARING
FARINHA S
FARINHAS
FARINOSE
FARL ES
FARLE S
FERAL FLARE
FARLES
FALSER
FERALS
FLARES
FARLS
FARM S
FARMABLE
FRAMABLE
FARMED
FRAMED
FARMER S
FRAMER
FARMERS
FRAMERS
FARMHAND S
FARMING S
FRAMING
FARMINGS
FRAMINGS
FARMLAND S
FARMS
FARMWIFE
FARMWORK S
FARMYARD S
FARNESOL S
FARNESS
FARO S
FORA
FAROLITO S
FAROS
SOFAR
FAROUCHE
FARRAGO
FARRIER SY
FARRIERS
FARRIERY
FARROW S
FARROWED
FARROWS
FARSIDE S
FARSIDES
FARTHER
FARTHEST
FARTHING S
FARTLEK S
FARTLEKS
FAS HT
FASCES
FASCIA ELS
FACIAS
FASCIAE
FASCIAL
FACIALS
FASCIAS
FASCIATE D
FASCICLE DS
FASCINE S
FANCIES
FIANCES
FASCINES
FASCISM S
FASCISMS
FASCIST S
FASCISTS
FASCITIS
FASH
FASHED
FASHES
SHEAFS
FASHING
FASHION S
FASHIONS
FASHIOUS
FAST S
FATS
FASTBACK S
FATBACKS
FASTBALL S
FASTED
DEFATS
FASTEN S
FASTENED
FASTENER S
FENESTRA
REFASTEN
FASTENS
FATNESS
FASTER
AFTERS
STRAFE
FASTEST
FASTING S
FASTINGS
FASTNESS
FASTS
FASTUOUS
FAT ES
AFT
FATAL
FATALISM S
FATALIST S
FATALITY
FATALLY
FATBACK S
FATBACKS
FASTBACK
FATBIRD S
FATBIRDS
FATE DS
FEAT FETA
FATED
DEFAT
FATEFUL
FATES
FEAST FEATS
FETAS
FATHEAD S
FATHEADS
FATHER S
HAFTER
TREFAH
FATHERED
FATHERLY
FATHERS
HAFTERS
FATHOM S
FATHOMED
FATHOMER S
FATHOMS
FATIDIC
FATIGUE DS
FATIGUED
FATIGUES
FATING
FATLESS
FALSEST
FATLIKE
FATLING S
FATLINGS
FATLY
FATNESS
FASTENS
FATS O
FAST
FATSTOCK S
FATTED
FATTEN S
FATTENED
FATTENER S
FATTENS
FATTER
FATTEST
FATTIER
FATTIES T
FATTIEST
FATTILY
FATTING
FATTISH
FATTY
FATUITY
FATUOUS
FATWA S
FATWAS
FATWOOD S
FATWOODS
FAUBOURG S
FAUCAL S
FACULA
FAUCALS
FAUCES
FAUCET S
FAUCETS
FAUCIAL
FAUGH
FAULD S
FAULDS
FAULT SY
FAULTED
DEFAULT
FAULTIER
FILATURE
FAULTILY
FAULTING
FAULTS
FLATUS
FAULTY
FAUN AS
FAUNA ELS
FAUNAE
FAUNAL
FAUNALLY
FAUNAS
FAUNLIKE
FAUNS
SNAFU
FAUTEUIL S
FAUVE S

FAUVES
FAUVISM S
FAUVISMS
FAUVIST S
FAUVISTS
FAUX
FAVA S
FAVAS
FAVE S
FAVELA S
FAVELAS
FAVELLA S
FAVELLAS
FAVES
FAVISM S
FAVISMS
FAVONIAN
FAVOR S
FAVORED
FAVORER S
OVERFAR
FAVORERS
FAVORING
FAVORITE S
FAVORS
FAVOUR S
FAVOURED
FAVOURER S
FAVOURS
FAVUS
FAVUSES
FAWN SY
FAWNED
FAWNER S
FAWNERS
FAWNIER
FAWNIEST
FAWNING
FAWNLIKE
FAWNS
FAWNY
FAX
FAXED
FAXES
FAXING
O FAY S
FAYALITE S
FAYED
FAYING
O FAYS
FAZE DS
FAZED
FAZENDA S
FAZENDAS
FAZES
FAZING
FE DEHMNRST
EF UWYZ
FEAL
ALEF FLEA
LEAF
FEALTIES
FETIALES
LEAFIEST
FEALTY
FEATLY
FEAR S
FARE FRAE
A FEARED
DEAFER
FEARER S
FEARERS
FEARFUL
FEARING
FEARLESS
FEARS
FARES SAFER
FEARSOME
FEASANCE S
FEASE DS
FEASED
FEASES
FEASIBLE
FEASIBLY
FEASING

FEAST S
FATES FEATS
FETAS
FEASTED
DEAFEST
DEFEATS
FEASTER S
AFREETS
FEASTERS
FEASTFUL
SUFFLATE
FEASTING
FEASTS
SAFEST
FEAT S
FATE FETA
FEATER
AFREET
FEATEST
FEATHER SY
TEREFAH
FEATHERS
FEATHERY
FEATLIER
FEATLY
FEALTY
FEATS
FATES FEAST
FETAS
FEATURE DS
FEATURED
FEATURES
FEAZE DS
FEAZED
FEAZES
FEAZING
FEBRIFIC
A FEBRILE
FECAL
FECES
FECIAL S
FACILE
FECIALS
FECK S
FECKLESS
FECKLY
FLECKY
FECKS
FECULA E
FECULAE
FECULENT
FECUND
FED S
DEF
FEDAYEE N
FEDAYEEN
FEDERACY
FEDERAL S
FEDERALS
FEDERATE DS
DEFEATER
REDEFEAT
FEDEX
FEDEXED
FEDEXES
FEDEXING
FEDORA S
FEDORAS
FEDS
FEE BDLST
FEEB S
BEEF
FEEBLE R
FEEBLER
FEEBLEST
FEEBLISH
FEEBLY
FEEBS
BEEFS
FEED S
FEEDABLE
BEFLEAED
FEEDBACK S
FEEDBAG S
FEEDBAGS
FEEDBOX
FEEDER S
REEFED
REFEED

FEEDERS
REFEEDS
FEEDHOLE S
FEEDING
FEIGNED
FEEDLOT S
FEEDLOTS
FEEDS
FEEDYARD S
DEFRAYED
FEEING
FEEL S
FLEE
FEELER S
REFEEL
FEELERS
REFEELS
FEELESS
FEELING S
FLEEING
FEELINGS
FEELS
FLEES
FEES
FEET
FETE
FEETLESS
FEEZE DS
FEEZED
FEEZES
FEEZING
FEH S
FEHS
FEIGN S
FEIGNED
FEEDING
FEIGNER S
FREEING
REEFING
FEIGNERS
FEIGNING
FEIGNS
FEIJOA S
FEIJOAS
FEINT S
FEINTED
FEINTING
FEINTS
FINEST
INFEST
FEIRIE
FEIST SY
FEISTIER
FERITIES
FIERIEST
FEISTILY
FEISTS
FEISTY
FELAFEL S
FELAFELS
FELDSHER S
FELDSPAR S
FELICITY
FELID S
FIELD FILED
FLIED
FELIDS
FIELDS
FELINE S
FELINELY
FELINES
FELINITY
FINITELY
FELL ASY
FELLA HS
FELLABLE
FELLAH S
FELLAHIN
FELLAHS
FELLAS
FELLATE DS
LEAFLET
FELLATED
FELLATES
LEAFLETS
FELLATIO NS
FELLATOR S
FELLED

FELLER S
REFELL
FELLERS
FELLEST
FELLIES
FELLING
FELLNESS
FELLOE S
FELLOES
FELLOW S
FELLOWED
FELLOWLY
FELLOWS
FELLS
FELLY
FELON SY
FELONIES
OLEFINES
FELONRY
FELONS
FELONY
FELSIC
FELSITE S
LEFTIES
LIEFEST
FELSITES
FELSITIC
FELSPAR S
FELSPARS
FELSTONE S
FELT S
LEFT
FELTED
FELTING S
FELTINGS
FELTLIKE
FELTS
LEFTS
FELUCCA S
FELUCCAS
FELWORT S
FELWORTS
FEM ES
FEMALE S
FEMALES
FEME S
FEMES
FEMINACY
FEMINIE
FEMININE S
FEMINISE DS
FEMINISM S
FEMINIST S
FEMINITY
FEMINIZE DS
FEMME S
FEMMES
FEMORA L
FOAMER
FEMORAL
FEMS
FEMUR S
FUMER
FEMURS
FUMERS
FEN DS
FENAGLE DS
FENAGLED
FENAGLES
FENCE DRS
FENCED
FENCER S
FENCEROW S
FENCERS
FENCES
FENCIBLE S
FENCING S
FENCINGS
FEND S
FENDED
DEFEND
FENDER S
FENDERED
DEFENDER
FENDERS
FENDING

FENDS
FENESTRA EL
FASTENER
REFASTEN
FENLAND S
FENLANDS
FENNEC S
FENNECS
FENNEL S
FENNELS
FENNIER
FENNIEST
FENNY
FENS
FENTANYL S
FENTHION S
FENURON S
FENURONS
FEOD S
FEODARY
FORAYED
FEODS
FEOFF S
FEOFFED
FEOFFEE S
FEOFFEES
FEOFFER S
FEOFFERS
FEOFFING
FEOFFOR S
FEOFFORS
FEOFFS
FER EN
REF
FERACITY
FERAL S
FARLE FLARE
FERALS
FALSER
FARLES
FLARES
FERBAM S
FERBAMS
FERE S
FREE REEF
FERES
FREES REEFS
FERETORY
FERIA ELS
AFIRE
FERIAE
FAERIE
FERIAL
FERIAS
FRAISE
FERINE
REFINE
FERITIES
FEISTIER
FIERIEST
FERITY
FERLIE S
LIEFER
REFILE
RELIEF
FERLIES
REFILES
REFLIES
RELIEFS
FERLY
FLYER REFLY
FERMATA S
FERMATAS
FERMATE
FERMENT S
FERMENTS
FERMI S
FERMION S
FERMIONS
ENSIFORM
FERMIS
FERMIUM S
FERMIUMS
FERN SY
FERNERY
FERNIER
REFINER
FERNIEST
INFESTER

FERNINST
FERNLESS
FLENSERS
FRESNELS
FERNLIKE
FERNS
FERNY
FEROCITY
FERRATE S
FERRATES
FERREL S
FERRELED
FERRELS
FERREOUS
FERRET SY
FERRETED
FERRETER S
FERRETS
FERRETY
FERRIAGE S
FERRIC
FERRIED
REFIRED
REFRIED
FERRIES
REFIRES
REFRIES
FERRITE S
FERRITES
FERRITIC
TERRIFIC
FERRITIN S
FERROUS
FURORES
FERRULE DS
FERRULED
FERRULES
FERRUM S
FERRUMS
FERRY
FRYER REFRY
FERRYING
REFRYING
FERRYMAN
FERRYMEN
FERTILE
FERULA ES
EARFUL
FERULAE
FERULAS
EARFULS
REFUSAL
FERULE DS
FUELER
REFUEL
FERULED
FERULES
FUELERS
REFUELS
FERULING
FERVENCY
FERVENT
FERVID
FERVIDLY
FERVOR S
FERVORS
FERVOUR S
FERVOURS
FES ST
EFS
FESCUE S
FESCUES
FESS E
FESSE DS
FESSED
FESSES
FESSING
FESSWISE
FEST S
EFTS FETS
FESTAL
FESTALLY
FESTER S
FREEST
FESTERED
FESTERS
FESTIVAL S
FESTIVE

FESTOON S
EFTSOON
FESTOONS
EFTSOONS
FESTS
FET AES
EFT
FETA LS
FATE FEAT
FETAL
FETAS
FATES FEAST
FEATS
FETATION S
FETCH
FETCHED
FETCHER S
FETCHERS
FETCHES
FETCHING
FETE DS
FEET
FETED
FETERITA S
FETES
FETIAL S
FETIALES
FEALTIES
LEAFIEST
FETIALIS
FILIATES
FETIALS
SEALIFT
FETICH
FETICHES
CHIEFEST
FETICIDE S
FETID
FETIDITY
FETIDLY
FETING
FETISH
FETISHES
FETLOCK S
FETLOCKS
FETOLOGY
FETOR S
FORTE OFTER
FETORS
FOREST
FORTES
FOSTER
SOFTER
FETS
EFTS FEST
FETTED
FETTER S
FETTERED
FETTERER S
FETTERS
FETTING
FETTLE DS
FETTLED
FETTLES
LEFTEST
FETTLING S
FETUS
FETUSES
FEU DS
FEUAR S
FEUARS
FEUD S
FEUDAL
FEUDALLY
FEUDARY
FEUDED
FEUDING
FEUDIST S
FEUDISTS
FEUDS
FUSED
FEUED
FEUING
FEUS
FUSE
FEVER S
FEVERED
FEVERFEW S
FEVERING

FEVERISH
FEVEROUS
FEVERS
FEW
FEWER
FEWEST
FEWNESS
FEWTRILS
FEY
FEYER
REEFY
FEYEST
FEYLY
FEYNESS
FEZ
FEZES
FEZZED
FEZZES
FEZZY
FIACRE S
FARCIE
FIACRES
FARCIES
FIANCE ES
FIANCEE S
FAIENCE
FIANCEES
FAIENCES
FIANCES
FANCIES
FASCINE
FIAR S
FAIR
FIARS
FAIRS
FIASCHI
FIASCO S
FIASCOES
FIASCOS
FIAT S
FIATS
FIB S
FIBBED
FIBBER S
FIBBERS
FIBBING
FIBER S
BRIEF FIBRE
FIBERED
BRIEFED
DEBRIEF
FIBERIZE DS
FIBERS
BRIEFS
FIBRES
FIBRANNE S
FIBRE S
BRIEF FIBER
FIBRES
BRIEFS
FIBERS
FIBRIL S
FIBRILLA ER
FIBRILS
FIBRIN S
FIBRINS
FIBROID S
FIBROIDS
FIBROIN S
FIBROINS
FIBROMA S
FIBROMAS
FIBROSES
FIBROSIS
FIBROTIC
FIBROUS
FIBS
FIBSTER S
FIBSTERS
FIBULA ERS
FIBULAE
FIBULAR
FIBULAS
FICE S
FICES
FICHE S
CHIEF
FICHES
CHIEFS
FICHU S
FICHUS
FICIN S
FICINS
FICKLE R
FICKLER
FLICKER
FICKLEST
FICKLY
FICO
COIF FOCI
FICOES
FICTILE
FICTION S
FICTIONS
FICTIVE
FICUS
CUIFS
FICUSES
FID OS
DIF
FIDDLE DRS
FIDDLED
FIDDLER S
FIDDLERS
FIDDLES
FIDDLING
FIDDLY
FIDEISM S
FIDEISMS
FIDEIST S
FIDEISTS
FIDELITY
FIDGE DST
FIDGED
FIDGES
FIDGET SY
GIFTED
FIDGETED
FIDGETER S
FIDGETS
FIDGETY
FIDGING
FIDO S
FIDOS
FIDS
DIFS
FIDUCIAL
FIE F
FIEF S
FIFE
FIEFDOM S
FIEFDOMS
FIEFS
FIFES
A FIELD S
FELID FILED
FLIED
FIELDED
DEFILED
FIELDER S
DEFILER
REFILED
FIELDERS
DEFILERS
FIELDING
DEFILING
FIELDS
FELIDS
FIEND S
FINED
FIENDISH
FINISHED
FIENDS
FIERCE R
FIERCELY
FIERCER
FIERCEST
FIERIER
REIFIER
FIERIEST
FEISTIER
FERITIES
FIERILY
FIERY
REIFY
FIESTA S
FIESTAS
FISSATE
FIFE DRS
FIEF
FIFED
FIFER S
FIFERS
FIFES
FIEFS
FIFING
FIFTEEN S
FIFTEENS
FIFTH S
FIFTHLY
FIFTHS
FIFTIES
IFFIEST
FIFTIETH S
FIFTY
FIFTYISH
FIG S
FIGEATER S
FIGGED
FIGGING
FIGHT S
FIGHTER S
FREIGHT
REFIGHT
FIGHTERS
FREIGHTS
REFIGHTS
FIGHTING S
FIGHTS
FIGMENT S
FIGMENTS
FIGS
FIGULINE S
FIGURAL
FIGURANT S
FIGURATE
FRUITAGE
FIGURE DRS
FIGURED
FIGURER S
FIGURERS
FIGURES
FIGURINE S
FIGURING
FIGWORT S
FIGWORTS
FIL AELMOS
FILA R
ALIF FAIL
FILAGREE DS
FILAMENT S
FILAR
FLAIR FRAIL
FILAREE S
LEAFIER
FILAREES
FILARIA ELN
FILARIAE
FILARIAL
FILARIAN
FILARIID S
FILATURE S
FAULTIER
FILBERT S
FILBERTS
FILCH
FILCHED
FILCHER S
FILCHERS
FILCHES
FILCHING
FILE DRST
LIEF LIFE
FILEABLE
FILED
FELID FIELD
FLIED
FILEFISH
FILEMOT
FILENAME S
FILER S
FLIER LIFER
RIFLE
FILERS
FLIERS
LIFERS
RIFLES
FILES
FLIES
FILET S
FLITE
FILETED
FILETING
FILETS
FLIEST
FLITES
ITSELF
STIFLE
FILIAL
FILIALLY
FILIATE DS
FILIATED
FILIATES
FETIALIS
FILIBEG S
FILIBEGS
FILICIDE S
FILIFORM
FILIGREE DS
FILING S
FILINGS
FILISTER S
FILL EOSY
FILLABLE
FALLIBLE
FILLE DRST
FILLED
FILLER S
REFILL
FILLERS
REFILLS
FILLES
FILLET S
FILLETED
FILLETS
FILLIES
FILLING S
FILLINGS
FILLIP S
FILLIPED
FILLIPS
FILLO S
FILLOS
FOLLIS
FILLS
FILLY
FILM ISY
FILMABLE
FILMCARD S
FILMDOM S
FILMDOMS
FILMED
FILMER S
REFILM
FILMERS
REFILMS
FILMGOER S
FILMI CS
FILMIC
FILMIER
FILMIEST
FILMILY
FILMING
FILMIS
FILMLAND S
FILMLESS
FILMLIKE
FILMS
FILMSET S
LEFTISM
FILMSETS
LEFTISMS
FILMY
FILO S
FOIL
FILOS E
FOILS
FILOSE
FILS
FILTER S
LIFTER
TRIFLE
FILTERED
FILTERER S
REFILTER
FILTERS
LIFTERS
STIFLER
TRIFLES
FILTH SY
FILTHIER
FILTHILY
FILTHS
FILTHY
FILTRATE DS
FILUM
FIMBLE S
FIMBLES
FIMBRIA EL
FIMBRIAE
FIMBRIAL
FIN DEKOS
FINABLE
FINAGLE DRS
LEAFING
FINAGLED
FINAGLER S
FINAGLES
FINAL ES
FINALE S
FINALES
FINALIS EMT
FINIALS
FINALISE DS
FINALISM S
FINALIST S
TAILFINS
FINALITY
FINALIZE DR S
FINALLY
FINALS
FINANCE DS
FINANCED
FINANCES
FINBACK S
FINBACKS
FINCA S
FINCAS
FINCH
FINCHES
FIND S
FINDABLE
FINDER S
FRIEND
REDFIN
REFIND
FINDERS
FRIENDS
REDFINS
REFINDS
FINDING S
FINDINGS
FINDS
FINE DRS
NEIF
FINEABLE
FINED
FIEND
FINELY
FINENESS
FINER Y
INFER
FINERIES
FINERY
FINES T
NEIFS
FINESPUN
FINESSE DS
FINESSED
FINESSES
FINEST
FEINTS
INFEST
FINFISH
FINFOOT S
FINFOOTS
FINGER S
FRINGE
FINGERED
FINGERER S
FINGERS
FRINGES
FINIAL S
FINIALED
FINIALS
FINALIS
FINICAL
FINICKIN G
FINICKY
FINIKIN G
FINIKING
FINING S
FININGS
FINIS H
FINISES
FINISH
FINISHED
FIENDISH
FINISHER S
REFINISH
FINISHES
FINITE S
FINITELY
FELINITY
FINITES
NIFTIES
FINITO
FINITUDE S
FINK S
FINKED
KNIFED
FINKING
KNIFING
FINKS
FINLESS
FINLIKE
FINMARK S
FINMARKS
FINNED
FINNICKY
FINNIER
FINNIEST
FINNING
FINNMARK S
FINNY
FINO S
FOIN INFO
FINOCHIO S
FINOS
FOINS INFOS
FINS
FIORD S
FIORDS
FIPPLE S
FIPPLES
FIQUE S
FIQUES
FIR EMNS
RIF
A FIRE DRS
REIF RIFE
FIREABLE
AFEBRILE
BALEFIRE
FIREARM S
FIREARMS
FIREBACK S
BACKFIRE
FIREBALL S
FIREBASE S
FIREBIRD S
FIREBOAT S
BIFORATE
FIREBOMB S
FIREBOX
FIREBRAT S
FIREBUG S
FIREBUGS
FIRECLAY S
FIRED
FRIED
FIREDAMP S
FIREDOG S
FIREDOGS
FIREFANG S
FIREFLY
FIREHALL S
FIRELESS
FIRELIT
FIRELOCK S
FLOCKIER
FIREMAN
FIREMEN
FIREPAN S
FIREPANS
PANFRIES
FIREPINK S
FIREPLUG S
FIREPOT S
PIEFORT
FIREPOTS
PIEFORTS
POSTFIRE
FIRER S
FRIER RIFER
FIREROOM S
FIRERS
FRIERS
FIRES
FRIES FRISE
REIFS SERIF
FIRESHIP S
FIRESIDE S
DEIFIERS
EDIFIERS
FIRETRAP S
FIREWALL S
FIREWEED S
FIREWOOD S
FIREWORK S
FIREWORM S
FIRING S
FIRINGS
FIRKIN S
FIRKINS
FIRM S
FIRMAN S
FIRMANS
FIRMED
FIRMER S
FIRMERS
FIRMEST
FIRMING
FIRMLY
FIRMNESS
FIRMS
FIRMWARE S
FIRN S
FIRNS
FIRRIER
FIRRIEST
FIRRY
FIRS T
RIFS
FIRST S
FRITS RIFTS
FIRSTLY
FIRSTS
FIRTH S
FRITH
FIRTHS
FRITHS
SHRIFT
FISC S
FISCAL S
CALIFS
FISCALLY
FISCALS
FISCS
FISH Y
FISHABLE
FISHBOLT S
FISHBONE S
BONEFISH
FISHBOWL S
BLOWFISH
FISHED
FISHER SY
SHERIF
FISHERS
SERFISH
SHERIFS
FISHERY
FISHES
FISHEYE S
FISHEYES

FISHGIG S
FISHGIGS
FISHHOOK S
FISHIER
FISHIEST
FISHILY
FISHING S
FISHINGS
FISHKILL S
FISHLESS
FISHLIKE
FISHLINE S
FISHMEAL S
FISHNET S
FISHNETS
FISHPOLE S
FISHPOND S
FISHTAIL S
FISHWAY S
FISHWAYS
FISHWIFE
FISHWORM S
FISHY
FISSATE
FIESTAS
FISSILE
FISSION S
FISSIONS
FISSIPED S
FISSURAL
FISSURE DS
FUSSIER
FISSURED
SURFSIDE
FISSURES
FIST S
FITS SIFT
FISTED
SIFTED
FISTFUL S
FISTFULS
FISTIC
FISTING
SIFTING
FISTNOTE S
FISTS
SIFTS
FISTULA ERS
FISTULAE
FISTULAR
FISTULAS
FIT S
FITCH Y
FITCHEE
FITCHES
FITCHET S
FITCHETS
FITCHEW S
FITCHEWS
FITCHY
FITFUL
FITFULLY
FITLY
FITMENT S
FITMENTS
FITNESS
INFESTS
FITS
FIST SIFT
FITTABLE
FITTED
FITTER S
TITFER
FITTERS
TITFERS
FITTEST
FITTING S
FITTINGS
FIVE RS
FIVEFOLD
FIVEPINS
FIVER S
FIVERS
FIVES
FIX T
FIXABLE
FIXATE DS

FIXATED
FIXATES
FIXATIF S
FIXATIFS
FIXATING
FIXATION S
FIXATIVE S
FIXED
FIXEDLY
FIXER S
REFIX
FIXERS
FIXES
FIXING S
FIXINGS
FIXIT Y
FIXITIES
FIXITY
FIXT
FIXTURE S
FIXTURES
FIXURE S
FIXURES
FIZ Z
FIZGIG S
FIZGIGS
FIZZ Y
FIZZED
FIZZER S
FIZZERS
FRIZZES
FIZZES
FIZZIER
FIZZIEST
FIZZING
FIZZLE DS
FIZZLED
FIZZLES
FIZZLING
FIZZY
FJELD S
FJELDS
FJORD S
FJORDIC
FJORDS
FLAB S
FLABBIER
FLABBILY
FLABBY
FLABELLA
FLABS
FLACCID
FLACK S
FLACKED
FLACKERY
FLACKING
FLACKS
FLACON S
FALCON
FLACONS
FALCONS
FLAG S
FLAGELLA R
FLAGGED
FLAGGER S
FLAGGERS
FLAGGIER
FLAGGING S
FLAGGY
FLAGLESS
FLAGMAN
FLAGMEN
FLAGON S
FLAGONS
FLAGPOLE S
FLAGRANT
FLAGS
FLAGSHIP S
FLAIL S
FLAILED
FLAILING
FLAILS
FLAIR S
FILAR FRAIL

FLAIRS
FRAILS
FLAK EY
FLAKE DRSY
FLAKED
FLAKER S
FLAKERS
FLAKES
FLAKEY
FLAKIER
FLAKIEST
FLAKILY
FLAKING
FLAKY
FLAM ESY
FLAMBE ES
FLAMBEAU SX
FLAMBEE D
FLAMBEED
FLAMBES
A FLAME DNRS
FLEAM
FLAMED
MALFED
FLAMEN S
FLAMENCO S
FLAMENS
FLAMEOUT S
FLAMER S
FLAMERS
FLAMES
FLEAMS
FLAMIER
FLAMIEST
FLAMINES
INFLAMES
FLAMING O
FLAMINGO S
FLAMMED
FLAMMING
FLAMS
FLAMY
FLAN KS
FLANCARD S
FLANERIE S
FLANES
FLANEUR S
FRENULA
FUNERAL
FLANEURS
FUNERALS
FLANGE DRS
FLANGED
FLANGER S
FLANGERS
FLANGES
FLANGING
FLANK S
FLANKED
FLANKEN
FLANKER S
FLANKERS
FLANKING
FLANKS
FLANNEL S
FLANNELS
FLANS
FLAP S
FLAPERON S
FLAPJACK S
FLAPLESS
FLAPPED
FLAPPER S
FLAPPERS
FLAPPIER
FLAPPING
FLAPPY
FLAPS
FLARE DS
FARLE FERAL
FLARED
FARDEL
FLARES
FALSER
FARLES
FERALS
FLAREUP S

FLAREUPS
FLARING
FLASH Y
FLASHED
FLASHER S
FLASHERS
FLASHES
FLASHGUN S
FLASHIER
FLASHILY
FLASHING S
FLASHY
FLASK S
FLASKET S
FLASKETS
FLASKS
FLAT S
FLATBED S
FLATBEDS
FLATBOAT S
FALTBOAT
FLATCAP S
FLATCAPS
FLATCAR S
FRACTAL
FLATCARS
FRACTALS
FLATFEET
FLATFISH
FLATFOOT S
FLATHEAD S
FLATIRON S
INFLATOR
FLATLAND S
FLATLET S
FLATLETS
FLATLINE DR S
FLATLING S
FLATLONG
FLATLY
FLATMATE S
FLATNESS
FLATS
FLATTED
FLATTEN S
FLATTENS
FLATTER SY
FLATTERS
FLATTERY
FLATTEST
FLATTING
FLATTISH
FLATTOP S
FLATTOPS
FLATUS
FAULTS
FLATUSES
SULFATES
FLATWARE S
FLATWASH
FLATWAYS
FLATWISE
FLAWIEST
FLATWORK S
FLATWORM S
FLAUNT SY
FLAUNTED
FLAUNTER S
FLAUNTS
FLAUNTY
FLAUTA S
FLAUTAS
FLAUTIST S
FLAVANOL S
FLAVIN ES
FLAVINE S
FLAVINES
FLAVINS
FLAVONE S
FLAVONES
FLAVONOL S
FLAVOR SY
FLAVORED
FLAVORER S
FLAVORS

FLAVORY
FLAVOUR SY
FLAVOURS
FLAVOURY
FLAW SY
FLAWED
FLAWIER
FLAWIEST
FLATWISE
FLAWING
FLAWLESS
FLAWS
FLAWY
FLAX Y
FALX
FLAXEN
FLAXES
FLAXIER
FLAXIEST
FLAXSEED S
FLAXY
FLAY S
FLAYED
DEAFLY
FLAYER S
FLAYERS
FLAYING
FLAYS
FLEA MS
ALEF FEAL
LEAF
FLEABAG S
FLEABAGS
FLEABANE S
FLEABITE S
FLEAM S
FLAME
FLEAMS
FLAMES
FLEAPIT S
FLEAPITS
FLEAS
ALEFS FALSE
LEAFS
FLEAWORT S
FLECHE S
FLEECH
FLECHES
FLECK SY
FLECKED
FLECKING
FLECKS
FLECKY
FECKLY
FLECTION S
FLED
DELF
FLEDGE DS
FLEDGED
FLEDGES
FLEDGIER
FLEDGING
FLEDGY
FLEE RST
FEEL
FLEECE DRS
FLEECED
FLEECER S
FLEECERS
FLEECES
FLEECH
FLECHE
FLEECHED
FLEECHES
FLEECIER
FLEECILY
FLEECING
FLEECY
FLEEING
FEELING
FLEER S
REFEL
FLEERED
FLEERING
FLEERS
REFELS
FLEES
FEELS

FLEET S
FLEETED
FLEETER
FLEETEST
FLEETING
FLEETLY
FLEETS
FLEHMEN S
FLEHMENS
FLEISHIG
FLEMISH
HIMSELF
FLENCH
FLENCHED
FLENCHES
FLENSE DRS
FLENSED
FLENSER S
FRESNEL
FLENSERS
FERNLESS
FRESNELS
FLENSES
FLENSING
FLESH Y
SHELF
FLESHED
FLESHER S
HERSELF
FLESHERS
FLESHES
FLESHIER
FLESHILY
ELFISHLY
FLESHING S
FLESHLY
FLESHPOT S
FLESHY
FLETCH
FLETCHED
FLETCHER S
FLETCHES
FLEURON S
FLEURONS
FLEURY
FLEW S
FLEWS
FLEX
FLEXAGON S
FLEXED
FLEXES
FLEXIBLE
FLEXIBLY
FLEXILE
FLEXING
FLEXION S
FLEXIONS
FLEXOR S
FLEXORS
FLEXTIME RS
FLEXUOSE
FLEXUOUS
FLEXURAL
FLEXURE S
FLEXURES
REFLUXES
FLEY S
FLEYED
FLEYING
FLEYS
FLIC KS
FLICHTER S
FLICK S
FLICKED
FLICKER SY
FICKLER
FLICKERS
FLICKERY
FLICKING
FLICKS
FLICS
FLIED
FELID FIELD
FILED
FLIER S
FILER LIFER
RIFLE

FLIERS
FILERS
LIFERS
RIFLES
FLIES T
FILES
FLIEST
FILETS
FLITES
ITSELF
STIFLE
FLIGHT SY
FLIGHTED
FLIGHTS
FLIGHTY
FLIMFLAM S
FLIMSIER
FLIMSIES T
MISFILES
FLIMSILY
FLIMSY
FLINCH
FLINCHED
FLINCHER S
FLINCHES
FLINDER S
FLINDERS
FLING S
FLINGER S
FLINGERS
FLINGING
FLINGS
FLINKITE S
FLINT SY
FLINTED
FLINTIER
FLINTILY
FLINTING
FLINTS
FLINTY
FLIP S
FLIPBOOK S
FLIPFLOP S
FLIPPANT
FLIPPED
FLIPPER S
FLIPPERS
FLIPPEST
FLIPPING
FLIPPY
FLIPS
FLIR ST
FLIRS
FLIRT SY
FLIRTED
TRIFLED
FLIRTER S
TRIFLER
FLIRTERS
TRIFLERS
FLIRTIER
FLIRTING
TRIFLING
FLIRTS
FLIRTY
FLIT ES
LIFT
FLITCH
FLITCHED
FLITCHES
FLITE DS
FILET
FLITED
LIFTED
FLITES
FILETS
FLIEST
ITSELF
STIFLE
FLITING
LIFTING
FLITS
LIFTS
FLITTED
FLITTER S
FLITTERS
FLITTING
FLIVVER S

FLIVVERS
A FLOAT SY
ALOFT FLOTA
FLOATAGE S
FLOATED
FLOATEL S
FLOATELS
FLOATER S
REFLOAT
FLOATERS
FORESTAL
REFLOATS
FLOATIER
FLOATING
FLOATS
FLOTAS
FLOATY
FLOC KS
FLOCCED
FLOCCI
FLOCCING
FLOCCOSE
FLOCCULE S
FLOCCULI
FLOCCUS
FLOCK SY
FLOCKED
FLOCKIER
FIRELOCK
FLOCKING S
FLOCKS
FLOCKY
FLOCS
FLOE S
FLOES
FLOG S
GOLF
FLOGGED
FLOGGER S
FLOGGERS
FLOGGING S
FLOGS
GOLFS
FLOKATI S
FLOKATIS
FLONG S
FLONGS
FLOOD S
FLOODED
FLOODER S
FLOORED
REFLOOD
FLOODERS
REFLOODS
FLOODING
FLOODLIT
FLOODS
FLOODWAY S
FLOOEY
FLOOIE
FLOOR S
FLOORAGE S
FLOORED
FLOODER
REFLOOD
FLOORER S
FLOORERS
FLOORING S
FLOORS
FLOOSIE S
FOLIOSE
FLOOSIES
FLOOSY
FLOOZIE S
FLOOZIES
FLOOZY
FLOP S
FLOPOVER S
FLOPPED
FLOPPER S
FLOPPERS
FLOPPIER
FLOPPIES T
FLOPPILY
FLOPPING
FLOPPY
FLOPS
FLORA ELS
FLORAE
LOAFER
FLORAL S
FLORALLY
FLORALS
FLORAS
SAFROL
FLORENCE S
FLORET S
LOFTER
FLORETS
LOFTERS
FLORID
FLORIDLY
FLORIGEN S
FLORIN S
FLORINS
FLORIST S
FLORISTS
FLORUIT S
FLORUITS
FLOSS Y
FLOSSED
FLOSSER S
FLOSSERS
FLOSSES
FLOSSIE RS
FLOSSIER
FLOSSIES T
FLOSSILY
FLOSSING
FLOSSY
FLOTA S
ALOFT FLOAT
FLOTAGE S
FLOTAGES
FLOTAS
FLOATS
FLOTILLA S
FLOTSAM S
FLOTSAMS
FLOUNCE DS
FLOUNCED
FLOUNCES
FLOUNCY
FLOUNDER S
UNFOLDER
FLOUR SY
FLUOR
FLOURED
FLOURING
FLOURISH
FLOURS
FLUORS
FLOURY
FLOUT S
FLOUTED
FLOUTER S
FLOUTERS
FLOUTING
FLOUTS
FLOW NS
FOWL WOLF
FLOWAGE S
FLOWAGES
FLOWED
FOWLED
WOLFED
FLOWER SY
FOWLER
REFLOW
WOLFER
FLOWERED
DEFLOWER
REFLOWED
FLOWERER S
REFLOWER
FLOWERET S
FLOWERS
FOWLERS
REFLOWS
WOLFERS
FLOWERY
FLOWING
FOWLING
WOLFING
FLOWN
FLOWS
FOWLS WOLFS
FLU BESX
FLUB S
FLUBBED
FLUBBER S
FLUBBERS
FLUBBING
FLUBDUB S
FLUBDUBS
FLUBS
FLUE DS
FUEL
FLUED
FLUENCY
FLUENT
UNFELT
FLUENTLY
FLUERIC S
LUCIFER
FLUERICS
LUCIFERS
FLUES
FUELS FUSEL
FLUFF SY
FLUFFED
FLUFFER S
FLUFFERS
FLUFFIER
FLUFFILY
FLUFFING
FLUFFS
FLUFFY
FLUID S
FLUIDAL
FLUIDIC S
FLUIDICS
FLUIDISE DS
FLUIDITY
FLUIDIZE DR S
FLUIDLY
FLUIDRAM S
FLUIDS
SULFID
FLUISH
FLUKE DSY
FLUKED
FLUKES
FLUKEY
FLUKIER
FLUKIEST
LUTEFISK
FLUKILY
FLUKING
FLUKY
FLUME DS
FLUMED
FLUMES
FLUMING
FLUMMERY
FLUMMOX
FLUMP S
FLUMPED
FLUMPING
FLUMPS
FLUNG
FLUNK SY
FLUNKED
FLUNKER S
FLUNKERS
FLUNKEY S
FLUNKEYS
FLUNKIE S
FLUNKIES
FLUNKING
FLUNKS
FLUNKY
FLUOR S
FLOUR
FLUORENE S
FLUORIC
FLUORID ES
FLUORIDE S
FLUORIDS
FLUORIN ES
FLUORINE S
FLUORINS
FLUORITE S
FLUORS
FLOURS
FLURRIED
FLURRIES
FLURRY
FLUS H
FLUSH
FLUSHED
FLUSHER S
FLUSHERS
FLUSHES T
FLUSHEST
FLUSHING
LUNGFISH
FLUSTER S
FLUTERS
RESTFUL
FLUSTERS
TURFLESS
FLUTE DRSY
FLUTED
FLUTER S
FLUTERS
FLUSTER
RESTFUL
FLUTES
FLUTEY
FLUTIER
FLUTIEST
FLUTING S
FLUTINGS
FLUTIST S
FLUTISTS
A FLUTTER SY
FLUTTERS
FLUTTERY
FLUTY
FLUYT
FLUVIAL
FLUX
FLUXED
FLUXES
FLUXGATE S
FLUXING
FLUXION S
FLUXIONS
FLUYT S
FLUTY
FLUYTS
FLY
FLYABLE
FLYAWAY S
FLYAWAYS
FLYBELT S
FLYBELTS
FLYBLEW
FLYBLOW NS
BLOWFLY
FLYBLOWN
FLYBLOWS
FLYBOAT S
FLYBOATS
FLYBOY S
FLYBOYS
FLYBY S
FLYBYS
FLYER S
FERLY REFLY
FLYERS
FLYING S
FLYINGS
FLYLEAF
FLYLESS
FLYMAN
FLYMEN
FLYOFF S
FLYOFFS
FLYOVER S
OVERFLY
FLYOVERS
FLYPAPER S
FLYPAST S
FLYPASTS
FLYSCH
FLYSCHES
FLYSHEET S
FLYSPECK S
FLYTE DS
LEFTY
FLYTED
DEFTLY
FLYTES
FLYTIER S
FLYTIERS
FLYTING S
FLYTINGS
FLYTRAP S
FLYTRAPS
FLYWAY S
FLYWAYS
FLYWHEEL S
FOAL S
LOAF
FOALED
LOAFED
FOALING
LOAFING
FOALS
LOAFS
FOAM SY
FOAMABLE
FOAMED
DEFOAM
FOAMER S
FEMORA
FOAMERS
FOAMIER
FOAMIEST
FOAMILY
FOAMING
FOAMLESS
FOAMLIKE
FOAMS
FOAMY
FOB S
FOBBED
FOBBING
FOBS
FOCACCIA S
FOCAL
FOCALISE DS
FOCALIZE DS
FOCALLY
FOCI
COIF FICO
FOCUS
FOCUSED
DEFOCUS
FOCUSER S
REFOCUS
FOCUSERS
FOCUSES
FUCOSES
FOCUSING
FOCUSSED
FOCUSSES
FODDER S
FORDED
FODDERED
FODDERS
FODGEL
GOLFED
FOE S
FOEHN S
FOEHNS
FOEMAN
FOEMEN
FOES
FOETAL
FOLATE
FOETID
FOETOR S
FOOTER
FOETORS
FOOTERS
FOETUS
FOETUSES
FOG SY
FOGBOUND
FOGBOW S
FOGBOWS
FOGDOG S
FOGDOGS
FOGEY S
FOGEYISH
FOGEYISM S
FOGEYS
FOGFRUIT S
FOGGAGE S
FOGGAGES
FOGGED
FOGGER S
FOGGERS
FOGGIER
FOGGIEST
FOGGILY
FOGGING
FOGGY
FOGHORN S
FOGHORNS
FOGIE S
FOGIES
FOGLESS
FOGS
FOGY
FOGYISH
FOGYISM S
FOGYISMS
FOH N
FOHN S
FOHNS
FOIBLE S
FOIBLES
FOIL S
FILO
FOILABLE
FOILED
FOILING
FOILS
FILOS
FOILSMAN
FOILSMEN
FOIN S
FINO INFO
FOINED
FOINING
FOINS
FINOS INFOS
FOISON S
FOISONS
FOIST S
FOISTED
FOISTING
FOISTS
FOLACIN S
FOLACINS
FOLATE S
FOETAL
FOLATES
FOLD S
FOLDABLE
FOLDAWAY S
FOLDBOAT S
FOLDED
FOLDER S
REFOLD
ROLFED
FOLDEROL S
FOLDERS
REFOLDS
FOLDING
FOLDOUT S
FOLDOUTS
FOLDS
FOLDUP S
UPFOLD
FOLDUPS
UPFOLDS
FOLEY S
FOLEYS
FOLIA R
FOLIAGE DS
FOLIAGED
FOLIAGES
FOLIAR
FOLIATE DS
FOLIATED
FOLIATES
FOLIC
FOLIO S
FOLIOED
FOLIOING
FOLIOS E
FOLIOSE
FLOOSIE
FOLIOUS
FOLIUM S
FOLIUMS
FOLK SY
FOLKIE RS
FOLKIER
FOLKIES T
FOLKIEST
FOLKISH
FOLKLIFE
FOLKLIKE
FOLKLORE S
FOLKMOOT S
FOLKMOT ES
FOLKMOTE S
FOLKMOTS
FOLKS Y
FOLKSIER
FOLKSILY
FOLKSONG S
FOLKSY
FOLKTALE S
FOLKWAY S
FOLKWAYS
FOLKY
FOLLES
FOLLICLE S
FOLLIES
FOLLIS
FILLOS
FOLLOW S
FOLLOWED
FOLLOWER S
FOLLOWS
FOLLOWUP S
FOLLY
FOMENT S
FOMENTED
FOMENTER S
FOMENTS
FOMITE S
FOMITES
FON DST
FOND SU
FONDANT S
FONDANTS
FONDED
FONDER
FONDEST
FONDING
FONDLE DRS
ENFOLD
FONDLED
FONDLER S
FONDLERS
FONDLES
ENFOLDS
FONDLING S
FONDLY
FONDNESS
FONDS
FONDU ES
FOUND
FONDUE DS
FONDUED
FOUNDED
FONDUES
FONDUING
FOUNDING
FONDUS
FOUNDS
FONS
FONT S
FONTAL
FONTANEL S
FONTINA S
FONTINAS
FONTS
FOOD S

FOODIE S
FOODIES
FOODLESS
FOODS
FOODWAYS
FOOFARAW S
FOOL S
LOOF
FOOLED
FOOLERY
FOOLFISH
FOOLING
FOOLISH
FOOLS
LOOFS
FOOLSCAP S
FOOSBALL S
A FOOT SY
FOOTAGE S
FOOTAGES
FOOTBAG S
FOOTBAGS
FOOTBALL S
FOOTBATH S
FOOTBOY S
FOOTBOYS
FOOTED
FOOTER S
FOETOR
FOOTERS
FOETORS
FOOTFALL S
FOOTGEAR S
FOOTHILL S
FOOTHOLD S
FOOTIE RS
FOOTIER
FOOTIES T
FOOTSIE
FOOTIEST
FOOTING S
FOOTINGS
FOOTLE DRS
FOOTLED
FOOTLER S
FOOTLERS
FOOTLES S
FOOTLESS
FOOTLIKE
FOOTLING
FOOTMAN
FOOTMARK S
FOOTMEN
FOOTNOTE DS
FOOTPACE S
FOOTPAD S
FOOTPADS
FOOTPATH S
FOOTRACE S
FOOTREST S
FOOTROPE S
FOOTS Y
FOOTSIE S
FOOTIES
FOOTSIES
FOOTSLOG S
FOOTSORE
FOOTSTEP S
FOOTSY
FOOTWALL S
FOOTWAY S
FOOTWAYS
FOOTWEAR
FOOTWORK S
FOOTWORN
FOOTY
FOOZLE DRS
FOOZLED
FOOZLER S
FOOZLERS
FOOZLES
FOOZLING
FOP S
FOPPED
FOPPERY

FOPPING
FOPPISH
FOPS
FOR ABDEKMT
FRO
FORA MY
FARO
FORAGE DRS
FORAGED
FORAGER S
FORAGERS
FORAGES
FORAGING
FORAM S
FORAMEN S
FOREMAN
FORAMENS
FORAMINA L
FORAMS
FORAY S
FORAYED
FEODARY
FORAYER S
FORAYERS
FORAYING
FORAYS
FORB SY
FORBAD E
FORBADE
FORBARE
FORBEAR
FORBEAR S
FORBARE
FORBEARS
FORBID S
FORBIDAL S
FORBIDS
FORBODE DS
FORBODED
FORBODES
FORBORE
FORBORNE
FORBS
FORBY E
FORBYE
FOREBY
FORCE DRS
FORCED
FORCEDLY
FORCEFUL
FORCEPS
FORCER S
FORCERS
FORCES
FRESCO
FORCIBLE
FORCIBLY
FORCING
FORCIPES
FORD OS
FORDABLE
FORDED
FODDER
FORDID
FORDING
FORDLESS
FORDO
FORDOES
FORDOING
FORDONE
FORDS
A FORE S
FROE
FOREARM S
FOREARMS
FOREBAY S
FOREBAYS
FOREBEAR S
FOREBODE DR S
FOREBODY
FOREBOOM S
FOREBY E
FORBYE
FOREBYE
FORECAST S
FOREDATE DS

FOREDECK S
FOREDID
FOREDO
ROOFED
FOREDOES
FOREDONE
FOREDOOM S
FOREFACE S
FOREFEEL S
FOREFEET
FOREFELT
FOREFEND S
OFFENDER
FOREFOOT
FOREGO
FOREGOER S
FOREGOES
FOREGONE
FOREGUT S
FOREGUTS
A FOREHAND S
FOREHEAD S
FOREHOOF S
FOREIGN
FOREKNEW
FOREKNOW NS
FORELADY
FORELAND S
FORELEG S
FORELEGS
FORELIMB S
FORELOCK S
FOREMAN
FORAMEN
FOREMAST S
FORMATES
FOREMEN
FOREMILK S
FOREMOST
FORENAME DS
FORENOON S
FORENSIC S
COINFERS
CONIFERS
FORNICES
FOREPART S
FOREPAST
FOREPAW S
FOREPAWS
FOREPEAK S
FOREPLAY S
FORERAN K
FORERANK S
FORERUN S
FORERUNS
FORES T
FROES
A FORESAID
FORESAIL S
FORESAW
FORESEE NRS
FORESEEN
FORESEER S
FORESEES
FORESHOW NS
FORESIDE S
FORESKIN S
FOREST S
FETORS
FORTES
FOSTER
SOFTER
FORESTAL L
FLOATERS
REFLOATS
FORESTAY S
FORESTED
DEFOREST
FOSTERED
FORESTER S
FOSTERER
REFOREST
FORESTRY
FORESTS
FOSTERS
FORETELL S
A FORETIME S

FORETOLD
FORETOP S
FORETOPS
FOREVER S
FOREVERS
FOREWARN S
FOREWENT
FOREWING S
FOREWORD S
FOREWORN
FOREYARD S
FORFEIT S
FORFEITS
FORFEND S
FORFENDS
FORGAT
FORGAVE
FORGE DRST
GOFER
FORGED
FORGER SY
FORGERS
FORGERY
FORGES
GOFERS
FORGET S
FORGETS
FORGING S
FORGINGS
FORGIVE NRS
FORGIVEN
FORGIVER S
FORGIVES
FORGO T
FORGOER S
FORGOERS
FORGOES
FORGOING
FORGONE
FORGOT
FORINT S
FORINTS
FORJUDGE DS
FORK SY
FORKBALL S
FORKED
FORKEDLY
FORKER S
FORKERS
FORKFUL S
FORKFULS
FORKSFUL
FORKIER
FORKIEST
FORKING
FORKLESS
FORKLIFT S
FORKLIKE
FORKS
FORKSFUL
FORKFULS
FORKY
FORLORN
FORM ES
FROM
FORMABLE
FORMABLY
FORMAL S
FORMALIN S
INFORMAL
FORMALLY
FORMALS
FORMANT S
FORMANTS
FORMAT ES
FORMATE S
FORMATES
FOREMAST
FORMATS
FORME DERS
FORMED
DEFORM
FORMEE
FORMER S
REFORM
FORMERLY

FORMERS
REFORMS
FORMES
FORMFUL
FORMIC A
FORMICA S
ACIFORM
FORMICAS
FORMING
FORMLESS
FORMOL S
FORMOLS
FORMS
FORMULA ES
FORMULAE
FUMAROLE
FORMULAS
FORMWORK S
FORMYL S
FORMYLS
FORNENT
FORNICAL
FORNICES
COINFERS
CONIFERS
FORENSIC
FORNIX
FORRADER
FORRIT
FORSAKE NRS
FORSAKEN
FORSAKER S
FORSAKES
FORSOOK
FORSOOTH
FORSPENT
FORSWEAR S
FORSWORE
FORSWORN
FORT EHSY
FORTE S
FETOR OFTER
FORTES
FETORS
FOREST
FOSTER
SOFTER
FORTH
FROTH
FORTIES
FORTIETH S
FORTIFY
FORTIS
FORTRESS
FORTS
FROST
FORTUITY
FORTUNE DS
FORTUNED
FORTUNES
FORTY
FORTYISH
FORUM S
FORUMS
FORWARD S
FROWARD
FORWARDS
FORWENT
FORWHY
FORWORN
S FORZANDI
S FORZANDO S
FOSS AE
FOSSA ES
SOFAS
FOSSAE
FOSSAS
FOSSATE
FOSSE S
FOSSES
FOSSETTE S
FOSSICK S
FOSSICKS
FOSSIL S
FOSSILS

FOSTER S
FETORS
FOREST
FORTES
SOFTER
FOSTERED
DEFOREST
FORESTED
FOSTERER S
FORESTER
REFOREST
FOSTERS
FORESTS
FOU LR
FOUETTE S
FOUETTES
FOUGHT
FOUGHTEN
A FOUL S
FOULARD S
FOULARDS
FOULED
FOULER
FOULEST
FOULING S
FOULINGS
FOULLY
FOULNESS
SULFONES
FOULS
SULFO
FOUND S
FONDU
FOUNDED
FONDUED
FOUNDER S
REFOUND
FOUNDERS
REFOUNDS
FOUNDING
FONDUING
FOUNDRY
FOUNDS
FONDUS
FOUNT S
FUTON
FOUNTAIN S
FOUNTS
FUTONS
FOUR S
FOURCHEE
FOUREYED
FOURFOLD
FOURGON S
FOURGONS
FOURPLEX
FOURS
FOURSOME S
FOURTEEN S
FOURTH S
FOURTHLY
FOURTHS
FOVEA ELS
FOVEAE
FOVEAL
FOVEAS
FOVEATE D
FOVEATED
FOVEOLA ERS
FOVEOLAE
FOVEOLAR
FOVEOLAS
FOVEOLE ST
FOVEOLES
FOVEOLET S
FOWL S
FLOW WOLF
FOWLED
FLOWED
WOLFED
FOWLER S
FLOWER
REFLOW
WOLFER
FOWLERS
FLOWERS
REFLOWS
WOLFERS

FOWLING S
FLOWING
WOLFING
FOWLINGS
FOWLPOX
FOWLS
FLOWS WOLFS
FOX Y
FOXED
FOXES
FOXFIRE S
FOXFIRES
FOXFISH
FOXGLOVE S
FOXHOLE S
FOXHOLES
FOXHOUND S
FOXHUNT S
FOXHUNTS
FOXIER
FOXIEST
FOXILY
FOXINESS
FOXING S
FOXINGS
FOXLIKE
FOXSKIN S
FOXSKINS
FOXTAIL S
FOXTAILS
FOXTROT S
FOXTROTS
FOXY
FOY S
FOYER S
FOYERS
FOYS
FOZIER
FOZIEST
FOZINESS
FOZY
FRABJOUS
FRACAS
FRACASES
FRACTAL S
FLATCAR
FRACTALS
FLATCARS
FRACTED
CRAFTED
FRACTI
FRACTION S
FRACTUR ES
FRACTURE DR S
FRACTURS
FRACTUS
FRAE
FARE FEAR
FRAENA
FRAENUM S
FRAENUMS
FRAG S
FRAGGED
FRAGGING S
FRAGILE
FRAGMENT S
FRAGRANT
FRAGS
FRAIL S
FILAR FLAIR
FRAILER
FRAILEST
FRAILLY
FRAILS
FLAIRS
FRAILTY
FRAISE S
FERIAS
FRAISES
FRAKTUR S
FRAKTURS
FRAMABLE
FARMABLE
FRAME DRS
FRAMED
FARMED

FRAMER S
FARMER
FRAMERS
FARMERS
FRAMES
FRAMING S
FARMING
FRAMINGS
FARMINGS
FRANC S
FRANCIUM S
FRANCIZE DS
FRANCS
FRANK S
FRANKED
FRANKER S
FRANKERS
FRANKEST
FRANKING
FRANKLIN S
FRANKLY
FRANKS
FRANTIC
INFARCT
INFRACT
FRAP S
FRAPPE DS
FRAPPED
FRAPPES
FRAPPING
FRAPS
FRASS
FRASSES
FRAT S
RAFT
FRATER S
RAFTER
FRATERS
RAFTERS
STRAFER
FRATS
RAFTS
FRAUD S
FRAUDS
FRAUGHT S
FRAUGHTS
FRAULEIN S
FRAY S
FRAYED
DEFRAY
FRAYING S
FRAYINGS
FRAYS
FRAZIL S
FRAZILS
FRAZZLE DS
FRAZZLED
FRAZZLES
FREAK SY
FAKER
FREAKED
FREAKIER
FREAKILY
FREAKING
FREAKISH
FREAKOUT S
FREAKS
FAKERS
FREAKY
FAKERY
FRECKLE DS
FRECKLED
FRECKLES
FRECKLY
FREE DRS
FERE REEF
FREEBASE DR S
FREEBEE S
FREEBEES
FREEBIE S
BEEFIER
FREEBIES
FREEBOOT S
FREEBORN
FREED
DEFER REFED
FREEDMAN
ENFRAMED

FREEDMEN
FREEDOM S
FREEDOMS
FREEFORM
FREEHAND
FREEHOLD S
FREEING
FEIGNER
REEFING
FREELOAD S
FREELY
FREEMAN
ENFRAME
FREEMEN
FREENESS
FREER S
FRERE REFER
FREERS
FRERES
REFERS
FREES T
FERES REEFS
FREESIA S
FAERIES
FREESIAS
FREEST
FESTER
FREEWARE S
FREEWAY S
FREEWAYS
FREEWILL
FREEZE RS
FREEZER S
FREEZERS
FREEZES
FREEZING
FREIGHT S
FIGHTER
REFIGHT
FREIGHTS
FIGHTERS
REFIGHTS
FREMD
FREMITUS
FRENA
FRENCH
FRENCHED
FRENCHES
FRENETIC S
INFECTER
REINFECT
FRENULA R
FLANEUR
FUNERAL
FRENULAR
FRENULUM S
FRENUM S
FRENUMS
SURFMEN
FRENZIED
FRENZIES
FRENZILY
FRENZY
FREQUENT S
FRERE S
FREER REFER
FRERES
FREERS
REFERS
FRESCO S
FORCES
FRESCOED
DEFORCES
FRESCOER S
FRESCOES
FRESCOS
A **FRESH**
FRESHED
FRESHEN S
FRESHENS
FRESHER
REFRESH
FRESHES T
FRESHEST
FRESHETS
FRESHET S
HEFTERS
FRESHETS
FRESHEST
FRESHING

FRESHLY
FRESHMAN
FRESHMEN
FRESNEL S
FLENSER
FRESNELS
FERNLESS
FLENSERS
FRET S
REFT TREF
FRETFUL
TRUFFLE
FRETLESS
FRETS
FRETSAW S
WAFTERS
FRETSAWS
FRETSOME
FRETTED
FRETTER S
FRETTERS
FRETTIER
FRETTING
FRETTY
FRETWORK S
FRIABLE
FRIAR SY
FRIARIES
RARIFIES
FRIARLY
FRIARS
FRIARY
RARIFY
FRIBBLE DRS
FRIBBLED
FRIBBLER S
FRIBBLES
FRICANDO
FRICTION S
FRIDGE S
FRIDGES
FRIED
FIRED
FRIEND S
FINDER
REDFIN
REFIND
FRIENDED
FRIENDLY
FRIENDS
FINDERS
REDFINS
REFINDS
FRIER S
FIRER RIFER
FRIERS
FIRERS
FRIES
FIRES FRISE
REIFS SERIF
FRIEZE S
FRIEZES
FRIG S
FRIGATE S
FRIGATES
FRIGES
GRIEFS
FRIGGED
FRIGGING
FRIGHT S
FRIGHTED
FRIGHTEN S
FRIGHTS
FRIGID
FRIGIDLY
FRIGS
FRIJOL E
FRIJOLE S
FRIJOLES
FRILL SY
FRILLED
FRILLER S
FRILLERS
FRILLIER
FRILLING S
FRILLS
FRILLY

FRINGE DS
FINGER
FRINGED
FRINGES
FINGERS
FRINGIER
REFIRING
FRINGING
FRINGY
FRYING
FRIPPERY
FRISBEE S
FRISBEES
FRISE ES
FIRES FRIES
REIFS SERIF
FRISEE S
FRISEES
FRISES
SERIFS
FRISETTE S
FRISEUR S
SURFIER
FRISEURS
FRISK SY
FRISKED
FRISKER S
FRISKERS
FRISKET S
FRISKETS
FRISKIER
FRISKILY
FRISKING
FRISKS
FRISKY
FRISSON S
FRISSONS
A **FRIT** HSTZ
RIFT
FRITES
REFITS
RESIFT
RIFEST
SIFTER
STRIFE
FRITH S
FIRTH
FRITHS
FIRTHS
SHRIFT
A **FRITS**
FIRST RIFTS
FRITT S
FRITTATA S
FRITTED
FRITTER S
FRITTERS
FRITTING
FRITTS
FRITZ
FRITZES
FRIVOL S
FRIVOLED
FRIVOLER S
FRIVOLS
FRIZ Z
FRIZED
FRIZER S
FRIZERS
FRIZES
FRIZETTE S
FRIZING
FRIZZ Y
FRIZZED
FRIZZER S
FRIZZERS
FRIZZES
FIZZERS
FRIZZIER
FRIZZIES T
FRIZZILY
FRIZZING
FRIZZLE DRS
FRIZZLED
FRIZZLER S
FRIZZLES
FRIZZLY
FRIZZY

FRO EGMW
FOR
FROCK S
FROCKED
DEFROCK
FROCKING
FROCKS
FROE S
FORE
FROES
FORES
FROG S
FROGEYE DS
FROGEYED
FROGEYES
FROGFISH
FROGGED
FROGGIER
FROGGING
FROGGY
FROGLET S
FROGLETS
FROGLIKE
FROGMAN
FROGMEN
FROGS
FROLIC S
FROLICKY
FROLICS
FROM
FORM
FROMAGE S
FROMAGES
FROMENTY
FROND S
FRONDED
FRONDEUR S
FRONDOSE
FRONDS
FRONS
FRONT S
FRONTAGE S
FRONTAL S
FRONTALS
FRONTED
FRONTER S
REFRONT
FRONTES
FRONTIER S
FRONTING
FRONTLET S
FRONTMAN
FRONTMEN
FRONTON S
FRONTONS
FRONTS
FRORE
FROSH
FROST SY
FORTS
FROSTBIT E
FROSTED S
DEFROST
FROSTEDS
DEFROSTS
FROSTIER
ROTIFERS
FROSTILY
FROSTING S
FROSTNIP S
FROSTS
FROSTY
FROTH SY
FORTH
FROTHED
FROTHER S
FROTHERS
FROTHIER
FROTHILY
FROTHING
FROTHS
FROTHY
FROTTAGE S
FROTTEUR S
FROUFROU S
FROUNCE DS

FROUNCED
UNFORCED
FROUNCES
FROUZIER
FROUZY
FROW NS
FROWARD
FORWARD
FROWN S
FROWNED
FROWNER S
FROWNERS
FROWNING
FROWNS
FROWS TY
FROWSIER
FROWST SY
FROWSTED
FROWSTS
FROWSTY
FROWSY
FROWZIER
FROWZILY
FROWZY
FROZE N
FROZEN
FROZENLY
FRUCTIFY
FRUCTOSE S
FRUG S
FRUGAL
FRUGALLY
FRUGGED
FRUGGING
FRUGS
FRUIT SY
FRUITAGE S
FIGURATE
FRUITED
FRUITER S
TURFIER
FRUITERS
FURRIEST
FRUITFUL
FRUITIER
FRUITILY
FRUITING
FRUITION S
FRUITLET S
FRUITS
FRUITY
FRUMENTY
FURMENTY
FRUMP SY
FRUMPIER
FRUMPILY
FRUMPISH
FRUMPS
FRUMPY
FRUSTA
FRUSTULE S
SULFURET
FRUSTUM S
FRUSTUMS
FRY
FRYABLE
FRYBREAD S
FRYER S
FERRY REFRY
FRYERS
FRYING
FRINGY
FRYPAN S
PANFRY
FRYPANS
FUB S
FUBBED
FUBBING
FUBS Y
FUBSIER
FUBSIEST
FUBSY
FUCHSIA S
FUCHSIAS
FUCHSIN ES
FUCHSINE S

FUCHSINS
FUCI
CUIF
FUCOID S
FUCOIDAL
FUCOIDS
FUCOSE S
FUCOSES
FOCUSES
FUCOUS
FUCUS
FUCUSES
FUD S
FUDDIES
FUDDLE DS
FUDDLED
FUDDLES
FUDDLING
FUDDY
FUDGE DS
FUDGED
FUDGES
FUDGING
FUDS
FUEHRER S
FUEHRERS
FUEL S
FLUE
FUELED
DEFUEL
FUELER S
FERULE
REFUEL
FUELERS
FERULES
REFUELS
FUELING
FUELLED
FUELLER S
FUELLERS
FUELLING
FUELS
FLUES FUSEL
FUELWOOD S
FUG SU
FUGACITY
FUGAL
FUGALLY
FUGATO S
FUGATOS
FUGGED
FUGGIER
FUGGIEST
FUGGILY
FUGGING
FUGGY
FUGIO S
FUGIOS
FUGITIVE S
FUGLE DS
FUGLED
GULFED
FUGLEMAN
FUGLEMEN
FUGLES
FUGLING
GULFING
FUGS
FUGU ES
FUGUE DS
FUGUED
FUGUES
FUGUING
FUGUIST S
FUGUISTS
FUGUS
FUHRER S
FUHRERS
FUJI S
FUJIS
FULCRA
CARFUL
FULCRUM S
FULCRUMS
FULFIL LS
FULFILL S
FULFILLS

FULFILS
FULGENT
FULGID
FULHAM S
FULHAMS
FULL SY
FULLAM S
FULLAMS
FULLBACK S
FULLED
FULLER SY
FULLERED
FULLERS
FULLERY
FULLEST
FULLFACE S
FULLING
FULLNESS
FULLS
FULLY
FULMAR S
ARMFUL
FULMARS
ARMFULS
ARMSFUL
FULMINE DS
FULMINED
UNFILMED
FULMINES
FULMINIC
FULNESS
FULSOME
FULVOUS
FUMARASE S
FUMARATE S
FUMARIC
FUMAROLE S
FORMULAE
FUMATORY
FUMBLE DRS
FUMBLED
FUMBLER S
FUMBLERS
FUMBLES
FUMBLING
FUME DRST
FUMED
FUMELESS
FUMELIKE
FUMER S
FEMUR
FUMERS
FEMURS
FUMES
FUMET S
FUMETS
FUMETTE S
FUMETTES
FUMIER
FUMIEST
FUMIGANT S
FUMIGATE DS
FUMING
FUMINGLY
FUMITORY
FUMULI
FUMULUS
FUMY
FUN DKS
FUNCTION S
FUNCTOR S
FUNCTORS
FUND IS
FUNDED
DEFUND
FUNDER S
REFUND
FUNDERS
REFUNDS
FUNDI C
FUNDIC
FUNDING
FUNDS
FUNDUS
FUNERAL S
FLANEUR
FRENULA
FUNERALS
FLANEURS
FUNERARY
FUNEREAL
FUNEST
FUNFAIR S
RUFFIAN
FUNFAIRS
RUFFIANS
FUNFEST S
FUNFESTS
FUNGAL S
FUNGALS
FUNGI C
FUNGIBLE S
FUNGIC
FUNGO
FUNGOES
FUNGOID S
FUNGOIDS
FUNGOUS
FUNGUS
FUNGUSES
FUNHOUSE S
FUNICLE S
FUNICLES
FUNICULI
FUNK SY
FUNKED
FUNKER S
FUNKERS
FUNKIA S
FUNKIAS
FUNKIER
FUNKIEST
FUNKILY
FUNKING
FUNKS
FUNKY
FUNNED
FUNNEL S
FUNNELED
FUNNELS
FUNNER
FUNNEST
FUNNIER
FUNNIES T
FUNNIEST
FUNNILY
FUNNING
FUNNY
FUNNYMAN
FUNNYMEN
FUNPLEX
FUNS
FUR LSY
FURAN ES
FURANE S
FURANES
FURANOSE S
FURANS
FURBELOW S
FURBISH
FURCATE DS
FACTURE
FURCATED
FURCATES
FACTURES
FURCRAEA S
FURCULA ER
FURCULAE
FURCULAR
FURCULUM
FURFUR
FURFURAL S
FURFURAN S
FURFURES
FURIBUND
FURIES
FURIOSO
FURIOUS
FURL S
FURLABLE
FURLED
FURLER S
FURLERS
FURLESS
FURLING
FURLONG S
FURLONGS
FURLOUGH S
FURLS
FURMENTY
FRUMENTY
FURMETY
FURMITY
FURNACE DS
FURNACED
FURNACES
FURNISH
FUROR ES
FURORE S
FURORES
FERROUS
FURORS
FURRED
FURRIER SY
FURRIERS
FURRIERY
FURRIEST
FRUITERS
FURRILY
FURRINER S
FURRING S
FURRINGS
FURROW SY
FURROWED
FURROWER S
FURROWS
FURROWY
FURRY
FURS
SURF
FURTHER S
FURTHERS
FURTHEST
FURTIVE
FURUNCLE S
FURY
FURZE S
FURZES
FURZIER
FURZIEST
FURZY
FUSAIN S
FUSAINS
FUSARIA
FUSARIUM
FUSCOUS
FUSE DELS
FEUS
FUSED
FEUDS
FUSEE S
FUSEES
FUSEL S
FLUES FUELS
FUSELAGE S
FUSELESS
FUSELIKE
FUSELS
FUSES
FUSIBLE
SUBFILE
FUSIBLY
FUSIFORM
FUSIL ES
FUSILE
FUSILEER S
FUSILIER S
FUSILLI S
FUSILLIS
FUSILS
FUSING
FUSION S
FUSIONAL
FUSIONS
FUSS Y
FUSSED
FUSSER S
FUSSERS
FUSSES
FUSSIER
FISSURE
FUSSIEST
FUSSILY
FUSSING
FUSSPOT S
FUSSPOTS
FUSSY
FUSTIAN S
FUSTIANS
FUSTIC S
FUSTICS
FUSTIER
SURFEIT
FUSTIEST
FUSTILY
FUSTY
FUSUMA
FUTHARC S
FUTHARCS
FUTHARK S
FUTHARKS
FUTHORC S
FUTHORCS
FUTHORK S
FUTHORKS
FUTILE
FUTILELY
FUTILITY
FUTON S
FOUNT
FUTONS
FOUNTS
FUTTOCK S
FUTTOCKS
FUTURAL
FUTURE S
FUTURES
FUTURISM S
FUTURIST S
FUTURITY
FUTZ
FUTZED
FUTZES
FUTZING
FUZE DES
FUZED
FUZEE S
FUZEES
FUZES
FUZIL S
FUZILS
FUZING
FUZZ Y
FUZZED
FUZZES
FUZZIER
FUZZIEST
FUZZILY
FUZZING
FUZZTONE S
FUZZY
FYCE S
FYCES
FYKE S
FYKES
FYLFOT S
FYLFOTS
FYNBOS
FYTTE S
FYTTES

G

GAB SY
BAG
GABBARD S
GABBARDS
GABBART S
GABBARTS
GABBED
GABBER S
GABBERS
GABBIER
GABBIEST
GABBING
GABBLE DRS
GABBLED
GABBLER S
GRABBLE
GABBLERS
GRABBLES
GABBLES
GABBLING
GABBRO S
GABBROIC
GABBROID
GABBROS
GABBY
GABELLE DS
GELABLE
GABELLED
BEGALLED
GABELLES
GABFEST S
GABFESTS
GABIES
GABION S
BAGNIO
GABIONS
BAGNIOS
GABLE DS
BAGEL BELGA
GLEBA
GABLED
BEGLAD
GABLES
BAGELS
BELGAS
GABLING
GABOON S
GABOONS
GABS
BAGS
GABY
E GAD IS
DAG
GADABOUT S
GADARENE
GADDED
GADDER S
GRADED
GADDERS
GADDI S
GADID
GADDING
GADDIS
GADIDS
GADFLIES
GADFLY
GADGET SY
TAGGED
GADGETRY
GADGETS
STAGGED
GADGETY
GADI DS
GADID S
GADDI
GADIDS
GADDIS
GADIS
GADOID S
GADOIDS
GADROON S
DRAGOON
GADROONS
DRAGOONS
E GADS
DAGS
GADWALL S
GADWALLS
GADZOOKS
GAE DNS
AGE
GAED
AGED EGAD
GAEING
AGEING
GAEN
GANE
GAES
AGES SAGE
GAFF ES
GAFFE DRS
GAFFED
GAFFER S
GAFFERS
GAFFES
GAFFING
GAFFS
GAG AES
GAGA
GAGAKU S
GAGAKUS
GAGE DRS
GAGED
GAGER S
AGGER EGGAR
GAGERS
AGGERS
EGGARS
SAGGER
SEGGAR
GAGES
GAGGED
GAGGER S
GAGGERS
GAGGING
GAGGLE DS
GAGGLED
GAGGLES
GAGGLING
GAGING
GAGMAN
GAGMEN
GAGS
GAGSTER S
GARGETS
STAGGER
TAGGERS
GAGSTERS
STAGGERS
GAHNITE S
HEATING
GAHNITES
GAIETIES
GAIETY
GAIJIN
GAILY
A GAIN S
AGIN
GAINABLE
GAINED
GAINER S
EARING
REAGIN
REGAIN
REGINA
GAINERS
EARINGS
ERASING
REAGINS
REGAINS
REGINAS
SEARING
SERINGA
GAINFUL
GAINING
GAINLESS
GLASSINE
LEASINGS
GAINLIER
GAINLY
LAYING
GAINS T
SIGNA
GAINSAID
GAINSAY S
GAINSAYS
ASSAYING
A GAINST
GIANTS
SATING
GAIT S
GAITED
GAITER S
AIGRET
TRIAGE
GAITERS
AIGRETS
SEAGIRT
STAGIER
TRIAGES
GAITING
GAITS
AGIST STAIG
E GAL AELS
LAG
GALA HSX
ALGA
GALABIA S
GALABIAS
GALABIEH S
GALABIYA HS
GALACTIC
GALAGO S
GALAGOS
GALAH S
GALAHS
GALANGA LS
GALANGAL S
GALANGAS
GALAS
ALGAS
GALATEA S
GALATEAS
GALAVANT S
GALAX Y
GALAXES
GALAXIES
GALAXY
GALBANUM S
GALE AS
EGAL
GALEA ES
ALGAE
GALEAE
GALEAS
GALEATE D
GALEATED
GALENA S
ANLAGE
GALENAS
ANLAGES
LASAGNE
GALENIC
ANGELIC
ANGLICE
GALENITE S
GELATINE
LEGATINE
GALERE S
REGALE
GALERES
REGALES
GALES
GALETTE S
GALETTES
GALILEE S
GALILEES
LEGALISE
GALIOT S
LATIGO
GALIOTS
LATIGOS
GALIPOT S
GALIPOTS
GALIVANT S
GALL SY
GALLANT S
GALLANTS
GALLATE S
GALLETA
TALLAGE
GALLATES
GALLETAS
TALLAGES
GALLEASS
GALLED
GALLEIN S
NIGELLA
GALLEINS
NIGELLAS
GALLEON S
ALLONGE
GALLEONS
ALLONGES
GALLERIA S
GALLERY
ALLERGY
LARGELY
REGALLY
GALLET AS

GALLETA S
GALLATE
TALLAGE
GALLETAS
GALLATES
TALLAGES
GALLETED
GALLETS
GALLEY S
GALLEYS
GALLFLY
GALLIARD S
GALLIASS
GALLIC A
GALLICA NS
GLACIAL
GALLICAN
GALLICAS
GALLIED
GALLIES
GALLING
GINGALL
GALLIOT S
GALLIOTS
GALLIPOT S
GALLIUM S
GALLIUMS
GALLNUT S
NUTGALL
GALLNUTS
NUTGALLS
GALLON S
GALLONS
GALLOON S
GALLOONS
GALLOOT S
GALLOOTS
GALLOP S
GALLOPED
GALLOPER S
GALLOPS
GALLOUS
GALLOWS
GALLS
GALLUS
GALLUSED
GALLUSES
SEAGULLS
SULLAGES
GALLY
GALLYING
GALOOT S
GALOOTS
GALOP S
GALOPADE S
GALOPED
GALOPING
GALOPS
GALORE S
GAOLER
GALORES
GAOLERS
GALOSH E
GALOSHE DS
GALOSHED
GALOSHES
GALS
LAGS SLAG
GALUMPH S
GALUMPHS
GALVANIC
GALYAC S
GALYACS
GALYAK S
GALYAKS
O GAM ABEPSY
MAG
A GAMA SY
AGMA
A GAMAS
AGMAS
GAMASHES
GAMAY S
GAMAYS
GAMB AES
GAMBA S
GAMBADE S
GAMBADES

GAMBADO S
GAMBADOS
GAMBAS
GAMBE S
GAMBES
GAMBESON S
GAMBIA S
GAMBIAS
GAMBIER S
GAMBIERS
GAMBIR S
GAMBIRS
GAMBIT S
GAMBITS
GAMBLE DRS
GAMBLED
GAMBLER S
GAMBREL
GAMBLERS
GAMBRELS
GAMBLES
GAMBLING
GAMBOGE S
GAMBOGES
GAMBOL S
GAMBOLED
GAMBOLS
GAMBREL S
GAMBLER
GAMBRELS
GAMBLERS
GAMBS
GAMBUSIA S
GAME DRSY
MAGE MEGA
GAMECOCK S
GAMED
GAMELAN S
GAMELANS
GAMELIKE
GAMELY
GLEAMY
GAMENESS
GAMER S
MARGE REGMA
GAMERS
MARGES
GAMES T
MAGES
GAMESMAN
GAMESMEN
GAMESOME
GAMEST
GAMESTER S
GAMETAL
A GAMETE S
METAGE
A GAMETES
METAGES
GAMETIC
GAMEY
A GAMIC
MAGIC
GAMIER
IMAGER
MAIGRE
MIRAGE
GAMIEST
SIGMATE
GAMILY
GAMIN EGS
GAMINE S
ENIGMA
GAMINES S
ENIGMAS
SEAMING
GAMINESS
GAMING S
GAMINGS
GAMINS
GAMMA S
MAGMA
GAMMADIA
GAMMAS
MAGMAS
GAMMED
GAMMER S
GRAMME
GAMMERS
GRAMMES

GAMMIER
GAMMIEST
GAMMING
GAMMON S
GAMMONED
GAMMONER S
GAMMONS
GAMMY
GAMODEME S
GAMP S
GAMPS
O GAMS
MAGS
GAMUT S
GAMUTS
GAMY
GAN EG
NAG
GANACHE S
GANACHES
GANDER S
DANGER
GARDEN
RANGED
GANDERED
DANGERED
DERANGED
GARDENED
GANDERS
DANGERS
GARDENS
GANE FV
GAEN
GANEF S
GANEFS
GANEV S
VEGAN
GANEVS
VEGANS
GANG S
GANGBANG S
GANGED
NAGGED
GANGER S
GRANGE
NAGGER
GANGERS
GRANGES
NAGGERS
GANGING
NAGGING
GANGLAND S
GANGLIA LR
GANGLIAL
GANGLIAR
GANGLIER
LAGERING
REGALING
GANGLING
GANGLION S
GANGLY
GANGPLOW S
GANGREL S
GANGRELS
GANGRENE DS
GANGS
GANGSTA S
GANGSTAS
GANGSTER S
GANGUE S
GANGUES
GANGWAY S
GANGWAYS
GANISTER S
ANGRIEST
ASTRINGE
GANTRIES
GRANITES
INGRATES
RANGIEST
GANJA HS
GANJAH S
GANJAHS
GANJAS
GANNET S
GANNETS
GANOF S
GANOFS
GANOID S

GANOIDS
GANTLET S
GANTLETS
GANTLINE S
LATENING
GANTLOPE S
GANTRIES
ANGRIEST
ASTRINGE
GANISTER
GRANITES
INGRATES
RANGIEST
GANTRY
GANYMEDE S
MEGADYNE
GAOL S
GOAL
GAOLED
GOALED
GAOLER S
GALORE
GAOLERS
GALORES
GAOLING
GOALING
GAOLS
GOALS
GAP ESY
A GAPE DRS
PAGE PEAG
GAPED
PAGED
GAPER S
GRAPE PAGER
PARGE
GAPERS
GASPER
GRAPES
PAGERS
PARGES
SPARGE
A GAPES
PAGES PEAGS
GAPESEED S
GAPEWORM S
GAPING
PAGING
GAPINGLY
GAPLESS
GAPOSIS
GAPPED
GAPPIER
GAPPIEST
GAPPING
GAPPY
GAPS
GASP
GAPY
A GAR BS
RAG
GARAGE DS
GARAGED
AGGRADE
GARAGES
GARAGING
GARB S
BRAG GRAB
GARBAGE SY
GARBAGES
GARBAGEY
GARBAGY
GARBANZO S
GARBED
BADGER
BARGED
GARBING
BARGING
GARBLE DRS
GARBLED
GARBLER S
GARBLERS
GARBLES S
GARBLESS
GARBLING
GARBOARD S
GARBOIL S
GARBOILS
GARBS
BRAGS GRABS
GARCON S

GARCONS
GARDA I
GARDAI
GARDANT
GARDEN S
DANGER
GANDER
RANGED
GARDENED
DANGERED
DERANGED
GANDERED
GARDENER S
DERANGER
GARNERED
GARDENIA S
DRAINAGE
GARDENS
DANGERS
GANDERS
GARDYLOO
GARFISH
GARGANEY S
GARGET SY
TAGGER
GARGETS
GAGSTER
STAGGER
TAGGERS
GARGETY
GARGLE DRS
LAGGER
RAGGLE
GARGLED
DRAGGLE
GARGLER S
GARGLERS
GARGLES
LAGGERS
RAGGLES
GARGLING
GARGOYLE DS
GARIGUE S
GARIGUES
GARISH
GARISHLY
GARLAND S
GARLANDS
GARLIC S
GARLICKY
GARLICS
GARMENT S
MARGENT
GARMENTS
MARGENTS
GARNER S
RANGER
GARNERED
DERANGER
GARDENER
GARNERS
RANGERS
GARNET S
ARGENT
GARNETS
ARGENTS
STRANGE
GARNI
GRAIN
GARNISH
SHARING
GAROTE DS
ORGEAT
GAROTED
GAROTES
ORGEATS
STORAGE
GAROTING
GAROTTE DRS
GAROTTED
GAROTTER S
GARROTTE
GAROTTES
GARPIKE S
GARPIKES
GARRED
GRADER
REGARD
GARRET S
GARTER
GRATER

GARRETED
GARTERED
REGRATED
GARRETS
GARTERS
GRATERS
GARRING
GARRISON S
ROARINGS
GARRON S
GARRONS
GARROTE DRS
GARROTED
GARROTER S
GARROTES
GARROTTE DS
GAROTTER
A GARS
RAGS
GARTER S
GARRET
GRATER
GARTERED
GARRETED
REGRATED
GARTERS
GARRETS
GRATERS
GARTH S
GARTHS
GARVEY S
GARVEYS
A GAS HPT
AGS
SAG
GASALIER S
GASBAG S
GASBAGS
GASCON S
CONGAS
GASCONS
GASEITY
GASELIER S
GASEOUS
GASES
SAGES
GASH
HAGS SHAG
GASHED
GASHER
GERAHS
GASHES T
GASHEST
GASHING
GASHOUSE S
GASIFIED
GASIFIER S
GASIFIES
GASIFORM
GASIFY
GASKET S
GASKETS
GASKIN GS
ASKING
KIANGS
GASKING S
GASKINGS
GASKINS
ASKINGS
GASLESS
GLASSES
GASLIGHT S
GASLIT
GASMAN
MANGAS
GASMEN
MANGES
GASOGENE S
GASOHOL S
GASOHOLS
GASOLENE S
GASOLIER S
GIRASOLE
SERAGLIO
GASOLINE S
GASP S
GAPS
GASPED

GASPER S
GAPERS
GRAPES
PAGERS
PARGES
SPARGE
GASPERS
SPARGES
GASPING
PAGINGS
GASPS
GASSED
GASSER S
SARGES
GASSERS
GRASSES
GASSES
GASSIER
GASSIEST
GASSILY
GASSING S
GASSINGS
GASSY
GAST S
GATS STAG
TAGS
GASTED
STAGED
GASTER S
GATERS
GRATES
GREATS
RETAGS
STAGER
TARGES
GASTERS
STAGERS
GASTIGHT
GASTING
GATINGS
STAGING
GASTNESS
GASTRAEA S
GASTRAL
GASTREA S
TEARGAS
GASTREAS
GASTRIC
TRAGICS
GASTRIN S
GRATINS
RATINGS
STARING
GASTRINS
GASTRULA ER S
GASTS
STAGS
GASWORKS
GAT ES
TAG
A GATE DRS
GETA
GATEAU SX
GATEAUS
GATEAUX
GATED
GATEFOLD S
GATELESS
GATELIKE
GATEMAN
MAGENTA
MAGNATE
NAMETAG
GATEMEN
GATEPOST S
POTTAGES
GATER S
GRATE GREAT
RETAG TARGE
TERGA
GATERS
GASTER
GRATES
GREATS
RETAGS
STAGER
TARGES
A GATES
GETAS STAGE
GATEWAY S
GETAWAY

GATEWAYS
GETAWAYS
GATHER S
GATHERED
GATHERER S
REGATHER
GATHERS
GATING S
GATINGS
GASTING
STAGING
GATOR S
ARGOT GROAT
GATORS
ARGOTS
GROATS
GATS
GAST STAG
TAGS
GAUCHE R
GAUCHELY
GAUCHER
GAUCHEST
GAUCHO S
GAUCHOS
GAUD SY
GAUDERY
GAUDIER
GAUDIES T
GAUDIEST
GAUDILY
GAUDS
GAUDY
GAUFFER S
GAUFFERS
SUFFRAGE
GAUGE DRS
GAUGED
GAUGER S
GAUGERS
GAUGES
GAUGING
GAULT S
GAULTS
GAUM S
GAUMED
GAUMING
GAUMS
MAGUS SAGUM
GAUN T
GUAN
GAUNT
GAUNTER
GAUNTEST
GAUNTLET S
GAUNTLY
GAUNTRY
GAUR S
GUAR RUGA
GAURS
ARGUS GUARS
SUGAR
GAUSS
GAUSSES
GAUZE S
GAUZES
GAUZIER
GAUZIEST
GAUZILY
GAUZY
GAVAGE S
GAVAGES
A **GAVE** L
GAVEL S
GAVELED
GAVELING
GAVELLED
GAVELOCK S
GAVELS
GAVIAL S
GAVIALS
GAVOT S
GAVOTS
GAVOTTE DS
GAVOTTED
GAVOTTES
GAWK SY
GAWKED
GAWKER S
GAWKERS
GAWKIER
GAWKIES T
GAWKIEST
GAWKILY
GAWKING
GAWKISH
GAWKS
GAWKY
GAWP S
GAWPED
GAWPER S
GAWPERS
GAWPING
GAWPS
GAWSIE
GAWSY
GAY S
YAG
GAYAL S
GAYALS
GAYDAR S
GAYDARS
GAYER
YAGER
GAYEST
STAGEY
GAYETIES
GAYETY
GAYLY
GAYNESS
GAYS
SAGY YAGS
GAYWINGS
GAZABO S
GAZABOES
GAZABOS
GAZANIA S
GAZANIAS
GAZAR S
GAZARS
A **GAZE** DRS
GAZEBO S
GAZEBOES
GAZEBOS
GAZED
GAZELLE S
GAZELLES
GAZER S
GRAZE
GAZERS
GRAZES
GAZES
GAZETTE DS
GAZETTED
GAZETTES
GAZING
GAZOGENE S
GAZPACHO S
GAZUMP S
GAZUMPED
GAZUMPER S
GAZUMPS
GEAR S
AGER RAGE
GEARBOX
GEARCASE S
ACREAGES
GEARED
AGREED
DRAGEE
GEARHEAD S
HEADGEAR
GEARING S
NAGGIER
GEARINGS
GREASING
SNAGGIER
GEARLESS
EELGRASS
LARGESSE
GEARS
AGERS RAGES
SAGER SARGE
GECK OS
GECKED
GECKING
GECKO S
GECKOES
GECKOS
GECKS
A **GED** S
GEDS
AO **GEE** DKSZ
GEED
EDGE
GEEGAW S
GEEGAWS
GEEING
GEEK SY
GEEKDOM S
GEEKDOMS
GEEKED
GEEKIER
GEEKIEST
GEEKS
GEEKY
GEEPOUND S
O **GEES** ET
GEESE
GEEST S
EGEST GESTE
GEESTS
EGESTS
GESTES
GEEZ
GEEZER S
GEEZERS
GEISHA S
GEISHAS
GEL DST
LEG
GELABLE
GABELLE
GELADA S
GELADAS
GELANT S
TANGLE
GELANTS
TANGLES
GELATE DS
EAGLET
LEGATE
TELEGA
GELATED
LEGATED
GELATES
EAGLETS
LEGATES
SEGETAL
TELEGAS
GELATI NS
AIGLET
LIGATE
GELATIN EGS
ATINGLE
ELATING
GENITAL
TAGLINE
GELATINE S
GALENITE
LEGATINE
GELATING
LEGATING
GELATINS
GENITALS
STEALING
TAGLINES
GELATION S
LEGATION
GELATIS
AIGLETS
LIGATES
GELATO S
LEGATO
GELATOS
LEGATOS
GELCAP S
GELCAPS
GELD S
GLED
GELDED
GELDER S
LEDGER
REDLEG
GELDERS
LEDGERS
REDLEGS
GELDING S
NIGGLED
GELDINGS
SLEDGING
SNIGGLED
GELDS
GLEDS
GELEE S
GELEES
GELID
GLIDE
GELIDITY
GELIDLY
GELLANT S
GELLANTS
GELLED
GELLING
GELS
LEGS
GELSEMIA
MILEAGES
GELT S
GELTS
GEM S
MEG
GEMATRIA S
GEMINAL
GEMINATE DS
GEMLIKE
GEMMA E
GEMMAE
GEMMATE DS
TAGMEME
GEMMATED
GEMMATES
TAGMEMES
GEMMED
GEMMIER
GREMMIE
IMMERGE
GEMMIEST
GEMMILY
GEMMING
GEMMULE S
GEMMULES
GEMMY
GEMOLOGY
GEMOT ES
GEMOTE S
GEMOTES
GEMOTS
GEMS
MEGS
GEMSBOK S
GEMSBOKS
GEMSBUCK S
GEMSTONE S
GEN ESTU
ENG
NEG
GENDARME S
GENDER S
GENDERED
DEGENDER
GENDERS
A **GENE** ST
GENERA L
ENRAGE
GENERAL S
ENLARGE
GLEANER
GENERALS
ENLARGES
GLEANERS
GENERATE DS
TEENAGER
GENERIC S
GENERICS
GENEROUS
A **GENES**
A **GENESES**
A **GENESIS**
SEEINGS
SIGNEES
GENET S
TENGE
A **GENETIC** S
GENETICS
GENETS
GENTES
GENETTE S
GENETTES
GENEVA S
AVENGE
GENEVAS
AVENGES
GENIAL
LINAGE
GENIALLY
GENIC
GENIE S
GENIES
SEEING
SIGNEE
GENII
GENIP S
GENIPAP S
GENIPAPS
GENIPS
GENITAL S
ATINGLE
ELATING
GELATIN
TAGLINE
GENITALS
GELATINS
STEALING
TAGLINES
GENITIVE S
GENITOR S
GENITORS
GENITURE S
GENIUS
GENIUSES
GENNAKER S
GENOA S
AGONE
GENOAS
AGONES
GENOCIDE S
GENOGRAM S
GENOISE S
SOIGNEE
GENOISES
GENOM ES
GNOME
GENOME S
GENOMES
GENOMIC S
GENOMICS
GENOMS
GNOMES
GENOTYPE S
GENRE S
GREEN
GENRES
GREENS
GENRO S
GONER
GENROS
GONERS
GENS
ENGS NEGS
GENSENG S
GENSENGS
A **GENT** S
GENTEEL
GENTES
GENETS
GENTIAN S
ANTEING
ANTIGEN
GENTIANS
ANTIGENS
GENTIL E
TINGLE
GENTILE S
GENTILES
SLEETING
STEELING
GENTLE DRS
GENTLED
GENTLER
GENTLES T
GENTLEST
GENTLING
GENTLY
GENTOO S
GENTOOS
GENTRICE S
ERECTING
A **GENTRIES**
INTEGERS
REESTING
STEERING
GENTRIFY
A **GENTRY**
A **GENTS**
GENU AS
GENUA
GENUINE
INGENUE
GENUS
NEGUS
GENUSES
NEGUSES
GEODE S
GEODES Y
GEODESIC S
GEODESY
GEODETIC S
GEODIC
GEODUCK S
GEODUCKS
GEOGNOSY
GEOID S
DOGIE
GEOIDAL
GEOIDS
DOGIES
GEOLOGER S
GEOLOGIC
GEOLOGY
GEOMANCY
GEOMETER S
GEOMETRY
GEOPHAGY
GEOPHONE S
GEOPHYTE S
GEOPONIC S
GEOPROBE S
GEORGIC S
GEORGICS
GEOTAXES
GEOTAXIS
GERAH S
GERAHS
GASHER
GERANIAL S
GERANIOL S
REGIONAL
GERANIUM S
GERARDIA S
GERBERA S
GERBERAS
GERBIL S
GERBILLE S
GERBILS
GERENT S
REGENT
GERENTS
REGENTS
GERENUK S
GERENUKS
GERM SY
GERMAN ES
ENGRAM
MANGER
RAGMEN
GERMANE
GERMANIC
AMERCING
CREAMING
GERMANS
ENGRAMS
MANGERS
GERMEN S
GERMENS
GERMFREE
GERMIER
GERMIEST
GERMINA L
MANGIER
REAMING
GERMINAL
MALIGNER
MALINGER
GERMLIKE
GERMS
GERMY
GERONTIC
GERUND S
NUDGER
GERUNDS
NUDGERS
GESNERIA D
ANERGIES
GESSO
SEGOS
GESSOED
GESSOES
E **GEST** ES
GETS TEGS
GESTALT S
GESTALTS
GESTAPO S
POSTAGE
POTAGES
GESTAPOS
POSTAGES
GESTATE DS
GESTATED
GESTATES
GESTE S
EGEST GEEST
GESTES
EGESTS
GEESTS
GESTIC
GESTICAL
E **GESTS**
GESTURAL
GESTURE DRS
GESTURED
GESTURER S
GESTURES
GET AS
TEG
GETA S
GATE
GETABLE
GETAS
GATES STAGE
GETAWAY S
GATEWAY
GETAWAYS
GATEWAYS
GETS
GEST TEGS
GETTABLE
GETTER S
GETTERED
GETTERS
GETTING
GETUP S
GETUPS
GEUM S
GEUMS
GEWGAW S
GEWGAWED
GEWGAWS
GEY
GEYSER S
GEYSERS
GHARIAL S
GHARIALS
GHARRI S
GHARRIES
GHARRIS
GHARRY
A **GHAST**
GHATS
GHASTFUL
GHASTLY
GHAT S
GHATS
GHAST
GHAUT S
AUGHT
GHAUTS
AUGHTS
GHAZI S
GHAZIES
GHAZIS
GHEE S
GHEES

GHERAO
GHERAOED
GHERAOES
GHERKIN S
GHERKINS
GHETTO S
GHETTOED
DOGTEETH
GHETTOES
GHETTOS
GHI S
GHIBLI S
GHIBLIS
GHILLIE S
GHILLIES
GHIS
SIGH
GHOST SY
GOTHS
GHOSTED
GHOSTIER
GHOSTING S
GHOSTLY
GHOSTS
GHOSTY
GHOUL S
LOUGH
GHOULIE S
GHOULIES
GHOULISH
GHOULS
LOUGHS
SLOUGH
GHYLL S
GHYLLS
GIANT S
GIANTESS
EASTINGS
SEATINGS
GIANTISM S
GIANTS
GAINST
SATING
GIAOUR S
GIAOURS
GIARDIA S
GIARDIAS
GIB ES
BIG
GIBBED
GIBBER S
GIBBERED
GIBBERS
GIBBET S
GIBBETED
GIBBETS
GIBBING
GIBBON S
GIBBONS
SOBBING
GIBBOSE
GIBBOUS
GIBBSITE S
GIBE DRS
GIBED
GIBER S
GIBERS
GIBES
GIBING
BIGGIN
GIBINGLY
GIBLET S
GIBLETS
GIBS
BIGS
GIBSON S
BINGOS
BOINGS
GIBSONS
BOSSING
GID S
DIG
GIDDAP
GIDDIED
GIDDIER
GIDDIES T
GIDDIEST
GIDDILY
GIDDY
GIDDYAP
GIDDYING
GIDDYUP
GIDS
DIGS
GIE DNS
GIED
GIEING
GIEN
GIES
EGIS
GIFT S
GIFTABLE S
GIFTED
FIDGET
GIFTEDLY
GIFTEE S
GIFTEES
GIFTING
GIFTLESS
GIFTS
GIFTWARE S
GIFTWRAP S
GIG AS
IGG
GIGA S
GIGABIT S
GIGABITS
GIGABYTE S
GIGAFLOP S
GIGANTIC
GIGAS
GIGATON S
GIGATONS
GIGAWATT S
GIGGED
GIGGING
GIGGLE DRS
GIGGLED
GIGGLER S
GIGGLERS
GIGGLES
GIGGLIER
GIGGLING
GIGGLY
GIGHE
GIGLET S
GIGLETS
GIGLOT S
GIGLOTS
GIGOLO S
GIGOLOS
GIGOT S
GIGOTS
GIGS
IGGS
GIGUE S
GIGUES
GILBERT S
GILBERTS
GILD S
GILDED
GLIDED
GILDER S
GIRDLE
GLIDER
REGILD
RIDGEL
GILDERS
GIRDLES
GLIDERS
REGILDS
RIDGELS
GILDHALL S
GILDING S
GLIDING
GILDINGS
GILDS
GILL SY
GILLED
GILLER S
GRILLE
GILLERS
GRILLES
GILLIE DS
GILLIED
GILLIES
GILLING
GILLNET S
TELLING
GILLNETS
GILLS
GILLY
GILLYING
GILT S
GILTHEAD S
ALIGHTED
GILTS
GIMBAL S
GIMBALED
GIMBALS
GIMCRACK S
GIMEL S
GLIME
GIMELS
GLIMES
GIMLET S
GIMLETED
GIMLETS
GIMMAL S
GIMMALS
GIMME S
GIMMES
GIMMICK SY
GIMMICKS
GIMMICKY
GIMMIE S
GIMMIES
GIMP SY
GIMPED
GIMPIER
GIMPIEST
GIMPING
GIMPS
GIMPY
PIGMY
A GIN KS
GINGAL LS
GINGALL S
GALLING
GINGALLS
GINGALS
GINGELEY S
GINGELI S
GINGELIS
GINGELLI S
GINGELLY
GINGELY
GLEYING
GINGER SY
GINGERED
RENIGGED
GINGERLY
GINGERS
SERGING
SNIGGER
GINGERY
GREYING
GINGHAM S
GINGHAMS
GINGILI S
GINGILIS
GINGILLI S
GINGIVA EL
GINGIVAE
GINGIVAL
GINGKO S
GINKGO
GINGKOES
GINKGOES
GINGKOS
GINKGOS
GINK S
KING
GINKGO S
GINGKO
GINKGOES
GINGKOES
GINKGOS
GINGKOS
GINKS
KINGS
GINNED
ENDING
A GINNER S
A GINNERS
GINNIER
REINING
GINNIEST
GINNING S
GINNINGS
GINNY
GINS
SIGN SING
GINSENG S
GINSENGS
GIP S
PIG
GIPON S
OPING PINGO
GIPONS
PINGOS
POSING
GIPPED
GIPPER S
GRIPPE
GIPPERS
GRIPPES
GIPPING
GIPS Y
PIGS
GIPSIED
GIPSIES
GIPSY
GIPSYING
GIRAFFE S
GIRAFFES
GIRASOL ES
GLORIAS
GIRASOLE S
GASOLIER
SERAGLIO
GIRASOLS
GIRD S
GRID
GIRDED
GRIDED
RIDGED
GIRDER S
GIRDERS
GIRDING
GRIDING
RIDGING
GIRDLE DRS
GILDER
GLIDER
REGILD
RIDGEL
GIRDLED
GRIDDLE
GIRDLER S
GIRDLERS
GIRDLES
GILDERS
GLIDERS
REGILDS
RIDGELS
GIRDLING
RIDGLING
GIRDS
GRIDS
GIRL SY
GIRLHOOD S
GIRLIE RS
GIRLIER
GIRLIES T
GIRLIEST
GIRLISH
GIRLS
GIRLY
GIRN S
GRIN RING
GIRNED
DINGER
ENGIRD
REDING
RINGED
GIRNING
RINGING
GIRNS
GRINS RINGS
GIRO NS
GIROLLE S
GIROLLES
GIRON S
GROIN
GIRONS
GRISON
GROINS
ROSING
SIGNOR
SORING
GIROS
GIROSOL S
GIROSOLS
GIRSH
GIRSHES
SIGHERS
GIRT HS
GRIT TRIG
GIRTED
GIRTH S
GRITH RIGHT
GIRTHED
RIGHTED
GIRTHING
RIGHTING
GIRTHS
GRITHS
RIGHTS
GIRTING
RINGGIT
GIRTS
GRIST GRITS
TRIGS
GISARME S
IMAGERS
MIRAGES
GISARMES
GISMO S
GISMOS
A GIST S
GITS
A GISTS
GIT ES
GITANO S
GITANOS
AGONIST
GITE S
GITES
GITS
GIST
GITTED
GITTERN S
RETTING
GITTERNS
GITTIN G
GITTING
O GIVE NRS
GIVEABLE
GIVEAWAY S
GIVEBACK S
GIVEN S
GIVENS
GIVER S
GIVERS
O GIVES
GIVING
GIZMO S
GIZMOS
GIZZARD S
GIZZARDS
GJETOST S
GJETOSTS
GLABELLA ER
GLABRATE
GLABROUS
GLACE S
GLACEED
GLACEING
CAGELING
GLACES
GLACIAL
GALLICA
GLACIATE DS
GLACIER S
GRACILE
GLACIERS
GRACILES
GLACIS
GLACISES
GLAD ESY
GLADDED
GLADDEN S
DANGLED
GLADDENS
GLADDER
GLADDEST
GLADDING
GLADE S
GLADES
GLADIATE
GLADIER
GLAIRED
GLADIEST
GLADIOLA RS
GLADIOLI
GLADLIER
GRILLADE
GLADLY
GLADNESS
GLADS
GLADSOME R
GLADY
GLAIKET
TAGLIKE
GLAIKIT
GLAIR ESY
ARGIL GRAIL
GLAIRE DS
GLAIRED
GLADIER
GLAIRES
GLAIRIER
GLAIRING
GLAIRS
ARGILS
GRAILS
GLAIRY
GLAIVE DS
VAGILE
GLAIVED
GLAIVES
GLAM S
GLAMOR S
GLAMORS
GLAMOUR S
GLAMOURS
GLAMS
GLANCE DRS
GLANCED
CLANGED
GLANCER S
CLANGER
GLANCERS
CLANGERS
GLANCES
GLANCING
CLANGING
GLAND S
GLANDERS
DANGLERS
GLANDES
DANGLES
LAGENDS
SLANGED
GLANDS
GLANDULE S
UNGALLED
GLANS
SLANG
A GLARE DS
ARGLE LAGER
LARGE REGAL
GLARED
ARGLED
GLARES
ARGLES
LAGERS
LARGES
GLARIER
GLARIEST
GLARING
ARGLING
GLARY
GYRAL
GLASNOST S
GLASS Y
SLAGS
GLASSED
GLASSES
GASLESS
GLASSFUL S
GLASSIE RS
LIGASES
SILAGES
GLASSIER
GLASSIES T
GLASSILY
GLASSINE S
GAINLESS
LEASINGS
GLASSING
GLASSMAN
GLASSMEN
GLASSY
GLAUCOMA S
GLAUCOUS
GLAZE DRS
GLAZED
GLAZER S
GLAZERS
GLAZES
GLAZIER SY
GLAZIERS
GLAZIERY
GLAZIEST
GLAZILY
GLAZING S
GLAZINGS
GLAZY
A GLEAM SY
GLEAMED
GLEAMER S
GLEAMERS
GLEAMIER
GLEAMING
GLEAMS
GLEAMY
GAMELY
GLEAN S
ANGEL ANGLE
GLEANED
ANGELED
GLEANER S
ENLARGE
GENERAL
GLEANERS
ENLARGES
GENERALS
GLEANING S
ANGELING
GLEANS
ANGELS
ANGLES
GLEBA E
BAGEL BELGA
GABLE
GLEBAE
BEAGLE
GLEBE S
GLEBES
O GLED ES
GELD
GLEDE S
GLEED LEDGE
GLEDES
GLEEDS
LEDGES
SLEDGE
GLEDS
GELDS
A GLEE DKST
GLEED S
GLEDE LEDGE
GLEEDS
GLEDES
LEDGES
SLEDGE
GLEEFUL
GLEEK S
GLEEKED
GLEEKING
GLEEKS
GLEEMAN
MELANGE
GLEEMEN
GLEES
LEGES
GLEESOME
GLEET SY
GLEETED
GLEETIER
GLEETING
GLEETS
GLEETY
GLEG

GLEGLY
GLEGNESS
GLEN S
GLENLIKE
GLENOID
GLENS
A GLEY S
GLEYED
GLEYING S
GINGELY
GLEYINGS
GLEYS
GLIA LS
GLIADIN ES
DIALING
GLIADINE S
GLIADINS
DIALINGS
GLIAL
GLIAS
SIGLA
GLIB
GLIBBER
GRIBBLE
GLIBBEST
GLIBLY
GLIBNESS
BLESSING
GLIDE DRS
GELID
GLIDED
GILDED
GLIDER S
GILDER
GIRDLE
REGILD
RIDGEL
GLIDERS
GILDERS
GIRDLES
REGILDS
RIDGELS
GLIDES
GLIDING
GILDING
GLIFF S
GLIFFS
GLIM ES
GLIME DS
GIMEL
GLIMED
MIDLEG
GLIMES
GIMELS
GLIMING
A GLIMMER S
GLIMMERS
GLIMPSE DRS
MEGILPS
GLIMPSED
GLIMPSER S
GLIMPSES
GLIMS
GLINT SY
GLINTED
TINGLED
GLINTIER
RETILING
TINGLIER
GLINTING
TINGLING
GLINTS
GLINTY
TINGLY
GLIOMA S
GLIOMAS
GLIOMATA
GLISSADE DR S
GLISTEN S
SINGLET
SNIGLET
TINGLES
GLISTENS
SINGLETS
SNIGLETS
GLISTER S
GRISTLE
GLISTERS
GRISTLES
GLITCH Y
GLITCHES
GLITCHY
A GLITTER SY
GLITTERS
GLITTERY
GLITZ Y
GLITZED
GLITZES
GLITZIER
GLITZING
GLITZY
GLOAM S
GLOAMING S
GLOAMS
GLOAT S
GLOATED
GLOATER S
LEGATOR
GLOATERS
LEGATORS
GLOATING
GLOATS
GLOB ES
BLOG
GLOBAL
GLOBALLY
GLOBATE D
GLOBATED
GLOBBIER
GLOBBY
GLOBE DS
BOGLE
GLOBED
GLOBES
BOGLES
GLOBIN GS
GOBLIN
GLOBING
GLOBINS
GOBLINS
GLOBOID S
GLOBOIDS
GLOBOSE
GLOBOUS
GLOBS
BLOGS
GLOBULAR S
GLOBULE S
GLOBULES
GLOBULIN S
GLOCHID S
GLOCHIDS
GLOGG S
GLOGGS
GLOM S
GLOMERA
GOMERAL
GLOMMED
GLOMMING
GLOMS
GLOMUS
MOGULS
GLONOIN S
GLONOINS
SNOOLING
GLOOM SY
GLOOMED
GLOOMFUL
GLOOMIER
OLIGOMER
GLOOMILY
GLOOMING S
GLOOMS
GLOOMY
GLOP S
GLOPPED
GLOPPIER
GLOPPING
GLOPPY
GLOPS
GLORIA S
GLORIAS
GIRASOL
GLORIED
GODLIER
GLORIES
GLORIFY
GLORIOLE S
GLORIOUS
GLORY
GLORYING
GLOSS AY
SLOGS
GLOSSA ELS
GLOSSAE
GLOSSAL
GLOSSARY
GLOSSAS
GLOSSED
GODLESS
GLOSSEME S
GLOSSER S
REGLOSS
GLOSSERS
GLOSSES
GLOSSIER
GLOSSIES T
GLOSSILY
GLOSSINA S
LASSOING
GLOSSING
GOSLINGS
GLOSSY
GLOST S
GLOSTS
GLOTTAL
GLOTTIC
GLOTTIS
GLOUT S
GLOUTED
GLOUTING
GLOUTS
GLOVE DRS
GLOVED
GLOVER S
GROVEL
GLOVERS
GROVELS
GLOVES
GLOVING
A GLOW S
GLOWED
GLOWER S
REGLOW
GLOWERED
REGLOWED
GLOWERS
REGLOWS
GLOWFLY
GLOWING
GLOWS
GLOWWORM S
GLOXINIA S
GLOZE DS
GLOZED
GLOZES
GLOZING
GLUCAGON S
GLUCAN S
GLUCANS
GLUCINIC
GLUCINUM S
CINGULUM
GLUCOSE S
GLUCOSES
GLUCOSIC
GLUE DRSY
LUGE
GLUED
LUGED
GLUEING
LUGEING
GLUELIKE
GLUEPOT S
GLUEPOTS
GLUER S
GRUEL LUGER
GLUERS
GRUELS
LUGERS
GLUES
GULES LUGES
GLUEY
GLUG S
GLUGGED
GUGGLED
GLUGGING
GUGGLING
GLUGS
GLUHWEIN S
GLUIER
LIGURE
REGULI
UGLIER
GLUIEST
UGLIEST
GLUILY
UGLILY
GLUINESS
UGLINESS
GLUING
LUGING
GLUM ES
GLUME S
GLUMES
GLUMLY
GLUMMER
GLUMMEST
GLUMNESS
GLUMPIER
GLUMPILY
GLUMPY
GLUMS
GLUNCH
GLUNCHED
GLUNCHES
GLUON S
GLUONS
GLUT ES
GLUTE INS
GLUTEAL
GLUTEI
GLUTELIN S
GLUTEN S
ENGLUT
GLUTENIN S
GLUTENS
ENGLUTS
GLUTES
GLUTEUS
GLUTS
GLUTTED
GUTTLED
GLUTTING
GUTTLING
GLUTTON SY
GLUTTONS
GLUTTONY
GLYCAN S
GLYCANS
GLYCERIC
GLYCERIN ES
GLYCEROL S
GLYCERYL S
GLYCIN ES
CLINGY
GLYCINE S
GLYCINES
GLYCINS
GLYCOGEN S
GLYCOL S
GLYCOLIC
GLYCOLS
GLYCONIC S
GLYCOSYL S
GLYCYL S
GLYCYLS
GLYPH S
GLYPHIC
GLYPHS
GLYPTIC S
GLYPTICS
GNAR LRS
GRAN RANG
GNARL SY
GNARLED
DANGLER
GNARLIER
GNARLING
GNARLS
GNARLY
GNARR S
GNARRED
GRANDER
GNARRING
GNARRS
GNARS
GRANS
GNASH
HANGS SANGH
GNASHED
GNASHES
GNASHING
HANGINGS
GNAT S
TANG
GNATHAL
GNATHIC
GNATHION S
GNATHITE S
GNATLIKE
GNATS
ANGST STANG
TANGS
GNATTIER
TREATING
GNATTY
GNAW NS
GNAWABLE
GNAWED
GNAWER S
GNAWERS
GNAWING S
GNAWINGS
GNAWN
GNAWS
SWANG
GNEISS
SINGES
GNEISSES
GNEISSIC
GNOCCHI
GNOME S
GENOM
GNOMES
GENOMS
GNOMIC
COMING
GNOMICAL
GNOMISH
MOSHING
GNOMIST S
GNOMISTS
GNOMON S
GNOMONIC
ONCOMING
GNOMONS
GNOSES
SEGNOS
GNOSIS
A GNOSTIC S
COSTING
A GNOSTICS
GNU S
GUN
GNUS
GUNS SNUG
SUNG
AE GO ABDORSTX Y
GOA DLST
AGO
GOAD S
GOADED
GOADING
GOADLIKE
GOADS
GOAL S
GAOL
GOALED
GAOLED
GOALIE S
GOALIES
SOILAGE
GOALING
GAOLING
GOALLESS
GOALPOST S
GOALS
GAOLS
GOALWARD
GOANNA S
GOANNAS
GOAS
SAGO
GOAT S
TOGA
GOATEE DS
GOATEED
GOATEES
GOATFISH
GOATHERD S
GOATISH
GOATLIKE
GOATS
TOGAS
GOATSKIN S
GOB OSY
BOG
GOBAN GS
BOGAN
GOBANG S
GOBANGS
GOBANS
BOGANS
GOBBED
GOBBET S
GOBBETS
GOBBING
GOBBLE DRS
GOBBLED
GOBBLER S
GOBBLERS
GOBBLES
GOBBLING
GOBIES
BOGIES
GOBIOID S
GOBIOIDS
GOBLET S
GOBLETS
GOBLIN S
GLOBIN
GOBLINS
GLOBINS
GOBO S
GOBOES
GOBONEE
GOBONY
GOBOS
GOBS
BOGS
GOBSHITE S
GOBY
BOGY
GOD S
DOG
GODCHILD
GODDED
DODGED
GODDESS
GODDING
DODGING
GODET S
GODETIA S
GODETIAS
GODETS
STODGE
GODHEAD S
GODHEADS
GODHOOD S
GODHOODS
GODLESS
GLOSSED
GODLIER
GLORIED
GODLIEST
GODLIKE
DOGLIKE
GODLILY
GODLING S
LODGING
GODLINGS
LODGINGS
GODLY
GODOWN S
GODOWNS
GODROON S
GODROONS
GODS
DOGS
GODSEND S
GODSENDS
GODSHIP S
GODSHIPS
GODSON S
GODSONS
GODWIT S
GODWITS
GOER S
ERGO GORE
OGRE
GOERS
GORES GORSE
OGRES
GOES
EGOS SEGO
GOETHITE S
GOFER S
FORGE
GOFERS
FORGES
GOFFER S
GOFFERED
GOFFERS
GOGGLE DRS
GOGGLED
GOGGLER S
GOGGLERS
GOGGLES
GOGGLIER
GOGGLING
GOGGLY
GOGLET S
TOGGLE
GOGLETS
LOGGETS
TOGGLES
GOGO S
GOGOS
GOING S
GOINGS
GOITER S
GOITRE
GOITERS
GOITRES
GORIEST
GOITRE S
GOITER
GOITRES
GOITERS
GORIEST
GOITROUS
GOLCONDA S
GOLD S
GOLDARN S
GOLDARNS
GOLDBUG S
GOLDBUGS
GOLDEN
DONGLE
LONGED
GOLDENER
GOLDENLY
GOLDER
LODGER
GOLDEST
GOLDEYE S
GOLDEYES
GOLDFISH
GOLDS
GOLDTONE
GOLDURN S
GOLDURNS
GOLEM S
GOLEMS
GOLF S
FLOG
GOLFED
FODGEL
GOLFER S
GOLFERS
GOLFING S
GOLFINGS
GOLFS
FLOGS
GOLGOTHA S
GOLIARD S
GOLIARDS
GOLIATH S
GOLIATHS
GOLLIWOG GS
GOLLY

GOLLYWOG S
GOLOSH E
GOLOSHE S
GOLOSHES
GOMBEEN S
GOMBEENS
GOMBO S
GOMBOS
GOMBROON S
GOMER S
GOMERAL S
GLOMERA
GOMERALS
GOMEREL S
GOMERELS
GOMERIL S
GOMERILS
GOMERS
GOMUTI S
GOMUTIS
GONAD S
DONGA
GONADAL
GONADIAL
DIAGONAL
GONADIC
GONADS
DONGAS
GONDOLA S
DONGOLA
GONDOLAS
DONGOLAS
A GONE FR
GONEF S
GONEFS
GONENESS
GONER S
GENRO
GONERS
GENROS
GONFALON S
GONFANON S
GONG S
NOGG
GONGED
NOGGED
GONGING
NOGGING
GONGLIKE
GONGS
NOGGS
GONIA
GONIDIA L
GONIDIAL
GONIDIC
GONIDIUM
GONIF FS
GONIFF S
OFFING
GONIFFS
OFFINGS
GONIFS
GONION
GONIUM
GONOCYTE S
GONOF S
GONOFS
GONOPH S
GONOPHS
GONOPORE S
GONZO
GOO DFKNPS
GOOBER S
BOOGER
GOOBERS
BOOGERS
GOOD SY
GOODBY ES
GOODBYE S
GOODBYES
GOODBYS
GOODIE S
GOODIES
GOODISH
GOODLIER
GOODLY
GOODMAN
GOODMEN
GOODNESS
GOODS
GOODWIFE
GOODWILL S
GOODY
GOOEY
GOOF SY
GOOFBALL S
GOOFED
GOOFIER
GOOFIEST
GOOFILY
GOOFING
GOOFS
GOOFY
GOOGLIES
GOOGLY
GOOGOL S
GOOGOLS
GOOIER
GOOIEST
GOOK SY
GOOKS
GOOKY
GOOMBAH S
GOOMBAHS
GOOMBAY S
GOOMBAYS
GOON SY
GOONEY S
OOGENY
GOONEYS
GOONIE RS
NOOGIE
GOONIER
GOONIES T
ISOGONE
NOOGIES
GOONIEST
GOONS
GOONY
GOOP SY
GOOPIER
GOOPIEST
GOOPS
GOOPY
GOORAL S
GOORALS
GOOS EY
GOOSE DSY
GOOSED
GOOSES
GOOSEY
GOOSIER
GOOSIEST
GOOSING
GOOSY
GOPHER S
GOPHERS
GOPIK
GOR EMPY
GORAL S
ALGOR ARGOL
LARGO
GORALS
ALGORS
ARGOLS
LARGOS
GORBELLY
GORBLIMY
GORCOCK S
GORCOCKS
GORDITA S
GORDITAS
GORE DS
ERGO GOER
OGRE
GORED
GORES
GOERS GORSE
OGRES
GORGE DRST
GREGO
GORGED
DOGGER
GORGEDLY
GORGEOUS
GORGER S
GORGERIN S
ROGERING
GORGERS
GORGES
GREGOS
GORGET S
GORGETED
GORGETS
GORGING
GORGON S
GORGONS
GORHEN S
GORHENS
GORIER
GORIEST
GOITERS
GOITRES
GORILLA S
GORILLAS
GORILY
GORINESS
GORING
GORM S
GORMAND S
GORMANDS
GORMED
GORMING
GORMLESS
GORMS
GORP S
PROG
GORPS
PROGS
GORSE S
GOERS GORES
OGRES
GORSES
OGRESS
GORSIER
GORSIEST
STRIGOSE
GORSY
GYROS
GORY
GYRO ORGY
E GOS H
GOSH
HOGS SHOG
GOSHAWK S
GOSHAWKS
GOSLING S
GOSLINGS
GLOSSING
GOSPEL S
GOSPELER S
GOSPELLY
GOSPELS
GOSPORT S
GOSPORTS
GOSSAMER SY
GOSSAN S
GOSSANS
GOSSIP SY
GOSSIPED
GOSSIPER S
SERPIGOS
GOSSIPRY
GOSSIPS
GOSSIPY
GOSSOON S
GOSSOONS
GOSSYPOL S
GOT H
TOG
GOTCHA S
GOTCHAS
GOTH S
GOTHIC S
GOTHICS
GOTHITE S
GOTHITES
GOTHS
GHOST
GOTTEN
GOUACHE S
GOUACHES
GOUGE DRS
GOUGED
GOUGER S
GOUGERS
GOUGES
GOUGING
GOULASH
GOURAMI S
GOURAMIS
GOURD ES
GOURDE S
DROGUE
ROGUED
ROUGED
GOURDES
DROGUES
GROUSED
GOURDS
GOURMAND S
GOURMET S
GOURMETS
GOUT SY
GOUTIER
GOUTIEST
GOUTILY
GOUTS
GUSTO
A GOUTY
GUYOT
GOVERN S
GOVERNED
GOVERNOR S
GOVERNS
GOWAN SY
WAGON
GOWANED
WAGONED
GOWANS
WAGONS
GOWANY
GOWD S
GOWDS
GOWK S
GOWKS
GOWN S
GOWNED
GOWNING
GOWNS
GOWNSMAN
GOWNSMEN
GOX
GOXES
GRAAL S
ARGAL
GRAALS
ARGALS
GRAB S
BRAG GARB
GRABBED
GRABBER S
GRABBERS
GRABBIER
GRABBING
GRABBLE DRS
GABBLER
GRABBLED
GRABBLER S
GRABBLES
GABBLERS
GRABBY
GRABEN S
BANGER
GRABENS
BANGERS
GRABS
BRAGS GARBS
GRACE DS
CAGER
GRACED
CADGER
GRACEFUL
GRACES
CAGERS
GRACILE S
GLACIER
GRACILES
GLACIERS
GRACILIS
GRACING
GRACIOSO S
GRACIOUS
GRACKLE S
GRACKLES
GRAD ES
DRAG
GRADABLE
GRADATE DS
GRADATED
GRADATES
GRADE DRS
RAGED
GRADED
GADDER
GRADER S
GARRED
REGARD
GRADERS
REGARDS
GRADES
GRADIENT S
DERATING
REDATING
TREADING
GRADIN EGS
DARING
GRADINE S
DERAIGN
GRAINED
READING
GRADINES
DERAIGNS
READINGS
GRADING
NIGGARD
GRADINS
DARINGS
GRADS
DRAGS
GRADUAL S
GRADUALS
GRADUAND S
GRADUATE DS
GRADUS
GUARDS
GRADUSES
DESUGARS
GRAECIZE DS
S GRAFFITI S
S GRAFFITO
GRAFT S
GRAFTAGE S
GRAFTED
GRAFTER S
REGRAFT
GRAFTERS
REGRAFTS
GRAFTING
GRAFTS
GRAHAM S
GRAHAMS
GRAIL S
ARGIL GLAIR
GRAILS
ARGILS
GLAIRS
GRAIN SY
GARNI
GRAINED
DERAIGN
GRADINE
READING
GRAINER S
ANGRIER
EARRING
RANGIER
REARING
GRAINERS
EARRINGS
GRAINIER
GRAINING
GRAINS
RASING
GRAINY
RAYING
GRAM APS
GRAMA S
GRAMARY E
GRAMARYE S
GRAMAS
GRAMERCY
GRAMMA RS
GRAMMAR S
GRAMMARS
GRAMMAS
GRAMME S
GAMMER
GRAMMES
GAMMERS
GRAMP AS
GRAMPA S
GRAMPAS
GRAMPS
GRAMPUS
GRAMS
GRAN ADST
GNAR RANG
GRANA
GRANARY
GRAND S
GRANDAD S
GRANDADS
GRANDAM ES
GRANDMA
GRANDAME S
GRANDAMS
GRANDMAS
GRANDDAD S
GRANDDAM S
GRANDEE S
ANGERED
DERANGE
ENRAGED
GRENADE
GRANDEES
DERANGES
GRENADES
GRANDER
GNARRED
GRANDEST
DRAGNETS
GRANDEUR S
GRANDKID S
GRANDLY
GRANDMA S
GRANDAM
GRANDMAS
GRANDAMS
GRANDPA S
GRANDPAS
GRANDS
GRANDSIR ES
GRANDSON S
GRANGE RS
GANGER
NAGGER
GRANGER S
GRANGERS
GRANGES
GANGERS
NAGGERS
GRANITA S
GRANITAS
GRANITE S
GRATINE
INGRATE
TANGIER
TEARING
GRANITES
ANGRIEST
ASTRINGE
GANISTER
GANTRIES
INGRATES
RANGIEST
GRANITIC
GRANNIE S
AGINNER
EARNING
ENGRAIN
NEARING
GRANNIES
AGINNERS
EARNINGS
ENGRAINS
GRANNY
GRANOLA S
GRANOLAS
GRANS
GNARS
GRANT S
GRANTED
DRAGNET
GRANTEE S
GREATEN
NEGATER
REAGENT
GRANTEES
ESTRANGE
GREATENS
NEGATERS
REAGENTS
SERGEANT
GRANTER S
REGRANT
GRANTERS
REGRANTS
STRANGER
GRANTING
GRANTOR S
GRANTORS
GRANTS
STRANG
GRANULAR
GRANULE S
GRANULES
GRANUM
GRAPE SY
GAPER PAGER
PARGE
GRAPERY
GRAPES
GAPERS
GASPER
PAGERS
PARGES
SPARGE
GRAPEY
GRAPH S
GRAPHED
GRAPHEME S
A GRAPHIC S
GRAPHICS
GRAPHING
GRAPHITE S
GRAPHS
GRAPIER
GRAPIEST
GRAPLIN ES
PARLING
GRAPLINE S
PEARLING
GRAPLINS
SPARLING
SPRINGAL
GRAPNEL S
GRAPNELS
GRAPPA S
GRAPPAS
GRAPPLE DRS
GRAPPLED
GRAPPLER S
GRAPPLES
GRAPY
GRASP S
SPRAG
GRASPED
SPARGED
GRASPER S
SPARGER
GRASPERS
SPARGERS
GRASPING
PARGINGS
SPARGING
GRASPS
SPRAGS
GRASS Y
GRASSED
GRASSES
GASSERS
GRASSIER
GRASSILY
GRASSING
GRASSY
GRAT E
GRATE DRS
GATER GREAT
RETAG TARGE
TERGA
GRATED
GRATEFUL

GRATER S
GARRET
GARTER
GRATERS
GARRETS
GARTERS
GRATES
GASTER
GATERS
GREATS
RETAGS
STAGER
TARGES
GRATIFY
GRATIN EGS
RATING
TARING
GRATINE E
GRANITE
INGRATE
TANGIER
TEARING
GRATINEE DS
INTERAGE
GRATING S
GRATINGS
GRATINS
GASTRIN
RATINGS
STARING
GRATIS
GRATUITY
GRAUPEL S
EARPLUG
PLAGUER
GRAUPELS
EARPLUGS
PLAGUERS
GRAVAMEN S
GRAVE DLNRS
GRAVED
GRAVEL SY
GRAVELED
GRAVELLY
GRAVELS
VERGLAS
GRAVELY
GRAVEN
GRAVER S
GRAVERS
GRAVES T
GRAVEST
GRAVID A
GRAVIDA ES
GRAVIDAE
GRAVIDAS
GRAVIDLY
GRAVIES
RIVAGES
GRAVING
GRAVITAS
STRAVAIG
GRAVITON S
GRAVITY
GRAVLAKS
GRAVLAX
GRAVURE S
GRAVURES
GRAVY
GRAY S
GRAYBACK S
GRAYED
GRAYER
GRAYEST
GYRATES
GRAYFISH
GRAYING
GRAYISH
GRAYLAG S
GRAYLAGS
GRAYLING S
RAGINGLY
GRAYLY
GRAYMAIL S
GRAYNESS
GRAYOUT S
GRAYOUTS
GRAYS
GRAZABLE
GRAZE DRS
GAZER
GRAZED
GRAZER S
GRAZERS
GRAZES
GAZERS
GRAZIER S
GRAZIERS
GRAZING S
GRAZINGS
GRAZIOSO
GREASE DRS
AGREES
EAGERS
EAGRES
RAGEES
GREASED
DRAGEES
GREASER S
REGEARS
GREASERS
GREASES
GREASIER
GREASILY
GREASING
GEARINGS
SNAGGIER
GREASY
GYRASE
YAGERS
GREAT S
GATER GRATE
RETAG TARGE
TERGA
GREATEN S
GRANTEE
NEGATER
REAGENT
GREATENS
ESTRANGE
GRANTEES
NEGATERS
REAGENTS
SERGEANT
GREATER
REGRATE
GREATEST
GREATLY
GREATS
GASTER
GATERS
GRATES
RETAGS
STAGER
TARGES
GREAVE DS
REGAVE
GREAVED
GREAVES
GREBE S
GREBES
GRECIZE DS
GRECIZED
GRECIZES
A GREE DKNST
EGER
A GREED SY
EDGER
GREEDIER
GREEDILY
GREEDS
EDGERS
SERGED
GREEDY
GREYED
GREEGREE S
A GREEING
GREEK
GREEN SY
GENRE
GREENBUG S
GREENED
RENEGED
GREENER Y
REGREEN
RENEGER
GREENERY
GREENEST
GREENFLY
GREENIE RS
GREENIER
GREENIES T
ENERGIES
ENERGISE
RESEEING
GREENING S
RENEGING
GREENISH
REHINGES
SHEERING
GREENLET S
GREENLIT
GREENLY
GREENS
GENRES
GREENTH S
GREENTHS
GREENWAY S
GREENY
ENERGY
GYRENE
A GREES
EGERS REGES
SERGE
GREET S
EGRET
GREETED
DETERGE
GREETER S
REGREET
GREETERS
REGREETS
GREETING S
GREETS
EGRETS
GREGO S
GORGE
GREGOS
GORGES
GREIGE S
GREIGES
GREISEN S
GREISENS
GREMIAL S
GREMIALS
GREMLIN S
MINGLER
GREMLINS
MINGLERS
GREMMIE S
GEMMIER
IMMERGE
GREMMIES
IMMERGES
GREMMY
GRENADE S
ANGERED
DERANGE
ENRAGED
GRANDEE
GRENADES
DERANGES
GRANDEES
GREW
GREWSOME R
GREY S
GYRE
GREYED
GREEDY
GREYER
GREYEST
GREYHEN S
GREYHENS
GREYING
GINGERY
GREYISH
GREYLAG S
GREYLAGS
GREYLY
GREYNESS
GREYS
GYRES
GRIBBLE S
GLIBBER
GRIBBLES
GRID ES
GIRD
GRIDDED
GRIDDER S
GRIDDERS
GRIDDLE DS
GIRDLED
GRIDDLED
GRIDDLES
GRIDE DS
DIRGE RIDGE
GRIDED
GIRDED
RIDGED
GRIDES
DIRGES
RIDGES
GRIDING
GIRDING
RIDGING
GRIDIRON S
GRIDLOCK S
GRIDS
GIRDS
GRIEF S
GRIEFS
FRIGES
GRIEVANT S
AVERTING
VINTAGER
GRIEVE DRS
REGIVE
GRIEVED
DIVERGE
GRIEVER S
GRIEVERS
GRIEVES
REGIVES
GRIEVING
REGIVING
GRIEVOUS
GRIFF ES
GRIFFE S
GRIFFES
GRIFFIN S
RIFFING
GRIFFINS
GRIFFON S
GRIFFONS
GRIFFS
GRIFT S
GRIFTED
GRIFTER S
GRIFTERS
GRIFTING
GRIFTS
GRIG S
GRIGRI S
GRIGRIS
GRIGS
GRILL ES
GRILLADE S
GLADLIER
GRILLAGE S
GRILLE DRS
GILLER
GRILLED
GRILLER SY
GRILLERS
GRILLERY
GRILLES
GILLERS
GRILLING
GRILLS
GRILSE S
LIGERS
GRILSES
GRIM EY
GRIMACE DRS
GRIMACED
DECIGRAM
GRIMACER S
GRIMACES
GRIME DS
GRIMED
GRIMES
GRIMIER
GRIMIEST
GRIMILY
GRIMING
GRIMLY
GRIMMER
GRIMMEST
GRIMNESS
GRIMY
GRIN DS
GIRN RING
GRINCH
GRINCHES
GRIND S
GRINDED
REDDING
GRINDER SY
REGRIND
GRINDERS
REGRINDS
GRINDERY
REDRYING
GRINDING
GRINDS
GRINNED
RENDING
GRINNER S
GRINNERS
GRINNING
GRINS
GIRNS RINGS
GRIOT S
TRIGO
GRIOTS
TRIGOS
GRIP ESTY
PRIG
GRIPE DRSY
GRIPED
GRIPER S
GRIPERS
GRIPES
GRIPEY
GRIPIER
GRIPIEST
GRIPING
GRIPMAN
RAMPING
GRIPMEN
IMPREGN
PERMING
GRIPPE DRS
GIPPER
GRIPPED
GRIPPER S
GRIPPERS
GRIPPES
GIPPERS
GRIPPIER
GRIPPING
GRIPPLE
GRIPPY
GRIPS
PRIGS SPRIG
GRIPSACK S
GRIPT
GRIPY
GRISEOUS
GRISETTE S
TERGITES
GRISKIN S
RISKING
GRISKINS
GRISLIER
GRISLY
GRISON S
GIRONS
GROINS
ROSING
SIGNOR
SORING
GRISONS
SIGNORS
SORINGS
GRIST S
GIRTS GRITS
TRIGS
GRISTER S
GRISTERS
GRISTLE S
GLISTER
GRISTLES
GLISTERS
GRISTLY
GRISTS
GRIT HS
GIRT TRIG
GRITH S
GIRTH RIGHT
GRITHS
GIRTHS
RIGHTS
GRITS
GIRTS GRIST
TRIGS
GRITTED
GRITTER S
GRITTERS
GRITTIER
GRITTILY
GRITTING
GRITTY
GRIVET S
GRIVETS
GRIZZLE DRS
GRIZZLED
GRIZZLER S
GRIZZLES
GRIZZLY
GROAN S
ARGON ORANG
ORGAN
GROANED
GROANER S
GROANERS
GROANING
GROANS
ARGONS
ORANGS
ORGANS
SARONG
GROAT S
ARGOT GATOR
GROATS
ARGOTS
GATORS
GROCER SY
GROCERS
GROCERY
GRODIER
GRODIEST
DIGESTOR
STODGIER
GRODY
GROG S
GROGGERY
GROGGIER
GROGGILY
GROGGY
GROGRAM S
GROGRAMS
GROGS
GROGSHOP S
GROIN S
GIRON
GROINED
ERODING
IGNORED
NEGROID
REDOING
GROINING
IGNORING
GROINS
GIRONS
GRISON
ROSING
SIGNOR
SORING
GROK S
GROKKED
GROKKING
GROKS
GROMMET S
GROMMETS
GROMWELL S
GROOM S
GROOMED
GROOMER S
REGROOM
GROOMERS
REGROOMS
GROOMING
GROOMS
GROOVE DRS
GROOVED
OVERDOG
GROOVER S
GROOVERS
GROOVES
GROOVIER
GROOVING
GROOVY
GROPE DRS
GROPED
GROPER S
GROPERS
GROPES
GROPING
GROSBEAK S
BROKAGES
GROSCHEN
GROSS
GROSSED
GROSSER S
GROSSERS
GROSSES T
GROSSEST
GROSSING
GROSSLY
GROSZ EY
GROSZE
GROSZY
GROT S
TROG
GROTS
TROGS
GROTTIER
GROTTO S
GROTTOED
GROTTOES
GROTTOS
GROTTY
GROUCH Y
GROUCHED
GROUCHES
CHOREGUS
COUGHERS
GROUCHY
A GROUND S
GROUNDED
UNDERDOG
UNDERGOD
GROUNDER S
REGROUND
GROUNDS
GROUP S
GROUPED
GROUPER S
REGROUP
GROUPERS
REGROUPS
GROUPIE S
PIROGUE
GROUPIES
PIROGUES
GROUPING S
GROUPOID S
GROUPS
GROUSE DRS
ERUGOS
ROGUES
ROUGES
RUGOSE
GROUSED
DROGUES
GOURDES
GROUSER S
GROUSERS
GROUSES
GROUSING
GROUT SY
GROUTED
GROUTER S
GROUTERS
GROUTIER
GROUTING
GROUTS
GROUTY
YOGURT
GROVE DLS
GROVED
GROVEL S
GLOVER
GROVELED
GROVELER S

GROVELS
GLOVERS
GROVES
GROW LNS
GROWABLE
GROWER S
REGROW
GROWERS
REGROWS
GROWING
GROWL SY
GROWLED
GROWLER S
GROWLERS
GROWLIER
GROWLING
GROWLS
GROWLY
GROWN
WRONG
GROWNUP S
UPGROWN
GROWNUPS
GROWS
GROWTH SY
GROWTHS
GROWTHY
GROYNE S
ERYNGO
GROYNES
ERYNGOS
GRUB S
BURG
GRUBBED
GRUBBER S
GRUBBERS
GRUBBIER
GRUBBILY
GRUBBING
GRUBBY
GRUBS
BURGS
GRUBWORM S
GRUDGE DRS
GURGED
RUGGED
GRUDGED
DRUGGED
GRUDGER S
GRUDGERS
GRUDGES
GRUDGING
DRUGGING
GRUE LS
URGE
GRUEL S
GLUER LUGER
GRUELED
REGLUED
GRUELER S
GRUELERS
GRUELING S
REGLUING
GRUELLED
GRUELLER S
GRUELS
GLUERS
LUGERS
GRUES
SURGE URGES
GRUESOME R
GRUFF SY
GRUFFED
GRUFFER
GRUFFEST
GRUFFIER
GRUFFILY
GRUFFING
GRUFFISH
GRUFFLY
GRUFFS
GRUFFY
GRUGRU S
GRUGRUS
GRUIFORM
GRUM EP
GRUMBLE DRS
GRUMBLED
GRUMBLER S
GRUMBLES
GRUMBLY
GRUME S
GRUMES
GRUMMER
GRUMMEST
GRUMMETS
GRUMMET S
GRUMMETS
GRUMMEST
GRUMOSE
MORGUES
GRUMOUS
GRUMP SY
GRUMPED
GRUMPHIE S
GRUMPHY
GRUMPIER
GRUMPILY
GRUMPING
GRUMPISH
GRUMPS
GRUMPY
GRUNGE RS
GRUNGER S
GRUNGERS
GRUNGES
SNUGGER
GRUNGIER
GRUNGY
GRUNION S
GRUNIONS
GRUNT S
GRUNTED
TRUDGEN
GRUNTER S
GRUNTERS
RESTRUNG
GRUNTING
GRUNTLE DS
GRUNTLED
GRUNTLES
GRUNTS
STRUNG
GRUSHIE
GUSHIER
GRUTCH
GRUTCHED
GRUTCHES
GRUTTEN
TURGENT
GRUYERE S
GRUYERES
GRYPHON S
GRYPHONS
GUACHARO S
GUACO S
GUACOS
GUAIAC S
GUAIACOL S
GUAIACS
GUAIACUM S
GUAIOCUM S
GUAN OS
GAUN
GUANACO S
GUANACOS
GUANASE S
GUANASES
GUANAY S
GUANAYS
GUANIDIN ES
GUANIN ES
GUANINE S
ANGUINE
GUANINES
SANGUINE
GUANINS
GUANO S
GUANOS
GUANS
GUAR DS
GAUR RUGA
GUARANA S
GUARANAS
GUARANI S
GUARANIS
GUARANTY
GUARD S
GUARDANT S
GUARDDOG S
GUARDED
GUARDER S
GUARDERS
GUARDIAN S
GUARDING
GUARDS
GRADUS
GUARS
ARGUS GAURS
SUGAR
GUAVA S
GUAVAS
GUAYULE S
GUAYULES
GUCK S
GUCKS
GUDE S
GUDES
GUDGEON S
GUDGEONS
GUENON S
GUENONS
GUERDON S
UNDERGO
GUERDONS
GUERIDON S
GUERILLA S
GUERNSEY S
GUESS
GUESSED
GUESSER S
GUESSERS
GUESSES
GUESSING
SNUGGIES
GUEST S
GUESTED
GUESTING
GUESTS
GUSSET
GUFF S
GUFFAW S
GUFFAWED
GUFFAWS
GUFFS
GUGGLE DS
GUGGLED
GLUGGED
GUGGLES
GUGGLING
GLUGGING
GUGLET S
GUGLETS
GUID ES
GUIDABLE
GUIDANCE S
GUIDE DRS
GUIDED
GUIDER S
GUIDERS
GUIDES
GUISED
GUIDEWAY S
GUIDING
GUIDON S
GUIDONS
DOUSING
GUIDS
GUILD S
GUILDER S
GUILDERS
SLUDGIER
GUILDS
GUILE DS
GUILED
GUILEFUL
GUILES
UGLIES
GUILING
GUILT SY
GUILTIER
GUILTILY
GUILTS
GUILTY
GUIMPE S
GUIMPES
GUINEA S
GUINEAS
GUIPURE S
GUIPURES
GUIRO S
GUIROS
GUISARD S
GUISARDS
GUISE DS
GUISED
GUIDES
GUISES
GUSSIE
GUISING
GUITAR S
GUITARS
GUITGUIT S
GUL FLPS
LUG
GULAG S
GULAGS
GULAR
RUGAL
GULCH
GULCHES
GULDEN S
LUNGED
GULDENS
GULES
GLUES LUGES
GULF SY
GULFED
FUGLED
GULFIER
GULFIEST
GULFING
FUGLING
GULFLIKE
GULFS
GULFWEED S
GULFY
GULL SY
GULLABLE
GULLABLY
GULLED
GULLET S
GULLETS
GULLEY S
GULLEYS
GULLIBLE
BLUEGILL
GULLIBLY
GULLIED
GULLIES
LIGULES
GULLING
GULLS
GULLWING
GULLY
GULLYING
GULOSITY
GULP SY
PLUG
GULPED
GULPER S
GULPERS
SPLURGE
GULPIER
GULPIEST
GULPING
GULPS
PLUGS
GULPY
GULS
LUGS SLUG
GUM S
MUG
GUMBALL S
GUMBALLS
GUMBO S
GUMBOIL S
GUMBOILS
GUMBOOT S
GUMBOOTS
GUMBOS
GUMBOTIL S
GUMDROP S
GUMDROPS
GUMLESS
GUMLIKE
GUMLINE S
LEGUMIN
GUMLINES
LEGUMINS
GUMMA S
GUMMAS
GUMMATA
GUMMED
GUMMER S
GUMMERS
GUMMIER
GUMMIEST
GUMMITES
GUMMING
GUMMITE S
GUMMITES
GUMMIEST
GUMMOSE S
GUMMOSES
GUMMOSIS
GUMMOUS
GUMMY
GUMPTION S
GUMS
MUGS SMUG
GUMSHOE DS
GUMSHOED
GUMSHOES
GUMTREE S
GUMTREES
GUMWEED S
GUMWEEDS
GUMWOOD S
GUMWOODS
GUN KS
GNU
GUNBOAT S
GUNBOATS
GUNDOG S
DUGONG
GUNDOGS
DUGONGS
GUNFIGHT S
GUNFIRE S
GUNFIRES
REFUSING
GUNFLINT S
GUNITE S
GUNITES
GUNK SY
GUNKHOLE DS
GUNKIER
GUNKIEST
GUNKS
GUNKY
GUNLESS
GUNSELS
GUNLOCK S
GUNLOCKS
GUNMAN
GUNMEN
GUNMETAL S
GUNNED
GUNNEL S
GUNNELS
GUNNEN
GUNNER SY
GUNNERS
GUNNERY
GUNNIES
ENSUING
GUNNING S
GUNNINGS
GUNNY
GUNNYBAG S
GUNPAPER S
GUNPLAY S
GUNPLAYS
GUNPOINT S
GUNROOM S
GUNROOMS
GUNS
GNUS SNUG
SUNG
GUNSEL S
LUNGES
GUNSELS
GUNLESS
GUNSHIP S
PUSHING
GUNSHIPS
GUNSHOT S
HOGNUTS
NOUGHTS
SHOTGUN
GUNSHOTS
SHOTGUNS
GUNSMITH S
GUNSTOCK S
GUNWALE S
GUNWALES
GUPPIES
GUPPY
GURGE DS
GURGED
GRUDGE
RUGGED
GURGES
GURGING
RUGGING
GURGLE DST
LUGGER
GURGLED
GURGLES
LUGGERS
SLUGGER
GURGLET S
GURGLETS
STRUGGLE
GURGLING
GURNARD S
GURNARDS
GURNET S
URGENT
GURNETS
GURNEY S
GURNEYS
GURRIES
GURRY
GURSH
SHRUG
GURSHES
GUSHERS
GURU S
GURUS
GURUSHIP S
GUSH Y
HUGS SUGH
UGHS
GUSHED
SUGHED
GUSHER S
GUSHERS
GURSHES
GUSHES
GUSHIER
GRUSHIE
GUSHIEST
GUSHILY
GUSHING
SUGHING
GUSHY
GUSSET S
GUESTS
GUSSETED
GUSSETS
GUSSIE DS
GUISES
GUSSIED
GUSSIES
GUSSY
GUSSYING
GUST OSY
GUTS TUGS
GUSTABLE S
GUSTED
DEGUST
GUSTIER
GUTSIER
GUSTIEST
GUTSIEST
GUSTILY
GUTSILY
GUSTING
GUSTLESS
GUSTO
GOUTS
GUSTOES
GUSTS
GUSTY
GUTSY
GUT S
TUG
GUTLESS
TUGLESS
GUTLIKE
GUTS Y
GUST TUGS
GUTSIER
GUSTIER
GUTSIEST
GUSTIEST
GUTSILY
GUSTILY
GUTSY
GUSTY
GUTTA E
GUTTAE
GUTTATE D
GUTTATED
GUTTED
GUTTER SY
GUTTERED
GUTTERS
GUTTERY
GUTTIER
TURGITE
GUTTIEST
GUTTING
GUTTLE DRS
GUTTLED
GLUTTED
GUTTLER S
GUTTLERS
GUTTLES
GUTTLING
GLUTTING
GUTTURAL S
GUTTY
GUV S
VUG
GUVS
VUGS
GUY S
GUYED
GUYING
GUYLINE S
GUYLINES
GUYOT S
GOUTY
GUYOTS
GUYS
GUZZLE DRS
GUZZLED
GUZZLER S
GUZZLERS
GUZZLES
GUZZLING
GWEDUC KS
GWEDUCK S
GWEDUCKS
GWEDUCS
GWINE
GYBE DS
GYBED
GYBES
GYBING
GYM S
GYMKHANA S
GYMNASIA L
GYMNAST S
SYNTAGM
GYMNASTS
SYNTAGMS
GYMS
GYNAECEA
GYNAECIA
GYNANDRY
GYNARCHY
GYNECIA
GYNECIC

GYNECIUM
GYNECOID
DECOYING
GYNIATRY
GYNOECIA
GYOZA S
GYOZAS
AZYGOS
GYP S
GYPLURE S
GYPLURES
GYPPED
GYPPER S
GYPPERS
GYPPING
GYPS Y
GYPSEIAN
GYPSEOUS
GYPSIED
GYPSIES
GYPSTER S
GYPSTERS
GYPSUM S
GYPSUMS
GYPSY
GYPSYDOM S
GYPSYING
GYPSYISH
GYPSYISM S
GYRAL
GLARY
GYRALLY
GYRASE S
GREASY
YAGERS
GYRASES
GYRATE DS
GYRATED
TRAGEDY
GYRATES
GRAYEST
GYRATING
GYRATION S
GYRATOR SY
GYRATORS
GYRATORY
GYRE DS
GREY
GYRED
GYRENE S
ENERGY
GREENY
GYRENES
GYRES
GREYS
GYRI
GYRING
GYRO NS
GORY ORGY
GYROIDAL
GYRON S
GYRONS
GYROS E
GORSY
GYROSE
GYROSTAT S
GYRUS
SURGY
GYTTJA S
GYTTJAS
GYVE DS
GYVED
GYVES
GYVING

H

ASW HA DEGHJMOP
AH STWY
HAAF S
HAAFS
HAAR S
HAARS
HABANERA S
HABANERO S
HABDALAH S
HABILE
HABIT S
BAITH
HABITAN ST
HABITANS
HABITANT S
HABITAT S
HABITATS
HABITED
HABITING
HABITS
HABITUAL
HABITUDE S
HABITUE S
HABITUES
HABITUS
HABOOB S
HABOOBS
HABU S
HABUS
SUBAH
HACEK S
HACEKS
HACHURE DS
HACHURED
HACHURES
HACIENDA S
STW HACK S
HACKABLE
HACKBUT S
HACKBUTS
STW HACKED
HACKEE S
HACKEES
W HACKER S
W HACKERS
HACKIE S
HACKIES
STW HACKING
S HACKLE DRS
S HACKLED
CHALKED
S HACKLER S
S HACKLERS
SHACKLER
S HACKLES
SHACKLE
HACKLIER
CHALKIER
S HACKLING
CHALKING
HACKLY
CHALKY
HACKMAN
HACKMEN
HACKNEY S
HACKNEYS
STW HACKS
SHACK
HACKSAW NS
KWACHAS
HACKSAWN
HACKSAWS
HACKWORK S
CS HAD EJ
DAH
HADAL
C HADARIM
HADDEST
S HADDOCK S
S HADDOCKS
SHADDOCK
S HADE DS
AHED HAED
HEAD
S HADED
S HADES
ASHED DEASH
HEADS SADHE
SHADE
S HADING
HADITH S
HADITHS
HADJ I
HADJEE S
HADJEES
HADJES
JEHADS
HADJI S
JIHAD
HADJIS
JADISH
JIHADS
HADRON S
HADRONIC
HADRONS
HADST
T HAE DMNST
HAED
AHED HADE
HEAD
HAEING
HAEM S
AHEM HAME
HAEMAL
HAEMATAL
HAEMATIC S
HAEMATIN S
ANTHEMIA
HAEMIC
HAEMIN S
HAEMINS
HAEMOID
HAEMS
HAMES SHAME
HAEN
HAEREDES
HAERES
HEARSE
HAES
SHEA
HAET S
EATH HATE
HEAT THAE
HAETS
HASTE HATES
HEATS
HAFFET S
HAFFETS
HAFFIT S
HAFFITS
HAFIZ
HAFIZES
HAFNIUM S
HAFNIUMS
S HAFT S
HAFTARA HS
HAFTARAH S
HAFTARAS
HAFTAROT H
S HAFTED
HAFTER S
FATHER
TREFAH
HAFTERS
FATHERS
S HAFTING
HAFTORAH S
HAFTOROS
HAFTOROT H
S HAFTS
SHAFT
S HAG S
HAGADIC
HAGADIST S
HAGBERRY
HAGBORN
HAGBUSH
HAGBUT S
HAGBUTS
HAGDON S
HAGDONS
SANDHOG
HAGFISH
HAGGADA HS
AGGADAH
HAGGADAH S
HAGGADAS
AGGADAHS
HAGGADIC
HAGGADOT H
AGGADOTH
HAGGARD S
HAGGARDS
S HAGGED
S HAGGING
HAGGIS H
HAGGISES
HAGGISH
HAGGLE DRS
HAGGLED
HAGGLER S
HAGGLERS
HAGGLES
HAGGLING
HAGRIDE RS
HAGRIDER S
HAGRIDES
HAGRODE
S HAGS
GASH SHAG
S HAH AS
HAHA S
HAHAS
HAHNIUM S
HAHNIUMS
S HAHS
HASH SHAH
HAIK ASU
HAIKA
HAIKS
HAIKU S
HAIKUS
HAIL S
HILA
HAILED
HALIDE
HAILER S
HAILERS
SHALIER
HAILING
NILGHAI
HAILS
HAIMISH
HAINT S
HAINTS
SHANTI
C HAIR SY
HAIRBALL S
HAIRBAND S
HAIRCAP S
CHARPAI
HAIRCAPS
CHARPAIS
HAIRCUT S
HAIRCUTS
HAIRDO S
HAIRDOS
C HAIRED
HAIRIER
HAIRIEST
HAIRLESS
HAIRLIKE
HAIRLINE S
HAIRLOCK S
HAIRNET S
INEARTH
THERIAN
HAIRNETS
INEARTHS
THERIANS
HAIRPIN S
HAIRPINS
C HAIRS
HAIRWORK S
HAIRWORM S
HAIRY
HAJ IJ
HAJES
HAJI S
HAJIS
HAJJ I
HAJJES
HAJJI S
HAJJIS
S HAKE S
HAKEEM S
HAKEEMS
S HAKES
SHAKE
HAKIM S
HAKIMS
HAKU S
HAKUS
HALACHA S
HALACHAS
HALACHIC
HALACHOT H
HALAKAH S
HALAKHA
HALAKAHS
HALAKHAS
HALAKHA HS
HALAKAH
HALAKHAH S
HALAKHAS
HALAKAHS
HALAKHIC
HALAKHOT H
HALAKOTH
HALAKIC
HALAKIST S
HALAKOTH
HALAKHOT
HALAL AS
HALALA HS
HALALAH S
HALALAHS
HALALAS
HALALS
HALATION S
HALAVAH S
HALAVAHS
HALAZONE S
HALBERD S
HALBERDS
HALBERT S
BLATHER
HALBERTS
BLATHERS
HALCYON S
HALCYONS
SW HALE DRS
HEAL
SW HALED
HALENESS
TW HALER SU
TW HALERS
ASHLER
LASHER
HALERU
HAULER
SW HALES T
HEALS LEASH
SELAH SHALE
SHEAL
HALEST
HASLET
LATHES
SHELTA
HALF
HALFBACK S
HALFBEAK S
HALFLIFE
HALFNESS
HALFPIPE S
HALFTIME S
HALFTONE S
HALFWAY
HALIBUT S
HALIBUTS
HALID ES
HALIDE S
HAILED
HALIDES
HALIDOM ES
HALIDOME S
HALIDOMS
HALIDS
W HALING
HALITE S
HALITES
HELIAST
HALITUS
THULIAS
S HALL OS
C HALLAH S
C HALLAHS
HALLAL
HALLEL S
HALLELS
HALLIARD S
HALLMARK S
HALLO AOSTW
HOLLA
HALLOA S
HALLOAED
HALLOAS
HALLOED
HOLLAED
HALLOES
HALLOING
HOLLAING
HALLOO S
HOLLOA
HALLOOED
HOLLOAED
HALLOOS
HOLLOAS
HALLOS
HOLLAS
CS HALLOT H
C HALLOTH
S HALLOW S
S HALLOWED
S HALLOWER S
S HALLOWS
SHALLOW
HALLS
SHALL
HALLUCAL
HALLUCES
HALLUX
HALLWAY S
HALLWAYS
HALM AS
HALMA S
ALMAH HAMAL
HALMAS
ALMAHS
HAMALS
HALMS
HALO NS
HALOED
HALOES
HALOGEN S
HALOGENS
HALOID S
HALOIDS
HALOING
HALOLIKE
HALON S
HALONS
HALOS
SHOAL
S HALT S
LATH
HALTED
DALETH
LATHED
HALTER ES
LATHER
THALER
HALTERE DS
LEATHER
HALTERED
LATHERED
HALTERES
LEATHERS
HALTERS
HARSLET
LATHERS
SLATHER
THALERS
HALTING
LATHING
HALTLESS
HALTS
LATHS SHALT
C HALUTZ
C HALUTZIM
HALVA HS
HALVAH S
HALVAHS
HALVAS
LAVASH
HALVE DS
HALVED
HALVERS
HALVES
HALVING
HALYARD S
HALYARDS
CSW HAM ES
HAMADA S
HAMADAS
HAMAL S
ALMAH HALMA
HAMALS
ALMAHS
HALMAS
HAMARTIA S
HAMATE S
HAMATES
HAMAUL S
HAMAULS
HAMBONE DS
HAMBONED
HAMBONES
HAMBURG S
HAMBURGS
S HAME S
AHEM HAEM
S HAMES
HAEMS SHAME
HAMLET S
HAMLETS
HAMMADA S
HAMMADAS
HAMMAL S
HAMMALS
HAMMAM S
HAMMAMS
SW HAMMED
S HAMMER S
HAMMERED
HAMMERER S
REHAMMER
S HAMMERS
SHAMMER
HAMMIER
HAMMIEST
HAMMILY
SW HAMMING
HAMMOCK S
HAMMOCKS
CSW HAMMY
C HAMPER S
HAMPERED
HAMPERER S
C HAMPERS
CSW HAMS
MASH SHAM
HAMSTER S
HAMSTERS
HAMULAR
HAMULATE
HAMULI
HAMULOSE
HAMULOUS
HAMULUS
HAMZA HS
HAMZAH S
HAMZAHS
HAMZAS
SHAZAM
HANAPER S
HANAPERS
C HANCE S
C HANCES
ENCASH
NACHES
HAND SY
HANDAX
HANDAXES
HANDBAG S
HANDBAGS
HANDBALL S
HANDBELL S
HANDBILL S
HANDBOOK S
HANDCAR ST
HANDCARS
HANDCART S
HANDCLAP S
HANDCUFF S
HANDED
HANDER S
HARDEN

HANDERS
HARDENS
HANDFAST S
HANDFUL S
HANDFULS
HANDSFUL
HANDGRIP S
HANDGUN S
HANDGUNS
HANDHELD S
HANDHOLD S
HANDICAP S
HANDIER
HANDIEST
HANDILY
HANDING
HANDLE DRS
HANDLED
C HANDLER S
C HANDLERS
HANDLES S
HANDSEL
HANDLESS
HANDSELS
HANDLIKE
HANDLING S
HANDLIST S
HANDLOOM S
HANDMADE
HANDMAID S
HANDOFF S
OFFHAND
HANDOFFS
HANDOUT S
HANDOUTS
THOUSAND
HANDOVER S
OVERHAND
HANDPICK S
HANDRAIL S
HANDS
HANDSAW S
HANDSAWS
HANDSEL S
HANDLES
HANDSELS
HANDLESS
HANDSET S
HANDSETS
HANDSEWN
HANDSFUL
HANDFULS
HANDSOME R
HANDWORK S
HANDWRIT E
S HANDY
HANDYMAN
HANDYMEN
BCW HANG S
HANGABLE
HANGAR S
HANGARED
HANGARS
HANGBIRD S
HANGDOG S
HANGDOGS
CW HANGED
C HANGER S
REHANG
C HANGERS
REHANGS
HANGFIRE S
CW HANGING S
HANGINGS
GNASHING
HANGMAN
HANGMEN
HANGNAIL S
HANGNEST S
HANGOUT S
HANGOUTS
HANGOVER S
OVERHANG
BCW HANGS
GNASH SANGH
HANGTAG S
HANGTAGS
HANGUL

HANGUP S
HANGUPS
HANIWA
ST HANK SY
ANKH KHAN
ST HANKED
T HANKER S
HARKEN
HANKERED
DAKERHEN
HARKENED
HANKERER S
HARKENER
T HANKERS
HARKENS
HANKIE S
HANKIES
ST HANKING
ST HANKS
ANKHS KHANS
SHANK
HANKY
HANSA S
HANSAS
HANSE LS
ASHEN
HANSEL S
HANSELED
HANSELS
HANSES
HANSOM S
HANSOMS
C HANT S
THAN
C HANTED
C HANTING
HANTLE S
THENAL
HANTLES
C HANTS
SNATH
HANUMAN S
HANUMANS
C HAO
CW HAP S
PAH
HAPAX
HAPAXES
HAPHTARA HS
HAPKIDO S
HAPKIDOS
HAPLESS
PLASHES
HAPLITE S
HAPLITES
HAPLOID SY
HAPLOIDS
SHIPLOAD
HAPLOIDY
HAPLONT S
NAPHTOL
HAPLONTS
NAPHTOLS
HAPLOPIA S
HAPLOSES
HAPLOSIS
ALPHOSIS
HAPLY
PHYLA
CW HAPPED
HAPPEN S
HAPPENED
HAPPENS
HAPPIER
HAPPIEST
EPITAPHS
HAPPILY
CW HAPPING
HAPPY
CW HAPS
HASP PASH
HAPTEN ES
HAPTENE S
HEPTANE
PHENATE
HAPTENES
HEPTANES
PHENATES
HAPTENIC
HAPTENS

HAPTIC
PHATIC
HAPTICAL
HARANGUE DR S
HARASS
HARASSED
HARASSER S
HARASSES
HARBOR S
HARBORED
ABHORRED
HARBORER S
ABHORRER
HARBORS
HARBOUR S
HARBOURS
CS HARD SY
HARDBACK S
HARDBALL S
HARDBOOT S
HARDCASE
CHARADES
HARDCORE S
HARDEDGE S
HARDEN S
HANDER
HARDENED
ADHEREND
HARDENER S
REHARDEN
HARDENS
HANDERS
HARDER
HARDEST
DEARTHS
HARDSET
HATREDS
THREADS
TRASHED
HARDHACK S
HARDHAT S
HARDHATS
HARDHEAD S
HARDIER
HARRIED
HARDIES T
AIRSHED
DASHIER
SHADIER
HARDIEST
HARDILY
HARDLINE
HARDLY
HARDNESS
HARDNOSE S
HARDPACK S
HARDPAN S
HARDPANS
CS HARDS
SHARD
HARDSET
DEARTHS
HARDEST
HATREDS
THREADS
TRASHED
HARDSHIP S
HARDTACK S
HARDTOP S
HARDTOPS
POTSHARD
HARDWARE S
HARDWIRE DS
HARDWOOD S
HARDY
HYDRA
CS HARE DMS
HEAR RHEA
HAREBELL S
CS HARED
HEARD
HAREEM S
HERMAE
HAREEMS
HARELIKE
HARELIP S
HARELIPS
EARLSHIP
PLASHIER

HAREM S
HERMA
HAREMS
MASHER
SHMEAR
CS HARES
HEARS RHEAS
SHARE SHEAR
HARIANA S
HARIANAS
HARICOT S
CHARIOT
HARICOTS
ACTORISH
CHARIOTS
HARIJAN S
HARIJANS
CS HARING
HARISSA S
SHARIAS
HARISSAS
CS HARK S
CS HARKED
HARKEN S
HANKER
HARKENED
DAKERHEN
HANKERED
HARKENER S
HANKERER
HARKENS
HANKERS
CS HARKING
CS HARKS
SHARK
HARL S
HARLOT S
HARLOTRY
HARLOTS
HARLS
CT HARM S
C HARMED
C HARMER S
C HARMERS
HARMFUL
HARMIN EGS
HARMINE S
HARMINES
CP HARMING
HARMINS
C HARMLESS
HARMONIC AS
OMNIARCH
HARMONY
CT HARMS
MARSH
HARNESS
S HARP SY
S HARPED
S HARPER S
S HARPERS
SHARPER
S HARPIES
SHARPIE
HARPIN GS
S HARPING S
HARPINGS
PHRASING
SHARPING
HARPINS
HARPIST S
HARPISTS
STARSHIP
HARPOON S
HARPOONS
S HARPS
SHARP
S HARPY
HARRIDAN S
HARRIED
HARDIER
C HARRIER S
HARRIERS
G HARRIES
HARROW S
HARROWED
HARROWER S
HARROWS
HARRUMPH S

CG HARRY
HARRYING
HARSH
HARSHEN S
HARSHENS
HARSHER
HARSHEST
THRASHES
HARSHLY
HARSLET S
HALTERS
LATHERS
SLATHER
THALERS
HARSLETS
SLATHERS
C HART S
RATH TAHR
HARTAL S
HARTALS
C HARTS
TAHRS TRASH
HARUMPH S
HARUMPHS
HARUSPEX
HARVEST S
THRAVES
HARVESTS
HAS HPT
AHS
ASH
SHA
HASH
HAHS SHAH
HASHED
HASHEESH
HASHES
HASHHEAD S
HASHING
HASHISH
HASLET S
HALEST
LATHES
SHELTA
HASLETS
HATLESS
SHELTAS
HASP S
HAPS PASH
HASPED
PASHED
PHASED
SHAPED
HASPING
PASHING
PHASING
SHAPING
HASPS
HASSEL S
HASSLE
LASHES
SELAHS
SHALES
SHEALS
HASSELS
ASHLESS
HASSLES
SLASHES
HASSIUM S
HASSIUMS
HASSLE DS
HASSEL
LASHES
SELAHS
SHALES
SHEALS
HASSLED
SLASHED
HASSLES
ASHLESS
HASSELS
SLASHES
HASSLING
LASHINGS
SLASHING
HASSOCK S
SHACKOS
HASSOCKS
G HAST EY
HATS
HASTATE

C HASTE DNS
HAETS HATES
HEATS
HASTED
DEATHS
HASTEFUL
C HASTEN S
SNATHE
THANES
C HASTENED
C HASTENER S
HEARTENS
C HASTENS
SNATHES
HASTES
HASTIER
HASTIEST
ATHEISTS
STAITHES
HASTILY
HASTING
HASTY
CGKPSTW HAT EHS
HATABLE
HATBAND S
HATBANDS
HATBOX
HATBOXES
T HATCH
HATCHECK S
CHATCHKE
T HATCHED
HATCHEL S
HATCHELS
T HATCHER SY
T HATCHERS
HATCHERY
THEARCHY
T HATCHES
CHETAHS
HATCHET S
HATCHETS
THATCHES
T HATCHING S
HATCHWAY S
HATE DRS
EATH HAET
HEAT THAE
HATEABLE
HEATABLE
HATED
DEATH
HATEFUL
HATER S
EARTH HEART
RATHE
HATERS
EARTHS
HEARTS
HATES
HAETS HASTE
HEATS
HATFUL S
HATFULS
HATSFUL
HATH
HATING
HATLESS
HASLETS
SHELTAS
HATLIKE
HATMAKER S
HATPIN S
HATPINS
HATRACK S
HATRACKS
HATRED S
DEARTH
THREAD
HATREDS
DEARTHS
HARDEST
HARDSET
THREADS
TRASHED
CGKW HATS
HAST
HATSFUL
HATFULS

C HATTED
CPS HATTER S
THREAT
HATTERIA S
CS HATTERS
SHATTER
THREATS
C HATTING
HAUBERK S
HAUBERKS
S HAUGH S
S HAUGHS
SHAUGH
HAUGHTY
S HAUL MS
HULA
HAULAGE S
HAULAGES
S HAULED
HAULER S
HALERU
HAULERS
HAULIER S
HAULIERS
S HAULING
NILGHAU
HAULM SY
HAULMIER
HAULMS
HAULMY
S HAULS
HULAS SHAUL
HAULYARD S
HAUNCH
HAUNCHED
HAUNCHES
C HAUNT S
UNHAT
C HAUNTED
C HAUNTER S
UNEARTH
URETHAN
C HAUNTERS
UNEARTHS
URETHANS
C HAUNTING
C HAUNTS
UNHATS
HAUSEN S
HAUSENS
HAUSFRAU S
G HAUT E
HAUTBOIS
HAUTBOY S
HAUTBOYS
HAUTE
HAUTEUR S
HAUTEURS
HAVARTI S
HAVARTIS
HAVDALAH S
S HAVE NRS
HAVELOCK S
S HAVEN S
HAVENED
HAVENING
HAVENS
SHAVEN
S HAVER S
HAVERED
HAVEREL S
HAVERELS
HAVERING
S HAVERS
SHAVER
S HAVES
SHAVE
S HAVING
HAVIOR S
HAVIORS
HAVIOUR S
HAVIOURS
HAVOC S
HAVOCKED
HAVOCKER S
HAVOCS
CST HAW KS
WHA

HAWALA S
HAWALAS
CST HAWED
HAWFINCH
CST HAWING
HAWK S
HAWKBILL S
HAWKED
HAWKER S
HAWKERS
HAWKEY S
HAWKEYED
HAWKEYS
HAWKIE S
HAWKIES
WEAKISH
HAWKING S
HAWKINGS
HAWKISH
HAWKLIKE
HAWKMOTH S
HAWKNOSE S
HAWKS
HAWKSHAW S
HAWKWEED S
CST HAWS E
SHAW SHWA
WASH
HAWSE RS
HAWSER S
REWASH
WASHER
HAWSERS
SWASHER
WASHERS
HAWSES
WASHES
HAWTHORN SY
CS HAY S
YAH
HAYCOCK S
HAYCOCKS
HAYED
HEADY
HAYER S
HAYERS
HAYEY
HAYFIELD S
HAYFORK S
HAYFORKS
HAYING S
HAYINGS
HAYLAGE S
HAYLAGES
HAYLOFT S
HAYLOFTS
HAYMAKER S
HAYMOW S
HAYMOWS
HAYRACK S
HAYRACKS
HAYRICK S
HAYRICKS
HAYRIDE S
HYDRIAE
HAYRIDES
CS HAYS
ASHY SHAY
HAYSEED S
HAYSEEDS
HAYSTACK S
HAYWARD S
HAYWARDS
HAYWIRE S
HAYWIRES
C HAZAN S
C HAZANIM
C HAZANS
HAZARD S
HAZARDED
HAZARDER S
HAZARDS
HAZE DLRS
HAZED
HAZEL S
HAZELHEN S
HAZELLY
HAZELNUT S
HAZELS
HAZER S
HAZERS
HAZES
HAZIER
HAZIEST
HAZILY
HAZINESS
HAZING S
HAZINGS
HAZMAT S
MATZAH
HAZMATS
MATZAHS
HAZY
C HAZZAN S
C HAZZANIM
C HAZZANS
ST HE HMNPRSTW
EH XY
A HEAD SY
AHED HADE
HAED
HEADACHE SY
HEADACHY
HEADBAND S
HEADED
HEADEND S
HEADENDS
HEADER S
ADHERE
HEADERS
ADHERES
HEARSED
SHEARED
HEADFISH
HEADFUL S
HEADFULS
HEADGATE S
HEADGEAR S
GEARHEAD
HEADHUNT S
HEADIER
HEADIEST
HEADILY
HEADING S
HEADINGS
DEASHING
HEADLAMP S
HEADLAND S
HEADLESS
HEADLINE DR
S
HEADLOCK S
HEADLONG
LONGHEAD
HEADMAN
HEADMEN
HEADMOST
HEADNOTE S
HEADPIN S
PINHEAD
HEADPINS
DEANSHIP
PINHEADS
HEADRACE S
HEADREST S
HEADROOM S
HEADS
ASHED DEASH
HADES SADHE
SHADE
HEADSAIL S
HEADSET S
HEADSETS
HEADSHIP S
HEADSMAN
HEADSMEN
HEADSTAY S
HEADWAY S
HEADWAYS
HEADWIND S
HEADWORD S
HEADWORK S
HEADY
HAYED
SW HEAL S
HALE
HEALABLE
HEALED
HEALER S
HEALERS
S HEALING
SW HEALS
HALES LEASH
SELAH SHALE
SHEAL
HEALTH SY
HEALTHS
HEALTHY
C HEAP SY
EPHA
HEAPED
C HEAPER S
HEAPERS
RESHAPE
HEAPING
C HEAPS
EPHAS PHASE
SHAPE
HEAPY
S HEAR DST
HARE RHEA
HEARABLE
HEARD
HARED
S HEARER S
REHEAR
S HEARERS
REHEARS
SHEARER
S HEARING S
S HEARINGS
HEARSING
SHEARING
HEARKEN S
HEARKENS
S HEARS E
HARES RHEAS
SHARE SHEAR
HEARSAY S
HEARSAYS
HEARSE DS
HAERES
HEARSED
ADHERES
HEADERS
SHEARED
HEARSES
HEARSING
HEARINGS
SHEARING
HEART HSY
EARTH HATER
RATHE
HEARTED
EARTHED
HEARTEN S
EARTHEN
HEARTENS
HASTENER
HEARTH S
HEARTHS
HEARTIER
EARTHIER
HEARTIES T
HEARTILY
EARTHILY
HEARTING
EARTHING
INGATHER
HEARTS
EARTHS
HATERS
HEARTY
EARTHY
CW HEAT HS
EATH HAET
HATE THAE
C HEATABLE
HATEABLE
C HEATED
HEATEDLY
CT HEATER S
AETHER
HEREAT
REHEAT
CT HEATERS
AETHERS
REHEATS
S HEATH SY
HEATHEN S
HEATHENS
ENSHEATH
S HEATHER SY
S HEATHERS
SHEATHER
HEATHERY
HEATHIER
S HEATHS
SHEATH
HEATHY
C HEATING
GAHNITE
W HEATLESS
CW HEATS
HAETS HASTE
HATES
HEAUME S
HEAUMES
S HEAVE DNRS
S HEAVED
HEAVEN S
HEAVENLY
HEAVENS
HEAVER S
HEAVERS
RESHAVE
S HEAVES
SHEAVE
HEAVIER
HEAVIES T
HEAVIEST
HEAVILY
S HEAVING
HEAVY
HEAVYSET
HEBDOMAD S
HEBETATE DS
HEBETIC
HEBETUDE S
HEBRAIZE DS
HECATOMB S
C HECK S
HECKLE DRS
HECKLED
HECKLER S
HECKLERS
HECKLES
HECKLING
C HECKS
HECTARE S
CHEATER
RECHEAT
RETEACH
TEACHER
HECTARES
CHEATERS
RECHEATS
TEACHERS
HECTIC
HECTICAL
HECTICLY
HECTOR S
ROCHET
ROTCHE
TOCHER
TROCHE
HECTORED
TOCHERED
HECTORS
ROCHETS
ROTCHES
TOCHERS
TORCHES
TROCHES
HEDDLE S
HEDDLES
C HEDER S
C HEDERS
HEDGE DRS
HEDGED
HEDGEHOG S
HEDGEHOP S
HEDGEPIG S
HEDGER S
HEDGEROW S
HEDGERS
HEDGES
HEDGIER
HEDGIEST
HEDGING
HEDGY
HEDONIC S
HEDONICS
HEDONISM S
MONISHED
HEDONIST S
HEED S
HEEDED
HEEDER S
HEEDERS
HEREDES
SHEERED
HEEDFUL
HEEDING
NEIGHED
HEEDLESS
HEEDS
HEEHAW S
HEEHAWED
HEEHAWS
W HEEL S
HEELBALL S
W HEELED
W HEELER S
REHEEL
W HEELERS
REHEELS
W HEELING S
W HEELINGS
W HEELLESS
HEELPOST S
PESTHOLE
TELESHOP
W HEELS
HEELTAP S
HEELTAPS
W HEEZE DS
W HEEZED
W HEEZES
W HEEZING
T HEFT SY
HEFTED
HEFTER S
HEFTERS
FRESHET
HEFTIER
HEFTIEST
HEFTILY
HEFTING
T HEFTS
HEFTY
HEGARI S
HEGIRA
HEGARIS
HEGIRAS
HEGEMON SY
HEGEMONS
HEGEMONY
HEGIRA S
HEGARI
HEGIRAS
HEGARIS
HEGUMEN ESY
HEGUMENE S
HEGUMENS
HEGUMENY
HEH S
HEHS
HEIFER S
HEIFERS
HEIGH T
HEIGHT HS
EIGHTH
HEIGHTEN S
HEIGHTH S
HEIGHTHS
HEIGHTS
EIGHTHS
HIGHEST
HEIL S
ELHI
HEILED
HEILING
HEILS
SHIEL
HEIMISH
HEINIE S
HEINIES
HEINOUS
T HEIR S
HIRE
HEIRDOM S
HEIRDOMS
HEIRED
HEIRESS
HEIRING
HEIRLESS
RELISHES
HEIRLOOM S
T HEIRS
HIRES SHIER
SHIRE
HEIRSHIP S
HEISHI
T HEIST S
HEISTED
HEISTER S
HEISTERS
HEISTING
NIGHTIES
T HEISTS
SHIEST
THESIS
HEJIRA S
HEJIRAS
HEKTARE S
HEKTARES
HELD
HELIAC
HELIACAL
ACHILLEA
HELIAST S
HALITES
HELIASTS
SHALIEST
HELICAL
CHALLIE
HELICES
LICHEES
HELICITY
HELICOID S
HELICON S
CHOLINE
HELICONS
CHOLINES
HELICOPT S
CHIPOTLE
HELILIFT S
HELIO S
HELIOS
HOLIES
ISOHEL
HELIPAD S
HELIPADS
HELIPORT S
HELISTOP S
HOPLITES
ISOPLETH
HELIUM S
HELIUMS
MUHLIES
HELIX
HELIXES
S HELL OS
HELLBENT
HELLBOX
HELLCAT S
HELLCATS
S HELLED
S HELLER ISY
HELLERI S
HELLERIS
SHELLIER
S HELLERS
SHELLER
HELLERY
S HELLFIRE S
HELLHOLE S
S HELLING
HELLION S
HELLIONS
HELLISH
HELLKITE S
HELLO S
HELLOED
HELLOES
HELLOING
HELLOS
S HELLS
SHELL
HELLUVA
W HELM S
W HELMED
HELMET S
HELMETED
HELMETS
W HELMING
HELMINTH S
HELMLESS
W HELMS
HELMSMAN
HELMSMEN
HELO ST
HOLE
HELOS
HOLES HOSEL
SHEOL
HELOT S
HOTEL THOLE
HELOTAGE S
HELOTISM S
HELOTRY
HELOTS
HOSTEL
HOTELS
THOLES
W HELP S
HELPABLE
W HELPED
HELPER S
HELPERS
HELPFUL
W HELPING S
HELPINGS
W HELPLESS
HELPMATE S
HELPMEET S
W HELPS
SHLEP
S HELVE DS
S HELVED
S HELVES
SHELVE
S HELVING
AT HEM EPS
HEMAGOG S
HEMAGOGS
HEMAL
ALMEH
HEMATAL
HEMATEIN S
HEMATINE
RT HEMATIC S
T HEMATICS
MASTICHE
MISTEACH
TACHISME
HEMATIN ES
HEMATINE S
HEMATEIN
HEMATINS
HEMATITE S
HEMATOID
HEMATOMA S
RT HEME S
RT HEMES
C HEMIC
CHIME MICHE
HEMIN S
HEMINS
INMESH
HEMIOLA S
HEMIOLAS
HEMIOLIA S
HEMIPTER S
HEMLINE S
HEMLINES
HEMLOCK S

HEMLOCKS
HEMMED
HEMMER S
HEMMERS
HEMMING
HEMOCOEL S
HEMOCYTE S
HEMOID
HEMOLYZE DS
C HEMOSTAT S
HEMP SY
HEMPEN
HEMPIE R
IMPHEE
HEMPIER
HEMPIEST
HEMPLIKE
HEMPS
HEMPSEED S
HEMPWEED S
HEMPY
HEMS
MESH
TW HEN ST
HENBANE S
HENBANES
HENBIT S
HENBITS
TW HENCE
HENCHMAN
HENCHMEN
HENCOOP S
HENCOOPS
HENEQUEN S
HENEQUIN S
HENIQUEN
HENGE S
HENGES
HENHOUSE S
HENIQUEN S
HENEQUIN
HENLEY S
HENLEYS
HENLIKE
HENNA S
HENNAED
HENNAING
HENNAS
HENNERY
HENNISH
HENPECK S
HENPECKS
HENRIES
INHERES
RESHINE
HENRY S
HENRYS
TW HENS
S HENT S
THEN
HENTED
HENTING
HENTS
SHENT THENS
HEP
PEH
HEPARIN S
HEPARINS
SERAPHIN
HEPATIC AS
APHETIC
HEPATICA ES
HEPATICS
PASTICHE
PISTACHE
HEPATIZE DS
HEPATOMA S
HEPCAT S
HEPCATS
PATCHES
HEPPER
HEPPEST
HEPTAD S
HEPTADS
SPATHED
HEPTAGON S
PATHOGEN
HEPTANE S
HAPTENE
PHENATE
HEPTANES
HAPTENES
PHENATES
HEPTARCH SY
HEPTOSE S
HEPTOSES
HER BDELMNO S
HERALD S
HERALDED
HERALDIC
HERALDRY
HERALDS
HERB SY
HERBAGE DS
HERBAGED
HERBAGES
HERBAL S
HERBALS
HERBARIA L
HERBED
HERBIER
HERBIEST
HERBLESS
HERBLIKE
HERBS
HERBY
HERCULES
S HERD S
HERDED
HERDER S
HERDERS
HERDIC S
CHIDER
DREICH
HERDICS
CHIDERS
HERDING
HERDLIKE
HERDMAN
HERDMEN
S HERDS
SHERD SHRED
HERDSMAN
HERDSMEN
TW HERE S
TW HEREAT
AETHER
HEATER
REHEAT
HEREAWAY S
TW HEREBY
HEREDES
HEEDERS
SHEERED
HEREDITY
TW HEREIN
INHERE
TW HEREINTO
TW HEREOF
TW HEREON
TW HERES Y
SHEER
HERESIES
HERESY
HERETIC S
ERETHIC
ETHERIC
TECHIER
HERETICS
CHESTIER
TW HERETO
HETERO
HERETRIX
TW HEREUNTO
TW HEREUPON
TW HEREWITH
HERIOT S
HERIOTS
HOISTER
SHORTIE
HERITAGE S
HERITOR S
HERITORS
HERITRIX
HERL S
LEHR
HERLS
LEHRS
T HERM AS
HERMA EI
HAREM
T HERMAE
HAREEM
HERMAEAN
HERMAI
HERMETIC
T HERMIT S
MITHER
HERMITIC
HERMITRY
T HERMITS
MITHERS
T HERMS
HERN S
HERNIA ELS
HERNIAE
HERNIAL
INHALER
HERNIAS
HERNIATE DS
HERNS
HERO NS
HOER
HEROES
RESHOE
HEROIC S
COHEIR
HEROICAL
HEROICS
COHEIRS
HEROIN ES
HEROINE S
HEROINES
HEROINS
INSHORE
HEROISM S
HEROISMS
HEROIZE DS
HEROIZED
HEROIZES
HERON S
HONER
HERONRY
HERONS
HONERS
NOSHER
SENHOR
HEROS
HOERS HORSE
HOSER SHOER
SHORE
HERPES
SPHERE
HERPETIC
W HERRIED
REHIRED
CSW HERRIES
REHIRES
HERRING S
HERRINGS
CSW HERRY
W HERRYING
HERS
RESH
HERSELF
FLESHER
HERSTORY
HERTZ
HERTZES
S HES T
SHE
HESITANT
HESITATE DR S
HESSIAN S
HESSIANS
ASHINESS
HESSITE S
HESSITES
ESTHESIS
C HEST S
ETHS HETS
C HESTS
KW HET HS
ETH
THE
HETAERA ES
HETAERAE
HETAERAS
HETAERIC
AETHERIC
HETAIRA IS
HETAIRAI
HETAIRAS
HETERO S
HERETO
HETEROS
CK HETH S
CK HETHS
HETMAN S
ANTHEM
HETMANS
ANTHEMS
KW HETS
ETHS HEST
S HEUCH S
S HEUCHS
SHEUCH
S HEUGH S
S HEUGHS
SHEUGH
CPS HEW NS
TW
C HEWABLE
CS HEWED
CS HEWER S
WHERE
CS HEWERS
SHEWER
WHERES
CS HEWING
WHINGE
S HEWN
WHEN
CST HEWS
W SHEW
HEX
HEXAD ES
HEXADE S
HEXADES
HEXADIC
HEXADS
HEXAGON S
HEXAGONS
HEXAGRAM S
HEXAMINE S
HEXANE S
HEXANES
HEXAPLA RS
HEXAPLAR
HEXAPLAS
HEXAPOD SY
HEXAPODS
HEXAPODY
HEXARCHY
HEXED
HEXER S
HEXEREI S
HEXEREIS
HEXERS
HEXES
HEXING
HEXONE S
HEXONES
HEXOSAN S
HEXOSANS
HEXOSE S
HEXOSES
HEXYL S
HEXYLIC
HEXYLS
TW HEY
YEH
HEYDAY S
HEYDAYS
HEYDEY S
HEYDEYS
ACG HI CDEMNPST
KP
HIATAL
HIATUS
HIATUSES
HIBACHI S
HIBACHIS
HIBERNAL
HIBISCUS
C HIC K
CHI
ICH
HICCOUGH S
HICCUP S
HICCUPED
HICCUPS
CT HICK S
HICKEY S
HICKEYS
HICKIE S
HICKIES
T HICKISH
C HICKORY
CT HICKS
CW HID E
HIDABLE
HIDALGO S
HIDALGOS
C HIDDEN
HIDDENLY
C HIDE DRS
HIED
HIDEAWAY S
C HIDED
HIDELESS
HIDEOUS
HIDEOUT S
HIDEOUTS
C HIDER S
HIRED
C HIDERS
C HIDES
SHIED SIDHE
C HIDING S
HIDINGS
DISHING
SHINDIG
HIDROSES
HIDROSIS
HIDROTIC S
TRICHOID
HIE DS
S HIED
HIDE
HIEING
HIEMAL
HIERARCH SY
HIERATIC
HIERURGY
S HIES
HIGGLE DRS
HIGGLED
HIGGLER S
HIGGLERS
HIGGLES
HIGGLING
T HIGH ST
HIGHBALL S
HIGHBORN
HIGHBOY S
HIGHBOYS
HIGHBRED
HIGHBROW S
HIGHBUSH
HIGHER
HIGHEST
EIGHTHS
HEIGHTS
HIGHJACK S
HIGHLAND S
HIGHLIFE S
HIGHLY
HIGHNESS
HIGHRISE S
HIGHROAD S
T HIGHS
HIGHSPOT S
HIGHTOPS
HIGHT HS
THIGH
HIGHTAIL S
HIGHTED
THIGHED
HIGHTH S
HIGHTHS
HIGHTING
HIGHTOP S
HIGHTOPS
HIGHSPOT
HIGHTS
THIGHS
HIGHWAY S
HIGHWAYS
HIJAB S
HIJABS
HIJACK S
HIJACKED
HIJACKER S
HIJACKS
HIJINKS
HIJRA HS
HIJRAH S
HIJRAHS
HIJRAS
HIKE DRS
HIKED
HIKER S
HIKERS
SHRIEK
SHRIKE
HIKES
SHEIK
HIKING
HILA R
HAIL
HILAR
HILARITY
C HILDING S
HILDINGS
C HILI
CST HILL OSY
CS HILLED
C HILLER S
C HILLERS
C HILLIER
C HILLIEST
CS HILLING
HILLO AS
HILLOA S
HILLOAED
HILLOAS
HILLOCK SY
HILLOCKS
HILLOCKY
HILLOED
HILLOES
HOLLIES
HILLOING
HILLOS
CST HILLS
SHILL
HILLSIDE S
SIDEHILL
HILLTOP S
HILLTOPS
C HILLY
HILT S
HILTED
HILTING
HILTLESS
HILTS
HILUM
HILUS
SW HIM S
HIMATIA
HIMATION S
SW HIMS
SHIM
HIMSELF
FLEMISH
CST HIN DST
W
HIND S
HINDER S
HINDERED
HINDERER S
HINDERS
NERDISH
SHRINED
HINDGUT S
HINDGUTS
HINDMOST
HINDS
W HINGE DRS
NEIGH
W HINGED
NIGHED
W HINGER S
NIGHER
W HINGERS
W HINGES
NEIGHS
W HINGING
NIGHING
C HINKIER
C HINKIEST
C HINKY
SW HINNIED
SW HINNIES
SW HINNY
SW HINNYING
CST HINS
W HISN SHIN
SINH
HINT S
THIN
HINTED
HINTER S
HINTERS
HINTING
C HINTS
THINS
CSW HIP S
PHI
HIPBONE S
HIPBONES
S HIPLESS
W HIPLIKE
HIPLINE S
HIPLINES
HIPLY
HIPNESS
HIPPARCH S
CSW HIPPED
CSW HIPPER
HIPPEST
C HIPPIE RS
CW HIPPIER
C HIPPIES T
CW HIPPIEST
CSW HIPPING
HIPPISH
HIPPO S
HIPPOS
CW HIPPY
CSW HIPS
PHIS PISH
SHIP
HIPSHOT
HIPSTER S
HIPSTERS
HIRABLE
HIRAGANA S
HIRCINE
S HIRE DERS
HEIR
HIREABLE
HIRED
HIDER
HIREE S
HIREES
HIRELING S
HIRER S
HIRERS
S HIRES
HEIRS SHIER
SHIRE
HIRING
HIRPLE DS
HIRPLED
HIRPLES
HIRPLING

HIRSEL S
HIRSLE
RELISH
HIRSELED
RELISHED
SHIELDER
HIRSELS
HIRSLES
HIRSLE DS
HIRSEL
RELISH
HIRSLED
HIRSLES
HIRSELS
HIRSLING
HIRSUTE
HIRUDIN S
HIRUDINS
ACG HIS NST
KPT
HISN
HINS SHIN
SINH
HISPID
HISS Y
HISSED
DISHES
HISSELF
SELFISH
HISSER S
SHIERS
SHIRES
HISSERS
HISSES
HISSIER
HISSIES T
HISSIEST
HISSING S
HISSINGS
HISSY
SW HIST S
HITS SITH
THIS
HISTAMIN ES
ISTHMIAN
THIAMINS
W HISTED
HISTIDIN ES
W HISTING
INSIGHT
HISTOGEN S
HISTOID
HISTONE S
ETHIONS
HISTONES
A HISTORIC
ORCHITIS
HISTORY
SW HISTS
SHIST
CSW HIT S
HITCH
HITCHED
HITCHER S
HITCHERS
HITCHES
HITCHING
TW HITHER
T HITHERTO
S HITLESS
HITMAN
HITMEN
CSW HITS
HIST SITH
THIS
HITTABLE
TITHABLE
CW HITTER S
TITHER
CW HITTERS
TITHERS
S HITTING
TITHING
CS HIVE DS
HIVED
HIVELESS
CS HIVES
SHIVE
HIVING
HIZZONER S
O HM M
HMM
MOR HO BDEGNPST
TW OH WY
HOACTZIN S
HOAGIE S
HOAGIES
HOAGY
HOAR DSY
HORA
HOARD S
HOARDED
HOARDER S
HOARDERS
HOARDING S
HOARDS
HOARIER
HOARIEST
HOARILY
HOARS E
HORAS
HOARSE NR
AHORSE
ASHORE
HOARSELY
HOARSEN S
SENHORA
HOARSENS
SENHORAS
HOARSER
HOARSEST
EARSHOTS
HOARY
HOATZIN S
HOATZINS
HOAX
HOAXED
HOAXER S
HOAXERS
HOAXES
HOAXING
HOB OS
HOBBED
HOBBER S
HOBBERS
HOBBIES
HOBBING
HOBBIT S
HOBBITS
HOBBLE DRS
HOBBLED
HOBBLER S
HOBBLERS
HOBBLES
HOBBLING
HOBBY
HOBBYIST S
HOBLIKE
HOBNAIL S
HOBNAILS
HOBNOB S
HOBNOBS
HOBO S
BOHO
HOBOED
HOBOES
HOBOING
HOBOISM S
HOBOISMS
HOBOS
BOHOS
HOBS
BOSH
CS HOCK S
CS HOCKED
CHOKED
S HOCKER S
CHOKER
S HOCKERS
CHOKERS
SHOCKER
HOCKEY S
CHOKEY
HOCKEYS
CS HOCKING
CHOKING
CS HOCKS
SHOCK
HOCKSHOP S
HOCUS
HOCUSED
CHOUSED
DOUCHES
HOCUSES
CHOUSES
HOCUSING
CHOUSING
HOCUSSED
HOCUSSES
S HOD S
HODAD S
HODADDY
HODADS
S HODDEN S
HODDENS
SHODDEN
HODDIN S
HODDINS
HODS
SHOD
S HOE DRS
HOECAKE S
HOECAKES
S HOED
OHED
HOEDOWN S
WOODHEN
HOEDOWNS
WOODHENS
S HOEING
HOELIKE
S HOER S
HERO
S HOERS
HEROS HORSE
HOSER SHOER
SHORE
S HOES
HOSE SHOE
S HOG GS
HOGAN S
HOGANS
HOGBACK S
HOGBACKS
HOGFISH
HOGG S
S HOGGED
HOGGER S
HOGGERS
HOGGET S
HOGGETS
S HOGGING
HOGGISH
HOGGS
HOGLIKE
HOGMANAY S
MAHOGANY
HOGMANE S
HOGMANES
HOGMENAY S
HOGNOSE S
HOGNOSES
HOGNUT S
NOUGHT
HOGNUTS
GUNSHOT
NOUGHTS
SHOTGUN
S HOGS
GOSH SHOG
HOGSHEAD S
HOGTIE DS
HOGTIED
HOGTIES
HOGTYING
HOGWASH
HOGWEED S
HOGWEEDS
HOICK S
HOICKED
HOICKING
HOICKS
HOIDEN S
HONIED
HOIDENED
HOIDENS
HOISE DS
HOISED
HOISES
HOISING
HOIST S
HOISTED
HOISTER S
HERIOTS
SHORTIE
HOISTERS
HORSIEST
SHORTIES
HOISTING
HOISTS
C HOKE DSY
OKEH
C HOKED
C HOKES
OKEHS
C HOKEY
C HOKIER
C HOKIEST
HOKILY
HOKINESS
C HOKING
HOKKU
HOKUM S
KHOUM
HOKUMS
KHOUMS
HOKYPOKY
HOLARD S
HOLARDS
A HOLD S
HOLDABLE
HOLDALL S
HOLDALLS
HOLDBACK S
HOLDDOWN S
HOLDEN
HONDLE
HOLDER S
HOLDERS
HOLDFAST S
HOLDING S
HOLDINGS
HOLDOUT S
HOLDOUTS
HOLDOVER S
OVERHOLD
A HOLDS
HOLDUP S
UPHOLD
HOLDUPS
UPHOLDS
DTW HOLE DSY
HELO
T HOLED
DHOLE
HOLELESS
DTW HOLES
HELOS HOSEL
SHEOL
HOLEY
HOYLE
HOLIBUT S
HOLIBUTS
HOLIDAY S
HYALOID
HYOIDAL
HOLIDAYS
HYALOIDS
HOLIER
HOLIES T
HELIOS
ISOHEL
HOLIEST
EOLITHS
HOSTILE
HOLILY
HOLINESS
T HOLING
W HOLISM S
W HOLISMS
HOLIST S
LITHOS
THIOLS
W HOLISTIC
HOLISTS
HOLK S
KOHL
HOLKED
HOLKING
HOLKS
KOHLS
C HOLLA S
HALLO
HOLLAED
HALLOED
HOLLAING
HALLOING
HOLLAND S
HOLLANDS
C HOLLAS
HALLOS
HOLLER S
HOLLERED
HOLLERS
HOLLIES
HILLOES
HOLLO AOSW
HOLLOA S
HALLOO
HOLLOAED
HALLOOED
HOLLOAS
HALLOOS
HOLLOED
HOLLOES
HOLLOING
HOLLOO S
HOLLOOED
HOLLOOS
HOLLOS
HOLLOW S
HOLLOWED
HOLLOWER
HOLLOWLY
HOLLOWS
W HOLLY
HOLM S
HOLMIC
HOLMIUM S
HOLMIUMS
HOLMS
HOLOCENE
HOLOGAMY
HOLOGRAM S
HOLOGYNY
HOLOTYPE S
HOLOZOIC
HOLP
HOLPEN
PHENOL
HOLS
HOLSTEIN S
HOTLINES
NEOLITHS
HOLSTER S
HOSTLER
HOLSTERS
HOSTLERS
HOLT S
LOTH
HOLTS
SLOTH
HOLY
HOLYDAY S
HOLYDAYS
HOLYTIDE S
HOMAGE DRS
OHMAGE
HOMAGED
HOMAGER S
HOMAGERS
HOMAGES
OHMAGES
HOMAGING
HOMBRE S
HOMBRES
HOMBURG S
HOMBURGS
HOME DRSY
HOMEBODY
HOMEBOY S
HOMEBOYS
HOMEBRED S
HOMEBREW S
HOMED
HOMEGIRL S
HOMELAND S
HOMELESS
HOMELIER
HOMELIKE
HOMELY
HOMEMADE
HOMEOBOX
HOMEOTIC
HOMEPAGE S
HOMEPORT S
HOMER S
HOMERED
HOMERIC
HOMERING
HOMEROOM S
HOMERS
MOSHER
HOMES
HOMESICK
HOMESITE S
HOMESPUN S
HOMESTAY S
HOMETOWN S
TOWNHOME
HOMEWARD S
HOMEWORK S
HOMEY S
HOMEYS
HOMICIDE S
HOMIE RS
HOMIER
HOMIES T
HOMIEST
HOMILIES
HOMILIST S
HOMILY
HOMINES S
HOMINESS
MONISHES
HOMING
HOMINIAN S
HOMINID S
HOMINIDS
HOMINIES
HOMININE
HOMINIZE DS
HOMINOID S
HOMINY
HOMMOCK S
HOMMOCKS
HOMMOS
HOMMOSES
HOMO S
HOMOGAMY
HOMOGENY
HOMOGONY
HOMOLOG SY
HOMOLOGS
HOMOLOGY
HOMONYM SY
HOMONYMS
HOMONYMY
HOMOS
HOMOSEX
HOMY
CP HON EGKS
NOH
HONAN S
HONANS
HONCHO S
HONCHOED
HONCHOS
HONDA S
HONDAS
HONDLE DS
HOLDEN
HONDLED
HONDLES
HONDLING
PS HONE DRSY
P HONED
HONER S
HERON
HONERS
HERONS
NOSHER
SENHOR
P HONES T
HOSEN SHONE
HONEST Y
ETHNOS
HONESTER
HONESTLY
HONESTY
HONEWORT S
P HONEY S
HONEYBEE S
HONEYBUN S
HONEYDEW S
P HONEYED
HONEYFUL
P HONEYING
HONEYPOT S
P HONEYS
T HONG IS
HONGI
OHING
HONGIED
HONGIES
SHOEING
HONGIING
T HONGS
P HONIED
HOIDEN
P HONING
HONK SY
HONKED
HONKER S
HONKERS
HONKING
HONKS
HONOR S
HONORAND S
HONORARY
HONORED
HONOREE S
HONOREES
HONORER S
HONORERS
HONORING
HONORS
HONOUR S
HONOURED
HONOURER S
HONOURS
P HONS
NOSH
HOOCH
HOOCHES
HOOCHIE S
HOOCHIES
HOOD SY
HOODED
HOODIE RS
HOODIER
HOODIES T
HOODIEST
DHOOTIES
HOODING
HOODLESS
HOODLIKE
HOODLUM S
HOODLUMS
HOODMOLD S
HOODOO S
HOODOOED
HOODOOS
HOODS
HOODWINK S
HOODY
P HOOEY S
HOOEYS
W HOOF S
HOOFBEAT S
W HOOFED
HOOFER S
HOOFERS
W HOOFING
HOOFLESS

HOOFLIKE
W HOOFS
CS HOOK ASY
HOOKA HS
HOOKAH S
HOOKAHS
HOOKAS
HOOKED
HOOKER S
HOOKERS
HOOKEY S
HOOKEYS
HOOKIER
HOOKIES T
HOOKIEST
HOOKING
HOOKLESS
HOOKLET S
HOOKLETS
HOOKLIKE
HOOKNOSE DS
CS HOOKS
SHOOK
HOOKUP S
HOOKUPS
HOOKWORM S
HOOKY
HOOLIE
HOOLIGAN S
D HOOLY
W HOOP S
POOH
W HOOPED
POOHED
W HOOPER S
W HOOPERS
W HOOPING
POOHING
W HOOPLA S
W HOOPLAS
HOOPLESS
HOOPLIKE
HOOPOE S
HOOPOES
HOOPOO S
HOOPOOS
W HOOPS
POOHS
HOOPSTER S
HOORAH S
HOORAHED
HOORAHS
HOORAY S
HOORAYED
HOORAYS
HOOSEGOW S
HOOSGOW S
HOOSGOWS
BS HOOT SY
HOOTCH
HOOTCHES
HOOTED
S HOOTER S
S HOOTERS
RESHOOT
SHEROOT
SHOOTER
SOOTHER
HOOTIER
HOOTIEST
S HOOTING
BS HOOTS
SHOOT SOOTH
HOOTY
HOOVED
HOOVER S
HOOVERED
HOOVERS
HOOVES
CSW HOP ES
POH
HOPE DRS
HOPED
EPHOD
HOPEFUL S
HOPEFULS

HOPELESS
HOPER S
EPHOR
HOPERS
EPHORS
POSHER
HOPES
HOPHEAD S
HOPHEADS
HOPING
HOPINGLY
HOPLITE S
HOPLITES
HELISTOP
ISOPLETH
HOPLITIC
CSW HOPPED
CSW HOPPER S
CSW HOPPERS
SHOPPER
C HOPPIER
C HOPPIEST
CSW HOPPING S
S HOPPINGS
SHOPPING
HOPPLE DS
HOPPLED
HOPPLES
HOPPLING
C HOPPY
CSW HOPS
POSH SHOP
SOPH
HOPSACK S
HOPSACKS
HOPTOAD S
HOPTOADS
HORA HLS
HOAR
HORAH S
HORAHS
C HORAL
HORARY
HORAS
HOARS
HORDE DS
C HORDED
HORDEIN S
HORDEINS
HORDEOLA
HORDES
HORSED
RESHOD
SHORED
C HORDING
HORIZON S
HORIZONS
HORMONAL
HORMONE S
MOORHEN
HORMONES
MOORHENS
HORMONIC
ST HORN SY
HORNBEAM S
HORNBILL S
HORNBOOK S
T HORNED
DEHORN
HORNET S
NOTHER
THRONE
HORNETS
SHORTEN
THRONES
HORNFELS
T HORNIER
T HORNIEST
ORNITHES
T HORNILY
T HORNING S
HORNINGS
HORNIST S
HORNISTS
HORNITO S
HORNITOS
T HORNLESS
T HORNLIKE

HORNPIPE S
HORNPOUT S
T HORNS
SHORN
HORNTAIL S
HORNWORM S
HORNWORT S
T HORNY
HOROLOGE RS
HOROLOGY
HORRENT
NORTHER
HORRIBLE S
HORRIBLY
HORRID
HORRIDER
HORRIDLY
HORRIFIC
HORRIFY
HORROR S
HORRORS
A HORSE DSY
HEROS HOERS
HOSER SHOER
SHORE
HORSECAR S
HORSED
HORDES
RESHOD
SHORED
HORSEFLY
HORSEMAN
MENORAHS
RHAMNOSE
HORSEMEN
HORSEPOX
HORSES
HOSERS
SHOERS
SHORES
HORSEY
HORSIER
HORSIEST
HOISTERS
SHORTIES
HORSILY
HORSING
SHORING
HORST ES
SHORT
HORSTE S
OTHERS
RESHOT
THROES
HORSTES
HORSTS
SHORTS
HORSY
HOSANNA HS
HOSANNAH S
HOSANNAS
CTW HOSE DLNRSY
HOES SHOE
HOSED
SHOED
HOSEL S
HELOS HOLES
SHEOL
HOSELIKE
HOSELS
SHEOLS
C HOSEN
HONES SHONE
HOSEPIPE S
HOSER S
HEROS HOERS
HORSE SHOER
SHORE
HOSERS
HORSES
SHOERS
SHORES
C HOSES
SHOES
HOSEY S
HOSEYED
HOSEYING
HOSEYS
HOSIER SY
HOSIERS

HOSIERY
HOSING
HOSPICE S
HOSPICES
HOSPITAL S
HOSPITIA
HOSPODAR S
G HOST AS
HOTS SHOT
SOTH TOSH
HOSTA S
OATHS SHOAT
HOSTAGE S
HOSTAGES
HOSTAS
SHOATS
G HOSTED
HOSTEL S
HELOTS
HOTELS
THOLES
HOSTELED
HOSTELER S
HOSTELRY
HOSTELS
HOSTESS
HOSTILE S
EOLITHS
HOLIEST
HOSTILES
G HOSTING
HOSTLER S
HOLSTER
HOSTLERS
HOLSTERS
G HOSTLY
G HOSTS
SHOTS SOTHS
PS HOT S
THO
HOTBED S
HOTBEDS
HOTBLOOD S
HOTBOX
HOTBOXES
HOTCAKE S
HOTCAKES
HOTCH
HOTCHED
HOTCHES
HOTCHING
HOTCHPOT S
HOTDOG S
HOTDOGS
HOTEL S
HELOT THOLE
HOTELDOM S
HOTELIER S
HOTELMAN
METHANOL
HOTELMEN
HOTELS
HELOTS
HOSTEL
THOLES
HOTFOOT S
HOTFOOTS
HOTHEAD S
HOTHEADS
HOTHOUSE DS
HOTLINE S
NEOLITH
HOTLINES
HOLSTEIN
NEOLITHS
HOTLINK S
HOTLINKS
HOTLY
HOTNESS
HOTPRESS
STROPHES
HOTROD S
HOTRODS
PS HOTS
HOST SHOT
SOTH TOSH
HOTSHOT S
HOTSHOTS

HOTSPOT S
POTSHOT
HOTSPOTS
POTSHOTS
HOTSPUR S
HOTSPURS
S HOTTED
HOTTER
TOTHER
HOTTEST
HOTTIE S
HOTTIES
S HOTTING
TONIGHT
HOTTISH
HOUDAH S
HOUDAHS
HOUND S
HOUNDED
HOUNDER S
HOUNDERS
ENSHROUD
UNHORSED
HOUNDING
HOUNDS
UNSHOD
HOUR IS
HOURI S
HOURIS
HOURLIES
HOURLONG
HOURLY
HOURS
C HOUSE DLRS
HOUSEBOY S
C HOUSED
HOUSEFLY
HOUSEFUL S
HOUSEL S
HOUSELED
HOUSELS
HOUSEMAN
HOUSEMEN
C HOUSER S
C HOUSERS
C HOUSES
HOUSESAT
HOUSESIT S
HOUSETOP S
POTHOUSE
C HOUSING S
HOUSINGS
S HOVE LR
S HOVEL S
S HOVELED
S HOVELING
S HOVELLED
S HOVELS
SHOVEL
S HOVER S
HOVERED
HOVERER S
HOVERERS
HOVERFLY
HOVERING
S HOVERS
SHOVER
SHROVE
CDS HOW EFKLS
WHO
HOWBEIT
HOWDAH S
HOWDAHS
HOWDIE DS
HOWDIED
HOWDIES
HOWDY
HOWDYING
HOWE S
HOWES
WHOSE
HOWEVER
WHOEVER
HOWF FS
HOWFF S
HOWFFS
HOWFS

HOWITZER S
HOWK S
HOWKED
HOWKING
HOWKS
HOWL S
HOWLED
HOWLER S
HOWLERS
HOWLET S
HOWLETS
HOWLING
HOWLS
CDS HOWS
SHOW
A HOY AS
HOYA S
AHOY
HOYAS
HOYDEN S
HOYDENED
HOYDENS
HOYLE S
HOLEY
HOYLES
HOYS
HRYVNA S
HRYVNAS
HRYVNIA S
HRYVNIAS
VARNISHY
HUARACHE S
HUARACHO S
C HUB S
HUBBIES
HUBBLY
HUBBUB S
HUBBUBS
C HUBBY
HUBCAP S
HUBCAPS
HUBRIS
HUBRISES
C HUBS
BUSH
CS HUCK S
C HUCKLE S
C HUCKLES
CS HUCKS
SHUCK
HUCKSTER S
HUDDLE DRS
HUDDLED
HUDDLER S
HURDLED
HUDDLERS
HUDDLES
HUDDLING
HUE DS
HUED
HUELESS
HUES
C HUFF SY
C HUFFED
C HUFFIER
C HUFFIEST
HUFFILY
C HUFFING
HUFFISH
C HUFFS
C HUFFY
CT HUG ES
UGH
HUGE R
HUGELY
HUGENESS
HUGEOUS
HUGER
HUGEST
HUGGABLE
C HUGGED
C HUGGER S
C HUGGERS
C HUGGING

CT HUGS
GUSH SUGH
UGHS
HUH
HUIC
HUIPIL S
HUIPILES
HUIPILS
HUISACHE S
HULA S
HAUL
HULAS
HAULS SHAUL
HULK SY
HULKED
HULKIER
HULKIEST
HULKING
HULKS
HULKY
A HULL OS
HULLED
HULLER S
HULLERS
HULLING
HULLO AOS
HULLOA S
HULLOAED
HULLOAS
HULLOED
HULLOES
HULLOING
HULLOO S
HULLOOED
HULLOOS
HULLOS
HULLS
C HUM PS
HUMAN ES
HUMANE R
HUMANELY
HUMANER
HUMANEST
HUMANISE DS
HUMANISM S
HUMANIST S
HUMANITY
HUMANIZE DRS
HUMANLY
HUMANOID S
HUMANS
HUMATE S
HUMATES
HUMBLE DRS
HUMBLED
HUMBLER S
HUMBLERS
HUMBLES T
HUMBLEST
HUMBLING
HUMBLY
HUMBUG S
HUMBUGS
HUMDRUM S
HUMDRUMS
HUMERAL S
HUMERALS
HUMERI
HUMERUS
HUMIC
HUMID
HUMIDEX
HUMIDIFY
HUMIDITY
HUMIDLY
HUMIDOR S
RHODIUM
HUMIDORS
RHODIUMS
HUMIFIED
HUMILITY
HUMITURE S
HUMMABLE
C HUMMED

HUMMER S
HUMMERS
C **HUMMING**
HUMMOCK SY
HUMMOCKS
HUMMOCKY
HUMMUS
HUMMUSES
HUMOR S
MOHUR
HUMORAL
HUMORED
HUMORFUL
HUMORING
HUMORIST S
THORIUMS
HUMOROUS
HUMORS
MOHURS
HUMOUR S
HUMOURED
HUMOURS
CTW **HUMP** HSY
HUMPBACK S
CTW **HUMPED**
T **HUMPER** S
T **HUMPERS**
HUMPH S
HUMPHED
HUMPHING
HUMPHS
HUMPIER
HUMPIEST
CTW **HUMPING**
HUMPLESS
CTW **HUMPS**
HUMPY
C **HUMS**
MUSH
HUMUS
HUMUSES
HUMVEE S
HUMVEES
S **HUN** GHKST
HUNCH
HUNCHED
HUNCHES
HUNCHING
HUNDRED S
HUNDREDS
HUNG
HUNGER S
REHUNG
HUNGERED
HUNGERS
HUNGOVER
OVERHUNG
HUNGRIER
HUNGRILY
HUNGRY
HUNH
CT **HUNK** SY
HUNKER S
HUNKERED
HUNKERS
C **HUNKIER**
C **HUNKIEST**
CT **HUNKS**
C **HUNKY**
HUNNISH
S **HUNS**
SHUN
S **HUNT** S
HUNTABLE
S **HUNTED**
HUNTEDLY
CS **HUNTER** S
CS **HUNTERS**
SHUNTER
S **HUNTING** S
HUNTINGS
SHUNTING
HUNTRESS
SHUNTERS
S **HUNTS**
SHUNT

HUNTSMAN
MANHUNTS
HUNTSMEN
W **HUP**
C **HUPPAH** S
C **HUPPAHS**
HURDIES
HURDLE DRS
HURLED
HURDLED
HUDDLER
HURDLER S
HURDLERS
HURDLES
HURDLING
HURDS
CT **HURL** SY
HURLED
HURDLE
HURLER S
HURLERS
HURLEY S
HURLEYS
HURLIES
HURLING S
HURLINGS
CT **HURLS**
HURLY
HURRAH S
HURRAHED
HURRAHS
HURRAY S
HURRAYED
HURRAYS
HURRIED
DHURRIE
HURRIER S
HURRIERS
D **HURRIES**
RUSHIER
HURRY
HURRYING
HURST S
HURTS RUTHS
HURSTS
HURT S
RUTH THRU
HURTER S
HURTERS
HURTFUL
RUTHFUL
HURTING
HURTLE DS
HURTLED
HURTLES S
HUSTLER
HURTLESS
HUSTLERS
RUTHLESS
HURTLING
HURTS
HURST RUTHS
HUSBAND S
HUSBANDS
S **HUSH**
HUSHABY
S **HUSHED**
HUSHEDLY
S **HUSHES**
HUSHFUL
S **HUSHING**
HUSK SY
HUSKED
HUSKER S
HUSKERS
HUSKIER
HUSKIES T
HUSKIEST
HUSKILY
HUSKING S
HUSKINGS
HUSKLIKE
HUSKS
HUSKY
HUSSAR S
SURAHS
HUSSARS

HUSSIES
HUSSY
HUSTINGS
UNSIGHTS
HUSTLE DRS
SLEUTH
HUSTLED
HUSTLER S
HURTLES
HUSTLERS
HURTLESS
RUTHLESS
HUSTLES
LUSHEST
SLEUTHS
HUSTLING
SUNLIGHT
HUSWIFE S
HUSWIFES
HUSWIVES
BPS **HUT** S
HUTCH
HUTCHED
HUTCHES
HUTCHING
HUTLIKE
HUTMENT S
HUTMENTS
BPS **HUTS**
SHUT THUS
TUSH
HUTTED
S **HUTTING**
C **HUTZPA** HS
C **HUTZPAH** S
C **HUTZPAHS**
C **HUTZPAS**
HUZZA HS
HUZZAED
HUZZAH S
HUZZAHED
HUZZAHS
HUZZAING
HUZZAS
HWAN
HYACINTH S
HYAENA S
HYAENAS
HYAENIC
HYALIN ES
HYALINE S
HYALINES
HYALINS
HYALITE S
HYALITES
HYALOGEN S
HYALOID S
HOLIDAY
HYOIDAL
HYALOIDS
HOLIDAYS
HYBRID S
HYBRIDS
HYBRIS
HYBRISES
HYDATID S
HYDATIDS
HYDRA ES
HARDY
HYDRACID S
HYDRAE
HYDRAGOG S
HYDRANT HS
HYDRANTH S
HYDRANTS
HYDRAS E
HYDRASE S
HYDRASES
HYDRATE DS
THREADY
HYDRATED
HYDRATES
HYDRATOR S
HYDRIA E
HYDRIAE
HAYRIDE
HYDRIC

HYDRID ES
HYDRIDE S
HYDRIDES
HYDRIDS
HYDRILLA S
HYDRO S
HYDROGEL S
HYDROGEN S
HYDROID S
HYDROIDS
HYDROMEL S
HYDRONIC
HYDROPIC
HYDROPS Y
HYDROPSY
HYDROS
HYDROSKI S
HYDROSOL S
HYDROUS
HYDROXY L
HYDROXYL S
HYENA S
HYENAS
HYENIC
HYENINE
HYENOID
HYETAL
HYGEIST S
HYGEISTS
HYGIEIST S
HYGIENE S
HYGIENES
HYGIENIC S
S **HYING**
P **HYLA** S
HYLAS
SHALY
HYLOZOIC
HYMEN S
HYMENAL
HYMENEAL S
HYMENIA L
HYMENIAL
HYMENIUM S
HYMENS
HYMN S
HYMNAL S
HYMNALS
HYMNARY
HYMNBOOK S
HYMNED
HYMNING
HYMNIST S
HYMNISTS
HYMNLESS
HYMNLIKE
HYMNODY
HYMNS
HYOID S
HYOIDAL
HOLIDAY
HYALOID
HYOIDEAN
HYOIDS
HYOSCINE S
HYP EOS
HYPE DRS
HYPED
HYPER S
HYPERGOL S
HYPERON S
HYPERONS
HYPEROPE S
HYPERS
SPHERY
SYPHER
HYPES
HYPHA EL
HYPHAE
HYPHAL
HYPHEMIA S
HYPHEN S
HYPHENED
HYPHENIC

HYPHENS
HYPING
HYPNIC
HYPNOID
HYPNOSES
HYPNOSIS
HYPNOTIC S
PHYTONIC
PYTHONIC
TYPHONIC
HYPO S
HYPOACID
HYPODERM AS
HYPOED
HYPOGEA LN
HYPOGEAL
HYPOGEAN
HYPOGENE
HYPOGEUM
HYPOGYNY
HYPOING
HYPONEA S
HYPONEAS
HYPONOIA S
HYPONYM SY
HYPONYMS
SYMPHONY
HYPONYMY
HYPOPNEA S
HYPOPYON S
HYPOS
SOPHY
HYPOTHEC S
HYPOXIA S
HYPOXIAS
HYPOXIC
HYPS
SYPH
HYRACES
HYRACOID S
HYRAX
HYRAXES
HYSON S
HYSONS
HYSSOP S
HYSSOPS
HYSTERIA S
HYSTERIC S
HYTE
THEY

I

IAMB IS
BIMA
IAMBI C
IAMBIC S
IAMBICS
IAMBS
BIMAS
IAMBUS
IAMBUSES
IATRIC
IATRICAL
IBEX
IBEXES
IBICES
IBIDEM
IBIS
IBISES
IBOGAINE S
BDF LMN PRS V **ICE** DS
ICEBERG S
ICEBERGS
ICEBLINK S
ICEBOAT S
ICEBOATS
ICEBOUND
ICEBOX
ICEBOXES
ICECAP S
IPECAC
ICECAPS
IPECACS

DRV **ICED**
CEDI DICE
ICEFALL S
ICEFALLS
ICEHOUSE S
ICEKHANA S
V **ICELESS**
ICELIKE
ICEMAKER S
ICEMAN
ANEMIC
CINEMA
ICEMEN
BDF RSV **ICES**
SICE
LRW **ICH** S
CHI
HIC
ICHNITE S
ICHNITES
ICHOR S
CHIRO CHOIR
ICHOROUS
ICHORS
CHIROS
CHOIRS
ORCHIS
ICHS
CHIS
ICHTHYIC
ICICLE DS
CILICE
ICICLED
ICICLES
CILICES
D **ICIER**
D **ICIEST**
CITIES
ICILY
ICINESS
INCISES
DRV **ICING** S
ICINGS
DHK LMN PRS TW **ICK** Y
BDK LNP STW **ICKER** S
BDK LNP TW **ICKERS**
SICKER
DKP **ICKIER**
DKP **ICKIEST**
EKISTIC
ICKILY
P **ICKINESS**
KINESICS
DKP **ICKY**
ICON S
CION COIN
CONI
ICONES
CONIES
COSINE
OSCINE
ICONIC
ICONICAL
ICONS
CIONS COINS
SCION SONIC
ICTERIC S
ICTERICS
ICTERUS
CURITES
ICTIC
R **ICTUS**
CUTIS
R **ICTUSES**
CUTISES
ICY
ABD FGH KLM RVY **ID** S
IDEA LS
AIDE
IDEAL S
AILED
IDEALESS
IDEALISE DS

IDEALISM S
MILADIES
IDEALIST S
IDEALITY
IDEALIZE DR S
IDEALLY
IDEALOGY
IDEALS
AISLED
DEASIL
LADIES
SAILED
IDEAS
AIDES ASIDE
IDEATE DS
IDEATED
IDEATES
IDEATING
IDEATION S
IODINATE
IDEATIVE
IDEM
DIME
IDENTIC
INCITED
IDENTIFY
IDENTITY
IDEOGRAM S
IDEOLOGY
ABH NRS TW **IDES**
DIES SIDE
IDIOCIES
IDIOCY
IDIOLECT S
IDIOM S
IMIDO
IDIOMS
IODISM
IDIOT S
IDIOTIC
IDIOTISM S
IDIOTS
IDIOTYPE S
S **IDLE** DRS
DEIL DELI
DIEL LIED
S **IDLED**
IDLENESS
LINSEEDS
S **IDLER** S
RILED
S **IDLERS**
SIDLER
SLIDER
S **IDLES** T
DEILS DELIS
ISLED SIDLE
SLIDE
IDLESSE S
DIESELS
SEIDELS
IDLESSES
IDLEST
DELIST
LISTED
SILTED
TILDES
S **IDLING**
IDLY
IDYL
IDOCRASE S
IDOL S
DIOL LIDO
LOID
IDOLATER S
TAILORED
IDOLATOR S
TOROIDAL
IDOLATRY
ADROITLY
DILATORY
IDOLISE DRS
DOILIES
IDOLISED
IDOLISER S
IDOLISES
IDOLISM S
IDOLISMS
IDOLIZE DRS

IDOLIZED
IDOLIZER S
IDOLIZES
IDOLS
DIOLS LIDOS LOIDS SLOID SOLDI SOLID
IDONEITY
IDONEOUS
ABFGKLMRVY **IDS**
DIS
IDYL LS
IDLY
IDYLIST S
IDYLISTS
IDYLL S
DILLY
IDYLLIC
IDYLLIST S
IDYLLS
IDYLS
DKR **IF** FS
BDJMRT **IFF** Y
M **IFFIER**
M **IFFIEST**
FIFTIES
M **IFFINESS**
BJM **IFFY**
DKR **IFS**
M **IGG** S
GIG
DFGJPRWZ **IGGED**
BDFGJPRWZ **IGGING**
M **IGGS**
GIGS
IGLOO S
LOGOI
IGLOOS
ISOLOG
IGLU S
IGLUS
IGNATIA S
IGNATIAS
L **IGNEOUS**
DLS **IGNIFIED**
DLS **IGNIFIES**
DLS **IGNIFY**
L **IGNITE** DRS
TIEING
IGNITED
DIETING EDITING
IGNITER S
TIERING
IGNITERS
RESITING STINGIER
L **IGNITES**
IGNITING
IGNITION S
IGNITOR S
RIOTING
IGNITORS
IGNITRON S
IGNOBLE
IGNOBLY
IGNOMINY
IGNORAMI
IGNORANT
S **IGNORE** DRS
ERINGO REGION
IGNORED
ERODING GROINED NEGROID REDOING
IGNORER S
IGNORERS
IGNORES
ERINGOS REGIONS SIGNORE

IGNORING
GROINING
IGUANA S
IGUANAS
IGUANIAN S
IGUANID S
IGUANIDS
IHRAM S
IHRAMS
MARISH
IKAT S
IKATS
IKEBANA S
IKEBANAS
E **IKON** S
KINO OINK
E **IKONS**
KINOS OINKS
P **ILEA** CL
ILEAC
ILEAL
ILEITIS
P **ILEUM**
P **ILEUS**
LIEUS
ILEUSES
S **ILEX**
S **ILEXES**
EXILES
CM **ILIA** CDL
ILIAC
CILIA
ILIAD S
ILIADS
SIALID
F **ILIAL**
CM **ILIUM**
BMS **ILK** AS
ILKA
KAIL
BMS **ILKS**
SILK
BDFGHJKMNPRSTVWYZ **ILL** SY
ILLATION S
ILLATIVE S
ILLEGAL S
ILLEGALS
BFGHKMSTW **ILLER**
RILLE
ILLEST
LISTEL
ILLICIT
ILLITIC
ILLINIUM S
ILLIQUID
T **ILLITE** S
T **ILLITES**
ILLITIC
ILLICIT
ILLNESS
ILLOGIC S
ILLOGICS
BDFGHJKMNPRSTVWYZ **ILLS**
SILL
ILLUDE DS
DUELLI
ILLUDED
ILLUDES
SULLIED
ILLUDING
ILLUME DS
ILLUMED
ILLUMES
ILLUMINE DS
ILLUMING
ILLUSION S
ILLUSIVE
ILLUSORY
ILLUVIA L
ILLUVIAL

ILLUVIUM S
BDFGHSW **ILLY**
LILY YILL
ILMENITE S
MELINITE TIMELINE
IMAGE DRS
IMAGED
DEGAMI
IMAGER SY
GAMIER MAIGRE MIRAGE
IMAGERS
GISARME MIRAGES
IMAGERY
IMAGES
AGEISM
IMAGINAL
IMAGINE DRS
IMAGINED
IMAGINER S
MIGRAINE
IMAGINES
IMAGING S
IMAGINGS
IMAGISM S
IMAGISMS
IMAGIST S
IMAGISTS
IMAGO S
AMIGO
IMAGOES
IMAGOS
AMIGOS
IMAM S
MAIM
IMAMATE S
IMAMATES
IMAMS
MAIMS MIASM
IMARET S
MATIER
IMARETS
MAESTRI MISRATE SMARTIE
IMAUM S
UMAMI
IMAUMS
UMAMIS
IMBALM S
IMBALMED
DIMMABLE
IMBALMER S
IMBALMS
IMBARK S
IMBARKED
IMBARKS
IMBECILE S
L **IMBED** S
BEDIM
IMBEDDED
IMBEDS
BEDIMS
IMBIBE DRS
IMBIBED
IMBIBER S
IMBIBERS
IMBIBES
IMBIBING
IMBITTER S
IMBLAZE DS
IMBLAZED
IMBLAZES
IMBODIED
IMBODIES
IMBODY
IMBOLDEN S
IMBOSOM S
IMBOSOMS
IMBOWER S
WOMBIER
IMBOWERS
IMBROWN S
IMBROWNS
IMBRUE DS
ERBIUM

IMBRUED
IMBRUES
ERBIUMS
IMBRUING
IMBRUTE DS
TERBIUM
IMBRUTED
IMBRUTES
RESUBMIT TERBIUMS
IMBUE DS
IMBUED
IMBUES
IMBUING
T **IMID** EOS
MIDI
IMIDE S
MEDII
IMIDES
IMIDIC
IMIDO
IDIOM
IMIDS
MIDIS
IMINE S
IMINES
IMINO
L **IMITABLE**
IMITATE DS
IMITATED
IMITATES
IMITATOR S
IMMANE
AMMINE
IMMANENT
IMMATURE S
IMMENSE R
IMMENSER
IMMERGE DS
GEMMIER GREMMIE
IMMERGED
IMMERGES
GREMMIES
IMMERSE DS
IMMERSED
SIMMERED
IMMERSES
IMMESH
IMMESHED
IMMESHES
GJ **IMMIES**
IMMINENT
IMMINGLE DS
IMMIX
IMMIXED
IMMIXES
IMMIXING
IMMOBILE
IMMODEST Y
IMMOLATE DS
IMMORAL
IMMORTAL S
IMMOTILE
IMMUNE S
IMMUNES
IMMUNISE DS
IMMUNITY
IMMUNIZE DRS
IMMURE DS
IMMURED
IMMURES
RUMMIES
IMMURING
J **IMMY**
GJLPSW **IMP** IS
IMPACT S
IMPACTED
IMPACTER S
IMPACTOR S
IMPACTS
IMPAINT S
TIMPANI
IMPAINTS
MISPAINT
IMPAIR S

IMPAIRED
IMPAIRER S
IMPAIRS
IMPALA S
IMPALAS
IMPALE DRS
IMPALED
IMPLEAD
IMPALER S
IMPEARL LEMPIRA PALMIER
IMPALERS
IMPEARLS LEMPIRAS
IMPALES
IMPALING
IMPANEL S
MANIPLE
IMPANELS
MANIPLES
IMPARITY
IMPARK S
IMPARKED
IMPARKS
IMPART S
ARMPIT
IMPARTED
PREADMIT
IMPARTER S
TRAMPIER
IMPARTS
ARMPITS MISPART
IMPASSE S
IMPASSES
IMPASTE DS
PASTIME
IMPASTED
IMPASTES
PASTIMES
IMPASTO S
IMPASTOS
IMPAVID
IMPAWN S
IMPAWNED
IMPAWNS
IMPEACH
IMPEARL S
IMPALER LEMPIRA PALMIER
IMPEARLS
IMPALERS LEMPIRAS
GLPW **IMPED** E
IMPEDE DRS
IMPEDED
IMPEDER S
DEMIREP EPIDERM
IMPEDERS
DEMIREPS EPIDERMS PREMISED SIMPERED
IMPEDES
IMPEDING
IMPINGED
IMPEL S
IMPELLED
MILLEPED
IMPELLER S
IMPELLOR S
IMPELS
SIMPLE
IMPEND S
IMPENDED
IMPENDS
IMPERIA L
IMPERIAL S
IMPERIL S
IMPERILS
LIMPSIER
IMPERIUM S
IMPETIGO S
IMPETUS
IMPUTES UPTIMES

IMPHEE S
HEMPIE
IMPHEES
IMPI S
IMPIETY
GLPW **IMPING** ES
IMPINGE DRS
IMPINGED
IMPEDING
IMPINGER S
IMPINGES
IMPINGS
IMPIOUS
IMPIS H
W **IMPISH**
IMPISHLY
IMPLANT S
IMPLANTS
MISPLANT
IMPLEAD S
IMPALED
IMPLEADS
MISPLEAD
DPRW **IMPLED**
DIMPLE LIMPED
IMPLEDGE DS
IMPLICIT
IMPLIED
IMPLIES
IMPLODE DS
IMPLODED
IMPLODES
IMPLORE DRS
IMPLORED
IMPLORER S
IMPLORES
DJLPS **IMPLY**
IMPLYING
IMPOLICY
IMPOLITE
IMPONE DS
IMPONED
IMPONES
PEONISM
IMPONING
IMPOROUS
IMPORT S
IMPORTED
IMPORTER S
REIMPORT
IMPORTS
TROPISM
IMPOSE DRS
IMPOSED
IMPOSER S
PROMISE SEMIPRO
IMPOSERS
PROMISES SEMIPROS
IMPOSES
IMPOSING
IMPOST S
IMPOSTED
IMPOSTER S
IMPOSTOR S
IMPOSTS
MISSTOP
IMPOTENT S
IMPOUND S
IMPOUNDS
IMPOWER S
IMPOWERS
IMPREGN S
GRIPMEN PERMING
IMPREGNS
IMPRESA S
IMPRESAS
MISPARSE

IMPRESE S
EMPIRES EMPRISE EPIMERS PREMIES PREMISE SPIREME
IMPRESES
EMPRISES PREMISES SPIREMES
IMPRESS
PREMISS SIMPERS SPIREMS
IMPREST S
PERMITS
IMPRESTS
IMPRIMIS
IMPRINT S
IMPRINTS
MISPRINT
IMPRISON S
IMPROPER
IMPROV ES
IMPROVE DRS
IMPROVED
IMPROVER S
IMPROVES
IMPROVS
GLPSW **IMPS**
MIPS SIMP
IMPUDENT
IMPUGN S
UMPING
IMPUGNED
IMPUGNER S
IMPUGNS
SPUMING
IMPULSE DS
IMPULSED
DISPLUME
IMPULSES
IMPUNITY
IMPURE R
UMPIRE
IMPURELY
IMPURER
IMPUREST
IMPUTERS STUMPIER
IMPURITY
IMPUTE DRS
UPTIME
IMPUTED
IMPUTER S
IMPUTERS
IMPUREST STUMPIER
IMPUTES
IMPETUS UPTIMES
IMPUTING
ABDFGHJKLPRSTWYZ **IN** KNS
INACTION S
INACTIVE
INANE RS
INANELY
INANER
NARINE
INANES T
INSANE SIENNA
INANEST
STANINE
INANITY
INAPT
PAINT PATIN PINTA
INAPTLY
PTYALIN
INARABLE
INARCH
INARCHED
INARCHES
ARCHINES

INARM S
INARMED
INARMING
INARMS
INBEING S
INBEINGS
INBOARD S
INBOARDS
INBORN
INBOUND S
INBOUNDS
INBRED S
BINDER
BRINED
REBIND
INBREDS
BINDERS
REBINDS
INBREED S
BENDIER
INBREEDS
INBUILT
INBURST S
INBURSTS
INBY E
INBYE
INCAGE DS
INCAGED
INCAGES
CEASING
INCAGING
INCANT S
TANNIC
INCANTED
INCANTS
STANNIC
INCASE DS
CASEIN
INCASED
CANDIES
INCASES
CASEINS
CASSINE
INCASING
INCENSE DS
INCENSED
INCENSES
NICENESS
INCENT S
INCENTED
INDECENT
INCENTER S
INCENTS
INCEPT S
PECTIN
INCEPTED
INCEPTOR S
ENTROPIC
INCEPTS
INSPECT
PECTINS
INCEST S
INSECT
NICEST
INCESTS
INSECTS
CFP INCH
W CHIN
CPW INCHED
CHINED
NICHED
PW INCHER S
ENRICH
RICHEN
PW INCHERS
RICHENS
CFP INCHES
W CHINES
NICHES
CPW INCHING
CHINING
NICHING
INCHMEAL
INCHOATE
INCHWORM S
INCIDENT S
INCIPIT S
INCIPITS
INCISAL
SALICIN
INCISE DS

INCISED
INDICES
INCISES
ICINESS
INCISING
INCISION S
INCISIVE
INCISOR SY
INCISORS
INCISORY
INCISURE S
SCIURINE
INCITANT S
Z INCITE DRS
INCITED
IDENTIC
INCITER S
CITRINE
CRINITE
NERITIC
INCITERS
CITRINES
CRINITES
Z INCITES
INCITING
INCIVIL
INCLASP S
CAPLINS
INCLASPS
INCLINE DRS
INCLINED
INCLINER S
INCLINES
INCLIP S
INCLIPS
INCLOSE DRS
CINEOLS
INCLOSED
INCLOSER S
LICENSOR
INCLOSES
INCLUDE DS
NUCLIDE
INCLUDED
INCLUDES
NUCLIDES
UNSLICED
INCOG S
COIGN
INCOGS
COIGNS
COSIGN
INCOME RS
INCOMER S
INCOMERS
SERMONIC
INCOMES
MESONIC
INCOMING S
INCONNU S
INCONNUS
INCONY
INCORPSE DS
CONSPIRE
INCREASE DR S
INCREATE
CENTIARE
CREATINE
ITERANCE
INCROSS
INCRUST S
INCRUSTS
INCUBATE DS
INCUBI
INCUBUS
INCUDAL
INCUDATE
INCUDES
INCUSED
INDUCES
INCULT
INCUMBER S
INCUR S
RUNIC
INCURRED
INCURS
INCURVE DS
INCURVED
INCURVES

INCUS E
INCUSE DS
INCUSED
INCUDES
INDUCES
INCUSES
INCUSING
INDABA S
INDABAS
INDAGATE DS
INDAMIN ES
INDAMINE S
INDAMINS
INDEBTED
INDECENT
INCENTED
INDEED
DENIED
INDENE S
INDENES
INDENT S
DENTIN
INTEND
TINNED
INDENTED
INTENDED
INDENTER S
INTENDER
INTERNED
INDENTOR S
INDENTS
DENTINS
INTENDS
INDEVOUT
INDEX
NIXED
INDEXED
INDEXER S
REINDEX
INDEXERS
INDEXES
INDEXING S
INDICAN ST
INDICANS
INDICANT S
V INDICATE DS
ACTINIDE
CTENIDIA
INDICES
INCISED
INDICIA S
INDICIAS
INDICIUM S
INDICT S
INDICTED
INDICTEE S
INDICTER S
INDIRECT
REINDICT
INDICTOR S
INDICTS
INDIE S
L INDIES
INSIDE
INDIGEN EST
INDIGENE S
INDIGENS
INDIGENT S
ENDITING
INDIGN
DINING
NIDING
INDIGNLY
W INDIGO S
INDIGOES
INDIGOID S
W INDIGOS
INDIRECT
INDICTER
REINDICT
INDITE DRS
TINEID
INDITED
INDITER S
NITRIDE
INDITERS
DISINTER
NITRIDES
INDITES
TINEIDS

INDITING
INDIUM S
INDIUMS
INDOCILE
INDOL ES
INDOLE S
INDOLENT
INDOLES
INDOLS
INDOOR S
INDOORS
SORDINO
INDORSE DER S
DINEROS
ORDINES
ROSINED
SORDINE
INDORSED
INDORSEE S
INDORSER S
INDORSES
SORDINES
INDORSOR S
W INDOW S
W INDOWED
W INDOWING
W INDOWS
DISOWN
INDOXYL S
INDOXYLS
INDRAFT S
INDRAFTS
INDRAWN
INDRI S
INDRIS
INDUCE DRS
INDUCED
INDUCER S
INDUCERS
INDUCES
INCUDES
INCUSED
INDUCING
INDUCT S
INDUCTED
INDUCTEE S
INDUCTOR S
INDUCTS
INDUE DS
NUDIE
INDUED
INDUES
NUDIES
UNDIES
INDUING
INDULGE DRS
DUELING
ELUDING
INDULGED
DELUDING
INDULGER S
INDULGES
INDULIN ES
INDULINE S
INDULINS
INDULT S
INDULTS
INDURATE DS
RUINATED
URINATED
INDUSIA L
INDUSIAL
INDUSIUM
INDUSTRY
INDWELL S
INDWELLS
INDWELT
WINTLED
INEARTH S
HAIRNET
THERIAN
INEARTHS
HAIRNETS
THERIANS
INEDIBLE
INEDIBLY
INEDITA
INEDITED

INEPT
INEPTLY
INEQUITY
EQUINITY
INERRANT
INERT S
INTER NITER
NITRE TRINE
INERTIA ELS
INERTIAE
INERTIAL
INERTIAS
RAINIEST
INERTLY
INERTS
ESTRIN
INSERT
INTERS
NITERS
NITRES
SINTER
TRIENS
TRINES
INEXACT
INEXPERT S
INFALL S
INFALLS
INFAMIES
INFAMOUS
INFAMY
INFANCY
INFANT AES
INFANTA S
INFANTAS
INFANTE S
INFANTES
INFANTRY
INFANTS
INFARCT S
FRANTIC
INFRACT
INFARCTS
INFRACTS
INFARE S
FAINER
INFARES
INFAUNA ELS
INFAUNAE
INFAUNAL
INFAUNAS
INFECT S
INFECTED
INFECTER S
FRENETIC
REINFECT
INFECTOR S
INFECTS
INFECUND
INFEOFF S
INFEOFFS
INFER S
FINER
INFERIOR S
INFERNAL
INFERNO S
INFERNOS
INFERRED
INFERRER S
INFERS
INFEST S
FEINTS
FINEST
INFESTED
INFESTER S
FERNIEST
INFESTS
FITNESS
INFIDEL S
INFIELD
INFIDELS
INFIELDS
INFIELD S
INFIDEL
INFIELDS
INFIDELS
INFIGHT S
INFIGHTS
SHIFTING
INFILL

INFINITE S
INFINITY
INFIRM S
INFIRMED
INFIRMLY
INFIRMS
INFIX
INFIXED
INFIXES
INFIXING
INFIXION S
INFLAME DRS
INFLAMED
INFLAMER S
RIFLEMAN
INFLAMES
FLAMINES
INFLATE DRS
INFLATED
INFLATER S
INFLATES
INFLATOR S
FLATIRON
INFLECT S
INFLECTS
INFLEXED
INFLICT S
INFLICTS
INFLIGHT
INFLOW S
INFLOWS
INFLUENT S
INFLUX
INFLUXES
INFO S
FINO FOIN
INFOBAHN S
P INFOLD S
P INFOLDED
INFOLDER S
P INFOLDS
INFORM S
INFORMAL
FORMALIN
INFORMED
INFORMER S
REINFORM
RENIFORM
INFORMS
INFOS
FINOS FOINS
INFOUGHT
INFRA
INFRACT S
FRANTIC
INFARCT
INFRACTS
INFARCTS
INFRARED S
INFRINGE DR S
REFINING
INFRUGAL
INFUSE DRS
INFUSED
INFUSER S
INFUSERS
INFUSES
INFUSING
INFUSION S
INFUSIVE
INGATE S
EATING
INGATES
EASTING
EATINGS
INGESTA
SEATING
TEASING
INGATHER S
EARTHING
HEARTING
INGENUE S
GENUINE
INGENUES
UNSEEING
INGEST AS
SIGNET
TINGES

INGESTA
EASTING
EATINGS
INGATES
SEATING
TEASING
INGESTED
SIGNETED
INGESTS
SIGNETS
DJM INGLE S
ST
DJM INGLES
ST SINGLE
INGOING
INGOT S
TIGON
INGOTED
INGOTING
INGOTS
STINGO
TIGONS
INGRAFT S
RAFTING
INGRAFTS
STRAFING
INGRAIN S
RAINING
INGRAINS
INGRATE S
GRANITE
GRATINE
TANGIER
TEARING
INGRATES
ANGRIEST
ASTRINGE
GANISTER
GANTRIES
GRANITES
RANGIEST
INGRESS
RESIGNS
SIGNERS
SINGERS
INGROUND
ROUNDING
INGROUP S
POURING
ROUPING
INGROUPS
INGROWN
INGROWTH S
THROWING
WORTHING
INGUINAL
INGULF S
INGULFED
INGULFS
INHABIT S
INHABITS
INHALANT S
INHALE DRS
INHALED
INHALER S
HERNIAL
INHALERS
INHALES
INHALING
INHAUL S
INHAULER S
INHAULS
INHERE DS
HEREIN
INHERED
INHERENT
INHERES
HENRIES
RESHINE
INHERING
INHERIT S
INHERITS
INHESION S
INHIBIN S
INHIBINS
INHIBIT S
INHIBITS
INHOLDER S
INHUMAN E
INHUMANE

INHUME DRS
INHUMED
INHUMER S
RHENIUM
INHUMERS
RHENIUMS
INHUMES
INHUMING
INIA
INIMICAL
MP INION S
MP INIONS
INIQUITY
INITIAL S
INITIALS
INITIATE DS
INJECT S
INJECTED
INJECTOR S
INJECTS
INJURE DRS
INJURED
INJURER S
INJURERS
INJURES
INJURIES
INJURING
INJURY
DFGJKLMOPRSW INK SY
KIN
INKBERRY
INKBLOT S
INKBLOTS
DFJKLOPW INKED
JLPSTW INKER S
REINK
JLPSTW INKERS
REINKS SINKER
INKHORN S
INKHORNS
DHK INKIER
DHK INKIEST
K INKINESS
DFJKLOPSW INKING
INKJET
TW INKLE S
LIKEN
TW INKLES S
LIKENS SILKEN
INKLESS
KINLESS
INKLIKE
TW INKLING S
KILNING LINKING
T INKLINGS
SLINKING
INKPOT S
INKPOTS
DFGJKLMOPRSW INKS
KINS SINK SKIN
INKSTAND S
INKSTONE S
INKWELL S
INKWELLS
INKWOOD S
INKWOODS
DHKLPZ INKY
INLACE DS
INLACED
INLACES
SANICLE SCALENI
INLACING
INLAID
INLAND S
INLANDER S

INLANDS
INLAY S
LAYIN
INLAYER S
INLAYERS
INLAYING
INLAYS
LAYINS
INLET S
ELINT
INLETS
ELINTS ENLIST LISTEN SILENT TINSEL
INLIER S
LINIER
INLIERS
RESILIN
INLY
LINY
INLYING
INMATE S
ETAMIN TAMEIN
INMATES
ETAMINS TAMEINS
INMESH
HEMINS
INMESHED
INMESHES
INMOST
MONIST
JL INN S
INNAGE S
INNAGES
INNARDS
P INNATE
P INNATELY
BDFGPSTW INNED
DGPSTW INNER S
RENIN
INNERLY
DGPSTW INNERS
RENINS SINNER
INNERVE DS
NERVINE
INNERVED
INNERVES
NERVINES
BDFGPRSTW INNING S
GW INNINGS
SINNING
INNLESS
INNOCENT S
INNOVATE DS
VENATION
JL INNS
INNUENDO S
INOCULA
INOCULUM S
INOSINE S
INOSINES
INOSITE S
INOSITES
NOISIEST
INOSITOL S
INPHASE
INPOUR S
INPOURED
INPOURS
INPUT S
INPUTS
INPUTTED
UNPITTED
INPUTTER S
INQUEST S
QUINTES
INQUESTS
INQUIET S
INQUIETS
INQUIRE DRS
INQUIRED

INQUIRER S
INQUIRES
INQUIRY
INRO
IRON NOIR NORI
INROAD S
ORDAIN
INROADS
ORDAINS SADIRON
INRUN S
INURN
INRUNS
INURNS
INRUSH
INRUSHES
ABDFGHJKLPRSTWYZ INS
SIN
INSANE R
INANES SIENNA
INSANELY
INSANER
INSNARE
INSANEST
STANINES
INSANITY
INSCAPE S
INSCAPES
INSCRIBE DRS
INSCROLL S
INSCULP S
SCULPIN UNCLIPS
INSCULPS
SCULPINS
INSEAM S
AMINES ANIMES MESIAN SEMINA
INSEAMS
SAMISEN
INSECT S
INCEST NICEST
INSECTAN
ANCIENTS CANNIEST INSTANCE
INSECTS
INCESTS
INSECURE
SINECURE
INSERT S
ESTRIN INERTS INTERS NITERS NITRES SINTER TRIENS TRINES
INSERTED
NERDIEST RESIDENT SINTERED TRENDIES
INSERTER S
REINSERT REINTERS RENTIERS TERRINES
INSERTS
ESTRINS SINTERS
INSET S
NEIST NITES SENTI STEIN TINES
INSETS
STEINS
INSETTED
DINETTES
P INSETTER S
INTEREST STERNITE TRIENTES

INSHEATH ES
INSHORE
HEROINS
INSHRINE DS
INSIDE RS
INDIES
INSIDER S
INSIDERS
INSIDES
INSIGHT S
HISTING
INSIGHTS
INSIGNE
SEINING
INSIGNIA S
INSIPID
INSIST S
INSISTED
TIDINESS
INSISTER S
SINISTER
INSISTS
INSNARE DRS
INSANER
INSNARED
INSNARER S
INSNARES
INSOFAR
INSOLATE DS
ELATIONS TOENAILS
INSOLE S
ELOINS LESION OLEINS
INSOLENT S
INSOLES
LESIONS LIONESS
INSOMNIA CS
INSOMUCH
INSOUL S
INSOULED
DELUSION UNSOILED
INSOULS
INSPAN S
PINNAS
INSPANS
INSPECT S
INCEPTS PECTINS
INSPECTS
INSPHERE DS
INSPIRE DRS
SPINIER
INSPIRED
INSPIRER S
INSPIRES
INSPIRIT S
INSTABLE
INSTAL LS
INSTALL S
INSTALLS
INSTALS
INSTANCE DS
ANCIENTS CANNIEST INSECTAN
INSTANCY
INSTANT S
INSTANTS
INSTAR S
SANTIR STRAIN TRAINS
INSTARS
SANTIRS STRAINS
INSTATE DS
SATINET
INSTATED
INSTATES
ANTSIEST NASTIEST SATINETS TITANESS

INSTEAD
DESTAIN DETAINS NIDATES SAINTED STAINED
INSTEP S
SPINET
INSTEPS
SPINETS
INSTIL LS
INSTILL S
INSTILLS
INSTILS
INSTINCT S
INSTROKE S
INSTRUCT S
INSULANT S
INSULAR S
URINALS
INSULARS
INSULATE DS
ALUNITES
INSULIN S
INULINS
INSULINS
INSULT S
SUNLIT
INSULTED
DILUENTS UNLISTED
INSULTER S
INSULTS
INSURANT S
INSURE DRS
INURES RUSINE URINES URSINE
INSURED S
INSUREDS
SUNDRIES
INSURER S
RUINERS
INSURERS
INSURES
SUNRISE
INSURING
INSWATHE DS
INSWEPT
INTACT
INTACTLY
INTAGLI O
TAILING
INTAGLIO S
LIGATION
INTAKE S
INTAKES
INTARSIA S
INTEGER S
TREEING
INTEGERS
GENTRIES REESTING STEERING
INTEGRAL S
ALERTING ALTERING RELATING TANGLIER TRIANGLE
INTEND S
DENTIN INDENT TINNED
INTENDED S
INDENTED
INTENDER S
INDENTER INTERNED
INTENDS
DENTINS INDENTS
INTENSE R
TENNIES
INTENSER
INTERNES
INTENT S
INTENTLY
INTENTS
TENNIST

HLMSTW INTER NS
INERT NITER NITRE TRINE
INTERACT S
INTERAGE
GRATINEE
INTERBED S
INTERCOM S
INTERCUT S
TINCTURE
INTEREST S
INSETTER STERNITE TRIENTES
INTERIM S
MINTIER TERMINI
INTERIMS
MINISTER MISINTER
INTERIOR S
INTERLAP S
TRAPLINE TRIPLANE
INTERLAY S
INTERMAT S
MARTINET
INTERMIT S
INTERMIX
INTERN ES
TINNER
INTERNAL S
INTERNE DES
INTERNED
INDENTER INTENDER
INTERNEE S
RETINENE
INTERNES
INTENSER
INTERNS
TINNERS
INTERRED
TRENDIER
INTERREX
INTERROW
HLMSTW INTERS
ESTRIN INERTS INSERT NITERS NITRES SINTER TRIENS TRINES
INTERSEX
INTERTIE S
RETINITE
INTERVAL ES
INTERWAR
INTHRAL LS
INTHRALL S
INTHRALS
INTHRONE DS
INTI S
INTIFADA HS
INTIMA ELS
INTIMACY
MINACITY
INTIMAE
INTIMAL
INTIMAS
ANIMIST SANTIMI
INTIMATE DRS
INTIME
INTIMIST S
INTINE S
INTINES
INTIS
INTITLE DS
INTITLED
INTITLES
LINTIEST
INTITULE DS
P INTO
INTOMB S
INTOMBED
INTOMBS

INTONATE DS
INTONE DRS
INTONED
INTONER S
TERNION
INTONERS
TERNIONS
INTONES
TENSION
INTONING
INTORT S
TRITON
INTORTED
INTORTS
TRITONS
INTOWN
INTRADAY
INTRADOS
DIATRONS
INTRANET S
INTRANT S
INTRANTS
INTREAT S
ITERANT NATTIER NITRATE TERTIAN
INTREATS
NITRATES STRAITEN TERTIANS
INTRENCH
INTREPID
INTRIGUE DRS
INTRO NS
NITRO
INTROFY
INTROIT S
INTROITS
INTROMIT S
INTRON S
INTRONS
INTRORSE
INTROS
NITROS
INTRUDE DRS
TURDINE UNTIRED UNTRIED
INTRUDED
INTRUDER S
INTRUDES
INTRUST S
INTRUSTS
INTUBATE DS
INTUIT S
INTUITED
INTUITS
INTURN S
INTURNED
INTURNS
INTWINE DS
INTWINED
INTWINES
INTWIST S
NITWITS
INTWISTS
INULASE S
INULASES
INULIN S
INULINS
INSULIN
INUNDANT
INUNDATE DS
INURBANE
INURE DS
URINE
INURED
RUINED
INURES
INSURE RUSINE URINES URSINE
INURING
RUINING
INURN S
INRUN
INURNED

INURNING
INURNS
INRUNS
INUTILE
INVADE DRS
INVADED
INVADER S
RAVINED
INVADERS
INVADES
INVADING
INVALID S
INVALIDS
INVAR S
RAVIN
INVARS
RAVINS
INVASION S
INVASIVE
INVECTED
INVEIGH S
INVEIGHS
INVEIGLE DR S
INVENT S
INVENTED
INVENTER S
REINVENT
INVENTOR SY
INVENTS
INVERITY
INVERSE DS
ENVIERS
VEINERS
VENIRES
VERSINE
INVERSED
INVERSES
VERSINES
INVERT S
INVERTED
INVERTER S
INVERTIN GS
INVERTOR S
INVERTS
STRIVEN
INVEST S
INVESTED
INVESTOR S
INVESTS
INVIABLE
INVIABLY
INVIRILE
INVISCID
INVITAL
INVITE DERS
INVITED
INVITEE S
INVITEES
VEINIEST
INVITER S
VITRINE
INVITERS
VITRINES
INVITES
VINIEST
INVITING
INVOCATE DS
CONATIVE
INVOICE DS
INVOICED
INVOICES
INVOKE DRS
INVOKED
INVOKER S
INVOKERS
INVOKES
INVOKING
INVOLUTE DS
INVOLVE DRS
INVOLVED
INVOLVER S
INVOLVES
INWALL S
INWALLED
INWALLS
INWARD S
INWARDLY

INWARDS
INWEAVE DS
INWEAVED
INWEAVES
INWIND S
INWINDS
INWOUND
INWOVE N
INWOVEN
INWRAP S
INWRAPS
RIPSAWN
IODATE DS
IODATED
TOADIED
IODATES
TOADIES
IODATING
IODATION S
IODIC
IODID ES
IODIDE S
IODIDES
IODISED
IODIDS
IODIN ES
IODINATE DS
IDEATION
IODINE S
IODINES
IONISED
IODINS
IODISE DS
IODISED
IODIDES
IODISES
IODISING
IODISM S
IDIOMS
IODISMS
IODIZE DRS
IODIZED
IODIZER S
IODIZERS
IODIZES
IODIZING
IODOFORM S
IODOPHOR S
IODOPSIN S
IODOUS
ODIOUS
IOLITE S
IOLITES
OILIEST
CLP ION S
BP IONIC S
IONICITY
B IONICS
L IONISE DS
L IONISED
IODINES
L IONISES
L IONISING
IONIUM S
IONIUMS
NIMIOUS
L IONIZE DRS
L IONIZED
L IONIZER S
IRONIZE
L IONIZERS
IRONIZES
L IONIZES
L IONIZING
IONOGEN S
IONOGENS
IONOMER S
MOONIER
IONOMERS
MOONRISE
IONONE S
IONONES
CLP IONS
B IOTA S
IOTACISM S
B IOTAS
OSTIA STOAI
IPECAC S
ICECAP

IPECACS
ICECAPS
IPOMOEA S
IPOMOEAS
IRACUND
T IRADE S
AIDER AIRED
DEAIR REDIA
T IRADES
AIDERS
DEAIRS
RAISED
REDIAS
RESAID
P IRATE R
RETIA TERAI
IRATELY
REALITY
TEARILY
IRATER
ARTIER
IRATEST
ARTIEST
ARTISTE
ATTIRES
RATITES
STRIATE
TASTIER
CDF HLM STW IRE DS
REI
AFH MST W IRED
DIRE RIDE
D IREFUL
D IREFULLY
FTW IRELESS
RESILES
E IRENIC S
E IRENICAL
IRENICS
SERICIN
CFH MST VW IRES
REIS RISE SIRE
V IRID S
IRIDES
IRISED
IRIDIC
IRIDIUM S
IRIDIUMS
IRIDS
AFH MST W IRING
IRIS
IRISED
IRIDES
IRISES
IRISING
IRITIC
IRITIS
IRITISES
BDK M IRK S
KIR
D IRKED
DIKER
D IRKING
BDK M IRKS
KIRS KRIS
RISK
IRKSOME
SMOKIER
IROKO S
IROKOS
G IRON ESY
INRO NOIR
NORI
IRONBARK S
IRONCLAD S
IRONE DRS
IRONED
DINERO
IRONER S
IRONERS
IRONES
NOSIER
SENIOR
IRONIC
IRONICAL

IRONIES
NOISIER
IRONING S
IRONINGS
NIGROSIN
ROSINING
IRONIST S
IRONISTS
IRONIZE DS
IONIZER
IRONIZED
IRONIZES
IONIZERS
IRONLIKE
IRONMAN
IRONMEN
IRONNESS
G IRONS
NOIRS NORIS
ORNIS ROSIN
IRONSIDE S
DERISION
RESINOID
IRONWARE S
IRONWEED S
IRONWOOD S
IRONWORK S
IRONY
IRREAL
RAILER
IRRIGATE DS
IRRITANT S
IRRITATE DS
IRRUPT S
IRRUPTED
IRRUPTS
STIRRUP
ABC DHK LMP QST VWX IS M
SI
ISAGOGE S
ISAGOGES
ISAGOGIC S
ISARITHM S
ISATIN ES
ISATINE S
ISATINES
SANITIES
SANITISE
TENIASIS
ISATINIC
ISATINS
ISBA S
BIAS
ISBAS
BASIS BASSI
ISCHEMIA S
ISCHEMIC
ISCHIA L
ISCHIAL
ISCHIUM
ISLAND S
ISLANDED
LANDSIDE
ISLANDER S
ISLANDS
AL ISLE DST
LEIS LIES
AM ISLED
DEILS DELIS
IDLES SIDLE
SLIDE
ISLELESS
AL ISLES
ISLET S
ISTLE STILE
TILES
ISLETED
ISLETS
ISTLES
SLIEST
STILES
ISLING
J ISM S
MIS
SIM
J ISMS
MISS SIMS

ISOBAR ES
ISOBARE S
ISOBARES
ISOBARIC
ISOBARS
ISOBATH S
ISOBATHS
ISOBUTYL S
ISOCHEIM S
ISOCHIME
ISOCHIME S
ISOCHEIM
ISOCHOR ES
ISOCHORE S
CHOOSIER
ISOCHORS
ISOCHRON ES
CHORIONS
ISOCLINE S
SILICONE
ISOCRACY
ISODOSE
ISOFORM S
ISOFORMS
M ISOGAMY
ISOGENIC
ISOGENY
ISOGLOSS
ISOGON ESY
ISOGONAL S
ISOGONE S
GOONIES
NOOGIES
ISOGONES
ISOGONIC S
ISOGONS
ISOGONY
ISOGRAFT S
ISOGRAM S
ISOGRAMS
ISOGRAPH S
ISOGRIV S
ISOGRIVS
ISOHEL S
HELIOS
HOLIES
ISOHELS
ISOHYET S
ISOHYETS
ISOLABLE
LOBELIAS
ISOLATE DS
ISOLATED
DIASTOLE
SODALITE
ISOLATES
ISOLATOR S
OSTIOLAR
ISOLEAD S
ISOLEADS
ASSOILED
ISOLINE S
ELISION
LIONISE
ISOLINES
ELISIONS
LIONISES
OILINESS
ISOLOG S
IGLOOS
ISOLOGS
ISOLOGUE S
ISOMER S
MOIRES
RIMOSE
ISOMERIC
ISOMERS
MOSSIER
ISOMETRY
ISOMORPH S
ISONOMIC
ISONOMY
ISOPACH S
ISOPACHS
ISOPHOTE S
ISOPLETH S
HELISTOP
HOPLITES
ISOPOD S

ISOPODAN S
ISOPODS
ISOPRENE S
PEREIONS
PIONEERS
ISOSPIN S
ISOSPINS
ISOSPORY
ISOSTACY
ISOSTASY
ISOTACH S
ISOTACHS
ISOTHERE S
THEORIES
THEORISE
ISOTHERM S
ISOTONE S
TOONIES
ISOTONES
ISOTONIC
COITIONS
ISOTOPE S
ISOTOPES
ISOTOPIC
ISOTOPY
ISOTROPY
POROSITY
ISOTYPE S
ISOTYPES
ISOTYPIC
ISOZYME S
ISOZYMES
ISOZYMIC
ISSEI S
ISSEIS
ISSUABLE
ISSUABLY
ISSUANCE S
ISSUANT
SUSTAIN
T ISSUE DRS
T ISSUED
DISUSE
ISSUER S
SIEURS
ISSUERS
RISUSES
T ISSUES
T ISSUING
ISTHMI C
MISHIT
ISTHMIAN S
HISTAMIN
THIAMINS
ISTHMIC
ISTHMOID
ISTHMUS
ISTLE S
ISLET STILE
TILES
ISTLES
ISLETS
SLIEST
STILES
ABD FGH KLN PST WZ IT S
TI
ITALIC S
ITALICS
ABD FHP W ITCH Y
CHIT
BDH PW ITCHED
ABD FHP W ITCHES
ETHICS
BPW ITCHIER
BPW ITCHIEST
CHITTIES
ETHICIST
THEISTIC
BP ITCHILY
BDH PW ITCHING S
W ITCHINGS
BFP W ITCHY

ITEM S
EMIT MITE
TIME
ITEMED
ITEMING
ITEMISE DS
ITEMISED
ITEMISES
ITEMIZE DRS
ITEMIZED
ITEMIZER S
ITEMIZES
ITEMS
EMITS METIS
MITES SMITE
STIME TIMES
ITERANCE S
CENTIARE
CREATINE
INCREATE
ITERANT
INTREAT
NATTIER
NITRATE
TERTIAN
L ITERATE DS
ARIETTE
ITERATED
L ITERATES
ARIETTES
TEARIEST
TREATIES
TREATISE
ITERUM
CDE HLM TWZ ITHER
THEIR
ABD FGH KLN PST WZ ITS
SIT TIS
ITSELF
FILETS
FLIEST
FLITES
STIFLE
IVIED
C IVIES
IVORIES
IVORY
JT IVY
IVYLIKE
K IWIS
IXIA S
IXIAS
IXODID S
DIOXID
IXODIDS
DIOXIDS
IXORA S
IXORAS
IXTLE S
IXTLES
S IZAR S
S IZARS
SIZAR
G IZZARD S
G IZZARDS

J

JAB S
JABBED
JABBER S
JABBERED
JABBERER S
JABBERS
JABBING
JABIRU S
JABIRUS
JABOT S
JABOTS
JABS
JACAL S
JACALES
JACALS
JACAMAR S
JACAMARS

JACANA S
JACANAS
JACINTH ES
JACINTHE S
JACINTHS
JACK SY
JACKAL S
JACKALS
JACKAROO S
JACKASS
JACKBOOT S
BOOTJACK
JACKDAW S
JACKDAWS
JACKED
JACKER S
JACKEROO S
JACKERS
JACKET S
JACKETED
JACKETS
JACKFISH
JACKIES
JACKING
JACKLEG S
JACKLEGS
JACKPOT S
JACKPOTS
JACKROLL S
JACKS
JACKSTAY S
JACKY
JACOBIN S
JACOBINS
JACOBUS
JACONET S
JACONETS
JACQUARD S
E JACULATE DS
JACUZZI S
JACUZZIS
JADE DS
JADED
JADEDLY
JADEITE S
JADEITES
JADELIKE
JADES
JADING
JADISH
HADJIS
JIHADS
JADISHLY
JADITIC
JAEGER S
JAEGERS
JAG GS
JAGER S
JAGERS
JAGG SY
JAGGARY
JAGGED
JAGGEDER
JAGGEDLY
JAGGER SY
JAGGERS
JAGGERY
JAGGHERY
JAGGIER
JAGGIES T
JAGGIEST
JAGGING
JAGGS
JAGGY
JAGLESS
JAGRA S
JAGRAS
JAGS
JAGUAR S
JAGUARS
JAIL S
JAILABLE
JAILBAIT
JAILBIRD S
JAILED
JAILER S
JAILERS
JAILING
JAILOR S
JAILORS
JAILS
JAKE S
JAKES
JALAP S
JALAPENO S
JALAPIC
JALAPIN S
JALAPINS
JALAPS
JALOP SY
JALOPIES
JALOPPY
JALOPS
JALOPY
JALOUSIE DS
JAM BS
JAMB ES
JAMBE DS
JAMBEAU X
JAMBEAUX
JAMBED
JAMBES
JAMBING
JAMBOREE S
JAMBS
JAMLIKE
JAMMABLE
JAMMED
JAMMER S
JAMMERS
JAMMIER
JAMMIES T
JAMMIEST
JAMMING
JAMMY
JAMS
JANE S
JEAN
JANES
JEANS
JANGLE DRS
JANGLED
JANGLER S
JANGLERS
JANGLES
JANGLIER
JANGLING
JANGLY
JANIFORM
JANISARY
JANITOR S
JANITORS
JANIZARY
JANTY
JAPAN S
JAPANIZE DS
JAPANNED
JAPANNER S
JAPANS
JAPE DRS
JAPED
JAPER SY
JAPERIES
JAPERS
JASPER
JAPERY
JAPES
JAPING
JAPINGLY
JAPONICA S
A JAR LS
RAJ
JARFUL S
JARFULS
JARSFUL
JARGON SY
JARGONED
JARGONEL S
JARGONS
JARGONY
JARGOON S
JARGOONS
JARHEAD S
JARHEADS
JARINA S
JARINAS
JARL S
JARLDOM S
JARLDOMS
JARLS
JAROSITE S
JAROVIZE DS
JARRAH S
JARRAHS
JARRED
JARRING
JARS
JARSFUL
JARFULS
JARVEY S
JARVEYS
JASMIN ES
JASMINE S
JASMINES
JASMINS
JASPER SY
JAPERS
JASPERS
JASPERY
JASSID S
JASSIDS
JATO S
JOTA
JATOS
JOTAS
JAUK S
JAUKED
JAUKING
JAUKS
JAUNCE DS
JAUNCED
JAUNCES
JAUNCING
JAUNDICE DS
JAUNT SY
JUNTA
JAUNTED
JAUNTIER
JAUNTILY
JAUNTING
JAUNTS
JUNTAS
JAUNTY
JAUP S
PUJA
JAUPED
JAUPING
JAUPS
PUJAS
JAVA S
JAVAS
JAVELIN AS
JAVELINA S
JAVELINS
JAW S
JAWAN S
JAWANS
JAWBONE DRS
JAWBONED
JAWBONER S
JAWBONES
JAWED
JAWING
JAWLESS
JAWLIKE
JAWLINE S
JAWLINES
JAWS
JAY S
JAYBIRD S
JAYBIRDS
JAYGEE S
JAYGEES
JAYS
JAYVEE S
VEEJAY
JAYVEES
VEEJAYS
JAYWALK S
JAYWALKS
JAZZ Y
JAZZBO S
JAZZBOS
JAZZED
JAZZER S
JAZZERS
JAZZES
JAZZIER
JAZZIEST
JAZZILY
JAZZING
JAZZLIKE
JAZZMAN
JAZZMEN
JAZZY
JEALOUS Y
JEALOUSY
JEAN S
JANE
JEANED
JEANS
JANES
D JEBEL S
D JEBELS
A JEE DPRSZ
JEED
JEEING
JEEP S
JEEPED
JEEPERS
JEEPING
JEEPNEY S
JEEPNEYS
JEEPS
JEER S
JEERED
JEREED
JEERER S
JEERERS
JEERING
JEERS
JEES
JEEZ
JEFE S
JEFES
JEHAD S
JEHADS
HADJES
JEHU S
JEHUS
JEJUNA L
JEJUNAL
JEJUNE
JEJUNELY
JEJUNITY
JEJUNUM
JELL OSY
D JELLABA S
D JELLABAS
JELLED
JELLIED
JELLIES
JELLIFY
JELLING
JELLO S
JELLOS
JELLS
JELLY
JELLYING
JELUTONG S
JEMADAR S
JEMADARS
JEMIDAR S
JEMIDARS
JEMMIED
JEMMIES
JEMMY
JEMMYING
JENNET S
JENNETS
JENNIES
JENNY
JEON
JEOPARD SY
JEOPARDS
JEOPARDY
JERBOA S
JERBOAS
JEREED S
JEERED
JEREEDS
JEREMIAD S
JERID S
JERIDS
JERK SY
JERKED
JERKER S
JERKERS
JERKIER
JERKIES T
JERKIEST
JERKILY
JERKIN GS
JINKER
JERKING
JERKINS
JINKERS
JERKS
JERKY
JEROBOAM S
JERREED S
JERREEDS
JERRICAN S
JERRID S
JERRIDS
JERRIES
JERRY
JERRYCAN S
JERSEY S
JERSEYED
JERSEYS
JESS E
JESSANT
JESSE DS
JESSED
JESSES
JESSING
JEST S
JETS
JESTED
JESTER S
JESTERS
JESTFUL
JESTING S
JESTINGS
JESTS
JET ES
JETBEAD S
JETBEADS
JETE S
JETES
JETFOIL S
JETFOILS
JETLAG S
JETLAGS
JETLIKE
JETLINER S
JETON S
JETONS
JETPORT S
JETPORTS
JETS
JEST
JETSAM S
JETSAMS
JETSOM S
JETSOMS
JETTED
JETTIED
JETTIER
JETTIES T
JETTIEST
JETTING
JETTISON S
JETTON S
JETTONS
JETTY
JETTYING
JETWAY S
JETWAYS
JEU X
JEUX
JEWEL S
JEWELED
JEWELER S
JEWELERS
JEWELING
JEWELLED
JEWELLER SY
JEWELRY
JEWELS
JEWFISH
JEZAIL S
JEZAILS
JEZEBEL S
JEZEBELS
JIAO
JIB BES
JIBB S
JIBBED
JIBBER S
JIBBERS
JIBBING
JIBBOOM S
JIBBOOMS
JIBBS
JIBE DRS
JIBED
JIBER S
JIBERS
JIBES
JIBING
JIBINGLY
JIBS
JICAMA S
JICAMAS
JIFF SY
JIFFIES
JIFFS
JIFFY
JIG S
JIGGED
JIGGER S
JIGGERED
REJIGGED
JIGGERS
JIGGIER
JIGGIEST
JIGGING
JIGGISH
JIGGLE DS
JIGGLED
JIGGLES
JIGGLIER
JIGGLING
JIGGLY
JIGGY
JIGLIKE
JIGS
JIGSAW NS
JIGSAWED
JIGSAWN
JIGSAWS
JIHAD S
HADJI
JIHADS
HADJIS
JADISH
JILL S
JILLION S
JILLIONS
JILLS
JILT S
JILTED
JILTER S
JILTERS
JILTING
JILTS
JIMINY
JIMJAMS
JIMMIE DS
JIMMIED
JIMMIES
JIMMINY
JIMMY
JIMMYING
JIMP Y
JIMPER
JIMPEST
JIMPLY
JIMPY
D JIN KNSX
JINGAL LS
JINGALL S
JINGALLS
JINGALS
JINGKO
JOKING
JINGKOES
JINGLE DRS
JINGLED
JINGLER S
JINGLERS
JINGLES
JINGLIER
JINGLING
JINGLY
JINGO
JINGOES
JINGOISH
JINGOISM S
JINGOIST S
JOISTING
JINK S
JINKED
JINKER S
JERKIN
JINKERS
JERKINS
JINKING
JINKS
D JINN IS
JINNEE
D JINNI S
JINNIS
D JINNS
D JINS
JINX
JINXED
JINXES
JINXING
JIPIJAPA S
JITNEY S
JITNEYS
JITTER SY
TRIJET
JITTERED
JITTERS
TRIJETS
JITTERY
JIUJITSU S
JIUJUTSU S
JIVE DRSY
JIVEASS
JIVED
JIVER S
JIVERS
JIVES
JIVEY
JIVIER
JIVIEST
JIVING
JIVY
JNANA S
JNANAS
JO BEGTWY
JOANNES
JOB S
JOBBED
JOBBER SY
JOBBERS
JOBBERY
JOBBING

JOBLESS
JOBNAME S
JOBNAMES
JOBS
JOCK OS
JOCKETTE S
JOCKEY S
JOCKEYED
JOCKEYS
JOCKO S
JOCKOS
JOCKS
JOCOSE
JOCOSELY
JOCOSITY
JOCULAR
JOCUND
JOCUNDLY
JODHPUR S
JODHPURS
JOE SY
JOES
JOEY S
JOEYS
JOG S
JOGGED
JOGGER S
JOGGERS
JOGGING S
JOGGINGS
JOGGLE DRS
JOGGLED
JOGGLER S
JOGGLERS
JOGGLES
JOGGLING
JOGS
JOHANNES
JOHN S
JOHNBOAT S
JOHNNIE S
JOHNNIES
JOHNNY
JOHNS
JOIN ST
JOINABLE
JOINDER S
JOINDERS
JOINED
JOINER SY
REJOIN
JOINERS
REJOINS
JOINERY
JOINING S
JOININGS
JOINS
JOINT S
JOINTED
JOINTER S
JOINTERS
JOINTING
JOINTLY
JOINTS
JOINTURE DS
JOIST S
JOISTED
JOISTING
JINGOIST
JOISTS
JOJOBA S
JOJOBAS
JOKE DRSY
JOKED
JOKER S
JOKERS
JOKES
JOKESTER S
JOKEY
JOKIER
JOKIEST
JOKILY
JOKINESS
JOKING
JINGKO

JOKINGLY
JOKY
JOLE S
JOLES
JOLLIED
JOLLIER S
JOLLIERS
JOLLIES T
JOLLIEST
JOLLIFY
JOLLILY
JOLLITY
JOLTILY
JOLLY
JOLLYING
JOLT SY
JOLTED
JOLTER S
JOLTERS
JOSTLER
JOLTIER
JOLTIEST
JOLTILY
JOLLITY
JOLTING
JOLTS
JOLTY
JOMON
JONES
JONESED
JONESES
JONESING
JONGLEUR S
JONQUIL S
JONQUILS
JORAM S
MAJOR
JORAMS
MAJORS
JORDAN S
JORDANS
JORUM S
JORUMS
JOSEPH S
JOSEPHS
JOSH
JOSHED
JOSHER S
JOSHERS
JOSHES
JOSHING
JOSS
JOSSES
JOSTLE DRS
JOSTLED
JOSTLER S
JOLTERS
JOSTLERS
JOSTLES
JOSTLING
JOT AS
JOTA S
JATO
JOTAS
JATOS
JOTS
JOTTED
JOTTER S
JOTTERS
JOTTING S
JOTTINGS
JOTTY
JOUAL S
JOUALS
JOUK S
JOUKED
JOUKING
JOUKS
JOULE S
JOULES
JOUNCE DS
JOUNCED
JOUNCES
JUNCOES
JOUNCIER
JOUNCING

JOUNCY
JOURNAL S
JOURNALS
JOURNEY S
JOURNEYS
JOURNO S
JOURNOS
SOJOURN
JOUST S
JOUSTED
JOUSTER S
JOUSTERS
JOUSTING
JOUSTS
JOVIAL
JOVIALLY
JOVIALTY
JOW LS
JOWAR S
JOWARS
JOWED
JOWING
JOWL SY
JOWLED
JOWLIER
JOWLIEST
JOWLS
JOWLY
JOWS
JOY S
JOYANCE S
JOYANCES
JOYED
JOYFUL
JOYFULLY
JOYING
JOYLESS
JOYOUS
JOYOUSLY
JOYPOP S
JOYPOPS
JOYRIDE RS
JOYRIDER S
JOYRIDES
JOYRODE
JOYS
JOYSTICK S
JUBA S
JUBAS
JUBBAH S
JUBBAHS
JUBE S
JUBES
JUBHAH S
JUBHAHS
JUBILANT
JUBILATE DS
JUBILE ES
JUBILEE S
JUBILEES
JUBILES
JUCO S
JUCOS
JUDAS
JUDASES
JUDDER S
JUDDERED
JUDDERS
JUDGE DRS
JUDGED
JUDGER S
JUDGERS
JUDGES
JUDGING
JUDGMENT S
JUDICIAL
JUDO S
JUDOIST S
JUDOISTS
JUDOKA S
JUDOKAS
JUDOS
JUG AS
A JUGA L

JUGAL
JUGATE
JUGFUL S
JUGFULS
JUGSFUL
JUGGED
JUGGING
JUGGLE DRS
JUGGLED
JUGGLER SY
JUGGLERS
JUGGLERY
JUGGLES
JUGGLING S
JUGHEAD S
JUGHEADS
JUGS
JUGSFUL
JUGFULS
JUGULA R
JUGULAR S
JUGULARS
JUGULATE DS
JUGULUM
JUGUM S
JUGUMS
JUICE DRS
JUICED
JUICER S
JUICERS
JUICES
JUICIER
JUICIEST
JUICILY
JUICING
JUICY
JUJITSU S
JUJUIST
JUJITSUS
JUJUISTS
JUJU S
JUJUBE S
JUJUBES
JUJUISM S
JUJUISMS
JUJUIST S
JUJITSU
JUJUISTS
JUJITSUS
JUJUS
JUJUTSU S
JUJUTSUS
JUKE DS
JUKEBOX
JUKED
JUKES
JUKING
JUKU S
JUKUS
JULEP S
JULEPS
JULIENNE DS
JUMBAL S
JUMBALS
JUMBLE DRS
JUMBLED
JUMBLER S
JUMBLERS
JUMBLES
JUMBLING
JUMBO S
JUMBOS
JUMBUCK S
JUMBUCKS
JUMP SY
JUMPABLE
JUMPED
JUMPER S
JUMPERS
JUMPIER
JUMPIEST
JUMPILY
JUMPING
JUMPOFF S
JUMPOFFS

JUMPS
JUMPSUIT S
JUMPY
JUN K
JUNCO S
JUNCOES
JOUNCES
JUNCOS
JUNCTION S
JUNCTURE S
JUNGLE DS
JUNGLED
JUNGLES
JUNGLIER
JUNGLY
JUNIOR S
JUNIORS
JUNIPER S
JUNIPERS
JUNK SY
JUNKED
JUNKER S
JUNKERS
JUNKET S
JUNKETED
JUNKETER S
JUNKETS
JUNKIE RS
JUNKIER
JUNKIES T
JUNKIEST
JUNKING
JUNKMAN
JUNKMEN
JUNKS
JUNKY
JUNKYARD S
JUNTA S
JAUNT
JUNTAS
JAUNTS
JUNTO S
JUNTOS
JUPE S
JUPES
JUPON S
JUPONS
JURA LT
JURAL
JURALLY
JURANT S
JURANTS
JURASSIC
JURAT S
JURATORY
JURATS
JUREL S
JURELS
JURIDIC
JURIED
JURIES
JURIST S
JURISTIC
JURISTS
JUROR S
JURORS
JURY
JURYING
JURYLESS
JURYMAN
JURYMEN
JUS T
JUSSIVE S
JUSSIVES
JUST S
JUTS
JUSTED
JUSTER S
JUSTERS
JUSTEST
JUSTICE S
JUSTICES
JUSTIFY
JUSTING
JUSTLE DS

JUSTLED
JUSTLES
JUSTLING
JUSTLY
JUSTNESS
JUSTS
JUT ES
JUTE S
JUTELIKE
JUTES
JUTS
JUST
JUTTED
JUTTIED
JUTTIES
JUTTING
JUTTY
JUTTYING
JUVENAL S
JUVENALS
JUVENILE S

K

OS KA BEFSTY
KAAS
KAB S
KABAB S
BABKA
KABABS
BABKAS
KABAKA S
KABAKAS
KABALA S
KABALAS
KABALISM S
KALIMBAS
KABALIST S
KABAR S
KABARS
KABAYA S
KABAYAS
KABBALA HS
KABBALAH S
KABBALAS
KABELJOU S
KABIKI S
KABIKIS
KABOB S
KABOBS
KABS
BASK
KABUKI S
KABUKIS
KACHINA S
KACHINAS
KADDISH
KADI S
KADIS
KAE S
KEA
KAES
KEAS SAKE
KAF S
KAFFIR S
KAFFIRS
KAFFIYAH S
KAFFIYEH S
KEFFIYAH
KAFIR S
FAKIR
KAFIRS
FAKIRS
KAFS
KAFTAN S
KAFTANS
KAGU S
KAGUS
KAHUNA S
KAHUNAS
KAIAK S
KAIAKS
KAIF S
KAIFS
KAIL S
ILKA
KAILS

KAILYARD S
KAIN S
AKIN KINA
KAINIT ES
KAINITE S
KAINITES
KAINITS
KAINS
KINAS
KAISER S
KAISERIN S
KAISERS
KAJEPUT S
KAJEPUTS
KAKA S
KAKAPO S
KAKAPOS
KAKAS
KAKEMONO S
KAKI S
KAKIEMON S
KAKIS
KALAM S
KALAMATA S
KALAMS
KALE S
LAKE LEAK
KALENDS
KALES
LAKES LEAKS
SLAKE
KALEWIFE
KALEYARD S
KALIAN S
KALIANS
KALIF S
KALIFATE S
KALIFS
KALIMBA S
KALIMBAS
KABALISM
KALIPH S
KALIPHS
KALIUM S
KALIUMS
KALLIDIN S
KALMIA S
KALMIAS
KALONG S
KALONGS
KALPA CKS
KALPAC S
KALPACS
KALPAK S
KALPAKS
KALPAS
KALYPTRA S
KAMAAINA S
KAMACITE S
KAMALA S
KAMALAS
KAME S
MAKE
KAMES
MAKES SAMEK
KAMI K
KAMIK S
KAMIKAZE S
KAMIKS
KAMPONG S
KAMPONGS
KAMSEEN S
KAMSEENS
KAMSIN S
KAMSINS
KANA S
KANAS
KANBAN S
KANBANS
KANE S
KANES
SKEAN SNAKE
SNEAK
KANGAROO S
KANJI S
KANJIS

KANTAR S
KANTARS
KANTELE S
KANTELES
KANZU S
KANZUS
KAOLIANG S
KAOLIN ES
KAOLINE S
KAOLINES
KAOLINIC
KAOLINS
KAON S
KOAN
KAONIC
KAONS
KOANS
KAPA S
KAPAS
KAPH S
KAPHS
KAPOK S
KAPOKS
KAPPA S
KAPPAS
KAPUT T
KAPUTT
KARAKUL S
KARAKULS
KARAOKE S
KARAOKES
KARAT ES
KARATE S
KARATES
KARATS
KARMA S
MAKAR MARKA
KARMAS
MAKARS
MARKAS
KARMIC
KARN S
KNAR NARK
RANK
KARNS
KNARS NARKS
RANKS SNARK
KAROO S
KAROOS
KAROSS
KAROSSES
KARROO S
KARROOS
KARST S
KARTS STARK
KARSTIC
KARSTS
KART S
KARTING S
KARTINGS
KARTS
KARST STARK
KARYOTIN S
OS KAS
ASK SKA
KASBAH S
KASBAHS
KASHA S
KASHAS
KASHER S
SHAKER
KASHERED
KASHERS
SHAKERS
KASHMIR S
KASHMIRS
KASHRUT HS
KASHRUTH S
KASHRUTS
IS KAT AS
KATA S
TAKA
KATAKANA S
KATAS
TAKAS
KATCHINA S
KATCINA S
KATCINAS
KATHODAL
KATHODE S
KATHODES
KATHODIC
KATION S
KATIONS
IS KATS
SKAT TASK
KATSURA S
KATSURAS
KATYDID S
KATYDIDS
KAURI S
KAURIES
KAURIS
KAURY
KAVA S
KAVAKAVA S
KAVAS S
KAVASS
KAVASSES
O KAY OS
YAK
KAYAK S
KAYAKED
KAYAKER S
KAYAKERS
KAYAKING S
KAYAKS
KAYLES
KAYO S
OAKY OKAY
KAYOED
OKAYED
KAYOES
KAYOING
OKAYING
KAYOS
OKAYS
O KAYS
YAKS
KAZACHKI
KAZACHOK
KAZATSKI
KAZATSKY
KAZOO S
KAZOOS
KBAR S
BARK
KBARS
BARKS
KEA S
KAE
KEAS
KAES SAKE
KEBAB S
KEBABS
KEBAR S
BAKER BRAKE
BREAK
KEBARS
BAKERS
BRAKES
BREAKS
KEBBIE S
KEBBIES
KEBBOCK S
KEBBOCKS
KEBBUCK S
KEBBUCKS
KEBLAH S
KEBLAHS
KEBOB S
KEBOBS
KECK S
KECKED
KECKING
KECKLE DS
KECKLED
KECKLES
KECKLING
KECKS
KEDDAH S
KEDDAHS
KEDGE DS
KEDGED
KEDGEREE S
KEDGES
KEDGING
KEEF S
KEEFS
KEEK S
KEEKED
KEEKING
KEEKS
KEEL S
LEEK LEKE
KEELAGE S
KEELAGES
KEELBOAT S
KEELED
KEELHALE DS
KEELHAUL S
KEELING
KEELLESS
KEELS
LEEKS SLEEK
KEELSON S
KEELSONS
S KEEN S
KNEE
KEENED
KEENER S
KEENERS
KEENEST
KETENES
KEENING
KNEEING
KEENLY
KEENNESS
S KEENS
KNEES SKEEN
SKENE
KEEP S
PEEK PEKE
KEEPABLE
KEEPER S
KEEPERS
KEEPING S
PEEKING
KEEPINGS
KEEPS
PEEKS PEKES
KEEPSAKE S
KEESHOND S
KEESTER S
SKEETER
KEESTERS
SKEETERS
S KEET S
S KEETS
SKEET STEEK
KEEVE S
KEEVES
KEF S
KEFFIYAH S
KAFFIYEH
KEFFIYEH S
KEFIR S
KEFIRS
KEFS
S KEG S
KEGELER S
KEGELERS
KEGGED
KEGGER S
KEGGERS
KEGGING
KEGLER S
KEGLERS
KEGLING S
KEGLINGS
S KEGS
SKEG
KEIR S
KIER
KEIRETSU S
KEIRS
KIERS SIKER
SKIER
KEISTER S
KIESTER
KEISTERS
KIESTERS
KEITLOA S
OATLIKE
KEITLOAS
KELEP S
KELEPS
KELIM S
KELIMS
KELLIES
KELLY
KELOID S
KELOIDAL
KELOIDS
S KELP SY
S KELPED
KELPIE S
KELPIES
S KELPING
S KELPS
SKELP
KELPY
KELSON S
KELSONS
KELT S
S KELTER S
S KELTERS
KESTREL
SKELTER
KELTS
KELVIN S
KELVINS
KEMP ST
KEMPS
KEMPT
KEN OST
KENAF S
KENAFS
KENCH
KENCHES
KENDO S
KENDOS
KENNED
KENNEL S
KENNELED
KENNELS
KENNING S
KENNINGS
KENO S
KENOS
KENOSIS
KENOTIC
KETONIC
KENOTRON S
KENS
KENT E
KENTE S
KENTES
S KEP IST
KEPHALIN S
KEPI S
PIKE
KEPIS
PIKES SPIKE
KEPPED
KEPPEN
KEPPING
S KEPS
SKEP
KEPT
KERAMIC S
KERAMICS
KERATIN S
KERATINS
KERATOID
KERATOMA S
KERATOSE S
KERB S
BERK
KERBED
KERBING
KERBS
BERKS
KERCHIEF S
KERCHOO
KERF S
KERFED
KERFING
KERFS
KERMES S
KERMESS E
KERMESSE S
KERMIS
KERMISES
KERN ES
KERNE DLS
KERNED
KERNEL S
KERNELED
KERNELLY
KERNELS
KERNES
KERNING
KERNITE S
KERNITES
KERNS
KEROGEN S
KEROGENS
KEROSENE S
KEROSINE S
KERPLUNK S
KERRIA S
KERRIAS
SARKIER
S KERRIES
S KERRY
KERSEY S
REKEYS
KERSEYS
KERYGMA S
KERYGMAS
KESTREL S
KELTERS
SKELTER
KESTRELS
SKELTERS
KETAMINE S
S KETCH
S KETCHES
KETCHUP S
KETCHUPS
KETENE S
KETENES
KEENEST
KETO L
TOKE
KETOL S
KETOLS
KETONE S
KETONES
KETONIC
KENOTIC
KETOSE S
KETOSES
KETOSIS
KETOTIC
KETTLE S
KETTLES
KEVEL S
KEVELS
KEVIL S
KEVILS
KEWPIE S
KEWPIES
KEX
KEXES
KEY S
KYE
KEYBOARD S
KEYCARD S
KEYCARDS
KEYED
KEYHOLE S
KEYHOLES
KEYING
KEYLESS
KEYNOTE DRS
KEYNOTED
KEYNOTER S
KEYNOTES
KEYSTONE
KEYPAD S
KEYPADS
KEYPAL S
KEYPALS
KEYPUNCH
KEYS
KYES SYKE
KEYSET S
KEYSETS
KEYSTER S
KEYSTERS
KEYSTONE S
KEYNOTES
KEYWAY S
KEYWAYS
KEYWORD S
KEYWORDS
KHADDAR S
KHADDARS
KHADI S
KHADIS
KHAF S
KHAFS
KHAKI S
KHAKIS
KISHKA
KHALIF AS
KHALIFA S
KHALIFAS
KHALIFS
KHAMSEEN S
KHAMSIN S
KHAMSINS
KHAN S
ANKH HANK
KHANATE S
KHANATES
KHANS
ANKHS HANKS
SHANK
KHAPH S
KHAPHS
KHAT S
KHATS
KHAZEN S
KHAZENIM
KHAZENS
KHEDA HS
KHEDAH S
KHEDAHS
KHEDAS
KHEDIVAL
KHEDIVE S
KHEDIVES
KHET HS
KHETH S
KHETHS
KHETS
KHI S
KHIRKAH S
KHIRKAHS
KHIS
KHOUM S
HOKUM
KHOUMS
HOKUMS
S KI DFNPRST
KIANG S
KIANGS
ASKING
GASKIN
KIAUGH S
KIAUGHS
KIBBE HS
KIBBEH S
KIBBEHS
KIBBES
KIBBI S
KIBBIS
KIBBITZ
KIBBLE DS
KIBBLED
KIBBLES
KIBBLING
KIBBUTZ
KIBE IS
BIKE
KIBEI S
BIKIE
KIBEIS
BIKIES
KIBES
BIKES
KIBITZ
KIBITZED
KIBITZER S
KIBITZES
KIBLA HS
KIBLAH S
KIBLAHS
KIBLAS
KIBOSH
KIBOSHED
KIBOSHES
KICK SY
KICKABLE
KICKBACK S
KICKBALL S
KICKBOX
KICKED
KICKER S
KICKERS
KICKIER
KICKIEST
KICKING
KICKOFF S
KICKOFFS
KICKS
KICKSHAW S
KICKUP S
KICKUPS
KICKY
S KID S
S KIDDED
S KIDDER S
DIRKED
S KIDDERS
SKIDDER
KIDDIE S
KIDDIES
S KIDDING
KIDDISH
KIDDO S
KIDDOES
KIDDOS
KIDDUSH
S KIDDY
KIDLIKE
KIDNAP S
KIDNAPED
KIDNAPEE S
KIDNAPER S
KIDNAPS
KIDNEY S
DINKEY
KIDNEYS
DINKEYS
S KIDS
DISK SKID
KIDSKIN S
KIDSKINS
KIDVID S
KIDVIDS
KIEF S
KIEFS
KIELBASA S
KIELBASI
KIELBASY
S KIER S
KEIR
S KIERS
KEIRS SIKER
SKIER
KIESTER S
KEISTER
KIESTERS
KEISTERS
KIF S
KIFS
KILIM S
KILIMS
S KILL S
KILLABLE
KILLDEE RS
KILLDEER S
KILLDEES
S KILLED

KILLER S
KILLERS
KILLICK S
KILLICKS
KILLIE S
KILLIES
S KILLING S
S KILLINGS
SKILLING
KILLJOY S
KILLJOYS
KILLOCK S
KILLOCKS
S KILLS
SKILL
KILN S
LINK
KILNED
KINDLE
LINKED
KILNING
INKLING
LINKING
KILNS
LINKS SLINK
KILO S
KILOBAR S
KILOBARS
KILOBASE S
KILOBAUD S
KILOBIT S
KILOBITS
KILOBYTE S
KILOGRAM S
KILOMOLE S
KILORAD S
KILORADS
KILOS
KILOTON S
KILOTONS
KILOVOLT S
KILOWATT S
KILT SY
KILTED
KILTER S
KIRTLE
KILTERS
KIRTLES
KLISTER
KILTIE S
KILTIES
KILTING S
KITLING
KILTINGS
KITLINGS
KILTLIKE
KILTS
KILTY
KIMCHEE S
KIMCHEES
KIMCHI S
KIMCHIS
KIMONO S
KIMONOED
KIMONOS
AS KIN ADEGKOS
INK
KINA S
AKIN KAIN
KINARA S
KINARAS
KINAS E
KAINS
KINASE S
KINASES
KIND S
DINK
KINDER
KIRNED
KINDEST
KINDLE DRS
KILNED
LINKED
KINDLED
KINDLER S
KINDLERS
KINDLES S
SLINKED
KINDLESS

KINDLIER
KINDLING S
KINDLY
DINKLY
KINDNESS
KINDRED S
KINDREDS
KINDS
DINKS
KINE S
KINEMA S
KINEMAS
KINES
SKEIN
KINESES
ENSKIES
KINESIC S
KINESICS
ICKINESS
KINESIS
A KINETIC S
KINETICS
KINETIN S
KINETINS
KINFOLK S
KINFOLKS
KINSFOLK
E KING S
GINK
KINGBIRD S
KINGBOLT S
KINGCUP S
KINGCUPS
KINGDOM S
KINGDOMS
KINGED
DEKING
KINGFISH
KINGHOOD S
KINGING
KINGLESS
KINGLET S
KINGLETS
KINGLIER
RINGLIKE
KINGLIKE
KINGLY
KINGPIN S
PINKING
KINGPINS
PINKINGS
KINGPOST S
KINGS
GINKS
KINGSHIP S
KINGSIDE S
KINGWOOD S
KININ S
KININS
S KINK SY
KINKAJOU S
S KINKED
KINKIER
KINKIEST
KINKILY
S KINKING
S KINKS
SKINK
KINKY
S KINLESS
INKLESS
KINO S
IKON OINK
KINOS
IKONS OINKS
S KINS
INKS SINK
SKIN
KINSFOLK
KINFOLKS
KINSHIP S
PINKISH
KINSHIPS
KINSMAN
KINSMEN
KIOSK S
KIOSKS
S KIP S
S KIPPED

KIPPEN
S KIPPER S
S KIPPERED
KIPPERER S
S KIPPERS
SKIPPER
S KIPPING
S KIPS
SKIP
KIPSKIN S
KIPSKINS
KIR KNS
IRK
KIRIGAMI S
KIRK S
KIRKMAN
KIRKMEN
KIRKS
KIRMESS
KIRN S
RINK
KIRNED
KINDER
KIRNING
KIRNS
RINKS
KIRS
IRKS KRIS
RISK
KIRSCH
CHIRKS
SCHRIK
KIRSCHES
SHICKERS
KIRTLE DS
KILTER
KIRTLED
KIRTLES
KILTERS
KLISTER
S KIS ST
SKI
KISHKA S
KHAKIS
KISHKAS
KISHKE S
KISHKES
KISMAT S
KISMATS
KISMET S
KISMETIC
KISMETS
KISS Y
SKIS
KISSABLE
KISSABLY
KISSED
KISSER S
KRISES
SKIERS
KISSERS
KISSES
KISSING
SKIINGS
KISSY
KIST S
KITS SKIT
KISTFUL S
LUTFISK
KISTFULS
LUTFISKS
KISTS
SKITS
S KIT EHS
KITBAG S
KITBAGS
KITCHEN S
THICKEN
KITCHENS
THICKENS
S KITE DRS
TIKE
S KITED
KITELIKE
KITER S
TRIKE
KITERS
STRIKE
TRIKES
S KITES
SKITE TIKES
KITH ES

KITHARA S
KITHARAS
KITHE DS
KITHED
KITHES
KITHING
KITHS
SHTIK
S KITING
KITLING S
KILTING
KITLINGS
KILTINGS
S KITS
KIST SKIT
KITSCH Y
SCHTIK
SHTICK
THICKS
KITSCHES
KITSCHY
SHTICKY
KITTED
KITTEL
KITTLE
KITTEN S
KITTENED
KITTENS
KITTIES
KITTING
S KITTLE DRS
KITTEL
KITTLED
KITTLER
S KITTLES T
SKITTLE
KITTLEST
KITTLING
KITTY
KIVA S
KIVAS
KIWI S
KIWIS
KLATCH
KLATCHES
KLATSCH
KLAVERN S
KLAVERNS
KLAXON S
KLAXONS
KLEAGLE S
KLEAGLES
KLEENEX
KLEPHT S
KLEPHTIC
KLEPHTS
KLEPTO S
KLEPTOS
KLEZMER S
KLEZMERS
KLICK S
KLICKS
KLIK S
KLIKS
KLISTER S
KILTERS
KIRTLES
KLISTERS
KLONDIKE S
KLONG S
KLONGS
KLOOF S
KLOOFS
KLUDGE DSY
KLUGED
KLUDGED
KLUDGES
KLUDGEY
KLUDGIER
KLUDGING
KLUDGY
KLUGE DS
KUGEL
KLUGED
KLUDGE
KLUGES
KUGELS
KLUGING

KLUTZ Y
KLUTZES
KLUTZIER
KLUTZY
KLYSTRON S
KNACK S
KNACKED
KNACKER SY
KNACKERS
KNACKERY
KNACKING
KNACKS
KNAP S
KNAPPED
KNAPPER S
KNAPPERS
KNAPPING
KNAPS
SPANK
KNAPSACK S
KNAPWEED S
KNAR S
KARN NARK
RANK
KNARRED
KNARRY
KNARS
KARNS NARKS
RANKS SNARK
KNAUR S
KNAURS
KNAVE S
KNAVERY
KNAVES
KNAVISH
KNAWE LS
WAKEN
KNAWEL S
KNAWELS
KNAWES
WAKENS
KNEAD S
NAKED
KNEADED
KNEADER S
NAKEDER
KNEADERS
KNEADING
KNEADS
SNAKED
KNEE DLS
KEEN
KNEECAP S
KNEECAPS
KNEED
KNEEHOLE S
KNEEING
KEENING
KNEEL S
KNEELED
KNEELER S
KNEELERS
KNEELING
KNEELS
KNEEPAD S
KNEEPADS
KNEEPAN S
KNEEPANS
KNEES
KEENS SKEEN
SKENE
KNEESIES
KNEESOCK S
KNELL S
KNELLED
KNELLING
KNELLS
KNELT
KNESSET S
KNESSETS
KNEW
KNICKERS
KNIFE DRS
KNIFED
FINKED
KNIFER S
KNIFERS

KNIFES
KNIFING
FINKING
KNIGHT S
KNIGHTED
KNIGHTLY
KNIGHTS
KNISH
KNISHES
KNIT S
KNITS
SKINT STINK
KNITTED
KNITTER S
TRINKET
KNITTERS
TRINKETS
KNITTING S
KNITWEAR
KNIVES
KNOB S
BONK
KNOBBED
KNOBBIER
KNOBBLY
KNOBBY
KNOBLIKE
KNOBS
BONKS
KNOCK S
KNOCKED
KNOCKER S
KNOCKERS
KNOCKING
KNOCKOFF S
KNOCKOUT S
KNOCKS
KNOLL SY
KNOLLED
KNOLLER S
KNOLLERS
KNOLLING
KNOLLS
KNOLLY
KNOP S
KNOPPED
KNOPS
KNOSP
KNOSP S
KNOPS
KNOSPS
KNOT S
KNOTHOLE S
KNOTLESS
KNOTLIKE
KNOTS
KNOTTED
KNOTTER S
KNOTTERS
KNOTTIER
KNOTTILY
KNOTTING S
KNOTTY
KNOTWEED S
KNOUT S
KNOUTED
KNOUTING
KNOUTS
KNOW NS
WONK
KNOWABLE
KNOWER S
KNOWERS
KNOWING S
KNOWINGS
KNOWN S
KNOWNS
KNOWS
WONKS
KNUBBIER
KNUBBY
KNUCKLE DRS
KNUCKLED
KNUCKLER S
KNUCKLES
KNUCKLY

KNUR LS
KNURL SY
KNURLED
RUNKLED
KNURLIER
KNURLING
RUNKLING
KNURLS
KNURLY
KNURS
KOA NS
OAK
OKA
KOALA S
KOALAS
KOAN S
KAON
KOANS
KAONS
KOAS
OAKS OKAS
SOAK
KOB OS
KOBO S
BOOK
KOBOLD S
KOBOLDS
KOBOS
BOOKS
KOBS
BOSK
KOEL S
KOELS
KOHL S
HOLK
KOHLRABI
KOHLS
HOLKS
KOI S
KOINE S
EIKON ENOKI
KOINES
EIKONS
ENOKIS
KOIS
KOJI S
KOJIS
KOKANEE S
KOKANEES
KOLA S
KOLACKY
KOLAS
SKOAL
KOLBASI S
KOLBASIS
KOLBASSI
KOLBASSI S
KOLBASIS
KOLHOZ Y
KOLHOZES
KOLHOZY
KOLINSKI
KOLINSKY
KOLKHOS Y
KOLKHOSY
KOLKHOZ Y
KOLKHOZY
KOLKOZ Y
KOLKOZES
KOLKOZY
KOLO S
LOOK
KOLOS
LOOKS SOKOL
KOMATIK S
KOMATIKS
KOMBU S
KOMBUS
KOMONDOR S
KONK S
KONKED
KONKING
KONKS
KOODOO S
KOODOOS
KOOK SY
KOOKIE R
KOOKIER
KOOKIEST

KOOKS
KOOKY
KOP HS
KOPECK S
KOPECKS
KOPEK S
KOPEKS
KOPH S
KOPHS
KOPIYKA S
KOPIYKAS
KOPJE S
KOPJES
KOPPA S
KOPPAS
KOPPIE S
KOPPIES
KOPS
KOR AES
KORA IST
OKRA
KORAI
KORAS
OKRAS
KORAT S
TAROK TROAK
KORATS
TAROKS
TROAKS
KORE
KORMA S
KORMAS
KORS
KORUN AY
KORUNA S
KORUNAS
KORUNY
KOS S
KOSHER S
KOSHERED
KOSHERS
KOSS
KOTO SW
TOOK
KOTOS
STOOK
KOTOW S
KOTOWED
KOTOWER S
KOTOWERS
KOTOWING
KOTOWS
KOUMIS S
KOUMISES
KOUMISS
KOUMYS S
KOUMYSES
KOUMYSS
KOUPREY S
KOUPREYS
KOUROI
KOUROS
KOUSSO S
KOUSSOS
KOWTOW S
KOWTOWED
KOWTOWER S
KOWTOWS
KRAAL S
KRAALED
KRAALING
KRAALS
KRAFT S
KRAFTS
KRAIT S
TRAIK
KRAITS
TRAIKS
KRAKEN S
KRAKENS
SKANKER
KRATER S
KRATERS
STARKER
KRAUT S
KURTA

KRAUTS
KURTAS
KREEP S
KREEPS
KREMLIN S
KREMLINS
KREPLACH
KREPLECH
KREUTZER S
KREUZER S
KREUZERS
KREWE S
KREWES
SKEWER
KRILL S
KRILLS
KRIMMER S
KRIMMERS
KRIS
IRKS KIRS
RISK
KRISES
KISSER
SKIERS
KRONA
KRONE NR
KRONEN
KRONER
KRONOR
KRONUR
KROON IS
KROONI
KROONS
KRUBI S
KRUBIS
KRUBUT S
KRUBUTS
KRULLER S
KRULLERS
KRUMHORN S
KRUMKAKE S
KRYOLITE S
KRYOLITH S
KRYPTON S
KRYPTONS
KUCHEN S
KUCHENS
KUDO S
KUDOS
KUDU S
KUDUS
KUDZU S
KUDZUS
KUE S
UKE
KUES
UKES
KUFI S
KUFIS
KUGEL S
KLUGE
KUGELS
KLUGES
KUKRI S
KUKRIS
KULAK IS
KULAKI
KULAKS
KULTUR S
KULTURS
KUMISS
KUMISSES
KUMMEL S
KUMMELS
KUMQUAT S
KUMQUATS
KUMYS
MUSKY
KUMYSES
KUNA
KUNE
NEUK NUKE
KUNZITE S
KUNZITES
KURBASH
KURGAN S
KURGANS

KURTA S
KRAUT
KURTAS
KRAUTS
KURTOSES
KURTOSIS
KURU S
KURUS
KUSSO S
SOUKS
KUSSOS
KUVASZ
KUVASZOK
KVAS S
KVASES
KVASS
KVASSES
KVELL S
KVELLED
KVELLING
KVELLS
KVETCH Y
KVETCHED
KVETCHER S
KVETCHES
KVETCHY
KWACHA S
KWACHAS
HACKSAW
KWANZA S
KWANZAS
KYACK S
KYACKS
KYAK S
KYAKS
KYANISE DS
KYANISED
KYANISES
KYANITE S
KYANITES
KYANIZE DS
KYANIZED
KYANIZES
KYAR S
KYARS
SARKY
KYAT S
KYATS
KYBOSH
KYBOSHED
KYBOSHES
KYE S
KEY
KYES
KEYS SYKE
KYLIKES
SKYLIKE
KYLIX
KYMOGRAM S
KYPHOSES
KYPHOSIS
KYPHOTIC
KYRIE S
KYRIES
KYTE S
TYKE
KYTES
TYKES
KYTHE DS
KYTHED
KYTHES
KYTHING

L

A LA BCDGMPRS
AL TVWXY
LAAGER S
AGLARE
ALEGAR
LAAGERED
LAAGERS
ALEGARS
LAARI
BFS LAB S
ALB
BAL
LABARA

LABARUM S
LABARUMS
LABDANUM S
LABEL S
LABELED
LABELER S
RELABEL
LABELERS
RELABELS
LABELING
FG LABELLA
LABELLED
LABELLER S
F LABELLUM
LABELS
LABIA L
LABIAL S
LABIALLY
LABIALS
LABIATE DS
LABIATED
LABIATES
SATIABLE
LABILE
ALIBLE
LIABLE
LABILITY
LABIUM
LABOR S
BOLAR BORAL
LOBAR
LABORED
LABORER S
LABORERS
LABORING
LABORITE S
LABORS
BORALS
LABOUR S
LABOURED
LABOURER S
RUBEOLAR
LABOURS
SUBORAL
LABRA
LABRADOR S
LARBOARD
LABRET S
LABRETS
BLASTER
STABLER
LABROID S
LABROIDS
LABRUM S
BRUMAL
LUMBAR
UMBRAL
LABRUMS
LUMBARS
LABRUSCA
BFS LABS
ALBS BALS
SLAB
LABURNUM S
ALBURNUM
LAC EKSY
GP LACE DRSY
ALEC
P LACED
CLADE DECAL
P LACELESS
LACELIKE
P LACER S
CARLE CLEAR
LACERATE DS
P LACERS
CARLES
CLEARS
SCALER
SCLERA
LACERTID S
ARTICLED
GP LACES
ALECS SCALE
LACEWING S
LACEWOOD S
LACEWORK S
LACEY
LYCEA
LACHES
CHELAS

G LACIER
ECLAIR
LACIEST
ELASTIC
LATICES
LACILY
LACINESS
SANICLES
P LACING S
LACINGS
SCALING
ABC LACK S
FPS CALK
A LACKADAY
BCF LACKED
S CALKED
BCS LACKER S
CALKER
RACKLE
LACKERED
CS LACKERS
CALKERS
SLACKER
LACKEY S
LACKEYED
LACKEYS
BCF LACKING
S CALKING
BCF LACKS
PS CALKS SLACK
LACONIC
CONICAL
LACONISM S
LIMACONS
LACQUER S
CLAQUER
LACQUERS
CLAQUERS
LACQUEY S
LACQUEYS
LACRIMAL S
LACROSSE S
ESCOLARS
SOLACERS
LACS
LACTAM S
LACTAMS
LACTARY
LACTASE S
ACETALS
LACTASES
LACTATE DS
LACTATED
LACTATES
LACTEAL S
LACTEALS
LACTEAN
LACTEOUS
LOCUSTAE
OSCULATE
LACTIC
LACTONE S
LACTONES
LACTONIC
LACTOSE S
LOCATES
TALCOSE
LACTOSES
COATLESS
LACUNA ELRS
CANULA
LACUNAE
CANULAE
LACUNAL
LACUNAR SY
CANULAR
LACUNARS
LACUNARY
LACUNAS
CANULAS
LACUNATE
CANULATE
TENACULA
LACUNE S
CUNEAL
LAUNCE
UNLACE
LACUNES
CENSUAL
LAUNCES
UNLACES

LACUNOSE
LACY
ACYL CLAY
CG LAD ESY
DAL
LADANUM S
LADANUMS
BG LADDER S
LARDED
RADDLE
LADDERED
B LADDERS
RADDLES
SADDLER
LADDIE S
DIALED
LADDIES
LADDISH
BCG LADE DNRS
DALE DEAL
LEAD
B LADED
ADDLE DEDAL
LADEN S
ELAND NALED
LADENED
LADENING
LADENS
ELANDS
NALEDS
SENDAL
B LADER S
ALDER
B LADERS
ALDERS
BCG LADES
DALES DEALS
LASED LEADS
LADHOOD S
LADHOODS
LADIES
AISLED
DEASIL
IDEALS
SAILED
B LADING S
LIGAND
B LADINGS
LIGANDS
LADINO S
LADINOS
LADLE DRS
LADLED
LADLEFUL S
LADLER S
LADLERS
LADLES
DALLES
LADLING
LADRON ES
LARDON
LADRONE S
LADRONES
SOLANDER
LADRONS
LARDONS
CG LADS
DALS
G LADY
YALD
LADYBIRD S
LADYBUG S
LADYBUGS
LADYFISH
LADYHOOD S
LADYISH
SHADILY
LADYKIN S
LADYKINS
LADYLIKE
LADYLOVE S
LADYPALM S
LADYSHIP S
LAETRILE S
LAEVO
CFS LAG S
GAL
LAGAN S
ALANG
LAGANS

LAGEND S
ANGLED
DANGLE
LAGENDS
DANGLES
GLANDES
SLANGED
LAGER S
ARGLE GLARE
LARGE REGAL
LAGERED
REGALED
LAGERING
GANGLIER
REGALING
LAGERS
ARGLES
GLARES
LARGES
LAGGARD S
LAGGARDS
CFS LAGGED
DAGGLE
F LAGGER S
GARGLE
RAGGLE
F LAGGERS
GARGLES
RAGGLES
BCF LAGGING S
S
BF LAGGINGS
SLAGGING
LAGNAPPE S
LAGOON S
LAGOONAL
LAGOONS
CFS LAGS
GALS SLAG
LAGUNA S
LAGUNAS
LAGUNE S
LANGUE
LAGUNES
ANGELUS
LANGUES
LAHAR S
LAHARS
ASHLAR
LAIC HS
LAICAL
LAICALLY
LAICH S
LAICHS
LAICISE DS
LAICISED
LAICISES
LAICISM S
LAICISMS
LAICIZE DS
LAICIZED
LAICIZES
LAICS
SALIC
P LAID
DIAL
LAIGH S
LAIGHS
BEP LAIN
S ANIL NAIL
FG LAIR DS
ARIL LARI
LIAR LIRA
RAIL RIAL
LAIRD S
DRAIL LIARD
LIDAR
LAIRDLY
LAIRDS
DRAILS
LIARDS
LIDARS
G LAIRED
ARILED
DERAIL
DIALER
RAILED
REDIAL
RELAID
G LAIRING
RAILING

FG **LAIRS**
ARILS LARIS LIARS LIRAS RAILS RIALS
LAITANCE S
ANALCITE
LAITH
LATHI
LAITHLY
LAITIES
LAITY
FS **LAKE** DRS
KALE LEAK
LAKEBED S
LAKEBEDS
FS **LAKED**
LAKELIKE
LAKEPORT S
FS **LAKER** S
FS **LAKERS**
SLAKER
FS **LAKES**
KALES LEAKS SLAKE
LAKESIDE S
LAKH S
LAKHS
F **LAKIER**
F **LAKIEST**
TALKIES
FS **LAKING** S
LAKINGS
SLAKING
F **LAKY**
ALKY
LALIQUE S
LALIQUES
SQUILLAE
LALL S
LALLAN DS
LALLAND S
LALLANDS
LALLANS
LALLED
LALLING
LALLS
LALLYGAG S
BCFGS **LAM** ABEPS
LU **LAMA** S
ALMA
LU **LAMAS**
ALMAS
LAMASERY
LAMB SY
BALM BLAM
LAMBADA S
LAMBADAS
LAMBAST ES
LAMBASTE DS
BLASTEMA
LAMBASTS
LAMBDA S
LAMBDAS
LAMBDOID
LAMBED
AMBLED BEDLAM BELDAM BLAMED
LAMBENCY
LAMBENT
C **LAMBER** ST
AMBLER BLAMER MARBLE RAMBLE
C **LAMBERS**
AMBLERS BLAMERS MARBLES RAMBLES
LAMBERT S
LAMBERTS
LAMBIE RS
LAMBIER
BALMIER
LAMBIES T
ABLEISM

LAMBIEST
BALMIEST BIMETALS TIMBALES
LAMBING
AMBLING BLAMING
LAMBKILL S
LAMBKIN S
LAMBKINS
LAMBSKIN
LAMBLIKE
BALMLIKE
LAMBS
BALMS BLAMS
LAMBSKIN S
LAMBKINS
LAMBY
BALMY
BF **LAME** DRS
ALME MALE MEAL
BF **LAMED** HS
MEDAL
LAMEDH S
LAMEDHS
LAMEDS
DAMSEL MEDALS
LAMELLA ERS
LAMELLAE
LAMELLAR
LAMELLAS
LAMELY
LAMENESS
MALENESS MANELESS NAMELESS SALESMEN
LAMENT S
MANTEL MANTLE MENTAL
LAMENTED
LAMENTER S
LAMENTS
MANTELS MANTLES
BF **LAMER**
REALM
BF **LAMES** T
ALMES MALES MEALS
LAMEST
METALS SAMLET
LAMIA ES
LAMIAE
LAMIAS
SALAMI
LAMINA ELRS
ANIMAL MANILA
LAMINAE
LAMINAL S
MANILLA
LAMINALS
MANILLAS
LAMINAR Y
LAMINARY
LAMINAS
ANIMALS MANILAS
LAMINATE DS
ANTIMALE
BF **LAMING**
LINGAM MALIGN
LAMININ S
LAMININS
LAMINOSE
SEMOLINA
LAMINOUS
LAMISTER S
MARLIEST MARLITES MISALTER
CFS **LAMMED**
CFS **LAMMING**
C **LAMP** S
PALM
LAMPAD S
LAMPADS

LAMPAS
PLASMA
LAMPASES
C **LAMPED**
PALMED
C **LAMPERS**
PALMERS SAMPLER
C **LAMPING**
PALMING
LAMPION S
LAMPIONS
LAMPOON S
LAMPOONS
LAMPPOST S
PALMTOPS
LAMPREY S
LAMPREYS
C **LAMPS**
PALMS PLASM PSALM
LAMPYRID S
BCFGS **LAMS**
ALMS SLAM
LAMSTER S
ARMLETS TRAMELS
LAMSTERS
TRAMLESS
LANAI S
LIANA
LANAIS
LIANAS NASIAL SALINA
P **LANATE** D
LANATED
G **LANCE** DRST
CLEAN
G **LANCED**
CANDLE
LANCELET S
G **LANCER** S
G **LANCERS**
G **LANCES**
CLEANS
LANCET S
CANTLE CENTAL
LANCETED
LANCETS
CANTLES CENTALS
LANCIERS
CARLINES
G **LANCING**
ABEG **LAND** S
LANDAU S
LANDAUS
LANDED
DANDLE
BS **LANDER** S
DARNEL RELAND
GS **LANDERS**
DARNELS RELANDS SLANDER SNARLED
LANDFALL S
LANDFILL S
LANDFORM S
LANDGRAB S
LANDING S
LANDINGS
SANDLING
LANDLADY
LANDLER S
LANDLERS
G **LANDLESS**
LANDLINE S
LANDLORD S
LANDMAN
LANDMARK S
LANDMASS
LANDMEN
AEG **LANDS**
LANDSIDE S
ISLANDED
LANDSKIP S

LANDSLID E
LANDSLIP S
LANDSMAN
LANDSMEN
LANDWARD S
AP **LANE** S
ELAN LEAN
LANELY
LEANLY
FP **LANES**
ELANS LEANS
LANEWAY S
LANEWAYS
ACS **LANG**
LANGLAUF S
LANGLEY S
LANGLEYS
LANGRAGE S
LANGREL S
LANGRELS
LANGSHAN S
LANGSYNE S
S **LANGUAGE** S
LANGUE ST
LAGUNE
LANGUES
ANGELUS LAGUNES
LANGUET S
LANGUETS
LANGUID
LAUDING
LANGUISH
NILGHAUS SHAULING
LANGUOR S
LANGUORS
LANGUR S
LANGURS
LANIARD S
NADIRAL
LANIARDS
LANIARY
LANITAL S
LANITALS
BCFPS **LANK** Y
BF **LANKER**
RANKLE
B **LANKEST**
ANKLETS
C **LANKIER**
C **LANKIEST**
LANKILY
B **LANKLY**
B **LANKNESS**
C **LANKY**
P **LANNER** S
LANNERET S
P **LANNERS**
ENSNARL
LANOLIN ES
LANOLINE S
LANOLINS
LANOSE
ANOLES
LANOSITY
LANTANA S
LANTANAS
LANTERN S
LANTERNS
LANTHORN S
LANUGO S
LANUGOS
LANYARD S
LANYARDS
LAOGAI S
LAOGAIS
CFS **LAP** S
ALP PAL
C **LAPBOARD** S
LAPDOG S
LAPDOGS
LAPEL S
LAPELED
LAPELLED
LAPELS

LAPFUL S
LAPFULS
LAPIDARY
LAPIDATE DS
LAPIDES
ALIPEDS ELAPIDS PALSIED PLEIADS
LAPIDIFY
LAPIDIST S
LAPILLI
LAPILLUS
LAPIN S
PLAIN
LAPINS
PLAINS SPINAL
LAPIS
PAILS SPAIL
LAPISES
ESPIALS LIPASES PALSIES
CFS **LAPPED**
DAPPLE PALPED
CFS **LAPPER** S
RAPPEL
LAPPERED
RAPPELED
CFS **LAPPERS**
RAPPELS SLAPPER
LAPPET S
APPLET
LAPPETED
LAPPETS
APPLETS
CFS **LAPPING**
PALPING
CFS **LAPS** E
ALPS PALS SALP SLAP
LAPSABLE
E **LAPSE** DRS
LEAPS PALES PEALS PLEAS SALEP SEPAL SPALE
E **LAPSED**
PADLES PEDALS PLEADS
LAPSER S
PARLES PEARLS
LAPSERS
E **LAPSES**
PASSEL SALEPS SEPALS SPALES
LAPSIBLE
E **LAPSING**
PALINGS SAPLING
LAPSUS
LAPTOP S
LAPTOPS
LAPWING S
LAPWINGS
A **LAR** DIKS
LARBOARD S
LABRADOR
LARCENER S
LARCENY
LARCH
LARCHEN
CHARNEL
LARCHES
CLASHER
LARD SY
LARDED
LADDER RADDLE
LARDER S
LARDERS
LARDIER
LARDIEST
DILATERS REDTAILS

LARDING
DARLING
LARDLIKE
LARDON S
LADRON
LARDONS
LADRONS
LARDOON S
LARDOONS
LARDS
LARDY
LYARD
LAREE S
LAREES
LEASER REALES RESALE RESEAL SEALER
BFG **LARES**
ARLES EARLS LASER LEARS RALES REALS SERAL
LARGANDO
LARGE RS
ARGLE GLARE LAGER REGAL
LARGELY
ALLERGY GALLERY REGALLY
LARGER
LARGES ST
ARGLES GLARES LAGERS
LARGESS E
LARGESSE S
EELGRASS GEARLESS
LARGEST
LARGISH
LARGO S
ALGOR ARGOL GORAL
LARGOS
ALGORS ARGOLS GORALS
LARI S
ARIL LAIR LIAR LIRA RAIL RIAL
LARIAT S
ATRIAL LATRIA
LARIATED
LARIATS
LATRIAS
LARINE
ALINER LINEAR NAILER RENAIL
LARIS
ARILS LAIRS LIARS LIRAS RAILS RIALS
LARK SY
LARKED
DARKLE
LARKER S
LARKERS
LARKIER
LARKIEST
STALKIER STARLIKE
LARKING
LARKISH
LARKS
LARKSOME
LARKSPUR S
LARKY
LARRIGAN S
LARRIKIN S
LARRUP S
LARRUPED
LARRUPER S
LARRUPS
LARS

A **LARUM** S
MURAL
A **LARUMS**
MURALS
LARVA ELS
ARVAL
LARVAE
LARVAL
LARVAS
LARYNGAL S
LARYNGES
LARYNX
LARYNXES
A **LAS** EHST
ALS SAL
LASAGNA S
LASAGNAS
LASAGNE S
ANLAGES GALENAS
LASAGNES
LASCAR S
CRAALS RASCAL SACRAL SCALAR
LASCARS
RASCALS SACRALS SCALARS
B **LASE** DRS
ALES LEAS SALE SEAL
LASED
DALES DEALS LADES LEADS
LASER S
ARLES EARLS LARES LEARS RALES REALS SERAL
LASERS
RASSLE
LASES
SALES SEALS
CFPS **LASH**
CFPS **LASHED**
SHALED
CFPS **LASHER** S
ASHLER HALERS
CFPS **LASHERS**
ASHLERS SLASHER
CFPS **LASHES**
HASSEL HASSLE SELAHS SHALES SHEALS
CFPS **LASHING** S
FS **LASHINGS**
HASSLING SLASHING
LASHINS
LASHKAR S
LASHKARS
LASING
ALGINS ALIGNS LIANGS LIGANS LINGAS SIGNAL
CG **LASS** IO
SALS
CG **LASSES**
LASSI ES
SAILS SIALS SISAL
G **LASSIE** S
AISLES
G **LASSIES**
C **LASSIS**
SISALS
LASSO S
LASSOED
ALDOSES

LASSOER S
OARLESS
SEROSAL
LASSOERS
LASSOES
LASSOING
GLOSSINA
LASSOS
BC LAST S
ALTS LATS
SALT SLAT
LASTBORN S
B LASTED
DELTAS
DESALT
SALTED
SLATED
STALED
BP LASTER S
ALERTS
ALTERS
ARTELS
ESTRAL
RATELS
SALTER
SLATER
STALER
STELAR
TALERS
BP LASTERS
ARTLESS
SALTERS
SLATERS
B LASTING S
SALTING
SLATING
STALING
B LASTINGS
SALTINGS
SLATINGS
LASTLY
BC LASTS
SALTS SLATS
BFP LAT EHISU
S ALT
LATAKIA S
LATAKIAS
KS LATCH
LATCHED
KS LATCHES
CHALETS
SATCHEL
LATCHET S
CHATTEL
LATCHETS
CHATTELS
LATCHING
LATCHKEY S
ABE LATE DNRX
PS TAEL TALE
TEAL TELA
AEP LATED
S DEALT DELTA
LATEEN S
LATEENER S
LATEENS
LEANEST
LATELY
LEALTY
P LATEN ST
LEANT
LATENCY
LATENED
LATENESS
LATENING
GANTLINE
P LATENS
LATENT S
LATTEN
TALENT
LATENTLY
LATENTS
LATTENS
TALENTS
EPS LATER
ALERT ALTER
ARTEL RATEL
TALER
LATERAD
LATERAL S
LATERALS

E LATERITE S
LITERATE
LATERIZE DS
LATEST S
LATTES
LATESTS
SALTEST
STALEST
LATEWOOD S
LATEX
EXALT
LATEXES
LATH EISY
HALT
LATHE DRS
LATHED
DALETH
HALTED
BS LATHER SY
HALTER
THALER
BS LATHERED
HALTERED
B LATHERER S
BS LATHERS
HALTERS
HARSLET
SLATHER
THALERS
LATHERY
EARTHLY
LATHES
HALEST
HASLET
SHELTA
LATHI S
LAITH
LATHIER
LATHIEST
LATHING S
HALTING
LATHINGS
LATHIS
LATISH
TAHSIL
LATHS
HALTS SHALT
LATHWORK S
LATHY
LATI
ALIT TAIL
TALI
LATICES
ELASTIC
LACIEST
LATIGO S
GALIOT
LATIGOES
OTALGIES
LATIGOS
GALIOTS
LATILLA S
LATILLAS
P LATINA S
P LATINAS
LATINITY
P LATINIZE DS
LATINO S
TALION
LATINOS
TALIONS
LATISH
LATHIS
TAHSIL
P LATITUDE S
ALTITUDE
LATKE S
LATKES
LATOSOL S
LATOSOLS
LATRIA S
ATRIAL
LARIAT
LATRIAS
LARIATS
LATRINE S
RATLINE
RELIANT
RETINAL
TRENAIL

LATRINES
ENTRAILS
RATLINES
RETINALS
TRENAILS
BFP LATS
S ALTS LAST
SALT SLAT
LATTE NRS
F LATTEN S
LATENT
TALENT
F LATTENS
LATENTS
TALENTS
BCF LATTER
P RATTLE
LATTERLY
LATTES
LATEST
LATTICE DS
TACTILE
LATTICED
LATTICES
LATTIN S
LATTINS
LATU
LAUAN S
LAUANS
LAUD S
AULD DUAL
LAUDABLE
LAUDABLY
LAUDANUM S
LAUDATOR SY
ADULATOR
LAUDED
LAUDER S
AULDER
LAUDERS
LAUDING
LANGUID
LAUDS
DUALS
LAUGH S
LAUGHED
LAUGHER S
LAUGHERS
LAUGHING S
LAUGHS
S LAUGHTER S
LAUNCE S
CUNEAL
LACUNE
UNLACE
LAUNCES
CENSUAL
LACUNES
UNLACES
LAUNCH
NUCHAL
LAUNCHED
LAUNCHER S
RELAUNCH
LAUNCHES
LAUNDER S
LURDANE
LAUNDERS
LURDANES
LAUNDRY
LAURA ES
AURAL
LAURAE
LAURAS
LAUREATE DS
LAUREL S
ALLURE
LAURELED
LAURELS
ALLURES
LAUWINE S
LAUWINES
LAV AES
LAVA S
LAVABO S
LAVABOES
LAVABOS
LAVAGE S
LAVAGES
SALVAGE
LAVALAVA S

LAVALIER ES
LAVALIKE
LAVAS H
VASAL
LAVASH
HALVAS
LAVASHES
C LAVATION S
LAVATORY
CS LAVE DRS
LEVA VALE
VEAL VELA
S LAVED
LAVEER S
LEAVER
REVEAL
VEALER
LAVEERED
REVEALED
LAVEERS
LEAVERS
REVEALS
SEVERAL
VEALERS
LAVENDER S
CS LAVER S
RAVEL VELAR
LAVEROCK S
CS LAVERS
RAVELS
SALVER
SERVAL
SLAVER
VELARS
VERSAL
CS LAVES
SALVE SELVA
SLAVE VALES
VALSE VEALS
S LAVING
S LAVISH
LAVISHED
LAVISHER S
SHRIEVAL
LAVISHES T
S LAVISHLY
LAVROCK S
LAVROCKS
LAVS
BCF LAW NS
S AWL
LAWBOOK S
LAWBOOKS
BCF LAWED
WALED WEALD
LAWFUL
LAWFULLY
LAWGIVER S
LAWINE S
LAWINES
BCF LAWING S
WALING
LAWINGS
CF LAWLESS
C LAWLIKE
LAWMAKER S
LAWMAN
LAWMEN
B LAWN SY
LAWNS
LAWNY
WANLY
BCF LAWS
S AWLS SLAW
LAWSUIT S
LAWSUITS
LAWYER S
LAWYERED
LAWYERLY
LAWYERS
F LAX
LAXATION S
LAXATIVE S
LAXER
RELAX
F LAXES T
AXELS AXLES
LAXEST
EXALTS
LAXITIES

LAXITY
LAXLY
LAXNESS
CFP LAY S
S
LAYABOUT S
LAYAWAY S
LAYAWAYS
CFP LAYED
S DELAY LEADY
FPS LAYER S
EARLY LEARY
RELAY
LAYERAGE S
LAYERED
DELAYER
RELAYED
LAYERING S
RELAYING
YEARLING
FPS LAYERS
RELAYS
SLAYER
LAYETTE S
LAYETTES
LAYIN GS
INLAY
CFP LAYING
S GAINLY
LAYINS
INLAYS
LAYMAN
LAYMEN
MEANLY
NAMELY
P LAYOFF S
P LAYOFFS
LAYOUT S
OUTLAY
LAYOUTS
OUTLAYS
LAYOVER S
OVERLAY
LAYOVERS
OVERLAYS
CFP LAYS
S SLAY
LAYUP S
LAYUPS
LAYWOMAN
LAYWOMEN
LAZAR S
LAZARET S
LAZARETS
LAZARS
BG LAZE DS
ZEAL
BG LAZED
BG LAZES
ZEALS
LAZIED
G LAZIER
LAZIES T
G LAZIEST
G LAZILY
G LAZINESS
BG LAZING
LAZULI S
LAZULIS
LAZULITE S
LAZURITE S
G LAZY
LAZYING
LAZYISH
FIO LEA DFKLNPR
P ALE S
BP LEACH Y
CHELA
LEACHATE S
BP LEACHED
B LEACHER S
B LEACHERS
BP LEACHES
LEACHIER
BP LEACHING
LEACHY
P LEAD SY
DALE DEAL
LADE

P LEADED
DELEAD
LEADEN S
ANELED
LEANED
LEADENED
LEADENLY
LEADENS
P LEADER S
DEALER
P LEADERS
DEALERS
LEADIER
LEADIEST
P LEADING S
ALIGNED
DEALING
P LEADINGS
DEALINGS
SIGNALED
LEADLESS
ALLSEEDS
LEADMAN
LEADMEN
LEADOFF S
LEADOFFS
P LEADS
DALES DEALS
LADES LASED
LEADSMAN
DALESMAN
LEADSMEN
DALESMEN
LEADWORK S
LEADWORT S
LEADY
DELAY LAYED
LEAF SY
ALEF FEAL
FLEA
LEAFAGE S
LEAFAGES
LEAFED
DEFLEA
LEAFIER
FILAREE
LEAFIEST
FEALTIES
FETIALES
LEAFING
FINAGLE
LEAFLESS
LEAFLET S
FELLATE
LEAFLETS
FELLATES
LEAFLIKE
LEAFS
ALEFS FALSE
FLEAS
LEAFWORM S
LEAFY
LEAGUE DRS
LEAGUED
LEAGUER S
LEAGUERS
LEAGUES
LEAGUING
B LEAK SY
KALE LAKE
LEAKAGE S
LEAKAGES
LEAKED
B LEAKER S
LEAKERS
LEAKIER
LEAKIEST
LEAKILY
LEAKING
LINKAGE
LEAKLESS
B LEAKS
KALES LAKES
SLAKE
LEAKY
I LEAL
LEALLY
LEALTIES
LEALTY
LATELY

CG LEAN ST
ELAN LANE
CG LEANED
ANELED
LEADEN
CG LEANER S
CG LEANERS
C LEANEST
LATEENS
CG LEANING S
ANELING
EANLING
G LEANINGS
EANLINGS
C LEANLY
LANELY
C LEANNESS
CG LEANS
ELANS LANES
LEANT
LATEN
LEAP ST
PALE PEAL
PLEA
LEAPED
PEALED
LEAPER S
REPEAL
LEAPERS
PLEASER
PRESALE
RELAPSE
REPEALS
LEAPFROG S
LEAPING
PEALING
LEAPS
LAPSE PALES
PEALS PLEAS
SALEP SEPAL
SPALE
LEAPT
LEPTA PALET
PETAL PLATE
PLEAT TEPAL
BC LEAR NSY
EARL RALE
REAL
B LEARIER
EARLIER
B LEARIEST
ATELIERS
EARLIEST
REALTIES
LEARN ST
RENAL
LEARNED
LEARNER S
RELEARN
LEARNERS
RELEARNS
LEARNING S
LEARNS
LEARNT
ANTLER
RENTAL
BC LEARS
ARLES EARLS
LARES LASER
RALES REALS
SERAL
B LEARY
EARLY LAYER
RELAY
FP LEAS EHT
ALES LASE
SALE SEAL
LEASABLE
SALEABLE
SEALABLE
P LEASE DRS
EASEL
P LEASED
SEALED
P LEASER S
LAREES
REALES
RESALE
RESEAL
SEALER
P LEASERS
EARLESS
RESALES
RESEALS
SEALERS

P **LEASES**
EASELS
LEASH
HALES HEALS
SELAH SHALE
SHEAL
LEASHED
LEASHES
LEASHING
SHEALING
P **LEASING** S
LINAGES
SEALING
LEASINGS
GAINLESS
GLASSINE
LEAST S
SETAL SLATE
STALE STEAL
STELA TAELS
TALES TEALS
TESLA
LEASTS
SLATES
STALES
STEALS
TASSEL
TESLAS
P **LEATHER** NSY
HALTERE
LEATHERN
P **LEATHERS**
HALTERES
LEATHERY
CS **LEAVE** DNRS
CS **LEAVED**
VEALED
LEAVEN S
LEAVENED
LEAVENS
ENSLAVE
C **LEAVER** S
LAVEER
REVEAL
VEALER
C **LEAVERS**
LAVEERS
REVEALS
SEVERAL
VEALERS
CS **LEAVES**
SLEAVE
LEAVIER
VEALIER
LEAVIEST
ELATIVES
VEALIEST
CS **LEAVING** S
VEALING
LEAVINGS
SLEAVING
LEAVY
VEALY
LEBEN S
LEBENS
LECH
LECHAYIM S
LECHED
LECHER SY
LECHERED
CHEERLED
LECHERS
LECHERY
CHEERLY
F **LECHES**
LECHING
LECHWE S
LECHWES
WELCHES
LECITHIN S
LECTERN S
LECTERNS
LECTIN S
CLIENT
LENTIC
LECTINS
CLIENTS
STENCIL
EF **LECTION** S
EF **LECTIONS**
TELSONIC
E **LECTOR** S
COLTER

E **LECTORS**
COLTERS
CORSLET
COSTREL
LECTURE DRS
LECTURED
RELUCTED
LECTURER S
LECTURES
CRUELEST
LECYTHI S
ETHYLIC
TECHILY
LECYTHIS
CHESTILY
LECYTHUS
BFG **LED**
PS DEL ELD
FPS **LEDGE** RS
GLEDE GLEED
P **LEDGER** S
GELDER
REDLEG
P **LEDGERS**
GELDERS
REDLEGS
FPS **LEDGES**
GLEDES
GLEEDS
SLEDGE
F **LEDGIER**
F **LEDGIEST**
F **LEDGY**
AFG **LEE** KRST
EEL
LEEBOARD S
ERODABLE
F **LEECH**
F **LEECHED**
F **LEECHES**
F **LEECHING**
CGS **LEEK** S
KEEL LEKE
CGS **LEEKS**
KEELS SLEEK
F **LEER** SY
REEL
F **LEERED**
REELED
LEERIER
LEERIEST
SLEETIER
STEELIER
LEERILY
F **LEERING**
REELING
F **LEERS**
REELS
LEERY
FG **LEES**
EELS ELSE
SEEL
FGS **LEET** S
TEEL TELE
FGS **LEETS**
SLEET STEEL
STELE TEELS
TELES
LEEWARD S
LEEWARDS
LEEWAY S
LEEWAYS
WEASELY
C **LEFT** SY
FELT
LEFTER
REFELT
REFLET
TELFER
LEFTEST
FETTLES
LEFTIES
FELSITE
LIEFEST
LEFTISH
LEFTISM S
FILMSET
LEFTISMS
FILMSETS
LEFTIST S
LEFTISTS
LEFTMOST S
LEFTOVER S

C **LEFTS**
FELTS
LEFTWARD S
LEFTWING
LEFTY
FLYTE
G **LEG** S
GEL
LEGACIES
ELEGIACS
LEGACY
LEGAL S
LEGALESE S
LEGALISE DS
GALILEES
LEGALISM S
MEGILLAS
MILLAGES
LEGALIST S
TILLAGES
LEGALITY
LEGALIZE DRS
LEGALLY
LEGALS
LEGATE DES
EAGLET
GELATE
TELEGA
LEGATED
GELATED
LEGATEE S
LEGATEES
LEGATES
EAGLETS
GELATES
SEGETAL
TELEGAS
LEGATINE
GALENITE
GELATINE
LEGATING
GELATING
LEGATION S
GELATION
LEGATO RS
GELATO
LEGATOR S
GLOATER
LEGATORS
GLOATERS
LEGATOS
GELATOS
LEGEND S
LEGENDRY
LEGENDS
LEGER S
LEGERITY
LEGERS
LEGES
GLEES
LEGGED
LEGGIER O
LEGGIERO
LEGGIEST
LEGGIN GS
NIGGLE
LEGGING S
LEGGINGS
LEGGINS
NIGGLES
SNIGGLE
LEGGY
LEGHORN S
LEGHORNS
LEGIBLE
LEGIBLY
LEGION S
ELOIGN
LEGIONS
ELOIGNS
LINGOES
LONGIES
E **LEGIST** S
LEGITS
E **LEGISTS**
E **LEGIT** S
E **LEGITS**
LEGIST
LEGLESS
LEGLIKE

LEGMAN
MANGEL
MANGLE
LEGMEN
LEGONG S
LEGONGS
LEGROOM S
LEGROOMS
LEGS
GELS
LEGUME S
LEGUMES
LEGUMIN S
GUMLINE
LEGUMINS
GUMLINES
LEGWORK S
LEGWORKS
LEHAYIM S
LEHAYIMS
LEHR S
HERL
LEHRS
HERLS
LEHUA S
LEHUAS
LEI S
LIE
LEIS
ISLE LIES
LEISTER S
RETILES
STERILE
LEISTERS
TIRELESS
LEISURE DS
LEISURED
LEISURES
LEK ESU
ELK
LEKE
KEEL LEEK
LEKKED
LEKKING
LEKS
ELKS
LEKU
LEKVAR S
LEKVARS
LEKYTHI
LEKYTHOI
LEKYTHOS
LEKYTHUS
LEMAN S
LEMANS
MENSAL
LEMMA S
LEMMAS
LEMMATA
LEMMING S
LEMMINGS
LEMNISCI
LEMON SY
MELON
LEMONADE S
LEMONISH
LEMONS
MELONS
SOLEMN
LEMONY
LEMPIRA S
IMPALER
IMPEARL
PALMIER
LEMPIRAS
IMPALERS
IMPEARLS
LEMUR S
LEMURES
RELUMES
LEMURINE
RELUMINE
LEMUROID S
MOULDIER
LEMURS
B **LEND** S
LENDABLE
BS **LENDER** S
RELEND

B **LENDERS**
RELENDS
SLENDER
B **LENDING**
B **LENDS**
LENES
LENSE
LENGTH SY
LENGTHEN S
LENGTHS
LENGTHY
THEGNLY
LENIENCE S
LENIENCY
LENIENT
LENIS
LIENS LINES
LENITE DS
LENITED
LENITES
LISENTE
SETLINE
TENSILE
LENITIES
LENITING
LENITION S
LENITIVE S
LENITY
LENO S
ENOL LONE
NOEL
LENOS
ENOLS NOELS
G **LENS** E
F **LENSE** DS
LENES
F **LENSED**
F **LENSES**
LESSEN
F **LENSING**
LENSLESS
LENSMAN
LENSMEN
B **LENT** O
LENTANDO
LENTEN
LENTIC
CLIENT
LECTIN
LENTICEL S
LENTIGO
LENTIL S
LINTEL
LENTILS
LINTELS
LENTISK S
TINKLES
LENTISKS
LENTO S
LENTOID S
LENTOIDS
LENTOS
STOLEN
TELSON
LEONE S
LEONES
LEONINE
LEOPARD S
PAROLED
PRELOAD
LEOPARDS
PRELOADS
LEOTARD S
DELATOR
LEOTARDS
DELATORS
LODESTAR
LEPER S
REPEL
LEPERS
REPELS
LEPIDOTE S
PETIOLED
LEPORID S
LEPORIDS
LEPORINE
LEPROSE
ELOPERS
LEPROSY
LEPROTIC
PETROLIC

LEPROUS
PELORUS
SPORULE
CS **LEPT** A
PELT
LEPTA
LEAPT PALET
PETAL PLATE
PLEAT TEPAL
LEPTIN S
PINTLE
LEPTINS
PINTLES
PLENIST
LEPTON S
LEPTONIC
LEPTONS
LESBIAN S
LESBIANS
LESION S
ELOINS
INSOLE
OLEINS
LESIONED
LESIONS
INSOLES
LIONESS
B **LESS**
SELS
LESSEE S
LESSEES
LESSEN S
LENSES
LESSENED
NEEDLESS
LESSENS
B **LESSER**
LESSON S
LESSONED
LESSONS
SONLESS
P **LESSOR** S
LOSERS
SORELS
P **LESSORS**
B **LEST**
LETS TELS
B **LET** S
TEL
F **LETCH**
F **LETCHED**
F **LETCHES**
F **LETCHING**
LETDOWN S
LETDOWNS
LETHAL S
LETHALLY
LETHALS
LETHARGY
LETHE S
LETHEAN
LETHES
B **LETS**
LEST TELS
LETTED
LETTER S
LETTERED
LETTERER S
RELETTER
LETTERS
SETTLER
STERLET
TRESTLE
LETTING
LETTUCE S
LETTUCES
LETUP S
LETUPS
LEU D
LEUCEMIA S
LEUCEMIC
LEUCIN ES
NUCLEI
LEUCINE S
LEUCINES
LEUCINS
LEUCITE S
LEUCITES
LEUCITIC
LEUCOMA S

LEUCOMAS
LEUD S
DUEL LUDE
LEUDES
ELUDES
LEUDS
DUELS DULSE
LUDES SLUED
LEUKEMIA S
LEUKEMIC S
LEUKOMA S
LEUKOMAS
LEUKON S
LEUKONS
LEUKOSES
LEUKOSIS
LEUKOTIC
LEV AOY
LEVA
LAVE VALE
VEAL VELA
LEVANT S
LEVANTED
LEVANTER S
RELEVANT
LEVANTS
E **LEVATOR** S
E **LEVATORS**
OVERSALT
LEVEE DS
LEVEED
LEVEEING
LEVEES
SLEEVE
LEVEL S
LEVELED
LEVELER S
LEVELERS
LEVELING
LEVELLED
LEVELLER S
LEVELLY
LEVELS
C **LEVER** S
ELVER REVEL
LEVERAGE DS
LEVERED
REVELED
LEVERET S
LEVERETS
LEVERING
REVELING
LEVERS
ELVERS
REVELS
LEVIABLE
LIVEABLE
LEVIED
VEILED
LEVIER S
EVILER
LIEVER
RELIVE
REVILE
VEILER
LEVIERS
RELIVES
REVILES
SERVILE
VEILERS
LEVIES
SLIEVE
LEVIGATE DS
A **LEVIN** S
LIVEN
A **LEVINS**
LIVENS
SNIVEL
LEVIRATE S
RELATIVE
C **LEVIS**
EVILS LIVES
VEILS
LEVITATE DS
LEVITIES
LEVITY
LEVO
LOVE VOLE
LEVODOPA S
LEVOGYRE
LEVULIN S

LEVULINS
LEVULOSE S
LEVY
LEVYING
LEWD
WELD
LEWDER
REWELD
WELDER
LEWDEST
LEWDLY
LEWDNESS
LEWIS
LWEIS WILES
LEWISES
LEWISITE S
LEWISSON S
FIP LEX
LEXEME S
LEXEMES
LEXEMIC
FIP LEXES
LEXICA L
LEXICAL
LEXICON S
LEXICONS
LEXIS
SILEX
FG LEY S
LYE
FG LEYS
LYES LYSE
LI BDENPST
P LIABLE
ALIBLE
LABILE
LIAISE DS
LIAISED
DAILIES
SEDILIA
LIAISES
SILESIA
LIAISING
LIAISON S
LIAISONS
LIANA S
LANAI
LIANAS
LANAIS
NASIAL
SALINA
LIANE S
ALIEN ALINE
ANILE ELAIN
LIANES
ALIENS
ALINES
ELAINS
SALINE
SILANE
LIANG S
ALGIN ALIGN
LIGAN LINGA
LIANGS
ALGINS
ALIGNS
LASING
LIGANS
LINGAS
SIGNAL
LIANOID
LIAR DS
ARIL LAIR
LARI LIRA
RAIL RIAL
LIARD S
DRAIL LAIRD
LIDAR
LIARDS
DRAILS
LAIRDS
LIDARS
LIARS
ARILS LAIRS
LARIS LIRAS
RAILS RIALS
G LIB S
LIBATION S
LIBECCIO S
LIBEL S
LIBELANT S
LIBELED
BELLIED
LIBELEE S
LIBELEES
LIBELER S
LIBELERS
LIBELING
LIBELIST S
LIBELLED
LIBELLEE S
LIBELLER S
LIBELOUS
LIBELS
LIBER S
BIRLE
LIBERAL S
BRAILLE
LIBERALS
BRAILLES
LIBERATE DS
LIBERS
BIRLES
LIBERTY
LIBIDO S
LIBIDOS
LIBLAB S
LIBLABS
LIBRA ES
BRAIL
LIBRAE
BAILER
LIBRARY
LIBRAS
BRAILS
BRASIL
LIBRATE DS
TRIABLE
LIBRATED
LIBRATES
BLASTIER
LIBRETTI
LIBRETTO S
BLOTTIER
LIBRI
LIBS
S LICE
CEIL
LICENCE DER S
LICENCED
LICENCEE S
LICENCER S
ENCIRCLE
LICENCES
LICENSE DER S
SELENIC
SILENCE
LICENSED
DECLINES
SILENCED
LICENSEE S
LICENSER S
RECLINES
SILENCER
LICENSES
SILENCES
LICENSOR S
INCLOSER
LICENTE
CENTILE
LICH IT
LICHEE S
LICHEES
HELICES
LICHEN S
LICHENED
LICHENIN GS
LICHENS
C LICHES
CHIELS
CHILES
CHISEL
LICHI S
CHILI
LICHIS
CHILIS
LICHT S
LICHTED
LICHTING
CHITLING
LICHTLY
LICHTS
E LICIT
LICITLY
CFK LICK S
S
CFS LICKED
CFS LICKER S
CFS LICKERS
SLICKER
CFS LICKING S
LICKINGS
SICKLING
SLICKING
CFK LICKS
S SLICK
LICKSPIT S
LIPSTICK
LICORICE S
LICTOR S
LICTORS
S LID OS
LIDAR S
DRAIL LAIRD
LIARD
LIDARS
DRAILS
LAIRDS
LIARDS
LIDDED
DIDDLE
LIDDING
LIDLESS
LIDO S
DIOL IDOL
LOID
LIDOS
DIOLS IDOLS
LOIDS SLOID
SOLDI SOLID
LIDS
SILD SLID
P LIE DFNRSU
LEI
FP LIED
DEIL DELI
DIEL IDLE
LIEDER
RELIED
LIEF
FILE LIFE
LIEFER
FERLIE
REFILE
RELIEF
LIEFEST
FELSITE
LEFTIES
LIEFLY
LIEGE S
LIEGEMAN
LIEGEMEN
LIEGES
A LIEN S
LINE
A LIENABLE
LINEABLE
LIENAL
LINEAL
A LIENS
LENIS LINES
LIENTERY
ENTIRELY
FPS LIER S
LIRE RIEL
RILE
LIERNE S
RELINE
LIERNES
RELINES
FP LIERS
RIELS RILES
SLIER
FP LIES
ISLE LEIS
LIEU S
LIEUS
ILEUS
S LIEVE R
LIEVER
EVILER
LEVIER
RELIVE
REVILE
VEILER
LIEVEST
EVILEST
VELITES
LIFE R
FILE LIEF
LIFEBOAT S
LIFECARE S
LIFEFUL
LIFELESS
LIFELIKE
LIFELINE S
LIFELONG
LIFER S
FILER FLIER
RIFLE
LIFERS
FILERS
FLIERS
RIFLES
LIFESPAN S
LIFETIME S
LIFEWAY S
LIFEWAYS
LIFEWORK S
C LIFT S
FLIT
LIFTABLE
LIFTED
FLITED
LIFTER S
FILTER
TRIFLE
LIFTERS
FILTERS
STIFLER
TRIFLES
LIFTGATE S
LIFTING
FLITING
LIFTMAN
LIFTMEN
LIFTOFF S
LIFTOFFS
C LIFTS
FLITS
LIGAMENT S
METALING
TEGMINAL
LIGAN DS
ALGIN ALIGN
LIANG LINGA
LIGAND S
LADING
LIGANDS
LADINGS
LIGANS
ALGINS
ALIGNS
LASING
LIANGS
LINGAS
SIGNAL
LIGASE S
SILAGE
LIGASES
GLASSIE
SILAGES
LIGATE DS
AIGLET
GELATI
LIGATED
LIGATES
AIGLETS
GELATIS
LIGATING
LIGATION S
INTAGLIO
LIGATIVE
LIGATURE DS
LIGER S
LIGERS
GRILSE
ABF PS LIGHT S
ABF PS LIGHTED
DELIGHT
LIGHTEN S
LIGHTENS
BPS LIGHTER S
RELIGHT
BPS LIGHTERS
RELIGHTS
SLIGHTER
S LIGHTEST
LIGHTFUL
ABF PS LIGHTING S
LIGHTISH
S LIGHTLY
ABF PS LIGHTS
SLIGHT
LIGNAN S
LIGNANS
LINSANG
LIGNEOUS
LIGNIFY
LIGNIN S
LINING
LIGNINS
LININGS
LIGNITE S
LIGNITES
LINGIEST
LIGNITIC
LIGROIN ES
ROILING
LIGROINE S
RELIGION
REOILING
LIGROINS
LIGULA ERS
LIGULAE
LIGULAR
LIGULAS
LUGSAIL
LIGULATE D
LIGULE S
LIGULES
GULLIES
LIGULOID
LIGURE S
GLUIER
REGULI
UGLIER
LIGURES
LIKABLE
A LIKE DNRS
LIKEABLE
LIKED
LIKELIER
LIKELY
LIKEN S
INKLE
LIKENED
A LIKENESS
LIKENING
LIKENS
INKLES
SILKEN
LIKER S
LIKERS
LIKES T
LIKEST
LIKEWISE
LIKING S
LIKINGS
SILKING
LIKUTA
LILAC S
LILACS
SCILLA
LILIED
LILIES
LILLIPUT S
LILO S
LILOS
LILT S
TILL
LILTED
TILLED
LILTING
TILLING
LILTS
STILL TILLS
S LILY
ILLY YILL
LILYLIKE
LIMA NS
MAIL
LIMACINE
LIMACON S
LIMACONS
LACONISM
LIMAN S
LIMANS
LIMAS
MAILS SALMI
C LIMB AIOSY
LIMBA S
LIMBAS
LIMBATE
BIMETAL
TIMBALE
LIMBECK S
LIMBECKS
C LIMBED
C LIMBER S
LIMBERED
LIMBERER
LIMBERLY
C LIMBERS
LIMBI C
LIMBIC
LIMBIER
LIMBIEST
C LIMBING
LIMBLESS
LIMBO S
LIMBOS
C LIMBS
LIMBUS
LIMBUSES
SUBLIMES
LIMBY
BLIMY
CGS LIME DNSY
MILE
LIMEADE S
EMAILED
LIMEADES
GS LIMED
LIMEKILN S
LIMELESS
LIMEN S
LIMENS
SIMNEL
LIMERICK S
CGS LIMES
MILES SLIME
SMILE
B LIMEY S
LIMEYS
SMILEY
S LIMIER
S LIMIEST
ELITISM
LIMITES
LIMINA L
LIMINAL
S LIMINESS
GS LIMING
LIMIT S
LIMITARY
MILITARY
LIMITED S
DELIMIT
LIMITEDS
DELIMITS
LIMITER S
MILTIER
LIMITERS
LIMITES
ELITISM
LIMIEST
LIMITING
LIMITS
MISLIT
GS LIMMER S
GS LIMMERS
SLIMMER
LIMN S
LIMNED
MILDEN
LIMNER S
MERLIN
LIMNERS
MERLINS
LIMNETIC
LIMNIC
LIMNING
LIMNS
LIMO S
MILO MOIL
LIMONENE S
LIMONITE S
LIMOS
MILOS MOILS
B LIMP AS
LIMPA S
MILPA
LIMPAS
MILPAS
LIMPED
DIMPLE
IMPLED
LIMPER S
PRELIM
RIMPLE
LIMPERS
PRELIMS
RIMPLES
SIMPLER
LIMPEST
LIMPETS
LIMPET S
LIMPETS
LIMPEST
LIMPID
LIMPIDLY
LIMPING
LIMPKIN S
LIMPKINS
LIMPLY
LIMPNESS
PLENISMS
B LIMPS Y
LIMPSEY
S LIMPSIER
IMPERILS
S LIMPSY
SIMPLY
LIMULI
LIMULOID S
LIMULUS
BS LIMY
B LIN EGKNOST
NIL Y
LINABLE
LINAC S
LINACS
LINAGE S
GENIAL
LINAGES
LEASING
SEALING
LINALOL S
LINALOLS
LINALOOL S
LINCHPIN S
LINDANE S
ANNELID
LINDANES
ANNELIDS
LINDEN S
LINDENS
LINDIES
LINDY
AC LINE DNRSY
LIEN
LINEABLE
LIENABLE
LINEAGE S
LINEAGES
ENSILAGE
LINEAL
LIENAL
LINEALLY
LINEAR
ALINER
LARINE
NAILER
RENAIL
LINEARLY
LINEATE D

LINEATED
DATELINE
ENTAILED
LINEBRED
RENDIBLE
LINECUT S
CUTLINE
TUNICLE
LINECUTS
CUTLINES
TUNICLES
A **LINED**
LINELESS
LINELIKE
LINEMAN
MELANIN
LINEMEN
LINEN SY
LINENS
LINENY
A **LINER** S
A **LINERS**
AC **LINES**
LENIS LIENS
LINESMAN
MELANINS
LINESMEN
LINEUP S
LUPINE
UNPILE
LINEUPS
LUPINES
SPINULE
UNPILES
LINEY
CFS **LING** AOSY
LINGA MS
ALGIN ALIGN
LIANG LIGAN
LINGAM S
LAMING
MALIGN
LINGAMS
MALIGNS
LINGAS
ALGINS
ALIGNS
LASING
LIANGS
LIGANS
SIGNAL
LINGCOD S
CODLING
LINGCODS
CODLINGS
SCOLDING
CFS **LINGER** S
LINGERED
ENGIRDLE
REEDLING
LINGERER S
LINGERIE S
CFS **LINGERS**
SLINGER
C **LINGIER**
C **LINGIEST**
LIGNITES
O **LINGO**
LOGIN
LINGOES
ELOIGNS
LEGIONS
LONGIES
CFS **LINGS**
SLING
LINGUA EL
NILGAU
LINGUAE
UNAGILE
LINGUAL S
LINGULA
LINGUALS
LINGUICA S
LINGUINE S
LINGUINI S
LINGUISA S
LINGUIST S
LINGULA ER
LINGUAL
LINGULAE
LINGULAR
ALLURING

C **LINGY**
LYING
LINIER
INLIER
LINIEST
LINIMENT S
LININ GS
A **LINING** S
LIGNIN
LININGS
LIGNINS
LININS
BCP **LINK** SY
S KILN
LINKABLE
BALKLINE
LINKAGE S
LEAKING
LINKAGES
SNAGLIKE
LINKBOY S
LINKBOYS
BCP **LINKED**
S KILNED
KINDLE
BCP **LINKER** S
RELINK
BCP **LINKERS**
RELINKS
BCP **LINKING**
S INKLING
KILNING
LINKMAN
LINKMEN
BCP **LINKS**
S KILNS SLINK
LINKSMAN
LINKSMEN
LINKUP S
UPLINK
LINKUPS
UPLINKS
LINKWORK S
S **LINKY**
LINN S
LINNET S
LINNETS
LINNS
LINO S
LION LOIN
NOIL
LINOCUT S
LINOCUTS
LINOLEUM S
LINOS
LIONS LOINS
NOILS
LINOTYPE DR S
LINS
NILS
LINSANG S
LIGNANS
LINSANGS
LINSEED S
ENISLED
ENSILED
LINSEEDS
IDLENESS
LINSEY S
LYSINE
LINSEYS
LYSINES
LINSTOCK S
EFG **LINT** SY
FG **LINTED**
DENTIL
LINTEL S
LENTIL
LINTELS
LENTILS
LINTER S
LINTERS
FG **LINTIER**
NITRILE
FG **LINTIEST**
INTITLES
FG **LINTING**
LINTLESS
LINTOL S
LINTOLS
EFG **LINTS**

FG **LINTY**
LINUM S
LINUMS
MUSLIN
LINURON S
LINURONS
LINY
INLY
LION S
LINO LOIN
NOIL
LIONESS
INSOLES
LESIONS
LIONFISH
LIONISE DRS
ELISION
ISOLINE
LIONISED
LIONISER S
LIONISES
ELISIONS
ISOLINES
OILINESS
LIONIZE DRS
LIONIZED
LIONIZER S
LIONIZES
LIONLIKE
LIONS
LINOS LOINS
NOILS
BCF **LIP** AES
S
LIPA
PAIL PIAL
LIPASE S
ESPIAL
LIPASES
ESPIALS
LAPISES
PALSIES
S **LIPE**
PILE PLIE
LIPID ES
LIPIDE S
LIPIDES
LIPIDIC
LIPIDS
LIPIN S
LIPINS
S **LIPLESS**
LIPLIKE
LIPOCYTE S
EPICOTYL
LIPOID S
LIPOIDAL
LIPOIDS
LIPOMA S
LIPOMAS
LIPOMATA
LIPOSOME S
BCF **LIPPED**
S
LIPPEN S
NIPPLE
LIPPENED
LIPPENS
NIPPLES
CFS **LIPPER** S
RIPPLE
S **LIPPERED**
CFS **LIPPERS**
RIPPLES
SLIPPER
S **LIPPIER**
S **LIPPIEST**
BCF **LIPPING** S
S
C **LIPPINGS**
SLIPPING
FS **LIPPY**
LIPREAD S
PREDIAL
LIPREADS
PARSLIED
SPIRALED
BCF **LIPS**
S LISP SLIP
LIPSTICK S
LICKSPIT

LIQUATE DS
TEQUILA
LIQUATED
LIQUATES
TEQUILAS
LIQUEFY
LIQUEUR S
LIQUEURS
LIQUID S
LIQUIDLY
LIQUIDS
LIQUIFY
LIQUOR S
LIQUORED
LIQUORS
LIRA S
ARIL LAIR
LARI LIAR
RAIL RIAL
LIRAS
ARILS LAIRS
LARIS LIARS
RAILS RIALS
LIRE
LIER RIEL
RILE
LIRI
LIRIOPE S
LIRIOPES
LIRIPIPE S
LIROT H
TRIOL
LIROTH
LIS PT
LISENTE
LENITES
SETLINE
TENSILE
LISLE S
LISLES
LISP S
LIPS SLIP
LISPED
DISPEL
SLIPED
SPILED
LISPER S
PERILS
PLIERS
LISPERS
LISPING
PILINGS
SLIPING
SPILING
LISPS
SLIPS
LISSOM E
LISSOME
LISSOMLY
A **LIST** S
LITS SILT
SLIT TILS
LISTABLE
BASTILLE
LISTED
DELIST
IDLEST
SILTED
TILDES
LISTEE S
ELITES
LISTEES
TELESIS
TIELESS
LISTEL S
ILLEST
LISTELS
G **LISTEN** S
ELINTS
ENLIST
INLETS
SILENT
TINSEL
G **LISTENED**
ENLISTED
TINSELED
LISTENER S
ENLISTER
REENLIST
SILENTER

G **LISTENS**
ENLISTS
SILENTS
TINSELS
BGK **LISTER** S
LITERS
LITRES
RELIST
TILERS
LISTERIA S
BGK **LISTERS**
RELISTS
LISTING S
SILTING
TILINGS
LISTINGS
LISTLESS
SLITLESS
LISTS
SILTS SLITS
AFS **LIT** ESU
TIL
LITAI
LITANIES
ALIENIST
LITANY
LITAS
ALIST TAILS
LITCHI S
LITHIC
LITCHIS
BEF **LITE** R
TILE
LITENESS
SETLINES
LITER S
LITRE RELIT
TILER
A **LITERACY**
LITERAL S
TALLIER
LITERALS
TALLIERS
LITERARY
A **LITERATE** S
LATERITE
LITERATI M
LITERS
LISTER
LITRES
RELIST
TILERS
LITHARGE S
THIRLAGE
B **LITHE** R
B **LITHELY**
LITHEMIA S
LITHEMIC
BS **LITHER**
B **LITHEST**
THISTLE
LITHIA S
LITHIAS
LITHIC
LITCHI
LITHIFY
LITHIUM S
LITHIUMS
LITHO S
THIOL
LITHOED
LITHOID
DITHIOL
LITHOING
LITHOPS
LITHOS
HOLIST
THIOLS
LITHOSOL S
LITIGANT S
LITIGATE DS
LITMUS
LITMUSES
C **LITORAL**
LITOTES
TOILETS
LITOTIC
LITRE S
LITER RELIT
TILER

LITRES
LISTER
LITERS
RELIST
TILERS
FS **LITS**
LIST SILT
SLIT TILS
LITTEN
FGS **LITTER** SY
TILTER
FG **LITTERED**
RETITLED
LITTERER S
FGS **LITTERS**
SLITTER
TILTERS
G **LITTERY**
TRITELY
LITTLE RS
LITTLER
LITTLES T
LITTLEST
LITTLISH
LITTORAL S
TORTILLA
LITU
LITURGIC S
LITURGY
LIVABLE
AO **LIVE** DNRS
EVIL VEIL
VILE
LIVEABLE
LEVIABLE
LIVED
DEVIL
LIVELIER
LIVELILY
LIVELONG
LIVELY
EVILLY
VILELY
LIVEN S
LEVIN
LIVENED
LIVENER S
LIVENERS
SNIVELER
A **LIVENESS**
EVILNESS
VEINLESS
VILENESS
LIVENING
LIVENS
LEVINS
SNIVEL
S **LIVER** SY
ERVIL LIVRE
VILER
S **LIVERED**
DELIVER
RELIVED
REVILED
LIVERIED
LIVERIES
S **LIVERING**
RELIVING
REVILING
LIVERISH
CS **LIVERS**
ERVILS
LIVRES
SILVER
SLIVER
LIVERY
LIVYER
VERILY
O **LIVES** T
EVILS LEVIS
VEILS
LIVEST
VILEST
LIVETRAP S
LIVID
LIVIDITY
LIVIDLY
LIVIER S
VIRILE
LIVIERS
LIVING S
LIVINGLY

LIVINGS
LIVRE S
ERVIL LIVER
VILER
LIVRES
ERVILS
LIVERS
SILVER
SLIVER
LIVYER S
LIVERY
VERILY
LIVYERS
SILVERY
LIXIVIA L
LIXIVIAL
LIXIVIUM S
LIZARD S
LIZARDS
LLAMA S
LLAMAS
LLANO S
LLANOS
LO BGOPTWX
LOACH
CHOLA
LOACHES
LOAD S
LOADED
LOADER S
ORDEAL
RELOAD
LOADERS
ORDEALS
RELOADS
LOADING S
LOADINGS
LOADS
LOADSTAR S
LOAF S
FOAL
LOAFED
FOALED
LOAFER S
FLORAE
LOAFERS
SAFROLE
LOAFING
FOALING
LOAFS
FOALS
G **LOAM** SY
MOLA
LOAMED
LOAMIER
LOAMIEST
G **LOAMING**
LOAMLESS
G **LOAMS**
MOLAS
LOAMY
LOAN S
LOANABLE
LOANED
LOANER S
RELOAN
LOANERS
RELOANS
LOANING S
LOANINGS
LOANS
SALON SOLAN
LOANWORD S
LOATH E
ALTHO LOTAH
LOATHE DRS
LOATHED
LOATHER S
RATHOLE
LOATHERS
RATHOLES
LOATHES
LOATHFUL
LOATHING S
LOATHLY
TALLYHO
LOAVES
BGS **LOB** EOS
LOBAR
BOLAR BORAL
LABOR

G **LOBATE** D
BOATEL
OBLATE
G **LOBATED**
BLOATED
LOBATELY
OBLATELY
LOBATION S
BOLTONIA
OBLATION
B **LOBBED**
CS **LOBBER** S
CS **LOBBERS**
SLOBBER
LOBBIED
BILOBED
LOBBIES
BILBOES
B **LOBBING**
GS **LOBBY**
LOBBYER S
LOBBYERS
SLOBBERY
LOBBYGOW S
LOBBYING
LOBBYISM S
LOBBYIST S
G **LOBE** DS
BOLE
G **LOBED**
LOBEFIN S
LOBEFINS
LOBELIA S
LOBELIAS
ISOLABLE
LOBELINE S
G **LOBES**
BOLES
LOBLOLLY
LOBO S
BOLO OBOL
LOBOS
BOLOS OBOLS
LOBOTOMY
BGS **LOBS**
SLOB
LOBSTER S
BOLSTER
BOLTERS
LOBSTERS
BOLSTERS
LOBSTICK S
G **LOBULAR**
LOBULATE D
G **LOBULE** S
BOULLE
G **LOBULES**
BOULLES
SOLUBLE
LOBULOSE
LOBWORM S
LOBWORMS
LOCA L
CALO COAL
COLA
LOCAL ES
LOCALE S
LOCALES
CALLOSE
LOCALISE DS
LOCALISM S
LOCALIST S
LOCALITE S
TEOCALLI
LOCALITY
COITALLY
LOCALIZE DR
S
LOCALLY
LOCALS
LOCATE DRS
LOCATED
LOCATER S
LOCATERS
SECTORAL
LOCATES
LACTOSE
TALCOSE
LOCATING
LOCATION S
LOCATIVE S

LOCATOR S
LOCATORS
LOCH S
LOCHAN S
LOCHANS
LOCHIA L
LOCHIAL
LOCHS
LOCI
COIL
BCF **LOCK** S
B **LOCKABLE**
B **LOCKAGE** S
B **LOCKAGES**
LOCKBOX
LOCKDOWN S
BCF **LOCKED**
BC **LOCKER** S
RELOCK
BC **LOCKERS**
RELOCKS
LOCKET S
LOCKETS
LOCKSET
BCF **LOCKING**
LOCKJAW S
LOCKJAWS
LOCKNUT S
LOCKNUTS
LOCKOUT S
LOCKOUTS
LOCKRAM S
ARMLOCK
LOCKRAMS
ARMLOCKS
BCF **LOCKS**
LOCKSET S
LOCKETS
LOCKSETS
LOCKSTEP S
LOCKUP S
LOCKUPS
LOCO S
COOL
LOCOED
COOLED
LOCOES
LOCOFOCO S
LOCOING
COOLING
LOCOISM S
LOCOISMS
LOCOMOTE DS
LOCOS
COOLS
LOCOWEED S
LOCULAR
LOCULATE D
LOCULE DS
LOCULED
COLLUDE
LOCULES
OCELLUS
LOCULI
LOCULUS
LOCUM S
LOCUMS
LOCUS T
LOCUST AS
CLOUTS
LOCUSTA EL
TALCOUS
LOCUSTAE
LACTEOUS
OSCULATE
LOCUSTAL
OUTCALLS
LOCUSTS
E **LOCUTION** S
LOCUTORY
LODE NS
DOLE
LODEN S
OLDEN
LODENS
LODES
DOLES SOLED
LODESTAR S
DELATORS
LEOTARDS

LODGE DRS
OGLED
LODGED
LODGER S
GOLDER
LODGERS
LODGES
LODGING S
GODLING
LODGINGS
GODLINGS
LODGMENT S
LODICULE S
LOESS
LOSES SLOES
SOLES
LOESSAL
LOESSES
LOESSIAL
A **LOFT** SY
LOFTED
LOFTER S
FLORET
LOFTERS
FLORETS
LOFTIER
TREFOIL
LOFTIEST
LOFTILY
LOFTING
LOFTLESS
LOFTLIKE
LOFTS
LOFTY
BCF **LOG** EOSY
S
S **LOGAN** S
ALONG ANGLO
LOGANIA
S **LOGANS**
ANGLOS
SLOGAN
LOGBOOK S
LOGBOOKS
LOGE S
OGLE
LOGES
OGLES
LOGGATS
CFS **LOGGED**
DOGLEG
BCF **LOGGER** S
S
BCF **LOGGERS**
S SLOGGER
LOGGETS
GOGLETS
TOGGLES
LOGGIA S
LOGGIAS
LOGGIE R
C **LOGGIER**
C **LOGGIEST**
BCF **LOGGING** S
S
BF **LOGGINGS**
SLOGGING
LOGGISH
C **LOGGY**
LOGIA
LOGIC S
A **LOGICAL**
LOGICIAN S
LOGICISE DS
LOGICIZE DS
LOGICS
LOGIER
LOGIEST
LOGILY
LOGIN S
LINGO
LOGINESS
LOGINS
LOSING
SOLING
LOGION S
LOOING
OLINGO

LOGIONS
LOOSING
OLINGOS
SOLOING
LOGISTIC S
LOGJAM S
LOGJAMS
LOGO INS
LOGOGRAM S
LOGOI
IGLOO
LOGOMACH SY
LOGON S
LOGONS
LOGOS
LOGOTYPE S
LOGOTYPY
TYPOLOGY
LOGROLL S
LOGROLLS
BCF **LOGS**
S SLOG
LOGWAY S
LOGWAYS
LOGWOOD S
LOGWOODS
O **LOGY**
S **LOID** S
DIOL IDOL
LIDO
LOIDED
DILDOE
DOILED
LOIDING
S **LOIDS**
DIOLS IDOLS
LIDOS SLOID
SOLDI SOLID
AE **LOIN** S
LINO LION
NOIL
AE **LOINS**
LINOS LIONS
NOILS
LOITER S
TOILER
LOITERED
DOLERITE
LOITERER S
LOITERS
ESTRIOL
TOILERS
LOLL SY
LOLLED
LOLLER S
LOLLERS
LOLLIES
LOLLING
LOLLIPOP S
LOLLOP SY
LOLLOPED
LOLLOPS
LOLLOPY
LOLLS
LOLLY
LOLLYGAG S
LOLLYPOP S
LOMEIN S
MOLINE
OILMEN
LOMEINS
LOMENT AS
MELTON
MOLTEN
LOMENTA
OMENTAL
TELAMON
LOMENTS
MELTONS
LOMENTUM S
AC **LONE** R
ENOL LENO
NOEL
LONELIER
LONELILY
LONELY
A **LONENESS**
C **LONER** S
ENROL NEROL

C **LONERS**
ENROLS
NEROLS
LONESOME S
OENOMELS
AFK **LONG** ES
LONGAN S
LONGANS
LONGBOAT S
LONGBOW S
LONGBOWS
LONGE DRS
LONGED
DONGLE
GOLDEN
LONGEING
LONGER S
LONGERON S
LONGERS
LONGES T
LONGEST
LONGHAIR S
LONGHAND S
LONGHEAD S
HEADLONG
LONGHORN S
LONGIES
ELOIGNS
LEGIONS
LINGOES
LONGING S
LONGINGS
LONGISH
LONGJUMP S
LONGLEAF
LONGLINE S
LONGLY
LONGNECK S
LONGNESS
FK **LONGS**
LONGSHIP S
LONGSOME
LONGSPUR S
LONGTIME
LONGUEUR S
LONGWAYS
LONGWISE
LOO FKMNPST
LOOBIES
LOOBY
LOOED
BF **LOOEY** S
LOOEYS
AK **LOOF** AS
FOOL
LOOFA HS
ALOOF
LOOFAH S
LOOFAHS
LOOFAS
K **LOOFS**
FOOLS
BF **LOOIE** S
LOOIES
LOOING
LOGION
OLINGO
LOOK S
KOLO
LOOKDOWN S
LOOKED
LOOKER S
RELOOK
LOOKERS
RELOOKS
LOOKING
LOOKISM S
LOOKISMS
LOOKSISM
LOOKIST S
LOOKISTS
LOOKOUT S
OUTLOOK
LOOKOUTS
OUTLOOKS
LOOKS
KOLOS SOKOL
LOOKSISM S
LOOKISMS

LOOKUP S
LOOKUPS
BG **LOOM** S
MOOL
BG **LOOMED**
BG **LOOMING**
BG **LOOMS**
MOOLS OSMOL
LOON SY
NOLO
LOONEY S
LOONEYS
LOONIE RS
LOONIER
LOONIES T
LOONIEST
OILSTONE
LOONILY
LOONS
NOLOS SNOOL
SOLON
LOONY
BS **LOOP** SY
POLO POOL
B **LOOPED**
POODLE
POOLED
B **LOOPER** S
POOLER
B **LOOPERS**
POOLERS
RESPOOL
SPOOLER
LOOPHOLE DS
LOOPIER
LOOPIEST
LOOPILY
B **LOOPING**
POOLING
BS **LOOPS**
POLOS POOLS
SLOOP SPOOL
LOOPY
LOOS E
SOLO
LOOSE DNRS
OLEOS
LOOSED
OODLES
SOLOED
LOOSELY
LOOSEN S
LOOSENED
LOOSENER S
LOOSENS
LOOSER
LOOSES T
LOOSEST
LOTOSES
LOOSING
LOGIONS
OLINGOS
SOLOING
C **LOOT** S
TOOL
LOOTED
TOLEDO
TOOLED
LOOTER S
RETOOL
ROOTLE
TOOLER
LOOTERS
RETOOLS
ROOTLES
TOOLERS
LOOTING
TOOLING
C **LOOTS**
LOTOS SOTOL
STOOL TOOLS
CFG **LOP** ES
PS POL
ES **LOPE** DRS
POLE
ES **LOPED**
POLED
ES **LOPER** S
POLER PROLE

ES **LOPERS**
POLERS
PROLES
SLOPER
SPLORE
ES **LOPES**
POLES SLOPE
ES **LOPING**
POLING
CFG **LOPPED**
PS
F **LOPPER** S
PROPEL
LOPPERED
F **LOPPERS**
PROPELS
FGS **LOPPIER**
FGS **LOPPIEST**
CFG **LOPPING**
PS
FGS **LOPPY**
POLYP
CFG **LOPS**
PS POLS SLOP
LOPSIDED
DISPLODE
LOPSTICK S
LOQUAT S
LOQUATS
F **LORAL**
LORAN S
LORANS
LORD S
LORDED
LORDING S
LORDINGS
LORDLESS
LORDLIER
LORDLIKE
LORDLING S
DROLLING
LORDLY
DROLLY
LORDOMA S
MALODOR
LORDOMAS
MALODORS
LORDOSES
DOORLESS
ODORLESS
LORDOSIS
LORDOTIC
LORDS
LORDSHIP S
LORE S
ORLE ROLE
LOREAL
LORES
LOSER ORLES
ROLES SOREL
LORGNON S
LORGNONS
LORICA E
CAROLI
LORICAE
CALORIE
CARIOLE
COALIER
LORICATE DS
EROTICAL
G **LORIES**
OILERS
ORIELS
REOILS
LORIKEET S
LORIMER S
LORIMERS
LORINER S
LORINERS
LORIS
ROILS
LORISES
RISSOLE
LORN
LORNNESS
LORRIES
LORRY
G **LORY**
C **LOSABLE**

C LOSE LRS
OLES SLOE SOLE
LOSEL S
LOSELS
C LOSER S
LORES ORLES ROLES SOREL
C LOSERS
LESSOR SORELS
C LOSES
LOESS SLOES SOLES
C LOSING S
LOGINS SOLING
LOSINGLY
C LOSINGS
FG LOSS Y
SOLS
FG LOSSES
LOSSLESS
FG LOSSY
G LOST
LOTS SLOT
LOSTNESS
BCPS LOT AHIS
F LOTA HS
ALTO TOLA
LOTAH S
ALTHO LOATH
LOTAHS
F LOTAS
ALTOS TOLAS
CS LOTH
HOLT
LOTHARIO S
LOTHSOME
LOTI C
TOIL
LOTIC
LOTION S
LOTIONS
SOLITON
LOTOS
LOOTS SOTOL STOOL TOOLS
LOTOSES
LOOSEST
BCPS LOTS
LOST SLOT
LOTTE DRS
BCPS LOTTED
DOTTEL DOTTLE
BPS LOTTER SY
BPS LOTTERS
SETTLOR SLOTTER
LOTTERY
LOTTES
BCPS LOTTING
B LOTTO S
LOTTOS
LOTUS
LOUTS TOLUS
LOTUSES
SOLUTES TOUSLES
LOUCHE
AC LOUD
LOUDEN S
NODULE
LOUDENED
LOUDENS
NODULES
LOUDER
LOURED
LOUDEST
TOUSLED
LOUDISH
LOUDLIER
LOUDLY
LOUDNESS
CPS LOUGH S
GHOUL
CPS LOUGHS
GHOULS SLOUGH

LOUIE S
LOUIES
LOUIS
LOUMA S
LOUMAS
LOUNGE DRS
LOUNGED
LOUNGER S
LOUNGERS
LOUNGES
LOUNGING
LOUNGY
LOUP ES
LOUPE DNS
LOUPED
LOUPEN
LOUPES
LOUPING
LOUPS
CF LOUR SY
CF LOURED
LOUDER
CF LOURING
CF LOURS
F LOURY
B LOUSE DS
OUSEL
B LOUSED
SOULED
B LOUSES
OUSELS SOLEUS
B LOUSIER
SOILURE
B LOUSIEST
B LOUSILY
B LOUSING
B LOUSY
CFG LOUT S
TOLU
CFG LOUTED
OUTLED
CFG LOUTING
LOUTISH
CFG LOUTS
LOTUS TOLUS
LOUVER S
LOUVRE VELOUR
LOUVERED
LOUVERS
LOUVRES VELOURS
LOUVRE DS
LOUVER VELOUR
LOUVRED
LOUVRES
LOUVERS VELOURS
LOVABLE
LOVABLY
LOVAGE S
LOVAGES
LOVAT S
VOLTA
LOVATS
CG LOVE DRS
LEVO VOLE
LOVEABLE
LOVEABLY
LOVEBIRD S
LOVEBUG S
LOVEBUGS
G LOVED
VOLED
LOVEFEST S
LOVELESS
LOVELIER
LOVELIES T
LOVELILY
LOVELOCK S
LOVELORN
LOVELY
VOLLEY
CGP LOVER S
LOVERLY
CGP LOVERS
SOLVER

CG LOVES
SOLVE VOLES
LOVESEAT S
LOVESICK
LOVESOME
LOVEVINE S
G LOVING
VOLING
LOVINGLY
ABFGPS LOW ENS
OWL
B LOWBALL S
B LOWBALLS
LOWBORN
P LOWBOY S
P LOWBOYS
LOWBRED
BOWLDER
LOWBROW S
LOWBROWS
BS LOWDOWN S
BS LOWDOWNS
SLOWDOWN
LOWE DRS
BFGPS LOWED
DOWEL
BFGPS LOWER SY
ROWEL
FG LOWERED
ROWELED
FG LOWERING
ROWELING
BFGP LOWERS
ROWELS SLOWER
F LOWERY
YOWLER
LOWES T
LOWSE
S LOWEST
OWLETS TOWELS
BFGPS LOWING S
LOWINGS
SLOWING
S LOWISH
OWLISH
P LOWLAND S
P LOWLANDS
LOWLIER
LOWLIEST
LOWLIFE RS
LOWLIFER S
LOWLIFES
LOWLIGHT S
LOWLILY
LOWLIVES
S LOWLY
BCF LOWN
S LOWNESS
LOWRIDER S
BFGPS LOWS E
OWLS SLOW
LOWSE
LOWES
LOX
LOXED
LOXES
LOXING
LOYAL
ALLOY
LOYALER
LOYALEST
LOYALISM S
LOYALIST S
LOYALLY
LOYALTY
LOZENGE S
LOZENGES
LUAU S
LUAUS
USUAL
BCFS LUBBER S
BURBLE RUBBLE
LUBBERLY

BCFS LUBBERS
BURBLES RUBBLES SLUBBER
LUBE DS
BLUE
LUBED
BLUED
LUBES
BLUES
LUBING
BLUING
LUBRIC
LUBRICAL
LUCARNE S
NUCLEAR UNCLEAR
LUCARNES
LUCE S
CLUE
LUCENCE S
LUCENCES
LUCENCY
LUCENT
LUCENTLY
LUCERN ES
LUCERNE S
LUCERNES
LUCERNS
LUCES
CLUES
LUCID
LUDIC
LUCIDITY
LUCIDLY
LUCIFER S
FLUERIC
LUCIFERS
FLUERICS
LUCITE S
LUETIC
LUCITES
LUETICS
CP LUCK SY
CP LUCKED
LUCKIE RS
P LUCKIER
LUCKIES T
P LUCKIEST
P LUCKILY
CP LUCKING
LUCKLESS
CP LUCKS
SCULK
P LUCKY
LUCRE S
CRUEL ULCER
LUCRES
ULCERS
LUCULENT
E LUDE S
DUEL LEUD
E LUDES
DUELS DULSE LEUDS SLUED
LUDIC
LUCID
BCFGS LUES
SLUE
LUETIC S
LUCITE
LUETICS
LUCITES
BFS LUFF AS
LUFFA S
LUFFAS
BFS LUFFED
DUFFEL DUFFLE
BFS LUFFING
BFS LUFFS
SLUFF
GPS LUG ES
GUL
K LUGE DRS
GLUE
K LUGED
GLUED
LUGEING
GLUEING
LUGER S
GLUER GRUEL

LUGERS
GLUERS GRUELS
K LUGES
GLUES GULES
LUGGAGE S
LUGGAGES
GPS LUGGED
PS LUGGER S
GURGLE
PS LUGGERS
GURGLES SLUGGER
LUGGIE S
LUGGIES
GPS LUGGING
K LUGING
GLUING
GPS LUGS
GULS SLUG
LUGSAIL S
LIGULAS
LUGSAILS
LUGWORM S
LUGWORMS
LUKEWARM
LULL S
LULLABY
LULLED
LULLER S
LULLERS
LULLING
LULLS
LULU S
LULUS
AGPS LUM APS
LUMA S
ALUM MAUL
LUMAS
ALUMS MAULS
P LUMBAGO S
P LUMBAGOS
LUMBAR S
BRUMAL LABRUM UMBRAL
LUMBARS
LABRUMS
CPS LUMBER S
RUMBLE
S LUMBERED
S LUMBERER S
LUMBERLY
CPS LUMBERS
RUMBLES SLUMBER
LUMEN S
LUMENAL
LUMENS
A LUMINA L
ALUMIN ALUMNI
LUMINAL
LUMINARY
LUMINISM S
LUMINIST S
A LUMINOUS
F LUMMOX
F LUMMOXES
CFPS LUMP SY
PLUM
CFPS LUMPED
PLUMED
P LUMPEN S
PLENUM
P LUMPENS
PLENUMS
P LUMPER S
RUMPLE
P LUMPERS
RUMPLES
LUMPFISH
CG LUMPIER
PLUMIER
CG LUMPIEST
PLUMIEST
G LUMPILY
CFPS LUMPING
PLUMING
CP LUMPISH

CFPS LUMPS
PLUMS SLUMP
CG LUMPY
PLUMY
AGPS LUMS
SLUM
LUNA RS
ULAN ULNA
LUNACIES
LUNACY
LUNAR S
ULNAR
LUNARIAN S
LUNARS
LUNAS
ULANS ULNAS
LUNATE D
ELUANT
LUNATED
LUNATELY
LUNATIC S
LUNATICS
SULTANIC
LUNATION S
G LUNCH
LUNCHBOX
G LUNCHED
LUNCHEON S
LUNCHER S
LUNCHERS
G LUNCHES
G LUNCHING
LUNE ST
LUNES
LUNET S
UNLET
LUNETS
LUNETTE S
LUNETTES
UNSETTLE
CFS LUNG EIS
LUNGAN S
LUNGANS
BP LUNGE DERS
BP LUNGED
GULDEN
LUNGEE S
LUNGEES
BP LUNGER S
BP LUNGERS
BP LUNGES
GUNSEL
LUNGFISH
FLUSHING
LUNGFUL S
LUNGFULS
LUNGI S
BP LUNGING
LUNGIS
SLUING
LUNGS
SLUNG
LUNGWORM S
LUNGWORT S
LUNGYI S
LUNGYIS
LUNIER
LUNIES T
LUNIEST
LUTEINS UTENSIL
CFPS LUNK S
CFP LUNKER S
RUNKLE
CFP LUNKERS
RUNKLES
LUNKHEAD S
CFP LUNKS
SLUNK
B LUNT S
B LUNTED
B LUNTING
B LUNTS
LUNULA ER
LUNULAE
LUNULAR
LUNULATE D
LUNULE S

LUNULES
LUNY
LUPANAR S
LUPANARS
LUPIN ES
LUPINE S
LINEUP UNPILE
LUPINES
LINEUPS SPINULE UNPILES
LUPINS
LUPOUS
LUPULIN S
LUPULINS
LUPUS
LUPUSES
LURCH
CHURL
LURCHED
LURCHER S
LURCHERS
LURCHES
LURCHING
LURDAN ES
LURDANE S
LAUNDER
LURDANES
LAUNDERS
LURDANS
LURE DRSX
RULE
LURED
RULED
LURER S
RULER
LURERS
RULERS
LURES
RULES
LUREX
LUREXES
LURID
LURIDLY
LURING
RULING
LURINGLY
LURK S
LURKED
LURKER S
LURKERS
LURKING
LURKS
LUSCIOUS
BFPS LUSH
SHUL
BFS LUSHED
BFP LUSHER
BFPS LUSHES T
FP LUSHEST
HUSTLES SLEUTHS
BFS LUSHING
P LUSHLY
FP LUSHNESS
LUST SY
SLUT
LUSTED
BCF LUSTER S
LUSTRE RESULT RUSTLE SUTLER ULSTER
BCF LUSTERED
DELUSTER RESULTED
BCF LUSTERS
LUSTRES RESULTS RUSTLES SUTLERS ULSTERS
LUSTFUL
LUSTIER
RULIEST RUTILES
LUSTIEST

LUSTILY
LUSTING
LUTINGS
LUSTRA L
ULTRAS
LUSTRAL
LUSTRATE DS
TUTELARS
LUSTRE DS
LUSTER
RESULT
RUSTLE
SUTLER
ULSTER
LUSTRED
RUSTLED
STRUDEL
LUSTRES
LUSTERS
RESULTS
RUSTLES
SUTLERS
ULSTERS
LUSTRING S
RUSTLING
LUSTROUS
LUSTRUM S
LUSTRUMS
LUSTS
SLUTS
LUSTY
LUSUS
SULUS
LUSUSES
LUTANIST S
EFG LUTE ADS
TULE
LUTEA L
G LUTEAL
LUTECIUM S
EF LUTED
LUTEFISK S
FLUKIEST
LUTEIN S
LUTEINS
LUNIEST
UTENSIL
LUTENIST S
LUTEOLIN S
LUTEOUS
EFG LUTES
TULES
LUTETIUM S
LUTEUM
MUTUEL
MUTULE
LUTFISK S
KISTFUL
LUTFISKS
KISTFULS
LUTHERN S
LUTHERNS
LUTHIER S
LUTHIERS
EF LUTING S
F LUTINGS
LUSTING
F LUTIST S
F LUTISTS
K LUTZ
K LUTZES
LUV S
LUVS
F LUX E
LUXATE DS
LUXATED
LUXATES
LUXATING
LUXATION S
LUXE S
F LUXES
LUXURIES
LUXURY
LWEI S
WILE
LWEIS
LEWIS WILES
LYARD
LARDY
LYART

LYASE S
LYASES
LYCEA
LACEY
LYCEE S
LYCEES
LYCEUM S
LYCEUMS
LYCH
LYCHEE S
LYCHEES
LYCHES
CHYLES
LYCHNIS
LYCOPENE S
LYCOPOD S
LYCOPODS
LYCRA S
CLARY
LYCRAS
LYDDITE S
LYDDITES
LYE S
LEY
LYES
LEYS LYSE
FP LYING S
LINGY
P LYINGLY
F LYINGS
LYSING
SINGLY
LYMPH S
LYMPHOID
LYMPHOMA S
LYMPHS
LYNCEAN
LYNCH
LYNCHED
LYNCHER S
LYNCHERS
LYNCHES
LYNCHING S
LYNCHPIN S
LYNX
LYNXES
LYOPHILE D
LYRATE D
ELYTRA
REALTY
LYRATED
LYRATELY
LYRE S
RELY
LYREBIRD S
LYRES
SLYER
LYRIC S
LYRICAL
LYRICISE DS
LYRICISM S
LYRICIST S
LYRICIZE DS
LYRICON S
CORNILY
LYRICONS
LYRICS
LYRIFORM
LYRISM S
LYRISMS
LYRIST S
LYRISTS
LYSATE S
SLATEY
LYSATES
LYSE DS
LEYS LYES
LYSED
LYSES
LYSIN EGS
LYSINE S
LINSEY
LYSINES
LINSEYS
LYSING
LYINGS
SINGLY
LYSINS

LYSIS
SYLIS
LYSOGEN SY
LYSOGENS
LYSOGENY
LYSOSOME S
LYSOZYME S
LYSSA S
SLAYS
LYSSAS
LYTIC
LYTTA ES
LYTTAE
LYTTAS

M

A MA CDEGNPRS
AM TWXY
MAAR S
MARA
MAARS
MARAS
MABE S
BEAM BEMA
MABES
BEAMS BEMAS
MAC EHKS
CAM
MACABER
MACABRE
MACABRE
MACABER
MACACO S
MACACOS
MACADAM S
MACADAMS
MACAQUE S
MACAQUES
MACARONI CS
ARMONICA
MAROCAIN
MACAROON S
MACAW S
MACAWS
MACCABAW S
MACCABOY S
MACCHIA
MACCHIE
MACCOBOY S
MACE DRS
ACME CAME
MACED
MACER S
CREAM
MACERATE DR
RACEMATE S
MACERS
CREAMS
SCREAM
MACES
ACMES CAMES
MACH EOS
CHAM
MACHE S
MACHES
SACHEM
SAMECH
SCHEMA
MACHETE S
MACHETES
MACHINE DS
MACHINED
MACHINES
MACHISMO S
MACHOISM
MACHO S
MOCHA
MACHOISM S
MACHISMO
MACHOS
MOCHAS
MACHREE S
MACHREES
CASHMERE
MARCHESE
MACHS
CHAMS CHASM
MACHZOR S
MACHZORS
MACING

S MACK S
MACKEREL S
MACKINAW S
MACKLE DS
MACKLED
MACKLES
MACKLING
S MACKS
SMACK
MACLE DS
CAMEL
MACLED
CALMED
MACLES
CAMELS
MESCAL
MACON S
MACONS
MASCON
SOCMAN
MACRAME S
MACRAMES
MACRO NS
CAROM
MACRON S
MACRONS
MACROS
CAROMS
MACRURAL
MACRURAN S
MACS
CAMS SCAM
MACULA ERS
MACULAE
MACULAR
MACULAS
CALAMUS
MACULATE DS
MACULE DS
ALMUCE
MACULED
MACULES
ALMUCES
MACULING
MACUMBA S
MACUMBAS
MAD ES
DAM
MADAM ES
MADAME S
MADAMES
MADAMS
MADCAP S
MADCAPS
MADDED
MADDEN S
DAMNED
DEMAND
MADDENED
DEMANDED
MADDENS
DEMANDS
MADDER S
MADDERS
MADDEST
MADDING
MADDISH
MADE
DAME MEAD
MADEIRA S
MADEIRAS
MADERIZE DS
MADHOUSE S
MADLY
MADMAN
MADMEN
MADNESS
DESMANS
MADONNA S
MADONNAS
MADRAS A
DAMARS
DRAMAS
MADRASA HS
ARMADAS
RAMADAS
MADRASAH S
MADRASAS
MADRASSA
MADRASES

MADRASSA HS
MADRASAS
MADRE S
ARMED DERMA
DREAM
MADRES
DERMAS
DREAMS
MADRIGAL S
MADRONA S
MONARDA
MADRONAS
MONARDAS
MADRONE S
MADRONES
RANSOMED
MADRONO S
DOORMAN
MADRONOS
MADS
DAMS
MADTOM S
MADTOMS
MADURO S
MADUROS
MADWOMAN
MADWOMEN
MADWORT S
MADWORTS
MADZOON S
MADZOONS
MAE S
MAENAD S
ANADEM
MAENADES
MAENADIC
MAENADS
ANADEMS
MAES
MESA SAME
SEAM
MAESTOSO S
OSTEOMAS
MAESTRI
IMARETS
MISRATE
SMARTIE
MAESTRO S
MAESTROS
MAFFIA S
MAFFIAS
MAFFICK S
MAFFICKS
MAFIA S
MAFIAS
MAFIC
MAFIOSI
MAFIOSO S
MAFIOSOS
MAFTIR S
MAFTIRS
MAG EIS
GAM
MAGALOG S
MAGALOGS
MAGAZINE S
MAGDALEN ES
I MAGE S
GAME MEGA
MAGENTA S
GATEMAN
MAGNATE
NAMETAG
MAGENTAS
MAGNATES
NAMETAGS
I MAGES
GAMES
MAGGOT SY
MAGGOTS
MAGGOTY
MAGI C
MAGIAN S
MAGIANS
SIAMANG
MAGIC S
GAMIC
MAGICAL
MAGICIAN S
MAGICKED

MAGICS
MAGILP S
MAGILPS
MAGISTER S
MIGRATES
RAGTIMES
STERIGMA
MAGLEV S
MAGLEVS
MAGMA S
GAMMA
MAGMAS
GAMMAS
MAGMATA
MAGMATIC
MAGNATE S
GATEMAN
MAGENTA
NAMETAG
MAGNATES
MAGENTAS
NAMETAGS
MAGNESIA NS
MAGNESIC
MAGNET OS
MAGNETIC S
MAGNETO NS
MEGATON
MONTAGE
MAGNETON S
MAGNETOS
MEGATONS
MONTAGES
MAGNETS
MAGNIFIC O
MAGNIFY
MAGNOLIA S
MAGNUM S
MAGNUMS
MAGOT S
MAGOTS
MAGPIE S
MAGPIES
MISPAGE
MAGS
GAMS
MAGUEY S
MAGUEYS
MAGUS
GAUMS SAGUM
MAHARAJA HS
MAHARANI S
MAHATMA S
MAHATMAS
MAHIMAHI S
MAHJONG GS
MAHJONGG S
MAHJONGS
MAHOE S
MAHOES
MAHOGANY
HOGMANAY
MAHONIA S
MAHONIAS
MAHOUT S
MAHOUTS
MAHUANG S
MAHUANGS
MAHZOR S
MAHZORIM
MAHZORS
MAIASAUR AS
MAID S
AMID
MAIDEN S
AIDMEN
DAIMEN
MEDIAN
MEDINA
MAIDENLY
MEDIANLY
MAIDENS
MEDIANS
MEDINAS
SIDEMAN
MAIDHOOD S
MAIDISH
MAIDS
AMIDS

MAIEUTIC
MAIGRE
GAMIER
IMAGER
MIRAGE
MAIHEM S
MAIHEMS
E MAIL ELS
LIMA
MAILABLE
MAILBAG S
MAILBAGS
MAILBOX
MAILE DRS
EMAIL
E MAILED
MEDIAL
MAILER S
REMAIL
MAILERS
REALISM
REMAILS
MAILES
EMAILS
MESIAL
SAMIEL
MAILGRAM S
E MAILING S
MAILINGS
MISALIGN
MAILL S
MAILLESS
MAILLOT S
MAILLOTS
MISALLOT
MAILLS
MAILMAN
MAILMEN
MAILROOM S
E MAILS
LIMAS SALMI
MAIM S
IMAM
MAIMED
MAIMER S
MAIMERS
MAIMING
MAIMS
IMAMS MIASM
A MAIN S
AMIN MINA
MAINLAND S
MAINLINE DR
S
MAINLY
MAINMAST S
MAINS
AMINS MINAS
MAINSAIL S
MAINSTAY S
MAINTAIN S
AMANITIN
MAINTOP S
PTOMAIN
TAMPION
TIMPANO
MAINTOPS
PTOMAINS
TAMPIONS
MAIOLICA S
MAIR S
AMIR RAMI
MAIRS
AMIRS SIMAR
MAIST S
TAMIS
MAISTS
MAIZE S
MAIZES
MAJAGUA S
MAJAGUAS
MAJESTIC
MAJESTY
MAJOLICA S
MAJOR S
JORAM
MAJORED
MAJORING
MAJORITY
MAJORLY

MAJORS
JORAMS
MAKABLE
MAKAR S
KARMA MARKA
MAKARS
KARMAS
MARKAS
MAKE RS
KAME
MAKEABLE
MAKEBATE S
BAKEMEAT
MAKEFAST S
MAKEOVER S
MAKER S
MAKERS
MASKER
MAKES
KAMES SAMEK
MAKEUP S
MAKEUPS
MAKIMONO S
MAKING S
MAKINGS
MASKING
MAKO S
AMOK
MAKOS
AMOKS
MAKUTA
MALACCA S
MALACCAS
MALADIES
MALADY
MALAISE S
MALAISES
MALAMUTE S
MALANGA S
MALANGAS
MALAPERT S
MALAPROP S
MALAR S
ALARM RAMAL
MALARIA LNS
MALARIAL
MALARIAN
MALARIAS
MALARKEY S
MALARKY
MALAROMA S
MALARS
ALARMS
MALATE S
MEATAL
TAMALE
MALATES
MALTASE
TAMALES
MALE S
ALME LAME
MEAL
MALEATE S
MALEATES
MALEDICT S
MALEFIC
MALEMIUT S
MALEMUTE S
MALENESS
LAMENESS
MANELESS
NAMELESS
SALESMEN
MALES
ALMES LAMES
MEALS
MALFED
FLAMED
MALGRE
MALIC E
CLAIM
MALICE S
MALICES
MALIGN S
LAMING
LINGAM
MALIGNED
MEDALING
MALIGNER S
GERMINAL
MALINGER

MALIGNLY
MALIGNS
LINGAMS
MALIHINI S
MALINE S
MENIAL
MALINES
MENIALS
SEMINAL
MALINGER S
GERMINAL
MALIGNER
MALISON S
MALISONS
MALKIN S
MALKINS
S **MALL** S
MALLARD S
MALLARDS
MALLED
MALLEE S
MALLEES
MALLEI
MALLEOLI
MALLET S
MALLETS
MALLEUS
MALLING S
MALLINGS
MALLOW S
MALLOWS
S **MALLS**
SMALL
MALM SY
MALMIER
MALMIEST
MALMS
MALMSEY S
MALMSEYS
MALMY
MALODOR S
LORDOMA
MALODORS
LORDOMAS
MALOTI
MALPOSED
S **MALT** SY
MALTASE S
MALATES
TAMALES
MALTASES
MALTED S
MALTEDS
MALTHA S
MALTHAS
MALTIER
MARLITE
MALTIEST
METALIST
SMALTITE
MALTING
MALTOL S
MALTOLS
MALTOSE S
MALTOSES
MALTREAT S
S **MALTS**
SMALT
MALTSTER S
MARTLETS
MALTY
MALVASIA NS
MAMA S
MAMALIGA S
MAMAS
MAMBA S
MAMBAS
MAMBO S
MAMBOED
MAMBOES
MAMBOING
MAMBOS
MAMELUKE S
MAMEY S
MAMEYES
MAMEYS
MAMIE S

MAMIES
MAMLUK S
MAMLUKS
MAMMA ELS
MAMMAE
MAMMAL S
MAMMALS
MAMMARY
MAMMAS
MAMMATE
MAMMATI
MAMMATUS
MAMMEE S
MAMMEES
MAMMER S
MAMMERED
MAMMERS
MAMMET S
MAMMETS
MAMMEY S
MAMMEYS
MAMMIE S
MAMMIES
MAMMILLA E
MAMMITIS
MAMMOCK S
MAMMOCKS
MAMMON S
MAMMONS
MAMMOTH S
MAMMOTHS
MAMMY
MAMZER S
MAMZERS
MAN AEOSY
NAM
MANA ST
MANACLE DS
MANACLED
MANACLES
MANAGE DRS
MANAGED
MANAGER S
MANAGERS
MANAGES
SAGAMEN
MANAGING
MANAKIN S
MANAKINS
MANANA S
MANANAS
MANAS
MANAT S
ATMAN MANTA
MANATEE S
EMANATE
ENEMATA
MANATEES
EMANATES
MANATOID
MANATS
ATMANS
MANTAS
MANCHE ST
MANCHES
MANCHET S
MANCHETS
MANCIPLE S
MANDALA S
MANDALAS
MANDALIC
MANDAMUS
MANDARIN S
MANDATE DS
MANDATED
MANDATES
MANDATOR SY
MANDIBLE S
MANDIOCA S
MANDOLA S
MONADAL
MANDOLAS
MANDOLIN ES
MANDRAKE S
MANDREL S
MANDRELS

MANDRIL LS
RIMLAND
MANDRILL S
MANDRILS
RIMLANDS
MANE DS
AMEN MEAN
NAME NEMA
MANED
ADMEN AMEND
MENAD NAMED
MANEGE S
MENAGE
MANEGES
MENAGES
MANELESS
LAMENESS
MALENESS
NAMELESS
SALESMEN
MANES
AMENS MANSE
MEANS MENSA
NAMES NEMAS
MANEUVER S
MANFUL
MANFULLY
MANGA S
MANGABEY S
MANGABY
MANGANIC
MANGANIN S
MANGAS
GASMAN
MANGE LRSY
MANGEL S
LEGMAN
MANGLE
MANGELS
MANGLES
MANGER S
ENGRAM
GERMAN
RAGMEN
MANGERS
ENGRAMS
GERMANS
MANGES
GASMEN
MANGEY
MANGIER
GERMINA
REAMING
MANGIEST
MINTAGES
MISAGENT
STEAMING
MANGILY
MANGLE DRS
LEGMAN
MANGEL
MANGLED
MANGLER S
MANGLERS
MANGLES
MANGELS
MANGLING
MANGO S
AMONG
MANGOES
MANGOLD S
MANGOLDS
MANGONEL S
MANGOS
MANGROVE S
VENOGRAM
MANGY
MANHOLE S
MANHOLES
MANHOOD S
MANHOODS
MANHUNT S
MANHUNTS
HUNTSMAN
MANIA CS
AMAIN AMNIA
ANIMA
MANIAC S
CAIMAN
MANIACAL
MANIACS
CAIMANS

MANIAS
ANIMAS
MANIC S
AMNIC
MANICS
MANICURE DS
MANIFEST OS
MANIFOLD S
MANIHOT S
MANIHOTS
MANIKIN S
MANIKINS
MANILA S
ANIMAL
LAMINA
MANILAS
ANIMALS
LAMINAS
MANILLA S
LAMINAL
MANILLAS
LAMINALS
MANILLE S
MANILLES
MANIOC AS
ANOMIC
CAMION
MANIOCA S
MANIOCAS
MANIOCS
ANOSMIC
CAMIONS
MASONIC
MANIPLE S
IMPANEL
MANIPLES
IMPANELS
MANITO SU
MANITOS
MANITOU S
TINAMOU
MANITOUS
TINAMOUS
MANITU S
MANITUS
SANTIMU
TSUNAMI
MANKIND
MANLESS
MANLIER
MARLINE
MINERAL
MANLIEST
AILMENTS
ALIMENTS
MELANIST
SMALTINE
MANLIKE
MANLILY
MANLY
MANMADE
MANNA NS
MANNAN S
MANNANS
MANNAS
MANNED
MANNER S
MANNERED
REMANNED
MANNERLY
MANNERS
MANNIKIN S
MANNING
MANNISH
MANNITE S
MANNITES
MANNITIC
MANNITOL S
MANNOSE S
MANNOSES
MANO RS
MOAN NOMA
MANOR S
ROMAN
MANORIAL
MORAINAL
MANORS
RAMSON
RANSOM
ROMANS

MANOS
MASON MOANS
MONAS NOMAS
SOMAN
MANPACK
PACKMAN
MANPOWER S
MANQUE
MANROPE S
MANROPES
MANS E
MANSARD S
MANSARDS
MANSE S
AMENS MANES
MEANS MENSA
NAMES NEMAS
MANSES
MENSAS
MESSAN
MANSION S
AMNIONS
ONANISM
MANSIONS
ONANISMS
MANTA S
ATMAN MANAT
MANTAS
ATMANS
MANATS
MANTEAU SX
MANTEAUS
MANTEAUX
MANTEL S
LAMENT
MANTLE
MENTAL
MANTELET S
MANTELS
LAMENTS
MANTLES
MANTES
AMENTS
STAMEN
MANTIC
MANTID S
MANTIDS
MANTILLA S
MANTIS
MATINS
MANTISES
MATINESS
MANTISSA S
SATANISM
STAMINAS
MANTLE DST
LAMENT
MANTEL
MENTAL
MANTLED
MANTLES
LAMENTS
MANTELS
MANTLET S
MANTLETS
MANTLING S
MANTRA MPS
MANTRAM S
MANTRAMS
MANTRAP S
RAMPANT
MANTRAPS
MANTRAS
MANTRIC
MANTUA S
MANTUAS
MANUAL S
ALUMNA
MANUALLY
MANUALS
MANUARY
MANUBRIA L
MANUMIT S
MANUMITS
MANURE DRS
MANURED
DURAMEN
MAUNDER
UNARMED
MANURER S

MANURERS
SURNAMER
MANURES
SURNAME
MANURIAL
MANURING
UNARMING
MANUS
MANWARD S
MANWARDS
MANWISE
MANY
MYNA
MANYFOLD
MAP S
AMP
PAM
MAPLE S
AMPLE
MAPLES
SAMPLE
MAPLIKE
MAPMAKER S
MAPPABLE
MAPPED
MAPPER S
PAMPER
PREAMP
MAPPERS
PAMPERS
PREAMPS
MAPPING S
MAPPINGS
MAPS
AMPS PAMS
SAMP SPAM
MAQUETTE S
MAQUI S
UMIAQ
MAQUILA S
MAQUILAS
MAQUIS
UMIAQS
MAR ACEKLST
ARM
RAM
MARA S
MAAR
MARABOU ST
MARABOUS
MARABOUT S
TAMBOURA
MARACA S
MARACAS
MARASCA
MASCARA
MARANTA S
MARANTAS
MARAS
MAARS
MARASCA S
MARACAS
MASCARA
MARASCAS
MASCARAS
MARASMIC
MARASMUS
MARATHON S
MARAUD S
MARAUDED
MARAUDER S
MARAUDS
MARAVEDI S
MARBLE DRS
AMBLER
BLAMER
LAMBER
RAMBLE
MARBLED
RAMBLED
MARBLER S
RAMBLER
MARBLERS
RAMBLERS
MARBLES
AMBLERS
BLAMERS
LAMBERS
RAMBLES
MARBLIER
MARBLING S
RAMBLING

MARBLY
MARC HS
CRAM
MARCATO S
MARCATOS
MARCEL S
CALMER
MARCELS
MARCH
CHARM
MARCHED
CHARMED
MARCHEN
MARCHER S
CHARMER
MARCHERS
CHARMERS
MARCHES AEI
MESARCH
SCHMEAR
MARCHESA
MARCHESE
CASHMERE
MACHREES
MARCHESI
CHIMERAS
MARCHING
CHARMING
MARCS
CRAMS SCRAM
MARE S
REAM
MAREMMA
MAREMME
MARENGO
MEGARON
MARES
MARSE MASER
REAMS SMEAR
MARGARIC
MARGARIN ES
MARGAY S
MARGAYS
MARGE S
GAMER REGMA
MARGENT S
GARMENT
MARGENTS
GARMENTS
MARGES
GAMERS
MARGIN S
ARMING
MARGINAL S
ALARMING
MARGINED
DREAMING
MIDRANGE
MARGINS
ARMINGS
MARGRAVE S
MARIA
MARIACHI S
MARIGOLD S
MARIMBA S
MARIMBAS
MARINA S
AIRMAN
MARINADE DS
MARINARA S
MARINAS
MARINATE DS
ANIMATER
MARINE RS
AIRMEN
REMAIN
MARINER S
MARINERS
MARINES
REMAINS
SEMINAR
MARIPOSA S
PAROSMIA
MARISH
IHRAMS
MARISHES
MISHEARS
MARITAL
MARTIAL
MARITIME
MARJORAM S
MARK AS

MARKA S
KARMA MAKAR
MARKAS
KARMAS
MAKARS
MARKDOWN S
MARKED
DEMARK
MARKEDLY
MARKER S
REMARK
MARKERS
REMARKS
MARKET S
MARKETED
MARKETER S
REMARKET
MARKETS
MARKHOOR S
MARKHOR S
MARKHORS
MARKING S
MARKINGS
MARKKA AS
MARKKAA
MARKKAS
MARKS
MARKSMAN
MARKSMEN
MARKUP S
MARKUPS
MARL SY
MARLED
DERMAL
MEDLAR
MARLIER
MARLIEST
LAMISTER
MARLITES
MISALTER
MARLIN EGS
MARLINE S
MANLIER
MINERAL
MARLINES
MINERALS
MISLEARN
MARLING S
MARLINGS
MARLINS
MARLITE S
MALTIER
MARLITES
LAMISTER
MARLIEST
MISALTER
MARLITIC
MARLS
MARLY
MYLAR
MARMITE S
MARMITES
RAMMIEST
MARMOSET S
MARMOT S
MARMOTS
MAROCAIN S
ARMONICA
MACARONI
MAROON S
ROMANO
MAROONED
MAROONS
ROMANOS
MARPLOT S
MARPLOTS
MARQUE ES
MARQUEE S
MARQUEES
MARQUES S
MASQUER
MARQUESS
MASQUERS
MARQUIS E
MARQUISE S
MARRAM S
MARRAMS
MARRANO S
MARRANOS
MARRED

MARRER S
MARRERS
MARRIAGE S
MARRIED S
ADMIRER
MARRIEDS
ADMIRERS
DISARMER
MARRIER S
MARRIERS
MARRIES
MARRING
MARRON S
MARRONS
MARROW SY
MARROWED
MARROWS
MARROWY
MARRY
MARRYING
MARS EH
ARMS RAMS
MARSALA S
MARSALAS
MARSE S
MARES MASER
REAMS SMEAR
MARSES
MASERS
SMEARS
MARSH Y
HARMS
MARSHAL LS
MARSHALL S
MARSHALS
MARSHES
MASHERS
SHMEARS
SMASHER
MARSHIER
MARSHY
MARSUPIA L
S MART S
TRAM
MARTAGON S
S MARTED
DREAMT
MARTELLO S
S MARTEN S
S MARTENS
SARMENT
SMARTEN
MARTIAL
MARITAL
MARTIAN S
TAMARIN
MARTIANS
TAMARINS
MARTIN GIS
MARTINET S
INTERMAT
S MARTING
MIGRANT
MARTINI S
MARTINIS
MISTRAIN
MARTINS
MARTLET S
MARTLETS
MALTSTER
S MARTS
SMART TRAMS
MARTYR SY
MARTYRED
MARTYRLY
MARTYRS
MARTYRY
MARVEL S
MARVELED
MARVELS
MARVY
MARYJANE S
MARZIPAN S
A MAS AHKST
O MASA S
AMAS
MASALA S
SALAAM
MASALAS
SALAAMS

MASAS
AMASS MASSA
MASCARA S
MARACAS
MARASCA
MASCARAS
MARASCAS
MASCON S
MACONS
SOCMAN
MASCONS
MASCOT S
MASCOTS
MASER S
MARES MARSE
REAMS SMEAR
MASERS
MARSES
SMEARS
S MASH Y
HAMS SHAM
S MASHED
EMDASH
SHAMED
S MASHER S
HAREMS
SHMEAR
S MASHERS
MARSHES
SHMEARS
SMASHER
S MASHES
SHAMES
MASHGIAH
MASHIE S
MASHIES
MESSIAH
S MASHING
SHAMING
MASHY
MASJID S
MASJIDS
MASK S
MASKABLE
MASKED
MASKEG S
MASKEGS
MASKER S
MAKERS
MASKERS
MASKING S
MAKINGS
MASKINGS
MASKLIKE
MASKS
MASON S
MANOS MOANS
MONAS NOMAS
SOMAN
MASONED
DAEMONS
MONADES
MASONIC
ANOSMIC
CAMIONS
MANIOCS
MASONING
MASONITE S
AMNIOTES
MISATONE
MASONRY
MASONS
SOMANS
MASQUE RS
MASQUER S
MARQUES
MASQUERS
MARQUESS
MASQUES
A MASS AEY
MASSA S
AMASS MASAS
MASSACRE DR S
MASSAGE DRS
MASSAGED
MASSAGER S
MASSAGES
MASSAS
MASSCULT S
MASSE DS
MESAS SEAMS

A MASSED
MASSEDLY
A MASSES
MASSETER S
SEAMSTER
STEAMERS
MASSEUR S
AMUSERS
ASSUMER
MASSEURS
ASSUMERS
MASSEUSE S
MASSICOT S
MASSIER
MASSIEST
MISSEATS
MASSIF S
MASSIFS
A MASSING
MASSIVE
MAVISES
MASSLESS
MASSY
MAST S
MATS TAMS
MASTABA HS
MASTABAH S
MASTABAS
MASTED
DEMAST
MASTER SY
ARMETS
MATERS
MATRES
RAMETS
STREAM
TAMERS
MASTERED
STREAMED
MASTERLY
MASTERS
STREAMS
MASTERY
STREAMY
MASTHEAD S
MASTIC S
MISACT
MASTICHE S
HEMATICS
MISTEACH
TACHISME
MASTICS
MISACTS
MISCAST
MASTIFF S
MASTIFFS
MASTING
MATINGS
MASTITIC
ATTICISM
MASTITIS
MASTIX
MASTIXES
MASTLESS
MASTLIKE
MASTODON ST
MASTOID S
DIATOMS
MASTOIDS
MASTS
MASURIUM S
MAT EHST
TAM
MATADOR S
MATADORS
MATCH
MATCHBOX
MATCHED
MATCHER S
REMATCH
MATCHERS
MATCHES
MATCHING
MATCHUP S
MATCHUPS
MATE DRSY
MEAT META
TAME TEAM
MATED
TAMED

MATELESS
MEATLESS
TAMELESS
MATELOT ES
MATELOTE S
MATELOTS
MATER S
ARMET RAMET
TAMER
MATERIAL S
MATERIEL S
MATERNAL
MATERS
ARMETS
MASTER
MATRES
RAMETS
STREAM
TAMERS
MATES
MEATS SATEM
STEAM TAMES
TEAMS
MATESHIP S
SHIPMATE
MATEY S
ETYMA MEATY
MATEYS
MAYEST
STEAMY
MATH S
MATHS
MATIER
IMARET
MATIEST
ETATISM
MATILDA S
MATILDAS
MATIN GS
MATINAL
MATINEE S
ETAMINE
MATINEES
ETAMINES
MISEATEN
MATINESS
MANTISES
MATING S
TAMING
MATINGS
MASTING
MATINS
MANTIS
MATLESS
SAMLETS
MATRASS
MATRES
ARMETS
MASTER
MATERS
RAMETS
STREAM
TAMERS
MATRICES
CERAMIST
MISTRACE
SCIMETAR
MATRIX
MATRIXES
MATRON S
MATRONAL
MATRONLY
MATRONS
TRANSOM
MATS
MAST TAMS
MATSAH S
ASTHMA
MATSAHS
ASTHMAS
MATT ES
MATTE DRS
MATTED
MATTEDLY
S MATTER SY
S MATTERED
S MATTERS
SMATTER
MATTERY
MATTES
TAMEST

MATTIN GS
TITMAN
MATTING S
MATTINGS
MATTINS
MATTOCK S
MATTOCKS
MATTOID S
MATTOIDS
MATTRASS
MATTRESS
SMARTEST
SMATTERS
MATTS
MATURATE DS
MATURE DRS
MATURED
MATURELY
MATURER S
ERRATUM
MATURERS
MATURES T
STRUMAE
MATUREST
MATURING
MATURITY
MATZA HS
MATZAH S
HAZMAT
MATZAHS
HAZMATS
MATZAS
MATZO HST
MATZOH S
MATZOHS
MATZOON S
MATZOONS
MATZOS
MATZOT H
MATZOTH
MAUD S
DUMA
MAUDLIN
MAUDS
DUMAS
MAUGER
MAUGRE
MAUGRE
MAUGER
MAUL S
ALUM LUMA
MAULED
ALMUDE
MAULER S
MAULERS
SERUMAL
MAULING
MAULS
ALUMS LUMAS
MAUMET S
MAUMETRY
MAUMETS
SUMMATE
MAUN D
MAUND SY
DUNAM
MAUNDER S
DURAMEN
MANURED
UNARMED
MAUNDERS
DURAMENS
SURNAMED
MAUNDIES
MAUNDS
DUNAMS
MAUNDY
MAUSOLEA N
MAUT S
MAUTS
MAUVE S
MAUVES
MAVEN S
MAVENS
MAVERICK S
MAVIE S
MAVIES
MAVIN S
MAVINS

MAVIS
MAVISES
MASSIVE
MAW NS
MAWED
MAWING
MAWKISH
MAWN
MAWS
SWAM
MAX I
MAXED
MAXES
EXAMS
MAXI MS
MAXICOAT S
MAXILLA ES
MAXILLAE
MAXILLAS
MAXIM AS
MAXIMA L
MAXIMAL S
MAXIMALS
MAXIMIN S
MINIMAX
MAXIMINS
MAXIMISE DS
MAXIMITE S
MAXIMIZE DR S
MAXIMS
MAXIMUM S
MAXIMUMS
MAXING
MAXIS
MAXIXE S
MAXIXES
MAXWELL S
MAXWELLS
MAY AOS
YAM
MAYA NS
MAYAN
MAYAPPLE S
MAYAS
MAYBE S
BEAMY EMBAY
MAYBES
EMBAYS
MAYBIRD S
MAYBIRDS
MAYBUSH
MAYDAY S
MAYDAYS
MAYED
MAYEST
MATEYS
STEAMY
MAYFLIES
MAYFLY
MAYHAP
MAYHEM S
MAYHEMS
MAYING S
MAYINGS
MAYO RS
MAYOR S
MORAY
MAYORAL
MAYORESS
MAYORS
MORAYS
MAYOS
MAYPOLE S
MAYPOLES
MAYPOP S
MAYPOPS
MAYS T
YAMS
MAYST
MAYVIN S
MAYVINS
MAYWEED S
MAYWEEDS
MAZAEDIA
MAZARD S
MAZARDS

AS MAZE DRS
A MAZED
A MAZEDLY
MAZELIKE
MAZELTOV
MAZER S
MAZERS
AS MAZES
SMAZE
MAZIER
MAZIEST
MESTIZA
MAZILY
MAZINESS
A MAZING
MAZOURKA S
MAZUMA S
MAZUMAS
MAZURKA S
MAZURKAS
MAZY
MAZZARD S
MAZZARDS
MBAQANGA S
MBIRA S
MBIRAS
E ME DGLMNTW
EM
MEAD S
DAME MADE
MEADOW SY
MEADOWS
MEADOWY
MEADS
DAMES
MEAGER
MEAGRE
MEAGERLY
MEAGRELY
MEAGRE
MEAGER
MEAGRELY
MEAGERLY
MEAL SY
ALME LAME
MALE
MEALIE RS
MEALIER
MEALIES T
MEALIEST
METALISE
MEALLESS
MEALS
ALMES LAMES
MALES
MEALTIME S
MEALWORM S
MEALY
MEALYBUG S
MEAN STY
AMEN MANE
NAME NEMA
MEANDER S
AMENDER
REEDMAN
RENAMED
MEANDERS
AMENDERS
MEANER S
RENAME
MEANERS
RENAMES
MEANEST
MEANIE S
MEANIES
MEANING S
MEANINGS
MEANLY
LAYMEN
NAMELY
MEANNESS
MEANS
AMENS MANES
MANSE MENSA
NAMES NEMAS
MEANT
AMENT MENTA
MEANTIME S
MEANY
YAMEN

MEASLE DS
MEASLED
MEASLES
MEASLIER
MEASLY
MEASURE DRS
MEASURED
MEASURER S
MEASURES
REASSUME
MEAT SY
MATE META
TAME TEAM
MEATAL
MALATE
TAMALE
MEATBALL S
MEATED
TEAMED
MEATHEAD S
MEATIER
EMERITA
EMIRATE
MEATIEST
ESTIMATE
TEATIMES
MEATILY
MEATLESS
MATELESS
TAMELESS
MEATLOAF
MEATMAN
MEATMEN
MEATS
MATES SATEM
STEAM TAMES
TEAMS
MEATUS
MUTASE
MEATUSES
MEATY
ETYMA MATEY
MECCA S
MECCAS
MECHANIC S
MECHITZA S
MECONIUM S
ENCOMIUM
MED S
MEDAKA S
MEDAKAS
MEDAL S
LAMED
MEDALED
MEDALING
MALIGNED
MEDALIST S
MISDEALT
MEDALLED
MEDALLIC
MEDALS
DAMSEL
LAMEDS
MEDDLE DRS
MELDED
MEDDLED
MEDDLER S
MEDDLERS
MEDDLES
MEDDLING
MEDEVAC S
MEDEVACS
MEDFLIES
MEDFLY
MEDIA DELNS
AIMED AMIDE
MEDIACY
MEDIAD
DIADEM
MEDIAE
MEDIAL S
MAILED
MEDIALLY
MEDIALS
MISDEAL
MISLEAD
MEDIAN ST
AIDMEN
DAIMEN
MAIDEN
MEDINA

MEDIANLY
MAIDENLY
MEDIANS
MAIDENS
MEDINAS
SIDEMAN
MEDIANT S
MEDIANTS
MEDIAS
AMIDES
MEDIATE DS
MEDIATED
MEDIATES
MEDIATOR SY
MEDIC KOS
DEMIC
MEDICAID S
MEDICAL S
CAMELID
CLAIMED
DECIMAL
DECLAIM
MEDICALS
CAMELIDS
DECIMALS
DECLAIMS
MEDICANT S
MEDICARE S
CERAMIDE
MEDICATE DS
DECIMATE
MEDICIDE S
MEDICINE DS
MEDICK S
MEDICKS
MEDICO S
MEDICOS
MISCODE
MEDICS
MEDIEVAL S
MEDIGAP S
MEDIGAPS
MISPAGED
MEDII
IMIDE
MEDINA S
AIDMEN
DAIMEN
MAIDEN
MEDIAN
MEDINAS
MAIDENS
MEDIANS
SIDEMAN
MEDIOCRE
MEDITATE DS
ADMITTEE
MEDIUM S
MEDIUMS
DUMMIES
MEDIUS
MEDIVAC S
MEDIVACS
MEDLAR S
DERMAL
MARLED
MEDLARS
MEDLEY S
MEDLEYS
MEDS
MEDULLA ERS
MEDULLAE
MEDULLAR Y
MURALLED
MEDULLAS
MEDUSA ELNS
AMUSED
MEDUSAE
MEDUSAL
ALMUDES
MEDUSAN S
MEDUSANS
MEDUSAS
ASSUMED
MEDUSOID S
MEED S
DEEM DEME
MEEDS
DEEMS DEMES
S MEEK
MEEKER

MEEKEST
MEEKLY
MEEKNESS
MEERKAT S
MEERKATS
MEET S
METE TEEM
MEETER S
REMEET
TEEMER
MEETERS
REMEETS
TEEMERS
MEETING S
TEEMING
MEETINGS
MEETLY
MEETNESS
MEETS
METES TEEMS
MEG AS
GEM
O MEGA
GAME MAGE
MEGABAR S
MEGABARS
MEGABIT S
MEGABITS
MEGABUCK S
MEGABYTE S
MEGACITY
MEGADEAL S
MEGADOSE S
MEGADYNE S
GANYMEDE
MEGAFLOP S
MEGAHIT S
MEGAHITS
MEGALITH S
MEGALOPS
MEGAPLEX
MEGAPOD ES
MEGAPODE S
MEGAPODS
MEGARA
MEGARON
MARENGO
MEGASS E
MEGASSE S
MESSAGE
MEGASSES
MESSAGES
MEGASTAR S
MEGATON S
MAGNETO
MONTAGE
MEGATONS
MAGNETOS
MONTAGES
MEGAVOLT S
MEGAWATT S
MEGILLA HS
MILLAGE
MEGILLAH S
MEGILLAS
LEGALISM
MILLAGES
MEGILP HS
MEGILPH S
MEGILPHS
MEGILPS
GLIMPSE
MEGOHM S
MEGOHMS
MEGRIM S
MEGRIMS
MEGS
GEMS
MEHNDI S
MEHNDIS
MEIKLE
MEINIE S
MEINIES
MEINY
MEIOSES
MEIOSIS
MEIOTIC

MEISTER S
METIERS
REEMITS
RETIMES
TRISEME
MEISTERS
MISSTEER
TRISEMES
MEL DLST
ELM
MELAMDIM
MELAMED
MELAMINE S
MELANGE S
GLEEMAN
MELANGES
MELANIAN
MELANIC S
MELANICS
MENISCAL
MELANIN S
LINEMAN
MELANINS
LINESMAN
MELANISM S
MELANIST S
AILMENTS
ALIMENTS
MANLIEST
SMALTINE
MELANITE S
MELANIZE DS
MELANOID S
MELANOMA S
MELANOUS
MELD S
MELDED
MEDDLE
MELDER S
MELDERS
MELDING
MINGLED
MELDS
MELEE S
MELEES
MELENA S
ENAMEL
MELENAS
ENAMELS
MELIC
CLIME
MELILITE S
MELILOT S
MELILOTS
MELINITE S
ILMENITE
TIMELINE
MELISMA S
MELISMAS
S MELL S
S MELLED
MELLIFIC
S MELLING
MELLOW S
MELLOWED
MELLOWER
MELLOWLY
MELLOWS
S MELLS
SMELL
MELODEON S
MELODIA S
MELODIAS
MELODIC A
MELODICA S
MELODIES
MELODISE
MELODISE DS
MELODIES
MELODIST S
MODELIST
MOLDIEST
MELODIZE DR S
MELODY
MELOID S
MOILED
MELOIDS
MIDSOLE
MELON S
LEMON

MELONS
LEMONS
SOLEMN
MELS
ELMS
S MELT SY
MELTABLE
MELTAGE S
MELTAGES
MELTDOWN S
S MELTED
S MELTER S
REMELT
S MELTERS
REMELTS
RESMELT
SMELTER
S MELTING
MELTON S
LOMENT
MOLTEN
MELTONS
LOMENTS
S MELTS
SMELT
MELTY
MEM EOS
MEMBER S
MEMBERED
MEMBERS
MEMBRANE DS
MEME S
MEMENTO S
MEMENTOS
MEMES
MEMETICS
MEMO S
MOME
MEMOIR S
MEMOIRS
MEMORIAL S
MEMORIES
MEMORISE
MEMORISE DS
MEMORIES
MEMORIZE DR S
MEMORY
MEMOS
MOMES
MEMS
MEMSAHIB S
AO MEN DOU
MENACE DRS
MENACED
MENACER S
MENACERS
MENACES
MENACING
MENAD S
ADMEN AMEND
MANED NAMED
MENADS
AMENDS
DESMAN
MENAGE S
MANEGE
MENAGES
MANEGES
MENARCHE S
MENAZON S
MENAZONS
AE MEND S
AE MENDABLE
AE MENDED
AE MENDER S
REMEND
AE MENDERS
REMENDS
MENDIGO S
DEMOING
MENDIGOS
SMIDGEON
AE MENDING S
MENDINGS
AE MENDS
MENFOLK S
MENFOLKS
MENHADEN S
MENHIR S

MENHIRS
MENIAL S
MALINE
MENIALLY
MENIALS
MALINES
SEMINAL
MENINGES
MENINX
MENISCAL
MELANICS
MENISCI
MENISCUS
MENO
NOME OMEN
MENOLOGY
MENORAH S
MENORAHS
HORSEMAN
RHAMNOSE
MENSA ELS
AMENS MANES
MANSE MEANS
NAMES NEMAS
MENSAE
ENEMAS
SEAMEN
MENSAL
LEMANS
MENSAS
MANSES
MESSAN
MENSCH Y
MENSCHEN
MENSCHES
CHESSMEN
MENSCHY
MENSE DS
MESNE NEEMS
SEMEN
MENSED
EMENDS
MENSEFUL
MENSES
MESNES
SEMENS
MENSH
MENSHEN
MENSHES
MENSING
MENSTRUA L
MENSURAL
NUMERALS
MENSWEAR
O MENTA L
AMENT MEANT
O MENTAL
LAMENT
MANTEL
MANTLE
MENTALLY
TALLYMEN
MENTEE S
MENTEES
MENTHENE S
MENTHOL S
MENTHOLS
MENTION S
MENTIONS
MENTOR S
MENTORED
ENTODERM
MENTORS
MONSTER
O MENTUM
MENU S
NEUM
MENUDO S
MENUDOS
MENUS
NEUMS
MEOU S
MOUE
MEOUED
MEOUING
MEOUS
MOUES MOUSE
MEOW S
MEOWED
MEOWING
MEOWS

MEPHITIC
MEPHITIS
MERC HSY
MERCAPTO
A MERCER SY
A MERCERS
MERCERY
A MERCES
CREMES
MERCH
MERCHANT S
MERCHES
SCHEMER
SCHMEER
MERCIES
MERCIFUL
MERCS
MERCURIC
MERCURY
MERCY
MERE RS
MERELY
MERENGUE S
MERER
MERES T
MEREST
METERS
METRES
RETEMS
E MERGE DERS
E MERGED
DEGERM
MERGEE S
EMERGE
MERGEES
EMERGES
E MERGENCE S
MERGER S
MERGERS
E MERGES
E MERGING
MERIDIAN S
MERINGUE S
MERINO S
MERINOS
MERISES
MESSIER
REMISES
MERISIS
MERISTEM S
STEMMIER
MERISTIC
SCIMITER
TRISEMIC
MERIT S
MITER MITRE
REMIT TIMER
MERITED
DEMERIT
DIMETER
MITERED
RETIMED
MERITING
MITERING
RETIMING
MERITS
MISTER
MITERS
MITRES
REMITS
SMITER
TIMERS
S MERK S
S MERKS
SMERK
MERL ES
MERLE S
MERLES
MERLIN S
LIMNER
MERLINS
LIMNERS
MERLON S
MERLONS
MERLOT S
MOLTER
MERLOTS
MOLTERS
MERLS
MERMAID S

MERMAIDS
MERMAN
MERMEN
MEROPIA S
EMPORIA
MEROPIAS
MEROPIC
MERRIER
MERRIEST
MITERERS
RIMESTER
TRIREMES
MERRILY
MERRY
MESA S
MAES SAME
SEAM
MESALLY
MESARCH
MARCHES
SCHMEAR
MESAS
MASSE SEAMS
MESCAL S
CAMELS
MACLES
MESCALS
MESCLUN S
MESCLUNS
MESDAMES
MESEEMED
MESEEMS
SEMEMES
MESH Y
HEMS
MESHED
MESHES
MESHIER
MESHIEST
MESHING
MESHUGA H
MESHUGAH
MESHUGGA H
MESHUGGE
MESHWORK S
MESHY
MESIAL
EMAILS
MAILES
SAMIEL
MESIALLY
MESIAN
AMINES
ANIMES
INSEAM
SEMINA
MESIC
MESMERIC
MESNALTY
MESNE S
MENSE NEEMS
SEMEN
MESNES
MENSES
SEMENS
MESOCARP S
CAPSOMER
COMPARES
MESODERM S
MESOGLEA LS
MESOMERE S
MESON S
NOMES OMENS
MESONIC
INCOMES
MESONS
MESOPHYL LS
MESOSOME S
MESOTRON S
MONTEROS
MESOZOAN S
MESOZOIC
MESQUIT ES
MESQUITE S
MESQUITS
MESS Y
MESSAGE DS
MEGASSE
MESSAGED

MESSAGES
MEGASSES
MESSAN S
MANSES
MENSAS
MESSANS
MESSED
MESSES
MESSIAH S
MASHIES
MESSIAHS
MESSIER
MERISES
REMISES
MESSIEST
METISSES
MESSILY
SMILEYS
MESSING
MESSMAN
MESSMATE S
MESSMEN
MESSUAGE S
MESSY
MESTEE S
ESTEEM
MESTEES
ESTEEMS
MESTESO S
MESTESOS
MESTINO S
MOISTEN
SENTIMO
MESTINOS
MOISTENS
SENTIMOS
MESTIZA S
MAZIEST
MESTIZAS
MESTIZO S
MESTIZOS
MET AEH
META L
MATE MEAT
TAME TEAM
METAGE S
GAMETE
METAGES
GAMETES
METAL S
METALED
METALING
LIGAMENT
TEGMINAL
METALISE DS
MEALIEST
METALIST S
MALTIEST
SMALTITE
METALIZE DS
METALLED
METALLIC S
METALS
LAMEST
SAMLET
METAMER ES
AMMETER
METAMERE S
METAMERS
AMMETERS
METAPHOR S
METATAG S
METATAGS
METATE S
METATES
METAZOA LN
METAZOAL
METAZOAN S
METAZOIC
AZOTEMIC
METAZOON
METE DRS
MEET TEEM
METED
METEOR S
EMOTER
REMOTE
METEORIC
METEORS
EMOTERS
REMOTES

METEPA S
METEPAS
METER S
METRE REMET
RETEM
METERAGE S
METERED
METERING
REGIMENT
METERS
MEREST
METRES
RETEMS
METES
MEETS TEEMS
METH S
THEM
METHADON ES
METHANE S
METHANES
METHANOL S
HOTELMAN
METHINKS
METHOD S
METHODIC
METHODS
METHOXY L
METHOXYL
METHS
METHYL S
METHYLAL S
METHYLIC
METHYLS
METICAIS
METICAL S
CLIMATE
METICALS
CLEMATIS
CLIMATES
METIER S
REEMIT
RETIME
METIERS
MEISTER
REEMITS
RETIMES
TRISEME
METING
METIS
EMITS ITEMS
MITES SMITE
STIME TIMES
METISSE S
METISSES
MESSIEST
METOL S
MOTEL
METOLS
MOLEST
MOTELS
METONYM SY
METONYMS
METONYMY
METOPAE
METOPE S
METOPES
METOPIC
METOPON S
METOPONS
METRAZOL S
METRE DS
METER REMET
RETEM
METRED
TERMED
METRES
MEREST
METERS
RETEMS
METRIC S
METRICAL
METRICS
METRIFY
METRING
TERMING
METRIST S
METRISTS
METRITIS
METRO S
METROS

METTLE DS
METTLED
METTLES
METUMP S
METUMPS
MEUNIERE
S MEW LS
MEWED
MEWING
MEWL S
MEWLED
MEWLER S
MEWLERS
MEWLING
MEWLS
S MEWS
SMEW
MEZCAL S
MEZCALS
MEZE S
MEZEREON S
MEZEREUM S
MEZES
MEZQUIT ES
MEZQUITE S
MEZQUITS
MEZUZA HS
MEZUZAH S
MEZUZAHS
MEZUZAS
MEZUZOT H
MEZUZOTH
MEZZO S
MEZZOS
MHO S
OHM
MHOS
MOSH OHMS
SHMO
A MI BCDGLMRS
X
MIAOU S
MIAOUED
MIAOUING
MIAOUS
MIAOW S
MIAOWED
MIAOWING
MIAOWS
MIASM AS
IMAMS MAIMS
MIASMA LS
MIASMAL
MIASMAS
MIASMATA
MIASMIC
MIASMS
MIAUL S
MIAULED
MIAULING
MIAULS
MIB S
MIBS
E MIC AES
MICA S
MICAS
MICAWBER S
A MICE
EMIC
MICELL AES
MICELLA ER
MICELLAE
MICELLAR
MILLRACE
MICELLE S
MICELLES
MICELLS
MICHE DS
CHIME HEMIC
MICHED
CHIMED
MICHES
CHIMES
MICHING
CHIMING
MICKEY S
MICKEYS

MICKLE RS
MICKLER
MICKLES T
MICKLEST
MICRA
MICRIFY
MICRO NS
MICROBAR S
MICROBE S
MICROBES
MICROBIC
MICROBUS
MICROCAP
MICRODOT S
MICROHM S
MICROHMS
MICROLUX
MICROMHO S
O MICRON S
O MICRONS
CRIMSON
MICROS
MICRURGY
MICS
AI MID IS
DIM
MIDAIR S
MIDAIRS
MIDBRAIN S
MIDCAP
MIDCULT S
MIDCULTS
MIDDAY S
MIDDAYS
MIDDEN S
MINDED
MIDDENS
MIDDIES
MIDDLE DRS
MILDED
MIDDLED
MIDDLER S
MIDDLERS
MIDDLES
MIDDLING S
MIDDY
MIDFIELD S
S MIDGE ST
S MIDGES
SMIDGE
MIDGET S
MIDGETS
MIDGUT S
MIDGUTS
MIDI S
IMID
MIDIRON S
MIDIRONS
MIDIS
IMIDS
MIDLAND S
MIDLANDS
MIDLEG S
GLIMED
MIDLEGS
MIDLIFE R
MIDLIFER S
MIDLINE S
MIDLINES
MIDLIST S
MIDLISTS
MIDLIVES
MISLIVED
MIDMONTH S
MIDMOST S
MIDMOSTS
MIDNIGHT S
MIDNOON S
MIDNOONS
MIDPOINT S
MIDRANGE S
DREAMING
MARGINED
MIDRASH
DIRHAMS
MIDRIB S
MIDRIBS

MIDRIFF S
MIDRIFFS
AI MIDS T
DIMS
A MIDSHIP S
A MIDSHIPS
MIDSIZE D
MIDSIZED
MIDSOLE S
MELOIDS
MIDSOLES
MIDSPACE S
A MIDST S
MIDSTORY
MIDSTS
MIDTERM S
TRIMMED
MIDTERMS
MIDTOWN S
MIDTOWNS
MIDWATCH
MIDWAY S
MIDWAYS
MIDWEEK S
MIDWEEKS
MIDWIFE DS
MIDWIFED
MIDWIFES
MIDWIVED
MIDWIVES
MIDYEAR S
MIDYEARS
MIEN S
MINE
MIENS
MINES
MIFF SY
MIFFED
MIFFIER
MIFFIEST
MIFFING
MIFFS
MIFFY
MIG GS
MIGG S
MIGGLE S
MIGGLES
MIGGS
MIGHT SY
MIGHTIER
MIGHTILY
MIGHTS
MIGHTY
MIGNON S
MIGNONNE
MIGNONS
MIGRAINE S
IMAGINER
E MIGRANT S
MARTING
E MIGRANTS
SMARTING
E MIGRATE DS
RAGTIME
E MIGRATED
E MIGRATES
MAGISTER
RAGTIMES
STERIGMA
MIGRATOR SY
MIGS
MIHRAB S
MIHRABS
MIJNHEER S
MIKADO S
MIKADOS
MIKE DS
MIKED
MIKES
MIKING
MIKRA
O MIKRON S
O MIKRONS
MIKVAH S
MIKVAHS
MIKVEH S
MIKVEHS

MIKVOS
MIKVOT H
MIKVOTH
MIL DEKLOST
MILADI S
MILADIES
IDEALISM
MILADIS
MISDIAL
MISLAID
MILADY
MILAGE S
MILAGES
MILCH
MILCHIG
MILD S
MILDED
MIDDLE
MILDEN S
LIMNED
MILDENED
MILDENS
MILDER
MILDEST
MILDEW SY
MILDEWED
MILDEWS
MILDEWY
MILDING
MILDLY
MILDNESS
MINDLESS
MILDS
S MILE RS
LIME
MILEAGE S
MILEAGES
GELSEMIA
MILEPOST S
POLEMIST
S MILER S
S MILERS
SMILER
S MILES
LIMES SLIME
SMILE
MILESIAN
ALIENISM
MILESIMO S
MILFOIL S
MILFOILS
MILIA
MILIARIA LS
MILIARY
MILIEU SX
MILIEUS
MILIEUX
MILITANT S
MILITARY
LIMITARY
MILITATE DS
MILITIA S
MILITIAS
MILIUM
MILK SY
MILKED
MILKER S
MILKERS
MILKFISH
MILKIER
MILKIEST
MILKILY
MILKING
MILKLESS
MILKMAID S
MILKMAN
MILKMEN
MILKS
MILKSHED S
MILKSOP S
MILKSOPS
MILKWEED S
MILKWOOD S
MILKWORT S
MILKY
MILL ES
MILLABLE

MILLAGE S
MEGILLA
MILLAGES
LEGALISM
MEGILLAS
MILLCAKE S
CLAMLIKE
MILLDAM S
MILLDAMS
MILLE DRST
MILLED
MILLEPED ES
IMPELLED
MILLER S
MILLERS
MILLES
MILLET S
MILLETS
MILLIARD S
MILLIARE S
RAMILLIE
MILLIARY
MILLIBAR S
MILLIEME S
MILLIER S
MILLIERS
MILLIGAL S
MILLILUX
MILLIME S
MILLIMES
MILLIMHO S
MILLIOHM
MILLINE RS
MILLINER SY
MILLINES
MILLING S
MILLINGS
MILLIOHM S
MILLIMHO
MILLION S
MILLIONS
MILLIPED ES
MILLIREM S
MILLPOND S
MILLRACE S
MICELLAR
MILLRUN S
MILLRUNS
MILLS
MILLWORK S
MILNEB S
NIMBLE
MILNEBS
MILO S
LIMO MOIL
MILORD S
MILORDS
MILOS
LIMOS MOILS
MILPA S
LIMPA
MILPAS
LIMPAS
MILREIS
SLIMIER
MILS
SLIM
MILT SY
MILTED
MILTER S
MILTERS
MILTIER
LIMITER
MILTIEST
MISTITLE
MILTING
MILTS
MILTY
MIM E
MIMBAR S
MIMBARS
MIME DORS
MIMED
MIMEO S
MIMEOED
MIMEOING
MIMEOS
MIMER S

MIMERS
SIMMER
MIMES
MIMESES
MIMESIS
MIMETIC
MIMETITE S
MIMIC S
MIMICAL
MIMICKED
MIMICKER S
MIMICRY
MIMICS
MIMING
MIMOSA S
MIMOSAS
MINA ES
AMIN MAIN
MINABLE
MINACITY
INTIMACY
MINAE
AMINE ANIME
MINARET S
RAIMENT
MINARETS
RAIMENTS
MINAS
AMINS MAINS
MINATORY
MINCE DRS
MINCED
MINCER S
MINCERS
MINCES
MINCIER
CREMINI
CRIMINE
MINCIEST
MINCING
MINCY
MIND S
MINDED
MIDDEN
MINDER S
REMIND
MINDERS
REMINDS
MINDFUL
MINDING
MINDLESS
MILDNESS
MINDS
MINDSET S
MISTEND
MINDSETS
MISTENDS
AI MINE DRS
MIEN
MINEABLE
MINED
DENIM
MINER S
MINERAL S
MANLIER
MARLINE
MINERALS
MARLINES
MISLEARN
MINERS
AI MINES
MIENS
MINGIER
MINGIEST
MINGLE DRS
MINGLED
MELDING
MINGLER S
GREMLIN
MINGLERS
GREMLINS
MINGLES
MINGLING
MINGY
MINI MS
MINIBAR S
MINIBARS
BINARISM
MINIBIKE RS
MINIBUS
MINICAB S

MINICABS
MINICAM PS
MINICAMP S
MINICAMS
MINICAR S
MINICARS
MINIDISC S
MINIFIED
MINIFIES
MINIFY
MINIKIN S
MINIKINS
MINILAB S
MINILABS
ALBINISM
MINIM AS
MINIMA LX
MINIMAL S
MINIMALS
MINIMAX
MAXIMIN
MINIMILL S
MINIMISE DS
MINIMIZE DR S
MINIMS
MINIMUM S
MINIMUMS
MINING S
MININGS
MINION S
MINIONS
MINIPARK S
MINIPILL S
MINIS H
MINISH
MINISHED
MINISHES
MINISKI S
MINISKIS
MINISTER S
INTERIMS
MISINTER
MINISTRY
MINIUM S
MINIUMS
MINIVAN S
MINIVANS
MINIVER S
MINIVERS
MINK ES
MINKE S
MINKES
MINKS
MINNIES
MINNOW S
MINNOWS
MINNY
MINOR S
MINORCA S
MINORCAS
MINORED
MINORING
MINORITY
MINORS
MINSTER S
MINTERS
REMINTS
MINSTERS
TRIMNESS
MINSTREL S
MINT SY
MINTAGE S
TEAMING
TEGMINA
MINTAGES
MANGIEST
MISAGENT
STEAMING
MINTED
MINTER S
REMINT
MINTERS
MINSTER
REMINTS

MINTIER
INTERIM
TERMINI
MINTIEST
MINTING
MINTS
MINTY
MINUEND S
UNMINED
MINUENDS
MINUET S
MINUTE
MUTINE
MINUETS
MINUTES
MISTUNE
MUTINES
MINUS
MUNIS
MINUSES
MINUTE DRS
MINUET
MUTINE
MINUTED
MUTINED
UNTIMED
MINUTELY
UNTIMELY
MINUTER
UNMITER
UNMITRE
MINUTES T
MINUETS
MISTUNE
MUTINES
MINUTEST
MINUTIA EL
MINUTIAE
MINUTIAL
MINUTING
MUTINING
MINX
MINXES
MINXISH
MINYAN S
MINYANIM
MINYANS
MIOCENE
MIOSES
MIOSIS
MIOTIC S
MIOTICS
SOMITIC
MIPS
IMPS SIMP
MIQUELET S
AE MIR EIKSY
RIM
MIRACLE S
CLAIMER
RECLAIM
MIRACLES
CLAIMERS
RECLAIMS
MIRADOR S
MIRADORS
MIRAGE S
GAMIER
IMAGER
MAIGRE
MIRAGES
GISARME
IMAGERS
MIRE DSX
EMIR RIME
MIRED
DIMER RIMED
MIREPOIX
MIRES
EMIRS MISER
RIMES
MIREX
MIXER REMIX
MIREXES
REMIXES
MIRI N
MIRIER
RIMIER
MIRIEST
MISTIER
RIMIEST
MIRIN GS

MIRINESS
RIMINESS
MIRING
RIMING
MIRINS
S MIRK SY
S MIRKER
MIRKEST
S MIRKIER
S MIRKIEST
S MIRKILY
S MIRKS
SMIRK
S MIRKY
MIRLITON S
MIRROR S
MIRRORED
MIRRORS
AE MIRS
RIMS
MIRTH S
MIRTHFUL
MIRTHS
MIRY
RIMY
MIRZA S
ZIRAM
MIRZAS
ZIRAMS
A MIS EOST
ISM
SIM
MISACT S
MASTIC
MISACTED
MISACTS
MASTICS
MISCAST
MISADAPT S
MISADD S
MISADDED
MISADDS
MISAGENT S
MANGIEST
MINTAGES
STEAMING
MISAIM S
MISAIMED
MISAIMS
MISALIGN S
MAILINGS
MISALLOT S
MAILLOTS
MISALLY
MISALTER S
LAMISTER
MARLIEST
MARLITES
MISANDRY
MISAPPLY
MISASSAY S
MISATE
MISEAT
SAMITE
MISATONE DS
AMNIOTES
MASONITE
MISAVER S
MISAVERS
MISAWARD S
MISBEGAN
MISBEGIN S
MISBEGOT
MISBEGUN
BEMUSING
MISBIAS
MISBILL S
MISBILLS
MISBIND S
MISBINDS
MISBOUND
MISBRAND S
MISBUILD S
MISBUILT
SUBLIMIT
MISCALL S
MISCALLS
MISCARRY

MISCAST S
MASTICS
MISACTS
MISCASTS
MISCHIEF S
MISCHOSE N
ECHOISMS
MISCIBLE
MISCITE DS
MISCITED
MISCITES
MISCLAIM S
MISCLASS
CLASSISM
MISCODE DS
MEDICOS
MISCODED
MISCODES
MISCOIN S
MISCOINS
MISCOLOR S
COLORISM
MISCOOK S
MISCOOKS
MISCOPY
MISCOUNT S
MISCUE DS
CESIUM
MISCUED
MISCUES
CESIUMS
MISCUING
MISCUT S
MISCUTS
MISDATE DS
DIASTEM
MISDATED
MISDATES
DIASTEMS
MISDEAL ST
MEDIALS
MISLEAD
MISDEALS
MISLEADS
MISDEALT
MEDALIST
MISDEED S
DEMISED
MISDEEDS
MISDEEM S
MISDEEMS
MISDIAL S
MILADIS
MISLAID
MISDIALS
MISDID
MISDO
MISDOER S
MISDOERS
MISDOES
MISDOING S
MISDONE
DOMINES
EMODINS
MISDOUBT S
MISDRAW NS
MISDRAWN
MISDRAWS
MISDREW
MISDRIVE NS
MISDROVE
MISE RS
SEMI
MISEASE S
SIAMESE
MISEASES
SIAMESES
MISEAT S
MISATE
SAMITE
MISEATEN
ETAMINES
MATINEES
MISEATS
MISSEAT
SAMITES
TAMISES
MISEDIT S
STIMIED
MISEDITS
MISENROL LS

MISENTER S
MISENTRY
MISER SY
EMIRS MIRES
RIMES
MISERERE S
MISERIES
MISERLY
MISRELY
MISERS
REMISS
MISERY
MISES
SEISM SEMIS
MISEVENT S
MISFAITH S
MISFED
MISFEED S
MISFEEDS
MISFIELD S
MISFILED
MISFILE DS
MISFILED
MISFIELD
MISFILES
FLIMSIES
MISFIRE DS
MISFIRED
MISFIRES
MISFIT S
MISFITS
MISFOCUS
MISFORM S
MISFORMS
MISFRAME DS
MISGAUGE DS
MISGAVE
MISGIVE NS
MISGIVEN
MISGIVES
MISGRADE DS
MISGRAFT S
MISGREW
MISGROW NS
MISGROWN
MISGROWS
MISGUESS
MISGUIDE DR S
MISHAP S
MISHAPS
MISHEAR DS
MISHEARD
SEMIHARD
MISHEARS
MARISHES
MISHIT S
ISTHMI
MISHITS
MISHMASH
MISHMOSH
MISINFER S
MISINTER S
INTERIMS
MINISTER
MISJOIN S
MISJOINS
MISJUDGE DS
MISKAL S
MISKALS
MISKEEP S
MISKEEPS
MISKEPT
MISKICK S
MISKICKS
MISKNEW
MISKNOW NS
MISKNOWN
MISKNOWS
MISLABEL S
MISLABOR S
MISLAID
MILADIS
MISDIAL
MISLAIN
MISLAY S
MISLAYER S

MISLAYS
MISLEAD S
MEDIALS
MISDEAL
MISLEADS
MISDEALS
MISLEARN ST
MARLINES
MINERALS
MISLED
SLIMED
SMILED
MISLIE S
SIMILE
MISLIES
MISSILE
SIMILES
MISLIGHT S
MISLIKE DRS
MISLIKED
MISLIKER S
MISLIKES
MISLIT
LIMITS
MISLIVE DS
MISLIVED
MIDLIVES
MISLIVES
MISLODGE DS
MISLYING
MISMADE
MISMAKE S
MISMAKES
MISMARK S
MISMARKS
MISMATCH
MISMATE DS
SEMIMAT
TAMMIES
MISMATED
MISMATES
MISMEET S
MISMEETS
MISMET
MISMOVE DS
MISMOVED
MISMOVES
MISNAME DS
AMMINES
MISNAMED
MISNAMES
MISNOMER S
MISO S
MISOGAMY
MISOGYNY
MISOLOGY
MISORDER S
MISOS
MISPAGE DS
MAGPIES
MISPAGED
MEDIGAPS
MISPAGES
MISPAINT S
IMPAINTS
MISPARSE DS
IMPRESAS
MISPART S
ARMPITS
IMPARTS
MISPARTS
MISPATCH
MISPEN S
MISPENS
MISPLACE DS
MISPLAN ST
PLASMIN
MISPLANS
PLASMINS
MISPLANT S
IMPLANTS
MISPLAY S
MISPLAYS
MISPLEAD S
IMPLEADS
MISPLED
DIMPLES
MISPOINT S
MISPOISE DS

MISPRICE DS
EMPIRICS
MISPRINT S
IMPRINTS
MISPRIZE DR S
MISQUOTE DR S
MISRAISE DS
MISRATE DS
IMARETS
MAESTRI
SMARTIE
MISRATED
READMITS
MISRATES
ASTERISM
SMARTIES
MISREAD S
ADMIRES
SEDARIM
SIDEARM
MISREADS
SIDEARMS
MISREFER S
MISRELY
MISERLY
MISROUTE DS
MOISTURE
MISRULE DS
MISRULED
MISRULES
A **MISS** Y
ISMS SIMS
MISSABLE
ABLEISMS
MISSAID
MISSAL S
SALMIS
MISSALS
MISSAY S
MYASIS
MISSAYS
MISSEAT S
MISEATS
SAMITES
TAMISES
MISSEATS
MASSIEST
MISSED
DEISMS
DISMES
MISSEL S
SLIMES
SMILES
MISSELS
MISSEND S
DIMNESS
MISSENDS
MISSENSE S
MISSENT
MISSES
SEISMS
MISSET S
SMITES
STIMES
TMESIS
MISSETS
MISSHAPE DN RS
EMPHASIS
MISSHOD
MISSIES
MISSILE S
MISLIES
SIMILES
MISSILES
MISSILRY
MISSING
EO **MISSION** S
EO **MISSIONS**
MISSIS
MISSISES
EO **MISSIVE** S
MISSIVES
MISSORT S
MISSORTS
MISSOUND S
MISSOUT S
SUMOIST
MISSOUTS
SUMOISTS

MISSPACE DS
ESCAPISM
SCAMPIES
MISSPEAK S
MISSPELL S
MISSPELT
SIMPLEST
MISSPEND S
MISSPENT
MISSPOKE N
MISSTAMP S
MISSTART S
MISSTATE DS
ETATISMS
MISSTEER S
MEISTERS
TRISEMES
MISSTEP S
MISSTEPS
MISSTOP S
IMPOSTS
MISSTOPS
MISSTYLE DS
MISSUIT S
MISSUITS
MISSUS
MISSUSES
MISSY
MIST SY
SMIT
MISTAKE NRS
MISTAKEN
MISTAKER S
MISTAKES
MISTBOW S
MISTBOWS
MISTEACH
HEMATICS
MASTICHE
TACHISME
MISTED
DEMITS
MISTEND S
MINDSET
MISTENDS
MINDSETS
MISTER MS
MERITS
MITERS
MITRES
REMITS
SMITER
TIMERS
MISTERM S
MISTERMS
MISTERS
SMITERS
MISTEUK
MISTHINK S
MISTHREW
MISTHROW NS
MISTIER
MIRIEST
RIMIEST
MISTIEST
SEMITIST
MISTILY
MISTIME DS
MISTIMED
MISTIMES
MISTING
SMITING
TIMINGS
MISTITLE DS
MILTIEST
MISTOOK
MISTOUCH
MISTRACE DS
CERAMIST
MATRICES
SCIMETAR
MISTRAIN S
MARTINIS
MISTRAL S
RAMTILS
MISTRALS
MISTREAT S
TERATISM
MISTRESS
MISTRIAL S

MISTRUST S
MISTRUTH S
MISTRYST S
MISTS
MISTUNE DS
MINUETS
MINUTES
MUTINES
MISTUNED
MISTUNES
MISTUTOR S
MISTY
STIMY
MISTYPE DS
MISTYPED
MISTYPES
MISUNION S
UNIONISM
MISUSAGE S
MISUSE DRS
MISUSED
MISUSER S
MUSSIER
SURMISE
MISUSERS
SURMISES
MISUSES
MISUSING
MISVALUE DS
MISWORD S
MISWORDS
MISWRIT E
MISWRITE S
MISWROTE
WORMIEST
MISYOKE DS
MISYOKED
MISYOKES
S **MITE** RS
EMIT ITEM
TIME
S **MITER** S
MERIT MITRE
REMIT TIMER
MITERED
DEMERIT
DIMETER
MERITED
RETIMED
MITERER S
TRIREME
MITERERS
MERRIEST
RIMESTER
TRIREMES
MITERING
MERITING
RETIMING
S **MITERS**
MERITS
MISTER
MITRES
REMITS
SMITER
TIMERS
S **MITES**
EMITS ITEMS
METIS SMITE
STIME TIMES
MITHER S
HERMIT
S **MITHERS**
HERMITS
MITICIDE S
MITIER
MITIEST
MITIGATE DS
MITIS
MITISES
STIMIES
MITOGEN S
EMOTING
MITOGENS
A **MITOSES**
SOMITES
A **MITOSIS**
A **MITOTIC**
MITRAL
RAMTIL

MITRE DS
MERIT MITER
REMIT TIMER
MITRED
MITRES
MERITS
MISTER
MITERS
REMITS
SMITER
TIMERS
MITRING
MITSVAH S
MITSVAHS
MITSVOTH
MITT S
S **MITTEN** S
TITMEN
MITTENED
MITTENS
SMITTEN
MITTIMUS
MITTS
A **MITY**
MITZVAH S
MITZVAHS
MITZVOTH
MIX T
MIXABLE
MIXED
MIXEDLY
MIXER S
MIREX REMIX
MIXERS
MIXES
MIXIBLE
MIXING
MIXOLOGY
MIXT
MIXTURE S
MIXTURES
MIXUP S
MIXUPS
MIZEN S
MIZENS
MIZUNA S
MIZUNAS
MIZZEN S
MIZZENS
MIZZLE DS
MIZZLED
MIZZLES
MIZZLING
MIZZLY
HU **MM**
MNEMONIC S
MO ABCDGLMN OM OPRSTW
MOA NST
MOAN S
MANO NOMA
MOANED
DAEMON
MOANER S
ENAMOR
MOANERS
ENAMORS
OARSMEN
MOANFUL
MOANING
MOANS
MANOS MASON
MONAS NOMAS
SOMAN
MOAS
SOMA
MOAT S
ATOM
MOATED
MOATING
MOATLIKE
MOATS
ATOMS STOMA
MOB S
MOBBED
BOMBED
MOBBER S
BOMBER

MOBBERS
BOMBERS
MOBBING
BOMBING
MOBBISH
MOBBISM S
MOBBISMS
MOBCAP S
MOBCAPS
MOBILE S
EMBOLI
MOBILES
OBELISM
MOBILISE DS
MOBILITY
MOBILIZE DR S
MOBLED
MOBOCRAT S
MOBS
MOBSTER S
MOBSTERS
MOC KS
MOCCASIN S
MOCHA S
MACHO
MOCHAS
MACHOS
MOCHILA S
MOCHILAS
S MOCK S
MOCKABLE
S MOCKED
MOCKER SY
MOCKERS
MOCKERY
S MOCKING
S MOCKS
SMOCK
MOCKTAIL S
MOCKUP S
MOCKUPS
MOCS
MOD EIS
DOM
MODAL S
DOLMA DOMAL
MODALITY
MODALLY
MODALS
DOLMAS
MODE LMS
DEMO DOME
MODEL S
MODELED
MODELER S
REMODEL
MODELERS
MORSELED
REMODELS
MODELING S
MODELIST S
MELODIST
MOLDIEST
MODELLED
MODELLER S
MODELS
SELDOM
MODEM S
MODEMED
MODEMING
MODEMS
MODERATE DS
MODERATO RS
MODERN ES
NORMED
RODMEN
MODERNE RS
MODERNER
MODERNES T
MODERNLY
MODERNS
RODSMEN
MODES T
DEMOS DOMES
MODEST Y
MODESTER
MODESTLY
MODESTY

MODI
MODICA
MODICUM S
MODICUMS
MODIFIED
MODIFIER S
MODIFIES
MODIFY
MODIOLI
MODIOLUS
MODISH
MODISHLY
MODISTE S
DISTOME
MODISTES
DISTOMES
MODS
DOMS
MODULAR S
MODULARS
MODULATE DS
MODULE S
MODULES
MODULI
MODULO
MODULUS
MODUS
DOUMS
MOFETTE S
MOFETTES
MOFFETTE S
S MOG S
MOGGED
MOGGIE S
MOGGIES
MOGGING
S MOGGY
MOGHUL S
MOGHULS
S MOGS
SMOG
MOGUL S
MOGULED
MOGULS
GLOMUS
MOHAIR S
MOHAIRS
MOHALIM
MOHAWK S
MOHAWKS
MOHEL S
MOHELIM
MOHELS
MOHUR S
HUMOR
MOHURS
HUMORS
MOIDORE S
DOOMIER
MOODIER
MOIDORES
MOIETIES
MOIETY
MOIL S
LIMO MILO
MOILED
MELOID
MOILER S
MOILERS
MOILING
MOILS
LIMOS MILOS
MOIRA I
MOIRAI
MOIRE S
MOIRES
ISOMER
RIMOSE
MOIST
OMITS
MOISTEN S
MESTINO
SENTIMO
MOISTENS
MESTINOS
SENTIMOS

MOISTER
EROTISM
MORTISE
TRISOME
MOISTEST
MOISTFUL
MOISTLY
MOISTURE S
MISROUTE
MOJARRA S
MOJARRAS
MOJO S
MOJOES
MOJOS
S MOKE S
S MOKES
SMOKE
MOL ADELSTY
MOLA LRS
LOAM
MOLAL
MOLALITY
MOLAR S
MORAL
MOLARITY
MORALITY
MOLARS
MORALS
MOLAS
LOAMS
MOLASSES
MOLD SY
MOLDABLE
MOLDED
S MOLDER S
REMOLD
S MOLDERED
REMOLDED
S MOLDERS
REMOLDS
SMOLDER
MOLDIER
MOLDIEST
MELODIST
MODELIST
MOLDING S
MOLDINGS
MOLDS
MOLDWARP S
MOLDY
A MOLE S
MOLECULE S
MOLEHILL S
A MOLES T
MOLESKIN S
MOLEST S
METOLS
MOTELS
MOLESTED
MOLESTER S
MOLESTS
MOLIES
MOLINE
LOMEIN
OILMEN
MOLL SY
MOLLAH S
MOLLAHS
MOLLIE S
MOLLIES
MOLLIFY
MOLLS
MOLLUSC AS
MOLLUSCA N
MOLLUSCS
MOLLUSK S
MOLLUSKS
MOLLY
MOLOCH S
MOLOCHS
MOLS
S MOLT OS
MOLTED
MOLTEN
LOMENT
MELTON
MOLTENLY
MOLTER S
MERLOT

MOLTERS
MERLOTS
MOLTING
MOLTO
S MOLTS
SMOLT
MOLY
MOLYBDIC
MOM EIS
MOME S
MEMO
MOMENT AOS
MOMENTA
MOMENTLY
MOMENTO S
MOMENTOS
MOMENTS
MOMENTUM S
MOMES
MEMOS
MOMI
MOMISM S
MOMISMS
MOMMA S
MOMMAS
MOMMIES
MOMMY
MOMS
MOMSER S
MOMSERS
MOMUS
MOMUSES
MOMZER S
MOMZERS
MON KOSY
NOM
MONACHAL
MONACID S
MONADIC
NOMADIC
MONACIDS
MONAD S
NOMAD
MONADAL
MANDOLA
MONADES
DAEMONS
MASONED
MONADIC
MONACID
NOMADIC
MONADISM S
NOMADISM
MONADS
DAMSON
NOMADS
MONANDRY
MONARCH SY
NOMARCH
MONARCHS
NOMARCHS
MONARCHY
NOMARCHY
MONARDA S
MADRONA
MONARDAS
MADRONAS
MONAS
MANOS MASON
MOANS NOMAS
SOMAN
MONASTIC S
MONAURAL
MONAXIAL
MONAXON S
MONAXONS
MONAZITE S
MONDE S
DEMON
MONDES
DEMONS
MONDO S
MONDOS
MONECIAN
MONELLIN S
MONERAN S
MONERANS
SONARMEN
MONETARY

MONETISE DS
SEMITONE
MONETIZE DS
ZONETIME
MONEY S
MONEYBAG S
BOGEYMAN
MONEYED
MONEYER S
MONEYERS
MONEYMAN
MONEYMEN
MONEYS
MONGEESE
MONGER S
MORGEN
MONGERED
MONGERS
MORGENS
MONGO ELS
MONGOE S
MONGOES
MONGOL S
MONGOLS
MONGOOSE S
MONGOS
MONGREL S
MONGRELS
A MONGST
MONICKER S
MONIE DS
MONIED
DOMINE
EMODIN
MONIES
EONISM
MONIKER S
MONIKERS
MONISH
MONISHED
HEDONISM
MONISHES
HOMINESS
MONISM S
NOMISM
MONISMS
NOMISMS
MONIST S
INMOST
MONISTIC
NOMISTIC
MONISTS
MONITION S
MONITIVE
MONITOR SY
MONITORS
MONITORY
MORONITY
MONK S
MONKERY
MONKEY S
MONKEYED
MONKEYS
MONKFISH
MONKHOOD S
MONKISH
MONKS
MONO S
MOON
MONOACID S
MONOCARP S
CRAMPOON
MONOCLE DS
MONOCLED
MONOCLES
MONOCOT S
MONOCOTS
MONOCRAT S
MONOCYTE S
MONODIC
MONODIES
DOMINOES
MONODIST S
MONODY
MONOECY
ECONOMY
MONOFIL S
MONOFILS
MONOFUEL S

MONOGAMY
MONOGENY
MONOGERM
MONOGLOT S
MONOGRAM S
NOMOGRAM
MONOGYNY
MONOHULL S
MONOKINE S
MONOLITH S
MONOLOG SY
MONOLOGS
MONOLOGY
NOMOLOGY
MONOMER S
MONOMERS
MONOMIAL S
MONOPOD ESY
MONOPODE S
MONOPODS
MONOPODY
MONOPOLE S
MONOPOLY
MONORAIL S
MONOS
MOONS NOMOS
MONOSOME S
MONOSOMY
MONOTINT S
MONOTONE S
MONOTONY
MONOTYPE S
MONOXIDE S
MONS
NOMS
MONSIEUR
MONSOON S
MONSOONS
MONSTER AS
MENTORS
MONSTERA S
ONSTREAM
TONEARMS
MONSTERS
MONTAGE DS
MAGNETO
MEGATON
MONTAGED
MONTAGES
MAGNETOS
MEGATONS
MONTANE S
NONMEAT
MONTANES
MONTE S
MONTEITH S
MONTERO S
MONTEROS
MESOTRON
MONTES
MONTH S
MONTHLY
MONTHS
MONUMENT S
MONURON S
MONURONS
MONY
MOO DLNRST
S MOOCH
S MOOCHED
S MOOCHER S
S MOOCHERS
SMOOCHER
S MOOCHES
S MOOCHING
MOOD SY
DOOM
MOODIER
DOOMIER
MOIDORE
MOODIEST
DOOMIEST
SODOMITE
MOODILY
DOOMILY
MOODS
DOOMS SODOM
MOODY
DOOMY

MOOED
MOOING
MOOL AS
LOOM
MOOLA HS
MOOLAH S
MOOLAHS
MOOLAS
MOOLEY S
MOOLEYS
MOOLS
LOOMS OSMOL
MOON SY
MONO
MOONBEAM S
MOONBOW S
MOONBOWS
MOONCALF
MOONDUST S
MOONED
MOONER S
MOONERS
MOONEYE S
MOONEYES
MOONFISH
MOONIER
IONOMER
MOONIEST
EMOTIONS
MOONILY
MOONING
MOONISH
MOONLESS
MOONLET S
MOONLETS
MOONLIKE
MOONLIT
MOONPORT S
MOONRISE S
IONOMERS
MOONROOF S
MOONS
MONOS NOMOS
MOONSAIL S
MOONSEED S
ENDOSOME
MOONSET S
MOONSETS
MOOTNESS
MOONSHOT S
MOONWALK S
MOONWARD S
MOONWORT S
MOONY
MOOR SY
ROOM
MOORAGE S
MOORAGES
MOORCOCK S
MOORED
ROOMED
MOORFOWL S
MOORHEN S
HORMONE
MOORHENS
HORMONES
MOORIER
ROOMIER
MOORIEST
MOTORISE
ROOMIEST
MOORING S
ROOMING
MOORINGS
MOORISH
MOORLAND S
MOORS
ROOMS
MOORWORT S
ROOTWORM
TOMORROW
WORMROOT
MOORY
ROOMY
MOOS E
MOOSE
MOOT S
TOOM
MOOTED
MOOTER S

MOOTERS
MOOTING
MOOTNESS
MOONSETS
MOOTS
MOP ESY
MOPBOARD S
MOPE DRSY
POEM POME
MOPED S
MOPEDS
MOPER SY
PROEM
MOPERIES
PROMISEE REIMPOSE
MOPERS
PROEMS
MOPERY
MOPES
POEMS POMES
MOPEY
MYOPE
MOPIER
MOPIEST
OPTIMES
MOPINESS
PEONISMS
MOPING
MOPINGLY
MOPISH
MOPISHLY
MOPOKE S
MOPOKES
MOPPED
MOPPER S
MOPPERS
MOPPET S
MOPPETS
MOPPING
MOPS
MOPY
MOQUETTE S
MOR AENST
ROM
MORA ELSY
ROAM
MORAE
MORAINAL
MANORIAL
MORAINE S
ROMAINE
MORAINES
ROMAINES ROMANISE
MORAINIC
A MORAL ES
MOLAR
MORALE S
MORALES
MORALISE DS
A MORALISM S
MORALIST S
A MORALITY
MOLARITY
MORALIZE DRS
A MORALLY
MORALS
MOLARS
MORAS S
ROAMS
MORASS Y
MORASSES
MORASSY
MORATORY
MORAY S
MAYOR
MORAYS
MAYORS
MORBID
BROMID
MORBIDLY
MORBIFIC
MORBILLI
MORCEAU X
MORCEAUX
MORDANCY
DORMANCY
MORDANT S
DORMANT

MORDANTS
MORDENT S
MORDENTS
MORE LS
OMER
MOREEN S
MOREENS
MOREL S
MORELLE S
MORELLES
MORELLO S
MORELLOS
MORELS
MORSEL
MORENESS
MOREOVER
MORES
MORSE OMERS
MORESQUE S
MORGAN S
MORGANS
MORGEN S
MONGER
MORGENS
MONGERS
MORGUE S
MORGUES
GRUMOSE
MORIBUND
MORION S
MORIONS
MORN S
NORM
MORNING S
MORNINGS
MORNS
NORMS
MOROCCO S
MOROCCOS
MORON S
MORONIC
OMICRON
MORONISM S
MORONITY
MONITORY
MORONS
MOROSE
ROMEOS
MOROSELY
MOROSITY
MORPH OS
MORPHED
MORPHEME S
MORPHIA S
MORPHIAS
APHORISM
MORPHIC
MORPHIN EGS
MORPHINE S
MORPHING S
MORPHINS
MORPHO S
MORPHOS
MORPHS
MORRION S
MORRIONS
MORRIS
MORRISES
MORRO SW
MORROS
MORROW S
MORROWS
MORS E
ROMS
MORSE L
MORES OMERS
MORSEL S
MORELS
MORSELED
MODELERS REMODELS
MORSELS
A MORT S
MORTAL S
MORTALLY
MORTALS
STROMAL
MORTAR SY
MORTARED

MORTARS
MORTARY
MORTGAGE DERS
MORTICE DS
MORTICED
MORTICES
MORTIFY
A MORTISE DRS
EROTISM MOISTER TRISOME
A MORTISED
MORTISER S
STORMIER
A MORTISES
EROTISMS TRISOMES
MORTMAIN S
MORTS
STORM
MORTUARY
MORULA ERS
MORULAE
MORULAR
MORULAS
MOS HKST
OMS SOM
MOSAIC S
MOSAICS
MOSASAUR S
MOSCHATE L
MOSEY S
MOSEYED
MOSEYING
MOSEYS
MYOSES
MOSH
MHOS OHMS SHMO
MOSHAV
MOSHAVIM
MOSHED
MOSHER S
HOMERS
MOSHERS
MOSHES
SHMOES
MOSHING S
GNOMISH
MOSHINGS
MOSK S
MOSKS
MOSQUE S
MOSQUES
MOSQUITO S
MOSS OY
SOMS
MOSSBACK S
MOSSED
MOSSER S
MOSSERS
MOSSES
MOSSIER
ISOMERS
MOSSIEST
MOSSING
MOSSLIKE
MOSSO
MOSSY
MOST ES
MOTS TOMS
MOSTE
MOTES SMOTE TOMES
MOSTEST S
MOSTESTS
MOSTLY
MOSTS
MOT EHST
TOM
ES MOTE LSTY
TOME
MOTEL S
METOL
MOTELS
METOLS MOLEST

E MOTES
MOSTE SMOTE TOMES
MOTET S
MOTTE TOTEM
MOTETS
MOTTES TOTEMS
MOTEY
MOTH SY
MOTHBALL S
S MOTHER SY
S MOTHERED
MOTHERLY
S MOTHERS
SMOTHER THERMOS
S MOTHERY
MOTHIER
MOTHIEST
MOTHLIKE
MOTHS
MOTHY
MOTIF S
MOTIFIC
MOTIFS
MOTILE S
MOTILES
MOTILITY
AE MOTION S
E MOTIONAL
MOTIONED
DEMOTION
MOTIONER S
REMOTION
AE MOTIONS
MOTIVATE DS
E MOTIVE DS
MOTIVED
VOMITED
MOTIVES
MOTIVIC
MOTIVING
VOMITING
E MOTIVITY
MOTLEY S
MOTLEYER
REMOTELY
MOTLEYS
MOTLIER
MOTLIEST
MOTMOT S
MOTMOTS
MOTOR S
MOTORBUS
MOTORCAR S
MOTORDOM S
MOTORED
MOTORIC
MOTORING S
MOTORISE DS
MOORIEST ROOMIEST
MOTORIST S
MOTORIZE DS
MOTORMAN
MOTORMEN
MOTORS
MOTORWAY S
MOTS
MOST TOMS
MOTT EOS
MOTTE S
MOTET TOTEM
MOTTES
MOTETS TOTEMS
MOTTLE DRS
MOTTLED
MOTTLER S
MOTTLERS
MOTTLES
MOTTLING
MOTTO S
MOTTOES
MOTTOS
MOTTS

MOUCH
MUCHO
MOUCHED
MOUCHES
MOUCHING
MOUCHOIR S
MOUE S
MEOU
MOUES
MEOUS MOUSE
MOUFFLON S
MOUFLON S
MOUFLONS
MOUILLE
MOUJIK S
MOUJIKS
MOULAGE S
MOULAGES
MOULD SY
MOULDED
S MOULDER S
S MOULDERS
SMOULDER
MOULDIER
LEMUROID
MOULDING S
MOULDS
MOULDY
MOULIN S
MOULINS
MOULT S
MOULTED
MOULTER S
MOULTERS
MOULTING
MOULTS
MOUND S
MOUNDED
MOUNDING
MOUNDS
OSMUND
A MOUNT S
MUTON NOTUM
MOUNTAIN SY
A MOUNTED
DEMOUNT
MOUNTER S
REMOUNT
MOUNTERS
REMOUNTS
A MOUNTING S
A MOUNTS
MUTONS
MOURN S
MOURNED
MOURNER S
MOURNERS
MOURNFUL
MOURNING S
MOURNS
MOUSAKA S
MOUSAKAS
MOUSSAKA
MOUSE DRSY
MEOUS MOUES
MOUSED
ODEUMS
MOUSEPAD S
MOUSER S
MOUSERS
MOUSES
MOUSSE
MOUSEY
MOUSIER
MOUSIEST
MOUSILY
MOUSING S
MOUSINGS
MOUSSING
MOUSSAKA S
MOUSAKAS
MOUSSE DS
MOUSES
MOUSSED
MOUSSES
MOUSSING
MOUSINGS
MOUSY
MOUTH SY

MOUTHED
MOUTHER S
MOUTHERS
MOUTHFUL S
MOUTHIER
MOUTHILY
MOUTHING
MOUTHS
MOUTHY
MOUTON S
MOUTONS
MOVABLE S
MOVABLES
MOVABLY
MOVE DRS
MOVEABLE S
MOVEABLY
MOVED
MOVELESS
MOVEMENT S
MOVER S
VOMER
MOVERS
VOMERS
MOVES
MOVIE S
MOVIEDOM S
MOVIEOLA S
MOVIES
MOVING
MOVINGLY
MOVIOLA S
MOVIOLAS
MOW NS
MOWED
MOWER S
MOWERS
MOWING S
MOWINGS
MOWN
MOWS
MOXA S
MOXAS
MOXIE S
OXIME
MOXIES
OXIMES
MOZETTA S
MOZETTAS
MOZETTE
MOZO S
ZOOM
MOZOS
ZOOMS
MOZZETTA S
MOZZETTE
MRIDANGA MS
AE MU DGMNST
UM
MUCH O
CHUM
MUCHACHO S
MUCHES
MUCHLY
MUCHNESS
MUCHO
MOUCH
MUCID
MUCIDITY
MUCILAGE S
MUCIN S
CUMIN
MUCINOID
CONIDIUM ONCIDIUM
MUCINOUS
MUCINS
CUMINS
A MUCK SY
MUCKED
MUCKER S
MUCKERS
MUCKIER
MUCKIEST
MUCKILY
MUCKING
MUCKLE S

MUCKLES
MUCKLUCK S
MUCKRAKE DRS
A MUCKS
MUCKWORM S
MUCKY
MUCLUC S
MUCLUCS
MUCOID S
MUCOIDAL
MUCOIDS
MUCOR S
MUCRO
MUCORS
MUCOSA ELS
MUCOSAE
MUCOSAL
MUCOSAS
MUCOSE
MUCOSITY
MUCOUS
MUCRO
MUCOR
MUCRONES
CONSUMER
MUCUS
MUCUSES
MUD S
MUDBUG S
MUDBUGS
MUDCAP S
MUDCAPS
MUDCAT S
MUDCATS
MUDDED
MUDDER S
MUDDERS
MUDDIED
MUDDIER
MUDDIES T
MUDDIEST
MUDDILY
MUDDING
MUDDLE DRS
MUDDLED
MUDDLER S
MUDDLERS
MUDDLES
MUDDLING
MUDDLY
MUDDY
MUDDYING
MUDFISH
MUDFLAP S
MUDFLAPS
MUDFLAT S
MUDFLATS
MUDFLOW S
MUDFLOWS
MUDGUARD S
MUDHEN S
MUDHENS
MUDHOLE S
MUDHOLES
MUDLARK S
MUDLARKS
MUDPACK S
MUDPACKS
MUDPUPPY
MUDRA S
MUDRAS
MUDROCK S
MUDROCKS
MUDROOM S
MUDROOMS
MUDS
MUDSILL S
MUDSILLS
MUDSLIDE S
MUDSTONE S
DEMOUNTS
MUEDDIN S
MUEDDINS
MUENSTER S

MUESLI S
MUESLIS
MUEZZIN S
MUEZZINS
MUFF S
MUFFED
MUFFIN GS
MUFFING
MUFFINS
MUFFLE DRS
MUFFLED
MUFFLER S
MUFFLERS
MUFFLES
MUFFLING
MUFFS
MUFTI S
MUFTIS
S MUG GS
GUM
MUGFUL S
MUGFULS
MUGG SY
MUGGAR S
MUGGARS
MUGGED
MUGGEE S
MUGGEES
S MUGGER S
MUGGERS
SMUGGER
MUGGIER
MUGGIEST
MUGGILY
MUGGING S
MUGGINGS
MUGGINS
MUGGS
MUGGUR S
MUGGURS
MUGGY
MUGHAL S
MUGHALS
MUGS
GUMS SMUG
MUGWORT S
MUGWORTS
MUGWUMP S
MUGWUMPS
MUHLIES
HELIUMS
MUHLY
MUJIK S
MUJIKS
MUKLUK S
MUKLUKS
MUKTUK S
MUKTUKS
MULATTO S
MULATTOS
MULBERRY
MULCH
MULCHED
MULCHES
MULCHING
MULCT S
MULCTED
MULCTING
MULCTS
MULE DSY
MULED
MULES
MULETA S
AMULET
MULETAS
AMULETS
MULETEER S
MULEY S
MULEYS
MULING
MULISH
MULISHLY
MULL AS
MULLA HS
MULLAH S

MULLAHS
MULLAS
MULLED
MULLEIN S
MULLEINS
MULLEN S
MULLENS
MULLER S
MULLERS
MULLET S
MULLETS
MULLEY S
MULLEYS
MULLIGAN S
MULLING
MULLION S
MULLIONS
MULLITE S
MULLITES
MULLOCK SY
MULLOCKS
MULLOCKY
MULLS
MULTIAGE
MULTICAR
MULTIDAY
MULTIFID
MULTIJET
MULTIPED ES
MULTIPLE ST X
MULTIPLY
MULTITON E
MULTIUSE R
MULTURE S
MULTURES
MUM MPSU
UMM
MUMBLE DRS
MUMBLED
MUMBLER S
MUMBLERS
MUMBLES
MUMBLING
MUMBLY
MUMM SY
MUMMED
MUMMER SY
MUMMERS
MUMMERY
MUMMIED
MUMMIES
MUMMIFY
MUMMING
MUMMS
MUMMY
MUMMYING
MUMP S
MUMPED
MUMPER S
MUMPERS
MUMPING
MUMPS
MUMS
MUMU S
MUMUS
MUN IS
MUNCH
MUNCHED
MUNCHER S
MUNCHERS
MUNCHES
MUNCHIES
MUNCHING
MUNCHKIN S
MUNDANE
UNNAMED
MUNDUNGO S
MUNGO S
MUNGOES
MUNGOOSE S
MUNGOS
MUNI S
MUNIMENT S

MUNIS
MINUS
MUNITION S
MUNNION S
MUNNIONS
MUNS
MUNSTER S
STERNUM
MUNSTERS
STERNUMS
MUNTIN GS
MUNTING S
MUNTINGS
MUNTINS
MUNTJAC S
MUNTJACS
MUNTJAK S
MUNTJAKS
MUON S
MUONIC
CONIUM
MUONIUM S
MUONIUMS
MUONS
MURA LS
ARUM
MURAENID S
MURAL S
LARUM
MURALED
MURALIST S
ALTRUISM
ULTRAISM
MURALLED
MEDULLAR
MURALS
LARUMS
MURAS
ARUMS RAMUS
MURDER S
MURDERED
DEMURRED
MURDEREE S
MURDERER S
DEMURRER
MURDERS
MURE DSX
MURED
DEMUR
MUREIN S
MURINE
MUREINS
MURINES
MURES
MUSER SERUM
MUREX
MUREXES
MURIATE DS
MURIATED
MURIATES
MURICATE D
MURICES
CERIUMS
MURID S
MURIDS
MURINE S
MUREIN
MURINES
MUREINS
MURING
MURK SY
MURKER
MURKEST
MURKIER
MURKIEST
MURKILY
MURKLY
MURKS
MURKY
MURMUR S
MURMURED
MURMURER S
MURMURS
MURPHIES
MURPHY
MURR AESY
MURRA S
MURRAIN S
MURRAINS

MURRAS
MURRE SY
MURRELET S
MURRES
MURREY S
MURREYS
MURRHA S
MURRHAS
MURRHINE
MURRIES
MURRINE
MURRS
MURRY
MURTHER S
MURTHERS
AE MUS EHKST
SUM
MUSCA ET
SUMAC
MUSCADEL S
MUSCADET S
MUSCAE
MUSCAT S
MUSCATEL S
CALUMETS
MUSCATS
MUSCID S
MUSCIDS
MUSCLE DS
MUSCLED
MUSCLES
MUSCLING
MUSCLY
CLUMSY
MUSCULAR
A MUSE DRS
EMUS
A MUSED
SEDUM
MUSEFUL
A MUSER S
MURES SERUM
A MUSERS
SERUMS
A MUSES
MUSETTE S
MUSETTES
MUSEUM S
MUSEUMS
S MUSH Y
HUMS
S MUSHED
MUSHER S
RHEUMS
MUSHERS
S MUSHES
MUSHIER
MUSHIEST
MUSHILY
S MUSHING
MUSHROOM S
MUSHY
MUSIC KS
MUSICAL ES
MUSICALE S
MUSICALS
MUSICIAN S
MUSICK S
MUSICKED
MUSICKS
MUSICS
A MUSING S
A MUSINGLY
MUSINGS
MUSSING
MUSJID S
MUSJIDS
MUSK SY
MUSKEG S
MUSKEGS
MUSKET S
MUSKETRY
MUSKETS
MUSKIE RS
MUSKIER
MUSKIES T
MUSKIEST

MUSKILY
MUSKIT S
MUSKITS
MUSKOX
MUSKOXEN
MUSKRAT S
MUSKRATS
MUSKROOT S
MUSKS
MUSKY
KUMYS
MUSLIN S
LINUMS
MUSLINS
MUSPIKE S
MUSPIKES
MUSQUASH
MUSS Y
SUMS
MUSSED
SEDUMS
MUSSEL S
MUSSELS
SUMLESS
MUSSES
MUSSIER
MISUSER
SURMISE
MUSSIEST
MUSSILY
MUSSING
MUSINGS
MUSSY
MUST HSY
MUTS SMUT
STUM
MUSTACHE DS
MUSTANG S
MUSTANGS
MUSTARD SY
DURMAST
MUSTARDS
DURMASTS
MUSTARDY
MUSTED
MUSTEE S
MUSTEES
MUSTELID S
MUSTER S
ESTRUM
MUSTERED
DEMUREST
MUSTERS
ESTRUMS
MUSTH S
MUSTHS
MUSTIER
MUSTIEST
MUSTILY
MUSTING
MUSTS
SMUTS STUMS
MUSTY
S MUT EST
MUTABLE
MUTABLY
MUTAGEN S
AUGMENT
MUTAGENS
AUGMENTS
MUTANT S
MUTANTS
MUTASE S
MEATUS
MUTASES
MUTATE DS
MUTATED
MUTATES
MUTATING
MUTATION S
MUTATIVE
S MUTCH
S MUTCHES
MUTCHKIN S
MUTE DRS
MUTED
MUTEDLY
MUTELY

MUTENESS
TENESMUS
MUTER
MUTES T
MUTEST
MUTICOUS
MUTILATE DS
ULTIMATE
MUTINE DS
MINUET
MINUTE
MUTINED
MINUTED
UNTIMED
MUTINEER S
MUTINES
MINUETS
MINUTES
MISTUNE
MUTING
MUTINIED
MUTINIES
MUTINING
MINUTING
MUTINOUS
MUTINY
MUTISM S
SUMMIT
MUTISMS
SUMMITS
MUTON S
MOUNT NOTUM
MUTONS
MOUNTS
S MUTS
MUST SMUT
STUM
MUTT S
MUTTER S
MUTTERED
MUTTERER S
MUTTERS
MUTTON SY
MUTTONS
MUTTONY
MUTTS
MUTUAL S
UMLAUT
MUTUALLY
MUTUALS
UMLAUTS
MUTUEL S
LUTEUM
MUTULE
MUTUELS
MUTULES
MUTULAR
TUMULAR
MUTULE S
LUTEUM
MUTUEL
MUTULES
MUTUELS
MUUMUU S
MUUMUUS
MUZHIK S
MUZHIKS
MUZJIK S
MUZJIKS
MUZZIER
MUZZIEST
MUZZILY
MUZZLE DRS
MUZZLED
MUZZLER S
MUZZLERS
MUZZLES
MUZZLING
MUZZY
MY C
MYALGIA S
MYALGIAS
MYALGIC
MYASES
MYASIS
MISSAY
MYC S
MYCELE S
MYCELES
MYCELIA LN

MYCELIAL
MYCELIAN
MYCELIUM
MYCELOID
MYCETOMA S
MYCOLOGY
MYCOSES
MYCOSIS
MYCOTIC
MYCS
MYELIN ES
MYELINE S
MYELINES
MYELINIC
MYELINS
MYELITIS
MYELOID
MYELOMA S
MYELOMAS
MYIASES
MYIASIS
MYLAR S
MARLY
MYLARS
MYLONITE S
MYNA HS
MANY
MYNAH S
MYNAHS
MYNAS
MYNHEER S
MYNHEERS
MYOBLAST S
MYOGENIC
MYOGRAPH S
MYOID
MYOLOGIC
MYOLOGY
MYOMA S
MYOMAS
MYOMATA
MYOPATHY
MYOPE S
MOPEY
MYOPES
MYOPIA S
MYOPIAS
MYOPIC
MYOPIES
MYOPY
MYOSCOPE S
MYOSES
MOSEYS
MYOSIN S
SIMONY
MYOSINS
MYOSIS
MYOSITIS
MYOSOTE S
MYOSOTES
MYOSOTIS
MYOTIC S
COMITY
MYOTICS
MYOTOME S
MYOTOMES
A MYOTONIA S
MYOTONIC
MYRIAD S
MYRIADS
MYRIAPOD S
MYRICA S
MYRICAS
MYRIOPOD S
MYRMIDON S
MYRRH S
MYRRHIC
MYRRHS
MYRTLE S
TERMLY
MYRTLES
MYSELF
MYSID S
MYSIDS
MYSOST S

MYSOSTS
MYSTAGOG SY
MYSTERY
MYSTIC S
MYSTICAL
MYSTICLY
MYSTICS
MYSTIFY
MYSTIQUE S
MYTH SY
MYTHIC
THYMIC
MYTHICAL
MYTHIER
THYMIER
MYTHIEST
THYMIEST
MYTHOI
MYTHOS
MYTHS
MYTHY
THYMY
MYXAMEBA ES
MYXEDEMA S
MYXOCYTE S
MYXOID
MYXOMA S
MYXOMAS
MYXOMATA

N

A NA BEGHMNPW
AN Y
NAAN S
ANNA NANA
NAANS
ANNAS NANAS
NAB ES
BAN
NABBED
NABBER S
NABBERS
NABBING
NABE S
BANE BEAN
NABES
BANES BEANS
NABIS
BASIN SABIN
NABOB S
NABOBERY
NABOBESS
NABOBISH
NABOBISM S
BAMBINOS
NABOBS
NABS
BANS
NACELLE S
NACELLES
NACHAS
ASHCAN
NACHES
ENCASH
HANCES
NACHO S
ANCHO
NACHOS
ANCHOS
NACRE DS
CANER CRANE
RANCE
NACRED
CEDARN
CRANED
DANCER
NACREOUS
NACRES
CANERS
CASERN
CRANES
RANCES
NADA S
NADAS
NADIR S
DINAR DRAIN
RANID
NADIRAL
LANIARD
NADIRS
DINARS
DRAINS
RANIDS
NAE
ANE
NAETHING S
NAEVI
NAIVE
NAEVOID
NAEVUS
NAFF S
NAFFED
NAFFING
NAFFS
S NAG S
GAN
NAGANA S
NAGANAS
S NAGGED
GANGED
NAGGER S
GANGER
GRANGE
NAGGERS
GANGERS
GRANGES
S NAGGIER
GEARING
S NAGGIEST
S NAGGING
GANGING
S NAGGY
S NAGS
SANG SNAG
NAH
NAIAD S
NAIADES
NAIADS
NAIF S
FAIN
NAIFS
S NAIL S
ANIL LAIN
S NAILED
ALINED
DENIAL
NAILER S
ALINER
LARINE
LINEAR
RENAIL
NAILERS
ALINERS
RENAILS
NAILFOLD S
NAILHEAD S
S NAILING
ALINING
S NAILS
ANILS SLAIN
SNAIL
NAILSET S
ELASTIN
ENTAILS
SALIENT
SALTINE
SLAINTE
TENAILS
NAILSETS
ELASTINS
SALIENTS
SALTINES
NAINSOOK S
NAIRA S
NAIRAS
NAIRU S
NAIRUS
NAIVE RS
NAEVI
NAIVELY
NAIVER
RAVINE
VAINER
NAIVES T
NAVIES
SAVINE
NAIVEST
NATIVES
VAINEST
NAIVETE S
NAIVETES
NAIVETY
S NAKED
KNEAD
NAKEDER
KNEADER
NAKEDEST
NAKEDLY
NAKFA S
NAKFAS
NALA S
ALAN ANAL
NALAS
ALANS ANLAS
NASAL
NALED S
ELAND LADEN
NALEDS
ELANDS
LADENS
SENDAL
NALOXONE S
NAM E
MAN
NAMABLE
NAME DRS
AMEN MANE
MEAN NEMA
NAMEABLE
AMENABLE
NAMED
ADMEN AMEND
MANED MENAD
NAMELESS
LAMENESS
MALENESS
MANELESS
SALESMEN
NAMELY
LAYMEN
MEANLY
NAMER S
RAMEN REMAN
NAMERS
REMANS
NAMES
AMENS MANES
MANSE MEANS
MENSA NEMAS
NAMESAKE S
NAMETAG S
GATEMAN
MAGENTA
MAGNATE
NAMETAGS
MAGENTAS
MAGNATES
NAMING
NAN AS
J NANA S
ANNA NAAN
J NANAS
ANNAS NAANS
NANDIN AS
NANDINA S
NANDINAS
NANDINS
O NANISM S
O NANISMS
NANKEEN S
NANKEENS
NANKIN S
NANKINS
NANNIE S
NANNIES
NANNY
NANNYISH
NANOGRAM S
NANOTECH S
NANOTUBE S
BUTANONE
NANOWATT S
NANS
NAOI
NAOS
KS NAP AES
PAN
NAPA S
NAPALM S
NAPALMED
NAPALMS
NAPAS
NAPE S
NEAP PANE
PEAN
NAPERIES
NAPERY
NAPES
ASPEN NEAPS
PANES PEANS
SNEAP SPEAN
NAPHTHA S
NAPHTHAS
NAPHTHOL S
NAPHTHYL S
NAPHTOL S
HAPLONT
NAPHTOLS
HAPLONTS
NAPIFORM
NAPKIN S
NAPKINS
S NAPLESS
NAPOLEON S
NAPPA S
NAPPAS
NAPPE DRS
KS NAPPED
APPEND
KS NAPPER S
RAPPEN
KS NAPPERS
SNAPPER
NAPPES
NAPPIE RS
S NAPPIER
NAPPIES T
PINESAP
S NAPPIEST
KS NAPPING
S NAPPY
NAPROXEN S
KS NAPS
PANS SNAP
SPAN
NARC OS
CARN
NARCEIN ES
CANNIER
NARCEINE S
NARCEINS
CRANNIES
NARCISM S
NARCISMS
NARCISSI
NARCIST S
NARCISTS
NARCO S
ACORN RACON
NARCOMA S
NARCOMAS
NARCOS E
ACORNS
RACONS
NARCOSE S
CANOERS
COARSEN
CORNEAS
NARCOSES
COARSENS
NARCOSIS
NARCOTIC S
CRATONIC
NARCS
CARNS
NARD S
DARN RAND
NARDINE
NARDS
DARNS RANDS
S NARES
EARNS NEARS
SANER SNARE
NARGHILE S
NARGILEH
NARGILE HS
ALIGNER
ENGRAIL
REALIGN
REGINAL
NARGILEH S
NARGHILE
NARGILES
ALIGNERS
ENGRAILS
REALIGNS
SIGNALER
SLANGIER
NARIAL
NARIC
CAIRN
NARINE
INANER
NARIS
AIRNS RAINS
RANIS SARIN
S NARK SY
KARN KNAR
RANK
NARKED
DANKER
DARKEN
RANKED
NARKING
RANKING
S NARKS
KARNS KNARS
RANKS SNARK
S NARKY
NARRATE DRS
NARRATED
NARRATER S
NARRATES
NARRATOR S
NARROW S
NARROWED
NARROWER
NARROWLY
NARROWS
NARTHEX
NARWAL S
NARWALS
NARWHAL ES
NARWHALE S
NARWHALS
U NARY
YARN
NASAL S
ALANS ANLAS
NALAS
NASALISE DS
NASALISM S
NASALITY
NASALIZE DS
NASALLY
ALANYLS
NASALS
NASCENCE S
NASCENCY
NASCENT
NASIAL
LANAIS
LIANAS
SALINA
NASION S
ANIONS
NASIONS
NASTIC
ACTINS
ANTICS
NASTIER
ANESTRI
ANTSIER
RATINES
RETAINS
RETINAS
RETSINA
STAINER
STEARIN
NASTIES T
ENTASIS
SEITANS
SESTINA
TANSIES
TISANES
NASTIEST
ANTSIEST
INSTATES
SATINETS
TITANESS
NASTILY
SAINTLY
NASTY
ANTSY TANSY
NATAL
ALANT
NATALITY
NATANT
NATANTLY
NATATION S
NATATORY
S NATCH
CHANT
E NATES
ANTES ETNAS
NEATS STANE
NATHLESS
E NATION S
ANOINT
NATIONAL S
E NATIONS
ANOINTS
ONANIST
NATIVE S
NATIVELY
VENALITY
NATIVES
NAIVEST
VAINEST
NATIVISM S
VITAMINS
NATIVIST S
VISITANT
NATIVITY
NATRIUM S
NATRIUMS
NATURISM
NATRON S
NONART
NATRONS
NONARTS
NATTER S
RATTEN
NATTERED
ATTENDER
RATTENED
NATTERS
RATTENS
G NATTIER
INTREAT
ITERANT
NITRATE
TERTIAN
G NATTIEST
NATTILY
G NATTY
NATURAL S
NATURALS
NATURE DS
NATURED
DAUNTER
UNRATED
UNTREAD
NATURES
SAUNTER
NATURISM S
NATRIUMS
NATURIST S
ANTIRUST
NAUGHT SY
NAUGHTS
NAUGHTY
NAUMACHY
NAUPLIAL
NAUPLII
NAUPLIUS
NAUSEA S
NAUSEANT S
NAUSEAS
NAUSEATE DS
NAUSEOUS
NAUTCH
CHAUNT
NAUTCHES
UNCHASTE
NAUTICAL
NAUTILI
NAUTILUS
NAVAID S
NAVAIDS
NAVAL
NAVALLY
NAVAR S
VARNA
NAVARS
VARNAS
K NAVE LS
VANE VENA
NAVEL S
VENAL
NAVELS
K NAVES
AVENS VANES
NAVETTE S
NAVETTES
NAVICERT S
NAVIES
NAIVES
SAVINE
NAVIGATE DS
VAGINATE
NAVVIES
NAVVY
NAVY
GS NAW
AWN WAN
NAWAB S
BWANA
NAWABS
BWANAS
NAY S
ANY
NAYS
NAYSAID
NAYSAY S
NAYSAYER S
NAYSAYS
NAZI S
NAZIFIED
NAZIFIES
NAZIFY
NAZIS
AO NE BEGTW
EN
S NEAP S
NAPE PANE
PEAN
S NEAPS
ASPEN NAPES
PANES PEANS
SNEAP SPEAN
A NEAR S
EARN
NEARBY
BARNEY
A NEARED
EARNED
ENDEAR
NEARER
EARNER
REEARN
NEAREST
EARNEST
EASTERN
A NEARING
AGINNER
EARNING
ENGRAIN
GRANNIE
NEARLIER
NEARLY
NEARNESS
ENSNARES
RENNASES
A NEARS
EARNS NARES
SANER SNARE
NEARSIDE S
ARSENIDE
NEAT HS
ANTE ETNA
U NEATEN S
NEATENED
NEATENS
NEATER
ENTERA
NEATEST
NEATH
THANE
NEATHERD S
ADHERENT
NEATLY
NEATNESS
NEATNIK S

NEATNIKS
NEATS
ANTES ETNAS
NATES STANE
NEB S
BEN
NEBBISH Y
NEBBISHY
NEBS
BENS
NEBULA ERS
UNABLE
UNBALE
NEBULAE
NEBULAR
NEBULAS
UNBALES
NEBULE
NEBULISE DS
NEBULIZE DRS
NEBULOSE
BLUENOSE
NEBULOUS
NEBULY
S **NECK** S
NECKBAND S
NECKED
NECKER S
NECKERS
NECKING S
NECKINGS
NECKLACE DS
NECKLESS
NECKLIKE
NECKLINE S
S **NECKS**
SNECK
NECKTIE S
NECKTIES
NECKWEAR
NECROPSY
NECROSE DS
ENCORES
NECROSED
CENSORED
ENCODERS
SECONDER
NECROSES
NECROSIS
NECROTIC
CONCERTI
NECTAR SY
CANTER
CARNET
CENTRA
RECANT
TANREC
TRANCE
NECTARS
CANTERS
CARNETS
RECANTS
SCANTER
TANRECS
TRANCES
NECTARY
NEDDIES
NEDDY
K **NEE** DMP
K **NEED** SY
DENE
NEEDED
NEEDER S
NEEDERS
SNEERED
NEEDFUL S
NEEDFULS
NEEDIER
NEEDIEST
NEEDILY
NEEDING
ENGINED
NEEDLE DRS
NEEDLED
NEEDLER S
NEEDLERS
NEEDLES S

NEEDLESS
LESSENED
NEEDLING S
NEEDS
DENES DENSE
NEEDY
NEEM S
NEEMS
MENSE MESNE
SEMEN
NEEP S
PEEN
NEEPS
PEENS PENES
NEG S
ENG
GEN
NEGATE DRS
NEGATED
AGENTED
NEGATER S
GRANTEE
GREATEN
REAGENT
NEGATERS
ESTRANGE
GRANTEES
GREATENS
REAGENTS
SERGEANT
NEGATES
NEGATING
AGENTING
NEGATION S
NEGATIVE DS
AGENTIVE
NEGATON S
TONNAGE
NEGATONS
TONNAGES
NEGATOR S
NEGATORS
ESTRAGON
NEGATRON S
NEGLECT S
NEGLECTS
NEGLIGE ES
NEGLIGEE S
NEGLIGES
NEGROID S
ERODING
GROINED
IGNORED
REDOING
NEGROIDS
NEGRONI S
NEGRONIS
NEGS
ENGS GENS
NEGUS
GENUS
NEGUSES
GENUSES
NEIF S
FINE
NEIFS
FINES
NEIGH S
HINGE
NEIGHBOR S
NEIGHED
HEEDING
NEIGHING
NEIGHS
HINGES
NEIST
INSET NITES
SENTI STEIN
TINES
NEITHER
THEREIN
NEKTON S
NEKTONIC
NEKTONS
NELLIE S
NELLIES
NELLY
NELSON S
NELSONS
NELUMBO S
NELUMBOS

E **NEMA** S
AMEN MANE
MEAN NAME
E **NEMAS**
AMENS MANES
MANSE MEANS
MENSA NAMES
NEMATIC
NEMATODE S
NEMESES
NEMESIS
SIEMENS
NENE S
NENES
NEOCON S
NEOCONS
NEOGENE
NEOLITH S
HOTLINE
NEOLITHS
HOLSTEIN
HOTLINES
NEOLOGIC
NEOLOGY
ENOLOGY
NEOMORPH S
NEOMYCIN S
NEON S
NONE
NEONATAL
NEONATE S
NEONATES
NEONED
DONNEE
NEONS
NONES
NEOPHYTE S
NEOPLASM S
PLEONASM
NEOPRENE S
NEOTENIC
NEOTENY
NEOTERIC S
ERECTION
NEOTYPE S
NEOTYPES
NEPENTHE S
NEPETA S
NEPETAS
PENATES
NEPHEW S
NEPHEWS
NEPHRIC
PHRENIC
PINCHER
NEPHRISM S
NEPHRITE S
TREPHINE
NEPHRON S
NEPHRONS
NEPOTIC
ENTOPIC
NEPOTISM S
PIMENTOS
NEPOTIST S
NERD SY
REND
NERDIER
DERNIER
NERDIEST
INSERTED
RESIDENT
SINTERED
TRENDIES
NERDISH
HINDERS
SHRINED
NERDS
RENDS
NERDY
NEREID S
DENIER
REINED
NEREIDES
REDENIES
NEREIDS
DENIERS
RESINED
NEREIS
SEINER
SEREIN
SERINE

NERITIC
CITRINE
CRINITE
INCITER
NEROL IS
ENROL LONER
NEROLI S
NEROLIS
NEROLS
ENROLS
LONERS
I **NERTS**
RENTS STERN
TERNS
NERTZ
E **NERVATE**
VETERAN
NERVE DS
NEVER
NERVED
VENDER
NERVES
NERVIER
VERNIER
NERVIEST
REINVEST
SIRVENTE
NERVILY
NERVINE S
INNERVE
NERVINES S
INNERVES
NERVING S
NERVINGS
NERVOUS
NERVULE S
NERVULES
NERVURE S
NERVURES
NERVY
NESCIENT S
NESS
NESSES
SENSES
NEST S
NETS SENT
TENS
NESTABLE
NESTED
TENSED
NESTER S
ENTERS
RENEST
RENTES
RESENT
TENSER
TERNES
TREENS
NESTERS
RENESTS
RESENTS
NESTING
TENSING
NESTLE DRS
NESTLED
NESTLER S
RELENTS
NESTLERS
NESTLES
NETLESS
NESTLIKE
NESTLING S
NESTOR S
NOTERS
STONER
TENORS
TENSOR
TONERS
TRONES
NESTORS
STONERS
TENSORS
NESTS
NET ST
TEN
NETHER
NETIZEN S
NETIZENS
NETLESS
NESTLES
NETLIKE
NETOP S

NETOPS
PONTES
NETS
NEST SENT
TENS
NETSUKE S
NETSUKES
NETT SY
TENT
NETTABLE
NETTED
DETENT
TENTED
NETTER S
TENTER
NETTERS
TENTERS
NETTIER
TENTIER
NETTIEST
TENTIEST
NETTING S
TENTING
NETTINGS
NETTLE DRS
TELNET
NETTLED
NETTLER S
NETTLERS
NETTLES
TELNETS
NETTLIER
NETTLING
NETTLY
NETTS
STENT TENTS
NETTY
TENTY
NETWORK S
NETWORKS
NEUK S
KUNE NUKE
NEUKS
NUKES
NEUM ES
MENU
P **NEUMATIC**
NEUME S
NEUMES
NEUMIC
NEUMS
MENUS
NEURAL
UNREAL
NEURALLY
UNREALLY
NEURAXON S
NEURINE S
NEURINES
NEURITIC S
NEURITIS
NEUROID
DOURINE
NEUROMA S
ENAMOUR
NEUROMAS T
ENAMOURS
NEURON ES
NEURONAL
NEURONE S
NEURONES
NEURONIC
NEURONS
NONUSER
NEUROSAL
ALEURONS
NEUROSES
NEUROSIS
RESINOUS
NEUROTIC S
UNEROTIC
NEURULA ERS
NEURULAE
NEURULAR
NEURULAS
NEUSTIC
NEUSTON S
NEUSTONS
SUNSTONE

NEUTER S
RETUNE
TENURE
TUREEN
NEUTERED
NEUTERS
RETUNES
TENURES
TUREENS
NEUTRAL S
NEUTRALS
NEUTRINO S
NEUTRON S
NEUTRONS
NEVE RS
EVEN
NEVER
NERVE
NEVES
EVENS SEVEN
NEVI
VEIN VINE
NEVOID
NEVUS
VENUS
AK **NEW** ST
WEN
NEWBIE S
NEWBIES
NEWBORN S
NEWBORNS
NEWCOMER S
NEWEL S
NEWELS
NEWER
RENEW
NEWEST
TWEENS
NEWFOUND
NEWIE S
NEWIES
NEWSIE
NEWISH
WHINES
NEWLY
NEWLYWED S
NEWMOWN
NEWNESS
NEWS Y
SEWN WENS
NEWSBEAT S
NEWSBOY S
NEWSBOYS
NEWSCAST S
NEWSDESK S
NEWSGIRL S
NEWSHAWK S
NEWSIE RS
NEWIES
NEWSIER
WEINERS
WIENERS
NEWSIES T
NEWSIEST
NEWSLESS
NEWSMAN
NEWSMEN
NEWSPEAK S
NEWSREEL S
NEWSROOM S
NEWSWIRE S
NEWSY
NEWT S
WENT
NEWTON S
NEWTONS
NEWTS
NEWWAVER S
NEXT
NEXTDOOR
NEXUS
UNSEX
NEXUSES
UNSEXES
NGULTRUM S
NGWEE
NIACIN S
NIACINS

S **NIB** S
BIN
S **NIBBED**
S **NIBBING**
NIBBLE DRS
NIBBLED
NIBBLER S
NIBBLERS
NIBBLES
NIBBLING
NIBLICK S
NIBLICKS
NIBLIKE
S **NIBS**
BINS SNIB
NICAD S
CANID CNIDA
NICADS
CANIDS
NICE R
CINE
NICELY
NICENESS
INCENSES
NICER
NICEST
INCEST
INSECT
NICETIES
NICETY
NICHE DS
CHINE
NICHED
CHINED
INCHED
NICHES
CHINES
INCHES
NICHING
CHINING
INCHING
S **NICK** S
S **NICKED**
NICKEL S
NICKLE
NICKELED
NICKELIC
NICKELS
NICKLES
SLICKEN
S **NICKER** S
S **NICKERED**
KS **NICKERS**
SNICKER
S **NICKING**
NICKLE DS
NICKEL
NICKLED
CLINKED
NICKLES
NICKELS
SLICKEN
NICKLING
CLINKING
NICKNACK S
NICKNAME DRS
S **NICKS**
SNICK
NICOISE
EOSINIC
NICOL S
COLIN
NICOLS
COLINS
NICOTIN ES
NICOTINE S
COTININE
NICOTINS
NICTATE DS
TETANIC
NICTATED
NICTATES
ENTASTIC
TETANICS
NIDAL
NIDATE DS
DETAIN
NIDATED

NIDATES
DESTAIN
DETAINS
INSTEAD
SAINTED
STAINED
NIDATING
NIDATION S
S NIDE DS
DENI DINE
NIDED
DINED
NIDERING S
NIDES
DINES SNIDE
NIDGET S
TINGED
NIDGETS
NIDI
NIDIFIED
NIDIFIES
NIDIFY
NIDING
DINING
INDIGN
NIDUS
NIDUSES
NIECE S
NIECES
NIELLI
NIELLIST S
NIELLO S
NIELLOED
NIELLOS
NIEVE S
NIEVES
ENVIES
S NIFFER S
NIFFERED
S NIFFERS
SNIFFER
NIFTIER
NIFTIES T
FINITES
NIFTIEST
NIFTILY
NIFTY
NIGELLA S
GALLEIN
NIGELLAS
GALLEINS
NIGGARD S
GRADING
NIGGARDS
S NIGGLE DRS
LEGGIN
S NIGGLED
GELDING
S NIGGLER S
S NIGGLERS
SNIGGLER
S NIGGLES
LEGGINS
SNIGGLE
NIGGLIER
S NIGGLING S
NIGGLY
NIGH ST
NIGHED
HINGED
NIGHER
HINGER
NIGHEST
NIGHING
HINGING
NIGHNESS
NIGHS
K NIGHT SY
THING
NIGHTCAP S
PATCHING
NIGHTIE S
NIGHTIES
HEISTING
NIGHTJAR S
K NIGHTLY
K NIGHTS
THINGS
NIGHTY
NIGRIFY

NIGROSIN ES
IRONINGS
ROSINING
NIHIL S
NIHILISM S
NIHILIST S
NIHILITY
NIHILS
A NIL LS
LIN
NILGAI S
AILING
NILGAIS
SAILING
NILGAU S
LINGUA
NILGAUS
NILGHAI S
HAILING
NILGHAIS
NILGHAU S
HAULING
NILGHAUS
LANGUISH
SHAULING
NILL S
NILLED
NILLING
NILLS
A NILS
LINS
NIM S
NIMBI
NIMBLE R
MILNEB
NIMBLER
NIMBLEST
NIMBLY
NIMBUS
NIMBUSED
NIMBUSES
NIMIETY
NIMIOUS
IONIUMS
NIMMED
NIMMING
NIMROD S
DORMIN
NIMRODS
DORMINS
NIMS
NINE S
NINEBARK S
NINEFOLD
NINEPIN S
NINEPINS
NINES
NINETEEN S
NINETIES
EINSTEIN
NINETY
NINJA S
NINJAS
NINNIES
NINNY
NINNYISH
NINON S
NINONS
NINTH S
NINTHLY
NINTHS
NIOBATE S
NIOBATES
BOTANIES
BOTANISE
OBEISANT
NIOBIC
BIONIC
NIOBITE S
NIOBITES
NIOBIUM S
NIOBIUMS
NIOBOUS
S NIP AS
PIN
NIPA S
PAIN PIAN
PINA

NIPAS
PAINS PIANS
PINAS
S NIPPED
S NIPPER S
S NIPPERS
SNIPPER
S NIPPIER
S NIPPIEST
S NIPPILY
S NIPPING
NIPPLE DS
LIPPEN
NIPPLED
NIPPLES
LIPPENS
S NIPPY
S NIPS
PINS SNIP
SPIN
NIRVANA S
NIRVANAS
NIRVANIC
NISEI S
NISEIS
SEISIN
NISI
NISUS
SINUS
KSU NIT ES
TIN
U NITE RS
TINE
U NITER SY
INERT INTER
NITRE TRINE
NITERIE S
NITERIES
U NITERS
ESTRIN
INERTS
INSERT
INTERS
NITRES
SINTER
TRIENS
TRINES
NITERY
U NITES
INSET NEIST
SENTI STEIN
TINES
NITID
NITINOL S
NITINOLS
NITON S
NITONS
NITPICK SY
NITPICKS
STICKPIN
NITPICKY
NITRATE DS
INTREAT
ITERANT
NATTIER
TERTIAN
NITRATED
NITRATES
INTREATS
STRAITEN
TERTIANS
NITRATOR S
NITRE S
INERT INTER
NITER TRINE
NITRES
ESTRIN
INERTS
INSERT
INTERS
NITERS
SINTER
TRIENS
TRINES
NITRIC
CITRIN
NITRID ES
NITRIDE DS
INDITER
NITRIDED

NITRIDES
DISINTER
INDITERS
NITRIDS
NITRIFY
NITRIL ES
NITRILE S
LINTIER
NITRILES
NITRILS
NITRITE S
NITTIER
NITRITES
NITRO S
INTRO
NITROGEN S
NITROLIC
NITROS O
INTROS
NITROSO
TORSION
NITROSYL S
NITROUS
TURIONS
KSU NITS
SNIT TINS
NITTIER
NITRITE
NITTIEST
NITTY
NITWIT S
NITWITS
INTWIST
NIVAL
ANVIL VINAL
NIVEOUS
ENVIOUS
NIX EY
NIXE DS
NIXED
INDEX
NIXES
NIXIE S
NIXIES
NIXING
NIXY
NIZAM S
NIZAMATE S
NIZAMS
O NO BDGHMORS
ON TW
KS NOB S
KS NOBBIER
KS NOBBIEST
S NOBBILY
NOBBLE DRS
NOBBLED
NOBBLER S
NOBBLERS
NOBBLES
NOBBLING
KS NOBBY
NOBELIUM S
NOBILITY
NOBLE RS
BELON
NOBLEMAN
NOBLEMEN
NOBLER
NOBLES T
BELONS
NOBLESSE S
BONELESS
NOBLEST
NOBLY
NOBODIES
NOBODY
KS NOBS
SNOB
NOCENT
K NOCK S
CONK
K NOCKED
CONKED
K NOCKING
CONKING
K NOCKS
CONKS
NOCTUID S
CONDUIT

NOCTUIDS
CONDUITS
DISCOUNT
NOCTULE S
NOCTULES
NOCTUOID
NOCTURN ES
NOCTURNE S
NOCTURNS
NOCUOUS
NOD EIS
DON
A NODAL
NODALITY
A NODALLY
NODDED
NODDER S
DRONED
NODDERS
NODDIES
NODDING
NODDLE DS
NODDLED
NODDLES
NODDLING
NODDY
A NODE S
DONE
A NODES
NOSED SONDE
NODI
DINO
NODICAL
NODOSE
NOOSED
ODEONS
NODOSITY
NODOUS
NODS
DONS
NODULAR
NODULE S
LOUDEN
NODULES
LOUDENS
NODULOSE
UNLOOSED
NODULOUS
NODUS
SOUND UDONS
NOEL S
ENOL LENO
LONE
NOELS
ENOLS LENOS
NOES
EONS NOSE
ONES SONE
NOESIS
ENOSIS
EOSINS
ESSOIN
NOISES
OSSEIN
SONSIE
NOESISES
ENOSISES
NOETIC
NOTICE
S NOG GS
NOGG S
GONG
S NOGGED
GONGED
NOGGIN GS
S NOGGING S
GONGING
NOGGINGS
SNOGGING
NOGGINS
NOGGS
GONGS
S NOGS
SNOG SONG
NOH
HON
NOHOW
NOIL SY
LINO LION
LOIN

NOILS
LINOS LIONS
LOINS
NOILY
NOIR S
INRO IRON
NORI
NOIRISH
NOIRS
IRONS NORIS
ORNIS ROSIN
NOISE DS
EOSIN
NOISED
DONSIE
ONSIDE
NOISES
ENOSIS
EOSINS
ESSOIN
NOESIS
OSSEIN
SONSIE
NOISETTE S
TEOSINTE
NOISIER
IRONIES
NOISIEST
INOSITES
NOISILY
NOISING
NOISOME
NOISY
YONIS
NOLO S
LOON
NOLOS
LOONS SNOOL
SOLON
NOM AES
MON
NOMA DS
MANO MOAN
NOMAD S
MONAD
NOMADIC
MONACID
MONADIC
NOMADISM S
MONADISM
NOMADS
DAMSON
MONADS
NOMARCH SY
MONARCH
NOMARCHS
MONARCHS
NOMARCHY
MONARCHY
NOMAS
MANOS MASON
MOANS MONAS
SOMAN
NOMBLES
NOMBRIL S
NOMBRILS
G NOME NS
MENO OMEN
NOMEN
G NOMES
MESON OMENS
NOMINA L
AMNION
NOMINAL S
NOMINALS
NOMINATE DS
ANTINOME
NOMINEE S
NOMINEES
NOMISM S
MONISM
NOMISMS
MONISMS
NOMISTIC
MONISTIC
NOMOGRAM S
MONOGRAM
NOMOI
NOMOLOGY
MONOLOGY
NOMOS
MONOS MOONS
NOMS
MONS

NONA S
ANON
NONACID S
NONACIDS
NONACTOR S
NONADULT S
NONAGE S
NONAGES
NONAGON S
NONAGONS
NONART S
NATRON
NONARTS
NATRONS
NONAS
NONBANK S
NONBANKS
NONBASIC
NONBEING S
NONBLACK S
NONBODY
NONBOOK S
NONBOOKS
NONBRAND
NONCASH
CHANSON
NONCE S
NONCES
NONCLASS
NONCLING
NONCOLA S
NONCOLAS
NONCOLOR S
NONCOM S
NONCOMS
NONCORE
NONCRIME S
NONDAIRY
NONDANCE RS
CANNONED
NONDRIP
NONDRUG
NONE ST
NEON
NONEGO S
NONEGOS
NONELECT
NONELITE
NONEMPTY
NONENTRY
NONEQUAL S
NONES
NEONS
NONESUCH
UNCHOSEN
NONET S
TENON TONNE
NONETS
SONNET
TENONS
TONNES
NONEVENT S
NONFACT S
NONFACTS
NONFAN S
NONFANS
NONFARM
NONFAT
NONFATAL
NONFATTY
NONFINAL
NONFLUID S
NONFOCAL
NONFOOD
NONFUEL
NONGAME
AGNOMEN
NONGAY S
NONGAYS
NONGLARE S
NONGREEN
NONGUEST S
NONGUILT S
NONHARDY
NONHEME
NONHERO
NONHOME

NONHUMAN S
NONIDEAL
NONIMAGE S
NONINERT
NONIONIC
NONIRON
NONISSUE S
UNSONSIE
NONJUROR S
NONJURY
NONLABOR
NONLEAFY
NONLEGAL
NONLEVEL
NONLIFE
NONLIVES
NONLOCAL S
NONLOYAL
NONLYRIC
NONMAJOR S
NONMAN
NONMEAT
MONTANE
NONMEN
NONMETAL S
NONMETRO
NONMODAL
NONMONEY
NONMORAL
NONMUSIC S
NONNASAL
NONNAVAL
NONNEWS
NONNOBLE
NONNOVEL S
NONOBESE
NONOHMIC
NONOILY
NONORAL
NONOWNER S
NONPAGAN S
NONPAID
DIPNOAN
NONPAPAL
NONPAR
NONPARTY
NONPAST S
NONPASTS
NONPEAK
NONPLAY S
NONPLAYS
NONPLUS
NONPOINT
NONPOLAR
NONPOOR
NONPRINT
NONPROS
NONQUOTA
NONRATED
NONRIGID
NONRIVAL S
NONVIRAL
NONROYAL
NONRURAL
NONSELF
NONSENSE S
NONSKED S
NONSKEDS
NONSKID
NONSKIER S
EINKORNS
NONSLIP
NONSOLAR
NONSOLID S
NONSTICK Y
NONSTOP S
PONTONS
NONSTOPS
NONSTORY
NONSTYLE S
NONSUCH
NONSUGAR S
NONSUIT S
NONSUITS
NONTAX
NONTAXES
NONTIDAL
NONTITLE
NONTONAL
NONTONIC
NONTOXIC
NONTRUMP
NONTRUTH S
NONUNION S
NONUPLE S
NONUPLES
NONURBAN
NONUSE RS
NONUSER S
NEURONS
NONUSERS
NONUSES
NONUSING
NONVALID
NONVIRAL
NONRIVAL
NONVITAL
NONVOCAL S
NONVOTER S
NONWAGE
NONWAR S
NONWARS
NONWHITE S
NONWOODY
NONWOOL
NONWORD S
NONWORDS
NONWORK
NONWOVEN S
NONYL S
NYLON
NONYLS
NYLONS
NONZERO
NOO KN
ONO
NOODGE DS
NOODGED
NOODGES
NOODGING
NOODLE DS
NOODLED
NOODLES
SNOOLED
NOODLING
NOOGIE S
GOONIE
NOOGIES
GOONIES
ISOGONE
S NOOK S
NOOKLIKE
S NOOKS
SNOOK
NOON S
NOONDAY S
NOONDAYS
NOONING S
NOONINGS
NOONS
NOONTIDE S
NOONTIME S
NOOSE DRS
NOOSED
NODOSE
ODEONS
NOOSER S
SOONER
NOOSERS
SOONERS
NOOSES
NOOSING
NOPAL S
NOPALES
ESPANOL
NOPALITO S
OPTIONAL
NOPALS
NOPE
OPEN PEON
PONE
NOPLACE
NOR IM
NORDIC
NORI AS
INRO IRON
NOIR
NORIA S
NORIAS
ARSINO
NORIS
IRONS NOIRS
ORNIS ROSIN
NORITE S
ORIENT
TONIER
NORITES
OESTRIN
ORIENTS
STONIER
NORITIC
NORLAND S
NORLANDS
E NORM S
MORN
NORMAL S
NORMALCY
NORMALLY
NORMALS
NORMANDE
NORMED
MODERN
RODMEN
NORMLESS
NORMS
MORNS
NORTH S
THORN
NORTHER NS
HORRENT
NORTHERN S
NORTHERS
NORTHING S
THORNING
THRONING
NORTHS
THORNS
O NOS EHY
ONS
SON
NOSE DSY
EONS NOES
ONES SONE
NOSEBAG S
NOSEBAGS
NOSEBAND S
NOSED
NODES SONDE
NOSEDIVE DS
NOSEDOVE
NOSEGAY S
NOSEGAYS
NOSELESS
SOLENESS
NOSELIKE
G NOSES
SONES
NOSEY
NOSH
HONS
NOSHED
NOSHER S
HERONS
HONERS
SENHOR
NOSHERS
SENHORS
NOSHES
NOSHING
NOSIER
IRONES
SENIOR
NOSIEST
NOSILY
NOSINESS
NOSING S
NOSINGS
NOSOLOGY
NOSTOC S
CONTOS
NOSTOCS
NOSTRIL S
NOSTRILS
NOSTRUM S
NOSTRUMS
NOSY
KS NOT AE
TON
NOTA L
NOTABLE S
NOTABLES
STONABLE
NOTABLY
NOTAL
TALON TOLAN
TONAL
NOTARIAL
RATIONAL
NOTARIES
SENORITA
NOTARIZE DS
NOTARY
AROYNT
NOTATE DS
NOTATED
NOTATES
NOTATING
NOTATION S
NOTCH
NOTCHED
NOTCHER S
CHORTEN
NOTCHERS
CHORTENS
NOTCHES
TECHNOS
NOTCHING
NOTE DRS
TONE
NOTEBOOK S
NOTECARD S
CARTONED
NOTECASE S
ACETONES
NOTED
TONED
NOTEDLY
NOTELESS
TONELESS
NOTEPAD S
NOTEPADS
NOTER S
TENOR TONER
TRONE
NOTERS
NESTOR
STONER
TENORS
TENSOR
TONERS
TRONES
NOTES
ONSET SETON
STENO STONE
TONES
A NOTHER
HORNET
THRONE
NOTHING S
NOTHINGS
NOTICE DRS
NOETIC
NOTICED
CTENOID
DEONTIC
NOTICER S
COINTER
NOTICERS
COINTERS
CORNIEST
NOTICES
SECTION
NOTICING
NOTIFIED
NOTIFIER S
NOTIFIES
NOTIFY
NOTING
TONING
NOTION S
NOTIONAL
NOTIONS
NOTORNIS
NOTTURNI
NOTTURNO
NOTUM
MOUNT MUTON
NOUGAT S
NOUGATS
OUTSANG
NOUGHT S
HOGNUT
NOUGHTS
GUNSHOT
HOGNUTS
SHOTGUN
NOUMENA L
NOUMENAL
NOUMENON
NOUN S
NOUNAL
NOUNALLY
NOUNLESS
NOUNS
NOURISH
NOUS
ONUS
NOUSES
ONUSES
NOUVEAU
NOUVELLE S
NOVA ES
NOVAE
NOVALIKE
NOVAS
NOVATION S
NOVEL S
NOVELISE DS
NOVELIST S
NOVELIZE DR
S
NOVELLA S
NOVELLAS
NOVELLE
NOVELLY
NOVELS
SLOVEN
NOVELTY
NOVENA ES
NOVENAE
NOVENAS
NOVERCAL
NOVICE S
NOVICES
EKS NOW ST
OWN
WON
NOWADAYS
NOWAY S
NOWAYS
NOWHERE S
WHEREON
NOWHERES
NOWISE
WINOES
NOWNESS
EKS NOWS
OWNS SNOW
SOWN WONS
NOWT S
TOWN WONT
NOWTS
TOWNS WONTS
NOXIOUS
NOYADE S
NOYADES
NOZZLE S
NOZZLES
NTH
G NU BNST
UN
NUANCE DS
NUANCED
NUANCES
S NUB S
BUN
KS NUBBIER
KS NUBBIEST
NUBBIN S
NUBBINS
NUBBLE S
NUBBLES
NUBBLIER
NUBBLY
KS NUBBY
NUBIA S
NUBIAS
NUBILE
NUBILITY
NUBILOSE
NUBILOUS
S NUBS
BUNS SNUB
NUBUCK S
NUBUCKS
NUCELLAR
NUCELLI
NUCELLUS
NUCHA EL
NUCHAE
NUCHAL S
LAUNCH
NUCHALS
NUCLEAL
NUCLEAR
LUCARNE
UNCLEAR
NUCLEASE S
E NUCLEATE DS
NUCLEI N
LEUCIN
NUCLEIN S
NUCLEINS
NUCLEOID S
UNCOILED
UNDOCILE
NUCLEOLE S
NUCLEOLI
NUCLEON S
NUCLEONS
NUCLEUS
NUCLIDE S
INCLUDE
NUCLIDES
INCLUDES
UNSLICED
NUCLIDIC
NUDE RS
DUNE UNDE
NUDELY
NUDENESS
NUDER
UNDER
NUDES T
DUNES
NUDEST
TENDUS
NUDGE DRS
NUDGED
DUNGED
NUDGER S
GERUND
NUDGERS
GERUNDS
NUDGES
NUDGING
DUNGING
NUDICAUL
NUDIE S
INDUE
NUDIES
INDUES
UNDIES
NUDISM S
NUDISMS
NUDIST S
NUDISTS
NUDITIES
DISUNITE
UNTIDIES
NUDITY
UNTIDY
NUDNICK S
NUDNICKS
NUDNIK S
UNKIND
NUDNIKS
NUDZH
NUDZHED
NUDZHES
NUDZHING
NUGATORY
NUGGET SY
NUGGETS
NUGGETY
NUISANCE S
NUKE DS
KUNE NEUK
NUKED
NUKES
NEUKS
NUKING
NULL S
NULLAH S
NULLAHS
NULLED
NULLIFY
NULLING
NULLITY
NULLS
NUMB S
NUMBAT S
NUMBATS
NUMBED
NUMBER S
NUMBERED
NUMBERER S
RENUMBER
NUMBERS
NUMBEST
NUMBFISH
NUMBING
NUMBLES
NUMBLY
NUMBNESS
NUMBS
NUMCHUCK S
NUMEN
NUMERACY
NUMERAL S
NUMERALS
MENSURAL
NUMERARY
E NUMERATE DS
NUMERIC S
NUMERICS
NUMEROUS
NUMINA
NUMINOUS
NUMMARY
NUMMULAR
NUMSKULL S
NUN S
NUNATAK S
NUNATAKS
NUNCHAKU S
NUNCIO S
NUNCIOS
NUNCLE S
NUNCLES
NUNLIKE
NUNNERY
NUNNISH
NUNS
SUNN
NUPTIAL S
UNPLAIT
NUPTIALS
UNPLAITS
NURD S
DURN
NURDS
DURNS
K NURL S
K NURLED
RUNDLE
K NURLING
K NURLS
NURSE DRS
RUNES
NURSED
SUNDER
NURSER SY
RERUNS
NURSERS
NURSERY
NURSES
NURSING S
NURSINGS
NURSLING S

NURTURAL
NURTURE DRS
UNTRUER
NURTURED
NURTURER S
NURTURES
AGO NUS
SUN UNS
NUT S
TUN
NUTANT
NUTATE DS
ATTUNE
TAUTEN
NUTATED
ATTUNED
TAUNTED
NUTATES
ATTUNES
TAUTENS
TETANUS
UNSTATE
NUTATING
ATTUNING
TAUNTING
NUTATION S
NUTBROWN
NUTCASE S
NUTCASES
NUTGALL S
GALLNUT
NUTGALLS
GALLNUTS
NUTGRASS
NUTHATCH
NUTHOUSE S
NUTLET S
NUTLETS
NUTLIKE
NUTMEAT S
NUTMEATS
NUTMEG S
NUTMEGS
NUTPICK S
NUTPICKS
NUTRIA S
NUTRIAS
NUTRIENT S
NUTS Y
STUN TUNS
NUTSEDGE S
NUTSHELL S
NUTSIER
TRIUNES
UNITERS
NUTSIEST
NUTSY
NUTTED
NUTTER S
NUTTERS
ENTRUST
NUTTIER
NUTTIEST
NUTTILY
NUTTING S
NUTTINGS
STUNTING
NUTTY
NUTWOOD S
NUTWOODS
NUZZLE DRS
NUZZLED
NUZZLER S
NUZZLERS
NUZZLES
NUZZLING
NYALA S
NYALAS
NYLGHAI S
NYLGHAIS
NYLGHAU S
NYLGHAUS
NYLON S
NONYL
NYLONS
NONYLS
NYMPH AOS
NYMPHA EL
NYMPHAE
NYMPHAL
NYMPHEAN
NYMPHET S
NYMPHETS
NYMPHO S
NYMPHOS
NYMPHS
NYSTATIN S

O

L OAF S
OAFISH
OAFISHLY
L OAFS
SOFA
S OAK SY
KOA
OKA
OAKEN
OAKIER
OAKIEST
OAKLIKE
OAKMOSS
S OAKS
KOAS OKAS
SOAK
OAKUM S
OAKUMS
OAKY
KAYO OKAY
BHR OAR S
S ORA
RS OARED
ADORE OREAD
B OARFISH
RS OARING
ONAGRI
ORIGAN
OARLESS
LASSOER
SEROSAL
OARLIKE
OARLOCK S
OARLOCKS
BHR OARS
S OSAR SOAR
SORA
OARSMAN
RAMONAS
OARSMEN
ENAMORS
MOANERS
OASES
OASIS
OSSIA
BCR OAST S
T OATS STOA
TAOS
BCR OASTS
T STOAS
BCD OAT HS
GM TAO
OATCAKE S
OATCAKES
OATEN
ATONE
BC OATER S
ORATE
BC OATERS
ORATES
OSETRA
L OATH S
OATHS
HOSTA SHOAT
BGM OATLIKE
KEITLOA
OATMEAL S
OATMEALS
BCD OATS
GM OAST STOA
TAOS
LS OAVES
SOAVE
S OBA S
BOA
S OBAS
BOAS SOBA
OBCONIC
OBDURACY
OBDURATE
TABOURED
LR OBE SY
OBEAH S
BOHEA
OBEAHISM S
BOHEMIAS
OBEAHS
BOHEAS
OBEDIENT
OBEISANT
BOTANIES
BOTANISE
NIOBATES
OBELI A
L OBELIA S
L OBELIAS
OBELISE DS
OBELISED
OBELISES
OBELISK S
OBELISKS
OBELISM S
MOBILES
OBELISMS
OBELIZE DS
OBELIZED
OBELIZES
OBELUS
BLOUSE
BOULES
OBENTO S
OBENTOS
LR OBES E
OBESE
OBESELY
OBESITY
OBEY S
OBEYABLE
OBEYED
OBEYER S
OBEYERS
OBEYING
BIOGENY
OBEYS
OBI AST
BIO
C OBIA S
C OBIAS
OBIISM S
OBIISMS
OBIS
BIOS
OBIT S
OBITS
OBITUARY
OBJECT S
OBJECTED
OBJECTOR S
OBJECTS
OBJET S
OBJETS
OBLAST IS
BLOATS
OBLASTI
OBLASTS
OBLATE S
BOATEL
LOBATE
OBLATELY
LOBATELY
OBLATES
BOATELS
OBLATION S
BOLTONIA
LOBATION
OBLATORY
OBLIGATE DS
OBLIGATI
OBLIGATO RS
OBLIGE DERS
OBLIGED
OBLIGEE S
OBLIGEES
OBLIGER S
OBLIGERS
OBLIGES
OBLIGING
OBLIGOR S
OBLIGORS
OBLIQUE DS
OBLIQUED
OBLIQUES
OBLIVION S
OBLONG S
OBLONGLY
OBLONGS
OBLOQUY
OBOE S
GH OBOES
OBOIST S
OBOISTS
OBOL EIS
BOLO LOBO
OBOLE S
OBOLES
OBOLI
OBOLS
BOLOS LOBOS
OBOLUS
OBOVATE
OBOVOID
OBSCENE R
OBSCENER
OBSCURE DRS
BESCOUR
OBSCURED
OBSCURER
OBSCURES T
BESCOURS
OBSEQUY
OBSERVE DRS
OBVERSE
VERBOSE
OBSERVED
OBSERVER S
OBSERVES
OBVERSES
OBSESS
BOSSES
OBSESSED
OBSESSES
OBSESSOR S
SORBOSES
OBSIDIAN S
OBSOLETE DS
OBSTACLE S
OBSTRUCT S
OBTAIN S
BONITA
OBTAINED
OBTAINER S
BARITONE
REOBTAIN
TABORINE
OBTAINS
BASTION
BONITAS
OBTECT
OBTECTED
OBTEST S
OBTESTED
BESOTTED
OBTESTS
OBTRUDE DRS
DOUBTER
OUTBRED
REDOUBT
OBTRUDED
OBTRUDER S
OBTRUDES
DOUBTERS
REDOUBTS
OBTUND S
OBTUNDED
OBTUNDS
OBTURATE DS
TABOURET
OBTUSE R
BUTEOS
OBTUSELY
OBTUSER
OBTUSEST
OBTUSITY
OBVERSE S
OBSERVE
VERBOSE
OBVERSES
OBSERVES
OBVERT S
OBVERTED
OBVERTS
OBVIABLE
OBVIATE DS
OBVIATED
OBVIATES
OBVIATOR S
OBVIOUS
OBVOLUTE
CLS OCA S
OCARINA S
OCARINAS
CS OCAS
SOCA
OCCASION S
OCCIDENT S
OCCIPITA L
OCCIPUT S
OCCIPUTS
OCCLUDE DS
OCCLUDED
OCCLUDES
OCCLUSAL
OCCULT S
OCCULTED
OCCULTER S
OCCULTLY
OCCULTS
OCCUPANT S
OCCUPIED
OCCUPIER S
OCCUPIES
OCCUPY
OCCUR S
OCCURRED
OCCURS
CROCUS
SUCCOR
OCEAN S
CANOE
OCEANAUT S
OCEANIC
COCAINE
OCEANS
CANOES
OCELLAR
OCELLATE D
OCELLI
COLLIE
OCELLUS
LOCULES
OCELOID
OCELOT S
OCELOTS
COOLEST
T OCHER SY
CHORE OCHRE
T OCHERED
COHERED
T OCHERING
COHERING
OCHEROUS
OCHREOUS
T OCHERS
CHORES
COSHER
OCHRES
OCHERY
OCHONE
OCHRE ADS
CHORE OCHER
OCHREA E
CHOREA
ORACHE
OCHREAE
OCHRED
CHORED
OCHREOUS
OCHEROUS
OCHRES
CHORES
COSHER
OCHERS
OCHRING
CHORING
OCHROID
CHOROID
OCHROUS
OCHRY
OCICAT S
OCICATS
CDH LMR OCKER S
CDH LMR OCKERS
OCOTILLO S
OCREA E
OCREAE
C OCREATE
OCTAD S
OCTADIC
CACTOID
OCTADS
OCTAGON S
OCTAGONS
OCTAL
OCTAN EST
CANTO COTAN
OCTANE S
OCTANES
OCTANGLE S
OCTANOL S
COOLANT
OCTANOLS
COOLANTS
OCTANS
CANTOS
COTANS
OCTANT S
OCTANTAL
OCTANTS
OCTARCHY
OCTAVAL
OCTAVE S
AVOCET
OCTAVES
AVOCETS
OCTAVO S
OCTAVOS
OCTET S
OCTETS
OCTETTE S
OCTETTES
OCTONARY
CARTOONY
OCTOPI
OCTOPOD S
OCTOPODS
OCTOPUS
COPOUTS
OCTOROON S
OCTROI S
OCTROIS
OCTUPLE DST
COUPLET X
OCTUPLED
OCTUPLES
COUPLETS
OCTUPLET S
OCTUPLEX
OCTUPLY
OCTYL S
OCTYLS
COSTLY
JL OCULAR S
J OCULARLY
OCULARS
CAROLUS
OSCULAR
L OCULI
OCULIST S
OCULISTS
L OCULUS
BCG HMN PRS TY OD ADES
DO
CS ODA HS
ADO
ODAH S
ODAHS
ODALISK S
ODALISKS
CS ODAS
ADOS SODA
ODD S
ODDBALL S
ODDBALLS
CDF N ODDER
ODDEST
ODDISH
ODDITIES
ODDITY
ODDLY
ODDMENT S
ODDMENTS
ODDNESS
SODDENS
ODDS
BCL MNR ODE AS
DOE
ODEA
ODEON S
ODEONS
NODOSE
NOOSED
BCL MNR ODES
DOES DOSE
ODEUM S
ODEUMS
MOUSED
IS ODIC
ODIOUS
IODOUS
ODIOUSLY
ODIST S
DOITS
ODISTS
PS ODIUM S
DUOMI
PS ODIUMS
SODIUM
ODOGRAPH S
ODOMETER S
I ODOMETRY
ODONATE S
ODONATES
ODONTOID S
ODOR S
DOOR ORDO
ROOD
ODORANT S
DONATOR
TANDOOR
TORNADO
ODORANTS
DONATORS
TANDOORS
TORNADOS
ODORED
ODORFUL
ODORIZE DS
ODORIZED
ODORIZES
ODORLESS
DOORLESS
LORDOSES
ODOROUS
ODORS
DOORS ORDOS
ROODS
ODOUR S
ODOURFUL
ODOURS
BCG HMN PRS TY ODS
DOS SOD
ODYL ES
OLDY
ODYLE S
YODEL YODLE
ODYLES
YODELS
YODLES
ODYLS
SLOYD
ODYSSEY S
ODYSSEYS
DFH JRT VW OE S
OECOLOGY
OEDEMA S
OEDEMAS

OEDEMATA
OEDIPAL
OEDIPEAN
OEILLADE S
P **OENOLOGY**
OENOMEL S
OENOMELS
LONESOME
OERSTED S
TEREDOS
OERSTEDS
DOSSERET
DFG HJN RTV W **OES**
OSE
OESTRIN S
NORITES ORIENTS STONIER
OESTRINS
OESTRIOL S
OESTRONE S
OESTROUS
OESTRUM S
OESTRUMS
STRUMOSE
OESTRUS
ESTROUS OUSTERS SOUREST SOUTERS STOURES TUSSORE
OEUVRE S
OEUVRES
OVERUSE
OF FT
BCD T **OFF** S
OFFAL S
OFFALS
OFFBEAT S
OFFBEATS
OFFCAST S
CASTOFF
OFFCASTS
CASTOFFS
OFFCUT S
CUTOFF
OFFCUTS
CUTOFFS
BD **OFFED**
OFFENCE S
OFFENCES
OFFEND S
OFFENDED
OFFENDER S
FOREFEND
OFFENDS
SENDOFF
OFFENSE S
OFFENSES
CDG **OFFER** S
CG **OFFERED**
OFFERER S
REOFFER
OFFERERS
REOFFERS
CG **OFFERING** S
OFFEROR S
OFFERORS
CDG **OFFERS**
OFFHAND
HANDOFF
OFFICE RS
COIFFE
OFFICER S
OFFICERS
OFFICES
COIFFES
OFFICIAL S
BCD **OFFING** S
GONIFF
OFFINGS
GONIFFS
OFFISH
OFFISHLY
OFFKEY
OFFLINE
OFFLOAD S
OFFLOADS
OFFPRINT S
OFFRAMP S
OFFRAMPS
BCD T **OFFS**
OFFSET S
SETOFF
OFFSETS
SETOFFS
OFFSHOOT S
OFFSHORE S
OFFSIDE S
DIEOFFS
OFFSIDES
OFFSTAGE S
OFFTRACK
CLS T **OFT**
S **OFTEN**
S **OFTENER**
OFTENEST
LS **OFTER**
FETOR FORTE
S **OFTEST**
OFTTIMES
OGAM S
OGAMS
OGDOAD S
OGDOADS
Y **OGEE** S
Y **OGEES**
OGHAM S
OGHAMIC
OGHAMIST S
OGHAMS
OGIVAL
OGIVE S
VOGIE
OGIVES
B **OGLE** DRS
LOGE
OGLED
LODGE
OGLER S
OGLERS
B **OGLES**
LOGES
OGLING
OGRE S
ERGO GOER GORE
OGREISH
OGREISM S
OGREISMS
OGRES S
GOERS GORES GORSE
OGRESS
GORSES
OGRESSES
OGRISH
OGRISHLY
OGRISM S
OGRISMS
FNO P **OH** MOS
HO
O **OHED**
HOED
OHIA S
OHIAS
O **OHING**
HONGI
OHM S
MHO
OHMAGE S
HOMAGE
OHMAGES
HOMAGES
OHMIC
OHMMETER S
OHMS
MHOS MOSH SHMO
BC **OHO**
OOH
O **OHS**
KP **OI** L
OIDIA
OIDIOID
OIDIUM
BCF MNR ST **OIL** SY
OILBIRD S
OILBIRDS
OILCAMP S
OILCAMPS
OILCAN S
ALNICO
OILCANS
ALNICOS
OILCLOTH S
OILCUP S
UPCOIL
OILCUPS
UPCOILS
BCD FMR ST **OILED**
OLDIE
BCM T **OILER** S
ORIEL REOIL
BCM T **OILERS**
LORIES ORIELS REOILS
OILHOLE S
OILHOLES
R **OILIER**
R **OILIEST**
IOLITES
OILILY
OILINESS
ELISIONS ISOLINES LIONISES
BCF MRS T **OILING**
OILMAN
OILMEN
LOMEIN MOLINE
OILPAPER S
OILPROOF
BCF MNR ST **OILS**
SILO SOIL SOLI
OILSEED S
OILSEEDS
OILSKIN S
OILSKINS
OILSTONE S
LOONIEST
OILTIGHT
OILWAY S
OILWAYS
DNR **OILY**
B **OINK** S
IKON KINO
B **OINKED**
B **OINKING**
B **OINKS**
IKONS KINOS
OINOLOGY
OINOMEL S
OINOMELS
SIMOLEON
OINTMENT S
OITICICA S
OKA SY
KOA OAK
OKAPI S
OKAPIS
OKAS
KOAS OAKS SOAK
T **OKAY** S
KAYO OAKY
OKAYED
KAYOED
OKAYING
KAYOING
T **OKAYS**
KAYOS
CHJ MPS TWY **OKE** HS
OKEH S
HOKE
OKEHS
HOKES
CHJ MPS TY **OKES**
SOKE
OKEYDOKE Y
OKRA S
KORA
OKRAS
KORAS
BCF GHM STW **OLD** SY
DOL
GH **OLDEN**
LODEN
BCF GHM PS **OLDER**
BCG **OLDEST**
STOLED
OLDIE S
OILED
OLDIES
SILOED SOILED
C **OLDISH**
BC **OLDNESS**
BCF GHM W **OLDS**
DOLS SOLD
OLDSQUAW S
OLDSTER S
OLDSTERS
OLDSTYLE S
OLDWIFE
OLDWIVES
M **OLDY**
ODYL
BCD HJM PRS TV **OLE** AOS
OLEA
ALOE
OLEANDER S
RELOANED
OLEASTER S
OLEATE S
OLEATES
OLEFIN ES
OLEFINE S
OLEFINES
FELONIES
OLEFINIC
OLEFINS
OLEIC
OLEIN ES
ELOIN
OLEINE S
OLEINES
OLEINS
ELOINS INSOLE LESION
OLEO S
OLEOS
LOOSE
BCD HJM PRS TV **OLES**
LOSE SLOE SOLE
OLESTRA S
OLESTRAS
OLEUM S
OLEUMS
OLIBANUM S
OLICOOK S
OLICOOKS
OLIGARCH SY
OLIGOMER S
GLOOMIER
OLIGURIA S
OLINGO S
LOGION LOOING
OLINGOS
LOGIONS LOOSING SOLOING
FP **OLIO** S
FP **OLIOS**
OLIVARY
OLIVE S
VOILE
OLIVES
VOILES
OLIVINE S
OLIVINES
OLIVINIC
H **OLLA** S
H **OLLAS**
SALOL
O **OLOGIES**
O **OLOGIST** S
O **OLOGISTS**
O **OLOGY**
D **OLOROSO** S
OLOROSOS
OLYMPIAD S
DMN PRS TY **OM** S
MO
OMASA
OMASUM
BCS **OMBER** S
BROME OMBRE
BC **OMBERS**
BROMES OMBRES SOMBER SOMBRE
HS **OMBRE** S
BROME OMBER
H **OMBRES**
BROMES OMBERS SOMBER SOMBRE
OMEGA S
OMEGAS
OMELET S
TELOME
OMELETS
TELOMES
OMELETTE S
NW **OMEN** S
MENO NOME
OMENED
OMENING
OMENS
MESON NOMES
LMT **OMENTA** L
OMENTAL
LOMENTA TELAMON
LMT **OMENTUM** S
LM **OMENTUMS**
CGH V **OMER** S
MORE
CGH V **OMERS**
MORES MORSE
OMICRON S
MORONIC
OMICRONS
OMIKRON S
OMIKRONS
OMINOUS
OMISSION S
OMISSIVE
V **OMIT** S
V **OMITS**
MOIST
OMITTED
OMITTER S
OMITTERS
OMITTING
OMNIARCH S
HARMONIC
OMNIBUS
OMNIFIC
OMNIFORM
OMNIMODE
OMNIVORA
OMNIVORE S
OMOPHAGY
OMPHALI
OMPHALOS
DMN PRS T **OMS**
MOS SOM
CDE FHI MST WY **ON** EOS
NO
ONAGER S
ORANGE
ONAGERS
ORANGES
ONAGRI
OARING ORIGAN
ONANISM S
AMNIONS MANSION
ONANISMS
MANSIONS
ONANIST S
ANOINTS NATIONS
ONANISTS
ONBOARD
BRADOON
NP **ONCE** T
CONE
ONCET
CENTO CONTE
ONCIDIUM S
CONIDIUM MUCINOID
ONCOGENE S
ONCOLOGY
ONCOMING S
GNOMONIC
ONDOGRAM S
BCD GHL NPS TZ **ONE** S
EON
ONEFOLD
ONEIRIC
DGL **ONENESS**
ONERIER
ONERIEST
SEROTINE
ONEROUS
ONERY
BCH JNP STZ **ONES**
EONS NOES NOSE SONE
ONESELF
Z **ONETIME**
ONGOING
GR **ONION** SY
R **ONIONS**
ONIONY
CGI **ONIUM**
ONLAY S
ONLAYS
ONLINE
ONLOAD S
ONLOADED
ONLOADS
ONLOOKER S
S **ONLY**
M **ONO** S
NOO
M **ONOS**
SOON
ONRUSH
ONRUSHES
UNHORSES
CDE FHI MPS TW **ONS**
NOS SON
ONSCREEN
ONSET S
NOTES SETON STENO STONE TONES
ONSETS
SETONS STENOS STONES
ONSHORE
ONSIDE
DONSIE NOISED
ONSTAGE
ONSTREAM
MONSTERA TONEARMS
ONTIC
TONIC
C **ONTO**
TOON
ONTOGENY
ONTOLOGY
BCT **ONUS**
NOUS
BNT **ONUSES**
NOUSES
ONWARD S
ONWARDS
ONYX
ONYXES
OOCYST S
OOCYSTS
OOCYTE S
COYOTE
OOCYTES
COYOTES
BDN P **OODLES**
LOOSED SOLOED
OODLINS
Z **OOGAMETE** S
OOGAMIES
OOGAMOUS
OOGAMY
Z **OOGENIES**
Z **OOGENY**
GOONEY
OOGONIA L
OOGONIAL
OOGONIUM S
P **OOH** S
OHO
P **OOHED**
P **OOHING**
P **OOHS**
SHOO
OOLACHAN S
OOLITE S
OOLITES
OSTIOLE STOOLIE
OOLITH S
THOLOI
OOLITHS
OOLITIC
Z **OOLOGIC**
Z **OOLOGIES**
Z **OOLOGIST** S
Z **OOLOGY**
OOLONG S
OOLONGS
OOMIAC KS
OOMIACK S
OOMIACKS
OOMIACS
OOMIAK S
OOMIAKS
OOMPAH S
OOMPAHED
OOMPAHS
SHAMPOO
OOMPH S
OOMPHS
Z **OOPHYTE** S
Z **OOPHYTES**
Z **OOPHYTIC**
CGH LPW **OOPS**
W **OORALI** S
W **OORALIS**
OORIE
Z **OOSPERM** S
Z **OOSPERMS**
N **OOSPHERE** S
Z **OOSPORE** S
Z **OOSPORES**
Z **OOSPORIC**
BCF HLM RST **OOT** S
TOO
OOTHECA EL
OOTHECAE
OOTHECAL
OOTID S

OOTIDS
BCF HLM RST **OOTS** SOOT
B **OOZE** DS
B **OOZED**
B **OOZES**
BW **OOZIER** ZOOIER
BW **OOZIEST** ZOOIEST
BW **OOZILY**
BW **OOZINESS** OZONISES
B **OOZING**
BDW **OOZY**
BCF HKL MPS TW **OP** EST

OPACIFY
OPACITY
OPAH S
OPAHS
CN **OPAL** S
OPALESCE DS ESCALOPE
OPALINE S
OPALINES
CN **OPALS**
OPAQUE DRS
OPAQUED
OPAQUELY
OPAQUER
OPAQUES T
OPAQUEST
OPAQUING
CDH LMN PRT **OPE** DNS
CDH LMR T **OPED** DOPE
C **OPEN** S NOPE PEON PONE
OPENABLE BEANPOLE
OPENCAST CAPSTONE
OPENED DEPONE
OPENER S PEREON REOPEN
OPENERS PEREONS REOPENS
OPENEST PENTOSE POSTEEN POTEENS
OPENING S
OPENINGS
OPENLY POLEYN
OPENNESS
C **OPENS** PEONS PONES
OPENWORK S
OPERA S PAREO
OPERABLE
OPERABLY
OPERAND S APRONED PADRONE PANDORE
OPERANDS PADRONES PANDORES
OPERANT S PRONATE PROTEAN
OPERANTS PRONATES PROTEANS
OPERAS PAREOS SOAPER
OPERATE DS

OPERATED
OPERATES PROTEASE
OPERATIC S
OPERATOR S
OPERCELE S
OPERCULA R
OPERCULE S RECOUPLE
OPERETTA S
OPERON S
OPERONS SNOOPER
OPEROSE
CDH LMP RT **OPES** EPOS PESO POSE
OPHIDIAN S
OPHITE S
OPHITES
OPHITIC
OPIATE DS
OPIATED
OPIATES ATOPIES
OPIATING
OPINE DS
OPINED PONIED
OPINES PONIES
CDH LMR T **OPING** GIPON PINGO
OPINING
OPINION S
OPINIONS
OPIOID S
OPIOIDS
OPIUM S
OPIUMISM S
OPIUMS
OPOSSUM S
OPOSSUMS
OPPIDAN S
OPPIDANS
OPPILANT
OPPILATE DS
OPPONENT S
OPPOSE DRS
OPPOSED
OPPOSER S PROPOSE
OPPOSERS PROPOSES
OPPOSES
OPPOSING POGONIPS
OPPOSITE S
OPPRESS
OPPUGN S POPGUN
OPPUGNED
OPPUGNER S
OPPUGNS POPGUNS
BCF HKL MOP STW **OPS** SOP
OPSIN S PIONS
OPSINS
OPSONIC POCOSIN
OPSONIFY
OPSONIN S
OPSONINS SPONSION
OPSONIZE DS
OPT S POT TOP
OPTATIVE S
OPTED DEPOT TOPED
OPTIC S PICOT TOPIC

OPTICAL CAPITOL COALPIT TOPICAL
OPTICIAN S
OPTICIST S
OPTICS PICOTS TOPICS
OPTIMA L
OPTIMAL
OPTIME S
OPTIMES MOPIEST
OPTIMISE DS
OPTIMISM S
OPTIMIST S
OPTIMIZE DRS
OPTIMUM S
OPTIMUMS
OPTING TOPING
OPTION S POTION
OPTIONAL S NOPALITO
OPTIONED
OPTIONEE S
OPTIONS POTIONS
OPTS POST POTS SPOT STOP TOPS
OPULENCE S
OPULENCY
OPULENT
OPUNTIA S UTOPIAN
OPUNTIAS UTOPIANS
OPUS SOUP
OPUSCULA R
OPUSCULE S
OPUSES SPOUSE
OQUASSA S
OQUASSAS
CDF GKM NT **OR** ABCEST
BFH KMS T **ORA** DL OAR
ORACH E ROACH
ORACHE S CHOREA OCHREA
ORACHES CHOREAS ROACHES
C **ORACLE** S COALER RECOAL
C **ORACLES** CLAROES COALERS ESCOLAR RECOALS SOLACER
ORACULAR
ORAD ROAD
BCG HLM **ORAL** S
M **ORALISM** S
M **ORALISMS** SOLARISM
M **ORALIST** S RIALTOS TAILORS
M **ORALISTS**
M **ORALITY**
M **ORALLY**
BCG M **ORALS** SOLAR
ORANG ESY ARGON GROAN ORGAN

ORANGE SY ONAGER
ORANGERY
ORANGES ONAGERS
ORANGEY
ORANGIER
ORANGISH
ORANGS ARGONS GROANS ORGANS SARONG
ORANGY
B **ORATE** DS OATER
B **ORATED**
B **ORATES** OATERS OSETRA
B **ORATING**
ORATION S
ORATIONS
ORATOR SY
ORATORIO S
ORATORS
M **ORATORY**
ORATRESS ASSERTOR ASSORTER REASSORT ROASTERS
ORATRIX
FS **ORB** SY BRO ROB
S **ORBED** BORED ROBED
ORBIER
ORBIEST
S **ORBING** BORING ROBING
ORBIT S
ORBITAL S
ORBITALS STROBILA
ORBITED DEORBIT
ORBITER S
ORBITERS
ORBITING
ORBITS BISTRO
ORBLESS
FS **ORBS** BROS ROBS SORB
CF **ORBY**
T **ORC** AS COR ROC
ORCA S ARCO
ORCAS
ORCEIN S COINER RECOIN
ORCEINS COINERS CRONIES RECOINS
ORCHARD S
ORCHARDS
ORCHID S RHODIC
ORCHIDS
ORCHIL S
ORCHILS
ORCHIS CHIROS CHOIRS ICHORS
ORCHISES
ORCHITIC
ORCHITIS HISTORIC
ORCIN S
ORCINOL S
ORCINOLS
ORCINS

T **ORCS** CORS ROCS
ORDAIN S INROAD
ORDAINED
ORDAINER S REORDAIN
ORDAINS INROADS SADIRON
ORDEAL S LOADER RELOAD
ORDEALS LOADERS RELOADS
BC **ORDER** S
B **ORDERED**
B **ORDERER** S REORDER
B **ORDERERS** REORDERS
B **ORDERING**
ORDERLY
BC **ORDERS** DORSER
ORDINAL S
ORDINALS
ORDINAND S
ORDINARY
ORDINATE S AROINTED RATIONED
S **ORDINES** DINEROS INDORSE ROSINED SORDINE
ORDNANCE S
F **ORDO** S DOOR ODOR ROOD
ORDOS DOORS ODORS ROODS
B **ORDURE** S DOURER
B **ORDURES**
ORDUROUS
BCD FGK LMP STW Y **ORE** S ROE
OREAD S ADORE OARED
OREADS ADORES SARODE SOARED
ORECTIC CEROTIC
ORECTIVE
OREGANO S
OREGANOS
OREIDE S
OREIDES OSIERED
OREODONT S
BCF GLM PST Y **ORES** EROS ROES ROSE SORE
ORFRAY S
ORFRAYS
M **ORGAN** AS ARGON GROAN ORANG
ORGANA ANGORA
ORGANDIE S
ORGANDY
ORGANIC S
ORGANICS
ORGANISE DRS
ORGANISM S
ORGANIST S ROASTING
ORGANIZE DRS
ORGANON S

ORGANONS
M **ORGANS** ARGONS GROANS ORANGS SARONG
ORGANUM S
ORGANUMS
ORGANZA S
ORGANZAS
ORGASM S
ORGASMED
ORGASMIC
ORGASMS
ORGASTIC
ORGEAT S GAROTE
ORGEATS GAROTES STORAGE
ORGIAC
ORGIAST S
ORGIASTS
ORGIC CORGI
P **ORGIES**
F **ORGONE** S
ORGONES
ORGULOUS
P **ORGY** GORY GYRO
ORIBATID S
ORIBI S
ORIBIS
ORIEL S OILER REOIL
ORIELS LORIES OILERS REOILS
ORIENT S NORITE TONIER
ORIENTAL S RELATION
ORIENTED
ORIENTER S REORIENT
ORIENTS NORITES OESTRIN STONIER
ORIFICE S
ORIFICES
ORIGAMI S
ORIGAMIS
ORIGAN S OARING ONAGRI
ORIGANS SIGNORA SOARING
ORIGANUM S
ORIGIN S
ORIGINAL S
ORIGINS SIGNIOR SIGNORI
ORINASAL S
ORIOLE S
ORIOLES
ORISHA S
ORISHAS
ORISON S
ORISONS
ORLE S LORE ROLE
ORLES LORES LOSER ROLES SOREL
ORLON S
ORLONS
ORLOP S
ORLOPS
DFW **ORMER** S
DFW **ORMERS**
ORMOLU S
ORMOLUS
ORNAMENT S

ORNATE ATONER
ORNATELY
ORNERIER
ORNERY
ORNIS IRONS NOIRS NORIS ROSIN
ORNITHES HORNIEST
ORNITHIC
OROGENIC
OROGENY
OROIDE S
OROIDES
H **OROLOGY**
OROMETER S
OROTUND
ORPHAN S
ORPHANED
ORPHANS
M **ORPHIC**
ORPHICAL
ORPHISM S ROMPISH
ORPHISMS
ORPHREY S
ORPHREYS
ORPIMENT S
ORPIN ES PRION
ORPINE S PERNIO
ORPINES
ORPINS PRIONS PRISON SPINOR
ORRA ROAR
ORRERIES
ORRERY
ORRICE S CORRIE
ORRICES CIRROSE CORRIES CROSIER
M **ORRIS**
M **ORRISES**
CDK MT **ORS**
BFM PST W **ORT** S ROT TOR
ORTHICON S
ORTHO THORO
ORTHODOX Y
ORTHOEPY
ORTHOSES RESHOOTS SHEROOTS SHOOTERS SOOTHERS
ORTHOSIS
ORTHOTIC S
ORTOLAN S
ORTOLANS
BFM PST W **ORTS** ROTS SORT TORS
ORYX
ORYXES
ORZO S
ORZOS
BCD GHK MNS W **OS** E SO
OSAR OARS SOAR SORA
OSCINE S CONIES COSINE ICONES
OSCINES CESSION COSINES

OSCININE
CONIINES
OSCITANT
TACTIONS
OSCULA R
OSCULANT
OSCULAR
CAROLUS
OCULARS
OSCULATE DS
LACTEOUS
LOCUSTAE
OSCULE S
COLEUS
OSCULES
OSCULUM
DHL NPR **OSE** S
OES
CDH LNP R **OSES**
OSETRA S
OATERS
ORATES
OSETRAS
OSSETRA
CHN R **OSIER** S
OSIERED
OREIDES
H **OSIERS**
SEISOR
OSMATIC
ATOMICS
SOMATIC
C **OSMIC** S
OSMICS
OSMIOUS
OSMIUM S
OSMIUMS
OSMOL ES
LOOMS MOOLS
OSMOLAL
OSMOLAR
OSMOLE S
OSMOLES
OSMOLS
OSMOSE DS
OSMOSED
C **OSMOSES**
OSMOSING
OSMOSIS
OSMOTIC
OSMOUS
OSMUND AS
MOUNDS
OSMUNDA S
OSMUNDAS
OSMUNDS
OSNABURG S
OSPREY S
OSPREYS
F **OSSA**
OSSATURE S
OSSEIN S
ENOSIS
EOSINS
ESSOIN
NOESIS
NOISES
SONSIE
OSSEINS
ESSOINS
SESSION
OSSEOUS
OSSETRA S
OSETRAS
OSSETRAS
OSSIA
OASIS
OSSICLE S
OSSICLES
OSSIFIC
OSSIFIED
OSSIFIER S
OSSIFIES
OSSIFY
OSSUARY
SUASORY

OSTEAL
SOLATE
OSTEITIC
OSTEITIS
OTITISES
OSTEOID S
OSTEOIDS
OSTEOMA S
OSTEOMAS
MAESTOSO
OSTEOSES
OSTEOSIS
OSTIA
IOTAS STOAI
OSTIARY
OSTINATI
OSTINATO S
OSTIOLAR
ISOLATOR
OSTIOLE S
OOLITES
STOOLIE
OSTIOLES
STOOLIES
OSTIUM
HJ **OSTLER** S
STEROL
HJ **OSTLERS**
STEROLS
P **OSTMARK** S
P **OSTMARKS**
OSTOMATE S
TOMATOES
OSTOMIES
OSTOMY
OSTOSES
OSTOSIS
OSTRACA
OSTRACOD ES
OSTRACON
CARTOONS
CORANTOS
OSTRAKA
OSTRAKON
OSTRICH
OTALGIA S
OTALGIAS
OTALGIC
OTALGIES
LATIGOES
OTALGY
BMN PT **OTHER** S
THROE
BMP **OTHERS**
HORSTE
RESHOT
THROES
L **OTIC**
OTIOSE
OTIOSELY
OTIOSITY
OTITIC
OTITIDES
OTITIS
OTITISES
OSTEITIS
OTOCYST S
OTOCYSTS
OTOLITH S
OTOLITHS
OTOLOGY
OTOSCOPE S
OTOSCOPY
OTOTOXIC
C **OTTAR** S
TAROT TORTA
C **OTTARS**
STATOR
TAROTS
TORTAS
OTTAVA S
OTTAVAS
CDH JLP RT **OTTER** S
ROTTE TORTE
TOTER
CDJ LPR T **OTTERS**
ROTTES
TORTES
TOTERS

LMP **OTTO** S
TOOT
OTTOMAN S
OTTOMANS
LMP **OTTOS**
TOOTS
OUABAIN S
OUABAINS
CMP TV **OUCH**
CDM PTV **OUCHED**
DOUCHE
CDM PRT V **OUCHES**
CHOUSE
CDM PTV **OUCHING**
L **OUD** S
DUO
UDO
OUDS
DUOS UDOS
BDF NS **OUGHT** S
TOUGH
OUGHTED
TOUGHED
OUGHTING
TOUGHING
N **OUGHTS**
SOUGHT
TOUGHS
OUGUIYA S
OUGUIYAS
OUISTITI S
BJP **OUNCE** S
BJP **OUNCES**
OUPH ES
OUPHE S
OUPHES
OUPHS
DFH LPS TY **OUR** S
OURANG S
OURANGS
OURARI S
OURARIS
OUREBI S
OUREBIS
OURIE
FHL PST Y **OURS**
SOUR
Y **OURSELF**
H **OUSEL** S
LOUSE
H **OUSELS**
LOUSES
SOLEUS
JR **OUST** S
OUTS
JR **OUSTED**
TOUSED
JR **OUSTER** S
OUTERS
ROUTES
SOUTER
STOURE
JR **OUSTERS**
ESTROUS
OESTRUS
SOUREST
SOUTERS
STOURES
TUSSORE
JR **OUSTING**
OUTINGS
OUTSING
TOUSING
JR **OUSTS**
BGL PRT **OUT** S
OUTACT S
OUTACTED
OUTACTS
OUTCAST
OUTADD S
OUTADDED
OUTADDS
OUTAGE S
OUTAGES

OUTARGUE DS
OUTASK S
OUTASKED
OUTASKS
OUTATE
OUTEAT
OUTBACK S
BACKOUT
OUTBACKS
BACKOUTS
OUTBAKE DS
OUTBAKED
OUTBAKES
OUTBARK S
OUTBARKS
OUTBAWL S
OUTBAWLS
OUTBEAM S
OUTBEAMS
OUTBEG S
OUTBEGS
OUTBID S
OUTBIDS
OUTBITCH
OUTBLAZE DS
OUTBLEAT S
OUTBLESS
OUTBLOOM S
OUTBLUFF S
OUTBLUSH
OUTBOARD S
OUTBOAST S
OUTBOUND
OUTBOX
OUTBOXED
OUTBOXES
OUTBRAG S
OUTBRAGS
OUTBRAVE DS
OUTBRAWL S
OUTBREAK S
BREAKOUT
OUTBRED
DOUBTER
OBTRUDE
REDOUBT
OUTBREED S
OUTBRIBE DS
OUTBUILD S
OUTBUILT
OUTBULGE DS
OUTBULK S
OUTBULKS
OUTBULLY
OUTBURN ST
BURNOUT
OUTBURNS
BURNOUTS
OUTBURNT
OUTBURST S
OUTBUY S
BUYOUT
OUTBUYS
BUYOUTS
OUTBY E
OUTBYE
OUTCALL S
OUTCALLS
LOCUSTAL
OUTCAPER S
OUTCAST ES
OUTACTS
OUTCASTE S
OUTCASTS
OUTCATCH
OUTCAVIL S
OUTCHARM S
OUTMARCH
OUTCHEAT S
OUTCHID E
OUTCHIDE DS
OUTCITY
OUTCLASS
OUTCLIMB S
OUTCLOMB
OUTCOACH
OUTCOME S

OUTCOMES
OUTCOOK S
COOKOUT
OUTCOOKS
COOKOUTS
OUTCOUNT S
OUTCRAWL S
OUTCRIED
OUTCRIES
CITREOUS
OUTCROP S
OUTCROPS
OUTCROSS
OUTCROW DS
OUTCROWD S
OUTCROWS
OUTCRY
OUTCURSE DS
COUTURES
OUTCURVE S
OUTDANCE DS
UNCOATED
OUTDARE DS
OUTREAD
READOUT
OUTDARED
OUTDARES
OUTREADS
READOUTS
OUTDATE DS
OUTDATED
OUTDATES
OUTDID
OUTDO
OUTDODGE DS
OUTDOER S
OUTRODE
OUTDOERS
OUTDOES
OUTDOING
OUTDONE
DUOTONE
OUTDOOR S
OUTDOORS Y
OUTDRAG S
OUTDRAGS
OUTDRANK
OUTDRAW NS
OUTWARD
OUTDRAWN
UNTOWARD
OUTDRAWS
OUTWARDS
OUTDREAM ST
OUTDRESS
OUTDREW
OUTDRINK S
OUTDRIVE NS
OUTDROP S
DROPOUT
OUTDROPS
DROPOUTS
OUTDROVE
OUTDRUNK
OUTDUEL S
OUTDUELS
OUTEARN S
OUTEARNS
OUTEAT S
OUTATE
OUTEATEN
OUTEATS
OUTECHO
LPR T **OUTED**
CPR ST **OUTER** S
OUTRE ROUTE
CPR ST **OUTERS**
OUSTER
ROUTES
SOUTER
STOURE
OUTFABLE DS
OUTFACE DS
OUTFACED
OUTFACES
OUTFALL S
FALLOUT
OUTFALLS
FALLOUTS

OUTFAST S
OUTFASTS
OUTFAWN S
OUTFAWNS
OUTFEAST S
OUTFEEL S
OUTFEELS
OUTFELT
OUTFENCE DS
OUTFIELD S
OUTFIGHT S
OUTFIND S
OUTFINDS
OUTFIRE DS
OUTFIRED
OUTFIRES
OUTFISH
OUTFIT S
OUTFITS
OUTFLANK S
OUTFLEW
OUTFLIES
OUTFLOAT S
OUTFLOW NS
OUTFLOWN
OUTFLOWS
OUTFLY
OUTFOOL S
OUTFOOLS
OUTFOOT S
OUTFOOTS
OUTFOUND
OUTFOX
OUTFOXED
OUTFOXES
OUTFROWN S
OUTGAIN S
AUTOING
OUTGAINS
OUTGAS
OUTGAVE
OUTGAZE DS
OUTGAZED
OUTGAZES
OUTGIVE NS
OUTGIVEN
OUTGIVES
OUTGLARE DS
OUTGLEAM S
OUTGLOW S
OUTGLOWS
OUTGNAW NS
OUTGNAWN
OUTGNAWS
OUTGO
OUTGOES
OUTGOING S
OUTGONE
OUTGREW
OUTGRIN S
OUTRING
ROUTING
TOURING
OUTGRINS
OUTRINGS
ROUSTING
TOURINGS
OUTGROSS
OUTGROUP S
OUTGROW NS
OUTGROWN
OUTGROWS
OUTGUESS
OUTGUIDE DS
OUTGUN S
OUTGUNS
OUTSUNG
OUTGUSH
OUTHAUL S
OUTHAULS
OUTHEAR DS
OUTHEARD
AUTHORED
OUTHEARS
OUTHIT S

OUTHITS
OUTHOMER S
OUTHOUSE S
OUTHOWL S
OUTHOWLS
OUTHUMOR S
OUTHUNT S
OUTHUNTS
LPR T **OUTING** S
OUTINGS
OUSTING
OUTSING
TOUSING
OUTJINX
OUTJUMP S
OUTJUMPS
OUTJUT S
OUTJUTS
OUTKEEP S
OUTKEEPS
OUTKEPT
OUTKICK S
OUTKICKS
OUTKILL S
OUTKILLS
OUTKISS
OUTLAID
OUTLAIN
OUTLAND S
OUTLANDS
OUTLAST S
OUTLASTS
OUTLAUGH S
OUTLAW S
OUTLAWED
OUTLAWRY
OUTLAWS
OUTLAY S
LAYOUT
OUTLAYS
LAYOUTS
OUTLEAD S
OUTLEADS
OUTLEAP ST
OUTLEAPS
PETALOUS
OUTLEAPT
OUTLEARN ST
OUTLED
LOUTED
OUTLET S
OUTLETS
OUTLIE RS
OUTLIER S
OUTLIERS
OUTLIES
OUTLINE DRS
ELUTION
OUTLINED
OUTLINER S
OUTLINES
ELUTIONS
OUTLIVE DRS
OUTLIVED
OUTLIVER S
OUTLIVES
OUTLOOK S
LOOKOUT
OUTLOOKS
LOOKOUTS
OUTLOVE DS
OUTLOVED
OUTLOVES
OUTLYING
OUTMAN S
AMOUNT
OUTMANS
AMOUNTS
OUTMARCH
OUTCHARM
OUTMATCH
OUTMODE DS
OUTMODED
OUTMODES
OUTMOST
OUTMOVE DS

OUTMOVED
OUTMOVES
OUTPACE DS
OUTPACED
OUTPACES
SAUCEPOT
OUTPAINT S
OUTPASS
OUTPITCH
PITCHOUT
OUTPITY
OUTPLACE DS
COPULATE
OUTPLAN S
OUTPLANS
OUTPLAY S
OUTPLAYS
OUTPLOD S
OUTPLODS
OUTPLOT S
OUTPLOTS
OUTPOINT S
OUTPOLL S
OUTPOLLS
OUTPORT S
OUTPORTS
OUTPOST S
OUTPOSTS
OUTPOUR S
OUTPOURS
OUTPOWER S
OUTPRAY S
OUTPRAYS
OUTPREEN S
OUTPRESS
POSTURES
SPOUTERS
OUTPRICE DS
OUTPULL S
PULLOUT
OUTPULLS
PULLOUTS
OUTPUNCH
OUTPUPIL S
OUTPUSH
OUTPUT S
PUTOUT
OUTPUTS
PUTOUTS
OUTQUOTE DS
OUTRACE DS
OUTRACED
AERODUCT
EDUCATOR
OUTRACES
OUTRAGE DS
OUTRAGED
RAGOUTED
OUTRAGES
OUTRAISE DS
SAUTOIRE
OUTRAN GK
OUTRANCE S
COURANTE
OUTRANG E
OUTRANGE DS
OUTRANK S
OUTRANKS
OUTRATE DS
OUTRATED
OUTTRADE
OUTRATES
OUTSTARE
SEATROUT
OUTRAVE DS
OUTRAVED
OUTRAVES
OUTRE
OUTER ROUTE
OUTREACH
OUTREAD S
OUTDARE
READOUT
OUTREADS
OUTDARES
READOUTS
OUTRIDE RS
OUTRIDER S

OUTRIDES
OUTSIDER
OUTRIG S
OUTRIGHT
OUTRIGS
OUTRING S
OUTGRIN
ROUTING
TOURING
OUTRINGS
OUTGRINS
ROUSTING
TOURINGS
OUTRIVAL S
OUTROAR S
OUTROARS
OUTROCK S
OUTROCKS
OUTRODE
OUTDOER
OUTROLL S
ROLLOUT
OUTROLLS
ROLLOUTS
OUTROOT S
OUTROOTS
OUTROW S
OUTROWED
OUTROWS
OUTRUN GS
RUNOUT
OUTRUNG
OUTRUNS
RUNOUTS
OUTRUSH
BGL OUTS
PRT OUST
OUTSAID
OUTSAIL S
OUTSAILS
OUTSANG
NOUGATS
OUTSAT
OUTSAVOR S
OUTSAW
OUTSAY S
OUTSAYS
OUTSCOLD S
OUTSCOOP S
OUTSCORE DS
ECOTOURS
OUTSCORN S
CONTOURS
CORNUTOS
CROUTONS
OUTSEE NS
OUTSEEN
OUTSEES
OUTSELL S
SELLOUT
OUTSELLS
SELLOUTS
OUTSERT S
STOUTER
TOUTERS
OUTSERTS
TUTORESS
OUTSERVE DS
OUTSET S
SETOUT
OUTSETS
SETOUTS
OUTSHAME DS
OUTSHINE DS
OUTSHONE
OUTSHOOT S
SHOOTOUT
OUTSHOT
OUTSHOUT S
OUTSIDE RS
TEDIOUS
OUTSIDER S
OUTRIDES
OUTSIDES
OUTSIGHT S
OUTSIN GS
OUTSING S
OUSTING
OUTINGS
TOUSING
OUTSINGS

OUTSINS
OUTSIT S
OUTSITS
OUTSIZE DS
OUTSIZED
OUTSIZES
OUTSKATE DS
OUTTAKES
STAKEOUT
TAKEOUTS
OUTSKIRT S
OUTSLEEP S
EELPOUTS
OUTSLEPT
OUTSPELT
OUTSLICK S
OUTSMART S
OUTSMELL S
OUTSMELT
OUTSMILE DS
OUTSMOKE DS
OUTSNORE DS
OUTSOAR S
OUTSOARS
OUTSOLD
OUTSOLE S
OUTSOLES
OUTSPAN S
OUTSPANS
OUTSPEAK S
OUTSPED
SPOUTED
OUTSPEED S
OUTSPELL S
POLLUTES
OUTSPELT
OUTSLEPT
OUTSPEND S
UNPOSTED
OUTSPENT
OUTSPOKE N
OUTSTAND S
STANDOUT
OUTSTARE DS
OUTRATES
SEATROUT
OUTSTART S
OUTSTATE DS
OUTSTAY S
OUTSTAYS
OUTSTEER S
OUTSTOOD
OUTSTRIP S
OUTSTUDY
OUTSTUNT S
OUTSULK S
OUTSULKS
OUTSUNG
OUTGUNS
OUTSWAM
OUTSWARE
OUTSWEAR
OUTWEARS
OUTSWEAR S
OUTSWARE
OUTWEARS
OUTSWEEP S
OUTWEEPS
OUTSWEPT
OUTSWIM S
OUTSWIMS
OUTSWING S
OUTSWORE
OUTSWORN
OUTSWUM
OUTSWUNG
OUTTAKE S
TAKEOUT
OUTTAKES
OUTSKATE
STAKEOUT
TAKEOUTS
OUTTALK S
OUTTALKS
OUTTASK S
OUTTASKS
OUTTELL S
OUTTELLS

OUTTHANK S
OUTTHINK S
OUTTHREW
OUTTHROB S
OUTTHROW NS
OUTTOLD
OUTTOWER S
OUTWROTE
OUTTRADE DS
OUTRATED
OUTTRICK S
OUTTROT S
OUTTROTS
OUTTRUMP S
OUTTURN S
TURNOUT
OUTTURNS
TURNOUTS
OUTVALUE DS
OUTVAUNT S
OUTVIE DS
OUTVIED
OUTVIES
OUTVOICE DS
OUTVOTE DS
OUTVOTED
OUTVOTES
OUTVYING
OUTWAIT S
OUTWAITS
OUTWALK S
WALKOUT
OUTWALKS
WALKOUTS
OUTWAR DS
OUTWARD S
OUTDRAW
OUTWARDS
OUTDRAWS
OUTWARS
OUTWASH
WASHOUT
OUTWASTE DS
OUTWATCH
WATCHOUT
OUTWEAR SY
OUTWEARS
OUTSWARE
OUTSWEAR
OUTWEARY
ROUTEWAY
OUTWEEP S
OUTWEEPS
OUTSWEEP
OUTWEIGH S
OUTWENT
OUTWEPT
OUTWHIRL S
OUTWILE DS
OUTWILED
OUTWILES
OUTWILL S
OUTWILLS
OUTWIND S
OUTWINDS
OUTWISH
OUTWIT HS
OUTWITH
WITHOUT
OUTWITS
OUTWORE
OUTWORK S
WORKOUT
OUTWORKS
WORKOUTS
OUTWORN
OUTWRIT E
OUTWRITE S
OUTWROTE
OUTTOWER
OUTYELL S
OUTYELLS
OUTYELP S
OUTYELPS
OUTYIELD S
OUZEL S
OUZELS
OUZO S
OUZOS

N OVA L
AVO
OVAL S
OVALITY
OVALLY
OVALNESS
OVALS
SALVO
OVARIAL
VARIOLA
OVARIAN
C OVARIES
OVARIOLE S
OVARITIS
C OVARY
OVATE
OVATELY
N OVATION S
N OVATIONS
CDR OVEN S
W
OVENBIRD S
OVENLIKE
CDW OVENS
OVENWARE S
CHL OVER ST
MR ROVE
C OVERABLE
OVERACT S
OVERACTS
OVERCAST
C OVERAGE DS
OVERAGED
C OVERAGES
C OVERALL S
ALLOVER
C OVERALLS
ALLOVERS
OVERAPT
OVERARCH
OVERARM S
OVERARMS
OVERATE
OVEREAT
OVERAWE DS
OVERAWED
REAVOWED
OVERAWES
OVERBAKE DS
OVERBEAR S
OVERBEAT S
OVERBED
OVERBET S
OVERBETS
OVERBID S
OVERBIDS
OVERBIG
OVERBILL S
OVERBITE S
OVERBLEW
OVERBLOW NS
OVERBOIL S
BOILOVER
OVERBOLD
OVERBOOK S
OVERBORE
OVERBORN E
OVERBRED
OVERBURN ST
OVERBUSY
OVERBUYS
OVERBUY S
OVERBUYS
OVERBUSY
OVERCALL S
COVERALL
OVERCAME
OVERCAST S
OVERACTS
OVERCOAT S
EVOCATOR
OVERCOLD
OVERCOME RS
OVERCOOK S
OVERCOOL S
OVERCOY
OVERCRAM S
OVERCROP S

OVERCURE DS
OVERCUT S
CUTOVER
OVERCUTS
CUTOVERS
OVERDARE DS
OVERDEAR
OVERDEAR
OVERDARE
OVERDECK S
OVERDID
OVERDO G
OVERDOER S
OVERRODE
OVERDOES
OVERDOSE
OVERDOG S
GROOVED
OVERDOGS
OVERDONE
OVERDOSE DS
OVERDOES
OVERDRAW NS
OVERDREW
OVERDRY
OVERDUB S
OVERDUBS
OVERDUE
OVERDYE DRS
OVERDYED
OVERDYER S
OVERDYES
OVEREASY
OVEREAT S
OVERATE
OVEREATS
CH OVERED
OVEREDIT S
OVERFAR
FAVORER
OVERFAST
OVERFAT
OVERFEAR S
OVERFED
OVERFEED S
OVERFILL S
OVERFISH
OVERFIT
OVERFLEW
OVERFLOW NS
H OVERFLY
FLYOVER
OVERFOND
OVERFOUL
OVERFREE
OVERFULL
OVERFUND S
OVERGILD S
OVERGILT
OVERGIRD S
OVERGIRT
OVERGLAD
OVERGOAD S
OVERGREW
OVERGROW N S
OVERHAND S
HANDOVER
OVERHANG S
HANGOVER
OVERHARD
OVERHATE DS
OVERHEAT
OVERHAUL S
OVERHEAD S
OVERHEAP S
OVERHEAR DS
OVERHEAT S
OVERHATE
OVERHELD
OVERHIGH
OVERHOLD S
HOLDOVER
OVERHOLY
OVERHOPE DS
OVERHOT
OVERHUNG
HUNGOVER
OVERHUNT S

OVERHYPE DS
OVERIDLE
EVILDOER
CH OVERING
OVERJOY S
OVERJOYS
OVERJUST
OVERKEEN
OVERKILL S
OVERKIND
OVERLADE DN S
OVERLAID
OVERLAIN
OVERLAND S
OVERLAP S
OVERLAPS
OVERLATE
ELEVATOR
OVERLAX
OVERLAY S
LAYOVER
OVERLAYS
LAYOVERS
OVERLEAF
OVERLEAP ST
OVERLEND S
OVERLENT
C OVERLET S
C OVERLETS
OVERLEWD
OVERLIE S
RELIEVO
OVERLIES
RELIEVOS
VOLERIES
OVERLIT
OVERLIVE DS
OVERLOAD S
OVERLONG
OVERLOOK S
OVERLORD S
OVERLOUD
OVERLOVE DS
OVERLUSH
L OVERLY
VOLERY
OVERMAN SY
OVERMANS
OVERMANY
OVERMEEK
OVERMELT S
OVERMEN
VENOMER
OVERMILD
OVERMILK S
OVERMINE DS
VOMERINE
OVERMIX
OVERMUCH
OVERNEAR
OVERNEAT
RENOVATE
OVERNEW
REWOVEN
OVERNICE
OVERPACK S
OVERPAID
OVERPASS
PASSOVER
OVERPAST
OVERPAY S
OVERPAYS
OVERPERT
OVERPLAN ST
OVERPLAY S
OVERPLOT S
OVERPLUS
OVERPLY
OVERPUMP S
OVERRAN K
OVERRANK
OVERRASH
OVERRATE DS
OVERRICH
OVERRIDE S
OVERRIFE

OVERRIPE
OVERRODE
OVERDOER
OVERRUDE
DEVOURER
OVERRUFF S
OVERRULE DS
OVERRUN S
RUNOVER
OVERRUNS
RUNOVERS
CHL OVERS
MR ROVES SERVO
VERSO
OVERSAD
SAVORED
OVERSALE S
OVERSALT S
LEVATORS
OVERSAVE DS
OVERSAW
AVOWERS
REAVOWS
OVERSEA S
OVERSEAS
OVERSEE DNR S
OVERSEED S
OVERSEEN
OVERSEER S
OVERSEES
OVERSELL S
OVERSET S
REVOTES
VETOERS
OVERSETS
ESTOVERS
OVERSEW NS
OVERSEWN
OVERSEWS
OVERSHOE S
OVERSHOT S
OVERSICK
OVERSIDE S
OVERSIZE DS
C OVERSLIP ST
SLIPOVER
OVERSLOW
OVERSOAK S
OVERSOFT
OVERSOLD
OVERSOON
OVERSOUL S
OVERSPIN S
OVERSTAY S
OVERSTEP S
OVERSTIR S
SERVITOR
OVERSUDS
OVERSUP S
OVERSUPS
OVERSURE
C OVERT
TROVE VOTER
OVERTAKE NS
TAKEOVER
OVERTALK S
OVERTAME
OVERTART
OVERTASK S
OVERTAX
OVERTHIN K
OVERTIME DS
OVERTIP S
OVERTIPS
SORPTIVE
SPORTIVE
OVERTIRE DS
C OVERTLY
OVERTOIL S
OVERTONE S
OVERTOOK
OVERTOP S
OVERTOPS
STOPOVER
OVERTRIM S
C OVERTURE DS
TROUVERE

OVERTURN S
TURNOVER
OVERURGE DS
OVERUSE DS
OEUVRES
OVERUSED
OVERUSES
OVERVIEW S
OVERVOTE DS
OVERWARM S
OVERWARY
OVERWEAK
OVERWEAR SY
OVERWEEN S
OVERWET S
OVERWETS
OVERWIDE
OVERWILY
OVERWIND S
OVERWISE
OVERWORD S
OVERWORE
OVERWORK S
OVERWORN
OVERZEAL S
OVIBOS
OVICIDAL
OVICIDE S
OVICIDES
OVIDUCAL
OVIDUCT S
OVIDUCTS
OVIFORM
B OVINE S
ENVOI
B OVINES
ENVOIS
OVIPARA
OVIPOSIT S
OVISAC S
OVISACS
OVOID S
OVOIDAL S
OVOIDALS
OVOIDS
OVOLI
OVOLO S
OVOLOS
OVONIC S
OVONICS
OVULAR Y
VALOUR
OVULARY
OVULATE DS
OVULATED
OVULATES
OVULE S
OVULES
OVUM
BCD HJL MNP RST VWY OW ELN
WO
HLY OWE DS
WOE
BCD JLM RST VWY OWED
HLY OWES
OWSE WOES
BCD JLM RST VWY OWING
BCF HJY OWL S
LOW
H OWLET S
TOWEL
H OWLETS
LOWEST
TOWELS
OWLISH
LOWISH
OWLISHLY
B OWLLIKE

BCF HJY OWLS
LOWS SLOW
DGL MST OWN S
NOW
WON
OWNABLE
DG OWNED
ENDOW
D OWNER S
REWON ROWEN
D OWNERS
RESOWN
ROWENS
WORSEN
DG OWNING
DGT OWNS
NOWS SNOW
SOWN WONS
BDL OWSE N
OWES WOES
OWSEN
ENOWS
BCF GLP SV OX OY
OXALATE DS
OXALATED
OXALATES
OXALIC
OXALIS
OXALISES
OXAZEPAM S
OXAZINE S
OXAZINES
OXBLOOD S
OXBLOODS
OXBOW S
OXBOWS
OXCART S
OXCARTS
OXEN
EXON
BCF GLP OXES
OXEYE S
OXEYES
OXFORD S
OXFORDS
OXHEART S
OXHEARTS
THORAXES
OXID ES
OXIDABLE
OXIDANT S
OXIDANTS
OXIDASE S
OXIDASES
OXIDASIC
OXIDATE DS
OXIDATED
OXIDATES
OXIDE S
DOXIE
OXIDES
DOXIES
OXIDIC
OXIDISE DRS
OXIDISED
DIOXIDES
OXIDISER S
OXIDISES
OXIDIZE DRS
OXIDIZED
OXIDIZER S
OXIDIZES
OXIDS
OXIM ES
OXIME S
MOXIE
OXIMES
MOXIES
OXIMETER S
OXIMETRY
OXIMS
SIXMO
BF OXLIKE
OXLIP S
OXLIPS
OXO

OXPECKER S
F OXTAIL S
F OXTAILS
OXTER S
OXTERS
OXTONGUE S
BDF P OXY
OXYACID S
OXYACIDS
OXYGEN S
OXYGENIC
OXYGENS
OXYMORA
OXYMORON S
OXYPHIL ES
OXYPHILE S
OXYPHILS
OXYSALT S
OXYSALTS
OXYSOME S
OXYSOMES
OXYTOCIC S
OXYTOCIN S
OXYTONE S
OXYTONES
BCF GHJ ST OY
YO
CFT OYER S
YORE
FT OYERS
YORES
OYES
OYESSES
OYEZ
OYEZES
R OYSTER S
STOREY
TOYERS
R OYSTERED
STOREYED
OYSTERER S
R OYSTERS
STOREYS
OZALID S
OZALIDS
OZONATE DS
ENTOZOA
OZONATED
OZONATES
OZONE S
OZONES
SNOOZE
OZONIC
OZONIDE S
OZONIDES
OZONISED
OZONISE DS
OZONISED
OZONIDES
OZONISES
OOZINESS
OZONIZE DRS
OZONIZED
OZONIZER S
OZONIZES
OZONOUS

P

S PA CDHLMNPR STWXY
PABLUM S
PABLUMS
PABULAR
PABULUM S
PABULUMS
PAC AEKSTY
CAP
PACA S
PACAS
AS PACE DRSY
CAPE
S PACED
CAPED
S PACER S
CAPER CRAPE
RECAP

S PACERS
CAPERS
CRAPES
ESCARP
PARSEC
RECAPS
SCRAPE
SECPAR
SPACER
S PACES
CAPES SCAPE
SPACE
S PACEY
PACHA S
PACHADOM S
PACHALIC S
PACHAS
PACHINKO S
PACHISI S
PACHISIS
PACHOULI S
PACHUCO S
CAPOUCH
PACHUCOS
S PACIER
S PACIEST
ASEPTIC
SPICATE
PACIFIC
O PACIFIED
O PACIFIER S
O PACIFIES
PACIFISM S
PACIFIST S
O PACIFY
S PACING
PACK S
PACKABLE
PACKAGE DRS
PACKAGED
PACKAGER S
PACKAGES
PACKED
PACKER S
REPACK
PACKERS
REPACKS
PACKET S
PACKETED
PACKETS
PACKING S
PACKINGS
PACKLY
PACKMAN
MANPACK
PACKMEN
PACKNESS
PACKS
PACKSACK S
PACKWAX
PACS
CAPS
E PACT S
PACTION S
CAPTION
PACTIONS
CAPTIONS
E PACTS
S PACY
PAD IS
DAP
PADAUK S
PADAUKS
PADDED
PADDER S
DRAPED
PADDERS
PADDIES
PADDING S
PADDINGS
PADDLE DRS
PADDLED
PADDLER S
PADDLERS
SPRADDLE
PADDLES
PADDLING S
PADDOCK S

PADDOCKS
PADDY
PADI S
PAID
PADIS
SAPID
PADISHAH S
PADLE S
PALED PEDAL
PLEAD
PADLES
LAPSED
PEDALS
PLEADS
PADLOCK S
PADLOCKS
PADNAG S
PADNAGS
PADOUK S
PADOUKS
PADRE S
DRAPE PARED
RAPED
PADRES
DRAPES
PARSED
RASPED
SPADER
SPARED
SPREAD
PADRI
PARDI RAPID
PADRONE S
APRONED
OPERAND
PANDORE
PADRONES
OPERANDS
PANDORES
PADRONI
PONIARD
PADS
DAPS
PADSHAH S
PADSHAHS
PADUASOY S
PAEAN S
APNEA
PAEANISM S
PAEANS
APNEAS
PAESAN
PAELLA S
PALEAL
PAELLAS
PAEON S
PAEONS
PAESAN IOS
APNEAS
PAEANS
PAESANI
PAESANO S
APNOEAS
PAESANOS
PAESANS
PAGAN S
PANGA
PAGANDOM S
PAGANISE DS
PAGANISH
PAGANISM S
PAGANIST S
PAGANIZE DR S
PAGANS
PANGAS
PAGE DRS
GAPE PEAG
PAGEANT S
PAGEANTS
PAGEBOY S
PAGEBOYS
PAGED
GAPED
PAGEFUL S
PAGEFULS
PAGER S
GAPER GRAPE
PARGE

PAGERS
GAPERS
GASPER
GRAPES
PARGES
SPARGE
PAGES
GAPES PEAGS
PAGINAL
PAGINATE DS
PAGING S
GAPING
PAGINGS
GASPING
PAGOD AS
PAGODA S
PAGODAS
PAGODS
PAGURIAN S
PAGURID S
PAGURIDS
O PAH
HAP
PAHLAVI S
PAHLAVIS
PAHOEHOE S
PAID
PADI
PAIK S
PIKA
PAIKED
PAIKING
PAIKS
PIKAS
S PAIL S
LIPA PIAL
PAILFUL S
PAILFULS
PAILSFUL
PAILLARD S
S PAILS
LAPIS SPAIL
PAILSFUL
PAILFULS
PAIN ST
NIPA PIAN
PINA
PAINCH
PAINCHES
PAINED
PAINFUL
PAINING
PAINLESS
SPANIELS
PAINS
NIPAS PIANS
PINAS
PAINT SY
INAPT PATIN
PINTA
PAINTED
DEPAINT
PATINED
PAINTER S
PERTAIN
REPAINT
PAINTERS
PANTRIES
PERTAINS
PINASTER
PRISTANE
REPAINTS
PAINTIER
PAINTING S
PATINING
PAINTS
PATINS
PINTAS
PTISAN
PAINTY
PAIR S
PAIRED
DIAPER
PARDIE
REPAID
PAIRING S
PAIRINGS
ASPIRING
PRAISING
PAIRS
PARIS
PAISA NS

PAISAN AOS
PAISANA S
PAISANAS
PAISANO S
ANOPIAS
ANOPSIA
PAISANOS
ANOPSIAS
PAISANS
PAISAS
PAISE
SEPIA
PAISLEY S
PAISLEYS
PAJAMA S
PAJAMAED
PAJAMAS
PAKEHA S
PAKEHAS
PAKORA S
PAKORAS
O PAL ELMPSY
ALP
LAP
PALABRA S
PALABRAS
PALACE DS
PALACED
PALACES
PALADIN S
PALADINS
PALAIS
PALAPA S
PALAPAS
PALATAL S
PALATALS
PALATE S
PALATES
PALATIAL
PALATINE S
PALAVER S
PALAVERS
PALAZZI
PALAZZO S
PALAZZOS
S PALE ADRST
LEAP PEAL
PLEA
PALEA EL
PALEAE
PALEAL
PAELLA
PALEATE
PALED
PADLE PEDAL
PLEAD
PALEFACE S
PALELY
PALENESS
PANELESS
PALEOSOL S
PALER
PARLE PEARL
S PALES T
LAPSE LEAPS
PEALS PLEAS
SALEP SEPAL
SPALE
PALEST
PALETS
PASTEL
PETALS
PLATES
PLEATS
SEPTAL
STAPLE
TEPALS
PALESTRA EL
S
PALET S
LEAPT LEPTA
PETAL PLATE
PLEAT TEPAL
PALETOT S
PALETOTS

PALETS
PALEST
PASTEL
PETALS
PLATES
PLEATS
SEPTAL
STAPLE
TEPALS
PALETTE S
PELTATE
PALETTES
PALEWAYS
PALEWISE
PALFREY S
PALFREYS
PALIER
PALIEST
APLITES
PLATIES
TALIPES
PALIKAR S
PALIKARS
PALIMONY
PALING S
PALINGS
LAPSING
SAPLING
PALINODE S
PALISADE DS
PALISH
PHIALS
S PALL SY
PALLADIA
PALLADIC
S PALLED
PALLET S
PALLETED
PETALLED
PALLETS
PALLETTE S
PLATELET
PALLIA L
PALLIAL
PALLIATE DS
PALLID
PALLIDLY
PALLIER
PERILLA
PALLIEST
PASTILLE
S PALLING
PALLIUM S
PALLIUMS
PALLOR S
PALLORS
S PALLS
SPALL
PALLY
PALM SY
LAMP
PALMAR Y
PALMARY
PALMYRA
PALMATE D
PALMATED
PALMED
LAMPED
PALMER S
AMPLER
PALMERS
LAMPERS
SAMPLER
PALMETTE S
TEMPLATE
PALMETTO S
PALMFUL S
PALMFULS
PALMIER
IMPALER
IMPEARL
LEMPIRA
PALMIEST
PALMING
LAMPING
PALMIST S
PALMISTS
PSALMIST
PALMITIN S
PALMLIKE

PALMS
LAMPS PLASM
PSALM
PALMTOP S
PALMTOPS
LAMPPOST
PALMY
AMPLY
PALMYRA S
PALMARY
PALMYRAS
PALOMINO S
PALOOKA S
PALOOKAS
PALP IS
PALPABLE
PALPABLY
PALPAL
APPALL
PALPATE DS
PALPATED
PALPATES
PALPATOR SY
PALPEBRA EL
S
PALPED
DAPPLE
LAPPED
PALPI
PIPAL
PALPING
LAPPING
PALPS
PALPUS
O PALS Y
ALPS LAPS
SALP SLAP
PALSHIP S
SHIPLAP
PALSHIPS
SHIPLAPS
PALSIED
ALIPEDS
ELAPIDS
LAPIDES
PLEIADS
PALSIES
ESPIALS
LAPISES
LIPASES
PALSY
PLAYS SPLAY
PALSYING
SPLAYING
PALTER S
PLATER
PALTERED
REPLATED
PALTERER S
PREALTER
PALTERS
PERSALT
PLASTER
PLATERS
PSALTER
STAPLER
PALTRIER
PRETRIAL
PALTRILY
PALTRY
PARTLY
RAPTLY
PALUDAL
PALUDISM S
PALY
PLAY
S PAM S
AMP
MAP
PAMPA S
PAMPAS
PAMPEAN S
PAMPEANS
PAMPER OS
MAPPER
PREAMP
PAMPERED
REMAPPED
PAMPERER S
PAMPERO S
PAMPEROS

PAMPERS
MAPPERS
PREAMPS
PAMPHLET S
S PAMS
AMPS MAPS
SAMP SPAM
S PAN EGST
NAP
PANACEA NS
PANACEAN
PANACEAS
PANACHE S
PANACHES
PANADA S
PANADAS
PANAMA S
PANAMAS
PANATELA S
PANBROIL S
PANCAKE DS
PANCAKED
PANCAKES
PANCETTA S
PANCHAX
PANCREAS
PANDA S
PANDANI
PANDANUS
PANDAS
PANDECT S
PANDECTS
PANDEMIC S
PANDER S
REPAND
PANDERED
PANDERER S
PANDERS
PANDIED
PANDIES
PANDIT S
PANDITS
SANDPIT
PANDOOR S
PANDOORS
PANDORA S
PANDORAS
PANDORE S
APRONED
OPERAND
PADRONE
PANDORES
OPERANDS
PADRONES
PANDOUR S
PANDOURS
PANDOWDY
PANDURA S
PANDURAS
PANDY
PANDYING
PANE DLS
NAPE NEAP
PEAN
PANED
PANEL S
PENAL PLANE
PLENA
PANELED
DEPLANE
PANELESS
PALENESS
PANELING S
PANELIST S
PANTILES
PLAINEST
PANELLED
PANELS
PLANES
PANES
ASPEN NAPES
NEAPS PEANS
SNEAP SPEAN
PANETELA S
PANFISH
PANFRIED
PANFRIES
FIREPANS

PANFRY
FRYPAN
PANFUL S
PANFULS
S PANG AS
PANGA S
PAGAN
PANGAS
PAGANS
PANGED
PANGEN ES
PENANG
PANGENE S
PANGENES
PANGENS
PENANGS
PANGING
PANGOLIN S
PANGRAM S
PANGRAMS
PANGS
SPANG
PANHUMAN
PANIC S
PANICKED
PANICKY
PANICLE DS
CAPELIN
PELICAN
PANICLED
PANICLES
CAPELINS
PELICANS
PANICS
PANICUM S
PANICUMS
PANIER S
RAPINE
PANIERS
RAPINES
PANINI
PANINO
PANMIXES
PANMIXIA S
PANMIXIS
PANNE DRS
PENNA
S PANNED
S PANNER S
S PANNERS
SPANNER
PANNES
PANNIER S
PANNIERS
PANNIKIN S
S PANNING
PANOCHA S
PANOCHAS
PANOCHE S
PANOCHES
PANOPLY
PANOPTIC
PANORAMA S
PANPIPE S
PANPIPES
S PANS Y
NAPS SNAP
SPAN
PANSIES
SAPIENS
PANSOPHY
PANSY
PANT OSY
PANTALET S
PANTED
PEDANT
PENTAD
PANTHEON S
PANTHER S
PANTHERS
PANTIE S
PATINE
PINETA
PANTIES
PATINES
SAPIENT
SPINATE
PANTILE DS
PANTILED

PANTILES
PANELIST
PLAINEST
PANTING
PANTO S
PANTOFLE S
PANTOS
PANTOUM S
PANTOUMS
PANTRIES
PAINTERS
PERTAINS
PINASTER
PRISTANE
REPAINTS
PANTRY
PANTS
PANTSUIT S
PANTY
PANZER S
PANZERS
PAP AS
APP
PAPA LSW
PAPACIES
PAPACY
PAPADAM S
PAPADAMS
PAPADOM S
PAPADOMS
PAPADUM S
PAPADUMS
PAPAIN S
PAPAINS
PAPAL
APPAL
PAPALLY
PAPAS
PAPAW S
PAPAWS
PAPAYA NS
PAPAYAN
PAPAYAS
PAPER SY
PAPERBOY S
PAPERED
PAPERER S
PREPARE
REPAPER
PAPERERS
PREPARES
REPAPERS
PAPERING
PAPERS
SAPPER
PAPERY
PREPAY
YAPPER
PAPHIAN S
PAPHIANS
PAPILLA ER
PAPILLAE
PAPILLAR Y
PAPILLON S
PAPOOSE S
PAPOOSES
PAPPADAM S
PAPPI
PAPPIER
PAPPIES T
PAPPIEST
PAPPOOSE S
PAPPOSE
PAPPOUS
PAPPUS
PAPPY
PAPRICA S
PAPRICAS
PAPRIKA S
PAPRIKAS
PAPS
APPS
PAPULA ER
PAPULAE
PAPULAR
PAPULE S
UPLEAP

PAPULES
APPULSE
UPLEAPS
PAPULOSE
PAPYRAL
PAPYRI
PAPYRIAN
PAPYRINE
PAPYRUS
S PAR ADEKRST
RAP
PARA ES
S PARABLE S
S PARABLES
PARSABLE
PREBASAL
SPARABLE
PARABOLA S
PARACHOR S
PARADE DRS
PARADED
PARADER S
PARADERS
PARADES
PARADIGM S
PARADING
PARADISE S
PARADOR S
PARADORS
PARADOS
PARADOX
PARADROP S
PARAE
AREPA
PARAFFIN ES
PARAFOIL S
PARAFORM S
PARAGOGE S
PARAGON S
PARAGONS
PARAKEET S
PARAKITE S
PARALLAX
PARALLEL S
PARALYSE DS
PARALYZE DR
S
PARAMENT AS
PARAMO S
PARAMOS
PARAMOUR S
PARANG S
PARANGS
PARANOEA S
PARANOIA CS
PARANOIC S
PARANOID S
PARAPET S
PARAPETS
PARAPH S
PARAPHS
PARAQUAT S
PARAQUET S
PARAS
PARASAIL S
PARASANG S
PARASHAH S
PARASHOT H
PARASITE S
ASPIRATE
SEPTARIA
PARASOL S
PARASOLS
PARAVANE S
PARAWING S
PARAZOAN S
PARBAKE DS
PARBAKED
PARBAKES
PARBOIL S
BIPOLAR
PARBOILS
PARCEL S
CARPEL
PLACER

PARCELED
REPLACED
PARCELS
CARPELS
CLASPER
PLACERS
RECLASP
SCALPER
PARCENER S
E **PARCH**
PARCHED
PARCHES I
EPARCHS
PARCHESI S
ASPHERIC
SERAPHIC
PARCHING
PARCHISI S
PARCLOSE S
PARD ISY
PARDAH S
PARDAHS
PARDEE
REAPED
PARDI E
PADRI RAPID
PARDIE
DIAPER
PAIRED
REPAID
PARDINE
PARDNER S
PARDNERS
PARDON S
PARDONED
PARDONER S
PARDONS
PARDS
PARDY
S **PARE** DORSU
APER PEAR
RAPE REAP
PARECISM S
SAPREMIC
S **PARED**
DRAPE PADRE
RAPED
PAREIRA S
PAREIRAS
PARENT S
ARPENT
ENRAPT
ENTRAP
TREPAN
PARENTAL
PARLANTE
PATERNAL
PRENATAL
PARENTED
PARENTS
ARPENTS
ENTRAPS
PASTERN
TREPANS
PAREO S
OPERA
PAREOS
OPERAS
SOAPER
S **PARER** S
RAPER
PARERGA
PARERGON
S **PARERS**
PARSER
RAPERS
RASPER
SPARER
S **PARES**
APERS APRES
ASPER PARSE
PEARS PRASE
PRESA RAPES
REAPS SPARE
SPEAR
PARESES
ASPERSE
SERAPES

PARESIS
ASPIRES
PARISES
PRAISES
SPIREAS
PARETIC S
PICRATE
PARETICS
CRISPATE
PICRATES
PRACTISE
PAREU S
PAREUS
PAUSER
PAREVE
REPAVE
PARFAIT S
PARFAITS
PARFLESH
PARFOCAL
S **PARGE** DST
GAPER GRAPE
PAGER
S **PARGED**
S **PARGES**
GAPERS
GASPER
GRAPES
PAGERS
SPARGE
PARGET S
PARGETED
PARGETS
S **PARGING** S
PARGINGS
GRASPING
SPARGING
PARGO S
PARGOS
PARHELIA
PARHELIC
PARIAH S
RAPHIA
PARIAHS
RAPHIAS
PARIAN S
PIRANA
PARIANS
PIRANAS
PARIES
ASPIRE
PRAISE
SPIREA
PARIETAL S
PARIETES
S **PARING** S
RAPING
PARINGS
PARSING
RASPING
SPARING
PARIS H
PAIRS
PARISES
ASPIRES
PARESIS
PRAISES
SPIREAS
PARISH
RAPHIS
PARISHES
SHARPIES
PARITIES
PARITY
S **PARK** AS
PARKA S
PARKADE S
PARKADES
PARKAS
S **PARKED**
S **PARKER** S
REPARK
S **PARKERS**
REPARKS
SPARKER
PARKETTE S
S **PARKING** S
PARKINGS
SPARKING
PARKLAND S
PARKLIKE

S **PARKS**
SPARK
PARKWAY S
PARKWAYS
PARLANCE S
PARLANDO
PARLANTE
PARENTAL
PATERNAL
PRENATAL
PARLAY S
PARLAYED
PARLAYS
PARLE DSY
PALER PEARL
PARLED
PEDLAR
PARLES
LAPSER
PEARLS
PARLEY S
PEARLY
PLAYER
REPLAY
PARLEYED
REPLAYED
PARLEYER S
PARLEYS
PARSLEY
PLAYERS
REPLAYS
SPARELY
S **PARLING**
GRAPLIN
PARLOR S
PARLORS
PARLOUR S
PARLOURS
SPORULAR
PARLOUS
PARMESAN S
SPEARMAN
PARODIC
PICADOR
PARODIED
PARODIES
DIASPORE
PARODIST S
PAROTIDS
PARODOI
PARODOS
PARODY
PAROL ES
POLAR
PAROLE DES
PAROLED
LEOPARD
PRELOAD
PAROLEE S
PAROLEES
PAROLES
REPOSAL
PAROLING
PAROLS
POLARS
SPORAL
PARONYM S
PARONYMS
PAROQUET S
PAROSMIA S
MARIPOSA
PAROTIC
APRICOT
APROTIC
PAROTID S
PAROTIDS
PARODIST
PAROTOID S
PAROUS
SAPOUR
UPSOAR
PAROXYSM S
PARQUET S
PARQUETS
PARR SY
PARRAL S
PARRALS
S **PARRED**
DRAPER
PARREL S
PARRELS

PARRIDGE S
PARRIED
RAPIDER
S **PARRIER** S
PARRIERS
SPARRIER
PARRIES
ASPIRER
PRAISER
RAPIERS
RASPIER
REPAIRS
S **PARRING**
PARRITCH
PHRATRIC
PARROKET S
PARROT SY
RAPTOR
PARROTED
PREDATOR
PRORATED
PROTRADE
TEARDROP
PARROTER S
PARROTS
RAPTORS
PARROTY
PORTRAY
PARRS
S **PARRY**
PARRYING
S **PARS** E
RAPS RASP
SPAR
PARSABLE
PARABLES
PREBASAL
SPARABLE
S **PARSE** CDRS
APERS APRES
ASPER PARES
PEARS PRASE
PRESA RAPES
REAPS SPARE
SPEAR
PARSEC S
CAPERS
CRAPES
ESCARP
PACERS
RECAPS
SCRAPE
SECPAR
SPACER
PARSECS
ESCARPS
SCRAPES
SECPARS
SPACERS
PARSED
DRAPES
PADRES
RASPED
SPADER
SPARED
SPREAD
S **PARSER** S
PARERS
RAPERS
RASPER
SPARER
PARSERS
RASPERS
SPARERS
SPARSER
PARSES
ASPERS
PASSER
PRASES
REPASS
SPARES
SPARSE
SPEARS
PARSING
PARINGS
RASPING
SPARING
PARSLEY S
PARLEYS
PLAYERS
REPLAYS
SPARELY

PARSLEYS
SPARSELY
PARSLIED
LIPREADS
SPIRALED
PARSNIP S
PARSNIPS
PARSON S
APRONS
PARSONIC
PARSONS
A **PART** SY
PRAT RAPT
TARP TRAP
PARTAKE NRS
PARTAKEN
PARTAKER S
PARTAKES
S **PARTAN** S
TARPAN
TRAPAN
PARTANS
SPARTAN
TARPANS
TRAPANS
PARTED
DEPART
PETARD
PRATED
PARTERRE S
PARTIAL S
PARTIALS
PARTIBLE
PARTICLE S
PRELATIC
PARTIED
DIPTERA
PIRATED
PARTIER S
PARTIERS
PARTIES
PASTIER
PIASTER
PIASTRE
PIRATES
TRAIPSE
PARTING S
PRATING
PARTINGS
PARTISAN S
ASPIRANT
SPARTINA
PARTITA S
PARTITAS
PARTITE
PARTIZAN S
PARTLET S
PLATTER
PRATTLE
PARTLETS
PLATTERS
PRATTLES
SPLATTER
SPRATTLE
PARTLY
PALTRY
RAPTLY
PARTNER S
PARTNERS
PARTON S
PATRON
TARPON
PARTONS
PATRONS
TARPONS
PARTOOK
PARTS
PRATS SPRAT
STRAP TARPS
TRAPS
PARTWAY
PARTY
PARTYER S
PARTYERS
PARTYING
PARURA S
PARURAS
PARURE S
UPREAR
PARURES
UPREARS

PARVE
PAVER
PARVENU ES
PARVENUE S
PARVENUS
PARVIS E
PARVISE S
PAVISER
PARVISES
PAVISERS
PARVO S
VAPOR
PARVOLIN ES
PARVOS
VAPORS
SU **PAS** EHST
ASP
SAP
SPA
PASCAL S
PASCALS
PASCHAL S
PASCHALS
PASE OS
APES APSE
PEAS SPAE
PASEO S
PSOAE
PASEOS
U **PASES**
APSES PASSE
SPAES
PASH A
HAPS HASP
PASHA S
PASHADOM S
PASHALIC S
CALIPASH
PASHALIK S
PASHAS
PASHED
HASPED
PHASED
SHAPED
PASHES
PHASES
SHAPES
PASHING
HASPING
PHASING
SHAPING
PASHMINA S
PASQUIL S
PASQUILS
PASS E
ASPS SAPS
SPAS
PASSABLE
PASSABLY
PASSADE S
PASSADES
PASSADO S
POSADAS
PASSADOS
PASSAGE DS
PASSAGED
PASSAGES
PASSANT
PASSBAND S
PASSBOOK S
PASSE DELRS
APSES PASES
SPAES
PASSED
SPADES
PASSEE
PEASES
PASSEL S
LAPSES
SALEPS
SEPALS
SPALES
PASSELS
SAPLESS
PASSER S
ASPERS
PARSES
PRASES
REPASS
SPARES
SPARSE
SPEARS

PASSERBY
PASSERS
PASSES
PASSIBLE
PASSIM
PASSING S
PASSINGS
PASSION S
PASSIONS
PASSIVE S
PAVISES
PAVISSE
SPAVIES
PASSIVES
PAVISSES
PASSKEY S
PASSKEYS
PASSLESS
PASSOVER S
OVERPASS
PASSPORT S
PASSUS
PASSUSES
PASSWORD S
PAST AESY
PATS SPAT
TAPS
PASTA S
ATAPS TAPAS
PASTAS
PASTE DLRS
PATES PEATS
SEPTA SPATE
TAPES TEPAS
PASTED
ADEPTS
PASTEL S
PALEST
PALETS
PETALS
PLATES
PLEATS
SEPTAL
STAPLE
TEPALS
PASTELS
STAPLES
PASTER NS
PATERS
PRATES
REPAST
TAPERS
TRAPES
PASTERN S
ARPENTS
ENTRAPS
PARENTS
TREPANS
PASTERNS
RAPTNESS
PASTERS
REPASTS
SPAREST
PASTES
SPATES
STAPES
PASTEUP S
PUPATES
PASTEUPS
PASTICCI O
PASTICHE S
HEPATICS
PISTACHE
PASTIE RS
PETSAI
PIETAS
PASTIER
PARTIES
PIASTER
PIASTRE
PIRATES
TRAIPSE
PASTIES T
PATSIES
PETSAIS
TAPISES
PASTIEST
PASTIL S
PLAITS
SPITAL
PASTILLE S
PALLIEST

PASTILS
SPITALS
PASTIME S
IMPASTE
PASTIMES
IMPASTES
PASTINA S
PATINAS
PINATAS
TAIPANS
PASTINAS
PASTING
PASTIS
SPAITS
PASTISES
PASTITSO S
PASTLESS
PASTNESS
PASTOR S
PASTORAL EI S
PASTORED
ADOPTERS
READOPTS
PASTORLY
PASTORS
PASTRAMI S
PASTRIES
PIASTERS
PIASTRES
RASPIEST
TRAIPSES
PASTROMI S
ATROPISM
PASTRY
PASTS
SPATS
PASTURAL
SPATULAR
PASTURE DRS
UPRATES
UPSTARE
UPTEARS
PASTURED
UPDATERS
UPSTARED
PASTURER S
RAPTURES
PASTURES
UPSTARES
PASTY
PATSY
S PAT EHSY
APT
TAP
PATACA S
PATACAS
PATAGIA L
PATAGIAL
PATAGIUM
PATAMAR S
PATAMARS
PATCH Y
CHAPT
PATCHED
PATCHER S
CHAPTER
REPATCH
PATCHERS
CHAPTERS
PATCHES
HEPCATS
PATCHIER
CHAPITER
PHREATIC
PATCHILY
PATCHING
NIGHTCAP
PATCHY
S PATE DNRS
PEAT TAPE
TEPA
PATED
ADEPT TAPED
PATELLA ERS
PATELLAE
PATELLAR
PATELLAS
PATEN ST
PATENCY
PATENS

PATENT S
PATTEN
PATENTED
PATTENED
PATENTEE S
PATENTLY
PATENTOR S
PATENTS
PATTENS
PATER S
APTER PEART
PRATE TAPER
PATERNAL
PARENTAL
PARLANTE
PRENATAL
PATERS
PASTER
PRATES
REPAST
TAPERS
TRAPES
S PATES
PASTE PEATS
SEPTA SPATE
TAPES TEPAS
PATH S
PHAT
A PATHETIC
PATHLESS
PATHOGEN ES
HEPTAGON Y
PATHOS
POTASH
PATHOSES
POTASHES
SPATHOSE
TEASHOPS
PATHS
STAPH
PATHWAY S
PATHWAYS
PATIENCE S
PATIENT S
PATIENTS
PATIN AES
INAPT PAINT
PINTA
PATINA ES
PINATA
TAIPAN
PATINAE D
PATINAED
PATINAS
PASTINA
PINATAS
TAIPANS
PATINATE DS
PATINE DS
PANTIE
PINETA
PATINED
DEPAINT
PAINTED
PATINES
PANTIES
SAPIENT
SPINATE
PATINING
PAINTING
PATINIZE DS
PATINS
PAINTS
PINTAS
PTISAN
PATIO S
PATIOS
PATOIS
PATLY
APTLY PLATY
TYPAL
PATNESS
APTNESS
PATOIS
PATIOS
PATOOTIE S
PATRIATE DS
PATRIOT S
PATRIOTS
PATROL S
PORTAL
PATROLS
PORTALS

PATRON S
PARTON
TARPON
PATRONAL
PATRONLY
PATRONS
PARTONS
TARPONS
PATROON S
PRONOTA
PATROONS
S PATS Y
PAST SPAT
TAPS
PATSIES
PASTIES
PETSAIS
TAPISES
PATSY
PASTY
PATTAMAR S
S PATTED
PATTEE
PATTEN S
PATENT
PATTENED
PATENTED
PATTENS
PATENTS
S PATTER NS
S PATTERED
PATTERER S
PRETREAT
PATTERN S
REPTANT
PATTERNS
TRANSEPT
TRAPNEST
S PATTERS
SPATTER
TAPSTER
PATTIE S
PATTIES
S PATTING
PATTY
PATTYPAN S
PATULENT
PETULANT
PATULOUS
PATY
PATZER S
PATZERS
PAUCITY
PAUGHTY
PAULDRON S
PAULIN S
PAULINS
SPINULA
PAUNCH Y
PAUNCHED
PAUNCHES
PAUNCHY
PAUPER S
PAUPERED
PAUPERS
PAUSAL
PAUSE DRS
PAUSED
PAUSER S
PAREUS
PAUSERS
PAUSES
UPASES
PAUSING
PAVAN ES
PAVANE S
PAVANES
PAVANS
PAVE DRS
PAVED
PAVEED
PAVEMENT S
PAVER S
PARVE
PAVERS
PAVES
PAVID
VAPID
PAVILION S
PAVILLON S

S PAVIN GS
PAVING S
PAVINGS
S PAVINS
SPAVIN
PAVIOR S
PAVIORS
PAVIOUR S
PAVIOURS
PAVIS E
PAVISE RS
SPAVIE
PAVISER S
PARVISE
PAVISERS
PARVISES
PAVISES
PASSIVE
PAVISSE
SPAVIES
PAVISSE S
PASSIVE
PAVISES
SPAVIES
PAVISSES
PASSIVES
PAVLOVA S
PAVLOVAS
PAVONINE
PAW LNS
WAP
PAWED
PAWER S
PAWERS
PAWING
PAWKIER
PAWKIEST
PAWKILY
PAWKY
PAWL S
PAWLS
S PAWN S
PAWNABLE
PAWNAGE S
PAWNAGES
S PAWNED
PAWNEE S
PAWNEES
S PAWNER S
ENWRAP
S PAWNERS
ENWRAPS
SPAWNER
S PAWNING
PAWNOR S
PAWNORS
S PAWNS
SPAWN
PAWNSHOP S
PAWPAW S
PAWPAWS
PAWS
SWAP WAPS
WASP
PAX
PAXES
PAXWAX
PAXWAXES
S PAY S
PYA
YAP
PAYABLE S
PAYABLES
PAYABLY
PAYBACK S
PAYBACKS
PAYCHECK S
PAYDAY S
PAYDAYS
S PAYED
PAYEE S
PAYEES
PAYER S
APERY REPAY
PAYERS
REPAYS
PAYGRADE S
S PAYING

PAYLOAD S
PAYLOADS
PAYMENT S
PAYMENTS
PAYNIM S
PAYNIMS
PAYOFF S
PAYOFFS
PAYOLA S
PAYOLAS
PAYOR S
PAYORS
PAYOUT S
PAYOUTS
AUTOPSY
PAYROLL S
PAYROLLS
S PAYS
PYAS SPAY
YAPS
PAZAZZ
PAZAZZES
AO PE ACDEGHNP RSTW
PEA GKLNRST
APE
PEACE DS
PEACED
PEACEFUL
PEACENIK S
PEACES
ESCAPE
PEACH Y
CHAPE CHEAP
PEACHED
PEACHER S
CHEAPER
PEACHERS
PREACHES
PEACHES
PEACHIER
PEACHING
PEACHY
PEACING
PEACOAT S
PEACOATS
PEACOCK SY
PEACOCKS
PEACOCKY
PEAFOWL S
PEAFOWLS
PEAG ES
GAPE PAGE
PEAGE S
PEAGES
PEAGS
GAPES PAGES
PEAHEN S
PEAHENS
AS PEAK SY
PEAKED
PEAKIER
PEAKIEST
S PEAKING
PEAKISH
PEAKLESS
PEAKLIKE
S PEAKS
SPAKE SPEAK
PEAKY
PEAL S
LEAP PALE
PLEA
PEALED
LEAPED
PEALIKE
APELIKE
PEALING
LEAPING
PEALS
LAPSE LEAPS
PALES PLEAS
SALEP SEPAL
SPALE
S PEAN S
NAPE NEAP
PANE

S PEANS
ASPEN NAPES
NEAPS PANES
SNEAP SPEAN
PEANUT S
PEANUTS
S PEAR LST
APER PARE
RAPE REAP
PEARL SY
PALER PARLE
PEARLASH
PEARLED
PEDALER
PLEADER
REPLEAD
PEARLER S
PEARLERS
RELAPSER
PEARLIER
PEARLING
GRAPLINE
PEARLITE S
PEARLS
LAPSER
PARLES
PEARLY
PARLEY
PLAYER
REPLAY
PEARMAIN S
S PEARS
APERS APRES
ASPER PARES
PARSE PRASE
PRESA RAPES
REAPS SPARE
SPEAR
PEART
APTER PATER
PRATE TAPER
PEARTER
TAPERER
PEARTEST
PRETASTE
PEARTLY
PEYTRAL
PTERYLA
PEARWOOD S
PEAS E
APES APSE
PASE SPAE
PEASANT S
ANAPEST
PEASANTS
ANAPESTS
PEASCOD S
PEASCODS
PEASE NS
PEASECOD S
PEASEN
PEASES
PASSEE
PEAT SY
PATE TAPE
TEPA
PEATIER
PEATIEST
PEATS
PASTE PATES
SEPTA SPATE
TAPES TEPAS
PEATY
PEAVEY S
PEAVEYS
PEAVIES
PEAVY
PEBBLE DS
PEBBLED
PEBBLES
PEBBLIER
PEBBLING
PEBBLY
S PEC HKS
CEP
PECAN S
PECANS
PECCABLE
PECCANCY
PECCANT
PECCARY

PECCAVI S
PECCAVIS
PECH S
PECHAN S
PECHANS
PECHED
PECHING
PECHS
S PECK SY
S PECKED
PECKER S
PECKERS
PECKIER
PICKEER
PECKIEST
S PECKING
PECKISH
S PECKS
SPECK
PECKY
PECORINI
PECORINO S
S PECS
CEPS SPEC
PECTASE S
PECTASES
S PECTATE S
S PECTATES
SPECTATE
PECTEN S
PECTENS
PECTIC
PECTIN S
INCEPT
PECTINES
PECTINS
INCEPTS
INSPECT
PECTIZE DS
PECTIZED
PECTIZES
PECTORAL S
S PECULATE DS
PECULIA R
PECULIAR S
PECULIUM
AOS PED S
PEDAGOG SY
PEDAGOGS
PEDAGOGY
PEDAL OS
PADLE PALED
PLEAD
PEDALED
PLEADED
PEDALER S
PEARLED
PLEADER
REPLEAD
PEDALERS
PLEADERS
RELAPSED
REPLEADS
PEDALFER S
PEDALIER S
PEDALING
PLEADING
PEDALLED
PEDALLER S
PREDELLA
PEDALO S
PEDALOS
DEPOSAL
PEDALS
LAPSED
PADLES
PLEADS
PEDANT S
PANTED
PENTAD
PEDANTIC
PEDANTRY
PEDANTS
PENTADS
PEDATE
PEDATELY
PEDDLE DRS
PEDDLED
PEDDLER SY

PEDDLERS
PEDDLERY
PEDDLES
PEDDLING
PEDERAST SY
PREDATES
REPASTED
TRAPESED
PEDES
DEEPS SPEED
PEDESTAL S
PEDICAB S
PEDICABS
PEDICEL S
PEDICLE
PEDICELS
ECLIPSED
PEDICLES
PEDICLE DS
PEDICEL
PEDICLED
PEDICLES
ECLIPSED
PEDICELS
PEDICURE DS
PEDIFORM
PEDIGREE DS
PEDIMENT S
PEDIPALP S
PEDLAR SY
PARLED
PEDLARS
PEDLARY
PEDLER SY
REPLED
PEDLERS
PEDLERY
PEDOCAL S
PEDOCALS
PEDOLOGY
PEDRO S
DOPER PORED
ROPED
PEDROS
DOPERS
PROSED
SPORED
PEDS
SPED
PEDUNCLE DS
E PEE KLNPRS
PEEBEEN S
PEEBEENS
A PEEK S
KEEP PEKE
PEEKABOO S
PEEKAPOO S
PEEKED
PEEKING
KEEPING
PEEKS
KEEPS PEKES
S PEEL S
PELE
PEELABLE
S PEELED
PEELER S
PEELERS
SLEEPER
S PEELING S
PEELINGS
SLEEPING
SPEELING
S PEELS
PELES SLEEP
SPEEL
PEEN S
NEEP
PEENED
DEEPEN
PEENING
PEENS
NEEPS PENES
PEEP S
PEEPED
PEEPER S
PEEPERS
PEEPHOLE S
PEEPING
PEEPS

PEEPSHOW S
PEEPUL S
PEEPULS
S PEER SY
PERE PREE
PEERAGE S
PEERAGES
S PEERED
DEEPER
PEERESS
PEERIE S
PEERIES
SEEPIER
S PEERING
PREEING
PEERLESS
SLEEPERS
S PEERS
PERES PERSE
PREES PRESE
SPEER SPREE
PEERY
E PEES
SEEP
PEESWEEP S
PEETWEET S
PEEVE DS
PEEVED
PEEVES
PEEVING
PEEVISH
PEEWEE S
PEEWEES
PEEWIT S
PEEWITS
PEG S
PEGBOARD S
PEGBOX
PEGBOXES
PEGGED
PEGGING
PEGLESS
PEGLIKE
PEGS
PEH S
HEP
PEHS
PEIGNOIR S
PEIN S
PINE
PEINED
PEINING
PEINS
PENIS PINES
SNIPE SPINE
S PEISE DS
PEISED
ESPIED
S PEISES
ESPIES
SPEISE
PEISING
PEKAN S
PEKANS
PEKE S
KEEP PEEK
PEKEPOO S
PEKEPOOS
PEKES
KEEPS PEEKS
PEKIN S
PEKINS
PEKOE S
PEKOES
PELAGE S
PELAGES
PELAGIAL
PELAGIC S
PELAGICS
PELE S
PEEL
PELERINE S
PELES
PEELS SLEEP
SPEEL
PELF S
PELFS

PELICAN S
CAPELIN
PANICLE
PELICANS
CAPELINS
PANICLES
PELISSE S
PELISSES
PELITE S
PELITES
EPISTLE
PELITIC
PELLAGRA S
PELLET S
PELLETAL
PELLETED
PELLETS
PELLICLE S
PELLMELL S
PELLUCID
PELMET S
TEMPLE
PELMETS
TEMPLES
PELON
PLEON
PELORIA NS
PELORIAN
PELORIAS
POLARISE
PELORIC
POLICER
PELORUS
LEPROUS
SPORULE
PELOTA S
PELOTAS
APOSTLE
PELOTON S
PELOTONS
S PELT S
LEPT
PELTAST S
PELTASTS
PELTATE
PALETTE
PELTED
S PELTER S
PETREL
PELTERED
DEPLETER
S PELTERS
PETRELS
RESPELT
SPELTER
PELTING
PELTLESS
PELTRIES
EPISTLER
PERLITES
REPTILES
PELTRY
PERTLY
S PELTS
SLEPT SPELT
PELVES
PELVIC S
PELVICS
PELVIS
PELVISES
PEMBINA S
PEMBINAS
PEMICAN S
PEMICANS
PEMMICAN S
PEMOLINE S
PEMPHIX
O PEN DST
PENAL
PANEL PLANE
PLENA
PENALISE DS
SEPALINE
PENALITY
PENALIZE DS
PENALLY
PENALTY
APLENTY
PENANCE DS
PENANCED

PENANCES
PENANG S
PANGEN
PENANGS
PANGENS
PENATES
NEPETAS
S PENCE L
PENCEL S
PENCELS
PENCHANT S
PENCIL S
PENCILED
PENCILER S
PENCILS
SPLENIC
SU PEND S
PENDANT S
PENDANTS
U PENDED
DEPEND
PENDENCY
PENDENT S
PENDENTS
SU PENDING
SU PENDS
SPEND
PENDULAR
UNDERLAP
UPLANDER
PENDULUM S
PENES
NEEPS PEENS
PENGO S
PENGOS
SPONGE
PENGUIN S
PENGUINS
PENIAL
ALPINE
PINEAL
PENICIL S
PENICILS
PENILE
PENIS
PEINS PINES
SNIPE SPINE
PENISES
PENITENT S
PENKNIFE
PENLIGHT S
PENLITE S
PENLITES
PLENTIES
PENMAN
PENMEN
PENNA E
PANNE
PENNAE
PENNAME S
PENNAMES
PENNANT S
PENNANTS
PENNATE D
PENTANE
PENNATED
PENNE DR
PENNED
PENNER S
PENNERS
PENNI AS
PENNIA
PINNAE
PENNIES
PINENES
PENNINE S
PENNINES
PENNING
PENNIS
PENNON S
PENNONED
PENNONS
PENNY
PENOCHE S
PENOCHES
PENOLOGY
PENONCEL S
PENPOINT S

O PENS
PENSEE S
PENSEES
PENSIL ES
SPINEL
SPLINE
PENSILE
PENSILS
SPINELS
SPLINES
PENSION ES
PINONES
PENSIONE DR S
PENSIONS
PENSIVE
VESPINE
PENSTER S
PRESENT
REPENTS
SERPENT
PENSTERS
PERTNESS
PRESENTS
SERPENTS
PENSTOCK S
S PENT
PENTACLE S
PENTAD S
PANTED
PEDANT
PENTADS
PEDANTS
PENTAGON S
PENTANE S
PENNATE
PENTANES
PENTANOL S
PENTARCH SY
PENTENE S
PENTENES
PENTODE S
PENTODES
PENTOMIC
PENTOSAN S
PENTOSE S
OPENEST
POSTEEN
POTEENS
PENTOSES
POSTEENS
PENTYL S
PLENTY
PENTYLS
PENUCHE S
PENUCHES
PENUCHI S
PENUCHIS
PENUCHLE S
PENUCKLE S
PENULT S
PENULTS
PENUMBRA EL S
PENURIES
RESUPINE
PENURY
PEON SY
NOPE OPEN
PONE
PEONAGE S
PEONAGES
PEONES
PEONIES
PEONISM S
IMPONES
PEONISMS
MOPINESS
PEONS
OPENS PONES
PEONY
PEOPLE DRS
PEOPLED
PEOPLER S
PEOPLERS
PEOPLES
PEOPLING
PEP OS
PEPERONI S
PEPINO S

PEPINOS
PEPLA
APPEL APPLE
PEPLOS
PEPLOSES
POPELESS
PEPLUM S
PEPLUMED
PEPLUMS
PEPLUS
SUPPLE
PEPLUSES
PEPO S
POPE
PEPONIDA S
PEPONIUM S
PEPOS
POPES
PEPPED
PEPPER SY
PEPPERED
PEPPERER S
PEPPERS
PEPPERY
PEPPIER
PREPPIE
PEPPIEST
PEPPILY
PEPPING
PEPPY
PEPS
PEPSIN ES
PEPSINE S
PEPSINES
PEPSINS
PEPTALK S
PEPTALKS
PEPTIC S
PEPTICS
PEPTID ES
TIPPED
PEPTIDE S
PEPTIDES
PEPTIDIC
PEPTIDS
PEPTIZE DRS
PEPTIZED
PEPTIZER S
PEPTIZES
PEPTONE S
PEPTONES
PEPTONIC
A PER EIKMPTV
REP
PERACID S
PERACIDS
PERCALE S
REPLACE
PERCALES
REPLACES
PERCEIVE DR S
PERCENT S
PRECENT
PERCENTS
PRECENTS
PERCEPT S
PRECEPT
PERCEPTS
PRECEPTS
PERCH
PERCHED
PERCHER S
PERCHERS
PERCHES
PERCHING
PERCOID S
PERCOIDS
PERCUSS
SPRUCES
PERDIE
PERDU ES
DRUPE DUPER
PRUDE URPED
PERDUE S
PUREED
PERDUES
PERUSED
SUPERED

PERDURE DS
PERDURED
PERDURES
PERDUS
DRUPES
DUPERS
PRUDES
PURSED
PERDY
PERE AS
PEER PREE
PEREA
PEREGRIN ES
PEREIA
PEREION S
PIONEER
PEREIONS
ISOPRENE
PIONEERS
PEREON S
OPENER
REOPEN
PEREONS
OPENERS
REOPENS
PEREOPOD S
PERES
PEERS PERSE
PREES PRESE
SPEER SPREE
PERFECT AOS
PREFECT
PERFECTA S
PRAEFECT
PERFECTO S
PERFECTS
PREFECTS
PERFIDY
PERFORCE
PERFORM S
PREFORM
PERFORMS
PREFORMS
PERFUME DRS
PERFUMED
PERFUMER SY
PERFUMES
PERFUMY
PERFUSE DS
PERFUSED
PERFUSES
PERGOLA S
PERGOLAS
PERHAPS
PERI LS
PIER RIPE
PERIANTH S
PERIAPT S
PERIAPTS
PERIBLEM S
PERICARP S
CRAPPIER
PERICOPE S
PERIDERM S
PERIDIA L
PERIDIAL
PERIDIUM
PERIDOT S
DIOPTER
DIOPTRE
PROTEID
PERIDOTS
DIOPTERS
DIOPTRES
PORTSIDE
PROTEIDS
RIPOSTED
TOPSIDER
PERIGEAL
PERIGEAN
PERIGEE S
PERIGEES
PERIGON S
PIROGEN
PERIGONS
REPOSING
SPONGIER
PERIGYNY
PERIL S
PLIER

PERILED
REPLIED
PERILING
PERILLA S
PALLIER
PERILLAS
PERILLED
PERILOUS
PERILS
LISPER
PLIERS
PERILUNE S
PERINEA L
PERINEAL
PERINEUM
PERIOD S
DOPIER
A PERIODIC
PERIODID S
PERIODS
PERIOTIC
PERIPETY
PERIPTER S
PERIQUE S
REEQUIP
PERIQUES
REEQUIPS
PERIS H
PIERS PRIES
PRISE RIPES
SPEIR SPIER
SPIRE
PERISARC S
PERISH
PISHER
RESHIP
PERISHED
PERISHES
PHERESIS
PERITI
PITIER
PERITUS
PERIWIG S
PERIWIGS
PERJURE DRS
PERJURED
PERJURER S
PERJURES
PERJURY
PERK SY
PERKED
PERKIER
PERKIEST
PERKILY
PERKING
PERKISH
PERKS
PERKY
PERLITE S
REPTILE
PERLITES
EPISTLER
PELTRIES
REPTILES
PERLITIC
S PERM S
PERMEANT
PERMEASE S
PERMEATE DS
PERMED
DEPERM
PREMED
PERMIAN
PERMING
GRIPMEN
IMPREGN
PERMIT S
PERMITS
IMPREST
S PERMS
SPERM
PERMUTE DS
PERMUTED
PERMUTES
PERNIO
ORPINE
PERNOD S
PONDER

PERNODS
PONDERS
RESPOND
PERONEAL
PERORAL
PREORAL
PERORATE DS
PEROXID ES
PEROXIDE DS
PEROXIDS
PEROXY
PERP S
PREP REPP
PERPEND S
PERPENDS
PERPENT S
PERPENTS
PERPLEX
PERPS
PREPS REPPS
PERRIES
PRISERE
REPRISE
RESPIRE
PERRON S
PERRONS
PERRY
PRYER
PERSALT S
PALTERS
PLASTER
PLATERS
PSALTER
STAPLER
PERSALTS
PLASTERS
PSALTERS
STAPLERS
PERSE S
PEERS PERES
PREES PRESE
SPEER SPREE
PERSES
SPEERS
SPREES
PERSIST S
ESPRITS
PRIESTS
SPRIEST
SPRITES
STIRPES
STRIPES
PERSISTS
PERSON AS
PERSONA ELS
PERSONAE
PERSONAL S
PSORALEN
PERSONAS
RESPONSA
PERSONS
PERSPEX
PERSPIRE DS
PERSPIRY
PERSUADE DR
S
PERT
PERTAIN S
PAINTER
REPAINT
PERTAINS
PAINTERS
PANTRIES
PINASTER
PRISTANE
REPAINTS
PERTER
PERTEST
PETTERS
PRETEST
PERTLY
PELTRY
PERTNESS
PENSTERS
PRESENTS
SERPENTS
PERTURB S
PERTURBS
PERUKE DS
PERUKED
PERUKES

PERUSAL S
PLEURAS
PERUSALS
PERUSE DRS
PUREES
RUPEES
PERUSED
PERDUES
SUPERED
PERUSER S
PERUSERS
PRESSURE
PERUSES
PERUSING
SUPERING
PERV S
PERVADE DRS
DEPRAVE
REPAVED
PERVADED
DEPRAVED
PERVADER S
DEPRAVER
PERVADES
DEPRAVES
PERVERSE
PRESERVE
PERVERT S
PERVERTS
PERVIOUS
PREVIOUS
VIPEROUS
PERVS
AO PES OT
PESADE S
PESADES
PESETA S
ETAPES
PESETAS
PESEWA S
PESEWAS
PESKIER
PESKIEST
PESKILY
PESKY
PESO S
EPOS OPES
POSE
PESOS
POSES POSSE
PESSARY
PEST OSY
PETS SEPT
STEP
PESTER S
PETERS
PRESET
PESTERED
PESTERER S
PESTERS
PRESETS
PESTHOLE S
HEELPOST
TELESHOP
PESTIER
RESPITE
PESTIEST
PESTLE DS
PESTLED
PESTLES
PESTLING
PESTO S
ESTOP POETS
STOPE TOPES
PESTOS
ESTOPS
POSSET
PTOSES
STOPES
PESTS
SEPTS STEPS
PESTY
TYPES
PET S
PETABYTE S
PETAL S
LEAPT LEPTA
PALET PLATE
PLEAT TEPAL
PETALED
PLEATED

PETALINE
TAPELINE
PETALLED
PALLETED
PETALODY
PETALOID
A PETALOUS
OUTLEAPS
PETALS
PALEST
PALETS
PASTEL
PLATES
PLEATS
SEPTAL
STAPLE
TEPALS
PETARD S
DEPART
PARTED
PRATED
PETARDS
DEPARTS
PETASOS
SAPOTES
PETASUS
PETCOCK S
PETCOCKS
PETECHIA EL
PETER S
PETERED
PETERING
PETERS
PESTER
PRESET
PETIOLAR
EPILATOR
PETIOLE DS
PETIOLED
LEPIDOTE
PETIOLES
PETIT E
PETTI
PETITE S
PETITES
PETITION S
PETNAP S
PETNAPER S
PETNAPS
PETRALE S
PLEATER
PRELATE
REPLATE
PETRALES
PLEATERS
PRELATES
REPLATES
PETREL S
PELTER
PETRELS
PELTERS
RESPELT
SPELTER
PETRIFY
PETROL S
REPLOT
PETROLIC
LEPROTIC
PETROLS
REPLOTS
PETRONEL S
PETROSAL
POLESTAR
PETROUS
POSTURE
POUTERS
PROTEUS
SPOUTER
TROUPES
PETS
PEST SEPT
STEP
PETSAI S
PASTIE
PIETAS
PETSAIS
PASTIES
PATSIES
TAPISES
PETTABLE
PETTED
PETTEDLY

PETTER S
PETTERS
PERTEST
PRETEST
PETTI
PETIT
PETTIER
PETTIEST
PETTIFOG S
PETTILY
PETTING S
PETTINGS
PETTISH
PETTLE DS
PETTLED
PETTLES
PETTLING
PETTO
PETTY
PETULANT
PATULENT
PETUNIA S
PETUNIAS
SUPINATE
PETUNTSE S
PETUNTZE S
S PEW S
PEWEE S
PEWEES
PEWIT S
PEWITS
S PEWS
SPEW
PEWTER S
PEWTERER S
PEWTERS
PEYOTE S
PEYOTES
EYESPOT
PEYOTL S
PEYOTLS
PEYTRAL S
PEARTLY
PTERYLA
PEYTRALS
PLASTERY
PSALTERY
PEYTREL S
PEYTRELS
PFENNIG ES
PFENNIGE
PFENNIGS
PFFT
PFUI
PHAETON S
PHONATE
PHAETONS
PHONATES
STANHOPE
PHAGE S
PHAGES
PHALANGE RS
PHALANX
PHALLI C
PHALLIC
PHALLISM S
PHALLIST S
PHALLUS
PHANTASM AS
PHANTAST S
PHANTASY
PHANTOM S
PHANTOMS
PHARAOH S
PHARAOHS
PHARISEE S
PHARMACY
PHARMING S
PHAROS
PHAROSES
PHARYNX
PHASE DS
EPHAS HEAPS
SHAPE
PHASEAL

PHASED
HASPED
PASHED
SHAPED
PHASEOUT S
TAPHOUSE
PHASES
PASHES
SHAPES
A PHASIC
PHASING
HASPING
PASHING
SHAPING
PHASIS
ASPISH
SPAHIS
PHASMID S
DAMPISH
PHASMIDS
PHAT
PATH
PHATIC
HAPTIC
PHATTER
PHATTEST
PHEASANT S
PHELLEM S
PHELLEMS
PHELONIA
APHELION
PHENATE S
HAPTENE
HEPTANE
PHENATES
HAPTENES
HEPTANES
PHENAZIN ES
PHENETIC S
PHENETOL ES
PHENIX
PHENIXES
PHENOL S
HOLPEN
PHENOLIC S
PINOCHLE
PHENOLS
PHENOM S
PHENOMS
SHOPMEN
PHENOXY
PHENYL S
PHENYLIC
PHENYLS
A PHERESES
A PHERESIS
PERISHES
PHEW
PHI SZ
HIP
PHIAL S
PHIALS
PALISH
PHILABEG S
PHILIBEG S
PHILOMEL AS
PHILTER S
PHILTRE
PHILTERS
PHILTRES
PHILTRA
PHILTRE DS
PHILTER
PHILTRED
PHILTRES
PHILTERS
PHILTRUM
PHIMOSES
PHIMOSIS
PHIMOTIC
A PHIS
HIPS PISH
SHIP
PHIZ
PHIZES
PHLEGM SY
PHLEGMS
PHLEGMY
PHLOEM S
PHLOEMS
PHLOX

PHLOXES
PHOBIA S
PHOBIAS
PHOBIC S
PHOBICS
PHOCINE
CHOPINE
PHOEBE S
PHOEBES
EPHEBOS
PHOEBUS
PHOENIX
PHON EOSY
PHONAL
PHONATE DS
PHAETON
PHONATED
PHONATES
PHAETONS
STANHOPE
PHONE DSY
PHONED
PHONEME S
PHONEMES
PHONEMIC S
PHONES
PHONETIC S
PHONEY S
PHONEYED
PHONEYS
A PHONIC S
CHOPIN
A PHONICS
CHOPINS
PHONIED
PHONIER
PHONIES T
PHONIEST
PHONILY
PHONING
PHONO NS
PHONON S
PHONONS
PHONOS
PHONS
PHONY
PHONYING
PHOOEY
E PHORATE S
E PHORATES
PHORESY
PHORONID S
PHOSGENE S
PHOSPHID ES
PHOSPHIN ES
PHOSPHOR EI
S
PHOT OS
TOPH
A PHOTIC S
PHOTICS
PHOTO GNS
PHOTOED
PHOTOG S
PHOTOGS
PHOTOING
PHOTOMAP S
PHOTON S
PHOTONIC S
PHOTONS
PHOTOPIA S
PHOTOPIC
PHOTOS
POTHOS
PHOTOSET S
PHOTS
TOPHS
PHPHT
PHRASAL
PHRASE DS
RAPHES
SERAPH
SHAPER
SHERPA
PHRASED
SHARPED

PHRASES
SERAPHS
SHAPERS
SHERPAS
PHRASING S
HARPINGS
SHARPING
PHRATRAL
PHRATRIC
PARRITCH
PHRATRY
PHREAK S
PHREAKED
PHREAKER S
PHREAKS
PHREATIC
CHAPITER
PATCHIER
PHRENIC
NEPHRIC
PINCHER
PHRENSY
PHT
PHTHALIC
PHTHALIN S
PHTHISES
PHTHISIC S
PHTHISIS
PHUT S
PHUTS
PHYLA ER
HAPLY
PHYLAE
PHYLAR
PHYLAXIS
PHYLE
PHYLESES
PHYLESIS
PHYLETIC S
PHYLIC
PHYLLARY
PHYLLITE S
PHYLLO S
PHYLLODE S
PHYLLOID S
PHYLLOME S
PHYLLOS
PHYLON
PHYLUM
PHYSED S
PHYSEDS
PHYSES
PHYSIC S
SCYPHI
PHYSICAL S
PHYSICS
PHYSIQUE DS
PHYSIS
PHYTANE S
PHYTANES
PHYTIN S
PHYTINS
PHYTOID
TYPHOID
PHYTOL S
PHYTOLS
PHYTON S
PYTHON
TYPHON
PHYTONIC
HYPNOTIC
PYTHONIC
TYPHONIC
PHYTONS
PYTHONS
TYPHONS
PI ACEGNPST
UX
PIA LNS
PIACULAR
PIAFFE DRS
PIAFFED
PIAFFER S
PIAFFERS
PIAFFES
PIAFFING
PIAL
LIPA PAIL

A PIAN OS
NIPA PAIN
PINA
PIANIC
PIANISM S
PIANISMS
SINAPISM
PIANIST S
PIANISTS
PIANO S
PIANOS
PIANS
NIPAS PAINS
PINAS
PIAS
PIASABA S
PIASABAS
PIASSABA
PIASAVA S
PIASAVAS
PIASSAVA
PIASSABA S
PIASABAS
PIASSAVA S
PIASAVAS
PIASTER S
PARTIES
PASTIER
PIASTRE
PIRATES
TRAIPSE
PIASTERS
PASTRIES
PIASTRES
RASPIEST
TRAIPSES
PIASTRE S
PARTIES
PASTIER
PIASTER
PIRATES
TRAIPSE
PIASTRES
PASTRIES
PIASTERS
RASPIEST
TRAIPSES
PIAZZA S
PIAZZAS
PIAZZE
PIBAL S
PIBALS
PIBROCH S
PIBROCHS
ES PIC AEKS
S PICA LS
PICACHO S
PICACHOS
PICADOR S
PARODIC
PICADORS
SPORADIC
AE PICAL
PLICA
PICANTE
PICARA S
PICARAS
PICARO S
PICAROON S
PICAROS
PROSAIC
S PICAS
ASPIC SPICA
PICAYUNE S
PICCATA
PICCOLO S
PICCOLOS
S PICE
EPIC
PICEOUS
PICIFORM
S PICK SY
PICKADIL S
PICKAX E
PICKAXE DS
PICKAXED
PICKAXES
PICKED
PICKEER S
PECKIER

PICKEERS
PICKER S
PICKEREL S
PICKERS
PICKET S
PICKETED
PICKETER S
PICKETS
SKEPTIC
PICKIER
PICKIEST
PICKING S
PICKINGS
PICKLE DS
PICKLED
PICKLES
PICKLING
PICKLOCK S
PICKOFF S
PICKOFFS
S PICKS
PICKUP S
PICKUPS
PICKWICK S
PICKY
PICLORAM S
PROCLAIM
PICNIC S
PICNICKY
PICNICS
PICOGRAM S
PICOLIN ES
CIPOLIN
PICOLINE S
PICOLINS
CIPOLINS
PSILOCIN
PICOMOLE S
PICOT S
OPTIC TOPIC
PICOTED
PICOTEE S
PICOTEES
PICOTING
PICOTS
OPTICS
TOPICS
PICOWAVE DS
PICQUET S
PICQUETS
PICRATE DS
PARETIC
PICRATED
PICRATES
CRISPATE
PARETICS
PRACTISE
PICRIC
PICRITE S
PICRITES
PRICIEST
E PICRITIC
ES PICS
PICTURE DS
CUPRITE
PICTURED
PICTURES
CUPRITES
PIECRUST
PICUL S
PICULS
PIDDLE DRS
PIDDLED
PIDDLER S
PIDDLERS
PIDDLES
PIDDLING
PIDDLY
PIDDOCK S
PIDDOCKS
PIDGIN S
PIDGINS
PIE DRS
PIEBALD S
BIPEDAL
PIEBALDS
A PIECE DRS

PIECED
PIECER S
PIERCE
RECIPE
PIECERS
PIERCES
PRECISE
RECIPES
PIECES
SPECIE
PIECING S
PIECINGS
PIECRUST S
CUPRITES
PICTURES
S PIED
PIEDFORT S
PROFITED
PIEDMONT S
PIEFORT S
FIREPOT
PIEFORTS
FIREPOTS
POSTFIRE
PIEHOLE S
PIEHOLES
PIEING
PIEPLANT S
S PIER S
PERI RIPE
PIERCE DRS
PIECER
RECIPE
PIERCED
PIERCER S
CREPIER
REPRICE
PIERCERS
PRECISER
REPRICES
PIERCES
PIECERS
PRECISE
RECIPES
PIERCING S
PIEROGI
PIERROT S
PRERIOT
PIERROTS
SPORTIER
S PIERS
PERIS PRIES
PRISE RIPES
SPEIR SPIER
SPIRE
S PIES
SIPE
PIETA S
PIETAS
PASTIE
PETSAI
PIETIES
PIETISM S
PIETISMS
PIETIST S
PIETISTS
STIPITES
TIPSIEST
PIETY
PIFFLE DS
PIFFLED
PIFFLES
PIFFLING
PIG S
GIP
PIGBOAT S
PIGBOATS
PIGEON S
EPIGON
PIGEONS
EPIGONS
PINGOES
PIGFISH
PIGGED
PIGGERY
PIGGIE RS
PIGGIER
PIGGIES T
PIGGIEST
PIGGIN GS
PIGGING

PIGGINS
PIGGISH
PIGGY
PIGLET S
PIGLETS
PIGLIKE
PIGMENT S
TEMPING
PIGMENTS
EMPTINGS
PIGMIES
PIGMY
GIMPY
PIGNOLI AS
PIGNOLIA S
PIGNOLIS
SPOILING
PIGNORA
PIGNUS
SPUING
PIGNUT S
PIGNUTS
PIGOUT S
PIGOUTS
PIGPEN S
PIGPENS
PIGS
GIPS
PIGSKIN S
SPIKING
PIGSKINS
PIGSNEY S
ESPYING
PIGSNEYS
PIGSTICK S
PIGSTIES
PIGSTY
PIGTAIL S
PIGTAILS
PIGWEED S
PIGWEEDS
PIING
PIKA S
PAIK
PIKAKE S
PIKAKES
PIKAS
PAIKS
S PIKE DRS
KEPI
S PIKED
PIKEMAN
PIKEMEN
S PIKER S
S PIKERS
SPIKER
S PIKES
KEPIS SPIKE
PIKI S
S PIKING
PIKIS
PILAF FS
PILAFF S
PILAFFS
PILAFS
PILAR
PILASTER S
PLAISTER
PLAITERS
PILAU S
PILAUS
PILAW S
PILAWS
PILCHARD S
S PILE ADIS
LIPE PLIE
PILEA
PILEATE D
EPILATE
PILEATED
DEPILATE
EPILATED
S PILED
PLIED
PILEI
PILELESS
ELLIPSES
PILEOUS

S PILES
PLIES SLIPE
SPEIL SPIEL
SPILE
PILEUM
PILEUP S
UPPILE
PILEUPS
UPPILES
PILEUS
PILEWORT S
PILFER S
PILFERED
PREFILED
PILFERER S
PILFERS
PILGRIM S
PILGRIMS
PILI S
PILIFORM
S PILING S
S PILINGS
LISPING
SLIPING
SPILING
PILIS
S PILL S
S PILLAGE DRS
PILLAGED
PILLAGER S
S PILLAGES
SPILLAGE
PILLAR S
PILLARED
PILLARS
PILLBOX
S PILLED
S PILLING
PILLION S
PILLIONS
PILLORY
PILLOW SY
PILLOWED
PILLOWS
PILLOWY
S PILLS
SPILL
PILOSE
POLEIS
POLIES
PILOSITY
PILOT S
PILOTAGE S
PILOTED
PILOTING S
PILOTS
PISTOL
SPOILT
PILOUS
POILUS
PILSENER S
PILSNER S
PILSNERS
PILULAR
PILULE S
PILULES
PILUS
PULIS
PILY
PIMA S
PIMAS
PIMENTO S
PIMENTOS
NEPOTISM
PIMIENTO S
PIMP S
PIMPED
PIMPING
PIMPLE DS
PIMPLED
PIMPLES
PIMPLIER
PIMPLY
PIMPS
S PIN AEGKSTY
NIP

PINA S
NIPA PAIN
PIAN
PINAFORE DS
PINANG S
PINANGS
PINAS
NIPAS PAINS
PIANS
PINASTER S
PAINTERS
PANTRIES
PERTAINS
PRISTANE
REPAINTS
PINATA S
PATINA
TAIPAN
PINATAS
PASTINA
PATINAS
TAIPANS
PINBALL S
PINBALLS
PINBONE S
PINBONES
PINCER S
PRINCE
PINCERS
CRISPEN
PRINCES
PINCH
PINCHBUG S
PINCHECK S
PINCHED
PINCHER S
NEPHRIC
PHRENIC
PINCHERS
PINSCHER
PINCHES
SPHENIC
PINCHING
PINDER S
PINDERS
S PINDLING
OS PINE DSY
PEIN
PINEAL S
ALPINE
PENIAL
PINEALS
ALPINES
SPANIEL
SPLENIA
PINECONE S
OS PINED
PINELAND S
S PINELIKE
PINENE S
PINENES
PENNIES
PINERIES
PINERY
OS PINES
PEINS PENIS
SNIPE SPINE
PINESAP S
NAPPIES
PINESAPS
PINETA
PANTIE
PATINE
PINETUM
PINEWOOD S
PINEY
PINFISH
PINFOLD S
PINFOLDS
AO PING OS
PINGED
PINGER S
PINGERS
SPRINGE
PINGING
PINGO S
GIPON OPING
PINGOES
EPIGONS
PIGEONS

PINGOS
GIPONS
POSING
PINGRASS
RASPINGS
PINGS
PINGUID
PINHEAD S
HEADPIN
PINHEADS
DEANSHIP
HEADPINS
PINHOLE S
PINHOLES
S **PINIER**
S **PINIEST**
PINITES
TIEPINS
O **PINING**
O **PINION** S
O **PINIONED**
O **PINIONS**
PINITE S
TIEPIN
PINITES
PINIEST
TIEPINS
PINITOL S
PINITOLS
PINK OSY
PINKED
PINKEN S
PINKENED
PINKENS
PINKER S
PINKERS
PINKEST
PINKEY ES
PINKEYE S
PINKEYES
PINKEYS
PINKIE S
PINKIES
PINKING S
KINGPIN
PINKINGS
KINGPINS
PINKISH
KINSHIP
PINKLY
PINKNESS
PINKO S
PINKOES
PINKOS
PINKROOT S
PINKS
PINKY
PINNA ELS
PINNACE S
PINNACES
PINNACLE DS
PINNAE
PENNIA
PINNAL
PINNAS
INSPAN
PINNATE D
PINNATED
PINNED
S **PINNER** S
S **PINNERS**
SPINNER
S **PINNIES**
S **PINNING**
PINNIPED S
PINNULA ER
PINNULAE
PINNULAR
PINNULE S
PINNULES
S **PINNY**
PINOCHLE S
PHENOLIC
PINOCLE S
PLEONIC
PINOCLES
PINOLE S
PINOLES
EPSILON

PINON S
PINONES
PENSION
PINONS
PINOT S
PINTO PITON
POINT
PINOTS
PINTOS
PISTON
PITONS
POINTS
POSTIN
SPINTO
PINPOINT S
PINPRICK S
S **PINS**
NIPS SNIP
SPIN
PINSCHER S
PINCHERS
PINT AOS
PINTA S
INAPT PAINT
PATIN
PINTADA S
PINTADAS
PINTADO S
PINTADOS
SATINPOD
PINTAIL S
PINTAILS
ALPINIST
ANTISLIP
TAILSPIN
PINTANO S
PINTANOS
PINTAS
PAINTS
PATINS
PTISAN
PINTLE S
LEPTIN
PINTLES
LEPTINS
PLENIST
S **PINTO** S
PINOT PITON
POINT
PINTOES
POINTES
S **PINTOS**
PINOTS
PISTON
PITONS
POINTS
POSTIN
SPINTO
PINTS
PINTSIZE D
PINUP S
PINUPS
PINWALE S
PINWALES
PINWEED S
PINWEEDS
PINWHEEL S
PINWORK S
PINWORKS
PINWORM S
PINWORMS
S **PINY**
PYIN
PINYIN
PINYON S
PINYONS
PIOLET S
POLITE
PIOLETS
PISTOLE
PION S
PIONEER S
PEREION
PIONEERS
ISOPRENE
PEREIONS
PIONIC
PIONS
OPSIN
PIOSITY
PIOUS

PIOUSLY
PIP ESY
PIPAGE S
PIPAGES
PIPAL S
PALPI
PIPALS
PIPE DRST
PIPEAGE S
PIPEAGES
PIPED
PIPEFISH
PIPEFUL S
PIPEFULS
PIPELESS
PIPELIKE
PIPELINE DS
PIPER S
PIPERINE S
PIPERS
SIPPER
PIPES
PIPESTEM S
PIPET S
PIPETS
SIPPET
PIPETTE DS
PIPETTED
PIPETTES
PIPIER
PIPIEST
PIPINESS
PIPING S
PIPINGLY
PIPINGS
SIPPING
PIPIT S
PIPITS
PIPKIN S
PIPKINS
PIPPED
PIPPIN GS
PIPPING
PIPPINS
PIPS
PIPY
PIQUANCE S
PIQUANCY
PIQUANT
PIQUE DST
EQUIP
PIQUED
PIQUES
EQUIPS
PIQUET S
PIQUETS
PIQUING
PIRACIES
PIRACY
PIRAGUA S
PIRAGUAS
PIRANA S
PARIAN
PIRANAS
PARIANS
PIRANHA S
PIRANHAS
PIRARUCU S
PIRATE DS
PIRATED
DIPTERA
PARTIED
PIRATES
PARTIES
PASTIER
PIASTER
PIASTRE
TRAIPSE
PIRATIC
PIRATING
PIRAYA S
APIARY
PIRAYAS
PIRIFORM
PIRN S
PIRNS
PIROG I

PIROGEN
PERIGON
PIROGHI
PIROGI
PIROGIES
PIROGUE S
GROUPIE
PIROGUES
GROUPIES
PIROJKI
PIROQUE S
PIROQUES
PIROSHKI
PIROZHKI
PIROZHOK
PIS HO
PSI
SIP
PISCARY
PISCATOR SY
APRICOTS
PISCINA ELS
PISCINAE
PISCINAL
PISCINAS
PISCINE
PISCO S
PISCOS
A **PISH**
HIPS PHIS
SHIP
PISHED
PISHER S
PERISH
RESHIP
PISHERS
RESHIPS
PISHES
PISHING
PISHOGE S
PISHOGES
PISHOGUE S
PISIFORM S
PISMIRE S
PRIMSIE
PISMIRES
PISO S
POIS
PISOLITE S
POLITIES
PISOLITH S
PISOS
PISSOIR S
PISSOIRS
PISTACHE S
HEPATICS
PASTICHE
PISTE S
SPITE STIPE
PISTES
SPITES
STIPES
PISTIL S
PISTILS
PISTOL ES
PILOTS
SPOILT
PISTOLE DS
PIOLETS
PISTOLED
PISTOLES
PISTOLS
PISTON S
PINOTS
PINTOS
PITONS
POINTS
POSTIN
SPINTO
PISTONS
POSTINS
SPINTOS
PISTOU S
PISTOUS
S **PIT** AHSY
TIP
PITA S
PITAHAYA S
PITAPAT S
PITAPATS

PITAS
SPAIT TAPIS
PITAYA S
PITAYAS
PITCH Y
PITCHED
PITCHER S
PITCHERS
PITCHES
PITCHIER
PITCHILY
PITCHING
PITCHMAN
PITCHMEN
PITCHOUT S
OUTPITCH
PITCHY
PITEOUS
PITFALL S
PITFALLS
PITH SY
PITHEAD S
PITHEADS
PITHED
PITHIER
PITHIEST
PITHILY
PITHING
PITHLESS
PITHS
PITHY
PITIABLE
PITIABLY
PITIED
PITIER S
PERITI
PITIERS
TIPSIER
PITIES
PITIFUL
PITILESS
PITMAN S
PITMANS
PITMEN
PITON S
PINOT PINTO
POINT
PITONS
PINOTS
PINTOS
PISTON
POINTS
POSTIN
SPINTO
S **PITS**
SPIT TIPS
PITSAW S
PITSAWS
PITTA S
PITTANCE S
PITTAS
S **PITTED**
S **PITTING** S
PITTINGS
SPITTING
PITY
PITYING
PIU
PIVOT S
PIVOTAL
PIVOTED
PIVOTING
PIVOTMAN
PIVOTMEN
PIVOTS
PIX Y
PIXEL S
PIXELS
PIXES
PIXIE S
PIXIEISH
PIXIES
PIXINESS
PIXY
PIXYISH
PIZAZZ Y
PIZZAZ

PIZAZZES
PIZZAZES
PIZAZZY
PIZZA SZ
PIZZAS
PIZZAZ Z
PIZAZZ
PIZZAZES
PIZAZZES
PIZZAZZ Y
PIZZAZZY
PIZZELLE S
PIZZERIA S
PIZZLE S
PIZZLES
PLACABLE
PLACABLY
PLACARD S
PLACARDS
PLACATE DRS
PLACATED
PLACATER S
PLACATES
PLACE DRST
PLACEBO S
PLACEBOS
PLACED
PLACEMAN
PLACEMEN T
PLACENTA EL S
PLACER S
CARPEL
PARCEL
PLACERS
CARPELS
CLASPER
PARCELS
RECLASP
SCALPER
PLACES
PLACET S
CAPLET
PLACETS
CAPLETS
PLACID
PLACIDLY
PLACING
PLACK S
PLACKET S
PLACKETS
PLACKS
PLACOID S
PLACOIDS
PLAFOND S
PLAFONDS
PLAGAL
PLAGE S
PLAGES
PLAGIARY
PLAGUE DRSY
PLAGUED
PLAGUER S
EARPLUG
GRAUPEL
PLAGUERS
EARPLUGS
GRAUPELS
PLAGUES
PLAGUEY
PLAGUILY
PLAGUING
PLAGUY
PLAICE S
EPICAL
PLICAE
PLAICES
SPECIAL
PLAID S
PLAIDED
PLAIDS
SALPID
PLAIN ST
LAPIN
PLAINED
PLAINER
PRALINE

PLAINEST
PANELIST
PANTILES
PLAINING
PLAINLY
PLAINS
LAPINS
SPINAL
PLAINT S
PLIANT
PLAINTS
PLAISTER S
PILASTER
PLAITERS
PLAIT S
PLAITED
TALIPED
PLAITER S
PLATIER
PLAITERS
PILASTER
PLAISTER
PLAITING S
PLAITS
PASTIL
SPITAL
PLAN EKST
PLANAR
PLANARIA NS
PLANATE
PLATANE
PLANCH E
PLANCHE ST
PLANCHES
PLANCHET S
PLANE DRST
PANEL PENAL
PLENA
PLANED
PLANER S
REPLAN
PLANERS
REPLANS
PLANES
PANELS
PLANET S
PLATEN
PLANETS
PLATENS
PLANFORM S
PLANGENT
PLANING
PLANISH
PLANK S
PLANKED
PLANKING S
PLANKS
PLANKTER S
PLANKTON S
PLANLESS
PLANNED
PLANNER S
PLANNERS
PLANNING S
PLANOSOL S
PLANS
PLANT S
PLANTAIN S
PLANTAR
PLANTED
PLANTER S
REPLANT
PLANTERS
REPLANTS
PLANTING S
PLANTLET S
PLANTS
PLANULA ER
PLANULAE
PLANULAR
PLAQUE S
PLAQUES
S **PLASH** Y
S **PLASHED**
S **PLASHER** S
SPHERAL
S **PLASHERS**
SPLASHER
S **PLASHES**
HAPLESS

S PLASHIER
EARLSHIP
HARELIPS
S PLASHING
S PLASHY
PLASM AS
LAMPS PALMS
PSALM
PLASMA S
LAMPAS
PLASMAS
PLASMIC
PSALMIC
PLASMID S
PLASMIDS
PLASMIN S
MISPLAN
PLASMINS
MISPLANS
PLASMOID S
DIPLOMAS
PLASMON S
PLASMONS
PLASMS
PSALMS
PLASTER SY
PALTERS
PERSALT
PLATERS
PSALTER
STAPLER
PLASTERS
PERSALTS
PSALTERS
STAPLERS
PLASTERY
PEYTRALS
PSALTERY
A PLASTIC S
PLASTICS
PLASTID S
PLASTIDS
PLASTRAL
PLASTRON S
PLASTRUM S
S PLAT ESY
PLATAN ES
PLATANE S
PLANATE
PLATANES
PLEASANT
PLATANS
SALTPAN
PLATE DNRS
LEAPT LEPTA
PALET PETAL
PLEAT TEPAL
PLATEAU SX
PLATEAUS
PLATEAUX
PLATED
PLATEFUL S
PLATELET S
PALLETTE
PLATEN S
PLANET
PLATENS
PLANETS
PLATER S
PALTER
PLATERS
PALTERS
PERSALT
PLASTER
PSALTER
STAPLER
PLATES
PALEST
PALETS
PASTEL
PETALS
PLEATS
SEPTAL
STAPLE
TEPALS
PLATFORM S
PLATIER
PLAITER
PLATIES T
APLITES
PALIEST
TALIPES
PLATIEST
PLATINA S
PLATINAS
PLATING S
PLATINGS
STAPLING
PLATINIC
PLATINUM S
PLATONIC
PLATOON S
PLATOONS
S PLATS
SPLAT
S PLATTED
S PLATTER S
PARTLET
PRATTLE
S PLATTERS
PARTLETS
PRATTLES
SPLATTER
SPRATTLE
S PLATTING
PLATY S
APTLY PATLY
TYPAL
PLATYPI
PLATYPUS
PLATYS
PLAUDIT S
PLAUDITS
PLAUSIVE
S PLAY AS
PALY
PLAYA S
PLAYABLE
PLAYACT S
PLAYACTS
PLAYAS
PLAYBACK S
PLAYBILL S
PLAYBOOK S
PLAYBOY S
PLAYBOYS
PLAYDATE S
PLAYDAY S
PLAYDAYS
PLAYDOWN S
DOWNPLAY
S PLAYED
PLAYER S
PARLEY
PEARLY
REPLAY
PLAYERS
PARLEYS
PARSLEY
REPLAYS
SPARELY
PLAYFUL
PLAYGIRL S
PLAYGOER S
S PLAYING
PLAYLAND S
PLAYLESS
PLAYLET S
PLAYLETS
PLAYLIKE
PLAYLIST S
PLAYMATE S
PLAYOFF S
PLAYOFFS
PLAYPEN S
PLAYPENS
PLAYROOM S
S PLAYS
PALSY SPLAY
PLAYSUIT S
PLAYTIME S
PLAYWEAR
PLAZA S
PLAZAS
PLEA DST
LEAP PALE
PEAL
PLEACH
CHAPEL
PLEACHED
PLEACHES
PLEAD S
PADLE PALED
PEDAL
PLEADED
PEDALED
PLEADER S
PEARLED
PEDALER
REPLEAD
PLEADERS
PEDALERS
RELAPSED
REPLEADS
PLEADING S
PEDALING
PLEADS
LAPSED
PADLES
PEDALS
PLEAS E
LAPSE LEAPS
PALES PEALS
SALEP SEPAL
SPALE
PLEASANT
PLATANES
PLEASE DRS
ASLEEP
ELAPSE
PLEASED
ELAPSED
SEPALED
PLEASER S
LEAPERS
PRESALE
RELAPSE
REPEALS
PLEASERS
PRESALES
RELAPSES
PLEASES
ELAPSES
PLEASING
ELAPSING
PLEASURE DS
PLEAT S
LEAPT LEPTA
PALET PETAL
PLATE TEPAL
PLEATED
PETALED
PLEATER S
PETRALE
PRELATE
REPLATE
PLEATERS
PETRALES
PRELATES
REPLATES
PLEATHER S
PLEATING
PLEATS
PALEST
PALETS
PASTEL
PETALS
PLATES
SEPTAL
STAPLE
TEPALS
PLEB ES
PLEBE S
BLEEP
PLEBEIAN S
PLEBES
BLEEPS
PLEBS
PLECTRA
PLECTRON S
PLECTRUM S
PLED
PLEDGE DERS T
PLEDGED
PLEDGEE S
PLEDGEES
PLEDGEOR S
PLEDGER S
PLEDGERS
PLEDGES
PLEDGET S
PLEDGETS
PLEDGING
PLEDGOR S
PLEDGORS
PLEIAD S
ALIPED
ELAPID
PLEIADES
PLEIADS
ALIPEDS
ELAPIDS
LAPIDES
PALSIED
PLENA
PANEL PENAL
PLANE
PLENARY
PLENCH
PLENCHES
PLENISH
PLENISM S
PLENISMS
LIMPNESS
PLENIST S
LEPTINS
PINTLES
PLENISTS
PLENTIES
PENLITES
A PLENTY
PENTYL
PLENUM S
LUMPEN
PLENUMS
LUMPENS
PLEON S
PELON
PLEONAL
PLEONASM S
NEOPLASM
PLEONIC
PINOCLE
PLEONS
PLEOPOD S
PLEOPODS
PLESSOR S
SLOPERS
SPLORES
PLESSORS
PLETHORA S
PLEURA ELS
PLEURAE
PLEURAL
PLEURAS
PERUSAL
PLEURISY
PLEURON
PLEUSTON S
PLEW S
PLEWS
PLEX
PLEXAL
PLEXES
EXPELS
PLEXOR S
PLEXORS
PLEXUS
PLEXUSES
EXPULSES
PLIABLE
PLIABLY
PLIANCY
PLIANT
PLAINT
PLIANTLY
PLICA EL
PICAL
PLICAE
EPICAL
PLAICE
PLICAL
PLICATE D
PLICATED
PLIE DRS
LIPE PILE
PLIED
PILED
PLIER S
PERIL
PLIERS
LISPER
PERILS
PLIES
PILES SLIPE
SPEIL SPIEL
SPILE
U PLIGHT S
U PLIGHTED
PLIGHTER S
U PLIGHTS
PLIMSOL ELS
PLIMSOLE S
PLIMSOLL S
PLIMSOLS
U PLINK S
U PLINKED
PLINKER S
PLINKERS
SPRINKLE
U PLINKING
U PLINKS
PLINTH S
PLINTHS
PLIOCENE
PLIOFILM S
PLIOTRON S
PLISKIE S
PLISKIES
PLISKY
PLISSE S
SLIPES
SPEILS
SPIELS
SPILES
PLISSES
PLOD S
PLODDED
PLODDER S
PLODDERS
PLODDING
PLODS
PLOIDIES
PLOIDY
DOPILY
PLONK S
PLONKED
PLONKING
PLONKS
PLOP S
PLOPPED
POPPLED
PLOPPING
POPPLING
PLOPS
PLOSION S
PLOSIONS
PLOSIVE S
PLOSIVES
PLOT SZ
PLOTLESS
PLOTLINE S
PLOTS
PLOTTAGE S
PLOTTED
PLOTTER S
PLOTTERS
PLOTTIER
PLOTTIES T
POLITEST
PLOTTING
PLOTTY
PLOTZ
PLOTZED
PLOTZES
PLOTZING
PLOUGH S
PLOUGHED
PLOUGHER S
PLOUGHS
PLOVER S
PLOVERS
PLOW S
PLOWABLE
PLOWBACK S
PLOWBOY S
PLOWBOYS
PLOWED
PLOWER S
REPLOW
PLOWERS
REPLOWS
PLOWHEAD S
PLOWING
PLOWLAND S
PLOWMAN
PLOWMEN
PLOWS
PLOY S
POLY
PLOYED
DEPLOY
PLOYING
PLOYS
POLYS
PLUCK SY
PLUCKED
PLUCKER S
PLUCKERS
PLUCKIER
PLUCKILY
PLUCKING
PLUCKS
PLUCKY
PLUG S
GULP
PLUGGED
PLUGGER S
PLUGGERS
PLUGGING
PLUGLESS
PLUGOLA S
PLUGOLAS
PLUGS
GULPS
PLUGUGLY
PLUM BEPSY
LUMP
PLUMAGE DS
PLUMAGED
PLUMAGES
PLUMATE
PLUMB S
PLUMBAGO S
PLUMBED
PLUMBER SY
REPLUMB
PLUMBERS
REPLUMBS
PLUMBERY
PLUMBIC
UPCLIMB
PLUMBING S
PLUMBISM S
PLUMBOUS
PLUMBS
PLUMBUM S
PLUMBUMS
PLUME DS
PLUMED
LUMPED
PLUMELET S
PLUMERIA S
PLUMES
PLUMIER
LUMPIER
PLUMIEST
LUMPIEST
PLUMING
LUMPING
PLUMIPED S
PLUMLIKE
PLUMMER
PLUMMEST
PLUMMETS
PLUMMET S
PLUMMETS
PLUMMEST
PLUMMIER
PLUMMY
PLUMOSE
PUMELOS
PLUMP S
PLUMPED
PLUMPEN S
PLUMPENS
PLUMPER S
PLUMPERS
PLUMPEST
PLUMPING
PLUMPISH
PLUMPLY
PLUMPS
PLUMS
LUMPS SLUMP
PLUMULAR
PLUMULE S
PLUMULES
PLUMY
LUMPY
PLUNDER S
PLUNDERS
PLUNGE DRS
PUNGLE
PLUNGED
PUNGLED
PLUNGER S
PLUNGERS
PLUNGES
PUNGLES
PLUNGING
PUNGLING
PLUNK SY
PLUNKED
PLUNKER S
PLUNKERS
PLUNKIER
PLUNKING
PLUNKS
PLUNKY
PLURAL S
PLURALLY
PLURALS
PLUS H
PULS
PLUSES
PULSES
PLUSH Y
PLUSHER
PLUSHES T
PLUSHEST
PLUSHIER
PLUSHILY
PLUSHLY
PLUSHY
PLUSSAGE S
PLUSSES
PLUTEI
PLUTEUS
PUSTULE
PLUTON S
PLUTONIC
PLUTONS
PLUVIAL S
PLUVIALS
PLUVIAN
PLUVIOSE
PLUVIOUS
PLY
PLYER S
REPLY
PLYERS
PLYING
PLYINGLY
PLYWOOD S
PLYWOODS
PNEUMA S
PNEUMAS
POACEOUS
POACH Y
POACHED
POACHER S
POACHERS
POACHES
CHEAPOS
SHOEPAC
POACHIER
POACHING
POACHY
POBLANO S
POBLANOS
POBOY S

POBOYS
POCHARD S
POCHARDS
POCK SY
POCKED
POCKET S
POCKETED
POCKETER S
POCKETS
POCKIER
POCKIEST
POCKILY
POCKING
POCKMARK S
POCKS
POCKY
POCO
COOP
POCOSEN S
POCOSENS
POCOSIN S
OPSONIC
POCOSINS
POCOSON S
POCOSONS
A POD S
PODAGRA LS
PODAGRAL
PODAGRAS
PODAGRIC
PODDED
PODDING
PODESTA S
PODESTAS
PODGIER
PODGIEST
PODGILY
PODGY
PODIA
PODIATRY
PODITE S
PODITES
DEPOSIT
DOPIEST
POSITED
SOPITED
TOPSIDE
PODITIC
PODIUM S
PODIUMS
PODLIKE
PODOCARP
PODOMERE S
A PODS
PODSOL S
PODSOLIC
PODSOLS
PODZOL S
PODZOLIC
PODZOLS
POECHORE S
POEM S
MOPE POME
POEMS
MOPES POMES
POESIES
POESY
SEPOY
POET S
TOPE
POETESS
POETIC S
POETICAL
POETICS
POETISE DRS
POETISED
EPIDOTES
POETISER S
POETRIES
POETISES
POETIZE DRS
POETIZED
POETIZER S
POETIZES
POETLESS
POETLIKE

POETRIES
POETISER
POETRY
POETS
ESTOP PESTO
STOPE TOPES
POGEY S
POGEYS
POGIES
POGONIA S
POGONIAS
POGONIP S
POOPING
POGONIPS
OPPOSING
POGROM S
POGROMED
POGROMS
POGY
POH
HOP
POI S
POIGNANT
POILU S
POILUS
PILOUS
POIND S
POINDED
POINDING
POINDS
POINT ESY
PINOT PINTO
PITON
POINTE DRS
POINTED
POINTER S
PROTEIN
TROPINE
POINTERS
PORNIEST
PROTEINS
TROPINES
POINTES
PINTOES
POINTIER
POINTING
POINTMAN
POINTMEN
POINTS
PINOTS
PINTOS
PISTON
PITONS
POSTIN
SPINTO
POINTY
POIS E
PISO
POISE DRS
POISED
POISER S
POISERS
PROSSIE
POISES
POSIES
POISHA
POISING
POISON S
POISONED
POISONER S
SNOOPIER
SPOONIER
POISONS
POITREL S
POLITER
POITRELS
POKABLE
S POKE DRSY
S POKED
POKER S
POKEROOT S
POKERS
S POKES
SPOKE
POKEWEED S
POKEY S
POKEYS
POKIER
POKIES T

POKIEST
POKILY
POKINESS
S POKING
POKY
POL ELOSY
LOP
POLAR S
PAROL
POLARISE DS
PELORIAS
POLARITY
POLARIZE DR S
POLARON S
POLARONS
POLARS
PAROLS
SPORAL
POLDER S
POLDERS
PRESOLD
POLE DRS
LOPE
POLEAX E
POLEAXE DS
POLEAXED
POLEAXES
POLECAT S
POLECATS
POLED
LOPED
POLEIS
PILOSE
POLIES
POLELESS
POLEMIC S
COMPILE
POLEMICS
COMPILES
COMPLIES
POLEMIST S
MILEPOST
POLEMIZE DS
POLENTA S
POLENTAS
POLER S
LOPER PROLE
POLERS
LOPERS
PROLES
SLOPER
SPLORE
POLES
LOPES SLOPE
POLESTAR S
PETROSAL
POLEWARD
POLEYN S
OPENLY
POLEYNS
POLICE DRS
POLICED
POLICER S
PELORIC
POLICERS
POLICES
POLICIES
POLICING
POLICY
POLIES
PILOSE
POLEIS
POLING
LOPING
POLIO S
POLIOS
POLIS H
SPOIL
POLISH
POLISHED
DEPOLISH
POLISHER S
REPOLISH
POLISHES
POLITE R
PIOLET
POLITELY
POLITER
POITREL
POLITEST
PLOTTIES

POLITIC KOS
POLITICK S
POLITICO S
POLITICS
COLPITIS
PSILOTIC
POLITIES
PISOLITE
POLITY
POLKA S
POLKAED
POLKAING
POLKAS
POLL S
POLLACK S
POLLACKS
POLLARD S
POLLARDS
POLLED
POLLEE S
POLLEES
POLLEN S
POLLENED
POLLENS
POLLER S
REPOLL
POLLERS
REPOLLS
POLLEX
POLLICAL
POLLICES
POLLING
POLLINIA
POLLINIC
POLLIST S
POLLISTS
POLLIWOG S
POLLOCK S
POLLOCKS
POLLS
POLLSTER S
POLLUTE DRS
POLLUTED
POLLUTER S
POLLUTES
OUTSPELL
POLLYWOG S
POLO S
LOOP POOL
POLOIST S
TOPSOIL
POLOISTS
TOPSOILS
POLONIUM S
POLOS
LOOPS POOLS
SLOOP SPOOL
POLS
LOPS SLOP
POLTROON S
POLY PS
PLOY
POLYBRID S
POLYCOT S
POLYCOTS
POLYENE S
POLYENES
POLYENIC
POLYGALA S
POLYGAMY
POLYGENE S
POLYGLOT S
POLYGON SY
POLYGONS
POLYGONY
POLYGYNY
POLYMATH SY
POLYMER S
POLYMERS
POLYNYA S
POLYNYAS
POLYNYI
POLYOL S
POLYOLS
POLYOMA S
POLYOMAS

POLYP IS
LOPPY
POLYPARY
POLYPED S
POLYPEDS
POLYPI
POLYPIDE S
POLYPNEA S
POLYPOD SY
POLYPODS
POLYPODY
POLYPOID
POLYPORE S
POLYPOUS
POLYPS
SLOPPY
POLYPUS
POLYS
PLOYS
POLYSEMY
POLYSOME S
POLYTENE
POLYTENY
POLYTYPE S
POLYURIA S
POLYURIC
CROUPILY
POLYZOAN S
POLYZOIC
POMACE S
POMACES
POMADE DS
POMADED
POMADES
POMADING
POMANDER S
POMATUM S
POMATUMS
POME S
MOPE POEM
POMELO S
POMELOS
POMES
MOPES POEMS
POMFRET S
POMFRETS
POMMEE
POMMEL S
POMMELED
POMMELS
POMO S
POMOLOGY
POMOS
POMP S
POMPANO S
POMPANOS
POMPOM S
POMPOMS
POMPON S
POMPONS
POMPOUS
POMPS
PONCE DS
COPEN
PONCED
PONCES
COPENS
PONCHO S
PONCHOED
CHENOPOD
PONCHOS
PONCING
POND S
PONDED
PONDER S
PERNOD
PONDERED
PONDERER S
PONDERS
PERNODS
RESPOND
PONDING
PONDS
PONDWEED S
PONE S
NOPE OPEN
PEON

PONENT
PONES
OPENS PEONS
PONG S
S PONGED
PONGEE S
PONGEES
PONGID S
DOPING
PONGIDS
DOPINGS
S PONGING
PONGS
PONIARD S
PADRONI
PONIARDS
PONIED
OPINED
PONIES
OPINES
PONS
PONTES
NETOPS
PONTIFEX
PONTIFF S
PONTIFFS
PONTIFIC
PONTIL S
PONTILS
PONTINE
PONTON S
PONTONS
NONSTOP
S PONTOON S
S PONTOONS
SPONTOON
PONY
PONYING
PONYTAIL S
POOCH
POOCHED
POOCHES
POOCHING
POOD S
POODLE S
LOOPED
POOLED
POODLES
SPOOLED
POODS
S POOF
POOH S
HOOP
POOHED
HOOPED
POOHING
HOOPING
POOHS
HOOPS
S POOL S
LOOP POLO
S POOLED
LOOPED
POODLE
S POOLER S
LOOPER
S POOLERS
LOOPERS
RESPOOL
SPOOLER
POOLHALL S
S POOLING
LOOPING
POOLROOM S
S POOLS
LOOPS POLOS
SLOOP SPOOL
POOLSIDE S
S POON S
S POONS
SNOOP SPOON
POOP S
POOPED
POOPING
POGONIP
POOPS
S POOR I
POORER
POOREST
STOOPER
POORI S

POORIS H
POORISH
POORLY
POORNESS
SNOOPERS
POORTITH S
POP ES
POPCORN S
POPCORNS
POPE S
PEPO
POPEDOM S
POPEDOMS
POPELESS
PEPLOSES
POPELIKE
POPES
PEPOS
POPEYED
POPGUN S
OPPUGN
POPGUNS
OPPUGNS
POPINJAY S
POPLAR S
POPLARS
POPLIN S
POPLINS
POPLITEI
POPLITIC
POPOVER S
POPOVERS
POPPA S
POPPADOM S
POPPADUM S
POPPAS
POPPED
POPPER S
POPPERS
POPPET S
POPPETS
POPPIED
POPPIES
POPPING
POPPLE DS
POPPLED
PLOPPED
POPPLES
POPPLING
PLOPPING
POPPY
POPS Y
POPSICLE S
POPSIE S
POPSIES
POPSY
SOPPY
POPULACE S
POPULAR
POPULATE DS
POPULISM S
POPULIST S
POPULOUS
PORCH
PORCHES
PORCINE
PORCINI S
PORCINIS
PORCINO
S PORE DS
REPO ROPE
S PORED
DOPER PEDRO
ROPED
S PORES
POSER PROSE
REPOS ROPES
SPORE
PORGIES
SERPIGO
PORGY
S PORING
ROPING
PORISM S
PRIMOS
PORISMS
PORK SY
PORKED

PORKER S
PORKERS
PORKIER
PORKIES T
PORKIEST
PORKING
PORKPIE S
PORKPIES
PORKS
PORKWOOD S
PORKY
PORN OSY
PORNIER
PORNIEST
POINTERS
PROTEINS
TROPINES
PORNO S
PORNOS
PORNS
PORNY
POROSE
POROSITY
ISOTROPY
POROUS
POROUSLY
PORPHYRY
PORPOISE DS
PORRECT
PORRIDGE S
PORRIDGY
AS PORT S
TROP
PORTABLE S
PORTABLY
PORTAGE DS
PORTAGED
PORTAGES
PORTAL S
PATROL
PORTALED
PORTALS
PATROLS
PORTANCE S
COPARENT
PORTAPAK S
S PORTED
DEPORT
REDTOP
PORTEND S
PROTEND
PORTENDS
PROTENDS
PORTENT S
PORTENTS
S PORTER S
PRETOR
REPORT
PORTERED
DEPORTER
REPORTED
S PORTERS
PRESORT
PRETORS
REPORTS
SPORTER
PORTHOLE S
PORTICO S
PORTICOS
PORTIERE S
S PORTING
PORTION S
PORTIONS
POSITRON
SORPTION
PORTLESS
PORTLIER
PORTLY
PROTYL
PORTRAIT S
PORTRAY S
PARROTY
PORTRAYS
PORTRESS
PRESORTS
SPORTERS
S PORTS
PROST SPORT
STROP
PORTSIDE
DIOPTERS
DIOPTRES
PERIDOTS
PROTEIDS
RIPOSTED
TOPSIDER
POSABLE
POSADA S
POSADAS
PASSADO
POSE DRS
EPOS OPES
PESO
POSED
DOPES SPODE
POSER S
PORES PROSE
REPOS ROPES
SPORE
POSERS
PROSES
SPORES
E POSES
PESOS POSSE
POSEUR S
UPROSE
POSEURS
POSH
HOPS SHOP
SOPH
POSHER
EPHORS
HOPERS
POSHEST
POSHLY
POSHNESS
POSIES
POISES
POSING
GIPONS
PINGOS
POSINGLY
SPONGILY
POSIT S
TOPIS
POSITED
DEPOSIT
DOPIEST
PODITES
SOPITED
TOPSIDE
POSITING
SOPITING
POSITION S
POSITIVE RS
POSITRON S
PORTIONS
SORPTION
POSITS
PTOSIS
POSOLE S
POSOLES
POSOLOGY
POSSE ST
PESOS POSES
POSSES S
POSSESS
POSSET S
ESTOPS
PESTOS
PTOSES
STOPES
POSSETS
POSSIBLE R
POSSIBLY
O POSSUM S
O POSSUMS
POST S
OPTS POTS
SPOT STOP
TOPS
POSTAGE S
GESTAPO
POTAGES
POSTAGES
GESTAPOS
POSTAL S
POSTALLY
POSTALS
POSTANAL
POSTBAG S
POSTBAGS
POSTBASE
POSTBOX
POSTBOY S
POTBOYS
POSTBOYS
POSTBURN
POSTCARD S
POSTCAVA EL S
POSTCODE S
POSTCOUP
POSTDATE DS
POSTDIVE
POSTDOC S
POSTDOCS
POSTDRUG
POSTED
DEPOTS
DESPOT
STOPED
POSTEEN S
OPENEST
PENTOSE
POTEENS
POSTEENS
PENTOSES
POSTER NS
PRESTO
REPOTS
RESPOT
STOPER
TOPERS
TROPES
POSTERN S
POSTERNS
POSTERS
PRESTOS
RESPOTS
STOPERS
POSTFACE S
POSTFIRE
FIREPOTS
PIEFORTS
POSTFIX
POSTFORM S
POSTGAME
POSTGRAD S
POSTHEAT S
POSTHOLE S
POTHOLES
POSTICHE S
POTICHES
POSTIE S
POTSIE
SOPITE
POSTIES
POTSIES
SOPITES
POSTIN GS
PINOTS
PINTOS
PISTON
PITONS
POINTS
SPINTO
POSTING S
STOPING
POSTINGS
SIGNPOST
POSTINS
PISTONS
SPINTOS
POSTIQUE S
POSTLUDE S
POSTMAN
TAMPONS
POSTMARK S
POSTMEN
POSTOP S
POSTOPS
POSTORAL
POSTPAID
POSTPONE DR S
POSTPOSE DS
POSTPUNK
POSTRACE
POSTRIOT
POSTS
SPOTS STOPS
POSTSHOW
POSTSYNC S
POSTTAX
POSTTEEN S
POTTEENS
POSTTEST S
POSTURAL
PULSATOR
POSTURE DRS
PETROUS
POUTERS
PROTEUS
SPOUTER
TROUPES
POSTURED
PROUDEST
SPROUTED
POSTURER S
RESPROUT
TROUPERS
POSTURES
OUTPRESS
SPOUTERS
POSTWAR
POSY
S POT S
OPT
TOP
POTABLE S
POTABLES
POTAGE S
POTAGES
GESTAPO
POSTAGE
POTAMIC
APOMICT
POTASH
PATHOS
POTASHES
PATHOSES
SPATHOSE
TEASHOPS
POTASSIC
POTATION S
POTATO
POTATOES
POTATORY
POTBELLY
POTBOIL S
POTBOILS
POTBOUND
POTBOY S
POTBOYS
POSTBOY
POTEEN S
POTEENS
OPENEST
PENTOSE
POSTEEN
POTENCE S
POTENCES
POTENCY
POTENT
POTENTLY
POTFUL S
TOPFUL
POTFULS
POTHEAD S
POTHEADS
POTHEEN S
POTHEENS
POTHER BS
THORPE
POTHERB S
POTHERBS
POTHERED
POTHERS
STROPHE
THORPES
POTHOLE DS
POTHOLED
POTHOLES
POSTHOLE
POTHOOK S
POTHOOKS
POTHOS
PHOTOS
POTHOUSE S
HOUSETOP
POTICHE S
POTICHES
POSTICHE
POTION S
OPTION
POTIONS
OPTIONS
POTLACH E
POTLACHE S
POTLATCH
POTLIKE
POTLINE S
TOPLINE
POTLINES
TOPLINES
POTLUCK S
POTLUCKS
POTMAN
TAMPON
POTMEN
POTPIE S
POTPIES
S POTS Y
OPTS POST
SPOT STOP
TOPS
POTSHARD S
HARDTOPS
POTSHERD S
POTSHOT S
HOTSPOT
POTSHOTS
HOTSPOTS
POTSIE S
POSTIE
SOPITE
POTSIES
POSTIES
SOPITES
POTSTONE S
TOPSTONE
POTSY
TYPOS
POTTAGE S
POTTAGES
GATEPOST
S POTTED
POTTEEN S
POTTEENS
POSTTEEN
S POTTER SY
POTTERED
REPOTTED
POTTERER S
S POTTERS
PROTEST
SPOTTER
POTTERY
S POTTIER
POTTIES T
TIPTOES
S POTTIEST
S POTTING
POTTLE S
POTTLES
POTTO S
POTTOS
S POTTY
POTZER S
POTZERS
POUCH Y
POUCHED
POUCHES
POUCHIER
EUPHORIC
POUCHING
POUCHY
POUF FS
POUFED
POUFF ESY
POUFFE DS
POUFFED
POUFFES
POUFFS
POUFFY
POUFS
POULARD ES
POULARDE S
POULARDS
POULT S
POULTER S
POULTERS
POULTICE DS
POULTRY
POULTS
POUNCE DRS
POUNCED
POUNCER S
POUNCERS
POUNCES
POUNCING
POUND S
POUNDAGE S
POUNDAL S
POUNDALS
POUNDED
POUNDER S
UNROPED
POUNDERS
POUNDING
POUNDS
POUR S
ROUP
POURABLE
POURED
ROUPED
POURER S
REPOUR
POURERS
REPOURS
POURING
INGROUP
ROUPING
POURS
ROUPS
POUSSIE S
POUSSIES
S POUT SY
S POUTED
S POUTER S
ROUPET
TROUPE
UPTORE
S POUTERS
PETROUS
POSTURE
PROTEUS
SPOUTER
TROUPES
POUTFUL
POUTIER
POUTIEST
POUTINE S
POUTINES
S POUTING
S POUTS
SPOUT STOUP
POUTY
POVERTY
POW S
POWDER SY
POWDERED
POWDERER S
POWDERS
POWDERY
POWER S
POWERED
POWERFUL
POWERING
POWERS
POWS
SWOP
POWTER S
POWTERS
PROWEST
POWWOW S
POWWOWED
POWWOWS
POX Y
POXED
POXES
EXPOS
POXIER
POXIEST
EXPOSIT
POXING
POXVIRUS
E POXY
POYOU S
POYOUS
POZOLE S
POZOLES
POZZOLAN AS
PRAAM S
PRAAMS
A PRACTIC E
PRACTICE DR S
PRACTISE DS
CRISPATE
PARETICS
PICRATES
PRAECIPE S
PRAEDIAL
PRAEFECT S
PERFECTA
PRAELECT S
PRAETOR S
PRORATE
PRAETORS
PRORATES
PRAHU S
PRAHUS
PRAIRIE S
PRAIRIES
U PRAISE DRS
ASPIRE
PARIES
SPIREA
U PRAISED
ASPIRED
DESPAIR
DIAPERS
U PRAISER S
ASPIRER
PARRIES
RAPIERS
RASPIER
REPAIRS
U PRAISERS
ASPIRERS
U PRAISES
ASPIRES
PARESIS
PARISES
SPIREAS
U PRAISING
ASPIRING
PAIRINGS
PRAJNA S
PRAJNAS
PRALINE S
PLAINER
PRALINES
PRAM S
RAMP
PRAMS
RAMPS
PRANCE DRS
PRANCED
PRANCER S
PRANCERS
PRANCES
PRANCING
PRANDIAL
S PRANG S
PRANGED
PRANGING
S PRANGS
SPRANG
PRANK S
PRANKED
PRANKING
PRANKISH
PRANKS
PRAO S
PROA
PRAOS
PROAS SAPOR
PRASE S
APERS APRES
ASPER PARES
PARSE PEARS
PRESA RAPES
REAPS SPARE
SPEAR

PRASES
ASPERS
PARSES
PASSER
REPASS
SPARES
SPARSE
SPEARS
S **PRAT** ES
PART RAPT
TARP TRAP
U **PRATE** DRS
APTER PATER
PEART TAPER
U **PRATED**
DEPART
PARTED
PETARD
PRATER S
PRATERS
U **PRATES**
PASTER
PATERS
REPAST
TAPERS
TRAPES
PRATFALL S
U **PRATING**
PARTING
PRATIQUE S
S **PRATS**
PARTS SPRAT
STRAP TARPS
TRAPS
S **PRATTLE** DRS
PARTLET
PLATTER
S **PRATTLED**
PRATTLER S
S **PRATTLES**
PARTLETS
PLATTERS
SPLATTER
SPRATTLE
PRAU S
PRAUS
SUPRA
PRAWN S
PRAWNED
PREDAWN
PRAWNER S
PREWARN
PRAWNERS
PREWARNS
PRAWNING
PRAWNS
PRAXES
PRAXIS
PRAXISES
S **PRAY** S
S **PRAYED**
DRAPEY
S **PRAYER** S
S **PRAYERS**
RESPRAY
SPRAYER
S **PRAYING**
S **PRAYS**
RASPY SPRAY
U **PREACH** Y
EPARCH
U **PREACHED**
PREACHER S
U **PREACHES**
PEACHERS
PREACHY
EPARCHY
PREACT S
CARPET
PREACTED
CARPETED
PREACTS
CARPETS
PRECAST
SPECTRA
PREADAPT S
PREADMIT S
IMPARTED
PREADOPT S
PREADULT S
PREAGED
PREALLOT S

PREALTER S
PALTERER
PREAMBLE DS
PREAMP S
MAPPER
PAMPER
PREAMPS
MAPPERS
PAMPERS
PREANAL
PREAPPLY
PREARM S
PREARMED
PREARMS
PREAUDIT S
EUPATRID
PREAVER S
PREAVERS
PREAXIAL
PREBADE
BEDRAPE
PREBAKE DS
BARKEEP
PREBAKED
PREBAKES
BARKEEPS
PREBASAL
PARABLES
PARSABLE
SPARABLE
PREBEND S
PREBENDS
PREBID S
PREBIDS
PREBILL S
PREBILLS
PREBIND S
PREBINDS
PREBIRTH S
PREBLESS
PREBOARD S
PREBOIL S
PREBOILS
PREBOOK S
PREBOOKS
PREBOOM
PREBOUND
UNPROBED
PREBUILD S
PREBUILT
PREBUY S
PREBUYS
PRECAST S
CARPETS
PREACTS
SPECTRA
PRECASTS
PRECAVA EL
PRECAVAE
PRECAVAL
PRECEDE DS
CREEPED
PRECEDED
PRECEDES
PRECENT S
PERCENT
PRECENTS
PERCENTS
PRECEPT S
PERCEPT
PRECEPTS
PERCEPTS
PRECESS
PRECHECK S
PRECHILL S
PRECHOSE N
PRECIEUX
PRECINCT S
PRECIOUS
PRECIPE S
PRECIPES
PRECIS E
CRIPES
PRICES
SPICER
PRECISE DRS
PIECERS
PIERCES
RECIPES

PRECISED
PRECISER
PIERCERS
REPRICES
PRECISES T
PRECITED
DECREPIT
DEPICTER
PRECLEAN S
PRECLEAR S
REPLACER
PRECLUDE DS
PRECODE DS
PROCEED
PRECODED
PRECODES
PROCEEDS
PRECOOK S
PRECOOKS
PRECOOL S
PRECOOLS
PRECOUP
PRECRASH
PRECURE DS
PRECURED
PRECURES
PRECUT S
PRECUTS
PREDATE DS
ADEPTER
RETAPED
TAPERED
PREDATED
DEPARTED
PREDATES
PEDERAST
REPASTED
TRAPESED
PREDATOR SY
PARROTED
PRORATED
PROTRADE
TEARDROP
PREDAWN S
PRAWNED
PREDAWNS
PREDEATH S
THREAPED
PREDELLA S
PEDALLER
PREDIAL
LIPREAD
PREDICT S
PREDICTS
SCRIPTED
PREDIVE
DEPRIVE
PREDRAFT
PREDRIED
PREDRIES
PRESIDER
REPRISED
RESPIRED
PREDRILL S
PREDRY
PREDUSK S
PREDUSKS
S **PREE** DNS
PEER PERE
PREED
PREEDIT S
PREEDITS
PRIESTED
RESPITED
PREEING
PEERING
PREELECT S
PREEMIE S
EPIMERE
PREEMIES
EMPERIES
EPIMERES
PREEMPT S
PREEMPTS
PREEN S
PREENACT S
PREENED
PREENER S
PREENERS
PREENING
PREENS

PREERECT S
S **PREES**
PEERS PERES
PERSE PRESE
SPEER SPREE
PREEXIST S
PREFAB S
PREFABS
PREFACE DRS
PREFACED
PREFACER S
PREFACES
PREFADE DS
PREFADED
PREFADES
PREFECT S
PERFECT
PREFECTS
PERFECTS
PREFER S
PREFERS
PREFIGHT
PREFILE DS
PRELIFE
PREFILED
PILFERED
PREFILES
PREFIRE DS
PREFIRED
PREFIRES
PREFIX
PREFIXAL
PREFIXED
PREFIXES
PREFLAME
PREFOCUS
PREFORM S
PERFORM
PREFORMS
PERFORMS
PREFRANK S
PREFROZE N
PREFUND S
PREFUNDS
PREGAME S
PREGAMES
PREGGERS
PREGNANT
PREGUIDE DS
PREHEAT S
PREHEATS
PREHUMAN S
PREJUDGE DR S
PRELACY
PRELATE S
PETRALE
PLEATER
REPLATE
PRELATES
PETRALES
PLEATERS
REPLATES
PRELATIC
PARTICLE
PRELAW
PRELECT S
PRELECTS
PRELEGAL
PRELIFE
PREFILE
PRELIM S
LIMPER
RIMPLE
PRELIMIT S
PRELIMS
LIMPERS
RIMPLES
SIMPLER
PRELIVES
PRELOAD S
LEOPARD
PAROLED
PRELOADS
LEOPARDS
PRELUDE DRS
PRELUDED
PRELUDER S

PRELUDES
REPULSED
PRELUNCH
PREMADE
PREMAN
PREMEAL
EMPALER
PREMED S
DEPERM
PERMED
PREMEDIC S
PREMEDS
DEPERMS
PREMEET
PREMEN
PREMIE RS
EMPIRE
EPIMER
PREMIER ES
PREMIERE DS
PREMIERS
SIMPERER
PREMIES
EMPIRES
EMPRISE
EPIMERS
IMPRESE
PREMISE
SPIREME
PREMISE DS
EMPIRES
EMPRISE
EPIMERS
IMPRESE
PREMIES
SPIREME
PREMISED
DEMIREPS
EPIDERMS
IMPEDERS
SIMPERED
PREMISES
EMPRISES
IMPRESES
SPIREMES
PREMISS
IMPRESS
SIMPERS
SPIREMS
PREMIUM S
PREMIUMS
PREMIX T
PREMIXED
PREMIXES
PREMIXT
PREMOLAR S
PREMORAL
PREMOLD S
PREMOLDS
PREMOLT
PREMORAL
PREMOLAR
PREMORSE
EMPERORS
PREMUNE
PRENAME S
PRENAMES
SPEARMEN
PRENATAL
PARENTAL
PARLANTE
PATERNAL
PRENOMEN S
PRENOON
PRENTICE DS
TERPENIC
PREOP S
PREOPS
PREORAL
PERORAL
PREORDER S
PREOWNED
PREP S
PERP REPP
PREPACK S
PREPACKS
PREPAID
PREPARE DRS
PAPERER
REPAPER

PREPARED
DAPPERER
PREPARER S
PREPARES
PAPERERS
REPAPERS
PREPASTE DS
PRETAPES
PREPAVE DS
PREPAVED
PREPAVES
PREPAY S
PAPERY
YAPPER
PREPAYS
YAPPERS
PREPENSE
PREPILL
PREPLACE DS
PREPLAN ST
PREPLANS
PREPLANT
PREPPED
PREPPIE RS
PEPPIER
PREPPIER
PREPPIES T
PREPPILY
PREPPING
PREPPY
PREPREG S
PREPREGS
PREPRESS
PREPRICE DS
PREPRINT S
PREPS
PERPS REPPS
PREPUBES
PREPUBIS
PREPUCE S
PREPUCES
PREPUNCH
PREPUPA ELS
PREPUPAE
PREPUPAL
PREPUPAS
PREQUEL S
PREQUELS
PRERACE
CAPERER
PRERADIO
PRERENAL
PRERINSE DS
REPINERS
RIPENERS
PRERIOT
PIERROT
PREROCK
PRESA
APERS APRES
ASPER PARES
PARSE PEARS
PRASE RAPES
REAPS SPARE
SPEAR
PRESAGE DRS
PRESAGED
PRESAGER S
PRESAGES
ASPERGES
PRESALE S
LEAPERS
PLEASER
RELAPSE
REPEALS
PRESALES
PLEASERS
RELAPSES
PRESCIND S
PRESCORE DS
PRESE T
PEERS PERES
PERSE PREES
SPEER SPREE
PRESELL S
RESPELL
SPELLER
PRESELLS
RESPELLS
SPELLERS

PRESENCE S
PRESENT S
PENSTER
REPENTS
SERPENT
PRESENTS
PENSTERS
PERTNESS
SERPENTS
PRESERVE DR S
PERVERSE
PRESET S
PESTER
PETERS
PRESETS
PESTERS
PRESHAPE DS
PRESHIP S
SHIPPER
PRESHIPS
SHIPPERS
PRESHOW NS
PRESHOWN
PRESHOWS
PRESIDE DRS
SPEIRED
SPIERED
PRESIDED
PRESIDER S
PREDRIES
REPRISED
RESPIRED
PRESIDES
DESPISER
DISPERSE
PRESIDIA L
PRESIDIO S
PRESIFT S
PRESIFTS
PRESLEEP
PRESLICE DS
ECLIPSER
RESPLICE
PRESOAK S
PRESOAKS
PRESOLD
POLDERS
PRESOLVE DS
PRESONG
SPONGER
PRESORT S
PORTERS
PRETORS
REPORTS
SPORTER
PRESORTS
PORTRESS
SPORTERS
PRESPLIT
RIPPLETS
STIPPLER
TIPPLERS
PRESS
PRESSED
DEPRESS
PRESSER S
REPRESS
PRESSERS
PRESSES
PRESSING S
SPRINGES
PRESSMAN
PRESSMEN
PRESSOR S
PROSERS
PRESSORS
PRESSRUN S
SPURNERS
PRESSURE DS
PERUSERS
PREST OS
STREP
PRESTAMP S
PRESTER S
PRESTERS
PRESTIGE S

PRESTO S
POSTER REPOTS RESPOT STOPER TOPERS TROPES
PRESTORE DS
PRESTOS
POSTERS RESPOTS STOPERS
PRESTS
STREPS
PRESUME DRS
SUPREME
PRESUMED
PRESUMER S
SUPREMER
PRESUMES
SUPREMES
PRETAPE DS
PRETAPED
PRETAPES
PREPASTE
PRETASTE DS
PEARTEST
PRETAX
PRETEEN S
TERPENE
PRETEENS
PRETENSE TERPENES
PRETELL S
PRETELLS
PRETENCE S
PRETEND S
PRETENDS
PRETENSE S
PRETEENS TERPENES
PRETERIT ES
PRETTIER
PRETERM S
PRETERMS
PRETEST S
PERTEST PETTERS
PRETESTS
PRETEXT S
PRETEXTS
PRETOLD
DROPLET
PRETOR S
PORTER REPORT
PRETORS
PORTERS PRESORT REPORTS SPORTER
PRETRAIN S
TERRAPIN
PRETREAT S
PATTERER
PRETRIAL S
PALTRIER
PRETRIM S
PRETRIMS
PRETTIED
PRETTIER
PRETERIT
PRETTIES T
PRETTIFY
PRETTILY
PRETTY
PRETYPE DS
PRETYPED
PRETYPES
PRETZEL S
PRETZELS
PREUNION S
PREUNITE DS
PREVAIL S
PREVAILS
PREVALUE DS
PREVENT S
PREVENTS
PREVERB S
PREVERBS
PREVIEW S
PREVIEWS
PREVIOUS
PERVIOUS VIPEROUS
PREVISE DS
PREVISED
DEPRIVES
PREVISES
PREVISIT S
PRIVIEST
PREVISOR S
PREVUE DS
PREVUED
PREVUES
PREVUING
PREWAR MN
REWRAP WARPER
PREWARM S
PREWARMS
PREWARN S
PRAWNER
PREWARNS
PRAWNERS
PREWASH
PREWEIGH S
PREWIRE DS
PREWIRED
PREWIRES
PREWORK S
PREWORKS
PREWORN
PREWRAP S
WRAPPER
PREWRAPS
WRAPPERS
PREX Y
PREXES
PREXIES
EXPIRES
PREXY
PYREX
PREY S
PYRE
PREYED
PREYER S
PREYERS
PREYING
PREYS
PYRES
PREZ
PREZES
PRIAPEAN
PRIAPI C
PRIAPIC
PRIAPISM S
PRIAPUS
PRICE DRSY
CRIPE
PRICED
PRICER S
PRICERS
CRISPER
PRICES
CRIPES PRECIS SPICER
PRICEY
PRICIER
PRICIEST
PICRITES
PRICILY
PRICING
PRICK SY
PRICKED
PRICKER S
PRICKERS
PRICKET S
PRICKETS
PRICKIER
PRICKING S
PRICKLE DS
PRICKLED
PRICKLES
PRICKLY
PRICKS
PRICKY
PRICY
PYRIC
PRIDE DS
PRIED REDIP RIPED
PRIDED
PRIDEFUL
PRIDES
PRISED REDIPS SPIDER SPIRED
PRIDING
PRIED
PRIDE REDIP RIPED
PRIEDIEU SX
S **PRIER** S
RIPER
PRIERS
SPRIER
PRIES T
PERIS PIERS PRISE RIPES SPEIR SPIER SPIRE
S **PRIEST** S
ESPRIT RIPEST SPRITE STRIPE TRIPES
PRIESTED
PREEDITS RESPITED
PRIESTLY
PRIESTS
ESPRITS PERSIST SPRIEST SPRITES STIRPES STRIPES
S **PRIG** S
GRIP
S **PRIGGED**
PRIGGERY
S **PRIGGING**
PRIGGISH
PRIGGISM S
S **PRIGS**
GRIPS SPRIG
PRILL S
PRILLED
PRILLING
PRILLS
PRIM AEIOPS
PRIMA LS
PRIMACY
PRIMAGE S
EPIGRAM
PRIMAGES
EPIGRAMS
PRIMAL
PRIMARY
PRIMAS
PRIMATAL S
PRIMATE S
PRIMATES
PRIME DRS
PRIMED
PRIMELY
PRIMER OS
PRIMERO S
PRIMEROS
PRIMROSE PROMISER
PRIMERS
PRIMES
SIMPER SPIREM
PRIMEVAL
PRIMI
PRIMINE S
PRIMINES
PRIMING S
PRIMINGS
PRIMLY
PRIMMED
PRIMMER
PRIMMEST
PRIMMING
PRIMNESS
PRIMO S
PRIMOS
PORISM
PRIMP S
PRIMPED
PRIMPING
PRIMPS
PRIMROSE S
PRIMEROS PROMISER
PRIMS
PRISM
PRIMSIE
PISMIRE
PRIMULA S
PRIMULAS
PRIMUS
PURISM
PRIMUSES
PRINCE S
PINCER
PRINCELY
PRINCES S
CRISPEN PINCERS
PRINCESS E
CRISPENS
PRINCIPE
PRINCIPI A
PRINCOCK S
PRINCOX
PRINK S
PRINKED
PRINKER S
PRINKERS
PRINKING
PRINKS
S **PRINT** S
S **PRINTED**
S **PRINTER** SY
REPRINT
S **PRINTERS**
REPRINTS SPRINTER
PRINTERY
S **PRINTING** S
PRINTOUT S
S **PRINTS**
SPRINT
PRION S
ORPIN
PRIONS
ORPINS PRISON SPINOR
PRIOR SY
PRIORATE S
PRIORESS
PRIORIES
A **PRIORITY**
PRIORLY
PRIORS
PRIORY
U **PRISE** DS
PERIS PIERS PRIES RIPES SPEIR SPIER SPIRE
PRISED
PRIDES REDIPS SPIDER SPIRED
PRISERE S
PERRIES REPRISE RESPIRE
PRISERES
REPRISES RESPIRES
U **PRISES**
SPEIRS SPIERS SPIRES
U **PRISING**
SPIRING
PRISM S
PRIMS
PRISMOID S
PRISMS
PRISON S
ORPINS PRIONS SPINOR
PRISONED
PRISONER S
PRISONS
SPINORS
PRISS Y
PRISSED
SPIDERS
PRISSES
PRISSIER
PRISSIES T
PRISSILY
PRISSING
PRISSY
PRISTANE S
PAINTERS PANTRIES PERTAINS PINASTER REPAINTS
PRISTINE
PRITHEE
PRIVACY
PRIVATE RS
PRIVATER
PRIVATES T
PRIVET S
PRIVETS
PRIVIER
PRIVIES T
PRIVIEST
PREVISIT
PRIVILY
PRIVITY
PRIVY
PRIZE DRS
PRIZED
PRIZER S
PRIZERS
PRIZES
PRIZING
PRO ADFGMPS W
PROA S
PRAO
PROAS
PRAOS SAPOR
PROBABLE S
PROBABLY
PROBAND S
PROBANDS
PROBANG S
PROBANGS
PROBATE DS
PROBATED
PROBATES
PROBE DRS
REBOP
PROBED
PROBER S
PROBERS
PROBES
REBOPS
PROBING
PROBIT SY
PROBITS
PROBITY
PROBLEM S
PROBLEMS
PROCAINE S
APOCRINE CAPONIER
PROCARP S
PROCARPS
PROCEED S
PRECODE
PROCEEDS
PRECODES
PROCESS
CORPSES
PROCHAIN
PROCHEIN
PROCLAIM S
PICLORAM
PROCTOR S
PROCTORS
PROCURAL S
PROCURE DRS
PROCURED
PRODUCER
PROCURER S
PROCURES S
PROD S
DORP DROP
PRODDED
PRODDER S
PRODDERS
PRODDING
PRODIGAL S
PRODIGY
PRODROME S
PRODRUG S
PRODRUGS
PRODS
DORPS DROPS
PRODUCE DRS
PRODUCED
PRODUCER S
PROCURED
PRODUCES
PRODUCT S
PRODUCTS
PROEM S
MOPER
PROEMIAL
PROEMS
MOPERS
PROETTE S
TREETOP
PROETTES
TREETOPS
PROF S
PROFANE DRS
PROFANED
PROFANER S
PROFANES
PROFESS
PROFFER S
PROFFERS
PROFILE DRS
PROFILED
PROFILER S
PROFILES
PROFIT S
PROFITED
PIEDFORT
PROFITER S
PROFITS
SPORTIF
PROFORMA
PROFOUND S
PROFS
PROFUSE
PROG S
GORP
PROGENY
PYROGEN
PROGERIA S
PROGGED
PROGGER S
PROGGERS
PROGGING
PROGNOSE DS
PROGRADE
DRAGROPE
PROGRAM S
PROGRAMS
PROGRESS
PROGS
GORPS
PROGUN
PROHIBIT S
PROJECT S
PROJECTS
PROJET S
PROJETS
PROLABOR
PROLAMIN ES
PROLAN S
PROLANS
PROLAPSE DS
SAPROPEL
PROLATE
PROLE GS
LOPER POLER
PROLEG S
PROLEGS
PROLES
LOPERS POLERS SLOPER SPLORE
PROLIFIC
PROLINE S
PROLINES
PROLIX
PROLIXLY
PROLOG S
PROLOGED
PROLOGS
PROLOGUE DS
PROLONG ES
PROLONGE DR S
PROLONGS
PROM OS
ROMP
PROMINE S
PROMINES
PROMISE DER S
IMPOSER SEMIPRO
PROMISED
PROMISEE S
MOPERIES REIMPOSE
PROMISER S
PRIMEROS PRIMROSE
PROMISES
IMPOSERS SEMIPROS
PROMISOR S
PROMO S
PROMOED
PROMOING
PROMOS
PROMOTE DRS
PROMOTED
PROMOTER S
PROMOTES
PROMPT S
PROMPTED
PROMPTER S
PROMPTLY
PROMPTS
PROMS
ROMPS
PROMULGE DS
PRONATE DS
OPERANT PROTEAN
PRONATED
PRONATES
OPERANTS PROTEANS
PRONATOR S
PRONE
PRONELY
PRONG S
PRONGED
PRONGING
PRONGS
PRONOTA
PATROON
PRONOTUM
PRONOUN S
PRONOUNS
PRONTO
PROTON
PROOF S
PROOFED
PROOFER S
REPROOF
PROOFERS
REPROOFS
PROOFING
PROOFS
PROP S
PROPANE S

PROPANES
PROPEL S
LOPPER
PROPELS
LOPPERS
PROPEND S
PROPENDS
PROPENE S
PROPENES
PROPENSE
PROPENOL S
PROPENSE
PROPENES
PROPENYL
PROPER S
PROPERER
PROPERLY
PROPERS
PROSPER
PROPERTY
PROPHAGE S
PROPHASE S
PROPHECY
PROPHESY
PROPHET S
PROPHETS
PROPINE DS
PROPINED
PROPINES
PROPJET S
PROPJETS
PROPMAN
PROPMEN
PROPOLIS
PROPONE DS
PROPONED
PROPONES
PROPOSAL S
PROPOSE DRS
OPPOSER
PROPOSED
PROPOSER S
PROPOSES
OPPOSERS
PROPOUND S
PROPPED
PROPPING
PROPRIA
PROPRIUM
PROPS
PROPYL AS
PROPYLA
PROPYLIC
PROPYLON
PROPYLS
PRORATE DS
PRAETOR
PRORATED
PARROTED
PREDATOR
PROTRADE
TEARDROP
PRORATES
PRAETORS
PROROGUE DS
PROS EOSTY
PROSAIC
PICAROS
PROSAISM S
PROSAIST S
AIRPOSTS
PROTASIS
U **PROSE** DRS
PORES POSER
REPOS ROPES
SPORE
PROSECT S
COPTERS
PROSECTS
PROSED
DOPERS
PEDROS
SPORED
PROSER S
REPROS
ROPERS
PROSERS
PRESSOR

PROSES
POSERS
SPORES
PROSIER
PROSIEST
PROSTIES
REPOSITS
RIPOSTES
TRIPOSES
PROSILY
PROSING
SPORING
PROSIT
RIPOST
TRIPOS
PROSO S
SOPOR SPOOR
PROSODIC
PROSODY
PROSOMA LS
PROSOMAL
PROSOMAS
PROSOS
SOPORS
SPOORS
PROSPECT S
PROSPER S
PROPERS
PROSPERS
PROSS
PROSSES
PROSSIE S
POISERS
PROSSIES
PROST
PORTS SPORT
STROP
PROSTATE S
PROSTIE S
REPOSIT
RIPOSTE
ROPIEST
PROSTIES
PROSIEST
REPOSITS
RIPOSTES
TRIPOSES
PROSTYLE S
PROTYLES
PROSY
PYROS
PROTAMIN ES
PROTASES
ESPARTOS
SEAPORTS
PROTASIS
AIRPOSTS
PROSAIST
PROTATIC
PROTEA NS
PROTEAN S
OPERANT
PRONATE
PROTEANS
OPERANTS
PRONATES
PROTEAS E
ESPARTO
SEAPORT
PROTEASE S
OPERATES
PROTECT S
PROTECTS
PROTEGE ES
PROTEGEE S
PROTEGES
PROTEI DN
PROTEID ES
DIOPTER
DIOPTRE
PERIDOT
PROTEIDE S
PROTEIDS
DIOPTERS
DIOPTRES
PERIDOTS
PORTSIDE
RIPOSTED
TOPSIDER
PROTEIN S
POINTER
TROPINE

PROTEINS
POINTERS
PORNIEST
TROPINES
PROTEND S
PORTEND
PROTENDS
PORTENDS
PROTEOME S
PROTEOSE S
PROTEST S
POTTERS
SPOTTER
PROTESTS
SPOTTERS
PROTEUS
PETROUS
POSTURE
POUTERS
SPOUTER
TROUPES
PROTIST S
PROTISTS
PROTIUM S
PROTIUMS
PROTOCOL S
PROTON S
PRONTO
PROTONIC
PROTONS
PROTOPOD S
PROTOXID ES
PROTOZOA LN
PROTRACT S
PROTRADE
PARROTED
PREDATOR
PRORATED
TEARDROP
PROTRUDE DS
PROTYL ES
PORTLY
PROTYLE S
PROTYLES
PROSTYLE
PROTYLS
PROUD
PROUDER
PROUDEST
POSTURED
SPROUTED
PROUDFUL
PROUDLY
PROUNION
PROVABLE
PROVABLY
PROVE DNRS
PROVED
PROVEN
PROVENLY
PROVER BS
PROVERB S
PROVERBS
PROVERS
PROVES
PROVIDE DRS
PROVIDED
PROVIDER S
PROVIDES
DISPROVE
PROVINCE S
PROVING
PROVIRAL
PROVIRUS
PROVISO S
PROVISOS
PROVOKE DRS
PROVOKED
PROVOKER S
PROVOKES
PROVOST S
PROVOSTS
PROW LS
PROWAR
PROWER
PROWESS
PROWEST
POWTERS

PROWL S
PROWLED
PROWLER S
PROWLERS
PROWLING
PROWLS
PROWS
PROXEMIC S
PROXIES
PROXIMAL
PROXIMO
PROXY
PRUDE S
DRUPE DUPER
PERDU URPED
PRUDENCE S
PRUDENT
UPTREND
PRUDERY
PRUDES
DRUPES
DUPERS
PERDUS
PURSED
PRUDISH
PRUINOSE
PRUNABLE
PRUNE DRS
PRUNED
PRUNELLA S
PRUNELLE S
PRUNELLO S
PRUNER S
PRUNERS
SPURNER
PRUNES
PRUNING
PRUNUS
PRUNUSES
PRURIENT
PRURIGO S
PRURIGOS
PRURITIC
PRURITUS
PRUSSIC
PRUTA H
PRUTAH
PRUTOT H
PRUTOTH
S **PRY**
S **PRYER** S
PERRY
PRYERS
SPRYER
PRYING
PRYINGLY
PRYTHEE
PSALM S
LAMPS PALMS
PLASM
PSALMED
SAMPLED
PSALMIC
PLASMIC
PSALMING
SAMPLING
PSALMIST S
PALMISTS
PSALMODY
PSALMS
PLASMS
PSALTER SY
PALTERS
PERSALT
PLASTER
PLATERS
STAPLER
PSALTERS
PERSALTS
PLASTERS
STAPLERS
PSALTERY
PEYTRALS
PLASTERY
PSALTRY
PSAMMITE S
PSAMMON S
PSAMMONS
PSCHENT S

PSCHENTS
PSEPHITE S
PSEUD OS
DUPES SPUED
PSEUDO S
SOUPED
PSEUDOS
SPOUSED
PSEUDS
PSHAW S
WHAPS
PSHAWED
PSHAWING
PSHAWS
PSI S
PIS
SIP
PSILOCIN S
CIPOLINS
PICOLINS
PSILOSES
PSILOSIS
PSILOTIC
COLPITIS
POLITICS
A **PSIS**
SIPS
PSOAE
PASEO
PSOAI
PSOAS
SOAPS
PSOATIC
PSOCID S
PSOCIDS
PSORALEA S
PSORALEN S
PERSONAL
PSST
PST
PSYCH EOS
PSYCHE DS
PSYCHED
PSYCHES
PSYCHIC S
PSYCHICS
PSYCHING
PSYCHO S
PSYCHOS
PSYCHS
PSYLLA S
PSYLLAS
PSYLLID S
PSYLLIDS
PSYLLIUM S
PSYOPS
PSYWAR S
PSYWARS
PTERIN S
PTERINS
PTEROPOD S
PTERYGIA L
PTERYLA E
PEARTLY
PEYTRAL
PTERYLAE
PTISAN S
PAINTS
PATINS
PINTAS
PTISANS
PTOMAIN ES
MAINTOP
TAMPION
TIMPANO
PTOMAINE S
PTOMAINS
MAINTOPS
TAMPIONS
PTOOEY
PTOSES
ESTOPS
PESTOS
POSSET
STOPES
PTOSIS
POSITS
PTOTIC
PTUI

PTYALIN S
INAPTLY
PTYALINS
PTYALISM S
PUB S
PUBERAL
PUBERTAL
PUBERTY
PUBES
PUBIC
PUBIS
PUBLIC S
PUBLICAN S
PUBLICLY
PUBLICS
PUBLISH
PUBS
PUCCOON S
PUCCOONS
PUCE S
PUCES
PUCK AS
PUCKA
PUCKER SY
PUCKERED
PUCKERER S
PUCKERS
PUCKERY
PUCKISH
PUCKS
S **PUD** S
DUP
S **PUDDING** S
PUDDINGS
SPUDDING
PUDDLE DRS
PUDDLED
PUDDLER S
PUDDLERS
PUDDLES
PUDDLIER
PUDDLING S
PUDDLY
PUDENCY
PUDENDA L
PUDENDAL
PUDENDUM
PUDGIER
PUDGIEST
PUDGILY
PUDGY
PUDIBUND
PUDIC
CUPID
S **PUDS**
DUPS SPUD
PUEBLO S
PUEBLOS
PUERILE
PUERPERA EL
PUFF SY
PUFFBALL S
PUFFED
PUFFER SY
PUFFERS
PUFFERY
PUFFIER
PUFFIEST
PUFFILY
PUFFIN GS
PUFFING
PUFFINS
PUFFS
PUFFY
PUG HS
PUGAREE S
PUGAREES
PUGGAREE S
PUGGED
PUGGIER
PUGGIEST
PUGGING
PUGGISH
PUGGREE S
PUGGREES

PUGGRIES
PUGGRY
PUGGY
PUGH
PUGILISM S
PUGILIST S
PUGMARK S
PUGMARKS
PUGREE S
PUGREES
PUGS
PUISNE S
SUPINE
PUISNES
SUPINES
PUISSANT
PUJA HS
JAUP
PUJAH S
PUJAHS
PUJAS
JAUPS
PUKE DS
PUKED
PUKES
PUKING
PUKKA
PUL AEILPS
PULA
PULE DRS
PULED
DUPLE
PULER S
PULERS
PULSER
PULES
PULSE
PULI KS
PULICENE
PULICIDE S
PULIK
PULING S
PULINGLY
PULINGS
PULSING
PULIS
PILUS
PULL S
PULLBACK S
PULLED
PULLER S
PULLERS
PULLET S
PULLETS
PULLEY S
PULLEYS
PULLING
PULLMAN S
PULLMANS
PULLOUT S
OUTPULL
PULLOUTS
OUTPULLS
PULLOVER S
PULLS
PULLUP S
PULLUPS
PULMONIC
PULMOTOR S
PULP SY
PULPAL
PULPALLY
PULPED
PULPER S
PURPLE
PULPERS
PURPLES
SUPPLER
PULPIER
PULPIEST
PULPILY
PULPING
PULPIT S
PULPITAL
PULPITS
PULPLESS
PULPOUS

PULPS
PULPWOOD S
PULPY
PULQUE S
PULQUES
PULS E
PLUS
PULSANT
PULSAR S
PULSARS
PULSATE DS
PULSATED
PULSATES
PULSATOR SY
POSTURAL
PULSE DRS
PULES
PULSED
PULSEJET S
PULSER S
PULERS
PULSERS
PULSES
PLUSES
PULSING
PULINGS
PULSION S
UPSILON
PULSIONS
UPSILONS
PULSOJET S
PULVILLI
PULVINAR
PULVINI
PULVINUS
PUMA S
PUMAS
PUMELO S
PUMELOS
PLUMOSE
PUMICE DRS
PUMICED
PUMICER S
PUMICERS
PUMICES
PUMICING
PUMICITE S
PUMMEL OS
PUMMELED
PUMMELO S
PUMMELOS
PUMMELS
PUMP S
PUMPED
PUMPER S
REPUMP
PUMPERS
REPUMPS
PUMPING
PUMPKIN S
PUMPKINS
PUMPLESS
PUMPLIKE
PUMPS
S PUN AGKSTY
PUNA S
PUNAS
PUNCH Y
PUNCHED
PUNCHEON S
PUNCHER S
PUNCHERS
PUNCHES
PUNCHIER
PUNCHILY
PUNCHING
PUNCHY
PUNCTATE D
PUNCTUAL
PUNCTURE DS
PUNDIT S
PUNDITIC
PUNDITRY
PUNDITS
PUNG S
PUNGENCY
PUNGENT
PUNGLE DS
PLUNGE
PUNGLED
PLUNGED
PUNGLES
PLUNGES
PUNGLING
PLUNGING
PUNGS
PUNIER
PURINE
UNRIPE
PUNIEST
PUNTIES
PUNILY
PUNINESS
PUNISH
UNSHIP
PUNISHED
PUNISHER S
PUNISHES
PUNITION S
PUNITIVE
PUNITORY
PUNJI S
PUNJIS
S PUNK ASY
PUNKA HS
PUNKAH S
PUNKAHS
PUNKAS
PUNKER S
PUNKERS
PUNKEST
PUNKEY S
PUNKEYS
S PUNKIE RS
S PUNKIER
S PUNKIES T
SPUNKIE
S PUNKIEST
PUNKIN S
PUNKINS
PUNKISH
S PUNKS
SPUNK
S PUNKY
PUNNED
PUNNER S
PUNNERS
PUNNET S
UNPENT
PUNNETS
UNSPENT
PUNNIER
PUNNIEST
PUNNING
PUNNY
PUNS
SPUN
PUNSTER S
PUNTERS
PUNSTERS
PUNT OSY
PUNTED
PUNTER S
PUNTERS
PUNSTER
PUNTIES
PUNIEST
PUNTING
PUNTO S
PUTON
PUNTOS
PUTONS
UNSTOP
PUNTS
PUNTY
PUNY
PUP ASU
PUPA ELS
PUPAE
PUPAL
PUPARIA L
PUPARIAL
PUPARIUM
PUPAS
PUPATE DS
PUPATED
PUPATES
PASTEUP
PUPATING
PUPATION S
PUPFISH
PUPIL S
PUPILAGE S
PUPILAR Y
PUPILARY
PUPILS
SLIPUP
PUPPED
PUPPET S
PUPPETRY
PUPPETS
PUPPIES
PUPPING
PUPPY
PUPPYDOM S
PUPPYISH
PUPS
PUPU S
PUPUS
S PUR EILRS
URP
PURANA S
PURANAS
PURANIC
PURBLIND
PURCHASE DR S
PURDA HS
PURDAH S
PURDAHS
PURDAS
PURE ER
PUREBRED S
PUREE DS
RUPEE
PUREED
PERDUE
PUREEING
PUREES
PERUSE
RUPEES
PURELY
PURENESS
PURER
PUREST
ERUPTS
PURFLE DRS
PURFLED
PURFLER S
PURFLERS
PURFLES
PURFLING S
S PURGE DRS
PURGED
PURGER S
PURGERS
S PURGES
SPURGE
PURGING S
PURGINGS
PURI NS
PURIFIED
PURIFIER S
PURIFIES
PURIFY
PURIN ES
UNRIP
PURINE S
PUNIER
UNRIPE
PURINES
UPRISEN
PURINS
UNRIPS
PURIS MT
SIRUP
PURISM S
PRIMUS
PURISMS
PURIST S
UPSTIR
PURISTIC
PURISTS
UPSTIRS
PURITAN S
PURITANS
PURITIES
PURITY
PURL S
PURLED
PURLIEU S
PURLIEUS
PURLIN EGS
PURLINE S
PURLINES
PURLING S
PURLINGS
SLURPING
PURLINS
PURLOIN S
PURLOINS
PURLS
SLURP
PURPLE DRS
PULPER
PURPLED
PURPLER
PURPLES T
PULPERS
SUPPLER
PURPLEST
PURPLING
PURPLISH
PURPLY
PURPORT S
PURPORTS
PURPOSE DS
PURPOSED
PURPOSES
SUPPOSER
PURPURA S
PURPURAS
PURPURE S
PURPURES
PURPURIC
PURPURIN S
PURR S
S PURRED
S PURRING
PURRS
S PURS EY
SPUR URPS
PURSE DRS
SPRUE SUPER
PURSED
DRUPES
DUPERS
PERDUS
PRUDES
PURSER S
PURSERS
PURSES
SPRUES
SUPERS
PURSIER
UPRISER
PURSIEST
PURSILY
PURSING
PURSLANE S
SUPERNAL
PURSUANT
PURSUE DRS
PURSUED
USURPED
PURSUER S
USURPER
PURSUERS
USURPERS
PURSUES
PURSUING
USURPING
PURSUIT S
PURSUITS
PURSY
SYRUP
PURTIER
PURTIEST
PUTTIERS
PURTY
PURULENT
PURVEY S
PURVEYED
PURVEYOR S
PURVEYS
PURVIEW S
PURVIEWS
O PUS HS
SUP
UPS
O PUSES
SPUES SUPES
PUSH Y
PUSHBALL S
PUSHCART S
PUSHDOWN S
PUSHED
PUSHER S
PUSHERS
PUSHES
PUSHFUL
PUSHIER
PUSHIEST
PUSHILY
PUSHING
GUNSHIP
PUSHOVER S
PUSHPIN S
PUSHPINS
PUSHROD S
PUSHRODS
PUSHUP S
PUSHUPS
PUSHY
PUSLEY S
PUSLEYS
PUSSLEY
PUSLIKE
PUSS Y
SUPS
PUSSES
PUSSIER
SUSPIRE
UPRISES
PUSSIES T
PUSSIEST
PUSSLEY S
PUSLEYS
PUSSLEYS
PUSSLIES
PUSSLIKE
PUSSLY
PUSSY
PUSSYCAT S
PUSTULAR
PUSTULE DS
PLUTEUS
PUSTULED
PUSTULES
PUT STZ
TUP
PUTAMEN
PUTAMINA
PUTATIVE
PUTDOWN S
PUTDOWNS
PUTLOG S
PUTLOGS
PUTOFF S
PUTOFFS
PUTON S
PUNTO
PUTONS
PUNTOS
UNSTOP
PUTOUT S
OUTPUT
PUTOUTS
OUTPUTS
PUTREFY
PUTRID
PUTRIDLY
PUTS
TUPS
PUTSCH
PUTSCHES
PUTT IOSY
PUTTED
PUTTEE S
PUTTEES
S PUTTER S
S PUTTERED
S PUTTERER S
S PUTTERS
SPUTTER
PUTTI E
PUTTIE DRS
PUTTIED
PUTTIER S
PUTTIERS
PURTIEST
PUTTIES
PUTTING
PUTTO
PUTTS
PUTTY
PUTTYING
PUTZ
PUTZED
PUTZES
PUTZING
PUZZLE DRS
PUZZLED
PUZZLER S
PUZZLERS
PUZZLES
PUZZLING
PYA S
PAY
YAP
PYAEMIA S
PYAEMIAS
PYAEMIC
PYAS
PAYS SPAY
YAPS
PYCNIDIA L
PYCNOSES
SYNCOPES
PYCNOSIS
PYCNOTIC
PYE S
YEP
PYELITIC
PYELITIS
PYEMIA S
PYEMIAS
PYEMIC
PYES
ESPY YEPS
PYGIDIA L
PYGIDIAL
PYGIDIUM
PYGMAEAN
PYGMEAN
PYGMIES
PYGMOID
PYGMY
PYGMYISH
PYGMYISM S
PYIC
PYIN S
PINY
PYINS
SPINY
PYJAMA S
PYJAMAS
PYKNIC S
PYKNICS
PYKNOSES
PYKNOSIS
PYKNOTIC
PYLON S
PYLONS
PYLORI C
ROPILY
PYLORIC
PYLORUS
PYODERMA S
PYOGENIC
PYOID
PYORRHEA LS
PYOSES
SEPOYS
PYOSIS
PYRALID S
RAPIDLY
PYRALIDS
PYRAMID S
PYRAMIDS
PYRAN S
PYRANOID
PYRANOSE S
PYRANS
PYRE SX
PREY
PYRENE S
PYRENES
PYRENOID S
PYRES
PREYS
A PYRETIC
PYREX
PREXY
PYREXES
PYREXIA LS
PYREXIAL
PYREXIAS
PYREXIC
PYRIC
PRICY
PYRIDIC
PYRIDINE S
PYRIFORM
PYRITE S
TYPIER
PYRITES
PYRITIC
PYRITOUS
PYRO S
ROPY
PYROGEN S
PROGENY
PYROGENS
PYROLA S
PYROLAS
PYROLIZE DS
PYROLOGY
PYROLYZE DR S
PYRONE S
PYRONES
PYRONINE S
PYROPE S
PYROPES
PYROS
PROSY
PYROSIS
PYROSTAT S
PYROXENE S
PYRRHIC S
PYRRHICS
PYRROL ES
PYRROLE S
PYRROLES
PYRROLIC
PYRROLS
PYRUVATE S
PYTHON S
PHYTON
TYPHON
PYTHONIC
HYPNOTIC
PHYTONIC
TYPHONIC
PYTHONS
PHYTONS
TYPHONS
PYURIA S
PYURIAS
PYX
PYXES
PYXIDES
PYXIDIA
PYXIDIUM
PYXIE S
PYXIES
PYXIS

Q

QABALA HS
QABALAH S
QABALAHS
QABALAS
QADI S
QAID

QADIS
QAIDS
QAID S
QADI
QAIDS
QADIS
QANAT S
QANATS
QAT S
QATS
QI S
QINDAR S
QINDARKA
QINDARS
QINTAR S
QINTARS
QIS
QIVIUT S
QIVIUTS
QOPH S
QOPHS
A QUA DGIY
QUAALUDE S
QUACK SY
QUACKED
QUACKERY
QUACKIER
QUACKING
QUACKISH
QUACKISM S
QUACKS
QUACKY
S QUAD S
S QUADDED
S QUADDING
QUADPLEX
QUADRANS
QUADRANT S
QUADRAT ES
QUADRATE DS
QUADRATS
QUADRIC S
QUADRICS
QUADRIGA E
QUADROON S
S QUADS
SQUAD
QUAERE S
QUAERES
QUAESTOR S
EQUATORS
QUAFF S
QUAFFED
QUAFFER S
QUAFFERS
QUAFFING
QUAFFS
QUAG S
QUAGGA S
QUAGGAS
QUAGGIER
QUAGGY
QUAGMIRE S
QUAGMIRY
QUAGS
QUAHAUG S
QUAHAUGS
QUAHOG S
QUAHOGS
QUAI LS
QUAICH S
QUAICHES
QUAICHS
QUAIGH S
QUAIGHS
QUAIL S
QUAILED
QUAILING
QUAILS
QUAINT
QUINTA
QUAINTER
ANTIQUER
QUAINTLY
QUAIS
QUASI
QUAKE DRS
QUAKED
QUAKER S
QUAKERS
QUAKES
SQUEAK
QUAKIER
QUAKIEST
QUAKILY
QUAKING
QUAKY
QUALE
EQUAL
QUALIA
QUALIFY
E QUALITY
QUALM SY
QUALMIER
QUALMISH
QUALMS
QUALMY
QUAMASH
QUANDANG S
QUANDARY
QUANDONG S
QUANGO S
QUANGOS
QUANT AS
QUANTA L
QUANTAL
QUANTED
QUANTIC S
QUANTICS
QUANTIFY
QUANTILE S
QUANTING
QUANTITY
QUANTIZE DRS
QUANTONG S
QUANTS
QUANTUM
S QUARE
S QUARK S
S QUARKS
SQUARK
QUARREL S
QUARRELS
QUARRIED
QUARRIER S
QUARRIES
QUARRY
QUART EOSZ
QUARTAN S
QUARTANS
QUARTE RST
QUATRE
QUARTER NS
QUARTERN S
QUARTERS
QUARTES
QUATRES
QUARTET S
QUARTETS
SQUATTER
QUARTIC S
QUARTICS
QUARTIER S
QUARTILE S
REQUITAL
QUARTO S
QUARTOS
QUARTS
QUARTZ
QUARTZES
QUASAR S
QUASARS
S QUASH
S QUASHED
S QUASHER S
S QUASHERS
SQUASHER
S QUASHES
S QUASHING
QUASI
QUAIS
QUASS
QUASSES
QUASSIA S
QUASSIAS
QUASSIN S
QUASSINS
E QUATE
QUATORZE S
QUATRAIN S
QUATRE S
QUARTE
QUATRES
QUARTES
QUAVER SY
QUAVERED
QUAVERER S
QUAVERS
QUAVERY
QUAY S
QUAYAGE S
QUAYAGES
QUAYLIKE
QUAYS
QUAYSIDE S
QUBIT S
QUBITS
QUBYTE S
QUBYTES
QUEAN S
QUEANS
QUEASIER
QUEASILY
QUEASY
QUEAZIER
QUEAZY
QUEEN S
QUEENDOM S
QUEENED
QUEENING
QUEENLY
QUEENS
QUEER S
QUEERED
QUEERER
QUEEREST
QUEERING
QUEERISH
QUEERLY
QUEERS
QUELEA S
QUELEAS
SEQUELA
QUELL S
QUELLED
QUELLER S
QUELLERS
QUELLING
QUELLS
QUENCH
QUENCHED
QUENCHER S
QUENCHES
QUENELLE S
QUERCINE
QUERIDA S
QUERIDAS
QUERIED
QUERIER S
REQUIRE
QUERIERS
REQUIRES
QUERIES
ESQUIRE
QUERIST S
QUERISTS
QUERN S
QUERNS
QUERY
QUERYING
QUEST S
QUESTED
QUESTER S
REQUEST
QUESTERS
REQUESTS
QUESTING
QUESTION S
QUESTOR S
QUOTERS
ROQUETS
TORQUES
QUESTORS
QUESTS
QUETZAL S
QUETZALS
QUEUE DRS
QUEUED
QUEUEING
QUEUER S
QUEUERS
QUEUES
QUEUING
QUEY S
QUEYS
QUEZAL S
QUEZALES
QUEZALS
QUIBBLE DRS
QUIBBLED
QUIBBLER S
QUIBBLES
QUICHE S
QUICHES
QUICK S
QUICKEN S
QUICKENS
QUICKER
QUICKEST
QUICKSET
QUICKIE S
QUICKIES
QUICKLY
QUICKS
QUICKSET S
QUICKEST
ES QUID S
QUIDDITY
QUIDNUNC S
ES QUIDS
SQUID
QUIET S
QUITE
QUIETED
QUIETEN S
QUIETENS
QUIETER S
REQUITE
QUIETERS
REQUITES
QUIETEST
QUIETING
QUIETISM S
QUIETIST S
QUIETLY
QUIETS
QUIETUDE S
QUIETUS
QUIFF S
QUIFFS
S QUILL S
QUILLAI AS
QUILLAIA S
QUILLAIS
QUILLAJA S
QUILLED
QUILLET S
QUILLETS
QUILLING S
S QUILLS
SQUILL
QUILT S
QUILTED
QUILTER S
QUILTERS
QUILTING S
QUILTS
QUIN ST
QUINARY
QUINATE
ANTIQUE
QUINCE S
CINQUE
QUINCES
CINQUES
QUINCUNX
QUINELA S
QUINELAS
QUINELLA S
QUINIC
QUINIELA S
AQUILINE
QUININ AES
QUININA S
QUININAS
QUININE S
QUININES
QUININS
QUINNAT S
QUINTAN
QUINNATS
QUINTANS
QUINOA S
QUINOAS
QUINOID S
QUINOIDS
QUINOL S
QUINOLIN ES
QUINOLS
QUINONE S
QUINONES
QUINS Y
QUINSIED
QUINSIES
QUINSY
S QUINT AES
QUINTA LNRS
QUAINT
QUINTAIN S
QUINTAL S
QUINTALS
QUINTAN S
QUINNAT
QUINTANS
QUINNATS
QUINTAR S
QUINTARS
QUINTAS
ASQUINT
QUINTE ST
QUINTES
INQUEST
QUINTET S
QUINTETS
QUINTIC S
QUINTICS
QUINTILE S
QUINTIN S
QUINTINS
S QUINTS
SQUINT
E QUIP SU
E QUIPPED
E QUIPPER S
E QUIPPERS
QUIPPIER
E QUIPPING
QUIPPISH
QUIPPU S
QUIPPUS
QUIPPY
E QUIPS
QUIPSTER S
QUIPU S
QUIPUS
S QUIRE DS
S QUIRED
S QUIRES
RISQUE
SQUIRE
S QUIRING
QUIRK SY
QUIRKED
QUIRKIER
QUIRKILY
QUIRKING
QUIRKISH
QUIRKS
QUIRKY
S QUIRT S
S QUIRTED
S QUIRTING
S QUIRTS
SQUIRT
QUISLING S
QUIT ES
QUITCH
QUITCHES
QUITE
QUIET
QUITRENT S
QUITS
QUITTED
QUITTER S
QUITTERS
QUITTING
QUITTOR S
QUITTORS
A QUIVER SY
QUIVERED
QUIVERER S
QUIVERS
QUIVERY
QUIXOTE S
QUIXOTES
QUIXOTIC
QUIXOTRY
QUIZ
QUIZZED
QUIZZER S
QUIZZERS
QUIZZES
QUIZZING
QUOD S
QUODS
QUOHOG S
QUOHOGS
QUOIN S
QUOINED
QUOINING
QUOINS
QUOIT S
QUOITED
QUOITING
QUOITS
QUOKKA S
QUOKKAS
QUOLL S
QUOLLS
QUOMODO S
QUOMODOS
QUONDAM
QUORUM S
QUORUMS
QUOTA S
QUOTABLE
QUOTABLY
QUOTAS
QUOTE DRS
TOQUE
QUOTED
QUOTER S
ROQUET
TORQUE
QUOTERS
QUESTOR
ROQUETS
TORQUES
QUOTES
TOQUES
QUOTH A
QUOTHA
QUOTIENT S
QUOTING
QURSH
QURSHES
QURUSH
QURUSHES
QWERTY S
QWERTYS

R

RABAT OS
RABATO S
ABATOR
RABATOS
ABATORS
RABATS
D RABBET S
BARBET
RABBETED
D RABBETS
BARBETS
STABBER
RABBI NST
RABBIES
BARBIES
RABBIN S
RABBINIC
RABBINS
RABBIS
RABBIT SY
RABBITED
RABBITER S
RABBITRY
RABBITS
RABBITY
BDG RABBLE DRS
BARBEL
BDG RABBLED
DABBLER
DRABBLE
BG RABBLER S
BG RABBLERS
BDG RABBLES
BARBELS
SLABBER
BDG RABBLING
RABBONI S
RABBONIS
A RABIC
BARIC
RABID
BRAID
RABIDITY
RABIDLY
RABIES
BRAISE
RABIETIC
RACCOON S
RACCOONS
BGT RACE DRS
ACRE CARE
BGT RACED
ACRED ARCED
CADRE CARED
CEDAR
RACEMATE S
MACERATE
RACEME DS
AMERCE
RACEMED
AMERCED
CREAMED
RACEMES
AMERCES
RACEMIC
CERAMIC
RACEMISM S
RACEMIZE DS
RACEMOID
COADMIRE
RACEMOSE
RACEMOUS
BT RACER S
CARER
BT RACERS
CARERS
SCARER
BGT RACES
ACRES CARES
CARSE ESCAR
SCARE SERAC
RACEWALK S
RACEWAY S
RACEWAYS
B RACHET S
RACHETED
DETACHER

B **RACHETS**
CHASTER
RATCHES
B **RACHIAL**
ACHIRAL
RACHIDES
RACHILLA E
RACHIS
CHAIRS
RACHISES
CASHIERS
RACHITIC
RACHITIS
RACIAL
RACIALLY
RACIER
RACIEST
ATRESIC
CRISTAE
STEARIC
RACILY
RACINESS
ARCSINES
ARSENICS
BGT **RACING** S
ARCING
CARING
BT **RACINGS**
SACRING
SCARING
RACISM S
RACISMS
RACIST S
CRISTA
TRIACS
RACISTS
SACRIST
CTW **RACK** S
CARK
CTW **RACKED**
ARCKED
CARKED
DACKER
CT **RACKER** S
RERACK
CT **RACKERS**
RERACKS
B **RACKET** SY
RETACK
TACKER
B **RACKETED**
RETACKED
B **RACKETS**
RESTACK
RETACKS
STACKER
TACKERS
RACKETY
W **RACKFUL** S
RACKFULS
CTW **RACKING**
ARCKING
CARKING
CG **RACKLE**
CALKER
LACKER
CTW **RACKS**
CARKS
RACKWORK S
RACLETTE S
RACON S
ACORN NARCO
RACONS
ACORNS
NARCOS
RACOON S
CORONA
RACOONS
CORONAS
RACQUET S
RACQUETS
RACY
BGO **RAD** S
T
RADAR S
RADARS
SARDAR
B **RADDED**
B **RADDING**
RADDLE DS
LADDER
LARDED
RADDLED

RADDLES
LADDERS
SADDLER
RADDLING
RADIABLE
RADIAL ES
RADIALE
RADIALIA
RADIALLY
RADIALS
RADIAN ST
RADIANCE S
RADIANCY
RADIANS
RADIANT S
RADIANTS
E **RADIATE** DS
AIRDATE
TIARAED
E **RADIATED**
E **RADIATES**
AIRDATES
DATARIES
RADIATOR S
RADICAL S
RADICALS
RADICAND S
E **RADICATE** DS
RADICEL S
DECRIAL
RADICLE
RADICELS
DECRIALS
RADICLES
RADICES
SIDECAR
RADICLE S
DECRIAL
RADICEL
RADICLES
DECRIALS
RADICELS
RADII
RADIO S
AROID
RADIOED
RADIOING
RADIOMAN
RADIOMEN
RADIOS
AROIDS
RADISH
SHAIRD
RADISHES
AIRSHEDS
RADIUM S
RADIUMS
RADIUS
RADIUSES
SUDARIES
RADIX
RADIXES
RADOME S
ROAMED
RADOMES
RADON S
ADORN ANDRO
RADONS
ADORNS
ANDROS
BG **RADS**
SARD
RADULA ERS
RADULAE
RADULAR
RADULAS
RADWASTE S
EASTWARD
D **RAFF** S
RAFFIA S
AFFAIR
RAFFIAS
AFFAIRS
D **RAFFISH**
RAFFLE DRS
FARFEL
RAFFLED
RAFFLER S
RAFFLERS
RAFFLES
FARFELS

RAFFLING
D **RAFFS**
CDG **RAFT** S
K FRAT
CDG **RAFTED**
DAFTER
CDG **RAFTER** S
FRATER
RAFTERED
CDG **RAFTERS**
FRATERS
STRAFER
CDG **RAFTING**
INGRAFT
CDG **RAFTS**
K FRATS
CD **RAFTSMAN**
CD **RAFTSMEN**
BCD **RAG** AEGIS
F GAR
RAGA S
AGAR
RAGAS
AGARS
RAGBAG S
RAGBAGS
RAGE DES
AGER GEAR
RAGED
GRADE
D **RAGEE** S
AGREE EAGER
EAGRE
D **RAGEES**
AGREES
EAGERS
EAGRES
GREASE
RAGES
AGERS GEARS
SAGER SARGE
RAGG SY
BCD **RAGGED** Y
F DAGGER
RAGGEDER
RAGGEDLY
RAGGEDY
RAGGEE S
REGGAE
RAGGEES
REGGAES
RAGGIES
SAGGIER
BDF **RAGGING**
D **RAGGLE** S
GARGLE
LAGGER
D **RAGGLES**
GARGLES
LAGGERS
RAGGS
BCD **RAGGY**
T **RAGI** S
RAGING
RAGINGLY
GRAYLING
RAGIS
RAGLAN S
RAGLANS
RAGMAN
RAGMEN
ENGRAM
GERMAN
MANGER
RAGOUT S
RAGOUTED
OUTRAGED
RAGOUTS
BCD **RAGS**
F GARS
RAGTAG S
TAGRAG
RAGTAGS
TAGRAGS
RAGTIME S
MIGRATE
RAGTIMES
MAGISTER
MIGRATES
STERIGMA
RAGTOP S
RAGTOPS

RAGWEED S
WAGERED
RAGWEEDS
RAGWORT S
RAGWORTS
RAH
RAI ADLNS
AIR
RIA
RAIA S
ARIA
RAIAS
ARIAS
B **RAID** S
ARID
B **RAIDED**
B **RAIDER** S
ARIDER
B **RAIDERS**
B **RAIDING**
B **RAIDS**
BDF **RAIL** S
GT ARIL LAIR
LARI LIAR
LIRA RIAL
RAILBIRD S
RAILBUS
BURIALS
RAILCAR S
RAILCARS
BT **RAILED**
ARILED
DERAIL
DIALER
LAIRED
REDIAL
RELAID
FT **RAILER** S
IRREAL
T **RAILERS**
T **RAILHEAD** S
BT **RAILING** S
LAIRING
RAILINGS
RAILLERY
RAILROAD S
BDF **RAILS**
GT ARILS LAIRS
LARIS LIARS
LIRAS RIALS
RAILWAY S
RAILWAYS
RAIMENT S
MINARET
RAIMENTS
MINARETS
BDG **RAIN** SY
T AIRN RANI
T **RAINBAND** S
RAINBIRD S
RAINBOW S
RAINBOWS
RAINCOAT S
RAINDROP S
BDG **RAINED**
T DENARI
RAINFALL S
BG **RAINIER**
BG **RAINIEST**
INERTIAS
B **RAINILY**
BDG **RAINING**
T INGRAIN
BG **RAINLESS**
RAINOUT S
RAINOUTS
BDG **RAINS**
T AIRNS NARIS
RANIS SARIN
B **RAINWASH**
RAINWEAR
BG **RAINY**
RAIS E
AIRS RIAS
SARI
RAISABLE
BFP **RAISE** DRS
ARISE SERAI

BP **RAISED**
AIDERS
DEAIRS
IRADES
REDIAS
RESAID
P **RAISER** S
AIRERS
SIERRA
P **RAISERS**
ARRISES
SIERRAS
BFP **RAISES**
ARISES
SERAIS
RAISIN GSY
BP **RAISING** S
AIRINGS
ARISING
RAISINGS
RAISINS
RAISINY
RAISONNE
RAITA S
ATRIA RIATA
TIARA
RAITAS
ARISTA
RIATAS
TARSIA
TIARAS
RAJ A
JAR
RAJA HS
AJAR
RAJAH S
RAJAHS
RAJAS
RAJES
BCD **RAKE** DERS
B **RAKED**
DRAKE
RAKEE S
RAKEES
RAKEHELL SY
RAKEOFF S
RAKEOFFS
RAKER S
RAKERS
BCD **RAKES**
ASKER ESKAR
SAKER
RAKI S
B **RAKING**
RAKIS H
RAKISH
SHIKAR
RAKISHLY
RAKU S
RAKUS
RALE S
EARL LEAR
REAL
RALES
ARLES EARLS
LARES LASER
LEARS REALS
SERAL
RALLIED
DALLIER
DIALLER
RALLIER S
RALLIERS
RALLIES
SALLIER
RALLINE
O **RALLY** E
RALLYE S
REALLY
RALLYES
RALLYING S
RALLYIST S
RALPH S
RALPHED
RALPHING
RALPHS
CDG **RAM** IPS
PT ARM
MAR
RAMADA S
ARMADA

RAMADAS
ARMADAS
MADRASA
RAMAL
ALARM MALAR
RAMATE
RAMBLA S
RAMBLAS
B **RAMBLE** DRS
AMBLER
BLAMER
LAMBER
MARBLE
B **RAMBLED**
MARBLED
RAMBLER S
MARBLER
RAMBLERS
MARBLERS
B **RAMBLES**
AMBLERS
BLAMERS
LAMBERS
MARBLES
B **RAMBLING**
MARBLING
RAMBUTAN S
RAMEE S
AMEER
RAMEES
AMEERS
SEAMER
RAMEKIN S
RAMEKINS
RAMEN
NAMER REMAN
RAMENTA
RAMENTUM
RAMEQUIN S
RAMET S
ARMET MATER
TAMER
RAMETS
ARMETS
MASTER
MATERS
MATRES
STREAM
TAMERS
RAMI E
AMIR MAIR
RAMIE S
AIMER
RAMIES
AIMERS
ARMIES
RAMIFIED
RAMIFIES
RAMIFORM
RAMIFY
RAMILIE S
RAMILIES
RAMILLIE S
MILLIARE
RAMJET S
RAMJETS
CDT **RAMMED**
DAMMER
C **RAMMER** S
C **RAMMERS**
RAMMIER
RAMMIEST
MARMITES
CDT **RAMMING**
RAMMISH
RAMMY
RAMONA S
RAMONAS
OARSMAN
RAMOSE
RAMOSELY
RAMOSITY
RAMOUS
AMOURS
CGT **RAMP** S
PRAM
RAMPAGE DRS
RAMPAGED
RAMPAGER S
RAMPAGES
RAMPANCY

RAMPANT
MANTRAP
RAMPART S
RAMPARTS
CT **RAMPED**
DAMPER
RAMPIKE S
RAMPIKES
CT **RAMPING**
GRIPMAN
RAMPION S
RAMPIONS
RAMPOLE S
RAMPOLES
CGT **RAMPS**
PRAMS
RAMROD S
RAMRODS
CDG **RAMS**
PT ARMS MARS
RAMSHORN S
RAMSON S
MANORS
RANSOM
ROMANS
RAMSONS
RANSOMS
RAMTIL S
MITRAL
RAMTILLA S
RAMTILS
MISTRAL
RAMULOSE
RAMULOUS
RAMUS
ARUMS MURAS
BG **RAN** DGIKT
PT **RANCE** S
CANER CRANE
NACRE
PT **RANCES**
CANERS
CASERN
CRANES
NACRES
BC **RANCH** O
BC **RANCHED**
ENDARCH
RANCHER OS
RANCHERO S
RANCHERS
BCT **RANCHES**
BC **RANCHING**
RANCHMAN
RANCHMEN
RANCHO S
ANCHOR
ARCHON
RANCHOS
ANCHORS
ARCHONS
RANCID
RANCIDLY
RANCOR S
RANCORED
RANCORS
RANCOUR S
RANCOURS
BG **RAND** SY
DARN NARD
RANDAN S
RANDANS
RANDIER
DRAINER
B **RANDIES** T
SANDIER
SARDINE
RANDIEST
DETRAINS
STRAINED
RANDOM S
RODMAN
RANDOMLY
RANDOMS
RODSMAN
BG **RANDS**
DARNS NARDS
B **RANDY**
RANEE S
ARENE

RANEES
ARENES
OPW **RANG** EY
GNAR GRAN
GO **RANGE** DRS
ANGER REGNA
P **RANGED**
DANGER
GANDER
GARDEN
G **RANGER** S
GARNER
G **RANGERS**
GARNERS
GO **RANGES**
ANGERS
SANGER
O **RANGIER**
ANGRIER
EARRING
GRAINER
REARING
O **RANGIEST**
ANGRIEST
ASTRINGE
GANISTER
GANTRIES
GRANITES
INGRATES
P **RANGING**
O **RANGY**
ANGRY
RANI DS
AIRN RAIN
RANID S
DINAR DRAIN
NADIR
RANIDS
DINARS
DRAINS
NADIRS
RANIS
AIRNS NARIS
RAINS SARIN
BCDFPT **RANK** S
KARN KNAR
NARK
CFP **RANKED**
DANKER
DARKEN
NARKED
CF **RANKER** S
F **RANKERS**
CF **RANKEST**
TANKERS
CFP **RANKING** S
NARKING
RANKINGS
CP **RANKISH**
C **RANKLE** DS
LANKER
C **RANKLED**
C **RANKLES** S
RANKLESS
C **RANKLING**
CF **RANKLY**
F **RANKNESS**
BCFPT **RANKS**
KARNS KNARS
NARKS SNARK
RANPIKE S
RANPIKES
RANSACK S
RANSACKS
T **RANSOM** S
MANORS
RAMSON
ROMANS
RANSOMED
MADRONES
RANSOMER S
T **RANSOMS**
RAMSONS
BG **RANT** S
TARN
G **RANTED**
ARDENT
G **RANTER** S
ERRANT
G **RANTERS**
ERRANTS
G **RANTING**

BG **RANTS**
TARNS TRANS
RANULA RS
ANURAL
G **RANULAR**
RANULAS
CFTW **RAP** EST
PAR
RAPACITY
CDG **RAPE** DRS
APER PARE
PEAR REAP
CD **RAPED**
DRAPE PADRE
PARED
D **RAPER** S
PARER
D **RAPERS**
PARERS
PARSER
RASPER
SPARER
CDGT **RAPES**
APERS APRES
ASPER PARES
PARSE PEARS
PRASE PRESA
REAPS SPARE
SPEAR
RAPESEED S
RAPHAE
RAPHE S
RAPHES
PHRASE
SERAPH
SHAPER
SHERPA
RAPHIA S
PARIAH
RAPHIAS
PARIAHS
RAPHIDE S
RAPHIDES
RAPHIS
PARISH
RAPID S
PADRI PARDI
RAPIDER
PARRIED
RAPIDEST
TRAIPSED
RAPIDITY
RAPIDLY
PYRALID
RAPIDS
SPARID
G **RAPIER** S
REPAIR
RAPIERED
REPAIRED
RAPIERS
ASPIRER
PARRIES
PRAISER
RASPIER
REPAIRS
RAPINE S
PANIER
RAPINES
PANIERS
CD **RAPING**
PARING
RAPINI
RAPIST S
TAPIRS
RAPISTS
RAPPAREE S
REAPPEAR
CFTW **RAPPED**
DAPPER
RAPPEE S
RAPPEES
RAPPEL S
LAPPER
RAPPELED
LAPPERED
RAPPELS
LAPPERS
SLAPPER
RAPPEN
NAPPER
CTW **RAPPER** S
CTW **RAPPERS**

CFTW **RAPPING**
RAPPINI
RAPPORT S
RAPPORTS
CFTW **RAPS**
PARS RASP
SPAR
TW **RAPT**
PART PRAT
TARP TRAP
RAPTLY
PALTRY
PARTLY
RAPTNESS
PASTERNS
RAPTOR S
PARROT
RAPTORS
PARROTS
RAPTURE DS
RAPTURED
RAPTURES
PASTURER
U **RARE** DRS
REAR
RAREBIT S
ARBITER
RAREBITS
ARBITERS
RARED
DARER DREAR
RAREFIED
RAREFIER S
RAREFIES
RAREFY
RARELY
RARENESS
RARER
RARERIPE S
REPAIRER
U **RARES** T
RASER REARS
RAREST
ARREST
RASTER
RATERS
STARER
TARRES
TERRAS
RARIFIED
RARIFIES
FRIARIES
RARIFY
FRIARY
RARING
RARITIES
RARITY
BE **RAS** EHP
ARS
RASBORA S
ARROBAS
RASBORAS
RASCAL S
CRAALS
LASCAR
SACRAL
SCALAR
RASCALLY
RASCALS
LASCARS
SACRALS
SCALARS
EPU **RASE** DRS
ARES EARS
ERAS SEAR
SERA
E **RASED**
DARES DEARS
READS
E **RASER** S
RARES REARS
E **RASERS**
CEPU **RASES**
ARSES SEARS
BCT **RASH**
BCT **RASHER** S
SHARER
CT **RASHERS**
SHARERS
BCT **RASHES** T
SHARES
SHEARS

B **RASHEST**
TRASHES
RASHLIKE
B **RASHLY**
B **RASHNESS**
E **RASING**
GRAINS
RASORIAL
G **RASP** SY
PARS RAPS
SPAR
G **RASPED**
DRAPES
PADRES
PARSED
SPADER
SPARED
SPREAD
G **RASPER** S
PARERS
PARSER
RAPERS
SPARER
G **RASPERS**
PARSERS
SPARERS
SPARSER
RASPIER
ASPIRER
PARRIES
PRAISER
RAPIERS
REPAIRS
RASPIEST
PASTRIES
PIASTERS
PIASTRES
TRAIPSES
G **RASPING** S
PARINGS
PARSING
SPARING
RASPINGS
PINGRASS
RASPISH
G **RASPS**
SPARS
RASPY
PRAYS SPRAY
W **RASSLE** DS
LASERS
W **RASSLED**
W **RASSLES**
W **RASSLING**
RASTER S
ARREST
RAREST
RATERS
STARER
TARRES
TERRAS
RASTERS
ARRESTS
STARERS
E **RASURE** S
URARES
E **RASURES**
ASSURER
BDFGP **RAT** EHOS
ART
TAR
RATABLE S
RATABLES
ARBALEST
RATABLY
RATAFEE S
RATAFEES
RATAFIA S
RATAFIAS
RATAL S
ALTAR ARTAL
TALAR
RATALS
ALTARS
ASTRAL
TALARS
TARSAL
RATAN SY
ANTRA
RATANIES
ANTISERA
SANTERIA
SEATRAIN

RATANS
RATANY
YANTRA
RATAPLAN S
RATATAT S
RATATATS
RATBAG S
RATBAGS
C **RATCH**
CHART
C **RATCHES**
CHASTER
RACHETS
RATCHET S
CHATTER
RATCHETS
CHATTERS
CGIOPU **RATE** DLRS
TARE TEAR
RATEABLE
TEARABLE
RATEABLY
BETRAYAL
CGOP **RATED**
DATER DERAT
TARED TRADE
TREAD
RATEL S
ALERT ALTER
ARTEL LATER
TALER
RATELS
ALERTS
ALTERS
ARTELS
ESTRAL
LASTER
SALTER
SLATER
STALER
STELAR
TALERS
CFGIKP **RATER** S
TARRE TERRA
CFGKP **RATERS**
ARREST
RAREST
RASTER
STARER
TARRES
TERRAS
CGOPU **RATES**
ASTER RESAT
STARE TARES
TEARS
RATFINK S
RATFINKS
RATFISH
W **RATH** E
HART TAHR
RATHE R
EARTH HATER
HEART
RATHER
RATHOLE S
LOATHER
RATHOLES
LOATHERS
RATICIDE S
G **RATIFIED**
G **RATIFIER** S
G **RATIFIES**
G **RATIFY**
G **RATINE** S
RETAIN
RETINA
RATINES
ANESTRI
ANTSIER
NASTIER
RETAINS
RETINAS
RETSINA
STAINER
STEARIN
CGOP **RATING** S
GRATIN
TARING
G **RATINGS**
GASTRIN
GRATINS
STARING

RATIO NS
O **RATION** S
AROINT
RATIONAL ES
NOTARIAL
RATIONED
AROINTED
ORDINATE
O **RATIONS**
AROINTS
RATIOS
AORIST
ARISTO
SATORI
RATITE S
ATTIRE
RATITES
ARTIEST
ARTISTE
ATTIRES
IRATEST
STRIATE
TASTIER
RATLIKE
TALKIER
RATLIN ES
TRINAL
RATLINE S
LATRINE
RELIANT
RETINAL
TRENAIL
RATLINES
ENTRAILS
LATRINES
RETINALS
TRENAILS
RATLINS
RATO S
ROTA TARO
TORA
RATOON S
RATOONED
RATOONER S
RATOONS
SANTOOR
RATOS
ROAST ROTAS
SORTA TAROS
TORAS
BDFP **RATS**
ARTS STAR
TARS TSAR
RATSBANE S
ANTBEARS
RATTAIL S
RATTAILS
RATTAN S
TANTRA
TARTAN
RATTANS
TANTRAS
TARTANS
D **RATTED**
TARTED
TETRAD
RATTEEN S
ENTREAT
TERNATE
RATTEENS
ENTREATS
RATTEN S
NATTER
RATTENED
ATTENDER
NATTERED
RATTENER S
RATTENS
NATTERS
RATTER S
TARTER
RATTERS
RESTART
STARTER
B **RATTIER**
TARTIER
B **RATTIEST**
ATTRITES
TARTIEST
TITRATES
TRISTATE
D **RATTING**
TARTING

B **RATTISH**
ATHIRST
TARTISH
BP **RATTLE** DRS
LATTER
BP **RATTLED**
P **RATTLER** S
P **RATTLERS**
STARTLER
BP **RATTLES**
STARLET
STARTLE
BP **RATTLING** S
RATTLY
TARTLY
RATTON S
ATTORN
RATTONS
ATTORNS
RATTOON S
ARNOTTO
RATTOONS
ARNOTTOS
RATTRAP S
RATTRAPS
B **RATTY**
TARTY
RAUCITY
RAUCOUS
C **RAUNCH** Y
C **RAUNCHES**
RAUNCHY
UNCHARY
RAVAGE DRS
RAVAGED
RAVAGER S
RAVAGERS
RAVAGES
SAVAGER
RAVAGING
BCDGT **RAVE** DLNRS
AVER VERA
BCG **RAVED**
DRAVE
GT **RAVEL** S
LAVER VELAR
GT **RAVELED**
T **RAVELER** S
T **RAVELERS**
REVERSAL
SLAVERER
RAVELIN GS
GT **RAVELING** S
RAVELINS
GT **RAVELLED**
T **RAVELLER** S
G **RAVELLY**
GT **RAVELS**
LAVERS
SALVER
SERVAL
SLAVER
VELARS
VERSAL
CG **RAVEN** S
C **RAVENED**
RAVENER S
RAVENERS
C **RAVENING** S
RAVENOUS
C **RAVENS**
BCG **RAVER** S
BCG **RAVERS**
BCGT **RAVES**
AVERS SAVER
RAVIGOTE S
RAVIN EGS
INVAR
RAVINE DS
NAIVER
VAINER
RAVINED
INVADER
RAVINES
BCG **RAVING** S
RAVINGLY
C **RAVINGS**
RAVINING
RAVINS
INVARS

RAVIOLI S
RAVIOLIS
RAVISH
RAVISHED
RAVISHER S
RAVISHES
BCD RAW S
WAR
RAWBONED
BD RAWER
B RAWEST
TAWERS
WASTER
WATERS
RAWHIDE DS
RAWHIDED
RAWHIDES
DISHWARE
RAWIN S
RAWINS
RAWISH
BCD RAWLY
RAWNESS
ANSWERS
BCD RAWS
WARS
RAX
RAXED
P RAXES
RAXING
BDF GPT RAY AS
RYA
YAR
RAYA HS
RAYAH S
RAYAHS
RAYAS
BDF GP RAYED
DEARY DERAY
READY
RAYGRASS
BDF GP RAYING
GRAINY
RAYLESS
SLAYERS
RAYLIKE
C RAYON S
C RAYONS
BDF GPT RAYS
RYAS
BCG RAZE DERS
BCG RAZED
RAZEE DS
RAZEED
RAZEEING
RAZEES
BG RAZER S
BG RAZERS
BCG RAZES
BCG RAZING
RAZOR S
RAZORED
RAZORING
RAZORS
RAZZ
RAZZED
RAZZES
RAZZING
AEI O RE BCDEFGIM ER PSTVX
P REABSORB S
ABSORBER
REACCEDE DS
REACCENT S
REACCEPT S
ACCEPTER
P REACCUSE DS
BP REACH
CHARE
BP REACHED
BP REACHER S
BP REACHERS
RESEARCH
SEARCHER
BP REACHES
BP REACHING

P REACT S
CARET CARTE
CATER CRATE
RECTA TRACE
REACTANT S
P REACTED
CATERED
CERATED
CREATED
P REACTING
ARGENTIC
CATERING
CREATING
REACTION S
ACTIONER
ANORETIC
CREATION
REACTIVE
CREATIVE
REACTOR S
CREATOR
REACTORS
CREATORS
P REACTS
CARETS
CARTES
CASTER
CATERS
CRATES
RECAST
TRACES
BDO T READ DSY
DARE DEAR
READABLE
READABLY
P READAPT S
ADAPTER
P READAPTS
ADAPTERS
READD S
ADDER DARED
DREAD
READDED
DREADED
READDICT S
READDING
DREADING
READDS
ADDERS
DREADS
SADDER
T READER S
DEARER
REARED
REDEAR
REREAD
READERLY
T READERS
REDEARS
REREADS
READIED
DEAIRED
READIER
READIES T
DEARIES
READIEST
SERIATED
STEADIER
READILY
BDT READING S
DERAIGN
GRADINE
GRAINED
READINGS
DERAIGNS
GRADINES
P READJUST S
ADJUSTER
P READMIT S
P READMITS
MISRATED
P READOPT S
ADOPTER
P READOPTS
ADOPTERS
PASTORED
READORN S
ADORNER
READORNS
ADORNERS
READOUT S
OUTDARE
OUTREAD

READOUTS
OUTDARES
OUTREADS
BDO T READS
DARES DEARS
RASED
B READY
DEARY DERAY
RAYED
READYING
REAFFIRM S
AFFIRMER
REAFFIX
AFFIXER
REAGENT S
GRANTEE
GREATEN
NEGATER
REAGENTS
ESTRANGE
GRANTEES
GREATENS
NEGATERS
SERGEANT
REAGIN S
EARING
GAINER
REGAIN
REGINA
REAGINIC
REAGINS
EARINGS
ERASING
GAINERS
REGAINS
REGINAS
SEARING
SERINGA
AU REAL MS
EARL LEAR
RALE
REALER
REALES T
LAREES
LEASER
RESALE
RESEAL
SEALER
REALEST
ELATERS
RELATES
RESLATE
STEALER
REALGAR S
REALGARS
REALIA
AERIAL
REALIGN S
ALIGNER
ENGRAIL
NARGILE
REGINAL
REALIGNS
ALIGNERS
ENGRAILS
NARGILES
SIGNALER
SLANGIER
REALISE DRS
REALISED
RESAILED
SIDEREAL
REALISER S
REALISES
REALISM S
MAILERS
REMAILS
REALISMS
REALIST S
RETAILS
SALTIER
SALTIRE
SLATIER
TAILERS
REALISTS
SALTIERS
SALTIRES
REALITY
IRATELY
TEARILY
REALIZE DRS
REALIZED
REALIZER S

REALIZES
SLEAZIER
P REALLOT S
P REALLOTS
ROSTELLA
A REALLY
RALLYE
REALM S
LAMER
REALMS
REALNESS
REALS
ARLES EARLS
LARES LASER
LEARS RALES
SERAL
P REALTER S
ALERTER
ALTERER
RELATER
P REALTERS
ALTERERS
RELATERS
REALTIES
ATELIERS
EARLIEST
LEARIEST
REALTOR S
RELATOR
REALTORS
RELATORS
RESTORAL
REALTY
ELYTRA
LYRATE
BCD REAM S
MARE
BCD REAMED
REMADE
CD REAMER S
CD REAMERS
SMEARER
BCD REAMING
GERMINA
MANGIER
BCD REAMS
MARES MARSE
MASER SMEAR
REANNEX
REANOINT S
ANOINTER
REAP S
APER PARE
PEAR RAPE
REAPABLE
REAPED
PARDEE
REAPER S
REAPERS
SPEARER
REAPHOOK S
REAPING
REAPPEAR S
RAPPAREE
P REAPPLY
REAPS
APERS APRES
ASPER PARES
PARSE PEARS
PRASE PRESA
RAPES SPARE
SPEAR
D REAR MS
RARE
REARED
DEARER
READER
REDEAR
REREAD
REARER S
REARERS
REARGUE DS
REARGUED
REDARGUE
REARGUES
REARING
ANGRIER
EARRING
GRAINER
RANGIER
P REARM S
ARMER

P REARMED
DREAMER
REDREAM
REARMICE
CREAMIER
RECAMIER
P REARMING
REARMOST
P REARMS
ARMERS
REAROUSE DS
REARREST S
ARRESTER
D REARS
RARES RASER
REARWARD S
REASCEND S
ASCENDER
REASCENT S
CENTARES
REENACTS
SARCENET
T REASON S
ARSENO
SENORA
REASONED
REASONER S
T REASONS
SENORAS
REASSAIL S
ASSAILER
SALARIES
REASSERT S
ASSERTER
SERRATES
TERRASES
REASSESS
P REASSIGN S
ASSIGNER
SERINGAS
REASSORT S
ASSERTOR
ASSORTER
ORATRESS
ROASTERS
REASSUME DS
MEASURES
P REASSURE DS
ERASURES
REATA S
REATAS
REATTACH
ATTACHER
REATTACK S
ATTACKER
REATTAIN S
ATTAINER
REAVAIL S
VELARIA
REAVAILS
G REAVE DRS
G REAVED
EVADER
P REAVER S
P REAVERS
G REAVES
AVERSE
REAVING
VINEGAR
REAVOW S
AVOWER
REAVOWED
OVERAWED
REAVOWS
AVOWERS
OVERSAW
REAWAKE DNS
REAWAKED
REAWAKEN S
AWAKENER
REAWAKES
REAWOKE N
REAWOKEN
REB S
REBAIT S
BAITER
BARITE
TERBIA
REBAITED
REBAITS
BAITERS
BARITES
TERBIAS

REBAR S
BARER BARRE
REBARS
BARRES
REBATE DRS
BEATER
BERATE
REBATED
BERATED
DEBATER
TABERED
REBATER S
REBATERS
REBATES
BEATERS
BERATES
REBATING
BERATING
TABERING
REBATO S
BOATER
BORATE
REBATOS
BOASTER
BOATERS
BORATES
SORBATE
REBBE S
REBBES
REBEC KS
REBECK S
REBECKS
REBECS
REBEGAN
REBEGIN S
REBEGINS
REBEGUN
REBEL S
REBELDOM S
REBELLED
REBELS
P REBID S
BIDER BRIDE
P REBIDDEN
P REBIDS
BIDERS
BRIDES
DEBRIS
P REBILL S
BILLER
P REBILLED
P REBILLS
BILLERS
P REBIND S
BINDER
BRINED
INBRED
P REBINDS
BINDERS
INBREDS
P REBIRTH S
P REBIRTHS
REBLEND S
BLENDER
REBLENDS
BLENDERS
REBLENT
REBLOOM S
BLOOMER
REBLOOMS
BLOOMERS
REBOANT
BARONET
P REBOARD S
ARBORED
BOARDER
BROADER
P REBOARDS
ADSORBER
BOARDERS
REBODIED
REBODIES
REBODY
P REBOIL S
BOILER
P REBOILED
ERODIBLE
P REBOILS
BOILERS
P REBOOK S
BOOKER
P REBOOKED

P REBOOKS
BOOKERS
REBOOT S
REBOOTED
REBOOTS
BOOSTER
REBOP S
PROBE
REBOPS
PROBES
REBORE DS
REBORED
REBORES
SOBERER
REBORING
REBORN
REBOTTLE DS
P REBOUGHT
P REBOUND S
BOUNDER
UNROBED
REBOUNDS
BOUNDERS
SUBORNED
REBOZO S
BOOZER
REBOZOS
BOOZERS
REBRANCH
REBRED
REBREED S
BREEDER
REBREEDS
BREEDERS
REBS
REBUFF S
BUFFER
REBUFFED
BUFFERED
REBUFFS
BUFFERS
P REBUILD S
BUILDER
P REBUILDS
BUILDERS
P REBUILT
REBUKE DRS
REBUKED
REBUKER S
REBUKERS
REBUKES
REBUKING
REBURIAL S
REBURIED
REBURIES
REBURY
REBUS
BURSE RUBES
SUBER
REBUSES
SUBSERE
REBUT S
BRUTE BURET
TUBER
REBUTS
BRUTES
BURETS
BUSTER
TUBERS
REBUTTAL S
REBUTTED
BUTTERED
REBUTTER S
REBUTTON S
BUTTONER
P REBUY S
BUYER
P REBUYING
P REBUYS
BUYERS
REC KS
RECALL S
CALLER
CELLAR
RECALLED
CELLARED
RECALLER S
CELLARER
RECALLS
CALLERS
CELLARS
SCLERAL

RECAMIER S
CREAMIER
REARMICE
RECANE DS
CAREEN
RECANED
RECANES
CAREENS
CASERNE
RECANING
RECANT S
CANTER
CARNET
CENTRA
NECTAR
TANREC
TRANCE
RECANTED
CANTERED
CRENATED
DECANTER
RECANTER S
RECREANT
RECANTS
CANTERS
CARNETS
NECTARS
SCANTER
TANRECS
TRANCES
RECAP S
CAPER CRAPE
PACER
RECAPPED
RECAPS
CAPERS
CRAPES
ESCARP
PACERS
PARSEC
SCRAPE
SECPAR
SPACER
RECARPET S
RECARRY
P **RECAST** S
CARETS
CARTES
CASTER
CATERS
CRATES
REACTS
TRACES
P **RECASTS**
ACTRESS
CASTERS
RECCE S
RECCES
P **RECEDE** DS
DECREE
P **RECEDED**
DECREED
P **RECEDES**
DECREES
SECEDER
P **RECEDING**
RECEIPT S
RECEIPTS
CREPIEST
RECEIVE DRS
RECEIVED
DECEIVER
RECEIVER S
RECEIVES
RECEMENT S
CEMENTER
CEREMENT
RECENCY
P **RECENSOR** S
P **RECENT**
CENTER
CENTRE
TENREC
RECENTER
RECENTLY
P **RECEPT** S
P **RECEPTOR** S

P **RECEPTS**
RESPECT
SCEPTER
SCEPTRE
SPECTER
SPECTRE
P **RECESS**
SCREES
P **RECESSED**
SECEDERS
P **RECESSES**
RECHANGE DS
P **RECHARGE** DR S
RECHART S
CHARTER
RECHARTS
CHARTERS
RECHEAT S
CHEATER
HECTARE
RETEACH
TEACHER
RECHEATS
CHEATERS
HECTARES
TEACHERS
P **RECHECK** S
CHECKER
P **RECHECKS**
CHECKERS
RECHEW S
CHEWER
RECHEWED
RECHEWS
CHEWERS
P **RECHOOSE** S
P **RECHOSE** N
CHEEROS
COHERES
ECHOERS
P **RECHOSEN**
P **RECIPE** S
PIECER
PIERCE
P **RECIPES**
PIECERS
PIERCES
PRECISE
RECIRCLE DS
P **RECISION** S
SORICINE
RECIT ES
CITER RECTI
TRICE
RECITAL S
ARTICLE
RECITALS
ARTICLES
STERICAL
RECITE DRS
CERITE
TIERCE
P **RECITED**
TIERCED
RECITER S
RECITERS
RECITES
CERITES
TIERCES
RECITING
RECITS
CITERS
STERIC
TRICES
DW **RECK** S
W **RECKED**
DECKER
W **RECKING**
RECKLESS
RECKON S
CONKER
RECKONED
RECKONER S
RECKONS
CONKERS
DW **RECKS**
RECLAD S
CRADLE
CREDAL
RECLADS
CRADLES

RECLAIM S
CLAIMER
MIRACLE
RECLAIMS
CLAIMERS
MIRACLES
RECLAME S
RECLAMES
RECLASP S
CARPELS
CLASPER
PARCELS
PLACERS
SCALPER
RECLASPS
CLASPERS
SCALPERS
P **RECLEAN** S
CLEANER
P **RECLEANS**
CLEANERS
CLEANSER
RECLINE DRS
RECLINED
DECLINER
RECLINER S
RECLINES
LICENSER
SILENCER
RECLOTHE DS
RECLUSE S
RECLUSES
CURELESS
RECOAL S
COALER
ORACLE
RECOALED
COLEADER
RECOALS
CLAROES
COALERS
ESCOLAR
ORACLES
SOLACER
RECOAT S
COATER
RECOATED
DECORATE
RECOATS
COASTER
COATERS
RECOCK S
COCKER
RECOCKED
COCKERED
RECOCKS
COCKERS
P **RECODE** DS
P **RECODED**
DECODER
P **RECODES**
RECODIFY
P **RECODING**
RECOIL S
COILER
RECOILED
RECOILER S
RECOILS
COILERS
RECOIN S
COINER
ORCEIN
RECOINED
RECOINS
COINERS
CRONIES
ORCEINS
RECOLOR S
COLORER
RECOLORS
COLORERS
RECOMB S
COMBER
RECOMBED
RECOMBS
COMBERS
RECOMMIT S
RECON S
CRONE
RECONFER S
CONFRERE
ENFORCER
RECONNED

RECONS
CENSOR
CRONES
RECONVEY S
CONVEYER
P **RECOOK** S
COOKER
P **RECOOKED**
P **RECOOKS**
COOKERS
RECOPIED
RECOPIES
RECOPY
RECORD S
CORDER
RECORDED
RECORDER S
RERECORD
RECORDS
CORDERS
RECORK S
CORKER
ROCKER
RECORKED
RECORKS
CORKERS
ROCKERS
RECOUNT S
CORNUTE
COUNTER
TROUNCE
RECOUNTS
CONSTRUE
COUNTERS
TROUNCES
P **RECOUP** ES
CROUPE
RECOUPE D
RECOUPED
RECOUPLE DS
OPERCULE
RECOUPS
CROUPES
RECOURSE S
RESOURCE
RECOVER SY
COVERER
RECOVERS
COVERERS
RECOVERY
RECRATE DS
CATERER
RETRACE
TERRACE
RECRATED
CRATERED
RETRACED
TERRACED
RECRATES
CATERERS
RETRACES
TERRACES
RECREANT S
RECANTER
RECREATE DS
RECROSS
CROSSER
SCORERS
RECROWN S
CROWNER
RECROWNS
CROWNERS
RECRUIT S
RECRUITS
CRUSTIER
RECS
RECTA L
CARET CARTE
CATER CRATE
REACT TRACE
RECTAL
CARTEL
CLARET
RECTALLY
RECTI
CITER RECIT
TRICE
RECTIFY
CERTIFY
RECTO RS
E **RECTOR** SY
E **RECTORS**
RECTORY

RECTOS
CORSET
COSTER
ESCORT
SCOTER
SECTOR
RECTRIX
RECTUM S
RECTUMS
RECTUS
CRUETS
CRUSET
CURETS
ERUCTS
RECUTS
TRUCES
RECUR S
CURER
RECURRED
RECURS
CURERS
CURSER
RECURVE DS
RECURVED
RECURVES
RECUSAL S
SECULAR
RECUSALS
SECULARS
RECUSANT S
CENTAURS
UNCRATES
RECUSE DS
CEREUS
CERUSE
RESCUE
SECURE
RECUSED
REDUCES
RESCUED
SECURED
SEDUCER
RECUSES
CERUSES
RESCUES
SECURES
RECUSING
RESCUING
SECURING
P **RECUT** S
CRUET CURET
CUTER ERUCT
TRUCE
P **RECUTS**
CRUETS
CRUSET
CURETS
ERUCTS
RECTUS
TRUCES
RECYCLE DRS
RECYCLED
RECYCLER S
RECYCLES
BCI **RED** DEOS
REDACT S
CARTED
CRATED
TRACED
REDACTED
REDACTOR S
REDACTS
SCARTED
REDAMAGE DS
REDAN S
DENAR
REDANS
DENARS
SANDER
SNARED
REDARGUE DS
REARGUED
P **REDATE** DS
DERATE
TEARED
P **REDATED**
DERATED
TREADED
P **REDATES**
DEAREST
DERATES
SEDATER

P **REDATING**
DERATING
GRADIENT
TREADING
REDBAIT S
TRIBADE
REDBAITS
TRIBADES
REDBAY S
BRAYED
BREADY
REDBAYS
REDBIRD S
REDBIRDS
REDBONE S
DEBONER
ENROBED
REDBONES
DEBONERS
REDBRICK S
REDBUD S
BUDDER
REDBUDS
BUDDERS
REDBUG S
BEDRUG
BUDGER
REDBUGS
BEDRUGS
BUDGERS
REDCAP S
CARPED
CRAPED
REDCAPS
SCARPED
SCRAPED
REDCOAT S
CORDATE
REDCOATS
REDD S
REDDED
REDDEN S
RENDED
REDDENED
REDDENS
REDDER S
REDDERS
REDDEST
TEDDERS
REDDING
GRINDED
REDDISH
T **REDDLE** DS
T **REDDLED**
T **REDDLES**
SLEDDER
T **REDDLING**
REDDS
B **REDE** DS
DEER DERE
DREE REED
REDEAR S
DEARER
READER
REARED
REREAD
REDEARS
READERS
REREADS
REDECIDE DS
REDED
DREED
REDEEM S
REDEEMED
REDEEMER S
REDEEMS
EMERSED
REDEFEAT S
DEFEATER
FEDERATE
REDEFECT S
REFECTED
REDEFIED
REDEFIES
P **REDEFINE** DS
REDEFY
REDEMAND S
DAMNEDER
DEMANDER
REMANDED
REDENIED

REDENIES
NEREIDES
REDENY
REDEPLOY S
DEPLOYER
B **REDES**
DEERS DREES
REEDS SEDER
SERED
REDESIGN S
DESIGNER
ENERGIDS
REEDINGS
RESIGNED
REDEYE S
REDEYES
REDFIN S
FINDER
FRIEND
REFIND
REDFINS
FINDERS
FRIENDS
REFINDS
REDFISH
REDHEAD S
ADHERED
REDHEADS
REDHORSE S
U **REDIA** ELS
AIDER AIRED
DEAIR IRADE
REDIAE
AERIED
DEARIE
PU **REDIAL** S
ARILED
DERAIL
DIALER
LAIRED
RAILED
RELAID
REDIALED
DEADLIER
DERAILED
REDIALS
DERAILS
DIALERS
REDIAS
AIDERS
DEAIRS
IRADES
RAISED
RESAID
REDID
DRIED
P **REDIGEST** S
DIGESTER
REDING
DINGER
ENGIRD
GIRNED
RINGED
REDIP ST
PRIDE PRIED
RIPED
REDIPPED
REDIPS
PRIDES
PRISED
SPIDER
SPIRED
REDIPT
TREPID
REDIRECT S
DIRECTER
REDIVIDE DS
REDLEG S
GELDER
LEDGER
REDLEGS
GELDERS
LEDGERS
REDLINE DRS
RELINED
REDLINED
REDLINER S
REDLINES
REDLY
REDNESS
RESENDS
SENDERS

CU **REDO** NSX
DOER DORE
RODE
REDOCK S
CORKED
DOCKER
ROCKED
REDOCKED
REDOCKS
DOCKERS
REDOES
ERODES
REDOING
ERODING
GROINED
IGNORED
NEGROID
REDOLENT
RONDELET
REDON ES
DRONE
REDONE
REDONNED
DONNERED
REDONS
DRONES
SNORED
SONDER
SORNED
CU **REDOS**
DOERS DOSER
RESOD RODES
ROSED SORED
REDOUBLE DR S
REDOUBT S
DOUBTER
OBTRUDE
OUTBRED
REDOUBTS
DOUBTERS
OBTRUDES
REDOUND S
ROUNDED
UNDERDO
REDOUNDS
REDOUT S
DETOUR
ROUTED
TOURED
REDOUTS
DETOURS
DOUREST
ROUSTED
REDOWA S
REDOWAS
REDOX
REDOXES
REDPOLL S
REDPOLLS
P **REDRAFT** S
DRAFTER
REDRAFTS
DRAFTERS
REDRAW NS
DRAWER
REWARD
WARDER
WARRED
REDRAWER S
REREWARD
REWARDER
REDRAWN
REDRAWS
DRAWERS
REWARDS
WARDERS
REDREAM ST
DREAMER
REARMED
REDREAMS
DREAMERS
REDREAMT
REDRESS
DRESSER
REDREW
P **REDRIED**
DERIDER
P **REDRIES**
DERRIES
DESIRER
RESIDER
SERRIED

P **REDRILL** S
DRILLER
P **REDRILLS**
DRILLERS
REDRIVE NS
DERIVER
REDRIVEN
REDRIVES
DERIVERS
REDROOT S
REDROOTS
REDROVE
P **REDRY**
DERRY DRYER
P **REDRYING**
GRINDERY
C **REDS**
REDSHANK S
REDSHIFT S
REDSHIRT S
REDSTART S
REDTAIL S
DILATER
TRAILED
REDTAILS
DILATERS
LARDIEST
REDTOP S
DEPORT
PORTED
REDTOPS
DEPORTS
SPORTED
REDUB S
REDUBBED
REDUBS
REDUCE DRS
REDUCED
REDUCER S
REDUCERS
CURSEDER
REDUCES
RECUSED
RESCUED
SECURED
SEDUCER
REDUCING
REDUCTOR S
REDUVIID S
REDUX
REDWARE S
REDWARES
REDWING S
WRINGED
REDWINGS
REDWOOD S
REDWOODS
REDYE DS
REEDY
REDYED
REDYEING
REDYES
BDF GPT **REE** DFKLS
ERE
REEARN S
EARNER
NEARER
REEARNED
REEARNS
EARNERS
REECHIER
CHEERIER
REECHO
CHEERO
COHERE
ECHOER
REECHOED
REECHOES
REECHY
CHEERY
BCD FGP T **REED** SY
DEER DERE
DREE REDE
REEDBIRD S
REEDBUCK S
REEDED
G **REEDIER**
G **REEDIEST**
REEDIFY
G **REEDILY**
YIELDER

B **REEDING** S
DREEING
ENERGID
REIGNED
B **REEDINGS**
DESIGNER
ENERGIDS
REDESIGN
RESIGNED
P **REEDIT** S
DIETER
RETIED
TIERED
P **REEDITED**
P **REEDITS**
DIESTER
DIETERS
RESITED
REEDLIKE
DEERLIKE
REEDLING S
ENGIRDLE
LINGERED
F **REEDMAN**
AMENDER
MEANDER
RENAMED
F **REEDMEN**
EMENDER
BCG **REEDS**
DEERS DREES
REDES SEDER
SERED
G **REEDY**
REDYE
REEF SY
FERE FREE
REEFABLE
REEFED
FEEDER
REFEED
REEFER S
REEFERS
REEFIER
REEFIEST
REEFING
FEIGNER
FREEING
REEFS
FERES FREES
REEFY
FEYER
REEJECT S
REEJECTS
CG **REEK** SY
REEKED
REEKER S
REEKERS
REEKIER
REEKIEST
REEKING
BC **REEKS**
ESKER
REEKY
REKEY
C **REEL** S
LEER
REELABLE
P **REELECT** S
P **REELECTS**
RESELECT
C **REELED**
LEERED
REELER S
REELERS
C **REELING** S
LEERING
REELINGS
C **REELS**
LEERS
REEMBARK S
REEMBODY
REEMERGE DS
REEMIT S
METIER
RETIME
REEMITS
MEISTER
METIERS
RETIMES
TRISEME

REEMPLOY S
EMPLOYER
P **REENACT** S
CENTARE
CRENATE
P **REENACTS**
CENTARES
REASCENT
SARCENET
REENDOW S
ENDOWER
REENDOWS
ENDOWERS
WORSENED
G **REENGAGE** DS
REENJOY S
ENJOYER
REENJOYS
ENJOYERS
REENLIST S
ENLISTER
LISTENER
SILENTER
REENROLL S
ENROLLER
REENTER S
ENTERER
TERREEN
TERRENE
REENTERS
ENTERERS
TERREENS
TERRENES
REENTRY
REEQUIP S
PERIQUE
REEQUIPS
PERIQUES
P **REERECT** S
ERECTER
P **REERECTS**
ERECTERS
SECRETER
BDF GPT **REES** T
SEER SERE
F **REEST** S
ESTER RESET
STEER STERE
TERSE TREES
REESTED
STEERED
REESTING
GENTRIES
INTEGERS
STEERING
REESTS
ESTERS
RESETS
SEREST
STEERS
STERES
REEVE DS
REEVED
VEERED
REEVES
SEVERE
REEVING
REGIVEN
VEERING
REEVOKE DS
REEVOKED
REEVOKES
REEXPEL S
REEXPELS
REEXPORT S
EXPORTER
P **REEXPOSE** DS
T **REF** ST
FER
P **REFACE** DS
P **REFACED**
DEFACER
P **REFACES**
P **REFACING**
REFALL S
FALLER
REFALLEN
REFALLS
FALLERS
REFASTEN S
FASTENER
FENESTRA
P **REFECT** S

REFECTED
REDEFECT
P **REFECTS**
REFED
DEFER FREED
REFEED S
FEEDER
REEFED
REFEEDS
FEEDERS
REFEEL S
FEELER
REFEELS
FEELERS
REFEL LST
FLEER
REFELL
FELLER
REFELLED
REFELS
FLEERS
REFELT
LEFTER
REFLET
TELFER
REFENCE DS
REFENCED
REFENCES
P **REFER** S
FREER FRERE
REFEREE DS
REFEREED
REFEREES
REFERENT S
REFERRAL S
P **REFERRED**
DEFERRER
P **REFERRER** S
P **REFERS**
FREERS
FRERES
REFFED
DEFFER
REFFING
P **REFIGHT** S
FIGHTER
FREIGHT
REFIGHTS
FIGHTERS
FREIGHTS
P **REFIGURE** DS
P **REFILE** DS
FERLIE
LIEFER
RELIEF
P **REFILED**
DEFILER
FIELDER
P **REFILES**
FERLIES
REFLIES
RELIEFS
P **REFILING**
REFILL S
FILLER
P **REFILLED**
REFILLS
FILLERS
REFILM S
FILMER
REFILMED
REFILMS
FILMERS
REFILTER S
FILTERER
REFIND S
FINDER
FRIEND
REDFIN
REFINDS
FINDERS
FRIENDS
REDFINS
REFINE DRS
FERINE
REFINED
DEFINER
REFINER SY
FERNIER
REFINERS
REFINERY
REFINES
REFINING
INFRINGE

REFINISH
FINISHER
P **REFIRE** DS
P **REFIRED**
FERRIED
REFRIED
P **REFIRES**
FERRIES
REFRIES
P **REFIRING**
FRINGIER
REFIT S
REFITS
FRITES
RESIFT
RIFEST
SIFTER
STRIFE
REFITTED
P **REFIX**
FIXER
P **REFIXED**
P **REFIXES**
P **REFIXING**
REFLAG S
REFLAGS
REFLATE DS
REFLATED
DEFLATER
FALTERED
REFLATES
REFLECT S
REFLECTS
REFLET S
LEFTER
REFELT
TELFER
REFLETS
TELFERS
REFLEW
REFLEX
REFLEXED
REFLEXES
REFLEXLY
REFLIES
FERLIES
REFILES
RELIEFS
REFLOAT S
FLOATER
REFLOATS
FLOATERS
FORESTAL
REFLOOD S
FLOODER
FLOORED
REFLOODS
FLOODERS
REFLOW NS
FLOWER
FOWLER
WOLFER
REFLOWED
DEFLOWER
FLOWERED
REFLOWER S
FLOWERER
REFLOWN
REFLOWS
FLOWERS
FOWLERS
WOLFERS
REFLUENT
REFLUX
REFLUXED
REFLUXES
FLEXURES
REFLY
FERLY FLYER
REFLYING
P **REFOCUS**
FOCUSER
REFOLD S
FOLDER
ROLFED
REFOLDED
REFOLDS
FOLDERS
REFOREST S
FORESTER
FOSTERER
REFORGE DS

REFORGED
REFORGES
P **REFORM** S
FORMER
P **REFORMAT** ES
P **REFORMED**
DEFORMER
REFORMER S
P **REFORMS**
FORMERS
REFOUGHT
REFOUND S
FOUNDER
REFOUNDS
FOUNDERS
REFRACT S
CRAFTER
REFRACTS
CRAFTERS
REFRAIN S
REFRAINS
REFRAME DS
REFRAMED
REFRAMES
P **REFREEZE** S
REFRESH
FRESHER
REFRIED
FERRIED
REFIRED
REFRIES
FERRIES
REFIRES
REFRONT S
FRONTER
REFRONTS
P **REFROZE** N
P **REFROZEN**
REFRY
FERRY FRYER
REFRYING
FERRYING
REFS
SERF
REFT
FRET TREF
REFUEL S
FERULE
FUELER
REFUELED
REFUELS
FERULES
FUELERS
REFUGE DES
REFUGED
REFUGEE S
REFUGEES
REFUGES
REFUGIA
REFUGING
REFUGIUM
P **REFUND** S
FUNDER
P **REFUNDED**
UNDERFED
REFUNDER S
P **REFUNDS**
FUNDERS
REFUSAL S
EARFULS
FERULAS
REFUSALS
REFUSE DRS
REFUSED
DEFUSER
REFUSER S
REFUSERS
REFUSES
REFUSING
GUNFIRES
REFUSNIK S
REFUTAL S
TEARFUL
REFUTALS
REFUTE DRS
REFUTED
REFUTER S
REFUTERS
REFUTES
REFUTING

D **REG** S
ERG
REGAIN S
EARING
GAINER
REAGIN
REGINA
REGAINED
REGAINER S
REGAINS
EARINGS
ERASING
GAINERS
REAGINS
REGINAS
SEARING
SERINGA
REGAL E
ARGLE GLARE
LAGER LARGE
REGALE DRS
GALERE
REGALED
LAGERED
REGALER S
REGALERS
REGALES
GALERES
REGALIA
REGALING
GANGLIER
LAGERING
REGALITY
REGALLY
ALLERGY
GALLERY
LARGELY
REGARD S
GARRED
GRADER
REGARDED
DEGRADER
REGRADED
REGARDS
GRADERS
REGATHER S
GATHERER
REGATTA S
REGATTAS
REGAUGE DS
REGAUGED
REGAUGES
REGAVE
GREAVE
REGEAR S
REGEARED
REGEARS
GREASER
REGELATE DS
EGLATERE
RELEGATE
REGENCY
REGENT S
GERENT
REGENTAL
REGENTS
GERENTS
REGES
EGERS GREES
SERGE
REGGAE S
RAGGEE
REGGAES
RAGGEES
REGICIDE S
REGILD S
GILDER
GIRDLE
GLIDER
RIDGEL
REGILDED
REGILDS
GILDERS
GIRDLES
GLIDERS
RIDGELS
REGILT
REGIME NS
EMIGRE
REGIMEN ST
REGIMENS
REGIMENT S
METERING

REGIMES
EMIGRES
REMIGES
REGINA ELS
EARING
GAINER
REAGIN
REGAIN
REGINAE
REGINAL
ALIGNER
ENGRAIL
NARGILE
REALIGN
REGINAS
EARINGS
ERASING
GAINERS
REAGINS
REGAINS
SEARING
SERINGA
REGION S
ERINGO
IGNORE
REGIONAL S
GERANIOL
REGIONS
ERINGOS
IGNORES
SIGNORE
REGISTER S
REGISTRY
REGIUS
REGIVE NS
GRIEVE
REGIVEN
REEVING
VEERING
REGIVES
GRIEVES
REGIVING
GRIEVING
REGLAZE DS
REGLAZED
REGLAZES
REGLET S
REGLETS
REGLOSS
GLOSSER
REGLOW S
GLOWER
REGLOWED
GLOWERED
REGLOWS
GLOWERS
REGLUE DS
REGLUED
GRUELED
REGLUES
REGLUING
GRUELING
B **REGMA**
GAMER MARGE
B **REGMATA**
REGNA L
ANGER RANGE
REGNAL
ANGLER
P **REGNANCY**
P **REGNANT**
REGNUM
REGOLITH S
REGORGE DS
REGORGED
REGORGES
REGOSOL S
REGOSOLS
REGRADE DS
REGRADED
DEGRADER
REGARDED
REGRADES
REGRAFT S
GRAFTER
REGRAFTS
GRAFTERS
REGRANT S
GRANTER
REGRANTS
GRANTERS
STRANGER

REGRATE DS
GREATER
REGRATED
GARRETED
GARTERED
REGRATES
REGREEN S
GREENER
RENEGER
REGREENS
RENEGERS
REGREET S
GREETER
REGREETS
GREETERS
REGRESS
SERGERS
REGRET S
REGRETS
REGREW
REGRIND S
GRINDER
REGRINDS
GRINDERS
REGROOM S
GROOMER
REGROOMS
GROOMERS
REGROOVE DS
REGROUND
GROUNDER
REGROUP S
GROUPER
REGROUPS
GROUPERS
REGROW NS
GROWER
REGROWN
WRONGER
REGROWS
GROWERS
P **REGROWTH** S
D **REGS**
ERGS
REGULAR S
REGULARS
REGULATE DS
REGULI
GLUIER
LIGURE
UGLIER
REGULINE
REGULUS
REHAB S
REHABBED
REHABBER S
REHABS
BASHER
REHAMMER S
HAMMERER
P **REHANDLE** DS
REHANG S
HANGER
REHANGED
REHANGS
HANGERS
P **REHARDEN** S
HARDENER
REHASH
REHASHED
REHASHES
REHEAR DS
HEARER
REHEARD
ADHERER
REHEARS E
HEARERS
SHEARER
REHEARSE DR S
P **REHEAT** S
AETHER
HEATER
HEREAT
P **REHEATED**
P **REHEATER** S
P **REHEATS**
AETHERS
HEATERS
REHEEL S
HEELER
REHEELED

REHEELS
HEELERS
REHEM S
RHEME
REHEMMED
REHEMS
RHEMES
REHINGE DS
REHINGED
REHINGES
GREENISH
SHEERING
REHIRE DS
REHIRED
HERRIED
REHIRES
HERRIES
P **REHIRING**
REHOBOAM S
REHOUSE DS
REHOUSED
REHOUSES
REHUNG
HUNGER
REI FNS
IRE
REIF SY
FIRE RIFE
REIFIED
DEIFIER
EDIFIER
REIFIER S
FIERIER
REIFIERS
REIFIES
REIFS
FIRES FRIES
FRISE SERIF
REIFY
FIERY
REIFYING
REIGN S
RENIG
REIGNED
DREEING
ENERGID
REEDING
REIGNING
REIGNITE DS
RETIEING
REIGNS
RENIGS
RESIGN
SERING
SIGNER
SINGER
REIMAGE DS
REIMAGED
REIMAGES
REIMPORT S
IMPORTER
P **REIMPOSE** DS
MOPERIES
PROMISEE
REIN KS
REINCITE DS
REINCUR S
REINCURS
REINDEER S
REINDEX
INDEXER
REINDICT S
INDICTER
INDIRECT
REINDUCE DS
REINDUCT S
REINED
DENIER
NEREID
REINFECT S
FRENETIC
INFECTER
P **REINFORM** S
INFORMER
RENIFORM
REINFUSE DS
REINING
GINNIER
REINJECT S
REINJURE DS
REINJURY

REINK S
INKER
REINKED
REINKING
REINKS
INKERS
SINKER
REINLESS
REINS
RESIN RINSE
RISEN SERIN
SIREN
P **REINSERT** S
INSERTER
REINTERS
RENTIERS
TERRINES
REINSMAN
REINSMEN
REINSURE DR S
REINTER S
RENTIER
TERRINE
REINTERS
INSERTER
REINSERT
RENTIERS
TERRINES
REINVADE DS
REINVENT S
INVENTER
REINVEST S
NERVIEST
SIRVENTE
P **REINVITE** DS
REINVOKE DS
REIS
IRES RISE
SIRE
REISSUE DRS
SEISURE
REISSUED
DIURESES
RESIDUES
REISSUER S
REISSUES
SEISURES
REITBOK S
REITBOKS
REIVE DRS
REIVED
DERIVE
REIVER S
RIEVER
VERIER
REIVERS
REVISER
RIEVERS
REIVES
REVISE
REIVING
REJACKET S
REJECT S
REJECTED
REJECTEE S
REJECTER S
REJECTOR S
REJECTS
REJIG S
REJIGGED
JIGGERED
REJIGGER S
REJIGS
REJOICE DRS
REJOICED
REJOICER S
REJOICES
REJOIN S
JOINER
REJOINED
REJOINS
JOINERS
P **REJUDGE** DS
P **REJUDGED**
P **REJUDGES**
REJUGGLE DS
REKEY S
REEKY
REKEYED
REKEYING

REKEYS
KERSEY
REKINDLE DS
RELINKED
REKNIT S
TINKER
REKNITS
STINKER
TINKERS
REKNOT S
REKNOTS
RELABEL S
LABELER
RELABELS
LABELERS
RELACE DS
CEREAL
RELACED
CLEARED
CREEDAL
DECLARE
RELACES
CEREALS
RESCALE
SCLERAE
RELACING
CLEARING
RELAID
ARILED
DERAIL
DIALER
LAIRED
RAILED
REDIAL
RELAND S
DARNEL
LANDER
RELANDED
RELANDS
DARNELS
LANDERS
SLANDER
SNARLED
RELAPSE DRS
LEAPERS
PLEASER
PRESALE
REPEALS
RELAPSED
PEDALERS
PLEADERS
REPLEADS
RELAPSER S
PEARLERS
RELAPSES
PLEASERS
PRESALES
P **RELATE** DRS
ELATER
RELATED
ALERTED
ALTERED
TREADLE
RELATER S
ALERTER
ALTERER
REALTER
RELATERS
ALTERERS
REALTERS
P **RELATES**
ELATERS
REALEST
RESLATE
STEALER
RELATING
ALERTING
ALTERING
INTEGRAL
TANGLIER
TRIANGLE
RELATION S
ORIENTAL
RELATIVE S
LEVIRATE
RELATOR S
REALTOR
RELATORS
REALTORS
RESTORAL
P **RELAUNCH**
LAUNCHER
RELAX
LAXER
RELAXANT S

RELAXED
RELAXER S
RELAXERS
RELAXES
RELAXIN GS
RELAXING
RELAXINS
RELAY S
EARLY LAYER
LEARY
RELAYED
DELAYER
LAYERED
RELAYING
LAYERING
YEARLING
RELAYS
LAYERS
SLAYER
RELEARN ST
LEARNER
RELEARNS
LEARNERS
RELEARNT
RELEASE DRS
RELEASED
RESEALED
RELEASER S
RELEASES
RELEGATE DS
EGLATERE
REGELATE
RELEND S
LENDER
RELENDS
LENDERS
SLENDER
RELENT S
RELENTED
RELENTS
NESTLER
RELET S
RELETS
STREEL
RELETTER S
LETTERER
RELEVANT
LEVANTER
RELEVE S
RELEVES
RELIABLE S
RELIABLY
BLEARILY
RELIANCE S
RELIANT
LATRINE
RATLINE
RETINAL
TRENAIL
RELIC ST
RELICS
SLICER
RELICT S
RELICTS
RELIED
LIEDER
RELIEF S
FERLIE
LIEFER
REFILE
RELIEFS
FERLIES
REFILES
REFLIES
RELIER S
RELIERS
RELIES
RESILE
RELIEVE DRS
RELIEVED
RELIEVER S
RELIEVES
RELIEVO S
OVERLIE
RELIEVOS
OVERLIES
VOLERIES
RELIGHT S
LIGHTER
RELIGHTS
LIGHTERS
SLIGHTER

RELIGION S
LIGROINE
REOILING
RELINE DS
LIERNE
RELINED
REDLINE
RELINES
LIERNES
RELINING
RELINK S
LINKER
RELINKED
REKINDLE
RELINKS
LINKERS
RELIQUE S
RELIQUES
RELISH
HIRSEL
HIRSLE
RELISHED
HIRSELED
SHIELDER
RELISHES
HEIRLESS
RELIST S
LISTER
LITERS
LITRES
TILERS
RELISTED
RELISTS
LISTERS
RELIT
LITER LITRE
TILER
RELIVE DS
EVILER
LEVIER
LIEVER
REVILE
VEILER
RELIVED
DELIVER
LIVERED
REVILED
P **RELIVES**
LEVIERS
REVILES
SERVILE
VEILERS
RELIVING
LIVERING
REVILING
RELLENO S
RELLENOS
P **RELOAD** S
LOADER
ORDEAL
P **RELOADED**
RELOADER S
P **RELOADS**
LOADERS
ORDEALS
RELOAN S
LOANER
RELOANED
OLEANDER
RELOANS
LOANERS
P **RELOCATE** DE
CORELATE S
RELOCK S
LOCKER
RELOCKED
RELOCKS
LOCKERS
RELOOK S
LOOKER
RELOOKED
RELOOKS
LOOKERS
RELUCENT
RELUCT S
CUTLER
RELUCTED
LECTURED
RELUCTS
CLUSTER
CUTLERS
RELUME DS
RELUMED

RELUMES
LEMURES
RELUMINE DS
LEMURINE
RELUMING
RELY
LYRE
RELYING
REM S
P **REMADE**
REAMED
REMAIL S
MAILER
REMAILED
REMEDIAL
REMAILS
MAILERS
REALISM
REMAIN S
AIRMEN
MARINE
REMAINED
C **REMAINS**
MARINES
SEMINAR
REMAKE RS
REMAKER S
REMAKERS
REMAKES
REMAKING
P **REMAN** DS
NAMER RAMEN
REMAND S
DAMNER
REMANDED
DAMNEDER
DEMANDER
REDEMAND
REMANDS
DAMNERS
REMANENT
REMANNED
MANNERED
REMANS
NAMERS
REMAP S
REMAPPED
PAMPERED
REMAPS
REMARK S
MARKER
REMARKED
REMARKER S
P **REMARKET** S
MARKETER
REMARKS
MARKERS
REMARQUE S
REMARRY
REMASTER S
STREAMER
REMATCH
MATCHER
C **REMATE** DS
RETEAM
C **REMATED**
C **REMATES**
RETEAMS
STEAMER
C **REMATING**
EMIGRANT
REMEDIAL
REMAILED
REMEDIED
REMEDIES
REMEDY
P **REMEET** S
METEER
TEEMER
REMEETS
MEETERS
TEEMERS
REMELT S
MELTER
REMELTED
REMELTS
MELTERS
RESMELT
SMELTER
REMEMBER S
REMEND S
MENDER
REMENDED

REMENDS
MENDERS
REMERGE DS
REMERGED
DEMERGER
REMERGES
REMET
METER METRE
RETEM
REMEX
REMIGES
EMIGRES
REGIMES
REMIGIAL
REMIND S
MINDER
REMINDED
REMINDER S
REREMIND
REMINDS
MINDERS
REMINT S
MINTER
REMINTED
REMINTS
MINSTER
MINTERS
P **REMISE** DS
P **REMISED**
P **REMISES**
MERISES
MESSIER
P **REMISING**
P **REMISS**
MISERS
REMISSLY
REMIT S
MERIT MITER
MITRE TIMER
REMITS
MERITS
MISTER
MITERS
MITRES
SMITER
TIMERS
REMITTAL S
REMITTED
REMITTER S
TRIMETER
REMITTOR S
P **REMIX** T
MIREX MIXER
P **REMIXED**
P **REMIXES**
MIREXES
P **REMIXING**
P **REMIXT**
REMNANT S
REMNANTS
REMODEL S
MODELER
REMODELS
MODELERS
MORSELED
P **REMODIFY**
REMOLADE S
P **REMOLD** S
MOLDER
P **REMOLDED**
MOLDERED
P **REMOLDS**
MOLDERS
SMOLDER
REMORA S
ROAMER
REMORAS
ROAMERS
REMORID
P **REMORSE** S
REMORSES
REMOTE RS
EMOTER
METEOR
REMOTELY
MOTLEYER
REMOTER
REMOTES T
EMOTERS
METEORS
REMOTEST
REMOTION S
MOTIONER

REMOUNT S
MOUNTER
REMOUNTS
MOUNTERS
REMOVAL S
REMOVALS
REMOVE DRS
REMOVED
REMOVER S
REMOVERS
REMOVES
REMOVING
REMS
REMUDA S
REMUDAS
T **RENAIL** S
ALINER
LARINE
LINEAR
NAILER
RENAILED
T **RENAILS**
ALINERS
NAILERS
RENAL
LEARN
P **RENAME** DS
MEANER
RENAMED
AMENDER
MEANDER
REEDMAN
P **RENAMES**
MEANERS
RENAMING
C **RENATURE** DS
T **REND** S
NERD
T **RENDED**
REDDEN
RENDER S
RENDERED
RENDERER S
RENDERS
RENDIBLE
LINEBRED
T **RENDING**
GRINDED
T **RENDS**
NERDS
RENDZINA S
RENEGADE DS
RENEGADO S
RENEGE DRS
RENEGED
GREENED
RENEGER S
GREENER
REGREEN
RENEGERS
REGREENS
RENEGES
RENEGING
GREENING
RENEST S
ENTERS
NESTER
RENTES
RESENT
TENSER
TERNES
TREENS
RENESTED
RESENTED
RENESTS
NESTERS
RESENTS
RENEW S
NEWER
RENEWAL S
RENEWALS
RENEWED
RENEWER S
RENEWERS
RENEWING
RENEWS
RESEWN
RENIFORM
INFORMER
REINFORM
RENIG S
REIGN

RENIGGED
GINGERED
RENIGS
REIGNS
RESIGN
SERING
SIGNER
SINGER
RENIN S
INNER
RENINS
INNERS
SINNER
RENITENT
RENMINBI
RENNASE S
ENSNARE
RENNASES
ENSNARES
NEARNESS
RENNET S
TENNER
RENNETS
TENNERS
RENNIN S
RENNINS
RENOGRAM S
P **RENOTIFY**
RENOUNCE DR
S
RENOVATE DS
OVERNEAT
RENOWN S
WONNER
RENOWNED
RENOWNS
WONNERS
B **RENT** ES
TERN
RENTABLE
RENTAL S
ANTLER
LEARNT
RENTALS
ANTLERS
SALTERN
STERNAL
RENTE DRS
ENTER TERNE
TREEN
RENTED
TENDER
RENTER S
RERENT
RENTERS
RERENTS
STERNER
RENTES
ENTERS
NESTER
RENEST
RESENT
TENSER
TERNES
TREENS
RENTIER S
REINTER
TERRINE
RENTIERS
INSERTER
REINSERT
REINTERS
TERRINES
RENTING
RINGENT
B **RENTS**
NERTS STERN
TERNS
P **RENUMBER** S
NUMBERER
RENVOI S
ENVIRO
RENVOIS
ENVIROS
VERSION
REOBJECT S
P **REOBTAIN** S
BARITONE
OBTAINER
TABORINE
P **REOCCUPY**
REOCCUR S
REOCCURS
SUCCORER

REOFFER S
OFFERER
REOFFERS
OFFERERS
REOIL S
OILER ORIEL
REOILED
REOILING
LIGROINE
RELIGION
REOILS
LORIES
OILERS
ORIELS
REOPEN S
OPENER
PEREON
REOPENED
REOPENS
OPENERS
PEREONS
REOPPOSE DS
P **REORDAIN** S
ORDAINER
P **REORDER** S
ORDERER
P **REORDERS**
ORDERERS
REORIENT S
ORIENTER
REOUTFIT S
REOVIRUS
P **REP** OPS
PER
REPACIFY
P **REPACK** S
PACKER
P **REPACKED**
P **REPACKS**
PACKERS
P **REPAID**
DIAPER
PAIRED
PARDIE
REPAINT S
PAINTER
PERTAIN
REPAINTS
PAINTERS
PANTRIES
PERTAINS
PINASTER
PRISTANE
REPAIR S
RAPIER
REPAIRED
RAPIERED
REPAIRER S
RARERIPE
REPAIRS
ASPIRER
PARRIES
PRAISER
RAPIERS
RASPIER
REPAND
PANDER
REPANDLY
REPANEL S
REPANELS
REPAPER S
PAPERER
PREPARE
REPAPERS
PAPERERS
PREPARES
REPARK S
PARKER
REPARKED
REPARKS
PARKERS
SPARKER
REPARTEE S
REPEATER
REREPEAT
REPASS
ASPERS
PARSES
PASSER
PRASES
SPARES
SPARSE
SPEARS

REPASSED
ASPERSED
RESPADES
REPASSES
ASPERSES
REPAST S
PASTER
PATERS
PRATES
TAPERS
TRAPES
P **REPASTED**
PEDERAST
PREDATES
TRAPESED
REPASTS
PASTERS
SPAREST
REPATCH
CHAPTER
PATCHER
P **REPAVE** DS
PAREVE
P **REPAVED**
DEPRAVE
PERVADE
P **REPAVES**
P **REPAVING**
P **REPAY** S
APERY PAYER
P **REPAYING**
P **REPAYS**
PAYERS
REPEAL S
LEAPER
REPEALED
REPEALER S
REPEALS
LEAPERS
PLEASER
PRESALE
RELAPSE
REPEAT S
RETAPE
REPEATED
DEPARTEE
REPEATER S
REPARTEE
REREPEAT
REPEATS
RETAPES
REPEG S
REPEGGED
REPEGS
REPEL S
LEPER
REPELLED
REPELLER S
REPELS
LEPERS
REPENT S
REPENTED
REPETEND
REPENTER S
REPENTS
PENSTER
PRESENT
SERPENT
REPEOPLE DS
REPERK S
REPERKED
REPERKS
REPETEND S
REPENTED
REPHRASE DS
RESHAPER
REPIN ES
RIPEN
REPINE DRS
REPINED
RIPENED
REPINER S
RIPENER
REPINERS
PRERINSE
RIPENERS
REPINES
EREPSIN
REPINING
RIPENING
REPINNED
REPINS
RIPENS
SNIPER

P **REPLACE** DRS
PERCALE
P **REPLACED**
PARCELED
REPLACER S
PRECLEAR
P **REPLACES**
PERCALES
P **REPLAN** ST
PLANER
P **REPLANS**
PLANERS
P **REPLANT** S
PLANTER
REPLANTS
PLANTERS
REPLATE DS
PETRALE
PLEATER
PRELATE
REPLATED
PALTERED
REPLATES
PETRALES
PLEATERS
PRELATES
REPLAY S
PARLEY
PEARLY
PLAYER
REPLAYED
PARLEYED
REPLAYS
PARLEYS
PARSLEY
PLAYERS
SPARELY
REPLEAD S
PEARLED
PEDALER
PLEADER
REPLEADS
PEDALERS
PLEADERS
RELAPSED
REPLED
PEDLER
REPLEDGE DS
REPLETE S
REPLETES
REPLEVIN S
REPLEVY
REPLICA S
CALIPER
REPLICAS E
CALIPERS
SPIRACLE
REPLICON S
REPLIED
PERILED
REPLIER S
REPLIERS
REPLIES
SPIELER
REPLOT S
PETROL
REPLOTS
PETROLS
REPLOW S
PLOWER
REPLOWED
REPLOWS
PLOWERS
REPLUMB S
PLUMBER
REPLUMBS
PLUMBERS
REPLUNGE DS
REPLY
PLYER
REPLYING
REPO ST
PORE ROPE
REPOLISH
POLISHER
REPOLL S
POLLER
REPOLLED
REPOLLS
POLLERS
REPORT S
PORTER
PRETOR
REPORTED
DEPORTER
PORTERED
REPORTER S
REPORTS
PORTERS
PRESORT
PRETORS
SPORTER
REPOS E
PORES POSER
PROSE ROPES
SPORE
REPOSAL S
PAROLES
REPOSALS
REPOSE DRS
REPOSED
DEPOSER
REPOSER S
REPOSERS
REPOSES
REPOSING
PERIGONS
SPONGIER
REPOSIT S
PROSTIE
RIPOSTE
ROPIEST
REPOSITS
PROSIEST
PROSTIES
RIPOSTES
TRIPOSES
REPOT S
TOPER TROPE
REPOTS
POSTER
PRESTO
RESPOT
STOPER
TOPERS
TROPES
REPOTTED
POTTERED
REPOUR S
POURER
REPOURED
REPOURS
POURERS
REPOUSSE S
ESPOUSER
REPOWER S
REPOWERS
REPP S
PERP PREP
P **REPPED**
P **REPPING**
REPPS
PERPS PREPS
P **REPRESS**
PRESSER
P **REPRICE** DS
CREPIER
PIERCER
P **REPRICED**
P **REPRICES**
PIERCERS
PRECISER
REPRIEVE DS
P **REPRINT** S
PRINTER
P **REPRINTS**
PRINTERS
SPRINTER
REPRISAL S
REPRISE DS
PERRIES
PRISERE
RESPIRE
REPRISED
PREDRIES
PRESIDER
RESPIRED
REPRISES
PRISERES
RESPIRES
REPRO S
ROPER
REPROACH
REPROBE DS
REPROBED
REPROBES
REPROOF S
PROOFER
REPROOFS
PROOFERS
REPROS
PROSER
ROPERS
REPROVAL S
REPROVE DRS
REPROVED
REPROVER S
REPROVES
P **REPS**
REPTANT
PATTERN
REPTILE S
PERLITE
REPTILES
EPISTLER
PELTRIES
PERLITES
REPTILIA N
REPUBLIC S
REPUGN S
REPUGNED
REPUGNS
REPULSE DRS
REPULSED
PRELUDES
REPULSER S
REPULSES
REPUMP S
PUMPER
REPUMPED
REPUMPS
PUMPERS
REPURIFY
REPURSUE DS
REPUTE DS
REPUTED
ERUPTED
REPUTES
REPUTING
ERUPTING
REQUEST S
QUESTER
REQUESTS
QUESTERS
REQUIEM S
REQUIEMS
REQUIN S
REQUINS
REQUIRE DRS
QUERIER
REQUIRED
REQUIRER S
REQUIRES
QUERIERS
REQUITAL S
QUARTILE
REQUITE DRS
QUIETER
REQUITED
REQUITER S
REQUITES
QUIETERS
RERACK S
RACKER
RERACKED
RERACKS
RACKERS
RERAISE DS
RERAISED
DREARIES
RERAISES
RERAN
REREAD S
DEARER
READER
REARED
REDEAR
REREADS
READERS
REDEARS
P **RERECORD** S
RECORDER
REREDOS
REREMICE
REREMIND S
REMINDER
RERENT S
RENTER
RERENTED
TENDERER
RERENTS
RENTERS
STERNER
REREPEAT S
REPARTEE
REPEATER
P **REREVIEW** S
REVIEWER
REREWARD S
REDRAWER
REWARDER
RERIG S
RERIGGED
DREGGIER
RERIGS
RERISE NS
SIRREE
RERISEN
RERISES
SERRIES
SIRREES
RERISING
REROLL S
ROLLER
REROLLED
REROLLER S
REROLLS
ROLLERS
REROOF S
ROOFER
REROOFED
REROOFS
ROOFERS
REROSE
REROUTE DS
REROUTED
REROUTES
RERUN S
RERUNS
NURSER
AIO **RES** HT
T ERS
SER
RESADDLE DS
RESAID
AIDERS
DEAIRS
IRADES
RAISED
REDIAS
RESAIL S
ARIELS
SAILER
SERAIL
SERIAL
RESAILED
REALISED
SIDEREAL
RESAILS
AIRLESS
SAILERS
SERAILS
SERIALS
P **RESALE** S
LAREES
LEASER
REALES
RESEAL
SEALER
P **RESALES**
EARLESS
LEASERS
RESEALS
SEALERS
RESALUTE DS
RESAMPLE DS
EMPALERS
RESAT
ASTER RATES
STARE TARES
TEARS
RESAW NS
SAWER SEWAR
SWARE SWEAR
WARES WEARS
RESAWED
DRAWEES
RESAWING
SWEARING
RESAWN
ANSWER
RESAWS
SAWERS
SEWARS
SWEARS
WRASSE
RESAY S
EYRAS SAYER
YEARS
RESAYING
SYNERGIA
RESAYS
SAYERS
RESCALE DS
CEREALS
RELACES
SCLERAE
RESCALED
DECLARES
RESCALES
CARELESS
P **RESCHOOL** S
P **RESCIND** S
CINDERS
DISCERN
P **RESCINDS**
DISCERNS
P **RESCORE** DS
P **RESCORED**
P **RESCORES**
P **RESCREEN** S
SCREENER
P **RESCRIPT** S
SCRIPTER
RESCUE DRS
CEREUS
CERUSE
RECUSE
SECURE
RESCUED
RECUSED
REDUCES
SECURED
SEDUCER
RESCUER S
SECURER
RESCUERS
SECURERS
RESCUES
CERUSES
RECUSES
SECURES
RESCUING
RECUSING
SECURING
RESCULPT S
RESEAL S
LAREES
LEASER
REALES
RESALE
SEALER
RESEALED
RELEASED
RESEALS
EARLESS
LEASERS
RESALES
SEALERS
RESEARCH
REACHERS
SEARCHER
P **RESEASON** S
SEASONER
RESEAT S
ARETES
EASTER
EATERS
SEATER
TEASER
RESEATED
RESEATS
EASTERS
SEAREST
SEATERS
TEASERS
TESSERA
RESEAU SX
UREASE
RESEAUS
UREASES
RESEAUX
RESECT S
CERTES
ERECTS
SECRET
TERCES
RESECTED
SECRETED
RESECTS
CRESSET
SECRETS
RESECURE DS
RESEDA S
ERASED
SEARED
RESEDAS
RESEE DKNS
RESEED S
SEEDER
RESEEDED
RESEEDS
SEEDERS
RESEEING
ENERGIES
ENERGISE
GREENIES
RESEEK S
SEEKER
RESEEKS
SEEKERS
RESEEN
SERENE
RESEES
RESEIZE DS
RESEIZED
RESEIZES
P **RESELECT** S
REELECTS
P **RESELL** S
SELLER
RESELLER S
P **RESELLS**
SELLERS
RESEMBLE DR S
RESEND S
DENSER
ENDERS
SENDER
RESENDS
REDNESS
SENDERS
P **RESENT** S
ENTERS
NESTER
RENEST
RENTES
TENSER
TERNES
TREENS
P **RESENTED**
RENESTED
P **RESENTS**
NESTERS
RENESTS
P **RESERVE** DRS
REVERES
REVERSE
SEVERER
P **RESERVED**
DESERVER
REVERSED
P **RESERVER** S
REVERERS
REVERSER
P **RESERVES**
REVERSES
P **RESET** S
ESTER REEST
STEER STERE
TERSE TREES
P **RESETS**
ESTERS
REESTS
SEREST
STEERS
STERES
RESETTER S
P **RESETTLE** DS
RESEW NS
EWERS SEWER
SWEER
RESEWED
SEWERED
WEEDERS
RESEWING
SEWERING
RESEWN
RENEWS
RESEWS
SEWERS
F **RESH**
HERS
P **RESHAPE** DRS
HEAPERS
P **RESHAPED**
EPHEDRAS
RESHAPER S
REPHRASE
P **RESHAPES**
RESHAVE DNS
HEAVERS
RESHAVED
RESHAVEN
RESHAVES
F **RESHES**
SHEERS
RESHINE DS
HENRIES
INHERES
RESHINED
RESHINES
P **RESHIP** S
PERISH
PISHER
P **RESHIPS**
PISHERS
RESHOD
HORDES
HORSED
SHORED
RESHOE DS
HEROES
RESHOED
RESHOES
RESHONE
RESHOOT S
HOOTERS
SHEROOT
SHOOTER
SOOTHER
RESHOOTS
ORTHOSES
SHEROOTS
SHOOTERS
SOOTHERS
RESHOT
HORSTE
OTHERS
THROES
P **RESHOW** NS
SHOWER
WHORES
P **RESHOWED**
SHOWERED
RESHOWER S
SHOWERER
P **RESHOWN**
P **RESHOWS**
SHOWERS
RESID ES
DRIES RIDES
SIRED
P **RESIDE** DRS
DESIRE
EIDERS
P **RESIDED**
DERIDES
DESIRED
P **RESIDENT** S
INSERTED
NERDIEST
SINTERED
TRENDIES
P **RESIDER** S
DERRIES
DESIRER
REDRIES
SERRIED
P **RESIDERS**
DERRISES
DESIRERS
DRESSIER
P **RESIDES**
DESIRES
P **RESIDING**
DESIRING
RINGSIDE
RESIDS

RESIDUA L
RESIDUAL S
RESIDUE S
UREIDES
RESIDUES
DIURESES
REISSUED
RESIDUUM S
P **RESIFT** S
FRITES
REFITS
RIFEST
SIFTER
STRIFE
P **RESIFTED**
P **RESIFTS**
SIFTERS
STRIFES
RESIGHT S
SIGHTER
RESIGHTS
SIGHTERS
RESIGN S
REIGNS
RENIGS
SERING
SIGNER
SINGER
RESIGNED
DESIGNER
ENERGIDS
REDESIGN
REEDINGS
RESIGNER S
RESIGNS
INGRESS
SIGNERS
SINGERS
RESILE DS
RELIES
RESILED
RESILES
IRELESS
RESILIN GS
INLIERS
RESILING
RIESLING
RESILINS
RESILVER S
REVILERS
SILVERER
SLIVERER
RESIN SY
REINS RINSE
RISEN SERIN
SIREN
RESINATE DS
ARENITES
ARSENITE
STEARINE
TRAINEES
RESINED
DENIERS
NEREIDS
RESINIFY
RESINING
RESINOID S
DERISION
IRONSIDE
RESINOUS
NEUROSIS
RESINS
RINSES
SERINS
SIRENS
RESINY
RESIST S
RESITS
SISTER
RESISTED
DIESTERS
EDITRESS
SISTERED
RESISTER S
TRESSIER
RESISTOR S
ROISTERS
SORRIEST
RESISTS
SISTERS
RESIT ES
RITES TIERS
TIRES TRIES

RESITE DS
RETIES
RESITED
DIESTER
DIETERS
REEDITS
RESITES
RESITING
IGNITERS
STINGIER
RESITS
RESIST
SISTER
RESIZE DS
SEIZER
RESIZED
RESIZES
SEIZERS
RESIZING
RESKETCH
SKETCHER
RESLATE DS
ELATERS
REALEST
RELATES
STEALER
RESLATED
DESALTER
TREADLES
RESLATES
STEALERS
TEARLESS
RESMELT S
MELTERS
REMELTS
SMELTER
RESMELTS
SMELTERS
TERMLESS
RESMOOTH S
SMOOTHER
P **RESOAK** S
ARKOSE
SOAKER
P **RESOAKED**
P **RESOAKS**
ARKOSES
SOAKERS
RESOD S
DOERS DOSER
REDOS RODES
ROSED SORED
RESODDED
RESODS
DOSERS
DOSSER
RESOFTEN S
SOFTENER
RESOJET S
RESOJETS
P **RESOLD**
DORSEL
SOLDER
RESOLDER S
SOLDERER
RESOLE DS
RESOLED
RESOLES
RESOLING
RESOLUTE RS
P **RESOLVE** DRS
P **RESOLVED**
RESOLVER S
P **RESOLVES**
RESONANT S
RESONATE DS
EARSTONE
RESORB S
BORERS
RESORBED
RESORBS
RESORCIN S
P **RESORT** S
RETROS
ROSTER
SORTER
STORER
P **RESORTED**
RESTORED
RESORTER S
RESTORER
RETRORSE

P **RESORTS**
ROSTERS
SORTERS
STORERS
RESOUGHT
ROUGHEST
RESOUND S
ENDUROS
SOUNDER
UNDOERS
RESOUNDS
DOURNESS
SOUNDERS
RESOURCE S
RECOURSE
RESOW NS
SEROW SOWER
SWORE WORSE
RESOWED
RESOWING
RESOWN
OWNERS
ROWENS
WORSEN
RESOWS
SEROWS
SOWERS
WORSES
RESPACE DS
ESCAPER
RESPACED
ESCARPED
RESPACES
ESCAPERS
RESPADE DS
SPEARED
RESPADED
RESPADES
ASPERSED
REPASSED
RESPEAK S
SPEAKER
RESPEAKS
SPEAKERS
RESPECT S
RECEPTS
SCEPTER
SCEPTRE
SPECTER
SPECTRE
RESPECTS
SCEPTERS
SCEPTRES
SPECTERS
SPECTRES
RESPELL S
PRESELL
SPELLER
RESPELLS
PRESELLS
SPELLERS
RESPELT
PELTERS
PETRELS
SPELTER
RESPIRE DS
PERRIES
PRISERE
REPRISE
RESPIRED
PREDRIES
PRESIDER
REPRISED
RESPIRES
PRISERES
REPRISES
RESPITE DS
PESTIER
RESPITED
PREEDITS
PRIESTED
RESPITES
RESPLICE DS
ECLIPSER
PRESLICE
P **RESPLIT** S
TRIPLES
RESPLITS
RESPOKE N
RESPOKEN
RESPOND S
PERNODS
PONDERS
RESPONDS

RESPONSA
PERSONAS
RESPONSE S
RESPOOL S
LOOPERS
POOLERS
SPOOLER
RESPOOLS
SPOOLERS
RESPOT S
POSTER
PRESTO
REPOTS
STOPER
TOPERS
TROPES
RESPOTS
POSTERS
PRESTOS
STOPERS
RESPRANG
RESPRAY S
PRAYERS
SPRAYER
RESPRAYS
SPRAYERS
RESPREAD S
SPREADER
RESPRING S
SPRINGER
RESPROUT S
POSTURER
TROUPERS
RESPRUNG
CDP **REST** S
W ERST RETS
TRES
RESTABLE DS
ARBELEST
BLEATERS
RETABLES
RESTACK S
RACKETS
RETACKS
STACKER
TACKERS
RESTACKS
STACKERS
RESTAFF S
STAFFER
RESTAFFS
STAFFERS
RESTAGE DS
ERGATES
RESTAGED
RESTAGES
P **RESTAMP** S
STAMPER
TAMPERS
P **RESTAMPS**
STAMPERS
RESTART S
RATTERS
STARTER
RESTARTS
STARTERS
RESTATE DS
ESTREAT
RETASTE
RESTATED
RETASTED
RESTATES
ESTREATS
RETASTES
CW **RESTED**
DESERT
DETERS
PW **RESTER** S
TERSER
PW **RESTERS**
RESTFUL
FLUSTER
FLUTERS
CW **RESTING**
STINGER
RESTITCH
CHITTERS
STITCHER
RESTIVE
SIEVERT
VERIEST
VERITES
C **RESTLESS**
TRESSELS

RESTOCK S
ROCKETS
STOCKER
RESTOCKS
STOCKERS
RESTOKE DS
RESTOKED
RESTOKES
RESTORAL S
REALTORS
RELATORS
P **RESTORE** DRS
P **RESTORED**
RESORTED
RESTORER S
RESORTER
RETRORSE
P **RESTORES**
RESTRAIN ST
RETRAINS
STRAINER
TERRAINS
TRAINERS
P **RESTRESS**
RESTRICT S
CRITTERS
STRICTER
P **RESTRIKE** S
RESTRING S
STRINGER
RESTRIVE NS
RIVETERS
RESTROOM S
RESTROVE
EVERTORS
RESTRUCK
TRUCKERS
RESTRUNG
GRUNTERS
CPW **RESTS**
TRESS
RESTUDY
RESTUFF S
STUFFER
TRUFFES
RESTUFFS
STUFFERS
RESTYLE DS
TERSELY
RESTYLED
RESTYLES
RESUBMIT S
IMBRUTES
TERBIUMS
RESULT S
LUSTER
LUSTRE
RUSTLE
SUTLER
ULSTER
RESULTED
DELUSTER
LUSTERED
RESULTS
LUSTERS
LUSTRES
RUSTLES
SUTLERS
ULSTERS
P **RESUME** DRS
P **RESUMED**
P **RESUMER** S
P **RESUMERS**
P **RESUMES**
P **RESUMING**
RESUMMON S
SUMMONER
RESUPINE
PENURIES
RESUPPLY
RESURGE DS
RESURGED
RESURGES
P **RESURVEY** S
FT **RET** ES
RETABLE S
BLEATER
RETABLES
ARBELEST
BLEATERS
RESTABLE

RETACK S
RACKET
TACKER
RETACKED
RACKETED
RETACKLE DS
RETACKS
RACKETS
RESTACK
STACKER
TACKERS
RETAG S
GATER GRATE
GREAT TARGE
TERGA
RETAGGED
RETAGS
GASTER
GATERS
GRATES
GREATS
STAGER
TARGES
RETAIL S
RETIAL
TAILER
RETAILED
DETAILER
ELATERID
RETAILER S
RETAILOR S
RETAILS
REALIST
SALTIER
SALTIRE
SLATIER
TAILERS
RETAIN S
RATINE
RETINA
RETAINED
DETAINER
RETAINER S
RETAINS
ANESTRI
ANTSIER
NASTIER
RATINES
RETINAS
RETSINA
STAINER
STEARIN
RETAKE NRS
RETAKEN
RETAKER S
RETAKERS
STREAKER
RETAKES
RETAKING
RETALLY
ALERTLY
P **RETAPE** DS
REPEAT
P **RETAPED**
ADEPTER
PREDATE
TAPERED
P **RETAPES**
REPEATS
P **RETAPING**
TAPERING
RETARD S
DARTER
TARRED
TRADER
RETARDED
RETARDER S
RETARDS
DARTERS
STARRED
TRADERS
RETARGET S
P **RETASTE** DS
ESTREAT
RESTATE
P **RETASTED**
RESTATED
P **RETASTES**
ESTREATS
RESTATES
RETAUGHT
P **RETAX**
EXTRA TAXER

RETAXED
RETAXES
RETAXING
W **RETCH**
CHERT
W **RETCHED**
W **RETCHES**
ETCHERS
RETCHING
A **RETE** M
TREE
RETEACH
CHEATER
HECTARE
RECHEAT
TEACHER
RETEAM S
REMATE
RETEAMED
RETEAMS
REMATES
STEAMER
RETEAR S
TEARER
TERRAE
RETEARS
SERRATE
TEARERS
P **RETELL** S
TELLER
P **RETELLS**
TELLERS
RETEM S
METER METRE
REMET
RETEMPER S
TEMPERER
RETEMS
MEREST
METERS
METRES
RETENE S
ENTREE
ETERNE
TEENER
RETENES
ENTREES
TEENERS
P **RETEST** S
SETTER
STREET
TESTER
P **RETESTED**
DETESTER
P **RETESTS**
SETTERS
STREETS
TERSEST
TESTERS
RETHINK S
THINKER
RETHINKS
THINKERS
RETHREAD S
THREADER
RETIA L
IRATE TERAI
RETIAL
RETAIL
TAILER
RETIARII
RETIARY
RETICENT
RETICLE S
TIERCEL
RETICLES
SCLERITE
TIERCELS
TRISCELE
RETICULA R
RETICULE S
RETIE DS
RETIED
DIETER
REEDIT
TIERED
RETIEING
REIGNITE
RETIES
RESITE
RETIFORM
RETILE DS
RETILED

RETILES
LEISTER
STERILE
RETILING
GLINTIER
TINGLIER
RETIME DS
METIER
REEMIT
RETIMED
DEMERIT
DIMETER
MERITED
MITERED
RETIMES
MEISTER
METIERS
REEMITS
TRISEME
RETIMING
MERITING
MITERING
RETINA ELS
RATINE
RETAIN
RETINAE
ARENITE
TRAINEE
RETINAL S
LATRINE
RATLINE
RELIANT
TRENAIL
RETINALS
ENTRAILS
LATRINES
RATLINES
TRENAILS
RETINAS
ANESTRI
ANTSIER
NASTIER
RATINES
RETAINS
RETSINA
STAINER
STEARIN
RETINE S
ENTIRE
TRIENE
RETINENE S
INTERNEE
RETINES
ENTIRES
ENTRIES
TRIENES
RETINITE S
INTERTIE
C **RETINOID** S
RETINOL S
RETINOLS
RETINT S
TINTER
RETINTED
RETINTS
STINTER
TINTERS
RETINUE DS
REUNITE
UTERINE
RETINUED
REUNITED
RETINUES
ESURIENT
REUNITES
RETINULA ER
AUNTLIER S
TENURIAL
RETIRANT S
RETIRE DERS
RETIRED
RETRIED
TIREDER
RETIREE S
RETIREES
RETIRER S
TERRIER
RETIRERS
TERRIERS
RETIRES
RETRIES
TERRIES
RETIRING
RETITLE DS

RETITLED
LITTERED
RETITLES
P **RETOLD**
RETOOK
RETOOL S
LOOTER
ROOTLE
TOOLER
RETOOLED
RETOOLS
LOOTERS
ROOTLES
TOOLERS
RETORE
RETORN
RETORT S
ROTTER
RETORTED
RETORTER S
RETORTS
ROTTERS
STERTOR
RETOTAL S
RETOTALS
RETOUCH
COUTHER
TOUCHER
RETRACE DRS
CATERER
RECRATE
TERRACE
RETRACED
CRATERED
RECRATED
TERRACED
RETRACER S
RETRACES
CATERERS
RECRATES
TERRACES
RETRACK S
TRACKER
RETRACKS
TRACKERS
RETRACT S
RETRACTS
P **RETRAIN** S
TERRAIN
TRAINER
P **RETRAINS**
RESTRAIN
STRAINER
TERRAINS
TRAINERS
RETRAL
RETRALLY
RETREAD S
TREADER
RETREADS
ARRESTED
SERRATED
TREADERS
P **RETREAT** S
TREATER
P **RETREATS**
TREATERS
RETRENCH
TRENCHER
P **RETRIAL** S
TRAILER
P **RETRIALS**
TRAILERS
RETRIED
RETIRED
TIREDER
RETRIES
RETIRES
TERRIES
RETRIEVE DRS
P **RETRIM** S
TRIMER
P **RETRIMS**
TRIMERS
RETRO S
RETROACT S
RETROFIT S
RETRONYM S
RETRORSE
RESORTER
RESTORER

RETROS
RESORT
ROSTER
SORTER
STORER
RETRY
TERRY
RETRYING
FT **RETS**
ERST REST
TRES
RETSINA S
ANESTRI
ANTSIER
NASTIER
RATINES
RETAINS
RETINAS
STAINER
STEARIN
RETSINAS
ARTINESS
STAINERS
STEARINS
F **RETTED**
F **RETTING**
GITTERN
RETUNE DS
NEUTER
TENURE
TUREEN
RETUNED
DENTURE
TENURED
RETUNES
NEUTERS
TENURES
TUREENS
RETUNING
TENURING
RETURN S
TURNER
RETURNED
RETURNEE S
RETURNER S
RETURNS
TURNERS
RETUSE
RETWIST S
TWISTER
RETWISTS
TWISTERS
RETYING
P **RETYPE** DS
P **RETYPED**
P **RETYPES**
P **RETYPING**
REUNIFY
P **REUNION** S
P **REUNIONS**
P **REUNITE** DRS
RETINUE
UTERINE
P **REUNITED**
RETINUED
REUNITER S
UNRETIRE
P **REUNITES**
ESURIENT
RETINUES
REUPTAKE S
REUSABLE S
REUSE DS
REUSED
REUSES
REUSING
REUTTER S
UTTERER
REUTTERS
UTTERERS
REV S
P **REVALUE** DS
P **REVALUED**
P **REVALUES**
REVAMP S
VAMPER
REVAMPED
REVAMPER S
REVAMPS
VAMPERS
REVANCHE S

REVEAL S
LAVEER
LEAVER
VEALER
REVEALED
LAVEERED
REVEALER S
REVEALS
LAVEERS
LEAVERS
SEVERAL
VEALERS
REVEHENT
REVEILLE S
REVEL S
ELVER LEVER
REVELED
LEVERED
REVELER S
REVELERS
REVELING
LEVERING
REVELLED
REVELLER S
REVELRY
REVELS
ELVERS
LEVERS
REVENANT S
REVENGE DRS
REVENGED
REVENGER S
REVENGES
REVENUAL
REVENUE DRS
UNREEVE
REVENUED
UNREEVED
REVENUER S
REVENUES
UNREEVES
P **REVERB** S
REVERBED
P **REVERBS**
REVERE DRS
REVERED
REVEREND S
REVERENT
REVERER S
REVERERS
RESERVER
REVERSER
REVERES
RESERVE
REVERSE
SEVERER
REVERIE S
REVERIES
REVERIFY
REVERING
REVERS EO
SERVER
VERSER
REVERSAL S
RAVELERS
SLAVERER
REVERSE DRS
RESERVE
REVERES
SEVERER
REVERSED
DESERVER
RESERVED
REVERSER S
RESERVER
REVERERS
REVERSES
RESERVES
REVERSO S
REVERSOS
REVERT S
REVERTED
REVERTER S
REVERTS
REVERY
REVEST S
EVERTS
REVETS
VERSET
VERSTE
REVESTED

REVESTS
VERSETS
VERSTES
BT **REVET** S
EVERT
BT **REVETS**
EVERTS
REVEST
VERSET
VERSTE
B **REVETTED**
P **REVIEW** S
VIEWER
REVIEWAL S
P **REVIEWED**
P **REVIEWER** S
REREVIEW
P **REVIEWS**
VIEWERS
REVILE DRS
EVILER
LEVIER
LIEVER
RELIVE
VEILER
REVILED
DELIVER
LIVERED
RELIVED
REVILER S
REVILERS
RESILVER
SILVERER
SLIVERER
REVILES
LEVIERS
RELIVES
SERVILE
VEILERS
REVILING
LIVERING
RELIVING
REVISAL S
REVISALS
P **REVISE** DRS
REIVES
P **REVISED**
DERIVES
DEVISER
DIVERSE
REVISER S
REIVERS
RIEVERS
REVISERS
P **REVISES**
P **REVISING**
P **REVISION** S
P **REVISIT** S
VISITER
P **REVISITS**
VISITERS
P **REVISOR** SY
P **REVISORS**
REVISORY
REVIVAL S
REVIVALS
REVIVE DRS
REVIVED
REVIVER S
REVIVERS
REVIVES
REVIVIFY
REVIVING
REVOICE DS
REVOICED
CODERIVE
DIVORCEE
REVOICES
REVOKE DRS
EVOKER
REVOKED
REVOKER S
REVOKERS
REVOKES
EVOKERS
REVOKING
REVOLT S
REVOLTED
REVOLTER S
REVOLTS

REVOLUTE
TRUELOVE
REVOLVE DRS
EVOLVER
REVOLVED
REVOLVER S
REVOLVES
EVOLVERS
REVOTE DS
VETOER
REVOTED
REVOTES
OVERSET
VETOERS
REVOTING
REVS
P **REVUE** S
P **REVUES**
REVUIST S
STUIVER
VIRTUES
REVUISTS
STUIVERS
REVULSED
REVVED
REVVING
REWAKE DNS
WEAKER
REWAKED
WREAKED
REWAKEN S
WAKENER
REWAKENS
WAKENERS
REWAKES
REWAKING
WREAKING
REWAN
REWARD S
DRAWER
REDRAW
WARDER
WARRED
REWARDED
REWARDER S
REDRAWER
REREWARD
REWARDS
DRAWERS
REDRAWS
WARDERS
P **REWARM** S
WARMER
P **REWARMED**
P **REWARMS**
SWARMER
WARMERS
P **REWASH**
HAWSER
WASHER
P **REWASHED**
P **REWASHES**
REWAX
WAXER
REWAXED
REWAXES
REWAXING
REWEAR S
WEARER
REWEARS
SWEARER
WEARERS
REWEAVE DS
REWEAVED
REWEAVES
BC **REWED** S
REWEDDED
REWEDS
P **REWEIGH** S
WEIGHER
P **REWEIGHS**
WEIGHERS
REWELD S
LEWDER
WELDER
REWELDED
REWELDS
WELDERS
REWET S
REWETS
WESTER
REWETTED

REWIDEN S
WIDENER
REWIDENS
WIDENERS
REWIN DS
REWIND S
WINDER
REWINDED
REWINDER S
REWINDS
WINDERS
REWINS
P **REWIRE** DS
P **REWIRED**
WEIRDER
P **REWIRES**
P **REWIRING**
REWOKE N
REWOKEN
REWON
OWNER ROWEN
REWORD S
REWORDED
REWORDS
REWORE
P **REWORK** S
WORKER
P **REWORKED**
P **REWORKS**
WORKERS
P **REWORN**
REWOUND
REWOVE N
REWOVEN
OVERNEW
P **REWRAP** ST
PREWAR
WARPER
P **REWRAPS**
WARPERS
REWRAPT
REWRITE RS
REWRITER S
REWRITES
REWROTE
P **REX**
P **REXES**
REXINE S
REXINES
REYNARD S
REYNARDS
REZERO S
REZEROED
REZEROES
REZEROS
REZONE DS
REZONED
REZONES
REZONING
RHABDOM ES
RHABDOME S
RHABDOMS
RHACHIS
RHAMNOSE S
HORSEMAN
MENORAHS
RHAMNUS
RHAPHAE
RHAPHE S
RHAPHES
RHAPSODE S
RHAPSODY
RHATANY
RHEA S
HARE HEAR
RHEAS
HARES HEARS
SHARE SHEAR
RHEBOK S
RHEBOKS
RHEMATIC
RHEME S
REHEM
RHEMES
REHEMS
RHENIUM S
INHUMER
RHENIUMS
INHUMERS

RHEOBASE S
RHEOLOGY
RHEOPHIL E
RHEOSTAT S
RHESUS
RHUSES
RUSHES
USHERS
RHESUSES
RHETOR S
RHETORIC S
TORCHIER
RHETORS
SHORTER
RHEUM SY
RHEUMIC
RHEUMIER
RHEUMS
MUSHER
RHEUMY
RHINAL
RHINITIS
RHINO S
RHINOS
RHIZOBIA L
RHIZOID S
RHIZOIDS
RHIZOMA
RHIZOME S
RHIZOMES
RHIZOMIC
RHIZOPI
RHIZOPOD S
RHIZOPUS
RHO S
RHODAMIN ES
RHODIC
ORCHID
RHODIUM S
HUMIDOR
RHODIUMS
HUMIDORS
RHODORA S
RHODORAS
RHOMB IS
RHOMBI C
RHOMBIC
RHOMBOID S
RHOMBS
RHOMBUS
RHONCHAL
RHONCHI
RHONCHUS
RHOS
RHOTIC
THORIC
RHUBARB S
RHUBARBS
RHUMB AS
RHUMBA S
RHUMBAED
RHUMBAS
SAMBHUR
RHUMBS
RHUS
RUSH
RHUSES
RHESUS
RUSHES
USHERS
RHYME DRS
RHYMED
RHYMER S
RHYMERS
RHYMES
RHYMING
RHYOLITE S
RHYTA
RHYTHM S
RHYTHMIC S
RHYTHMS
RHYTON S
THORNY
RHYTONS
A **RIA** LS
AIR
RAI

TU **RIAL** S
ARIL LAIR
LARI LIAR
LIRA RAIL
TU **RIALS**
ARILS LAIRS
LARIS LIARS
LIRAS RAILS
RIALTO S
TAILOR
RIALTOS
ORALIST
TAILORS
RIANT
TRAIN
RIANTLY
A **RIAS**
AIRS RAIS
SARI
RIATA S
ATRIA RAITA
TIARA
RIATAS
ARISTA
RAITAS
TARSIA
TIARAS
CD **RIB** S
RIBALD S
BRIDAL
RIBALDLY
BRIDALLY
RIBALDRY
RIBALDS
BRIDALS
RIBAND S
RIBANDS
RIBBAND S
RIBBANDS
CD **RIBBED**
BRIBED
DIBBER
C **RIBBER** S
BRIBER
C **RIBBERS**
BRIBERS
RIBBIER
RIBBIEST
CD **RIBBING** S
BRIBING
C **RIBBINGS**
RIBBON SY
ROBBIN
RIBBONED
RIBBONS
ROBBINS
RIBBONY
RIBBY
BT **RIBES**
BIERS BIRSE
BRIES
RIBGRASS
RIBIER S
RIBIERS
RIBLESS
D **RIBLET** S
D **RIBLETS**
BLISTER
BRISTLE
RIBLIKE
RIBOSE S
RIBOSES
BOSSIER
RIBOSOME S
RIBOZYME S
CD **RIBS**
BRIS
RIBWORT S
RIBWORTS
PT **RICE** DRS
CIRE
RICEBIRD S
PT **RICED**
CIDER CRIED
DICER
P **RICER** S
CRIER
RICERCAR EI S
P **RICERS**
CRIERS

PT **RICES**
CIRES CRIES
RICH
RICHEN S
ENRICH
INCHER
RICHENED
ENRICHED
RICHENS
INCHERS
RICHER
CHIRRE
RICHES T
RICHEST
CITHERS
RICHLY
RICHNESS
RICHWEED S
RICIN GS
PT **RICING**
RICINS
RICINUS
BCP **RICK** S TW
BCP **RICKED** TW
DICKER
CP **RICKETS**
STICKER
TICKERS
RICKETY
C **RICKEY** S
CRIKEY
RICKEYS
BCP **RICKING** TW
RICKRACK S
BCP **RICKS** TW
RICKSHA SW
RICKSHAS
RICKSHAW S
RICOCHET S
RICOTTA S
CITATOR
RICOTTAS
CITATORS
RICRAC S
RICRACS
RICTAL
CITRAL
RICTUS
CITRUS
RUSTIC
RICTUSES
CITRUSES
CURTSIES
AGI **RID** ES
RIDABLE
BEDRAIL
BRAILED
RIDDANCE S
CANDIDER
G **RIDDED**
RIDDEN
RINDED
G **RIDDER** S
G **RIDDERS**
RIDDING
G **RIDDLE** DRS
DIRLED
DREIDL
G **RIDDLED**
DIDDLER
RIDDLER S
RIDDLERS
G **RIDDLES**
DREIDLS
G **RIDDLING**
BGP **RIDE** RS
DIRE IRED
RIDEABLE
T **RIDENT**
TINDER
TRINED
A **RIDER** S
DIRER DRIER
RIDERS
DERRIS
DRIERS
BGI **RIDES** P
DRIES RESID
SIRED

BF **RIDGE** DLS
DIRGE GRIDE
B **RIDGED**
GIRDED
GRIDED
RIDGEL S
GILDER
GIRDLE
GLIDER
REGILD
RIDGELS
GILDERS
GIRDLES
GLIDERS
REGILDS
BF **RIDGES**
DIRGES
GRIDES
RIDGETOP S
RIDGIER
RIDGIEST
RIDGIL S
RIDGILS
B **RIDGING**
GIRDING
GRIDING
RIDGLING S
GIRDLING
RIDGY
RIDICULE DR S
GP **RIDING** S
RIDINGS
RIDLEY S
DIRELY
RIDLEYS
RIDOTTO S
RIDOTTOS
GI **RIDS**
AO **RIEL** S
LIER LIRE
RILE
AO **RIELS**
LIERS RILES
SLIER
RIESLING S
RESILING
G **RIEVER** S
REIVER
VERIER
G **RIEVERS**
REIVERS
REVISER
RIF EFST
FIR
RIFAMPIN S
RIFE R
FIRE REIF
RIFELY
RIFENESS
RIFER
FIRER FRIER
RIFEST
FRITES
REFITS
RESIFT
SIFTER
STRIFE
G **RIFF** S
RIFFED
DIFFER
RIFFING
GRIFFIN
RIFFLE DRS
RIFFLED
RIFFLER S
RIFFLERS
RIFFLES
RIFFLING
RIFFRAFF S
G **RIFFS**
T **RIFLE** DRS
FILER FLIER LIFER
T **RIFLED**
RIFLEMAN
INFLAMER
RIFLEMEN
T **RIFLER** SY
T **RIFLERS**
RIFLERY

T **RIFLES**
FILERS
FLIERS
LIFERS
T **RIFLING** S
T **RIFLINGS**
RIFLIP S
RIFLIPS
RIFS
FIRS
DG **RIFT** S
FRIT
DG **RIFTED**
DG **RIFTING**
RIFTLESS
STIFLERS
DG **RIFTS**
FIRST FRITS
BFG **RIG** S PT
RIGADOON S
RIGATONI S
RIGAUDON S
FPT **RIGGED**
DIGGER
T **RIGGER** S
T **RIGGERS**
FPT **RIGGING** S
RIGGINGS
ABF **RIGHT** OSY W
GIRTH GRITH
F **RIGHTED**
GIRTHED
B **RIGHTER** S
RIGHTERS
B **RIGHTEST**
F **RIGHTFUL**
RIGHTIES
TIGERISH
F **RIGHTING**
GIRTHING
RIGHTISM S
RIGHTIST S
B **RIGHTLY**
RIGHTO
BFW **RIGHTS**
GIRTHS
GRITHS
RIGHTY
F **RIGID**
RIGIDIFY
F **RIGIDITY**
F **RIGIDLY**
RIGOR S
RIGORISM S
RIGORIST S
RIGOROUS
RIGORS
RIGOUR S
RIGOURS
BFG **RIGS** PT
RIKISHA S
SHIKARI
RIKISHAS
SHIKARIS
RIKSHAW S
RIKSHAWS
RILE DSY
LIER LIRE
RIEL
A **RILED**
IDLER
RILES
LIERS RIELS
SLIER
RILEY
RILIEVI
RILIEVO
RILING
BDF **RILL** ES GKP T
G **RILLE** DST
ILLER
DFG **RILLED** PT
G **RILLES**
SILLER

RILLET S
TILLER
RILLETS
STILLER
TILLERS
TRELLIS
DFG **RILLING** PT
BDF **RILLS** GKP T
BGP **RIM** ESY T
MIR
CGP **RIME** DRS
EMIR MIRE
GP **RIMED**
DIMER MIRED
PT **RIMER** S
PT **RIMERS**
CGP **RIMES**
EMIRS MIRES
MISER
T **RIMESTER** S
MERRIEST
MITERERS
TRIREMES
RIMFIRE S
RIMFIRES
G **RIMIER**
MIRIER
G **RIMIEST**
MIRIEST
MISTIER
G **RIMINESS**
MIRINESS
GP **RIMING**
MIRING
RIMLAND S
MANDRIL
RIMLANDS
MANDRILS
B **RIMLESS**
SMILERS
BPT **RIMMED**
DIMMER
BCG **RIMMER** S KPT
BCK **RIMMERS** T
BPT **RIMMING**
RIMOSE
ISOMER
MOIRES
RIMOSELY
RIMOSITY
RIMOUS
C **RIMPLE** DS
LIMPER
PRELIM
C **RIMPLED**
C **RIMPLES**
LIMPERS
PRELIMS
SIMPLER
C **RIMPLING**
RIMROCK S
RIMROCKS
BPT **RIMS**
MIRS
RIMSHOT S
RIMSHOTS
G **RIMY**
MIRY
BG **RIN** DGKS
G **RIND** SY
BG **RINDED**
RIDDEN
RINDLESS
G **RINDS**
RINDY
BIW **RING** S
GIRN GRIN
RINGBARK S
RINGBOLT S
RINGBONE S
ENROBING
RINGDOVE S
CFW **RINGED**
DINGER
ENGIRD
GIRNED
REDING

RINGENT
RENTING
BCW **RINGER** S
ERRING
BCW **RINGERS**
RINGGIT S
GIRTING
RINGGITS
RINGHALS
BCF **RINGING** W
GIRNING
RINGLET S
TINGLER
RINGLETS
STERLING
TINGLERS
RINGLIKE
KINGLIER
RINGNECK S
BW **RINGS**
GIRNS GRINS
RINGSIDE S
DESIRING
RESIDING
RINGTAIL S
TRAILING
RINGTAW S
RINGTAWS
STRAWING
RINGTOSS
RINGWORM S
BDP **RINK** S
KIRN
BDP **RINKS**
KIRNS
G **RINNING**
BG **RINS** E
RINSABLE
RINSE DRS
REINS RESIN
RISEN SERIN
SIREN
RINSED
DINERS
SNIDER
RINSER S
RINSERS
RINSES
RESINS
SERINS
SIRENS
RINSIBLE
RINSING S
RINSINGS
RIOJA S
RIOJAS
G **RIOT** S
ROTI TIRO
TORI TRIO
RIOTED
DOTIER
EDITOR
TRIODE
RIOTER S
RIOTERS
ROISTER
RIOTING
IGNITOR
RIOTOUS
G **RIOTS**
ROTIS TIROS
TORSI TRIOS
TROIS
DGT **RIP** ES
RIPARIAN
RIPCORD S
RIPCORDS
CGT **RIPE** DNRS
PERI PIER
G **RIPED**
PRIDE PRIED
REDIP
RIPELY
RIPEN S
REPIN
RIPENED
REPINED
RIPENER S
REPINER
RIPENERS
PRERINSE
REPINERS

RIPENESS
EREPSINS
RIPENING
REPINING
RIPENS
REPINS
SNIPER
G **RIPER**
PRIER
CGT **RIPES** T
PERIS PIERS
PRIES PRISE
SPEIR SPIER
SPIRE
RIPEST
ESPRIT
PRIEST
SPRITE
STRIPE
TRIPES
RIPIENI
RIPIENO S
RIPIENOS
G **RIPING**
RIPOFF S
RIPOFFS
RIPOST ES
PROSIT
TRIPOS
RIPOSTE DS
PROSTIE
REPOSIT
ROPIEST
RIPOSTED
DIOPTERS
DIOPTRES
PERIDOTS
PORTSIDE
PROTEIDS
TOPSIDER
RIPOSTES
PROSIEST
PROSTIES
REPOSITS
TRIPOSES
RIPOSTS
RIPPABLE
DGT **RIPPED**
DIPPER
DGT **RIPPER** S
DGT **RIPPERS**
DGT **RIPPING**
CG **RIPPLE** DRST
LIPPER
C **RIPPLED**
C **RIPPLER** S
C **RIPPLERS**
C **RIPPLES**
LIPPERS
SLIPPER
RIPPLET S
TIPPLER
RIPPLETS
PRESPLIT
STIPPLER
TIPPLERS
RIPPLIER
C **RIPPLING**
RIPPLY
RIPRAP S
RIPRAPS
DGT **RIPS**
RIPSAW NS
RIPSAWED
RIPSAWN
INWRAPS
RIPSAWS
RIPSTOP S
RIPSTOPS
RIPTIDE S
TIDERIP
RIPTIDES
SPIRITED
TIDERIPS
AFP **RISE** NRS
IRES REIS
SIRE
A **RISEN**
REINS RESIN
RINSE SERIN
SIREN

RISER S
RISERS
ABC **RISES**
FIK SIRES
P
RISHI S
RISHIS
RISIBLE S
RISIBLES
RISIBLY
AIP **RISING** S
SIRING
RISINGS
BF **RISK** SY
IRKS KIRS
KRIS
BF **RISKED**
DIKERS
BF **RISKER** S
F **RISKERS**
F **RISKIER**
F **RISKIEST**
F **RISKILY**
BF **RISKING**
GRISKIN
RISKLESS
BF **RISKS**
F **RISKY**
RISOTTO S
RISOTTOS
RISQUE
QUIRES
SQUIRE
RISSOLE S
LORISES
RISSOLES
RISTRA S
RISTRAS
RISUS
RISUSES
ISSUERS
RITARD S
RITARDS
TW **RITE** S
TIER TIRE
FW **RITES**
RESIT TIERS
TIRES TRIES
CFG **RITTER** S
TERRIT
TRITER
CFG **RITTERS**
TERRITS
RITUAL S
RITUALLY
RITUALS
F **RITZ** Y
F **RITZES**
RITZIER
RITZIEST
RITZILY
RITZY
RIVAGE S
RIVAGES
GRAVIES
RIVAL S
VIRAL
RIVALED
RIVALING
VIRGINAL
RIVALLED
RIVALRY
RIVALS
D **RIVE** DNRST
VIER
RIVED
DIVER DRIVE
D **RIVEN**
D **RIVER** S
RIVERBED S
RIVERINE
D **RIVERS**
D **RIVES**
SIVER VIERS
VIRES
GPT **RIVET** S
RIVETED
RIVETER S

RIVETERS
RESTRIVE
RIVETING
GPT **RIVETS**
STIVER
STRIVE
VERIST
RIVETTED
RIVIERA S
RIVIERAS
RIVIERE S
RIVIERES
D **RIVING**
VIRGIN
RIVULET S
RIVULETS
RIVULOSE
RIYAL S
RIYALS
B **ROACH**
ORACH
B **ROACHED**
B **ROACHES**
CHOREAS
ORACHES
B **ROACHING**
B **ROAD** S
ORAD
ROADBED S
BOARDED
ROADBEDS
ADSORBED
ROADEO S
ROADEOS
ROADIE S
ROADIES
ROADKILL S
ROADLESS
B **ROADS**
DORSA SAROD
ROADSHOW S
B **ROADSIDE** S
ROADSTER S
ROADWAY S
ROADWAYS
ROADWORK S
ROAM S
MORA
ROAMED
RADOME
ROAMER S
REMORA
ROAMERS
REMORAS
ROAMING
ROAMS
MORAS
G **ROAN** S
G **ROANS**
ARSON SONAR
ROAR S
ORRA
ROARED
ADORER
ROARER S
ROARERS
ROARING S
ROARINGS
GARRISON
ROARS
ROAST S
RATOS ROTAS
SORTA TAROS
TORAS
ROASTED
TORSADE
ROASTER S
ROASTERS
ASSERTOR
ASSORTER
ORATRESS
REASSORT
ROASTING
ORGANIST
ROASTS
ASSORT
ROB ES
BRO
ORB
ROBALO S
ROBALOS

P **ROBAND** S
P **ROBANDS**
ROBBED
DOBBER
ROBBER SY
ROBBERS
ROBBERY
ROBBIN GS
RIBBON
ROBBING
ROBBINS
RIBBONS
P **ROBE** DS
BORE
P **ROBED**
BORED ORBED
P **ROBES**
BORES BROSE
SOBER
ROBIN GS
P **ROBING**
BORING
ORBING
ROBINS
ROBLE S
ROBLES
ROBORANT S
ROBOT S
ROBOTIC S
ROBOTICS
ROBOTISM S
ROBOTIZE DS
ROBOTRY
ROBOTS
ROBS
BROS ORBS
SORB
ROBUST A
TURBOS
ROBUSTA S
ABORTUS
RUBATOS
TABOURS
ROBUSTAS
ROBUSTER
ROBUSTLY
C **ROC** KS
COR
ORC
ROCAILLE S
C **ROCHET** S
HECTOR
ROTCHE
TOCHER
TROCHE
C **ROCHETS**
HECTORS
ROTCHES
TOCHERS
TORCHES
TROCHES
BCF **ROCK** SY
T CORK
ROCKABLE
ROCKABY E
ROCKABYE S
ROCKAWAY S
CFT **ROCKED**
CORKED
DOCKER
REDOCK
ROCKER SY
CORKER
RECORK
ROCKERS
CORKERS
RECORKS
C **ROCKERY**
BC **ROCKET** S
C **ROCKETED**
ROCKETER S
ROCKETRY
BC **ROCKETS**
RESTOCK
STOCKER
ROCKFALL S
ROCKFISH
ROCKIER
CORKIER

ROCKIEST
CORKIEST
STOCKIER
CFT **ROCKING**
CORKING
F **ROCKLESS**
ROCKLIKE
CORKLIKE
ROCKLING S
ROCKOON S
ROCKOONS
ROCKROSE S
BCF **ROCKS**
T CORKS
ROCKWEED S
ROCKWORK S
ROCKY
CORKY
ROCOCO S
ROCOCOS
C **ROCS**
CORS ORCS
PT **ROD** ES
DOR
P **RODDED**
DODDER
P **RODDING**
ET **RODE** OS
DOER DORE
REDO
E **RODENT** S
RODENTS
SNORTED
RODEO S
RODEOED
RODEOING
RODEOS
ROOSED
E **RODES**
DOERS DOSER
REDOS RESOD
ROSED SORED
RODLESS
DORSELS
SOLDERS
RODLIKE
RODMAN
RANDOM
RODMEN
MODERN
NORMED
P **RODS**
DORS SORD
RODSMAN
RANDOMS
RODSMEN
MODERNS
F **ROE** S
ORE
ROEBUCK S
ROEBUCKS
ROENTGEN S
F **ROES**
EROS ORES
ROSE SORE
ROGATION S
ROGATORY
ROGER S
ROGERED
ROGERING
GORGERIN
ROGERS
BD **ROGUE** DS
ERUGO ROUGE
ROGUED
DROGUE
GOURDE
ROUGED
ROGUEING
B **ROGUERY**
BD **ROGUES**
ERUGOS
GROUSE
ROUGES
RUGOSE
ROGUING
ROUGING
B **ROGUISH**
B **ROIL** SY
B **ROILED**
ROILIER
ROILIEST

B **ROILING**
LIGROIN
B **ROILS**
LORIS
ROILY
ROISTER S
RIOTERS
ROISTERS
RESISTOR
SORRIEST
ROLAMITE S
AMITROLE
P **ROLE** S
LORE ORLE
P **ROLES**
LORES LOSER
ORLES SOREL
ROLF S
ROLFED
FOLDER
REFOLD
ROLFER S
ROLFERS
ROLFING
ROLFS
DT **ROLL** S
ROLLAWAY S
ROLLBACK S
DT **ROLLED**
DT **ROLLER** S
REROLL
T **ROLLERS**
REROLLS
ROLLICK SY
ROLLICKS
ROLLICKY
DT **ROLLING** S
T **ROLLINGS**
ROLLMOP S
ROLLMOPS
ROLLOUT S
OUTROLL
ROLLOUTS
OUTROLLS
ROLLOVER S
DT **ROLLS**
ROLLTOP
TROLLOP
ROLLWAY S
ROLLWAYS
FP **ROM** PS
MOR
ROMAINE S
MORAINE
ROMAINES
MORAINES
ROMANISE
ROMAJI S
ROMAJIS
ROMAN OS
MANOR
ROMANCE DRS
ROMANCED
ROMANCER S
ROMANCES
ROMANISE DS
MORAINES
ROMAINES
ROMANIZE DS
ROMANO S
MAROON
ROMANOS
MAROONS
ROMANS
MANORS
RAMSON
RANSOM
ROMANTIC S
ROMAUNT S
ROMAUNTS
ROMEO S
ROMEOS
MOROSE
T **ROMP** S
PROM
T **ROMPED**
ROMPER S
ROMPERS
T **ROMPING**
ROMPISH
ORPHISM

T **ROMPS**
PROMS
P **ROMS**
MORS
RONDEAU X
RONDEAUX
RONDEL S
RONDELET S
REDOLENT
RONDELLE S
ENROLLED
RONDELS
RONDO S
DONOR
RONDOS
DONORS
RONDURE S
ROUNDER
RONDURES
ROUNDERS
RONION S
RONIONS
RONNEL S
RONNELS
RONTGEN S
RONTGENS
RONYON S
RONYONS
B **ROOD** S
DOOR ODOR
ORDO
B **ROODS**
DOORS ODORS
ORDOS
P **ROOF** S
P **ROOFED**
FOREDO
P **ROOFER** S
REROOF
P **ROOFERS**
REROOFS
ROOFIE S
ROOFIES
P **ROOFING** S
ROOFINGS
ROOFLESS
ROOFLIKE
ROOFLINE S
P **ROOFS**
ROOFTOP S
ROOFTOPS
ROOFTREE S
BC **ROOK** SY
BC **ROOKED**
C **ROOKERY**
B **ROOKIE** RS
ROOKIER
B **ROOKIES** T
ROOKIEST
BC **ROOKING**
BC **ROOKS**
ROOKY
BGV **ROOM** SY
MOOR
BGV **ROOMED**
MOORED
G **ROOMER** S
G **ROOMERS**
ROOMETTE S
ROOMFUL S
ROOMFULS
ROOMIE RS
B **ROOMIER**
MOORIER
ROOMIES T
B **ROOMIEST**
MOORIEST
MOTORISE
ROOMILY
BGV **ROOMING**
MOORING
ROOMMATE S
BGV **ROOMS**
MOORS
B **ROOMY**
MOORY
ROORBACH S
ROORBACK S
ROOSE DRS

ROOSED
RODEOS
ROOSER S
ROOSERS
ROOSES
ROOSING
ROOST S
ROOTS ROTOS
TOROS TORSO
ROOSTED
ROOSTER S
ROOTERS
TOREROS
ROOSTERS
ROOSTING
ROOSTS
TORSOS
ROOT SY
ROTO TORO
ROOTAGE S
ROOTAGES
ROOTCAP S
ROOTCAPS
COPASTOR
ROOTED
ROOTER S
TORERO
ROOTERS
ROOSTER
TOREROS
ROOTHOLD S
ROOTIER
ROOTIEST
TORTOISE
ROOTING
ROOTLE DST
LOOTER
RETOOL
TOOLER
ROOTLED
ROOTLES S
LOOTERS
RETOOLS
TOOLERS
ROOTLESS
ROOTLET S
TOOTLER
ROOTLETS
TOOTLERS
ROOTLIKE
ROOTLING
ROOTS
ROOST ROTOS
TOROS TORSO
ROOTWORM S
MOORWORT
TOMORROW
WORMROOT
ROOTY
ROPABLE
GT **ROPE** DRSY
PORE REPO
G **ROPED**
DOPER PEDRO
PORED
ROPELIKE
GP **ROPER** SY
REPRO
ROPERIES
GP **ROPERS**
PROSER
REPROS
ROPERY
GT **ROPES**
PORES POSER
PROSE REPOS
SPORE
ROPEWALK S
ROPEWAY S
ROPEWAYS
ROPEY
ROPIER
ROPIEST
PROSTIE
REPOSIT
RIPOSTE
ROPILY
PYLORI
ROPINESS
G **ROPING**
PORING

ROPY
PYRO
ROQUE ST
ROQUES
C **ROQUET** S
QUOTER
TORQUE
C **ROQUETED**
C **ROQUETS**
QUESTOR
QUOTERS
TORQUES
C **ROQUETTE** S
RORQUAL S
RORQUALS
ROSACEA S
ROSACEAS
ROSARIA N
ROSARIAN S
ROSARIES
ROSARIUM S
ROSARY
ROSCOE S
COOERS
ROSCOES
ABE **ROSE** DST
P EROS ORES
ROES SORE
ROSEATE
ROSEBAY S
ROSEBAYS
ROSEBUD S
ROSEBUDS
ROSEBUSH
P **ROSED**
DOERS DOSER
REDOS RESOD
RODES SORED
ROSEFISH
ROSEHIP S
ROSEHIPS
ROSELIKE
ROSELLE S
ROSELLES
ROSEMARY
ROSEOLA RS
AEROSOL
ROSEOLAR
ROSEOLAS
AEROSOLS
ROSERIES
ROSEROOT S
ROSERY
BEP **ROSES**
SORES
ROSESLUG S
ROSET S
ROTES STORE
TORES TORSE
ROSETS
SOREST
STORES
TORSES
TOSSER
TSORES
ROSETTE S
ROSETTES
ROSEWOOD S
ROSHI S
ROSHIS
CP **ROSIER**
P **ROSIEST**
SORITES
SORTIES
STORIES
TRIOSES
P **ROSILY**
ROSIN GSY
IRONS NOIRS
NORIS ORNIS
ROSINED
DINEROS
INDORSE
ORDINES
SORDINE
P **ROSINESS**

P **ROSING**
GIRONS
GRISON
GROINS
SIGNOR
SORING
ROSINING
IRONINGS
NIGROSIN
ROSINOL S
ROSINOLS
ROSINOUS
ROSINS
ROSINY
ROSOLIO S
ROSOLIOS
ROSTELLA R
REALLOTS
ROSTER S
RESORT
RETROS
SORTER
STORER
ROSTERS
RESORTS
SORTERS
STORERS
ROSTRA L
SARTOR
ROSTRAL
P **ROSTRATE**
ROSTRUM S
ROSTRUMS
ROSULATE
BP **ROSY**
GT **ROT** AEILOS
ORT
TOR
ROTA S
RATO TARO
TORA
ROTARIES
ROTARY
ROTAS
RATOS ROAST
SORTA TAROS
TORAS
ROTATE DS
ROTATED
ROTATES
TOASTER
ROTATING
ROTATION S
ROTATIVE
ROTATOR SY
ROTATORS
ROTATORY
C **ROTCH** E
TORCH
ROTCHE S
HECTOR
ROCHET
TOCHER
TROCHE
C **ROTCHES**
HECTORS
ROCHETS
TOCHERS
TORCHES
TROCHES
W **ROTE** S
TORE
ROTENONE S
ROTES
ROSET STORE
TORES TORSE
ROTGUT S
ROTGUTS
ROTI S
RIOT TIRO
TORI TRIO
ROTIFER S
ROTIFERS
FROSTIER
ROTIFORM
ROTIS
RIOTS TIROS
TORSI TRIOS
TROIS
ROTL S
ROTLS

ROTO RS
ROOT TORO
ROTOR S
ROTORS
ROTOS
ROOST ROOTS
TOROS TORSO
ROTOTILL S
GT **ROTS**
ORTS SORT
TORS
ROTTE DNRS
OTTER TORTE
TOTER
T **ROTTED**
DOTTER
ROTTEN
TORTEN
ROTTENER
ROTTENLY
T **ROTTER** S
RETORT
T **ROTTERS**
RETORTS
STERTOR
ROTTES
OTTERS
TORTES
TOTERS
T **ROTTING**
O **ROTUND** A
UNTROD
ROTUNDA S
ROTUNDAS
ROTUNDLY
ROTURIER S
T **ROUBLE** S
T **ROUBLES**
ROUCHE S
CG **ROUCHES**
CHOUSER
ROUE NS
EURO
ROUEN S
ROUENS
ROUES
EUROS ROUSE
ROUGE DS
ERUGO ROGUE
ROUGED
DROGUE
GOURDE
ROGUED
ROUGES
ERUGOS
GROUSE
ROGUES
RUGOSE
T **ROUGH** SY
ROUGHAGE S
ROUGHDRY
ROUGHED
ROUGHEN S
ROUGHENS
ROUGHER S
ROUGHERS
ROUGHEST
RESOUGHT
ROUGHHEW N S
ROUGHIES
ROUGHING
ROUGHISH
ROUGHLEG S
ROUGHLY
T **ROUGHS**
ROUGHY
ROUGING
ROGUING
ROUILLE S
ROUILLES
ROULADE S
ROULADES
ROULEAU SX
ROULEAUS
ROULEAUX
ROULETTE DS
AG **ROUND** S

G **ROUNDED**
REDOUND
UNDERDO
ROUNDEL S
ROUNDELS
UNSOLDER
G **ROUNDER** S
RONDURE
G **ROUNDERS**
RONDURES
ROUNDEST
TONSURED
UNSORTED
G **ROUNDING**
INGROUND
ROUNDISH
ROUNDLET S
ROUNDLY
G **ROUNDS**
ROUNDUP S
ROUNDUPS
CG **ROUP** SY
POUR
GT **ROUPED**
POURED
ROUPET
POUTER
TROUPE
UPTORE
C **ROUPIER**
C **ROUPIEST**
C **ROUPILY**
GT **ROUPING**
INGROUP
POURING
CG **ROUPS**
POURS
C **ROUPY**
ACG **ROUSE** DRS
EUROS ROUES
AG **ROUSED**
DOUSER
SOURED
UREDOS
AGT **ROUSER** S
SOURER
AGT **ROUSERS**
AG **ROUSES**
SEROUS
AG **ROUSING**
SOURING
T **ROUSSEAU** S
ROUST S
ROUTS STOUR
TORUS TOURS
ROUSTED
DETOURS
DOUREST
REDOUTS
ROUSTER S
ROUTERS
TOURERS
TROUSER
ROUSTERS
TRESSOUR
TROUSERS
ROUSTING
OUTGRINS
OUTRINGS
TOURINGS
ROUSTS
STOURS
TUSSOR
GT **ROUT** EHS
TOUR
C **ROUTE** DRS
OUTER OUTRE
G **ROUTED**
DETOUR
REDOUT
TOURED
ROUTEMAN
ROUTEMEN
G **ROUTER** S
TOURER
G **ROUTERS**
ROUSTER
TOURERS
TROUSER
C **ROUTES**
OUSTER
OUTERS
SOUTER
STOURE

ROUTEWAY S
OUTWEARY
D **ROUTH** S
D **ROUTHS**
ROUTINE S
ROUTINES
SNOUTIER
G **ROUTING**
OUTGRIN
OUTRING
TOURING
GT **ROUTS**
ROUST STOUR
TORUS TOURS
ROUX
DGP **ROVE** DNRS
T OVER
DGP **ROVED**
DROVE
P **ROVEN**
DPT **ROVER** S
DPT **ROVERS**
DGP **ROVES**
T OVERS SERVO
VERSO
DP **ROVING** S
ROVINGLY
ROVINGS
BCF **ROW** S
GPT
V
G **ROWABLE**
ROWAN S
ROWANS
ROWBOAT S
ROWBOATS
ROWDIER
WORDIER
WORRIED
C **ROWDIES** T
DOWRIES
WEIRDOS
ROWDIEST
WORDIEST
ROWDILY
WORDILY
C **ROWDY**
DOWRY WORDY
ROWDYISH
ROWDYISM S
BCT **ROWED**
DOWER
T **ROWEL** S
LOWER
T **ROWELED**
LOWERED
T **ROWELING**
LOWERING
T **ROWELLED**
WELLDOER
T **ROWELS**
LOWERS
SLOWER
ROWEN S
OWNER REWON
ROWENS
OWNERS
RESOWN
WORSEN
CGP **ROWER** S
CG **ROWERS**
WORSER
CGT **ROWING** S
ROWINGS
ROWLOCK S
ROWLOCKS
BCF **ROWS**
GPT
V
GT **ROWTH** S
THROW WHORT
WORTH WROTH
GT **ROWTHS**
THROWS
WHORTS
WORTHS
ROYAL S
ROYALISM S
ROYALIST S
SOLITARY
ROYALLY
ROYALS

ROYALTY
ROYSTER S
STROYER
ROYSTERS
STROYERS
ROZZER S
ROZZERS
RUANA S
RUANAS
DG **RUB** ESY
BUR
URB
RUBABOO S
RUBABOOS
RUBACE S
RUBACES
SUBRACE
RUBAIYAT
RUBASSE S
ABUSERS
SURBASE
RUBASSES
SURBASES
RUBATI
RUBATO S
TABOUR
RUBATOS
ABORTUS
ROBUSTA
TABOURS
RUBBABOO S
DG **RUBBED**
DUBBER
DG **RUBBER** SY
RUBBERED
DG **RUBBERS**
RUBBERY
RUBBIES
DG **RUBBING** S
D **RUBBINGS**
RUBBISH Y
RUBBISHY
RUBBLE DS
BURBLE
LUBBER
RUBBLED
BLURBED
BURBLED
RUBBLES
BURBLES
LUBBERS
SLUBBER
RUBBLIER
BURBLIER
RUBBLING
BLURBING
BURBLING
RUBBLY
BURBLY
RUBBOARD S
G **RUBBY**
RUBDOWN S
RUBDOWNS
RUBE LS
RUBEL S
BLUER RUBLE
RUBELLA S
RULABLE
RUBELLAS
RUBELS
RUBLES
RUBEOLA RS
RUBEOLAR
LABOURER
RUBEOLAS
RUBES
BURSE REBUS
SUBER
RUBICUND
RUBIDIC
RUBIDIUM S
RUBIED
BURDIE
BURIED
RUBIER
BURIER
RUBIES T
BRUISE
BURIES
BUSIER
RUBIEST
BUSTIER

RUBIGO S
RUBIGOS
RUBIOUS
RUBLE S
BLUER RUBEL
RUBLES
RUBELS
RUBOFF S
RUBOFFS
RUBOUT S
RUBOUTS
RUBRIC S
RUBRICAL
RUBRICS
DG RUBS
BURS URBS
RUBUS
RUBY
BURY
RUBYING
BURYING
RUBYLIKE
RUCHE DS
RUCHED
RUCHES
RUCHING S
RUCHINGS
CRUSHING
CT RUCK S
T RUCKED
DUCKER
T RUCKING
T RUCKLE DS
T RUCKLED
T RUCKLES
SCULKER
SUCKLER
T RUCKLING
CT RUCKS
RUCKSACK S
RUCKUS
RUCKUSES
RUCTION S
RUCTIONS
RUCTIOUS
RUDD SY
RUDDER S
RUDDERS
C RUDDIER
C RUDDIEST
STURDIED
RUDDILY
RUDDLE DS
RUDDLED
RUDDLES
RUDDLING
RUDDOCK S
RUDDOCKS
RUDDS
C RUDDY
CP RUDE R
DURE RUED
C RUDELY
C RUDENESS
C RUDER Y
RUDERAL S
RUDERALS
P RUDERIES
P RUDERY
RUDESBY
C RUDEST
DUSTER
RUSTED
RUDIMENT S
UNMITRED
GT RUE DRS
T RUED
DURE RUDE
RUEFUL
RUEFULLY
T RUER S
RUERS
SURER
GT RUES
RUSE SUER
SURE USER
G RUFF ES
T RUFFE DS

G RUFFED
DUFFER
T RUFFES
SUFFER
RUFFIAN S
FUNFAIR
RUFFIANS
FUNFAIRS
G RUFFING
T RUFFLE DRS
T RUFFLED
RUFFLER S
RUFFLERS
T RUFFLES
RUFFLIER
RUFFLIKE
RUFFLING
G RUFFLY
G RUFFS
RUFIYAA
RUFOUS
DFT RUG AS
RUGA EL
GAUR GUAR
RUGAE
ARGUE AUGER
F RUGAL
GULAR
RUGALACH
RUGATE
RUGBIES
RUGBY
RUGELACH
DF RUGGED
GRUDGE
GURGED
RUGGEDER
RUGGEDLY
RUGGER S
RUGGERS
DF RUGGING
GURGING
RUGLIKE
A RUGOLA S
A RUGOLAS
RUGOSA S
RUGOSAS
RUGOSE
ERUGOS
GROUSE
ROGUES
ROUGES
RUGOSELY
RUGOSITY
RUGOUS
DFT RUGS
RUGULOSE
B RUIN GS
RUINABLE
RUINATE DS
TAURINE
URANITE
URINATE
RUINATED
INDURATE
URINATED
RUINATES
TAURINES
URANITES
URINATES
RUINED
INURED
RUINER S
RUINERS
INSURER
T RUING
UNRIG
RUINING
INURING
RUINOUS
URINOUS
B RUINS
RULABLE
RUBELLA
RULE DRS
LURE
RULED
LURED
RULELESS
RULER S
LURER

RULERS
LURERS
RULES
LURES
RULIER
RULIEST
LUSTIER
RUTILES
RULING S
LURING
RULINGS
T RULY
ADG RUM PS
RUMAKI S
RUMAKIS
RUMBA S
UMBRA
RUMBAED
RUMBAING
RUMBAS
SAMBUR
UMBRAS
CDG RUMBLE DRS
LUMBER
CDG RUMBLED
DRUMBLE
G RUMBLER S
G RUMBLERS
CDG RUMBLES
LUMBERS
SLUMBER
CDG RUMBLING S
CG RUMBLY
RUMEN S
RUMENS
RUMINA L
RUMINAL
RUMINANT S
RUMINATE DS
RUMMAGE DRS
RUMMAGED
RUMMAGER S
RUMMAGES
DG RUMMER S
D RUMMERS
G RUMMEST
C RUMMIER
C RUMMIES T
IMMURES
C RUMMIEST
C RUMMY
RUMOR S
RUMORED
RUMORING
RUMORS
RUMOUR S
RUMOURED
RUMOURS
CFG RUMP S
T
C RUMPLE DS
LUMPER
C RUMPLED
C RUMPLES S
LUMPERS
RUMPLESS
C RUMPLIER
C RUMPLING
C RUMPLY
CFG RUMPS
T
RUMPUS
RUMPUSES
AD RUMS
RUN EGST
URN
RUNABOUT S
RUNAGATE S
RUNAWAY S
RUNAWAYS
RUNBACK S
RUNBACKS
T RUNDLE ST
NURLED
T RUNDLES
RUNDLET S
TRUNDLE
RUNDLETS
TRUNDLES

RUNDOWN S
RUNDOWNS
P RUNE S
RUNELIKE
P RUNES
NURSE
BW RUNG S
RUNGLESS
RUNGS
RUNIC
INCUR
RUNKLE DS
LUNKER
RUNKLED
KNURLED
RUNKLES
LUNKERS
RUNKLING
KNURLING
RUNLESS
RUNLET S
RUNLETS
T RUNNEL S
T RUNNELS
RUNNER S
RUNNERS
RUNNIER
RUNNIEST
RUNNING S
RUNNINGS
RUNNY
RUNOFF S
RUNOFFS
RUNOUT S
OUTRUN
RUNOUTS
OUTRUNS
RUNOVER S
OVERRUN
RUNOVERS
OVERRUNS
RUNROUND S
RUNS
URNS
BG RUNT SY
TURN
RUNTIER
RUNTIEST
RUNTISH
BG RUNTS
TURNS
RUNTY
RUNWAY S
UNWARY
RUNWAYS
RUPEE S
PUREE
RUPEES
PERUSE
PUREES
RUPIAH S
RUPIAHS
RUPTURE DS
RUPTURED
RUPTURES
C RURAL
RURALISE DS
RURALISM S
RURALIST S
RURALITE S
RURALITY
RURALIZE DS
RURALLY
RURBAN
CD RUSE S
RUES SUER
SURE USER
CDU RUSES
SUERS USERS
BC RUSH Y
RHUS
BC RUSHED
RUSHEE S
RUSHEES
BC RUSHER S
BC RUSHERS
BC RUSHES
RHESUS
RHUSES
USHERS

B RUSHIER
HURRIES
B RUSHIEST
BC RUSHING S
RUSHINGS
RUSHLIKE
B RUSHY
RUSINE
INSURE
INURES
URINES
URSINE
B RUSK S
RUSKS
RUSSET SY
ESTRUS
SUREST
TUSSER
RUSSETS
TRUSSES
TUSSERS
RUSSETY
RUSSIFY
CT RUST SY
RUTS
T RUSTABLE
BALUSTER
CT RUSTED
DUSTER
RUDEST
RUSTIC S
CITRUS
RICTUS
RUSTICAL S
CURTAILS
RUSTICLY
CRUSTILY
RUSTICS
CT RUSTIER
CT RUSTIEST
TRUSTIES
CT RUSTILY
CT RUSTING
RUSTLE DRS
LUSTER
LUSTRE
RESULT
SUTLER
ULSTER
RUSTLED
LUSTRED
STRUDEL
RUSTLER S
RUSTLERS
RUSTLES S
LUSTERS
LUSTRES
RESULTS
SUTLERS
ULSTERS
CT RUSTLESS
RUSTLING
LUSTRING
CT RUSTS
TRUSS
CT RUSTY
YURTS
B RUT HS
RUTABAGA S
T RUTH S
HURT THRU
RUTHENIC
T RUTHFUL
HURTFUL
T RUTHLESS
HURTLESS
HUSTLERS
T RUTHS
HURST HURTS
RUTILANT
RUTILE S
RUTILES
LUSTIER
RULIEST
RUTIN S
RUTINS
B RUTS
RUST
RUTTED
RUTTIER
RUTTIEST
RUTTILY

RUTTING
RUTTISH
RUTTY
RYA S
RAY
YAR
RYAS
RAYS
RYE S
RYEGRASS
RYES
RYKE DS
YERK
RYKED
RYKES
YERKS
RYKING
RYND S
RYNDS
RYOKAN S
RYOKANS
RYOT S
TORY TROY
TYRO
RYOTS
STORY STROY
TROYS TYROS

S

SAB ES
ABS
BAS
SABAL S
ALBAS BAALS
BALAS BALSA
BASAL
SABALS
BALSAS
SABATON S
SABATONS
SABAYON S
SABAYONS
SABBAT HS
SABBATH S
SABBATHS
SABBATIC S
SABBATS
SABBED
SABBING
SABE DRS
BASE
SABED
BASED BEADS
SABEING
SABER S
BARES BASER
BEARS BRAES
SABRE
SABERED
BEADERS
DEBASER
SABERING
BEARINGS
SABERS
SABRES
SABES
BASES
SABIN ES
BASIN NABIS
SABINE S
SABINES
SABINS
BASINS
SABIR S
ABRIS
SABIRS
U SABLE S
ABLES BALES
BLASE
SABLES
SABOT S
BOAST BOATS
BOTAS
SABOTAGE DS
SABOTEUR S
SABOTS
BOASTS
SABRA S
SABRAS

SABRE DS
BARES BASER
BEARS BRAES
SABER
SABRED
ARDEBS
BARDES
BEARDS
BREADS
DEBARS
SERDAB
SABRES
SABERS
SABRING
SABS
BASS
SABULOSE
SABULOUS
SAC KS
SACATON S
SACATONS
SACBUT S
SACBUTS
SACCADE S
CASCADE
SACCADES
CASCADES
SACCADIC
SACCATE
SACCULAR
ACCRUALS
CARACULS
SACCULE S
SACCULES
SACCULI
SACCULUS
SACHEM S
MACHES
SAMECH
SCHEMA
SACHEMIC
SACHEMS
SAMECHS
SCHEMAS
SACHET S
CHASTE
CHEATS
SCATHE
TACHES
SACHETED
DETACHES
SACHETS
SCATHES
SACK S
CASK
SACKBUT S
SACKBUTS
SACKED
CASKED
SACKER S
CRAKES
CREAKS
SCREAK
SACKERS
SCREAKS
SACKFUL S
SACKFULS
SACKSFUL
SACKING S
CASKING
SACKINGS
SACKLIKE
SACKS
CASKS
SACKSFUL
SACKFULS
SACLIKE
SACQUE S
CASQUE
SACQUES
CASQUES
SACRA L
SACRAL S
CRAALS
LASCAR
RASCAL
SCALAR
SACRALS
LASCARS
RASCALS
SCALARS
SACRARIA L

SACRED
CADRES CEDARS SCARED
SACREDLY
SACRING S
RACINGS SCARING
SACRINGS
SACRIST SY
RACISTS
SACRISTS
SACRISTY
SACRUM S
SACRUMS
SACS
SAD EI
ADS
SADDEN S
DEDANS DESAND SANDED
SADDENED
DESANDED
SADDENS
DESANDS
SADDER
ADDERS DREADS READDS
SADDEST
SADDHU S
SADDHUS
SADDLE DRS
ADDLES
SADDLED
DADDLES
SADDLER SY
LADDERS RADDLES
SADDLERS
SADDLERY
SADDLES
SADDLING
T **SADE** S
T **SADES**
SADHE S
ASHED DEASH HADES HEADS SHADE
SADHES
DASHES SASHED SHADES
SADHU S
SADHUS
T **SADI** S
AIDS DAIS SAID
SADIRON S
INROADS ORDAINS
SADIRONS
T **SADIS** MT
SAIDS
SADISM S
SADISMS
SADIST S
TSADIS
SADISTIC
SADISTS
SADLY
SADNESS
SAE
SEA
SAFARI S
SAFARIED
FARADISE
SAFARIS
SAFE RS
SAFELY
SAFENESS
SAFER
FARES FEARS
SAFES T
SAFEST
FEASTS
SAFETIED
SAFETIES
SAFETY
SAFFRON S
SAFFRONS
SAFRANIN ES
SAFROL ES
FLORAS
SAFROLE S
LOAFERS
SAFROLES
SAFROLS
SAG AEOSY
AGS GAS
SAGA S
AGAS
SAGACITY
SAGAMAN
SAGAMEN
MANAGES
SAGAMORE S
SAGANASH
SAGAS
SAGBUT S
SAGBUTS
U **SAGE** RS
AGES GAES
SAGELY
SAGENESS
SAGER
AGERS GEARS RAGES SARGE
U **SAGES** T
GASES
SAGEST
STAGES
SAGGAR DS
SAGGARD S
SAGGARDS
SAGGARED
AGGRADES
SAGGARS
SAGGED
SAGGER S
AGGERS EGGARS GAGERS SEGGAR
SAGGERED
SAGGERS
AGGRESS SEGGARS
SAGGIER
RAGGIES
SAGGIEST
STAGGIES
SAGGING
SAGGY
SAGIER
SAGIEST
AGEISTS
SAGITTAL
SAGO S
GOAS
SAGOS
SAGS
SAGUARO S
SAGUAROS
SAGUM
GAUMS MAGUS
SAGY
GAYS YAGS
SAHIB S
SAHIBS
SAHIWAL S
SAHIWALS
SAHUARO S
SAHUAROS
SAICE S
SAICES
SAID S
AIDS DAIS SADI
SAIDS
SADIS
SAIGA S
SAIGAS
SAIL S
AILS SIAL
SAILABLE
SAILBOAT S
SAILED
AISLED DEASIL IDEALS LADIES
SAILER S
ARIELS RESAIL SERAIL SERIAL
SAILERS
AIRLESS RESAILS SERAILS SERIALS
SAILFISH
SAILING S
NILGAIS
SAILINGS
SAILLESS
SAILOR S
SAILORLY
SAILORS
SAILS
LASSI SIALS SISAL
SAIMIN S
ANIMIS SIMIAN
SAIMINS
SIMIANS
SAIN ST
AINS ANIS
SAINED
SAINFOIN S
SINFONIA
SAINING
SAINS
SASIN
SAINT S
ANTIS SATIN STAIN TAINS
SAINTDOM S
SAINTED
DESTAIN DETAINS INSTEAD NIDATES STAINED
SAINTING
STAINING
SAINTLY
NASTILY
SAINTS
SATINS STAINS
SAITH E
SAITHE
SAIYID S
SAIYIDS
SAJOU S
SAJOUS
SAKE RS
KAES KEAS
SAKER S
ASKER ESKAR RAKES
SAKERS
ASKERS ESKARS
SAKES
SAKI S
SIKA
SAKIS
SIKAS
SAL ELPST
ALS LAS
SALAAM S
MASALA
SALAAMED
ALAMEDAS
SALAAMS
MASALAS
SALABLE
SALABLY
BASALLY
SALACITY
SALAD S
SALADANG S
SALADS
SALAL S
SALALS
SALAMI S
LAMIAS
SALAMIS
SALARIAT S
SALARIED
SALARIES
ASSAILER REASSAIL
SALARY
SALCHOW S
SALCHOWS
SALE PS
ALES LASE LEAS SEAL
SALEABLE
LEASABLE SEALABLE
SALEABLY
SLAYABLE
SALEP S
LAPSE LEAPS PALES PEALS PLEAS SEPAL SPALE
SALEPS
LAPSES PASSEL SEPALS SPALES
SALEROOM S
SALES
LASES SEALS
SALESMAN
SALESMEN
LAMENESS MALENESS MANELESS NAMELESS
SALIC
LAICS
SALICIN ES
INCISAL
SALICINE S
SALICINS
SALIENCE S
SALIENCY
SALIENT S
ELASTIN ENTAILS NAILSET SALTINE SLAINTE TENAILS
SALIENTS
ELASTINS NAILSETS SALTINES
SALIFIED
SALIFIES
SALIFY
SALINA S
LANAIS LIANAS NASIAL
SALINAS
SALINE S
ALIENS ALINES ELAINS LIANES SILANE
SALINES
SILANES
SALINITY
SALINIZE DS
SALIVA S
AVAILS SALVIA
SALIVARY
SALIVAS
SALVIAS
SALIVATE DS
AESTIVAL
SALL Y
ALLS
SALLET S
STELLA
SALLETS
STELLAS
SALLIED
DALLIES
SALLIER S
RALLIES
SALLIERS
SALLIES
SALLOW SY
ALLOWS
SALLOWED
SALLOWER
SALLOWLY
SALLOWS
SALLOWY
SALLY
SALLYING
SIGNALLY SLANGILY
SALMI S
LIMAS MAILS
SALMIS
MISSAL
SALMON S
SALMONID S
SALMONS
SALOL S
OLLAS
SALOLS
SALON S
LOANS SOLAN
SALONS
SOLANS
SALOON S
SOLANO
SALOONS
SOLANOS
SALOOP S
SALOOPS
SALP AS
ALPS LAPS PALS SLAP
SALPA ES
SALPAE
SALPAS
SALPIAN S
SALPIANS
SALPID S
PLAIDS
SALPIDS
SALPINX
SALPS
SLAPS
SALS A
LASS
SALSA S
SALSAS
SALSIFY
SALSILLA S
SALT SY
ALTS LAST LATS SLAT
SALTANT
SALTBOX
SALTBUSH
SALTED
DELTAS DESALT LASTED SLATED STALED
P **SALTER** NS
ALERTS ALTERS ARTELS ESTRAL LASTER RATELS SLATER STALER STELAR TALERS
SALTERN S
ANTLERS RENTALS STERNAL
SALTERNS
P **SALTERS**
ARTLESS LASTERS SLATERS
SALTEST
LATESTS STALEST
SALTIE RS
STELAI
SALTIER S
REALIST RETAILS SALTIRE SLATIER TAILERS
SALTIERS
REALISTS SALTIRES
SALTIES T
SALTIEST
SLATIEST
SALTILY
SALTINE S
ELASTIN ENTAILS NAILSET SALIENT SLAINTE TENAILS
SALTINES
ELASTINS NAILSETS SALIENTS
SALTING S
LASTING SLATING STALING
SALTINGS
LASTINGS SLATINGS
SALTIRE S
REALIST RETAILS SALTIER SLATIER TAILERS
SALTIRES
REALISTS SALTIERS
SALTISH
TAHSILS
SALTLESS
SALTLIKE
SALTNESS
SALTPAN S
PLATANS
SALTPANS
SALTS
LASTS SLATS
SALTWORK S
SALTWORT S
SALTY
SLATY
SALUKI S
SALUKIS
SALUTARY
SALUTE DRS
SALUTED
AULDEST
SALUTER S
ESTRUAL
SALUTERS
SALUTES
TALUSES
SALUTING
SALVABLE
SALVABLY
SALVAGE DER
LAVAGES S
SALVAGED
SALVAGEE S
SALVAGER S
SALVAGES
SALVE DRS
LAVES SELVA SLAVE VALES VALSE VEALS
SALVED
SLAVED
SALVER S
LAVERS RAVELS SERVAL SLAVER VELARS VERSAL
SALVERS
SERVALS SLAVERS
SALVES
SELVAS SLAVES VALSES
SALVIA S
AVAILS SALIVA
SALVIAS
SALIVAS
SALVIFIC
SALVING
SLAVING
SALVO RS
OVALS
SALVOED
SALVOES
SALVOING
SALVOR S
VALORS
SALVORS
SALVOS
SAMADHI S
SAMADHIS
SAMARA S
ASRAMA
SAMARAS
ASRAMAS SAMSARA
SAMARIUM S
SAMBA LRS
SAMBAED
SAMBAING
SAMBAL S
BALSAM
SAMBALS
BALSAMS
SAMBAR S
SAMBARS
SAMBAS
SAMBHAR S
BRAHMAS
SAMBHARS
SAMBHUR S
RHUMBAS
SAMBHURS
SAMBO S
AMBOS
SAMBOS
SAMBUCA S
SAMBUCAS
SAMBUKE S
SAMBUKES
SAMBUR S
RUMBAS UMBRAS
SAMBURS
SAME K
MAES MESA SEAM
SAMECH S
MACHES SACHEM SCHEMA
SAMECHS
SACHEMS SCHEMAS
SAMEK HS
KAMES MAKES
SAMEKH S
SAMEKHS
SAMEKS
SAMENESS
SAMIEL S
EMAILS MAILES MESIAL
SAMIELS
AIMLESS SEISMAL
SAMISEN S
INSEAMS
SAMISENS
SAMITE S
MISATE MISEAT
SAMITES
MISEATS MISSEAT TAMISES
SAMIZDAT S

SAMLET S
LAMEST
METALS
SAMLETS
MATLESS
SAMOSA S
SAMOSAS
SAMOVAR S
SAMOVARS
SAMOYED S
SOMEDAY
SAMOYEDS
SAMP S
AMPS MAPS
PAMS SPAM
SAMPAN S
SAMPANS
SAMPHIRE S
SERAPHIM
SAMPLE DRS
MAPLES
SAMPLED
PSALMED
SAMPLER S
LAMPERS
PALMERS
SAMPLERS
SAMPLES
SAMPLING S
PSALMING
SAMPS
SPAMS SPASM
SAMSARA S
ASRAMAS
SAMARAS
SAMSARAS
SAMSHU S
SHAMUS
SAMSHUS
SAMURAI S
SAMURAIS
SANATIVE
SANCTA
SANCTIFY
SANCTION S
ACTINONS
CANONIST
CONTAINS
SONANTIC
SANCTITY
SANCTUM S
SANCTUMS
SAND SY
ANDS DANS
SANDABLE
SANDAL S
ALANDS
SANDALED
SANDALS
SANDARAC S
SANDBAG S
SANDBAGS
SANDBANK S
SANDBAR S
SANDBARS
SANDBOX
SANDBUR RS
SANDBURR S
SANDBURS
SANDDAB S
SANDDABS
SANDED
DEDANS
DESAND
SADDEN
SANDER S
DENARS
REDANS
SNARED
SANDERS
SANDFISH
SANDFLY
SANDHI S
DANISH
SANDHIS
SANDHOG S
HAGDONS
SANDHOGS

SANDIER
RANDIES
SARDINE
SANDIEST
DESTAINS
SANDING
SANDLESS
SANDLIKE
SANDLING S
LANDINGS
SANDLOT S
DALTONS
SANDLOTS
SANDMAN
SANDMEN
SANDPEEP S
SANDPILE S
SANDPIT S
PANDITS
SANDPITS
SANDS
SANDSHOE S
SANDSOAP S
SANDSPUR S
SANDWICH
SANDWORM S
SWORDMAN
SANDWORT S
SANDY
SANE DRS
ANES
SANED
DEANS SEDAN
SANELY
SANENESS
SANER
EARNS NARES
NEARS SNARE
SANES T
SENSA
SANEST
ASSENT
STANES
SANG AH
NAGS SNAG
SANGA RS
ANGAS
SANGAR S
SANGAREE S
SANGARS
SANGAS
SANGER S
ANGERS
RANGES
SANGERS
SANGH S
GNASH HANGS
SANGHS
SANGRIA S
SANGRIAS
SANGUINE S
GUANINES
SANICLE S
INLACES
SCALENI
SANICLES
LACINESS
SANIDINE S
SANIES
ANISES
SANSEI
SANING
SANIOUS
SUASION
SANITARY
SANITATE DS
ASTATINE
SANITIES
ISATINES
SANITISE
TENIASIS
SANITISE DS
ISATINES
SANITIES
TENIASIS
SANITIZE DR S
SANITY
SATINY
SANJAK S
SANJAKS
SANK

SANNOP S
SANNOPS
SANNUP S
UNSNAP
SANNUPS
UNSNAPS
SANNYASI NS
SANS
SANSAR S
SARANS
SANSARS
SANSEI S
ANISES
SANIES
SANSEIS
SANSERIF S
FAIRNESS
SANTALIC
SANTALOL S
SANTERA S
SANTERAS
SANTERIA S
ANTISERA
RATANIES
SEATRAIN
SANTERO S
ATONERS
SENATOR
TREASON
SANTEROS
ASSENTOR
SENATORS
STARNOSE
TREASONS
SANTIMI
ANIMIST
INTIMAS
SANTIMS
SANTIMU
MANITUS
TSUNAMI
SANTIR S
INSTAR
STRAIN
TRAINS
SANTIRS
INSTARS
STRAINS
SANTO LS
SANTOL S
STANOL
TALONS
TOLANS
SANTOLS
STANOLS
SANTONIN S
SANTOOR S
RATOONS
SANTOORS
SANTOS
SANTOUR S
SANTOURS
SANTUR S
SANTURS
SAP S
ASP
PAS
SPA
SAPAJOU S
SAPAJOUS
SAPHEAD S
SAPHEADS
SAPHENA ES
SAPHENAE
SAPHENAS
SAPID
PADIS
SAPIDITY
SAPIENCE S
SAPIENCY
SAPIENS
PANSIES
SAPIENT S
PANTIES
PATINES
SPINATE
SAPIENTS
STEAPSIN
SAPLESS
PASSELS

SAPLING S
LAPSING
PALINGS
SAPLINGS
SAPONIFY
SAPONIN ES
SAPONINE S
SAPONINS
SAPONITE S
SAPOR S
PRAOS PROAS
SAPOROUS
SAPORS
SAPOTA S
SAPOTAS
SAPOTE S
SAPOTES
PETASOS
SAPOUR S
PAROUS
UPSOAR
SAPOURS
UPSOARS
SAPPED
SAPPER S
PAPERS
SAPPERS
SAPPHIC S
SAPPHICS
SAPPHIRE S
SAPPHISM S
SAPPHIST S
SAPPIER
APPRISE
SAPPIEST
SAPPILY
SAPPING
SAPPY
SAPREMIA S
SAPREMIC
PARECISM
SAPROBE S
SAPROBES
SAPROBIC
SAPROPEL S
PROLAPSE
SAPS
ASPS PASS
SPAS
SAPSAGO S
SAPSAGOS
SAPWOOD S
SAPWOODS
SARABAND ES
SARAN S
SARANS
SANSAR
SARAPE S
AREPAS
SARAPES
SARCASM S
SARCASMS
SARCENET S
CENTARES
REASCENT
REENACTS
SARCINA ES
ACRASIN
ARNICAS
CARINAS
SARCINAE
ACARINES
CANARIES
CESARIAN
SARCINAS
ACRASINS
SARCOID S
SARCOIDS
SARCOMA S
SARCOMAS
SARCOUS
SOUCARS
SARD S
RADS
SARDANA S
SARDANAS
SARDAR S
RADARS
SARDARS

SARDINE DS
RANDIES
SANDIER
SARDINED
SARDINES
ARIDNESS
SARDIUS
SARDONIC
SARDONYX
SARDS
SAREE S
ERASE
SAREES
ERASES
SARGASSO S
SARGE S
AGERS GEARS
RAGES SAGER
SARGES
GASSER
SARGO S
SARGOS
SARI NS
AIRS RAIS
RIAS
SARIN S
AIRNS NARIS
RAINS RANIS
SARINS
SARIS
ARSIS
SARK SY
ARKS
SARKIER
KERRIAS
SARKIEST
ASTERISK
SARKS
SARKY
KYARS
SARMENT AS
MARTENS
SMARTEN
SARMENTA
SARMENTS
SMARTENS
SAROD ES
DORSA ROADS
SARODE S
ADORES
OREADS
SOARED
SARODES
SARODIST S
SARODS
SARONG S
ARGONS
GROANS
ORANGS
ORGANS
SARONGS
SAROS
SOARS SORAS
SAROSES
SEROSAS
SARSAR S
SARSARS
SARSEN S
SNARES
SARSENET S
ASSENTER
EARNESTS
SARSENS
SARSNET S
SARSNETS
SARTOR S
ROSTRA
SARTORII
SARTORS
SASH
SASHAY S
SASHAYED
SASHAYS
SASHED
DASHES
SADHES
SHADES
SASHES
SASHIMI S
SASHIMIS
SASHING
SASHLESS

SASIN S
SAINS
SASINS
SASS Y
SASSABY
SASSED
SASSES
ASSESS
SASSIER
SASSIES T
SASSIEST
SASSILY
SASSING
ASSIGNS
SASSWOOD S
SASSY
SASTRUGA
SASTRUGI
SAT EI
TAS
SATANG S
SATANGS
SATANIC
SATANISM S
MANTISSA
STAMINAS
SATANIST S
SATARA S
SATARAS
SATAY S
SATAYS
SATCHEL S
CHALETS
LATCHES
SATCHELS
SLATCHES
SATE DMS
ATES EAST
EATS ETAS
SEAT SETA
TEAS
SATED
DATES STADE
STEAD TSADE
SATEEN S
ENATES
SENATE
SATEENS
ENTASES
SENATES
SENSATE
SATEM
MATES MEATS
STEAM TAMES
TEAMS
SATES
ASSET EASTS
SEATS TASSE
SATI NS
AITS
SATIABLE
LABIATES
SATIABLY
SATIATE DS
SATIATED
SATIATES
SATIETY
I **SATIN** GSY
ANTIS SAINT
STAIN TAINS
SATINET S
INSTATE
SATINETS
ANTSIEST
INSTATES
NASTIEST
TITANESS
SATING
GAINST
GIANTS
SATINPOD S
PINTADOS
I **SATINS**
SAINTS
STAINS
SATINY
SANITY
SATIRE S
AIREST
STRIAE
TERAIS
SATIRES

SATIRIC
SATIRISE DS
SATIRIST S
SITARIST
SATIRIZE DR S
SATIS
SATISFY
SATORI S
AORIST
ARISTO
RATIOS
SATORIS
AORISTS
ARISTOS
SATRAP SY
SATRAPS
SATRAPY
SATSUMA S
SATSUMAS
SATURANT S
SATURATE DR S
TUATERAS
SATYR S
ARTSY STRAY
TRAYS
SATYRIC
SATYRID S
SATYRIDS
SATYRS
STRAYS
SAU L
SAUCE DRS
CAUSE
SAUCEBOX
SAUCED
CAUSED
SAUCEPAN S
SAUCEPOT S
OUTPACES
SAUCER S
CAUSER
CESURA
SAUCERS
ARCUSES
CAUSERS
CESURAS
SUCRASE
SAUCES
CAUSES
SAUCH S
SAUCHS
SAUCIER S
SAUCIERS
SAUCIEST
SUITCASE
SAUCILY
SAUCING
CAUSING
SAUCY
YUCAS
SAUGER S
ARGUES
AUGERS
SAUGERS
ARGUSES
SAUGH SY
SAUGHS
SAUGHY
SAUL ST
SAULS
SAULT S
TALUS
SAULTS
TUSSAL
SAUNA S
SAUNAED
SAUNAING
SAUNAS
SAUNTER S
NATURES
SAUNTERS
ANESTRUS
SAUREL S
SAURELS
SAURIAN S
ANURIAS
URANIAS
SAURIANS
SAURIES
SAUROPOD S

SAURY
SAUSAGE S
ASSUAGE
SAUSAGES
ASSUAGES
SAUTE DS
SAUTED
SAUTEED
SAUTEING
UNITAGES
SAUTERNE S
SAUTES
SAUTOIR ES
SAUTOIRE S
OUTRAISE
SAUTOIRS
SAVABLE
SAVAGE DRS
AGAVES
SAVAGED
SAVAGELY
SAVAGER Y
RAVAGES
SAVAGERY
SAVAGES T
AVGASES
SAVAGEST
SAVAGING
SAVAGISM S
SAVANNA HS
SAVANNAH S
SAVANNAS
SAVANT S
SAVANTS
SAVARIN S
SAVARINS
SAVATE S
SAVATES
SAVE DRS
AVES VASE
SAVEABLE
SAVED
DEVAS
SAVELOY S
SAVELOYS
SAVER S
AVERS RAVES
SAVERS
SAVES
VASES
SAVIN EGS
VINAS
SAVINE S
NAIVES
NAVIES
SAVINES
VINASSE
SAVING S
SAVINGLY
SAVINGS
SAVINS
SAVIOR S
SAVIORS
SAVIOUR S
VARIOUS
SAVIOURS
SAVOR SY
ARVOS
SAVORED
OVERSAD
SAVORER S
SEROVAR
SAVORERS
SEROVARS
SAVORIER
SAVORIES T
SAVORILY
SAVORING
SAVOROUS
SAVORS
SAVORY
SAVOUR SY
SAVOURED
SAVOURER S
SAVOURS
SAVOURY
SAVOY S
SAVOYS
SAVVIED
SAVVIER
SAVVIES T
SAVVIEST
SAVVILY
SAVVY
SAVVYING
SAW NS
WAS
SAWBILL S
SAWBILLS
SAWBONES
SAWBUCK S
BUCKSAW
SAWBUCKS
BUCKSAWS
SAWDUST SY
SAWDUSTS
SAWDUSTY
SAWED
WADES
SAWER S
RESAW SEWAR
SWARE SWEAR
WARES WEARS
SAWERS
RESAWS
SEWARS
SWEARS
WRASSE
SAWFISH
SAWFLIES
SAWFLY
SAWHORSE S
SAWING
WIGANS
SAWLIKE
SAWLOG S
SAWLOGS
SAWMILL S
SAWMILLS
SAWN
AWNS SNAW
SWAN WANS
SAWNEY S
SAWNEYS
SAWS
SAWTEETH
SAWTOOTH
SAWYER S
SWAYER
SAWYERS
SWAYERS
SAX
SAXATILE
SAXES
SAXHORN S
SAXHORNS
SAXONIES
SAXONY
SAXTUBA S
SUBTAXA
SAXTUBAS
SAY S
AYS
SAYABLE
SAYED S
SAYEDS
SAYER S
EYRAS RESAY
YEARS
SAYERS
RESAYS
SAYEST
YEASTS
SAYID S
DAISY
SAYIDS
SAYING S
SAYINGS
SAYONARA S
SAYS T
SAYST
STAYS
SAYYID S
SAYYIDS
SCAB S
CABS
SCABBARD S
SCABBED
SCABBIER
SCABBILY
SCABBING
SCABBLE DS
SCABBLED
SCABBLES
SCABBY
SCABIES
ABSCISE
SEBASIC
SCABIOSA S
SCABIOUS
SCABLAND S
SCABLIKE
SCABROUS
SCABS
SCAD S
CADS
SCADS
SCAFFOLD S
SCAG S
SCAGS
SCALABLE
SCALABLY
E SCALADE S
ALCADES
E SCALADES
SCALADO S
SCALADOS
SCALAGE S
SCALAGES
SCALAR ES
CRAALS
LASCAR
RASCAL
SACRAL
SCALARE S
SCALARES
SCALARS
LASCARS
RASCALS
SACRALS
SCALAWAG S
SCALD S
CLADS
SCALDED
SCALDIC
SCALDING
SCALDS
SCALE DRS
ALECS LACES
SCALED
CLADES
DECALS
SCALENE
CLEANSE
ENLACES
SCALENI
INLACES
SANICLE
SCALENUS
SCALEPAN S
CAPELANS
SCALER S
CARLES
CLEARS
LACERS
SCLERA
SCALERS
CARLESS
CLASSER
SCLERAS
SCALES
SCALEUP S
CAPSULE
SPECULA
UPSCALE
SCALEUPS
CAPSULES
UPSCALES
SCALIER
CLARIES
ECLAIRS
SCALIEST
ELASTICS
SCALING
LACINGS
SCALL S
CALLS
SCALLION S
E SCALLOP S
E SCALLOPS
SCALLS
SCALP S
CLAPS CLASP
SCALPED
CLASPED
SCALPEL S
SCALPELS
SCALPER S
CARPELS
CLASPER
PARCELS
PLACERS
RECLASP
SCALPERS
CLASPERS
RECLASPS
SCALPING
CLASPING
SCALPS
CLASPS
SCALY
ACYLS CLAYS
SCAM PS
CAMS MACS
SCAMMED
SCAMMER S
SCAMMERS
SCAMMING
SCAMMONY
SCAMP IS
CAMPS
SCAMPED
DECAMPS
SCAMPER S
CAMPERS
SCAMPERS
SCAMPI
SCAMPIES
ESCAPISM
MISSPACE
SCAMPING
CAMPINGS
SCAMPISH
SCAMPS
SCAMS
SCAMSTER S
SCAN ST
CANS
SCANDAL S
SCANDALS
SCANDENT
SCANDIA S
SCANDIAS
SCANDIC
SCANDIUM S
SCANNED
SCANNER S
CANNERS
SCANNERS
SCANNING S
CANNINGS
SCANS
SCANSION S
SCANT SY
CANST CANTS
SCANTED
DECANTS
DESCANT
SCANTER
CANTERS
CARNETS
NECTARS
RECANTS
TANRECS
TRANCES
SCANTEST
SCANTIER
CANISTER
CERATINS
CISTERNA
CREATINS
TACRINES
SCANTIES T
CINEASTS
SCANTILY
SCANTING
SCANTLY
SCANTS
SCANTY
E SCAPE DS
CAPES PACES
SPACE
E SCAPED
SPACED
E SCAPES
SPACES
SCAPHOID S
E SCAPING
SPACING
SCAPOSE
SCAPULA ERS
SCAPULAE
SCAPULAR SY
CAPSULAR
SCAPULAS
E SCAR EFPSTY
ARCS CARS
SCARAB S
BARCAS
SCARABS
SCARCE R
SCARCELY
SCARCER
SCARCEST
SCARCITY
SCARE DRSY
ACRES CARES
CARSE ESCAR
RACES SERAC
A SCARED
CADRES
CEDARS
SACRED
SCAREDER
SCARER S
CARERS
RACERS
SCARERS
CRASSER
SCARES
CARESS
CARSES
CRASES
ESCARS
SERACS
SCAREY
CREASY
SCARF S
SCARFED
SCARFER S
FARCERS
SCARFERS
SCARFING
SCARFPIN S
SCARFS
SCARIER
CARRIES
SCARIEST
SCARIFY
SCARILY
SCARING
RACINGS
SACRING
SCARIOSE
SCARIOUS
SCARLESS
CLASSER
SCARLET S
CARTELS
CLARETS
CRESTAL
SCARLETS
E SCARP HS
CARPS CRAPS
SCRAP
E SCARPED
REDCAPS
SCRAPED
SCARPER S
CARPERS
SCRAPER
SCARPERS
SCRAPERS
SCARPH S
SCARPHED
SCARPHS
E SCARPING
CARPINGS
SCRAPING
E SCARPS
SCRAPS
SCARRED
CARDERS
SCARRIER
CARRIERS
SCARRING
SCARRY
E SCARS
CRASS
SCART S
CARTS
SCARTED
REDACTS
SCARTING
TRACINGS
SCARTS
SCARVES
SCARY
SCAT ST
ACTS CAST
CATS
SCATBACK S
BACKCAST
SCATHE DS
CHASTE
CHEATS
SACHET
TACHES
SCATHED
SCATHES
SACHETS
SCATHING
SCATS
CASTS
SCATT SY
TACTS
SCATTED
SCATTER S
SCATTERS
SCATTIER
CITRATES
CRISTATE
SCATTING
SCATTS
SCATTY
SCAUP S
SCAUPER S
APERCUS
SCAUPERS
SCAUPS
SCAUR S
ARCUS
SCAURS
SCAVENGE DR S
SCENA S
ACNES CANES
SCENARIO S
SCENAS
A SCEND S
A SCENDED
DESCEND
A SCENDING
A SCENDS
SCENE S
CENSE
SCENERY
SCENES
CENSES
SCENIC S
SCENICAL
CALCINES
SCENICS
A SCENT S
CENTS
SCENTED
DESCENT
SCENTING
A SCENTS
SCEPTER S
RECEPTS
RESPECT
SCEPTRE
SPECTER
SPECTRE
SCEPTERS
RESPECTS
SCEPTRES
SPECTERS
SPECTRES
SCEPTIC S
SCEPTICS
SCEPTRAL
SPECTRAL
SCEPTRE DS
RECEPTS
RESPECT
SCEPTER
SPECTER
SPECTRE
SCEPTRED
SCEPTRES
RESPECTS
SCEPTERS
SPECTERS
SPECTRES
SCHAPPE S
SCHAPPES
SCHAV S
SCHAVS
SCHEDULE DR S
SCHEMA S
MACHES
SACHEM
SAMECH
SCHEMAS
SACHEMS
SAMECHS
SCHEMATA
SCHEME DRS
SCHEMED
SCHEMER S
MERCHES
SCHMEER
SCHEMERS
SCHMEERS
SCHEMES
SCHEMING
SCHERZI
SCHERZO S
SCHERZOS
SCHILLER S
CHILLERS
SCHISM S
SCHISMS
SCHIST S
STICHS
SCHISTS
SCHIZIER
SCHIZO S
SCHIZOID S
SCHIZONT S
SCHIZOS
SCHIZY
SCHIZZY
SCHLEP PS
SCHLEPP S
SCHLEPPS
SCHLEPS
SCHLIERE N
CHISELER
SCHLOCK SY
SCHLOCKS
SCHLOCKY
SCHLUB S
SCHLUBS
SCHLUMP SY
SCHLUMPS
SCHLUMPY
SCHMALTZ Y
SCHMALZ Y
SCHMALZY
SCHMATTE S
SCHMEAR S
MARCHES
MESARCH
SCHMEARS
SCHMEER S
MERCHES
SCHEMER
SCHMEERS
SCHEMERS
SCHMELZE S
SCHMO ES
SCHMOE S
CHEMOS
SCHMOES
SCHMOOS E
SCHMOOSE DS
SMOOCHES

SCHMOOZE DR S
SCHMOOZY
SCHMOS
SCHMUCK S
SCHMUCKS
SCHNAPPS
SCHNAPS
SCHNECKE N
SCHNOOK S
SCHNOOKS
SCHNOZ Z
SCHNOZES
SCHNOZZ
SCHOLAR S
CHORALS
SCHOLARS
SCHOLIA
SCHOLIUM S
SCHOOL S
CHOLOS
SCHOOLED
SCHOOLS
SCHOONER S
SCHORL S
SCHORLS
SCHRIK S
CHIRKS
KIRSCH
SCHRIKS
SCHROD S
CHORDS
SCHRODS
SCHTICK S
SCHTICKS
SCHTIK S
KITSCH
SHTICK
THICKS
SCHTIKS
SHTICKS
SCHUIT S
SCHUITS
SCHUL NS
SCHULN
SCHULS
SCHUSS
SCHUSSED
SCHUSSER S
SCHUSSES
SCHWA S
CHAWS
SCHWAS
SCIAENID S
SCIATIC AS
ASCITIC
SCIATICA S
SCIATICS
SCIENCE S
SCIENCES
SCILICET
SCILLA S
LILACS
SCILLAS
SCIMETAR S
CERAMIST
MATRICES
MISTRACE
SCIMITAR S
SCIMITER S
MERISTIC
TRISEMIC
SCINCOID S
SCIOLISM S
SCIOLIST S
SOLICITS
SCION S
CIONS COINS
ICONS SONIC
SCIONS
SONICS
SCIROCCO S
SCIRRHI
SCIRRHUS
SCISSILE
SCISSION S
SCISSOR S
SCISSORS

SCISSURE S
SCIURID S
SCIURIDS
SCIURINE S
INCISURE
SCIUROID
SCLAFF S
SCLAFFED
SCLAFFER S
SCLAFFS
SCLERA ELS
CARLES
CLEARS
LACERS
SCALER
SCLERAE
CEREALS
RELACES
RESCALE
SCLERAL
CALLERS
CELLARS
RECALLS
SCLERAS
CARLESS
CLASSER
SCALERS
SCLEREID S
SCLERITE S
RETICLES
TIERCELS
TRISCELE
SCLEROID
SCLEROMA S
SCLEROSE DS
CORELESS
SCLEROUS
CLOSURES
SCOFF S
COFFS
SCOFFED
SCOFFER S
COFFERS
SCOFFERS
SCOFFING
SCOFFLAW S
SCOFFS
SCOLD S
CLODS COLDS
SCOLDED
CODDLES
SCOLDER S
SCOLDERS
CORDLESS
SCOLDING S
CODLINGS
LINGCODS
SCOLDS
SCOLECES
SCOLEX
SCOLICES
SCOLIOMA S
SCOLLOP S
COLLOPS
SCOLLOPS
SCOMBRID S
SCONCE DS
SCONCED
SCONCES
SCONCING
SCONE S
CONES
SCONES
SCOOCH
SCOOCHED
SCOOCHES
SCOOP S
COOPS
SCOOPED
SCOOPER S
COOPERS
SCOOPERS
SCOOPFUL S
SCOOPING
SCOOPS
SCOOT S
COOTS
SCOOTCH
SCOOTED

SCOOTER S
COOTERS
SCOOTERS
SCOOTING
SCOOTS
SCOP ES
COPS
SCOPE DS
COPES COPSE
SCOPED
SCOPES
COPSES
SCOPING
COPINGS
SCOPS
SCOPULA ES
COPULAS
CUPOLAS
SCOPULAE
SCOPULAS
SCORCH
SCORCHED
SCORCHER S
SCORCHES
SCORE DRS
CEROS CORES
CORSE
SCORED
CODERS
CREDOS
DECORS
SCOREPAD S
SCORER S
CORERS
CRORES
SCORERS
CROSSER
RECROSS
SCORES
CORSES
CROSSE
SCORIA E
SCORIAE
SCORIFY
SCORING
SCORN S
CORNS
SCORNED
SCORNER S
CORNERS
SCORNERS
SCORNFUL
SCORNING
SCORNS
SCORPION S
AE SCOT S
COST COTS
SCOTCH
SCOTCHED
SCOTCHES
SCOTER S
CORSET
COSTER
ESCORT
RECTOS
SECTOR
SCOTERS
CORSETS
COSTERS
ESCORTS
SECTORS
SCOTIA S
COATIS
SCOTIAS
SCOTOMA S
SCOTOMAS
SCOTOPIA S
SCOTOPIC
AE SCOTS
COSTS
SCOTTIE S
SCOTTIES
SCOUR S
SCOURED
COURSED
SOURCED
SCOURER S
COURSER
SCOURERS
COURSERS

SCOURGE DRS
SCROUGE
SCOURGED
SCROUGED
SCOURGER S
SCOURGES
SCROUGES
SCOURING S
COURSING
SOURCING
SCOURS
SCOUSE S
SCOUSES
SCOUT HS
SCOUTED
SCOUTER S
COUTERS
CROUTES
SCOUTERS
CRUSTOSE
SCOUTH S
COUTHS
SCOUTHER S
TOUCHERS
SCOUTHS
SCOUTING S
SCOUTS
CUSTOS
SCOW LS
COWS
SCOWDER S
SCOWDERS
SCOWED
SCOWING
SCOWL S
COWLS
SCOWLED
SCOWLER S
SCOWLERS
SCOWLING
COWLINGS
SCOWLS
SCOWS
SCRABBLE DR S
CLABBERS
SCRABBLY
SCRAG S
CRAGS
SCRAGGED
SCRAGGLY
SCRAGGY
SCRAGS
SCRAICH S
SCRAICHS
SCRAIGH S
SCRAIGHS
SCRAM S
CRAMS MARCS
SCRAMBLE DR S
CLAMBERS
SCRAMJET S
SCRAMMED
SCRAMS
SCRANNEL S
SCRAP ES
CARPS CRAPS
SCARP
SCRAPE DRS
CAPERS
CRAPES
ESCARP
PACERS
PARSEC
RECAPS
SECPAR
SPACER
SCRAPED
REDCAPS
SCARPED
SCRAPER S
CARPERS
SCARPER
SCRAPERS
SCARPERS
SCRAPES
ESCARPS
PARSECS
SECPARS
SPACERS
SCRAPIE S
SPACIER

SCRAPIES
SCRAPING S
CARPINGS
SCARPING
SCRAPPED
SCRAPPER S
SCRAPPLE S
CLAPPERS
SCRAPPY
SCRAPS
SCARPS
SCRATCH Y
SCRATCHY
SCRAWL SY
CRAWLS
SCRAWLED
SCRAWLER S
CRAWLERS
SCRAWLS
SCRAWLY
SCRAWNY
SCREAK SY
CRAKES
CREAKS
SACKER
SCREAKED
SCREAKS
SACKERS
SCREAKY
SCREAM S
CREAMS
MACERS
SCREAMED
SCREAMER S
AMERCERS
CREAMERS
SCREAMS
SCREE DNS
CERES
SCREECH Y
CRECHES
SCREECHY
SCREED S
CEDERS
CREEDS
SCREEDED
SCREEDS
SCREEN S
CENSER
SECERN
SCREENED
SECERNED
SCREENER S
RESCREEN
SCREENS
CENSERS
SECERNS
SCREES
RECESS
SCREW SY
CREWS
SCREWED
SCREWER S
SCREWERS
SCREWIER
SCREWING
SCREWS
SCREWUP S
SCREWUPS
SCREWY
SCRIBAL
SCRIBBLE DR S
SCRIBBLY
A SCRIBE DRS
A SCRIBED
SCRIBER S
SCRIBERS
A SCRIBES
A SCRIBING
SCRIED
CIDERS
DICERS
SCRIES
CRISES
SCRIEVE DS
SERVICE
SCRIEVED
SERVICED
SCRIEVES
SERVICES

SCRIM PS
SCRIMP SY
CRIMPS
SCRIMPED
SCRIMPER S
CRIMPERS
SCRIMPIT
SCRIMPS
SCRIMPY
SCRIMS
SCRIP ST
CRISP
SCRIPS
CRISPS
SCRIPT S
SCRIPTED
PREDICTS
SCRIPTER S
RESCRIPT
SCRIPTS
SCRIVE DS
SCRIVED
SCRIVES
SCRIVING
SCROD S
CORDS
SCRODS
SCROFULA S
SCROGGY
SCROLL S
SCROLLED
SCROLLS
SCROOCH
SCROOGE S
SCROOGES
SCROOP S
SCROOPED
SCROOPS
SCROOTCH
SCROTA L
ACTORS
CASTOR
COSTAR
TAROCS
SCROTAL
SCROTUM S
SCROTUMS
SCROUGE DS
SCOURGE
SCROUGED
SCOURGED
SCROUGES
SCOURGES
SCROUNGE DR S
SCROUNGY
SCRUB S
CURBS
SCRUBBED
SCRUBBER S
SCRUBBY
SCRUBS
SCRUFF SY
SCRUFFS
SCRUFFY
SCRUM S
SCRUMMED
SCRUMS
SCRUNCH Y
SCRUNCHY
SCRUPLE DS
SCRUPLED
SCRUPLES
SCRUTINY
SCRY
SCRYING
SCUBA S
SCUBAED
ABDUCES
SCUBAING
SCUBAS
SCUD IOS
CUDS
SCUDDED
SCUDDING
SCUDI
E SCUDO
SCUDS

SCUFF S
CUFFS
SCUFFED
SCUFFER S
SCUFFERS
SCUFFING
SCUFFLE DRS
SCUFFLED
SCUFFLER S
SCUFFLES
CUFFLESS
SCUFFS
SCULCH
SCULCHES
SCULK S
LUCKS
SCULKED
SUCKLED
SCULKER S
RUCKLES
SUCKLER
SCULKERS
SUCKLERS
SCULKING
SUCKLING
SCULKS
SCULL S
CULLS
SCULLED
SCULLER SY
CULLERS
SCULLERS
SCULLERY
SCULLING
SCULLION S
CULLIONS
SCULLS
SCULP ST
SCULPED
SCULPIN GS
INSCULP
UNCLIPS
SCULPING
SCULPINS
INSCULPS
SCULPS
SCULPT S
SCULPTED
SCULPTOR S
SCULPTS
SCULTCH
SCUM S
SCUMBAG S
SCUMBAGS
SCUMBLE DS
SCUMBLED
SCUMBLES
SCUMLESS
SCUMLIKE
SCUMMED
SCUMMER S
CUMMERS
SCUMMERS
SCUMMIER
CRUMMIES
SCUMMILY
SCUMMING
SCUMMY
SCUMS
SCUNNER S
CUNNERS
SCUNNERS
SCUP S
CUPS CUSP
SCUPPAUG S
SCUPPER S
CUPPERS
SCUPPERS
SCUPS
CUSPS
SCURF SY
CURFS
SCURFIER
SCURFS
SCURFY
SCURRIED
SCURRIES
CRUISERS
SCURRIL E
SCURRILE

SCURRY
SCURVIER
SCURVIES T
CURSIVES
SCURVILY
SCURVY
SCUT AES
CUTS
SCUTA
SCUTAGE S
SCUTAGES
SCUTATE
ACUTEST
SCUTCH
SCUTCHED
SCUTCHER S
CRUTCHES
SCUTCHES
SCUTE S
CUTES
SCUTELLA R
SCUTES
CESTUS
SCUTS
SCUTTER S
CURTEST
CUTTERS
SCUTTERS
SCUTTLE DS
CUTLETS
CUTTLES
SCUTTLED
SCUTTLES
SCUTUM
SCUTWORK S
CUTWORKS
SCUZZ Y
SCUZZES
SCUZZIER
SCUZZY
SCYPHATE
SCYPHI
PHYSIC
SCYPHUS
SCYTHE DS
CHESTY
SCYTHED
SCYTHES
SCYTHING
A **SEA** LMRST
SAE
SEABAG S
SEABAGS
BAGASSE
SEABEACH
SEABED S
DEBASE
SEABEDS
DEBASES
SEABIRD S
ABIDERS
BRAISED
DARBIES
SIDEBAR
SEABIRDS
SIDEBARS
SEABOARD S
SEABOOT S
SEABOOTS
SEABORNE
SEACOAST S
SEACOCK S
SEACOCKS
SEACRAFT S
SEADOG S
DOSAGE
SEADOGS
DOSAGES
SEADROME S
SEAFARER S
SEAFLOOR S
SEAFOOD S
SEAFOODS
SEAFOWL S
SEAFOWLS
SEAFRONT S
SEAGIRT
AIGRETS
GAITERS
STAGIER
TRIAGES
SEAGOING
SEAGULL S
SULLAGE
ULLAGES
SEAGULLS
GALLUSES
SULLAGES
SEAHORSE S
SEASHORE
SEAL S
ALES LASE
LEAS SALE
SEALABLE
LEASABLE
SALEABLE
SEALANT S
SEALANTS
SEALED
LEASED
SEALER SY
LAREES
LEASER
REALES
RESALE
RESEAL
SEALERS
EARLESS
LEASERS
RESALES
RESEALS
SEALERY
SEALIFT S
FETIALS
SEALIFTS
SEALING
LEASING
LINAGES
SEALLIKE
SEALS
LASES SALES
SEALSKIN S
SEAM SY
MAES MESA
SAME
SEAMAN
SEAMANLY
SEAMARK S
SEAMARKS
SEAMED
ADEEMS
EDEMAS
SEAMEN
ENEMAS
MENSAE
SEAMER S
AMEERS
RAMEES
SEAMERS
SEAMIER
SERIEMA
SEAMIEST
SEAMING
ENIGMAS
GAMINES
SEAMLESS
SEAMLIKE
SEAMOUNT S
SEAMS
MASSE MESAS
SEAMSTER S
MASSETER
STEAMERS
SEAMY
SEANCE S
ENCASE
SENECA
SEANCES
CASSENE
ENCASES
SENECAS
SEAPIECE S
SEAPLANE S
SPELAEAN
SEAPORT S
ESPARTO
PROTEAS
SEAPORTS
ESPARTOS
PROTASES
SEAQUAKE S
SEAR S
ARES EARS
ERAS RASE
SERA
SEARCH
ARCHES
CHARES
CHASER
ESCHAR
SEARCHED
SEARCHER S
REACHERS
RESEARCH
SEARCHES
SEARED
ERASED
RESEDA
SEARER
ERASER
SEAREST
EASTERS
RESEATS
SEATERS
TEASERS
TESSERA
SEARING
EARINGS
ERASING
GAINERS
REAGINS
REGAINS
REGINAS
SERINGA
SEAROBIN S
BARONIES
SEARS
ARSES RASES
SEAS
SEASCAPE S
SEASCOUT S
SEASHELL S
SEASHORE S
SEAHORSE
SEASICK
SEASIDE S
DISEASE
SEASIDES
DISEASES
SEASON S
SEASONAL S
SEASONED
ADENOSES
SEASONER S
RESEASON
SEASONS
SEAT S
ATES EAST
EATS ETAS
SATE SETA
TEAS
SEATBACK S
BACKSEAT
SEATBELT S
TESTABLE
SEATED
SEDATE
TEASED
SEATER S
ARETES
EASTER
EATERS
RESEAT
TEASER
SEATERS
EASTERS
RESEATS
SEAREST
TEASERS
TESSERA
SEATING S
EASTING
EATINGS
INGATES
INGESTA
TEASING
SEATINGS
EASTINGS
GIANTESS
SEATLESS
SEATMATE S
SEATRAIN S
ANTISERA
RATANIES
SANTERIA
SEATROUT S
OUTRATES
OUTSTARE
SEATS
ASSET EASTS
SATES TASSE
SEATWORK S
SEAWALL S
SEAWALLS
SEAWAN ST
SEAWANS
SEAWANT S
SEAWANTS
SEAWARD S
SEAWARDS
SEAWARE S
SEAWARES
SEAWATER S
TEAWARES
SEAWAY S
SEAWAYS
SEAWEED S
SEAWEEDS
SEESAWED
SEBACIC
SEBASIC
ABSCISE
SCABIES
SEBUM S
SEBUMS
SEC ST
SECALOSE S
SECANT S
ASCENT
CENTAS
ENACTS
STANCE
SECANTLY
SECANTS
ASCENTS
STANCES
SECATEUR S
SECCO S
COSEC
SECCOS
COSECS
SECEDE DRS
SECEDED
SECEDER S
DECREES
RECEDES
SECEDERS
RECESSED
SECEDES
SECEDING
SECERN S
CENSER
SCREEN
SECERNED
SCREENED
SECERNS
CENSERS
SCREENS
SECLUDE DS
SECLUDED
SECLUDES
SECONAL S
SECONALS
SECOND EIOS
CODENS
SECONDE DRS
ENCODES
SECONDED
SECONDER S
CENSORED
ENCODERS
NECROSED
SECONDES
SECONDI
CODEINS
SECONDLY
CONDYLES
SECONDO
CONDOES
SECONDS
SECPAR S
CAPERS
CRAPES
ESCARP
PACERS
PARSEC
RECAPS
SCRAPE
SPACER
SECPARS
ESCARPS
PARSECS
SCRAPES
SPACERS
SECRECY
SECRET ES
CERTES
ERECTS
RESECT
TERCES
SECRETE DRS
SECRETED
RESECTED
SECRETER
ERECTERS
REERECTS
SECRETES T
SESTERCE
SECRETIN GS
ENTERICS
ENTICERS
SECRETLY
SECRETOR SY
ERECTORS
SECRETS
CRESSET
RESECTS
SECS
CESS
SECT S
SECTARY
SECTILE
SECTION S
NOTICES
SECTIONS
SECTOR S
CORSET
COSTER
ESCORT
RECTOS
SCOTER
SECTORAL
LOCATERS
SECTORED
CORSETED
ESCORTED
SECTORS
CORSETS
COSTERS
ESCORTS
SCOTERS
SECTS
SECULAR S
RECUSAL
SECULARS
RECUSALS
SECUND
DUNCES
SECUNDLY
SECUNDUM
SECURE DRS
CEREUS
CERUSE
RECUSE
RESCUE
SECURED
RECUSED
REDUCES
RESCUED
SEDUCER
SECURELY
SECURER S
RESCUER
SECURERS
RESCUERS
SECURES T
CERUSES
RECUSES
RESCUES
SECUREST
SECURING
RECUSING
RESCUING
SECURITY
SEDAN S
DEANS SANED
SEDANS
SEDARIM
ADMIRES
MISREAD
SIDEARM
SEDATE DRS
SEATED
TEASED
SEDATED
DEADEST
STEADED
SEDATELY
SEDATER
DEAREST
DERATES
REDATES
SEDATES T
SEDATEST
SEDATING
STEADING
SEDATION S
ASTONIED
SEDATIVE S
DEVIATES
SEDER S
DEERS DREES
REDES REEDS
SERED
SEDERS
SEDERUNT S
DENTURES
UNDERSET
UNRESTED
SEDGE S
EDGES
SEDGES
SEDGIER
SEDGIEST
SEDGY
SEDILE
DIESEL
EDILES
ELIDES
SEIDEL
SEDILIA
DAILIES
LIAISED
SEDILIUM
SEDIMENT S
SEDITION S
EDITIONS
SEDUCE DRS
DEUCES
EDUCES
SEDUCED
DEDUCES
SEDUCER S
RECUSED
REDUCES
RESCUED
SECURED
SEDUCERS
SEDUCES
SEDUCING
SEDUCIVE
SEDULITY
SEDULOUS
SEDUM S
MUSED
SEDUMS
MUSSED
SEE DKLMNPR S
SEEABLE
SEECATCH
SEED SY
DEES
SEEDBED S
SEEDBEDS
SEEDCAKE S
SEEDCASE S
DECEASES
SEEDED
SEEDER S
RESEED
SEEDERS
RESEEDS
SEEDIER
SEEDIEST
SEEDILY
EYELIDS
SEEDING
SEEDLESS
SEEDLIKE
SEEDLING S
SEEDMAN
DEMEANS
SEEDMEN
DEMESNE
SEEDPOD S
DEPOSED
SEEDPODS
SEEDS
SEEDSMAN
SEEDSMEN
DEMESNES
SEEDTIME S
SEEDY
SEEING S
GENIES
SIGNEE
SEEINGS
GENESIS
SIGNEES
SEEK S
EKES SKEE
SEEKER S
RESEEK
SEEKERS
RESEEKS
SEEKING
SKEEING
SEEKS
SKEES
SEEL SY
EELS ELSE
LEES
SEELED
SEELING
SEELS
SEELY
SEEM S
EMES SEME
SEEMED
SEEMER S
EMEERS
SEEMERS
SEEMING S
SEEMINGS
SEEMLIER
SEEMLY
SEEMS
SEMES
SEEN
ESNE SENE
SEEP SY
PEES
SEEPAGE S
SEEPAGES
SEEPED
SEEPIER
PEERIES
SEEPIEST
EPEEISTS
SEEPING
SEEPS
SEEPY
SEER S
REES SERE
SEERESS
SEERS
ERSES SERES
SEES
ESES
SEESAW S
SEESAWED
SEAWEEDS
SEESAWS
SEETHE DS
SEETHED
SHEETED
SEETHES
SEETHING
SHEETING
SEG OS
SEGETAL
EAGLETS
GELATES
LEGATES
TELEGAS

SEGGAR S
AGGERS EGGARS GAGERS SAGGER
SEGGARS
AGGRESS SAGGERS
SEGMENT S
SEGMENTS
SEGNI
SENGI SINGE
SEGNO S
SEGNOS
GNOSES
SEGO S
EGOS GOES
SEGOS
GESSO
SEGS
SEGUE DS
SEGUED
SEGUEING
SEGUES
SEI FS
SEICENTO S
SEICHE S
SEICHES
SEIDEL S
DIESEL EDILES ELIDES SEDILE
SEIDELS
DIESELS IDLESSE
SEIF S
SEIFS
SEIGNEUR SY
SEIGNIOR SY
SEIGNORY
SEINE DRS
SEINED
DENIES DIENES
SEINER S
NEREIS SEREIN SERINE
SEINERS
SEREINS SERINES
SEINES
SENSEI
SEINING
INSIGNE
SEIS EM
SEISABLE
SEISE DRS
SEISED
DIESES
SEISER S
SERIES SIREES
SEISERS
SEISES
SEISIN GS
NISEIS
SEISING S
SEISINGS
SEISINS
SEISM S
MISES SEMIS
SEISMAL
AIMLESS SAMIELS
SEISMIC
SEISMISM S
SEISMS
MISSES
SEISOR S
OSIERS
SEISORS
SEISURE S
REISSUE
SEISURES
REISSUES
SEITAN S
TENIAS TINEAS TISANE
SEITANS
ENTASIS NASTIES SESTINA TANSIES TISANES
SEIZABLE
SIZEABLE
SEIZE DRS
SEIZED
SEIZER S
RESIZE
SEIZERS
RESIZES
SEIZES
SEIZIN GS
SEIZING S
SEIZINGS
SEIZINS
SEIZOR S
SEIZORS
SEIZURE S
SEIZURES
SEJANT
SEJEANT
SEL FLS
ELS
SELADANG S
SELAH S
HALES HEALS LEASH SHALE SHEAL
SELAHS
HASSEL HASSLE LASHES SHALES SHEALS
SELAMLIK S
SELCOUTH
SELDOM
MODELS
SELDOMLY
SELECT S
ELECTS
SELECTED
DESELECT
SELECTEE S
ELECTEES
SELECTLY
SELECTOR S
CORSELET ELECTORS ELECTROS
SELECTS
SELENATE S
SELENIC
LICENSE SILENCE
SELENIDE S
SELENITE S
ENLISTEE
SELENIUM S
SELENOUS
SELF S
SELFDOM S
SELFDOMS
SELFED
SELFHEAL S
SELFHOOD S
SELFING
SELFISH
HISSELF
SELFLESS
SELFNESS
SELFS
SELFSAME
FAMELESS
SELFWARD S
SELKIE S
SELKIES
SELL ES
ELLS
SELLABLE
SELLE RS
SELLER S
RESELL
SELLERS
RESELLS
SELLES
SELLING
SELLOFF S
SELLOFFS
SELLOUT S
OUTSELL
SELLOUTS
OUTSELLS
SELLS
SELS
LESS
SELSYN S
SELSYNS
SLYNESS
SELTZER S
SELTZERS
SELVA S
LAVES SALVE SLAVE VALES VALSE VEALS
SELVAGE DS
SELVAGED
SELVAGES
SELVAS
SALVES SLAVES VALSES
SELVEDGE DS
SELVES
VESSEL
SEMANTIC S
AMNESTIC
SEMATIC
SEME NS
EMES SEEM
SEMEME S
SEMEMES
MESEEMS
SEMEMIC
SEMEN S
MENSE MESNE NEEMS
SEMENS
MENSES MESNES
SEMES
SEEMS
SEMESTER S
SEMI S
MISE
SEMIARID
SEMIBALD
SEMICOMA S
SEMIDEAF
SEMIDOME DS
SEMIDRY
SEMIFIT
SEMIGALA
SEMIHARD
MISHEARD
SEMIHIGH
SEMIHOBO S
SEMILLON S
SEMILOG
SEMIMAT T
MISMATE TAMMIES
SEMIMATT E
SEMIMILD
SEMIMUTE
SEMINA LR
AMINES ANIMES INSEAM MESIAN
SEMINAL
MALINES MENIALS
SEMINAR SY
MARINES REMAINS
SEMINARS
SEMINARY
SEMINOMA DS
SEMINUDE
SEMIOPEN
SEMIOSES
SEMIOSIS
SEMIOTIC S
COMITIES
SEMIOVAL
SEMIPRO S
IMPOSER PROMISE
SEMIPROS
IMPOSERS PROMISES
SEMIRAW
SEMIS
MISES SEISM
SEMISES
SEMISOFT
SEMITIST S
MISTIEST
SEMITONE S
MONETISE
SEMIWILD
SEMOLINA S
LAMINOSE
SEMPLE
SEMPLICE
SEMPRE
SEN DET
ENS
SENARII
SENARIUS
ANURESIS
SENARY
YEARNS
SENATE S
ENATES SATEEN
SENATES
ENTASES SATEENS SENSATE
SENATOR S
ATONERS SANTERO TREASON
SENATORS
ASSENTOR SANTEROS STARNOSE TREASONS
SEND S
DENS ENDS SNED
SENDABLE
SENDAL S
ELANDS LADENS NALEDS
SENDALS
SENDED
SENDER S
DENSER ENDERS RESEND
SENDERS
REDNESS RESENDS
SENDING
ENDINGS
SENDOFF S
OFFENDS
SENDOFFS
SENDS
SNEDS
SENDUP S
UPENDS UPSEND
SENDUPS
SUSPEND UPSENDS
SENE
ESNE SEEN
SENECA S
ENCASE SEANCE
SENECAS
CASSENE ENCASES SEANCES
SENECIO S
SENECIOS
SENEGA S
AGENES
SENEGAS
SENGI
SEGNI SINGE
SENHOR AS
HERONS HONERS NOSHER
SENHORA S
HOARSEN
SENHORAS
HOARSENS
SENHORES
SENHORS
NOSHERS
SENILE S
ENISLE ENSILE
SENILELY
SENILES
ENISLES ENSILES
SENILITY
SENIOR S
IRONES NOSIER
SENIORS
SONSIER
SENITI
SENNA S
SENNAS
SENNET S
SENNETS
SENNIGHT S
SENNIT S
TENNIS
SENNITS
SENOPIA S
EPINAOS
SENOPIAS
SENOR AS
SNORE
SENORA S
ARSENO REASON
SENORAS
REASONS
SENORES
SENORITA S
NOTARIES
SENORS
SENSOR SNORES
SENRYU
SENSA
SANES
SENSATE DS
ENTASES SATEENS SENATES
SENSATED
ASSENTED STANDEES
SENSATES
SENSE DIS
ESNES
SENSED
SENSEFUL
SENSEI S
SEINES
SENSEIS
SENSES
NESSES
SENSIBLE RS
SENSIBLY
SENSILLA E
AINSELLS
SENSING
ENSIGNS
SENSOR SY
SENORS SNORES
SENSORIA L
ERASIONS
SENSORS
SENSORY
SENSUAL
UNSEALS
SENSUM
SENSUOUS
SENT EI
NEST NETS TENS
SENTE
TEENS TENSE
SENTENCE DR S
SENTI
INSET NEIST NITES STEIN TINES
SENTIENT S
SENTIMO S
MESTINO MOISTEN
SENTIMOS
MESTINOS MOISTENS
SENTINEL S
SENTRIES
SENTRY
SEPAL S
LAPSE LEAPS PALES PEALS PLEAS SALEP SPALE
SEPALED
ELAPSED PLEASED
SEPALINE
PENALISE
SEPALLED
SEPALOID
SEPALOUS
ESPOUSAL
SEPALS
LAPSES PASSEL SALEPS SPALES
SEPARATE DS
ASPERATE
SEPIA S
PAISE
SEPIAS
SEPIC
EPICS SPICE
SEPOY S
POESY
SEPOYS
PYOSES
SEPPUKU S
SEPPUKUS
A **SEPSES**
A **SEPSIS**
SPEISS
SEPT AS
PEST PETS STEP
SEPTA L
PASTE PATES PEATS SPATE TAPES TEPAS
SEPTAGE S
SEPTAGES
SEPTAL
PALEST PALETS PASTEL PETALS PLATES PLEATS STAPLE TEPALS
SEPTARIA N
ASPIRATE PARASITE
SEPTATE
SEPTET S
SEPTETS
SEPTETTE S
A **SEPTIC** S
SEPTICAL
TIECLASP
SEPTICS
CESSPIT
SEPTIME S
EMPTIES
SEPTIMES
SEPTS
PESTS STEPS
SEPTUM S
SEPTUMS
SEPTUPLE DS T
SEQUEL AS
SEQUELA E
QUELEAS
SEQUELAE
SEQUELS
SEQUENCE DR S
SEQUENCY
SEQUENT S
SEQUENTS
SEQUIN S
SEQUINED
SEQUINS
SEQUITUR S
SEQUOIA S
SEQUOIAS
U **SER** AEFS
ERS RES
SERA CIL
ARES EARS ERAS RASE SEAR
SERAC S
ACRES CARES CARSE ESCAR RACES SCARE
SERACS
CARESS CARSES CRASES ESCARS SCARES
SERAGLIO S
GASOLIER GIRASOLE
SERAI LS
ARISE RAISE
SERAIL S
ARIELS RESAIL SAILER SERIAL
SERAILS
AIRLESS RESAILS SAILERS SERIALS
SERAIS
ARISES RAISES
SERAL
ARLES EARLS LARES LASER LEARS RALES REALS
SERAPE S
SERAPES
ASPERSE PARESES
SERAPH S
PHRASE RAPHES SHAPER SHERPA
SERAPHIC
ASPHERIC PARCHESI
SERAPHIM S
SAMPHIRE
SERAPHIN
HEPARINS
SERAPHS
PHRASES SHAPERS SHERPAS
SERDAB S
ARDEBS BARDES BEARDS BREADS DEBARS SABRED
SERDABS
BRASSED
SERE DRS
REES SEER
SERED
DEERS DREES REDES REEDS SEDER
SEREIN S
NEREIS SEINER SERINE
SEREINS
SEINERS SERINES
SERENADE DR S

SERENATA S
ARSENATE
SERENATE
SERENE RS
RESEEN
SERENELY
SERENER
SNEERER
SERENES T
SERENEST
SERENITY
SERER
SERES T
ERSES SEERS
SEREST
ESTERS
REESTS
RESETS
STEERS
STERES
SERF S
REFS
SERFAGE S
SERFAGES
SERFDOM S
DEFORMS
SERFDOMS
SERFHOOD S
SERFISH
FISHERS
SHERIFS
SERFLIKE
SERFS
SERGE DRS
EGERS GREES
REGES
SERGEANT SY
ESTRANGE
GRANTEES
GREATENS
NEGATERS
REAGENTS
SERGED
EDGERS
GREEDS
SERGER S
SERGERS
REGRESS
SERGES
EGRESS
SERGING S
GINGERS
SNIGGER
SERGINGS
SNIGGERS
SERIAL S
ARIELS
RESAIL
SAILER
SERAIL
SERIALLY
SERIALS
AIRLESS
RESAILS
SAILERS
SERAILS
SERIATE DS
AERIEST
SERIATED
READIEST
STEADIER
SERIATES
SERIATIM
AIRTIMES
SERICIN S
IRENICS
SERICINS
SERIEMA S
SEAMIER
SERIEMAS
SERIES
SEISER
SIREES
SERIF S
FIRES FRIES
FRISE REIFS
SERIFED
DEFIERS
SERIFFED
SERIFS
FRISES

SERIN EGS
REINS RESIN
RINSE RISEN
SIREN
E **SERINE** S
NEREIS
SEINER
SEREIN
E **SERINES**
SEINERS
SEREINS
SERING A
REIGNS
RENIGS
RESIGN
SIGNER
SINGER
SERINGA S
EARINGS
ERASING
GAINERS
REAGINS
REGAINS
REGINAS
SEARING
SERINGAS
ASSIGNER
REASSIGN
SERINS
RESINS
RINSES
SIRENS
SERIOUS
SERJEANT SY
SERMON S
SERMONIC
INCOMERS
SERMONS
SEROLOGY
SEROSA ELS
SEROSAE
SEROSAL
LASSOER
OARLESS
SEROSAS
SAROSES
SEROSITY
SEROTINE S
ONERIEST
SEROTINY
TYROSINE
SEROTYPE DS
SEROUS
ROUSES
SEROVAR S
SAVORER
SEROVARS
SAVORERS
SEROW S
RESOW SOWER
SWORE WORSE
SEROWS
RESOWS
SOWERS
WORSES
SERPENT S
PENSTER
PRESENT
REPENTS
SERPENTS
PENSTERS
PERTNESS
PRESENTS
SERPIGO S
PORGIES
SERPIGOS
GOSSIPER
SERRANID S
DRAINERS
SERRANO S
SERRANOS
SERRATE DS
RETEARS
TEARERS
SERRATED
ARRESTED
RETREADS
TREADERS
SERRATES
ASSERTER
REASSERT
TERRASES

SERRIED
DERRIES
DESIRER
REDRIES
RESIDER
SERRIES
RERISES
SIRREES
SERRY
SERRYING
U **SERS**
SERUM S
MURES MUSER
SERUMAL
MAULERS
SERUMS
MUSERS
SERVABLE
SERVAL S
LAVERS
RAVELS
SALVER
SLAVER
VELARS
VERSAL
SERVALS
SALVERS
SLAVERS
SERVANT S
TAVERNS
VERSANT
SERVANTS
VERSANTS
SERVE DRS
SEVER VEERS
VERSE
SERVED
VERSED
SERVER S
REVERS
VERSER
SERVERS
VERSERS
SERVES
SEVERS
VERSES
SERVICE DRS
SCRIEVE
SERVICED
SCRIEVED
SERVICER S
SERVICES
SCRIEVES
SERVILE
LEVIERS
RELIVES
REVILES
VEILERS
SERVING S
VERSING
SERVINGS
SERVITOR S
OVERSTIR
SERVO S
OVERS ROVES
VERSO
SERVOS
VERSOS
SESAME S
SESAMES
SESAMOID S
SESSILE
SESSION S
ESSOINS
OSSEINS
SESSIONS
SESSPOOL S
SESTERCE S
SECRETES
SESTET S
TESTES
TSETSE
SESTETS
TSETSES
SESTINA S
ENTASIS
NASTIES
SEITANS
TANSIES
TISANES
SESTINAS
SESTINE S
SESTINES

SET AST
SETA EL
ATES EAST
EATS ETAS
SATE SEAT
TEAS
SETAE
TEASE
SETAL
LEAST SLATE
STALE STEAL
STELA TAELS
TALES TEALS
TESLA
SETBACK S
BACKSET
SETBACKS
BACKSETS
SETENANT S
SETIFORM
SETLINE S
LENITES
LISENTE
TENSILE
SETLINES
LITENESS
SETOFF S
OFFSET
SETOFFS
OFFSETS
SETON S
NOTES ONSET
STENO STONE
TONES
SETONS
ONSETS
STENOS
STONES
SETOSE
SETOUS
TOUSES
SETOUT S
OUTSET
SETOUTS
OUTSETS
SETS
SETSCREW S
SETT S
STET TEST
TETS
SETTEE S
TESTEE
SETTEES
TESTEES
SETTER S
RETEST
STREET
TESTER
SETTERS
RETESTS
STREETS
TERSEST
TESTERS
SETTING S
TESTING
SETTINGS
SETTLE DRS
SETTLED
SETTLER S
LETTERS
STERLET
TRESTLE
SETTLERS
STERLETS
TRESTLES
SETTLES
SETTLING S
SETTLOR S
LOTTERS
SLOTTER
SETTLORS
SLOTTERS
SETTS
STETS TESTS
SETULOSE
SETULOUS
SETUP S
STUPE UPSET
SETUPS
STUPES
UPSETS
SEVEN S
EVENS NEVES
SEVENS

SEVENTH S
SEVENTHS
SEVENTY
SEVER ES
SERVE VEERS
VERSE
SEVERAL S
LAVEERS
LEAVERS
REVEALS
VEALERS
SEVERALS
SEVERE DR
REEVES
SEVERED
DESERVE
SEVERELY
SEVERER
RESERVE
REVERES
REVERSE
SEVEREST
SEVERING
SEVERITY
SEVERS
SERVES
VERSES
SEVICHE S
CHEVIES
SEVICHES
SEVRUGA S
SEVRUGAS
SEW NS
SEWABLE
SEWAGE S
SEWAGES
SEWAN S
WANES WEANS
SEWANS
SEWAR S
RESAW SAWER
SWARE SWEAR
WARES WEARS
SEWARS
RESAWS
SAWERS
SWEARS
WRASSE
SEWED
SWEDE WEEDS
SEWER S
EWERS RESEW
SWEER
SEWERAGE S
SEWERED
RESEWED
WEEDERS
SEWERING
RESEWING
SEWERS
RESEWS
SEWING S
SWINGE
SEWINGS
SWINGES
SEWN
NEWS WENS
SEWS
SEX TY
SEXED
DESEX DEXES
SEXES
SEXIER
SEXIEST
SEXILY
SEXINESS
SEXING
SEXISM S
SEXISMS
SEXIST S
EXISTS
SIXTES
SEXISTS
SEXLESS
SEXOLOGY
SEXPOT S
SEXPOTS
SEXT OS
SEXTAIN S
ANTISEX
SEXTAINS

SEXTAN ST
SEXTANS
SEXTANT S
SEXTANTS
SEXTARII
SEXTET S
SEXTETS
SEXTETTE S
SEXTILE S
SEXTILES
EXITLESS
SEXTO NS
SEXTON S
SEXTONS
SEXTOS
SEXTS
SEXTUPLE DS T
SEXTUPLY
A **SEXUAL**
A **SEXUALLY**
SEXY
SFERICS
SFORZATO S
SFUMATO S
SFUMATOS
A **SH** AEHY
SHA DGHMWY
AHS
ASH
HAS
SHABBIER
SHABBILY
SHABBY
SHACK OS
HACKS
SHACKED
SHACKING
SHACKLE DRS
HACKLES
SHACKLED
SHACKLER S
HACKLERS
SHACKLES
SHACKO S
SHACKOES
SHACKOS
HASSOCK
SHACKS
SHAD ESY
DAHS DASH
SHADBLOW S
SHADBUSH
SHADCHAN S
SHADDOCK S
HADDOCKS
SHADE DRS
ASHED DEASH
HADES HEADS
SADHE
SHADED
DASHED
SHADER S
DASHER
SHARED
SHADERS
DASHERS
SHADES
DASHES
SADHES
SASHED
SHADFLY
SHADIER
AIRSHED
DASHIER
HARDIES
SHADIEST
DASHIEST
SHADILY
LADYISH
SHADING S
DASHING
SHADINGS
SHADKHAN S
SHADOOF S
SHADOOFS
SHADOW SY
SHADOWED
SHADOWER S

SHADOWS
SHADOWY
SHADRACH S
SHADS
SHADUF S
SHADUFS
SHADY
DASHY
SHAFT S
HAFTS
SHAFTED
SHAFTING S
SHAFTS
SHAG S
GASH HAGS
SHAGBARK S
SHAGGED
SHAGGIER
SHAGGILY
SHAGGING
SHAGGY
SHAGREEN S
SHAGS
SHAH S
HAHS HASH
SHAHDOM S
SHAHDOMS
SHAHS
SHAIRD S
RADISH
SHAIRDS
SHAIRN S
ARSHIN
SHAIRNS
ARSHINS
SHAITAN S
SHAITANS
SHAKABLE
SHAKE NRS
HAKES
SHAKEN
SHAKEOUT S
SHAKER S
KASHER
SHAKERS
KASHERS
SHAKES
SHAKEUP S
SHAKEUPS
SHAKIER
SHAKIEST
SHITAKES
SHAKILY
SHAKING
SHAKO S
SHAKOES
SHAKOS
SHAKY
SHALE DSY
HALES HEALS
LEASH SELAH
SHEAL
SHALED
LASHED
SHALES
HASSEL
HASSLE
LASHES
SELAHS
SHEALS
SHALEY
SHALIER
HAILERS
SHALIEST
HELIASTS
SHALL
HALLS
SHALLOON S
SHALLOP S
SHALLOPS
SHALLOT S
SHALLOTS
SHALLOW S
HALLOWS
SHALLOWS
SHALOM S
SHALOMS
SHALT
HALTS LATHS

SHALY
HYLAS
SHAM ES
HAMS MASH
SHAMABLE
SHAMABLY
SHAMAN S
ASHMAN
SHAMANIC
SHAMANS
SHAMAS
SHAMBLE DS
SHAMBLED
SHAMBLES
SHAME DS
HAEMS HAMES
A **SHAMED**
EMDASH
MASHED
SHAMEFUL
SHAMES
MASHES
SHAMING
MASHING
SHAMISEN S
SHAMMAS H
SHAMMASH
SHAMMED
SHAMMER S
HAMMERS
SHAMMERS
SHAMMES
SHAMMIED
SHAMMIES
SHAMMING
SHAMMOS
SHAMMY
SHAMOIS
SHAMOS
SHAMOSIM
SHAMOY S
SHAMOYED
SHAMOYS
SHAMPOO S
OOMPAHS
SHAMPOOS
SHAMROCK S
SHAMS
SMASH
SHAMUS
SAMSHU
SHAMUSES
SHANDIES
DANISHES
SHANDY
SHANGHAI S
SHANK S
ANKHS HANKS
KHANS
SHANKED
SHANKING
SHANKS
SHANNIES
SHANNY
SHANTEY S
ASTHENY
SHANTEYS
SHANTI HS
HAINTS
SHANTIES
ANTHESIS
SHEITANS
STHENIAS
SHANTIH S
SHANTIHS
SHANTIS
SHANTUNG S
SHANTY
SHAPABLE
SHAPE DNRS
EPHAS HEAPS
PHASE
SHAPED
HASPED
PASHED
PHASED
SHAPELY
SHAPEN

SHAPER S
PHRASE
RAPHES
SERAPH
SHERPA
SHAPERS
PHRASES
SERAPHS
SHERPAS
SHAPES
PASHES
PHASES
SHAPEUP S
UPHEAPS
SHAPEUPS
SHAPING
HASPING
PASHING
PHASING
SHARABLE
SHARD S
HARDS
SHARDS
SHARE DRS
HARES HEARS
RHEAS SHEAR
SHARED
DASHER
SHADER
SHARER S
RASHER
SHARERS
RASHERS
SHARES
RASHES
SHEARS
SHARIA HS
SHARIAH S
SHARIAHS
SHARIAS
HARISSA
SHARIF S
SHARIFS
SHARING
GARNISH
SHARK S
HARKS
SHARKED
SHARKER S
SHARKERS
SHARKING
SHARKS
SHARN SY
SHARNS
SHARNY
SHARP SY
HARPS
SHARPED
PHRASED
SHARPEN S
SHARPENS
SHARPER S
HARPERS
SHARPERS
SHARPEST
SHARPIE S
HARPIES
SHARPIES
PARISHES
SHARPING
HARPINGS
PHRASING
SHARPLY
SHARPS
SHARPY
SHASHLIK S
SHASLIK S
SHASLIKS
SHATTER S
HATTERS
THREATS
SHATTERS
SHAUGH S
HAUGHS
SHAUGHS
SHAUL S
HAULS HULAS
SHAULED
SHAULING
LANGUISH
NILGHAUS
SHAULS

SHAVABLE
SHAVE DNRS
HAVES
SHAVED
SHAVEN
HAVENS
SHAVER S
HAVERS
SHAVERS
SHAVES
SHAVIE S
SHAVIES
SHAVING S
SHAVINGS
P **SHAW** LMNS
HAWS SHWA
WASH
P **SHAWED**
WASHED
P **SHAWING**
WASHING
SHAWL S
SHAWLED
SHAWLING
WHALINGS
SHAWLS
SHAWM S
WHAMS
SHAWMS
SHAWN
P **SHAWS**
SHWAS SWASH
SHAY S
ASHY HAYS
SHAYS
SHAZAM
HAMZAS
SHE ADSW
HES
SHEA FLRS
HAES
SHEAF S
SHEAFED
SHEAFING
SHEAFS
FASHES
SHEAL S
HALES HEALS
LEASH SELAH
SHALE
SHEALING S
LEASHING
SHEALS
HASSEL
HASSLE
LASHES
SELAHS
SHALES
SHEAR S
HARES HEARS
RHEAS SHARE
SHEARED
ADHERES
HEADERS
HEARSED
SHEARER S
HEARERS
REHEARS
SHEARERS
SHEARING S
HEARINGS
HEARSING
SHEARS
RASHES
SHARES
SHEAS
ASHES
SHEATH ES
HEATHS
SHEATHE DRS
SHEATHED
SHEATHER S
HEATHERS
SHEATHES
SHEATHS
SHEAVE DS
HEAVES
SHEAVED
SHEAVES
SHEAVING
SHEBANG S
SHEBANGS

SHEBEAN S
BANSHEE
SHEBEANS
BANSHEES
SHEBEEN S
SHEBEENS
A **SHED** S
EDHS
SHEDABLE
SHEDDED
SHEDDER S
SHEDDERS
SHEDDING
SHEDLIKE
SHEDS
SHEEN SY
SHEENED
SHEENFUL
SHEENIER
SHEENING
SHEENS
SNEESH
SHEENY
SHEEP
SHEEPCOT ES
SHEEPDOG S
SHEEPISH
SHEEPMAN
SHEEPMEN
SHEER S
HERES
SHEERED
HEEDERS
HEREDES
SHEERER
SHEEREST
SHEETERS
SHEERING
GREENISH
REHINGES
SHEERLY
SHEERS
RESHES
SHEESH
SHEET S
THESE
SHEETED
SEETHED
SHEETER S
SHEETERS
SHEEREST
SHEETFED
SHEETING S
SEETHING
SHEETS
THESES
SHEEVE S
SHEEVES
SHEIK HS
HIKES
SHEIKDOM S
SHEIKH S
SHEIKHS
SHEIKS
SHEILA S
SHEILAS
SHEITAN S
STHENIA
SHEITANS
ANTHESIS
SHANTIES
STHENIAS
SHEKALIM
SHEKEL S
SHEKELIM
SHEKELS
SHELDUCK S
SHELF
FLESH
SHELFFUL S
SHELL SY
HELLS
SHELLAC KS
SHELLACK S
SHELLACS
SHELLED
SHELLER S
HELLERS
SHELLERS

SHELLIER
HELLERIS
SHELLING
SHELLS
SHELLY
SHELTA S
HALEST
HASLET
LATHES
SHELTAS
HASLETS
HATLESS
SHELTER S
SHELTERS
SHELTIE S
SHELTIES
SHELTY
ETHYLS
SHELVE DRS
HELVES
SHELVED
SHELVER S
SHELVERS
SHELVES
SHELVIER
SHELVING S
SHELVY
SHEND S
SHENDING
SHENDS
SHENT
HENTS THENS
SHEOL S
HELOS HOLES
HOSEL
SHEOLS
HOSELS
SHEPHERD S
SHEQALIM
SHEQEL S
SHEQELS
SHERBERT S
SHERBET S
SHERBETS
SHERD S
HERDS SHRED
SHERDS
SHREDS
SHEREEF S
SHEREEFS
SHERIF FS
FISHER
SHERIFF S
SHERIFFS
SHERIFS
FISHERS
SERFISH
SHERLOCK S
SHEROOT S
HOOTERS
RESHOOT
SHOOTER
SOOTHER
SHEROOTS
ORTHOSES
RESHOOTS
SHOOTERS
SOOTHERS
SHERPA S
PHRASE
RAPHES
SERAPH
SHAPER
SHERPAS
PHRASES
SERAPHS
SHAPERS
SHERRIES
SHERRIS
SHERRY
A **SHES**
SHETLAND S
SHEUCH S
HEUCHS
SHEUCHS
SHEUGH S
HEUGHS
SHEUGHS
SHEW NS
HEWS

SHEWED
SHEWER S
HEWERS
WHERES
SHEWERS
SHEWING
WHINGES
SHEWN
WHENS
SHEWS
SHH
SHIATSU S
SHIATSUS
SHIATZU S
SHIATZUS
SHIBAH S
SHIBAHS
SHICKER S
SHICKERS
KIRSCHES
SHIED
HIDES SIDHE
SHIEL DS
HEILS
SHIELD S
DELISH
SHIELDED
SHIELDER S
HIRSELED
RELISHED
SHIELDS
SHIELING S
SHIELS
A **SHIER** S
HEIRS HIRES
SHIRE
SHIERS
HISSER
SHIRES
SHIES T
A **SHIEST**
HEISTS
THESIS
SHIFT SY
SHIFTED
SHIFTER S
SHIFTERS
SHIFTIER
SHIFTILY
SHIFTING
INFIGHTS
SHIFTS
SHIFTY
SHIGELLA ES
SHIITAKE S
SHIKAR IS
RAKISH
SHIKAREE S
SHIKARI S
RIKISHA
SHIKARIS
RIKISHAS
SHIKARS
SHIKKER S
SHIKKERS
SHILINGI
SHILL S
HILLS
SHILLALA HS
SHILLED
SHILLING S
SHILLS
SHILPIT
SHILY
SHIM S
HIMS
SHIMMED
SHIMMER SY
SHIMMERS
SHIMMERY
SHIMMIED
SHIMMIES
SHIMMING
SHIMMY
SHIMS
SHIN ESY
HINS HISN
SINH
SHINBONE S

SHINDIES
SHINDIG S
DISHING
HIDINGS
SHINDIGS
SHINDY S
SHINDYS
SHINE DRS
SHINED
SHINER S
SHRINE
SHINERS
SHRINES
SHINES
SHINGLE DRS
ENGLISH
SHINGLED
SHINGLER S
SHINGLES
SHINGLY
SHINIER
SHINIEST
SHINILY
SHINING
SHINLEAF S
SHINNED
SHINNERY
SHINNEY S
SHINNEYS
SHINNIED
SHINNIES
SHINNING
SHINNY
SHINS
SINHS
SHINY
SHIP S
HIPS PHIS
PISH
SHIPLAP S
PALSHIP
SHIPLAPS
PALSHIPS
SHIPLESS
SHIPLOAD S
HAPLOIDS
SHIPMAN
SHIPMATE S
MATESHIP
SHIPMEN T
SHIPMENT S
SHIPPED
SHIPPEN S
SHIPPENS
SHIPPER S
PRESHIP
SHIPPERS
PRESHIPS
SHIPPING S
SHIPPON S
SHIPPONS
SHIPS
SHIPSIDE S
SHIPWAY S
SHIPWAYS
SHIPWORM S
SHIPYARD S
SHIRE S
HEIRS HIRES
SHIER
SHIRES
HISSER
SHIERS
SHIRK S
SHIRKED
SHIRKER S
SHIRKERS
SHIRKING
SHIRKS
SHIRR S
SHIRRED
SHIRRING S
SHIRRS
SHIRT SY
SHIRTIER
SHIRTING S
SHIRTS

SHIRTY
THYRSI
YIRTHS
SHIST S
HISTS
SHISTS
SHITAKE S
SHITAKES
SHAKIEST
SHITTAH S
SHITTAHS
SHITTIM S
SHITTIMS
SHIV AES
SHIVA HS
SHIVAH S
SHIVAHS
SHIVAREE DS
SHIVAS
SHIVE RS
HIVES
SHIVER SY
SHRIVE
SHIVERED
SHRIEVED
SHIVERER S
SHIVERS
SHRIVES
SHIVERY
SHIVES
SHIVITI S
SHIVITIS
SHIVS
SHLEMIEL S
SHLEP PS
HELPS
SHLEPP S
SHLEPPED
SHLEPPS
SHLEPS
SHLOCK SY
SHLOCKS
SHLOCKY
SHYLOCK
SHLUB S
BLUSH BUHLS
SHLUBS
SHLUMP SY
SHLUMPED
SHLUMPS
SHLUMPY
SHMALTZ Y
SHMALTZY
SHMEAR S
HAREMS
MASHER
SHMEARS
MARSHES
MASHERS
SMASHER
SHMO
MHOS MOSH
OHMS
SHMOES
MOSHES
SHMOOZE DS
SHMOOZED
SHMOOZES
SHMUCK S
SHMUCKS
SHNAPPS
SHNAPS
SHNOOK S
SHNOOKS
SHNORRER S
SHOAL SY
HALOS
SHOALED
SHOALER
SHOALEST
SHOALIER
AIRHOLES
SHOALING
SHOALS
ASLOSH
SHOALY
SHOAT S
HOSTA OATHS

SHOATS
HOSTAS
SHOCK S
HOCKS
SHOCKED
SHOCKER S
CHOKERS
HOCKERS
SHOCKERS
SHOCKING
SHOCKS
SHOD
HODS
SHODDEN
HODDENS
SHODDIER
SHODDIES T
SHODDILY
SHODDY
SHOE DRS
HOES HOSE
SHOEBILL S
SHOEBOX
SHOED
HOSED
SHOEHORN S
SHOEING
HONGIES
SHOELACE S
SHOELESS
SHOEPAC KS
CHEAPOS
POACHES
SHOEPACK S
SHOEPACS
SHOER S
HEROS HOERS
HORSE HOSER
SHORE
SHOERS
HORSES
HOSERS
SHORES
SHOES
HOSES
SHOETREE S
SHOFAR S
SHOFARS
SHOFROTH
SHOG IS
GOSH HOGS
SHOGGED
SHOGGING
SHOGI S
SHOGIS
SHOGS
SHOGUN S
SHOGUNAL
SHOGUNS
SHOJI S
SHOJIS
SHOLOM S
SHOLOMS
SHONE
HONES HOSEN
SHOO KLNST
OOHS
SHOOED
SHOOFLY
SHOOING
SHOOK S
HOOKS
SHOOKS
SHOOL S
SHOOLED
SHOOLING
SHOOLS
SHOON
SHOOS
SHOOT S
HOOTS SOOTH
SHOOTER S
HOOTERS
RESHOOT
SHEROOT
SOOTHER

SHOOTERS
ORTHOSES
RESHOOTS
SHEROOTS
SOOTHERS
SHOOTING S
SOOTHING
SHOOTOUT S
OUTSHOOT
SHOOTS
SOOTHS
SHOP S
HOPS POSH
SOPH
SHOPBOY S
SHOPBOYS
SHOPGIRL S
SHOPHAR S
SHOPHARS
SHOPLIFT S
SHOPMAN
SHOPMEN
PHENOMS
SHOPPE DRS
SHOPPED
SHOPPER S
HOPPERS
SHOPPERS
SHOPPES
SHOPPING S
HOPPINGS
SHOPS
SOPHS
SHOPTALK S
SHOPWORN
SHORAN S
SHORANS
A SHORE DS
HEROS HOERS
HORSE HOSER
SHOER
SHORED
HORDES
HORSED
RESHOD
SHORES
HORSES
HOSERS
SHOERS
SHORING S
HORSING
SHORINGS
SHORL S
SHORLS
SHORN
HORNS
SHORT SY
HORST
SHORTAGE S
SHORTCUT S
SHORTED
DEHORTS
SHORTEN S
HORNETS
THRONES
SHORTENS
SHORTER
RHETORS
SHORTEST
SHORTIA S
AIRSHOT
THORIAS
SHORTIAS
AIRSHOTS
SHORTIE S
HERIOTS
HOISTER
SHORTIES
HOISTERS
HORSIEST
SHORTING
SHORTISH
SHORTLY
SHORTS
HORSTS
SHORTY
SHOT EST
HOST HOTS
SOTH TOSH
SHOTE S
ETHOS THOSE

SHOTES
TOSHES
SHOTGUN S
GUNSHOT
HOGNUTS
NOUGHTS
SHOTGUNS
GUNSHOTS
SHOTHOLE S
SHOTS
HOSTS SOTHS
SHOTT S
SHOTTED
SHOTTEN
SHOTTING
TONIGHTS
SHOTTS
SHOULD
SHOULDER S
SHOULDST
SHOUT S
SOUTH THOUS
SHOUTED
SOUTHED
SHOUTER S
SOUTHER
SHOUTERS
SOUTHERS
SHOUTING
SOUTHING
SHOUTS
SOUTHS
SHOVE DLRS
SHOVED
SHOVEL S
HOVELS
SHOVELED
SHOVELER S
SHOVELS
SHOVER S
HOVERS
SHROVE
SHOVERS
SHOVES
SHOVING
SHOW NSY
HOWS
SHOWABLE
SHOWBIZ
SHOWBOAT S
SHOWCASE DS
SHOWDOWN S
SHOWED
SHOWER SY
RESHOW
WHORES
SHOWERED
RESHOWED
SHOWERER S
RESHOWER
SHOWERS
RESHOWS
SHOWERY
SHOWGIRL S
SHOWIER
SHOWIEST
SHOWILY
SHOWING S
SHOWINGS
SHOWMAN
SHOWMEN
SHOWN
SHOWOFF S
SHOWOFFS
SHOWRING S
SHOWROOM S
SHOWS
SHOWTIME S
SHOWY
SHOYU S
SHOYUS
SHRANK
SHRAPNEL
SHRED S
HERDS SHERD
SHREDDED
SHREDDER S
SHREDS
SHERDS
SHREW DS

SHREWD
SHREWDER
SHREWDIE S
SHREWDLY
SHREWED
SHREWING
WHINGERS
SHREWISH
SHREWS
SHRI S
SHRIEK SY
HIKERS
SHRIKE
SHRIEKED
SHRIEKER S
SHRIEKS
SHRIKES
SHRIEKY
SHRIEVAL
LAVISHER
SHRIEVE DS
SHRIEVED
SHIVERED
SHRIEVES
SHRIFT S
FIRTHS
FRITHS
SHRIFTS
SHRIKE S
HIKERS
SHRIEK
SHRIKES
SHRIEKS
SHRILL SY
SHRILLED
SHRILLER
SHRILLS
SHRILLY
SHRIMP SY
SHRIMPED
SHRIMPER S
SHRIMPS
SHRIMPY
SHRINE DS
SHINER
SHRINED
HINDERS
NERDISH
SHRINES
SHINERS
SHRINING
SHRINK S
SHRINKER S
SHRINKS
SHRIS
SHRIVE DLNR
SHIVER S
SHRIVED
DERVISH
SHRIVEL S
SHRIVELS
SHRIVEN
SHRIVER S
SHRIVERS
SHRIVES
SHIVERS
SHRIVING
SHROFF S
SHROFFED
SHROFFS
SHROUD S
SHROUDED
SHROUDS
SHROVE
HOVERS
SHOVER
SHRUB S
BRUSH BUHRS
SHRUBBY
SHRUBS
SHRUG S
GURSH
SHRUGGED
SHRUGS
SHRUNK
SHRUNKEN
SHTETEL S
SHTETELS
SHTETL S

SHTETLS
SHTICK SY
KITSCH
SCHTIK
THICKS
SHTICKS
SCHTIKS
SHTICKY
KITSCHY
SHTIK S
KITHS
SHTIKS
SHUCK S
HUCKS
SHUCKED
SHUCKER S
SHUCKERS
SHUCKING S
SHUCKS
SHUDDER SY
SHUDDERS
SHUDDERY
SHUFFLE DRS
SHUFFLED
SHUFFLER S
SHUFFLES
SHUL NS
LUSH
SHULN
SHULS
SLUSH
SHUN ST
HUNS
SHUNNED
SHUNNER S
SHUNNERS
SHUNNING
SHUNPIKE DR S
SHUNS
SHUNT S
HUNTS
SHUNTED
SHUNTER S
HUNTERS
SHUNTERS
HUNTRESS
SHUNTING
HUNTINGS
SHUNTS
SHUSH
SHUSHED
SHUSHER S
SHUSHERS
SHUSHES
SHUSHING
SHUT ES
HUTS THUS
TUSH
SHUTDOWN S
SHUTE DS
SHUTED
TUSHED
SHUTES
TUSHES
TUSSEH
SHUTEYE S
SHUTEYES
SHUTING
TUSHING
UNSIGHT
SHUTOFF S
SHUTOFFS
SHUTOUT S
SHUTOUTS
SHUTS
SHUTTER S
SHUTTERS
SHUTTING
SHUTTLE DRS
SHUTTLED
SHUTTLER S
SHUTTLES
SHWA S
HAWS SHAW
WASH
SHWANPAN S
SHWAS
SHAWS SWASH

A SHY
SHYER S
SHYERS
SHYEST
SHYING
SHYLOCK S
SHLOCKY
SHYLOCKS
SHYLY
SHYNESS
SHYSTER S
THYRSES
SHYSTERS
P SI BCMNPRST
IS X
SIAL S
AILS SAIL
SIALIC
SILICA
SIALID S
ILIADS
SIALIDAN S
SIALIDS
SIALOID
SIALS
LASSI SAILS
SISAL
SIAMANG S
MAGIANS
SIAMANGS
AMASSING
SIAMESE S
MISEASE
SIAMESES
MISEASES
SIB BS
BIS
SIBB S
BIBS
SIBBS
SIBILANT S
SIBILATE DS
SIBLING S
SIBLINGS
BLISSING
SIBS
SIBYL S
SIBYLIC
SIBYLLIC
SIBYLS
SIC EKS
CIS
SICCAN
SICCED
SICCING
SICE S
ICES
SICES
SICK OS
SICKBAY S
SICKBAYS
SICKBED S
SICKBEDS
SICKED
SICKEE S
SICKEES
SICKEN S
SICKENED
SICKENER S
SICKENS
SICKER
ICKERS
SICKERLY
SICKEST
SICKIE S
SICKIES
SICKING
SICKISH
SICKLE DS
SICKLED
SLICKED
SICKLES
SICKLIED
DISCLIKE
SICKLIER
SICKLIES T
SICKLILY

SICKLING
LICKINGS
SLICKING
SICKLY
SICKNESS
SICKO S
SICKOS
SICKOUT S
SICKOUTS
SICKROOM S
SICKS
SICS
SIDDUR S
DRUIDS
SIDDURIM
DRUIDISM
SIDDURS
A **SIDE** DS
DIES IDES
SIDEARM S
ADMIRES
MISREAD
SEDARIM
SIDEARMS
MISREADS
SIDEBAND S
SIDEBAR S
ABIDERS
BRAISED
DARBIES
SEABIRD
SIDEBARS
SEABIRDS
SIDECAR S
RADICES
SIDECARS
SIDED
SIDEHILL S
HILLSIDE
SIDEKICK S
SIDELINE DR S
SIDELING
SIDELONG
SIDEMAN
MAIDENS
MEDIANS
MEDINAS
SIDEMEN
SIDEREAL
REALISED
RESAILED
SIDERITE S
A **SIDES**
SIDESHOW S
SIDESLIP S
SIDESPIN S
SIDESTEP S
DESPITES
SIDEWALK S
SIDEWALL S
SIDEWARD S
SIDEWAY S
WAYSIDE
SIDEWAYS
WAYSIDES
SIDEWISE
SIDH E
DISH
SIDHE
HIDES SHIED
SIDING S
SIDINGS
DISSING
SIDLE DRS
DEILS DELIS
IDLES ISLED
SLIDE
SIDLED
SIDLER S
IDLERS
SLIDER
SIDLERS
SLIDERS
SIDLES
SLIDES
SIDLING
SLIDING
SIEGE DS
SIEGED
SIEGES
EGISES

SIEGING
SIEMENS
NEMESIS
SIENITE S
SIENITES
SIENNA S
INANES
INSANE
SIENNAS
SIEROZEM S
SIERRA NS
AIRERS
RAISER
SIERRAN
SIERRAS
ARRISES
RAISERS
SIESTA S
TASSIE
SIESTAS
TASSIES
SIEUR S
SIEURS
ISSUER
SIEVE DS
SIEVED
DEVISE
VISEED
SIEVERT S
RESTIVE
VERIEST
VERITES
SIEVERTS
VESTRIES
SIEVES
SIEVING
VISEING
SIFAKA S
SIFAKAS
SIFFLEUR S
SIFT S
FIST FITS
SIFTED
FISTED
SIFTER S
FRITES
REFITS
RESIFT
RIFEST
STRIFE
SIFTERS
RESIFTS
STRIFES
SIFTING S
FISTING
SIFTINGS
SIFTS
FISTS
SIGANID S
SIGANIDS
SIGH ST
GHIS
SIGHED
SIGHER S
SIGHERS
GIRSHES
SIGHING
SIGHLESS
SIGHLIKE
SIGHS
SIGHT S
SIGHTED
SIGHTER S
RESIGHT
SIGHTERS
RESIGHTS
SIGHTING S
SIGHTLY
SIGHTS
SIGHTSAW
SIGHTSEE NR S
SIGIL S
SIGILS
SIGLA
GLIAS
SIGLOI
SIGLOS
SIGLUM
SIGMA S
AGISM

SIGMAS
AGISMS
SIGMATE
GAMIEST
SIGMOID S
SIGMOIDS
SIGN AS
GINS SING
SIGNA L
GAINS
SIGNAGE S
AGEINGS
SIGNAGES
SIGNAL S
ALGINS
ALIGNS
LASING
LIANGS
LIGANS
LINGAS
SIGNALED
DEALINGS
LEADINGS
SIGNALER S
ALIGNERS
ENGRAILS
NARGILES
REALIGNS
SLANGIER
SIGNALLY
SALLYING
SLANGILY
SIGNALS
SIGNED
DEIGNS
DESIGN
DINGES
SINGED
SIGNEE S
GENIES
SEEING
SIGNEES
GENESIS
SEEINGS
SIGNER S
REIGNS
RENIGS
RESIGN
SERING
SINGER
SIGNERS
INGRESS
RESIGNS
SINGERS
SIGNET S
INGEST
TINGES
SIGNETED
INGESTED
SIGNETS
INGESTS
SIGNIFY
SIGNING
SINGING
SIGNIOR ISY
ORIGINS
SIGNORI
SIGNIORI
SIGNIORS
SIGNIORY
SIGNOR AEIS Y
GIRONS
GRISON
GROINS
ROSING
SORING
SIGNORA S
ORIGANS
SOARING
SIGNORAS
ASSIGNOR
SOARINGS
SIGNORE
ERINGOS
IGNORES
REGIONS
SIGNORI
ORIGINS
SIGNIOR
SIGNORS
GRISONS
SORINGS
SIGNORY

SIGNPOST S
POSTINGS
SIGNS
SINGS
SIKA S
SAKI
SIKAS
SAKIS
SIKE RS
SIKER
KEIRS KIERS
SKIER
SIKES
SKIES
SILAGE S
LIGASE
SILAGES
GLASSIE
LIGASES
SILANE S
ALIENS
ALINES
ELAINS
LIANES
SALINE
SILANES
SALINES
SILD S
LIDS SLID
SILDS
SILENCE DRS
LICENSE
SELENIC
SILENCED
DECLINES
LICENSED
SILENCER S
LICENSER
RECLINES
SILENCES
LICENSES
SILENI
SILENT S
ELINTS
ENLIST
INLETS
LISTEN
TINSEL
SILENTER
ENLISTER
LISTENER
REENLIST
SILENTLY
TINSELLY
SILENTS
ENLISTS
LISTENS
TINSELS
SILENUS
SILESIA S
LIAISES
SILESIAS
SILEX
LEXIS
SILEXES
SILICA S
SIALIC
SILICAS
SILICATE S
CILIATES
SILICIC
SILICIDE S
SILICIFY
SILICIUM S
SILICLE S
SILICLES
SILICON ES
SILICONE S
ISOCLINE
SILICONS
SILICULA E
SILIQUA E
SILIQUAE
SILIQUE S
SILIQUES
SILK SY
ILKS
SILKED
SILKEN
INKLES
LIKENS
SILKIE RS
SILKIER

SILKIES T
SILKIEST
SILKILY
SILKING
LIKINGS
SILKLIKE
SILKS
SILKWEED S
SILKWORM S
SILKY
SILL SY
ILLS
SILLABUB S
SILLER S
RILLES
SILLERS
SILLIBUB S
SILLIER
SILLIES T
SILLIEST
SILLILY
SILLS
SILLY
SLILY YILLS
SILO S
OILS SOIL
SOLI
SILOED
OLDIES
SOILED
SILOING
SOILING
SILOS
SOILS
SILOXANE S
SILT SY
LIST LITS
SLIT TILS
SILTED
DELIST
IDLEST
LISTED
TILDES
SILTIER
SILTIEST
ELITISTS
SILTING
LISTING
TILINGS
SILTS
LISTS SLITS
SILTY
STYLI
SILURIAN
SILURID S
SILURIDS
SILUROID S
SILVA ENS
VAILS VIALS
SILVAE
VALISE
SILVAN S
ANVILS
VINALS
SILVANS
SILVAS
SILVER NSY
ERVILS
LIVERS
LIVRES
SLIVER
SILVERED
DELIVERS
DESILVER
SLIVERED
SILVERER S
RESILVER
REVILERS
SLIVERER
SILVERLY
SILVERN
SILVERS
SLIVERS
SILVERY
LIVYERS
SILVEX
VEXILS
SILVEXES
SILVICAL
SILVICS

SIM APS
ISM
MIS
SIMA RS
AIMS AMIS
SIMAR S
AMIRS MAIRS
SIMARS
SIMARUBA S
SIMAS
AMISS
SIMAZINE S
SIMIAN S
ANIMIS
SAIMIN
SIMIANS
SAIMINS
SIMILAR
SIMILE S
MISLIE
SIMILES
MISLIES
MISSILE
SIMIOID
SIMIOUS
SIMITAR S
SIMITARS
SIMLIN S
SIMLINS
SIMMER S
MIMERS
SIMMERED
IMMERSED
SIMMERS
SIMNEL S
LIMENS
SIMNELS
SIMOLEON S
OINOMELS
SIMONIAC S
SIMONIES
EMISSION
SIMONIST S
SIMONIZE DS
SIMONY
MYOSIN
SIMOOM S
SIMOOMS
SIMOON S
SOMONI
SIMOONS
SIMP S
IMPS MIPS
SIMPER S
PRIMES
SPIREM
SIMPERED
DEMIREPS
EPIDERMS
IMPEDERS
PREMISED
SIMPERER S
PREMIERS
SIMPERS
IMPRESS
PREMISS
SPIREMS
SIMPLE RSX
IMPELS
SIMPLER
LIMPERS
PRELIMS
RIMPLES
SIMPLES T
SIMPLEST
MISSPELT
SIMPLEX
SIMPLIFY
SIMPLISM S
SIMPLIST S
SIMPLY
LIMPSY
SIMPS
SIMS
ISMS MISS
SIMULANT S
SIMULAR S
SIMULARS
SIMULATE DS
SIN EGHKS
INS

SINAPISM S
PIANISMS
SINCE
CINES
SINCERE R
SINCERER
SINCIPUT S
SINE SW
SINECURE S
INSECURE
SINES
SINEW SY
SWINE WINES
SINEWED
ENDWISE
SINEWING
SINEWS
SINEWY
SINFONIA S
SAINFOIN
SINFONIE
SINFUL
SINFULLY
SULFINYL
U **SING** ES
GINS SIGN
SINGABLE
SINGE DRS
SEGNI SENGI
SINGED
DEIGNS
DESIGN
DINGES
SIGNED
SINGEING
SINGER S
REIGNS
RENIGS
RESIGN
SERING
SIGNER
SINGERS
INGRESS
RESIGNS
SIGNERS
SINGES
GNEISS
SINGING
SIGNING
SINGLE DST
INGLES
SINGLED
DINGLES
ENGILDS
SINGLES
SINGLET S
GLISTEN
SNIGLET
TINGLES
SINGLETS
GLISTENS
SNIGLETS
SINGLING
SLINGING
SINGLY
LYINGS
LYSING
SINGS
SIGNS
SINGSONG SY
SINGULAR S
SINH S
HINS HISN
SHIN
SINHS
SHINS
SINICIZE DS
SINISTER
INSISTER
SINK S
INKS KINS
SKIN
SINKABLE
SINKAGE S
SINKAGES
SINKER S
INKERS
REINKS
SINKERS
SINKHOLE S
SINKING
SINKS
SKINS

SINLESS
SINNED
SINNER S
INNERS
RENINS
SINNERS
SINNING
INNINGS
SINOLOGY
SINOPIA S
SINOPIAS
SINOPIE
SINS
SINSYNE
SINTER S
ESTRIN
INERTS
INSERT
INTERS
NITERS
NITRES
TRIENS
TRINES
SINTERED
INSERTED
NERDIEST
RESIDENT
TRENDIES
SINTERS
ESTRINS
INSERTS
SINUATE DS
AUNTIES
SINUATED
AUDIENTS
SINUATES
SINUOUS
SINUS
NISUS
SINUSES
SINUSOID S
SIP ES
PIS
PSI
SIPE DS
PIES
SIPED
SPIED
SIPES
SPIES
SIPHON S
SIPHONAL
SIPHONED
SPHENOID
SIPHONIC
SIPHONS
SONSHIP
SIPING
SIPPED
SIPPER S
PIPERS
SIPPERS
SIPPET S
PIPETS
SIPPETS
SIPPING
PIPINGS
SIPS
PSIS
SIR ES
SRI
SIRDAR S
SIRDARS
SIRE DENS
IRES REIS
RISE
SIRED
DRIES RESID
RIDES
SIREE S
SIREES
SEISER
SERIES
SIREN S
REINS RESIN
RINSE RISEN
SERIN
SIRENIAN S
SIRENS
RESINS
RINSES
SERINS
SIRES
RISES
SIRING
RISING
SIRLOIN S
SIRLOINS
SIROCCO S
SIROCCOS
SIRRA HS
ARRIS
SIRRAH S
SIRRAHS
SIRRAS
SIRREE S
RERISE
SIRREES
RERISES
SERRIES
SIRS
SRIS
SIRUP SY
PURIS
SIRUPED
UPDRIES
SIRUPIER
SIRUPING
UPRISING
SIRUPS
SIRUPY
SIRVENTE S
NERVIEST
REINVEST
P **SIS**
SISAL S
LASSI SAILS
SIALS
SISALS
LASSIS
SISES
SISKIN S
SISKINS
SISSES
SISSIER
SISSIES T
SISSIEST
SISSY
SISSYISH
SISTER S
RESIST
RESITS
SISTERED
DIESTERS
EDITRESS
RESISTED
SISTERLY
STYLISER
SISTERS
RESISTS
SISTRA
SITARS
STAIRS
SISTROID
SISTRUM S
TRISMUS
TRUISMS
SISTRUMS
SIT EHS
ITS
TIS
SITAR S
AIRTS ASTIR
STAIR STRIA
TARSI
SITARIST S
SATIRIST
SITARS
SISTRA
STAIRS
SITCOM S
SITCOMS
COSMIST
SITE DS
TIES
SITED
DEIST DIETS
DITES EDITS
STIED TIDES
SITES
STIES
SITH
HIST HITS
THIS
SITHENCE
SITHENS
SITING
SITOLOGY
SITS
SITTEN
SITTER S
TETRIS
TITERS
TITRES
TRISTE
SITTERS
SITTING S
SITTINGS
SITUATE DS
SITUATED
SITUATES
SITUP S
SITUPS
SITUS
SUITS
SITUSES
TISSUES
SITZMARK S
SIVER S
RIVES VIERS
VIRES
SIVERS
SIX
XIS
SIXES
SIXFOLD
SIXMO S
OXIMS
SIXMOS
SIXPENCE S
SIXPENNY
SIXTE S
EXIST EXITS
SIXTEEN S
SIXTEENS
SIXTES
EXISTS
SEXIST
SIXTH S
SIXTHLY
SIXTHS
SIXTIES
SIXTIETH S
SIXTY
XYSTI
SIXTYISH
SIZABLE
SIZABLY
SIZAR S
IZARS
SIZARS
SIZE DRS
SIZEABLE
SEIZABLE
SIZEABLY
SIZED
SIZER S
SIZERS
SIZES
SIZIER
SIZIEST
SIZINESS
SIZING S
SIZINGS
SIZY
SIZZLE DRS
SIZZLED
SIZZLER S
SIZZLERS
SIZZLES
SIZZLING
SJAMBOK S
SJAMBOKS
SKA GST
ASK
KAS
SKAG S
SKAGS
SKALD S
SKALDIC
SKALDS
SKANK SY
SKANKED
SKANKER S
KRAKENS
SKANKERS
SKANKIER
SKANKING
SKANKS
SKANKY
SKAS
ASKS
SKAT ES
KATS TASK
SKATE DRS
STAKE STEAK
TAKES TEAKS
SKATED
STAKED
TASKED
SKATER S
STRAKE
STREAK
TAKERS
SKATERS
STRAKES
STREAKS
SKATES
STAKES
STEAKS
SKATING S
STAKING
TAKINGS
TASKING
SKATINGS
SKATOL ES
SKATOLE S
SKATOLES
SKATOLS
SKATS
TASKS
SKEAN ES
KANES SNAKE
SNEAK
SKEANE S
AKENES
SKEANES
SKEANS
SNAKES
SNEAKS
SKEE DNST
EKES SEEK
SKEED
DEKES
SKEEING
SEEKING
SKEEN S
KEENS KNEES
SKENE
SKEENS
SKENES
SKEES
SEEKS
SKEET S
KEETS STEEK
SKEETER S
KEESTER
SKEETERS
KEESTERS
SKEETS
STEEKS
SKEG S
KEGS
SKEGS
SKEIGH
SKEIN S
KINES
SKEINED
ENSKIED
SKEINING
SKEINS
SKELETAL
SKELETON S
SKELL S
SKELLS
SKELLUM S
SKELLUMS
SKELM S
SKELMS
SKELP S
KELPS
SKELPED
SKELPING
SKELPIT
SKELPS
SKELTER S
KELTERS
KESTREL
SKELTERS
KESTRELS
SKENE S
KEENS KNEES
SKEEN
SKENES
SKEENS
SKEP S
KEPS
SKEPS
SKEPSIS
SKEPTIC S
PICKETS
SKEPTICS
SKERRIES
SKERRY
SKETCH Y
SKETCHED
SKETCHER S
RESKETCH
SKETCHES
SKETCHY
A **SKEW** S
SKEWBACK S
SKEWBALD S
SKEWED
SKEWER S
KREWES
SKEWERED
SKEWERS
SKEWING
A **SKEWNESS**
SKEWS
SKI DMNPST
KIS
SKIABLE
SKIAGRAM S
SKIBOB S
SKIBOBS
SKID S
DISK KIDS
SKIDDED
SKIDDER S
KIDDERS
SKIDDERS
SKIDDIER
SKIDDING
SKIDDOO S
SKIDDOOS
SKIDDY
SKIDOO S
SKIDOOED
SKIDOOS
SKIDS
DISKS
SKIDWAY S
SKIDWAYS
SKIED
DIKES
SKIER S
KEIRS KIERS
SIKER
SKIERS
KISSER
KRISES
SKIES
SIKES
SKIEY
YIKES
SKIFF S
SKIFFLE DS
SKIFFLED
SKIFFLES S
SKIFFS
SKIING S
SKIINGS
KISSING
SKIJORER S
SKILFUL
SKILL S
KILLS
SKILLED
SKILLESS
SKILLET S
SKILLETS
SKILLFUL
SKILLING S
KILLINGS
SKILLS
SKIM PS
SKIMMED
SKIMMER S
SKIMMERS
SKIMMING S
SKIMP SY
SKIMPED
SKIMPIER
SKIMPILY
SKIMPING
SKIMPS
SKIMPY
SKIMS
SKIN KST
INKS KINS
SINK
SKINFUL S
SKINFULS
SKINHEAD S
SKINK S
KINKS
SKINKED
SKINKER S
SKINKERS
SKINKING
SKINKS
SKINLESS
SKINLIKE
SKINNED
SKINNER S
SKINNERS
SKINNIER
SKINNING
SKINNY
SKINS
SINKS
SKINT
KNITS STINK
SKIORING S
SKIP S
KIPS
SKIPJACK S
SKIPLANE S
SKIPPED
SKIPPER S
KIPPERS
SKIPPERS
SKIPPET S
SKIPPETS
SKIPPING
SKIPS
SKIRL S
SKIRLED
SKIRLING
SKIRLS
SKIRMISH
SKIRR S
SKIRRED
SKIRRET S
SKIRTER
STRIKER
SKIRRETS
SKIRTERS
STRIKERS
SKIRRING
SKIRRS
SKIRT S
STIRK
SKIRTED
SKIRTER S
SKIRRET
STRIKER
SKIRTERS
SKIRRETS
STRIKERS
SKIRTING S
STRIKING
SKIRTS
STIRKS
SKIS
KISS
SKIT ES
KIST KITS
SKITE DS
KITES TIKES
SKITED
SKITES
SKITING
SKITS
KISTS
SKITTER SY
SKITTERS
SKITTERY
SKITTISH
SKITTLE S
KITTLES
SKITTLES
SKIVE DRS
SKIVED
SKIVER S
SKIVERS
SKIVES
SKIVING
VIKINGS
SKIVVIED
SKIVVIES
SKIVVY
SKIWEAR
SKLENT S
SKLENTED
SKLENTS
SKOAL S
KOLAS
SKOALED
SKOALING
SKOALS
SKOOKUM
SKORT S
STORK TORSK
SKORTS
STORKS
TORSKS
SKOSH
SKOSHES
SKREEGH S
SKREEGHS
SKREIGH S
SKREIGHS
SKUA S
AUKS
SKUAS
SKULK S
SKULKED
SKULKER S
SKULKERS
SKULKING
SKULKS
SKULL S
SKULLCAP S
SKULLED
SKULLING
SKULLS
SKUNK SY
SKUNKED
SKUNKIER
SKUNKING
SKUNKS
SKUNKY
SKY
SKYBOARD S
SKYBORNE
SKYBOX
SKYBOXES
SKYCAP S
SKYCAPS
SKYDIVE DRS
SKYDIVED
SKYDIVER S
SKYDIVES
SKYDOVE
SKYED
DYKES
SKYEY
SKYHOOK S
SKYHOOKS
SKYING
SKYJACK S
SKYJACKS
SKYLARK S
SKYLARKS
SKYLIGHT S

SKYLIKE
KYLIKES
SKYLINE S
SKYLINES
SKYLIT
SKYMAN
SKYMEN
SKYPHOI
SKYPHOS
SKYSAIL S
SKYSAILS
SKYSURF S
SKYSURFS
SKYWALK S
SKYWALKS
SKYWARD S
SKYWARDS
SKYWAY S
SKYWAYS
SKYWRITE RS
SKYWROTE
SLAB S
ALBS BALS
LABS
SLABBED
DABBLES
SLABBER SY
BARBELS
RABBLES
SLABBERS
BARBLESS
SLABBERY
SLABBING
SLABLIKE
SLABS
SLACK S
CALKS LACKS
SLACKED
SLACKEN S
SLACKENS
SLACKER S
CALKERS
LACKERS
SLACKERS
SLACKEST
TACKLESS
SLACKING
CALKINGS
SLACKLY
SLACKS
SLAG S
GALS LAGS
SLAGGED
DAGGLES
SLAGGIER
SLAGGING
LAGGINGS
SLAGGY
SLAGS
GLASS
SLAIN
ANILS NAILS
SNAIL
SLAINTE
ELASTIN
ENTAILS
NAILSET
SALIENT
SALTINE
TENAILS
SLAKABLE
SLAKE DRS
KALES LAKES
LEAKS
SLAKED
SLAKER S
LAKERS
SLAKERS
SLAKES
SLAKING
LAKINGS
SLALOM S
SLALOMED
SLALOMER S
SLALOMS
SLAM S
ALMS LAMS
SLAMMED
SLAMMER S
SLAMMERS
SLAMMING S
SLAMS
I **SLANDER** S
DARNELS
LANDERS
RELANDS
SNARLED
I **SLANDERS**
SLANG SY
GLANS
SLANGED
DANGLES
GLANDES
LAGENDS
SLANGIER
ALIGNERS
ENGRAILS
NARGILES
REALIGNS
SIGNALER
SLANGILY
SALLYING
SIGNALLY
SLANGING
ANGLINGS
SLANGS
SLANGY
SLANK
A **SLANT** SY
SLANTED
DENTALS
SLANTING
SLANTLY
SLANTS
SLANTY
SLAP S
ALPS LAPS
PALS SALP
SLAPDASH
SLAPJACK S
SLAPPED
DAPPLES
SLAPPER S
LAPPERS
RAPPELS
SLAPPERS
SLAPPING
SLAPS
SALPS
SLASH
SLASHED
HASSLED
SLASHER S
ASHLERS
LASHERS
SLASHERS
SLASHES
ASHLESS
HASSELS
HASSLES
SLASHING S
HASSLING
LASHINGS
SLAT ESY
ALTS LAST
LATS SALT
SLATCH
SLATCHES
SATCHELS
SLATE DRSY
LEAST SETAL
STALE STEAL
STELA TAELS
TALES TEALS
TESLA
SLATED
DELTAS
DESALT
LASTED
SALTED
STALED
SLATER S
ALERTS
ALTERS
ARTELS
ESTRAL
LASTER
RATELS
SALTER
STALER
STELAR
TALERS
SLATERS
ARTLESS
LASTERS
SALTERS
SLATES
LEASTS
STALES
STEALS
TASSEL
TESLAS
SLATEY
LYSATE
SLATHER S
HALTERS
HARSLET
LATHERS
THALERS
SLATHERS
HARSLETS
SLATIER
REALIST
RETAILS
SALTIER
SALTIRE
TAILERS
SLATIEST
SALTIEST
SLATING S
LASTING
SALTING
STALING
SLATINGS
LASTINGS
SALTINGS
SLATS
LASTS SALTS
SLATTED
SLATTERN S
SLATTING S
SLATY
SALTY
SLAVE DRSY
LAVES SALVE
SELVA VALES
VALSE VEALS
SLAVED
SALVED
SLAVER SY
LAVERS
RAVELS
SALVER
SERVAL
VELARS
VERSAL
SLAVERED
SLAVERER S
RAVELERS
REVERSAL
SLAVERS
SALVERS
SERVALS
SLAVERY
SLAVES
SALVES
SELVAS
VALSES
SLAVEY S
SYLVAE
SLAVEYS
SLAVING
SALVING
SLAVISH
SLAW S
AWLS LAWS
SLAWS
SLAY S
LAYS
SLAYABLE
SALEABLY
SLAYED
DELAYS
SLAYER S
LAYERS
RELAYS
SLAYERS
RAYLESS
SLAYING
SLAYS
LYSSA
SLEAVE DS
LEAVES
SLEAVED
SLEAVES
SLEAVING
LEAVINGS
SLEAZE S
SLEAZES
SLEAZIER
REALIZES
SLEAZILY
SLEAZO
AZOLES
SLEAZOID S
DIAZOLES
SLEAZY
I **SLED** S
DELS ELDS
SLEDDED
SLEDDER S
REDDLES
SLEDDERS
SLEDDING S
SLEDGE DS
GLEDES
GLEEDS
LEDGES
SLEDGED
SLEDGES
SLEDGING
GELDINGS
SNIGGLED
SLEDS
SLEEK SY
KEELS LEEKS
SLEEKED
SLEEKEN S
SLEEKENS
SLEEKER S
SLEEKERS
SLEEKEST
SLEEKIER
SLEEKING
SLEEKIT
SLEEKLY
SLEEKS
SLEEKY
A **SLEEP** SY
PEELS PELES
SPEEL
SLEEPER S
PEELERS
SLEEPERS
PEERLESS
SLEEPIER
SLEEPILY
SLEEPING S
PEELINGS
SPEELING
SLEEPS
SPEELS
SLEEPY
SLEET SY
LEETS STEEL
STELE TEELS
TELES
SLEETED
DELETES
STEELED
SLEETIER
LEERIEST
STEELIER
SLEETING
GENTILES
STEELING
SLEETS
STEELS
STELES
SLEETY
STEELY
SLEEVE DS
LEVEES
SLEEVED
SLEEVES
SLEEVING
SLEIGH ST
SLEIGHED
SLEIGHER S
SLEIGHS
SLEIGHT S
SLEIGHTS
SLENDER
LENDERS
RELENDS
SLEPT
PELTS SPELT
SLEUTH S
HUSTLE
SLEUTHED
SLEUTHS
HUSTLES
LUSHEST
SLEW S
SLEWED
WEDELS
SLEWING
SWINGLE
SLEWS
SLICE DRS
CEILS
SLICED
SLICER S
RELICS
SLICERS
SLICES
SLICING
SLICK S
LICKS
SLICKED
SICKLED
SLICKEN S
NICKELS
NICKLES
SLICKENS
SLICKER S
LICKERS
SLICKERS
SLICKEST
STICKLES
SLICKING
LICKINGS
SICKLING
SLICKLY
SLICKS
SLID E
LIDS SILD
SLIDABLE
SLIDDEN
DINDLES
SLIDE RS
DEILS DELIS
IDLES ISLED
SIDLE
SLIDER S
IDLERS
SIDLER
SLIDERS
SIDLERS
SLIDES
SIDLES
SLIDEWAY S
SLIDING
SIDLING
SLIER
LIERS RIELS
RILES
SLIEST
ISLETS
ISTLES
STILES
SLIEVE S
LEVIES
SLIEVES
SLIGHT S
LIGHTS
SLIGHTED
DELIGHTS
SLIGHTER S
LIGHTERS
RELIGHTS
SLIGHTLY
SLIGHTS
SLILY
SILLY YILLS
SLIM ESY
MILS
SLIME DS
LIMES MILES
SMILE
SLIMED
MISLED
SMILED
SLIMES
MISSEL
SMILES
SLIMIER
MILREIS
SLIMIEST
ELITISMS
SLIMILY
SLIMING
SMILING
SLIMLY
SLIMMED
SLIMMER S
LIMMERS
SLIMMERS
SLIMMEST
SLIMMING
SLIMNESS
SLIMPSY
SLIMS Y
SLIMSIER
SLIMSY
SLIMY
I **SLING** S
LINGS
SLINGER S
LINGERS
SLINGERS
SLINGING
SINGLING
SLINGS
SLINK SY
KILNS LINKS
SLINKED
KINDLES
SLINKIER
SLINKILY
SLINKING
INKLINGS
SLINKS
SLINKY
SLIP EST
LIPS LISP
SLIPCASE DS
SPECIALS
SLIPE DS
PILES PLIES
SPEIL SPIEL
SPILE
SLIPED
DISPEL
LISPED
SPILED
SLIPES
PLISSE
SPEILS
SPIELS
SPILES
SLIPFORM S
SLIPING
LISPING
PILINGS
SPILING
SLIPKNOT S
SLIPLESS
SLIPOUT S
SLIPOUTS
SLIPOVER S
OVERSLIP
SLIPPAGE S
SLIPPED
SLIPPER SY
LIPPERS
RIPPLES
SLIPPERS
SLIPPERY
SLIPPIER
SLIPPILY
SLIPPING
LIPPINGS
SLIPPY
SLIPS
LISPS
SLIPSHOD
SLIPSLOP S
SLIPSOLE S
SLIPT
SPILT SPLIT
SLIPUP S
PUPILS
SLIPUPS
SLIPWARE S
SLIPWAY S
WASPILY
SLIPWAYS
SLIT S
LIST LITS
SILT TILS
SLITHER SY
SLITHERS
SLITHERY
SLITLESS
LISTLESS
SLITLIKE
SLITS
LISTS SILTS
SLITTED
STILTED
SLITTER S
LITTERS
TILTERS
SLITTERS
SLITTIER
SLITTING
STILTING
SLITTY
SLIVER S
ERVILS
LIVERS
LIVRES
SILVER
SLIVERED
DELIVERS
DESILVER
SILVERED
SLIVERER S
RESILVER
REVILERS
SILVERER
SLIVERS
SILVERS
SLIVOVIC
SLOB S
LOBS
SLOBBER SY
LOBBERS
SLOBBERS
SLOBBERY
LOBBYERS
SLOBBIER
SLOBBISH
SLOBBY
SLOBS
SLOE S
LOSE OLES
SOLE
SLOES
LOESS LOSES
SOLES
SLOG S
LOGS
SLOGAN S
ANGLOS
LOGANS
SLOGANS
SLOGGED
DOGLEGS
SLOGGER S
LOGGERS
SLOGGERS
SLOGGING
LOGGINGS
SLOGS
GLOSS
SLOID S
DIOLS IDOLS
LIDOS LOIDS
SOLDI SOLID
SLOIDS
DOSSIL
SOLIDS
SLOJD S
SLOJDS
SLOOP S
LOOPS POLOS
POOLS SPOOL
SLOOPS
SPOOLS
SLOP ES
LOPS POLS
A **SLOPE** DRS
LOPES POLES
SLOPED
SLOPER S
LOPERS
POLERS
PROLES
SPLORE

SLOPERS PLESSOR SPLORES
SLOPES
SLOPING
SLOPPED
SLOPPIER
SLOPPILY
SLOPPING
SLOPPY POLYPS
SLOPS
SLOPWORK S
A SLOSH Y
SLOSHED
SLOSHES
SLOSHIER
SLOSHING
SLOSHY
SLOT HS LOST LOTS
SLOTBACK S
SLOTH S HOLTS
SLOTHFUL
SLOTHS
SLOTS
SLOTTED DOTTELS DOTTLES
SLOTTER S LOTTERS SETTLOR
SLOTTERS SETTLORS
SLOTTING
SLOUCH Y
SLOUCHED
SLOUCHER S
SLOUCHES
SLOUCHY CHYLOUS
SLOUGH SY GHOULS LOUGHS
SLOUGHED
SLOUGHS
SLOUGHY
SLOVEN S NOVELS
SLOVENLY
SLOVENS
SLOW S LOWS OWLS
SLOWDOWN S LOWDOWNS
SLOWED DOWELS
SLOWER LOWERS ROWELS
SLOWEST
SLOWING LOWINGS
SLOWISH
SLOWLY
SLOWNESS SNOWLESS
SLOWPOKE S
SLOWS
SLOWWORM S
SLOYD S ODYLS
SLOYDS
SLUB S
SLUBBED
SLUBBER S BURBLES LUBBERS RUBBLES
SLUBBERS
SLUBBING S
SLUBS
SLUDGE DS
SLUDGED
SLUDGES
SLUDGIER GUILDERS
SLUDGING
SLUDGY
SLUE DS LUES
SLUED DUELS DULSE LEUDS LUDES
SLUES
SLUFF S LUFFS
SLUFFED DUFFELS DUFFLES
SLUFFING
SLUFFS
SLUG S GULS LUGS
SLUGABED S
SLUGFEST S
SLUGGARD S
SLUGGED
SLUGGER S GURGLES LUGGERS
SLUGGERS
SLUGGING
SLUGGISH
SLUGS
SLUICE DS
SLUICED
SLUICES
SLUICING
SLUICY
SLUING LUNGIS
SLUM PS LUMS
SLUMBER SY LUMBERS RUMBLES
SLUMBERS
SLUMBERY
SLUMGUM S
SLUMGUMS
SLUMISM S
SLUMISMS
SLUMLORD S
SLUMMED
SLUMMER S
SLUMMERS
SLUMMIER
SLUMMING
SLUMMY
SLUMP S LUMPS PLUMS
SLUMPED
SLUMPING
SLUMPS
SLUMS
SLUNG LUNGS
SLUNK LUNKS
SLUR BPS
SLURB S BLURS BURLS
SLURBAN
SLURBS
SLURP S PURLS
SLURPED
SLURPING PURLINGS
SLURPS
SLURRED
SLURRIED
SLURRIES
SLURRING
SLURRY
SLURS
SLUSH Y SHULS
SLUSHED
SLUSHES
SLUSHIER
SLUSHILY
SLUSHING
SLUSHY
SLUT S LUST
SLUTS LUSTS
SLUTTIER SURTITLE
SLUTTISH
SLUTTY
SLY
SLYBOOTS
SLYER LYRES
SLYEST STYLES
SLYLY
SLYNESS SELSYNS
SLYPE S YELPS
SLYPES
SMACK S MACKS
SMACKED
SMACKER S
SMACKERS
SMACKING
SMACKS
SMALL S MALLS
SMALLAGE S
SMALLER
SMALLEST
SMALLISH
SMALLPOX
SMALLS
SMALT IOS MALTS
SMALTI
SMALTINE S AILMENTS ALIMENTS MANLIEST MELANIST
SMALTITE S MALTIEST METALIST
SMALTO S ALMOST STOMAL
SMALTOS
SMALTS
SMARAGD ES
SMARAGDE S DAMAGERS
SMARAGDS
SMARM SY
SMARMIER
SMARMILY
SMARMS
SMARMY
SMART SY MARTS TRAMS
SMARTASS
SMARTED
SMARTEN S MARTENS SARMENT
SMARTENS SARMENTS
SMARTER ARMREST
SMARTEST MATTRESS SMATTERS
SMARTIE S IMARETS MAESTRI MISRATE
SMARTIES ASTERISM MISRATES
SMARTING MIGRANTS
SMARTLY
SMARTS
SMARTY
SMASH SHAMS
SMASHED
SMASHER S MARSHES MASHERS SHMEARS
SMASHERS
SMASHES
SMASHING
SMASHUP S
SMASHUPS
SMATTER S MATTERS
SMATTERS MATTRESS SMARTEST
SMAZE S MAZES
SMAZES
SMEAR SY MARES MARSE MASER REAMS
SMEARED
SMEARER S REAMERS
SMEARERS
SMEARIER
SMEARING
SMEARS MARSES MASERS
SMEARY
SMECTIC
SMECTITE S
SMEDDUM S
SMEDDUMS
SMEEK S
SMEEKED
SMEEKING
SMEEKS
SMEGMA S
SMEGMAS
SMELL SY MELLS
SMELLED
SMELLER S
SMELLERS
SMELLIER
SMELLING
SMELLS
SMELLY
SMELT S MELTS
SMELTED
SMELTER SY MELTERS REMELTS RESMELT
SMELTERS RESMELTS TERMLESS
SMELTERY
SMELTING
SMELTS
SMERK S MERKS
SMERKED
SMERKING
SMERKS
SMEW S MEWS
SMEWS
SMIDGE NS MIDGES
SMIDGEN S
SMIDGENS
SMIDGEON S MENDIGOS
SMIDGES
SMIDGIN S
SMIDGINS
SMILAX
SMILAXES
SMILE DRSY LIMES MILES SLIME
SMILED MISLED SLIMED
SMILER S MILERS
SMILERS RIMLESS
SMILES MISSEL SLIMES
SMILEY S LIMEYS
SMILEYS MESSILY
SMILING SLIMING
SMIRCH CHIRMS CHRISM
SMIRCHED
SMIRCHES
SMIRK SY MIRKS
SMIRKED
SMIRKER S
SMIRKERS
SMIRKIER
SMIRKILY
SMIRKING
SMIRKS
SMIRKY
SMIT EH MIST
SMITE RS EMITS ITEMS METIS MITES STIME TIMES
SMITER S MERITS MISTER MITERS MITRES REMITS TIMERS
SMITERS MISTERS
SMITES MISSET STIMES TMESIS
SMITH SY
SMITHERS
SMITHERY
SMITHIES
SMITHS
SMITHY
SMITING MISTING TIMINGS
SMITTEN MITTENS
SMOCK S MOCKS
SMOCKED
SMOCKING S
SMOCKS
SMOG S MOGS
SMOGGIER
SMOGGY
SMOGLESS
SMOGS
SMOKABLE ABELMOSK
SMOKE DRSY MOKES
SMOKED
SMOKEPOT S
SMOKER S
SMOKERS
SMOKES
SMOKEY
SMOKIER IRKSOME
SMOKIEST
SMOKILY SOYMILK
SMOKING
SMOKY
SMOLDER S MOLDERS REMOLDS
SMOLDERS
SMOLT S MOLTS
SMOLTS
SMOOCH Y
SMOOCHED
SMOOCHER S MOOCHERS
SMOOCHES SCHMOOSE
SMOOCHY
SMOOSH
SMOOSHED
SMOOSHES
SMOOTH SY
SMOOTHED
SMOOTHEN S
SMOOTHER S RESMOOTH
SMOOTHES T
SMOOTHIE S
SMOOTHLY
SMOOTHS
SMOOTHY
SMOTE MOSTE MOTES TOMES
SMOTHER SY MOTHERS THERMOS
SMOTHERS
SMOTHERY
SMOULDER S MOULDERS
SMUDGE DS DEGUMS
SMUDGED
SMUDGES
SMUDGIER
SMUDGILY
SMUDGING
SMUDGY
SMUG GUMS MUGS
SMUGGER MUGGERS
SMUGGEST
SMUGGLE DRS
SMUGGLED
SMUGGLER S
SMUGGLES
SMUGLY
SMUGNESS
SMUSH
SMUSHED
SMUSHES
SMUSHING
SMUT S MUST MUTS STUM
SMUTCH Y
SMUTCHED
SMUTCHES
SMUTCHY
SMUTS MUSTS STUMS
SMUTTED
SMUTTIER
SMUTTILY
SMUTTING
SMUTTY
SNACK S
SNACKED
SNACKER S CANKERS
SNACKERS
SNACKING
SNACKS
SNAFFLE DS
SNAFFLED
SNAFFLES
SNAFU S FAUNS
SNAFUED
SNAFUING
SNAFUS
SNAG S NAGS SANG
SNAGGED
SNAGGIER GEARINGS GREASING
SNAGGING
SNAGGY
SNAGLIKE LINKAGES
SNAGS
SNAIL S ANILS NAILS SLAIN
SNAILED DENIALS
SNAILING
SNAILS
SNAKE DSY KANES SKEAN SNEAK
SNAKEBIT E BEATNIKS
SNAKED KNEADS
SNAKEPIT S
SNAKES SKEANS SNEAKS
SNAKEY SNEAKY
SNAKIER
SNAKIEST
SNAKILY
SNAKING
SNAKY YANKS
SNAP S NAPS PANS SPAN
SNAPBACK S
SNAPLESS SPANLESS
SNAPPED APPENDS
SNAPPER S NAPPERS
SNAPPERS
SNAPPIER
SNAPPILY
SNAPPING
SNAPPISH
SNAPPY
SNAPS SPANS
SNAPSHOT S
SNAPWEED S
SNARE DRS EARNS NARES NEARS SANER
SNARED DENARS REDANS SANDER
SNARER S
SNARERS
SNARES SARSEN
SNARF S
SNARFED
SNARFING
SNARFS
SNARING
SNARK SY KARNS KNARS NARKS RANKS
SNARKIER
SNARKILY
SNARKS
SNARKY
SNARL SY
SNARLED DARNELS LANDERS RELANDS SLANDER
SNARLER S
SNARLERS
SNARLIER
SNARLING
SNARLS
SNARLY
SNASH
SNASHES
SNATCH Y CHANTS STANCH
SNATCHED STANCHED

SNATCHER S
CHANTERS
STANCHER
TRANCHES
SNATCHES
CHASTENS
STANCHES
SNATCHY
SNATH ES
HANTS
SNATHE S
HASTEN
THANES
SNATHES
HASTENS
SNATHS
SNAW S
AWNS SAWN
SWAN WANS
SNAWED
DEWANS
SNAWING
AWNINGS
SNAWS
SWANS
SNAZZIER
SNAZZY
SNEAK SY
KANES SKEAN
SNAKE
SNEAKED
SNEAKER S
SNEAKERS
SNEAKIER
SNEAKILY
SNEAKING
SNEAKS
SKEANS
SNAKES
SNEAKY
SNAKEY
SNEAP S
ASPEN NAPES
NEAPS PANES
PEANS SPEAN
SNEAPED
SPEANED
SNEAPING
SPEANING
SNEAPS
ASPENS
SPEANS
SNECK S
NECKS
SNECKS
SNED S
DENS ENDS
SEND
SNEDDED
SNEDDING
SNEDS
SENDS
SNEER SY
ERNES
SNEERED
NEEDERS
SNEERER S
SERENER
SNEERERS
SNEERFUL
SNEERIER
SNEERING
SNEERS
SNEERY
SNEESH
SHEENS
SNEESHES
SNEEZE DRS
SNEEZED
SNEEZER S
SNEEZERS
SNEEZES
SNEEZIER
SNEEZING
SNEEZY
SNELL S
SNELLED
SNELLER
SNELLEST
SNELLING
SNELLS

SNIB S
BINS NIBS
SNIBBED
SNIBBING
SNIBS
SNICK S
NICKS
SNICKED
DICKENS
SNICKER SY
NICKERS
SNICKERS
SNICKERY
SNICKING
SNICKS
SNIDE R
DINES NIDES
SNIDELY
SNIDER
DINERS
RINSED
SNIDEST
DISSENT
SNIFF SY
SNIFFED
SNIFFER S
NIFFERS
SNIFFERS
SNIFFIER
SNIFFILY
SNIFFING
SNIFFISH
SNIFFLE DRS
SNIFFLED
SNIFFLER S
SNIFFLES
SNIFFLY
SNIFFS
SNIFFY
SNIFTER S
SNIFTERS
SNIGGER S
GINGERS
SERGING
SNIGGERS
SERGINGS
SNIGGLE DRS
LEGGINS
NIGGLES
SNIGGLED
GELDINGS
SLEDGING
SNIGGLER S
NIGGLERS
SNIGGLES
SNIGLET S
GLISTEN
SINGLET
TINGLES
SNIGLETS
GLISTENS
SINGLETS
SNIP ES
NIPS PINS
SPIN
SNIPE DRS
PEINS PENIS
PINES SPINE
SNIPED
SPINED
SNIPER S
REPINS
RIPENS
SNIPERS
SNIPES
SPINES
SNIPING
SNIPPED
SNIPPER S
NIPPERS
SNIPPERS
SNIPPET SY
SNIPPETS
SNIPPETY
SNIPPIER
SNIPPILY
SNIPPING
SNIPPY
SNIPS
SPINS

SNIT S
NITS TINS
SNITCH
CHINTS
SNITCHED
SNITCHER S
CHRISTEN
CITHERNS
CITHRENS
SNITCHES
CHINTSES
SNITS
SNIVEL S
LEVINS
LIVENS
SNIVELED
SNIVELER S
LIVENERS
SNIVELS
SNOB S
NOBS
SNOBBERY
SNOBBIER
SNOBBILY
SNOBBISH
SNOBBISM S
SNOBBY
SNOBS
SNOG S
NOGS SONG
SNOGGED
SNOGGING
NOGGINGS
SNOGS
SONGS
SNOOD S
SNOODED
SNOODING
SNOODS
SNOOK S
NOOKS
SNOOKED
SNOOKER S
SNOOKERS
SNOOKING
SNOOKS
SNOOL S
LOONS NOLOS
SOLON
SNOOLED
NOODLES
SNOOLING
GLONOINS
SNOOLS
SOLONS
SNOOP SY
POONS SPOON
SNOOPED
SPOONED
SNOOPER S
OPERONS
SNOOPERS
POORNESS
SNOOPIER
POISONER
SPOONIER
SNOOPILY
SPOONILY
SNOOPING
SPOONING
SNOOPS
SPOONS
SNOOPY
SPOONY
SNOOT SY
TOONS
SNOOTED
SNOOTIER
SNOOTILY
SNOOTING
SNOOTS
SNOOTY
TOYONS
SNOOZE DRS
OZONES
SNOOZED
SNOOZER S
SNOOZERS
SNOOZES
SNOOZIER
SNOOZING
SNOOZLE DS

SNOOZLED
SNOOZLES
SNOOZY
SNORE DRS
SENOR
SNORED
DRONES
REDONS
SONDER
SORNED
SNORER S
SORNER
SNORERS
SORNERS
SNORES
SENORS
SENSOR
SNORING
SORNING
SNORKEL S
SNORKELS
SNORT S
SNORTED
RODENTS
SNORTER S
SNORTERS
SNORTING
SNORTS
SNOT S
TONS
SNOTS
SNOTTIER
TENORIST
TRITONES
SNOTTILY
SNOTTY
SNOUT SY
TONUS
SNOUTED
SNOUTIER
ROUTINES
SNOUTING
SNOUTISH
SNOUTS
SNOUTY
SNOW SY
NOWS OWNS
SOWN WONS
SNOWBALL S
SNOWBANK S
SNOWBELL S
SNOWBELT S
SNOWBIRD S
SNOWBUSH
SNOWCAP S
SNOWCAPS
SNOWCAT S
SNOWCATS
SNOWDROP S
SNOWED
ENDOWS
SNOWFALL S
SNOWIER
SNOWIEST
SNOWILY
SNOWING
SNOWLAND S
SNOWLESS
SLOWNESS
SNOWLIKE
SNOWMAN
SNOWMELT S
SNOWMEN
SNOWMOLD S
SNOWPACK S
SNOWPLOW S
SNOWS
SNOWSHED S
SNOWSHOE DR S
SNOWSUIT S
SNOWY
SNUB S
BUNS NUBS
SNUBBED
SNUBBER S
SNUBBERS
SNUBBIER
SNUBBING

SNUBBY
SNUBNESS
SNUBS
SNUCK
SNUFF SY
SNUFFBOX
SNUFFED
SNUFFER S
SNUFFERS
SNUFFIER
SNUFFILY
SNUFFING
SNUFFLE DRS
SNUFFLED
SNUFFLER S
SNUFFLES
SNUFFLY
SNUFFS
SNUFFY
SNUG S
GNUS GUNS
SUNG
SNUGGED
SNUGGER Y
GRUNGES
SNUGGERY
SNUGGEST
SNUGGIES
GUESSING
SNUGGING
SNUGGLE DS
SNUGGLED
SNUGGLES
SNUGLY
SNUGNESS
SNUGS
SNYE S
SYNE YENS
SNYES
SO BDLMNPST
OS UWXY
SOAK S
KOAS OAKS
OKAS
SOAKAGE S
SOAKAGES
SOAKED
SOAKER S
ARKOSE
RESOAK
SOAKERS
ARKOSES
RESOAKS
SOAKING
SOAKS
ASKOS
SOAP SY
APOS
SOAPBARK S
SOAPBOX
SOAPED
SOAPER S
OPERAS
PAREOS
SOAPERS
SOAPIER
SOAPIEST
SOAPILY
SOAPING
SOAPLESS
SOAPLIKE
SOAPS
PSOAS
SOAPSUDS Y
SOAPWORT S
SOAPY
SOAR S
OARS OSAR
SORA
SOARED
ADORES
OREADS
SARODE
SOARER S
SOARERS
SOARING S
ORIGANS
SIGNORA

SOARINGS
ASSIGNOR
SIGNORAS
SOARS
SAROS SORAS
SOAVE S
OAVES
SOAVES
SOB AS
BOS
SOBA S
BOAS OBAS
SOBAS
BASSO
SOBBED
SOBBER S
SOBBERS
SOBBING
GIBBONS
SOBEIT
BOITES
TOBIES
SOBER S
BORES BROSE
ROBES
SOBERED
BEDSORE
SOBERER
REBORES
SOBEREST
SOBERING
SOBERIZE DS
SOBERLY
SOBERS
BROSES
SOBFUL
SOBRIETY
SOBS
BOSS
SOCA S
OCAS
SOCAGE RS
SOCAGER S
CARGOES
CORSAGE
SOCAGERS
CORSAGES
SOCAGES
SOCAS
SOCCAGE S
SOCCAGES
SOCCER S
SOCCERS
SOCIABLE S
SOCIABLY
A **SOCIAL** S
SOCIALLY
A **SOCIALS**
SOCIETAL
COALIEST
SOCIETY
SOCK OS
SOCKED
SOCKET S
SOCKETED
SOCKETS
SOCKEYE S
SOCKEYES
SOCKING
SOCKLESS
SOCKMAN
SOCKMEN
SOCKO
COOKS
SOCKS
SOCLE S
CLOSE COLES
SOCLES
CLOSES
SOCMAN
MACONS
MASCON
SOCMEN
SOD AS
DOS
ODS
SODA S
ADOS ODAS
SODALESS
SODALIST S

SODALITE S
DIASTOLE
ISOLATED
SODALITY
SODAMIDE S
SODAS
SODDED
SODDEN S
SODDENED
SODDENLY
SODDENS
ODDNESS
SODDIES
SODDING
SODDY
SODIC
DISCO
SODIUM S
ODIUMS
SODIUMS
SODOM SY
DOOMS MOODS
SODOMIES
SODOMIST S
SODOMITE S
DOOMIEST
MOODIEST
SODOMIZE DS
SODOMS
SODOMY
SODS
DOSS
SOEVER
SOFA RS
OAFS
SOFABED S
SOFABEDS
SOFAR S
FAROS
SOFARS
SOFAS
FOSSA
SOFFIT S
SOFFITS
SOFT ASY
SOFTA S
SOFTAS
SOFTBACK S
SOFTBALL S
SOFTCORE
SOFTEN S
SOFTENED
SOFTENER S
RESOFTEN
SOFTENS
SOFTER
FETORS
FOREST
FORTES
FOSTER
SOFTEST
SOFTHEAD S
SOFTIE S
SOFTIES
SOFTISH
SOFTLY
SOFTNESS
SOFTS
SOFTWARE S
SOFTWOOD S
SOFTY
SOGGED
SOGGIER
SOGGIEST
SOGGILY
SOGGY
SOIGNE E
SOIGNEE
GENOISE
SOIL S
OILS SILO
SOLI
SOILAGE S
GOALIES
SOILAGES
SOILED
OLDIES
SILOED

SOILING
SILOING
SOILLESS
SOILS
SILOS
SOILURE S
LOUSIER
SOILURES
SOIREE S
SOIREES
SOJA S
SOJAS
SOJOURN S
JOURNOS
SOJOURNS
SOKE S
OKES
SOKEMAN
SOKEMEN
SOKES
SOKOL S
KOLOS LOOKS
SOKOLS
SOL ADEIOS
SOLA NR
ALSO
SOLACE DRS
SOLACED
COLEADS
SOLACER S
CLAROES
COALERS
ESCOLAR
ORACLES
RECOALS
SOLACERS
ESCOLARS
LACROSSE
SOLACES
SOLACING
SOLAN DOS
LOANS SALON
SOLAND S
SOLDAN
SOLANDER S
LADRONES
SOLANDS
SOLDANS
SOLANIN ES
SOLANINE S
SOLANINS
SOLANO S
SALOON
SOLANOS
SALOONS
SOLANS
SALONS
SOLANUM S
SOLANUMS
SOLAR
ORALS
SOLARIA
SOLARISE DS
SOLARISM S
ORALISMS
SOLARIUM S
SOLARIZE DS
I **SOLATE** DS
OSTEAL
I **SOLATED**
I **SOLATES**
SOLATIA
I **SOLATING**
ANTILOGS
I **SOLATION** S
SOLATIUM
SOLD IO
DOLS OLDS
SOLDAN S
SOLAND
SOLDANS
SOLANDS
SOLDER S
DORSEL
RESOLD
SOLDERED
SOLDERER S
RESOLDER
SOLDERS
DORSELS
RODLESS

SOLDI
DIOLS IDOLS
LIDOS LOIDS
SLOID SOLID
SOLDIER SY
SOLIDER
SOLDIERS
SOLDIERY
SOLDO
SOLE DIS
LOSE OLES
SLOE
SOLECISE DS
SOLECISM S
SOLECIST S
SOLSTICE
SOLECIZE DS
SOLED
DOLES LODES
SOLEI
SOLELESS
SOLELY
SOLEMN
LEMONS
MELONS
SOLEMNER
SOLEMNLY
SOLENESS
NOSELESS
SOLENOID S
EIDOLONS
SOLERET S
SOLERETS
SOLES
LOESS LOSES
SLOES
SOLEUS
LOUSES
OUSELS
SOLEUSES
SOLFEGE S
SOLFEGES
SOLFEGGI O
SOLGEL
SOLI D
OILS SILO
SOIL
SOLICIT S
COLITIS
SOLICITS
SCIOLIST
SOLID IS
DIOLS IDOLS
LIDOS LOIDS
SLOID SOLDI
SOLIDAGO S
SOLIDARY
SOLIDER
SOLDIER
SOLIDEST
SOLIDI
SOLIDIFY
SOLIDITY
SOLIDLY
SOLIDS
DOSSIL
SLOIDS
SOLIDUS
SOLING
LOGINS
LOSING
SOLION S
SOLIONS
SOLIQUID S
SOLITARY
ROYALIST
SOLITON S
LOTIONS
SOLITONS
SOLITUDE S
TOLUIDES
SOLLERET S
SOLO NS
LOOS
SOLOED
LOOSED
OODLES
SOLOING
LOGIONS
LOOSING
OLINGOS

SOLOIST S
SOLOISTS
SOLON S
LOONS NOLOS
SNOOL
SOLONETS
SOLONETZ
SOLONS
SNOOLS
SOLOS
SOLS
LOSS
SOLSTICE S
SOLECIST
SOLUBLE S
BOULLES
LOBULES
SOLUBLES
SOLUBLY
SOLUM S
SOLUMS
SOLUNAR
SOLUS
SOULS
SOLUTE S
TOUSLE
SOLUTES
LOTUSES
TOUSLES
SOLUTION S
SOLVABLE
SOLVATE DS
SOLVATED
SOLVATES
SOLVE DRS
LOVES VOLES
SOLVED
SOLVENCY
SOLVENT S
SOLVENTS
SOLVER S
LOVERS
SOLVERS
SOLVES
SOLVING
SOM AES
MOS
OMS
SOMA NS
MOAS
SOMAN S
MANOS MASON
MOANS MONAS
NOMAS
SOMANS
MASONS
SOMAS
SOMATA
SOMATIC
ATOMICS
OSMATIC
SOMBER
BROMES
OMBERS
OMBRES
SOMBRE
SOMBERLY
SOMBRELY
SOMBRE
BROMES
OMBERS
OMBRES
SOMBER
SOMBRELY
SOMBERLY
SOMBRERO S
SOMBROUS
SOME
SOMEBODY
SOMEDAY
SAMOYED
SOMEDEAL
SOMEHOW
SOMEONE S
SOMEONES
SOMERSET S
SOMETIME S
SOMEWAY S
SOMEWAYS
SOMEWHAT S

SOMEWHEN
SOMEWISE
SOMITAL
SOMITE S
SOMITES
MITOSES
SOMITIC
MIOTICS
SOMONI
SIMOON
SOMS
MOSS
SON EGS
NOS
ONS
SONANCE S
ANCONES
SONANCES
CANONESS
SONANT S
SONANTAL
SONANTIC
ACTINONS
CANONIST
CONTAINS
SANCTION
SONANTS
SONAR S
ARSON ROANS
SONARMAN
SONARMEN
MONERANS
SONARS
ARSONS
SONATA S
SONATAS
SONATINA S
SONATINE
ENATIONS
SONDE RS
NODES NOSED
SONDER S
DRONES
REDONS
SNORED
SORNED
SONDERS
SONDES
SONE S
EONS NOES
NOSE ONES
SONES
NOSES
SONG S
NOGS SNOG
SONGBIRD S
BIRDSONG
SONGBOOK S
SONGFEST S
SONGFUL
SONGLESS
SONGLIKE
SONGS
SNOGS
SONGSTER S
SONHOOD S
SONHOODS
SONIC S
CIONS COINS
ICONS SCION
SONICATE DS
ACONITES
CANOEIST
SONICS
SCIONS
SONLESS
LESSONS
SONLIKE
SONLY
SONNET S
NONETS
TENONS
TONNES
SONNETED
ENDNOTES
SONNETS
SONNIES
SONNY
SONOBUOY S
SONOGRAM S
SONORANT S
SONORITY

SONOROUS
SONOVOX
SONS Y
SONSHIP S
SIPHONS
SONSHIPS
SONSIE R
ENOSIS
EOSINS
ESSOIN
NOESIS
NOISES
OSSEIN
SONSIER
SENIORS
SONSIEST
STENOSIS
SONSY
SOOCHONG S
SOOEY
SOOK S
SOOKS
SOON
ONOS
SOONER S
NOOSER
SOONERS
NOOSERS
SOONEST
SOOT HSY
OOTS
SOOTED
SOOTH ES
HOOTS SHOOT
SOOTHE DRS
SOOTHED
SOOTHER S
HOOTERS
RESHOOT
SHEROOT
SHOOTER
SOOTHERS
ORTHOSES
RESHOOTS
SHEROOTS
SHOOTERS
SOOTHES T
SOOTHEST
SOOTHING
SHOOTING
SOOTHLY
SOOTHS
SHOOTS
SOOTHSAY S
SOOTIER
SOOTIEST
TOOTSIES
SOOTILY
SOOTING
SOOTS
SOOTY
TOYOS
SOP HS
OPS
SOPH SY
HOPS POSH
SHOP
SOPHIES
SOPHISM S
SOPHISMS
SOPHIST S
SOPHISTS
SOPHS
SHOPS
SOPHY
HYPOS
SOPITE DS
POSTIE
POTSIE
SOPITED
DEPOSIT
DOPIEST
PODITES
POSITED
TOPSIDE
SOPITES
POSTIES
POTSIES
SOPITING
POSITING
SOPOR S
PROSO SPOOR

SOPORS
PROSOS
SPOORS
SOPPED
SOPPIER
SOPPIEST
SOPPING
SOPPY
POPSY
SOPRANI
SOPRANO S
SOPRANOS
SOPS
SORA S
OARS OSAR
SOAR
SORAS
SAROS SOARS
SORB S
BROS ORBS
ROBS
SORBABLE
BELABORS
SORBATE S
BOASTER
BOATERS
BORATES
REBATOS
SORBATES
BOASTERS
SORBED
DESORB
SORBENT S
SORBENTS
SORBET S
STROBE
SORBETS
STROBES
SORBIC
SORBING
BORINGS
SORBITOL S
SORBOSE S
SORBOSES
OBSESSOR
SORBS
SORCERER S
SORCERY
SORD S
DORS RODS
SORDID
DROIDS
SORDIDLY
SORDINE S
DINEROS
INDORSE
ORDINES
ROSINED
SORDINES
INDORSES
SORDINI
SORDINO
INDOORS
SORDOR S
SORDORS
SORDS
DROSS
SORE DLRS
EROS ORES
ROES ROSE
SORED
DOERS DOSER
REDOS RESOD
RODES ROSED
SOREHEAD S
SOREL SY
LORES LOSER
ORLES ROLES
SORELS
LESSOR
LOSERS
SORELY
SORENESS
SORER
T **SORES** T
ROSES
SOREST
ROSETS
STORES
TORSES
TOSSER
TSORES

SORGHO S
SORGHOS
SORGHUM S
SORGHUMS
SORGO S
SORGOS
SORI
SORICINE
RECISION
SORING S
GIRONS
GRISON
GROINS
ROSING
SIGNOR
SORINGS
GRISONS
SIGNORS
SORITES
ROSIEST
SORTIES
STORIES
TRIOSES
SORITIC
SORN S
SORNED
DRONES
REDONS
SNORED
SONDER
SORNER S
SNORER
SORNERS
SNORERS
SORNING
SNORING
SORNS
SOROCHE S
CHOOSER
SOROCHES
CHOOSERS
SORORAL
SORORATE S
SORORITY
SOROSES
SOROSIS
SORPTION S
PORTIONS
POSITRON
SORPTIVE
OVERTIPS
SPORTIVE
SORREL S
SORRELS
SORRIER
SORRIEST
RESISTOR
ROISTERS
SORRILY
SORROW S
SORROWED
SORROWER S
SORROWS
SORRY
SORT AS
ORTS ROTS
TORS
SORTA
RATOS ROAST
ROTAS TAROS
TORAS
SORTABLE
BLOATERS
STORABLE
SORTABLY
SORTED
DOTERS
STORED
STRODE
SORTER S
RESORT
RETROS
ROSTER
STORER
SORTERS
RESORTS
ROSTERS
STORERS
SORTIE DS
TORIES
TRIOSE

SORTIED
EDITORS
STEROID
STORIED
TRIODES
SORTIES
ROSIEST
SORITES
STORIES
TRIOSES
SORTING
STORING
TRIGONS
SORTS
SORUS
SOURS
SOS
SOT HS
SOTH S
HOST HOTS
SHOT TOSH
SOTHS
HOSTS SHOTS
SOTOL S
LOOTS LOTOS
STOOL TOOLS
SOTOLS
STOOLS
SOTS
TOSS
SOTTED
SOTTEDLY
SOTTISH
SOU KLPRS
SOUARI S
SOUARIS
SOUBISE S
SOUBISES
SOUCAR S
SOUCARS
SARCOUS
SOUCHONG S
SOUDAN S
SOUDANS
SOUFFLE DS
SOUFFLED
SOUFFLES
SOUGH ST
SOUGHED
SOUGHING
SOUGHS
SOUGHT
OUGHTS
TOUGHS
SOUK S
SOUKOUS
SOUKS
KUSSO
SOUL S
SOULED
LOUSED
SOULFUL
SOULLESS
SOULLIKE
SOULMATE S
SOULS
SOLUS
SOUND S
NODUS UDONS
SOUNDBOX
SOUNDED
SOUNDER S
ENDUROS
RESOUND
UNDOERS
SOUNDERS
DOURNESS
RESOUNDS
SOUNDEST
SOUNDING S
UNDOINGS
SOUNDLY
SOUNDMAN
SOUNDMEN
SOUNDS
SOUP SY
OPUS
SOUPCON S
COUPONS
SOUPCONS
SOUPED
PSEUDO
SOUPIER
SOUPIEST
SOUPING
SOUPLESS
SOUPLIKE
SOUPS
SOUPY
SOUR S
OURS
SOURBALL S
SOURCE DS
CEROUS
COURSE
CROUSE
SOURCED
COURSED
SCOURED
SOURCES
COURSES
SUCROSE
SOURCING
COURSING
SCOURING
SOURDINE S
DOURINES
SOURED
DOUSER
ROUSED
UREDOS
SOURER
ROUSER
SOUREST
ESTROUS
OESTRUS
OUSTERS
SOUTERS
STOURES
TUSSORE
SOURING
ROUSING
SOURISH
SOURLY
SOURNESS
SOURPUSS
SOURS
SORUS
SOURSOP S
SOURSOPS
SOURWOOD S
SOUS E
SOUSE DS
SOUSED
DOUSES
SOUSES
SOUSING
SOUSLIK S
SOUSLIKS
SOUTACHE S
CATHOUSE
SOUTANE S
SOUTANES
SOUTER S
OUSTER
OUTERS
ROUTES
STOURE
SOUTERS
ESTROUS
OESTRUS
OUSTERS
SOUREST
STOURES
TUSSORE
SOUTH S
SHOUT THOUS
SOUTHED
SHOUTED
SOUTHER NS
SHOUTER
SOUTHERN S
SOUTHERS
SHOUTERS
SOUTHING S
SHOUTING
SOUTHPAW S
SOUTHRON S
SOUTHS
SHOUTS
SOUVENIR S
SOUVLAKI AS
SOVIET S
SOVIETS
SOVKHOZ Y
SOVKHOZY
SOVRAN S
SOVRANLY
SOVRANS
SOVRANTY
SOW NS
WOS
SOWABLE
SOWANS
SOWAR S
SOWARS
SOWBELLY
SOWBREAD S
SOWCAR S
SOWCARS
SOWED
DOWSE
SOWENS
SOWER S
RESOW SEROW
SWORE WORSE
SOWERS
RESOWS
SEROWS
WORSES
SOWING
SOWN
NOWS OWNS
SNOW WONS
SOWS
SOX
SOY AS
SOYA S
SOYAS
SOYBEAN S
SOYBEANS
SOYMILK S
SMOKILY
SOYMILKS
SOYS
SOYUZ
SOYUZES
SOZIN ES
SOZINE S
SOZINES
SOZINS
SOZZLED
SPA EMNRSTY
ASP
PAS
SAP
SPACE DRSY
CAPES PACES
SCAPE
SPACED
SCAPED
SPACEMAN
SPACEMEN
SPACER S
CAPERS
CRAPES
ESCARP
PACERS
PARSEC
RECAPS
SCRAPE
SECPAR
SPACERS
ESCARPS
PARSECS
SCRAPES
SECPARS
SPACES
SCAPES
SPACEY
SPACIAL
APICALS
SPACIER
SCRAPIE
SPACIEST
ESCAPIST
SPACING S
SCAPING
SPACINGS
SPACIOUS
SPACKLE DS
SPACKLED
SPACKLES
SPACY
SPADE DRS
SPAED
SPADED
SPADEFUL S
SPADER S
DRAPES
PADRES
PARSED
RASPED
SPARED
SPREAD
SPADERS
SPREADS
SPADES
PASSED
SPADICES
SPADILLE S
SPADING
SPADIX
SPADIXES
SPADO
APODS DOPAS
SPADONES
DAPSONES
SPAE DS
APES APSE
PASE PEAS
SPAED
SPADE
SPAEING S
SPINAGE
SPAEINGS
SPINAGES
SPAES
APSES PASES
PASSE
SPAETZLE S
SPAGYRIC S
SPAHEE S
SPAHEES
APHESES
SPAHI S
APHIS APISH
SPAHIS
ASPISH
PHASIS
SPAIL S
LAPIS PAILS
SPAILS
SPAIT S
PITAS TAPIS
SPAITS
PASTIS
SPAKE
PEAKS SPEAK
SPALDEEN S
DEPLANES
SPALE S
LAPSE LEAPS
PALES PEALS
PLEAS SALEP
SEPAL
SPALES
LAPSES
PASSEL
SALEPS
SEPALS
SPALL S
PALLS
SPALLED
SPALLER S
SPALLERS
SPALLING
SPALLS
SPALPEEN S
SPAM S
AMPS MAPS
PAMS SAMP
SPAMBOT S
SPAMBOTS
SPAMMED
SPAMMER S
SPAMMERS
SPAMMING
SPAMS
SAMPS SPASM
SPAN GKS
NAPS PANS
SNAP
SPANCEL S
ENCLASP
SPANCELS
ENCLASPS
SPANDEX
EXPANDS
SPANDREL S
SPANDRIL S
SPANG
PANGS
SPANGLE DS
SPANGLED
SPANGLES
SPANGLY
SPANIEL S
ALPINES
PINEALS
SPLENIA
SPANIELS
PAINLESS
SPANK S
KNAPS
SPANKED
SPANKER S
SPANKERS
SPANKING S
SPANKS
SPANLESS
SNAPLESS
SPANNED
SPANNER S
PANNERS
SPANNERS
SPANNING
SPANS
SNAPS
SPANSULE S
SPANWORM S
SPAR EKS
PARS RAPS
RASP
SPARABLE S
PARABLES
PARSABLE
PREBASAL
SPARE DRS
APERS APRES
ASPER PARES
PARSE PEARS
PRASE PRESA
RAPES REAPS
SPEAR
SPARED
DRAPES
PADRES
PARSED
RASPED
SPADER
SPREAD
SPARELY
PARLEYS
PARSLEY
PLAYERS
REPLAYS
SPARER S
PARERS
PARSER
RAPERS
RASPER
SPARERIB S
SPARERS
PARSERS
RASPERS
SPARSER
SPARES T
ASPERS
PARSES
PASSER
PRASES
REPASS
SPARSE
SPEARS
SPAREST
PASTERS
REPASTS
SPARGE DRS
GAPERS
GASPER
GRAPES
PAGERS
PARGES
SPARGED
GRASPED
SPARGER S
GRASPER
SPARGERS
GRASPERS
SPARGES
GASPERS
SPARGING
GRASPING
PARGINGS
SPARID S
RAPIDS
SPARIDS
SPARING
PARINGS
PARSING
RASPING
SPARK SY
PARKS
SPARKED
SPARKER S
PARKERS
REPARKS
SPARKERS
SPARKIER
SPARKILY
SPARKING
PARKINGS
SPARKISH
A **SPARKLE** DRS T
SPARKLED
SPARKLER S
SPARKLES
SPARKLET S
SPARKLY
SPARKS
SPARKY
SPARLIKE
SPARLING S
GRAPLINS
SPRINGAL
SPAROID S
SPAROIDS
SPARRED
DRAPERS
SPARRIER
PARRIERS
SPARRING
SPARROW S
SPARROWS
SPARRY
SPARS E
RASPS
SPARSE R
ASPERS
PARSES
PASSER
PRASES
REPASS
SPARES
SPEARS
SPARSELY
PARSLEYS
SPARSER
PARSERS
RASPERS
SPARERS
SPARSEST
TRESPASS
SPARSITY
SPARTAN
PARTANS
TARPANS
TRAPANS
SPARTINA S
ASPIRANT
PARTISAN
SPAS M
ASPS PASS
SAPS
SPASM S
SAMPS SPAMS
SPASMED
SPASMING
SPASMS
SPASTIC S
SPASTICS
SPAT ES
PAST PATS
TAPS
SPATE S
PASTE PATES
PEATS SEPTA
TAPES TEPAS
SPATES
PASTES
STAPES
SPATHAL
ASPHALT
SPATHE DS
SPATHED
HEPTADS
SPATHES
SPATHIC
SPATHOSE
PATHOSES
POTASHES
TEASHOPS
SPATIAL
SPATS
PASTS
SPATTED
SPATTER S
PATTERS
TAPSTER
SPATTERS
TAPSTERS
SPATTING
SPATULA RS
SPATULAR
PASTURAL
SPATULAS
SPATZLE S
SPATZLES
SPAVIE ST
PAVISE
SPAVIES
PASSIVE
PAVISES
PAVISSE
SPAVIET
SPAVIN S
PAVINS
SPAVINED
SPAVINS
SPAWN S
PAWNS
SPAWNED
SPAWNER S
ENWRAPS
PAWNERS
SPAWNERS
SPAWNING
WINGSPAN
SPAWNS
SPAY S
PAYS PYAS
YAPS
SPAYED
SPAYING
SPAYS
SPEAK S
PEAKS SPAKE
SPEAKER S
RESPEAK
SPEAKERS
RESPEAKS
SPEAKING S
SPEAKS
SPEAN S
ASPEN NAPES
NEAPS PANES
PEANS SNEAP
SPEANED
SNEAPED
SPEANING
SNEAPING
SPEANS
ASPENS
SNEAPS
SPEAR S
APERS APRES
ASPER PARES
PARSE PEARS
PRASE PRESA
RAPES REAPS
SPARE
SPEARED
RESPADE
SPEARER S
REAPERS
SPEARERS
ASPERSER

SPEARGUN S
SPEARING
SPEARMAN
PARMESAN
SPEARMEN
PRENAMES
SPEARS
ASPERS
PARSES
PASSER
PRASES
REPASS
SPARES
SPARSE
SPEC KS
CEPS PECS
SPECCED
SPECCING
E **SPECIAL** S
PLAICES
SPECIALS
SLIPCASE
SPECIATE DS
SPECIE S
PIECES
SPECIES
SPECIFIC S
SPECIFY
SPECIMEN S
SPECIOUS
SPECK S
PECKS
SPECKED
SPECKING
SPECKLE DS
SPECKLED
SPECKLES
SPECKS
SPECS
SPECTATE DS
PECTATES
SPECTER S
RECEPTS
RESPECT
SCEPTER
SCEPTRE
SPECTRE
SPECTERS
RESPECTS
SCEPTERS
SCEPTRES
SPECTRES
SPECTRA L
CARPETS
PREACTS
PRECAST
SPECTRAL
SCEPTRAL
SPECTRE S
RECEPTS
RESPECT
SCEPTER
SCEPTRE
SPECTER
SPECTRES
RESPECTS
SCEPTERS
SCEPTRES
SPECTERS
SPECTRUM S
CRUMPETS
SPECULA R
CAPSULE
SCALEUP
UPSCALE
SPECULAR
SPECULUM S
SPED
PEDS
SPEECH
CHEEPS
SPEECHES
SPEED OSY
DEEPS PEDES
SPEEDED
SPEEDER S
SPEERED
SPEEDERS
SPEEDIER
SPEEDILY
SPEEDING S

SPEEDO S
DEPOSE
EPODES
SPEEDOS
DEPOSES
SPEEDS
SPEEDUP S
SPEEDUPS
SPEEDWAY S
SPEEDY
SPEEL S
PEELS PELES
SLEEP
SPEELED
SPEELING
PEELINGS
SLEEPING
SPEELS
SLEEPS
SPEER S
PEERS PERES
PERSE PREES
PRESE SPREE
SPEERED
SPEEDER
SPEERING S
SPEERS
PERSES
SPREES
SPEIL S
PILES PLIES
SLIPE SPIEL
SPILE
SPEILED
SPIELED
SPEILING
SPIELING
SPEILS
PLISSE
SLIPES
SPIELS
SPILES
SPEIR S
PERIS PIERS
PRIES PRISE
RIPES SPIER
SPIRE
SPEIRED
PRESIDE
SPIERED
SPEIRING
SPIERING
SPEIRS
PRISES
SPIERS
SPIRES
SPEISE S
ESPIES
PEISES
SPEISES
SPEISS
SEPSIS
SPEISSES
SPELAEAN
SEAPLANE
SPELEAN
SPELL S
SPELLED
SPELLER S
PRESELL
RESPELL
SPELLERS
PRESELLS
RESPELLS
SPELLING S
SPELLS
SPELT SZ
PELTS SLEPT
SPELTER S
PELTERS
PETRELS
RESPELT
SPELTERS
SPELTS
SPELTZ
SPELTZES
SPELUNK S
SPELUNKS
SPENCE RS
SPENCER S
SPENCERS
SPENCES

SPEND SY
PENDS
SPENDER S
SPENDERS
SPENDIER
SPENDING
SPENDS
SPENDY
SPENSE S
SPENSES
SPENT
SPERM S
PERMS
SPERMARY
SPERMIC
SPERMINE S
SPERMOUS
SUPREMOS
SPERMS
SPEW S
PEWS
SPEWED
SPEWER S
SPEWERS
SPEWING
SPEWS
SPHAGNUM S
SPHENE S
SPHENES
SPHENIC
PINCHES
SPHENOID S
SIPHONED
SPHERAL
PLASHER
SPHERE DS
HERPES
SPHERED
SPHERES
A **SPHERIC** S
CERIPHS
CIPHERS
SPHERICS
SPHERIER
SPHERING
SPHEROID S
SPHERULE S
SPHERY
HYPERS
SYPHER
SPHINGES
SPHINGID S
SPHINX
SPHINXES
SPHYGMIC
SPHYGMUS
SPHYNX
SPHYNXES
SPICA ES
ASPIC PICAS
SPICAE
APICES
SPICAS
ASPICS
SPICATE D
ASEPTIC
PACIEST
SPICATED
SPICCATO S
SPICE DRSY
EPICS SEPIC
SPICED
SPICER SY
CRIPES
PRECIS
PRICES
SPICERS
SPICERY
SPICES
SPICEY
SPICIER
SPICIEST
SPICILY
SPICING
SPICULA ER
SPICULAE
SPICULAR
SPICULE S
SPICULES

SPICULUM
SPICY
SPIDER SY
PRIDES
PRISED
REDIPS
SPIRED
SPIDERS
PRISSED
SPIDERY
E **SPIED**
SIPED
SPIEGEL S
SPIEGELS
SPIEL S
PILES PLIES
SLIPE SPEIL
SPILE
SPIELED
SPEILED
SPIELER S
REPLIES
SPIELERS
SPIELING
SPEILING
SPIELS
PLISSE
SLIPES
SPEILS
SPILES
SPIER S
PERIS PIERS
PRIES PRISE
RIPES SPEIR
SPIRE
SPIERED
PRESIDE
SPEIRED
SPIERING
SPEIRING
SPIERS
PRISES
SPEIRS
SPIRES
E **SPIES**
SIPES
SPIFF SY
SPIFFED
SPIFFIED
SPIFFIER
SPIFFIES T
SPIFFILY
SPIFFING
SPIFFS
SPIFFY
SPIGOT S
SPIGOTS
SPIKE DRSY
KEPIS PIKES
SPIKED
SPIKELET S
STEPLIKE
SPIKER S
PIKERS
SPIKERS
SPIKES
SPIKEY
SPIKIER
SPIKIEST
SPIKILY
SPIKING
PIGSKIN
SPIKY
SPILE DS
PILES PLIES
SLIPE SPEIL
SPIEL
SPILED
DISPEL
LISPED
SLIPED
SPILES
PLISSE
SLIPES
SPEILS
SPIELS
SPILIKIN S
SPILING S
LISPING
PILINGS
SLIPING
SPILINGS

SPILL S
PILLS
SPILLAGE S
PILLAGES
SPILLED
SPILLER S
SPILLERS
SPILLING
SPILLS
SPILLWAY S
SPILT H
SLIPT SPLIT
SPILTH S
SPILTHS
SPIN ESY
NIPS PINS
SNIP
SPINACH Y
SPINACHY
SPINAGE S
SPAEING
SPINAGES
SPAEINGS
SPINAL S
LAPINS
PLAINS
SPINALLY
SPINALS
SPINATE
PANTIES
PATINES
SAPIENT
SPINDLE DRS
SPLINED
SPINDLED
SPLENDID
SPINDLER S
SPINDLES
SPINDLY
SPINE DLST
PEINS PENIS
PINES SNIPE
SPINED
SNIPED
SPINEL S
PENSIL
SPLINE
SPINELLE S
SPINELS
PENSILS
SPLINES
SPINES
SNIPES
SPINET S
INSTEP
SPINETS
INSTEPS
SPINIER
INSPIRE
SPINIEST
SPINIFEX
SPINLESS
SPINNER SY
PINNERS
SPINNERS
SPINNERY
SPINNEY S
SPINNEYS
SPINNIES
SPINNING S
SPINNY
SPINOFF S
SPINOFFS
SPINOR S
ORPINS
PRIONS
PRISON
SPINORS
PRISONS
SPINOSE
SPINOUS
SPINOUT S
SPINOUTS
SPINS
SNIPS
SPINSTER S

SPINTO S
PINOTS
PINTOS
PISTON
PITONS
POINTS
POSTIN
SPINTOS
PISTONS
POSTINS
SPINULA E
PAULINS
SPINULAE
SPINULE S
LINEUPS
LUPINES
UNPILES
SPINULES
SPLENIUS
SPINY
PYINS
SPIRACLE S
CALIPERS
REPLICAS
SPIRAEA S
SPIRAEAS
SPIRAL S
SPIRALED
LIPREADS
PARSLIED
SPIRALLY
SPIRALS
A **SPIRANT** S
A **SPIRANTS**
A **SPIRE** ADMS
PERIS PIERS
PRIES PRISE
RIPES SPEIR
SPIER
SPIREA S
ASPIRE
PARIES
PRAISE
SPIREAS
ASPIRES
PARESIS
PARISES
PRAISES
A **SPIRED**
PRIDES
PRISED
REDIPS
SPIDER
SPIREM ES
PRIMES
SIMPER
SPIREME S
EMPIRES
EMPRISE
EPIMERS
IMPRESE
PREMIES
PREMISE
SPIREMES
EMPRISES
IMPRESES
PREMISES
SPIREMS
IMPRESS
PREMISS
SIMPERS
A **SPIRES**
PRISES
SPEIRS
SPIERS
SPIRIER
SPIRIEST
SPIRILLA
A **SPIRING**
PRISING
SPIRIT S
SPIRITED
RIPTIDES
TIDERIPS
SPIRITS
SPIROID
SPIRT S
SPRIT STIRP
STRIP TRIPS
SPIRTED
STRIPED
SPIRTING
STRIPING

SPIRTS
SPRITS
STIRPS
STRIPS
SPIRULA ES
SPIRULAE
SPIRULAS
SPIRY
SPIT ESZ
PITS TIPS
SPITAL S
PASTIL
PLAITS
SPITALS
PASTILS
SPITBALL S
SPITE DS
PISTE STIPE
SPITED
STIPED
SPITEFUL
SPITES
PISTES
STIPES
SPITFIRE S
SPITING
SPITS
SPITTED
SPITTER S
TIPSTER
SPITTERS
TIPSTERS
SPITTING
PITTINGS
SPITTLE S
SPITTLES
SPITTOON S
SPITZ
SPITZES
SPIV S
SPIVS
SPIVVY
SPLAKE S
SPLAKES
SPLASH Y
SPLASHED
SPLASHER S
PLASHERS
SPLASHES
SPLASHY
SPLAT S
PLATS
SPLATS
SPLATTED
SPLATTER S
PARTLETS
PLATTERS
PRATTLES
SPRATTLE
SPLAY S
PALSY PLAYS
SPLAYED
SPLAYING
PALSYING
SPLAYS
SPLEEN SY
SPLEENS
SPLEENY
SPLENDID
SPINDLED
SPLENDOR S
SPLENIA L
ALPINES
PINEALS
SPANIEL
SPLENIAL
SPLENIC
PENCILS
SPLENII
SPLENIUM
SPLENIUS
SPINULES
SPLENT S
SPLENTS
SPLICE DRS
SPLICED
SPLICER S
SPLICERS
SPLICES
SPLICING

SPLIFF S
SPLIFFS
SPLINE DS
PENSIL
SPINEL
SPLINED
SPINDLE
SPLINES
PENSILS
SPINELS
SPLINING
SPLINT S
SPLINTED
SPLINTER SY
SPLINTS
SPLIT S
SLIPT SPILT
SPLITS
SPLITTER S
TRIPLETS
SPLODGE DS
SPLODGED
SPLODGES
SPLORE S
LOPERS
POLERS
PROLES
SLOPER
SPLORES
PLESSOR
SLOPERS
SPLOSH
SPLOSHED
SPLOSHES
SPLOTCH Y
SPLOTCHY
SPLURGE DRS
GULPERS
SPLURGED
SPLURGER S
SPLURGES
SPLURGY
SPLUTTER SY
SPODE S
DOPES POSED
SPODES
SPODOSOL S
SPOIL ST
POLIS
SPOILAGE S
SPOILED
DESPOIL
DIPLOES
DIPOLES
SPOILER S
SPOILERS
SPOILING
PIGNOLIS
SPOILS
SPOILT
PILOTS
PISTOL
SPOKE DNS
POKES
SPOKED
SPOKEN
SPOKES
SPOKING
SPOLIATE DS
SPONDAIC S
SPONDEE S
DEPONES
SPONDEES
SPONGE DRS
PENGOS
SPONGED
SPONGER S
PRESONG
SPONGERS
SPONGES
SPONGIER
PERIGONS
REPOSING
SPONGILY
POSINGLY
SPONGIN GS
SPONGING
SPONGINS
SPONGY
SPONSAL

SPONSION S
OPSONINS
SPONSON S
SPONSONS
SPONSOR S
SPONSORS
SPONTOON S
PONTOONS
SPOOF SY
SPOOFED
SPOOFER SY
SPOOFERS
SPOOFERY
SPOOFING
SPOOFS
SPOOFY
SPOOK SY
SPOOKED
SPOOKERY
SPOOKIER
SPOOKILY
SPOOKING
SPOOKISH
SPOOKS
SPOOKY
SPOOL S
LOOPS POLOS
POOLS SLOOP
SPOOLED
POODLES
SPOOLER S
LOOPERS
POOLERS
RESPOOL
SPOOLERS
RESPOOLS
SPOOLING S
SPOOLS
SLOOPS
SPOON SY
POONS SNOOP
SPOONED
SNOOPED
SPOONEY S
SPOONEYS
SPOONFUL S
SPOONIER
POISONER
SNOOPIER
SPOONIES T
SPOONILY
SNOOPILY
SPOONING
SNOOPING
SPOONS
SNOOPS
SPOONY
SNOOPY
SPOOR S
PROSO SOPOR
SPOORED
SPOORING
SPOORS
PROSOS
SOPORS
SPORADIC
PICADORS
SPORAL
PAROLS
POLARS
SPORE DS
PORES POSER
PROSE REPOS
ROPES
SPORED
DOPERS
PEDROS
PROSED
SPORES
POSERS
PROSES
SPORING
PROSING
SPOROID
SPOROZOA LN
SPORRAN S
SPORRANS
SPORT SY
PORTS PROST
STROP

SPORTED
DEPORTS
REDTOPS
SPORTER S
PORTERS
PRESORT
PRETORS
REPORTS
SPORTERS
PORTRESS
PRESORTS
SPORTFUL
SPORTIER
PIERROTS
SPORTIF
PROFITS
SPORTILY
SPORTING
SPORTIVE
OVERTIPS
SORPTIVE
SPORTS
STROPS
SPORTY
SPORULAR
PARLOURS
SPORULE S
LEPROUS
PELORUS
SPORULES
SPOT S
OPTS POST
POTS STOP
TOPS
SPOTLESS
SPOTLIT
SPOTS
POSTS STOPS
SPOTTED
SPOTTER S
POTTERS
PROTEST
SPOTTERS
PROTESTS
SPOTTIER
SPOTTILY
SPOTTING
SPOTTY
E SPOUSAL S
E SPOUSALS
E SPOUSE DS
OPUSES
E SPOUSED
PSEUDOS
E SPOUSES
E SPOUSING
SPOUT S
POUTS STOUP
SPOUTED
OUTSPED
SPOUTER S
PETROUS
POSTURE
POUTERS
PROTEUS
TROUPES
SPOUTERS
OUTPRESS
POSTURES
SPOUTING S
SPOUTS
STOUPS
TOSSUP
UPTOSS
SPRADDLE DS
PADDLERS
SPRAG S
GRASP
SPRAGS
GRASPS
SPRAIN S
SPRAINED
SPRAINS
SPRANG S
PRANGS
SPRANGS
SPRAT S
PARTS PRATS
STRAP TARPS
TRAPS
SPRATS
STRAPS

SPRATTLE DS
PARTLETS
PLATTERS
PRATTLES
SPLATTER
SPRAWL SY
SPRAWLED
SPRAWLER S
SPRAWLS
SPRAWLY
SPRAY S
PRAYS RASPY
SPRAYED
SPRAYER S
PRAYERS
RESPRAY
SPRAYERS
RESPRAYS
SPRAYING
SPRAYS
SPREAD S
DRAPES
PADRES
PARSED
RASPED
SPADER
SPARED
SPREADER S
RESPREAD
SPREADS
SPADERS
SPREE S
PEERS PERES
PERSE PREES
PRESE SPEER
SPREES
PERSES
SPEERS
SPRENT
SPRIER
PRIERS
SPRIEST
ESPRITS
PERSIST
PRIESTS
SPRITES
STIRPES
STRIPES
SPRIG S
GRIPS PRIGS
SPRIGGED
SPRIGGER S
SPRIGGY
SPRIGHT S
SPRIGHTS
SPRIGS
SPRING ESY
SPRINGAL DS
GRAPLINS
SPARLING
SPRINGE DRS
PINGERS
SPRINGED
SPRINGER S
RESPRING
SPRINGES
PRESSING
SPRINGS
SPRINGY
SPRINKLE DR S
PLINKERS
SPRINT S
PRINTS
SPRINTED
SPRINTER S
PRINTERS
REPRINTS
SPRINTS
E SPRIT ESZ
SPIRT STIRP
STRIP TRIPS
SPRITE S
ESPRIT
PRIEST
RIPEST
STRIPE
TRIPES

SPRITES
ESPRITS
PERSIST
PRIESTS
SPRIEST
STIRPES
STRIPES
E SPRITS
SPIRTS
STIRPS
STRIPS
SPRITZ
SPRITZED
SPRITZER S
SPRITZES
SPROCKET S
SPROUT S
STUPOR
SPROUTED
POSTURED
PROUDEST
SPROUTS
STUPORS
SPRUCE DRS
SPRUCED
SPRUCELY
SPRUCER
SPRUCES T
PERCUSS
SPRUCEST
SPRUCIER
SPRUCING
SPRUCY
CYPRUS
SPRUE S
PURSE SUPER
SPRUES
PURSES
SUPERS
SPRUG S
SPRUGS
SPRUNG
SPRY
SPRYER
PRYERS
SPRYEST
SPRYLY
SPRYNESS
SPUD S
DUPS PUDS
SPUDDED
SPUDDER S
SPUDDERS
SPUDDING
PUDDINGS
SPUDS
SPUE DS
SUPE
SPUED
DUPES PSEUD
SPUES
PUSES SUPES
SPUING
PIGNUS
SPUME DS
SPUMED
SPUMES
SPUMIER
UMPIRES
SPUMIEST
SPUMING
IMPUGNS
SPUMONE S
SPUMONES
SPUMONI S
SPUMONIS
SPUMOUS
SPUMY
SPUN K
PUNS
SPUNK SY
PUNKS
SPUNKED
SPUNKIE RS
PUNKIES
SPUNKIER
SPUNKIES T
SPUNKILY
SPUNKING
SPUNKS

SPUNKY
SPUR NST
PURS URPS
SPURGALL S
SPURGE S
PURGES
SPURGES
SPURIOUS
SPURN S
SPURNED
SPURNER S
PRUNERS
SPURNERS
PRESSRUN
SPURNING
SPURNS
SPURRED
SPURRER S
SPURRERS
SPURREY S
SPURREYS
SPURRIER S
SPURRIES
SURPRISE
UPRISERS
SPURRING
SPURRY
SPURS
SPURT S
TURPS
SPURTED
SPURTER S
SPURTERS
SPURTING
SPURTLE S
SPURTLES
SPURTS
SPUTA
STUPA
SPUTNIK S
SPUTNIKS
SPUTTER SY
PUTTERS
SPUTTERS
SPUTTERY
SPUTUM
E SPY
SPYGLASS
E SPYING
SQUAB S
SQUABBLE DR S
SQUABBY
SQUABS
SQUAD S
QUADS
SQUADDED
SQUADRON S
SQUADS
SQUALENE S
SQUALID
SQUALL SY
SQUALLED
SQUALLER S
SQUALLS
SQUALLY
SQUALOR S
SQUALORS
SQUAMA E
SQUAMAE
SQUAMATE S
SQUAMOSE
SQUAMOUS
SQUANDER S
SQUARE DRS
SQUARED
SQUARELY
SQUARER S
SQUARERS
SQUARES T
SQUAREST
SQUARING
SQUARISH
SQUARK S
QUARKS
SQUARKS

SQUASH Y
SQUASHED
SQUASHER S
QUASHERS
SQUASHES
SQUASHY
SQUAT S
SQUATLY
SQUATS
SQUATTED
SQUATTER S
QUARTETS
SQUATTY
SQUAWK S
SQUAWKED
SQUAWKER S
SQUAWKS
SQUEAK SY
QUAKES
SQUEAKED
SQUEAKER S
SQUEAKS
SQUEAKY
SQUEAL S
EQUALS
SQUEALED
SQUEALER S
SQUEALS
SQUEEGEE DS
SQUEEZE DRS
SQUEEZED
SQUEEZER S
SQUEEZES
SQUEG S
SQUEGGED
SQUEGS
SQUELCH Y
SQUELCHY
SQUIB S
SQUIBBED
SQUIBS
SQUID S
QUIDS
SQUIDDED
SQUIDS
SQUIFFED
SQUIFFY
SQUIGGLE DS
SQUIGGLY
SQUILGEE DS
SQUILL AS
QUILLS
SQUILLA ES
SQUILLAE
LALIQUES
SQUILLAS
SQUILLS
SQUINCH
SQUINNY
A SQUINT SY
QUINTS
SQUINTED
SQUINTER S
SQUINTS
SQUINTY
E SQUIRE DS
QUIRES
RISQUE
E SQUIRED
SQUIREEN S
ENQUIRES
E SQUIRES
E SQUIRING
SQUIRISH
SQUIRM SY
SQUIRMED
SQUIRMER S
SQUIRMS
SQUIRMY
SQUIRREL SY
SQUIRT S
QUIRTS
SQUIRTED
SQUIRTER S
SQUIRTS

SQUISH Y
SQUISHED
SQUISHES
SQUISHY
SQUOOSH Y
SQUOOSHY
SQUUSH
SQUUSHED
SQUUSHES
SRADDHA S
SRADDHAS
SRADHA S
SRADHAS
SRI S
SIR
SRIS
SIRS
STAB S
BAST BATS
TABS
STABBED
STABBER S
BARBETS
RABBETS
STABBERS
STABBING
STABILE S
ABLEIST
ALBITES
ASTILBE
BASTILE
BESTIAL
BLASTIE
STABILES
ABLEISTS
ASTILBES
BASTILES
BLASTIES
STABLE DRS
ABLEST
BLEATS
TABLES
STABLED
BALDEST
BLASTED
STABLER S
BLASTER
LABRETS
STABLERS
BLASTERS
STABLES T
STABLEST
STABLING S
BLASTING
E **STABLISH**
STABLY
BLASTY
STABS
BASTS
STACCATI
STACCATO S
STOCCATA
TOCCATAS
STACK S
TACKS
STACKED
STACKER S
RACKETS
RESTACK
RETACKS
TACKERS
STACKERS
RESTACKS
STACKING
STACKS
STACKUP S
STACKUPS
STACTE S
STACTES
STADDLE S
STADDLES
STADE S
DATES SATED
STEAD TSADE
STADES
STEADS
TSADES
STADIA S
STADIAS
STADIUM S
STADIUMS

STAFF S
STAFFED
STAFFER S
RESTAFF
STAFFERS
RESTAFFS
STAFFING
STAFFS
STAG ESY
GAST GATS
TAGS
STAGE DRSY
GATES GETAS
STAGED
GASTED
STAGEFUL S
STAGER S
GASTER
GATERS
GRATES
GREATS
RETAGS
TARGES
STAGERS
GASTERS
STAGES
SAGEST
STAGEY
GAYEST
STAGGARD S
STAGGART S
STAGGED
GADGETS
STAGGER SY
GAGSTER
GARGETS
TAGGERS
STAGGERS
GAGSTERS
STAGGERY
STAGGIE RS
STAGGIER
STAGGIES T
SAGGIEST
STAGGING
STAGGY
STAGIER
AIGRETS
GAITERS
SEAGIRT
TRIAGES
STAGIEST
STAGILY
STAGING S
GASTING
GATINGS
STAGINGS
STAGNANT
STAGNATE DS
STAGS
GASTS
STAGY
STAID
ADITS DITAS
TSADI
STAIDER
ARIDEST
ASTRIDE
DIASTER
DISRATE
TARDIES
TIRADES
STAIDEST
DISTASTE
STAIDLY
STAIG S
AGIST GAITS
STAIGS
AGISTS
STAIN S
ANTIS SAINT
SATIN TAINS
STAINED
DESTAIN
DETAINS
INSTEAD
NIDATES
SAINTED

STAINER S
ANESTRI
ANTSIER
NASTIER
RATINES
RETAINS
RETINAS
RETSINA
STEARIN
STAINERS
ARTINESS
RETSINAS
STEARINS
STAINING
SAINTING
STAINS
SAINTS
SATINS
STAIR S
AIRTS ASTIR
SITAR STRIA
TARSI
STAIRS
SISTRA
SITARS
STAIRWAY S
STAITHE S
ATHEIST
STAITHES
ATHEISTS
HASTIEST
STAKE DS
SKATE STEAK
TAKES TEAKS
STAKED
SKATED
TASKED
STAKEOUT S
OUTSKATE
OUTTAKES
TAKEOUTS
STAKES
SKATES
STEAKS
STAKING
SKATING
TAKINGS
TASKING
STALAG S
STALAGS
STALE DRS
LEAST SETAL
SLATE STEAL
STELA TAELS
TALES TEALS
TESLA
STALED
DELTAS
DESALT
LASTED
SALTED
SLATED
STALELY
STALER
ALERTS
ALTERS
ARTELS
ESTRAL
LASTER
RATELS
SALTER
SLATER
STELAR
TALERS
STALES T
LEASTS
SLATES
STEALS
TASSEL
TESLAS
STALEST
LATESTS
SALTEST
STALING
LASTING
SALTING
SLATING
STALK SY
TALKS
STALKED
STALKER S
TALKERS
STALKERS

STALKIER
LARKIEST
STARLIKE
STALKILY
STALKING S
TALKINGS
STALKS
STALKY
STALL S
TALLS
STALLED
STALLING
STALLION S
STALLS
STALWART S
STAMEN S
AMENTS
MANTES
STAMENED
STAMENS
STAMINA LS
STAMINAL
TALISMAN
STAMINAS
MANTISSA
SATANISM
STAMMEL S
STAMMELS
STAMMER S
STAMMERS
STAMP S
TAMPS
STAMPED E
DAMPEST
STAMPEDE DR
STEPDAME S
STAMPER S
RESTAMP
TAMPERS
STAMPERS
RESTAMPS
STAMPING
STAMPS
STANCE S
ASCENT
CENTAS
ENACTS
SECANT
STANCES
ASCENTS
SECANTS
STANCH
CHANTS
SNATCH
STANCHED
SNATCHED
STANCHER S
CHANTERS
SNATCHER
TRANCHES
STANCHES T
CHASTENS
SNATCHES
STANCHLY
STAND S
STANDARD S
STANDBY S
STANDBYS
STANDEE S
STANDEES
ASSENTED
SENSATED
STANDER S
STANDERS
STANDING S
STANDISH
STANDOFF S
STANDOUT S
OUTSTAND
STANDPAT
STANDS
STANDUP S
DUSTPAN
UPSTAND
STANDUPS
DUSTPANS
UPSTANDS
STANE DS
ANTES ETNAS
NATES NEATS
STANED

STANES
ASSENT
SANEST
STANG S
ANGST GNATS
TANGS
STANGED
STANGING
STANGS
ANGSTS
STANHOPE S
PHAETONS
PHONATES
STANINE S
INANEST
STANINES
INSANEST
STANING
ANTINGS
STANK S
TANKS
STANKS
STANNARY
STANNIC
INCANTS
STANNITE S
STANNOUS
STANNUM S
STANNUMS
STANOL S
SANTOL
TALONS
TOLANS
STANOLS
SANTOLS
STANZA S
STANZAED
STANZAIC
STANZAS
STAPEDES
STAPELIA S
STAPES
PASTES
SPATES
STAPH S
PATHS
STAPHS
STAPLE DRS
PALEST
PALETS
PASTEL
PETALS
PLATES
PLEATS
SEPTAL
TEPALS
STAPLED
STAPLER S
PALTERS
PERSALT
PLASTER
PLATERS
PSALTER
STAPLERS
PERSALTS
PLASTERS
PSALTERS
STAPLES
PASTELS
STAPLING
PLATINGS
STAR EKST
ARTS RATS
TARS TSAR
STARCH Y
CHARTS
STARCHED
STARCHES
STARCHY
STARDOM S
TSARDOM
STARDOMS
TSARDOMS
STARDUST S
STARE DRS
ASTER RATES
RESAT TARES
TEARS
STARED
DATERS
DERATS
TRADES
TREADS

STARER S
ARREST
RAREST
RASTER
RATERS
TARRES
TERRAS
STARERS
ARRESTS
RASTERS
STARES
ASSERT
ASTERS
STARETS
STATERS
TASTERS
STARFISH
STARGAZE DR S
STARING
GASTRIN
GRATINS
RATINGS
STARK
KARST KARTS
STARKER S
KRATERS
STARKERS
STARKEST
STARKLY
STARLESS
STARLET S
RATTLES
STARTLE
STARLETS
STARTLES
STARLIKE
LARKIEST
STALKIER
STARLING S
STARLIT
STARNOSE S
ASSENTOR
SANTEROS
SENATORS
TREASONS
STARRED
DARTERS
RETARDS
TRADERS
STARRIER
TARRIERS
STARRING
STARRY
STARS
TRASS TSARS
STARSHIP S
HARPISTS
START S
TARTS
STARTED
TETRADS
STARTER S
RATTERS
RESTART
STARTERS
RESTARTS
STARTING
STARTLE DRS
RATTLES
STARLET
STARTLED
STARTLER S
RATTLERS
STARTLES
STARLETS
STARTS Y
STARTSY
STARTUP S
UPSTART
STARTUPS
UPSTARTS
STARVE DRS
AVERTS
TRAVES
VASTER
STARVED
ADVERTS
STARVER S
STARVERS
STARVES
STARVING
STARWORT S

STASES
ASSETS
TASSES
STASH
STASHED
STASHES
STASHING
STASIMA
STASIMON
STASIS
ASSIST
STAT ES
TATS
STATABLE
ABETTALS
TASTABLE
STATAL
STATANT
E **STATE** DRS
TASTE TATES
TEATS TESTA
E **STATED**
TASTED
STATEDLY
STATELY
STYLATE
STATER S
TASTER
TATERS
TETRAS
TREATS
STATERS
STARETS
TASTERS
E **STATES**
TASSET
TASTES
A **STATIC** ES
ATTICS
STATICAL
CATTAILS
STATICE S
CATTIES
STATICES
STATICKY
STATICS
STATIN GS
TAINTS
TANIST
TITANS
E **STATING**
TASTING
STATINS
TANISTS
STATION S
STATIONS
STATISM S
STATISMS
STATIST S
STATISTS
STATIVE S
STATIVES
VASTIEST
STATOR S
OTTARS
TAROTS
TORTAS
STATORS
STATS
STATUARY
STATUE DS
ASTUTE
STATUED
STATUES
STATURE S
STATURES
STATUS Y
SUTTAS
STATUSES
STATUSY
STATUTE S
TAUTEST
STATUTES
STAUMREL S
STAUNCH
CANTHUS
CHAUNTS
STAVE DS
VESTA
STAVED
STAVES
VESTAS

STAVING
STAW
SWAT TAWS
TWAS WAST
WATS
STAY S
STAYED
STEADY
STAYER S
ESTRAY
YAREST
STAYERS
ESTRAYS
STAYING
STYGIAN
STAYS
SAYST
STAYSAIL S
STEAD SY
DATES SATED
STADE TSADE
STEADED
DEADEST
SEDATED
STEADIED
STEADIER S
READIEST
SERIATED
STEADIES T
STEADILY
STEADING S
SEDATING
STEADS
STADES
TSADES
STEADY
STAYED
STEAK S
SKATE STAKE
TAKES TEAKS
STEAKS
SKATES
STAKES
O **STEAL** S
LEAST SETAL
SLATE STALE
STELA TAELS
TALES TEALS
TESLA
STEALAGE S
STEALER S
ELATERS
REALEST
RELATES
RESLATE
STEALERS
RESLATES
TEARLESS
STEALING S
GELATINS
GENITALS
TAGLINES
STEALS
LEASTS
SLATES
STALES
TASSEL
TESLAS
STEALTH SY
STEALTHS
STEALTHY
STEAM SY
MATES MEATS
SATEM TAMES
TEAMS
STEAMED
STEAMER S
REMATES
RETEAMS
STEAMERS
MASSETER
SEAMSTER
STEAMIER
EMERITAS
EMIRATES
STEAMILY
TALEYSIM
STEAMING
MANGIEST
MINTAGES
MISAGENT
STEAMS
STEAMY
MATEYS
MAYEST
STEAPSIN S
SAPIENTS
STEARATE S
STEARIC
ATRESIC
CRISTAE
RACIEST
STEARIN ES
ANESTRI
ANTSIER
NASTIER
RATINES
RETAINS
RETINAS
RETSINA
STAINER
STEARINE S
ARENITES
ARSENITE
RESINATE
TRAINEES
STEARINS
ARTINESS
RETSINAS
STAINERS
STEATITE S
STEDFAST
STEED S
DEETS
STEEDS
STEEK S
KEETS SKEET
STEEKED
STEEKING
STEEKS
SKEETS
STEEL SY
LEETS SLEET
STELE TEELS
TELES
STEELED
DELETES
SLEETED
STEELIE RS
EELIEST
STEELIER
LEERIEST
SLEETIER
STEELIES T
STEELING
GENTILES
SLEETING
STEELS
SLEETS
STELES
STEELY
SLEETY
STEENBOK S
BETOKENS
STEEP S
STEEPED
DEEPEST
STEEPEN S
STEEPENS
STEEPER S
STEEPERS
STEEPEST
STEEPING
STEEPISH
STEEPLE DS
STEEPLED
DEPLETES
STEEPLES
STEEPLY
STEEPS
STEER S
ESTER REEST
RESET STERE
TERSE TREES
STEERAGE S
EAGEREST
ETAGERES
STEERED
REESTED
STEERER S
STEERERS
STEERING
GENTRIES
INTEGERS
REESTING
STEERS
ESTERS
REESTS
RESETS
SEREST
STERES
STEEVE DS
VESTEE
STEEVED
STEEVES
VESTEES
STEEVING S
STEGODON S
STEIN S
INSET NEIST
NITES SENTI
TINES
STEINBOK S
STEINS
INSETS
STELA EIR
LEAST SETAL
SLATE STALE
STEAL TAELS
TALES TEALS
TESLA
STELAE
ELATES
TEASEL
STELAI
SALTIE
STELAR
ALERTS
ALTERS
ARTELS
ESTRAL
LASTER
RATELS
SALTER
SLATER
STALER
TALERS
STELE S
LEETS SLEET
STEEL TEELS
TELES
STELENE
STELES
SLEETS
STEELS
STELIC
STELLA RS
SALLET
STELLAR
STELLAS
SALLETS
STELLATE D
STELLIFY
STELLITE S
STEM S
STEMLESS
STEMLIKE
STEMMA S
STEMMAS
STEMMATA
STEMMED
STEMMER SY
STEMMERS
STEMMERY
STEMMIER
MERISTEM
STEMMING
STEMMY
STEMS
STEMSON S
STEMSONS
STEMWARE S
STENCH Y
STENCHES
STENCHY
STENCIL S
CLIENTS
LECTINS
STENCILS
STENGAH S
STENGAHS
STENO S
NOTES ONSET
SETON STONE
TONES
STENOKY
STENOS
ONSETS
SETONS
STONES
STENOSED
STENOSES
STENOSIS
SONSIEST
STENOTIC
TONETICS
STENT S
NETTS TENTS
STENTOR S
STENTORS
STENTS
STEP S
PEST PETS
SEPT
STEPDAME S
STAMPEDE
STEPLIKE
SPIKELET
STEPPE DRS
STEPPED
STEPPER S
STEPPERS
STEPPES
STEPPING
STEPS
PESTS SEPTS
STEPSON S
STEPSONS
STEPWISE
STERE OS
ESTER REEST
RESET STEER
TERSE TREES
STEREO S
STEREOED
STEREOS
STERES
ESTERS
REESTS
RESETS
SEREST
STEERS
STERIC
CITERS
RECITS
TRICES
STERICAL
ARTICLES
RECITALS
STERIGMA S
MAGISTER
MIGRATES
RAGTIMES
STERILE
LEISTER
RETILES
STERLET S
LETTERS
SETTLER
TRESTLE
STERLETS
SETTLERS
TRESTLES
STERLING S
RINGLETS
TINGLERS
A **STERN** AS
NERTS RENTS
TERNS
STERNA L
ANTRES
ASTERN
A **STERNAL**
ANTLERS
RENTALS
SALTERN
STERNER
RENTERS
RERENTS
STERNEST
STERNITE S
INSETTER
INTEREST
TRIENTES
STERNLY
STERNS
STERNSON S
STERNUM S
MUNSTER
STERNUMS
MUNSTERS
STERNWAY S
A **STEROID** S
EDITORS
SORTIED
STORIED
TRIODES
A **STEROIDS**
STEROL S
OSTLER
STEROLS
OSTLERS
STERTOR S
RETORTS
ROTTERS
STERTORS
STET S
SETT TEST
TETS
STETS
SETTS TESTS
STETSON S
TESTONS
STETSONS
STETTED
STETTING
STEW SY
TEWS WEST
WETS
STEWABLE
STEWARD S
STRAWED
STEWARDS
STEWBUM S
STEWBUMS
STEWED
TWEEDS
STEWING
TWINGES
WESTING
STEWPAN S
STEWPANS
STEWS
WESTS
STEWY
WYTES
STEY
STYE TYES
A **STHENIA** S
SHEITAN
A **STHENIAS**
ANTHESIS
SHANTIES
SHEITANS
A **STHENIC**
ETHNICS
STIBIAL
STIBINE S
STIBINES
STIBIUM S
STIBIUMS
STIBNITE S
STICH S
CHITS
STICHIC
STICHS
SCHIST
STICK SY
TICKS
STICKED
DETICKS
STICKER S
RICKETS
TICKERS
STICKERS
STICKFUL S
STICKIER
STICKIES T
EKISTICS
STICKILY
STICKING
TICKINGS
STICKIT
STICKLE DRS
TICKLES
STICKLED
STICKLER S
STRICKLE
TICKLERS
TRICKLES
STICKLES
SLICKEST
STICKMAN
STICKMEN
STICKOUT S
STICKPIN S
NITPICKS
STICKS
STICKUM S
STICKUMS
STICKUP S
UPTICKS
STICKUPS
STICKY
STICTION S
STIED
DEIST DIETS
DITES EDITS
SITED TIDES
STIES
SITES
STIFF S
TIFFS
STIFFED
STIFFEN S
STIFFENS
STIFFER
STIFFEST
STIFFING
STIFFISH
STIFFLY
STIFFS
STIFLE DRS
FILETS
FLIEST
FLITES
ITSELF
STIFLED
STIFLER S
FILTERS
LIFTERS
TRIFLES
STIFLERS
RIFTLESS
STIFLES
STIFLING
STIGMA LS
STIGMAL
STIGMAS
STIGMATA
STILBENE S
TENSIBLE
STILBITE S
STILE S
ISLET ISTLE
TILES
STILES
ISLETS
ISTLES
SLIEST
STILETTO S
STILL SY
LILTS TILLS
STILLED
STILLER
RILLETS
TILLERS
TRELLIS
STILLEST
STILLIER
STILLING
STILLMAN
STILLMEN
STILLS
STILLY
STILT S
TILTS
STILTED
SLITTED
STILTING
SLITTING
STILTS
STIME S
EMITS ITEMS
METIS MITES
SMITE TIMES
STIMES
MISSET
SMITES
TMESIS
STIMIED
MISEDIT
STIMIES
MITISES
STIMULI
STIMULUS
STIMY
MISTY
STIMYING
STING OSY
TINGS
STINGER S
RESTING
STINGERS
TRIGNESS
STINGIER
IGNITERS
RESITING
STINGILY
STINGING
STINGO S
INGOTS
TIGONS
STINGOS
TOSSING
STINGRAY S
STRAYING
STINGS
STINGY
STYING
STINK OSY
KNITS SKINT
STINKARD S
STINKBUG S
STINKER S
REKNITS
TINKERS
STINKERS
STINKIER
STINKING
STINKO
STINKPOT S
STINKS
STINKY
STINT S
TINTS
STINTED
DENTIST
DISTENT
STINTER S
RETINTS
TINTERS
STINTERS
STINTING
TINTINGS
STINTS
STIPE DLS
PISTE SPITE
STIPED
SPITED
STIPEL S
STIPELS
TIPLESS
STIPEND S
DIPNETS
STIPENDS
STIPES
PISTES
SPITES
STIPITES
PIETISTS
TIPSIEST
STIPPLE DRS
TIPPLES
STIPPLED
STIPPLER S
PRESPLIT
RIPPLETS
TIPPLERS
STIPPLES
STIPULAR
STIPULE DS
STIPULED
STIPULES
A **STIR** KPS
STIRK S
SKIRT
STIRKS
SKIRTS

STIRP S
SPIRT SPRIT
STRIP TRIPS
STIRPES
ESPRITS
PERSIST
PRIESTS
SPRIEST
SPRITES
STRIPES
STIRPS
SPIRTS
SPRITS
STRIPS
STIRRED
STRIDER
STIRRER S
STIRRERS
STIRRING S
STIRRUP S
IRRUPTS
STIRRUPS
STIRS
STITCH
STITCHED
STITCHER SY
CHITTERS
RESTITCH
STITCHES
STITHIED
DITHEIST
STITHIES
STITHY
STIVER S
RIVETS
STRIVE
VERIST
STIVERS
STRIVES
VERISTS
STOA EIST
OAST OATS
TAOS
STOAE
TOEAS
STOAI
IOTAS OSTIA
STOAS
OASTS
STOAT S
TOAST
STOATS
TOASTS
STOB S
BOTS
STOBBED
STOBBING
STOBS
STOCCADO S
STOCCATA S
STACCATO
TOCCATAS
STOCK SY
STOCKADE DS
STOCKAGE S
STOCKCAR S
STOCKED
DOCKETS
STOCKER S
RESTOCK
ROCKETS
STOCKERS
RESTOCKS
STOCKIER
CORKIEST
ROCKIEST
STOCKILY
STOCKING S
STOCKISH
STOCKIST S
STOCKMAN
STOCKMEN
STOCKPOT S
STOCKS
STOCKY
STODGE DS
GODETS
STODGED
STODGES
STODGIER
DIGESTOR
GRODIEST
STODGILY
STODGING
STODGY
STOGEY S
STOGEYS
STOGIE S
EGOIST
STOGIES
EGOISTS
STOGY
STOIC S
STOICAL
CITOLAS
STOICISM S
STOICS
STOKE DRS
TOKES
STOKED
STOKER S
STROKE
TOKERS
TROKES
STOKERS
STROKES
STOKES
STOKESIA S
STOKING
STOLE DNS
TELOS TOLES
STOLED
OLDEST
STOLEN
LENTOS
TELSON
STOLES
STOLID
STOLIDER
STOLIDLY
STOLLEN S
STOLLENS
STOLON S
STOLONIC
COLONIST
STOLONS
STOLPORT S
STOMA LS
ATOMS MOATS
STOMACH SY
STOMACHS
STOMACHY
STOMAL
ALMOST
SMALTO
STOMAS
STOMATA L
A **STOMATAL**
O **STOMATE** S
O **STOMATES**
STOMATIC
STOMODEA L
STOMP S
STOMPED
STOMPER S
TROMPES
STOMPERS
STOMPING
STOMPS
STONABLE
NOTABLES
STONE DRSY
NOTES ONSET
SETON STENO
TONES
STONED
STONEFLY
STONER S
NESTOR
NOTERS
TENORS
TENSOR
TONERS
TRONES
STONERS
NESTORS
TENSORS
STONES
ONSETS
SETONS
STENOS
STONEY
STONIER
NORITES
OESTRIN
ORIENTS
STONIEST
STONILY
TYLOSIN
STONING
A **STONISH**
A **STONY**
STOOD
STOOGE DS
STOOGED
STOOGES
STOOGING
STOOK S
KOTOS
STOOKED
STOOKER S
STOOKERS
STOOKING
STOOKS
STOOL S
LOOTS LOTOS
SOTOL TOOLS
STOOLED
TOLEDOS
STOOLIE S
OOLITES
OSTIOLE
STOOLIES
OSTIOLES
STOOLING
TOOLINGS
STOOLS
SOTOLS
STOOP S
TOPOS
STOOPED
STOOPER S
POOREST
STOOPERS
STOOPING
STOOPS
E **STOP** EST
OPTS POST
POTS SPOT
TOPS
STOPBANK S
STOPCOCK S
STOPE DRS
ESTOP PESTO
POETS TOPES
STOPED
DEPOTS
DESPOT
POSTED
STOPER S
POSTER
PRESTO
REPOTS
RESPOT
TOPERS
TROPES
STOPERS
POSTERS
PRESTOS
RESPOTS
STOPES
ESTOPS
PESTOS
POSSET
PTOSES
STOPGAP S
STOPGAPS
STOPING
POSTING
STOPOFF S
STOPOFFS
STOPOVER S
OVERTOPS
E **STOPPAGE** S
E **STOPPED**
STOPPER S
TOPPERS
STOPPERS
E **STOPPING**
TOPPINGS
STOPPLE DS
TOPPLES
STOPPLED
STOPPLES
E **STOPS**
POSTS SPOTS
STOPT
STOPWORD S
STORABLE S
BLOATERS
SORTABLE
STORAGE S
GAROTES
ORGEATS
STORAGES
STORAX
STORAXES
STORE DRSY
ROSET ROTES
TORES TORSE
STORED
DOTERS
SORTED
STRODE
STORER S
RESORT
RETROS
ROSTER
SORTER
STORERS
RESORTS
ROSTERS
SORTERS
STORES
ROSETS
SOREST
TORSES
TOSSER
TSORES
STOREY S
OYSTER
TOYERS
STOREYED
OYSTERED
STOREYS
OYSTERS
STORIED
EDITORS
SORTIED
STEROID
TRIODES
STORIES
ROSIEST
SORITES
SORTIES
TRIOSES
STORING
SORTING
TRIGONS
STORK S
SKORT TORSK
STORKS
SKORTS
TORSKS
STORM SY
MORTS
STORMED
STORMIER
MORTISER
STORMILY
STORMING
STORMS
STORMY
STORY
RYOTS STROY
TROYS TYROS
STORYING
STROYING
STOSS
STOT ST
TOST TOTS
STOTIN S
STOTINKA
STOTINKI
STOTINOV
STOTINS
STOTS
STOTT S
STOTTED
STOTTING
STOTTS
A **STOUND** S
DONUTS
A **STOUNDED**
A **STOUNDS**
STOUP S
POUTS SPOUT
STOUPS
SPOUTS
TOSSUP
UPTOSS
STOUR ESY
ROUST ROUTS
TORUS TOURS
STOURE S
OUSTER
OUTERS
ROUTES
SOUTER
STOURES
ESTROUS
OESTRUS
OUSTERS
SOUREST
SOUTERS
TUSSORE
STOURIE
STOURS
ROUSTS
TUSSOR
STOURY
STOUT S
TOUTS
STOUTEN S
TENUTOS
STOUTENS
STOUTER
OUTSERT
TOUTERS
STOUTEST
STOUTISH
STOUTLY
STOUTS
STOVE RS
VOTES
STOVER S
STROVE
TROVES
VOTERS
E **STOVERS**
VOTRESS
STOVES
STOW PS
SWOT TOWS
TWOS WOST
WOTS
STOWABLE
BESTOWAL
TEABOWLS
STOWAGE S
TOWAGES
STOWAGES
STOWAWAY S
TOWAWAYS
STOWED
STOWING
STOWP S
STOWPS
STOWS
SWOTS
A **STRADDLE** DR S
STRAFE DRS
AFTERS
FASTER
STRAFED
STRAFER S
FRATERS
RAFTERS
STRAFERS
STRAFES
STRAFING
INGRAFTS
STRAGGLE DR S
STRAGGLY
STRAIGHT S
STRAIN S
INSTAR
SANTIR
TRAINS
STRAINED
DETRAINS
RANDIEST
STRAINER S
RESTRAIN
RETRAINS
TERRAINS
TRAINERS
STRAINS
INSTARS
SANTIRS
STRAIT S
ARTIST
STRATI
TRAITS
STRAITEN S
INTREATS
NITRATES
TERTIANS
STRAITER
TARRIEST
STRAITLY
STRAITS
ARTISTS
TSARIST
STRAKE DS
SKATER
STREAK
TAKERS
STRAKED
DARKEST
STRAKES
SKATERS
STREAKS
STRAMASH
STRAMONY
STRAND S
STRANDED
DARNDEST
STRANDER S
STRANDS
STRANG E
GRANTS
E **STRANGE** RS
ARGENTS
GARNETS
E **STRANGER** S
GRANTERS
REGRANTS
E **STRANGES** T
STRANGLE DR
TANGLERS S
STRAP S
PARTS PRATS
SPRAT TARPS
TRAPS
STRAPPED
STRAPPER S
TRAPPERS
STRAPPY
STRAPS
SPRATS
STRASS
STRASSES
STRATA LS
ATTARS
TATARS
STRATAL
STRATAS
STRATEGY
STRATH S
STRATHS
STRATI
ARTIST
STRAIT
TRAITS
STRATIFY
STRATOUS
STRATUM S
STRATUMS
STRATUS
STRAVAGE DS
STRAVAIG S
GRAVITAS
STRAW SY
SWART WARTS
STRAWED
STEWARD
STRAWHAT
STRAWIER
STRAWING
RINGTAWS
STRAWS
STRAWY
SWARTY
WASTRY
AE **STRAY** S
ARTSY SATYR
TRAYS
E **STRAYED**
STRAYER S
STRAYERS
E **STRAYING**
STINGRAY
E **STRAYS**
SATYRS
STREAK SY
SKATER
STRAKE
TAKERS
STREAKED
STREAKER S
RETAKERS
STREAKS
SKATERS
STRAKES
STREAKY
STREAM SY
ARMETS
MASTER
MATERS
MATRES
RAMETS
TAMERS
STREAMED
MASTERED
STREAMER S
REMASTER
STREAMS
MASTERS
STREAMY
MASTERY
STREEK S
STREEKED
STREEKER S
STREEKS
STREEL S
RELETS
STREELED
STREELS
TRESSEL
STREET S
RETEST
SETTER
TESTER
STREETS
RETESTS
SETTERS
TERSEST
TESTERS
STRENGTH S
STREP S
PREST
STREPS
PRESTS
STRESS
STRESSED
DESSERTS
STRESSES
STRESSOR S
STRETCH Y
STRETCHY
STRETTA S
TARTEST
TATTERS
STRETTAS
STRETTE
TETTERS
STRETTI
TITTERS
TRITEST
STRETTO S
TOTTERS
STRETTOS
STREUSEL S
STREW NS
TREWS WREST
STREWED
WRESTED
STREWER S
WRESTER
STREWERS
WRESTERS
STREWING
WRESTING
STREWN

STREWS
WRESTS
STRIA E
AIRTS ASTIR
SITAR STAIR
TARSI
STRIAE
AIREST
SATIRE
TERAIS
STRIATA
STRIATE DS
ARTIEST
ARTISTE
ATTIRES
IRATEST
RATITES
TASTIER
STRIATED
TARDIEST
STRIATES
ARTISTES
ARTSIEST
STRIATUM
STRICK S
TRICKS
STRICKEN
STRICKLE DS
STICKLER
TICKLERS
TRICKLES
STRICKS
A **STRICT**
STRICTER
CRITTERS
RESTRICT
STRICTLY
STRIDDEN
A **STRIDE** RS
DIREST
DRIEST
STRIDENT
TRIDENTS
STRIDER S
STIRRED
STRIDERS
STRIDES
DISSERT
STRIDING
STRIDOR S
STRIDORS
STRIFE S
FRITES
REFITS
RESIFT
RIFEST
SIFTER
STRIFES
RESIFTS
SIFTERS
STRIGIL S
STRIGILS
STRIGOSE
GORSIEST
STRIKE RS
KITERS
TRIKES
STRIKER S
SKIRRET
SKIRTER
STRIKERS
SKIRRETS
SKIRTERS
STRIKES
STRIKING
SKIRTING
STRING SY
A **STRINGED**
STRINGER S
RESTRING
STRINGS
STRINGY
STRIP ESTY
SPIRT SPRIT
STIRP TRIPS
STRIPE DRS
ESPRIT
PRIEST
RIPEST
SPRITE
TRIPES
STRIPED
SPIRTED

STRIPER S
STRIPERS
STRIPES
ESPRITS
PERSIST
PRIESTS
SPRIEST
SPRITES
STIRPES
STRIPIER
STRIPING S
SPIRTING
STRIPPED
STRIPPER S
TRIPPERS
STRIPS
SPIRTS
SPRITS
STIRPS
STRIPT
STRIPY
STRIVE DNRS
RIVETS
STIVER
VERIST
STRIVED
DIVERTS
STRIVEN
INVERTS
STRIVER S
STRIVERS
STRIVES
STIVERS
VERISTS
STRIVING
STROBE S
SORBET
STROBES
SORBETS
STROBIC
STROBIL AEI S
BRISTOL
STROBILA ER
ORBITALS
STROBILE S
STROBILI
STROBILS
BRISTOLS
STRODE
DOTERS
SORTED
STORED
STROKE DRS
STOKER
TOKERS
TROKES
STROKED
STROKER S
STROKERS
STROKES
STOKERS
STROKING
STROLL S
TROLLS
STROLLED
DROLLEST
STROLLER S
TROLLERS
STROLLS
STROMA L
STROMAL
MORTALS
STROMATA
STRONG
STRONGER
STRONGLY
STRONGYL
STRONGYL ES
STRONGLY
STRONTIA NS
STRONTIC
STROOK
STROP S
PORTS PROST
SPORT
STROPHE S
POTHERS
THORPES
STROPHES
HOTPRESS
STROPHIC
STROPPED

STROPPER S
STROPPY
STROPS
SPORTS
STROUD S
STROUDS
STROVE
STOVER
TROVES
VOTERS
STROW NS
TROWS WORST
WORTS
STROWED
WORSTED
STROWING
WORSTING
STROWN
STROWS
WORSTS
STROY S
RYOTS STORY
TROYS TYROS
STROYED
DESTROY
STROYER S
ROYSTER
STROYERS
ROYSTERS
STROYING
STORYING
STROYS
STRUCK
TRUCKS
STRUCKEN
STRUDEL S
LUSTRED
RUSTLED
STRUDELS
STRUGGLE DR S
GURGLETS
E **STRUM** AS
STRUMA ES
STRUMAE
MATURES
STRUMAS
STRUMMED
STRUMMER S
STRUMOSE
OESTRUMS
STRUMOUS
STRUMPET S
TRUMPETS
E **STRUMS**
STRUNG
GRUNTS
STRUNT S
STRUNTED
STRUNTS
STRUT S
STURT TRUST
STRUTS
STURTS
TRUSTS
STRUTTED
STRUTTER S
STUB S
BUST BUTS
TUBS
STUBBED
STUBBIER
SUBTRIBE
STUBBILY
STUBBING
STUBBLE DS
STUBBLED
STUBBLES
STUBBLY
STUBBORN
STUBBY
STUBS
BUSTS
STUCCO S
STUCCOED
STUCCOER S
STUCCOES
STUCCOS
STUCK
TUCKS
STUD SY
DUST

STUDBOOK S
STUDDED
STUDDIE S
STUDIED
STUDDIES
STUDDING S
STUDENT S
STUNTED
STUDENTS
STUDFISH
STUDIED
STUDDIE
STUDIER S
DUSTIER
STUDIERS
DIESTRUS
STURDIES
STUDIES
TISSUED
STUDIO S
STUDIOS
STUDIOUS
STUDLIER
DILUTERS
STUDLY
STUDS
DUSTS
STUDWORK S
STUDY
DUSTY
STUDYING
STUFF SY
TUFFS
STUFFED
STUFFER S
RESTUFF
TRUFFES
STUFFERS
RESTUFFS
STUFFIER
STUFFILY
STUFFING S
STUFFS
STUFFY
STUIVER S
REVUIST
VIRTUES
STUIVERS
REVUISTS
STULL S
STULLS
STULTIFY
STUM PS
MUST MUTS
SMUT
STUMBLE DRS
TUMBLES
STUMBLED
STUMBLER S
TUMBLERS
TUMBRELS
STUMBLES
STUMMED
STUMMING
STUMP SY
TUMPS
STUMPAGE S
STUMPED
STUMPER S
SUMPTER
STUMPERS
SUMPTERS
STUMPIER
IMPUREST
IMPUTERS
STUMPING
STUMPS
STUMPY
STUMS
MUSTS SMUTS
STUN GKST
NUTS TUNS
STUNG
TUNGS
STUNK
STUNNED
DUNNEST
STUNNER S
STUNNERS
STUNNING
STUNS

STUNSAIL S
STUNT S
STUNTED
STUDENT
STUNTING
NUTTINGS
STUNTMAN
STUNTMEN
STUNTS
STUPA S
SPUTA
STUPAS
STUPE S
SETUP UPSET
STUPEFY
STUPES
SETUPS
UPSETS
STUPID S
STUPIDER
DISPUTER
STUPIDLY
STUPIDS
STUPOR S
SPROUT
STUPORS
SPROUTS
STURDIED
RUDDIEST
STURDIER
STURDIES T
DIESTRUS
STUDIERS
STURDILY
STURDY
STURGEON S
STURT S
STRUT TRUST
STURTS
STRUTS
TRUSTS
STUTTER S
STUTTERS
STY E
STYE DS
STEY TYES
STYED
STYES
STYGIAN
STAYING
STYING
STINGY
A **STYLAR**
STYLATE
STATELY
STYLE DRST
STYLED
STYLER S
STYLERS
STYLES
SLYEST
STYLET S
STYLETS
STYLI
SILTY
STYLING S
STYLINGS
STYLISE DRS
STYLISED
STYLISER S
SISTERLY
STYLISES
STYLISH
STYLIST S
STYLISTS
STYLITE S
TESTILY
STYLITES
STYLITIC
STYLIZE DRS
ZESTILY
STYLIZED
STYLIZER S
STYLIZES
STYLOID
STYLUS
STYLUSES
STYMIE DS
STYMIED
STYMIES

STYMY
STYMYING
STYPSIS
STYPTIC S
STYPTICS
STYRAX
STYRAXES
STYRENE S
YESTERN
STYRENES
SUABLE
USABLE
SUABLY
USABLY
SUASION S
SANIOUS
SUASIONS
SUASIVE
SUASORY
OSSUARY
SUAVE R
UVEAS
SUAVELY
SUAVER
SUAVEST
SUAVITY
SUB AS
BUS
T **SUBA** HS
SUBABBOT S
SUBACID
SUBACRID
SUBACUTE
SUBADAR S
SUBADARS
SUBADULT S
SUBAGENT S
SUBAH S
HABUS
SUBAHDAR S
BAHADURS
SUBAHS
SUBALAR
SUBAREA S
SUBAREAS
SUBARID
SUBAS
SUBATOM S
SUBATOMS
SUBAURAL
SUBAXIAL
SUBBASE S
SUBBASES
SUBBASIN S
SUBBASS
SUBBED
SUBDEB
SUBBING S
SUBBINGS
SUBBLOCK S
SUBBREED S
SUBCASTE S
SUBCAUSE S
SUBCELL S
SUBCELLS
SUBCHIEF S
SUBCLAIM S
SUBCLAN S
SUBCLANS
SUBCLASS
SUBCLERK S
BUCKLERS
SUBCODE S
SUBCODES
SUBCOOL S
COLOBUS
SUBCOOLS
SUBCULT S
SUBCULTS
SUBCUTES
SUBCUTIS
SUBDEAN S
UNBASED
SUBDEANS
SUBDEB S
SUBBED
SUBDEBS
SUBDEPOT S

SUBDUAL S
SUBDUALS
SUBDUCE DS
SUBDUCED
SUBDUCES
SUBDUCT S
SUBDUCTS
SUBDUE DRS
SUBDUED
SUBDUER S
SUBDUERS
SUBDUES
SUBDUING
SUBDURAL
SUBDWARF S
SUBECHO
SUBEDIT S
SUBEDITS
SUBENTRY
SUBEPOCH S
SUBER S
BURSE REBUS
RUBES
SUBERECT
SUBERIC
SUBERIN S
BURNIES
SUBERINS
SUBERISE DS
SUBERIZE DS
SUBEROSE
SUBEROUS
SUBERS
BURSES
SUBFIELD S
SUBFILE S
FUSIBLE
SUBFILES
SUBFIX
SUBFIXES
SUBFLOOR S
SUBFLUID
SUBFRAME S
SUBFUSC S
SUBFUSCS
SUBGENRE S
SUBGENUS
SUBGOAL S
SUBGOALS
SUBGRADE S
SUBGRAPH S
SUBGROUP S
SUBGUM S
SUBGUMS
SUBHEAD S
SUBHEADS
SUBHUMAN S
SUBHUMID
SUBIDEA S
SUBIDEAS
DISABUSE
SUBINDEX
SUBITEM S
SUBITEMS
SUBITO
SUBJECT S
SUBJECTS
SUBJOIN S
SUBJOINS
SUBLATE DS
SUBLATED
SUBLATES
SUBLEASE DS
SUBLET S
BLUEST
BLUETS
BUSTLE
BUTLES
SUBTLE
SUBLETS
BUSTLES
SUBLEVEL S
SUBLIME DRS
SUBLIMED
SUBLIMER S

SUBLIMES T
LIMBUSES
SUBLIMIT SY
MISBUILT
SUBLINE S
SUBLINES
SUBLOT S
SUBLOTS
SUBLUNAR Y
SUBMENU S
SUBMENUS
SUBMERGE DS
SUBMERSE DS
SUBMISS
SUBMIT S
SUBMITS
SUBNASAL
SUBNET S
SUBNETS
SUBNICHE S
SUBNODAL
SUBOCEAN
SUBOPTIC
SUBTOPIC
SUBORAL
LABOURS
SUBORDER S
BORDURES
SUBORN S
BOURNS
SUBORNED
BOUNDERS
REBOUNDS
SUBORNER S
SUBORNS
SUBOVAL
SUBOVATE
SUBOXIDE S
SUBPANEL S
SUBPAR T
SUBPART S
SUBPARTS
SUBPENA S
SUBPENAS
SUBPHASE S
SUBPHYLA R
SUBPLOT S
SUBPLOTS
SUBPOENA S
SUBPOLAR
SUBPUBIC
SUBRACE S
RUBACES
SUBRACES
SUBRENT S
BRUNETS
BUNTERS
BURNETS
SUBRENTS
SUBRING S
SUBRINGS
SUBRULE S
SUBRULES
SUBS
BUSS
SUBSALE S
SUBSALES
SUBSCALE S
BASCULES
SUBSEA
ABUSES
SUBSECT S
SUBSECTS
SUBSENSE S
SUBSERE S
REBUSES
SUBSERES
SUBSERVE DS
SUBSET S
SUBSETS
SUBSHAFT S
SUBSHELL S
SUBSHRUB S
SUBSIDE DRS
SUBSIDED
SUBSIDER S
DISBURSE
SUBSIDES
SUBSIDY
SUBSIST S
SUBSISTS
SUBSITE S
BUSIEST
SUBSITES
SUBSKILL S
SUBSOIL S
SUBSOILS
SUBSOLAR
SUBSONIC
SUBSPACE S
SUBSTAGE S
SUBSTATE S
SUBSUME DS
SUBSUMED
SUBSUMES
SUBTASK S
SUBTASKS
SUBTAXA
SAXTUBA
SUBTAXON S
SUBTEEN S
BUTENES
SUBTEENS
SUBTEND S
SUBTENDS
SUBTEST S
SUBTESTS
SUBTEXT S
SUBTEXTS
SUBTHEME S
SUBTILE R
SUBTILER
BURLIEST
SUBTILIN S
SUBTILTY
SUBTITLE DS
SUBTLE R
BLUEST
BLUETS
BUSTLE
BUTLES
SUBLET
SUBTLER
BLUSTER
BUSTLER
BUTLERS
SUBTLEST
SUBTLETY
SUBTLY
BUTYLS
SUBTONE S
SUBTONES
SUBTONIC S
SUBTOPIA S
SUBTOPIC S
SUBOPTIC
SUBTOTAL S
SUBTRACT S
SUBTREND S
SUBTRIBE S
STUBBIER
SUBTUNIC S
SUBTYPE S
SUBTYPES
SUBULATE
SUBUNIT S
SUBUNITS
SUBURB S
SUBURBAN S
SUBURBED
SUBURBIA S
SUBURBS
SUBVENE DS
SUBVENED
SUBVENES
SUBVERT S
SUBVERTS
SUBVICAR S
SUBVIRAL
SUBVIRUS
SUBVOCAL
SUBWAY S
SUBWAYED
SUBWAYS
SUBWORLD S
SUBZERO
SUBZONE S
SUBZONES
SUCCAH S
SUCCAHS
SUCCEED S
SUCCEEDS
SUCCESS
SUCCINCT
SUCCINIC
SUCCINYL S
SUCCOR SY
CROCUS
OCCURS
SUCCORED
SUCCORER S
REOCCURS
SUCCORS
SUCCORY
SUCCOTH
SUCCOUR S
SUCCOURS
SUCCUBA ES
SUCCUBAE
SUCCUBAS
SUCCUBI
SUCCUBUS
SUCCUMB S
SUCCUMBS
SUCCUSS
SUCH
SUCHLIKE
SUCHNESS
SUCK SY
CUSK
SUCKED
SUCKER S
SUCKERED
SUCKERS
SUCKFISH
SUCKIER
SUCKIEST
SUCKING
SUCKLE DRS
SUCKLED
SCULKED
SUCKLER S
RUCKLES
SCULKER
SUCKLERS
SCULKERS
SUCKLES S
SUCKLESS
SUCKLING S
SCULKING
SUCKS
CUSKS
SUCKY
YUCKS
SUCRASE S
ARCUSES
CAUSERS
CESURAS
SAUCERS
SUCRASES
SUCRE S
CRUSE CURES
CURSE ECRUS
SUCRES
CRUSES
CURSES
CUSSER
SUCROSE S
COURSES
SOURCES
SUCROSES
SUCTION S
SUCTIONS
SUDARIA
SUDARIES
RADIUSES
SUDARIUM
SUDARY
SUDATION S
SUDATORY
SUDD S
DUDS
SUDDEN S
SUDDENLY
SUDDENS
SUDDS
SUDOR S
DUROS
SUDORAL
SUDORS
SUDS Y
SUDSED
SUDSER S
DRUSES
DURESS
SUDSERS
SUDSES
SUSSED
SUDSIER
DISEURS
SUDSIEST
SUDSING
SUDSLESS
SUDSY
SUE DRST
USE
SUED E
DUES USED
SUEDE DS
SUEDED
SUEDES
SUEDING
SUER S
RUES RUSE
SURE USER
SUERS
RUSES USERS
SUES
USES
SUET SY
UTES
SUETS
SUETY
SUFFARI S
SUFFARIS
SUFFER S
RUFFES
SUFFERED
SUFFERER S
SUFFERS
SUFFICE DRS
SUFFICED
SUFFICER S
SUFFICES
SUFFIX
SUFFIXAL
SUFFIXED
SUFFIXES
SUFFLATE DS
FEASTFUL
SUFFRAGE S
GAUFFERS
SUFFUSE DS
SUFFUSED
SUFFUSES
SUGAR SY
ARGUS GAURS
GUARS
SUGARED
DESUGAR
SUGARER S
ARGUERS
SUGARERS
SUGARIER
SUGARING
SUGARS
SUGARY
SUGGEST S
SUGGESTS
SUGH S
GUSH HUGS
UGHS
SUGHED
GUSHED
SUGHING
GUSHING
SUGHS
SUICIDAL
SUICIDE DS
SUICIDED
SUICIDES
SUING
USING
SUINT S
UNITS
SUINTS
SUIT ES
TUIS
SUITABLE
SUITABLY
SUITCASE S
SAUCIEST
SUITE DRS
ETUIS
SUITED
DUTIES
SUITER S
SUITERS
SUITES
TISSUE
SUITING S
SUITINGS
TISSUING
SUITLIKE
SUITOR S
SUITORS
TSOURIS
SUITS
SITUS
SUK S
SUKIYAKI S
SUKKAH S
SUKKAHS
SUKKOT H
SUKKOTH
SUKS
SULCAL
CALLUS
SULCATE D
SULCATED
SULCI
SULCUS
SULDAN S
SULDANS
SULFA S
SULFAS
SULFATE DS
SULFATED
DEFAULTS
SULFATES
FLATUSES
SULFID ES
FLUIDS
SULFIDE S
SULFIDES
SULFIDS
SULFINYL S
SINFULLY
SULFITE S
SULFITES
SULFITIC
SULFO
FOULS
SULFONE S
SULFONES
FOULNESS
SULFONIC
SULFONYL S
SULFUR SY
SULFURED
DESULFUR
SULFURET S
FRUSTULE
SULFURIC
SULFURS
SULFURY L
SULFURYL S
SULK SY
SULKED
SULKER S
SULKERS
SULKIER
SULKIES T
SULKIEST
SULKILY
SULKING
SULKS
SULKY
SULLAGE S
SEAGULL
ULLAGES
SULLAGES
GALLUSES
SEAGULLS
SULLEN
UNSELL
SULLENER
SULLENLY
SULLIED
ILLUDES
SULLIES
SULLY
SULLYING
SULPHA S
SULPHAS
SULPHATE DS
SULPHID ES
SULPHIDE S
SULPHIDS
SULPHITE S
SULPHONE S
SULPHUR SY
SULPHURS
SULPHURY
SULTAN AS
SULTANA S
SULTANAS
SULTANIC
LUNATICS
SULTANS
SULTRIER
SULTRILY
SULTRY
SULU S
ULUS
SULUS
LUSUS
SUM OPS
MUS
SUMAC HS
MUSCA
SUMACH S
SUMACHS
SUMACS
SUMLESS
MUSSELS
SUMMA ES
SUMMABLE
SUMMAE
SUMMAND S
SUMMANDS
SUMMARY
SUMMAS
SUMMATE DS
MAUMETS
SUMMATED
SUMMATES
SUMMED
SUMMER SY
SUMMERED
SUMMERLY
SUMMERS
SUMMERY
SUMMING
SUMMIT S
MUTISM
SUMMITAL
SUMMITED
SUMMITRY
SUMMITS
MUTISMS
SUMMON S
SUMMONED
SUMMONER S
RESUMMON
SUMMONS
SUMO S
SUMOIST S
MISSOUT
SUMOISTS
MISSOUTS
SUMOS
SUMP S
UMPS
SUMPS
SUMPTER S
STUMPER
SUMPTERS
STUMPERS
SUMPWEED S
SUMS
MUSS
SUN GKNS
NUS
UNS
SUNBACK
SUNBAKED
SUNBATH ES
SUNBATHE DR S
SUNBATHS
SUNBEAM SY
SUNBEAMS
SUNBEAMY
SUNBELT S
UNBELTS
UNBLEST
SUNBELTS
SUNBIRD S
SUNBIRDS
SUNBLOCK S
UNBLOCKS
SUNBOW S
SUNBOWS
SUNBURN ST
SUNBURNS
SUNBURNT
SUNBURST S
SUNCHOKE S
UNCHOKES
SUNDAE S
SUNDAES
SUNDECK S
SUNDECKS
A SUNDER S
NURSED
SUNDERED
DENUDERS
SUNDERER S
ENDURERS
SUNDERS
UNDRESS
SUNDEW S
SUNDEWS
SUNDIAL S
SUNDIALS
SUNDOG S
SUNDOGS
SUNDOWN S
SUNDOWNS
SUNDRESS
SUNDRIES
INSUREDS
SUNDRILY
SUNDROPS
SUNDRY
SUNFAST
SUNFISH
SUNG
GNUS GUNS
SNUG
SUNGLASS
SUNGLOW S
SUNGLOWS
SUNK
SUNKEN
SUNKET S
SUNKETS
SUNLAMP S
SUNLAMPS
SUNLAND S
SUNLANDS
SUNLESS
SUNLIGHT S
HUSTLING
SUNLIKE
SUNLIT
INSULT
SUNN ASY
NUNS
SUNNA HS
SUNNAH S
SUNNAHS
SUNNAS
SUNNED
SUNNIER
UNRISEN
SUNNIEST

SUNNILY
SUNNING
SUNNS
SUNNY
SUNPORCH
SUNPROOF
SUNRAY S
SYNURA
SUNRAYS
SUNRISE S
INSURES
SUNRISES
SUNROOF S
UNROOFS
SUNROOFS
SUNROOM S
UNMOORS
SUNROOMS
SUNS
SUNSCALD S
SUNSET S
UNSETS
SUNSETS
SUNSHADE S
SUNSHINE S
SUNSHINY
SUNSPOT S
UNSTOPS
SUNSPOTS
SUNSTONE S
NEUSTONS
SUNSUIT S
SUNSUITS
SUNTAN S
SUNTANS
SUNUP S
SUNUPS
SUNWARD S
UNDRAWS
SUNWARDS
SUNWISE
SUP ES
PUS
UPS
SUPE RS
SPUE
SUPER BS
PURSE SPRUE
SUPERADD S
SUPERB
SUPERBAD
SUPERBER
SUPERBLY
SUPERBUG S
SUPERCAR S
SUPERCOP S
SUPERED
PERDUES
PERUSED
SUPEREGO S
SUPERFAN S
SUPERFIX
SUPERHIT S
SUPERHOT
SUPERING
PERUSING
SUPERIOR S
SUPERJET S
SUPERLAY
SUPERLIE S
SUPERMAN
SUPERMEN
SUPERMOM S
SUPERNAL
PURSLANE
SUPERPRO S
SUPERS
PURSES
SPRUES
SUPERSEX
SUPERSPY
SUPERTAX
SUPES
PUSES SPUES
SUPINATE DS
PETUNIAS
SUPINE S
PUISNE
SUPINELY
SUPINES
PUISNES
SUPPED
SUPPER S
UPPERS
SUPPERS
SUPPING
UPPINGS
SUPPLANT S
SUPPLE DRS
PEPLUS
SUPPLED
SUPPLELY
SUPPLER
PULPERS
PURPLES
SUPPLES T
SUPPLEST
SUPPLIED
SUPPLIER S
SUPPLIES
SUPPLING
SUPPLY
SUPPORT S
SUPPORTS
SUPPOSAL S
SUPPOSE DRS
SUPPOSED
SUPPOSER S
PURPOSES
SUPPOSES
SUPPRESS
SUPRA
PRAUS
SUPREME RS
PRESUME
SUPREMER
PRESUMER
SUPREMES T
PRESUMES
SUPREMO S
SUPREMOS
SPERMOUS
SUPS
PUSS
SUQ S
SUQS
SURA HLS
URSA
SURAH S
SURAHS
HUSSAR
SURAL
SURAS
SURBASE DS
ABUSERS
RUBASSE
SURBASED
SURBASES
RUBASSES
SURCEASE DS
SURCOAT S
CUATROS
TURACOS
SURCOATS
SURD S
URDS
SURDS
SURE R
RUES RUSE
SUER USER
SUREFIRE
SURELY
SURENESS
U SURER
RUERS
SUREST
ESTRUS
RUSSET
TUSSER
SURETIES
SURETY
TUYERS
SURF SY
FURS
SURFABLE
SURFACE DRS
SURFACED
SURFACER S
FARCEURS
SURFACES
SURFBIRD S
SURFBOAT S
SURFED
SURFEIT S
FUSTIER
SURFEITS
SURFIEST
SURFER S
SURFERS
SURFFISH
SURFIER
FRISEUR
SURFIEST
SURFEITS
SURFING S
SURFINGS
SURFLIKE
SURFMAN
SURFMEN
FRENUMS
SURFS
SURFSIDE
FISSURED
SURFY
SURGE DRS
GRUES URGES
SURGED
SURGEON S
SURGEONS
SURGER SY
URGERS
SURGERS
SURGERY
SURGES
SURGICAL
SURGING
SURGY
GYRUS
SURICATE S
SURIMI S
SURIMIS
SURLIER
SURLIEST
SURLILY
SURLY
SURMISE DRS
MISUSER
MUSSIER
SURMISED
SURMISER S
SURMISES
MISUSERS
SURMOUNT S
SURNAME DRS
MANURES
SURNAMED
DURAMENS
MAUNDERS
SURNAMER S
MANURERS
SURNAMES
SURPASS
SURPLICE DS
SURPLUS
SURPRINT S
SURPRISE DR S
SPURRIES
UPRISERS
SURPRIZE DS
SURRA S
SURRAS
SURREAL
SURREY S
SURREYS
SURROUND S
SURROYAL S
SURTAX
SURTAXED
SURTAXES
SURTITLE S
SLUTTIER
SURTOUT S
SURTOUTS
SURVEIL S
SURVEILS
SURVEY S
SURVEYED
SURVEYOR S
SURVEYS
SURVIVAL S
SURVIVE DRS
SURVIVED
SURVIVER S
SURVIVES
SURVIVOR S
SUSHI S
SUSHIS
SUSLIK S
SUSLIKS
SUSPECT S
SUSPECTS
SUSPEND S
SENDUPS
UPSENDS
SUSPENDS
SUSPENSE RS
SUSPIRE DS
PUSSIER
UPRISES
SUSPIRED
SUSPIRES
SUSS
SUSSED
SUDSES
SUSSES
SUSSING
SUSTAIN S
ISSUANT
SUSTAINS
SUSURRUS
SUTLER S
LUSTER
LUSTRE
RESULT
RUSTLE
ULSTER
SUTLERS
LUSTERS
LUSTRES
RESULTS
RUSTLES
ULSTERS
SUTRA S
SUTRAS
TARSUS
TUSSAR
SUTTA S
TAUTS
SUTTAS
STATUS
SUTTEE S
TUTEES
SUTTEES
SUTURAL
SUTURE DS
UTERUS
SUTURED
SUTURES
SUTURING
SUZERAIN S
SVARAJ
SVARAJES
SVEDBERG S
SVELTE R
SVELTELY
SVELTER
SVELTEST
SWAB S
WABS
SWABBED
SWABBER S
SWABBERS
SWABBIE S
SWABBIES
SWABBING
SWABBY
SWABS
SWACKED
SWADDLE DS
DAWDLES
WADDLES
SWADDLED
SWADDLES
SWAG ES
WAGS
SWAGE DRS
WAGES
SWAGED
SWAGER S
WAGERS
SWAGERS
SWAGES
SWAGGED
SWAGGER S
WAGGERS
SWAGGERS
SWAGGIE S
SWAGGIES
SWAGGING
SWAGING
SWAGMAN
SWAGMEN
SWAGS
SWAIL S
WAILS
SWAILS
SWAIN S
WAINS
SWAINISH
SWAINS
SWALE S
WALES WEALS
SWALES
AWLESS
SWALLOW S
WALLOWS
SWALLOWS
SWAM IPY
MAWS
SWAMI S
SWAMIES
SWAMIS
SWAMP SY
SWAMPED
SWAMPER S
SWAMPERS
SWAMPIER
SWAMPING
SWAMPISH
SWAMPS
SWAMPY
SWAMY
SWAN GKS
AWNS SAWN
SNAW WANS
SWANG
GNAWS
SWANHERD S
SWANK SY
SWANKED
SWANKER
SWANKEST
SWANKIER
SWANKILY
SWANKING
SWANKS
SWANKY
SWANLIKE
SWANNED
SWANNERY
SWANNING
SWANNY
SWANPAN S
SWANPANS
SWANS
SNAWS
SWANSKIN S
SWAP S
PAWS WAPS
WASP
SWAPPED
SWAPPER S
SWAPPERS
SWAPPING
SWAPS
WASPS
SWARAJ
SWARAJES
SWARD S
DRAWS WARDS
SWARDED
WADDERS
SWARDING
DRAWINGS
SWARDS
SWARE
RESAW SAWER
SEWAR SWEAR
WARES WEARS
SWARF S
SWARFS
A SWARM S
WARMS
SWARMED
SWARMER S
REWARMS
WARMERS
SWARMERS
SWARMING
SWARMS
SWART HY
STRAW WARTS
SWARTH SY
THRAWS
WRATHS
SWARTHS
SWARTHY
SWARTY
STRAWY
WASTRY
SWASH
SHAWS SHWAS
SWASHED
SWASHER S
HAWSERS
WASHERS
SWASHERS
SWASHES
SWASHING
WASHINGS
SWASTICA S
SWASTIKA S
SWAT HS
STAW TAWS
TWAS WAST
WATS
SWATCH
SWATCHES
SWATH ES
THAWS WHATS
SWATHE DRS
WHEATS
SWATHED
SWATHER S
THAWERS
WREATHS
SWATHERS
SWATHES
SWATHING
SWATHS
SWATS
WASTS
SWATTED
SWATTER S
SWATTERS
SWATTING
SWAY S
WAYS YAWS
SWAYABLE
SWAYBACK S
SWAYED
SWAYER S
SAWYER
SWAYERS
SAWYERS
SWAYFUL
SWAYING
SWAYS
SWEAR S
RESAW SAWER
SEWAR SWARE
WARES WEARS
SWEARER S
REWEARS
WEARERS
SWEARERS
SWEARING
RESAWING
SWEARS
RESAWS
SAWERS
SEWARS
WRASSE
SWEAT SY
TAWSE TWAES
WASTE
SWEATBOX
SWEATED
SWEATER S
SWEATERS
SWEATIER
WASTERIE
WEARIEST
SWEATILY
SWEATING
SWEATS
TAWSES
WASTES
SWEATY
SWEDE S
SEWED WEEDS
SWEDES
SWEENEY S
SWEENEYS
SWEENIES
SWEENY
WEENSY
SWEEP SY
WEEPS
SWEEPER S
WEEPERS
SWEEPERS
SWEEPIER
SWEEPING S
WEEPINGS
SWEEPS
SWEEPY
SWEER
EWERS RESEW
SEWER
SWEET S
WEEST WEETS
SWEETEN S
SWEETENS
TWEENESS
SWEETER
SWEETEST
SWEETIE S
SWEETIES
SWEETING S
SWEETISH
SWEETLY
SWEETS
SWEETSOP S
SWELL S
WELLS
SWELLED
SWELLER
SWELLEST
SWELLING S
SWELLS
SWELTER S
WELTERS
WRESTLE
SWELTERS
WRESTLES
SWELTRY
SWEPT
SWERVE DRS
SWERVED
SWERVER S
SWERVERS
SWERVES
SWERVING
SWEVEN S
SWEVENS
SWIDDEN S
SWIDDENS
SWIFT S
SWIFTER S
SWIFTERS
SWIFTEST
SWIFTLET S
SWIFTLY
SWIFTS
SWIG S
WIGS
SWIGGED
SWIGGER S
SWIGGERS
SWIGGING
WIGGINGS
SWIGS
SWILL S
WILLS

SWILLED
SWILLER S
WILLERS
SWILLERS
SWILLING
SWILLS
SWIM S
SWIMMER S
SWIMMERS
SWIMMIER
SWIMMILY
SWIMMING S
SWIMMY
SWIMS
SWIMSUIT S
SWIMWEAR
SWINDLE DRS
WINDLES
SWINDLED
DWINDLES
SWINDLER S
SWINDLES
WILDNESS
WINDLESS
SWINE
SINEW WINES
SWINEPOX
SWING ESY
WINGS
SWINGBY S
SWINGBYS
SWINGE DRS
SEWING
SWINGED
SWINGER S
WINGERS
SWINGERS
SWINGES
SEWINGS
SWINGIER
SWINGING S
SWINGLE DS
SLEWING
SWINGLED
SWINGLES
WINGLESS
SWINGMAN
SWINGMEN
SWINGS
SWINGY
SWINISH
SWINK S
WINKS
SWINKED
SWINKING
SWINKS
SWINNEY S
SWINNEYS
SWIPE DS
WIPES
SWIPED
WISPED
SWIPES
SWIPING
WISPING
SWIPLE S
SWIPLES
SWIPPLE S
SWIPPLES
A SWIRL SY
SWIRLED
WILDERS
SWIRLIER
SWIRLING
SWIRLS
SWIRLY
SWISH Y
SWISHED
SWISHER S
WISHERS
SWISHERS
SWISHES
SWISHIER
SWISHING
SWISHY
SWISS
SWISSES
SWITCH
SWITCHED
SWITCHER S
SWITCHES
SWITH E
WHIST WHITS
SWITHE R
WHITES
WITHES
SWITHER S
WITHERS
WRITHES
SWITHERS
SWITHLY
SWIVE DLST
VIEWS WIVES
SWIVED
SWIVEL S
SWIVELED
SWIVELS
SWIVES
SWIVET S
SWIVETS
SWIVING
SWIZZLE DRS
SWIZZLED
SWIZZLER S
SWIZZLES
SWOB S
BOWS
SWOBBED
SWOBBER S
SWOBBERS
SWOBBING
SWOBS
SWOLLEN
A SWOON SY
SWOONED
SWOONER S
SWOONERS
SWOONIER
SWOONING
SWOONS
SWOONY
SWOOP SY
WOOPS
SWOOPED
WOOPSED
SWOOPER S
SWOOPERS
SWOOPIER
SWOOPING
WOOPSING
SWOOPS
SWOOPY
SWOOSH
SWOOSHED
SWOOSHES
SWOP S
POWS
SWOPPED
SWOPPING
SWOPS
SWORD S
WORDS
SWORDMAN
SANDWORM
SWORDMEN
SWORDS
SWORE
RESOW SEROW
SOWER WORSE
SWORN
SWOT S
STOW TOWS
TWOS WOST
WOTS
SWOTS
STOWS
SWOTTED
SWOTTER S
SWOTTERS
SWOTTING
SWOUN DS
SWOUND S
WOUNDS
SWOUNDED
SWOUNDS
SWOUNED
UNSOWED
SWOUNING
SWOUNS
SWUM
SWUNG
SYBARITE S
BESTIARY
SYBO
BOYS YOBS
SYBOES
SYCAMINE S
SYCAMORE S
SYCE ES
SYCEE S
SYCEES
CYESES
SYCES
SYCOMORE S
SYCONIA
SYCONIUM
SYCOSES
SYCOSIS
SYENITE S
SYENITES
SYENITIC
SYKE S
KEYS KYES
SYKES
SYLI S
SYLIS
LYSIS
SYLLABI C
A SYLLABIC S
SYLLABLE DS
SYLLABUB S
SYLLABUS
SYLPH SY
SYLPHIC
SYLPHID S
SYLPHIDS
SYLPHISH
SYLPHS
SYLPHY
SYLVA ENS
SYLVAE
SLAVEY
SYLVAN S
SYLVANS
SYLVAS
SYLVATIC
SYLVIN ES
VINYLS
SYLVINE S
SYLVINES
SYLVINS
SYLVITE S
SYLVITES
SYMBION ST
SYMBIONS
SYMBIONT S
SYMBIOT ES
SYMBIOTE S
SYMBIOTS
SYMBOL S
SYMBOLED
SYMBOLIC
SYMBOLS
A SYMMETRY
SYMPATHY
SYMPATRY
SYMPHONY
HYPONYMS
SYMPODIA L
SYMPOSIA C
SYMPTOM S
SYMPTOMS
SYN CE
SYNAGOG S
SYNAGOGS
SYNANON S
SYNANONS
SYNAPSE DS
SYNAPSED
DYSPNEAS
A SYNAPSES
SYNAPSID S
A SYNAPSIS
SYNAPTIC
SYNC HS
SYNCARP SY
SYNCARPS
SYNCARPY
SYNCED
SYNCH S
SYNCHED
SYNCHING
SYNCHRO S
SYNCHROS
SYNCHS
SYNCING
SYNCLINE S
SYNCOM S
SYNCOMS
SYNCOPAL
SYNCOPE S
SYNCOPES
PYCNOSES
SYNCOPIC
SYNCS
SYNCYTIA L
SYNDESES
SYNDESIS
SYNDET S
A SYNDETIC
SYNDETS
SYNDIC S
SYNDICAL
SYNDICS
SYNDROME S
SYNE
SNYE YENS
SYNECTIC
SYNERGIA S
RESAYING
SYNERGIC
SYNERGID S
SYRINGED
SYNERGY
SYNESIS
SYNFUEL S
SYNFUELS
SYNGAMIC
SYNGAMY
SYNGAS
SYNGASES
SYNGENIC
ENSIGNCY
SYNKARYA
SYNOD S
DONSY
SYNODAL
SYNODIC
SYNODS
SYNONYM ESY
SYNONYME S
SYNONYMS
SYNONYMY
SYNOPSES
SYNOPSIS
SYNOPTIC
SYNOVIA LS
SYNOVIAL
SYNOVIAS
SYNTAGM AS
GYMNAST
SYNTAGMA S
SYNTAGMS
GYMNASTS
SYNTAX
SYNTAXES
SYNTH S
SYNTHPOP S
SYNTHS
SYNTONIC
SYNTONY
SYNURA E
SUNRAY
SYNURAE
SYPH S
HYPS
SYPHER S
HYPERS
SPHERY
SYPHERED
SYPHERS
SYPHILIS
SYPHON S
SYPHONED
SYPHONS
SYPHS
SYREN S
SYRENS
SYRETTE S
SYRETTES
SYRINGA S
SYRINGAS
SYRINGE DS
SYRINGED
SYNERGID
SYRINGES
SYRINX
SYRINXES
SYRPHIAN S
SYRPHID S
SYRPHIDS
SYRUP SY
PURSY
SYRUPED
SYRUPIER
SYRUPING
SYRUPS
SYRUPY
SYSADMIN S
SYSOP S
SYSOPS
SYSTEM S
SYSTEMIC S
SYSTEMS
SYSTOLE S
TOYLESS
SYSTOLES
SYSTOLIC
SYZYGAL
SYZYGIAL
SYZYGIES
SYZYGY

T

EU TA BDEGJMNO
AT PRSTUVWX
S TAB SU
BAT
TABANID S
TABANIDS
TABARD S
TABARDED
TABARDS
BASTARD
TABARET S
TABARETS
S TABBED
TABBIED
TABBIES
BABIEST
S TABBING
TABBIS
TABBISES
TABBY
TABBYING
TABER S
TABERED
BERATED
DEBATER
REBATED
TABERING
BERATING
REBATING
TABERS
BAREST
BASTER
BREAST
TABES
ABETS BASTE
BATES BEAST
BEATS BETAS
TABETIC S
TABETICS
TABID
TABLA S
TABLAS
BASALT
S TABLE DST
BLATE BLEAT
TABLEAU SX
TABLEAUS
TABLEAUX
S TABLED
TABLEFUL S
S TABLES
ABLEST
BLEATS
STABLE
TABLET S
BATTLE
TABLETED
TABLETOP S
TABLETS
BATTLES
S TABLING
TABLOID S
TABLOIDS
TABOO S
TABOOED
TABOOING
TABOOLEY S
TABOOS
TABOR S
ABORT BOART
TABORED
ABORTED
BORATED
TABORER S
ABORTER
TABORERS
ABORTERS
TABORET S
ABETTOR
TABORETS
ABETTORS
TABORIN EGS
TABORINE S
BARITONE
OBTAINER
REOBTAIN
TABORING
ABORTING
BORATING
TABORINS
TABORS
ABORTS
BOARTS
TABOULEH S
TABOULI S
BAILOUT
TABOULIS
BAILOUTS
TABOUR S
RUBATO
TABOURED
OBDURATE
TABOURER S
TABOURET S
OBTURATE
TABOURS
ABORTUS
ROBUSTA
RUBATOS
S TABS
BAST BATS
STAB
TABU NS
ABUT TUBA
TABUED
TABUING
ANTIBUG
TABULAR
TABULATE DS
TABULI S
TABULIS
TABUN S
TABUNS
TABUS
ABUTS TSUBA
TUBAS
TACE ST
CATE
TACES
CASTE CATES
CESTA
TACET
TECTA
TACH ES
CHAT
TACHE S
CHEAT TEACH
THECA
TACHES
CHASTE
CHEATS
SACHET
SCATHE
TACHINID S
TACHISM ES
TACHISME S
HEMATICS
MASTICHE
MISTEACH
TACHISMS
TACHIST ES
CATTISH
TACHISTE S
TACHISTS
TACHS
CHATS
TACHYON S
TACHYONS
TACIT
ATTIC
TACITLY
CATTILY
TACITURN
URTICANT
S TACK SY
S TACKED
S TACKER S
RACKET
RETACK
S TACKERS
RACKETS
RESTACK
RETACKS
STACKER
TACKET S
TACKETS
TACKEY
TACKIER
TACKIEST
TACKIFY
TACKILY
S TACKING
TACKLE DRS
TACKLED
TALCKED
TACKLER S
TACKLERS
TACKLES S
S TACKLESS
SLACKEST
TACKLING S
TALCKING
S TACKS
STACK
TACKY
TACNODE S
TACNODES
ENDOCAST
TACO S
COAT
TACONITE S
TACOS
ASCOT COAST
COATS COSTA
TACRINE S
CERATIN
CERTAIN
CREATIN
TACRINES
CANISTER
CERATINS
CISTERNA
CREATINS
SCANTIER
TACT S
TACTFUL
A TACTIC S
TICTAC
TACTICAL
TACTICS
TICTACS
TACTILE
LATTICE
TACTION S
TACTIONS
OSCITANT
TACTLESS

TACTS
SCATT
TACTUAL
TAD S
TADPOLE S
TADPOLES
TADS
TAE L
ATE
EAT
ETA
TEA
TAEL S
LATE TALE
TEAL TELA
TAELS
LEAST SETAL
SLATE STALE
STEAL STELA
TALES TEALS
TESLA
TAENIA ES
TAENIAE
TAENIAS
ENTASIA
TAFFAREL S
TAFFEREL S
TAFFETA S
TAFFETAS
TAFFIA S
TAFFIAS
TAFFIES
TAFFRAIL S
TAFFY
TAFIA S
TAFIAS
S TAG S
GAT
TAGALONG S
TAGBOARD S
TAGGANT S
TAGGANTS
S TAGGED
GADGET
S TAGGER S
GARGET
S TAGGERS
GAGSTER
GARGETS
STAGGER
S TAGGING
TAGLIKE
GLAIKET
TAGLINE S
ATINGLE
ELATING
GELATIN
GENITAL
TAGLINES
GELATINS
GENITALS
STEALING
TAGMEME S
GEMMATE
TAGMEMES
GEMMATES
TAGMEMIC S
TAGRAG S
RAGTAG
TAGRAGS
RAGTAGS
S TAGS
GAST GATS
STAG
TAHINI S
TAHINIS
TAHR S
HART RATH
TAHRS
HARTS TRASH
TAHSIL S
LATHIS
LATISH
TAHSILS
SALTISH
TAIGA S
AGITA
TAIGAS
AGITAS
TAIGLACH

TAIL S
ALIT LATI
TALI
TAILBACK S
TAILBONE S
TAILCOAT S
COATTAIL
TAILED
DETAIL
DILATE
TAILER S
RETAIL
RETIAL
TAILERS
REALIST
RETAILS
SALTIER
SALTIRE
SLATIER
TAILFAN S
FANTAIL
TAILFANS
FANTAILS
TAILFIN S
TAILFINS
FINALIST
TAILGATE DR
S
TAILING S
INTAGLI
TAILINGS
TAILLAMP S
TAILLE S
TELIAL
TAILLES S
TALLIES
TAILLESS
TALLISES
TAILLEUR S
TAILLIKE
TAILOR S
RIALTO
TAILORED
IDOLATER
TAILORS
ORALIST
RIALTOS
TAILPIPE S
TAILRACE S
TAILS
ALIST LITAS
TAILSKID S
TAILSPIN S
ALPINIST
ANTISLIP
PINTAILS
TAILWIND S
S TAIN ST
ANTI
S TAINS
ANTIS SAINT
SATIN STAIN
TAINT S
TITAN
TAINTED
TAINTING
TAINTS
STATIN
TANIST
TITANS
TAIPAN S
PATINA
PINATA
TAIPANS
PASTINA
PATINAS
PINATAS
TAJ
TAJES
TAKA S
KATA
TAKABLE
TAKAHE S
TAKAHES
TAKAS
KATAS
S TAKE NRS
TEAK
TAKEABLE
TAKEAWAY S
TAKEDOWN S
TAKEN
TAKEOFF S

TAKEOFFS
S TAKEOUT S
OUTTAKE
S TAKEOUTS
OUTSKATE
OUTTAKES
STAKEOUT
TAKEOVER S
OVERTAKE
TAKER S
TAKERS
SKATER
STRAKE
STREAK
S TAKES
SKATE STAKE
STEAK TEAKS
TAKEUP S
UPTAKE
TAKEUPS
UPTAKES
TAKIN GS
S TAKING S
TAKINGLY
TAKINGS
SKATING
STAKING
TASKING
TAKINS
TALA RS
TALAPOIN S
TALAR S
ALTAR ARTAL
RATAL
TALARIA
TALARS
ALTARS
ASTRAL
RATALS
TARSAL
TALAS
ATLAS
TALC S
TALCED
TALCING
CATLING
TALCKED
TACKLED
TALCKING
TACKLING
TALCKY
TALCOSE
LACTOSE
LOCATES
TALCOUS
LOCUSTA
TALCS
CLAST
TALCUM S
TALCUMS
S TALE RS
LATE TAEL
TEAL TELA
TALEGGIO S
TALENT S
LATENT
LATTEN
TALENTED
TALENTS
LATENTS
LATTENS
S TALER S
ALERT ALTER
ARTEL LATER
RATEL
TALERS
ALERTS
ALTERS
ARTELS
ESTRAL
LASTER
RATELS
SALTER
SLATER
STALER
STELAR
S TALES
LEAST SETAL
SLATE STALE
STEAL STELA
TAELS TEALS
TESLA
TALESMAN

TALESMEN
TALEYSIM
STEAMILY
TALI
ALIT LATI
TAIL
TALION S
LATINO
TALIONS
LATINOS
TALIPED S
PLAITED
TALIPEDS
TALIPES
APLITES
PALIEST
PLATIES
TALIPOT S
TALIPOTS
TALISMAN S
STAMINAL
S TALK SY
TALKABLE
TALKBACK S
S TALKED
S TALKER S
S TALKERS
STALKER
TALKIE RS
S TALKIER
RATLIKE
TALKIES T
LAKIEST
S TALKIEST
S TALKING S
S TALKINGS
STALKING
S TALKS
STALK
S TALKY
S TALL SY
TALLAGE DS
GALLATE
GALLETA
TALLAGED
TALLAGES
GALLATES
GALLETAS
TALLBOY S
TALLBOYS
TALLER
TALLEST
TALLIED
TALLIER S
LITERAL
TALLIERS
LITERALS
TALLIES
TAILLES
TALLIS H
TALLISES
TAILLESS
TALLISH
TALLISIM
TALLIT HS
TALLITH S
TALLITHS
TALLITIM
TALLITS
TALLNESS
TALLOL S
TALLOLS
TALLOW SY
TALLOWED
TALLOWS
TALLOWY
TOLLWAY
S TALLS
STALL
TALLY
TALLYHO S
LOATHLY
TALLYHOS
TALLYING
TALLYMAN
TALLYMEN
MENTALLY
TALMUDIC
E TALON S
NOTAL TOLAN
TONAL

TALONED
E TALONS
SANTOL
STANOL
TOLANS
TALOOKA S
TALOOKAS
TALUK AS
TALUKA S
TALUKAS
TALUKS
TALUS
SAULT
TALUSES
SALUTES
TAM EPS
MAT
TAMABLE
TAMAL ES
TAMALE S
MALATE
MEATAL
TAMALES
MALATES
MALTASE
TAMALS
TAMANDU AS
TAMANDUA S
TAMANDUS
TAMARACK S
TAMARAO S
TAMARAOS
TAMARAU S
TAMARAUS
TAMARI NS
AMRITA
TAMARIN DS
MARTIAN
TAMARIND S
TAMARINS
MARTIANS
TAMARIS K
AMRITAS
TAMARISK S
TAMASHA S
TAMASHAS
TAMBAC S
TAMBACS
TAMBAK S
TAMBAKS
TAMBALA S
TAMBALAS
TAMBOUR AS
TAMBOURA S
MARABOUT
TAMBOURS
TAMBUR AS
TAMBURA S
TAMBURAS
TAMBURS
TAME DRS
MATE MEAT
META TEAM
TAMEABLE
TAMED
MATED
TAMEIN S
ETAMIN
INMATE
TAMEINS
ETAMINS
INMATES
TAMELESS
MATELESS
MEATLESS
TAMELY
TAMENESS
TAMER S
ARMET MATER
RAMET
TAMERS
ARMETS
MASTER
MATERS
MATRES
RAMETS
STREAM

TAMES T
MATES MEATS
SATEM STEAM
TEAMS
TAMEST
MATTES
TAMING
MATING
TAMIS
MAIST
TAMISES
MISEATS
MISSEAT
SAMITES
TAMMIE S
TAMMIES
MISMATE
SEMIMAT
TAMMY
S TAMP S
TAMPALA S
TAMPALAS
TAMPAN S
TAMPANS
S TAMPED
S TAMPER S
TAMPERED
TAMPERER S
S TAMPERS
RESTAMP
STAMPER
S TAMPING
TAMPION S
MAINTOP
PTOMAIN
TIMPANO
TAMPIONS
MAINTOPS
PTOMAINS
TAMPON S
POTMAN
TAMPONED
TAMPONS
POSTMAN
S TAMPS
STAMP
TAMS
MAST MATS
TAN GKS
ANT
TANAGER S
TANAGERS
TANBARK S
TANBARKS
TANDEM S
TANDEMS
TANDOOR IS
DONATOR
ODORANT
TORNADO
TANDOORI S
TANDOORS
DONATORS
ODORANTS
TORNADOS
S TANG AOSY
GNAT
TANGA
S TANGED
TANGELO S
TANGELOS
TANGENCE S
TANGENCY
TANGENT S
TANGENTS
TANGIBLE S
BLEATING
TANGIBLY
TANGIER
GRANITE
GRATINE
INGRATE
TEARING
TANGIEST
ESTATING
S TANGING
TANGLE DRS
GELANT
TANGLED
TANGLER S

TANGLERS
STRANGLE
TANGLES
GELANTS
TANGLIER
ALERTING
ALTERING
INTEGRAL
RELATING
TRIANGLE
TANGLING
TANGLY
TANGO S
TONGA
TANGOED
TANGOING
TANGOS
TONGAS
TANGRAM S
TRANGAM
TANGRAMS
TRANGAMS
S TANGS
ANGST GNATS
STANG
TANGY
TANIST S
STATIN
TAINTS
TITANS
TANISTRY
TANISTS
STATINS
S TANK AS
TANKA S
TANKAGE S
TANKAGES
TANKARD S
TANKARDS
TANKAS
ASKANT
TANKED
TANKER S
TANKERS
RANKEST
TANKFUL S
TANKFULS
TANKING
TANKINI S
TANKINIS
TANKLESS
TANKLIKE
S TANKS
STANK
TANKSHIP S
TANNABLE
TANNAGE S
TANNAGES
TANNATE S
TANNATES
TANNED
TANNER SY
TANNERS
TANNERY
TANNEST
TENANTS
S TANNIC
INCANT
TANNIN GS
TANNING S
TANNINGS
TANNINS
TANNISH
TANNOY S
TANNOYS
TANREC S
CANTER
CARNET
CENTRA
NECTAR
RECANT
TRANCE
TANRECS
CANTERS
CARNETS
NECTARS
RECANTS
SCANTER
TRANCES

TANS Y
ANTS
TANSIES
ENTASIS
NASTIES
SEITANS
SESTINA
TISANES
TANSY
ANTSY NASTY
TANTALIC
TANTALUM S
TANTALUS
TANTARA S
TARTANA
TANTARAS
TARANTAS
TARTANAS
TANTIVY
TANTO
TANTRA S
RATTAN
TARTAN
TANTRAS
RATTANS
TARTANS
TANTRIC
TANTRISM S
TRANSMIT
TANTRUM S
TANTRUMS
TANUKI S
TANUKIS
TANYARD S
TANYARDS
TAO S
OAT
TAOS
OAST OATS
STOA
A TAP AES
APT
PAT
TAPA S
ATAP
TAPADERA S
TAPADERO S
TAPALO S
TAPALOS
TAPAS
ATAPS PASTA
E TAPE DRS
PATE PEAT
TEPA
TAPEABLE
TAPED
ADEPT PATED
TAPELESS
TAPELIKE
TAPELINE S
PETALINE
TAPENADE S
TAPER S
APTER PATER
PEART PRATE
TAPERED
ADEPTER
PREDATE
RETAPED
TAPERER S
PEARTER
TAPERERS
TAPERING
RETAPING
TAPERS
PASTER
PATERS
PRATES
REPAST
TRAPES
ES TAPES
PASTE PATES
PEATS SEPTA
SPATE TEPAS
TAPESTRY
TAPETA L
TAPETAL
TAPETUM
TAPEWORM S
TAPHOLE S
TAPHOLES
TAPHOUSE S
PHASEOUT
TAPING
TAPIOCA S
TAPIOCAS
TAPIR S
ATRIP
TAPIRS
RAPIST
TAPIS
PITAS SPAIT
TAPISES
PASTIES
PATSIES
PETSAIS
TAPPABLE
TAPPED
TAPPER S
TAPPERS
TAPPET S
TAPPETS
TAPPING S
TAPPINGS
TAPROOM S
TAPROOMS
TAPROOT S
TAPROOTS
A TAPS
PAST PATS
SPAT
TAPSTER S
PATTERS
SPATTER
TAPSTERS
SPATTERS
TAQUERIA S
S TAR ENOPST
ART
RAT
TARAMA S
TARAMAS
TARANTAS
TANTARAS
TARTANAS
TARBOOSH
TARBUSH
TARDIER
TARRIED
TARDIES T
ARIDEST
ASTRIDE
DIASTER
DISRATE
STAIDER
TIRADES
TARDIEST
STRIATED
TARDILY
TARDIVE
TARDO
TARDY
TARDYON S
TARDYONS
S TARE DS
RATE TEAR
S TARED
DATER DERAT
RATED TRADE
TREAD
S TARES
ASTER RATES
RESAT STARE
TEARS
TARGE ST
GATER GRATE
GREAT RETAG
TERGA
TARGES
GASTER
GATERS
GRATES
GREATS
RETAGS
STAGER
TARGET S
TARGETED
TARGETS
TARIFF S
TARIFFED
TARIFFS
S TARING
GRATIN
RATING
TARLATAN S
TARLETAN S
ALTERANT
TARMAC S
AMTRAC
TARMACS
AMTRACS
TARN S
RANT
TARNAL
ANTRAL
TARNALLY
TARNISH
TARNS
RANTS TRANS
TARO CKST
RATO ROTA
TORA
TAROC S
ACTOR
TAROCS
ACTORS
CASTOR
COSTAR
SCROTA
TAROK S
KORAT TROAK
TAROKS
KORATS
TROAKS
TAROS
RATOS ROAST
ROTAS SORTA
TORAS
TAROT S
OTTAR TORTA
TAROTS
OTTARS
STATOR
TORTAS
TARP S
PART PRAT
RAPT TRAP
TARPAN S
PARTAN
TRAPAN
TARPANS
PARTANS
SPARTAN
TRAPANS
TARPAPER S
TARPON S
PARTON
PATRON
TARPONS
PARTONS
PATRONS
TARPS
PARTS PRATS
SPRAT STRAP
TRAPS
TARRAGON S
ARROGANT
TARRE DS
RATER TERRA
S TARRED
DARTER
RETARD
TRADER
TARRES
ARREST
RAREST
RASTER
RATERS
STARER
TERRAS
TARRIED
TARDIER
S TARRIER S
TARRIERS
STARRIER
TARRIES T
ARTSIER
TARSIER
S TARRIEST
STRAITER
S TARRING
S TARRY
TARRYING
S TARS T
ARTS RATS
STAR TSAR
TARSAL S
ALTARS
ASTRAL
RATALS
TALARS
TARSALS
ASTRALS
TARSI A
AIRTS ASTIR
SITAR STAIR
STRIA
TARSIA S
ARISTA
RAITAS
RIATAS
TIARAS
TARSIAS
ARISTAS
TARSIER S
ARTSIER
TARRIES
TARSIERS
TARSUS
SUTRAS
TUSSAR
S TART SY
TARTAN AS
RATTAN
TANTRA
TARTANA S
TANTARA
TARTANAS
TANTARAS
TARANTAS
TARTANS
RATTANS
TANTRAS
TARTAR ES
TARTARE
TARTARIC
TARTARS
S TARTED
RATTED
TETRAD
S TARTER
RATTER
TARTEST
STRETTA
TATTERS
TARTIER
RATTIER
TARTIEST
ATTRITES
RATTIEST
TITRATES
TRISTATE
TARTILY
S TARTING
RATTING
TARTISH
ATHIRST
RATTISH
TARTLET S
TATTLER
TARTLETS
TATTLERS
TARTLY
RATTLY
TARTNESS
TARTRATE DS
S TARTS
START
TARTUFE S
TARTUFES
TARTUFFE S
TARTY
RATTY
TARWEED S
DEWATER
WATERED
TARWEEDS
DEWATERS
TARZAN S
TARZANS
EU TAS KS
SAT
TASK S
KATS SKAT
TASKBAR S
TASKBARS
TASKED
SKATED
STAKED
TASKING
SKATING
STAKING
TAKINGS
TASKS
SKATS
TASKWORK S
TASS E
TASSE LST
ASSET EASTS
SATES SEATS
TASSEL S
LEASTS
SLATES
STALES
STEALS
TESLAS
TASSELED
DATELESS
DETASSEL
TASSELS
TASSES
ASSETS
STASES
TASSET S
STATES
TASTES
TASSETS
TASSIE S
SIESTA
TASSIES
SIESTAS
TASTABLE
ABETTALS
STATABLE
TASTE DRS
STATE TATES
TEATS TESTA
TASTED
STATED
TASTEFUL
TASTER S
STATER
TATERS
TETRAS
TREATS
TASTERS
STARETS
STATERS
TASTES
STATES
TASSET
TASTIER
ARTIEST
ARTISTE
ATTIRES
IRATEST
RATITES
STRIATE
TASTIEST
TASTILY
TASTING
STATING
TASTY
S TAT ES
ATT
TATAMI S
TATAMIS
TATAR S
ATTAR
TATARS
ATTARS
STRATA
S TATE RS
TEAT
S TATER S
TETRA TREAT
S TATERS
STATER
TASTER
TETRAS
TREATS
S TATES
STATE TASTE
TEATS TESTA
TATOUAY S
TATOUAYS
S TATS
STAT
TATSOI S
TATSOIS
TATTED
TATTER S
TATTERED
TATTERS
STRETTA
TARTEST
TATTIE RS
TATTIER
ATTRITE
TITRATE
TATTIES T
ETATIST
TATTIEST
TATTILY
TATTING S
TATTINGS
TATTLE DRS
TATTLED
TATTLER S
TARTLET
TATTLERS
TARTLETS
TATTLES
TATTLING
TATTOO S
TATTOOED
TATTOOER S
TATTOOS
TATTY
TAU ST
UTA
TAUGHT
TAUNT S
TAUNTED
ATTUNED
NUTATED
TAUNTER S
TAUNTERS
TAUNTING
ATTUNING
NUTATING
TAUNTS
TAUON S
TAUONS
TAUPE S
TAUPES
TAURINE S
RUINATE
URANITE
URINATE
TAURINES
RUINATES
URANITES
URINATES
TAUS
UTAS
TAUT S
TAUTAUG S
TAUTAUGS
TAUTED
TAUTEN S
ATTUNE
NUTATE
TAUTENED
TAUTENS
ATTUNES
NUTATES
TETANUS
UNSTATE
TAUTER
TAUTEST
STATUTE
TAUTING
TAUTLY
TAUTNESS
UNSTATES
TAUTOG S
TAUTOGS
TAUTOMER S
TAUTONYM SY
TAUTS
SUTTA
TAV S
VAT
TAVERN AS
TAVERNA S
TAVERNAS
TSAREVNA
TAVERNER S
TAVERNS
SERVANT
VERSANT
TAVS
VAST VATS
S TAW S
TWA
WAT
TAWDRIER
TAWDRIES T
TAWDRILY
TAWDRY
TAWED
TAWER S
WATER
TAWERS
RAWEST
WASTER
WATERS
TAWIE
TAWING
TAWNEY S
TAWNEYS
TAWNIER
TINWARE
TAWNIES T
WANIEST
TAWNIEST
TAWNILY
TAWNY
TAWPIE S
TAWPIES
TAWS E
STAW SWAT
TWAS WAST
WATS
TAWSE DS
SWEAT TWAES
WASTE
TAWSED
WADSET
WASTED
TAWSES
SWEATS
WASTES
TAWSING
WASTING
TAX AI
TAXA
TAXABLE S
TAXABLES
TAXABLY
TAXATION S
TAXED
TAXEME S
TAXEMES
TAXEMIC
TAXER S
EXTRA RETAX
TAXERS
EXTRAS
TAXES
TEXAS
TAXI S
TAXICAB S
TAXICABS
TAXIED
A TAXIES
AXITES
TAXIING
TAXIMAN
TAXIMEN
TAXING
TAXINGLY
TAXIS
TAXITE S
TAXITES
TAXITIC
TAXIWAY S
TAXIWAYS
TAXLESS
TAXMAN
TAXMEN
TAXOL S
TAXOLS
TAXON S
TAXONOMY
TAXONS
TAXPAID
TAXPAYER S
TAXUS

TAXWISE
WAXIEST
TAXYING
TAZZA S
TAZZAS
TAZZE
TEA KLMRST
ATE
EAT
ETA
TAE
TEABERRY
BETRAYER
TEABOARD S
TEABOWL S
TOWABLE
TEABOWLS
BESTOWAL
STOWABLE
TEABOX
TEABOXES
TEACAKE S
TEACAKES
TEACART S
TEACARTS
CASTRATE
TEACH
CHEAT TACHE
THECA
TEACHER S
CHEATER
HECTARE
RECHEAT
RETEACH
TEACHERS
CHEATERS
HECTARES
RECHEATS
TEACHES
ESCHEAT
TEACHING S
CHEATING
TEACUP S
TEACUPS
CUSPATE
TEAHOUSE S
S **TEAK** S
TAKE
S **TEAKS**
SKATE STAKE
STEAK TAKES
TEAKWOOD S
S **TEAL** S
LATE TAEL
TALE TELA
TEALIKE
S **TEALS**
LEAST SETAL
SLATE STALE
STEAL STELA
TAELS TALES
TESLA
S **TEAM** S
MATE MEAT
META TAME
TEAMAKER S
S **TEAMED**
MEATED
S **TEAMING**
MINTAGE
TEGMINA
TEAMMATE S
S **TEAMS**
MATES MEATS
SATEM STEAM
TAMES
TEAMSTER S
TEAMWORK S
WORKMATE
TEAPOT S
TEAPOTS
TEAPOY S
TEAPOYS
TEAR SY
RATE TARE
TEARABLE
RATEABLE
TEARAWAY S
TEARDOWN S
DANEWORT

TEARDROP S
PARROTED
PREDATOR
PRORATED
PROTRADE
TEARED
DERATE
REDATE
TEARER S
RETEAR
TERRAE
TEARERS
RETEARS
SERRATE
TEARFUL
REFUTAL
TEARGAS
GASTREA
TEARIER
TEARIEST
ARIETTES
ITERATES
TREATIES
TREATISE
TEARILY
IRATELY
REALITY
TEARING
GRANITE
GRATINE
INGRATE
TANGIER
TEARLESS
RESLATES
STEALERS
TEAROOM S
TEAROOMS
TEARS
ASTER RATES
RESAT STARE
TARES
TEARY
TEAS E
ATES EAST
EATS ETAS
SATE SEAT
SETA
TEASABLE
EATABLES
TEASE DLRS
SETAE
TEASED
SEATED
SEDATE
TEASEL S
ELATES
STELAE
TEASELED
TEASELER S
TEASELS
TEASER S
ARETES
EASTER
EATERS
RESEAT
SEATER
TEASERS
EASTERS
RESEATS
SEAREST
SEATERS
TESSERA
TEASES
TEASHOP S
TEASHOPS
PATHOSES
POTASHES
SPATHOSE
TEASING
EASTING
EATINGS
INGATES
INGESTA
SEATING
TEASPOON S
TEAT S
TATE
TEATED
TEATIME S
TEATIMES
ESTIMATE
MEATIEST

TEATS
STATE TASTE
TATES TESTA
TEAWARE S
TEAWARES
SEAWATER
TEAZEL S
TEAZLE
TEAZELED
TEAZELS
TEAZLES
TEAZLE DS
TEAZEL
TEAZLED
TEAZLES
TEAZELS
TEAZLING
TECH SY
ECHT ETCH
TECHED
ETCHED
TECHIE RS
TECHIER
ERETHIC
ETHERIC
HERETIC
TECHIES T
TECHIEST
ESTHETIC
TECHILY
ETHYLIC
LECYTHI
A **TECHNIC** S
TECHNICS
TECHNO S
TECHNOS
NOTCHES
TECHS
CHEST
TECHY
TECTA L
TACET
TECTAL
CATTLE
TECTITE S
TECTITES
TECTONIC S
TECTRIX
TECTUM S
TECTUMS
TED S
TEDDED
TEDDER S
TEDDERED
TEDDERS
REDDEST
TEDDIES
TEDDING
TEDDY
TEDIOUS
OUTSIDE
TEDIUM S
TEDIUMS
TEDS
TEE DLMNS
S **TEED**
DEET
TEEING
S **TEEL** S
LEET TELE
S **TEELS**
LEETS SLEET
STEEL STELE
TELES
TEEM S
MEET METE
TEEMED
TEEMER S
MEETER
REMEET
TEEMERS
MEETERS
REMEETS
TEEMING
MEETING
TEEMS
MEETS METES
TEEN SY
TEENAGE DR
TEENAGED
TEENAGER S
GENERATE

TEENER S
ENTREE
ETERNE
RETENE
TEENERS
ENTREES
RETENES
TEENFUL
TEENIER
TEENIEST
TEENS Y
SENTE TENSE
TEENSIER
ETERNISE
TEENSY
YENTES
TEENTSY
TEENY
YENTE
TEENYBOP
TEEPEE S
TEEPEES
TEES
TEETER S
TERETE
TEETERED
TEETERS
TEETH E
TEETHE DRS
TEETHED
TEETHER S
TEETHERS
TEETHES
ESTHETE
TEETHING S
TEETOTAL S
TEETOTUM S
TEFF S
TEFFS
TEFILLIN
TEFLON S
TEFLONS
TEG GS
GET
TEGG S
TEGGS
TEGMEN
TEGMENTA L
TEGMINA L
MINTAGE
TEAMING
TEGMINAL
LIGAMENT
METALING
TEGS
GEST GETS
TEGUA S
TEGUAS
TEGULAR
TEGUMEN T
TEGUMENT S
TEGUMINA
UMANGITE
TEIGLACH
TEIID S
TEIIDS
TIDIES
TEIND S
TINED
TEINDS
TEKKIE S
TEKKIES
TEKTITE S
TEKTITES
TEKTITIC
TEL AELS
LET
S **TELA** E
LATE TAEL
TALE TEAL
S **TELAE**
ELATE
TELAMON
LOMENTA
OMENTAL
TELCO S
TELCOS
CLOSET
S **TELE** SX
LEET TEEL

TELECAST S
TELECOM S
TELECOMS
TELEDU S
ELUTED
TELEDUS
TELEFAX
TELEFILM S
TELEGA S
EAGLET
GELATE
LEGATE
TELEGAS
EAGLETS
GELATES
LEGATES
SEGETAL
TELEGONY
TELEGRAM S
TELEMAN
TELEMARK S
TELEMEN
ELEMENT
TELEOST S
TELEOSTS
TELEPATH SY
TELEPLAY S
TELEPORT S
TELERAN S
ENTERAL
ETERNAL
TELERANS
ETERNALS
S **TELES**
LEETS SLEET
STEEL STELE
TEELS
TELESES
TELESHOP S
HEELPOST
PESTHOLE
TELESIS
LISTEES
TIELESS
TELESTIC HS
TESTICLE
TELETEXT S
TELETHON S
TELETYPE DS
TELEVIEW S
TELEVISE DS
TELEX
TELEXED
TELEXES
TELEXING
TELFER S
LEFTER
REFELT
REFLET
TELFERED
TELFERS
REFLETS
TELFORD S
TELFORDS
TELIA L
TELIAL
TAILLE
AS **TELIC**
TELIUM
TELL SY
TELLABLE
TELLER S
RETELL
TELLERS
RETELLS
TELLIES
TELLING
GILLNET
TELLS
TELLTALE S
TELLURIC
TELLY S
TELLYS
TELNET S
NETTLE
TELNETED
TELNETS
NETTLES
TELOI
TOILE

TELOME S
OMELET
TELOMERE S
TELOMES
OMELETS
TELOMIC
TELOS
STOLE TOLES
TELPHER S
TELPHERS
TELS
LEST LETS
TELSON S
LENTOS
STOLEN
TELSONIC
LECTIONS
TELSONS
TEMBLOR S
TEMBLORS
TEMERITY
TEMP IOST
TEMPED
TEMPEH S
TEMPEHS
TEMPER AS
TEMPERA S
TEMPERAS
TEMPERED
TEMPERER S
RETEMPER
TEMPERS
TEMPEST S
TEMPESTS
TEMPI
TEMPING
PIGMENT
TEMPLAR S
TRAMPLE
TEMPLARS
TRAMPLES
TEMPLATE S
PALMETTE
TEMPLE DST
PELMET
TEMPLED
TEMPLES
PELMETS
TEMPLET S
TEMPLETS
TEMPO S
A **TEMPORAL** S
TEMPOS
TEMPS
TEMPT S
TEMPTED
TEMPTER S
TEMPTERS
TEMPTING
TEMPTS
TEMPURA S
TEMPURAS
UPSTREAM
TEN DST
NET
TENABLE
TENABLY
TENACE S
CETANE
TENACES
CETANES
TENACITY
TENACULA
CANULATE
LACUNATE
TENAIL S
ENTAIL
TINEAL
TENAILLE S
TENAILS
ELASTIN
ENTAILS
NAILSET
SALIENT
SALTINE
SLAINTE
TENANCY
TENANT S
TENANTED
TENANTRY

TENANTS
TANNEST
S **TENCH**
S **TENCHES**
TEND SU
DENT
TENDANCE S
TENDED
DENTED
TENDENCE S
TENDENCY
TENDER S
RENTED
TENDERED
TENDERER S
RERENTED
TENDERLY
TENDERS
TENDING
DENTING
TENDON S
TENDONS
TENDRIL S
TRINDLE
TENDRILS
TRINDLES
TENDS
DENTS
TENDU S
TUNED
TENDUS
NUDEST
TENEBRAE
TENEMENT S
TENESMIC
CENTIMES
TENESMUS
MUTENESS
TENET S
TENETS
TENFOLD S
TENFOLDS
TENGE
GENET
TENIA ES
ENTIA TINEA
TENIAE
TENIAS
SEITAN
TINEAS
TISANE
TENIASES
ETESIANS
TENIASIS
ISATINES
SANITIES
SANITISE
TENNER S
RENNET
TENNERS
RENNETS
TENNIES
INTENSE
TENNIS T
SENNIT
TENNISES
TENNIST S
INTENTS
TENNISTS
TENON S
NONET TONNE
TENONED
ENDNOTE
TENONER S
ENTERON
TENONERS
ENTERONS
TENONING
TENONS
NONETS
SONNET
TONNES
TENOR S
NOTER TONER
TRONE
TENORIST S
SNOTTIER
TRITONES
TENORITE S

TENORS
NESTOR NOTERS STONER TENSOR TONERS TRONES
TENOTOMY
TENOUR S
TENOURS
TONSURE
TENPENCE S
TENPENNY
TENPIN S
TENPINS
TENREC S
CENTER CENTRE RECENT
TENRECS
CENTERS CENTRES
TENS E
NEST NETS SENT
TENSE DRS
SENTE TEENS
TENSED
NESTED
TENSELY
TENSER
ENTERS NESTER RENEST RENTES RESENT TERNES TREENS
TENSES T
TENSEST
TENSIBLE
STILBENE
TENSIBLY
TENSILE
LENITES LISENTE SETLINE
TENSING
NESTING
TENSION S
INTONES
TENSIONS
TENSITY
TENSIVE
TENSOR S
NESTOR NOTERS STONER TENORS TONERS TRONES
TENSORS
NESTORS STONERS
S **TENT** HSY
NETT
TENTACLE DS
TENTAGE S
TENTAGES
TENTED
DETENT NETTED
TENTER S
NETTER
TENTERED
TENTERS
NETTERS
TENTH S
TENTHLY
TENTHS
TENTIE R
TENTIER
NETTIER
TENTIEST
NETTIEST
TENTING
NETTING
TENTLESS
TENTLIKE
TENTORIA L
S **TENTS**
NETTS STENT

TENTY
NETTY
TENUES
TENUIS
UNITES UNTIES
TENUITY
TENUOUS
TENURE DS
NEUTER RETUNE TUREEN
TENURED
DENTURE RETUNED
TENURES
NEUTERS RETUNES TUREENS
TENURIAL
AUNTLIER RETINULA
TENURING
RETUNING
TENUTI
TENUTO S
TENUTOS
STOUTEN
TEOCALLI S
LOCALITE
TEOPAN S
TEOPANS
TEOSINTE S
NOISETTE
TEPA LS
PATE PEAT TAPE
TEPAL S
LEAPT LEPTA PALET PETAL PLATE PLEAT
TEPALS
PALEST PALETS PASTEL PETALS PLATES PLEATS SEPTAL STAPLE
TEPAS
PASTE PATES PEATS SEPTA SPATE TAPES
TEPEE S
TEPEES
TEPEFIED
TEPEFIES
TEPEFY
TEPHRA S
TERAPH THREAP
TEPHRAS
THREAPS
TEPHRITE S
TEPID
TEPIDITY
TEPIDLY
TEPOY S
TEPOYS
TEQUILA S
LIQUATE
TEQUILAS
LIQUATES
TERABYTE S
TERAFLOP S
TERAI S
IRATE RETIA
TERAIS
AIREST SATIRE STRIAE
TERAOHM S
TERAOHMS
TERAPH
TEPHRA THREAP
TERAPHIM
TERATISM S
MISTREAT
TERATOID

TERATOMA S
AMARETTO
TERAWATT S
TERBIA S
BAITER BARITE REBAIT
TERBIAS
BAITERS BARITES REBAITS
TERBIC
TERBIUM S
IMBRUTE
TERBIUMS
IMBRUTES RESUBMIT
TERCE LST
ERECT
TERCEL S
TERCELET S
ELECTRET
TERCELS
TERCES
CERTES ERECTS RESECT SECRET
TERCET S
TERCETS
TEREBENE S
TEREBIC
TEREDO S
TEREDOS
OERSTED
TEREFAH
FEATHER
TERETE
TEETER
TERGA L
GATER GRATE GREAT RETAG TARGE
TERGAL
TERGITE S
TERGITES
GRISETTE
TERGUM
TERIYAKI S
TERM S
TERMED
METRED
TERMER S
TERMERS
TERMINAL S
TRAMLINE
TERMING
METRING
TERMINI
INTERIM MINTIER
TERMINUS
UNMITERS UNMITRES
TERMITE S
EMITTER
TERMITES
EMITTERS
TERMITIC
TERMLESS
RESMELTS SMELTERS
TERMLY
MYRTLE
TERMOR S
TREMOR
TERMORS
TREMORS
TERMS
TERMTIME S
S **TERN** ES
RENT
TERNARY
TERNATE
ENTREAT RATTEEN
E **TERNE** S
ENTER RENTE TREEN

TERNES
ENTERS NESTER RENEST RENTES RESENT TENSER TREENS
TERNION S
INTONER
TERNIONS
INTONERS
S **TERNS**
NERTS RENTS STERN
TERPENE S
PRETEEN
TERPENES
PRETEENS PRETENSE
TERPENIC
PRENTICE
TERPINOL S
TERRA ES
RATER TARRE
TERRACE DS
CATERER RECRATE RETRACE
TERRACED
CRATERED RECRATED RETRACED
TERRACES
CATERERS RECRATES RETRACES
TERRAE
RETEAR TEARER
TERRAIN S
RETRAIN TRAINER
TERRAINS
RESTRAIN RETRAINS STRAINER TRAINERS
TERRANE S
TERRANES
TERRAPIN S
PRETRAIN
TERRARIA
TERRAS
ARREST RAREST RASTER RATERS STARER TARRES
TERRASES
ASSERTER REASSERT SERRATES
TERRAZZO S
TERREEN S
ENTERER REENTER TERRENE
TERREENS
ENTERERS REENTERS TERRENES
TERRELLA S
TERRENE S
ENTERER REENTER TERREEN
TERRENES
ENTERERS REENTERS TERREENS
TERRET S
TERRETS
TERRIBLE
TERRIBLY
TERRIER S
RETIRER
TERRIERS
RETIRERS
TERRIES
RETIRES RETRIES

TERRIFIC
FERRITIC
TERRIFY
TERRINE S
REINTER RENTIER
TERRINES
INSERTER REINSERT REINTERS RENTIERS
TERRIT S
RITTER TRITER
TERRITS
RITTERS
TERROR S
TERRORS
TERRY
RETRY
TERSE R
ESTER REEST RESET STEER STERE TREES
TERSELY
RESTYLE
TERSER
RESTER
TERSEST
RETESTS SETTERS STREETS TESTERS
TERTIAL S
TERTIALS
TERTIAN S
INTREAT ITERANT NATTIER NITRATE
TERTIANS
INTREATS NITRATES STRAITEN
TERTIARY
TERYLENE S
TESLA S
LEAST SETAL SLATE STALE STEAL STELA TAELS TALES TEALS
TESLAS
LEASTS SLATES STALES STEALS TASSEL
TESSERA E
EASTERS RESEATS SEAREST SEATERS TEASERS
TESSERAE
ESTERASE
TEST ASY
SETT STET TETS
TESTA E
STATE TASTE TATES TEATS
TESTABLE
SEATBELT
TESTACY
TESTAE
ESTATE
TESTATE S
TESTATES
TESTATOR S
ATTESTOR
TESTED
DETEST
TESTEE S
SETTEE
TESTEES
SETTEES
TESTER S
RETEST SETTER STREET

TESTERS
RETESTS SETTERS STREETS TERSEST
TESTES
SESTET TSETSE
TESTICLE S
TELESTIC
TESTIER
TESTIEST
TESTIFY
TESTILY
STYLITE
TESTING
SETTING
TESTIS
TESTON S
TESTONS
STETSON
TESTOON S
TESTOONS
TESTS
SETTS STETS
TESTUDO S
TESTUDOS
TESTY
YETTS
S **TET** HS
TETANAL
TETANIC S
NICTATE
TETANICS
ENTASTIC NICTATES
TETANIES
ANISETTE TETANISE
TETANISE DS
ANISETTE TETANIES
TETANIZE DS
TETANOID
ANTIDOTE
TETANUS
ATTUNES NUTATES TAUTENS UNSTATE
TETANY
TETCHED
TETCHIER
TETCHILY
TETCHY
TETH S
TETHER S
TETHERED
TETHERS
TETHS
TETOTUM S
TETOTUMS
TETRA DS
TATER TREAT
TETRACID S
CITRATED TETRADIC
TETRAD S
RATTED TARTED
TETRADIC
CITRATED TETRACID
TETRADS
STARTED
TETRAGON S
TETRAMER S
TETRAPOD S
TETRARCH SY
TETRAS
STATER TASTER TATERS TREATS
TETRI S
TITER TITRE TRITE
TETRIS
SITTER TITERS TITRES TRISTE

TETRODE S
TETRODES
TETROXID ES
TETRYL S
TETRYLS
S **TETS**
SETT STET TEST
TETTER S
TETTERS
STRETTE
TEUCH
CHUTE
TEUGH
TEUGHLY
TEVATRON S
S **TEW** S
WET
S **TEWED**
TWEED
S **TEWING**
TWINGE
S **TEWS**
STEW WEST WETS
TEXAS
TAXES
TEXASES
TEXT S
TEXTBOOK S
TEXTILE S
TEXTILES
TEXTLESS
TEXTS
TEXTUAL
TEXTUARY
TEXTURAL
TEXTURE DS
TEXTURED
TEXTURES
THACK S
THACKED
THACKING
THACKS
THAE
EATH HAET HATE HEAT
THAIRM S
THIRAM
THAIRMS
THIRAMS
THALAMI C
THALAMIC
THALAMUS
THALER S
HALTER LATHER
THALERS
HALTERS HARSLET LATHERS SLATHER
THALLI C
THALLIC
THALLIUM S
THALLOID
THALLOUS
THALLUS
THALWEG S
THALWEGS
THAN EK
HANT
THANAGE S
THANAGES
THANATOS
E **THANE** S
NEATH
E **THANES**
HASTEN SNATHE
THANK S
THANKED
THANKER S
THANKERS
THANKFUL
THANKING
THANKS
THARM S
THARMS

THAT
THATAWAY
THATCH Y
THATCHED
DETHATCH
THATCHER S
THATCHES
HATCHETS
THATCHY
THAW S
WHAT
THAWED
THAWER S
WREATH
THAWERS
SWATHER
WREATHS
THAWING
THAWLESS
THAWS
SWATH WHATS
THE EMNWY
ETH
HET
THEARCHY
HATCHERY
THEATER S
THEATRE
THEREAT
THEATERS
EARTHSET
THEATRES
THEATRE S
THEATER
THEREAT
THEATRES
EARTHSET
THEATERS
THEATRIC S
CHATTIER
THEBAINE S
THEBE S
THEBES
BEHEST
THECA EL
CHEAT TACHE
TEACH
THECAE
THECAL
CHALET
THECATE
THEE
THEELIN S
THEELINS
THEELOL S
THEELOLS
THEFT S
THEFTS
THEGN S
THEGNLY
LENGTHY
THEGNS
THEIN ES
THINE
THEINE S
THEINES
THEINS
THEIR S
ITHER
THEIRS
A THEISM S
A THEISMS
A THEIST S
TITHES
A THEISTIC
CHITTIES
ETHICIST
ITCHIEST
A THEISTS
THELITIS
THEM E
METH
THEMATIC S
THEME DS
THEMED
THEMES
THEMING
THEN S
HENT
THENAGE S
THENAGES

THENAL
HANTLE
THENAR S
ANTHER
THENARS
ANTHERS
THENCE
THENS
HENTS SHENT
THEOCRAT S
THEODICY
THEOGONY
THEOLOG SY
THEOLOGS
THEOLOGY
ETHOLOGY
THEONOMY
THEORBO S
THEORBOS
THEOREM S
THEOREMS
THEORIES
ISOTHERE
THEORISE
THEORISE DS
ISOTHERE
THEORIES
THEORIST S
THORITES
THEORIZE DR S
THEORY
THERAPY
THERE S
ETHER THREE
THEREAT
THEATER
THEATRE
THEREBY
THEREFOR E
THEREIN
NEITHER
THEREMIN S
THEREOF
THEREON
THERES
ETHERS
THREES
THERETO
THERIAC AS
THERIACA LS
THERIACS
CHARIEST
THERIAN S
HAIRNET
INEARTH
THERIANS
HAIRNETS
INEARTHS
THERM ES
THERMAE
THERMAL S
THERMALS
THERME LS
THERMEL S
THERMELS
THERMES
THERMIC
THERMION S
THERMIT ES
THERMITE S
THERMITS
THERMOS
MOTHERS
SMOTHER
THERMS
THEROID
THEROPOD S
THESAURI
THESE S
SHEET
THESES
SHEETS
THESIS
HEISTS
SHIEST
THESP S
THESPIAN S
THESPS
THETA S

THETAS
THETIC
THETICAL
ATHLETIC
THEURGIC
THEURGY
THEW SY
WHET
THEWIER
THEWIEST
THEWLESS
THEWS
WHETS
THEWY
THEY
HYTE
THIAMIN ES
THIAMINE S
THIAMINS
HISTAMIN
ISTHMIAN
THIAZIDE S
THIAZIN ES
THIAZINE S
THIAZINS
THIAZOL ES
THIAZOLE S
THIAZOLS
THICK S
THICKEN S
KITCHEN
THICKENS
KITCHENS
THICKER
THICKEST
THICKETS
THICKSET
THICKET SY
THICKETS
THICKEST
THICKSET
THICKETY
THICKISH
THICKLY
THICKS
KITSCH
SCHTIK
SHTICK
THICKSET S
THICKEST
THICKETS
THIEF
THIEVE DS
THIEVED
THIEVERY
THIEVES
THIEVING
THIEVISH
THIGH S
HIGHT
THIGHED
HIGHTED
THIGHS
HIGHTS
THILL S
THILLS
THIMBLE S
THIMBLES
THIN EGKS
HINT
THINCLAD S
THINDOWN S
THINE
THEIN
THING S
NIGHT
THINGS
NIGHTS
THINK S
THINKER S
RETHINK
THINKERS
RETHINKS
THINKING S
THINKS
THINLY
THINNED
THINNER S
THINNERS
THINNESS

THINNEST
THINNING
THINNISH
THINS
HINTS
THIO L
THIOL S
LITHO
THIOLIC
THIOLS
HOLIST
LITHOS
THIONATE S
THIONIC
THIONIN ES
E THIONINE S
THIONINS
THIONYL S
THIONYLS
TONISHLY
THIOPHEN ES
THIOTEPA S
THIOUREA S
THIR DL
THIRAM S
THAIRM
THIRAMS
THAIRMS
THIRD S
THIRDLY
THIRDS
THIRL S
THIRLAGE S
LITHARGE
THIRLED
THIRLING
THIRLS
A THIRST SY
THIRSTED
THIRSTER S
THIRSTS
THIRSTY
THIRTEEN S
THIRTIES
THIRTY
THIS
HIST HITS
SITH
THISAWAY
THISTLE S
LITHEST
THISTLES
THISTLY
THITHER
THO U
HOT
THOLE DS
HELOT HOTEL
THOLED
THOLEPIN S
THOLES
HELOTS
HOSTEL
HOTELS
THOLING
THOLOI
OOLITH
THOLOS
THONG S
THONGED
THONGS
THORACAL
THORACES
THORACIC
TROCHAIC
THORAX
THORAXES
OXHEARTS
THORIA S
THORIAS
AIRSHOT
SHORTIA
THORIC
RHOTIC
THORITE S
THORITES
THEORIST
THORIUM S

THORIUMS
HUMORIST
THORN SY
NORTH
THORNED
THRONED
THORNIER
THORNILY
THORNING
NORTHING
THRONING
THORNS
NORTHS
THORNY
RHYTON
THORO N
ORTHO
THORON S
THORONS
THOROUGH
THORP ES
THORPE S
POTHER
THORPES
POTHERS
STROPHE
THORPS
THOSE
ETHOS SHOTE
THOU S
THOUED
THOUGH T
THOUGHT S
THOUGHTS
THOUING
THOUS
SHOUT SOUTH
THOUSAND S
HANDOUTS
THOWLESS
THRALDOM S
THRALL S
THRALLED
THRALLS
THRASH
THRASHED
THRASHER S
THRASHES
HARSHEST
THRAVE S
THRAVES
HARVEST
THRAW NS
WRATH
THRAWART
THRAWED
WRATHED
THRAWING
WRATHING
THRAWN
THRAWNLY
THRAWS
SWARTH
WRATHS
THREAD SY
DEARTH
HATRED
THREADED
THREADER S
RETHREAD
THREADS
DEARTHS
HARDEST
HARDSET
HATREDS
TRASHED
THREADY
HYDRATE
THREAP S
TEPHRA
TERAPH
THREAPED
PREDEATH
THREAPER S
THREAPS
TEPHRAS
THREAT S
HATTER
THREATED
THREATEN S

THREATS
HATTERS
SHATTER
THREE PS
ETHER THERE
THREEP S
THREEPED
THREEPS
THREES
ETHERS
THERES
THRENODE S
DETHRONE
THRENODY
THRESH
THRESHED
THRESHER S
THRESHES
THREW
THRICE
CITHER
THRIFT SY
THRIFTS
THRIFTY
THRILL S
THRILLED
THRILLER S
THRILLS
THRIP S
THRIPS
THRIVE DNRS
THRIVED
THRIVEN
THRIVER S
THRIVERS
THRIVES
THRIVING
THRO BEW
THROAT SY
THROATED
THROATS
THROATY
THROB S
BROTH
THROBBED
THROBBER S
THROBS
BORSHT
BROTHS
THROE S
OTHER
THROES
HORSTE
OTHERS
RESHOT
THROMBI N
THROMBIN S
THROMBUS
THRONE DS
HORNET
NOTHER
THRONED
THORNED
THRONES
HORNETS
SHORTEN
THRONG S
THRONGED
THRONGS
THRONING
NORTHING
THORNING
THROSTLE S
THROTTLE DR S
THROUGH
THROVE
THROW NS
ROWTH WHORT
WORTH WROTH
THROWER S
THROWERS
THROWING
INGROWTH
WORTHING
THROWN

THROWS
ROWTHS
WHORTS
WORTHS
THRU M
HURT RUTH
THRUM S
THRUMMED
THRUMMER S
THRUMMY
THRUMS
THRUPUT S
THRUPUTS
UPTHRUST
THRUSH
THRUSHES
THRUST S
TRUTHS
THRUSTED
THRUSTER S
THRUSTOR S
THRUSTS
THRUWAY S
THRUWAYS
THUD S
THUDDED
THUDDING
THUDS
THUG S
THUGGEE S
THUGGEES
THUGGERY
THUGGISH
THUGS
THUJA S
THUJAS
THULIA S
THULIAS
HALITUS
THULIUM S
THULIUMS
THUMB S
THUMBED
THUMBING
THUMBKIN S
THUMBNUT S
THUMBS
THUMP S
THUMPED
THUMPER S
THUMPERS
THUMPING
THUMPS
THUNDER SY
THUNDERS
THUNDERY
THUNK S
THUNKED
THUNKING
THUNKS
THURIBLE S
THURIFER S
THURL S
THURLS
THUS
HUTS SHUT
TUSH
THUSLY
THUYA S
THUYAS
THWACK S
THWACKED
THWACKER S
THWACKS
A THWART S
THWARTED
THWARTER S
THWARTLY
THWARTS
THY
THYME SY
THYMES
THYMEY
THYMI C
THYMIC
MYTHIC

THYMIER
MYTHIER
THYMIEST
MYTHIEST
THYMINE S
THYMINES
THYMOL S
THYMOLS
THYMOSIN S
THYMUS
THYMUSES
THYMY
MYTHY
THYREOID
THYROID S
THYROIDS
THYRSOID
THYROXIN ES
THYRSE S
THYRSES
SHYSTER
THYRSI
SHIRTY
YIRTHS
THYRSOID
THYROIDS
THYRSUS
THYSELF
TI CELNPST
IT
TIARA S
ATRIA RAITA
RIATA
TIARAED
AIRDATE
RADIATE
TIARAS
ARISTA
RAITAS
RIATAS
TARSIA
TIBIA ELS
TIBIAE
S TIBIAL
TIBIAS
EO TIC KS
TICAL S
TICALS
TICCED
TICCING
S TICK S
S TICKED
DETICK
S TICKER S
S TICKERS
RICKETS
STICKER
TICKET S
TICKETED
TICKETS
S TICKING S
TICKINGS
STICKING
S TICKLE DRS
S TICKLED
S TICKLER S
TRICKLE
S TICKLERS
STICKLER
STRICKLE
TRICKLES
S TICKLES
STICKLE
S TICKLING
TICKLISH
S TICKS
STICK
S TICKSEED S
TICKTACK S
TICKTOCK S
TICS
CIST
TICTAC S
TACTIC
TICTACS
TACTICS
TICTOC S
TICTOCS
TIDAL
TIDALLY
TIDBIT S
TIDBITS
TIDDLER S
TIDDLERS
TIDDLY
TIDE DS
DIET DITE
EDIT TIED
TIDED
TIDELAND S
TIDELESS
TIDELIKE
TIDEMARK S
TIDERIP S
RIPTIDE
TIDERIPS
RIPTIDES
SPIRITED
TIDES
DEIST DIETS
DITES EDITS
SITED STIED
TIDEWAY S
TIDEWAYS
TIDIED
TIDIER S
TIDIERS
DIRTIES
DITSIER
TIDIES T
TEIIDS
TIDIEST
DITTIES
TIDILY
TIDINESS
INSISTED
TIDING S
TIDINGS
TIDY
TIDYING
DIGNITY
TIDYTIPS
TIE DRS
TIEBACK S
TIEBACKS
TIEBREAK S
TIECLASP S
SEPTICAL
S TIED
DIET DITE
EDIT TIDE
TIEING
IGNITE
TIELESS
LISTEES
TELESIS
TIEPIN S
PINITE
TIEPINS
PINIEST
PINITES
TIER S
RITE TIRE
TIERCE DLS
CERITE
RECITE
TIERCED
RECITED
TIERCEL S
RETICLE
TIERCELS
RETICLES
SCLERITE
TRISCELE
TIERCES
CERITES
RECITES
TIERED
DIETER
REEDIT
RETIED
TIERING
IGNITER
TIERS
RESIT RITES
TIRES TRIES
S TIES
SITE
S TIFF S
TIFFANY
S TIFFED
TIFFIN GS
TIFFINED
S TIFFING
TIFFINS
S TIFFS
STIFF
TIGER S
TIGEREYE S
TIGERISH
RIGHTIES
TIGERS
TIGHT S
TIGHTEN S
TIGHTENS
TIGHTER
TIGHTEST
TIGHTLY
TIGHTS
TIGHTWAD S
TIGLON S
TOLING
TIGLONS
TIGON S
INGOT
TIGONS
INGOTS
STINGO
TIGRESS
TIGRISH
TIKE S
KITE
TIKES
KITES SKITE
TIKI S
TIKIS
TIKKA S
TIKKAS
TIL ELST
LIT
TILAK S
TILAKS
TILAPIA S
TILAPIAS
TILBURY
TILDE S
TILED
TILDES
DELIST
IDLEST
LISTED
SILTED
SU TILE DRS
LITE
TILED
TILDE
TILEFISH
TILELIKE
TILER S
LITER LITRE
RELIT
TILERS
LISTER
LITERS
LITRES
RELIST
S TILES
ISLET ISTLE
STILE
TILING S
TILINGS
LISTING
SILTING
S TILL S
LILT
TILLABLE
TILLAGE S
TILLAGES
LEGALIST
S TILLED
LILTED
S TILLER S
RILLET
TILLERED
TILLERS
RILLETS
STILLER
TRELLIS
S TILLING
LILTING
TILLITE S
TILLITES
S TILLS
LILTS STILL
TILS
LIST LITS
SILT SLIT
AS TILT HS
TILTABLE
S TILTED
TITLED
TILTER S
LITTER
TILTERS
LITTERS
SLITTER
TILTH S
TILTHS
S TILTING
TITLING
S TILTS
STILT
TILTYARD S
TIMARAU S
TIMARAUS
TIMBAL ES
TIMBALE S
BIMETAL
LIMBATE
TIMBALES
BALMIEST
BIMETALS
LAMBIEST
TIMBALS
TIMBER SY
TIMBRE
TIMBERED
TIMBERS
TIMBRES
TIMBERY
TIMBRAL
TIMBRE LS
TIMBER
TIMBREL S
TIMBRELS
TIMBRES
TIMBERS
S TIME DRS
EMIT ITEM
MITE
TIMECARD S
TIMED
DEMIT
TIMELESS
TIMELIER
TIMELINE S
ILMENITE
MELINITE
TIMELY
TIMEOUS
TIMEOUT S
TIMEOUTS
TITMOUSE
TIMER S
MERIT MITER
MITRE REMIT
TIMERS
MERITS
MISTER
MITERS
MITRES
REMITS
SMITER
S TIMES
EMITS ITEMS
METIS MITES
SMITE STIME
TIMEWORK S
TIMEWORN
TIMID
TIMIDER
TIMIDEST
TIMIDITY
TIMIDLY
TIMING S
TIMINGS
MISTING
SMITING
TIMOLOL S
TIMOLOLS
TIMOROUS
TIMOTHY
TIMPANA
TIMPANI
IMPAINT
TIMPANO
MAINTOP
PTOMAIN
TAMPION
TIMPANUM S
TIN EGSTY
NIT
TINAMOU S
MANITOU
TINAMOUS
MANITOUS
TINCAL S
CATLIN
TINCALS
CATLINS
TINCT S
TINCTED
TINCTING
TINCTS
TINCTURE DS
INTERCUT
TINDER SY
RIDENT
TRINED
TINDERS
TINDERY
TINE ADS
NITE
TINEA LS
ENTIA TENIA
TINEAL
ENTAIL
TENAIL
TINEAS
SEITAN
TENIAS
TISANE
TINED
TEIND
TINEID S
INDITE
TINEIDS
INDITES
TINES
INSET NEIST
NITES SENTI
STEIN
TINFOIL S
TINFOILS
TINFUL S
TINFULS
S TING ES
TINGE DS
TINGED
NIDGET
TINGEING
TINGES
INGEST
SIGNET
S TINGING
A TINGLE DRS
GENTIL
TINGLED
GLINTED
TINGLER S
RINGLET
TINGLERS
RINGLETS
STERLING
TINGLES
GLISTEN
SINGLET
SNIGLET
TINGLIER
GLINTIER
RETILING
TINGLING
GLINTING
TINGLY
GLINTY
S TINGS
STING
TINHORN S
TINHORNS
TINIER
TINIEST
TINILY
TININESS
TINING
S TINKER S
REKNIT
TINKERED
TINKERER S
S TINKERS
REKNITS
STINKER
TINKLE DRS
TINKLED
TINKLER S
TINKLERS
TINKLES
LENTISK
TINKLIER
TINKLING S
TINKLY
TINLIKE
TINMAN
TINMEN
TINNED
DENTIN
INDENT
INTEND
TINNER S
INTERN
TINNERS
INTERNS
TINNIER
TINNIEST
TINNILY
TINNING
TINNITUS
TINNY
TINPLATE S
TINPOT
TINS
NITS SNIT
TINSEL S
ELINTS
ENLIST
INLETS
LISTEN
SILENT
TINSELED
ENLISTED
LISTENED
TINSELLY
SILENTLY
TINSELS
ENLISTS
LISTENS
SILENTS
TINSMITH S
TINSNIPS
TINSTONE S
TONTINES
S TINT S
S TINTED
S TINTER S
RETINT
S TINTERS
RETINTS
STINTER
S TINTING S
TINTINGS
STINTING
TINTLESS
S TINTS
STINT
TINTYPE S
TINTYPES
TINWARE S
TAWNIER
TINWARES
TINWORK S
TINWORKS
TINY
TYIN
TIP IS
PIT
TIPCART S
TIPCARTS
TIPCAT S
TIPCATS
TIPI S
TIPIS
TIPLESS
STIPELS
TIPOFF S
TIPOFFS
TIPPABLE
TIPPED
PEPTID
TIPPER S
TIPPERS
TIPPET S
TIPPETS
TIPPIER
TIPPIEST
TIPPING
S TIPPLE DRS
S TIPPLED
S TIPPLER S
RIPPLET
S TIPPLERS
PRESPLIT
RIPPLETS
STIPPLER
S TIPPLES
STIPPLE
S TIPPLING
TIPPY
TIPPYTOE DS
TIPS Y
PITS SPIT
TIPSHEET S
EPITHETS
TIPSIER
PITIERS
TIPSIEST
PIETISTS
STIPITES
TIPSILY
TIPSTAFF S
TIPSTER S
SPITTER
TIPSTERS
SPITTERS
TIPSTOCK S
TIPSY
TIPTOE DS
TIPTOED
TIPTOES
POTTIES
TIPTOP S
TIPTOPS
TIRADE S
AIRTED
TIRADES
ARIDEST
ASTRIDE
DIASTER
DISRATE
STAIDER
TARDIES
TIRAMISU S
TIRE DS
RITE TIER
TIRED
TRIED
TIREDER
RETIRED
RETRIED
TIREDEST
TIREDLY
TIRELESS
LEISTERS
TIRES
RESIT RITES
TIERS TRIES
TIRESOME
TIRING
TIRL S
TIRLED
TIRLING
TIRLS
TIRO S
RIOT ROTI
TORI TRIO
TIROS
RIOTS ROTIS
TORSI TRIOS
TROIS
TIRRIVEE S
TIS
ITS SIT
TISANE S
SEITAN
TENIAS
TINEAS

TISANES
ENTASIS
NASTIES
SEITANS
SESTINA
TANSIES
TISSUAL
TISSUE DSY
SUITES
TISSUED
STUDIES
TISSUES
SITUSES
TISSUEY
TISSUING
SUITINGS
TISSULAR
TIT IS
TITAN S
TAINT
TITANATE S
TITANESS
ANTSIEST
INSTATES
NASTIEST
SATINETS
TITANIA S
TITANIAS
TITANIC
TITANISM S
TITANITE S
TITANIUM S
TITANOUS
TITANS
STATIN
TAINTS
TANIST
TITBIT S
TITBITS
TITER S
TETRI TITRE
TRITE
TITERS
SITTER
TETRIS
TITRES
TRISTE
TITFER S
FITTER
TITFERS
FITTERS
TITHABLE
HITTABLE
TITHE DRS
TITHED
TITHER S
HITTER
TITHERS
HITTERS
TITHES
THEIST
TITHING S
HITTING
TITHINGS
TITHONIA S
TITI S
TITIAN S
TITIANS
O **TITIS**
TITIVATE DS
TITLARK S
TITLARKS
TITLE DS
TITLED
TILTED
TITLES
TITLING
TILTING
TITLIST S
TITLISTS
TITMAN
MATTIN
TITMEN
MITTEN
TITMICE
TITMOUSE
TIMEOUTS
TITRABLE
TITRANT S
TITRANTS

TITRATE DS
ATTRITE
TATTIER
TITRATED
ATTRITED
TITRATES
ATTRITES
RATTIEST
TARTIEST
TRISTATE
TITRATOR S
TITRE S
TETRI TITER
TRITE
TITRES
SITTER
TETRIS
TITERS
TRISTE
TITS
TITTER S
TITTERED
TITTERER S
TITTERS
STRETTI
TRITEST
TITTIE S
TITTIES
TITTLE S
TITTLES
TITTUP S
TITTUPED
TITTUPPY
TITTUPS
TITTY
TITUBANT
TITULAR SY
TITULARS
ALTRUIST
ULTRAIST
TITULARY
TIVY
TIZZIES
TIZZY
TMESES
TMESIS
MISSET
SMITES
STIMES
TO DEGMNOPR TWY
TOAD SY
DATO DOAT
TOADFISH
TOADFLAX
TOADIED
IODATED
TOADIES
IODATES
TOADISH
TOADLESS
TOADLIKE
TOADS
DATOS DOATS
TOADY
TODAY
TOADYING
TOADYISH
TOADYISM S
TOAST SY
STOAT
TOASTED
TOASTER S
ROTATES
TOASTERS
TOASTIER
TOASTING
TOASTS
STOATS
TOASTY
TOBACCO S
TOBACCOS
TOBIES
BOITES
SOBEIT
TOBOGGAN S
TOBY
S **TOCCATA** S

S **TOCCATAS**
STACCATO
STOCCATA
TOCCATE
TOCHER S
HECTOR
ROCHET
ROTCHE
TROCHE
TOCHERED
HECTORED
TOCHERS
HECTORS
ROCHETS
ROTCHES
TORCHES
TROCHES
TOCOLOGY
TOCSIN S
TONICS
TOCSINS
CONSIST
TOD SY
DOT
TODAY S
TOADY
TODAYS
TODDIES
TODDLE DRS
TODDLED
TODDLER S
TODDLERS
TODDLES
TODDLING
TODDY
TODIES
TODS
DOST DOTS
TODY
DOTY
TOE ADS
TOEA S
TOEAS
STOAE
TOECAP S
CAPOTE
TOECAPS
CAPOTES
TOED
DOTE
TOEHOLD S
TOEHOLDS
TOOLSHED
TOEING
TOELESS
TOELIKE
TOENAIL S
ELATION
TOENAILS
ELATIONS
INSOLATE
TOEPIECE S
TOEPLATE S
TOES
TOESHOE S
TOESHOES
TOFF SY
TOFFEE S
TOFFEES
TOFFIES
TOFFS
TOFFY
TOFT S
TOFTS
TOFU S
TOFUS
TOFUTTI S
TOFUTTIS
TOG AS
GOT
TOGA ES
GOAT
TOGAE D
TOGAED
DOTAGE
TOGAS
GOATS
TOGATE D
TOGATED
TOGETHER

TOGGED
TOGGERY
TOGGING
TOGGLE DRS
GOGLET
TOGGLED
TOGGLER S
TOGGLERS
TOGGLES
GOGLETS
LOGGETS
TOGGLING
TOGS
TOGUE S
TOGUES
TOIL ES
LOTI
E **TOILE** DRST
TELOI
TOILED
TOILER S
LOITER
TOILERS
ESTRIOL
LOITERS
E **TOILES**
TOILET S
TOILETED
TOILETRY
TOILETS
LITOTES
TOILETTE S
TOILFUL
TOILING
TOILS
TOILSOME
TOILWORN
TOIT S
TOITED
TOITING
TOITS
TOKAMAK S
TOKAMAKS
TOKAY S
TOKAYS
S **TOKE** DNRS
KETO
S **TOKED**
TOKEN S
TOKENED
TOKENING
TOKENISM S
TOKENS
S **TOKER** S
TROKE
S **TOKERS**
STOKER
STROKE
TROKES
S **TOKES**
STOKE
S **TOKING**
TOKOLOGY
TOKOMAK S
TOKOMAKS
TOKONOMA S
TOLA NRS
ALTO LOTA
TOLAN ES
NOTAL TALON
TONAL
TOLANE S
ETALON
TOLANES
ETALONS
TOLANS
SANTOL
STANOL
TALONS
TOLAR S
TOLARJEV
TOLARS
TOLAS
ALTOS LOTAS
TOLBOOTH S
TOLD
DOLT
S **TOLE** DS
S **TOLED** O

TOLEDO S
LOOTED
TOOLED
TOLEDOS
STOOLED
TOLERANT
TOLERATE DS
S **TOLES**
STOLE TELOS
TOLIDIN ES
TOLIDINE S
TOLIDINS
TOLING
TIGLON
A **TOLL** S
TOLLAGE S
TOLLAGES
TOLLBAR S
TOLLBARS
TOLLED
TOLLER S
TOLLERS
TOLLGATE S
TOLLING
TOLLMAN
TOLLMEN
A **TOLLS**
TOLLWAY S
TALLOWY
TOLLWAYS
TOLU S
LOUT
TOLUATE S
TOLUATES
TOLUENE S
TOLUENES
TOLUIC
TOLUID ES
TOLUIDE S
TOLUIDES
SOLITUDE
TOLUIDIN ES
DILUTION
TOLUIDS
TOLUOL ES
TOLUOLE S
TOLUOLES
TOLUOLS
TOLUS
LOTUS LOUTS
TOLUYL S
TOLUYLS
TOLYL S
TOLYLS
A **TOM** BES
MOT
TOMAHAWK S
TOMALLEY S
TOMAN S
TOMANS
TOMATO
TOMATOES
OSTOMATE
TOMATOEY
TOMB S
TOMBAC KS
COMBAT
TOMBACK S
TOMBACKS
BACKMOST
TOMBACS
COMBATS
TOMBAK S
TOMBAKS
TOMBAL
TOMBED
TOMBING
TOMBLESS
TOMBLIKE
TOMBOLA S
TOMBOLAS
TOMBOLO S
TOMBOLOS
TOMBOY S
TOMBOYS
TOMBS
TOMCAT S
TOMCATS

TOMCOD S
TOMCODS
TOME S
MOTE
TOMENTA
TOMENTUM
TOMES
MOSTE MOTES
SMOTE
TOMFOOL S
TOMFOOLS
TOMMIES
TOMMY
TOMMYROT S
TOMOGRAM S
TOMORROW S
MOORWORT
ROOTWORM
WORMROOT
TOMPION S
TOMPIONS
A **TOMS**
MOST MOTS
TOMTIT S
TOMTITS
TON EGSY
NOT
A **TONAL**
NOTAL TALON
TOLAN
A **TONALITY**
A **TONALLY**
TONDI
TONDO S
TONDOS
AS **TONE** DRSY
NOTE
TONEARM S
TONEARMS
MONSTERA
ONSTREAM
AS **TONED**
NOTED
TONELESS
NOTELESS
TONEME S
TONEMES
TONEMIC
CENTIMO
AS **TONER** S
NOTER TENOR
TRONE
AS **TONERS**
NESTOR
NOTERS
STONER
TENORS
TENSOR
TRONES
AS **TONES**
NOTES ONSET
SETON STENO
STONE
TONETIC S
TONETICS
STENOTIC
TONETTE S
TONETTES
S **TONEY**
TONG AS
TONGA S
TANGO
TONGAS
TANGOS
TONGED
TONGER S
TONGERS
TONGING
TONGMAN
TONGMEN
TONGS
TONGUE DS
TONGUED
TONGUES
TONGUING S
A **TONIC** S
ONTIC
A **TONICITY**
A **TONICS**
TOCSIN

S **TONIER**
NORITE
ORIENT
S **TONIEST**
TONIGHT S
HOTTING
TONIGHTS
SHOTTING
AS **TONING**
NOTING
S **TONISH**
TONISHLY
THIONYLS
TONLET S
TONLETS
TONNAGE S
NEGATON
TONNAGES
NEGATONS
TONNE RS
NONET TENON
TONNEAU SX
TONNEAUS
TONNEAUX
TONNER S
TONNERS
TONNES
NONETS
SONNET
TENONS
TONNISH
TONS
SNOT
TONSIL S
TONSILAR
TONSILS
TONSURE DS
TENOURS
TONSURED
ROUNDEST
UNSORTED
TONSURES
TONTINE S
TONTINES
TINSTONE
TONUS
SNOUT
TONUSES
AS **TONY**
TOO KLMNT
OOT
S **TOOK**
KOTO
S **TOOL** S
LOOT
TOOLBAR S
TOOLBARS
BARSTOOL
TOOLBOX
S **TOOLED**
LOOTED
TOLEDO
TOOLER S
LOOTER
RETOOL
ROOTLE
TOOLERS
LOOTERS
RETOOLS
ROOTLES
TOOLHEAD S
S **TOOLING** S
LOOTING
TOOLINGS
STOOLING
TOOLLESS
TOOLROOM S
S **TOOLS**
LOOTS LOTOS
SOTOL STOOL
TOOLSHED S
TOEHOLDS
TOOM
MOOT
TOON S
ONTO
TOONIE S
TOONIES
ISOTONE
TOONS
SNOOT
TOOT HS
OTTO

TOOTED
TOOTER S
TOOTERS
TOOTH SY
TOOTHED
TOOTHIER
TOOTHILY
TOOTHING
TOOTHS
TOOTHY
TOOTING
TOOTLE DRS
TOOTLED
TOOTLER S
ROOTLET
TOOTLERS
ROOTLETS
TOOTLES
TOOTLING
TOOTS Y
OTTOS
TOOTSES
TOOTSIE S
TOOTSIES
SOOTIEST
TOOTSY
AS **TOP** EHIOS
OPT
POT
TOPAZ
TOPAZES
TOPAZINE
TOPCOAT S
TOPCOATS
TOPCROSS
S **TOPE** DERS
POET
S **TOPED**
DEPOT OPTED
TOPEE S
TOPEES
S **TOPER** S
REPOT TROPE
S **TOPERS**
POSTER
PRESTO
REPOTS
RESPOT
STOPER
TROPES
S **TOPES**
ESTOP PESTO
POETS STOPE
TOPFUL L
POTFUL
TOPFULL
TOPH EIS
PHOT
TOPHE S
TOPHES
TOPHI
TOPHS
PHOTS
TOPHUS
UPSHOT
TOPI CS
TOPIARY
A **TOPIC** S
OPTIC PICOT
TOPICAL
CAPITOL
COALPIT
OPTICAL
TOPICS
OPTICS
PICOTS
S **TOPING**
OPTING
TOPIS
POSIT
TOPKICK S
TOPKICKS
TOPKNOT S
TOPKNOTS
TOPLESS
TOPLINE S
POTLINE
TOPLINES
POTLINES
TOPLOFTY

TOPMAST S
TOPMASTS
TOPMOST
TOPNOTCH
TOPO IS
TOPOI
TOPOLOGY
TOPONYM SY
TOPONYMS
TOPONYMY
TOPOS
STOOP
TOPOTYPE S
S **TOPPED**
S **TOPPER** S
S **TOPPERS**
STOPPER
S **TOPPING** S
TOPPINGS
STOPPING
S **TOPPLE** DS
S **TOPPLED**
S **TOPPLES**
STOPPLE
S **TOPPLING**
S **TOPS**
OPTS POST
POTS SPOT
STOP
TOPSAIL S
APOSTIL
TOPSAILS
APOSTILS
TOPSIDE RS
DEPOSIT
DOPIEST
PODITES
POSITED
SOPITED
TOPSIDER S
DIOPTERS
DIOPTRES
PERIDOTS
PORTSIDE
PROTEIDS
RIPOSTED
TOPSIDES
DEPOSITS
TOPSOIL S
POLOIST
TOPSOILS
POLOISTS
TOPSPIN S
TOPSPINS
TOPSTONE S
POTSTONE
TOPWORK S
TOPWORKS
TOQUE ST
QUOTE
TOQUES
QUOTES
TOQUET S
TOQUETS
TOR ACEINOR
ORT STY
ROT
TORA HS
RATO ROTA
TARO
TORAH S
TORAHS
TORAS
RATOS ROAST
ROTAS SORTA
TAROS
TORC HS
TORCH Y
ROTCH
TORCHED
TORCHERE S
TORCHES
HECTORS
ROCHETS
ROTCHES
TOCHERS
TROCHES
TORCHIER ES
RHETORIC
TORCHING
TORCHON S

TORCHONS
TORCHY
TORCS
S **TORE** S
ROTE
TOREADOR S
TORERO S
ROOTER
TOREROS
ROOSTER
ROOTERS
S **TORES**
ROSET ROTES
STORE TORSE
TOREUTIC S
TORI CI
RIOT ROTI
TIRO TRIO
TORIC S
TORICS
S **TORIES**
SORTIE
TRIOSE
TORII
TORMENT S
TORMENTS
TORN
TORNADIC
TORNADO S
DONATOR
ODORANT
TANDOOR
TORNADOS
DONATORS
ODORANTS
TANDOORS
TORNILLO S
TORO ST
ROOT ROTO
TOROID S
TOROIDAL
IDOLATOR
TOROIDS
DISROOT
TOROS E
ROOST ROOTS
ROTOS TORSO
TOROSE
TOROSITY
TOROT H
TOROTH
TOROUS
TORPEDO S
TROOPED
TORPEDOS
DOORSTEP
TORPID S
TRIPOD
TORPIDLY
TORPIDS
DISPORT
TRIPODS
TORPOR S
TORPORS
TORQUATE
TORQUE DRS
QUOTER
ROQUET
TORQUED
TORQUER S
TORQUERS
TORQUES
QUESTOR
QUOTERS
ROQUETS
TORQUING
TORR S
TORREFY
TORRENT S
TORRENTS
TORRID
TORRIDER
TORRIDLY
TORRIFY
TORRS
TORS EIKO
ORTS ROTS
SORT
TORSADE S
ROASTED

TORSADES
ASSORTED
TORSE S
ROSET ROTES
STORE TORES
TORSES
ROSETS
SOREST
STORES
TOSSER
TSORES
TORSI
RIOTS ROTIS
TIROS TRIOS
TROIS
TORSION S
NITROSO
TORSIONS
TORSK S
SKORT STORK
TORSKS
SKORTS
STORKS
TORSO S
ROOST ROOTS
ROTOS TOROS
TORSOS
ROOSTS
TORT AES
TROT
TORTA S
OTTAR TAROT
TORTAS
OTTARS
STATOR
TAROTS
TORTE NS
OTTER ROTTE
TOTER
TORTEN
ROTTEN
TORTES
OTTERS
ROTTES
TOTERS
TORTILE
TRIOLET
TORTILLA S
LITTORAL
TORTIOUS
TORTOISE S
ROOTIEST
TORTONI S
TORTONIS
TORTRIX
TORTS
TROTS
TORTUOUS
TORTURE DRS
TORTURED
TORTURER S
TORTURES
TORULA ES
TORULAE
TORULAS
TORUS
ROUST ROUTS
STOUR TOURS
S **TORY**
RYOT TROY
TYRO
TOSH
HOST HOTS
SHOT SOTH
TOSHES
SHOTES
S **TOSS**
SOTS
TOSSED
TOSSER S
ROSETS
SOREST
STORES
TORSES
TSORES
TOSSERS
TOSSES
TOSSING
STINGOS
TOSSPOT S
TOSSPOTS

TOSSUP S
SPOUTS
STOUPS
UPTOSS
TOSSUPS
TOST
STOT TOTS
TOSTADA S
TOSTADAS
TOSTADO S
TOSTADOS
S **TOT** ES
TOTABLE
TOTAL S
TOTALED
TOTALING
TOTALISE DS
TOTALISM S
TOTALIST S
TOTALITY
TOTALIZE DR S
TOTALLED
ALLOTTED
TOTALLY
TOTALS
TOTE DMRS
TOTEABLE
TOTED
TOTEM S
MOTET MOTTE
TOTEMIC
TOTEMISM S
TOTEMIST S
TOTEMITE S
TOTEMS
MOTETS
MOTTES
TOTER S
OTTER ROTTE
TORTE
TOTERS
OTTERS
ROTTES
TORTES
TOTES
TOTHER
HOTTER
TOTING
S **TOTS**
STOT TOST
S **TOTTED**
TOTTER SY
TOTTERED
TOTTERER S
TOTTERS
STRETTO
TOTTERY
S **TOTTING**
TOUCAN S
TOUCANS
CONATUS
TOUCH EY
COUTH
TOUCHE DRS
TOUCHED
TOUCHER S
COUTHER
RETOUCH
TOUCHERS
SCOUTHER
TOUCHES
TOUCHIER
COUTHIER
TOUCHILY
TOUCHING
TOUCHPAD S
TOUCHUP S
TOUCHUPS
TOUCHY
TOUGH SY
OUGHT
TOUGHED
OUGHTED
TOUGHEN S
TOUGHENS
TOUGHER
TOUGHEST
TOUGHIE S

TOUGHIES
TOUGHING
OUGHTING
TOUGHISH
TOUGHLY
TOUGHS
OUGHTS
SOUGHT
TOUGHY
TOUPEE S
TOUPEES
S **TOUR** S
ROUT
TOURACO S
TOURACOS
TOURED
DETOUR
REDOUT
ROUTED
TOURER S
ROUTER
TOURERS
ROUSTER
ROUTERS
TROUSER
TOURING S
OUTGRIN
OUTRING
ROUTING
TOURINGS
OUTGRINS
OUTRINGS
ROUSTING
TOURISM S
TOURISMS
TOURIST ASY
TOURISTA S
TOURISTS
TOURISTY
TOURNEY S
TOURNEYS
S **TOURS**
ROUST ROUTS
STOUR TORUS
TOUSE DS
TOUSED
OUSTED
TOUSES
SETOUS
TOUSING
OUSTING
OUTINGS
OUTSING
TOUSLE DS
SOLUTE
TOUSLED
LOUDEST
TOUSLES
LOTUSES
SOLUTES
TOUSLING
S **TOUT** S
TOUTED
S **TOUTER** S
TOUTERS
OUTSERT
STOUTER
TOUTING
S **TOUTS**
STOUT
TOUZLE DS
TOUZLED
TOUZLES
TOUZLING
TOVARICH
TOVARISH
S **TOW** NSY
TWO
WOT
S **TOWABLE**
TEABOWL
S **TOWAGE** S
S **TOWAGES**
STOWAGE
TOWARD S
TOWARDLY
TOWARDS
S **TOWAWAY** S
S **TOWAWAYS**
STOWAWAY
TOWBOAT S

TOWBOATS
S **TOWED**
TOWEL S
OWLET
TOWELED
TOWELING S
TOWELLED
TOWELS
LOWEST
OWLETS
TOWER SY
WROTE
TOWERED
TOWERIER
TOWERING
TOWERS
WORSET
TOWERY
TOWHEAD S
TOWHEADS
TOWHEE S
TOWHEES
TOWIE S
TOWIES
S **TOWING**
TOWLINE S
TOWLINES
TOWMOND S
TOWMONDS
TOWMONT S
TOWMONTS
TOWN SY
NOWT WONT
TOWNEE S
TOWNEES
TOWNFOLK
TOWNHOME S
HOMETOWN
TOWNIE S
TOWNIES
TOWNISH
TOWNLESS
TOWNLET S
TOWNLETS
TOWNS
NOWTS WONTS
TOWNSHIP S
TOWNSMAN
TOWNSMEN
TOWNWEAR
TOWNY
TOWPATH S
TOWPATHS
TOWPLANE S
TOWROPE S
TOWROPES
S **TOWS**
STOW SWOT
TWOS WOST
WOTS
TOWSACK S
TOWSACKS
TOWY
TOXAEMIA S
TOXAEMIC
TOXEMIA S
TOXEMIAS
TOXEMIC
TOXIC S
TOXICAL
TOXICANT S
TOXICITY
TOXICS
TOXIN ES
TOXINE S
TOXINES
TOXINS
TOXOID S
TOXOIDS
TOY OS
TOYED
TOYER S
TOYERS
OYSTER
STOREY
TOYING

TOYISH
TOYLESS
SYSTOLE
TOYLIKE
TOYO NS
TOYON S
TOYONS
SNOOTY
TOYOS
SOOTY
TOYS
TOYSHOP S
TOYSHOPS
TRABEATE D
TRACE DRS
CARET CARTE
CATER CRATE
REACT RECTA
TRACED
CARTED
CRATED
REDACT
TRACER SY
CARTER
CRATER
TRACERS
CARTERS
CRATERS
TRACERY
TRACES
CARETS
CARTES
CASTER
CATERS
CRATES
REACTS
RECAST
TRACHEA ELS
TRACHEAE
TRACHEAL
TRACHEAS
TRACHEID S
TRACHLE DS
TRACHLED
TRACHLES
TRACHOMA S
ACHROMAT
TRACHYTE S
CHATTERY
TRACING S
CARTING
CRATING
TRACINGS
SCARTING
TRACK S
TRACKAGE S
TRACKED
TRACKER S
RETRACK
TRACKERS
RETRACKS
TRACKING S
TRACKMAN
TRACKMEN
TRACKPAD S
TRACKS
TRACKWAY S
TRACT S
TRACTATE S
TRACTILE
TRACTION S
TRACTIVE
TRACTOR S
TRACTORS
TRACTS
TRAD E
DART DRAT
TRADABLE
TRADE DRS
DATER DERAT
RATED TARED
TREAD
TRADED
DARTED
TRADEOFF S
TRADER S
DARTER
RETARD
TARRED
TRADERS
DARTERS
RETARDS
STARRED
TRADES
DATERS
DERATS
STARED
TREADS
TRADING
DARTING
TRADITOR
TRADUCE DRS
CURATED
TRADUCED
TRADUCER S
TRADUCES
TRAFFIC S
TRAFFICS
TRAGEDY
GYRATED
TRAGI C
TRAGIC S
TRAGICAL
TRAGICS
GASTRIC
TRAGOPAN S
TRAGUS
TRAIK S
KRAIT
TRAIKED
TRAIKING
TRAIKS
KRAITS
TRAIL S
TRIAL
TRAILED
DILATER
REDTAIL
TRAILER S
RETRIAL
TRAILERS
RETRIALS
TRAILING
RINGTAIL
TRAILS
TRIALS
S TRAIN S
RIANT
S TRAINED
ANTIRED
DETRAIN
TRAINEE S
ARENITE
RETINAE
TRAINEES
ARENITES
ARSENITE
RESINATE
STEARINE
S TRAINER S
RETRAIN
TERRAIN
S TRAINERS
RESTRAIN
RETRAINS
STRAINER
TERRAINS
TRAINFUL S
S TRAINING S
TRAINMAN
TRAINMEN
S TRAINS
INSTAR
SANTIR
STRAIN
TRAINWAY S
TRAIPSE DS
PARTIES
PASTIER
PIASTER
PIASTRE
PIRATES
TRAIPSED
RAPIDEST
TRAIPSES
PASTRIES
PIASTERS
PIASTRES
RASPIEST
S TRAIT S
TRAITOR S
TRAITORS
S TRAITS
ARTIST
STRAIT
STRATI
TRAJECT S
TRAJECTS
TRAM PS
MART
TRAMCAR S
TRAMCARS
TRAMEL LS
ARMLET
TRAMELED
TRAMELL S
TRAMELLS
TRAMELS
ARMLETS
LAMSTER
TRAMLESS
LAMSTERS
TRAMLINE S
TERMINAL
TRAMMED
TRAMMEL S
TRAMMELS
TRAMMING
TRAMP SY
TRAMPED
TRAMPER S
TRAMPERS
TRAMPIER
IMPARTER
TRAMPING
TRAMPISH
TRAMPLE DRS
TEMPLAR
TRAMPLED
TRAMPLER S
TRAMPLES
TEMPLARS
TRAMPS
TRAMPY
TRAMROAD S
TRAMS
MARTS SMART
TRAMWAY S
TRAMWAYS
TRANCE DS
CANTER
CARNET
CENTRA
NECTAR
RECANT
TANREC
TRANCED
TRANCES
CANTERS
CARNETS
NECTARS
RECANTS
SCANTER
TANRECS
TRANCHE S
CHANTER
TRANCHES
CHANTERS
SNATCHER
STANCHER
TRANCING
TRANGAM S
TANGRAM
TRANGAMS
TANGRAMS
TRANK S
TRANKS
TRANNIES
ENTRAINS
TRANNY
TRANQ S
TRANQS
TRANQUIL
TRANS
RANTS TARNS
TRANSACT S
TRANSECT S
TRANSEPT S
PATTERNS
TRAPNEST
TRANSFER S
TRANSFIX T
TRANSHIP S
TRANSIT S
TRANSITS
TRANSMIT S
TANTRISM
TRANSOM S
MATRONS
TRANSOMS
TRANSUDE DS
DAUNTERS
UNTREADS
S TRAP ST
PART PRAT
RAPT TARP
TRAPAN S
PARTAN
TARPAN
TRAPANS
PARTANS
SPARTAN
TARPANS
TRAPBALL S
TRAPDOOR S
TRAPES
PASTER
PATERS
PRATES
REPAST
TAPERS
TRAPESED
PEDERAST
PREDATES
REPASTED
TRAPESES
TRAPEZE S
TRAPEZES
TRAPEZIA L
TRAPEZII
TRAPLIKE
TRAPLINE S
INTERLAP
TRIPLANE
TRAPNEST S
PATTERNS
TRANSEPT
TRAPPEAN
APPARENT
S TRAPPED
S TRAPPER S
S TRAPPERS
STRAPPER
S TRAPPING S
TRAPPOSE
TRAPPOUS
TRAPROCK S
S TRAPS
PARTS PRATS
SPRAT STRAP
TARPS
TRAPT
TRAPUNTO S
TRASH Y
HARTS TAHRS
TRASHED
DEARTHS
HARDEST
HARDSET
HATREDS
THREADS
TRASHER S
TRASHERS
TRASHES
RASHEST
TRASHIER
TRASHILY
TRASHING
TRASHMAN
TRASHMEN
TRASHY
S TRASS
STARS TSARS
S TRASSES
ASSERTS
TRAUCHLE DS
TRAUMA S
TRAUMAS
TRAUMATA
TRAVAIL S
TRAVAILS
TRAVE LS
AVERT
TRAVEL S
VARLET
TRAVELED
TRAVELER S
TRAVELOG S
TRAVELS
VARLETS
VESTRAL
TRAVERSE DR
AVERTERS S
TRAVES
AVERTS
STARVE
VASTER
TRAVESTY
TRAVOIS E
VIATORS
TRAVOISE S
VIATORES
VOTARIES
TRAWL S
TRAWLED
TRAWLER S
TRAWLERS
WARSTLER
TRAWLEY S
TRAWLEYS
TRAWLING
TRAWLNET S
TRAWLS
S TRAY S
ARTY
TRAYFUL S
TRAYFULS
S TRAYS
ARTSY SATYR
STRAY
TREACLE S
TREACLES
CLEAREST
TREACLY
TREAD S
DATER DERAT
RATED TARED
TRADE
TREADED
DERATED
REDATED
TREADER S
RETREAD
TREADERS
ARRESTED
RETREADS
SERRATED
TREADING
DERATING
GRADIENT
REDATING
TREADLE DRS
ALERTED
ALTERED
RELATED
TREADLED
TREADLER S
TREADLES S
DESALTER
RESLATED
TREADS
DATERS
DERATS
STARED
TRADES
TREASON S
ATONERS
SANTERO
SENATOR
TREASONS
ASSENTOR
SANTEROS
SENATORS
STARNOSE
TREASURE DR
AUSTERER S
TREASURY
TREAT SY
TATER TETRA
TREATED
TREATER S
RETREAT
TREATERS
RETREATS
TREATIES
ARIETTES
ITERATES
TEARIEST
TREATISE
TREATING
GNATTIER
TREATISE S
ARIETTES
ITERATES
TEARIEST
TREATIES
TREATS
STATER
TASTER
TATERS
TETRAS
TREATY
YATTER
TREBLE DS
BELTER
TREBLED
TREBLES
BELTERS
TREBLING
TREBLY
TRECENTO S
TREDDLE DS
TREDDLED
TREDDLES
TREE DNS
RETE
TREED
DETER
TREEING
INTEGER
TREELAWN S
TREELESS
TREELIKE
TREEN S
ENTER RENTE
TERNE
TREENAIL S
ELATERIN
ENTAILER
TREENS
ENTERS
NESTER
RENEST
RENTES
RESENT
TENSER
TERNES
TREES
ESTER REEST
RESET STEER
STERE TERSE
TREETOP S
PROETTE
TREETOPS
PROETTES
TREF
FRET REFT
TREFAH
FATHER
HAFTER
TREFOIL S
LOFTIER
TREFOILS
TREHALA S
TREHALAS
TREK S
TREKKED
TREKKER S
TREKKERS
TREKKING
TREKS
TRELLIS
RILLETS
STILLER
TILLERS
A TREMBLE DRS
TREMBLED
TREMBLER S
TREMBLES
TREMBLY
TREMOLO S
TREMOLOS
TREMOR S
TERMOR
TREMORS
TERMORS
TRENAIL S
LATRINE
RATLINE
RELIANT
RETINAL
TRENAILS
ENTRAILS
LATRINES
RATLINES
RETINALS
TRENCH
TRENCHED
TRENCHER S
RETRENCH
TRENCHES
TREND SY
TRENDED
TRENDIER
INTERRED
TRENDIES T
INSERTED
NERDIEST
RESIDENT
SINTERED
TRENDILY
TRENDING
TRENDOID S
TRENDS
TRENDY
TREPAN GS
ARPENT
ENRAPT
ENTRAP
PARENT
TREPANG S
TREPANGS
TREPANS
ARPENTS
ENTRAPS
PARENTS
PASTERN
TREPHINE DS
NEPHRITE
TREPID
REDIPT
TRES S
ERST REST
RETS
TRESPASS
SPARSEST
S TRESS Y
RESTS
S TRESSED
DESERTS
DESSERT
TRESSEL S
STREELS
TRESSELS
RESTLESS
S TRESSES
TRESSIER
RESISTER
TRESSOUR S
ROUSTERS
TROUSERS
TRESSURE S
TRESSY
TRESTLE S
LETTERS
SETTLER
STERLET
TRESTLES
SETTLERS
STERLETS
TRET S
TRETS
TREVALLY S
TREVET S
VETTER
TREVETS
VETTERS
S TREWS
STREW WREST
TREY S
TYER TYRE
TREYS
TYERS TYRES
TRIABLE
LIBRATE
TRIAC S

TRIACID S
TRIADIC
TRIACIDS
CARDITIS
TRIADICS
TRIACS
CRISTA
RACIST
TRIAD S
TRIADIC S
TRIACID
TRIADICS
CARDITIS
TRIACIDS
TRIADISM S
TRIADS
TRIAGE DS
AIGRET
GAITER
TRIAGED
TRIAGES
AIGRETS
GAITERS
SEAGIRT
STAGIER
TRIAGING
A **TRIAL** S
TRAIL
TRIALS
TRAILS
TRIANGLE DS
ALERTING
ALTERING
INTEGRAL
RELATING
TANGLIER
TRIARCHY
TRIASSIC
TRIAXIAL
TRIAZIN ES
TRIAZINE S
TRIAZINS
TRIAZOLE S
TRIBADE S
REDBAIT
TRIBADES
REDBAITS
TRIBADIC
TRIBAL S
TRIBALLY
TRIBALS
TRIBASIC
TRIBE S
BITER
TRIBES
BESTIR
BISTER
BISTRE
BITERS
TRIBRACH S
TRIBUNAL S
TURBINAL
TRIBUNE S
TURBINE
TRIBUNES
TURBINES
TRIBUTE S
TRIBUTES
TRICE DPS
CITER RECIT
RECTI
TRICED
CREDIT
DIRECT
TRICEP S
TRICEPS
TRICES
CITERS
RECITS
STERIC
TRICHINA EL S
TRICHITE S
TRICHOID
HIDROTIC
TRICHOME S
CHROMITE
TRICING
S **TRICK** SY
TRICKED
TRICKER SY
TRICKERS
TRICKERY
TRICKIE R
TRICKIER
TRICKILY
TRICKING
TRICKISH
S **TRICKLE** DS
TICKLER
S **TRICKLED**
S **TRICKLES**
STICKLER
STRICKLE
TICKLERS
TRICKLY
S **TRICKS** Y
STRICK
TRICKSY
TRICKY
TRICLAD S
TRICLADS
TRICOLOR S
TRICORN ES
TRICORNE S
TRICORNS
TRICOT S
TRICOTS
TRICTRAC S
TRICYCLE S
S **TRIDENT** S
TRIDENTS
STRIDENT
TRIDUUM S
TRIDUUMS
TRIED
TIRED
TRIENE S
ENTIRE
RETINE
TRIENES
ENTIRES
ENTRIES
RETINES
TRIENNIA L
TRIENS
ESTRIN
INERTS
INSERT
INTERS
NITERS
NITRES
SINTER
TRINES
TRIENTES
INSETTER
INTEREST
STERNITE
TRIER S
TRIERS
TRIES
RESIT RITES
TIERS TIRES
TRIETHYL
TRIFECTA S
TRIFID
TRIFLE DRS
FILTER
LIFTER
TRIFLED
FLIRTED
TRIFLER S
FLIRTER
TRIFLERS
FLIRTERS
TRIFLES
FILTERS
LIFTERS
STIFLER
TRIFLING S
FLIRTING
TRIFOCAL S
TRIFOLD
TRIFORIA
TRIFORM
TRIG OS
GIRT GRIT
TRIGGED
TRIGGER S
TRIGGERS
TRIGGEST
TRIGGING
TRIGLY
TRIGLYPH S
TRIGNESS
STINGERS
TRIGO NS
GRIOT
TRIGON S
TRIGONAL
TRIGONS
SORTING
STORING
TRIGOS
GRIOTS
TRIGRAM S
TRIGRAMS
TRIGRAPH S
TRIGS
GIRTS GRIST
GRITS
TRIHEDRA L
TRIJET S
JITTER
TRIJETS
JITTERS
S **TRIKE** S
KITER
S **TRIKES**
KITERS
STRIKE
TRILBIES
TRILBY
TRILITH S
TRILITHS
TRILL S
TRILLED
TRILLER S
TRILLERS
TRILLING
TRILLION S
TRILLIUM S
TRILLS
TRILOBAL
TRILOBED
TRILOGY
TRIM S
TRIMARAN S
TRIMER S
RETRIM
TRIMERIC
TRIMERS
RETRIMS
TRIMETER S
REMITTER
TRIMLY
TRIMMED
MIDTERM
TRIMMER S
TRIMMERS
TRIMMEST
TRIMMING S
TRIMNESS
MINSTERS
TRIMORPH S
TRIMOTOR S
TRIMS
TRINAL
RATLIN
TRINARY
TRINDLE DS
TENDRIL
TRINDLED
TRINDLES
TENDRILS
TRINE DS
INERT INTER
NITER NITRE
TRINED
RIDENT
TINDER
TRINES
ESTRIN
INERTS
INSERT
INTERS
NITERS
NITRES
SINTER
TRIENS
TRINING
TRINITY
TRINKET S
KNITTER
TRINKETS
KNITTERS
TRINKUMS
TRINODAL
TRIO LS
RIOT ROTI
TIRO TORI
TRIODE S
DOTIER
EDITOR
RIOTED
TRIODES
EDITORS
SORTIED
STEROID
STORIED
TRIOL S
LIROT
TRIOLET S
TORTILE
TRIOLETS
TRIOLS
TRIOS E
RIOTS ROTIS
TIROS TORSI
TROIS
TRIOSE S
SORTIE
TORIES
TRIOSES
ROSIEST
SORITES
SORTIES
STORIES
TRIOXID ES
TRIOXIDE S
TRIOXIDS
AS **TRIP** ES
TRIPACK S
TRIPACKS
TRIPART
S **TRIPE** S
TRIPEDAL
DIPTERAL
S **TRIPES**
ESPRIT
PRIEST
RIPEST
SPRITE
STRIPE
TRIPHASE
TRIPLANE S
INTERLAP
TRAPLINE
TRIPLE DSTX
TRIPLED
TRIPLES
RESPLIT
TRIPLET S
TRIPLETS
SPLITTER
TRIPLEX
S **TRIPLING**
TRIPLITE S
TRIPLOID SY
TRIPLY
TRIPOD SY
TORPID
TRIPODAL
DIOPTRAL
TRIPODIC
DIOPTRIC
DIPROTIC
TRIPODS
DISPORT
TORPIDS
TRIPODY
TRIPOLI S
TRIPOLIS
TRIPOS
PROSIT
RIPOST
TRIPOSES
PROSIEST
PROSTIES
REPOSITS
RIPOSTES
S **TRIPPED**
S **TRIPPER** S
S **TRIPPERS**
STRIPPER
TRIPPET S
TRIPPETS
TRIPPIER
S **TRIPPING** S
TRIPPY
S **TRIPS**
SPIRT SPRIT
STIRP STRIP
TRIPTAN ES
TRIPTANE S
TRIPTANS
TRIPTYCA S
TRIPTYCH S
TRIPWIRE S
TRIREME S
MITERER
TRIREMES
MERRIEST
MITERERS
RIMESTER
TRISCELE S
RETICLES
SCLERITE
TIERCELS
TRISECT S
TRISECTS
TRISEME S
MEISTER
METIERS
REEMITS
RETIMES
TRISEMES
MEISTERS
MISSTEER
TRISEMIC
MERISTIC
SCIMITER
TRISHAW S
WRAITHS
TRISHAWS
TRISKELE S
TRISMIC
TRISMUS
SISTRUM
TRUISMS
TRISOME S
EROTISM
MOISTER
MORTISE
TRISOMES
EROTISMS
MORTISES
TRISOMIC S
TRISOMY
TRISTATE
ATTRITES
RATTIEST
TARTIEST
TITRATES
TRISTE
SITTER
TETRIS
TITERS
TITRES
TRISTEZA S
TRISTFUL
TRISTICH S
TRITE R
TETRI TITER
TITRE
TRITELY
LITTERY
TRITER
RITTER
TERRIT
TRITEST
STRETTI
TITTERS
TRITHING S
TRITICUM S
TRITIUM S
TRITIUMS
TRITOMA S
TRITOMAS
TRITON ES
INTORT
TRITONE S
TRITONES
SNOTTIER
TENORIST
TRITONS
INTORTS
TRIUMPH S
TRIUMPHS
TRIUMVIR IS
TRIUNE S
UNITER
TRIUNES
NUTSIER
UNITERS
TRIUNITY
TRIVALVE S
TRIVET S
TRIVETS
TRIVIA L
TRIVIAL
TRIVIUM
TROAK S
KORAT TAROK
TROAKED
TROAKING
TROAKS
KORATS
TAROKS
TROCAR S
CARROT
TROCARS
CARROTS
TROCHAIC S
THORACIC
TROCHAL
TROCHAR S
TROCHARS
TROCHE ES
HECTOR
ROCHET
ROTCHE
TOCHER
TROCHEE S
TROCHEES
TROCHES
HECTORS
ROCHETS
ROTCHES
TOCHERS
TORCHES
TROCHIL IS
TROCHILI
TROCHILS
TROCHLEA ER S
CHELATOR
CHLORATE
TROCHOID S
TROCK S
TROCKED
TROCKING
TROCKS
TROD E
TRODDEN
S **TRODE**
DOTER
TROFFER S
TROFFERS
TROG S
GROT
TROGON S
TROGONS
TROGS
GROTS
TROIKA S
TROIKAS
TROILISM S
TROILITE S
TROILUS
TROIS
RIOTS ROTIS
TIROS TORSI
TRIOS
S **TROKE** DS
TOKER
S **TROKED**
S **TROKES**
STOKER
STROKE
TOKERS
S **TROKING**
TROLAND S
TROLANDS
S **TROLL** SY
S **TROLLED**
S **TROLLER** S
S **TROLLERS**
STROLLER
TROLLEY S
TROLLEYS
TROLLIED
TROLLIES
S **TROLLING** S
TROLLOP SY
ROLLTOP
TROLLOPS
TROLLOPY
S **TROLLS**
STROLL
TROLLY
TROMBONE S
TROMMEL S
TROMMELS
TROMP ES
TROMPE DS
TROMPED
TROMPES
STOMPER
TROMPING
TROMPS
TRONA S
TRONAS
TRONE S
NOTER TENOR
TONER
TRONES
NESTOR
NOTERS
STONER
TENORS
TENSOR
TONERS
TROOP S
TROOPED
TORPEDO
TROOPER S
TROOPERS
TROOPIAL S
TROOPING
TROOPS
TROOZ
S **TROP** E
PORT
TROPE S
REPOT TOPER
TROPES
POSTER
PRESTO
REPOTS
RESPOT
STOPER
TOPERS
AS **TROPHIC**
A **TROPHIED**
A **TROPHIES**
A **TROPHY**
TROPIC S
TROPICAL S
TROPICS
A **TROPIN** ES
A **TROPINE** S
POINTER
PROTEIN
A **TROPINES**
POINTERS
PORNIEST
PROTEINS
A **TROPINS**
A **TROPISM** S
IMPORTS
A **TROPISMS**
TROPONIN S
TROT HS
TORT
TROTH S
TROTHED
TROTHING
TROTHS
TROTLINE S
TROTS
TORTS

TROTTED
TROTTER S
TROTTERS
TROTTING
TROTYL S
TROTYLS
TROUBLE DRS
TROUBLED
TROUBLER S
TROUBLES
TROUGH S
TROUGHS
TROUNCE DRS
CORNUTE
COUNTER
RECOUNT
TROUNCED
CORNUTED
TROUNCER S
TROUNCES
CONSTRUE
COUNTERS
RECOUNTS
TROUPE DRS
POUTER
ROUPET
UPTORE
TROUPED
TROUPER S
TROUPERS
POSTURER
RESPROUT
TROUPES
PETROUS
POSTURE
POUTERS
PROTEUS
SPOUTER
TROUPIAL S
TROUPING
TROUSER S
ROUSTER
ROUTERS
TOURERS
TROUSERS
ROUSTERS
TRESSOUR
TROUT SY
TUTOR
TROUTIER
TROUTS
TUTORS
TROUTY
TRYOUT
TROUVERE S
OVERTURE
TROUVEUR S
S TROVE RS
OVERT VOTER
TROVER S
TROVERS
TROVES
STOVER
STROVE
VOTERS
S TROW S
WORT
S TROWED
TROWEL S
TROWELED
TROWELER S
TROWELS
S TROWING
S TROWS
STROW WORST
WORTS
TROWSERS
TROWTH S
TROWTHS
S TROY S
RYOT TORY
TYRO
S TROYS
RYOTS STORY
STROY TYROS
TRUANCY
TRUANT S
TRUANTED
TRUANTLY
TRUANTRY

TRUANTS
TRUCE DS
CRUET CURET
CUTER ERUCT
RECUT
TRUCED
TRUCES
CRUETS
CRUSET
CURETS
ERUCTS
RECTUS
RECUTS
TRUCING
S TRUCK S
TRUCKAGE S
TRUCKED
TRUCKER S
TRUCKERS
RESTRUCK
TRUCKFUL S
TRUCKING S
TRUCKLE DRS
TRUCKLED
TRUCKLER S
TRUCKLES
TRUCKMAN
TRUCKMEN
TRUCKS
STRUCK
TRUDGE DNRS
TRUDGED
TRUDGEN S
GRUNTED
TRUDGENS
TRUDGEON S
TRUDGER S
TRUDGERS
TRUDGES
TRUDGING
TRUE DRS
TRUEBLUE S
TRUEBORN
TRUEBRED
TRUED
TRUEING
TRUELOVE S
REVOLUTE
TRUENESS
TRUER
TRUES T
TRUEST
UTTERS
TRUFFE S
TRUFFES
RESTUFF
STUFFER
TRUFFLE DS
FRETFUL
TRUFFLED
TRUFFLES
TRUG S
TRUGS
TRUING
UNGIRT
TRUISM S
TRUISMS
SISTRUM
TRISMUS
TRUISTIC
TRULL S
TRULLS
TRULY
TRUMEAU X
TRUMEAUX
TRUMP S
TRUMPED
TRUMPERY
S TRUMPET S
S TRUMPETS
STRUMPET
TRUMPING
TRUMPS
TRUNCATE DS
TRUNDLE DRS
RUNDLET
TRUNDLED
TRUNDLER S

TRUNDLES
RUNDLETS
TRUNK S
TRUNKED
TRUNKFUL S
TRUNKS
TRUNNEL S
TRUNNELS
TRUNNION S
TRUSS
RUSTS
TRUSSED
DUSTERS
TRUSSER S
TRUSSERS
TRUSSES
RUSSETS
TUSSERS
TRUSSING S
TRUST SY
STRUT STURT
TRUSTED
TRUSTEE DS
TRUSTEED
TRUSTEES
TRUSTER S
TURRETS
TRUSTERS
TRUSTFUL
TRUSTIER
TRUSTIES T
RUSTIEST
TRUSTILY
TRUSTING
TRUSTOR S
TRUSTORS
TRUSTS
STRUTS
STURTS
TRUSTY
TRUTH S
TRUTHFUL
TRUTHS
THRUST
TRY
TRYING
TYRING
TRYINGLY
TRYMA
TRYMATA
TRYOUT S
TROUTY
TRYOUTS
TRYPSIN S
TRYPSINS
TRYPTIC
TRYSAIL S
TRYSAILS
TRYST ES
TRYSTE DRS
TRYSTED
TRYSTER S
TRYSTERS
TRYSTES
TRYSTING
TRYSTS
TRYWORKS
TSADDIK
TSADE S
DATES SATED
STADE STEAD
TSADES
STADES
STEADS
TSADI S
ADITS DITAS
STAID
TSADIS
SADIST
TSAR S
ARTS RATS
STAR TARS
TSARDOM S
STARDOM
TSARDOMS
STARDOMS
TSAREVNA S
TAVERNAS

TSARINA S
ANTIARS
ARTISAN
TSARINAS
ARTISANS
TSARISM S
TSARISMS
TSARIST S
ARTISTS
STRAITS
TSARISTS
TSARITZA S
TSARS
STARS TRASS
TSATSKE S
TSATSKES
TSETSE S
SESTET
TESTES
TSETSES
SESTETS
TSIMMES
TSK S
TSKED
TSKING
TSKS
TSKTSK S
TSKTSKED
TSKTSKS
TSOORIS
TSORES
ROSETS
SOREST
STORES
TORSES
TOSSER
TSORIS
TSORRISS
TSOURIS
SUITORS
TSUBA
ABUTS TABUS
TUBAS
TSUNAMI CS
MANITUS
SANTIMU
TSUNAMIC
TSUNAMIS
TSURIS
TUATARA S
TUATARAS
TUATERA S
TUATERAS
SATURATE
S TUB AES
BUT
TUBA ELS
ABUT TABU
TUBAE
BEAUT
TUBAIST S
TUBAISTS
TUBAL
TUBAS
ABUTS TABUS
TSUBA
TUBATE
BATTUE
TUBBABLE
S TUBBED
TUBBER S
TUBBERS
S TUBBIER
S TUBBIEST
S TUBBING
S TUBBY
TUBE DRS
BUTE
TUBED
DEBUT
TUBELESS
TUBELIKE
TUBENOSE S
TUBER S
BRUTE BURET
REBUT
TUBERCLE S
TUBEROID
TUBEROSE S
TUBEROUS

TUBERS
BRUTES
BURETS
BUSTER
REBUTS
TUBES
BUTES
TUBEWORK S
TUBEWORM S
TUBFUL S
TUBFULS
TUBIFEX
TUBIFORM
TUBING S
TUBINGS
BUSTING
TUBIST S
TUBISTS
TUBLIKE
S TUBS
BUST BUTS
STUB
TUBULAR
TUBULATE DS
TUBULE S
TUBULES
TUBULIN S
UNBUILT
TUBULINS
TUBULOSE
TUBULOUS
TUBULURE S
TUCHUN S
TUCHUNS
S TUCK S
TUCKAHOE S
TUCKED
TUCKER S
TUCKERED
TUCKERS
TUCKET S
TUCKETS
TUCKING
TUCKS
STUCK
TUCKSHOP S
TUFA S
TUFAS
S TUFF S
TUFFET S
TUFFETS
S TUFFS
STUFF
TUFOLI
TUFT SY
TUFTED
TUFTER S
TUFTERS
TUFTIER
TUFTIEST
TUFTILY
TUFTING S
TUFTINGS
TUFTS
TUFTY
TUG S
GUT
TUGBOAT S
TUGBOATS
TUGGED
TUGGER S
TUGGERS
TUGGING
TUGHRIK S
TUGHRIKS
TUGLESS
GUTLESS
TUGRIK S
TUGRIKS
TUGS
GUST GUTS
EP TUI S
TUILLE S
TUILLES
E TUIS
SUIT
TUITION S

TUITIONS
TULADI S
TULADIS
DUALIST
TULE S
LUTE
TULES
LUTES
TULIP S
UPLIT
TULIPS
TULLE S
TULLES
TULLIBEE S
S TUMBLE DRS
S TUMBLED
S TUMBLER S
TUMBREL
S TUMBLERS
STUMBLER
TUMBRELS
S TUMBLES
STUMBLE
S TUMBLING S
TUMBREL S
TUMBLER
TUMBRELS
STUMBLER
TUMBLERS
TUMBRIL S
TUMBRILS
TUMEFIED
TUMEFIES
TUMEFY
TUMESCE DS
TUMESCED
TUMESCES
TUMID
TUMIDITY
TUMIDLY
TUMMIES
TUMMLER S
TUMMLERS
TUMMY
TUMOR S
TUMORAL
TUMOROUS
TUMORS
TUMOUR S
TUMOURS
S TUMP S
S TUMPED
S TUMPING
TUMPLINE S
S TUMPS
STUMP
TUMULAR
MUTULAR
TUMULI
TUMULOSE
TUMULOUS
TUMULT S
TUMULTS
TUMULUS
S TUN AEGS
NUT
TUNA S
AUNT
TUNABLE
ABLUENT
TUNABLY
TUNAS
AUNTS
TUNDISH
TUNDRA S
TUNDRAS
TUNE DRS
TUNEABLE
TUNEABLY
TUNED
TENDU
TUNEFUL
TUNELESS
UNSTEELS
TUNER S
TUNERS
UNREST
TUNES
UNSET

TUNEUP S
TUNEUPS
S TUNG S
TUNGS
STUNG
TUNGSTEN S
TUNGSTIC
CUTTINGS
TUNIC AS
CUTIN
TUNICA E
TUNICAE
TUNICATE DS
TUNICLE S
CUTLINE
LINECUT
TUNICLES
CUTLINES
LINECUTS
TUNICS
CUTINS
TUNING
TUNNAGE S
TUNNAGES
S TUNNED
TUNNEL S
TUNNELED
TUNNELER S
TUNNELS
TUNNIES
S TUNNING
TUNNY
S TUNS
NUTS STUN
TUP S
PUT
TUPELO S
TUPELOS
TUPIK S
TUPIKS
TUPPED
TUPPENCE S
TUPPENNY
TUPPING
TUPS
PUTS
TUQUE S
TUQUES
TURACO SU
CUATRO
TURACOS
CUATROS
SURCOAT
TURACOU S
TURACOUS
TURBAN S
TURBANED
BREADNUT
TURBANS
TURBARY
TURBETH S
TURBETHS
TURBID
TURBIDLY
TURBINAL S
TRIBUNAL
TURBINE S
TRIBUNE
TURBINES
TRIBUNES
TURBIT HS
TURBITH S
TURBITHS
TURBITS
TURBO ST
TURBOCAR S
TURBOFAN S
TURBOJET S
TURBOS
ROBUST
TURBOT S
TURBOTS
TURDINE
INTRUDE
UNTIRED
UNTRIED

TUREEN S
NEUTER
RETUNE
TENURE
TUREENS
NEUTERS
RETUNES
TENURES
TURF SY
TURFED
TURFIER
FRUITER
TURFIEST
TURFING
TURFLESS
FLUSTERS
TURFLIKE
TURFMAN
TURFMEN
TURFS
TURFSKI S
TURFSKIS
TURFY
TURGENCY
TURGENT
GRUTTEN
TURGID
TURGIDLY
TURGITE S
GUTTIER
TURGITES
TURGOR S
TURGORS
TURION S
TURIONS
NITROUS
TURISTA S
TURISTAS
TURK S
TURKEY S
TURKEYS
TURKOIS
TURKS
TURMERIC S
TURMOIL S
TURMOILS
TURN S
RUNT
TURNABLE
TURNCOAT S
TURNDOWN S
DOWNTURN
TURNED
TURNER SY
RETURN
TURNERS
RETURNS
TURNERY
TURNHALL S
TURNING S
TURNINGS
UNSTRING
TURNIP S
TURNIPS
TURNKEY S
TURNKEYS
TURNOFF S
TURNOFFS
TURNON S
UNTORN
TURNONS
TURNOUT S
OUTTURN
TURNOUTS
OUTTURNS
TURNOVER S
OVERTURN
TURNPIKE S
TURNS
RUNTS
TURNSOLE S
TURNSPIT S
TURNUP S
UPTURN
TURNUPS
UPTURNS
TURPETH S
TURPETHS
TURPS
SPURT

TURQUOIS E
TURRET S
TURRETED
TURRETS
TRUSTER
TURRICAL
TURTLE DRS
TURTLED
TURTLER S
TURTLERS
TURTLES
TURTLING S
TURVES
VERTUS
TUSCHE S
CHUTES
TUSCHES
TUSH Y
HUTS SHUT
THUS
TUSHED
SHUTED
TUSHERY
TUSHES
SHUTES
TUSSEH
TUSHIE S
TUSHIES
TUSHING
SHUTING
UNSIGHT
TUSHY
TUSK S
TUSKED
TUSKER S
TUSKERS
TUSKING
TUSKLESS
TUSKLIKE
TUSKS
TUSSAH S
TUSSAHS
TUSSAL
SAULTS
TUSSAR S
SUTRAS
TARSUS
TUSSARS
TUSSEH S
SHUTES
TUSHES
TUSSEHS
TUSSER S
ESTRUS
RUSSET
SUREST
TUSSERS
RUSSETS
TRUSSES
TUSSES
TUSSIS
TUSSISES
TUSSIVE
TUSSLE DS
TUSSLED
TUSSLES
TUSSLING
TUSSOCK SY
TUSSOCKS
TUSSOCKY
TUSSOR ES
ROUSTS
STOURS
TUSSORE S
ESTROUS
OESTRUS
OUSTERS
SOUREST
SOUTERS
STOURES
TUSSORES
TUSSORS
TUSSUCK S
TUSSUCKS
TUSSUR S
TUSSURS
TUT SU
TUTEE S

TUTEES
SUTTEE
TUTELAGE S
TUTELAR SY
TUTELARS
LUSTRATE
TUTELARY
TUTOR S
TROUT
TUTORAGE S
TUTORED
TUTORESS
OUTSERTS
TUTORIAL S
TUTORING
TUTORS
TROUTS
TUTOYED
TUTOYER S
TUTOYERS
TUTS
TUTTED
TUTTI S
TUTTIES
TUTTING
TUTTIS
TUTTY
TUTU S
TUTUED
TUTUS
TUX
TUXEDO S
TUXEDOED
TUXEDOES
TUXEDOS
TUXES
TUYER ES
TUYERE S
TUYERES
TUYERS
SURETY
TWA ES
TAW
WAT
TWADDLE DRS
TWADDLED
TWADDLER S
TWADDLES
TWAE S
TWAES
SWEAT TAWSE
WASTE
A **TWAIN** S
WITAN
TWAINS
WITANS
TWANG SY
TWANGED
TWANGER S
TWANGERS
TWANGIER
WATERING
TWANGING
TWANGLE DRS
TWANGLED
TWANGLER S
TWANGLES
TWANGS
TWANGY
TWANKIES
TWANKY
TWAS
STAW SWAT
TAWS WAST
WATS
TWASOME S
TWASOMES
TWATTLE DS
TWATTLED
TWATTLES
TWEAK SY
TWEAKED
TWEAKIER
TWEAKING
TWEAKS
TWEAKY
E **TWEE** DNT
WEET

TWEED SY
TEWED
TWEEDIER
TWEEDLE DS
TWEEDLED
TWEEDLES
TWEEDS
STEWED
TWEEDY
A **TWEEN** SY
TWEENER S
TWEENERS
TWEENESS
SWEETENS
TWEENIES
WEENIEST
TWEENS
NEWEST
TWEENY
TWEET S
TWEETED
TWEETER S
TWEETERS
TWEETING
TWEETS
TWEEZE DRS
TWEEZED
TWEEZER S
TWEEZERS
TWEEZES
TWEEZING
TWELFTH S
TWELFTHS
TWELVE S
TWELVEMO S
TWELVES
TWENTIES
TWENTY
TWERP S
TWERPS
TWIBIL LS
TWIBILL S
TWIBILLS
TWIBILS
TWICE
TWIDDLE DRS
TWIDDLED
TWIDDLER S
TWIDDLES
TWIDDLY
TWIER S
WRITE
TWIERS
WRIEST
WRITES
TWIG S
TWIGGED
TWIGGEN
TWIGGIER
TWIGGING
TWIGGY
TWIGLESS
TWIGLIKE
TWIGS
TWILIGHT S
TWILIT
TWILL S
TWILLED
TWILLING S
TWILLS
TWIN ESY
TWINBORN
TWINE DRS
TWINED
TWINER S
WINTER
TWINERS
WINTERS
TWINES
WISENT
TWINGE DS
TEWING
TWINGED
TWINGES
STEWING
WESTING
TWINGING

TWINIER
TWINIEST
TWINIGHT
TWINING
TWINJET S
TWINJETS
TWINKIE S
TWINKIES
TWINKLE DRS
TWINKLED
TWINKLER S
TWINKLES
TWINKLY
TWINNED
TWINNING S
TWINS
TWINSET S
ENTWIST
TWINSETS
ENTWISTS
TWINSHIP S
TWINY
TWIRL SY
TWIRLED
TWIRLER S
TWIRLERS
TWIRLIER
TWIRLING
TWIRLS
TWIRLY
TWIRP S
TWIRPS
TWIST SY
TWITS
TWISTED
TWISTER S
RETWIST
TWISTERS
RETWISTS
TWISTIER
TWISTING S
WITTINGS
TWISTS
TWISTY
TWIT S
TWITCH Y
TWITCHED
TWITCHER S
TWITCHES
TWITCHY
TWITS
TWIST
TWITTED
A **TWITTER** SY
TWITTERS
TWITTERY
TWITTING
TWIXT
TWO S
TOW
WOT
TWOFER S
TWOFERS
TWOFOLD S
TWOFOLDS
TWOONIE S
TWOONIES
TWOPENCE S
TWOPENNY
TWOS
STOW SWOT
TOWS WOST
WOTS
TWOSOME S
TWOSOMES
TWYER S
TWYERS
WRYEST
TYCOON S
TYCOONS
S **TYE** ERS
YET
TYEE S
TYEES
TYER S
TREY TYRE
TYERS
TREYS TYRES

S **TYES**
STEY STYE
TYIN G
TINY
S **TYING**
TYIYN
TYKE S
KYTE
TYKES
KYTES
TYLOSIN S
STONILY
TYLOSINS
TYMBAL S
TYMBALS
TYMPAN AIOS
Y
TYMPANA L
TYMPANAL
TYMPANI C
TYMPANIC
TYMPANO
TYMPANS
TYMPANUM S
TYMPANY
TYNE DS
TYNED
TYNES
TYNING
TYPABLE
TYPAL
APTLY PATLY
PLATY
TYPE DSY
TYPEABLE
TYPEBAR S
TYPEBARS
TYPECASE S
TYPECAST S
TYPED
TYPEFACE S
TYPES
PESTY
TYPESET S
TYPESETS
TYPEY
TYPHOID S
PHYTOID
TYPHOIDS
TYPHON S
PHYTON
PYTHON
TYPHONIC
HYPNOTIC
PHYTONIC
PYTHONIC
TYPHONS
PHYTONS
PYTHONS
TYPHOON S
TYPHOONS
TYPHOSE
TYPHOUS
TYPHUS
TYPHUSES
A **TYPIC**
A **TYPICAL**
TYPIER
PYRITE
TYPIEST
TYPIFIED
TYPIFIER S
TYPIFIES
TYPIFY
TYPING
TYPIST S
TYPISTS
TYPO S
TYPOLOGY
LOGOTYPY
TYPOS
POTSY
TYPP S
TYPPS
TYPY
TYRAMINE S
TYRANNIC
TYRANNY

TYRANT S
TYRANTS
TYRE DS
TREY TYER
TYRED
TYRES
TREYS TYERS
TYRING
TRYING
TYRO S
RYOT TORY
TROY
TYRONIC
TYROS
RYOTS STORY
STROY TROYS
TYROSINE S
SEROTINY
TYTHE DS
TYTHED
TYTHES
TYTHING
TZADDIK
TZAR S
TZARDOM S
TZARDOMS
TZAREVNA S
TZARINA S
TZARINAS
TZARISM S
TZARISMS
TZARIST S
TZARISTS
TZARITZA S
TZARS
TZETZE S
TZETZES
TZIGANE S
TZIGANES
TZIMMES
TZITZIS
TZITZIT H
TZITZITH
TZURIS

U

UAKARI S
UAKARIS
D **UBIETIES**
D **UBIETY**
UBIQUE
UBIQUITY
BJM **UDDER** S
R DURED
BJM **UDDERS**
R
JK **UDO** NS
DUO
OUD
UDOMETER S
UDOMETRY
UDON S
UNDO
UDONS
NODUS SOUND
JK **UDOS**
DUOS OUDS
UFOLOGY
PSV **UGH** S
HUG
SV **UGHS**
GUSH HUGS
SUGH
UGLIER
GLUIER
LIGURE
REGULI
UGLIES T
GUILES
UGLIEST
GLUIEST
UGLIFIED
UGLIFIER S
UGLIFIES
UGLIFY
UGLILY
GLUILY
UGLINESS
GLUINESS

UGLY
UGSOME
DH UH
UHLAN S
UHLANS
UNLASH
UINTAITE S
UKASE S
UKASES
CDJ NP UKE S
KUE
UKELELE S
UKELELES
CDJ NP UKES
KUES
UKULELE S
UKULELES
ULAMA S
ULAMAS
Y ULAN S
LUNA ULNA
Y ULANS
LUNAS ULNAS
ULCER S
CRUEL LUCRE
ULCERATE DS
ULCERED
ULCERING
ULCEROUS
ULCERS
LUCRES
ULEMA S
ULEMAS
ULEXITE S
ULEXITES
S ULLAGE DS
ULLAGED
S ULLAGES
SEAGULL
SULLAGE
ULNA DERS
LUNA ULAN
ULNAD
ULNAE
ULNAR
LUNAR
ULNAS
LUNAS ULANS
ULPAN
ULPANIM
ULSTER S
LUSTER
LUSTRE
RESULT
RUSTLE
SUTLER
ULSTERS
LUSTERS
LUSTRES
RESULTS
RUSTLES
SUTLERS
ULTERIOR
ULTIMA S
ULTIMACY
ULTIMAS
ULTIMATA
ULTIMATE DS
MUTILATE
ULTIMO
ULTRA S
ULTRADRY
ULTRAHIP
ULTRAHOT
ULTRAISM S
ALTRUISM
MURALIST
ULTRAIST S
ALTRUIST
TITULARS
ULTRALOW
ULTRARED S
ULTRAS
LUSTRA
LS ULU S
ULULANT
ULULATE DS
ULULATED
ULULATES
LS ULUS
SULU
V ULVA S
V ULVAS
BCG HLM RSV Y UM MP
MU
UMAMI S
IMAUM
UMAMIS
IMAUMS
UMANGITE S
TEGUMINA
UMBEL S
BLUME
UMBELED
UMBELLAR
UMBRELLA
UMBELLED
UMBELLET S
UMBELS
BLUMES
UMBLES
CDL N UMBER S
BRUME
CLN UMBERED
EMBRUED
CLN UMBERING
EMBRUING
CLN UMBERS
BRUMES
UMBILICI
BFH JMN RT UMBLES
BLUMES
UMBELS
DGJ UMBO S
UMBONAL
UMBONATE
UMBONES
UMBONIC
DGJ UMBOS
UMBRA ELS
RUMBA
UMBRAE
UMBRAGE S
UMBRAGES
UMBRAL
BRUMAL
LABRUM
LUMBAR
UMBRAS
RUMBAS
SAMBUR
UMBRELLA S
UMBELLAR
UMBRETTE S
UMIAC KS
UMIACK S
UMIACKS
UMIACS
AMICUS
UMIAK S
UMIAKS
UMIAQ S
MAQUI
UMIAQS
MAQUIS
UMLAUT S
MUTUAL
UMLAUTED
UMLAUTS
MUTUALS
M UMM
MUM
BDH JLM PRS T UMP S
BDH JLM PT UMPED
BDH JLM PT UMPING
IMPUGN
UMPIRAGE S
UMPIRE DS
IMPURE
UMPIRED
DUMPIER
UMPIRES
SPUMIER
UMPIRING
BDH JLM PRS T UMPS
SUMP
UMPTEEN
UMTEENTH
BDF GHJ MNP RST UN S
NU
UNABATED
T UNABLE
NEBULA
UNBALE
UNABUSED
UNACIDIC
UNACTED
UNADDED
UNADEPT
UNADULT
UNAFRAID
UNAGED
AUGEND
UNAGEING
UNAGILE
LINGUAE
UNAGING
UNAGREED
DUNGAREE
UNDERAGE
UNAI S
UNAIDED
UNAIMED
UNAIRED
URANIDE
UNAIS
UNAKIN
UNAKITE S
UNAKITES
UNALIKE
UNALLIED
UNAMAZED
UNAMUSED
UNANCHOR S
UNANELED
UNAPT
UNAPTLY
UNARCHED
UNARGUED
UNARM S
UNARMED
DURAMEN
MANURED
MAUNDER
UNARMING
MANURING
UNARMS
UNARTFUL
UNARY
UNASKED
UNATONED
UNAU S
UNAUS
UNAVOWED
UNAWAKE D
UNAWAKED
UNAWARE S
UNAWARES
UNAWED
UNAXED
UNBACKED
S UNBAKED
UNBALE DS
NEBULA
UNABLE
UNBALED
UNBALES
NEBULAS
UNBALING
UNBAN S
UNBANDED
UNBANNED
UNBANS
UNBAR S
BURAN URBAN
UNBARBED
UNBARRED
UNBARS
BURANS
UNBASED
SUBDEAN
UNBASTED
UNBATED
S UNBATHED
UNBE
UNBEAR S
URBANE
UNBEARED
UNBEARS
UNBEATEN
UNBEING
UNBELIEF S
S UNBELT S
UNBELTED
S UNBELTS
SUNBELT
UNBLEST
UNBEND S
UNBENDED
UNBENDS
UNBENIGN
UNBENT
UNBIASED
UNBID
UNBIDDEN
UNBILLED
UNBIND S
UNBINDS
UNBITTED
UNBITTEN
UNBITTER
UNBLAMED
UNBLEST
SUNBELT
UNBELTS
S UNBLOCK S
S UNBLOCKS
SUNBLOCK
UNBLOODY
UNBOBBED
UNBODIED
UNBOILED
UNILOBED
UNBOLT S
UNBOLTED
UNBOLTS
UNBONDED
UNBONED
BOUNDEN
S UNBONNET S
UNBOOTED
UNBORN
UNBOSOM S
UNBOSOMS
UNBOTTLE DS
UNBOUGHT
UNBOUNCY
UNBOUND
UNBOWED
UNBOWING
UNBOX
UNBOXED
UNBOXES
UNBOXING
UNBRACE DS
UNBRACED
UNBRACES
UNBRAID S
UNBRAIDS
UNBRAKE DS
UNBRAKED
UNBRAKES
UNBRED
BURDEN
BURNED
UNBREECH
UNBRIDLE DS
UNBRIGHT
UNBROKE N
UNBROKEN
UNBUCKLE DS
UNBUILD S
UNBUILDS
UNBUILT
TUBULIN
UNBULKY
UNBUNDLE DS
UNBURDEN S
UNBURNED
UNBURIED
S UNBURNED
UNBURDEN
S UNBURNT
UNBUSTED
UNBUSY
UNBUTTON S
UNCAGE DS
CANGUE
UNCAGED
UNCAGES
CANGUES
UNCAGING
UNCAKE DS
UNCAKED
UNCAKES
UNCAKING
UNCALLED
UNCANDID
UNCANNED
UNCANNY
UNCAP S
UNCAPPED
UNCAPS
UNCARDED
UNCARING
UNCARTED
UNCRATED
UNDERACT
UNTRACED
UNCARVED
UNCASE DS
USANCE
UNCASED
UNCASES
USANCES
UNCASHED
UNCASING
UNCASKED
UNCAST
CANTUS
UNCATCHY
UNCAUGHT
UNCAUSED
UNCEDED
UNCHAIN S
UNCHAINS
ANCHUSIN
UNCHAIR S
UNCHAIRS
UNCHANCY
UNCHARGE DS
UNCHARY
RAUNCHY
UNCHASTE R
NAUTCHES
UNCHEWED
UNCHIC
UNCHICLY
S UNCHOKE DS
UNCHOKED
S UNCHOKES
SUNCHOKE
UNCHOSEN
NONESUCH
UNCHURCH
UNCI A
UNCIA EL
UNCIAE
UNCIAL S
UNCIALLY
UNCIALS
UNCIFORM S
CUNIFORM
UNCINAL
R UNCINATE
UNCINI
UNCINUS
UNCIVIL
UNCLAD
UNCLAMP S
UNCLAMPS
UNCLASP S
UNCLASPS
UNCLASSY
UNCLAWED
N UNCLE S
UNCLEAN
UNCLEAR
LUCARNE
NUCLEAR
UNCLEFT
UNCLENCH
N UNCLES
UNCLINCH
UNCLIP S
UNCLIPS
INSCULP
SCULPIN
UNCLOAK S
UNCLOAKS
UNCLOG S
UNCLOGS
UNCLOSE DS
COUNSEL
UNCLOSED
UNCLOSES
CLONUSES
COUNSELS
UNCLOTHE DS
UNCLOUD SY
UNCLOUDS
UNCLOUDY
UNCLOYED
BJ UNCO SY
UNCOATED
OUTDANCE
UNCOCK S
UNCOCKED
UNCOCKS
UNCODED
UNCOFFIN S
UNCOIL S
UNCOILED
NUCLEOID
UNDOCILE
UNCOILS
UNCOINED
UNCOMBED
UNCOMELY
UNCOMIC
UNCOMMON
UNCOOKED
UNCOOL
UNCOOLED
UNCORK S
UNCORKED
UNCORKS
BJ UNCOS
CONUS
UNCOUPLE DR S
UNCOUTH
UNCOVER S
UNCOVERS
UNCOY
UNCRATE DS
CENTAUR
UNCRATED
UNCARTED
UNDERACT
UNTRACED
UNCRATES
CENTAURS
RECUSANT
UNCRAZY
UNCREATE DS
UNCREWED
UNCROSS
UNCROWN S
UNCROWNS
FJ UNCTION S
FJ UNCTIONS
UNCTUOUS
UNCUFF S
UNCUFFED
UNCUFFS
UNCURB S
UNCURBED
UNCURBS
UNCURED
UNCURL S
UNCURLED
UNCURLS
UNCURSED
UNCUS
UNCUT E
UNCUTE
UNDAMPED
UNDARING
UNDATED
DAUNTED
UNDE ER
DUNE NUDE
UNDEAD
UNDECKED
UNDEE
ENDUE
UNDENIED
UNDENTED
UNTENDED
FS UNDER
NUDER
UNDERACT S
UNCARTED
UNCRATED
UNTRACED
UNDERAGE DS
DUNGAREE
UNAGREED
UNDERARM S
UNMARRED
UNDERATE
DENATURE
UNDEREAT
UNDERBID S
UNDERBUD S
UNDERBUY S
UNDERCUT S
UNDERDID
UNDERDO G
REDOUND
ROUNDED
UNDERDOG S
GROUNDED
UNDERGOD
UNDEREAT S
DENATURE
UNDERATE
UNDERFED
REFUNDED
UNDERFUR S
UNDERGO D
GUERDON
UNDERGOD S
GROUNDED
UNDERDOG
UNDERJAW S
UNDERLAP S
PENDULAR
UPLANDER
UNDERLAY S
UNDERLET S
UNDERLIE S
UNDERLIP S
UNDERLIT
UNDERPAY S
UNDERPIN S
UNDERRAN
UNDERRUN S
UNDERSEA S
UNERASED
UNSEARED
UNDERSET S
DENTURES
SEDERUNT
UNRESTED
UNDERTAX
UNDERTOW S
UNDERUSE DS
UNDERWAY
UNDEVOUT
UNDID
UNDIES
INDUES
NUDIES
UNDIMMED
UNDINE S
UNDINES

UNDO
UDON
UNDOABLE
UNDOCILE
NUCLEOID
UNCOILED
UNDOCK S
UNDOCKED
UNDOCKS
UNDOER S
ENDURO
UNDOERS
ENDUROS
RESOUND
SOUNDER
UNDOES
UNDOING S
UNDOINGS
SOUNDING
UNDONE
UNDOTTED
UNDOUBLE DS
UNDRAPE DS
UNDRAPED
UNDRAPES
UNDRAW NS
UNDRAWN
UNDRAWS
SUNWARD
UNDREAMT
S UNDRESS
SUNDERS
UNDREST
UNDREW
UNDRIED
UNDRUNK
UNDUBBED
UNDUE
UNDULANT
UNDULAR
UNDULATE DS
UNDULLED
UNDULY
UNDY
UNDYED
UNDYING
UNEAGER
UNEARNED
UNEARTH S
HAUNTER
URETHAN
UNEARTHS
HAUNTERS
URETHANS
UNEASE S
AENEUS
UNEASES
UNEASIER
UNEASILY
UNEASY
UNEATEN
UNEDIBLE
UNEDITED
UNENDED
UNENDING
UNENVIED
UNVEINED
UNEQUAL S
UNEQUALS
UNERASED
UNDERSEA
UNSEARED
UNEROTIC
NEUROTIC
UNERRING
UNEVADED
UNEVEN
UNEVENER
UNEVENLY
UNEXOTIC
UNEXPERT
UNFADED
UNFADING
F UNFAIR
UNFAIRER
UNFAIRLY
UNFAITH S
UNFAITHS
UNFAKED
UNFALLEN
UNFAMOUS
UNFANCY
UNFASTEN S
UNFAZED
UNFEARED
UNFED
UNFELT
FLUENT
UNFELTED
UNFENCE DS
UNFENCED
UNFENCES
UNFETTER S
UNFILIAL
UNFILLED
UNFILMED
FULMINED
UNFIRED
UNFISHED
UNFIT S
UNFITLY
UNFITS
UNFITTED
UNFIX T
UNFIXED
UNFIXES
UNFIXING
UNFIXT
UNFLASHY
UNFLAWED
UNFLEXED
UNFLUTED
UNFOILED
UNFOLD S
UNFOLDED
UNFOLDER S
FLOUNDER
UNFOLDS
UNFOND
UNFORCED
FROUNCED
UNFORGED
UNFORGOT
UNFORKED
UNFORMED
G UNFOUGHT
UNFOUND
UNFRAMED
UNFREE DS
UNFREED
UNFREES
UNFREEZE S
UNFROCK S
UNFROCKS
UNFROZE N
UNFROZEN
UNFUNDED
UNFUNNY
UNFURL S
UNFURLED
UNFURLS
UNFUSED
UNFUSSY
UNGAINLY
UNLAYING
UNGALLED
GLANDULE
UNGARBED
UNGATED
UNGAZING
UNGELDED
UNGENIAL
UNGENTLE
P UNGENTLY
UNGIFTED
UNGIRD S
DURING
UNGIRDED
UNGIRDS
UNGIRT
TRUING
UNGIVING
UNGLAZED
UNGLOVE DS
UNGLOVED
UNGLOVES
UNGLUE DS
UNGLUED
UNGLUES
UNGLUING
UNGODLY
UNGOT
UNGOTTEN
UNGOWNED
UNGRACED
UNGRADED
UNGREEDY
UNGROUND
UNGUAL
UNGULA
UNGUARD S
UNGUARDS
UNGUENT AS
UNGUENTA
UNGUENTS
UNGUES
UNGUIDED
UNGUIS
UNGULA ER
UNGUAL
UNGULAE
UNGULAR
UNGULATE S
UNHAILED
UNHAIR S
UNHAIRED
UNHAIRER S
UNHAIRS
UNHALLOW S
UNHALVED
UNHAND SY
UNHANDED
UNHANDS
UNHANDY
UNHANG S
UNHANGED
UNHANGS
UNHAPPY
UNHARMED
UNHASTY
UNHAT S
HAUNT
UNHATS
HAUNTS
UNHATTED
UNHEALED
UNHEARD
UNHEATED
UNHEDGED
UNHEEDED
UNHELM S
UNHELMED
UNHELMS
UNHELPED
UNHEROIC
UNHEWN
UNHINGE DS
UNHINGED
UNHINGES
UNHIP
UNHIRED
UNHITCH
UNHOLIER
UNHOLILY
UNHOLY
UNHOOD S
UNHOODED
UNHOODS
UNHOOK S
UNHOOKED
UNHOOKS
UNHOPED
UNHORSE DS
UNHORSED
ENSHROUD
HOUNDERS
UNHORSES
ONRUSHES
F UNHOUSE DS
UNHOUSED
F UNHOUSES
UNHUMAN
UNHUNG
UNHURT
UNHUSK S
UNHUSKED
UNHUSKS
UNIALGAL
UNIAXIAL
UNIBODY
UNICOLOR
UNICORN S
UNICORNS
UNICYCLE DS
UNIDEAED
UNIDEAL
ALIUNDE
UNIFACE S
UNIFACES
UNIFIC
UNIFIED
UNIFIER S
UNIFIERS
UNIFIES
UNIFILAR
C UNIFORM S
C UNIFORMS
UNIFY
UNIFYING
UNILOBED
UNBOILED
UNIMBUED
B UNION S
UNIONISE DS
UNIONISM S
MISUNION
UNIONIST S
UNIONIZE DRS
B UNIONS
UNISON
UNIPOD S
UNIPODS
UNIPOLAR
UNIQUE RS
UNIQUELY
UNIQUER
UNIQUES T
UNIQUEST
UNQUIETS
UNIRONED
UNIRONIC
UNISEX
UNISEXES
UNISIZE
UNISON S
UNIONS
UNISONAL
UNISONS
UNISSUED
UNIT ESY
UNITAGE S
UNITAGES
SAUTEING
UNITARD S
UNITARDS
UNITARY
DG UNITE DRS
UNTIE
UNITED
DUNITE
UNTIED
UNITEDLY
UNITER S
TRIUNE
UNITERS
NUTSIER
TRIUNES
DG UNITES
TENUIS
UNTIES
UNITIES
UNITING
P UNITIVE
UNITIZE DRS
UNITIZED
UNITIZER S
UNITIZES
UNITRUST S
UNITS
SUINT
UNITY
UNIVALVE DS
UNIVERSE S
UNIVOCAL S
UNJADED
UNJAM S
UNJAMMED
UNJAMS
UNJOINED
UNJOINT S
UNJOINTS
UNJOYFUL
UNJUDGED
UNJUST
UNJUSTLY
UNKEELED
UNKEMPT
UNKEND
UNKENNED
UNKENNEL S
UNKENT
UNKEPT
UNKIND
NUDNIK
UNKINDER
UNKINDLY
UNKINGLY
UNKINK S
UNKINKED
UNKINKS
UNKISSED
UNKNIT S
UNKNITS
UNKNOT S
UNKNOTS
UNKNOWN S
UNKNOWNS
UNKOSHER
UNLACE DS
CUNEAL
LACUNE
LAUNCE
UNLACED
UNLACES
CENSUAL
LACUNES
LAUNCES
UNLACING
UNLADE DNS
UNLEAD
UNLADED
UNLADEN
UNLADES
UNLEADS
UNLADING
UNLAID
UNLASH
UHLANS
UNLASHED
UNLASHES
UNLATCH
UNLAWFUL
UNLAY S
YULAN
UNLAYING
UNGAINLY
UNLAYS
YULANS
UNLEAD S
UNLADE
UNLEADED S
UNLEADS
UNLADES
UNLEARN ST
UNLEARNS
UNLEARNT
UNLEASED
UNSEALED
UNLEASH
UNLED
GRS UNLESS
R UNLET
LUNET
UNLETHAL
UNLETTED
UNLEVEL S
UNLEVELS
UNLEVIED
UNVEILED
UNLICKED
NS UNLIKE D
UNLIKED
UNLIKELY
UNLIMBER S
UNLINED
UNLINK S
UNLINKED
UNLINKS
UNLISTED
DILUENTS
INSULTED
S UNLIT
UNTIL
UNLIVE DS
UNVEIL
UNLIVED
UNLIVELY
UNLIVES
UNVEILS
UNLIVING
UNLOAD S
UNLOADED
DUODENAL
UNLOADER S
UNLOADS
UNLOBED
G UNLOCK S
UNLOCKED
G UNLOCKS
UNLOOSE DNS
UNLOOSED
NODULOSE
UNLOOSEN S
UNLOOSES
UNLOVED
UNLOVELY
UNLOVING
UNLUCKY
UNMACHO
UNMADE
UNMAILED
UNMAKE RS
UNMAKER S
UNMAKERS
UNMASKER
UNMAKES
UNMAKING
G UNMAN S
UNMANFUL
UNMANLY
UNMANNED
UNMANS
UNMAPPED
UNMARKED
UNMARRED
UNDERARM
UNMASK S
UNMASKED
UNMASKER S
UNMAKERS
UNMASKS
UNMATED
UNTAMED
UNMATTED
UNMEANT
UNMEET
UNMEETLY
UNMELLOW
UNMELTED
UNMENDED
UNMERRY
UNMESH
UNMESHED
UNMESHES
UNMET
UNMEW S
UNMEWED
UNMEWING
UNMEWS
UNMILLED
UNMINED
MINUEND
UNMINGLE DS
UNMITER S
MINUTER
UNMITRE
UNMITERS
TERMINUS
UNMITRES
UNMITRE DS
MINUTER
UNMITER
UNMITRED
RUDIMENT
UNMITRES
TERMINUS
UNMITERS
UNMIX T
UNMIXED
UNMIXES
UNMIXING
UNMIXT
UNMODISH
UNMOLD S
UNMOLDED
UNMOLDS
UNMOLTEN
UNMOOR S
UNMOORED
UNMOORS
SUNROOM
UNMORAL
UNMOVED
UNMOVING
UNMOWN
UNMUFFLE DS
UNMUZZLE DS
UNNAIL S
ANNULI
UNNAILED
UNNAILS
UNNAMED
MUNDANE
UNNEEDED
UNNERVE DS
UNNERVED
UNNERVES
UNNOISY
UNNOTED
UNOILED
UNOPEN
UNOPENED
UNORNATE
UNOWNED
ENWOUND
UNPACK S
UNPACKED
UNPACKER S
UNPACKS
UNPADDED
UNPAGED
UNPAID
UNPAIRED
UNREPAID
UNPARTED
UNPAVED
UNPAYING
UNPEELED
UNPEG S
UNPEGGED
UNPEGS
UNPEN ST
UNPENNED
UNPENS
UNPENT
PUNNET
UNPEOPLE DS
UNPERSON S
UNPICK S
UNPICKED
UNPICKS
UNPILE DS
LINEUP
LUPINE
UNPILED

UNPILES
LINEUPS
LUPINES
SPINULE
UNPILING
UNPIN S
UNPINNED
UNPINS
UNPITIED
UNPITTED
INPUTTED
UNPLACED
UNPLAIT S
NUPTIAL
UNPLAITS
NUPTIALS
UNPLAYED
UNPLIANT
UNPLOWED
UNPLUG S
UNPLUGS
UNPOETIC
UNPOISED
UNPOLITE
UNPOLLED
UNPOSED
UNPOSTED
OUTSPEND
UNPOTTED
UNPRETTY
UNPRICED
UNPRIMED
UNPRIZED
UNPROBED
PREBOUND
UNPROVED
UNPROVEN
UNPRUNED
UNPUCKER S
UNPURE
UNPURELY
UNPURGED
UNPUZZLE DS
UNQUIET S
UNQUIETS
UNIQUEST
UNQUOTE DS
UNQUOTED
UNQUOTES
UNRAISED
DENARIUS
URANIDES
UNRAKED
UNRANKED
UNRATED
DAUNTER
NATURED
UNTREAD
UNRAVEL S
VENULAR
UNRAVELS
UNRAZED
UNREAD Y
UNREADY
UNREAL
NEURAL
UNREALLY
NEURALLY
UNREASON S
UNREEL S
UNREELED
UNREELER S
UNREELS
UNREEVE DS
REVENUE
UNREEVED
REVENUED
UNREEVES
REVENUES
UNRENT
UNRENTED
UNREPAID
UNPAIRED
UNREPAIR S
UNREST S
TUNERS

UNRESTED
DENTURES
SEDERUNT
UNDERSET
UNRESTS
UNRETIRE DS
REUNITER
UNRHYMED
UNRIBBED
UNRIDDLE DR S
UNRIFLED
UNRIG S
RUING
UNRIGGED
UNRIGS
UNRIMED
UNRINSED
UNRIP ES
PURIN
UNRIPE R
PUNIER
PURINE
UNRIPELY
UNRIPER
UNRIPEST
UNRIPPED
UNRIPS
PURINS
UNRISEN
SUNNIER
UNROBE DS
BOURNE
UNROBED
BOUNDER
REBOUND
UNROBES
BOURNES
UNSOBER
UNROBING
UNROLL S
UNROLLED
UNROLLS
S **UNROOF** S
UNROOFED
S **UNROOFS**
SUNROOF
UNROOT S
UNROOTED
UNROOTS
UNROPED
POUNDER
UNROUGH
R **UNROUND** S
R **UNROUNDS**
UNROVE N
UNROVEN
UNRULED
UNRULIER
UNRULY
UNRUSHED
UNRUSTED
BDF GHM NPR ST **UNS**
NUS SUN
UNSADDLE DS
UNSAFE
UNSAFELY
UNSAFETY
UNSAID
UNSALTED
UNSATED
UNSAVED
UNSAVORY
UNSAWED
UNSAWN
UNSAY S
YUANS
UNSAYING
UNSAYS
UNSCALED
UNSCREW S
UNSCREWS
UNSEAL S
UNSEALED
UNLEASED
UNSEALS
SENSUAL

UNSEAM S
UNSEAMED
UNSEAMS
UNSEARED
UNDERSEA
UNERASED
UNSEAT S
UNSEATED
UNSEATS
UNSEEDED
UNSEEING
INGENUES
UNSEEMLY
UNSEEN
UNSEIZED
UNSELL S
SULLEN
UNSELLS
UNSENT
UNSERVED
UNVERSED
S **UNSET** S
TUNES
S **UNSETS**
SUNSET
UNSETTLE DS
LUNETTES
UNSEW NS
UNSEWED
UNSEWING
UNSEWN
UNSEWS
UNSEX Y
NEXUS
UNSEXED
UNSEXES
NEXUSES
UNSEXING
UNSEXUAL
UNSEXY
UNSHADED
UNSHAKEN
UNSHAMED
UNSHAPED
UNSHAPEN
UNSHARED
UNSHARP
UNSHAVED
UNSHAVEN
UNSHED
UNSHELL S
UNSHELLS
UNSHIFT S
UNSHIFTS
G **UNSHIP** S
PUNISH
G **UNSHIPS**
UNSHOD
HOUNDS
UNSHORN
UNSHOWY
UNSHRUNK
UNSHUT
UNSICKER
UNSIFTED
UNSIGHT S
SHUTING
TUSHING
UNSIGHTS
HUSTINGS
UNSIGNED
UNSILENT
UNSINFUL
UNSIZED
UNSLAKED
UNSLICED
INCLUDES
NUCLIDES
UNSLICK
UNSLING S
UNSLINGS
UNSLUNG
UNSMART
ANTRUMS
UNSMOKED
UNSNAG S
UNSNAGS

UNSNAP S
SANNUP
UNSNAPS
SANNUPS
UNSNARL S
UNSNARLS
UNSOAKED
UNSOBER
BOURNES
UNROBES
UNSOCIAL
UNSOILED
DELUSION
INSOULED
UNSOLD
UNSOLDER S
ROUNDELS
UNSOLID
UNSOLVED
UNSONCY
UNSONSIE
NONISSUE
UNSONSY
UNSORTED
ROUNDEST
TONSURED
UNSOUGHT
UNSOUND
UNSOURED
UNSOWED
SWOUNED
UNSOWN
UNSPEAK S
UNSPEAKS
UNSPENT
PUNNETS
UNSPHERE DS
UNSPILT
UNSPLIT
UNSPLIT
UNSPILT
UNSPOILT
UNSPOKE N
UNSPOKEN
UNSPOOL S
UNSPOOLS
UNSPRUNG
UNSPUN
UNSTABLE R
ABLUENTS
UNSTABLY
UNSTACK S
UNTACKS
UNSTACKS
UNSTATE DS
ATTUNES
NUTATES
TAUTENS
TETANUS
UNSTATED
UNTASTED
UNSTATES
TAUTNESS
UNSTAYED
UNSTEADY
UNSTEADY
UNSTAYED
UNSTEEL S
ELUENTS
UNSTEELS
TUNELESS
UNSTEP S
UPSENT
UNSTEPS
UNSTICK S
UNSTICKS
UNSTITCH
UNSTONED
UNSTOP S
PUNTOS
PUTONS
UNSTOPS
SUNSPOT
UNSTRAP S
UNSTRAPS
UNSTRESS
UNSTRING S
TURNINGS
UNSTRUNG
UNSTUCK
UNTUCKS

UNSTUFFY
UNSTUNG
UNSUBTLE
UNSUBTLY
UNSUITED
UNSUNG
UNSUNK
UNSURE
UNSURELY
UNSWATHE DS
UNSWAYED
UNSWEAR S
UNSWEARS
UNSWEPT
UNSWORE
UNSWORN
UNTACK S
UNTACKED
UNTACKS
UNSTACK
UNTAGGED
UNTAKEN
UNTAME D
UNTAMED
UNMATED
UNTANGLE DS
S **UNTANNED**
UNTAPPED
UNTASTED
UNSTATED
UNTAUGHT
UNTAXED
UNTEACH
UNTENDED
UNDENTED
UNTENTED
UNTESTED
UNTETHER S
UNTHAWED
UNTHINK S
UNTHINKS
UNTHREAD S
UNTHRONE DS
UNTIDIED
UNTIDIER
UNTIDIES T
DISUNITE
NUDITIES
UNTIDILY
UNTIDY
NUDITY
A **UNTIE** DS
UNITE
UNTIED
DUNITE
UNITED
UNTIEING
AP **UNTIES**
TENUIS
UNITES
UNTIL
UNLIT
UNTILLED
UNTILTED
UNTITLED
UNTIMED
MINUTED
MUTINED
UNTIMELY
MINUTELY
UNTINGED
UNTIPPED
UNTIRED
INTRUDE
TURDINE
UNTRIED
UNTIRING
UNTITLED
UNTILTED
JP **UNTO**
UNTOLD
UNTORN
TURNON
UNTOWARD
OUTDRAWN
UNTRACED
UNCARTED
UNCRATED
UNDERACT

UNTRACK S
UNTRACKS
UNTREAD S
DAUNTER
NATURED
UNRATED
UNTREADS
DAUNTERS
TRANSUDE
UNTRENDY
UNTRIED
INTRUDE
TURDINE
UNTIRED
UNTRIM S
UNTRIMS
UNTROD
ROTUND
UNTRUE R
UNTRUER
NURTURE
UNTRUEST
UNTRULY
UNTRUSS
UNTRUSTY
UNTRUTH S
UNTRUTHS
UNTUCK S
UNTUCKED
UNTUCKS
UNSTUCK
UNTUFTED
UNTUNE DS
UNTUNED
UNTUNES
UNTUNING
UNTURNED
UNTWINE DS
UNTWINED
UNTWINES
UNTWIST S
UNTWISTS
UNTYING
UNUNBIUM S
UNUNITED
UNURGED
UNUSABLE
UNUSED
UNUSUAL
UNVALUED
UNVARIED
UNVEIL S
UNLIVE
UNVEILED
UNLEVIED
UNVEILS
UNLIVES
UNVEINED
UNENVIED
UNVERSED
UNSERVED
UNVESTED
UNVEXED
UNVEXT
UNVIABLE
UNVOCAL
UNVOICE DS
UNVOICED
UNVOICES
UNWALLED
UNWANING
UNWANTED
UNWARIER
UNWARILY
UNWARMED
UNWARNED
UNWARPED
UNWARY
RUNWAY
UNWASHED S
UNWASTED
UNWAXED
UNWEANED
UNWEARY
UNWEAVE S
UNWEAVES
UNWED

UNWEDDED
UNWEEDED
UNWEIGHT S
UNWELDED
UNWELL
UNWEPT
UNWET
UNWETTED
UNWHITE
UNWIELDY
UNWIFELY
UNWILLED
UNWIND S
UNWINDER S
UNWINDS
UNWISDOM S
S **UNWISE** R
UNWISELY
UNWISER
UNWISEST
UNWISH
UNWISHED
UNWISHES
UNWIT S
UNWITS
UNWITTED
UNWON
UNWONTED
UNWOODED
UNWOOED
UNWORKED
UNWORN
UNWORTHY
UNWOUND
UNWOVE N
UNWOVEN
UNWRAP S
UNWRAPS
UNWRUNG
UNYEANED
UNYOKE DS
UNYOKED
UNYOKES
UNYOKING
UNYOUNG
UNZIP S
UNZIPPED
UNZIPS
UNZONED
CDH PST Y **UP** OS
P **UPAS**
UPASES
PAUSES
UPBEAR S
C **UPBEARER** S
UPBEARS
UPBEAT S
UPBEATS
UPBIND S
UPBINDS
UPBOIL S
UPBOILED
UPBOILS
UPBORE
UPBORNE
UPBOUND
UPBOW S
UPBOWS
UPBRAID S
UPBRAIDS
UPBUILD S
BUILDUP
UPBUILDS
BUILDUPS
UPBUILT
UPBY E
UPBYE
UPCAST S
CATSUP
UPCASTS
CATSUPS
UPCHUCK S
UPCHUCKS

UPCLIMB S
PLUMBIC
UPCLIMBS
UPCOAST
UPCOIL S
OILCUP
UPCOILED
CLUPEOID
UPCOILS
OILCUPS
UPCOMING
UPCOURT
UPCURL S
UPCURLED
UPCURLS
UPCURVE DS
UPCURVED
UPCURVES
UPDART S
UPDARTED
UPDARTS
UPDATE DRS
UPDATED
UPDATER S
UPRATED
UPDATERS
PASTURED
UPSTARED
UPDATES
UPDATING
UPDIVE DS
UPDIVED
UPDIVES
UPDIVING
UPDO S
UPDOS
UPDOVE
UPDRAFT S
UPDRAFTS
UPDRIED
UPDRIES
SIRUPED
UPDRY
UPDRYING
UPEND S
UPENDED
UPENDING
UPENDS
SENDUP
UPSEND
UPFIELD
UPFLING S
UPFLINGS
UPFLOW S
UPFLOWED
UPFLOWS
UPFLUNG
UPFOLD S
FOLDUP
UPFOLDED
UPFOLDS
FOLDUPS
UPFRONT
UPGATHER S
UPGAZE DS
UPGAZED
UPGAZES
UPGAZING
UPGIRD S
UPGIRDED
UPGIRDS
UPGIRT
UPGOING
UPGRADE DS
UPGRADED
UPGRADES
UPGREW
UPGROW NS
UPGROWN
GROWNUP
UPGROWS
UPGROWTH S
UPHEAP S
UPHEAPED
UPHEAPS
SHAPEUP
UPHEAVAL S
UPHEAVE DRS
UPHEAVED
UPHEAVER S
UPHEAVES
UPHELD
UPHILL S
UPHILLS
UPHOARD S
UPHOARDS
UPHOLD S
HOLDUP
UPHOLDER S
UPHOLDS
HOLDUPS
UPHOVE
E UPHROE S
E UPHROES
UPKEEP S
UPKEEPS
UPLAND S
UPLANDER S
PENDULAR
UNDERLAP
UPLANDS
UPLEAP ST
PAPULE
UPLEAPED
UPLEAPS
APPULSE
PAPULES
UPLEAPT
UPLIFT S
UPLIFTED
UPLIFTER S
UPLIFTS
UPLIGHT S
UPLIGHTS
UPLINK S
LINKUP
UPLINKED
UPLINKS
LINKUPS
UPLIT
TULIP
UPLOAD S
UPLOADED
UPLOADS
UPMARKET
UPMOST
UPO N
JY UPON
CDP UPPED
ST
CS UPPER S
UPPERCUT S
CS UPPERS
SUPPER
UPPILE DS
PILEUP
UPPILED
UPPILES
PILEUPS
UPPILING
CDP UPPING S
ST
C UPPINGS
SUPPING
UPPISH
UPPISHLY
UPPITY
UPPROP S
UPPROPS
UPRAISE DRS
UPRAISED
UPRAISER S
UPRAISES
UPRATE DS
UPTEAR
UPRATED
UPDATER
UPRATES
PASTURE
UPSTARE
UPTEARS
UPRATING
UPREACH
UPREAR S
PARURE
UPREARED
UPREARS
PARURES
UPRIGHT S
UPRIGHTS
UPRISE NRS
UPRISEN
PURINES
UPRISER S
PURSIER
UPRISERS
SPURRIES
SURPRISE
UPRISES
PUSSIER
SUSPIRE
UPRISING S
SIRUPING
UPRIVER S
UPRIVERS
UPROAR S
UPROARS
UPROOT S
UPROOTAL S
UPROOTED
UPROOTER S
UPROOTS
UPROSE
POSEUR
UPROUSE DS
UPROUSED
UPROUSES
UPRUSH
UPRUSHED
UPRUSHES
CDP UPS
STY PUS SUP
UPSCALE DS
CAPSULE
SCALEUP
SPECULA
UPSCALED
CAPSULED
UPSCALES
CAPSULES
SCALEUPS
UPSEND S
SENDUP
UPENDS
UPSENDS
SENDUPS
SUSPEND
UPSENT
UNSTEP
UPSET S
SETUP STUPE
UPSETS
SETUPS
STUPES
UPSETTER S
UPSHIFT S
UPSHIFTS
UPSHOOT S
UPSHOOTS
UPSHOT S
TOPHUS
UPSHOTS
UPSIDE S
UPSIDES
UPSILON S
PULSION
UPSILONS
PULSIONS
UPSIZE DS
UPSIZED
UPSIZES
UPSIZING
UPSLOPE
UPSOAR S
PAROUS
SAPOUR
UPSOARED
UPSOARS
SAPOURS
UPSPRANG
UPSPRING S
UPSPRUNG
UPSTAGE DRS
UPSTAGED
UPSTAGER S
UPSTAGES
UPSTAIR S
UPSTAIRS
UPSTAND S
DUSTPAN
STANDUP
UPSTANDS
DUSTPANS
STANDUPS
UPSTARE DS
PASTURE
UPRATES
UPTEARS
UPSTARED
PASTURED
UPDATERS
UPSTARES
PASTURES
UPSTART S
STARTUP
UPSTARTS
STARTUPS
UPSTATE RS
UPSTATER S
UPSTATES
UPSTEP S
UPSTEPS
UPSTIR S
PURIST
UPSTIRS
PURISTS
UPSTOOD
UPSTREAM
TEMPURAS
UPSTROKE S
UPSURGE DS
UPSURGED
UPSURGES
UPSWEEP S
UPSWEEPS
UPSWELL S
UPWELLS
UPSWELLS
UPSWEPT
UPSWING S
UPSWINGS
UPSWUNG
UPTAKE S
TAKEUP
UPTAKES
TAKEUPS
UPTALK S
UPTALKED
UPTALKS
UPTEAR S
UPRATE
UPTEARS
PASTURE
UPRATES
UPSTARE
UPTEMPO S
UPTEMPOS
UPTHREW
UPTHROW NS
UPTHROWN
UPTHROWS
UPTHRUST S
THRUPUTS
UPTICK S
UPTICKS
STICKUP
UPTIGHT
UPTILT S
UPTILTED
UPTILTS
UPTIME S
IMPUTE
UPTIMES
IMPETUS
IMPUTES
UPTORE
POUTER
ROUPET
TROUPE
UPTORN
UPTOSS
SPOUTS
STOUPS
TOSSUP
UPTOSSED
UPTOSSES
UPTOWN S
UPTOWNER S
UPTOWNS
UPTREND S
PRUDENT
UPTRENDS
UPTURN S
TURNUP
UPTURNED
UPTURNS
TURNUPS
UPWAFT S
UPWAFTED
UPWAFTS
UPWARD S
UPWARDLY
UPWARDS
UPWELL S
UPWELLED
UPWELLS
UPSWELL
UPWIND S
WINDUP
UPWINDS
WINDUPS
URACIL S
CURIAL
URACILS
URAEI
AUREI
URAEMIA S
URAEMIAS
URAEMIC
URAEUS
AUREUS
URAEUSES
R URALITE S
R URALITES
URALITIC
URANIA S
ANURIA
URANIAS
ANURIAS
SAURIAN
P URANIC
ANURIC
URANIDE S
UNAIRED
URANIDES
DENARIUS
UNRAISED
URANISM S
URANISMS
URANITE S
RUINATE
TAURINE
URINATE
URANITES
RUINATES
TAURINES
URINATES
URANITIC
URANIUM S
URANIUMS
URANOUS
ANUROUS
URANYL S
URANYLIC
CULINARY
URANYLS
C URARE S
C URARES
RASURE
CO URARI S
CO URARIS
URASE S
AURES UREAS
URSAE
URASES
ASSURE
AC URATE S
C URATES
URATIC
BC URB S
BUR
RUB
RT URBAN E
BURAN UNBAR
URBANE R
UNBEAR
URBANELY
URBANER
URBANEST
URBANISE DS
URBANISM S
URBANIST S
URBANITE S
BRAUNITE
URBANITY
URBANIZE DS
URBIA S
URBIAS
AIRBUS
BC URBS
BURS RUBS
URCHIN S
URCHINS
BCN URD S
ST
BCH URDS
NST SURD
UREA LS
UREAL
UREAS E
AURES URASE
URSAE
UREASE S
RESEAU
UREASES
RESEAUS
UREDIA L
UREDIAL
UREDINIA L
UREDIUM
UREDO S
UREDOS
DOUSER
ROUSED
SOURED
UREIC
CURIE
UREIDE S
UREIDES
RESIDUE
UREMIA S
UREMIAS
UREMIC
CERIUM
URETER S
URETERAL
URETERIC
URETERS
URETHAN ES
HAUNTER
UNEARTH
URETHANE S
URETHANS
HAUNTERS
UNEARTHS
URETHRA ELS
URETHRAE
URETHRAL
URETHRAS
URETIC
CURITE
GPS URGE DRS
GRUE
GPS URGED
T URGENCY
T URGENT
GURNET
URGENTLY
BPS URGER S
BPS URGERS
SURGER
GPS URGES
GRUES SURGE
GPS URGING
URGINGLY
BC URIAL S
B URIALS
A URIC
URIDINE S
URIDINES
URINAL S
URINALS
INSULAR
URINARY
URINATE DS
RUINATE
TAURINE
URANITE
URINATED
INDURATE
RUINATED
URINATES
RUINATES
TAURINES
URANITES
URINATOR S
MP URINE S
INURE
URINEMIA S
URINEMIC
MP URINES
INSURE
INURES
RUSINE
URSINE
URINOSE
URINOUS
RUINOUS
BCD URN S
T RUN
URNLIKE
BCD URNS
T RUNS
UROCHORD S
URODELE S
URODELES
DELOUSER
UROLITH S
UROLITHS
UROLOGIC
UROLOGY
UROPOD S
UROPODAL
UROPODS
UROPYGIA L
UROSCOPY
UROSTYLE S
ELYTROUS
B URP S
PUR
B URPED
DRUPE DUPER
PERDU PRUDE
B URPING
BT URPS
PURS SPUR
B URSA E
SURA
B URSAE
AURES URASE
UREAS
URSID S
URSIDS
B URSIFORM
URSINE
INSURE
INURES
RUSINE
URINES
URTEXT S
URTEXTS
URTICANT S
TACITURN
URTICATE DS
GK URUS
URUSES
URUSHIOL S
BJM US E
NP
USABLE
SUABLE
USABLY
SUABLY
USAGE S
AGUES
USAGES
USANCE S
UNCASE
USANCES
UNCASES
USAUNCE S
USAUNCES
FMR USE DRS
SUE
USEABLE
USEABLY
BFM USED
DUES SUED
M USEFUL

USEFULLY
F USELESS
M USER S
RUES RUSE SUER SURE
USERNAME S
M USERS
RUSES SUERS
BFMPR USES
SUES
BGLMPR USHER S
USHERED
USHERING
BGMPR USHERS
RHESUS RHUSES RUSHES
BFM USING
SUING
USNEA S
USNEAS
ANUSES
USQUABAE S
USQUE S
USQUEBAE S
USQUES
P USTULATE
USUAL S
LUAUS
USUALLY
USUALS
USUFRUCT S
USURER S
USURERS
USURIES
USURIOUS
USURP S
USURPED
PURSUED
USURPER S
PURSUER
USURPERS
PURSUERS
USURPING
PURSUING
USURPS
USURY
BCGHJMNOPRT UT AES
UTA S
TAU
UTAS
TAUS
BCJLM UTE S
UTENSIL S
LUNIEST LUTEINS
UTENSILS
UTERI
UTERINE
RETINUE REUNITE
UTERUS
SUTURE
UTERUSES
BCJLM UTES
SUET
FR UTILE
UTILIDOR S
UTILISE DRS
UTILISED
UTILISER S
UTILISES
F UTILITY
UTILIZE DRS
UTILIZED
UTILIZER S
UTILIZES
O UTMOST S
UTMOSTS
UTOPIA NS
UTOPIAN S
OPUNTIA
UTOPIANS
OPUNTIAS
UTOPIAS

UTOPISM S
UTOPISMS
UTOPIST S
UTOPISTS
UTRICLE S
UTRICLES
CURLIEST
UTRICULI
BCGHJMNOPRT UTS
BCGMNP UTTER S
BGMP UTTERED
MP UTTERER S
REUTTER
MP UTTERERS
REUTTERS
BGMP UTTERING
UTTERLY
BCGMNP UTTERS
TRUEST
UVEA LS
UVEAL
VALUE
UVEAS
SUAVE
UVEITIC
UVEITIS
UVEOUS
UVULA ERS
UVULAE
UVULAR S
UVULARLY
UVULARS
UVULAS
UVULITIS
UXORIAL
UXORIOUS

V

VAC S
VACANCY
VACANT
VACANTLY
VACATE DS
CAVEAT
VACATED
VACATES
CAVEATS
VACATING
VACATION S
VACCINA LS
VACCINAL
VACCINAS
VACCINE ES
VACCINEE S
VACCINES
VACCINIA LS
VACS
VACUA
VACUITY
VACUOLAR
VACUOLE S
VACUOLES
VACUOUS
VACUUM S
VACUUMED
VACUUMS
VADOSE
VAGABOND S
VAGAL
VAGALLY
VAGARIES
VAGARY
VAGI
VIGA
VAGILE
GLAIVE
VAGILITY
VAGINA ELS
VAGINAE
VAGINAL
VAGINAS

E VAGINATE D
NAVIGATE
VAGOTOMY
VAGRANCY
VAGRANT S
VAGRANTS
VAGROM
VAGUE R
VAGUELY
VAGUER
VAGUEST
VAGUS
VAHINE S
VAHINES
EVANISH
A VAIL S
VIAL
A VAILED
VIALED
A VAILING
VIALING
A VAILS
SILVA VIALS
VAIN
VINA
VAINER
NAIVER RAVINE
VAINEST
NAIVEST NATIVES
VAINLY
VAINNESS
VAIR S
VAIRS
VAKEEL S
VAKEELS
VAKIL S
VAKILS
VALANCE DS
VALANCED
VALANCES
VALE ST
LAVE LEVA VEAL VELA
VALENCE S
ENCLAVE
VALENCES
ENCLAVES
VALENCIA S
VALIANCE
VALENCY
VALERATE S
VALERIAN S
VALERIC
CAVILER CLAVIER
VALES
LAVES SALVE SELVA SLAVE VALSE VEALS
VALET S
VALETED
VALETING
VALETS
VESTAL
VALGOID
VALGUS
VALGUSES
VALIANCE S
VALENCIA
VALIANCY
VALIANT S
VALIANTS
VALID
VALIDATE DS
VALIDITY
VALIDLY
VALINE S
ALEVIN ALVINE VEINAL VENIAL VINEAL
VALINES
ALEVINS
VALISE S
SILVAE
VALISES
VALKYR S

VALKYRIE S
VALKYRS
VALLATE
VALLEY S
VALLEYED
VALLEYS
VALONIA S
VALONIAS
VALOR S
VOLAR
VALORISE DS
VARIOLES
VALORIZE DS
VALOROUS
VALORS
SALVOR
VALOUR S
OVULAR
VALOURS
VALSE S
LAVES SALVE SELVA SLAVE VALES VEALS
VALSES
SALVES SELVAS SLAVES
E VALUABLE S
VALUABLY
E VALUATE DS
E VALUATED
E VALUATES
E VALUATOR S
VALUE DRS
UVEAL
VALUED
VALUER S
VALUERS
VALUES
AVULSE
VALUING
VALUTA S
VALUTAS
VALVAL
VALVAR
VALVATE
VALVE DS
VALVED
VALVELET S
VALVES
VALVING
VALVULA ER
VALVULAE
VALVULAR
VALVULE S
VALVULES
VAMBRACE DS
VAMOOSE DS
VAMOOSED
VAMOOSES
VAMOSE DS
VAMOSED
VAMOSES
VAMOSING
VAMP SY
VAMPED
VAMPER S
REVAMP
VAMPERS
REVAMPS
VAMPIER
VAMPIRE
VAMPIEST
VAMPING
VAMPIRE S
VAMPIER
VAMPIRES
VAMPIRIC
VAMPISH
VAMPS
VAMPY
VAN EGS
VANADATE S
VANADIC
VANADIUM S
VANADOUS
VANDA LS

VANDAL S
VANDALIC
VANDALS
VANDAS
VANDYKE DS
VANDYKED
VANDYKES
VANE DS
NAVE VENA
VANED
DAVEN
VANES
AVENS NAVES
VANG S
VANGS
VANGUARD S
VANILLA S
VANILLAS
VANILLIC
VANILLIN S
E VANISH
E VANISHED
VANISHER S
ENRAVISH
E VANISHES
VANITIED
VANITIES
VANITORY
VANITY
VANLOAD S
VANLOADS
VANMAN
VANMEN
VANNED
VANNER S
VANNERS
VANNING
VANPOOL S
VANPOOLS
VANQUISH
VANS
VANTAGE S
VANTAGES
VANWARD
VAPID
PAVID
VAPIDITY
VAPIDLY
VAPOR SY
PARVO
VAPORED
VAPORER S
VAPORERS
VAPORING S
VAPORISE DS
VAPORISH
VAPORIZE DRS
VAPOROUS
VAPORS
PARVOS
VAPORY
VAPOUR SY
VAPOURED
VAPOURER S
VAPOURS
VAPOURY
VAQUERO S
VAQUEROS
VAR ASY
VARA S
VARACTOR S
VARAS
VARIA S
VARIABLE S
VARIABLY
VARIANCE S
VARIANT S
VARIANTS
VARIAS
VARIATE DS
VARIATED
VARIATES
A VARICES
VISCERA

VARICOSE DS
COVARIES
VARIED
VARIEDLY
VARIER S
ARRIVE
VARIERS
ARRIVES
O VARIES
AIVERS
VARIETAL S
VARIETY
VARIFORM
VARIOLA RS
OVARIAL
VARIOLAR
VARIOLAS
O VARIOLE S
O VARIOLES
VALORISE
VARIORUM S
VARIOUS
SAVIOUR
VARISTOR S
VARIX
VARLET S
TRAVEL
VARLETRY
VARLETS
TRAVELS VESTRAL
VARMENT S
VARMENTS
VARMINT S
VARMINTS
VARNA S
NAVAR
VARNAS
NAVARS
VARNISH Y
VARNISHY
HRYVNIAS
VAROOM S
VAROOMED
VAROOMS
VARS
VARSITY
VARUS
VARUSES
VARVE DS
VARVED
VARVES
O VARY
VARYING
K VAS AET
VASA L
VASAL
LAVAS
VASCULA R
A VASCULAR
VASCULUM S
VASE S
AVES SAVE
VASELIKE
VASELINE S
K VASES
SAVES
VASIFORM
VASOTOMY
VASSAL S
VASSALS
A VAST SY
TAVS VATS
VASTER
AVERTS STARVE TRAVES
VASTEST
VASTIER
VERITAS
VASTIEST
STATIVES
VASTITY
VASTLY
VASTNESS
VASTS
VASTY
VAT SU
TAV
VATFUL S

VATFULS
VATIC
VATICAL
VATICIDE S
CAVITIED
VATS
TAVS VAST
VATTED
VATTING
VATU S
VATUS
VAU S
VAULT SY
VAULTED
VAULTER S
VAULTERS
VESTURAL
VAULTIER
VAULTING S
VAULTS
VAULTY
A VAUNT SY
VAUNTED
VAUNTER S
VAUNTERS
VAUNTFUL
VAUNTIE
VAUNTING
VAUNTS
VAUNTY
VAUS
VAV S
VAVASOR S
VAVASORS
VAVASSOR
VAVASOUR S
VAVASSOR S
VAVASORS
VAVS
VAW S
VAWARD S
VAWARDS
VAWNTIE
VAWS
U VEAL SY
LAVE LEVA VALE VELA
VEALED
LEAVED
VEALER S
LAVEER LEAVER REVEAL
VEALERS
LAVEERS LEAVERS REVEALS SEVERAL
VEALIER
LEAVIER
VEALIEST
ELATIVES LEAVIEST
VEALING
LEAVING
VEALS
LAVES SALVE SELVA SLAVE VALES VALSE
VEALY
LEAVY
VECTOR S
CORVET COVERT
VECTORED
VECTORS
CORVETS COVERTS
VEDALIA S
AVAILED
VEDALIAS
VEDETTE S
VEDETTES
VEE PRS
EVE
VEEJAY S
JAYVEE
VEEJAYS
JAYVEES
VEENA S
VENAE

VEENAS
VEEP S
VEEPEE S
VEEPEES
VEEPS
VEER SY
EVER
VEERED
REEVED
VEERIES
VEERING
REEVING
REGIVEN
VEERS
SERVE SEVER
VERSE
VEERY
EVERY
VEES
EVES
VEG
VEGAN S
GANEV
VEGANISM S
VEGANS
GANEVS
VEGES
VEGETAL
VEGETANT
VEGETATE DS
VEGETE
VEGETIST S
VEGETIVE
VEGGED
VEGGIE S
VEGGIES
VEGGING
VEGIE S
VEGIES
VEHEMENT
VEHICLE S
VEHICLES
VEIL S
EVIL LIVE
VILE
VEILED
LEVIED
VEILEDLY
VEILER S
EVILER
LEVIER
LIEVER
RELIVE
REVILE
VEILERS
LEVIERS
RELIVES
REVILES
SERVILE
VEILING S
VEILINGS
VEILLIKE
VEILS
EVILS LEVIS
LIVES
VEIN SY
NEVI VINE
VEINAL
ALEVIN
ALVINE
VALINE
VENIAL
VINEAL
VEINED
DEVEIN
ENDIVE
ENVIED
VEINER S
ENVIER
VENIRE
VEINERS
ENVIERS
INVERSE
VENIRES
VERSINE
VEINIER
VEINIEST
INVITEES
VEINING S
VEININGS

VEINLESS
EVILNESS
LIVENESS
VILENESS
VEINLET S
VEINLETS
VEINLIKE
VEINS
VINES
VEINULE ST
VEINULES
VEINULET S
VEINY
VELA R
LAVE LEVA
VALE VEAL
VELAMEN
VELAMINA
VELAR S
LAVER RAVEL
VELARIA
REAVAIL
VELARIUM
VELARIZE DS
VELARS
LAVERS
RAVELS
SALVER
SERVAL
SLAVER
VERSAL
VELATE
VELCRO S
CLOVER
VELCROS
CLOVERS
VELD ST
VELDS
VELDT S
VELDTS
VELIGER S
VELIGERS
VELITES
EVILEST
LIEVEST
VELLEITY
VELLUM S
VELLUMS
VELOCE
VELOCITY
VELOUR S
LOUVER
LOUVRE
VELOURS
LOUVERS
LOUVRES
VELOUTE S
EVOLUTE
VELOUTES
EVOLUTES
VELUM
VELURE DS
VELURED
VELURES
VELURING
VELVERET S
VELVET SY
VELVETED
VELVETS
VELVETY
VENA EL
NAVE VANE
VENAE
VEENA
VENAL
NAVEL
VENALITY
NATIVELY
VENALLY
VENATIC
VENATION S
INNOVATE
VEND S
VENDABLE S
VENDACE S
VENDACES
VENDED
VENDEE S
EVENED
VENDEES

VENDER S
NERVED
VENDERS
VENDETTA S
VENDEUSE S
VENDIBLE S
VENDIBLY
VENDING
VENDOR S
VENDORS
VENDS
VENDUE S
VENDUES
VENEER S
EVENER
VENEERED
VENEERER S
VENEERS
EVENERS
VENENATE DS
VENENE S
VENENES
VENENOSE
VENERATE DS
ENERVATE
VENEREAL
VENERIES
VENERY
VENETIAN S
A VENGE DS
A VENGED
A VENGEFUL
A VENGES
A VENGING
VENIAL
ALEVIN
ALVINE
VALINE
VEINAL
VINEAL
VENIALLY
VENIN ES
VENINE S
VENINES
VENINS
VENIRE S
ENVIER
VEINER
VENIRES
ENVIERS
INVERSE
VEINERS
VERSINE
VENISON S
VENISONS
VENOGRAM S
MANGROVE
VENOLOGY
VENOM S
VENOMED
VENOMER S
OVERMEN
VENOMERS
VENOMING
VENOMOUS
VENOMS
VENOSE
VENOSITY
VENOUS
VENOUSLY
E VENT S
VENTAGE S
VENTAGES
A VENTAIL S
A VENTAILS
VENTED
VENTER S
VENTERS
VENTING
E VENTLESS
VENTRAL S
VENTRALS
E VENTS
VENTURE DRS
VENTURED
VENTURER S
VENTURES

VENTURI S
VENTURIS
A VENUE S
A VENUES
VENULAR
UNRAVEL
VENULE S
VENULES
VENULOSE
VENULOUS
VENUS
NEVUS
VENUSES
VERA
AVER RAVE
VERACITY
VERANDA HS
VERANDAH S
VERANDAS
VERATRIA S
VERATRIN ES
VERATRUM S
VERB S
VERBAL S
VERBALLY
VERBALS
VERBATIM
AMBIVERT
VERBENA S
VERBENAS
VERBIAGE S
O VERBID S
O VERBIDS
VERBIFY
VERBILE S
VERBILES
VERBLESS
VERBOSE
OBSERVE
OBVERSE
VERBOTEN
VERBS
VERDANCY
VERDANT
VERDERER S
VERDEROR S
VERDICT S
VERDICTS
VERDIN S
DRIVEN
VERDINS
VERDITER S
DIVERTER
VERDURE DS
VERDURED
VERDURES
VERECUND
VERGE DRS
VERGED
VERGENCE S
VERGER S
VERGERS
VERGES
VERGING
VERGLAS
GRAVELS
VERIDIC
VERIER
REIVER
RIEVER
VERIEST
RESTIVE
SIEVERT
VERITES
VERIFIED
VERIFIER S
VERIFIES
VERIFY
VERILY
LIVERY
LIVYER
VERISM OS
VERMIS
VERISMO S
VERISMOS
VERISMS

VERIST S
RIVETS
STIVER
STRIVE
VERISTIC
VERISTS
STIVERS
STRIVES
VERITAS
VASTIER
VERITE S
VERITES
RESTIVE
SIEVERT
VERIEST
VERITIES
VERITY
VERJUICE S
VERMEIL S
VERMEILS
VERMES
VERMIAN
VERMIN
VERMIS
VERISM
VERMOULU
VERMOUTH S
VERMUTH S
VERMUTHS
VERNACLE S
VERNAL
VERNALLY
VERNICLE S
VERNIER S
NERVIER
VERNIERS
VERNIX
VERNIXES
VERONICA S
VERRUCA ES
VERRUCAE
VERRUCAS
VERSAL
LAVERS
RAVELS
SALVER
SERVAL
SLAVER
VELARS
VERSANT S
SERVANT
TAVERNS
VERSANTS
SERVANTS
A VERSE DRST
SERVE SEVER
VEERS
VERSED
SERVED
VERSEMAN
VERSEMEN
VERSER S
REVERS
SERVER
VERSERS
SERVERS
VERSES
SERVES
SEVERS
O VERSET S
EVERTS
REVEST
REVETS
VERSTE
O VERSETS
REVESTS
VERSTES
VERSICLE S
VERSIFY
VERSINE S
ENVIERS
INVERSE
VEINERS
VENIRES
VERSINES
INVERSES
VERSING
SERVING
AE VERSION S
ENVIROS
RENVOIS

AE VERSIONS
VERSO S
OVERS ROVES
SERVO
VERSOS
SERVOS
VERST ES
VERTS
VERSTE S
EVERTS
REVEST
REVETS
VERSET
VERSTES
REVESTS
VERSETS
VERSTS
VERSUS
AEO VERT SU
VERTEBRA EL
S
VERTEX
VERTEXES
VERTICAL S
VERTICES
VERTICIL S
VERTIGO S
VERTIGOS
AE VERTS
VERST
VERTU S
VERTUS
TURVES
VERVAIN S
VERVAINS
VERVE ST
VERVES
VERVET S
VERVETS
E VERY
VESICA EL
CAVIES
VESICAE
VESICAL
VESICANT S
VESICATE DS
VESICLE S
VESICLES
CLEVISES
VICELESS
VESICULA ER
VESPER S
VESPERAL S
VESPERS
VESPIARY
VESPID S
VESPIDS
VESPINE
PENSIVE
VESSEL S
SELVES
VESSELED
VESSELS
VEST AS
VETS
VESTA LS
STAVE
VESTAL S
VALETS
VESTALLY
VESTALS
VESTAS
STAVES
VESTED
DEVEST
VESTEE S
STEEVE
VESTEES
STEEVES
VESTIARY
VESTIGE S
VESTIGES
VESTIGIA L
VESTING S
VESTINGS
VESTLESS
VESTLIKE
VESTMENT S

VESTRAL
TRAVELS
VARLETS
VESTRIES
SIEVERTS
VESTRY
VESTS
VESTURAL
VAULTERS
VESTURE DS
VESTURED
VESTURES
VESUVIAN S
VET OS
K VETCH
K VETCHES
VETERAN S
NERVATE
VETERANS
VETIVER ST
VETIVERS
VETIVERT S
VETO
VOTE
VETOED
DEVOTE
VETOER S
REVOTE
VETOERS
OVERSET
REVOTES
VETOES
VETOING
VETS
VEST
VETTED
VETTER S
TREVET
VETTERS
TREVETS
VETTING
VEX T
VEXATION S
VEXED
VEXEDLY
VEXER S
VEXERS
VEXES
VEXIL S
VEXILLA R
VEXILLAR Y
VEXILLUM
VEXILS
SILVEX
VEXING
VEXINGLY
VEXT
VIA L
VIABLE
VIABLY
VIADUCT S
VIADUCTS
VIAL S
VAIL
VIALED
VAILED
VIALING
VAILING
VIALLED
VIALLING
VIALS
SILVA VAILS
VIAND S
DIVAN
VIANDS
DIVANS
A VIATIC A
VIATICA L
AVIATIC
VIATICAL S
VIATICUM S
A VIATOR S
VIATORES
TRAVOISE
VOTARIES
A VIATORS
TRAVOIS
VIBE S
VIBES
VIBIST S

VIBISTS
VIBRANCE S
VIBRANCY
VIBRANT S
VIBRANTS
VIBRATE DS
VIBRATED
VIBRATES
VIBRATO RS
VIBRATOR SY
VIBRATOS
VIBRIO NS
VIBRIOID
VIBRION S
VIBRIONS
VIBRIOS
VIBRISSA EL
VIBRONIC
VIBURNUM S
VICAR S
VICARAGE S
VICARATE S
VICARIAL
VICARLY
VICARS
VICE DS
VICED
VICELESS
  CLEVISES
  VESICLES
VICENARY
VICEROY S
VICEROYS
VICES
VICHIES
  CHIVIES
VICHY
  CHIVY
VICINAGE S
VICINAL
VICING
VICINITY
VICIOUS
VICOMTE S
VICOMTES
VICTIM S
VICTIMS
E VICTOR SY
VICTORIA S
E VICTORS
VICTORY
VICTRESS
VICTUAL S
VICTUALS
VICUGNA S
VICUGNAS
VICUNA S
VICUNAS
A VID ES
VIDE O
  DIVE VIED
VIDEO S
VIDEOS
VIDEOTEX T
VIDETTE S
VIDETTES
VIDICON S
VIDICONS
VIDS
VIDUITY
VIE DRSW
I VIED
  DIVE VIDE
VIER S
  RIVE
VIERS
  RIVES SIVER
  VIRES
I VIES
  VISE
VIEW SY
  WIVE
VIEWABLE
VIEWDATA
VIEWED
VIEWER S
  REVIEW
VIEWERS
  REVIEWS
VIEWIER
VIEWIEST
VIEWING S
VIEWINGS
VIEWLESS
VIEWS
  SWIVE WIVES
VIEWY
VIG AS
VIGA S
  VAGI
VIGAS
VIGIA S
VIGIAS
VIGIL S
VIGILANT E
VIGILS
VIGNERON S
VIGNETTE DR S
VIGOR S
VIGORISH
VIGOROSO
VIGOROUS
VIGORS
VIGOUR S
VIGOURS
VIGS
VIKING S
VIKINGS
  SKIVING
VILAYET S
VILAYETS
VILE R
  EVIL LIVE
  VEIL
VILELY
  EVILLY
  LIVELY
VILENESS
  EVILNESS
  LIVENESS
  VEINLESS
E VILER
  ERVIL LIVER
  LIVRE
E VILEST
  LIVEST
VILIFIED
VILIFIER S
VILIFIES
VILIFY
VILIPEND S
VILL AIS
VILLA ES
VILLADOM S
VILLAE
VILLAGE RS
VILLAGER SY
VILLAGES
VILLAIN SY
VILLAINS
VILLAINY
VILLAS
VILLATIC
VILLEIN S
VILLEINS
VILLI
VILLOSE
VILLOUS
VILLS
VILLUS
VIM S
VIMEN
VIMINA L
VIMINAL
VIMS
VINA LS
  VAIN
VINAL S
  ANVIL NIVAL
VINALS
  ANVILS
  SILVAN
VINAS
  SAVIN
VINASSE S
  SAVINES
VINASSES
VINCA S
VINCAS
E VINCIBLE
VINCIBLY
VINCULA
VINCULUM S
VINDALOO S
O VINE DS
  NEVI VEIN
VINEAL
  ALEVIN
  ALVINE
  VALINE
  VEINAL
  VENIAL
VINED
VINEGAR SY
  REAVING
VINEGARS
VINEGARY
VINERIES
VINERY
O VINES
  VEINS
VINEYARD S
VINIC
VINIER
VINIEST
  INVITES
VINIFERA S
VINIFIED
VINIFIES
VINIFY
VINING
VINO S
VINOS
VINOSITY
VINOUS
VINOUSLY
VINTAGE RS
VINTAGER S
  AVERTING
  GRIEVANT
VINTAGES
VINTNER S
VINTNERS
VINY L
VINYL S
VINYLIC
VINYLS
  SYLVIN
VIOL AS
VIOLA S
  VOILA
VIOLABLE
VIOLABLY
VIOLAS
VIOLATE DRS
VIOLATED
  DOVETAIL
VIOLATER S
VIOLATES
VIOLATOR S
VIOLENCE S
VIOLENT
VIOLET S
VIOLETS
VIOLIN S
VIOLINS
VIOLIST S
VIOLISTS
VIOLONE S
VIOLONES
VIOLS
VIOMYCIN S
VIPER S
VIPERINE
VIPERISH
VIPEROUS
  PERVIOUS
  PREVIOUS
VIPERS
VIRAGO S
VIRAGOES
VIRAGOS
VIRAL
  RIVAL
VIRALLY
VIRELAI S
VIRELAIS
VIRELAY S
VIRELAYS
VIREMIA S
VIREMIAS
VIREMIC
VIREO S
VIREOS
VIRES
  RIVES SIVER
  VIERS
VIRGA S
VIRGAS
VIRGATE S
VIRGATES
VIRGIN S
  RIVING
VIRGINAL S
  RIVALING
VIRGINS
VIRGULE S
VIRGULES
VIRICIDE S
VIRID
VIRIDIAN S
VIRIDITY
VIRILE
  LIVIER
VIRILELY
VIRILISM S
VIRILITY
VIRILIZE DS
VIRION S
VIRIONS
VIRL S
VIRLS
VIROID S
VIROIDS
  DIVISOR
VIROLOGY
VIROSES
VIROSIS
VIRTU ES
VIRTUAL
VIRTUE S
VIRTUES
  REVUIST
  STUIVER
VIRTUOSA S
VIRTUOSE
  VITREOUS
VIRTUOSI C
VIRTUOSO S
VIRTUOUS
VIRTUS
VIRUCIDE S
A VIRULENT
VIRUS
VIRUSES
VIRUSOID S
VIS AE
VISA S
VISAED
  ADVISE
  DAVIES
VISAGE DS
VISAGED
VISAGES
VISAING
VISARD S
VISARDS
VISAS
VISCACHA S
VISCERA L
  VARICES
VISCERAL
  CAVILERS
  CLAVIERS
VISCID
VISCIDLY
VISCOID
VISCOSE S
VISCOSES
VISCOUNT SY
VISCOUS
VISCUS
VISE DS
  VIES
VISED
  DIVES
VISEED
  DEVISE
  SIEVED
VISEING
  SIEVING
VISELIKE
VISES
VISIBLE
VISIBLY
VISING
VISION S
VISIONAL
VISIONED
VISIONS
VISIT S
VISITANT S
  NATIVIST
VISITED
VISITER S
  REVISIT
VISITERS
  REVISITS
VISITING
VISITOR S
VISITORS
VISITS
VISIVE
VISOR S
VISORED
  DEVISOR
  DEVOIRS
  VOIDERS
VISORING
VISORS
VISTA S
VISTAED
  DATIVES
VISTAS
VISUAL S
VISUALLY
VISUALS
VITA EL
VITAE
VITAL S
VITALISE DS
VITALISM S
VITALIST S
VITALITY
VITALIZE DR S
VITALLY
VITALS
VITAMER S
VITAMERS
VITAMIN ES
VITAMINE S
VITAMINS
  NATIVISM
VITELLIN ES
VITELLUS
VITESSE S
VITESSES
VITIABLE
VITIATE DS
VITIATED
VITIATES
VITIATOR S
VITILIGO S
VITRAIN S
VITRAINS
VITREOUS
  VIRTUOSE
VITRIC S
VITRICS
VITRIFY
VITRINE S
  INVITER
VITRINES
  INVITERS
VITRIOL S
VITRIOLS
VITTA E
VITTAE
VITTATE
VITTLE DS
VITTLED
VITTLES
VITTLING
VITULINE
VIVA S
VIVACE S
VIVACES
VIVACITY
VIVARIA
VIVARIES
VIVARIUM S
VIVARY
VIVAS
VIVE
VIVERRID S
VIVERS
VIVID
VIVIDER
VIVIDEST
VIVIDLY
VIVIFIC
VIVIFIED
VIVIFIER S
VIVIFIES
VIVIFY
VIVIPARA
VIVISECT S
VIXEN S
VIXENISH
VIXENLY
VIXENS
VIZARD S
VIZARDED
VIZARDS
VIZCACHA S
VIZIER S
VIZIERS
VIZIR S
VIZIRATE S
VIZIRIAL
VIZIRS
VIZOR S
VIZORED
VIZORING
VIZORS
VIZSLA S
VIZSLAS
VOCAB S
E VOCABLE S
VOCABLES
VOCABLY
VOCABS
VOCAL S
VOCALESE S
VOCALIC S
VOCALICS
VOCALISE DS
VOCALISM S
VOCALIST S
VOCALITY
VOCALIZE DR S
VOCALLY
VOCALS
AE VOCATION S
E VOCATIVE S
VOCES
  COVES
VOCODER S
  CODROVE
VOCODERS
VODKA S
VODKAS
VODOU NS
VODOUN S
  VOUDON
VODOUNS
  VOUDONS
VODOUS
VODUN S
VODUNS
VOE S
VOES
VOGIE
  OGIVE
VOGUE DRS
VOGUED
VOGUEING S
VOGUER S
VOGUERS
VOGUES
VOGUING S
VOGUINGS
VOGUISH
VOICE DRS
VOICED
VOICEFUL
VOICER S
VOICERS
VOICES
VOICING S
VOICINGS
AO VOID S
A VOIDABLE
A VOIDANCE S
A VOIDED
  DEVOID
A VOIDER S
  DEVOIR
A VOIDERS
  DEVISOR
  DEVOIRS
  VISORED
A VOIDING
VOIDNESS
AO VOIDS
VOILA
  VIOLA
VOILE S
  OLIVE
VOILES
  OLIVES
VOLANT E
VOLANTE
VOLAR
  VALOR
VOLATILE S
VOLCANIC S
VOLCANO S
VOLCANOS
VOLE DS
  LEVO LOVE
VOLED
  LOVED
VOLERIES
  OVERLIES
  RELIEVOS
VOLERY
  OVERLY
VOLES
  LOVES SOLVE
VOLING
  LOVING
VOLITANT
VOLITION S
VOLITIVE
VOLLEY S
  LOVELY
VOLLEYED
VOLLEYER S
VOLLEYS
VOLOST S
VOLOSTS
VOLPLANE DS
VOLT AEIS
VOLTA
  LOVAT
VOLTAGE S
VOLTAGES
VOLTAIC
VOLTAISM S
VOLTE S
VOLTES
VOLTI
VOLTS
VOLUBLE
VOLUBLY
VOLUME DS

VOLUMED
VOLUMES
VOLUMING
E VOLUTE DS
VOLUTED
E VOLUTES
VOLUTIN S
VOLUTINS
E VOLUTION S
VOLVA S
VOLVAS
VOLVATE
VOLVOX
VOLVOXES
VOLVULI
VOLVULUS
VOMER S
MOVER
VOMERINE
OVERMINE
VOMERS
MOVERS
VOMICA E
VOMICAE
VOMIT OS
VOMITED
MOTIVED
VOMITER S
VOMITERS
VOMITING
MOTIVING
VOMITIVE S
VOMITO S
VOMITORY
VOMITOS
VOMITOUS
VOMITS
VOMITUS
VOODOO S
VOODOOED
VOODOOS
VORACITY
VORLAGE S
VORLAGES
VORTEX
VORTEXES
VORTICAL
VORTICES
EVICTORS
VOTABLE
VOTARESS
VOTARIES
TRAVOISE
VIATORES
VOTARIST S
VOTARY
VOTE DRS
VETO
VOTEABLE
VOTED
VOTELESS
VOTER S
OVERT TROVE
VOTERS
STOVER
STROVE
TROVES
VOTES
STOVE
VOTING
VOTIVE S
VOTIVELY
VOTIVES
VOTRESS
STOVERS
A VOUCH
A VOUCHED
VOUCHEE S
VOUCHEES
A VOUCHER S
A VOUCHERS
A VOUCHES
A VOUCHING
VOUDON S
VODOUN
VOUDONS
VODOUNS
VOUDOUN S
VOUDOUNS
VOUSSOIR S
VOUVRAY S
VOUVRAYS
A VOW S
A VOWED
VOWEL S
VOWELIZE DS
VOWELS
WOLVES
A VOWER S
A VOWERS
A VOWING
VOWLESS
A VOWS
VOX
VOYAGE DRS
VOYAGED
VOYAGER S
VOYAGERS
VOYAGES
VOYAGEUR S
VOYAGING
VOYEUR S
VOYEURS
VROOM S
VROOMED
VROOMING
VROOMS
VROUW S
VROUWS
VROW S
VROWS
VUG GHS
GUV
VUGG SY
VUGGIER
VUGGIEST
VUGGS
VUGGY
VUGH S
VUGHS
VUGS
GUVS
VULCANIC
VULGAR S
VULGARER
VULGARLY
VULGARS
VULGATE S
VULGATES
VULGO
VULGUS
VULGUSES
VULPINE
VULTURE S
VULTURES
VULVA ELRS
VULVAE
VULVAL
VULVAR
VULVAS
VULVATE
VULVITIS
O VUM
VYING
VYINGLY

W

S WAB S
WABBLE DRS
WABBLED
WABBLER S
WABBLERS
WABBLES
WABBLIER
WABBLING
WABBLY
S WABS
SWAB
WACK EOSY
WACKE RS
WACKER
WACKES T
WACKEST
WACKIER
WACKIEST
WACKILY
WACKO S
WACKOS
WACKS
WACKY
WAD EISY
DAW
WADABLE
WADDED
WADDER S
WARDED
WADDERS
SWARDED
WADDIE DS
WADDIED
WADDIES
WADDING S
WADDINGS
ST WADDLE DRS
DAWDLE
ST WADDLED
DAWDLED
T WADDLER S
DAWDLER
DRAWLED
T WADDLERS
DAWDLERS
ST WADDLES
DAWDLES
SWADDLE
ST WADDLING
DAWDLING
WADDLY
WADDY
WADDYING
WADE DRS
AWED
WADEABLE
WADED
DAWED
WADER S
DEWAR WARED
WADERS
DEWARS
WADES
SAWED
WADI S
WADIES
WADING
DAWING
WADIS
WADMAAL S
WADMAALS
WADMAL S
WADMALS
WADMEL S
WADMELS
WADMOL LS
WADMOLL S
WADMOLLS
WADMOLS
WADS
DAWS
WADSET S
TAWSED
WASTED
WADSETS
WADY
T WAE S
AWE
WAEFUL
WAENESS
T WAES
AWES
WAESUCK S
WAESUCKS
WAFER SY
WAFERED
WAFERING
WAFERS
WAFERY
WAFF S
WAFFED
WAFFIE S
WAFFIES
WAFFING
WAFFLE DRS
WAFFLED
WAFFLER S
WAFFLERS
WAFFLES
WAFFLIER
WAFFLING S
WAFFLY
WAFFS
WAFT S
WAFTAGE S
WAFTAGES
WAFTED
WAFTER S
WAFTERS
FRETSAW
WAFTING
WAFTS
WAFTURE S
WAFTURES
S WAG ES
S WAGE DRS
S WAGED
WAGELESS
S WAGER S
WAGERED
RAGWEED
WAGERER S
WAGERERS
WAGERING
S WAGERS
SWAGER
S WAGES
SWAGE
S WAGGED
S WAGGER SY
S WAGGERS
SWAGGER
WAGGERY
S WAGGING
WAGGISH
WAGGLE DS
WAGGLED
WAGGLES
WAGGLIER
WAGGLING
WAGGLY
WAGGON S
WAGGONED
WAGGONER S
WAGGONS
S WAGING
WAGON S
GOWAN
WAGONAGE S
WAGONED
GOWANED
WAGONER S
WAGONERS
WAGONING
WAGONS
GOWANS
S WAGS
SWAG
WAGSOME
WAGTAIL S
WAGTAILS
WAHCONDA S
WAHINE S
WAHINES
WAHOO S
WAHOOS
WAIF S
WAIFED
WAIFING
WAIFISH
WAIFLIKE
WAIFS
S WAIL S
WAILED
WAILER S
WAILERS
WAILFUL
WAILING
S WAILS
SWAIL
WAILSOME
ST WAIN S
ST WAINS
SWAIN
WAINSCOT S
WAIR S
WAIRED
WAIRING
WAIRS
WAIST S
WAITS
WAISTED
DAWTIES
WAISTER S
WAITERS
WARIEST
WASTRIE
WAISTERS
WAITRESS
WASTRIES
WAISTING S
WAITINGS
WAISTS
A WAIT S
A WAITED
DAWTIE
A WAITER S
WAITERED
A WAITERS
WAISTER
WARIEST
WASTRIE
A WAITING S
WAITINGS
WAISTING
WAITLIST S
WAITRESS
WAISTERS
WASTRIES
WAITRON S
WAITRONS
A WAITS
WAIST
WAIVE DRS
WAIVED
WAIVER S
WAVIER
WAIVERS
WAIVES
WAVIES
WAIVING
WAKAME S
WAKAMES
WAKANDA S
WAKANDAS
A WAKE DNRS
WEAK WEKA
A WAKED
WAKEFUL
WAKELESS
A WAKEN S
KNAWE
A WAKENED
A WAKENER S
REWAKEN
A WAKENERS
REWAKENS
A WAKENING S
A WAKENS
KNAWES
WAKER S
WREAK
WAKERIFE
WAKERS
WREAKS
A WAKES
ASKEW WEKAS
WAKIKI S
WAKIKIS
A WAKING
S WALE DRS
WEAL
WALED
LAWED WEALD
WALER S
WALERS
WARSLE
S WALES
SWALE WEALS
WALIES
WALING
LAWING
WALK S
WALKABLE
WALKAWAY S
WALKED
WALKER S
WALKERS
WALKING S
WALKINGS
WALKOUT S
OUTWALK
WALKOUTS
OUTWALKS
WALKOVER S
WALKS
WALKUP S
WALKUPS
WALKWAY S
WALKWAYS
WALKYRIE S
WALL ASY
WALLA HS
WALLABY
WALLAH S
WALLAHS
WALLAROO S
WALLAS
WALLED
WALLET S
WALLETS
WALLEYE DS
WALLEYED
WALLEYES
WEASELLY
WALLIE S
WALLIES
WALLING
WALLOP S
WALLOPED
WALLOPER S
WALLOPS
S WALLOW S
S WALLOWED
S WALLOWER S
S WALLOWS
SWALLOW
WALLS
WALLY
WALNUT S
WALNUTS
WALRUS
WALRUSES
WALTZ
WALTZED
WALTZER S
WALTZERS
WALTZES
WALTZING
WALY
YAWL
WAMBLE DS
WAMBLED
WAMBLES
WAMBLIER
WAMBLING
WAMBLY
WAME S
WAMEFOU S
WAMEFOUS
WAMEFUL S
WAMEFULS
WAMES
WAMMUS
WAMMUSES
S WAMPISH
WAMPUM S
WAMPUMS
WAMPUS
WAMPUSES
WAMUS
WAMUSES
HS WAN DEKSTY
AWN
NAW
WAND S
DAWN
WANDER S
WARDEN
WARNED
WANDERED
WANDERER S
WANDEROO S
WANDERS
WARDENS
WANDLE
WANDS
DAWNS
WANE DSY
ANEW WEAN
WANED
AWNED DAWEN
DEWAN
WANES
SEWAN WEANS
WANEY
WANGAN S
WANGANS
T WANGLE DRS
T WANGLED
T WANGLER S
WRANGLE
T WANGLERS
WRANGLES
T WANGLES
T WANGLING
WANGUN S
WANGUNS
WANIER
WANIEST
TAWNIES
WANIGAN S
WANIGANS
WANING
AWNING
WANION S
WANIONS
WANLY
LAWNY
WANNABE ES
WANNABEE S
WANNABES
S WANNED
WANNER
WANNESS
WANNEST
WANNIGAN S
S WANNING
S WANS
AWNS SAWN
SNAW SWAN
WANT S
WANTAGE S
WANTAGES
WANTED
WANTER S
WANTERS
WANTING
WANTON S
WANTONED
WANTONER S
WANTONLY
WANTONS
WANTS
WANY
AWNY YAWN
S WAP S
PAW
WAPITI S
WAPITIS
S WAPPED
S WAPPING
S WAPS
PAWS SWAP
WASP
WAR DEKMNPS
RAW TY
WARBLE DRS
BAWLER
WARBLED
BRAWLED
WARBLER S
BRAWLER
WARBLERS
BRAWLERS
WARBLES
BAWLERS

WARBLING
BRAWLING
WARCRAFT S
AS WARD S
DRAW
AS WARDED
WADDER
WARDEN S
WANDER
WARNED
WARDENRY
WARDENS
WANDERS
A WARDER S
DRAWER
REDRAW
REWARD
WARRED
A WARDERS
DRAWERS
REDRAWS
REWARDS
AS WARDING
DRAWING
WARDLESS
WRASSLED
WARDRESS
WARDROBE DS
DRAWBORE
WARDROOM S
AS WARDS
DRAWS SWARD
WARDSHIP S
AS WARE DS
WEAR
WARED
DEWAR WADER
WAREROOM S
WARES
RESAW SAWER
SEWAR SWARE
SWEAR WEARS
WARFARE S
WARFARES
WARFARIN S
WARHEAD S
WARHEADS
WARHORSE S
WARIER
WARIEST
WAISTER
WAITERS
WASTRIE
WARILY
WARINESS
WARING
WARISON S
WARISONS
WARK S
WARKED
WARKING
WARKS
WARLESS
WARSLES
WRASSLE
WARLIKE
WARLOCK S
WARLOCKS
WARLORD S
WARLORDS
S WARM S
WARMAKER S
S WARMED
S WARMER S
REWARM
S WARMERS
REWARMS
SWARMER
WARMEST
S WARMING
WARMISH
WARMLY
WARMNESS
WARMOUTH S
S WARMS
SWARM
WARMTH S
WARMTHS
WARMUP S
WARMUPS
WARN S
WARNED
WANDER
WARDEN
WARNER S
WARREN
WARNERS
WARRENS
WARNING S
WARNINGS
WARNS
WARP S
WRAP
WARPAGE S
WARPAGES
WARPATH S
WARPATHS
WARPED
WARPER S
PREWAR
REWRAP
WARPERS
REWRAPS
WARPING
WARPLANE S
WARPOWER S
WARPS
WRAPS
WARPWISE
WARRAGAL S
WARRANT SY
WARRANTS
WARRANTY
WARRED
DRAWER
REDRAW
REWARD
WARDER
WARREN S
WARNER
WARRENER S
WARRENS
WARNERS
WARRIGAL S
WARRING
WARRIOR S
WARRIORS
WARS
RAWS
WARSAW S
WARSAWS
WARSHIP S
WARSHIPS
WARSLE DRS
WALERS
WARSLED
WARSLER S
WARSLERS
WARSLES
WARLESS
WRASSLE
WARSLING
WARSTLE DRS
WASTREL
WRASTLE
WARSTLED
WRASTLED
WARSTLER S
TRAWLERS
WARSTLES
WARTLESS
WASTRELS
WRASTLES
S WART SY
WARTED
WARTHOG S
WARTHOGS
WARTIER
WARTIEST
WARTIME S
WARTIMES
WARTLESS
WARSTLES
WASTRELS
WRASTLES
WARTLIKE
WARTS
STRAW SWART
S WARTY
WARWORK S
WARWORKS
WARWORN
WARY
AWRY
T WAS HPT
SAW
WASABI S
WASABIS
AS WASH Y
HAWS SHAW
SHWA
WASHABLE S
WASHBOWL S
WASHDAY S
WASHDAYS
S WASHED
SHAWED
S WASHER S
HAWSER
REWASH
S WASHERS
HAWSERS
SWASHER
S WASHES
HAWSES
WASHIER
WEARISH
WASHIEST
S WASHING S
SHAWING
WASHINGS
SWASHING
WASHOUT S
OUTWASH
WASHOUTS
WASHRAG S
WASHRAGS
WASHROOM S
WASHTUB S
WASHTUBS
WASHUP S
WHAUPS
WASHUPS
WASHY
WASP SY
PAWS SWAP
WAPS
WASPIER
WASPIEST
WASPILY
SLIPWAY
WASPISH
WASPLIKE
WASPS
SWAPS
WASPY
YAWPS
WASSAIL S
WASSAILS
WAST ES
STAW SWAT
TAWS TWAS
WATS
WASTABLE
WASTAGE S
WASTAGES
WASTE DRS
SWEAT TAWSE
TWAES
WASTED
TAWSED
WADSET
WASTEFUL
WASTELOT S
WASTER SY
RAWEST
TAWERS
WATERS
WASTERIE S
SWEATIER
WEARIEST
WASTERS
WASTERY
WASTES
SWEATS
TAWSES
WASTEWAY S
WASTING
TAWSING
WASTREL S
WARSTLE
WRASTLE
WASTRELS
WARSTLES
WARTLESS
WRASTLES
WASTRIE S
WAISTER
WAITERS
WARIEST
WASTRIES
WAISTERS
WAITRESS
WASTRY
STRAWY
SWARTY
WASTS
SWATS
ST WAT ST
TAW
TWA
WATAP ES
WATAPE S
WATAPES
WATAPS
S WATCH
WATCHCRY
WATCHDOG S
DOGWATCH
WATCHED
WATCHER S
WATCHERS
S WATCHES
WATCHEYE S
WATCHFUL
WATCHING
WATCHMAN
WATCHMEN
WATCHOUT S
OUTWATCH
WATER SY
TAWER
WATERAGE S
WATERBED S
WATERBUS
WATERDOG S
WATERED
DEWATER
TARWEED
WATERER S
WATERERS
WATERHEN S
WREATHEN
WATERIER
WATERILY
WATERING S
TWANGIER
WATERISH
WATERJET S
WATERLOG S
WATERLOO S
WATERMAN
WATERMEN
WATERS
RAWEST
TAWERS
WASTER
WATERSKI S
WATERWAY S
WATERY
ST WATS
STAW SWAT
TAWS TWAS
WAST
WATT S
WATTAGE S
WATTAGES
WATTAPE S
WATTAPES
S WATTER
WATTEST
WATTHOUR S
T WATTLE DS
T WATTLED
T WATTLES S
WATTLESS
T WATTLING
WATTS
WAUCHT S
WAUCHTED
WAUCHTS
WAUGH T
WAUGHT S
WAUGHTED
WAUGHTS
WAUK S
WAUKED
WAUKING
WAUKS
WAUL S
WAULED
WAULING
WAULS
WAUR
WAVE DRSY
WAVEBAND S
WAVED
WAVEFORM S
WAVELESS
WAVELET S
WAVELETS
WAVELIKE
WAVEOFF S
WAVEOFFS
WAVER SY
WAVERED
WAVERER S
WAVERERS
WAVERING
WAVERS
WAVERY
WAVES
WAVEY S
WAVEYS
WAVICLE S
WAVICLES
WAVIER
WAIVER
WAVIES T
WAIVES
WAVIEST
WAVILY
WAVINESS
WAVING
WAVY
WAW LS
WAWL S
WAWLED
WAWLING
WAWLS
WAWS
WAX Y
WAXABLE
WAXBERRY
WAXBILL S
WAXBILLS
WAXED
DEWAX
WAXEN
WAXER S
REWAX
WAXERS
WAXES
WAXIER
WAXIEST
TAXWISE
WAXILY
WAXINESS
WAXING S
WAXINGS
WAXLIKE
WAXPLANT S
WAXWEED S
WAXWEEDS
WAXWING S
WAXWINGS
WAXWORK S
WAXWORKS
WAXWORM S
WAXWORMS
WAXY
AS WAY S
YAW
WAYBILL S
WAYBILLS
WAYFARER S
WAYGOING S
WAYLAID
WAYLAY S
WAYLAYER S
WAYLAYS
WAYLESS
WAYPOINT S
S WAYS
SWAY YAWS
WAYSIDE S
SIDEWAY
WAYSIDES
SIDEWAYS
WAYWARD
WAYWORN
AEO WE BDENT
T WEAK
WAKE WEKA
WEAKEN S
WEAKENED
WEAKENER S
WEAKENS
WEAKER
REWAKE
WEAKEST
WEAKFISH
WEAKISH
HAWKIES
WEAKLIER
WEAKLING S
WEAKLY
WEAKNESS
WEAKON S
AWOKEN
WEAKONS
WEAKSIDE S
WEAL DS
WALE
WEALD S
LAWED WALED
WEALDS
WEALS
SWALE WALES
WEALTH SY
WEALTHS
WEALTHY
WEAN S
ANEW WANE
WEANED
DEEWAN
WEANER S
WEANERS
WEANING
WEANLING S
WEANS
SEWAN WANES
WEAPON S
WEAPONED
WEAPONRY
WEAPONS
S WEAR SY
WARE
WEARABLE S
S WEARER S
REWEAR
S WEARERS
REWEARS
SWEARER
WEARIED
WEARIER
WEARIES T
WEARIEST
SWEATIER
WASTERIE
WEARIFUL
WEARILY
S WEARING
WEARISH
WASHIER
S WEARS
RESAW SAWER
SEWAR SWARE
SWEAR WARES
A WEARY
WEARYING
WEASAND S
WEASANDS
WEASEL SY
WEASELED
WEASELLY
WALLEYES
WEASELS
AWELESS
WEASELY
LEEWAYS
WEASON S
WEASONS
A WEATHER S
WHEREAT
WREATHE
WEATHERS
WREATHES
WEAVE DRS
WEAVED
WEAVER S
WEAVERS
WEAVES
WEAVING
WEAZAND S
WEAZANDS
WEB S
WEBBED
WEBBIER
WEBBIEST
WEBBING S
WEBBINGS
WEBBY
WEBCAM S
WEBCAMS
WEBCAST S
WEBCASTS
WEBER S
WEBERS
WEBFED
WEBFEET
WEBFOOT
WEBLESS
WEBLIKE
WEBLOG S
BOWLEG
WEBLOGS
BOWLEGS
WEBPAGE S
WEBPAGES
WEBS
WEBSITE S
WEBSITES
WEBSTER S
BESTREW
WEBSTERS
BESTREWS
WEBWORK S
WEBWORKS
WEBWORM S
WEBWORMS
WECHT S
WECHTS
AO WED S
DEW
WEDDED
WEDDER S
WEDDERS
WEDDING S
WEDDINGS
WEDEL NS
WEDELED
WEDELING
WEDELN S
WEDELNS
WEDELS
SLEWED
WEDGE DS
WEDGED
WEDGES
WEDGIE RS
WEDGIER
WEDGIES T
WEDGIEST
WEDGING
WEDGY
WEDLOCK S
WEDLOCKS
WEDS
DEWS
AT WEE DKLNPRS
EWE T

T WEED SY
WEEDED
WEEDER S
WEEDERS
RESEWED
SEWERED
T WEEDIER
T WEEDIEST
WEEDILY
WEEDING
WEEDLESS
WEEDLIKE
T WEEDS
SEWED SWEDE
T WEEDY
WEEK S
WEEKDAY S
WEEKDAYS
WEEKEND S
WEEKENDS
WEEKLIES
WEEKLONG
WEEKLY
WEEKS
WEEL
T WEEN SY
WEENED
WEENIE RS
WEENIER
ST WEENIES T
WEENIEST
TWEENIES
WEENING
T WEENS Y
WEENSIER
WEENSY
SWEENY
ST WEENY
S WEEP SY
S WEEPER S
S WEEPERS
SWEEPER
WEEPIE RS
S WEEPIER
WEEPIES T
S WEEPIEST
S WEEPING S
S WEEPINGS
SWEEPING
S WEEPS
SWEEP
S WEEPY
S WEER
EWER WERE
WEES T
EWES
WEEST
SWEET WEETS
ST WEET S
TWEE
T WEETED
ST WEETING
ST WEETS
SWEET WEEST
WEEVER S
WEEVERS
WEEVIL SY
WEEVILED
WEEVILLY
WEEVILS
WEEVILY
WEEWEE DS
WEEWEED
WEEWEES
WEFT S
WEFTS
WEFTWISE
WEIGELA S
WEIGELAS
WEIGELIA S
A WEIGH ST
WEIGHED
WEIGHER S
REWEIGH
WEIGHERS
REWEIGHS
WEIGHING
WEIGHMAN
WEIGHMEN
WEIGHS
WEIGHT SY
WEIGHTED
WEIGHTER S
WEIGHTS
WEIGHTY
WEINER S
WIENER
WEINERS
NEWSIER
WIENERS
WEIR DS
WIRE
WEIRD OSY
WIDER WIRED
WRIED
WEIRDED
WEIRDER
REWIRED
WEIRDEST
WEIRDIE S
WEIRDIES
WEIRDING
WEIRDLY
WEIRDO S
WEIRDOES
DOWERIES
WEIRDOS
DOWRIES
ROWDIES
WEIRDS
WEIRDY
WEIRS
WIRES WISER
WRIES
WEKA S
WAKE WEAK
WEKAS
ASKEW WAKES
WELCH
WELCHED
WELCHER S
WELCHERS
WELCHES
LECHWES
WELCHING
WELCOME DRS
WELCOMED
WELCOMER S
WELCOMES
WELD S
LEWD
WELDABLE
WELDED
WELDER S
LEWDER
REWELD
WELDERS
REWELDS
WELDING
WELDLESS
WELDMENT S
WELDOR S
WELDORS
WELDS
WELFARE S
WELFARES
WELKIN S
WINKLE
WELKINS
WINKLES
DS WELL SY
WELLADAY S
WELLAWAY S
WELLBORN
WELLCURB S
WELLDOER S
ROWELLED
DS WELLED
S WELLHEAD S
WELLHOLE S
WELLIE S
WELLIES
DS WELLING
WELLNESS
DS WELLS
SWELL
WELLSITE S
WELLY
WELSH
WELSHED
WELSHER S
WELSHERS
WELSHES
WELSHING
D WELT S
WELTED
S WELTER S
S WELTERED
S WELTERS
SWELTER
WRESTLE
WELTING S
WINGLET
WELTINGS
WINGLETS
WELTS
WEN DST
NEW
WENCH
WENCHED
WENCHER S
WENCHERS
WRENCHES
WENCHES
WENCHING
WEND S
WENDED
WENDIGO S
WIDGEON
WENDIGOS
WIDGEONS
WENDING
WENDS
WENNIER
WENNIEST
ENTWINES
WENNISH
WENNY
WENS
NEWS SEWN
WENT
NEWT
S WEPT
WERE
EWER WEER
WEREGILD S
WEREWOLF
WERGELD S
WERGELDS
WERGELT S
WERGELTS
WERGILD S
WERGILDS
WERT
WERWOLF
WESKIT S
WESKITS
WESSAND S
WESSANDS
WEST S
STEW TEWS
WETS
WESTER NS
REWETS
WESTERED
WESTERLY
WESTERN S
WESTERNS
WESTERS
WESTING S
STEWING
TWINGES
WESTINGS
WESTMOST
WESTS
STEWS
WESTWARD S
WET S
TEW
WETHER S
WETHERS
WETLAND S
WETLANDS
WETLY
WETNESS
WETPROOF
WETS
STEW TEWS
WEST
WETSUIT S
WETSUITS
WETTABLE
WETTED
WETTER S
WETTERS
WETTEST
WETTING S
WETTINGS
WETTISH
WHITEST
WETWARE S
WETWARES
WHA MPT
HAW
WHACK OSY
WHACKED
WHACKER S
WHACKERS
WHACKIER
WHACKING
WHACKO S
WHACKOS
WHACKS
WHACKY
WHALE DRS
WHEAL
WHALED
WHALEMAN
WHALEMEN
WHEELMAN
WHALER S
WHALERS
WHALES
WHEALS
WHALING S
WHALINGS
SHAWLING
WHAM OS
WHAMMED
WHAMMIES
WHAMMING
WHAMMO
WHAMMY
WHAMO
WHAMS
SHAWM
WHANG S
WHANGED
WHANGEE S
WHANGEES
WHANGING
WHANGS
WHAP S
WHAPPED
WHAPPER S
WHAPPERS
WHAPPING
WHAPS
PSHAW
WHARF S
WHARFAGE S
WHARFED
WHARFING
WHARFS
WHARVE S
WHARVES
WHAT S
THAW
WHATEVER
WHATNESS
WHATNOT S
WHATNOTS
WHATS
SWATH THAWS
WHATSIS
WHATSIT S
WHATSITS
WHAUP S
WHAUPS
WASHUP
WHEAL S
WHALE
WHEALS
WHALES
WHEAT S
WHEATEAR S
AWEATHER
WHEATEN S
WHEATENS
ENSWATHE
WHEATS
SWATHE
WHEE LNP
WHEEDLE DRS
WHEELED
WHEEDLED
WHEEDLER S
WHEEDLES
WHEEL S
WHEELED
WHEEDLE
WHEELER S
WHEELERS
WHEELIE S
WHEELIES
WHEELING S
WHEELMAN
WHALEMEN
WHEELMEN
WHEELS
WHEEN S
WHEENS
WHEEP S
WHEEPED
WHEEPING
WHEEPLE DS
WHEEPLED
WHEEPLES
WHEEPS
WHEEZE DRS
WHEEZED
WHEEZER S
WHEEZERS
WHEEZES
WHEEZIER
WHEEZILY
WHEEZING
WHEEZY
WHELK SY
WHELKIER
WHELKS
WHELKY
WHELM S
WHELMED
WHELMING
WHELMS
WHELP S
WHELPED
WHELPING
WHELPS
WHEN S
HEWN
WHENAS
WHENCE
WHENEVER
WHENS
SHEWN
WHERE S
HEWER
WHEREAS
WHEREAT
WEATHER
WREATHE
WHEREBY
WHEREIN
WHEREOF
WHEREON
NOWHERE
WHERES
HEWERS
SHEWER
WHERETO
WHEREVER
WHERRIED
WHERRIES
WHERRY
WHERVE S
WHERVES
WHET S
THEW
WHETHER
WHETS
THEWS
WHETTED
WHETTER S
WHETTERS
WHETTING
WHEW S
WHEWS
WHEY S
WHEYEY
WHEYFACE DS
WHEYISH
WHEYLIKE
WHEYS
WHICH
WHICKER S
WHICKERS
WHID S
WHIDAH S
WHIDAHS
WHIDDED
WHIDDING
WHIDS
WHIFF S
WHIFFED
WHIFFER S
WHIFFERS
WHIFFET S
WHIFFETS
WHIFFING
WHIFFLE DRS
WHIFFLED
WHIFFLER S
WHIFFLES
WHIFFS
WHIG S
WHIGS
A WHILE DS
WHILED
WHILES
WHILING
WHILOM
WHILST
WHIM S
WHIMBREL S
WHIMPER S
WHIMPERS
WHIMS Y
WHIMSEY S
WHIMSEYS
WHIMSIED
WHIMSIES
WHIMSY
WHIN ESY
WHINCHAT S
WHINE DRSY
WHINED
WHINER S
WHINERS
WHINES
NEWISH
WHINEY
WHINGE DRS
HEWING
WHINGED
WHINGER S
WHINGERS
SHREWING
WHINGES
SHEWING
WHINGING
WHINIER
WHINIEST
WHINING
WHINNIED
WHINNIER
WHINNIES T
WHINNY
WHINS
WHINY
WHIP ST
WHIPCORD S
WHIPLASH
WHIPLIKE
WHIPPED
WHIPPER S
WHIPPERS
WHIPPET S
WHIPPETS
WHIPPIER
WHIPPING S
WHIPPY
WHIPRAY S
WHIPRAYS
WHIPS
WHIPSAW NS
WHIPSAWN
WHIPSAWS
WHIPT
WHIPTAIL S
WHIPWORM S
WHIR LRS
A WHIRL SY
WHIRLED
WHIRLER S
WHIRLERS
WHIRLIER
WHIRLIES T
WHIRLING
WHIRLS
WHIRLY
WHIRR SY
WHIRRED
WHIRRIED
WHIRRIES
WHIRRING
WHIRRS
WHIRRY
WHIRS
WHISH T
WHISHED
WHISHES
WHISHING
WHISHT S
WHISHTED
WHISHTS
WHISK SY
WHISKED
WHISKER SY
WHISKERS
WHISKERY
WHISKEY S
WHISKEYS
WHISKIES
WHISKING
WHISKS
WHISKY
WHISPER SY
WHISPERS
WHISPERY
WHIST S
SWITH WHITS
WHISTED
WHISTING
WHITINGS
WHISTLE DRS
WHISTLED
WHISTLER S
WHISTLES
WHISTS
WHIT ESY
WITH
WHITE DNRSY
WITHE
WHITECAP S
WHITED
WITHED
WHITEFLY
WHITELY
WHITEN S
WHITENED
WHITENER S
WHITENS
WHITEOUT S
WHITER
WITHER
WRITHE
WHITES T
SWITHE
WITHES

WHITEST
WETTISH
WHITEY
WHITHER
WHITIER
WITHIER
WHITIEST
WITHIEST
WHITING S
WITHING
WHITINGS
WHISTING
WHITISH
WHITLOW S
WHITLOWS
WHITRACK S
WHITS
SWITH WHIST
WHITTER S
WHITTERS
WHITTLE DRS
WHITTLED
WHITTLER S
WHITTLES
WHITTRET S
WHITY
WITHY
WHIZ Z
WHIZBANG S
WHIZZ Y
WHIZZED
WHIZZER S
WHIZZERS
WHIZZES
WHIZZIER
WHIZZING
WHIZZY
WHO AMP
HOW
WHOA
WHODUNIT S
WHOEVER
HOWEVER
WHOLE S
WHOLES
WHOLISM S
WHOLISMS
WHOLLY
WHOM P
WHOMEVER
WHOMP S
WHOMPED
WHOMPING
WHOMPS
WHOMSO
WHOOF S
WHOOFED
WHOOFING
WHOOFS
WHOOP S
WHOOPED
WHOOPEE S
WHOOPEES
WHOOPER S
WHOOPERS
WHOOPIE S
WHOOPIES
WHOOPING
WHOOPLA S
WHOOPLAS
WHOOPS
WHOOSH
WHOOSHED
WHOOSHES
WHOOSIS
WHOP S
WHOPPED
WHOPPER S
WHOPPERS
WHOPPING
WHOPS
WHORE DS
WHORED
WHOREDOM S

WHORES
RESHOW
SHOWER
WHORESON S
WHORING
WHORISH
WHORL S
WHORLED
WHORLS
WHORT S
ROWTH THROW
WORTH WROTH
WHORTLE S
WHORTLES
WHORTS
ROWTHS
THROWS
WORTHS
WHOSE
HOWES
WHOSEVER
WHOSIS
WHOSISES
WHOSO
WOOSH
WHUMP S
WHUMPED
WHUMPING
WHUMPS
WHUP S
WHUPPED
WHUPPING
WHUPS
WHY S
WHYDAH S
WHYDAHS
WHYS
WICCA NS
WICCAN S
WICCANS
WICCAS
WICH
WICHES
WICK S
WICKAPE S
WICKAPES
WICKED
WICKEDER
WICKEDLY
WICKER S
WICKERS
WICKET S
WICKETS
WICKING S
WICKINGS
WICKIUP S
WICKIUPS
WICKLESS
WICKS
WICKYUP S
WICKYUPS
WICOPIES
WICOPY
WIDDER S
WIDDERS
WIDDIE S
WIDDIES
T WIDDLE DS
WILDED
T WIDDLED
T WIDDLES
T WIDDLING
WIDDY
WIDE NRS
WIDEBAND
WIDEBODY
WIDELY
DEWILY
WIELDY
WIDEN S
DWINE WINED
WIDENED
WIDENER S
REWIDEN
WIDENERS
REWIDENS

WIDENESS
DEWINESS
WIDENING
WIDENS
DWINES
WIDEOUT S
WIDEOUTS
WIDER
WEIRD WIRED
WRIED
WIDES T
WISED
WIDEST
WISTED
WIDGEON S
WENDIGO
WIDGEONS
WENDIGOS
WIDGET S
WIDGETS
WIDISH
WIDOW S
WIDOWED
WIDOWER S
WIDOWERS
WIDOWING
WIDOWS
WIDTH S
WIDTHS
WIDTHWAY S
WIELD SY
WILED
WIELDED
WIELDER S
WIELDERS
WIELDIER
WIELDING
WIELDS
WIELDY
DEWILY
WIDELY
WIENER S
WEINER
WIENERS
NEWSIER
WEINERS
WIENIE S
WIENIES
EISWEIN
WIFE DSY
WIFED
WIFEDOM S
WIFEDOMS
WIFEHOOD S
WIFELESS
WIFELIER
WIFELIKE
WIFELY
WIFES
WIFEY S
WIFEYS
WIFING
WIFTIER
WIFTIEST
WIFTY
ST WIG S
WIGAN S
AWING
WIGANS
SAWING
WIGEON S
WIGEONS
ST WIGGED
WIGGERY
T WIGGIER
T WIGGIEST
ST WIGGING S
WIGGINGS
SWIGGING
WIGGLE DRS
WIGGLED
WIGGLER S
WRIGGLE
WIGGLERS
WRIGGLES
WIGGLES
WIGGLIER
WIGGLING
WIGGLY

T WIGGY
WIGHT S
WIGHTS
T WIGLESS
WIGLET S
WIGLETS
T WIGLIKE
WIGMAKER S
ST WIGS
SWIG
WIGWAG S
WIGWAGS
WIGWAM S
WIGWAMS
WIKIUP S
WIKIUPS
WILCO
WILD S
WILDCARD S
WILDCAT S
WILDCATS
WILDED
WIDDLE
WILDER S
WILDERED
WILDERS
SWIRLED
WILDEST
WILDFIRE S
WILDFOWL S
WILDING S
WILDINGS
WILDISH
WILDLAND S
WILDLIFE
WILDLING S
WILDLY
WILDNESS
SWINDLES
WINDLESS
WILDS
WILDWOOD S
WILE DS
LWEI
WILED
WIELD
WILES
LEWIS LWEIS
WILFUL
WILFULLY
WILIER
WILIEST
WILILY
WILINESS
WILING
ST WILL SY
WILLABLE
ST WILLED
S WILLER S
S WILLERS
SWILLER
WILLET S
WILLETS
WILLFUL
WILLIED
WILLIES
ST WILLING
WILLIWAU S
WILLIWAW S
WILLOW SY
WILLOWED
WILLOWER S
WILLOWS
WILLOWY
ST WILLS
SWILL
WILLY
WILLYARD
WILLYART
WILLYING
WILLYWAW S
WILT S
WILTED
WILTING
WITLING
WILTS

WILY
WIMBLE DS
WIMBLED
WIMBLES
WIMBLING
WIMMIN
WIMP SY
WIMPED
WIMPIER
WIMPIEST
WIMPING
WIMPISH
WIMPLE DS
WIMPLED
WIMPLES
WIMPLING
WIMPS
WIMPY
T WIN DEGKOSY
WINCE DRSY
WINCED
WINCER S
WINCERS
WINCES
WINCEY S
WINCEYS
WINCH
WINCHED
WINCHER S
WINCHERS
WINCHES
WINCHING
WINCING
WIND SY
WINDABLE
WINDAGE S
WINDAGES
WINDBAG S
WINDBAGS
WINDBELL S
WINDBURN ST
WINDED
DWINED
WINDER S
REWIND
WINDERS
REWINDS
WINDFALL S
WINDFLAW S
WINDGALL S
WINDIER
WINDIEST
WINDIGO S
WINDIGOS
WINDILY
WINDING S
DWINING
WINDINGS
WINDLASS
DS WINDLE DS
DS WINDLED
DWINDLE
DS WINDLES S
SWINDLE
WINDLESS
SWINDLES
WILDNESS
DS WINDLING S
WINDMILL S
WINDOW SY
WINDOWED
WINDOWS
WINDOWY
WINDPIPE S
WINDROW S
WINDROWS
WINDS
WINDSOCK S
WINDSURF S
WINDUP S
UPWIND
WINDUPS
UPWINDS
WINDWARD S
WINDWAY S
WINDWAYS

WINDY
DGS WINE DSY
T
DT WINED
DWINE WIDEN
WINELESS
WINERIES
WINERY
DT WINES
SINEW SWINE
WINESAP S
WINESAPS
WINESHOP S
WINESKIN S
WINESOP S
WINESOPS
WINEY
AOS WING SY
WINGBACK S
WINGBOW S
WINGBOWS
WINGDING S
ST WINGED
DEWING
WINGEDLY
S WINGER S
S WINGERS
SWINGER
S WINGIER
S WINGIEST
ST WINGING
WINGLESS
SWINGLES
WINGLET S
WELTING
WINGLETS
WELTINGS
WINGLIKE
S WINGMAN
S WINGMEN
WINGOVER S
S WINGS
SWING
WINGSPAN S
SPAWNING
WINGTIP S
WINGTIPS
S WINGY
T WINIER
T WINIEST
DT WINING
S WINISH
S WINK S
S WINKED
WINKER S
WINKERS
S WINKING
T WINKLE DS
WELKIN
T WINKLED
T WINKLES
WELKINS
T WINKLING
S WINKS
SWINK
WINLESS
WINNABLE
T WINNED
ENWIND
WINNER S
WINNERS
T WINNING S
T WINNINGS
WINNOCK S
WINNOCKS
WINNOW S
WINNOWED
WINNOWER S
WINNOWS
WINO S
WINOES
NOWISE
WINOS
T WINS
WINSOME R
WINSOMER
WINTER SY
TWINER

WINTERED
WINTERER S
WINTERLY
WINTERS
TWINERS
WINTERY
WINTLE DS
WINTLED
INDWELT
WINTLES
WINTLING
WINTRIER
WINTRILY
WINTRY
T WINY
WINZE S
WIZEN
WINZES
WIZENS
S WIPE DRS
S WIPED
WIPEOUT S
WIPEOUTS
WIPER S
WIPERS
S WIPES
SWIPE
S WIPING
WIRABLE
BRAWLIE
WIRE DRS
WEIR
WIRED
WEIRD WIDER
WRIED
WIREDRAW NS
WIREDREW
WIREHAIR S
WIRELESS
WIRELIKE
WIREMAN
WIREMEN
WIRER S
WRIER
WIRERS
WIRES
WEIRS WISER
WRIES
WIRETAP S
WIRETAPS
WIREWAY S
WIREWAYS
WIREWORK S
WIREWORM S
WIRIER
WIRIEST
WIRILY
WIRINESS
WIRING S
WIRINGS
WIRRA
WIRY
IY WIS EHPST
WISDOM S
WISDOMS
WISE DRS
WISEACRE S
WISEASS
WISED
WIDES
WISEGUY S
WISEGUYS
WISELIER
WISELY
WISENESS
WISENT S
TWINES
WISENTS
WITNESS
WISER
WEIRS WIRES
WRIES
WISES T
WISEST
S WISH A
WISHA
WISHBONE S
S WISHED

S **WISHER** S
S **WISHERS**
SWISHER
S **WISHES**
WISHFUL
S **WISHING**
WISHLESS
WISING
WISP SY
WISPED
SWIPED
WISPIER
WISPIEST
WISPILY
WISPING
SWIPING
WISPISH
WISPLIKE
WISPS
WISPY
S **WISS**
WISSED
S **WISSES**
WISSING
T **WIST** S
WITS
WISTARIA S
T **WISTED**
WIDEST
WISTERIA S
WISTFUL
T **WISTING**
T **WISTS**
T **WIT** EHS
WITAN S
TWAIN
WITANS
TWAINS
ST **WITCH** Y
ST **WITCHED**
WITCHERY
ST **WITCHES**
T **WITCHIER**
ST **WITCHING** S
T **WITCHY**
WITE DS
WITED
WITES
S **WITH** EY
WHIT
WITHAL
WITHDRAW NS
WITHDREW
S **WITHE** DRS
WHITE
WITHED
WHITED
S **WITHER** S
WHITER
WRITHE
S **WITHERED**
WITHERER S
WITHEROD S
S **WITHERS**
SWITHER
WRITHES
WITHES
SWITHE
WHITES
WITHHELD
WITHHOLD S
WITHIER
WHITIER
WITHIES T
WITHIEST
WHITIEST
WITHIN GS
WITHING
WHITING
WITHINS
WITHOUT S
OUTWITH
WITHOUTS
WITHY
WHITY
WITING
WITLESS
WITLING S
WILTING

WITLINGS
WITLOOF S
WITLOOFS
WITNESS
WISENTS
WITNEY S
WITNEYS
T **WITS**
WIST
T **WITTED**
WITTIER
WITTIEST
WITTILY
T **WITTING** S
WITTINGS
TWISTING
WITTOL S
WITTOLS
WITTY
S **WIVE** DRS
VIEW
S **WIVED**
WIVER NS
WIVERN S
WIVERNS
WIVERS
S **WIVES**
SWIVE VIEWS
S **WIVING**
WIZ
WIZARD S
WIZARDLY
WIZARDRY
WIZARDS
WIZEN S
WINZE
WIZENED
WIZENING
WIZENS
WINZES
WIZES
WIZZEN S
WIZZENS
WIZZES
T **WO** EKNOSTW
OW
WOAD S
WOADED
WOADS
WOADWAX
WOALD S
WOALDS
WOBBLE DRS
WOBBLED
WOBBLER S
WOBBLERS
WOBBLES
WOBBLIER
WOBBLIES T
WOBBLING
WOBBLY
BLOWBY
WOBEGONE
WODGE S
WODGES
WOE S
OWE
WOEFUL
WOEFULLY
WOENESS
WOES
OWES OWSE
WOESOME
WOFUL
WOFULLER
WOFULLY
WOK ES
A **WOKE** N
A **WOKEN**
WOKS
WOLD S
WOLDS
WOLF S
FLOW FOWL
WOLFED
FLOWED
FOWLED

WOLFER S
FLOWER
FOWLER
REFLOW
WOLFERS
FLOWERS
FOWLERS
REFLOWS
WOLFFISH
WOLFING
FLOWING
FOWLING
WOLFISH
WOLFLIKE
WOLFRAM S
WOLFRAMS
WOLFS
FLOWS FOWLS
WOLVER S
WOLVERS
WOLVES
VOWELS
WOMAN S
WOMANED
ADWOMEN
WOMANING
WOMANISE DS
WOMANISH
WOMANISM S
WOMANIST S
WOMANIZE DR S
WOMANLY
WOMANS
WOMB SY
WOMBAT S
WOMBATS
WOMBED
WOMBIER
IMBOWER
WOMBIEST
WOMBS
WOMBY
WOMEN
WOMERA S
WOMERAS
WOMMERA S
WOMMERAS
WOMYN
WON KST
NOW
OWN
WONDER S
DOWNER
WONDERED
WONDERER S
WONDERS
DOWNERS
WONDROUS
WONK SY
KNOW
WONKIER
WONKIEST
WONKS
KNOWS
WONKY
WONNED
WONNER S
RENOWN
WONNERS
RENOWNS
WONNING
WONS
NOWS OWNS
SNOW SOWN
WONT S
NOWT TOWN
WONTED
WONTEDLY
WONTING
WONTON S
WONTONS
WONTS
NOWTS TOWNS
WOO DFLS
WOOD SY
WOODBIN DES
WOODBIND S
WOODBINE S

WOODBINS
WOODBOX
BOXWOOD
WOODCHAT S
WOODCOCK S
WOODCUT S
WOODCUTS
WOODED
WOODEN
WOODENER
WOODENLY
WOODHEN S
HOEDOWN
WOODHENS
HOEDOWNS
WOODIE RS
WOODIER
WOODIES T
WOODIEST
WOODING
WOODLAND S
DOWNLOAD
WOODLARK S
WORKLOAD
WOODLESS
WOODLORE S
WOODLOT S
WOODLOTS
WOODMAN
WOODMEN
WOODNOTE S
WOODTONE
WOODPILE S
WOODRUFF S
WOODS Y
WOODSHED S
WOODSIA S
WOODSIAS
WOODSIER
WOODSMAN
WOODSMEN
WOODSY
WOODTONE S
WOODNOTE
WOODWAX
WOODWIND S
WOODWORK S
WOODWORM S
WORMWOOD
WOODY
WOOED
WOOER S
WOOERS
WOOF S
WOOFED
WOOFER S
WOOFERS
WOOFING
WOOFS
WOOING
WOOINGLY
WOOL SY
WOOLED
DEWOOL
WOOLEN S
WOOLENS
WOOLER S
WOOLERS
WOOLFELL S
WOOLHAT S
WOOLHATS
WOOLIE RS
WOOLIER
WOOLIES T
WOOLIEST
WOOLLED
WOOLLEN S
WOOLLENS
WOOLLIER
WOOLLIES T
WOOLLIKE
WOOLLILY
WOOLLY
WOOLMAN
WOOLMEN
WOOLPACK S

WOOLS
WOOLSACK S
WOOLSHED S
WOOLSKIN S
WOOLWORK S
WOOLY
WOOMERA S
WOOMERAS
S **WOOPS**
SWOOP
WOOPSED
SWOOPED
WOOPSES
WOOPSING
SWOOPING
WOORALI S
WOORALIS
WOORARI S
WOORARIS
WOOS H
S **WOOSH**
WHOSO
S **WOOSHED**
S **WOOSHES**
S **WOOSHING**
WOOZIER
WOOZIEST
WOOZILY
WOOZY
S **WORD** SY
WORDAGE S
DOWAGER
WORDAGES
DOWAGERS
WORDBOOK S
WORDED
WORDIER
ROWDIER
WORRIED
WORDIEST
ROWDIEST
WORDILY
ROWDILY
WORDING S
WORDINGS
DROWSING
WORDLESS
S **WORDPLAY** S
S **WORDS**
SWORD
WORDY
DOWRY ROWDY
S **WORE**
WORK S
WORKABLE
WORKABLY
WORKADAY
WORKBAG S
WORKBAGS
WORKBOAT S
WORKBOOK S
WORKBOX
WORKDAY S
DAYWORK
WORKDAYS
DAYWORKS
WORKED
WORKER S
REWORK
WORKERS
REWORKS
WORKFARE S
WORKFLOW S
WORKFOLK S
WORKHOUR S
WORKING S
WORKINGS
WORKLESS
WORKLOAD S
WOODLARK
WORKMAN
WORKMATE S
TEAMWORK
WORKMEN
WORKOUT S
OUTWORK
WORKOUTS
OUTWORKS
WORKROOM S

WORKS
WORKSHOP S
WORKUP S
WORKUPS
WORKWEEK S
WORLD S
WORLDLY
WORLDS
WORM SY
WORMED
DEWORM
WORMER S
WORMERS
WORMGEAR S
WORMHOLE S
WORMIER
WORMIEST
MISWROTE
WORMIL S
WORMILS
WORMING
WORMISH
WORMLIKE
WORMROOT S
MOORWORT
ROOTWORM
TOMORROW
WORMS
WORMSEED S
WORMWOOD S
WOODWORM
WORMY
S **WORN**
WORNNESS
WORRIED
ROWDIER
WORDIER
WORRIER S
WORRIERS
WORRIES
WORRIT S
WORRITED
WORRITS
WORRY
WORRYING
WORSE NRST
RESOW SEROW
SOWER SWORE
WORSEN S
OWNERS
RESOWN
ROWENS
WORSENED
ENDOWERS
REENDOWS
WORSENS
WORSER
ROWERS
WORSES
RESOWS
SEROWS
SOWERS
WORSET S
TOWERS
WORSETS
WORSHIP S
WORSHIPS
WORST S
STROW TROWS
WORTS
WORSTED S
STROWED
WORSTEDS
WORSTING
STROWING
WORSTS
STROWS
WORT HS
TROW
WORTH SY
ROWTH THROW
WHORT WROTH
WORTHED
WORTHFUL
WROTHFUL
WORTHIER
WORTHIES T
WORTHILY

WORTHING
INGROWTH
THROWING
WORTHS
ROWTHS
THROWS
WHORTS
WORTHY
WORTS
STROW TROWS
WORST
T **WOS** T
SOW
WOST
STOW SWOT
TOWS TWOS
WOTS
S **WOT** S
TOW
TWO
S **WOTS**
STOW SWOT
TOWS TWOS
WOST
S **WOTTED**
S **WOTTING**
WOULD
WOULDEST
WOULDST
S **WOUND** S
S **WOUNDED**
S **WOUNDING**
S **WOUNDS**
SWOUND
WOVE N
WOVEN S
WOVENS
WOW S
WOWED
WOWING
WOWS
WOWSER S
WOWSERS
WRACK S
WRACKED
WRACKFUL
WRACKING
WRACKS
WRAITH S
WRAITHS
TRISHAW
WRANG S
WRANGLE DRS
WANGLER
WRANGLED
WRANGLER S
WRANGLES
WANGLERS
WRANGS
WRAP ST
WARP
WRAPPED
WRAPPER S
PREWRAP
WRAPPERS
PREWRAPS
WRAPPING S
WRAPS
WARPS
WRAPT
WRASSE S
RESAWS
SAWERS
SEWARS
SWEARS
WRASSES
WRASSLE DS
WARLESS
WARSLES
WRASSLED
WARDLESS
WRASSLES
WRASTLE DS
WARSTLE
WASTREL
WRASTLED
WARSTLED
WRASTLES
WARSTLES
WARTLESS
WASTRELS

WRATH SY
THRAW
WRATHED
THRAWED
WRATHFUL
WRATHIER
WRATHILY
WRATHING
THRAWING
WRATHS
SWARTH
THRAWS
WRATHY
WREAK S
WAKER
WREAKED
REWAKED
WREAKER S
WREAKERS
WREAKING
REWAKING
WREAKS
WAKERS
WREATH ESY
THAWER
WREATHE DNR
WEATHER S
WHEREAT
WREATHED
WREATHEN
WATERHEN
WREATHER S
WREATHES
WEATHERS
WREATHS
SWATHER
THAWERS
WREATHY
WRECK S
WRECKAGE S
WRECKED
WRECKER S
WRECKERS
WRECKFUL
WRECKING S
WRECKS
WREN S
WRENCH
WRENCHED
WRENCHER S
WRENCHES
WENCHERS
WRENS
WREST S
STREW TREWS
WRESTED
STREWED
WRESTER S
STREWER
WRESTERS
STREWERS
WRESTING
STREWING
WRESTLE DRS
SWELTER
WELTERS
WRESTLED
WRESTLER S
WRESTLES
SWELTERS
WRESTS
STREWS
WRETCH
WRETCHED
WRETCHES
WRICK S
WRICKED
WRICKING
WRICKS
WRIED
WEIRD WIDER
WIRED
WRIER
WIRER
WRIES T
WEIRS WIRES
WISER
WRIEST
TWIERS
WRITES
WRIGGLE DRS
WIGGLER

WRIGGLED
WRIGGLER S
WRIGGLES
WIGGLERS
WRIGGLY
WRIGHT S
WRIGHTS
WRING S
WRINGED
REDWING
WRINGER S
WRINGERS
WRINGING
WRINGS
WRINKLE DS
WRINKLED
WRINKLES
WRINKLY
WRIST SY
WRITS
WRISTIER
WRISTLET S
WRISTS
WRISTY
WRIT ES
WRITABLE
WRITE RS
TWIER
WRITER S
WRITERLY
WRITERS
WRITES
TWIERS
WRIEST
WRITHE DNRS
WHITER
WITHER
WRITHED
WRITHEN
WRITHER S
WRITHERS
WRITHES
SWITHER
WITHERS
WRITHING
WRITING S
WRITINGS
WRITS
WRIST
WRITTEN
WRONG S
GROWN
WRONGED
WRONGER S
REGROWN
WRONGERS
WRONGEST
WRONGFUL
WRONGING
WRONGLY
WRONGS
WROTE
TOWER
WROTH
ROWTH THROW
WHORT WORTH
WROTHFUL
WORTHFUL
WROUGHT
WRUNG
A WRY
WRYER
WRYEST
TWYERS
WRYING
WRYLY
WRYNECK S
WRYNECKS
WRYNESS
WUD
WURST S
WURSTS
WURTZITE S
WURZEL S
WURZELS
WUSHU
WUSS Y
WUSSES

WUSSIER
WUSSIES T
WUSSIEST
WUSSY
WUTHER S
WUTHERED
WUTHERS
WYCH
WYCHES
WYE S
YEW
WYES
YEWS
WYLE DS
WYLED
WYLES
WYLING
WYN DNS
WYND S
WYNDS
WYNN S
WYNNS
WYNS
WYTE DS
WYTED
WYTES
STEWY
WYTING
WYVERN S
WYVERNS

X

XANTHAN S
XANTHANS
XANTHATE S
XANTHEIN S
XANTHINE
XANTHENE S
XANTHIC
XANTHIN ES
XANTHINE S
XANTHEIN
XANTHINS
XANTHOMA S
XANTHONE S
XANTHOUS
XEBEC S
XEBECS
XENIA LS
XENIAL
ALEXIN
XENIAS
A XENIC
XENOGAMY
XENOGENY
XENOLITH S
XENON S
XENONS
XENOPUS
XERARCH
XERIC
XEROSERE S
XEROSES
XEROSIS
XEROTIC
EXCITOR
XEROX
XEROXED
XEROXES
XEROXING
XERUS
XERUSES
XI S
XIPHOID S
XIPHOIDS
A XIS
SIX
XU
XYLAN S
XYLANS
XYLEM S
XYLEMS
XYLENE S
XYLENES
XYLIDIN ES
XYLIDINE S
XYLIDINS
XYLITOL S
XYLITOLS
XYLOCARP S
XYLOID
XYLOL S
XYLOLS
XYLOSE S
XYLOSES
XYLOTOMY
XYLYL S
XYLYLS
XYST IS
XYSTER S
XYSTERS
XYSTI
SIXTY
XYSTOI
XYSTOS
XYSTS
XYSTUS

Y

PR YA GHKMPRWY
AY
YABBER S
YABBERED
YABBERS
YABBIE S
YABBIES
YABBY
YACHT S
YACHTED
YACHTER S
YACHTERS
YACHTING S
YACHTMAN
YACHTMEN
YACHTS
K YACK S
CAKY
YACKED
YACKING
K YACKS
CASKY
YAFF S
YAFFED
YAFFING
YAFFS
YAG IS
GAY
YAGER S
GAYER
YAGERS
GREASY
GYRASE
YAGI S
YAGIS
YAGS
GAYS SAGY
A YAH
HAY
YAHOO S
YAHOOISM S
YAHOOS
YAHRZEIT S
YAIRD S
DAIRY DIARY
YAIRDS
K YAK S
KAY
YAKITORI S
YAKKED
YAKKER S
YAKKERS
YAKKING
K YAKS
KAYS
YAKUZA
YALD
LADY
YAM S
MAY
YAMALKA S
YAMALKAS

YAMEN S
MEANY
YAMENS
YAMMER S
YAMMERED
YAMMERER S
YAMMERS
YAMS
MAYS
YAMULKA S
YAMULKAS
YAMUN S
YAMUNS
YANG S
YANGS
YANK S
YANKED
YANKING
YANKS
SNAKY
YANQUI S
YANQUIS
YANTRA S
RATANY
YANTRAS
YAP S
PAY
PYA
YAPOCK S
YAPOCKS
YAPOK S
YAPOKS
YAPON S
YAPONS
YAPPED
YAPPER S
PAPERY
PREPAY
YAPPERS
PREPAYS
YAPPING
YAPS
PAYS PYAS
SPAY
K YAR DEN
RAY
RYA
L YARD S
DRAY
YARDAGE S
DRAYAGE
YARDAGES
DRAYAGES
YARDARM S
YARDARMS
YARDBIRD S
YARDED
DRAYED
YARDER S
DREARY
YARDERS
YARDING
DRAYING
YARDLAND S
YARDMAN
DRAYMAN
YARDMEN
DRAYMEN
YARDS
DRAYS
YARDWAND S
YARDWORK S
YARE R
AERY EYRA
YEAR
YARELY
YEARLY
YARER
YAREST
ESTRAY
STAYER
YARMELKE S
YARMULKE S
YARN S
NARY
YARNED
DENARY
YARNER S
YARNERS
YARNING
YARNS

YARROW S
ARROWY
YARROWS
YASHMAC S
YASHMACS
YASHMAK S
YASHMAKS
YASMAK S
YASMAKS
YATAGAN S
YATAGANS
YATAGHAN S
YATTER S
TREATY
YATTERED
YATTERS
YAUD S
YAUDS
YAULD
YAUP S
YAUPED
YAUPER S
YAUPERS
YAUPING
YAUPON S
YAUPONS
YAUPS
YAUTIA S
YAUTIAS
YAW LNPS
WAY
YAWED
YAWEY
YAWING
YAWL S
WALY
YAWLED
YAWLING
YAWLS
YAWMETER S
YAWN S
AWNY WANY
YAWNED
YAWNER S
YAWNERS
YAWNING
YAWNS
YAWP S
YAWPED
YAWPER S
YAWPERS
YAWPING S
YAWPINGS
YAWPS
WASPY
YAWS
SWAY WAYS
YAY S
YAYS
YCLAD
YCLEPED
YCLEPT
ABD YE AHNPSTW
EKL
PRT
W
YEA HNRS
AYE
YEAH S
YEAHS
YEALING S
YEALINGS
YEAN S
YEANED
YEANING
YEANLING S
YEANS
YEAR NS
AERY EYRA
YARE
YEARBOOK S
YEAREND S
DEANERY
YEARNED
YEARENDS
YEARLIES

YEARLING S
LAYERING
RELAYING
YEARLONG
YEARLY
YARELY
YEARN S
YEARNED
DEANERY
YEAREND
YEARNER S
YEARNERS
YEARNING S
YEARNS
SENARY
YEARS
EYRAS RESAY
SAYER
YEAS T
AYES EASY
EYAS
YEASAYER S
YEAST SY
YEASTED
YEASTIER
YEASTILY
YEASTING
YEASTS
SAYEST
YEASTY
YECCH S
YECCHS
YECH SY
YECHS
YECHY
YEELIN S
YEELINS
YEGG S
EGGY
YEGGMAN
YEGGMEN
YEGGS
YEH
HEY
YELD
YELK S
YELKS
YELL S
YELLED
YELLER S
YELLERS
YELLING
YELLOW SY
YELLOWED
YELLOWER
YELLOWLY
YELLOWS
YELLOWY
YELLS
YELP S
YELPED
DEEPLY
YELPER S
YELPERS
YELPING
YELPS
SLYPE
E YEN S
YENNED
YENNING
YENS
SNYE SYNE
YENTA S
YENTAS
YENTE S
TEENY
YENTES
TEENSY
YEOMAN
YEOMANLY
YEOMANRY
YEOMEN
YEP S
PYE
YEPS
ESPY PYES
YERBA S
BARYE

YERBAS
BARYES
YERK S
RYKE
YERKED
YERKING
YERKS
RYKES
ABD YES
EKL
OPR
TW
C YESES
YESHIVA HS
YESHIVAH S
YESHIVAS
YESHIVOT H
YESSED
O YESSES
YESSING
YESTER N
YESTERN
STYRENE
YESTREEN S
YET IT
TYE
YETI S
YETIS
YETT S
YETTS
TESTY
YEUK SY
YEUKED
YEUKING
YEUKS
YEUKY
YEW S
WYE
YEWS
WYES
YIELD S
YIELDED
YIELDER S
REEDILY
YIELDERS
YIELDING
YIELDS
YIKES
SKIEY
YILL S
ILLY LILY
YILLS
SILLY SLILY
APT YIN S
YINCE
AP YINS
YIP ES
YIPE S
YIPES
YIPPED
YIPPEE
YIPPIE S
YIPPIES
YIPPING
YIPS
YIRD S
YIRDS
YIRR S
YIRRED
YIRRING
YIRRS
YIRTH S
YIRTHS
SHIRTY
THYRSI
X YLEM S
ELMY
X YLEMS
YO BDKMNUW
OY
YOB S
BOY
YOBBO S
BOOBY
YOBBOES
YOBBOS
YOBS
BOYS SYBO
YOCK S
COKY

YOCKED
YOCKING
YOCKS
YOD HS
YODEL S
ODYLE YODLE
YODELED
YODELER S
YODELERS
YODELING
YODELLED
YODELLER S
YODELS
ODYLES
YODLES
YODH S
YODHS
YODLE DRS
ODYLE YODEL
YODLED
YODLER S
YODLERS
YODLES
ODYLES
YODELS
YODLING
YODS
YOGA S
YOGAS
YOGEE S
YOGEES
YOGH S
YOGHOURT S
YOGHS
YOGHURT S
YOGHURTS
YOGI CNS
YOGIC
YOGIN IS
YOGINI S
YOGINIS
YOGINS
YOGIS
YOGURT S
GROUTY
YOGURTS
YOHIMBE S
YOHIMBES
YOICKS
YOK ES
YOKE DLS
YOKED
YOKEL S
YOKELESS
YOKELISH
YOKELS
YOKEMATE S
YOKES
YOKING
YOKOZUNA S
YOKS
YOLK SY
YOLKED
YOLKIER
YOLKIEST
YOLKS
YOLKY
YOM
YOMIM
YON DI
YOND
YONDER
YONI CS
YONIC
YONIS
NOISY
YONKER S
YONKERS
YORE S
OYER
YORES
OYERS
YOU RS
YOUNG S
YOUNGER S
YOUNGERS

YOUNGEST
YOUNGISH
YOUNGS
YOUNKER S
YOUNKERS
YOUPON S
YOUPONS
YOUR NS
YOURN
YOURS
YOURSELF
YOUS E
YOUSE
YOUTH S
YOUTHEN S
YOUTHENS
YOUTHFUL
YOUTHS
YOW ELS
YOWE DS
YOWED
YOWES
YOWIE S
YOWIES
YOWING
YOWL S
YOWLED
YOWLER S
LOWERY
YOWLERS
YOWLING
YOWLS
YOWS
YPERITE S
YPERITES
YTTERBIA S
YTTERBIC
YTTRIA S
YTTRIAS
YTTRIC
YTTRIUM S
YTTRIUMS
YUAN S
YUANS
UNSAY
YUCA S
YUCAS
SAUCY
YUCCA S
YUCCAS
YUCCH
YUCH
YUCK SY
YUCKED
YUCKIER
YUCKIEST
YUCKING
YUCKS
SUCKY
YUCKY
YUGA S
YUGAS
YUK S
YUKKED
YUKKIER
YUKKIEST
YUKKING
YUKKY
YUKS
YULAN S
UNLAY
YULANS
UNLAYS
YULE S
YULES
YULETIDE S
YUM
YUMMIER
YUMMIES T
YUMMIEST
YUMMY
YUP S
YUPON S
YUPONS
YUPPIE S

YUPPIES
YUPPIFY
YUPPY
YUPS
YURT AS
YURTA
YURTS
RUSTY
YUTZ
YUTZES
YWIS

Z

ZA GPSX
ZABAIONE S
ZABAJONE S
ZACATON S
ZACATONS
ZADDICK
T ZADDIK
T ZADDIKIM
ZAFFAR S
ZAFFARS
ZAFFER S
ZAFFRE
ZAFFERS
ZAFFRES
ZAFFIR S
ZAFFIRS
ZAFFRE S
ZAFFER
ZAFFRES
ZAFFERS
ZAFTIG
ZAG S
ZAGGED
ZAGGING
ZAGS
ZAIBATSU
ZAIKAI S
ZAIKAIS
ZAIRE S
ZAIRES
ZAMARRA S
ZAMARRAS
ZAMARRO S
ZAMARROS
ZAMIA S
ZAMIAS
ZAMINDAR IS
ZANANA S
ZANANAS
ZANDER S
ZANDERS
ZANIER
ZANIES T
AZINES
ZANIEST
ZEATINS
ZANILY
ZANINESS
ZANY
ZANYISH
ZANZA S
ZANZAS
ZAP S
ZAPATEO S
ZAPATEOS
ZAPPED
ZAPPER S
ZAPPERS
ZAPPIER
APPRIZE
ZAPPIEST
ZAPPING
ZAPPY
ZAPS
ZAPTIAH S
ZAPTIAHS
ZAPTIEH S
ZAPTIEHS
ZARATITE S
ZAREBA S
ZAREBAS
ZAREEBA S

ZAREEBAS
ZARF S
ZARFS
ZARIBA S
ZARIBAS
ZARZUELA S
ZAS
ZASTRUGA
ZASTRUGI
ZAX
ZAXES
ZAYIN S
ZAYINS
ZAZEN S
ZAZENS
ZEAL S
LAZE
ZEALOT S
ZEALOTRY
ZEALOTS
ZEALOUS
ZEALS
LAZES
ZEATIN S
ZEATINS
ZANIEST
ZEBEC KS
ZEBECK S
ZEBECKS
ZEBECS
ZEBRA S
BRAZE
ZEBRAIC
ZEBRANO S
ZEBRANOS
ZEBRAS S
BRAZES
ZEBRASS
ZEBRINE S
ZEBRINES
ZEBROID
ZEBU S
ZEBUS
ZECCHIN IOS
ZECCHINI
ZECCHINO S
ZECCHINS
ZECHIN S
ZECHINS
ZED S
ZEDOARY
ZEDS
ZEE S
ZEES
ZEIN S
ZINE
ZEINS
ZINES
ZEK S
ZEKS
ZELKOVA S
ZELKOVAS
ZEMINDAR SY
ZEMSTVA
ZEMSTVO S
ZEMSTVOS
ZENAIDA S
ZENAIDAS
ZENANA S
ZENANAS
ZENITH S
ZENITHAL
ZENITHS
ZEOLITE S
ZEOLITES
ZEOLITIC
ZEP S
ZEPHYR S
ZEPHYRS
ZEPPELIN S
ZEPPOLE S
ZEPPOLES
ZEPPOLI
ZEPS
ZERK S

ZERKS
ZERO S
ZEROED
ZEROES
ZEROING
ZEROS
ZEROTH
ZEST SY
ZESTED
ZESTER S
ZESTERS
ZESTFUL
ZESTIER
ZESTIEST
ZESTILY
STYLIZE
ZESTING
ZESTLESS
ZESTS
ZESTY
ZETA S
ZETAS
ZEUGMA S
ZEUGMAS
ZIBELINE S
ZIBET HS
ZIBETH S
ZIBETHS
ZIBETS
ZIG S
ZIGGED
ZIGGING
ZIGGURAT S
ZIGS
ZIGZAG S
ZIGZAGGY
ZIGZAGS
ZIKKURAT S
ZIKURAT S
ZIKURATS
ZILCH
ZILCHES
ZILL S
ZILLAH S
ZILLAHS
ZILLION S
ZILLIONS
ZILLS
ZIN CEGS
ZINC SY
ZINCATE S
ZINCATES
ZINCED
DEZINC
ZINCIC
ZINCIFY
ZINCING
ZINCITE S
CITIZEN
ZINCITES
CITIZENS
ZINCKED
ZINCKING
ZINCKY
ZINCOID
ZINCOUS
ZINCS
ZINCY
A ZINE BS
ZEIN
ZINEB S
ZINEBS
A ZINES
ZEINS
ZING SY
ZINGANI
ZINGANO
ZINGARA
ZINGARE
ZINGARI
ZINGARO
ZINGED
ZINGER S
ZINGERS
ZINGIER

ZINGIEST
ZINGING
ZINGS
ZINGY
ZINKIFY
ZINKY
ZINNIA S
ZINNIAS
ZINS
ZIP S
ZIPLESS
ZIPLOCK
ZIPPED
ZIPPER S
ZIPPERED
ZIPPERS
ZIPPIER
ZIPPIEST
ZIPPING
ZIPPY
ZIPS
ZIRAM S
MIRZA
ZIRAMS
MIRZAS
ZIRCALOY S
ZIRCON S
ZIRCONIA S
ZIRCONIC
ZIRCONS
ZIT IS
ZITHER NS
ZITHERN S
ZITHERNS
ZITHERS
ZITI S
ZITIS
ZITS
ZIZIT H
ZIZITH
ZIZZLE DS
ZIZZLED
ZIZZLES
ZIZZLING
ZLOTE
ZLOTIES
ZLOTY S
ZLOTYCH
ZLOTYS
ZOA
AZO
ZOARIA L
ZOARIAL
ZOARIUM
ZOCALO S
ZOCALOS
ZODIAC S
ZODIACAL
ZODIACS
ZOEA ELS
ZOEAE
ZOEAL
AZOLE
ZOEAS
ZOECIA
ZOECIUM
ZOFTIG
A ZOIC
ZOISITE S
ZOISITES
ZOMBI ES
ZOMBIE S
ZOMBIES
ZOMBIFY
ZOMBIISM S
ZOMBIS
ZONA EL
AZON
ZONAE
A ZONAL
AZLON
ZONALLY
ZONARY
O ZONATE D
O ZONATED

O ZONATION S
O ZONE DRS
ZONED
DOZEN
ZONELESS
ZONER S
ZONERS
O ZONES
ZONETIME S
MONETIZE
ZONING
ZONK S
ZONKED
ZONKING
ZONKS
ZONULA ERS
ZONULAE
ZONULAR
ZONULAS
ZONULE S
ZONULES
ZOO MNS
ZOOCHORE S
ZOOECIA
ZOOECIUM
ZOOEY
ZOOGENIC
ZOOGENY
ZOOGLEA ELS
ZOOGLEAE
ZOOGLEAL
ZOOGLEAS
ZOOGLOEA EL S
ZOOID S
ZOOIDAL
ZOOIDS
ZOOIER
OOZIER
ZOOIEST
OOZIEST
ZOOKS
ZOOLATER S
ZOOLATRY
ZOOLOGIC
ZOOLOGY
ZOOM S
MOZO
ZOOMANIA S
ZOOMED
ZOOMETRY
ZOOMING
ZOOMORPH S
ZOOMS
MOZOS
ZOON S
ZOONAL
ZOONED
ZOONING
ZOONOSES
ZOONOSIS
ZOONOTIC
ZOONS
ZOOPHILE S
ZOOPHILY
ZOOPHOBE S
ZOOPHYTE S
ZOOS
ZOOSPERM S
ZOOSPORE S
ZOOTIER
ZOOTIEST
ZOOTOMIC
ZOOTOMY
ZOOTY
ZORI LS
ZORIL S
ZORILLA S
ZORILLAS
ZORILLE S
ZORILLES
ZORILLO S
ZORILLOS
ZORILS
ZORIS
ZOSTER S
ZOSTERS
ZOUAVE S
ZOUAVES
ZOUK S
ZOUKS
ZOUNDS
ZOWIE
ZOYSIA S
ZOYSIAS
ZUCCHINI S
ZUGZWANG S
ZUZ
ZUZIM
ZWIEBACK S
ZYDECO S
ZYDECOS
ZYGOID
ZYGOMA S
ZYGOMAS
ZYGOMATA
ZYGOSE S
A ZYGOSES
ZYGOSIS
ZYGOSITY
ZYGOTE S
ZYGOTENE S
ZYGOTES
ZYGOTIC
ZYMASE S
ZYMASES
ZYME S
ZYMES
ZYMOGEN ES
ZYMOGENE S
ZYMOGENS
ZYMOGRAM S
ZYMOLOGY
ZYMOSAN S
ZYMOSANS
ZYMOSES
ZYMOSIS
ZYMOTIC
ZYMURGY
ZYZZYVA S
ZYZZYVAS
ZZZ

Made in the USA
Lexington, KY
18 January 2014